ISBN 978-0-266-66497-0
PIBN 10877199

ITALIAN AND ENGLISH DICTIONARY

WITH PRONUNCIATION AND BRIEF ETYMOLOGIES

BY

HJALMAR EDGREN, PH.D.

Recent professor of Romance Languages in the University of Nebraska; member of the Nobel Institute of the Swedish Academy in Stockholm; author of various works on Romance, Germanic, and Indo-European Philology, etc.

ASSISTED BY

GIUSEPPE BICO, D.C.L.
University of Rome

JOHN L. GERIG, A.M.
Instructor, University of Nebraska

NEW YORK
HENRY HOLT AND COMPANY

PREFACE

It is the aim of this work to meet the long-felt need of an Italian and English dictionary, based on the foremost recent authorities, and embodying a copious selection of modern words, as well as important obsolete ones, presented in a practical and yet etymological form.

The main features of the work are explained below.

I. THE ITALIAN-ENGLISH PART

The chief authority followed has been Petrocchi's *Novo dizionario scolastico.* But at its side have been consulted especially Petrocchi's *Dizionario universale della lingua italiana*, Rigutini-Fanfani's *Vocabolario italiano*, Zambaldi's *Vocabolario etimologico italiano*, and Baretti's, Millhouse's, and James-Grassi's well-known dictionaries.

The vocabulary embodies a considerably larger number of Italian words than ordinary dictionaries of a similar size, and many more than Rigutini-Fanfani's large Italian dictionary. Almost every modern word contained in Petrocchi's 'scholastic' dictionary is quoted, and also a large number of rare or obsolete words, especially such as are indispensable in reading Italian classics. These are mainly from Petrocchi's 'lingua fuori d' uso,' and are marked with a dagger (†). It should be noted here, however, that the obsolete abstracts in *-tate*, *-tade*, and *-tute*, *-tude*, as identical with the modern in *-tà* and *-tù*, have been consistently omitted as unnecessary repetitions.

Irregular forms of inflection are noted with their words, and also largely as titles in their alphabetical order. The full conjugation of each simple irregular verb is given below the verb, and the conjugation of their compounds by proper reference, either directly or by pointing out the composition.

Idiomatic phrases are usually given only when not self-explanatory; and, on the whole, space for idioms has been economized in favor of a large vocabulary.

The pronunciation is marked principally by subscript signs (as explained p. vi), such a method being the most direct, unequivocal, and free from confusion.

Etymologically related words are grouped together, observing the requirements of convenience and absolute alphabetical sequence. Such grouping will serve the threefold purpose of both etymological and mnemonic association, of space-saving, and of facilitating the search for words, by enabling the student to pass easily from one group to another.

The division of the group-words is made chiefly with reference to Italian spelling and pronunciation, and to space-saving. This is done with some disregard of etymological division, which could not be consistently carried out.

The words are not grouped with reference to immediate derivation from each other, which would have necessitated very numerous groups, but simply with reference to near relationship of some kind. Hence the etymological word of the group is not necessarily the actual source-word from which the others are derived, though it may be so, and, as a rule, comes nearer to it than the others.

The derivation of current Italian words, when known, is briefly denoted in brackets after each word occurring singly, or after that word in the group which comes nearest the etymological source. This latter word is divided by a heavy hyphen (**-**), or, in case of compounds, by double heavy hyphens (**=**); and, besides, if not found first in the group, preceded, for ease of reference, by double bars (‖). Other words are divided by slight single or (for compounds) double hyphens (-, or =). These conventional division-marks can cause no confusion, as Italian ordinarily uses no hyphens at all.

When the derivation of a word is unknown or questionable, this is denoted by an interrogation-mark above or before the suggested etymology. Suggestions are purposely rare. Besides the more immediate source of the Italian word, sometimes a remoter source is also indicated in parenthesis, especially when this may help t… …he present meaning, or to suggest a familiar form. To … …cal students, the meaning of source-words, when … …immediate sense of the Italian word, is given. …n Greek words are transliterated. For rare and …hose marked †) no etymologies are given, except …s, as when they underlie current forms.

English cognates, from whatever source, when not evident at first sight, are in SMALL CAPITALS, but only once, and under the Italian head-word, provided the English cognate occurs there, and in a form also sufficiently suggestive for derivative words.

II. THE ENGLISH-ITALIAN PART,

though more immediately based on previous works of a similar scope and purpose, yet, like the Italian-English part, has indications of pronunciation (cf. page iv), and etymological connections (by grouping). Light hyphens (-) are here conventional, while the heavy (-) stand for English hyphens between the members of a composite word. The requirements of the varied utterance and accentuation of English words have here necessitated a less rigorous grouping of kindred words than in the Italian-English part; and, as the source of the Germanic elements of English is unfamiliar to the ordinary student, no etymologies (except as suggested by the grouping and by the frequent Italian cognates) are attempted.

Also here a large number of obsolete words (marked †) are given as an aid to the Italian student of English classics.

Dr. Giuseppe Bico has assisted me in revising the manuscript of the entire Italian-English part, and my pupil, Mr. J. L. Gerig, by much secretarial work, as well as aid in reading the proofs.

It is in the hope that this dictionary, though imperfect, may contribute its share to a scholarly study of a language whose literary treasures, besides their intrinsic value, have had so great an influence on the shaping of English literature, that it is now submitted to the public.

HJALMAR EDGREN.

LINCOLN, NEB., May 1901.

PRONUNCIATION

A. SIGNS OF ITALIAN PRONUNCIATION

☞ To know Italian sounds well, a correct pronunciation of the examples in the lists below will be of service.

1. *Accent-marks.* Though usage varies, Italian is ordinarily written without any other accent-sign than the grave (ˋ) for accented final vowels (whether pronounced close or open). Accent-signs on other vowels are therefore conventional in this work, to mark the accented vowel, and, in part, its pronunciation.

2. The Italian accent is less energetic than the English, and all syllables are uttered more evenly.

3. *Silent letters* are in *italics* (e.g., *i* in **ágio**, *g* in **légno**).

VOWELS

4. Italian vowels are uttered with a clear, full sound, and rarely dimmed like the English unaccented vowels.

5. An accent-vowel is ordinarily long before another vowel, or one consonant, or a mute + *r*, *l*; otherwise short. Unaccented vowels are short.

6. List of the vowels with pronunciation signs :—

ACC.	UNACC.		LONG	SHORT
á	a	= *a* in *ask* (Webster); § 5:	**áma** ;	**pálla**
é	e	= *e* " *bey* (without vanish : French *é*); § 5:	**méno** ;	**détto**
è		= *e* " *met;* § 5:	**tèma** ;	**tèrra**
í	i	= *i* " *police;* § 5:	**vídi** ;	**íllico**
ó	o	= *o* " *no* (without vanish); § 5:	**lóro** ;	**sótto**
ò		= *o* " *orb;* § 5:	**òro** ;	**pòrto**
ú	u	= *u* " *rue;* § 5:	**úno** ;	**usúrpo**
	y	= Ital. *i* before vowel (cf. below):	**yard**	

vowel-compounds : each vowel has its own sound, though unaccented *i*, *u* are lightly uttered : . . . . **leóne** ; **fióre** ; **cuòre**

CONSONANTS

7. Consonants omitted below are pronounced as in English (unless in italics, § 3), observing that *d*, *t* are dental (formed near the base of the upper teeth) ; and that in uttering double consonants the tongue-contact is protracted (as if to allow for two consonants) before it is broken.

8. List of consonants with their pronunciation signs :—

c = *k*:	**cáro**	s = *s* in *so* :	**suòno**
c ... :	**céra**	ș = *s* in *rose* (*z*) :	**ròșa, șbárra**
	górgo	ș = *sh* in *shall* :	**șcélta, cáșcia**
	gènte	z = *ts* :	**nazióne**
	gli, fíglio	ẓ = Eng. *ds* :	**ẓèro, mánẓo**
	légno (*lén'yo*)		

| (sharply as initial or after consonant) : **paròla, rícco, pádre**

B. SEGNI DELLA PRONUNZIA INGLESE

☞ **Per conoscere bene i suoni inglesi bisogna imparare la pronunzia corretta degli esempi inglesi nelle liste sottostanti.**

1. I segni di pronunzia delle vocali accentate sono messi SOPRA le vocali; gli altri segni (- di **e** e **th** eccettuato) SOTTO le lettere; **accūmulạte.**

2. Le lettere corsive (come *e* di **accūmulạte**) sono mute: **āble, făttẹn, thōugh** (*ugh* mute).

VOCALI

3. Le vocali non accentate con un segno sottoscritto si pronunziano come le vocali accentate collo stesso segno, benchè meno distintamente (ed **ạ, ẹ, ọ** senza sdrucciolamento).

4. Le vocali senza segni si pronunziano come le vocali col segno breve (**a, e,** ecc. = **ă, ĕ,** ecc.), benchè meno distintamente.

5. L' accento inglese è discendente e più energico dell' accento italiano.

6. La pronunzia delle parole ripetute non è indicata, fuorchè per ragioni speciali.

7. Vocali coi loro segni convenzionali: —

ACC.	NON ACC.		ESEMPI
â		= *a* del ital. *la:*	**dânce**
ă	a	= â, più piatta:	**ăt; attĕst**
ä	ạ	= â, più guttur. e lungo:	**härmony; hạrmōnious**
a̤	ạ	= fra â ed ŏ:	**a̤ll; a̤lthōugh**
ȧ	ạ	= ŏ:	**wȧs; quạlificātiọn**
ā	ạ(ạ)	= *e* chiusa, sdrucciol. in *i* (*é^i*):	**fāte; ĕmanạte, sĕnạte**
â	ạ	= ê:	**câre; wĕlfạre**
ă		= ĕ:	**agăin**
	ẹ	= ẹ, più indistinto:	**tĕmplạr**
ĕ	e	= *e* aperto in *del:*	**mĕt; cŏncept**
ê	ẹ	= ĕ, ma lungo:	**whêre; whẹrein**
ê	ẹ	= *e* chiusa, sdrucciol. in *i* (*é^i*):	**êight; ŏsprẹy**
ē	ẹ(ẹ)	= ĭ:	**mē; concrēte, ẹvĕnt**
ẽ	ẹ	= *eu* del francese *leur:*	**tẽrm; tẹrminātiọn**
ēw	ew	= ū:	**fēw; nĕphew**
ĭ	i	= *i* breve, avvicin. ad *e:*	**ĭn; infẽr**
ï	ị	= *i* lungo:	**mïen; quărantịne**
ī	ị	= ă'y:	**fīne; ĕmpịre**
ĩ	ị	= ẽ:	**fĩr; nădịr**
ị		= y:	**ŏnịọn**
ŏ	o	= *o* di *notte*, avvicin. a â ingl.:	**hŏt; dogmătic**
ō	ọ(ọ)	= *o* di *loro*, sdrucciol. in *u* (*o^u*):	**nō; lọcălity; dọminịọn**
ô	ọ	= a̤:	**ôrb; ọrdāin**
ö	ọ	= *u* lungo:	**möve, fööl; hălf-mọọn**
ȯ	ọ	= *u* breve:	**bȯsọm, fȯot; nĕedfụl**
ó	ọ	= ŭ:	**cóme; hăndsọme**
õ	ọ	= ẽ:	**wõrkẹr; ŏpẹrạtọr**
ŏị	oị	= ă'y:	**ŏịl; cōal-oịl**
ŏụ	oụ	= ă'ụ:	**ŏụt; hŏthouse**

ACC.	NON ACC.		ESEMPI
ŏw		= ŏu̧:	nŏw
ū	u̧	= u lungo:	rūle; fĕrru̧le
u̇	u̧	= u breve:	fu̇ll; -fu̧l
ŭ	u	= fra ŏ e ŏ breve:	bŭt; submit
ū	u̧	= y'ū (dopo *d*, *t*, *s*, *l* quasi ū):	ūse, beaūty; u̧nite
û	u̧	= ŏ:	ûrn; sŏjou̧rn
ȳ	y̠	= ī:	mȳ; dĕify̠
ỹ		= ĩ:	fỹrd

CONSONANTI

8. Le consonanti omesse si pronunziano in inglese come in italiano, osservando tuttavia che *d*, *t* si formano più in dietro.

c	= *k*:	cärt
ċ	= *s*:	cĕll
ç	= sh:	ferōçious
ch	= *c* di *ce*: . . .	chăp, chĕst
g	= *g* di *gala*:	gāme
ġ	= *j*:	ġĕm
h	= *h* aspirata:	hăve
j	= *j* ital.:	jōke
ŋ	= *n* palatale: . . .	sŏŋ*g*, liviŋ*g*
q	= *k*:	pīque
qu	= *qu* ital.:	quĕst
r	= senza vibrazione distinta, e formata contro il palato anteriore (-*r* finale è muta nel sud dell' Inghilterra): .	rōll, rē*a*r, fäthẹr
s	= *s* di *se*:	sĕll
ş	= *s* di *rosa*:	rōşe, ăş
ș	= sh:	șūre
ș	= ș sonoro:	plĕ*a*șu̧re
sh	= *sc* di *scelta*:	shē, shŭn
ţ	= sh:	ŏpţiọn
ţ	= ch:	quĕsţiọn
th	= *t* colla punta della lingua fra i denti:	thin
th	= th sonoro:	thē, bāthe
w	= *u*- di *uovo*:	wāş
wh	= ʰw:	whàt
x̧	= gz:	ex̧ist
x	= k'sh:	lŭxu̧ry
x	= gʒ:	lux̧ūrious
z	= ş:	gāze
z̧	= ʒ:	ăz̧u̧re

LIST OF ABBREVIATIONS

ADJ., adjective.
ADV., adverb.
agr., agriculture.
alch., alchemy.
Am., American.
anat., anatomy.
antiq., antiquity.
Ar(ab.), Arabic.
arch., architecture.
arith., arithmetic.
ART., article.
artil., artillery.
astrol., astrology.
astron., astronomy.
aug., augmentative.
auxil., auxiliary.
Bav., Bavarian.
bot., botany.
car., caressing (endearing).
car. dim., caressing diminutive.
Cath. rel., Catholic religion.
carp., carpentry.
chem., chemistry.
coll., collective.
com., commerce.
CONJ., conjunction.
contr., contraction.
cook., cookery.
dial., dialectic.
dim., diminutive.
disp., disparaging.
disp. aug., disparaging augmentative.
disp. dim., disparaging diminutive.
dy., dyeing.
eccl., ecclesiastical.
echoic, onomatopoetic.
Eng., English.
engr., engraving.
ent., entomology.
F., feminine.
fam., familiar.
fenc., fencing.
fig., figuratively.
fort., fortification.
Fr., French.
Fut., Future.
gard., gardening.
geol., geology.
geom., geometry.
Ger., German.
Gr., Greek.
her., heraldry.
horol., horology.
hort., horticulture.
hunt., hunting.
hydr., hydraulics.
ichth., ichthyology.
IMP., impersonal.
I(nd.), Indicative.
invar., invariable.
INTR., intransitive.
INTERJ., interjection.
iron., ironically.
Impf., Imperfect.
IRR., irregular.
It., Italian.
I've, Imperative.
jest., jestingly.
jur., jurisprudence.
L., Latin.
leg., legal.
lit., literature.
l. L., late Latin (vulgar or scholastic).
log., logic.
M., masculine.
mam., mammalogy.
man., manege.
mar., marine.
math., mathematics.
mech., mechanics.
med., medicine.
metal., metallurgy.
mil(it)., military art.
min., mineralogy.
mus., music.
myth., mythology.
N., noun-substantive.
nav., naval.
OFr., Old French.
OGer., Old German.
OHG., Old High German
opt., optics.
orni., ornithology.
P., Past.
paint., painting.
Part., PART., participle
pers., person.
pharm., pharmacy.
phil(os.), philosophy.
phys., physics.
pl., plural.
p. L., popular Latin.
poet., poetic.
pol., politics.
pop., popular.
Pres., Present.
PREF., prefix.
PREP., preposition.
Pret., PRET., Preterit.
print., printing.
PRON., pronoun.
REFL., reflexive.
rel., religion.
rhet., rhetoric.
Scand., Scandinavian.
sculpt., sculpture.
s(ing)., singular.
S(ubj.), Subjunctive.
Swed., Swedish.
Sp., Spanish.
surg., surgery.
Syr., Syriac.
tech., technology.
theat., theatre.
theol., theology.
TR., transitive.
triv., trivial.
typ., typography.
vet., veterinary art.
vulg., vulgar.
zoöl., zoölogy.

†, obsolete word or meaning.

* before a word, hypothetical form.

‖, sign to help find the etymology-word within a group.

–, in Part I, division-sign of the etymology-word of a group; in Part II English hyphens between members of compound.

-, division-sign of other than etymology-words.

=, division-sign between members of a compound.

≡, division-sign between members of a compound which is also the etymology-word.

ITALIAN-ENGLISH

a1 [L.], F.: a (the letter).
a 2, before vowel **ad** [L. *ad*], PREP.: at; to; for; (*occas'ly*) by, with, in; on; according to, as: — *casa*, at home; — *cavallo*, on horseback; — *mente*, by heart; — *poco* — *poco*, little by little, gradually; — *quanto penso*, as I think; — *che pro?* of what use?
a', for *ai* = *a i*, 'to the.'
aba.., for words not found under *aba..*, cf. *abba..*
aba-déssa† = *badessa*. **-día**† = *abbadia*. **-táccio**, *disp.* of *-te*. ‖**abá-te** [L. *abbas* (Syr. *abbâ*, father)], M.: abbot; (Rom. Cath.) priest (clergyman). **-tíno**, *dim.* of *-te*. **-tóne**, *augm.* of *-te*. **-tónzolo**, **-túccio**, **-tuccîáccio**, **-túcolo**, *disp.* of *-te*. **-zía**, **-ziále** = *abbazia*, *-ziale*.
abba-caménto, M.: musing; raving. ‖**-cáre** [*-co*], INTR.: compute†; muse (fancy); puzzle one's head; rave.
abbac-chiaménto, M.: knocking down (fruit); lowering (of price). ‖**-chiáre** [*bacchio*], TR.: knock down with a pole (as fruit, etc.); knock down; sell cheap: — *una ragazza*, marry a girl poorly (merely to get her married). **-chiáta**, F.: knocking down; cudgeling. **-chiáto**, PART.: knocked down; dejected; humiliated. **-chiatúra**, F.: knocking down.
abba-chíno [*-co*], M.: simple arithmetic. **-chísta**, M.: arithmetician (us'ly *disp.*).
abbaci-náre [*bacino*], TR.: blind by torture; †dim (obfuscate, eclipse). **-náto**, PART.: injured (of the eyes).
ábba-co [L. *abacus*, counting-board], M.: arithmetic; counting: *aver poco* —, be a poor computer.
abbadáre† = *badare*.
abbadía = *abbazia*.
abba-gliaménto, M., **-gliánza**, F.: blindness; delusion. ‖**-gliáre** [*bagliore*], TR.: dazzle; beguile; INTR.: be dazzled (be blinded), REFL.: make a mistake.
abbai-aménto, M.: barking. ‖**-áre** [*bau*], INTR.: BAY (bark, howl); sing poorly; carp. **-áta**, F.: barking (yelp); yell. **-atóre**, M., **-atóra**, **-atríce**, F.: barker; babbler.
abbáino [?], M.: dormer-window.
ab-báio [*-are*], M.: barking. **-baío**, M.: much barking. **-baióne**, M.: loud barker.

abbal-láre [*balla*], TR.: emBALE (pack up). **-latóre**, M.: embaler (packer). **-lináre**, TR.: roll up (a mattress for airing the bed). **-lottáre** [*ballotta*], TR.: handle, fumble with; manage; put to the vote. **-lottatúra**, F.: handling. **-lottío**, M.: much or frequent handling.
abbalordíre [*balordo*], TR.: stun (dull).
abbamboláto [*bambola*], ADJ.: doll-eyed (with expressionless eyes, languid-eyed).
abban-donáre, TR.: abandon (relinquish, forsake); REFL.: give one's self up (yield). **-donataménte**, ADV.: in an abandoned manner; hopelessly. **-donáto**, ADJ.: abandoned (forsaken); hopeless. **-donatóre**, M.: deserter. ‖**-dóno** [cf. OFr. *bandon*, power], M.: abandonment (forsaking, desertion): *in* —, in utter neglect *or* disorder.
abbar-bagliaménto, M.: dazzling; delusion. ‖**-bagliáre** [*bagliore*], TR.: dazzle (daze, stupify). **-báglio**, M.: dazzling; delusion.
abbarbicáre [*barba*], INTR.: take root.
abbarcáre [*barca*], TR.: load up (pile up).
abbarráre† = *sbarrare*.
abba-ruffaménto, M.: scuffle; quarrel. ‖**-ruffáre** [*baruffa*], TR.: put in confusion (jumble together); REFL.: scuffle (wrangle). **-ruffío**, M.: violent wrangle.
ab-bassaménto, M.: lowering; debasing. ‖**-bassáre** [*basso*], TR.: lower (depress; diminish, reduce); deBASE; cast down; INTR.: abate. **-bassáta**, F.: lowering; reduction; humiliation. **-básso**, ADV. PREP.: below; down; down-stairs: — *i cappelli!* hats off! — *i tiranni!* down with the tyrants!
abba-stánte, (*vulg.*) = *bastante*. **-stánza** [cf. *bastanza*], ADV.: sufficiently (enough).
abbáto†, etc. = *abate*, etc.
abbát-tere [*battere*], TR.: beat or knock down (BATTER down, overthrow); cut down, ABATE (lower, humble); REFL.: be downcast (be distressed); hit or happen upon. **-timénto**, M.: beating down (overthrow); dejection; faintness; languidness; debasement.
abbatufoláre [*batufolo*], TR.: make a bundle of; throw into a heap (throw in confusion).

abbattúto [part. of *abbattere*], ADJ.: struck down; downcast (depressed); humbled.

abba-zía [*abate*], F.: abbey; abbotship. **-ziále**, ADJ.: abbatial.

abbecedário [*a, b, c, d*], M.: spelling-book.

abbelláre† = *abbellire*.

abbel-liménto, M.: embellishment. **-líre** [*bello*], TR.: embellish. **-litúra**, F.: embellishment; ornamented story.

abbenchè†, (*vulg.*) = *benchè*.

abbendáre†, TR.: gather; join; crowd together.

abbertescáre†, TR.: fortify with battlements.

abbeve-ráre [*bevere*], TR.: water, give drink to (animals); soak; REFL.: drink. **-ratóio**, M.: watering-trough; horse-pound.

abbiadáre [*biada*], TR.: feed with oats.

abbicáre [*bica*], TR.: heap up; join.

abbìcci [*a, b, c*], M.: alphabet.

abbiènte [*abbiare*† = *avere*], M.: possessor.

abbiett..† = *abiett..*

abbi-gliaménto, M.: attire (dress). ‖**-gliáre** [L. *habilis*, ABLE], TR.: attire (dress, HABIT, array). **-gliatúra**, F.: attiring; attire.

abbindo-laménto, M.: deceit (cheat, trick). ‖**-láre** [*bindolo*], TR.: deceive (delude, beguile, cheat); reel†. **-latúra**, F.: deceit (artifice). **-latóre**, M.: deceiver (beguiler). **-latúra**, F.: artifice.

abbiosciáre†, TR.: cast down (deject).

abbiso-gnáre [*bisognare*], TR.: need. **-gnévole**, ADJ.: needing, needy.

abbiur..† = *abiur..*

abboc-caménto, M.: interview. ‖**-cáre** [*bocca*], TR.: snatch (with the mouth); fill to the brim ('mouth'); RECIPR.: have an interview; confer. **-cáto**, ADJ.: filled (full); brimful; palatable (toothsome, delicate, of agreeable flavour); sweetish; eating anything (easily satisfied). **-catúra**, F.: snatching; filling (to the brim). **-conáre**, TR.: cut into morsels ('mouthfuls').

abbom..† = *abom..*

abbonac-ciaménto, M.: calm. ‖**-ciáre** [*bonaccia*], TR.: calm (pacify); REFL.: grow calm.

abbo-naménto, M.: subscription. ‖**-náre**¹ [Fr. *abonner* (*borne*, limit)], TR.: (agree to pay limited sum, *hence*) subscribe; contract: REFL.: subscribe.

a... **-re**² [*buono*], TR.: assent to, ac... ve (grant); allow (deduct); ... ve; grow calm.

...**ménte**, ADV.: abundantly. ... M.: abundance. **-dánza**, ...; flood†. **-dánzia**†, F.: abundance. ‖**-dáre** [*onda*], INTR.: abound. **-dévole**†, ADJ.: abundant. **-dézza**†, F., **-dézzo**†, M.: abundance. **-dóne**, M.: big talker; wiseacre.

ab-boníre [*buono*], TR.: appease (pacify, calm); meliorate; mature. **-bòno**, M.: deduction.

ab-bordággio, M.: boarding (of a ship); approach. ‖**-bordáre** [*bordo*], TR.: board (a ship); approach (accost). **-bórdo** = *-bordaggio*. **-bordóne**, M.: boarder.

abborrac-ciaménto, M.: bungling. ‖**-ciáre** [*borra*], TR.: bungle (botch). **-ciatúra**, F.: botch-work. **-cióne**, M., **-cióna**, F.: bungler.

abborráre†, TR.: fill with stuff; super-add; INTR.: err.

abborri..†, **abbort..**† = *aborri..*, *abort..*

abbotti-naménto†, M.: plunder (booty). ‖**-náre**†, TR.: plunder; REFL.: mutiny. **-natóre**†, M.: plunderer.

abbotto-náre [*bottone*], TR.: button. **-natúra**, F.: buttoning.

abboz-zaménto, M.: rough draught, (sketch). ‖**-záre** [*bozza*], TR.: sketch (outline); rough-cast; rough-hew; shadow forth. **-zataménte**, ADV.: roughly (in outline). **-zatíccio**, ADJ.: half-sketched; half-blown. **-zatóre**, M., **-zatríce**, F.: sketcher. **-zatúra**, F., **abbòz-zo**, M.: sketch(ing); rough draught; outline; embryo.

abbozzoláre [*bózzolo*], REFL.: agglomerate; form its cocoon.

abbrac-ciaménto, M.: embrace. ‖**-ciáre** [*braccio*], TR.: emBRACE; devote one's self to; contain. **-ciáta**, F.: embrace. **-ciatóre**, M.: embracer. **-cia-tútto**, M.: meddler-in-everything. **-cio**, M.: embrace.

abbra-ciáre†, TR.: set on fire. **-ciaménto**†, M.: setting on fire.

abbran-cáre [*branca*], TR.: seize firmly (grasp); clasp. **-catóre**, M.: grasper.

abbre-viaménto, M.: abridgment. ‖**-viáre** [*breve*], TR.: abbreviate (abridge, shorten): *per* —, in short. **-viataménto**, ADV.: in an abridged manner. **-viatívo**, ADJ.: abbreviatory. **-viatóre**, M., **-viatríce**, F.: abridger. **-viatúra**, **-viazióne**, F.: abbreviation (shortening).

ab-briváre [*riva*], INTR.: (*nav.*) sail or steam out (be under way): *-briva*, 'forward!' **-brívo**, M.: sailing; course: *prender l'* —, set out.

abbrividáre†, **-díre**† = *rabbrividire*.

abbron-zacchiáre, TR.: tan slightly. **-zaménto**, M.: bronzing; tanning. ‖**-záre** [*bronzo*], TR., INTR.: bronze; scorch; tan (sunburn). **-zatèllo**, **-zatíccio**, ADJ.: slightly sunburnt. **-zatúra**, F.:

scorching. **-ẓíre** [*bronzo*], INTR.: be bronzed or sunburnt.
abbrost. .† *abbrust..*
abbruciábile† = *bruciabile.*
abbru-ciacchiménto, M.: slight burn. **-ciacchiáre**, TR.: burn slightly. **-ciaménto**, M.: burning. ‖**-ciáre** [*bruciare*], TR.: burn; consume. **-ciatíccio**†, M.: burning.
abbru-naménto, M.: mourning. ‖**-náre** [*bruno*], TR.: drape in mourning; REFL.: put on mourning. **-níre** [*bruno*], TR.: imbrown; INTR.: be sunburnt; grow dusk.
abbrus-tiáre†, **-tíre**†, TR.: singe (scorch). **-toliménto**, M.: scorching; toasting. **-toláre**†, ‖**-tolíre** [L. *perustulare* (*urere*, burn)], TR.: scorch; toast (crisp). **-tolíta**, F.: slight toasting.
abbru-timénto, M.: brutalization. ‖**-tíre** [*bruto*], TR., INTR.: brutalize.
ab-buiaménto, M.: darkening. ‖**-buiáre** [*buio*], TR.: darken (dim); conceal.
abbuòno = *abbono.*
abburat-taménto, M.: bolting (sifting). ‖**-táre** [*buratto*], TR.: bolt (sift); abuse; INTR.: talk tediously; REFL.: †fidget. **-táta**, F.: sieveful of flour. **-tatóne**, M.: great babbler. **-tatóre**, M.: bolter (sifter). **-tatúra**, F.: bolting.
abbuzzíre [*buzzo*], TR., REFL.: overload (the stomach); be cloudy.
abdi-cáre [*dicare*], INTR.: abdicate (resign). **-cazióne**, F.: abdication.
aber-ráre [*errare*], INTR.: err; deviate. **-razióne**, F.: aberration (deviation); error of judgment.
abé-te [L. *abies*], M.: fir-tree. **-táia**† = *-tina.* **-tèlla**, F.: felled fir-tree. **-tí(n)a**, F.: fir-forest. **-tíno**, ADJ.: seasoned with fir-leaves (of drinks). **-to**†, for *abete.*
ab-iettaménte, ADV.: abjectly. **-iettáre**† TR.: cast down. **-iettézza**, F.: abjectness. ‖**-iètto** [L. *-jectus*, cast off], ADJ.: abject (despicable); unpleasant. **-iezióne**, F.: abjection (meanness).
ab-igeáto [L. *-igere*, carry off], M.: cattle-stealing. **-ígeo**, M.: cattle-stealer.
ábi-le [L. *habilis*], ADJ.: ABLE (capable, skilful). **-lità**, F.: ability (skill). **-litáre**, TR.: enable; qualify. **-litazióne**, F.: enabling; qualification. **-lménte**, ADV.: ably (skilfully).
a-bissáre, TR.: throw into an abyss (engulf). ‖**-bísso** [Gr. *á-bussos*, bottomless], M.: abyss.
abi-tábile, ADJ.: inhabitable. **-tácolo**, M.: habitation. **-tánte**, ADJ.: inhabiting; M.: inhabitant. ‖**-táre** [L. *habitare*], TR.; inHABIT; INTR.: reside. **-táto**, PART.: inhabited; M.: inhabited place. **-tatóre**, M., **-tatríce**, F.: inhabitant. **-tazióne**, F.: habitation, (dwelling).
ábi-to [L. *habitus*], M.: HABIT (custom); dress (garment, clothes; PL. suit of clothes); temperament: *pigliar l' —*, take the cowl (go into a monastery). **-tíno**, M.: scapular (shoulder-scarf). **-tuále**, ADJ.: habitual. **-tualménte**, ADV.: habitually; usually. **-tuáre**, TR.: habituate (accustom). **-tuatózza**†, F.: state of being accustomed (custom, habitualness). **-tuazióne**† (*vulg.*) = *-túdine.* **-tudinário**, ADJ.: habitual. **-túdine**, F.: habit. **-túro**, M.: (*poet.*) humble abode.
ab-iuráre [L. *jurare*, swear], TR.: abjure; renounce (recant). **-iúra**, F.: abjuration. **-iurazióne**†, F.: abjuration.
ablatívo [L. *-vus*], M.: ablative.
ablu-ènte [L. *-ens*], ADJ.: abluent. **-zióne**, F.: ablution; cleansing.
abne-gáre [L.], TR.: abnegate (deny). **-gazióne**, F.: abnegation.
abo-líre [L. *ab-olere*], TR.: abolish; annul. **-litívo**, ADJ.: abolishing. **-lizióne**, F.: abolition.
abólla [?], F.: (old) military dress.
abomáṣo [L. *ab*, *omasum*, tripe], M.: abomasum (fourth stomach of a ruminant).
abomi-nábile, **-nándo**, ADJ.: abominable. ‖**-náre** [L. *-nari*], TR.: abominate (abhor, detest). **-nazióne**, F.: abomination (detestation). **-névole**, ADJ.: abominable (execrable). **abomí-nio**, M.: abomination. **-nóso**†, ADJ.: abominable.
aborígeno, ADJ. or S.: aboriginal; PL.: aborigines (natives).
abor-rènte, **-révole**†, ADJ.: abhorrent (repugnant, detestable). **-riménto**, M.: horror. ‖**-ríre** [L. *ab-horrere*], TR.: abhor (loathe).
ab-ortáre, or **-ortíre**, INTR.: be abortive (miscarry). **-ortívo**, ADJ.: abortive. ‖**-òrto** [L. *-tus*], M.: abortion; abortive child.
abrá-dere† = *radere.* **-ṣióne**†, F.: abrasion (rubbing off).
abro-gáre [L.], TR.: abrogate (repeal). **-gazióne**, F.: abrogation (repeal).
absènte† = *assente.*
ábside [L. *-da* (Gr. *apsís*, curve)], F.: APSE.
abst. .† = *ast..*
abu-ṣáre, TR.: abuse (misuse); impose on. **-ṣazióne**, F.: abuse. **-ṣióne**†, F.: desertion. **-ṣívo**, ADJ.: abusive; base. ‖**-ṣo** [L. *-sus*], M.: abuse; disuse†. **-ṣivaménte**, ADV.: abusively.
ac- = *ad-.*
acácia [L. (*acus*, sharp)], F.: acacia.
acánto [L. *-thus*], M.: acanthus.
acatalèttico [Gr. *-tikós* 'not defective'], ADJ.: acatalectic

acata-lessía [Gr. *-lepsía*, 'in-comprehensibleness'], F.: acatalepsy. **-lèttico**, M.: acataleptic.

acattòlico [Gr. *a-*, not, *c.* ..], ADJ.: non-Catholic.

àcca, F.: h (the letter): *un'* —, a nothing; *non vale un'* —, he is worthless.

acca-dèmia [L.], F.: academy; university. **-dèmico**, ADJ.: academical; M.: academician. **-demicaménte**, ADV.: for fun, by the way.

acca-dére [L. *cádere*, fall], IRR. (cf. *cadere*), INTR.: befall (happen); (esp. with *non*) import (be of importance); REFL.: fit (become). **-diméntо**†, M.: accident (chance). **-dúto**, PART.: happened; M.: happening (incident).

accaffáre†, TR.: snatch away.

accagio-naménto, M.: imputation. ‖**-náre** [*cagione*], impute (ACCUSE of). **-natóre**†, M.: imputer (accuser).

acca-gliaménto, M.: coagulation. ‖**-gliáre** [*caglio*], INTR.: COAGULATE. **-gliatúra**, F.: coagulation.

accalap-piacáni [*cane*], M.: municipal catcher of unmuzzled dogs, dog-catcher; scamp (cheat). ‖**-piáre** [*calappio*], TR.: insnare (inveigle). **-piatóre**, M.: cheat (deceiver). **-piatúra**, F.: insnaring, deceit.

accalcáre [*calca*], TR.: crowd.

accaldáre [*caldo*], REFL.: be flushed with fatigue.

accaloráre†, TR.: heat.

accambiáre†, TR.: exchange.

accampanáre [*campana*], TR.: shape like a bell.

accam-paménto, M.: encampment. ‖**-páre** [*campo*], INTR.: encamp; REFL. encamp (pitch one's camp).

accampio-naménto, M.: registering (registry). ‖**-náre** [*campione*], TR.: register (real estate).

accanaláre [*canale*], TR.: channel.

acca-náre†, **-neggiáre**† = *-nire*.

acca-niménto, M.: fury; pertinacity. ‖**-níre** [*cane*], TR.: infuriate; INTR.† or REFL.: be infuriated (grow mad); persist. **-nitaménte**, ADJ.: furiously (rabidly). **-níto**, ADJ.: infuriated (furious, rabid).

accannel-laménto, M.: winding up bobbins. ‖**-láre** [*cannello*], TR.: wind up bobbins.

accánto [*a*, *canto*], PREP. or ADV.: aside; beside; near.

accapac-ciaménto, M.: (mental) weariness. ‖**-ciáre** [*capaccio*], INTR. or REFL.: (..)... one's head weary, be (mentally) wea-
...to, ADJ.: (mentally) wearied.
...: (mental) weariness.
...e [*caparra*], TR.: engage or
...g earnest; buy up (forestall).

accapezzáre [*capo*], TR.: level; place even (stones); fit; finish off†.

accapi-gliaménto, M.: scuffle. ‖**-gliáre** [*capello*], REFL.: take one another by the hair; scuffle. **-gliatúra**, F.: scuffling; hair-pulling.

accappatóio [*cappa*], M.: mantle; combing-cloth.

accap-piáre [*cappio*], TR.: tie; gin (snare). **-piatúra**, F.: running knot (snare). **-piettáre**, TR.: ensnare.

accappo-náre [*cappone*], TR.: capon; REFL.: shiver (shudder). **-natúra**, F.: caponing.

accapric-ciáre†, INTR.: shudder.

accarez-zaménto†, M.: caressing. ‖**-záre** [*carezza*], TR.: caress (fondle); flatter. **-zatívo**†, ADJ.: caressing. **-zatóre**, M., **-zatríce**, F.: caresser; flatterer. **-zévole**, ADJ.: flattering.

accarnáre†, **-níre**†, TR.: pierce (into the flesh of).

accarpionáre [*carpione*], TR.: cook like carps.

accartoccláre [*cartoccio*], TR.: wrap up in a cornet; curl up.

acca-saménto, M.: wedding (marriage). ‖**-sáre** [*casa*], TR.: wed; REFL.: marry; begin housekeeping; build (houses)†.

accascáre†, INTR.: chance (happen).

acca-sciaménto, M.: debility; decay. ‖**-sciáre** [?], TR.: weaken (debilitate); REFL.: become feeble (by age, etc.) or dejected; decay.

accastelláre [*castello*], TR.: arrange in a pyramid; fortify†; provide with a forecastle†.

accatar-raménto†, M.: catarrh; cold. ‖**-ráre**, INTR.: contract a catarrh. **-ratúra**, F. = *-ramento*.

accata-staménto, M.: piling up. ‖**-stáre** [*catasta*], TR.: pile up.

accat-tabrighe [*briga*], M.: (*indecl.*) quarrelsome fellow (brawler). **-taménto**†, M.: begging. **-ta-pane**†, M.: beggar. ‖**-táre** [L. *captare*, take], TR., INTR.: ask alms (of); beg; borrow; get. **-tatóre**, M.: beggar. **-tatózzi**†, M.: professional beggar. **-tería**, F.: borrowing; begging. **-tíno**, M.: one asking for alms (alms-collector). **accátto**, M.: loan; sum collected; gain: *pigliar ad* —, borrow. **-tòlica** (*all'* —), ADV.: beggingly; by way of borrowing. **-tóne**, M.: vile beggar; impostor. **-tonággio**, M.: professional begging (beggary).

accaval-cáre†, TR.: mount upon. ‖**-ciáre**] *cavallo*], TR.: stand astraddle of (straddle); span. **-cióne** or **-cióni**, ADV.: astride: *stare* —, be mounted. **-laménto**, M.: skipping over, omission; superposing. **-láre**, TR.: skip (a stich in knitting), pass over; superpose. **-latúra,** F.: omission (skipping); superposition.

accaviglíare [*caviglia*], TR.: wind (on bobbins).

acce-caménto, M.: blindness; error; obstruction. ||**-cáre** [*cieco*], TR.: blind, dim; INTR. become blind; tarnish. **-catóre,** M.: blinder; deceiver. **-catúra,** F.: blinding; cavity.

accèdere [L.], TR.: draw near (approach).

acceffáre†, TR.: seize (with the teeth).

accéggia†, F.: woodcock.

accele-raménto, M.: acceleration; swiftness (haste). ||**-ráre** [*celere*], TR.: accelerate (speed); REFL.: make haste. ADV.: swiftly (in a hurry). **-ratívo,** ADJ.: accelerating. **-ratóre,** M., **-ratríce,** F.: accelerator. **-razióne,** *f.:* acceleration (speed).

accèn-dere [L. (*candere*, shine)], IRR.§; TR.: kindle (light, set on fire); inCENSE (excite); REFL.: kindle (catch fire). **-díbile,** ADJ.: that may be kindled (inflammable, combustible). **-diménto**†, M.: kindling (setting on fire). **-ditóio,** M.: lighting-stick. **-ditóre,** M.: kindler (inflamer).

§ Pret. *accé-si, -se; -sero.* Part. *-céso.*

ac-cennáre, TR.: make a sign to (nod to); beckon; indicate; hint; feign (pretend). **-cennatúra**†, F.: nodding. ||**-cénno** [*cenno*], M.: sign (nod).

ac-censíbile, ADJ.: inflammable (combustible). **-censióne,** F.: burning (conflagration). **-cènso** [poet. for *-ceso*, part. of *-cendere*], kindled (inflamed).

ac-centáre, TR.: accent. **-centáto,** PART.: accented. **-centatúra,** F.: accentuation. ||**-cènto** [L. *ac-centus* (*canere*, sing)], M.: accent; tone; voice; (*mus.*) expression.

accentráre [*centro*], TR.: concentrate (center).

accen-tuáre [*-to*], TR.: accentuate. **-tuáto,** ADJ.: accentuated; pronounced. **-tuazióne,** F.: accentuation.

accer-chiaménto, M.: encircling. ||**-chiáre** [*cerchio*], TR.: encircle (encompass); hoop.

accerító [? *cera*], ADJ.: red-faced (flushed).

accer-tamento, M.: ASSURANCE; ascertainment (confirmation). **-táre** [*certo*], TR.: make certain (assure); ascertain. **-tataménte**†, ADV.: assuredly.

ac-cesaménte†, ADV.: ardently. ||**-céso,** PART. of *-cendere.*

acces-síbile, ADJ.: accessible (approachable). **-sibilità,** F.: accessibility. **-sióne,** F.: accession; access; fit. ||**accèsso** [*accedere*], M.: access (approach, road); fit; suffrage. **-sòrio,** M.: accessory. **-soriaménte,** ADV.: accessorily.

acces-timénto, M.: tufting. ||**-tíre** [*cesto*], TR.: tuft.

accétta [old *accia* = *azza*], F.: HATCHET; *fatto coll'* —, rough-hewn.

accet-tábile, ADJ.: acceptable. **-tabilità,** F.: acceptability. ||**-táre** [L. *acceptare* (*capere*, take)], TR.: accept (receive).

accettáta [*accetta*], F.: blow of the hatchet.

accet-tatóre, M., **-tatríce** [*-tare*], F.: accepter. **-tazióne,** F.: acceptation; acceptance. **-tévole,** ADJ.: acceptable (agreeable).

accettíno or **-na,** *dim.* of *accetta.*

accezióne [L. *ac-ceptio*], F.: acceptation (of a meaning).

acche-taménto, M.: quieting (calming). ||**-táre** [*chetare*], TR.: quiet (hush; appease, calm).

acchiap-páre [*chiappa*], TR.: snatch (catch, seize); cheat (trick). **-patèllo** or **-parèllo,** M.: artifice (catch).

acchináre† = *chinare.*

acchiocciolàre [*chiocciola*], TR.: wind (twist like 'snail'); cause to crouch or squat; REFL.: squat; sit cowering; cuddle up.

ac=chiúdere†, TR.: enCLOSE. **-chiúsi**†, *pret.* **-chiúso**†, *part.*

áccia [L. *acia*], F.: thread (in skeins).

acciabat-taménto, M.: botching (bungling). ||**-táre** [*ciabatta*], TR.: cobble (botch, fix carelessly). **-tío,** M.: frequent botching. **-tóne,** M., **-tóna,** F.: botcher.

acciac-caménto, M.: squashing. ||**-cáre** [*-co*], TR.: squash (bruise, pound). **-cáta,** F.: squashing. **-catúra,** F.: squashing.

acciaccináre [? ak. to L. *agere*, act], REFL.: bestir (busy) one's self, work hurriedly.

acciácco [? *ciacco*], M.: illness (indisposition); misfortune.

accia-iáre, TR.: convert into steel; tip with steel. **-iatúra,** F.: conversion into steel; steeling. **-iería,** F.: steel-works. ||**acciá-io** [L. *acies*, sharp edge], M.: steel; sword†. **-iolíno,** M.: small file; steel-bead (for lady's dress). **-i(u)òlo,** M.: file; steel (for sharpening knives).

acciambelláre [*ciambella*], TR.: form into a cake.

acciappináre [?], REFL.: act hastily, be angry.

ac-ciaríno, M.: steel (to strike fire with). ||**-ciáro** [*-ciaio*], M.: (*poet.*) steel; sword.

acciar-paménto, M.: botching. ||**-páre** [*ciarpa*], TR.: do slovenly (botch). **-pataménte,** ADV.: slovenly. **-patóre,** M.: botcher. **-pío,** M.: botching. **-póne,** M., **-póna,** F.: botcher.

acci-dentále, ADJ.: accidental. **-dentalità,** F.: accidentality. **-dental-**

ménte, ADV.: accidentally. **-dentáto**, M.: apoplectic fit; stroke. ‖**-dènte** [L. *-dens, -dent-* (*cadere*, fall)], M.: accident (chance; mishap; property of a word); apoplectic fit. **-dentúccio**†, M.: little accident.

accí-dia [Gr. *a-kedía*, carelessness], F.: indolence (idleness, sloth). **-diosaménte**, ADV.: lazily (idly). **-dióso**, ADJ.: indolent (idle, lazy); M.: sluggard.

acci-gliaménto, M.: gloom; sadness. ‖**-gliáre** [*ciglio*], REFL.: knit one's brows (frown); look sullen or gloomy. **-gliataménte**, ADV.: sullenly; sadly. **-gliáto**, ADJ.: sullen; gloomy; sad. **-gliatúra**, F.: sullenness; gloom. **-glionáre**, TR.: provide with brows.

accí-gnere† = *accingere*. **-gniménto**†, M.: preparation.

accileccáre [*cilecca*], TR.: mock (delude); tantalize; flatter.

accincignáre [*incignare*], TR.: rumple.

ac-cíngere [L. *cingere*], IRR. (cf. *c.*); REFL.: gird up one's loins; prepare one's self; set about. **-cinto**, PART.: girt; prepared (ready).

acciò [*a ciò*], CONJ.: to the end that; that. **-cchè** [*che*], or — **che**, CONJ.: in order that.

acciotto-láre [*ciottolo*], TR.: pave with pebbles; clatter. **-latúra**, F.: stone paving.

acciroondáre†, TR.: surround.

accismáre†, TR.: cut asunder.

acciuffáre [*ciuffo*], TR.: take by the hair; catch.

acciúga [?], F.: anchovy.

accivettá-re [*civetta*], TR.: (*hunt.*) lure (birds) with the owl; entice (seduce). **-to**, PART.: excited; ADJ.: tried; cautious.

acci-viménto†, M.: provision. **-víre**†, TR.: provide.

accla-máre [L. (*clamare*, call)], INTR.: acclaim (shout applause); TR.: acclaim; elect by acclamation. **-mazióne**, F.: acclamation (acclaim).

acclimáre or **-matáre** [*clima*], TR.: acclimate, -matise.

acclináre†, **-no**† = *inclináre, -no*.

acclí-ve [*clivo*], ADJ.: declivous (sloping). **-vitá**, F.: acclivity.

ac-clúdere [L. (*claudere*, CLOSE)], IRR. §; TR.: enclose. **-clúso**, *part.* **-clusa**, F.: enclosed letter.

§ Pret. *acclú-si, -se; -sero.* Part. *acclúso.*

accoccáre [*cocca*], TR.: fix (the thread) on the spindle; adjust, give (a blow, etc.); strike; cheat, †fix: *accoccarla a uno*, cheat, entrap one.

accoccoláre [Sp. *acloear* (ak. to *cluck*)], REFL.: sit, squat; stoop down.

acco-daménto, M.: tying together. ‖**-dáre** [*coda*], TR.: tie (horses, etc.) together by the tail; REFL.: tie one's self to (follow closely). **-datúra**, F.: tying together.

ac-coglièmza, F.: reception (welcome). ‖**=cògliere**, IRR.; TR.: receive (welcome); accept (approve, consent to); COLLECT (assemble); INTR.: happen; REFL.: assemble (meet). **-coglimentáccio**†, M.: cool reception. **-coglimènto**†, M.: gathering (assemblage); reception. **-coglitíccio**†, M.: picking up. **-coglitóre**†, M.: gatherer.

accòlito [Gr. *akólouthos*, following], M.: acolyte.

accol-láre [*collo*], TR.: put on the back ("neck"), load; yoke; REFL.: take charge of. **-latário**, M.: public contractor. **-latúra**, F.: upper part of a dress. **accòl-lo**, M.: load (on the neck of a beast of burden); contract.

accòlta [*-cogliere*], F.: assembly.

accoltel-lánte†, M.: stabber. ‖**-láre** [*coltello*], TR.: stab. **-latóre**, M.: stabber; gladiator.

accòlto, PART. of *cogliere*.

acco-mánda†, F.: trust; share. **-mandánte**, M.: sleeping partner (shareholder). ‖**-mandáre**† [L. *mandare*, intrust], TR.: RECOMMEND; give in charge; fasten. **-mandatário**, M.: trustee; agent. **-mandígia**, F.: trust; protection (guardianship). **-mándita**, F.: partnership; stock company.

accomandoláre [*comandolo*], TR.: tie up (the broken thread in a warp).

accomiatáre [*comiato*], TR.: dismiss (let go); bid good-bye; REFL.: take one's leave.

accomignoláre†, TR.: join like the rafters of a roof; combine.

accomo-dábile, ADJ.: accommodable (adjustable). **-daménto**, M.: accommodation (adjustment); agreement. ‖**-dáre** [*comodo*], TR.: accommodate (adjust, arrange); compromise; suit (please); REFL.: conform one's self; come to an agreement; make one's self comfortable (sit down): *la s' accomodi*, please be seated. **-dataménte**, ADV.: suitably (justly); seasonably. **-datívo**, ADJ.: suitable; seasonable. **-dáto**, ADJ.: adapted; convenient (suitable). **-datóre**, M., **-datríce**, F.: accommodator (fitter); F.: tire-woman (milliner). **-datúra**, F.: adjustment; agreement. **-dazióne**†, F.: accommodation (adjustment). **-devolménte**†, ADV.: conveniently.

accompa-gnábile, ADJ.: that may be accompanied or matched. **-gnaménto**, M.: accompaniment; suite (retinue). ‖**-gnáre** [*compagno*], TR.: accompany (attend, escort); join with (match); REFL.: accompany one's self; join one's self; marry. **-*gn*atóre,** M., **-*gn*atríce,** F.: accompanist; companion (attendant). **-*gn*atúra,** F.: accompaniment; train.

accomu-naménto, M.: community; participation. ‖**-náre** [*comune*], TR.: make common (put in common); REFL.: make one's self familiar; mingle freely (with people); accompany.

accon-ciézza, F.: suitableness; finery. **-ciaménte,** ADJ.: properly. **-ciaménto,** M.: adjustment; skill. ‖**-ciáre** [p. L. **comptiare* (L. *comere*, *co-emere*, put together)], TR.: fit (together); set in order; adorn (deck); settle; reconcile†; marry†; (*cook.*) preserve†; REFL.: adapt one's self; deck one's self; settle; go in service: *—ragioni*, settle disputed accounts; *—rsi dell' anima*, prepare for death. **-ciatamente†,** ADV.: properly. **-ciatóre,** M.: adjuster; hair-dresser. **-ciatríce,** F.: tire-woman (milliner). **-ciatúra,** F.: adornment, head-dress: *perdere l' —*, be frustrated (miss one's aim). **-cime,** M.: repair.

accón-cio, ADJ.: adapted (fitted); opportune; ADV.: suitably: *in —*, suitably, seasonably; M.†: convenience; gain.

accondiscéndere† = *condiscendere*.

acconigliáre†, TR.: draw up (the oars).

acconsen-timénto†, M.: consent. ‖**-tíre** [*consentire*], TR.: consent or agree to (approve).

accontáre†, TR.: balance (level); (fill up).

accónto [*conto*], M.: part paid.

accoppáre [*coppa*], TR.: give a death-blow to (on the 'head,' knock down).

accop-piábile, ADJ.: matchable. **-piaménto,** M.: coupling (copulation, match). ‖**-piáre** [*coppia*], TR.: couple (join, yoke, match): REFL.: form a couple (pair); walk two by two. **-piatóre,** M.: coupler; match-maker. **-piatúra,** F.: coupling; (pairing).

acco-raménto, M.: affliction (grief). ‖**-ráre** [*core*], IRR.†§; TR.: grieve (to the 'heart'), afflict; REFL.: be deeply grieved. **-ratòio,** ADJ.†: heart-rending; M.: knife for killing hogs. **-razióne†,** F.: grief.

§ †Pr. *accuòro*, etc.: *uò*, where accented.

accor-ciábile, ADJ.: that may be shortened. **-ciaménto,** M.: shortening (contraction). ‖**-ciáre** [*corto*], TR.: shorten (CURTail, abridge); contract; REFL.: grow short (decrease, shrink). **-ciataménte†,** ADJ.: briefly (in a word). **-ciatívo,** ADJ.: shortening. **-ciatúra** = *-ciamento*.

accor-dábile, ADJ.: that may be accorded; agreeable. **-daménto,** M.: accordance (accord, agreement). **-dánte,** ADJ.: accordant (agreeing, harmonious). **-dánza,** F.: accordance. ‖**-dáre** [L. *cor*, HEART], TR.: accord (make agree, reconcile; grant); tune; REFL.: agree; harmonize (be in tune). **-dataménte,** ADV.: harmoniously; unanimously. **-datóre,** M.: reconciler (peace-maker); tuner. **-datríce,** F.: mediatrix. **-datúra,** F.: accord; consonance (harmony). **-dévole†,** ADJ.: agreeable. **accòr-do,** M.: accord (harmony); agreement; (compact): *essere d' —*, be agreed (agree); harmonize; *mettere d' —*, reconcile.

accòr-gere [L. *ad*, *cor-rigere*, correct], IRR.§; REFL.: infer (conclude); discover (perceive, observe). **-giménto,** M.: sagacity (providence, prudence).

§ Pret. *accòr-si*, *-se*; *-sero*. Part. *accòrto*.

accòrre, *abbrev.* of *accogliere*.

ac-córrere, IRR.; INTR.: run or hasten to; run after (pursue): *accorr'uomo!* help! **-córsi,** PRET. of *-correre* or *-corgere*. **-córso,** PART. of *-correre*.

accortaménte [*corto*], ADV.: prudently; cunningly

accortáre† = *accorciare*.

ac-cortézza, F.: prudence; sagacity (cunning). ‖**-còrto** [*-corgere*], PART.: perceived, etc.; ADJ.: prudent (provident); wary (cunning): *male —*, imprudent; *fare —*, warn, advise; *star —*, be attentive.

accosciáre [*coscia*], REFL.: squat; cower.

acco-staménto, M.: approach (access). **-stánte,** ADJ.: approaching (near); nearly like; pliant (supple): *persona —*, near relative. ‖**-stáre** [*costa*], TR.: ACCOST (approach); bring near; be like; REFL.: approach (draw near); conform or ally one's self. **-statúra,** F.: approach; connection. **-stévole†,** ADJ.: of easy approach.

accòs-to, PREP. or ADV.: beside; near (close to). **-tolatúra,** F.: wrinkle (crease).

accostu-mánza†, F.: custom; practice. ‖**-máre** [*costume*], TR.†: accustom (inure); REFL.: accustom or inure one's self. **-mataménte†,** ADV.: usually. **-máto,** ADJ.: accustomed (customary, usual); civil.

accoto-náre [*cotone*], TR.: raise the nap of.

accovac-ciáre [*covaccio*], REFL.: lie down in a lair; cower down; crouch. **-cioláre,** REFL.: nestle (squat down).

accovonáre [*covone*], TR.: bind up in sheaves.

accoz-zábile, ADJ.: that may be gathered. **-zágl̤ia,** F.: congregation (mass, mob). **-zaménto,** M.: gathering (collection, mass). ‖**-záre** [*cozzo*], TR.: throw together (join indiscreetly); gather; REFL.: congregate (gather). **-zatóre,** M.: gatherer. **accòz-zo,** M.: gathering (crowd).

accredi-táre [*credito*], TR.: accredit.

-táto, ADJ.: accredited; authorized; worthy.

ac-creşcènza†, F.: increase. ‖**=créşcere**, IRR.; TR.: INCREASE (augment). **-creşciménto**, M.: increase (growth). **-creşcitivaménte**, ADV.: increasingly. **-creşcitívo**, ADJ.: increasing. **-creşcitóre**, M.: increaser. **-creşciúto**, PART.: increased (grown).

accrespáre†, TR.: crisp (curl).

accuc-ciáre [*cuccia*], REFL.: **-cioláre**, REFL.: crouch (lie down).

accudíre [L. *-dere* (*cudere*, forge), join], INTR.: attend (to work); apply one's self.

accu-láre [*culo*], TR.: place with the back against; move back; place; REFL.: rear; sit on the haunches (squat down); take one's lodgings. **-lattáre**, TR.: dump down on the back.

accumu-laménto, M.: accumulation. ‖**-láre** [*cumulo*], TR.: accumulate (heap up). **-latóre**, M., **-latríce**, F.: accumulator. **-lazióne**, F.: accumulation.

accu-rataménte, ADV.: accurately. **-ratézza**, F.: accuracy; diligence. ‖**-ráto** [*cura*], ADJ.: accurate (careful).

accú-şa, F.: accusation (charge). **-şábile**, ADJ.: accusable. **-şaménto**, M.: accusation. **-şánte**, M., F.: accuser. ‖**-şáre** [L. (*causa*, CAUSE)], TR.: accuse (impeach); reproach; confess (i.e. accuse one's self); acknowledge (a letter); own; REFL.: accuse or blame one's self; confess. **-şatívo**, M.: accusative (case). **-şatóre**, M., **-şatóra**, F.: accuser. **-şatòrio**, ADJ.: accusatory. **-şatríce**, F.: accuser. **-şazióne†**, F.: accusation. **-şánza†**, F.: imputation.

acèfalo [Gr. *a-*, not, *kephalé*, head], ADJ.: acephalous.

acer-baménte, ADV.: with acerbity (sharply); prematurely. **-bétto**, ADJ.: sourish (tartish). **-bézza**, F.: acerbity (asperity); tartness. **-bità**, F.: acerbity (asperity). ‖**acèr-bo** [L. *-bus* (*acer*, sharp)], ADJ.: acerb (sour); harsh (severe).

ácero [L. *acer*], M.: maple-tree.

acèrrimo [sup. of *acre*], ADJ.: most sour.

acertèllo [?], M.: kestrel (hawk).

acèrvo†, M.: heap (pile).

ace-tábolo, **-tábulo**, M.: vinegar cruet. **-táto**, ADJ.: acid (sour); tart. **-tificazióne**, F.: acetification. **-tíre†**, become acid (sour). ‖**acé-to** [L. *-tum* (*acer*, sharp)], M.: VINEGAR. **-tósa**, F.: acid drink; sorrel (plant). **-tosèlla**, F.: wild sorrel (plant). **-tosità**, F.: acidity. **-tóso**, ADJ.: acetous (acid, sourish).

Acherón-te, F.: Acheron (river in the Nether World); infernal regions. **-tèo**, ADJ.: Acherontic (infernal).

Achille, M.: Achilles.

aci-détto, *dim.* of *-do.* **-dézza**, F.: acidity. **-dificáre**, TR.: acidify. **-dificazióne**, F.: acidification. **-díno**, ADJ.: sourish. **-dità**, F.: acidity. ‖**áci-do** [L. *-dus* (root *ac-*, be sharp)], ADJ.: acid (sour, tart); M.: acid. **-duláre**, TR.: acidulate. **ací-dulo**, ADJ.: slightly acid (sourish). **-dúme**, M.: acid matter.

áci-no [L. *-nus*], M.: grape-stone. **-nóso†**, ADJ.: full of grape-stones.

acònito [L. *-tum*], M.: aconite (plant).

acotilèdone [Gr. *a-*, not, *kotyledón*, cup-shaped], ADJ.: acotyledonous.

ác-qua [L. *aqua*], F.: water; rain: — *cedrata*, lemonade; — *concia*, perfumed water; — *dolce*, fresh water; — *di latte*, buttermilk; whey; — *morta*, stagnant water; — *pazza*, diluted wine; — *rosa* (or *rosata*), rose-water; — *viva*, spring water; *far* —, (*nav.*) leak. **-quacchiáre†**, REFL.: hide one's self. **-quáccia**, F.: *disp.* of *-qua:* bad (muddy, putrid) water. **-quacedratáio** [*cedro*, citron], M.: (ambulant) vender of drinks (as lemonades, etc.). **-quagliáre**, TR.: curdle. **-quáio**, M.: water-pipe (conduit); draining ditch; sink; greed. **-quaiòlo**, M., **-quaiòla**, F.: water-vender; ADJ.: aquatic. **-quamarína**, F.: aquamarine (gem). **-qua=pendènte†**, M.: declivity. **-qua=pèndere**, INTR.: slope towards the water, be declivous; M.: declivity. **-quáre†**, TR.: water; (*nav.*) take in water. **-quarèllo** = *-querello.*

acquartie-raménto, M.: lodging. ‖**-ráre** [*quartiere*], TR.: provide with quarters or lodging (lodge).

acqu- [*acqua*]: **=arzènto†**, M.: brandy. **-astríno†**. M.: marsh (bog); ADJ.: marshy. **-áta**, F.: heavy shower; (*nav.*) water-supply. **-ático**, ADJ.: aquatic. **-átile**, ADJ.: aquatic (watery). **-áto†**, PART.: watered.

acquattáre [*quatto*], REFL.: squat (cower).

acqua=víte, F.: brandy. **-zzóne**, M.: heavy burst of rain. **-zzóso†**, ADJ.: rainy.

acque- [*acqua*]: **-dótto** [L. *ductus*, led], M.: aqueduct. **´-o**, ADJ.: aqueous (watery). **-réccia**, F.: ewer; basin. **-rèlla**, F.: light rain; water-colours†. **-relláre**, TR.: paint in water-colours. **-rèllo**, M.: aquarelle (painting in water-colours); watery or diluted wine†. **-rúgiola**, F.: drizzling rain.

acquetáre, poet. for *acquietare.*

acquétta [*acqua*], F.: light shower; poison.

acqui- [*acqua*]: **-cèlla**, F.: light rain. **-dóccio** [*ducere*, lead], M.: drain (water-conduit); AQUEDUCT†. **-dóso**†, ADJ.: aqueous: humid (damp). **-dótto** = *aquedotto*. **-drinóso**† = *acquitrinoso*.

acquie-scènza, F.: acquiescence. **-taménto**, M.: quieting; quiet (tranquillity). ||**-táre** [L. *quietus*, QUIET], TR.: quiet (calm, appease, pacify).

acqui-rènte [L. *-rere* (*quærere*, seek), acquire], M.: acquirer (buyer). **-síre**, TR.: acquire (purchase). **-sitívo**, ADJ.: entitling (to acquire or possess). **-síto**, ADJ.: acquired; M.: acquisition. **-stábile**, ADJ.: acquirable (obtainable). **-staménto**†, M.: acquest (purchase). **-stáre**, TR.: acquire (purchase); †conquer. **-statóre**, M.: purchaser. **-stévole**, ADJ.: acquirable. **-sto**, M.: acquisition (purchase).

acqu-itríno, M.: marsh (bog). **-itrinóso**, ADJ.: marshy (boggy). **-olína**, F.: light rain. **-ositá**, F.: aquosity (wateriness). ||**-óso** [*acqua*], ADJ.: aqueous (watery).

á-cre [L. *acer*], ADJ.: acrid (pungent, sharp, harsh). **-crèdine**, F.: acrimony (sharpness). **-creménte**, ADV.: sharply (harshly). **-crézza**, F.: sharpness. **-crimònia**, F.: acrimony (sharpness). **-mònico**†, ADJ.: acrimonious.

acrò-bata [Gr. *ákros*, high, *báinein*, go], M.: acrobat. **-baticaménte**, ADV.: acrobatically. **-bático**, ADJ.: acrobatic.

acromático [Gr. *a-*, not, *chrôma*, colour], ADJ.: achromatic.

acròpoli [Gr. *-lis*], F.: acropolis (high citadel).

acròstico [Gr. *ákros*, extreme, *stíchos*, line], M.: acrostic.

acrotèrio [Gr. *ákros*, high], M.: acroterium (pedestal).

a-cuíre [L. *acus*, sharp point], TR.; sharpen (whet). **-cuitá**†, **-cuitáde**†, **-cuitáte**†, F.: acuteness (sharpness). **-cúleo**, M.: goad (sting); prickle. **-cúme**, M.: acumen; sharp point†. **-cumináre**, TR.: sharpen.

acústica [Gr. *akoúein*, hear], F.: acoustics.

acu-taménte, ADJ.: acutely (sharply). **-t=ángolo**, ADJ.: with acute angles. **-tézza**, F.: acuteness (sharpness, wit). ||**-to** [L. *acus*, sharp point], ADJ.: acute (pointed, sharp; shrill). **-ziángolo**† = *-tangolo*.

ad [L.], PREP.: for *a* before vowel sound.

ad-aquaménto, M.: watering (irrigation). ||**=acquáre**, TR.: water; irrigate. **-acquatúra**, F.: watering.

ad-agiare, TR.: place gently or with care; lay down; make comfortable; REFL.: lie down (comfortably). **-agiáto**†, ADJ.: laid down; comfortable (easy); in an easy position. **-agíno**, ADJ.: very gently or softly. ||**=ágio**, ADV.: slowly; gently; leisurely.

adamánte [Gr. *-mas*], M.: diamond. **-tino**, ADJ.: adamantine.

Adá-mo, M.: Adam. **-mítico**, ADJ.: Adamitic.

adasperáre†, TR.: exasperate.

adastáre†, TR.: hasten.

ad-astiaménto†, M.: spite; envy. ||**=astiáre**, TR.: envy.

adat-tábile, ADJ.: adaptable. **-tabilitá**, F.: adaptability. **-taménto**, M.: **-tánza**†, F.: adaptation. ||**-táre** [L. *aptus*, apt], TR.: ADAPT (adjust, fit, accommodate). **-tazióne**†, F.: adaptation. **-táto**, ADJ.: adapted (fit, proper); skilful. **adát-to**, ADJ.: apt (fit).

ad=dáre, IRR.; REFL.: addict one's self; perceive.

addaziáre [*dazio*], TR.: subject to toll or duty.

ad-debitáre, TR.: indebt; impute. ||**=débito**, M.: imputation.

addebolíre†, **-bilire**† = *indebolire*.

addecimáre†, TR.: TITHE.

adden-saménto, M.: thickening. ||**-sáre** [*denso*], make dense (thicken).

adden-táre [*dente*], TR.: seize with the teeth (bite). **-tatúra**, F.: seizing with the teeth; notch. **-telláre**, TR.: indent (dovetail); provide with toothing-stones. **-telláto**, M.: toothing-stone; cornerstone.

ad=déntro, ADV.: inwardly; within. **-dentráre**, REFL.: ENTER (into).

adde-strábile, ADJ.: teachable. **-straménto**, M.: preparing (instruction). ||**-stráre** [*destro*], make skilful (drill, instruct; prepare); break in (a horse); REFL.: practice (exercise). **-stratóre**†, M.: teacher; gentleman usher; groom.

addétto [*addire*], ADJ.: assigned; pertaining; attached.

addì or *a dì*: 'at the day'; date.

addiacciáre†, etc. = *agghiacciare*, etc.

addiacènte†, ADJ.: adjacent.

ad=dietro, ADV.: behind; backwards: *per l'* —, formerly (heretofore); *essere — con*, be behind in; *dare* —, go backwards; *mettere* —, neglect; *tenere* —, hold back (retard).

addimand. .† = *addomand*. .

addimest. .† = *addomest*. .

ad=dío, ADV.: ADIEU (farewell).

addíre [L. *ad-decere*], REFL.: be proper or suitable; become (suit).

addirimpetto†, PREP.: over against.

ad=dirittúra, ADV.: directly; openly; absolutely.

addiriz-zaménto, M.: straightening; direction. ||**-záre** [*diritto*], TR.: make straight (straighten); set right (correct); instruct; raise†; direct†, apply†; dedicate; REFL.: become straight (straighten out); mend. **-zatóio**, M.: bodkin (to dress the hair). **-zatóre**, M., **-zatríce**, F.: straightener; arranger. **-zatúra**, F.: straightening (correcting); parting of the hair.

addi-taménto, M.: pointing out. ||**-táre** [*dito*], TR.: point out (indicate). **-tatóre**, M.: pointer out (indicator).

addítto†, ADJ.: assigned; dedicated; destined.

addiveníre† = *avvenire*.

addi-zionále, ADJ.: additional. **-zionáre**, TR.: add together (sum up). **-zióne** [L. *ad-dere*, ADD], F.: addition.

addob-baménto, M.: ornament; attire. **-báre** [?], TR.: adorn (deck, decorate); adapt. **-batóre**, M.: ornamenter. **addòb-bo**, M.: decoration (finery); ornamental furniture.

addocilíre [*docile*], TR.: render docile; soften.

addogáre†, TR.: stripe.

addol-cáre [*dolco*], TR.: soften (turn mild). **-ciménto**, M.: sweetening (softening). **-círe** [*dolce*], TR.: sweeten (soften); alleviate; content. **-citívo**, ADJ.: softening; lenitive.

addoloráre [*dolore*], TR.: afflict; torment; REFL.: be afflicted (grieve).

addomand..† = *domand..*

addòme [L. *abdomen*], M.: ABDOMEN.

addomesti-cábile, ADJ.: that may be domesticated (tamable). **-caménto**, M.: domesticating (taming). ||**-cáre** [*domestico*], TR.: domesticate (tame); cultivate; civilize; soften; familiarize: — *con*, be domesticated, etc.; grow familiar. **-cáto**, ADJ.: domesticated (tame); familiar. **-catóre**, M.: tamer. **-catúra**, F.: domestication (taming); civilizing. **-chíre**, TR.: render less rough (soften); domesticate.

ad-dominále, ADJ.: abdominal. ||**-dòmine** = *-dome*.

addoppáre [*dopo*], REFL.: hide one's self behind.

addop-piaménto, M.: doubling. ||**-piáre** [*doppio*], TR.: double, †redouble; fold. **-piatóre**, M., **-piatóra**, F.: one who doubles. **-piatúra**, F.: (re)doubling.

addormen-táre [*addormire*], TR.: put to sleep (lull); make drowsy or lazy; assuage; REFL.: go to sleep; be benumbed; die: *-tarsi nel Signore*, die in the Lord (die in peace). **-táto**, ADJ.: sleepy (drowsy); lazy. **-tatóre**, M.: one that lulls asleep; tiresome person; opiate.

addormíre†, REFL.: fall asleep.

ad-dossaménto, M.: burdening; burden (charge). **-dossáre**, TR.: load upon one's back (load, charge); REFL.: take upon one's shoulder, or upon one's self; take charge of. ||**=dòsso**, ADV.: upon (one's) back; upon or about (one); at: *abbaiare* —, bark at; *dare* —, fall upon; assail; accuse; *mettere* —, charge with (impute); *mettere le mani* —, lay hold of, apprehend; *porre gli occhi* —*r a*, cast an eye upon; *dare* — *a*, assail; harm, wrong; accuse.

addótto, PART. of *addurre*.

addotto-raménto, M.: making a doctor. ||**-ráre** [*dottore*], TR.: make or create a doctor; doctor; (*iron.*) doctor (= teach evil). **-ráto**, ADJ.: created doctor.

addottri-naménto, M.: instruction; erudition. ||**-náre** [*dottrinare*], TR.: instruct (teach); REFL.: study. **-natamente**, ADV.: learnedly. **-náto**, ADJ.: instructed; learned. **-natúra**†, F.: learning.

addrappelláre†, TR.: form in line of battle.

addr(i)ètto† = *addietro*.

adduáre†, TR.: couple.

ad=dúcere [L.] = *addurre*. **-ducíbile**, ADJ.: adducible.

adduráre = *indurare*.

ad-dúrre [L. *ad-ducere*], IRR.§; TR.: bring (on); produce; convey; cite; allege. **-dússi**, *pret.* **-duttóre**, M.: abductor.

§ Pret. *addússi, -se; -sero.* Fut. *addurrò.* Cond. *addurrèi.* Part.: *addótto.*

ad-eguaménto, M.: equalizing; evenness. ||**-eguáre** [L. *æquare*, make EQUAL), TR.: equalize (balance); proportion; level. **-eguataménte**, ADJ.: equally; proportionally.

ad-empíbile, ADJ.: feasible. ||**=émpiere** or **=empíre**, IRR.; TR.: fulfil (accomplish, execute). **-empiménto**†, M.: fulfilling. **-empitóre**†, M.: accomplisher. **-empiúto**, ADJ.: fulfilled (accomplished).

adéntro†, ADJ.: entered; ADV.: within.

adequ..† = *adegu..*

aderbáre†, TR.: feed with grass.

ade-rènte [*aderire*], ADJ.: adherent; M.: adherent; favourer. **-rènza**, F.: adherence; attachment.

ad=èrgere, IRR.; TR.: raise up, extol.

ad-eriménto†, M.: adherence. ||**-eríre** [L. *ad-hærere*], INTR.: ADHERE (stick); consent; approve. **-eríto**, ADJ.: attached (to a party, etc.); consented to.

ad-escaménto, M.: bait (allurement). ||**-escáre** [*esca*], TR.: bait (allure, entice). **-escatóre**, M.: allurer.

ad-esióne [*-erire*], F.: adhesion (adherement); consent. **-esívo**, ADJ.: adhesive (adherent). **-èso**, ADJ.: attached.

adèspoto [Gr. *a-* not, *despótes*, master]; ADJ.: without the author's name (said of books, etc.).

adèsso [L. *ad ipsum*, 'at same,' sc. *tem-*

pus, time], ADV.: at the instant; now; always†: *adess'* —, just now, presently.
adia-cènte [L. *jacere*, lie], ADJ.: adjacent (contiguous). **-cènza**, F.: adjacency (nearness).
adiánto [L. *-tus*], M.: maidenhair (fern).
adiettiv.. † = *aggettiv..*
adimáre†, TR.: bring or cast down; bend.
ádi-pe [L. *adeps*], M.: fat (grease). **-posità**, F.: adiposity (fatness). **-póso**, ADJ.: adipose (fat).
adi-raménto, M.: anger. ‖**-ráre** [*ira*], REFL.: grow angry or IRATE. **-rataménte**, ADV.: angrily. **-ráto**, ADJ.: angry.
adíre [L. *ad-ire*, go to], TR.: come into the possession of (an inheritance); inherit.
adiróso†, ADJ.: irascible (hasty).
adí-to, PART. of *adire*. **ádi-to**, M.: access (entry); opportunity.
adiut..†, **adiuv..** = *aiut..*
adizióne [*adire*], F.: accession (to property); inheritance.
adizzáre† = *aizzare*.
adoffáre† = *addobbare*.
adoc-chiaménto, M.: look (glance, gaze). ‖**-chiáre** [*occhio*, eye], TR.: eye (look or stare at).
adole-scènte [L. *-scens*], ADJ.: adolescent; M.: youth; young man. **-scènza**, F.: youth.
adom-braménto, M.: shadowing (umbrage). ‖**-bráre** [*ombra*], TR.: shade; overshadow; obfuscate; blind; shadow forth (sketch, delineate); fancy; suspect; †symbolize. **-brazióne**, F.: adumbration; umbrage; faint sketch.
adonáre†, TR.: subdue; oppress; REFL.: be subdued (be humbled); surrender.
Adóne, M.: Adonis.
ad=onestáre, TR.: make appear honest; palliate.
adónide [*-ne*], F.: adonide (plant).
adon-táre [*onta*], REFL.: be indignant (be offended). **-tóso**†, ADJ.: insulting (offensive).
adop(e)-rábile, ADJ.: that can be used: **-raménto**, M.: use. ‖**-ráre** [*opera*], TR.: make use of (employ); REFL.: exert one's self (endeavour). **-ráto**, ADJ.: used (employed). **-ratóre**†, M.: operator. **-razióne**†, F.: use; exertion.
ado-rábile, ADJ.: adorable. **-rabilità**, F.: adorableness. **-raménto**, M.: adoration. **-ránte**, M.: adorer; worshipper. ‖**-ráre** [L. (*orare*, pray)], TR.: adore, worship. **-ratóre**, M.: adorer; worshipper. **-ratòrio**†, M.: oratory; temple (for idols). **-ratríce**, F.: (female) adorer or worshipper. **-razióne**, F.: adoration (worship).
adordináre†, REFL.: prepare one's self.
adorezzáre, INTR.: be shady.
ador-nábile, ADJ.: that may be adorned. **-naménte**, ADV.: elegantly; neatly. **-naménto**, M.: adornment (ornament). ‖**-náre** [*ornare*], TR.: adorn (deck, embellish). **-nataménte**, ADV.: in an ornamental manner (elegantly). **-náto**, ADJ.: adorned; M.†: adornments. **-natóre**, M.: adorner.
adot-taménto, M.: adoption. **-tánte**, ADJ.: adopting; M.: adopter. ‖**-táre** [cf. *ottare*], TR.: ADOPT. **-(ta†)tívo**, ADJ.: adoptive. **-zióne**, F.: adoption.
adovrare† = *adoprare*.
adro† = *atro*.
adug-giaménto, M.: blighting shade. ‖**-giare** [*uggia*], TR.: overshade; blight.
adugnare† = *augnare*.
adu-lánte, ADJ.: flattering (adulatory): †flatterer. ‖**-láre** [L. *-lari*], TR.: flatter. **-latóre**, M.: flatness. **-latòrio**, ADJ.: adulatory (flattering). **-latríce**, F.: flatterer. **-lazióne**, F.: adulation (flattery).
adulte-raménto, M.: adulteration. **-rare**, TR.: adulterate; falsify; †INTR.: commit adultery. **-ratóre**, M.; adulterer. **-ratríce**, F.: adulteress. **-razióne**, F.: adulteration (corruption); forgery. **-rino**, ADJ.: adulterine; counterfeit. **adultèrio**, M.: adultery. ‖**adúlte-ro** [L. *ad* to, *ulter* for *alter*, another], ADJ.: adulterous; M.†: adulterer.
adúlto [L. *-tus* (*ad-olescere*, grow)], ADJ.: adult (grown up).
adu-naménto, M.: uniting (assembling); collection **-nánza**, F.: meeting (assembly). ‖**-náre** [L. *ad*, to *unus*, one], TR.: UNITE (bring together, assemble, convoke); REFL.: come together (assemble, meet). **-náta**, F.: assembly (meeting). **-natóre**, M.: collector. **-nazióne**†, F.: union (collection).
ad-uncáre†, TR.: bend into a hook (curve). ‖**-únco** [L. *uncus*, hook], ADJ.: aduncous (hooked).
adúnque [L. *ad tunc*], CONJ.: then, therefore.
adu-stáre†, TR.: scorch. **-stézza**†, F.: scorching, dryness. **-stivaménte**†, ADV.: scorchingly; in a dry manner. **-stívo**†, ADJ.: scorching; dry. ‖**adú-sto** [L. *-stus* (*urere*, burn)], ADJ.: adust (scorched, burnt).
áe-re [L. *aer*], M.: (*poet.*) AIR, wind. **-reáto**†, ADJ.: aired. **aè-reo**, ADJ.: aerial. **-reolíto** or **-reòlito** [*lithos*, stone], M.: aerolite. **-r(e)onáuta** [Gr. *naútes*, navigator], M.: aeronaut. **-reonáutica**, F.: aeronautics. **-reonáutico**, ADJ.: aeronautic(al). **-reòstato** [Gr. *statós*, placed], M.: aerostat (balloon).

'-rimanzía, -romanzía [Gr. manteía, divination], F.: aeromancy. -ro., cf. -reo., -réoo, ADJ.: airy; sprightly; polite.
aescáre† = adescare.
af- for Lat. ad, 'to,' in composition.
á-fa [? Gr. haphé, kindling], F.: sultry or suffocating heat (sultriness): fare —, annoy, tire, disgust. -fáto, ADJ.: withered (blighted); weak. -fatúccio†, ADJ.: languid (sickly).
afèlio [Gr. apó, from, hélios, sun], M.: aphelion.
afèresi [Gr. apó, from, airein, take], M.: aphaeresis.
affábi-le [L. fari, speak], ADJ.: affable (easy of approach). -lità, F.: affability. -lménte, ADV.: affably (courteously).
affaccen-daménto, M.: busy occupation (diligence). ‖-dáre [faccenda], REFL.: be very busy (hustle about). -dáto, ADJ.: very busy; occupied. -dóna, F., -dóne, M.: very busy person.
affaccettáre = sfaccettáre.
affacchináre [facchino], REFL.: work hard (like a 'porter'); toil (drudge).
affac-ciaménto, M.: smoothing. ‖-ciáre [faccia], REFL.: show one's self; look out; appear; present one's self; aspire. -ciataménte, ADV.: boldly. -ciáto, ADJ.: bold.
affagottáre [fagotto], TR.: bundle up.
affaitáre†, REFL.: adorn one's self; conform one's self.
affal-dáre [falda], TR.: fold up (plait). -delláre, TR.: fold, wrap up.
affalsáre†, TR.: falsify, adulterate.
affa-máre [fame], TR.: FAMISH; starve; make hungry. -máto, ADJ.: famished (starved); needy; wretched. -matóre, M.: famisher. -matúzzo†, ADJ.: starved-looking (object). -míre†, INTR.: starve.
affangáre†, TR.: splash with mud (soil).
affan-naménto, M.: anxiety; vexation. -nánte, ADJ.: suffocating; grievous. -náre, TR.: suffocate; afflict (grieve, overcome); REFL.: grieve (vex one's self); strain; strive. -nataménte, ADV.: anxiously; grievously. -náto, ADJ.: suffocated; grieved; anxious. -natóre, M.: vexer. ‖affán-no [?], M.: shortness of breath; anguish; anxiety; pain. -nóna, F., -nóne, M.: troublesome person (busybody). -noneria†, F.: meddlesomeness. -nosaménte, ADV.: with [illegible]lty (of breathing); painfully; anx[illegible] -nóso, ADJ.: suffocating (sultry); [illegible] (troublesome).
[illegible]lláre [fardello], TR.: make up [illegible] bundle (bundle or pack up).
[illegible]e†, M.: AFFAIR (business); quality [illegible]n, rank): casa di mal —, brothel; donna di mal —, prostitute. =fáre† 2, IRR.; IMPERS., REFL.: suit (become). -faráccio, M.: wretched affair. -faríno, M.: trifling affair (trifle). -faróne, M.: big affair; good affair. -faráccio, -farucciáccio, M.: wretched affair.
affasciáre†, TR.: tie in fagots (bundle).
affasci-naménto, M.: fascination. -nánte, ADJ.: fascinating (bewitching). ‖-náre [fascino], TR.: fascinate (charm). -natóre, M.: charmer (bewitcher). -natríce, F.: charmer; sorceress. -nazióne†, F.: fascination.
affa-stelláre [fastello], TR.: make a bundle of; jumble together. -stellío, M.: jumble.
affastidi(a)re†, TR.: trouble (vex).
affatáre†, TR.: charm; render invulnerable; bewitch; embellish.
affati-caménto, M.: fatiguing; tiredness; toil. ‖-cáre [fatica], TR.: fatigue (tire); harass; REFL.: toil; strive. -cáto, ADJ.: fatigued (weary); harassed. -chévole†, ADJ.: fatiguing (wearisome); painstaking. -cóso†, ADJ.: fatiguing; laborious.
af=fátto, ADV.: perfectly; entirely; quite; at all: niente —, nothing at all.
affattu-raménto†, M.: sorcery. ‖-ráre [fattura], TR.: charm (bewitch). -razióne†, F.: sorcery.
affazo-naménto†, M.: ornament. ‖-náre† [fazione], TR.: adorn (embellish).
af=fè†, ADV.: in faith; upon my faith.
affegatáre†, REFL.: be afflicted.
affer-maménto†, M.: affirmation. -mánte, ADJ.: affirmative. ‖-máre [firmare], TR.: affirm (assert); REFL.†: become firm or strong; be confirmed. -mataménte, ADV.: affirmatively; assuredly. -matívo, ADJ.: affirmative (positive). -matíva, F.: affirmative. -matóre, M., -matríce, F.: a person who affirms (maintainer). -mazióne, F.: affirmation.
affer-raménto, M.: grasping. -ránte, ADJ.: grasping; M.: battle horse†. ‖-ráre [ferro], TR.: grapple (grasp, gripe); comprehend; hold; (nav.) land. -ratóio†, M.: grappling-iron; tongs. -ratóre, M., -ratríce, F.: grappler.
affet-taménto†, M.: affectation; adornment. ‖-táre [1. -to; 2. fetta], TR.: 1. affect (pretend); pretend to (covet); adorn; REFL.: be affected; 2. cut in slices (slice, cut up). -tataménte, ADV.: affectedly; eagerly. -táto, ADJ.: 1. affected; 2. sliced. -tatóre†, M., -tatríce†, F.: affected person. -tatúra, F.: slicing. -tatúzzo, ADJ.: much affected. -tazióne, F.: affectation.
affet-tívo, ADJ.: affecting (touching).

‖ **affèt-to** [L. *affectus* (*af-ficere*, touch)], ADJ.: AFFECTED (touched); burdened; M.: affection (passion, tenderness); desire. **-tuosaménte**, ADV.: affectionately (tenderly). **-tuosità**, F.: affectionateness (affection). **-tuòso**, ADJ.: affectionate (tender).

affezio-náre, TR.: make affectionate or fond (enamour); REFL.: get fond of (become attached to, fall in love). **-natamente**, ADV.: affectionately (fondly). **-náto**, ADJ.: affectionate (fond). **-neèlla**, F.: slight affection. ‖**affezió-ne** [*affetto*], F.: affection (tenderness; morbid condition); (*math.*)† property; (*gram.*)† inflection. **-névole**†, ADJ.: affectionate, fond.

affiammáre† = *inflammare*.

affiatáre [*fiato*], REFL.: become confident or familiar.

affib-biáglio†, M.: buckle (clasp). **-biaménto**, M.: buckling. ‖**-biáre** [*fibbia*], TR.: buckle (clasp); button: *-biarla ad uno*, play one a trick. **-biatóio**†, M.: buckle. **-biatúra**, F.: buckling (clasping); clasping part (of a dress); hooks and eyes†; buttons†.

af=ficcáre†, TR.: thrust in; fix.

affi-dáre [*fede*], TR.: CONFIDE; entrust; REFL.: confide (one's self); trust; rely. **-dáto**, ADJ.: confided; trusty; certain; M.: confidant, trusty friend. **-dataménte**†, ADV.: confidently.

affiebolíre†, INTR.: debilitate.

affie-náre [*fieno*], TR.: fodder; forage. **-náta**, F.: foraging. **-níre**, INTR.: sprout.

affievo-liménto, M.: weakness. ‖**-líre** [*fievole*], TR.: enfeeble (weaken); INTR., REFL.: grow weak (weaken).

af=figgere, IRR.; TR.: stick up (placards, etc.); post; fix; fasten†; nail†; REFL.†: look fixedly (stare); apply one's self.

affiguráre† [*figura*], TR.: recognize; recollect; REFL.: fancy.

affi-laménto, M.: arranging in files; whetting. ‖**-láre** [*fila*], TR.: arrange in a file or row; file (sharpen, whet); INTR.†: file (march in files). **-láta**, F.: slight sharpening (setting). **-láto**, ADJ.: arranged in a file; sharp(ened); long and thin (face). **-latúra**, F.: sharpening; sharp edge. **-lettáre**, TR.: (*mas.*) smooth (the points between brick with the trowel); tie (the threads of a net). **-lettatúra**, F.: smoothing, etc. (cf. *-lettare*).

affi-liáre [L. *filius*, son], TR.: take in as a member (in a society, etc.); associate; REFL.: join. **-liazióne**, F.: association; society.

affi-naménto, M.: refinement. ‖**-náre** [*fine*], TR.: refine; purify; sharpen; REFL.: become refined or purified. **-natóio**, M.: crucible (melting-pot). **-natóre**, M.: refiner. **-natúra**, F.: refinement.

affin-chè† [*a fine che*], ADV.: to the end that; in order to; that. **-e** 1 **di** = *a fine di*, in order that.

affí-ne 2 [L. *af-finis* ('to-border'), neighbouring], ADJ.: kindred (akin); M.: kinsman (relation). **-níssimo**, ADJ.: very closely akin. **-nità**, F.: affinity (kindred).

affio-caménto†, M.: hoarseness. ‖**-cáre**† [*fioco*], INTR.: get hoarse. **-cáto**†, ADJ.: hoarse. **-catúra**†, F.: hoarseness. **-chiménto**, M.: becoming hoarse (hoarseness). **-chíre**, INTR., REFL.: get hoarse.

affioráto†, ADJ.: ornamented or embroidered with flowers; damasked.

affirmáre† = *affermare*.

af-fissáre = *fissare*. **-fissaménto**†, M.: gazing at. =**fissáre**†, TR.: affix; fix one's eyes upon (gaze at); REFL.: apply one's self. **-físsi**, PRET. of *-figgere*. **-fissióne**, F.: affixing. ‖**-físso** [PART. of *-figgere*], ADJ.: fixed (fastened); eager; M.: placard (bill); affix.

affit-tai(u)òlo, M.: tenant (lease-holder). **-tánte**, M.: landlord. **-táre**, TR.: lease (rent); hire; freight; REFL.: be let (let). **-tatóre**, M.: leaser; landlord; freighter. **-tazióne**†, F.: leasing. **-tévole**†, ADJ.: to be leased or let out. **-tíre**, TR.: render thick or frequent; INTR., REFL.: grow thick or frequent. ‖**affít-to** [*fitto*], ADJ.: affixed (fastened); M.: lease; rent. **-tuále**†, M.: tenant; farmer. **-tuário**, M., **-tuária**, F.: lease-holder; tenant (renter).

af-fliggènte, ADJ.: afflicting (painful). ‖**-fliggere** [L. *fligere*, strike], IRR.§; TR.: afflict, grieve, torment; REFL.: be afflicted (grieve). **-flíssi**, PRET. of *-fliggere*. **-flittívo**, ADJ.: afflicted; grievous. **-flítto**, PART. of *-fliggere*. **-flizióne**, F.: affliction. **-flizioncèlla**, F.: *dim.* of *-flizione*.

§ Pret. *afflis-si, -se; -sero.* Part. *afflitto.*

afflosciíre [*floscio*], INTR.: become flabby or loose.

afflu-ènte, ADJ.: affluent (abundant). **-enteménte**, ADV.: abundantly. **-ènza**, F.: affluence (abundance). ‖**-íre** [L. *fluere*, flow], INTR.: flow on or together; flow in abundance (abound). **'-sso**, M.: afflux; congestion.

affocáre [*fuoco*], TR.: set on fire (inflame).

affo-gággine† or **-gagióne**†, F., **-gaménto**, M.: suffocation. ‖**-gáre** [*fogo*], TR.: SUFFOCATE (smother); drown; REFL.: be suffocated or stifled. **-gáto**, ADJ.: suffocated; extinguished; overloaded; furious†: *uova —te*, poached eggs. **-gatóio**, M.: place of suffocation, (*fig.*) oven.

affol-láre [*folla*], TR.: crowd together; throng; stuff. **-latamónte**, ADV.: in a crowd; greedily.

affol-tamónto†, M.: thickening; precipitation. ‖**-táre**†, TR.: crowd or press upon; INTR.: hurry. **-táta**†, F.: haste, eagerness.

affon-daménto, M.: foundering (sinking). ‖**-dáre** [*fondo*], INTR.: FOUNDER (go to the 'bottom,' sink); TR.: sink. **-dáto**, ADJ.: sunk; shipwrecked; ruined. **-datóre**, M.: sinker; wrecker. **-datúra**, F.: sinking. **-do**† for *a fondo*.

afforestieráre [*forestiere*], INTR.: become a stranger.

af=fortificáre, TR.: fortify.

af=fortunáto, ADJ.: fortunate.

affór-za†, ADV.: by force. **-zaménto**†, M.: fortifying. **-záre**†, TR.: strengthen, fortify.

affos-saménto, M.: ditch; trench (intrenchment). ‖**-sáre** [*fossa*], TR.: ditch; intrench. **-satúra**, F.: intrenchment.

affrágnere† = *affrangere*.

affra-láre†, **-líre**†, TR.: enfeeble.

affran-cábile, ADJ.: capable of being freed. **-caménto**, M.: freeing (emancipating). ‖**-cáre** [*franco*], TR.: free (FRANCHIZE, emancipate); REFL.: be freed; become vigorous. **-cáto**, ADJ.: freed; M.: freeman.

af=frángere†, IRR.; TR.: break; violate. **-fránto**, PART.: broken; fatigued.

affrappáre†, TR.: cut (mince).

affratel-laménto, M.: brotherly affection (intimacy). ‖**-láre** [*fratello*], TR.: make brothers; REFL.: become brothers (in affection).

affreddáre†, TR.: cool.

affre-naménto†, M.: check (restraint). **-náre**†, TR.: bridle (curb, check).

af=frésco, M.: fresco.

affret-taménto, M.: hurry (speed). **-tánza**, F.: hurry. ‖**-táre** [*fretta*], TR.: urge (hurry, speed, despatch). **-tataménte**†, ADV.: hurriedly. **-tóso**†, ADJ.: hasty (hurried).

áffrico [L. *-cus*], M.: south-wind.

affritt... [*f*...*ittello*], TR.: fry (eggs); kill

... L.: affront; assault.
... L.: affront; assault
... set face to face; as-
... **-táta**†, F.: assault;
..., ADJ.: affronted; as-
...ace. **affrón-to**, M.:

...o, M.: fumigation. ‖**-cá-**
... fumigate; smoke dry.
...dity. **-catúra**, F.: fumi-
...).
...o], TR.: form into a spindle

or shaft (taper). **-sáto**, PART.: tapering. **-selláre** or **-selláre** = *-sare*.

af=fústo, M.: gun-carriage.

afonía, F.: aphony. ‖**áfono** [Gr. *a-*, not, *phoné*, voice], ADJ.: aphonous (voiceless).

afo-rísmo [Gr. *aphorismós*, definition], M.: aphorism. **-rístico**, ADJ.: aphoristic(al). **-risticaménte**, ADV.: aphoristically.

afóso [*afa*], ADJ.: suffocating (sultry).

a-fréttо†, ADJ.: sourish. **-frézza**†, F.: sourness; asperity. ‖**-fro**†, ADJ.: sour (acrid).

afrodisíaco [*Afrodite*], ADJ.: aphrodisiacal.

agáme [Gr. *a-*, not, *gámos*, marriage], F.: acotyledons.

ágape [Gr. *agápe*, love], F.: love-feast.

agárico [L. *-cum*] M.: agaric.

ágata [Gr. *Achátes* in Sicily], F.: agate.

agáta [*ago*], F.: needleful.

ágave [L.], F.: agave (plant).

a-gènda [L., 'to be done'], F.: note-book (memorandum). ‖**-gènte** [*-gire*], ADJ.: acting; active; M.: agent; manager. **-genzía**, F.: agency.

agevo-laménto, M.: facilitation (ease). **-láre**, TR.: facilitate (help). ‖**agévole** [L. *agibilis* (L. *agere*, act)] ADJ.: easy (manageable, practicable). **-lézza**, F.: facility (ease); civility (courtesy). **-líno**, ADJ.: easy, manageable. **-lménte**, ADV.: easily (readily).

aggaffáre† = *accaffare*

aggalláto [*galla*], M.: marshy ground.

aggan-ciáre [*gancio*], TR.: hook. **-gheráre** [*ganghero*], TR.: hinge.

aggavignáre†, TR.: grasp (seize).

aggecchíre†, REFL.: respond.

ag-geggiáre, INTR.: (*pop.*) muse; TR.: arrange; dress, put on. ‖**-géggio** [?], M.: trifle (worthless thing); perplexity.

ag-geláre†, TR.: congeal (freeze). **-gelazióne**†, F.: congealment; jelly.

aggentilíre† = *ingentilire*.

ag-gettáre, INTR.: project (jut out). **-gettívo**, ADJ., M.: adjective. ‖**-gètto** [L. *ad-jectus*, 'thrown upon,' joined], M.: projection (prominence, jutting).

agghermigliáre†, TR.: grasp.

agghiac-ciaménto, F.: frost. ‖**-ciáre** [*ghiaccio*], TR.: freeze (congeal).

ag-ghiadáre†, INTR.: be frozen or benumbed with cold; be horrified. **-ghiádo**†, M.: horror.

agghindáre [ak. to Eng. *wind*], TR.: trim (adorn).

aggia-cénza†, F.: adjacency. ‖**-cére**†, IRR.; INTR.: be adjacent; suit.

agginocchiáre†, REFL.: KNEEL.

ággio† 1, for *ho*, I have.

ággio 2 [*agio*], M.: exchange; discount.

aggiogáre [*giogo*], TR.: put the yoke on (yoke).
aggioglįáto†, ADJ.: mixed with tares.
aggior-naménto, M.: adjournment; dawn. ‖**-náre** [*giorno*], TR.: adjourn; illumine†; appoint†; INTR., REFL.: dawn.
aggi-raménto, M.: surrounding (circumventing); evasion. ‖**-ráre** [*girare*], TR.: surround (enclose); take in (deceive); INTR.: go or roam about; REFL.: go around (ramble). **-ráta**†, F.: turning round; dwindling. **-ratóre**, M., **-ratríce**, F.: rambler; deceiver (swindler); bewitcher.
aggiudi-cánte, ADJ.: adjudicating; M.: adjudicator. ‖**-cáre** [*giudicare*], TR.: adjudge (award). **-catário**, M.: beneficiary (to whom a thing is adjudged). **-cazióne**, F.: adjudication (award).
aggiugn. .† = *aggiung*. .
aggiúngere, IRR.; TR.: join; add; reach; REFL.: join (meet together). **-giungiménto**, M.: joining; addition; supplement. **-giúnsi**, PRET. of *-giungere*. **-giúnta**, F.: addition. **-giuntáre**, TR.: join; add; sew together. **-giuntatúra**, F.: joining; joint, seam. **-giúnto**, PART. of *giungere*: joined (added); adjunct (assistant). **-giunzióne**†, F.: joining; addition.
aggiuráre†, TR.: swear; conjure.
aggiu-stábile, ADJ.: adjustable. **-staménto**, M.: adjustment. ‖**-stáre** [*giusto*], TR.: adjust (set to rights); direct; REFL.: adjust one's self; agree. **-statamente**, ADV.: rightly (properly). **-statézza**, F.: justice. **-statóre**, M.: adjuster (regulator). **-statúra**, F.: adjustment, settlement.
agglome-raménto, M.: agglomeration. ‖**-ráre** [L. *glomus*, ball], TR.: agglomerate.
aggluti-naménto, M.: agglutination (gluing). ‖**-náre** [*glutine*], TR.: agglutinate (glue together). **-nazióne**, F.: agglutination (gluing; joining of words).
aggobbíre [*gobbo*], TR.: make hunchbacked.
aggomitolá-re [*gomitolo*], TR.: make into a clew or coil (wind up); REFL.: form into clews or groups. **-túra**, F.: forming into clews.
aggottá-re [*gotto*], TR.: bail (a boat); pump. **-túra**, F.: bailing.
aggra-dáre [*grado* I], INTR.: be agreeable (please). **-dévole**, ADJ.: agreeable (pleasing). **-devolménte**, ADV.: agreeably. **-diménto**, M.: agreeableness, pleasure. **-díre**, TR. (3 Sing. *-da*, impers.): accept with pleasure (receive kindly); like. **-díto**, ADJ.: gladly accepted; agreeable (acceptable). **-duíre**†, REFL.: make one's self agreeable.
aggraffáre†, TR.: clasp.
aggraffignáre [*granfia*], TR.: claw, clutch; rob.
aggrampáre† = *aggrappare*.
aggranáre†, TR.: grain (form into grains); INTR.: seed.
aggranchi(á)re [*granchio*], TR.: benumb with cold.
aggran-diménto, M.: aggrandizement; increase (rise). ‖**-díre** [*grande*], TR.: increase (enlarge); REFL.: grow.
aggran-fiáre [*granfia*], TR.: claw, grapple. **-fignáre**, TR.: rob.
aggrappáre [*grappa*], TR.: grapple; grasp (catch); REFL.: clutch (cling).
aggratíre† = *aggradire*.
aggraticciáre [*graticcio*], TR.: entwine; REFL.: become interwoven; be entangled.
aggratigliáre†, TR.: fetter; imprison.
aggra-vaménto, M.: aggravation. **-vánte**, ADJ.: aggravating; overcharging. ‖**-váre** [*grave*], TR.: overload (overcharge); aggravate; aggrieve; accuse; REFL.: grow heavy, be aggravated; be aggrieved. **-vazióne**†, F.: overloading; aggravation. **'-vio**, M.: excessive burden, weight; aggravation; injury; imputation.
aggra-ziáre [*grazia*], TR.: be grateful or pleasing to (please). **-ziataménte**, ADV.: gratefully; pleasingly. **-ziatíno**, ADJ.: pleasing (nice). **-ziáto**, ADJ.: pleasing; graceful; genteel.
aggredíre [L. *gradior*, advance], TR.: assault; offend, (Eng.†) AGGRESS.
aggre-gaménto, M.: aggregation. ‖**-gáre** [L. *grex*, flock], TR.: aggregate. **-gáto**, PART.: aggregated; M.: aggregate; assemblage. **-gazióne**, F.: aggregation; assembly. **-ggiáre**†, TR.: collect; REFL.: herd together.
aggres-sióne [*aggredire*], F.: aggression (assault). **-sóre**, M.: aggressor.
aggrezzáre†, or **-zíre**†, INTR.: be benumbed with cold.
aggricchiáre†, TR.: cramp with cold.
aggrin-záre, or **-zíre** [*grinza*], TR.: wrinkle (shrivel).
aggrizzáre†, REFL.: be stiff with cold.
aggrommáre†, INTR.: get covered with tartar (incrustate).
aggroppáre†, TR.: wrap (tie); heap.
aggrottáre [*grotta*], TR.: — *le ciglia*, knit one's brows (frown), embank† (a ditch); repair†.
aggrotte-scáre†, INTR.: fall into the grotesque. **-scáto**†, M.: grotesque.
aggrovi-gliáre, or **-glioláre** [*groviglia*], TR.: curl up (twist up); entangle.
aggru-máre [*grumo*], REFL.: curdle (coagulate). **-moláre** [*grumolo*], REFL.: form into bunches,
aggrup-paménto, M.: grouping; union;

forming a bunch or knot. ||**-páre** [*gruppo*], TR.: group, collect, heap up; knot (tie).

aggruzzoláre [*gruzzolo*], TR.: scrape together (hoard up).

aggua-gliaménto, M.: equalizing. **-gliánza**†, F.: equality; conformity; resemblance. ||**-gliáre** [L. *æqualis*, EQUAL], TR.: equalize; make even or smooth; compare; REFL.: become equal or even; compare one's self (with). **-gliatamén-te**, ADV.: equally (proportionally). **-gliatóre**, M.: equalizer. **-gliazióne**†, F.: equality; conformity. **agguá-glio**, M.: comparison.

agguantáre [*guanto*], TR.: clutch (catch suddenly); rob; reef.

agguard..† = *guard..*

ag-guatáre† [OGer. *wahten*, WATCH], TR.: lie in wait for; spy. **-guáto**, M.: ambush.

aggueffáre†, TR.: join.

agguerríre [*guerra*], TR.: inure to war (harden, train).

agguindo-laménto, M.: reeling off; artifice. ||**-láre** [*guindolo*], TR.: reel off; wind up; lead by the nose (trick). **ag-guíndolo**† = *guindolo*.

aggustáre [*gusto*], INTR.: give pleasure (please).

ághero [L. *acer*], ADJ.: sour (sharp).

aghétto [*ago*], M.: shoe-string (with metal point).

aghiácelo†, M.: helm (rudder).

aghiróne† = *airone*.

agiá-re† [*agio*], TR.: adapt; accommodate; place. **-taménte**, ADV.: commodiously (with ease). **-tézza**, F.: ease (comfort); wealth. **'-to**, ADJ.: adapted; convenient; in easy circumstances (wealthy); lazy.

agíbile†, ADJ.: feasible.

ági-le [L. *-lis*], ADJ.: agile (nimble), lively. **-lità**, F.: agility. **-lménte**, ADV.: nimbly.

ágio [?], M.: ease; convenience; comfort; leisure: *dar* ––, give time (to pay); *prender* —, take one's ease.

agí-re [L. *agere*], TR.: ACT; operate; proceed. **-taméntó**†, F.: action; agitation (stir). **-táre**, TR.: agitate (stir, excite); molest; plead; REFL.: be agitated (be disturbed): – *una lite*, carry on a law-suit. **-tatóre**, M., **-tatríce**, F.: agitator. **-tazioncèlla**, F.: slight agitation. **-tazióne**, F.: agitation.

ágli, for *a gli*, to the.

agli-áta, F.: garlic sauce. **-áio**, M.: garlic bed. **-étto**, M.: small or young garlic. **-ettíno**, M.: little bit of a garlic. ||**ágli-o** [L. *allium*], M.: garlic.

ágna†, F.: she-lamb.

agná-to [L. *-tus* (*natus*, born)], M.: agnate (kinsman by the father's side). **-tízio**, ADJ.: agnatic. **-zióne**, F.: agnation.

agnèl-la, F.: little she-lamb. **-láio**, M.: dealer in mutton, etc. **-latúra**, F.: lambing time. **-létto**, M.: lambkin. **-lína**, F.: little she-lamb. **-líno**, M.: lambkin; ADJ.: of lamb (lamb-). ||**agnèl-lo** [L. *agnus*, lamb], M.: lamb(kin). **-lòt-to**, M.: big lamb; PL.: (perh. from *anello*) dumpling stuffed with meats.

agnizióne†, F.: recognition.

ágno†, M.: lamb; swelling.

agnusdèi [L. *Agnus Dei*, 'Lamb of God'], M.: Agnus Dei (image of the Lamb; prayer at Mass).

ágo [L. *acus*], M.: needle; hand (of a clock); stile (of a dial); sting (of a bee, etc.); spire; compass needle: — *da testa*, bodkin.

agognáre [*agonia*], TR.: desire anxiously or eagerly (long for), aspire to.

agó-ne [Gr. *agṓn* (*ágein*, lead)], M.: agon (contest for a prize at the public games in Greece); (*poet.*) contest, fight; wrestling ground; battle-field. **-nía**, F.: agony. **-nísta**, M.: wrestler. **-nística**, F.: agonistics (athletic exercise). **-nístico**, ADJ.: agonistic(al). **-nizzánte**, ADJ.: agonizing; in agony (dying). **-nizzáre**, INTR.: writhe with agony, agonize, be dying.

agoráio [*ago*], M.: needle-case; needle-maker or seller.

ago-stiniáno, ADJ.: Augustinian. **-stí-no**, ADJ.: of August (born or ripening in A.). ||**agó-sto** [L. *Augustus*], M.: August (the month).

agraménte [*agro*], ADV.: sharply.

agr-ária, F.: (science of) agriculture. **-ário** [L. *ager*, field], ADJ.: agrarian (agricultural). **-èste**, ADJ.: agrestic (rural, rustic). **-estemónte**†, ADV.: rurally (rustically). **-estézza**†, F.: rusticity.

agr-estíno†, ADJ.: sourish (tartish). ||**-èste** [*agro* I], M.: kind of sour grape; sour grape juice (verjuice). **-estéso**†, ADJ.: sourish. **-estúme**†, M.: acid thing, acids. **-ettíno**, *dim.* of *-etto*. **-étto**, ADJ.: sourish (somewhat acid); M.: acidity. **-ézza**, F.: sourness (acidity).

agri- [L. *ager*, field]: **-cola**†, M.: tiller, farmer (husbandman). **-coltóre**, M.: agriculturer (farmer). **-coltúra**, F.: agriculture (farming). **-fòglio**, M.: holly. **-mensóre**, M.: field-surveyor (-'MEASURER'). **-mensúra**, F.: field-surveying (mensuration).

agrimónia†, F.: agrimony (liverwort).

agri-òtta†, F.: egriot: — *persa*, marjoram.

ágro 1 [L. *acer*, sharp], ADJ.: sour (ACID, ACRID); sharp (severe); disagreeable (cross-grained).
ágro 2 [L. *ager*, field], M.: territory (esp. of a city).
agro=dólce, ADJ.: sweet and sour.
agro-nomía [*agro* 2], F.: agronomy (science of agriculture). **-nòmico**, ADJ.: agronomical. **agrò-nomo**, M.: agronomist (agriculturist).
agrúme†, M.: acid herbs (pot-herbs).
aguagliánza† = *eguaglianza*.
aguardáre†, TR.: guard (take care of).
aguastáre†, TR.: WASTE; spoil.
aguat†.. = *agguat*..
agúc-chia† [*ago*], F.: knitting-needle. **-chiáre**, TR.: stitch (sew).
agú-glia†, F.: eagle; Roman standard; obelisk; steeple; needle. **-gliácelo**†, M.: standard. **-gliáre**†, TR.: sew (stitch). **-gliáta**†, F.: needleful. **-glióne**†, M.: sting; incentive. **-gliòtto**†, M.: young eagle.
agugnáre† = *agognare*.
agumentáre† = *aumentare*.
agunáre† = *adunare*.
agur..† = *augur*..
agu-tèllo, **-tétto**, ADJ.: rather sharp; M.: tack. **-tézza**, F.: acuteness. ||**agúto** [L. *acutus*, sharp], M.: long nail. **-zzaménto**, M.: sharpening. **-zzáre**, TR.: sharpen (whet). **-zzáta**, F.: rapid sharpening. **-zzatóre**†, M.: whetter. **-zzatúra**, F.: sharpening (whetting).
aguzzíno [Sp. *alguacil*], M.: guardian of galley-slaves; tyrant, hard fellow.
agúzzo† = *acúto*.
ahí, **-mè**, INTERJ.: oh! alas!
ái, for *a i*, to the.
áia 1 [L. *area*], F.: threshing-floor; garden-plot†; AREA†; halo†: *menare il can per l'* —, drag out (a discourse, etc.) in aimless length.
áia 2 [*aio*], F.: perceptress (governess).
aiáta [*aia* 1], F.: sheaves on the threshing-floor; threshing-floor full of sheaves: *romper l'* —, begin threshing.
aiáto†, ADJ.: rambling: *andar* —, ramble about.
aiétta†, F.: hotbed.
aimè† = *ahimè*,
áio, pl. *ai* [Sp. *ayo*, master], M.: preceptor, tutor (in a private house).
aióne†, M.: rambler.
a=íre, M.: leap; run, free course; direction.
airóne [OGer. *heigero*], M.: HERON.
ait.. (*poet.*) = *aiut*..
ai(u)ò-la [*areola*], F.: garden-plot†. **-lo**†, M.: bird-net.
aiu-taménto, M.: aid (help). **-tánte**, ADJ.: aiding (helpful); strong; M.: helper (assistant); adjutant: — *di campo*, aide-de-camp. **-táre**, TR.: aid (help, assist); REFL.: help one's self (avail or help one's self). **-táto**†, M.: help. **-tatóre**, M. **-tatríce**, F.: helper (assistant). **-tévole**, ADJ.: aiding (helpful); favorable. ||**aiú-to** [L. *ad-jutum* (*juvare*, help)], M.: AID (help, assistance); PL.: auxiliary troops. **-tóre**, M., **-tríce**, F.: helper.
aiz-zaménto, M.: incitement; provocation. ||**-záre** [Ger. *hetzen*], TR.: incite; set (dogs) upon; irritate (provoke). **-zatóre**, M., **-zatríce**, F.: inciter (instigator). **-zóso**†, ADJ.: provoking.
al, for *a il*, to the.
ála, pl. *-li* (poet. *-le*) [L.], F.: wing (of a bird, structure, or army): *far(e)* —, form a line (to honour some one passing); *stare sull'* —*e*, be just going.
alabár-da [Ger. *helm-barte*, 'helmet-splitter'], F.: HALBERD. **-dáta**, F.: halberd thrust. **-dière**, M.: hallebardier.
ala-bastríno, ADJ.: of alabaster. ||**-bástro** [L. *-bastrum*], M.: alabaster.
alá-cre or **ála-cre** [L. *-cris*], ADJ.: alacrious (brisk, lively). **-creménte**, ADV.: with alacrity (briskly). **-critá**, F.: alacrity.
alamár(r)i [Sp. *-mdr*], M.: ornamented button-hole.
aláno [*Alani*], M.: bulldog.
aláre [L. *ad larem*, 'to Lar' (domestic deity)], M.: andiron.
aláta [*ala*], F.: stroke of the wing.
alatèrno [L. *-nus*], M.: privet (shrub); prim.
aláto [*ala*], ADJ.: winged; flighty†.
álba [L. *-bus*, white], F.: break of day (early dawn).
alba-gía [?], F.: great vanity (conceit). **-gióso**, ADJ.: conceited.
albána [*albo*], F.: kind of white grape.
albanése, M.: light cavalryman.
álbatro 1 [L. *arbutus*], M.: (*bot.*) arbutus.
álbatro 2 [fr. Ar.], M.: albatross.
al-bazzáno [*albo*], M.: limestone. **-bèdine**, F.: whiteness. **-beggiaménto**, M.: dawning. **-beggiáre**, INTR.: dawn; break (of day).
albe-ráre [*albero*], TR.: plant with trees; mast (a ship). **-ratúra**, F.: tree-plantation; masts. **-rèllo** 1, M.: sort of mushroom.
alberèllo 2 [?], M.: earthen vase (pot).
alberése [*albo*], M.: limestone.
albe-réta [*-ro*], F., or **-réto**, M.: tree-plantation (grove). **-rétto**, M.: small tree (shrub).
alber-gagióne†, F., **-gaménto**†, M.: staying at a hotel; lodging. **-gáro**, TR.: lodge; harbour; INTR.: lodge (reside, stop). **-gáto**, PART.: lodged; M.: lodger†

[illegible]gatore, M., -gatrice, F.: innkeeper; [illegible]. -gheria†, F.: [illegible]. -ghetto, M.: small inn. ||albèr-go [illegible], 'army-shelter'], inn, hotel.

albe[illegible]rino, dim. of [illegible]. álbe-ro [L. [illegible]], M.: tree; poplar; mast; (mec.) shaft; shafting. [illegible] da trinchetto, fore-mast. [illegible]róne, M.: big tree.

al[illegible]bicante, -biccio [albo], ADJ.: whitish.

albi[illegible]cocca, F.: apricot. -cocco [Sp. al-[illegible]], M.: APRICOT-tree.

al[illegible]bino, [illegible]: whitish†, M.: albino. -bis: [illegible] Sunday after Easter. [illegible] ADJ.: white†; fig-like [illegible] special whitish fig); tipsy†: [illegible] borare†, INTR.: [illegible]. -bore, M.: dawn (aurora). -bugi-[illegible], F.: albugo. -bum, M.: album. -bu-[illegible], M.: white of the egg. -bumina, [illegible], F.: albumen. -buminato, ADJ.: albuminous. -burno, M.: white hazel-tree.

alcaico [L. [illegible]cus], M.: alcaic (meter).

alca-lescente, ADJ.: alkalescent. -lescenza, F.: alkalescence. ||álca-li, [Ar.], M.: alkali. -lino, ADJ.: alkaline. -lizzare, TR.: alkalize.

álco [Gr. alkḗ], M.: ELK.

alcèa [L.], F.: vervain (plant).

alchèrmes [fr. Ar.], M.: sort of sweet drink.

alchi-mia [fr. Ar.], F.: alchemy. -'mico, ADJ.: alchemical. -mista, -misti, M.: alchemist. -mizzare†, INTR.: practice alchemy.

alcióne [Gr. alkyon], M.: HALCYON; king-fisher.

alco-ol [fr. Ar.], M.: alcohol. -òlico, ADJ.: alcoholic. -olismo, M.: alcoholism.

alcorano [fr. Ar.], M.: Alcoran.

alcòva [fr. Ar.], F.: alcove (recess).

al[illegible] [illegible]: something. ||-cúno [L. aliquis unus], [illegible]: some one (somebody). [illegible] volta, sometimes.

al[illegible] [illegible] al dio, dióne, M.: [illegible] ball fired out.

alea [L. [illegible]], F.: fate.

aleàtico [illegible], M.: sort of black grape; wine made from it.

aleatòrio [alea], ADJ.: contingent, uncertain.

aleggiare [ala], INTR.: ... the wings [illegible].

alè-n[illegible] [illegible]: breath (respiration). [illegible] breathing. [illegible]are†, INTR. [illegible] panting. [illegible] = [illegible] [illegible] [illegible] [illegible] small wing, fin, [illegible] [illegible] with ... [illegible]

álfa, F.: alpha (Greek a). -betica-ménte, ADV.: alphabetically. -bético, ADJ.: alphabetical. -bèto [Gr. *beta*, β], M.: alphabet.

alfána†, F.: mare.

alfière [L. *aquili-fer*, EAGLE-BEARER], M.: ensign-bearer (ensign); bishop (at chess).

alfíne [*alla fine*], ADV.: finally.

álli-ga [L. *alga*], F.: alga; seaweed. -góso, ADJ.: full of seaweeds.

ál-gebra [fr. Ar.], F.: algebra. -gè-brico, ADJ.: algebraic. -gebricamén-te, ADV.: algebraically. -gebrísta, M.: algebraist.

algènte†, ADJ.: algid (freezing). ál-gere†, IRR.: INTR.: freeze. álgere†, M.: extreme cold.

algóso = *aligoso*.

ália, vulg. for *ala*, wing of a building.

aliáre†, INTR.: fly.

álias [L.], ADV.: otherwise: also called.

álibi [L.], M.: alibi.

alíce†, F.: anchovy.

alidáda†, F.: alidade (quadrant).

áli-do [*arido*], ADJ.: arid (dry); M.: dryness. -dézza, F.: aridness. -dóre, M.: dry season (dryness).

alidoráto [*ala*, *dorato*], ADJ.: gold-winged.

alieggiáre† = *aleggiare*.

alie-nábile, ADJ.: alienable. -nabilità, F.: alienability. -naménto, M.: alienation: separation†. -náre, TR.: alienate; transfer; REFL.: become alienated or estranged; withdraw. -nata-ménte, ADV.: giddily. -natária, F., —o, M.: receiver of alienated property. -náto, ADJ.: alienated (estranged); distracted (mad). -natóre, M.: alienator. -nazióne, F: alienation; estrangement; distraction; separation†. ||aliè-no [L. *alienus*], ADJ.: alien† (foreign); disinclined (reluctant, averse).

alifloríto [*ala*, *fiorito*], ADJ.: with flowery wings.

áliga = *alga*.

alígero†, ADJ.: winged.

alimen-taménto, M.: nourishing (aliment). -táre 1, TR.: nourish (feed). -táre 2, -tário, ADJ.: alimentary: *pensione* [illegible], maintenance. -tatóre, M., -tatrice, F.: nourisher. -tízio, ADJ.: alimentary. ||alimén-to [L. -*tum* (*alere*, nourish)], M.: aliment (food, nourishment). -tóso†, ADJ.: nutritious.

alína [*ala*], F.: little wing.

alínea [L. *ab*, from, *linea*, line], F.: subparagraph; clause.

alìosso†, M.: ossicle; cockle.

aliòtto†, M.: ruffle.

alípede [*ala*, *piede*], ADJ.: with winged feet.

aliquánto†, ADJ.: aliquant; unequal.
aliquóto [L. *alia-quota*], ADJ.: aliquot.
aliseo [?], ADJ.: trade-: *venti —ei*, trade-winds.
ali-táre, INTR.: breathe gently; pant; M.: panting. ||**áli-to** [L. *halitus*], M.: breath (breathing); breeze; odour†. **-t(u)òso**†, ADJ.: bad smelling.
all', **álla** 1, for *a la*, to the.
álla 2†, F.: market-place; ell.
allac-ciaménto, M.: lacing; allurement. ||**-ciáre** [*laccio*], TR.: lace; bind (tie up); catch with a lasso or snare; catch; allure; entangle. **-ciatívo**†, ADJ.: catching; alluring. **-ciatúra**, F.: lacing; buttoning; bandage.
alla-gaménto, M.: deluge (inundation). ||**-gáre** [*lago*], TR.: deluge (overflow, inundate). **-gazióne**†, F.: overflowing (flood).
allampanáto [*lámpana*], ADJ.: emaciated ('transparent like a lamp'), very thin.
allampáre [*lampo*], INTR.: burn with thirst (parch).
allar-gaménto, M.: enlargement; extension. ||**-gáre** [*largo*], TR.: enlarge (widen, extend, dilate): — *la mano*, be open-handed. **-gáta**, F.: enlargement or stretching (made in haste). **-gatína**, F.: poor enlargement or stretch. **-gatóio**, M.: instrument for enlarging; stretcher. **-gatóne**, M.: enlarger (amplifier). **-gatúra**, F.: enlargement.
allar-máre, TR.: alarm; REFL.: be alarmed. ||**allár-me** [*all'arme*, 'to arms!'], M.: alarm. **-mánte**, ADJ.: alarming.
allas-saménto†, M.: LASSITUDE, weariness. ||**-sáre**†, TR.: fatigue (tire).
al=láto, ADV., PREP.: beside; by: — —, close by.
allat-taménto, M.: giving suck. ||**-táre** [*latte*], TR.: suckle (give suck to). **-tatríce**, F.: nurse.
álle = *a le*, to the.
alle-ánza, F.: alliance. ||**-áre** [Fr. *allier* (L. *ligare*, bind)]; REFL.: ally one's self. **-áto**, ADJ.: allied (confederate); M.: ally.
alleccorníre [*leccornia*], TR.: allure; excite.
allefìcáre†, INTR.: take root; cultivate friendship.
alle-gábile, ADJ.: that may be alleged. **-gaménto**, M.: allegation; setting on edge. ||**-gáre** [*legare*], TR.: ALLEGE (adduce); ALLOY; TR., INTR.: promise well (of fruits, etc.); set (the teeth) on edge; REFL.†: league one's self (form an alliance). **-gatóre**, M.: alleger. **-gazióne**, F.: allegation, quotation†; alloy†.

alleggera. . † = *alleggeri*. .
allegge-riménto, M.: lightening (easing, relief). ||**-ríre** [*leggero*], TR.: lighten (ease); ALLEVIATE (reLIEVE, mitigate); REFL.: remove one's clothes.
alleggiáre† = *alleggerire*.
alle-goría [Gr. *állos*, other, *agoréin*, speak], F.: allegory. **-goricaménte**, ADV.: allegorically. **-gòrico**, ADJ.: allegoric(al). **-goríst a**, M.: allegorist. **-gorizzáre**, INTR.: allegorize.
alle-graménte, ADV.: cheerfully (gaily). **-gránte**†, ADJ.: cheerful. **-gránza**†, F.: cheerfulness. **-gráre**, TR.: gladden (cheer). **-grétto**, *dim.* of *-gro*. **-grézza**, F.: cheerfulness (joyousness). **-gría**, F.: gladness (merriment). ||**allé-gro** [L. *alacer*], ADJ.: cheerful (merry, gay); brisk (ALACRIOUS); tipsy. **-gròccio**, **-grúccio**, ADJ.: jovial (good-humoured).
allelúia [fr. Heb.], M.: hallelujah: *vecchio quanto* —, old as hallelujah (very old).
alle-naménto†, M.: respite (delay). **-náre**†, INTR.: decay; slacken; take breath; TR.: strengthen (fortify); REFL.: take breath. **-níre**†, TR.: soften; mitigate; INTR.: be gentle.
allen-tagióne, F.: hernia (rupture). **-taménto**, M.: relaxation; slowness. ||**-táre** [*lento*], TR.: render more loose (relax, slacken); rarefy; REFL.: be relaxed (get slack); have a rupture (hernia). **-tatúra**, F.: hernia (rupture).
allen-zaménto†, M.: ligature (bandage). ||**-záre**†, TR.: bandage; swathe.
alles-saménto†, M.: boiling. ||**-sáre**†, TR.: boil (stew). **allés-so** [*lesso*], ADJ.: boiled; M.: boiled meat.
alle-stiménto, M.: preparation. ||**-stíre** [*lesto*], TR.: make ready (prepare).
alletamáre†, TR.: manure (dung).
allettaiuòlo†, M.: decoy-bird.
allet-taménto, M.: allurement (charm). **-tánte**, ADJ.: alluring (attractive). ||**-táre** [1. L. *al-lectare* (*lacere*, allure); 2. *letto*], TR.: 1. allure (entice, attract); invite; 2. cause to lie down (lay); strike down; REFL.: lie down (of grains, etc.); take to one's bed; nestle. **-tatíva**, F.: allurement (charm). **-tatívo**, ADJ.: alluring (attractive). **-táto**, ADJ.: 1. allured (attracted); 2. bed-ridden. **-tatóre**, M.: enticer.
alletteráto [*lettera*], ADJ.: lettered (learned).
alle-vaménto, M.: bringing up (education). ||**-váre** [*levare*], TR.: bring up (educate; foster, raise). **-váto**, ADJ.: educated; M.: pupil. **-vatóre**, M., **-vatríce**, F.: educator; raiser. **-vatúra**, F.: bringing up (education); fostering

(raising). **-viagióne**†, F.: alleviation. **-viáre**, TR.: alleviate (ease); REFL.: lie in. **-viazióne**†, F.: alleviation.

alliánza† = *alleanza*.

allib(b)íre [*livido*], INTR.: be amazed.

alli-bramént o, M.: booking. ‖**-bráre** [*libro*], TR.: book (register). **-brazióne**, F.: booking (registration).

alliccїáre [*liccio*], TR.: pass (the woof) through the warp; set (the teeth of a saw).

alliccre†, TR.: allure (entice).

allietáre [*lieto*], TR.: gladden.

alliè-va, F., **-vo** [*allevare*], M.: pupil (scholar); foster-child; foal; calf.

alligáta†, F.: enclosed letter.

alligatóre [Eng. *-tor*], M.: alligator.

alligпáre [*legno*], INTR.: take root (grow, thrive).

allin-dáre†, TR.: make nice or spruce (deck). **-datóre**†, M.: embellisher.

alli-neaménto, M.: alignment. ‖**-neáre** [*linea*], TR.: ALIGN.

allinguáto†, ADJ.: talkative.

alliqui-dáre†, TR.: render liquid (melt).

allisçiáre† = *lisciare*.

allistáre†, TR.: lace (embroider).

allitterazióne [L. *ad*, to, *litera*, letter], F.: alliteration.

allivellá-re [*livello*], TR.: level. **-zióne**, F.: levelling.

allividíre [*livido*], INTR.: grow livid or pale (pale).

állo, for *a lo*, to the.

allocáre†, TR.: locate (place).

al-loccáccio, M.: big ugly owl; stupid loon. ‖**-lòcca**, F., **-lòcco** [L. *alucus*]: M.: owl. **-loccóne** = *-locaccio*.

allocuzióne [L. *loqui*, speak], F.: allocution (address).

al-lodiále, ADJ.: allodial. **-lòdio** [? OHG. *al-ōd*, 'all-free'], M.: allodium (freehold).

allòdola [L. *alauda*], F.: skylark.

allo-gaménto, M.: lease. ‖**-gáre** [*luogo*], TR.: LOCATE (place); settle; employ; invest (money); give in marriage (marry). **-gatóre**, M.: landlord. **-gatríce**, F.: landlady. **-gazióne**, F.: employment.

allog-giaménto†, M.: lodging. **-giáre**, TR.: lodge; INTR., REFL.: lodge (dwell): — *alla prim' osteria*, yield to the first reason. **-giatóre**, M., **-giatríce**, F.: landlord; landlady. ‖**allòg-gio** [*loggia*], M.: lodging-place (lodging-house, inn).

alloglíáto [*loglio*], ADJ.: mixed with cockle-weed; stupid.

allongáre†, TR.: remove.

allonta-naménto, M.: removal; remoteness. ‖**-náre** [*lontano*], TR.: remove (send away); repel; REFL.: go away (depart). **-náto**, ADJ.: removed; remote (distant; far-off).

allo-patía [Gr. *állos*, other, *páthos*, suffering], F.: allopathy. **-pático**, ADJ.: allopathic.

allop-piaménto, M.: drugging. **-piáre**, TR.: mix with opium; drug; REFL.: drowse (fall asleep; slumber). **-picáre**†, INTR.: drowse (slumber). ‖**allòp-pio**† = *oppio*.

allór-a [*all' ora*], ADV.: at that time (then); recently: — *quando*, when; whilst; — —, just then; *d'* —, of that time; then; *da* —, from that time (thence); *d'* — *in poi*, thenceforward (from that time on); *per* —, by that time. **=chè**, **=quándo**, ADV.: when.

allòro [L. *laurus*], M.: LAUREL.

allòtta†, ADV.: at that time; then.

allottáre [*lotto*], TR.: put on lottery.

allu-ciáre [*luce*], TR.: gaze at (eye). **-cignoláre** [*lucignolo*], TR.: make a wick of; twist; rumple. **-cináre**, TR.: dazzle; beguile; REFL.: be hallucinated; err. **-cinazióne**, F.: hallucination.

allúda [L. *-luta*], M.: sheep's skin.

allúdere [L. *ludere*, play], IRR.§; INTR.: allude, hint.

§ Pret. *allúsi, -se; -sero*. Part. *allúso*.

allumacá-re [*lumaca*], TR.: mark with a snail-track; stripe. **-túra**, F.: snail-track.

allumáre† 1, TR.: kindle (light).

allu-máre 2, TR.: alumize. ‖**allú-me** [L. *-men*], M.: alum(en). **-mièra**, F.: alum-mine. **-mína**, F.: alumine.

allumi-náre, vulg. for *illuminare*. **-náto**, ADJ.: bright (clear). **-nazióne**, vulg. for *illuminazione*.

allumí-nio [*allumina*], M.: aluminium. **-nóso**, ADJ.: aluminous.

allun-gaménto, M.: lengthening (prolongation, extension). ‖**-gáre** [*lungo*], TR.: lengthen (prolong, extend, stretch); REFL.: stretch one's self; extend; remove. **-gatívo**, ADJ.: lengthening (extending). **-gáto**, ADJ.: lengthened (extended); distant. **-gatúra**, F.: lengthening (prolongation, extension); added piece.

allupáre [*lupo*], INTR.: be hungry as a wolf.

al-lusingáre†, TR.: flatter (wheedle).

allu-sióne [*-dere*], F.: allusion. **-sívo**, ADJ.: allusive.

alluvióne [L. *luere*, wash], F.: alluvion.

álma [*anima*], F.: (*poet.*) soul.

almagèsto [fr. Ar.], M.: almagest.

alma-naccáre, INTR.: puzzle one's brains; cast about; build air-castles. ‖**-nácco** [?], M.: almanac: *far -nacchi* = *almanaccare*. **-nácchio**, M.: constant puzzling. **-naccóna**, F., **-naccóne**, M.: great muser (phantast).

al=máno o, ADV.: at least.

al=méno, ADV.: at least.
almirágliot†, -rántet† = *ammiraglio.*
álmo [L. *-mus*], ADJ.: nourishing; great (immortal); soul†.
álo-e [Gr.], M.: aloe. **-ètico†,** ADJ.: aloetic.
alóne [*ala*], M.: HALO.
alòecia†, F.: hydromel.
alpáca [Sp. (Peruv.)], F.: (*zoöl.*) alpaca; alpaca (fabric).
ál-pe [Celt.], F.: alp; PL.: alps. **-pè-stre,** (*poet.*) **-pèstro,** ADJ.: Alpine, mountainous; rugged. **-pigiáno,** ADJ.: Alpine. **-pinísmo,** M.: love of (climbing the) Alps. **-pinísta,** pl. *-ti,* M.: Alpinist, (alp-climber, mountaineer). **-píno,** ADJ.: Alpine; PL.: alp-soldier; mountain-guard.
alquán-to [L. *ali-quantum*], ADV.: some what; ADJ.: some (some few). **=túne** = *alcune.*
alsì†, ADV.: also; too.
altalé-na [L. *tolleno*], F.: seesaw; swing. **-náre,** INTR.: seesaw; swing. **-no,** M.: swing-gate; lever.
altaménte [*alto*], ADV.: highly; greatly; nobly.
altá-re [L. (? *altus,* high)], M.: altar; *sacrifizio dell'* —, mass. **-rèllo, -ríno,** M.: small altar; family altar: *scoprire gli —i,* reveal the tricks.
altassóso†, ADJ.: haughty (proud).
altèa [Gr. *-thaia*], F.: marshmallow.
alte-rábile [*-rare*], ADJ.: alterable. **-rabilità,** F.: alterability.
alteraménte [*altero*], ADV.: haughtily (proudly).
alte-raménto†, M.: alteration. ‖**-rá-re** [*altro*], TR.: alter (change); deteriorate; upset (the stomach); REFL.: change; grow worse; be excited; grow angry. **-rataménte†,** ADV.: angrily. **-ratívo,** ADJ.: alterative. **-razióne,** F.: alteration (change). **-razioncèlla,** F.: little change.
alter-cáre [L. *-ri* (*alter,* other)], INTR.: altercate (wrangle). **-cazióne,** F.: altercation. **altèr-co,** M.: wrangle.
alterègo [L. *alter,* other, *ego,* I], M.: alter ego (close representative).
alte-rèllo [*-ro*], ADJ.: somewhat high. **-rézza,** F.: haughtiness (arrogance, disdain). **-rígia,** F.: arrogance.
alter-naménte, ADV.: alternately. **-ná-re,** TR.: alternate. **-nataménte,** ADV.: alternately. **-natíva,** F.: alternative. **-nativaménte,** ADV.: alternatively. **-natívo,** ADV.: alternate; reciprocal. ‖**altèr-no** [*-nus* (*alter,* other)], ADJ.: altern (alternate); successive.
al-tèro [*alto*], ADJ.: haughty (proud). **-tétto,** ADJ.: somewhat high. **-tézza,** F.: highness; height (elevation). **-tezzó-so,** ADJ.: arrogant. **-tíccio,** ADJ.: rather high or tall; gay (slightly intoxicated). **-tieraménte,** ADV.: haughtily; nobly. **-tierézza,** F.: haughtiness. **-tiè-ro,** ADJ.: haughty (arrogant, proud); lofty. **-timetría,** F.: altimetry. **-tí=metro,** ADJ.: measuring the height. **-ti=piáno,** M.: elevated plain. **-ti=só-no, -ti=sonánte,** ADJ.: high-sounding. **-tíssimo,** ADJ.: most high; the Most High. **-ti=tonánte,** ADJ.: sounding from on high. **-titúdine,** F.: altitude (height). **-ti=volánte,** ADJ.: high-flying. ‖**ál-to** 1 [L. *-tus*], ADJ.: high (elevated, lofty; upper; tall; loud); deep; ADV.: loud; M.: height; (*mus.*) treble; full sea; abyss: *in — mare,* on the open sea; *ad — voce,* aloud; *fare — e basso,* play the lord; *avere degli —ti e bassi,* have ups and downs.
álto 2 [Ger. *halt*], M.: halt: *fare* —, halt (stop).
altóre, M., **-tríce** [L. *alere,* feed], F.: nourisher.
al-traménte†, —ti = *altrimenti.* **-tre=sì†,** ADV.: likewise; too. **-trettále†,** ADJ.: such like, similar. **-tre=tánte,** ADV.: as much; as much again. ‖**ál-tri** [L. *-ter*], PRON.: another; some one, anybody. **-trièri†,** M.: day before yesterday. **-triménti,** ADV.: otherwise. **ál-tro,** ADJ.: other; different; M.: another thing: *-tra cosa,* something else; *per* —, in other respects, however; *se — avviene,* if something new happens; — *che,* except that; *se non* —, at least. **-tro=chè†,** ADV.: except that (unless). **-tróndе** or *d'* — [*onde*], ADV.: on the other hand; elsewhere. **-tróve** [*ove*], ADV.: elsewhere. **-trúi** [L. *-ter-huic*], PRON.: other people (others): *l'* —, other people's property.
altúra [*alto*], F.: height (high place); height† (elevation, loftiness); latitude†; haughtiness†.
alturità† = *autorità.*
alúnna, F., **-no** [L. *alere,* nourish], M.: alumna, -nus (in sense of pupil, scholar).
al-veáre, M.: beehive (alveary). **ál-veo,** M.: river-bed; channel; alveus. **-vèolo,** M.: socket; bee cell, alveole; cup (of a flower). **-víno,** ADJ.: alvine. ‖**-vo** [*-vus,* cavity], M.: belly; womb; centre†.
alzábile [*-zare*], ADJ.: that may be raised.
alzáia [L. *helcium*], F.: towing cable.
al-zaménto, M.: raising (lifting). ‖**-zá-re** [*alto*], TR.: raise (lift, elevate, hoist); INTR., REFL.: rise. **-záta,** F.: elevation (rise). **-záto,** ADJ.: raised (lifted up); risen (got up). **-zatúra,** F.: elevation (rise).
am- [L. *ad,* to], PREF.

amá-bile [*amare*], ADJ.: amiable (agreeable). **-bilità**, F.: amiableness. **-bilménte**, ADV.: amiably.

amáca [Sp.], F.: hammock.

amadó-ra†, F., **-re**, M.: lover.

amadría-da or **-de** [Gr. *háma*, together, *drûs*, oak], F.: hamadryad (tree nymph).

amálga-ma [Gr. *málgama*, emollient], F.: amalgam. **-máre**, TR.: amalgamate. **-mazióne†**, F.: amalgamation.

amán-te [*amare*], ADJ.: loving; M.: lover; sweetheart. **-teménte**, ADV.: lovingly.

amanuènse [L. *-sis*], M.: amanuensis; secretary.

amánza†, F.: love; mistress; desire.

ama-ráccio [*-ro*], ADJ.: very bitter. **-ráccìola**, F.: genet (broom).

amáraco [Gr. *-rakos*], M.: MARJORAM.

amaraménte [*-ro*], ADV.: bitterly.

amarán-to [Gr. *a-márantos*, undying], M.: amaranth. **-tíno**, ADJ.: amaranthine. **-tàidi**, M.: family of amaranths.

amará-sca, F.: egriot. ‖**-sco** [*amaro*], M.: egriot (sour cherry) tree.

amáre [L.], TR.: love, like: — *meglio*, like better, have rather.

ama-reggiáre, TR.: embitter; INTR. or REFL.: grow bitter. **-réggiola†**, F.: motherwort. **-rétto**, ADJ.: somewhat bitter (tart); M.: almond-cake. **-rézza**, F.: bitterness (rancour). **-rezzáre†**, TR.: embitter. **-ricánte†**, M.: bitter medicine; PL.: bitters. **-ricáre†**, TR.: embitter; INTR: grow bitter. **-ríccio**, ADJ.: somewhat bitter (tart). **-ríno**, ADJ.: somewhat bitter; M.: almond-cake; egriot†. **-ríre†** = *-reggiare*. **-ritúdine**, F.: bitterness, grief. ‖**amá-ro** [L. *-rus*], ADJ.: bitter; M.: bitter(ness). **-rógnole**, ADJ.: somewhat bitter. **-róre†**, M.: bitterness; severity. **-rulènto†**, ADJ.: bitter. **-ráme**, M.: very bitter thing.

amá-sio, M., **-sia**, F.: lover (paramour). ‖**-ta** [*-re*], F.: lady-love.

amatísta [Gr. *-thustos*], F.: amethyst.

amá-to [*-re*], ADJ.: beloved (dear). **-tóre**, M.: lover. **-tòrio**, ADJ.: loving; amatory. **-tríce**, F.: sweetheart; paramour.

amauròşi [Gr. *-rosis* (*-rós*, dark)], F.: (*med.*) amaurosis.

amáz-zone [Gr. *-zon*], F.: amazon. **-zonèo**, **-zònio**, ADJ.: amazonian.

ambági [L. *-ges*], F. PL.: ambages (circumlocution): *senz'* —, without uncertainty, clearly.

ambasceria = *ambasciata*.

ambáscia [?], F.: pain (grief); anxiety; shortness of breath.

ambasciadóre† = *-sciatore*.

ambasciáre†, INTR.: grieve; be short of breath (pant).

amba-sciáta [L. L. *-ctia*], F.: embassy; commission. **-sciatóra**, F., **—e**, M.: ambassadress, -dor; commissioner. **-sciatríce**, F.: ambassador's wife.

ambásciot = *-scia*.

ámbe† [L. *-bo*], PRON.: both. **=dúe**, **=dúi†**, **=dúo†**, PRON.: both.

ambiáre† [L. *-blare*, walk], INTR.: AMBLE; pace.

ambidúe† = *ambedue*.

ambiènte [*-bire*], ADJ.: ambient (enclosing); M.: surrounding air.

ambi-guaménte, ADV.: ambiguously. **-guità**, F.: ambiguity. **ambí-guo** [L. *-guus* (*amb-igere*, drive about)], ADJ.: ambiguous.

ámbio [*-biare*], M.: AMBLE.

ambí-re [L. (*ire*, go, go round)], TR.: desire eagerly (covet); Eng.† AMBITION. **ambí-to**, ADJ.: coveted. **ámbi-to†**, M.: ambit (circuit), intrigue. **-zioncèlla**, F.: slight ambition. **-zióne**, F.: ambition; eagerness. **-zionáccio**, ADJ.: possessed of low ambition. **-ziosaménte**, ADV.: ambitiously. **-ziosétto**, **-ziosíno**, **-ziosèllo**, ADJ.: somewhat ambitious. **-zióso**, ADJ.: ambitious; desirous.

ámbo [L.], PRON.: both. **=dúe†**, **-dúo†**, PRON.: both.

ám-bra [? Ar.], F.: amber. **-bráre†**, TR.: amber. **-brétta**, F.: sort of mallows.

ambro-gétta [?], F.: paving-brick. **-gíno**, M.: old coin.

am-bròşia [Gr. *-brosía* (*á-mbrotos*, IMMORTAL)], F.: ambrosia. **-broşiáno**, ADJ.: Ambrosian. **-bròşio**, ADJ.: ambrosial.

ambu-lánte, ADJ.: ambulant; ambulatory. ‖**-láre** [L., walk], INTR.: (*jest.*) go or run away. **-lánza**, F.: ambulance. **-latòrio†**, M.: walk.

ame-naménte, ADV.: agreeably. **-nità**, F.: amenity. ‖**amè-no** [L. *amœnus* (*amare*, love)], ADJ.: pleasing (agreeable).

ametisto† = *amatista*.

amfíbio = *anfibio*.

amènte† = *demente*.

amiánto [Gr. *-tos*, in-corrupt], M.: amianth (asbestos).

amí-ca, F.: lady-friend; sweetheart. **-cábile†**, ADJ.: friendly; AMIABLE (affable). **-cabménte**, ADV.: amicably. **-cáre**, REFL.: form a friendship. **-chévole**, ADJ.: AMIABLE (affable). **-chevolézza**, F.: amicableness (amiability). **-chevolménte**, ADV.: amicably. **-císsimo**, ADV.: most friendly. **-cízia**, F.: friendship. ‖**amí-co** [L. *-cus* (*amare*)], M.: friend; ADJ.: friendly. **-cóne**, M.: great friend.

ámido [Gr. *á-mulos*, 'un-ground'], M.: amidin (starch).

amistà [L. *amicitas*], F.: AMITY (friendship).
amítto† = *ammitto.*
ammac-caménto†, M.: bruise. ‖**-cáre** [*macca*], TR.: pound (bruise, crush); depress. **-catúra,** F.: bruise (contusion).
ammacchiáre†, REFL.: hide in a bush.
ammae-strábile, ADJ.: teachable (docile). ‖**-stráre** [*maestro*], TR.: teach; train (discipline). **-stratívo,** ADJ.: instructive. **-stratóre,** M., **-stratríce,** F.: teacher (trainer). **-strazióne**†, F.: teaching. **-strévole**†, ADJ.: teachable (docile).
ammagliá-re [*maglia*], TR.: cord; bind or tie up. **-túra,** F.: tying up (binding).
ammaiáre†, TR.: deck with leaves and flowers.
ammaináre [?], TR.: take in or lower (sails).
ammalá-re [*male*], INTR., REFL.: fall sick; TR.: make sick; infect. **-tíccio**†, ADJ.: sickly. **-ta,** F., **-to,** M.: sick person (patient); ADJ.: sick (diseased). **-túccio**†, **-zzáto**†, ADJ.: sickly.
amma-liaménto, M.: bewitching. ‖**-liáre** [*malia*], TR.: bewitch (charm). **-liatóre,** M.: enchanter (magician). **-liatóra, -liatríce,** F.: enchantress (sorceress). **-liatúra,** F.: witchcraft, charm. **-liazióne,** F.: witchcraft (sorcery).
ammali-ziáre†, **-zíre** [*malizia*], TR.: make malicious. **-zi(a)to,** ADJ.: (grown) malicious.
ammandorláto [*mandorlato*], ADJ.: lozenged; M.: lozenged wall.
ammanettáro [*manetta*], TR.: MANACLE (shackle).
ammanie-raménto, M.: mannerism; studied ornamentation. **-ráre** [*maniera*], TR.: work or embellish in a mannered style; decorate studiously. **-ratúra,** F.: embellishment.
ammanaiáre†, TR.: behead.
amman-náre [*manna*, sheaf], TR.: gather in sheafs; collect; arrange. **-naménto**† = *-nimento.* **-nelláre,** TR.: bundle. **-niménto,** M.: gathering. **-níre,** TR.: put in order (arrange). **-nitúra,** F.: gathering; arrangement.
amman-sáre, -síre [*manso*], domesticate (tame); soften; appease.
amman-táre, TR.: cloak; palliate; disguise. **-tatúra**†, F.: cloaking. **-telláre**†, TR.: cover with a mantle; palliate. ‖**ammán-to** [*manto*], M.: (*poet.*) mantle (cloak).
ammarcíre†, INTR.: putrefy.
ammarginàre†, REFL.: = *marginare.*
ammartelláre† = *martellare.*
ammas-saménto, M.: massing (accumulation). ‖**-sáre** [*massa*], amass (heap up, accumulate). **-satóre,** M.: accumulator. **-sicciáre,** TR.: make massive or compact; REFL.: get compact. **ammás-so,** M.: mass (accumulation, heap).
ammatassáre [*matassa*], TR.: wind into skeins.
ammat-timénto, M.: maddening trouble. ‖**-tíre** [*matto*], INTR.: go mad (be distracted). **-títo,** ADJ.: maddened (distracted, crazy).
ammatto-naménto, M.: brick paving. ‖**-náre** [*mattone*], TR.: pave with bricks. **-náto,** ADJ.: brick-paved; M.: pavement; paved square. **-natúra,** F.: brick paving.
ammaz-za=gátti, M.: old worthless gun or weapon. **-zaménto,** M.: massacre; murder. ‖**-záre** [*mazza*], TR.: murder (massacre); kill; overcome; bore; outdo (at cards); REFL.: kill one's self; toil hard. **-za=sètto,** M.: bully (swaggerer). **-zatóio,** M.: slaughter-house; toilsome work; ADJ.: toilsome. **-zatóre,** M., **-zatríce,** F.: murderer.
ammazzeráre† = *mazzerare.*
ammazzoláre [*mazzo*], TR.: form into bunches or nosegays.
ammelmáre†, **-memmáre**†, REFL.: sink into the mire.
ám(m)en, -ne [Heb.], INTR.: amen.
am=menáre, TR.: bring; give.
ammencíre [*mencio*], TR.: thin.
ammèn-da [*menda*], F.: amends; reform; penalty. **-dábile,** ADJ.: amendable. **-daménto**†, M.: amendment. **-dáre**†, TR.: amend; reform; repair; REFL.: improve. **-dazióne**†, F.: amendment; amelioration.
amme(n)-nicoláre, TR., INTR.: support by trifling or fanciful argument; trifle; indulge in fancies. ‖**-nícolo** [L. *ad-miniculum* (*manus*, hand), light support], M.: trifle (plaything); fanciful word (play of word). **-nicolóna,** F., **-nicólone,** M.: trifler; phantast.
ammensáre [*mensa*, sc. *espiscopale*], TR.: add to a bishop's income.
ammentáre† = *rammentare.*
am-mésso, PART. of *-mettere.* ‖**=méttere,** IRR.; TR.: ADMIT; receive.
ammez-zaménto, M.: division; half. ‖**-záre** [*mezzo*], TR.: divide in two; do half; half complete; cut short (words); meet half-ways†; INTR. or REFL.: be divided in two; be half completed. **-zatóre**†, M.: divider in halves; MEDIATOR. **-zíre,** INTR.: be divided in the middle; be half completed.
am-miccáre [? *mica*], INTR.: wink; beckon. **-mícco,** M.: winking; nod.
ammiglioráre† = *migliorare*
ammi(n)nicol. . † = *amme(n)nicol. .*

ammini-stragióne† = *-strazione*. ‖**-stráre** [*ministro*], TR.: administer. **-strativo**, ADJ.: administrative. **-stratóre**, M.: administrator. **-stratóra**, **-stratríce**, F.: administratrix. **-stratòrio**, ADJ.: administrative. **-strazióne**, F.: administration.

amminuíre† = *diminuire*.

amminutáre†, TR.: MINCE (hash).

ammi-rábile [*-rare*], ADJ.: admirable; wonderful. **-rabilità**, F.: admirability. **-rabilménte**, ADV.: admirably; wonderfully.

ammi-ragliáto, M.: admiralty; admiralship. ‖**-rágllo** [Ar. *al-emir*], M.: admiral; prince†; governor†.

ammi-raméntо†, M.: wonder; admiration. **-rándo**, ADJ.: wonderful; admirable. **-ránza**†, F.: wonder (marvel). ‖**-ráre** [L. *-rari* (*mirari*, wonder)], TR.: regard with wonder (*cf.* arch. Eng. admire; marvel at; admire); REFL.: be astonished (marvel). **-ratívo**, ADJ.: marvellous; admirative. **-ráto**, ADJ.: regarded with wonder (marvellous); admired. **-ratóre**, M., **-ratríce**, F.: admirer. **-razióne**, F.: wonder (surprise; admiration).

ammí-si, PRET. of *ammettere*. **-ssíbile**, ADJ.: admissible. **-ssibilità**, F.: admissibility. **-ssióne**, F.: admission.

ammistióne†, F.: mixture.

ammisu-ráre†, TR.: measure. **-ráto**†, ADJ.: moderate. **-rataménte**†, ADV.: moderately.

ammítto [L. *am-ictus* (*jacere*, throw), mantle], M.: upper vestment of a priest; AMICE (white linen worn about the neck and shoulders at Mass).

ammobi-liaménto, M.: furnishing; furniture. ‖**-liáre** [*mobile*], TR.: furnish.

ammodernáre [*moderno*], TR.: modernize.

ammo-gliaménto, M.: marriage. ‖**-gliáre** [*moglie*], TR.: give a wife to; marry (a son); REFL.: marry (get married).

ammoi-naménto†, M.: dalliance. ‖**-náre**†, TR.: caress (fondle).

ammol-laménto†, M.: steeping; softening. ‖**-láre** [*molle*], TR.: unstretch (loosen); soften (mollify); (us'ly *immollare*) soak (steep); cudgel; answer sharply. **-liènte**, ADJ.: emollient; softening. **-ménto**, M.: softening. **-líre**, TR.: (mollify); relax; REFL.: be softened; calm. **-litívo**, ADJ.: softening; ent; laxative.

-níaca [Gr. *-niaka*], F.: ammonia. **-cále**, ADJ.: ammoniac(al). **-nía-**L.: ammoniac.

ammonigióne† = *ammonizione*.

ammo-niménto, M.: admonishment, etc. ‖**-níre** [L. *monere*, teach], TR.: admonish; warn; (*hist.*) tax; forbid. **-níto**, PART.: admonished, etc.; M.: admonishment; prohibition. **-nitóre**, M., **-nitríce**, F.: admonisher. **-nizioncèlla**, F.: light admonition. **-nizióne**, F.: admonition (warning; reproof); prohibition.

ammon-tataménte, ADV.: confusedly. **-taménto**, M.: massing. ‖**-táre** [*monte*], TR.: pile or heap up (amass); INTR.: amount. **-ticchiáre**, TR.: heap up. **-ticelláre**, TR.: form into small heaps.

ammor-bánte, ADJ.: sickening; stinking. ‖**-báre** [*morbo*], TR.: affect; sicken; INTR., REFL.: sicken; stink. **-bidaménto**, M.: softness; effeminacy. **-bidáre**†, **-bidíre**, TR.: soften; enervate (render effeminate); REFL.: grow soft or effeminate.

ammorsellátо†, M: minced meat and eggs.

ammor-taméntо†, **-táre** = *-timento*, *-tire*. **-timénto**, M.: extinction (quenching); swoon. ‖**-tíre** [*morte*], TR.: MORTIFY (deaden); extinguish; lame; wither; make swoon; Eng.† amortize; INTR.: be extinguished; decay; swoon. **-tizzaménto**, M.: extinguishing; withering. **-tizzáre**, TR.: pay by instalments (amortize). **-tizzazióne**, F.: redemption; amortization: *cassa d'* —, sinking fund.

ammorvidíre [*morvido*], TR.: weaken (soften, render effeminate).

ammorz. . = *smorz. .*

ammoscíre [*moscio*], INTR.: wither (fade, languish).

ammos-fèra [Gr. *atmós*, vapor, *sphaira*, sphere], F.: atmosphere. **-fèrico**, ADJ.: atmospheric.

ammostá-re [*mosto*], TR.: press (the grape). **-tóio**, M.: wine-press. **-tóre**, M.: grape-presser; vintager. **-túra**, F.: grape-pressing; vintage.

ammott. .†, **ammov. .** = *smott. .*, *mov. .*

ammozzicáre†, TR.: cut to pieces.

ammuc-chiaménto, M.: piling up; heap. ‖**-chiáre** [*mucchio*], TR.: heap or pile up.

ammucidíre [*mucido*], INTR.: grow musty or rancid.

ammuf-fáre†, **-fíre** [*muffa*], INTR.: become musty or mouldy.

ammuin. .† = *ammoin. .*

ammulináre [*mulino*], TR.: whirl.

ammun. .† = *ammon. .*

ammusáre, INTR.: pout; REFL.†: meet face to face.

ammu-táre†, **-toláre**† = *ammutire*.

ammuti-naménto, M.: mutiny. ‖**-náre** [?], REFL.: mutiny (revolt).

ammu-tíre, -tolíre [*muto(lo)*], INTR.: become mute or dumb; be embarrassed or nonplussed. **-tolíto,** ADJ.: dumb (speechless).
ámnio [Gr. *-nios*], M.: amnion (membrane round the fœtus).
amni-stía [Gr. *-nestia* (*a-*, not, *mnâsthai*, remember)], F.: amnesty. **-stiáre,** TR.: amnesty.
ámo [L. *hamus*], M.: fish-hook.
amoèrre = *moerre*.
amòmo [Gr. *-on*], M.: amomum (plant).
amoráccia†, F.: horse-radish.
amo-rázzo, M.: light or illicit love. ||**amó-re** [L. *amor*], M.: love (affection; beloved person or thing); regard; charity: — *proprio*, self-love; *per — mio*, for my sake; *per l' — di Dio*, for God's sake; *essere in —*, be in favor with; *andare in —*, be in heat, rut (of animals). **-reggiaménto,** M.: love-affair. **-reggiáre,** TR.: make love to (flirt with); fondle. **-rétto,** M.: slight love or affection (inclination). **-révole,** ADJ.: loving (affectionate, affable): *all' —*, affectionately. **-revoleggiáre**† = *-reggiare*. **-revolézza,** F.: affability (cordiality); kindness. **-revolménte,** ADV.: affectionately; kindly. **-revolóne,** *aug.* of *-revole*.
amòrfo [Gr. *a-*, not *morphé*, form], ADJ.: amorphous.
amo-ríno [*-re*], M.: little Cupid; charming baby; mignonette; tête-à-tête (S-shaped) sofa. **-rosaménte,** ADV.: lovingly. **-rosèllo**†, ADJ.: amiable (pleasing). **-rosíno,** ADJ.: nice. ||**-róso** [*-re*], ADJ.: loving (amorous, affectionate); M.: lover (gallant, wooer). **-ròtto**†, M.: nascent love.
amoscíno [L. *damascenus*], M.: DAMSON plum.
amovíbi-le [*movere*], ADJ.: movable. **-lità,** F.: movableness.
am-piaménte, ADV.: amply. **-piáre**†, TR.: amplify (enlarge, extend). **-piézza,** F.: ampleness (largeness, extent). ||**ám-pio** [L. *-plus*], ADJ.: AMPLE (large). **-piogiovánte**†, ADJ.: very helpful. **-pioveggènte**†, ADJ.: broad-sighted. **-pióso**†, ADJ.: ample, vast.
amplaménte = *ampiamente*.
amplèsso [L. *-plexus* (*plectere*, wind)], M.: (*jest.*) embrace.
ampli-aménto, M.: enlargement. **-áre,** TR.: enlarge (extend). **-atívo,** ADJ.: enlarging. **-atóre,** M., **-atríce,** F.: extender, amplifier. **-azióne,** F.: enlargement. **-ficaménto,** M.: amplification. **-ficáre,** TR.: amplify (enlarge); exaggerate. **-ficatóre,** M., **-ficatríce,** F.: amplifier, magnifier. **-ficazióne,** F.: amplification; exegesis. **-túdine,** F.: amplitude. ||**ámpl(i)-o** [L. *amplus*], ADJ.: ample (broad).
ampól-la [L. *ampulla*], F.: ampulla (cruet, vial); bubble; inflated expression. **-létta**†, F.: small vial; hour-glass. **-lína,** *dim.* of *-la*. **-losaménte,** ADV.: in an inflated or bombastic manner. **-losità,** F.: bombast; fustian. **-lóso,** ADJ.: inflated; bombastic. **-lúzza**†, F.: small vial; hour-glass.
ampu-táre [L. *putare*, prune], TR.: amputate. **-tazióne,** F.: amputation.
amuèrre = *moerre*.
amuléto [L. *-tum*], M.: amulet.
anabattísta [Gr. *aná*, again, *baptízein*, baptize], M.: anabaptist.
anacárd(i)o [l. L.], M.: ancardium (plant).
ána-ce, -cio [Gr. *ánison*], M.: anise. **-ciáto,** ADJ.: anise-flavoured. **-cíno,** M.: sugar pill (with anise-seed).
anacolúto [Gr. *a-*, not, *akóluthos*, following], M.: anacoluthon (want of gram. sequence).
anaco-rèta [Gr. *ana-chorein*, retire], M.: anchoret, -rite. **-rètico,** ADJ.: anchoretic(al).
ana-creòntica [poet *Anacreon*], F.: anacreontic. **-creòntico,** ADJ.: anacreontic.
anacronismo [Gr. *aná*, back, *chrónos*, time], M.: anachronism.
an-áfora [Gr. *aná*, back, *phérein*, carry], F.: anaphora.
anaglifo [Gr. *aná*, up, *glúphein*, engrave], M.: anaglyph (ornament in light relief).
ana-gogía [Gr. *aná*, up, *ágein*, lead], F.: anagogics (spiritual interpretation). **-gogicaménte,** ADV.: anagogically. **-gògico,** ADJ.: anagogic(al).
anagrám-ma [Gr. *aná*, again, *gráphein*, write], M.: anagram. **-mático,** ADJ.: anagrammatic(al). **-maticaménte,** ADV.: anagrammatically. **-matismo,** M.: anagrammatism. **-matísta,** pl. *—ti*, M.: anagrammatist. **-matizzáre,** TR.: anagrammatize.
analèttì†, M. PL.: analects.
an=alfabèto [Gr. *an-*, not], ADJ.: unable to read; illiterate; M. (*—ta*, f.): illiterate.
aná-lisi [Gr. *aná*, back, *lúein*, loose], F.: analysis. **-lísta,** pl. *-listi*, M.: analyzer. **-lítica,** F.: analytics. **-lítico,** ADJ.: analytical. **-liticaménte,** ADV.: analytically. **-lizzáre,** TR.: analyze.
ana-logaménte, ADV.: analogously. **-logía,** F.: analogy. **-logicaménte,** ADV.: analogically. **-lògico,** ADJ.: analogic(al). **-logismo,** M.: analogism. ||**aná-logo** [Gr. *aná*, after, *lógos*, ratio], ADJ.: analogous.
ananásso [fr. Peruv.], M.: ananas, pine-apple.

ana-pèsto [Gr. *ana-paíein*, strike back, reverse], M.: anapest (⏑ ⏑ —, i.e. a 'reversed' dactyl). **-pèstico**, ADJ.: anapestic.

an-archía [Gr. *a*-, not, *arché*, head], F.: anarchy. **-árchico**, ADJ.: anarchic(al). **-archísta**, pl. *-archisti*, M.: anarchist.

anástrofe [Gr. *aná*, back, *stréphein*, turn], F.: anastrophe (reversed construction).

aná-tema or **-tèma** [Gr. *aná-thema*, setting up], F.: anathema (ban). **-temizzáre**, TR.: anathematize (excommunicate).

ana-tomía [Gr. *ana-tomé*, dis-section], F.: anatomy. **-tomicaménte**, ADV.: anatomically. **-tòmico**, ADJ.: anatomic(al). **-tomísta**, pl. *—ti*, M.: anatomist. **-tomizzáre**, TR.: anatomize (dissect); investigate.

ána-tra [L. *anas*] F.: duck. **-trèlla**, F., **-tríno**, M.: young duck. **-tròccolo**, M.: young duck; short fellow. **-tròtto**, M.: young duck.

ánca [? Ger. *hanke*, HAUNCH], F.: haunch; hip: *dare d'anche*, run away.

ancèlla [L. *-cilla*], F.: maid-servant.

ánche [L. *hanc*, this, sc. *horam*, hour], ADV.: also, too, even: *ne* —, not even; neither; *quand'* —, although.

anchilòsi [Gr *ankulósis*], F.: anchylosis.

anci d.† = *uccid.*.

ancíle [L.], M.: ancile (sacred shield).

ancílla† = *ancella*.

ancípite†, ADJ.: uncertain; amphibious.

ancíso†, PART. of *ancidere*.

ánco = *anche*: *per* —, as yet.

ancói†, ADV.: to-day.

ancóra [L. *hanc horam*, this hour], ADV.: yet, still; now; even; again: — *che* or *ancor(a)chè*, even though; although.

áncora [L.], F.: anchor.

ancorachè†, see *ancóra*.

anco-rággio [*-ra*], M.: anchorage. **-ráre**, TR.: anchor.

ancor-chè, see *ancóra*.

ancorétta, *dim.* of *áncora*.

ancúdine [L. *in-cus* (*cudere*, beat)], F.: anvil.

an-damentáccio†, M.: bad walk. **-daménto**, M.: walk (gait, carriage); proceeding. **-dánte**, ADJ.: going; easy†; M.: andante (easy gait). **-danteménte**, ADV.: continuously (without interruption). **-dantíno**, M.: andantino. ||**-dáre** [?], IRR. §; TR.: go; move; M.: walking, gait; PL. garden-walks; alleys: — *rsene*, go away; disappear; decline; — *in collera*, get angry; — *(all')incontro*, go to meet; — *a marito*, marry; — *a monte*, interrupt; — *pelegrino*, go wandering; — *a seconda*, go with the stream (prosper); *al peggio* —, at the worst.

-dáta, F.: going away; walk; movement (of the bowels), stool. **-dáto**, ADJ.: gone; past; ruined; wasted. **-datóre**†, M., **-datríce**†, F.: walker: — *di notte*, nightwalker. **-datúra**, F.: manner of walking (gait). **-dazzáccio**†, M.: violent disease. **-dázzo**, M.: passing or superficial fashion; epidemical disease. **-dir-i-vièni**, PL.: going and coming; meander (windings); digressions.

§ Ind.: Pres. *vò* or *vádo*, *vài*, *vá*; *andiámo*, *andáte*, *vánno*. Fut. *and(e)rò*. Cond. *and(e)rèi*. Subj.: Pres. *váda*, etc.: *andiámo*, *andiáte*, *vádano*. I've *vá*, *andáte*. With *tras-*, and *ri-*, regular.

ándito [L. *ad-itus* (*ire*, go)], M.: entrance; passage; landing (of a staircase).

andriènne [Fr.], M.: (*jest.*) old garment.

andrògino [Gr. *anér*, man, *guné*, woman], ADJ.: androgynous.

andróne [?], M.: palace entrance (portal); entrance†; avenue; waiting-room.

anèd-doto [Gr. *an*-, not, *ék-dotos*, given out, published], M.: anecdote. **-dòtico**, ADJ.: anecdotic(al).

ane-lánte, ADJ.: panting†; desirous. ||**-láre** [L. (*halare*, breathe)]; INTR.: breathe strongly† (pant, Eng.† ANHELE); be breathlessly eager, desire eagerly (long ardently). **-lánza**†, F.: ardent desire.

anè-lito, M.: strong breathing (panting).

anel-láre†, TR.: provide with rings; curl. **-latúra**†, F.: curliness; curled hair. **-létto**, **-líno**, M.: little ring. ||**anèl-lo**, pl. *-li* or (*lit.*) *-la* [dim. of L. *anus*, ring], M.: ring; ringlet; link; thimble (ring-like): *dar* (*prender*) *l'* —, marry (be married); *giorno dell'* —, wedding-day.

anè-lo [*-lare*], M.: (*poet.*) panting; breathless. **-lóso**†, ADJ.: short-breathed (asthmatic).

ane-mía [Gr. *an*-, not, *háima*, blood], F.: anæmia. **-èmico**, ADJ.: anæmic.

anèmone [L.], **-molo**†, M.: anemone.

anes-tesía [Gr. *an*-, not, *aísthesis*, feeling], F.: anæsthesia. **-tètico**, ADJ.: anæsthetic.

anfa-naménto, M.: rambling, incoherent speech. ||**-náre** [variant of *affanare*], TR.: ramble about; talk at random†. **-natóre**†, M.: pratter. **-neggiáre**†, INTR.: talk foolishly. **-nía**†, F.: talk; nonsense.

anfíbio [Gr. *amphi*, both, *bíos*, life], ADJ.: amphibious.

anfi-bología [Gr. *amphi-bólos*, casting about, ambiguous, *lógos*, speech], F.: amphibology. **-bologicaménte**, ADV.: ambiguously. **-bològico**, ADJ.: amphibolic (ambiguous, doubtful).

anfiteátro [Gr. *amphi*, around, *théatron*], M.: amphitheatre.

anfi-zióne [Gr. *amphiktúones*], M.: Am-

phictyons. **-ziònico**, ADJ.: Amphictyonic.
ánfora [L. *amphora*], F.: amphora (Rom. vase).
anfrátto†, M.: narrow place.
angá-ria† [L.], F.: forced service. **-riáre, -rieggiáre**, TR.: overtax (burden).
ánge-la, F.: angel. **-létta**, F.: little angel. **-licaménte**, ADV.: angelically.
angè-lico, ADJ.: angelical. ||**ánge-lo** [Gr. *ángelos*, messenger], M.: angel: — *custode*, tutelar angel; *pane* (or *cibo*) *degli* —*i*, communion. **-lòtto**†, M.: old coin. **-lúccio**, M.: little angel.
ángere [L.], TR.: lighten; anguish.
angheria [fr. Pers.], F.: hateful tax; imposition; violence.
angí-na [*angere*], F.: quinsy. **-nóso**, ADJ.: quinsy (as adj.)
ángio-la, -lo, (*pop.*) for *angela, -lo*. **-létta, -létto, -líno**, *dim.*; dead child.
angipòrto†, M.: portal; blind alley; brothel.
angli-canísmo, M.: Anglicanism. ||**-cáno**, ADJ.: Anglican. **-cismo**, M.: Anglicism.
ango-láre, ADJ.: angular. **-larménte**, ADV.: angularly. **-larità**, F.: angularity. **-létto**, M.: small angle. ||**ángolo** [L. *-lus*], M.: angle; corner. **-lóso**, ADJ.: angulous (full of corners).
an-gonía (*vulg.*) = *agonia*. **-góre**†, M.: anguish.
ango-scévole†, ADJ.: painful. ||**angòscia** [L. *angustia*, narrowness], F.: ANGUISH. **-sciaménte**, ADV.: painfully. **-sciaménto**†, M.: anguish (affliction). **-sciáre**, TR.: anguish; distress (grieve); REFL.: be grieved (grieve); fret. **-sciáto**, ADJ.: in anguish (grieved, distressed); anxious. **-sciosaménte**, ADV.: distressedly (with grief). **-scióso**, ADJ.: distressed (grieved); anxious.
án-gue [L. *-guis*], M.: (*poet.*) serpent. **-gui=criníto**, ADJ.: snake-haired. **-guílla**, F.: eel. **-guilláia**, F.: place where eels are found. **-guillétta, -guillína**, F.: small eel.
anguináia [L. *inguinalia*], F.: groin.
angúria†, F.: watermelon.
angú-stia, F.: narrowness; distress. **-stiáre**, TR.: compress; distress, pain; REFL.: be distressed. **-stióso**, ADJ.: distressed; anxious. ||**angú-sto** [L. *-stus*], ADJ.: narrow, tight; close; stingy; miserable.
áni-ce†, **-cio**† = *anaccio*.
aníle†, ADJ.: (*poet.*) aged (old).
áni-ma [L.], F.: soul; life; breastplate: *render l'* —, give up the ghost. **-maccína**, F.: poor soul; wretch. **-maláccio**, M.: great ugly animal; stupid dunce. **-mále**, M: animal. **-malescaménte**, ADV.: like an animal; beastly. **-malésco**, ADJ.: animal. **-malétto**, M.: small animal; animalcule. **-malettuccíáccio**, M.: ugly little animal. **-malità**†, F.: animality. **-malóne**, M.: big animal. **-malúccio, -malúzzo**, M.: ugly animal. **-mánte**, ADJ.: animating; being† (animal). **-máre**, TR.: animate; encourage. **-mataménte**, ADV: animately. **-máto**, ADJ.: animated (lively). **-matóre**, M., **-matríce**, F.: animator. **-mavversióne**†, F.: animadversion; chastisement. **-mazióne**, F.: animation. **-mèlla**, F.: sweet-bread; sucker (of a pump). **ánimo** [L. *-mus*], M.: soul, esp. as heart; mind (understanding); sentiment; affection; courage: *di buon* —, with all my heart; *farsi* —, pick up courage. **-mosaménte**, ADV.: courageously (boldly). **-mosità**, F.: animosity. **-móso**, ADJ.: animated; courageous (valiant); Eng.† animose; hostile. **-muccíno**†, M.: small mind.
anisétta [*anace*], F.: anisette (cordial).
áni-tra†, etc., **-tròccolo** = *anatra*, etc.
annac-quaménto, M.: watering. ||**-quáre** [*acqua*], TR.: mix with water (water); temper; mitigate. **-quatíccio**, ADJ.: somewhat mixed with water (dilute); M.: admixture of water.
annaf-fiaménto, M.: sprinkling. ||**-fiáre** [L. *in-ad*, *flare*, blow], TR.: sprinkle (water). **-fiáta**, F.: sprinkling. **-fiatína**, F.: light sprinkling. **-fiatóio**, M.: watering-pot (sprinkler). **-fiatúra**, F.: sprinkling.
anná-le [*anno*], ADJ.†: annual. **-li**, M. PL.: annals. **-lísta**, M.: annalist.
annasáre† = *annusare*.
anna-spáre, TR.: reel into skeins. **-spío**, M.: violent gesticulation; agitation. ||**anná-spo** [OHG. *haspa*, HASP, spindle], M.: reel (for winding yarn). **-spóna**, F., —**e**, M.: busybody; jack-of-all-trades
anná-ta [*anno*], F.: year (esp. with reference to products); year's profits or interest. **-táccia**, F.: bad year. **-tína**, F.: (*iron.*) little yearly interest. **-túccia**, F.: bad year.
anneb-biaménto, M.: cloudiness; gloom. ||**-biáre** [*nebbia*], TR.: surround with a mist or fog (befog); cloud; obfuscate; mildew; REFL: become obfuscated or turbid.
anne-gaménto, M.: smothering; drowning. ||**-gáre** [L. *necare*, kill], TR.: smother; drown.
annegazióne = *abnegazione*.
anneghit-timénto†, M.: laziness. **-tíre** [*neghittoso*], INTR.: grow lazy.
anne-ráre [*nero*], TR.: blacken. **-ri-**

ménto, M.: blackening; blackness. **-ríre**, TR.: blacken (darken); tarnish; INTR., REFL.: grow black; darken. **-ritúra**, F.: blackness.

an-mèssi, PRET. of *-nettere*. **-nessióne**, F.: annexation. ‖**-mèsso**, PART. of *-nèttere:* ANNEXED (joined); M.: annex; part.

anne-stamènto, M.: grafting; inoculation. ‖**-stáre** [variant of *innestare*], TR.: (in)graft, insert. **-statúra**, F.: grafting; insertion. **annè-sto**, M.: grafting.

an-nèttere [L. *nectere*, bind], IRR.§; TR.: combine; bind together.

§ Pret. *an-nettèi* or *-nèssi*, *-nettè* or *-nèsse*, etc. Part. *annèsso*.

annétto, *dim.* of *anno*.

annichi-lamènto, M.: annihilation. ‖**-láre** [L. *nihil*, nothing], TR.: ANNIHILATE; annul; dismay; humble. **-lazióne**†, F.: annihilation. **-líre** = **-láre**.

annidáre [*nido*], TR.: build (a nest)†; nestle†; harbour (have in mind); REFL.: nestle; settle (get into).

annien-tamènto, M.: reduction to nothing (annihilation). ‖**-táre** [*niente*], TR.: reduce to nothing (annihilate).

annighitt..† = *anneghitt..*

annistía† = *amnistía*.

anniversário [L. *-rius*], M.: anniversary.

ánno [L. *-nus*], M.: year: *d' — in —*, from year to year: *capo d' —*, new year.

annobilíre† = *nobilitare*.

anno-damènto, M.: tying; knot. ‖**-dáre** [*nodo*], TR.: tie (knot); join. **-datúra**, F.: tying. **-dicchiáto**, ADJ.: lightly tied.

annoi-amènto, M.: annoyance; weariness. ‖**-áre** [*noia*], TR.: annoy; weary; REFL.: be annoyed; grow weary. **-atóre**, M.: annoyer. **-óso**†, ADJ.: annoying (tedious).

annoláre† = *noleggiare*.

annomáre† = *nominare*.

annò-na [L. *annus*, year], F.: (a year's) provisions (victuals). **-nário**, ADJ.: pertaining to provisions (of provisions). **annó-so**, ADJ.: of years (old; ancient).

annotá-re [*nota*], TR.: annotate (note). **-riáre**, TR.: fit or qualify for a notary. **-tóre**, M.: annotator. **-zióne**, F.: annotation; observation (remark).

annot-táre [*notte*], IMP.: become night; grow dark; pass the night. **-tíre**† = *-tare*.

annovelláre†, TR.: misinform; beguile.

annove-ramènto, M.: enumeration. ‖**-ráre** [*novero*], TR.: number (count). ...**-re**†, M.: counter. **-révole**†, ADJ.: ...y be counted (computable). **an-**...**o**†, M.: reckoning (calculation). ...**lo** [*anno*], ADJ.: annual (yearly); year's profit or allowance†; year†; anniversary†. **-almènte**, ADV.: annually. **-ário**, M.: annuary, year-book. **annuáccio**, M.: bad year.

annugoláre† = *annuvolare*.

annu-íre [L. *ad-nuere*, nod to], INTR.: nod assent; assent. **-ènte**, ADJ.: assenting. **-ènza**, F.: consent.

annul-lamènto, M.: annulment. ‖**-láre** [*nullo*], TR.: annul (render null; nullify; cancel). **-latívo**, ADJ.: annulling. **-latóre**, M.: annuller (abolisher). **-lagióne**†, **-lazióne**†, F.: annulment. **-líre**† = *-lare*.

annumeráre† = *annoverare*.

annunci.. = *annunzi..*

annun-ziáre [*nunzio*], TR.: announce; predict. **-ziáta**, F.: the Virgin Mary receiving the Annunciation; picture of the Annunciation. **-ziatóre**, M., **-ziatríce**, F.: announcer; foreboder. **-ziazióne**, F.: annunciation; Lady-day. **annún-zio**, M.: announcement; advertisement.

ánnuo [*anno*], ADJ.: annual (yearly).

annusáre [*naso*], TR.: bring under the nose (for smelling, etc.); smell at; test; (smell out) guess; suspect; REFL.: find each other by smelling (of dogs); grow attached to one another.

annuvo-lamènto, M.: clouding up; cloudiness. ‖**-láre** [*nuvola*], TR.: cloud; INTR., REFL.: cloud up (grow cloudy). **-láto**, PART.: cloudy. **-líre**† = *-lare*.

áno [L. *-nus*, ring], M.: anus.

anodíno [Gr. *an-*, not, *odúne*, pain], M.: anodyne.

an-omalía, F.: anomaly. ‖**-òmalo** [Gr. *an-*, not, *homalós*, even], ADJ.: anomalous.

anònimo [Gr. *an-*, not, *ónuma*, NAME], ADJ.: anonymous.

anormá-le [Gr. *a-*, not, *nórma*, RULE], ADJ.: abnormal; irregular. **-lità**, F.: abnormality.

án-sa [L.], F.: handle (of a vase): *dare* (*prender*) —, give (take) boldness; encourage, take courage. **-sáto**, ADJ.: provided with a handle.

an-samènto, M.: shortness of breath. ‖**-sáre** [*-sio*], INTR.: pant (breathe short).

anseático [Ger. *hanse*], ADJ.: Hanseatic.

án-sia, **-sietà**, F.: anxiety. ‖**án-sio** [L. *-xius*], ADJ.: anxious.

ánsi-ma [*asma*], F.: difficulty of breathing (asthma). **-máre**, INTR.: breathe with difficulty.

an-siosamènte, ADV.: anxiously. ‖**-sióso** [*-sio*], ADJ.: anxious.

ánsola [L. *-sula* (*-sa*)], F.: clapper hook (of a bell).

antago-nísmo, M.: antagonism. ‖**-ní-**

-sta [Gr. *anti*, against, *agonistés*, combattant], M.: antagonist.
antártico [L. *-cus*], ADJ.: antarctic.
ánte [L.], PREP.: before.
ante-cedènte, ADJ.: antecedent (preceding). **-cedentemẽnte,** ADV.: antecedently. **-cedènza**†, F.: antecedency (priority). ‖**-cèdere**† [L. *cedere*, go], TR.: go before (antecede; precede). **-cessóra,** F., **-cessóre,** M.: predecessor.
ante=fátto, M.: Eng.† antefact; previous act.
antelmíntico [Gr. *anti*, against, *élmins*, worm], M.: vermifuge.
antelucáno [L. *ante*, *lux*, LIGHT], ADJ.: preceding daybreak.
antelunáre [L. *ante*, *luna*, moon], ADJ.: preceding the appearance of the moon.
antemuràle [*antimuro*], M.: rampart.
ante=náto, M.: forefather (ancestor).
antén-na [L.], F.: sail-yard; lance; log (trunk); antenna (feeler); sail†. **-náre**†, TR.: provide with feelers. **-nétta,** *dim.* of *-na*.
Antenòra [*Antenora*, Trojan deemed a traitor], F.: 'Antenora' (place of punishment for traitors, in Dante's Inferno).
antepenúltimo† = *antipenultimo*.
ante=pórre, IRR.; TR.: put before; prefer. **-pósi,** PRET. of *-porre*. **-posizióne,** F.: placing before; preference. **-pósto,** PART. of *-porre*.
ántera or **antèra** [Gr. *antherós*, flowery], F.: anther.
anterió-re [L. *-r*], ADJ.: anterior (prior, former). **-rità,** F.: anteriority (priority). **-rménte,** ADV.: anteriorly (previously, before).
ante=scrítto, ADJ.: written before or above.
antesignáno [L. *ante*, SIGNUM, sign], M.: standard-bearer.
ante=veníre†, IRR.; INTR.: come before or first.
ánti- [L. *ante* or Gr. *antí*], PREF.: before; against.
anti=andáre†, IRR.; INTR.: go before.
anti=bágno, M.: bath-room cabinet.
anti=bráccio, M.: forearm.
anticá-glia [*antico*], F.: antiquities†; worthless old stuff; old person. **-ménte,** ADJ.: anciently (formerly).
anti=cámera, F.: antechamber (waiting-room); servants in waiting: *fare* —, wait to be received.
anti-cáto† [*-co*] = *antiquato*. **-cheggiáre**†, INTR.: follow ancient customs. **-chétto,** ADJ.: rather ancient or old-fashioned. **-chézza**† = *-chità*. **-chi,** PL. of *-co*. **-chità,** F.: antiquity (ancientness; ancient relics or customs); (*jest.*) old person.

antici-paménto = *-pazione*. ‖**-páre** [L. *ante*, *capere*, take], TR.: anticipate; pay in advance; pay out; INTR.: come beforehand; REFL.: act quickly or promptly. **-pataménte,** ADV.: by anticipation (beforehand, in advance). **-páto,** PART.: anticipated, etc.; precocious†, out of tune†; M.: sum paid in advance. **-pazióne,** F.: anticipation; foresight; sum paid in advance. **-pazioncèlla,** *dim.* of *-pazione*.
antí-co [L. *-quus*], ADJ.: antique (ancient, old); M.: antique (ancient art and manners); **-chi,** PL.: ancients (esp. Greeks and Romans); ancestors. **-cúccio,** *dim.* of *-co*.
anti=cognizióne†, F.: precognition. **=cognóscere**†, IRR.; TR.: foreknow; foresee.
anticolèrico [*anti colera*], ADJ.: counter-active of cholera.
anti=córrere†, IRR.; TR.: run before; outrun. **-corrière**†, M.: forerunner.
anticórte†, F.: fore-court.
anti=cristiáno†, ADJ.: antichristian. **-crísto**†, M.: antichrist.
anticursóre†, M.: forerunner.
anti=dáta, F.: antedate.
antidétto†, ADJ.: foretold, aforesaid.
anti-diciménto†, M.: prediction. **=díre**†, IRR.; TR.: predict.
anti=diluviáno, ADJ.: antediluvian.
anti-dotário†, M.: dispensatory. **antí-doto** [Gr. *-doton* (*didónai*, give)], M.: antidote.
anti=febbríle, ADJ.: antifebrile.
antí-fona [Gr. *phoné*, sound], F.: antiphon, anthem. **-fonário,** M.: anthem-book.
antífrasi [Gr. *-phrasis*], F.: antiphrasis.
anti=giudicáre, TR.: prejudge.
antígrafo [Gr. *-phé*], M.: antigraph (transcript).
anti=guardáre†, TR.: foresee. **-guárdia**†, F., **-guárdo**†, M.: vanguard.
antilogía [Gr.], F.: antilogy.
antílope [?], F.: antelope.
anti=meridiáno, ADJ.: antemeridian.
anti=méttere†, IRR.; TR.: place before; prefer.
antimò-nio [?], M.: antimony. **-niále,** ADJ.: antimonic.
anti=múro, M.: front-walk; parapet.
anti=náto, ADJ.: born before; first-born.
anti=nóme, M.: first name.
antinomía [Gr. *anti*, against, *nómos*, law], F.: antinomy.
anti=pápa, M.: antipope.
anti=párte, F.: first settlement (of a will).
anti=passáto, ADJ.: past (last, ult.).
anti=pásto, M.: course served after the

meat; (in some countries) side-dish served before table.
anti-patía [Gr. *antí*, against, *pathein*, suffer], F.: antipathy. **-pático**, ADJ.: antipathetic(al).
anti=pensáre†, TR.: premeditate.
anti=penúltimo, ADJ.: antepenultimate; M.: antepenult.
antípode [Gr. *antí*, against, *poús*, FOOT], M.: antipode.
anti=pónere†, **=pórre†** = *anteporre*.
anti=pòrta, F.: (us'ly) **-pòrto**, M.: anteport (outer gate); vestibule; outwork (before the gate of a city); (*typ.*) half-title, bastard title.
anti=prèndere†, IRR.; TR.: seize beforehand.
anti-quária, F.: antiquarian science; antiquities. **-quário**, M.: antiquarian. **-quáto**, ADJ.: antiquated. ‖**antí-quo** [L. *-quus* (*ante*, before)], ADJ.: antique (ancient, old).
anti=sála, F.: front hall or parlour.
anti=sapére†, IRR.; TR.: foreknow. **-sapévole†**, ADJ.: foreknowing (prognostic). **-sapúta†**, F.: foreknowledge, foresight. **-sapúto†**, PART.: foreknown.
anti=scrítto, ADJ.: written before (aforesaid).
antisèttico [Gr. *antí*, against, *septikós*, putrefying], ADJ.: antiseptic.
antistèrico, ADJ.: anti-hysteric.
antí-sta†, **-ste†**, **-stite**, M.: head; chief; prelate.
antí=strofe, F.: antistrophe.
antí=tesi, F.: antithesis.
antitopèia [Gr. *antí*, against, *tópos*, place], F.: change of place by poetical license.
anti=vanguárdia, F.: scouts preceding the vanguard.
anti=vedére, IRR.; TR.: foresee. **-vediménto†**, M.: foreseeing. **-veditóre†**, M.: foreseer (foreboder). **-vedutaménte**, ADV.: with precaution. **-vedúto**, PART. of *-vedere*. **-veggènte**, ADJ.: foreseeing. **-veggènza**, F.: foresight (prevision).
anti-vegnènte†, ADJ.: preventing. **=veníre†**, IRR.; TR.: come beforehand with (anticipate); forestall; prevent. **-venúto†**, PART. of *-venire*.
anti=vigília, F.: day before the eve.
antología [Gr. *ánthos*, flower, *légein*, gather], F.: anthology.
antono-másia [Gr. *antí*, instead, *ónoma*, NAME], F.: antonomasia. **-mástico**, ADJ.: antonomastic.
antráce [Gr. *-thrax*], M.: anthrax.
ántro [L. *-trum*], M.: cave; den; grotto.
antropo- [Gr. *ánthropos*, man]: **-fagía** [*-fago*], F.: anthropophagy. **antropòfago** [Gr. *phagein*, eat], M.: cannibal; PL.: anthropophagi. **-logía** [Gr. *lógos*, discourse], F.: anthropology. **-morfiṣmo** [*-morfo*], M.: anthropomorphism. **-mòrfo** [Gr. *morphé*, form], M.: manlike animal; PL.: anthropomorpha.
anuláre [L. *-lus*, little ring], M.: ring-finger; stone set in a ring; ring-shaped eclipse; ADJ.: for a ring.
ánzi [L. *ante*], ADV.: instead; on the contrary; rather, nay; before†.
anzi-†, often for *anti-*.
anzia-nità, F.: ancientness (antiquity): *per* —, by seniority. **-nítico**, M.: seniority (eldership). ‖**anziá-no** [l. L. *antianus* (*ante*, before)], ADJ.: old; senior; M.: senior; elder. **-nòtto**, ADJ.: rather old (oldish).
anzi=chè, CONJ.: before that; rather than; besides†.
anzidétto [*ante detto*], ADJ.: aforesaid.
aocchiáre, etc. = *adocchiare*, etc.
aoliáto = *oliato*.
aombráre [*ombra*], TR.: shade; INTR.: be shaded.
aònio [*Aonia*], ADJ.: Aonian (pertaining to the Muses).
aorcáre†, TR.: hang.
aorísto [Gr. *a-*, not, *horízein*, define], M.: aorist.
aormáre†, TR.: trace.
aòrta [Gr. *-té*], F.: aorta.
ap- [L. *ad*, to], PREF.: ap-.
apa-tía [Gr. *a-*, not, *pathein*, suffer], F.: apathy. **-tísta**, pl. *-tisti*, M.: apathist, cold person. **-tisticaménte**, ADV.: apathetically. **-tístico**, pl. —*ci*, ADJ.: apathetic.
ápe [L. *apis*], F.: bee.
a-períre† = *aprire*. **-peritívo**, ADJ.: aperitive (opening). **-pertaménte**, ADV.: openly (publicly). **-pèrto**, PART. of *-p(e)rire*. **-pertóne†**, ADV.: wide open. **-pertóre**, M.: opener. **-pertúra**, F.: aperture (opening).
apètalo [Gr. *a-*, not, *p..*], ADJ.: apetalous.
apiário [*ape*], M.: apiary.
ápi-ce [L. *apex*], M.: apex (summit, top), climax; tonic accent: *un* —, a smallest bit. **apí-colo†**, M.: small peak.
api=cultóre, M.: bee-breeder. **=cultúra**, F.: apiculture.
ápiro [Gr. *a-*, not, *pûr*, FIRE], ADJ.: incombustible.
aplústre [L.] or **-stro**, M.: poop-ornament.
apo- [Gr. *apó*, from, away], PREF.: apo-.
apocalisse [Gr. *apo-kalúptein*, un-cover], F.: Apocalypse.
apòcope [Gr. *apó*, *kóptein*, cut], F.: apocope.
apòcrifo [Gr. *apó*, *krúptein*, hide], ADJ. apocryphal (doubtful).

apodíttico [Gr. *apo-deiktúnai*, point out], ADJ.: apodictic(al).
ápodo [Gr. *a-*, not, *poús*, FOOT], ADJ.: footless.
apòdosi [Gr. *apó-dosis*, giving back], F.: apodosis.
apofisi [Gr. *apó-physis*, off-growth], F.: apophysis,
apoftègma, -tèmma [Gr. *apó*, *phthéngesthai*, speak], M.: apo(ph)thegm.
apogèo [Gr. *apó*, *gaia*, earth], M.: apogee.
apògrafo [Gr. *apó*, *gráphein*, write], M.: apograph (copy).
Apòl-line [*-lo*], M.: (*lit.*) Apollo: *stare in* —, fare (eat) sumptuously. **-líneo,** ADJ.: Apollonic.
apolo-gètico, ADJ.: apologetic. ‖**-gía** [Gr. *apó*, *lógos*, speech], F.: apology (defense). **-gísta,** M.: apologist. **-gizzáre,** INTR.: make apology. **apòlo-go,** M.: apologue; allegory.
apo-plessía [Gr. *apó*, *plêssein*, strike], apoplexy. **-plèt(t)ico,** ADJ.: apoplectic.
apo-stasía [Gr. *apo-stasía*, STANDING OFF], F.: apostasy. **apò-stata,** pl. *-stati*, M.: apostate. **-statáre,** INTR.: apostatize. **-statrícet,** F.: apostate.
apo-stèma† [Gr. *apo-stênai*, stand off], F.: aposteme (abcess). **-stemáre,** INTR.: suppurate. **-stemáto,** ADJ.: affected with an abscess. **-stemazióne,** F.: apostemation (formation of an abscess).
apostílla† = *postilla*.
apo-stoláto, M.: apostleship. **-stolicaménte,** ADV.: apostolically. **-stòlico,** ADJ.: apostolic. ‖**apò-stolo** [Gr. *apo-stéllein*, send off], M.: apostle.
apòstro-fa† = *-fo*. **-fáre,** TR.: apostrophize. ‖**apòstro-fe** [Gr. *apo-strophé*, turning off], F.: apostrophe (rhetorical address). **apòstro-fo,** M.: (*gram.*) apostrophe.
apotègma, -tèmma = *apoftegma*.
apoteòsi [Gr. *apó*, *theoûn*, deify], F.: apotheosis.
appa-cetáre†, -cificáre [*pace*], TR.: pacify (appease, calm).
appadiglionáre [*padiglione*], TR.: use as a pavilion or tent; pitch (a tent).
appa-gábile, ADJ.: that may be appeased or satisfied. **-gaménto†,** M.: pacification: contentment. ‖**-gáre** [*pagare*], TR.: appease (satisfy, content). **appágo†,** M.: contentment.
appagliaiáre [*paglia*], TR.: stack (hay).
appai-aménto, M.: coupling (matching). ‖**-áre** [*paio*], TR.: pair (couple, match); join. **-áto,** PART.: paired (matched, suited to one another). **-atúra,** F.: coupling (matching).
ap-palesáre, TR.: discover (reveal).
appallidíre† = *impallidire*.
appallott(ol)áre [*pallottola*], TR.: form into small balls or pellets.
ap-paltáre, TR.: contract (bargain), lease. **-paltatóre,** M.: contractor; leaser. ‖**-pálto** [root *pact-* in L. *pactum*], M.: PACT (contract, agreement, lease); place for making contracts; tobacco-shop. **-paltóne,** M.: big talker, intriguer (meddling fellow).
appanáre [*pane*], TR.: reduce to the use of bread.
appanicáre [*panico*], TR.: accustom (birds) to millet.
appannággio† [l. L. *ap-panare* (L. *panis*, bread), furnish with bread], M.: appanage; income.
appan-naménto, M.: dimness, tarnish. ‖**-náre** [*panno*], TR.: cover with a piece of cloth†; dim; tarnish (dull); veil; catch in a spider's web†; ensnare†. **-náto,** ADJ.: dimmed, etc.; abundant. **-natóio,** M.: that which dims; veil†; rubbing cloth (for horses). **-natòtto,** ADJ.: rather fat or fleshy. **-natúra,** F.: covering (with cloth)†; veiling; dimming.
ap-paraménto† = *paramento*. ‖**-paráre†,** TR.: prepare; adorn; vest; meet. **-paráto,** PART.†: prepared, etc.; M.: preparation; adornment; pomp; apparatus.
apparec-chiaménto†, M.: preparation; PL.: goods. ‖**-chiáre** [*parecchio*], TR.: arrange; prepare; set (the table); REFL.: prepare one's self (get ready). **-chiáta†** = *-chio*. **-chiatóre†,** M., **-chiatrícet,** F.: preparer, dresser. **-chiatúra** = *-chio*. **apparéc-chio,** M.: arrangement (preparative); apparatus (implements); preparation; (*paint.*) grounding.
appareggiáre† = *pareggiare*.
apparenta..† = *imparenta..*
appa-rènte [*-rire*], ADJ.: apparent; visible. **-renteménte,** ADV.: apparently. **-rènza,** F.: appearance; apparition: *per* —, for appearance's sake. ‖**-rére†** = *rire*.
apparigliáre [*pariglia*], TR.: match or brace (horses); REFL.: combine (for an evil purpose).
appa-ríre [L. *-rere*], IRR.§; INTR.: APPEAR. **-riscènte,** ADJ.: apparent; visible; striking (splendid); graceful. **-riscènza,** F.: appearance; splendid appearance (splendor, stateliness). **-ríta,** F.: first appearance. **-rizióne, -rsióne†,** F.: apparition. **-rso,** PART. of *-rire*; ADJ.: evident.

§ Ind.: Pres. *ap-parisco* or *-páio*, *-parisci*, *-pári*, *-parisce* or *-páre*; *-paiámo* (rare), *-parite*, *-pariscono* or *-páiono*. Pret. *ap-parli* or *-pàrsi* or *-pàrvi*, etc. (opt'ly *-parv-*, *-parv-* in 1, 3 sing., 3 pl.). Subj.: Pres. *ap-parisca* or (rare) *-paia*, etc.

appar-taménto, M.: apartment. ‖**-táre** [*parte*], TR.: set apart (separate); REFL.: withdraw one's self (retire). **-tataménte**, ADV.: apart (separately).

apparte-nènte, **-gnèntet†**, ADJ.: pertaining (belonging); suitable. **-nènza**, F.: pertaining; appurtenance. ‖**-nére**, [L. *ad*, *per-tinere*, hold to, belong], IRR. (cf. *tenere*); INTR.: pertain; belong; be related; be a member; concern; become (agree): *questo non m' appartiene*, that does not concern me. **appartè-nni**, PRET., **-núto**, PART. of *-nere*.

appas-sáre† = *-sire*. **-siménto**, M.: withering.

appassio-naménto, M.: growing passionate; passion. **-náre**, REFL.: conceive a passion, or ardent desire (desire eagerly). **-nataménte**, ADV.: passionately. **-náto**, M.: impassioned (passionate); strongly affected.

appas-síre [*passo*], INTR.: wither (fade); become stale or old. **-síto**, ADJ.: withered; stale (old).

appastáre† = *impastare*.

appel-lábile, ADJ.: appealable. **-labilità**, F.: liability of appeal. **-lagióne†**, F., **-laménto†**, M.: appeal. **-lánte**, ADJ.: appealing; M.: appellant. ‖**-láre** [L.], TR.: call; summon; cite; INTR.: APPEAL. **-latívo**, ADJ.: appellatory; M.: (*gram.*) appellative: *lasciare il proprio per l' —*, leave the certain for the uncertain. **-latòrio**, ADJ.: appellatory. **-lazióne**, F.: appellation. **appèl-lo**, M.: call; roll-call; appeal; challenge.

ap=péna, ADV.: hardly (scarcely): *— che*, as soon as, no sooner than. **-penáre†**, TR.: pain (distress).

ap=pèndere, IRR.§; TR.: append; hang up; suspend†; weigh†. **-pendíce**, F.: appendix; feuilleton (serial story at the foot of a newspaper). **-pendízio**, F. PL.: gratuity (of eggs, poultry, etc.) to the lord.

§ Pret. *ap-pési* or (rare) *-pendéi*. Part. *ap-péso*.

appennecchiáre†, TR.: fill the distaff.

Appennino, M.: Apennines; ADJ.: Apennine.

ap=pensáre†, TR.: think out; foresee. **-pensataménte†**, ADV.: on purpose (designedly).

appéso, PART. of *-pendere*.

appestáre [*peste*], TR.: infect.

appe-tènte = *-titoso*. **-tènza** = *-tito*. **-tèto-re†** [L. *petere*, seek] = *-petire*. **-tíbile**, ADJ.: desirable; pleasing. **-tíre**, desire; INTR.: feel a desire; have appetite. **-títo**, M.: appetite; strong desire. **-titosaménte**, ADV.: with appetite; eagerly. **-titóso**, ADJ.: appetizing; attractive. **-titóre†**, M.: appetizer. **-tizióne**, F.: appetite; desire.

appettáre [*petto*], TR.: have at heart; attribute.

ap=pètto, PREP.: opposite (in comparison).

appez-zaménto, M.: detached piece of land. ‖**-záre** [*pezzo*], TR.: piece together. **-zatúra**, F.: piece; piecing; jointure.

appiacére† = *piacere*.

appiacevolíre [*piacevole*], TR.: render agreeable; soften.

appia-naménto, TR.: levelling; smoothing. ‖**-náre** [*piano*], TR.: render level or smooth (level; plane).

appia-stráre [*impiastro*], TR.: stick (fasten); fit; REFL.: adhere. **-striccia-ménto**, M.: sticking (conglutination). **-stricciáre**, TR.: stick (glue).

appiatt.. = *rimpiatt..*

appi-ccágnolo, M.: hook; crook. **-ccaménto†**, M.: hanging up; fastening. **-ccánte**, ADJ.: sticking (glutinous). ‖**-ccáre** [L. *picare* (*pix*, pitch), tar], TR.: stick†; join†; attach†; hang up, kindle (a fire); REFL.: join†; meet†; catch†; hang one's self; kindle: *— il fuoco*, kindle the fire (fire). **-ccatíccio†** ADJ.: sticky; contagious; M.: importunate fellow. **-ccatívo†**, ADJ.: sticky; contagious. **-ccatóio†**, M.: hook; hold-fast. **-ccatúra**, F.: fastening; hanging. **-cciatúra**, F.: candle fee (paid for candle burned).

appiccio-laménto†, M.: diminution. ‖**-láre†**, **-líre** [*piccolo*], TR.: diminish (lessen).

ap=piè, PREP.: at the foot or bottom.

ap=pièno, ADV.: completely (quite).

appi-gionaménto, M.: house-rent (rent). ‖**-gionáre** [*pigione*], TR.: let; rent out (a house, etc.) **-giònasi**, M.: ('for rent') placard or notice (announcing a house for rent).

ap=pigliáre, REFL.: attach one's self to (choose). **-píglio**, M.: pretext; trick.

appigríre† = *impigrire*.

appillottáre†, REFL.: linger (loiter).

appin-záre [*pinzo*], TR.: sting. **-zatúra**, F.: sting.

áppio†, M.: parsley; celery.

appiòla, F., **-lo** [Gr. *ápion*], M.: pippin (apple).

ap=piómbo [or *a piombo*], ADV.: perpendicularly (PLUMB).

appioppáre [*pioppo*], TR.: tie (a vine) to a poplar; join; apply; give (a blow, etc.); fix.

ap=pisoláre [*pisola*], REFL.: take a nap (slumber).

applau-dènte, ADJ.: applauding; M.:

applauder. ‖'-**deret**†, **-díre** [L. *plaudere*], TR.: clap the hands; applaud. **-ditóre,** M.: applauder. **appláu-ṣo,** M.: applause (plaudit); noise. **-ṣóret**†, M.: applauder.
appli-cábile, ADJ.: applicable. **-caménto**†, M.: application. ‖**-cáre** [L. *plicare*, fold], TR.: APPLY (fit); REFL.: apply or devote one's self. **-cataménte,** ADV.: diligently (intently). **-cáto,** ADJ.: applied; prone. **-catóre,** M.: applier; fitter. **-cazióne,** F.: application; assiduity.
áppo†, PREP.: near; by; with; ADV.: in comparison.
appode-raménto, M.: farming. ‖**-ráre**† [*podere*], TR.: farm; REFL.: take to farming.
appo-diaménto†, M.: enfeoffment. ‖**-diáre**†, TR.: enfeoff.
appog-giaménto†, M.: elbow prop; support. ‖**-giáre** [l. L. *ap-podiare* (L. *podium*, elevation)], TR.: support (against some elevated object); lean; prop; REFL.: support one's self (lean); seek protection; trust. **-giatóio,** M.: support (prop). **-giatúra,** F.: support(ing); leaning; appoggiatura (passing tone). **appòggio,** M.: support (prop); protection.
appollaiáre [*pollo*], REFL.: roost; lodge.
appomiciáre†, TR.: rub with pumice.
ap-pónere† = *apporre*. **-poniménto**†, M., **-ponizióne**†, F.: addition (supplement). ‖**=pórre,** IRR.; TR.: put; affix; impute (attribute); object; blame; REFL.: guess (conjecture).
ap=portáre, TR.: bring; cause; announce†; allege†. **-portatóre,** M., **-portatríce,** F.: bringer.
ap-poṣitaménte, ADV.: on purpose; appositely†. **-poṣitívo**†, **-poṣitízio**†, ADJ.: put on (fictitious). ‖**=pòṣito,** ADJ.: intentional; subjoined†. **-poṣizióne,** F.: addition; apposition.
appoṣoláre [*posola*], TR.: harness; burden.
ap=pòsta, ADV.: on purpose (expressly). **-postaménto,** M.: lying in wait (ambush). **-postáre,** TR.: watch or lie in wait for. **-postatóre**†, M.: waylayer.
appósto, PART. of *apporre*.
appostol. .† = *apostol*. .
appozzáre [*pozza*], TR.: make pools of; REFL.: fill with water.
appra-timénto, M.: making into a meadow. ‖**-tíre** [*prato*], TR.: make a meadow of.
appregiáre† = *apprezzare*.
appren-dènte, ADJ.: learning; M.: learner; apprentice. ‖**apprèn-dere** [L. *ad-prehendere*, seize], IRR. (cf. *prendere*): TR.: learn (Eng.† apprehend); seize†; apprehend†; REFL.†: hold to; take root; kindle. **-dévole,** ADJ.: that may be learned. **-diménto,** M.: learning; apprehension†. **-dísta,** pl. *-disti*, M.: apprentice. **-síbile**†, ADJ.: conceivable. **-sióne,** F.: apprehension. **-sioníre,** REFL.: apprehend. **-síva**†, F.: faculty of conception. **-sívo,** ADJ.: apprehensive (fearful).
appreṣentáre†, TR.: represent (show); REFL.: appear.
appréso, PART. of *apprendere*.
ap-pressaménto, M.: approach. **-pressáre,** TR.: put or draw near; REFL.: approach. ‖**=prèsso,** ADV.: near (hard by); almost (nearly); a little later (soon); afterwards: *l'anno* —, the following year; — *a poco*, about; *poco* —, soon afterwards; — *che*, after that (since).
appre-staménto, M.: preparation. ‖**-stáre** [*presto*], TR.: make ready (prepare); provide; REFL.: prepare one's self (get ready). **-státo,** ADJ.: prepared (ready). **apprè-sto**†, ADJ.: prepared; M.: preparation.
apprezia. .† = *apprezza*. .
apprez-zábile, ADJ.: appreciable; valuable. **-zaménto,** M.: appreciation; estimate. ‖**-záre** [*pregio*], TR.: appreciate; value (rate). **-zatívo**†, ADJ.: to be appreciated (commendable). **-zatóre,** M.: valuer (appraiser).
approb. .† = *approv*. .
ap-prociáre [L. *propius*, nearer], REFL.: approach†; make approaches to (a fort). **-pròccio,** M.: (besieger's) advanced work (approaches).
ap-prodáre [*proda*], INTR.: come to shore (land); profit; (*agr.*) bank; border (with vines).
approfittáre [*profitto*], INTR.: profit.
approfon-daménto, -diménto, M.: deepening; investigation. ‖**-dáre** [*fondo*], TR.: deepen; go deep(er) into (examine thoroughly, investigate).
approntáre [*pronto*], TR.: prepare well,
appro-piaménto, M.: adaptation; appropriation. ‖**-p(r)iáre** [*prop(r)io*], TR.: apply properly or fitly (adapt); compare†; apply†; imitate†; REFL.: appropriate; approach†. **-piataménte,** ADV.: with propriety; conveniently. **-piáto,** ADJ.: adapted; convenient (suitable). **-piazióne,** F.: adaptation; appropriation.
appropinquáre†, TR.: approach.
appropòṣito = *a proposito*.
appropria. .† = *appropia*. .
approssi-maménto, M.: approach. ‖**-máre** [*prossimo*], TR.: approach; REFL.: approach (draw near). **-mativaménte,** ADV.: approximatively. **-matívo,** ADJ.: approximate. **-mazióne,** F.: approach; approximation.

[illegible] [illegible]

[illegible] [illegible] [illegible]

[illegible] [illegible] [illegible]

[illegible] ...ato. [illegible]

[illegible] era.

[illegible] ...cere.

[illegible] ...lureo.

[illegible]

arcanaménte [*arcano*], ADV.: mysteriously (secretly).
arc=ángelo, -ángiolo, M.: archangel.
arcáno [L. *-nus* (*arca*, chest)], M.: arcanum (mystery); ADJ.: hidden (secret).
ar-cáre† [*-co*], TR.: dart, shoot (an arrow); ARCH; cheat. **-cáta,** F.: arch; touch with the fiddle-bow; bow-shot† (distance); interval†. **-cáto,** ADJ.: arched (curved). **-catóre,** M.: archer (bowman); cheat.
arc=ávola, F.: great-great-grandmother. **-ávolo,** M.: great-great-grandfather.
árce [L.], F.: fort.
archeggiáre†, TR.: arch (bend).
archeò-logía [Gr. *archaîos*, old, *lógos*, discourse], F.: archeology. **-logicaménte,** ADV.: archeologically. **-lògico,** ADJ.: archeologic(al). **archeò-logo,** M.: archeologist.
archètipo [Gr. *arche-*, chief, *túpos*, stamp], M.: archetype.
ar-chettíno, -chétto [*arco*], M.: small arch; bird-pole (to catch birds); trick; fiddlestick.
archi- [Gr. *archi-*, chief, first], PREF.: archi-: for words not found under *archi-*, cf. *arci-*.
archiacúto [*arco, acuto*], ADJ.: with a pointed or Gothic arch.
archiátro [Gr. *archi-*, chief, *iatrós*, physician], M.: archiater.
archibugi.. = *archibus..*
archi-busáre†, TR.: shoot. **-busáta,** F.: arquebuse-shot; gun-shot. **-busièra**†, F.: loop-hole. **-busière,** M.: arquebusier. ‖**-búso** [?], arquebuse.
archi=diácono = *arcidiacono.*
archi=ginnásio, M.: first university (so called in Rome and Boulogne).
archi=mandríta, M.: archimandrite.
archim†.. = *alchim..*
archi=pèndolo or **=pènsolo,** M.: plummet.
archi-tètta, F.: architect; architect's wife. **-tettáre,** TR.: build (construct); contrive. ‖**-tètto** [Gr. *archi-*, chief, *tékton*, workman], M.: architect. **-tettonicaménte,** ADV.: architectonically. **-tettònico,** ADJ.: architectonic(al). **-tettóne**† = *-tetto.* **-tettúra,** F.: architecture.
archi=trá-ve, M.: architrave. **-váta,** F.: arrangement of architraves. **-váto,** ADJ.: architraved. **-vatúra,** F.: placing of architraves; architraves (*collect.*)
archi-viábile, ADJ.: to be (or that may be) registered. **-viáre,** TR.: register (record). **-viatúra, -viazióne,** F.: registration. ‖**archí-vio** [L. *-vum*], M.: archive (record office). **-vísta,** pl. *-visti*, M.: archivist (recorder).
arci-, PREF. = *archi-*: **=bèllo,** very beautiful. **=beníssimo,** ADJ.: exceedingly well. **=briccóne,** M.: scoundrel. **=buffóne,** M.: archfool. **=diácono,** M.: archdeacon. **-dúca,** M.: archduke. **-ducále,** ADJ.: archducal. **-ducáto,** M.: archdukedom. **-duchéssa,** F.: archduchess.
arcière [*arco*], M.: archer.
arci=fánfano, M.: great boaster (swaggerer).
ar-cignaménte, ADV.: gruffly. **-cignézza,** gruffness (crossness). ‖**-cígno** [?], ADJ.: gruff (grouty, harsh).
arci=mástro, M.: head-master.
arcióne [*arco*], M.: saddle-bow.
arcipèlago [Gr. *aigio-pélago*, Ægean Sea], M.: archipelago.
arci=prète, M.: archpriest. **-pretúra,** F.: office of archpriest; archpresbytery
arci=spedále, M.: chief hospital.
arci-vescovádo, M.: archbishop's residence. **-vescovíle, -vescovále**†, ADJ.: archiepiscopal. **-vescováto,** M.: archbishopry. ‖**=vèscovo,** M.: archbishop.
árco [L. *-cus*], M.: arc(h); bow (the weapon); fiddle-bow; eyebrow: *coll'— dell' osso o della schiena*, with all force or energy; *ad* —, like an arch. **=baléno,** M.: rainbow. **=balèstro,** M., **=balísta,** F.: ar(cu)balist.
arcoláio [?], M.: reel, winder; phantast; juggler†: PL.: whims (castles in the air).
ar-concèllo†, *dim.* of *arco.* **-cóne,** M.: great bow.
arcónte [Gr. *árchon*, ruler], M.: archon.
ar-cuáto [*arco*], ADJ.: curved (bent). **-cúccio,** M.: cradle tester.
ar-dènte, ADJ.: burning (ardent, passionate). **-denteménte,** ADV.: ardently. **-dènza,** F.: ardour; heat; burning desire. ‖**ár-dere** [L.], IRR.§; INTR.: burn.
§ Pret. *ársi, -se; -sero.* Part. *árso.*
ardèsia†, F.: slate.
ardiglióne [Fr.: *harde*, stick], M.: tongue of a buckle.
ardi-ménto, M.: boldness (impudence). **-mentóso,** ADJ.: bold (impudent). **-mentosaménte,** ADV.: boldly. ‖**ardí-re** [OGer. *hardi*, HARD], INTR.: be bold (dare, venture); M.: boldness (daring); impudence. **-taménte,** ADV.: boldly. **-tèllo,** ADJ.: rather bold. **-tézza,** F.: boldness (daring); HARDihood, impudence. **ardíto,** ADJ.: bold (daring).
ardóre [L. *-dor*], M.: ardour (fervour); passionate desire.
ar-duaménte, ADJ.: arduously. **-duità**†, F.: arduousness. ‖**ár-duo** [L. *arduus*, steep], ADJ.: arduous (difficult).
ardúra† = *arsura.*
área [L.], F.: area.
árem [fr. Ar.], M.: harem.

arè-na [L.], F.: sand; arena (amphitheatre); shore†; land†. **-náccio**, ADV.: sandy. **-nário**, ADJ.: sandy; M.: sandstone; PL. gladiators: *grotta —a*, catacomb. **-nosità**, F.: sandiness. **-nóso**, ADJ.: sandy.

arèntet†, ADJ.: arid (dry).

arèola [*area*], F.: small area (spot).

areo..† = *aero..*

areo-pagíta, M.: areopagite. ‖**-págo** [Gr. *-pagos*], M.: areopagus.

arfa-sattèllo, -sátto [?], M.: vulgar thing or fellow.

arganèllo, *dim.* of *-gano*. **árgano** [?], M.: lever (windlass, capstan).

argen-táio† = *-tiere*. **-tále**† = *-tino*. **-táre**†, TR.: silver (plate with silver). **-táto**, ADJ.: silvered (plated with silver); silvery. **-tatóre**†, M.: one that silvers over. **argèn-teo**, ADJ.: silvery. **-tería**, silver-plate. **-tièra**, F.: silver-mine. **-tière**, M.: silver-smith. **-tiféra**, F.: silver-mine. **-tífero**, ADJ.: argentiferous. **-tíno**, ADJ.: silver-coloured (silvery). ‖**argèn-to** [L. *-tum*], M.: silver; money†: *— vivo*, quicksilver (mercury).

argigli..† = *argill..*

argil-la [L.], F.: argil (potter's clay). **-láceo**, ADJ.: argillaceous. **-lóso**, ADJ.: clayey.

argi-nále, M.: long dam or causeway. **-naménto**, M.: embankment. **-náre**, TR.: build (an embankment or causeway). **-natúra**, F.: embankment. ‖**árgi-ne** [L. *ag-ger* (*ad*, *gerere*, bring), heap], M.: embankment (bank, causeway); barrier. **-nèllo, -nétto, -níno**, *dim.* of *-ne*. **-nóne**, *aug.* of *-ne*.

argógli.. = *inorgogli..*

argomen-tábile, ADJ.: subject to argument (debatable). **-táccio**, M.: bad argument. **-táre**, INTR.: argue (reason); conclude†; REFL.†: strive. **-tatóre**, M.: arguer (reasoner). **-tazióne**, F.: argumentation. ‖**argomén-to** [L. *-tum*], M.: argument; proof; subject (plot). **-tóso**†, ADJ.: persuasive.

argonáuta [Gr. *-tes*], M.: (*myth.*) argonaut; (*zoöl.*) -ta.

argu-íre [L. *-ere*], INTR.: argue (infer, conclude); reprimand.† **-ment..** = *argoment..*

argu-taménte, ADV.: ingeniously. **-tézza**, F.: subtlety (finesse, witty conceit). ‖**argú-to** [L. *-tus* (*-ere*, argue)], ADJ.: sharp-witted (subtle, ingenious). **argúzia**, F.: quick-wittedness; subtility; witticism.

ária [L. *aer*, AIR.], F.: AIR (atmosphere); style); (*mus.*) aria (air, song): *colpo* old (catarrh); *non esser —*, be in-w; *darsi —*, put on airs (pretend); *fare —*, clear; *aver l' — di*, look like; *a —*, at about.

ari-daménte, ADV.: dryly. **-dézza**, F.: aridity. ‖**ári-do** [L. *-dus* (*arere*, dry)], ADJ.: arid (dry).

arieggiáre [*aria*], INTR.: resemble.

arien..† = *argent..*

ar-ietáre, TR.: batter (ram). ‖**-íete** [L. *aries*], M.: ram; battering-ram; aries.

ariétta [*aria*], F.: arietta (short aria).

arimm.. = *aritm..*

arínga [OGer. *harinc*], F.: HERRING.

aring†.. = *arring..*

ariòlo†, M.: diviner.

arióso [*aria*], ADJ.: airy.

arism†.. = *aritm..*

árista [L.], F.: chine of pork.

arí-sta† = *resta*.

aristárco [*Aristarchus*], M.: severe critic.

aristo-crático, aristò-crate, ADJ.: aristocratic(al). ‖**-crazía** [Gr. *áristos*, best, *kratein*, rule], F.: aristocracy.

arit-mètica [Gr. *-mós*, number], F.: arithmetic. **-meticaménte**, ADV.: arithmetically. **-mètico**, ADJ.: arithmetic(al); M.: arithmetician.

arlec-chináta, F.: buffoonery. **-chinésco**, ADJ.: buffoon. ‖**-chíno** [?], M.: harlequin (buffoon).

arlòtto†, M.: stupid fool.

árma† = *arme*. **-còllo**†, ADV.: *ad —*, over the shoulder; across.

armad..† = *armad..*

armadiétto, M.: small clothes-press. ‖**armá-dio** [L. *-rium* (*arma*, weapon)], M.: clothes-press. **-dióne**, M.: large press.

armadíllo [Sp.], M.: (*zoöl.*) armadillo.

ar-mai(u)òlo, M.: armorer; gunsmith. **-mamentário**†, M.: surgical instruments. **-maménto**, M.: armament. **-máre**, TR.: arm (equip). **-mário** = *-madio*. **-máta**, F.: armament (military forces, land and naval); force, troop; (*rare*) army; navy (fleet): *— di mare*, fleet; *— di terra*, army. **-mataménte**, ADV.: with arms. **-matèlla**, F.: small fleet. **-matóre**, M.: equipper (of ships); privateer. **-matúra**, F.: armour (breastplate); armament; framework, timberwork. ‖**ár-me** [L. *-ma*], F.: arm (weapon); armour: *— bianca*, bare weapon; *— corta*, 'short weapon' (dagger, pistol, etc.); *— da fuoco*, fire-arm; *— d'asta*, spear, lance; *viso dell' —*, sullen look; *far d' —*, fight. **-meggería**†, F.: tournament (joust). **-meggévole**, ADJ.: fighting. **-meggiaménto, -meggiáre**, INTR.: wield weapon†; fight†; joust†; fumble; be confused; be puzzled, puzzle one's self. **-meggiatóre**, M.: fighter†; tilter†; agitator. **-méggio**, M.: agitation; brawl.

-meggióne, M., **-meggióna,** F.: busy-body (meddling fellow).
armellína†, -no† = *ermellino.*
ar-mentário†, ADJ.: of cattle, M.: herdsman. ‖**-ménto** [L. *-mentum*], M.: herd of cattle.
ar-meria [*arme*], F.: armory (arsenal). **-mígero,** ADJ.: warlike.
armíl-la [*armo*], F.: bracelet (armlet, armilla). **-láre,** ADJ.: armillary.
armistízio [l. L. *-stitium*], M.: armistice.
ármo† [L. *-mus*], M.: shoulder.
armo-nía [Gr. *harmonía*], F.: harmony. **-niále†** = *-nico.* **armò-nica,** F.: harmonica. **-nicaménte,** ADV.: harmoniously. **armò-nico,** ADJ.: harmoni(cal); harmonious. **-niosaménte,** ADV.: harmoniously. **-nióso,** ADJ.: harmonious. **-nizzaménto,** M.: harmonizing. **-nizzáre,** TR.: harmonize; accord.
armoráccio†, M.: horse-radish.
arnése [Eng. *harness*], M.: HARNESS (armour†; gear); implement (utensil); apparatus; vestment, dress; baggage†; bad fellow: *male in* —, poorly attired.
ár-nia [?], F.: bee-hive. **-niáio,** M.: place for bee-hives.
árnica [?], F.: (*pharm.*) arnica.
arnióne [L. *renio*], M.: kidney; PL.: REINS.
áro [*area*], M.: ARE (100 square meters).
arò-ma [Gr.], F.: aroma. **-matário†,** M.: seller of aromas (druggist). **-matichézza†, -maticità†,** F.: aromatic quality (fragrance). **-mático,** ADJ.: aromatic; spicy†; extravagant†; M.: aroma† (perfume). **-matizzáre,** TR.: aromatize (perfume). **-mato†,** ADJ.: aromatic; M.: aroma.
árpa [O.Ger. *harpha*], F.: HARP.
arpa-gonáre†, TR.: harpoon; grapple. ‖**-góne†,** M.: harpoon.
arpeg-giaménto, M.: harping. ‖**-giáre** [*arpa*], INTR.: play on the harp; harp.
arpég-gio, M.: harping; arpeggio.
arpése [L. *harpa*, hook], M.: crampiron.
arpía [L. *harpya*], M.: harpy; miser.
arpicáre [Fr. *harpe*, claw (Gr., sickle)], TR.: climb up.
arpicòrdo, M.: harpsichord.
arpióne [L. *harpa*, hook], M.: hinge; hook.
arpísta, M.: harpist (harper).
árra [L. *harra*], F.: earnest-money.
arrabattáre [? Ger. *arbeiten*, work], REFL.: work hard (strive).
arrab-biaménto, M.: madness. ‖**-biáre** [*rabbia*], INTR.: be infected with rabies; be mad or furious; be much troubled; REFL.: get troubled or vexed: — *dalla fame,* die of hunger; starve; — *dalla sete,* die of thirst. **-biataménte,** ADV.: madly. **-biatèllo,** ADJ.: vexed (irate). **-biáto,** ADJ.: seized with rabies (mad, furious); too salt; in a hurry; meagre.
arraff(i)áre [*raffio*], TR.: snatch; grapple.
arramaccíare†, TR.: drive in a sledge.
arrampicáre [*rampare*], REFL.: climb out.
arrancáre [*ranca*], INTR.: hobble along; row with full speed†.
arrancidíre†, INTR.: become rancid.
arrandelláre [*randello*], TR.: fling away; (beat down); sell cheap; tighten (with a packing-stick).
arrangoláre†, INTR.: fret; be uneasy; be angry.
arrantoláto†, ADJ.: hoarse; rough.
arrapi-náre [*rapina*], REFL.: toil hard (strive). **-náto,** ADJ.: passionate; eager.
arrappá-re† = *arraffare.* **-tóre†,** M.: robber.
arraspáre† = *raspare.*
arráta† = *arra.*
ar=recáre, TR.: bring; cause; reduce†; attribute†; allege†.
ar-redáre, TR.: ornament; furnish. ‖**-rèdo** [?], M.: ornament; equipment†.
arrem-bággio, M.: boarding (a ship). ‖**-báre** [Gr. *rhémbein*, wrench], INTR.: be boarded. **-báto,** ADJ.: boarded; jaded. **-batúra,** F.: boarding.
arre-naménto, M.: running aground (stranding). ‖**-náre** [*rena*], INTR.: run aground or ashore (strand); fail.
arren-daménto, M.: lease. **-datóre†,** M.: renter. ‖**ar=rèndere,** IRR.; REFL.: surrender (give up; yield); comply. **-dévole,** ADJ.: yielding; flexible (supple); docile. **-devolézza,** F.: flexibility; docility. **-devolménte,** ADV.: pliantly; submissively. **-diménto†,** M.: yielding (surrender).
arrequiáre† = *requiare.*
arréso, PART. of *arrendere.*
arre=staménto†, M.: arresting (arrest). ‖**-stáre** [*resta*], TR.: arrest; seize (catch); REFL.: stop; restrain one's self. **-stazióne†,** F., **arrè-sto,** M.: arrest.
arre-táre, -ticáre† [*rete*], TR.: catch in a net (ensnare).
arre-tráre [*retro*], TR.: hold back (check); REFL.: go back (recoil). **-tráto,** ADJ.: drawn back; checked; left behind; unpaid; M.: arrears.
arrettízio†, ADJ.: possessed (by demons).
arrezzáre†, TR.: shade (screen).
árri or **arri là** [?], INTERJ.: get up! (to horses).
arric-chiménto, M.: enrichment; ornamentation. ‖**-chíre** [*ricco*], TR.: enrich; ornament; INTR., REFL.: become rich; be enriched (be adorned).
arric-ciaménto, M.: frizzle; shiver;

horror (fright). ‖**-ciáre** [*riccio*], TR.: bristle or curl up (put on end); frizzle: — *il muso*†, get furious; — *un muro*, rough-cast a wall. **-ciatúra**, F.: bristling; curling; rough-cast. **arríc-cio**, M.: rough-cast wall. **-ciolaménto**, M.: curling; curls. **-ciolare** [*ricciolo*], TR.: curl. **-cioláto**, ADJ.: curled; curly. **-ciolin**. .† = *-ciol*. .

arricorda. .† = *ricorda*. .

ar-rídere, IRR.; TR.: smile upon (favour).

arriffáre†, TR.: raffle; stake.

arrín-ga [OGer. *hring*, RING], F.: HARANGUE (public oration); pleading. **-gaménto**, M.: (*jest.*) harangue (long speech). **-gáre**, TR.: harangue; plead before. **-gatóre**†, M.: haranguer. **-ghería**†, F.: harangue (pleading). **arrín-go**, M.: ists; bar†: *difender l'* —†, accept a challenge.

arripáre†, INTR.: land.

arris-chiánte, ADJ.: risking (venturous). ‖**-chiáre** [*rischio*], TR., REFL.: risk (hazard; venture). **-chiataménte**, ADV.: hazardously; daringly. **-chiáto**, ADJ.: risked; risky (hazardous; venturesome). **-chiévole**†, ADJ.: venturesome (rash). **arrís-chio**† = *rischio*.

arrí-si, PRET., **-so**, PART. of *arridere*.

arrisic. . = *arrischi*. .

arrissáre†, INTR.: wrangle (quarrel).

arristia. . (*vulg.*) = *arrischia*. .

arri-vaménto† = *-vo*. ‖**-váre** [L. *ad ripam*, 'to the shore'], INTR.: come ashore†; arrive; come to the end; reach†; suffice; succeed; hit; TR.: join; overtake; equal: — *bene*, succeed well; be well received; *non ci -vo*, I cannot reach it; it is beyond me. **-váto**, PART.: arrived, etc.: *ben* —, welcome! **arrí-vo**, M.: arrival.

arrizzáre† = *rizzare*.

arrobbiáre†, TR.: dye with madder.

arrocáre†, INTR.: grow hoarse.

arroccáre [*rocca*], INTR.: castle (at chess).

arrocchiáre [*rocchio*], TR.: cut to pieces; cobble; botch.

arrochíre [*roco*], TR.: make hoarse.

arro-gantáccio, ADJ.: very arrogant; M.: arrogant fool. **-gantáre**†, TR.: treat with arrogance. **-gánte**, ADJ.: arrogant; M.: arrogant fellow. **-ganteménte**, ADV.: arrogantly. **-gantóne**, ADJ.: very arrogant. **-gánza**, F.: arrogance. ‖**-gáre** [*rogare*], TR.: adopt; REFL.: arrogate; claim (assume). **-gazióne**, F.: adoption. **arrò-gere**, IRR.; TR.: join (add, give to boot). **-giménto**†, M.: addition.

arro-laménto, M.: enrolment. ‖**-láre**† [*r(u)olo*], TR.: enroll (enlist, register).

arrómpere† = *rompere*.

arroncáre†, TR.: weed (root out).

arronciglíáre [*ronciglio*], TR.: grapple; REFL.: writhe (twist).

arros-saménto, M.: making or turning red. ‖**-sáre** [*rosso*], TR.: make red; INTR.: turn red. **-siménto**, M.: blush(ing). **-síre**, INTR.: turn red; blush.

arrostáre† [*rosta*], TR.: fan away (flies); fan; agitate; twist.

arro-stiménto†, M.: roasting. **-stíre**, TR.: roast; toast; cheat: *manzo -stito*, roast-beef. ‖**arrò-sto** [OGer. *rost*, gridiron], M.: roast meat†; blunder.

arrò-ta† [*-to*], F.: addition; overplus: *per* —, in addition, moreover.

arro-taménto, M.: whetting. **-tánte**, ADJ.: whetting; whetter (knife-grinder); whetstone†. ‖**-táre** [*rota*], TR.: grind (on a grindstone), whet (sharpen); smooth; grind; murmur; rack (stretch on the wheel); REFL.: strain one's self (strive); clash by the wheels (of carriages). **-táto**, PART.: ground, etc.; dappled. **-tatúra**, F.: grinding (whetting; smoothing). **-tíno**, M.: knife-grinder.

arròto, PART. of *arrogere*; M.: aid; addition.

arrotoláre [*rotolo*], TR.: make a roll of (roll).

arrovel-láre [*rovello*], TR.: make angry (infuriate); REFL.: get angry. **-lataménte**, ADV.: furiously. **-láto**, ADJ.: angered (furious).

arroven-táre [*rovente*], TR.: make red-hot. **-tatúra**, F.: heating red; glow. **-timénto**, M.: getting red-hot. **-tíre**, TR.: make red-hot (us'ly *-tare*), INTR.: grow red-hot. **-títo**, ADJ.: red-hot (glowing).

arrove-sciaménto, M.: overthrow. ‖**-sciáre** [*rovesciare*], TR.: turn upside down or about, overthrow; REFL.: get upset; turn the wrong way, take a bad turn. **-sciatúra**, F.: overthrow. **arrovèscio** or *a rovescio*†, ADV.: on the wrong side, contrary to expectation, contrariously, badly.

arrozzíre [*rozzo*], INTR.: become rough; TR.: make rough.

arrubináre [*rubino*], TR.: redden, RUBY.

arruf-fáre [*ruffa*], TR.: dishevel, ruffle. **-fataménte**, ADV.: in a ruffled or disorderly way. **-fáto**, ADJ.: dishevelled (disorderly). **-fío**, M.: great disorder. **-fóna**, F., **-fóne**, M.: great disturber.

arrugginíre [*ruggine*], INTR.: grow rusty; rust (of iron, plants or grain); be set on edge (of teeth).

arruol. .†, **arruot**. . = *arrol*. ., *arrot*. .

arruvidíre [*ruvido*], TR.: make rough; INTR., REFL.: grow rough.

arsenále [*darsena*], M.: arsenal.
arseni-cále, ADJ.: arsenic(al). **-cáto,** ADJ.: arsenicated (arsenic).
arsèni-co [L. *-cum*], M.: arsenic.
ársi 1 [Gr. *-sis*], M.: arsis.
ár-si 2, PRET. of *-dere.* **-síbile†,** ADJ.: combustible. **-sicciáre†,** TR.: scorch. **-síccio,** ADJ.: scorched. **-sióne,** F.: conflagration. ‖**-so,** PART. of *ardere:* burnt. **-súra,** F.: burning heat; smart.
ar-táre [L.], TR.: constrain (force). **-taménte,** ADV.: with constraint (artfully).
ár-te [L. *ars*], F.: art; skill; artifice (cunning): *ad —,* on purpose. **-te=fátto,** ADJ.: artificial. **-téfice,** M.: artificer, artisan (mechanic). **-tefìcèllo†,** *disp.* of *-téfice* **-teficiáto†,** ADJ.: artificial; fictitious. **-tefício†** = *artifizio.* **-teggiáre†,** INTR.: use artifice.
artè-ria [Gr.], F.: artery. **-riále,** ADJ.: arterial. **-rióso,** ADJ.: arterial.
artesiáno [*Artois*, in France], ADJ.: artesian.
artet..† = *artrit..*
artézza†, F.: narrowness; want.
articèlla†, F.: small art; poor trade.
ártico [Gr. *arktikós* (*árktos*, bear)], ADJ.: Arctic.
artico-láre 1, TR.: articulate (joint; utter); pronounce. **-lare** 2, ADJ.: articular. **-lataménte,** ADV.: articularly (jointly). **-láto,** ADJ.: articulated, etc.; contracted (like *a il* to *al*, etc.); M.: series of (legal) articles; articulate. **-lazióne,** F.: articulation. **-lísta,** pl. *-listi,* M.: author of articles (writer). ‖**artíco-lo** [L. *articulus* (*artus*, member)], M.: article: *— di fondo,* leading article (leader).
arti-ère [*arte*], M.: artisan (mechanic). **-ficiále,** ADJ.: artificial. **-ficialménte,** ADV.: artificially. **-ficiáto,** ADJ.: artificial. **-fício,** M.: artifice (cunning). **-ficiosaménte,** ADV.: artfully (cunningly). **-ficiosità,** F.: artifice (cunning). **-ficióso,** ADJ.: artificial; artful (cunning, crafty, astute). **-fizi..** = *-fici..* (*z* more common in *-fizio, -fiziato*). **-gianèllo,** *disp.* of *-giano.* **-giáno,** M.: artisan (mechanic); ADJ.: of an artisan or mechanic (workman).
artigliáre†, TR.: seize with the claws.
artiglìè-re [*arte*], M.: artilleryman (gunner). **-ría,** F.: artillery. **-ro†** = *-re.*
artí-glio [L. *articulus*, joint], M.: claw (talon); clutch. **-glióso,** ADJ.: clawed.
artimóne†, M.: mizzen-sail.
ar-tísta, pl. *-tisti* [*-te*], M.: artist. **-tisticaménte,** ADV.: artistically. **-tístico,** ADJ.: artistic(al).
árto 1 [L. *-tus*], M.: joint.
árto† 2, ADJ.: narrow (cramped).
ar-trítico, ADJ.: arthritic(al). ‖**-trít(id)e** [Gr. *árthron*, joint], F.: arthritis (gout).
Artúro [Gr. *Arkt-oûros*, 'bear-ward'], M.: Arcturus; (*poet.*) Great Bear.
arú-spice [L. *haru-spex*, 'entrail-observer'], M.: aruspex (augur, soothsayer). **-spício†,** M.: augury. **-spicína,** F.: augur's art (aruspicy).
arzen..† = *arsen..*
arzènte = *ardente.*
arzigo-golánte, ADJ.: fanciful (fantastic). **-goláre,** INTR.: fancy; be fanciful or fantastic. **arzigò-golo** [cf. *girigogolo*], M.: captious remark; quibble; sophistry; deceitful word. **-golóna,** F., **-golóne,** M.: cunning fellow.
arzíllo [?], ADJ.: brisk (sprightly); juvenile; pungent; tipsy.
as- [L. *abs*, for *ab*, OFF, from; *ads*, for *ad*, to], PREF.: abs-, as-; *as-*, to, by.
asbèsto [Gr. *-tos*], M.: asbestos.
ásce = *ascia.*
ascèlla [L. *axilla*], F.: armpit.
ascen-dentále, ADJ.: ascendant. **-dènte,** ADJ.: ascending; ascendant; M.: ascendant (ancestor). **-dènza,** F.: ascent; ancestry. ‖**ascén-dere** [L. (*scandere*, climb)]; IRR. (cf. *scendere*); TR.: ascend (mount); amount; surpass†; approach. **-diménto†,** M.: ascent. **-sióne,** F.: ascent (rising); Ascension (-day). **-sionále,** ADJ.: ascensional. **ascèn-so†,** M.: ascent. **-sóre,** M.: elevator, lift.
ascé-si, PRET., **-so,** PART. of *ascendere.* **-sa†,** F.: ascent.
ascèsso [L. *abs-cessus*, 'OFF-going'], M.: abscess.
a-scèta [Gr. *asketes* (*askein*, exercise)], M.: ascetic. **-scètico,** ADJ., M.: ascetic. **-scetismo,** M.: ascetism.
áschio = *astio*
á-scia [?], F.: AXE: *fatto con —,* roughly made; *sentenza coll' —,* blind sentence. **-sciáre,** TR.: shape with the axe (cut, smooth). **-sciáta,** F.: stroke of the axe or hatchet; careless sentence.
a=sciògliere†, IRR.; TR.: dissolve (resolve); untie; accomplish (fulfill). **-sciòlto,** PART. =**sciòlvere,** IRR.; TR.: breakfasting; breakfast; M.: collation (breakfast).
ascíssa [L. *ab-scissus* (*scindere*, cut)], F.: abscissa.
ascitízio [L. *sciscere*, seek to know], ADJ.: adscititious.
asciu-gággine†, F.: dryness. **-ga=máno,** M.: towel. **-gaménto,** M.: wiping; dryness. ‖**-gáre** [L. *ex-succare* (*succus*, juice)], TR.: dry up; wipe away; console; rob; INTR.: dry. **-gatóio,** M.: towel. **-gatúra,** F.: drying; wiping. **-tta-**

-ménto, ADV.: dryly. **-ttáre** = *-gare*. **-ttézza**, F.: dryness. **asciú-tto** (for *-gato*), ADJ.: dry (arid); lean (emaciated); reserved; M.: dryness; dry land. **-ttóre**, M.: drought.

ascól-ta†, F.: listening; sentinel. **-tamémto†**, M.: hearing (listening). **-tánte**, ADJ.: listening; M.: listener (auditor). ‖**-táre** [L. *auscultare* (*auris*, EAR)], TR.: listen to, hear; lend an ear to (attend to, heed); auscultate. **-tatóre**, M., **-tatríce**, F.: listener (auditor). **-tazióne**, listening; auscultation. **ascólto**, M.: hearing; heed, attention: *dar* (*porgere*) —, give heed (attend); *mettersi in* —, become attentive; *stare in* —, be listening (be an eavesdropper).

a-scóndere = *nascondere*. **-scos..†** = *nascos..*

a-scríssi, PRET., **-scrítto**, PART. of *-scrívere*. **=scrívere**, IRR.; TR.: ascribe (assign, attribute); reckon (number); enroll; REFL.: rank one's self: — *a onore*, consent as an honour (be honoured by).

as-fáltico, ADJ.: asphaltic (of asphalt). ‖**-fálto** [Gr. *ásphaltos*], M.: asphalt.

as-fissía [Gr. *a-sphuxía*, 'non-throbbing'], F.: asphyxia. **-fissiáto**, ADJ.: asphyxiated. **-fíttico**, ADJ.: asphyctic (asphyxal).

asfo-dèlo, **-díllo†** [Gr. *asphodelós*], M.: asphodel, DAFFODIL.

asiático [*Asia*], ADJ.: Asiatic.

asílo [Gr. *-ásulon*, 'in-violable'], M.: asylum.

ásima† = *asma*.

ási-na, F.: she-ass. **-náccio**, *disp.* of *-no*. **-naggine**, F.: asininity (ignorant stupidity). **-náio**, M.: ass-driver. **-náre†**, TR., INTR.: travel on an ass. **-náta**, F.: asinine act; riding or journey on an ass. **-nèlla**, F.: young she-ass. **-nèllo**, M.: little ass (young ass); rafter. **-nería**, F.: asininity (stupidity, stupid act or words). **-nescaménte**, ADV.: stupidly. **-nésco**, ADJ.: asinine (stupid, dull). **-nétto**, M.: little ass. **-níno**, ADJ.: asinine; stupid; rude. **-nità**, F.: asininity (stupidity); rudeness. ‖**ási-no** [L. *-nus*], M.: ASS (donkey): — *salito* (or *bardato*), person who has become rich and haughty, upstart; *buscar dell'* —, be called ignorant; *far come l'* — *del pentolaio*, do as the potter's ass, shut one's self up against an approach. **-nóne**, M.: great ass (blockhead).

ás-ma [Gr. *ásthma* (*áein*, blow)], F.: asthma. **-mático**, ADJ.: asthmatic.

asoláre [*esalare*], INTR.: breathe gently; REFL.: take an airing. **ásolo**, M.: breath of air: *dare* —, dry in the air or sun; *prender* —, take an airing.

aspálto† = *asfalto*.

asparagéto = *sparagiaia*.

áspe† = *aspide*.

asper-áre†, TR.: exasperate (provoke). **=artèria**, F.: windpipe (us'ly *trachea*). **-èlla**, F.: horse-tail (plant). ‖**-étto** [*aspero*], ADJ.: rather harsh.

a-spèrgere [L. *spargere*, strew], IRR. §; TR.: sprinkle; besprinkle with holy water. **-spèrges** = *aspersorio*. **-spèrgine†**, M.: sprinkling; sign. **-spergitóre†**, M.: sprinkler.

§ Pret. *aspèr-si*, *-se*; *-sero*. Part. *aspèrso*.

aspe-rità†, **-ritádine†** = *asprezza*.

áspe-ro† = *aspro*.

a-spèrsi, PRET. of *-spergere*. **-spersióne**, F.: sprinkling (aspersion). ‖**-spèrso**, PART. of *-spergere*. **-spersòrio**, M.: aspergill (holy-water brush).

aspet-tamènto† = *-tazione*. **-tánte**, ADJ.: expecting, etc.; M.: spectator (bystander). **-tánza†** = *-tativa*. ‖**-táre** [L. *a-spectare* (*specere*, look)], INTR.: expect (wait for, await); look for, (desire); linger (stay); REFL.: appertain, belong: — *a gloria* (or *a braccia aperte*), expect or wait contentedly. **-tatíva**, F.: expectance (hope, expectative): *metter in* —, retire (an officer, etc.) for the time being (until possibly called into service again). **-tatóre†**, M.: expecter. **-tazióne**, F.: expectation, hope (confidence). **aspèt-to**, M.: ASPECT (sight); air, view; watch.

áspi-de [Gr. *aspis*], **-de†**, M.: aspic.

aspi-ránte, ADJ.: aspiring, etc.; M.: aspirant (candidate): *tromba* —, suction-pump. ‖**-ráre** [L. *spirare*, breathe], TR.: breathe; aspirate (pronounce with a breathing); aspire to (wish for); INTR.: (be a candidate). **-rataménte**, ADV.: with aspiration. **-ráto**, ADJ.: breathed; aspirate(d); aspired to (desired). **-razióne**, F.: aspiration (breathing; aspiring).

áspo [OGer. *haspa*], M.: reel (HASP, spindle).

aspor-táre [L. *a(b)s-portare*], TR.: carry away (transport); cut away (tumours, etc.). **-tazióne**, F.: transportation; cutting away; operation.

a-spraménte, ADV.: harshly. **-spraménto**, M.: difficulty; fear. **-spreggiaménto**, M.: exasperation. **-spreggiáre**, TR.: exasperate (provoke). **-sprétto**, ADJ.: somewhat harsh. **-sprézza**, F.: asperity; harshness; tartness. **-sprigníno**, ADJ.: tartish: *vino* —, sort of white wine. **-sprígno**, ADJ.: sharp (tart, sourish). **-sprità†** = *-sprezza*. ‖**á-spro** [L. *asper*], ADJ.: harsh (rough sharp; fierce); acrid (sour); shrill.

assáccia [*asse*], F.: bad board.
assaccommannáre†, TR.: plunder.
assaet-taménto, M.: sharp pain; eagerness. **-táre** [*saettare*], INTR.: give a sharp pain; sting, offend; suffer; REFL.: strive eagerly.
assa [Pers.], or =**fètida**, F.: assafœtida.
assag-giaménto, M.: tasting; assay. ‖**-giáre** [*a-*, *saggiare*], TR.: taste; begin eating; get a drubbing; test (assay). **-giatóre**, M.: taster; assayer. **-giatúra**, F.: tasting; assaying. **asság-gio**, M.: tasting; assaying.
ass-ái [L. *ad*, *satis*, enough], ADV.: enough; very, quite (pretty); much; ADJ.: much (many); M.: (*pop.*) enough; great quantity; weight: — *più*, much (many) more; — *per tempo*, very early; — *volte*, many times; *parer* —, seem strange; *uomo d'* —, man of weight, valiant man. **-aíssimo**, ADV.: very much (extremely).
assále† [*asse*], M.: axle, axle-tree.
assa-liménto, M.: assault. ‖**-líre** [*salire*], IRR.§; TR.: ASSAIL (ASSAULT, attack). **-líta**†, F.: assault. **-litóre**, M., **-litríce**, F.: assailant (assaulter). **-ltábile**, ADJ.: assailable. **-ltánte**, ADJ.: assailing, M.: assailant. **-ltáre** [intens. of *-lire*], TR.: ASSAULT. **-ltatóre**, M.: assailant; assaulter. **assá-lto**, M.: assault (onset).

§ Ind.: Pres. *as-salisco* or *-sálgo*, etc.; *-saliámo* or *-salghiámo*, *-salite*, *-saliscono*, *-sálgono*. Pret. *as-sálsi* or *-salii*; *-salse* or *-salì*; *-sálsero*, *-salirono*. Subj.: Pres. *as-salisca* or *-sálga*; etc. Part. *assalito*. — Poet. forms: Pres. Ind. *asságlio*; Sub. *asságlia*.

assannáre† = *azzanare*.
assapére† = *sapere*.
assapo-raménto, M.: tasting; savour. ‖**-ráre** [*sapore*], TR.: savour (taste); enjoy. **-ríre**, TR.: savour.
assas-sinaménto, M.: assassination. **-sináre**, TR.: assassinate (murder); ruin. **-sínio**, M.: assassination. ‖**-síno** [fr. Ar., 'drinkers of *hashish*'], M.: assassin (murderer).
assavor. .† = *assapor*. .
assaziáre† = *saziare*.
ásse 1 [L. *axis*, axis], F.: board (for building), plank; AXLE-tree; AXIS; diameter; hand (of a quadrant); lever.
ásse 2 [L. *as*], M.: small Roman coin; (*leg.*) property.
assec-cáre† = *seccare*. **-chíre** [*secco*], INTR.: become dry (dry).
assecondáre = *secondare*.
assecuráre† = *assicurare*.
assecut. .† = *esecut*. .
as=sedére†, IRR.; INTR.: sit down; reside; be; live; TR.: seat; REFL.: sit down (be seated). **-sediaménto**†, M.: siege. **-sediáre**, TR.: beSIEGE. **-sediatóre**, M., **-sediatríce**, F.: besieger. **-sèdio**, M.: SIEGE; importunity (teasing): — *largo*, blockade.
asse-gnábile, ADJ.: assignable. **-gnaménto**, M.: assignment; allowance; expectation: *far* — *sopra*, rely upon. ‖**-gnáre** [L. *ad-signare*, 'SIGN or mark out'], TR.: assign, allow (a certain sum, etc.); determine, fix (a condition, etc.), attribute; consign†; allege†; note†; limit†). **-gnataménte**, ADV.: economically; thriftily. **-gnatézza**, F.: economy; thrift; reservedness. **-gnáto**, ADJ.: assigned, etc.; reserved; economical; thrifty. **-gnazióne**, F.: assignment; allowance; fixing. **assé-gno**, M.: assignment; allowance.
assegui. .† = *consegui*. .
assem-bia. .†, **-bla**. .† = *assembra*. . **-blèa**, F.: assembly (meeting). **-brágli a**†, F.: clash (combat). **-braménto**, M.: assembly (union). ‖**-bráre** [L. *ad*, *simul* (*similis*, alike), together], TR., REFL.: ASSEMBLE (unite); INTR.†: seem; resemble; imitate. **-brèa** = *-blea*.
assempráre†, TR.: copy.
assen-náre† [*senno*], TR.: advise (warn); make sensible or prudent. **-nataménte**, ADV.: judiciously (wisely). **-natézza**, F.: sense (judgment). **-náto**, ADJ.: sensible (judicious, prudent). **-níre**†, TR.: make sensible; REFL.: be prudent (act judiciously).
as-sensióne†, **-sènso** [*-sentire*], M.: assent (approbation, consent).
as-sentáre 1 [*-sente*], TR.: absent; remove; REFL.: absent one's self (be off).
assen-táre 2 †, TR.: flatter; INTR.: = *-tire*; sit down. **-tatóre**, M.: flatterer (fawner). **-tazióne**†, F.: adulation.
assènte [L. *abs-ens*, 'off-being'], ADJ.: ABSENT.
assen-timénto, M.: assent (consent). **-tíre** [L. (*sentire*, feel)], INTR.: assent (consent); approve; feel†; TR.: inform. **-títo**, ADJ.: assented; judicious (wary): *andare* (or *stare*) —, be all attentive; be upon one's guard. **-to**† = *-so*.
assènza [*assente*], F.: absence.
assènzio [L. *absinthium*], M.: absinth(e); wormwood.
asseráre [*sera*], INTR., REFL.: get late; grow dark.
asserèlla, F.: *dim.* of *asse* (little board, etc.); PL.: mattress-boards.
asserenáre† = *rasserenare*.
asse-rènte, ADJ.: asserting; M.: asserter (maintainer). **-riménto**† = *-rzióne*. ‖**-ríre** [L. *as-serere*, join to], TR.: ASSERT; affirm.
asserpoláre [*serpe*], REFL.: worm (twist).
asserragliáre [*serraglio*], TR.: barricade (obstruct).

[illegible]

-ránta [illegible] **-rantemónte.** [illegible] **-ránza** [illegible] **-ráre** [illegible] **-ratívo** [illegible]

ass... cúra-mento, M.: assurance; security, trust, boldness. **-ránza†,** F.: assurance (security), trust. ‖**-ráre** [*sicuro*], TR.: secure (assure, guarantee), fix; insure, take in tender; REFL.: make one's self sure (assure one's self, take courage†). **-ratamente,** ADV.: securely (with certainty). **-ratóre,** M.: securer; insurer. **-razióne,** F.: assurance (security); insurance; *società d'* —, insurance company.

assiduità, F.: assiduity, presence.

assidera-ménto, M.: benumbment. ‖**-ráre** [L. *sidere* (*sidus*, *star*), be influenced by the star], INTR., REFL.: be benumbed with cold (be frozen); TR.: benumb with cold (chill). **-razióne,** F.: benumbment (numbness).

as-sidere, INTR., REFL.: seat; be... set down.

[illegible] Part. *assiso*

assiduamente, ADV.: assiduously. **-duità,** F.: assiduity. ‖**assi-duo** [L. *duus*] ADJ.: assiduous.

assième [L. *ad, simul*, together], ADV.: together.

[illegible]

-sistire† = [illegible] **-sistére†,** M.: [illegible]

[illegible] Part. *assistito*

assi-táre [illegible] TR.: smell, scent; give [illegible] REFL.: accustom [illegible] **-táto,** ADJ.: scented; bad-[illegible]

assito [illegible], M.: (partition-board); floor-[illegible]

ásso [illegible], M.: ACE: *è asso fisso*, it is perfectly certain; *è l'* —, he is number one; it is excellent; *restare in* —, be forsaken.

assoc-cidménto, M.: (giving) partnership in cattle. ‖**-ciáre** [*soccio*], TR.: lease out (cattle).

asso-ciábile, ADJ.: associable. ‖**-ciáre** [*socio*], TR.: associate (make an associate, take into partnership; join); attend (a funeral procession); bring; REFL.: become a partner; subscribe. **-ciáto,** ADJ.: associat(ed); M.: associate; subscriber. **-ciatóre,** M.: solicitor for subscriptions. **-ciazióne,** F.: association; funeral procession.

asso-daménto, M.: consolidation. ‖**-dáre** [*sodo*], TR.: make solid (consolidate, strengthen); REFL.: get compact; persist.

assogget-táre [*soggetto*], TR.: subject (subdue). **-timénto†,** M.: subjection. **-tíre†,** TR.: subject; INTR.: be subjected.

assoláre1 [*solo*, ground], TR.: beat or pick down.

assoláre2 [*suolo*, alone], TR.: place or leave alone.

asso-láre3† [*sole*], TR.: expose to the sun. **-látio,** ADJ.: sunny (southern). **-láto†,** ADJ.: exposed to the sun (sunny)

assolcáre [*solco*], TR.: furrow (plough).

assol-daménto, M.: enrollment (of soldiers). ‖**-dáre** [*soldo*], TR.: enlist; REFL.: enlist (enter as a volunteer).
assolfoníre†, INTR.: grow sulphurous.
assolid. .† = *consolid*. .
as-sòlsi, PRET., **-sòlto**, PART. of *-solvere*. **-solutaménte**, ADV.: absolutely. **-solutézza**, F.: absoluteness. **-solutísmo**, M.: absolutism. **-solúto**, ADJ.: absolute (positive). **-solutóre**, M.: absolver. **-solutòrio**, ADJ.: absolutory (clearing). **-soluzióne**, F.: absolution (acquittal). **-solvènte**, ADJ.: absolving. =**sòlvere**, IRR.§; TR.: absolve (acquit); free.
§ Pret. *as-solvèi* or *-solvètti* or *-sòlsi*. Part. *as-solúto* or *-sòlto*.
assomáre†1, TR.: load.
assomáre†2, TR.: conclude; finish.
assomi-gliánte, ADJ.: resembling (similar). **-gliaménto**, M., **-gliánza**, **-gliazióne**†, F.: resemblance. ‖**-gliáre** [L. *similis*, alike], TR.: compare; INTR., REFL.: resemble (be like). **assomí-glio**†, M.: similarity.
as-sonánte, ADJ.: assonant (concordant). **-sonánza**, F.: assonance (harmony). ‖=**sonáre**†, INTR.: sound (resound).
assóne [*asse*], M.: big board (plank).
asson-náre† [*sonno*], TR.: lull asleep (make drowsy); REFL.: fall asleep. **-náto**, **-níto**, ADJ.: asleep; sleepy; dull.
as-sopiménto, M.: drowsiness. ‖=**sopíre**, INTR: become sleepy or drowsy.
assor-bènte, ADJ.: absorbing (absorbent). **-biménto**, M.: absorption. ‖**-bíre** [L. *-bere* (*sorbere*, suck)], IRR.§; TR.: absorb (suck up).
§ Pres. *as-sorbisco* or *-sòrbo*, etc. Part. *assorbito* or *-sòrto*.
assor-daménto, M.: stunning. ‖**-dáre**, **-díre** [*sordo*], TR.: stun (deafen); INTR., REFL.: become deaf.
as=sórgere, IRR.; INTR.: rise politely.
assor-timénto, M.: assortment; lot†. ‖**-tíre** [*sortire*], TR.: assort (furnish, equip); sort (match); draw lots for† (raffle off).
assòrto, PART. of *assorbire*.
assotti-gliaménto, M.: subtilization (thinning, refinement). ‖**-gliáre** [*sottile*], TR.: subtilize (thin, refine); render thin or lean; sharpen; REFL.: grow thin; be sharpened. **-gliatívo**, ADJ.: attenuating. **-gliatóre**, M.: subtilizer. **-gliatúra**, F.: subtilization (thinning); sharpening; refinement.
assozzáre† = *insozzare*.
assue-fáre [L. *-facere*, make accustomed], TR.: accustom (inure). **-fátto**, ADJ.: accustomed (inured). **-fazióne**, F.: accustoming (Eng.† assuefaction), custom.
‖**assuè-to**† [*-tus*], ADJ.: accustomed. **-túdine**, F.: custom.
assuggettíre† = *assoggettare*.
as-súmere [L. *-sumere* (take)], IRR.§; TR.: assume (undertake); raise up (exalt). **-súnsi**, PRET. of *-sumere*. **-súnta**, F.: Virgin Mary (Madonna); Assumption (festival of the Virgin Mary taken into heaven). **-súnto**, PART. of *-sumere*: assumed; M.: undertaking, task; charge. **-sunzióne**, F.: assumption; elevation (exaltation).
§ Pret. *assún-si*, *-se*; *-sero*. Part. *assúnto*
assur-daménte, ADV.: absurdly. **-dità**, F.: absurdity. ‖**assúr-do** [L. *ab-surdus*], ADJ.: absurd; M.: absurdity.
assúrgere = *assorgere*.
ásta [L. (*h*)*asta*], F.: spear†; lance; (us'ly) staff (pole); handle; auction (a staff being set up as a token of authority); stroke (in writing); growth; form: — *di bandiera*, flagstaff; *mettere all'* —, sell at auction; *bell'* — *di donna*, well-formed lady.
ásta-co, **-co**† [L. *-cus*], M.: astacus (crawfish).
astal-laménto†, M.: abode. ‖**-láre**†, REFL.: install one's self; set up one's abode (put up).
a-stánte, ADJ.: standing by (present); bystander (spectator); attendant (assistant). ‖=**stáre**, INTR.: stand by (be present); insist.
a-státa†, F.: thrust of a lance. **-státo**, ADJ.: armed with a lance; M.: (*Rom.*) lance-soldier. ‖**-ste**† = *asta*. **-steggiáre**, INTR.: make strokes or flourishes (in writing). **-steggiatúra**, F.: forming strokes (in writing).
astegn. .† = *astin*. .
astèmio [L. *abs-temius* (*temum*, wine)], ADJ.: abstemious.
as-tenènte, ADJ.: abstinent. ‖=**tenére** [L. *abs-tinere*, hold off], IRR.; TR.: ABSTAIN. **-tensióne**, F.: abstention (forbearing).
as-tergènte, ADJ.: abstergent (cleansing). ‖=**tèrgere**, IRR.; TR.: absterge (cleanse), polish.
aste-rísco [*astro*], M.: asterisk. **-rísmo**, M.: asterism. **áste-ro**, M.: (*bot.*) aster, starwort. **-ròide**, M.: asteroid.
as-tersióne, F.: abstersion (cleansing). **-tersívo**, ADJ.: abstersive (cleansing). **-tèrsi**, PRET., **-tèrso**, PART. of *tergere*.
astétta, *dim.* of *asta*.
astiáre [*astio*], TR.: envy (grudge).
astie-ciòla, **-èllo**†, *dim.* of *asta*.
asti-nènte [L. *abs-tinens*, 'off-holding'], ADJ.: abstinent. **-nènza**, F.: abstinence.

á-stio [?], M.: envy; grudge; spite. **-stiosaménte,** ADV.: enviously. **-stióso,** ADJ.: envious (spiteful).
astivaméntet†, ADV.: hastily (promptly).
astóre [?], M.: goshawk.
astráere† = *astrarre.*
astrágalo† [Gr. *-los*], M.: ankle-bone; astragal.
astrággo, PRES. of *-trarre.*
astrále†, ADJ.: astral.
as=trárre, IRR.; TR., INTR.: abstract; REFL.: turn away one's mind. **-trássi,** PRET. of *-trarre.* **-trattággine†,** F.: abstraction; absent-mindedness. **-trattaménte,** ADV.: abstrac(ted)ly; absent-mindedly. **-trattézza,** F.: abstractness. **-trattívo†,** ADJ.: abstractive. **-trátto,** ADJ.: abstracted (abstract); absent-minded; eccentric†: *in* —, in the abstract (abstractly). **-trazióne,** F.: abstraction; absent-mindedness.
a-strétto, PART. of *-stringere.* **-strign..** = *-string..* **-stringènte,** ADJ.: astringent. ‖**=stríngere,** IRR.; TR.: astringe† (constrict, reduce); CONSTRAIN (force). **-strínsi,** PRET. of *stringere.*
ástro [Gr. *-stron*], M.: heavenly body; STAR. **=lábio** [Gr. *lambánein*, take], M.: astrolabe. **-logáre,** INTR.: astrologize; prognosticate. **-logía** [Gr. *lógos*, speech], F.: astrology. **-lògico,** ADJ.: astrological. **astrò-logo,** M.: astrologer. **-nomía** [Gr. *nómos*, law], F.: astronomy. **-nomicaménte,** ADV.: astronomically. **-nòmico,** ADJ.: astronomical. **astrònomo,** M.: astronomer.
as-truşería, F.: abstruse thing (abstrusity). ‖**-tráşo** [L. *abs-trusus* (*trudere*, thrust)], ADJ.: abstruse (hidden, obscure).
astúccio [?], M.: case (box).
astu-taménte, ADV.: astutely (craftily). **-tézza,** F.: astuteness (craftiness, cunning). ‖**astú-to** [L. *-tus*], ADJ.: astute (crafty, cunning). **astú-zia,** F.: astuteness (craftiness, art). **-ziétta,** F.: cunning, trick.
at- [L. *at-* for *ad*, to], PREF.: at, etc.
a-tánte†, ADJ.: helpful; vigorous. **-táre†,** TR.: help. **-tatóre†,** M.: helper.
áta-va, F.: great-grandmother. **-vişmo,** M.: atavism. ‖**áta-vo** [L. *ad*, *avus*, grandfather], M.: great-grandfather.
ate-íşmo [-o], M.: atheism. **-ísta,** M.: atheist. **-ístico,** ADJ.: atheistic.
atenèo [Gr. *athénaion*, temple of Athene], M.: athenæum; university.
...eo [Gr. *a-*, not, *theós*, god], M.: atheist.
...ròma, -òmata [Gr. *athéroma*], M.: ...roma (tumour).
...te [Gr. *Atlas*], M.: ATLAS.
...a [Gr. *athletés* (*áthlos*, prize], M.: ... **-lètico,** ADJ.: athletic.
atmosfer..† = *ammosfer..*
ato-métto, ADJ.: small atom. **-míşmo,** M.: atomism. **-místa,** M.: atomist. **-místico,** ADJ.: atomistic. ‖**áto-mo** [Gr. *á-tomos*, uncut], M.: atom (particle); moment.
atonía [Gr. *a-*, not, *tónos*, tone, strength], F.: atony.
atra-bíle [L. *ater*, black, *bilos*, bile], F.: black bile (spleen). **-biliáre, -biliário,** ADJ.: atrabilious (melancholic).
atra-mentário, ADJ.: black. ‖**-ménto†** [L. *-mentum*, ink], M.: black colour.
átrio [L. *atrium*], M.: atrium (vestibule); porch.
átro [L. *ater*], ADJ.: black; horrible.
atró-ce [L. *atrox*], ADJ.: atrocious (heinous). **-ceménte,** ADV.: atrociously. **-cità,** F.: atrocity.
a-trofía [Gr. *a-*, not, *tréphein*, nourish], F.: atrophy. **-tròfico,** ADJ.: atrophic. **-trofizzáre,** TR.: atrophy; REFL.: be consumed.
attac-cábile, ADJ.: that may be attacked (assailable). **-cágnolo,** M.: hook; cavil (pretext). **-ca-líte,** M.: litigious person (wrangler). **-caménto,** M.: attachment. **-ca=pánni** [*panno*], M.: clothes-rack. ‖**-cáre** [*tacca*], TR.: ATTACH (fix, stick); harness; communicate (disease, etc.); begin; ATTACK (assail); INTR.: stick (adhere); be united; be attached; take root (thrive); stutter; REFL.: be attached (unite); stick (adhere); litigate: — *un avviso*, post a bill; — *gli abiti*, hang up clothes: — *il dente*, eat what is agreeable; — *il fuoco a*, set fire to; *-carla con*, litigate (quarrel, come to blows) with. **-catézza,** F.: attachment. **-catíccio,** ADJ.: sticky (viscous). **-catíva,** F.: attaching quality; stickiness. **-catóio,** M.: attaching instrument. **-catúra,** F.: attachment; adhesion. **-chíno,** M.: litigious person, quarrelsome person.
attác-co, M.: attack; attachment; point of attachment; hold; span (of horses), turn-out.
atta-gliáre [*taglio*], TR.†: cut; REFL.: fit (suit); comply. **-glioláre,** TR.: chop (mince).
attalentáre†, TR.: please; agree with.
attaménte†, ADV.: aptly (fitly).
attanagliáre [*tanaglia*], TR.: tear with red-hot pincers (torture).
attapi-naménto, M.: dejection (wretchedness). ‖**-náre** [*tapino*], REFL.: toil hard; lament.
attapezzáto† = *tappezzato.*
attard..† = *tard..*
attáre† = *adattare.*
attastáre = *tastare.*
attec-chiménto, M.: thriving (growth).

||-**chíre** [*tecchire*], INTR.: grow (grow well); TR.: prosper.
attediáre† = *tediare.*
atteg-giaménto, M.: attitude (posture). ||-**giáre** [*atto*], TR.: ADAPT (give the right expression or position to); REFL.: (*a*) enact; gesticulate; imitate. -**giatóre**†, M.: gesticulator. -**giévole**, ADJ.: imitating; gesticulating.
attegnènza†, F.: continence; calmness.
atteláre†, TR.: draw in battle-array.
attem-páre† [*tempo*], INTR.: grow older; delay. -**patèllo**, -**patétto**, ADJ.: somewhat old. -**páto**, ADJ.: in years (growing old). -**patòtto**, ADJ.: rather old. -**patúccio**, ADJ.: not very old (young).
attempora. .† = *tempera*. .
atten-daménto, M.: encampment. ||-**dáre** [*tenda*]; REFL.: pitch one's tents (encamp, settle).
at-tendènte, ADJ.: attending; M., F.: attendant; agent. ||=**tèndere**, IRR.; TR.: pay attention to; INTR.: attend; pay attention (mind); await; expect: — *a fare*, continue; — *la promessa*, keep one's word. -**tendíbile**, ADJ.: worthy of attention. -**tendiménto**†, M.: attention.
attenebráre [*tenebra*], INTR.: grow dark.
at-tenènte, ADJ.: holding to; belonging to; M.: kinsman. -**tenènza**, F.: appurtenance; relationship. ||=**tenére**, IRR.; INTR.: (ap)pertain, belong; REFL.: belong; hold on (stick to); follow.
attentaménte [-*tento*], ADV.: attentively.
at=tentáre, TR.: attempt (venture); REFL.: venture (have the courage); take the risk. -**tentáto**, ADJ.: attempted; M.: criminal attempt (crime). -**tentatòrio**, ADJ.: unlawful.
attènto [L. -*tus*], ADJ.: attentive; diligent.
atte-nuaménto, M.: attenuating. -**nuánte**, ADJ.: attenuating (diluent). ||-**nuáre** [*tenue*], TR.: attenuate (THIN); weaken. -**nuazióne**, F.: attenuation; emaciation; weakening.
attenúto, PART. of *attenere.*
atten-zioncèlla, F.: little attention. ||-**zióne** [-*dere*], F.: attention; application.
attergáre [*terga*], TR.: place behind; withdraw; REFL.: get behind; go back.
atter-raménto, M.: overthrow. ||-**ráre** [*terra*], TR.: cast to the ground or down (overthrow; prostrate); humble; REFL.: humble one's self; debase one's self†. -**riménto**† 1, M.: deposit.
atter-riménto† 2, M.: terror. ||-**ríre** [L. *terrere*], TR.: terrify (dismay); REFL.: be frightened; despond.
atterzáre†, TR.: reduce to a third.
atté-sa, F.: expectation. -**saménte**, ADV.: attentively. ||-**si**, PRET. of -*ndere.* ||-**so**, PART. of -*ndere;* attended, etc.; awaiting; cautious (careful): — *che*, seeing that; because.
attestáre† 1 [*testa*], TR.: join end to end; REFL.: press close; come to blows.
attes-táre 2 [*teste*], TR.: attest (testify to); call to witness. -**táto**, PART. of -*tare;* M.: attestation (certificate). -**tóre**, M., -**tríce**, F.: attester (witness). -**tatúra**, F.: jointure. -**tazióne**, F.: attestation (testimony).
attézza†, F.: aptness; ability.
atticaménte [-*co*], ADV.: in an Attic style; elegantly.
atticciáto [?], ADJ.: thick; sturdy.
atti-císmo, M.: Atticism; elegance. -**císta**, M.: writer in the Attic style. -**cizzáre**, INTR.: atticize (use the Attic style). ||**átti-co** [Gr. -*kós*], ADJ.: Attic; elegant; M.: (*arch.*) attic.
attiepidáre†, -**díre** [*tepido*], TR.: render tepid or lukewarm (cool).
attign. .† = *atting*. .
attíguo [L. -*guus* (*tangere*, TOUCH)], ADJ.: contiguous (adjacent).
attillá-re [? *atto*], REFL.: dress one's self with pedantic or studied care; fit well. -**taménte**, ADV.: affectedly; elegantly. -**to**, ADJ.: affectedly dressed (dandyish); well-fitting. -**tézza**, F.: affectation in dress. -**tíno**, ADJ.: neatly dressed; becoming. -**túra**, F.: affectation in dressing; studied elegance.
áttimo [variant of *átomo*], M.: moment (instant).
atti-nènte [L. *at-tinere*, hold to], ADJ.: pertaining (relating); M. PL.: relatives (kindred). -**nènza**, F.: relationship (kinship); PL.: appurtenances; relatives.
at-tíngere [L. (*tangere*, TOUCH)], IRR.; TR.: ATTAIN† (reach); draw (water, etc.), raise; derive; learn; perceive: — *cogli occhi*, discern (perceive). -**tingiménto**, M.: drawing (water, etc.), raising; learning. -**tingitóio**, M.: instrument for raising, bucket. -**tingitóre**, M.: raiser. -**tingitúra**, F.: drawing of water; raising. -**tínsi**, PRET., -**tínto**, PART. of -*tingere.*
attirágli̱o†, M.: equipment (equipage)
at=tiráre, TR.: ATTRACT, draw; REFL.: draw upon one's self (attract, win).
attitáre [L. *actitare* (*agere*, ACT)], TR.: proceed with (a legal action); treat.
attitúdine [*atto* 2], F.: APTITUDE (talent); attitude.
atti-vaménte, ADV.: actively. -**vità**, F.: activity. ||**attí-vo** [L. -*vus*], ADJ.: active: *debiti -vi*, outstanding debts.
attiz-zaménto, M.: stirring up the fire;

enticing: *forza -trattiva*, force
-trátto, PART. of *-trarre*.
-trattore†, M., -trattrice†, F.: at-
charmer; inveigler.

attra-versaménto, M.: traversing; im-
-versáre, TR.: traverse (cross);
REFL.: oppose one's self (to).
-versato, traversed; crossed out;
-vèrso [*traverso*], ADV., PREP.:
across (through);

attrazione [...], F.: attraction.

attrezzare, TR.: equip. ‖**-trázzo**
M.: trifling or worth-
less ...

attrecciare† = *intrecciare*.

attrezzista, M.: stage-furnisher. ‖**-tréz-**
zo ... implement (tool).

attribuíbile, ADJ.: attributable. **-bui-**
mento, M.: attributing (imputation).
-buire [... *tribuere*, bestow)], TR.: attribute; impute; REFL.: claim
-butivo, ADJ.: attributa-
-búto, M.: attribute.
-buzione, F.: attribution.

attrice, F.: actress; defendant†.

attristare, ... **-stire** [*tristo*],
grow sad (be affected); be-

attritare† ... **-trito**, ADJ.:
M.: attrition (fric-
-trizione, F.: attrition (compunc-

attruppamento, M.: gathering. ‖**-pá-**
re, ... gather in troops or
gather.

attuale, ... actual; effec-
-lità, F.: actuality.
-almente, ... really; at this

attuare, TR.: actuate;
constraint; con-
one's self intently.

attuario, ... 's office or dignity.
attuario, ... notary, clerk).

attutare, ... safe], TR.: calm
REFL.: grow
-tatore†, M.: pacifier. **-tíre**,
silence. **-titóre**†,

aucupio [... bird)], M.: bird-

au-dace [...], ADJ.: audacious (bold).
-dacemente, ADV.: audaciously. **-dá-**
cia, F.: audacity (boldness).

audi. .† = *udi*. . **-tóre,** M.: presiding judge; auditor (in a court). **-tòrio†,** M.: auditory; audience chamber; court-room.

áufo = *ufo*.

áuge [? Ar. *aug*, apogee], F.: high credit (glory): *vivere in* —, live as a great lord; live in glory.

au-gellatóre†, M.: bird-catcher. **-gèllo,** pl. *-gelli* or *-gei* [L. *-cellus* (*avis*, bird)], M.: (*poet.*) bird.

auggiáre [*uggia*], TR.: shade.

augná-re [*ugna*], TR.: claw; clutch; cut slanting. **-túra,** F.: slanting.

augument. .† = *aument*. .

augu-ràle, ADJ.: augurial. **-ráre,** TR.: augur (foretell); have a presentiment of†. **-ráto,** ADJ.: augured; M.: augurer's office: *bene* —, well begun or finished. **-ratóre,** M., **-ratríce,** F.: augurer (soothsayer). ‖**áugu-re** [L. *augur* (*avis*, bird)], M.: augur (Rom. diviner, orig'ly by the flight of birds, etc.). **-riáre†** = *-rare*. **augú-rio,** M.: augury (omen). **-rosaménte,** ADV.: by (good or bad) augury; ominously. **-róso,** ADJ.: augural (significant, ominous).

augústo [L. *-tus* (*augere*, increase)], ADJ.: august (solemn).

áula [L.], F.: assembly-hall.

aulédo†, M.: flute-player.

aulènte†, ADJ.: fragrant.

áulico [*-la*], ADJ.: aulic (of the court, court).

aulíre†, TR.: perfume.

aumen-taménto† = *-to*. **-táre,** TR.: augment (increase). **-tatívo,** ADJ.: augmentative. **-tatóre,** M., **-tatríce,** F.: increaser. **-tazióne†** = *-to*. ‖**auménto** [L. *augere*, increase], M.: augmentation (increase, growth).

aumettáre† = *umettare*.

aumil. .† = *umil*. .

auna. .† = *aduna*. .

auncicáre†, TR.: rob.

auncináre = *uncinare*.

aunghia. . = *augna*. .

áura [L.], F.: gentle breeze; air; aura†; — *popolare*, popular favour.

au-ráre†, TR.: gild. **-rèlia†,** F.: chrysalis. **-reáto†,** ADJ.: woven in gold. ‖**áureo** [L. *-reus*], ADJ.: of gold (golden); glorious. **-rèola,** F.: aureole (halo, glory).

aurétta [*-ra*], F.: light breeze (zephyr).

auri-coláre [L. *-cula*, dim. of *auris*, EAR], ADJ.: auricular.

auréfero [*auro*], ADJ.: auriferous.

auríga [L. (*aurea*, bridle, *ago*, lead)], M.: coachman.

auríno†, ADJ.: gold-coloured (golden).

aurispic. .† = *aruspic*. .

áuro (*poet.*) = *oro*.

auróra, pop. **-ròra** [L.], F.: aurora (dawn).

auṣáre†, TR.: accustom (inURE).

auṣi-liáre, -liário, ADJ.: auxiliary; M.: auxiliary verb; PL.: auxiliaries. **-liatóre,** M.: helper. ‖**auṣí-lio†** [L. *auxilium*], M.: assistance (help).

auṣo†, ADJ.: bold (daring).

au-spicáto, ADJ.: augured. ‖**áu-spice** [L. *-spex* (*avis*, bird, *specere*, view)], M.: augur (diviner); protector (patron). **-spício, -spízio,** M.: auspice (presage; protection).

auste-raménte, ADV.: austerely. **-rità,** F.: austerity. ‖**austè-ro** [L. *-rus* (Gr. *aúrein*, parch)], ADJ.: austere (severe); morose; poor (of food); sour (of wine).

au-stràle, -stríno†, ADJ.: austral (southern). ‖**áu-stro** [L. *-ster*], M.: south; south wind (auster). **-stríaco** [Austria], pl. *-ci*, M.: Austrian.

aut, aut [L.], ADV.: either, or.

autènti-ca, F.: authentic proof. **-caménte,** ADV.: authentically. **-cáre,** TR.: authenticate (prove). **-cazióne,** F.: authentication. **-cità,** F.: authenticity. ‖**autènti-co** [Gr. *autós*, self], ADJ.: authentic; authoritative†; *per* —†, authentically.

aúto 1 (*vulg.*) = *avuto* (cf. *avere*).

áuto 2 **da fe** [Port. 'ACT of FAITH'], M.: auto-da-fé.

auto= [Gr. *autós*, self], PREF.: auto-.

auto=biografía, F.: autobiography.

autò=crata, F., **-crate** [Gr. *krátos*, strength], M.: autocrat. **-crático,** ADJ.: autocratic(al). **-crazía,** F.: autocracy.

autodafé = *auto da fe*.

auto=grafía, F.: autography. **autò=grafo,** M.: autograph.

autò=ma [Gr. *mátos*, force], M.: automaton (self-moving machine). **-mático,** ADJ.: automatic(al).

auto-nomía, F.: autonomy. **autò=nomo** [*nómos*, law], ADJ.: autonomous.

autopsía = *autossia*.

autó-re [L. *auctor* (*augere*, produce)], M.: author. **-révole,** ADJ.: authoritative. **-revolézza,** F.: authoritativeness. **-revolménte,** ADV.: authoritatively. **-rità,** F.: authority. **-toritatívo,** ADJ.: authoritative. **-rizẓáre,** TR.: authorize. **-rizẓazióne,** F.: authorization. **-róne,** M.: great author. **-rúccio,** M.: wretched author.

autossía, [Gr. *autós*, self, *ópsis*, view], F.: AUTOPSY.

autríce [*-tore*], F.: authoress.

au-tunnále, ADJ: autumnal. ‖**-túnno** [L. *-tumnus*], M.: autumn.

auẓẓ. . = *auguzz*. .

av- [L. ad, or ab, from], PREF. ad-, ab-.
áva [avo], F.: grandmother.
avac-cévole†, ADJ.: solicitous, swift. **-cézza**†, F.: solicitude, hurry. **-ciáre**†, TR.: hasten. **avác-cio**†, M.: solicitude; hurry; ADV.: in haste, quickly: o tardi o —, sooner or later.
avále†, ADV.: soon, presently.
aván† = avanti. **-guárdia**, F.: vanguard.
avanía [fr. Turk.], F.: imposition (orig. by the Turks on the Christians): exaction; affront.
avannòtto [ugnauno], M.: young fry: simpleton.
avantággio† = vantaggio.
aván-te (poet.), **-ti** [L. ab, ante, before], PREP. or ADV.: before (of place or time); forward: d'ora (or da qui) in —, henceforward, andare —, go before: go on (proceed), essere —, be advanced: farsi —, present or introduce one's self: passare —, pass beyond (leave behind). **-ti-cámera**† = anticamera. **-chè**†, CONJ.: before that. **-ti-guárdia**† = avanguardia. **-zaménto**, M.: advancement (progress). **-záre**, TR.: advance; present; pass beyond† (outstrip, surpass); INTR.: advance, proceed; be over and above, remain; escape; REFL.: advance; be ready; anticipate†; take courage†: mi basta e me n' avanza, I have enough and to spare. **-zaticcio**, M.: remnant (scrap). **-záto**, ADJ.: advanced; over and above; left, remaining. **-zatóre**†, M.: advancer. **-zétto**†, M.: trifling remnant. **-zévole**†, ADJ.: superfluous. **aván-zo**, M.: (what is over and above) remnant; remainder, rest; saving (profit); PL.: old remains (ruins): d' —, over and above, more than enough. **-zúccio**, **-zúglio**, **-zúgliolo**, **-zúme**, M.: disp. of -zo; poor remnants or scraps, etc.
ava-ráccio [-ro], ADJ.: very avaricious (niggardly). **-raménte**, ADV.: avariciously. **-rétto**, M.: little miser. **-rézza**† = -rizia.
ava-ría [Ger. haferei], F.: particular AVERAGE (damage to ship or cargo). **-riáre**, TR.: cause damage to ship or cargo. **-riáto**, ADJ.: damaged.
ava-rízia, F.: avarice. **-rizzáre**†, INTR.: be niggardly. ||**avá-ro** [L. avarus], ADJ.: avaricious (greedy); sparing; M.: miser. **-ronáccio**, M.: wretched miser. **-róne**, M.: great miser.
áve [L.], INTERJ.: ave! all hail!
avellá-na [L.], F.: filbert. **-no**†, M.: filbert-tree.
avèllere† = svellere.
avèllo [lavello, tub], M.: grave (tomb).
avemmaría [ave Maria], F.: Ave-Maria.

avèna [L.], F.: OATS; shepherd's pipe.
avére [L. habere], IRR. §: TR.: HAVE; sometimes with an abstract noun to be rendered by 'be' and an adject.; M.: possession, property; PL.: riches: — caldo (freddo, fame, paura, etc.), be warm (cold, hungry, afraid, etc.); (also) have warmth, etc.; — bisogno, need; — faccia, be like; — agio, be at leisure, have time; — sospetto, have a mind; — a caro, be glad; — a dispetto, disdain (despise); — al sole, have landed property; — in costume, be accustomed; — in grado, accept; — in odio, hate; — in pregio, value (esteem); — per buono, take in good part: averla con, be angry with.

§ Ind. Pres. ho or ò, hai or ài, ha or à; abbiamo, avete, hanno or anno. Pret. ebbi, avesti, ebbe, avemmo, aveste, ebbero. Fut. avrò. Cond. avrei. Subj.: abbia; pl. abbiamo abbiate, abbiano. Impv. abbi; abbiate.

Rare forms: Pr. I. 1. aggio, 3. àve; 4. avémo. S. 1. aggia; 6. aggiano. Pret. 6. ébbono. Fut. averò. Cond. 1. 3. averia; 6. (avr)ieno. Ger. abbiendo. Part. auto.

Avèrno [L. -nus], M.: Avernus (lake in Campania with poisonous vapours); (poet.) hell; ADJ.: Avernian.
aversi..† = avversi..
avèrso†, PART. of avertere: avert.
avi-daménte, ADV.: greedily; eagerly. **-dézza**, **-dità**, F.: avidity; eagerness. ||**ávi-do** [L. -dus (avere, wish)], ADJ.: avid (greedy): eager.
avironáre†, TR.: environ (surround).
av-íto, ADJ.: ancestral (hereditary). **áv-o** [L. avus], M.: grandfather; PL.: ancestors.
a=vocáre, TR.: appeal; (Eng.† avocate); take up. **-vocazióne**, F.: appealing.
avogad..† = avvocat..
ávo-la, F.: grandmother. ||**-lo** [avo], M.: grandfather.
avolt(e)r..† = adulter..
avoltóio†, M.: vulture.
avòrio [L. eboreus, of ivory], M.: IVORY.
avòrnio†, M.: laburnum.
avúlso, PART. of avellere: torn up.
avúncolo†, M.: uncle.
avú-to, PART. of avere. **-ta**, F.: gain.
avval-laménto, M.: sinking down; low ground; cavity. ||**-láre** [valle], INTR.: sink or crumble down (cave in); flow down; TR.: let down (sink); sign as security (at the bottom of a note). **-latúra**, F.: hollowness.
avvalo-raménto, M.: strengthening; valour. ||**-ráre** [valore], TR.: strengthen (invigorate, animate); REFL.: be strengthened (be encouraged).
avvam-paménto, M.: burning; flame. ||**-páre** [vampa], INTR.: flame (blaze, burn).
avvan-taggiaménto, M.: advantage (gain). ||**-taggiáre** [vantaggio], TR.:

advantage; improve; increase; REFL.: derive advantage; get the better. **-tàggio**, M.: advantage: *d'* —, more. **-taggióso**, ADJ.: advantageous.
avvantáre† = *vantare.*
av=vedére, IRR.; INTR., REFL.: perceive; foresee. **-vediménto**, M.: perception; foresight; prudence; cunning. **-vedutaménte**, ADV.: providently (prudently). **-vedutézza**, F.: foresight (sagacity). **-vedúto**, ADJ.: provident (prudent, cautious).
avvegna-chè†, **-dioche**†, CONJ.: although.
avvele-naménto, M.: empoisonment. ‖**-náre** [*veleno*], TR.: poison. **-natóre**, M., **-natríce**, F.: poisoner.
avve-nènte, ADJ.: graceful (genteel, pleasing). **-nenteménte**†, ADV: gracefully. **-nènza**, F.: grace (elegance). **-névole**, ADJ.: graceful (genteel). **-nevolézza**, F.: grace (elegance). **-nevolménte**, ADV.: gracefully. **-niènte**, ADJ.: coming (future). **-niménto**, M.: EVENT (incident); success†; coming†; access†. ‖**-nire** [L. *ad-venire*], IRR. (cf. *venire*); INTR.: come to pass, happen; arrive†; derive†; succeed†; REFL.: become (suit, fit, be adapted); fall in with†; M.: future (futurity); grace† (elegance): *per l'* —, henceforth. **-nitíccio**† = *-ntizio.*
avven-taménto, M.: blowing out; rush. ‖**-táre** [*vento*], TR.: blow out; pronounce boldly; shoot† (hurl); INTR.: make a big impression; impose; REFL.: rush upon. **-tággine**, F.: rashness. **-tataménte**, ADV.: rashly (inconsiderately). **-tatèllo**, ADJ.: hair-brained. **-tatézza**, F.: rashness (temerity, imprudence). **-táto**, ADJ.: rash (inconsiderate, hasty).
avven-tíccio†, **-tízio** [*-ire*], ADJ.: adventitious. **avvèn-to**, M.: advent; arrival. **-tóra**, F., **-tóre**, M.: customer.
avventrináre [*ventre*], INTR., REFL.: get belly-ache.
avventú-ra [*avvenire*], F.: adventure (occurrence; risk†); good luck†. **-ráre**, TR.: adventure (hazard); REFL.: run the risk (venture). **-rataménte**†, ADV.: fortunately; at a risk. **-ráto**, ADJ.: hazarded; fortunate (lucky). **-revolménte**†, ADV.: luckily. **-rière** or **-rièro**, M.: adventurer; soldier of fortune. **-rosaménte**†, ADV.: luckily. **-róso**, ADJ.: lucky (fortunate); adventurous.
avvenúto, PART. of *avvenire.*
avve-raménto, M.: averment (confirmation). ‖**-ráre** [*vero*], TR.: aver (confirm).
av-verbiále, ADJ.: adverbial. **-verbialménte**, ADV.: adverbially. **-vèrbio** [*verbo*], M.: adverb.
avverdíre [*verde*], INTR.: become green or verdant.
avverificáre† = *verificare.*
avverrò, FUT. of *avvenire.*
avver-saménte, ADV.: adversely; unfortunately. **-sáre**, TR.: turn against (oppose). **-sário**, ADJ.: adverse (contrary); M.: adversary (opponent). **-satívo**, ADJ.: adversative. **-satóre**, M., **-satríce**, F.: opposer (adversary). **-sazióne**†, F.: opposition. **-sióne**, F.: aversion. **-sità**, F.: adversity. ‖**avvèr-so** [L. *ad-versus* (*vertere*, turn)], ADJ.: adverse (contrary; hostile); hurtful; PREP.†: against; opposite; M.†: adversity: *per* —, on the contrary.
avver-tènte, ADJ.: advertent (careful, circumspect). **-tenteménte**, ADV.: advertently (carefully). **-tènza**, F.: advertency (heedfulness, care). **-timénto**, M.: advice (counsel); (Eng.† advertisement). ‖**-tíre** [L. *ad-vertere* (turn)], Pr. *-to* or *-tisco*, TR.: advise (apprise, inform; Eng.† advertise); admonish; observe (pay attention to). **-titaménte**, ADV.: advertently (carefully). **-títo**, ADJ.: advised, etc.: *stare* —, be upon one's guard.
av-vezzaménto†, M.: custom. ‖**-vezzáre** [*vezzo*], TR.: accustom (train). **-vezzáto**, or pop. **-vézzo**, PART.: accustomed; trained. **-vezzatúra**†, F.: habit.
av-viaménto, M.: beginning. ‖**-viáre** [*via*], TR.: start (begin); set on foot; prepare; REFL.: set out. **-viáto**, ADJ.: started; introduced. **-viatúra**, F.: beginning; preparation; first kindling.
avvicen-daménto, M.: alternation. ‖**-dáre** [*vicenda*], TR.: alternate; REFL.: alternate (change bv turns). **-dévole**†, ADJ.: alternate.
avvici-naménto, M.: approach(ment). **-nánza**†, F.: approach. ‖**-náre** [*vicino*], TR., REFL.: approach. **-náto**, ADJ.: approached; near (close).
avvignáre [*vigna*], TR.: plant with vines.
avvi-liménto, M.: abasement; humiliation. ‖**-líre** [*vile*], TR.: degrade (debase, Eng.† vilify); deject (discourage); REFL.: degrade one's self (be degraded); lose courage. **-litívo**, ADJ.: degrading (debasing); depreciative; discouraging. **-líto**, ADJ.: degraded, etc.; weakened.
avvilup-paménto, M.: entanglement. ‖**-páre** [*viluppo*], TR.: envelop (wrap up); entangle (confuse); REFL.: get entangled (get bewildered). **-páta**, F.: confusion: *all'* —, helter-skelter. **-pataménte**, ADV.: confusedly. **-patóre**, M., **-patríce**, F.: wrapper; entangler; cheat. **-patúra**, F.: entanglement.
avvi-nacciáto† = *-nazzáto.* ‖**-náre**

[illegible] imbue with wine (as casks. [illegible] -**máto**, ADJ.: [illegible] wine-coloured. [illegible] getting tipsy. -**nar**- [illegible] get tipsy. [illegible]

[illegible] -**vinchiá**- [illegible] fasten [illegible] REFL.: [illegible] set out.

[illegible] petty fight). [illegible] advice, observation. [illegible] show], [illegible] to apprise, in- [illegible] guess†; aim at†; [illegible] REFL.†: perceive; [illegible] face, have an encoun- [illegible] -**patamente**†, ADV.: advisedly. [illegible] adviser, informer; (theat.) [illegible] **avviso**, M.: advice; [illegible] advertisement, placard; a mio —, [illegible] opinion; stare [illegible] be upon one's guard.

[illegible] judge at view [illegible] appearance to [illegible] -**tato**, ADJ.: attrac- [illegible]

[illegible] -**tic**- [illegible] -**tic**- [illegible] -**tire**, INTR.: [illegible] TR.: [illegible] -**vare** [illegible] be [illegible] become [illegible] soft [illegible]

mistaken†. -**volgiménto**, M.: wrapping or turning round; winding; tortuosity; deception. -**volgoláre**†, TR.: entangle.

avvolon-tataménte†, ADV.: willingly. -**táto**†, ADJ.: willing; arbitrary.

avvolpacchiáre†, REFL.: bewilder one's self.

avvolpináre†, TR.: deceive.

avvòlsi, PRET. of *avvolgere*.

avvol-tacchiáre†, INTR.: turn to and fro; ramble. ‖-**táre** [*voltare*], TR.: wrap up; turn around. -**táto**, ADJ.: wrapped up; twisted (entangled). -**tatúra**, F.: wrapping; winding. -**tecchiáre**, TR.: entangle.

avvòlto, PART. of *avvolgere*.

avvolto-láre [*volto*], TR., REFL.: roll (round); whirl; ramble; wallow. -**lata**-**ménte**, ADV.: confusedly. -**latúra**, F.: rolling or rambling about.

aziènda [? Span. *hacienda*, farm], F.: public or private administration (management).

ázimut [fr. Ar.], M.: azimuth.

azio-náccia, *disp.* of -**ne**. -**ncèlla**, *dim.* of -**ne**. ‖**azió-ne** [L. *actio*], F.: action; act (deed); subject (of a play); (*leg.*) cause; stock, share. -**nísta**, M.: shareholder. -**núccia**, F.: mean little act.

azòto [Gr. *a*-, not, *zoé*, life], M.: azote (nitrogen).

ázza [cf. *ascia*], F.: battle-axe.

azzampáto [*zampa*], ADJ.: provided with claws.

azzan-naménto, M.: seizing with the teeth. ‖-**náre** [*zanna*], TR.: seize with the teeth.

azzar-dáre, TR.: hazard. ‖-'**do** [fr. Ar.], M.: hazard. -**dóso**, ADJ.: hazardous.

azzeccáre [*zecca*], TR.: hit (strike); hurl; catch, guess.

azzeròlo = *lazzarolo*.

azzi-cáre†, TR.: move; REFL.: stir; be busy. -**catóre**†, M.: bustler.

ázzi-ma, F.: unleavened dough. -**máre**, TR.: perfume; adorn; polish. -**mèlla**, F.: unleavened wafer. ‖**ázzi-mo** [Gr. *ázymos*, un-leavened], ADJ.: unleavened; [illegible], M. PL.: Easter (of the Jews) or seven days after Easter.

azzit-táre†, -**tíre**†, TR.: silence (stop).

azzollare†, TR.: kill with clods.

azzop-páre†, -**píre** [*zoppo*], TR.: make limp; INTR.: limp (hobble). -**páto**†, -**píto**, ADJ.: lame (crippled).

azzuf-faménto†, M.: strife. ‖-**fáre** [*zuffa*], REFL.: come to blows (fight, join battle). -**fatóre**, M.: wrangler. -**físo**†, M.: [illegible].

azzuolo†, ADJ.: dark-blue.

azzur-reggiáre, INTR.: incline to azure-colour. **-riccio, -rigno**, ADJ.: slightly azured (sky-coloured). ‖**azzúr-ro** [l. L. *lazur* (fr. Pers.)], M.: AZURE.

B

b, bi [L.], M.: b (the letter).
ba-, *disp. pref.* (cf. *bis*).
babáu [*bau*], M.: bugbear.
bab-b.. [*ba-ba*, infantile BAB-ling]: **-báccio**, *disp.* of *-bo*; ADJ.: silly. **-baccióne†**, M.: fool. **-balèo**, ADJ.: silly. **-balòcco**, ADJ.: dull, heavy. **-bèo**, ADJ.: silly; M. (*bea, f.*): silly person (fool). **-bíno**, *car.* of *-bo*. **-bióne**, *aug.* of *-beo*. **-bo**, M.: (*fam.*) father (dad). **-buassággine**, F.: silliness. **-buásso**, ADJ.: foolish (stupid).
babbúccia [fr. Ar.], F.: toe-slipper.
babbuíno [?], M.: BABOON; fool.
babbúsco†, ADJ.: big and tall.
Ba-bèl(l)e [fr. Assyr.], F.: Babylon (city of Assyria); babel, confusion. **-bilònia**, = *Babèle*.
ba-cáccio, *disp.* of *baco*. **-cáio**, M.: silkworm raiser. **-cáre**, INTR.: be worm-eaten. **-caròzzo**, M.: little worm (grub); robber. **-catíccio**, ADJ.: worm-eaten; somewhat unhealthy. **-cáto**, ADJ.: having worms; sick.
báoca [L.], F.: berry; pearl.
bac-calà, -caláro† [Sp. *-alao*], M.: dried cod, stockfish.
bacca-láre [L. *-larius*], M.: wiseacre, pretender to wisdom. **-lería†**, F.: bachelor's degree; arrogance.
bacca-nále [*Bacco*], M.: bacchanal (feast in honour of Bacchus). **-nária**, F.: feast of Bacchus. **-'no**, M.: loud talking. **-'nte**, F.: bacchante (priestess of Bacchus). **-'re†**, TR.: dance; revel. **-'to†**, ADJ.: drunk.
bac-cèlla [*-cello*], F.: silly woman. **-celláio**, M.: bean-field. **-cellétto**, *dim.* of *-cello*.
bac-cellière [Fr. *bachelier*], M.: bachelor's degree; bachelor; wiseacre†. **-cellieráto**, M.: bachelor's degree.
bac-cellíno, ADJ.: of the bean variety; like a bean. ‖**-cèllo** [*-ca*], M.: bean or pea (with the pod); pod (shell); simpleton. **-cellóne** *aug.* of *-cello*.
bacchét-ta [*bacchio*], F.: stick; rod. **-táre**, TR.: beat with a stick: — *una cosa*, sell a thing for very little. **-táta**, F.: blow with a stick. **-tína**, *car. dim.* of *-ta*. **-tíno**, *dim.* of *-to*. **-to**, M.: rather large stick. **-tóna**, F., **-tóne**, M.: devotee (penitents being touched with a rod, by the priest); bigot; hypocrite. **-toneria**, F., **-tonismo** [cf. *-tone*], M.: bigotry; hypocrisy.
bac-chiáre [*bacchio*], TR.: knock down (with a 'pole'); kill†, murder. **-chiáta**, F.: beating.
bácchico, ADJ.: Bacchian (drunken).
bacchil(l)ón-a, F., **-e** [?], M.: simpleton; idler.
bácchio [*baculo*], M.: big stick; pole; young lamb†.
baccífero [*bacca*], ADJ.: producing berries; bacciferous.
Bácco, M.: Bacchus (god of wine); wine; love†.
bachè-ca†, F.: show-case. **-co†**, M., **-ca†**, F.: showy person.
bache-rèllo, *dim.* of *baco*. **bacheròzzo, -ròzzolo**, M.: worm (grub).
bacia=básso, M.: profound reverence; humility. **-máno**, M.: kiss on the hand; compliment. **-ménto**, M.: kissing (salute). **=píle** [*pila*, font of holy water], M.: bigot; hypocrite. **=pólvere**, M.: hypocrite. ‖**baciá-re** [*bacio* 1], TR.: kiss (salute); REFL.: kiss one another; M.†: kiss. **=sánti** [*santi*, saints], M.: devotee; hypocrite. **bacígno**, M.: kiss.
ba-cíle, M.: basin. **-cinèlla**, F.: small basin. **-cinétto**, M.: helmet-piece. ‖**-císno** 1 [l. L. *bassinus*], M.: BASIN, vase.
ba-cíno 2, *dim.* of *-cio*. ‖**-'cio** 1 [L. *basium*], M.: kiss (salute).
bácio 2 [l. L. *opacivus*, OPAQUE], ADJ.†: shady (in the shade).
ba-cióne, -ciòzzo, *aug.* of *-cio* 1. **-cucchiáre**, TR.: kiss repeatedly. **-cucchío**, M.: repeated kissing.
bá-co [L. *-cus*], M.: worm; silkworm. **-colíno**, *dim.*
bácolo† = **-culo**.
bacúcco, M.: cowl (hood).
báculo [L. *-lum*], M.: stick; staff.
bá-da [*-dare*], F.: delay: only in *stare* (*tener*) *a* —, delay, detain, keep expectant. **-dággio**, M.: expectation, hope.
bada-lícchio†, -lischio†, -lísco†, M.: basilisk.
bada-lóne, ADJ.†: idle; M.: great idler or trifler; choir-desk; large fig.† **-lucáre**, INTR.: loiter, watch; skirmish; assault†; invest†. **-luccatóre†**, M.: assailant. **-lúcco†**, M.: slight skirmish; trifling diversion; trifle. **-ménto†**, M.: delay. ‖**badá-re** [?], INTR.: observe carefully (be attentive); mind; lose time†; REFL.: avoid danger.
badèrla†, F.: frivolous woman.
ba-déssa [L. *abbatissa* (cf. *abate*)], F.: ABBESS. **-día**, F.: abbey. **-diále**, ADJ.: (*jest.*) large, fat.
badigliaménto†, -díglio†, M.: yawning.
badíle [L. *batillo*], M.: shovel.

baf-fétto, **-fíno**, *dim.* of *-fo.* ‖**-fo** [?], (us'ly pl.), M.: mustache. **-fóna**, F.: bearded woman. **-fóne**, ADJ., M.: heavy-bearded (man).

bága†[1] [Fr. *bague* = It. *bacca*], F.: gem.

bá-ga†[2] [l. L.], F.: leather bottle. **-gá-gl̤io**, M.: baggage; knapsack. **-gagl̤iú-me**, M.: mass of baggage. **-gáscia**, F.: strumpet.

bagat-tèlla [? *baga* 1], F.: bagatelle (trifle). **-tíno**, M.: small coin; worthless fellow.

bag-gèo [?], M.: fool; ADJ.: foolish. **-gianáta**, F.: foolish act. **-giáno**, M.: fool (simpleton).

baggioláre†, TR.: support, rest.

bágher [Ger. *wagen*], M.: four-wheeled carriage (or WAGON).

bághe-ro [? *baga*], M.: coin (farthing). **-róne**, M.: big copper coin.

bágio†, M.: kiss.

bagl̤ióre [? *ba-*, *lucore*], M.: flash.

ba-gnaiòlo, M.: bath-attendant. **-gna-ménto**, M.: bathing (wetting). **-gnán-te**, M., F. (us'ly pl.): bather. **-gnáre**, TR.: bathe (sprinkle, wash, moisten; REFL.: bathe. **-gnatúra**, F.: course of baths; time for bathing. **-gnétto**, *dim.* of *-gno.* ‖**-gno** [L. *balneum*], M.: bath. **-gnòlo**, M.: bathing with water, etc. (to ease pain).

ba-gordáre, INTR.: revel; tilt† (joust). ‖**-górdo** [l. L. *bufurdium*], M.: revelling company; lance (pike)†.

bái=a 1 [?], F.: BAY. **-étta**†, *dim.*

bái=a 2 [?], F.: joke. **-étta**†, *dim.*

baiettóne [*baio*], M.: lining goods (chestnut coloured).

baiáre† = *abbaiare.*

bailámme [Turk.], M.: hubbub.

bái-lo [L. *-ulus*, porter: ak. to Eng. bailiff], M.: city magistrate; official. **-líre**†, TR.: rule (govern).

bái-o [L. *badius*], M.: chestnut colour. **-òc-co**, M.: four farthings† (from the colour); worthless man; boor. **-occóne**, *aug.* of *-occo.*

bai-onáccio†, *disp.* of *-one.* ‖**-óne** [*aug.* of *baia* 2], M.: big or bad joke; joker (banterer).

baionét-ta [*Bayonne*, Fr. city], F.: bayonet. **-táta**, F.: bayonet thrust.

baióso†, M.: lover of jokes.

baiúca†, F.: nonsense, trifle.

ba-lásc̤io or **-lásso** [l. L. *-lascius*], M.: kind of ruby.

baláu-sta†, F., **-sto**†, M.: pomegranate flower.

baláu-stro [Gr. *-stion*], M.: small balustrade. **-stráta**, F.: balustrade. **-stráto**, ADJ.: balustraded.

bal-bettaménto, M.: stammering. **-bet-tánte**, M.: stutterer (stammerer). **-bet-táre**, TR., INTR.: stutter (stammer). **-bet-tío**, M.: continued stammering. **-bezzá-re**†, INTR.: stammer. ‖**-bo** [L. *-bus*], ADJ.: stammering. **-botíre**†, **-buzzáre**†, **-butíre**†, **-buzzáre**†, INTR.: stammer. **-búzie**, F.: stammering. **-buzziènte**, ADJ.: stammering; M., F.: stammerer. **-buzzíre**†, INTR.: stammer.

Balcáno, ADJ., M.: Balcan.

bal-cò† [L. *-cus*], M.: floor; scaffold; horns of a stag. **-cóne**, M.: balcony.

baldacchíno [*Bagdad*], M.: baldachin (canopy).

bal-danzménte, ADV.: boldly. **-dánza**, F.: boldness (self-confidence). **-danzeg-giáre**†, INTR.: possess boldness; act boldly. **-danzosaménte**, ADV.: boldly. **-danzosétto**, *dim.* of *-danzoso.* **-dan-zóso**, ADJ.: bold (courageous). **-dàllo**†, ADJ.: bold. **-diménto**†, M.: boldness. ‖**-do** [Ger. *bald*], ADJ.: BOLD. **-dòria**, F.: bonfire.

baldràcca [?], F.: harlot.

ba-léna [L. *-læna*], F.: whale; whalebone.

bale-naménto, M.: lightning. ‖**-ná-re** [*-leno*], INTR.: flash.

balenière [*-lena*], ADJ.: whaling; M.: whaling-vessel.

ba-lenío, M.: frequent lightning. ‖**-lé-no** [?], M.: lightning (flash).

balenòtto [*-lena*], M.: young whale.

balè-stra [L. *balista*], F.: cross-bow; (*typ.*) galley. **-stráio**, M.: bow-man. **-stráre**, TR., INTR.: shoot (hurl); transpierce†. **-stráta**, F.: bow-shot; length of a bow-shot†; gun-shot†. **-strière**, M.: bowman. **-stríno**†, *dim.* of *-stro.* **-'stro**, M.: crossbow. **-stróne**, *aug.* of *-stro;* kind of bread†. **-strúccio**, M.: kind of swallow.

ba-lì [L. *baiulus*, 'carrier,' ak. to Eng. *bailiff*], M.: commander (in knighthood). **-lía** 1, F.: authority (power). **bá-lia** 2, F.: wet-nurse. **-liáccia**, *disp.* of *-lia* 2. **-liággio**, M.: office of a commander; magistrate; BAILIWICK. **-liático** [cf. *-lia* 2], M.: nurse's pay. **-liáto**†, M.: bailiff's rank. **bá-lio** [*-lia* 2], M.: husband of a nurse; preceptor†. **-lióna**, *aug.* of *-lia* 2.

balí-sta [L.], F.: ballista. **balí-stica**, F.: ballistics.

bálla [OGer. *balla*], F.: BALE, sack: *a balle*, in abundance.

bal-lábile†, M.: ballet (dance). **-ladó-re**†, M.: gallery of a ship. **-laménto**†, M.: wavering; dancing. ‖**-láre** [ak. to Eng. *ball*], INTR.: dance, waver. **-láta**, F.: BALLAD; intrigue†. **-latèlla**, **-la-tétta**, *dim.* of *-lata.* **-latína**, *dim.* of *-lata.* **-latóio**, M.: gallery, terrace. **-la-tóre**, M., **-latríce**, F.: dancer. **-lería**†,

[illegible]

[illegible] rdamente [illegible]

[illegible]

bálta [illegible]

bálteo [illegible]

Báltico [illegible]

baluárd[illegible]

ba-lug[illegible]

balu[illegible]

bál-za

bál-za [illegible]

bandolièra [*banda*], M.: shoulder-belt; soldier's belt.
bándolo [*-da*], M.: head of a skein.
bára [OGer. *bara*], F.: BIER, coffin; litter.
barabúffa [*baruffa*], F.: scuffling; riot (confusion).
baráo-ca [*barra*], F.: barrack; bath-house. **-chière**†, M.: sutler. **-cúccia**, *dim.* and *disp.* of *-ca*.
baragòzzo [? Afr.], M.: trifle.
baraónda [Sp. *-rahunda*], F.: confusion (hubbub).
ba-ráre [*-ro*], INTR.: cheat (at play).
báratro [L. *-trum*], M.: deep, dark place; abyss (hell).
barátta†, F.: contention.
barat-taménto, M.: exchanging. ||**-tá-re** [Gr. *práttein*], TR.: exchange (BARTER); cheat; deal with swindlers†; embroil one's self†. **-tatóre**, M.: exchanger. **-tazió-ne**†, F.: exchanging. **-tería**, F.: bartering. **-tière**, M.: swindler; huckster†. **-to**, M.: exchange; swindle.
baráttola†, F.: water-fowl.
baráttolo [? l. L. *veratrum*], M.: vase; pot (for medicines, conserves, etc.).
bár-ba [L.], F.: beard; force (strength); root; uncle†: *in, alla* —, in spite of. **-babiètola**, F.: beet-root. **-bacáne**, M.: barbacan, fortification. **-báccia**, F.: rough beard. **-bagiánni** [Fr. *barbe à Jean*], M.: owl; simpleton.
barbáglio [*bagliore*], M.: dazzling; dizziness.
bar-baláocchio†, M.: dotard. **-bandròc-co**†, M.: lazy person. **-báno**†, M.: uncle.
barbaraménte [*-ro*], ADV.: barbarously.
barbáre [*-ba*], TR.: take root; play a trick.
bar-bareggiáre, INTR.: speak or act barbarously; commit barbarisms. **-ba-rescaménte**, ADV.: barbarously. **-ba-résco**, ADJ.: barbarous. **bár-bari**, M. PL.: barbarians (northern nations not under Roman rule). **-bárico**, ADJ.: barbarous. **-bárie**, F.: barbarity (cruel act); barbarous manner of speaking or writing. **-barísmo**, M.: barbarism; solecism. **bár-baro** [Gr. *-baros*], ADJ.: barbarous (fierce, cruel); M.: barbarian.
barbaróssa [*-ba*], F.: sort of grape.
barbassòro [*varvassoro*, vassal of low rank], M.: wiseacre.
bar-báta [*-ba*], F.: roots. **-batèlla**, F.: layer, sprig; kind of herb (eaten in salad). **-báto**†, ADJ.: rooted; wise; valiant. **-bazzále**, M.: curb (check); fetter.
bar-beráre†, INTR.: play horse; whirl (of a peg-top). **-berésco**, M.: † barbery horses; barbery horse†. **-sro** [*Barberia*], M.: BARBERY **-ce-horse**.

barbétta [*-ba*], F.: small, thin beard.
bar-bicamánto, M.: taking root. ||**-bi-cáre** [*-ba*], INTR.: take root; grow.
bárbicoe†, ADJ.: pertaining to a sheep; F.: sheep; ewe.
bar-bicèlla, **-bicína**, *dim.* of **-ba** (in sense of root). **-bícola**†, *dim.* of **-ba**. **-bicóne**, M.: large, coarse beard; main root. **-bière**, M.: barber (hair-dresser). **-bieria**†, F.: barber's shop. **-bigi**, M. PL.: whiskers. ||**-bíno** [*-ba*], M.: small beard; piece of cloth to polish razors; miser†; ADJ.: lacking ability. **-bio**, **-bo**, M.: barbel (kind of fish). **-bi=ton-sóre**, M.: barber. **-bògio**, ADJ.: old, imbecile; M.: dotard. **-bolína**, F.: very small root. **-bóne**, M.: *aug.* of **-ba**; long thick beard; water-spaniel. **-bòzza**, F.: horse's under-jaw; = **-bòzzo**†, M.: helmet-front (for cheek and chin). **-bucíno**†, ADJ.: slightly bearded.
barbu-gliaménto, M.: stammering. ||**-gliáre** [ak. to *barbottare*], INTR.: stammer; speak confusedly.
bar-búta [*-ba*], F.: helmet with a deep visor; helmeted soldier. **-búto**, ADJ.: heavily bearded.
bár-ca [L.], F.: bark (small boat); affair; confused heap. **-cáccia**, *disp.* of *-ca*. **-caiòlo**, M.: boatman; ferryman. **-ca-menáre**, REFL.: save one's self. **-ca-ròla**, F.: barcarolle (gondolier's song). **-cáta**, F.: boat-load (boatful). **-cheg-giáre**, INTR.: ride in a boat (for pleasure)†; REFL.: save one's self. **-chég-gio**†, M.: boat-riding. **-cheréccio**†, M.: large number of boats. **-chétta**, F.: small boat; pleasure-boat. **-chettaiòlo**, M.: boatman. **-chettína**, **-chettíno**, **-chétto**, **-chettúccio**, *dim.* of *-ca*. **-chíno**, M.: hunting-boat (used in marshes). **-collaménto**, M.: wavering. **-colláre**, INTR.: stagger, waver (totter). **-collio**, M.: continuous wavering. **-còl-lo**†, M.: wavering. **-cóne**, *aug.* of *-ca*. **-culláre** = *-collare*. **-cullóne**, **-cul-lóni**, ADV.: waveringly.
bár-da [l. L.], F.: caparison. **-damen-táre**†, TR.: caparison. **-daménto**†, M.: trappings (of a horse). **-dáre**, TR.: caparison; harness.
bardána [l. L.], F.: burdock.
bardássa [?], M.: naughty or ill-bred boy; rogue.
bar-datúra, F.: caparison (trappings of a horse). **-dèlla** [*-da*], F.: pack-saddle. **-delláre**†, TR.: put on a pack-saddle. **-dellóne**, M.: large saddle (used in training colts). **-díglio** [Fr. *-de*, piece of bacon], M.: kind of marble (white and cerulean).
bár-do [Celt. *-dus*], M.: bard (poet, esp.

of the north). **-doccucúllo**†, M.: bard's garment.
bardòtto [-*da*], M.: mule; apprentice.
ba-rèlla [-*ra*], F.: handbarrow, litter; PL.: eye-glasses. **-rellàre**, INTR.: rest; carry on a handbarrow†. **-rellóne**, M.: wavering.
barería†, F.: cheat; swindle.
bar-gagnàre†, INTR.: bargain. **-gágno**†, M.: negotiation.
bar-gèlla, F.: crafty or talkative woman. **-gellíno**, M.: small coin (coined under the first *Bargelli*). ‖**-gèllo** [l. L. *barigildus* (Ger.)], M.: commander (in Italian city); chief of bailiffs; sheriff; residence of the commander; slanderer.
bár-gia† [-*ba*], F.: dew-lap (of oxen); beard (of goats). **-gíglio**, M. (us'ly pl.): gills (of a cock). **-gigliáto**†, ADJ.: having gills.
barigèllo† = *bargello*.
ba-rígli oncíno, *dim.* of *-riglione*. **-riglióne**, M.: barrel (cask). **-rila**†, F.: = *-rile*. **-riláia**, F.: place where barrels are (cooperage). **-riláio**, M.: cooper. ‖**-ríle** [l. L. *-rilus*], M.: BARREL; beehive; old Florentine coin†. **-rilétto**, *dim.* of *-rile*. **-rilòtto**, M.: medium-sized barrel. **-rlétto**†, M.: small barrel. **-rlióne**†, M.: small barrel.
barí-tono [Gr. *barús*, heavy, *tónos*, tone], M.: barytone voice; barytone singer. **-tonále**, ADJ.: barytone. **-toneggiáre**, INTR.: possess or imitate a barytone voice.
barláccio [*bis-*, L. *laxus*, lax], ADJ.: spoiled (egg); slightly ill.
bar-létta [for *-iletta*, of *-ile*], F.: traveller's flask (barrel-shaped). **-lettáio**, M.: cooper. **-lòtta**† = *-letta*. **-lòzzo**, M.: small barrel.
barlúme [*bis-*, L. *lumen*, light], M.: dim, uncertain light; (*fig.*) weak idea.
barnabíta [*Barnaba*], M.: Barnabite (member of a religious order); ADJ.: of a Barnabite.
báro [?], M.: cheat, swindler (at cards).
baroccohísmo [-*rocco*], M.: awkward (clumsy) work; uncouthness.
ba-rocciáio, M.: carter (drayman). **-rocciáta**, F.: cartload; very fat woman. **-roccinàio**, M.: cart-lender; street-vender. **-roccíno**, M.: small vehicle (cart). ‖**-ròccio** [L. *bi-roteus*] M.: 'TWO-wheeled' waggon (cart, handcart); great quantity.
ba-ròcco [-*roco*, in sense of oddness], ADJ.: BAROQUE; awkward; much ornamented; kind of usury†. **-ròccolo**†, M.: kind of usury. **-roccúme**, M.: quantity of odd, strange things. **-ròco** [mnemonic word], M.: baroko (kind of syllogism).

ba - romètrico, ADJ.: barometric(al). ‖**-ròmetro** [Gr. *báros*, weight, *metrón*, MEASURE], M.: barometer.
ba-ronággio, M.: barony. **-ronále**, ADJ.: baronial. **-ronáre**†, INTR.: play the knave. **-ronáta**, F.: wicked deed; despicable thing. **-roncèllo**, M.: idle (good for nothing) boy. **-roncíno**, M.: son of a baron. ‖**-róne** [Fr. *-ron*], M.: baron; game (with dice); knave (vagabond); title given to saints and to Christ†; great lord†. **-ronería**†, F.: wicked action. **-ronescaménte**, ADV.: knavishly. **-ronésco**, ADJ.: knavish. **-ronéssa**, F.: baroness. **-ronétto**, M.: baronet. **-ronévole**†, ADJ.: noble, valiant. **-ronía**, F.: barony; company of barons†; company of noble, valiant men†; rank (honour)†.
bár-ra, [l. L.], F.: BAR (in a court-room; metal plate†). **-ráre**†, TR.: bar; cheat. **-rería**, F.: deceit, fraud. **-ricáre**, TR.: barricade; REFL.: protect one's self by a barricade. **-ricáta**, F.: barricade. **-rièra**†, F.: barrier (balustrade); palisade.
bar-ríre [L.], INTR.: roar (of elephants). **-ríto**, M.: roaring.
barròccio and *der.*, cf. *baroccio*.
barúf-fa [*ruffa*], F.: quarrel. **-fo**†, M.: quarrel; intrigue.
barúgioli [?], in: *tra ugioli e* —, all in all, altogether.
barul - láre†, TR.: retail; roll. **-'lo**†, M.: *disp.*: huckster; simpleton.
barzellét-ta [?] F.: joke; funny story. **-táre**, INTR.: joke.
báza† = *base*.
baza-líschio†, **-lísco**†, M.: basilisk.
bazál-te, **-to** [L. *-tes*], M.: basalt.
ba-zaménto, M.: base (foundation). **-záre** [-*se*], TR., REFL.: found (establish).
baz ciá, M.: pop. for *pasciá*.
ba - zciáre†, TR.: kiss. ‖**-zcio**†, M.: kiss.
báze [Gr. *-sis*], F.: base (foundation); support.
bazèo†, ADJ.: stupid (dull); M.: simpleton.
bazét-ta [?], F.: mustache; whiskers. **-tíni**†, M. PL.: whiskers. **-tóne**, M.: big-whiskered man.
ba-zílica [Gr. *-siliké* (*-sileús*, king), royal palace], F.: basilica (Roman public hall; cathedral). **-zilicále**, ADJ.: pertaining to a cathedral. **-zílico** [Gr. *-silikón*, king plant], M.: sweet basil. **-zilísco** [Gr. *-siliskós*, king lizard], M.: basilisk.
baziménto [-*sire*], M.: fainting.
bazína†, F.: pottage.
bazíno [for *bombasino*], M.: bombasin.
bazíre [Celt. *bas*, dead], INTR.: die, faint.
basóffia†, F.: pottage.

bagéso†, ADJ.: stupid, dull.
bas-saménte [*basso*], ADV.: humbly; basely. **-saménto†**, **-sánza†** = *abbassamento*, *abbassanza*. **-sáre†** = *abbassare*. **-sétta**, F.: skin of a slaughtered sheep†; broken flask; (*fig.*) dwarf; basset (game of cards). **-settáre**, TR.: kill. **-sétto**, ADJ.: *dim.* of *-so*†; small violin. **-sézza**, F.: lowness, humility; abjectness; base thing†. ‖**-so** [L. L. *-sus*, thick], ADJ.: low, short; shallow (of water); base (mean); wretched; ADV.: below, down; basely; M.: profundity (depth, bottom); bass; bass viol. **-so=rilièvo**, M.: basrelief. **-sòtto**, M.: *dim.* of *-so*; short person; mess of macaroni†. **-súra**, F.: low place or condition.
básta 1 [OFr. *-stir*, BASTE], F.: basting; wide fold (to lengthen a garment).
básta 2 [*-stáre*], INTERJ.: enough! stop!
bastágio†, M.: porter.
bastáio [*-to*], M.: pack-saddle maker.
ba-stánte [*-stare*], ADJ.: sufficient. **-stanteménte**, ADV.: sufficiently. **-stánza**, F.: in *a* —, usually *abbastanza*, in sufficiency, sufficiently, enough; duration†; competence†.
ba-stárda†, F.: small galley. **-stardèlla**, F.: stew-pan; sauce-pan. **-stardèllo**, M.: foundling. **-stardígia†**, F.: being a bastard. ‖**-stárdo** [*-sto*], ADJ.: bastard (illegitimate; false); borrowed; M.: bastard. **-stardúme**, M.: (*disp.*) number of bastards; false things; useless growth (of plants).
bastáre [?], INTR.: suffice; last; subsist†.
bastèrna [? *-stare*], F.: ancient chariot.
ba-stévole [*-stare*], ADJ.: sufficient. **-stevolézza†**, F.: sufficiency. **-stevolménte**, ADV.: sufficiently.
bastía†, F.: bastion; fortress.
bastière†, M.: pack-saddle maker.
bastiménto [OFr. *-tir*, build], M.: ship.
bastína [*-to*], F.: light pack-saddle.
ba-stionáre, TR.: fortify with bastions; REFL. **-stionáta**, F.: defense of bastions. **-stióne**, M.: fortification; bastion. ‖**-stíre†** [OFr. *-stir*], TR.: build. **-stíta†**, F.: palisade; fortification.
básto [?], M.: pack-saddle; troublesome weight; heavy care.
basto-náre, TR.: beat, cudgel, BASTINADE ("cane"); sell cheaply. **-náta**, F.: beating. **-natúra**, F.: beating. **-ncèllo**, *dim.* of *-ne*. **-ncíno**, M.: cloth (of wool and lace); tea-roll. **-ncióne**, *aug.* of *-ne*. ‖**bastó-ne** [? *basto*], M.: stick (cane), staff; chicken-roost; emblem of rank; staff of command† (cf. Eng. baton); PL.: clubs (at cards). **-nière†**, M.: mace-bearer; lictor.
-stracóne†, M.: fat man.
bastorovèscio [*basto*], M.: gutter.
ba-tácchia†, F.: bastinade. **-tacchiáre**, TR., REFL.: beat (cudgel). **-tacchiáta†**, F.: bastinade; blow. ‖**-tácchio** [L. *-*taculum* (-*tuere*, hit)], M.: bell-clapper; big stick; pole.
batassáre†, TR.: shake.
batáta†, F.: sweet potato.
batísta [*Baptiste* of Cambrai, inventor], ADJ.: of fine cambric, lawn, batist.
batòcchio†, M.: blindman's staff.
bátolo [?], M.: priest's mantle; fold of the cowl†; foundation†.
ba-tòsta [?], F.: agitation (disturbance); contention; battle† (combat). **-tostáre†**, INTR.: dispute (quarrel).
bat-táglia [L. L. *-ualia* (L. *-tuere*, strike)], F.: BATTLE; battalion†. **-tagliáre**, INTR.: wage battle (us'ly in fig. sense); TR.: fight†; beat in walls†. **-tagliáta†**, F.: blow in battle. **-taglièra†**, F.: bastion, fortress. **-taglière†**, ADJ.: fond of battle. **-taglièro**, ADJ.: accustomed to battle; fond of battle. **-taglierésco†**, **-tagliévole†**, ADJ.: warlike. **-tágllo**, M.: bell-clapper. **-taglióne**, M.: battalion; crowd; soldier of a battalion†. **-tagliésco†**, ADJ.: warlike; quarrelsome. **-taglísta†**, M.: battle-painter. **-tagliuòla†**, *dim.* of *-taglia*. **-tagliuzza†**, *dim* of *-taglia*.
batteggiáre†, TR.: baptize.
bat-telláta, F.: boat-load. **-tellétto**, *dim.* of *-tello*. **-tellière**, M.: boatman. ‖**-tèllo** [*-to*], M.: small boat: — *di salvamento*, life-boat.
bat-ténte, M.: folding-door; frame (of a mirror, etc.); knocker. ‖**bát-tere** [L. *-tuere*], TR.: beat (strike, knock; overcome); chatter; scour; REFL.: fight; fight a duel; — *i denti*, chatter (from cold, fever); — *le dieci*, strike ten; — *le mani*, applaud; — *moneta*, coin money. **-tería**, F.: battery; quantity of merchandise; breach†; artillery fire†: — *da cucina*, kitchen utensils.
bat-tesimále, ADJ.: baptismal. ‖**-tésimo** [Gr. *baptismos*], M.: BAPTISM. **-tésmo†**, M.: baptism. **-tessaménto†**, M.: baptizing. **-tessáre**, TR.: baptise; name (a thing); REFL.: receive baptism; — *il vino*, thin, adulterate the wine. **-tessatóre**, M.: baptiser. **-tessatòrio**, M.: baptismal font. **-tessière**, M.: baptizer.
batti- [*battere*]: **=baléno**, *in un* —, in a moment. **=códa**, F.: titmouse. **=cuòre**, M.: cf. *-cuore*. **-cúlo†**, M.: thigh armor; kind of sail. **=cuòre**, M.: palpitation (of the heart); fear. **=fiánco**, M.: partition board (of a stable). **=f(u)òco**, M.: steel (to strike fire).

battifòlle†, M.: citadel.
battifrédo†, M.: tower; rampart; movable tower (for attacking a fort).
batti- [*battere*]: **-ṣi†** or **-ṣie†**, F.: falling sickness; convulsions. =**láno**, M.: wool-carder. **-lòro** [*l' oro*], M.: gold or silver beater. =**máno**, or =**máni**, M.: applause. **-ménto†**, M.: beating (esp. applause). **battí-o**, M.: beating. =**pòrto†**, M.: entrance (into a ship). =**sóffia†**, F.: sudden fear.
battis-tèrio†, **-tèro** [Gr. *baptistérion*], M.: baptismal chapel; bath†.
batti- [*battere*]: =**stráda**, M.: outrider.
bátti-to, M.: beating (of the heart), pulsation; trembling (fear). **-tóio**, M.: club; folding-door. **-tóre**, M.: beater. **-túra**, F.: beating (thrashing); imprint of the hammer; punishment.
bátto†, M.: rowboat.
bát-tola† [*-tere*], F.: clatterboard. **-toláre†**, INTR.: chatter.
battú-ta, F.: pulse-beat; beating time (in music). ‖**-'to** [*battere*], ADJ.: beaten, M.: condiment; pavement†, Tuscan coin†.
batúf-fo, or **-(f)òlo** [?], M.: heap.
bau [echoic], M.: dog's bark; one who causes fear (fright).
báudo†, ADJ.: bold.
baú-le [? L. *baiulus*, 'carrier'], M.: coffer, trunk. **-létto**, **-líno**, M.: *dim.* of *-le;* jewel or workbox.
bausètte [*bau, sette*], M.: fear.
baútta [?], F.: domino.
bá-va [?], F.: saliva; slobbering; poor silk; profile. **-vaglíno**, *dim.* of *-vaglio.* **-váglio**, M.: bib; gag.
Ba-varése, M., F., **-váro**, M.: Bavarian.
ba-vèlla [*-va*], F.: kind of silk. **-'vera**, F.: cape. **-veríua**, F.: embroidered collar. **-'vero**, M.: collar, cape. **-vétta**, F.: *dim.*† of *-va;* scum. **-vettíne**, F. PL.: dough; broth. **-vóso** [*-va*], ADJ.: slobbering.
baẓẓa [OGer. *baze*, gain, ak. to Eng. *better*], F.: bargain (cheap purchase); good luck; winning card; projecting chin; trick† (at cards).
baẓẓána [Ar.] F.: tanned sheepskin.
baẓẓár [Ar.], M.: bazar.
baẓẓár-a†, or **-o†**, cf. *baratto.*
baẓ-ẓècola [dim. of *-za*], F.: folly; trifle. **-zésco†**, ADJ.: low; clownish (coarse). **-'zica**, F.: game of cards. **-zicáre**, INTR.: play *-zica;* fight duels; frequent (of a place). **-ẓicatúra†**, F.: folly; trifle. **-zicòtto**, M.: making a point (at *-zica*). **-zicottóne**, M.: term in card-playing. **baẓ-ẓína**, F., **baẓ-ẓíno**, M.: small purchase.
baẓẓòffia [*zuffa*], F.: coarse food (thick pottage); long, confused composition.
baẓẓòtto [? Ger. *besotten*, boiled], ADJ.: soft boiled (of eggs); half-done; unskilled.
bè [echoic], M.: bleating.
bè', ADV.: for *bene.*
beá-re [L.], TR.: beatify (make happy); bless; REFL.: take pleasure in. **-taménte**, ADV.: blessedly. **-tánza**, F.: bliss, beatitude. **-tificáre**, TR.: bless (beatify); magnify†. **-tificazióne**, F.: beatification; function of the high priest (at mass). **-tífico**, ADJ.: beatific. **-titúdine**, F.: beatitude (bliss); title of the pontiff. **-to**, ADJ.: happy (contented); beatifier (elect of Paradise).
béca [*-co*], F.: woman of low rank; slattern.
bécca†, F.: scarf (worn by university professor); band; garter.
bec-cábile [*-co* I, BEAK], ADJ.: that may be picked. **-cáccia**, F.: woodcock. **-caccíno**, M.: snipe. **-cáccio**, *disp.* of *-co.* **-caffco**, M.: fig-pecker.
beccáio [*becco* 2], M.: butcher.
becca=mòrti, M.: grave-digger. **becca=péṣci** [*pesce*], M.: sea-bird. ‖**beccá-re** [*becco* I], TR.: peck (eat); strike with the beak; win; obtain by cunning; REFL.: catch: *-carsi il cervello*, puzzle one's brain.
beccarèllo†, M.: kid.
beccastríno†, M.: mattock.
bec-cáta [*-co* I], F.: blow with the beak; beakful. **-catèlla†**, F.: hawk's lure; trifle. **-catèllo**, M.: bracket. **-catína**, *dim.* of *-cata.* **-catóio**, M.: food-box (in bird-cages). **-catúra**, F.: pecking.
becche-rèllo†, M.: *dim.* of *becco* 2; kid. ‖**-ría** [*becco* 2], F.: butcher's shop; killing†.
bécchico†, ADJ.: good for coughs; pectoral.
becchíno [*becco* 2, in anal. with *beccaio*], M.: grave-digger.
bécco I [?], M.: BEAK; mouth; point (of various objects, as lip or spout of a pitcher, etc.); beak of a ship; mallet: *aver paglia in* —, share a secret.
béc-co 2 [?], M.: goat; cuckold. **-cóne**, *aug.*
bec-cúccio [dim. of *-co* I], M.: spout. **-cuzzáre**, TR.: *freq.* of *-care.*
be-ceráta, F.: insolent word or act. ‖**-'cero** [*pecoro*], M.: vulgar man; cynical, insolent man. **-ceróna**, **-ceróne**, *aug.* **-cerúme**, M.: vulgar crowd; mob.
béco [L. *pecus*], M.: dull (stupid); rustic.
be-fána [*Epifania*], F.: Epiphany; goblin (bringing gifts to children at Epiphany); gift; ugly woman. **-fanáccia**, *disp.* of *-fana.* **-fanía**, F.: Epiphany.
bèf-fa [?], F.: derision (scorn). **-fárdo**, ADJ.: jesting; M.: jester (banterer). **-fa-**

re, TR.: ridicule (jeer at, scorn): *-farsi d'una cosa*, not to care for a thing, scorn a thing. **-fatóre**, M., **-fatríce**, F.: mocker. **-feggiaménto**, M.: derision (ridicule). **-feggiáre**, TR.: *freq.* of *-fare*. **-févole†**, **-fívile†**, ADJ.: ridiculous; contemptible.

bèga [?], F.: contention, trouble.

beghína [l. L. *-gardus* (ak. to Eng. *beg*)], F.: lay-sister; beguine; bigot.

bègli, PL. of *bello* before vowel or *s* impure.

begli-(u)òmini, M. PL.: garden balsam (plant).

begoláre†, INTR.: trifle. ‖**bègole†**, F. PL.: foolish talk; trifles.

bèi 1, PL. of *bello* before consonants (exc. *s* impure).

béi 2 or **bei** [Turk.], M.: bey (Turkish ruler).

bèl for *bello* before consonants.

be-laménto, M.: bleating. ‖**-láre** [L.], INTR.: bleat; cry; call†. **-láto**, M.: bleating. **-latóre**, M., **-latríce**, F.: bleater, crier.

bélgico, ADJ.: Belgian.

belío [*-lare*], M.: continued bleating.

belguíno†, M.: benzoin.

bell' = *bello*.

bella=dònna, F.: belladonna.

bellaménte [*-llo*], ADV.: gracefully, well; beautifully†; gently†.

bel-láre†, INTR.: wage war. **-latóre†**, M.: warrior.

bellétta [?], F.: sediment; mud (mire).

bellétto [*-llo*], M.: paint (rouge).

bel-lézza [*-lo*], F.: beauty; abundance. **-lezzína**, *dim.* of *-lezza*.

bellíco [*umbilico*], M.: navel.

bèllico [L. *-um*], pl. *-ci*. ADJ.: pertaining to war.

bellicóncio, M.: umbilical cord.

bellicóne†, M.: beaker (bumper).

bel-licóso [L. *-lum*], ADJ.: warlike (martial); inciting to war†. **-ligeránte**, ADJ.: belligerant. **-lígero**, ADJ.: warlike.

bellimbústo [*bello in busto*], M.: dandy (fop).

bellíno [*bello*], ADJ.: rather pretty.

bellírico†, M.: myrobolan (plant).

bèl-lo [L. *-lus*], ADJ.: beautiful (fine; gracious); gentle; M.: beauty; fine opportunity; (fine) thing. **-lòccio**, *dim. car.* of *-lo*. **-lóne**, *aug.* of *-lo*. **-lóso†**, ADJ.: beautiful. **-lo=spírito**, M.: wit: *far il —*, act insipidly. **-l=umóre**, M., F.: gay person. **-lúria**, F.: superficial beauty.

…† [*-lare*], M.: bleating, crying. **-lóne**, … wailing person (esp. child).

… = *bellezza*.

… [L. *-lua*], F.: wild beast.

bèl=vedére, M.: belvedere (point commanding a fine prospect).

belzebù [Heb. *Baal*, lord], M.: Beelzebub.

belzuíno [?], M.: benzoin.

bembè [*bene-bene*], ADV.: well, well.

bemòlle, cf. *bimolle*.

ben-, for *bene* in compounds.

ben=andáta, F.: farewell-money. **=augurato** or **bèn auguráto**, ADJ.: auspicious. **=avventuránza**, F.: good luck; prosperity. **=chè** [*che*], CONJ.: (al)though.

bén-da [cf. *banda*], F.: band; veil. **-dáre**, TR.: blindfold. **-datúra**, F.: bandaging; blindfolding. **-dóne**, M.: bonnet-strings; trimming. **-dúccio†**, M.: child's handkerchief.

bène [L. *bene*], ADV.: well; M.: good (advantage); property (wealth); peace (quiet); PL.: goods, property (possessions): *farsi —*, sell well; *operare —*, work, act uprightly; *trattar —*, have good manners; *— spesso*, very often; *sì —*, most certainly; *— vestito*, decently, becomingly dressed; *vestito —*, dressed in rich garments.

bene-détta, F.: electuary; thunderbolt. **-dettíno** [*Benedetto*, Benedict], ADJ.: Benedictine, M.: drink made by the Benedictines. **-détto**, ADJ.: blessed; longed for; M.: slight convulsion. **=dícere†**, cf. *-dire*. **-dícite** [L.], grace (at table). **-dícola**, F.: trifling ecclesiastical office. ‖**=díre** [*dire*], IRR.§; TR.: bless, consecrate; exalt; become spoiled (of things): *mandar uno a farsi —*, send any one to perdition. **-ditóre†**, M., **-ditríce†**, F.: blesser. **-dizióne**, F.: benediction; consecration: *dar la —*, wish to know no more of a thing.

§ Like *dire*, except: Pres. *bene-dico* or (pop.) *-disco*. I've *benedici*. Impf. *bene-dicéva* or (pop.) *-diva*; Subj.: *bene-dicéssi*. Pret. *bene-dissi* or (pop.) *-dii*, 3. *-disse*, *-dì*; 6. *-dissero*, *-dirono*.

bene=fáre, IRR.; INTR.: act honestly; BENEFIT. **-fattívo†**, ADJ.: benefiting. **-fátto**, M.: benefit; service. **-fattóre**, M.: benefactor (philanthropist). **-fattríce**, F.: benefactress. **-ficáre**, TR.: benefit (do good to). **-ficatóre†**, M.: benefactor. **-ficènte†**, ADJ.: beneficent. **-ficènza**, F.: beneficence. **-ficiále†**, ADJ.: pertaining to an ecclesiastical benefice. **-ficiáre†**, TR.: benefit (do kindnesses to). **-ficiáta**, F.: benefit (for an actor). **-ficiáto**, cf. *-fiziato*. **-fício**, M.: kindness; benefice. **benè-fico**, ADJ.: beneficent; benefiting. **-fiziáre†**, TR.: benefit. **-fiziáto**, M.: beneficiary. **-fízio**, M.: kindness (service); benefice; gain; utility; advantage. **-fiziòtto**, M.: benefice.

bene-merènza, us'ly pl., F.: merit (de-

sert). ‖=**mèrito**, ADJ.: well-merited; M.: man of merit; service†.
beneplácito [L. *-citum*(*placere*, PLEASE)], M.: approbation (consent; will, option).
ben=èssere or **ben essere**, M.: prosperous condition (of health, fortune, etc.); well-being.
bene-stánte, ADJ.: well-conditioned, comfortable; healthy. ‖=**stáre**, M.: approval (of accounts, etc.).
bene-voglièntet†, ADJ.: benevolent. **-vogliènza**†, F.: benevolence. **benè-volet**†, cf. *-volo*. **-voleménte**†, ADV.: benevolently. **-volentemènte**†, ADV.: with benevolence. **-volènza**, F.: benevolence. **-volménte**, ADV.: with benevolence. ‖**benè=volo**, ADJ.: benevolent (kind).
ben=fátto, ADJ.: well made; good featured: *cuore* —, kind; generous.
beniamíno [*Beniamino*, Benjamin], M.: beloved, favorite child.
beni-ficáre†, **-ficènza**†, **-fício**†, cf. *bene-ficare*, etc.
be-nignaménte, ADV.: benignantly (kindly). **-nignità**, F.: benignity (goodness; kindness). ‖**-nígno** [L. *-nignus*], ADJ.: benign (kind); mild (of weather); not dangerous (of sickness); propitious.
beníno [*dim.* of *bene*], ADV.: pretty well; well: *per* —, quite well, good.
benivogl.. = *benevol..*
bénna†, F.: mountain cart or sled; fold; diadem.
ben=náto, ADJ.: well born; happy†; fortunate†.
benóne [*bene*], ADV.: very well (excellently).
ben=servíto, M.: testimonial; recommendation; recompense†.
ben=sì, ADV.: certainly; but.
ben=tornáto, M.: welcome.
ben=trováto, M.: welcome (greeting, salute).
ben=venúto, M.: welcome: *dar il* —, welcome.
ben-voglièntet†, ADJ.: benevolent. ‖=**voléro**, IRR.; TR.: wish well, love; M.: benevolence, love: *farsi* —, make one's self loved; *prender a* —, take under one's protection†, adopt; love. **-volúto**, PART.: beloved.
benzína [*belzuino*], F.: benzine.
be-óne, pop. for *-vone*, M.: tippler, drunkard.
bèrbero or **-ri**, M.: barberry.
bèrbice†, F.: sheep; lamb.
beretáre [?], INTR.: howl (shriek).
bercilòcchio†, M.: squint-eyed; near-sighted person.
bèrcio [*-ciare*], M.: howl; scream.
bére or *bevere* [L *bibere*], IRR. (cf. *bevere*); TR.: drink: — *grosso*, be very credulous; *dare a* —, make (any one) believe; *bersela*, *berselo*, believe blindly; — *una cosa*†, believe a thing readily ('swallow').
bergamásca [*Bergamo*, Italian province], F.: kind of dance.
berga-mòtta [Turk.], F.: bergamot. **-mòtto**, ADJ.: bergamot.
berghinèlla†, F.: gossip; low woman.
bergolináre†, TR.: quiz, rally. **bèrgolo**†, M.: blockhead; big talker; fickle person; willow-basket.
beri-cocoláio†, M.: honey-cake (or gingerbread) seller. **-c(u)òcolo**†, M.: honey-cake (gingerbread).
beríllo [L. *-ryllus*], M.: beryl.
berlícche [?], M.: (*jest.*) devil (dickens).
berlina 1 [?], F.: pillory; gallows†.
berlí-na 2 [*Berlino*, Berlin], F.: berlin (coach). **-nése**, ADJ.: Berlinian.
berlin-gaccíno, M.: second Thursday before Lent. ‖**-gáccio** [?], M.: fat Thursday (last Thursday of the carnival); fat person. **-gaiuòlo**†, M.: big talker; big eater. **-gaménto**†, M.: babbling. **-gáre**†, INTR.: babble, chat (after a meal). **-gatóre**†, M.: big babbler. **-ghièro**†, M.: big eater. **-gòzza**†, F.: country-dance. **-gòzzo**, M.: big cake.
bernabíta = *barnabita*.
bernácla†, F.: barnacle.
bernòcche [L. *ebronicus*], M.: *essere, andare in* —, be a little intoxicated.
ber-neggiáre [*Berni*, Ital. humorist], INTR.: write in a humorous vein. **-nésco**, ADJ.: burlesque.
bèrnia†, F.: woman's cloak.
ber-nòcchio†, **-nòccolo** [*bis-*, *nocchio*], M.: protuberance, knob: *aver il — di qualcosa*, have a mind (inclination) for a thing. **-noccolétto**, **-noccolíno**, *dim.* **-noccolúto**, ADJ.: full of knobs.
berrét-ta [l. L. (L. *birrus*, 'red,' viz. cloth)], F.: barretta (priest's cap); lady's bonnet; cap; red berries of shrubs: — *rossa*, cardinal's hat; *aver il cervello sopra la* —, be without judgment; *far di* —, salute a person. **-táccia**, *disp.* of *-ta*. **-táccio**, *disp.* of *-to*. **-táio**, M.: maker or seller of bonnets. **-tíno**, *dim.* of *-to;* ADJ.: malignant; wretched. **berrét-to**, M.: cap (with a vizor): — *frigio*, republican emblem; — *ducale*, ducal coronet; — *da notte*, nightcap; *far di* —, salute a person. **-tóne**, *aug.* **-túccia**, **-túccio**, *disp. dim.* of *-to*.
berriuòla†, F.: *dim.* of *berretta*; house-cap.
berro-váglia, F.: crowd of armed men. ‖**-vière** [OFr. *-vier*, inhabitant of Berry], M.: armed man; bailiff; audacious soldier.
ber-sagliáre, TR.: shoot at a target;

(*fig.*) torment through enmity. **-saglière**, M.: sharpshooter. ‖**-ságlio** [?], M.: bull's-eye, target; mark, butt; encounter† (fight).
bèrta [?], F.: pile-driver; trick; trifle†: *dar la —*, deride, scorn.
bertabèllo, M.: same as *bertuello*.
berteggiáre [-*ta*], TR.: deride, ridicule.
bertés-ca [?], F.: parapet; bricklayer's hod†; bench†. **-tescáre†**, INTR.: fortify with parapets; puzzle one's self.
bertòldo [*Bertoldo*], M.: foolish man.
bertóne†, M.: cropped horse; high ship.
bertovèllo† = *bertuello*.
ber-túccia [-*ta*], F.: monkey; ugly gossiping woman. **-tuccináta**, F.: foolish act. **-tuccina**, *dim.* of *-tuccia*. **-túccio†**, M.: monkey, baboon. **-tuccióne**, *aug.* of *-tuccio*.
bertuèllo [l. L. *vertebolum* (*-tere*, turn)], M.: fishing-net.
berúzzo†, M.: peasant's breakfast.
bèrza†, F.: calf of the leg.
berzáglio† = *bersaglio*.
bes-sággine†, F.: foolishness. **bès-so†**, ADJ.: foolish; stolid.
bestém-mia [Gr. *blasphemía*], F.: BLASPHEMY; false judgment. **-miamènto†**, M.: blaspheming. **-miáre**, TR., INTR.: blaspheme. **-miatóra**, F., **-miatóre**, M.: blasphemer. **-mióne**, M.: continuous blasphemer.
bé-stia [L.], F.: BEAST; cruel man; ignorant person: *andare* (*entrare, saltare*) *in —*, fly into a rage; *conoscere l'umor della —*, know with whom one has to do. **-stiáccia**, *disp.* of *-stia*. **-stiáio**, keeper of animals. **-stiále**, ADJ.: bestial (brutal); enormous. **-stialità**, F.: bestiality; stupidity. **-stialménte**, ADV.: in a bestial manner. **-stiáme**, M.: herd of cattle, horses, etc. **-stiecciuòla†**, *dim.* = *-stioluccia*. **-stilità†**, F.: same as *-stialita*. **-stiòla**, F.: small animal; ignorant person. **-stiolina**, **-stiolino**, **-stiolúccia**, *dim.* of *-stia*. **-stionáccio**, *disp.* (applied to persons). **-stióne**, M.: *aug.* of *-stia*; coarse, wicked man; very ignorant man. **-stiuòla** = *-stiola*. **-stiuòlo**, M.: small animal; ignorant person.
bét-tola [for *bevettola* (*bevere*, drink)], F.: ale-house, tavern. **-tolánte**, M.: frequenter of ale-houses; tippler. **-tolière**, M.: ale-house keeper.
bettònica [L.], F.: betony (plant): *esser più conosciuto della —*, be very well known.
bè-tula or **-túlla** [L.], F.: birch-tree.
...ucch.., **-ut..** = *be-vucch.., -ut..*
...**'a**, F.: time when a wine is fit to drink; ...lity of wine, savour; (*fig.*) true ele-...forto, gift: *i sonetti son la sua —*, sonnets are his forte. **-vánda**, F.: drink; potion. **-verággio**, M.: drink (esp. for animals); drink-money; recompense†. **-veratóio**, same as *abbeveratoio*. ‖**bé-vere**, or *bere* [L. *bibere*], IRR.§; TR.: drink (cf. *bere*). **-vería†**, F.: drinking (merry-making). **-veríno**, M.: drinking cup in bird-cages.

§ Pres. *bèvo* or (pop.) *bèo*, etc. Pret. *bèvvi* (*bevv-* in 1., 3., 6.) or (pop.) *bevètti*. Fut. *beverò* or (pop.) *berrò*, etc. — Rare forms: Pret. *bevéi* or *bébbi*, *bésti*, etc.

bévero, M.: BEAVER.
be-veróne [-*vere*], M.: drink (for horses and cattle); medicinal drink. **-víbile**, ADJ.: drinkable. **-viléoqua†**, M.: water-drinker. **-viménto†**, M.: drinking. **-vitóre**, M., **-vitríce**, F.: drinker. **-vitúra†**, **-vizióne†**, F.: drinking. **-vóne**, M.: hard drinker; tippler. **-vucchiáre**, INTR.: *freq.* of *-re*. **-vúta**, F.: drinking. **-vutina**, *dim.* of *-vuta*.
bezzi-cáre [*becco* 1], TR., REFL.: peck; TR., INTR.: peck (food); dispute (quarrel). **-cáta**, F.: blow with the beak. **-catúra**, F.: wound from a beak.
bèzzo [L. *bi-assis*, double coin], M.: small Venetian coin; PL.: money.
bi- [L. *bis*, TWICE], PREF.: bi-, TWO-, double [cf. *bis-*], also disparaging.
biácca [Ger. *bleich*, pale], F.: white lead.
biácco [? ak. to *black*], M.: species of non-poisonous snake (*coluber milo*).
biá-da [?], F.: horse-feed, oats, etc.; PL.: grains in general. **-daiòlo**, M.: grain-seller. **-dáre**, TR.: feed (animals).
biadétto†, ADJ.: clear azure; M.: blue paint.
bian-cástro, ADJ.: whitish. **-castróne**, *aug.* **-cheggiaménto**, M.: whitening. **-cheggiáre**, INTR.: become white or pale; grow hoary or gray. **-chería**, F.: linen or cotton clothes. **-cheríaccia**, *dim.* and *disp.* **-chézza**, F.: whiteness, paleness. **-chiccio**, ADJ.: whitish. **-chiménto**, M.: whitening, bleaching. **-chire**, TR.: whiten; bleach; polish.
‖**bián-co** [OGer. *blanc*], ADJ.: white; pale; hoary; M.: whiteness, brightness; blank. **-comangiáre†**, M.: blanc-mange. **-cóne**, ADJ.: white-skinned; M.†: kind of falcon. **-córe†**, M.: whiteness, paleness. **-cóso†**, ADJ.: very white. **-cospino** [-*co*, *spino*], M.: white thorn, hawthorn. **-cúme**, M.: quantity of white things.
biánte†, M.: vagabond.
biá-scia, F.: saliva, slaver. **-sciaménto**, M.: chewing. **-scia=midèllo**, M., F.: chewer. ‖**-sciáre** [? L. *blæsare*], TR.: eat slowly (chew, munch); eat without appetite; mumble (words): *— una lingua*, speak a language badly. **-scia=roçári**,

M.: mumbler of prayers; bigot; hypocrite. **-sciáre**, same as *-sciare*.

biasi-mábile, ADJ.: blamable. ‖**-máre** [L. *blasphemare*, BLASPHEME], TR.: BLAME (censure); grieve (lament). **-matóre**, M.: blamer. **-mévole**, ADJ.: blamable (reprehensible). **-mevolménte**, ADV.: reprehensibly. **biási-mo**, M.: censure, blame; reproof.

biasmáre†, **biásmo**†, same as *biasimare*, *biasimo*.

biastemáre†, INTR.: same as *bestemmiare*.

bibáce†, ADJ.: bibacious; M.: drinker.

Bíbbia [Gr. *biblia*], F.: Bible; tiresome writing.

bíbere†, same as *bevere*.

bíbita [*-bere*], F.: drink (of medicinal waters).

bíblico [*Bibbia*], ADJ.: Biblical, scriptural; reader in church†.

biblio- [Gr. *biblíon*, book]: **-filo** (Gr. *phílos*, friend], M.: bibliophile. **bibliò-grafo** [Gr. *gráphein*, write], M.: bibliographer. **-grafía**, F.: bibliography. **-gráfico**, ADJ.: bibliographical. **-graficaménte**, ADV.: bibliographically. **bibliò-mane**, **-mano**, M.: bibliomaniac. **-manía**, F.: bibliomania. **-tèca** [Gr. *théke*, box], F.: library; collection of books (bearing on a particular subject). **-tecário**, M.: librarian. **-techétta**, *dim.* and *car.* of *-teca*. **-techína**, *car. dim.* of *-teca*; collection of small books (in the same edition).

bíca [OGer. *biga*], F.: heap, pile.

bic-chieráio†, M.: maker or seller of beakers. ‖**-chière** [Ger. *becher*], M.: BEAKER, drinking-glass; beakerful, calyx (of lichens)†. **-chierétto**, *dim.* **-chieríno**, M.: *dim.*; choice liquor or wine. **-chièro**† = *-chiere*. **-chieróne**, *aug.* of *-chiere*. **-chieròtto**, M.: medium-sized glass. **-chierúccio**, *dim.* and *disp.* of *-chiere*.

biccia cúto†, M.: offensive weapon.

bicciocúcca [ak. to *bicocca*], F.: worthless house or thing.

bi-ciclétta, M.: safety bicycle. **-ciclísta**, M.: bicyclist. ‖**-cíclo** [*bi-*, Gr. *kúklos*, circle], M.: bicycle (old style).

bicípite [L. *bi-ceps*, TWO-HEADED], ADJ.: bicipital.

bicòcca [?], F.: small fortress or castle (us'ly upon a height); worthless house†; belvedere†.

bicolóre [*bi-*, L. *color*], ADJ.: two-coloured.

bi-còrne, **-còrno** [*bi-*, L. *cornu*, HORN], ADJ.: bicornous, TWO-HORNED. **-còrnia**, F.: double-pointed anvil. **-cornúto**, ADJ.: having two horns.

bicúspide [*bi-*, L. *cuspis*, point], ADJ.: (*arch.*) double-pointed.

bidále†, M.: foot-soldier.

bidèl-la, F., [l. L. *bidellus* (Ger.)], **-lo**, M.: custodian of a university, etc. (BIDEL, BEADLE).

bidènte [L. *bi-dens*, TWO-TOOTHED], M.: pitch-fork; mattock; two-pointed sceptre (of Pluto).

bi-ecaménte, ADV.: squintingly. ‖**-èco** [*obliquo*], ADJ.: squinting; sad.

bi-ennále, ADJ.: lasting two years; biennial. ‖**-ènne** [*bi-*, L. *annus*, year], ADJ.: two years; second year (of a University student). **-ènnio**, M.: space of two years.

biè-tola [L. *beta*], F.: beet. **-tolággine**, F.: fool, simpleton. **-tolína**, *dim.* of *-tola*. **-tolóne**, M.: stupid person; spinach†.

biétta [?], F.: wedge; (*typ.*) wooden quoin.

bíf-fa [?], F.: levelling-stake. **-fáre**, TR.: mark off with levelling stakes.

bi-folcheria, F.: tillage (husbandry); state of a ploughman†. ‖**-fólco** [L. *bubulcus* (*bos*, ox), plougher with oxen], M. **-fólca**, F.: ploughman (tiller, farm-labourer); boor.

bifonchiáre = *bofonchiare*.

bifor-caménto, M.: bifurcation. ‖**-cáre** [*bi-*, L. *forca*], REFL.: bifurcate. **-cáto**, PART.: bifurcated. **-catúra**, F.: point of bifurcation. **bifór-co**†, M.: double harness.

bifórme [*bi-*, L. *forma*], ADJ.: having two forms or shapes.

bifrónte [*bi-*, L. *frons*], ADJ.: having two fronts or faces; two-faced (deceitful).

bifúlco = *bifolco*.

bíga [L. *biga* (*bis*, TWICE)], F.: ancient two-horsed coach.

biga-mía, F.: bigamy. ‖**bíga-mo** [L. *-mus* (*bis*, TWICE, Gr. *gámos*, marriage)], M.: bigamist.

bi-gattièra, F.: silk-worm establishment. ‖**-gátto**† [? ak. to *baco*], **-gáttolo**, M.: silk-worm.

bi-gèllo†, M.: coarse gray cloth. **-gerógnolo**†, ADJ.: grayish.

bighel-lonáre, INTR.: loiter about. ‖**-lóna**, F., **-lóne** [?], M.: aimless person (gawky idler; dolt).

bigheráio†, M.: buffoon.

bighe-ráto, PART.: trimmed with lace. **-ríno**, M.: lace. ‖**bíghe-ro**† [?], M.: thread-lace; fringe.

bighína†, **-no** = *begh*..

bi-gíccio†, ADJ.: grayish. ‖**-gío** [?], ADJ.: gray; sad†. **-giógnolo**, ADJ.: grayish.

bigióne†, M.: figpecker.

bigiù [Fr. *bijou*, jewel], M.: beautiful thing.

bilaterale

bile

bilia

bília

biliárdo

bi-liáre -liá-

rio

bilicáre

bi-

lico

lingue [illegible] bilingual.

[illegible] linguoi -lingue.

[illegible] million

[illegible]).

bidello [illegible] -lé-

[illegible] -lino, *dim.*

bindo-lo [illegible], -ló-

ne

[illegible] EYE].

[illegible] M.:

[illegible] biòcco-

[illegible] M.: FLOCK of

[illegible] — di

[illegible] eaves-

-luto.

biòdolo

bio-grafia [illegible] write], -grafico, ADJ.: b. graph-

bio-grafo, M.: [illegible]grapher.

biondaccio, [illegible] -deggiáre, [illegible] fair; ripen (of corn). -dèllo [illegible] -do. -dótto, ADJ.: [illegible] -dózza, F.: being fair. -diccio, -dicce, ADJ.: inclined to be [illegible] -díno, *dim.* and *car.* of *-do.*

biόn-do [illegible orig.], ADJ.: BLOND, fair; [illegible] -dóna, -dóne, *aug.*

biordáro [illegible] *bajordare.*

bi-òscia [*doscio*], F.: wet snow; thin, [illegible] soap. -òsciot = *-oscia;* ADJ.: [illegible], loose; [illegible], indistinct; athwart.

biòttot, ADJ.: poor, miserable.

bi partíre, TR.: divide in two.

bípede [L. *bi-pes*], ADJ.: biped (TWO-FOOTED).
bipinèlla†, F.: (*bot.*) pimpernel.
bi-qquádro [*bi*, *quadro*], M.: (*mus.*) natural sign. **-quadráto**, ADJ.: biquadratic; M.: fourth power of a number.
biráccʰhio [? disp. of *birro*], M.: rag, tatter.
bír-ba, F.: idling youth; rascal; malice†; fraud†: *far la* —, go idling, play the street Arab; *battere la* —, go a-begging. **-bacchiòla**, *dim.* and *car.* of *-ba.* **-báccia**, *disp.* of *-ba.* **-baccióna**, **-baccióne**, *aug.* of *-ba.* **-bánte**, M.: rogue. **-bantería**, F.: roguery (fraud); vice. **-bantésco**, ADJ.: roguish (dishonest). **-barèlla**, **-berèlla**, *dim.* of *-ba.* **-báta**, F.: roguish act or word. **-bería**, F.: deception (fraud). **-bésco**, ADJ.: idle, worthless; fraudulent. ‖**-bo** [ak. to *furbo*], M.: knave, cheat. **-bonáio**, M.: haunt of knaves. **-bonáta**, F.: knavery (fraud); piece of botchery. **-bonccèllo**, **-boncèlla**, *disp. dim.* of *-bone.* **-bóna**, F., **-bóne**, M.: wicked person; ADJ.: wicked (fraudulent). **-boneggiáre**, INTR.: be wicked or fraudulent. **-bonería**, F.: knavery.
bírcio [?], ADJ.: short-sighted; squint-eyed.
birèmo [L. *-mis* (*remus*, oar)], F.: bireme (double-oared ship).
biribára†, M.: intricate game; squabble.
biri-bissáia, F.: winning card (at biribi). **-bissáio**, M.: stake-holder (at biribi). ‖**-bíssi** [?], M.: biribi (game).
biri-chináta, F.: impertinent act. ‖**-china**, F., **-chíno**, M.: [**bricchino*, dim. of *bricco*]; impudent girl or boy; street urchin; rascal.
biríllo [?], M.: billiard-ball (placed with five others forming a cross).
biróldo [L. *-rotulus*], M.: kind of sausage.
bírra [Ger. *bier*], F.: BEER.
birráccʰhio†, M.: calf a year old.
bir-racchiòlo [*-ro*], *dim.* of *-ro.* **-ráccio**, *disp.* of *-ro.* **-rágʟia** = *sbirraglia.*
bir-ráio [*-ra*], M.: brewer. **-rería**, F.: brewery; saloon; number of bailiffs†.
bir-résco, ADJ.: pertaining to a bailiff. ‖**-ro** [l. L. *-rus*], M.: bailiff, policeman: *dar le sue ragioni a' birri*, give one's account to one unwilling to hear it.
birróne [*birra*], M.: strong beer.
birrovière† = *berroviere.*
bis [L.], ADV.: TWICE. **bis-**, *ber-*, *ba(r)-* [? L. *bis*, or *vix*, hardly], *disp. pref.* (very, badly, perversely, etc.).
bisáccia [*bi-*, *sacca*], F.: large purse, wallet.
bisán-te [*Bisanzio*], M.: ancient Byzantian coin; spangle; tinsel ornament. **-tíno**, M.: small spangle.
bis=arcávolo, M.: great-great-grandfather.
bis=ávo or **-ávolo**, M.: great-grandfather.
bisbètico [?], ADJ.: grumbling; dissatisfied; strange, difficult.
bis-bigʟiaménto, M.: whispering. ‖**-bigʟiáre** [echoic], INTR.: whisper; buzz. **-bígʟio**, M.: whispering.
bísca [?], F.: gambling-house.
bis=cantáre, TR.: sing low; hum. **-cantarèllo**†, M.: low singing; humming. ‖**-cánto** 1, M.: duet.
biscánto 2 [*bis*, *canto* (ak. to Eng. *cant*, corner)], M.: two-cornered nook; retired corner.
biscáz-za†, *disp.* of *bisca.* ‖**-záre** [*bisca*], INTR.: frequent gambling-houses. **-zière**, M.: gambler.
biscázzo†, M.: mean joke or trick.
bischénco [?], M.: impoliteness; mean joke or trick.
bis-cherétto†, M.: small peg. **bís-chero**†, M.: peg (of a stringed instrument).
bischétto [for *deschetto*], M.: shoemaker's table.
bischiz-záre†, INTR.: muse; pun. **bischízo**†, M.: caprice, whim; pun, play on words.
bíscia [?], F.: serpent, snake.
bisció-la, **-lóna**, F.: kind of cherry. **-lína**, *dim.* and *car.* of *-la.* **-líno**, *dim.* and *car.* of *-lo.* ‖**bíscio-lo** 1 [?], M.: cherry-tree.
bísciolo 2 [echoic], ADJ., M.: lisping.
bi-scióne, *aug.* of *-scia.*
biscolóre†, ADJ.: two-coloured.
bis-cottáre, TR.: bake hard. **-cottería**, F.: biscuit or cake shop. **-cottíno**, M.: little sugar cake; light slap. ‖**=còtto**, ADJ.: hard-baked; M.: BISCUIT; sugar cake. **-cottóne**, *aug.* of *-to.*
bis=cròma, F.: (*mus.*) demi-semiquaver.
bis=cugína, F., **=cugíno**, M.: second or third cousin.
bises-táre, INTR.: be leap-year. **-tíle**, ADJ.: bissextile. ‖**bisès-to** [*bis-*, L. *sextus*], ADJ.: bissextile.
bisgènero†, M.: grand-daughter's husband.
bisíllabo [*bi-*, *sillaba*], ADJ., M.: dissyllabic.
bislác-co, ADJ.: whimsical; odd; M.: whimsical person. **-cóne**, *aug.*
bisleále†, ADJ.: disloyal; M.: traitor.
bislessáre†, TR.: scald; boil.
bis=lúngo, ADJ.: oblong.
bismúto [?], M.: bismuth.
bis=nipóte, M., F.: grandnephew, grandniece; PL.: descendants.
bis-nònna, F.: great-grandmother. ‖**=nònno**, M.: great-grandfather.

bi-sógna, F.: affair; business. **-sogna-ménto**† = -sogno. **-sognáre**, IMPERS. INTR.: be necessary; be needed, etc.; cf. [illegible] — [illegible] is necessary for me; I need; I want; I am in want of. **-so-gnévole**, ADJ.: necessary. **-sognino**, dim. and [illegible] of -sogno: [illegible] — [illegible] want. when poverty [illegible] at the door. ‖**-ógno** [illegible], M.: want; need; necessary amount; [illegible] -sogni [illegible] the month's expenses: [illegible] — , keep as much as one requires. **-sognóso**, ADJ.: needy; poor; M.: poor person.

bispénto [illegible], M.: [illegible].

bissíllabo = bisillabo.

bissénte† = bisestile.

bísso [L. byssus, [illegible]], M.: fine linen (used by the ancients).

bistánte†, M.: instant.

bistécca [Eng. beefsteak], F.: beefsteak.

bis-tentáre†, INTR.: hesitate; put off. ‖**-tènto**†, M.: procrastination; pain.

bis-ticciáre [?], INTR., RECIP.: contend; dispute. **-tíccio**, M.: dispute.

bistínto†, ADJ.: twice dyed.

bis-tondáto, ADJ.: roundish (somewhat round). **=tóndo**, ADJ.: round.

bistornáre†, TR.: divert; (fig.) overturn.

bis-tòrta†, F.: winding; distortion; medicinal plant. ‖**=tòrto**, ADJ.: twisted; crooked.

bis=trattáre, TR., RECIPR.: treat badly; wrong.

bistu-rì [*Pistorium*, Pistoja, where made], **-ríno**, M.: bistoury (surgeon's knife).

bisúlco [L. *-cus* (*sulcus*, furrow)], ADJ.: bisulcous (two-furrowed); cloven-footed.

bis=únto, ADJ.: very greasy; filthy.

bitontóne†, M.: large fig.

bi-tórzo† [*bi-*, L. *tortus*, twisted] = *-torzolo*. **-torzoláto**†, ADJ.: having warts; knotty. **-tórzolo**, M.: wart; knot. **-torzolúto**, ADJ.: having warts or knots.

bítter [Ger. *bitter*], M.: bitters (alcoholic drink).

bitú-me [L. *-men*], M.: bitumen; chalk†. **-minóso**, ADJ.: bituminous.

bivac-cáre, INTR.: bivouac. ‖**bivác-co** [Fr. *bivac* (Ger. *bei-wache*, 'by-watch')], M.: bivouac.

bivál-ve, **-o**, ADJ.: bivalve.

bívaro†, M.: beaver.

bívio [L. *bivium* (*bis*, *via*, road)], M.: cross-roads; uncertainty.

bizantíno [*Bisanzio*, Byzantium], ADJ.: Byzantine.

bízza [?], F.: slight, passing anger.

bizzar-raménte, ADV.: strangely (oddly). **-ría**, F.: strangeness, oddness. ‖**biz-zár-ro** [?], ADJ.: bizarre (strange, odd; fantastic); spirited (of horses); irascible†.

bizzéffe (a) [?], M., ADV.: in great quantity.

bizzò-chero†, ‖**bizzò-co**†, ADJ.: bigoted; hypocritical; M.: bigot; hypocrite. **-cóne**†, M.: big fool.

bizzo-sétto, **-síno**, *dim.* of -so. ‖**biz-zó-so** [*bizza*], ADJ.: quick-tempered.

biz-zúca†, **-zúga**†, F.: tortoise; turtle.

blan-diménte, ADV.: blandly. **-di-ménto**, M.: blandishment (caress; flattery). **-díre**, TR.: allure, caress; flatter. **-dízie**, F. PL.: blandishments (caresses; flattery). ‖**-do** [L. *-dus*], ADJ.: BLAND (gentle; mild).

blas=fémia† = *bestemmia*. **-fèmio**† = *bestemmiatore*.

blasmáre† = *biasimare*.

bla-sóne [OGer. *blas*, torch, ak. to Eng. *blaze*], M.: blazonry; coat of arms. **-sò-nico**, ADJ.: pertaining to blazonry.

blateráre [L.], INTR.: babble (prate continuously).

blátta†, F.: cockroach.

blèso [L. *blæsus*], ADJ.: tongue-tied; lisping.

bloc-cáre, TR.: blockade. ‖**blòc-co** [Ger. *block*], M.: block; blockade.

blú [Fr. *bleu*], INVAR. ADJ.: blue; M.: the colour blue.

bòa [L.], M.: boa (serpent; woman's neck-scarf).

boá-to [L. *-re*], M.: roar (bellowing). **-ttière**†, M.: grazier.

bòbbia [ak. to *bombo*], F.: loose, wobbly mass.

bobólco† = *bifolco*.

bócca [L. *bucca*], F.: mouth; opening: *acqua in —!* hush!

boccac-césco [*Boccaccio*], ADJ.: like Boccaccio. **-cévole**, *disp.* of *-cesco*. **-cevolménte**, ADV.: after the manner of Boccaccio.

boccáccia, *disp.* of *bocca*.

bocca-láccio, *disp.* of *-le*. ‖**boccá-le** [L. *baucalis*], M.: bocal; decanter; liquid in the decanter.

bocca=pòrta, F., **-pòrto**, M.: hatchway (of a ship).

boccáta [*bocca*], F.: mouthful; slap (on the face)†.

boccétta [dim. of *boccia*], F.: phial.

boccheg-giaménto, M.: gasping. ‖**-giá-re** [*bocca*], TR.: gasp (for breath).

boc-chétta [*bocca*], F.: small mouth; small opening. **-chíno**, M.: *car.* of *-ca*: pout; mouthpiece (cigar-holder).

bòc-cia [?], F.: glass (goblet); bud; false invention; PL.: wooden balls. **-ciáre**, TR.: smash; fail (in an examination).

boccíno†, ADJ.: bovine; M.: calf.

bòc-cio [*-cia*], M.: goblet; bud. **-cio-létto**, *dim.* of *-ciolo*. **-ci(u)òlo**, M.:

section of a windpipe; pipe; socket, burner (gas-); graft†; = -*cio*. **-ciolóso**†, ADJ.: full of buds. **-ciónа**, *aug.* of *-cia* (vase). **-cióne**, M.: large glass. **-ciuòla**, F.: small rosebud.
bòcco [?], M.: chestnut (used in playing); worthless fellow; fool.
boc-cóna [-*ca*], **-cóne**, *aug.* of *-ca*. **-concèllo**, *dim.* of *-cone*. **-concíno**, M.: *dim.* of *-cone;* any pleasing thing. **-cóne**, M.: mouthful; big pill†: *dare il —*, corrupt with bribes; *lavorar a bocconi*, work amid interruptions; rarely = *-coni*. **-cóni**, or *a -coni*, ADV.: lying upon one's face. **-cúccia**, *car.* of *-ca*. **-cúzza**† = *-cuccia*.
bó-cе† [= *voce*], F.: voice; vote. **-ciáre**, INTR.: call out; give a bad reputation. **-cio**, M.: continued calling. **-cióne**, M., **-cióna**, F.: loud talker.
bòdola [?], F.: trap-door.
bodoniáno [publisher *Bodoni*], ADJ.: pertaining to Bodoni: *edizione —a*, Bodoni's edition.
boèmo, M.: Bohemian.
bòf-fice [? *soffice*], ADJ.: soft, delicate; plump (woman or boy): *pane —*, raised bread. **-ficióna**, **-ficióne**, *aug.* of *-fice*.
bo-fonchiáre, INTR.: mutter, grumble. ||**-fónchio**† [?], M.: wasp, hornet.
bóga†, F.: chain; prison.
bògia [?], F.: mark, blemish on the skin.
bogliènte†, PART. of *bollire*.
bò-ia [L., string of cow-hide], M., INVAR.: hangman. **-iéssa**†, F.: hangman's wife.
bol-cionáre†, TR.: strike with a battering-ram. ||**-cióne**†, **-zóne**†, M.: battering-ram.
bol-dronáio†, M.: seller of hides. ||**-dróne**†, M.: hide; fleece.
bol-gétta, F.: *dim.* of *-gia;* large bag for carrying letters. ||**bòl-gia** [L. *bulga*], F.: large wallet or valise: *le bolge dell'Inferno*, the circles of Dante's Inferno; the ten trenches of the eighth circle.
bòlide [Gr. *-lis*, missile], M.: meteor.
bolíno† = *bulino*.
ból-la [L. *bulla*], F.: bubble; boil; pimple; ball; BULL (Pope's letter); PL.: seals (of ancient emperors). **-láre**, TR.: seal: stamp. **-lário**, M.: collection of Papal bulls. **-latóre**, M.: sealer; stamper. **-latúra**, F.: sealing (stamping). **-lènte**, PART. of- *lire:* boiling, hot. **-létta**, and derivatives = *bulletta*. **-li -li**, M.: ebullition; uproar. **-licaménto**†, M.: swarming. **-licáre**†, INTR.: swarm. **-licèlla**, *dim.* of *-la*. **-liciáttola**, F.: *dim.* of *-la* (esp. pimple). **-licína**, *dim.* of *-la*. **-liménto**, M.: boiling; bubbling. **-líre** (Pres. *-lo*), INTR.: boil, bubble. **-líto**, ADJ.: boiled. **-litúra**, F.: ebullition; decoction. **-lo**, M.: seal; stamp. **-lóre**, M.: boiling; anger (rage). **-loríno**, *dim.* of *-lore*. **-lóso**, ADJ.: pimpled. **-lúccia**, *dim.* of *-la*.
bòlo†, M.: bole (clay); (*med.*) bolus.
bolognino [*Bologna*], M.: Bolognese coin.
bol-sággine, F.: pursiness (esp. of horses). ||**-so** [L. *pulsus*], ADJ.: asthmatic; weak-lunged.
bolzo-náre†, TR.: strike with a battering-ram. **-náta**†, F.: blow with a battering-ram. ||**bolzó-ne**†, M.: battering-ram; stamping-iron (for medallions, etc.).
bómba [?], F.: bomb; boasting; idle story; mark (butt); game (similar to game of 'tag'): *stare, tornare a —*, come back to the subject.
bombánza, F.: boldness; pomp (magnificence).
bombár-da [*bomba*], F.: bombard (mortar; part of an organ). **-daménto**, M.: bombardment. **-dáre**, TR.: bombard. **-dièra**, F.: embrasure (for a bombard); gun-boat. **-dière**, M.: bombardier. **-dièro**† = *beone*. **-dóne**, M.: bombardo.
bòmbero [?], M.: blockhead.
bombettáre†, TR.: tipple.
bómbice [Gr. *-byx*], M.: silkworm.
bómbo [?], M.: (*child.*) drink.
bómbo-la, F.: decanter (short-necked bellying vessel). **-létta**, *dim.*
bom-bóna, F., **-bóne** [-*ba*], M.: boaster; foolish talker.
bómere†, **-ro**†, M.: ploughshare.
bomicáre† = *vomitare*.
bomprèsso [Eng. *bowsprit*], M.: bowsprit.
bo-náccia [*buono*], F.: calm (at sea); time of tranquillity, happiness; good-nature†. **-nacciáre**, INTR., REFL.: become calm. **-náccio**, ADJ.: good-natured (kind-hearted). **-naccióne**, *aug.* of *-naccio*. **-naccióso**, ADJ.: calm, tranquil. **-na=máno**, F.: extra fee, tip. **-naménte**†, ADV.: kindly; truly; as well as possible. **-nariaménte**, ADV.: kindly, in good faith. **-narietà**, F.: good-nature, affability. **-nário** [*buono*], ADJ.: good-natured; candid; credulous. **-narità**† = *-narietà*. **-na=vòglia**, M.: young doctor (esp. student-doctor in a hospital).
boncinèllo [*bolcione*], M.: staple (of a lock).
bon=gustáio [*gusto*], M.: person of good taste. **-ífica**, F.: cultivating. **-ificaménto**, M.: improving, cultivating. **-ificáre** [ak. to Eng. *boni-fy*], TR.: render fit for cultivation; redeem (lands); credit an account†. **-ità**† = *-tà*. **-íno**, *dim.* and *car.* of *bono*. ||**bòn-o** [L. *-us*], ADJ.: good (pop. for *buono*); 'good,' as in — per

500 *lire*, good for 500 lire. **-omía** [*-omo*], F.: good-nature. **-omáccio**, *disp.* or *car.* of *-omo*. **-òmini** [*-omo*], M. PL.: pl. of *-omo*; ancient Florentine tribunal (of twelve men). =**òmo**, M.: good-natured man. **-óne**, *aug.* of *bono*. **-tà**, F.: goodness (kindness); good† (advantage); wealth†.
bónzo†, M.: bonze (Chinese or Japanese priest).
bòra†, F.: kind of serpent.
bo-ráce [Ar.], ADJ., F.: borax. **-rácico**, ADJ.: boracic.
borbígi†, M.: lisper; blockhead.
bor-bogliaménto†, M.: muttering. ||**-bogliáre**†, TR.: murmur; whisper. **-bóglio**, M.: muttering; uproar.
borbot-taménto, M.: muttering (grumbling). ||**-táre** [*barbottare*, disp. of *balbettare*], INTR.: grumble (mutter); TR.: speak (a language) badly; REFL.: speak low.
borbottíno [?], M.: ragout; dish; narrow-necked vase†.
borbot-tío [*-tare*], M.: continued grumbling. **-tóna**, F., **-tóne**, M.: constant grumbler.
bòr-chia [?], F.: stud; boss; ornament. **-chiáio**, M.: maker or seller of studs, etc. **-chiétta**, **-chiettína**, **-chína**, *dim.* of *chia*. **-chióna**, *aug.* of *-chia*.
bor-dáglia, F.: rabble (populace). ||**-dáre** [from a lost *-da*, cudgel], TR.: beat; work hard.
bor-datíno or **-dáto** [*-do*], M.: blue and white linen cloth. **-deggiáre**, INTR.: beat (against the wind), tack.
bordellería†, F.: trifle.
bordèllo [Fr. *-del*], M.: brothel; tumult.
bórdo [OGer. *bort*], M.: (*nar.*) board; border†: *andar a* —, go aboard; *persona di alto* —, person of great authority and importance.
bordò [*Bordeaux*], M.: bordeaux (claret).
bordóne [aug. of *-da* (cf. *-dare*)], M.: pilgrim's staff; first wing-feathers; beam† (plank); (*mus.*) bass†.
bò-rea [Gr. *Boréas*], M.: (*poet.*) north; north-wind. **-reále**, ADJ.: boreal, northern.
bor-gáta, F.: borough. **-gatèlla**, *dim.* of *-gata*. **-ghése**, M.: burgess (burgher, citizen). **-ghesía**, F.: burgesship (burghership); the citizens. **-ghesúccio**, *disp. dim.* of *-ghese*. **-ghettíno**, *dim.* of *-ghetto*. **-ghétto**, *dim.* of *-go*. **-ghicciòlo**, *dim.* of *-go*. **-ghigiána**, F.: villager. **-ghigiáno**, M.: burgher (villager). ||**bór-go** [Ger. *burg*], M.: BOROUGH; town; suburb. **-gomástro** [Ger. *meister*], M.: burgomaster. **-gúccio**, *dim.* of *-go*.
bò-ria [*-rea*], F.: inflation, vanity; arrogance, pride. **-riáre**, REFL.: be arrogant or proud. **-rióne**, M.: very arrogant person. **-riosaménte**, ADV.: arrogantly. **-riosétto**, *dim.* of *-rioso*. **-riosità**, F.: arrogance, pride. **-rióso**, ADJ.: inflated (arrogant, proud). **-riúccia**, *disp. dim.* of *-ria*.
bòrnio†, ADJ.: short-sighted; squint-eyed.
bòrniola†, F.: unjust decision.
bór-ra [l. L. *burra*], F.: clippings (of rags, hair, etc.); stuffing; shabby coat; trash, worthless thing; (*pop.*) strength. **-ráccia**, F.: *disp.* of *-ra*; canteen. **-raccína**, F.: lichen. **-rág(g)ine**†, F.: borage. **-rána**, F.: borage (plant.).
bor-ratèllo, *dim.* of *-ro*. ||**bór-ro** [Gr. *bóthros*, trench], M.: ravine, hollow (formed by a flood). **-róne** = *burrone*.
bór-sa [Gr. *búrsa*, hide], F.: PURSE; bag (for money); portmanteau; swelling; exchange: *far* —, hoard money. **-saio**†, M.: maker or seller of purses. **-saiòlo**, M.: pickpocket. **-sellíno**, M.: purse. **-sèllo**, **-sétta**, *dim.* of *-sa*. **-settína**, *dim.* of *-setta*. **-síglio**, M.: extra money. **-sína**, *dim.* of *-sa*. **-sóne**, M.: large purse. **-sòtto**†, M.: rather large purse.
borzacchíno†, M.: buskin.
bos-cáglia, F.: woods, forest. **-cagliáccia**†, *disp.* of *-caglia*. **-caiòla**, F.: forester's wife. **-caiòlo**, M.: forester. **-caiuòlo**†, M.: forester. **-cáta**†, F.: boscage (grove). **-cáto**†, ADJ.: woody. **-cheréccio**, ADJ.: pertaining to woods; forest-; dweller† in a forest. **-chettíno**, *dim.* of *-co*. **-chétto**, M.: grove; place for snaring birds. **-chívo**, ADJ.: wooded; planted with trees. ||**bòs-co** [l. L. *buscus*], M.: forest (woods); grove; (*fig.*) confusion. **-cóso**, ADJ.: full of woods.
bos-síno†, *dim.* of *-so*. ||**bòs-so**† [L. *buxus*] = *-solo*. **-solétto**, **-solíno**, *dim.* of *-solo*. **bòs-solo**, M.: box-tree; small box; poor-box.
bo-tánica [Gr. *botáne*, pasture], F.: botany. **-tánico**, ADJ.: botanical; M.: botanist.
bo-táre†, TR.: vow (consecrate). **bo-to**†, M.: VOTE; simpleton.
bòtola†, F.: trap-door.
bòtolo [?], M.: small, snappish dog; (*fig.*) furious man.
bótro [cf. *borro*], M.: mountain-pool: *esser un* —, be a big eater.
bòtta [? OGer. *butze*, knock], F.: swelling (from a blow); blow; shot; toad (as 'swelled up'); fat person.
bot-tacciáta, F.: bottleful of water. **-taccíno**, M.: small bottle. ||**-táccio**

[-*te*], M.: BOTTLE (flagon); kind of thrush†. -**taccidlo**, M.: small bottle.
bottágl̥ie†, F. PL.: water-tight boots.
bot-táio [-*te*], M.: cooper. -**táme**, M.: quantity of casks.
bottárga [?], F.: kind of caviar.
bottáta [*botta*], F.: sharp word or phrase; obscure phrase; harm; blow† (of firearm).
bótte [L. *buttis*], F.: cask, barrel.
botté-ga [Gr. *apó*, from, *théke*, repository], F.: shop. -**gáccia**, *disp.* of -*ga*. -**gáia**, F., -**gáio**, M.: shop-keeper; provision-dealer. -**gánte**, M.: shop-attendant, clerk. -**ghétta**, *car. dim.* of -*ga*. -**ghíno**, M.: *dim.* of -*ga*; place of illicit traffic; lottery. -**góna**, *aug.* of -*ga*. -**gúccia**, *disp. dim.* of -*ga*.
botti-cèlla [*botte*], *dim.* of *botte*; *dim.*† of *botta*. -**cèllo**, *dim.* of *botte*. -**cína** 1, *dim.* of *botte*.
botticína 2 [*botta*], *dim.* of *botta*.
bot-ticíno, *dim.* of -*te*. -**tígl̥ia** [-*te*], F.: BOTTLE; wine. -**tigl̥ière**†, M.: BUTLER (steward); maker or seller of liquors. -**tigl̥iería**, F.: wine-cellar; wines; wine-shop. -**tigl̥ína**, *dim.* of -*tiglia*. -**tigl̥ióna**, *aug.* of -*tiglia*.
botti-náio [*botte*], M.: well-digger. **bottíno** 1, M.: dark pool.
bottíno 2 [Fr. *butin*], M.: BOOTY (plunder).
bòt-to [-*ta*], M.: blow: *di* —, suddenly; *ad un* —, together.
botto-náio, M.: maker or seller of buttons. -**natúra**, F.: buttonholes. -**ncèllo**, -**ncíno**, *dim.* of -*tone*; PL.: very small earrings. ‖**bottó-ne** [*botta*, swelling], M.: BUTTON; BUD; earring. -**tonièra**, F.: row of buttons.
bò-ve [L. *bos*], pl. -*vi* or *buoi*, M.: ox. -**víle**†, M.: ox-stall. -**vína**, F.: dung. -**víno**, ADJ.: bovine.
bòzza [ak. to OGer. *butze*, knock], F.: rough dressing-stone; freestone; rough sketch; swelling†; foolish story†; PL.: proof-sheets.
boz-zácchio, -**zacchióne** [*borza*], M.: withered, swollen plum.
bozzáccia, *disp.* of *bozza*.
boz-zágo†, -**zágro**†, M.: buzzard.
boz-záto [-*za*], M.: (*mas.*) bossage. -**zétto**, M.: rough sketch or draft.
bòẓẓima [?], F.: gum-water; weaver's starch; poor mixture.
bozzína†, F.: boiling, cooking.
bozzíninga†, F.: rattlesnake.
bòzzo 1 [*bozza*], M.: rough sketch.
bòẓẓo 2 [ak. to *pozzo*], M.: pool; rough stone, freestone.
bozzo-láio, M.: dealer in silk-worms. -**láre** = *sbozzolare*. -**láro**, M.: sugar-cake seller. ‖**bòzzo-lo** [L. *bombucius*], M.: chrysalis (cocoon); knot in wool; lump in flour; measure of grain that the miller takes as his pay for grinding. -**lóso**, ADJ.: knotty, lumpy. -**lúto**, ADJ.: knotty.
brá-ca [L.], F.: leg of breeches; breech-cloth (diaper); (*nav.*) stopper, cord used on board ship. -**che**, PL.: BREECHes; small-clothes. -**calóne**, M.: loose-breeched fellow (who wears the breeches hanging slovenly), sloven: *a* — or -*caloni*, hanging slovenly; negligently. -**cáre**, INTR.: be a busybody. -**cáto**, PART.: *grasso* —, very fat.
braccáre [*bracco*], TR.: scent (of dogs); (*fig.*) hunt for (aspire to, seek).
braccétto [-*ccio*], M.: *dim.* of -*ccio*: *a* —, arm in arm.
brac-cheggiáre [-*co*], TR.: *freq.* of -*care*. -**chéggio**, M.: scenting (seeking). -**chería**†, F.: pack of dogs. -**chétto**, *dim.* of *bracco*. -**chière**†, -**chièro**† M.: keeper of dogs.
brác-cia, PL. of -*cio*. -**ciaiuòla**†, F. = -*ciale*. -**ciále**, M.: armed plate; bar; ancient armor for the arm; bracelet. -**cialétto**, M.: bracelet. -**ciánte**, M.: ('arm-worker') labourer. -**ciáre**†, TR. = *abbracciare*. -**ciáta**, F.: armful; embrace†. -**ciatèlla**, F.: small armful. -**ciatèllo**†, M.: kind of cake. -**ciatúra**, F.: measure of the arm. -**cière**, M.: one that gives a lady his arm; lady's escort. -**cíno**, pl. -*na* or -*ni*, *dim.* and *car.* of -*cio*. ‖-**cio**, pl. -*cia* (lit. sense), or -*ci* [L. *brachium*], M.: arm; length-measure (cubit). -**ciòlo**, M.: arm of a chair; baluster. -**cióne**, *aug.* of -*cio*. -**ciòtto**, *aug.* of -*cio*; plump arm. -**ciuòlo**† = -*ciolo*.
bràcco [Ger. *bracke*], M.: BRACH (hunting-dog); police-officer.
bráce [? Ger. -*sa*, fire], M.: live coals; coke.
brá-che [-*ca*], F. PL.: see -*ca*. -**chettóne**, M.: (*arch.*) ornament of an arch. -**chieráio**, M.: truss-maker. -**chière**, M.: truss. -**chína**, *dim.* of -*ca*. -**chíno**, M.: busybody; gossip.
brá-cia† [-*ce*], F.: live coals. -**ciaiòlo**, M., -**ciaiòla**, F.: maker or seller of coke. -**cière**, M.: brasier. -**cína**, F., -**cíno**, M.: kindling-seller; dirty person; bad painter. -**ciòla**, F.: fry. -**ciolétta**, *dim.* of -*ciola*. -**ciolína**, *car. dim.* of -*ciola*. -**ciuòla**† = -*ciola*.
brácco†, M.: mire, mud.
bracóne, *aug.* of -*chino*.
brádo [L. *bravus*], ADJ.: untamed, wild.
brádipo [Gr. *bradupoûs*, slow-footed], M.: (*zoöl.*) sloth.
bradóne†, M.: loose sleeve.
bradúme†, M.: herd of wild cattle.
bráge†, F.: live coals.

bra-ghésse† = *-che*. **-ghière†** = *-chiere*.

brágia†, F.: smoldering coals.

brágo [Ger. *brack*], M.: mire (mud); swamp.

brá-ma [?], F.: great desire. **-mangière†**, M.: appetizing dish. **-máre**, TR., INTR.: desire (wish).

bramíno [Hindoo], M.: Brahmin.

brámito†, M.: cry or howl of animals.

bra-mosaménte, ADV.: eagerly. **-mosía**, F.: great desire, eagerness. **-mosità** = *-mosia*. ‖**-móso** [*brama*], ADJ.: desirous (eager).

brán-ca [L.], F.: claw; clutch; BRANCH (part of anything, as branch of science, etc.); paw†. **-cáre†**, TR.: clutch, snatch. **-cáta**, F.: handful. **-catína**, *dim.* of *-cata*. **-chettíno**, *dim.* of *-chetto*. **-chétto**, *dim.* of *-co*.

bránchia [Gr.], F.: branchia, gill of fishes.

bran-cicaménto, M.: handling. ‖**-cicáre** [*-ca*], TR.: touch, handle. **-cicatúra**, F.: touching; sign, mark. **-cicóne**, M.: touch-all; meddler; = *-colone†*. **-co**, M.: herd (flock); assemblage. **-coláre**, INTR.: grope along. **-colóne**, **-colóni**, ADV.: gropingly. **-cúccia**, *dim.* of *-ca*.

brán-da [?], F.: camp-bed (cot). **-dellétto**, **-dellíno**, *dim.* of *-dello*. **-dèllo**, M.: tatter; bit (fragment).

bran-díre, TR.: BRANDISH; INTR.†: be excited. **-ditóre**, M.: brandisher. **-do** [OGer. *brant*], M.: BRAND (sword).

brandóne†, M.: rag; piece.

bráno [?], M.: piece (bit, esp. of goods).

brásca†, F.: cabbage.

bra-vàccio, M.: *disp.* of *-vo*; bully. **-vaccióne**, *disp. aug.* of *bravaccio*. **-vaménte**, ADV.: bravely; resolutely. **-váre**, TR., INTR.: brave (defy); threaten. **-váta**, F.: defying; severe reproof†. **-vatòrio†**, ADJ.: threatening. **-vazzáta**, F.: boasting. **-vázzo†** = *-vaccio*. **-vazzóne**, M.: bully (swaggerer). **-veggiáre**, INTR., FREQ.: bluster (bully); prance (of horses). **-vería**, F.: braving; bravery (courage). **-vière** [?], M.: yellow-hammer. ‖**-vo** [L. *-vus*], ADJ.: skilful (expert, excellent: *usly after the noun*); brave (courageous); M.: bandit, ruffian: *alla -va*, in a few moments. **-vúra**, F.: bravery; skill; fierceness†. **-vúria** = *-vura*.

bréccia [OGer. *brecha*], F.: BREACH (opening in a wall): *far —*, (*fig.*) persuade, make an impression.

brémma [?], F.: jade (worn-out horse).

brènta [?], F.: bowl (cup).

brétto†, ADJ.: miserable; foolish; sordid.

brè-ve [L. *-vis*], ADJ.: BRIEF (short); M.: BRIEF; papal letter; charm worn around the neck (trinket); (*mus.*) note held two beats; statute; ADV.†: briefly; *in* (*fra*) *—*, shortly. **-veménte**, ADV.: briefly (shortly). **-vettáre**, TR.: patent. **-vétto**, M.: decree; patent. **-viáre†**, TR.: abbreviate. **-viário**, M.: breviary. **-vicèllo†**, M.: lime-twig. **-viloquènza**, F.: brevity (conciseness of speech). **-vilòquio†**, M.: compendium; brief discourse. **-vità**, F.: brevity.

bréz-za [? *orezzo*], F.: cool breeze. **-zétta**, **-zettína**, **-zolína**, *dim.* of *-za*. **-zóne**, M.: strong breeze.

bría†, F.: measure.

briachézza†, F.: trouble (affair); drunkenness.

briá-co [*ubriaco*], ADJ.: drunk. **-cóne**, M.: drunkard.

bríccа†, F.: precipice (steep place).

bricchétto†, M.: little mule; ass.

brícci-ca [ak. to *brincello*], F.: trifle. **-cáre**, INTR.: be absorbed in trifles.

bríccо 1 [Ar.], M.: coffee-pot.

bríccо† 2, M.: ass.

brícсola†, F.: catapult.

bricco-náccio, *disp.* of *-ne*. **-náta**, F.: knavishness (roguery). **-ncèllo**, *dim.* and *car.* of *-ne*. ‖**briccó-ne** [?], ADJ.: knavish (roguish); M.: knave (rogue). **-neggiáre†**, INTR.: be a knave. **-nería**, F.: roguery.

brí-cia†, F.: crumb of bread. **bri-ciola**, *dim.* of *-cia*. **-ciolíno**, *dim.* of *-ciolo*. **brí-ciolo**, M.: bit (very small part).

brièvе† = *breve*.

brí-ga [?], F.: trouble; noise†. **-gadière**, M.: non-commissioned officer; brigadier. **-gantággio**, M.: brigandage. **-gánte**, M.: brigand; hired soldier; rascal; PART.†: intriguing. **-gantèllo**, *dim.* of *-gante*. **-gantíno**, M.: brigantine. **-gáre**, INTR.: scheme, intrigue; TR.: scheme for. **-gáta**, F.: company (troop); friends; flock of birds; crowd†; family†; bundle† (mass of things). **-gatáccia**, *disp.* of *-gata*. **-gatèlla**, **-gatína**, *dim.* of *-gata*. **-ghèlla**, M.: mask in Italian theatre.

brigidíno [made by nuns of *St. Brigida*], M.: small cake; tassel.

brí-glia [OGer. *brittil*], F.: BRIDLE; PL.: reins. **-gliáio**, M.: maker or seller of bridles. **-gliétta**, **-gliettína**, *dim.* of *-glia*. **-glióne**, *aug.* of *-glia*. **-gliòsa†**, M.: snaffle (muzzle).

brigóso†, ADJ.: quarrelsome; difficult; fatiguing.

brílla [?], F.: rice-mill.

bril-laménto, M.: brilliancy. **-lantáre**, TR.: cut into facets; sprinkle with sugar. **-lánte,** M.: brilliant; the funny man; ADJ.: brilliant. ‖**-láre** [?], INTR.: be brilliant (scintillate, shine, sparkle). **-latóio,** M.: rice-sieve. **-latúra,** F.: cleaning.

brillo [?], ADJ.: tipsy.

brí-na [L. *pruina*], F.: white-frost (rime). **-náre,** INTR.: fall as white frost. **-náta,** F.: fall of frost; frost. **-náto,** ADJ.: frosted, whitened (hair, beard).

brin-cèllo [variant of *brandello*], M.: crumb, bit. **-dèllo,** M.: piece, rag (of clothing). **-dellóne,** M.: ragamuffin (slovenly person).

brin-dáre, INTR.: propose a toast. ‖**brín-disi** [Ger. *Ich bring' dir's*, 'I bring it to thee'], M.: toast (health); poem read at a banquet.

brinóso†, ADJ.: hoary.

brí-o [?], M.: vivacity (spirit); courage†. **-osaménte,** ADV.: vivaciously. **-osétto,** *dim.* of *-oso*. **-óso,** ADJ.: vivacious (spirited; frisky); gay.

brisciaménto†, M.: shuddering, shivering.

brí-scola [? Ger. *pritschen*, strike], F.: trick at cards; PL.: blows. **-scoláre,** TR.: strike. **-scolína, -scolíno,** *dim.* of *-scola*.

bri-vidío, M.: continued shivering or chill. ‖**brí-vido** [? L. *frigidus*], M.: shivering.

brizzolá-to [?], ADJ.: speckled. **-túra,** F.: speckled appearance; checker-work.

bròb-bio†, **-brio**†, M.: opprobrium.

bròcca 1 [Gr. *próchous*, cup], F.: pitcher (jar); contents of a jar.

bròc-ca† 2, F.: twig. **-cáre**† 1, TR.: urge (stimulate).

broc-cáre† 2 [l. L.], TR.: stitch. **-catèllo,** M.: brocatel; variegated marble. **-catíno,** *dim.* of *-cato*. **-cáto,** M.: brocade; stockade†; palisade†.

broc-chétta [*-ca* 1], F., **-chétto, -chíno,** M.: small pitcher.

brocchière [l. L. *buccularius*], M.: buckler.

bròc-co [*-ca* 2], M.: splinter; sprout†. **bròc-colo,** M.: broccoli; blockhead. **-colétto,** *dim.* of *-colo*. **-colóso**†, **-colúto,** ADJ.: having sprouts.

brò-da, F.: thin soup; wish-wash; miry water: *dare la — addosso a uno*, give a person all the blame. **-dáio,** M.: soup-seller. **-dettáto,** ADJ.: done in broth. **-détto,** M.: egg-soup; Spartan soup. **-dícchio,** M.: thin soup; (*fig.*) heavy dew; mud. **-díglia,** F.: more commonly *-dicchio*. ‖**brò-do** [OGer. *brod*], M.: BROTH (soup); (*fig.*) insipid composition. **-dolíno,** M.: dirty child. **-dolóne,** M.: slovenly eater. **-dolóso,** ADJ.: of broth (broth-); dirty† (greasy).

brodóne†, M.: sleeve ornament.

bròzio [?], M.: dullard.

bro-gliáre, INTR.: scheme (plot, intrigue); be agitated†. ‖**brò-glio** [? *brolo*], M.: scheme (plot, intrigue); sedition†; tumult†.

bróllo†, ADJ.: naked; miserable.

bròlo [Celt.], M.: garden; park; garland†.

brò-mo [Gr. *brômos*, bad smell], M.: bromine. **-múro,** M.: bromide.

brón-chi, PL.: cf. *-co*. **-chiále,** ADJ.: bronchial. **-chíte,** F.: bronchitis.

bróncio [?], M.: grudge; anger.

brón-co [?], M.: sprout: stem; trunk: *-chi*, bronchial tubes. **-cóne,** M.: big branch.

bronto-láre [ak. to Gr. *brontáo*, sound], INTR.: muttor (rumble); grumble. **-lío,** M.: continued muttering, rumbling. **-lóne,** M.: grumbler.

bron-záre, TR.: bronze. **-zatúra,** F.: bronzing. **-zíno,** ADJ.: bronzed (bronze-coloured). **-zísta,** M.: bronze-worker. ‖**brón-zo** [?], M.: bronze; PL.: bronze works (objects of art).

bròscia, more commonly *sbroscia*.

bru-cáre [*-co*], TR.: eat off leaves (said of worms, sheep, etc.); gather leaves. **-catóre,** M.: one that strips off leaves. **-catúra,** F.: stripping off leaves.

bru-cènte, ADJ.: burning. **-ciacchiáre,** *freq.* of *-ciare*. **-ciaménto,** M.: burning; conflagration. **-cia=pélo** ('burn-hair'): (*a* —), ADV.: *tirare a* —, fire at close range; *prendere a* —, suddenly. ‖**-ciáre** [ak. to L. *perurere*, 'burn up'], TR.: burn; cauterize; INTR.: burn, be hot. **-ciáta,** F.: roasted chestnut. **-ciatáio,** M.: seller of roasted chestnuts. **-ciatíccio,** M.: bits of anything burned. **-ciatína,** *car. dim.* of *-ciata*. **-ciatúra,** F.: cauterization.

brúcio = *bruco*.

brucío = *bruciore*.

bru-ciolátо†, ADJ.: worm-eaten. ‖**brú-ciolo**†, M.: small worm; chip (bit).

bruciόre [*-ciare*], M.: itch, smart.

brúco [L. *-chus*], M.: little worm (grub); button-loop; button-hole.

bruíre†, INTR.: rumble (of the bowels).

brulláσσο†, ADJ.: blear-eyed.

bruli-cáme, M.: swarm (multitude). ‖**-cáre** [*bollicare*], INTR.: swarm. **-chío,** M.: swarming.

brul-laménte†, ADV.: miserably. ‖**-lo** [?], ADJ.: naked (bare); very poor (miserable).

brulòtto [Fr. *-lot* (*-ler*)], M.: fire-ship.

brúma† 1, F.: ship-worm.

brú-ma 2 [L., 'fog'], F.: (*poet.*) winter; (*fig.*) old age. **-máio,** M.: Brumaire (2d month in the first French republic). **-mále,** ADJ.: (*poet.*) brumal, wintry.

bru-názzo†, ADJ.: slightly brown. **-nèllo**, ADJ.: brownish. **-nellúccio**, *dim.* of *-no.* **-nettíno**, *car. dim.* of *-netto.* **-nézza**, F.: brownness (swarthiness). **-niménto**, M.: burnishing. **-níre**, TR.: burnish (polish); clean†. **-nitóio**, M.: burnishing (polishing) tool. **-nitóre**, M.: burnisher (polisher). **-nitúra**, F.: burnishing (polishing). ‖**-no** [OGer. *brûn*], ADJ.: BROWN, dusky (poorly lighted; dark); M.: brown; mourning. **-nòtto, nòzzo**†, *dim.* of *-no.*

bruòlo† = *brolo.*

brúsca [OGer. *brusta*], F.: BRUSH for horses.

bruscaménte [*-sco*], ADV.: brusquely (abruptly).

bruscáre†, TR.: prune (trim).

bruschétte [*-ca*], F. PL.: game of cuts played by children.

bru-schétto, *dim.* of *-sco.* **-schézza**, F.: brusqueness (rudeness). ‖**-sco** [?], ADJ.: brusque (rough, rude, abrupt); harsh; sour.

brusco-líno, *dim.* of *-scolo.* ‖**brúscolo** [*-sca*], M.: mote, particle (in the eye).

brusío [ak. to *bruire*], M.: buzz (confused murmur); uproar; praise (applause); great quantity.

brustoláre†, TR.: toast, grill.

bru-tále, ADJ.: brutal. **-talità**, F.: brutality. **-talménte**, ADV.: brutally. **-teggiáre**†, INTR.: act, live as a beast. ‖**-to** [L. *-tus*, stupid], M.: brute (beast); ADJ.: without reason. **-ttacchiòlo**, *dim.* of *-tto.* **-ttáccio**, *disp.* of *-tto.* **-ttaménte**, ADV.: meanly. **-ttáre**, TR.: soil, stain. **-tterèllo**, ADJ.: rather ugly. **-ttézza**, F.: ugliness. **-ttíno**, *dim.* of *-tto.* **-tto**, ADJ.: ugly; disagreeable; gloomy; thoughtful. **-ttóre**†, M., **-ttúra**, F.: ugly thing.

bruum [echoic], INTERJ.: boom (of guns).

bruzzáglia [?], F.: mass (mob, rabble); confusion†.

brúz-zico [*bar-luzzico*, 'twi-light'], **-zo**†, **brúz-zolo**, M.: morning-twilight, dawn.

búa [Sp.], F.: childish word for pain

bu-áccio†, M.: *disp.* of *-e*, dunce. ‖**-acciòla** [*bue*], F., **-acciòlo**, M.: dunce. **-acciolàta**, F.: foolish acts or words. **-ággine**, **-assággine**, F.: stupidity; awkwardness (clownishness).

bubalíno†, M.: young buffalo.

búbbola 1 [?], F.: HOOPOE (crested bird).

búb-bola 2 [Gr. *boubón*, swelling], F.: trifle (nonsense); foolish story. **-boláre**, INTR.: thunder; hum; shiver; TR.†: squander one's means. **-boláta**, F.: nonsense, trifle. **-bolièra**, F.: bridle-rein. **búb-bolo**, M.: bell (on a horse or dog). **-bolóne**, M.: babbler. **-bóne**, M.: bubo. **-bònico**, ADJ.: bubonic. **-bula**† = *bubbola.*

bu bu [echoic], bow-wow; noise, cry.

bubúlca†, F.: acre of land; kind of measure.

bú-ca [OGer. *bûch* = Ger. *bauch*, paunch], F.: cave; narrow valley; hollow (pit, hole). **-cacchiáre**, *freq.* of *-care.* **-cáccia**, *disp.* of *-ca.* **-cáre**, TR.: pierce (perforate, bore); REFL.: prick one's self.

buca-táia, F.: washerwoman. **-táio**, M.: washerman. **-tíno**, *dim.* of *-to.* ‖**bucáto** [?], M.: BUCKing (washing); washing (things to be washed). **-túra**, F.: bucking (washing). **-turína**, *dim.* of *-tura.*

búcchero [Gr. *boúkaros*], M.: reddish clay (used in making vases); vase (jar); dark red colour.

búc-cia [?], F.: bark; peel (hull); skin. **-ciáta**, F.: blow from a peeling.

buccicáta [?], F., as in: *non sapere una* —, know nothing of the matter.

buccidòre†, M.: butcher.

búcci-na [L.], F.: trumpet (of the ancients). **-náre**†, INTR.: trumpet; divulge.

búccino [L. *-nus*], M.: buccinum (whelk).

búccio [*-cia*], M.: surface of hides (skin).

bucciòlo†, M.: reed; length of a joint.

buccióso†, ADJ.: having skin.

búccola [L. *bucula*], F.: earring.

buc-còlica [Gr. *boukolikós*, pastoral], F.: bucolic. **-còlico**, ADJ.: bucolic.

bucèfalo [Gr. *Bouképhalos*, Alexander's horse], M.: (*jest.*) Bucephalus (charger, horse).

bucèllo†, M.: young ox.

bucen-tòrio†, **-tòro**†, M.: bucentaur.

bucherámе†, M.: buckram (coarse cloth).

bu-cheráre† [*-co*], TR.: make holes, pierce. **-cheráto**, ADJ.: full of holes. **-cherèlla**, F.: small hole. **-cherelláre**, TR.: pierce. **-cherèllo**, M.: small hole. **-chétta**, *dim.* of *-ca.* **-chétto**, *dim.* of *-co.* **-chína**, *dim.* of *-ca.* **-chíno**, *dim.* of *-co.*

buciácchio†, M.: young ox.

bú-ci, INTERJ.: hush. ‖**-cicáre** [*-lica-re*], INTR., REFL.: stir (move gently).

bucináre [*buccina*], INTR.: sound abroad, rumor.

búcine [?], F.: fishing-net; partridge-net.

bucintòro [Gr. *boukéntauros*], M.: bucentaur (Venetian state barge).

bú-co [*-ca*], M.: hole; small, dark room. **-colína**, *dim.* of *-ca.* **-colíno**, *dim.* of *-co.* **-cóne**, *aug.* of *-co.* **-cúccio**, *dim.* and *disp.* of *-co.*

bu-dellámе†, M.: entrails, bowels. **-dellíno**, pl. —*ne* or —*na*, *dim.* of *-dello.* ‖**-dèllo** [L. *botellus*, little sausage], M.: BOWEL (intestine); us'ly pl. **-dellóne**, *aug.* of *-dello.*

budrièrе†, M.: shoulder-belt.
bú-e [L. *bos*], pl. *-oi*, M.: ox; (*fig.*) dunce. **-éssa**†, F.: cow.
búfa-la, F. of *-lo*. **-láta**, F.: buffalo-race (held at Florence); poetry written for this occasion. **-líno**, ADJ.: of buffaloes, buffalo. ‖**búfa-lo** [Gr. *boúbalos*], M.: buffalo (wild ox); blockhead. **-lóne**, *aug.* of *-lo*.
bu-fáre, INTR.: storm and snow. **-fèra**, F.: hurricane; hailstorm. **-ffa**, F.: blast†; jest† (trifle); hood, cowl, vizor. **-ffáre**, INTR.: blow; jest†; banter. **-ffettáre**†, INTR.: pant. **-ffétto**, M.: BUFFET, light slap; ADJ.: *pan* —, light bread. ‖**-ffo** [?], M.: puff (gust of wind, blast); ADJ.: curious; comical; M.: comic actor or singer. **-ffonáre**†, INTR.: play the buffoon. **-ffonáta**, F.: buffoon's trick, buffoonry. **-ffoncèlla**, F., **-ffoncèllo**, M.: *dim.* of *-ffona* and *-ffone*. **-ffóna**, F., **-ffóne**, M.: BUFFOON, jester. **-ffoneggiáre**, INTR.: play the buffoon. **-ffonería**, F.: buffoonry. **-ffonescaménte**, ADV.: as a buffoon. **-ffonésco**, **-ffonévole**†, ADJ.: buffoon.
búfolo†, M.: buffalo.
bufonchiáre = *bofonchiare*.
bugía 1 [ak. to Ger. *böse*, bad], F.: lie (falsehood).
bugía 2 [*Bugia*, Algerian city], F.: flat candlestick.
bu-giáccia [*-gia* 1], *disp.* of *-gia* 1. **-giardáccio**, *disp.* of *-giardo*. **-giardaménte**, ADV.: falsely. **-giardèllo**, *dim.* of *-giardo*. **-giardería**, F.: lie. **-giardíno**, *dim.* of *-giardo*. **-giárdo**, ADJ.: lying (false); M.: liar: *pero* —, kind of pear. **-giardòlo**, *dim.* of *-giardo*. **-giardóne**, *aug.* of *-giardo*. **-giétta**, *dim.* of *-gia*.
bu-gigáttolo [disp. dim. of *-gio*], M.: small room; hiding-place. ‖**-gio**†, M.: hole; ADJ.: pierced.
bu-gióne [*-gia* 1], M.: big liar. **-giúccia**, **-giúzza**, *dim.* of *-gia*.
bugliáre†, INTR.: be agitated; come to blows.
bugliòlo [ak. to *buiolo*], M.: small barrel; tub (bucket).
buglióne [Fr. *bouillon*], M.: broth†; confused mass.
bugliuòlo† = *bugliolo*.
bú-gna 1 [?], F.: bossage. **-gnáto**, M.: bossed.
bú-gna† 2 = *-gnola*. ‖**-gno** [?], M.: bee-hive; small, restricted place. **bú-gnola**, F.: straw basket, etc.; pulpit. **-gnolétta**, **-gnolína**, *dim.* of *-gnola*. **búgnolo**, M.: small basket for fruits, etc. **-gnolóne**†, *aug.* of *-gnolo*.
buíccio†, M.: slight darkness.
buína [*bue*], F.: cow-dung.
buíno†, ADJ.: bovine.
bu-ío [?], ADJ.: dark (obscure); M.: darkness, obscurity; night; (*jest.*) lockup. **-ióre**†, M.: darkness.
búlbo† 1, ADJ.: austere, morose.
búl-bo 2 [L. *-bus*], M.: BULB; eye-ball. **-bóso**, ADJ.: bulbous.
bulè-gia†, F., **-gio**†, M.: pastern.
búlgaro [*Bulgaria*], M.: kind of dark red leather.
buli-cáme†, M.: bubbling springs, source; crowd. **-cáre**†, INTR.: boil; bubble up; swarm.
búlima†, F.: crowd, throng.
búlimo†, M.: bulimy (illness which causes hunger).
buli-náre†, TR.: engrave. **-nísta**, M.: burinist (engraver). ‖**bulí-no** [OGer. *bora*, auger], M.: burin (graver); engraver; engraving.
búl-la [L.], F.: neck ornament worn by Roman boys; = *bolla*†. **-létta**, F.: small nail; shoe-tack; upholsterer's nail; passport†; lottery ticket†. **-lettáio**, M.: nail-seller. **-lettáme**, M.: quantity of nails. **-lettáre**†, TR.: embellish, strengthen with nails. **-lettína**, *dim.* of *-letta*. **-lettináio**, M.: ticket-seller. **-lettíno**, M.: bulletin; billet†; permit† (passport); theatre ticket. **-lettóne**, M.: large upholsterer's nail (for decorating).
bulsíno†, M.: pursiness; shortness of breath.
bum [echoic], M.: boom of cannons.
buòi, PL. of *bue*.
buonaccòrdo†, M.: harpsichord.
buòn for *buono* before consonants (exc. *s* impure). **-amáno** = *bonamano*. **-améнте**† = *bonamente*. **-auguráto**†, ADJ.: auspicious; fortunate. **-a=vòglia** = *bonavoglia*. **=dáto**†, ADJ.: abundant. **=fátto**†, M.: benefit. **=gustáio**† = *bongustaio*. ‖**buòn-o** [L. *bonus*], ADJ.: good (excellent; kind; docile, strong; genuine); M.: good; advantage: *di buon' ora*, early; *far buon viso*, give a kind welcome; *una buona volta*, at last; *essere in buone acque*, be favourably situated. **=òmini**† = *bonomini*.
burat-táre, TR.: bolt, sift. **-tèllo**†, M.: sieve, bolter. **-tináio**, M.: puppet showman. **-tináta**, F.: poor dramatic performance. **-tíno**, ADJ.: as in *birba -tina*, rabble; M.: puppet; puppet-show; *dim.*† of *-to*. ‖**burát-to**† [? ak. to L. *burrus*, red; red texture], M.: thin goods (bombazin); sieve, bolter
burbán-za [?], F.: pride, vanity. **-záre**†, INTR.: boast. **-zésco**†, ADJ.: proud. **-zosaménte**, ADV.: proudly. **-zóso**, ADJ.: proud, vain.

búrbe-ra [?], F.: crane for raising weights; capstan. **-ro**, ADJ.: severe (austere); sullen.
burchiellésco [*Burchiello*], ADJ.: in the style of Burchiello (comic poet).
bur-chiellétto, -chiellino, -chièllo, *dim.* of *-chio.* ‖**-chio** [ak. to *rimorchio*], M.: transport-boat.
búre [L. *-ris*], F.: plough-handle.
burèlla†, F.: prison (dungeon).
Bur-gógna, F.: Burgundy. **-gognèse, -gognóne**, ADJ.: Burgundian.
buriáno†, M.: kind of wine.
buriásso†, M.: instructor (of tilters); prompter.
buríceo [l. L. *-ricus*], M.: ass.
búr-la [?], F.: deceit (trick); joke. **-láre**, TR.: deceiver; INTR.: joke (banter); REFL.: laugh at. **-latóre†**, M.: joker (wag; banterer). **-lescaménte,** ADV.: jokingly (banteringly). **-lésco,** ADJ.: burlesque (ludicrous); bantering (facetious). **-létta**, F.: *dim.* of *-la*; farce (light opera). **-lévole†**, ADJ.: jesting. **-lièro†**, ADJ.: jesting, facetious. **-lonáccio,** *disp.* of *-lone.* **-lóna**, F., **-lóne**, M.: joker (wag).
búro†, ADJ.: dark.
burocrá-tico, ADJ.: bureaucratic. ‖**-zía** [Fr. *bureau*, Gr. *kratein*, govern], F.: bureaucracy.
burráio [*-rro*], M.: butterman.
burrá-sca [? *borea*], F.: hurricane; storm; misfortune. **-schétta**, *dim.* of *-sca.* **-scóso**, ADJ.: stormy, threatening.
bur-ráto, ADJ.: with butter, buttered. ‖**-ro** [*butirro*], M.: butter.
bur-roncèllo, *dim.* of *-ne.* ‖**-róne** [ak. to *borro*], M.: deep ravine; precipice.
burróso†, ADJ.: buttered; buttery.
buṣáre†, TR.: pierce.
buṣbac-cáre†, INTR.: deceive. **-cheria†**, F.: deceit (cheating). **-'co†**, M.: deceiver.
buṣbería†, F.: imposture.
bús-ca, F.: search; inquiry: *andare in* (*alla*) —, go searching at random. **-cacchiáre**, TR.: go in search of. **-c=alfána**, F.: miserable nag. ‖**-cáre** [Sp. *-car* (*-co*, BUSH)], TR.: seek or hunt after (of dogs); (*fig.*) win by effort; hunt up (find, get); REFL.: procure one's self: — *di botte*, or *-carne*, get a drubbing.
buscherío [?], M.: noise (bustle); crowd.
buschétta† = *bruschette.*
bu-sciónе†, M.: thorny bush; jungle. **-sco†**, M.: straw. **-scolíno†**, *dim.* of *-co.*
busécchia [Lomb. *-ca* (*busso*), stomach], F., **busécchio**, M.: intestine; sausage.
busnága [Sp. *bisnaga*], F.: fennel-like plant.
búṣo†, M.: hole; ADJ.: pierced; empty, useless.
bús-sa†, F.: blow (stroke): trouble; sorrow. **-samento†**, M.: beating. ‖**-sáre** [? L. *pulsare*], INTR.: beat (strike), knock at a door. **-sáta**, F.: (*fig.*) hurt; quarrel. **-satína**, *dim.* of *-sata.* **-satóre†**, M.: beater, knocker. **-se**, F. PL.: slap; hurt.
bus-sétto, M.: polisher (shoemaker's tool). ‖**-so†** [L. *buxus*], M.: BOX-tree; little box; noise. **bús-sola**, F.: mariner's compass; hand-cart; horse-brush; house-door. **bússolo†**, M.: little box. **-solètto**, M.: little box.
bussóne†, M.: BASSOON.
bú-sta [*-xida* (L. *-xus*, BOX-wood)], F.: paper-BOX; box (case); envelope. **-stáia** [*-aio*], F.: maker of stays. **-stáio**, M.: maker of stays. **-sto**, M.: BUST; stays (corset); trunk† of the body; monument†; bodice†.
butír-ro [L. *butyrum*], M.: BUTTER. **-róso**, ADJ.: containing butter; butyraceous.
butta=fuòri, M.: call-boy in a theatre. **=là**, F.: closet, wardrobe. ‖**buttá-re** [OGer. *bozen*, knock], TR.: throw; decry; REFL.: let one's self down; be discouraged. **-ta**, F.: sprout, shoot.
butteráto, ADJ.: pock-marked. ‖**bútter 1** [?], M.: pock-mark.
bútter 2 [?], M.: cow-boy.
butteróso†, ADJ.: pock-marked.
buzzicáre [ak. to *bucicare*], INTR.: move, stir.
buzzi-chèllo†, M.: little noise. **-cchío†**, M.: whispers.
búẓ-zo [OGer. *butze*], M.: stomach; pin-cushion†; ADJ.: cloudy: *è tempo* —, it is cloudy weather. **-zóne**, M.: *aug.* of *-zo*; one who has a large stomach.
buẓẓárro [?], M.: Swiss who sells roasted chestnuts, polenta, etc.

C

c *ci* [L.], M.: c (the letter).
ca'†, for *casa*, house.
cába-la [Heb.], F.: cabala (Jewish doctrine); cabal (intrigue). **-láre**, INTR.: cabal (plot); form wild projects; circumvent (deceive). **-létta**, F.: lively melody (at the end of a song). **-lísta**, M.: cabalist. **-lístico**, ADJ.: cabalistic. **-lóne**, M.: plotter (meddler).
cabína [Eng. *cabin*], F.: cabin in a ship.
caca=dúbbi, M.: (*vulg.*) eternal waverer. **-iòla**, F.: diarrhœa. **=pensièri†**, M.: suspicious fellow. ‖**cacá-re** [L.], INTR.: void (the bowels, CACK). **-rèlla**, F.: diarrhœa. **=sòdo**, M.: important pretender; pedant. **=stécchi**, M.: miser.
cacá-ta, F.: evacuation. **-tóio**, M.:

water-closet. **-túra,** F.: excrement of insects. **cácca,** F.: (*child.*) excrement. **cacca-báldole,** F. PL.: blandishments, flatteries.
cac-cáo, -cáos [Mex.], M.: cocoa (palm or nut).
cac-chiatèlla, F.: small white loaf. ‖**-chio**†, M.: vine-sprout or shoot. **-chióne,** M.: worm of the bee; PL.: flies' eggs. **-chionóso**†, ADJ.: full of worms.
các-cia, F.: CHASE (hunt, hunting); game. **-cia=diávoli**†, M.: conjurer. **-ciagióne,** F.: game (prey). **-ciaménto**†, M.: chasing away. ‖**-ciáre** [l. L. *captiare* (L. *capere,* take)], INTR.: CHASE (hunt); spur on; expel; pursue†; REFL.: intrude one's self. **-ciáta,** F.: hunt (pursuit); expulsion. **-ciatóia,** F.: punch; driver. **-ciatóra,** F.: hunting-coat: *alla* —, in the manner of hunters. **-ciatóre,** M.: hunter (sportsman); light-armed soldier. **-ciatríce,** F.: huntress. **-cia=víte,** F.: screw-driver.
caccicúcco [?], M.: highly seasoned fish-soup.
cácco-la [*cacca*], F.: dirt in sheep's wool; rheum. **-lóso,** ADJ.; rheumy (bleared).
caccétto [*-cio*], M.: small cheese.
cache-rèllo [*cacca*], M.: dung (of sheep, etc.). **-róso,** ADJ.: awkward; disagreeable.
ca-chessía [Gr. *kach-exía,* bad condition], F.: (*med.*) cachexy. **-chèttico,** M.: sufferer from cachexy.
cachinno†, M.: burst of laughter.
ca-ciáia, F.: place for keeping cheese. **-ciáia,** F., **-ciáio,** M.: cheese-maker. **-ciaiòla,** F., —**lo,** M.: cheesemonger. =**cimpèr(i)o,** M.: cheese-custard. ‖**-cio** [L. *-seus*], M.: CHEESE: *essere pane e* —, be very intimate; *essere come il — su' maccheroni,* be useful, opportune. **-ciòla,** F.: small round cheese. **-ciolíno,** M.: small fresh cheese. **-cióso,** ADJ.: caseous, cheesy.
caco- [Gr. *kakós,* bad]: **-fonía** [Gr. *phoné,* sound], F.: cacophony (disagreeable sound). **-fònico,** ADJ.: cacophonic (harsh-sounding). **-grafía** [Gr. *gráphein,* write], F.: cacography (bad spelling).
cacúme†, M.: summit.
ca-dávere [L. *-daver*], **-dávero**†, M., corpse (cadaver). **-davèrico, -daveróso**†, ADJ.: cadaverous.
cadaúno†, PRON.: every one (each).
cáddi, PRET. of *cadere.*
ca-dènte, PART., ADJ.: cadent (falling); failing†. **-dènza,** F.: cadence; pause. **-denzáto,** ADJ.: having cadences. ‖**-dére** [L. *cadere*], IRR.§; INTR.: fall.

§ Pret. *cád-di, -de; -dero.* Fut. *cadrò.* Poet. forms: *cág-gi, -giono; cággia; cadèi, cadé.*

cadétto [L. **capitettus* (*caput,* head)], M.: cadet (younger son; military student); ADJ.: younger.
ca-dévole†, ADJ.: frail; falling. **-diménto**†, M.: fall. **-ditóia**†, F.: (*fort.*) portcullis; loophole. **-ditóio**†, ADJ.: falling.
cádmio [Gr. *kadmeía*], M.: cadmium.
cadúceo [L. *-duceus*], M.: caduceus (wand of Mercury, carried also by heralds).
ca-ducità, F.: caducity (frailty); lapsed will or contract. **-dúco** [L. *-ducus*], ADJ.: caducous; frail, transitory: *mal* —, falling sickness (epilepsy). **-dúta** [*-dere*], F.: fall; relapse; mistake, transgression. ‖**-dúto,** PART. of *cadere.*
caèndo†, GER.: seeking: *andare* —, seek for.
caf-fè [Fr. *café* (Ar.)], M.: coffee (plant, berry, or drink); café (coffee-shop). **-feáccio,** *disp.* of *-fè.* **-fe=aus** [*-fe,* Ger. *haus*], M.: COFFEE-HOUSE. **-feíno,** *car. dim.* of *-fè.* **-feísta,** pl. —*sti,* M.: coffee-drinker. **-fettièra,** F.: wife of a coffee-house keeper; coffee-pot. **-fettière,** M.: coffee-house keeper.
caf-fétto, *dim.* of *-fè.* ‖**-fo** [? *capo*], M.: odd number; fortune; ADJ.: odd.
Caffro, N.: Caffre.
cáfura†, F.: camphor.
caggènte†, ADJ.: falling.
ca-gionaménto†, M.: cause. **-gionáre,** TR.: cause (occasion). **-gionatóre,** M.: causer. **-gioncèlla,** F.: slight cause. ‖**-gióne** [*occasione*], F.: OCCASION (cause, reason). **-gionévole** [who gets sick from slight 'cause'], ADJ.: weak (sickly). **-gionóso,** ADJ.: sickly (infirm).
cáglia SUBJ. of *calere.*
ca-gliáre, INTR.: curdle (coagulate); quail†. ‖**-glio** [L. *coagulum*], M.: rennet.
cá-gna [L. *-nia* (*-nis,* dog)], F.: bitch; low woman. **-gnáccio, -gnáccia,** *disp.* of *-ne.* **-gnaia, -gnára,** F.: barking of a pack of dogs; (*fig.*) uproar. **-gnázzo**†, M.: big ugly dog; ADJ.: dog-like, ugly; violet-coloured. **-gnescaménte,** ADV.: surlily, threateningly. **-gnésco,** ADJ.: doggish: *guardare* (*stare*) *in* —, look at angrily. **-gnétto,** *dim.* of *-ne.* **-gnína**†, F., **-gníno**†, M.: little dog. **-gnòla,** *dim.* of *-gna.* **-gnolétto, -gnolína, -gnolíno,** *dim.* of *-gna, -ne.* **-gnòtto,** M.: hireling ('serving dog'), tool; hired bully.
caícco [Turk.], M.: caïque.
caimáno [Carib.], M.: cayman (alligator).
Ca-ína, F.: place in the last circle of Dante's Inferno. ‖**-íno,** M.: Cain; traitor.
cála [*-lare*], F.: bay, cove.
calabráche [?], M., INVAR.: game of cards (between two).

calabré-se [*Calabria*], M.: pointed felt hat. **-sèlla** [?], F.: game of cards (one against two). **-sellísta**, pl. —*sti*, M.: skilful player of *-sella*.

calabróne [L. *crabronis*], M.: hornet (wasp).

cala-fáo†, M.: calker. ‖**-fatáre** [Ar.], TR.: calk. **-fáto**, M.: calker.

cala-maiáta, F.: blow with an inkstand. **-maiétto**, **-maíno**, *dim.* of *-maio*. ‖**-máio** [L. *-marium* (*-mus*, reed)], M.: inkstand; ink-fish. **-maiúccio**, *disp. dim.* of *-maio*. **-mandrèa**†, F.: germander (plant). **-marétto**, M.: little ink-fish. **-máro** = *-maio*.

calaménto†, M.: going down.

calamístro [*-mo*], M.: curling iron.

calamità [L. *-tas*], F.: calamity (misfortune).

calamí-ta [? *calamo*, reed; ref. to the pivot of the needle], F.: loadstone (magnet); magnet needle (of a compass). **-táre**, TR.: magnetize. **-tazióne**, F.: magnetization.

calami-tosaménte, ADV.: disastrously. ‖**-tóso** [*-tà*], ADJ.: calamitous (wretched).

cálamo [L. *-mus*], M.: cane (reed).

calándra [Gr.], F.: woodlark.

calandríno [character in Boccaccio], M.: simpleton.

calándro [cf. *-dra*], M.: mocking-lark.

caláppio [OGer. *klappa*], M.: snare; (*fig.*) deceit.

cala-pránzi [*-re*, *pranzo*], M., INVAR.: dumb-waiter. **calá-re** [Gr. *chalân*, slacken], TR.: lower; INTR.: decrease; go down (in price). **calá-ta**, F.: going down, fall; declivity. **-tína**, F.: lowering of the voice.

calbígia [?], F.: kind of fine grain.

cál-ca [*-care*], F.: crowd, multitude. **-cábile**, ADJ.: that may be trodden under foot. **-ca-fògli**, M.: paper-weight. **-cagníno**, M.: heel (of a shoe, etc.). **-cágno**, pl. *-cagni* or *-cagna* [L. *-neum*], M.: heel. **-ca-lèttere**, M.: paper-weight. **-ménto**, M.: trampling. ‖**-cáre** 1 [L. (*calx*, heel)], TR.: trample (tread upon); oppress.

cal-cáre 2 [*-ce* 1], M.: calcite (carbonate of lime). **-cáreo**, **-cário**†, ADJ.: calcareous.

calcá-ta [*-re*], F.: trampling; highway†. **-taménte**†, ADV.: closely. **-tóio**, M.: copying instruments; gun sponge; charger for loading cannons. **-tóre**† = *-toio*.

calcatríce†, F.: cockatrice (fabled serpent).

calcatúra [*-care*], F.: trampling, crushing.

cálce 1 [L. *calx*], F.: lime, CHALK.

cálce 2 [L. *calx*, HEEL], M.: now only in *in* —, at the foot of the page; butt-end† (of a lance, gun, etc.).

calcedònio [*Kalkedon*, Chalcedon], M.: chalcedony.

calcése†, M.: (*nav.*) topmast.

calcestrúzzo [? *calce* 1, L. *structus*, piled up], M.: cement, mortar.

cal-cétto [*-ce* 2, heel], M.: low shoe, pump; cloth shoe†. **-ciánte**†, M.: football player. **-cicáre**†, TR.: trample upon.

calcí-na [ak. to *calce* 1], F: lime; mortar. **-nábile**, ADJ.: calcinable. **-náccio**, M.: rubbish (in old walls); broken bricks. **-náio**, M.: lime pit; lime-trough. **-náre**, TR.: calcine, pulverize; scatter lime (to fertilize land); REFL.: become lime. **-natòrio**†, ADJ.: pertaining to calcination. **-natúra**, F.: calcination. **-nazióne**, F.: calcinating. **-nosità**, F.: liminess. **-nóso**, ADJ.: of lime; like lime.

cálcio [L. *calx*, HEEL], M.: kick; butt-end of a gun; staff of a lance; game at foot-ball.

calcistrúzzo [*calce*], M.: mortar.

calci-tráre [L. (*calx*, heel)], INTR.: kick (calcitrate). **-trazióne**†, F.: kicking, (*fig.*) resistance. **-tróso**†, ADJ.: kicking.

cálco [*-care*], M.: counter-drawing; light sketch.

cal-cografía, F.: calcography (engraving in brass); calcographical studio. **-cográfico**, ADJ.: calcographical. ‖**-cògrafo** [Gr. *chalkós*, copper, *gráphein*, write], M.: calcographer (engraver in copper or brass); printer or seller of prints.

cálcola [*-care*], F.: weaver's treadle.

calco-lábile, ADJ.: calculable. **-láre**, TR.: calculate; suppose (think); INTR.: compute by calculus. **-latóre**, M.: calculator. **-lazióne**†, F.: calculation. **-létto**, *dim.* of *-lo*. ‖**cálco-lo** [L. *calculus*, 'pebble,' used in reckoning], M.: calculation; stone in the bladder. **-lóso**†, ADJ.: calculous (stony). **calcò-sa**†, F.: street (road).

calcul. † = *calcol.*.

cál-da† [*-do*], F.: heating. **-dáia** [L. *-daria*], F.: CALDRON; kettle; boiler. **-dáio**†, M.: kettle; boiler. **-daiáta**, F.: kettleful. **-daiétta**, *dim.* of *-da*. **-daíno**, M.: brasier (warming-pan). **-daióna**, **-daióne**, *aug.* of *-daia*, *-daio*. **-daiuòla**†, *dim.* of *-daia*. **-daménte**, ADV.: warmly, vehemently (used only in fig. sense). **-dána**, F.: burning in the face or head; warm room where bread may rise; heat of summer†; pleurisy†. **-daníno**, M.: small brasier. **-dáno**, M.: brasier. **-danúccio**, *disp. dim.* of *-dano*. **-dáre**† = *-daia*. **-deggiáre**, TR.: favour. **-deráio**, M.: brasier.

calde-rèllo†, ‖**-ríno** [*cardellino*], M.: goldfinch.

calderóne†, M.: large kettle.
calde-rottíno, M.: small tea-kettle. ||**-ròtto** [*caldaro*], M.: small kettle; tea-kettle.
calderúgio†, M.: goldfinch.
cal-deruòla†, F.: small kettle or boiler. **-détto**, ADJ.: rather warm. **-dézza**†, F.: heat; passion. **-dicciuòlo**†, M.: slight heat. **-dímo**†, M.: sunny spot. ||**-do** [L. *-idus*], ADJ.: warm, hot; M.: heat. **-duccino**, *car. dim.* of *-duccio*. **-dúccio**, *dim.* of *-do*. **-dúra**, F.: heat, heat of summer.
cá-le [3. Sing. of *-lere*]: it imports: *avere in non* —, pay no heed to.
calefa-ciènte†, **-ttívo**†, ADJ.: calefacient, heating. **-zióne**†, F.: calefaction.
caleidoscòpio [Gr. *kalós*, beautiful, *skopéin*, see], M.: kaleidoscope.
ca-lèn for *-lende*. **-lendário**, **-lendáro**†, M.: calendar. ||**-lènde** [L. *-lare*, call], F. PL.: calends. **-lendinággio**, M.: Florentine festival, May 1.
calèndula†, F.: calendula (marigold).
calenzòlo [?], M.: greenfinch.
calepíno [author *Calepio*], M.: first Latin dictionary; big volume.
calére†, DEFECT.§; INTR.: care, be concerned for: *non me ne cale*, I don't care about it.

§ Ind.: Pres. *cále*; (poet.) Impf. *calèva*. Pret. *cálse*. Subj.: Pres. *cáglia*. Impf. *calésse*. Ger. *caléndo*. Part. *calúto*.

cales-sábile, ADJ.: passable for carriages. **-sáccio**, *disp.* of *-se*. **-sánte**, M.: driver. **-sáta**, F.: calashful. ||**calèsso** [Bohem.], M.: calash (light carriage). **-sína**, **-síno**, *dim.* of *-se*. **calès-so**, M.: calash.
calèstro = *galestro*.
caléttа†, F.: slice, bit.
calet-táre [?], TR.: join closely (close up); adjust.
calía [*-lare*], F.: gold or silver filings; rubbish; tiresomeness.
cá-libe†, M.: (*med.*) steel.
cali-bráre, TR.: calibrate (find calibre of); proportion. **-bratóio**, M.: calibre compasses. **calí-bro** [Ar.], M.: calibre; instrument for measuring the bore of a cannon; (*fig.*) quality (character).
cáli-ce [L. *-x*], M.: chalice (communion cup; cup; calix). **-cétto**, **-cíno**, *dim.* of *-ce*. **-cióne**, M.: large cup; kind of cake†.
cálico [city *Calicut*], M.: calico.
calidità†, F.: calidity, heat.
ca-liffáto, M.: caliphate. ||**-líffo** [Ar.], M.: caliph.
ca-ligáre†, INTR.: become dark. ||**-lígine** [L. *-ligo*], F.: mist (fog); darkness. **-liginóso**, ADJ.: dark (caliginous).
cál-la†, F.: field-path. **-láia**, F.: path; opening†; sluice†. **-lai(u)òla**†, F.: snare for rabbits. ||**-le** [L. *-lis*], M.: (*poet.*) path, by-way.
calli-dità†, F.: cunning. **cálli-do**†, ADJ.: crafty (callid).
calli-grafía, F.: calligraphy. **-gráfico**, ADJ.: calligraphic. ||**callí-grafo** [Gr. *kalós*, beautiful, *gráphein*, write], M.: calligrapher.
cal-lísta, M.: chiropodist (remover of corns, etc.). ||**-lo** [L. *-lum*], M.: callosity, corn.
callóne [*calla*], M.: sluice, lock (in canals).
cal-losità, F.: callosity. ||**-lóso** [*-lo*], ADJ.: callous.
callòtta [*Callott*, Italian painter], M.: as in *figura del* —, grotesque person.
cál-ma [Gr. *kaûma*, heat], F.: CALM (at sea); tranquillity. **-mánte**, M.: anodyne (soothing medicine). **-máre**, TR.: calm, quiet; REFL.: become calm. **-mo** 1, ADJ.: calm.
cálmo† 2, M.: twig, graft.
cálo [*-lare*], M.: diminution, descent.
calógna†, F.: calumny.
calomelá-no [Gr. *kalós*, beautiful, *mélas*, black], *-'no*s, M.: calomel.
calònaco = *canonico*.
ca-lóre [L. *-lor*], M.: heat; (*fig.*) enthusiasm. **-loría**, F.: improving land (by manuring or rotation of crops). **-lòrico**, M.: caloric, principle of heat. **-lorífero**, M.: heater, furnace. **-loríficо**†, ADJ.: calorific, heating. **-loríno**, M.: slight heat. **-lorosaménte**, ADV.: ardently. **-lorosità**, F.: heat. **-loróso**, ADJ.: hot; fiery. **-lorúccio**, M.: slight heat.
calòscia [Fr.], F.: GALOSHE (overshoe).
calòscio†, ADJ.: weak, feeble.
cal-pestaménto†, M.: trampling upon. ||**-pestáre** [*-ce*, *pestare*], TR.: trample upon. **-pestatóre**, M., **-pestatríce**, F.: trampler. **-pestío**, M.: stamping.
calte-ríre†, TR.: injure. **-ritúra**†, F.: scratch.
calúco†, ADJ.: miserable, frail.
calúggine†, F.: down (of birds).
calumáre†, TR.: (*nav.*) let out the rope, drag.
calún-nia [L. *calumnia*], F.: calumny (slander). **-niáre**, TR.: calumniate (slander). **-niatóre**, M., **-niatríce**, F.: calumniator. **-niazióne**†, F.: calumny. **-niosaménte**, ADV.: slanderously. **-nióso**, ADJ.: calumnious.
calváre†, TR.: make bald.
calvèllo†, ADJ.: fine (said of grains).
calvézza [*-vo*], F.: baldness.
calvi-nísmo [*Calvin*], M.: Calvinism. **-nísta**, M.: Calvinist; (*jest.*) bald person.

cal-vízie, F.: baldness. ||**cál-vo** [L. *-vus*], ADJ.: bald.

cál-za [L. *-cea* (cf. *-cio*)], F.: stocking; strainer; blow-pipe: *di — disfatta*, very thin or weak; *tagliare le -ze a*, speak ill of; *tirar su le -ze a*, worm out a secret from. **-záccia**, *disp.* of *-za*. **-zai(u)òlo**†, M.: hosier. **-zaménto**, M., pl. *—ti* and *—ta*: shoes and stockings. **-zánte**, ADJ.: (*fig.*) neat, suitable. **-záre**, TR.: put shoes, gloves, etc., on, put or fit on; REFL.: put or fit on (shoes, gloves, etc.); INTR.: fit smoothly, look well; M.: shoes and stockings. **-zatóia**, F.: prop; shoe-horn. **-zatóio**†, M.: shoe-horn. **-zatúra**, F.: covering for the feet; shoes and stockings. **-zeróne**†, M.: coarse stockings. **-zerótto**, M.: half-hose. **-zétta**, *dim.* of *-za*. **-zettáia**, F., **-zettáio**, M.: hosier. **-zíno**, M.: half-hose, sock. **-zoláio**, M.: shoemaker. **-zolaiúccio**, M.: poor shoemaker. **-zolería**, F.: shoemaker's shop. **-zonácci**, *disp.* of *-zoni*. **-zoncíni**, *car. dim.* of *-zoni*. **-zoncióni**, *aug.* of *-zoni*. **-zóne**, us'ly in pl. **-zóni**, M.: breeches. **-zonúcci**, *disp.* of *-zoni*. **-zuòlo**†, M.: wedge, prop; ferrule.

camáglio [*cap(o)*, head, *maglia*, armour], M.: CAMAIL (neck-armor).

camaleón-te [Gr. *chamaí*, on the ground, *léon*, lion], M.: chameleon (lizard with shifting colour); (*fig.*) one who has no colour in his politics. **-tèo**, ADJ.: pertaining to the chameleon. **-téssa**, F.: female of the chameleon.

camangiáre†, M.: esculent herbs.

camarlin-ga, F.: convent-matron; lady in waiting†. **-gáto**, M.: office of chamberlain. **-ghería**, F.: office of chamberlain. **-'go** [Ger. *kämmerling* (*kammer*, CHAMBER)], M.: CHAMBERLAIN; treasurer, administrator.

camáto, us'ly *scamato*.

camáuro [?], M.: Pope's cap.

cambellòtto = *cammellotto*.

cam-biále, F.: bill of exchange. **-bialétta**, **-bialína**, **-bialúccia**, *dim.* of *-le*. **-biaménto**, M.: change. **-bia=monéte**, M.: money-changer. ||**-biáre** [l. L.], INTR.: CHANGE (transform); TR.: exchange; REFL.: change colour. **-biário**, ADJ.: of exchange (CAMBIAL). **-biatóre**, M.: banker. **-biatúra**†, F.: change. **-bia=valúte**, M.: money-changer. **cám-bio**, M.: exchange: *libero —*, free trade. **-bísta**, M.: banker (cambist).

cam-bráia†, F.: cambric. ||**-brì** (*Cambrai*, where made], M.: cambric.

camèlia [Jesuit *Camelli*], F.: camellia.

cáme-ra [L., vault], F.: CHAMBER (bed-room); chamber (of commerce), etc. **-rále**, ADJ.: of a chamber (deliberative body). **-ráta** 1, pl. *—ti*, M.: comrade (companion). **-ráta** 2, F.: division (of students in a school); dormitory (for each division). **-rèlla**, F.: *dim.* of *-ra*; cell containing the seed of grain. **-rièra**, F.: lady's maid. **-rieráccia**, *disp.* of *-riera*. **-rière**, M.: valet, gentleman's servant; prelate's title. **-rierína**, *car. dim.* of *-riere*. **-rína**, F.: small, pleasant room. **-ríno**, M.: dressing-room in a theatre. **-rísta**, F.: maid of honour. **-róna**, *aug.* of *-ra*. **-róne**, M.: very large room; *disp.*: large uncomfortable room. **-ròtto**† = *-retta*. **-rúccia**, **-rúzza**†, *disp. dim.* of *-ra*.

cá-mice [l. L. *-misia*, cf. Eng.† *camis*], M.: alb (priest's garment). **-micétta**, *dim.* of *-micia*. **-mícia**, F.: shirt, smock. **-miciáccia**, *disp.* of *-micia*. **-miciáta**, F.: profuse perspiration (as causing change of 'shirt'); night-attack (by soldiers in white shirts, Eng.† CAMISADE). **-micína**, F.: child's shirt. **-micíno**, M.: smock, CHEMISE. **-miciòla**, F.: flannel waistcoat. **-micioláia**, F., **-micioláio**, M.: waistcoat seller. **-miciolína**, *dim.* of *-miciola*. **-micioléne**, M.: heavy waistcoat. **-micióne**, M.: coarse shirt. **-miciòtto**, M.: blouse. **-miciuòla**†, F.: flannel waistcoat. **-míscia**†, F.: shirt.

camin. = *cammin.*.

cammeista [*cammeo*], M.: engraver of cameos.

cammellíno†, M.: camlet.

cammèllo [Gr. *kámelos*], M.: camel.

cammel-lòtto [l. L. *camelotum*, camel's hair], M.: camlet (a fabric). **-lopárdo**†, M.: camelopard.

cammèo [l. L. *camæus*], M.: cameo.

cammi-nábile, ADJ.: fit for travel. ||**-náre** [Celt., ak. to Fr. *chemin*, road], INTR.: walk; travel; M.: walking; gait. **-náta**, F.: walk; ball†. **-natóra**, F., **-natóre**, M.: walker (pedestrian, rambler); traveller. **-natúra**, F.: walk, gait.

cammi-nétto, M.: small fire-place (grate, Eng.† CHIMNEY). **-nièra**, F.: fire-screen; mantel-mirror. **cammí-no** 1 [Gr. *káminos*], M.: hearth (fire-place); chimney.

cammíno 2 [*-nare*], M.: walk, road.

cámo†, M.: rein; bridle.

camomílla [Gr. *chamaí-melon*, earth-apple], F.: camomile.

ca-mòrra, F.: name of a secret (self-seeking) Ital. society. **-morrísta**, M.: schemer. ||**-mòrro** [Sp. *chamorro*, bald], M.: weak, languid person; bore.

cámo-sciáre†, TR.: dress chamois leather. **-sciatúra**†, F.: dressing chamois

leather. -**scíno**†, ADJ.: of chamois leather ||**camò-scio** 1 [?], M.: CHAMOIS; chamois leather.
camóscio† 2, ADJ.: flat-nosed (Eng.† CAMOUS).
camòzza [-*moscio* 1], F.: female of the chamois.
campacchiáre†, INTR.: live in want, be poor.
cam-págna [-*po*], F.: open country or field, country, CAMPAIGN, campagna). -**pagn(u)òlo**, ADJ.: of the country, country-, (rustic); M.: countryman. -**paiuòlo**†, ADJ.: rural. -**pále**, ADJ.: in the field; (*fig.*) fatiguing: *battaglia* —, pitched battle; *giornata* —, fatiguing day. -**paménto** [-*pare* 2], M.: provisions.
campá-na [*Campania* (where first made?)], F.: bell (church-bell); glass-shade (to protect from dust); alembic: *avere le -ne grosse*, be hard of hearing; *far la — tutta d' un pezzo*, do a thing without interruption. -**náccia**, *disp.* of -*na*. -**náccio**, M.: cow-bell (ram's bell, etc.). -**náio**, -**náro**†, M.: bell-ringer. -**nèlla**, F.: little bell; campanula (bell-flower); door-bell; door-clapper (in form of a ring); nose-ring (of animals); ear-ring. -**nellína**, *dim.* of -*nella*. -**nellíno**, *dim.* of -*nello*. -**nèllo**, M.: hand-bell; little bell. -**niláccio**, *disp.* of -*nile*. -**níle**, M.: campanile (bell-tower); belfry: *idee di* —, intense love of one's town or neighbourhood. -**nilétto**, -**nilíno**, *dim.* of -*nile*. -**nilísta**, M.: love of one's own town. -**nína**, F.: small bell. -**níno** = -*naccio*. -**nóne**, M.: big bell.
cam-páre 1 [-*po*], TR.: us'ly *scampare*, save; INTR.: escape. ||-**páre** 2 [-*po*], INTR.: live (more pop. than *vivere*); TR.: nourish (maintain); (*paint.*) paint the ground of; sculpture in relief. -**peggiaménto**, M.: encampment; camp. -**peggiáre**, INTR.: encamp; set off in relief; besiege†.
campéggio [*Campeche*], M.: Campeachy wood, logwood.
cam-perécció†, ADJ.: rural. -**perèllo**, M.: small field. ||-**pèstre** [-*po*], ADJ.: campestral, rustic. -**pettíno**, -**pétto**, *dim.* of -*po*. -**picchiáre**, INTR.: live in want. -**picèllo**, M.: small field.
campigiána [?], F.: very large brick.
cam-pío†, ADJ.: of the country. -**pionário**, M.: sample-book. -**pioncíno**, M.: small sample. -**pióne**, M.: champion; sample; registry-book; ledger; rule, model. -**píre**†, TR.: (*paint.*) paint the ground of. -**pitèllo**†, M.: small field. ||-**po** [L. -*pus*], M.: field (plain); (*fig.*) freedom; camp; field of battle; field of a shield; ground of a picture. -**poraiòlo**, M.: farmer on shares. -**poréccio**, ADJ.: of the country. -**po=sánto**, M.: cemetery; devastated place. -**pucchiáre**, INTR.: be poor. -**púccio**, M.: small field.
camuffáre [*capo muffare*], TR., REFL.: muffle up (mask, disguise); cheat†.
camúso†, ADJ.: camous (flat-nosed).
ca-náccio, M.: big ugly dog. ||-**náglia** [-*ne*], F.: canaille (rabble). -**nagliáccia**, *disp.* of -*naglia*. -**nagliáta**, F.: act of the rabble. -**nagliésco**, ADJ.: pertaining to the rabble. -**nagliúme**, M.: rabble; gathering place of the rabble. -**náio**, M.: keeper of dogs. -**nai(u)òlo**, M.: kind of sweet grape.
caná-le [L. -*lis*], M.: canal; channel; irrigating-ditch. -**létto**, -**líno**, *dim.* of -*le*. -**lúccio**, M.: little canal, gutter.
cána-pa [L. *cannabis*], F.: HEMP. -**páia**, F.: hemp-field. -**páio**, M.: dresser and seller of hemp. -**pále**†, M.: rope, halter.
cána-pe†, M.: hemp-rope.
cana-pè [Fr.; ak. to Eng. *canopy*], M.: sofa. -**peíno**, M.: small sofa.
canapétto [-*po*], M.: small rope.
canapíglia†, F.: kind of wild duck.
cana-píno, ADJ.: hempen; M.: hemp-dresser. ||**cána-po** [-*pa*], M.: big rope, cable. -**púccia**†, F.: hemp-seed. -**púle**, M.: stalk of hemp.
canarí-na, F. [*Canarie*], -**no**, M.: canary-bird; singer with a small voice; ADJ.: yellow.
caná-ta [*cane*], F.: reproof. -**ttería**†, F.: pack of dogs. -**ttière**†, M.: dog-keeper.
canaváccio = *canovaccio*.
cancán [Fr.], M.: cancan (vulgar French dance).
cancel-lábile, ADJ.: that can be cancelled. -**laménto**†, M.: cancelling. -**láre**, TR.: cancel (erase). -**láta**, F.: railing (rail-fence). -**latína**, *dim.* of -*lata*. -**láto**, PART., M.: railing (rail-fence). -**latóre**, M., -**latríce**, F.: canceller. -**latúra**, -**lazióne**†, F.: cancelling (erasure). -**lerésco**, ADJ.: belonging to chancery. -**lería**, F.: chancery; chancellor's residence. -**lièra**, F.: chancellor's wife. -**lieráto**, M.: chancellorship. -**lière**, M.: registrar, chancellor. -**líno**, M.: small lattice. ||**cancèl-lo** [L. -*lus* (dim. of *cancer*, lattice)], M.: cancel, enclosure, lattice, chancel-bar.
can-ceróso, ADJ.: cancerous. -**cheríno**, M.: small canker. ||**cán-chero** [L. -*cer*, crab], M.: cancer (us'ly -*cro*); (*fig.*) evil (trouble), plague; wretch; INTERJ.: misery! fudge! -**cheróne**, M.: big canker. -**cheróso**, ADJ.: cancerous.

can-crèna [Gr. *gángraina* (*grain-*, gnaw)], F.: GANGRENE. **-crenáre**, INTR., REFL.: gangrene. **-crenóso**, ADJ.: gangrenous.
cáncro [L. *-cer*, crab], M.: cancer (ulceration; sign of the zodiac).
candé-la [L. (*-re*, be white)], F.: candle. **-lábro**, M.: chandelier. **-láia**, **-lára**, F.: Candlemas. **-létta**, F.: small candle; (*med.*) bougie. **-(l)lière**, M.: candlestick, candelabrum. **-lóna**, F., **-lóne**, M.: large candle. **-lòra**, F.: Candlemas. **-lòtto**, M.: thick, short candle. **candè-nte**†, ADJ.: shining, candent.
candi-daménte, ADV.: candidly. **-daménto**, M.: whiteness. **-dáto**, ADJ.†: attired in white; M.: candidate (Rom. candidates dressed in white). **-dézza**, F.: whiteness. **-díssimo**, ADJ.: very white. ||**cándi-do** [L. *-dus*], ADJ.: white, pure; ingenuous (sincere). **-ficáre**†, TR.: make very hot.
can-díre [Turk.], TR.: candy, preserve. **-díto**, PART.: candied; M. PL.: sweetmeats.
cán-do†, ADJ.: white. ||**-dóre** [L. *-dor*], M.: whiteness; purity, simplicity.
cá-ne [L. *-nis*], M.: dog; low person (rascal); dentist's key; cock of a gun; dog-star (Sirius); **-nèa**, F.: barking of a pack of dogs.
canè-fora [Gr. *phóros*, bearer], F.: girl who brought baskets of flowers, etc., to Pallas. **canè-stra** [L. *canistra* (Gr. *káneon*, basket)], F.: small willow basket; light carriage. **-stráccia**, **-stráccio**, *disp.* of *-stro*. **-stráta**, F.: basketful. **-strína**, **-stríno**, *dim.* of *-stra*, *-stro*. **canè-stro**, M.: basket (pannier). **-strúccio**, *disp. dim.* of *-stro*.
canétto [*cane*], M.: small dog.
cánfo-ra [Ar.], F.: camphor. **-ráto**, ADJ.: camphorated.
can-giábile, ADJ.: changeable. **-giaménto**, M.: change. **-giánte**, ADJ.: changing; changeable (of colours). ||**-giáre** [*cambiare*], TR.: CHANGE (exchange); REFL.: change one's mind. **cán-gio** = *-giante*.
cangrèna†, F.: gangrene.
ca-nicciáta, F.: batch. ||**-níccio** [*-nna*], M.: bed of reeds or pipes; drying-bed (for chestnuts).
ca-nicídio, M.: killing of dogs. ||**-nícola** [*-ne*], F.: Canicula (dog-star): dog-days. **-nicoláre**, ADJ.: canicular. **-nícula**†, F.: dog-star.
cánido†, ADJ.: white; candid.
ca-níle [*-ne*], M.: KENNEL; miserable room or bed. **-nína**, F.: small bitch. **-ninaménte**, ADV.: like a dog. **-níno**, *car. dim.* of *cane*; ADJ.: canine.
canizie [L. *-nities*], F.: white hairs of age.

canízza [*-ne*], F.: bay (of dogs).
cán-na [L.], F.: cane, reed; stick (staff); pipe (tube); barrel of a gun; measure of length. **-náio**†, M.: weaver's drawer; reed basket for grains. **-namèle**†, F., M.: sugar-cane. **-náta**, F.: blow with a cane. **-neggiáre**, TR.: measure with a rod, survey. **-neggiatóre**, M.: surveyor's assistant. **-nèlla**, F.: small waterpipe (conduit); tube; faucet; bad practice; cinnamon. **-nelláto**†, ADJ.: cinnamon-; seasoned with cinnamon. **-nellétta**, *dim.* of *-nella*. **-nellétto**, **-nellíno**, *dim.* of *-nello*. **-nellína** = *-nelletta*. **-nèllo**, M.: joint of cane; weaver's reel; small tube, syphon. **-nellóne**, *aug.* of *-nello*. **-néto**, M.: place full of reeds. **-nétta**, *dim.* of *-na*.
canníbale [*-ba*, Caribbean word], M.: cannibal.
canníccі. . = *caniccі*. .
can-nonáta, F.: cannon-shot; idle story. **-noncèllo**†, **-noncíno**, M.: small cannon. ||**-nóne** [*-na*], M.: big cane or tube; cannon. **-noneggiaménto**, M.: cannonading. **-noneggiáre**, TR.: cannonade. **-nonièra**, F.: embrasure; porthole; gunboat: ADJ.: of a gunboat. **-nonière**, M.: cannoneer, gunner. **-nóso**†, ADJ.: reedy. **-núccia**, *disp. dim.* of *-na*.
cannutíglia = *canutiglia*.
cáno†, ADJ.: gray-haired.
canòa†, F.: canoe.
ca-nocchiále [*canna occhiale*], M.: telescope. **-nòcchio**†, M.: vine-prop.
canóne1 [*cane*], M.: big dog.
cá-none2 [Gr. *kanón*, rod, rule (*kánє*, reed)], M.: canon (church law); land-rent; PL.: catalogue of Greek classics (by Alexandrian grammarians). **-nònica**, F.: priest's residence. **-nonicále**, ADJ.: canonical. **-nonicaménte**, ADV.: canonically. **-nonicáto**, M.: canonry. **-nonichéssa**, F.: canoness. **-nonicità**, F.: canonicalness. **-nònico**, ADJ.: canonical; M.: canon (member of a cathedral chapter). **-nonísta**, M.: canonist. **-nonizzáre**, TR.: canonize; authorize. **-nonizzazióne**, F.: canonization.
canopè†, M.: sofa.
canòro [L. *-rus* (*-ere*, sing)], ADJ.: melodious (canorous).
canòsc. . † = *conosc*. .
ca-nottière, M.: canoe-man. ||**-nòtto** [Sp. *canoa* (Carib.)], M.: canoe.
cánova [L. *-naba*, hut], F.: wine-shop; provision-shop.
canováccio [*-napa*], M.: rough cloth for dusting or polishing, dusting-rag; embroidery-cloth; CANVAS.
cano-váia, F. [*-va*], **-váio**, M.: storekeeper in a convent.

can-sáre [L. *campsare*], TR.: remove, set aside. **-satéia**†, F., **-satóio**†, M.: refuge (shelter).
can-tábile [*-tare*], ADJ.: that may be sung; M.: cantibile (passage in music). **-tacchiáre**†, TR.: sing low (hum). **-ta=fávola**, F.: idle story. **-tafèra** [variant of *tantafera*], F.: tiresome song. **-taiòlo**, ADJ.: singing (of birds); M.: decoy-bird. **-tam=bánca**, F., **-tambánco**, M.: mountebank (humbug). **-tánte**, M., F.: singer. ||**-táre** [L.], INTR.: sing; celebrate (praise); TR.: sing; M.†: song.
cantáride, F. = *canterella*.
cantáre [Gr. *-tharos*, cup], M.: cantaro (anc. weight).
canta=stòrie [*-re*], M., INVAR.: singing beggar. **cantá-ta**, F.: cantata. **-tóre**, M.: cantor (singer).
canterèlla [Gr. *kantharis*, beetle], F.: cantharis (blister-fly).
canterelláre [*-tare*], INTR.: sing low, hum; warble.
canterèllo† [*-tero*], M.: small vase; tinsel.
canteríno [*-tare*], ADJ.: singing; M.: (*jest.*) singer.
cántero [Gr. *kántharos*], M.: vase, chamber utensil.
canterúto†, ADJ.: angular (cornered).
cán-tica [*-to* I], F.: song (poem in parts). **-ticchiáre**, TR., INTR.: sing low. **cántico**, M.: canticle (religious song).
cantière [L. *-terius*], M.: dockyard.
canti-lèna [*-tare*], F.: tiresome music. **-lenáre**†, TR.: compose poor music.
cantimplòra [L. *canna impletoria*], F.: wine or water-cooler.
cantí-na [? ak. to *canova*], F.: wine-cellar; sutler's shop; wine; cave†. **-nétta**, *dim.* of *-na*. **-nière**, M.: butler.
can-tíno, M.: treble string of a violin, etc. ||**-to** I [L. *-tus*], M.: singing; song; canto (part of a poem); ballad.
cán-to 2 [?], M.: corner (angle, CANT); side: *a* —, near, beside. **-tonále**, ADJ.: cantonal. **-tonáre**†, TR.: divide in parts; REFL.: withdraw. **-tonáta**, F.: angle, corner. **-tóne** [aug. of *-to*], M.: part, side; cornerstone; canton. **-tonièra**, F.: corner closet. **-tonière**, M.: custodian of a high road. **-tonúto**, ADJ.: angular.
can-tóra [*-tare*], F.: nun singing in a choir. **-tóre**, M.: singer; choir-leader. **-toría**, F.: singer's gallery. **-toríno**, M.: hymn-book. **-tucchiáre**, TR., INTR.: sing low.
can-tucciáio, M.: biscuit maker or seller. **-tuccíno**, *dim.* of *-tuccio*. ||**-túccio** [*dim.* of *-to* 2], M.: corner; small piece or part; bit of bread; biscuit.
ca-nuccíáccio, **-núccio**, *disp.* of *-ne*.
canu-taménte†, ADV.: with judgment, prudently. ||**-tézza** [L. *canities*], F.: gray hairs, hoariness of age.
canutíglia [*canna*], F.: gold or silver embroidery; spangles.
canúto [L. *-tus*], ADJ.: gray-haired.
can-zóna, F.: song. **-zonáccia**, F.: bad song. **-zonáre**, TR.: banter, make fun of. **-zonatóre**, M., **-zonatríce**, F.: banterer. **-zonatoriaménte**, ADV.: banteringly. **-zonatòrio**, ADJ.: bantering, quizzing. **-zonatúra**, F.: bantering. **-zoncína**, F., **-zoncíno**, M.: canzonet. **-zoncióna**, **-zoncióne**, *aug.* of *-zone*. ||**-zóne** [L. *-tio* (*-ere*, sing)], M.: song (CHANT); ballad: *mettere in* —, make fun of, deride. **-zonèlla**, F.: *mettere* (*mandare*) *in* —, make fun of, deride. **-zonétta**, *dim.* of *-zone*. **-zonière**, M.: collection of songs; song-book. **-zonúccia**, *disp. dim.* of *-zone*.
cáo-s, **-sse** [Gr. *cháos*, space], M.: chaos.
ca-paccína [*-po*], F.: pain in the head; confused feeling. **-páccio**, M.: bad man. **-paccíúto**, ADJ.: big-headed (said of vegetables, etc.).
capá-ce [*capire*], ADJ.: capacious; capable (able). **-císsimo**, ADJ.: superl. of *-ce*. **-cità**, F.: capacity; ability. **-citáre**, TR.: capacitate; persuade; INTR.: be or become capable: *non mi -cita*, it is not to my taste. **-citáto**, PART.: convinced.
capagúto†, M.: sharp-pointed weapon.
capamèno or *capo ameno*, M.: gay, whimsical person.
capán-na [Celt. *caban*], F.: barn (shed); CABIN (hut). **-náccia**, F.: miserable hut. **-nèlla**, *dim.* of *-na*. **-nèllo**, M.: group (talking in secret); small hut†. **-nétto**†, M.: small cabin. **=niscóndere**, M.: game of hide-and-seek. **-no**, M.: hut used as hiding-place by fowlers; hut; cupola. **-nòla**†, F.: small hut. **-nóne**, M.: hay-loft; large room. **-núccia**, F.: *disp. dim.* of *-na*; representation of the birth of Christ (hut of wood, figures of wax, etc.). **-núccio**, *disp. dim.* of *-no*.
capar-biággine, F.: stubbornness, obstinacy. **-biaménte**, ADV.: stubbornly. **-biería**, F.: stubbornness (obstinacy). ||**capár-bio** [*capo*], ADJ.: stubborn (head-strong); M.: obstinate fellow. **-biòlo**, ADJ.: rather stubborn.
capár-ra [? *cape*, take, *arra*, pledge], F.: earnest-money (pledge). **-ráre**, TR.: give earnest to; hire; engage.
capá-ta [*capo*], F.: blow with the head; inclination of the head. **-tína**, *dim.* of *-ta*.
cápe [3. Sing. of *capere*], find room: *nel baule non ci* — (does not find place in the trunk), cannot be packed in the trunk.

ca-pecchiáccio, M.: rubbish. ‖**-pécchio** [L. *-pillus*, hair], M.: flock (coarse part of flax or hemp).

capèlla†, F.: she-goat.

capel-lácci, M. PL.: ugly hair. **-latúra**, F.: head of hair. **-lièra**, F.: hair of the head. **-líno**, *dim.* of *-lo*. ‖**capél-lo** [L. *capillus*], pl. *-li* or *capegli*, M.: hair. **-lúto**†, ADJ.: hairy, having much hair. =**vènere**, or **capél vènere**, M.: maidenhair (plant).

ca-peròzzolo, M.: rounded head or extremity. **-pestrería**, F.: strangeness, whim. ‖**-pèstro** or *é* [L. *-pistrum* (*-put*, head)], M.: halter; rope for hanging criminals; monk's girdle; criminal. **-pestrúzzo**, *dim.* of *-pestro*. **-pettáccio**, *disp. dim.* of *-petto*. **-pétto**, M.: headstrong (capricious) fellow. **-pettucciáccio**, *disp.* of *-pettaccio*.

capévole†, ADJ.: capacious; intelligent.

capezzále [*capo*], M.: bolster; pillow.

capézzolo [Sp. *cabezo* (L. *caput*, head), hill-top)], M.: nipple.

capi-dòglia†, F., ‖**-dòglio** [*capo olio*], M.: sperm-whale.

capíglia†, F.: quarrel (scuffle).

capi-gliatúra, F.: hair, head of hair. ‖**-lláre** [L. *-llus*, hair], ADJ.: capillary. **-llarità**, F.: capillarity.

capiménto†, M.: (*fig.*) capacity (comprehension).

capi=néra, F., =**néro**, M.: black-headed linnet. **capí-no**, *car. dim.* of *capo*.

capíre [L. *-pere*], INTR.: contain (IRR.§); comprehend (understand).

§ Pres. *cá-pe*; *-pano*: in sense of 'contain.'

capi-tále [*capo*], ADJ.: capital (principal; mortal); M.: capital, stock. **-talétto**, **-talíno**, *dim.* of *-tale*. **-talísta**, M.: capitalist. **-talizzáre**, TR.: capitalize (convert into capital); INTR.: amass capital. **-talménte**†, ADV.: capitally; mortally. **-talúccio**, *disp. dim.* of *-tale*. **-tána**, F.: admiral's ship; (*jest.*) captain's wife. **-tanáre**, TR.: lead, command. **-tanáto**, PART.: provided with commanders; M.: captaincy. **-taneggiáre**, TR.: command; INTR.: be captain. **-tanería**, F.: coast region under a sea-officer's command; officer's residence; captaincy†. **-táno**, M.: captain; chief (commander of an army). **-táre**, INTR.: arrive; (*fig.*) come into the mind; with *di* and inf.: happen. **-tazióne**, F.: poll-tax. **cápi-te** (*in*), ADV.: in chief: *generale in* —, general-in-chief. **-tèllo**, M.: capital of a column. **-toláre** 1, ADJ.: capitular. **-toláre** 2, INTR.: capitulate; parley; divide into chapters†. **-tolarménte**, ADV.: capitularly. **-toláto**, M.: capitulation, document containing terms for surrender. **-tolazióne**, F.: term of surrender; capitulation; enlistment. **-tolétto**, *dim.* of *-tolo*. **-tolíno**, ADJ.: *dim.* of *-tolo*; capitoline. **capí-tolo**, M.: CHAPTER; head (subject); poem of triplets; chapter (body of canons); assembling-place or assemblage of monks. **-tolúccio**, **-tolúzzo**, *disp. dim.* of *-tolo*.

capi-tomboláre, INTR.: fall head over heels (tumble). ‖=**tómbolo** [*capo tombolo*], M.: tumble. **-tombolóni**, ADV.: in tumbles. **-tóndolo** = *capitombolo*.

capi-tóne [L. *caput*, head], M.: tangle of silk-thread; thick eel. **-tóso**†, ADJ.: headstrong, obstinate. **-tòzza** F.: pollard. **-tozzáre** = *scapitozzare*.

cápo [L. *-put*], M.: head; mind; chief; summit, origin, end; promontory: *a* (*in*) — *al mondo*, to the end of the world; *in* — *a* (*di*) *tre anni*, at the end of three years; *far* —, arrive at. =**bánda**, M.: leader of a band of musicians. =**bandíto**, M.: chief of banditti. =**brigánte**, M.: chief of brigands. =**cáccia**, M.: head huntsman. =**caníno**, ADJ.: having a head like a dog's. **capò-cchia**, F.: head of pins or nails. **capò-cchio**, M.: blockhead. **-cchióne**, M.: big dunce. **capò-ccia**, pl. *-cci* or *-ccia*, M.: head of a country-family; foreman (boss). =**còco**, M.: head cook. =**còmico**, M.: head comedian. =**cuòco**, M.: head cook. =**d'òpera**, M.: masterpiece; gay person. =**fíla**, M.: first soldier of the file. =**fítto**, ADJ. (ADV.): head downwards. **-gátto**, M.: staggers (vertigo). **-gírlo**†, =**gíro**, M.: dizziness. =**lavóro**, M.: masterpiece. =**lètto**, M.: tapestry (hangings originally behind head of bed). **-leváre**†, INTR.: fall head foremost. **-líno**, M.: *dim.* of *-po*; dot over the i: *il sole oggi fa* —, the sun is hardly visible today. =**lísta**, M.: head of the list. =**luògo**, M.: chief place or town (residence place). =**maèstro**, M.: master-mason; architect†. =**mándria**, M.: herder, shepherd. **capó-na**, F.: stubborn woman. **-nággine**, F.: stubbornness (obstinacy). **capó-ne**, M.: big head; stubborn fellow; blockhead. **-nería**, F.: stubbornness. =**parte**, M.: head of a party or faction. =**piède** or =**piè**, ADV.: as *far* —, turn upside down. =**pòpolo**, M.: head of the popular party. =**pósto**, M.: chief of a guard. **-rála**, F.: hospital matron. **-raláto**, M.: corporalship. **-rále**, M.: CORPORAL; overseer, foreman; ADJ.†: principal. **-ralétto**, M.: young corporal. **-ralúccio**, *disp. dim.* of *-rale*. **-ráme**†, M.: chief (master). **-ríccio**†, M.: fright, horror. =**rióna**, F., =**rióne**, M.: chief,

al (term of reproach). =**rovèscio**, ead downwards, topsy-turvy. =**scá-** head of the stairs. =**sc(u)òla**, nder of a school (in art or letters). , =**settário**, M.: head of a sect. †, M.: increase of pay; soldier tra pay. =**squádra**, M.: com- of a squadron (commodore). =**stre-** M.: (*jest.*) chief of sorcerers. **áro**, M.: head-drum. =**tásto**, (of stringed instruments). =**tá-** M.: head of the table; us'ly per- the head of the table. =**vèrso**, ginning of a verse; verse. =**vòl-** TR.: turn upside down; REFL.; n. =**vòlto**, PART. of *-volgere*.
[Gr. *kappa*], M., INVAR.: k (the

[L. L.], F.: CAPE (hooded cloak); cloak: *sotto la — del sole* (*del cie-* this world. =**mágna**, F.: state- f cardinals, etc.
ᴇ†, TR.: choose.
lla [*-pa*, cape (of St. Martin, kept apel)], F.: CHAPEL; oratory; chap- ; band of choristers; head of ails: *maestro di* —, director of music. **-pelláccia**, F.: kind of **-pelláccio**, *disp.* of *-llo*. **-pel-** F.: hatter's wife. **-pelláio**, M.: **-pellanáto**, M.: office of chap- **pellanía**, F.: chaplainship, living. **no**, M.: chaplain; assistant priest. **ta**, F.: blow with the hat; hatful: *te*, in great quantity. **-pellétta**, *-pella*. **-pellétto**, M.: small hat. **ra**, F.: hatbox. **-pellína**, *dim.* *a*; of *-pello*†. **-pellináio**, M.: clothes rack. **-pellíno**, *car. dim.* o. ||**-pèllo** [*-pa*, cape (part used], M.: hat; head of a still; head **-pellóne**, *aug.* of *-pello*; *aug.* *a*. **-pellúccia**, *dim.* of *-pelle*. **ccio**, *disp.* of *-pello*. **-pellúto**, rested, tufted (used of birds).
réto, M.: caper-bed. **cáp-peri**, : exclamation of surprise. ||**cáp-** Gr. *kápparis*], M.: CAPER (spice).
réme†, M.: large peasant's or car- hood. **-perúccio**†, M.: hood.
[*-pa*], F.: small cape; light cloak.
tto [*cappio*], M.: small knot; small of ribbons.
a [*cappa*], F.: small cape.
[L. *capulum*], M.: knot; knot or of ribbons.
a, **-terína** = *capperi*.
náia, F.: capon-coop. **-nare**, **pon**. **-ncèllo**, M.: young capon.
ó-ne [L. *capo*], M.: capon. **-niè-** (*fort.*) caponiere (covered way).
étta [*-pa*], F.: long cloak; woollen cap; woman's hat. **-pòtto**, M.: capote, long cloak; capot (at the game of piquet). **-puccáio**†, M.: hoodmaker or seller. **-puccína**, F.: Capuchin nun: *insalata* —, kind of salad. **-puccíno**, M.: Capuchin friar: *i -puccini*, the church and monastery. **-púccio**, M.: CAPOCH (cowl, hood); 'headed cabbage.'
cá-pra [L.], F.: she-goat; goat-skin. **-prággine**, F.: goat's-rue (plant). **-práio**, M., **-práia**, F.: goat-herd. **-prétta**, F.: kid. **-prettína**, F., **-prettíno**, M.: small kid. **-prétto**, M.: kid. **-prézzo**†, M.: CAPER; CAPRICE, whim. **-pricciáre** = *rac-capricciare*. **-príccio**, M.: CAPRICE (whim); shivering†. **-pricciosaménte**, ADV.: capriciously. **-pricciosétto**, M.: capricious fellow. **-pricciòso**, ADV.: capricious; M.: capricious, whimsical fellow. **-pri=còrno**, M.: Capricorn. **-pri=fíco**, M.: wild fig-tree. **-pri=fòglio**, M.: honeysuckle, woodbine; caprifole. **-prígno**†, ADJ.: goatish. **-prína**, F.: kid. **-prí-no**, ADJ.: caprine, pertaining to a goat. **-prio**†, M.: roebuck. **-priòla**, F.: roe; caper; capriole. **-priolétta**, (*iron.*) *dim.* of *-riola*. **-priolétto**, M.: fawn. **-priò-lo**, M.: roebuck. ||**-pro** [L. *caper*], M.: goat: — *emissario*, — *espiatorio*, scape-goat. **-próne**, M.: large goat.
ca-prugginàre, TR.: notch (the staves of a cask). **-prugginatóio**, M.: instrument for marking notches. ||**-prúggine** [?], F.: notch (in the staves of a barrel, for fixing the bottom).
cápsula [dim. of L. *capsa*, case], F.: capsule, case; pod: — *da fucile*, cap (primer of a gun).
capzióso†, ADJ.: deceitful.
carabáttole [L. *grabatulus*, couch], F. PL.: in *pigliar le* —, take one's belongings (in leaving a place).
cárabe†, F.: yellow amber.
carabí-na [?], F.: carbine. **-nière**, M.: carbineer.
caràcca [Dutch *kraeke*], F.: carack (large ship).
cara-colláre [Ar.], INTR.: caracole, wheel. **-còllo**, M.: caracole, turning about.
caráf-fa [? Ar.], F.: carafe (glass bottle). **-fína**, F., **-físo**, M.: small carafe.
cara-mèlla [? Ar.], F.: candied fru . **-melláio**, M.: maker or seller of candied fruits. **-melláre**, TR.: crystallize sugar.
caraménte [*caro*], ADV.: dearly.
caramògio†, M.: dwarf.
caratáre†, TR.: weigh very carefully.
cara-tèllo [*carro*], M.: keg (cask). **-tel-létto**, **-tellíno**, *dim.* of *-tello*.
caráto [Ar.], M.: carat; twenty-fourth part.

carátte-re [Gr. *charaktḗr*], M.: character (letter; handwriting; type; quality). **-rísta**, M.: actor who creates a part. **-rística**, F.: characteristic. **-rístico**, ADJ.: characteristic. **-rizzáre**, TR.: characterize. **-róne**, *aug.* of *-re*. **-rúccio**, *disp. dim.* of *-re*.

caravèlla [L. *-rabus*], F.: caravel (ship).

carbo-náia [*-ne*], F.: charcoal-place (charcoal-stack); pile of wood; (*jest.*) prison; moat†. **-náio**, M.: charcoal-maker or seller. **-narísmo**, M.: carbonarism. **-náro**, M.: carbonaro (member of the 'Carbonari' revolutionary society, 1808–15). **-náta**†, F.: carbonado (salt fried pork). **-náto**, M.: carbonate. **-ncèllo**, *dim.* of *-bone*.

carbón-chio [L. *carbunculus*], M.: carbuncle (gem; boil); smut, mildew. **-chióso**†, ADJ.: affected with mildew.

carbo-ncíno, *dim.* of *-ne*. ||**carbó-ne** [L. *carbo*], M.: coal; charcoal; mildew, smut; carbuncle†: *a misura di* —, measuring by wholesale; in abundance; — *fossile*, pit-coal. **-nèlla**, F.: small coal; burning coal. **-nería**, F.: Carbonarism.

carbò-nico, ADJ.: carbonic. **-nièra**, F.: charcoal-shed or depot. **-nífero**, ADJ.: carboniferous. **carbò-nio**, M.: carbon. **-nizzáre**, TR.: carbonize; REFL.: become carbon.

carbúncolo†, M.: carbuncle.

carcáme [?], M.: carcass.

carcáre†, TR.: load.

carcássa [*carne cassa*], F.: carcass; breast of a chicken; hulk of a ship.

carcásso†, M.: quiver.

carce-raménto†, M.: imprisonment. **-ráre**, TR.: incarcerate (imprison). **-rário**, ADJ.: of a prison (carceral). **-razióne**, F.: incarceration. ||**cárce-re** [L. *carcer*], M. or (us'ly pl.) F.: prison. **-rière**, M.: jailer.

car-ciofáia, F.: field of artichokes. **-ciòfano**†, M.: artichoke. **-ciofétto**, **-ciofíno**, M.: small artichoke. ||**-ciòfo** [Ar.], M.: artichoke; dunce. **-ciòfola**†, F.: artichoke.

cárco†, ADJ.: loaded.

cardamòmo [Gr. *-mon*], M.: cardamom.

car-dáre [*cardo*], TR.: card (wool); slander†. **-datóre**, M.: carder. **-datúra**, F.: carding. **-deggiáre**†, TR.: card; slander.

cardellíno [?], M.: goldfinch.

cár-dia [Gr. *kardía*], M.: cardia (HEART). **-díaco**, ADJ.: cardiac. **-diálgia**, F.: cardialgy, heartburn.

cardina-láto, M.: cardinalate. ||**cardiná-le** [*cardine*], ADJ.: cardinal; M.: cardinal; cardinal bird (finch); hinge†. **-lésco**, ADJ.: pertaining to a cardinal. **-létto**, *dim.* of *-le*. **-lísta**, M.: adherent of a cardinal. **-lízio**, ADJ.: of a cardinal.

cárdine [L. *-do*], M.: hinge; foundation: *cardini del mondo*, poles of the earth.

car-déto, M.: field of thistles. **-díno**, *dim.* of *-do*. ||**-do** [L. *-duus*], M.: thistle; card (for combing wool). **-doncèllo**†, **-dóne**, **-dúccio**, M.: artichoke sprout.

careggiáre†, TR.: caress; esteem.

carèllo†, M.: pillow, cushion.

carè-na [L. *carina*], F.: keel. **-náre**†, TR.: CAREEN (for repairs).

ca-rènte†, ADJ.: wanting. ||**-restía** [L. *-rere*, want], F.: scarcity, famine. **-restóso**†, ADJ.: dear, expensive.

carétto†, M.: reed (rush).

ca-rézza 1 [L. *-rus*, dear], F.: caress; attention (care). **-rézza** 2 [*-ro*], F.: dearness (costliness). **-rezzáre**, TR.: caress, fondle. **-rezzatóre**, M.: caresser. **-rezzévole**, ADJ.: caressing. **-rezzevolménte**, ADV.: caressingly. **-rezzína**, *dim.* of *-rezza* 1.

cariággio = *carriaggio*.

cariáre [*carie*], TR., INTR.: make or become carious.

cariátide [Gr. *Karuátides*, priestess], F.: caryatid; (*jest.*) clumsy support or prop.

cári-ca [*-co*], F.: CHARGE (office); burden (care); charge (of a gun): — *a fondo*, determined attack. **-cáre**, TR.: CHARGE, load; add to; accuse. **-cataménte**, ADV.: affectedly. **-cáto**, ADJ.: affected (insincere). **-catóre**, M.: loader, freighter. **-catúra**, F.: charge (load); affectation; caricature. **-caturína**, *dim.* of *-catura*. **-caturísta**, M.: caricaturist.

cárice†, F.: reed, rush.

cárico [*carro*], ADJ.: pop. for *caricato*; M.: load (burden); blame; CHARGE†.

cárie [L. *-ries*], F.: caries (disease of bone); decay.

caríno [*-ro*], M.: darling (dear).

cariòla [*carro*], F.: wheelbarrow; knife-grinder's cart.

carióso†, ADJ.: carious (decaying).

cari-tà [*caro*], F.: CHARITY; love; favour. **-tatévole**, ADJ.: charitable. **-tatevolménte**, **-tativaménte**†, ADV.: charitably. **-tatívo**†, **-tévole**†, ADJ.: charitable. **-tevolménte**†, ADV.: charitably.

carlíno [*Carlo*], M.: carline (small coin).

cárme [L. *-men*], M.: (*poet.*) verse, poem.

carmelitáno [*Carmelo*, where the order was founded], ADJ.: Carmelite; M.: Carmelite friar.

carmi-náre†, TR.: card (wool); (*med.*) expel wind. **-natívo**†, ADJ.: carminative, expelling wind.

carmínio [l. L. *-mesinus*], M.: carmine.

car-náccia, *disp.* of *-ne*. **-naccé-**

sot, -naccitátot, ADJ.: fleshy. -nággiot, M.: meat; carnage. -nagióne, F.: carnation, flesh colour. -náio, M.: (jest.) charnel house. -naiuòlo†, M.: game-bag; bag. -nále, ADJ.: carnal; of same blood (related). -nalità, F.: carnality. -nalménte, ADV.: carnally. -náme, M.: mass of human limbs or corpses; quantity of bad meat. -nascialáre† [-ne scialare], INTR.: give one's self up to excesses. -nasciále [-nascialare], M.: carnival. -nascialésco, ADJ.: pertaining to the carnival. -náto, M.: carnation, flesh colour. ||-ne [L. caro], F.: flesh; meat; PL.: appearance (complexion); health; pulp of fruit†. -néfice [L. carni-fex], M.: executioner (hangman); cruel man. -neficína, F.: carnage; torture. cár-neo†, ADJ.: carneous, fleshy. -ne=sécca, F.: salt-meat. -nevaláta, F.: carnival pleasure. -ne=vále, M.: carnival; festival, merry-making. -nevalésco, ADJ.: belonging to the carnival. -nevalíno, M.: amusement, small pleasure; first Sunday of Lent (which is a continuation of the Carnival). -nevalóne, M.: gay festival. -níccio, M.: fleshy side of raw skins; scrapings or shreds of skins. -nicíno, ADJ.: flesh-coloured; pale rose-coloured. -nièra, F., -nière†, M.: game bag. -nificína, F.: carnage; torment. -nívoro, ADJ.: carnivorous; M.: carnivorous animal. -nosità, F.: fleshiness; (med.) carnosity (fleshy excrescence). -nóso, ADJ.: fleshy (carnous): muscoli -nosi, large muscles. -noval. . (pop.) = carneval. . -núto†, ADJ.: fleshy.

cáro [L. -rus], ADJ.: dear (valued, costly); M.: dearness; scarcity†; ADV.: dearly; at a high price.

caró-gna [L. caro, flesh], F.: poor horse (jade); corpse†; CARRION†. -gnáccia, F.: worn-out horse.

carò-la, F.: dance (ballet). ||-láre [L. caraulare], INTR.: dance a ballet.

carosèllo [?], M.: exhibition on horseback (by several persons); merry-go-round.

caròta [L.], F.: carrot; idle story, fib: piantare (vender) -te, tell foolish tales. -táccia, disp. of -ta. -táio, M.: foolish talker. -táre†, INTR.: tell foolish stories; fib. -tière†, M.: foolish talker.

caròtide [Gr. -tides], F.: carotid artery.

carována [Ar.], F.: caravan; large company.

carpáre†, INTR.: walk upon all-fours; TR.: snatch; arrest.

carpentière†, M.: carpenter.

cárpi-ne [L. -nus], M.: hornbeam (tree). -néta, F.: place planted with hornbeams. cárpi-no, M.: hornbeam.

cár-pio [l. L. -pa], M.: carp. -pióne, M.: carp.

carpíre [L. -pere], TR.: obtain unlawfully (snatch); wrest†.

carpíta†, F.: woolly cloth; woolly covering.

cár-po [Gr. karpós], M.: wrist (carpus). -póne or -póni, ADV.: on hands and feet, on all-fours.

car-radóre, -ráio, M.: cartwright. -ráta, F.: cart-load; great quantity. -ratèllo†, M.: keg (cask). -reggiábile, ADJ.: passable for wagons. -reggiáre, TR.: convey by carts or wagons. -reggiáta, F.: wagon track (cart-road). -reggiatóre†, M.: driver, carter. -réggio, M.: carting, conveying by wagons; M.†: great number of carts. -rétta, F.: cart; carriage†; gun-carriage. -rettáio, M.: carter. -rettáta, F.: cartful. -rettèlla, F.: small four-wheeled carriage. -rettière, M.: carter, teamster. -rettíno, M.: small pushcart. -rétto, M.: pushcart. -rettonáio, M.: carter, teamster. -rettonáta, F.: large wagon-load. -rettóne, M.: tilt-cart, large wagon (dray). -riággio, M.: baggage wagon; baggage of an army. -ricèllo†, M.: small wagon. -rièra, F.: career, race; career (life). -ri(u)òla, F.: wheelbarrow; trundle bed†; litter. ||cár-ro [L. -rus (= currus)], pl. -ri, or -ra (ref. to the contents), M.: wagon, CAR; wagonload: il — di Boote, Charles' Wain, Great Bear. -ròccio, M.: war chariot (of Italian republics). -ròzza, F.: coach, carriage. -rozzábile, ADJ.: passable for carriages. -rozzáccia, disp. of -rozza. -rozzáio, M.: carriage-maker. -rozzáta, F.: carriageful. -rozzétta, F.: light carriage. -rozzière, M.: carriage-maker; (jest.) coachman. -rozzíno, M.: small carriage. -rozzóne, M.: aug. of -rozza; big profit.

ca(r)-rúba, F.: carob-bean, St. John's bread. ||-rúbbio [Ar.], M.: carob-tree.

carrúca†, F.: pulley.

carrúccio [carro], M.: go-cart for children.

carrúco-la [carruca], F.: pulley: unger le -le, flatter, bribe. -láre†, TR.: draw up with pulleys. -lína, F.: small pulley.

cár-ta [L. charta], F.: paper (leaf of paper); card; printed paper; chart; legal document; map; playing-card. -tabèllo†, M.: pamphlet. -táccia, F.: bad paper. -táceo, ADJ.: of paper, paper. -ta=glòria, F.: altar-scrolls. -táio, M.: paper-maker. -ta=pècora, F.: parchment; documents written on parchment. -ta=pésta, F.: papier-mâché. -táro†, M.: paper maker. -ta=stráccia [c. straccio], F.: wrapping-paper; worthless writing. **-teggiáre**, INTR.: keep up a correspondence; TR.†: study (a nautical chart); glance over†. **-téggio**, M.: correspondence by letter; collection of letters. **-tèlla**, F.: label; bond, government bond; ticket (in lottery). **-tellét-ta**, **-tellína**, *dim.* of *-tella*. **-tellíno**, *dim.* of *-tello*. **-tèllo**, M.: posting-bill, placard; sign-board. **-telléne**, *aug.* of *-tello*. **-tiçíno**, M.: pamphlet of additions and corrections. **-tièra**, F.: paper-mill.

carti-lágine [L. *-lago*], F.: cartilage (gristle). **-lagíneo**, **-lagineóso**, ADJ.: cartilaginous (gristly).

car-tína, F.: *dim.* of *-ta*; worthless card (in a certain game); (*mus.*) solo: — *di spilli*, paper of pins. **-tòccio**, M.: paper-cornet (cornet); CARTOUCH (cartridge); (*arch.*) scroll. **-toláio**, M.: stationer, paper seller. **-toláre**, M.: copy-book; TR.†: page a book. **-toláro**, M.: stationer. **-tolería**, F.: stationer's shop. **-tolína**, F.: small strip of paper; label; post(al) card (or — *postale*). **-tonác-cio**, *disp.* of *-tone*. **-toncíno**, *dim.* of *-tone*. **-tóne**, M.: pasteboard; cartoon. **-túccia**, F.: CARTOUCH (cartridge); small piece of paper. **-tuccièra**, F.: cartridge-box.

carúbo†, M.: pop. form for *carrubbio*.

carúccio [*-ro*], ADJ.: very dear.

carún-cola [L. *caro*], **-cula**, F.: CARBUNCLE.

cárvi†, M.: caraway plant.

cása [L.], F.: house; household, family; home: — *di campagna*, country house; — *di commercio*, mercantile house, firm; — *di correzione*, bridewell; *faccende di* —, household affairs; *a* —, home.

caşácca [?], F.: kind of coat or jacket; CASSOCK.

casáccia, *disp.* of *casa*.

caşáccio [*-so*], M.: mischance: *a* —, botchingly, carelessly.

caşaccóne, *aug.* of *-cca*.

ca-sále [*-sa*], M.: hamlet, village. **-sa-língo**, ADJ.: domestic: *pane* —, home-made bread. **-sa=mátta** [*matto*], F.: casemate. **-saménto**, M.: large apartment house (block, tenement-house). **-sá-re**† = *accasare*. **-saréccio** = *case-reccio*. **-sáta**, F.: family, race. **-sáto**, M.: family name.

cas-cággine, F.: weakness; drowsiness. **-caménto**†, M.: falling, fall. **-ca=mòr-to**, M.: in *fare il* —, make passionate love to a woman. **-cánte**, ADJ.: falling; weak, failing. ‖**-cáre** [? ak. to *cadere*], INTR.: fall; fail; TR.†: fell (throw down): — *le braccia*, discourage; more common than *cadere*. **-cáta**, F.: fall; waterfall (CASCADE). **-catèlla**, F.: *dim.* of *-cata*; little cascade. **-catíccio**, ADJ.: frail, perishable. **-catóio** = **-caticcio**.

caschétto [*-co*], M.: small or light helmet.

caşcimírra [*Cascemir*], F.: cashmere.

caşcí-na, F.: cow pasture and dairy; cheese-form (of beech-wood); thin board (of beech). **-náio**, M.: dairy superintendent. ‖**cáşci-o**† [*cacio*], M.: cheese.

cásco [Sp.], M.: casque (helmet).

ca-seggiáto [*case*], M.: group of scattered houses, hamlet. **-sèlla**, F.: little compartment (in pods, etc.); small square (made by ruling, etc.); closet. **-seréc-cio**, ADJ.: domestic. **-şèrma**, F.: cavern, barracks. **-sétta**, F.: pretty little house. **-settína**, **-sicciòla**, F.: very small house. **-sière**, M., **-sièra**, F.: one that has charge of a house; steward, housekeeper. **-sigliáno**, M., **-sigliá-na**, F.: in the same house as another. **-síle**, M.: wretched hut. **-sinína**†, F.: small cottage. ‖**-síno** [*-sa*], M.: country or suburban residence; club-house; public house. **-sípola**, F.: miserable little house; hovel.

ca-şíssimo, ADJ.: superl. of *-so*; very suitable, or capable. **-şísta**, M.: casuist. **-şística**, F.: casuistry. ‖**-şo** [L. *-sus*], M.: case (chance); accident; case of a noun: *a — pensato*, with premeditation.

ca-sòccia† [*-sa*], F.: large, ugly house. **-soláre**, M.: lonely hovel; hamlet. **-só-na**, F.: large house. **-sóne**[1], M.: very large plain house.

ca-şóne[2] [*-so*], M.: casuist; pessimist. **-şóso**, ADJ.: fearful, afraid.

ca-sòtta [*-sa*], rather large house. **-sòt-to**, M.: sentry-box.

cáspita = *cappita*.

cás-sa [L. *capsa*], F.: CASE; chest; trunk; coffin; treasury; (*typ.*) type-case. **-sáio**, M.: trunk-maker or seller.

cassále†, ADJ.: mortal, deadly.

cassa=mádia†, F.: kneading-trough.

cassaménto†, M.: cancelling, annulling.

cassa=pánca, F.: chest used as a bench.

cas-sáre [L. (*-sus*, empty)], TR.: erase; cancel (abolish, Eng.† CASSATE); dismiss. **-satúra**, F.: cancelling (cassation). **-sa-zióne**, F.: cassation†: *corte di* —, court of cassation.

cássero [Sp. *alcázar*], M.: citadel (fortress); (*nav.*) poop.

cassét-ta [*cassa*], F.: small box (casket); drawer; cash-drawer; letter-box; alms-box; coach-box; dust-pan. **-táccia**, *disp.* of *-ta*. **-táio**†, M.: box-maker. **-táta**, F.: boxful. **-tína**, *dim.* of *-ta*. **-tíno**, M.: (*typ.*) box, compartment of case. **cassét-to**, M.: small box, casket; drawer. **-toncíno**, *dim.* of *-tone*. **-tóne**, M.: bureau, commode.

cássia [L. *casia*], F.: (*med.*) cassia.
cassiè-ra, F., **-re** [*cassa*], M.: CASHIER.
cassilìgnea†, F.: cassia bark.
cassína [*cassa*], F.: small box; salt-box.
cassi-nènse [*Cassino*], **-nése**, ADJ.: of the order of Mount Cassino; M.: monk (of that order).
cas-síno [-*sa*], M.: small dust-cart. **-so**†1, M.: chest (thorax).
cásso†2, ADJ.: vain; annulled.
cas-sonáccio, *disp.* of -*sone*. **-soncèllo**, **-soncíno**, *dim.* of -*sone*. ||**-sóne** [-*sa*], M.: large chest or box (esp. for grain, flour, etc.); tool-box; packing-box; munition-wagon.
cássula = *capsula*.
cásta [Sp., pure race (L. -*tus*, 'chaste')], F.: caste, class.
castá-gna [L. -*nea*], F.: CHESTNUT. **-gnacciáio**, M.: seller of chestnut-cakes. **-gnáccio**, M.: chestnut-pudding. **-gnéto**, M.: grove of chestnut-trees. **-gnétta**, F.: small chestnut; CASTANET. **-gno**, M.: chestnut-tree; chestnut-wood; ADJ.: chestnut or bay-coloured. **-gnúccia**, *disp.* of -*gna*. **-gn(u)òlo**†, ADJ.: chestnut-coloured.
castal-deria†, F.: stewardship. ||**-'do** [l. L. *gastaldius*], M.: majordomo (steward).
castaménte [-*sto*], ADV.: chastely.
castel-láccio, *disp.* of -*lo*. **-lána**, F.: castellan's wife. **-lanería**, **-lanía**, F.: (office of castellan); castellany. **-láno**, ADJ.: of a castle or castellan; M.: castellan. **-láre**†, M.: old ruined castle. **-létto**, M.: *dim.* of -*lo*; bank register of good clients. ||**castèl-lo**, pl. -*li*, (rare) -*la* [L. -*lum* (*castrum*, camp)], M.: castle (fortified place; fortress, fort); engine of war; capstan; deck. **-lòtto**, *aug.* of -*lo*. **-lúccio**, *disp.* of -*lo*.
castiga.. = *gastiga*..
castigliáno [prov. *Castiglia*], ADJ.: Castilian; Castilian coin.
castiglióne† = *castelletto*.
castígo = *gastigo*.
ca-stimònia, **-stità**, F.: chastity (purity). ||**-sto** [L. -*stus*], ADJ.: CHASTE (pure).
castóne [?], M.: bezel or collet of a ring.
ca-stòrio†, M.: castoreum. ||**-stòro** [L. -*stor*], M.: castor (beaver).
castrametazióne [L. *castra*, camp, *metari*, MEASURE], F.: castrametation (art of camping).
ca-straporcèlli, **-strapòrci** [*porco*], M.: gelder. ||**-stráre** [root *kas*, cut], TR.: castrate. **-stráto**, M.: castrate (eunuch); mutton. **-stratúra**, **-strazióne**, F.: castration.
ca-strènse, ADJ.: pertaining to a camp, camp-. ||**-stro**† [L. -*strum*, camp], M.: castle.
ca-stronáccio, *disp.* of -*strone*. **-stroncèllo**, **-stroncíno**, M.: young wether; simpleton. ||**-stróne** [-*strare*], M.: wether; blockhead. **-stronería**, F.: stupidity; silly talk.
casuá-le [*caso*], ADJ.: casual (accidental). **-lità**, F.: casualty. **-lménte**, ADV.: casually (by chance).
casú-ccia [*casa*], **casú-cola**, **casúpola**, F.: small wretched house, hovel.
cata- [Gr. *katá*, down, under, mis-], PREF.: cata-: **-clísma**, pl. -*clismi* [Gr. *klúzein*, wash], **-clísmo**, M.: cataclysm. **-cómba** [Gr. *kómbe*, vault], F.: catacomb (burial vault). **-crèsi** [Gr. *chrésthai*, use], F.: catachresis. **-fálco** [?], M.: catafalque; scaffold†. **-lèssi** [Gr. -*lepsis*, 'down-taking'], **-lessía**, F.: catalepsy. **-lèttico**1, ADJ.: cataleptic. **-lèttico**2 [Gr. -*légein*, leave], ADJ.: catalectic. =**lètto**, M.: litter; bier. **-logáre** [-*go*], TR.: catalogue. **-loghíno**, M.: small catalogue. **catá-logo** [Gr. *légein*, say, count], M.: catalogue, list. **-pécchia** [?], F.: miserable hut; deserted place†. **-plásma** [Gr. *plássein*, mould], M.: cataplasm (poultice). **-púlta** [Gr. *pállein*, hurl], F.: catapult. **-rrále**, ADJ.: catarrhal. -'**rro** [Gr. *hrein*, flow], M.: catarrh. **-rróso**, ADJ.: catarrhous.
catártico [Gr. *katharós*, pure], ADJ.: cathartic(al); M.: cathartic.
catárzo [?], M.: coarse silk (used for tassels, etc.).
catá-sta [Gr. *katá-stasis*, 'down-setting'], F.: pile of wood; pile, mass; funeral pile†. **-stále**, ADJ.: pertaining to taxes, tax. **-stáre**† = *accatastare*. **catá-sto**, M.: impost (tax); tax-book.
catástrofe [Gr. -*phe* (*strephéin*, turn)], F.: catastrophe.
cataúno†, PRON.: each one.
cate-[=*cata*-]: **-chèsi** [Gr. *echéin*, sound], F.: (*theol.*) explanation of doctrine. **-chismo**, M.: catechism. **-chista**, M.: catechist. **-chístico**, ADJ.: catechistic(al). **-chizzáre**, TR.: catechise. **-císmo**† = -*chismo*. **-cúmeno**, M.: catechumen. **-goría** [Gr.], F.: category. **-goricaménte**, ADV.: categorically. **-gòrico**, ADJ.: categorical; positive.
catelàno [*Catalogna*], M.: Catalan plum.
ca-tellíno†, **-tèllo**†, M.: little dog, puppy. **-tellón**†, **-tellóne**†, ADV.: very softly. **-tellóne**, M.: rather large dog.
caté-na [L.], F.: CHAIN; ridge; key, iron band to strengthen walls. **-náccio**, M.: bolt. **-náre**† = *incatenare*. **-nèlla**, **-nína**, F.: small chain. **-nóna**, F., **-nóne**, M.: large chain. **-núzza**†, F.: small chain.

caterát-ta [Gr. *katarráktes*], F.: sluice, flood-gate; cataract (fall; eye-disease); portcullis. **-táio†**, M.: sluice-guard.

catèrva [L.], F.: troop, division of an army; contempt; crowd.

catèto [L. *-thetus*], M.: cathetus (perpendicular line).

cati-náccio, *disp.* of *-no*. **-náio**, M.: crockery or earthenware seller; potter†. **-nèlla**, F.: wash-handbasin; basinful. **-nelláta**, F.: basinful. **-nellétta**, F., **-nellíno**, M.: small handbasin. **-nétto**, M.: small basin. ‖**catí-no** [L. *-nus*, dish], M.: basin, vase (bowl).

catoneggiáre, INTR.: do as Cato.

catòrbia [?], F.: (*jest.*) prison.

ca-tòrcio [l. L. *-thucium*], M.: bolt. **-tòrzolo**, M.: knot (in wood). **-torzolúto**, ADJ.: knotty.

catragímoro†, M.: vertigo, dizziness.

catráme [Ar.], M.: tar.

catriòsso [?], M.: carcass, skeleton.

cattabríga† = *accattabrighe*.

cattáno†, M.: CAPTAIN.

cattáre†, TR.: procure, acquire.

cátte-dra [Gr. *kathédra*, seat], F.: cathedra (instructor's chair; bishop's seat); CHAIR†. **-drále**, ADJ., F.: cathedral. **-dránte**, M.: (*iron.*) professor, lecturer. **-draticaménte**, ADV.: (*iron.*) as a lecturer. **-drático**, ADJ.: (*iron.*) instructive; authoritative; M.: professor.

catti-vàccio, ADJ.: very wicked, bad. **-vággio†**, M.: captivity. **-vaménte†**, ADV.: wickedly; badly. **-vánza†**, F.: captivity; rascality. **-vanzuòla†**, F.: roguery. ‖**-váre** [l. L. *captivare*], REFL.: CAPTIVATE (charm); TR.†: imprison, subdue. **-veggiáre†**, INTR.: lead a wicked life. **-velláccio†**, M.: miserable wretch. **-vèllo**, *dim.* of *-vo*. **-vèria**, **-vería**, **-vézza**, F.: wickedness, rascality. **-vità**, F.: wickedness; idleness†; captivity†. **cattí-vo** [L. *captivus*, captive, slave], ADJ.: bad, wicked; unfortunate; M.: bad man, CAITIFF.

cátto [Gr. *káktos*], M.: (*bot.*) cactus.

cat-tolicaménte, ADV.: according to the Catholic doctrine. **-tolicísmo**, M.: Catholicism. **-tolicità**, F.: catholicity; Catholic world. ‖**-tòlico** [Gr. *katholikós*, universal], ADJ.: catholic; of the Roman Catholic faith; universal†; M.: Catholic.

cattú-ra [L. *captura*], F.: CAPTURE; arrest. **-ráre**, TR.: seize; arrest.

cau-dále [L. *-da*, tail], ADJ.: caudal. **-datário**, M.: prelate's train-bearer. **-dáto**, ADJ.: having a tail.

cáule†, M.: stem (stalk).

cáu-ça [L.], F.: cause (reason); suit (action at law; case); interest. **-çáccia**, F.: bad cause. **-çále**, ADJ.: causal. **-çalità**, F.: causality. **-çalménte**, ADV.: causally. **-çáre**, TR.: cause (occasion). **-çatóre†**, M.: author, agent. **-çídico**, M.: counsellor (advocate).

cáusti-ca, F.: caustic curve. **-cità**, F.: causticity. ‖**cáusti-co** [Gr. *-kós* (*kaíein*, burn)], ADJ.: caustic(al), burning; M.: caustic.

cau-taménte, ADV.: cautiously. ‖**-tèla** [*-to*], F.: caution; guarantee (surety). **-teláre**, INTR.: use caution; REFL.: take precautions. **-telativo**, ADJ.: cautionary.

cautè-rio [Gr. *-térion* (*kaíein*, burn)], M.: cautery. **-rizzáre**, TR.: cauterize. **-rizzazióne**, F.: cauterization.

cáu-to [L. *-tus*], ADJ.: CAUTIOUS; insured. **-zióne**, F.: guarantee (security); caution†.

cáva [*cavo* 1], F.: cave†; quarry; mine. **-dènti** [*cavare dente*], M.: dentist. **-fángo** [*cavare*], M.: dredging-machine. **caváguo**, M.: kind of basket.

ca-valcábile, ADJ.: that can be ridden. **-valcánte†**, M.: postilion. **-valcáre**, INTR.: ride horseback; TR.: ride (a horse); domineer†. **-valcáta**, F.: riding on horseback; cavalcade. **-valcatóio†**, M.: mounting-block. **-valcatóre**, M.: horseman. **-valcatúra**, F.: horse, any riding animal. **-valca=vía**, F.: covered passageway. **-valcheréscо†** = *-valleresco*. **-valciáre** = *accavalciare*. **-valcióne**, **-valcióni** = *accavalcione*. **-valeggièro†**, **-valeggièro†**, M.: light horseman. **-valieráto**, M.: knighthood. **-valière**, M.: cavalryman (horseman); knight; cavalier: — *d'industria*, sharper. **-valièri** = *-valiere*. **-valieríno**, M.: young cavalier. **-valieròtto†**, M.: great lord. **-válla**, F.: mare. **-valláccio**, *disp.* of *-vallo*. **-valláro**, M.: one in charge of a herd of horses; driver†. **-valleggièro**, **-valleggière†**, M.: light horseman. **-valleréccio†**, ADJ.: fit to be carried by horses. **-vallerescaménte**, ADV.: chivalrously. **-valleréscо**, ADJ.: chivalrous. **-vallería**, F.: cavalry; knighthood (chivalry); valour. **-vallerízza**, M.: riding-school; horsemanship. **-vallerízzo†**, M.: riding-master; esquire. **-vallétta**, F.: locust (grasshopper); fraud. **-vallétto**, M.: small horse; saw-horse; wooden frame; easel. **-vallína**, F.: filly. **-vallíno**, M.: colt; ADJ.: caballine (of a horse). ‖**-vállo** [L. *-ballus*, nag], M.: horse; knight at chess; horse-soldier; lively boy; dune†. **-vallóne**, M.: large horse; wave, billow. **-vallúccio**, M.: sorry horse: *a* —, on the shoulders, astride.

cava=lòcchio [*l'occhio*, as attacking the eyes], M.: wasp; hedge-lawyer (pettifogger); dishonest official; exactor†. **-ménto**†, M.: excavating. ||**cavá-re** [*cavo* I], TR.: dig out, raise or bring out (from anything deep), draw (water), lift up; remove, free; excavate†: — *gli occhi a*, treat badly, abuse; — *le penne maestre*, pick out the feathers; pick; — *un vizio a*, correct, reproach. =**stiváli**, M.: bootjack. =**strácci**, M.: wormscrew; gunworm. **cavá-ta**, F.: taking away, blood-letting. =**táppi**, M.: corkscrew. **-tína**, F.: cavatina, short air. **cavá-to**†, M.: cavity. **-tóre**†, M.: digger, miner. **-túra**, F.: excavation. =**turáccioli**, M.: corkscrew.

cavèlle†, F.: trifle, nothing.

caverèlla†, F.: small hole or cavity.

cavèr-na [L.], F.: cavern. **-nèlla**†, **-nétta**, F.: small cavern. **-nosità**, F.: hollowness (concavity). **-nóso**, ADJ.: cavernous, hollow. **-núzza**†, F.: small cavern. **-òzzola**, F.: very small (quarry).

cavéz-za [L. *caput*, head], F.: halter, bridle. **-záta**, F.: blow with a halter. **-zína**, F.: small halter. **-zóne**, M.: cavezon; snaffle. **-zuòla**†, F.: small halter.

caviále [fr. Turk.], M.: caviar.

ca-vícchia, F.: large peg or hook. ||**-vícchio** [L. *claviculus* (*clavis*, key)], M.: peg, hook; pile. **-vìglia**, F.: peg, hinge; ankle. **-vìglio**† = *-vicchio*. **-vigliuòlo**†, M.: small peg.

cavil-láre, INTR.: cavil; seek excuses. **-latóre**, M., **-latríce**, F.: caviller. **-lazióne**, F.: cavilling, carping. **-lità**†, F.: sophism. ||**cavíl-lo** [L. *-lum*, jest], M.: sophism (false argument). **-losaménte**, ADV.: cavillingly. **-lóso**, ADJ.: cavilling; sophistical.

ca-vità, F.: cavity. ||**cá-vo** I [L. *-vus*], ADJ.: hollow, concave; M.: hollow; mould; open needlework.

cávo 2 [? L. *capere*, take], M.: cable, hawser.

cavo-láia, F.: planting of cabbages. **-láio**, M.: cabbage field. **-l=fióre**, M.: CAULIFLOWER. **-líno**, M.: small cabbage. ||**cávo-lo** [L. *caulis*, stalk], M.: cabbage, COLE. **-lóne**, *aug.* of *-lo*.

ca-vréttо† = *-pretto*. **-vri(u)òla**† = *-priola*. **-vriuòlo**† = *-priolo*.

cazióso†, ADJ.: captious, insidious.

cázza†, F.: crucible; ladle.

cazzáre†, TR.: haul in the cable.

cazzaròla [*cazza*], F.: stewpan.

cázzica = *cappita*.

cazzòla [*cazza*], F.: trowel.

caz-zottáre, TR.: fisticuff. ||**-zòtto** [?], M.: fist; box (cuff).

cazzuòla [*cazza*], F.: trowel; scent-bottle†.

ce [*ci*], PRON.: us, to us; ADV.: here.

ce-cággine [*-co*], F.: (*contempt.*) CECITY, blindness. **-cáre**† = *accecare*.

cécca I [abbr. of *Francesca*], F.: magpie.

cécca 2 [echoic], F.: click.

céce [L. *cicer*], M.: CHICKpea; small fleshy excrescence.

cécero†, M.: swan.

cechézza†, M.: blindness.

ce-ciáto [*-ce*], ADJ.: chickpea-coloured. **-cína**, F.: young, graceful woman. **-cíno**, *dim.* of *-ce*. **-cio** = *-ce*.

ce-cità, F.: cecity, blindness; infatuation. ||**cè-co** [L. *cæcus*], ADJ.: blind; infatuated; dark; M.: blind man. **-colína**, F., **-colíno**, M.: blind young person; eel†.

ce-dènte, ADJ.: yielding, flexible. ||**cè-dere** [L., go (away); yield], (IRR.)§; INTR.: CEDE, yield; resign; TR.: give up. **-dévole** [*-dere*], ADJ.: flexible; yielding. **-devolézza**, F.: flexibility. **-diménto**, M.: yielding. **-dizióne**†, F.: cession, yielding. **-dobònis** [L. *bonus*], M.: yielding one's property.

§ Pret. reg. or (poet.) *cès-si, -se; -sero*. Part. *cedúto* or *cèsso*. (So *con-, inter-, retro-, suc-*; others only reg.)

cèdo-la [l. L. *schedula*], F.: note, bill, commission. **-lóne**, M.: big bill, placard; monitory.

cedornèlla† = *cedronella*.

ce-drángola†, F.: (*bot.*) lucern. **-dráre**†, TR.: flavour with lemon. ||**-dráto** [*-dro*], ADJ.: of lemon taste or odour; M.: cedrat.

cedriuòlo† = *cetriolo*.

cé-dro [L. *-drus*], M.: cedar; lime. **-dróne**, ADJ.: of a colour like cedar. **-dronèlla**, F.: (*bot.*) balm-mint.

cèduo [L. *cædere*, cut down], ADJ.: fit to be felled (Eng.† ceduous).

cedúto, PART. from *cedere*.

ce-falálgia [Gr. *álgos*, pain], F.: cephalalgia (headache). **-fálico**, ADJ.: cephalic. ||**cè-falo** [Gr. *kephalê*, head], M.: mullet (fish).

cef-fáre† = *acciuffare*. **-fáta**, F.: slap. **-fatóne**†, M.: severe blow. ||**cèf-fo** [L. *caput*, head], M.: muzzle, snout; ugly face. **-fonáre**, TR.: strike, slap. **-fóne**, M.: slap on the face.

cèlabro† = *cervello*.

ce-laménto, M.: concealing. ||**-láre** [L.], TR.: conCEAL, secrete. **-láta**† I, F.: ambuscade.

celáta 2 [L. *cælare*, chisel], F.: helmet.

cela-taménte [*-re*], ADV.: secretly. **-túra**†, F.: concealing.

cèle-be† = *-bre*. **-bèrrimo**, ADJ.: superl. of *-bre*. **-brábile**, ADJ.: worthy to be celebrated. **-braménto**, M.: celebration. **-bránte**, PART. of *-brare;* M.: celebrant, officiating priest. **-bráre**, TR.: praise; celebrate; perform. **-bratóre**, M.: celebrator, praiser. **-brazióne**, F.: celebration, performance. ‖**cèle-bre** [L. *-ber*], ADJ.: celebrated (famous). **-brévole**†, ADJ.: worthy of being celebrated. **-brità**, F.: celebrity; famous man (fame).

cèlebro†, M.: brain.

cèle-re [L. *celer*], ADJ.: quick (swift). **-reménte**, ADJ.: in haste; swiftly. **-rità**, F.: celerity (speed).

celè-ste [L. *cœlestis*], ADJ.: celestial; skyblue-coloured; M.: skyblue. **-stiále**, ADJ.: celestial. **-stialménte**, ADJ.: divinely. **-stíno**, ADJ.: skyblue (azure); M.: azure.

cè-lia [comedian *Celia*], F.: jest, joke. **-liáccia**, F.: bad joke. **-liáre**, INTR.: joke, banter. **-liatóre**, M., **-liatríce**, F.: joker.

celibáto, M.: celibacy. ‖**-èlibe** [L. *cœlebs*], ADJ.: celibate (unmarried); M.: celibate (bachelor).

celidònia†, F.: (*bot.*) celandine.

ce-lína [*-lia*], F.: little joke; slight trick. **-lióna**, F.: big joke. **-lióne**, ADJ.: fond of joking; M.: joker.

cèl-la [L.], F.: CELL; (*jest.*) small room; cell of a beehive; wine-cellar†. **-láio**†, M.: wine-cellar. **-leráio**†, M.: cellarer. **-létta**, F.: small cell. **-lièro**†, M.: wine-cellar; pantry. **-lína**, F.: small cell. **-lòria**†, F.: brain; head. **-lula**, F.: cellule; small cell. **-luláre**, ADJ.: cellular. **-lulóso**, ADJ.: cellular.

celo-máio†, M.: upholsterer. **celó-ne**†, M.: counterpane; carpet.

celsitúdine†, F.: celsitude, height.

cémbalo [L. *cymbalum*], M.: cymbal (harpsichord).

cembanèlla† = *cennamella*.

cémbolo, pop. for *cembalo*.

cemen-táre, TR.: cement. **-tazióne**, F.: cementation. ‖**cemén-to** [L. *cœmentum*, chip], M.: cement.

cempén-na, M., F.: (inept) person. ‖**-náre** [variant of *tentennare*], INTR.: stumble, be inept.

cèn, for *cento*.

cé-na [L. *cœna*], F.: supper. **-nácolo**, M.: supper-room; room where Christ gave the Last Supper; Last Supper (painting). **-náre**, INTR.: sup. **-náta**†, F.: supper.

cen-cerèllo†, M.: little rag. **-cería**†, F.: pile of rags. **-ciáia**, F.: heap of rags; trifle, worthless thing. **-ciáio**, M., **-ciaiòlo**, M.: ragman. **-ciáta**, F.: blow with a rag. **-cíno**, M.: small rag; very little. ‖**cén-cio** [? L. *-to*, patchwork], M.: rag (tatter); dust-rag; old dress; pl. *-ci*, dough, with eggs: *dare in -ci*, disappoint; *esser ne' suoi -ci*, be in the bloom of health and youth; *venir dal —*, loathe, disdain. **-cióso**, ADJ.: ragged, tattered.

cene-ráccio, M.: buck ashes. **-ráccíolo**, M.: bucking cloth. **-rário**† = *cinerario*. **-ráta**, F.: lye. ‖**cénere** [L. *cinis*], F.: CINDERS; ashes; (*poet.*) M., or *le -ri*: remains; *il giorno delle —*, *Le Ceneri*, Ash-Wednesday. **-ríno**, ADJ.: ash-coloured. **-rógnolo**, ADJ.: slightly ash-coloured (used in rather disp. sense). **-róne**, M.: remains of ashes in the bucking cloth. **-róso**, ADJ.: scattered over with ashes.

ce-nétta [*cena*], F.: delicious little supper. **-nína**, F.: light supper.

cennamèlla [L. *calamus*, reed], F.: pipe, wind instrument; flageolet.

cénnamo†, M.: cinnamon.

cénno [L. *cinnus*], M.: nod, sign; command.

ce-nòbio [Gr. *koinó-bios*, 'common-life'], M.: monastery. **-nobíta**, M.: monk (cenobite). **-nobítico**, ADJ.: cenobitic (monastic).

cenotáfio [Gr. *kénos*, empty, *táphos*, tomb], M.: cenotaph.

censalíto† = *cencioso*.

cen-siménto, M.: census. **-síto**, ADJ.: taxable. ‖**cèn-so** [L. *-sus* (*-sere*, value)], M.: patrimony; rent (tribute); census. **-sóre**, M.: censor (Roman magistrate; censor, of the press); critic. **-sòria**†, F.: censure. **-sòrio**, ADJ.: censorious. **-suário**, ADJ.: censual; taxable; M.: tenant (renter). **-suáto**†, ADJ.: taxed. **-súra**, F.: censorship; penance established by the sacred canons. **-surábile**, ADJ.: censurable. **-suráre**, TR.: censure, criticise. **-suratóre**, M.: censurer.

cen-táurea, F.: (*bot.*) centaury. ‖**-táuro** [Gr. *kéntauros*], M.: centaur (fabulous monster; constellation).

cen-telláre, TR.: sip. **-tellináre**, *freq.* of *-tellare*. **-tellíno**, M.: small sip: *a -tellini*, in sips. ‖**-tèllo** [*-to*], M.: small draught (sip).

cen-tenário [*-to*], ADJ.: centenary (centennial); M.: centennial. **-tèsimo**, ADJ.: hundredth; M.: centime. **-tí=grado**, ADJ.: centigrade. **-tí=grámmo**, M.: centigram. **-tí=litro**, M.: centiliter. **-tí=mano**, ADJ.: having a hundred hands. **-tí=metro**, M.: centimeter.

cèntina [Fr. *cintre*], F.: (*arch.*) mould (support) for an arch.

centináio, pl. *-naí*, *-naia* (*f.*) [*cento*], M.: hundred: *a —*, by hundreds, abundantly.

centi-náre [*-na*], TR.: arch (bend into an arch). **-natúra**, F.: arching.

cèn-to [L. *-tum*], ADJ.: HUNDRED; many;

M.: hundred; great number. **-to=gámbe** [*gamba*], M.: galleyworm. **-to=míla**, ADJ.: hundred thousand; great many. **-to=millèşimo**, ADJ.: hundred thousandth. **-tónochio**, M.: centinody, knotgrass. **-tóne**, M.: cento. **-to=novèlle** [*novella*], M.: book composed of a hundred tales.

cen-trále, ADJ.: central. **-trí=fugo** [*fugere*, flee], ADJ.: centrifugal. **-trína†**, F.: seahog. **-trí=peto** [*petere*, seek], ADJ.: centripetal. ||**cèn-tro** [L. *-trum*], M.: centre, middle.

centúmviro [L. *-vir*, 'hundred-man'], M.: centumvir.

centu-plicáre, TR.: centuplicate. ||**cèn-tu-plo** [L. *-plex*], M.: centuple, hundredfold.

centúra† = *cintura*.

cen-túria [L. (*-tum*, 100)], F.: CENTURY (a hundred; company of 100 men). **-tu-rióne**, M.: centurion.

ce-núccia [*-na*], **-núzza†**, F.: poor supper.

cep-páia, **-páta†**, F.: stump. **-patèllo**, **-perèllo**, *dim.* of *-po*. **-picóne**, M.: (*jest.*) head. ||**cép-po** [L. *cippus*], M.: trunk (stump); block: — *di Natale*, yule-log; PL.: fetters.

cé-ra [L.], F.: wax; wax-candle; face (countenance): *far buona* —, be in good health; make one welcome; — *di Spagna* = *-ralacca*. **-raiòlo**, M.: chandler. **-ra=lácca**, F.: sealing-wax.

ceramèlla† = *cennamella*.

ce-rámica [Gr. *kéramos*, earthenware], F.: ceramics. **-rámico**, ADJ.: ceramic.

ceráşa† = *ciliegia*.

cerásta [Gr. *kerástes*, horned], F.: cerastes (horned viper).

cerbáia†, F.: forest of oaks.

cer-biátto, M.: fawn. **-biattolíno**, M.: very young fawn; timid person. ||**cèr-bio†** [*-vo*], M.: stag.

cerbonèca [?], F.: very bad wine.

cerbottána [Ar.], F.: tube; ear-trumpet†: *sapere una cosa per* —, know a thing indirectly.

cér-ca, F.: search. **-ca=brighe** [*briga*], M., INVAR.: quarrelsome fellow. ||**-cáre** [L. *circare*, go about], TR.: SEARCH (seek); inquire. **-cáta**, F.: search. **-catóre**, M.: searcher; inquirer. **-catúra†**, F.: search.

cér-chia, F.: circle of walls about a city. **-chiáio**, M.: cooper. **-chiaménto†**, M.: hooping. **-chiáre**, TR.: encircle, hoop. **-chiatúra**, F.: hooping. **-chiellíno**, M.: very small circle. **-chièllo**, **-chiétto**, M.: small circle. ||**cér-chio** [*circolo*], M.: CIRCLE; hoop; small earring; ring; assemblage; garland†. **-chiolíno**, M.: small circle or hoop. **-chióne**, *aug.* of *-chio*. **cér-cine**, M.: porter's head-cushion; padded cap. **-co†** = *-chio*. **-concèllo†**, M.: cress. **-cóne**, M.: turned wine. **-cúito†** = *circuito*.

cereále [L. *-lis* (*Ceres*)], ADJ.: cereal.

cere-bèllo†, M.: cerebellum. **-brále**, ADJ.: cerebral. ||**cère-bro** [L. *-brum*], M.: cerebrum (brain).

ceremo.. = *cerimo..*

cè-reo [*-ra*], ADJ.: cereous (waxen); M.: wax-candle. **-rería**, F.: chandler's shop. **-rétta**, F.: tube of hair-wax.

cerfòglio [L. *cære-folium*], M.: CHERVIL (plant); loose lock of hair†.

ceri-mònia [L. (*cerus*, god)], F.: rite (ceremony); formality (politeness). **-moniále**, ADJ.: ceremonial; M.: ceremonial; book of ceremonies. **-monière**, M.: master of ceremonies. **-moniosaménte**, ADV.: ceremoniously. **-monióso**, ADJ.: ceremonious.

ceríno [*cera*], M.: taper, tube of hair-wax.

cerín-ta [L. *-tha*], F., **-to**, M.: honey-wort.

cèr-na†, F.: choice; worthless fellow. **-necchiáre†**, INTR.: *freq.* of *-nere*.

cer-nécchio [?], M.: disordered lock of hair. **-necchióna**, F., **-necchióne**, M.: person with disordered hair.

cèrnere†, TR.: choose; sift; discern.

cernièra [Fr. *cerne* (L. *circus*, CIRCLE)], F.: hinge.

cernitóre [*cernere*], M.: sifter.

cè-ro [L. *-reus*], M.: large wax candle. **-róna**, F.: *aug.* of *-ra*; large fat face. **-róso**, ADJ.: waxy. **-rottíno**, *dim.* of *-ro*. **-ròtto** [Gr. *kerotós*], M.: CERATE (unctuous plaster); botch-work; languid person.

cerpell..† = *scerpell..*

cerrac-chiòlo [*cerro*], M.: young bitter oak. **-chióne**, M.: large or old oak.

cerretáno [?], M.: charlatan, cheat.

cèrro [L. *cerrus*], M.: cerris (bitter oak).

certáme [L. *-men*], M.: (*poet.*) combat.

cer-taménte [*-to*], ADV.: certainly. **-taménto†** = *accertamento*. **-táno†**, ADJ.: certain.

certáre†, INTR.: fight, contend.

cer-tézza, F.: certainty; assurance. **-tificaménto**, M.: certification. **-tificáre**, TR.: assure, certify. **-tificáto**, M.: certificate. **-tificazióne†**, F.: certification. ||**cèr-to** [L. *-tus*], ADJ.: CERTAIN, assured; M.: some one; ADV.: certainly, in truth; *al* —, *di* —, *per* —, certainly.

certó-şa [Fr. *Chartreuse*, first place], F.: Carthusian monastery. **-şíno**, ADJ.: Carthusian; M.: Carthusian monk.

certúni [*certo uno*], PRON., M. PL.: some.

cerúccia, F.: *disp.* of *-ra*: unhealthy countenance.

cerú-leo [L. *cæruleus*], **cèru-lo**, ADJ.: (*poet.*) cerulean (sky-blue).

cerúme [-ra], M.: cerumen (earwax).

ce-ruṣia† = *chirurgia*. **-rúṣico** = *chirurgo*.

cerússa†, F.: ceruse, white lead.

cèrva [-vo], F.: hind.

cervel-láccio, M.: madcap. **-lággine**†, F.: caprice, freak. **-láta**, F.: sausage containing pig's brains, spices, etc. **-létto**, M.: part back of the brain: freakish person†. **-lièra**, F.: casque. **-linággine**†, F.: foolishness. **-líno**, M.: little brain; giddy person; ADJ.: freakish, harebrained. **cervèl-lo** [L. *cerebellum*], M.: brain; intellect. **-lóne**, M.: great brain; (*fig.*) obstinate fellow. **-loticaménte**, ADV.: fantastically. **-lòtico**, ADJ.: fantastic. **-lúto**, ADJ.: (*jest.*) brained. **-lúzzo**, M.: giddy person.

cer-vétta [-vo], F.: young hind. **-vettíno**, **-vétto**, M.: young stag. **cèr-via**, pop. for -va. **-viátto**, M.: fawn.

cervíce [L. *-vix*], F.: cervix, neck.

cer-vière†, M.: lynx. ‖**-vièro** [L. *-varius*], ADJ.: of the lynx, lynx-.

cer-viótto, M.: young stag. **-víno**, ADJ.: of the stag. **cèr-vio** = *-vo*. **-viòtto**, M.: rather large stag. ‖**cèr-vo** [L. *-rus*], M.: stag.

cervògia [L. *cervisia*], F.: (*jest.*) beer.

cerzio-ráre [L. *certior*, more certain], TR.: give notice (of a legal proceeding); instruct; ASCERTAIN; assure; REFL.: assure one's self. **-razióne**†, F.: notice; assurance.

ceṣá-reo [L. *Cæsar*], ADJ.: Cæsarean (imperial). **-ríṣmo**, M.: Cæsarism.

ceṣárie [L. *cæsaries*], F.: long, loose hair.

ceṣel-laménto, M.: chiseling. **-láre**, TR.: chisel, sculpture. **-latóre**, M.: worker with the chisel, sculptor. **-latúra**, F.: chisel work. **-létto**, **-líno**, M.: small chisel. ‖**ceṣèl-lo** [L. *cædere*, *cæs-*, cut], M.: chisel, graver.

cèṣio†, ADJ.: blue-eyed.

ce-ṣoiáta, F.: blow or cut with scissors. ‖**-ṣóie** [L. *cædere*, cut], F. PL.: SCISSORS. **-ṣoiétte**, F. PL. **-ṣoíne**, F. PL.: small scissors. **-ṣoióne**, F. PL.: big shears. **-ṣoiúccce**, F.: wretched little scissors.

cespicáre† = *incespicare*.

cès-pite [L. *cæspes*], M.: (*poet.*) = *cespo*. **cés-po**, M.: heap of grass, etc.; turf. **-pugliáto**†, ADJ.: made of shrubs. **-puglíétto**, M.: small shrub. **-púglio**, M.: shrub, bush. **-puglióso**, ADJ.: full of bushes.

cessagióne†, F.: cessation.

cessáme†, M.: filth; scum of the people, mob.

ces-saménto†, M.: cessation. **-sánte**, PART. of *-sare*; M.†: debtor. **-sáre** [L. *cedere*, withdraw], INTR.: CEASE; remove†; escape†. **-sazióne**, F.: cessation. **cès-si**, PRET. of *cedere*. **-sionário**, M.: one who has surrendered his effects, bankrupt. **-sióne**, F.: cession (surrender of property). ‖**cès-so** 1, PART. of *cedere*; M.: cessation.

cèsso 2 [*secesso*], M.: water-closet; excrement, dung.

cé-sta [Gr. *kístē*, 'CHEST'], F.: basket (hamper); basket carriage. **-stáio**, M.: basket-maker. **-stèlla**†, *dim.* of *-sta*. **-stellíno**, *dim.* of *-stello*. **-stèllo**, M.: small basket, fishing basket. **-stína**, *dim.* of *-sta*. **-stináre**, TR.: throw into the waste-basket. **-stíno**, M.: small basket; fishing basket; go-cart. **-stíre** = *accestire*. **cé-sto** 1, M.: bushy head, tuft of plants, etc.

cèsto 2 [L. *cæstus*], M.: cestus (gauntlet of Roman boxers); cestus-play.

cèsto 3 [L. *-tus*], M.: girdle; girdle of Venus.

ce-stóne [*-sta*], M.: big basket (hamper). **-stúto**, ADJ.: tufted; bushy.

ceṣúra [L. *cæsura* (*cædere*, cut)], F.: cæsura (pause in a verse).

cetáceo [L. *-tus*], ADJ.: cetaceous; M.: cetacean.

cétera 1 [L. *cithara*], F.: CITHERN (lyre).

cètera (e -) = *eccetera*.

cete-ratóre†, **-rísta**†, M.: cithern-player. **-rizzáre**, INTR.: play on the cithern.

cèto 1 [L. *cœtus*], M.: order (class of people).

cèto† 2, M.: whale.

cétra = *cetera*.

cetriòlo [L. *citrus*], M.: cucumber; ninny.

che 1 *-é* [L. *quem*], PRON.: who, whom; which, that; what? ADJ.: which, what; CONJ.: that; than; as: — *che* or *-chè*, whatever. **che** 2 *-è*, INTERJ.: what! (excl. of doubt, scorn, etc.), why! *—! —!* impossible! **chè** 3 *-é*, CONJ.: abbrev. of *perchè*, *poichè*, *affinchè*: because (since); in order that (that); ADV.: till (until).

che=chè *é*, PRON.: whatever. **-che=ssía**, PRON.: anything whatever.

chelídro†, M.: poisonous sea-serpent.

chelonite†, F.: toadstone.

chèn-te†, ADJ.: what(ever). **-túnque**†, ADJ.: whatever.

chepì [Fr. *képi*], M.: 'kepi' (*mil.* parade CAP).

chéppia [L. *clipea*], F.: shad fish.

chérca† = *cherica*.

chèrere†, TR.: seek, desire.

chéri-ca, F.: tonsure. **-cále**†, ADJ.:

clerical. **-cáto**, M.: clergy. **-chétto**, **-chíno**, *dim.* of *-co*. **chéri-co** [L. *clericus*, clerk], M.: CLERGYman, priest. **-cúccio**, *disp.* of *-co*. **-cúto**, ADJ.: one that wears the tonsure. **-cúzzo** = *-cuccio*. **-zía**†, F.: clergy.

chèr-mes [Ar.], M.: chermes (kind of insect used as a dye). **-misi**, M.: CRIMSON. **-misíno**, ADJ.: crimson coloured; M.: crimson.

cherú-bico, ADJ.: cherubic. ||**-rubíno** [Heb.], M.: cherub.

chèsta† = *chiesta*.

che-taménte†, ADV.: quietly; secretly. **-tánza**†, F.: quittance; calm from storm. **-táre**, TR.: quiet; REFL.: become quiet, grow calm. **-tézza**†, F.: quiet. **-tíno**, M.: quiet little fellow. ||**ché-to** [L. *quietus*], ADJ.: QUIET; silent: — —, very quietly. **-tóne**†, ADV.: very silent.

cheúnque† = *chiunque*.

chi [L. *quis*], PRON.: who, whom, whoever.

chiácchie-ra [Fr. *claque*], F.: chat (idle talk); false saying; chattering woman. **-raménto**†, M.: chat. **-ráre**, INTR.: chat (babble); mumble. **-ráta**, F.: chatting; tiresome talk. **-ratóre**, M.: chatterer. **-ríno** 1, F.: chatter (babbling). **-rína** 2, F., **-ríno**, M.: prattler (chatterbox). **-río**, M.: confused chatter (babble). **-róna**, F., **-róne**, M.: big talker; gossip. **chiacchilláre**†, INTR.: waste time in chattering.

chiá-ma, F.: calling the roll, calling off names. **-maménto**†, M.: calling; appeal. ||**-máre** [L. *clamare*, 'CLAIM'], TR.: call; call to; name; REFL.: be named. **-máta**, F.: calling; election†. **-matóre**, M.: one that calls or appeals. **-mazióne**†, F.: calling.

chiána†, F.: swamp (marsh).

chiantáre†, TR.: deceive.

chiáp-pa, F.: CAPTure (catch); acquisition (gain). ||**-páre** [L. *capere*], TR.: (*pop.*) CATCH (snatch); surprise. **chiáppola**†, F.: trifle; frivolous man. **-poláre**†, TR.: snatch; discard. **-poleríа**† = *-la*. **-políno**, M.: (*jest.*) worthless man. **chiáppo-lo**†, M.: mass of trifles.

chiá-ra, F.: white of an egg. **-raménte**, ADV.: clearly; faithfully†. **-ráre**†, TR.: make clear. **-ráta**, F.: beaten whites of eggs used for bruises, etc. **-rèllo**†, M.: wine with much water. **-rétto**, ADJ.: rather clear. **-rézza**, F.: clearness, brightness. **-rificáre**, TR.: clarify, clear. **-rificazióne**, F., **-riménto**†, M.: clarification, clearing. **-rína**†, F., **-ríno**†, M.: clarion. **-ríre**, TR.: make clear; explain. **-ríssimo**, ADJ.: most or very clear; title given to men of letters. **-ritá**, F.: clearness, splendour; explanation. **-ritóre**, M.: one who clears; explainer. **-ritúra**, F.: clarification. ||**-ro** [L. *clarus*], ADJ.: CLEAR (bright, sparkling; evident); ADV.: clearly; M.†: light. **-róre**, M.: bright light in a dark place. **-ro=scúro**, M.: (*paint.*) chiaroscuro. **-róso**†, ADJ.: (*jest.*) clear. **-ro=veggènza** [*veggenza*, sight], F.: clairvoyance.

chiassaiuòlo†, M.: trench (ditch).

chiassáta [*chiasso*], F.: noise, clatter; loud cries; jest, joke.

chiassatèllo† = *chiassolo*.

chiásso 1 [L. *classicum*, trumpet sound], M.: noise (uproar); jest.

chiás-so 2† [Ger. *gasse*], M.: alley; brothel. **-sòlo**, M.: narrow street, alley.

chias-sóne [*-so*], M.: noisy person. **-sóso**, ADJ.: noisy.

chiát-ta, F.: ferry boat. ||**-to** [dial. form of *piatto*], ADJ.: flattened, crushed.

chia-váccio [*-vo*], M.: large bolt. **-vacuòre**†, M.: gold or silver clasp. **-váio**†, **-vaiuòlo**, M.: turnkey; locksmith. **-várda**, F.: screw-bolt. **-vardáre**, TR.: bolt. **-vardétta**, *dim.* of *-varda*. **-váro**† = *-vaio*.

chiá-ve [L. *clavis* (*clau-*, CLOSE)], F.: key; tuning-key; stop-cock; (*mus.*) CLEF: *sante -vi*, pontifical coat of arms; pontifical authority.

chia-velláre, TR.: nail. **-velláta**†, F.: hurt from a nail. **-vèllo**†, M.: nail. **-verína**, F.: javelin.

chiavétta, F.: *dim.* of *-ve;* valve; key of a flute, etc.

chiá-vica [L. *clavaca* (cf. *cloaca*)], F.: common sewer, drain. **-vichétta**, **-vichína**, F.: *dim.* of *-vica*.

chia-vicína [*-ve*], **-vína**, F.: small key.

chia-vistellíno, M.: small bolt. **-vistèllo**, M.: bolt. ||**-vo**† [L. *clavus* (*clau-*, CLOSE)], M.: nail.

chiás-za [Ger. *kletz*], F.: scab. **-záto**, ADJ.: scabby.

chíc-ca [*-co*], F.: sweetmeat (confection). **-cáio**, M.: seller of sweetmeats.

chícche-ra [Sp. *jícara* (Mexic.)], F.: small cup for coffee and chocolate. **-rétta**, F.: very small cup. **-róne**, M.: large cup.

chicchessía†, PRON.: whoever.

chicchi-riáta, F.: continued crowing. ||**-richì** [echoic], M.: crowing of the cock. **-rilláre**†, INTR.: jest, trifle away one's time.

chícco [Gr. *kíkkos*, husk], M.: grain (seed).

chiè-dere [L. *quærere*, seek], IRR.§; TR.: ask (beg, reQUEST). **-diménto**†, M.: demand; petition. **-ditóre**, M., **-ditríce**, F.: petitioner.

§ Ind.: Pres. reg. or *chiéggo; -gono*. Pret. *chiési, -se; -sero*. Subj.: Pres. reg. or *chiègga*, etc. Part. *chièsto*. — Poet. forms *chièggio, -giámo, -giono; chièggia*, etc.

chièggia†, F.: precipice.
chièrere† = *chiedere*.
chiérica and deriv. = *cherica* and deriv.
chiè-ṣa [L. *ecclesia*], F.: church. **-ṣétta**, F., **-ṣettína**, *dim.* of *-sa*. **-ṣiccióla**, *disp. dim.* of *-sa*. **-ṣína**, **-ṣíno**, **-ṣòla**, *dim.* of *-sa*. **-ṣóna**, **-ṣóne**, *aug.* of *-sa* (*-sone* esp. of large, simple structure).
chiè-sta [*-dere*], F.: request, petition. **-sto**, PART. of *-dere*.
chie-ṣúccia [*-sa*], F., **-ṣúcola**, F.: small ugly church.
chilídro† = *chelidro*.
chilí-fero, ADJ.: chyliferous. **-fica-méntо**†, M.: = *-ficazione*. **-ficáre**†, INTR.: chylify, form chyle. **-ficazióne**, F.: (*med.*) chylification. ‖**chílo** [Gr. *chulós*], M.: chyle.
chi-lográmmo [Gr. *chílioi*, thousand, *gramma*, gram], M.: kilogram. **-lòlitro** [Gr. *lítra*, pound], M.: kiloliter. **-lòmetro** [Gr. *métron*, measure], M.: kilometer.
chi-mèra [Gr. *chímaira*, she-goat], F.: chimera (fabulous monster); wild fancy (illusion). **-mericaménte**, ADV.: chimerically. **-mèrico**, ADJ.: chimerical. **-meriṣṣáre**†, INTR.: indulge in wild fancies. **-meriṣṣatóre**†, M.: visionary.
chími-ca [Gr. *chumía* (*-mós*, juice)], F.: chemistry. **-caménte**, ADV.: chemically.
chími-co, ADJ.: chemical; M.: chemist.
chína 1, —*china* [*China*], F.: QUININE.
chí-na 2, F., **-naménto**†, M.: incline (slope). ‖**-náre** [L. *clinare*], TR.: INCLINE (bend); lower; bow; REFL.: bend (stoop). **-náta**†, F.: declivity. **-nataménte**†, ADV.: in curves. **-natézza**†, F.: curvity. **-natúra**†, F.: inclination.
chin-cáglie [Fr. *quincaille* (? ak. to Eng. *clink*)], F. PL.: ironware, hardware. **-caglière**, M.: ironmonger, hardware merchant. **-caglierÍa**, F.: hardware store.
chinchessía†, PRON.: whoever.
chinchína† = *chinachina*.
chinèa†, F.: ambling nag.
chiníno [*china*], M.: quinine.
chíno [*-nare*], ADJ.: bent (inclined); cast down; M.†: declivity.
chiòc-ca†, F.: blow. ‖**-cáre** [*cloc*, echoic], INTR.: crack, swing (a whip); TR.: beat, cuff.
chiocchétta†, F.: small clump or tuft.
chiòc-cia, F.: brooding hen. ‖**-ciáre** [L. *glocire*, echoic], INTR.: CLUCK. **-ciáta**, F.: brood of young chicks.
chiòcciо†, ADJ.: sick (indisposed).
chiòccio-la [L. *coclea*], F.: snail; screw-bolt†: *scala a* —, spiral staircase. **-láio**, M.: one that seeks snails. **-létta**, **-lína**, **-líno**, M., *dim.* of *-la*; twist. **-lóna**, **lóne**, M.: *aug.* of *-la*; old-style watch.

chiòcco [echoic *cloc*], M.: crack of a whip.
chio-dáia, F.: nail mould. **-daiòlo**, M.: nailmaker. **-dáme**, M.: assortment of nails. **-dáre**† = *inchiodare*. **-derÍa**, F.: forge where nails are made; assortment of nails. **-détto**, M.: small nail. ‖**chiò-do** [L. *clavus* (*claud-*, CLOSE)], M.: nail: *aver fisso il* —, be determined.
chiò-ma [L. *coma*], F.: hair; head of hair; lion's mane; leaves of trees; tail of a COMET. **-máto**, ADJ.: (*poet.*) hairy.
chiò-ṣa [Gr. *glôssa*, tongue, language], F.: GLOSS (comment); spot. **-ṣáre**, TR.: gloss, explain. **-ṣatóre**, M., **-ṣatríce**, F.: commentator, explainer.
chiòsco [Turk.], M.: kiosk (summer house); small booth.
chiò-stra† = *-stro*. **-strétto**, **-stríno**, M.: small court or garden. ‖**chiò-stro** [L. *claustrum* (*claud-*, CLOSE)], M.: CLOISTER (covered court of a convent; convent).
chiòtto [?], ADJ.: silent (taciturn, reserved).
chio-váre† = *inchiodare*. **-vatúra**† = *inchiodatura*. **-vèllo**†, **chiò-vo**† = *chiodo*.
chir- [Gr. *cheír*, hand]: **-ágra** [Gr. *ágra*, seizure)], F.: chiragra (gout in the hand). **-ágrico**†, ADJ.: chiragrical. **-ografário**, M.: creditor or debtor by virtue of a chirograph; ADJ.: chirographic(al). **-ògrafo** [Gr. *gráphein*, write], M.: chirograph (bond under one's own hand). **-ománte**†, M.: chiromancer. **-omanzía**†, F.: chiromancy (palmistry). **-urgía** [*érgon*, work], F.: SURGERY. **-urgicaménte**, ADV.: surgically. **-úrgico**, ADJ.: surgical. **-úrgo**, M.: surgeon.
chiṣciáre†, TR.: weed, hoe.
chissisía [*chi si sia*], PRON.: whosoever.
chitáre†, TR.: quit; abandon.
chitár-ra [Gr. *kithára*], F.: GUITAR. **-rína**, **-ríno**, *dim.* of *-ra*. **-rísta**, M.: guitar-player. **-róne**, *aug.* of *-ra*.
chiù [echoic], M.: horned owl.
chiucchiurláia [echoic], F.: confused chatter.
chiu-dènda, F.: enclosure; hedge. ‖**chiú-dere** [L. *claudere*], IRR.§; TR.: CLOSE (shut up; finish, stop). **-diménto**†, M.: enclosing; enclosure.

§ Pret. *chiú-si*, *-se*; *-sero*. Part. *chiúso*.

chiúnque [L. *qui-cumque*], PRON.: whosoever.
chiúr-la, F.: foolish, trifling woman. **-láre**, INTR.: hoot as the owl. ‖**-lo** [*chiù*], M.: small owl; CURLEW; bird-catching (with owls, bird-lime, etc.); simpleton.
chiú-sa, F.: enclosure; close (end of a letter, etc.). **-saménte**†, ADV.: secret-

ly. **-si**, PRET. of *-dere*. **-síno**, M.: stopper, lid, cover. ‖**-so**, PART. of *-dere*: closed; enclosed; (*fig.*) reserved; M.: enclosure. **-súra**, F.: close of schools, etc.; lock†.

ci [L. *ecce hic*, 'to here'], ADV.: here, there; PRON.: us, to us.

cià†, F., INVAR.: tea.

ciá-ba, M.: cobbler. ‖**-bátta** [?], F.: house-shoe (slipper); old shoe; jaded woman. **-battáio**† = *-battino*. **-battáta**, F.: blow with a shoe. **-battière**†, **-battíno**, M.: cobbler. **-battinúccio**, *disp.* of *-battino*.

ciácche [echoic], M.: crack, cracking sound.

ciac-cherímo, M.: insolent youth. ‖**ciácchero** [*ciacco*], M.: insolent, ill-bred person.

ciac-ciáre [*-che*], INTR.: talk without understanding; chatter. **-cíno**, M.: foolish talker, chatterer.

ciácco†, M.: hog; ADJ.: dirty, slovenly.

ciál-da [Fr. *chaude* (L. *calidus*, warm)], F.: small cake; wafer. **-donáio**, M.: wafer seller. **-dóne**, M.: cornet-formed wafer.

cialtró-na, F. [*geldrone* (aug. of *geldra*)], **-ne**, M.: slovenly, vile person; rogue. **-nería**, F.: slovenliness; vile deed.

ciam-bèlla [?], F.: round cake; roll. **-belláia**, F., **-belláio**, M.: cake-seller. **-bellétta**, **-bellína**, *dim.* of *bella*.

ciambellòtto† = *cammellotto*.

ciamber-lanáto, M.: chamberlainship. ‖**-láno** [OFr. *chamber-lain*, 'chamberling'], M.: CHAMBERLAIN.

ciambo-láre [L.* *clamulare* (*clamare*, shout)], INTR.: talk much nonsense, tell foolish stories. **-lío**, M.: foolish talker. **-lóne**, M.: foolish talker.

ciamméngola†, F.: trifle.

ciam-panèlla†, ‖**-panèlle**, F.: in *dare in -panelle*, make a slip; do foolish things. ‖**-páre**† [*zampa*], INTR.: stumble. **-picáre**, INTR.: stumble, trip. **-picóne**, M.: stumbler.

ciá-na [?], F.: ill-bred woman. **-náta**, F.: act of an ill-bred woman.

cian-cerèlla, **-cerélla**†, **-cétta**†, *dim.* of *-cia*. ‖**cián-cia** [echoic], F.: nonsensical talk (fiddlefaddle), idle story; trifle (worthless thing). **-cia=frúscole**, F. PL.: trifles (worthless things; fooleries). **-ciaménto**†, M.: prating; trifling. **-ciáre**, INTR.: tell foolish stories; prate: trifle. **-ciatóre**, M., **-ciatríce**, F.; idle talker, trifler. **-cicáre**, INTR.: stutter; drawl; eat or work slowly. **-cièro**†, ADJ.: prattling. **-ciolína**†, *dim.* of *-cia*. **-cióne**, M.: great talker or trifler; ribald. **-ciosaménte**†, ADV.: in jest. **-ciósо**†, ADJ.: prating; trifling. **-cian-gliáre**, TR.: mumble, talk indistinctly; INTR.: stammer. **-fruscáglia** = *cianciafruscole*.

ciangot-táre [? L. *singultare*, hiccup], INTR.: pronounce badly; talk as a child. **-tío**, M.: jabbering (indistinct talk).

cianína [*ciano* 2], F.: cyanin, blue colouring matter of flowers.

ciáno 1 [*-na*], M.: ill-bred man.

ciano 2 [Gr. *kúanos*, dark blue], M.: bluebottle (corn-flower).

cián-ta [? *pianta*], F.: sole (of the foot). **-tèlla**, F.: house shoe, slipper; (*jest.*) too large a shoe.

ciappe-róne†, F.: CHAPERON (hood). **-ròtto**†, M.: mantle, cloak.

ciáppo-la [Fr. *échoppe* (Ger. *schüppe*, SHOVEL)], M.: flat graver. **-létta**, *dim.* of *-la*.

ciara-mèlla†, F.: = *cennamella*; big talker, babbler. **-melláre**, INTR.: chatter; trifle.

ciár-la, F.: idle talk, gossip. ‖**-láre** [disp. of *parlare*], INTR.: chatter (prattle, gossip). **-láta**, F.: continued chatter.

ciarla-tanáta, F.: trick, deceit. **-tanería**, F.: charlatanism. **-tanésco**, ADJ.: quackish. **-tanísmo**, M.: charlatanism. ‖**-táno** [? *ciarlare*], M.: CHARLATAN (mountebank).

ciar-latóre [*-lare*], M.: prattler (big talker). **-lería**†, F.: chatter. **-lière**, **-lièro**, ADJ.: talkative, gossipy. **-lóne**, M.: babbler (big talker).

ciár-pa [? l. Ger. *schrap*, pocket], F.: SCARF; light wrap; baldric; old worn-out gown. **-páme**, M.: old clothes, pile of rags. **-páre**†, INTR.: bungle. **-pétta**, **-pettína**, F.: small light scarf. **-pière**†, **-póne**, M.: bungler.

ciasc(hed)úno [L. *quisque unus*], PRON.: each one, every one.

ci-bále†, ADJ.: pertaining to food, nutritive. **-baménto**†, M.: food, nutriment. **-báre**, TR.: nourish, feed; REFL.: eat, nourish one's self. **-bária**, F.: victuals, food in general. **-bário**, ADJ.: cibarious, pertaining to food. **-bazióne**†, F.: nourishing one's self. ‖**-bo** [L. *-bus*], M.: food (nourishment). **-bòrio**, M.: ciborium (case containing the host). **-bóso**†, ADJ.: fruitful.

cibrèo [?], M.: giblet, ragout.

cíca [L., bits, trifles], F.: a bit (the slightest thing): *non* . . . —, not a bit, nothing.

cicá-da† [L.], **-la**, F.: cicada (kind of locust); tiresome prater. **-láio**, M.: noisy place. **-laménto**†, M.: chattering. **-láre**, INTR.: chatter (babble). **-láta**, F.: babbling (tiresome talk). **-latóre**†, M.: prater. **-latòrio**†, ADJ.:

chattering. **-léccio**, M., **-leria†**, F.: chattering, hum of voices. **-lína**, F., **-líno**, M.: *dim.* of *-la;* prattler (chatterer). **-lío**, M.: chatter, confused buzz of voices. **-lóna**, F., **-lóne**, M.: gossip.
cica-trice [L. *-trix*], F.: cicatrice (scar); fraud†. **-trizzáre**, INTR.: cicatrize. **-trizzazióne**, F.: cicatrization.
cíc-ca [*cica*], F.: cigar stub. **-caiòlo**, M.: gatherer of cigar stubs.
ciccantóne†, M.: buffoon.
cicchéra† = *chicchera.*
cíc-cia [? L. *in-sicia* (root *see*, cut), minced meat], F.: (*child.* or *jest.*) meat; flesh: *far* —, slay, murder. **cic-ciolo**, M.: small bit of bacon; proud flesh in a wound. **-cióne**, M.: fat man; tumour (boil)†. **-cióso**, ADJ.: plump.
cicérbita [L. *cicer*, CHICKpea], F.: herb used in salads. **-cérchia**, F.: lathyrus sativus (sort of vegetable).
cíce-ro [L. *Cicero*], M.: pica type (in which Cicero was first printed). **-róna**, F.: learned woman. **-róne**, M.: (*fig.*) big talker, wiseacre; cicerone, guide. **-roniáno**, ADJ.: Ciceronian.
cichíno†, M.: very little.
ciciégna†, F.: small lizard.
cici-sbèa†, F.: coquette. **-sbeáre†**, INTR.: play the gallant. **-sbeáto†**, M.: gallantry. ||**-sbèo** [?], M.: cicisbeo (gallant).
cíc-lico, ADJ.: cyclic. ||**-lo** [Gr. *kúklos*, circle], M.: cycle. **-lòide**, F.: cycloid. **-lóne**, M.: cyclone, wind storm.
ciclòpe [Gr. *kúkl-ops*, 'round-EYED'], M.: Cyclop (one-eyed giant).
cicó-gna [L. *-nia*], F.: stork; beam of a bell†. **-gníno**, M.: young stork.
ci-coráceo, ADJ.: extracted from chicory; chicory-. ||**-còria** [Gr. *kíchora*], F.: chicory.
cicúta [L.], F.: cicuta, hemlock.
cieo..† = *cec..*
cièlo [L. *cælum*], M.: sky; heaven; atmosphere.
cí-fera†, F., ||**-fra** [Ar.], F.: cipher; sum (amount); device (monogram). **-fráre†**, TR.: sign with one's initials.
cí-glio, pl. *-gli* or *-glia* [L. *-lium*, eyelid], M.: eyebrow; eye, face; wink, nod; edge, embankment; grassy rampart; PL.: view. **-glionáre**, TR.: embank. **-glióne**, M.: raised edge of a ditch, embankment, bank. **-gliúto**, ADJ.: heavy-eyebrowed.
cígna [*cinghia*], F.: girth (CINGLE): *le cigne della carrozza*, springs of a coach; *esser sulle cigne*, be ill or be out of funds.
cignále, more pop. than *cinghiale.*
ci-gnáta [*-gna*], F.: blow with a girth. **-gnere†** = *cingere.*
cígno [L. *cygnus*], M.: swan; poet.
cignóne [*cigna*], M.: large girth.

cigo-laménto, M.: creaking ||**-láre** [?], INTR.: creak, rattle (as wheels). **-lío**, M.: continued creaking.
cí-golo†, **-gulo†**, ADJ.: little.
cilécca [?], F.: trick.
cilestríno† = *celestino.*
ci-liccíno†, ADJ.: of haircloth. **-liccio†**, **-licio†**, M.: haircloth.
ci-liègia [L. *cerasa*], F.: CHERRY. **-liegiáio**, M.: cherry seller. **-liègio**, M.: cherry-tree; cherry wood. **-liegióna**, *aug.* of *-liegia.*
ci-lindrétto, M.: small cylinder. **-lindricaménte**, ADV.: cylindrically. **-líndrico**, ADJ.: cylindrical. ||**-líndro** [Gr. *kúlindros*], M.: cylinder; roller.
cilízio [*Cilicia*, in Asia Minor], M.: cilice (haircloth worn by penitents); torment (torture).
cí-ma [L. *cyma*, cabbage sprout], F.: top (summit); eminence. **-máre**, TR.: shear (cloth); cut off†, lop. **-másа**, F.: (*arch.*) cyma (moulding). **-masétta**, **-masína**, *dim.* of *-masa.* **-máta**, F.: cloth-shearing. **-matóre**, M.: cloth shearer. **-matúra**, F.: cloth-shearing; shearings of cloth. **-mázio†** = *-masa.*
címba†, F.: bark, boat.
címbalo† = *cembalo†.*
cimbelláre†, INTR.: fall.
címberli [*cimbalo*]: *in* —, in high spirits (merry; tipsy).
cim-bottoláre†, INTR.: fall down. **-bòttolo†**, M.: tumble.
cimbráccola [echoic], F.: slut.
cimè-lio, **-llo** [Gr. *keimélion* (root *kei-*, lie), treasure], M.: valuable relic (antiquity).
cimen-táccio, *disp.* of *-to.* **-táre**, TR.: (*fig.*) risk, try; REFL.: prove one's self. **-tatóre**, M.: one that tries. ||**ciménto** [?], M.: risk (trial, proof). **-tóso**, ADJ.: hazardous.
cími-ce [L. *cimex*], F.: bedbug. **-ciáio**, M.: place full of bugs. **-cióne**, M.: big bug. **-cióso**, ADJ.: infested with bugs.
ci-mièro†, ||**-mièro** [*-ma*], M.: crest of a helmet.
cimíno [L. *cuminum*], M.: cumin (plant).
cími-tèrio†, ||**-tèro** [Gr. *koimetérion* (*koimân*, sleep)], M.: cemetery (churchyard); silent place.
ci-mólo [*-ma*], M.: head of greens. **-mósa**, F.: selvage of cloth.
cimúrro [Gr. *kumórrhous*], M.: glanders.
cina-brése, ADJ.: cinnabarine; M.: cinnabar. ||**ciná-bro** [Gr. *kinnábari*], M.: cinnabar, vermillion.
cín-cia [echoic], **-ciallégra**, F.: titmouse.
cin-cíglio†, M.: belt. **-cínno†**, M.: ringlet, lock of hair.

cin-cischiáre [?], TR.: hack (slash); mumble; INTR.: dawdle. **-císchio†**, M.: hacking; shred. **-cischióne**, M.: dawdler.

cinematògrafo [Gr. *kinetós*, movable, *grápheín*, write], M.: kinetoscope.

cine-rário [L. *-rarius*], ADJ.: cinerary. **-rízio†**, ADJ.: ash-coloured.

cingallégra = *cinciallegra*.

cin-gere [L.], IRR.§; TR.: gird; surround, enclose. **cín-ghia** [L. *-gulum*], F.: girth, CINGLE.

§ Pret. *cin-si, -se; -sero.* Part. *cinto.*

cinghiále [L. *singularis*, lone], M.: wild boar.

cin-ghiáre†, TR.: gird; enclose. **-ghiatúra†**, F.: girding. **cín-ghio†**, M.: circle. ‖**cín-golo** [L. *-gulum*], M.: girdle, belt; CINCture.

cinguet-táre [ak. to *ciangottare*], INTR.: lisp; mumble (mutter); chirp. **-tatóre**, M.: lisper; mumbler. **-toría**, F.: lisping; mumbling; chit-chat. **-tièra**, F., **-tière**, M.: lisper; chatterer.

cini-caménte, ADV.: cynically. ‖**cínico** [Gr. *kun-ikós*, dog-like], ADJ.: cynical; M.: cynic.

cinígia [L. *cinisia*], F.: CINDER (ember).

cinígl̤ia [Fr. *chenille*], F.: chenille.

ciníşmo [*cinico*], M.: cynicism.

cinná-mo†, **-mòmo** [Gr. *-mòmon*], M.: cinnamon.

cino†, M.: kind of plum.

cino-glòssa [Gr. *kúon*, dog, *glossa*, tongue], F.: hound's-tongue (plant). **-şúra†**, F.: (*astr.*) cynosure (in Little Bear).

cin-quánta, ADJ.: fifty. **-quantèşimo**, ADJ.: fiftieth. **-quantína**, F.: about fifty. ‖**-que** [L. *quinque*], ADJ.: FIVE. **-quecentísta**, ADJ.: belonging to the sixteenth century; M.: person of the sixteenth century. **-que=cènto**, ADJ.: five hundred; M.: *il* —, sixteenth century. **-que=fògl̤ie** [*foglia*], M.: cinquefoil (plant). **-que=míla**, ADJ.: five thousand. **-quènnio†**, M.: space of five years. **-que=rème**, F.: quinquereme. **-quína**, F.: five (at dice). **-quíno**, M.: five-cent coin.

cín-si, PRET. of *-gere*. **-ta**, F.: enclosure, circumference; girdle†. **-tíno**, M.: priest's tunic. ‖**-to** [*-gere*], PART., ADJ.: girded; M.: girdle, cincture. **cín-tola**, F.: waist; girdle. **-tolíno**, *dim.* of *-tolo*. **cín-tolo**, M.: string; garter, band; list of cloth. **-túra**, F.: cincture; sash. **-turétta**, *dim.* of *-tura*. **-turíno**; M.: small cincture; narrow belt. **-turóne**, M.: leather belt.

ciò [L. *ecce hoc*, 'lo this'], PRON.: this, that.

ciòcca [Ger. *schock*, bunch], F.: bunch (of flowers, etc.), tuft.

ciocchè -é [*ciò che*], PRON.: that which.

ciocchét-ta, **-tína**, F.: small bunch or tuft. ‖**ciòcco** [Ger. *schock*, bunch], M.: stump, log of wood; (*fig.*) blockhead.

cioccо-láta [Sp. *chocolate* (ak. to *caccaos*)], F.: chocolate. **-latière**, M.: chocolate maker or seller. **-latíno**, M.: piece or square of chocolate. **-látte†**, M.: chocolate. **-lattièra**, F., **-lattièro**, M.: chocolate-pot.

cioc-colína [*-ca*], F.: small bunch or tuft. **-cúto†**, ADJ.: tufted, having clusters.

cioè [*ciò è*], ADV.: that is, namely.

ciom-pería†, F.: stupid trick. ‖**ciómpo** [?], M.: wool carder; simpleton.

cioncáre† 1 = *troncare*.

cioncá-re 2 [?], INTR.: tipple. **-tóre**, M.: tippler.

cióncо [*cioncare* 1], ADJ.: maimed (mutilated); cut off†.

ciondo-laménto†, M.: swinging. ‖**-láre** [L. *ex undulare*], INTR.: dangle (swing); loiter about; trifle. **-líno**, M.: small pendant or ear-ring. **cióndo-lo**, M.: dangling thing; pendant; ear-ring. **-lóne**, M.: procrastinator; lounger: *a -loni*, dangling.

ciónno†, ADJ.: worthless.

ciónta†, F.: blow, beating.

ciòppa [?], F.: (*jest.*) kind of petticoat.

ciòto-la [?], F.: cup or bowl; contents of a cup. **-lótta**, **-lettína**, F.: small cup. **-lóna**, F., **-lóne**, M.: large bowl.

ciottáre†, TR.: frustrate.

ciòtto†, M.: pebble; cripple; ADJ.: lame. **-láre**, TR.: pave; throw stones†. **-láta**, F.: blow with a stone. **-láto**, M.: paved road. **-létto**, M.: small stone. ‖**ciòttolo** [?], M.: pebble (flintstone). **-lóne**, M.: large stone.

ciovétta† = *civetta*.

ci-pigl̤iáccio, M.: severe frown. ‖**-pígl̤io** [L. *super-cilium*, eyebrow], M.: frown. **-pigl̤ióso**, ADJ.: frowning, angry.

cipól-la [L. *cæpulla*], F.: onion; (*jest.*) head; large watch; bulb; gizzard of fowls. **-láio**, M.: onion-field; onion seller. **-láta†**, F.: ragout of onions; mixture. **-láto**, ADJ.: knotty (said of wood). **-latúra**, F.: knottiness. **-lótta**, **-lína**, *dim.* of *-la*. **-líno**, M.: little onion; veined marble. **-lóna**, *aug.* of *-la*.

cipòrro†, M.: crab.

cíppo [L. *cippus*], M.: cippus (half-column for marking something).

ci-pressáia, F., **-presséto**, M.: plantation of cypress trees. **-prèsso**, M.: cypress; cypress wood. **-pressóne**, M.: large cypress tree. **cí-pria**, F.: face-powder. **-prígna**, ADJ.: Cyprian; F.: Venus, Cyprian goddess. **cí-prio** = *-pria*. ‖**cí-pro** [*Cipro*, Cyprus], M.: Cyprus wine.

cirágra† = *chiragra*.

círca [L.], ADV.: about; around; PREP.: concerning.

cir-cènsi, ADJ.: circensian (of the Roman Circus). ‖**-co** [L. *-cus*, circle], M.: circus. **-coláre¹**, ADJ.: circular: *lettera* —, circular. **-coláre²**, INTR.: circulate; argue†, dispute. **-colarménte**, ADV.: circularly. **-colatòrio†**, ADJ.: circulatory. **-colazióne**, F.: circulation. **-colétto**, M.: small circle. **cír-colo**, M.: circle; circuit; club.

circon- [L. *circum*, around]: **-cídere** [L. *cædere*, cut], IRR. (cf. *decidere*); TR.: CIRCUMCISE. **-cidiménto†**, M.: circumcision. =**cingere**, IRR.; TR.: gird. **-císi**, PRET. of *-cidere*. **-cisióne**, F.: circumcision. **-císo**, PART. of *-cidere*. **-daménto†**, M.: surrounding. =**dáre**, TR.: surround, enclose. **-dário**, M.: boundary, district. **-dazióne†**, F.: surrounding. =**dúrre**, IRR.; TR.: lead around. **-ferènza** [L. *ferre*, bring], F.: circumference. **-flèsso** [L. *flexus*, bent], ADJ.: bent; M.: circumflex accent. =**flèttere**, IRR.; TR.: twist around; circumflex. =**fóndere†**, IRR.; TR.: circumfuse, pour around. **-fúso**, PART., ADJ.: scattered. =**locuzióne** [L. *circum-locutio*], F.: circumlocution. **-scr. .†**, **-sp. .†**, **-st. .†** = *circo-scr.* ., etc. **-valláre** [L. *vallum*, wall], TR.: circumvallate. **-vallazióne**, F.: circumvallation. =**veníre**, IRR.; TR.: circumvent. **-venzióne†**, F.: circumvention. =**vicíno**, ADJ.: neighbouring, adjacent. **-voluzióne†**, F.: circumvolution.

circo- [*circon-*]: **-scritto**, PART. of *-scrivere*. =**scrívere** [L. *circum-scribere*], IRR.; TR.: circumscribe, restrict. **-scrizióne**, F.: circumscription, bounding. **-spettaménte**, ADV.: circumspectly. **-spètto** [L. *specere*, look], ADJ.: circumspect. **-spezióne**, F.: circumspection. =**stánte**, ADJ.: circumstant, surrounding; M.: bystander. **-stánza**, F.: circumstance, particularity. **-stanziáre**, TR.: circumstantiate. **-stanziataménte**, ADV.: circumstantially.

cir-cuíre [L. *circum-ire*], TR.: surround, enclose; go around†. **-cúito**, M.: circuit, extent. **-cuizióne†**, F.: circuition; circuit.

círcula. . = *circola*. .

ci-regéto†, M.: cherry orchard. **-riègio†** = *ciliegio*. **-riegiuòlo†**, ADJ.: cherry-coloured.

cirimòni. . = *cerimoni*. .

cirindóne†, M.: present.

círro†, M.: ringlet.

ciságlio†, M.: ridge, landmark.

ciscrán-na [*arci-*, *scranna*], F.: armchair; old furniture. **-'no†**, M.: bookshelf.

císio [L. *-sium*], M.: two-wheeled carriage

císma† = *scisma*.

ciséi. . = *cesoi*. .

cí-spa [?], F.: blearedness; rheum (from the eyes). **-spárdo†** = *-sposo*. **-spellíno**, ADJ.: blear-eyed. **-spositá**, F.: blearedness. **-spóso**, ADJ.: blear-eyed; rheumy.

císte, pl. *-sti* or *-stidi* [Gr. *kústis*, bag], F.: cyst.

cistercènse [L. *Cistercium*, where founded], ADJ.: Cistercian; M.: Cistercian monk.

cistèr-na [L.], F.: cistern. **-nétta**, F.: small tank. **-nóne**, M.: large cistern or reservoir.

cístico [*ciste*], ADJ.: cystic. **-fèllea**, F.: gall-bladder.

cístio†, M.: rock rose.

citábile [*citare*], ADJ.: citable.

cítara† [L. *cithara*], F.: cithera (kind of lute).

citáre [L.], TR.: CITE (summon; quote).

cita-rèdico, ADJ.: citharistic (of the cithern). ‖**-rèdo** [*-re*], M.: cithara or cithern-player. **-reggiáre†**, INTR.: play upon the cithara. **-rísta** = *-redo*. **-rizzáre** = *-reggiare*.

cita-tóre [*-re*], M.: citer. **-tòria†**, F.: summons, writ. **-zióne**, F.: summons, citation; quoting.

cítera† = *citara*.

citerióre [L. *citerior*], ADJ.: on this side (hither).

citèrna†, F.: cistern.

cítiso [L. *cytisus*], M.: cytisus (a shrub, heath).

citrággine†, F.: balm-mint.

ci-tráto [L. *-trus*, citron-tree], M.: citrate. **cí-trico**, ADJ.: citric. **-trinézza†**, F.: yellow. **-tríno†**, ADJ.: citrine. **-trí(u)òlo†**, M.: cucumber.

ci-trullággine, F.: stupidity. ‖**-trúllo** [L. *-trus*, disp. of L. *-trus*, citron (cf. Fr. *citrouille*, pumpkin)], M.: simpleton, dunce; fop; ADJ.: stupid.

cítta†, F.: girl.

città [L. *civitas*], F.: CITY (town). **-dèlla**, F.: citadel. **-détta**, *dim.* of *-tà*. **-dína**, F.: citizen's wife. **-dináme**, M.: crowd of citizens, mob. **-dinaménte†**, ADV.: as a citizen, civilly. **-dinánza**, F.: citizens; citizenship. **-dináre†**, TR.: people a city. **-dinático†**, M.: right of citizenship. **-dinèllo**, M.: young citizen. **-dinescaménte**, ADV.: like a citizen. **-dinésco**, ADJ.: of a citizen or a city. **-díno**, ADJ.: of a citizen, civic; M.: citizen. **-dóne**, M.: large city. **-dúccia**, F.: ugly town.

c-ítto†, M.: boy. **-íttola†**, F.: little girl. **-íttolo†**, M.: little boy.

ciú-co, M.: ass. **-cággine**, F.: obstinacy. **-cáio**, M.: ass-driver. **-carèllo**, *dim.* of *-co*. **-cherèllo** = *-chetto*. **-cheria**, F.: obstinacy. **-chésco**, ADJ.: stupid, obstinate. **-chétto**, *dim.* of *-co*. ‖**-co** [?], M.: ass; dunce.

ciuf-fágno†, ADJ.: griping, snatching. **-fáre**, TR.: snatch by the hair; grasp, seize. **-fétto**, M.: small tuft of hair. ‖**-fo** [Ger. *schopf*], M.: tuft of hair, forelock, toupee; mane; tuft. **-fóna**, F., **-fóne**, M.: bushy hair; person with bushy hair.

ciúffolo†, F. PL.: trifles, nonsense.

ciúlla† = *fanciulla*.

ciúr-ma [? (Gr. *kéleusma*, oarsmen's song)], F.: ship's crew; crowd. **-madóre**† = *-matore*. **-máglia**, F.: rabble, mob. **-máre**, TR.: cheat, deceive; charm†. **-matóre**, M.: cheat, wizzard. **-meria**, F.: trick; charm.

ciúschero†, ADJ.: tipsy.

ci-váia [L. *-baria*, food], F.: all kinds of pulse. **-vaiòlo**, M.: seller of pulse, rice, etc.

civán-za† = *-zo*. **-záre**†, TR.: provide; advance, procure. **civán-zo** [? *avanza*], M.: advantage, benefit.

cíve†, M.: citizen.

civèa†, F.: osier sledge.

civét-ta [Fr. *chouette* (ak. to Eng. *caw*)], F.: owl; coquette: *far la* —, hunt with the owl; allure. **-táre**, INTR.: hunt with the owl; play the coquette. **-teria**, F.: coquetry. **-tína**, *dim.* of *-ta*. **-tíno**, M.: young owl; dandy†, fop. **-tòla**, F.: coquettish girl. **-tóne**, M.: absurd fop.

cívi-co [L. *-cus*], ADJ.: civic. **-'le**, ADJ.: civil; courteous; civilized; M.: register. **-lísta**†, M.: jurisconsult. **-lità**† = *-lta*. **-lizzáre**, TR.: civilize. **-lizzatóre**, M.: civilizer. **-lizzazióne**, F.: civilization. **-lménte**, ADV.: civilly. **-ltà**, F.: civilization; civility, politeness.

civíre†, TR.: procure, supply.

civòrio† = *ciborio*.

cláde†, F.: slaughter.

clamazióne†, F.: invocation.

clámide [L. *chlamys*], F.: chlamys (kind of cloak).

clamó-re [L. *clamor*], M.: clamour. **-rosaménte**, ADV.: clamorously. **-róso**, ADJ.: clamorous.

clandes-tinaménte, ADV.: clandestinely. ‖**-tíno** [L. *-tinus*], ADJ.: clandestine (secret).

clangóre†, M.: clangor, sound of trumpets.

cla-réttot†, M.: claret. **-rificáre** = *chiarificare*.

cla-rinettísta, M.: player on the clarinet. **-rinétto**, M.: clarinet: clarinet-player. ‖**-ríno** [L. *-rus*, clear], M.: clarinet.

clá-ro† = *chiaro*. **-róre**† = *chiarore*.

clás-se [L. *-sis*], F.: class (order, grade). **-sicaménte**, ADV.: classically. **-sicísmo**, M.: classicalism. **-sicísta**, M.: classicist. **clás-sico**, ADJ.: classical. **-sificábile**, ADJ.: classifiable. **-sificáre**, TR.: classify. **-sificazióne**, F.: classification.

cláuso-la [L. *clausula* (*claudere*, 'close')], F.: clause. **-létta**, *dim.*

clau-stràle, ADJ.: claustral; retired. ‖**cláu-stro**† [L. *-strum* (*-dere*, CLOSE)], M.: CLOISTER.

cláusula† = *clausola*.

clausúra [L. (*claudere*, 'close')], F.: enclosure, cloister.

cláva [L.], F.: Hercules' club; mace, club.

clavi- [L. *-s*, key]: **-cémbalo**, M.: harpsichord. **claví-cola**, F.: clavicle. **-còrd(i)o**, M.: clavichord.

clemátide [L. *-tis*], F.: clematis (plant).

cle-mènte [L. *-mens*], ADJ.: clement (mild). **-menteménte**, ADV.: mildly. **-mentíssimo**, ADJ.: superl. of *-mente*. **-mènza**, **-mènzia**†, F.: clemency.

cleri-cále, ADJ.: clerical. **-cáto**, M.: clergy. ‖**clèro** [Gr. *klêros*, lot; election], M.: clergy.

clèssidra [Gr. *kleps-údra* 'hide-water'], F.: clepsydra (water-clock).

cliè̀n-te [L. *cliens*], M.: client; adherent. **-tèla**, F.: clientship; clientele. **clièntolo**†, **-tulo**†, M.: client (dependent).

clí-ma [Gr. *klíma*, inCLINE], M.: climate. **-matèrico**, ADJ.: climacteric. **clímato**†, M.: climate. **-matología**, F.: climatology.

clíni-ca, F.: clinic. **-caménte**, ADV.: clinically. ‖**clíni-co** [Gr. *klíne*, bed], ADJ.: clinical.

cli-peáto, ADJ.: armed with a shield. ‖**clí-peo** [L. *-peus*], M.: shield.

clistère [Gr. *klúdzein*, wash out], M.: clyster.

clívo [L. *clivus*], M.: (*poet.*) declivity, hillock; ADJ.†: sloping.

clízia [Gr. *klínein*, incline], F.: sunflower.

cloáca [L.], F.: sewer.

clo-ráto, ADJ.: chloric. ‖**clò-ro** [Gr. *klorós*, yellowish green], M.: chlorine. **-rofòrmio**, M.: chloroform.

club [Eng.], M.: club, association.

co', for *con i*, with the.

coabi-táre [*con abitare*], INTR.: cohabit. **-tatóre**†, M.: cohabitant. **-tazióne**, F.: cohabitation.

coadesióne [*con adesione*], F.: cohesion.

coadiu-toráto, M.: coadjutorship. **-tóre**, M.: coadjutor. **-toría**, F.: coadjutorship. ‖**-váre** [L. (*juvare*, help)], TR.: AID, assist.

coaduná-re [L. (*unus*, ONE)], TR.: UNITE, collect, gather up. **-nazióne**†, F.: coadunation.

coá-golo† = *caglio.* **-gulábile,** ADJ.: coagulable. **-gulaménto†,** M.: coagulation. ||**-guláre** [L.], TR.: coagulate. **-gulatívo,** ADJ.: coagulative. **-gulazióne,** F.: coagulation, curdling. **coágulo†,** M.: coagulum; rennet.
coar-táre [L.], TR.: force, compel. **-tazióne,** F.: forcing.
co=attívo, ADJ.: coactive, restraining. ||**=átto** [L. *-actus* (*cogere,* force)], ADJ.: forced. **-azióne,** F.: coaction, force.
cobálto [Ger. *kobalt*], M.: cobalt.
còcca [?], F.: corner or tip (of a handkerchief, apron, etc.); tip or end (of a spindle, where the end is fastened); peak (of a mountain)†; notch of an arrow; arrow†; bowstring†; cockboat†.
coccárda [Fr. *cocarde* (*coq,* cock; cock's crest)], F.: COCKADE.
coccáro, TR.: = *accoccare;* jeer.
coccerèllo [*-ccio*], M.: small shard, fragment.
coc-chiáta [*-chio*], F.: carriage-drive; serenade (orig. in a coach). **-chière,** M.: coachman (esp. of private persons).
cocchína†, F.: country-dance.
còc-chio [? Gr. *kóchlos,* 'cockle'], M.: COACH. **-chióne,** M.: large coach. **-chiumáre,** TR.: bung; quiz (banter). **-chiúme,** M.: bung, bung-hole.
còccia [?], F.: hilt; (*jest.*) head; swelling†; pimple.
coccinìglia [Gr. *kókkos,* berry], F.: coccus; cochineal.
coc-cíno, *dim.* of *-cio.* ||**còc-cio** [?], M.: shard (potsherd). **-ci(u)òla,** F.: swelling; bite of a gnat.
cocciu-tággine [*coccia,* head], F.: stubbornness. **cocciú-to,** ADJ.: stubborn.
còcco 1 = *coccarda* and *cucco.*
còcco 2 [Gr. *kókkos,* kernel], M.: cocoa (palm or nut); cochineal†; egg†.
coccodè [echoic], M.: cackling.
coccodrillo [Gr. *krokódeilos*], M.: crocodile.
còcco-la [Gr. *kókkos,* berry], F.: berry; (*jest.*) head. **-lársi,** INTR.: enjoy one's self. **-létta, -lettína,** F.: small berry. **-lína†,** ADJ.: in *tosse* —, whooping-cough. **-líno,** M.: plump child. **còcco-lo,** M.: enjoying one's self; fat boy. **-lóne,** M.: apoplectic stroke. **-lóni,** ADV.: squatting.
coccovég-gia†, F.: coquette. **-giáre†,** INTR.: coquet.
co-centeménte, ADV.: hotly, sharply. **-cènte,** ADJ.: burning (hot). ||**cò-cere** [L. *-quere*], IRR.§; TR.: COOK; (*fig.*) displease, grieve.

§ Pres. *c(u)ò-cio, -ci, -ce; cociámo,* etc. (*cuòc-* or *còc-* accented, *coc-* unaccented). Pret. *còs-si, -se; -sero.* Part. *còtto* (rarely *cocinto,* 'grieved').

cochíglia†, F.: shell.
co-ciménto, M.: heat; scalding; coction, digestion. ||**-cióre** [*-cere*], M.: burning pain, smart. **-citóio†,** ADJ.: easily cooked. **-citúra,** F.: cooking, decoction. **-ciúto** for the ordinary *cotto,* PART. of *-cere;* (*fig.*) grieved, displeased.
coclearia†, F.: scurvy grass.
còco [L. *coquus* (*-quere* 'cook')], M.: COOK.
cocòlla [l. L. *cuculla*], F.: COWL, hood.
co-comeráio, M.: watermelon patch; watermelon seller. **-comeríno,** M.: small watermelon. ||**-cómero** [pop. form of *cucurbita,* gourd], M.: watermelon; secret hard to keep: *non saper tenere un — all' erta,* be unable to keep a secret. **-comeróne,** M.: large watermelon. **-cúzza** [pop. for *cucurbita*], F.: (*jest.*) head. **-cúzzo†, -cúzzolo,** M.: crown of the head; summit, top.
có-da [L. *cauda*], F.: tail; end; file; train. **-dardaménte,** ADV.: basely. **-dardía,** F.: cowardice. **-dárdo,** ADJ.: COWARDly, base; M.: coward. **-dáto,** ADJ.: tailed. **-dázzo,** M.: train (attendants). **-deáre†,** TR.: follow, dog.
codésto [L. *eccu-tibi-iste*], PRON.: that, this.
co-détta [*-da*], F.: little tail. **-diáre†,** TR.: follow at one's heels, spy. **-diatóre†,** M.: spy.
cò-dice [L. *-dex* (orig. trunk, tablet of wood)], M.: code, codex; ancient manuscript: — *della lingua,* dictionary. **-dicilláre,** ADJ.: codicillary. **-dicíllo,** M.: codicil; addition to a writing. **-dificazióne,** F.: codification.
codi- [*coda*]: **=lúngo,** M.: tomtit. **=mózzo†,** ADJ.: docked, clipped. **codí-na,** F.: little tail. **codí-no,** M.: stumpy tail; braid, coil of hair. **codí-nzolo,** M.: very little tail. **-óne,** M.: rump of birds. **=rósso,** M.: redstart, redtail.
codognáto† = *cotognato.*
co-dóne [*-da*], M.: large tail. **-drióne,** M.: rump of birds. **-dúto†** = *codato.*
co=eguále, ADJ.: coequal.
co=erède, M.: co-heir.
co-erènte [L. *co-hærens* (*hærere,* stick)], ADJ.: coherent. **-erenteménte,** ADV.: coherently. **-erènza,** F.: coherence. **-esióne,** F.: cohesion.
co=esístere, INTR.: coexist. **-esistènza,** F.: coexistence.
coetáneo [L. *co-ætaneus* (*ætas,* AGE)], ADJ.: coetaneous (contemporaneous).
co=etèrno, ADJ.: coeternal.
coèvo [L. *co-ævus* (*ævum,* age)], ADJ.: coeval.
cofác-cia†, F.: pie. **-cína†,** F.: small pie.
cofa-náio†, M.: cabinet-maker. **-nétto,** M.: small coffer or basket. ||**còfa-no**

[L. *cophinus*, basket], M.: COFFER, cabinet; basket†.
còffa†, F.: (*nav.*) small basket (for biscuit).
cogita-bóndo, ADJ.: cogitabund, thoughtful. ||**cogitá-re**† [L.], INTR.: cogitate. **-tíva**, F.: cogitative faculty; thought. **-tívo**†, ADJ.: musing. **-zióne**†, F.: cogitation; contemplation.
cógli, for *con gli*, with the.
cóglia [Gr. *koleón*, sheath], F.: (*anat.*) scrotum; (*fam.*) coxcomb, fop: *in* —, well dressed; in good order (fine).
cògliere [L. *col-ligere*], IRR.§; TR.: COLLECT (CULL, gather); strike; catch; comprehend.

§ Ind.: Pres. *còlgo, cògli, còglie; cogliámo* or *colghiámo, cogliéte, còlgono.* Pret. *còl-si, -se; -sero.* Fut. Cond. reg. or *cor-rò; -rèi.* Subj.: Pres. *còlga.* Part. *còlto.*—Poet. forms: *còglio*, etc.; *còglia*, etc.

còglio† = *collo.*
coglióne [*-glia*], M.: testicle.
cogli-tóre [*cogliere*], M.: gatherer. **-túra**, F.: gathering, collecting.
cognná-ta, F.: sister-in-law. ||**cognná-to** [L. *cognatus*, "with-born," cognate], M.: brother-in-law; ADJ.†: cognate (kindred). **-zióne**, F.: cognation (kindred).
cògni-to [L. *-tus*, (*g*)*noscere*, KNOW], ADJ.: KNOWN. **-tóre**†, M.: one who knows, discerner. **-zionèlla**, *dim.* of *-zione.* **-zióne**, F.: cognition; knowledge; PL.: intelligence, instruction.
còguo [L. *congius*], M.: congius (liquid measure).
cognó-me [L. *-men*], M.: cognomen (surname). **-mináre**, TR.: surname; REFL.: take a surname. **-minazióne**†, F.: cognomen.
cognosce..† = *conosce*..
cogoláría†, F.: sweep-net.
còi, for *con i*, with the.
coi-áio [*coio*], M.: leather seller. **-áme**, M.: quantity of leather. **-áro**† = *coiaio.* **-áttolo**, M.: leather-scrap. **-étto**†, M.: leather jerkin.
co-incidènte, PART., ADJ.: coincident. **-incidènza**, F.: coincidence. ||=**incídere**, IRR.; INTR.: coincide.
còio [L. *corium*], M.: hide (skin); leather.
còito [L. *-itus* (*ire*, go)], M.: coition.
coitóso†, ADJ.: thoughtful.
col for *con il*, *collo* (*con lo*), with the.
cóla [L. *-lum*], F.: colander (strainer).
colà [L. *eccu-illac*, 'lo-there'], ADV.: there.
cola=brèdo, M.: soup-strainer.
colafizzáre†, TR.: cuff; vex, irritate.
colag-giù†, **-giúso**†, ADV.: below, down there.
cola-ménto†, M.: colation, straining; thing strained. ||**colá-re** [L.], TR.: percolate (strain); sift; melt: — *a fondo*, sink (a ship).
colascióne [?], M.: Italian lute.
colassù†, ADV.: up there.
cola-tíccio, M.: strainings; dregs, residue. **-tío**†, ADJ.: perishable. **-tívo**†, ADJ.: strainable; dissolving. ||**colá-to**, PART. of *-re*; M.†: percolation, colature. **-tóio**, M.: strainer, filter. **-túra**, F.: straining (colature, filtration).
colazio-náccia, *disp.* of *-ne.* **-ncèlla**, **-ncína**, *dim.* of *-ne.* **colazió-ne** [*collezione*], F.: collation, breakfast. **-nétta**, *dim.* of *-ne.* **-núccia**, *disp.* of *-ne.*
colcáre†, TR.: lay down; INTR.: set (said of the sun).
colèi [*f.* of *-lui*], PRON.: (*disp.*) she, that one.
colendíssimo [*colere*], ADJ.: most worshipful.
colèra [? Gr. *cholé*, bile], F.: cholera.
còlere†, DEFECT.§; TR.: venerate, worship.

§ Pres. *cò-li, -le.* Part. *cólto* or *cúlto.*

colezióne† = *colazione.*
colibéto†, M.: equivocal talk; gossip.
co-librì or **-líbri** [Carib.], M.: humming-bird.
còlica [L. *-cus* (Gr. *kólon*, colon)], F.: colic. **còlico**, ADJ.: colic, affecting the bowels.
coliséo = *colosseo.*
colizióne = *colazione.*
còlla 1 [Gr. *kólla*], F.: GLUE; cord† (used in torture); torture†.
cólla 2, for *con la*, with the.
collaborá-re [L.], INTR.: collaborate, coöperate. **-tóre**, M., **-tríce**, F.: collaborator, fellow-worker. **-zióne**, F.: collaboration.
collacrimáre†, INTR.: weep with.
collá-na [*collo*], F.: necklace; collection (of cognate literary works). **-nèlla**, *dim.* of *-na.* **-nóne**, *augm.* of *-na.* **-núccia**, *disp.* of *-na.* **-re** 1, M.: yoke, collar (for animals); collar.
colláre 2, TR.: torture; lower with a rope; raise up.
colla-rétto [*-na*], **-ríno**, M.: small collar; collar band.
colláta†, F.: blow on the neck; accolade.
col=laterále, ADJ.: collateral (indirect); M.: collateral relative.
collatóre†, M.: collator, patron.
collattáneo†, M.: foster-brother.
colla-zionáre, TR.: collate, compare. ||**-zióne** [L. *col-latio*, bringing together], F.: collation (presentation of a benefice); contribution†; conference†; comparing†.
cólle 1, for *con le*, with the.
còlle 2 [L. *collis*], M.: little hill; mound.
collèga [L. (*legare*, choose)], M.: colleague (associate); league†.
colle-gaménto, M.: joining. **-gánza**,

F.: joining; alliance†. ‖**-gáre** [L. *colligare*], TR.: join (unite); REFL.: alLY or LEAGUE one's self. **-gáto**, ADJ.: allied; M.: ally. **-gatóre**, M.: uniter. **-gazióne**†, F.: joining; alliance.
colle-giále, ADJ.: collegial; M.: collegian. **-gialménte**, ADV.: in common. **-giáre**†, INTR.: consult. **-giáta**, F.: collegiate church. **-giáto**, ADJ.: collegiate. ‖**collè-gio** [L. *-gium* (*-ga*, colleague)], M.: college; society (assembly).
colleppoláre†, INTR.: shake; dance for joy.
còl-lera [Gr. *cholé*, bile], F.: choler (anger); cholera†. **-lericaménte**, ADV.: angrily. **-lèrico**, ADJ.: choleric (irritable). **-leróso**† = *-lerico*.
collèt-ta [L. *collecta* (*legere*, gather)], F.: collection; contribution; collect. **-táre**, TR.: collect. **-tivaménte**, ADV.: collectively. **-tívo**, ADJ.: collective. **-tízio**, ADJ.: collected; picked up.
collétto [*colle*], M.: hillock.
colle-ttóre [*-tta*], M.: collector; compiler. **-ttoría**†, F.: collectorship. **-zioncèlla**, **-zioncína**, F.: small collection. **-zióne**, F.: collection (mass); impost†.
collicáre = *coricare*.
collicèllo 1 [*collo*], M.: little neck.
colli-cèllo 2 [*colle*], M.: little hill. **-giáno**, ADJ.: inhabiting hills.
collimáre [L. *limus*, oblique], INTR.: have a common aim, agree; harmonize.
collí-na [*colle*], F.: hill. **-nétta**, F., **nétto**†, M.: hillock.
collíno [*collo*], M.: little neck.
colliquá-re†, TR.: dissolve, melt. **-zióne**†, F.: colliquation.
collírio [Gr. *kollúrion*], M.: collyrium, eye-water.
collisióne [L. *collisio* (*lædere*, strike)], F.: collision.
cóllo 1, for *con lo*, with the.
còllo 2 [L. *-llum*], M.: neck; mountain-top†.
còllo 3 [Eng. *coil*], M.: large package or bundle.
collo-cábile, ADJ.: collocatable. **-caménto**, M.: collocation (placing). ‖**-cáre** [L. (*locus*, place)], TR.: collocate; place. **-cazióne**, F.: collocation.
collocuzióne†, F.: collocution (parley).
collòdio [Gr. *kollódes*, like glue], M.: collodion.
collòquio [L. *-loquium* (*loqui*, speak)], M.: colloquy (conference).
col-losità, F.: stickiness. ‖**-lóso** [*-la* 1], ADJ.: gluey (sticky).
collo=tòrto, M.: hypocrite. **collò-ttola**, F.: nape of the neck.
collu-sióne [L. *col-ludere*, play with], F.: collusion. **-sívo**, ADJ.: collusive.
collúvie [L. *col-luere*, wash, together], F.: mass, heap (of filth); throng.
col-máre, TR.: fill up, heap up. **-máta**, F.: filling up; embankment. **-matúra**, F.: overfulness. **-mígno**†, M.: covering, projecting. **-mígnolo**†, M.: ridge, top. ‖**cól-mo** [L. *-umen*], M.: top (summit, CULMEN); height, culmination; ADJ.: overflowing; overloaded; convex.
cólo = *cola*.
colofònia†, F.: colophony; resin.
colóm-ba, F.: pigeon (dove). **-bàccio**, M.: ringdove, wood-pigeon. **-báia**, F., **-báio**†, M.: dove-cote. **-báno**, M.: sweet white grape. **-bára**†, F.: dove-cote. **-bário**, M.: columbarium. **-bèlla**, F.: young pigeon. **-bína**, F.: young pigeon; pigeon's dung. **-bíno**, ADJ.: columbine: *sasso -bino*, *pietra -bina*, limestone. ‖**colómbo** [L. *columbus*], M.: pigeon.
còlon [Gr. *kólon*], M.: (*anat.*) colon.
colò-nia [L. (*colere*, cultivate)], F.: colony. **-niále**, ADJ.: colonial. **-nizzáre**, TR.: colonize.
colón-na [L. *columna*], F.: column (pillar); division of a page; support (stay). **-náto**, M.: colonnade. **-nèlla**, F. (*jest.*): colonel's wife. **-nèllo**, M.: *dim.* of *-na*; COLONEL. **-nétta**, F.: small pillar. **-níno**, M.: small column; gallery or balustrade pillar.
colòno [L. *-lonus* (*-lere*, cultivate)], M.: planter (colonist).
colo-ráccio, *disp.* of *-re*. **-raménto**†, M.: colour. **-ráre**, TR.: colour, tinge; disguise; REFL.†: paint, rouge. **-rataménte**, ADV.: with pretence, speciously. **-ráto**, PART.: coloured; specious, feigned. ‖**coló-re** [L. *-r*], M.: colour; pretence; appearance. **-rétto**, **-rettíno**, M.: slight colour, tint. **-ríre**, TR.: colour. **-rísta**, M.: colourist, painter. **-ríto**, PART.: coloured; M.: colouring, complexion. **-ritóre**, M.: colourist.
colóro, PL. of *colei* and *colui*.
colo-róno [*-re*], M.: deep, bright colour. **-rúccio**, M.: bad colour; pallor.
colos-sále, ADJ.: colossal. **-sèo**, M.: Roman Coliseum. ‖**colòs-so** [Gr. *kolossós*], M.: colossus, giant.
cól-pa [L. *culpa*], F.: fault (guilt); sin: *chiamarsi in* —, own one's guilt. **-pábile**†, ADJ.: culpable. **-páre**†, TR.: inculpate, blame; INTR.: be faulty.
col-peggiáre†, INTR.: beat, strike. **-pettíno**, M.: slight blow, slap. ‖**-pétto** [*-po*], M.: light blow.
colpévo-le [*colpa*], ADJ.: culpable. **-lézza**, F.: culpability. **-líssimo**, ADJ.: superl. of *-le*: most guilty. **-lménte**, ADV.: culpably.
col-píre, TR.: hit, beat, strike. **-pitóre**,

M.: beater. ||**cól-po** [Gr. *kólaphos*, cuff], M.: blow (stroke): — *di fucile*, gunshot; — *di mare*, big wave, breaker.
colpóso [*colpa*], ADJ.: culpable, offensive.
còl-si, PRET. of *cogliere*. **còl-ta** 1 [*cogliere*], F.: collecting, gathering; harvest, crop; harvest-time; collection†; mill-dam†; impost†.
còl-ta 2 [? for *-pita* (*-pire*), blow], in *di* —, suddenly: *far* —†, hit.
coltáre† = *coltivare*.
coltèl-la, F.: big knife (carving-knife, butcher's knife, hunting-knife). **-láccio**, M.: *disp.* of *-la*; (*nav.*) studding sail. **-láme**, M.: quantity of knives. **-láta**, F.: cut, stab. **-létto**, *dim.* of *-lo*. **-lièra**, F.: knife-box, sheath. **-lína**, *dim.* of *-la*. **-lináio**, M.: cutler. ||**coltèl-lo**, pl. *-li* or *-la* [L. *cultellus* (*culter*, colter)], M.: knife; poniard† (dagger); severe criticism: — *a molla*, clasp-knife; — *da tavola*, table-knife; *per* —, edgewise. **-lóne**, *aug.* of *-lo*.
colti-vábile, ADJ.: cultivable, tillable. **-vabilità**, F.: being cultivable. **-vaménto**, M.: culture; veneration. ||**-váre** [l. L. (L. *colere*)], TR.: till, cultivate. **-váto**, PART., ADJ.: cultivated; M.: cultivated land. **-vatóre**, M.: cultivator (tiller). **-vatríce**, F.: encourager. **-vatúra**†, **-vazióne**, F.: cultivation. **coltívo**†, ADJ.: cultivable; cultivated.
cólto 1, PART. of *coltivare*: cultivated; M.: cultivated land†; worship†.
còlto 2, PART. of *cogliere*: gathered.
coltóre†, M.: cultivator.
coltráre [*coltro*], TR.: plough.
cól-tre [L. *culcitra*, mattress], F.: pall; coverlet†. **-tríce**†, F.: feather-bed, mattress: F.† of *-tore*. **-tricèlla**, **-tricétta**, F.: small pall; small coverlet†. **-tricióna**†, F.: large mattress or feather-bed.
cóltro [L. *culter*], M.: colter.
col-troncíno, M.: light quilt. ||**-tróne** [*-tre*], M.: quilt.
coltúra [*cultura*], F.: cultivation; culture; veneration†.
colu-brína, F.: CULVERIN (long cannon, 16th Cent.). ||**colú-bro** [L. *-ber*], M.: (*poet.*) serpent.
colúi [l. L. **eccu-illui*, 'lo-that'], PRON.: that one.
columbária†, F.: vervain (plant).
com- [L. *cum*, with], PREF.: com-.
còma 1 [Gr. *koimân*, put to sleep], F.: coma.
còma† 2, F.: head of hair.
còma† 3, F.: comma.
co=mádre†, F.: godmother.
coman-daménto, M.: command. **-dánte**, M.: military commander. ||**-dáre** [*mandare*], TR.: command. **-dáta**†, F.: royal command. **-datívo**†, ADJ.: commanding. **-datóre**†, M.: commander. **-dígia**†, F.: recommendation. **comándo**, M.: command.
comáre [*comadre*], F.: godmother.
comá-re†, TR.: deceive. **-tóre**†, M.: deceiver.
comatóso [*coma* 1], ADJ.: comatose.
com-baciaménto, M.: joining together; junction. ||=**baciáre**, INTR.: join together; TR.: fit together (cause to join); REFL.†: kiss each other. **-bagiaménto**† = *-baciamento*.
combat-tènte, PART.: fighting; M.: combatant. ||**combát-tere** [*battere*], INTR.: fight (COMBAT); resist; TR.: contend against. **-timénto**, M.: battle. **-titóre**, M.: combatant. **-titríce**†, F.: virago.
com-biatáre†, TR.: dismiss. **-biáto**†, M.: dismission.
combi-naménto†, M.: combination. ||**-náre** [l. L. (L. *binus*, two and two)], TR.: combine (unite). **-natóre**, M.: combiner. **-nazióne**, F.: combination; happy chance.
com=bríccola, F.: conventicle; assemblage, noisy crowd.
combú-rere [? L. *co-amb-urere* ('burn')], TR.: burn. **-stíbile**, ADJ.: combustible; M.: combustible. **-stibilità**, F.: combustibility. **-stióne**, F.: combustion; scalding. **combú-sto**, ADJ.: burned.
combútta [? *buttare*], F.: crowd, confusion.
cóme [L. *quo-modo*, in what manner], ADV.: as (like); how (in what manner); because (why); when. =**c(c)hè**† *-é*, CONJ.: although, notwithstanding.
coment. . = *comment. .*
comé-ta [L. (Gr. *kóme*, hair)], F.: comet. **-tário**†, ADJ.: cometary.
comiáto = *commiato*.
còmi-ca, F.: art of gesturing; comédienne. **-caménte**, ADV.: comically. ||**còmi-co** [L. *-cus* (Gr. *kômos*, revel)], ADJ.: comical (ludicrous); M.: comic actor.
comígnolo [*colmignolo*], M.: ridge (of a roof); ridge-pole; top of a rick.
comin-ciaménto, M.: commencement. ||**-ciáre** [L. *cum*, *initiare*, begin], TR.: commence (begin). **-ciáto**†, M.: beginning. **-ciatóre**†, M.: founder. **comíncio**†, M.: commencement.
comíno†, M.: cumin (plant or seed).
comitánte†, PART.: accompanying.
comi-táto, M.: junta, commission; assembly. **-tíva**, F.: party. **-ziále**, ADJ.: comitial. ||**comí-zio** [L. *-tium* (*ire*, go)], M.: comitia, assembly.
còmma [L. (Gr. *kop-*, cut)], F.: comma;

head (paragraph); (*mus.*) comma (small interval).
commacoláre†, TR.: stain.
commè-dia [L. *comœdia*], F.: comedy. **-diáio**†, M.: (*disp.*) comedy-writer. **-diánte**, M., F.: comedian, comédienne. **-diáre**†, INTR.: write comedies. **-diétta**, **-dína**, *dim.* of *-dia*. **-diògrafo** [Gr. *gráphein*, write], M.: comedy-writer. **-diòla**, F.: short comedy. **-dióna**, F., **-dióne**, M.: long comedy. **-diúccia**, *disp.* of *-dia*.
commemo-rábile, ADJ.: commemorable. **-raménto**†, M.: commemoration. ‖**-ráre** [L.], TR.: commemorate (celebrate). **-ratívo**, ADJ.: commemorative. **-razióne**, F.: commemoration; memorial.
commèn-da, F.: benefice, revenue (from some order). **-dábile**, ADJ.: commendable. **-dabilménte**†, ADV.: commendably. **-daménto**†, M.: praise. ‖**-dáre** [L.], TR.: commend; recommend†. **-datário**, M.: commendator. **-datízia**, F.: letter of recommendation; recommendation. **-datízio**, ADJ.: recommendatory. **-datóre**, M.: commander; elder (in an order). **-dazióne**†, F.: commendation. **-dévole**, ADJ.: commendable. **-devolménte**, ADV.: commendably.
commensále [*con mensa*], M., F.: table-companion.
commensu-rábile, ADJ.: commensurable. **-rabilità**, F.: commensurability. ‖**-ráre**† [L.], TR.: commensurate; adjust.
commen-táre [L. explain (*mens*, mind)], TR.: comment; annotate. **-tariétto**, M.: brief commentary. **-tário**, M.: commentary. **-tatóre**, M.: commentator.
commén-to, M.: comment, annotation.
commer-ciábile, ADJ.: that can be traded. **-ciále**, ADJ.: commercial. **-cialménte**, ADV.: commercially. **-ciánte**, M.: trader. **-ciáre**, INTR.: trade, carry on business; TR.: sell. ‖**commèr-cio** [L. *-cium*], M.: commerce, business; affair; intercourse. **commèr-zio**† = *-cio*.
com-méssa†, F.: commission, order. **-messária**†, F.: commissaryship. **-messário**†, M.: commissary.
commessazióne†, F.: orgy, debauch.
com-messióne†, F.: commission. ‖**-mésso** [*-mettere*], PART.: committed; M.: employee; commissioner; fellow-boarder†: *lavoro di* —, mosaic, inlaid work. **-messúra**, F.: commissure (joint).
commo-stíbile [L. *comestus* (*edere*, EAT)], M. (us'ly pl.): comestible (food); ADJ.: eatable. **-stióne**, F.: fast-day food (allowed by the church); mixture†.
-m-mettènte†, M.: committer, one who [...]es an order. ‖**=méttere**, IRR.; TR.: join, unite; entrust, commit; perpetrate. **-metti=mále**, M.: mischief-maker; slanderer. **-mettitóre**, M.: committer, employer. **-mettitúra**, F.: joining.
commiáto [L. *com-meatus* (*meare*, go)], M.: leave, permission; furlough†; dismissal†: *prender* —, take leave, bid farewell.
commilitóne [*con milite*], M.: fellow-soldier.
commi-náre [L. *-nari*], TR.: MENACE (threaten). **-natòria**, F.: threat; prohibition. **-natòrio**, ADJ.: comminatory. **-nazióne**, F.: commination, menace.
commischia. . = *mischia*. .
commiṣe-rándo, ADV.: pitiable. ‖**-ráre** [L. *-rari*], TR.: commiserate (pity). **-razióne**, F.: commiseration. **-révole**†, ADJ.: miserable.
commí-ṣi, PRET. of *commettere*.
commis-sariáto, M.: commissaryship. ‖**-sário** [*commettere*], M.: commissary; commissioner, trustee. **-sionário**, M.: agent, broker. **-sióne**, F.: commission, charge.
com-mistióne†, F.: mixture. ‖**=místo**, ADJ.: mixed.
com-miṣúra†, F.: proportion (fitness). ‖**=miṣuráre**, TR.: commensurate (regulate).
committènte, PART. of *commettere*.
còmmodo† = *comodo*.
commoránte†, ADJ.: dwelling, residing.
com-mòsso, PART.: moved. **-mòto**† = *-mosso*. ‖**=mòvere**, IRR.; TR.: move (affect, touch); agitate (disturb); REFL.: be affected. **-moviménto**†, M.: disturbance. **-movitóre**, M.: mover, exciter. **-mozióne**, F.: commotion, perturbation.
communíre†, TR.: strengthen, fortify.
commuòvere† = *commovere*.
commu-tábile, ADJ.: commutable. **-taménto**†, M.: commutation. ‖**-táre** [L. (*mutare*, change)], TR.: commute (exchange). **-tatívo**†, ADJ.: commutative. **-tazióne**, F.: commutation.
como-daménte, ADV.: commodiously; without effort. **-dáre**, TR.: accommodate; adjust (fit); lend. **-dáto**†, M.: gratuitous loan. **-datóre**†, M.: lender. **-devolménte**†, ADV.: conveniently. **-dézza**† = *-dità*. **-díno**, M.: commode (chest of drawers). **-dità**, F.: convenience; opportunity. ‖**còmo-do** [L. *-dus* (*modus*, mode)], ADJ.: commodious; proper; easy, comfortable; M.: commodity; convenience, leisure: *esser* —, be well off. **-dóne**, M.: easy-going person.
compadróne†, M.: joint proprietor.
com=paeṣána, F., **paeṣáno**, M.: compatriot (fellow-countrywoman, -man).

compa-ginàre†, TR.: hold together, unite. ||**compá-gine** [L. *compages* (*pangere*, fasten)], F.: compages (joined structure, contexture).

compá-gna, F.: female companion; company†. *-gnáccio*, M.: bad companion. *-gnésco*†, ADJ.: companionable; of a companion. *-gnévole*, ADJ.: companionable, sociable. *-gnevolménte*, ADV.: companionably. *-gnía*, F.: company, society; association; brotherhood; company of soldiers. *-gníno*, M.: dear little companion. *-gniúccia*, *disp. dim.* of *-gnia*. ||**compá-gno** [l. L. *-nio*], M.: companion (associate; partner; fellow-worker); ADJ.: like, equal. *-gnóne*, M.: boon companion. *-gnúccia*, *-gnúccio*, *car. dim.* of *-gna* and *-gno*.

companáti-ca†, F., **-co** [*con pane*], M.: any food eaten with bread.

comparábile [*comparare*], ADJ.: comparable.

comparággio† = *comparatico*.

compa-ragióne†, F.: comparison. ||**-ráre** [L.], TR.: compare; REFL.: compare one's self.

comparático [*compare*], M.: standing godfather.

compara-tivaménte, ADV.: comparatively. ||**-tívo** [*-re*], ADJ.: comparative; M.: (*gram.*) comparative. **-zióne**, F.: comparison.

compáre [*con padre*], M.: godfather (sponsor); companion.

com-parigióne†, F.: appearance. **-parìi**, PRET. of *-parire*. ||**-paríre** [L. *-parere*], IRR. (cf. *apparire*); INTR.: appear, show one's self; appear in court. **-parigcènza**†, F.: appearance. **-parigcióne**†, F.: comparison. **-paríta**, F.: appearance; outside show. **-parizióne**, F.: appearance in court; court-summons.

comparóne [*-pare*], M.: (*jest.*) large godfather.

com-pársa [*-parire*], F.: appearance, show; PL.: silent characters (in a play). **-párso**, PART. of *-parire*.

com=partecipáre, INTR.: participate with another. **-partecipazióne**, F.: participating with. **-partécipe**, M.: participator, sharer.

com-partiménto, M.: division, compartment. ||**=partíre**, TR.: divide (compart); impart; grant. **-partitóre**, M.: divider.

compárvi, PRET. of *comparire*.

compáscuo†, M.: pasture.

compas-sáre [*-so*], TR.: measure with the compass; weigh (consider).

com-passionaménto†, M.: compassion. **-passionáre**, TR.: compassionate, pity. **-passionatóre**, M.: compassionate person. ||**=passióne**, F.: compassion (pity). **-passionévole**, ADJ.: merciful; piteous, miserable. **-passionevolménte**, ADV.: pitifully. **-passívo**†, ADJ.: compassionate, merciful.

com=pásso, M.: compass; compartment†: *a* —, measuredly; *parlare col* —, speak in measured terms.

compatí-bile, ADJ.: worthy of pardon; compatible. **-bilità**, F.: compatibility. **-bilménte**, ADV.: compatibly. **-ménto**, M.: indulgence, pardon. ||**compatíre** [*patire*], TR.: excuse; pity.

com=patriòtta, M., F., **=patriòtto**, M.: compatriot.

com=patròno, M.: patron saint; patron of a benefice.

com-pattézza, F.: compactness. ||**-pátto** 1 [L. *-pactum* (*pingere*, fix)], ADJ.: compact, dense, solid; (*typ.*) solid (unleaded); M.†: compactness.

compátto† 2, M.: compact, covenant.

compazienteménte†, ADV.: patiently.

compen-diáre, TR.: shorten, epitomize. **-diatóre**, M.: abridger. ||**compèndio** [L. *-dium*], M.: compendium (epitome). **-diosaménte**, ADV.: compendiously. **-diosità**, F.: compendiousness. **-dióso**, ADJ.: compendious.

compen-sábile, ADJ.: that may be compensated. **-sagióne**† = *-sazione*. **-saménto**†, M.: recompense. ||**-sáre** [L.], TR.: compensate (recompense). **-satívo**, ADJ.: compensatory. **-satóre**, M.: compensator. **-sazióne**, F.: compensation.

compèn-so, M.: compensation.

cómpera.. = *compra*..

compe-tènte, PART., ADJ.: competent. **-tenteménte**, ADV.: competently. **-tentíssimo**, ADJ.: most competent. **-tènza**, F.: competency: *stare a* —, compete. ||**compè-tere** [L. (*petere*, seek)], INTR.: compete; dispute; belong to (concern); be convenient†. **-titóre**, M.: competitor.

compia-cènte, ADJ.: complaisant, amiable. **-centíssimo**, ADJ.: superl. of *-cente*. **-cènza**, F.: complaisance; complacency. ||**-céro** [*piacere*], IRR.; INTR.: PLEASE (satisfy); REFL.: take pleasure in; be pleased (condescend). **-cévole**†, ADJ.: complaisant; delightful. **-ciménto**, M.: pleasure; condescension; approbation. **compiá-cqui**, PRET. of *-cere*. **-ciúto**, PART. of *-cere*.

com=piángere, IRR.; TR.: pity; bewail. **-piánsi**, PRET. **-piánto**, PART.: pitied; M.: lamentation.

com=piegáre, TR.: fold together, enclose.

com-piéi, PRET. of *-pire*. ||**cóm-piere** = *-pire*. **-pièta**, F.: complin (last canonical hour). **-piì**, PRET. of *-pire*.

compigliáre†, TR.: understand; REFL.: coagulate.

compíglio†, M.: beehive.

compila-ménto†, M.: compilation. ‖**compilá-re** [L. (*pilare*, plunder)], TR.: compile (collect). **-tóre**, M., **-tríce**, F.: compiler. **-lazióne**, F.: compilation.

com-piménto, M.: completion, perfection. ‖**-píre** [L. *com-plere*, FILL], IRR.§; TR.: COMPLETE, ACCOMPLISH. **-pitaménte**, ADV.: completely; politely.

§ Ind.: Pres. *cóm-pio* or *-pìsco*. Ipf. *com-piva* or *-plìva*. Subj.: Pres. *cóm-pia* or *-pìsca*. Impf. *com-pissi* or *-pìssi*. I've *cóm-pi* or *-pìsci*. Ger. *compièndo*. Part. *com-pito* or *-pìsito*.

compi-táre [variant of *computare*], INTR.: spell; TR.†: compute. **-tazióne**, F.: spelling.

com-pitézza [*-pire*], F.: completion†; politeness. **-pitíssimo**, ADJ.: superl. of *-pito* 1. **-píto** 1, PART. of *-pire*: completed; accomplished (polite).

cómpito 2 [variant of *computo*], M.: task; account†: *a* —, scantily, barely.

com-pitóre, M.: finisher. **-piutaménte**, ADV.: completely. ‖**-piáto**, PART. of *-pire*.

complacènza† = *compiacenza*.

comple=ánno, M.: birth-day; ANNIVersary. **-ménto** [L. *-mentum* (*plere*, FILL)], M.: complement.

comples-sionáto, ADJ.: complexioned. **-sióne**, F.: complexion; constitution. **-sità**, F.: complexity. **-sivaménte**, ADV.: complexly. **-sívo**, ADJ.: together (generally). ‖**complès-so** [L. *com-plexus* (*plectere*, twist)], ADJ.: complex; strong; M.: mass, generality: *in* —, in general.

comple-táre, TR.: complete. **-tívo**, ADJ.: completive. ‖**complè-to** [L. *-tus* (*plere*, FILL)], ADJ.: complete, entire. **-tòrio**, ADJ.: complementary.

compli-cáre [L. (*plicare*, fold)], TR.: complicate; REFL.: become complicated. **-cazióne**, F.: complication.

cómpli-ce [L. *com plectere*, twist], ADJ.: participating; M.: accomplice. **-cità**, F.: complicity.

compli-mentáre, TR.: compliment. **-mentário**, ADJ.: complimentary; M.: complimenter (envoy). **-mentíno**, M.: delicate compliment. ‖**-ménto** [*complemento*], M.: compliment (courtesy). **-mentosaménte**, ADV.: in a complimentary manner. **-mentóso**, ADJ.: complimentary; M.: flatterer. **complí-re**†, TR.: fulfil; complete.

compluvio [L. *-rium*], M.: (*arch.*) compluvium (opening for 'rain' in Rom. buildings).

com-ponènte, PART.: composing, forming; M.: component, ingredient. ‖**-pónere**, pop. for *-porre*. **-poniménto**, M.: composition; modesty†. **-ponitóre**†, M., **-ponitríce**†, F.: author; (*mus.*) composer. =**pórre**, IRR.; TR.: COMPOUND (COMPOSE); form (arrange); conciliate†; REFL.: be composed.

compor-tábile, ADJ.: supportable. **-tabilménte**, ADV.: supportably. ‖**-táre** [L. (*portare*, carry)], TR.: bear (endure, tolerate, Eng. comport†); permit (allow); REFL.: conduct one's self; contain one's self. **-tevolménte**†, ADV.: sufficiently. **compòr-to**, M.: days of grace.

compósi, PRET. of *comporre*.

compòsi-to [L. *-tus* (*ponere*, put)], ADJ.: (*arch.*) composite. **-tóio**, M.: printer's composing-stick. **-tóre**, M.: composer; compositor. **-túra**†, F.: composition. **-zioncèlla**, **-zioncína**, F.: little composition. **-zióne**, F.: composing; composition; agreement; component parts. **-zionúccia**, F.: poor composition.

com=possessióne, F., =**possèsso**, M.: joint possession. =**possessóre**, M.: joint possessor.

compó-sta, F.: compote. **-staménte**, ADV.: composedly. **-stézza**, F.: composure. ‖**compó-sto** [*-rre*], PART.: composed (mixed); sedate (serious); artificial; M.: composition (mixture).

cómpra, F., **-ménto**†, M.: purchase. ‖**comprá-re** [L. *com-parare*, procure], TR.: buy (purchase). **-tóre**, M.: purchaser.

compren-dènza†, F.: comprehension. ‖**comprèn-dere** [*com-*, *p*. .], IRR.; TR.: COMPRISE (contain); comprehend (understand). **-díbile**†, ADJ.: comprehensible. **-diménto**, M.: comprehension; district†. **-ditívo**†, ADJ.: comprehensive. **-ditóre**, M.: he that comprehends. **-dònio**, M.: (*jest.*) understanding. **-síbile**, ADJ.: comprehensible. **-sióne**, F.: comprehension. **-síva**, F.: understanding, intelligence. **-sivaménte**, ADV.: comprehensibly. **-sívo**, ADJ.: comprehensive.

com-prési, PRET., **-préso**, PART. of *-prendere*.

com-prèssa, F.: compress. **-prèssi**, PRET. of *-primere*. **-pressióne**, F.: compression. **-prèsso**, PART. of *-primere*. **-primènte**, PART., ADJ.: compressing. ‖**-prímere** [L.], IRR.§; TR.: COMPRESS; repress.

§ Pret. *comprès-si*, *-se*; *-sero*. Part. *compresso*.

cómpro, pop. for *comprato*.

comprobáre† = *comprovare*.

compro-mésso, PART., ADJ.: compromised; M.: compromise (arbitration). **-mettènte**, PART., ADJ.: compromising.

[com]mèttere [*pro-mettere*], IRR.; TR.: compromise, endanger; REFL.: compromise one's self. **-mísi**, PRET. of *-mettere*. **-missário**, M.: arbitrator; referee. **-mittènte**, PART., ADJ.: compromising.

com=proprietà, F.: joint proprietorship. **=proprietário**, M.: joint proprietor.

compro-vábile, ADJ.: approvable. **-vaménto†**, M.: approbation. ‖**-váre** [L. *-bare*], TR.: approve (accept). **-vatóre**, M.: approver. **-vazióne†**, F.: approbation, attest.

compugn.. = *compung..*

compulsáre†, TR.: compel (summon to court).

com=púngere, IRR.; TR.: prick hard; afflict, grieve. **-púnsi**, PRET. of *pungere*. **-puntaménto**, ADV.: with compunction. **-puntívo**, ADJ.: touching, compunctious. **-púnto**, PART.: grieved, repentant. **-punzióne**, F.: compunction (remorse).

compu-tábile, ADJ.: computable. ‖**-táre** [L. (*putare*, reckon)], TR.: compute, calculate. **-tísta**, M.: computer (accountant). **-tistería**, F.: accountantship. **-tístico**, ADJ.: of an accountant. **còmpu-to**, M.: computation: — *ecclesiastico*, church calendar.

comú-na† = *-ne* (*f.*). ‖**-nále** [*-ne*], ADJ.: common (public); common† (ordinary). **-nalménte†**, ADV.: in common. **-nalità**, F.: community. **-nánza**, F.: community (participation); society. **-nárdo**, M.: communist.

comúnche† = *comunque*.

comú-ne [L. *communis*], ADJ.: COMMON (general; ordinary); M.: majority; general public; F.: community, town. **-nèlla**, F.: community†; common cause (in *far* —, combine, connive). **-nèllo**, M.: small community. **-neménte**, ADV.: generally. **-nicábile**, ADJ.: communicable; affable†. **-nicabilità**, F.: communicability. **-nicándo**, ADJ.: communicating; M.: communicant (for the first time). **-nicáre**, TR.: communicate; REFL.: receive the communion (commune); INTR.: have intercourse. **-nicatíva**, F.: faculty in imparting one's thoughts. **-nicatívo**, ADJ.: communicable. **-nicazióne**, F.: communication; communion†. **-nichíno†**, M.: host (consecrated wafer). **-nióne**, F.: communion, participation; sacrament. **-nísmo**, M.: communism. **-nísta**, M.: communist. **-nità**, F.: community. **-natívo**, more us'ly *-nale*. **-náne†** = *-ne*.

común-que [L. *quomodo*, how, *utcumque*, soever], **-queménte**, ADV.: in whatever manner; however.

con [L. *-cum*], PREP.: with; against: — *ciò sia che* = *conciossiachè*.

conáto [L. *-nari*, attempt], M.: attempt, endeavour.

cón-ca [L. *-cha*, conch], F.: washing-vessel, basin, tub; tubful; low place, valley; shell†. **-cáio**, M.: tub maker or seller.

con=cámbio, M.: exchange; recompense.

concamerâre†, TR.: (*arch*) concamerate.

concáta [*-ca*], F.: tubful.

concate-naménto, M.: concatenation. ‖**-náre** [*catena*], TR.: concatenate (link together). **-natúra**, **-nazióne**, F.: concatenation, chain.

con=cáusa, F.: concause, joint cause.

conca-vità, F.: concavity. ‖**cònca-vo** [L. *-vus* (*cavus*, hollow)], ADJ.: concave; M.: concavity.

concè-dere [*con-*, *e..*], IRR.; TR.: concede (grant; admit). **-díbile**, ADJ.: admissible. **-diménto**, M.: concession. **-ditóre**, M.: granter. **-dúto**, PART.

concènto [L. *-tus* (*com-canere*, sing)], M.: harmony (concert).

concen-traménto, M.: concentration. ‖**-tráre** [*centro*], TR.: concentrate; INTR.: meet in a centre. **-trazióne**, F.: concentration. **-tricaménte**, ADV.: concentrically. **concèn-trico**, ADJ.: concentric.

conce-píbile, ADJ.: conceivable. **-píi**, PRET. of *-pire*. **-piménto**, M.: conception. ‖**-píre** [L. *con-cipere* (*capere*, take)], IRR.§; TR.: CONCEIVE; form, imagine.

§ Reg.: or (poet.) Pres. *concè-pe*; *-pono*. Part. *conce-púto*.

concer-nènte, PART., ADJ.: concerning, relating to. **-nènza†**, F.: concernment, interest. ‖**concèr-nere** [L., mix together], TR.: concern (regard). **-névole†**, ADJ.: concerning. **-táre** [*-to*], TR.: concert (bring into harmony); direct a rehearsal; REFL.: agree to. **-táto**, PART. of *-tare*; M.: agreement, concert. **-tatóre**, M., **-tatríce**, F.: concerter, planner. **-tíno**, M.: little concert. **-tísta**, M.: concert-giver, concert-artist. **concèr-to** [part. of *-nere*], M.: concert (concerto, musicale); agreement: *di* —, by agreement, jointly.

concès-si, PRET. of *concedere*. **-sionário**, M.: grantee. **-sióne**, F.: concession; grant; permission. **-sívo**, ADJ.: concessive. ‖**concès-so**, PART. of *concedere*. **-sóre**, M.: granter.

concèt-ta, F.: concept. **-táccio**, M.: poor idea. **-tíno**, M.: idea. **-tívo**, ADJ.: conceptive. **-tizzáre†**, INTR.: find ideas, utter witticisms. ‖**concèt-to** [L. *conceptus* (*capere*, take)], M.: conceit, thought, idea, opinion; mind. **-tóne**, M.: (*jest.* or *iron.*) good idea; great imagination. **-tosaménte**, ADV.: thoughtfully. **-tóso**,

ADJ.: full of ideas. **-tuále**, ADJ.: conceptual. **-tismo**, M.: conceptualism. **-túccio**, **-túzzo**, *disp.* of *-cetto*. **concezióne**, F.: conception; Lady-day; thought, comprehension.

con-chétta, F.: small shell. ||**-chiglia** [Gr. *konchílion* (*kónche*)], F.: CONCH, shell. **-chigliétta**, **-chiglína**, *dim.* of *-chiglia*. **-chiliáceo**, ADJ.: composed of shells. **-chili=fórme**, ADJ.: formed like shells.

conchiud. . = *conclud.* .

cón-cia, F.: tanning, dressing; tannery; adulteration of wines†. **-ciáia** = *concimaia*. **-ciaiòlo**, M.: tanner. **-cialána**, F.: wool-comber. ||**-ciáre** [l. L. *comptiare* (L. *comptus*, PART. of *comere*, prepare, adorn)], TR.: dress (skins), tan; comb (wool, etc.); prepare, fix; belabour, whip; spoil, soil. **-ciatóre**, M.: tanner. **-ciatúra**, F.: dressing.

concièro†, M.: emendation, correction.

conci-glio† = *-lio*. **-liábile**, ADJ.: conciliable. **-liabilità**, F.: possibility of conciliating. **-liábolo**, M.: assembly (for an evil purpose); conciliabule. **-liaménto**, M.: conciliation. **-liáre**, TR.: conciliate; REFL.: become reconciled; settle (an affair). **-liáre†**, ADJ.: conciliary. **-liatívo**, ADJ.: conciliatory. **-liatóre**, M.: conciliator. **-liatríce**, F.: peacemaker. **-liazióne**, F.: conciliation. ||**concí-lio** [L. *-lium* (*calare*, call)], M.: council; church council; deliberation.

conci-máia, F.: dung yard. **-máre**, TR.: dung, manure land. ||**concí-me** [*concio*], M.: manure, compost.

concinni-tà†, F.: concinnity (elegance).

con-círo [*-ciare*], M.: tan-bark. **cóncio**, PART.: pop. for *conciato*, dressed; M.: dung; worthless thing or person; ornament (gilding†).

conciofossecosachè = *conciossiacosache*.

concio-náre, INTR.: preach; harangue. **-natóre**, M.: concionator, preacher. **-natòrio**, ADJ.: pertaining to preaching; M.: preacher. **-natríce**, F.: preacher. ||**concióne** [L. *contio* for *con-ventio*], F.: CONVENTION (assembly), congregation; sermon; speech.

con=ciò=ssia(=cosa)=chè *-é* [*ssia* for *sia*], CONJ.: inasmuch as†; now used to mock stilted or pedantic language.

conci-samónte, ADV.: concisely. **-sióne**, F.: concision. ||**concí-so** [L. *-sus*, (*cædere*, cut)], ADJ.: concise (brief).

conci-storiále, ADJ.: consistorial. **-stòrio†**. ||**-stòro** [L. *con-sistorium*], M.: consistory; assembly.

concita-ménto, M.: agitation. ||**concitá-re** [L. (*-cire*, stir)], TR.: excite (agitate, Eng. concite†); provoke†. **-taménte**, ADV.: agitatedly. **-tívo**, ADJ.: exciting, stimulating. **-tóre**, M.: inciter. **-zióne**, F.: agitation.

concitta-dína, F.: fellow-citizeness. **-dinánza**, F.: fellow-citizenship. ||**-díno** [*cittadino*], M.: fellow-citizen.

conclá-ve [L. (*clavis*, key)], M.: conclave (rooms where the cardinals are 'secluded' when choosing a pope; the body of cardinals). **conclá-vio†**, M.: closet, cabinet. **-vísta**, M.: member of the conclave.

conclu-dènte, PART., ADJ.: concluding. **-denteménte**, ADV.: conclusively. **-dènza**, F.: conclusiveness. ||**conclú-dere** [L. (*claudere*, CLOSE)], IRR. (cf. *accludere*); TR.: conclude, finish; press†, enclose. **conclú-si**, PRET. of *-dere*. **-sionáccia**, F.: bad conclusion. **-sionále**, ADJ.: conclusive. **-sioncèlla**, *dim.* of *-sione*. **-sióne**, F.: conclusion; consequence: *in —*, in fine. **-sivaménte**, ADV.: conclusively. **-sívo**, ADJ.: conclusive. **conclú-so**, PART. of *-dere*.

con-cò́cere, IRR.; TR.: digest (Eng.† concoct); INTR., REFL.: change into nourishment.

cóncola†, F.: small shell; small hand basin.

concomi-tánte [L. *-tans* (*comes*, companion)], ADJ.: concomitant. **-tánza**, F.: concomitance.

concor-dábile, ADJ.: concordable. **-dánte**, PART., ADJ.: concordant, harmonious. **-danteménte†**, ADV.: concordantly, suitably. **-dánza**, F.: concordance, agreement. **-dáre**, INTR.: agree; TR.: reconcile. **-dataménte†**, ADV.: harmoniously. **-dáto**, PART., ADJ.: agreed, harmonious; M.: agreement; concordat. ||**concòr-de** [L. *-s* (*cor*, HEART)], ADJ.: concordant (harmonious, unanimous). **-deménte**, ADV.: harmoniously, unanimously. **-dévole†**, ADJ.: conformable. **-devolménte†**, ADV.: harmoniously. **concòr-dia**, F.: concord (harmony).

concor-rènte, PART., ADJ.: concurrent; M.: competitor. **-rènza**, F.: competition. ||**concór-rere** [*con-*, *c.*], IRR.; INTR.: run together; concur; contribute (said of causes). **concór-si**, PRET. of *-rere*. **concór-so**, PART. of *-rere*; M.: concourse, throng.

concòtto, PART. of *concocere*.

con=creáre, TR.: concreate (create together). **-creáto**, PART.: innate (inherent).

concre-taménte, ADV.: concretely. **-táre**, TR.: come to concrete terms; conclude. **-tézza**, F.: concreteness. ||**concrè-to** [L. *-tus* (*crescere*, grow)], ADJ.:

concrete (specific); M.: concrete. **-zióne,** F.: concretion.

concubí-na [L. (*cubare*, lie down)], F.: concubine. **-nário,** M.: concubinary. **-nàto,** M.: concubinage. **concúbi-to,** M.: lying together.

conculcá-bile, ADJ.: fit to be trampled upon. ||**-'re** [L. (*calx*, heel)], TR.: conculcate, trample upon. **-tóre,** M., **-tríce,** F.: trampler. **-zióne**†, F.: trampling upon.

concuòcere = *concocere.*

concupí-re [L. *con-cupere*], TR.: desire ardently. **-çcènza, -çcènzia**†, F.: concupiscence. **-'çcere**† = *-re.* **-çcévole**†, ADJ.: concupiscible.

concus-sáre†, TR.: concuss, shake. **-satóre**†, M.: shaker. ||**concus-sióne** [L. *-sio* (*con quatere*, shake)], F.: concussion†; extortion. **-sívo**†, ADJ.: concussive.

condán-na, F.: condemnation, sentence; fine. **-nábile,** ADJ.: condemnable. **-nagióne**†, F., **-naménto**† = *-na.* ||**-náre** [*con-*, *d.* .], TR.: condemn (sentence; reject); compel. **-náto,** PART. of *-nare;* M.: condemned person (prisoner). **-natóre,** M.: condemner. **-natòrio,** ADJ.: condemnatory. **-nazióne,** F.: condemnation. **-névole,** ADJ.: condemnable.

condecèn-te†, ADJ.: decent. **-teménte**†, ADV.: decently.

con-degnaménte, ADV.: condignly. **-degnità**†, **-degnitáde**†, **-degnitáte**†, F.: condignness. ||**-dégno** [L. *-dignus* (worthy)], ADJ.: condign (suitable).

condenn..† = *condann..*

conden-sábile, ADJ.: condensable. **-saménto,** M.: condensation. ||**-sáre** [L. (*densus*, dense)], TR.: condense; INTR.: become condensed. **-satóre,** M.: condenser. **-sazióne,** F.: condensation. **condèn-so**†, ADJ.: condensed.

condeçcend.. = *condiscend..*

con-diménto, M.: condiment. ||**-díre** [L.], TR.: season; assuage; provide abundantly; soil (by spilling); preserve (pickle, cf. Eng.† CONDITE).

condi-çcendènte, ADJ.: condescending. **-çcendènza,** F.: condescension. ||**-çcéndere** [*con*, *d.* .], IRR.; INTR.: condescend, yield.

con=diçcépola, F., **-diçcépolo,** M.: schoolfellow.

condi-çcési, PRET., **-çcéso,** PART. of *-scendere.*

condíto[1] [*condire*], PART.: seasoned.

còndi-to[2]†, ADJ.: built, formed. **-tóre**†, M.: founder, author.

conditúra [*condire*], F.: seasoning, condiment.

con=divídere, IRR.; TR.: share, divide with.

condizio-nále, ADJ.: conditional. **-nalménte,** ADV.: conditionally. **-náre,** TR.: season, prepare (said of food); prepare, arrange. **-nataménte,** ADV.: conditionally. **-náto,** PART., ADJ.: prepared, fit; conditioned. **-ncèlla,** *dim.* of *-ne.* ||**condizió-ne** [L. *condicio*], F.: condition (state); rank: *a — che*, on condition that.

condo-gliánza, **-gliènza**†, **-lènza**†, F.: condolence. ||**-lére** [*con-*, *d.* .], IRR.; REFL.: condole with. **condò-lsi,** PRET. of *-lere.*

con=domínio, M.: joint dominion.

condo-nábile, ADJ.: pardonable. ||**-náre** [*con-*, *d.* .], TR.: condone (pardon; remit). **-natóre,** M.: pardoner. **-nazióne,** F.: condonation (pardon).

condóre [Sp. (Peruv.)], M.: condor.

con-dótta, F.: conduct; transportation, management; escort†. **-dottière, -dottièro,** M.: (*mil.*) leader (captain); condottiere†, pl. *-ri* (leader of adventurers: 14th Cent.); carrier†. **-dótto,** PART. of *-durre;* M.: CONDUIT (aqueduct; channel); conduct†. **-dúcere**† = *-durre.* **-ducévole**†, ADJ.: conductive. **-duciménto**†, M.: conduct; proceeding. **-ducitóre**†, M.: conductor; instructor.

conduplicazióne†, F.: redoubling.

con-dúrre [L. *-ducere* (lead)], IRR. (cf. *addurre*); TR.: conduct (guide); (*a*) lead to (result in); induce†; REFL.: come to; conduct one's self. **-dússi,** PRET. of *-durre.* **-dútto**† = *-dotto;* M.: guide. **-duttóre,** M., **-duttríce,** F.: conductor (manager); lessee; ADJ.: conducting. **-duttúra**†, F.: conducting; coach. **-duzióne,** F.: lease; water-conveyance.

conestá-bile [L. *comes stabuli*, COUNT of the STABLE], M.: constable (superior militia-officer; court-officer). **-bolería**†, F.: constableship.

confabulá-re [L. *-ri* (*fabulari*, speak)], INTR.: chat together (confabulate). **-tòrio,** ADJ.: confabulatory. **-zióne,** F.: familiar talk.

confa-cènte [*-re*], ADJ.: convenient (fit). **-centeménte,** ADV.: conveniently. **-cènza**†, F.: suitability. **-cévole**†, ADJ.: suitable. **-cevolézza**†, F.: suitability. **-ciménto**†, M.: conformity.

confar-r(e)azióne [L. *-reatio* (*far*, spelt)], F.: confarreation (Rom. marriage ceremony).

con=fáre, IRR.; INTR., REFL.: suit, befit; agree with; harmonize.

confastidiáre†, INTR., REFL.: grow tired of (be annoyed).

confede-raménto†, M.: confederation, league. ||**-ráre** [L. (*fœdus*, league)], INTR., REFL.: confederate, form a league;

TR.: join together. **-ráto**, ADJ.: confederate; M.: confederate. **-ratívo**, ADJ.: confederative. **-razióne**, F.: confederation.

confe-rènte, PART., ADJ.: conferring. **-rènza**, F.: conference. **-renzière**, M.: conferree. **-riménto**, M.: conferring. ‖**-ríre** [L. *con-ferre* (bear)], TR.: confer (bestow); INTR.: confer (consult); contribute; TR.†: compare. **-ritóre**, M., **-ritríce**, F.: conferrer (giver).

confér-ma, **-magióne**†, F.: confirmation. ‖**-máre** [L. *con-firmare*], TR.: confirm (strengthen, ratify). **-matívo**, ADJ.: confirmative. **-matóre**, M.: confirmer. **-matòrio**, ADJ.: confirmatory. **-matríce**, F.: confirmer. **-mazióne**, F.: confirmation. **confér-mo**, ADJ.: confirmed.

confes-saménto†, M.: confession. **-sáre**, TR.: confess; declare; REFL.: make confession (to a priest). **-satóre**, M.: confessor. **-sionále**, ADJ.: of the confession; M.: confessional. **-sionário**, M.: confessional; office of confessor. **-sioncèlla**, *dim.* of *-sione*. **-sióne**, M.: confession. ‖**confès-so** [L. *-sus*], ADJ.: confessed. **-soráto**, M.: office of confessor; hour of confession (in convents, etc.). **-sóre**†, **-sòre**, M.: father confessor.

confet-táre, TR.: candy; preserve. **-tatóre**, M.: confectioner. **-tièra**, F.: candy-box. **-tière** = *-turiere*. **-tíno**, M.: small comfit. ‖**confèt-to** [L. *confectus* (*facere*, make)], ADJ.: candied; M.: COMFIT (CONFECTION): (*jest.*) *-ti di montagna*, dry chestnuts. **-túra**, F.: comfit, sugarplum. **-turería**, F.: confectionery shop. **-turière**, M.: confectioner. **confezionáre**, TR.: make confections. **confezióne**, F.: mixture; artificial composition; comfit†.

conficca-ménto, M.: nailing. ‖**conficcá-re** [*ficcare*], TR.: fasten; nail. **-túra**, F.: nailing, driving in.

confi-daménto†, M., **-dánza**, F.: confidence. ‖**-dáre** [L. *con-fidere* (trust)], TR.: confide (entrust); INTR.: CONFIDE (trust; feel sure). **-dènte**, ADJ.: confiding; M.: confidant. **-denteménte**, ADV.: confidently. **-dènza**, F.: confidence; familiarity (intimacy). **-denziále**, ADJ.: confidential; familiar. **-denzialménte**, ADV.: confidentially. **confí-do**†, ADJ.: confident.

con=fíggere, IRR.; TR.: nail.

configu-ráre [*figura*], TR.: configure, represent in a figure. **-razióne**, F.: configuration.

confi-nánte, ADJ.: near, contiguous. **-náre**, TR.: banish; confine; INTR.: border upon; REFL.: limit one's self. ‖**confí-ne** [L. (*finis*, end)], M.: confine (border); boundary-stone.

con=fíngere†, IRR.; TR.: counterfeit.

confíno, pop. for *confine*.

confi-sca, F.: confiscation. ‖**-scáre** [L. (*fiscus*, basket)], TR.: confiscate. **-scazióne**†, F.: confiscation.

confíssi, PRET. of *configgere*.

con-fitènte†, ADJ.: confessing. ‖**-fíteor** [L., 'I CONFESS'], M.: confiteor (Catholic prayer): *dire* (*recitare*) *il* —, confess one's self.

confítto, PART. of *-figgere*.

conflitto [L. *-flictus* (*fligere*, strike)], M.: conflict; opposition.

con-fluènte, PART.: flowing together; M.: confluence. **-fluènza**, F.: flowing together. ‖**-fluíre** [L. *-fluere* (FLOW)], INTR.: flow together (meet).

confón-dere [*con-*, *f.*. (pour)], IRR.; TR.: CONFOUND (CONFUSE, mistake); REFL.: become confused. **-díbile**, ADJ.: confusing. **-diménto**, M.: confusion. **-ditéra**, F., **-ditóre**, M.: confounder.

confor-mábile, ADJ.: conformable. **-máre**, TR.: conform; REFL.: adapt one's self (comply). **-matívo**†, ADJ.: conformable. **-mazióne**, F.: conformation; conformity. ‖**confór-me** [L. *-mis*], ADJ.: conformable, resembling; ADV.: conformably to (according as). **-meménte**, ADV.: conformably (suitably). **-mévole**†, ADJ.: conformable; like. **-místa**, M.: conformist. **-mità**, F.: conformity.

confor-tábile, ADJ.: that can be comforted. **-tabilménte**, ADV.: comfortingly. **-tagióne**†, F.: comfort (relief). **-tánte**, ADJ.: comforting. **-tánti**, M.: stomachics (cordials for the stomach). ‖**-táre** [L. (*fortis*, strong)], TR.: comfort (strengthen, encourage); REFL.: take courage. **-tatívo**, ADJ.: comforting; M.: remedy (relief). **-tatóre**, M., **-tatríce**, F.: comforter (of the condemned). **-tazióne**†, F.: comfort. **-tévole**, ADJ.: that can be comforted. **-tináio**†, M.: maker or seller of spiced cakes. **-tíno**, M.: kind help; kind of sweet spice cake†.

confòr-to, M.: comfort (consolation); exhortation; relief, last sacraments.

con=fráte†, **-fratèllo**, M.: brother (fellow-member). **-fraternità**, F.: confraternity (religious brotherhood).

confri-caménto, M.: rubbing. ‖**-cáre** (L. (*fricare*, rub)], TR.: rub; INTR.: rub off (FRAY). **-cazióne**, F.: rubbing; friction.

confronta-ménto†, M.: confronting. ‖**confrontá-re** [*fronte*], TR.: confront (compare); INTR.: be like, conform. **-zióne**†, F.: confronting, meeting. **confrónto**, M.: confronting (comparison);

a —, compared to, comparatively; *star a* —, be equal to.

confuggíre, INTR.: flee for refuge.

confu-ṣaménte, ADV.: confusedly. **-ṣét-to**, ADJ.: slightly confused. **confú-ṣi**, PRET. of *confondere*. ||**-ṣióne** [*confondere*], F.: confusion (perturbation); shame. **-ṣíssimo**, ADJ.: superl. of *-so*. **confú-ṣo**, PART.: confused, indistinct: *alla -sa*, confusedly.

confu-tábile, ADJ.: confutable. **-ta-ménto**, M.: confutation. ||**-táre** [L.], TR.: confute (disprove): *-tarsi da sè*, contradict one's self. **-tatívo**, ADJ.: confutative. **-tatóre**, M.: confuter. **-ta-tòrio**, ADJ.: confutative. **-tazióne**, F.: confutation.

con-gedáre, TR.: give leave to depart; dismiss. ||**-gèdo** [Fr. *-gé* (cf. *commiato*)], M.: leave (permission); farewell; leave of absence (furlough); discharge: *dar* —, dismiss; (*mil.*) discharge; *prendere* —, take one's leave, bid farewell.

conge-gnaménto, M.: joining, union. **-gnáre**, TR.: connect (join); adjust (put together, arrange skilfully). ||**congé-gno** [*ingegno*], M.: joining (connection); machine.

congela-ménto, M.: congelation. ||**congelá-re** [*con-*, *g*. .], INTR., REFL.: congeal, freeze. **-tóre**, M.: freezer. **-zió-ne**†, F.: coagulation.

con-gènere, ADJ.: congeneric (of the same kind). ||**-gènito** [L. *-genitus* (*gignere*, beget)], ADJ.: congenital (innate).

congè-rie [L. *-ries* (*gerere*, bring)], F.: congeries (heap). ||**-stióne** [L. *-stio*], F.: congestion.

congettú-ra [L. *conjectura* (*jacere*, throw)], F.: conjecture. **-rábile**, ADJ.: conjecturable. **-rále**, ADJ.: conjectural. **-ralménte**, ADV.: conjecturally. **-ráre**, TR.: conjecture. **-ratóre**, M.: guesser.

conghiettur. . = *congettur*. .

congio†, M.: leave of absence.

congiug. .† = *coniug*. .

congiugn. .† = *congiung*. .

congiún-gere [*con-*, *g*. .], IRR.; TR.: conjoin (unite); REFL.: unite one's self; †add, annex. **-giménto**, M.: conjunction. **-si**, PRET. of *-gere*. **-'ta**†, F.: wife. **-taménte**, ADV.: conjointly. **-tíva**, F.: (*med.*) conjunctiva. **-tivíte**, F.: (*med.*) conjunctivitis. **-tívo**, ADJ., M.: conjunctive (subjunctive). **-'to**, PART. of *-gere*; M. PL.: relations. **-túra**, F.: juncture; circumstance. **-zióne**, F.: conjunction.

congiú-ra, F.: conspiracy. ||**-ráre** [L. (*jurare*, swear)], INTR.: conspire, conjure; plot. **-ráto**, PART.; M.: conspirator. **-ratóre**, M.: conspirator. **-ra-zióne**†, F.: conspiracy.

conglobáre [L. (*globus*, ball)]. TR.: conglobate.

conglomerá-re†, TR.: conglomerate. **-zióne**†, F.: conglomeration.

conglutin. . = *agglutin*. .

congratulá-re [*con g*. .], REFL.: rejoice (with others, be glad); congratulate one's self†; INTR.†: give congratulation. **-tò-rio**, ADJ.: congratulatory. **-zióne**, F.: congratulation.

congrè-ga, F.: assembly (gathering). **-gaménto**†, M.: aggregation (union). **-gánza**†, F.: congregation. ||**-gáre** [L. (*grex*, flock)], TR.: congregate. **-ga-zióne**, F.: congregation (assemblage); charitable association; assembling place.

congrèsso [L.], M.: congress (convention).

còn-grua, F.: endowment, allowance (for a parish). **-gruaménte**, ADV.: congruously. **-gruáto**, ADJ.: endowed. **-gruènte**, ADJ.: congruent, suitable. **-gruènza**, F.: congruence, consistency. **-gruità**, F.: congruity. ||**còn-gruo** [L. *-gruere*, coincide], ADJ.: congruous (suitable).

con-guagliáre [*con-*, *agguagliare*], TR.: equalize; INTR.: be equal. **-guáglio**, M.: equalization.

cònia [? *-nio* 2], F.: fun (joke): *uomo di* —, jolly fellow (boon companion); *far la* —, joke, jest.

coniá-re [*cuneo*], TR.: COIN (mint; originate words). **-tóre**, M.: coiner. **-túra**, F.: coinage.

coni-caménte, ADV.: conically. **-cità**, F.: conicalness. ||**còni-co** [*cono*], ADJ.: conic(al).

coniettur. .† = *congettur*. .

conifero [*cono*], ADJ.: coniferous.

co-nigliáccio, *disp.* of *-niglio*. **-ni-glièra**, F.: rabbit-warren. ||**-níglio** [L. *cuniculus*], M.: CONEY (rabbit); coward. **-nigliolo**, pop. for *-niglio*.

cònio 1 [*cuneo*], M.: COIN (wedge); stamp.

cònio 2 = *cogno*.

coniu-gábile, ADJ.: able to be conjugated. **-gále**, ADJ.: conjugal. **-gal-ménte**, ADV.: conjugally. ||**-gáre** [L. (root *jug-*, JOIN)], TR.: conjugate (verbs); marry, unite. **-gáto**, PART., ADJ.: conjugate. **-gazióne**, F.: conjugation. **cò-niu-ge**, M.: spouse (consort). **coniú-gio**†, M.: marriage.

coniun. .† = *congiun*. .

con meco, pop. for *meco*.

connaturá-le [*natura*], ADJ.: connatural (natural, proper). **-lità**, F.: connaturality. **-'re**, TR.: render of the same nature, adapt.

connazionále [*nazione*], ADJ.: of the same nation; M.: native.

con-nessaménte, ADV.: connectedly.

-nèssi, PRET. of *-nettere*. **-nessióne, -nessità**, F.: connection (continuity). ‖**-nèsso**, PART. of *-nettere*.
connestábile = *conestabile*.
connèttere [*co-*, *n*..], IRR.; TR.: connect (unite).
conni-vènte [L. *-vere*, wink], ADJ.: conniving. **-vènza**, F.: connivance.
connotáto [*notare*], M.: personal description (on a passport, etc.).
con-nubiále, ADJ.: connubial. ‖**-núbio** [L. *-bium* (*nubere*, veil)], M.: marriage.
connume-ráre [*numero*], TR.: number. **-razióne**, F.: connumeration.
còno [L. *-nus*], M.: CONE.
conóbbi, PRET. of *conoscere*.
co-nòcchia, F.: bunch of flax, etc., on the distaff; (*poet.*) distaff. **-noidále**, ADJ.: conoidal. ‖**-nòide** [Gr. *kônos*, cone, *eidos*, form], F.: conoid.
conopèo [Gr. *konopeîon*], M.: mosquito net; woman's baptismal veil.
cono-scènte, ADJ.: knowing; M.: acquaintance. **-scentemènte†**, ADV.: thankfully. **-scènza**, F.: cognizance (knowledge); acquaintance. ‖**conó-scere** [L. *co-gnoscere* (KNOW)] IRR.§; TR.: KNOW (cognize); comprehend; experience; taste; REFL.: acknowledge one's self. **-scíbile**, ADJ.: knowable (cognoscible). **-scibilità**, F.: cognoscibility. **-sciménto**, M.: reason, knowledge. **-scitívo**, ADJ.: perceptible. **-scitóre**, M., **-scitríce**, F.: connoisseur. **-scitúra†**, F.: knowledge. **-sciutaménte**, ADV.: knowingly. **-sciúto**, PART. of *-scere*.

§ Pret. *conób-bi, -be; -bero.* Part. *conosciuto.*

conquas-saménto† = *-so*. ‖**-sáre** [L. (*quassare*, shake)], TR.: shake; dash. **-sazióne†**, F., **conquás-so**, M.: shaking; discord (tumult).
con-quídere [L. *con-quirere*, seek for], IRR.§; TR.: importune (with QUESTIONS etc.), annoy; afflict; CONQUER; REFL.: fret one's self, grieve. **-quísi**, PRET., **-quíso**, PART. of *-quidere*. **-quísta**, F.: conquest. **-quistábile**, ADJ.: conquerable. **-quistaménto†**, M.: conquest. **-quistáre**, TR.: conquer (overcome). **-quistatóre**, M., **-quistatríce**, F.: conqueror.

§ Defect.: Perf. *conqui-si, -se; -sero.* Part. *conquiso.*

consa-crábile, ADJ.: that can be consecrated. **-cránte**, M.: consecrator. ‖**-cráre** [L. *con-secrare* (*sacer*, sacred)], TR.: consecrate; authorize; REFL.: devote one's self. **-crazióne**, F.: consecration.
consagra.. = *consacra..*
consan-guineità, F.: consanguinity. ‖**-guíneo** [L. *-guineus* (*sanguis*, blood)], ADJ.: consanguineous; M.: kinsman. **-guinità**, F.: consanguinity.
consapévo-le [*con-*, *s*..], ADJ.: conscious of: *far — uno*, inform a person. **-lézza**, F.: consciousness. **-lménte**, ADV.: consciously.
consçéndere† = *condiscendere*.
consçiènzia† = *coscienza*. ‖**cònsçio** [L. *-scius* (*scire*, know)], ADJ.: conscious.
consecri†.. = *coscri..*
consecra†.. = *consacra..*
consecu-tivaménte, ADV.: consecutively; consequently. ‖**-tívo** [L. *-tus* (*sequi*, follow)], ADJ.: consecutive. **-zióne†**, F.: consecution.
consé-gna, F.: consignment (commission); command; slight military punishment: *dar un bimbo in —*, put a child out to nurse. ‖**-gnáre** [*con-*, *s*..], TR.: consign, deliver; intrust: *— alla memoria*, commit to memory. **-gnazióne†** = *-gna*.
conse-guènte, PART., ADJ.: ensuing, consistent; M.: consequence. **-guentemènte**, ADV.: consequently. **-guènza**, F.: consequence (result); authority. **-guíbile**, ADJ.: obtainable. **-guiménto**, M.: attainment. ‖**-guíre** [*con-*, *s*..], TR.: acquire (obtain); INTR.: follow (result); happen. **-guitáre**, INTR.: follow (ensue); TR.†: follow; obtain (wrongly).
consèn-so, M.: consent. **-táneo**, ADJ.: consentaneous (consistent, corresponding). **-timénto**, M.: accord; consent. ‖**-tíre** [*con-*, *s*..], TR.: allow (grant); INTR.: consent (agree, permit). **-titaménte**, ADV.: consentingly. **-titóre**, M.: consenter. **-ziènte**, PART., ADJ.: consenting.
consequen.. = *conseguen..*
consèrba†, F.: store-room.
consèrto [L. *-serere*, join], ADJ.: intertwined, joined; M.† = *concerto*.
consèr-va, F.: preserve; store-room; store, pantry, etc.: *— d' acqua*, reservoir of water; *— de' pesci*, fish-pond; *andar di —*, go together. **-vábile**, ADJ.: conservable. **-vadóre†** = *-vatore*. **-vagióne†** = *-vazione*. ‖**-váre** [L. *servare*, SAVE], TR.: preserve (keep; maintain); REFL.: keep (last). **-vatívo**, ADJ.: conservative. **-vatóre**, M.: preserver; conservative: *liquidi -vatori*, preserving liquids (alcohol, etc.). **-vatòrio**, M.: refuge; workhouse; conservatory; academy; ADJ.: preservative. **-vatríce**, F.: preserver. **-vazióne**, F.: conservation. **-vévole†**, ADJ.: conservable.
consèsso [L. *-ssum* (*sedere*, SIT)], M.: assembly (assemblage).
consettainòlo†, M.: fellow-sectary.
conside-rábile, ADJ.: considerable. **-rabilménte**, ADV.: considerably. **-ra-**

a —, compared to, comparatively; *star a* —, be equal to.
confuggíre, INTR.: flee for refuge.
confu-ṣaménte, ADV.: confusedly. **-ṣétto**, ADJ.: slightly confused. **confúṣi**, PRET. of *confondere*. ‖**-ṣióne** [*confondere*], F.: confusion (perturbation); shame. **-ṣíssimo**, ADJ.: superl. of *-so*. **confú-ṣo**, PART.: confused, indistinct: *alla -sa*, confusedly.
confu-tábile, ADJ.: confutable. **-taménto**, M.: confutation. ‖**-táre** [L.], TR.: confute (disprove): *-tarsi da sè*, contradict one's self. **-tatívo**, ADJ.: confutative. **-tatóre**, M.: confuter. **-tatòrio**, ADJ.: confutative. **-tazióne**, F.: confutation.
con-ġedáre, TR.: give leave to depart; dismiss. ‖**-ġèdo** [Fr. *-gé* (cf. *commiato*)], M.: leave (permission); farewell; leave of absence (furlough); discharge: *dar* —, dismiss; (*mil.*) discharge; *prendere* —, take one's leave, bid farewell.
conge-gnaménto, M.: joining, union. **-gnáre**, TR.: connect (join); adjust (put together, arrange skilfully). ‖**congégno** [*ingegno*], M.: joining (connection); machine.
congela-ménto, M.: congelation. ‖**congelá-re** [*con-*, *g*. .], INTR., REFL.: congeal, freeze. **-tóre**, M.: freezer. **-zióne**†, F.: coagulation.
con=gènere, ADJ.: congeneric (of the same kind). ‖**-gènito** [L. *-genitus* (*gignere*, beget)], ADJ.: congenital (innate).
congè-rie [L. *-ries* (*gerere*, bring)], F.: congeries (heap). ‖**-stióne** [L. *-stio*], F.: congestion.
congettú-ra [L. *conjectura* (*jacere*, throw)], F.: conjecture. **-rábile**, ADJ.: conjecturable. **-rále**, ADJ.: conjectural. **-ralménte**, ADV.: conjecturally. **-ráre**, TR.: conjecture. **-ratóre**, M.: guesser.
conghiettur. . = *congettur*. .
congìo†, M.: leave of absence.
congiug. .† = *coniug*. .
congiugn. .† = *congiung*. .
congiún-gere [*con-*, *g*. .], IRR.; TR.: conjoin (unite); REFL.: unite one's self; †add, annex. **-giménto**, M.: conjunction. **-si**, PRET. of *-gere*. **-'ta**†, F.: wife. **-taménte**, ADV.: conjointly. **-tíva**, F.: (*med.*) conjunctiva. **-tivíte**, F.: (*med.*) conjunctivitis. **-tívo**, ADJ., M.: conjunctive (subjunctive). **-'to**, PART. of *-gere*; M. PL.: relations. **-túra**, F.: juncture; circumstance. **-zióne**, F.: conjunction.
congiú-ra, F.: conspiracy. ‖**-ráre** [L. (*jurare*, swear)], INTR.: conspire, conjure; plot. **-ráto**, PART.; M.: conspirator. **-ratóre**, M.: conspirator. **-razióne**†, F.: conspiracy.
conglobáre [L. (*globus*, ball)]. TR.: conglobate.
conglomerá-re†, TR.: conglomerate. **-zióne**†, F.: conglomeration.
conglutin. . = *agglutin*. .
congratulá-re [*con g*. .], REFL.: rejoice (with others, be glad); congratulate one's self†; INTR.†: give congratulation. **-tòrio**, ADJ.: congratulatory. **-zióne**, F.: congratulation.
congrè-ga, F.: assembly (gathering). **-gaménto**†, M.: aggregation (union). **-gánza**†, F.: congregation. ‖**-gáre** [L. (*grex*, flock)], TR.: congregate. **-gazióne**, F.: congregation (assemblage); charitable association; assembling place.
congrèsso [L.], M.: congress (convention).
còn-grua, F.: endowment, allowance (for a parish). **-gruaménte**, ADV.: congruously. **-gruáto**, ADJ.: endowed. **-gruènte**, ADJ.: congruent, suitable. **-gruènza**, F.: congruence, consistency. **-gruità**, F.: congruity. ‖**còn-gruo** [L. *-gruere*, coincide], ADJ.: congruous (suitable).
con-guagliáre [*con-*, *agguagliare*], TR.: equalize; INTR.: be equal. **-guáglio**, M.: equalization.
cònia [? *-nio* 2], F.: fun (joke): *uomo di* —, jolly fellow (boon companion); *far la* —, joke, jest.
coniá-re [*cuneo*], TR.: COIN (mint; originate words). **-tóre**, M.: coiner. **-túra**, F.: coinage.
coni-caménte, ADV.: conically. **-cità**, F.: conicalness. ‖**còni-co** [*cono*], ADJ.: conic(al).
coniettur. .† = *congettur*. .
conífero [*cono*], ADJ.: coniferous.
co-nigliáccio, *disp*. of *-niglio*. **-niglièra**, F.: rabbit-warren. ‖**-níglio** [L. *cuniculus*], M.: CONEY (rabbit); coward. **-nígliolo**, pop. for *-niglio*.
cònio 1 [*cuneo*], M.: COIN (wedge); stamp.
cònio 2 = *cogno*.
coniu-gábile, ADJ.: able to be conjugated. **-gále**, ADJ.: conjugal. **-galménte**, ADV.: conjugally. ‖**-gáre** [L. (root *jug-*, JOIN)], TR.: conjugate (verbs); marry, unite. **-gáto**, PART., ADJ.: conjugate. **-gazióne**, F.: conjugation. **còniu-ge**, M.: spouse (consort). **coniúgio**†, M.: marriage.
coniun. .† = *congiun*. .
con meco, pop. for *meco*.
connaturá-le [*natura*], ADJ.: connatural (natural, proper). **-lità**, F.: connaturality. **-'re**, TR.: render of the same nature, adapt.
connazionále [*nazione*], ADJ.: of the same nation; M.: native.
con-nessaménte, ADV.: connectedly.

worn out; ruined. **-nzióne**, F.: consumption; decay.

§ Reg.; or Pret. *consún-si, -se; -sero*. Part. *consúnto*.

consuònare† = *consonare*.

consúrgere = *sorgere*.

consustanziá-le [*sostanza*], ADJ.: consubstantial. **-lità**, F.: consubstantiality. **-lménte**, ADV.: consubstantially.

conta-dína, F.: country-woman. **-dinàccio**, M.: rude peasant. **-dináme**, M.: country crowd. **-dináta**, F.: stupidity, foolish act. **-dinèlla**, F.: pretty country girl. **-dinescaménte**, ADV.: in a countrified way. **-dinésco**, ADJ.: rustic, countrified. **-dinétta**, F.: pretty village girl. **-dinétto**, F.: country boy. **-díno**, ADJ.: country; M.: countryman; peasant; rustic, boor. **-dinóna**, **-dinóne**, *aug.* of **-no**. **-dinòtto**, M.: strong country boy. ‖**contá-do** [L. *comitatus* (*comes*, COUNT)], M.: COUNTY†; country; peasant (villager).

contá-ge†, F., ‖**contá-gio** [L. *-gio* (*tangere*, touch)], M.: contagion. **-giosaménte**, ADV.: contagiously. **-gióso**, ADJ.: contagious.

contagócce [*contare goccia*], M., INVAR.: dropping tube.

contaménto†, M.: counting; account.

contami-nábile, ADJ.: contaminable. **-naménto†**, M.: contamination. ‖**-náre** [L. *tangere*, touch], TR.: contaminate, defile. **-natóre**, M.: defiler. **-nazióne**, F.: contamination. **-nóso**, ADJ.: easily contaminated.

con-tánte, ADJ.: counting; cash: *danaro* —, ready money, cash. ‖**-táre** [*computare*], INTR.: COUNT; be esteemed; count (for); TR.: esteem; relate. **-táta**, F.: enumeration. **-tatóre**, M.: counter.

contátto [L. *-tactus* (*tangere*, TOUCH)], M.: contact (touch).

contazióne [*contare*], F.: counting.

cón-te [L. *com-es* (*ire*, go)], M.: COUNT (earl). **-tèa**, F.: county; count's estate.

conteggiáre [*-to*], INTR.: count up; cast accounts. **contéggio**, M.: casting accounts.

contégna†, F.: demeanour; proud demeanour (haughtiness). **-gnènza†**, F.: circuit of a town (territory). ‖**contégno** [*-nere*], M.: demeanour (esp. dignified); behaviour (conduct); gravity; contents†; circuit†: *in* —, with gravity; *stare in* —, assume dignity. **-gnosaménte**, ADV.: gravely. **-gnóso**, ADJ.: dignified, grave.

contempe-raménto, M., **-ránza**, F.: tempering; proportion. ‖**-ráre** [L.], TR.: temper, regulate.

contemplá-bile, ADJ.: that can be contemplated. **-ménto†**, M.: contemplation. ‖**-re** [L. *-ri* (*templum*, temple, where auspices were taken)], TR.: contemplate, reflect upon. **-tíva†**, F.: contemplative faculty. **-tívo**, ADJ.: contemplative. **-tóre**, M., **-tríce**, F.: contemplator. **-zióne**, F.: contemplation: *a — di*, in consideration of.

contempo-raneaménte, ADV.: contemporaneously. **-raneità**, F.: contemporaneity. ‖**-ráneo** [L. *-raneus* (*tempus*, time)], ADJ.: contemporary.

contemprárе† = *contemperare*.

conten-dènza, F.: dispute. ‖**contèndere** [*con-, t. .*], IRR.; INTR.: contend (contest); quarrel; cry out; TR.: contest (prohibit); combat†. **-devolménte†**, ADV.: wranglingly. **-diménto†**, M.: contest, quarrel. **-ditóre**, M.: disputant.

con-tenènte, ADJ.: containing; ADV.†: immediately. **-tenènza†**, F.: contents; gravity. ‖**=tenére**, IRR.; INTR.: CONTAIN (comprise); REFL.: contain or restrain one's self (refrain, forbear); demean one's self (behave); be dignified. **-teniménto†**, M.: contents; continence. **-tenitóre**, M.: restrainer.

contènnere†, TR.: contemn.

contén-ni, PRET. of *-ere*. **-tábile**, ADJ.: easily contented. **-taménto**, M.: content, satisfaction. ‖**-táre** [*-to*], TR.: content; gain the approval of; REFL.: content one's self. **-tatúra**, F.: contentment. **-tévole†**, ADJ.: satisfying. **-tézza**, F.: content: *mala* —, discontent.

contentíbile†, ADJ.: contemptible.

conten-tíno, M.: addition, overweight, extra. **-tívo†**, ADJ.: containing. ‖**contèn-to** [L. *-tus* (*tenere*, hold)], ADJ.: content, satisfied, pleased; contained†; M.: contentment; contents†. **-tóne**, ADJ.: exceedingly content. **-úto**, PART. of *-ere*; M.: contents.

conten-zióne† [L. *-tio* (cf. *-dere*)], F.: contention. **-ziosaménte†**, ADV.: contentiously. **-zióso**, ADJ.: contentious.

contería†, F.: glass beads.

contermi-nále†, ADJ.: conterminous. **-náre†**, INTR.: confine (lie contiguous).

conterrá-neo [L. *-neus* (*terra*, land)], ADJ.: of the same country or village; M.: fellow-countryman. **-náme** = **-neo**.

con-tésa, F.: contest (dispute, quarrel). **-tési**, PRET. of *-tendere*. ‖**-téso** [*-tendere*], PART.: contested, disputed; forbidden.

contéssa [*conte*], F.: countess.

contèssere [*con-, t. .*], TR. (part. *-tessúto* or *-tèsto*): weave together; entwine; compound (compose).

contessína [*contessa*], F.: young countess; count's daughter.

contestábile = *conestabile*.

contestá-re [L. *-ri* (*testis*, witness)], TR.:

notify (legally); CONTEST. **-zióne**, F.: notification; contest.
con-tèsto [*-tessere*], PART.: interwoven; M.: context. **-testuále**, ADJ.: pertaining to the context.
contézza [*conto* 2], F.: notice, cognition.
conticíno [*conto* 1], M.: small account.
contí-gia†, F.: ornament; pretty trifle. **-giáto**†, ADJ.: much ornamented.
con-tiguità, F.: contiguity. ||**-tíguo** [L. *-tiguus* (*tangere*, touch)], ADJ.: contiguous (adjacent).
conti-nentále, ADJ.: continental. ||**-nènte** [L. *-nens* (*tenere*, hold)], ADJ.: continent; containing†; M.: continent; contents†; continuance†. **-nentemén-te**†, ADV.: continently. **-nènza**, F.: continence.
contin-gènte [L. *-gens* (*tangere*, touch)], ADJ.: contingent; M.: proportion (quota). **-gentemènte**†, ADV.: contingently. **-gènza**, F.: contingency. **contín-gere**†, INTR.: happen. **-gíbile**, ADJ.: possible; casual. **-gibilità**†, F.: contingency.
contíno [*conte*], M.: young count; count's son.
conti-nováre = *-nuare*. **contí-novo**, pop. for *-nuo*. **contí-nua**, F.: continuation. **-nuábile**, ADJ.: continuable. **-nuaménte**, ADJ.: continually. **-nua-ménto**†, M., **-nuánza**†, F.: continuation. **-nuáre**, INTR.: continue. **-nuatamente**, ADV.: continuously. **-nuatívo**, ADJ.: continuative. **-nuatóre**, M.: continuer. **-nuazióne**, F.: continuation. **-nuità**, F.: continuity. ||**contí-nuo** [L. *-nuus* (*tenere*, hold)], ADJ.: continuous; M.: continuity.
cónto 1 [*computo*], M.: computation; (bill; ACCOUNT; report, information); cause: *aver uno in — di*, regard a person as; *uomo di —*, man of worth; *far —*, intend; substitute; *fatto il —*, all things considered; *a buon —*, in conclusion; *metter* (*tornar*) —, be profitable.
cónto† 2, ADJ.: known; ready; skilled; graceful, polite.
con=tòrcere, IRR.; TR.: CONTORT (twist, wring); REFL.: contort one's self, writhe. **-torciménto**, M.: contortion.
contor-náre, TR.: surround; trace the contours of (sketch); REFL.: resort to. **-níno**, M.: slight contour. ||**contór-no** [*torno*], M.: contour (outline); PL.: environs.
contòr-si, PRET. of *-cere*. **-sióne**, F.: contortion. **-taménte**, ADV.: with contortions. ||**contòr-to**, PART. of *-cere*.
cóntra [L.], PREP.: against, contra-; PREF.: (following single cons't us'ly doubled). **-bbandière**, M.: contrabandist. **=bbán-do**, M.: contraband; contraband goods: *di —*, clandestinely. **-bbassísta**, M.: contra-basso player. **=bbásso**, M.: contra-basso. **-bbattènte**†, ADJ.: repercussive. **=ccambiáre**, TR.: exchange; reward†. **=ccámbio**, M.: exchange; recompense. **=ccássa**, F.: extra case or covering. **=ccáva** = *controcava*. **=cchiáve** [*chiave*], F.: inner key; duplicate key; false key. **=ccífra** = *controcifra*. **=ccólpo**, M.: rebound. **=ccuòre**, M.: heartbreak. **contrá-da** [L. *contra*, over against], F.: street; region, COUNTRY. **=ddánza** [*danza*], F.: contradance. **-ddétto**, **-ddíre** = *-detto*, *-dire*. **=ddirítto**†, M.: fine, penalty. **=ddistínguere**, IRR.; TR.: (contra)distinguish; label. **-ddistínsi**, PRET., **-ddistínto**, PART. of *-ddistinguere*. **=ddivièto**†, M.: contraband goods. **-ddizióne**†, F.: contradiction. **=ddòte**, F.: marriage portion (bestowed by the husband). **-détto**, PART. of *-dire*. **-diáre**† = *-riare*. **-dicènte**, PART.: contradicting. **-dícere**† = *-dire*. **=díre**, IRR.; TR.: contradict; REFL.: contradict one's self. **-díssi**, PRET. of *-dire*. **-dittóre**, M.: contradicter. **-dittòria**, F.: contradictory proposition. **-dittoriaménte**, ADV.: contradictorily. **-dittòrio**, ADJ.: contradictory. **-dizioncèlla**, F.: slight contradiction. **-dizióne**, F.: contradiction; opposition†.
con-traènte, PART. of *-trarre*. **-tráere**† = *-trarre*.
contra- [cf. the word]: **-ffacènte**, PART.: counterfeiting; disobeying. **-ffaciménto**, M.: counterfeit. ||**=ffáre**, IRR.; TR.: counterfeit, imitate; disobey; REFL.: disguise one's self. **-ffátto**, PART., ADJ.: counterfeited; deformed. **-ffattóre**, M.: counterfeiter. **-ffattúra**†, **-ffazióne**, F.: counterfeiting; forgery. **-ffèci**, PRET. of *-fare*. **=ffòrte**, M.: counterfort; iron bar. **-ffòrza**†, F.: counterforce. **=ggènio** [*contra genio*], M.: antipathy, dislike. **=íre**†, INTR.: be contrary, oppose. **=llèttera**†, F.: countermand. **-contrá-lta** = *contralto*. **-ltáre** = *altare*. **contrá=lto** [*contra alto*], M.: contralto. **-mmandáre**†, TR.: countermand. **-mmandáto**†, M.: countermand. **=mmárcia**†, F.: countermarch. **=mmína**†, F.: countermine. **-mmináre**†, TR.: countermine. **=mmirágl̲io** [*ammiraglio*], M.: rear-admiral. **=mmoménto**†, M.: counteraction. **=nnaturále**†, ADJ.: against nature. **=ppásso**†, M.: retaliation. **=ppélo**, M.: against the hair: *fare il — a una persona*, criticise a person thoroughly. **-pposaménto**†, M.: counterpoise. **=ppesáre**, TR.: counterpoise; examine; REFL.:

balance one's self. **-ppéso**, M.: counterpoise. **-pponiméntoꝉ**, M.: opposition. **-ppórre** [*porre*], IRR.; TR.: oppose; REFL.: oppose, resist. **-ppósi**, PRET. of *-pporre*. **-pposizioncèlla**, F.: slight opposition. **-pposizióne**, F.: opposition, resistance; antithesis. **-ppósto**, PART. of *-porre*: opposed; M.: opposition. **-ppuntísta**, M.: contrapuntist. ||**=ppúnto**, M.: (*mus.*) counterpoint.

contrárgine [*contra, a..*], M.: double dike, extra levee.

contra-riaménte, ADV.: contrarily. **-riáre**, TR.: counteract (oppose; thwart, Eng. CONTRARYꝉ); contradict. **-rietà**, F.: contrariety, resistance; adversity. ||**contrá-rio** [L. *-rius* (*contra*, against)], ADJ.: contrary (adverse); M.: opposite: *al* (*per lo*) —, on the contrary. **-ríssimo**, ADJ.: very contrary.

con=trárre, IRR.; TR.: CONTRACT.

contra=scárpa ꝉ, F.: counterscarp. **-scri..ꝉ** = *controscri..* **=sfòrzoꝉ**, M.: opposite force. **=ssegnáre**, TR.: note, countersign. **=sségno**, M.: sign (mark, token); pl. *-ssegni*, personal description (identification).

contrássi, PRET. of *contrarre*.

contra-stábile [*-stare*], ADJ.: contestable. **-stabilménte**, ADV.: opposingly. **-staméntoꝉ**, M.: dispute. **=stámpa**, F.: counter-proof. **-stampáre**, TR.: counterprove. **-stánzaꝉ**, F.: dispute. **=stáre**, TR.: resist (oppose, dispute); deny. **-statóre**, M.: opponent. **contrá-sto**, M.: opposition, dispute; contrast.

contrattábile [*-tto*], ADJ.: contractile.

contrattácco [*contra attacco*], M.: (*mil.*) counter-guard.

contrattá-re [*-tto*], TR.: contract, bargain. **-zióne**, F.: negotiation; commerce.

contrattèmpo [*contra tempo*], M.: contretemps (untoward accident): *di* —, unseasonably.

contrát-tile, ADJ.: contractile. **-tilità**, F.: contractility. ||**contrát-to** [*contrarre*], PART.: contracted; M.: contract, agreement. **-tóne**, M.: profitable contract. **-tuále**, ADJ.: concerning contracts. **-túraꝉ**, F.: contraction.

contra-urtáreꝉ, TR.: strike against. **-vvallazióneꝉ**, F.: contravallation. **-vvedéreꝉ**, IRR.; TR.: regard with displeasure. **-vveléno**, M.: counterpoison. **=vveníre**, IRR.; INTR.: contravene (offend against, break). **-vventóre**, M.: contravener. **-vvenzióne**, F.: contravention (violation). **-vversitàꝉ**, F.: controversy, contrariety.

contrazióne [*contrarre*], F.: contraction.

contri-buènte, PART.: contributing; M.: contributor. ||**-buíre** [L. *con-tribuere* (grant)], INTR.: contribute; coöperate (concur). **-búto**, M.: contribution. **-butóreꝉ**, M.: contributor. **-buzioncèlla**, F.: small contribution. **-buzióne**, F.: contribution; impost, tax.

contrimboscáta [*contra imboscata*], F.: counter-ambuscade.

contríreꝉ, TR.: bruise; feel contrition.

contristá-bile, ADJ.: saddening. **-ménto**, M.: sadness. ||**contristá-re** [L. *tristis*, sad)], TR.: afflict (sadden); REFL.: be afflicted. **-tóre**, M., **-tríce**, F.: afflicter. **-zióneꝉ**, F.: sadness.

contri-taménte, ADV.: contritely. **-táreꝉ**, TR.: crush (pulverize). ||**contrí-to** [L. *-tus* (*terere*, grind)], ADJ.: crushedꝉ; contrite. **-zioncèlla**, F.: slight contrition. **-zióne**, F.: contrition.

cóntro [L. *contra*], PREP.: against; opposite to; M.: contrary: *il pro e il* —, the pro and the con; *darsi* —, contradict one's self. **=cássa**, F.: outside case. **=cáva**, F.: countermine. **=cífra**, F.: key of a cipher. **=dáta**, F.: revised date, letter, poem. **=finèstra**, F.: opposite window. **=fòdera**, F.: stiffening; quilting. **=fòrza**, F.: counter-force, etc. **=légge**, F.: counter-law. **=lèva**, F.: counter-lever. **=lúce**, F.: unfavorable light. **=márcia**, F.: countermarch. **=mína**, F.: countermine. **=mináre**, TR.: countermine, frustrate. **=nòta**, F.: answering note. **=párte**, F.: opposing side. **-perazióne** [*operazione*], F.: counter-operation. **=pòrta**, F.: extra door; heavy door. **=pròva**, F.: counter-proof.

contró-rdine [*ordine*], M.: countermand. **=scárpa**, F.: counterscarp. **=scèna**, F.: silent part of an actor (when some one else speaks). **=scrítta**, F.: duplicate, copy. **=scrívereꝉ**, TR.: write against. **=sènso**, M.: opposite meaning. **=stampáre** = *contrastampare*. **=stímolo**, M.: debilitant drug, whatever weakens. **=stòmaco**, ADV.: with great repugnance, unwillingly.

con=trováreꝉ, TR.: invent, feign.

contro-vèrsi, PRET. of *-vertere*. **-vèrsia**, F.: controversy. **-versísta**, M.: controversialist. **-vèrso**, PART. of *-vertere*; ADJ.: controversial, doubtful. ||**=vèrtere**, IRR.; INTR.: controvert, dispute. **-vertíbile**, ADJ.: controvertible.

contu-bernále, ADJ.: contubernal, living together. **-bèrnia**, F., ||**-bèrnio** [L. *-bernium* (*taberna*, hut)], M.: (*mil.*) tent-companionship; messmates; ADJ.: contubernal.

contu-máce, ADJ.: contumacious. ||**-mácia** [L.], F.: contumacy (wilful defiance);

(*nav.*) quarantine: *fare la* —, put under quarantine. **-macïále**, ADJ.: contumacious. **-mèlia**, F.: contumely. **-melióso**, ADJ.: contumelious.
contúndere [L. (*tundere*, beat)], IRR.§; TR.: contuse, bruise.
§ Pret. *contú-si, -se; -sero*. Part. *contúso*.
conturba-zióne†, -'**nza**, F., **-ménto**, M.: perturbation, agitation. ‖**conturbá-re** [*con-*, *t.* .], TR.: disturb, alarm; REFL.: be disturbed. **-tívo**, ADJ.: disquieting. **-tóre**, M.: disturber. **-zióne**, F.: perturbation, trouble.
con-túsi, PRET. of *-tundere*. **-tusióne**, F.: contusion. ‖**-túso**, PART. of *-tundere*.
con=tutóre, M.: fellow-tutor.
con=tutto=chè, CONJ.: although.
con=tutto=ciò, ADV.: nevertheless, yet.
con=tutto=quésto, ADV.: notwithstanding that.
convale-scènte [L. *-scere* (*validus*, strong)], ADJ., M.: convalescent. **-scènza**, F.: convalescence.
convali-dáre [L. (*validus*, strong)], TR.: render valid (strengthen). **-dazióne**, F.: strengthening (authentication).
con=válle, F.: valley (vale); us'ly pl.
con-vègna†, F.: convention. **-vègno**, ‖**-végno** [L. **venium* (*venire*, COME)], M.: convention; compact†.
con-vellènte, ADJ.: CONVULSIVE. ‖**-vèllere**† [L. (*vellere*, tear)], TR.: tear or pull away, twist.
conve-nènte†, M.: fact; state; way; agreement; condition. **-nènza**†, F.: agreement; convention. **-névole**, ADJ.: suitable; M.: convenience (conformity); PL. compliments. **-nevolézza**, F.: suitableness (propriety). **-nevolménte**, ADV.: suitably. **-niènte**, ADJ.: convenient, fit; M.: suitableness. **-nientemente**, ADV.: suitably. **-niènza**, F.: convenience, propriety; compliments; advantage. ‖**-níre** [*con-*, *v.* .], IRR.; TR.: convene; summon; INTR.: agree (harmonize); suit; be convenient; be necessary. **convénni**, PRET. of *-nire*. **convè-no**†, M.: need. **-ntáre**†, TR.: covenant; become; admit as a doctor; crown with laurel. **-ntazióne**†, F.: crowning of poets. **-ntícola**, F., **-ntícolo**†, M.: conventicle. **-ntíno**, M.: small convent; asylum (retreat). **convè-nto**, M.: convent; assembly. **-ntuále**, ADJ.: conventual; M., F.: monk, nun. **-núto**, PART.: assembled; M.: assemblage. **-nzionále**, ADJ.: conventional. **-nzionáre**†, TR.: stipulate. **-nzióne**, F.: covenant (treaty; agreement); convention (assembly).
conver-gènte, ADJ.: convergent. **-gènza**, F.: convergence. ‖**convèr-gere** [L. (*vergere*. turn)], INTR.: converge.
convèr-sa, F.: lay sister. **-saménto**†, M.: conversation. **-sáre**, INTR.: converse; frequent†. **-satívo**†, ADJ.: conversative. **-satóre**, M.: converser. **-sazioncèlla**, **-sazioncína**, F.: short conversation; small assemblage. **-sazióne**, F.: assembly; conversation; social gathering (party): *tener* —, hold a reception. **-sévole**, ADJ.: conversable; sociable. **-sevolménte**, ADV.: sociably. **convèr-si**, PRET. of *-tire*. **-sióne**, F.: conversion, change. **convèr-so**, ADJ.: converted; M.: lay brother: *per* —†, on the contrary. **convèr-tere**† = *-tire*. **-tíbile**, ADJ.: convertible. **-timénto**†, M.: conversion. ‖**-tíre** [L. *-tere* (*vertere* turn)], IRR.§; TR. (Pr. *-to*): convert (change); (Pr. *-tisco*) turn†; REFL.: become converted. **-títo**, PART., M.: convert. **-titóre**, M.: converter.
§ Ind.: Pres. *convèr-to* or *-tisco*†. Pret. *convèrsi*†. Part. *convèrso*†.
con-vessità, F.: convexity. ‖**con-vèsso** [L. *-vexus* (*vehere*, carry)], ADJ.: convex; M.: convexity.
conviáre†, TR.: convoy (escort).
convicíno†, ADJ.: adjacent (VICINAL).
convin-centeménte, ADV.: convincingly. **-cènte**, PART., ADJ.: convincing. ‖**convín-cere** [*con-*, *v.* .], IRR.; TR.: convince; REFL.: be convinced. **-ciménto**, M.: persuasion. **-citívo**†, ADJ.: convincing. **convin-si**, PRET. of *-cere*. **-tíssimo**, ADJ.: perfectly convinced. **convín-to**, PART.: convinced, convicted. **-zióne**, F.: conviction.
con-víssi, PRET., **-vissúto**, PART. of *-vivere*.
convi-tánte, PART.: inviting; M.: host. ‖**-táre** [*co-invitare*], TR.: invite (to a repast). **-táto**, PART.: invited; M.: guest. **-tatóre**, M.: inviter.
convitígia†, F.: covetousness, avarice.
conví-to [*-tare*], M.: dinner, banquet.
con-vítto, M.: school where students live and board (boarding-school, college); student of such a school. **-vittóre** [cf. *-vitto*], M., **-vittríce**, F.: boarding student (*f.* boarding-school miss), collegian. **-víva**†, M.: boarder. **-vivále**†, ADJ.: convivial. **-viváre**†, INTR.: eat at the same table. **-vivatóre**†, M.: fellow-boarder. **-vivènza**, F.: living together. ‖**=vívere**, IRR.; INTR.: live together. **-vívio**†, M.: feast.
convi-ziáre†, TR.: injure. **-ziatóre**†, M.: injurer.
conviziόso, ADJ.: desirous.
convoca-ménto, M.: assembly. ‖**convocá-re** [*con-*, *v.* .], TR.: convoke, assemble. **-zióne**, F.: convocation.
con-vogliáre, TR.: convoy, escort.

‖**-vòglio** [Fr. -voi (L. *via*, WAY)], M.: CONVOY (escort); procession; train: — *funebre*, funeral procession.

convoláre†, INTR.: fly together; run fast.

convòlgere†, TR.: roll.

convòlvolo [L. -*vulus* (*volvere*, twine)], M.: convolvulus (plant).

convul-saménte, ADV.: convulsively. **-sionária**, F., **-sionário**, M.: convulsionist. **-sioncèlla**, F.: slight convulsion. **-sióne**, F.: convulsion. **-sívo**, ADJ.: convulsive. ‖**convúl-so** [L. -*sus* (*vellere*, tear)], ADJ.: convulsed; M.: convulsion.

coone-staménto, M.: excuse, pretext. ‖**-stáre** [*co-*, *o.* .], TR.: palliate, cloak.

coopera-ménto†, M.: coöperation. **coo-perá-re** [*co-*, *o.* .], INTR.: coöperate, concur. **-tívo**, ADJ.: coöperative. **-tóre**, M., **-tríce**, F.: coöperator. **-zióne**, F.: coöperation.

coordina-ménto, M.: coördination. ‖**coordiná-re** [*co-*, *o.* .], TR.: coördinate. **-tóre**, M., **-tríce**, F.: adjuster (classifier). **-zióne**†, F.: coördination.

coortáre†, TR.: comfort, exhort.

coòrte [L. *co-hors*, YARD, pen], F.: cohort (tenth of a Rom. legion); crowd.

coper-chiáre†, TR.: cover. **-chiàlla**†, F.: small cover; fraud. **-chiétto**, M.: *dim.* of -*chio*. **copèr-chio**, M.: lid (cover). **copèr-si**, PRET. of *coprire*. **copèr-ta**, F.: cover; excuse (pretext): *d'una lettera*, envelope; *alla* —, secretly. **-taménte**, ADV.: secretly. **-tína**, F.: small cover. ‖**copèr-to**, PART. of *coprire*: covered: *al* —, in safety; *parlar* —, speak ambiguously. **-tóia**, F., **-tóio**, M.: large lid. **-tóne**, M.: large cover. **-túra**, F.: cover; mask†.

còpia 1 [L. (*ops*, riches)], F.: copiousness (plenty).

còpia 2 [*coppia*], F.: copy, reproduction; book; imitation. **-lèttere**, M.: letter-book; copying-press. ‖**copiá-re** [*copia* 2], TR.: copy; imitate. **-tívo**, ADJ.: copying. **-tóre**, M.: copier. **-túra**, F.: copying.

copíglio, M.: beehive.

copio-saménte, ADV.: copiously. **-sità**, F.: copiousness, abundance. ‖**copió-so** [*copia* 1], ADJ.: copious.

copí-sta [*copiare*], M.: copyist. **-stería**, F.: copyist's office.

còp-pa [L. *cupa*, cask], F.: CUP, bowl; oil vase (of a lamp); back of the head†: — *d'oro*, excellent character; *servir di* —, be a cup-bearer. **-páia**, F.: room for oil-jars.

coppále [from Mex.], ADJ., M.: copal.

copparòsa†, F.: copperas.

cop-pèlla [-*pa*], F.: COPPEL (cupel, crucible): *oro di* —, pure gold. **-pelláre**, TR.: cupel, refine. **-pétta**, F.: cupping glass. **-pettóne**, M.: large cupping-glass.

còppia [*copula*], F.: couple, pair: *una* — *di pane*, kind of fine bread, oblong loaf.

cop-pière [-*pa*], **-pièro**†, M.: cupbearer.

coppiétta [-*pia*], F.: small couple; small oblong loaf.

cóppo [*coppa*], M.: vase (us'ly for oil; jar); pantile (~shaped tile).

copri-ménto†, M.: covering. ‖**coprí-re** [L. *co-operire*, cover], IRR.§; TR.: COVER; conceal, palliate; REFL.: cover one's self, put on one's hat. **-tóre**, M.: coverer. **-túra**, F.: cover; pretext†. =**vivánde**, M.: cover for dishes.

§ = *aprire*; but poet. also accent. *cuòpr-* for *còpr-*.

còpu-la [L.], F.: copulation; conjunction. **-láre**†, TR.: couple. **-latívo**, ADJ.: copulative.

cor- = *con* (before *r*.)

corá-ccio, M.: bad heart. ‖**corá-ggio** [*core*], M.: courage, desire†. **-ggiosaménte**, ADV.: courageously. **-ggióso**, ADJ.: courageous; M.: courageous man.

corále 1 [*coro*], ADJ., M.: choral.

corále† 2 [*core*], ADJ.: CORDIAL.

coral-láio, M.: worker in coral. **-lífero**, ADJ.: coralliferous. **-lína**, F.: sea-moss. **-líno**, ADJ.: coralline. **corál-lo** [Gr. *korállion*], M.: coral.

coralménte†, ADV.: cordially.

coráme [L. -*rium*, leather], M.: dressed leather.

corampò-polo, **-pulo** [L. *coram*, before, *populus*, people], ADV.: PUBLICLY.

coramvòbis†, M.: pompous man.

coráno [fr. Ar.], M.: Koran.

corá-ta [*core*], **-tèlla**, F.: pluck, liver.

corás-za [L. *coriacea* (*corium*, leather)], CUIRASS, armour; cuirassier. **-záio**, M.: cuirass-maker. **-záre**, TR.: arm with a cuirass. **-záta**, F., or *nave* —: ironclad. **-zato**, PART.: cuirassed, ironclad. **-zatúra**, F.: arming with a cuirass. **-zière**, M.: cuirassier; royal guard. **-zína**†, F.: breastplate. **-zóne**, M.: large cuirass.

còrba [L. -*bis*], F.: basket; basketful†.

cor-bacchíno†, *dim.*, **-bacchióne**†, *aug.* of -*bo*. **-báre**†, INTR.: caw (like a crow).

corbel-láio, M.: basket-maker or seller. **-láre**, TR.: joke, rally. **-latóra**, F., **-latóre**, M.: jester. **-latòrio**, ADJ.: jesting, ridiculous. **-latúra**, F.: raillery. **-lería**, F.: nonsense; absurdity; trifle, jest. **-létto**, *dim.* of -*lo*. **-líno**, M.: small basket: *portare il* —, be a bricklayer; *a -lini*, in quantities. ‖**corbèl-**

-lo [*corba*], M.: round basket; silly person (fool); testicle: *a -li*, 'basketfuls,' in great quantities; *o -li!* exclamation of impatience; pshaw! **-lóna**, F.: simpleton. **-lóne**, *aug.* of *-lo*.

cor-bézzola, F.: arbute berry. ||**-bézzolo** [Ger. *kürbiss*, gourd], M.: arbute. **-bezzolóne**, M.: large arbute tree.

corbicíno†, *dim.* of *corbo*. **còrbo**† = *corvo*.

còrbona [fr. Heb.], F.: corban, alms-box.

corcáre† = *coricare*.

còr-da [L. *chorda*], F.: cord (thin rope); torture: *a —*, in a line; *dar — a uno*, make a person talk. **-dáio**†, M.: ropemaker. **-dáme**, M.: cordage. **-deggiáre**†, INTR.: be on a line (with). **-dèlla**†, **-dellína**, F.: small cord. **-dellóne**, M.: corded cloth. **-dettína**, F.: twine (string).

cordía-co†, ADJ.: cardiac. ||**cordiá-le** [L. *cor*, HEART], ADJ.: cordial (affectionate); M.: cordial. **-lità**, F.: cordiality. **-lménte**, ADV.: cordially. **-lóne**, ADJ.: very cordial.

cor-dicèlla [*-da*], **-dicína**, F.: small cord. **-dièra**, F.: tailpiece (of a violin, etc.). **-diglièro**, M.: cordelier (monk). **-díglio**, M.: monk's girdle. **-díno**, M.: string.

cor-dogliáre†, TR.: pity; INTR.: grieve. ||**-dòglio** [L. *-dolium* (*cor*, HEART, *dolere*, suffer)], M.: heart-grief (great sorrow); lament. **-dogliosaménte**†, ADV.: painfully. **-doglióso**, ADJ.: sorrowful (painful).

cordo-náre, TR.: cord; quiz. **-náta**, F., **-náto**, M.: inclined plane (for steps). **-natúra**, F.: quizzing. **-ncèllo**, **-ncíno**, M.: small cord; twine. ||**cordó-ne** [*corda*], M.: cord; coping of a wall; cordon (of troops): *o -ni!* pshaw! **-nería**, F.: nonsense, trifle.

cordo-vanière†, M.: shoemaker (Eng.† cordwainer). **-váno**†, M.: cordwain (cordovan leather).

còre, us'ly *cuore* [L. *cor*], M.: HEART.

coréggia [L. *corrigia* (*corium*, leather)], F.: strap, leather-thong; shoe-tie†; (*vulg.*) breaking of wind, fart. **-giáio**, M.: strapmaker. **-giáto**, M.: flail. **-giòla**†, F.: small leather-strap. **-giòlo**, M.: kind of olive-tree; band of a book; PL.: shoestrings or straps. **-giuòla**†, *dim.* of *-gia*. **-giuòlo** [1]†, M.: kind of olive-tree; strap.

coreggiuòlo† [2] = *crogiolo*.

corèo [*choreios* (*chorós*, dance)], ADJ.: trochaic; M.: choree (Gr. meter = trochee). **-grafía**, F.: composing dances. **-gráfico**, ADJ.: dance. **coreò-grafo**, M.: dance composer.

corétto [1] [*coro*], M.: choir-room; church-annex.

corétto† [2] [*-rio*], M.: breastplate.

còri [*cuore*], F.: hearts (suit at cards).

coriáceo [*corio*], ADJ.: coriaceous (of leather).

co-riámbico, ADJ.: choriambic. ||**-riámbo** [L. *chor-iambo* (cf. *coreo*, *iambo*)], M.: choriambus (—⏑⏑—).

coriándolo, **coriándro** [L. *-drum*], M.: coriander (plant or seed).

cori-bánte [Gr. *korúbas*], M.: Corybant (priest of Cybele). **-bántico**, ADJ.: Corybantic.

coricáre [L. *col-locare*], INTR.: lay down (COUCH); REFL.: go to bed; set (of the sun); spread.

cori-ciáttolo [*core*], M.: bad heart. **-cíno**, M.: little heart.

corifèo [L. *coryphæus* (Gr. *-phé*, head)], M.: corypheus (dramatic chorus leader); (*disp.*) chief.

corilèto†, M.: hazelnut grove. **còrilo**†, M.: hazelnut bush.

co-rimbífero, ADJ.: corymbiferous. ||**-rímbo** [L. *-rymbus*], M.: corymb.

corín-tio [L. *-thus*, Corinth], **-zio**, ADJ.: Corinthian; M.: (*arch.*) Corinthian order.

còrio† [L. *-rium*], M.: hide, leather.

corísta [*coro*], M.: chorister (chorus singer); tuning-fork.

corízza†, F.: cold, rheum.

corláia†, F.: parts about the heart; pluck.

còrna = *corniola*.

cornác-chia [L. *cornicula* (*cornix*, crow)], F.: crow; chatterer. **-chiaménto**†, M.: foolish chatter. **-chiáre**†, INTR.: croak, chatter. **-chíno**†, *dim.* of *-chia*. **-chióne**, *aug.* of *-chia*. **-chiúccia**, *disp. dim.* of *-chia*.

cornággine [*corno*], F.: obstinacy.

cornaménto†, M.: buzzing in the ears.

cornamú-sa [L. *cornu*, HORN, *musa*, muse], F.: bagpipe. **-sáre**†, TR.: play upon the bagpipe.

cor-náre† [*-no*], TR.: sound the horn. **-náta**, F.: blow with a horn; bugle-note. **-natóre**†, M.: who sounds the horn. **-natúra**, F.: shape or quality of animal's horns: *esser di tale —*, be of such a disposition; *esser di — gentile*, have a delicate constitution. **còr-nea**, F.: cornea. **còr-neo**, ADJ.: corneous (hard). **-nétta**, F.: cornet (mus. instrument; cavalry-flag borne by the bugler†; flag-bearer, young officer; troop of cavalry). **-nettíno**, F.: little horn. **-nétto**, pl. *-netti* or *-netta* (horns of animals), M.: small horn; postilion's horn; ear-trumpet; cupping-glass; (*mus.*) cornet†. **còr-nia**†, F.: cornelian cherry.

cornìce [l. L. *-ronix* (ak. *-rona*, crown)], F.: frame; cornice.

cornicèllo†, *dim.* of *corno*.
corni-cétta, F.: small cornice or frame. ||**-ciáme** [*-ce*], M.: cornice-work. **-cia-ménto**, M.: cornice-work. **-ciáre**, more commonly *scorniciare*. **-ciáto**, M.: corniced building, door, etc. **-ciatúra**, F.: cornice-work; framework. **-cína**, F.: small cornice or frame.
cornicíno [*corno*], M.: small horn.
cornicióne [*-nice*], M.: (*arch.*) entablature.
cor-níno, pl. *-nini* or *-nina; dim.* of *-no*.
còr-nio† = *-niolo*. **còr-niola** 1, F.: cornelian cherry. **-niòla** 2, F.: cornelian (variety of chalcedony). **còr-niolo**, M.: cornus or dogwood tree; cornelian cherry; ADJ.: cornus-, dogwood-. **-ní-pode**, ADJ.: horn-foot, hoofed; M.: (*poet.*) horse. ||**còr-no**, pl. (*f.*) *-na* or *-ni* (instrument), [L. *-nu*, HORN], M.: HORN; arm of a river or street; wing of an army; end; tip (of a flame); PL. (*-na*): infidelity (in marriage); impertinences: *fiaccar le -na a*, lower the pride of; humble; *far le -na a*, make a cuckold; *portar le -na*, be a cuckold; *non valere un —*, be of no value.
cor-nucòpia [L. *cornu*, HORN, *copia*, plenty], F.: cornucopia (horn of plenty). **-núto**, ADJ.: cornute; horned; M.: cuckold.
còro [L. *chorus*, choral dance], M.: CHOIR (chorus).
coro-grafía [Gr. *chôros*, place, *gráphein*, write], F.: chorography. **-gráfico**, ADJ.: chorographical. **coròg-rafo**, M.: chorographer.
coró-lla, F.: corolla. **-llário**, M.: corollary. ||**coró-na** [L.], F.: CROWN; royal dignity; garland; tonsure; chaplet, beads. **-náio**, M.: chaplet-maker or seller. **-nále**, ADJ.: (*anat.*) coronal. **-naménto**, M.: crowning. **-náre**, TR.: crown. **-nazióne**, F.: coronation. **-ncí-na**, *dim.* of *-na*. **-ncióna**, **-ncióne**, (*jest.*) *aug.* of *-na*. **-nèlla**, F.: small tumor.
cor-paccíáta, F.: stomachful. **-pác-cio**, M.: clumsy body. **-paccíúto**, ADJ.: corpulent; capacious. **-pettíno**, *dim.* of *-petto*. **-pétto**, M.: under-waist-coat. **-picciòlo**, M.: little body. **-pi-cèllo**, M.: small body. **-piciáttolo**, M.: weak body. **-piíno**, *dim.* and *car.* of *-po*. ||**còr-po** [L. *-pus*], M.: body; substance; stomach; society (order); corps of soldiers; hulk of a ship. **-póne**, M.: large body. **-poràle**, ADJ.: corporal, corporeal; M.: corporal (altar linen). **-poralità**†, F.: corporality (materiality). **-poralménte**, ADV.: corporally, bodily. **-poratúra**, F.: constitution, size. **-po-razióne**, F.: corporation. **-poreità**†, F.: corporeity. **-pòreo**, ADJ.: corporeal, bodily. **-púccio**, *disp.* of *-po*. **-pulèn-to**, ADJ.: corpulent. **-pulènza**, F.: corpulence. **-puscoláre**, ADJ.: corpuscular. **-púscolo**, M.: corpuscle (atom). **-pusdòmini** [L., 'Lord's body'], M.: eucharist; Corpus Christi day. **-púto**†, ADJ.: corpulent. **-púzzo**†, M.: ugly body.
còrre = *cogliere*.
corre-daménto, M.: furniture, equipment. **-dáre**, TR.: furnish, equip. ||**cor-rè-do** [?], M.: equipment (outfit, necessaries); complete assortment; feast†.
corrèg-gere [*cor-*, *r.*.], IRR.; TR.: CORRECT, chastise; improve; REFL.: correct one's self. **-gévole**†, ADJ.: corrigible. **-gíbile**, ADJ.: corrigible. **-giménto**†, M.: correction; direction (guidance). **-gi-tóre**, M.: corrector. **-gitúra**†, F.: correction.
corregnáre†, INTR.: reign together.
correla-tívo [*relativo*], ADJ.: correlative. **-zióne**, F.: correlation.
correligionário [*con*, *religione*], M.: coreligionist.
corrèn-te [*correre*], PART., ADJ.: current; general; ready, quick; F.: current, stream; M.: (*arch.*) scantling, crosspiece; ADV.: freely, fluently. **-teménte**, ADV.: currently; fluently. **-tézza**, F.: currency. **-tía**†, F.: current. **corrèn-zia**†, F.: rush of water.
còr-reo or **cor-rèo**, M.: accomplice.
cór-rere 1 [L. *currere*], IRR.§; INTR.: run, flow; TR.: run, pass through: *-re voce* (*fama*), they say; *— per le poste*, travel by post. **-rère** 2 = *corriere*. **-re-ría**†, more commonly *scorrería*.

§ Pret. *còr-si*, *-se*; *-sero*. Part. *córso*.

corrispet-tività, F.: mutual relation, equivalence. ||**-tívo** [*respettivo*], ADJ.: correspondent, equivalent; M.: equivalent.
corressi, PRET. of *correggere*.
corret-taménte, ADV.: correctly. **-téz-za**, F.: correctness. **-tívo**, M., ADJ.: corrective. ||**corrèt-to** [*correggere*], PART.: corrected; ADJ.: correct. **-tóre**, M.: corrector; rector. **-toría**†, F.: office of corrector or rector. **-tríce**, F.: she who corrects. **-túra**†, F.: correction. **corre-zionále**, ADJ.: of correction. **-zioncèlla**, **-zioncína**, F.: slight correction. **-zióne**, F.: correction; censure: *— di lingua*, correctness of language.
corríbo† = *corrivo*.
cor-ridóio [*-rere*], **-ridóre**, M.: corridor; swift horse, courser; scout; ADJ.: running, swift. **-rièra**, F., **-rière**, **-rièro**†, M.: courier, messenger.

corrigíbile†, ADJ.: corrigible.
corrimènto†, M.: running (course).
corri-spondènte, PART.: corresponding. **-spondentemènte**, ADV.: correspondingly. **-spondènza**, F.: correspondence; affinity: *a* —, opposite to, over against. ‖**-spóndere** [*rispondere*], IRR.; INTR.: correspond, agree with; suit; answer for, go security. **-spósi**, PRET., **-spósto**, PART. of *-dere*.
corrit.. = *corrid*.., M.: runner. **corrivamènte**, ADV.: readily. ‖**=rívo**, ADJ.: ready; (prone); ready of belief (credulous); ready to admit (yielding); free; M.†: dupe.
corrobo-ráre [L. (*robur*, strength)], TR.: corroborate (strengthen, confirm). **-ramènto**, M.: corroboration. **-ratívo**, ADJ., M.: corroborative. **-razióne**†, F.: confirmation.
cor=ródere, IRR.; TR.: corrode (wear away). **-rodimènto**, M.: corrosion.
corróm-pere [*cor-*, *r*..], IRR.; TR.: CORRUPT (spoil); infect; bribe; REFL.: become corrupt, putrify. **-pévole**†, ADJ.: corruptible. **-pimènto**, M.: corruption. **-pitóre**, M., **-pitrice**, F.: corrupter.
corró-si, PRET. of *-dere*. **-sióne**, F.: corrosion. **-sívo**, ADJ., M.: corrosive. ‖**corró-so**, PART. of *-dere*.
cor-rottamènte, ADV.: corruptly. **-rottíbile**† = *corruttibile*. ‖**-rótto** [*corrompere*], PART.: corrupted (corrupt); mourning†.
corruc-ciáre, INTR., REFL.: be (become) angry. **-ciatamènte**, ADV.: angrily. **-ciáto**, PART., ADJ.: angry. ‖**corrúccio** [ak. to *corrotto*], M.: anger (wrath). **-ciosamènte**†, ADV.: angrily. **-cióso**†, ADJ.: choleric, irritable.
corrugáre [*ruga*], TR., REFL.: corrugate (wrinkle, frown).
corrúppi, PRET. of *corrompere*.
corru-scáre, INTR.: coruscate (flash). **-scazióne**, F.: coruscation (glitter). ‖**corrú-sco** [L. *coruscus*, shaking], ADJ.: coruscant (flashing).
corrut-tèla [*corrotto*], F.: corruption. **-tévole**†, **-tíbile**, ADJ.: corruptible. **-tibilità**, F.: corruptibility. **-tívo**†, ADJ.: corruptive. **-tóre**, M., **-trice**, F.: corrupter. **corruzióne**, F.: corruption; putrefaction.
cór-sa [*-so*], F.: running; course, race: *a* (*di*) —, very swiftly. **-sále**† = *-saro*.
corsalètto [Fr. *-selet* (L. *corpus*, body)], M.: corselet.
cor-saréSco, ADJ.: pertaining to a corsair. ‖**-sáro** [*-so*], M.: corsair (pirate). **-seggiáre**†, INTR.: be a corsair. **-seggiatóre**†, M.: corsair. **-serèlla**, F.: short run or course.
corsé-sca†, F.: javelin (spear). **-scáta**†, F.: spear-thrust.
cor-settína, F.: short course. **cór-si**, PRET. of *-rere*. **-sía**, F.: current of a stream; way, passage; gangway. **-sière**, **-sièro**, M.: (*poet.*) courser, steed. **-sína**, *dim.* of *-sa*. **-sío**, ADJ.: running, flowing (said of water). **-sivamènte**†, ADV.: cursorily. **-sívo**, ADJ.: running, cursive: *carattere* —, running hand; italics. ‖**cór-so** 1 [*-rere*], PART.: run, etc.; passed (last); M.: running; COURSE (progress; career; period); currency; race-course ('corso'; public drive-way); carriage-ride; cruise: *aver* —, have a run; be in vogue (be fashionable); *fare un — di studi*, pursue a course of studies; *andare in* —, be a pirate.
còrso 2 [*Corsica*], ADJ.: Corsican.
corsóio†, ADJ.: running, sliding.
cortáldo†, M.: bob-tailed horse.
cortamènte†, ADV.: briefly.
córte [*co-hors*, YARD, pen], F.: court-yard; court; court-room: *tener* —, entertain, banquet.
cortéc-cia [L. *cortex*], F.: bark (outside); crust: *guardare alla — delle cose*, look at things superficially. **-cína**, F.: thin bark or crust. **-cióna**, F.: thick bark. **-cióso**, ADJ.: having a thick bark. **-ciuòla** † = *-cina*.
cor-teggiamènto, M.: paying court. ‖**-teggiáre** [*-te*], TR.: court. **-teggiatóre**, M.: courtier; flatterer. **-téggio**, M.: cortege (retinue). **-tegianésco**†, ADJ.: of a courtier. **-tegianía**† = *-tigianeria*. **-tèo**, M.: retinue; bridal or baptismal train. **-tése**, ADJ.: courteous. **-teseggiamènto**†, M.: liberality. **-teseggiáre**†, INTR.: be courteous or liberal. **-tesemènte**, ADV.: courteously. **-tesía**, F.: courtesy (politeness; affability); gratuity (drink-money). **-tesiòla**, F.: slight courtesy.
cortézza [*corto*], F.: shortness.
còrtice†, M.: bark, crust.
corti-cèlla [*corte*], **-cína**, F.: small court (of a house). **-giána**†, F.: court lady; courtesan. **-gianamènte**, ADV.: courteously; in a courtly manner. **-gianáta**, F.: act of a courtier. **-gianèllo**, M.: young courtier. **-gianería**, F.: manner of a courtier (Eng.† courtiery); adulation, finesse (flattery). **-gianésco**, ADJ.: courtier-like; fawning. **-giáno**, M.: courtier; flatterer; ADJ.: of the court. **cortí-le**, M.: large inner court (court-yard). **-lètto**, M.: small court. **-lóne**, *aug.* of *-le*.
cortí-na [?], F.: curtain; bed-curtain; (*mil.*) curtain (part of wall between two bastions). **-nággio**, M.: bed-curt[ain]. **-náre**†, TR.: furnish with curtains.

córto [L. *curtus*], ADJ.: short (CURT); ADV.: shortly: *di* —, shortly; *venire alle corte*, come to a conclusion; *alle corte*, in short.
corúccio 1 [*coro*], M.: poor choir.
corúccio 2 [*core*], M.: bad heart.
corusc. . = *corrusc. .*
corvátta = *cravatta*.
cor-vétta 1 [L. *corbita* (*-bis*, basket)], F.: corvette (small war vessel).
corvét-ta 2 [L. *curvus*, curved], F.: curvet (leap). **-táre**, INTR.: curvet (leap). **-tatóre**, M.: curveting horse.
cor-víno, ADJ.: raven (jet black). ||**còrvo** [L. *-vus*], M.: raven: *aspettare il* —, wait for what never comes.
cò-sa [L. *causa*, cause], F.: thing; matter; affair, business; use, service: *-se da nulla*, trifles. **-sáccia**, F., **-sáccio**, M.: bad thing.
cosácco [fr. Russ.], M.: Cossack; barbarous soldier.
cosarèlla = *coserella*.
coscéndere† = *condiscendere*.
coscon - ziosaménte, ADV.: conscientiously. ||**-zióso** [*coscienza*], ADJ.: conscientious.
co-scétta, *dim.* of *-scia*. **-scétto**, M.: haunch (of meat). ||**cò-scia**, pl. *-sce* [L. *coxa*, hip], F.: thigh, haunch: — *del ponte*, abutment of a bridge. **-sciále**, M.: CUISH (armour for the thigh); axle-tree of a coach†.
co-sciènza [L. *con-scientia* (*scire*, know)], F.: conscience: *in* —, in truth, truly. **-scienzióso**, ADJ.: conscientious.
coscína, *dim.* of *coscia*.
coscíno † = *cuscino*.
còscio [*coscia*], M.: leg, haunch of meat.
co-scritto, PART. of *-scrivere*; M.: conscript. ||**=scrívere**, IRR.; TR.: conscript, enroll. **-scrizióne**, F.: conscription.
cose-llína [*cosa*], **-llúccia**, F.: little bit of a thing, trifle.
co séno, M.: (*geom.*) cosine.
cose-rèlla, **-rellína**, **-rellúccia**, *car. dim.* of *cosa*. **cosé-tta**, *dim.* of *cosa*. **-ttáccia**, F.: ugly little thing.
così [L. *eccu-sic*, 'lo-thus'], ADV.: thus, in this way: — *come*, as, so; — *fatto*, such; — —, so so, moderately; — *e* —, so and so. **-cchè**, CONJ.: so that.
co-sicciuòla [*-sa*], F.: small, little thing. **-sína**, *car. dim.* of *-sa*. **-síno**, *dim.* of *coso*.
cosmètico, ADJ., M.: cosmetic.
cos - micaménte, ADV.: cosmically. ||**còs - mico** [Gr. *kosmikós* (cf. *-mo*)], ADJ.: cosmic.
còsmo [Gr. *kósmos*, order, world], M.: cosmos, universe. **-gonía** [Gr. *gonos*, birth], F.: cosmogony. **-gònico**, ADJ.: cosmogonic. **-grafía**, F.: cosmography. **-gráfico**, ADJ.: cosmographical. **cosmògrafo**, M.: cosmographer. **-logía**, F.: cosmology. **-lògico**, ADJ.: cosmological. **-políta** [Gr. *-polites* (citizen)], M.: cosmopolite. **-polítíco**, ADJ.: cosmopolitan. **-politísmo**, M.: cosmopolitanism.
còso [disp. of *cosa*], M.: (*indef.*) thing (matter); simpleton (blockhead); money, measure: *un* — *d' otto metri*, a matter of eight metres.
cosóffiola †, F.: great confusion.
co=spárgere, IRR.; TR.: sprinkle, scatter. **-spársi**, PRET., **-spárso**, PART. of *-spargere*. **-sper. .**† = *-spar. .*
co-spettáccio, INTERJ.: zounds! confound it! M.: swagger†. **-spètto**, M.: presence; aspect (sight); INTERJ.: zounds! **-spettóne**, INTERJ.: plague on it! **-spicuità**, F.: conspicuousness, distinction. ||**-spícuo** [L. *-spicuus* (root *spec*, see)], ADJ.: conspicuous, distinguished.
cospi - ráre [*co-*, *s. .*], INTR.: conspire; combine. **-ratóre**, M., **-ratríce**, F.: conspirator. **-razioncèlla**, F.: little plot. **-razióne**, F.: conspiracy.
cóssi, PRET. of *cocere*.
còsso [L. *cossus*, wood-worm], M.: pimple, wart.
còsta [L. (rib, side)], F.: declivity, hillock; COAST: — —, along the coast.
co-stà [L. *eccu-istac*, 'lo-there'], ADV.: there, in that place: — *fuori*, there, outside. **-staggiù**, ADV.: there below.
co-stánte, ADJ.: constant. **-stantemónte**, ADV.: constantly. **-stánza**, F.: constancy, firmness. ||**-stáre** [L. *constare*, stand at], INTR.: COST; be evident†.
costassù [*costà*, *su*], ADV.: there above.
co-státo [*-sta*], M.: chest, ribs; side†. **-steggiáre**, INTR.: coast along; TR.: follow, wind along. **-steggiatóre**, M.: coaster.
costèi [L. *eccu-iste-hæc*, 'lo-this-here'], PRON. F.: that one, that, she.
costellá-re [*stella*], TR.: (*poet.*) sprinkle with stars. **-zióne**, F.: constellation.
coste-réccio [*costa*], M.: pickled pork-ribs. **-rèlla**, F.: pretty little slope.
coster-náre† [L. *con-sternere* (ak. to STREW)], TR.: throw down; REFL.: be in consternation, be confused. **-náto**, ADJ.: astonished, confounded. **-nazióne**, F.: consternation.
costì [L. *eccu-istic*, 'lo-there'], ADV.: in that place, there: — *poi*, in that case.
co-stièra [*-sta*], F.: shore, sea-coast; hillock. **-stièro**†, ADJ.: sidelong, slanting.
costi-paménto, M.: constipation. ||**-páre** [L. *con-stipare* (crowd)], TR.: consti-

pate. **-pazióne**, F.: severe cold (rheum); constipation.

costi-tuènte, ADJ.: constituent; M.: constituent assembly. ‖**-tuíre** [L. *constituere*], TR.: constitute; organize (establish); REFL.: surrender (submit). **-tutívo**, ADJ.: constitutive. **-túto**, M.: hearing, examination (in court). **-tutóre†**, M.: constituter. **-tuzionále**, ADJ.: constitutional. **-tuzióne**, F.: constitution; law.

còsto [*costare*], M.: cost (expense): *a nessun* —, at no price, in no way.

còsto-la [L. *costula* (*costa*, rib)], F.: rib; main filament in leaves; back of a knife. **-latúra**, F.: the ribs. **-létta**, F.: small rib; CUTLET, chop. **-lière†**, M.: broadsword. **-lína**, F.: small rib. **-lóne**, M.: large rib; coarse man. **-lúto**, ADJ.: (*bot.*) costal-nerved.

costóro [*-tui*], PRON. PL.: those, these.

costóso [*-to*], ADJ.: costly, expensive.

co-strettívo†, ADJ.: coercive; constringent. **-strétto**, PART., ADJ.: constrained, obliged. **-strígnere†**, ‖**=stríngere**, IRR.; TR.: constrict†; CONSTRAIN (oblige, compel); bind†. **-stringiménto**, M.: constraint, force. **-strínsi**, PRET. of *stringere*. **-strittívo**, ADJ.: constrictive (binding). **-strizióne†**, F.: constriction.

co-struíre [L. *con-struere* (pile)], IRR.§; TR.: construct, erect; construe. **-strútto**, PART.: constructed; M.: (*gram.*) construction; advantage, consequence. **-struttóre**, M., **-struttríce**, F.: constructer. **-struttúra†**, **-struzióne**, F.: structure; construction.

§ Reg. or Pret. *costrús-si, -se; -sero.* Part. *costrútto.*

costúi [L. *eccu-iste-hic*, 'lo-this-here'], PRON.: this fellow (in disp. sense).

costú-ma†, F.: custom. **-máccio**, M.: bad custom. **-mánza**, F.: custom (us'ly ancient); good breeding; way†. **-máre**, INTR.: be customary (be wont); TR.†: educate; accustom; practice. **-mataménte**, ADV.: politely. **-matézza**, F.: good breeding. **-máto**, PART.: educated, polite; habituated†. **-mazióne†**, F.: teaching. ‖**costú-me** [L. *con-suetudo* (*suus*, one's own)], M.: custom (usage); way; morals, habit; costume.

costúra [*cucitura*], F.: seam.

co-súccia [*-sa*], **-súzza†**, F.: trifle (nonsense).

cotá-le [L. *eccu-tale*, 'lo-such'], PRON.: such a one; ADJ.: such; ADV.†: so, thus. **-lménte†**, ADV.: in such a way (thus).

cotánto [L. *eccu-tantus*, 'lo-as-much'], ADV.: so much; so long†; ADJ.†: as much, as many: *due cotanti*, twice as many.

còte [L. *cos*], F.: whetstone; stimulus.

co-teghíno, M.: kind of pork sausage. ‖**-ténna** [L. *cutis*, skin], F.: rind of bacon; (*jest.*) skin of the head: *metter su* —, fatten. **-tennóso**, ADJ.: swardlike.

co-tésto [*-desto*], PRON.: that (one). **-testúi†**, PRON.: this fellow.

coti-chíno [L. *cutis*, skin], M.: kind of pork sausage. **-cóne**, M.: hard-skinned person; rude fellow.

cotidian.. = *quotidian..*

cotilèdone [Gr. *kotuledṓn* (*kotulḗ*, hollow cup)], M.: (*bot.*) cotyledon.

còto†, M.: thought.

cotó-gna, F.: quince (sort of apple). **-gnáto**, M.: quince preserve or marmalade. **-gníno**, ADJ.: smelling and tasting like quince. ‖**cotó-gno** [L. *cydonius*, quince-tree], M.: QUINCE-tree.

cotó-ne [fr. Ar.], M.: cotton: — *fulminante*, gun cotton. **-neríe**, F. PL.: cotton goods. **-nína**, F.: calico, canvas. **-nóso**, ADJ.: cottony, downy.

cotorníce†, F.: quail, partridge.

còtta 1 [?], F.: tunic (tabard); surplice.

còt-ta 2 [*cotto*], F.: cooking; baking; quantity cooked; drunkenness; infatuation: *di tre* —, most complete, arrant; *pigliare una* —, get drunk. **-tíccio**, ADJ.: half-cooked or baked; half-tipsy; somewhat in love.

còttimo [L. *quotumus*, of what number], M.: work by contract; contract: *lavorare a* —, work by contract.

còt-to [*cocere*], PART.: cooked; M.: cooked food. **-tóia**, F.: cooking; preparation; disposition. **-tóio**, ADJ.: easily cooked; easily falling in love. **-túra**, F.: cooking.

co-turnáto, ADJ.: wearing the buskin, buskined. ‖**-túrno** [Gr. *kóthornos*], M.: cothurn (buskin): *calzare il* —, write tragedies.

có-va, F.: brooding (hatching); hatching-place; den†. **-vaccíno**, M.: thin hard cake (baked in ashes). **-váccio†**, **-váccíolo** [*-vo*], M.: cave, den; (*jest.*) bed. ‖**-váre** [L. *cubare*, lie down], TR.: brood (hatch; plot); INTR.: sit brooding; linger idly; smoulder; stagnate (of water). **-váta**, F.: COVEY (brood). **-vatúra**, **-vazióne†**, F.: brooding (hatching).

cover-chiáre = *coperchiare*. ‖**covèr-ta** [*coperta*], F.: deck; covert†, lid. **-tína†**, F.: saddle-cloth.

covi-dáre†, TR.: covet. **-dóso†**, ADJ.: covetous.

covigliáre†, INTR.; REFL.: shelter one's self.

covíglio†, M.: beehive.

co-víle, M.: lair (den); (*jest.*) room; bed. ‖**có-vo** [*-vare*], **có-volo†**, M.: lair, haunt; (*jest.*) bed.

covon-cèllo, **-cíno**, M.: small sheaf. ||**covóne** [?], M.: sheaf.

covr.. = *copr*..

cozióne†, F.: cooking.

coz-záre [?], TR.: butt (strike with the horns); INTR.: dispute (contend): — *col muro*, struggle in vain. **-záta**, F.: butting (blow with the horns). **còz-zo**, M.: butting (shock): *dar di* —, run against.

cozzóne [L. *coctio*, cooking], M.: matrimonial agent; agent.

cra cra [echoic], F.: caw-caw of ravens.

craí† = *cra cra*.

crá-nio [L. *-nium*], M.: cranium (skull). **-niología**, F.: craniology.

cráp-ola†, **cráp-ula** [L.], F.: gluttony; debauch (cf. Eng. *crapula*, surfeit). **-ulá-re**, INTR.: indulge in debauch. **-ulóne**, M.: glutton, debauchee. **-ulosità**† = *-la*.

cráşi [Gr. *krâsis*, mixture], F.: crasis (contraction of vowels; *med.*: mixture).

cras-sézza†, F.: fatness. **-sízie**†, F.: (thickness). ||**-so** [L. *-sus*], ADJ.: crass (thick, gross, coarse).

cra-tèra†, F.: cup; crater. ||**-tère** [L. *-ter*], M.: crater.

cravát-ta [Fr. *-e* (*Cravate*, Croat)], F.: cravat. **-táio**, M.: maker or seller of cravats.

crázia [Ger. *kreuzer* (*kreuz*, cross)], F.: small Tuscan coin.

creá-nza, F.: education, good breeding. **-nzáto**, ADJ.: (*jest.*) well-bred. ||**creá-re** [L.], TR.: create (produce). **-tívo**, ADJ.: creative. **creá-to**, PART., ADJ.: created; M.†: creature (servant): *il* —, the world. **-tóre**, M.: creator. **-tríce**, F.: creatress. **-túra**, F.: creature; dependent. **-turína**, F.: dear little creature. **-zióne**, F.: creation; appointment; world.

crébbi, PRET. of *crescere*.

crèbro†, ADJ.: close (frequent).

cre-dènte, PART., ADJ.: believing. **-dèn-za**, F.: credence, faith; confidence; credit; pantry; cupboard: *lettere di* —, letters of credit; *a* —, on credit. **-den-zétta**, F.: small cupboard or pantry. **-denziále**, ADJ., M.: credential. **-den-zièra**† = *-denza*. **-denzière**, M.: butler; confidant†. **-denzína**, F.: small cupboard. **-denzóne**, M.: credulous man. ||**cré-dere** [L.], TR.: believe; imagine (suppose). **-dévole**†, ADJ.: credible: credulous. **-díbile**, ADJ.: credible; ...ous†. **-dibilità**, F.: credibility. ...**ménte**, ADV.: credibly. **cré-di**... credit; reputation. **-ditóre**, M., ...**e**, F.: creditor. **crè-do**, M.: ... *un* —, in an instant. **-dulità**, ...lity. **crè-dulo**, ADJ.: credu-

crè-ma, F.: cream (dish made of eggs, milk, sugar, etc.). ||**-máre** [L., burn], TR.: cremate. **-matóio**, M.: crematory. **-ma-tòrio**, ADJ.: crematory. **-mazióne**, F.: cremation.

cremiş.. = *chermis*..

cremóre†, M.: cream, essence.

creò-la, F., **-lo**, M. [?]: creole.

creoşòto [Gr. *kréas*, flesh, *sódzein*, preserve], M.: creosote.

crè-pa, F.: cleft; large opening (in walls). **-páccia**, F.: large crack. **-pacciáto**†, ADJ.: full of gaps or cracks. **-páccio**, M.: large cleft or gap; crepance. **-pac-ciòlo**, M.: gap. **-pa=c(u)òre**, M.: heartbreak. ||**-páre** [L.], INTR.: crack (split). **-patúra**, F.: crack.

crèpida [L.], F.: kind of sandal.

crepi-táre [L.], INTR.: crepitate (crackle). **crèpi-to**, M.: crepitation.

crepoláre, us'ly *screpolare*.

crepóre†, M.: hatred, scorn.

crepúnde†, M. or F. PL.: toys.

cre-puscoláre, ADJ.: crepuscular. ||**-pú-scolo** [L. *-pusculum*], M.: twilight (Eng.† crepuscle).

cre-şcèndo, M.: (*mus.*) crescendo. **-şcènte**, PART., ADJ.: growing, crescent; F.†: crescent moon. **-şcènza**, F.: increase, growth. ||**cré-şcere** [L.], IRR.§; INTR.: grow, inCREASE; TR.: augment. **-şciménto**, M.: increase, augmentation.

§ Pret. *crèb-bi*, *-be*; *-bero*. Part. *cresciúto*.

creşcióne [?], M.: cress.

cre-şcitóre, M., **-şcitríce**, F.: increaser. **-şciúta**, F.: growth. ||**-şciúto** [*crescere*], PART. of *-scere*.

crèş(i)-ma [cf. *crisma*], F.: CHRISMATION (sacrament of confirmation of faith by applying the chrism or holy oil). **-mán-do**, M.: person about to be confirmed (cf. *-ma*). **-máre**, TR.: confirm (cf. *-ma*); REFL.: be confirmed.

crésо†, PART. of *credere*.

cré-spa, F.: wrinkle, crease. **-spáre**†, TR.: crisp (curl); INTR.: curl. **-spàllo**†, M.: small wrinkle; fritter. **-spézza**†, F.: wrinkling. ||**cré-spo** [L. *crispus*], ADJ.: crisp (curled). **-spáto**, ADJ.: curled; wrinkled.

cré-sta [L. *crista*], F.: crest (tuft; summit); (*jest.*) woman's head-dress. **-stáia**, F.: milliner. **-staína**, *dim.* of *-staia*.

crestomazía [Gr. *chrestós*, useful, *ma-thein*, learn], F.: chrestomathy.

cre-stóso†, **-stúto**†, ADJ.: crested, tufted.

cré-ta, pop. *crè-ta* [L. (*Creta*, Crete)], F.: chalk, clay. **-tácco**, ADJ.: cretaceous; clayey. **crè-tico**, ADJ.: cretic (—⏑—). **-tína**, F., **-tíno** [from the colour of the skin], M.: cretin (idiot). **-tóso**, ADJ.: chalky.

crètto [*crepito*], M.: crack (chink).

cri [echoic], M.: crick, crack (sound): *cri-cri*, cricket's chirp.

criáre† = *creare*.

cri-bráre, TR.: sift; cleanse. **-brazióne**†, F.: sifting. **-bro** [L. *-brum*], M.: sieve.

cric [echoic], M.: crick, crack. **-ca**, F.: company of plotters, conspirators; flush of cards†; kind of game. **-che** = *cric*. **-chiáre**, us'ly *scricchiare*. **cric-chio**, M.: crack; caprice†.

cri-me†, M.: crime. **-men=lèṣe** [L. *-men læsæ* sc. *majestatis*, 'crime of offended majesty'], M.: LEZE-majesty (high treason). **-mināle**, ADJ.: criminal. **-minalísta**, M.: criminalist. **-minalità**, F.: criminality. **-minalménte**, ADV.: criminally. **-mináre**†, TR.: criminate, accuse. **-minazióne**†, F.: crimination (accusation). **crí-mine**, M.: crime. **-minosità**, F.: criminality. **-minóso**, ADJ.: criminal.

cri-nále, M.: comb; hair ornament. ‖**-ne** [L. *-nis*], M.: hair; mane: *il — d'un monte*, summit of a mountain; *i -ni del cavallo*, horse's mane and tail. **-nièra**, F.: horse's mane. **-níto**, ADJ.: (*poet.*) crinated (hairy). **-no**, M.: horse-hair (for stuffing).

cricca†, F.: crowd; clique.

crípta = *critta*.

criṣálide [Gr. *chrusallís* (*chrusós*, gold)], F.: chrysalis.

criṣantèmo [Gr. *chrusós*, gold, *ánthemon*, flower], M.: chrysanthemum.

crí-ṣe, -ṣi [Gr. *-sis*], F.: crisis.

críṣma [Gr. *chrísma*, unction], M.: chrism (consecrated oil used in some sacraments).

criṣòlito [Gr. *chrusós*, gold, *líthos*, stone], M.: chrysolite; (*fig.*) good wine.

cristal-láio, M.: maker or seller of glassware. **-láme**, M.: glassware. **-líno**, ADJ.: crystalline; M.: crystalline. **-lizzáre**, TR.: crystallize; REFL.: become crystallized. **-lizzazióne**, F.: crystallization. ‖**cristál-lo** [L. *-lum* (Gr. *krúos*, frost)], M.: crystal. **-lografía**, F.: crystallography. **-lògrafo**, M.: crystallographer.

cristátо†, ADJ.: crested.

cristèo†, M.: clyster.

cri-stianáccio, *disp.* of *-stiano*. **-stianaménte**, ADV.: as a Christian. **-stianeggiáre**, INTR.: approach Christianity. **-stianèllo**, *disp.* of *-stiano*. **-stianésimo**, M.: Christianity. **-stianíssimo**, ADJ.: most Christian; title of French kings. **-stianità**, F.: Christendom; Christianity. **-stiáno**, M.: Christian; civilized man; ADJ.: Christian: (*jest.*) *ogni fedel* —, every man, everybody. ‖**Crí-sto** [Gr. *christós* (*chríein*, anoint)], M.: Christ; image of Christ (crucifix).

cri-tèrio [Gr. *kri-térion* (*-nein*, separate)], M.: criterion (discernment, judgment). **crí-tica**, F.: criticism; critique, censure. **-ticábile**, ADJ.: criticisable. **-ticaménte**, ADV.: critically. **-ticáre**, TR.: criticise; censure. **-ticatóre**, M.: critic. **-tichétto**, *disp.* of *-tico*. **-ticíṣmo**, M.: criticism. **crí-tico**, ADJ.: critical; M.: critic. **-ticóne**, *aug.* of *-tico*.

crít-ta [Gr. *krúp-te* (*-tein*, hide)], F.: GROTTO; subterraneous place; CRYPT. **-tògama** [Gr. *gámos*, marriage], ADJ.: cryptogamian; F.: cryptogamia.

cri-vellàre, TR.: cribble; sift. ‖**-vèllo** [L. *-brum*], M.: sieve, bolter; CRIBBLE.

croc-cánte, ADJ.: crackling, brittle (said of food); M.: kind of almond cake. ‖**-cáre**† = *-chiare*.

cròcchia [?], F.: tresses.

croc-chiáre [root *cro-*, ak. to 'crow'], INTR.: rattle; cluck; chatter†. **cròcchio**, M.: circle (of conversing people); clique; conversation: *mettersi a* —, converse. **-chióne**†, M.: chatterer.

cròccia†, F.: oyster.

crocciáre†, INTR.: cluck.

cròcco†, M.: iron hook.

cró-ce [L. *crux*], F.: CROSS; trouble, sorrow. **-cellína**, *car. dim* of *-ce*.

cròceo [L. *-ceus* (*-cus*, saffron)], ADJ.: (*poet.*) saffron-coloured.

cro-cería†, F.: multitude of crusaders. ‖**-ce=signáto** = *crucesignato*. **-cétta**, F.: crosslet. **-ciaménto**†, M.: affliction. **-ciáre**, TR.†: join a crusade; mark with a cross; REFL.: assume the cross. **-ciáta**, F.: crusade: — *di strade*, cross-road. **-ciáto**, M.: crusader; torment†; ADJ.†: marked with the cross. **-ciòcchio**, M.: cross-road.

crocidáre [L. *crocitare* (*crocire*)], INTR.: caw, croak.

crocièra [*croce*], F.: crossing (intersection); constellation.

croci- [L. *crux*, CROSS]. ‖**=fíggere**, IRR. TR.: crucify; torment; REFL.: mortify one's self. **-fissáio**, M.: maker or seller of crucifixes. **-físsi**, PRET. of *-figgere*. **-fissíne**, F. PL.: religious association. **-fissíno**, M.: small crucifix. **-fissióne**, F.: crucifixion. **-físso**, PART.: crucified; M.: crucifix. **-fissóre**, M.: crucifier.

crocióne [*-ce*], M.: great cross.

crociuòlo† = *crogiolo*.

cròco [L. *crocus*], M.: (*poet.*) crocus, saffron.

cro-giáre† [?], TR.: roast. **-gioláre**, TR.: roast; REFL.: give one's self up to, pamper one's self. **-gioletto**, M.: small

crucible. **-giòlo**¹, M.: crucible. **crò-giolo**², M.: roasting; slow cooking.
cròio†, ADJ.: hard (unyielding); clownish.
crol=láre [*co-rotulare* (L. *rota*, wheel)], INTR.: shake, fall; REFL.: fall headlong. **cròl-lo**, M.: shaking, jog: *dar l'ultimo* —, die; go to ruin.
crò-ma [Gr. *chróma*, colour], F.: (*mus.*) quaver. **-maticaménte**, ADV.: chromatically. **-mático**, ADJ.: chromatic. **-molitografía**, F.: chromolithography.
crò-naca [Gr. *chrónos*, time], F.: chronicle. **-nachétta**, F.: short chronicle. **crò-nica**† = *-naca*. **-nicaménte**, ADV.: in a chronic manner. **-nichísta**†, M.: chronicler. **-nicismo**, M.: (*med.*) chronic illness. **-nicità**, F.: being chronic. **crò-nico**, ADJ.: chronic, lingering. **-nísta**, **-nògrafo**, M.: chronicler. **-nología**, F.: chronology. **-nologicaménte**, ADV.: chronologically. **-nològico**, ADJ.: chronological. **-nologísta**, **-nòlogo**, M.: chronologist. **-nòmetro**, M.: chronometer.
crosci. . = *scrosci*. .
cròsta [L. *crusta*], F.: CRUST (scale); crust of bread; outside. **-stáceo**, ADJ.: crustacean; M.: crustacea. **-státa**, F.: pie, tart. **-sterèlla**, F.: very small crust. **-stíno**, M.: slice of bread. **-stóne**, M.: large crust. **-stóso**, **-státo**†, ADJ.: crusty.
cròtalo [L. *-talum*], M.: rattlesnake (of the 'crotalus' species); crotalum (sacred to Cybele).
cruccévo-le†, ADJ.: irritable. **-lménte**†, ADV.: irritably.
crúccia† = *gruccia*.
cru-cciáre [L. *-ciare* (*crux*, cross)], INTR., REFL.: grieve; TR.: torment, afflict. **-cciataménte**, ADV.: angrily; sorrowfully. **-cciáto**†, ADJ.: angry, provoked. **crúccio** [cf. *corruccio*], M.: anger (passion wrath); torment. **-cciosaménte**, ADV.: angrily. **-ccióso**, ADJ.: angry. **-cesignáto**, ADJ.: with the cavalier's cross; M.: cavalier with a cross. **-ciaménto**, M.: torment. **-ciársi**, REFL.: mortify one's self. **-cícchio**† = *crocicchio*. **-cifiggere**† = *crocifiggere*.
cru-daménte, ADV.: crudely. **-deláccio**, ADJ.: barbarous. **-dèle**, ADJ.: cruel; painful. **-delézza**†, **-delità**†, F.: cruelty. **-delménte**, ADV.: cruelly. **-deltà**, F.: cruelty. **-dère**†, ADJ.: cruel. **-détto**, ADJ.: somewhat crude. **-dézza**, **-dità**, F.: crudity. ‖**crú-do** [L. *-dus*], ADJ.: crude (raw; immature); harsh; (*poet.*) cruel. **-entáre**†, TR.: make bloody. **-ènto**, ADJ.: bloody.
crúna [*corona*], F., **crúno**†, M.: eye of a needle.

crú-sca [OGer. *grüsche*], F.: bran; freckle; Florentine Academy (whose device, a sieve, denoted a sifting out of the 'bran'): *parlare in* —, talk affectedly, pedantically. **-scáio**, M.: pedant. **-scánte**, M.: (*jest.*) member of the Della Crusca Academy; purist. **-scáta**†, F.: tiresome speech, jumble. **-schèllo**, M.: fine bran. **-scherèlla**, F.: child's game. **-scóne**†, M.: ninny. **-scóso**, ADJ.: branny (full of bran).
crustáceo† = *crostaceo*.
cubáre [*cubo*], TR.: (*math.*) cube.
cubáre†², REFL.: lie down.
cu-báttolo†, M., **-báttola**†, F.: bird-trap.
cubatúra [*cubo*], F.: cubature.
cubèbe [fr. Ar.], M., F.: cubeb.
cubi-caménte, ADV.: cubically. **cúbico** [*cubo*], ADJ.: cubic. **-culário**†, M.: chamberlain. **-tále**, ADJ.: cubital: *lettere -tali*, uncial letters.
cúbi-to [L. *-tum*], M.: elbow; cubit.
cubitóso†, ADJ.: desirous.
cúbo [Gr. *kúbos*], M.: cube; ADJ.: cubic.
cuccá-gna [?], F.: great abundance; COCAGNE (land of luxury, Utopia); feast of climbing the greased pole (for prizes): *albero di* —, greased pole. **-gnáre**, TR.: make one believe, deceive.
cuccáia†, F.: owl's nest.
cuccétta [*-ccia*], F.: sailor's bed.
cuc-chiáia, F.: drag; rammer. **-chiaiáta**, F.: spoonful. **-chiaiatína**, F.: teaspoonful. **-chiaièra**†, F.: quantity of spoons (in a case). **-chiaíno**, M.: teaspoon. ‖**-chiáio** [L. *cochliarium* (*concha*, shell)], M.: spoon; spoonful. **-chiaióne**, M.: large spoon; soup-ladle. **-chiára**, F.: trowel; large spoon; ladle for cannon.
cúc-cia, F.: dog's bed; (*jest.*) bed. ‖**-cciáre** [Fr. *coucher*, COUCH], INTR.: crouch, squat. **cúc-cio**† = *-cciolo*. **-cciolíno**, ADJ.: puppyish; inexperienced; M.: little dog; simpleton. **cúc-ciolo**, ADJ.: puppyish; simple; M.: puppy; ninny. **-cciolòtto** = *-cciolino*.
cúcco [ak. to *coccodè*], M.: egg; darling (favourite).
cuccù [echoic], M.: horned owl; horned owl's hoot.
cuccuíno†, M.: cuckoo.
cúccuma [L. *cucuma* (*coquere* 'cook')], F.: kettle, coffee-pot: *aver la* —, be furious.
cucimènto [*cucire*], M.: sewing.
cucí-na [L. (*coquere* 'cook')], F.: KITCHEN; cookery, victuals. **-nábile**, ADJ.: that can be cooked. **-náre**, INTR.: cook, prepare food: (*fig.*) — *una cosa*, arrange a thing. **-nário**, ADJ.: of the kitchen (culinary). **-natóra**, F., **-natóre**, M.:

cook. **-natúra**, F.: cooking. **-nièra**, F., **-nière**, M.: convent cook; cookery-book. **-nína**, **-níno**, *dim.* of *-na*. **-nóna**, **-nóne**, *aug.* of *-na*. **-núccia**, *disp.* of *-na*.

cu-círe [L. *con-suere* (SEW)], TR. (Pres. *-cisco*, or *-cio*): sew, stitch; — *menzogne*, weave lies. **-cíto**, M.: sewing; seam (suture). **-citóra**, F., **-citóre**, M.: sewer. **-citríce**, F.: seamstress. **-citúra**, F.: sewing; stitches.

cu-culiáre, TR.: tease (banter). **-liatúra**, F.: banter. **-cúlio**, **-cúlo** [L. *-lus* (echoic)], M.: CUCKOO.

cucúrbi-ta [L.], F.: gourd; cucurbit (distilling vessel). **-tácee**, F. PL.: cucurbitaceous plants.

cu-cúzz.. = *cocuzz..*

cúf-fia [l. L. *cofea* (ak. to *cupo*)], F.: COIF (woman's bonnet). **-fiáccia**, *disp.* of *-fia*. **-fiétta**, **-fína**, *dim.* of *-fia*. **-fióne**, *aug.* of *-fia*. **-fiòtto**†, M.: man's cap.

cúfico [*Cufa*, city in Bagdad], ADJ.: cufic.

cugí-na [L. *con sobrinus* (ak. to *soror*, sister)], F., **-no**, M.: COUSIN.

cúi [L., 'to whom'], PRON.: whom, which: *da* —, from whom, from which; *di* —, whose.

cu-laccíno [*-lo*], M.: end, bottom; remains (in a glass, etc.). **-látta**, F.: hinder part; breech of a cannon, etc. **-leggiáre**†, INTR.: strut.

cúlice [L. *-lex*], M.: culex (gnat).

cúl-la [L. *cunæ*], F.: cradle; (*fig.*) native place. **-laménto**, M.: rocking the cradle. **-láre**, TR.: cradle, lull.

culmífero [*-mo*], ADJ.: culmiferous.

cúlmine [L. *-men*], M.: culmen (summit).

cúlmo [L. *-mus*, stalk (ak. to *calamus*, reed)], M.: stalk (stem).

cúlo [L. *-lus*], M.: bottom (breech, buttocks; bottom of glasses, etc.).

cultèll.. = *coltell..*

cul-tiva..† = *coltiva..* ‖**-to** [L. *-tus* (*colere*, till)], M.: cult (religion); veneration; ADJ.: cultured. **-tóre**, M., **-tríce**, F.: cultivator. **cúl-tro**, M.: sacrificial knife. **-túra**, F.: cultivation; culture; civilization.

cumíno† = *comino*.

cúmolo = *cumulo*.

cumu-láre, TR.: heap up (accumulate). **-lataménte**, **-lativaménte**, ADV.: in a heap (collectively). **-latívo**, ADJ.: cumulative. **-latóre**, M.: accumulator. **-lazióne**, F.: accumulation. ‖**cúmu-lo** [L. *-lus*, heap], M.: heap (accumulation).

cúna, poet. for *culla*.

cu-neifórme, ADJ.: cuniform. ‖**cú-neo** [L. *cuneus*], M.: wedge; kind of torture.

cuní-colo, M.: (*mil.*) mine, tunnel. **cuní-culo**† [L. *-culus*, 'cony'], M.: rabbit.

cúnta†, F.: delay.

cún-zia [?], F.: sweet rush (plant). **-zièra**†, F.: scent-bottle.

cuoc.. = *coc..*

cuoi.. = *coi..*

cuopríre† = *coprire*.

cuò-re [L. *cor*], M.: HEART; feeling, disposition; courage: *di buon* —, willingly; *far tanto di* —, be completely satisfied. **-ri**, F.: hearts (suit at cards). **-ricíno**†, M.: little heart.

cu-paménte [*-po*], ADV.: deeply. **-pézza**, F.: depth.

cupi-daménte, ADV.: eagerly. **-dígia**, **-dità**, F.: cupidity (greed). ‖**cúpi-do** [L. *-dus*], ADJ.: desirous; greedy.

cúpo [L. *cupa*, tub], ADJ.: obscure (dark); deep; silent, reserved; M. PL.: obscurity: *voce cupa*, deep voice. **cúpo-la**, F.: cupola (dome). **-létta**, **-líno**, *dim.* of *-la*. **cúpo-lo**, ADJ.: slightly dome-shaped. **-lóne**, *aug.* of *-lo*.

cú-ra [L.], F.: care (management); treatment (of diseases); CURE, parish; curate's residence. **-rábile**, ADJ.: curable. **-radènti**†, M.: toothpick. **-ragióne**†, F.: care; treatment. **-randáio**, M.: bleacher. **-ránte**, ADJ.: careful: *medico* —, attending physician. **-ráre**, TR.: care for; esteem (value); treat, cure; cleanse, bleach; REFL.: pay attention to (heed); care to (desire); INTR.: suffer.

curá-ta†, **-tèlla** = *cora-ta*, *-tella*.

cura-tívo, ADJ.: curative. ‖**curá-to** [*-re*], M.: curate (parish priest). **-tóre**, M.: curator, guardian. **-tríce**, F.: guardian.

curattière†, M.: second-hand dealer; huckster.

curazióne† = *curagione*.

cú-ria [L.], F.: curia (division of Roman people); justice-court; advocates (lawyers); bishop's court or residence. **-riále**, ADJ.: of a court, curialistic; M.: court. **-rialésco**, *disp.* of *-riale*: ADJ.: *cavilli -rialeschi*, court sophistry or fallacies. **-rialità**†, F.: courtesy.

curiándolo† = *coriandolo*.

curiáto [*curia*], ADJ.: pertaining to the curia: *comizi* —*ti*, assembly of the curia.

curietáttola†, F.: bad care; bad remedy.

curio-sáccio, ADJ.: inquisitive; impertinent; ridiculous. **-saménte**, ADV.: curiously. **-sétto**, M.: somewhat curious man. **-sità**, F.: curiosity; rarity. ‖**curió-so** [L. *-sus* (*cura*, care)], ADJ.: curious (anxious; inquisitive); odd (comical); M.: curious, queer man.

cúr-ro†, M.: cart; roller. ‖**-sóre** [L. *-sor* (*-rere*, run)], M.: messenger; porter; usher.

curúle [L. *-lis*], ADJ.: curule, official; M.: magistrate: *sedia* —, curule chair.

cúr-va, F.: curve. **-váre**, TR.: bend (curve); REFL.: stoop. **-vatúra**, F.: curvature. **-vétto**, M.: small curve. **-vézza†** = *-vita*. **-vi-líneo**, ADJ.: curvilinear. **-vità†**, F.: gibbousness, being hunchbacked. ||**-vo** [L. *-vus*], ADJ.: curved; crooked (stooping).

cuşáre†, TR.: accuse (blame); REFL.: accuse one's self.

cu-şcinétto, M.: small cushion. ||**-şcíno** [l. L. *culcitinum* (L. *culcita*, mattress)], M.: CUSHION (pillow).

cuşcíre† = *cucire*.

cúscuta [L.], F.: monk's rhubarb.

cusòffiola†, F.: momentary fright.

cuşolière†, M.: spoon.

cuspi-dále, ADJ.: (*arch.*) cuspidated. ||**cúspi-de** [L. *cuspis*, point], F.: cusp; point†; vertex.

custò-de [L. *custos*], M.: custodian (watchman). **custò-dia**, F.: custody (charge; care). **-diménto**, M.: custody. **-díre**, TR.: have in custody (guard); maintain (support); REFL.: nourish one's self well. **-ditaménte†**, ADV.: accurately (carefully). **-ditóre**, M.: custodian.

cu-táneo, ADJ.: cutaneous. ||**cú-te** [L. *-tis*], F.: skin. **-ticágna**, F.: nape of the neck. **-tícola†**, F.: cuticule (pellicle).

cu-trétta†, **-tréttola** [? *coda trepida*], F.: wagtail.

czar, **-ína** [Russ. *tzar* (L. *Cæsar*)], M., F.: czar.

D

d *di* [L.], M.: d (the letter).

da [L. *de*], PREP.: from; by, near; *with infinit. denotes* fitness, capacity, etc.; *after the verb* '*avere*' *denotes* obligation, convenience: — *padre*, as a father; — *beffe*, in jest; — *che*, since; *lo farà — sè*, he will do it by himself; *far — padre*, act as a father; — *per tutto*, everywhere; — *quello in poi* (or *in fuori*), aside from that, that accepted; — *poi in qua*, since that time; — *vero*, truly, indeed.

dabbe-náccio, *aug.* of *-ne*. **-nággine**, F.: ingenuousness; simplicity. ||**dabbè-ne** [*da bene*], ADJ.: good, honest: *uomo* —, upright man; *dabben uomo*, blockhead.

daccápo [*da capo*], ADV.: once more; from the beginning.

dacchè [*da che*], ADV.: since.

dáddo-lo [infant's '*da*'], M.: affected caress; affectation; nonsense. **-lóna**, F., **-lóne**, M.: affected person. **-lóso**, ADJ.: affected, foolish.

daddovéro†, ADV.: in truth, seriously.

da-díno, M.: small die or cube. ||**dá-do** [? *dato* (*dare*, throw)], M.: DIE; cube; pedestal. **-dolíno**, *dim.* of *-do*.

daffáre, no pl. [*da fare*], M.: occupation (work).

dá-ga [l. L.], F.: dagger. **-ghétta**, F.: small dagger; stiletto.

dágli, for *da gli*, *da i*, from the; by the.

dái-na†, F.: doe. **-no** [L. *dama*, deer], M.: deer.

dallàto†, ADV.: by the side of, by.

dalmática [*Dalmazia*], F.: dalmatica (long white tunic).

dáma [L. *domina*, mistress], F.: dame (lady); sweetheart; game of draughts: *bocca di* —, kind of sweet cake.

damággio†, M.: damage.

damáre [*dama*], TR.: crown (a man at draughts).

dama-scáto, ADJ.: damasked (decorated). **-schétto**, M.: damask cloth or silk. **-schína**, F.: damaskin (Damascus blade). **-schíno**, ADJ.: damascene, damask. ||**da-má-sco** [*Damasco*, Damascus], M.: damask silk.

da-meggiáre†, TR.: play the dandy. **-meríno** [*-ma*], M.: gallant (dandy). **-migèlla**, F.: young lady; maid of honour. **-migèllo†**, M.: youth. **-mi-giána** [Fr. *dame*, lady, *Jeanne*, Jane], F.: demijohn. **-mína**, *car. dim.* of *-ma*.

dámma†, F.: deer.

dámo [*dama*], M.: (*vulg.*) lover; betrothed.

da-naiáccio†, M.: bad money. **-náio†** = *-naro*. **-naióso†**, ADJ.: rich in money. ||**-náro** [L. *denarius* (*deni*, ten), denary], M.: money; small coin (farthing); twenty-fourth part of an ounce; PL.: diamonds at cards. **-naróso**, ADJ.: rich in cash money.

dánda [Eng. *dandle*], F.: support-band (for children beginning to walk); mode of division.

dan-gièro†, M.: damage. **-nággio†**, M.: damage. **-náre**, REFL.: deserve the torments of hell; torment one's self†; TR.: condemn; cancel: *far* —, cause to despair. **-náto**, PART.: condemned, damned; M.: *i -nati*, the damned. **-na-tóre**, M.: condemner. **-nazióne**, F.: damnation, condemnation. **-neggia-ménto†**, M.: damage. **-neggiáre**, TR.: damage (hurt); REFL.: harm one's self. **-neggiatóre**, M.: who harms or damages. **-névole†**, ADJ.: blamable; harmful. **-nevolménte†**, ADV.: blamably. **-nificáre†**, TR.: damage; condemn. **-nío†**, ADJ.: harmful. ||**dán-no** [L. *damnum*], M.: DAMAGE (harm):

loss, prejudice: *mio* —, the worse for me; *recar* —, damage; be prejudicial. **-nosaménto,** ADV.: harmfully, with damage. **-nóso,** ADJ.: hurtful (noxious).

dánte [L. *dama*, deer], M.: tanned deer-skin.

dan-teggiáre [*Dante*], INTR.: imitate Dante. **-tésco,** ADJ.: Dantean. **-tísta,** M.: student of Dante.

dán-za, F.: dance. ‖**-záre** [Ger. *tanzen*], INTR.: dance. **-zatóre,** M., **-zatríce,** F.: dancer.

dápe†, F.: food.

dappertútto [*da per tutto*], ADV.: everywhere.

dap-piè†, **-piède** [*da piede*], ADV.: from the foot; from the bottom.

dappo-cággine, -chézza †, F.: worthlessness; idleness. ‖**dappò-co** [*da poco*], ADJ.: worthless, idle.

dap-pòi [*da poi*], ADV.: afterwards; after. **-poi=chè,** ADV.: since then, since.

dapprèsso [*da presso*], ADV.: close to (near).

dapprima [*da prima*], ADV.: at first.

dar-deggiáre, TR.: dart, hurl. **-dière**†, M.: darter; archer. ‖**dár-do** [ASax. *daradh*], M.: DART; javelin.

dáre [L.], IRR.§; TR.: give, present; devote; grant; commit, assign; produce, yield; strike (shine upon); come upon, meet; REFL.: give one's self up to, occupy one's self with: *dar da fare*, cause annoyance, grief; *dar da pensare*, cause to think; *villa che dà a mezzogiorno*, house facing south; *dar di capo*, — *in*, fall in with, light upon; — *'in*, incline to; *dar giù*, be in failing health, lose one's means; *darsela a gambe*, take to one's heels; *darsi*, happen, be possible; *darsi attorno*, work for a thing; *darsi a conoscere*, show one's self; *può darsi*, it is possible, it may be; — *del tu*, use thee and thou.

§ Ind. Pres. *dò, dai, dà, diámo, dáte, dánno*. Impf. *dávo*. Pret. *détti* or *diédi, désti dètte* or *dième*; *démmo, déste, dèttero* or *dièdero*. Fut. *darò*. Cond. *darèi*. Subj.: Pres. *día*, etc. Impf. *déssi*, etc. Ive *da'*, *date*. Ger. *dándo*. Part. *dáto*. — Old or poet. forms: *dièi, die*; *dierono*; *diássi*, etc.; (Subj.) *dia*!

dársena [fr. Ar.], F.: wet dock.

das-sái†, ADJ.: sufficient. **-saiézza**†, F.: sufficiency (ability).

dassézzo†, ADV.: lastly.

dá-ta, F.: date; patronage (of ecclesiastical benefices); nature† (quality); strike†; blow (in ball games). **-táre,** TR.: date. **-taría**† = *-teria*. **-tariáto,** M.: office or rank of datary. **-tário,** M.: datary (officer of Roman chancery). **-tería,** F.: dataria (Roman chancery). **-tívo,** M.: (*gram.*) dative case; ADJ.: dative (given by a magistrate). ‖**dá-to** [*-re*], PART.: given; given to; M.: gift; datum: *esser* —, be in one's power; *in buon* —, in great quantity. **-tóre,** M.: giver.

dát-tero, M.: DATE (fruit). **-tílico,** ADJ.: dactylic. ‖**dát-tilo** [Gr. *dáktulos*, finger], M.: dactyl (—⏑⏑, i.e. like the three finger-joints).

dattórno [*da torno*], us'ly *dintorno*, *intorno*.

da-vánte†, **-vánti** [L. *de, ab*, from, *ante*, before], ADJ.: front; ADV.: in front of (before). **-vanzále,** M.: (*arch.*) window-cornice. **-vánzo,** M.: rest (remainder). **-vvantággio**†, ADV.: moreover.

davvéro [*da vero*], ADV.: in truth.

da-ziáre, TR.: tax. **-ziário,** ADJ.: of a tax or impost. ‖**dá-zio** [L. *-tio* (*dare*, give)], M.: custom (duty; toll); custom-place. **-zióne,** F.: giving (donation); surrender (dedition†). **-zaiòlo,** M.: collector of customs.

de- [L. *de*, of, from], PREF.: de-.

de', for *dei*, of the.

dèa [L. (*deus*, god)], F.: goddess.

debaccá-re†, INTR.: rage; REFL.: be furious. **-tóre**†, M.: raving man.

dèbbio†, M.: wood-ashes (for manure).

debel-laménto, M.: conquest (subjugation). ‖**-láre** [L. (*bellum*, war)], TR.: conquer (vanquish). **-latóre,** M.: conqueror.

débi-le [L. *-lis*], ADJ.: weak (Eng.† debile); pop. for *debole*. **-lézza, -lità,** F.: debility. **-litaménto,** M.: weakening (debilitation). **-litáre,** TR.: debilitate (weaken).

debi-taménte, ADV.: justly (duly). **-tarèllo,** M.: small duty or debt. ‖**débi-to** [L. *-tus* (*debere*, owe)], ADJ.: DUE (proper); M.: DEBT; DUTY: *a* —, without paying. **-tòlo,** M.: little debt. **-tóra,** F., **-tóre,** M., **-tríce,** F.: debtor. **-tuòlo** = *-tolo*. **-túccio,** *disp.* of *-to*.

débo-le [L. *debilis*], ADJ.: weak (feeble, Eng.† debile); defective; of little worth; M.: failing (foible, defect). **-létto,** M.: *dim.* of *-le*. **-lézza,** F.: debility (weakness); fault. **-líno,** *dim.* of *-le*. **-líssimo,** ADJ.: very weak or faint. **-lménte,** ADV.: weakly. **-lóna,** F., **-lóne,** M.: very feeble woman or man. **-lòtto,** ADJ.: somewhat weak. **-lúccio,** *disp. dim.* of *-le*.

dè-ca [Gr. *déka*], F.: group of ten; decade. ‖**-cacòrdo** [*chordé*, string], M.: decachord.

decáddi, PRET. of *decadere*.

decáde = *deca*.

deca-dènza, F.: decadence (decline). ‖**-dére** [*de-, c.*.], IRR.; INTR.: fall off; DECAY. **-diménto,** M.: decay (ruin).

deca=èdro [*hédra*, base], M.: decahedron. **decá-gono** [Gr. *gonía*, angle], M.: decagon. **-grámmo**, M.: decagram. **decá=litro**, M.: decaliter. **decá=logo** [Gr. *logos*, speech], M.: decalogue.

decalváre†, TR.: render bald.

Decameróne [Gr. *déka*, ten, *heméra*, day], M.: Decameron (tales by Boccaccio).

decá=metro, M.: decameter. **-náto** [-*no*], M.: deanship. ‖**decá-no** [chief of ten], M.: DEAN; senior (of an organization); decurion.

de=cantáre 1, TR.: extol (laud).

decantá-re 2 [*canto*], TR.: decant (pour off). **-zióne**, F.: decantation.

decapitá-re [L. *caput*, head], TR.: decapitate. **-zióne**, F.: decapitation.

deca=síllabo, ADJ.: decasyllabic; M.: verse of ten syllables. **-stèro** [Gr. *stereós*, solid], M.: decastere.

de-cèmbre [L. *-cember* (*decem*, TEN)], M.: December. **-cemvirále**, ADJ.: decemviral. **-cemviráto**, M.: decemvirate. **-cèmviro** [L. *vir*, man], M.: decemvir. **-cennále**, ADJ.: decennial; M.: ten years' history. **-cènne**, ADJ.: decennial. **-cènnio** [L. *annus*, year], M.: decennium.

de-cènte [L. *-cere*, be fitting], ADJ.: decent (suitable). **-centeménte**, ADV.: suitably. **-cènza**, F.: decency (propriety). **-cévole**†, ADJ.: suitable. **-cevolézza**, F.: suitability.

decezióne†, F.: deception; error.

dechiaráre = *dichiarare*.

dechináre†, INTR.: descend; decline.

dèci- [L. *decem*, ten], PREF.: deci-, tenth part.

decídere [L. (*de*, from, *cædere*, cut)], IRR.§; TR.: decide, determine; REFL.: form a determination.

§ Pret. *deci-si*, *-se*; *-sero*. Part. *deciso*.

deci-feráre, more commonly *-frare*. **-feratóre**, M.: decipherer. **-frábile**, ADJ.: decipherable. ‖**-fráre** [L. *de*, from, It. *cifra*], TR.: decipher (make out).

deci=grámmo, M.: tenth of a gramme.

decí-litro, M.: tenth of a liter. **dèci-ma**, F.: tithe; (*mus.*) tenth. **-mále**, ADJ.: decimal. **-máre**, TR.: (*mil.*) decimate; destroy. **-matóre**, M.: tithe-gatherer. **-mazióne**, F.: decimation. **-mino**†, M.: TITHE-book. ‖**dèci-mo** [L. *-mus* (*decem*, TEN)], ADJ.: TENTH; foolish†; M.: tenth part; ninny†. **-mottávo** [*ottavo*], ADJ.: eighteenth.

decípula, F.: snare, trap.

-si, PRET. of *-dere*. **-sióne**, F.: de- **-sivaménte**, ADV.: decidedly. ADJ.: decisive (conclusive). ‖**de-** PART. of *-dere*. **-sóre**†, M.: de-

-re [*de*, *c*. .], INTR.: declaim (recite; speak affectedly). **-tóre**, M.: declaimer. **-tòrio**, ADJ.: declamatory. **-zióne**, F.: declamation.

declaratòrio [L. *-clarare*, declare], ADJ.: declaratory (explanatory).

decliná-bile, ADJ.: declinable. **-ménto**†, M.: declination. ‖**decliná-re** [L.], INTR.: decline (sink; diminish, fail); TR.: lower; (*gram.*) decline. **-zióne**, F.: declension; declination. **declíno**†, M.: declension; decline.

de-clíve [L. *de*, from, *clivus*, slope], ADJ.: sloping; M.: slope. **-clívio**, M.: declivity. **-clività**, F.: declivity. **-clívo**†, ADJ.: sloping.

decollá-re [L. (*de*, from, *collum*, neck)], TR.: behead (decollate). **-zióne**, F.: decollation.

decom-pórre [*de*, *c*. .], IRR.; TR.: DECOMPOSE (separate); INTR.: decompose (decay). **-pósi**, PRET. of *-porre*. **-pósto**, PART. of *-porre*. **-posizióne**, F.: decomposition.

deco-ráre, TR.: decorate. **-ratívo**, ADJ.: decorative. **-ratóre**, M.: decorator. **-razióne**, F.: decoration. ‖**decò-ro** [L. *decus*, ornament], M.: dignity (decorum); ornament; ADJ.†: decorous. **-rosaménte**, ADV.: decorously. **-róso**, ADJ.: decorous; proper.

de-corrènza, F.: passing away. ‖**=cór-rere**, IRR.; INTR.: pass away (elapse). **-córsi**, PRET. of *-correre*. **-córso**, PART.: passed (elapsed); M.†: course; end.

de-cottáccio, *disp.* of *-cotto*. **-cottíno**, *dim.* of *-cotto*. ‖**-cótto** [L. *-coctus* (*coquere*, 'cook')], M.: decoction; ADJ.†: boiled. **-cottóre**†, M.: bankrupt. **-cozióne**, F.: boiling; decoction.

de-crébbi, PRET. of *-crescere*. ‖**-creménto** [*-crescere*], M.: decrement (decrease).

decrepi-tà†, **-tézza**, F.: decrepitude. ‖**decrèpi-to** [L. *-tus*], ADJ.: decrepit (broken with age).

de=créscere, IRR.; INTR.: DECREASE (diminish). **-cresciménto**, M.: decrease. **-cresciúto**, PART. of *-crescere*.

decre-tále, ADJ.: decretal; F.: decretal (papal letter); PL. M. or F.: decretal (body of canonical laws). **-talista**, M.: decretist. **-táre**, TR.: decree, ordain. ‖**de-cré-to** [L. *-tum*], M.: decree (order).

decúbito [L. *-tus* (*cumbere*, lie)], M.: lying down (decumbence; decubitus).

decu-mána [L. *decem*, TEN], ADJ.: (*Rom.*) of the tenth legion: *i decumani*, soldiers of the tenth legion. **dècu-plo**, ADJ.: tenfold; M.: decuple. **decú-ria**, F.: band of ten soldiers. **-rionále**, ADJ.: of a decurion. **-rionáto**, M.: decurionate. **-rióne**, M.: decurion.

dedá-leo, *poet.* **-lèo** [Gr. *daídalos*], ADJ.: dædalian (ingenious).

dèdi-ca, F.: dedication (address). **-caménte**† = *-cazione*. ‖**-cáre** [L.], TR.: dedicate (consecrate); REFL.: devote one's self. **-catèria**, F.: dedicatory letter; ADJ.: dedicatory. **-cazióne**, F.: dedication (consecration).

dedignazióne†, F.: indignation.

dèdi-to [*-tus* (*dare*, give)], ADJ.: addicted (devoted). **-zióne**, F.: surrender (dedition).

de-dótto, PART.: deduced, inferred. ‖**-dúrre** [L. (*ducere*, lead)], IRR. (cf. *addurre*); TR.: deduce (conclude); deduct. **-duttivaménte**, ADV.: deductively. **-duttívo**, ADJ.: deductive. **-duzióne**, F.: deduction; proposition.

defal-cáre [?], TR.: take away. **defálco**, M.: defalcation (taking away).

defatigáre†, TR.: fatigue.

defátto [*di fatti*], ADV.: in fact.

defensóre†, M.: defender.

defe-rènza, F.: deference. ‖**-ríre** [L. *de*, down, *ferre*, 'bear'], TR.: defer (delay); defer (yield).

defésso†, ADJ.: weary.

defet. . = *difet*. .

de-fezióne [L. *-fectio* (*de*, from, *facere*, make)], F.: defection; desertion. **-ficiènte**, ADJ.: deficient. **-ficiènza**, F.: deficiency. **dè-ficit** [L., 'it is wanting'], M.: deficit.

defi-níbile, ADJ.: definable. ‖**-níre** [L. (*finis*, end)], TR.: define; determine. **-nitivaménte**, ADV.: definitively. **-nitívo**, ADJ.: definitive (conclusive). **-nitóre**, M.: definer. **-nizióne**, F.: definition.

deflorá-re [l. L. (L. *flos*, flower)], TR.: deflower. **-zióne**, F.: defloration.

deflússo†, M.: defluxion.

defor-máre, TR.: deform (disfigure). **-mazióne**, F.: deformation. ‖**defór-me** [L. *-mis*], ADJ.: deformed. **-meménte**, ADV.: deformedly. **-mità**, F.: deformity.

defrau-dáre [L.], TR.: defraud. **-datóre**, M.: defrauder.

defúnto [L. *-functus* (*fungi*, perform)], ADJ.: defunct (dead); M.: deceased.

degene-ráre, INTR.: degenerate. **-razióne**, F.: degeneration; debasement. ‖**degène-re** [L. *-r* (*genus*, race)], ADJ.: degenerate.

dégli, for *di*, *gli*, of the.

deglutizióne [L. *-titio*], F.: deglutition.

de-gnaménte, ADV.: worthily. **-gnánte**, ADJ.: courteous. **-gnáre**, TR.: deign; INTR.: condescend; REFL.: be pleased to. **-gnazióne**, F.: condescension, courtesy. **-gnévole**†, ADJ.: polite. **-gnevolménte**†, ADV.: politely. **-gnificáre**†, TR.: make worthy. **-gníssimo**, SUPERL. ADJ.: most worthy. **-gnità**†, F.: dignity. ‖**dé-gno** [L. *dignus* (*decere*, be fitting)], ADJ.: worthy; excellent.

degra-dánte, PART., ADJ.: degrading. ‖**-dáre** [L.], TR.: degrade, disgrace; REFL.: degrade one's self. **-dazióne**, F.: degradation.

dèh [l. L. *dee*, God !], INTERJ.: alas ! ah !

dèi 1 [L. pl.], M. PL.: gods.

déi 2, for *di i*, of the.

deì [fr. Turk.], M.: dey.

dei-cídio†, M.: deicide. **-ficaménto**†, M.: deification. **-ficáre**, TR.: deify. **-ficazióne**, F.: deification. **deí-fico**†, ADJ.: divine. ‖**dei-smo** [L. *deus*, god], M.: deism. **deí-sta**, M.: deist. **-tà**, F.: deity (divinity).

del, for *di il*, of the.

dela-tóre [L. *-tor* (*de*, from, *ferre*, 'bear')], M.: accuser (delator). **-zióne**, F.: accusation (delation).

delèbile [L. *delere*, destroy], ADJ.: deleble (erasable).

dele-gáre [L. (*legare*, depute)], TR.: delegate, commit. **-gáto**, PART., ADJ.: delegated; M.: delegate, representative. **-gazióne**, F.: delegation.

deletèrio [L. *delere*, destroy], ADJ.: deleterious (hurtful).

de-lettáre† = *dilettare*. **-lètto**†, M.: choice.

delfíno [L. *delphinus*], M.: dolphin; DAUPHIN (title of crown prince of France).

delibáre [L.], TR.: (*poet.*) taste (try, Eng.† delibate).

deliberá-re [L. (*librare*, weigh)], INTR.: deliberate (take counsel); TR.: ponder (weigh). **-taménte**, ADV.: deliberately. **-tíva**, F.: deliberative faculty. **-tívo**, ADJ.: deliberative; M.: deliberative. **-zióne**, F.: deliberation.

delica-ménto† = *-tezza*. **-taménte**, ADV.: delicately; daintily. **-tézza**, F.: delicacy; softness; refinement; PL.: best comforts. **-tíno**, *car. dim.* of *-to*. ‖**delicá-to** [L. *-tus* (*deliciæ*, delight)], ADJ.: delicate, tender; refined, sensitive. **-túccio**, ADJ.: somewhat delicate. **-túra**, F.: delicacy, nicety.

delimáre†, TR.: consume; corrode.

delinea-ménto, M.: delineation. ‖**delineá-re** [L.], TR.: delineate; trace. **-tóre**, M., **-trice**, F.: delineator.

de-linquènte, PART., ADJ.: delinquent; M.: culprit. ‖**-línquere** [L.], INTR.: be delinquent (offend). **-líquio**, M.: swoon.

de-liraménto†, M.: delirium. ‖**-lirá-re** [L.], INTR.: be delirious (rave). **-lírio**, M.: delirium (frenzy). **-líro**†, ADJ.: delirious; doting.

delít-to [L. *delictum* (*linquere*, fail)], M.:

crime (transgression; DELICT). **-tuóso,** ADJ.: criminal.

delivráre†, TR.: deliberate; deliver.

delí-zia [L. *-ciæ*], F.: delight. **-ziaménto†,** M.: delight. **-ziáre,** TR.: delight; REFL.: delight in. **-ziosaménte,** ADV.: deliciously (delightfully). **-zióso,** ADJ.: delicious (delightful).

délla, délle, for *di la, di le,* of the.

dèl-ta [Gr.], M.: delta (Gr. letter Δ; Δ-shaped tract of land between rivers). **-tòide,** M.: deltoid muscle.

delúbro [L. *-lubrum* (*-luere,* wash = expiate)], M.: (*poet.*) temple.

delú-dere [L. (*ludere,* mock)]; IRR. (cf. *alludere*); TR.: delude (frustrate, disappoint). **-diménto†,** M.: delusion. **delú-si,** PRET. of *-dere.* **-ditóre†,** M.: deluder. **-sióne,** F.: delusion. **delú-so,** PART. of *-dere.* **-sóre,** M.: deceiver. **-sòrio,** ADJ.: delusory.

dema-gogía, F.: demagogy. **-gògico,** ADJ.: demagogic(al). ||**-gògo** [Gr. *dêmos,* people, *ágein,* lead], M.: demagogue.

demandáre [L. (*mandare,* intrust)], TR.: delegate, intrust.

de-maniále, ADJ.: of a domain. ||**-mánio** [OFr. *demaine*], M.: public DOMAIN, state lands; superintendent of lands.

de-mentáre†, TR.: dementate, make insane. ||**-mènte** [L. *-mens* (*mens,* mind)], ADJ.: demented, insane; M.: demented man. **-mènza†,** F.: dementia, imbecility (esp. from age).

demèrgere†, TR.: submerge; INTR.: sink.

demeri-táre [L. *merere,* deserve], INTR.: be unworthy of; TR.: forfeit, no longer deserve. **-tévole,** ADJ.: undeserving.

demèri-to, M.: demerit; misconduct. **-tòrio,** ADJ.: undeserving.

demèrso†, PART. of *demergere.*

demèrto† = *demerito.*

demo-craticaménte, ADV.: democratically. **-crático,** ADJ.: democratic. ||**-crazía** [Gr. *-kratía* (*-s,* people, *kratein,* rule)], F.: democracy.

demolí-re [L. *-rī*], TR.: demolish (destroy). **-tóre,** M.: demolisher. **-zióne,** F.: demolition.

dèmo-ne [Gr. *daímon,* divinity], M.: demon (divinity; evil spirit). **-niáccio,** M.: wicked spirit. **-níaco,** ADJ.: demoniac(al); wicked. **-niétto,** M., *car.* of *-nio:* cunning imp. **demò-nio,** M.: demon (evil spirit, devil).

demoraliz-záre [*de-, m..*], TR.: demoralize. **-zazióne,** F.: demoralization.

demòtico [Gr. *dêmos,* people], ADJ.: demotic.

de-náio† = *danaro.* ||**-nário** [L. *-narius* (*deni,* ten)], M.: denarius (Roman coin). **-naro..** = *danaro..*

denegáre [L.], TR.: DENY.

denigrá-re [L. (*de,* from, *niger,* black)], TR.: blacken (denigrate, defame). **-zióne,** F.: defamation (slander).

denominá-re [L.], TR.: denominate (NAME). **-tívo†,** ADJ.: denominative. **-tóre,** M.: denominator. **-zióne,** F.: denomination.

denotá-re [L.], TR.: denote (indicate). **-zióne†,** F.: denotation.

den-sáre† = *condensare.* **-sità,** F.: density. ||**dèn-so** [L. *-sus*], ADJ.: dense.

den-tále, ADJ.: dental; M.: ploughshare. **-táme†,** M.: quantity of teeth; teeth. **-táre†,** INTR.: cut teeth; indent. **-táta,** F.: bite. **-táto,** PART.: indented (notched). **-tatúra,** F.: set of teeth. ||**dèn-te** [L. *dens*], M.: TOOTH; notch: *non toccare un —,* not to suffice; *la lingua batte dove il — duole,* the tongue speaks what is in the heart. **-tecchiáre†,** TR.: nibble. **-telláto,** ADJ.: notched. **-tellatúra,** F.: indentation. **-tellièro†,** M.: toothpick. **-tèllo,** M.: notch; (*arch.*) dentil. **dèn-tice,** M.: dentex (fish). **-tièra,** F.: set of false teeth. **-tíno,** M.: little tooth: *metter un —,* grow in dignity. **-tísta,** M.: dentist. **-tizióne,** F.: dentition. **-tóne,** *aug.* of *-te.*

déntro [L. *de, intro,* within], PREP.: within, inside of; ADV.: within, inwardly: *esser — a una cosa,* occupy one's self about a thing.

dentúccio, *disp.* of *-te.*

denudá-re [L.], TR.: denude; make manifest† (expose). **-zióne,** F.: denudation.

denun-ciáre = *-ziare.* **denún-zia,** F.: denunciation; report; PL.: bans. ||**-ziáre** [L. *-tiare* (*nuntius,* messenger)], TR.: denounce; impeach. **-ziatóre,** M., **-ziatríce,** F.: denouncer.

depauperáre [L. (*pauper,* poor)], TR.: pauperize, make poor.

dependènte† = *dipendente.*

depennáre [*penna*], TR.: cancel, erase.

de=períre, INTR.: lose one's health; grow worse, deteriorate.

depilatòrio [L. *pilus,* hair], M.: depilatory (hair-removing).

deplo-rábile, ADJ.: deplorable. ||**-ráre** [L. *plorare,* lament], TR.: deplore; INTR.: lament. **-ratóre,** M.: deplorer. **-razióne†,** F.: deploration, lamentation. **-révole,** ADJ.: deplorable.

deponènte [*deporre*], ADJ.: disposing; (*gram.*) deponent.

depopulazióne†, F.: devastation (pillage).

de=pórre, IRR.; TR.: put down, lay aside; DEPOSE (remove; bear witness).

depor-táre [L.], TR.: deport (exile). **-tazióne,** F.: deportation (banishment).

de-póşi, PRET. of *deporre*. **-poşitáre**, TR.: deposit, commit. **-poşitário**, M.: depositary. **-poşitoría**, F.: depository, treasury. ‖**-pòşito** [L. *-positum* (*ponere*, put)], M.: deposit; layer. **-poşizióne**, F.: deposition, testimony. **-pósto**, PART. of *deporre*; M.: testimony.

depravá-re [L. (*pravus*, distorted)], TR.: deprave. **-tóre**, M.: depraver. **-zióne**, F.: depravation.

deprecá-bile†, ADJ.: deprecable, pitiful. **-tivaménte**, ADV.: deprecatively. ‖**-tívo** [L. *-tivus* (*precari*, pray)], ADJ.: deprecative. **-tòrio**, ADJ.: deprecatory. **-zióne**, F.: deprecation; entreaty.

depreda-ménto†, M.: pillage. ‖**depredá-re** [L. *-ri* (*præda*, prey)], TR.: depredate (plunder). **-tóre**, M.: depredator. **-zióne**, F.: depredation.

de-prèmere† = *-primere*. **-premúto**†, PART., ADJ.: depressed. **-prèssi**, PRET. of *-primere*. **-pressióne**, F.: depression, dejection. **-prèsso**, PART.: depressed; humbled. **-priménte**, PART.: depriment (depressing); M.: (*med.*): depressomotor. ‖**-prímere** [L. (*premere*, PRESS)], IRR. (cf. *comprimere*); TR.: lower; depress.

depura-ménto, M.: depuration. ‖**depurá-re** [L. (*purus*, pure)], TR.: purify, depurate. **-tívo**, ADJ., M.: depurative. **-tóre**, M.: depurator. **-tòrio**, ADJ.: depuratory; M.: reservoir (for depurating). **-zióne**, F.: depuration.

depu-táre [L.], TR.: depute (appoint). **-táto**, PART.; M.: deputy (envoy). **-tazióne**, F.: deputation.

dere-lítto [L. *-lictus* (*relinquere*, LEAVE behind)], ADJ.: derelict (abandoned). **-lizióne**†, F.: dereliction.

deretáno [L. *de*, of, *retro*, back], M.: hind part.

derí-dere [*de-*, *r*. .], IRR.; TR.: deride (scoff at). **-ditóre**† = *-sore*. **-şi**, PRET. of *-dere*. **-şíbile**, ADJ.: ridiculous. **-şióne**, F.: derision, scorn. **-şivaménte**, ADV.: derisively. **-şívo**, ADJ.: derisive. **derí-şo**, PART.: ridiculed†; M.: derision. **-şóre**, M.: derider. **-şòrio**, ADJ.: derisory.

deriva-ménto, M.: derivation. ‖**derivá-re** [L. (*rivus*, stream)], INTR.: derive (have its source); TR.: derive. **-tívo**, ADJ.: derivative. **-zióne**, F.: derivation (origin; etymology).

derivièni†, M. PL.: windings; digressions.

dèro-ga, F.: derogation, annulment. **-gábile**, ADJ.: that can be derogated. ‖**-gáre** [*de-*, *r*. .], INTR: derogate (repeal); disparage (slander)†. **-gatívo**, ADJ.: derogative. **-gatòrio**, ADJ.: derogatory. **-gazióne**, F.: derogation (repeal).

derrá-ta [L. *denarius*, coin (cf. Fr. *denrée*)], F: farm-produce (in the market: provisions, commodities); substance; prize†: *è buona* —, it is very cheap; *far gran — di*, sell dog-cheap; *fare — di sè*, prostitute one's self. **-táccia** *disp.* of *-ta*.

de=rubáre, TR.: rob (despoil).

dèrvis [fr. Pers.], M.: dervish.

deşcen. .† = *discen*. .

de-schétto, M.: *dim.* of *-sco;* cobbler's bench. ‖**dé-sco** [L. *discus*], M.: dining-table; butcher's table; bench (desk†); discus†.

descrí-ssi, PRET. of *-vere*. **-ttíbile**†, ADJ.: describable. **-ttivaménte**, ADV.: descriptively. **-ttívo**, ADJ.: descriptive. **-'tto**, PART. of *-vere*, described. **-ttóre**, M.: describer. ‖**descrí-vere** [*de-*, *s*. .], IRR.; TR.: describe (depict). **-víbile**, ADJ.: describable. **-zioncèlla**, *disp. dim.* of *-zione*. **-zioncína**, *car. dim.* of *-zione*. **-zióne**, F.: description.

de-şertáre† = *disertare*. ‖**-şèrto** [L. *-sertus* (*serere*, join)], ADJ.: desert (barren); solitary; M.: desert: *parlare al* —, speak without hearers.

deservíre† = *servire*.

deşerzióne† = *diserzione*.

deşia. . = *deside*. .

desiccáre† = *disseccare*.

deside-rábile, ADJ.: desirable. **-rabilménte**, ADV.: desirably. **-ránte**, ADJ.: desirous. ‖**-ráre** [L.], TR.: DESIRE. **-ratívo**, ADJ.: (*gram.*) desiderative; desirable†. **-ratóre**, M., **-ratríce**, F.: desirer. **desidè-rio**, M.: desire, wish. **-rosaménte**, ADV.: desirously. **-rosíssimo**, ADJ.: very desirous. **-róso**, ADJ.: desirous.

desídia†, F.: idleness.

desigņá-re [L. (*signum*, sign)], TR.: design (intend). **-zióne**, F.: intention.

deşiná-re [? L. *cœna*, supper], INTR.: dine; M.: dinner. **-ríno**, M.: little dinner. **-róne**, M.: elaborate dinner. **-tóre**†, M.: diner.

deşi-nènte [L. *-nens*], ADJ.: desinent, ending. **-nènza**, F.: ending (desinence).

de-şío, M.: (*lit.*) desire; (*pop.*) any welcome thing. **-şiosaménte**, ADV.: eagerly. **-şióso**, ADJ.: (*poet.*) desirous (eager). ‖**-şíre** [*desiderio*], **-şíro**†, M.: (*poet.*) desire.

desí-stere [L. (*stare*, stand)], INTR.: (part. *-stito*) desist, cease.

deşola-ménto†, M.: desolation. ‖**deşolá-re** [L. (*solus*, alone)], TR.: desolate, ruin. **-tóre**†, M.: desolater. **-zióne**, F.: desolation.

despera. .† = *dispera*. .

despètto† = *dispetto*.

des-pota [Gr. -pótēs, master], M.: despot. **-pòti** = despoti. **dès-pote**† = despota.

dés-sa, -so [ipsu], PRON.: only with stesso, proprio: she, he, herself, himself, the same.

desta-ménto†, M.: waking. ||**destà-re** [L. de-, ex-, rouse, shake], TR.: wake (rouse), excite; REFL.: awaken. **-tóre**, M.: awakener (rouser).

desterità†, F.: dexterity.

desti-náre [L.], TR.: destine, intend. **-natário**, M.: addressee (person to whom a thing is addressed). **-nazióne**, F.: destination (design). **desti-no**, M.: destiny (fate).

desti-tuire [L. -tuere (statuere, set)], TR.: dismiss (remove from office): abandon†. **-tuíto, -túto**†, PART.: dismissed, etc.; ADJ.: destitute. **-tuzióne**, F.: dismissal (removal from office): destitution (lack).

désto [destare], ADJ.: awake, lively.

dè-stra, F.: right hand: right side: a —, to the right. **-stràle**†, M.: ornament for the right hand. **-straménte**, ADV.: dexterously. **-streggiáre**, INTR.: use reserve; be skilful. **-streggiatóre**, M.: contriver. **-strézza**, F.: dexterity (cleverness). **-strière, -strière**, M.: charger (steed, Eng. destrer†: as led by the squire on the right hand). ||**dè-stro** [L. dexter], ADJ.: dexterous (nimble): right: propitious†: M.: opportunity (occasion, convenience): privy.

destru...† = *distru...*

de-súmere [L. (*sumere*, take)], IRR. (cf. *assumere*); TR.: infer, conclude. **-súnsi**, PRET., **-súnto**, PART. of *-sumere*.

dete-nére† [*de*, *t*...], IRR.; TR.: detain, impede. **-ntóre**, M.: detainer. **-núto**, PART. of *-nere*; M.: prisoner. **-nzióne**, F.: detention, imprisonment.

de-torgènte, PART., ADJ.: cleansing; M.: detergent. ||**-tèrgere**, IRR.; TR.: deterge (cleanse).

deterio-raménto, M.: deterioration. ||**-ráre** [L. *deterior*, worse], TR.: deteriorate, impair. **-razióne**, F.: deterioration.

determiná-bile, ADJ.: determinable. ||**-´re** [L. (*terminus*, limit)], TR.: determine (fix, limit); induce (lead); REFL.: determine (decide). **-taménte**, ADV.: determinately (resolutely). **-tézza**, F.: determinateness. **-tívo**, ADJ.: determitive. **-zióne**, F.: determination.

-tèrsi, PRET. of *-tergere*. **-tersívo**, M.: detersive. ||**-tèrso**, PART. of *-tergere*.

detestábile, ADJ.: detestable. **-stán-do**, ADJ.: execrable. ||**-stáre** [L.], TR.: detest (abhor). **-stazióne**, F.: detestation.

de-tráerre, IRR.; TR.: DETRACT (take away): disparage; lessen. **-trássi**, PRET. of *-trarre*. **-trátto**, PART. of *-trarre*. **-trattóre**, M.: detractor. **-trazióne**, F.: detraction.

detrimén-to [L. -tum (*terere*, rub)], M.: detriment (disadvantage). **-tóso**†, ADJ.: detrimental.

detronizzáre [trono], TR.: dethrone.

de-trúdere†, IRR. (cf. *intrudere*); TR.: thrust down (detrude). **-trúso**†, PART. of *-trudere*.

détta¹ = *debito*.

dét-ta² [-*to*], F.: saying, talk: good luck (at cards†): *esser in* — *con uno*, be in an agreement with one.

dettagli-ánte, M.: retailer. ||**-áre** [*de-*, *tagliare*], TR.: detail (particularise). **-ataménte**, ADV.: in detail, minutely. **dettágli-o**, M.: detail (particular); retail: *vendita a* (*or in*) —, retail sale.

det-táme, M.: precept, dictates. **-táre** [L. *dictare*, intens. of *dicere*], TR.: dictate; suggest; command. **-táto**, PART.; M.: style of writing: word†, saying. **-tatóre**, M.: dictator. **-tatúra**, F.: dictation; dictatorship. **-tazióne**†, F.: dictate. ||**dét-to**, PART. of *dire*: said; named; M.: word; saying: — *fatto*, no sooner said than done.

deturpa-ménto, M.: disfiguration, defilement. ||**-páre** [L. (*turpis*, foul)], TR.: defile (pollute). **-patóre**, M.: defiler. **-pazióne**, F.: defilement.

deutero-canònico [Gr. *deúteros*, second], ADJ.: deuterocanonical. **-nòmio** [Gr. *nómos*, law], M.: Deuteronomy.

devasta-ménto, M.: devastation. ||**devastá-ro** [L.], TR.: devastate (lay waste, destroy). **-tóre**, M.: devastator. **-zióne**, F.: devastation.

de-veníre, IRR.; INTR.: arrive at, become. **-vénni**, PRET., **-venúto**, PART. of *-venire*.

devia-ménto = *-zione*. ||**deviá-re** [L. (*via*, WAY)], INTR.: deviate (stray, wander). **-zióne**, F.: deviation (departure).

de-vòlsi, PRET. of *-volvere*. **-volúto**, ADJ.: devolved, transferred. **-voluzió-ne**, F.: devolution, transference (of claims). ||**-vòlvere** [L. (*volvere*, roll)], TR.: devolve; roll down; REFL.: pass by transmission.

devo-taménto, ADV.: devotedly, devoutly. **-tíssimo**, ADJ.: very devoted. ||**devò-to** [L. -*tus* (-*vovere*, vow)], ADJ.: devoted (zealous, devout); M.: devotee. **-zióne**, F.: devotion (attachment; piety).

di [L. *de*, from], PREP.: of, from; by, with; to (before an infin.); than (in compar.);

some, any (often with def. art.): — *certo*, for certain; — *giorno*, by day; *quella strega* — *donna*, (that) witch of a woman; *è più bravo* — *lui*, he is braver than he; *m' importa* — *molto*, it matters much to me.
dì [L. *dies*], M.: DAY.
dia- [Gr. *diá*, through, across], PREF.: dia-: **-bète** [Gr. *baínein*, go], M.: (*med.*) diabetes. **-bètico**, ADJ.: diabetic. **-bolicaménte**, ADV.: diabolically. **-bòlico**, ADJ.: diabolic. **diá-bolo** = *-volo*.
diac-ciáia, F.: ice-cellar, ice-house. **-ciáre**, INTR.: become ice, freeze; REFL.: freeze. **-ciáto**, PART.: frozen; M.: frost. **-ciatúra**, F.: freezing; cold weather (winter); blemish in ice. ||**diác-cio** [*ghiaccio*], M.: ice; ADJ.: frozen. **-ci(u)òlo**, M.: icicle; ADJ.: fragile: *dente* —, sensitive tooth.
diacé.., **diaci..** pop. = *giace..*, *giaci..*
diaco-nále, ADJ.: diaconal. **-náto**, M.: diaconate, deaconship. **-néssa**, F.: deaconess. **-nía**, F.: rank of cardinal deacon. ||**diáco-no** [Gr. *diákonos*, servant], M.: DEACON.
dia-: **-dèma** [Gr. (*deín*, bind)], M.: diadem; aureole; white fillet. **-fanità†**, F.: diaphaneity, transparency. **diá-fano** [Gr. *phaínein*, show], ADJ.: diaphanous (transparent). **-forètico** [Gr. *phoreín*, carry], ADJ.: diaphoretic. **-frámma** [Gr. *phrássein*, inclose], M.: diaphragm. **-frammático**, ADJ.: diaphragmatic. **diá-gnosi** [Gr. *gignóskein*, KNOW], F.: diagnosis. **-gnòstico**, ADJ.: diagnostic. **-gonále** [Gr. *gonía*, angle], ADJ., M.: diagonal. **-gonalménte**, ADV.: diagonally. **-lettále**, ADJ.: dialectal. **-lèttica**, F.: dialectics. **-letticaménte**, ADV.: dialectically. **-lèttico**, ADJ.: dialectical. **-lètto** [Gr. *légein*, speak], M.: dialect. **-logáre** = *-logizzare*. **-loghétto**, M.: short dialogue. **-lògico**, ADJ.: dialogistic. **-logísmo**, M.: dialogism. **-logísta**, M.: writer of dialogues. **-logístico**, ADJ.: dialogistic. **-logizzáre**, TR.: give the form of dialogue. **diá-logo** [Gr. *lógos*, speech], M.: dialogue.
diamán-te [L. *adamas*, adamant], M.: diamond: *essere un* (*di*) —, be very hard; be of a firm character. **-tíno**, ADJ.: diamond, adamantine; M.: small diamond.
diame-trále, ADJ.: diametral, diametrical. **-tralménte**, ADV.: diametrically. ||**diáme-tro** [Gr. *diá*, through, *métron*, measure], M.: diameter: *in* (*per*) —, diametrically.
diámine [euphem. for *diavolo*], INTERJ.: the dickens (the deuce).
diána [L. *Diana* (*dies*, DAY)], F.: reveille: *batter la* —, beat the reveille.
di=ánzi, ADV.: just now, a little while ago.
diápaşon [Gr. (*pâs*, all)], M.: diapason (compass or concord of tones).
diá-rio [L. *-rium* (*dies*, day)], M.: diary (JOURnal). **-rísta**, M.: diarist.
dia-rrèa [Gr. *-rroia* (*hreín*, flow)], **-rría†**, F.: diarrhœa.
diáscolo [euphem. for *diavolo*], M.: the deuce.
di-aspríno, **-áspro** [Gr. *íaspis*], M.: JASPER.
diástole [Gr. (*stéllein*, set)], F.: diastole.
diá- [Gr. *the-*, put]: **-teşi**, F.: diathesis. **-tònico** [Gr. *teínein*, stretch], ADJ.: diatonic. **-tríba** [Gr. *tríbein*, rub], F.: diatribe; dissertation.
diávo-la, F.: shrew: *una buona* —, a good creature. **-láccio**, M.: *disp.* of *-lo*; *buon* —, good-natured fellow. **-lería**, F.: deviltry; confused affair; fantastic composition. **-lésco**, ADJ.: devilish. **-léssa**, F.: wicked woman, termagant. **-léto**, M.: great tumult. **-létto**, M.: little devil; good-hearted fellow; curl-papers. **-líno**, M.: *car. dim.* of *-lo*; mischievous little imp. **-lío**, M.: great crowd, great confusion, hubbub. ||**diávo-lo** [Gr. *diá-bolos*, slanderer], M.: devil, evil spirit; good-natured fellow: *avere il* — *addosso*, be furious; *entrare il* —, appearance of discord; *fare il* — *e peggio*, take great pains to prevent or undo a thing; *sapere dove il* — *ha* (*tiene*) *la coda*, be very astute; *un* — *scaccia l' altro*, a fresh misfortune causes forgetfulness of the old ones; — *scatenato*, lively boy. **-lóne**, *aug.* of *-lo*.
dibar-báre†, **-bicáre†**, TR.: uproot.
dibassa.. = *sbassa..*
dibastáre†, TR.: unsaddle.
dibát-tere [*di-*, *b..*], TR.: shake, chatter (said of teeth); debate; be enraged, agitated. **-timénto**, M.: public trial; shaking†; dispute†. **-títo**, M.: debate. **-titóre**, M.: debater. **-'to†**, M.: dispute. **-túto**, PART. of *-tere*; ADJ.†: afflicted (cast down).
dibona-riaménte†, ADV.: courteously (Eng.† debonairly). **-rietà**, F.: courtesy (debonairness).
dibo-scaménto, M.: thinning of forests. ||**-scáre** [*bosco*], TR.: deforest; cut out (trees).
dibottáre† = *dibattere*.
dibrancáre†, TR.: lop off, separate.
dibrucáre†, TR.: prune, lop.
dibuc-ciaménto†, M.: barking (of trees). **-ciáre†**, TR.: remove the bark from, peel.
dicá-ce [L. *-x* (*dicere*, talk)], ADJ.: chatty (Eng.† dicacious); pert. **-cità**, F.: dicacity, pertness.

dicadére† = *decadere*.
dicalváre†, TR.: render bald.
dicapitáre† = *decapitare*.
dicastèro [Gr. *díke*, justice], M.: dicast.
dicáre† = *dedicare*.
dicátti [L. *de capto*, taken = gain], M.: as in *aver* —, come off fortunately, be lucky enough.
dícco†, M.: dike, defense.
dicèmbre, pop. for *decembre*.
dice-re† [L.] = *dire*. **-ría**, F.: tiresome talk; harangue.
dicervelláre [*di cervello*], TR.: tire the brain of (tire to death, bore); REFL.: rack one's brain; overwork one's brain.
dicessáre†, TR.: stop.
dicé-vole [L. *decere*, be proper], ADJ.: DECENT (proper), decorous. **-volézza**†, F.: suitableness. **-volménto**, ADV.: decorously.
dichiara-zióne†, F., **-ménto**†, M.: explanation. ‖**dichiará-re** [L. *de-clarare*], TR.: DECLARE; explain; REFL.: declare one's intention; reveal one's self. **-tamente**, ADV.: avowedly (openly). **-tívo**, ADJ.: declarative (explanatory). **-tóre**, M.: declarer (expounder). **-tòrio**, ADJ.: explanatory. **-zioncèlla**, F.: short explanation. **-zióne**, F.: declaration (explanation). **dichiaríre**†, TR.: clear, explain.
dichinaménto†, M.: decline; stooping. **-náre**†, INTR.: DECLINE; stoop. **dichíno**†, M.: going down (decline).
dician-nòve [*dieci nove*], NUM.: NINETEEN. **-nnovèsimo**, ADJ.: nineteenth. **-nnovíno**, M.: papal coin (in Tuscany). **-ssètte**, NUM.: SEVENTEEN. **-ssettèsimo**, ADJ.: seventeenth.
dicíbile [*dire*], ADJ.: utterable.
dicifráre† = *decifrare*.
dicimáre†, TR.: remove the top, clip.
diciocca-re [*ciocca*], TR.: thin out the branches of (hop). **-túra**, F.: thinning out.
diciottènne, ADJ.: eighteen years old. **-ottésimo**, ADJ.: eighteenth. **-ótto** [*dieci otto*], NUM.: EIGHTEEN.
dici-tóre [*dire*], M.: speaker. **-túra**, F.: speech (manner of expression).
diciullare† [illegible]
dicol-láto [illegible] **dicollazione**†, F.: decollation.
[illegible]

didótto†, ADJ.: deducted.
díe†, M.: day.
diè for *diede*, PRET. of *dare*.
dièci, **-ce**† [L. *decem*], NUM.: ten. **-cemíla**, NUM.: ten thousand. **-cína**, F.: group of ten, half a score.
diédi, PRET. of *dare*.
dièresi [Gr. *diá*, apart, *hairein*, take], F.: diæresis.
diesíre [L. *dies*, day, *iræ*, of wrath], M.: Dies Iræ (hymn); day of wrath (Judgment Day).
dièsis [Gr. *diá*, through, *hiénai*, let go], M.: (*mus.*) sharp.
dièta 1 [l. L. (L. *dies*, day)], F.: diet (assembly).
dièta 2 [Gr. *díaita*, way of living], F.: diet (course of food).
dietaménte†, ADV.: quickly.
die-tètica [*dieta* 2], F.: dietetics. **-tètico**, ADJ.: dietetic.
dietreggiáre†, INTR.: draw back.
diètro [L. *de*, from, *retro*, back], PREP.: behind, after; ADV.: afterwards; behind; ADJ., M.: back, rear: — —, without interruption, very close; *farsi correr* —, cause one's self to be entreated. **-guárdia**†, F.: rearguard.
difalc. . = *defalc*. .
difálta† = *diffalta*.
difèn-dere [L. *de-fendere* (strike)], IRR.§; TR.: defend, guard; uphold. **-dévole**†, ADJ.: defensive; defensible. **-díbile**, ADJ.: defendable. **-diménto**†, M.: defence. **-ditóre**†, M.: defender. **-síbile**† = *-dibile*. **-sióne**†, F.: defence. **-síva**, F.: as in *stare sulla* —, be on the defensive. **-sívo**, ADJ.: defensive. **-sóre**, M.: defender.

§ Pret. *difé-si*, *-se*; *-sero*. Part. *difeso*.

di-fésa, F.: defence; fortification. **-fési**, PRET. ‖**-féso**, PART. of *-fendere*.
difet-táre, INTR.: be defective, be lacking in. **-tivaménte**†, ADV.: defectively. **-tívo**, ADJ.: defective. ‖**difètto** [L. *de-fectus*], M.: DEFECT (imperfection). **-tosaménte**, ADV.: defectively. **-tóso**, ADJ.: defective (wanting). **-tuccio**, *disp. dim.* of *-to*.
dif-falcáre†, TR.: defalcate (deduct). **-fálco**†, M.: deduction.
dif-fálta†, F.: default. **-faltáre**†, INTR.: fail.
diffama-ménto†, M.: defamation. ‖**diffamá-re** [*fama*], TR.: defame. **-tóre**, M.: defamer. **-tòrio**, ADJ.: defamatory. **-tríce**, F.: defamer. **-zióne**, F.: defamation, slander.
diffe-rènte, ADJ.: different. **-renteménte**, ADV.: differently. **-rènza**, F.: difference, dissimilarity. **-renziále**, ADJ.: differential. **-renziáre**, TR.: distin-

guish; differentiate; REFL.: be different, differ. **-renzúccia**, F.: slight difference. **-ríbile**, ADJ.: easily deferred. **-riménto**, M.: deferring (delay). ||**-ríre** [L. *dif-ferre* (BEAR)], INTR.: be different; TR.: defer. **-ritóre**, M.: one that differs; one that defers.

differ-maménto†, M.: confutation. **-máre†**, TR.: confute.

diffi-cile [L. *-cilis* (*facilis*, easy)], ADJ.: difficult; crabbed. **-cilétto**, ADJ.: somewhat difficult. **-cilménte**, ADV.: with difficulty. **-coltà**, F.: difficulty; obstacle. **-coltáre**, TR.: make difficult; INTR.: raise a difficulty. **-coltóso**, ADJ.: difficult. **-cult. .** = *-colt. .*

diffi-daménto†, M., **-dánza†**, F.: distrust. ||**-dáre** [L. *dif-fidere*, trust], INTR.: distrust (doubt). **-dènte**, ADJ.: diffident (distrustful). **-dènza**, F.: diffidence (distrust).

diffini. . = *defini. .*

diffón-dere [*dis-*, *f. .*], IRR.; TR.: DIFFUSE (pour out); REFL.: abound; enlarge upon. **-ditóre**, M.: diffuser.

diffor-máre = *sformare*. **-mataménte†**, ADV.: deformedly. **diffór-me** = *disforme*; deformed†. **-mità** = *disformità*; deformity†.

dif-fusaménte [*-fuso*], ADV.: diffusely. **-fúsi**, PRET. of *-fondere*. **-fusióne**, F.: diffusion. **-fusívo**, ADJ.: diffusive, ample. ||**-fúso**, PART. of *-fondere*; ADJ.: diffuse (prolix).

difícío† = *edifizio*.

difi-láre [*di filo*], INTR.: defile, go straight. **-láto**, PART., ADJ.: straight; ADV.: directly (straight ahead).

difini. .†, **diform. .†** = *defini. .*, *deform. .*

diftè-rico, ADJ.: diphtheritic. ||**-ríte** [Gr. *diphthéra*, membrane], F.: diphtheria.

díga [Dutch *dyk*], F.: dike, bank.

digámma [Gr. *dis*, twice, *gámma*], F.: digamma (old Greek letter).

digeneráre† = *degenerare*.

dige-ríbile, ADJ.: digestible. **-ribilità**, F.: digestibility. **-riménto†**, M.: digestion. ||**-ríre** [L. *di-gerere* (carry)], TR.: DIGEST; endure; comprehend. **-ritóre**, M.: digester. **-stíbile†** = *-ribile*. **-stióne**, F.: digestion; comprehension. **-stíre†** = *-rire*. **-stívo**, ADJ.: digestive. **digè-sto**, M.: digest (of law); PART.†: digested.

dighiacci. . = *didiacci. .*

digiogáre†, TR.: unyoke.

digi-tále, F.: digitalis (plant); ADJ.: digital. ||**dígi-to†** [L. *-tus*], M.: finger; inch.

digiúgnere = *digiungere*.

digiu-náre [*-no*], INTR.: fast (abstain from food). **-natóre**, M.: faster. **digiú-ne†**, F. PL.: fasting; ember weeks.

digiúngere†, TR.: disjoin.

digiúno [L. *jejunus*, dry, fasting], M.: fast (abstinence from food); ADJ.: fasting; jejune.

digiúnto†, PART. of *-giungere*.

digni-tà [L. *-tas* (*dignus*, worthy)], F.: rank; honour; dignity. **-tário**, M.: dignitary. **-tosaménte**, ADV.: worthily (with dignity). **-tóso**, ADJ.: dignified.

digoccioláre†, TR.: pour drop by drop.

digozzáre†, TR.: cut the throat.

digrada-ménto, M.: gradation (of tints). ||**digradá-re** [L. *gradus*, degree], INTR.: descend gradually; go to the bad†; TR.: blend colours; lessen objects. **-taménte†**, ADV.: gradually (by degrees). **-zióne**, F.: gradation (of colours, objects, etc.); degradation.

digranáre†, TR.: husk.

digrassáre [*grasso*], TR.: remove fat from: — *il brodo*, skim the broth.

digre-díre [L. *de-gredi* (*gradus*, step)], INTR.: DIGRESS (turn aside). **-díto**, PART.: digressed. **-ssioncèlla**, **-ssioncína**, F.: slight digression. **-ssióne**, F.: digression. **-ssívo**, ADJ.: digressive. **digrè-sso†**, PART.: digressed; digression.

digrignáre [Prov. *grinar*], TR.: gnash, snarl: — *i denti*, gnash the teeth.

digros-saménto, M.: rough-cast; rubbing off. ||**-sáre** [*grosso*], TR.: rough-hew, give shape to (a statue); polish (instruct).

digrumá-re [*ruminare*], TR.: RUMINATE (chew over again); INTR.: ruminate (chew the cud); eat much; consider†. **-tóre**, M.: ruminator.

diguastáre†, TR.: WASTE, spoil; dissipate.

diguazzáre [*guazzo*], TR.: shake, mix (a liquid).

digusciáre†, TR.: husk, shell.

dilaccáre†, REFL.: cut, lacerate.

dilacciáre†, TR.: unlace, unfasten.

dilacera. . = *lacera. .*

dilagá-re [*lago*], INTR., REFL.: form a lake. **-taménte†**, ADV.: like an overflow; furiously.

dilaniáre [L. (*lanius*, butcher)], TR.: tear (lacerate, dilaniate).

dilapidá-re [*lapidare*], TR.: dilapidate; squander. **-zióne**, F.: dilapidation; waste.

dilargáre†, TR.: enlarge.

diláta†, F.: delay. **-ménto**, M.: dilation. ||**dilatá-re** [L. (*latus*, wide)], TR.: dilate (widen, expand); REFL.: dilate (expand). **-tóre**, M.: dilator. **-tòrio**, ADJ.: dilatory (delaying). **-zioncèlla**, *dim.* of *-zione*. **-zióne**, F.: dilation (expansion).

dile-[illegible], [illegible]. [illegible] away. ‖**-[illegible]re** [illegible], TR.: [illegible] away, wear away [illegible]. [illegible]. **-[illegible]**, PART. [illegible] pale. [illegible].

dile-[illegible], F.: [illegible] decay. ‖**-[illegible]re** [illegible], F.: decay [illegible].

dilegare†, TR.: [illegible].

dileg-giabile, ADJ.: [illegible]. **-gia-mento**, M.: [illegible]. ‖**-giá-re** [illegible], TR.: [illegible]. **-giatore**†, F.: [illegible]. **-giatore**, M.: [illegible]. **-gone**†, M.: [illegible]. **diléggio**, M.: [illegible].

dilégine†, ADJ.: [illegible].

dile-guáre [illegible], TR.: make disappear, disperse; REFL.: disappear [illegible] away. **-guo**, M.: disappearance; [illegible] — disappear.

dilèmma, [illegible], M.: dilemma.

di-leticare†, TR.: [illegible]. **-lético**†, M.: [illegible].

dilet-tábile, ADJ.: delectable (pleasing). **-tabilità**, F.: delectableness. **-taménto**, M.: delectation (delight). **-tante**, M., F.: amateur, dilettante. **-tánza**†, F.: delight. **-táre**, TR.: delight; REFL.: delight in, find pleasure in. **-tato**†, M.: delight. **-tatóre**, M.: [illegible]. **-tazióne**†, F.: delectable pleasure. **-té-vole** = [illegible]. **-tevolménte**, ADV.: delectably, pleasingly. **-tivo**†, ADJ.: [illegible]. ‖**dilèt-to** [L. *dilectus* (*di-ligere*, love)], ADJ.: beloved; M.: lover; [illegible], pleasure; a [illegible] —, for pleasure; *andare a* —, walk about for pleasure. **-tosaménte**, ADV.: delightfully. **-tóso**, ADJ.: delightful.

dile-zióne [-tio], F.: kindness; spiritual love.

dillibora†. . = *delibera*. .

dillibráre†, INTR., REFL.: tumble, fall.

dillica†. . = *delica*. .

dili-gènte [L. *-gens* (*diligere*, love)], ADJ.: diligent (attentive). **-genteménte**, ADV.: diligently. **-gènza**, F.: diligence (attention); diligence (stage-coach).

diligióne†, F.: jest; ridicule.

diliquidáre†, INTR.: become liquid.

diliscáre†, TR.: bone (a fish).

dilitic. . = *diletic*. .

diliver. .† = *deliber*. .

dilizi. .† = *delizi*. .

diloggiáre [*alloggio*], TR.: DISLODGE; INTR.: move (change one's lodging).

[illegible]**báre** [*lombo*], REFL.: strain one's [illegible]**báto**, PART.: weak-backed, fee[illegible]. [illegible]**túra**, F.: lumbar strain.

[illegible]**áre** [*lontano*], TR.: send away; [illegible] away (withdraw).

[illegible]**méntet**†, ADV.: lucidly, plainly. [illegible] [*lucido*], TR.: elucidate (explain).

-dazióne, F.: [illegible]. **dilúci-do**†, ADJ.: [illegible] clear.

di-luénte, ADJ., M.: diluent. ‖**-luíre** [L. *diluere* (wash)], TR.: dilute, weaken.

dilun-gaménto†, M.: delay; remoteness. ‖**-gáre**† [*lungo*], TR.: stretch; remove, [illegible]; REFL.: withdraw; wander away.

dilusióne† = *illusione*.

dilu-viáne†, ADJ.: diluvian. **-viáre**, IMPERS.: rain hard, be a deluge; TR., INTR.: devour, eat greedily. **-viatóre**, M.: glutton. ‖**dilú-vio** [L. *-vium* (root *lu-*, wash)], M.: DELUGE (flood); abundance; gluttony. **-vióne**, M.: glutton. **-vió-so**†, ADJ.: fluvial.

dimacchiáre [*macchia*], TR.: clear of [illegible]; clear of trees.

dima-gheráre, ‖**-gráre** [*magro*], INTR.: become lean; TR.: make lean. **-grazió-ne**†, F.: becoming lean.

dimand. . = *domand*. .

dimáne†, **dimáni** = *domani*.

dimembráre†, TR.: dismember; tear apart.

dime-naménto† = *-nio*. ‖**-náre** [*menare*], TR.: agitate (shake); jolt. **-na-zióne**†, F., **dime-nio**, M.: shaking (jolting).

dimensióne [L. *-sio*], F.: dimension.

dimentáre†, TR.: dementate (deprive of reason).

dimenti-cággine, F., **-caménto**†, M.: absent-mindedness (forgetfulness). **-cán-za**, F.: forgetting, forgetfulness. ‖**-cá-re** [*mente*], TR.: forget; disregard; REFL.: forget one's self. **-catóio**, M.: forgetfulness (oblivion): *lasciare* (*mettere*) *nel* —, forget. **-chévole**†, ADJ.: very forgetful. **diménti-co**, ADJ.: neglectful. **-cóne**, ADJ.: very forgetful or absent-minded; M.: forgetful man.

dimentire†, TR.: give the lie to (contradict).

dimeritáre† = *demeritare*.

di-messaménto, ADV.: humbly. **-més-si**, PRET. of *-mettere*. **-messióne**†, F.: humiliation. ‖**-mésso**, PART. of *-mette-re*; ADJ.: humble, dispirited.

dimestic. . = *domestic*. .

dimetro [Gr. *di(s)*, twice, *métron*, measure], ADJ.: dimeter.

di-méttere, IRR.; TR.: DISMISS (discharge); forget; pardon; abandon†; cease†; REFL.: resign (give up).

dimez-zaménto, M.: halving, division. ‖**-záre** [*mezzo*], TR.: divide in the middle (halve).

dimíno†, M.: dominion; will.

dimi-nuèndo†, M.: (*mus.*) diminuendo. **-nuiménto**†, M.: diminution. ‖**-nuí-re** [L. *-nuere*], TR.: diminish, reduce;

INTR.: lessen, decrease. **-nutivaménte†**, ADV.: diminutively. **-nutívo**, ADJ., M.: diminutive. **-nuzióne**, F.: diminution.

dimí-si, PRET. of *dimettere*. **-ssióne**, F.: dismission, resignation. **-ssòria**, ADJ.: dimissory; F.: dimissory letter.

dimoiáre [*molle*], INTR.: liquefy; thaw.

dimól-to [*molto*], ADV.: very much, a great deal. **-tóne**, ADV.: (*fam. jest.*) excessively.

dimònio† = *demonio*.

dimò-ra, F.: stay, habitation, abode; delay. **-ragióne†**, F.: stay, abode. **-raménto†**, M.: residence. **-ránza†** = *-ra*. ||**-ráre** [L. *demorari* (*mora*, delay)], INTR.: reside, stay. **-razióne†**, **dimò-ro†** = *-ra*.

dimorsáre†, TR.: let go from one's teeth.

dimo-strábile, ADJ.: demonstrable. **-straménto**, M.: demonstration. **-stránza†** = *-strazione*. ||**-stráre** [L. *de-monstrare* (show)], TR.: demonstrate (prove); REFL.: show one's self. **-stratíva**, F.: demonstrative faculty. **-strativaménte**, ADV.: demonstratively. **-stratívo**, ADJ.: demonstrative. **-stratóre**, M.: demonstrator. **-strazioncèlla**, **-strazioncína**, F.: short demonstration. **-strazióne**, F.: demonstration; sign; manifestation. **dimó-stro†** = *-strato*.

di-múgnere†, **-múngere†**, TR.: milk dry; empty. **-múnto†**, PART., ADJ.: dried.

di-námica [Gr. *dúnamis*, power], F.: dynamics. **-námico**, ADJ.: dynamic. **-namíte**, F.: dynamite. **-namòmetro** [Gr. *métron*, measure], M.: dynamometer.

dinánzi [*di in anzi*], PREP., ADV.: before (in presence of, in front of); preceding†; ADJ.: front; M.: front.

di-nastía [Gr. *dunástes*, ruler], F.: dynasty. **-nástico**, ADJ.: dynastic.

dindérlo†, M.: tasselled ornament, fringe.

díndo [echoic], M.: farthing (coin).

dindòn [echoic], ding-dong (of bells).

dinegá-re†, TR.: deny. **-zióne†**, F.: denial.

dinerváre†, TR.: unnerve; enervate.

dinfignimento†, M.: fiction.

diniègo [*dinegare*], M.: denial.

dinigráre†, TR.: blacken.

dinoc-cáre† [*nocca*], TR.: put out of joint; break the neck of; INTR., REFL.: put out of joint. **-coláto**, ADJ.: unjointed (broken); languid (listless).

dinodáre†, INTR., REFL.: become separated (joint from joint).

dinom. .†, **dinon. .†**, **dinot. .†** = *denom. .*, etc.

din-tornaménto†, M.: drawing contours, environs. **-náre†**, TR.: outline. ||**d' intór-no** 1, PREP.: around. **-tór-ni** 2, M. PL.: environs; contour†, outline.

dinudáre†, TR.: denude; uncover.

dinumerá-re†, TR.: enumerate. **-zióne†**, F.: enumeration.

dinunzia. .† = *denuncia. .*

Dío, pl. *dei* (of antiquity) or *dii* [L. *deus*], M.: God; ADJ.†: divine: *lavorare per l'amor di* —, work without compensation; *faccia* —, — *voglia*, God grant; — *me ne guardi*, God forbid.

di-ocesáno, ADJ.: diocesan; M.: diocesan. ||**-òcesi** [Gr. *dioíkesis* (*diá*, through, *oíkos*, house)], F.: diocese.

diòt-tra [Gr. *díoptra* (*diá*, through, root *op-*, see)], F., M.: dioptra. **diòt-trica**, F.: dioptrics. **diòt-trico**, ADJ.: dioptric.

dipaná-re [L. *panus*, ball of thread], TR.: wind, reel; (*fig.*) clear up a confused matter; eat heartily. **-túra**, F.: reeling, winding.

diparére†, INTR.: appear.

dipar-tènza, F.: as in *far le -tenze*, bid farewell; departure†. **-timénto**, M.: department; division; departure†. ||**-tíre** [*partire*], TR.†: part (divide); INTR., REFL.: depart (leave). **-títa** = *-tenza*.

dipeláre†, TR.: make bald; scorch.

dipelláre†, TR.: skin (flay).

di-pendènte, ADJ. or M.: dependent. **-pendenteménte**, ADV.: dependently. **-pendènza**, F.: dependence; PL.: dependent states. ||**=pèndere**, IRR.; INTR.: depend. **-pendúto**, **-péso**, PART. of *-pendere*.

di-pígnere†, ||**=píngere**, IRR.; TR.: PAINT; DEPICT (represent); REFL.: use rouge. **-pínsi**, PRET. of *-pingere*. **-pínto**, PART. of *-pingere*; M.: painting, picture. **-pintóre**, M.: painter. **-pintúra**, F.: painting.

diplò-ma [Gr. (*diplóos*, TWOFOLD)], M.: document; diploma. **-mática**, F.: diplomatics. **-maticaménte**, ADV.: diplomatically. **-mático**, ADJ: diplomatic; M.: diplomat(ist). **-mazía**, F.: diplomacy.

dipopoláre†, TR.: depopulate.

dipórre† = *deporre*.

di-portaménto†, M.: deportment, conduct. ||**=portáre**, REFL.: carry or deport one's self; divert one's self†. **-pòrto**, M.: amusement, recreation; solace†.

dipos. .†, **diput. .** = *depos. .*, *deput. .*

diradáre [*rado*], TR.: thin (plants, etc.); REFL.: become thin.

diradicáre†, TR.: eradicate, rout out.

diramá-re [*ramo*], TR.: thin off branches (thin out); separate, divide into branches. **-zioncèlla**, F.: slight division. **-zióne**, F.: branching (ramification).

diramcáre†, TR.: spoil, root up.

dirazzáre [*razza*], INTR.: lose one's race (or family) qualities.

díre [L. *dicere*], IRR.§; TR.: say, tell; mean, signify; call; M.: saying: *dir la sua*, add one's opinion; *dir bene d'uno*, speak well of one; *non mi vuol* —, I do not succeed; I have no good fortune; *voler* —, mean.

§ Ind.: Pres. *di-co, -ci* or *di', -ce; -ciámo, -te, di-cono.* Impf. *dicéva.* Pret. *dissi, dicésti, disse; dicémmo, dicéste, dissero.* Subj.: Pres.: *dica*, etc. Impf. *dicessi.* Fut. *dirò.* Cond. *direi.* Ipve *di', dite.* Ger. *dicendo.* Part. *détto.* Old form: *ditto.* — Of compounds *benedire* and *maledire* have Impf. in *-dicéva* or *-diva*; Pret. in *-disse, -dissero* or *-di, -dirono†.*

diredáre = *diseredare.*

direnáre†, TR.: sprain the back.

direptióne†, F.: rapine; destruction.

dirèssi, PRET. of *dirigere.*

diretáno† ADJ.: hind, last.

diretáre† = *diseredare.*

dirètro†, M.: hinder, back part; ADJ., ADV.: behind.

diret-taménte, ADV.: directly. **-tívo**, ADJ.: directing. ‖**dirèt-to**, PART. of *dirigere;* ADJ.: direct (straight); directed (addressed); ADV.: directly. **-tóre**, M.: director. **-tòrio**, M.: Directory of France. **-tríce**, F.: directress. **direzióne**, F.: office of director; official title or residence; direction; address.

diricciáre [*riccio*], TR.: shell (chestnuts).

diridere† = *deridere.*

dirièto†, PREP., ADV.: behind, after.

dirígere [L. *regere*, guide)], IRR.§; TR.: direct, manage; address; REFL.: go.

§ Pret. *dirès-si, -se; -sero.* Part. *dirètto.*

dir-imènte, ADJ.: annulling, invalidating (a marriage). ‖**-imére†** [L. *dis-imere*], TR.: divide; break, annul.

di=rimpètto, PREP., ADV.: opposite (to), over against.

dirincóntro†, ADV.: opposite to; on the contrary.

diripáta†, F.: precipice.

dirişióne† = *derisione.*

dirit-ta, F.: right hand; direct road. **-taménte**, ADV.: directly, straight. **-tánza†**, **-tézza**, F.: straightness; justice, uprightness. ‖**dirít-to** [*diretto*], ADJ.: DIRECT (straight); just (upright); M.: right side; right; claim; law; title; level†; ADV.: straight, directly: *a* —, rightly, with reason; *ogni — ha il suo rovescio*, all good things have their bad sides. **-túra**, F.: straightness; judgment; impost†, tax.

diriva.. = *deriva..*

dirivièni†, M., INVAR.: windings, meanderings.

dirizza-crine† = *-zatoio.* **-zaménto†**, M.: directing. ‖**-záre** [*diritto*], TR.: straighten; reform; direct (turn); REFL.†: arise. **-zatóio**, M.: bodkin for the hair. **-zatóre**, M.: manager. **-zatríce**, F.: directress. **-zatúra**, F.: straightening. **-zóne**, M.: thoughtless action; whim; stubborn insistence.

díro†, ADJ.: impious, dire, cruel.

dirocc-aménto, M.: destruction, demolition. ‖**-cáre** [*rocca*], TR.: destroy (ruin). **-catóre**, M.: destroyer.

diroccciáre†, INTR.: fall from a rock.

diroga..† = *deroga..*

di=rómpere, IRR.; TR.: soften (loosen, relax); interrupt†, break†; REFL.: become angry. **-rompiménto**, M.: relaxation; interruption†. **-rótta†**, F.: hard rubbing, friction.

di-rottaménte, ADV.: excessively. ‖**-rótto 1** [*-rompere*], PART., ADJ.: relaxed; excessive: *a* —, excessively, heavily.

dirótto†2, ADJ.: broken, steep.

dirovináre†, TR.: ruin.

diroz-zaménto, M.: polishing; instruction. ‖**-záre** [*rozzo*], TR.: rough-hew; polish, instruct.

dirubáre†, TR.: rob.

diruggi-náre† = *-nire.* **-nío**, M.: grinding, gnashing. ‖**-níre** [*ruggine*], TR.: remove the rust from: — *i denti*, gnash the teeth.

diru-paménto†, M.: falling down; precipice. ‖**-páre** [*rupe*], INTR.: fall from a precipice (be precipitated); TR.†: precipitate. **-páto**, PART.; M.: precipice. **-pináre†** = *-pare.* **dirú-po**, us'ly pl., **-pi**, M.: precipice; craggy place.

diruppi, PRET. of *dirompere.*

dirúto†, ADJ.: ruined.

di(s)- [L., apart], PREF.: dis-.

dis=abbellíre, TR., REFL.: lose one's beauty.

dişabilità†, F.: inability.

dişabi-táre†, TR.: depopulate. ‖**-táto** [*abitato*], ADJ.: uninhabited. **-tazióne†**, F.: being uninhabited.

dis=accentáre, TR.: remove the accent from.

dişaccéso†, ADJ.: extinguished.

dis=accètto, ADJ.: unaccepted, unwelcome.

dis-acconciaménte, ADV.: unsuitably, improperly. ‖**=accóncio**, ADJ.: unfitted (ill-adapted).

dis-accordáre†, REFL.: disagree. ‖**=accòrdo**, M.: disagreement.

dis=accuráto, ADJ.: inaccurate.

dişacerbáre [*acerbo*], TR.: appease (quiet); REFL.: become calm.

dişacquistáre†, TR.: lose.

dis-adattággine, F.: unfitness. **-adattaménte**, ADV.: unsuitably. ‖**=adátto**, ADJ.: unadapted (unsuitable, awkward).
dis=adornáre, TR.: deprive of ornaments; adorn unsuitably. **=adórno**, ADJ.: unadorned.
disaffaticáre†, REFL.: rest one's self.
disaffe-zionáre, TR.: disaffect. ‖**-zióne** [*affezione*], F.: disaffection, unfriendliness.
disagévo-le [*agevole*], ADJ.: difficult, uneasy. **-lézza**, F.: uneasiness. **-lménte**, ADV.: with difficulty.
disaggra-dáre†, INTR.: be displeasing. **-dévole**, ADJ.: disagreeable. ‖**-díre** [*aggradire*], TR.: displease; INTR.: be disagreeable.
disagguagli..† = *disuguagli*..
dis-agiáre, TR.: deprive of ease (disturb, incommode). **-agiáto**, PART., ADJ.: troubled; needy. **-agiatóre**, M.: disturber. ‖**=ágio**, M.: discomfort (inconvenience); trouble; want. **-agióso**, ADJ.: inconvenient, troubled: *tenere a* —, keep waiting.
disagráre†, TR.: desecrate.
dis-aiutáre†, TR.: hinder. **-aiúto**†, M.: hindrance, impediment.
disalberáre†, TR.: dismast.
disalbergáre†, INTR.: leave home.
disalloggiáre†, TR.: dislodge.
dis-amábile, ADJ.: unamiable. **-amánte**†, PART., ADJ.: unloving. ‖**=amáre**, TR.: cease to love; dislike.
disambizióso†, ADJ.: unambitious.
dis-amenità, F.: disagreeableness. ‖**=améno**, ADJ.: disagreeable.
disamicízia†, F.: unfriendliness.
disami-na, F., **-naménto**†, M.: examination. **-nánte**†, M.: examiner. ‖**-náre**† [L. *examinare*], TR.: examine carefully. **-nazióne**†, F.: examination.
disammirazióne†, F.: lack of admiration.
disamo-ráre, TR.: cause to lose affection; REFL.: lose liking for. **-ráto**, PART., ADJ.: indifferent. **-ratáccio**, ADJ.: hard-hearted, cold. ‖**disamó-re** [*amore*], M.: want of affection (indifference, dislike). **-révole**, ADJ.: unkind. **-revolézza**, F.: lack of affection, unkindness. **-róso**† = *-revole*.
dis=animáre, TR.: dishearten, discourage; REFL.: become discouraged.
disapparáre†, TR.: unlearn.
disapparisciénto†, ADJ.: ugly.
disappeténza, F.: lack of appetite.
disappli-cáre [*applicare*], REFL.: not apply one's self (be inattentive). **-catézza**, F.: lack of application (inattention). **-cáto**, ADJ.: indolent. **-cazióne**, F.: inattention.
dis=apprèndere, IRR.; TR.: unlearn. **-apprensióne**, F.: fearlessness. **-appresi**, PRET. of *-apprendere*. **-appréso**, PART. of *-apprendere*.
dis=approváre, TR.: disapprove. **-approvazióne**, F.: disapprobation.
disarboráre† = *disalberare*.
disarginàre [*argine*], TR.: break down the banks of (said of rivers, etc.).
dis-armaménto†, M.: disarming. ‖**=armáre**, TR.: disarm; appease. **-ármo**, M.: disarming.
disar-monía [*armonia*], F.: lack of harmony, discord. **-mònico**, ADJ.: inharmonious. **-monizzáre**, INTR.: be out of harmony.
disarticoláre [*articolo*], TR.: (*surg.*) amputate at the joints.
disascóso†, ADJ.: disclosed, manifest.
disaspríre†, TR.: mitigate (relieve).
disassue-fáre [*dis-*, *a*..], IRR.; TR.: disaccustom; REFL.: become disaccustomed. **-fátto**, PART., **-féci**, PRET. of *-fare*.
dis-astráre, TR.: hurt; prejudice; REFL.: damage one's business. ‖**=ástro**, M.: disaster; damage. **-astróso**, ADJ.: disastrous.
disattèn-to [*attento*], ADJ.: inattentive. **-zióne**, F.: inattention.
disauto-ráre [L. *auctorare*], TR.: remove from authority; REFL.: be deprived of authority. **-rizzáre** = *-rare*.
dis-avanzáre, INTR.: cease to advance; lose ground (suffer loss). ‖**=avánzo**, M.: deficit, loss.
disavvan-taggiáre [*avvantaggiare*], TR.: lose an advantage. **-tággio**, M.: disadvantage. **-taggiosaménte**†, ADV.: at a disadvantage. **-taggióso**, ADV.: disadvantageous.
disavve-diménto†, M.: inadvertence. **-dutaménte**, ADV.: heedlessly. **-dutézza**, F.: inconsiderateness, imprudence. ‖**-dúto** [*dis-*, *a*..], ADJ.: improvident (imprudent); inconsiderate (heedless).
disavve-nènte [*avvenente*], ADJ.: unprepossessing (charmless, graceless). **-nentézza**†, **-nènza**, F.: want of grace, of charm. **-névole**† = *-nente*. **-níre**†, INTR.: come inconveniently. **-ntúra**, F.: mishap, misfortune. **-nturataménte**, ADV.: unfortunately. **-nturáto**, **-nturóso**†, ADJ.: unfortunate, unlucky.
dis=avvertènza, F.: inadvertency.
dis-avvezzaménto†, M.: disuse. ‖**=avvezzáre**, TR.: disaccustom; REFL.: become disaccustomed.
disavvisaménto†, M.: negligence.
disban-deggiáre†, **-díre**†, TR.: banish.
disbarattáre†, TR.: dissipate.
disbarbáre†, TR.: root up.
disbarcáre†, TR., INTR.: disembark; unload.

disbassáre = *sbassare*.
di=sbórso, M.: disbursement.
dis=bramáre†, TR.: gratify.
disbrancáre†, TR.: strip of branches (disbranch).
di=sbrigáre, TR.: extricate, clear up; REFL.: rid or free one's self of.
di-scacciaménto, M.: dismissal; expulsion. ‖**=scacciáre**, TR.: send away (dismiss). **-scacciatívo**, ADJ.: dismissive, expulsive. **-scacciatóre**, M.: expeller.
disca-déré†, INTR.: fall away; waste; fall or return to (said of property). **-diménto†**, M.: falling away; decay. **-dúto†**, ADJ.: fallen.
dis-calzáre†, TR.: strip of shoes and stockings. **-cálzo†**, ADJ.: barefooted.
discánso†, M.: escape.
discapezzáre†, TR.: lop off; decapitate.
di=scapitáre, INTR.: undergo loss. **-scápito**, M.: loss; injury.
discarcáre†, TR.: unload.
discarceráre†, TR.: release from prison.
dis-caricaménto† = *-carico*. ‖**=caricáre**, TR.: unload; relieve; REFL.: ease one's self. **-cárico**, M.: unloading; exculpation.
discarnáre†, TR.: strip of flesh; REFL.: become thin.
dis=cáro, ADJ.: unpleasant (offensive).
discatenáre†, TR.: unchain.
discavalcáre†, TR.: unhorse, throw; INTR.: dismount.
discèdere†, IRR.; INTR.: go away.
di-scendènte, ADJ.: descending; M.: descendant. **-scendènza**, F.: descent, lineage. ‖**=scéndere**, IRR.; INTR.: descend (go down; spring from); TR.: descend. **-scendiménto†**, M., **-scensióne†**, F.: descent, origin. **-scensóre†**, M.: descendant.
discènte†, M.: learner.
dis-centraménto, M.: decentralization. ‖**-centráre** [*centro*], TR.: decentralize.
di-scépola, F.: pupil. **-scepoláto†**, M.: pupilage. ‖**-scépolo** [L. *discipulus* (*discere*, learn)], M.: disciple (pupil).
discer-nènte, PART., ADJ.: discerning, understanding. **-nènza†**, F.: discernment; sign. ‖**discèr-nere** [*cernere*], TR.; discern (distinguish; perceive). **-névole†**, ADJ.: distinctive. **-níbile**, ADJ.: discernible. **-niménto**, M.: discernment. **-nitóre**, M.: discerner.
discèrpere†, TR.: tear to pieces.
…cervelláre = *dicervellare*.
…**-sa**, F.: descent (going down; de…ity). **discé-si**, PRET., ‖**discé-so**, …of **-ndere**.
…**ttá-re†**, TR.: dispute (contend). …**o†**, F.: contention.

discevE-ránza†, F.: separation. **-ráre†**, INTR.: dissever.
dischiaráre† = *dichiarare*.
dischiattáre†, INTR.: degenerate.
dischiavacciáre†, TR.: unlock.
dischiaváre†, TR.: open (with a key), unlock.
dischièdere†, TR.: refuse.
dischieráre†, TR.: break the ranks of, disorder; REFL.: quit the ranks.
dischièsta†, F.: indigence.
dischiodáre = *schiodare*.
dischiomáre†, TR.: disorder the hair of.
dis=chiúdere, IRR.; TR.: disclose (open).
dischiumáre†, TR.: scum, skim.
dis-chiúsi, PRET., **-chiúso**, PART. of *-chiudere*.
di-scígnere†, ‖**-scíngere** [*dis-, c. .*], IRR.; TR.: ungird (untie). **-scínsi**, PRET.; **-scínto**, PART. of *-scingere*.
di=sciògliere, IRR.; TR.: DISSOLVE; unfasten (loosen); REFL.: melt. **-sciogliménto**, M.: solution. **-scioglitóre**, M.: dissolver. **-sciòlsi**, PRET. of *-sciogliere*. **-scioltaménte†**, ADV.: freely, loosely. **-sciòlto**, PART. of *-sciogliere*: dissolved, loose, free. **-scièrre†** = *-sciogliere*.
discipli-na [L. (*discere*, learn)], F.: discipline (system of rules; subjection to rule; training, instruction; science; chastisement, penance); scourge (flagellant's lash, whipcord). **-nábile**, ADJ.: disciplinable. **-nabilità**, F.: disciplinableness. **-nánti**, M. PL.: penitents. **-náre¹**, ADJ.: disciplinary. **-náre²**, TR.: discipline; REFL.: do penance. **-nataménte**, ADV.: according to rule or discipline. **-natézza**, F.: observance of discipline. **-névole†**, ADJ.: disciplinable.
discípulo† = *discepolo*.
dís-co [Gr. *-kos*], M.: discus (quoit); disk. **-còbolo**, M.: discus-thrower.
discoccáre† = *scoccare*.
disco-laménte†, ADV.: dissolutely. **-létto**, M.: idle youth. ‖**dísco-lo** [Gr. *dúskolos*, hard to cultivate], ADJ.: disorderly (dissolute, wild, vile); M.: dissolute person (libertine).
discolorá-re†, TR.: discolour. **-zióne†**, F.: paleness.
discól-pa [*colpa*], F., **-paménto†**, M.: exculpation, vindication. **-páre**, TR.: exculpate.
discom. .† = *scom. .*
dis-concíáre†, TR.: disarrange. **-cóncio†**, ADJ.: disarranged; unsuited; rude.
dis=confessáre, TR.: disavow (disown).
disconf. .† = *sconf. .*
disco-nòbbi, PRET. of *-noscere*. **-noscènza†**, F.: mistaken knowledge; lack of recognition, ingratitude. ‖**-nóscere**

[*dis-*, *c.* .], IRR.; TR.: not recognize. **-nosçiutaménte**†, ADV.: ungratefully; without being known. **-nosçiúto**, PART. of *-noscere;* ADJ.†: unknown.

dis-consentiménto, M.: dissent. ‖=**consentíre**, TR.: dissent (disagree).

disconsi-gliaménto†, M.: dissuasion. **-gliáre**†, TR.: dissuade.

discons. .†, **discont.** .† = *scons.* ., *scont.* .

discon-tinuáre†, TR.: discontinue. **-tinuataménte**†, ADV.: interruptedly. **-tinuazióne**†, F.: discontinuation. ‖**-tínuo** [*continuo*], ADJ.: discontinuous.

dis-convenévole, ADJ.: unsuitable, unbecoming. **-conveniènza**, F.: unsuitability, incongruity. ‖=**convenire**, IRR.; INTR.: misbecome, be unsuitable. **-convénni**, PRET. of *-connire*. **-convenúto**, PART. of *-convenire*.

discop. .†, **discora.** .† = *scop.* ., *scora.* .

discor-daménto†, M., **-dánza**, F.: discord; dissension. **-dáre**, INTR.: be discordant (disaccord); disagree; (Eng.† discord); cause discord†; be distant†. **-datóre**†, M.: disputant. ‖**discòr-de** [L. *dis*, *cor*, HEART], ADJ.: discordant (dissonant); disagreeing†. **-deménte**, ADV.: discordantly. **-dévole**†, ADJ.: discordant. **discòr-dia**, F.: discord (strife). **-dióso**†, ADJ.: quarrelsome.

discor-rèndo, GER.: discoursing: *e via* —, and so on. ‖**-'rere** [*dis-*, *c.* .], IRR.; INTR.: DISCOURSE (talk); run or ramble about†: *far* — *i morti*, change a testament. **-révole**†, ADJ.: flowing. **-riménto**†, M.: discourse; flowing; concourse; running about. **-ritóre**, M., **-ritrice**, F.: discourser (talker). **discór-sa**, F.: tedious talk (nonsense); affected wittiness. **-sáccio**, M.: stupid discourse. **-sétto**, **-síno**, M.: pretty little speech. **discór-si**, PRET. of *-rere*. **-sívo**†, ADJ.: discursive. **discór-so**, PART. of *-rere:* discoursed, etc.; M.: discourse; reasoning. **-sóne**, M.: long discourse.

discortése† = *scortese*.

discoscéso = *scosceso*.

discosciáre†, TR.: disjoint the thigh; INTR.: be rugged or steep.

disco-staménto, M.: removal, departure. ‖**-stáre** [*costa*], TR.: remove, put away; REFL.: go away, withdraw. **-státo**, **di-scò-sto** 1, ADJ.: removed; distant. **di-scò-sto** 2, ADV.: far off.

discovríre† = *scoprire*.

discrasía [Gr. *dus*, bad, *krâsis*, mixture], F.: (*med.*) dyscrasia.

discre-dènte†, ADJ.: incredulous. **-dènza**†, F.: incredulity. ‖**discré-dere** [*dis-*, *c.* .], TR.: discredit (disbelieve); REFL.: change one's opinion. **-ditaménto**†, M.: discredit. **-ditáre**, TR.: discredit (deprive of credibility; disgrace); REFL.: disgrace one's self. **discré-dito**, M.: discredit, loss of favor.

dis-crepánte†, ADJ.: discrepant. **-crepánza**, F.: discrepancy, difference. ‖=**crepáre**, INTR.: be discrepant (differ, be at variance).

discresce. .† = *decresce.* .

discre-taménte, ADV.: discreetly. **-tézza** = *-zione*. **-tivaménte**, ADV.: discretively. **-tívo**, ADJ.: discretive (discerning). ‖**discré-to** [L. *-tus* (*cernere*, separate)], ADJ.: discreet (prudent, just, fair); moderate (mediocre); fair (quite considerable). **-zióne**, F.: discretion.

discriminále†, M.: bodkin for the hair.

discrít. .†, **discriz.** . = *descrit.* ., *descriz.* .

discrolláre†, TR.: shake, toss.

discucíre†, TR.: unsew, rip out.

disculmináre†, TR.: remove the top, unroof.

discuoiáre†, TR.: skin.

dis-cussáre† = *-cutere*. **-cússi**, PRET. of *-cutere*. **-cussióne**, F.: discussion, debate. **-cússo**, PART. of *-cutere*. ‖**-cútere** [L. *quatere*, shake], IRR.§; TR.: DISCUSS.

§ Pret. reg.; or *discús-si*, *-se*; *-sero*. Part. *discùsso*.

diṣ-degnaménto, M.: scorn, anger. **-degnánza**†, F.: disdain. ‖=**degnáre**, TR.: disdain (scorn); INTR.: be disdainful. **-dégno**, M.: disdain. **-degnosaménte**, ADV.: disdainfully. **-degnóso**, ADJ.: disdainful, angry.

diṣ-détta, F.: refusal; denial; (*fam.*) bad luck (esp. at play). ‖**-détto** [*-dire*], PART.: refused; M.†: refusal, bad luck.

diṣdicé-vole†, ADJ.: indecent; improper. **-volézza**†, F.: impropriety. **-volménte**†, ADV.: improperly.

diṣ=dire 1, IRR.; TR.: unsay (retract); deny; forbid; withdraw: — *il fitto* (or *la casa*), give notice to quit.

diṣdire 2 [L. *dis decere*, be fitting], INTR.: be unbecoming (be unsuitable).

diṣdíssi, PRET. of *disdire* 1.

diṣdòro [L. *de-decorus*, shameful], M.: dishonour, shame.

diṣebbriáre†, INTR.: become sober again.

disecc. .† = *dissecc.* .

dise-gnaménto† = *-gno*. ‖**-gnáre** [*di-*, *s.* .], TR.: design (delineate, draw; describe; plan, intend). **-gnatóio**, M.: crayon-case. **-gnatóre**, M., **-gnatrice**, F.: designer. **-gnatúra**†, F.: design. **-gnétto**, **-gníno**, M.: pretty little sketch. **disé-gno**, M.: design (sketch; intention); art of drawing: *colorire un* —, put an idea into practice.

diṣegual. . = *disugual.* .

disellare†, TR.: unsaddle.

diş=enfiáre, TR.: disinflate; reduce the swelling of.
disennáto†, ADJ.: out of one's mind, foolish.
disensáto†, ADJ.: dull, insensate.
disenteria† = *dissenteria.*
diş=equilíbrio, M.: disequilibrium.
diş=eredáre, TR.: disinherit. **-eredazióne**, F.: disinheriting. **-erède**†, ADJ.: disinherited; M.: disinherited person. **-ereditáre**† = *-dare.*
diserráre†, TR.: open, unlock.
dişer-taménto, M.: desolation. ||**-táre** [ak. to *deserto*], TR.: destroy (ruin); INTR.: desert. **-tatóre**, M.: destroyer.
dişèr-to†, ADJ.: deserted (solitary); M.: desert. **-tóre**, M.: deserter.
diser-vígio†, M.: bad turn (unkindness). **-víre**†, TR.: disserve, harm.
disfaci-ménto [*disfare*], M.: undoing (destruction). **-tóre**, M.: undoer (destroyer). **-túra**, F.: undoing.
disfamáre = *sfamare.*
dis=fáre, IRR.; TR.: undo (destroy, defeat); REFL.: dissolve; rid one's self (*di*, of): *-farsi in lacrime*, burst into tears. **-fátta**, F.: defeat (rout of an army). **-fattíbile**, ADJ.: that can be undone or destroyed. **-fátto**, PART of *-fare.* **-fattóre**†, M.: destroyer.
disfavilláre†, INTR.: sparkle.
disfavor.. = *sfavor..*
dis-fazióne†, F.: destruction, ruin. **-féci**, PRET. of *disfare.*
disferenziáre [*differente*], TR.: distinguish.
disfermáre†, TR.: weaken, make less firm.
disferr..†, **disfid..**†, **disfig..**† = *sferr..*, *sfid..*, *sfig..*
dis=fíngere†, IRR.; INTR.: dissemble. **-fingiménto**†, M.: dissembling.
disfiníre† = *definire.*
disfio†.., **disfog..**† = *sfio..*, *sfog..*
dis-formáre = *sformare.* ||**-fórme** [*forma*], ADJ.: unlike, different. **-formità**, F.: diversity, difference.
disforníre†, TR.: unfurnish.
disfortunáto = *sfortunato.*
disfrancáre†, TR.: disfranchise.
disfren..†, **dişgann..**† = *sfren..*, *disingann..*
disgiugn..† = *disgiung..*
dis=giúngere, IRR.; TR.: disjoin (separate); distinguish; unyoke. **-giungiménto**, M.: disjunction (separating). **-giúnsi**, PRET. of *-giungere.* **-giuntaménte**, ADV.: disjointedly (separately). **-giuntivaménte**, ADV.: disjunctively. **-giuntívo**, ADJ.: (*gram.*) disjunctive. **-giúnto**, PART. of *-giungere.* **-giunzióne**, F.: disjunction, separation.

dişgo..† = *sgo..*
dişgra-dáre [*grado*], TR.: put to shame; degrade (disgrace†); descend by steps or degrees†. **-dévole**, ADJ.: unpleasant. **-diménto**, M.: disapprobation, contempt. **-díre**, TR.: dislike. **dişgrá-do**, M.: despite: *avere a —*, dislike, have an aversion for; *a —*, in spite of.
dişgraticoláre†, TR.: deprive of grating or bars.
dişgráto†, ADJ.: disagreeable.
dişgrava.. = *sgrava..*
dişgravidáre†, INTR.: bring forth.
diş=grázia, F.: misfortune (ill luck, mischance); disgrace (disfavour): *per —*, unfortunately. **-graziáre**† = *disgradare.* **-graziataménte**, ADV.: unfortunately. **-graziáto**, ADJ.: unfortunate, unhappy (wretched). **-grazióso**†, ADJ.: quarrelsome.
dişgre-gábile, ADJ.: that can be separated. **-gánza**† = *-gazione.* ||**-gáre** [L. *grex*, flock], TR.: separate (disunite, Eng.† disgregate). **-gatívo**, ADJ.: separating. **-gazióne**, F.: separation.
dişgrev..†, **dişgrign..**† = *disgrev..*, *digrign..*
dişgroppáre†, TR.: undo.
dişgross..† = *sgross..*
diş-guagliánza†, F., **-guáglio**†, M.: inequality.
disgu-stáre, TR.: disgust; offend; REFL.: be disgusted. **-stévole**, ADJ.: disgusting. **-stevolézza**, F.: disgustfulness. ||**dişgú-sto** [*gusto*], M.: disgust (aversion, dislike). **-stóso**, ADJ.: disgusting.
di-şía†, F.: desire. **-şiáre**†, TR.: desire.
disid.., **disig..** = *desid..*, *dissig..*
diş=impacciáre, TR.: disencumber (disembarrass).
diş=imparáre, TR.: unlearn (forget).
dişim-pegnáre [*impegno*], TR.: disengage (release); perform (achieve); REFL.: get through, get off: *-pegnarsi di sua parola*, keep one's word. **-pégno**, M.: disengagement (release).
dişináre† = *desinare.*
diş=incantáre, TR.: disenchant.
dişinclinazióne†, F.: disinclination.
dişinènza = *desinenza.*
diş-infettánte, ADJ., M.: disinfectant. ||**=infettáre** [*infetto*], TR.: disinfect. **-infezióne**, F.: disinfection.
diş=infíngere†, IRR.; TR.: dissemble.
diş=ingannáre, TR.: disillusion (undeceive); REFL.: be disillusioned (be undeceived). **-ingánno**, M.: disillusion.
diş-innamoraménto, M.: ceasing to love. ||**=innamoráre**, REFL.: cease being enamoured.
diş=insegnáre, TR.: unteach; teach the opposite of.

diş-interessáto, ADJ.: disinterested. ‖**=interèsse**, M.: disinterestedness.

dişinvitáre†, TR.: countermand.

diş-involtaménto, ADV.: easily, gracefully. ‖**=invòlto**, ADJ.: unembarrassed (self-possessed, easy; graceful). **-involtúra**, F.: self-possession (ease, grace); boldness; levity.

dişío, **dişíro**† = *desire*, *desio*.

dişistancáre†, REFL.: rest one's self.

dişistí-ma [*dis-*, *stima*], F.: disesteem; disrepute. **-máre**, TR.: disesteem.

dişlaccetáre [*laccio*], TR.: unlace.

dişlagáre†, REFL.: overflow.

dişle. ., **dişloc**. . = *sle*. ., *slog*. .

diş=lodáre, TR.: dispraise.

dişloga. . = *sloga*. .

dişmagáre†, TR.: err; deviate; REFL.: separate one's self.

dişmagliáre†, TR.: break the meshes; (*fig.*) tear flesh with the nails.

dişmaláre†, TR.: cure.

dişmantáre†, REFL.: remove one's cloak.

dişmarr. .†, **dişmem**. .† = *smarr*. ., *smem*. .

dişmemoráto†, ADJ.: unmindful.

dişmen-táre†, **-ticáre** = *dimenticare*.

dişméttere = *smettere*.

dişmişú-ra [*dis-*, *m*. .], F.: excess: *a* —, excessively. **-ránza**† = *-ra*. **-ráre**†, INTR.: exceed the measure.

dişmodáto = *smodato*.

dişmonacáre†, TR.: uncloister; REFL.: leave a cloister.

dişmontáre = *smontare*.

dişmuòvere†, TR.: dissuade; disturb; REFL.: change one's mind.

dişnatura. . = *snatura*. .

dişnebbiáre [*nebbia*], TR.: free from mist or clouds.

dişnerváre†, TR.: enervate.

dişnidáre†, TR.: take from the nest; REFL.: leave the nest.

dişno-dáre [*nodo*], TR.: unknot, undo. **-dévole**†, ADJ.: that can be untied.

dişnore† = *disonore*.

diş=nudáre, TR.: denude.

dişobbedi. . = *disubbidi*. .

diş-obbligánte, PART., ADJ.: disobliging. **=obbligáre**, TR.: free from obligation (Eng.† disoblige). **-òbbligo**, M.: release from obligation.

diş=occupáre, TR.: disengage (release); REFL.: rest from labor (take one's ease). **-occupáto**, ADJ.: unoccupied (at leisure). **-occupazióne**, F.: leisure.

dişolaménto†, M.: desolation.

diş-onestà, F.: dishonesty. **-onestaménte**, ADV.: dishonestly. **-onestáre**†, TR.: dishonour; REFL.: disgrace one's self. ‖**=onèsto**, ADJ.: dishonest; indecent.

dişonnáre†, REFL.: awake.

dişono-raménto, M., **-ránza**†, F.: dishonour, disgrace. **-ráre**, TR.: dishonour (disgrace); REFL.: disgrace one's self. **-ratóre**, M.: he who dishonours. ‖**dişonó-re** [*onore*], M.: dishonour (disgrace). **-révole**, ADJ.: dishonourable. **-revolménte**, ADV.: dishonourably.

dişoppi-lánte, ADJ., M.: deoppilative. ‖**-láre** [*dis-*, *o*. .], TR.: clear (Eng.† deoppilate). **-latívo** = *-lante*.

di=sópra, ADV.: over; above. **=sopra=più**, ADV.: over and above, besides.

dişorbi-tánte, ADJ.: exorbitant. **-tanteménte**, ADV.: exorbitantly. **-tánza**, F.: exorbitance. ‖**-táre** [*orbita*], TR.: exceed.

dişordi-náccio, M.: great disorder. **-naménto**, M., **-nánza**†, F.: disorder. **-náre**, TR.: disorder (disturb); INTR.: exceed, be immoderate; REFL.†: be confused. **-nataménte**, ADV.: in a disorderly way; lawlessly. **-náto**, PART., ADJ.: disorderly; irregular; dissolute†. **-nazióne**†, F.: disorder. ‖**dişórdi-ne** [*ordine*], M.: disorder (confusion); irregularity.

diş=organizzáre, TR.: disorganize; REFL.: be confused.

dişormeggiáre†, TR.: uncable.

dişornáre†, TR.: disadorn.

dişorpelláre [*orpello*], TR.: strip of tinsel; bare (unmask).

dişossáre [*osso*], TR.: bone.

dişossidáre [*ossido*], TR.: reduce the oxides.

disottáno†, ADJ.: lower (inferior).

disotterráre = *dissotterrare*.

di=sótto, PREP., ADV.: below, beneath.

disp. ., often = *sp*. .

dispac-ciaménto†, M.: speed. ‖**-ciáre** [L. *pedica* (*pes*, foot), fetter], TR.: DISPATCH (telegraph); exPEDite. **dispáccio**, M.: dispatch (message, official letter; telegram); course†, expedition†.

dispaiáre [*paio*], TR.: unmatch (disunite, separate).

dis=paráre†, TR.: unmatch; unlearn, forget. **-paráto**, ADJ.: disparate (dissimilar).

disparécchi†, PRON. (M. PL.): a great many.

disparènza†, F.: disappearance.

dis=parére 1, M.: slight dissension, dispute.

dispa-rére† 2, INTR.: disappear. **-révole**†, ADJ.: passing, fleeting.

di=spárgere†, IRR.; TR.: DISPERSE. **-spargiménto**†, M.: dispersion.

dispari [L. *dis-par* (*par*, equal)], ADJ.: unequal (odd, uneven); different†. **-ménte**†, ADV.: unequally.

disparíre and deriv. = *sparire* and deriv.

disparità [*dispari*], F.: disparity (difference).

disparménte†, ADV.: unequally.

dispár-si†, PRET., **-so**†, PART. of *-gere*.

dispár-te, ADV.: apart: *in* —, in a place apart; *tenersi* (*stare*) *in* —, not aspire to honours, etc. ‖**-tíre** [L.], TR.: part, separate (disputants); divide: — *l'amistà*†, break the friendship. **-titaménte**†, ADV.: separately. **-titóre**, M.: divider.

disparut..† = *sparut..*

dispassionaménto†, M.: dispassion, apathy.

dispastoiáre†, TR.: unfetter a horse; free.

dispaventáre† = *spaventare*.

dispèn-dere [L. (*pendere*, weigh)], IRR. (cf. *spendere*); TR.: dispend; spend. **dispèn-dio**, M.: expense, costs. **-diosaménte**, ADV.: expensively. **-dióso**, ADJ.: expensive. **-ditóre**†, M.: spendthrift. **dispèn-sa**, F.: dispensation; distribution; privilege; instalment (part, number of a book); pantry (larder). **-sábile**†, ADJ.: dispensable. **-sagióne**†, F., **-saménto**†, M.: distribution; immunity. **-sáre**, TR.: dispense, distribute; exempt; REFL.: dispense with. **-satóre**, M., **-satríce**, F.: dispenser. **-sazióne**†, F.: distribution; dispensation. **-sièra**, F.: housekeeper. **-sière**, M.: steward, butler.

dispènto†, ADJ.: extinguished; destroyed.

dispe-rábile†, ADJ.: desperate, despaired of. **-ragióne**†, **-ránza**†, F.: desperation. ‖**-ráre** [*spero*], TR.: not hope for; deprive of hope†; INTR.: despair; REFL.: be desperate. **-rataménte**, ADV.: desperately. **-ratézza**†, F.: despair. **-ráto**, PART., ADJ.: desperate (beyond hope); M.: desperate person; madman: *alla -rata*, desperately. **-razióne**, F.: desperation (despair); sorrow.

dis=pèrdere, TR.: waste (squander, scatter). **-perdiménto**, M.: waste (dissipation). **-perditóre**, M.: squanderer.

di=spèrgere, IRR.; TR.: DISPERSE (scatter, diffuse); waste. **-spergiménto**†, M.: dispersion. **-spergitóre**, M.: waster.

dis=per=sè, ADV.: by one's self, alone, apart.

dis-pèrsi, PRET. of *-pergere*. **-persióne**, F.: dispersion. **-pèrso**, PART. of *-pergere*.

dispéso†, PART. of *dispendere*.

dispet-tábile†, ADJ.: despicable. **-táccio**, M.: despicable affront. **-táre**†, TR.: despise; REFL.: be vexed. **-tévole**†, ADJ.: disdainful. **-tivaménte**†, ADV.: disdainfully. ‖**dispèt-to** [L. *despicere* (look)], M.: DESPITE (malignity; anger); contempt†: *a* (*per*) —, in spite of; *avere in* —, despise. **-tosáccio**, disp. of *-toso*. **-tosaménte**, ADV.: despitefully. **-tóso**, ADV.: despiteful; saucy. **-tosúccio**, **-tosúzzo**†, dim. of *-toso*. **-túccio**, M.: sauciness.

dispia-cènte, ADJ.: displeasing. **-centíssimo**, ADJ.: most (very) displeasing. **-cènza**, F.: displeasure; grief. ‖**-cére** [*dis-*, *p..*], IRR.; TR.: DISPLEASE; VEX; REFL.: be displeased; feel sorry. **-cévole**, ADJ.: unpleasing. **-cevolézza**, F.: displeasure. **-cevolménte**, ADV.: unpleasingly (disagreeably). **-ciménto**, M.: vexation, grief. **-ciúto**, PART. of *-cere*.

dispiá-cqui, PRET. of *-cere*.

dispianáre†, TR.: level; REFL.: stretch out (lie down).

dispiant..†, **dispicc..** = *spiant..*, *spicc..*

dispicciáre†, TR.: dispatch, hasten.

dispieg.. = *spieg..*

dispie-tánza†, F.: inhumanity. **-tataménte**†, ADV.: pitilessly, inhumanly. **-táto**†, ADJ.: pitiless, cruel.

dis=pígnere†, **=píngere**†, IRR.; TR.: cancel, blot out. **-pínsi**†, PRET., **-pínto**†, PART. of *-pingere*.

displicènza† = *dispiacenza*.

dispod.., **dispogl..**, **dispol..** = *spod..*, *spogl..*, *spol..*

dis-ponènte, PART. of *-porre*; M.: disposer. ‖**=pónere** = *-porre*. **-poníbile**, ADJ.: disposable. **-poniménto**†, M.: disposal, order. **-ponitívo**, more commonly *-positivo*. **-ponitóre**, M.: regulator, bestower. **=pórre**, IRR.; TR.: DISPOSE (arrange, put in order); persuade; REFL.: prepare one's self. **-pósi**, PRET. of *-porre*. **-positivaménte**, ADV.: disposingly. **-positívo**, ADJ.: disposing, enacting; F.: enactment. **-positóre**, M., **-positríce**, F.: disposer. **-posizióne**, F.: disposition; intent; order. **-pósta**, F.: disposition. **-postaménte**†, ADV.: with order. **-postézza**, F.: disposedness, readiness. **-pósto**, PART. of *-porre*; ADJ.: disposed, adapted; well made†, nimble.

di-spoticaménte, ADV.: despotically. ‖**-spòtico** [*despota*], ADJ.: despotic. **-potísmo**, M.: despotism.

dispre-gévole, ADJ.: despicable. **-gevolménte**, ADV.: slightingly. **-giábile**, ADJ.: contemptible. **-giaménto**, M.: contempt. ‖**-giáre** [*dis-*, *p..*], TR.: DEPRECIATE (hold to be of little value); look down upon (despise). **-giatívo**, ADJ.: depreciating; M.: depreciative suffix. **-giatóre**, M.: scorner. **disprègio**, M.: scorn (contempt). **-zzábile**, ADJ.: contemptible. **-zzanteménte**, ADV.: scornfully. **-zzáre** [*prezzo*], TR.: deprecate (hold to be of small value); look down upon (despise). -**zzatóre**, M., -**zzatríce**, F.: scorner. -**zzévole**†, ADJ.: despicable. -**zzevolménte**†, ADV.: scornfully. **disprè-zzo**, M.: contempt.

dispri.., **dispro..** = *spri..*, *spro..*

dispúro†, ADJ.: impure.

dispu-ta, F.: dispute, discussion. -**tábile**, ADJ.: disputable. -**tánte**, M.: disputant. ‖-**táre** [L. (*putare*, clean)], INTR.: dispute; discuss; REFL.: contest. -**tatívo**, ADJ.: disputative. -**táto**, ADJ.: disputed, controverted. -**tatóre**, M., -**tatríce**, F.: disputer, arguer. -**tazióne**, F.: disputation; argument.

disquisizióne [L. -*sitio* (*quærere*, seek)], F.: disquisition (dissertation).

disradicáre†, TR.: eradicate.

disrag..†, **disreg..** = *srag..*, *sreg..*

dis=rómpere†, IRR.; TR.: break off.

disrugginíre†, TR.: remove the rust, polish.

dissacráre†, TR.: desecrate.

dissaláre [*sale*], INTR.: freshen salt meat.

dissan-guáre [*sangue*], TR.: remove blood, bleed. -**guináre**, TR.: wash off blood (from skins, etc.).

dissa-píto†, ADJ.: insipid. ‖-**póre** [*sapore*], M.: disagreement (quarrel). -**porí-to**†, -**voróso**†, ADJ.: unsavory, tasteless.

disseccá-re [L. (*secare*, cut)], TR.: dissect. -**zióne**, F.: dissection.

dissecca-ménto, M.: desiccation. ‖-**cáre** [L. *siccus*, dry], TR.: desiccate; REFL.: become dry. -**catívo**, ADJ.: desiccative (drying).

disselciáre [*selce*], TR.: tear up the pavement of.

dissemin-áre [*semino*], TR.: disseminate (scatter). -**tóre**, M.: disseminator. -**zióne**, F.: dissemination.

dissennáre [*senno*], TR.: deprive of sense.

dis-sensióne, F.: dissension. ‖=**sènso**, M.: dissent (discord).

dissen-tería [Gr. *dus*, ill, *énteron*, intestine], F.: dysentery. -**tèrico**, ADJ.: dysenteric.

dis-sentiménto, M.: dissent. ‖=**sentíre**, INTR.: dissent. -**senziènte**, PART., ADJ.: dissentient.

dissepara.. = *separa..*

dis=seppellíre, TR.: unbury, disinter.

dis=serráre, TR.: unlock.

dissertá-re [L. *dis-serere* (join)], INTR.: discuss (dissert). -**zioncèlla**, F.: brief discussion. -**zióne**, F.: dissertation.

disser-vígio† = -*vizio*. -**víre**†, TR.: disserve (harm). -**vízio**†, M.: disservice (ill turn).

dissestáre, TR.: derange; REFL.: be in disorder. -**sèsto**, M.: disorder.

dissetáre [*sete*], INTR.: quench thirst.

dis-settóre [L. -*sector* (*secare*, cut)], M.: dissector (anatomist). -**sezióne**, F.: dissection.

díssi, PRET. of *dire*.

dis-sidènte [L. -*dens* (*sedere*, SIT)], ADJ.: dissident (disagreeing); M.: dissenter (in religion). -**sídio**, M.: dissension.

dis=sigilláre, TR.: unseal.

dis-síllabo, ADJ.: dissyllabic; M.: dissyllable.

dissimiglia..† = *dissomiglia..*

dissími-le [*dis-*, *s..*], ADJ.: dissimilar, unlike. -**litúdine**, F.: dissimilitude, unlikeness.

dissimulá-re [*dis-*, *s..*], TR.: dissimulate (pretend). -**taménte**, ADV.: dissemblingly. -**tóre**, M., -**tríce**, F.: dissembler. -**zióne**, F.: dissimulation.

dissi-pábile, ADJ.: dissipable. -**paménto**, M.: dissipation. ‖-**páre** [L. (*sipare*, throw)], TR.: dissipate (disperse). -**pataménte**, ADV.: wastefully. -**patézza**, F.: dissipation. -**páto**, ADJ.: dissipated; scattered. -**patóre**, M., -**patríce**, F.: squanderer. -**pazióne**, F.: dissipation.

dissipíto†, ADJ.: insipid.

dissodáre [*sodo*], TR.: till (plough).

dissollecitúdine†, F.: slowness.

disso-lúbile, ADJ.: dissoluble. -**lubilità**, F.: dissolubility. -**lutaménte**, ADV.: dissolutely. -**lutézza**, F.: dissoluteness. -**lutívo**, ADJ.: dissolvent. -**lúto**, PART. of -*lvere*; ADJ.: dissolute. -**luzióne**, F.: dissolution. **disso-lvéi**, PRET. of -*lvere*. -**lvènte**, ADJ., M.: dissolvent. ‖**dissò-lvere** [*dis-*, *s..*], IRR.; TR.: dissolve; REFL.: dissolve, melt. -**lviménto**, M.: dissolving, melting.

dis-somigliánza, F.: unlikeness. ‖=**somigliáre**, INTR., REFL.: be unlike, be different.

dis-sonánte, ADJ.: dissonant. -**sonánza**, F.: dissonance; incongruity. ‖=**sonáre**, INTR.: be dissonant.

dissonnáre [*sonno*], TR., REFL.: awake.

dis=sono [L. *sonus*, sound], ADJ.: dissonant.

dis-sotterraménto, M.: exhumation. ‖=**sotterráre**, TR.: disinter, dig up.

dis=sovveníre†, IRR.; INTR.: forget.

dis=suadére, IRR.; TR.: dissuade. -**suási**, PRET. of -*suadere*. -**suasióne**, F.: dissuasion. -**suasívo**, ADJ.: dissuasive. -**suáso**, PART. of -*suadere*. -**suasòrio** = -*suasivo*.

dissuetúdine [L. -*do* (*suescere*, be used)], F.: desuetude (disuse).

dissugáre [*sugo*], TR.: deprive of juice or sap.

dissuggelláre = *dissigillare*.

dissúria [Gr. *dus-*, bad, *oûron*, urine], F.: dysury.

di-staccaménto, M.: detaching; d

tachment. **-staccánza**† = *-staccamento*. ‖=**staccáre**, TR.: detach, pull away. **-staccatúra**†, F.: detaching, separating. **-stácco**, M.: separation, parting.

dista-gliáre†, INTR., REFL.: intersect; TR.: cut apart. **-gliatúra**†, F.: cut, division.

di-stánte, ADJ.: distant (far). **-stánza**, **-stánzia**†, F.: distance. ‖=**stáre**, IRR.; INTR.: be distant (be remote).

distasáre†, TR.: unstop.

distemperáre = *stemperare*.

dis=tèndere, IRR.; TR.: distend (stretch or spread out); REFL.: dwell or enlarge upon. **-tendíbile**, ADJ.: distensible. **-tendiménto**, M.: distension.

distenebráre [*tenebra*], TR.: clear up.

dis=tenére†, IRR.; TR.: hold back, detain. **-teniménto**†, M.: detention.

dis-tensióne [*-tendere*], F.: distension (expansion).

distenúto†, PART. of *distenere*.

disterminare† = *sterminare*.

dis-tésa, F.: extent; expansion: *alla* —, at large; diffusedly. **-tesaménte**, ADV.: extensively. **-tési**, PRET. of *-tendere*. ‖**-téso**, PART. of *-tendere*.

disti-chétto, *dim.* of *-co*. ‖**dísti-co** [Gr. *dis*, twice, *stíkos*, row, verse], M.: distich (epigram of two verse-lines).

distil-laménto, M.: distilling. ‖**-láre** [L. (*stillare*, drop)], TR.: distill. **-latóio**, M.: still, distillery. **-latóre**, M.: distiller. **-latòrio**, M.: still. **-lazióne**, F.: distillation. **-lería**, F.: distillery.

di-stínguere [L.], IRR.§; TR.: distinguish, separate; REFL.: distinguish one's self. **-stinguíbile**, ADJ.: distinguishable. **-stínsi**, PRET. of *-stinguere*. **-stintaménte**, ADV.: distinctly. **-stintívo**, ADJ.: distinctive; M.: sign, characteristic. **-stínto**, PART. of *-stinguere*; ADJ.: clear, distinct. **-stinzioncèlla**, F.: slight distinction. **-stinzióne**, F.: difference; distinction, honour.

§ Pret. *distin-si, -se; -sero*. Part. *distinto*.

dis=tògliere, IRR.; TR.: dissuade, divert. **-togliménto**, M.: dissuasion. **-tòlsi**, PRET., **-tòlto**, PART. of *-togliere*.

diston..†, **distore..**†, **distorn..**† = *ston..*, *store..*, *storn..*

distòrre = *distogliere*.

dis-torsióne, F.: distortion, contorsion. ‖**-tòrto**† [L. *-tortus* (*torquere*, twist)], ADJ.: distorted; unjust.

dis-tráere†, =**trárre**, IRR.; TR.: distract (divert); REFL.: divert one's mind. **-trássi**, PRET. of *-trarre*. **-trattaménte**, ADV.: distractedly. **-trátto**, PART. of *-trarre*. **-trazioncèlla**, F.: slight distraction. **-trazióne**, F.: distraction (diversion).

di-strétta†, F.: distress (need). **-strettaménte**†, ADV.: severely. **-strettézza**†, F.: severity. ‖**-strétto** [*-stringere*], PART.†, ADJ.: pressed, needy; M.: district, province. **-strettuále**, ADJ.: territorial.

distri-buiménto†, M.: distribution. ‖**-buíre** [L. *dis-tribuere* (*tribus*, tribe)], TR.: distribute; range. **-butivaménte**, ADV.: distributively. **-butívo**, ADJ.: distributive. **-butóre**, M., **-butríce**, F.: distributer. **-buzióne**, F.: distribution.

distrigáre = *strigare*.

di-strígnere†, **-stríngere**†, TR.: bind close; pinch. **-stringiménto**†, M.: binding, pinching.

di=strúggere, IRR.; TR.: DESTROY (demolish). **-struggíbile**, ADJ.: destructible. **-struggiménto**†, M.: destruction. **-struggitívo** = *-struttivo*. **-struggitóre**, M., **-struggitríce**, F.: destroyer. **-strússi**, PRET. of *-struggere*. **-struttíbile**† = *-struggibile*. **-struttívo**, ADJ.: destructive. **-strútto**, PART. of *-struggere*. **-struttóre**, M.: destroyer. **-struzióne**, F.: destruction, demolition.

disturáre†, TR.: uncork.

dis-turbánza†, F.: disturbance. ‖**-turbáre** [L. (*turba*, disorder)], TR.: disturb. **-turbatóre**, M., **-turbatríce**, F.: disturber. **-túrbo**, M.: disturbance.

disubbi-diènte, ADJ.: disobedient. **-dienteménte**, ADV.: disobediently. **-diènza**, F.: disobedience. ‖**-díre** [*obedire*], TR.: disobey; INTR.: be disobedient.

disudíre†, TR.: appear not to hear.

disuggelláre†, TR.: unseal.

dis-uguagliánza, F.: inequality. **-uguagliáre**, TR.: render unequal. ‖=**uguále**, ADJ.: unequal, unlike. **-ugualità**, F.: inequality. **-ugualménte**, ADV.: unequally.

dis-umanáre†, TR.: divest of humanity; REFL.: become inhuman. ‖=**umáno**, ADJ.: inhuman.

disumidíre [*umido*], TR.: remove the humidity.

dis=úngere, TR.: free from grease.

dis-unióne, F.: disunion, division. ‖=**uníre**, TR.: disunite (separate); REFL.: be separated. **-unitaménte**, ADJ.: separately. **-unito**, PART.; ADJ.: separate.

disúnto†, ADJ.: empty (vain).

disúria = *dissuria*.

disurpáre = *usurpare*.

dis-usánza†, F.: disuse. **-usáre**, TR.: disaccustom. **-usataménte**†, ADV.: against custom. **-usáto**, ADJ.: disused, obsolete; unusual. ‖**dis-úso**, M.: disuse, desuetude.

dis-utiláccio, ADJ.: utterly useless, good for nothing. ‖**=útile**, ADJ.: useless. **-utilità**, F.: inutility, uselessness. **-utilménte**, ADV.: uselessly.

disva-lére†, TR.: harm. **-lóre†**, M.: little value.

disvantággio = *svantaggio*.

disvariáre†, INTR.: vary.

disvel(l).., **disvi..** = *svel(l)..*, *svi..*

dis=volére, INTR.: unwill (will the reverse).

dí-ta, PL. of *-to*. **-tále**, M.: finger-stall; thimble. **-táta**, F.: slap with the finger; sign, mark (left by the fingers).

ditèllo†, M.: arm-pit.

diten..†, **diter..†** = *deten..*, *deter..*

diti-rambeggiáre, INTR.: write dithyrambs. **-rámbico**, ADJ.: dithyrambic. ‖**-rámbo** [Gr. *dithúrambos*, name of Bacchus], M.: dithyramb (hymn to Bacchus).

dí-to [L. *-gitus*], pl. *-ti* or (*f.*) *-ta*, M.: finger, inch: — *grosso*, thumb; — *mignolo*, little finger; *legarsela a* —, not to forget (an injury); *mordersi il* — *per una cosa*, repent a thing; *mostrare a* —, point at. **dí-tola**, F. PL.: fungus (mushroom). **-tóne**, *aug.* of *-to*.

dítono [Gr. *dis*, two, *tónos*, tone], M.: interval of two notes.

ditrappáre†, TR.: rob (swindle).

di=tràrre†, IRR.; TR.: take away; DETRACT (defame). **-trazióne†**, F.: detraction.

ditrinciáre†, TR.: cut, hash.

dítta [*ditto*, old part. of *-dire*], F.: firm (commercial house).

dittá-re† [L. *dictare*], TR.: dictate. **dittá-to†**, M.: dictation; adage. **-tóre**, M.: dictator. **-tòrio**, ADJ.: dictatorial. **-túra**, F.: dictatorship.

dítto†, M.: saying, maxim.

dit-tongáre, TR.: diphthongize. ‖**-tòngo** [Gr. *dis-*, twice, *phthóngos*, sound], M.: diphthong.

diturpáre†, TR.: defile (Eng.† diturpate).

diú-rno [L. *-rnus* (*dies*, DAY)], ADJ.: diurnal (daily); M.: diurnal (prayer-book); (*zoöl.*) diurnal bird. **-turnaménto**, ADV.: for a long time. **-turnità**, F.: diuration. **-túrno**, ADJ.: lasting (Eng.† diuturnal).

diva [L.], F.: goddess.

diva-gaménto, M.: roving (divagation). ‖**-gáre** [L. *-vagari* (rove)], INTR., REFL.: rove (ramble, wander); TR.: distract (divert).

dival-laménto†, M.: descent, going down. **-láre†**, INTR., REFL.: descend (decline).

divam-paménto, M.: shining, blaze. ‖**-páre** [*di-*, *v..*], INTR.: burn (blaze).

divàno [Ar. *daiwan*, council], M.: divan (Turk. council; couch; assembly hall).

di-variáre†, TR., INTR.: vary. **-vário†**, M.: distraction; interruption.

divastazióne†, F.: devastation.

divecchiáre†, TR.: make young; renew; INTR.: grow young.

di=vedére, IRR.; TR.: let see (show): *dare a* —, demonstrate. **-vedúto**, PART. of *-vedere*.

di-vèglere†, **=vèllere**, TR.: uproot. **-velliménto†**, M.: uprooting. **-vèlto**, ADJ.: uprooted; ploughed; M.: deep digging; ploughed ground.

di=veníre, IRR.; INTR.: become; derive. **-vénni**, PRET. of *-venire*. **-ventáre**, INTR.: become. **-venúto**, PART. of *-venire*.

divèrbio [*verbo*], M.: dispute.

di-vergènte, PART.: diverging. **-vergènza**, F.: divergence. ‖**=vèrgere**, IRR.; INTR.: diverge.

divèrre†, TR.: uproot, dig out.

di-versaménte, ADV.: diversely. **-versáre†**, INTR.: be different. **-versificáre**, INTR.: vary; TR.: diversify. **-versificazióne**, F.: variation, change. **-versióne†**, F.: diversion (amusement; stratagem). **-versità**, F.: diversity. **-vèrso**, ADJ.: diverse; strange†, horrible. **-versòrio†**, M.: lodging, inn. **-vèrtere†**, TR.: divert. **-vertícolo†**, M.: subterfuge; digression. **-vertiménto**, M.: diversion (pastime). ‖**-vertíre** [L. *divertere*, turn], TR. (Pres. *-verto*): distract, divert; REFL.: be diverted.

divestíre†, TR.: undress, divest.

divettáre [*di vetta*], TR.: prune.

divez-záre [*vezzo*], TR.: disaccustom; wean (children); REFL.: disaccustom one's self. **-záto**, **divéz-zo**, PART., ADJ.: disaccustomed.

di-viáre† [*via*], TR.: deviate. **-viáto**, ADJ.: direct; quick; ADV.: hurriedly, right AWAY.

di-vidèndo, M.: dividend, share. ‖**-vídere** [L.], IRR.§; TR.: divide; part (separate). **-vidévole†**, ADJ.: divisible. **-viditóre†**, M.: divider.

§ Pret. *divi-si*, *-se*; *-sero*. Part. *diviso*.

di-vietaménto† = *-vieto*. ‖**=vietáre**, TR.: prohibit, forbid. **-vietazióne†**, F., **-vièto**, M.: prohibition, forbidding.

divimáre†, TR.: untie (loosen); REFL.: disentangle one's self.

divi-naménte, ADV.: divinely. ‖**-náre** [*-no*], TR., INTR.: divine (predict, presage). **-natóre**, M.: diviner. **-natòrio**, ADJ.: divining. **-nazióne**, F.: divination.

divinco-lábile, ADJ.: that can be twisted. **-laménto**, M.: twisting. ‖**-láre** [*di-*, *v..*], TR.: twist, wring; REFL.: writhe.

divi-nità, F.: [illegible]. **-nizzáre**, TR.: [illegible]. **-nizzazióne**, F.: [illegible]. ||**di-vi-no** [L. -nus], ADJ.: [illegible].

divi-ṣa, F.: [illegible] share, manner [illegible]. **-ṣaménte**, [illegible] separately. **-ṣaménto**, M.: [illegible] [illegible]. **-ṣáre**, TR.: [illegible] consider, [illegible]. **-ṣataménte**, [illegible] distinctly. **-ṣáto**[illegible] ADJ.: variegated; disfigured. **divi-ṣi**, PART. of -dere. **-ṣi-bile**, ADJ.: divisible. **-ṣibilità**, F.: divisibility. **-ṣióne**, F.: division. **-ṣivo**†, ADJ.: divisible. **divi-ṣo** [-dere], PART.: separated. **-ṣóre**, M.: divider; divisor. **-ṣòrio**, ADJ.: dividing.

di-vízia†, F.: abundance; PL.: riches. **-vi-zióso**†, ADJ.: rich.

dívo [L. -vus (deus, god)], ADJ.: (poet.) divine.

divolga[illegible]† = [illegible].

di=vòlgere†, TR. [illegible]: [illegible] wrap. **-vòl-to**†, PART.

divora-cità†, F.: voracity. **-ménto** [-re], M.: voracity, gluttony. **=mónti**†, M., INVAR.: braggart. **-re** [L. devo-rare], TR.: devour. **-tóre**, M., **-trice**, F.: devourer. **-zióne**†, F.: devouring.

divòrzio [L. -tium (vertere, turn)], M.: divorce.

dívot. = [illegible].

divul-gaménto, M.: divulging, publication. **-gáre** [L. vulgus, crowd], TR.: divulge (publish). **-gatóre**, M., **-gatrí-ce**, F.: divulger. **-gazióne**† = *-ga-mento*.

divúlso†, PART. of *divellere*.

di-zionário, M.: dictionary. **-zióne** [L. *dictio* (*dicere*, say)], F.: diction (phrase, word); district†; power†.

dò1, PRES. IND. of *dare*.

dò2, M.: do (first note of the scale).

doána† = *dogana*.

dó-bla = *doppia*. **-blétto**, M.: kind of cotton stuff. **-bblóne** [Sp.], M.: doubloon (Spanish coin). **dó-blo**† = *doppio*.

dóc-cia, F.: CONDUIT (duct); canal; shower-bath. ||**-ciáre** [l. L. *ductiare* (*du-cere*, lead)], TR., INTR.: pour down; take shower-baths†. **-ciatúra**, F.: lotion; shower-bath. **dóc-cio**† = *-cia*. **-cio-náta**, F.: conduit. **-cióne**, M.: large conduit-pipe.

dòci-le [L. *-lis* (*docere*, teach)], ADJ.: docile (tractable). **-lità**, F.: docility. **-lmé**[illegible] [illegible] tractably.

doc[illegible] [illegible] TR.: provide with doc-[illegible] ||**-ménto** [L. *-men*-[illegible]], M.: document; pre-[illegible]

[illegible] ka, twelve]: **-èdro** [Gr. [illegible]] dodecahedron. **-'gono** [Gr. [illegible] angle], M.: dodecagon. **-sil-labo**, ADJ.: dodecasyllabic; M.: dodeca-syllable.

dodi=cènne†, ADJ.: twelve years old. **-cèṣimo**, ADJ.: twelfth. ||**dódi-ci** [L. *duodecim*], NUM.: twelve. **-ci=mila**, M.: twelve thousand. **-cina**, F.: dozen.

dóga [Gr. *doché*, cask], F.: stave (of a cask, etc.).

dogále [*doge*], ADJ.: dogal.

dogáme [*doga*], M.: quantity of staves.

dogá-na [?], F.: custom-house or office; administration of customs. **-nále**, ADJ.: of customs. **-nière**, M.: custom-house officer.

dogáre [*doga*], TR.: put the staves on (a barrel).

do-garéssa, F.: spouse of the doge. **-gá-to**, M.: dogate, office of doge. ||**dò-ge** [L. *dux*, leader], M.: doge.

doghétto†, M.: young mastiff.

dò-glia [L. *-lor*], F.: pain, grief; PL.: pains of labour. **-gliánza**, F.: lamentation, complaint. **-gliarèlla**, F.: slight pain. **-glie**, cf. *-glia*. **-gliènte**†, ADJ.: doleful.

do-gliétto†, *dim.* of *-glio*. ||**dò-glio**†, M.: cask.

do-gliosaménte, ADV.: sorrowfully. **-glióso** [*-glia*], ADJ.: sorrowful (painful). **-gliúccia**, F.: slight grief.

dogma. = *domma*.

dógo†, M.: mastiff.

dól-ce [L. *dulcis*], ADJ.: sweet (mild, gentle); ADV.: softly; M.: sweetness. **-ceménte**, ADV.: sweetly (softly). **-céz-za**, F.: sweetness; PL.: pleasures. **dól-ci**, M. PL.: sweets (confits). **dól-cia**†, F.: swine's blood. **-ciástro**, ADJ.: sweetish; sickening. **-ciáto**†, ADJ.: sweet (charming). **-ciosonòro**†, ADJ.: melodious. **-cificáre**, TR.: sweeten, dulcify. **-cificazióne**, F.: dulcification. **-cígno**, ADJ.: somewhat sweet. **-cióne**, ADJ.: very sweet; dull†, silly. **-cióre**†, M., **-ci-túdine**†, F.: sweetness. **-ciúme**, M.: sweetmeats. **dól-co**, ADJ.: mild, pleasant (said of weather).

do-lènte, PART., ADJ.: doleful (sorrowful). **-lenteménte**, ADV.: sorrowfully. **-lèn-zia**†, F.: pain, sorrow. ||**-lére** [L., suffer], IRR.§; INTR.: give pain (*dat.* pain, ache); REFL.: suffer (grieve); complain: *mi* (*dat.*) *-le il capo*, my head aches. **-licchiáre**, **-licciáre**, INTR.: feel a slight pain or grief.

§ Ind.: Pres. *dòlgo, duòli, duòle; dogliámo* or *dolghiámo, doléte, dòlgono.* Pret. *dòlsi, -ésti, -se; -émmo, -éste, -sero.* Fut. *dorrò.* Cond. *dorrèi.* Subj.: Pres. *dòlga*, etc. Ipve *duòli; doléte.* Part. *doluto.* — Poet. forms: *dogl-*.

dòllaro [fr. Eng.], M.: dollar.

dòlo [L. *dolus*], M.: fraud (trick).
dolo-ránza†, F.: pain. **-ráre†**, TR.: give pain, afflict; REFL.: suffer, complain. **-razióne†**, F.: pain. ‖**doló-re** [L. *dolor*], M.: pain (anguish, sorrow). **-rétto**, *dim.* of *-re.* **-ríflco†**, ADJ.: painful. **-rosaménto**, ADV.: sorrowfully. **-róso**, ADJ.: painful (sad; dolorous). **-rúccio**, M.: slight grief.
dolo-saménto [*dolo*], ADV.: fraudulently, deceitfully. **-sità**, F.: fraud, artifice. **doló-so**, ADJ.: fraudulent.
dòl-si, PRET., **-sáto†**, **-úto**, PART. of *dolere.*
dolz..† = *dolc..*
domábile, ADJ.: tamable.
domán-da, **-dagióne†**, F.: demand, requisition. **-dánte**, M.: demandant. ‖**-dáre** [L. *de-mandare*], TR.: DEMAND (ask). **-datóre†**, M.: demander. **domán-do†**, M.: demand.
domá-ne†, **-ni** [L. *de*, *mane*, morning], ADV.: to-morrow: *doman a sera*, to-morrow evening; *doman l'altro*, day after to-morrow.
domá-re [L.], TR.: TAME (break, subdue). **-tóre**, M., **-tríce**, F.: tamer.
domattína [*di mattina*], ADV.: to-morrow morning.
domatúra [*-mare*], F.: taming.
Domeneddío [L. *dominus*, lord, *Dio*], M.: God.
doméni-ca [L. *dominus*, lord, master], F.: Sunday. **-cále**, ADJ.: dominical, of Sunday; M.: Sunday clothes. **-cána**, F.: Dominican nun. **-cáno**, ADJ.: Dominican; M.: Dominican friar.
do-mèstica, F.: domestic, maid. **-mesticaménte**, ADV.: familiarly. **-mesticáre**, TR.: tame, domesticate. **-mestichézza**, F.: domesticity, familiarity. ‖**-mèstico** [L. *-mesticus* (*-mus*, house)], ADJ.: domestic, familiar, tame; M.: domestic, valet.
doméVole†, ADJ.: tamable.
domi-ciliáre, INTR., REFL.: install one's self, take up one's abode. ‖**-cílio** [L. *-cilium* (*domus*, house)], M.: domicile (residence).
domi-nánte, ADJ.: dominant, ruling. ‖**-náre** [L. *-nari* (*dominus*, master)], TR.: dominate, rule over; INTR.: be dominant. **-náto**, ADJ.: dominated, ruled; M.†: power, dominion. **-natóre**, M., **-natríce**, F.: ruler. **-nazióne**, F.: domination (sway). **dòmi-ne** [L. voc. of *-nus*, lord], M.: Lord. **-neddío** = *domeneddio.* **domí-nico†**, ADJ.: of God; dominical. **domí-nio**, M.: dominion. **dòmi-no**, **-nò**, M.: dominoes (game); domino (mask).
dòmito†, PART.: tamed.

dòm-ma [Gr. *dógma*, opinion], M.: dogma (tenet). **-mática** [*-ma*], F.: dogmatics. **-maticaménte**, ADV.: dogmatically. **-mático**, ADJ.: dogmatical. **-matizzáre**, INTR.: dogmatize.
dómo 1 [for *domato*], ADJ.: tamed.
dòmo 2 [L. *domus*], M.: house†; dome (cathedral): *in — Petri*, in prison.
dón or **dòn** [L. *dominus*, lord], M.: don (Span.), Sir, lord.
dona-zióne†, M.: donation. **-ménto†**, M.: gift. ‖**doná-re** [L.], TR.: donate. **-tário**, M.: receiver of a gift (donee). **-tívo**, M.: donative (gift). **-tóre**, M., **-tríce**, F.: donor (giver). **-túra†**, F.: gift. **-zióne**, F.: donation.
dónde [L. *de*, from, *unde*, whence], ADV.: from whence; why. =**chè** **-é**, ADV.: whatsoever be the reason.
dondo-láre [?], TR.: swing; dally; REFL.: loiter about. **-lío**, M.: continued swinging. **dóndo-lo**, M.: swinging object; pendulum; delay†: *voler il —†*, love a joke. **-lóna**, F.: lounging, idle woman. **-lóne**, M.: dangler; lounger. **-lóni**, ADJ.: as in *a -loni*, dangling.
dondúnque† = *dondechè.*
dòn-na [L. *domina*, mistress], F.: woman; wife; mistress: *— da camera*, maid, waiting-woman. **-nácchera**, *disp.* of *-na.* **-náccia**, *disp.* of *-na.* **-naccína**, *dim.* of *-na.* **-naccináta**, F.: young woman's act. **-náccola**, F.: gossip. **-naiòlo**, **-naiuòlo†**, M.: admirer of women. **-neáre†**, INTR.: court, flirt. **-neggiáre†**, INTR.: lord it (domineer). **-nescaménte**, ADV.: like a woman. **-nésco**, ADJ.: womanly. **-nétta**, *car. dim.* of *-na.* **-nicciòla**, *disp. dim.* of *-na.* **-nicciioláta**, F.: act of silly woman. **-nína**, *car. dim.* of *-na.* **-níno**, M.: little graceful woman. **-'no†**, M.: master, lord; ADJ.: good, kind. **dón-nola**, F.: weasel. **-nóna**, F., **-nóne**, M.: large, well-formed woman. **-nòtta**, F.: disgraceful woman. **-núccia**, *dim.* of *-na.* **-nucciáccia**, *disp.* of *-nuccia.* **-núcola**, F.: poor, wretched woman.
dó-no [L. *-num*], M.: gift (present; talent): *in —*, as a gift, free. **dó-nora†**, F. PL.: bride's clothes.
dónque† = *dunque.*
donúzzo(lo)†, *dim* of *-no.*
don-zèlla [*-na*], F.: DAMSEL (young girl). **-zellétta**, F.: *dim.* of *-zella;* cookey. **-zèllo**, M.: bailiff (constable); knight's esquire†; valet. **-zellóne†**, M.: loiterer (idler).
dopiáre†, TR.: redouble.
dópo [*de*, *poi*], PREP.: after; behind†; ADV.: since, afterwards: *— che* or **-chè** **-é**, ADV., CONJ.: after that, when.

dóp-pia, F.: flounce; pistole (coin). **-piaménte**, ADV.: doubly; deceitfully. **-piáre**, TR.: double. **-piatúra**, F.: doubling. **-pière** [because having double candle], **-pièro**†, M.: chandelier. **-pierúzzo**†, M.: small torch. **-piézza**, F.: being double; duplicity (deceit). ||**dóppio** [L. *duplus*], ADJ.: DOUBLE; deceitful (crafty); M.: double; chime. **-pióne**, M.: double (second copy of a book in libraries); doubloon† (coin).

do-raménto†, M.: gilding. ||**-ráre** [L. *de-aurare* (*aurum*, gold)], TR.: gild. **-ratóre**, M.: gilder. **-ratúra**, F.: gilding; PL.: ornaments. **-rè**, INVAR. ADJ.: gold colour. **-reria**†, F.: things of gold, gold plate, etc.

dori-cíşmo, M.: doricism. ||**dòri-co** [Gr. *-kós*], ADJ.: Doric.

dor-malfuòcco†, M.: drone (sluggard). **-mentòrio**, M.: dormitory. **-micchiáre**, INTR.: nap, doze. **-miènte**, PART., ADJ.: sleeping, dormant; M.: sleeper. **-migliáre**† = *-micchiare*. **-miglióna**, F., **-miglióne**, M.: great sleeper (sluggard). **-miglióso**†, ADJ.: sleepy (drowsy). ||**-míre** [L.], INTR. (Pres. *-mo*): sleep; M.: sleep (repose); sleeping-place: — *al fuoco*, be negligent. **-míta**, F.: long continued sleep, rest. **-mitóre**†, M.: sleeper. **-mitòrio**, M.: dormitory. **-mitríce**†, F.: sluggard. **-mizióne**†, F.: sleeping.

dor-sále, ADJ.: dorsal (of the back). ||**dò-rso** [L. *-sum*], M.: back.

do-şáre, TR.: mix doses, dose. ||**dò-şe** [Gr. *dósis*, giving], F.: dose.

dossière†, **dossièro**†, M.: coverlet; blanket.

dòsso [L. *dorsum*], M.: back; pl. *dossi*, skins of animals.

dò-ta = *-te*. **-tále**, ADJ.: dotal (pertaining to a dower). **-táre**, TR.: ENDOW (bestow). **-tatóre**, M.: bestower; giver of a dowry. **-tazióne**, F.: dotation (bestowing a dowry). ||**dò-te** [L. *dos*], F.: gift; dowry (portion); talent. **-tóna**, F.: large dowry.

dòtta† 1, F.: hour, good opportunity.

dót-ta† 2, F., **-tággio**†, M.: fear.

dottaménte [*dotto*], ADV.: learnedly.

dottáre†, INTR.: be afraid, be suspicious.

dòt-to [L. *doctus* (*docere*, teach)], ADJ.: learned: *alla dotta*, in a learned manner. **-toráccio**, M.: pitiful doctor. **-torággine**, M.: (*jest.*) doctorship. **-torále**, ADJ.: doctoral. **-toráre**†, R.: give the degree of doctor; REFL.: take the doctor's degree. **-toráto**, M.: doctorate. **-tóre**, M.: doctor. **-toreggiáre**, INTR.: act the doctor, display one's learning. **-torèllo**, *disp. dim.* of *-tore*. **-torésco**, ADJ.: doctoral. **-toréssa**, F.: learned woman, doctoress. **-torétto**, **-toríno**, *car. dim.* of *-tore*. **-toróne**, M.: great doctor. **-toruccíáccio**, *disp.* of *-toruccio*. **-torúccio**, *disp.* of *-tore*.

dottóso†, ADJ.: doubtful.

dottri-na [*dotto*], F.: learning, erudition; doctrine†. **-nále**, ADJ.: learned; doctrinal. **-nalménte**, ADV.: doctrinally. **-naménto**†, M.: instruction. **-náre**†, TR.: instruct. **-nário**, M.: doctrinaire. **-natóre**†, M.: instructor.

dóve [L. *de*, from, *ubi*, where], ADV.: where, whither. **=chè**, CONJ.: although. **=cchessía**, ADV.: wherever.

do-vére [L. *debere*], IRR.§; INTR.: owe (be obliged, must, be to), M.: DUTY, task: *egli deve venire domani*, he is to come tomorrow. **-verosaménte**, ADV.: rightfully. **-veróso**, ADJ.: DUE (proper).

§ Ind.: Pres. *dèvo* or *dèbbo*, *dèvi* or *dèi*, *dève* or *dèbbe* or *dèe*; *dobbiámo*, *dovéte*, *dèvono*, *dèbbono*. Pret. *dovéi* or *dovétti*. Fut. *dovrò*. Cond. *dovrèi*. Subj.: Pres. *dèva* or *dèbba*, etc. I've lacking. — Poet. forms: *dèg-gio*, *-giono* or *dèuno*. (S.) *dèb-bia*, *-biano* or *dèg-gia*, *-giano*.

dovi-zia [L. *-tia* (*dives*, wealthy)], F.: abundance (wealth). **-ziosaménte**, ADV.: abundantly. **-zióso**, ADJ.: rich (abundant).

dovúnque [*dove* (L. *unquam*, ever)], ADV.: wherever.

do-vutaménte, ADV.: DULY (rightly). ||**-vúto**, PART. of *dovere*.

dozzí-na [*dodicina*], F.: dozen; boarding: *stare a* —, board; *tenere a* —, keep boarders; *di* —, of the dozen (= little value). **-nále**, ADJ.: common (ordinary). **-nalménte**, ADV.: commonly; meanly. **-nánte**, F., M.: boarder.

draghétto†, M.: cock of a gun.

draghinássa†, F.: rapier.

drágo [Gr. *drákon*], M.: dragon.

dragománno [Ar.], M.: dragoman (interpreter).

dra-góna, F.: ensign (standard). ||**-góne** [*-go* (troops carried an ensign with a dragon on it)], M.: dragoon.

drámma 1 [Gr. *drachmé*, handful], F.: dram: *a — a* —, little by little.

drám-ma 2 [Gr. *drâma* (*drân*, do, act)], F.: drama. **-mática**, F.: dramatic art. **-maticaménte**, ADV.: dramatically. **-mático**, ADJ.: dramatic. **-matizzáre**, TR.: dramatize. **-maturgía**, M.: dramaturgy. **-matúrgo**, M.: dramatist.

drap-pellétto, M.: small band, or troop. ||**-pèllo** [OProv. *tropel* (dim. of *troupe*)], M.: small TROOP of soldiers (band).

drap-pellóne, M.: tapestry, hangings. **-pería**, F.: silk draperies. **-pétto**, M.: light silk stuff. **-pière**†, M.: silk-weaver.

‖-po [L. L. *-pus*], M.: silks; mercery; dress (clothes)†.
drénto, drètto = *dentro, dietro.*
dría-da or **-de** [Gr. *druás* (*drûs*, tree)], F.: dryad.
dringoláre†, TR.: jog, shake.
dritt.., **drizz..** = *diritt..*, *dirizz..*
drò-ga [? Dutch *droog*, dry substance], F.: drug; PL.: drugs; spices, groceries. **-gáre**, TR.: spice (season). **-ghería**, F.: drug-store; spice-store. **-ghière**, M.: druggist.
dromedário [L. *-rius* (Gr. *dramein*, run)], M.: dromedary.
drú-da, F.: mistress, sweetheart. **-dería†**, F.: fondling, amourous caresses. **‖-do** [OGer. *drut*, friend], M.: lover; gallant; ADJ.†: amourous.
druí-dico, ADJ.: druidic(al). **‖drúi-do** [L. *Druides* (fr. Celt.)], M.: druid (ancient Celtic priest).
druşciáre = *strusciare.*
duá-le [L. *duo*, 'two'], ADJ.: dual. **-lísmo**, M., **-lità**, F.: dualism; duality.
du-bbiaménte, ADV.: irresolutely. **-bbiáre†**, INTR.: doubt; fear. **-bbietà†**, **-bbiézza**, F.: doubt; irresolution; suspense. **‖dú-bbio** [L. *-bius* (*duo*, 'two')], ADJ.: doubtful (uncertain); M.: doubt. **-bbiosaménte**, ADV.: dubiously. **-bbiosità†**, F.: dubiousness. **-bbióso**, ADJ.: doubtful (dubious); irresolute. **dú-bio†**, M.: doubt. **-bitábile**, ADJ.: uncertain (dubitable). **-bitaménto†**, M., **-bitánza†**, F.: doubt. **-bitáre**, INTR.: be doubtful. **-bitativaménte**, ADV.: doubtfully. **-bitatívo**, ADJ.: doubtful. **-bitazioncèlla**, *dim.* of *-bitazione*. **-bitazióne**, F.: doubt. **-bitevolménte†**, ADV.: doubtfully. **-bitóso**, ADJ.: doubtful.
dú-ca [L. *dux* (*ducere*, lead)], M.: leader, chief; DUKE. **-cále**, ADJ.: ducal. **-cáto**, M.: dukedom (duchy); ducat (coin). **-catóne**, M.: big ducat. **-ce**, M.: captain (military leader); guide. **-cèa†**, F.: duchy. **-chésco**, ADJ.: (*disp.*) ducal. **-chéssa**, F.: duchess. **-chessína**, F.: young duchess. **-chétto**, *dim.* of *-ca*. **-chíno**, M.: young duke.
dúo [L. *duo*], NUM.: TWO; M.: two: *essere* (*stare*) *fra* —, be uncertain; *tener tra* —, hold in suspense. **=cènto**, ADJ., M.: two hundred.
duel-lánte, ADJ.: duelling, fighting; M.: duellist. **-láre**, INTR.: fight a duel. **-latóre**, M.: duellist. **-lísta**, M.: expert duellist. **‖duèl-lo** [L. *-lum* (*duo*, TWO)], M.: duel.
due=míla, ADJ., M.: two thousand. **-nnále** [*anno*], ADJ.: biennial. **dué-tto**, M.: duet.
du-gentèsimo, ADJ.: two hundredth.
‖-gènto [L. *ducenti* (*duo*, two, *centum*, hundred)], ADJ., M.: two hundred. **-gento=míla**, ADJ., M.: two hundred thousand.
duíno†, M.: two aces.
dulcamára [man *D.*], M.: quack (charlatan).
dulcificáre† = *dolcificare.*
dulía [Gr. *douleía*, servitude], F.: dulia (worship of angels and saints).
dumíla [*due mila*], ADJ., M.: two thousand.
dú-mo [L. *-mus*], M.: thornbush (briers). **-móso**, ADJ.: dumose (full of briers).
dúna [Celt.], F.: DOWN (sand hill).
dúnque [L. *ad*, to, *tunc*, then], ADV.: then; what?
dúo [*due*], M.: duet (duo). **-dècimo**, ADJ.: twelfth. **-dècuplo**, ADJ.: twelve times more. **-denário**, ADJ.: duodenary, of twelve. **-dèno**, M.: duodenum (first of the small intestines).
duòle, cf. *dolere*. **d(u)òlo**, M.: pain, grief.
duòmo = *domo.*
dupli-cáre, TR.: duplicate. **-cataménte**, ADV.: doubly. **-cáto**, PART.: doubled; M.: double, duplicate; (*typ.*) doublet. **-cazióne**, F.: duplication. **‖dúpli-ce** [L. *du-plex*, double], ADJ.: double (twofold). **-cità**, F.: duplicity (dissimulation). **dúplo**, ADJ., M.: double.
dú-ra†, F.: duration; obstinacy. **-rábile** [*-rare*], ADJ.: durable. **-rabilità**, F.: durability. **-rabilménte**, ADV.: perpetually. **-rácine** [L. *-racinus*, berry], ADJ.: hard, tough, clinging (said of fruit). **-raménte**, ADV.: hardly, harshly. **-raménto†**, M.: durability, continuance. **-ránte**, PART., ADJ.: during, lasting. **-ránza†**, F.: duration. **-ráre**, INTR.: endure (last), resist (hold out): — *fatica*, bear labour; *chi la dura la vince*, he who holds out, conquers. **-rástro**, ADJ.: somewhat hard. **-ráta**, F.: duration. **-ratúro**, ADJ.: durable, continuing. **-razióne†**, F.: duration. **-rétto**, ADJ.: tough, hardish. **-révole**, ADJ.: durable, lasting. **-revolézza**, F.: durability, lastingness. **-revolménte**, ADV.: lastingly. **-rézza**, F.: induration, hardness. **-rità†**, F.: hardness. **-rlindána** [?], F.: Rowland's sword; sword. **‖dú-ro** [L. *-rus*], ADJ.: hard (strong; rude, cruel); stubborn; M.: hardness: *capo* —, blockhead; — *di bocca*, hard-mouthed (said of horses); *star* (*tener*) —, be firm. **-ròtto**, ADJ.: slightly hard.
dút-tile [L. *ductilis* (*ducere*, lead)], ADJ.: ductile (flexible, malleable). **-tilità**, F.: ductility. **dút-to†**, M.: duct (canal). **-tóre†**, M.: leader (guide).
du-umviráto, M.: duumvirate. **‖-úmviro** [L. *-um-vir*, 'TWO-man'], M.: duumvir.

E

e 1 [L.], F.: e (the letter).
e 2 [L. *et*], CONJ.: and; then; both: *e* ... *e*, both ... and.
e', pop. for *egli*, *essi*.
è [L. *est*]: is.
e- [L. *ex*, from], PREF.: e-, ex-.
eba-nísta, pl. *—ti*, M.: ebonist (cabinet-maker). ‖**èba-no** [L. *ebenus*], M.: ebony.
eb-bè for ‖**-bène** [*e bene*], ADV.: ah well, well now.
ébbio [L. *ebulum*], M.: dwarf-elder.
eb-brézza, F.: drunkenness (inebriety); intoxication. **-briachézza**, F.: drunkenness. **-briácco†**, ADJ.: drunk. **-brietà†**, F.: drunkenness. **-brióso** = *-bro*. ‖**èb-bro** [L. *ebrius*], ADJ.: drunk (inEBRIATE); infatuated.
ebdom. .† = *eddom.* .
èbeno† = *ebano*.
èbe=re†, INTR.: grow weak, faint. **-tág-gine**, F.: stupidity. **-tazióne†**, F.: bluntness; thickness. ‖**èbe-te** [L. *hebes*], ADJ.: blunt (dull, HEBETATE, stupid). **-tísmo**, M.: dullness (stupidity).
ebol-liménto†, M.: boiling. ‖**-líre†**, INTR.: BOIL (cf. *bollire*). **-lizióne**, F.: boiling; ebullition.
ebr-aicaménte, ADV.: Hebraically. **-ái-co**, ADJ.: Hebraic(al). **-aísmo**, M.: Hebraism. **-aísta**, pl. *—ti*, M.: Hebraist. **-aizzáre**, TR., INTR.: Hebraize. ‖**-èo** [L. *hebræus*], ADJ., M.: Hebrew.
ebrézza†, **ebri.** .† = *ebbrezza*, *ebbri.* .
èbulo, *poet.* = *ebbio*.
èb-ure† [L. *ebur*], M.: IVORY. **-úrneo**, **-úrno†**, ADJ.: ivory, ivory-white.
ecatómbe [Gr. *hekatón*, HUNDRED, *boûs*, ox], F.: hecatomb (sacrifice of '100 oxen'), slaughter.
ec-cedènte, ADJ.: exceeding. **-ceden-teménte**, ADV.: exceedingly. **-cedèn-za**, F.: excess (superfluity). ‖**-cèdere** [L. *ex-cedere* (*c.*, go from)], IRR. (cf. *cedere*); TR.: exceed (go beyond, surpass). **-cedúto**, PART. of *-cedere*.
ec-cellènte, ADJ.: excellent. **-cellen-teménte**, ADV.: excellently. **-cellen-tíssimo**, ADJ.: most excellent (a title). **-cellènza**, **-cellènzia†**, F.: excellence; excellency. ‖**-cèllere** [L. *ex-cellere* (root *cel-*, rise)], TR.: excel. **-celsaménte**, ADV.: in a lofty manner; highly. **-cel-situdine†**, F.: highness (title). **-cèlso**, ADJ.: lofty (sublime); M.: God.
ec-centricaménte, ADV.: in an eccen-[tric] manner. **-centricità**, F.: eccen-[tricity.] ‖**-cèntrico** [L. *-centros* (Gr. of, *kéntron*, center], ADJ.: eccen-
ec-cessivaménte, ADV.: excessively. **-cessività**, F.: excessiveness. **-cessí-vo**, ADJ.: excessive. ‖**-cèsso** [L. *ex-cessus* (*cedere*, go away)], M.: excess (immoderateness); passion; exaltation (ecstacy)†: *all'* —, excessively.
eccètera [L. *et cætera*], F.: et cetera (and so on).
ec-cettáre†, TR.: except. **-cètto** [L. *ex-ceptus* (*capere*, take)], ADJ.†: excepted; PREP., CONJ.: except (save; unless); M.†: exception. **-cettuábile**, ADJ.: exceptable. **-cettuáre**, TR.: except. **-cet-tuatívo**, ADJ.: exceptive. **-cettuá-to**, ADJ.: excepted; PREP.: except. **-cet-tuazióne†**, F.: exception. **-cezioná-le**, ADJ.: exceptional. **-cezióne**, F.: exception; censure.
ecchimòsi or **ecchímosi** [Gr. *ek-chýmo-sis*], F.: ecchymosis (livid spot).
eccídio [L. *ex-cidium* (*cædere*, cut)], M.: slaughter (carnage); ruin.
ecci-tábile, ADJ.: excitable. **-tabili-tà**, F.: excitability. **-taménto**, M.: excitation; incitement. **-tánte**, ADJ.: exciting. ‖**-táre** [L. *ex-citare* (*citare*, rouse)], TR.: excite, incite (provoke; stimulate). **-tatívo**, ADJ.: exciting; stimulating. **-tatóre**, M., **-tatríce**, F.: exciter; instigator; (*electr.*) excitator. **-ta-zióne**, F.: excitation; excitement; stimulation.
ecclè-sia† [Gr. *ek-klesía* (*kalein*, call), assembly†], F.: church. **-siasticamén-te**, ADV.: ecclesiastically. **-siástico**, ADJ.: ecclesiastic(al); ecclesiastic person (priest).
ec-clissaménto, M.: eclipsing. **-clis-sáre**, TR.: eclipse (obscure). ‖**-clisse** [L. *-lipsis* (Gr. *ek-leípein*, LEAVE out)], M.: eclipse.
ècco 1 [L. *ecce*, lo!], ADV.: lo, behold, here (is, are), there (is, are); *combines with pers. and demonstr. pron.*: *—mi* (lo me! here I am), *—ci*, *—ti*, *—velo*; *— che†*, since.
ècco† 2 = *eco*.
echeggiáre [*eco*], INTR.: echo (resound).
echíno†, M.: hedgehog (esp. sea-).
èchio†, M.: heart's-tongue (plant).
eclèttico [Gr. *ek-lektikos* (*-legein*, SELECT)], ADJ., M.: eclectic.
ecliss. .† = *eccliss.* .
eclíttica [Gr. *ek-leiptikós* (*leípein*, LEAVE)], F.: ecliptic.
èco [Gr. *echṓ*], M., F.: echo.
eco-nomáto, M.: stewardship; steward's office; administration of ecclesiastical goods. ‖**-nomía** [L. *œconomia* (Gr. *oîkos*, house, *nómos*, rule)], F.: economy. **-no-micaménte**, ADV.: economically. **-nò-mico**, ADJ.: economic(al); frugal. **-no-**

-místa, pl. —*ti*, M.: economist (student of political economy). **ecò-nomo**, M.: steward; manager; economizer; parsimonious fellow.
ecúleo [L. *equus*, horse], M.: rack (instrument of torture).
ecumènico [Gr. *oikoumenikós* (*-méne*, 'inhabited,' sc. world)], ADJ.: ecumenic(al).
ed = *e*, and.
edá-ce [L. *edax* (*edere*, EAT)], ADJ.: eating (consuming); voracious. **-cità**, F.: edacity.
eddomadário [L. *hebdomadarius* (Gr. *hébdomos*, SEVENth)], ADJ.: hebdomadal, -madary (weekly).
ède-ma [Gr. *oídema* (*oideín*, swell)], M.: œdema (tumour). **-mático**, ADJ.: œdematous. **-matóso**, ADJ.: œdematose.
Eden [Heb., 'garden'], M.: Eden.
éde-ra [L. *hedera*], F.: ivy. **-ráceo**, ADJ.: of ivy. **-róso**, ADJ.: ivied (full of ivy).
edícola [L. *ædicula* (*ædes*, temple)], F.: little chapel; shrine; cell; kiosk.
edifi-caménto†, M.: building. **-cánte**, ADJ.: edifying (upbuilding). ‖**-cáre** [L. *ædi-ficare* (*ædes*, building, *facere*, make)], TR.: build, build up, construct; EDIFY (upbuild). **-cáta**†, F.: edifice. **-catívo**†, ADJ.: upbuilding; edifying. **-cáto**, ADJ.: edified. **-catóre**, M., **-catríce**, F.: builder; edifier. **-catòrio**, ADJ.: edifying. **-cazióne**, F.: building; edification (upbuilding). **edifí-cio**, **-zio**, M.: edifice (building; structure).
edí-le [L. *ædilis* (*ædes*, building)], M.: ædile (edile, Roman magistrate superintending public buildings, etc.); ADJ.†: of an ædile. **-lità**, F.: ædileship. **-lízio**, ADJ.: of an ædile.
èdi-to [L. *e-dere*, give out], ADJ.: edited; published. **-tóre**, M., **-tríce**, F.: editor, publisher.
editto [L. *e-dictum* (*dicere*, say)], M.: edict (decree).
edi-zionáccia, *disp.* of *-zione*. **-zioncína**, *disp. dim.* of *-zione*. ‖**-zióne** [L. *-tio* (*e-dere*, give out)], F.: edition; publication.
édra† = *edera*.
educá-nda, F.: boarding-school miss. ‖**educá-re** [L. (*ex*, out, *ducere*, lead)], TR.: educate. **-tívo**, ADJ.: educating. **-tóre**, M., **-tríce**, F.: educator; instructor (teacher). **-tòrio**, M.: girls' school (female institute). **-zióne**, F.: education.
edúlio†, M.: relish; victuals (eaten with bread); (Scotch) kitchen.
efemèride† = *effemeride*.
effábile†, ADJ.: effable (utterable).
èffe, F.: f (the letter).
effemèride [Gr. *ephémeros* (*heméra*, day)], F.: ephemeris.
ef(f)em(m)i-naménto, M.: effeminacy. ‖**-náre** [L. *femina*, woman], TR.: effeminate (weaken). **-nataménto**, ADV.: effeminately. **-natézza**, F.: effeminacy. **-náto**, ADJ.: effeminate (unmanly). **-natóre**, M., **-natríce**, F.: effeminating.
effe-rataménte, ADV.: inhumanly. **-ratézza**, F.: ferocity. ‖**-ráto** [L. *-ratus* (*ferus*, wild)], ADJ.: FEROcious (inhuman, barbarous, cruel). **-rità**†, F.: ferocity.
efferve-scènte [L. *-scens* (*fervere*, boil)], ADJ.: effervescent. **-scènza**, F.: effervescence; fervor.
effet-tivaménte, ADJ.: effectively, in fact. **-tività**, F.: effectiveness (efficiency); efficacy. **-tívo**, ADJ.: effective (efficient); reàl. ‖**effèt-to** [L. *ef-fectus* (*facere*, do)], M.: effect; impression; ware; result (end); execution (accomplishment): *recare ad* —, carry out, accomplish; *in* —, in fact; *per* — *di*, by reason (virtue) of; *per questo* —, to that purpose, therefore. **-tóne**, *aug.* of *-to*. **-tóre**†, M., **-tríce**†, F.: effector, agent; actor. **-tuále**, ADJ.: effectual; real. **-tualménte**, ADV.: effectually; really (in fact). **-tuáre**, TR.: effect (accomplish, carry out). **-tuazióne**, F.: effecting; accomplishment (execution).
effi-cáce, ADJ.: efficacious (effectual, potent). **-caceménte**, ADV.: efficaciously. **-cácia**, F.: efficacy. **-cacíssimo**, ADJ.: very efficacious (most efficient). ‖**-ciènte** [L. *ef-ficiens* (*facere*, do)], ADJ.: efficient; effective (operative). **-ciènza**, F.: efficiency, efficacy†.
effi-giaménto, M.: image (likeness). **-giáre**, TR.: image (represent). **effí-gi(e)** [L. *-gies* (*fingere*, FEIGN)], F.: effigy; representation; aspect. **-giétta**, *car. dim.* of *-gie*.
effímero [cf. *effemeride*], ADJ.: ephemeral.
efflorescènza [L. *ef-florescere*, bloom out], F.: efflorescence.
ef-flússo, M.: efflux (effusion). ‖**-flúvio** [L. *-fluvium* (*fluere*, FLOW)], M.: effluvium; exhalation.
effón-dere [L. *ef-fundere*], TR.: pour out (EFFUSE, shed). **-diménto**, M.: effusion.
effrazióne [*frangere*], F.: (*leg.*) breaking into; burglary.
effrenat. .† = *efrenat*. .
effumazióne [L. *-mare*, FUME], F.: fuming (reeking).
effú-si, PRET. of *effondere*. **-sioncèlla**, *dim.* of *-sione*. **-sióne**, F.: effusion. ‖**effú-so**, PART. of *effondere*.
efímero† = *effímero*.

èfod [Heb.]. M.: ephod (high priest's girdle).
èforo [L. *ephorus* (Gr. *horân*, see)]. M.: ephor (Spartan magistrate).
egènte†, ADJ.: needy, indigent.
egestióne [L. -*tio* (*gerere*, lead)]. F.: egestion (evacuation; excrements).
ègida [L. *aegida* (Gr. *aigís*, goat-skin)]. F.: ægis (shield; protection).
egira [fr. Ar.]. F.: hegira.
Egi-tto, M.: Egypt. **-ziaco**, M.: kind of ointment. **-ziáno**, ADJ.: Egyptian.
egí-zio, ADJ.: Egyptian.
égli [L. *ille*]. PRON.: he; it.
églino [*egli*]. PRON.: they.
ègloga [L. (Gr. *ek-légein*, pick out)]. F.: eclogue.
ego-ísmo [L. *ego*, I]. M.: egotism (selfishness). **-ísta**, pl. —*ti*, M., F.: egotist. **-ístico**, ADJ.: egotistical (selfish).
egraménte†, ADV.: reluctantly.
e-gregiaménte, ADV.: egregiously. ‖**-grègio** [L. *e-gregius* (*grex*, crowd)]. ADJ.: egregious (uncommon).
egrèsso [-*ssus* (*gradior*, go)]. M.: egress (outlet).
egritúdine†, F.: infirmity (sickness).
ègro [L. *aeger*], ADJ.: sick.
eguagl.. = *uguagl*..
egual.. = *ugual*..
éh or **èh**, **éhi**, **èhm** [echoic]. INTERJ.: ah! ha! so! hallo! hem! ahem!
éi, for *egli* (pop. also for *eglino*).
éia†, INTERJ.: come! courage!
eiacula-tóre, **-tòrio** [L. -*ri* (*jacere*, throw)], ADJ.: ejaculatory. **-zióne**, F.: ejaculation.
el†, for *egli*, *lui*, *per il*.
ela†, INTERJ.: oh! alas!
elaborá-re [L. (*labor*, work)]. TR.: elaborate. **-tézza**, F.: elaborateness; refinement. **-zióne**, F.: elaboration.
elargíre, TR.: give liberally.
elasti-cità, F.: elasticity. ‖**elásti-co** [Gr. *elaúnein*, drive], ADJ.: elastic.
ela-tèria or usly **-tèridi** [Gr. -*térion* (-*tére*, driver)], PL.: family elateridæ (elaters, beetles). **-tèrio** or **-tère**, M.: power of expansion (elasticity).
elá-to†, ADJ.: elate (haughty). **-zióne**†, F.: elation (haughtiness).
élce [L. *ilex*], M.: holm-oak.
eldorádo [Sp. *el dorado*, 'the golden' land]. M.: El Dorado (imaginary rich country).
elefán-te [L. *elephas*], M.: elephant. **-co**, ADJ.: elephantine. **-téssa**, F.: elephant. **-tíaco**, ADJ.: elephantine; ... **-tíasi**, F.: elephantiasis. M.: small (young) elephant: ADJ.: ...
... [L. *-gans* (*e-ligere*, elect)], ADJ.: elegant; graceful. **-gantemente**, ADV.: elegantly. **-gánza**, **-gánzia**†, F.: elegance.
elèg-gere [*e-*, *l.*.]. IRR. (cf. *leggere*); TR.: ELECT, choose. **-gènte**, ADJ.: electing. **-gíbile**, ADJ.: eligible. **-gibilità**, F.: eligibility. **-giménto**, M.: election.
ele-gía [L. (Gr. *élegos*, plaint)], F.: elegy. **-gíaco**, ADJ.: elegiac; M.: elegiac poet. **-giétta**, *dim.* of *-gia*. **-giúccia**, **-giúzza**, *disp. dim.* of *-gia*.
elèi-son or **-sònne** [Gr. *eléeson*, 'have mercy']. M.: 'eleeson' (part of the Mass or Litany).
elembíccot = *lambicco*.
elemen-tále† = *-tare*. **-táre** I, ADJ.: elementary. **-táre**† 2, TR.: compose of elements. **-tário**†, ADJ.: elementary. ‖**elemén-to** [L. -*tum*]. M.: element.
elemòsi-na [Gr. *eleemosúne* (*eleein*, pity), charity]. F.: ALMS (charity). **-náre** = *limosinare*. **-nário**†, M.: almoner. **-nière** (*f.* -*niera*), ADJ.: eleemosynary (charitable); M. (F.): almoner (alms-giver). **-núzza**, *dim.* of *-na*.
elènco [Gr. -*chos*, control], M.: index (register).
elèt-ta, F.: election (choice). **-tivaménte**, ADV.: electively (by election). **-tívo**, ADJ.: elective. ‖**elèt-to**, PART. of *eleggere*. **-torále**, ADJ.: electoral. **-toráto**, M.: electorate (electorship). **-tóre**, M.: elector. **-tríce**, F.: electress.
elettovário† = *elettuario*.
elet-tricaménte, ADV.: electrically. **-tricísmo**, M.: electricity. **-tricità**, F.: electricity. **elèt-trico**, ADJ.: electric(al). **-trizzáre**, TR.: electrify. **-trizzatóre**, M., **-trizzatríce**, F.: electrifier. ‖**elèt-tro** [Gr. *élektron*, amber (the friction of which revealed electricity)], M.: amber; electro- (in many compounds, as): **-tròforo**, M.: electrophore. **-tròmetro**, M.: electrometer, etc.
elettuário [L. -*rium* (? Gr. *leíchein*, LICK)], M.: electuary (medicine).
eleva-ménto, M.: elevation. ‖**eleváre** [L.], TR.: elevate (lift up; raise); promote; exalt. **-tézza**, F.: height (eminence). **-to**, PART.: elevated, etc.; lofty, sublime. **-tóre**, M.: elevator; ADJ.: lifting. **-zióne**, F.: elevation (raising; height).
ele-zionáre†, TR.: elect. ‖**-zióne** [L. -*tio* (*legere*, choose)], F.: election (choice).
elíaco [Gr. *heliakós* (*hélios*, sun)], ADJ.: heliac(al).
èli-ca or **-ce** I [Gr. *hélix*, 'twisted'], F.: helix (non-plane curve; rim of the ear); screw (propeller); (*astron.*) Great Bear; *scala a* —, steep spiral staircase.

éli-ce†2 = *elce*. **-céto**†, M.: holm-grove.

e-lícere†, TR.: elicit. **-lícito**, PART.

Eli-cóna [Gr. *Helikón*], M.: Helicon (mount of Apollo and the Muses). **-cònio**, ADJ.: Heliconian.

elídere [L. (*lædere*, hurt)], IRR.§; TR.: elide; suppress (annul, neutralize).

§ Pret. *elí-si*, *-se*; *-sero*. Part. *eliso*.

elig.. = *elegg..*

eliminá-re [L.(*ex*, *limen*, threshold)], TR.: eliminate. **-nazióne**, F.: elimination.

elimosin.. = *elemosin..*

eliò- [Gr. *hélios*, sun]: **-metro**, M.: heliometer. **-scòpio** [Gr. *skopeín*, examine], M.: helioscope. **-tipía** [Gr. *túpos*, type], F.: heliotypy. **-tròpia** [cf. *tropio*], F.: sort of heliotrope. **-tròpio** [Gr. *trópos*, turn], M.: heliotrope (turnsole; bloodstone).

elísi, PRET. of *elidere*.

Elísio, poet. for *Eliso*; ADJ.: Elysian.

elisióne [*elidere*], F.: elision.

elí-sir or **-sí(r)re** [Ar. *eliksir*], M.: elixir.

Elíso [Gr. *Elúsion*], M.: Elysium.

elíso, PART. of *elidere*.

elitrop.. = *eliotrop..*

élla 1 [L. *illa*], PRON.: she; it.

èlla†2, F.: starwort.

èlle, name for *l*, which see.

ellèboro [Gr. *-ros*], M.: hellebore (herb).

ellè-nico [Gr. *Héllenes*, Greeks], ADJ.: Hellenic. **-nísmo**, M.: Hellenism. **-nísta**, M.: Hellenist (one versed in Greek).

èlleno [*ella*], PRON., F.: they.

éllera [cf. *edera*], F.: ivy.

élli†, for *egli*, *eglino*.

el-lísse [Gr. *-leipsis* (*leípein*, LEAVE)], F.: ellipse. **-lissi**, F.: elipsis (omission). **-litticaménte**, ADV.: eliptically, by omission. **-líttico**, ADJ.: eliptic(al).

el-máto†, ADJ.: helmed. **-métto**, M.: *dim.* of *-mo*; helmet. ||**él-mo** [Ger. *helm*], M.: HELM(et).

elocuzióne [L. *-cutio*], F.: elocution.

elo-gétto, *dim.* of *-gio*. **-giáre**, TR.: eulogize. **-giatóre**, M.: eulogizer. ||**elò-gio** [L. *-gium* (Gr. *eû*, well, *légein*, speak)], M.: eulogy. **-gísta**, pl. *—ti*, M.: eulogist (writer of eulogies). **-gístico**, ADJ.: eulogistic(al).

elo-quènte [L. *-quens* (*loqui*, speak)], ADJ.: eloquent. **-quenteménte**, ADV.: eloquently. **-quènza**, F.: eloquence. **elò-quio**, M.: (manner of) speaking, address; discourse.

él-sa [OGer. *helza*], F., **-so**†, M.: HILT.

elucubrá-re [L., work out by lamplight (*lux*, light)], TR.: lucubrate; elaborate. **-zióne**, F.: lucubration; elaboration.

e=lúdere, IRR.; TR.: elude. **-ludènte**, ADJ.: eluding. **-lúsi**, PRET. **-lúso**, PART.

ema-ciaménto, M.: emaciation. ||**-ciáre** [L. (*macer*, lean, MEAGER)], TR.: emaciate; REFL.: emaciate (grow thin). **-ciazióne**, F.: emaciation (leanness).

emaná-re [L. (*manare*, flow)], INTR.: emanate, flow; TR.: send out (publish). **-zióne**, F.: emanation; promulgation.

emancipá-re [L. (*m-*, transfer)], TR.: emancipate (a minor, etc.), free. **-tóre**, M., **-tríce**, F.: emancipator. **-zióne**, F.: emancipation.

ematòsi [Gr. *haimátosis* (*haîma*, blood)], M.: hematosis.

emblè-ma [Gr. (*em-bállein*, throw in)], M.: emblem. **-maticaménte**, ADV.: emblematically. **-mático**, ADJ.: emblematic.

émbri-ce [L. *imbrex* (*imber*, rain)], M.: roof tile: *scoprire un* —, reveal a secret. **-ciáta**, F.: blow of a tile.

em-brióne [Gr. *-bruon* (*brúein*, swell)], M.: embryo. **-briònico**, ADJ.: embryonic.

emèn-da, F.: emendation. **-dábile**, ADJ.: emendable (corrigible). **-daménto**, M.: emendation. ||**-dáre** [L. (*menda*, fault)], TR.: emend (amend, correct). **-datívo**, ADJ.: emendatory. **-datóre**, M., **-datríce**, F.: emendator. **-datòrio**, ADJ.: emendatory. **-dazióne**, F.: emendation; revisal.

e-mergènte, ADJ.: emergent. **-mergènza**, F.: emergency. ||**=mèrgere**, IRR.; TR.: emerge, rise up.

emèrito [L. *-tus* (*merere*, merit)], ADJ.: emeritus (honorably discharged).

e-mèrsi, PRET. of *-mergere*. **-mersióne**, F.: emersion. ||**-mèrso**, PART. of *-mergere*.

emètico [Gr. *-kós* (*emeîn*, VOMIT)], ADJ., M.: emetic.

e=méttere, IRR.; TR.: emit (give forth; send forth). **-mésso**, PART.

emi= [Gr. *hemi-*, half]: **-cíclo**, M.: hemicycle. **-cránia** [Gr. *kránion*, skull], F.: (*med.*) hemicrania (MEGRIM, MIGRAINE).

emi-gráre [L. (*migrare*, pass)], INTR.: emigrate. **-gráto**, PART.: emigrated; M.: emigrant (specif. political, as the French emigrants after the Revolution). **-grazióne**, F.: emigration.

emi-nènte [L. *-nens* (*-nere*, stand out)], ADJ.: eminent (lofty). **-nenteménte**, ADV.: eminently. **-nentíssimo**, ADJ.: most eminent (title of cardinals). **-nènza**, F.: eminence (elevation; title of cardinals).

emi=plegía [Gr. *plegé*, stroke], F.: hemiplegia (palsy of one side). **-sfèrico**, ADJ.: hemispheric(al). **-sfèro**, **-sfèrio**† [*sphaîra*, ball], M.: hemisphere.

emis-sário [L. *-sarium* (*mittere*, send)

M.: emissary; spy; outlet, drain; stallion, stone-horse. **-sióne**, F.: emission; letting (of blood).
emistichio [Gr. *hemi-stichion*, half-line], M.: hemistich.
èmme, name of the letter **m**, which see.
emolliènte [L. *-liens* (*mollire*, soften)]. ADJ., M.: emollient.
emoluménto [L. *-tum* (*e-moliri*, bring out)]. M.: emolument (pay).
émo- [Gr. *haima*, blood]: **-rragía** [*hregnúnai*, burst], F.: hemorrhage. **-rroidále**, ADJ.: hemorrhoidal. **-rròidi** [Gr. *hrein*, flow], F. PL.: hemorrhoids. **-ttísi** [Gr. *ptúein*, spit], F.: hemoptysis. **-ttòico**, ADJ.: affected with hemoptysis.
emozióne [L. *e-motio*], F.: emotion.
empetíggine [L. *im-petigo* (*im-petere*, attack)], F.: impetigo (pustular eruption).
empiaménte [*-pio*], ADV.: impiously.
empiastr. .† = *impiastr*. .
em-piènte, PART.: filling. ‖**ém-piere** = *-pire*.
em-pietà, **-piézza** [*-pio*], F.: impiety.
empiménto [*-pire*], M.: filling up.
émpio [L. *im-pius*], ADJ.: impious, inhuman.
empíre, or less com. *-piere* [L. *implere*], IRR. (cf. *compire*); TR.: FILL up; COMPLETE.
empíreo [Gr. *em-púrios* (*pûr*, FIRE), in fire, fiery], ADJ.: empyreal; M.: empyrean (supposed highest heaven of pure fire).
empi-ricaménte, ADV.: empirically. ‖**empí-rico** [L. *-ricus* (Gr. *peira*, trial)] ADJ.: empiric(al). **-rísmo**, M.: empir(ic)ism.
émpito, pop. for *impeto*
em-píto or **-piúto**, PART. of *empi(e)re*.
empòrio [Gr. *-rion* (*ém-poros*, "on the road," trader)], M: emporium (mart; storehouse).
emugn. .† = *emung*. .
emu-lánte, ADJ.: emulating; emulous. ‖**-láre** [L. *æmulari*], TR.: emulate (vie with). **-latóre**, M., **-latríce**, F.: emulator (competitor). **-lazióne**, F.: emulation (rivalry).
e-mulgènte, ADJ.: emulgent. ‖**-múlgere**† [L. (*mulgere*, MILK)]; IRR.§; TR.: emulge (milk out); drain.

§ Pret. *emúl-si, -se; -sero* Part. *emúlso*.

èmulo [L. *æmulus*], ADJ.: emulous; M.: competitor, rival.
emulsióne [*emulgere*], F.: emulsion.
e-múngere†, TR.: milk out; drain.
enarmònico [Gr. *-kós*], ADJ.: enharmonic(al).
encefa-líte, **-lítide** [*enképhalos*, brain], F.: encephalitis (inflammation of the brain).
enchirídio [Gr. *-cheiridion* (*cheir*, hand)], M.: manual.
enci-clica [Gr. *enkúklios*, 'circular'], F.: encyclic (esp. papal letter or circular). **-clopedía** [Gr. *paidéia*, instruction], F.: encyclopædia. **-clopèdico**, ADJ.: encyclopedic(al). **-clopedísta**, pl. **—ti**, M.: encyclopedist.
enclítico [Gr. *-klitikós* (*klínein*, LEAN)], ADJ., F.: enclitic.
enco-miáre, TR.: laud, praise. **-miásta**†, M.: encomiast. **-miástico**, ADJ.: encomiastic(al). **-miatóre**, M., **-miatríce**, F.: encomiast (panegyrist). ‖**encò-mio** [Gr. *-mion* (*kômos*, revel), festive song to Bacchus], M.: encomium (praise).
éndet = *indi*.
endecasíllabo [Gr. *héndeka*, eleven], M.: endecasyllable.
en-demía [Gr. (*dêmos*, people)], F.: endemic. **-dèmico**, ADJ.: endemic(al).
éndi-ca†, F.: magazine; purchase; forestalling. **-caiuòlo**†, M.: forestaller. **-cáre**†, TR.: buy up, forestall.
éndice [pop. for *indice*], M.: nest-egg; bait†.
èneo†, ADJ.: of bronze.
en-ergía [Gr. *-érgeia* (*érgon*, WORK)], F.: energy. **-ergicaménte**, ADV.: energetically. **-èrgico**, ADJ.: energetic(al).
energúmeno [Gr. *-goúmenos* (*érgein*, WORK)], ADJ.: possessed by an evil spirit; M.: energumen.
enerv. . = *snerv*. .
èn-fasi [Gr. *émphasis* (*phainein*, show)], F.: emphasis. **-faticaménte**, ADV.: emphatically. **-fático**, ADJ.: emphatic(al).
en-fiagioncèlla, **-fiagioncína**, *dim.* of *-fiagione*. **-fiagióne**, F.: inflation (swelling). **-fiaménto**, M.: inflation; pride†. ‖**-fiáre** [L. *in-flare* (BLOW)], INTR.: INFLATE (swell, puff up); TR.†: inflate; embolden. **-fiáto**, PART.: swollen, etc.; proud†. **-fiatúra**, F.: inflation (swelling; pride†). **-fiaturína**, *dim.* of *-fiatura*. **-fiatúzzo**†, *dim.* of *-fiato*. **-fiazióne**†, F.: inflation (swelling; pride). **én-fio**†, ADJ.: swelling; swollen. **-fióre**, M.: inflation, swelling.
enigm. .† = *enimm*. .
ením-ma [Gr. *aínigma* (*aînos*, tale)], M.: enigma. **-maticaménte**, ADV.: enigmatically. **-mático**, ADJ.: enigmatic(al).
ènne, the letter *n* (which see).
enne(a)- [Gr. *ennéa*, NINE]: **-'gono**, M.: enneagon, etc.
ènnico† = *etnico*.
enología [Gr. *oînos*, WINE], F.: science of wine-production.
enór-me [L. *-mis* (*norma*, rule)], ADJ.: enormous. **-meménto**, ADV.: enormously. **-mézza**, **-mità**, F.: enormity.

ensifórme [L. *ensis*, sword], ADJ.: (*bot.*) ensiform.
ènte [L. *ens* (*esse*, be)], M.: being.
en-tèrico [Gr. *énteron*, intestine], ADJ.: enteric (intestinal). **-terítide, -tèrite,** F.: (*med.*) enteritis.
entità [*ente*], F.: entity; importance.
entò-mata†, F., **entò-mo**† [Gr. *én-to-mon* (*témein*, cut), in-sect (as nearly cut in two)], M.: insect. **-mología,** F.: entomology. **-mològico,** ADJ.: entomologic(al). **-mòlogo,** M.: entomologist.
entrá̤gna†, F., **-gno**†, M.: inside; entrails (bowels): *di buona* —, of good heart.
entrám-bi, -bo† [L. *inter*, between, *ambo*, both], ADJ.: both.
en-traménto, M.: entrance. **-tránto,** ADJ.: entering; beginning; penetrative, meddlesome; M.: entrance; beginning; meddlesome person: *il mese* —, next month. **-tráre,** INTR.: enter; begin; penetrate; TR.†: enter, make enter; M.: entering, etc.: — *in ballo*, engage one's self; — *in bestia*, fly into a passion; — *in parola*, open a discourse; — *in santo*, be churched (of women after childbirth). **-tráta,** F.: entrance; beginning; prelude; income; rent. **-tratáccia,** *disp.* of *-trata*. **-tratóre,** M.: enterer. **-tratúra,** F.: entrance; access; entrance fee; familiarity: *avere — con*, be familiar with. ‖**én-tro** [L. *intro*], ADV., PREP.: within. **-tro=méttere**†, IRR.; TR.: introduce.
entusi-asmáre, TR.: make enthusiastic (enthuse). ‖**-ásmo** [Gr. *enthousiasmós* (*theós*, god)], M.: enthusiasm. **-ásta,** pl. **-asti,** M.: enthusiast. **-ástico,** ADJ.: enthusiastic.
ènula†, F.: starwort.
enumerá-re [L.], TR.: enumerate. **-zióne,** F.: enumeration.
enunciá-re [L. *enuntiare* (*nuntio*, messenger)], TR.: enunciate (express; pronounce). **-tívo,** ADJ.: enunciative. **-zióne,** F.: enunciation.
enunzia. . = *enuncia*. .
enviáre†, TR.: show the way.
éo† = *io*.
eòo†, ADJ.: eastern (morning).
è-pa [? Gr. *hépar*, liver], F.: paunch (belly). **-páccia**†, *disp.* of *epa*. **èpa-to**†, M.: liver. **-pática**†, F.: liverwort. **-pático**†, ADJ.: hepatic.
epàn-teşi [Gr. *-thesis* (*epí*, by, *en-tithénai*, put in)], F.: epenthesis (insertion). **-tètico,** ADJ.: epenthetic(al).
epi- [Gr. *epí*, upon, by], PREF.
epicaménte [*-co*], ADV.: epically.
epi=ciclo, M.: epicycle.
èpico [L. *-cus* (Gr. *épos*, tale)], ADJ., M.: epic.

epicrá-şi [Gr. *krâsis*, mixture], F.: cure by refrigerants or lenitives. **-ticaménte,** ADV.: now and then, at intervals. **-'tico,** ADJ.: applied (medicines) at intervals.
epicurèo [philosopher *Epicurus*], ADJ.: Epicurean; M.: epicure.
epi-demía [Gr. (*epí-demos*, 'among-people')], F.: epidemy. **-dèmico,** ADJ.: epidemic(al).
epidèrmide [Gr. *-mis* (*dérma*, skin)], F.: epidermis.
epifanía [Gr. *epi-phánia*, ap-pearance], F.: Epiphany (church festival, 6th of Jan.).
epigástrico [Gr. *gastér*, belly], ADJ.: epigastric.
epí-grafe [Gr. *-graphe* (*gráphein*, write)], F.: epigraph (inscription). **-grafía,** F.: epigraphy. **-gráfico,** ADJ.: epigraphic(al). **-grafísta,** pl. *—ti*, M.: epigraphist. **-grámma,** M.: epigram. **-grammático,** ADJ.: epigrammatic(al). **-grammétto,** *dim.* of *-gramma*.
epi-lessía [Gr. *-lepsía* (*lambánein*, take)], F.: epilepsy. **-lèttico,** ADJ., M.: epileptic.
epilo-gaménto†, M.: epilogue, summary. **-gáre**†, TR.: sum up. **-gazióne**†, F.: epilogue. **epílo-go** [Gr. *-gos* (*epí*, after, *légein*, say)], M.: epilogue.
epi-scopále, ADJ.: episcopal. **-scopáto,** M.: bishopric. **-scòpio,** M.: bishopric; bishop's palace. ‖**epí-scopo**† [cf. *vescovo*], M.: BISHOP.
epi-şodicaménte, ADV.: episodically. **-şòdico,** ADJ.: episodical. ‖**-şòdio** [Gr. *ep-eís-odos*, 'by-in-way'], F.: episode.
epistílio [L. *-lium* (Gr. *stûlos*, column)], M.: epistyle (architrave)
epísto-la [L. (Gr. *stéllein*, send)], F.: epistle; letter. **-láre,** ADJ.: epistolary. **-lário,** M.: letter-book. **-larménte,** ADV.: in epistolary way. **-létta,** *dim.* of *-la*.
epitáf(f)io [Gr. *-táphios* (*táphos*, tomb)], M.: epitaph.
epita-lámico, ADJ.: epithalamic. ‖**-lámio** [Gr. *-lámios* (*thálamos*, bride-chamber)], M.: epithalamium (nuptial song).
epíteto [Gr. *-thetos* (*the-*, put)], M.: epithet.
epito-máre, TR.: epitomize, abridge. **-matóre**†, M.: epitomizer, abridger. ‖**epíto-me** [Gr. *-mé* (*témnein*, cut)], M., F.: epitome.
època [L. *-cha*], F.: epoch (culminating point); period; (*pop.*) time.
ep-òdico, ADJ.: epodic. ‖**-òdo** [Gr. *-odé* (*odé*, song)], M.: epode (after-song).
epo-pèa, -pèia† [Gr. *epo-poiía*, epos-poem], F.: epopee (epopœia).
eppúre [or *e pure*], CONJ.: nevertheless (however).
èpu-la† [L. *-lum*], F.: feast. **-lonáccio,** *disp.* of *-lone*. **-lóne,** M.: great

feaster (luxurious feeder). **-lonésco,** ADJ.: feasting. **-lonísmo,** M.: excessive feasting.

equa- [L. *æquus*, equal]: **-ábile,** ADJ.: equable. **-abilità,** F.: equability. **-abilménte,** ADV.: equably. **-ále†,** ADJ.: equal. **-alità†,** F.: equality. **-aménte,** ADV.: equally (equably). **-ánimo** [L. *animus*, soul], ADJ.: equanimous, just. **-animità,** F.: equanimity. **-atóre,** M.: equator. **-atoriále,** ADJ.: equatorial. **-azióne,** F.: equation.

equèstre [L. *-tris* (*equus*, horse)], ADJ.: equestrian.

equi- [L. *æquus*, equal]: **-ángolo,** ADJ.: equiangular. **-distánte,** ADJ.: equidistant. **-distantemènte,** ADV.: equidistantly. **-distánza,** F.: equidistance. **-látero,** ADJ.: equilateral. **-libráre,** TR.: equilibrate (balance equally). **-líbrio** [L. *libra*, balance], M.: equilibrium, equipoise.

equíno [L. *-nus*], ADJ.: equine.

equi-noziále, ADJ.: equinoctial. **‖-nòzio** [L. *-noctium* (*nox*, NIGHT)], M.: equinox.

equi-paggiáre, TR.: equip, fit out; man. **-pággio** [Fr. *-page*, ak. to Eng. *skiff*], M.: equipage (baggage); equipment (outfit); crew.

equi- [cf. above]: **-paráre,** TR.: equal; compare. **-pollènte** [L. *pollens*, strong], ADJ.: equipollent (of equal power). **-pollènza,** F.: equipollence. **-ponderánte†,** ADJ.: of equal weight. **-ponderáre†,** INTR.: equiponderate (be of equal weight). **-tà,** F.: equity (justness).

equi-táre, INTR.: ride on horseback. **-tazióne,** F.: equitation (riding on horseback). **‖èqui-te** [L. *eques* (*equus*, horse)], M.: rider.

equi- [L. *æquus*, equal]: **-valènte,** ADJ., M.: equivalent. **-valentemènte,** ADV.: equivalently. **-valènza,** F.: equivalence. **-valére,** IRR.; INTR.: be equivalent (be of equal value). **-vocále†,** ADJ.: equivocal. **-vocamènte,** ADV.: equivocally. **-vocaménto,** M.: ambiguity. **-vocáre,** INTR.: equivocate (mistake). **equí-voco** [L. *vox*, VOICE], ADJ.: equivocal (ambiguous); M.: misunderstanding, mistake: *prendere* —, be mistaken, misunderstand. **-vocóso,** ADJ.: ambiguous.

... [L. *æquus*, equal], ADJ.: equitable

... PERF. of *essere*.

... *æra*], F.: era, epoch.

... = *sradicare*.

... *ærarium* (*æs*, copper)], M.: treasury (exchequer).

... *herba*], F.: herb (grass): *mala* —, weeds: — *trastulla*, procrastinating; *in* —, growing, young (e.g., *dottore in* —, one studying to become a doctor; *mangiare il grano in* —, consume anything by anticipation or before fully gotten possession of). **-báccia,** F.: *disp.* of *-ba*; weed. **-báceo,** ADJ.: herbaceous (grassy). **-bággio,** M.: esculent plants, pot herbs. **-báio,** M.: weedy place. **-baiuòlo,** M.: herbalist (gatherer or seller of herbs). **-bále,** ADJ.: herbaceous, grassy. **-bário,** M.: herbarium. **-bátat,** F.: corn in the blade. **-báto,** ADJ.: grassy. **-bétta, -biccinola,** *dim.* of *-ba*. **-bicína, -bína,** F.: small esculent herb. **-bívoro** [L. *vorare*, eat], ADJ.: herbivorous. **-bolálo†,** M.: herbalist. **-bolína,** car. *dim.* of *-ba*. **-boráre†** = *-borizzáre*. **-borísta,** M.: herborist (collector of herbs). **-borizzáre,** INTR.: herborize (collect herbs). **-borizzatóre,** M.: herborist. **-bosétto,** *dim.* of *-boso*. **-bóso,** ADJ.: herbose (grassy, grass-covered). **-buccia,** F.: *disp. dim.* of *-ba*; scanty grass. **-buccína,** *dim.* of *-buccia*.

Er-cole, M.: Hercules. **-colíno,** ADJ.: bow-legged. **-cúleo,** ADJ.: herculean.

erè-da† = *-de*. **-dáre,** TR.: inherit. **‖erè-de** [L. *heres*], M., F.: HEIR. **-dità,** F., **-ditággio†,** M.: heirship; heritage (inheritance). **-ditáre,** TR.: inherit. **-ditariaménte,** ADV.: by inheritance. **-ditário,** ADJ.: hereditary. **-ditièra,** F.: rich heiress.

erèggere† = *erigere*.

ere-míta, pl. *-miti*, M.: hermit. **-mitággio,** M.: hermitage. **-mitáno,** M.: sort of religious order. **-mítico,** ADJ.: hermitic, solitary. **‖èré-mo** [Gr. *hérēmos*, solitary], M.: hermitage; lonely place.

eresí-a [Gr. *haíresis*, taking for one's self, choice], F.: heresy. **-árca** pl. **-archi** [Gr. *archós*, ruler], M.: heresiarch.

erèssi, PRET. of *erigere*.

eretággio, M.: heritage.

ereti-cáccio, *disp.* of *-co*. **-cále,** ADJ.: heretical. **-ca(l)ménte,** ADV.: heretically. **‖erèti-co** [L. *hæreticus* (cf. *eresia*)], ADJ.: heretic(al).

erè-tto, PART. of *erigere*; ADJ.: ERECT (upright, straight). **-ttóre,** M.: erector. **-zióne,** F.: erection; establishment (institution).

ergástolo [L. *-tulum*, WORKHOUSE], M.: prison, penitentiary.

èrgere [*erigere*], IRR.§; TR.: ERECT (raise).

§ Pret. *èr-si, -se; -sero*. Part. *èrto*.

èrgo [L.], CONJ.: ergo (therefore).

e-rigènza†, F.: erection; establishment.

‖-rigere [L.], IRR. (cf. *dirigere*); TR.: ERECT (raise; construct).

èrma [L. *herma* (Gr. *Hermês*, Gr. deity)], F.: herma, hermes (small column with a Hermes-head, or other head). **-frodíto** [L. *-phrodítus* (*Hermês*, *Aphrodite*, in one body)], M.: hermaphrodite.

ermellíno [l. L. *armellinus* (*Armenia*)], M.: ERMINE.

ermenèuti-ca [Gr. *hermeneutikê*, interpreting], F.: hermeneutics. **-co**, ADJ.: hermeneutic(al).

ermeşíno† = *ermişino*.

er-meticaménte, ADV.: hermetically. ||**-mètico** [Gr. god *Hermês*, inventor of alchemy], ADJ.: hermetic(al).

ermişíno [island *Ormus*], M.: sarcenet.

èrmo [*eremo*], ADJ.: solitary; M.†: hermitage.

èr-nia [L. *hernia*], F.: hernia (rupture). **-niária**, F.: rupturewort. **-niário**, ADJ.: hernial. **-nióso**, ADJ.: affected with hernia.

e-rodènte†, ADJ.: corrosive. **-ródere**† = *rodere*.

erò-e [L. *heros*], M.: HERO. **-éssa**† = *-ina*.

ero-gábile, ADJ.: that can be bestowed or laid out. ||**-gáre** [L. (*rogare*, ask)], TR.: appropriate (money), bestow (Eng.† erogate). **-gazióne**, F.: bestowal (disposal, Eng.† erogation).

ero-icaménte, ADV.: heroically. **-iciş-şáre**, TR.: make a hero of, lionize. ||**erò-ico** [*eroe*], ADJ.: heroic(al). **-i=cò-mico**, ADJ.: heroi-comic. **-íde**†, M.: heroic person. **-ína**, F.: heroine. **-i=satírico**, ADJ.: heroi-satiric. **-íşmo**, M.: heroism.

e=rómpere, IRR.; INTR.: burst forth.

ero-şióne [L. *-sio* (*rodere*, gnaw)], F.: erosion (corrosion). **-şívo**, ADJ.: erosive, corrosive.

eròtico [Gr. *-kós* (*éros*, love)], ADJ.: erotic(al).

èr-pete [Gr. *herpes* (*hérpein*, creep)], M.: herpes (skin eruption). **-pètico**, ADJ.: herpetic.

erpi-caménto, M.: harrowing; clambering†. **-cáre**, TR.: harrow; clamber†. **-catóio**†, M.: net for quails. **-catúra**, F.: harrowing. **érpi-ce** [L. *hirpex*], M.: harrow.

er-rabóndo, ADJ.: errant (vagrant). **-raménto**, M.: error. **-ránte**, ADJ.: erring (roving); in error: *cavaliere* —, knight-errant. ||**-ráre** [L.], INTR.: err (roam, wander); mistake. **-ráta** or **-rata-còrrige**, F.: errata (list of errors); for *-rata*†. **-rataménte**, ADV.: erratically. **-rático**†, ADJ.: errant (roaming); erratic. **-ráto**, PART.: erred, etc.; mistaken, confused.

èrre, F.: the letter *r* (which see): *perder l'* —, get confused; be tipsy.

èr-ro [*-rare*], M.: vulg. for *-rore*. **-roneaménte**, ADV.: erroneously. **-roneità**, F.: erroneousness (error). **-ròneo, -rò-nico**†, ADJ.: erroneous; rambling. **-roráccio**, *disp.* of *-rore*. **-róre**, M.: error, mistake; blunder. **-rorétto, -rorúc-cio**, *dim.* of *-rore*.

èrsi, PRET. of *ergere*.

ér-ta, F.: ascent (acclivity); (*fig.*) attention, guard (as from a hill): *stare all'* —, be upon one's guard, keep a sharp lookout; *all'* — *!* look out! challenge of sentinels; *confortare i cani all'* —, stir up one to something unpleasant. **-tézza**, F.: steepness. ||**ér-to** [*-gere*], PART.: erected; ADJ.: steep; arduous.

erube-şcènte†, ADJ.: erubescent. **-şcèn-z(i)a**†, F.: erubescence (blush).

erúca†, F.: ROCKET (plant); caterpillar.

eru-diménto, M.: erudition; instruction. ||**-díre** [L. (*ex*, *rudis*, RUDE)], TR.: instruct, teach. **-ditaménte**, ADV.: eruditely (learnedly). **-díto**, ADJ.: erudite (learned). **-dizióne**, F.: erudition.

e-rúmpere† = *-rompere*. **-rútto**, PART. **-ruttáre**, TR.: erupt (eject); ERUCT (belch). **-ruttazióne**, F.: eruption; eructation. **-ruttívo**, ADJ.: eruptive. **-ruzióne**, F.: eruption; efflorescence.

eşacer-baménto, M.: exasperation. ||**-báre** [L. *ex-acerbare* (*asper*, rough)], TR.: irritate. **-bazióne**, F.: irritation.

eşacòrdo [Gr. *hex*, SIX, *chordé*, string], M.: hexachord (old mus. instrument).

eşagerá-re [L. *ex-aggerare* (*ag-ger*, heap)], M.: exaggerate. **-tívo**, ADJ.: exaggerative (exaggerated). **-tóre**, M., **-tríce**, F.: exaggerator. **-zióne**, F.: exaggeration.

eşagi-táre†, TR.: agitate; vex (torment). **-tazióne**, F.: agitation; vexation.

eş-agonáto, ADJ.: hexagonal. ||**-ágono** [Gr. *hex*, SIX, *gonía*, angle], M.: hexagon.

eşa-lábile, ADJ.: exhalable; evaporable. **-laménto**, M.: exhalation; recreation†, diversion†. ||**-láre** [L. *ex-halare* (breathe)], INTR.: exhale, evaporate; TR.: breathe out or forth. **-lazióne**, F.: exhalation; evaporation.

eşaldíre† = *esaudire*.

eşálo† = *esalazione*.

eşal-taménto, M.: exaltation. ||**-táre** [L. *ex-altare* (*altus*, high)], TR.: exalt (magnify, extol). **-táto**, ADJ.: exalted; excited. **-tazióne**, F.: exaltation.

eşáme 1 [L. *ex-amen*, weighing], M.: examination (examen).

eşáme 2 [L. *ex-amen* (*agmen*, troop)], M.: swarm of bees.

eşámetro [Gr. *hexá-metros*, 'six-metric'], ADJ.: hexametric(al); M.: hexameter.

eṣámi-na [*esame* I], **-nánza**†, F.: examination. **-náre**, TR.: examine. **-nánte**, ADJ.: examining. **-náto**, PART.: examined; person examined. **-natóre**, M., **-natríce**, F.: examiner. **-nazióne**, F., **-ne**†, M.: examination.

eṣángue [L. *sanguis*, blood], ADJ.: bloodless.

eṣ-animáre, TR.: dishearten. ‖**-ánimo** [L. *ex-animis* (*anima*, soul)], ADJ.: soulless, lifeless.

eṣantèma [Gr. *ex-ánthema*, 'out-blooming'], F.: (*med.*) exanthema (eruption).

eṣár-ca or **-co**† [Gr. *éx-archos* (*árchein*, rule)], M.: exarch; viceroy. **-cáto**, M.: exarchate.

eṣaspe-raménto, M.: exasperation. ‖**-ráre** [L. *ex-asperare* (*asper*, rough)], exasperate (provoke). **-razióne**, F.: exasperation.

eṣat-taménte, ADV.: exactly. **-tézza**, F.: exactness. ‖**eṣát-to** [part. of *esigere*], ADJ.: exacted; exact (precise, accurate). **-tóre**, M.: tax-gatherer, collector. **-toría**, F.: collector's office.

eṣau-díbile, ADJ.: grantable. **-diménto**, M.: hearing and granting. ‖**-díre** [L. *ex-audire* (hear)], TR.: hear favorably and grant (grant). **-ditóre**, M., **-ditríce**, F.: granter. **-disióne**†, F.: granting.

eṣau-ríbile, ADJ.: exhaustible. ‖**-ríre** [L. *ex-haurire* (draw water)], TR.: EXHAUST (use up). **-ríto** or **eṣáu-sto**, PART.: exhausted.

eṣ=autoráre, TR.: exauthorize.

eṣazióne [*esatto*], F.: exaction.

és-ca [L. (*ed-*, EAT)], F.: victuals†; bait (decoy); tinder. **-caiòlo**, M.: tinder-seller.

escande-ṣcènte [L. *ex-candescens* (*candescere*, glow)], ADJ.: kindling with wrath (flying into a passion); flashing. **-ṣcènza**, F.: sudden wrath (violent passion, anger).

escándola†, F.: (*nav.*) cabin.

ésca-ra [Gr. *eschára*], F.: ESCHAR, SCAR. **-ròtico**, ADJ.: escharotic.

escáto [*esca*], M.: decoy-place; snare (allurement).

escavazióne [L. *ex-cavatio* (*cavare*, hollow)], F.: excavation.

eschétta†, *dim.* of *esca*.

èschio†, M.: beech-tree.

eṣciáme† = *sciame*.

eṣcídio† = *eccidio*.

eṣc-iménto†, **-íre**, **-íta** = *usc-imento, -ire, -ita*.

esclamá-re [L. *ex-clamare*], TR.: exclaim. **-tívo**, ADJ.: exclamatory. **-zióne**, F.: exclamation.

es-cludènte, ADJ.: excluding. ‖**-clúdere** [L. *ex-cludere* (close)], TR. (cf. *accludere*); TR.: exclude (except). **-clúṣi**, PRET. of *-cludere*. **-cluṣióne**, F.: exclusion. **-cluṣíva**, F.: exclusion; excluding vote (veto, at papal election). **-cluṣivaménte**, ADV.: exclusively. **-cluṣivíṣmo**, M.: exclusiveness. **-cluṣívo**, ADJ.: exclusive. **-clúṣo**, PART. of *-cludere*. **-cluṣòrio**, ADJ.: exclusory.

escogi-tábile, ADJ.: devisable. ‖**-táre** [L. *ex-cogitare* (think)], TR.: excogitate (think out, devise, contrive). **-tatíva**†, F.: thinking faculty.

escolpazióne†, F.: exculpation.

escomunic. .† = *scomunic*. .

escoriá-re [L. *ex-coriare* (*corium*, skin)], TR.: (*med.*) excoriate, abrade. **-tívo**, ADJ.: abrading. **-zióne**, F.: excoriation.

escre-mentízio, ADJ.: excrementitious. **-ménto** [L. *ex-crementum* (*cernere*, sift)], M.: excrement.

escreṣcènza [L. *ex-crescere*, grow out], F.: excrescence.

escre-tóre or **-tòrio** [L. *ex-cernere* (sift), excrete], ADJ.: excretory. **-zióne**, F.: excretion.

esculènto†, ADJ.: esculent.

escursióne [L. *ex-cursio* (*currere*, run)], F.: excursion; raid.

escuṣ. .† = *scus*. .

eṣecrá-bile, ADJ.: execrable. **-bilità**, F.: execrableness. **-bilménte**, ADV.: execrably. ‖**eṣecrá-re** [L. *ex-(s)ecrare* (*sacer*, holy)], TR.: execrate, abhor. **-zióne**, F.: execration.

eṣecu-táre [L. *ex-sequere*, follow out], TR.: execute. **-tívo**, ADJ.: executive. **-tóre**, M., **-tríce**, F.: executor, -trix; executive; executioner (hangman). **-zióne**, F.: execution.

eṣè-geṣi or **-gèṣi** [Gr. *ex-égesis* (*ágein*, lead)], F.: exegesis (interpretation). **-gèta**, pl. *-geti*, M.: exegete. **-gètico**, ADJ.: exegetic(al).

eṣe-guíbile, ADJ.: executable (feasible). **-guiménto**, M.: execution. ‖**-guíre** [L. *ex-sequi* (follow)], TR.: EXECUTE (perform). **-guitóre**†, M.: executor.

eṣem-pi=grázia, ADV., F.: for instance, e. g. ‖**eṣèm-pio** [L. *ex-emplum* (*emere*, take)], M.: example. **-pláre**, ADJ.: exemplary; M.: pattern (model); specimen (copy); TR.†: copy (imitate). **-plarità**, F.: exemplarity, exemplariness. **-plarménte**, ADV.: exemplarily. **-platívo**†, ADJ.: exemplary. **-plificáre**, TR.: exemplify. **-plificataménte**†, ADV.: by way of example. **-plificatívo**, ADJ.: exemplifying. **-plificatóre**†, M.: exemplifier; copier. **-plificazióne**, F.: exemplification. **-pli=grázia** = *-pigrazia*. **eṣèm-plo**† = *-pio*.

eṣen-táre, TR.: exempt; excuse. ||**eṣèn-te** [L. *ex-emptum* (*emere*, take)], ADJ.: EXEMPT. **-zionáre**†, TR.: exempt. **-zióne,** F.: exemption.

eṣèquie = *-quie*. **-quiále**†, ADJ.: exequial, funeral. **-quiáre**†, TR.: bury. ||**eṣè-quie** [L. *exequiæ* (*sequi*, follow)], F. PL., **-'quio**†, M.: exequies (obsequies, funeral rites).

eṣequíre† = *eseguire*.

eṣer-cènte, ADJ.: exercising (practicing); following (a profession). ||**eṣèr-cere**† [L. *ex-ercere* (*arcere*, shut up)], TR.: exercise. **-citábile,** ADJ.: exercisable. **-citaménto,** M.: exercise; effort. **-citáre,** TR.: exercise (practice; train). **-citatívo**†, ADJ.: exercising. **-citatóre,** M., **-citatríce,** F.: exerciser. **-citazióne,** F.: exercise. **eṣèr-cito,** M.: army; host. **-círio,** M.: exercise (practice); pursuit; theme: *far l'* —, exercise; drill.

eṣered(it)áre†, TR.: disinherit.

eṣ-ibíre [L. *ex-hibere* (*habere*, have)], TR.: exhibit (present); REFL.: offer one's self. **-íbita,** F.: exhibition. **-ibitóre,** M.: exhibitor. **-ibizióne,** F.: exhibition.

eṣi-gènte, ADJ.: exigent; pretentious. **-gènza,** F.: exigency. ||**eṣí-gere** [L. *ex-igere* (*agere*, drive)], IRR. (part. *esatto*); TR.: EXACT (require peremptorily). **-gíbile,** ADJ.: that may be exacted. **-gibilità,** F.: capability of being exacted.

eṣíglio = *esilio*.

eṣíguo [L. *exiguus* (*ag-*, weigh)], ADJ.: small (thin, exiguous).

eṣila-ránte, ADJ.: exhilarating. ||**-ráre** [L. *ex-hilarare* (cheer)], TR.: exhilarate (cheer).

eṣíle or **èṣile** [L. *exilis*], ADJ.: slender, feeble.

e-ṣiliáre, TR.: exile, banish. **-ṣiliáto,** PART.: exiled; M.: exile. ||**-ṣílio** [L. *ex-(s)ilium* (*solum*, SOIL)], M.: exile; banishment: *terra d'* —, world.

eṣilità [*esile*], F.: slenderness; feebleness.

eṣ-ímere [L. *ex-imere* (*emere*, take)], IRR.§; TR.: EXEMPT (free). **-ímio,** ADJ.: select (excellent, Eng.† eximious); famous.

§ Pret. *esi-mèi*, *-mèsti*, etc. Part. *esènto*.

eṣis-tènte, ADJ.: existing. **-tènza,** F.: existence. ||**eṣís-tere** [L. *ex-(s)istere* (*stare*, stand)], IRR. (Part. *-tito*); INTR.: exist. **-títo,** PART. of *-tere*.

eṣistim.. † = *stim..*

eṣitábile 1 [*-tare* 2], ADJ.: salable.

eṣi-tábile 2, ADJ.: dubious. **-taméntot**†, M.: h-sitation. **-tánza,** F.: hesitancy, besi:ation. ||**-táre** 1 [L. *hæsitare* (*hæs-*, sti:k)], INTR.: hesitate.

eṣitáre 2 [*-to*], TR.: turn out, retail, sell.

eṣitazióne [*-tare* 1], F.: hesitation.

èṣi-to [L. *ex-itus* (*i-*, go)], M.: exit, issue; event; success; sale; dénouement (of a drama). **-ziále,** ADJ.: of fatal issue, fatal.

èṣodo [L. *ex-odus* (Gr. *hodós*, road)], M.: exodus.

eṣòfago [L. L. *-gus*], M.: œsophagus.

eṣoneráre [L. *ex-onerare*], TR.: exonerate.

eṣorbi-tánte, ADJ.: exorbitant. **-tanteménte,** ADV.: exorbitantly. **-tánza,** F.: exorbitancy. ||**-táre** [L. *ex-orbitare* (*orbita*, track)], INTR.: go beyond the limit (Eng.† exorbitate).

eṣor-cíṣmo [L. *ex-orcismus* (Gr. *hórkos*, oath)], M.: exorcism. **-císta,** pl. *—ti*, M.: exorcist. **-cistáto,** M.: third minor clerical order. **-cizzáro,** TR.: exorcise.

eṣor-diènte, ADJ.: beginning; M.: beginner; debutant. **eṣòr-dio,** M.: exordium. ||**-díre** [L. *ex-ordiri*], INTR.: begin.

eṣorná-re†, TR.: adorn. **-tívo,** ADJ.: ornamental.

eṣor-tánte, ADJ.: exhorting. ||**-táre** [L. *ex-hortari* (excite)], TR.: exhort. **-tatívo,** ADJ.: exhortative. **-tatóre,** M., **-tatríce,** F.: exhorter. **-tatòrio,** ADJ.: exhortatory. **-tazioncèlla,** *dim.* of *-tazione*. **-tazióne,** F.: exhortation.

eṣòṣo [L. *ex-osus* (*odi*, hate)], ADJ.: hateful, detestable.

eṣotèrico [Gr. *-rikós* (*éso*, within), inner], ADJ.: esoteric(al).

eṣòtico [Gr. *exotikós* (*éxo*, outside)], ADJ.: exotic.

espán-dere† [L. *ex-pandere* (spread)], IRR. (cf. *spandere*); TR.: expand. **-síbile,** ADJ.: expansible. **-sibilità,** F.: expansibility. **-sióne,** F.: expansion; effusive sentiment (confidential manifestation of sentiments).

espe-diènte, ADJ.: expedient; fit (proper). ||**-díre**† = *spedire*. **-dit..**† = *spedit..*

espèllere [L. *ex-pellere* (drive)], IRR.§; TR.: expel.

§ Pret. reg.; or *espúl-si*, *-se*; *-sero*. Part. *espúlso*.

espe-riènza, F.: experience; experiment. **-rienzúccia,** *dim.* of *-rienza*. **-rimentále** (us'ly *sperimentale*), ADJ.: experimental. **-rimentáre,** TR.: experiment; experience. **-rimentatóre,** M.: experimenter. **-riménto,** M.: experiment; exhibition (proof); examination; experience. ||**-ríre** [L. *ex-periri* (*per-ire*, go through)], TR.: try. **-rtaménte,** ADV.: expertly. **espè-rto,** ADJ.: expert (skilful).

espet-tíbile†, ADJ.: desirable. **-tánte**†, ADJ.: expecting. ||**-táre** [L. *ex-(s)pectare*], TR.: expect (look for: us'ly *aspettare*). **-tazióne,** F.: expectation.

espetto-ránte, ADJ., M.: (*med.*) expectorative. ||**-ràre** [L. *ex-pectorare* (*pectus*, breast)], TR.: expectorate. **-razióne**, F.: expectoration.

espiá-re [L. *ex-piare* (*pius*, pious)], TR.: expiate (orig'ly by 'pious' rites), atone for (= *spiare*†). **-tóre**, M., **-tríce**, F.: expiator. **-tòrio**, ADJ.: expiatory. **-zióne**, F.: expiation.

espilá-re [L. *ex-pilare* (rob)], TR.: appropriate unlawfully (things held in trust), swindle (rob). **-tóre**, M., **-tríce**, F.: swindler. **-zióne**, F.: swindling (robbery).

espirá-re [L. *ex-*(*s*)*pirare* (breathe)], INTR.: breathe out (expire). **-zióne**, F.: expiration.

espletívo [L. *ex-pletivus* (*plere*, FILL)], ADJ.: expletive.

espli-cábile, ADJ.: explicable. ||**-cáre** [L. *ex-plicare* (fold)], TR.: explicate (explain). **-catívo**, ADJ.: explicative. **-catóre**, M.: explicator; explainer. **-cazióne**, F.: explication (explanation). **-citaménte**, ADV.: explicitly. **esplí-cito**, ADJ.: explicit.

es-plodènte, ADJ.: exploding. **-plòdere** [L. *ex-plodere* (clap)], IRR.§; TR.: explode.

§ Pret. *esplò-si, -se; -sero.* Part. *esplóso.*

esplorá-re [L. *ex-plorare* (*plo-*, FLOW)], explore (search, sound). **-tóre**, M., **-tríce**, F.: explorer. **-zióne**, F.: exploration.

esplo-sióne, F.: explosion. **esplò-si**, PRET. of *-dere*. **-sívo**, ADJ.: explosive. **esplò-so**, PART. of *-dere*.

espo-nènte, ADJ.: exposing; M.: exponent. **espò-ngo**, **espò-ni**, etc., PRES. of *-rre*. **-níbile**, ADJ.: that may be exposed. **-nitóre**, M.: exposes. ||**espó-rre** [L. *exponere* (put)], IRR. (cf. *porre*); TR.: EXPOSE; risk; represent; relate; explain (interpret); REFL.: expose one's self.

esportá-re [L. *ex-portare*], TR.: export. **-zióne**, F.: exportation.

espó-si, PRET. of *-rre*. **-sitívo**, ADJ.: expositive (explaining). **-sitóre**, M., **-sitríce**, F.: expositor (interpreter). **-sizióne**, F.: exposition; explanation. ||**espó-sto**, PART. of *-rre:* exposed, etc.: *fanciullo* —, foundling.

espres-saménte, ADV.: expressly. **-sióne**, F.: expression. **-síva**, F.: expression, force of expression. **-sivaménte**, ADV.: express(ive)ly. **-sívo**, ADJ.: expressive. **esprès-si**, PRET. of *esprimere*. ||**esprès-so**, PART. of *esprimere:* expressed, etc.; express; explicit (precise); ADV.†: expressly.

es-primènte, ADJ.: expressing; expressive. **-prímere** [L. *ex-primere* (press)], IRR. (cf. *comprimere*); TR.: EXPRESS; declare.

esprob..† = *rimprover..*

espropriá-re [L. *expropriu*, own], TR.: expropriate. **-zióne**, F.: expropriation.

espu-gnábile, ADJ.: expugnable. ||**-gná-re** [L. *ex-pugnare* (*pugna*, fight)], TR.: expugn; take by assault. **-gnatóre**, M.: expugner. **-gnazióne**, F.: taking by assault.

espúl-si, PRET. of *espellere*. **-sióne**, F.: expulsion. **-sívo**, ADJ.: expulsive. ||**espúl-so**, PART. of *espellere:* expelled. **-sóre**, M.: expeller.

espún-gere [L. *ex-pungere* (prick)], IRR. (cf. *pungere*); TR.: expunge; cancel. **espún-si**, PRET., **-to**, PART. of *-gere*.

espur-gábile, ADJ.: that may be expurgated. ||**-gáre** [L. *ex-purgare* (purge)], TR.: purge (clean); expurgate. **-gatòrio**†, ADJ.: cleansing. **-gazióne**†, F.: purging; spitting.

esquisi-t..† = *squisi-t..*; **-tóre**†, M.: searcher.

èsse, F.: s (the letter). Cf. also *esse*.

essecr..†, **esseg..**†, **essemp..**† = *esecr..*, etc.

es-sèndo, GER.: being: — *che* or **-sendo-chè** *-è*, CONJ.: inasmuch as (since). **-sènte**, ADJ.: existent (existing). **-sènza**, F.: essence. **-senziále**, F.: essential; M.: essential part. **-senzialménte**, ADV.: essentially. ||**ès-sere** [L. *esse*], IRR.§; INTR.: be (exist); become; be about; being; M.: being (existence); state (condition): — *per*, be about, be near, be ready; — *altrove*, be absent, be inattentive; — *di sua signoria*, be one's own master; — *fatto fare*, — *fatto il messere*, be led by the nose; — *in sè*, be in one's senses; *esserci per la sua*, be concerned in it, have to do with it: *che c'è?* what's the matter? *che è stato?* what was the matter? *s'io fossi in voi*, if I were you; *sia pure*, be it so; — *per*, be about, be near; *dar l'* —, call into being, create.

§ Ind.: Pres. *sóno, sèi, è; siámo, siète, sóno.* Impf. *èra* (*èro*), *èri, èra; eravámo, eraváte, èrano.* Pret. *fúi, fósti, fù; fúmmo, fóste, fúrono.* Fut. *sarò.* Cond. *sarèi.* Subj.: Pres. *sia, sii*, etc. Impf. *fóssi*, etc. I've *sii; siáte.* Part.: Pres. lacking. P. *státo.*—Poet. forms: Pres. 2. *sièi*; pl. *sé-mo, -te, èmo.* (S.) *sie; sieno.* Impf. *èramo, èrate.* (S.) *fóssi*; 6. *fússero* or *fóssimo.* Fut. 3. *fia* or *fie*; 6. *fiano.* Cond. 1., 3. *saría* or *fóra*; 6. *saríano* or *fórano.* Pret. 2. *fústi*, 3. *fúe*; 5. *fúste*, 6. *fúr(u)o, fóro.* Ger. *sèndo.* Part. *súto.*

éssi, PL. of *esso*.

essi-cánte, ADJ.: drying up. ||**-cáre** [L. *ex-siccare* (dry)], TR.: dry up (exsiccate.

ésso [L. *ipse*, self), PRON.: this; he (*f.* she), it.

essotèrico = *esoterico*.

èst [Germ. = Eng. EAST], F.: east.

està † = *estate*.

estánte† = *essente.*
èstasi [Gr. *ék-stasis,* 'EX-STATE' (being beside one's self)], F.: ecstasy.
estáte [L. *æstas*], F.: summer.
estático [*estasi*], ADJ.: ecstatic.
estempo-ràle† = *-ráneo.* **-raneaménte,** ADV.: extemporaneously. **-ráneo,** ADJ.: extemporaneous. **estèmpo-re** or **ex tèmpore** [L. *ex tempore,* 'out of time'], ADV.: extempore.
estèn-dere [L. *ex-tendere* (stretch)], IRR.; TR.: extend. **-díbile** = *-síbile.* **-diménto,** M.: extension. **-síbile,** ADJ.: extensible. **-sióne,** F.: extension. **-sivaménte,** ADV.: extensively. **-sívo,** ADJ.: extensive. **-'so†** = *esteso.* **-sóre,** M.: extender; (*anat.*) extensor; compiler.
estenuá-re [L. *ex-tenuare* (THIN)], TR.: extenuate; emaciate; impoverish. **-tívo,** ADJ.: emaciating. **-zióne,** F.: extenuation; emaciation.
esterió-re [L. *exterior*], ADJ.: exterior, external; M.: exterior; outward appearance. **-rità,** F.: outside. **-rménte,** ADV.: externally, outwardly.
estermin. . = *stermin.* .
ester-naménte, ADV.: externally. **-náre†,** TR.: manifest. **estèr-no,** ADJ.: external (outward); foreign†; of yesterday†: *scolari -ni,* day-scholars. ||**èster-o** [L. *exterus*], ADJ.: external; foreign (esp. of goods); M.: foreign countries: *all'* —, abroad.
esterrefátto [L. *ex-terre-facere,* terri-fy], ADJ.: terrified (frightened).
estersívo†, ADJ.: detersive (cleansing).
es-tesaménte, ADV.: extensively. **-tési,** PRET., **-téso,** PART. of *-tendere:* extended (enlarged).
estèti-ca, F.: æsthetics. ||**-co** [Gr. *aisthetikós,* perceptive], ADJ.: æsthetic(al).
estí-ma† = *stima.* **-mábile†** = *stimabile.* ||**-máre** [L. *æstimare*], TR.: esteem. **-matíva†,** F.: estimate; fancy. **-mazióne,** F.: esteem, regard. **èsti-mo,** M.: appraisement, tax-register; impost†, tax†.
estín-guere [L. *ex-(s)tinguere* (quench)], IRR. (cf. *distinguere*); TR.: extinguish. **-guíbile,** ADJ.: extinguishable. **-guiménto,** M.: extinction. **-guitóre,** M.: extinguisher. **estín-si,** PRET. of *-guere.* **-tívo,** ADJ.: extinctive. **estín-to,** PART. of *-tinguere.* **-zióne,** F.: extinction.
estir-paménto, M.: extirpation. ||**-páre** [L. *ex-(s)tirpare* (*stirpes,* root)], TR.: extirpate. **-patóre,** M., **-patríce,** F.: extirpator. **-pazióne,** F.: extirpation.
estí-vo, -vále† [L. *æstivus* (*æstas,* summer)], ADJ.: æstival (summer-).
ésto† = *questo.*
es-tògliere† = *-tollere.* **-tollànz(i)a†,** F.: pride. ||**-tòllere** [L. *ex-tollere* (lift)], IRR.; TR.: extol (exalt). **-tòlsi,** PRET., **-tòlto,** PART.
es-tòrcere or **-tòrquere†** [L. *ex-torquere* (twist)], IRR.; TR.: extort (wrest).
estòrre†, IRR.; TR.: take away; except.
es-tòrsi, PRET. of *-torcere.* **-torsióne,** F.: extorsion. **-tòrto,** PART. of *-torcere.*
estragiudiciále = *stragiudiciale.*
es-traneaménte, ADV.: extraneously. ||**-tráneo** [L. *extraneus* (*extra,* outside)], ADJ.: extraneous (foreign, strange); M.: stranger; foreigner.
estraord. .† = *straord.* .
es-trárre, IRR.; TR.: extract, DRAW. **-trássi,** PRET. **-trátto,** PART.: extracted; M.: extract; abridgment.
estravag. .† = *stravag.* .
estrazióne [*estrarre*], F.: extraction.
estre-maménte, ADV.: extremely. **-mità,** F.: extremity. **estrè-mo** [L. *extremus*], ADJ.: extreme, utmost; M.: extremity; (gen'ly pl.) point of death: *essere all'* — or *agli -mi* or *in extremis,* be at the point of death; *fino all'* —, until the last.
estrinse-caménte, ADJ.: extrinsically. **-caménto,** M., **-cazióne,** F.: the making extrinsical. **estrínse-co** [L. *extrinsecus* (*exter,* outside, *secus,* beside)], ADJ.: extrinsic.
è-stro [Gr. *oîstros,* horsefly; rage], M.: poetic rage or inspiration; freak; martial fury†. **-stróso,** ADJ.: freakish.
estrúdere†, IRR.; TR.: extrude (expel).
e-strúere†, TR.: build up. **-strútto†,** PART.
estu-ánte†, ADJ.: fervent. ||**-áre†** [L. *æstuare*], INTR.: estuate (boil up, swell). **-ário,** M.: estuary.
esturbáre†, TR.: expel; fling off.
esuber-ánte, ADJ.: exuberant. **-anteménte,** ADV.: exuberantly. **-ánza,** F.: exuberance. ||**-áre** [L. *ex-uberare* (*uber,* udder)], INTR.: exuberate, abound.
èsu-la†, F.: milk-thistle. **-láre,** TR.: go into exile.
esulce-raménto, M.: exulceration. ||**-ráre** [L. *ex-ulcerare*], TR.: exulcerate. **-razióne,** F.: exulceration.
èsule [L. *exul*], M.: voluntary exile.
esul-tánte, ADJ.: exulting. **-tánza,** F.: exultation. ||**-táre** [L. *ex-(s)ultare* (*salire,* leap)], INTR.: exult (leap for joy). **-tazióne,** F.: exultation.
esumá-re [L. *ex-humare* (*humus,* soil)], TR.: exhume. **-zióne,** F.: exhumation.
esuríre†, INTR.: be hungry.
esústo†, ADJ.: burnt; consumed.
èt = *ette.*
età [L. *ætas*], F.: AGE; epoch (generation, century).

è-tere or **-tera**† [L. *æther* (root *aith-*, burn)], M.: ether. **-tèreo**, ADJ.: ethereal. **-tèrico**, ADJ.: ethoreous. **-terío** = *-tèreo*. **-terizzáre**, TR.: etherize.

eter-nále† = *-no*. **-nal(e)ménte**†, **-naménte**, ADV.: eternally. **-náre**, TR.: eternize. **-nità**, F.: eternity. ||**etèrno** [L. *æternus*], ADJ.: eternal; ADV.: eternally; M.: eternal; time everlasting: *ab* —, from time immemorial; *in* —, forever; *l'* —, the Eternal, God; *mai in* —, never.

etero- [Gr. *héteros*, other]: **-'olito** [Gr. *klínein*, bend], ADJ.: heteroclitic (irregular). **-dossía** [see next], F.: heterodoxy. **-dòsso** [Gr. *dóxa*, opinion], ADJ.: heterodox. **-geneità** [see next], F.: heterogeneity. **-gèneo** [Gr. *génos*, KIND], ADJ.: heterogeneous.

e-tèsia [L. *-siæ* (Gr. *étos*, year)], F. PL.: trade winds. **-tèsio**, ADJ.: etesian (periodical).

ètica [*-co*], F.: ethics; also F. of *-co*. **-ménte**, ADV.: ethically.

etichétta [Fr. *étiquette* (l. Ger. *stikke*, stick, tack affixed as a label)], F.: label; etiquette (ceremony).

ètico 1 [Gr. *ethikós* (*éthos*, custom)], ADJ.: ethic(al).

ètico 2 [Gr. *hektikós* (*héxis*, habit)], ADJ.: hectic(al); M.: hectic.

ètimo [Gr. *étumos*, true], M.: etymon. **-logía**, F.: etymology. **-logicaménte**, ADV.: etymologically. **-lògico**, ADJ.: etymological. **-logista**, pl. *—ti*, M.: etymologist. **-logizzáre**, INTR.: etymologize.

etiología [Gr. *aitio-logía*, 'cause-description'], F.: ætiology.

èt-nico [Gr. *ethnikós* (*éthnos*, people)], ADJ.: ethnic(al); pagan†; M. PL.: pagan writers. **-nografía**, F.: ethnography. **-nográfico**, ADJ.: ethnographic(al). **-nògrafo**, M.: ethnograph.

ètra†, F.: ether; air.

ettágono [Gr. *heptá*, SEVEN, *gonía*, angle], M.: heptagon.

ètte [L. *et*, and], M.: mere trifle.

ettòlitro [Gr. *he-katón*, 'HUNDred,' *lítra*, measure], M.: hectolitre.

eu- [Gr. *eû-*, well]: **-carestía** or **-caristía** [Gr. *cháris*, grace, thanks], F.: eucharist; communion. **-carístico**, ADJ.: eucharistic(al). **-femismo** [Gr. *phánai*, speak], M.: euphemism. **-fonía** [Gr. *phoné*, sound], F.: euphony. **-fònico**, ADJ.: euphonic(al).

eunúco [Gr. *euné*, bed, *échein*, keep], M.: eunuch (in the Orient having charge of the women's apartments).

eu-rimmía, **-ritmía** [Gr. *eû-*, well, *hruthmós*, rhythm], F.: eurythmy, symmetry.

evacua-ménto, M.: evacuation. ||**-'re** [L.], TR.: evacuate. **-zioncèlla**, *dim.* of *-zione*. **-zióne**, F.: evacuation.

evádere [L. *e-vadere* (go)], IRR. (cf. *invadere*); INTR.: evade (escape).

evag.† = *svag.*.

evan-gelicaménte, ADV.: evangelically. **-gèlico**, ADJ.: evangelical. **-gèl(i)o** [Gr. *eu-angélion*, 'good-message'], M.: gospel (evangel). **-gelísta**, pl. *-gelisti*, evangelist. **-gelizzáre**, TR.: evangelize.

evapo-rábile, ADJ.: evaporable. **-raménto**, M.: evaporation. ||**-ráre** [L.], TR.: evaporate; vanish. **-ratívo**, ADJ.: evaporative. **-zióne**, F.: evaporation.

evá-si, PRET., **evá-so**, PART. of *-dere*. **-sióne**, F.: evasion. **-sivaménte**, ADV.: evasively. **-sívo**, ADJ.: evasive.

evòllere† = *svellere*.

even-iménto†, **evèn-to** [L. *-tus* (*venire*, COME)], M.: event. **-tuále**, ADJ.: eventual. **-tualità**, F.: eventuality.

e-versióne†, F.: overthrow. **-vèrso**†, ADJ.: opposed. **-versóre**†, M.: overthrower (destroyer).

evi-dènte [L. *e-videns* (*videre*, see)], ADJ.: evident; clear. **-dentemènte**, ADV.: evidently. **-dènza**, F.: evidence; clearness.

e-víncere†, IRR.; TR.: vindicate.

evirá-re [L. (*vir*, man)], TR.: emasculate (Eng.† evirate). **-zióne**, F.: emasculation.

evi-tábile, ADJ.: evitable (avoidable). ||**-táre** [L. (*vitare*, shun)], TR.: AVOID; escape. **-tazióne**†, F.: avoiding.

evizióne [L. *e-victio*], F.: eviction.

èvo [L. *ævum*], M.: AGE, time.

evocá-re [L.], TR.: evoke (conjure). **-zióne**, F.: evocation.

evoè [L. *euoe* (Gr. *euoí*)], INTERJ.: euoe! (exclamation in honour of Bacchus).

evoluzióne [L. *-lutio*], F.: evolution.

evvíva [*e viva*], INTERJ.: long live! hail!

ex [L.], PREF.: ex, ex-; by: — *professo*, by profession; — *proposito*, on purpose, designedly. **-trèmis**, *essere in* —, be in agony; be dying.

eziandío [L. *etiam*, also, It. *dio*], ADV.: even, yet, also: — *che*, although, however.

F

f *èffe* [L.], M., F.: f (the letter).

fa [L. *fa-muli*, in a hymn], M.: fa (mus. note).

fábbri-ca [L. *fabrica* (cf. *fabbro*)], F.: fabric (building); FACTory; manufactory. **-cábile**, ADJ.: that can be built. **-caménto**, M.: building (fabric, structure).

-cánte, M.: manufacturer. **-cáre**, TR.: build (construct); make (manufacture). **-cáto**, ADJ.: built; M.: building. **-ca-tóre**, M., **-catríce**, F.: manufacturer. **-catòrio**, ADJ.: manufacturing. **-cazió-ne**, F.: fabrication. **-chétta**, *dim.* of *-ca*. **-cière**, M.: workman (operative); (*eccl.*) administrator; maker†. **-cóne**, *aug.* of *-ca*. **-cúccia**, *disp.* of *-ca*. **fab-brí-le**, ADJ.: fabrile.

fábbro [L. *faber* (root *fac*, do)], M.: blacksmith; inventor†.

fabul-† = *favol-*.

faccell-† = *facell-*†.

faccèn-da [L. *facienda* (*facere*, do)], F.: business (afFAIR). **-deria**†, F.: housework; fussiness. **-détta**†, *dim.* of *faccenda*. **-dièra**, F., **-dière**, M.: busybody, intriguer. **-dína**, **-dòla**, *dim.* of *faccenda*. **-dóna**, F., **-dóne**, M.: busy person. **-dóso**†, ADJ.: busy (bustling). **-dúccio**, **-dúccia**, *disp.* of *faccenda*. **-duòla** = *-dola*. **faccèn-te** = *facente*.

faccét-ta [dim. of *faccia*], F.: small face; facet. **-táre**, TR.: facet. **-táto**, ADJ.: faceted. **-tína**, *dim.* of *faccia*.

facchi-náccio, *disp.* of *facchino*. **-nág-gio**, M.: custom-house porter's fee. **-náta** = *-neria*. **-neggiáre**, INTR.: work as porter. **-nería**, F.: porter's act or word; rude act or word (rudeness). **-nésco**, ADJ.: porter-like. ‖**facchí-no** [?], M.: porter; rude fellow.

fác-cia [L. *facies*, face], F.: FACE; appearance; outside; page; impudence; wall†: *voltar* —, change sides; *non guardare in — nessuno*, be impartial; *far* —, grow impudent, dare; *a — fresca*, without getting disturbed; *di* —, opposite. **-ciác-cia**, *disp.* of *-cia*: *fare una* —, be humiliated. **-ciále** = *-iale*. **-ciáta**, F.: façade; page. **-cio**, PRES. of *fa(ce)re*. **-ciòla**, F.: magistrate's collar (with pendent starched slips in front); eighth part of sheet of paper†. **-cióna**, **-cióne**, *aug.* of *-cia*. **-ciuòla**† = *-ciola*. **fác-e**† 1 = *-cia*.

fá-ce 2 [L. *fax*, torch], F.: torch; light†. **-cèlla**†, **-cellína**, *dim.* of *-ce*.

fa-cènte, ADJ.: doing; busy; (= *confacente*) fit (proper). ‖**fá-cere**† = *fare*.

fa-cetaménte, ADV.: humorously, FACETiously. **-cetáre**, INTR.: jest, be facetious. ‖**-cèto** [L. *-cetus*], ADJ.: facetious (Eng.† FACETE, humorous). **-cèzia**, F.: facetious saying (waggery). **-cezió-la**, *dim.* of *-cezia*.

facciál-e [L. *facies*, face], ADJ.: facial. **-ménte**†, ADV.: face to face.

facidánno [*facere*, *danno*], M.: rural thief; knave.

fáci-le [L. *-lis*], ADJ.: facile (easy); convenient; probable: *uomo* —, good-natured man. **-líno**, *dim.* of *-le*. **-lità**, F.: facility. **-litáre**, TR.: facilitate (make easy). **-litazióne**, F.: facility; reduction in price. **-lménte**, ADV.: easily. **-lóne**, ADJ.: *aug.* of *-le*; ready to yield.

faci-mále†, M.: mischievous fellow. **-ménto**†, M.: doing (performance). **fa-cí-mola**†, F., **-molo**†, M.: sorcery. **-no-róso**, ADJ.: addicted to violence, outrageous. **-tóio**†, ADJ.: FEAsible. ‖**-tóre**, M., **-tríce** [*facere*], F.: maker, FACTOR, agent. **-túra**† = *fattura*.

fácola†, F.: small torch.

facol-tà [L. *facultas*], F.: faculty (power); PL.: goods, riches. **-tatívo**, ADJ.: in one's power; optional. **-tóso**, ADJ.: wealthy.

fa-condaménte, ADV.: eloquently. **-cóndia**, F.: eloquence (fluency). **-con-dióso**†, ADJ.: eloquent (fluent). **-condi-tà**†, etc. = *-condia*, etc. ‖**-cóndo** [L. *-cundus* (*fari*, speak)], ADJ.: eloquent.

facsímile = *fassimile*.

factòtum = *fattotum*.

facult. .† = *facolt.* .

fádo†, ADJ.: insipid.

fag-géta, F., **-géto**, M.: beech-grove. ‖**-gio** [L. *-us*], M.: BEECH-tree. **-giòla**, **-giuòla**†, F.: beech-nut.

fagiá-na, F. of *-no*. **-náia**, F.: pheasantry. **-no** [Gr. *phasianós* (*Phâsis*, river)], M.: PHEASANT. **-nòtto**, *dim.* of *-no*.

fagio-láta, F.: mess of beans; silliness. **-létto**, *car. dim.* of *-lo*. **-líno**, *dim.* of *-lo*. ‖**fagi(u)ò-lo** [L. *phaseolus*], M.: kidney-bean; blockhead.

fa-gliáre, TR.: discard (at cards) ‖**-glio** [Sp. *fallo*, FAILure], M.: discard (at cards).

fágn-o†, ADJ.: dissembling (cunning but pretending awkwardness). **-óne**†, *aug.*

fa-gottíno, *dim.* of *-gotto*. **-gottísta**, M.: bassoon-player. ‖**-gòtto** [?], M.: bundle; (*mus.*) bassoon: *far* —, pack up; die. **-gottóne**, *aug.* of *-gotto*.

faína [?], F.: polecat.

falánge [Gr. *phálanx*], F.: phalanx; great number; digital bone.

falárica [L.], F.: heavy dart.

falásco, M.: bog grass.

fal-cáre†, TR.: bend over. **-cástro**†, M.: bill-hook. **-cáto**, ADJ.: with a scythe. **-catóre**†, M.: **-catríce**†, F.: armed with scythes. ‖**-ce** [L. *falx*], F.: sickle, scythe. **-cétto**, *dim.* of *-ce*. **-ciáre**, TR.: mow. **-ciáta**, F.: scythe-cut. **-cia-tóre**, M., **-ciatríce**, F.: reaper, mower. **-ciatúra**, F.: mowing time. **-cífero**†, ADJ.: armed with a scythe.

fal-cinèllo [*falco*], M.: speckled magpie.

fal-cíno, **-ciòlo** [*falce*], M.: grass-sickle. **-cióne**, M.: large forage cutter moun'.d on a bench.

fál-co [l. L.], M.: falcon: è un —, he's a daring one. **-conáre†**, INTR.: hawk. **-concèllo**, *dim.* of *-cone.* **-cóne**, M.: *aug.* of *-co;* hawk; (*mil.*†) falconet (small cannon). **-coneria†**, F.: hawk-training. **-conétto**, M.: falconet. **-conière**, M.: falconer.

fál-da [OHG. *fald*], F.: FOLD, plait; stratum; flake (of snow); streamer (of flame); tail (of dress-coat); dress-coat; brim (of hat); base (of mountain); loin (of beef): *a — a —*†, little by little; *di — in —*†, everywhere. **-dáta†**, F.: quantity of plaits; lint. **-dèlla**, F.: lint, salved bandage; ten pounds of wool†; cheat†. **-delláta†**, **-dellína†**, F.: small plait, lint. **-delláto**, ADJ.: plaited (folded); made into lint. **-dí*gl*ia**, F.: hoop-petticoat. **-díno**, M.: (*iron.*) short-skirted coat, scant coat. **-distòro** [OHG. *falt-stuol*], **-distòrio†**, M.: (*eccl.*) bishop's chair. **-dolína**, *dim.* of *-da..* **-dóna**, **-dóne**, *aug.* of *-da.* **-dóso**, ADJ.: folded, folding.

falegnáme [*fare, legname*], M.: carpenter; joiner.

faléna [Gr. *phálaina*], F.: moth; ashes (on burning coal; of paper); puffball; flighty person.

fálere [Gr. *phálara*], F. PL.: metal cornice-plates.

falèrno [mount *Falernus*, Italy], M.: Falernian wine.

falimbèllo†, M.: unsteady fellow.

fál-la, F.: leak (in ship); FAULT†. **-lábile†**, ADJ.: deceitful. **-láce**, ADJ.: fallacious (deceitful); disappointing. **-laceménte†**, ADV.: fallaciously (deceitfully). **-lácia**, F.: fallacy (deceit; sophistry; error); trick. **-lánte†**, ADJ.: failing; deceitful. **-lánza†**, F.: error; defect. **-láre**, INTR.: be mistaken; FAIL† (miss); sin (err). **-latóre†**, M., **-latríce,†** F.: transgressor. **-lènte†**, ADJ.: failing; missing, etc. **-lènza†** = *-lanza.* **-líbile**, ADJ.: fallible. **-libilità**, F.: fallibility. **-lig*l*óne†** = **-lo.** **-liménto**, M.: failure; bankruptcy. ‖**-líre** [L. *fallere*], INTR.: FAIL, mistake; want; go bankrupt; sin†; TR.: miss (blow, shot); omit (in copying)†; err; deceive; offend; M.†: error, fault. **-líto**, ADJ.: failed: *— di mente*†, insane; imbecile; M.: bankrupt. **-litóre†**, M.: transgressor. **-lo**, M.: FAULT, error; miss: *senza —*, without fail. **-lóre†**, **-lúra** = *-lo.*

falò [? Gr. *phalós*, shining], M.: bonfire: *fare un —*, waste a fortune quickly.

falòp-pa [?], F.: unfinished cocoon; lying braggart. **-póne**, *aug.* of *-pa.*

fa-lotich*e*ría†, F.: extravagance; fantasticalness. **-lòtico†**, ADJ.: extravagant (eccentric).

falpalà [Fr. *falbala*], M.: FURBELOW.

fal-saménte, ADV.: falsely. **-saménto**, M.: falsehood. **-sa=monéte**, M., INVAR.: counterfeiter (of money). **-sárda†**, F.: sorceress. **-sárdo†**, M.: sorcer. **-sáre**, TR.: falsify, counterfeit; alter; violate†; deceive†. **-sa=rèdine**, F.: false-rein. **-sa=ríga**, F.: ruled sheet to put under unruled paper. **-sário**, ADJ.: falsifying; M.: forger; counterfeiter. **-satóre**, M., **-satríce**, F.: falsifier; counterfeiter. **-satúra**, F.: insertion (lady's dress). **-seggiáre†**, TR.: falsify. **-sétto**, M.: falsetto. **-sídico†**, ADJ.: false-speaking. **-sificábile**, ADJ.: falsifiable. **-sificaménto**, M.: falsification; counterfeiting (forgery). **-sificáre**, TR.: falsify; counterfeit; show to be false†. **-sificáto**, ADJ.: falsified. **-sificatóre**, M., **-sificatríce**, F.: falsifier. **-sificazióne**, F.: falsification. **-sità**, F.: falsity; lie; imposture. ‖**-so** [L. *-sus*], ADJ.: false (deceitful; lying); counterfeit; ADV.: falsely; M.: falsehood. **-súra†** = *-sità.*

fál-ta†, F.: FAULT; want (need). **-táre†**, INTR.: want (lack).

fá-ma [L. (*fari*, speak)], F.: fame (reputation). **-máre†**, TR.: divulge.

fá-me [L. *-mes*], F.: hunger; craving (eagerness); famine (dearth): *avere —*, be hungry, long for. **-mèlico**, ADJ.: famished; hungry.

famigeráto [*fama*], ADJ.: notorious; famous (in bad way).

famí-*gl*ia [L. *-lia*], F.: family; household. **-*gl*iáccia**, *disp.* of *-glia.* **-*gl*iár..** = *-miliar..* **famí-*gl*io**, M.: bailiff (sergeant); servant. **-*gl*iòla**, *disp. dim.* of *-glia.* **-*gl*ióna**, F.: *aug.* of *-glia* (numerous; rich; powerful). **-*gl*iuòla†** = *-gliòla.* **-liáre**, ADJ.: familiar (intimate); M.: intimate†; servant. **-liarità**, F.: familiarity. **-liarizzáre**, REFL.: become familiar. **-liarménte**, ADV.: familiarly.

fa-mosaménte, ADV.: famously; notoriously. **-mosità†**, F.: fame; renown. ‖**-móso** [*fama*], ADJ.: famous; splendid: *libello —*, defamatory pamphlet.

fa-múccia, F.: *joc. dim.* of *fame;* small appetite. **-mulènto†**, ADJ.: famished.

faná-le [Gr. *phanós*, lantern], M.: lighthouse, lantern or tower; street-lamp; carriage-lamp; lamp for illuminations. **-létto**, *dim.* of *-le.*

faná-tico [L. *-ticus*, inspired (*fanum*, temple)], ADJ.: fanatic; M.: fanatic. **-tísmo**, M.: fanaticism. **-tizzáre**, TR.: make fanatic.

fancél.. = *fanciul..*

fanciúl-la, F.: girl. **-láccia**, *disp.* of *-lo.* **-lággine**, F.: childishness. **-láia†**, F.: troop of boys and girls. **-leggiáre**,

INTR.: be childish. **-lería†** = *-laggine*. **-lésco, -lescaménte**, ADV.: childishly. **-lésco**, ADJ.: childish. **-létta**, F.: little girl. **-létto**, M.: little boy. **-lézza**, F.: childhood; childishness. **-líno**, *car. dim.* of *-lo*. ‖**fanciúl-lo** [*fante*], M.: young child, boy. **-lóne**, *aug.* of *-lo*. **-lúzzo** = *-lino*.

fandò-nia [Fr. *fantôme*, phantom], F.: bragging lie; fable. **-nióna**, F., **-nióne**, M.: bragging liar.

fanèllo [?], M.: linnet.

fanfaléoco†, M.: childish, affected action.

fanfalúca [L. L. *famfaluca* (Gr. *pomphóluks*, bubble)], F.: fable (idle story); trifle (gewgaw); spark†.

fán-fano [?], M.: malicious babbler. **-fára**, F.: band (of music). **-faronáta**, F.: braggardism (boasting). **-faróne**, M.: braggart. **fán-fera**: *a* —, by chance. **-ferína†**, F.: joke.

fán-ga [Goth. *fani*], F.: soft mud, mire. **-gáccio**, *pop.* of *-go*. **-gáia**, F.: muddy street. **-gatúra**, F.: (*med.*) mud-bath. **-ghiccio**, *dim.* of *-go*. **-ghíglia**, F., *dim.* of *-go*: mud in grinder's trough. **-go**, M.: mud, (*fig.*) slime (of vice): *uscir del* —, get out of a scrape; *far — d'una cosa*, misuse. **-gosità**, F.: muddiness. **-góso**, ADJ.: muddy.

fangòtto† = *fagotto*.

fannul-lóna, F., **-lóne** [*fare, nulla*], M.: do-nothing.

fan-táccia†, F.: *disp.* of *-te*; scullion. ‖**-taccíno** [*fante*], M.: (*joc.*) private infantry soldier. **-táio†**, M.: lover of servant-girls.

fan-tasía, F.: FANCY, imagination; caprice, whim; (*mus.*) fantasia: *a* —, at pleasure; *di* —, improvising. **-tasiáccia**, *disp.* of *-tasia*. **-tásima**, M.: (*pop.*) phantom (spectre). **-tasióso**, ADJ.: capricious. **-tasiúccia**, *disp. dim.* of *-tasia*. ‖**-tásma** [Gr. *phántasma*, apparition (*phaínein*, appear)], M.: FANCY (conceit, imagining); phantom (ghost). **-tasmagoría** [Gr. *ageírein*, gather], F.: phantasmagoria. **-tasmagòrico**, ADJ.: phantasmagorical. **-tasticàggine**, F.: fantasy, whim. **-tasticaménte**, ADV.: fantastically (visionarily; oddly). **-tasticáre**, INTR.: build air-castles; fancy (imagine; devise). **-tasticatóre†**, M.: muser (imaginer). **-tasticheria**, F.: fancy. **-tastichétto**, *car. dim.* of *-tastico*. **-tástico**, ADJ.: fantastic (visionary, odd; whimsical); M.: whimsical person. **-tasticóna**, F., **-tasticóne**, M.: visionary (dreamer).

fán-te 1 [L. *infans*, child], M.: infantry soldier; knave (at cards); ridiculous bully; servant†. **-te 2**, F.: servant-maid. **-teggiáre†**, INTR.: serve, wait upon. **-tería**, F.: infantry. **-tésca**, F.: servant-maid. **-ticèlla†**, F., **-ticèllo†**, M.: (*dim.*) servant. **-ticíno†**, **-tigíno†**, M.: little boy; baby. **-tilità†**, F.: infancy; childishness. **-tinería†**, F.: malice; cunning, trick. **-tinézza†**, F.: infancy. **-tíno**, M.: jockey; crafty man; little boy†. **-toccináta**, F.: silliness; puppet-show (silly spectacle). **-toccíno**, *dim.* of *-toccio*. **-tòccio**, M.: puppet; booby. **-toccióna**, **-toccióne**, *aug.* of *-toccio*. **-tolíno**, M.: (*poet.*) babe; little boy.

fara-bolóna, F., **-bolóne**, **-bulóne** [Gr. *parabolé*, parabola], M.: great talker (who does little).

farabútto [Sp. *faraute* (Fr. *héraut*), HERALD; meddler], M.: rascal.

Faraóne, M.: Pharaoh; faro (game).

far-chétola†, F., **-ciglióne†**, M.: teal duck.

fár-da†, F.: dirty thing; phlegm. **-dàggio†**, M.: baggage. **-dáta†**, F.: blow with dirty rag; bundle of dirty rags. **-dellétto**, **-dellíno**, *dim.* of *-dello*. **-dèllo**, M., *dim.* of *fardo*; bundle. ‖**-do†** [Ar.], M.: spice-bag (skin bag to contain cloth bag of spices, etc.).

fáre [L. *facere*], IRR.§; TR.: do (make, compose); act (personate); cause; command; be; concern (matter); be enough (suffice); fit (suit); crack (wall); REFL.: make one's self; become; approach: *farla ad uno*, play one a trick; *questo non fa per me*, this doesn't suit me; *due mesi fa*, two months ago; *Milano fa da* 400,000 *abitanti*, Milan has 400,000 inhabitants; — *fagotto*, depart; *che vi fa egli che venga o non venga?* what is it to you if he comes or not? *al — del giorno*, at break of day; *al — della notte*, at dusk; *la luna fece ieri*, it was new moon yesterday; — *acqua*, (*nav.*) leak; — *aiuto*, lend assistance, aid; — (or *farsi*) *la barba*, shave (one's self); — *bello*, set off, adorn; — *bocca da ridere*, smile; — *caldo*, be hot weather; — *capo ad uno*, have recourse to one; — *le carte*, deal (at cards); — *caso di*, make account of; clear up; *fatti con Dio*, good-by, adieu, farewell; — *l'erba*, mow; — *faccia*, grow impudent; *farle ad uno*, cheat one; — *fiasco*, fail (play); — *le forche*, feign; *non fa forza*, no matter; — *forza di vela*, crowd sail; — *freddo*, be cold (weather); — *furore*, make a hit (play); — *il Giorgio*, strut, give one's self airs; — *del grande*, put on style or state; — *grazia a*, forgive, pardon; — *lontano*, send, drive away; — *a metà*, go by halves; — *motto di*, mention, speak of;

— *le nonе*†, secure beforehand; — *osteria*, keep inn; — *a pugni*, box; — *la quaresima*, keep Lent; — *scala*, touch at a port; — *sera* (*e sabato*), pass one's time; idle; — *sicurtà*, give bail for; — *silenzio*, be quiet; *ogni prun fa siepe*, every little helps; — *un sonno*, take a nap; — *spese ad uno*, keep, maintain one; — *testa a*, oppose, resist; — *torto a*, be unjust to; wrong; — *vago uno* (*di*), make one charmed (with), make one enamoured (of); charm one; — *vista*, feign; — *vela*, set sail; — *vento*, be windy; — *vita*, live; — *voglia a*, induce, entice; *fateci a me*, come here; *farsi beffe di*, make fun of, jeer, make light of; *farsi alla finestra*, look out of the window; *farsi alla porta*, go to the door; *farsi alle scale*, come to the stairs; *farsi sera*, draw towards night; *farsi tardi*, grow late.

§ *fáre* (*fácere*†): Ind.: Pres. *fò* or *fáccio*, *fái*, *fà*; *facciámo*, *fáte*, *fánno*. Impf. *facéva*. Pret. *féci*, *facésti*, *féce* or *fé'*; *facémmo*, *facéste*, *fécero*. Fut. *farò*. Cond. *farèi*. Subj.: Pres. *fáccia*. Impf. *facéssi*. Ive *fà*; *fáte*. Part.: Pres. *facènte*. Past. *fátto*. Ger. *facèndo*. — Poet. forms: Ind.: Pres. 2. *fáci*, 3. *fáce*. Impf. *féa*. Pret. *féi*, *fésti*; *fémmo*, *féste*, *féro*(*no*). Subj.: Impf. *féssi*.

farè-tra [Gr. *pharétra* (*phérein*, BEAR)], F.: quiver (for arrows). **-tráto**, ADJ.: bearing a quiver.

farfál-la [L. *papilio*], F.: butterfly. **-lét-ta**, **-lína**, *car. dim.* of *-là*. **-líno**, M.: small butterfly (which damages grain); volatile person. **-lóne**, M.: *aug.* of *-la*; great blunder; dandy.

farfanícchio [*fanfano*], M.: little bully; upstart boy.

fárfa-ra, F., **-ro** [L. *far*, grain, meal], M.: (*bot.*) coltsfoot.

farí-na [L. (*far*, grain, meal)], F.: flour (meal): — *lattea*, malted milk; *fior di* —, finest flour; *non essere schietta* —, not be sincere; *esser* — *propria*, be one's own work, words or deeds; *questo non fa* —, this doesn't pay. **-máceo**, ADJ.: farinaceous, mealy. **-naiuòlo**†, M.: seller of legumes, oil, etc. **-náta**, F.: porridge, mush. **-nèllo**†, ADJ.: roguish; M.: rogue.

fa-ringe [Gr. *phárunx*], F.: pharynx. **-ríngeo**, ADJ.: pharyngeal.

farinóso [*farina*], ADJ.: yielding much flour; floury; whitened.

fari-sáico, ADJ.: pharisaical. **-seísmo**, M.: pharisaism. ‖**-sèo** [Gr. *pharisaios* (Heb. *parash*, separate)], M.: pharisee (hypocrite).

farlingòtto†, ADJ.: speaking confusedly; jabbering; M.: jabberer.

farma-ceútica, F.: pharmaceutics. **-ceútico**, ADJ.: pharmaceutical. **-cía**, F.: pharmacy. **-císta**, M.: pharmacist. ‖**fárma-co** [Gr. *phármakon*], M.: drug, **-cología**, F.: pharmaceutics. **-copèa**, F.: pharmacopœia.

farneti-caménto, ADV.: frantically. **-caménto**, M.: frenzy. **-cáre**, INTR.: rave, dote. ‖**farnèti-co** [*frenetico*], ADJ.: frenetic (mad, doting); M.: frenzy (raving, doting).

fárnia [L. *-nea*], F.: large-leaved oak.

fáro [Gr. *Pháros*, island off Alexandria], M.: pharos (lighthouse; guide).

farragg. †= *farrag*..

far-raginare†, TR.: mix, jumble. ‖**-rá-gine** [L. *-rago* (*far*, grain, meal)], F.: mixed fodder; mixture (hodge-podge). **-raginóso**, ADJ.: farraginous; mixed. **-rágo**†, F.: farrago (medley, jumble). **-ráta**, F.: cake made of *farro* (a grain). **-ricèllo**†, M.: coarse meal. **-ro**, M.: a grain (eaten roasted without grinding, in pottage).

fár-sa [L. *-cire*, stuff], F.: FARCE (ludicrous comedy); doublet† (quilted); stuffed food†. **-sáta**†, F.: doublet-lining. **-sétta**, F.: *dim.* of *-sa*; doublet†. **-settáio**†, M.: doublet-maker. **-settína**, *dim.* of *-sa*. **-sétto**, M.: doublet (quilted). **-settóne**, *aug.* of *-setto*.

fa-scétta, F.: *dim.* of *-scia*; corset; metal strips binding barrel to gun-stock. **-scet-táia**, F.: corset-maker. **-scettíno**, **-scétto**, *dim.* of *-scio*. ‖**-scia** [L. (root *fasc-*, twist: cf. *fascio*)], F.: bandage; swaddling band†; outside bark: *in* —, *in fasce*, in infancy; — *bruciata*†, torrid zone. **-sciáre**, TR.: swathe; bind; environ. **-sciáta**†, F.: binding; bandaging. **-sciáto**, ADJ.: bound; swathed. **-scia-túra**, F.: binding; bandage; ligature; truss. **-scicoláre**†, TR.: bind in fagots; ADJ.: fascicular. **-scicoláto**†, ADJ.: FASCICLED (of roots). **-scicolétto**, *dim.* of *-scicolo*. **-scícolo**, M.: part (of book); fascicle†. **-scína**, F.: small fagot; fascine. **-scináia**, F.: place to keep fagots. **-scináio**, M.: maker or seller of fagots. **-scináme**, M.: fagot-wood. **-scináre**†[1], INTR.: make fascines.

fascináre[2] [L. (? connected with root *fasc-* of *fascia*, etc.)], TR.: fascinate.

fascináta [*-nare*[1]], F.: revetment of fascines.

fasci-natóre†, M., **-natrice**†[2], F.: sorcerer; sorceress; charmer. **-nazióne**†, F.: fascination; sorcery.

fasci-nétta, **-nétto**, *dim.* of *-na*.

fáscino [L. *-num*], M.: fascination (charm, witchery).

fa-scinettáio, M.: kindling-seller. **-sci-nòtto**, M.: kindling-fagot. ‖**fá-scio** [L. *-scis* (root *fasc-*, twist; cf. *-scia*)], M.: bunch, bundle of twigs, grass, etc.; fascine (fagot); PL.: fasces; ancient triple-barrelled gun: *fare d' ogni erba* (*un*) —, mix everything confusedly; mix good and bad; abuse everything; live recklessly; *andare in un* —, go to ruin. **-sciòla**, *dim.* of *-scio.* **-sciolína**, *dim.* of *-sciola.* **-sciáccio†**, *dim.* of *-scio.* **-sciúme†**, M.: rubbish-heap. **-sciuòla†**, F., **-sciuòlo†**, M.: *dim.* of *-scia;* fillet.

fáse [Gr. *phásis* (*phainein*, show)], F.: phase (of planet).

fasservízi [*fare, servizi*], M.: common servant; chore-boy.

fassímile [*fare, simile*], M.: facsimile.

fastèl-la, cf. *-lo.* **-láccio**, *disp.* of *-lo.* **-létto**, **-líno**, *dim.* of *-lo.* ||**fastèl-lo** [*fascio*], M. (pl. —*li* or as f. —*la*): bundle, fagot (of corn, wood, to carry on back). **-lóne**, *aug.* of *-lo.*

fásti [L.], M. PL.: fasti (Rom. calendar; records).

fasti-diáre†, TR.: disgust (annoy); REFL.: be disgusted, fastidious; loathe. ||**fastídio** [L. *-dium*, loathing], M.: weariness (tediousness, vexation); anxiety (care); disgust (aversion, loathing); filthiness†; (*euph.*) lice: *aver in* —, loathe. **-diosáccio**, *aug.* of *-dioso.* **-diosággine**, F.: annoyance, troublesomeness. **-diosaménte**, ADV.: tediously, tiresomely. **-diosèllo**, **-diosétto**, *disp. dim.* of *-dioso.* **-diosità†** = *-diosaggine;* FASTIDIOUSNESS. **-dióso**, ADJ.: wearying (bothersome, importunate); FASTIDIOUS†; insatiable†. **-díre**, TR.: annoy (importune, weary, disgust); INTR.†: be disgusted (be annoyed). **-diúccio**, *dim.* of *-dio.* **-diúme†**, M.: quantity of troubles.

fastígio [L. *-gium*], M.: (*arch.*) coping; top (summit); loftiness.

fastigióso† 1 [*fastidio*], ADJ.: wearying, FASTIDIOUS.

fa-stigióso† 2, ADJ.: pompous; proud. ||**-sto** 1 [L. *-stus*, pride], M.: pomp (luxury, ostentation).

fásto 2 [L. *-tus*], ADJ.: *giorno* —, court-day; propitious day.

fa-stosaménte, ADV.: pompously. **-stosità**, F.: pompousness. ||**-stóso** [*-sto* 1], ADJ.: pompous.

fá-ta [L. *-tum*], F.: FAY (elf). **-tagióne†**, F.: enchantment. **-tále**, ADJ.: fatal (predestined). **-talísmo**, M.: fatalism. **-talísta**, M.: fatalist. **-talità**, F.: fatality (destiny). **-talménte**, ADV.: fatally. **-táre†**, TR.: decree (destine); charm; make invulnerable. **-tataménte†**, ADV.: fatally. **-táto**, ADJ.: fated; invulnerable. **-tatúra**, F.: sorcery, enchantment (charm).

fatí-ca, F.: FATIGUE (hardship); labour†; wages; reward. **-cábile†**, ADJ.: capable of fatigue, Eng.† fatigable. **-cáccia**, F.: painful work. ||**-cáre** [L. *-gare*], TR.: fatigue; exhaust; annoy; REFL.: exert one's self, strive. **-catóre**, M., **-catríce**, F.: hard worker. **-chétta**, *dim.* of *-co.* **-chévole†**, ADJ.: industrious; toilsome. **-cosaménte**, ADV.: laboriously. **-cosétto**, ADJ.: rather fatiguing. **-cóso**, ADJ.: fatiguing; difficult. **-cúccia**, *dim.* of *-ca.*

fatídico [L. *-cus*], ADJ.: prophetic.

fatig. .† = *fatic.* .

fáto [L. *-tum*], M.: fate, destiny.

fát-ta [*-to*], F.: kind (sort, species; fashion); dung of wild beasts; scent (of game): *esser sulla* — *di*, be on the track of. **-táccio**, *disp.* of *-to.* **-taménte**, ADV.: *sì* (or *così*) —, in such a manner, so (Fr. *tellement*). **-terèllo**, M.: triple; nothing. **-tévole†**, ADJ.: FEASIBLE. **-tézza†**, F.: form, feature. **-tézze**, F. PL.: features (lineaments); make†; shape. **-tía†**, F.: witchcraft (charm). **-tibèllo†**, M.: rouge. **-tíbile**, ADJ.: feasible (possible). **-tíccio**, ADJ.: robust. **-ticcióne**, *aug.* of *-ticcio.*

fattispècie [L. *facti species*, kind of fact], M.: (*leg.*) case in question; report of a case.

fat-tívo†, ADJ.: efficacious; Eng.† FACTIVE. **-tízio†**, ADJ.: artificial. ||**-to** [*fare*], ADJ.: made; complete; grown-up; ripe; M.: FACT (deed, action); business; behaviour; case (matter, affair): — *d' armi*, small combat; *detto* —, no sooner said than done; *di* —, really, indeed; *a gran* —, a great deal; *in sul* —, immediately; *tanto* —, so big (indicating size); — (adverbially before a noun), after; *sino a* — *aprile*, till after April.

fat-toiáno, M.: (*pop.*) olive-oil presser. ||**-tóio** [*frantoio*], M.: olive-press.

fat-tóra, F.: factor's wife. ||**-tóre** [*fare*], M.: FACTOR; steward; author†; artisan†; broker†; shop-boy†; peg-top†: — *supremo*, God. **-torésse**, F.: factor or steward's wife; housekeeper. **-torétto†**, M.: shop-boy. **-toría**, F.: stewardship; steward's establishment. **-toríno**, M.: shop-boy; messenger-boy; spit-jack. **-toriúccia**, *disp.* of *-toria.*

fattòtum [L. *fac-totum*, 'do-all'], M.: factotum.

fattucchiè-ra, F., **-re**, **-ro** [? L. *facticius*, artificial], M.: sorcerer, -ess; witch. **-ría**, F.: sorcery (witchcraft); FETICHISM.

fattú-ra [*fare*], F.: work (of artisan); making; cost (of work); charge; wages; invoice; creature†; witchcraft†. **-ráre**, TR.: falsify; adulterate (wines, etc.); bewitch†. **-ráto**, ADJ.: adulterated; bewitched†. **-rína**, *car. dim.* of *-ra.* **-'ro†**, ADJ.: to be done.

fatu-ità, F.: fatuity. ||**fátu-o** [L. *-us*], ADJ.: fatuous (silly); flighty: *fuoco* —, ignis fatuus.

fáuci [L. *fauces*], F. PL.: jaws (throat).

fáu-na, F.: fauna. ||**fáu-no** [L. *-nus*], M.: faun.

fau-staménte, ADV.: fortunately, prosperously. ||**fáu-sto** [L. *-stus* (*favere*, favour)], ADJ.: auspicious (FAVOURable, happy, propitious). **-tóre**, M., **-tríce**, F.: FAVOURer; accomplice.

fá-va [L. *-ba*], F.: bean; ballot-marble; foolish pride†; trifle†: *metter alle -ve*, put to vote; *a — cruda*†, without examination; *uccellare a -ve*†, deceive. **-vagèllo**, M.: (*bot.*) celandine. **-vággine**, F.: plant (used as vermifuge). **-varèlla**, F.: bean-pottage. **-váta**, F.: vain boasting; bean-meal†.

favèl-la [L. *fabella* (*fari*, speak)], F.: speech; tongue (dialect); nation†: *tener — a uno*†, be unwilling to speak to one, be angry. **-laménto**†, M.: speech. **-láre**, M.: speak; TR.: say. **-latóre**†, M., **-latríce**†, F.: prattler. **-lío**†, M.: prattle.

fa-verèlla = *-varella*. **-véto**, M.: bean-field. ||**-vétta**, F.: *car. dim.* of *-va*; bean-pottage†; pride†.

favíl-la [L.], F.: spark (cinder). **-láre**†, INTR.: sparkle, scintillate. **-létta**, **-lína**, *dim.* of *-la*. **favíl-lo**†, M.: spark.

fávo [L. *favus*], M.: honeycomb.

fávo-la [L. *fabula* (*fari*, speak)], F.: FABLE (story; invention). **-láccia**, *disp.* of *-la*. **-láre**†, INTR.: tell stories; talk. **-leggevolménte**†, ADV.: fabulously. **-leggiáre**, TR.: fable (tell stories, fable): — *di*†, laugh at, mock. **-leggiatóre**†, M., —**tríce**†, F.: fabler. **-lésco**†, ADJ.: fabulous. **-létta**, *car. dim.* of *-la*. **-lóne**†, M.: bragging liar. **-losaménte**, ADV.: fabulously. **-lóso**, ADJ.: FABULOUS.

fa-vomèle†, M.: honeycomb. **-vóne**†, M.: honeycomb; very proud man.

favònio†, M.: (*poet.*) west wind.

favo-rábile†, ADJ.: favourable. **-ráre**†, TR.: favour. **-ratóre**†, M., **-ratríce**, F.: favourer, protector. ||**favó-re** [L. *-r*], M.: favour; sympathy (kindness); approval; aid: *lettere di* —, letters of recommendation. **-reggévole**†, **-reggiánte**†, ADJ.: favourable. **-reggiáre**, TR.: favour, aid. **-reggiatóre**, M., **-reggiatríce**, F.: favourer, aider. **-révole**, ADJ.: favourable. **-revolménte**, ADV.: favourably. **-ríre**, TR.: favour (help): *-risca di dirmi*, please tell me. **-ríta**, F.: prince's mistress. **-ríto**, ADJ., M.: favourite. **-ritóre**†, M., **-ritríce**†, F.: favourer. **-róso**†, ADJ.: favourable. **-ráccio**, *disp. dim.* of *-re*.

favále [*fava*], M.: bean-field; bean-sowing (for improving lands); beanstraw.

Fázio [*Bonifazio*]: *esser Fra —*, *fare —*, exercise charity; spend freely for others.

fa-zionário†, M.: factionist. **-zionáto**, ADJ.: FASHIONed (formed). ||**-zióne** [L. *factio* (root *fac-*, do)], F.: FACTION; FEAT (exploit); battle; military service; sentinel; action†; tax†: *esser in* —, be on duty. **-ziosaménte**, ADV.: seditiously, factiously. **-zióso**, ADJ.: factious (seditious, rebellious); M.: factionist (rebel).

faz-zolétto, **-zòlo**† [? *faccia*], M.: handkerchief.

fè (pron. *fè*), (*poet.*) for *-de*.

febbráccia, *disp.* of *-bre*.

febbráio [L. *februarius*], M.: February.

fèb-bre [L. *febris*], F.: fever. **-brétta**, *dim.* of *-bre*. **-brettáccia**, *disp. dim.* of *-bre*. **-bricèlla**†, *dim.* of *-bre*. **-briciáttola**, *dim.* of *-bre*. **-bricína**, *dim.* of *-bre*. **-bricità**†, F.: feverishness. **-bricitánte**, ADJ.: feverish. **-bricitáre**†, INTR.: be attacked by fever. **-bricóne**, M.: violent fever. **-bricóso**, ADJ.: giving fever. **-brifúgo**, ADJ., M.: febrifuge. **-bríle**, ADJ.: febrile. **-brína**, *dim.* of *-bre*. **-bróna**, **-bróne**, *aug.* of *-bre*. **-bróso**† = *-bricoso*. **-brúccia**, **-brúzza**†, *dim.* of *-bre*.

fe-bèo, ADJ.: poetical. ||**Fè-bo** [Gr. *Phoibos* ('bright')], M.: Phœbus (Apollo; sun). **-be**†, **-bèa**†, F.: Phœbe (moon).

fe-cále, ADJ.: fecal. ||**fè-ccia** [L. *fæx*], F.: sediment; dung; PL.: dregs, lees. **-cciáia**†, F.: faucet hole (for emptying the dregs of a barrel). **-ccióso**, ADJ.: dreggy, feculent. **-cciúme**, M.: mass of dregs; rabble.

féci, PRET. of *fare*.

feciále [L. *-lis*], M. PL.: fecials (Roman priests, sanctioning treaties, etc.).

fècola [L. *fæx*, sediment], F.: fecula; starch.

fecon-dábile, ADJ.: fecundable. **-daménte**, ADV.: fruitfully, prolifically. **-dáre**, TR.: fecundate (make fruitful). **-datívo**, ADJ.: fecundating. **-datóre**, M., **-datríce**, F.; ADJ.: fecundating (fertilizing). **-dazióne**, F.: fecundation. **fecón-dia**†, **-dità**, F.: fecundity. **-dévole**†, ADJ.: fruitful. ||**fecón-do** [L. *fecundus*], ADJ.: fecund (fruitful).

fé-de [L. *fides*], F.: FAITH; credit; certificate: *mani in* —, ring representing clasped hands; *atto di* —, prayer (Catholic); *fare atto di* —, take on faith.

fedecom-messário†, M.: trustee. ||**-mésso** [L. *fidei-commissum*, committed to FAITH or trust], M.: trust deed, feoffment. **-méttere**†, TR.: deed in trust.

fe-déle [*-de*], ADJ.: faithful; M. (esp. pl.):

devotee, believer; vassal†. **-delménte**, ADV.: faithfully. **-delóne**, *joc. aug.* of *-dele*. **-deltà**, F.: fidelity.

fèdera [Ger. *feder*, feather], F.: pillow-case.

federá-le [L. *fœderalis* (*fœdus*, league)], ADJ.: federal. **-lísmo**, M.: federalism. **-lísta**, M.: federalist. **-'to**, ADJ.: federated. **-zióne**, F.: federation.

fedífrago [L. *fœdi-fragus*, league-breaking], ADJ.: promise-breaking; M.: promise-breaker.

fediménto† = *ferimento*.

fedí-na [?], F. (us'ly pl.): mutton-chop whiskers. **-nóna**, **-nóne**, *aug.* of *-na*.

feditóre†, M.: 1. kind of soldier; 2. = *feritore*; ADJ.: predatory (of birds).

fega-táccio, M.: daredevil. **-tèllo**, M.: cooked liver. **-tíno**, *dim.* of *-to*. ||**féga-to** [l. L. *ficatum* (L. *ficus*, FIG), 'fig-fattened,' applied to goose liver], liver; (*fig.*) courage (boldness). **-tóso**, ADJ.: bilious; having liver-spots, moth-patches; liver-coloured; M.: bilious person.

fèi†, PRET. of *fare*.

fél-ce [L. *filix*], F.: fern. **-céta**, F., **-céto**, M.: fernery; ferny place.

fèle† = *fiele*.

felí-ce [L. *-x*], ADJ.: happy. **-ceménte**, ADV.: happily, fortunately. **-cità**, F.: felicity (prosperity). **-citáre**, TR.: felicitate; make happy†.

felíno [L. *-lis*, cat], ADJ.: feline.

fèlle† = *fiele*.

fèl-lo, ADJ.: wicked; melancholy (doleful)†. **-lonaménte**†, ADV.: wickedly. ||**-lóne** [l. L. *-o*, felon], ADJ.: (*poet.*) rebellious, perfidious; felonious. **-lonería**†, F.: rebelliousness, treachery. **-lonescaménte**, ADV.: rebelliously, treacherously. **-lonésco**, ADJ.: rebellious, perfidious; felonious; cruel†. **-lonéssa**†, F.: perfidious, cruel woman. **-lonía**, F.: conspiracy, rebellion; treachery; infidelity; infamy; felony. **-lonéso**†, ADJ.: rebellious; felonious.

fèlpa [?], F.: plush.

fel-tráre, TR.: full (thicken in a mill); cover with felt†; filter†. **-tratúra**, F.: fulling. ||**fél-tro** [l. L. *filtrum* (OHG. *filz*)], M.: felt; (*rare*) filter.

felúca [fr. Ar.], F.: boat (for sail or oars).

fem. .† = *femm..*

fémmi-na [L. *femina*, woman], F.: female (woman); wife†; socket. **-náccio**, *disp.* of *-na*. **-nèlla**, F.: *dim.* of *-na*; eyelet, eye (for book); false shoots (of pruned vine). **femminé-sco**, ADJ.: (*poet.*) feminine; effeminate†. **-nescaménte**, ADV.: like a woman. **-nésco**, ADJ.: womanish, effeminate. **-nétta**, *dim.* of *-na*. **-néz-za**†, F.: femininity. **-nièra**†, F.: woman's apartment; PL.: women-folks. **-níle**, ADJ.: feminine. **-nilménte**, ADV.: femininely. **-nilità**†, F.: effeminacy. **-níno**, ADJ.: feminine; effeminate†. **-nóccia**, *car. aug.* of *-na*. **-núccia**, **-núzza**†, *disp.* of *-na*.

fe-morále, ADJ.: femoral. ||**fè-more** [L. *-mur*], M.: thigh-bone.

fen-dènte, M.: cut (with sabre, etc.). ||**fèn-dere** [L. *findere*], IRR.§; TR.: split (cleave); cut (as air, water); REFL.: crack, split (as stones, etc.). **-díbile**, ADJ.: cleavable. **-diménto**†, M.: fissure, split. **-ditóio**, M.: cutting-block for quill-pens; splitting-blade of grafting-knife. **-ditóre**, M., **-ditríce**, F.: splitter. **-ditúra**, F.: split (cleft, fissure).

§ Pret. *fendèi* or *fendètti*. Part. *fendúto* or *fèsso*.

feneratóre†, M.: usurer.

fenice [Gr. *phoînix*], F.: phœnix; (*fig.*) rare thing.

fenicòttero [Gr. *phoinikó-pteros*, red-winged], M.: flamingo.

feníle†, M.: hay-loft.

fenòmeno [Gr. *phainómenon* (root *pha*, shine)], M.: phenomenon.

fèra† = *fiera*.

ferá-ce [L. *-x* (root *fer*, BEAR)], ADJ.: FERtile. **-cità**, F.: fertility.

ferá-le [L. *-lis* (root *fer*, BEAR)], funereal (orig. pall-bearing); cf. Eng.† *feral*, funereal; ADJ.: funereal (deadly, dismal, sad). **-lménte**†1, ADV.: funereally.

feralménte†2, ADV.: FIERcely (cruelly).

ferentári [L.], M. PL.: light-armed Roman troops.

fèrere† = *ferire*.

ferètrio [L. *-trius* (root *fer*, BEAR)], ADJ.: *Giove* —, Jupiter Feretrius (to whom were BORNE trophies).

fèretro [L. *-trum* (root *fer*, BEAR)], M.: BIER.

fè-ria [L.], F.: holiday (Eng.† ferie); (*eccl.*) week-day (ordinary day): — *terza*, Tuesday. **-riále**, ADJ.: ferial; week-day; (*eccl.*) ordinary. **-rialménte**, ADV.: commonly. **-riáre**, INTR.: make holiday, have vacation. **-riáto**, M.: vacation (esp. of courts); ADJ.: holiday.

feridóre = *feritore*.

feríg̃no†1, ADJ.: coarse-grained (bread).

feríg̃no†2, ADJ.: ferine (savage).

feriménto [*-rire*], M.: wounding.

fe-rinità, F.: ferocity (savageness, cruelty). ||**-ríno** [L. *-rus*, wild beast], ADJ.: ferine (savage; FERocious).

fe-ríre [L.], TR.: wound: *non so dove voglia andar a* , I do not know what he aims at. **-ríto**, ADJ.: wounded. **-ríta**1, F.: wound (hurt).

ferità 2 [-rime], F.: savagery (cruelty).
feri-tóia, F.: embrasure: loophole. **-tóre** [-re], M., **-tríce**, F.: assailant.
fér-ma, F.: enlistment: confirmation†; agreement†; assurance†. **-máglio**, M.: clasp, hasp. **-maménte**, ADV.: firmly (tenaciously). **-maménto**†, M.: FIRMness; confirmation (fortification): stoppage; firmament. **-mánza**†, F.: confirmation; bail. ‖**-máre** [L. *firmare*, make FIRM], TR.: stop, stay, impede; contract (as service, engagement of actor, singer): fasten; cook slightly (to prevent taint): attract (*Roma -ma per la sua grandezza*); lock†; establish†; resolve†; strengthen†; fix†; REFL.: stop; linger; stay; fortify one's self; wed†; endure†: — *l'animo*, make up one's mind; decide; — *la voce sopra una parola*, emphasize a word. **-máta**, F.: stop (halt; pause); camp (of soldiers). **-matína**, *dim.* of *-mata*. **-máto**, ADJ.: stopped; written; M.†: agreement. **-matúra**, F.: stoppage; clasp.
fermen-táre, INTR.: ferment. **-tatívo**, ADJ.: fermentative. **-tazióne**, F.: fermentation. ‖**fermén-to** [L. *-tum*], M.: ferment (yeast).
fer-mézza, F.: firmness (steadiness); clasp (of necklace, etc.); stability†; security†; ratification†; rigorousness† (of laws); assurance†. **-mezzína**, *car. dim.* of *-mezza*. **-míno**, *car. dim.* of *-mo*. ‖**férmo** [L. *firmus*], ADJ.: FIRM; (fixed; constant, resolute); still; sound† (in mind); M: certainty; steadiness; agreement; ADV.†: firmly, certainly: — *là*, sentinel's call, steady there! (to angry person): *cane da* —, setter-dog; *canto* —, plain (Gregorian) chant; *dare un — a una cosa*, establish certain conditions; *dare un — alle carni*, cook to prevent taint; *s'era* —, he had stopped; *notte -ma*, deep night; *per* —, certainly, "sure thing"; *punto* —, period (punctuation); *tenere il* —, hold to opinions strongly; *terra -ma*, continent; *viso* —†, serious, resolute face; — *in posta*, general delivery, poste restante.
fèro†, *poet.* for *fiero*.
fe-róce [L. *-rox*], ADJ.: ferocious; fierce (cruel); fiery; (*joc.*) severe. **-rocemén-te**, ADV.: ferociously; fiercely (cruelly). **-ròcia**, **-rocità**, **-rocitáde**†, **-rocitáte**†, F.: ferocity.
ferrác-cia [*ferro*], F.: sting-ray (fish); gilder's crucible; gold-leaf box. **-cio**, M.: worthless iron.
ferragósto [L. *feriæ Augusti*], M.: first day of August.
fer-raiétto, *dim.* of *-raio*. ‖**-ráio** [*-ro*], M.: ironworker, smith: *fabbro* —, ironworker, locksmith, blacksmith.
ferra-iolíno, M.: strip of silk or cloth worn by priests about their necks and hanging behind. ‖**-i(u)òlo** 1 [?], M.: large cloak; anything large, bothersome: *fare un* — (said of hunters who kill game instantly); (*vulg.*) *accidente a* —, apoplectic stroke. **-i(u)oláccio**, *disp. dim.* of *-i(u)olo*.
ferra-iuòlo† 2 [*ferro*], M.: locksmith. **-ménta**, F., **-ménti**, **-ménto**†, M.: hardware, ironmongery.
ferrána [*farragine*], F.: maslin (mixture of grasses).
fer-ráre, TR.: iron (bind with iron); shoe (a horse); shackle†; nail†; REFL.†: arm (for war): *lasciarsi* —, be under another's thumb. **-raréccia**, F.: coarse hardware; implements. **-ráta**, F.: iron grating; prison†; hoof-print. **-ráto**, ADJ.: ironed; shod; iron†; resolute†: *strada -rata*, railroad; — *a diaccio* (*ghiaccio*), (fig. of horses), hard-bitted; not afraid of misfortune, (of people) very rich†. **-ratóre**†, M.: FARRIER. **-ratúra**, F.: ironwork; implements; horse-shoeing (FARRIERY). **-ravècchio**, M.: old iron-seller, second-hand dealer. **-razzòlo**, M.: ironworker. **fèr-reo**, ADJ.: (*lit.*) iron; robust. **-rería**†, F.: implements. **-rettíno**, *dim.* of *-retto*. **-rétto**, M., *dim.* of *-ro*: small brace; ADJ.: gray (of hair). **-riáta**, F.: iron grating. **-rièra**, F.: smithy; iron-works; blacksmith-pouch; iron-mine†. **-rigno**, ADJ.: ferreous (esp. of colour or taste); iron-gray; obstinate†; strong†. **-ríno**, *dim.* of *-ro*. ‖**fèr-ro** [L. *-rum*], M.: iron; implement (tool, lit. and fig.); weapon; flat-iron; curling-iron; horseshoe; PL.: shackles; skates: *mettere a — e fuoco un paese*, destroy everything; *venire a' ferri*, come to conclusions. **-rolíno**, *dim.* of *-ro*. **-rovía**, F.: railroad. **-roviário**, ADJ.: railroad. **-rugíneo**, ADJ.: ferruginous (rust-coloured). **-ruginosità**, F.: ferruginosity. **-ruginóso**, ADJ.: ferruginous (containing iron in solution). **-ruminaménto**†, M.: solder. **-ruminá-re**†, TR.: solder, unite. **-ruzzíno**, *dim.* of *-ruzzo*. **-rúzzo**, *disp. dim.* of *-ro*: *adoprare, aguzzare i* —, sharpen the wits.
fèrti-le [L. *-lis* (root *fer-*, BEAR)], ADJ.: fertile. **-lità**, F.: fertility. **-lizzáre**, TR.: fertilize. **-lménte**, ADV.: fruitfully.
ferúcola†, F.: little wild beast; disgusting insect.
fèrula [L.], F.: ferule; umbelliferous plant.
ferúta†, F.: wound.
fer-vènte, ADJ.: fervent; boiling. **-venteménte**, ADV.: fervently. **-ventézza**†, **-vènza**, F.: fervency.

fèr-vere [L.], DEFECT.§; INTR.: be fervent (evince ardour, burn); boil†. **-vézza†**, F.: heat. **-vidaménte**, ADV.: fervidly. **-vidézza**, M.: fervor. **fèr-vido**, ADJ.: fervid (ardent). **-vóre**, M.: heat; fervor (zeal); boiling†. **-voríno**, M.: mild reproof; short, fervid speech. **-voresaménte**, ADV.: fervently (warmly). **-voróso**, ADJ.: fervent (zealous).

§ Ind.: Pres. 3. *fèr-ve*; 6. *-vono*. Impf. *fervéva*. Subj.: Impf. *fervèsse*. Part. Pres. *fervènte*. Ger. *fervèndo*.

fèr-za†, F.: whip-lash: — *del sole*, sun's heat. **-záre†**, TR.: whip.

fescen-níno [city *Fescennio*], ADJ.: fescennine (referring to obscene Latin poetry).

fèscera†, F.: (*bot.*) bryony.

féssi†, IMPERF. SUBJ. of *fare*.

fés-so [part. of *fendere*], ADJ.: split (cracked); M.: FISSURE, crack; cleft. **-solíno**, *dim.* of *-so*. **-súra**, F.: fissure (split); narrow passage. **-suríua**, *dim.* of *-sura*.

fè-sta [L. (sc. *dies*, day)], F.: holiday; FEAST; rejoicing (gaiety); *far — a*, feast; welcome; *far la — a*, slaughter (animals); rot; eat; *far — a una cosa*, enjoy a thing much; *far la — a una cosa*, consume a thing; *conciare* (*accomodare*) *per il dì delle -ste*, give a drubbing, thrash. **-stáccia**, *disp.* of *-sta*. **-staiòlo**, M.: (*eccl.*) feast-director. **-stánte**, ADJ.: joyful. **-stánza†**, F.: festival; joy. **-stáre**, TR., INTR.: feast. **-steggévole†**, ADJ.: festive (joyful). **-steggiaménto**, M.: rejoicing; fête. **-steggiáre**, TR.: celebrate (events); feast. **-steggiánte**, ADJ.: feasting. **-steggiáto**, ADJ.: feasted, fêted. **-steggiatóre**, M., **-steggiatríce**, F.: feaster; celebrator. **-stéggio†**, M.: rejoicing. **-steréccio**, ADJ.: festal (holiday). **-stévole**, ADJ.: festive (merry). **-stevolézza**, F.: festivity (rejoicing). **-stevolménte**, ADV.: festively (joyfully).

festichíno, ADJ.: bright green.

fe-sticciòla, *dim.* of *-sta*. **-sticina**, *car. dim.* of *-sta*. **-stína**, *car. dim.* of *-sta* (esp. religious).

festi-nanménte†, ADV.: quickly. **-nánza†**, F.: haste. **-náre†**, INTR.: hasten. **-nataménte†**, ADV.: quickly (hurriedly). **-naziône†**, F.: haste. ‖**festí-no†**1, ADJ.: quick (hasty, Eng. festinate†).

fe-stíno2 [*-sta*], M.: entertainment; evening party. **-stivaménte**, ADV.: festively. **-stività**, F.: church festival; joyous welcome. **-stívo**, ADJ.: festal; *abiti -stivi*, Sunday clothes. **-stòccia**, F.: kind welcome. **-stoncíno**, *car. dim.* of *-stone*. **-stóne**, M.: FESTOON (garland). **-stosaménte**, ADV.: festively (joyfully). **-stosétto**, ADJ.: rather festive. **-stóso**, ADJ.: festive (joyful).

festú-ca [L.], F., **-co**, M.: FESCUE; bit of straw; mote.

festúccia, *dim.* of *festa*.

fe-tènte, ADJ.: stinking. ‖**fè-tere†** [L. *-tidus*, stinking], INTR.: stink.

fe-tíccio [Port. *-tiço*, magic], M.: fetich. **-ticísmo**, M.: fetichism.

feti-daménte, ADV.: fetidly. ‖**fèti-do**, **-dóso** [L. *fœtidus*], ADJ.: fetid; *assa —*, assafœtida. **-dúme**, M.: mass of corruption.

fèto [L. *-tus*], M.: fœtus.

fetóre [L. *-tor*], M.: fetor (disgusting smell).

fét-ta [? L. *vitta*, band], M.: cut, slice (us'ly of food): *fare* (*tagliare*) *a -te*, cut up; massacre. **-tína**, **-tolína**, *dim.* of *-ta*. **-tóna**, **-tóne**, *aug.* of *-ta*. **-túccc**, **-túccia**, *disp. dim.* of *-ta*. **-tuccína**, *dim.* of *-ta*.

feu-dále, ADJ.: feudal. **-dalísmo**, M.: feudalism. **-dalità**, F.: feudality. **-datário**, M.: feudatory (vassal). ‖**fèu-do** [l. L. *-dum* (OHG. *feod*)], M.: FEUD (allotment of land, fief); FEE for same.

fèz [fr. Turk], M.: fez (Turkish cap).

fiába [*fabula*], F.: fib; story.

fiác-ca, F.: languidness; low act (meanness); noise (disturbance†). **-cábile**, ADJ.: breakable. **-ca-còllo**, M.: dangerous person; *a —*, in break-neck manner. **-caménte**, ADV.: flabbily; wearily (weakly). **-caménto**, M.: fracture (break, rupture). **-cáre**, TR.: break; fracture; weaken; debilitate. **-cáto**, ADJ.: broken. **-catóio**, ADJ.: breaking. **-catúra**, F.: fracture (breaking). **-chétto**, ADJ.: rather tired. **-chézza**, F.: weakness; lassitude; imbecility. ‖**fiác-co** [L. *flaccus*, flabby, flap-eared (? root, *frac-*, break)], ADJ.: FLACCID; weak (weary); M.: bruising; drubbing; ruin†; ravage†.

fiácco-la [L. *facula* (dim. of *fax*)], F.: torch. **-létta**, **-lína**, *dim.* of *-la*. **-lóna**, *aug.* of *-la*.

fiac-cóna, F.: exhaustion: lassitude. ‖**-cóne**, ADJ.: *aug.* of *-co*; M.: languid person.

fiadóne†, M.: honeycomb.

fiála†, F.: phial.

fiále†, F.: honeycomb.

fiám-ma [L. *flamma*], F.: FLAME; passion; sweetheart; forked pennant. **-mánte**, ADJ.: flaming (fiery red). **-máre**, INTR.: flame (burn). **-ma=sálsa†**, F.: itching (of salt rheum). **-máta**, F.: bonfire. **-matèlla**, **-matína**, *dim.* of *-ma*. **-meggiáre**, INTR.: flame, shine;

sparkle; glitter. **-meggiánte**, ADJ.: flaming. **-mèlla**, *dim.* of *-ma.* **-mésco**, ADJ.: flaming; bright. **-métta, -mettína**, *dim.* of *-ma.* **-miferáio**, M.: match-seller. **-mífero**, M.: friction-match; ADJ.†: flammiferous; kindling; burning. **-mína, -molína**, *car. dim.* of *-ma.* **-mórе†**, M.: inflammation.

fian-cáre, TR.: strengthen the sides of (arches, etc.), flank (guard the flank of). **-cáta**, F.: spur-blow (in flank); cutting saying; side (of building or piece of furniture); (*nav.*) broadside. **-cheggiaménto**, M.: reinforcement. **-cheggiáre**, TR.: reinforce; flank (stand alongside). **-cheggiánte**, ADJ.: flanking. **-cheggiáto**, ADJ.: flanked. **-chétta**, F.: waist (of garments). ‖**fián-co** [? L. *flaccus*, soft, viz., part], M.: FLANK, side. **-cúto†**, ADJ.: long or broad-sided.

fiá-sca, F.: (large, short-necked) FLASK. **-scáccia, -scáccio**, *disp. aug.* of *-sca.* **-scáia**, F., **-scáio**, M.: flask-seller or re-coverer. **-scheggiáre**, INTR.: fail (in an undertaking or play): buy by the bottle†. **-schétta**, F.: small flask; powder-flask. **-schettería**, F.: wine-shop. **-schettína**, *dim.* of *-schetta.* **-schettíno**, *dim.* of *-schetto.* **-schétto, -schíno**, *dim.* of *sco.* ‖**fiá-sco** [l. L. *flasco* (L. *vas*, vase)], M.: (long-necked) FLASK; *far* —, make a failure (vase-maker, who spoils glass-lump, makes bottle of it). **-scóne**, *aug.* of *-sco.* **-scúccio**, *disp.* of *-sco.*

fiáta [? ak. to *vice*], F.: time; *spesse fiate*, many times.

fia-taméntо†, M.: breathing. **-táre**, INTR.: breathe; puff†. **-táta**, F.: bad breath. **-tíno**, *car. dim.* of *-to.* ‖**fiá-to** [L. *flatus* (*flare*, blow)], M.: breath; wind; strength: *non mangio* —, I eat nothing; *strumenti a* —, wind-instruments; *a un* —, *d' un* —, in a moment; in a breath; very quickly; *un* —, a trifle; *rimetter il* — *in corpo*, encourage; cheer up.

fiátolo†, M.: VASSAL.

fiató-re†, M.: FETIDNESS. **-'so†**, ADJ.: FETID.

fíb-bia [L. *-ula* (*figere*, FIX)], F.: buckle. **-biáio†**, M.: buckle-maker. **-biáre†**, TR.: buckle; fasten. **-biétta, biettína**, *car. dim.* of *-bia.* **-bióna**, *aug.* of *bia.* **-bióne**, M.: harness-buckle.

fí-bra [L.], F.: fibre; force; will. **-brílla**, F.: (*bot.*) fibrilla; fibril. **-brína**, F.: fibrine. **-brosità**, F.: fibrousness. **-bróso**, ADJ.: fibrous.

fíbula [L.], F.: fibula.

fí-ca [*-co*], F.: fig†; female pudenda: *far le -che*, show contempt (by pointing at with the thumb between index and long finger); affront. **-cáccio**, *disp.* of *-ca.* **-cáia†**, F.: fig-tree. **-c=álbo**, M.: kind of fig. **-cáto**, ADJ.: full of figs or fig-trees; M.: fig-cake.

fic-cábile, ADJ.: that can be fixed. **-caménto†**, M.: thrusting in; setting. **-ca=náso**, M.: busybody (meddler; inquisitive person). ‖**-cáre** [L. *figere*], TR.: drive in; (FIX, set); stick in; make believe; INTR.: meddle; REFL.: intrude one's self: *-carsi in testa* (or *nella mente*), be obstinate; persist. **-catúra†**, F.: thrusting in; (fixing).

fiche-réto†, -'to†, M.: fig-plantation.

fic-chíno [*-care*], M.: intruder (meddler).

fí-co [L. *-cus*], M.: fig; fig-tree; grimace; compliment: *cercare de' -chi in vetta*, puzzle over difficulties; *far* —, miss, fail. **-co=sécco**, pl. *fichisecchi*, M.: dried fig. **-cóso**, ADJ.: grimacing; affected, complaining.

fi-da†, F.: security; safe-conduct; pasture. **-dánza**, F.: faith, CONFIDENCE. **-danzáre**, TR.: betroth; guarantee†. **-danzáta**, F., **danzáto**, M.: betrothed. **-dáre** [L. *-dere*], TR.: trust; CONFIDE: — *i bestiami*, guarantee pasture for cattle; — *de' denari*, give credit for money; *-darsi*, trust one's self; *-darsi di*, trust in; rely upon. **-dáta†**, F.: oath of allegiance. **-dataménte†**, ADV.: confidently. **-datézza**, F.: trustiness. **-dáto**, ADJ.: trusted; faithful. ‖**-de. .** [L. *-des*, FAITH]: **-de=comméssо**, M.: deed of trust. **-de=commissário**, M.: trustee. **-de=iussióne** [L. *iussio*, command], F.: security (surety). **-de=iussóre**, M.: guarantor (surety). **-lità†**, F.: fidelity. **-del. .** = *fedel. .*† **-do** [L. *-dus*], ADJ.: FAITHful. **-dúcia**, F.: CONFIDENCE; trust. **-duciále†**, ADJ.: fiducial. **-ducialménte**, ADV.: fiducially, confidently. **-duciariaménte**, ADV.: fiducially. **-duciário**, ADJ., M.: fiduciary. **-duciosaménte**, ADV.: confidently. **-ducióso**, ADJ.: confident.

fièbo-le†, ADJ.: FEEBLE. **-lézza†**, F.: feebleness.

fiè-dere†, TR.: strike; wound. **-ditóre†**, M.: striker.

fièle [L. *fel*], M.: GALL (bile; malignity, rancour); jaundice.

fie-náia, ADJ.: pertaining to hay: *falce* —, scythe. **-níle**, M.: hayloft. ‖**fiè-no** [L. *fenus*], M.: hay; forage. **-nóso**, ADJ.: full of hay (as grain, straw).

fièra 1 [L. *fera*, wild], F.: wild beast.

fiè-ra 2 [L. *feria*, feast], F.: large FAIR; market; gift bought at fair: — *fredda*, poor fair; *è* — *rotta*, it's a ruined affair. **-raiòlo**, M.: seller at fairs.

fie-raménte, ADV.: fiercely. **-rézza**,

F.: intrepidity; spiritedness (liveliness). **||fiè-ro** [L. *ferus*, wild], ADJ.: FEROcious†; FIERCE; intrepid; severe; vivacious (lively; spirited). **-rúcola**† 1, F.: little wild beast.

fierúco-la† 2 [*fiera* 1], F.: poor little fair. **-léna**, F.: torch-lantern (at fairs).

fièvo-le [L. *flebilis*], ADJ.: FEEBLE, weak. **-lézza**, F.: feebleness, debility. **-lménte**, ADV.: feebly (faintly).

fífa†, F.: lapwing.

fíggere, fígere† [L. *figere*], IRR.§; TR.: FIX; drive in; determine: *-gersi in capo*, be obstinate; — *baci*, imprint kisses.

§ Pret. *fis-si; -sero.* Part. *fisso* or *fitto.*

fí-glia, F.: daughter. **-gliáre**, TR.: bring forth (young). **-gliástra**, F., **-gliástro**, M.: step-child. **-gliáta**, F.: litter (of dogs, etc.). **-gliatíccia**, ADJ.: prolific (of beasts). **-gliatúra**, F.: delivery; birth; breeding time. **||fí-glio** [L. *-lius*], M.: son (boy; child): *-gli della terra*, (legendary) giants; *-gli della luce*, (*eccl.*) God's elect. **-gliòccia**, F.: god-daughter. **-glioccíno**†, **-gliòccio**, M.: godson. **-gliòla**, *dim.* of *-glia*. **-glioláme**, M.: flock of sons; plant-shoots. **-gliolánza**, F.: progeny. **-gliolétto**, **-gliolíno**, *dim.* of *-gliolo*. **-gliòlo**, M.: *dim.* of *-glio; esser fuori di -glioli*, be past the age of conception; *entrare in -glioli*, begin to have children; *buon* —, good-natured fellow. **-glioléna**, F., **-glioló-ne**, M.: big, fat child. **-gliolúccia**, **-glioláccio**, *disp. dim.* of *-gliola*, *-gliola*. **-gliuòla** = *-gliola*. **-gliuoláccio**†, = *-gliolaccio;* filiation. **-gliuolággio**†, M.: filiation.

figménto†, M.: figment; fiction.

fignere† = *fingere*.

fignoláre† = *frignare*.

fignu-olo [OHG. *fane*], M.: felon; boil. **-lóso**, ADJ.: having boils.

figu-lína [L. vessel (*fingere*, form)], F.: pottery-making. **-líno**, ADJ.: ceramic.

figu-lo†, M.: potter.

figú-ra [L. (*fingere*, form)], F.: figure; body; shape; face; portrait; statue; model; type; character (in novel); face-card: *far* —, appear well; dance-figure; *far buona* —, distinguish one's self; keep one's obligations; *far la* — *di*, have appearance of; *poniam* —†, let us suppose, for example. **-rábile**, ADJ.: figurable. **-rabilità**, F.: figurability. **-ráccia**, *disp.* of *-ra*. **-ráccio**, *disp.* of *-ro*. **-rále**†, ADJ.: figurative. **-ralménte**†, ADV.: figuratively. **-raménto**†, M.: figuration; figure; representation. **-ránte**, ADJ.: figuring; M., F.: (*theat.*) figurante. **-ráre**, TR.: figure, represent (in art); symbolize; resemble; INTR.: appear; feign; REFL.: imagine. **-ráto**, ADJ.: figured; represented (in art); figurative (of language): *canto* —, chant with full score music. **-rataménte**, **-rativaménte**, ADV.: figuratively. **-ratívo**, ADJ.: figurative; mystical. **-ratóre**, M., **-ratríce**, F.: figurer; former. **-razióne**†, F.: figuration. **-reggiáre**, INTR.: be rhetorical, use figures of speech. **-rétta**, *dim.* of *-ra*. **-rettína**, *car. dim.* of *-retta*. **-rína**, F.: *dim.* of *-ra;* statuette. **-rináio**, M.: image-vender. **-ríno**, M.: fashion-plate; dandy. **-rísta**, M.: figure-painter. **figú-ro**, M.: bad, ugly person. **-róna**, *aug.* of *-ra*. **-róne**, *disp. aug.* of *-ra*. **-rúccia**, *disp.* of *-ra*.

fí-la [L. *-lum*], F.: file (row, suit): *alla* (or *di*)—, consecutively. **-lábile**, ADJ.: that may be spun. **-láccc**, **-láccia**, **-láccica**†, F. PL.: threads, ravellings. **-lacciòso**, ADJ.: likely to ravel. **-lacciòne**, M.: sort of fish-line. **-la=òro**, M.: gold or silver wire-drawer. **-laménto**, M.: filament, fibre. **-lamentóso**, ADJ.: filamentous. **-lánda**, F.: silk-spinnery. **-landáia**, F.: silk-spinner. **-lándra**, F.: worms in hawks; marine plants (attaching to ships).

filan-tropía, F.: philanthropy. **-tropicaménte**, ADV.: philanthropically. **-tròpico**, ADJ.: philanthropic. **||filán-tropo** [Gr. *phil-ánthropos*, friend of man], M.: philanthropist.

fi-laráta, F.: long row. **-láre** 1 [*-la*], M.: row (of plants, teeth, houses, etc.). **||-láre** 2 [*-lo*], TR.: spin; wire-draw; spin out (discourse); pay out (cable); shed (blood); INTR.: leak (as casks); rope (as liquids): —*grosso*, be prodigal or unscrupulous; — *sottile*, be shrewd. **-larétto**, **-laríno**, M.: *dim.* of *-re* 1; sandstone strata.

filarmònico [Gr. *phílos*, loving, *harmonía*, harmony]; M.: music-lover; ADJ.: philharmonic.

fila-stròcca [*fila*], F.: rigmarole. **-taménte** [*-lo*], ADV.: as if spun (of speech, excuses). **fila-tèssa**, F.: file; rigmarole. **-tíccio**, M.: coarse silk (drawn from hatched cocoons). **||filá-to** [*-re* 2], ADJ.: spun; M.: thread: *il* — *de' ragnateli*, spider's web. **-tóio**, M.: spinning-wheel; candle-wick machine; spinning-room; spinning-mill. **-tóra**, F.: spinning-girl. **-tóre**, M.: **-tríce**, F.: spinner.

filat-tèra, F., **-tèrio** [Gr. *phúlax*, guard], M.: PHYLACTery; amulet.

fi-latúra [*-lare* 2], F.: spinning. **-lettáre**, TR.: stripe (in weaving); insert (in sewing). **-lettatúra**, F.: striping; insertion. **-lettíno**, *dim.* of *-letto*. **-lét-**

to, M.: *car. dim.* of *-lo*; (fowler's) net-line; snaffle; fillet (of beef); ligament (of tongue, etc.); fine wire (holding gem in setting); bezel (of watch, etc.).
filiá-le [L. *filius*, son], ADJ.: filial. **-lménte**, ADV.: filially. **-zióne**, F.: filiation.
filibustière [Sp. *-ter* (Eng. *freebooter*)], M.: filibuster (pirate).
filice† = *felice*.
fi-lièra [*filo*], F.: wire-drawing iron. **-liffórme**, ADJ.: filiform.
filig-gine [L. *fuligo*], F.: soot. **-ginóso**, ADJ.: fuliginous (sooty).
fi-ligrána [*-lo*], F.: filigree. **-ligranáto**, ADJ.: filigree-like. **-líno**, *dim.* of *-lo*.
filip-pica [*-po*], F.: philippic (invective). **-píno**, ADJ.: oratorian; M.: Oratorian monk (order founded by Philip Neri). ‖**filip-po** [*Filippo*, Philip], M.: silver coin (with head of King Philip).
fí-lo, pl. *-li* or *-la* [L. *-lum*], M.: thread; string; wire; series (of ideas, etc.); edge (of sword, etc.); bit; particle; long, narrow loaf; PL.: lint: — — or *di* —, at all costs; *fil* —, trickling (of liquids); — *dell' acqua*, current of the stream; — *d' acqua*, tiny stream of water; *andare per il — della sinopia*, 'chalk walk,' act or speak to the purpose; *battere il* — (or — *della sinopia*), snap the chalk-line; *esser un* —, be a rail (very lean); *esser in* —, (of seasons) be well advanced, (of persons) well-disposed; — *d' erba*, spear of grass; *far le -la*, be ropy (liquids, cheese); — *di legno*, grain of wood; *mandare* (or *mettere*) *a — di spada*, put to the sword; *mettere uno in* (or *sul*) *suo*† —, put one on his right road; *per* —, exactly; — *delli reni*, spine.
filodrammático [Gr. *phílos*, loving, *drâma*, play], M.: amateur actor; ADJ.: dramatic (society).
filògo = *filologo*.
filolíno, *dim.* of *filo*.
filo-logía, F.: philology. **-lògico**, ADJ.: philological. ‖**filò-logo** [Gr. *philo-lógos*, word-lover], M.: philologist.
filo-mèla, **-mèna** [Gr. *Philomḗla* (who was changed to a nightingale)], F.: (*poet*). nightingale.
fi-londènte [*filo*, *dente*], M.: embroidery canvas (one thread to each loom-tooth). **-lóne**, M.: *aug.* of *-lo*; vein (of ore, water, etc.). **-lóso**, ADJ.: thread-like.
filòso-fa, F.: female philosopher; would-be wise woman. **-fále**, ADJ.: philosophic: *pietra* —, philosopher's stone. **-fánte**, *disp.* of *-fo*. **-fáre**, INTR.: philosophize. -f... ro, *disp.* of *-fo*. **-feggiáre**, INTR.: ...e. **-feccaménte**, ADV.: so... **-físco**, ADJ.: sophistical. ...: female doctor of philosophy. ...F. or *disp. dim.* of *-fo*. **-fía**, F.: philosophy; (*typ.*) small pica. **filosòfica** (*alla* —), ADV.: philosophically. **-ficáre**, INTR.: philosophize. **-ficaménte**, ADV.: philosophically. **filosò-fico**, ADJ.: philosophic. **-físno**, *disp.* or *iron.* of *-fo*. ‖**filòso-fo** [Gr. *philó-sophos*, friend of wisdom], M.: philosopher. **-fóne**, *aug.* of *-fo*. **-fúccio**, **-fúzzo**, *disp. dim.* of *-fo*.
filosomía [*fisonomia*], F.: (*vulg.*) physiognomy.
fil-tráre, TR.: filter. ‖**-tro** 1 [l. L. *-trum* (Ger. *-z*)], M.: filter; filter paper.
filtro 2 [Gr. *phíltron*], M.: philter.
filugèllo [? L. *filucellum*], M.: silkworm.
filunguèllo = *fringuello*.
fil-úzzo, *dim.* of *filo*. ‖**fil-za** [l. L. *-itium* (L. *-um*, thread)], F.: row, string (of things); pamphlet; basting.
fim-bria [L.], F.: fringe (hem, border). **-briáto**, ADJ.: fringed (bordered).
fí-mo, **-mo**† [L. *-mus*, dung], M.: manure.
fin = *fino*.
finá-le [*fine*], ADJ.: final (definitive); M.: (*mus.*) finale; (*typ.*) tailpiece: *prigione* —, life imprisonment. **-lità**, F.: finality. **-lménte**, ADV.: finally. **-ménte**, ADV.: finely.
finán-za [Fr. *-ce*], F.: finance. **-ziariaménte**, ADV.: financially. **-ziário**, ADJ.: financial. **-zière**, M.: financier.
fi-náre†, INTR.: finish (cease): *far* —, kill. **-nattantochè** *-é*, [or *fin a tanto che*], ADV.: until, as long as. ‖**-ne** [L. *-nis*], M., F.: end (extremity); M.: aim (intention); ADJ.: fine (minute, exact); superior; expert†; brave†: *alla* —, finally; *non lo fa per nessun* —, he does not do it for ulterior ends; *stare in* —, be dying. **-neménte**†, ADV.: finely.
finè-stra [L. *fenestra* (ROOT *fa-*, show)], F.: window; opening; breach; (*jest.*) eye: *fare una — sul tetto a uno*, get what has been denied by resorting to higher authority; secure that desired by another. **-stráccia**, *disp.* of *-stra*. **-stráta**, F.: 'window-slam' (in contempt); sun-burst. **-stráto**†, ADJ.: windowed; M.: row of windows. **-strèlla**, **-strétta**, **-stríno**, *car. dim.* of *-stra*. **-stríno**, *dim.* of *-stra*. **-stróne**, *aug.* of *-stra*. **-struccia**, *disp. dim.* of *-stra*.
fi-nétto [*-ne*], M.: fine wool cloth. **-nézza**, F.: fineness; excellence; politeness; finesse; artifice.
fingènte†, ADJ.: feigning. ‖**fin-gere** [L.], IRR.§; INTR.: FEIGN; TR.: simulate; dissimulate. **-giménto**†, M.: feint (deceit): **-gitóre**†, M.: feigner.

§ Pret. *fin-si*, *-se*; *-sero*. Part. *finto*.

fi-niènte†, ADJ.: finishing. **-niménto**, M.: finishing off, conclusion, end, finish, (last) ornament; jewelry set; service (of china, etc.); PL.: harness (of draught horses). **-ni=móndo**, M.: end of the world; final destruction. **-níre**, TR.: finish (end, complete; use up); kill; INTR.: end (cease); die; REFL.: be out of patience: *sentirsi* —, be famished or used up. **-nità†**, F.: end; death. **-nitaménte**, ADV.: finitely. **-nitézza**, F.: perfection. **-nítimo**, ADJ.: adjoining; M.: bordering countries. **-níto**, ADJ.: finished; bounded; perfected; hopeless; tired out. **-nitúra**, F.: end; finishing touches. ||**fí-no** [L. *-nis*, end], PREP.: until; as far as; ADJ.†: fine, subtle; skilful; brave: *fin a luglio*, until July; *fin anche*, even; *fin a (tanto) che*, as long as; *fin che* or *finchè*, until; *fin da*, since, from; *fin allora* or *fin d'allora*, even then, then; *fin a qui*, until now, to this point; *fino a ora* or *finora*, hitherto; until now; *fin da quando?* since when? *fin da*, since.

finoc-chiétto, **-chiettíno**, *dim.* of *-chio*. ||**finòc-chio** [L. *fœniculum*], M.: FENNEL. **-'chi**, INTERJ.: zounds! good heavens! **-chióna**, F.: fennel-sausage. **-chióne**, *aug.* of *-chio*.

finóra = *fino a ora*: until now.

finsi, PRET. of *fingere*.

fin-ta [*-to*], F.: FEINT; feigned blow; false-pocket; pocket-flap. **-táccio**, *disp.* of *-to*. **-taménte**, ADV.: deceitfully.

fintantochè = *fin a tanto che*.

fin-tíno, *dim.* of *-to*; half-wig. ||**fín-to**, PART. of *-gere*: feigned; false. **-zióne**, F.: FICTION; feint; invention.

fio [OHG. *feod*], M.: FIEF†: *pagare il* —, pay dear (for).

fiocággine [*-co*], F.: hoarseness.

fiòc-ca, ADJ., F. of *-co*; F.: instep of shoe or foot (i.e., place for the bow-knot). **-cáre**, INTR.: fall in flakes; abound. **-cáto**, PART. of *-care*; ADJ.: adorned with bows. **-chettáto**, ADJ.: adorned with little bows. **-chétto**, *car. dim.* of *-co*. ||**fiòc-co** [L. *floccus*], M.: bow-knot (bow); flock (lock of wool); flake (of snow); tassel†; tuft†: *co' -chi*, in pomp; of excellence (tip-top, of high grade); *in -chi*, richly and affectedly dressed. **-cóso†**, ADJ.: flaky; hoary.

fio-chétto, *dim.* of *-co*. **-chézza**, F.: hoarseness.

fiòcina [L. *fuscina* (ak. to *fork*)], F.: fish-spear; trident.

fiòcine [L. *floces*, dregs], M.: skins and seeds of grapes, etc.

fiòco [?], ADJ.: hoarse; weak (of sound); faint (of light).

fiónda [L. *funda*], F.: sling. **-tóre**, M.: slinger.

fio-ráia, F., **-ráio**, pl. *-rai*, M.: flower-seller. **-ralíso†** = *fiordaliso*. **-ráme**, F.: flowers (esp. painted or sculptured). **-r=cappúccio**, M.: larkspur. **-rdalíso** [Fr. *fleur de lis*], M.: fleur-de-lis. ||**fió-re** [L. *flos*], M.: FLOWER (flowering-plant; bloom; choicest part; virginity); mould (on wine); a particle (the least); PL.: clubs (at cards): *a — di*, at the level of (on the surface of); *— di latte*, cream; *— d' ogni mese*, marigold; *— di rame*, verdigris; *non piovve* —, it has not rained a bit; *se tu mi volessi un — di bene*, if you loved me a little; *— di zolfo*, flowers of sulphur. **-reggiáre**, M.: bloom, FLOURish. **-rellíno**, **-rèllo†**, M.: floweret. **-rènte**, ADJ.: flowering; flourishing. **-rentinaménte** (cf. *-rentino*), ADV.: in Florentine way. **-rentineggiáre**, INTR.: affect Florentine speech. **-rentinésco**, ADJ.: Florentine. **-rentinísmo**, M.: Florentine idiom. **-rentinità**, F.: Florentinism. **-rentíno** [*Firenze* (L. *Florentia*, "the flowering"), Florence], ADJ.: Florentine; M.: Florentine dialect: *alla -rentina*, in Florentine fashion. **-rettáre**, TR.: be extravagantly flowery. **-rétto**, M.: *dim.* of *-re*; (*mus.*) turn, grace-note; (*lit.*) choice passage; fencing foil (Eng.† floret); (dance) fleurett†; kind of sugar†. **-ricíno**, *car. dim.* of *-re*. **-ríno**, M.: florin. **-ríre**, INTR.: flower; flourish; scatter flowers. **-riscènte**, ADJ.: flowering; flourishing. **-rísta**, F. artificial-flower seller or maker; M.: flower-painter. **-ríta**, F.: flower decoration; flowers strewn before a procession. **-ritézza†**, F.: florescence. **-ríto**, ADJ.: flowered: *abito* —, new suit; *-rita truppa* picked troops. **-ritúra**, F.: flowering; flourishing. **-rrancíno** [*-r-rancio*], M.: gold-crested wren. **-r=ráncio**, M.: marigold. **-rúme**, M.: hay-chaff.

fiòsso [?], M.: narrow part of shoe-sole.

fiòtola†, F.: FLUTE.

fiot-táre, INTR.: gurgle; murmur; grumble; sob. **-tío**, M.: continual sobbing. ||**fiòt-to** [*flutto*], M.: surge, wave; crowd†; fury†. **-tòso†**, ADJ.: billowy (tempestuous).

fír-ma [*-mare*], F.: signature. **-maménto**, M.: firmament; foundation†.

firmáno [Pers. *-man*], M.: firman (edict).

firmá-re [L., strengthen], TR.: sign; approve. **-tário**, M.: signatory.

fisa. . = *fissa*. .

fisarmònica [Gr. *phûsa*, breath, *harmonía*, harmony], F.: harmonium.

fiscá-le [*fisco*], ADJ.: fiscal; M.: chancellor of exchequer: *avvocato* —, public prosecutor. **-leggiáre**, INTR.: be cross-examined. **-lménte**, ADV.: fiscally.

fiscèlla†, F.: wicker-basket (curd-basket).

fischi-áre [L. *fistula*, reed], INTR.: whistle; whiz (hiss); have buzzing in the ears; be penniless. **-áta**, F.: whistling; hissing. **-atóre**, M.: whistler; hisser. **-erèlla**, F.: bird-whistle; bird-decoying. **-ettáre**, INTR.: whistle in snatches. **-ettío**, M.: continual whistling. **-étto**, M.: little whistle. **físchi-o**, M.: whistling (whistle); hiss. **-ióne**, M.: whistling-duck; curlew.

fisciù [Fr. *fichu*], M., INVAR.: lady's neck-handkerchief.

fi-scína†, F.: wicker-basket. ‖**-sco** [L. *-scus*, basket, thin purse], M.: FISC; public treasury.

físi-ca [Gr. *phusikós* (*phúsis*, nature)], F.: physics; science of medicine. **-cággine†**, F.: sophistry; whim. **-cále**, ADJ.: physical. **-caménte**, ADV.: physically. **-cáre†**, INTR.: sophisticate; fancy. **-císmo†**, M.: physician. **físi-co**, ADJ.: physical, natural; M.: physicist. **-cóso**, ADJ.: sophistical; fanciful.

físima [Gr. *phusēma*], F.: caprice (fancy).

fisio-logía [Gr. *phusio-logía*, 'nature-discourse'], F.: physiology. **-lògico**, ADJ.: physiological. **fisiò-logo**, M.: physiologist. **-mánte** [Gr. *mántis*, diviner], M.: soothsayer by faces. **-nom.** . = *fisonom.* .

fiso [*fisso*], ADJ.: fixed; attentive; ADV.: fixedly.

fiso-gnomonía [Gr. *phusio-gnomonía*, 'nature-KNOWledge'], F.: physiognomy. **-nomía** [Gr. *nómos*, law], F.: physiognomy (countenance). **-nomísta**, M.: physiognomist.

fis-saménte, ADV.: fixedly. **-sáre**, TR.: FIX; stare at: *-sarsi sur una cosa*, think too intently on a thing. **-sáto**, ADJ.: fixed; M.: agreed thing. **-sazióne**, F.: fixation; "brown study"; obstinate, strange opinion. **-si**, PRET. of *figgere*. **-sióne†**, F.: fixing; driving in. ‖**-so**, PART. of *figgere*: fixed (firm; constant).

fistèlla†, F.: basket.

fistia. . = *fischia*. .

físto-la [L. *fistula*, reed], F.: reed-pipe; fistula. **-láre**, ADJ.: fistular (hollow); INTR.: fistulate. **-lazióne**, F.: becoming fistular. **físto-lo†**, M.: fistula. **-lóso†**, ADJ.: fistulous. **-tulatóre†**, M.: piper.

fít-ta, F.: mud-hole (sticky place, hole); crack; dig of the spade (spade's depth); (*disp.*) crowd (gang, herd; heap); dent. **-taiòlo**, M.: tenant farmer. **-taménte**, ADV.: thickly. **-tézza**, F.: thickness. **fít-tile**, ADJ.: fictile (of clay). **-tívo†**, ADJ.: fictive. **-tiziaménte**, ADV.: fictitiously. **-tízio**, ADJ.: fictitious. ‖**-to** 1, PART. of *figgere*; ADJ.: FIXED; transfixed; crowded; thick; close-woven; M.: rent (hire, "fixed price"); ADV.: quickly: *a capo* —, with head downwards; *dare a* —, rent; *di — meriggio*, at high noon; *di -ta notte*, at dead of night; *di — verno*, in depth of winter; *rincarare il* —, be indifferent to threats.

fitto† 2, PART. of *fingere*.

fittóne [Gr. *phutón*, plant], M.: tap-root.

fitton. .† = *piton*. .

fittuário†, M.: tenant farmer.

fiu-máccio, *disp.* of *-me*. **-mále†**, ADJ.: FLUMINAL. **-mána**, F.: swelled river. ‖**fiú-me** [L. *flumen*], M.: river; great flow (eloquence, tears, etc.). **-métto**, **-micèllo**, M.: rivulet. **-miciáttolo**, *disp. dim.* of *-me*. **-micíno**, *dim.* of *-me*.

fiu-táre [L. *flutare*], TR.: snuff (for odours); smell; scent; try†. **-ta-sepólcri**, M.: (*disp.*) antiquarian. **-táta**, F.: smelling (snuffing). **-tatína**, F.: gentle smelling. -'**to**, M.: sense of smell; act of smelling. **-tóne**, M.: tattler.

fizióne† = *finzione*.

flabèllo [L. *-llum*], M.: feather-fan in papal procession.

flacci-dità†, F.: flaccidity. **fláccido†**, ADJ.: flaccid.

flagel-laménto†, M.: flagellation. **-láre**, TR.: whip (scourge); inveigh against; REFL.: discipline one's self. **-latóre**, M., **-latríce**, F.: flagellator. **-lazióne**, F.: flagellation; picture representing scourging of Christ. **-létto**, M.: small whip. ‖**flagèl-lo** [L. *-lum*], M.: whip (scourge); scourging; calamity: *a* —, in great quantity.

flagi-ziosaménte†, ADV.: flagitiously. **-zióso†**, ADJ.: flagitious.

fla-gránte [L. *-grans* (root *flag-*, blaze)], ADJ.: flagrant (notorious). **-gráre†**, INTR.: be inflamed.

fla-mináto, M.: office of flamen. ‖**flámine** [L. *-men*], M.: flamen (Rom. priest). **-mínica**, F.: flamen's wife.

flanèlla [Fr. *-nelle*], F.: flannel.

flá-to [L. *-tus*, BLOWing], M.: flatus (wind from stomach, belch). **-tulènte**, ADJ.: flatulent. **-tulènza**, **-tuosità**, F.: flatulence. **-tuóso**, ADJ.: flatulent; windy.

flau-tíno, *car. dim.* of *-uto*. **-utísta**, M.: flutist. **fláuto**, M.: FLUTE: *a* —, obliquely (of cuts in timber).

flávo†, ADJ.: yellow.

flèbi-le [L. *-lis* (*flere*, weep)], ADJ.: mournful. **-lménte**, ADV.: mournfully.

fle-bítide, **-bíte** [Gr. *phlebîtis* (*phléps*, vein)], F.: inflammation of veins. **-botomáre†**, TR.: let blood. **-botomía**, F.: phlebotomy. **-bòtomo**, M.: phlebotomist.

flèm-ma [Gr. *phlégma*, inFLAMMation], F.: phlegm. **-maticaménte**, ADV.: phleg-

matically. **-maticità†**, F.: quality of phlegm; coolness. **-mático**, ADJ.: phlegmatic. **flèm-mone**, M.: phlegmon (tumour). **-monóso**, ADJ.: inflammatory.
fles-síbile [L. *flexibilis*], ADJ.: flexible. **-sibilità**, F.: flexibility. **-sióne**, F.: flexion. **flès-so†**, PART. of *flettere*. **-sóre**, ADJ.: flexor (muscle); M.: flexor muscle. **-suosità**, F.: flexibility. **-suóso**, ADJ.: flexuous. **-súra†**, F.: flexure.
flèto†, M.: weeping (tears).
flèttere†, IRR. (part. *flesso*); TR.: bend (curve).
flibustièro†, M.: filibuster.
flobotomía† = *flebotomia*.
flòccido†, ADJ.: flabby.
flo-r(e)ále [L. *flos*, FLOWER], ADJ.: floral; F. PL.: festival for Flora. **-ridaménte**, ADV.: floridly. **-ridézza**, F.: floridness. **flò-rido**, ADJ.: florid. **-rífero†**, ADJ.: floriferous. **-rilègio**, M.: anthology.
flo-scézza, F.: flaccidity. **-sciaménte**, ADV.: flaccidly. ‖**flò-scio** [L. *fluxus* (root *flu-*, FLOW)], ADJ.: soft (of paper or cloth), flaccid; weak (in character).
flòt-ta [L. *fluctus* (*flu-*, FLOW)], F.: fleet. **-taménto†**, M.: ship's gauge. **-táre†**, TR.: float. **-tíglia**, F.: flotilla.
flu-ènte, ADJ.: fluent; copious; bordering on a river (of towns)†; M.†: river. **-idézza**, **-idità**, F.: fluidity. **flú-ido**, ADJ.: fluid, flowing; M.: fluid. ‖**-íre** [L. *-ere*], INTR.: FLOW, run. **-óre**, M.: fluor-spar; gonorrhœa.
flus-síbile†, ADJ.: flowing, fusible. **-sibilità†**, F.: fluidity; fusibility. **-sióne**, F.: fluxion. ‖**-so** [L. *fluxus*, FLOWing], M.: flux; tide; tide-like movement; ADJ.†: transitory, fleeting.
flút-to [L. *fluctus* (root *flu-*, FLOW)], M.: surge (billow). **-tuaménto**, M.: fluctuation. **-tuáre**, INTR.: move as a wave; fluctuate (waver). **-tuánte**, ADJ.: fluctuating. **-tuazióne**, F.: fluctuation; uncertainty. **-tuóso**, ADJ.: billowy; tempestuous.
fluviále [L. *-alis* (root *flu-*, FLOW)], ADJ.: fluvial.
fòca [Gr. *phóke*], F.: (*zoöl.*) seal.
fo-cáccia [*-co*], F.: flat, hard cake: *render pane per —*, render like for like. **-cacciuòla**, *dim.* of *-caccio*. **-cáce†**, ADJ.: ardent (fiery). **-cáia**, F.: flint. **-cára**, F.: kindling instrument (of iron). **-caríno**, **-caròlo**, M.: fireman. **-cático**, M.: hearth-tax. **-cáto**, ADJ.: fiery red.
fóce [L. *fauces*, throat], F.: river-mouth; gorge; street-opening.
fo-cherèllo, *dim.* of *-co*. **-chista**, pl. *—ti*, M.: seller or maker of fire-works; fireman. **-chèttolo†**, M.: hearth; house. ‖**fò-co** [L. *-cus*], M.: fire; family; hearth; passion; poetic fire; caustic; acidity (of wine); funeral pile; focus: *arder uno a — lento*, cause one to pine away; *dare — al cannone*, fire a cannon; *dire* (*fare*) *cose di —*, say (do) strange, terrible things; *fare — nell' orcio*, hatch a plot secretly; *— di leone*, fierce fire; *mettere troppa carne a —*, have too many irons in the fire; *— di paglia*, fleeting ardour; *— salvatico*, ring-worm. **-coláre**, M.: fire-place; (*lit.*) = *-co*. **-colíno**, *car. dim.* of *-co*. **-cóne**, M.: *aug.* of *-co*; priming-pan; touch-hole. **-cosaménte**, ADV.: ardently. **-cosétto**, *dim.* of *-coso*. **-cóso**, ADJ.: fiery, ardent, amourous.
fòde-ra, F.: lining. **-ráre**, TR.: line. **-ráto**, ADJ.: lined. **-ratóre†**, M.: rafts-man. **-ratúra**, F.: lining. **-rétta†**, F.: pillow-case. **-rína**, *car. dim.* of *-ra*. ‖**fòde-ro** [Goth. *fōdr*], M.: scabbard (sheath); raft; pelisse†; fur for lining†.
fóga [*fuga*], F.: impetuosity.
fog-géttа†, F.: small cap. ‖**fòg-gia** [?], F.: manner (fashion, custom); ancient cowl†. **-giáre**, TR.: fashion, form.
fò-glia, F.: leaf (esp. of mulberry); petal; FOIL; silvering (for mirrors): *— d'oro*, gold-leaf; *— a —*, one by one. **-gliáccia**, *disp.* of *-glia*. **-gliáccio**, M.: *disp.* of *-glio*; waste-paper. **-gliáceo**, ADJ.: foliaceous. **-gliáme**, F.: foliage; leaf-work. **-gliáre†**, INTR.: produce leaves. **-gliáta**, F.: sheet of paper and that wrapped in it. **-gliáto†**, ADJ.: foliaged, leafy. **-gliatúra**, F.: leaf-work. **-gliétta**, F.: *dim.* of *-glia*; snuff made of stems; wine measure. **-gliettína**, *dim.* of *-glietta*. **-gliétto**, *dim.* of *-glio*. **-glína**, *car. dim.* of *-glia*. ‖**fò-glio** [L. *-lium*, leaf], M.: sheet of paper; FOLIO; gazette: *— bianco*, carte blanche; *— a —*, one by one; *aprire il —*, explain, make known. **-gliolína**, *car. dim.* of *-glia*. **-gliolíno**, *car. dim.* of *-glio*. **-glióna**, *aug.* of *-glia*. **-glióne**, *aug.* of *-glio*. **-glióso**, ADJ.: leafy. **-gliúccia**, *dim.* of *-glia*. **-gliúccio**, *disp.* of *-glio*. **-gliúto**, ADJ.: leafy.
fó-gna [? (ak. to L. *fundus*, bottom)], F.: sewer; drain; drain-hole (in flower-pots); greedy eater. **-gnáre**, TR.: provide with sewers (drain); elide (letters): *— le misure* (or *le castagne*), give short measure (by leaving empty spaces). **-gnatúra**, F.: sewer-making; elision (of letters). **-gnóne**, *aug.* of *-gna*.
fógo [*fauci*], M.: choking by food.
fòia [L. *furia*], F.: lust (rut).
fòla I [L. *fabula*], F.: joke, idle story.
fòla† 2 = *folla*.
fòla-ga [L. *fulica*], F.: moor-hen. **-ghétta**, *car. dim.* of *-ga*.

foláta [*volata*], F.: gust (of wind); flight (of birds).

folcire†, TR.: prop, support.

folgo-ránte, ADJ.: flashing. **-ráre**, INTR.: flash (lighten); TR.: fulminate; do with lightning speed†. **-ráto†**, ADJ.: quick, hasty; splendid. ‖**fólgo-re** [L. *fulgur*], M., F.: thunderbolt; splendor†. **-reggiáre**, INTR.: flash (lighten); do with lightning speed.

fòlio: *in* —, of folio size.

fòl-la, F.: 'press' of people; crowd; multitude. ‖**-láre** [l. L. *fullare* (L. *fullo*, fuller)], TR.: full or work (felt); press (hides).

fòl-le [L. *-lis*, bellows (later, grimace of puffed cheeks)], ADJ.: foolish. **-leggiaménto**, M.: foolishness. **-leggiáre**, INTR.: act foolishly. **-leggiatóre**, M.: one who plays the fool. **-leménte**, ADV.: foolishly. **-létto**, M.: hobgoblin: *è un vero* —, he's a regular imp. **-lézza†**, **-lía**, F.: folly; insanity.

follíco-la† = *-lo*. **-láre**, ADJ.: follicular. **-láto**, ADJ.: in form of follicle. ‖**follíco-lo** [L. *folliculus*, little sack], M.: follicle; capsule.

follóne†, M.: fuller, dyer.

folléro†, M.: folly.

fól-ta†, F.: crowd. **-taménte**, ADV.: thickly, in crowds. **-tézza**, F.: thickness. ‖**-to** [L. *fultus*], ADJ.: thick; numerous; M.: thick, crowded part.

fomén-ta [L. *-tum*], F.: fomentation; poultice. **-táre**, TR.: foment (excite). **-tatóre**, M., **-tatríce**, F.: fomenter. **-tazióne**, F., **fomén-to†**, M.: fomentation.

fòmi-te [L. *fomes*, tinder], M.: evil incentive. **-to†**, M.: tinder; incentive.

fónda 1 [L. *funda*, sling, purse], F.: holster; purse.

fónda† 2 = *-do*.

fondacáio [*-daco*], M.: cloth-seller, draper.

fondáccio [*-do*], M.: dregs, remnants.

fonda-chétto, *car. dim.* of *-co*. **-chière†**, M.: cloth-seller, draper. ‖**fóndaco** [Ar. *fonduq*, shop], M.: draper's shop; provision shop; draper (cloth-seller).

fon-damentále, ADJ.: fundamental. **-damentalménte†**, ADV.: fundamentally. **-damentáre**, TR.: lay foundations of; found. **-daménto**, M.: foundation; basis. **-dáre** [L. *fundare*], TR.: FOUND; lay the foundations of; REFL.: *-darsi in* (*sur*) *una lingua*, know a language well. **-dáta**, F.: dregs (grounds; sediment); remnant. **-dataménte**, ADV.: with foundation; justly. **-dáto**, PART. of *-dare*; ADJ.: versed in; deep†. **-datóre**, M., **-datríce**, F.: founder. **-dazióne**, F.: foundation; founding.

fónde-re [L. *fundere*, pour], IRR.§; TR.: FUSE (cast); blend (colours). **-ría**, F.: foundry; essence factory.

§ Pret. *fú-si*, *-se*; *-sero*. Part. *fúso*.

fon-dézza [*-do*], F.: depth. **-diário**, ADJ.: that concerns ground, funded: *libri -diari*, deed-books.

fondíbile [*-dere*], ADJ.: fusible.

fon-diería [*fondo*], F.: ground-tax. **-digliuo**, **-digliuòlo** [*-do*], M.: dregs (lees, refuse).

fonditóre [*-dere*], M.: caster in metals.

fón-do [L. *fundus*], M.: bottom; depth; bed (of river); back part; conclusion; ground-colour; fund; ADJ.: deep (PROFOUND): *a* —, profoundly; *andare a* —, sink; *articolo di* —, leading article; *dar* —, waste; cast anchor; *-di del caffè*, coffee-grounds; *-di di magazzino*, unsold goods, remnants; *in* —, in conclusion, finally; *lati -di*, large rural estates; *dar* —, dissipate, ruin. **-dúra†**, F.: deep hollow; depth.

fondúto†, PART. of *-dere*.

fo-neticaménte, ADV.: phonetically. ‖**-nètico** [Gr. *phoné*, voice], ADJ.: phonetic. **fò-nica**, F.: phonics. **fò-nico**, ADJ.: phonic. **-nò-grafo** [Gr. *grápho*, I write], M.: phonograph. **-no-logía** [Gr. *lógos*, discourse], F.: phonology.

fon-tále†, ADJ.: original. **-talménte†**, ADV.: originally. **-tána**, F.: fountain. **-tanèlla**, F.: *car. dim.* of *-tana*; (*anat.*) fontanel; issue: — *di gola*, pit of the throat. **-tánco†**, ADJ.: belonging to a fountain. **-tanière**, M.: fountain-keeper or custodian. **-tanína**, *dim.* of *-tana*. **-táno†**, ADJ.: belonging to a fountain. **-tanóne**, *aug.* of *-tana*. **-tanóso†**, ADJ.: that has fountains. ‖**fón-te** [L. *fons*], F. (M.): fount (spring; source; origin): *sacro* —, baptismal font; *levare al — un bambino*, stand sponsor for a child. **-ticèlla**, *dim.* of *-te*. **-ticína**, *car. dim.* of *-te*.

fòra = *fuori*.

foracchiáre [L. *forare*], TR.: BORE full of holes.

forag-gère, M.: forager. **-giaménto**, M.: foraging. **-giáre**, INTR.: forage. **-g(i)ère**, M.: forager. ‖**foràg-gio** [Fr. *fourrage* (Goth. *fôdr*)], M.: forage; fodder (horse's rations).

foráme [L. *-men* (cf. *forare*)], M.: small hole (aperture).

foráneo [L. *foris*, outside], ADJ.: (*eccl.*) *vicario* —, priest (with authority in rural parishes); forensic†.

forá-re [L.], TR.: BORE. **-sácco**, M.: brome-grass. **-sièpe**, M.: wren. **-túra**, F.: aperture (hole). **-tèrra†**, F.: dibble.

-tíni, M. PL.: kind of macaroni. **-'to**, PART. of *-re: animo* —, ungrateful disposition; *capo* —, hair-brained person; *aver le mani -te*, be extravagant. **-tóio**, M.: drill, auger. **-tóre†**, M.: borer; auger. **-túra**, F.: boring, piercing.

fòrbi-ci, (*pop.*) **-ce** [L. *forfex*], F. PL.: scissors; metal-shears; claws (of crabs, scorpions, etc.); vine-grub; (*fig.*) obstinate person: *-ci!* obstinate one! *le sono state* —, they persisted in spite of all. **-ciáio†**, M.: scissors-maker or seller. **-ciáta**, F.: scissor-cut. **-cíno**, *car. dim.* of *-ce*. **-cióne**, M. PL.: *aug.* of *-ci*; shears.

forbí-re [OHG. *furban*], TR.: furbish, polish; clean: — *gli occhi*, rub the eyes; — *le lagrime*, wipe away the tears. **-tamènte**, ADV.: in polished manner. **-tézza**, F.: neatness; polish; purity of style.

forbí-to, PART. of *-re;* (of writings) elegant, faultless. **-tóio†**, M.: polishing tool. **-tóre**, M., **-tríce**, F.: polisher; cleaner.

forbottáre†, TR.: beat; revile.

fór-ca [L. *furca*], F.: fork (pitchfork, hayfork); gallows (gibbet); anything forked; mischievous boy†; forked road: *da* —, villainous; *far* —, play truant; *far le -che*, pretend poverty or pretend ignorance (of something). **-cáta**, F.: forkful; crotch of the legs. **-catèlla**, F.: small forkful. **-cáto†**, ADJ.: forked. **-catúra†**, F.: forkedness. **-cèlla**, F.: *dim.* of *-ca;* sternum; wishbone. **-che**, F PL.: gallows.

forchè -é [*fore che*], CONJ.: except.

for-chétta [*-ca*], F.: table-fork; musket-rest†: *parlare* (*favellare*) *in punta di* —, talk with affectation. **-chettáta**, F.: table-forkful; fork-thrust. **-chettièra**, F.: fork-case. **-chétto**, M.: two-pronged iron fork (for hanging or unhooking things); forked twig. **-chettóne**, M.: carving-fork.

forchiúdere†, IRR.; TR.: EXCLUDE (shut out).

forcína [*-ca*], F.: hairpin; harpoon†; musket-rest†.

fórcipe [L. *-ceps*, tongs], M.: forceps.

for-conáta, F.: pitchfork-thrust. ‖**-cóne** [*-ca*], M.: pitchfork; fork of roads†.

forcostumánza†, F.: bad custom.

for-cúto [*-ca*], ADJ.: forked. **-cutamènte†**, ADV.: forkedly. **-cúzza†**, F.: *dim.* of *-ca;* rascal.

fó-ro† =*fuori*. **-rellíno**, *dim.* of *-ro* I. **-résot†**, M.: peasant; ADJ.: rustic. **-resèllo†**, *dim.* of *-rese*. **-rènse** [*-ro* 2], ADJ.: forensic. **-resòzza†**, F.: (pretty) peasant girl. **-resòzzo†**, M.: (handsome) peasant lad.

forè-sta [L. *foras*, outdoor], F.: forest. **-stále**, ADJ.: pertaining to forest. **-staría†**, **-stería**, F.: guest-quarters in convent; crowd of foreigners. **-stieráio**, M.: convent guestmaster. **-stieramèntet†**, ADV.: in foreign manner. **-stière**, **-stièro**, M.: FOReigner; outsider; guest.

forè-sto†, ADJ.: wild, savage; uninhabited.

for=fáre†, IRR.; INTR.: transgress; TR.: deceive. **-fátto†**, M.: misdeed. **-fattúra†**, F.: knavery.

for-fic..† =*forbic..* **-fécchia**, F.: fruit-worm (maggot); earwig.

fórfo-ra [L. *furfur*, bran], F.: dandruff; scurf. **-róso**, ADJ.: scurvy.

fòri =*fuori*.

forié-re [l. L. *fodrarius* (Goth. *fôdr*, forage)], M.: quartermaster; forerunner.

fór-ma [L.], F.: form (shape); manner (style); formula; model; mould; cheese-mould; cheese: — *di calzetta*, stocking-frame; — *di cappello*, hat-block; — *di scarpe*, shoe-last; *a* (*in*) — *di*, in shape of, like; *per* — *che*, in manner that. **-mábile**, ADJ.: shapable. **-maggiáio**, M.: cheese-monger. **-mággio**, M.: cheese. **-maggiòlo**, *dim.* of *-maggio*. **-máio**, M.: last-maker. **-mále**, ADJ.: formal. **-malísta**, M.: formalist. **-malità**, F.: formality. **-malizzáre**, INTR.: wonder at (be surprised or scandalized at); define†. **-malménte**, ADV.: formally. **-maménto†**, M.: formation. **-máre**, TR.: form (fashion, design, make); make up; mould (cast); REFL.: be formed; grow; imagine (conceive). **-mataménte**, ADV.: in due form; well made. **-matèllo**, ADJ.: round (of handwriting). **-matívo**, ADJ.: formative. **-máto**, PART. of *-mare;* well-built (of persons); M.: size of book; form†: *ben* —, of regular form. **-matóre**, M., **-matríce**, F.: shaper; caster in plaster. **-mazióne**, F.: formation. **-mèlla**, F.: hole to plant trees in; spavin; PL.: tinder-cake; tessera; floor-tile; tesselated ornament. **-melláto**, ADJ.: tesselated.

for-mentáre†, INTR.: ferment. ‖**-ménto** I [L. *fermentum*], M.: yeast.

forménto† 2 [*frumento*], M.: wheat. ‖**-tóne**, M.: Indian corn.

forméttа, *dim.* of *-ma*.

formí-ca [L.], F.: ant; St. Anthony's fire (erysipelas). **-cáio**, M.: ant-hill. **-cáre†**, INTR.: swarm. **-chétta**, *dim.* of *-ca*. **formí-cola**, F.: ant. **-coláio**, M.: ant-hill; crowd: *stuzzicare il* —, stir up a hornet's nest. **-colaménto†**, M.: pricking (tingling). **-colánte**, PART. of *-colare*. **-coláre**, INTR.: swarm; tingle (as benumbed flesh, like ants' biting); M.

-*cola questo piede*, my foot's asleep. **-colétta, -colína,** *dim.* of *-cola.* **-colío,** M.: FORMICation, tingling; swarming. **-colóne,** M.: large winged ant: *essere* (or *fare*) *il — di sorbo,* be firm; be unmoved. **-cúccia,** *dim.* of *-ca.*
formi-dábile [L. *-dabilis*], ADJ.: formidable. **-dabilménte,** ADV.: formidably.
formí-dine†, F.: fear.
fòrmola = *formula.*
for-mosità, F.: shapeliness (beauty). ||**-móso** [L. *-mosus*], ADJ.: shapely (beautiful).
fòrmu-la [L.], F.: formula. **-láre,** TR.: formulate. **-lário,** M.: formulary.
for-náce [L. *-nax*], F.: FURNACE; kiln. **-nacèlla, -nacétta,** *dim.* of *-nace.* **-naciáio,** M.: furnace-tender; kiln-man: *— della calcina,* lime-kiln. **-naciáta,** F.: furnaceful. **-nacina,** *dim.* of *-nace.* **-náia,** F.: baker's wife. **-naina,** *dim.* of *-naia.* **-naino,** *dim.* of *-naio.* **-náio,** M.: baker: *assicurarsi il —,* find sure means of support. **-náta,** F.: batch. **-nèllo,** M.: cooking-stove; camp-stove; chemist's furnace; sauce-pan.
fornicá-re [L. (*-nix*, arch; later brothel, because under arches)], INTR.: fornicate; TR.: falsify. **-tóre,** M., **-tríce,** F.: fornicator. **-zióne,** F.: fornication.
for-niménto, M.: furnishing; thing furnished; furniture†; harness†; adornment. **-nimentúzzo,** *dim.* of *-nimento.* ||**-níre** [?], TR.: FURNISH (provide†); finish; execute†. **-níto,** PART. of *-nire;* ADJ.: adult†: *è ben —,* he's well fixed; M.†: furniture; trimming. **-nitóre,** M., **-nitríce,** F.: furnisher; wholesaler. **-nitúra,** F.: furnishing; contract to furnish.
fór-no [L. *furnus*], M.: oven; bake-shop. **-nuòlo†,** M.: lantern.
fó-ro 1 [*-rare*], M.: hole (aperture).
fò-ro 2 [L. *-rum* (*-ras*, outside)], M.: forum (tribunal). **-rosétta** [L. *-ras*], F.: peasant-girl.
fór-ra [OFr. *feurre*], F.: ravine (gorge). **-róne,** *aug.* of *-ra.*
fórse [L. *-san*], ADV.: perhaps: *essere in —,* be in doubt; *— di sì,* it may be so; *ivi — a tre miglia,* about three miles from here; *— —,* possibly (not probably); *senza —,* certainly; *— che* or *—chè,* perhaps that; it may be that.
for-sennáre† [*fuor senno*], INTR.: rave. **-sennatággine,** F.: madness; extravagance. **-sennataménte,** ADV.: madly. **-sennáto,** ADJ.: mad; SENseless; extravagant. **-senneria†,** F.: madness; extravagance.
fórsi† = *forse.*
fòr-te [L. *-tis*], ADJ.: strong (robust, firm); brave; energetic (arduous); strong-flavoured; ADV.: vigorously; loudly; soundly; M.: forte (specialty); fort; strongest; best portion or person; highest number: *colore —,* fast colour: *nel — della mischia,* in the thick of the fight: *non ti paia —,* may it not seem hard to you; *tempo —,* bad, stormy weather; *fuggir* (or *andar*) *—,* run away fast. **-teménte,** ADV.: strongly; stoutly; bravely; vigorously; loudly. **-terúzzo†, -tétto,** *dim.* of *-te.* **-tézza,** F.: fortitude; force; constancy; fortress: *andare in —,* sour (of liquids). **-tíccio,** ADJ.: rather strong-flavoured. **-tificábile,** ADJ.: fortifiable. **-tificaménto†,** M.: fortification. **-tificáre,** TR.: fortify; strengthen. **-tificánte, -tificatívo,** ADJ.: fortifying. **-tificatóre,** M.: fortifier. **-tificazióne,** F.: fortification. **-tígno,** ADJ.: sourish. **-tilízio, -tíno,** M.: small fort (redoubt). **-titúdine†,** F.: fortitude. **-tóre†,** M.: strength (of odour or taste); sourness; **-tóri,** PL.: sourness of stomach.
for-tuitaménte, ADV.: fortuitously. ||**-túito** [L. *-tuitus* (*fors,* chance)], ADJ.: fortuitous (casual).
fortúme [*-te*], M.: strong, savoury stuff.
fortú-na [L.], F.: fortune; chance (accident, luck); prosperity; tempest: *darsi alla —,* give one's self to despair; *tener la — per il ciuffo,* be prosperous. **-náccia,** F.: ill luck. **-nággio,** M.: storm. **-nále†,** ADJ.: accidental; tempestuous. **-náre†,** INTR.: suffer storm at sea; TR.: bless, make fortunate. **-nataménte,** ADV.: fortunately (luckily). **-náto,** ADJ.: fortunate. **-neggiáre,** INTR.: hazard. **-névole,** ADJ.: fortuitous. **-nóna,** *aug.* of *-na.* **-nosaménte,** ADV.: happily; by chance. **-nóso,** ADJ.: hazardous; unexpected.
for-túra†, F.: force (strength); valour. **-túzzo,** ADJ.: sourish.
forúncolo [L. *furunculus* (*fur,* thief)], M.: boil (felon).
forviáre [*fori, via*], INTR.: wander from the road; stray.
fòrvici† = *forbici.*
forvòglia†, ADV.: against one's will.
fòr-za [*-te*], F.: FORCE (strength); PL.: forces; troops; gymnastics, equestrian sports: *a —,* or *a viva —,* by violence; *far —,* force, constrain; *per —,* against one's will; *per — di,* by strength of, with the aid of. **-zaménto†,** M.: constraint. **-záre,** TR.: force (compel); REFL.: strive. **-zataménte,** ADV.: constrainedly. **-záto,** PART. of *-zare;* ADJ.: constrained; excessive; M.: galley-slave; convict: *lavori -zati,* galley labour. **-zatóre,** M., **-zatríce,** F.: gymnast. **-ze-**

rináio, M.: coffer-maker. **-zévole**†, ADJ.: FORCIBLE. **-zevolménte**†, ADV.: forcibly. **-zière**, M.: coffer (strong-box). **-zierétto**, **-ziercttíno**, *dim.* of *-ziere.* **fòr-zo**†, M.: force; effort. **-zóre**†, M.: strength (of flavour); sourness. **-zosaménte**, ADV.: vigorously; imposed by the law. **-zóso**, **-zúto**, ADJ.: sturdy (vigorous); valiant.

foscaménte, ADV.: obscurely, gloomily. ||**fó-sco** [L. *fuscus*], ADJ.: dark (obscure, gloomy, Eng.† obFUSCATE): *guardatura* *-sca*, sad look.

fosfático, ADJ.: phosphatic. **-sfáto**, M.: phosphate. **-sforescènte**, ADJ.: phosphorescent. **-sforescènza**, F.: phosphorescence. **-sfòrico**, ADJ.: phosphoric. ||**fò-sforo** [Gr. *phosphóros* (*phôs*, light)], M.: phosphorus.

fòs-sa [L.], F.: ditch (trench); grave; granary cut in tufa-rock. **-sáccia**, *disp.* of *-sa.* **-sarèllo**, *dim.* of *-sato.* **-satáccio**†, *disp.* of *-sato.* **-satèllo**, *dim.* of *-sato.* **-sáto**, M.: small torrent; drain. **-serèlla**, **-serèllo**, *dim.* of *-sa.* **-sétta**, *car. dim.* of *-sa.* **-settíno**, *dim.* of *-setto.* **-sétto**, *dim.* of *-so.* **-sicèlla**, **-sicina**, *car. dim.* of *-sa.* **fòs-sile**, ADJ., M.: fossil. **-silizzáre**, TR., REFL.: fossilize. **-silizzazióne**, F.: fossilization. **fòs-so**, M.: large open ditch. **-sóna**, *aug.* of *-sa.* **-sóne**, *aug.* of *-so.*

fotografáre, TR.: photograph; REFL.: have one's self photographed. ||**-grafía** [Gr. *phôs*, light, *gráphein*, write], F.: photography; photograph. **-gráfico**, ADJ.: photographic. **fotò-grafo**, M.: photographer.

fotti=vènto†, M.: kestrel, wind-hover (bird).

fra 1 [*frate*], M.: FRIAR (BROTHer).

fra 2, **fra-** [*infra*], PREP.: between, among, in: — *noi altri*, among ourselves; — *tre giorni*, in three days; — *poco*, in a short time; — *quanto?* in what time? — *tanto*, in the meanwhile; — *via*, in the road.

fracassaménto, M.: crash (smash, noisy breaking). ||**-sáre** [*fra*, L. *quassare*], TR.: crash (break violently); REFL.: ruin one's self. **-sáto**, PART., ADJ.: smashed; very poor: — *dalle fatiche*, broken with fatigue. **-satúra**†, F.: crash; smashing. **-síο**, M.: uproar, clatter. **fracás-so**, M.: uproar; great quantity: *far* —, make great noise in the world.

fraccurrádo†, M.: legless puppet: *fare i —di*, make faces, grimaces.

fracidáre†, INTR.: putrefy. **-cidézza**, F.: rottenness. **-cidíccio**, ADJ.: soaking; rotting; M.: soaking; rottenness. **frá-cido** [L. *-cidus* (root *frac-*, BREAK), soft], ADJ.: soaked; soft (Eng.† fracid), decayed: *tu m' hai* —, you have wearied me. **-cidúme**†, M.: putrid mass; weariness; wearisome person. **-diccézza**†, F.: rottenness. **frá-dicio** [by metath. fr. *-cido*], ADJ.: soaked; decayed; corrupt; M.: soaking (wet condition, wetness); corruption: *innamorato* —, deeply in love; *malato* — (*vulg.*), very ill. **-diciúme**, M.: soakage; mass of rottenness.

frága†, F.: strawberry.

fragel. .† = *flagel.* .

frá-gile [L. *-gilis*], ADJ.: fragile; delicate (of persons). **-gilézza**†, F.: fragility; weakness. **-gilità**, F.: fragility, frailty (weakness); changeableness. **-gilménte**, ADV.: fragilely. **-gménto**†, M.: fragment. ||**-gnere**† = *frangere.*

frágola [L. *-ga*], F.: strawberry.

fragóre† 1, M.: FRAgrance.

fra-góre 2 [L. *-gor* (root *frag-*, break)], M.: crashing noise. **-gorío**, M.: clatter. **-goróso**, ADJ.: noisy. **-góso**, ADJ.: noisy (tumultuous); sonorous.

fra-gránte [L. *-grans*], ADJ.: fragrant. **-gránza**, F.: fragrance.

frá(i)-le [L. *fragilis*], ADJ.: fragile; M.: (*poet.*) human body. **-lézza**, F.: frailty.

fra=mescoláre, TR.: interMIX (mingle).

fra=mezzáre, TR.: interpose.

frammén-to [L. *fragmentum*], M.: fragment. **-túccio**, *dim.* of *-to.*

frammescoláre = *framescolare.*

fram-mésso, PART. of *-mettere;* ADJ.: inserted; M.: insertion. **-mettènte**, ADJ.: meddling (troublesome). ||**-méttere** [*fra, mettere*], IRR.; TR.: interpose, insert; REFL.: mediate: — *la lingua*, lisp. **-mettiménto**†, M.: interposition.

frammischiáre [*fra, mischiare*], TR.: intermix.

frá-na [? L. *fragmina*, fragments], F.: landslide. **-náre**, INTR.: slide (of earth or rocks).

fran-cagióne†, F.: exemption. **-caménte**, ADV.: frankly (freely). **-caménto**, M.: franking, freeing. **-cáre**, TR.: frank; free. **-catúra**, F.: franking; postage. **-cescaménte**†, ADV.: in French fashion. **-cescáno**, ADJ., M.: Franciscan. **-cheggiáre**, TR.: assure; encourage. **-chézza**, F.: frankness; boldness; freedom; exemption†. **-chígia**, pl. *-ge* or *-gie*, F.: franchise (exemption; privilege); sanctuary† (for criminals). ||**fràn-co** [OHG. *francho*, Frank, also free man], M.: Frank; franc; sanctuary†; ADJ.: frank; bold; privileged; duty-free; speedy, expert: — *di porto*, postage paid. **-co=bóllo**, pl. —*i* or (rare) *-chibolli*, M.: postage-stamp. **-colíno**, M.: heathcock.

fran-gènte, PART. of *-gere;* M.: unforeseen accident, difficult case; breaker†. ‖**frán-gere** [L.], IRR.§; TR.: break, smash; crush (olives, etc.); INTR.: break (as a wave).

§ Pret. *frán-si, -se; -sero.* Part. *fránto.*

fran-gétta, *dim.* of *-gia.* ‖**frán-gia** [Fr. *-ge* (L. *fimbria*)], F.: FRINGE; untrue additions to a story. **-giáia**, F., **-giáio**, M.: fringe-maker or seller. **-giáre**†, TR.: fringe.

fran-gíbile [*-gere*], ADJ.: frangible (brittle). **-gibilità**, F.: frangibility (brittleness). **-giménto**†, M.: breaking; weakness; fragment.

frangióne, *aug.* of *frangia.*

frammassóne†, M.: Freemason.

frannónnolo†, M.: dotard.

franóso [*-nare*], ADJ.: liable to slip or slide (of earth).

fránsi, PRET. of *frangere.*

fran-tèndere [*fra, intendere*], IRR.; TR.: misunderstand. **-téso**, PART. of *-tendere;* ADJ.: misunderstood.

frán-to, PART. of *-gere;* ADJ.: crushed, etc. **-tóio**, M.: olive-crusher; place where olives are crushed. **-toiáno**, M.: olive-crusher tender. **-tumáre**, TR.: crush to pieces. **-túme**†, M., **-túmi**, M. PL.: mass of fragments.

franz. † = *franc.*

fraóre†, M.: fragrance.

fráp-pa, F.: foliage-painting; fringe†: scalloping (of dresses)†. **-páre** [?], TR.†: cut fine (mince, slash); fringe; cheat; INTR.: paint or draw foliage; chatter†. **-patóre**†, M.: chatterer; cheat. **-peggiáre**, INTR.: paint or draw foliage.

frap-poniménto, M.: interposition. ‖**-pórre** [*fra, porre*], IRR.; TR.: insert, interpose; REFL.: mediate. **-pósto**, PART. of *-porre.* **-posizióne**, F.: interposition; mediation.

fraşário [*-se*], M.: collection of phrases; pet phrases.

frá-sca [? ak. to L. root *frag-*, BREAK, split], F.: bough, bush; tavern-sign bush; inconstant person; PL.: idle stories; gewgaws; vanities: *saltare di palo in —*, digress from the matter, talk ramblingly; *metter la —*, open an inn. **-scáme**, M.: quantity of branches. **-scáto**, M.: shady recess made with boughs (bower): thick copse. **-scheggiáre**, INTR.: rustle; jest†, play fool. **-schéggio**, M.: rustling. **-scherèlla**, *dim.* of *-sca.* **-schería**, F.: trifles (gewgaws). **-schétta**, F.: *dim.* of *-sca;* twigs arranged for fowlers' nets; (*typ.*) FRISKET. **-schière**†, M.: frivolous man. **-scolína**, *dim.* of *-sca.* **-sconáia**, F.: place for fowlers' nets; ground too bushy; tree too much branched; anything too much ornamented. **-scóne**, M.: *aug.* of *-sca;* *seminare i -sconi*, (of chickens) stretch wings through weakness; (of persons) feel weak or used up. **-scúme**, M.: quantity of boughs.

frá-şe [Gr. *phrásis*], F.: phrase. **-şeggiaménto**, M.: phraseology. **-şeggiáre**, INTR.: phrase; use many phrases. **-şeggiatóre**, M.: phraser. **-şeología**, F.: phraseology. **-şétta**, **-şettína**, **-şína**, *dim.* of *-se.*

fras-sinèlla, F.: false dittany; bone. **-síneo**, ADJ.: ashen. **-sinéto**, M.: ash-grove. ‖**frás-sino** [L. *fraxinus*], M.: ash-tree.

frasta-gliáme†, **-gliaménto**, M.: cutting (slashing); cut (slash, notch). ‖**-gliáre** [*fra, tagliare*], TR.: cut (cut up, slash); notch; stammer†; talk confusedly†. **-gliáta**†, F.: cutting; confusion. **-gliataménte**, ADV.: fragmentarily; confusedly. **-gliatúra**†, F.: notch; eyelet. **frastá-glie**, F. PL.: entrails. **frastá-glio**, M.: open work (fret-work). **-gliúme**, *disp.* of *-glio.*

fras=tenére†, IRR.; TR.: keep waiting.

frastòno [*fra, tono*], M.: din (noise).

fra=stornáre, TR.: frustrate (impede); disturb. **-stornío**, M.: disturbance.

fra-stuòlo†, **-stuòno** = *-stono.*

fraşúccia, *disp. dim.* of *-se.*

fra-tacchióne, M.: big fat monk; (*jest.*) *disp. aug.* of *-te.* **-tacchiòtto**, M.: stocky, heavy-set monk. **-táccio**, *disp.* of *-te.* **-táglia**, F.: crowd of monks (*disp.*). **-táio**, ADJ.: fond of monks: *zucca -taia*, winter pumpkin. **-táta**, F.: monkish misdeed. ‖**frá-te** [L. *-ter*, BROTHER], M.: FRIAR; hood-like tile for ventilating; silk worm failing to make cocoon; kind of fish; brother†; PL.: doughnut. **-telláme**, *disp.* of *-telli.* **-tellánza**, F.: brotherhood (fraternity). **-tellástro**, M.: half-brother. **-tellésco**, ADJ.: (*disp.*) brotherly. **-tellévole**, ADJ.: brotherly. **-tellevolménte**, ADV.: fraternally. **-tellíno**, *car. dim.* of *-tello.* **-tèllo**, M.: brother: *— carnale* (or *germano*), full brother; *— di padre*, half brother by father's side; *— di madre* (or *uterino*), half brother by mother's side; *-telli cugini*, first cousins; *— di latte*, foster-brother. **-tellúccio**, *dim.* of *-tello.* **-tèlmo**†, M.: my brother. **-tèlto**†, M.: thy brother. **-tería**, F.: brotherhood; friary (community of monks). **-ternále**†, ADJ.: fraternal. **-ternalménte**†, **-ternaménte**, ADV.: fraternally. **-ternità**1, F.: fraternity (brotherliness). **-tèrnitá**†2, F.: (*rel.*) fraternity. **-ternizzáre**, INTR.: fraternise. **-tèrno**, ADJ.: brotherly. **-tescaménte**, ADV.:

monkishly. **-tésco**, ADJ.: monkish. **-ticèllo**, *dim.* of *-te.* **-ticída†**, M.: fratricide (person). **-ticídio**, M.: fratricide (crime). **-ticíno**, *dim.* of *-te.* **-tíle†**, ADJ.: monkish. **-tíno**, ADJ.: (*disp.*) monkish; M.: *dim.* of *-te.* **-tíşmo**, M.: monkery. **-tóne**, *aug.* of *-te.* **-tricída**, M., F.: fratricide (person). **-tricídio**, M.: fratricide (crime). **frá-tria**, F.: Greek phratria.

frátta [Gr. *phraktē*, hedge], F.: thorny hedge; briar patch: *esser per le —te*, be penniless.

frattá-glia [L. *fractus*, broken], F. (us'ly pl.): entrail; medley (rubbish). **-gliáio**, M.: entrail-seller.

frattánto [*fra, tanto*], ADV.: meanwhile.

frattèmpo [*fra, tempo*], M.: interval.

frát-to, *part.* of *frangere: canto —*, partaking both of Gregorian chant and music. **-túra**, F.: fracture; (*geol.*) fault. **-turáre**, TR., REFL.: fracture.

fratúccio, *dim.* of *-te.*

frau-dánte†, M.: defrauder. **-dáre**, TR.: defraud. **-datóre†**, M., **-datríce†**, F.: defrauder. ‖**fráu-de** [L. *fraus*], F.: fraud. **-dévole†**, ADJ.: fraudulent. **-dolènte†** = *-dolento.* **-dolenteménte**, ADV.: fraudulently. **-dolènto**, ADJ.: fraudulent. **-dolènza**, F.: fraudulency (fraud).

frávo-la [*fragola*], F.: strawberry. **-láia**, F., **-láio**, M.: strawberry-patch.

fraziéne [L. *frangere*, BREAK], F.: FRACTION (morsel).

frèc-cia [Ger. *flitsch*], F.: arrow; compass-needle; (*geom.*) versed sine of an arc: *dare la —†*, cheat, cozen. **-ciáre**, INTR.: shoot an arrow; dart; TR.: cozen, cheat. **-ciáta**, F.: arrow-shot (arrow-wound); sharp word. **-ciatína**, *dim.* of *-ciata.* **-ciatóre†**, M.: archer. **-ciósе†**, ADJ.: quick (prompt).

fred-daménte, ADV.: coldly (indifferently). **-dáre**, TR.: make cold; kill; REFL.: grow cold: *non la lasciate —*, make haste, "strike while the iron's hot." **-dáto**, *part.* of *-dare.* **-dézza**, F.: coldness (indifference); slowness. **-díccio**, ADJ.: coolish. **-díno**, *dim.* of *-do.* ‖**fréd-do** [L. *frigidus*], ADJ.: FRIGID (cold); phlegmatic (indifferent); M.: cold; indifference; PL.: cold viands. **-dolóso**, ADJ.: chilly; sensitive to cold; M.: chilly person. **-dóre†**, M.: coldness, cold. **-dóso†**, ADJ.: chilly. **-dòtto**, ADJ.: coolish; M.: coolness. **-dúra**, F.: coldness; cold weather; silly repartee: *dire -dure*, talk nonsense. **-duráio**, **-durísta**, M.: silly talker.

fré-ga, F.: desire; spawning†; rubbing: *essere in —*, be in heat, be amourous. **-gáccio**, *disp.* of *-go.* **-gacciolá-re**, TR.: rub gently. **-gácciolo**, *disp. dim.* of *-go.* **-gagióne**, M.: FRICtion; rubbing, massage. **-gaménto**, M.: rubbing. ‖**-gáre** [L. *fricare*], TR.: rub; cancel (by lines): *— uno*, swindle one; *-garsi intorno a uno*, curry favour with one. **-gáta** 1, F.: rubbing, polishing; dusting.

fregáta 2 [?], F.: frigate.

frega-tína [*-re*], F.: slight rubbing. **-túra**, F.: rubbing, friction.

fregétto, *dim.* of *-gio.*

freghétto, *dim.* of *-go.*

fre-giaménto, M.: ornament. **-giáre**, TR.: ornament (decorate). **-giatúra**, F.: decorating; border. ‖**fré-gio** [l. L. *frigium* (*Phrygiæ*, Phrygians)], M.: carved, embroidered or painted ornament; border; decoration (medal).

fré-go [*-gare*], M.: line (stroke); erasure: *dare* (or *fare*) *un —*, cancel; erase; *fare un — ad uno†*, to injure one. **fré-gola**, F.: spawning; longing, desire. **frégolo†**, M.: shoal of spawning fish.

fre-ménte, ADJ.: raging, fuming, chafing. ‖**frè-mere** [L.], INTR.: roar, howl; chafe, fret; tremble with rage or passion†. **-mitáre†**, INTR.: *freq.* of *-mere.* **frè-mito**, M.: roaring, raging; trembling; neighing.

fre-nábile, ADJ.: restrainable. **-náio†**, M.: bit-maker; (*rail.*) brakesman. ‖**-náre** [L.], TR.: curb (restrain; brake). **-natóre**, M., **-natríce**, F.: restrainer, brakesman. **-nèlla†** 1, F.: bit (curb).

frenèlla 2 = *flanella.*

fre-nèllo [*-nare*], M.: ligament (esp. of tongue); muzzle†; necklace†; bracelet†.

fre-neşía [Gr. *phrenēsis* (*phrēn*, mind)], F.: FRENZY (delirium). **-neticaménte**, ADV.: frantically. **-neticaménto**, M.: frenzy. **-neticánte**, PART., ADJ.: frantic (raving). **-neticáre**, INTR.: rave (be delirious). **-netichézza**, F.: frenzy. **-nètico**, ADJ.: phrenetic; frantic (mad); M.: madman. **frè-nico**, ADJ.: phrenic. **-níte**, F.: inflammation of diaphragm. **-nítide**, F.: phrenitis.

fréno [L. *-num*], M.: bit; restraint; brake: *a — sciolto*, with loose rein; *allargare* (or *rallentare*) *il —*, allow more liberty; *tenere a* (or *in*) *—*, restrain, hold to one's place.

freno-logía [Gr. *phrēn*, mind; *lógos*, discourse], F.: phrenology. **-lògico**, ADJ.: phrenological. **frenò-logo**, M.: phrenologist.

frènulo [*-no*], M.: ligament.

frequen-táre, TR.: frequent. **-tatívo**, ADJ.: (*gram.*) frequentative. **-táto**, PART.: frequented, crowded. **-tatóre**,

M., **-tatríce**, F.: frequenter. **-tazióne**, F.: frequenting, haunting; (*rhet.*) résumé. ‖**frequèn-te** [L. *frequens*], ADJ.: frequent (ordinary). **-teménte**, ADV.: frequently. **frequèn-za**, F.: frequency; throng.

fres-caménte, ADV.: freshly (recently). **-cánte**, M.: fresco-painter. **-chétto**, *dim.* of *-co*. **-chézza**, F.: freshness (coolness). **-chíno**, *dim.* of *-co*. ‖**frés-co** [OHG. *frisc*], ADJ.: FRESH (cool; recent, new-made); ruddy; M.: coolness: *di* —, recently, just now; *dipingere a* —, paint in fresco; *forze* (or *milizie*) *fresche*, raw troops; *prendere il* —, enjoy coolness, take the air; *per il* —, very early, after dawn. **-cóccio**, ADJ.: ruddy. **-colíno**, *dim.* of *-co* **-cúra**, F.: coolness, sharpness (of air): *prender una* —, get chilled, catch cold.

frèto†, M.: the sea.

frét-ta, F.: haste, hurry. ‖**-táre** [L. *fricare*], TR.: scrape (ship's bottom). **-tázza**, F.: (*nav.*) hog, scouring brush. **-teríа**†, F.: haste. **-tévole**, ADJ.: hasty; nimble. **-tolosaménte**, ADV.: quickly, hastily. **-tolóso**, **-tóso**†, ADJ.: quick, hasty, nimble.

friábi-le [L. *-lis*], ADJ.: friable. **-lità**, F.: friability.

fricassèa [Fr. *-cassée*], F.: fricasee.

frière†, M.: friar; Christian knight.

fríg-gere [L. *frigere*], IRR.§; TR.: FRY; INTR.: sputter; whine (pule): *buone parole e -gi*, fair words but no fulfillment; *mandare a farsi* —, send or bring to ruin; be ruined (lost); *non avere di quel che si -ge*, not to have brains or good sense. **-gi=búco**, M.: child's whining. **-gío**, M.: sound of frying, hissing. **-gitóre**, M.: frier; vender of fried viands.

§ Pret. *fris-si, -se; -sero.* Part. *fritto.*

frigi-dário, M.: cold-bath room. **-dézza**, **-dità**, F.: frigidity; ague; indifference; impotence. ‖**frígi-do** [L. *-dus*], ADJ.: frigid (cold, chilly); infertile; impotent.

frigióne†, M.: Friesland horse.

frignáre [Ger. *flennen*, grimace], INTR.: whine, pule.

fringuèllo [L. *frigilla*], M.: chaffinch.

frinzèllo [?], M.: botched mending; scar.

fri-sáre [Fr. *-ser*], TR.: hit foul (billiards, tennis, etc.). **-sáto**, M.: striped cloth. **-so**, M.: foul stroke.

friscèllo†, M.: mill-dust.

fríssi, PRET. of *friggere*.

frít-ta, F.: frit. **-táta**, F.: omelet: — *cogli zoccoli*, stuffed omelet; *fare una* —, make a mess of it; *rivoltare la* —, correct one's self, contradict one's self. **-tatína**, **-tatíno**, *car. dim.* of *-tata*. **-tatóne**, *aug.* of *-tata*. **-tèlla**, F.: fritter; grease-spot (on clothing); fop†. **-tellétta**, **-tellína**, *car. dim.* of *-tella*. **-tellóna**, **-tellóne**, *aug.* of *-tella*. ‖**frít-to**, PART. of *friggere*; ADJ.: undone, ruined; M.: fried eatables. **-túme**†, M., **-túra**, F.: frying; fry, mess; fried things.

frívo-lo†, ADJ.: frivolous. **-lézza**, F.: frivolity. ‖**frívo-lo** [L. *-lus*], ADJ.: frivolous.

friz-zaménto†, M.: smarting; sharp witticism. **-zánte**, PART. of *-zare*; ADJ.: pungent (sharp). ‖**-záre** [?], INTR.: smart (sting; be pungent); be witty. **-zo**, M.: sharp, witty saying; smarting (pricking).

frò-da†, F., **-daménto**, M.: fraud (cheating). **-dáre**, TR.: defraud. **-datóre**, M., **-datríce**, F.: defrauder. ‖**frò-de** [L. *fraus*], F.: FRAUD (deception). **-'do**, M.: smuggling; smuggled goods. **-dolènte**†, ADJ.: fraudulent. **-dolenteménte**, ADV.: fraudulently. **-dolènto**, ADJ.: fraudulent. **-dolènza**, F.: fraud (fraudulence).

frol-laménto, M.: making tender (of meat). ‖**-láre** [L. **friculare* (*fricare*, rub)], TR.: make tender or "high" (of meat); INTR.: become tender. **-latúra**, F.: tendering (of meat). **fròl-lo**, ADJ.: tender, "high," enervated.

fróm-ba†, F.: sling. **-batòre**, M.: slinger. **-bo**†, M.: whizzing, crash. ‖**fróm-bola** [?], F.: sling; slingstone. **-boláre**, TR.: sling. **-bolatóre**†, **-bolière**, M.: slinger.

frón-da [L. *frons*], F.: leafy branch, bough, twig; cf. Eng. FROND; leaf. **-deggiánte**, PART. of *-deggiare*; ADJ.: leafy. **-deggiáre**, INTR.: bring forth leaves. **-dicèlla**, *dim.* of *-da*. **-dífero**†, ADJ.: frondiferous. **-díre**†, INTR.: leaf out. **-díto**†, PART. of *-dire*; ADJ.: leafy. **-dosità**, F.: leafiness. **-dóso**, ADJ.: leafy. **-dúra**†, F.: foliage. **-dúto**†, ADJ.: leafy.

fron-tále, ADJ.: frontal; M.: frontal bone; frontlet. ‖**frón-te** [L. *frons*], F.: front; forehead; face: *a* —, or *alla* —, opposite; *alla — dell' esercito*, at the head of the army; *da* —, facing, opposite; *far* —, resist; *andare a* —, *scoperta*, not to be afraid (or ashamed) of anything; *stare a* —, cope with, resist; *voltar* —, turn face. **-teggiáre**, TR.: front, face. **-tespízio**, M.: frontispiece; fronton (pediment). **-tichináto**†, ADJ.: downcast; abashed. **-ticína**, *car. dim.* of *-te*. **-tièra**, F.: frontier, boundary. **-tispízio**† = *-tespizio*. **-tísta**, M.: proprietor of water or street frontage. **-tóne**, M.: frontal; chimney-back. **-tóso**†, ADJ.: bold (cheeky).

fronzíre† = *-dire.*
frón-zolo [L. *-deolus,* little leaf], M.: ribbons; tassels; ornaments. **-zúto**, ADJ.: leafy.
frosóne [Fr. *frinson*], M.: bullfinch.
fròt-ta [*flutto*], F., **-to**†, M.: crowd, throng. **fròt-tola**, F.: idle jest; nonsense; ballad. **-toláre**†, INTR.: jest, banter; write ballads. **-tolóna, -toló-ne**, ADJ.: bantering (jesting); F., M.: banterer.
fru fru [echoic], M.: frou-frou (rasping, rustling).
fru-cáre [L. **furcare* (*furca,* FORK)], INTR.: grope; search; sound with a stick; TR.: search (seek diligently); excite†, incite†. **-cáta**, F.: groping; searching; blow†. **-ciándolo**, M.: oven-mop. **-cóne**†, M.: pole; sounding-stick; pike-pole; club; fist-blow.
fru-gacchiaménto [*frucare*], M.: searching; sounding. **-gacchiáre**, TR.: sound with stick, search; INTR.: grope.
frugá-le [L. *-lis*], ADJ.: frugal. **-lità**, F.: frugality. **-lménte**, ADV.: frugally.
fru-gaménto, M.: groping. ‖**-gáre** [*-care*], INTR.: grope (fumble); TR.: sound (feel with stick); search; excite†, goad†. **-gáta**, F.: groping; goading†, poking†. **-gatóio**†, M.: fish-driving pole. **-gatóre**, M., **-gatríce**, F.: groper, searcher.
fru-gífero [L. *frux,* fruit], ADJ.: grain-bearing. **-gívoro**, ADJ.: vegetarian.
fru-gnoláre, INTR.: go fowling with lantern; explore with a lantern. **-gno-latóre**, M.: lantern-fowler. ‖**-gnòlo** [*fornuolo*], M.: fowling lantern: *andare a —,* be night-prowling; *entrare nel —,* fly into rage. **-gnuo.. =** *-gno..*
frugo-láre [*frugare*], INTR.: search with the snout. **-létto, -líno**, *car. dim.* of *-lo.* **frúgo-la**, F., **-lo**, M.: restless, mischievous child.
frú-i†, M.: enjoyment. ‖**-íre** [L. *fruor*], TR.: enjoy. **-itívo**, ADJ.: (*theol.*) enjoyable. **-izióne**, F.: fruition; enjoyment.
frúl-la, F.: trifle. **-lána**, F.: scythe. ‖**-láre** [?], INTR.: whiz (whir); REFL.: hasten; TR.: beat up (as eggs, chocolate): *far —,* make go, run, keep to one's duty; *far — uno,* make one hasten. **-líno**, M.: egg-beater; whirligig; trifle†. **frúl-lo**, M.: whirring; hand-mill†; toy†. **-lon-cíno**, *dim.* of *-lone.* **-lóne**, M.: bolting-chest; hand-mill†; four-wheeled calash†.
frumen-tário, ADJ.: relating to grain: *legge -taria,* corn-law. **-tière**†, M.: victualler. ‖**fruménto** [L. *-tum*], M.: grain. **-tóne**, M.: maize. **-tóso**†, ADJ.: grain-producing.
frummiáre†, INTR.: fuss.
fru-sciáre†, INTR.: pry around; TR.: annoy (importune). **-scio**, M.: rustle. ‖**frú-sco**† [?], M.: dead twig (on tree).
frusóne [Fr. *frinson*], M.: bullfinch.
frússi 1 = *flussi.*
frús-si† 2, M.: primero (card-game); flush: *stare a —,* hold a flush. **-so**†, M.: = *-si*; noise.
frústa [L. *fustis*], F.: whip (scourge); whipping.
frustágno [*Fostat,* city in Egypt], M.: FUSTIAN.
fru-stáre [*-sta*], TR.: whip (scourge; lash); wear out: *farsi —,* make one's self laughed at. **-státa**, F.: scourging (castigation); censure. **-statína**, *dim.* of *-stata.* **-statóre**, M.: scourger (flogger). **-statúra**, F.: whipping, scourging. **-stíno**, M.: switch (riding-whip); fop; snapper†. **frú-sto**, ADJ.: worn out; ragged; M.: bit (morsel): *a — a —,* bit by bit. **-stóne**, M.: large, green switch.
frú-stra† [L.], ADV.: in vain. **-strá-neo**, ADJ.: vain (fruitless). **-stráre**, TR.: frustrate, baffle. **-stratòrio**, ADJ.: frustrative.
frú-tice [L. *-tex*], M.: shrub. **-ticèllo, -ticétto**, *dim.* of *-tice.*
frút-ta, pl. *-ta* or *-te,* F.: FRUIT. **-taiò-lo, -taiuòlo**†, M.: fruit-seller. **-táme**, M.: fruit. **-táre**, INTR.: bear fruit; be proliferous; produce profit. **-táto**, PART.: fructified; planted with fruit; M.: produce. **-terèlla**, *car. dim.* of *-ta.* **-této**, M.: fruit-patch, orchard. **-tévole**†, ADJ.: fruitful (fertile). **-ticèllo**, *car. dim.* of *-to.* **-tidòro**, M.: Fructidor (12th Fr. Rev. month). **-tièra**, F.: fruit-dish (dessert-dish). **-tífero, -tiferóso**†, ADJ.: fruitful (fertile). **-tificáre**, INTR.: fructify, bear fruit; produce; yield profit. **-tificáto**, PART. of *-tificare.* **-tifica-zióne**, F.: fructification, production; profit, advantage. **-tífico**, ADJ.: fruitful. ‖**frút-to** [L. *fructus*], M.: fruit (produce); fruit-tree; profit; rent: *-ti fuor di stagione,* (*fig.*) inopportune happenings; *— del denaro,* interest; *-ti di mare,* small shellfish. **-tuáre**† = *-tare.* **-tuosa-ménte**, ADV.: fruitfully (profitably, lucratively). **-tuosità**†, **-tuositáde**†, **-tuositáte**†, F.: fertility (abundance). **-tuòso**, ADJ.: fruitful (profitable).
fu 1 **fu** [echoic], M.: confusion (disorder).
fu† 2, F.: valerian (herb).
fu 3 [Pret. of *essere*], ADJ.: deceased (late).
fucáto†, ADJ.: feigned (affected).
fuci-láre, TR.: fusillade. **-táta**, F.: fusillade. **-lazióne**, F.: fusillading (*mil. sentence*). ‖**fucí-le** [*focile* (*foco,* fire)], M.: fire-steel; fire-lock gun; musket (rifle) **-lière**, M.: fusileer. **fucí-na**, F

forge: — *infernale*, hell. **-máta†**, F.: great quantity. **-nétta**, *dim.* of *-na*.

fúco 1 [L. *-cus*], M.: drone-bee.

fuco 2 [L. *-cus*], M.: fucus, rock-lichen; red dye.

fú-ga [L.], F.: flight (escape); fugue: — *di stanze*, suite of rooms. **-gáce**, ADJ.: fugitive, transient. **-gaceménte**, ADV.: fugitively, transiently. **-gacità**, F.: fugacity. **-gáre**, TR.: put to flight (rout). **-gatóre**, M., **-gatrice**, F.: putter to flight, pursuer. **-gga†** = *fuga*.

fug-gènte, PART. of *-gire*; ADJ.: swift (fleeting); M.: runaway. **fúg-gere** †= *-gire*. **-gévole**, ADJ.: fugitive (flying; transient). **-giascaménte**, ADV.: fugitively. **-giásco**, ADJ.: fugitive; M.: fugitive: *alla -giasca*, as a fugitive. **-gíbile**, ADJ.: avoidable. **-gi=fatica**, M., INVAR.: work-shunner (idler). **-gilòzio**, M.: pastime (recreation). **-giménto**, M.: flight. ‖**-gíre** [L. *fugere*], IRR.§; INTR.: flee, move swiftly; take refuge; TR.: shun (eschew); run away with†, elope; conceal†: smuggle†. **-gíta†**, F.: flight. **-gitíccio†**, ADJ.: fugitive. **-gitivaménte**, ADV.: fugitively; transiently. **-gitívo**, **-gíto†**, ADJ.: fugitive; transient; M.: deserter (runaway). **-gitóre**, M., **-gitríce**, F.: fleer (fugitive, deserter).

§ Pres. *fúggo*, *fúggi*, etc. (Subj.) *fúgga*. I've *fúggi*. — Poet.: Pres. Subj. *fúggia*.

fúio†, M.: thief; villain; ADJ.: thievish; hidden (dark, obscure).

fulcíre†, TR.: prop (sustain).

ful-gènte, ADJ.: shining (brilliant). ‖**fúlgere†** [L.], INTR.: be refulgent (glitter, shine, blaze). **-gidézza**, **-gidità†**, F.: fulgency (splendour). **fúl-gido**, ADJ.: fulgent (brilliant, resplendent). **-goráto†**, ADJ.: refulgent. **-góre**, M.: splendour.

fulig-. . = *filigg*. .

fulmi=cotóne [Fr. *-coton*], M.: guncotton. **-naménto**, M.: fulmination. **-nánte†**, PART. of *-nare*; M.: sulphur match; percussion-cap (capsule). **-náre**, TR.: strike with lightning; fulminate; anathematize. **-nário†**, ADJ.: thundering. **-náto**, PART. of *-nare*; dumfounded. **-nazióne**, F.: fulmination; anathematization. ‖**fúlmi-ne** [L. *fulmen*], M.: lightning, thunderbolt. **fulmí-neo**, ADJ.: thundering; fulmineous.

fúl-vido†, ADJ.: brilliant (shining). ‖**-vo** [L. *-vus* (*-gere*, shine)], ADJ.: fulvid (fawn-coloured, tawny).

fumácchio, M.: smoky charcoal; volcanic smoke-jets or pools; fumigation. **-maiòlo**, M.: chimney-pot; smoky char[coal]. **-málo†**, ADJ.: smoky. **-mánte**, PART. of *-mare*; M.: fire†. **-máre**, INTR.: smoke, fume; steam; be enraged; TR.: smoke (tobacco). **-mária**, F.: (*bot.*) fumitory. **-máta**, F.: smoke-signal; smudge against frost; tobacco-smoking. **-matína**, *car. dim.* of *-mata*. **-matóre**, M.: smoker. **-mèa†**, F.: fumes from the stomach. **-micáre**, INTR.: *freq.* of *-mare*; TR.: fume, smoke. **-micazióne†**, F.: fumigation. **-micóso**, **fú-mido**, ADJ.: smoky; steaming; fuming (of wine). **-migazióne**, F.: fumigation. **fu-mm**. . = *fum*. . ‖**fú-mo** [L. *-mus*], M.: fume (smoke; vapour); vanity (pride); nothing (a trifle). **-mosèllo**, **-mosétto**, *dim.* of *-moso* (*fig.*) **-mosità**, F.: smokiness. **-móso**, ADJ.: smoky; smoking; fuming (of liquors); haughty (vain): *vino* —, rich wine. **-mostèrno**, M.: (*bot.*) FUMITORY.

fu-náio, **-naiòlo** [*-ne*], M.: rope-maker or seller: *far come i -nai*, retrograde, go backwards. **-námbolo**, **-námbulo**, M.: funambulist (rope-walker). **-náme**, M.: ship-tackle (cordage). **-náta**, F.: a ropeful: *fare una* —, get many prisoners, make a raid.

funditóre†, M.: metal founder.

fúne [L. *-nis*], F.: rope; torture-rack; *un po' più* —, a little more help; *stare sulla* —, be in suspense.

fú-nebre [L. *-nebris*], ADJ.: funereal. ‖**-neràle** [L. *-nus*], M.: funeral. **-nèreo**, ADJ.: funereal. **-nestáre**, TR.: sadden (afflict). **-nèsto**, ADJ.: calamitous (sad; fatal).

fún-ga [*-go*], F.: mould. **-gáia**, F.: mushroom-bed; (*disp.*) swarm (crowd).

fúngere [L. *-gi*], TR.: perform (exercise).

fun-ghettíno, *car. dim.* of *-go*. **-ghétto**, *dim.* of *-go*. **-ghíre**, INTR.: get mouldy. ‖**fún-go** [L. *-gus*], M.: fungus (mushroom; tumour); candle-snuff: *far le nozze co' funghi*, be niggardly. **-golíno**, *dim.* of *-go*. **-gosità**, F.: fungosity. **-góso**, ADJ.: fungous, mouldy; snuffy (of candle).

funi-cèlla, F., **-cèllo**, M., **-cína**, F.: *dim.* of *fune*; twine. **-coláre**, ADJ.: funicular; umbilical. **funí=colo**, M.: umbilical cord.

fún-si, PRET. of *fungere*. **-zionáre**, INTR.: perform functions, officiate. **-zionário**, M.: functionary. **-zioncèlla**, **-zioncína**, *dim.* of *-zione*. ‖**-zióne** [L. *-ctio* (*-gor*, perform)], M.: FUNCTION (duty, office).

fuoc. . = *foc*. .

fuò-ra = *-ri*. **-rchè -è**, PREP.: excepted (save). **-rchiúdere†**, TR.: shut out (exclude). **-rchiúso†**, PART.: shut out (excluded). **-re†** = *-ri*. ‖**fuò-ri** [L. *fo-*

ras], PREP.: without; out; beyond; except: — *di*, except; *di —re* (*-ra*), outdoors; *fuor —*, through and through, quite through; *in —*, except, saving; *fuor di maniera*, extraordinary, extraordinarily; — *di mano*, out of the way, rather distant; *fuor di modo* (*d' ordine*), extraordinarily; *esser — di sè*, be delirious; — *di strada*, out of the road, lost; — *di tempo*, inopportune, (*mus.*) out of time; — *d'* (*dell'*) *uso*, obsolete; — *via*, out of the way, distant; *fuor voglia*, unwillingly. **-r-uscíto**, M.: exile.

furá-ce†, ADJ.: thieving. **-ménto†**, M.: theft (robbery). ‖**furá-re** [L. *furari* (*fur*, thief)], TR.: rob; REFL.: steal away (abscond). **-tóre†**, M.: thief (robber).

fur-bacchiòla, **-bacchiòlo**, *car. dim.* of *-bo*. **-bacchióna**, **-bacchióne**, *aug.* of *-bo*. **-bacchiòtta**, **-bacchiòtto**, *dim.* of *-bo*. **-báccio**, *aug.* of *-bo*. **-baccióna**, **-baccióne**, *aug.* of *-bo*. **-baménte**, ADV.: slyly. **-bería**, F.: shrewdness (slyness; astuteness). **-berièla**, *car. dim.* of *-beria*. **-bescaménte**, ADV.: astutely (shrewdly). **-bésco**, ADJ.: shrewd (sly, astute): *lingua* (or *parlare*) *-besca* (or *-besco*), thieves' slang, cant. **-bétto**, *dim.* of *-bo*. ‖**fúr-bo** [OHG. *-ban*, polish], ADJ.: shrewd (sly); swindling†; rascally†; M.: shrewd fellow; rogue† (scoundrel†). **-bóne**, *aug.* of *-bo*.

furènte [L. *-rens*], ADJ.: FURious.

furétto†, M.: ferret.

fur-fantáccio, *disp.* of *-fante*. **-fantággine**, F.: knavery. **-fantáre**, INTR.: live vicious life. **-fánte**, PART. of *-fare*; M.: rascal (knave); ADJ.: wretched (vile); false†. **-fantèllo**, *dim.* of *-fante*. **-fantería**, F.: knavery. **-fantésco**, ADJ.: rascally. **-fantíno**, ADJ.: rascally: *lingua -fantina*, rascals' slang. **-fantóne**, *aug.* of *-fante*. ‖**-fáre** [L. *foris facere*, act beyond (the right)], TR.: cheat; extort.

fúri-a [L.], F.: fury (passion; impetuosity); hurry. **-áccia**, *disp. aug.* of *-a*. **-alménte†**, ADV.: furiously. **-áre†**, INTR.: be infuriated. **-áto†**, PART.: furious. **-bondáre†**, INTR.: be furious, frantic. **-bóndo**, ADJ.: furious (raging, frantic).

furière = *foriere*.

furi-étta, *dim.* of *-a*. **-osaménte**, ADV.: furiously (vehemently). **-osétto**, *dim.* of *-oso*. **-osità**, F.: furiousness. **-óso**, ADJ.: furious.

furlána (and vulg. *frullana*) [district of *Friuli*], F.: furlanian dance.

fú-ro†, M.: thief. **-roncèllo†**, *dim.* of *-ro*. **-róne†**, *aug.* of *-ro*.

furó-re [L. *-r*], M.: fury (rage; vehemence); furore ("hit"): *far —*, arouse enthusiasm. **-reggiáre**, INTR.: make a hit.

fur-tarèllo, *dim.* of *-to*. **-tivaménte**, ADV.: furtively. **-tívo**, ADJ.: furtive. ‖**fúr-to** [L. *-tum* (*fur*, thief)], M.: theft, booty: *di* (*per*) —, furtively, secretly.

furúncolo†, M.: boil.

fu-sáccio, *disp.* of *-so 2*. **-sággine**, F.: spindle-tree. **-sáio**, M.: spindle maker or seller. **-saiòla**, F.: spindle-rack. **-saiòlo**, **-saiuòlo†**, M.: whirl for a spindle. **-saròla** = *-saiola*. **-sáta**, F.: spindleful. **-sáto**, ADJ.: spindling (tapering).

fuscel-létto, **-líno**, M.: *dim.* of *-lo*: *cercare col —*, search with minuteness or pedantry; *rompere il —*, break friendship. ‖**fuscèl-lo** [*fusto*], M.: twig (stick): *-li impaniati*, limed twigs; *rompere il —*, break friendship. **-líno**, *dim.* of *-lo*: *cercar col —*, search diligently, hunt for.

fusciác-ca [Ger. *fusshacke*, heel (to which sash hangs)], F.: wide sash; pendent ends. **-co**, M.: canopy for crucifix.

fusciárra [? *fustiaria*, flogging], F.: scamp.

fúsco†, ADJ.: dark, gloomy.

fusel-láto, ADJ.: spindling (tapering). **-latúra**, F.: tapering (giving spindle-form). ‖**fusèl-lo** [*fuso 2*], M.: axle-end; wooden cylinder in paper-mill.

fú-si, PRET. of *fondere*. **-síbile**, ADJ.: fusible. **-sibilità**, F.: fusibility.

fu-sièra [*-so 2*], F.: spindle-holder. **-si-fórme**, ADJ.: spindle-form.

fu-sióne, F.: fusion (melting). ‖**fú-so 1**, PART. of *fondere*: fused (melted, liquefied).

fú-so 2, pl. *-si* or *-sa* [L. *-sus*], M.: spindle; shaft; custom-officer's sounding-stick; bell-founder's wooden model; arbour of mill; pl. *-sa*, purr: *fare le -sa*, purr; *far le -sa torte*, be unfaithful to one's husband. **fú-solo**, M.: *dim.* of *-so*; shin-bone; axle of millstone.

fusóne†, M.: two-year-old stag: *a —*, in quantity.

fusòrio [*-so 1*], ADJ.: relating to metal-melting: *forno —*, fusing-furnace.

fústa 1 [L. *-tis*], F.: light galley.

fústa† 2, F.: small torch.

fustágno [*Fostat*, in Egypt], M.: FUSTIAN.

fu-stáio, M.: saddle-frame maker. **-sticèllo**, M.: small stalk. **-stigáre**, TR.: flog. **-stigazióne**, F.: flagellation. ‖**fú-sto** [L. *-stis*, club], M.: stalk; trunk; framework (of furniture, etc.): — *della chiave*, barrel of a key; — *della stadera*, arm of steelyard. **-stúccio**, *dim.* of *-sto*.

fúta†, F.: flight.

fúti-le [L. *-lis*], ADJ.: futile (vain). **-li-**

tà, F.: futility. **-lménte**, ADV.: futilely.

futu-raménte†, ADV.: in future. ||**futú-ro** [L. *-rus*], ADJ., M.: future: *anno* —, next year; *i -ri*, posterity.

G

g *gi* [L.], M.: g (the letter).

gabba=dèo [*-re*], M.: bigot, hypocrite. **-ménto**, M.: deceit. **=móndo**, M., INVAR.: deceiver (Eng.† gabber).

gabba-nèlla, F.: hospital blouse. **-nét-to**, *dim.* of *-no*. ||**gabbá-no** [? cf. Eng. *gabardine*, Sp. *gabán*)], M.: rustic cloak or frock; clumsy overcoat. **-nóne**, *aug.* of *-no*.

gab-báre [*-bo*], TR.: deceive (cheat), disappoint (Eng.† GAB); deride†; beguile†: *-barsi d' uno*, jeer at. **-ba=sánti**, M., INVAR.: bigot; hypocrite. **-batóre**, M., **-batríce**, F.: deceiver, impostor (cf. Eng.† gabber). **-bévole**, ADJ.: deceitful, contemptible.

gáb-bia [L. *cavea*, cavity], F.: CAGE, aviary; prison; olive or grape bag; ox-muzzle; (*nav.*) top (for top-mast rigging). **-biáio**, M.: cage-maker.

gabbiáno [L. *gavia*, sea-mew], M.: gull; (*fig.*) fool.

gab-biáta [*-bia*], F.: cageful (of birds). **-bière**, **-bièro**, M.: (*nav.*) top-man. **-biétta**, **-biettína**, **-biòla**, **-biolína**, *dim.* of *-bia*. **-bionáta**, F.: large cageful (of animals); (*fort.*, *hydr.*) gabionade (structure of gabions). **-bioncèllo**, *dim.* of *-bione*. **-bióne**, M.: large cage (esp. compartment owl cage); (*mil.*, *hydr.*) gabion. **-biúccia**, *dim.* of *-bia*.

gábbo [Fr. *gaber* (ASax. *gabban*, mock, GAB)], M.: mocking: *pigliare* (*prendere*) *a* — or *farsi* — *di*, laugh at, mock, make light of; (*fig.*) veil.

gabèl-la [Fr. *-le*], F.: excise-tax ("octroi"); excise custom-house; government salt-house†: *fare il minchion per non pagar* —, pretend ignorance to avoid trouble or expense. **-lábile**, ADJ.: taxable, dutiable; (*fig.*) approvable, admissible. **-láre**, TR.: assess, levy tax on; pay (tax); credit: — *una cosa per*, make a thing pass as or for; — *una cosa*, accept a thing as true. **-lière**, M.: exciseman; tax farmer†. **-líno**, **-lòtto**, *disp.* of *-liere*.

gabi-nettíno, *car. dim.* of *-netto*. ||**-nét-to** [Fr. *cabinet*], M.: cabinet; private study; closet; cabinet† (chest of drawers).

gabrína, F.: hag (from character in Ariosto).

gábro [?], M.: (*min.*) serpentine.

gag-gía [Gr. *akakía*, thorn-tree], F.: acacia-flower. **-gío** 1, M.: acacia.

gággio 2†, M.: GAGE (pledge); hostage; salary; reward: — *morto*, lost capital.

gagliár-da, F.: old dance. **-daménte**, ADV.: vigorously. **-dázzo†**, *disp.* of *-do*. **-dézza**, F.: strength (esp. of liquors). **-día**, F.: robustness, vigour. ||**gagliár-do** [Celt. *gall*, strength], ADJ.: strong, robust; powerful: *alla -da*, vigorously, valiantly; *borsa -da*†, full purse; *vino* —, rich wine.

gáglio†, M.: rennet.

gagliof-fáccio, *disp.* of *-fo*. **-fággine**, F.: worthlessness, doltishness. **-faménte**, ADV.: doltishly. **-fería**, F.: worthlessness; scurrility†. ||**gagliòf-fo** [?], M.: worthless fellow; dolt; ADJ.: coarse, brutal; worthless; knavish. **-fóne**, *aug.* of *-fo*.

gaglióso†, ADJ.: containing rennet.

gagliuòlo†, M.: seed-vessel (pod shell).

gágno†, M.: lair (of wild beast); stable, fold; intrigue; abdomen.

gagno-laménto, M.: yelping. ||**-láre** [?], INTR.: yelp, whine. **-lío**, M.: whining, yelping.

ga-iaménte, ADV.: gayly (merrily). **-iét-to**, *dim.* of *-io*. **-iézza**, F.: gaiety, joyous temper. ||**gá-io** [OHG. *gahi*], ADJ.: GAY (merry, joyful, bright); well provided.

gá-la [OFr. *-le*], F.: strip of galoon or lace; finery (ornament); gala (pomp): *con* —, gracefully; *di* —, merrily, cheerfully; frankly; *far* —, be merry, feast; *giorno di* —, gala day; *star sulle -le*, love dress and finery; follow the fashion. **-láno**, M.: elegant bow(-knot). **-lánte**, ADJ.: gallant (showy, gay in dress, elegant); given to love (amourous); M.†: gallant (lady's man, cicisbeo); ADV.: = *-lantemente*. **-lanteggiáre**, INTR.: play the galant. **-lanteménte**, ADV.: elegantly; gallantly (in a gallant or polite manner). **-lantería**, F.: finery (elegant thing, trinket, small article of jewelry, Eng.† gallantry); gallantry, politeness, attention.

galantína [L. L. *-latina*, JELLY], F.: capon pie.

galant-íno, *dim.* of *galante*. **-ominó-ne**, *disp. aug.* of *-omo*. **-omísmo**, M.: act of a man of honour, honourableness. **=òmo**, M.: man of honour, honest man. **-omóno**, *aug.* of *-omo*. **=uòmo** = *-omo*.

galáppio [*calappio*], M.: trap (snare, noose).

galássia†, F.: GALAXY; milky way.

galatèo [*Galata*, suburb of Constantinople], M.: Galateo (book by Casa, which teaches manners); civility (good breeding).

galá-tida†, ‖**-ttíte** [Gr. *gála*, milk], F.: galactite (milk-stone†). **-ttòfago**†, M.: one who eats milky foods.

gal-baníforo†, ADJ.: producing galbanum. ‖**-báno** [L. *-banum*], M.: galbanum (gum of Syriac plant).

gald. .† = *gaud*. .

gálea 1 [L. (cf. Eng. *galea*)], F.: helmet.

galèa 2 [?], F.: GALLEY.

galeáre†, TR.: deceive (cheat, impose upon); make fun of (laugh at).

galeáto [*galea* 1], PART.: GALEATED (wearing a helmet).

galeatóre†, M.: deceiver (cheater).

galeázza [*galea* 2], F.: large galley.

galeffáre†, TR.: ridicule; laugh at.

ga-leóne [*-lea* 2], M.: galleon (Span. ship), large galley; (*fig.*) vagabond, cheat (knave). **-leòtta**†, F.: (*nav.*) galliot. **-leòtto**, M.: galley-slave (convict); cheat; pimp†; pilot†. **-lèra**, F.: galley; punishment; place of punishment.

ga-leríeulo†, *dim.* of *-lero*. ‖**-lèro** [L. *-lerum* (*-lea*, helmet), cap], M.: fur cap; pontiff's cap; priest's cap.

ga-lestríno, ADJ.: of clay. ‖**-lèstro** [?], M.: kind of clay. **-lestróso**, ADJ.: of clay.

gali-gáio [L. *caliga*, shoe], M.: tanner (currier).

gali-gaménto†, M.: dimness (of sight). ‖**-gáre**†, INTR.: be dim-sighted, be involved in a mist.

galióne† = *galeone*.

galiòsso†, M.: skittles, nine-pins.

gálla [L.], F.: gall-nut; tumour; bubble; gland†; acorn†; pill†; berry†: *star a* —, float.

galláre† 1 [? *galla*], INTR.: float; exult (be elated); be proud.

gal-láre 2 [*-lo*], TR.: fecundate (of the cock). **-lastróne** = *-lerone*.

galleg-giaménto, M.: action of floating. ‖**-giáre** [? *galla*], INTR.: float; be very gay (have excessive joy).

gallería [l. L.], F.: GALLERY; tunnel.

galleróne [*gallo*], M.: large cock.

gallétta 1, F.: kind of grape.

gallétta† 2, F.: goblet.

gal-lettíno, *dim.* of *-letto*. ‖**-létto** [*-lo*], M.: young cock; leguminous plant†.

gallétti [*galetta*], M.: thin cake.

gallicínio [*gallo*], M.: cock-crow; midnight (when the cock crows).

galli-cíşmo [*Gallia*], M.: gallicism. **gál-li-co**, pl. *-ci*, ADJ.: Gallic (French): *morbo* —, syphilis.

gal-lína [*gallo*], F.: hen: — *di Faraone*, — *prataiola*, Guinea hen; — *gobba*, Indian hen; — *regina*, wood-hen; *latti di* —, beverage composed of eggs, milk and sugar, something rare and exquisite; — *mugellese*, one who looks younger than he really is; *giuoco delle -line*, private lottery; *andare a* —, die, go to ruin; *mandare a* —, fling away, ruin. **-lináccia**, *disp.* of *-lina*. **-lináccio**, M.: turkey-cock; mushroom. **-lináceo**, ADJ.: gallinaceous. **-lináio**, M.: chicken-coop; chicken-thief; one who runs a private lottery. **-lióne**†, M.: bad capon; blockhead. ‖**gál-lo** [L. *-lus*], M.: cock; = *-loria*†: — *d'India*, turkey-cock; — *di montagna*, heath-cock; *far il* —, *mettere su* —, put on airs (be arrogant); *il* — *della checca*, ladies' man; *più largo d'un* —†, avaricious man; *più bugiardo che un* —†, great liar; *più scoperto d'un* —, great boaster.

gal-lonáre, TR.: ornament with galloon (lace). **-loneíno**, *dim.* of *-lone*. ‖**-lóne** [? *-a*], M.: GALLOON (lace); flank (side)†.

gal-lòria [*-lo*], F.: clamour (noise, exaltation): *far* —, be haughty. **-loriáre**†, INTR.: be clamorous (exultant).

gal-lòzza [*-la*], **-lòzzola**, F.: gall-nut; swelling; bubble. **-luzzáre**†, INTR.: thrill with joy (exult).

galop-páre [?], INTR.: gallop. **-páta**, F.: galloping; race. **-patóre**, M.: galloper. **-píno**, M.: useful person, errand boy. **galòp-po**, M.: gallop; (*of persons*) *andare a* —, go in great haste.

galòscia [?], F.: galoche.

galúppo†, M.: kind of soldier; (*fig.*) abject man.

galvá-nico, ADJ.: galvanic. ‖**-níşmo** [inventor *Galvani*], M.: galvanism. **-nişáre**, TR.: galvanize.

gám-ba [L.], F.: leg (*lit.* or *fig.*); (*mus.*) bar: *andare a -be alzate* (or *-bate*), go to ruin; *andar di buona o mala* —, go willingly or unwillingly; *aver* — *a una cosa*, know how to do a thing, have much practice; *darla a -be*, take to one's heels; *dare alle -be a uno*, hurt one with words and actions; *esser in -be*, be well, though old; *fare di sotto* —, do with much ease; *guardar la* —, take care; *mandar a -be levate*, trip up one's heels, ruin; *mettersi la coda, o la via, fra le -be*, walk fast; *mettersi, rimettersi in -be*, recover; *mettersi il capo fra le -be*, go away for shame; *raddrizzare, addrizzare le -be a' cani*, fatigue one's self in vain; *non reggersi in -be*, be very weak on account of sickness or old age; *stare bene, o male, in -be*, be strong or weak. **-báccia**, *disp.* of *-ba*. **-bále**, M.: shoe-last; stock, trunk (of tree)†; cuish†. **-bàta**, F.: kick (blow with the leg): *dar la* —, supplant another in love. **-beráccia**, F.: ulcerated leg.

gam-berèllo†, *dim.* of *-bero*. ‖**gám**

bero [L. *-barus* (*camera*, arch), sea-crab], M.: crayfish; (*typ.*) doublet: — *di mare*, lobster; *far come i -beri*, go backwards (be unprogressive).

gam-beróne, M.: varicose or swollen leg; long-legged fellow. **-beruòlo**, M.: greave (leg armour). **-bétta**, *disp. dim.* of *-ba*. **-bettáre†**, INTR.: kick the legs about. **-bétto**, M.: *dare a uno il —*, trip up one's heels; (*fig.*) injure. **-bièra** = *-bale*. **-bína**, **-bíno**, *car. dim.* of *-ba*, *-bo*. ‖**-bo** [L. *-ba*, hoof], M.: stalk (stem); joint; trunk† (of tree); limb (of letter, stroke)†. **-bóna**, **-bóne**, *aug.* of *-ba*, *-bo*: *dare —*, grow insubordinate. **-búccia**, *disp.* of *-be*. **-búle†**, M.: cuish (thigh-guards). **-búto†**, ADJ.: thin-stalked; long-legged.

gamèlla [Fr. *-lle* (L. *camera*, vault)], F.: (*mil.*) tin-can used for mess.

gám-ma [Gr.], F.: gamma (third letter of Greek alphabet). **-maútte**, **-máut**, M.: (*surg.*) bistoury (small knife).

ga(m)már-ra [? Sp. *camarro*], F., **-ríno**, M.: petticoat; woollen cloth.

gána†, F.: (*pop.*) *di —*, willingly (with pleasure); *di mala —*, unwillingly.

ga-náscia [L. *gena*, cheek], F.: jaw-bone (jaw); PL.: jaws (of pincers, vise, etc.); part of a gun which holds the flint (flint-box). **-nascíno**, *car. dim.* of *-nascia*. **-nascióne†**, M.: slap on the face; (*mus.*) Italian lute.

gan-cétto, *dim.* of *-cio*. **-ciáta**, F.: grasping with a hook. ‖**gán-cio** [? L. *cancer*, crab], M.: metal-hook (hasp).

ganghe-ráre, TR.: fasten to or set on hinges. **-ratúra**, F.: place where a thing is hinged **-rèlla**, *fem.* of *-ro*: — *maglietta*, stitch or mesh in netting. **-rétto**, **-ríno**, *dim.* of *-ro*. ‖**gánghe-ro** [? L. *cancer*, crab], M.: hook (clasp); hinge: *stare ne' -ri*, take heed (be on one's guard); *cavar de' -ri*, take off one's guard; *dare*, *fare un —*, give the slip (run away); *uscir de' -ri*, *esser fuori de' -ri*, get angry; *uomo fatto a -ri*, grumbler.

gánglio [Gr. *-glion*], M.: GANGLION (nerve-knot).

gángo-la [*glandula*], F.: gland; king's evil: *far — a uno*, spite one with a certain action. **-lóso**, ADJ.: glandulous; scrofulous.

Ganimè-de [L. *Ganymedes*], M.: Ganymede; dandy (fop). **-dúzzo**, *disp.* of *-de*.

gannire†, INTR.: yelp.

gán-za [?], F.: mistress. **-záre**, INTR.: be in love. **-zeríno**, M.: spark. **-zo**, M.: lover (paramour).

[g]ára [?], F.: competition (rivalry): *a —*, [i]n competition with; *vincere la —*, carry [o]ff the prize.

garaballáre†, (IN)TR.: confuse (disarrange); deceive (defraud); be idle.

garagol†. . = *caracol*. .

gara-moncíno, M.: bourgeois (kind of printing type). ‖**-móne** [printer *Garamond*], M.: long primer type.

gar-ánte [MHG. *werens*], M.: WARRANT, GUARANTEE; surety; (*naut.*) rope's end. **-antíre**, TR.: GUARANTEE (act surety); save (render secure). **-ánzia**, F.: guaranty (security, warranty).

garavína†, F.: sea-gull.

gar-báccio, M.: *disp.* of *-bo*; impoliteness (incivility; impolite action). **-báre** [*-bo*], INTR.: please (be agreeable, suit); be graceful†. **-batamente**, ADV.: gracefully; politely. **-batézza**, F.: politeness (gracefulness, gentility). **-batíno**, *car. dim.* of *-bato*. **-báto**, PART.: graceful, pleasing; polite (civil): *un lavoro —*, work done elegantly, skilfully; *troppo —*, too kind (expression of thanks to one who has done a kindness); (*iron.*) — *il signorino*, impolite, uncivil man. **-beggiáre†**, INTR.: please (suit, be agreeable). **-bíno 1**, *car. dim.* of *-bo*. **-bíno 2**, M.: south-west wind. ‖**gár-bo 1** [?], M.: manner, esp. graceful manner (grace, elegance); taste; skill; ornament: *uomo di —*, courteous man; *a —*, good (excellent); well; gracefully.

gárbo 2 [OHG. *harw* (= Ger. *herb*)], ADJ.: tart (sharp, bitter); harsh (rude).

garbúglio [?], M.: confusion, intrigue; agitation: — *di venti †*, whirlwind; *metter in — †*, embroil (disorder, confuse).

gareg-giaménto, M.: contention, emulation. ‖**-giáre** [*gara*], INTR.: compete (rival). **-giatóre**, M., **-giatríce**, F.: competitor (rival). **garég-gio†**, M.: contention. **-gióso**, ADJ.: contentious.

garent. . = *garant*. .

garétto [OFr. *-ret*], M.: Achilles' tendon; (*naut.*) top-rim.

garga-gliáre† [ak. to *gorgo*], INTR.: sing noisily. **-gliáta†**, F.: clamour. **-mèlla**, used ADV.: *bere a —*, drink without putting the vessel to the lips, gulp down. **-ntíglia†**, F.: neck-lace. **-rísmo**, M.: gargle (GARGARISM). **-rizzáre**, TR.: gargle (Eng.† gargarise). **-rózzo**, M.: throat (crop, craw). **-'tta†**, F: throat.

gárgia [? *cardia*], F.: gill (of fish).

gárgo [? OHG. *karg*, bad], ADJ.: crafty (knavish, sly).

gargòtta [Fr. *-gote* (root *garg-*, swallow)], F.: chop-house (paltry eating-house).

garíbo†, M.: dance (ball).

garò-fána, ADJ.: of October pears; of cloves. **-fanáre†**, TR.: give or impart the odour of cloves. **-fanáta**, F.: plant good for wounds. **-fanáto**, ADJ.: which smells like carnation or cloves: *viola* —, kind of gillyflower. ||**garò-fano** [Gr. *karuó-phullon*, 'nut-leaf'], M.: aroma of cloves or carnation; clove; gillyflower.

garóne = *gherone*.

ga-rontoláre, TR.: (*vulg.*) strike with the fist. ||**-róntolo** [Gr. *grónthos*, fist], M.: fisticuff (blow under armpit).

garopàllo† = *carosello*.

garóso†, ADJ.: contentious.

gárpa†, F.: spavin; PL.: galls.

garrése [?], M. PL.: withers, shoulders (of domestic animals).

garrét-ta†, **-to** = *garetto*.

gar-révole†, ADJ.: menacing; scolding (rebuking). **-riménto**†, M.: chiding (rebuking, reprimand). ||**-ríre** [L.], INTR.: warble (chirp, chatter); TR.: scold (reprove, reprimand, chide). **-rissário**†, ADJ.: garrulous (talkative). **-ríto**, M.: (*poet.*) chirping (warbling); rebuff (reprimand). **-ritóre**, M.: scold (grumbler).

garru-laménte, ADV.: in a prattling manner. **-lità**†, F.: garrulity (loquacity); slander (calumny). ||**gárru-lo** [L. *-lus*], ADJ.: GARRULOUS (talkative).

gárza [Sp. (L. *ardea*)], F.: white heron.

gar-záre, TR.: card cloth. **-zatóre**, M.: one who cards cloth. **-zèlla**, F.: instrument for carding cloth. ||**-zo** [*cardo*], M.: card†; carding of cloth: *dare il* —, card. **-zòlo**, M.: heart of lettuce or cabbage; wax drawn and bleached; fine hemp.

garzo-líno†, M.: little boy (child). ||**gar-zó-na**, F., **-no** [ak. to Fr. *garçon* (der.?)], M.: farm-servant; shop-boy; boy; bachelor†. **-nástro**†, *disp.* of *-ne*. **-ncèllo**, **-ncíno**, *dim.* of *-ne*. **-neggiáre**†, INTR.: make one's self young. **-nétto**, *car. dim.* of *-ne*. **-nevolménte**†, ADV.: boyishly (childishly); like a young man. **-nézza**†, F.: boyhood (childhood); youth. **-nile**†, ADJ.: boyish (childish). **-nòtto**†, *aug.* of *-ne*.

garzuòlo† = *garzolo*.

gás, (*vulg.*) **gásso** [word made by v. Helmont], M.: gas. **-òmetro**, M.: gasometer. **-ósa**, F.: drink, potion. **-óso**, ADJ.: gaseous.

gasti-gagióne†, F.: CASTIGATION (punishment, chastisement). **-gamátti**, M.: whip; chastiser. **-gaménto**†, M.: punishment (chastisement). ||**-gáre** [L. *castigare*], TR.: CASTIGATE (chastise, punish); correct†; reprimand† (reprove). **-gatézza**, F.: purity of style. **-gatóre**, M., **-gatríce**, F.: CASTIGATOR (chastiser). **-gatúra**†, **-gazióne**†, F.: castigation (chastisement). **gastí-go**, M.: castigation (punishment, correction); annoying musical instrument.

ga-stralgía, F.: gastralgia. **-strici-smo**, M.: gastric affections. ||**gá-strico** [Gr. *gastér*, stomach], ADJ.: gastric; of gastric fever: *sughi* —*ci*, gastric juice. **-stronomía** [Gr. *-stér*, *-nomós*, law], F.: gastronomy. **-stronòmico**, ADJ.: gastronomic. **-stròmomo**, M.: GASTRONOME (gastronomer).

gát-ta [*-to*], F.: female cat: *chiamar la* — —, call things by their right name (speak plain): *far la* — *morta* (or *la* — *di Masino*), "play possum" (pretend innocence); *uscire di* — *morta*, or *mogia*, quit deceit and show clearly one's intentions; — *ci cova!* there is a snake in the grass! *non portar* — *in sacco*, speak freely; *voler la* —, act seriously, be in earnest; *nè cane nè* —, neither one thing nor the other. **-táccio**, *disp.* of *-to*. **-táia**, **-taiòla**, F.: hole in a door for cats (cat's hole). **-ta=mòrta**, pl. *gattemorte*, F.: "playing possum": *far la* —, "play possum." **-tésco**, ADJ.: cat-like. **gát-tice**, M.: kind of tree. **-ticída**, M.: cat-killer. **-tigliáre**, TR., RECIPR.: litigate; vex one's self on account of nothing. **-tíno**, M.: *dim.* of *-to*; kitten. ||**gát-to** [L. *cat(t)us*], M.: cat; engine of war for battering walls (battering-ram); machine for driving in piles (pile-driver): *essere il* — *di casa*, be in great confidence with a family, go and come freely; *esser quattro -ti*, be few persons in a family (be few); — *frugato*†, gaping countryman. **-to=mammóne**, M.: marmoset (species of ape). **-tóne**, M.: *aug.* of *-to*; tomcat; (*fig.*) cunning fellow: *far il* —, play the simpleton.

gattóni [*gotoni*], M. PL.: mumps (inflammation of glands).

gat-to=párdo, M.: ferocious beast. **-to=sibétto**, M.: civet cat. ||**-táccio**, M.: *disp.* of *-to*; sea-dog (kind of fish); hand-saw.

gau-deámus [L., 'let us rejoice']: *stare*, *vivere in* —, live joyously. **-dènte**, ADJ.: rejoicing: *frati* —, monastic order. **-dentóne**, *aug.* of *-dente*. ||**gáu-dio** [L. *-dium*], M.: joy (gladness, rejoicing). **-diosaménte**, ADV. of *-dioso*; (*lit.*) with pleasure. **-dióso**, ADJ.: joyful (very glad): *misteri* —, part of the Rosary which records the happiness of Virgin Mary.

gaváz-za, F., **-zaménto**, M.: immoderate merriment (excessive joy). ||**-záre** [L. *gaudere*, rejoice], INTR.: jump for joy (rejoice exceedingly). **-zière**†, M.: loud or noisy rejoicer.

gaveg-giáre†, TR.: court (woo). **-gíno**†, M.: wooer (lover).

gavétta [?], F.: bundle of musical strings; wooden bowl† (porringer).

ga-vígne [*cavo*], F. PL.: cavity beneath the armpits where wrestlers grasp one another. **-vìn.** . = *gangol.* .
gavónchio [?], M.: marine eel.
gavòtta [*Garots*, inhabitant of Gap, in France], F.: kind of sea-fowl or sea-fish; gavot (a dance).
gáz-za [OHG. *agalastra* (= Ger. *elster*)], F.: magpie; (*fig.*) babbler (chatterer): *pelare la — senza farla stridere*, take advantage of one without his perceiving it; — *che ha pelata la coda*†, great cunning. **-zárra**, F.: joyous uproar. **-zèlla**, F.: *dim.* of *-za;* gazelle (antelope). **gáz-zera**, F.: magpie. **-zeròtto**†, M.: *disp.* of *-za;* stupid fellow.
gazzét-ta [orig. a coin, the cost of the paper (L. *gaza*, treasure)], F.: GAZETTE (newspaper): *battere le -te*, tremble with cold. **-tánte**, M.: (*disp.*) eager newspaper reader; newspaper writer. **-tière**, M.: (*disp.*) journalist. **-tíno**, M.: *dim.* of *-ta: fare un —, essere un —*, relate indiscreetly.
gèbo†, M.: he-goat.
ge-laménto, M.: congelation (freezing). ||**-láre** [*-lo*], TR., INTR.: freeze (congeal); quail; curdle†. **-láta**, F.: frost. **-lataménte**, ADV.: frostily (coldly). **-latína**, F.: jelly. **-latinóso**, ADJ.: GELATINOUS (gelatine). **-láto**, ADJ.: frozen; cold (chilly); terrified (frightened); M.: sherbet (ice-cream).
gèldra†, F.: crowd.
ge-licídio†, M.: frosty weather. **-lidézza**, F.: state of being frozen; insensibility. **gè-lido**, ADJ.: GELID (cold, chilly, frozen). ||**gè-lo** [L. *gelu*, cold], M.: freezing weather; coolness†; sugar crust†. **-lóne**, M.: chilblain; *aug.* of *gelo*†.
gelo-sáccio, *aug.* of *-so.* **-saménte**, ADV.: jealously; carefully; anxiously. **-sía**, F.: jealousy; care; lattice (Persian); apprehension† (anxiety). ||**geló-so** [L. *zelosus* (*zelus*, zeal)], ADJ.: jealous (envious); solicitous; careful; delicate: *affari -si*, delicate affairs; — *consuetudine*, scrupulous habit.
gèl-sa†, F.: mulberry. **-séta**, F., **-séto**, M.: land planted with mulberry trees. **-síno**, *dim.* of *-so.* ||**gèl-so** [L. *celsus* (*cellere*, rise)], M.: mulberry-tree.
gelsomíno [Ar. *jasmin*], M.: JASMINE (JESSAMINE).
geme-bóndo [*-re*], ADJ.: lamenting (plaintive).
gemèl-lo [L. *-lus*], M., ADJ.: twin: *-li*, (*astron.*) Gemini.
gè-mere [L.], INTR.: moan (lament, groan); drop (trickle down); creak; print (stamp). **-micáre**, INTR.: trickle lightly.
gemi-náre [L. *-ni*, twins], TR.: geminate (double). **-natúra**, F.: action or effect of geminating. **-nazióne**, F.: gemination (reduplication, doubling). **-gè-mi-no**, ADJ.: geminous (double); M. PL.: (*astron.*) twins.
gemíre† = *gemere.*
ge-mítio [*-mere*], M.: trickling, sweating. **gè-mito**, M.: moan.
gèm-ma [L.], F.: GEM; eye (of a peacock feather); bud. **-máre**†, INTR.: bud (sprout); gem. **-máto**, PART.: jewelled (studded with gems). **-métta**, *dim.* of *-ma.* **-mièra**, F.: gem (jewel). **-mífero**, ADJ.: gemmiferous; of soil producing precious stones.
gemònie [L. *-monia*, sighs], F. PL.: *scale* —, stairway of great prison at Campidoglio.
gèna†, F.: cheek.
gendár-me [Fr. *gens d'armes*, 'men at arms'], M.: gendarme; (*pop.*) carabinier. **-mería**, F.: gendarmery.
genea-logía [L.], genealogy. **-lògico**, ADJ.: genealogical. **-logísta**, M.: genealogist.
generábi-le [*generare*], ADJ.: that may be engendered. **-lità**, F.: productiveness.
gené-bro†, M.: juniper-tree.
genera-láto, M.: generalship; rank of general. ||**generá-le** [L. *-lis*], ADJ.: general (universal); M.: general (commander): *spacciare pel* —, deal in generals (avoid details); *uscir de'* —, come to particulars. **-líssimo**, ADJ.: superl. of *-le;* M.: generalissimo (general-in-chief). **-lità**, F.: GENERALITY. **-lizzáre**, TR.: GENERALIZE. **-lménte**, ADV.: generally (almost always); in the greater part.
gene-raménto†, M.: generation. **-ránte**, PART. of *-rare.* **-ráre**, TR.: generate (produce, engender). **-rativaménte**, ADV. of *-rativo.* **-ratívo**, ADJ.: generative. **-ratóre**, M.: generator. **-razióne**, F.: generation (progeny); kind (race, species); quality; genesis; proceeding of second person of Trinity from the Father. ||**gène-re** [L. *genus*], M.: GENUS (kind); (*gram.*) GENDER; species (nature); system: *in* — (opposed to species), in general; *un — di vita*, coarse kind of life. **-ricaménte**, ADV.: GENERICALLY. **genè-rico**, ADJ.: generic, common: *attore* —, generic actor. **-ríno**, *car. dim.* of *-re.* **gène-ro** [L. *gener*], M.: son-in-law.
genero-saménte, ADV.: generously. **-sità**, F.: GENEROSITY (magnanimity). ||**generó-so** [L. *-sus*, noble], ADJ.: generous (noble, magnanimous): *vino* —, strong wine, *terreno* —, very fertile land.

gènesi [Gr. *génesis*], F.: genesis; generation (birth).

genetlíaco [Gr. *genethliakós* (*genéthle*, birth)], ADJ.: genethliacal (of or pertaining to nationalities); M.: nativity (birthday); calculator of nativities, astrologer.

gengía = *gengiva*.

gengiòvo†, M.: ginger.

gengí-va [L. *gingiva*, gum], F.: (*anat.*) gum. **-vétta**, *car. dim.* of *-va*.

genía [Gr. *geneá*, birth], F.: (*disp.*) race; multitude†.

ge-niáccio, *disp.* of *-nio*. **-niále**, ADJ.: genial (pleasing). **-nialità**, F.: geniality (sympathy). **-nialménte**, ADV.: genially. ‖**gè-nio** [L. *genius*], M.: genius (spirit, demon); genius (talent); inclination (character, temper): *andare a* —, please; *con* —, with satisfaction. **-nitábile†**, ADJ.: generative. **-nitále**, ADJ.: genital: *terra* —, native land. **-nitívo**, M.: genitive case. **gè-nito**, ADJ.: generated (born); M.: child (son). **-nitóre**, M.: father. **-nitríce**, F.: mother. **-nitúra**, F.: generation (birth); seed.

gennáio [L. *Janus*], M.: January: *sudar di* —, give one's self much trouble; *fare sudar di* —, cause one to think.

genelogía†, F.: GENEALOGY.

gènevo†, F. PL.: ceremonies.

genoví-na [*Genova*], F., **-no**, M.: Genoese coin.

gensomíno = *gelsomino*.

gen-táccia, **-táglia**, F., **-táme**, M.: *disp.* of *-te*; rabble (mob). ‖**gèn-te** [L. *gens*], F.: nation (people, family); men (persons): *far* —, assemble; *smettere di far* —, cease making one's self noticed; cease being eccentric; — *grande, camicia corta*, one who pretends to be rich and is really not; — *di scarriera*, vagabonds; — *a piede, o a cavallo*, militia. **-terèlla**, *disp.* of *-te*. **-til=dònna**, F.: lady. **-tíle**, ADJ.: genteel (courteous, pleasing); gentle (tame); delicate (weak, tender); M.: gentile (heathen, pagan): *colore* —, rather pale; *panno molto* —, very soft cloth; *terra* —, fruitful earth; *fico* —, fig of delicate flavour; *carne* —, tender meat. **-tilescaménte**, ADV.: heathenly. **-tilésco**, pl. —*schi*, ADJ.: pagan. **-tilésimo**, M.: gentilism (paganism). **-tilétto**, ADJ.: pretty (nice, neat). **-tilézza**, F.: gentility (nobility); courtesy (affability); grace; paganism (gentilism). **-tilíno**, *car. dim.* of *-tile*. **-tilíre**, TR.: ennoble (make genteel). **-tilità**, F.: gentilism (heathenism). **-tilízia**, F.: gentility (nobility). **-tilízio**, ADJ.: of a noble family. **-tilménte**, ADV.: gently (nobly, courteously, gracefully). **-tilòmo**, **-tiluòmo**, M.: gentleman (nobleman). **-tilòtto†**, M.: gentleman. **-tína**, *dim.* of *-te*. **-túccia**, *disp.* of *-te*. **-tucciáccia**, —**ccc**, F.: *disp.* of *-tuccia*; dregs of the rabble.

genu-flessióne, F.: genuflection (kneeling). **-flèsso**, PART.: kneeling. ‖**-flèttere** [l. L. *-flectere* (*genus*, knee, *flectere*, bend)], IRR.; INTR.: kneel (bend one's knees).

ge-nuinaménte, ADV.: genuinely (truly). **-nuinità**, F.: genuineness. ‖**-nuíno** [L. *-nuinus*], ADJ.: genuine (natural, true): *andare, venir* —, be sincere.

genziá-na [L. *gentiana*], F.: gentian, bitterwort. **-nína**, F.: gentianin (extract of gentian).

geo- [Gr. *gaia*, earth]: **-desía** [Gr. *daisía*, division], F.: geodesy. **-dètico**, ADJ.: geodetical. **-gonía** [Gr. *goné*, generation], F.: geogony. **-grafía** [Gr. *gráphein*, write], F.: geography. **-gráfico**, ADJ.: geographical. **geò-grafo**, M.: geographer. **-logía** [Gr. *lógos*, science], F.: geology. **-lògico**, ADJ.: geological. **geò-logo**, M.: geologist. **-mánte** [Gr. *manteía*, divination], M.: geomancer. **-mántico**, ADJ.: geomantic. **-manzía**, F.: geomancy (kind of divination). **geò-metra**, M.: geometrician; land-surveyor. **-metría** [Gr. *métron*, measure], F.: geometry. **-metricaménte**, ADV.: geometrically. **-mètrico**, ADJ.: geometrical. **geò-metro†**, M.: geometrician. **geò-rgica** [Gr. *érgon*, work], F.: Georgic (treatise on agriculture); Georgics (poems of Virgil). **-rgichétta**, *dim.* of *-rgica*. **geò-rgico**, ADJ.: georgic. **-rgòfilo** [Gr. *érgon*, work, *philós*, lover], M.: one who is fond of agriculture. **-stática** [Eng. *static*], F.: geostatics.

geránio [L. *-nium*], M.: geranium.

ge-rárca [Gr. *hierárches*], M.: HIERARCH (high-priest, head): *supremo* —, pope. **-rarchía**, F.: hierarchy (church-government); order of angels; intrigue†. **-rárchico**, ADJ.: hierarchical.

gere-mía [*Jeremiah*], M.: one who laments; one who predicts misfortunes. **-miáta**, F.: long sorrowful discourse.

gerènte [L. *gerens*, carrying], M.: manager.

gerfálco†, M.: gerfalcon.

gèrgo [OFr. *gargon*], M.: jargon (slang, cant, argot).

gèrla [L. *gerula*, porter], F.: buck-basket (dorser, pannier).

ger-mána, F.: sister (full sister). **-manaménte†**, ADV.: sincerely (truly); brotherly. ‖**-máno** [L. *-manus*], ADJ.: real (true, sincere); M.: brother; wild-duck: *cugino* —, cousin-german.

gèr-me [L. *-men*], M.: germ, seed (*fig.*) son (offspring, descendant). **-mináre**,

TR., INTR.: germinate (sprout): procreate (produce). **-minatívo**, ADJ.: capable of germinating (germinative). **-minazióne**, F.: germination. **-mogliaménto**, M.: budding (sprouting). **-mogliáre**, INTR.: bud (sprout, blossom). **-móglio**, M.: bud (sprout, shoot, blossom).

gero-glificáre, INTR.: make hieroglyphics. ||**-glífico** [L. *hieroglyphicus* (Gr. *hierós*, sacred, *glúphein*, carve)], ADJ.: HIEROGLYPHIC; M.: hieroglyph.

gerrettièra† = *giarrettiera*.

gèrsa†, F.: kind of rouge or paint.

gerúndio [L. *-dium*], M.: gerund.

gesmíno† = *gelsomino*.

ges-sáio, M.: plaster-vender; maker of plaster figures. **-saiòlo**, M.: maker of plaster. **-sáre**, TR.: plaster; chalk (of wine). **-sáto**, PART.: plastered. **-sétto**, M.: chalk. ||**gès-so** [L. *gypsum*], M.: gypsum; plaster. **-sóso**, ADJ.: plastered.

gès-ta, F. PL.: GESTS (notable actions, achievements, exploits); SING.: expedition (enterprise); army†; race (progeny)†: *le Canzoni di Gesta*, les Chansons de Geste (OFr. Romances). **-táre**, TR.: bear (carry). **-tazióne**, F.: gestation. **-teggiáre**†, INTR.: gesticulate. **-ticolaménto**, M.: gesticulation. **-ticoláre**, INTR.: gesticulate (make gestures). **-ticolazióne**, F.: gesticulation. **-tióne**, F.: management (administration of affairs). **-tíre**, INTR.: make gestures.

gès-to [L. *-tus* (*gerere*, bear, perform)], M.: gesture (movement); achievement (exploit); management† (care, administration). **-tóre**, M.: manager (administrator).

Gesù, M.: Jesus Christ: *buona notte* —, good-bye to it (when a thing is lost or ruined); *far* —, join the hands in an attitude of prayer. **-áto**, M.: member of the order of St. Jerome. **-íta**, M.: Jesuit (member of Society of Jesus); impostor. **-iticaménte**, ADV.: jesuitically; craftily. **-ítico**, ADJ.: jesuitical (belonging to the Jesuits); crafty (false, deceitful).

get-taménto†, M.: throwing (hurling). ||**-táre** [L. *jactare*], TR.: throw (fling; cast); cast out; vomit; REFL.: throw one's self (upon); let one's self fall (from); give†: — *in carta*, *sulla carta*, write; — *fuori*, vomit; — *un sospiro*, heave a sigh; — *via*, cast off, give away; — *le parole al vento*, lament in vain; — *il proprio*, squander one's money; — *motto*, mention (talk of); — *l'abaco*, cast accounts; — *l'occhio*, glance; — *a tergo*, take no account of; — *buona o mala ragione*, adduce good or bad reasons; — *l'inchiostro*, write nonsense; — *in preghiera*, pray; *gettarsi via*, go mad, get angry. **-táta**, F.: cast (throw); sprout, shoot (of a plant). **-tatèllo**, M.: foundling (bastard). **-táto**, PART.: thrown: *abito che par — a suo dosso*, dress which suits one exactly. **-tatóre**, M.: squanderer; caster (of metals). **gèt-tito**†, M.: throwing (casting); vomiting; expectoration (spitting). **gèt-to**, M.: throw (cast); jet (gushing-forth); sprout (shoot of a plant); stalk (stem of flowers); plaster† (mortar); incrustation†: *far — d'una cosa*, throw a thing away (waste or squander a thing); *far* —, lighten a ship in a storm (throw overboard); *fare il* —†, divide, share (of calculators); *il primo* —, rough copy (first draught); *far di* —, cast metals. **-tóne**, M.: counter (at cards).

ghèffo†, M.: balcony (projection).

ghéppio [?], M.: kestrel, bird of prey.

gheríglio [Gr. *kárion*], M.: kernel of a nut.

gher-minèlla, F.: juggler's trick (legerdemain). ||**-míre** [*gremire*], TR.: catch; snatch (with claws or talons). **-mitóre**, M., **-mitríce**, F.: catcher (snatcher).

gherofan. .† = *garofan*. .

gheróne [OHG. *gero*, point of a lance], M.: gusset (bit, piece): *pigliarsela per un* —, run away.

ghétta [?], F.: gaiter (leggins).

ghétto [Heb. *ghet*, divorce], M.: ghetto (Jews' quarter); Jews of a city: *fare un* —, make a great tumult by all speaking at once.

ghézzo [?], ADJ.: black, swarthy (of a grape about to mature); M.: kind of mushroom; filth; kind of crow; negro.

ghiabaldána†, F.: toy (trifle).

ghiac-césco†, ADJ.: icy (frozen, cold). **-ciáia**, F.: ice-house. **-ciáio**, M.: GLACIER. **-ciáre**, TR., INTR.: freeze (congeal). ||**ghiác-cio** [L. *glacies*, ice], ADJ.: icy (frozen); M.: ice. **-ciuòlo**†, M.: icicle; split or crack (in jewels).

ghiacére† = *giacere*.

ghiádo†, M.: excessive cold; ice; knife.

ghiaggiuòlo†, M.: iris (sword-grass).

ghiá-ia [L. *glarea*], F.: gravel (pebble). **-iáta**, F.: act of scattering gravel; gravel-road. **-ióso**, ADJ.: gravelly (sandy). **-iòttolo**, M.: small gravel (sand). **-iúzza**, *dim.* of *-ia*.

ghián-da [L. *glans*], F.: acorn; mast; acorn-formed projectile; manner of curing†: — *unguentaria*, medicinal fruit. **-dáia**, F.: jay, jackdaw. **-daiòtto**, *dim.* of *-daia*. **-dellíno**†, *dim.* of *-da*. **-dífero**, ADJ.: producing acorns. **-dína**, F.: *dim.* of *-da*; vase for odorous essences. **ghián-dola**†, F.: gland. **-dúccia**, **-dúzza**†, *disp.* of *-da*.

ghiára† = *ghiaia*.

ghiarabaldána†, F.: nothing (trifle).
ghiaréto [*ghiaia*], M.: pebbly bed (of a river).
ghiazzerino†, M.: cuirass (coat of mail, habergeon).
ghiazzeruòla†, F.: pinnace (kind of an ancient ship).
ghibellíno [emperor of *Weibelingen*], ADJ., M.: Ghibelline (favourer of the German emperor: 12–13. Cent.).
ghièra [?], F.: ferrule, ring of iron; kind of dart†; medicine composed of aloes†.
ghierabaldána† = *ghiarabaldana*.
ghieráto [*ghiera*], ADJ.: furnished with ferrule.
ghièva† = *ghiova*.
ghigliottí-na [Dr. *Guillotin*], F.: guillotine. **-náre**, TR.: guillotine.
ghi-gna, F.: sinister, bad face; bold, impudent face. **-gnáccia**, *disp.* of *-gna*. ‖**-gnáre** [?], INTR.: sneer; grin. **-gná-ta**, F.: burst of derisive laughter. **-gnatóre**†, M.: sneerer. **-gnazzáre**, INTR.: laugh loudly (burst out laughing). **-gnettíno**, *dim. of -gnetto*. **-gnétto**, *dim.* of *-gno*. **-gno**, M.: sarcastic or malicious laugh (sneer); jester (banterer); flattering, fawning smile†.
ghin-dáre†, TR.: hoist. **-dázzo**†, M.: top-rope.
ghinèa [*Guinea*], F.: guinea; kind of dimity cloth.
ghingheri [*agghindare*], ADV.: badly knocked; clothed finely.
ghio [?], M.: boom-sail.
ghiót-ta, F.: dripping-pan. **-táccio**, *disp.* of *-to*. **-tamènte**, ADV.: greedily (gourmandly). **-terèllo**, *dim.* of *-to*. **-terellíno**, *dim.* of *-terello*. ‖**ghiótto** [L. *glut(t)o*], M.: gourmand (GLUTTON); ADJ.: gluttonous; covetous: *cibo* —, food for gourmands; *un boccone* —, good dish. **-toncèllo**, *dim.* of *-tone*. **-tóne**, *aug.* of *-to*. **-tonería**, F.: glutton's food; gluttony; wickedness (iniquity). **-tornía**, F.: gluttony (avidity, greediness). **-túme**, M.: glutton's food.
ghiòzzo [L. *gobius*], M.: gudgeon (small fresh-water fish); blockhead (clown); drop†: — *d'acqua*†, nothing, very small drop.
ghiribiz-záre, INTR.: fancy (imagine). **-zatóre**, M.: whimsical, fantastical person. **ghiribíz-zo** [*ghiro, bizzarro*], M.: whim (caprice, fancy). **-zóso**, ADJ.: whimsical (fantastical, capricious).
ghirigèro [*ghiro*], M.: flourish (with the pen): *camminare a* —, walk in a zigzag manner.
ghirlán-da [?], F.: garland (wreath); (*astron.*†) constellation (crown): *morire colla* —, die a virgin (die unmarried). **-dáio**, M.: one who makes or sells garlands. **-dáre**†, TR.: crown with a garland. **-dèlla**†, F.: small garland. **-détta**, *car. dim.* of *-da*.
ghíro [L. *glis*], M.: dormouse.
ghirónda [*giro*], F.: hurdy-gurdy.
ghíṣa [Ger. *giessen*, pour], F.: cast-iron.
gía, IMPERF. of *gire*, go.
già [L. *jam*], ADV.: formerly, once (in former days); already, now; yes; certainly (truly): *di* —, formerly; *al tempo di* —†, in the most ancient time; —†, of dead people, late. **-cchè** -é, ADV.: since that, since; because; now that.
giácchera†, F.: trick (joke); spavin.
giacchiáta [*giacchio*], F.: cast of the net.
giácchio [L. *jaculum*, javelin], M.: casting-net (trammel): *gettare il* — *tondo*, be impartial; *gettare il* — *sulla siepe*, do a thing without profit.
giáccio†, M.: ice; den of the stag or hart.
gia-cènte, PART.: situated; lying extended: *eredità* —, unclaimed estate. ‖**-cére** [L. *jacere*], IRR.§; INTR.: lie down; be situated; depend†, consist: *qui giace*, (of a discourse) the point. **-cíglio**, M.: paillasse (straw-bed); kennel. **-ciméntо**†, M.: lying down; (*fig.*) forgetfulness.

§ Ind.: Pres. *giáccio, giáci, giáce; giac(c)iámo, giacéte, giácciono.* Pret. *giác-qui, -que; -quero.* Subj.: Pres. *giáccia.*

gia-cintíno, M.: kind of precious stone. ‖**-cínto** [Gr. *huákinthos*], M.: hyacinth.
giaci-tóio, M.: place for lying down (bed, lair). ‖**-túra** [*giacere*], F.: act of lying down (posture); manner, place and position of lying down; (*poet.*) placing of the accent; attitude†, movement†. **giaci-úto**, PART.: lying down (stretched out).
giáco [?], M.: coat of mail (cuirass).
giacula-tòria [L. *jaculatorius*], F.: short prayer.
giaggiòlo [L. *gladiolus*, little sword], M.: iris.
giaguáro [Braz. *yaguara*], M.: JAGUAR.
giallamína [L. *calamina*], F.: calamine.
gial-lástro, ADJ.: yellowish. **-leggiánte**, PART.: yellowish. **-leggiáre**, INTR.: grow yellow (turn yellow, be yellowish). **-létto**, *dim.* of *-lo*. **-lézza**, F.: yellowness (yellow). **-líccio**, ADJ., M.: yellow. **-ligno**, ADJ.: pale yellow. **-líno**, *car. dim.* of *-lo*. ‖**giál-lo** [L. *galbus*], ADJ., M.: YELLOW. **-lógno, -lógnolo**, ADJ.: of a faint or pale yellow. **-lolíno**, M.: dry colour used in mixtures. **-lóre**†, M.: yellowness (paleness, sallowness); JAUNDice. **-lo-sánto**, M.: JAUN-

dice. **-lo-sánte**, M.: yellow colour extracted from a plant. **-lúccio**, *dim.* of *-lo*. **-lúme**, M.: excessive yellowness; yellow-spot; gold money.
giam-báre†, INTR.: jest (jeer, laugh at). **-beggiáre**, TR.: mock. **giám-bico**, ADJ.: iambic. ‖**-bo** [Gr. *íambos*, stroke], M.: iambic: *dare il — a uno*, deride (laugh at); *volere il — di qualcuno*, have sport with one.
giammái [*già, mai*], ADJ.: never (at no time).
giamméngola†, F.: bagatelle (trifle, toy).
giandarm. . (*pop.*) = *gendarm..*
gian-nétta [?], F.: lance (spear, dart); cane. **-nettário**† = *-nettiere*. **-nettáta**, F.: blow with the lance or spear. **-nettière**, M.: lancer (spearman, pikeman). **-nettina**, *dim.* of *-netta*.
giannétto†, M.: genet (kind of Spanish stallion).
giannettóne, *aug.* of *giannetta*.
giannízzero [fr. Turk.], M.: janissary (Turkish soldier); official of the Roman chancery.
gianse-nísmo [*Giansenio*], M.: Jansenism. **-nísta**, M.: Jansenist; rigorist.
giára [fr. Ar.], F.: JAR; cup (vase).
giárda†, F.: spavin (puffed sinews); mockery (joke); trick.
giardi-nággio, M.: art of cultivating gardens. **-nétto**, M.: *car. dim.* of *-no*; fruit (in a lodging-house pastry); ice-cream of different colours. **-nièra**, F.: gardener's wife; herb-woman; pot of flowers (flower-stand); kind of carriage; necklace†. **-nière**, M.: GARDENER. **giardí-no** [Ger. *garten*], M.: GARDEN; paradise (lovely country); cesspool (water-closet)†.
giardóne†, *aug.* of *giarda*.
giarétta, *dim.* of *-giara*.
giarrettièra [Fr. *jarretière*], F.: GARTER: *ordine della —*, order of the garter.
giárro†, M.: JAR (pitcher).
giat-tánza†, **-tánzia**, F.: JACTANCY (vainglory, brag). **-túra**†, F.: ill-luck; destruction (loss).
giáva†, F.: store-room of a ship.
giavázzo [Gr. *gagátes*], M.: black bitumen.
giavellòtto [?], M.: javelin.
gíb-ba†, F., **-bo**† [L. *-bus*], M.: hunch (protuberance, hump); eminence (height). **-bosità**, F.: gibbousness. **-bóso**, ADJ.: humped (gibbous; hunchbacked); elevated (raised).
gibèrna [?], F.: cartridge-box; pouch.
gioche-ro [Sp. *chícharo*, pea], M.: colocassia. **-róso**, ADJ.: full of colocassia.
gíga [Ger. *geige*], F.: ancient musical instrument; jig (dancing air).
gigan-táccio, *aug.* of *-te*. ‖**gigán-te** [L. *gigans*], M.: giant: *entrare nel —*, oppose a thing, be obstinate. **-teggiáre**, INTR.: be gigantic; (*fig.*) surpass (surmount)†. **-tèo**†, ADJ.: gigantic. **-tescaménte**, ADV.: in a giantlike manner. **-tésco**, ADJ.: gigantic; disproportionate. **-téssa**, F.: giantess.
gigli-áceo, ADJ.: lilaceous (like a lily). **-áto**, ADJ.: lilied; marked or strewn with lilies; sowed with lilies†. **-éto**, M.: bed of lilies. **-étto**, M.: *dim.* of *-o*; kind of lace. ‖**gígli-o** [L. *lilium*], M.: lily; flower-de-luce; (*fig.*) emblem of purity.
gílda [*Gilda*, cap. of Libbia], F.: kind of odourous water.
gin [Eng.], M.: gin.
ginecèo [Gr. *gunaikeîon* (*guné*, woman)], M.: gynæceum (part of a house for women); feminine conservatory†.
gi-néprа†, F.: juniper-berry. **-nepráio**, M.: place planted with juniper trees; labyrinth (intrigue, intricacy). ‖**-népro** [L. *juniperus*], M.: juniper-tree.
ginè-stra [L. *genista*], F.: broom-plant (GENET). **-strèlla**, F.: dying broom. **-stréto**, M.: place abounding in genets. **-strévole**, ADJ.: broomy (full of broom). **-strína** = *-strella*. **-stróne**, M.: kind of broom.
gingía† = *gengiva*.
gingil-láre, INTR., REFL.: waste one's time on trifles (procrastinate). **-líno**, M.: one who makes his way through baseness or hypocrisy. ‖**gingíl-lo** [L. *cingillum*, small girdle], M.: trifle (toy, plaything); trifling-work; small picklock†. **-lóne**, M.: one who wastes his time (trifler).
gingíva = *gengiva*.
gin-nasiále, *adj.* of *-nasio*. ‖**-násio** [L. *gumnasium*], M.: gymnasium (school below the lyceum; *class*. gymnastic school). **-nástica** [Gr. *gumnastés*], F.: gymnastics. **-nástico**, ADJ.: gymnastic.
ginnétto [?], M.: genet (Spanish stallion).
gín-nico [Gr. *gumnikós*], ADJ.: gymnic (of athletic exercises). **-nosofísta** [Gr. *gumno-sophistés*], M.: gymnosophist.
ginoc-chiáta, F.: blow with the knee. **-chièllo**, M.: hog's foot; knee-plate; wound in the knee of a horse. **-chíno**, *car. dim.* of *-chio*. ‖**ginòc-chio**, pl. *-chi* or (*f.*) *-chia* [L. *genuculum*, dim. of *genu*], M.: knee. **-chióne**†, **-chióni**, ADV.: kneeling (upon one's knees).
giò†, INTERJ.: get up, go on (to horses): *andare —*, go softly or gently.
giocacchiáre = *giocucchiare*.
gio-cáre, IRR. §; TR.: play (sport); wager (stake); risk losing (lose); joke (jest); rob (cheat)†; speak jestingly (rail): — *di*

bastone, know how to use a stick, beat (cudgel); — *di furberia, d' ingegno, di malizia*, play with sagacity; — *di maestria*, play in a masterly manner; — *di mano*, play with skill; (jesting) cheat; — *netto*, fair play; — *sul sicuro*, be sure of winning; — *di spada*, know how to handle a sword; — *d' autorità*, use authority, act by authority; — *d' una cosa*, make fun of a thing. **-cáta**, F.: continual game; stake; manner of playing. **-catáccia**, *disp.* of *-cata*. **-catína**, *car. dim.* of *-cata*. **-catoráccio**, *disp.* of *-catore*. **-catóre**, M., **-catríce**, F.: player (gamester). **-catoróne**, *aug.* of *-catore*. **-cáttolo**, M.: useful toys or trinkets. **-cherelláre**, INTR.: play little and at intervals. **-chettíno**, *dim.* of *-chetto*. **-chétto**, *dim.* of *-co*. ||**giò-co** [L. *jocus*], M.: game (play, diversion); athletic exercise; JOKE (jest); mode of action or proceeding; art (artifice, trick): *far* —, deride (make fun of); *brutto* or *cattivo* —, base trick; *ogni bel* — *dura poco*, continued jesting wearies; *chi ha cattivo* — *rimescola le carte*, who is poor desires a revolution of things; — *di parole*, pun; — *marziale*†, war; *a buon* —†, seriously; *a* —, for a joke (for fun); — *della cieca*, blindman's-buff. **-co = fòrza**, ADV.: *esser* —, be necessary. **-coláre**, INTR.: play tricks (amuse one's self). **-colatóre**, M., **-colatríce**, F.: jumper. **-colíno**, *dim.* of *-co*. **giòco-lo**†, M.: sport (jest).

§ Ind.: Pres. *gi(u)ò-co, -chi*, etc.: (*u*)*ò* accented; *uo*, unaccented.

giocon-daménte, ADV.: merrily (joyfully). **-dáre**, TR.: render joyful (rejoice); enjoy one's self. **-dévole**†, ADJ.: pleasing (delightful, rejoicing)†. **-dézza**, **-dità**, F.: jocundity (joy, mirth). ||**gio-cón-do** [L. *jucundus*, pleasant, agreeable], ADJ.: jocund (joyful, gay, merry†); flourishing (of plants).

gio-cosaménto, ADV.: JOCOSELY (merrily). **-cosità**, F.: jocoseness (mirth, gaiety). ||**-cóso** [*-co*], ADJ.: jocose (playful, merry); burlesque (of writers); (*mus.*) comic, cheerful (allegro); content. **-cucchiáre**, INTR.: play (freq.); play some. **-cúccio**, M.: little sport; little diversion.

giocul.. = *giocol*..

gio-gáia [L. *jugalia*], F.: dewlap (of oxen); chain (of mountains); nape of the neck†. **-gático**, M.: amount paid neighbours for ploughing a field with their own oxen.

giogant.. = *gigant*..

gio-gliáto, ADJ.: mixed with darnel.

giò-glio†, M.: darnel.

gió-go [L. *jugum*], M.: yoke; (*fig.*); slavery (servitude); tutelage, guardianship; peak of a mountain. **-góso**†, ADJ.: mountainous (girded with mountains).

giò-ia [L. *gaudia*, pl. of *gaudium*], F.: JOY (gladness, delight); precious stone (JEWEL); (*iron.*) jewel; a reinforce of the mouth of a cannon: *bella, cara* —, tiresome person; — *mia*, my love (my jewel); *far* —†, rejoice; *far* — *a uno*†, entertain or feast one. **-iále**, ADJ.: joyous (happy). **-ialità**, F.: joyousness. **-iánte**, PART.: joyful (merry). **-ielláre**, TR.: ornament with jewels; set or embellish jewels. **-ielláto**, ADJ.: adorned or ornamented with jewels. **-iellería**, F.: jeweler's art; jewel-store. **-iellière**, M.: jeweler. **-iellíno**, *dim.* of *-iello*. **-ièllo**, M.: jewel; an excellent, lovable person; very valuable thing. **-iétta**, *dim.* of *-ia*. **-ióre**†, M.: joy (contentment, mirth). **-iosaménte**, ADV.: joyfully. **-iosétto**, ADJ.: somewhat joyful. **-ióso**, ADJ.: joyful (merry); vigorous (flourishing†). **-íre**, INTR.: be in joy (rejoice).

giòlito†, M.: enjoyment (pleasure); repose.

giolláro†, M.: buffoon.

giomèlla†, F.: two handfuls.

giorgería†, F.: bravery (valour).

giorgína [*Georgi*, Russian scientist], F.: dahlia (a flower).

gior-náccio, *disp.* of *-no*. **-naláccio**, *disp.* of *-nale*. **-nále** [*-no*], M.: journal (newspaper; diary); day-book; ADJ.: DIURNAL† (daily). **-nalétto**, **-nalíno**, *car. dim.* of *-nale*. **-nalière**, M.: day-labourer (workman); ADJ.: daily. **-nalièro**, ADJ.: daily. **-nalísta**, M.: journalist. **-nalménte**, ADV.: daily. **-nalúccio**, *disp.* of *-nale*. **-nánte**, F.: day-girl; turn at service (in the Brothers of Mercy). **-narèllo**, *iron.* or *car. dim.* of *-no*. **-náta** [*-no*], F.: term of a day; day's work; daily gain (daily income or revenue); day's journey; field-battle (fight); epoch, period, day (of Bible); life (human existence): *le Cinque -nate*, battles against Austrians in 1848; *far* —, come to a battle; *compiere la sua* —, die; *vivire alla* —, live without thought of the future; *alla* —, *in* —, daily (every day, by the day); *a gran* —, swiftly (quickly). **-natáccia**, *disp.* of *-nata*. **-natína**, *car.* or *iron. dim.* of *-nata*. **-nèa** [Fr. *journée* from *-nata*], F.: ancient coat; soldier's cloak; robe (clerical vestment): *mettersi la* —, undertake to maintain a thing with great arrogance. ||**giór-no** [L. *diurnus*, of the DAY]; M.: day; midday; daybreak; time; life (existence); *a* —, at daybreak; *a -ni*, some days, at times; *a' miei* —, in my day (in my youth); *buon* —, good day (good morning); *di — in* —, from day to day; *di* —, during the day; *essere, stare in* —, be up-to-date (be posted on daily events); *farsi* —, become daylight; *fare di notte* —, work at night and sleep during the day; — *critico*, critical day (of the sick); — *nero* or *magro*, fish-day; *il gran* —, judgment day; *ogni — ne passa uno*, gently life passes away; *tutt' i -ni*, every day (always, continually).

giò-stra [Prov. *jostar* (L. *juxta*, near)], F.: JOUST (tournament); trick† (deception); jest†; skirmish†. **-tránte**, M.: tilter. **-tráre**, INTR.: have a joust, tilt; roam about, dispute, strive; cheat (deceive); combat†; wound†. **-tratóre**, M.: combatant (champion, tilter). **-tróne**, M.: one who roams about.

Giòtto, M.: Giotto (famous painter): *fare un O come* —, draw a circle with a steady hand; *tondo come l'O di* —, round as the O of — (i.e. dull in comprehending, credulous).

giovaménto [*giovare*], M.: aid (relief); utility, advantage.

gio-vanáccio, M.: *disp.* of *-vane;* wild young man. **-vanáglia**†, F.: multitude of youths; youth. **-vanástro**, M.: wild, reckless youth. ‖**gió-vane** [L. *juvenis*], ADJ.: youthful (young); tender; new; careless (incautious); M., F.: young man (youth); young woman: — *tempo*†, spring. **-vaneggiáre**†, INTR.: play the youth (act a boy). **-vanèllo**†, **-vanésco**†, ADJ.: young (youthful). **-vanétto**, ADJ.: youthful; M.: youth; young man. **-vanézza**, F.: youth; thoughtlessness†; juvenile pleasure†. **-vaníle**, ADJ.: JUVENILE (young). **-vanilménte**, ADV.: youthfully (in a youthful manner). **-vaníno**, *car. dim.* of *-vane*. **-vanottíno**, *car.* or *iron. dim.* of *-vanotto*. **-vanòtto**, M.: *aug.* of *-vane* or *-vine:* bachelor.

giová-re [L. *juvare*], INTR.: be useful; be of use; AID (help; favour); please†: *a che giova?* of what use? to what purpose? *mi giova credere*, I am ready to believe; *giova sperare*, it is well to hope. **-tívo**†, ADJ.: useful; pleasing. **-tóre**†, M., **-tríce**, F.: helper (aider).

Giòve [L. *Jovem*], M.: Jove (Jupiter).

giove-dì [L. *Jovis dies*, day of Jove], M.: Thursday.

gio-vènca, F.: heifer. ‖**-vènco** [L. *ju-**us*], M.: young steer (bullock). **-nézza**, F.: youth. **-níle**, ADJ.: lle (of a youth). ‖**-ntà** [L. *juven-*.: youth; youths (number of young n).

gio-veréccio [*-vare*], ADJ.: pleasing (agreeable). **-vévole**, ADJ.: helpful (profitable). **-vevolézza**†, F.: utility (use, advantage). **-vevolménte**, ADV.: usefully (profitably, advantageously).

gio-viále [*Giove*], ADJ.: jovial (pleasant); of Jove†. **-vialità**, F.: jovialty (gaiety). **-vialóne**, *aug.* of *-viale*.

giovin.. = *giovan..*

gira [*girare*], F.: indorsement (of a promissory note); turning† (turn, revolution). **-cápo** [*-re, capo*, head], M.: dizziness (vertigo). **-díto** [*-re, dito*, turning about the finger], M.: whitlow.

giráffa [Ar. *garráfah*], F.: giraffe.

gira-ménto [*-re*], M.: vertigo; rotation† (revolution). **-móndo** [*-re*, rove, *mondo*, world], M.: vagabond (tramp). **girá-ndola**, F.: catherine-wheel (firework); voluble and fickle person; turning or wheeling round; intrigue (perplexity, maze); fancy (chimera, fanciful conceit); strange thought (caprice): *dar foco alla* —, say what one thinks, decide or resolve on a certain proposition; *dar nelle -ndole* go mad. **-randoláre**, INTR.: roam about (rove); turn† (wheel); fancy† (muse); craftily find†. **-ndolétta**, **-ndolína**, *dim.* of *-ndola*. **-ndolíno**, M.: fickle person; weathercock. **-ndolóna**, F., **-ndolóne**, M.: roamer.

giránio = *geranio*.

gi-ránte, M.: indorser. ‖**-ráre** [*-ro*], TR.: turn (wheel, whirl); encircle (surround, enclose); revolve; (*fig.*) be careful or cautious; circulate (of money); wind (of streets); get spoiled (of wine); feel giddy; have extravagant ideas (be capricious); get angry†: — *una cambiale*, indorse a note; — *di bordo*, — *largo*, avoid a difficulty; — *nella memoria, nella mente*, remember. **-rarròsto** [*-rare, arrosto*], M.: spit (roasting-jack). **-rasóle** [*-rare, sole*], M.: sunflower; girasole† (opal-stone). **-ráta**, F.: turn (revolution); hand (at cards); circulation; indorsement. **-ratário**, M.: the person in whose favour a note is indorsed; first indorser. **-ratína**, F.: *dim.* of *-rata;* short walk. **-ratívo**†, ADJ.: circular (that turns about). **-ráto**, PART.: *arrosto* —, cooked on the spit. **-ratóna**, *aug.* of *-rata*. **-ravòlta** [*-rare, volta*], F.: quick turn (turning); gyration (winding). **-ravoltáre**, INTR.: turn about. **-razióne**†, F.: gyration (turning around).

gíre [L. *ire*], DEFECT.§; INTR.: (*poet.*) go; (*fig.*)† die.

§ Ind.: Pres. *gíamo, gíte*. Impf. *gíva* or *gía*. Pret. *gísti; gímmo, gíste, gírono*. Fut. *girò*. Cond. *girèi*. Subj.: Pres. *gíssi*. Part. *gíto*.

gi-rèlla [*-ro*], F.: disc (to play with);

pulley; (*fig.*) voluble person; political backslider; rowel of a spur†; wheel† (of cheese); caprice† (whim); weathercock†: *dare nelle -relle*, go crazy. **-rellaio†**, M.: maker or vender of discs or pulleys; (*fig.*) inconstant fellow. **-rellare**, INTR.: take short walks for diversion. **-rellina**, *dim.* of *-rella*. **-rèllo**, M.: heart or bottom of an artichoke; round-steak; ring; circlet†; whitlow†. **-rellonáre**, INTR.: walk about continually (loaf). **-rellóna**, F., **-rellóne**, M.: loafer. **-rettíno**, *dim.* of *-retto*. **-rétto**, *dim.* of *-ro*. **-révole**, ADJ.: that can turn, easily turning; fickle (inconstant, voluble).

girifálco, **girfálco†** [Ger. *geier*, vulture, *falk*, hawk], M.: gerfalcon.

girigògolo [?], M.: flourish with the pen.

gí-ro [L. *gyrus*, circle], M.: GYRE (circular motion, turn, rotation); circle (circumference, circuit); complete turn; circular voyage or journey; circulation (of money, etc.); brim (of a vase); circular rows: *in* —, about, around, by turns; *il — del viso*, contour of one's face; — *del periodo*, disposition of words in a sentence; *per* —, roundabout. **-rónda** = *ghironda*. **-róne**, M.: *aug.* of *-ro*: *andar a* — or *-roni*, ramble about. **-ronzáre**, **-ronzoláre**, INTR.: ramble or wander about. **-ròvago**, ADJ.: vagabond (roving or rambling).

gí-ta [*gire*], F.: excursion; jaunt: *far* —† take exercise (walk about). **-terèlla**, *car. dim.* of *-ta*.

gito†, PART.: gone.

gittaiéne†, M.: (*bot.*) coriander.

gitta. . = *getta*. .

git-to†, M.: throw; jet; mortar; ADV.: precisely (exactly, directly).

gittóne†, M.: coriander-seed.

giù [*giuso*], ADV.: down, below; down with: — *di lì*, about there; approximately; *andar* —, go down; go out of use; grow worse in health; lose interest; *mandar* —, swallow; believe; ruin†; *ridar* —, get sick again, get worse; *tirarla — a uno*, slander one behind his back.

giúb-ba [fr. Ar.], F.: swallow-tailed coat (dress-coat); mane; petticoat†. **-báccia**, *disp.* of *-ba*. **-berèllo†** = *-bettino*; *dim.* of *-betto*. **-bétta** = *-betto*. **-bétte**, F. PL.: gibbet (gallows). **-bettína**, **-bettíno**, *car. dim.* of *-betta*, *-betto*. **-bétto**, M.: dressing-jacket; gibbet.

giub-biláre [L. *jubilare*], INTR.: rejoice; TR.: grant a pension (give a sinecure). **-bilazióne**, F.: rejoicing (feasting, jubilation). **-bilèo**, M.: jubilee. **-biléo†**, ADJ.: overjoyed.

giub-boncèllo, *dim.* of *-bone*. ‖**-bóne** [*-ba*], M.: coat of coarse cloth.

giubil. . = *giubbil*. .

giuca. .† = *gioca*. .

giuc-carèllo, **-cherèllo**, *dim.* of *-co*. **-cáta**, F: foolish action. **-chería**, F.: senselessness. **giúc-co** [?], ADJ.: foolish (silly).

giu-dáico, ADJ.: Jewish. **-daísmo**, M.: Judaism. **-daizzáre**, INTR.: judaize. ‖**-dèo** [*Judæa*], M.: Jew (Israelite); ADJ.: Judaic.

giudi-cábile, ADJ.: judicable (which can be judged). **-caménto†**, M.: judgment (decree, opinion); penalty (punishment). **-cáre**, TR.: judge (pass judgment upon, decide); condemn†; leave, will (bequeath in testaments)†; desire to be. **-catívo**, ADJ.: judicative, judiciary. **-cáto†**, M.: judgment; jurisdiction; district of a judge. **-catóre**, M., **-catríce**, F.: judge (decider)†. **-catòrio**, ADJ.: judicatory (judicial); of judiciary astrology. **-catúra**, F.: judicature, office, dignity (of a judge). **-cazióne**, F.: judgment (sentence). ‖**giúdi-ce** [L. *judex*], M.: judge (magistrate); doctor of laws†; jurisprudent. **-chevolménte†**, ADV.: justly (judiciously). **-ci**. . = **-zi**. . **-ziále**, ADJ.: judicial; of judicial astrology†. **-zialménte**, ADV.: judicially. **-ziária†**, F.: jurisdiction of a judge. **-ziário**, ADJ.: judiciary (judicial); M.: astrologer. **giudí-zio**, M.: judgment (reasoning, understanding); court of justice (tribunal)†; indication† (sign). **-zióso**, ADJ.: judicious (prudent). **-ziosaménte†**, ADV.: judiciously.

giuggiáre†, TR.: judge (decide).

giúggio-la [L. *jujuba*], F.: fruit of the jujube-tree: *andare in broda di -le*, show great content. **-lèna**, F.: (*uncom.*) the plant sesame. **-líno**, ADJ.: jujube-coloured (yellowish-red). **giúggio-lo**, M.: jujube-tree.

giúgnere, etc. = *giungere*, etc.

giú-gno [L. *Junius*], M.: June.

giu-goláre, **-guláre** [L. *jugularis*], ADJ.: jugular.

giuládro = *giullare*.

giu-lebbáre, TR.: cook in sugar (of fruit); sweeten too much. ‖**-lèbbe** [l. L. *julapium*], **-lèbbo†**, M.: julep: *-lebbo lungo* †, prolix discourse.

giú-lia†, F.: kind of odorous herb. **-liána†**, F.: soup of herbs and vegetables; gillyflower.

giuliánza†, F.: jollity (joy).

giúlio 1 [Pope *Julius*], M.: jule (small silver coin); July†.

giulí-o† 2, ADJ.: gay (joyous); M.: joy (happiness). **-vaménte**, ADV.: gladly (joyously). **-vétto†**, *dim.* of *-vo*. **-vità†**, F.: joy (gayety). ‖**giulí-vo** [OF *jolif*, ak. to Eng. *jolly*], ADJ.: joyous (jolly, content).

giul-láre [L. *joculator*], M.: merry-andrew (buffoon, jester). **-laréseo**, ADJ.: comical (antic, foolish); of a buffoon. **-leria**†, F.: buffoonery.

giumèlla [*gemello*], F.: measure of two handfuls.

giu-ménta, F.: mare; prostitute†: *legar la* —†, tie the mare, sleep well. **-mentière**†, M.: ass-driver; stud-keeper. ‖**-ménto** [L. *jumentum*], M.: beast of burden.

giunáre† = *digiunare*.

giun-cáia, F.: place of rushes. **-cáre**†, TR.: strew with rushes and flowers. **-cáta**, F.: junket. **-chíglia**, F.: jonquil (species of the narcissus or daffodil). ‖**giún-co** [L. *juncus*], M.: rush (bulrush): *cercare il nodo nel* —, seek difficulties and defects where there are none.

giún-gere [L. *jungere*], IRR.§; INTR.: arrive; TR.: JOIN (unite); overtake; induce†; reduce†; cheat†; hit†. **-gi-ménto**†, M.: joining (junction, union).

Ind.: Pret. *giún-si, -se; -sero.* Part. *giún-to.* — Poet. *giugn..*

giuníparo†, M.: juniper-tree.

giún-ta, F.: addition (increase); appendix (to a book); junta (assembly, council); joint†; arrival†: *di* —, into the bargain (to boot); *a prima, di prima* —, at first (in the beginning). **-táre**, TR.: sew together (unite); deceive (cheat). **-tató-re**†, M.: cheat (rascal). **-teria**, F.: cozening (fraud, cheating). ‖**giún-to** [*-gere*], PART.: arrived; swindled† (deceived). **-túra**, F.: articulation (joining); conjunction†.

giuoc.. = *gioc..*

giu-raddína, **-raddiána** (vulg. euphemism) = *-raddio*. **-raddío** [*giuro, a, Dio*], INTERJ.: (angry) oath. **giú-ra**†, F.: oath; conspiracy (plot). **-raménto**, M.: oath: *dar il* —, administer the oath. **-ranto-ménte**†, ADV.: on oath. **-ráre**, INTR.: take an oath; TR.: swear; affiance (betroth): *giurarla a uno*, swear revenge against one; — *un ufficio, un magistrato*, swear to exercise an office conscientiously. **-ráto**, PART.: bound by an oath (sworn); M.: juror (jury-man); conspirator†: *donna -ta*, fiancée (bride-elect). **-ratóre**†, M., **-ratríce**, F.: swearer. **-ratòrio**, ADJ.: JURATORY (sworn): *cauzione —ria*, oath to put one's property at the disposal of the government. **-razióne**† = *-ramento*. ‖**giú-re** [L. *jus*, law], M.: law (jurisprudence): *in* —, according to law. **-consúlto**, M.: jurisconsult; civilian. **-**, M.: jury. **-ridicaménte**, ADV.: juridically (lawfully). **-ridicità**, F.: jurisdiction. **-rídico**, ADJ.: juridical (lawful, legal). **-risdizionále**, ADJ.: jurisdictional. **-risdizióne**, **-ridizióne** [L. *jurisdictio*], F.: jurisdiction; power (authority); place over which jurisdiction is exercised: — *di sangue*†, power of condemning to death. **-risperíto** [L. *juris-peritus*], M.: jurisconsult (learned lawyer). **-risprudènte**† = *-risperito*. **-risprudènza** [L. *juris-prudentia*], F.: jurisprudence. **-rísta**, M.: jurist; civilian. **giú-ro**, M.: oath: *far — d'assassino*, take a desperate oath. ‖**giú-s** [L. *jus*], M.: law (jurisprudence); right (justice). **-sdicènte**, M.: judge.

giúso† [L. *de-orsum*, 'down-turned'], ADV.: down, below.

gius=patronáto, M.: right to confer a benefice.

giusquiámo [fr. Gr.], M.: (*bot.*) henbane.

giústa [L. *iuxta*, near], PREP.: according to, inasmuch as, conformably to; near† (hard by); with†.

giustac(u)òre [Fr. *just-au-corps*], M.: close coat.

gius-taménte, ADV.: justly (rightly). **-tézza**, F.: justness (precision); punctuality; (*typ.*) the equal length of a line. **-tificábile**, ADJ.: justifiable. **-tificánte**, ADJ.: justifying. **-tificáre**, TR.: justify; prove; regulate: clear† (justify, exculpate); REFL.: justify or clear one's self (prove one's innocence). **-tificataménte**, ADV.: rightly (justifiably, in a justifying manner). **-tificatívo**, ADJ.: justificative. **-tificatóre**, M., **-tificatríce**, F.: justifier (defender). **-tificatòrio**, ADJ.: justificatory; justificative†. **-tificazióne**, F.: justification (vindication). **-tízia** [L. *justitia*], F.: justice; execution; (*pl.*) judges (tribunal); gallows† (gibbet): *far la — coll'ascia, coll'accetta*, render justice freely; *chiamar in* —, sue at law; *andare alla* —, go to execution; — *originale*, state of innocence. **-tiziáre** [*-tizia*], TR.: execute (put to death): — *una persona*, reduce one to a most pitiful state. **-tiziáto**, PART.: judged (executed, punished). **-tizieráto**†, M.: jurisdiction. **-tizière**, **-tizièro**†, M.: hangman (executioner); judge†. **-tizióso**†, ADJ.: just (upright). ‖**giús-to** [L. *justus*], ADJ.: just (equitable); upright; precise (exact; opportune); necessary; useful; ADV.: precisely (justly): *per dirla -ta*, to speak the truth; *conto* —, exact account; — *appunto*, precisely for that.

glába†, F.: sprout (twig, shoot).

glaciále [L. *-lis*], ADJ.: glacial (icy).

gladia-tóre [L. *-tor* (*gladius*, sword)], M.: gladiator. **-tòrio**, ADJ.: gladia-

torial. **gládio†**, M.: sword (poniard, dagger).
glán-dula, **-dola†** [L. (*dim.* of *glans*)], F.: gland; kernel. **-duláre**, ADJ.: glandular. **-dulétta**, *dim.* of *-dula*. **-duli=fórme**, ADJ.: glandiform. **-dulóso**, ADJ.: glandulous.
glásto†, **glástro†**, M.: (*bot.*) woad (a plant used for dyeing).
gláu-co [L. *-cus*], ADJ.: sea-green (cerulean). **-chi**, M. PL.: kind of fish popular among the Romans. **-cóma**, M.: glaucoma (disease of the eyes).
glávo†, M.: swordfish.
glèba [L.], F.: turf (clod): *servi della* —, serfs.
gli [L. *illi*], ART., M. PL.: the; PRON.: to him; (*fam.*) to her; to them; them; it (that); ADV.†: there (yonder).
glicerina [Gr. *glukerós*, sweet], F.: glycerine.
glicònio [fr. poet *Glúkon*], M.: kind of verse.
glie-, for *gli* before *lo, la, le, ne*.
glifo [Gr. *glúphos*], M.: glyph.
glit-tica [Gr. *gluptikḗ*], F.: art of carving precious stones. **-to=grafía**, F.: glyptography.
glò, us'ly — — [echoic], M.: gurgle (in pouring from a bottle): *fare* — —, drink.
glo-bettíno, *dim.* of *-bétto*. **-bétto**, M.: *dim.* of *-bo*; globule. ‖**glò-bo** [L. *-bus*], M.: globe (sphere, earth, ball); band of soldiers†. **-bosità**, F.: globosity (rotundity). **-bóso**, ADJ.: globular (globose, round). **-buláre** = *-boso*. **-bulétto**, *dim.* of *-bulo*. **glò-bulo**, *dim.* of *-bo*.
glòri-a [L.], F.: glory (reputation, honour, praise); heaven; verse of a prayer; kind of grape†: *andare a* —, have great satisfaction or delight; *aspettare a* —, await with great anxiety; *farsi* — *d' una cosa*, boast of a thing; *sonare a* —, ring the bells for joy; *non tutti i salmi finiscon in* —, not all hazardous undertakings are successful. **-riáre**, REFL.: take pride in; boast; hold one's self in esteem; TR.†: glorify (praise, make glorious). **-riáto†**, M.: glory; PART.: glorious (magnificent). **-riazióne†**, F.: vainglory (ostentation, pride). **-rificaménto†**, M.: glorification (act of glorifying). **-rificáre**, TR.: glorify (praise); take pride† (boast, brag). **-rificatívo**, ADJ.: able to glorify. **-rificatóre**, M., **-rificatríce**, F.: glorifier. **-rificazióne**, F.: glorification. **-riosaménte**, ADV.: gloriously; vainly (haughtily, conceitedly). **-riosétto**, *dim.* of *-rioso*. **-rióso**, ADJ.: glorious (famous, illustrious); vainglorious (proud, haughty): *vino* —, generous wine; *misteri -osi*, glorious mysteries (of the rosary). **-riúccia**, **-riúzza**, *disp. dim.* of *-ria*.
glòs-a†, **-sa** [L., tongue], F.: gloss (note, exposition). **-áre†**, **-sare**, TR.: gloss (expound, comment upon). **-sário**, M.: glossary (vocabulary). **-atóre†**, **-satóre**, M.: glosser (commentator). **-sèma**, M.: explanatory word. **-sografía**, F.: glossography. **-sògrafo**, M.: glossographer. **-sologia**, F.: glossology.
glòt-ta, **-tide** [Gr. *glótta*, tongue], F.: glottis. **-tologia**, F.: glottology. **-tològico**, ADJ.: glottological.
glucòsio [Gr. *glukerós*, sweet], M.: glucose.
glúma [L., hull, husk], F.: glume.
glúti-ne [L. *gluten*], M.: glue; coagulum (clot of blood); any viscous substance. **-nosità**, F.: glutinosity. **-nóso**, ADJ.: glutinous (viscous, sticky). **glúti-no†** = *-ne*.
gnácchera = *nacchera*.
gnáffa†, F.: prostitute.
gnáffe†, ADV.: in truth! by my troth!
gnatóne†, M.: glutton.
gná-o, *-u* [echoic], M.: mewing (of a cat). **-uláre**, INTR.: mew. **-uláta**, F.: mewing. **-ulío**, M.: continued mewing. *gnáu-lo*, M.: mewing.
gnòcco [?], M.: dumpling; dunce (blockhead, simpleton).
gnò-me†, F.: gnome (maxim). **gnò-mico**, ADJ.: gnomic. ‖**gnò-mo** [Gr. *gnóme*, intelligence], M.: gnome (genius). **-móne** [Gr. *gnómon*], M.: gnomon, index (of a sun dial). **-mònica**, F.: gnomonics. **-mònico**, ADJ.: gnomonical.
gnòrri [*ignoro*], M., INVAR.: *far lo* —, feign ignorance.
gnòs-tici [Gr. *-is*, cognition], M.: gnostics. **-tico**, ADJ.: nobody; none.
gòb-ba, F.: hump (hunch, prominence). **-báccio**, *disp.* of *-bo*. **-bétto**, *car. dim.* of *-bo*. ‖**gòb-bo** [L. *gibbus*], ADJ.: humped (humpbacked; hunched; GIBBOUS); curved; winding; M.: hunchback; hunch (hump; bulge); artichoke plant. **-bóne**, (*fam.*) *andar* —, go bent. **-búzzo†**, *dim.* of *-bo*.
góc-cia, **-ciola** [**guttea* (L. *gutta*)], F.: drop; earring; (*arch.*) guttæ; crack†: *a* — *a* —, drop by drop; *accidente a -ciola*, apoplexy. **-ciáre**, **-cioláre**, TR.: drop (pour out by drops); INTR.: drip (fall by drops); be desperately in love with†. **-ciolaménto†**, M.: dropping. **-ciolatóio**, M.: gutter (drain). **-ciolatúra**, F.: dropped wax. **-ciolétta**, **-ciolína**, *dim.* of *-ciola*. **-ciolíno**, *dim.* of *-ciolo*. **góc-ciolo**, M.: drop (small quantity of liquid, the least drop); least bit†. **-ciolóne**, M.: *aug.* of *-ciola* and *-ciolo*; (*fi*

dunce (ninny). **-ciolóso†**, ADJ.: dropping. **-ciolòtti**, M. PL.: munitions or provisions for hunting.

go-dènte, PART.: enjoying; possessing; PL.: of monks belonging to a religious order of knighthood. ‖**-dére** [L. *gaudere*], (IRR.§); INTR.: enjoy (take pleasure; rejoice); possess: — *la vita*, spend life in enjoyment; — *un podere*, receive the rents of an estate; — *le tasse*, be exempt from taxes; *godersela*, enjoy one's self. **-derèccio**, **-dévole**, ADJ.: pleasant (giving pleasure, agreeable). **-devolménte**, ADV.: agreeably (pleasantly, with joy). **-díbile**, ADJ.: enjoyable. **-diménto**, M.: enjoyment (pleasure). **-dióso†**, ADJ.: joyful (merry). **-ditóre**, M.: good fellow (jovial companion). **-dúta†**, F.: gaiety (revelry, enjoyment). **-dúto**, PART.: enjoyed.

§ Fut. *goderò* or *godrò*. Cond. *god(e)rèi*.

gof-fàggine, F.: awkwardness (stupidity). **-faménte**, ADV.: awkwardly (ungracefully). **-feggiáre**, INTR.: act awkwardly. **-fería**, **-fézza†**, F.: awkwardness. ‖**gòf-fo** [?], ADJ.: awkward; astonished†; M.: awkward person; kind of game at cards. **-fóne**, *aug.* of *-fo*. **-fòtto**, ADJ.: a little awkward.

gógna [?], F.: iron collar or band; pillory; (*fig.*) rogue.

gó-la [L. *gula*], F.: throat; gluttony; gluttonous or greedy person; conduit (pipe); defile; appetite (desire): *sentirsi un nodo alla* —, want to cry; *far un peccato di* —, want a thing badly; *mentire per* —, lie in the throat; *parlare in* —, speak low; — *di monte*, defile (gorge). **-láccia**, *disp.* of *-la*. **-láre†**, **-leggiáre†**, INTR.: covet (want, desire). **-létta†**, F.: *car. dim.* of *-la*; collar; (*fig.*) gluttonous person; necklace†; moulding†.

golétta2 [Fr. *goélette*], F.: schooner (small brig).

golétto [*gola*], M.: neckband (of a shirt), collar.

goliárdo [?], M.: student (in the Middle Ages).

gólfo [L. Gr. *kólphos*], M.: GULF (bay): *navigare a — lanciato*, sail in the main sea.

go-líno [*-la*], M.: fillip in the throat. **-losaménte**, ADV.: greedily. **-losità**, F.: gluttony (lust). **-lóso**, ADJ.: greedy (gluttonous, desirous).

gol-páto†, ADJ.: of a fox: mildewed (blasted, blighted). ‖**gól-pe†** [*volpe*], F.: fox; blight (mildew). **-póne†**, M.: cunning fox; old wily fox.

gombína [?], F.: thong (of a flail); ridge† (between furrows).

gómbito† = *gomito*.

gómena [?], F.: cable.

gomíre† = *vomitare*.

go-mitáta, F.: blow with the elbow. ‖**gó-mito**, pl. *-i* or *-a* [*cubito*], M.: elbow; arm; angle (corner); cubit (measure)†: *alzar il* —, be fond of drink.

gomi-toláre†, TR.: reel (wind); REFL.: gather into groups or clusters. **-tolíno**, *dim.* of *-tolo*. ‖**gomí-tolo** [L. *glomus*], M.: ball or clew of thread; cluster of bees; subterfuge†: — *della terra*, globe.

gomitó-ne†, **-ni**, ADV.: leaning on the elbows.

góm-ma [L. *gummi*], F.: gum; kind of venereal disease (bubo)†: — *turea*, incense; — *arabica*, gum arabic. **-mífero**, ADJ.: gum-producing. **-móso**, ADJ.: gummous (gummy).

gómo-na†, F.: cable. **-nétta†**, F.: *dim.* of *-na*; tackling of great guns.

gón-da† [Gr. *kóndu*, cup], F.: bark (boat). **gón-dola**, F.: gondola. **-dolétta**, *car. dim.* of *-dola*. **-dolière**, M.: gondolier (boatman).

gonfaló-ne [OHG. *gund-fano*, battle-flag], M.: gonfanon (standard, banner, flag): *tenere il* —, direct (be at the head). **-nieráto**, M.: dignity or office of the standard-bearer; time which that office lasts. **-nière**, **-nièro†**, M.: standard-bearer (ensign); supreme magistrate of the Florentine republic; head (chief)†.

gón-fia†, M.: glass-blower. **-fiággine†**, **-fiagióne†**, F.: swelling, tumour. **-fiaménto**, M.: swelling; pride (haughtiness)†. **-fianúvoli**, M. PL.: vainglorious, boasting man. ‖**-fiáre** [L. *conflare*, blow up], TR.: swell, blow out; puff up (with pride); INTR.: swell; become proud (be puffed up with pride); be swollen with anger. **-fiáto†**, M.: swelling; pride. **-fiatóio**, M.: instrument for filling with gas or air; syringe (squirt). **-fiatóre**, M.: puffer (flatterer); inflater. **-fiatúra**, F.: effect of swelling; haughtiness; flattery. **-fiétto**, *dim.* of *-fio*. **-fiézza**, F.: swelling; pride. **gón-fio**, ADJ.: swollen; proud (conceited); bombastic, turgid (style); M.: swelling, tumour: *andar* —, show vainglory. **-fióre**, M.: small swelling. **-fiòtto†**, M.: swimming-bladder.

gón-ga [?], F.: tonsil, gland; swelling of the tonsils (sore throat). **-goláre** [*-gola*], INTR.: jump for joy; be transported. **-góso**, ADJ.: glandulous; of sore throat.

góngro†, M.: conger-eel.

goniòmetro [Gr. *gonía*, angle, *métron*, measure], M.: goniometer.

gón-na [? ak. to Eng. *gown*], **-nèlla**, F.: petticoat (skirt); coat†; vest†; human body†. **-nelláccia**, *disp.* of *-nella*. **-nellétta**, **-nellína**, *dim.* of *-nella*.

-nellíno, M.: child's dress. **-nèllo**, M.: kilts, tunic. **-nellóne**, *aug.* of *-nello*. **-nellúccia**, *disp. dim.* of *-nella*.

gonorrèa [Gr. *-rrhoia* (*gónos*, genital, *rhéin*, flow)], F.: gonorrhœa.

gónzo [?], ADJ.: credulous (simple); too good.

góra [?], F.: conduit, trench; mill-race: *una — di sangue*, flow of blood.

gòrbia, F.: ferrule (at lower end of a cane); chisel; gouge†.

gordiáno [*Gordio*], ADJ.: Gordian.

gorèllo, M.: *dim.* of *gora*; small water-conduit.

gòr-ga†, F.: throat (gullet, windpipe). **-gèra**, F.: collar or ruff of fine cloth; gorget (armour for the neck). **-gerétta**, **-geríne**, *dim.* of *-gera*. **-gheggiaménto**, M.: trilling (quave, shaking). **-gheggiáre**, INTR.: trill (quaver, shake); warble; grumble†, rattle (of the intestines). **-gheggiatóre**, M.: triller; warbler. **-ghéggio**, M.: trill (shake). **-ghétto**, *dim.* of *-go*. **gòr-gia**, F.: prolonged and aspirated pronunciation of consonants; gullet (throat)†; tremulo (trill)†. **-gièra**, F.: = *-gera*; throat†; cover (lid). **-gierétta**, *dim.* of *-giera*. **-giéne**†, M.: drunkard (toper). ||**gór-go** [L. *gurges*], M.: vortex (whirlpool); gulf (abyss). **-gogliaménto**, M.: gurgling. **-gogliáre**, INTR.: gurgle (bubble up, boil); get wormy†. **-gogliáto**, PART.: worm-eaten (wormy). **-góglio**, M.: gurgling (bubbling); rumbling or rattling in the throat or intestines. **-goglióne**, M.: (*zoöl.*) weevil (mite); kind of bird†.

gor-góne, **gòr-gone** [L. *-gona* (Gr. *-gós*, terrible)], F.: (*myth*) gorgon; shield of Minerva. **-gòneo**, **-gònio**, ADJ.: gorgonian; (*fig.*) hard; fierce.

gorgoráno†, M.: grogram (silk stuff).

gorgòz-za† [*gargozza*], F.: throat (gullet). **-zále**, *disp.* of *-za*.

gorílla [fr. Afr.], M.: gorilla.

gòrna†, F.: gutter (drain).

gòrra†, F.: kind of ozier; coarse woollen cap.

gor-zarétto†, **-zaríno**†, **-zeríno**†, M.: collarette (small ruff).

gò-ta [? L. *gabata*, platter], F.: cheek; cheek-piece† (of a helmet): *stare in -te*, be reserved or grave; *cappuccio a -te*, hood (cowl). **-táccia**, *disp.* of *-ta*. **-táta**, F.: slap (cuff). **-tellína**†, *dim* of *-ta*.

gòtico [*Goti*], ADJ.: Gothic; (*typ.*) Old-English (black-letter).

gotína, *car. dim.* of *-ta*.

gòto, ADJ.: Gothic; M.: Goth.

go-tóna, **-tóne**, *aug.* of *-ta*.

gót-ta [L. *gutta*, drop], F.: GOUT; drop†: — *serena*, disease of the eyes. **-táto**, ADJ.: spotted. **-tázza**, F.: scoop (skeet).

gòt-to [L. *guttus*, vase], M.: goblet (bowl, cup). **-tóso**, ADJ.: gouty. **-túccia**, **-túzza**, *-dim.* of *-ta*.

gover-nále†, M.: helm (rudder); helmsman. **-naménto**†, M.: government (direction). **-nánte**, ADJ.: governing; F.: governess. ||**-náre** [L. *gubernare*], TR.: govern (manage); steer (pilot); take care of; manure; season: — *uno*†, dress one. **-nativo**, ADJ.: of government. **-natóra**, *disp.* or *iron.* of *-natore*. **-natóre**, M.: governor; helmsman†. **-natríce**, F.: governess. **-nazióne**†, F.: government. **-níme**†, M.: soil (manure).

govèr-no, M.: government; supreme administration, constitution; state; strengthening (of wines); manure: *sbarra di* —, hand-gear-rod (reversing lever).

goz-záia, F.: matter gathered in the throat; goitre† (wen); inveterate hatred†. ||**góz-zo** [*gargozzo*], M.: crop (craw, ingluvies); goitre; watering-trough†; cruse† (kind of cup); kind of fishing barque.

gozzo-víglia [*gaudibilia*], F.: revelling. **-vigliáre**, INTR.: feast (revel, stuff). **-vigliáta**, F.: revelry (stuffing). **-víglio** = *-viglia*.

gozzúto [*gozzo*], ADJ.: having a wen or goitre.

grácchi-a, F.: crow, jackdaw; chatterer (babbler). **-aménto**, M.: croaking; prattle. ||**-áre** [L. *graculus*, jackdaw], INTR.: croak; prate (chatter); scream; grumble; say vain or untrue things about another. **-áta**, F.: croaking; chat. **-atóre**, **-óne**, M.: croaker; prattler (babbler). **grácchi-o**, M.: noise of croaking or prattling. **grácculo**†, M.: jackdaw, crow.

graci-dáre [L. *-llare*, cackle], INTR.: CROAK; cluck† (cackle). **-datóre**, M., **-datríce**, F.: croaker; prater; slanderer. **-dazióne**, F.: croaking; clucking†; cackling†. **-dóso**, ADJ.: croaking; chatty, noisy.

gráci-le [L. *-lis*], ADJ.: slender (small, thin); weak, delicate. **-létto**, **-líno**, *dim.* of *-le*. **-lità**, F.: slenderness (thinness); weakness, delicacy.

gracímolo [*racimolo*], M.: bunch of grapes; glean.

gráda†, F.: gridiron.

gra-dággio†, M.: favour; pleasure. ||**-dáre**† [*-do*], INTR.: be divided by degrees; descend by degrees, TR.: grade; graduate.

gra-dassáta, F.: bullying. ||**-dásso** [knight *G.*], M.: cowardly bully.

grada-taménte [*grado*], ADV.: gradually (by degrees). **-zióne**, F.: gradation.

gradèlla†, F.: fishing-basket (hurdle).

gra-dévole [-*dire*], ADJ.: pleasant, agreeable (acceptable). **-devolménte,** ADV.: agreeably; gratefully; with pleasure. **-diménto,** M.: acceptance; satisfaction; pleasure.

gra-dína, F.: fine dented chisel; indentation. **-dinàre,** TR.: smooth with the chisel. **-dináta,** F.: flight of steps. **-dinatúra,** F.: chiselling; indentations made by it. ||**-díno** [-*do* 2], M.: step (stair); large step; chisel†.

gra-díre, TR.: accept with pleasure; approve of; have desire; please (satisfy, content); recompense† (reward); INTR.†: advance forward, ascend by steps. **-díto,** ADJ.: agreeable (welcome). **-divaménte†,** ADV.: with much pleasure. ||**grádo** 1 [L. *gratus*, pleasing], M.: pleasure (gratification, gratefulness); will; favour: *di buon* —, with pleasure (willingly); *a mal* or *mal* —, unwillingly; *vi saprò* —, I shall be obliged to you; *venire in* —†, have better luck; *quando vi sarà a* —†, when you please; *sentir* —†, feel grateful; *a tuo* —†, at your pleasure.

grá-do 2 [L. -*dus*], M.: grade (step, degree); rank (dignity); (*math.*) degree; stair†; species, nature†: *tener il* —, preserve one's dignity; *avere in* —, have in esteem; *a — a* —, gradually (little by little); *di* —†, spontaneously; *di — in* —, successively. **-duále,** ADJ.: gradual; M.: prayers after the epistle. **-dualménte,** ADV.: gradually (by degrees). **-duáre,** TR.: graduate. **-duáto,** PART.: graduated; having rank or degrees. **-duataménte** = -*datamente*. **-duatòria,** F.: document containing graduated list of creditors. **-duazióne,** F.: graduation. **-duíre†,** TR.: ennoble.

graf-fiaménto, M.: scratch (scratching). **-fiáre** [-*fio*], TR.: scratch (claw); cut: — *roba*, steal things. **-fiasánti,** M.: bigot, hypocrite. **-fiáta,** F.: scratching; mark of scratch. **-fiatína,** *dim.* of -*fiata*. **-fiatúra,** F.: scratch (slight tear]. **-fiétto,** M.: *dim.* of -*fio*; little scratch; marking iron. ||**gráf-fio** [OFr. *graffe* (OGer. *krapfo*, hook, clasp)], M.: scratch; hook.

gr-áffito [Gr. *gráphein*, write], M.: graffito (kind of fresco painting). **-áfia,** F.: mode of representing words in writing. **-aficaménte,** ADV.: graphically. **-áfico,** ADJ.: graphic. **-áfite,** F.: graphite (plumbago, blacklead).

gra-gn(u)òla [-*ndine*], F.: hail; small hail†; great quantity†: *conoscer la — della treggea*, distinguish the good from bad. **-gnoláre,** INTR.: hail.

-mágli̦a [Sp. -*malla*, coat of mail], F.: -ming clothes; (*fig.*)† darkness.

-náre†, TR.: grieve (afflict, vex).

gramatica. .† = *grammatica*. .

graméssa†, F.: sorrow (misery).

gramí-gna [L. -*nea*], F.: dog's-grass: *sentir nascer la* —, hear the slightest noises. **gramí-gno†, -gnòlo,** M.: species of the olive; ADJ.: covered with dog's-grass. **-gnóso,** ADJ.: full of dog's-grass. **-náceo,** ADJ.: gramineous.

grám-ma [Gr., letter; small weight], F.: gram(me).

grammáti-ca [L. (Gr. *gramma*, letter)], F.: grammar; Latin language†. **-cále,** ADJ.: grammatical. **-calménte, -caménte,** ADV.: grammatically. **-cástro,** M.: (*disp.*) wretched or poor grammarian. **-cherìa,** F.: pedantic grammatical minuteness. **grammáti-co,** M.: grammarian; Latinist†. **-cúccia,** *disp.* of -*ca*.

grám-mo = -*ma*.

grámo [OHG. *gram*], ADJ.: wretched (miserable).

grámo-la, F.: hemp-brake; kneading apparatus. ||**-láre** [?], TR.: mash (hemp, etc.); knead. **-láta** = *granita*. **-latúra,** F.: mashing flax or hemp; kneading.

grámpa†, F.: claw (paw, talon).

gramúffa†, F.: grammar.

gran = *grande*.

grá-na [-*no*], F.: grain; cochineal; roughness of the surface; kind of bad tobacco. **-nágli̦a,** F.: fusion of gold and silver into grains. **-nágli̦e,** F. PL.: grains in general. **-náio,** M.: granary; of corn (cereal). **-naiòlo,** M.: corn-merchant (corn-chandler). **-náre,** INTR.: uncom. form of -*nire*; TR.†: reduce to grains. **-náta,** F.: broom; grenade; sort of a late plum†: *esser di casa più che la* —, be very familiar with; *pigliar la* —, send away every one from an office; *saltar la* —†, be free from the superintendence of parents or tutors. **-natáio,** M.: broom maker or seller. **-natáta,** F.: blow with a broom. **-natétta, -natína,** *dim.* of -*nata*. **-natière,** M.: grenadier. **-natíno,** M.: small broom; daisy†. **-náto,** M.: pomegranate; garnet; granulated†; vigorous†; hard†. **-natóna, -natóne,** *aug.* of -*nata*. **-natúzza†,** *disp.* of -*nata*.

granbéstia or **gran béstia,** F.: elk.

gran=cancellière, M.: lord high chancellor.

gran=cáne, M.: title of nobility in the Orient.

gran=cássa, F.: one who beats the bass drum in a band.

gran-cèvola†, F.: crab. **-chiescaménte,** ADV.: backwardly. **-chiésco,** ADJ.: crab-like, backward. **-chiéssa,** F. of -*chio*. **-chiétto,** *dim.* of -*chio*.

grán-chio [dim. of L. *cancer*], M.: crustacea gen'ly (crayfish; crab); CANCER; cramp-iron (carpenter's holdfast); claw of a hammer; cramp: — *di mare*, lobster; *avere il — alla scarsella*, spend money unwillingly; — *a secco*, pinch; *prendere* (or *pigliare*) *un* — (*a secco*), be deceived, make a mistake; *più lunatico de' -chi*, madder than a March hare. **-chiolíno**, *dim.* of *-chio*. **-chióne**, *aug.* of *-chio*. **-ci=pòrro**, M.: grample (very large crab); great error (blunder): *pigliar un* —, make a blunder. **-círe†**, TR.: seize (grasp, snatch); rob (steal).

gran-dáccio, *disp.* of *-de*. ‖**grán-de** [L. *-dis*], ADJ.: great (large, huge); tall (high); grand (sublime; eminent); principal; noble; M.: adult; nobleman, grandee; ADV.: greatly: *nel più gran verno*, in midwinter; — *di età*, old; *venir — in alcuna cosa*, perfect one's self in a thing; *essere — con uno†*, be a greatly esteemed favourite; *notte —†*, long nights; *vino —†*, strong wine; *vita —†*, severe, austere life; *gran mercato†*, cheap; *gran pezzo†*, great while; *stare in sul —*, be grave and serious; *stare alla —†*, live in great style. **-deggiáre**, INTR.: play the great man; show pride (put on airs). **-deménte**, ADV.: greatly (much); nobly†; valorously†. **-détto**, ADJ.: *dim.* of *-de*; rather large. **-dézza**, F.: greatness (largeness); grandeur (nobility, sublimity); excess (luxury): *dare — a uno†*, render homage to one. **-dezzáta**, F.: ostentatious luxury. **-dicèllo**, **-dicellíno**, **-dicetuòlo†**, *car. dim.* of *-de*. **-dígia**, F.: pride (haughtiness); greatness†. **-digióne**, M.: large overgrown boy. **-diloquènza** [*-de, eloquenza*], F.: grandiloquence.

grandi-náre [*-ne*], IMPERS.; INTR.: hail. **-náta**, F.: shower of hail; hailstorm. ‖**grándi-ne** [L. *grando*], F.: hail; kind of pottage; storm; calamity (great misfortune); small tumour†. **-nína**, *dim.* of *-ne*; bit of pottage.

grandíno, *car. dim.* of *grande*.

grandinóso†, ADJ.: of hail; full of hail; tempestuous.

gran-diosaménte, ADV.: grandly (magnificently); haughtily. **-diosità**, F.: grandeur (magnificence, sumptuousness). **-dióso** [*-de*], ADJ.: grand (imposing, majestic); grandiose (pompous, ostentatious). **-díre†**, TR.: enlarge (increase); raise. **-do** = *-dine*. **-dóne**, *aug.* of *-de*. **-dóre†** = *-dezza*. **-dòtto**, ADJ.: rather large. **-dúca** [*-de, duca*], M.: grand-duke. **-ducále**, ADJ.: grand-ducal. **-ducáto**, M.: grand-duchy. **-duchéssa**, F.: grand-duchess.

gra-nellétto, **-nellíno**, *dim.* of *-nello*. ‖**-nèllo** [dim. of *-no*], M.: grain (corn); seed or kernel (of fruits); testicles; bit (very small portion); dunce† (blockhead). **-nellóso**, ADJ.: granulous (granular).

gran=fárro [L. *far*, grain], M.: spelt.

gran=fátto, ADV.: great deal (much): — *fia*, is it possible that?

grán-fia [OHG. *kramph*], F.: claw (clutch, talon). **-fiáta**, F.: scratch (pinch, cut).

gran=guárdia, F.: guard (grand guard, militia).

gra-nífero [*grano*, grain, L. *ferre*, bear], ADJ.: graniferous. **-nigióne**, F., **-niménto†**, M.: act of becoming seed (running to seed). **-níre**, INTR.: seed (become seed); TR.: yield seed or grain. **-níta**, F.: ice (of lemon, orange, coffee, etc.). **-nítico**, ADJ.: granitic. **-nitifórme** [*-nito, forma*], ADJ.: granitiform. **-níto**, ADJ.: granitic (grainy); solid (stout, firm); M.: granite; form of seed†; stone-chisel†. **-nitóio**, M.: stone-chisel. **-nitóre**, M.: one who grains metals, etc. **-nitúra**, F.: going to seed; graining; milling (of a coin). **-nívoro** [*-no*, L. *vorare*, devour], ADJ.: granivorous.

gran=maéstro, M.: grand master; very learned† or very able man.

granmercè, **gran mercè -é**, ADV.: gramercy, I thank you.

gráno [L. *granum*], M.: GRAIN (corn); seed; granule; grain-weight; very small quantity: *ogni uccello conosce il —*, every one knows what is good.

gra-nòcchia [*ranocchia*], F., **-nòcchio**, M.: frog.

gra-nóne [*-no*], M.: gold or silver twist sewn on embroidery (pearl). **-nóso†**, ADJ.: full of grains (well-grained, grainy, granulous). **-n=túrco**, M.: Indian corn. **-nuláre**, ADJ.: granular; TR.: granulate (reduce to grains). **-nulatóio**, M.: place where metals are granulated; granulating sieve. **-nulazióne**, F.: granulation. **-nulóso**, ADJ.: granulous.

gran=visír, **=visíre**, M.: grand vizier.

gráp-pa [OGer. *grapfo*], F.: hook, GRAPpling-iron (grapple); brace, crotchet (in printing); fine brandy; stem of cherries†. **-páre†**, TR.: grapple (seize, catch). **-píno**, M.: grappling-iron; grapnel: — *a mano†*, hand-grapple. **-po†**, M.: grapping (snatching, catching). **-polétto**, **-políno**, *dim.* of *-polo*. **gráp-polo**, M.: bunch or cluster of grapes: *nuovo* —, *dolce* —, fool (blockhead); *a —li†*, in quantities. **-polúccio**, *disp.* of *-polo*.

grá-scia†, F.: fat (lard, grease); provisions; gain (advantage, profit). ‖**grá-sce** [OFr. *granche*, GRANary], F. PL.: provisions (victuals); magistrate who superintends the markets. **-scéta**, F.: rk

grass land. **-scère, -scière, -scíno,** M.: commissary (superintendent of the market).
gráspo†, M.: grape-stalk.
grassá-ccio, *disp.* of *grasso.* **-ménte,** ADV.: with fatness; largely.
gras-satóre [L. *-sari,* go about], M.: highwayman (assassin). **-sazióne,** F.: highway robbery.
gras-sèllo, M.: bit of fat; flower of lime; kind of fig†. **-sétto,** ADJ.: pretty fat. **-sézza,** F.: fatness (embonpoint, plumpness); richness (opulence); density† (thickness). **-síno,** *car. dim.* of *-so.* ‖**-so** [*crasso*], ADJ.: fat (greasy, plump); wealthy (rich); advantageous; fertile; M.: fat (flesh); abundance: *è — che cola,* he is excessively fat; *discorsi -si,* slippery (wanton) discourses; *terreno —,* fertile land; *riso —,* loud burst of laughter; *patto —,* good bargain; *giorno di —,* meat day; *stare sul —,* live in plenty (be wealthy); *parola -sa,* obscure word; *alla -sa*†, with advantage; *il più — d' un paese,* most fertile part of a province. **-sòccio,** ADJ.: rather fat. **-soccióne,** *aug.* of *-soccio.* **-sottíno,** ADJ.: *dim.* of *-sotto;* rather fat. **-sòtto,** ADJ.: pretty fat. **-sottóne,** ADJ.: *aug.* of *-sotto;* rather fat.
grássula†, F.: fine, delicate fig.
grassúme, M.: *disp.* of *-so;* fat substance; manure.
grásta†, F.: flower-pot.
gráta [L. *crates,* hurdle], F.: grate (of a convent, etc.); grate†; gridiron†.
grataménte [*grato*], ADV.: graciously (gratefully).
gra-tèlla [*-ta*], F.: gridiron (small grate); fish-basket. **-tíccia,** F.: bow-net. **-ticciáta,** F.: trellis-work. **-tíccio,** M.: hurdle; lattice-work. **-ticciuòla**†, F.: small hurdle. **-tícola,** F.: grate; grating; gridiron†. **-ticoláre**†, TR.: graticulate, form a network. **-ticoláto,** M.: grating; trellis-work. **-ticolétta, -ticolína,** *dim.* of *-ticola.*
gratificá-re [L. *-ri* (*-tus,* favor)], TR.: gratify (favour, oblige); benefit; bestow on. **-zióne,** F.: gratification; gratuity (bounty).
grá-tis [L.], ADV.: gratis (gratuitously, for nothing). **-tis=dáto,** ADJ.: given gratuitously. **-titúdine** [L. *-titudo*], F.: gratitude (gratefulness); grateful and gratuitous thing†. **-tívo**†, ADJ.: gratuitous. ‖**grá-to** [L. *-tus*], ADJ.: grateful, pleasing, welcome; obliging (kind, affable); acceptable (agreeable); M.†: will, inclination; pleasure: *di buon —*†, willingly; *a —*†, gratis; *contra —,* unwillingly.
grat-ta=bùgia†, F.: scratching or scraping brush. **-ta=cápo,** M.: (*fam.*) trouble (vexation, care); scratching of the head†. **-taménto,** M.: scratching (scraping). ‖**-táre** [Ger. *kratzen*], TR.: scratch (scrape, GRATE); grind; tickle (flatter): *— la tigna a uno,* beat one; *— dove pizzica, dove prude,* scratch where it itches; *egli avrà da —,* he will have enough to do; *— il corpo, la pancia,* do nothing; *— gli orecchi*†, flatter. **-táta,** F.: scratching. **-tatíccio**†, M.: act of scratching. **-tatína,** *car. dim.* of *-tata.* **-tatúra,** F.: scratch (scar). **-tíno,** M.: engraver's tool. **-tugétta, -tugína,** *dim.* of *-tugia.* **-túgia,** F.: grater: *esser un cacio fra due —,* be weak between two dangers. **-tugiáre,** TR.: grate. **-tugína,** *dim.* of *-tugia.*
gra-tuíre† = *-tificare.* **-tuitaménte,** ADV.: gratuitously. **-túito, -tuíto** [L. *-tuitus*], ADJ.: gratuitous (without recompense, gratis); voluntary, without excuse.
gratu-láre† [L. *-lari*], INTR.: congratulate. **-latòrio,** ADJ.: congratulatory. **-lazióne**†, F.: congratulation.
gra-váccio, ADJ.: dull (heavy). **-vacciòlo,** ADJ.: somewhat heavy. **-vaccióne** *disp.* of *-ve.* **-váme,** M.: burden; taxation. **-vaménto,** M.: grievance, oppression; imposition (tax); seizure; weight (burden)†; aggravation (surcharge)†; extortion†. **-vánte,** ADJ.: heavy (burdensome). **-vánza**†, F.: heaviness; anguish (grief). **-váre,** TR., INTR.: press with a weight (load, burden); be sorry; seize in execution; trouble (aggravate, vex, wrong)†; weigh heavy†; complaint† (moan): *— coll' accento,* accentuate. **-vatívo**†, ADJ.: heavy (grievous). **-vazióne**†, F.: weight (heaviness, gravity). ‖**grá-ve** [L. *-vis*], ADJ.: grave (serious, dangerous); heavy (weighty, ponderous); strong (great); slow (dull, idle)†; ADV.: gravely; M.†: gravity (weight): *esser — ad alcuno,* be troublesome to any one; *— d' età* or *d' anni,* old; *capitelli troppo -ri,* (*arch.*) capitals with too much ornament; *— di suono,* deep, low sound; *— in famiglia,* with a large family; *aver a — una cosa,* be displeased, take a thing amiss; *parlare sul —,* speak seriously (speak about serious things). **-vèdine**†, F.: heaviness or cold in the head. **-veménte,** ADV.: heavily. **-vèmza**†, F.: torment, anguish (grief). **-vétto,** *dim.* of *-ve.* **-vézza,** F.: gravity (heaviness, weight); impost (toll, tax); rigidity, roughness; injury†; seriousness†; trouble (vexation)†: *recarsi a —,* take it as an affront. **-vicciuòlo**†, ADJ.: somewhat heavy.

gravicémbalo [*clavicembalo*], M.: old piano-forte.
gra-vidaménto, M., **-vidánza**, **-vidézza†**, F.: gravity†; pregnancy; fulness. ‖**grá-vido** [*-ve*], ADJ.: pregnant; very full; laden. **-vína**, F.: mason's hammer. **-vi-sonánte†**, ADJ.: loud-sounding. **-vità**, F.: gravity; austere dignity (majesty, graveness). **-vitáre**, INTR.: gravitate, weigh. **-vitazióne**, F.: gravitation. **-vosaménte**, ADV.: heavily (hardly, severely). **-vosíno**, *dim.* of *-voso*. **-véso**, ADJ.: heavy (ponderous); troublesome (tiresome, fatiguing); severe (rigid); grave (momentous). **-vúccio**, *dim.* of *-ve*.
grá-zia [L. *-tia*], F.: GRACE (elegance, comeliness; forgiveness, pardon; favour; sympathy (love, affection); service. **-zie!** thanks! thank you: *dar* —, confer a benefit or favour; *salva tua* —, with your permission; *colpo di* —, death-blow; *far* —, pardon; *in* — *vostra*, for your love; *di* —, pray; *trovar* —, be pleased; *le Grazie*, the Graces. **-ziábile†**, **-ziále†**, ADJ.: worthy of pardon or favour. **-ziáccia**, *disp.* of *-zia*. **-ziáre**, TR.: pardon (absolve); grant a favour to. **-ziáto**, PART.: absolved (acquitted); ADJ.: graceful. **-ziétta**, *car.* of *-zia*. **-ziòla†**, F.: (*bot.*) water-hyssop. **-ziosaménte**, ADV.: graciously. **-ziosétto**, **-ziosettíno**, ADJ.: *car. dim.* of *-zioso*; pretty, nice. **-ziosità**, F.: elegance (gracefulness); gracious act. **-zióso**, ADJ.: graceful (agreeable, elegant); gracious (kind); grateful† (pleasing, acceptable).
grè-ca [*-co*], F.: kind of ornament; woman's dress. **-cále**, M.: north-east wind. **gre-caménte**, ADV.: in the manner of the Greeks. **-cheggiáre**, INTR. = *-cizzare*; incline to the northeast. **-chétto**, **-chíno**, *dim.* of *-co*. **-císmo**, M.: grecism or Greek idiom; erudition in Greek things†. **-císta**, M.: Hellenist (one learned in Greek). **-cità**, F.: Greek; knowledge of Greek. **-cizzáre**, TR.: give a Greek form to speech; use grecisms. ‖**grè-co** [L. *græcus*], ADJ.: Greek, of Greece; M.: north-east wind; Greek language; Greek wine; place where Greek wine is drunk†.
gre-gário [L. *-garius*], ADJ.: gregarious; low (common): *soldati -gari*, common soldiers. ‖**gré-gge** [L. *grex*], M., **-ggia**, F.: flock (herd, crowd): — *barbuto*, goats; *uscir di -ggia*, depart from established customs.
grèggio [?], ADJ.: rough (raw, unpolished, uneducated, clownish): *seta -gia*, raw silk.
greggiuòla†, *dim.* of *greggia*.
gregoriáno [Pope *Gregory*], ADJ.: Gregorian.
grem-bialáta, **-biuláta**, F.: apronful (lapful). **-biále** = *-biule*. **-biáta**, F.: apronful; small quantity. **grèm-bio** (*vulg.*) = *-bo*. **-biúle**, M.: apron: *uomo di* —†, artisan (workman). **-biulíno**, *dim.* of *-bo*. ‖**grèm-bo** [L. *-ium*], M.: lap (bosom); middle; uterus (womb); apron†; apronful†: *gettarsi in* — *a uno*, rely completely on one; *gli si può metter il capo in* —, he can rest assured on his account; *andare a* — *aperto†*, proceed with liberality or ingenuity.
gremígna† = *gramigna*.
gre-míre [OHG. *krimman*], TR.: CRAM, fill; REFL.: be filled, fill up. **-míto**, ADJ.: full (thick, covered with).
gréppia [OHG. *krippa*], F.: CRIB (manger; rack): *buona* —, good food for filling up; *alzare la* —, take away the manger; (*fig.*) measure the food for a family (give with measure).
gréppo [OHG. *klēp*, CLIFF], M.: steep (side of a mound or ditch); steep place; broken earthen vase: *far* — or *greppino†*, pout.
grès [Fr. *grès*], M.: sandstone (GRIT).
gréto [*ghiareto*], M.: sandbank (shoal); shore.
grétola [L. *craticola*], F.: bar (of a cage), chicanery (cavilling); pretense; splinter or chip†.
gretóso [*greto*], ADJ.: shoaly; sandy.
gret-taménte, ADV.: miserly (niggardly). **-tería**, **-tézza**, F.: stinginess (penuriousness). **-tíno**, *dim.* of *-to*. ‖**grét-to** [OHG. *grit*, avarice], ADJ.: parsimonious (stingy).
grève [L. *gravis*, (stingy)], ADJ.: (*lit.*) grave.
grézzo = *greggio*.
gríe-ciolo†, M.: whim (fancy, caprice). ‖**-cióne†**, M.: kind of water-fowl.
grí-da, F.: ban (proclamation); report†; reproof† (reprimand); cry†, shriek (of several persons). **-daménto†**, M.: outcry (clamour). ‖**-dáre** [L. *quiritari*, wail], INTR.: cry out (bawl); TR.: reprove (scold); show† (divulge); murmur† (purl); M.†: act of crying out; rebuke: — *accorr' uomo*, call for help; — *la croce addosso sopra uno*, speak ill of one. **-dáta**, F.: outcry; reprimand (rebuke). **-datóre**, M.: crier (public crier, proclaimer); bawler. **-dío**, M.: bawling (clamour). **-do**, M.: cry (shriek); bird of rapine; reputation† (fame, renown): *alzare*, *levare* —, acquire great fame, raise a noise; *metter in* —, spread a report; *dar* —, abuse; *a* —†, crying.
grièvo†, ADJ.: (*poet.*) heavy; grievous.

-ménte†, ADV.: heavily; grievously (sadly).
gri-fáccio, *disp.* of *-fo 1*. **-fágno**, ADJ.: of a rapacious bird. **-fáre†**, TR.: rub the snout against. **-fáta**, F.: injury made by muzzle. **grí-fo 1** [OFr. *grif*, ak. to Eng. *gripe*], M.: snout (muzzle, mouth): *voltare*, *torcere il* —, frown (show anger, disgust); *ungere il — alle spalle d' altri*, eat at others' expense.
grí-fo 2, **-fóne** [OFr. *grif* (L. *gryphus*)], M.: griffin; slap in the face.
grígio [l. L. *griseus* (OGer. *gris*, gray)], ADJ.: GRAY (GRIZzly).
grillája [*grillo*], F.: barren, unfruitful place.
grillánda = *ghirlanda*.
gril-láre [*-lo*], INTR.: simmer (boil with a hissing): — *il cuore a un uomo†*, begin to get enamoured. **-lettáre** = *-lare*. **-létto**, M.: trigger; spring of a Jew's-harp; (*vulg.*) clitoris. **-líno**, *car. dim.* of *-lo*. ‖**gril-lo** [L. *gryllus*], M.: cricket; whim (fancy); block to play bowls with; movable or swing bridge†; engine of war†: *indovinala* —, fortune book; *pigliare* or *toccare il* —†, get cross, be provoked. **-lolíno†**, *car. dim.* of *-lo*. **-lóne†**, M.: *aug.* of *-lo*; down: *fare a bel* —, waste one's time. **-lóso**, ADJ.: capricious (whimsical). **-lo=tálpa**, M.: gryllotalpa (mole-cricket). **-lòtti**, M.: (*mil.*) silk of the epaulets; fringe of the ornaments.
grimaldèllo [?], M.: pick-lock.
grímo†, ADJ.: wrinkled.
grínfia = *granfia*.
grín-ta [Ger. *grimm*, GRIM], F.: sinister face. **-za**, F.: wrinkle: *cavare il corpo di -ze*, eat one's bellyful (after having suffered with hunger). **-zétta**, *dim.* of *-za*. **-zolína**, *car. dim.* of *-zo*. **-zóso**, **-zo†**, ADJ.: wrinkled.
gríppe [Fr. (ak. to Eng. *gripe*)], M.: la grippe (influenza).
gríșo†, ADJ.: GRAY (GRIZzly).
grișòli-ta†, F., **-to** [*crisolito*], M.: chrysolite.
grișopázio [L. *chrysoprasus*], M.: green emerald.
grispígnolo†, M.: sow-thistle.
grissíno [fr. Piedm. *grissin*], M.: very thin bread (like sticks).
-ròfano† = *garofano*.
-giolàre [*crogiolare*], TR., REFL.: be used with.
-ma [?], F.: tartar (crust, argal); ments (of water). **-máto**, **-móso**, : full of tartar (tartarized, incrusted).
-da [L. *grunda*], F.: eaves (gutter, pout); pantile; ADV.: *a* —, jutting eaves; inclined. **-dáia**, F., **-dáio**, eaves; water which falls from the eaves: *fuggire l'acqua sotto le* —, jump from the frying pan into the fire. **-dáre**, INTR.: drop (fall in drops). **-datóio**, M.: brow or coping of a wall. **-dàa†** = *-da*. **-deggiáre†**, INTR.: *freq.* of *-dare*. **-dóne**, M.: terra cotta placed under the eaves. **-dón -dóni**, ADV.: *andare*, *camminare -don -doni*, walk slowly with the body bent.
grónge [L. *congrus*], M.: conger.
gròp-pa [Fr. *croupe* (Ger. *kropf*, protuberance)], F.: crupper (rump): *aver degli anni sulla* —, be many years old; *andar in* —†, be an accessory; *non portar in* —†, not to bear an affront. **-páta**, F.: sudden start of a horse. **-pièra**, F.: crupper (saddle-strap). **-po**, M.: (*lit.*) knot: group†; bag (packet)†; gust† (hurricane). **-póne**, M.: (*fam.*) crupper (rump, back): *non ne volere sul* —, not desire to work. **-póso**, ADJ.: knotty.
gròs-sa [*-so*], F.: gross (twelve dozen); quantity† (mass): *alla* —, by the lump; *dormir la* —, sleep profoundly†. **-sáccio**, *disp. aug.* of *-so*. **gròs-sa-gràna†**, F.: gros-de-Naples (cloth made of silk and mohair). **-samente**, ADV.: roughly. **-seggiáre†**, INTR.: be proud. **-serèllo**, *car. dim.* of *-so*. **-sería†**, F.: working large articles in gold and silver; dulness (awkwardness). **-sèro†** = *-siere*. **-sétto**, **-settíno**, *dim.* of *-so*. **-sézza**, F.: bulk (volume); bigness; coarseness; clownishness. **-siére**, **-sièro†**, M.: wholesale merchant; ADJ.†: gross (solid); stupid (clownish). **-sísta**, M.: wholesale merchant. ‖**gròs-so** [L. *-sus*], ADJ.: big (great, large); gross (coarse, rough); fat (corpulent); pregnant; M.: thickest part of a body (bulk); piece of money; thickness† (bigness); pregnancy†; ADV.: in great quantity, heavily; coarsely (grossly): *udito* — —, little deaf; *vino* —, muddy wine; *star* — *con uno*, maintain a reserved demeanour towards one; *negoziante in* —, wholesale merchant. **-solanaménte**, ADV.: in a coarse manner. **-soláno**, ADJ.: ugly (coarse, homely); dull. **-sóne**, M.: *aug.* of *-so*; piece of money†. **-sòtto**, ADJ.: rather thick†. **-súme**, M., **-súra**, F.: coarse, thick material; bulk (bigness); ignorance (rudeness).
gròt-ta [L. *crypta* (cf. *cripta*)], F.: grotto (cave); bank (dam, ridge)†; steep†, precipitous place. **-terèlla**, *car. dim.* of *-ta*. **-tésca**, F.: grotesque painting. **-tescaménte**, ADV.: grotesquely (strangely). **-tésco**, ADJ.: grotesque (strange, odd); M.: grotesqueness. **-ticèlla**, **-ticellína**, *car. dim.* of *-to*. **gròt-to†**, M.: grotto (cave); pelican. **-tóso**, ADJ.: full of grottoes; hollow (cavernous): *ciglia -tosa*, frown.

gro-víglíola [*garbuglio*], F.: twining (twisting). **-víglíolo**, M.: knot.

gru, grue, grua† [L. *grus*], F.: crane.

gruc-cétta, -cettína, *dim.* of *-cia.* **grúc-cia** [L. *crucea** (*crux*, CROSS)], F.: crutch; kind of dibble; door-handle (door-knob); instrument for planting sprigs of trees; clothes-hook; wooden leg†: *te-ner sulla* —, keep in suspense. **-ciáta**, F.: blow with a crutch.

grue = *gru.*

gruèra [*Gruyère*, in Switz.], M.: kind of thick cheese.

grufoláre [? *grifo*], TR.: grub up; REFL.: roll about (like a hog); INTR.†: grunt.

grugáre [echoic], INTR.: coo (like pigeons).

gru-gnáccio, *disp.* of *-gno* **-gnétto, -gníno**, *dim.* of *-gno.* ‖**-gníre** [L. *grunnire*], INTR.: grunt. **-gníto**, M.: grunting. **-gnitóre**, M.: grunter. **-gno**, M.: snout (muzzle): *far* —, *far il* —, *te-ner* —, frown, pout. **-gnóna, -gnóne**, *disp.* of *-gno.*

grul-lággine, F.: silliness; depression. **-lería**, F.: act or speech of a simpleton. ‖**-lo** [?], ADJ.: silly; depressed; M: simpleton.

grú-ma [*gromma*], F.: tartar (crust). **-máto**†, M.: kind of mushroom. **-meróccio**, M.: after or second crop of hay.

gru-métto, *dim.* of *-mo.* ‖**-mo** [L. *-mus*, little heap], M.: clot of blood; bud of a flower†. **-molétto, -molíno**, *dim.* of *-molo.* **grú-molo**, M.: core or pulp of cabbage, lettuce, etc. **-molóso**, ADJ.: pulpy. **-móso**, ADJ.: grumous (clotted, curdled).

gruògo†, M.: saffron.

grup-pétto, M.: *dim.* of *-po*; (*mus.*) little group. **-píto**, ADJ.: naturally polished (of diamonds). ‖**-po** [*groppo*], M.: group; packet† (parcel); wreath†; knot†.

grús-so†, M.: hoard; heap (pile). ‖**grúzzolo** [?], M.: hoard of money.

guadábile [*guadare*], ADJ.: fordable (passable).

guadá-gna† = *-gno.* **-gnábile**†, ADJ.: attainable; fruitful (productive). **-gnaménto**†, M.: gain (lucre). ‖**-gnáre** [OHG. *waidan-jan* (Ger. *weiden*), pasture], TR.: GAIN (win, acquire; earn); beget (generate)†. **-gnáta**, F.: winning. **-gnatóre**, M., **-gnatríce**, F.: gainer (winner). **-gnería**†, F.: ill-gotten gain; covetousness (avarice). **-gnétto**, M.: small gain. **guadá-gno**, M.: gain (profit): *mettere a* —, put out at interest; *mettersi a* —, prostitute one's self. **-gnucchiáre**, TR.: make small gains; begin to gain. **-gnáccio**†, **-gnúzzo**†, M.: small gain.

gua-dáre, TR.: ford (wade). **-de**†, F. PL.: kind of a net. ‖**-do** [Germ'c, ak. to Eng. *wade*], M.: ford (shallow passage): *rompere il* —, break the ice; *entrare nel* —, examine (try). **-dóso**†, ADJ.: fordable (passable).

guaglíanza† = *uguaglianza.*

guagnèlo† = *evangelo.*

guái = *guaio.*

guái [L. *vai*], INTERJ.: beware! woe!

guaíme†, M.: after-grass.

guaí-na [L. *vagina*], F.: sheath (scabbard); lace-string (of a garment or shoe); coffer† (casket, purse). **-náio**, M.: scabbard-maker. **-nèlla**, F.: carob-tree.

guá-io [L. *væ*, alas!], M.: WOE (calamity, misfortune); wailing (howling); yelp† (of a dog): *guai a te!* woe to you; *a* —, cruelly (fiercely, barbarously). **-ioláre**†, INTR.: grieve (lament, moan); yelp (howl). **-íre**, INTR.: howl (yelp, wail); ADV.†: scarcely. **-íto**, PART.: wailing; M.: howling (yelping).

gual-cáro [OHG. *walchan*], TR.: press cloth. **-chièra**, F.: fuller's mill (cloth-press). **-chieráio, -chierái**, M.: fuller (cloth-presser).

gualcíre = *sgualcire.*

gualdána [OHG. *woldan*, assault], F.: hostile incursion.

guáldo†, M.: defect (imperfection); wood or forest for birds.

gualdráppa [?], F.: horse-cloth (saddle-blanket, caparison).

guale. .† = *uguale*. .

gualèr-cio†, **-chio**, ADJ.: loathsome (filthy, slovenly).

gualopp. .† = *galopp*. .

guanáco [fr. Peruv.], M.: llama (Peruvian sheep).

guán-cia [OGer. *wankia* (= Ger *wange*)], F.: cheek; side; facet†. **-cialáta**, F.: blow with a pillow. **-ciále**, M.: pillow. **-cialétto**, *dim.* of *-ciale.* **-cialíno**, *dim.* of *-ciale.* **-cialóne**, *aug.* of *-ciale.* **-ciáta**, F.: cuff (slap, blow on the face). **-ciatína**, *dim.* of *-ciata.* **-cióne**†, M.: sound slap.

gua-nína, F.: extract of guano. ‖**-no** [fr. Peruv.], M.: guano.

guan-táio, M.: glove-maker (glover). **-tièra**, F.: glove-basin. ‖**-to** [Swed. *vante*], M.: glove: *gettare il* —, challenge; *dare*† or *donare il* —, give security for one's promise; *dar nel* —†, fall into one's clutches, fall in the snares.

guarágno†, M.: stallion.

guaraguáto†, M.: guard (sentinel).

guarantíre† = *garantire.*

guár-da = *-dia.* **-da=bòschi**, M.: wood-ranger (forest-keeper). **-da=cartòcci**†, M.: fire-guard. **-da=còrpo**†, M.: bodyguard (life-guardsman). **-da=còste**, M.: coast-guard (preventive-man). **-da=cuòre**, M.: corset (bodice). **-da dònna†**, F.: midwife. **-da=gòte†**, M.: cheek covering. **-da=mácchia**, F.: guard (of a gun). **-da=máno**, M.: hilt (guard of a sword). **-da=ménto†**, M.: look (glance); guard (repository); consideration; respect. **-da=náppa**, F., **—po**, M.: napkin (towel). **-da=náso†**, M.: nose-guard. **-danfánte** [*-da*, *infante*], M.: hoop (hoop-petticoat). **-da=nídio**, M.: nest-egg. **-da=portóne**, M.: porter. ‖**-dáre** [OHG. *wartên*], TR.: GUARD (watch; WARD, defend, protect); regard (behold, perceive); face; (*law*) have retroactive effect; REFL.: abstain from; take care of† (care for); avoid† (shun); retain†; refer† (allude): *-date a' fatti vostri*, mind your own business; — *le feste*, keep holidays; — *in sù*, look up; — *a traverso*, look askance; — *spesa*, be parsimonious; — *di*, abstain from. **-da=ròba**, F.: wardrobe; wardrobe keeper. **-da=sigílli**, M.: minister of justice; keeper of the seals. **-dáta**, F.: hasty look (glance). **-datáccia**, *disp.* of *-data*. **-datína**, *car. dim.* of *-data*. **-datóre**, M., **-datríce**, F.: guardian (defender, inspector). **-datúra**, F.: look (regard); guard (protection). **-da=vivánde**, M.: pantry. **guár-dia**, F.: guard (watch); assistant, nurse; sentinel; protection (defence); fang-tooth of a dog†: *esser di* —, be on guard; *far la* —, watch; *prender* —, take care of (have care); — *di spada*, hilt of a sword; — *morta*, scarecrow; *aver* —, be careful, attentive; *avere a* —, guard (have in custody). **-diána**, F.: shepherdess. **-dianáto**, M.: duty of the guardian. **-dianería†**, F.: guardianship. **-diáno**, M.: guardian or superior of a monastery; keeper of a flock or herd; vine shoot with two buds: — *della strada ferrata*, line-keeper. **-d=infánte**, M.: hoop-skirt. **-dingaménte†**, ADV.: cautiously (warily). **-díngo**, ADJ.: cautious (wary); diligent†; M.†: citadel (fortress). **-diòlo**, M.: guard-house (sentry-box). **-do**, M.: look (regard); view (aspect).

guaren-tía†, **-tígia**, F.: guaranty (surety). **-tíre** = *garantire*.

guári [OFr. *guaires* (Fr. *guère*)], ADV.: much, long: — *non è*, it is not long since.

gua-ríbile [*-rire*], ADJ.: curable (remediable). **-rigióne**, F., **-riménto†**, M.: cure (healing); recovery. ‖**-ríre** [OFr. *-rir* (OHG. *warjan*, WARD)], INTR.: recover one's health, cure; TR.: cure (heal); cleanse (purge)†; defend (protect)†.

guar-nácca, **-náccia†**, F.: dressing-gown (morning-gown). **-nacchíno**, *dim.* of *-nacca*. **-naccóne**, *aug.* of *-nacca*. **-nellétto†**, *dim.* of *-nello*. **-nèllo†**, M.: fustian; fustian gown. **-nigióne**, F.: garrison. **-niménto**, M.: equipment (munition, provision); garrison†; defense†. ‖**-níre** [OFr. *-nir* (OHG. *warnon*, provide)], TR.: furnish (equip; rig; fortify; GARNISH). **-nitúra**, F.: furnishing (trimming). **-nizióne**, F.: furnishing (esp. trimming, garnish, garniture).

guascherino†, ADJ.: belonging to the nest; young (little).

guas-conáta, F.: gasconade (boasting). ‖**-cóne** [Fr. *Gascogne*], M.: Gascon; boaster.

guascòtto†, ADJ.: half-cooked (half-done).

guastá-da†, F.: decanter (phial). **-détta†**, **-dína**, *dim.* of *-da*.

guasta=fèste, M.: feast-disturber. **-taménto**, M.: spoiling, destruction. **-ta=mestièri**, M.: trade-spoiler; bungler. ‖**-táre** [L. *vastare*], TR.: WASTE, spoil (ruin, deteriorate, destroy) corrupt; fall in love†; REFL.: get spoiled; grow rotten (putrefy). **-tatóre**, M., **-tatríce**, F.: spoiler; pioneer; kind of soldier. **-tatúra**, F.: devastation (wasting, spoiling). **-to**, ADJ.: spoiled (ruined); abused; enamoured with†; M.: ruin (destruction, havoc); bewitching creature†; food composed of boiled fruit: *aver il sangue — con uno*, hate a person; *stomaco* —, stomach out of order; *cane* —†, mad dog; *uomo* —, man in love; *dar il* —†, lay waste, desolate†; *menare a* —, spoil.

gua-taménto†, M.: watching (observing, spying). ‖**-táre†**, TR.: look at (watch, spy); observe; consider. **-tatóre†**, M., **-tatríce†**, F.: watcher (spy, gazer). **-tatúra**, F.: look, gazing; guard. **-to†**, M.: ambush (trap, snare).

guatter.. = *sguatter..*

guattíre†, INTR.: yelp (bark, howl).

guáz-za, F.: dew. **-zabugliáre**, INTR.: confuse (mix). **-zabúglio**, M.: medley (confusion, mixture). **-záre**, TR.: ford (wade); lead a beast through water; shake (agitate, stir); INTR.: be agitated. **-záta**, F.: fording (wading); shaking. **-zatóio**, M.: watering-place. **-zeróne†**, M.: gusset (gore); shred (bit, piece). **-zettíno**, *dim.* of *-zetto*. **-zétto**, M.: hash (minced-meat, ragout). ‖**-zo** [?], M.: dampness; distemper, water-colours; ford†; watering-place†; mud (mire). **-zóso**, ADJ.: splashy (damp, wet); muddy.

gúbbia [?], F.: team of three; big cart.

gubernácolo†, M.: rudder (helm).

guèffa†, F.: cage; prison; small mass of iron.

guèffo† = *gheffo*.

guèlfo [*Welf*, German family], M.: Guelph (supporter of the Pope: 12–13. Cent.); Florentine coin; ADJ.: Guelphian.

guer-ciáccio, *disp.* of *-cio.* ‖**guèr-cio** [?], ADJ.: squint-eyed.

guerigióne† = *guarigione.*

guerni. = *guarni.*

guèr-ra [OHG. *werra*], F.: WAR (strife); discord; hindrance (obstacle): *far — alla strada*, assassinate; *far posar la —*, intermit war (make a truce). **-reggévole**†, ADJ.: warlike (martial). **-reggevolménte**†, ADV.: in a warlike manner. **-reggiaménto**†, M.: act of making war (fighting). **-reggiáre**, TR.: make war (contend, fight). **-reggiatóre**, M., **—trice**, F.: warrior (fighter). **-résco**, ADJ.: warlike (fit for war). **-riáre**† = *-reggiare.* **-riáto**, ADJ.: *guerra —ta*, skirmish. **-ricciòla**, F.: *dim.* of *-ra;* small war. **-rièra**, F. of *-riero.* **-rière**†, M.: warrior (soldier). **-rièro**, ADJ.: warlike (valiant); contending; M.: warrior (fighter). **-ríglia**, F.: guerrilla-warfare. **-riglièro**, M.: guerrilla (bushwhacker).

gu-fáccio, *disp.* of *-fo.* **-fáre**†, TR.: mock (scoff). **-feggiáre**†, INTR.: hoot or screech like an owl. ‖**-fo** [OHG. *hûf*], M.: owl (screech-owl); amice (priest's vestment).

gú-glia [*aguglia*], F.: obelisk. **-gliáta**, F.: needleful. **-gliatina**, *dim.* of *-gliata.* **-gliétta**, *dim.* of *-glia.*

gugnolino, M.: small acorn-bud.

guí-da [*-dare*], F.: guide (conductor); cicerone (guide-book); (*mil.*) guide; guide-rein; rut (track of a wheel); rail (of a railroad): *a — di*, under the direction of. **-dábile**, ADJ.: that can be guided or led. **-dággio**†, M.: toll (excise); turnpike. **-daiòla**, F., **-daiòlo**, M.: leader of the flock (bellwether); ringleader.

guidalésco [?], M.: ulcer or sore on the back of a horse; trouble; ailment (malady); grief.

guidaménto†, M.: guiding, conduct.

guidardonáre† = *guiderdonare.*

guidá-re [Germ. root *wit-*, know], TR.: guide (lead, conduct); rule; REFL.: conduct one's self, be guided by: *— la vita*, live. **-rménti**, M.: herdsman (shepherd). **-tóre**, M., **-trice**, F.: guide (conductor).

guider-donaménto†, M.: recompense. **-donáre**, TR.: reward (recompense). **-donatóre**, M.: rewarder. ‖**-dóne** [l. L. *wider-donum* (OGer. *widar*, again, *lon*, reward)]. **-dóno**†, M.: GUERDON (reward, recompense, remuneration).

guidé-ne†, M.: guide; flag (standard); rogue (cheat). **-nería**†, F.: roguery (cheating).

guíndolo [OFr. *guindal* (OGer. *windan*, wind)], M.: spindle (reel).

guin-zagliétto, *dim.* of *-zaglio.* **-zá-glio** [?], M.: leash (string): *stare in —*, have patience.

guirminèlla† = *gherminella.*

guísa [OHG. *wisa*], F.: WISE (GUISE, mode, manner, fashion); proportion†: *a —*, *in —*, after the manner (like); *in nessuna —*, by no means; *in assoluta —*†, absolutely.

guit-tería, F.: stinginess. ‖**-to** [?], ADJ.: miserable; penurious (stingy).

guiz-zaménto, M.: gliding. **-zánte**, ADJ.: gliding. ‖**-záre** [Ger. *quitschen*], INTR.: glide, dart; quiver (flicker). **-zo**, M.: gliding, frisking; oscillation; vibration; ADJ.†: flaccid (withered, wrinkled).

gumèdra†, F.: great ninny.

gúmina† = *pomena.*

gúrge†, M.: gorge; gulf.

gu-scétto, *dim.* of *-scio.* ‖**gú-scio** [?], M.: shell (husk, bark); wiseacre, cunning boy; scales (balance); case, pillow-case; bark (skiff); body (of a coach); bulk (of a ship): *tristo fin nel —*, bad from one's birth; *trar l'anima nel —*, kill. **-scióne**, *aug.* of *-scio.*

gus-tábile, ADJ.: gustable (tastable). **-táccio**, *disp.* of *-to.* **-taménto**†, M.: taste (tasting); pleasure. **-táre**, TR.: taste (relish); try (assay); please (afford pleasure). **-táto**†, M.: relish (taste). **-tatóre**, M., **-tatrice**, F.: taster; trier. **-tévole**, ADJ.: pleasing to the taste (savoury, agreeable). **-tevolménte**, ADV.: tastefully (agreeably). ‖**-to** [L. *-tus*], M.: taste (GUST; satisfaction, pleasure, desire); inclination; kind, quality, manner (of taste): *a mio —*, to my mind; *con —*, with delight, voluptuously. **-tosaménte**, ADV.: pleasantly, agreeably. **-tosità**, F.: savouriness (agreeableness). **-tóso**, ADJ.: savoury; agreeable (pleasant).

guttapèrca [Malay.], F.: gutta-percha.

gutturá-le [L. (*guttur*, throat)], ADJ.: guttural. **-lménte**, ADV.: gutturally.

H

h *acca* [L.], F.: h (the letter).

hòmo = *ecce homo.*

hi, INTERJ.: pugh!

hui, INTERJ.: ah! alas!

I

i 1 [L.], M., F.: i (the letter).

i 2, PL. of *il.*

i', PRON. for *io*, I.

i-, prothetic sound before *s* + consonant.
iacèa†, F.: (*bot.*) heart's-ease.
iacére = *giacere*.
iáculo†, M.: flying-serpent; dart.
iadi [Gr. *huádes*], F. PL.: hyades.
Iágo [character in *Othello*], M.: traitor; rogue.
ialíno [Gr. *húalos*, glass], ADJ.: hyaline (transparent).
iámbo [Gr. *íambos*], M.: iambus.
iáspide [L. *iaspis*], M.: jasper.
iáto [L. *hiatus*, aperture], M.: hiatus, opening.
iat-tánza [L. *jactantia* (*jacere*, throw)], F.: boasting (bragging; Eng.† JACTANCY). **-túra**, F.: misfortune; loss.
ibèrno†, ADJ.: hibernal.
ibi, ibis [L. *ibis*], M.: ibis-bird.
ibísco [Gr. *ibískos*], M.: marshmallows.
ibri-dișmo, M.: hybridism. ||**íbri-do** [L. *hibrida*], ADJ.: hybrid (mongrel).
Icaro [son of *Dædalus*], PR. N.: *volo d'* —, foolish impudence or boldness.
icásti-ca [Gr. *eikastikós* (*eikós*, like), designer], F.: realism. **-co**, ADJ.: imitative of the true or real.
iccas(s)e [Gr.], M.: consonant x, as a letter of the alphabet.
icnèumone [Gr. *ichneúmon*, tracker], M.: ichneumon (carnivorous mammal).
icno-grafía [Gr. *íchnos*, track, *gráphein*, write], F.: ichnography. **-gráfico**, ADJ.: ichnographic.
icóne [Gr. *eikón*], F.: sacred image.
icono- [Gr. *eikón*, image]: **-clásto, -clásta** [Gr. *eikono-klastés* (*klân*, break)], M.: iconoclast. **-clástico**, ADJ.: iconoclastic. **-grafía** [Gr. *gráphein*, write], F.: iconography. **-gráfico**, ADJ.: iconographic. **-logía** [Gr. *lógos*, discourse], F.: iconology. **-lògico**, ADJ.: iconological. **-logista**, M.: iconologist.
icònomo†, M.: economist (manager).
icó-re [Gr. *ichór*], M.: ichor (thin discharge). **-róso**, ADJ.: ichorous (serous).
icosa-èdrico, ADJ.: icosahedral. ||**-èdro** [Gr. *eíkosi*, twenty, *hédra*, base], M.: icosahedron.
ictiología [Gr. *ichthus*, fish, *lógos*, discourse], F.: ichthyology.
idátide [Gr. *hudatís*], F.: hydatid (membraneous bladder).
Iddío [L. *Deus*], M.: God.
idè-a [L.], F.: idea (opinion); conception (fancy, imagination); manner (style). **-éc-cia**, F.: *disp.* of *-a*; evil intention. **-ále**, ADJ.: ideal; fantastical (imaginary); M.: ideal. **-alișmo**, M.: idealism. **-alísta**, M.: idealist. **-alità**, F.: ideality. **-almente**, ADV.: ideally. **-áre**, TR.: imagine (conceive); REFL.: represent or imagine one's self. **-ína**, *car. dim.* of *-a*.
idem [L.], M.: same, same thing: *un* — *per* —, same thing over again.
identi-caménte, ADV.: identically. ||**idènti-co** [L. *idem*, same], ADJ.: identical (self-same). **-ficáre**, TR.: identify; REFL.: identify one's self with; become identical. **-ficazióne**, F.: identification. **-tà** [L. *-tas*], F.: identity.
ide-ografía [Gr. *idéa*, *gráphein*, write], F.: ideography. **-ográfico**, ADJ.: ideographic. **-ología** [Gr. *idéa*, *lógos*, discourse], F.: ideology. **-ològico**, ADJ.: ideological. **-òlogo**, M.: ideologist. **-óna**, *aug.* of *-a*.
idest(e) [L. *id est*, that is], ADV.: that is to say, i.e.
idi [L. *idus*], M. PL.: ides.
idil-liaco, ADJ.: idyllic. ||**idíl-lio** [L. *idyllium* (Gr. *eîdos*, form)], M.: idyl.
idi-òma [Gr. *-oma* (*-os*, special, particular)], M.: language (idiom). **-òta**, M.: idiot; ADJ.: idiotic (silly). **-otàggine**, F.: idiocy (foolishness). **-otaménte**, ADV.: idiotically. **-òtico**, M.: idiot. **-otișmo**, M.: idiotism.
ido-la† = *-lo*. **-láre**†, TR.: idolise. **-latóre**†, M.: idolater. **-látra** [L.], M.: idolater. **-latraménto**†, M.: idolatry. **-latráre**, TR.: worship idols; love desperately (idolize). **-latría**, F.: idolatry. **-látrico**, ADJ.: idolatrous. **-látro**†, M.: idolater. **-létto**, *car. dim.* of *-lo*. ||**ido-lo** [L. *-lum*], M.: idol (image).
idone-aménte, ADV.: fitly (aptly). **-ità**, F.: aptness (suitableness). ||**idòneo** [L. *-us*], ADJ.: idoneous (apt, suitable).
idr.. [Gr. *húdor*, water]: **idr-a** [Gr. *húdra*], F.: hydra. **-áto**, M.: hydrate. **-áulica**, F.: hydraulics. **-áulico** [Gr. *hudraulis*, water organ], ADJ.: hydraulic.
idr-ia, F.: hydria (water-jar). **idr-o**, M.: aquatic serpent. **-ocarbúro**, M.: hydro-carbon. **-ocèfalo** [Gr. *kephalé*, head], M.: hydrocephalous. **-ocèle** [Gr. *kéle*, tumour], M.: hydrocele. **-oclorato**, M.: hydrochlorate. **-odinámica** [Gr.], F.: hydrodynamics. **-ofobía** [Gr. *phóbos*, fear], F.: hydrophobia. **-òfobo**, ADJ.: afraid of water; M.: one afflicted with hydrophobia. **-ògene, -ògeno** [Gr. *génos*, origin], M.: hydrogen. **-ografía** [Gr. *gráphein*, write], F.: hydrography. **-ográfico**, ADJ.: hydrographical. **-ògrafo**, M.: hydrographer. **-ología**, M.: hydrology. **-òlogo**, M.: hydrologist. **-ománte** [Gr. *mántis*, diviner, foreteller], M.: hydromant (one who foretells events by means of water). **-omanzía**, F.: hydromancy. **-omèle** [Gr. *méli*, honey], M.: hydromel. **-òmetra** [Gr. *métron*, measure], M.: professor of hydrometry. **-ometría**, F.: hydrometry. **-omètrico**,

ADJ.: hydrometric. **-òmetro**, M.: hydrometer. **-ónfalo** [Gr. *omphálion*, navel], M.: kind of tumour or rupture. **-òpico**, ADJ.: dropsical; M.: dropsical person. **-opisía** [Gr. *húdrops*], F.: DROPSY. **-ostática**, F.: hydrostatics. **-ostático**, ADJ.: hydrostatical. **-oterapía** [Gr. *therapeía*, cure], F.: hydrotherapy (hydropathy). **-oterápico**, ADJ.: hydropathic.

iemále [L. *hiems*, winter], ADJ.: hyemal (wintery).

ièna [Gr. *húaina*, sow], F.: hyena.

ierático [Gr. *ierós*, sacred], ADJ.: hieratic.

ièri [L. *heri*], ADV.: yesterday: *ier l'altro*, day before yesterday; *l' altr' —*, some days ago; *ier mattina*, yesterday morning.

ierofánte [Gr. *iero-phántes* (*hierós*, sacred, *phaínein*, show)], M.: hierophant.

ieròfila†, F.: gillyflower; violet.

ieroglífico [Gr. *-glyphos* (*hierós*, sacred, *glúphein*, carve)], ADJ.: hieroglyph.

igiè-ne [Gr. *hugíeia*, health], F.: hygiene. **igiè-nico**, ADJ.: hygeian (healthy). **-nísta**, M.: hygienist.

ignáro [L. *-rus*], ADJ.: ignorant.

ignatóne†, M.: great eater (glutton, gourmand); sluggard.

ign-ávia, F.: sloth (indolence). ‖**-ávo** [L. *-avus*], ADJ.: slothful (idle, lazy); vile (contemptible).

ígn-eo [L. *-eus* (*-is*, fire)], ADJ.: igneous (fiery). **-ícolo** [L. *-iculus* (*dim.* of *-is*)], M.: spark of fire; excitation† (encouragement). **-íto**, ADJ.: ignited (inflamed). **-ívomo**†, ADJ.: ignivomous (vomiting flames). **-izióne**, F.: ignition.

ignò-bile [L. *-bilis*], ADJ.: ignoble (vulgar). **-bilità** = *-biltà*. **-bilménte**, ADV.: ignobly (basely). **-biltà**, F.: ignobility (baseness).

ignòcco = *gnocco*.

ignomí-nia [L.], F.: ignominy (dishonour). **-niosaménte**, ADV.: ignominiously. **-nióso**, ADJ.: ignominious.

igno-rantáccio, *disp.* of *-rante*. **-rantággine**, F.: ignorance; action of an ignorant person. **-ránte**, ADJ.: ignorant (illiterate); inexperienced; impolite (stupid); M.: ignorant fellow. **-rantèllo**, *dim.* of *-rante*. **-rantemente**, ADV.: ignorantly. **-rantóne**, *disp. aug.* of *-rante*. **-rantúccio**, **-rantúzzo**, *dim.* of *-rante*. **-ránza**, F.: ignorance; unskilfulness; rudeness. **-ránzia**†, F.: ignorant act. ‖**-ráre** [L.], TR.: be ignorant of (not know). **ignò-scere**†, IRR.; TR.: pardon (forgive). **-taménte**, ADV.: secretly (clandestinely). **ignò-to**, ADJ.: unknown; ignorant.

ignu-daménte, ADV.: nakedly. **-dáre**, TR.: strip naked (undress). ‖**-do** [*nudo*], ADJ.: nude (naked); deprived of; necessitous; manifest†; M.†: nude.

igro- [Gr. *hugrós*, wet], PREF.: humid. **-metría**, F.: hygrometry. **-mètrico**, ADJ.: hygrometrical. **igrò-metro** [Gr. *métron*, measure], M.: hygrometer. **-scopía**, F.: art of measuring the humidity of the atmosphere. **-scòpio** [Gr. *skopéo*, look], M.: hygroscope.

igual. † = *egual.*

iguána [Sp.], F.: iguana (large lizard).

ih! INTERJ. of anger or wrath.

il [L. *ille*], ART.: the; PRON.: that; him; it.

ila-re [L. *hilaris*], ADJ.: hilarious (joyful). **-rità**, F.: hilarity (cheerfulness).

íleo [Gr. *eileín*, roll up], M.: ileum (last part of intestine).

Iliade [Gr. *Iliás* (*Ilion*, Troy)], F.: Iliad; (*fig.*) long succession of misfortunes.

ílio [L. *ilium*, groin], M.: ilium (a portion of the hip-bone).

illaccciáre†, TR.: entangle (tie).

illacri-mábile [L. *-mabilis*], ADJ.: illachrymable (not to be cried about). **-máto**, ADJ.: unwept.

illaidíre [*in*, *laido*], TR.: make ugly; contaminate (soil).

illangui-diménto, M.: act of becoming weak. ‖**-díre** [*in*, *languido*], TR: render languid; INTR.: become weak or languid.

illaqueáre [L.], TR.: illaqueate (ensnare); enslave.

illa-tivaménte, ADV.: illatively (consequently). ‖**-tívo** [L. *-tivus*], ADJ.: illative (inferential).

illau-dábile, **-dévole** [*in-*, *l.*.], ADJ.: illaudable. **-dáto**, ADJ.: unworthy of praise.

illazióne [L. *illatio*], F.: illation (conclusion, inference).

illéce-bra†, F.: allurement (attraction). **-bróso**†, ADJ.: illecebrous (attractive, alluring).

il-lecitaménte, ADV.: illicitly. ‖**-lécito** [*in-*, *lecito*], ADJ.: illicit.

illegá-le [*in-*, *l.*.], ADJ.: illegal. **-lità**, F.: illegality. **-lménte**, ADV.: illegally (unlawfully).

illeggiadríre [*in*, *leggiadro*], TR.: beautify (embellish, adorn).

illeggíbile [*in-*, *l.*.], ADJ.: illegible.

illegitti-maménte, ADV.: illegitimately. **-mità**, F.: illegitimacy. ‖**illegítti-mo** [*in-*, *l.*.], ADJ.: illegitimate.

illéso [*in-*, *l.*.], ADJ.: unhurt (safe).

illetteráto [*in-*, *l.*.], ADJ.: illiterate (ignorant); M.: illiterate.

illi-batézza, F.: purity (integrity). ‖**-báto** [L. *in-*, *libatus*, harmed], ADJ.: immaculate (stainless, pure).

illiberále [*in-*, *l.*.], ADJ.: illiberal: *arti —li*, mechanical arts.

illicit. .† = *illecit*. .
illimi-tatamente, ADV.: unboundedly. ‖**-tato** [*in-*, *L.* .], ADJ.: unlimited (boundless): *fiducia -tata*, absolute faith.
illiquidire [*in*, *liquido*], INTR.: become liquid (dissolve).
illitterato = *illetterato*.
illividire [*in*, *livido*], INTR.: make livid; bruise.
illodabile†, ADJ.: illaudable.
il-logicamente, ADV.: illogically. ‖**-logico** [*in-*, *L.* .], ADJ.: illogical.
illudere [L.], IRR. (cf. *alludere*); TR.: delude (deceive).
illumi-nabile, ADJ.: illuminable. **-namento**, M.: illumination; enlightenment. ‖**-nare** [L.], TR.: illuminate (enlighten); cause to see; (*fig.*) make manifest or clear; REFL.: enlighten one's self. **-nativo**, ADJ.: illuminative (enlightening). **-nato**, PART.: illuminated, etc. **-natore**, M., **-natrice**, F.: enlightener (illuminator); illustrator†. **-nazione**, F.: illumination (light); (*fig.*) mental enlightenment (inspiration).
illu-sione [*-dere*], F.: illusion (deception); vain idea; derision† (mockery). **illuso**, PART. of *-dere;* deluded. **-sore**, M.: deceiver (deluder); derider. **-soriamente**, ADV.: deceptively; derisively. **-sorio**, ADJ.: illusory (vain, deceptive).
illu-stramento†, M.: illustration; clearness. **-strare** [L.], TR.: illustrate; explain (make clear); make famous. **-strativo**, ADJ.: illustrative. **-stratore**, M., **-stratrice**, F.: illustrator (explainer). **-strazione**, F.: illustration (explanation); enlightenment. ‖**illustre** [L. *-tris*], ADJ.: illustrious (famous, renowned). **-stremente**†, ADV.: illustriously.
il-luvie [L. *-luvies* (*luere*, wash)], F.: filthiness (sordidness). **-luvione**, F.: inundation (flood of waters).
im- = *in-*, prefix.
imag. . = *immag*. .
imano [Turk.], M.: iman (Turkish priest).
imbaca. . = *baca*. .
imbacchettonire [*bacchettone*], INTR.: become a devotee.
imbacuccare [*bacucco*], TR.: cover with a hood; wrap up (muffle up); REFL.: wrap about one's self.
imbagna. .† = *bagna*. .
imbalconato [*in*, *balcone*, calyx of a rose], ADJ.: of a rosy colour.
imbal-danzire [*in*, *baldanza*], INTR.: [illegible]d (take courage). **-dire**†, INTR.: [illegible]ld: become proud.
[illegible]gio, M.: act of packing bales; [illegible]d in embaling. ‖**-lare** [*in*, [illegible]] pack up (embale). **-latore**, M.: man employed to pack up (embaler). **-latura**, F.: act of packing up.
imbalordito†, ADJ.: stupified (stunned).
imbal-samare [*in*, *balsamo*], TR.: embalm (preserve). **-samatore**, M.: embalmer. **-samazione**, F.: embalming. **-simire**, INTR.: become balm.
imbamba-gellato†, ADJ.: smooth(ed); soft. **-giare**†, TR.: wrap up in cotton; line with cotton.
imbambo-lare†, TR.: soften (move to tears); INTR.: be affected. ‖**-lato** [*in*, *bambola*], ADJ.: softened (affected). **-lire**†, INTR.: become childish.
imbandie-ramento, M.: adornment (ornamentation. ‖**-rare** [*in*, *bandiera*], TR.: ornament with flags (adorn).
imban-digione, F., **-dimento**†, M.: dishes served up. ‖**-dire** [*in*, *bando*, feast], TR.: prepare (a feast); serve up. **-ditore**, M.: preparer of a feast.
imba-razzare, TR.: embarrass (confuse); hinder; REFL.: intermeddle. ‖**-razzo** [Sp. *embarazo*, obstacle], M.: embarrassment (confusion, disorder); obstacle.
imbarbarescatore†, M.: one who reminds or suggests; keeper of the barbs or race-horses.
imbarba-rimento, M.: act of becoming barbarous. ‖**-rire** [*in*, *barbaro*], INTR.: grow barbarous.
imbarbogire [*in*, *barbogio*], INTR.: grow senile or childish (fall into second childhood).
imbar-camento†, M.: embarcation. ‖**-care** [*in*, *barca*], TR.: embark; undertake (engage in); INTR.: grow angry; warp; be crooked or humped; REFL.†: fall in love; enter in: — *senza biscotto*, (*fig.*) embark in an undertaking without any preparation whatever; — *uno in un' impresa*, put one in a dangerous undertaking. **-catore**, M.: embarker; freighter. **-cazione**, F.: vessel with oars; embarcation. **imbar-co**, M.: embarcation; enterprise (undertaking); vessel; act of falling in love†.
imbardare†, TR.: caparison (harness); undertake (begin); allure; REFL.: fall in love
imbarrare†, TR.: bar (barricade); perplex.
imbarilare [*in*, *barile*], TR.: put in barrels.
imba-samento, M.: foundation (basis, basement). ‖**-sare** [*in*, *base*], TR.: put on a foundation or basis. **-satura** = *-samento*.
imba-sceria†, ‖**-sciata** [cf. *ambasciata*], F.: embassy. **-sciatore**, M.: ambassador.
imbastar-dimento, M.: corruption (de-

generation). ‖-**díre** [*in, bastardo*], TR.: corrupt (bastardize); INTR.: degenerate.
imbastáre†, TR.: put a pack-saddle upon.
imba-stiménto† = *-stitura*. ‖-**stíre** [*in, bas-ta, -tia*], TR.: baste (sew with long stitches); serve up†: — *un libro*, make a rough draft of a book. -**stitúra**, F.: basting (slight stitching); thing thus stitched.
imbásto†, M.: pack-saddle.
imbát-tere [*in, b.*], REFL.: meet with by chance. **imbát-to**†, M.: unexpected meeting; obstacle (hindrance). -**táto**, PART. of *-tere*.
imbauláre [*in, baule*], TR.: put into a trunk (pack).
imbavagliáre [*in, bavaglio*], TR.: put on a bib; gag; muffle up.
imbaváre [*in, bava*], TR.: slobber.
imbec-cáre [*in, becco*], TR.: feed (like a young bird); (*fig.*) instruct privately. -**cáta**, F.: billful; (*fig.*) instruction; agreement; bribe: *pigliare un'* —, catch a cold; *pigliare l'* —, take a bribe.
imbeccheráre [*-beverare*], TR.: suborn (bribe).
imbecíl-le [L. *-lis*, weak], ADJ.: imbecile (weak-minded). -**líre**, TR.: become imbecile or stupid. -**lità**, F.: imbecility (weakness of mind).
imbèlle [L. *im-bellis* (*bellum*, war)], ADJ.: unfit for war (unwarlike; Eng.† imbellic); cowardly.
imbellettáre [*in, belletto*], TR., REFL.: fard (paint one's self).
imbellíre [*in, bello*], INTR.: become beautiful; TR.†: embellish (beautify).
imbendáre†, TR.: bind put on a fillet.
imbèrbe [L. *im-berbis* (*barba*, beard)], ADJ.: beardless.
imber-ciáre [*in-, b.*], TR.: hit the mark; attain. -**ciatóre**, M.: one that hits the mark.
imbére† = *imbevere*; TR.: (*fig.*) desire earnestly.
imberret-táre [*in, berretta*], TR.: put a cap or bonnet on.
imbertescáre [*in, bertesca*], TR.: fortify with parapets or battlements.
imberto-náre†, ‖-**níre** [*in, bertone*, amourous], INTR., REFL.: be enamoured (fall in love).
imbe-stialíre [*in, bestiale*], INTR.: become brutal or cruel; look like a beast. -**stialíto**, PART.: furious (raging). -**stiáre** [*in, bestia*], INTR.: become brutish; TR.†: brutify (reduce to the state of a beast).
imbé-vere [*in-, b.*], IRR.; TR.: imbibe (absorb); inspire; instruct; REFL.: become imbibed; be imbued. -**viménto**, M.: imbibition (absorption). -**vúto**, PART.: imbibed (instilled); imbued (impressed).
imbiac-caménto, M.: coating with white lead. ‖-**cáre** [*in, biacca*], TR.: coat with white lead; REFL.: paint one's face. -**cáto**, PART. of *-care*; ADJ.: feigned (dissembled).
imbiadáto†, ADJ.: sown with corn.
imbian-caménto, M.: painting; whitewashing; bleaching; fraud (deceit)†. ‖-**cáre** [*in, bianco*], TR.: whiten (whitewash); disapprove; INTR.: become white (grow gray). -**catóre**, M.: whitewasher (whitener). -**catúra**, F.: whitewashing (whitening). -**chíno** = *-catore*. -**chíre**, TR.: whiten (blanch, wash white); INTR.: grow white; be confused†.
imbietolíre [*in, bietola*], INTR.: become a beet; (of persons) be affected or rejoice over nothing.
imbiettáre [*in, bietta*], TR.: put a wedge into; split.
imbion-díre [*in, biondo*], INTR.: become fair; turn yellowish†; TR.: make fair. -**díto**, PART.: grown fair; ripened.
imbirboníre [*in, birbone*], INTR.: become a rascal.
imbisacciáre†, TR.: put into a sack or wallet.
imbisognáto†, ADJ.: busy (occupied).
imbitumáre [*in, bitume*], TR.: cover with bitumen.
imbiutáre = *impiastrare*.
imbizzar-riménto, M.: liveliness (spiritedness); anger (wrath). ‖-**ríre** [*in, bizzarro*], INTR.: fly into a passion (rail); become spirited, lively; show great ardour. -**ríto**, PART.: raging, spirited.
imbizzíre [*in, bizza*]: INTR.: take fits of rage, become capricious or whimsical.
imboc-caménto, M.: feeding; instruction. ‖-**cáre** [*in, bocca*], TR.: feed; instruct (prepare, prompt); fit (join); disembogue; empty; (*art.*) disable: — *col cucchiaio vuoto*, pretend to instruct, but not do so; — *una cosa a uno*, make one understand a thing. -**catúra**, F.: mouth of a river; mouthpiece; bit of a bridle; entrance of a street; manner of blowing an instrument.
imboc-ciáre [*in, boccia*], INTR.: bud. -**cioláre** [*in, bocciolo*], TR.: put in a reed.
imbócco [*-ccare*], M.: entrance of a street.
imbociáre†, TR.: publish (spread abroad); blame publicly.
imboináre = *imbovinare*.
imbo-láre†, TR.: take away (steal, rob); gain; surprise. -**lío**†, M.: robbery (theft) *d'* —, by surprise.
imbolli-caménto†, M.: blister (pimp

‖**-cáre**†, INTR.: produce pimples or blisters; break out into pimples.
imbol-siménto, M.: pursiness (shortness of breath). ‖**-síre** [*in, bolso*], INTR.: grow pursy; render negligent or careless†. **-síto**, PART.: asthmatical.
imbonire = *abbonire*.
imbor-chiáre [?], TR.: (*nav.*) emboss (moor against the wind). **-chiatúra**, F.: (*nav.*) spring.
imborgáre†, REFL.: be filled with villages (be populous).
imborsá-re [*in, borsa*], TR.: purse (pocket); put into the ballot-box; understand†. **-zióne**, F.: laying up in a purse, pocketing money.
imbos-caménto†, M.: ambush (ambuscade). ‖**-cáre** [*in, bosco*], INTR.: hide in a wood; lay in ambush. **-cáta**, F.: ambuscade (ambush). **-chiménto** = *rimboschimento*. **-chíre**, INTR.: grow woody.
imbot-táre [*in, botte*], TR.: put into a hogshead or cask or vat; drink much. **-tatóio**, M.: funnel. **-tatúra**, F.: putting wine into casks. **-tavíno**, M.: funnel for a bunghole. **imbót-te**, F.: archivault (concave part of a vault or bridge). **-tigliáre**, TR.: put into bottles. **-tináre**, TR.: (*agr.*) compost. **-tíre**, TR.: wad (stuff). **-titúra**, F.: wadding.
imbovináre [*in, bovina*], TR.: spread with cow's dung.
imbozzacchíre [*in, bozzacchio*], INTR.: be stunted in growth (wither, thrive ill).
imbozzimá-re [*in, bozzima*], TR.: starch; daub with sticky stuff. **-túra**, F.: starching; daubing (soiling).
imbrá-ca [*in, b. .*], F.: breeching of a horse's harness; discouraged person; denier. **-cáre**, TR.: gird (tie around). **-catúra**, F.: tying around with a cord.
imbrac-ciáre [*in, braccio*], TR.: put on one's arm; embrace†. **-ciatúra**, F.: handle; braces of a shield.
imbrachettáre [*in, brachetta*], TR.: put breeches on; glue (fasten).
imbrancáre [*in, branco*], TR.: put into the flock; REFL.: enter or return into the flock; get into bad company.
imbrandíre†, TR.: brandish (a sword).
imbrat-taménto†, M.: foulness (nastiness). ‖**-táre** [*in, bratta*, dregs], TR.: soil (spoil). **-táto**, PART.: soiled; filled; obstructed; indebted†. **-tatóre**, M.: dauber. **-tatúra**, F.: slovenliness; stain ...); sketch (draught). **imbrátto**, ... daub; wash, hog's wash; dirt; ... cooked dish.
...**-ciáre** [*in, breccia*], TR.: gravel; hit the mark. **-ciáta**, F.: grav-

imbrènti-na, -ne [?], F.: rockrose; intrigue† (embarrassment).
imbria-caménto†, M.: intoxication (drunkenness). **-cáre**, TR.: intoxicate; REFL.: get drunk; (*fig.*) fall in love with. **-cáto**, PART.: drunk (tipsy). **-catúra**, **-chézza**†, F.: intoxication. ‖**imbriáco**† [*in-, b. .*], ADJ.: drunk (fuddled); M.: drunkard. **-cóne**, *aug.* of *-co*.
imbricconíre [*in, briccone*], INTR.: grow knavish (become a rascal).
imbri-gaménto†, M.: confusion (intricacy, perplexity); obstacle. ‖**-gáre**†, TR.: embroil (confuse); REFL.: intrigue; strive.
imbrigliá-re [*in, briglia*], TR.: bridle; restrain (repress). **-túra**, F.: bridling; restraint.
imbroc-cáre [*in, brocca*], TR.: hit (the mark); aim at; thwart† (hinder); INTR.†: perch upon a tree. **-cáta**, F.: blow with the sword; hit. **-ciáre**† = *-care*.
imbro-dáre [*in, broda*], **-doláre**, TR.: grease (soil with broth or grease); REFL.: soil one's self.
imbro-gliáre, TR.: embroil (perplex); ruffle up (entangle); covert†; REFL.: get bewildered; meddle in another's affairs (intrigue): — *le vele*, brail up the sails (reef); — *la Spagna*, turn things topsy-turvy. **-gliáto**, PART.: confused, etc.: *essere bene* —, be in many troublesome affairs. **-gliataménte**, ADV.: troublesomely (in a perplexing manner). **-gliatèllo**, *dim.* of *-gliato*. **-gliatóre**, M., **-gliatríce**, F.: troubler; intriguer (busybody). **imbrò-glio** [*in, b. .*], M.: perplexity (confusion, embarrassment); intrigue. **-glióna**, F., **-glióne**, M.: meddler (marplot).
imbron-ciáre, **-círe** [*in, broncio*], INTR.: pout (get angry).
imbru-náre [*in, bruno*], **-níre**, TR.: burnish (brown); INTR.: grow brown; become dark or gloomy. **-nitúra**, F.: burnishing; sun-burning.
imbrus-chíre†, INTR.: be sour or vexed. **-chíto**†, PART.: vexed (angry).
imbrutíre [*in, bruto*], INTR.: become brutish.
imbrut-táre†, TR.: daub (soil, bespatter). ‖**-tíre** [*in, brutto*], INTR.: grow ugly; TR.: make ugly.
imbubboláre [*in, bubbola*], REFL.: matter little (be of little import); TR.†: jest (banter); fool.
imbucáre [*in, buca*], TR.: put in a hole; REFL.: enter or creep into a hole.
imbucatáre [*in, bucato*], TR.: buck or wash with lye.
imbufonchiáre†, INTR.: murmur (grumble).

imbuíre [*in*, *bue*], INTR.: become a dunce (get stupid).

imbullettáre [*in*, *bulletta*], TR.: fasten with tacks; drive tacks into.

imbuondáto†, ADV.: plentifully (abundantly).

imbuonire = *imbonire*.

imburchiáre†, TR.: assist in a composition (prompt); instruct; plagiarize.

imburiassá-re†, TR.: instruct (teach). **-tóre**†, M., **-tríce**†, F.: teacher (instructor).

imburráre [*in*, *burro*], TR.: cover with butter.

imbuscheráre [*in*, *buschera*], INTR.: not care; laugh (at, *di*).

imbusecchiáre [*in*, *busecchia*], TR.: put (sausage) into the skin; (*fig.*) stuff (with food).

imbústo [*busto*], M.: *fare il bell' —*, act the dandy (be a fop); bust (trunk)†; corset†.

im-butíno, M.: funnel-shaped flower. ‖**-búto** [L. *-butus* (*-buere*, fill)], M.: funnel: *mangiare coll' —*, *pigliare l' —*, eat in great haste. **-butóne**, *aug.* of *-buto*.

imbuzzáre [*in*, *buzzo*], TR.: stuff (with food), overfeed; REFL.: eat too much.

imè-ne [Gr. *humén*, membrane], M.: hymen; marriage; god of marriage. **-nèo**, M.: marriage. **-nòtteri** [Gr. *humén*, membrane, *pterón*, winged], M. PL.: hymenoptera (order of insects).

imi-tábile, ADJ.: imitable. ‖**-táre** [L. *-tari*], TR.: imitate (copy, counterfeit). **-tatívo**, ADJ.: imitative. **-tatóre**, M., **-tatríce**, F.: imitator (counterfeiter). **-tatòrio**†, ADJ.: imitatory. **-tazióne**, F.: imitation (copy).

immacchiáre [*in*, *macchia*], REFL.: hide one's self in a bush (conceal one's self).

immaco-láre† [*in*, *m.*.], TR.: stain (soil, bespot). **-láta**, F.: Virgin Mary. **-lataménte**, ADV.: immaculately. **-láto**, ADJ.: immaculate (spotless, pure).

immagazzináre [*in*, *magazzino*], TR.: put in a magazine or shop.

immagi-nábile, ADJ.: imaginable. **-naménto**†, M.: imagination; idea (thought). **-náre** [L. *imaginari*], TR.: imagine (fancy, conceive); suppose; devise (plan). **-nariaménte**, ADV.: imaginarily. **-nário**, ADJ.: imaginary (ideal). **-natíva**, F.: imaginative faculty (imagination). **-nativaménte**, ADV.: in imagination. **-natívo**, ADJ.: imaginative. **-náto**, ADJ.: imagined (figured); M.†: imagination; idea. **-natóre**, M.: imaginer (conceiver). **-nazióne**, F.: imagination (fancy); affirmation (belief). ‖**immági-ne** [L. *imago*], F.: image (figure); likeness; appearance; picture. **-nétta**, *car. dim.* of *-ne*. **-névole**†, ADJ.: imaginable. **-nevolménte**, ADV.: fantastically. **-nosaménte**, ADV.: in a very imaginative manner. **-nóso**, ADJ.: full of fancies or imagination.

immágo† = *immagine*.

immagríre = *dimagrare*.

immalinco-nicáre†, **-nichíre**†, TR.: make melancholy (grieve); INTR.: become melancholy (be afflicted). ‖**-níre**† [*in*, *malinconia*], INTR.: become melancholy.

immalizzíre [*in*, *malizia*], INTR.: be malicious, crafty; TR.: make malicious.

immalsaníre†, TR.: weaken (enfeeble, sicken).

immancábi-le [*in*, *m.*.], ADJ.: unfailing; infallible. **-lménte**, ADV.: unfailingly; infallibly.

immáne [L. *-nis*], ADJ.: IMMENSE (enormous, Eng.† immane); cruel (inhuman).

im-maneggiábile, ADJ.: unmanageable.

imma-nènte [L. *-nere*, remain], ADJ.: immanent (inherent). **-nènza**, F.: immanence (inherence).

immanifèsto†, ADJ.: not manifest.

immanità [*-ne*], F.: ferocity.

immansuèto†, ADJ.: wild (savage).

immantinènte [L. *in manu tenente*, 'holding in the hand'], ADV.: immediately (instantly).

immar-cescíbile [L. *-cescibilis*], ADJ.: incorruptible. **-círe**†, INTR.: rot (spoil); corrupt.

immargináre†, TR.: fasten or join together (stitch together); REFL.: heal (cicatrize).

immasche-raménto†, M.: act of masking (disguisement). ‖**-ráre** [*in*, *maschera*], REFL.: disguise or mask one's self; (*fig.*) feign (dissemble).

immateriá-le [*in-*, *m.*.], ADJ.: immaterial. **-lità**, F.: immateriality. **-lménte**, ADV.: immaterially.

immatricoláre [*in*, *matricola*], TR.: register (matriculate).

imma-turaménte, ADV.: immaturely (prematurely). **-turità**, F.: immaturity (unripeness). ‖**-túro** [*in-*, *m.*.], ADJ.: immature (unripe, unseasonable).

immedesimáre [*in*, *medesimo*], TR.: identify.

imme-diataménte, **-diáte**, ADV.: immediately. ‖**-diáto** [L. *-diatus*], ADJ.: immediate; present.

immedicábi-le [*in-*, *m.*.], ADJ.: immedicable, incurable. **-lménte**, ADV.: incurably.

immeditáto [*in-*, *m.*.], ADJ.: unmeditated.

immeglíáre†, TR.: better (improve); REFL.: get better.

immelanconíre = *immalinconire*.

imme-láre†, TR.: give the taste of, or sweeten with (honey). **-latúra†**, F.: sweetening with honey.
im=memorábile, ADJ.: immemorable; immemorial. **=mèmore**, ADJ.: unmindful (forgetful).
immen-samènte, ADV.: immensely. **-sità**, F.: immensity (infiniteness). ‖**immènso** [L. *-sus*], ADJ.: immense (immeasurable). **-surábile**, ADJ.: immensurable. **-surabilità**, F.: immensurability.
immercantíre [*in*, *mercante*], REFL.: become a merchant.
im=mèrgere, IRR.; TR.: immerse (dip, plunge); REFL.: immerse one's self (dive). **-mergíbile**, ADJ.: immersible. **-mergimènto**, M.: immersion.
immeri-tamènte, ADV.: undeservedly. **-táto**, ADJ.: unmerited. **-tévole**, ADJ.: undeserving (unworthy). **-tevolmènte**, ADV.: unworthily. ‖**immèri-to†** [*in-*, *m.*.], ADJ.: unmerited (undeserved); ADV.: undeservedly.
im-mersióne, F.: immersion (plunging). ‖**-mèrso**, PART. of *-mergere;* ADJ.: immersed (ducked, plunged).
im=méttere, IRR.; TR.: make to enter; put in (insert).
immez-záre†, ‖**-zíre** [*in*, *mezzo*], INTR.: become overripe or musty; wither.
immigrá-re [L.], INTR.: immigrate. **-zióne**, F.: migration.
immilláre†, REFL.: multiply by thousands.
immi-nènte [L. *-nere*, overhang], ADJ.: imminent (pending). **-nènza**, F.: imminence.
immischiáre [*in*, *m.*.], INTR.: become mixed; mix one's self up with.
immisericordióso [*in-*, *m.*.], ADJ.: unmerciful.
immise-rimènto, M.: misery (wretchedness). ‖**-ríre** [*in*, *misero*], TR.: make miserable or wretched.
immis-sário [*immettere*], M.: flood-gate. **-sióne**, F.: immission (act of forcing in).
immísto†, ADJ.: unmixed; pure (uncorrupt).
immisurábile†, ADJ.: immeasurable (immense).
immí-te [L. *-tis* (*in-mitis*, not soft)], ADJ.: merciless (cruel, pitiless). **-tigábile**, ADJ.: immitigable (implacable).
immòbi-le [L. *-lis*], ADJ.: immovable: *beni -li*, real estate. **-lità**, F.: immobility. **-litáre**, **-lizzáre**, TR.: render immovable. **-lmènte**, ADV.: immovably.
immode-ránza†, F.: intemperance (immoderation). **-ratamènte**, ADV.: immoderately. **-ratézza**, F.: excess (immoderateness). ‖**-ráto** [L. *-ratus*], ADJ.: immoderate (intemperate).
immo-destamènte, ADV.: immodestly. **-dèstia**, F.: immodesty (wantonness). ‖**-dèsto** [L. *-destus*], ADJ.: immodest (bold, impudent).
immo-lamènto = *-lazione*. ‖**-láre** [L.], TR.: immolate (sacrifice). **-latóre**, M., **-latríce**, F.: sacrificer. **-lazióne**, F.: immolation (sacrifice).
immol-lamènto, M.: mollifying; softening (soaking). ‖**-láre** [*in*, *molle*], TR.: soak (moisten, bathe); mollify: *ogni acqua -la*, each cause produces its own effect, everything is of use; *ogni acqua l'-la*, every small thing injures him.
immon-damènte, ADV.: impurely (uncleanly). **-dézza**, **-dízia**, F.: immundicity (filthiness); dirt (filth); obscenity. ‖**immón-do** [L. *in-mundus* un-clean], ADJ.: filthy (unclean, impure); obscene.
immorá-le [*in-*, *m.*.], ADJ.: immoral. **-lità**, F.: immorality. **-lmènte**, ADV.: immorally.
immorbi-díre, **-dáre** = *ammorbidire*.
immorsáre [*in*, *morso*], TR.: bit (bridle).
immor-taláre, **-talizzáre†**, TR.: immortalize; REFL.: become immortal; immortalize one's self†. ‖**-tále** [*in-*, *m.*.], ADJ.: immortal (eternal). **-talità**, F.: immortality. **-talmènte**, ADV.: immortally (forever).
immortíre† = *ammortire*.
immoscadáre†, TR.: perfume with musk (scent).
immotáre [*in*, *mota*], TR.: soil with mud or dirt.
immòto [L. *-motus*], ADJ.: unmoved (steadfast).
immucidíre [*in*, *mucido*], INTR.: become mouldy or musty.
immundízia† = *immondizia*.
immú-ne [L. *-nis*], ADJ.: immune (exempt). **-nità**, F.: immunity (exemption).
immu-tábile [*in*, *m.*.], ADJ.: immutable (unchangeable). **-tabilità**, F.: immutability. **-tabilmènte**, ADV.: immutably (invariably). **-táre†**, TR.: change (alter, commute). **-tazióne**, F.: immutation (change).
ímo [L. *imus* (superl. of *inferus*, low)], ADJ.: low (inferior); abject (vile); M.: bottom (lowest part): *da sommo a —*, from head to foot; *ad —†*, down below. **-scápo** [Gr. *skápos*, prop], M.: thickness of the lowest part of a column.
impac-cáre [*in*, *pacco*], TR.: put in a package (pack). **-chettáre**, TR.: make into a small package (bundle up).
impac-ciamènto† = *-cio*. **-ciánte**, M.: busybody. ‖**-ciáre** [L. *in-pactiare*], TR.: encumber (embarrass, perplex); REFL.: intermeddle. **-ciatívo**, ADJ.: troublesome (perplexing). **-ciatóre**, M.: tire-

some fellow (bore). **impác-cio**, M.: trouble (impediment, perplexity); vexation; pain: *darsi gl' -ci del Mar Rosso*†, meddle in a thing that does not concern one. **-ciána**, F., **-ciòne**, M.: one who is always in the way. **-cióso**, ADJ.: troublesome (meddling).

impadronire [*in*, *padrone*], TR.: make master of (put in possession of); REFL.: seize for one's self (make one's self master of).

impaduláre [*in*, *padule*], INTR.: grow marshy.

impagábile [*in-*, *p.* .], ADJ.: that cannot be paid (invaluable).

impaginá-re [*in*, *pagina*], TR.: put in pages. **-tóre**, M.: one who pages. **-túra**, **-zióne**, F.: pagination (putting in pages).

impa-gliáre [*in*, *paglia*], TR.: cover with straw. **-gliáto**, PART.: strawy (covered with straw); mixed with straw†; straw-coloured†. **-gliatíno**, M.: straw seat of a chair. **-gliatóre**, M.: chair-mender; bird-stuffer. **-gliatúra**, F.: stuffing with straw.

impalancáto [*in*, *p.* .], M.: stockade (palisade).

impalandranáto†, ADJ.: wrapped up in a cloak.

impalá-re [*in*, *palo*], TR.: impale; fence with stakes: — *la vigna*, stake vines. **-'to**, PART.: impaled, etc.; erect (straight). **-túra**, **-zióne**, F.: impalement (impaling).

impal-caménto, M.: ceiling; flooring; boarding. ‖**-cáre** [*in*, *palco*], TR.: ceil (plank). **-catúra**, F.: ceiling; flooring.

impalizzáre†, TR.: palisade (enclose with stockade).

impalláre [*in*, *palla*], TR.: play at billiards or bowls.

impalli-dáre†, **-díre** [*in*, *pallido*], INTR.: become pale.

impallináre [*in*, *pallino*], TR.: wound with small shot.

impal-maménto† M.: joining of hands. ‖**-máre** [*in*, *palma*], TR.: give the hand to (grasp†); marry; REFL.†: promise one's self.

impalpábi-le [*in*, *palpare*], ADJ.: impalpable. **-litá**, F.: impalpability. **-lménte**†, ADV.: impalpably.

impalu-daménto, M.: forming of marshes. ‖**-dáre** [*in*, *palude*], INTR.: become marshy or fenny.

impaná-re [*in*, *pane*], TR.: impanate (embody in bread). **-túra**, F.: doctrine of impanation.

impancáre [*in*, *panca*], REFL.: push one's self with presumption (presume, arrogate); sit or lie down on a bench†.

impaniá-re [*in*, *pania*], TR.: daub with bird-lime; REFL.: be ensnared or entangled; be in love. **-tóre**, M.: one who daubs with bird-lime; lover. **-túra**, F.: act of alluring (ensnaring)

impaniccíáre [*in*, *paniccia*], TR.: plaster; paste; (*fig.*) embroil (confuse).

impáccio†, M.: hindrance; perplexity (confusion).

impan-náre [*in*, *panno*], TR.: stuff (wad); put cloth or paper into (a broken window-glass); cover with cloth or paper. **-náta**, F.: paper-window. **-náto**, PART.: covered with a cloth, etc. **-natúra**, F.: act of covering with cloth, etc.

impantanáre [*in*, *pantano*], TR.: cover with mud; put in the mire; REFL.: sink in the mire (be mired); get muddy.

impappafioáre†, TR.: hood (put on a hood or cowl).

impappináre [*in*, *pappa*], TR.: confuse with questions (perplex, mix up).

imparacchiáre = *imparucchiare*.

imparadisáre [*in*, *paradiso*], TR.: imparadise.

imparagonábile [*in-*, *p.* .], ADJ.: incomparable (excellent).

impará-re [L. *in*, *parare*, prepare], TR.: learn; teach: — *a mente*, *a memoria*, learn by heart. **-ticcio**, M.: bad learning; ADJ.: badly learned.

impareggiábi-le [*in-*, *p.* .], ADJ.: incomparable. **-lménte**, ADV.: incomparably.

imparentáre [*in*, *parente*], TR.: cause to become a parent; marry into; become domesticated†.

impa-ri [L. *im-par*], ADJ.: unequal (inferior, uneven). **-riménte**†, ADV.: unequally (not alike). **-ritá**†, F.: imparity (inequality).

impar-tíbile†, ADJ.: inseparable (indivisible). ‖**-tíre** [L. *-tiri*, share], TR.: share justly (impart, communicate).

imparucchiáre [*imparare*], TR.: learn a little or poorly.

imparziá-le [*in-*, *p.* .], ADJ.: impartial (just). **-litá**, F.: impartiality (justice). **-lménte**, ADV.: impartially (justly).

impassí-bile [L. *-bilis*], ADJ.: impassible (inalterable). **-bilitá**, F.: impassibility. **-bilménte**, ADV.: impassibly.

impassionáre†, TR.: impassion (torment).

impa-staménto, M.: impastation (act of mixing into paste). ‖**-stáre** [*in*, *pasta*], TR.: knead; paste (stick with paste); (*fig.*) put together; mix colours on a pallet; fatten†: *male -tato*, of a bad complexion; *è -tato di vizi*, he is very vicious. **-statóre**, M.: kneader; paster. **-statúra**, F.: impastation. **-sticciáre**, TR.: make a medley of; do (a thing) badly

impá-sto, M.: impasting; paste; fasting†. **-stocchiáre,** TR.: make believe (deceive). **-stoiáre** [*in, pastoia*], TR.: shackle; fetter; fasten. **-stúra**†, F.: pastern of a horse.
impastranáre [*in, pastrano*], REFL.: wrap one's self up in a cloak.
impataccáre [*in, patacca*], TR.: spot (stain, soil).
impatíbile†, ADJ.: impatible (intolerable).
impatriáre [*in, patria*], INTR.: return to one's own country.
impattáre [*in, patta*], TR.: make even.
impau-rànte†, ADJ.: frightful (horrible). **-ráre**†, ||**-ríre** [*in, paura*], TR.: terrify (frighten); INTR.: be afraid.
im-pavidaménte, ADV.: intrepidly (fearlessly). ||**-pávido** [*in-, p..*], ADJ.: intrepid (fearless).
impa-zientáre = *-zientire.* ||**-zièntе** [*in-, p..*], ADJ.: impatient (eager). **-zientеménte,** ADV.: impatiently. **-zientíre,** INTR.: lose patience. **-ziènza, -ziènzia**†, F.: impatience.
impaz-zaménto, M.: madness (insanity). ||**-záre, -zíre** [*in, pazzo*], INTR.: go mad (be crazed; become insane); curdle; TR.†: make crazy; render vain: — *d' alcuno,* be madly in love with some one. **-záto,** PART.: mad, crazy; *all' -zata,* crazily, heedlessly.
impeccábi-le [*in-, p..*], ADJ.: impeccable (sinless). **-lità,** F.: impeccability.
impe-cettáre [*in, pecetta*], TR.: daub (with pitch or tar); stain (soil). **-ciaménto,** M.: daubing with pitch. ||**-ciáre** [*in pece*], TR.: daub with tar or pitch: *dovunque va vi s' -cia,* he sticks wherever he goes; *-ciarsi gli orecchi,* stop one's ears (refuse to listen). **-ciatúra,** F.: pitching (tarring).
impecoríre [*in, pecora*], INTR.: become stupid.
impedaláre†, INTR.: thicken in the trunk or stem.
impedantíre [*in, pedante*], INTR.: become a pedant.
impe-díbile, ADJ.: that can be hindered. **-dicáre**†, TR.: allure; clog (shackle): impede. **-dièntе,** PART.: hindering (preventing). **-dimentáre**†, **-dimentíre**†, TR.: hinder (prevent). **-diménto** [L. *-dimentum*], M.: impediment (obstacle); infirmity (sickness)†; baggage†. ||**-díre** [L. *-dire*], TR.: impede (annoy, hinder): — *uno da una cosa*†, keep a thing far off from one. **-ditívo,** ADJ.: impeditive (obstructive). **-díto,** PART.: hindered; paralytic. **-ditóre,** M., **-ditríce,** F.: impeder (obstructor).
impe-gnáre [*in, pegno*], TR.: pawn (pledge): engage; REFL.: pledge: — *la fede,* give one's word; *-gnarsi a uno*†, do everything for one. **-gnáto,** PART.: promised; betrothed. **-gnatívo**†, ADJ.: obliging (engaging). **impé-gno,** M.: engagement (obligation, promise); debt; bond; trouble (contention, strife). **-gnóso,** ADJ.: troublesome (contentious); rash (precipitate).
impegoláre [*in, pegola*], TR.: pitch (smear with tar).
impelagáre [*in, pelago*], REFL.: be engulfed in.
impeláre [*in, pelo*], TR.: cover with hair.
im-pellènte, ADJ.: that which incites or impels. ||**-pèllere** [L.], IRR.§; TR.: impel (force on). **-púlso,** PART. of *-pellere.*
§ Pret. *impúlsi.* Part. *impúlso.*
impelliccіáre [*in, pelliccia*], TR.: dress in furs and skins.
im-pendènte†, ADJ.: impending (imminent); dubious (doubtful). ||**-pèndere**†, TR.: impend (hang, suspend); spend (lay out).
impenetrábi-le [*in-, p..*], ADJ.: impenetrable; incomprehensible; inscrutable. **-lità,** F.: impenetrability. **-lménte,** ADV.: impenetrably.
impeni-tènte [*in-, p..*], ADJ.: impenitent (unrepenting). **-tènza,** F.: impenitence.
impennacchiáre [*in, pennacchio*], TR.: adorn with feathers; REFL.: put on feathers (become fledged).
impen-náre [*in, penna*], TR.: cover with feathers; debit†; describe (write)†; INTR.: become fledged (get feathered); (of horses) rear; (*fig.*) resent; soar†: — *il piede*†, run swiftly; — *una saetta*†, feather an arrow. **-náta,** F.: penful of ink; rearing of a horse; written verse or words†. **-náto,** PART.: feathered (winged). **-natúra**†, F.: mulct (penalty).
impennelláre†, TR.: use the pen (or paint-brush); stroke with a pencil; hit (strike).
impen-sábile [*in-, p..*], ADJ.: unthinkable (unimaginable). **-sataménte,** ADV.: unexpectedly (suddenly). **-sáto,** ADJ.: unexpected (sudden): *all'* —, unexpectedly (all of a sudden). **-sieríre,** TR.: give thoughts to (make thoughtful); cause trouble (worry); REFL.: become thoughtful (muse deeply). **-sieríto,** PART.: thoughtful (pensive).
impepáre [*in, pepe*], TR.: pepper (season with pepper).
impe-radóre† = *-ratore.* **-radríce** = *-ratrice.* **-ránte,** M.: commander. ||**-ráre** [L.], INTR.: have empire (rule, command, govern); TR.†: impose (enjoin, lay on). **-rativaménte,** ADV.: imperatively. **-ratívo,** ADJ.: imperative (commanding); M.: imperative mood. **-rató-**

re, M.: emperor; commander (general). **-ratòrio**, ADJ.: imperatorial (imperial). **-ratrice**, F.: empress.

impercettíbi-le [*in-*, *p.* .], ADJ.: imperceptible. **-lità**, F.: imperceptibility. **-lménte**, ADV.: imperceptibly.

imper-chè† *-é*, ADV.: because; therefore; M.: reason (cause): *fare lo* —, give occasion. **-ciò**†, ADV.: therefore. **-cio=cchè** *-é*, ADV.: whereas (because); to the end that†; in order to†.

imperdonábile [*in-*, *p.* .], ADJ.: unpardonable (irremissible).

imper-fettaménte, ADV.: imperfectly. ‖**-fètto** [*in-*, *p.* .], ADJ.: imperfect (defective); M.: (*gram.*) imperfect; defect (imperfection)†. **-fezioncèlla**, *dim.* of *-fezione*. **-fezióne**, F.: imperfection (defect); lack (want). **-fezionúccia**, *dim.* of *-fezione*.

imperiá-le [*imperio*], ADJ.: imperial (sovereign); superior; excellent; eminent; beautiful (majestic)†; M.: imperial (roof of a coach). **-lésco**, ADJ.: imperialistic. **-lísta**, M.: imperialist. **-lménte**, ADV.: like an emperor. **imperiáre**† = *imperare*.

impericolosíre†, INTR.: hazard (incur danger, run a risk); TR.: put in danger.

impè-rio [L. *-rium*], M.: empire (dominion); command (order). **-riosaménte**, ADV.: imperiously; haughtily. **-riosità**, F.: haughtiness (imperiousness). **-rióso**, ADJ.: imperious (commanding).

impe-ritaménte, ADV.: unskilfully; ignorantly. ‖**-ríto** [L. *-ritus*], ADJ.: INEXPERIENCED (ignorant, raw). **-ritúra**, ADJ.: imperishable (immortal); M.: immortal. **-rízia**, F.: inexpertness (ignorance).

imperlaqualcòsa†, ADV.: therefore; wherefore.

imperláre [*in*, *perla*], TR.: impearl (adorn with pearls).

impermalíre [*in*, *per*, *male*], TR.: cause to be offended; INTR.: be offended; show wrath or disdain.

impermísto†, ADJ.: unmixed (genuine).

impermeábi-le [*in-*, *p.* .], ADJ.: impermeable; M.: waterproof. **-lità**, F.: impermeability.

impermutábi-le [*in-*, *p.* .], ADJ.: immutable (unchangeable). **-lità**, F.: immutability. **-lménte**, ADV.: immutably.

imper-náre, **-niáre** [*in*, *perno*, *pernio*], TR.: poise (place upon a pivot or axis). **-niatúra**, F.: poising or fixing upon a pivot.

impèro [L. *imperium*], M.: empire; power.

impe-rò [*in*, *però*], ADV.: (*vulg.*) therefore; notwithstanding. **-ro=cchè**, ADV.: because (whereas, since).

imperscrittíbile†, ADJ.: imprescriptible.

imperscrutábi-le [L. *-lis*], ADJ.: imperscrutable (inconceivable); unsearchable. **-lità**, F.: inconceivableness; unsearchableness.

imperseve-ránte†, ADJ.: changeable (inconstant). **-ránza**†, F.: inconstancy (want of perseverance). ‖**-ráre**†, INTR.: be inconstant (fickle).

imperso-nále [*in-*, *p.* .], ADJ.: impersonal. **-nalménte**, ADV.: impersonally. **-náre**, REFL.: personify.

impersuasíbile [*in-*, *p.* .], ADJ.: unpersuasible.

impertánto [*in*, *per*, *tanto*], ADV.: notwithstanding, however; (*vulg.*) insomuch as.

impertèrrito [L. *-rritus*], ADJ.: unterrified (undaunted, intrepid).

imperti-nènte [L. *-nens* (*per-tinens*, belonging)], ADJ.: impertinent (insolent, nonsensical); unseasonable†; importunate (troublesome)†. **-nentèllo**, *dim.* of *-nente*. **-nenteménte**, ADV.: impertinently. **-nènza**, F.: impertinence; extravagance (ostentation); affront (insult).

impertur-bábile [L. *-babilis*], ADJ.: imperturbable. **-babilità**, F.: imperturbability (tranquillity). **-báto**, ADJ.: undisturbed (tranquil, serene).

imperver-saménto, M.: perverseness; rage (fury). **-sáre** [*in*, *perverso*], INTR.: become furious (rage like a madman). ‖**-tíre**† [*in*, *p.* .], TR.: pervert (deprave); INTR.: become perverse (grow wicked).

impèrvio†, ADJ.: impervious.

impéso†, PART. of *impendere;* hanged (suspended).

impestáre [*in*, *peste*], TR.: infect.

impetecchíto [*in*, *petecchia*], ADJ.: covered with purple spots.

impe-tígine [L. *-tigo* (*-tere*, attack), F.: impetigo (cutaneous eruption). **-tiginóso**, ADJ.: having impetigo.

ímpeto [L. *-tus*], M.: mere impetuosity (violence, impetus): *a* —†, impetuously.

impe-trábile, ADJ.: impetrable (obtainable). **-tragióne**†, F.: obtaining by entreaty or prayer. ‖**-tráre** [L. *-trare*, obtain], TR.: impetrate (obtain by prayer or entreaty); merit (deserve)†; gain†; INTR.: petrify (harden). **-tratóre**†, M.: suppliant. **-trazióne**†, F.: impetration (prayer). **-tricáto**†, ADJ.: hard as stone (petrified).

impettíto [*in*, *petto*], ADJ.: straight (erect).

impe-tuosaménte, ADV.: impetuously (violently). **-tuosità**, F.: impetuosity (violence, fury). ‖**-tuóso** [L. *-tuosus*], ADJ.: impetuous (vehement).

impeveráto [*in*, *pevere*], ADJ.: peppered.

impiacevolíre†, TR.: appease (pacify, mitigate); render agreeable; INTR.: become agreeable; REFL.: show one's self polite.

impia-gáre [*in*, *piaga*], TR.: wound (hurt, cover with wounds); plough†. **-gatóre**, M., **-gatrice**, F.: wounder (hurter). **-gatúra**, F.: wounding; wound (hurt).

impiallacciá-re [*in*, *piallaccio*], TR.: inlay wood (veneer). **-túra**, F.: inlaying (veneering).

impianelláre [*in*, *pianella*], TR.: tile (a roof or floor).

impian-táre [*in*, *pianta*], TR.: implant; infix; put (place)†; REFL.: place one's self. **-títo**, M.: floor (flooring). **impián-to**, M.: establishment of a work or business; infixing; putting.

impia-stráccio, *disp.* of *-stro*. **-strafògli** [*foglio*], M.: scribbler (scrawler). **-stragióne**†, F.: inoculation (ingrafting). **-straménto**, M.: act of plastering. **-stráre**, TR.: plaster (apply a plaster); daub (besmear); blotch; inoculate (ingraft)†; reconcile (adjust)†; REFL.: paint or daub one's self. **-stratóre**, M.: plasterer; dauber. **-strazióne**† = *-stramento*. **-strícciaménto** = *-stramento*. **-stricciáre**, TR.: plaster badly (daub). **-stríno**, *car. dim.* of *-stro*. ‖**impiá-stro** [L. *emplastrum* (Gr. *plássein*, mould)], M.: plaster (poultice); remedy†.

impiattáre = *rimpiattare*.

impic-cagióne, F., **-caménto**, M.: act of hanging. ‖**-cáre** [L. *picare* (*pix*, pitch) stick], TR.: hang (execute); suspend (hang up); REFL.: hang one's self; attach one's self; join: *-carla ad uno*, fasten it on to one, show one the wrong or his falseness. **-catèllo**, *dim.* of *-cato*. **-cáto**, PART.: hanged, etc.; M.: rogue (hangdog): *stare —*, stand idling; *ognuno ha il suo — all' uscio*, every one has his faults (afflictions). **-catóio**†, ADJ.: ripe for the gallows; old enough to be hanged. **-catúra**, F.: hanging (execution).

impicciáre [OFr. *enpigier* (L. *in*, *pix*, pitch)], TR.: embarrass, obstruct; embroil (confuse); REFL.: intermeddle.

impiccinire [*in*, *piccino*], TR.: make little; INTR.: become little.

impíc-cio [*-ciare*], M.: perplexity (trouble). **-cióna**, F., **-cióne**, M.: troubler (intermeddler).

impiccolíre [*in*, *piccolo*], TR.: cause to become small (make little); INTR.: become (diminish); REFL.: become less.

loc-chiáre [*in*, *pidocchio*], TR.: fill lice. **-chíre**, INTR.: breed lice lousy).

impie-gábile, ADJ.: usable. ‖**-gáre** [L. *implicare*, infold], TR.: EMPLOY (use); give employment; spend (occupy). **-gáto**, PART.: employed, etc.; M.: employee. **-gatáccio**, *disp.* of *-gato*. **impiè-go**, M.: public office; employment (work); use. **-gáccio**, *disp.* of *-go*.

impiere† = *empire*.

im-pietà†, F.: impiety (irreligion). **-pietosíre** [*pietoso*], TR.: move to pity (touch, affect); REFL.: be affected or touched.

impie-triménto, M.: petrification. ‖**-tríre** [*in*, *pietra*], TR., INTR.: petrify.

impiézza†, F.: impiety.

impi-gliáre [*in*, *p*..], TR.: confuse (embroil); seize with force†; undertake†; light†; REFL.†: intermeddle (mix one's self up with). **-gliatóre**, M.: intermeddler (obstructor). **impí-glio**†, M.: perplexity (trouble).

impígnere† = *impingere*.

impigríre [*in*, *pigro*], INTR.: become lazy or idle.

impillaccheráre [*in*, *pillacchera*], TR.: soil with mud or dirt.

im-píngere†, IRR.; TR.: impel (push forward); charge (the enemy); REFL.: push one's self against.

impin-guáre [*in*, *pingue*], TR.: make fat or plump; ornament (adorn); REFL.: fatten (become fat). **-guíre**, INTR.: grow fat.

impínto†, PART. of *impingere*.

impinzáre [L. *in*, *pinsus*, bruised], TR.: fill; overfill.

impío†, ADJ.: impious (irreligious).

impioláre [*in*, *piolo*], INTR.: sprout (grow).

impiom-báre [*in*, *piombo*], TR.: lead (cover with lead); plumb: — *i denti*, fill the teeth. **-báto**, PART. of *-bare*: *mazza -bata*, loaded club. **-batúra**, F.: soldering or covering with lead.

impipáre [*in*, *pipa*], REFL.: (*pop.*) make light of (laugh at).

impiumáre [*in*, *piuma*], TR.: fledge (feather).

impiúto, PART. of *impiere*: filled; accomplished.

impla-cábile [*in-*, *p*..], ADJ.: implacable. **-cabilità**, F.: implacability. **-cabilménte**, ADV.: implacably. **-cidíre**, TR.: appease (calm).

impli-cánza†, F.: contradiction (obstacle). ‖**-cáre** [L. (*plicare*, fold)], TR.: implicate (entangle, embarrass); REFL.: mix one's self up in. **-cazióne**†, F.: implication (entanglement). **-citaménte**, ADV.: implicitly. **implí-cito** [L. *-citus*], ADJ.: implicit; entangled (confused)†.

implo-rábile, ADJ.: that can be implored. **||-ráre** [L.], TR.: implore (beseech).

implúme [L. *im-plumis*], ADJ.: unfledged (unfeathered).

implúvio [L. *-vium* (*pluere*, rain)], M.: impluvium (cistern in Rom. atrium to receive the rain); atrium (open court).

impo-liticaménte, ADV.: impolitically. **||-lítico** [*in-*, *p.* .], ADJ.: impolitic.

im-polito, ADJ.: unpolite (rude).

impolmonáto†, ADJ.: asthmatic; consumptive.

impoltronire [*in*, *poltrone*], TR.: make lazy; INTR.: become idle.

impolveráre [*in*, *polvere*], TR.: powder (cover with dust).

impomatáre [*in*, *pomata*], TR.: daub with pomatum.

impomáto†, ADJ.: planted with apple-trees; full of fruit.

impomiciáre [*in*, *pomice*], TR.: rub or polish with pumice stone.

imponde-rábile [*in-*, *p.* .], ADJ.: imponderable. **-rabilità**, F.: imponderability.

impo-nènte, ADJ.: imposing. **||impónere** [L.], = *-rre*. **-níbile**, ADJ.: imposable. **-nitóre†**, M.: imposer (enjoiner).

impopolá-re [*in-*, *p.* .], ADJ.: unpopular. **-rità**, F.: unpopularity.

imporcáre†, TR.: furrow (make ridges in).

imporporáre [*in*, *porpora*], TR.: dye purple; blush†; paint with rouge†.

imporráre [*in*, *porro*], INTR.: mould (become musty).

im-pórre, IRR.; TR.: impose (place upon); enjoin (command); wrap; attribute (impute to)†; bring†; fatten†; cover (copulate)†.

imporríre = *imporrare*.

impor-tábile†, ADJ.: intolerable (insufferable). **-tánte**, ADJ.: important (of great concern). **-tánza**, F.: importance. **||-táre** [L.], INTR.: import (matter); denote; amount; TR.: cost; heap up; signify (denote); bear†: *questo -ta a me*, that is my concern; — *poco*, be of little consequence. **-tazióne**, F.: importation. **-tévole†** = *-tabile*. **impòr-to**, M.: amount (cost, sum).

importu-naménte, ADV.: importunately. **-nánza†** = *-nità*. **-náre**, **-níre**, TR.: importune (trouble, irritate). **-namènte**, ADV.: importunately. **-nità**, F.: importunity. **||importú-no** [L. *-nus*], ADJ.: importune (troublesome, vexatious); sensible†; inopportune (unseasonable)†; auguring evil†.

imposi-tóre [*imporre*], M.: imposer (orderer). **-zióne**, F.: imposition; import (gravity); tax.

impossessáre [*in*, *possesso*], REFL.: take possession of (seize); make one's self master of.

impossíbi-le [*in-*, *p.* .], ADJ.: impossible; difficult; absurd; M.: impossible: *ridurre uno all'* —†, be unable to respond without falling into contradiction. **-lità**, F.: impossibility; impotence. **-litáre**, TR.: render impossible. **-ménte**, ADV.: impossibly.

impó-sta [*imporre*], F.: impost (duty, tax); order (command)†. **impò-sta**, F.: door or window shutter; (*arch.*) impost. **-stáme**, M.: window-shutters and doors of a house. **-stáre**, TR.: place upon or set up (an arch); post up (accounts); post (a letter); REFL.: be ready to throw one's self upon. **-statúra**, F.: arching (setting up); haughty attitude; impost†. **-stazióne**, F.: posting (posting up).

impostemíre [*in*, *postema*], INTR.: imposthumate (suppurate, swell up).

impó-sto, PART. of *imporre*; imposed; ordered. **-stóre** [L.], M.: impostor (deceiver). **-stúra**, F.: imposture (fraud, imposition). **-sturáre**, TR.: deceive (cheat); calumniate (slander).

impo-tènte [L. *-tens*], ADJ.: impotent (weak, powerless); incapable of generating; very potent (powerful)†. **-tènza**, **-tènzia†**, F.: impotence (weakness); profligacy (licentiousness).

impove-riménto, M.: impoverishment. **||-ríre** [*in*, *povero*], TR.: impoverish (make poor); INTR.: become poor: *durar fatica per* —, work for nothing.

impraticábi-le [*in-*, *p.* .], ADJ.: impracticable. **-lità**, F.: impracticability.

impratichíre [*in*, *pratica*], TR.: practise (exercise); REFL.: exercise one's self in.

imprecá-re [L. *-ri* (*precari*, PRAY)], TR.: invoke evil (*contro*, imprecate, curse). **-tívo**, ADJ.: imprecatory (cursing). **-tóre**, M.: curser (execrator). **-tòrio** = *-tivo*. **-zióne**, F.: imprecation (malediction).

imprecisióne [*in-*, *p.* .], F.: imprecision.

impregionáre† = *imprigionare*.

impregiudicáto [*in-*, *p.* .], ADJ.: unprejudicate (unprejudiced).

impre-gnaménto†, M.: impregnation (fecundation). **||-gnáre** [*in*, *pregno*], TR.: impregnate; INTR.: saturate; conceive. **-gnatúra**, F.: pregnancy.

impremeditáto [*in-*, *p.* .], ADJ.: unpremeditated.

imprèn-dere [*in*, *p.* .], IRR.; TR.: undertake (begin); learn†; understand†; take (seize)†: — *briga*, seek quarrel. **-díbile** [*in-*, *p.* .], ADJ.: that cannot be

taken (impregnable). **-diménto†**, M.: undertaking (attempt); learning; instruction. **-ditóre**, M., **-ditríce**, F.: undertaker; learner. **-sióne†**, F.: idea (opinion).
imprenta. .† = *impronta*. .
impreparáto [*in-*, *p.* .], ADJ.: unprepared.
impré-sa [*-ndere*], F.: enterprise (undertaking); company; device (emblem). **-sáccia**, *disp.* of *-sa*. **-sário**, M.: undertaker; manager; impresario (theatre-manager).
imprescindíbile [*in-*, *p.* .], ADJ.: that cannot be prescinded or omitted.
imprescrittíbi-le [*in-*, *p.* .], ADJ.: imprescriptible. **-lità**, F.: imprescriptibility.
impréso, PART. of *imprendere*; undertaken (begun), etc.
impres-sionábile, ADJ.: impressionable. **-sionabilità**, F.: impressionability. **-sionáre**, TR.: impress. ||**-sióne** [L. *-sio*], F.: impression; edition; stamp (mark); influence†. **imprès-so**, PART. of *imprimere*: impressed; imprinted. **-sóre**, M.: printer.
impre-stánza, F.: loan (lending). ||**-stáre** [*in*, *p.* .], TR.: lend. **-stíto**, M.: loan.
impretendènte†, ADJ.: unpretending.
impreteríbi-le†, ADJ.: unfailing (certain). **-lménte†**, ADV.: infallibly (unfailingly).
impre-vedíbile [*in-*, *p.* .], ADJ.: that cannot be foreseen. **-vedibilménte**, ADV.: in an unforeseen manner. **-vedúto**, ADJ.: unforeseen. **-vidènte**, ADJ.: lacking foresight. **-visto**, ADJ.: unforeseen (unanticipated).
impre-ziosíre [*in*, *prezioso*], TR.: render precious or valuable. **-ziábile†**, **-zzábile†**, ADJ.: inestimable (beyond all price).
imprigio-naménto, M.: imprisonment (incarceration). ||**-náre** [*in*, *prigione*], TR.: imprison (incarcerate). **-natóre**, M.: imprisoner.
imprímа†, ADV.: firstly (in the first place).
imprímere [L.], IRR. (cf. *comprimere*); TR.: imprint (stamp); impress.
imprimieraménte†, ADV.: first (in the first place).
imprimitúra†, F.: preparation used as a ground-work for paint; impression; coloured print.
improbábi-le [*in-*, *p.* .], ADJ.: improbable. **-lità**, F.: improbability. **-lménte**, ADV.: improbably.
-bаménte, ADV.: excessively; extraordinarily; wickedly. **-bità**, F.: improbity (wickedness)]. ||**impro-bo** [L. *in-*, not, *probus*, good)], ADJ.: excessive (extraordinary); long (continuous); wicked.
improcciáre†, TR.: reproach.
improdut-tíbile [*in-*, *p.* .], ADJ.: that cannot produce. **-tivo**, ADJ.: unproductive.
impro-méssa, F.: promise. ||**-méttere** [*in*, *p.* .], IRR.; TR.: promise.
imprón-ta, F.: impression (imprint, mark). **-táccio**, *disp.* of *-ta*. **-taménte**, ADV.: importunately. **-taménto†**, M.: importunity (incitement). ||**-táre** [L. *imprimitare* (*primere*, PRESS)], TR.: IMPRESS (IMPRINT, mark); lend; borrow. **-titúdine**, **-tézza†**, F.: importunity; efficacy†; entreaty†. **imprón-to**, ADJ.: importunate; M.†: impression (print, stamp).
impro-peráre†, TR.: reproach, blame. ||**-pèrio** [L. *-perium* (*probrum*, disgrace)], M.: reproach (blame).
impropi. . = *impropri*. .
improporzio-nále, ADJ.: disproportional. **-nalità**, F.: disproportionality. **-nalménte**, ADV.: disproportionally. **-náto**, ADJ.: disproportionate.
impro-priaménte, ADV.: improperly; inopportunely; inconveniently. **-prietà**, F.: impropriety; unfitness. ||**imprò-prio** [L. *-prius*], ADJ.: improper, inopportune; inconvenient.
improrogábile [*in-*, *p.* .], ADJ.: not to be put off.
improsciuttire [*in*, *prosciutto*], INTR.: dry like bacon; become emaciated or thin.
improspe-raménte [*in-*, *p.* .], ADV.: unprosperously. **-ríre†**, INTR.: prosper (become prosperous). **-ríto†**, ADJ.: prosperous.
improva-tívo†, ADJ.: disapproving. **-zióne†**, F.: disapprobation.
improveráre†, TR.: reprove (reproach).
improvi. . = *improvvi*. .
improvve-dutaménte†, ADV.: unprovidedly (unexpectedly). **-dúto†**, ADJ.: unforeseen (unexpected).
improvvi-daménte†, ADV.: imprudently (inconsiderately)†. **-dènza†**, F.: improvidence (imprudence). ||**impròvvi-do** [L. *im-pro-vidus*, 'un-for-seeing'], ADJ.: improvident (imprudent).
improvvi-saménte, ADV.: suddenly (unexpectedly). **-saménto**, M.: impromptu; improvisation. **-sáre**, TR.: improvise (extemporize); ask for artfully†. **-sáta**, F.: pleasant surprise; impromptu (extempore composition). **-satóre**, M., **-satríce**, F.: improvisatore. **-sazióne**, F.: improvisation. ||**improvvi-so** [L. *-sus* (*in*, not, *pro-videre*, fore-see)], ADJ.: unforeseen (unexpected, sudden); unprovided; ADV.: suddenly (unexpectedly); M.: impromptu. **-staménte** = **-saménte**.

improvvi-sto†, ADJ.: unprovided (unprepared).
impru-dènte [*in-, p.* .], ADJ.: imprudent (inconsiderate). **-denteménte**, ADV.: imprudently (incautiously). **-dènza**, **-dènzia†**, F.: imprudence.
imprunáre [*in, pruno*], TR.: hedge (obstruct with briars); measure beforehand†.
im-púbe, **-púbere** [L. *-pubes*], ADJ.: under age.
impu-dènte [L. *-dens*], ADJ.: impudent (bold, saucy). **-denteménte**, ADV.: impudently. **-dènza**, F.: impudence (shamelessness).
impu-dicaménte, ADV.: indecently (unchastely). **-dicízia**, F.: impudicity (immodesty). ||**-díco** [L. *-dicus* (*pudicus*, chaste)], ADJ.: lascivious (lewd, unchaste).
impu-gnábile, ADJ.: impugnable. **-gnaménto†**, M.: opposition (hindrance); grasping. ||**-gnáre** [L. *in, pugnare*, fight], TR.: seize (grasp, catch); IMPUGN (assail, attack); deny; take (choose)†; make (a fist)†: — *la spada*, draw the sword. **-gnatóre**, M.: impugner; antagonist. **-gnatúra**, F.: grasping; hilt (handle). **-gnazióne**, F.: grasping; opposition (combat).
impulciáre [*in, pulce*], TR.: cover with fleas.
impu-litaménte, ADV.: impolitely (rudely). **-litézza**, F.: incivility (impoliteness). ||**-líto** [*in-, p.* .], ADJ.: impolite (uncivil, rude); unpolished (rough)†.
im-pulsióne [L. *-sio*], F.: impulsion (thrust, push). **-pulsívo**, ADJ.: impulsive (impellent). ||**-púlso** [L. *-pulsus* (*pellere*, push)], M.: impulse (incentive, instigation).
impú-ne [L.], ADJ.: impune (unpunished). **-neménte**, ADV.: impunibly (with impunity). **-níbile**, ADJ.: not punishable. **-nità**, F.: impunity. **-nitaménte†** = *-nemente*. **-níto**, ADJ.: unpunished.
impuntáre [*in, punta*], INTR.: stop (halt); break off in a discourse; balk; TR.: pierce (point).
impun-tíre [*in, punto*], TR.: stitch (sew closely). **-titúra**, F.: stitching (sewing). **-túra**, F.: needle-work.
impu-raménte, ADV.: impurely (uncleanly). **-rità**, F.: impurity; obscenity (lasciviousness). ||**impú-ro** [L. *-rus*], ADJ.: impure (foul); lewd.
imputábile, ADJ.: imputable. **-tabilità**, F.: imputableness. **-taménto†**, M.: imputation (charge). ||**-táre** [L.], TR.: impute (attribute); accuse; repute (believe)†: — *a male*, blame. **-tatóre**, M.: imputer (accuser). **-táto**, PART.: imputed, etc.; M.: accused. **-tazióne**, F.: imputation (charge).
imputridíre [*in, putrido*], INTR.: putrefy.
impuz-záre†, ||**-zíre** [*in, puzzo*], INTR.: become stinking (or offensive to the smell, begin to smell; putrefy). **-solíre†** = *-zare*.
in [L.], PREP.: in (into); at; on (upon); to (towards); like; instead of: *stare* —, depend on; — *quanto a me*, as for me.
in- [L.], PREF.: in-, un-, not.
inábi-le [L. *in-habilis*], ADJ.: incapable (UNABLE, unskilful). **-lità**, F.: inability (incapacity). **-litáre**, TR.: render incapable (disable).
inabis-saménto, M.: engulfing (ruining); act of falling into an abyss. ||**-sáre** [*in, abisso*], TR.: throw into an abyss; engulf (ruin); REFL.: fall into an abyss; get ruined.
inabi-tábile [*in-, a.* .], ADJ.: uninhabitable. **-táre†**, TR.: inhabit. **-táto†**, PART.: uninhabited. **-tévole†** = *-tabile*.
inac-cessíbile [*in-, a.* .], ADJ.: inaccessible (out of reach). **-cessibilità**, F.: inaccessibility. **-cèsso**, ADJ.: inaccessible.
in=accettábile, ADJ.: unacceptable.
inacciaiá-re, **-ríre** [*in, acciaio*], TR.: steel.
in=accordábile, ADJ.: that cannot be granted.
inacer-báre†, **-bíre** [*in, acerbo*], TR.: exasperate (irritate).
inace-táre†, TR.: bathe or sprinkle with vinegar; INTR.: become sour. ||**-tíre** [*in, aceto*], INTR.: become sour. **-títo**, PART.: sour (bitter).
inaci-diménto, M.: act of becoming acid. ||**-díre** [*in, acido*], INTR.: become acid.
inacqua. . = *annacqua*. .
inacutíre†, TR.: make sharper (sharpen); REFL.: become sharper; TR.: (*mus.*) pass from the grave to the acute.
in=adattábile, ADJ.: unadaptable.
in addiétro, ADV.: formerly.
inade-guataménte, ADV.: inadequately. ||**-guáto** [*in-, a.* .], ADJ.: inadequate.
inadem-píbile [*in-, a.* .], ADJ.: that cannot be accomplished. **-piménto**, M.: non-accomplishment. **-píto**, **-piúto**, ADJ.: unaccomplished.
in=adombrábile, ADJ.: that cannot be fancied or imagined.
in=adoprábile, ADJ.: that cannot be used (useless).
inaffiatóio = *annaffiatoio*.
inaggua-gliábile [*in-, a.* .], ADJ.: unequable. **-gliánza†**, F.: inequality.
inagitáto†, ADJ.: not agitated.
inagráre†, INTR.: become sour.
inagrestíre [*in, agresto*], INTR.: grow sour (as grapes).

inaiáre [illegible], TR.: lay out on the threshing floor.

inaiáre [illegible], TR.: [illegible].

inal-bamánto, M.: whitening (whiteness). ||**-báre** [illegible], INTR.: become white; TR.: whiten.

inalbe-ramánto, M.: act of hoisting flags (hoisting them). ||**-ráre** [illegible], TR.: hoist (a flag); mast. REFL.: of horses: rear up; grow proud, become angry [illegible] a tree, be filled with trees.

inalidíre [in, alido], INTR.: become arid (dry up).

inalienábi-le [in-, a. .], ADJ.: inalienable. ||**-lità**, F.: unalienableness. **-lménte**, ADV.: inseparably.

inaltera-bile [in-, a. .], ADJ.: unalterable (immutable). **-rabilità**, F.: unalterableness (immutability). **-rabilménte**, ADV.: unalterably. **-ráto**, ADJ.: unaltered.

inalveá-re [in, alveo], TR.: lead waters into the beds of the rivers or canals. **-aióne**, F.: [illegible] of a canal.

inal zamánto, M.: elevation (exaltation); advancement (preferment). ||**-záre** [in, a. .], TR.: raise (elevate); REFL.: rise (ascend), place oneself. **-zatúra**†, F.: elevation (rise).

in amábile, ADJ.: unamiable (disagreeable).

inamáre†, TR.: catch with a hook; ensnare (captivate).

inamaríre†, TR.: make bitter (embitter); INTR.: become bitter.

in amóno, ADJ.: unpleasing (disagreeable).

inamidáre [in, amido], TR.: starch. **-áto**, ADJ.: starched, stiff (proud). **-atúra**, F.: starching.

inamistáre†, REFL.: form a friendship with.

in ammendábile†, ADJ.: incorrigible.

inammissíbi-le [in-, a. .], ADJ.: inadmissible. **-lità**, F.: inadmissibility.

inamovíbi-le [in-, a. .], ADJ.: that cannot be removed from office. **-lità**, F.: unremovableness.

ináne [L. inanis], ADJ.: inane (vain).

inanellá-re [in, anello], TR.: curl (frizzle) [illegible], put or insert in [illegible].

inanimá-re [in, a. .], TR.: animate (encourage [illegible]). ||**-máto** [in-, a. .], ADJ.: inanimate (lifeless, dead). **-ma**[illegible] [illegible] **inani**[illegible] [illegible] discouraged. **-mi**[illegible] [illegible] (stimulate), REFL.: be [illegible].

inanità [illegible], F.: inanity (futility). **-ziáne**, F.: inanition.

in-antennáre†, TR.: [illegible] hoist the sails to the yards.

in-appagábile, ADJ.: that cannot be satisfied.

in-appannábile, ADJ.: that cannot be dimmed or obscured.

in-appassionáre†, TR.: cause passion (put in a passion).

inappelláb-ile [in-, a. .], ADJ.: unappealable. **-ilménte**, ADV.: without appeal.

inappe-ténte†, ADJ.: without appetite (listless, disgusted). ||**-ténza** [in-, a. .], ADJ.: inappetence (want of appetite).

in-apprensíbile†, ADJ.: incomprehensible.

in-apprezzábile, ADJ.: inestimable (beyond all value).

in-appuntábile, ADJ.: that cannot be blamed or censured.

in-apparábile, ADJ.: that cannot be [illegible].

in-arábile, ADJ.: inarable. **-aráto**, ADJ.: unploughed.

in-arboráre†, TR.: = *inalberare*: plant with trees (fill with trees).

inar-camánto, M.: act of arching or bending like a bow. ||**-cáre** [in, arco], TR.: arch (bend); REFL.: grow curved or arched: — *le ciglia*, raise the eyebrows (amaze). **-catóre**, M.: one who looks amazed. **-catúra**, F.: arching (curving).

inarenáre†, TR.: fill or cover with sand.

inargen-táre [in, argento], TR.: silver (wash or plate with silver). **-tatúra**, F.: washing with silver.

inari-dáre†, ||**-díre** [in, arido], TR.: make arid (dry up); consume† (diminish); INTR.: become arid. **-díto**, PART.: withered (dried up).

inarientáre† = *inargentare*.

in armònico, ADJ.: inharmonious.

inarpicare† = *inerpicare*.

in arrendévole†, ADJ.: inflexible.

inarrivábi-le [in-, a. .], ADJ.: inaccessible (unattainable). **-lménte**, ADV.: beyond reach.

in arsicciáto†, ADJ.: parched (burnt); M.: burnt edge.

inartico-lataménte, ADV.: inarticulately. ||**-láto** [in-, a. .], ADJ.: inarticulate: *corpo* —, jointless body.

in artificióso†, ADJ.: unartful (not artificial).

inasiníre [in, asino], INTR.: become asinine or stupid.

inaspáre† = *innaspare*.

inaspet-tataménte, ADV.: unexpectedly. ||**-táto** [in-, a. .], ADJ.: unexpected (sudden).

ina spráre†, ||**-spríre** [in, aspro], TR.: exasperate (exacerbate); make churlish or crost†; increase†; INTR.: become cruel or sour†.

in=astáre, TR.: put on the staff.

in=attaccábile, ADJ.: unassailable (inexpugnable).

inat-tendíbile [*in-*, *a.* .], ADJ.: unworthy of attention. **-téso,** ADJ.: unexpected.

in=attitúdine, F.: inaptitude (incapacity). **=átto,** ADJ.: unfit (unsuitable).

inat-tività, F.: inactivity. ‖**-tívo** [*in-*, *a.* .], ADJ.: inactive.

inattuábi-le [*in-*, *a.* .], ADJ.: that cannot be executed or performed. **-lità,** F.: inability to do a thing.

in=attutíbile, ADJ.: unconquerable (indomitable).

in=avaríre†, INTR.: become avaricious.

inau-díbile†, ADJ.: inaudible. ‖**-díto** [L. *-ditus*], ADJ.: unheard of (wonderful, marvellous).

inaveráre†, TR.: pierce through; wound (hurt).

inaugu-rále, ADJ.: inaugural. ‖**-ráre** [*in*, *a.* .], TR.: inaugurate; consecrate†; take (the omen)†. **-razióne,** F.: inauguration.

in=auráto†, ADJ.: gilt (gilded).

inavve-dutaménte, ADV.: without shrewdness. **-dutézza,** F.: imprudence. ‖**-dúto** [*in-*, *a.* .], ADJ.: imprudent (unwary, indiscreet).

in=avventúra†, F.: misfortune (mishap).

inavver-tènte [*-tire*], ADJ.: inadvertent (imprudent). **-tenteménte,** ADV.: inadvertently (inconsiderately). **-tènza,** F.: inadvertence (thoughtlessness); lack of shrewdness. **-titaménto,** ADV.: inconsiderately (rashly).

in=azióne, F.: inaction.

in=caccíáre†, TR.: give chase (pursue).

incaciáre [*in*, *cacio*], TR.: season with grated cheese.

incadaveríre [*in*, *cadavere*], INTR.: become like a skeleton (grow thin).

in cadére, IRR.; INTR.: fall into; fall into sin or error.

in=cagionáre†, TR.: cause (occasion); lay the fault on.

inca-gliaménto, M.: obstacle (obstruction). ‖**-gliáre** [*in*, *caglio*], INTR.: strand (run aground); hinder; stammer. **incá-glio,** M.: stranding; obstacle (impediment).

inca-gnáre†, *-gníre*†, INTR.: be as enraged as a mad dog. *-gnáto*†, ADJ.: angry (mad); growling.

incalappiáre [*in*, *calappio*], TR.: cnsnare (inveigle); confuse (embroil).

in=calcàre†, TR.: trample (tread under foot); follow close (pursue hotly); cram (fill).

incalcia..† = *incalza..*

incalciná-re [*in*, *calcina*], TR.: calcine (cover with lime). **-túra,** F.: calcination.

in=calcitráre†, INTR.: make resistance: — *nel pungello*, kick against the pricks.

in=calcolábile, ADJ.: incalculable.

incaligináto [*in*, *caligine*], ADJ.: caliginous (obscure, dark).

incal-liménto, M.: callosity (induration). ‖**-líre** [*in*, *callo*], INTR.: grow callous (indurate). **-líto,** PART.: callous (hard).

incaloríre [*in*, *calore*], TR.: warm (heat); REFL.: warm one's self.

incalvíre [*in*, *calvo*], INTR.: grow bald.

incal-zaménto, M.: pursuit (chase). ‖**-záre** [*in*, *c.* .], TR.: pursue (chase). **-zatóre,** M.: pursuer.

incalzonáre†, REFL.: put on one's breeches.

incamatáto†, ADJ.: as straight as a stick; upright.

incame-rábile, ADJ.: that can be absorbed into the public treasury. **-raménto,** M.: incameration; imprisonment†. ‖**-ráre** [*in*, *camera*], TR.: absorb into the public treasury; imprison (confine)†; put in the chamber of firearms†. **-razióne**† = *-ramento*. **-relláto,** ADJ.: made into small rooms.

incami-ciáre [*in*, *camicia*], TR.: plaster; REFL.: put on one's shirt. **-ciáta,** F.: camisade (night-attack). **-ciáto,** ADJ.: shirted; plastered†; rough-cast†. **-ciatúra,** F.: plastering; rough-casting.

incammi-naménto†, M.: beginning; pushing forward; direction. ‖**-náre** [*in*, *c.* .], TR.: direct; set on foot (begin); push or send forward; REFL.: set out.

incamuffa.. = *camuffa..*

incamutáto†, ADJ.: quilted (stuffed, wadded).

incanaglíre [*in*, *canaglia*], INTR.: become like the rabble.

incana-laménto, M.: canalization. ‖**-láre** [*in*, *canale*], TR.: lead (water) into canals: — *un affare*, put an affair in the regular course, well-arrange. **-latúra,** F.: canalization; groove (canal).

incanáto†, ADJ.: enraged (mad, furious).

incancellábi-le [*in-*, *c.* .], ADJ.: that cannot be cancelled (indelible). **-lménte,** ADV.: indelibly.

incanche-ráre†, ‖**-ríre** [*in*, *canchero*], TR.: cause to fester; INTR.: fester (gangrene).

incancreníre [*in*, *cancrena*], INTR.: become gangrenous.

incande-scènte [L. *-scere*, become red hot], ADJ.: incandescent. **-scènza,** F.: incandescence.

incan-nággio, M.: winding up. ‖**-náre** [*in*, *canna*], TR.: wind on bobbins; take good aim at; tie in a roll†; put into the throat†. **-nátc**†, F.: stick of cherries; intrigue (snare). **-natóio**, M.: reel (spindle). **-natóra**, F., **-natóre**, M.: spinner. **-natúra**, F.: operation of spinning or winding into a skein. **-nucciáre**, TR.: enclose or cover with reeds; make into a trellis; (*surg.*) splint. **-nucciáta**, F.: splint (for a fracture); trellis. **-nuccia-túra**, F.: act of splinting.

incan-tagióne, F.: incantation. **-ta-ménto**, M.: enchantment. ‖**-táre** [L. (*cantare*, sing)], TR.: ENCHANT (fascinate, bewitch); delight; sell at auction†; REFL.: be enchanted, etc., be diverted; come to a standstill (of wheels, etc.): — *la nebbia*, eat and drink (feast). **-tatóre**, M., **-tatríce**, F.: enchanter (sorcerer). **-tatòrio**, ADJ.: enchanting (charming). **-tazióne**†, F., **-tésimo**, M.: enchantment (charm); allurement. **-tévole**, ADJ.: enchanting (bewitching). **incánto** 1, M.: enchantment (sorcery, charm): *andare come la biscia all'* —, do a thing against one's will; *guastar l'* —, frustrate one's plans.

incánto 2 [*mettere all' inquantum* (how much)], M.: auction.

incantucciáre = *rincantucciare*.

incanu-timénto†, M.: hoariness (growing gray). ‖**-tíre** [*in*, *canuto*], INTR.: become gray or hoary. **-títo**, PART.: hoary; gray-headed.

incapacciatúra = *accapacciatura*.

incapá-ce [*in*-, *c.*.], ADJ.: incapable (unable); inept (unfit)†. **-cità**, F.: incapacity (incompetence).

inca-paménto†, M.: obstinacy (stubbornness). ‖**-parbíre** [*in*, *caparbio*], INTR.: be obstinate, or headstrong. **-par-bíto**, PART.: obstinate (stubborn). **-pá-re**†, TR.: persuade; INTR.: be obstinate.

incaparráre = *accaparrare*.

incapestrá-re [*in*, *capestro*], REFL.: get tangled in the halter; TR.†: halter (*snare*). **-túra**, F.: tying on a halter; mark of a halter.

incaponíre [*in*, *capone*], REFL.: grow obstinate or stubborn.

incappáre [*in*, *cappa*], TR.: put on a cloak; snatch†; tie†; INTR.: fall into snares (be caught); injure one's self†; stumble†.

incappel-láre [*in*, *cappello*], REFL.: put on one's hat (cover one's self); be offended; ...n one's self with a garland†; become ...linal†. **-láto**, ADJ.: hatted (cov... offended.

...ucciáre† TR.: muffle up; wrap one's self in a hood or cowl.

incappiáre [*in*, *cappio*], TR.: tie with a knot (fasten); entangle.

incáppo†, M.: snare (trap); stumbling.

incappottáre [*in*, *cappotto*], REFL.: wrap one's self up well in a cloak.

incappucciáre [*in*, *cappuccio*], TR.: put on a hood; mask (disguise).

incapriccíre [*in*, *capriccio*], REFL.: take a great fancy for; fall in love with (be smitten).

incaráre† = *rincarare*.

incarbonchíre [*in*, *carbonchio*], INTR.: become like a carbuncle; get the smut, as corn.

incarboníre [*in*, *carbone*], INTR.: become charcoal.

incarcáre† = *incaricare*.

incarce-ragióne† = *-razione*. **-ra-ménto**, M.: imprisonment. ‖**-ráre** [*in*, *carcere*], TR.: incarcerate (imprison). **-ra-zióne**, F.: incarceration (imprisonment).

incárco = *incarico*.

incardináre [*in*, *cardine*], REFL.: determine on certain principles.

incardíre [*in*, *cardo*], REFL.: become like a thistle.

incári-ca†, F.: charge (load, burden). **-cáre**, TR.: charge (with); blame (accuse)†; invest (the enemy)†; vilify (abuse). **-cáto**, PART.: charged with, etc.; M.: envoy. ‖**incári-co** [*in*, *c.*.], M.: charge (duty); burden (load)†; care (trouble)†; injury†; blame†; imposition (tax)†: *prender l'* — *di*, take care of, take command of; *prender l'* —, take upon one's self.

incar-nagióne = *carnagione*. ‖**-ná-re** [*in*, *carne*], TR.: incarnate; wound (stick into the flesh)†; heal†; REFL.: assume human nature (become flesh). **-na-tíno**, ADJ.: incarnadine. **-natívo**†, ADJ.: incarnative. **-náto**, ADJ.: incarnate; flesh-coloured. **-nazióne**, F.: incarnation; flesh-colour. **-níre**, INTR.: stick the nails or claws into the flesh; REFL.: take flesh on one's self. **-níto**, PART.: rooted in the flesh.

incaro-gnáre†, **-gníre** [*in*, *carogna*], INTR.: become carrion; become worthless; be mad in love†.

incarrucoláre [*in*, *carrucola*], TR.: put (the rope) into the pulley.

incartaménto [*incartare*], M.: putting in paper; documents.

incartapecoríre [*in*, *cartapecora*], INTR.: become yellow (of skins); grow old.

incar-táre [*in*, *carta*], TR.: put or wrap in paper; put on paper†; (*fig.*†) hit the mark (attain). **-teggiáre**†, TR.: put upon paper (write). **incár-to**, M.: a bundle of papers; cocoons. **-tocciáre**, TR.: put in a cornet of paper; REFL.†:

twist up (curl, shrivel). **-tocciáto**, ADJ.: wrapped in paper; twisted. **-tonáre**, TR.: put in boards.

incasciáre = *incaciare*.

incas-saménto†, M.: packing in a box; collecting. ‖**-sáre** [*in, cassa*], TR.: put in a chest (case); cash (receive money); dike; set (gems); INTR.†: be joined. **-satúra**, F.: putting up in a case; cavity (hollow); enchasing (setting). **incás-so**, M.: cash.

incastagnáre†, TR.: wainscot (strengthen with boards); INTR.: get confused.

incastel-laménto, M.: battlement. ‖**-láre†**, TR.: fortify with castles or forts; fill with redoubts.

in-castità†, F.: unchasteness (incontinence). **-cásto†**, ADJ.: unchaste (incontinent).

incastoná-re [*in, castone*], TR.: enchase (set in). **-túra**, F.: enchasing (setting in).

inca-straménto, M.: enchasing. ‖**-stráre** [?], TR.: fix or join firmly; mortise; commit to memory. **-stratúra**, F.: enchasing (mortising). **incá-stro**, M.: junction (groove); hoof-parer (butteris).

incatar-raménto, M.: cold (catarrh). **-ráre**, ‖**-ríre** [*in, catarro*], INTR.: catch a cold.

incate-nacciáre [*in, catenaccio*], TR.: fasten with a padlock. **-naménto**, M.: incatenation (enchaining). ‖**-náre** [*in, catena*], TR.: enchain (shackle); draw a chain across (a harbour). **-natúra**, F.: chaining (concatenation); joining (union).

incatorbiáre [*in, catorbia*], TR.: put in prison.

incatorzo-liménto†, M.: blasting or withering of trees. ‖**-líre** [*in, catorzolo*], INTR.: blast (wither).

incatramáre [*in, catrame*], TR.: tar.

incattivíre [*in, cattivo*], TR., INTR.: become or cause to become wicked.

incau-taménte†, ADV.: imprudently. **-tèla†**, F.: imprudence (carelessness). ‖**incáu-to** [*in-, c.*.], ADJ.: inconsiderate (negligent).

incavalcá-re [*in, c.*.], TR.: place astride (mount); ride upon; drop a stitch. **-túra†**, F.: setting one thing over another; (*her.*) quartering.

incavalláre†, INTR.: furnish one's self with horses; TR.: place upon.

incavá-re [*in, cavo*], TR.: hollow out (excavate). **-túra**, F.: excavation; hollow (cavity).

incavernáre [*in, caverna*], TR.: make a cavern of; REFL.: sink into a hollow (said of waters, sink deep down): *occhi —nati*, deep-sunk eyes.

incavezzáre [*in, cavezza*], TR.: put on a halter.

incavicchiáre [*in, cavicchia*], TR.: peg (fasten with a peg, pin).

incaviglìáre [*in, caviglia*], TR.: put on pegs; fasten with pins or pegs.

incávo [*incavare*], M.: cavity (hole); hollowing out.

incèdere [L.], INTR.: PROCEED (go forward); stride on.

incelèbre†, ADJ.: obscure (unknown).

incèn-dere [L. (*candere*, glow)], IRR. (cf. *accendere*); TR.: kindle (light, set on fire, Eng.† INCEND); torment (vex); displease; cauterize; wish (desire); INTR.: burn; be inflamed with anger. **-dévole†**, ADJ.: combustible (inflammable). **-diaménto†** = *-dimento*. **-diário**, ADJ., M.: incendiary. **-diménto†** = *-dio*. **incèn-dio**, M.: conflagration (great fire). **incèn-dito†**, M.: conflagration; heart-burn (indigestion). **-ditóre†**, M., **-ditríce**, F.: incendiary. **-dóre†** = *ardore*.

incene-ráre [*in, cenere*], TR.: sprinkle with ashes; burn to ashes†. **-ríre**, TR.: reduce to ashes.

incen-saménto, M.: perfuming with incense. **-sáre**, TR.: incense (perfume with incense); praise (laud). **-sáta**, F.: act of giving incense. **-satóre**, M.: one who offers incense. **-satúra**, **-sazióne** = *-samento*. **-sière**, M.: thurible (censer). **-sióne†**, F.: conflagration (burning). **-sívo†**, ADJ.: incensive (inflammatory). ‖**incèn-so** [L. *-sum* (*-dere*, burn)], M.: incense; praise; ADJ.: inflamed (kindled): *dar — ad uno*, flatter or praise one; *dare l' — a' morti*, have useless care, "make almanacs for last year."

in-censurábile, ADJ.: uncensurable.

incentívo [L. *-vus* (*in-cinere*, set the tune)], M.: incentive (incitement, stimulus).

incentráre [*in, centro*], TR.: centralize.

incep-paménto, M.: act of impeding. ‖**-páre** [*in, ceppo*], TR.: fetter (impede); entangle (embroil, embarrass); benumb (stun); fuddle. **-patúra**, F.: heaviness (in the head).

ince-ráre [*in, cera*], TR.: wax (cover wit hwax); unite with wax; INTR.: turn yellow. **-ratíno**, *dim.* of *-rato*. **-ráto**, M.: tarpaulin (oilcloth); waxing; ADJ.: waxed; yellow; strong. **-ratúra**, F.: waxing; waxed point.

incerchiáre [*in, cerchio*], TR.: encircle (surround with a circle).

incercináre [*in, cercine*], INTR.: put a pad on.

incerconíre [*in, cercone*], INTR.: turn bad.

incerráre†, TR.: join (fasten together); hire.

incer-taménte, ADV.: uncertainly (doubtfully). **-tarèllo**, *dim.* of *-to*.

-tézza, **-titúdine**, F.: uncertainty (doubtfulness, incertitude). ||**incèr-to** [L. *-tus*], ADJ.: uncertain (doubtful); M.: uncertainty; perquisite. **-túccio**, *disp.* of *-to*.

incésot, M.: cautery; ADJ.: inflamed (burnt).

inces-páre, **-picáre** [*in*, *cespo*], INTR.: be entangled (stumble); grow broad (spread)†; cover with turfs.

inces-sábile [*in*, *cessare*], ADJ.: incessant (continual); inevitable†. **-sabilménte**, ADV.: incessantly (continually). **-sánte**, ADJ.: incessant (continual). **-santeménte**, ADV.: incessantly. **-sánza**†, F.: continuance.

incèsso [L. *-ssus* (*cedere*, move)], M.: lofty motion; progress (PROCESS).

incestáre†, TR.: put in a basket.

incès-to [L. *-tus* (*castus*, pure)], M.: incest. **-tuosaménte**, ADV.: incestuously. **-tuòso**, ADJ.: incestuous.

incèt-ta, F.: collection (or purchase) of rare things: *far* —, make a collection; buy†; *per* —, voluntarily. ||**-táre** [L. *in-ceptare*, undertake], TR.: collect (valuables, for retail); forestall (monopolize, engross). **-tatóre**, M., **-tatríce**, F.: collector; wholesale buyer; forestaller.

inchiavacciáre [*in*, *chiavaccio*], TR.: fasten with the padlock (bolt).

inchiavardáre [*in*, *chiavarda*], TR.: fasten with large nails or bolts.

inchia-váre†, TR.: lock. **-velláre**†, TR.: nail up (fasten with nails). **-vistelláre**†, TR.: fasten with a padlock; bolt.

in-chièdere†, IRR.; TR.: inquire (demand, make inquiry about); investigate. **-chieditóre**†, M., **-chieditríce**†, F.: seeker (inquirer). **-chièrere**†, TR.: ask (demand). **-chièsta**†, F.: inquest (search).

inchi-naménto, M.: inclination (bowing); abasement (humiliation); propensity (proneness), ||**-náre** [L. *inclinare*], TR.: incline (bend; have a propensity; bow); nod (assent); INTR.: nap; REFL.: make a bow: — *le orecchie*, give ear. **-náta**, F.: bow (reverence); humiliation. **-nazióne**†, F.: humiliation; disposition (attitude). **-névole**, ADJ.: inclinable (prone). **-nevolménte**, ADV.: respectfully (humbly). **inchíno**, M.: bow (salutation); nod; ADJ.: inclined; humbled (lowered). **-nósso**, *disp* of *-no*.

inchiodaménto, M.: nailing. ||**-dáre** [*in*, *chiodo*], TR.: nail (fasten with nails); ...nail); spike, sacrifice; (*fam.*) ... **-datóre**, M.: one who nails. ... nailing; prick (of a nail): ... discover a hidden truth. ...**e**, TR.: daub with ink ...n ink†; shut in (enclose)†.

||**-chiòstro** [L. *en-caustum* (Gr. *én-causton*, burnt in)], M.: INK; writing (composition); humour of the cuttlefish; cloister (convent)†: *opera d'* —, literary works; *scrivere a uno di buon* —, explain one's self clearly, with resentment; *raccomandare di buon* —, recommend warmly; *il suo* — *non corre*, his credit is not good.

inchiovatúra†, F.: nailing; prick or wound caused by a nail.

inchi-údere [*in*, *c*. .], IRR.; TR.: include (contain, comprehend); REFL.†: be enclosed or encompassed.

incialdáre†, TR.: roll in a wafer-biscuit (roll in batter); REFL.: become like batter; dress one's self in white.

inciam-páre [*in*, *c*. .], INTR.: stumble (trip); chance (— *in*), meet by chance (chance upon, fall in with). **-páta**, F.: stumbling. **-picáre**, INTR.: stumble often. **-picóne**, *aug.* of *-pone*. **inciámpo**, M.: stumbling (tripping); impediment (obstacle); difficulty (danger). **-póne**, *aug.* of *-po*.

inci-dènte [L. *incidere* (*cadere*, fall)], ADJ.: incidental; M.: incident (casual event). **-denteménte**, ADV.: incidentally. **-dènza**, F.: incidence; chance; digression.

in-cídere [L. (*cædere*, cut)], IRR.§; TR.: cut into (gash, INCISE); engrave; cut off† (retrench, amputate, Eng. INCIDE†); digress†; (*med.*†) open the bowels. **-císo**, PART. of *-cidere*.

§ Ind.: Pret. *incì-si*, *-se*; *-sero*. Part. *inciso*.

inci-feráto†, **-fráto**, ADJ.: done in cipher.

incignáre [L. *en-cœniare* (Gr. *kainós*, new), install], TR.: begin to use; taste (test wine, etc.); try on.

in-cignere†, IRR.; TR.: enclose (encompass); INTR.: be pregnant.

incíle [L. *in-cile* (*cædere*, cut), cut], M.: trench (drain).

incimiciáto [*in*, *cimice*], ADJ.: full of bedbugs.

incimur-riménto, M.: glanders. ||**-ríre** [*in*, *cimurro*], INTR.: have the glanders; (*disp.*) take a bad cold.

incincignáre [*in*, *cincinno*], TR.: rumple (a dress or coat).

incinciscchiáto [*in*, *cinciscchio*], ADJ.: hacked; stammering.

incinerazióne [*-rare*], F.: incineration.

incínta [L. *in-cincta*, un-girded], ADJ.: pregnant (ENCEINTE).

incipiènte [L. *incipere*, begin], ADJ.: incipient (beginning); M.: beginner (novice).

incipol-latúra, F.: softening (of wood). ||**-líre** [*in*, *cipolla*], INTR.: soften; crack.

incipriáre [*in*, *cipria*], TR.: powder with Cyprus dust.
incipriguire [*in*, *ciprigno*], INTR.: grow malignant (exasperate).
incírca [*in*, *circa*], ADV.: about (concerning).
in=circoncíso, ADJ.: uncircumcised.
incirco-scrittíbile, ADJ.: illimitable. ‖**-scrítto** [*in-*, *circoscrivere*], ADJ.: unbounded (illimited).
incischiáre† = *cincischiare*.
inci-sióne, F.: incision (cut); engraving; syncope (elision)†. **-sívo**, ADJ.: incisive (cutting). ‖**incí-so**, PART. of *-dere:* cut (engraved); M.: member or part of a discourse. **-sóre**, ADJ.: incisory (cutting); M.: engraver. **-súra**†, F.: incision (cut, gap).
inci-tábile, ADJ.: that can be incited. **-taménto**, M.: incitement (impulse). ‖**-táre** [L.], TR.: incite (spur on, provoke). **-tatívo**, ADJ.: inciting. **-tatóre**, M., **-tatríce**, F.: inciter (provoker). **-tazióne**†, F.: incitation (inducement).
incitrullíre [*in*, *citrullo*], INTR.: become a blockhead.
incittadináre [*in*, *cittadino*], REFL.: imitate manners of citizens.
inciuchíre [*in*, *ciuco*], INTR.: become an ass.
inciuscheráre†, TR.: intoxicate; REFL.: fill one's self with wine (get tipsy).
incivettíre [*in*, *civetta*], INTR.: become a flirt or coquette; become bold†; be ominous or unpropitious†.
incivi-le [*in-*, *c. .*], ADJ.: uncivil (rude, ill-bred). **-liménto**, M.: civilizing. **-lire** [*in*, *. .*], TR.: render civil (civilize); INTR.: become civil or polite. **-lménte**, ADV.: uncivilly (impolitely). **-lità**†, **-ltà**, F.: incivility (rudeness).
incle-mènte [*in-*, *c. .*], ADJ.: inclement; merciless (rigorous). **-mènza**, F.: inclemency (severity).
incli-nábile, ADJ.: inclinable (leaning). **-naménto**†, M.: inclination; propensity. **-nataménte**, ADV.: with inclination. ‖**-náre** [L.], TR.: incline (bend); INTR.: be inclined to (be prone). **-nazióne**, F.: inclination (propensity); disposition (bent); declination† (decadence). **-névole**, ADJ.: disposed to (prone).
inclito [L. *-tus* (*cluere*, be heard of)], ADJ.: celebrated (illustrious).
in-clúdere [L.], IRR. (cf. *chiudere*); TR.: include (comprehend). **-clúsa**, F.: enclosure; inclosed letter. **-clusióne**, F.: inclusion. **-clusíva**, F.: act of including. **-clusivaménte**, **-clusívo**, ADV.: inclusively. **-clúso**, PART. of *-dere*.
incoá-re [L. *inchoare*], TR.: commence (begin). **-tívo**, ADJ.: inchoative (inceptive). **-zióne**, F.: inchoation.
incoccáre [*in*, *cocca*], TR.: notch (an arrow); cock up; REFL.: stammer (hesitate).
incocciáre [*in*, *coccio* (cf. *pigliare i cocci*)], TR.: make mad; INTR., REFL.: get mad; grow obstinate or stubborn.
incodardíre [*in*, *codardo*], INTR.: become a coward (lose courage).
in=coercíbile, ADJ.: not coercible.
incoe-rènte [*in-*, *c. .*], ADJ.: incoherent (discordant). **-renteménte**, ADV.: incoherently. **-rènza**, F.: incoherency (discrepancy).
incogitábile†, ADJ.: incogitable (inconceivable).
in=cògliere, =**còrre**, IRR.; INTR.: happen (turn out); TR.: surprise (catch).
in-cognitaménte, ADV.: in an unknown manner. ‖=**cògnito**, ADJ.: unknown (incognito). **-cognoscíbile**†, ADJ.: unknowable (inscrutable).
incoiáre [*in*, *coio*], INTR.: grow hard or tough as leather.
incóla†, M.: inhabitant of a country.
incol-laménto, M.: gluing (joining, fastening). ‖**-láre** [*in*, *colla*], TR.: glue (paste together). **-láto**, PART.: glued (stuck to). **-latúra**, F.: gluing (sticking).
incolleríre [*in*, *collera*], INTR., REFL.: fly into a passion (get angry).
incoloráre [*in*, *colore*], INTR.: become coloured.
incol-pábile, ADJ.: inculpable (unblamable). **-pabilità**, F.: inculpability. **-pabilménte**, ADV.: inculpably. ‖**-páre** [*in*, *colpa*], TR.: inculpate (blame); censure†. **-páto**, PART.: inculpated; ADJ., M.: (*in*, 'not') faultless: *-pata tutela*, right of self-defence. **-patóre**, M.: accuser. **-pazióne**, F.: inculpation (blame). **-pévole**, ADJ.: unblamable (inculpable). **-pevolménte**, ADV.: inculpably.
incol-taménte, ADV.: impolitely (slovenly). **-tézza**, F.: want of culture. ‖**incól-to** 1 [*in-*, *c. .*], ADJ.: uncultivated; sloven (rude); neglected; desert (waste).
incòlto 2, PART. of *incogliere*.
incòlu-me [L. *-mis*], ADJ.: uninjured (unimpaired). **-mità**, F.: safety.
incombattíbile†, ADJ.: incontestable.
incom-bènte, ADJ.: incumbent. **-bènza**, F.: incumbency (charge, office). **-benzáre**, TR.: give an office or a charge to. ‖**incóm-bere** [L. *incumbere*, lie upon], INTR.: be imminent; belong to (regard).
incom-bustíbile [*in-*, *c. .*], ADJ.: incombustible. **-bustibilità**, F.: incombustibility. **-bústo**†, ADJ.: unburnt (not consumed).
incomin-ciaménto, M.: commenceme

(beginning). **-ciánte**, M.: novice (beginner). **-ciánza**† = *-ciamento*. ||**-ciáre** [*in*, *c.* .], TR.: commence (begin). **-ciáto**† = *-ciamento*. **-ciatóre** = *-ciante*. **incomín-cio**†, M.: commencement (beginning).
incommendáre [*in*, *commenda*], TR.: give or reduce 'in commendam.'
incommensurábi-le [*in-*, *c.* .], ADJ.: incommensurable. **-lità**, F.: incommensurability.
incommod. .† = *incomod. .*
incommutábi-le [*in-*, *c.* .], ADJ.: incommutable (immutable). **-lità**, F.: immutability (unchangeableness). **-lménte**, ADV.: immutably.
incomo-daménte, ADV.: incommodiously (inconveniently). **-dáre**, TR.: incommode (trouble, annoy). **-dáto**, ADJ.: disturbed (inconvenienced); sickly (indisposed). **-dézza**† = *-dita*. **-dità**, F.: incommodity (inconvenience); indisposition. ||**incòmodo** [*in-*, *c.* .], ADJ.: incommodious (inconvenient); M.: inconvenience (trouble); slight illness.
incomparábi-le [*in-*, *c.* .], ADJ.: incomparable. **-lménte**, ADV.: incomparably.
incompartíbile†, ADJ.: indivisible (inseparable).
incompassióne†, F.: inhumanity (cruelty).
incompatíbi-le [*in-*, *c.* .], ADJ.: incompatible. **-lità**, F.: incompatibility. **-lménte**, ADV.: incompatibly (inconsistently).
incompensábile [*in-*, *c.* .], ADJ.: not compensable.
incompe-tènte [*in-*, *c.* .], ADJ.: incompetent (unqualified). **-tenteménte**, ADV.: incompetently. **-tènza**, F.: incompetency (insufficiency)
incompiánto [*in-*, *c.* .], ADJ: unmourned (unpitied).
incompiúto [*in-*, *c* .], ADJ.: incomplete (unfinished, imperfect).
incomplèsso†, ADJ.: incomplex (simple).
incomplèto [*in-*, *c.* .], ADJ.: incomplete.
incompor-tábile [*in-*, *c.* .], ADJ.: insupportable (intolerable). **-tabilménte**, ADV.: insupportably (intolerably). **-tévole**† = *-tabile*.
incom-postaménte, ADV.: in a disordered or neglected manner. **-postézza**, F.: disorder (discomposure). ||**-pósto** [*in-*, *c.* .], ADJ.: disordered (ill-arranged, neglected).
incom-prensíbile [*in-*, *c.* .], ADJ.: incomprehensible. **-prensibilità**, F.: incomprehensibility. **-prensibilménte**, ADV.: incomprehensibly. **-préso**, ADJ.: not comprehended or understood.
incompressíbi-le [*in-*, *c.* .], ADJ.: incompressible. **-lità**, F.: incompressibility.

in=computábile, ADJ.: incomputable (incalculable).
incomunicábile†, ADJ.: incommunicable.
inconcáre [*in*, *conca*], TR.: put in a washtub.
inconcepíbi-le [*in-*, *c.* .], ADJ.: inconceivable. **-lità**, F.: inconceivableness.
inconciliábi-le [*in-*, *c.* .], ADJ.: incompatible. **-lità**, F.: irreconcilability. **-lménte**, ADV.: irreconcilably.
inconcludèn-te [*in-*, *c.* .], ADJ.: inconclusive (indecisive). **-teménte**, ADV.: inconclusively.
inconclúso†, ADJ.: unconcluded.
inconcússo [L. *-ssus* (*cutere*, shake)], ADJ.: unshaken (undisturbed, firm).
incòndito†, ADJ.: incondite (confused).
in=confusaménte, ADV.: confusedly.
incon-giungíbile [*in-*, *c.* .], ADJ.: that cannot be joined. **-giúnto**†, ADJ.: disjoined (disunited).
incon-gruènte [*in-*, *c.* .], ADJ.: incongruent (inconsistent). **-gruenteménte**, ADV.: incongruently (inconsistently). **-gruènza**, F.: incongruity (inconsistency); absurdity. **-gruità**, F.: incongruity (disproportion). **incòn-gruo** [L. *-gruus*], ADJ.: incongruous.
inconocchiáre [*in*, *conocchia*], TR.: put on the distaff.
inconosciúto†, ADJ.: unknown.
inconquassábile†, ADJ.: that cannot be broken (unshaken).
inconsapévo-le [*in-*, *c.* .], ADJ.: uninformed (unconscious). **-lézza**, F.: ignorance (unconsciousness). **-lménte**, ADV.: ignorantly.
incònscio [L. *-scius*], ADJ.: unconscious.
inconse-guènte [L. *-quens* (*sequere*, follow)], ADJ.: inconsequent. **-guènza**, F.: inconsequence (inconclusiveness).
inconside-rábile [*in-*, *c.* .], ADJ.: inconsiderable. **-rataménte**, ADV.: inconsiderately (rashly). **-ratézza**, F.: inadvertence (rashness). **-ráto**, ADJ.: inconsiderate (imprudent, foolish). **-razióne**, F.: inconsideration (imprudence).
in=consistènte, ADJ.: inconsistent.
inconso-lábile [*in-*, *c.* .], ADJ.: inconsolable. **-labilménte**, ADV.: inconsolably. **-láto**, ADJ.: disconsolate (sad). **-lazióne**†, F.: affliction (tribulation).
inconstánte = *incostante*.
inconsuèto [L. *-tus* (*consuetus*, accustomed)], ADJ.: unaccustomed (unusual, extraordinary).
incon-sultaménte, ADV.: inconsiderately (imprudently). ||**-súlto** [L. *-sultus* (*consulere*, consult)], ADJ.: unadvised; thoughtless (rash).
inconsu-mábile [*in-*, *c.* .], ADJ.: in-

consumable. **-máto**, ADJ.: unconsumed (remaining).

inconsútile [L. *-lis* (*suere*, sew)], ADJ.: seamless.

incontami-nábile [*in-*, *c.* .], ADJ.: that cannot be defiled (incorruptible). **-nataménte**, ADV.: incorruptibly. **-natézza**, F.: purity (chastity). **-náto**, ADJ.: undefiled (pure).

incontanènte [*incontinente*], ADV.: immediately.

incontestábile†, ADJ.: incontestable (indisputable).

incontempláb ile [*in-*, *c.* .], ADJ.: that cannot be contemplated.

incontenènto† = *incontanente*.

incontentábi-le [*in-*, *c.* .], ADJ.: insatiable; discontented. **-lità**, F.: insatiability, discontentedness. **-lménte**, ADV.: insatiably; discontentedly.

incontestábi-le [*in-*, *c.* .], ADJ.: INCONTESTABLE (unquestionable). **-lménte**, ADV.: incontestably (unquestionably).

inconti-nènte [L. *-nens*, not containing], ADJ.: incontinent (unchaste). **-nentaménte**, ADV.: incontinently (unchastely). **-nènza**, **-nènzia†**, F.: incontinence (lasciviousness).

incòlto†, ADJ.: unadorned (inelegant); uncultivated (illiterate).

incóntra†, PREP.: against; towards; over against (opposite): *all'* —, on the contrary.

incon-traménto†, M.: meeting; conference (interview). ‖**-tráre** [*in-*, *contro*], TR.: meet (hit upon, find); please (satisfy); INTR.: happen; REFL.: meet (fall in with).

incontras-tábile [*in-*, *c.* .], ADJ.: incontestable (indisputable). **-tabilménte**, ADV.: incontestably (unquestionably) **-táto**, ADJ.: uncontested (undisputed, evident).

in=cóntro, PREP.: against; over against (opposite); towards†; M.: meeting (encounter); accident (chance): *andare all'* —, go to meet; *farsi* —, advance, go further; *fare* —, be liked.

incontrovèr-so [*in-*, *c.* .], ADJ.: uncontroverted. **-tíbile**, ADJ.: incontrovertible. **-tibilménte**, ADV.: incontrovertibly.

inconturbábile†, ADJ.: imperturbable (tranquil).

inconve-névole [*in-*, *c.* .], ADJ.: unsuitable (inconvenient). ‖**-niènte** [*in-*, *c.* .], ADJ.: inconvenient; M.: inconvenience (trouble). **-nienteménte**, ADV.: inconveniently. **-niènza**, F.: inconvenience (difficulty).

inconvertíbi-le [*in-*, *c.* .], ADJ.: inconvertible; not convertible. **-lità**, F.: inconvertibility.

in=convincíbile, ADJ.: that cannot be convinced.

incorag-giaménto, M.: encouragement. ‖**-giáre** [*in*, *coraggio*] = *-gire*. **-giménto** = *-giamento*. **-gíre**, TR.: encourage (excite); INTR., REFL.: take courage.

inco-ráre [*in*, *core*], TR.: encourage (incite); put in mind (inspire, persuade)†. **-ráto**, ADJ.: inspired (persuaded).

incor-dáre [*in*, *corda*], TR.: string (an instrument); REFL.: become stiff. **-dáto**, PART.: strung; stiff. **-datúra**, F.: stringing of an instrument; crick (stiff neck).

incorná-re [*in*, *corna*], TR.: cuckold (Eng.† HORN); REFL.: be(come) obstinate (persist). **-túra**, F.: obstinacy (stubbornness); nature (inclination).

incorniciá-re [*in*, *cornice*], TR.: frame (border). **-túra**, F.: act or cost of framing.

incoro-náre [*in*, *corona*], TR.: crown (adorn); fill: — *il marito*, do the husband wrong. **-nazióne**, F.: coronation (crowning).

incorpo-rábile, ADV.: that can be incorporated. **-rále†**, ADJ.: incorporeal (immaterial). **-ralità†**, F.: incorporality (immateriality). **-ralménte†**, ADV.: without a body. **-raménto**, M.: incorporation. ‖**-ráre** [L.], TR.: incorporate (embody); confiscate (seize)†; REFL.: become incorporated; INTR.†: become a body (become material). **-razióne**, F: incorporation. **-reità**, F.: incorporeity. **incorpò-reo**, ADJ.: incorporeal (spiritual). **incòrpo-ro**, M.: incorporation (fusion).

incòrre = *incogliere*.

incorreggíbi-le [*in-*, *c.* .], ADJ.: incorrigible. **-lità**, F.: incorrigibility (obduracy). **-lménte**, ADV.: incorrigibly.

incorren-táre [*in*, *corrente*], TR.: (*arch.*) provide with scantlings; lath. **-tíre**, INTR.: become as stiff as a beam.

in=córrere, INTR.: incur (run into); take place (happen)†: — *in errore*, commit faults.

incor-rettaménte, ADV.: incorrectly. **-rettézza**, F.: incorrectness. ‖**-rètto** [*in-*, *c.* .], ADJ.: incorrect.

incor-rottaménte, ADV.: uprightly (purely). ‖**-rótto** [*in-*, *c.* .], ADJ.: incorrupt (unstained, pure). **-ruttíbile**, ADJ.: incorruptible. **-ruttibilità**, F.: incorruptibility (integrity). **-ruttibilménte**, ADV.: incorruptibly. **-ruzióne†**, F.: incorruption.

incórso, PART. of *incorrere*.

incortináre [*in*, *cortina*], TR.: surround with curtains.

incospícuo†, ADJ.: inconspicuous; indiscernible.

incos-tánte [in-, c..], ADJ.: inconstant (fickle). **-tanteménte**, ADV.: inconstantly. **-tánza**, F.: inconstancy.

incostituzioná-le [in-, c..], ADJ.: unconstitutional. **-lità**, F.: unconstitutionality. **-lménte**, ADV.: unconstitutionally.

incòtto, PART. of *incocere*; M.: bad spot.

incoverchiáre†, TR.: cover (put a lid upon).

increánza†, F.: rudeness (incivility).

increáto [in-, c..], ADJ.: increate (eternal).

incredíbi-le [in-, c..], ADJ.: incredible. **-lità**, F.: incredibility. **-lménte**, ADV.: incredibly.

increditáre [in, *credito*], TR.: accredit (give credit to, trust).

in=credulità, F.: incredulity. **=crèdu-lo**, ADJ.: incredulous.

increménto [L. -*tum*], M.: increment (increase).

incre-páre†, TR.: increpate (rebuke, chide). **-pazioncèlla†**, *dim.* of *-pazione*. **-pazióne†**, F.: reprimand (rebuke).

incre-scènza, F.: sorrow (vexation). ||**incré-scere** [L. -*scere*, increase], IRR. (cf. *crescere*); INTR.: be sorry; be weary: pity (commiserate). **-scévole**, ADJ.: tiresome (wearisome); saddening. **-scevolménte†**, ADV.: tediously; offensively. **-sciménto†**, M.: regret (vexation, sorrow). **-scióso**, ADJ.: annoying (troublesome).

incres-paménto, M.: curling (etc.), frowning. ||**-páre** [in, *crespo*], TR.: curl (crisp, ruffle, frizzle; shrivel); frown. **-patúra** = -*pamento*.

incretáre†, TR.: cover with clay.

incretinire [in, *cretino*], INTR.: become a cretin.

incrimi-nábile, ADJ.: that can be incriminated. **-nazióne**, F.: incrimination. ||**-náre** [L. (*crimen*, crime)], TR.: incriminate.

incri-náre [in, *crine*], TR.: crack (split). **-natúra**, F.: crack(ing).

in=criticábile, ADJ.: not to be criticised.

incro-ciaménto, M.: crossing (intersection). ||**-ciáre** [in, *croce*], TR.: cross (lay across); cruise. **-ciatóre**, M.: cruiser. **-ciatúra**, F.: crossing (intersection). **-cicchiaménto** = -*ciatura*. **-cicchiáre**, TR.: cross (intersect).

incroiáre†, TR.: wrinkle; INTR.: grow hard or tough as leather; grow rude; become stubborn.

in=crollábile, ADJ.: immovable (unshaken).

incronicáre†, TR.: chronicle; REFL.: meddle in (be troublesome).

incros-taménto, M.: incrusting. ||**-táre** [in, *crosta*], INTR.: be covered with a crust; TR.: incrust (form a crust over); plaster. **-tatúra**, **-tazióne**, F.: incrustation (incrusting).

incrude-liménto, M.: act of becoming cruel. ||**-líre** [in, *crudele*], INTR.: grow cruel or inhuman; become rough or hard†; TR.†: render cruel (exasperate); make rough.

incrudíre [in, *crudo*], INTR.: harden; become rigorous; TR.: make harsh or rough.

incruènto [L. -*tus*], ADJ.: bloodless.

incruscáre [in, *crusca*], TR.: fill with bran.

incu-bazióne [L. -*bare*, lie upon], F.: incubation. **incu-bo**, M.: incubus (nightmare).

in-cúde, **-cúdine** [L. -*cus* (*cudere*, beat)], F.: anvil. **-cudinétta**, *dim.* of -*cudine*.

inculcá-re [L.], TR.: inculcate. **-taménte**, ADV.: earnestly; urgently (instantly).

in=cúlto, ADJ.: uncultivated (untilled); unadorned†; not honoured with religious rite (not worshipped)†.

incumbènza = *incombenza*.

incu-náboli, **-nábuli** [L. -*nabula*, cradle], M.: first printed edition.

in=cuòcere, IRR.; TR.: cook (boil, roast, bake).

incupíre [in, *cupo*], INTR.: become dark or deep.

incu-rábile [in-, c..], ADJ.: incurable (irremediable); M.: chronic malady. **-rabilità**, F.: incurability. **-ránte**, ADJ.: negligent (not caring). **-ránza**, F.: negligence (carelessness). **-ráto†**, ADJ.: not cured; neglected (uncared for). **incúria** [L.], F.: negligence.

incu-riosaménte, ADV.: without curiosity. ||**-rióso** [in-, c..], ADJ.: incurious (not caring).

incursióne [L. -*sio*], F.: incursion (invasion); inundation (flood).

incur-vábile [in-, c..], ADJ.: that cannot be curved (uncurvable). **-vaménto**, M.: incurvation. ||**-váre** [in, c..], TR.: incurvate (bend, crook); REFL.: become bent or curved; (*pers.*) prostrate one's self. **-vatúra**, **-vazióne**, F.: incurvation (crookedness). **-víre**, INTR.: become bent. **incúr-vo**, ADJ.: curved (bent, crooked).

incuşáre†, TR.: accuse (blame).

incustodíto†, ADJ.: unguarded.

in-cútere [L.], IRR.§; TR.: strike into; inspire (instil). **-cússo**, PART. of -*cutere*.

§ Ind.: Pret. 1. *incutèi* or *incússi*, 3. *incutè* or *incússe*, 6. *incutèrono* or *incússero*. Part. *incússo*.

indaco [L. *-dicus*, Indian], M.: indigo.
inda-gábile, ADJ.: that cannot be investigated. ‖**-gáre** [L. *-gare*, track], TR.: investigate (search into, Eng.† indagate). **-gatóre**, M., **-gatríce**, F.: investigator. **-gazióne**† = *-gine*. **indágine**, F.: investigation (search).
indanaiáre, TR.: spot (speckle, stain).
indárno [OGer. *andarn*], ADV.: (*poet.*) in vain.
indebilíre† = *indebolire*.
in=debitaménte, ADV.: unduly.
indebi-taménto, M.: running into debt. **-táre**, ‖**-tíre** [*in*, *debito*], REFL.: contract debts. **-táto**, PART.: indebted.
in=débito, ADJ.: undue (unjust, unlawful).
indebo-liménto, M.: debilitation (weakness). ‖**-líre** [*in*, *debole*], TR.: render weak (debilitate); INTR.: become weak.
inde-cènte [*in-*, *d.* .], ADJ.: indecent. **-centeménte**, ADV.: indecently. **-cènza**, F.: indecency (immodesty).
indeci-frábile [*in-*, *d.* .], ADJ.: that cannot be deciphered. **-fráto**, ADJ.: not deciphered.
inde-cisióne [*in-*, *d.* .], F.: indecision. **-císo**, ADJ.: undecided (undetermined).
indeclinábi-le [*in-*, *d.* .], ADJ.: indeclinable. **-lità**, F.: quality of being indeclinable. **-lménte**, ADV.: indeclinably.
in=decomponíbile, ADJ.: that cannot be decomposed.
inde-coraménte, ADV.: indecorously.
indè-coro†, ADJ.: dishonoured (slighted). ‖**-còro**†, [*in-*, *d.* .], ADJ.: indecorous (indecent). **-corosaménte**, ADV.: indecorously. **-coróso**, ADJ.: indecorous (unbecoming).
indefensibilménte†, ADV.: indefensibly.
inde-fessaménte, ADV.: indefatigably (assiduously). ‖**-fèsso** [L. *-fessus* (*fatisci*, tire)], ADJ.: INDEFATigable (unwearied, assiduous).
indefettíbi-le [*in-*, *d.* .], ADJ.: indefectible. **-lità**, F.: indefectibility.
indefi-ciènte [*in-*, *d.* .], ADJ.: indeficient (continuous). **-cienteménte**†, ADV.: continuously. **-ciènza**, F.: indeficiency (abundance, plenty).
indefi-níbile, ADJ.: indefinable. **-nitaménte**, ADV.: indefinitely. **-nitézza**, F.: indefiniteness (indetermination). ‖**-níto** [*in-*, *d.* .], ADJ.: indefinite (undetermined).
inde-gnaménte, ADV.: unworthily (basely, infamously). **-gnaménto**†, M.: indignation (wrath); aversion (disdain). **-gnáre**†, INTR., REFL.: be angry (fret, fume). **-gnatívo**†, ADJ.: provoking (vexing). **-gnáto**†, PART.: indignant. **-gnazióne**†, F.: indignation (anger, rage); disease of the stomach. **-gnità**, F.: indignity (baseness); affront. ‖**indé-gno** [*in-*, *d.* .], ADJ.: unworthy (base); hurtful (pernicious)†.
indelèbi-le [L. *-lis* (L. *delere*, destroy)], ADJ.: indelible. **-lménte**, ADV.: indelibly.
indeliberá-to [*in-*, *d.* .], ADJ.: indeliberate (unpremeditated). **-zióne**, F.: want of deliberation.
indeli-cataménte, ADV.: indelicately. **-catézza**, F.: indelicacy. ‖**-cáto** [*in-*, *d.* .], ADJ.: indelicate.
indemaniáre [*in*, *demanio*], TR.: incorporate in the public domain.
indemo-niáre [*in*, *demonio*], INTR.: be possessed with a devil. **-niáto**, ADJ.: possessed with an evil spirit; raging (raving).
indèn-ne [L. *indemnis* (*in*, not, *damnum*, hurt)], ADJ.: indemnified; unhurt (safe); innocuous (harmless)†. **-nità**, F.: indemnity (security). **-nizzáre**, TR.: indemnify (reimburse). **-nizzazióne**, F: indemnification.
inden-táre [*in*, *dente*], INTR.: indent (mark with the teeth). **-tatúra**, F.: indentation.
indéntro = *dentro*.
independ. .† = *indipend.* .
indescrivíbi-le [*in-*, *d.* .], ADJ.: indescribable. **-lménte**, ADV.: indescribably.
indetermi-nábile, ADJ.: indeterminable. **-nabilménte**, ADV.: indeterminably. **-nataménte**, ADV.: indeterminately. ‖**-náto** [*in-*, *d.* .], ADJ.: indeterminate (undetermined, uncertain); perplexed (undecided). **-nazióne**, F.: indetermination.
indet-táre [*in-*, *d.* .], TR.: suggest. **-tatúra**, F.: suggestion.
indevò-to [*in-*, *d.* .], ADJ.: indevout (ungodly). **-zióne**, F.: indevotion.
indi [L. *inde*], ADV.: thence; after (afterwards); from thence: — *a pochi giorni*, few days after.
indiá-na [*India*], F.: printed cotton stuff. **-nísta**, M.: one versed in the Indian languages. **indiá-no**, ADJ., M.: Indian: *far l'* —, play Indian, "play possum."
india-scoláre = *-volare*.
india-volaménto†, M.: sorcery (witchcraft); furious rage. ‖**-voláre** [*in*, *diavolo*], INTR.: make a great noise or confusion; put upside down; get furious†. **-voláto**, ADJ.: devilish; mad (furious); intricate (very difficult).
indicá-bile, ADJ.: that can be indicated or pointed out. **-ménto**, M.: indication (sign). ‖**indicá-re** [L.], TR.: indicate (show, point out); intimate (signify)†. **-tívo**, ADJ.: indicative (demonstrative); M.: indicative mood. **-tóre**, M., **-tríce**, F.: indicator. **-zióne** = *-mento*.

indice [L. *index*], M.: index; forefinger; ADJ.†: indicating.
indicevol. .† = *indicibil.* .
indicíbil-e [*in-*, *d.* .], ADJ.: indicible (unspeakable). **-ménte,** ADV.: ineffably (unspeakably).
in-dietreggiáre, INTR.: go back (recede, recoil). ‖**=dietro,** ADV.: back (backwards); after (behind): *tempo* —, sometime ago; *rendere* —, push back (repel); *tirarsi* —, fall or draw backwards; *volgersi* —, look back.
indi-fendíbile, -fensíbile† [*in-*, *d.* .], ADJ.: indefensible. **-féso,** ADJ.: undefended (unguarded).
indiffe-rènte [L. *-rens*], ADJ.: indifferent (careless); not different (equal)†. **-renteménto,** ADV.: indifferently. **-rènza,** F.: indifference (impartiality); equality.
in-differíbile, ADJ.: that cannot be deferred or put off.
indiffinit. .† = *indefinit.* .
indígeno [L. *-nus*], ADJ.: indigenous; M.: indigene.
indi-gènte [L. *-gens*], ADJ.: indigent (poor). **-gènza,** F.: indigence (poverty, destitution). **indí-gere†,** INTR.: be indigent (be in want).
indi gerìbile [*in-*, *d.* .], ADJ.: indigestible. **-geribilità,** F.: indigestibility. **-gestaménte,** ADV.: in an undigested manner. **-gestíbile†** = *-geribile.* **-gestióne,** F.: indigestion. ‖**-gèsto** [*in-*, *d.* .], ADJ.: indigested (crude).
indígete [L. *-ges*], M.: divine hero; divinity.
indigná-re [L. *-ri*, disDAIN], TR.: excite indignation in, anger; REFL.: be indignant (be angry). **-to,** PART.: indignant, angered. **-zióne,** F.: indignation.
in di gròsso, ADV.: (*pop.*) thereabout, about; greatly†.
indiligènza†, F.: negligence (carelessness).
in dimenticábile, ADJ.: that cannot be forgotten.
indimos-trábile [*in-*, *d.* .], ADJ.: not demonstrable. **-trabilità,** F.: indemonstrability. **-tráto,** ADJ.: undemonstrated.
indipen-dènte [*in-*, *d.* .], ADJ.: independent. **-denteménte,** ADV.: independently. **-dènza,** F.: independence.
in díre, IRR.; TR.: announce (proclaim, intimate).
i-rettaménte, ADV.: indirectly. **-tto** [*in-*, *d.* .], ADJ.: indirect. **-itto,** ADJ.: directed (addressed); over against (opposite to). **-riz-ato** = *-rizzo.* ‖**-rizzáre** [*in-*, *d.* .]: direct (guide); address (a letter); REFL.: direct one's steps (begin one's journey, set out); apply (to). **-rizzatóre,** M.: director (guide). **-rizzo,** M.: direction (management); address.
in=discerníbile, ADJ.: indiscernible.
indisciplí-na [*in-*, *d.* .] = *-natezza.* **-nábile,** ADJ.: indisciplinable (indocile). **-natèzza,** F.: indiscipline. **-náto,** ADJ.: undisciplined; untaught (ignorant)†.
indiscre-taménte, ADV.: indiscreetly. **-tézza,** F.: indiscretion (imprudence, rashness). ‖**indiscré-to** [*in-*, *d.* .], ADJ.: indiscreet (imprudent). **-zióne** = *-tezza.*
in=discússo, ADJ.: undiscussed.
indisiáre†, TR.: excite (a desire).
indispensábi-le [*in-*, *d.* .], ADJ.: indispensable. **-lità,** F.: indispensability. **-lménte,** ADV.: indispensably.
indisporáto†, ADJ.: irregular (disorderly, immoderate).
indispettíre [*in*, *dispetto*], TR.: vex (enrage); REFL.: be vexed (get angry).
indis-pórre [*in-*, *d.* .], IRR.; TR.: indispose. **-posizioncèlla,** *dim.* of *-posizione.* **-posizióne,** F.: indisposition (illness); disinclination†; defect†. **-pósto,** ADJ.: indisposed (ill); inept (unfit)†; disinclined†.
indisputábi-le [*in-*, *d.* .], ADJ.: indisputable. **-lménte,** ADV.: indisputably.
indissolúbi-le [L. *-lis*], ADJ.: indissoluble. **-lità,** F.: indissolubility. **-lménte,** ADV.: indissolubly.
indistin-guíbile, ADJ.: indistinguishable. **-taménte,** ADV.: indistinctly. ‖**indistin-to** [*in-*, *d.* .], ADJ.: indistinct; M.†: indistinction. **-zióne†,** F.: indistinction (confusion).
indistruttíbi-le, ADJ.: indestructible. **-lità,** F.: indestructibility.
indívia [L. *intibus*], F.: (*bot.*) endive.
indivi-duále, ADJ.: individual (personal, special). **-dualísmo,** M.: individualism. **-dualità,** F.: individuality. **-dualménte,** ADV.: individually (separately). **-duáre,** TR.: individuate (discriminate). **-duazióne,** F.: individuation. ‖**indiví-duo** [L. *-duus*, undivided], ADJ.: individual; indivisible (inseparable)†; M.: individual; individuality†: **in —, singly** (one by one).
indivin. .† = *indovin.* .
indivi-saménte†, ADV.: indivisibly (indistinctly). **-síbile,** ADJ.: indivisible (inseparable). **-sibilità,** F.: indivisibility. **-síbilménte,** ADV.: indivisibly. ‖**indiví-so** [*in-*, *d.* .], ADJ.: undivided (whole).
indivò-to [*in-*, *d.* .], ADJ.: indevout. **-zióne,** F.: indevotion.
in-diziáre, TR.: hint (cause suspicion); indicate. ‖**-dízio** [L. *-dicium*], M.: sign

(index, mark). **-dizióne**, F.: indiction (cycle of fifteen years); declaration (proclamation)†; sign (token)†.
indo [L. *Indus*], ADJ.: Indian.
indòci-le [*in-*, *d.* .], ADJ.: indocile (unapt). **-líre**, TR.: render docile (mitigate, sweeten). **-lità**, F.: indocility. **-lménte**, ADV.: unteachably (intractably.
indol-círe [*in*, *dolce*], TR.: sweeten (mitigate); make pliable†; soften; INTR.: become soft. **-cíto**, ADJ.: sweetened; softened.
índole [L. *indoles*], F.: indoles (natural disposition, bent, temper).
indo-lènte [L. *-lens* (*in*, not, *dolere*, feel pain)], ADJ.: indolent (lazy, slothful). **-lenteménte**, ADV.: indolently. **-lènza**, **-lènzia**†, F.: indolence (laziness). **-lenzíre**, TR.: benumb; pain slightly; INTR.: be benumbed. **-liménto**, M.: slight pain; numbness.
in=domábile, ADJ.: untamable; that cannot be chiseled.
indomandáto†, ADJ.: unasked (undemanded).
in=dománi, M.: next day (day after).
in=domáto, ADJ.: indomite (uncurbed, untamed). **-dòmito**, **-dómo**†, ADJ.: indomite; indomitable.
indonnáre†, REFL.: make one's self master; make one's self a mistress.
indopáre†, REFL.: yield place (draw back); place one's self after.
indoppia. .† = *addoppia*. .
indo-raménto, M.: gilding. ||**-ráre** [*in*, *d.* .], TR.: gild; (*cook.*) dip into beaten eggs: — *la pillola*, *il boccone*, sweeten bad news. **-ratóre**, M.: gilder. **-ratúra**, F.: gilding; (*fig.*) appearance.
indor-mentáto†, ADJ.: sleepy (drowsy). **-mentiménto**†, M.: numbness. ||**-mentíre**†, TR.: stupefy (benumb). **-míre**†, TR.: disesteem; INTR.: fall asleep; be unconcerned. **-míto**†, ADJ.: sleepy; lulled asleep.
indos-sánte, M.: indorser. **-sáre**, TR.: put on the back; indorse. **-sáta**, F.: act of trying, or putting on. ||**indòs-so** [*in*, *d.* .], ADV.: upon one's back: *non ho denaro* —, I have no money about me.
indotáto†, ADJ.: remunerated (recompensed); dowerless.
indótta†, F.: inducement (persuasion).
indottaménte [*indotto*], ADV.: unlearnedly.
indottívo†, M.: impulsion; ADJ.: persuasive (inducing).
in=dòtto 1, ADJ.: unlearned (ignorant).
indótto 2, PART. of *indurre*; induced (persuaded); M.†: inducement (motive).
indottri-nábile†, ADJ.: indocible (unteachable). ||**-náre**†, TR.: indoctrinate (teach).
indováre†, INTR.: place one's self (adjust or adapt one's self).
indoverosaménte†, ADV.: unduly (unjustly).
indovi-nábile, ADJ.: that can be divined or predicted. **-naménto**†, M.: divination (prognostication). ||**-náre** [*in*, *divinare*], TR.: divine (predict, conjecture); guess. **-nático**† = *-namento*. **-natóre**†, M.: prophet (prognosticator). **-nazióne**† = *-namento*. **-nèllo**, M.: enigma (riddle). **indoví-no**, M.: diviner (soothsayer); ADJ.: prophetical (foretelling).
in-dovutaménte, ADV.: unduly (unjustly). ||=**dovúto**, ADJ.: undue (unjust).
indoz-zaménto†, M.: wasting away (consumption, sickness); sorcery (witchcraft). ||**-záre**†, INTR.: thrive poorly (fall away); enchant (bewitch).
indra-cáre†, **-gáre**†, TR.: make fierce (like a DRAGON); INTR.: grow fierce (get furious).
indrap-páre†, TR.: make (cloth). **-pelláre**†, TR.: draw up in line of battle.
in-drèto, **-drièto**† = *indietro*.
indrizzáre = *indirizzare*.
indrudíre†, INTR.: become amourous.
induáre†, TR.: divide into two; REFL.: double one's self (make one's self two); marry.
indúb-bio [*in-*, *d.* .], ADJ.: not doubtful (certain). **-itábile** [*in-*, *d.* .], ADJ.: indubitable. **-itabilità**, F.: certainty. **-itabilménte**, **-itataménte**†, ADV.: undoubtedly (certainly). **-itáto**, ADJ.: certain (sure).
indu-cènte, ADJ.: inducing (inciting). ||**indú-cere**† = *indurre*. **-ciménto**, M.: inducement. **-citóre**, M., **-citríce**, F.: inducer.
indu-gévole†, ADJ.: tardy (slow, procrastinating). ||**indú-gia** [L. *-tiæ*], F., **-giaménto**, M.: delay (stop); hindrance. **-giáre**, INTR.: delay (tarry); TR.: put off; make one wait†. **-giatóre**, M.: delayer (procrastinator). **indú-gio**, M.: delay (procrastination): *mettere ad* —, put off.
in-dul-gènte, ADJ.: indulgent (tolerant). **-dulgènza**, F.: indulgence (toleration). ||**-dúlgere** [L.], TR. indulge (allow, grant); pardon. **-dùlto**, PART. of *-dulgere*; M.: indult (pardon, amnesty).
induménto [L. *-tum*, covering], M.: clothing (raiment).
indu-rábile, ADJ.: that may be indurated. **-raménto**, M.: induration (hardness); obduracy. ||**-ráre** [*in*, *duro*], TR.: indurate (harden); make strong; INTR.†:

become hardened; become obdurate. **-ráto**, ADJ.: indurated. **-riménto** = *-ramento*. **-ríre**, TR.: harden.

indùrre [L. *in-ducere*, lead in], IRR. (cf. *addurre*); TR.: induce (entice); reason (deduce); occasion†; introduce†; dress†; REFL.: resolve (determine).

indús-tre = *-trioso*. ‖**indú-stria** [L.], F.: industry (labour); art; skill: *compare d' —*, make small gains by great labour. **-striále**, ADJ.: industrial; M.: one devoted to labour. **-striánte**, M.: one who lives by industry (labourer). **-striáre**, REFL.: strive hard (try one's best). **-striòla**, *dim.* of *-tria*. **-striosaménte**, ADV.: industriously. **-strióso**, ADJ.: industrious (diligent).

in-duttivaménte, ADV.: inductively. ‖**-duttívo** [L. *-ductivus* (*-ducere*, lead in)], ADJ.: inductive (persuasive). **-duzióne**, F.: induction.

ineb-briaméntо†, M.: inebriation; exhilaration. -(**b**)**riánza**†, F.: inebriety (drunkenness). ‖-(**b**)**riáre** [*in*, *ebbro*], TR.: inebriate (intoxicate).

in=eccitábile, ADJ.: inexcitable.

inèdia [L. (*in*, not, *edere*, EAT)], F.: fasting (abstinence from food).

in=èdito, ADJ.: inedited (unpublished).

inedu-cábile [*in-*, *e.* .], ADJ.: not educable. **-cáto**, ADJ.: uneducated.

ineffábi-le [L. *-lis* (*fari*, speak)], ADJ.: ineffable (unspeakable). **-lità**, F.: ineffability. **-lménte**, ADV.: ineffably (unspeakably).

ineffettuá-bile [*in-*, *e.* .], ADJ.: unfeasible (impractical). **-zióne**, F.: impracticableness.

ineffi-cáce [*in-*, *e.* .], ADJ.: inefficacious. **-cácia**, F.: inefficacy (inefficiency).

inegua-*gl*iánza, F.: inequality (disparity). ‖**ineguá-le** [*in-*, *e.* .], ADJ.: unequal (uneven); incapable (inept, unfit)†. **-lità** = *-glianza*. **-lménte**, ADV.: unequally.

inele-gánte [*in-*, *e.* .], ADJ.: inelegant (coarse, unpolished). **-ganteménte**, ADV.: inelegantly. **-gánza**, F.: inelegance.

ine-leggíbile, -ligíbile [*in-*, *e.* .], ADJ.: ineligible. **-leggibilità**, F.: ineligibility.

in=eloquènte, ADJ.: ineloquent.

ineluttábile [L. *-eluctabilis* (*e-luctor*, struggle out)], ADJ.: ineluctable (irresistible, unavoidable).

inemen-dábile [*in-*, *e.* .], ADJ.: incorrigible. **-dabilménte**, ADV.: incorrigibly. **-dáto**, ADJ.: not amended (uncorrected).

inenarrábile [L. *-lis* (*narrare*, relate)], ADJ.: ineffable (unutterable).

inéntro†, ADV.: within; inwardly.

inequa. .† = *inegua. .*

inequivalènte [*in-*, *e.* .], ADJ.: not equivalent (unequal).

inerbáre†, TR.: cover with grass.

ine-rènte [L. *in-hærere*, hang in], ADJ.: inherent (innate). **-rènza**, F.: inherence (innateness).

inèrme [L. *-mis* (*arma*, weapons)], ADJ.: UNARMED.

inerpicáre [?], REFL.: climb (clamber up).

inèrte [L. *in-ers* (*ars*, skill)], ADJ.: inert (sluggish); powerless; lifeless; useless.

inerudíto [*in-*, *e.* .], ADJ.: inerudite (unlearned).

inèrzia [L. *in-ertia* (*ars*, skill)], F.: inertia.

ine-ṣattaménte, ADV.: inexactly. **-ṣattézza**, F.: inexactness. ‖**-ṣátto** [*in-*, *e.* .], ADJ.: inexact.

in=eṣaudíto, ADJ.: not heard (not listened to).

in=eṣauríbile, ADJ.: inexhaustible. **-eṣauribilménte**, ADV.: inexhaustibly. **-eṣáusto**, ADJ.: inexhausted.

ines-caménto, M.: allurement (baiting, enticement). ‖**-cáre** [*in*, *esca*], TR.: allure (bait, Eng.† inescate).

inescogi-tábile, ADJ.: unimaginable. ‖**-táto**† [*in-*, *e.* .], ADJ.: unthought of.

in=escrutábile, ADJ.: inscrutable.

inescuṣábi-le [*in-*, *e.* .], ADJ.: inexcusable. **-lménte**, ADV.: inexcusably.

in=eṣeguíbile, ADJ.: inexecutable.

ineṣerci-tábile, ADJ.: not exercisable. ‖**-táto** [*in-*, *e.* .], ADJ.: unexercised (unpractised); ignorant.

ineṣigíbi-le [*in-*, *e.* .], ADJ.: that cannot be exacted or collected. **-lità**, F.: impossibility of exacting.

ineṣióne [L. *inhæsio*], F.: inhesion (inherence).

ineṣis-tènte [*in-*, *e.* .], ADJ.: inexistent. **-tènza**, F.: inexistence.

ineṣorábi-le [L. *in-ex-orabilis*], ADJ.: inexorable (implacable). **-lità**, F.: inexorability. **-lménte**, ADV.: inexorably.

ines-periènza [*in-*, *e.* .], F.: inexperience. **-pertaménte**, ADV.: not expertly. **-pèrto**, ADJ.: inexpert (inexperienced, raw).

ines-piábile [*in-*, *e.* .], ADJ.: inexpiable. **-piáto**, ADJ.: inexpiate.

inesplèbile†, ADJ.: insatiable.

inesplicábi-le [*in-*, *e.* .], ADJ.: inexplicable. **-lménte**, ADV.: inexplicably.

in=espirábile, ADJ.: not breathable.

inesplo-rábile [*in-*, *e.* .], ADJ.: inexplorable. **-ráto**, ADJ.: unexplored.

inesprimíbile [*in-*, *e.* .], ADJ.: inexpressible (unspeakable).

inespugnábi-le [*in-*, *e.*.], ADJ.: inexpugnable (impregnable). **-lità**, F.: quality of being inexpugnable. **-lménte**, ADV.: inexpugnably.

inessiccábile†, ADJ.: that cannot be dried up (perennial, inexhaustible).

inestéso [*in-*, *e.*.], ADJ.: inextended.

inesti-mábile [*in-*, *e.*.], ADJ.: inestimable. **-mabilménte**, ADV.: inestimably. **-máto**, ADJ.: unesteemed (not valued).

inestinguíbi-le [*in-*, *e.*.], ADJ.: inextinguishable. **-lménte**, ADV.: inextinguishably.

in=estirpábile, ADJ.: inextirpable.

inestri-cábile [L. *inextricabilis*], ADJ.: inextricable. **-cabilménte**, ADV.: inextricably. **-cáto**, ADJ.: entangled.

inet-taménte, ADV.: ineptly (unsuitably). **-tézza**, **-titúdine**, F.: ineptitude (unfitness). ‖**inètto** [L. *ineptus* (*aptus*, fit)], ADJ.: inept (unfit, improper).

inevitábi-le [*in-*, *e.*.], ADJ.: inevitable. **-lménte**, ADV.: inevitably.

inèzia [L. *in-eptia* (*aptus*, fit)], F.: worthless thing, trifle, nothing; platitude; stupidity (nonsense, folly).

infacèto†, ADJ.: insipid (dull, witless).

infa-cóndia, F.: want of eloquence. ‖**-cóndo** [*in-*, *f.*.], ADJ.: ineloquent.

infagottáre [*in*, *fagotto*], TR.: make into a bundle; wrap up hastily; REFL.: wrap one's self up like a bundle.

infal-lanteménte = *-libilmente.* ‖**-líbile** [L. *-libilis*], ADJ.: infallible (certain, sure). **-libilità**, F.: infallibility. **-libilménte**, ADV.: infallibly.

infa-maménto†, M.: infamy (disgrace). ‖**-máre** [L.], TR.: defame (slander); render infamous; divulge (report)†; REFL.: acquire renown. **-matóre**, M., **-matríce**, F.: defamer. **-matòrio**, ADJ.: defamatory. ‖**infá-me** [L. *-mis*], ADJ.: infamous (base, scandalous): *dito* —, middle finger. **-meménte**, ADV.: infamously (disgracefully). **infá-mia**, F.: infamy (shame, opprobrium).

infamigliáre†, REFL.: live together in a family.

infamíre†, INTR.: become very hungry or ravenous.

infamità [*-fame*], F.: infamy (infamous action).

infanatichíre [*in*, *fanatico*], TR., INTR.: make or become fanatic.

infanciullíre [*in*, *fanciullo*], INTR.: grow childish (play the child).

infándo†, ADJ.: unspeakable.

infan-gáre [*in*, *fango*], TR.: soil or bespatter with mud (besmirch); REFL.: soil one's self. **-gáto**, ADJ.: soiled (besmirched, dirty).

infan-táre†, TR.: bring forth (give birth to). **-ta**, cf. *-te*. **infán-te** [L. *in-fans*, not speaking], ADJ.: infant (young); M.: infant (babe); infante (younger Spanish prince); foot-soldier†; F. (*-ta*): infanta. **-tería**, F.: infantry (foot-soldiers). **-ticída**, F.: infanticide (killer of infants). **-ticídio**, M.: infanticide. **-tíle**, ADJ.: infantile (childish). **infán-zia**, F.: infancy (childhood); beginning.

infaonáto†, ADJ.: livid (black and blue).

infar-ciménto, M.: stuffing. ‖**-círe** [L.], TR.: stuff (Eng.† infarce).

infardáre†, TR.: daub (besmear); foul; REFL.: paint one's face (fard); marry into; contract familiarity with.

infari-nacchiáto, ADJ.: with a smattering of science. ‖**-náre** [*in*, *farina*], TR.: sprinkle with flour; (*fig.*) whitewash (whiten). **-náto**, ADJ.: powdered; (*fig.*) superficially informed. **-natúra**, F.: act of powdering (whitening); (*fig.*) smattering.

infasti-diáre†, TR.: disgust (tire); INTR.: be disgusted with (nauseate). **-diménto**, M.: disgust; vexation (annoyance). ‖**-díre** [*in*, *fastidio*], TR.: annoy (trouble, vex); importune.

infati-cábile [L. *-gabilis*], ADJ.: indefatigable. **-cabilità**, F.: indefatigability. **-cabilménte**, ADV.: indefatigably. **-gábile**† = *-cabile.*

in=fátti, ADV.: in effect (in short).

infa-tuáre [L.], TR.: infatuate. **-tuazióne**, F.: infatuation.

in-faustaménte, ADV.: unluckily (inauspiciously). ‖**-fáusto** [L. *-faustus* (*favere*, favour)], ADJ.: unlucky (unpropitious, Eng.† infaust).

infe-condaménte, ADV.: unfruitfully (unproductively). **-condità**, F.: infecundity (sterility). ‖**-cóndo** [*in-*, *f.*.], ADJ.: infecund (unfruitful, barren).

infedél-e [*in-*, *f.*.], ADJ.: unfaithful (disloyal); infidel (unbelieving); M.: infidel (sceptic). **-ménte**, ADV.: unfaithfully. **-tà**, F.: infidelity; disloyalty.

infederáre [*in*, *federa*], TR.: put on a pillow-case.

infelí-ce [*in-*, *f.*.], ADJ.: unhappy (wretched, unfortunate). **-ceménte**, ADV.: unhappily (unfortunately). **-cità**, F.: infelicity (misfortune).

infellonire [*in*, *fellone*], INTR.: grow cruel (become barbarous or inhuman).

infeltríre [*in*, *feltro*], INTR.: become like felt.

infemminíre [*in*, *femmina*], TR.: effeminate (enervate); INTR.: become effeminate (womanish).

infèrie [L. *-feriæ* (*-ferus*, beneath)], F. PL.: inferiæ (sacrifices for the dead).

inferígno, ADJ.: of bran and flour: *pane* —, brown bread.

inferió-re [L. *-r*], ADJ.: inferior; subordinate; M.: nether regions (hell). **-rità**, F.: inferiority; subordination. **-rménte**, ADV.: inferiorly.
inferíre [L. *in-ferre*, bring in], TR.: infer (conclude); bring (cause).
infer-máre [*-mo*], INTR., REFL.: become infirm (get sick); TR.: render ill (make sick): weaken; nullify. **-mazióne**, F.: (*leg.*) invalidation. **-mería**, F.: infirmary; epidemic†; infirmity†. **-míccio**, ADJ.: rather infirm (somewhat sick). **-mièra**, F.: nurse. **-mière**, M.: superintendent of a hospital; nurse. **-mità**, F.: infirmity (sickness); (*fig.*) weakness. ||**infér-mo** [L. *-firmus*], ADJ.: infirm (sick, weak); faint-hearted†; unhealthy†; insecure†; M.: sick person; (*lit.*) infirmity (weakness).
infer-nále, ADJ.: infernal (hellish); (*hyperb.*), very sad; M.†: inhabitant of hell: *pietra* —, nitrate of silver (lunar caustic). **-nalità**, F.: (*fig.*) great confusion (disturbance). ||**infèr-no** [L. *-nus* (*infer*, below)], M.: hell (infernal regions); place beneath an oil-press; horrid place; ADJ.: inferior; infernal.
infero-círe [*in, feroce*], INTR.: become ferocious. **-cíto**, ADJ.: ferocious (cruel).
inferraioláre [*in, ferraiolo*], REFL.: wrap one's self up in a cloak.
infer-ráre†, **-riáre**†, TR.: chain (shackle, bind in chains). **-ráta**† = *-riata*. ||**-riáta** [*in-, f..*], F.: iron bars (grating).
infertà† = *infermità*.
infèrti-le†, ADJ.: unfertile (barren). ||**inferti-líre** [*in, fertile*], TR.: fertilize (render fertile).
infervo-raménto, M.: fervor (heat); incitement to fervor. ||**-ráre** [*in, fervore*], TR.: fill with fervor (animate, encourage); REFL.: be animated. **-rataménte**, ADV.: with fervor. **-ráto**, ADJ.: fervent (ardent, zealous). **-ríre** = *-rare*.
inferzáto†, ADJ.: whip-like.
infe-stagióne† = *-stamento*. **-staménte**, ADV.: importunately (annoyingly). **-staménto**, M.: infestation (trouble). **-stáre**, TR.: infest (annoy); importune†. **-statóre**, M., **-statríce**, F.: infester, molester. **-stazióne**, F.: vexation (molestation). **-stévole**, ADJ.: troublesome (annoying). **infè-sto** [L. *-stus* (*fendere*, strike) unsafe], ADJ.: troublesome (annoying, Eng.† infestuous); dangerous; hostile; injurious (corrupting).
infestúto†, M.: (*vet.*) foundering.
-ménto, M.: infection (corrup-
-áre, TR.: infect (spoil, corrupt).
M., **-tatríce**, F.: corrupter
-tor). **-tazióne** = *-tamento*.
.: infective (catching, tainting).

||**infèt-to** [L. *in-fectus*], ADJ.: infected (spoiled, corrupted).
infeu-daménto = *-dazione*. ||**-dáre** [*in, feudo*], TR.: ENFEOFF. **-dazióne**, F.: infeudation (enfeoffment, investiture).
infezióne [*infetto*], F.: infection (contagion).
infiac-chiménto, M.: weakness (faintness). ||**-chíre** [*in, fiacco*], TR.: weaken (enervate); INTR.: become weak.
infiam-mábile, ADJ.: inflammable. **-mabilità**, F.: inflammability. **-magióne**†, F., **-maménto**†, M.: inflammation; heat (flame); fervour. ||**-máre** [*in-, f..*], TR.: INFLAME (burn, light); (*fig.*) excite (stir up, animate); REFL.: become inflamed. **-mataménte**, ADV.: with heat. **-matívo**, ADJ.: inflammatory. **-matóre**, M., **-matríce**, F.: inflamer (inciter). **-matòrio**, ADJ.: inflammatory. **-mazióne**, F.: inflammation.
infiascá-re [*fiasco*], TR.: bottle (put into bottles). **-túra**, F.: bottling (putting into bottles).
infiáto†, ADJ.: swollen (puffed up); proud (haughty).
infi-daménte, ADV.: unfaithfully (treacherously). **-delità**† = *-deltà*. ||**infí-do** [L. *-dus*], ADJ.: unfaithful (treacherous); unbelieving (infidel)†.
infieboliré† = *infievolire*.
infieláre†, TR.: make bitter with gall.
infieríre [*in, fiero*], INTR.: grow cruel (become ferocious).
infievo-liménto, M.: weakening (debilitation). ||**-líre** [*in, fievole*], TR.: weaken (debilitate); REFL.: become weak.
in-fíggere, IRR.; TR.: thrust (drive in).
infígnere† = *infingere*.
infiguràbile†, ADJ.: that cannot be figured, imagined or conceived.
infila-cáppi [*cappio*], **-guaíne** [*guaine*], M.: bodkin (tape-needle). ||**infilá-re** [*in, filo*], TR.: thread (string); pierce; block (a door, etc.); slip on (clothes); REFL.: put on (slip on): — *gli aghi al buio*, be very shrewd; — *i polli, gli uccelli*, put chickens or birds on spits to roast; — *uno*, pierce one (wound one severely); *le chiacchiere non -lano*, idle talk is worth nothing; — *le pentole*, become tired. **-'ta**, F.: file (row). **-túra**, F.: act of threading.
infiltrá-re [*in, f.*], INTR., REFL.: infiltrate. **-zióne**, F.: infiltration.
infil-záre [*in, filza*], TR.: thread (string); arrange in rows; stitch slightly; REFL.†: introduce one's self; intermeddle; fall into a trap; pierce one's self: *le parole non -zano*, words are not deeds. **-záta**, F.: string; file; series. **-zatúra**, F.: threading; piercing (enfilade); row; string (thread).

in-fimaménto, ADV.: abjectly. ||**in-fimo** [L. *-fimus*], ADJ.: lowest (utmost); vilest (basest).

in=fin=a=tanto=chè *-é*, PREP.: until (until that).

in=fin=chè† *-é*, ADV.: until; since; since when?

in=fine, ADV.: in short (finally, in conclusion).

infinochè† = *infinchè*.

infinestrá-re [*in, finestra*], TR.: make (a new margin) to a torn leaf. **-túra**, F.: paper-border.

infingar-dáccio, *disp.* of *-do*. **-dággine**, F.: laziness (idleness). **-damén-te**, ADV.: lazily (slothfully). **-dería**, **-dézza** = *-dia*. **-día**, F.: sloth (laziness); dissimulation (hypocrisy)†. **-díre**, TR.: cause to grow lazy (make lazy); INTR.: become lazy. ||**infingár-do** [*in-, fingere*, make†], ADJ.: lazy (slothful); M.: lazy fellow. **-dóne**, *aug.* of *-do*.

infin-gere [*in, f.* .], IRR.; REFL.: feign (pretend). **-gèvole**†, ADJ.: deceitful (feigning). **-giménto**, M.: dissimulation. **-gitóre**, M.: dissembler (pretender).

infini-tà, F.: infinity. **-taménte**, ADV.: infinitely (exceedingly). **-tesimále**, ADJ.: infinitesimal: *calcolo* —, infinitesimal calculus (fluxions). **-tèsimo**, ADJ., M.: infinitesimal. **-tívo**, M.: infinitive mood. ||**infini-to** [*in-, f.* .], ADJ.: infinite (unlimited, eternal); M.: infinitive mood; infinity.

in=fino, PREP.: as far as; till (until): — *ad ora*, till now; — *allora*, till then; — *a qui*, hitherto; — *a quando?* till when? how long? — *dal principio*, from the beginning: *mi levò* — *alla camicia*, he took away even my shirt.

infinocchiá-re [*in, finocchio*], TR.: spice with fennel; make to believe (impose upon, deceive). **-túra**, F.: deceit (imposition).

infin-taménte, ADV.: deceitfully. **-tivaménte**, ADV.: fictitiously (craftily). ||**infin-to**, PART. of *-gere*; feigned (pretended); M.: pretence. **-túra**†, **-zióne**, F.: dissimulation.

infioccáre [*in, fiocco*], TR.: ornament with bows.

infiochíre [*in, fioco*], INTR.: become hoarse or faint.

infio-ráre [*in, fiore*], TR.: ornament with flowers; (*fig.*) embellish (beautify); REFL.: adorn one's self with flowers. **-razióne**, F.: blossom time. **-ríre**† = *-rare*.

infirm. .† = *inferm*. .

infiscáre†, TR.: confiscate.

infischiáre [*fischio*], REFL.: whistle at (make light of).

infisso†, PART. of *infiggere*; infixed (fastened); wounded (pierced)†.

infistolire [*in, fistola*], INTR., REFL.: turn to a fistula.

infittíre [*in, fitto*], INTR.: become crowded or thick.

infilzáre† = *infilzare*.

infiammatòrio [L. *inflammare*, inflame], ADJ.: inflammatory.

in-flessíbile [*in-, f.* .], ADJ.: inflexible; inexorable. **-flessibilità**, F.: inflexibility. **-flessibilménte**, ADV.: inflexibly.

in-flessióne, F.: inflection (bending); variation. **-flèsso**, PART. of *-flettere*. ||**=flèttere**, IRR.; TR.: inflect (bend, curve); REFL.: bend one's self; become crooked.

in-flíggere [L. *-fligere* (strike)], IRR. (cf. *affliggere*); TR.: inflict upon. **-fliggiménto**, M.: infliction. **-flítto**, PART. of *-fliggere*. **-flizióne**, F.: infliction.

in-fluènte, ADJ.: influential. **-fluènza**, F.: influence (power); influenza; evil eye (omen)†; influx (fluxion)†. **-fluenzáre**, TR.: influence. ||**-fluíre** [L. *-fluere* (*fluere*, run)], TR.: influence (affect, have power over); INTR.†: abound (be plentiful). **-flússo**, M.: influence (virtue, power); influx (fluxion)†; PART.† of *-fluire*.

info-caménto, M.: inflammation; zeal (heat, fervour). ||**-cáre** [*in, foco*], IRR.§; TR.: heat (inflame); make zealous; REFL.: take fire (burn); influence one's self (fall into a passion). **-cataménte**, ADV.: hotly; angrily. **-cazióne**† = *-camento*.

§ Ind.: Pres. *inf(u)ò-co*, *-chi*, etc.: (*u*)*ò* accented, *o* unaccented.

infognáre [*in, fogna*], REFL.: stick in the mire; be involved (be entangled); plunge.

infola = *infula*.

infollíre†, TR.: make mad; INTR.: become mad.

infoltíre [*in, folto*], INTR.: become thick or crowded.

in-fondáto, ADJ.: unfounded.

in=fóndere, IRR.; TR.: INFUSE (instil); pour into; soak (steep)†; enlarge† (dilate); water†; bathe†. **-fondiménto**, M.: infusion (instillation).

inforábile†, ADJ.: impierceable.

infor-cáre [*in, forca*], TR.: catch with a fork; bestride (straddle); hang†. **-cáta**, F.: forkful. **-catúra**, F.: forking; fork (branching).

inforestie-ráre, **-ríre** [*in, forestiero*], TR.: speak like a foreigner; REFL.: become a stranger.

infor-magióne† = *-mazione*. ||**-máre** [*in, forma*], TR.: give form or shape to; inform (instruct); get information from; render suitable (fit, qualify)†; REFL.: inform one's self (get instructed); inquire;

M.†: personification. **-matívo,** ADJ.: informing; informative; M.: inquest; information. **-máto,** ADJ.: informed (acquainted with); strong-limbed (well-formed)†. **-matóre,** M., **-matríce,** F.: informer. **-mazióne,** F.: information; notice; instruction.

infór-me [L. *-mis*], ADJ.: formless (shapeless); ugly (deformed). **-meménte,** ADV.: shapelessly; deformedly.

informicco-laménto, M.: going asleep (of a limb); pricking. **-láre,** ‖**-líre** [*in, f.* .], INTR.: be asleep (of limbs).

informità†, F.: informity (shapelessness).

inforna-ciáre [*in, fornace*], TR.: put into a furnace. **-ciáta,** F.: putting into a furnace; ovenful.

infornapáne†, M.: baker's peel or shovel.

infor-náre [*in, forno*], TR.: put into the oven. **-máta,** F.: putting into the oven; batch (ovenful); batch of officers.

inforsáre†, TR.: put in doubt.

infortíre [*in, forte*], INTR.: become strong; grow sour; TR.: strengthen.

infor-tunáre, INTR.: be unfortunate; get shipwrecked; run the risk. **-tunataménte**†, ADV.: unfortunately. **-tunáto**†, ADJ.: unfortunate (unlucky). **-túnio** [L. *-tunium*], M.: misfortune (disaster, ill luck).

infor-záre [*in, f.* .], INTR.: turn strong (turn sour); TR.†: fortify (strengthen, reinforce). **-záto,** ADJ.: sour (bitter); fortified†; M.†: name of a law-book of Justinian.

info-scaménto†, M.: offuscation. ‖**-scáre** [*in, fosco*], TR.: offuscate (make dark); INTR.: become dark. **-scáto,** ADJ.: offuscated (dark).

infos-saménto, M.: hollow (depression); act of putting in the grave†. ‖**-sáre** [*in, fossa*], TR.: hide in the ground; cover up (grain, to preserve it); REFL.: become hollow (sink in). **-sáto,** ADJ.: hollow (concave).

infra = *fra.*

infra-cidaménto†, M.: putrefaction (corruption). **-cidáre**†, INTR.: putrefy (corrupt): — *uno*, bore one. **-cidatúra,** F.: putrescence. **-cidíre** = *-cidare.* **-diciaménto**† = *-cidamento.* ‖**-diciáre** [*in, fradicio*], TR.: wet (soak; moisten); REFL.: get wet or soaked; putrefy (rot). **-diciáta,** F.: putrefaction.

infragg. . = *infrang.* .

infragrántit†, ADV.: in the act.

infra-liménto, M.: frailness (feebleness). ‖**-líre** [*in, frale*], INTR.: become frail (grow weak or feeble). **-líto,** ADJ.: enfeebled (weakened).

infram-méssa†, F., **-mésso**†, M.: interposition (interference); interval (intermission); (*gram.*) interjection; ADJ.: intermeddled (interposed). **-mettènte**†, ADJ.: interposing. **-mettenteménte**†, ADV.: interruptedly (at intervals). ‖**-(m)méttere**† [*infra, mettere*], IRR.; TR.: interpose (insert); REFL.: meddle with; interfere.

infran-cesáre [*in, francese*, French], **-cescáre, -ciosáre,** TR.: make French (frenchify, gallicize); REFL.: become French (conform to the French mode or idiom).

infrán-gere [*in, f.* .], IRR.; TR.: break (bruise, crush); (*fig.*) transgress (infringe). **-gíbile,** ADJ.: infrangible. **infrán-to,** PART. of *-gere;* ADJ.: bruised (crushed). **-toiáta,** F.: as many olives as can be ground at one time. **-tóio,** M.: oil mill; kind of olive tree; olive. **-túra,** F.: breaking (crushing).

infra=ppórre, TR.: interpose (insert).

infra-scaménto, M.: covering with branches. ‖**-scáre** [*in, frasca*], TR.: cover with branches or bushes; support with bushes; (*fig.*) load with too many ornaments; REFL.: hide in the bushes; digress (be prolix); deceive. **-scatúra** = *-scamento.* **-sconáre,** TR.: cover with boughs or large branches.

infra-scrítto, ADJ.: subscribed; underwritten. ‖**=scrívere,** IRR.; TR.: underwrite (sign); subscribe.

infratíre [*in, frate*], INTR.: not to make a cocoon (be a drone).

infrattánto = *frattanto.*

infrazióne [*-frangere*], F.: infraction (infringement, violation).

infred-dagióne [*in, freddo*], F.: light cold. **-daménto**†, M.: cold. **-dáre,** INTR.: catch cold; TR.†: cool (make cold); REFL.†: come less often. **-datívo**†, ADJ.: that gives cold (cooling). **-datúra,** F.: cold (rheum). **-dolíre,** INTR., REFL.: shiver or tremble with cold.

infrèmere† = *fremere.*

in=frenáre, TR.: bridle; rein in; restrain.

infrene-síre†, ‖**-ticáre** [*in, frenetico*], TR.: render frantic; INTR.: become frantic or mad. **-ticáto,** ADJ.: phrenetic.

infre-quènte [*in-, f.* .], ADJ.: infrequent (rare). **-quènza,** F.: infrequency (rareness).

infre-scaménto†, M.: refreshment (cooling). ‖**-scatóio** [*in, fresco*], M.: cooler; wine-cooler.

infrigi-dáre†, TR.: infrigidate (cool, make cold); INTR., REFL.: become cold. **-diménto,** M.: cooling, refreshing. ‖**-díre** [*in, frigido*], TR.: make cold; REFL.: get cool.

infrignáto†, ADJ.: wrinkled (plaited).

infrollíre [*in*, *frollo*], INTR.: become tender.

infron-dáre†, TR.: cause to become leafy. ||**-díre** [*in*, *f*..], INTR.: become leafy (leaf).

infruscáre [*infoscare*], TR.: mix (mingle, confuse).

infrut-tífero [*in-*, *f*..], ADJ.: unfruitful (barren). **-tuosaménte**, ADV.: fruitlessly (unprofitably). **-tuosità**, F.: unfruitfulness. **-tuóso** = *-tifero*.

ínfula [L.], F.: infula (fillet).

infuná-re [*in*, *fune*], TR.: tie with a rope. **-túra**, F.: binding with a rope.

infundí-bolo†, **-bulo**, M.: funnel.

infunghíre [*in*, *fungo*], INTR.: be covered with must or mould.

infuocáre = *infocare*.

infur-bíre [*in*, *furbo*], INTR.: become shrewd. **-fantíre**†, INTR.: turn rogue (become roguish). **-fantíto**, ADJ.: roguish (cheating).

infu-riènto, ADJ.: furious. ||**-riáre** [*in*, *f*..], INTR., REFL.: rage (be furious, be angry); TR.: enrage (provoke). **-riataménte**, ADV.: furiously (angrily). **-riáto**, ADJ.: infuriated (enraged). **-ríre**† = *-riare*.

infusaménte†, ADV.: confusedly.

infu-seráto†, ADJ.: moistened (infused). **-síbile**†, ADJ.: infusible. **-sióne**, F.: infusion; liquor made by infusion. ||**infúso**, PART. of *infondere*; ADJ.: infused. **-sòrio**, M.: infusory animalcule.

infuturáre†, TR.: cause to live in the future; REFL.: extend into the future (last to futurity).

ingabbanáre [*in*, *gabbano*], REFL.: wrap one's self in an overcoat.

ingab-biáre [*in*, *gabbia*], TR.: cage (shut up, confine). **-biáta**, F.: caging.

ingag-giaménto, M.: engagement (attack). ||**-giáre** [*in*, *gaggio*], TR.: enlist; engage; attack; pawn (pledge)†; REFL.: enlist: — *a usura*, pawn. **-giatóre**, M.: enlister; pawner†. **ingág-gio**, M.: enlistment; enlisting-money.

ingagliar-día [*in-*, *g*..], F.: weakness (lassitude). **-díre** [*in*, *gagliardo*], TR.: invigorate (strengthen, reinforce); INTR., REFL.: grow strong (recover strength).

ingalappiáre†, TR.: trap (ensnare).

ingalluzzíre = *ringalluzzire*.

ingaloppáre†, TR.: (*nav.*) hoist (a mast).

ingambáre†, INTR.: stumble (trip up); run away (take to one's heels).

ingangheráre [*in*, *ganghero*], TR.: put on or fasten with hinges.

ingan-nábile, ADJ.: deceitful. **-nacontadíni**, M.: coarse but pleasing (or showy) work of art; showy artist. **-naménto**†, M.: deceit (fraud). **-nánte**, ADJ.: deceiving (cheating); M.: deceiver (cheat). **-náre**, TR.: deceive (cozen, cheat); REFL.: mistake (be deceived): *se non m' -no*, if I be not mistaken. **-natóre**, M., **-natríce**, F.: deceiver (cozener). **-nerèllo**, *dim.* of *-no*. **-névole**, ADJ.: deceitful (false). **-nevolménte**, ADV.: deceitfully. ||**ingán-no** [OFr. *engain* (ak. to Eng. *game*, 'sport')], M.: deceit (fraud); mistake (blunder); illusion: *a* —, deceitfully; *tirar d'* —, undeceive; *cosa fatta a* —, thing done to hide an evil. **-nóso** = *-nevole*. **-núzzo**†, *dim.* of *-no*.

ingarabu-gliáre, **-lláre** = *ingarbugliare*.

ingarbáre†, TR.: adjust with grace (set off); adapt; (*fig.*) adjust: — *una cosa*, give a thing a graceful form.

ingarbugliáre [*in*, *garbuglio*], TR.: confuse (confound, embroil).

ingarzullíre [*in*, *gazzarra*], TR.: gladden; INTR., REFL.: rejoice (be hilarious).

ingastá-da†, **-ra**†, F.: decanter.

in=gastigáto, ADJ.: unchastised (unpunished).

ingazzullíre = *ingarzullire*.

inge-gnáccio, *disp.* of *-gno*. **-gnaménto**, M.: cunning (craft, sagacity); ingenuity (industry). **-gnáre**, INTR., REFL.: strain one's self (strive, do one's best); TR.: contrive (devise)†. **-gnèra**, F.: female engineer; ingenious woman. **-gnère**, **-gnèro**†, M.: civil engineer. **-gnería**, F.: engineering. **-gnétto**, *dim.* of *-gno*. **-gníno**, *car. dim.* of *-gno*. ||**ingé-gno** [L. *-nium*], M.: natural talent (genius); craftiness (subtility); spring; artificer (operator)†: *a* —, cunningly (slily); *uomo d'* —, witty or ingenious man. **-gnóne**, *iron. aug.* of *-gno*. **-gnosaménte**, ADV.: ingeniously. **-gnosità**, F.: ingeniousness (cunning). **-gnóso**, ADJ.: ingenious; cunning (subtle, crafty): *fuoco* —†, fireworks. **-gnuòlo**, *disp. dim.* of *-gno*.

ingelosíre [*in*, *geloso*], TR.: make jealous; INTR., REFL.: become jealous.

ingem-maménto†, M.: setting or adorning with jewels; mineral crystals. ||**-máre** [*in*, *gemma*], TR.: adorn with gems or jewels; (*agr.*) inoculate (graft); REFL.: adorn one's self.

ingene-rábile†, ADJ.: ingenerable. **-raménto**, M.: generation (production). ||**-ráre** [*in*, *g*..], TR.: engender (beget). **-ratóre**†, M., **-ratríce**, F.: begetter (progenitor, producer). **-razióne**†, F.: generation; kind (sort, species).

in=generóso, ADJ.: ungenerous (illiberal).

ingenio.† = *ingegno*.

in=gènito, ADJ.: ingenite (inborn,

nate); not engendered†: *per* —, by natural instinct, naturally.

ingènte [L. *-gens*], ADJ.: enormous; bulky.

ingentilíre [*in*, *gentile*], TR.: ennoble (make noble); make better; INTR.: become noble or genteel.

inge-nuaménte, ADV.: ingenuously. **-nuità**, F.: ingenuousness (candor). ‖**ingè-nuo** [L. *-nuus*], ADJ.: ingenuous (sincere, candid): free from one's birth.

inge-rènza, F.: act of intermeddling; duty; office; charge. **-riménto†**, M.: intromission (intervention). ‖**-ríre** [L. *-rere* (*gerere*, bear)], TR.: adduce; insinuate (hint)†; REFL.: meddle with (interpose): — *sospetto*, awake suspicion.

inges-sáre [*in*, *gesso*], TR.: daub with plaster or chalk. **-satúra**, F.: chalking (plastering).

ingèsto†, ADJ.: inserted (placed within).

inghermíre† = *ghermire*.

inghiai-áre [*in*, *ghiaia*], TR.: gravel (cover with gravel). **-áto**, M.: gravelled place.

inghiot-timénto, M.: swallowing (absorption); abyss (gulf)†. ‖**-tíre** [*in*, *ghiotto*], IRR.§; TR.: swallow; bury (inter): — *un' ingiuria*, pocket an affront; — *altrui*, have the upper hand of a person. **-titóio**, M.: gullet (throat). **-titóre**, M.: one that swallows (glutton).

§ Ind.: Pres. *inghiottisco* or *inghiótto*, etc.; so also in Pres. Subj. and Ipv.

inghirlan-daménto, M.: crowning with a garland. ‖**-dáre** [*in*, *ghirlanda*], TR.: garland (deck with a garland); (*fig.*) environ; crown.

ingiacoáre†, TR.: put on a cuirass.

ingial-láre† = *-lire*. **-liménto**, M.: act of making yellow. ‖**-líre** [*in*, *giallo*], TR.: make or dye yellow; INTR.: become yellow.

ingiardináre†, TR.: provide with gardens.

ingieláre [*in*, *gielo*], TR.: freeze; INTR.: be frozen.

ingigantíre [*in*, *gigante*], TR.: (*hyperb.*) exaggerate.

inginoc-chiaménto, M.: genuflexion (kneeling). ‖**-chiáre** [*in*, *ginocchio*], REFL.: kneel down; TR.†: make to kneel. **-chiáta†** = *-chiamento*. **-chiatóio**, M.: kneeling-stool. **-chiatúra**, F.: curve ...ng). **-chiazióne†** = *-chiamento*. ...†, **-chióni**, ADV.: upon one's ...eeling).

...udo, ADJ.: unhappy (sorrowful, ...).

...e [*in*, *gioia*], TR.: deck with ...oice (exhilarate)†; REFL.: adorn ...ith jewelry; rejoice (be glad)†. TR.: deck with jewels.

ingiovaníre = *ringiovanire*.

in=giù, ADV.: down; downward; below.

ingiucchíre [*in*, *giucco*], TR., INTR.: become or cause to become silly.

in=giudicáto, ADJ.: unjudged.

ingiúggere† = *ingiungere*.

ingiuncáre [*in*, *giunco*], TR.: fasten or bind with rushes.

in=giúngere, IRR.; TR.: enjoin (command, order); join†. **-giúnto**, PART. of *-giungere*. **-giunzióne**, F.: injunction; junction.

ingiú-ria [L. *injuria* (*jus*, justice)], F.: injury (wrong, offence). **-riánte**, ADJ.: injurious (abusive). **-riáre**, TR.: injure (abuse, offend). **-riatívo**, ADJ.: that can injure. **-riatóre**, M.: injurer; abuser; insulter. **-riosaménte**, ADV.: injuriously; unjustly (outrageously). **-rióso**, ADJ.: injurious (unjust; dishonourable).

ingiu-staménte, ADV.: unjustly (wrongly). **-stificábile**, ADJ.: unjustifiable. **-stízia**, F.: injustice (injury, wrong). ‖**ingiú-sto** [*in-*, *g.*.], ADJ.: unjust (unreasonable, wrong); M.: injustice; unjust person.

inglése, ADJ.: English.

inglo-riosaménte, ADV.: ingloriously. ‖**-rióso** [*in-* *g.*.], ADJ.: inglorious.

in-gluviatóre†, M.: glutton (devourer). ‖**-glúvie†**, F.: gluttony (voraciousness).

ingobbíre [*in*, *gobbo*], INTR.: become humpbacked.

ingof-fáre†, TR.: strike (beat); INTR.: box one's ears (cuff). ‖**-fíre** [*in*, *goffo*], TR.: make awkward, stupid or dull; INTR.: become awkward. **ingòf-fo†**, M.: cuff (blow); bribe.

ingo-iaménto, M.: act of swallowing. ‖**-iáre** [*ingollare*], TR.: swallow voraciously (bolt); ingulf. **-iatóre**, M.: glutton (devourer).

ingol-faménto, M.: ingulfing. ‖**-fáre** [*in*, *golfo*], REFL.: be ingulfed (get deep into, plunge); enter into a gulf. **-fáto**, ADJ.: ingulfed.

ingól-la, F.: pole with a basket on one end for gathering fruit. ‖**-láre** [*in*, *gola*], TR.: swallow without mastication (gobble up).

ingolosíre [*in*, *goloso*], TR.: cause appetite or desire for (make the mouth water for).

ingom-beráre† = *-brare*. **-braménto†**, M.: incumbrance (hindrance). **-bráre**, TR.: incumber (hinder); occupy†; confiscate†. ‖**ingóm-bro** [l. L. *in-combrum* (*cumulus*, heap)], M.: incumbrance (hindrance, impediment); nuisance; ADJ.: incumbered.

ingommáre [*in*, *gomma*], TR.: gum.

ingonnelláto†, ADJ.: dressed in a gown.

ingorbiá-re†, TR.: put (a ferule) on a cane. **-túra†**, F.: putting on a ferule; hollow of a ferule (iron ring).

ingor-dággine = *-digia*. **-daménte**, ADV.: greedily (gluttonously). **-dézza†** = *-digia*; (*fig.*) excess (superfluity). **-dígia**, F.: insatiableness (greediness). **-díma**, F.: file; rasp. ||**ingór-do** [?], ADJ.: greedy (eager; covetous); exorbitant; M.: covetousness.

ingor-gaménto, M.: engorging (stoppage). ||**-gáre** [*in*, *gorgo*], REFL.: be choked up (engorged); TR.†: put in the throat. **-giaménto†**, M.: swallowing down. **-giáre†**, TR.: put in the throat (gorge; swallow down); pronounce in the throat. **ingór-go** = *-giamento*.

in-governábile, ADJ.: ungovernable.

ingoz-záre [*in*, *gozzo*], TR.: swallow (gorge, cram; put up with, endure; *fig.*: swallow an affront); force in, beat in; seize (appropriate to one's self)†. **-záta**, **-zatúra**, F.: forcing or beating in.

ingracilíre [*in*, *gracile*], INTR.: become slender or thin; TR.: make slender.

ingradáre†, INTR.: go on gradually (proceed by degrees); arrive; ascend.

ingramignáre†, INTR.: spread like weeds.

ingra-nággio [Fr. *engrenage*], M.: gear catching (wheels catching one another; sprocket). ||**-náre** [Fr. *engrener*], INTR.: (*mech.*) catch; tooth; indent; TR.†: reduce to grains.

ingranchíre = *aggranchire*.

ingran-diménto, M.: aggrandizement (enlargement); rise (growth); improvement (progress). ||**-díre** [*in*, *grande*], TR.: aggrandize (enlarge, increase); magnify; exaggerate; ameliorate†; REFL.: grow greater (increase); rise; INTR.: become large. **-ditóre**, M.: magnifier (enlarger, increaser).

ingras-sabúe, M.: kind of herb. **-saménto**, M.: fattening (cramming, stuffing); fatness. ||**-sáre** [L. *incrassare* (*crassus*, fat)], TR.: fatten (make fat); manure; INTR.: become fat (get fat); (*fig.*) grow rich: *il piè del padrone -ssa il campo*, vigilance is prosperity; — *in checchessia*, take pleasure in. **-satívo**, ADJ.: fattening. **-satóre**, M.: fattener. **ingrás-so**, M.: manure (dung). **-socchiáre**, INTR.: fatten slowly.

ingra-táccio, *disp.* of *-to*. **-taménte**, ADV.: ungratefully. **-tézza†** = *-titudine*.

ingraticciá-re [*in*, *graticcio*], TR.: enclose with lattice or hurdles. **-túra**, F.: enclosing with lattice-work.

ingraticola-ménto, M.: railing; grate; enclosure. ||**-láre** [*in*, *graticola*], TR.: enclose with a grate (rail, shut in with a railing). **-láta**, F., **-láto**, M.: grating (railing).

ingra-tífero, ADJ.: ungrateful. **-titúdine**, F.: ingratitude. ||**ingrá-to** [L. *-tus*], ADJ.: ungrateful (unthankful); unprofitable; displeasing (disagreeable); M.: ingrate (ungrateful person). **-tóne**, *aug.* of *-to*.

ingravi-daménto, M.: ingravidation; conceiving. ||**-dáre** [*in*, *gravido*], TR.: ingravidate (impregnate); INTR.: be pregnant. **-dáto**, ADJ.: pregnant.

ingra-ziáre [*in*, *grazia*], REFL.: ingratiate one's self. **-ziáto**, ADJ.: ingratiated in favour. **-zioníre**, REFL.: *intens.* of *-ziare*.

ingrecáre†, INTR.: grow very angry (get furious).

ingrediènte [L. *-diens*], M.: ingredient.

ingremíre† = *ghermire*.

ingrèsso [L. *-ssus*], M.: ingress (entrance); ADJ.†: rough; cruel.

ingriffáto†, ADJ.: snatched (seized); tormented (afflicted).

ingrillandáre = *inghirlandare*.

ingro-gnáre†, INTR.: fume (be angry, fret). **-gnáto**, ADJ.: angered (gruff, surly).

ingrommáre†, REFL.: form tartar (get incrusted); concrete.

ingroppáre†, TR.: group (form in groups, tie in knots); attach (unite); suggest immediately; carry on the crupper; INTR.: ride astraddle (be astride); speak swiftly.

ingros-saménto, M.: swelling; increase. ||**-sáre** [*in*, *grosso*], TR.: swell (make big, increase); impregnate†; INTR.: engross (become big, swell); conceive (become impregnated); grow obstinate: — *la coscienza*, become ever less scrupulous; — *la memoria*, render the memory slow at retaining; — *la voce*, make the voice rough or hoarse; — *il cervello*, become stupid; — *l' udito*, become a little deaf. **-satívo**, ADJ.: apt to swell or enlarge. **-satúra** = *-samento*. **ingròs-so** (*all'*), ADV.: in great quantity (by wholesale); in general (generally); plentifully (abundantly)†.

ingru-gnáre, **-gníre** [*in*, *grugno*], INTR.: pout; look gruff; be angry. **-gnatèllo**, ADJ.: somewhat angry. **-gnáto**, ADJ.: sullen; pouting; angry.

ingrullíre [*in*, *grullo*], INTR.: become a simpleton.

inguainàre [*in*, *guaina*], TR.: sheathe (put into the sheath).

ingualdrappáre [*in*, *gualdrappa*], TR.: put in a horsecloth; caparison.

inguan-táre [*in*, *guanto*], REFL.: put on one's gloves. **-tàto**, ADJ.: with one gloves on; enclosed (enveloped).

in=guaribile, ADJ.: incurable (irremediable).

ingubbiáre†, TR.: gorge; swallow; stuff.

inguiderdonáto†, ADJ.: without a guerdon (unrequited).

inguiggiáre†, TR.: fit on (a pair of shoes or slippers).

ingui-náia = *-ne*. **-nále**, ADJ.: inguinal (belonging to the groin). ‖**ínguine** [L. *inguen*], M.: groin.

inguistára†, F.: phial; decanter; glass-bottle.

ingurgi-taménto†, M.: ingurgitation (gorging). ‖**-táre**†, INTR.: ingurgitate (cram, stuff).

ingustábile, ADJ.: ingustable (not tastable).

ini-bíre [L. *inhibere* (*habere*, hold) keep back], TR.: inhibit (forbid, prohibit). **-bíta**† = *-bizione*. **-bitòria**, F.: decree that inhibits. **-bitòrio**, pl. *-ri*, ADJ.: inhibitory (prohibitory). **-bizióne**, F.: inhibition (prohibition).

in-iettáre [L. *jectare*], TR.: inject. **-iettáto**, ADJ.: injected. **-iezióne**, F.: injection.

inimi-cáre, TR.: treat as an enemy: REFL.: make a person one's enemy (become an enemy). **-chévole**†, ADJ.: inimical (hostile); contrary. **-chevolménte**†, ADV.: like an enemy. **-cízia**, F.: enmity (hostility); aversion. ‖**inimí-co** [L. *-cus* (*in-*, *amicus*, friend)], ADJ.: (*poet.*) inimical (hostile); adverse; M.: enemy.

inimitábi-le [*in-*, *i.* .], ADJ.: inimitable. **-lménte**, ADV.: inimitably. **-lità**, F.: inimitability.

in=immaginábile, ADJ.: unimaginable.

inintelli-gènte [*in-*, *i.* .], ADJ.: unintelligent. **-gènza**, F.: unintelligence. **-gíbile**, ADJ.: unintelligible. **-gibilità**, F.: unintelligibility.

in=investigábile, ADJ.: uninvestigable.

ini-quaménte, ADV.: iniquitously (unjustly). **-quità**, F.: iniquity (injustice); inequality (of land†). **-quitánza**† = *-quità*. **-quitíre**†, INTR.: become iniquitous or wicked. **-quitóso**, ADJ.: iniquitous or wicked. **-quízia**†, F.: iniquity (crime). ‖**iní-quo** [L. *-quus* (*in-*, *aequus*, equal)], ADJ.: iniquitous (unjust, wicked); grave (sad); very bad (of wine, etc.).

intúria† = *ingiuria*.

iniustízia† = *ingiustizia*.

ini-ziále ADJ., M.: initial. **-ziaménto**, M.: initiation. **-ziáre**, TR.: initiate (begin, originate): — *in una lingua, scienza*, … into, or teach the first rudi… a language or science. **-ziáto**, … initiated. **-ziatíva**, F.: initia… **-tívo**, ADJ.: initiative (apt to … **-ziatóre**, M., **-ziatríce**, F.: initiator (beginner). **-zióne**, F.: initiation (the ceremony). ‖**iní-zio** [L. *-tium*], M.: beginning (commencement, first principles): *dar* —, initiate (originate).

inizza. .† = *aizza*. .

in=l. .† = *ill*. .

in=m. .† = *imm*. .

innabissáre† = *inabissare*.

innacerbíre† = *inacerbire*.

innacqua. . = *annacqua*. .

innaffia. . = *annaffia*. .

innagrestíre† = *inagrestire*.

innalbáre = *inalbare*.

innalberáre = *inalberare*.

innalza. . = *inalza*. .

innamicáre†, REFL.: make one's self a friend (become friends).

innamidáre†, TR.: starch.

innamo-racchiaménto, M.: little love affair. **-racchiáre**, REFL.: be slightly in love. **-raménto**, M.: falling in love; love; love affair. **-ramentúzzo**†, *dim.* of *-ramento*. **-ránte**, ADJ.: lovely. ‖**-ráre** [*in*, *amore*], TR.: inflame with love (enamour, captivate); REFL.: become enamoured; fall in love. **-ráta**, F.: sweetheart (flame; mistress). **-rataménte**, ADV.: lovingly (tenderly). **-ratèllo**, *car.* of *-rato*. **-ratíno**, *dim.* of *-rato*. **-ratívo**, ADJ.: charming (lovely). **-ráto**, PART.: enamoured (in love, amourous); M.: inamorato (sweetheart). **-razzáre**†, REFL.: become slightly enamoured.

innanel-laménto†, M.: curling; curl. ‖**-láre**†, TR.: curl (frizzle); give (the ring) in marriage.

innani-máre†, TR.: animate (encourage); REFL.: take courage. **-máto**†, ADJ.: animated; angry (mad); inanimate (lifeless). **-míre**† = *-mare*.

innán-te†, **-ti**† = *-zi*. **-ti che**† *-é*, CONJ.: before that; ADV.: rather than. ‖**innán-zi** [*in*, *ante*], PREP.: before; in presence of; in preference to; above; without; ADV.: sooner (rather); better; before (forward); after; afterwards; hereafter; M.: exemplar (copy, pattern): — *tratto*, first of all, beforehand; *venire* —, present one's self before; *esser* —, be before; be a favourite; *andare* — *ad uno*, go to meet one; *andare* —, thrive (grow, prosper); *esser molto* or *poco* —, have much or little progressed; *metter* —, propose (lay before); *tirarsi* — *per avvocato*, study to become a lawyer; *più* —, farther, more; — —†, first of all, above all; — *a te*†, in your judgment; *gl'* — *a uno*†, the predecessors of one.

innaridíre† = *inaridire*.

innário†, M.: HYMN-book.

innarpicáre†, TR.: climb.

innarrábile† = *inenarrabile*.

innarráre†, TR.: narrate (relate); give earnest; bespeak.
innarsicciáto†, M.: burn (burning); ADJ.: burnt (parched); tanned (sunburnt).
innascóndere† = *nascondere*.
innaspáre†, TR.: reel or wind (yarn, etc.); (*fig.*) hesitate; get confused; be puzzled.
innas-priménto†, M.: exasperation (irritation). ‖**-príre**†, TR.: exasperate (irritate); make rough or hard; INTR.: grow rough.
innáto [L. *-tus* (*natus*, born)], ADJ.: innate (natural, inborn).
in=naturále, ADJ.: unnatural.
in=navigábile, ADJ.: innavigable.
innebbiáre†, REFL.: become cloudy; grow dark.
innebriáre† = *inebbriare*.
in=negábile, ADJ.: undeniable.
inneggiáre [*inno*], INTR.: sing hymns; praise.
innequízia†, F.: iniquity (wickedness).
innerpicáre†, INTR.: climb up.
inne-stábile, ADJ.: that can be grafted or inoculated. **-stagióne**, F., **-staménto**, M.: grafting; graft. **-stáre**, TR.: graft (inoculate); attach (join). **-statóio**, M.: grafting knife. **-statóre**, M.: grafter (inoculator). **-statúra**, F.: grafting (inoculation); graft; junction. ‖**innè-sto** [L. *in-situs* (*serere*, bind)], M.: grafting; graft (junction); ADJ.: grafted (inoculated).
inno [L. *hymnus*], M.: hymn: — *ambrosiano*, Te Deum.
innobbediènza† = *disobbedienza*.
innobiltà†, F.: ignobility.
inno-cènte [L. *-cens*], ADJ.: innocent (pure); harmless; ignorant (simple)†; M.: innocent person; harmless animal: *gl' -centi*, innocents (hospital or home for the illegitimate). **-centeménte**, ADV.: innocently. **-centíno**, *iron. dim.* of *-cente*; M. PL.: illegitimate children. **-cènza**, **-cènzia**†, F.: innocence (purity); harmlessness†; simplicity†. **-cuaménte**, ADV.: innocuously. **-cuità**, F.: innocuousness (harmlessness). **innòcuo**, ADJ.: innocuous (harmless).
innodiáre† = *inodiare*.
innoliáre† = *inoliare*.
innoltráre† = *inoltrare*.
innomi-nábile [*in-*, *n.* .], ADJ.: that cannot be named. **-náre**†, TR.: nominate (name, call). **-nataménte**, ADV.: namelessly (anonymously). **-náto**, ADJ.: unnamed; anonymous.
innondáre† = *inondare*.
inno-ránza†, F.: honour. **-ráre**†, TR.: 1. gild (gild over); 2. honour.
innòxio†, ADJ.: innoxious (harmless).
innostráre†, TR.: ornament with purple; (*fig.*) adorn.

innottusíre†, INTR.: become obtuse or blunt.
inno-váre [*in*, *novo*], TR.: innovate (renew, change); REFL.: become like new (have a new look). **-vatóre**, M., **-vatríce**, F.: innovator. **-vazióne**, F.: innovation. **-velláre**†, TR.: renew.
innubbidiènza† = *disobbedienza*.
innume-rábile [*in-*, *n.* .], ADJ.: innumerable (infinite). **-rabilménte**, ADV.: innumerably. **-ráre**†, TR.: enumerate (number, count); describe; make (a census). **-révole** = *-rabile*. **-revolménte** = *-rabilmente*.
innuováre = *innovare*.
innuzzolíre†, TR.: excite a wish or desire for; solicit.
inobbedien. . = *disobbedien. .*
inocchiáre [*in*, *occhio*], TR.: graft in the bud; inoculate.
in=occupáto, ADJ.: unoccupied.
inocu-lábile, ADJ.: that can be grafted or inoculated. ‖**-láre** [L.], TR.: inoculate. **-láto**, ADJ., M.: inoculated. **-lazióne**, F.: inoculation.
inodiáre†, TR.: hate.
ino-dorábile†, ‖**-dòro** [L. *-dorus*], ADJ.: inodorous (scentless).
inof-fensíbile [*in-*, *o.* .], ADJ.: unassailable (invulnerable); inoffensive. **-féso**, ADJ.: inoffensive (uninjured).
in=officióso, ADJ.: inofficious (discourteous, uncivil).
inoliáre [*in*, *olio*], TR.: anoint with oil.
in-oltráre, TR.: send before; present; REFL.: advance forward (go beyond). ‖**=óltre**, ADV.: beyond; besides (moreover).
inombráre†, TR.: shade (shadow).
inon-daménto† = *-dazione*. ‖**-dáre** [L. *inundare*], TR.: inundate (overflow); (*fig.*) overrun; irrigate†. **-datóre**, M., **-datríce**, F.: one who inundates. **-dazióne**, F.: inundation (submersion); invasion.
ino-nestà†, F.: dishonesty; unchasteness. **-nestaménte**, ADV.: dishonestly; indecently. ‖**-nèsto** [*in-*, *o.* .], ADJ.: dishonest; unchaste (indecent).
in=onoráto, ADJ.: unhonoured.
inópe†, ADJ.: poor (indigent).
inoperánte†, ADJ.: inoperative.
inope-rosaménte, ADV.: idly. **-rosità**, F.: idleness. ‖**-róso** [*in-*, *o.* .], ADJ.: idle (not working).
inòpia [L.], F.: want (poverty, indigence).
inopi-nábile [*in-*, *o.* .], ADJ.: unimaginable. **-nataménte**, ADV.: unexpectedly (suddenly). **-náto**, ADJ.: inopinate (sudden).
inoppor-tunaménto, ADV.: inopportunely. **-tunità**, F.: unseasonablen

‖**-túno** [*in-*, *o.* .], ADJ.: inopportune (unseasonable).
im=oppugnábile, ADJ.: unassailable.
inoráre†, TR.: 1. honour (adore, worship); 2. gild.
inordi-nataménte, ADV.: confusedly. **-natézza**, F.: irregularity (disorder, confusion). ‖**-nàto** [*in-*, *o.* .], ADJ.: inordinate (out of order, irregular).
inor-ganicaménte, ADV.: inorganically. ‖**-gánico** [*in-*, *o.* .], ADJ.: inorganic.
inorgo-gliáre†, ‖**-glire** [*in*, *orgoglio*], TR.: make proud; INTR., REFL.: become proud.
inor-nataménte, ADV.: inelegantly. ‖**-náto** [*in-*, *o.* .], ADJ.: unadorned (inelegant).
inorpel-laménto, M.: tinselling; disguise. ‖**-láre** [*in-*, *o.* .], TR.: tinsel; counterfeit (disguise). **-latúra**, F.: covering with tinsel.
inorridíre [*in*, *orrido*], TR.: horrify; make frightful; frighten; INTR.: be afraid (shiver with fear).
inospi-tále [*in-*, *o.* .], ADJ.: inhospitable; barbarous. **-talità**, F.: inhospitality. **inòspi-te**, ADJ.: rude; barbarous; solitary (uninhabited).
inosser-vábile [*in-*, *o.* .], ADJ.: unobservable (undistinguishable). **-vabilità**, F.: unobservability. **-vabilménte**, ADV.: without being observed. **-vánte**, ADJ.: unobservant (inattentive). **-vánza**, F.: inattention, neglect; violation. **-váto**, ADJ.: unobserved; concealed.
inossíre†, INTR.: ossify.
inqueríre†, TR.: INQUIRE (examine); impeach.
inquie-taménte, ADV.: unquietly (impatiently). **-táre** [L.], TR.: disquiet (perplex, trouble); REFL.: be vexed or angry (be uneasy); torment one's self. **-táto**, ADJ.: angry; disturbed. **-tatóre**, M.: disquieter (troubler). **-tazióne**†, F.: troubling (vexing). **-tézza**, F.: uneasiness; perplexity. **-tíno**, *dim.* of *-to*. **inquiè-to** [L. *-tus*], ADJ.: unquiet (restless, uneasy); troublesome. **-túccio**, *disp. dim.* of *-to*. **-túdine**, F.: inquietude (trouble).
inquilíno [L. *-nus* (*in-colere*, inhabit)], M.: tenant; lodger; inmate; inhabitant.
inqui-naménto, M.: defilement (soiling). ‖**-náre** [L.], TR.: defile (soil, stain); disgrace.
inqui-rènte [L. *-rens* (*quærere*, seek)], ADJ.: inquiring; seeking. **-ṣíre**, TR.: prosecute criminally (impeach, accuse); [..]t out (seek out). **-ṣitívo**, ADJ.: inquisitive. **-ṣitòre**, M., **-ṣitrice**, F.: in[..]; inquisitor; coroner: *faccia da —*, [..]us, savage face. **-ṣitoriále**, ADJ.: inquisitorial. **-ṣitòrio**, pl. *—ri*, ADJ.: inquisitory. **-ṣizióne**, F.: inquisition (examination; inquiry); search†; accusation†.
im=r. .† = *irr.* .
inrossáre [*in*, *rosso*], TR.: make red (redden).
inrugginíre†, INTR.: rust (grow rusty).
inrugiadáre†, TR.: bedew (cover with dew); sprinkle (water).
inruvidíre [*in*, *ruvido*], TR.: render rigid or hard; irritate (make angry).
insac-caménto, M.: act of putting in the sack. ‖**-cáre** [*in*, *sacco*], TR.: put in the sack (sack up); lay up in a purse (pocket money); put in skins; eat with avidity; shut up closely; REFL.: lock one's self up in a place. **-cáto**, PART. of *-care*: *carne -cata*, sausage, etc.; *pare —*, be clothed awkwardly. **-catúra** = *-camento*.
insafardáre [*in*, *gifardare* (OHG. *gifarwit*, tint)], TR.: soil with grease (spot).
insalamáre [*in*, *salame*], TR.: (*jest.*) wrap up like salame or bologna sausage.
insa-láre† [*in*, *s.* .], TR.: salt (corn); REFL.: grow brinish; become salty or pickled. **-láta**, F.: salad. **-latáia**, F., **-latáio**, M.: salad-seller. **-latièra**, F.: salad-bowl. **-latína**, *car. dim.* of *-lata*. **-láto**, ADJ.: salted (seasoned). **-latóna**, *aug.* of *-lata*. **-latúccia**, *disp.* of *-lata*. **-latúra**, F.: salting (pickling); season for salting; salt.
insal-dábile [*in-*, *s.* .], ADJ.: that cannot be starched or soldered. ‖**-dáre** [*in-*, *s.* .], TR.: starch; solder†; strengthen†; consolidate†; heal up†. **-datóra**, F.: starcher. **-datúra**, F.: starching; soldering; starched part of a shirt (bosom).
insaleggiáre†, TR.: salt slightly.
insalsáre†, REFL.: become salt (grow brinish).
insalvábile†, ADJ.: that cannot be saved.
insalvaticáre† = *insalvatichire*.
insalú-bre [*in-*, *s.* .], ADJ.: insalubrious (unhealthy). **-brità**, F.: insalubrity (unhealthiness).
in=salutáto, ADJ.: not saluted.
insalvati. . = *inselvati.* .
insaná-bile [*in-*, *s.* .], ADJ.: insanable (incurable). **-bilménte**, ADV.: insanably. **-ménte**, ADV.: insanely (foolishly).
insangui-naménto, M.: shedding or spilling of blood. ‖**-náre** [*in*, *s.* .], TR.: ensanguine (make bloody, stain with blood).
in-sánia [L.], F.: insanity (madness). **-saníre**, INTR.: become insane. ‖**-sáno** [L. *-sanus*], ADJ.: insane (mad).
insapiènza†, F.: ignorance.

insapo-naménto, M.: act of washing with soap. ‖**-náre** [*in, sapone*], TR.: soap (wash with soap); (*vulg.*) flatter. **-natúra** = *-namento*.
insaporáre†, TR.: give or impart a flavour to; REFL.: become tasty.
insapúta [*in, saputo*], ADV.: *all'* —, without one's knowledge.
insassáre†, TR.: cause to petrify; REFL.: become stone; (*fig.*) remain as if senseless.
in=satolláblle, ADJ.: insatiable.
in=saturábile, ADJ.: insaturable.
insa-ziábile [*in-, s.*.], ADJ.: insatiable. **-ziabilità**, F.: insatiableness. **-ziabilménte**, ADV.: insatiably. **-zietà**† = *-ziabilità*.
inscampábile†, ADJ.: inevitable (unavoidable).
inschiavíre†, TR.: enslave (make a slave of).
inschidionáre†, TR.: put upon the spit.
inscièn-te [*in-, s.*.], ADJ.: without knowledge, ignorant; unconscious. **-teménte**, ADV.: ignorantly. **insciènza**, F.: ignorance (inexperience); unconsciousness.
in-scrítto, PART.: inscribed. ‖**=scrívere**, IRR.; TR.: inscribe; dedicate; register. **-scrivíbile**, ADJ.: that cannot be inscribed. **-scrizióne**, F.: inscription; superscription; direction (address); title.
inscru-tábile [*in-, s.*.], ADJ.: inscrutable; impenetrable. **-tabilità**, F.: inscrutability; impenetrability.
insculto†, PART. of *insculpere*; sculptured; engraved.
in=scusábile, ADJ.: inexcusable.
insecchíre [*in, secco*], INTR.: become dry.
insediáre [*in, sedia*], TR.: put in the possession of (install).
insegáre [*in, sego*], TR.: grease with tallow.
insé-gna [L. *insigne*], F.: SIGN (token, mark); ENSIGN (standard); insignia; PL.: arms; countersign (signal)†; ensign-bearer (standard-bearer)†. **-gnábile**, ADJ.: teachable. **-gnaménto**, M.: admonition; teaching (instruction). **-gnánte**, PART.: teaching, etc.; M.: master. **-gnáre**, TR.: teach (instruct); show (indicate, point out). **-gnatívo**, ADJ.: instructive (informing). **-gnatóre**, M., **-gnatríce**, F.: instructor (teacher). **-gnévole**, ADJ.: docile (tractable, teachable).
inse-guiménto, M.: pursuit. ‖**-guíre** [*in, s.*.], TR.: pursue (run after). **-guènte**, ADJ.: pursuing.
inselicíáto†, M.: pavement (paving).
in=selláre, TR.: saddle (put on the saddle).
insel-váre [*in, selva*], REFL.: take refuge in a wood (fly to the woods); grow woody†. **-vaticáre**, **-vatichíre** [*selvatico*], INTR.: become SAVAGE (or wild); grow rude; TR.: make savage or brutish, brutify.
insembr-a, **-e** = *insieme*.
in=semináto, ADJ.: unsown.
insemitáre†, REFL.: enter on the road (begin one's journey).
insempráre†, REFL.: eternize one's self (make one's self immortal).
inseñá-re†, TR.: put in one's bosom; (*fig.*) recollect. ‖**-túra** [*in, seno*], F.: small bay or gulf; curving of a river.
insen-satággine = *-satezza*. **-sataménte**, ADV.: insensately (foolishly). **-satézza**, F.: folly (stupidity, madness). ‖**-sáto** [*in-, s.*.], ADJ.: insensate (foolish).
insensíbi-le [*in-, s.*.], ADJ.: insensible; imperceptible. **-lità**, F.: insensibility. **-lménte**, ADV.: insensibly; gradually.
insepa-rábile [*in-, s.*.], ADJ.: inseparable. **-rabilménte**, ADV.: inseparably. **-ráto**, ADJ.: separated (joined).
insepól-to [*in-, s.*.], ADJ.: unburied. **-túra**†, F.: privation of burial.
in=sequestrábile, ADJ.: that cannot be sequestrated.
inserenáre†, TR.: clear up; INTR.: grow serene or clear; rejoice.
inse-riménto, M.: insertion ‖**-ríre** [L. *-rere*], TR.: INSERT (put in, add); ingraft†.
inserpentíto†, PART.: envenomed.
inserráre†, TR.: shut up (lock up); enclose (contain).
insèrto, PART. of *inserire*; M.: brief (Fr. *dossier*); evidence (proof); graft†.
inser-víbile [*in-, s.*.], ADJ.: unserviceable (useless). ‖**-viènte** [L. *servire*, serve], M.: servant; ADJ.†: serviceable (useful). **-vigiáto**†, ADJ.: officious; kind; obliging.
inserzióne [*inserire*], F.: insertion.
inse-táre†, TR.: 1. cover with silk; 2. ingraft. **-tatúra**†, F.: grafting of vines, etc. **-tazióne**†, F.: ingraftment.
inset-ticída, pl. —*di*, ADJ.: insect-killing. **-tívoro**, ADJ.: insectivorous. ‖**insèt-to** [L. *insectum* (*-secare*, cut)], M.: insect; (*fig.*) worthless fellow. **-tología**, F.: entomology. **-tològico**, ADJ.: entomological. **-tòlogo**, M.: entomologist.
inseveríto†, ADJ.: grown severe.
insí-dia [L. *-diæ* (*in-sidere*, set in)], F.: ambush (deceit, snare, plot). **-diáre**, TR.: lay snares for (machinate, plot). **-diatóre**, M., **-diatríce**, F.: insidiator (plotter). **-diosaménte**, ADV.: insidiously. **-dióso**, ADJ.: insidious (treacherous).

insième [L. *in*, *simul*, together], ADV.: together; in company; at the same time; one with another (with each other); all together; equally†; M.: whole (entirety): — —, jointly (closely together); *a poco* —, little at a time. **-ménte†**, ADV.: together; likewise; at the same time; in company with.

insiepáre†, REFL.: hide one's self in a bush or hedge.

insígne [L. *insignis*], ADJ.: eminent (distinguished); famous.

in=significánte, ADJ.: insignificant.

insignire [L. (*signis*, mark)], TR.: honour (with titles, decorations, etc.; decorate; signalize); endow.

insignoríre [*in*, *signore*], INTR., REFL.: become a master; make one's self a master.

insino. . =*fino*. .

insinquà†, ADV.: so far; as far as here.

insi-nuábile, ADJ.: able to insinuate. **-nuabilità**, F.: susceptibility of being insinuated. **-nuánte**, ADJ.: insinuating. ‖**-nuáre** [L. *-nuare* (*sinus*, bosom), thrust into], TR.: introduce little by little; insinuate; suggest; REFL.: insinuate one's self. **-nuazióne**, F.: insinuation; creeping in; suggestion.

insipi-daménte, ADV.: insipidly. **-dézza**, F.: insipidity. **-dire†**, INTR.: become insipid. ‖**insípi-do** [L. *-dus* (*in*, not, *sapidus*, tasteful)], ADJ.: insipid (unsavoury; tedious).

insi-piènte [L. *-piens* (*in*, not, *sapiens*, knowing)], ADJ.: insipient (unwise, stupid). **-pienteménte**, ADV.: foolishly. **-piènza**, **-piènzia**, F.: insipience (folly).

insipilláre† = *insipillare*.

insis-tènza, F.: insistence; perseverance. ‖**insís-tere** [L. (*stare*, stand)], IRR. (cf. *assistere*); INTR.: insist (stand much upon); be above†. **-títo**, PART.: insisted, etc.

insíto, **insito** [L. *-tus* (*serere*, sow), implanted], ADJ.: innate (natural, inborn).

insmorzábile†, ADJ.: inextinguishable.

insoá-ve [*in-*, *s.* .], ADJ.: unpleasant (disagreeable). **-vità**, F.: insuavity.

insoccórso†, ADJ.: unhelped (unassisted).

inso-ciábile [*in-*, *s.* .], ADJ.: unsociable. **-ciabilità**, F.: unsociableness. **-ciabilménte**, ADV.: unsociably. **-ciále** [*in-*, *s.* .], ADJ.: unsocial.

in=soddisfátto, ADJ.: unsatisfied.

insof-ferènza [*in-*, *s.* .], F.: intolerance. **-fríbile**, ADJ.: intolerable. **-fribilità**, F.: intolerability. **-fribilménte**, ADV.: insufferably (intolerably).

insofficien. . = *insufficien*. .

. . **-spottábile†**, ADJ.: unconquerable.

. . **-gnáre†**, REFL.: dream; imagine false-

. . **-ógno†**, M.: dream (fancy, chimera).

. . **-zióne** [*in*, *sole*], F.: sunstroke.

insolcáre†, TR.: furrow (plough).

inso-lentáccio, *disp. aug.* of *-lente*. ‖**-lènte** [L. *-lens* (*in*, not, *solens*, accustomed)], ADJ.: insolent (impertinent, arrogant); unaccustomed (unusual)†. **-lenteménte**, ADV.: insolently (arrogantly). **-lentíre**, INTR.: become insolent or haughty; TR.: illtreat (abuse). **-lentóne**, *aug.* of *-lente*. **-lènza**, **-lènzia†**, F.: insolence (impudence, haughtiness).

in-solfáre [*in*, *zolfo*], TR.: daub with sulphur.

in-solitaménte, ADV.: unusually (rarely). ‖**-sòlito** [*in-*, *s.* .], ADJ.: unaccustomed (rare).

insol-láre†, ‖**-líre** [*in*, *sollo*], TR.: make soft; ruin†; INTR.: become flabby or soft; rise up† (revolt).

inso-lúbile [*in-*, *s.* .], ADJ.: insoluble (indissoluble). **-lubilménte**, ADV.: indissolubly. **-lubilità**, F.: insolubility. **-lúto**, ADJ.: not free (unsolved).

insol-vènte [*in-*, *s.* .], ADJ.: insolvent. **-vènza**, F.: insolvency.

in=sómma, ADV.: in fine (in short); finally; after all.

in=sommergíbile, ADJ.: that cannot be submerged.

in-sonnáre†, TR.: induce sleep upon (lull to sleep). ‖**-sònne** [L. *somnis* (*in-*, *somnus*, sleep)], ADJ.: sleepless (unsleeping). **-sònnia**, F.: insomnia (sleeplessness).

insònte†, ADJ.: innocent (innocuous).

insopportábi-le [*in-*, *s.* .], ADJ.: insupportable. **-lménte**, ADV.: insupportably.

insordíre [*in*, *sordo*], INTR.: become deaf.

insór-gere [*in-*, *s.* .], IRR.; INTR.: rise up (revolt). **-giménto**, M.: insurrection (rebellion).

insormontábile, ADJ.: insurmountable.

in=sorto, PART. of *insorgere*; risen up.

insospettíre [*in*, *sospetto*], TR.: cause to be suspected (make suspicious); INTR.: grow suspicious.

in=sostenibile, ADJ.: unsustainable.

insoz-záre [*in*, *sozzo*], **-zíre†**, TR., INTR.: soil (foul, pollute).

inspe-rábile [*in-*, *s.* .], ADJ.: not to be hoped for. **-rataménte**, ADV.: unexpectedly. **-ráto**, ADJ.: unhoped for (unexpected). **-ranzíre†**, INTR.: conceive some hopes (begin to hope).

inspèrgere = *aspergere*.

inspes-saménto†, M.: condensation. **-sáto†**, ADJ.: condensed (thickened).

inspe-tt. ., **-z**. . = *ispe-tt*. ., **-z**. .

inspi-rábile, ADJ.: inspirable. **-raménto†** = *-razione*. ‖**-ráre** [L.], TR.: breathe into; inhale (inspire); also = *ispirare*. **-razióne**, F.: inspiration.

inspontáneo†, ADJ.: not spontaneous (involuntary).

instábi-le [*in-*, *s.* .], ADJ.: unstable (infirm). **-lità**, F.: instability (inconstancy). **-lménte**, ADV.: inconstantly.
instal-láre [l. L.], TR.: install. **-lazióne**, F.: installation.
instancábi-le [*in-*, *s.* .], ADJ.: indefatigable. **-lità**, F.: indefatigability. **-lménte**, ADV.: indefatigably.
in-stant.. = *istant..* **-stanz..** = *istanz..*
instáre [L.], INTR.: be instant (be pressing or urgent).
instau-ráre [L., build], TR.: initiate. **-ratóre**, M.: initiation. **-razióne**, F.: initiation.
in-sterilíre, TR.: cause to become sterile; INTR.: become sterile or barren.
insti-gaménto = *-gazione*. ‖**-gáre** [L.], TR.: instigate (urge, stimulate). **-gatóre**, M., **-gatríce**, F.: instigator. **-gazióne**, F.: instigation.
in-stilláre, TR.: instill; insinuate.
instínto [L. *-stinctus*], M.: instinct.
institu.. = *istitu..*
in-stivaláto, ADJ.: booted (in boots).
in-stolidíre, INTR.: become stolid; grow stupid.
instruíre [L. *in-struere* (build)], TR.: instruct (teach).
instrument.. = *istrument..*
in-strutt.. = *istrutt..* **-strux..** = *istrux..*
instupidíre [*in*, *stupido*], INTR.: become stupid.
in-sù, ADV.: up, on high; PREP.: upon, above, over; near (by).
insuá-ve†, ADJ.: unsavoury (disagreeable). **-vità†**, F.: insuavity (unpleasantness).
insuberdi-nataménte, ADV.: insubordinately. **-natézza** = *-nazione*. ‖**-náto** [*in-*, *s.* .], ADJ.: insubordinate (rebellious). **-nazióne**, F.: insubordination.
in-succèsso, M.: insuccess.
insu-cidáre† = *-diciare*. ‖**-diciáre** [*in*, *sudicio*], TR.: foul (make dirty, spoil); INTR.: become dirty or filthy.
insuèto†, ADJ.: unusual (rare).
insuffi-ciènte [*in-*, *s.* .], ADJ.: insufficient (inadequate). **-cienteménte**, ADV.: insufficiently. **-ciènza**, **-ciènzia**, F.: insufficiency (want, scarcity).
insufflá-re [L.], TR.: inspire; blow (puff). **-zióne**, F.: insufflation.
insuláre [L. *-laris* (*-la*, ISLE)], ADJ.: insular.
insul-sággine, F.: insipidity. **-saménte**, ADV.: insipidly. **-sità**, F.: insulsity; vapidity. **insúl-so** [L. *-sus* (*in*, not, *salsus*, salted)], ADJ.: insipid (stupid, Eng.† insulse).
insul-táre [L. (*in-silire*, jump upon)], TR.: insult (abuse). **-tatóre**, M., **-tatríce**, F.: insulter. **insúl-to**, M.: insult (affront, outrage); (*med.*) attack.
insuperábi-le [*in-*, *s.* .], ADJ.: insuperable. **-lità**, F.: insuperability. **-lménte**, ADV.: insuperably.
insuper-báre†, **-biáre** = *-bire*. **-biménto**, M.: pride (vanity). ‖**-bíre** [*in*, *superbo*], TR.: make proud; REFL.: grow proud or haughty. **-bíto**, ADJ.: proud (vain).
insúrgere = *insorgere*.
in-surrezióne [L. *-surrectio*], F.: insurrection. **-súrto**, PART. of *-surgere*; risen up (rebelled).
in-suṣáre†, REFL.: raise one's self up (mount). **-súṣo†**, ADV.: above; over; up.
insussis-tènte [*in-*, *s.* .], ADJ.: not subsistent (chimerical, vain). **-tènza**, F.: inconsistency (invalidity).
insusurráre†, TR.: whisper (murmur).
intabaccáre [*in*, *tabacco*], TR.: soil with tobacco; make enamoured†; REFL.†: be engulfed.
intabarráre [*in*, *tabarro*], TR.: wrap up in a great coat.
intac-cábile, ADJ.: that can be notched, etc. **-caménto**, M.: slight cut (notch); offense. ‖**-cáre** [*in*, *tacca*], TR.: cut slightly (notch); wound; cut out (a dress); touch (money); offend (hurt). **-catúra**, F.: notch; detriment. **intác-co†**, M.: notch; offence; prejudice; hurt.
inta-gliaménto, M.: incision (cut, notch). ‖**-gliáre** [*in-*, *t.* .], TR.: carve (engrave); cut†; wound†; notch†: — *ad acqua forte*, etch. **-gliáto**, ADJ.: engraved; cut: *bene — di membra*, well formed or proportioned. **-gliatóre**, M., **-gliatríce**, F.: carver; engraver. **-gliatúra**, F.: cutting, carving; cut (incision). **intá-glio**, M.: intaglio (engraving); carving; profile†; design† (cut): — *in rame*, copper-plate engraving. **-gliuzzáre†**, TR.: cut into small bits (mince, hash).
intalen-táre†, INTR.: become desirous; TR.: awake an ardent wish for (cause a longing for). **-táto†**, ADJ.: very desirous (anxious for).
intamáto†, ADJ.: putrified.
intamburáre†, TR.: accuse; impeach; denounce.
intanáre [*in*, *tana*], REFL.: hide in a den; hide or conceal one's self (shut one's self up).
intan-fáre†, ‖**-fíre** [*in*, *tanfo*], INTR.: acquire a mouldy smell; become musty; (*pers.*) be tightly shut up.
intangíbi-le [*in-*, *t.* .], ADJ.: intangible. **-lità**, F.: intangibility.
intán-to [*in-*, *t.* .], ADV.: in the mean time (in the interim); so; so much;

(until); whilst; however. **-tochè** [*-to, che*], ADV.: till (until); whilst; so that†.
intar-laménto, M.: rottenness in wood (worm-eaten). ‖**-láre** [*in, tarlo*], INTR.: be worm-eaten; breed worms. **-láto**, ADJ.: worm-eaten (carious); infirm (old). **-latúra**, F. = *-lamento.*
intar-máre [*in, tarma*], INTR.: be moth-eaten or pock-fretten. **-matúra**, F.: moth-eating (eating of wood-lice).
intar-siáre [*in, tarsia*], TR.: inlay (chequer). **-siatóra**, F., **-siatóre**, M., **-siatríce**, F.: inlayer. **-siatúra**, F.: inlaid-work (marquetry). **intár-sio**, M.: inlaid-work; inlay.
intartaríre [*in, tartaro*], INTR.: cover with tartar.
inta-saménto = *-satura.* ‖**-sáre** [*in, taso*], INTR.: be full of tartar; TR.: fill with tartar (fill up, obstruct). **-satúra**, **-sazióne**, F.: stopping (obstruction).
intascáre [*in, tasca*], TR.: pocket (put in the pocket).
intassáre†, TR.: bend (a bow); string (a bow).
intátto [L. *in-tactus* (touched)], ADJ.: intact (untouched); pure (undefiled); unchanged.
intavo-láre [*in, tavola*], TR.: arrange (the pieces) at chess; make a counter (make a drawn game); wainscot (rail or table about with boards); propose (move); set in notes. **-láto**, ADJ.: wainscotted; set on foot; M.: wainscotting (planking). **-latúra**, F.: wainscot (lathing); rule (instruction); tablature (music-book).
integamáre [*in, tegame*], TR.: put in an earthen pan.
inte-gèrrimo, ADJ.: superl. of *-gro.* **-grále**, ADJ.: integral (essential, principal). **-gralménte**, ADV.: integrally (completely). **-graménte**, ADV.: with integrity (honestly). **-gránte**, ADJ.: integrant. **-gráre**, TR.: integrate (make entire, complete). **-gráto**, ADJ.: complete (whole). **-grazióne**, F.: integration. **-grità**, F.: integrity (entireness); honesty (uprightness); perfection (purity). **-grízia**† = *-grità.* ‖**ínte-gro**, **intè-gro** [L. *in-teger*, untouched], ADJ.: upright (honest); integral (whole, entire)†.
integuménto [L. *-mentum* (*tegere*, cover)], M.: integument (covering).
intela-iáre [*in, telaio*], TR.: put upon the loom (weave); propose (move). **-iatúra**, F.: framework (skeleton).
intel-lettíva, F.: intellectual faculty (understanding). **-lettivaménte**, ADV.: intellectually. **-lettívo**, ADJ.: intellective. **-lètto** [L. *-lectus*], M.: intellect (understanding); genius (talent); imagination†; conception†; sense (meaning)†; PART.† of *-ligere;* understood. **-lettóre**†, M., **-lettríce**†, F.: one who easily understands. **-lettuále**, ADJ.: intellectual. **-lettualità**, F.: intellectuality. **-lettualménte**, ADV.: intellectually (intelligently). **-lezióne**†, F.: intellection (intelligence). **-ligènte**, ADJ.: intelligent (sensible): — *di*, learned in (skilled in). **-ligenteménte**, ADV.: intelligently. **-ligènz(i)a**, F.: intelligence (knowledge); ability (skill); PL.: intelligences (spirits); artifice†; cunning. ‖**-lígere**† [L.], IRR. (cf. *leggere*); TR.: understand (comprehend). **-ligíbile**, ADJ.: intelligible (conceivable). **-ligibilità**, F.: intelligibility. **-ligibilménte**, ADV.: intelligibly.
inteme-ráta, F.: tedious discourse; long reprimand; prayer to the virgin†; ADJ.: cf. *-rato.* **-rataménte**, ADV.: in a pure manner. ‖**-ráto** [L. *-ratus*], ADJ.: immaculate (pure, Eng.† intemerate).
intempelláre†, TR.: delay (protract).
intempe-ránte [*in-, t.*.], ADJ.: intemperate (immoderate). **-ranteménte**, ADV.: intemperately. **-ránz(i)a**, F.: intemperance. **-ráre**†, TR.: moderate; regulate; REFL.: become temperate. **-rataménte**, ADV: intemperately. **-ráto**†, ADJ.: intemperate. **-ratúra**† = *-rie.*
intempè-rie [L. *-ries*], F.: intemperateness; inclemency; intemperance.
intempes-tivaménto, ADV.: unseasonably. **-tività**, F.: unseasonableness. ‖**-tívo** [L. *-tivus*], ADJ.: untimely (inopportune, Eng.† intempestive).
inten-dacchiáre†, TR.: know superficially. **-dánza** = *-denza.* **-dènte**, ADJ.: intelligent (skilful, learned); prudent (mindful); M.: intendant (steward). **-denteménte**†, ADV.: intelligently; attentively. **-dènza**, F.: intendant, office or dignity of an intendant; intelligence (understanding)†; love†; mistress (sweetheart)†. ‖**intèn-dere** [*in, t.*.], IRR.; TR.: understand (comprehend); hear; intend (aim); make believe; think (imagine); attend†; REFL.: have a secret understanding; agree with; be in love with: — *gli occhi*, fix one's eyes upon; *dare ad* —, give to understand; *non -do a quel che dite*, I don't mind what you say; *dirlo come s' -dene*, say it clearly. **-dévole**†, ADJ.: intelligible (clear). **-devolménte**, ADV.: intelligibly (clearly); learnedly. **-diménto**, M.: intention (knowledge); sense (signification)†; object loved (sweetheart)†: *dar effetto al suo* —, put one's plan in execution; *dare* —, give hope (make one believe); *recare al suo* —, bring one over to one's side; *essere d'— insieme*, understand each other. **-ditóre**, M.: intelligent man.

intene-braménto, M.: darkening (obfuscation. ‖**-bráre** [*in*, *tenebre*], TR.: darken (obfuscate); damage†. **-bríre**†, INTR.: darken (grow dark); be confused or troubled.

intene-riménto, M.: inteneration (softening); compassion (sympathy). ‖**-ríre** [*in*, *tenero*], TR.: make tender (intenerate): move to pity; INTR., REFL.: be moved (become compassionate). **-ríto**, ADJ.: softened; affected.

inten-saménte, ADV.: intensely; excessively; powerfully. **-sióne**†, F.: intension. **-sità**, F.: intensity. **-sivaménte**, ADV.: intensively. **-sívo** [L. *-sivus*], ADJ.: intensive (vehement, penetrating). ‖**intèn-so** [L. *-sus* (*tendere*, stretch)], ADJ.: intense (excessive; very great).

inten-tábile, ADJ.: not attemptable. **inten-taménte**, ADV.: intently (attentively). ‖**-táre** [L., EXTEND; attack], TR.: bring on (a suit, etc., institute); attempt (try)†. **-táto**, PART.: instituted; attempted; [*in-*, not] untried. **-tazióne**†, F.: attempt (trial); law-suit. **-tivaménte**†, ADV.: attentively (intentively). ‖**intèn-to** [L. *-tus* (*tendere*, stretch)], ADJ.: intent (attentive, diligent); straight†; M.: intent (design); object of the attention†. **intèn-sa**†, F.: instinct (inclination); intention; love (darling). **-zionále**, ADJ.: intentional. **-zionalménte**, ADV.: intentionally. **-zionáto**, ADJ.: intended. **-zióne**, F.: intention (meaning); tendency (propensity)†; intelligence†; opinion†. **-zionúccia**, **-ce**, *disp. dim.* of *-zione*.

intepidíre† = *intiepidire*.

inter- [L.], PREF.: between.

interáme†, M.: entrails (intestines).

interaménte [*intero*], ADV.: entirely (completely).

interáto†, ADJ.: stiffened or benumbed with cold.

intercalá-re [L. *-ris* (*inter*, between, *calare*, call)], ADJ.: intercalary (inserted); oft repeated; M.: intercalary verse; TR.: intercalate (insert). **-zióne**, F.: intercalation.

intercapèdine [L. *-do* (*capere*, take)], F.: interval (between walls, etc.).

inter=cèdere, IRR.; TR.: entreat (beg); INTR.: intercede (intervene); oppose†. **-ceditóre**†, **-ceditríce**† = *-ccesore*, *-cessora*. **-cedúto**, **-cèsso**, PART. of *-cedere*. **-cessióne**, F.: intercession. **-cessóra**, F., **-cessóre**, M.: intercessor (mediator).

inter-cettaménto, M.: interception. **-cettáre**, TR.: intercept (stop); impede (interrupt)†. ‖**-cètto** [L. *-ceptus*], PART.: intercepted; precluded; lost†; unespoused†. **-cezióne** = *-cettamento*.

inter=chiúdere, IRR.; TR.: INTERCLUDE (enCLOSE). **-chiúso**, PART.: enclosed.

inter-cídere [L. (*cædere*, cut)], TR.: cut in two; divide†; interrupt†; hinder†. **-cisaménte**†, ADV.: interruptedly. **-cisióne**†, F.: intercision; interruption. **-císo**†, PART.: cut (divided); interrupted; (*bot.*) indented; (*med.*) intermittent (pulse or fever).

intercolu. . = *interchiu*. .

interco-lónnio, **-lúnnio** [L. *-lumnium*], M.: (*arch.*) intercolumniation.

intercostále [*inter*, *costa*], ADJ.: (*anat.*) intercostal.

inter=cutáneo, ADJ.: intercutaneous.

inter-dètto, PART. of *-dire*; M.: interdict (suspension); forbidding (prohibition)†. **-dícere**† = *-dire*. **-dicimento**†, M.: act of interdicting or prohibiting. ‖**=díre** IRR.; TR.: interdict (suspend); prohibit (inhibit); banish; hinder (obstruct). **-dizióne**, F.: interdiction (prohibition).

interes-saménto, M.: interest (concern, care). **-sánte**, PART.: interesting. **-sáre**, TR.: interest (concern); affect; REFL.: interest one's self: *non -sa*, it matters not. **-sataménte**, ADV.: interestedly. **-sáto**, PART.: interested (affected); selfish; covetous; concerned in a business. ‖**interès-se** [L. *inter-esse*, be between], M.: interest (advantage); concern (solicitude); interest (use of money): *senz' —*, gratuitously; *andarne dell' —*, come off a loser; *badate a' vostri -si*, mind your own business. **-sosaménte**, ADV.: interestedly. **-sóso**, ADJ.: interested; greedy of gain. **-súccio**, *dim.* of *-se*.

interézza [*intero*], F.: entirety; vigour (strength); integrity.

interferènza [L. *inter*, *ferre*, bear], F.: (*phys.*) interference.

interfogliá-re [*inter*, *foglio*], TR.: interfoliate (interleave). **-túra**, F.: interleaving.

interiezióne [L. *inter-jectio*], F.: interjection.

ínterim [L.], ADV.: in the meantime, meanwhile.

interi-nále, ADJ.: temporal. **-nalménte**, ADV.: temporarily. **-náre**, TR.: make temporary; (*leg.*) ratify (an act). **-náto**, M.: temporary office; time one holds that office. **-nazióne**, F.: temporariness. ‖**interí-no** [*interim*], ADJ.: temporary.

inte-rióra, ADJ.: interior; F. PL.†: entrails. ‖**-rióre** [L. *-rior*], ADJ.: interior (internal); M.: interior (inward part); heart (breast); mind; PL.: viscera (bowels). **-riorità**†, F.: inwardness. **-riorménte**, ADV.: internally (inwardly).

[illegible]

[illegible] -[illegible]ere = -[illegible] [illegible] [illegible] [illegible] L. [illegible]

[illegible] L. [illegible] F. [illegible]

[illegible]

[illegible]

zio [-*stitium*, standing between], M.: interstice; interval.
inter=tenére, IRR.; TR.: entertain (amuse); maintain (support); arrest (stop); REFL.: amuse one's self; sojourn. **-teniménto**, M.: entertainment (amusement); conference; familiar conversation.
intertropicále [*inter*, *tropico*], ADJ.: intertropical.
inter-valláto†, ADJ.: divided into intervals. ‖**-vállo** [L. -*vallum* (wall)], M.: interval (space); (*mus.*) stop (rest); delay: *lucido* —, lucid interval (of a mad person).
inter-veniménto †, M.: accident (chance); help; intervention; means. **-venire**, IRR.; TR.: intervene; happen (befall): — *in checchessia*, be present. **-vènto**, M.: intervention (interposition); assistance. **-venúto**, PART.: intervened; arrived. **-venzióne** = -*vento*.
interzáto†, ADJ.: (*heral.*) tierced.
inté-sa [-*ndere*], F.: understanding: *star sull'* —, be on one's guard. **-saménte**†, ADV.: intently (diligently).
intesc*h*iáto†, ADJ.: obstinate (stubborn).
intéso, PART. of *intendere;* intent; understood; M.: idea (opinion); compact (agreement).
intès-sere [L. *in-texere*], TR.: interweave (weave into); intermingle. **-súto**, PART.: interwoven; intermingled.
intestábile†, ADJ.: (*law.*) intestable.
intes-táre [*in*, *testa*], TR.: write; entitle; inscribe: — *una catena*, fasten a chain in a wall in order to strengthen it. **-táre**, REFL.: be headstrong (grow obstinate).
intestáto [L. -*tus* (*in*-, not, *testari*, make a will)], ADJ.: intestate.
intesta-túra [-*re*], F.: title (head, beginning); stubbornness. **-zióne**, F.: title; inscription.
intes-tinále, ADJ.: intestinal. ‖**-tíno** [L. -*tinus*], ADJ.: intestinal (internal); M.: intestinal canal (bowels): *guerra* -*tina*, civil war.
intésto†, ADJ.: interwoven.
in-tiepidáre†, ‖**-tiepidíre** [*in*, *tiepido*], TR.: render tepid; INTR.: cool (grow lukewarm); become tepid; grow indifferent (cool).
intier.. = *inter..*
inti-*g*náre [*in*, *tigna*], INTR.: become worm-eaten; get a scald head. **-*g*náto**, PART.: worm-eaten. **-*g*natúra**, F.: moth-hole.
intí*g*nere† = *intingere*.
inti*g*nosíre†, TR.: cause to become scabby (give a scald head to).
inti-maménte, ADV.: intimately. ‖**-máre** [L.], TR.: order (command, Eng.† intimate); make intimate. **-matóre**, M.: informer. **-mazióne**, F.: order (summons).
intimi-dazióne, F.: intimidation. ‖**-díre** [*in*, *timido*], TR.: intimidate; REFL.: grow fearful or timid. **-dità**, F.: fearlessness (courage). **intími-do**†, ADJ.: courageous (intrepid, brave).
in-timità, F.: internality; intimacy. ‖**ín-timo** [L. -*timus*], ADJ.: inmost (internal); secret (hidden); intimate; M.: interior.
intimo-riménto, M.: intimidation. ‖**-ríre** [*in*, *timore*], TR.: intimidate (frighten); REFL.: be afraid. **-ríto**, PART.: frightened.
intimpaníre [*in*, *timpano*], INTR.: become like a drum.
intín-gere [*in*-, *t*..], IRR.; TR.: dip (soak, steep); involve. **-golétto**, *car. dim.* of -*golo*. **intín-golo**, M.: kind of ragout. **intín-to**, PART.: immersed (soaked); concerned; M.: gravy (juice, sauce). **-túra**†, F.: immersing (dipping).
intiranníre [*in*, *tiranno*], INTR.: become a tyrant over (usurp).
intiriz-zaménto† = -*zimento*. **-záre**† = -*zire;* INTR.: become stiff or insensible (*fig.*) be proud. **-záto**†, PART.: benumbed; proud. **-ziménto**, M.: stiffness (numbness). ‖**-zíre** [*interezza*], TR.: render inflexible; benumb (make stiff); INTR., REFL.: grow stiff; be benumbed. **-zíto**, PART.: benumbed; stiffened (dried up).
intirizzo† = -*zimento*.
intisic*h*íre [*in*, *tisico*], INTR.: grow consumptive; despond (pine away); TR.: make consumptive; waste.
intito-laménto, M.: act of giving a title. ‖**-láre** [*in*-, *t*..], TR.: entitle (intitule); dedicate; ascribe; REFL.: be called (denominated). **-lazióne**, F.: title (claim); dedication.
intoccábile†, ADJ.: untouchable (intangible).
intolle-rábile [*in*-, *t*..], ADJ.: intolerable (insufferable). **-rabilità**, F.: intolerability. **-rabilménte**, ADV.: intolerably (unbearably). **-rándo**, ADJ.: unbearable. **-ránte**, ADJ.: intolerant; impatient. **-ránza**, F.: intolerance.
intona-cáre, TR.: plaster. **-cáto**, PART.: plastered; M.: plaster. **-catúra**, F.: act of plastering. ‖**intòna-co** (*in*, *tonaca*], M.: plaster; rough-cast.
into-náre [*in*, *tono*], TR. intonate (begin to sing); (*fig.*) compose; sing (chant); tune; call from afar†; resound (ring)†; set to music. **-natóre**, M.: tuner; singer. **-natúra**, F.: intonation; (*fig.*) intimation; commencement of an enterprise; gravity (seriousness); pride (haught-

iness). **-nazióne**, F.: intonation (tuning); tune.

intonochiáre [*in*, *tonchio*], INTR.: be full of mites.

intonico. .† = *intonac*. .

in=tònso, ADJ.: unshorn; (of books) uncut.

intontíre [*in*, *tonto*], TR., INTR.: make or become astonished.

intòp-pa = *-po*. **-paménto**, M.: obstacle (hindrance). **-páre**, TR.: meet with; INTR., REFL.: stumble. ||**intòp-po** [*in-*, *t.* .], M.: obstacle (hindrance); meeting (encounter).

into-ráre†, INTR., REFL.: rage like a bull. **-ráto**†, ADJ.: furious as a bull.

intor-báre [*in*, *torbo*], TR.: make muddy or turbid. **-bidaménto**, M.: turbidness; disturbance. **-bidáre** [*in*, *torbido*], TR.: make turbid (inturbidate); vex (annoy); INTR., REFL.: get muddy; darken. **-bidáto**, PART.: troubled; muddy. **-bidatóre**, M., **-bidatríce**, F.: troubler. **-bidazióne**†, F. = *-bidamento*. **-bidíre** = *-bidare*. **-bidíto** = *-bidato*.

intormen-timénto, M.: numbness. ||**-tíre** [*in*, *tormento*], TR.: make numb; bewilder (confuse)†; INTR.: grow stiff or benumbed with cold.

intor-neáre†, TR.: enclose (surround); provide (furnish). **-niaménto**†, M.: surrounding (encompassing); enclosure. **-niáre**, TR.: environ. ||**intór-no** [*in*, *t.* .], PREP.: about; around; near; concerning (touching); ADV.: round about; circularly; M.†: circuit: outline: *essere* — *a*(*d*) *uno*, beg importunately; *guardare* —, look about; *d' ogni* —, from all sides; *lù* —, thereabout; — —, from all sides, everywhere.

intorpi-diménto, M.: act of growing torpid or dull. ||**-díre** [*in*, *torpido*], INTR.: become torpid (get dull). **-díto**, PART.: torpid (dull, heavy).

intòrto†, ADJ.: twisted; folded.

intoscaníre [*in*, *toscano*], TR.: affect (Tuscan pronunciation); INTR.: become Tuscan in manners, etc.

intossicáre = *attossicare*.

intostíre [*in*, *tosto*], INTR.: become hard or indurate.

intoz-záre† = *-zire*; (*fig.*) grow virulent (become angry). ||**-zíre** [*in*, *tozzo*], INTR.: become thick, clumsy or short. **-zíto**, PART.: clumsy; short.

intra [L.], PREP.: between; among; in; within: — *due*, in suspense (undecided).

intrabescáre†, REFL.: fall in love.

intraccíglio†, M.: space between the eyebrows.

intra=chiúdere, IRR.; TR.: enclose (surround); forbid; disturb. **-chiúso**, PART.: enclosed, etc.

intra-cídere†, TR.: cut in the middle (divide into two); interrupt. **-císo**†, PART.: divided; interrupted.

intra-détto = *interdetto*. **-díre** = *interdire*.

intraducíbi-le [*in-*, *t.* .], ADJ.: untranslatable. **-lménte**, ADV: in an untranslatable manner.

intradúe†, ADJ.: doubtful (uncertain); ADV.: doubtfully (in suspense); M.: doubt (uncertainty).

intrafátto†, ADV.: quite; thoroughly; altogether (entirely).

intra=fine=fátto, ADV.: suddenly (without losing time).

intraguardáre†, TR.: guard (defend).

intrala-sciaménto, M.: intermission (interruption). ||**-sciáre** [*in-*, *t.* .], TR.: interrupt; delay (suspend). **-sciánza** = *-sciamento*.

intral-ciaménto, M.: intricacy; embarrassment (perplexity); intrigue. ||**-ciáre** [*in*, *tralcio*], TR.: interweave (interlace); entangle (embarrass); REFL.: intrigue; get entangled. **-ciataménte**, ADV.: confusedly.

intrám-bo†, **-endúe**†, PRON.: both (both together).

intra-ménto, M.: entrance; commencement. **-méssa**†, F.: interposition (mediation); digression. **-mésso**†, M.: dainty dish (side-dish); PART.: interposed; intermeddled. ||**=méttere**, IRR.; TR.: introduce (insert); intermit (interrupt); REFL.: intermeddle; submit. **-mettiménto**†, M.: interposition; intermeddling.

intramezzáre = *tramezzare*.

intra-mischiánza, F.: intermixture. ||**=mischiáre**, TR.: mix together (intermix).

intramissióne†, F.: intermission (intervention).

intransgredíbile†, ADJ.: inviolable.

intransi-gènte [*in-*, *transigere*], ADJ.: intransigent (irreconcilable). **-gènza**, F.: irreconcilability.

intransi-tivaménto, ADV.: intransitively. ||**-tívo** [*in-*, *t.* .], ADJ.: intransitive.

intránte, PART. of *intrare*; entering.

intra-pórre†, **-ppórre** = *interporre*.

intra-prendènte, ADJ.: enterprising (energetic). **-prendènza**, F.: enterprise (undertaking). ||**=prèndere**, IRR.; TR.: undertake; intercept (catch)†; understand†; choose†; surprise†. **-prendiménto**, M.: undertaking (enterprise). **-prenditóre**, M., **-prenditríce**, F.: undertaker (contractor). **=prensóre** = *-prenditore*. **-présa**, F.: enterprise. **-préso**, PART.: undertaken, etc.

intráre†, INTR.: enter; engage in; M.: entrance (ingress); mien (appearance).

intrarómpere† = *interrompere*.
intraségna†, F.: ensign (banner); emblem; PL.: arms.
in=traggredibile, ADJ.: intransgressible (inviolable).
intráta†, F.: entrance (ingress); prelude; income (revenue).
intratèssere†, TR.: intermix; interweave.
intrattábi-le [*in*-, *t.*.], ADJ.: intractable (ungovernable); whimsical; unsociable; (of metals) unmanageable (difficult to work). **-lità**, F.: intractability.
intrattánto†, ADV.: meanwhile (in the meantime).
intratte-nére [*in*, *t.*.], IRR.; TR.: entertain (amuse); maintain†; hold in comfidence; REFL.: dwell on; expatiate. **-niménto†**, M.: amusement (recreation); delay; maintaining; enlisting. **-nitóre**, M., **-nitríce**, F.: entertainer; enlister.
intravedére [*in*, *t.*.], TR.: have a glimpse of (dimly foresee).
intraven..† = *interven..*.
intraver-sáre [*in*-, *t.*.], TR.: cross; plough across; cross-plane; REFL.†: go astray (err); deviate; oppose (withstand). **-sáto**, PART.: crossed, etc. **-satúra**, F.: crossing; opposition (resistance).
intravved.., **-vven..** = *intraved..*, *interven..*.
intreáre†, REFL.: make one's self into three.
intrec-ciaménto, M.: interlacing; ‖**-ciáre** [*in*, *treccia*], TR.: interlace (intertwine, braid); wreathe; collect (put together). **-ciataménto**, ADV.: in interlaced manner. **-ciatóio†**, M.: ornament for the hair; head-dress; (*nav.*) splicing fid (marlingspike). **-ciatúra**, F.: wreathing; braiding. **intréccio**, M.: mingling; intrigue or plot of a novel or drama.
intreguáre†, TR.: make a truce.
intremíre†, REFL.: tremble with fear.
intrepi-daménte, ADV.: intrepidly. **-dézza**, **-dità**, F.: intrepidity (fearlessness). ‖**intrèpi-do** [L. *-dus*], ADJ.: intrepid (dauntless).
intrescáre†, TR.: perplex (entangle); INTR.: be confounded.
intrica.. = *intriga..*.
intrídere [L. *in-terere* (rub)], IRR.§; TR.: knead; dirty (stain)†; soak (dilute, steep)†.

§ Ind.: Pret. *intri-si*, *-se*; *-sero*. Part. *intriso*.

intri-gaménto†, M.: intrigue (entanglement). **-gánte**, PART.: intriguing (perplexing); M.: intriguer (intermeddler). ‖**-gáre** [L. *-care* (*trica*, trick)], TR.: entangle (confound, Eng.† intrigue); obstruct; REFL.: be tangled, be entangled. **-gataménte**, ADV.: in a tangled manner. **-gatóre**, M.: intriguer. **intrígo**, M.: intrigue (design); confusion (perplexity). **-góne** = *-gatore*.
intrin-secaménte, ADV.: intrinsically. **-secáre**, REFL.: (*lit.*) become intimate (penetrate deeply). **-secáto**, PART.: intimate (familiar). **-sechézza**, F.: intimacy (friendship). ‖**intrín-seco** [L. *-secus*, inward], ADJ.: intrinsic; genuine (real); intimate; M.†: interior.
intríso, PART. of *intridere*: kneaded; M.: dough (batter, pap); plaster. **intristá-re†** = *-tire*. **-timénto**, M.: melancholy (sadness, sorrow); rotting; wasting. ‖**-tíre** [*in*, *tristo*], INTR.: become sad or sorrowful; become wicked; thrive ill (waste, rot).
intròcque†, ADV.: in the meantime.
intro-dótto†, PART.: introduced; M.: introduction; insinuation. ‖**-dúcere†** [L.] = *-durre*. **-ducimento**, M.: introduction; rudiment. **-ducitóre†** = *-duttore*. **-dúrre** [*-ducere*], IRR. (cf. *addurre*); TR.: introduce (bring in); narrate†. **-duttívo**, ADJ.: introductive. **-dútto**, PART. of *-durre*: introduced. **-duttóre**, M., **-duttríce**, F.: introducer; usher. **-duzioncèlla**, **-duzioncína**, *dim.* of *-duzione*. **-duzióne**, F.: introduction; preface (beginning); (*com.*) introduction of merchandise; insertion (interposition)†; mediation.
introgo-láre [*in*, *trogolo*], TR.: soil with liquid materials. **-lóna**, F., **-lóne**, M.: dirty child.
in-troitáre [L. *-tro-itus*, going in], TR.: **-tròito**, M.: introit (beginning of the mass); drawings; exordium (beginning).
intro-méssa, **-messióne** = *-missione*. **-mésso**, PART.: introduced (inserted); M.†: side-dish (entremets). ‖=**méttere**, IRR.; TR.: insert (put in); introduce (present)†; REFL.: meddle (intermeddle); interpose illegally. **-mettitóre**, M.: introducer; meddler. **-mettitúra**, **-missióne**, F.: introduction (insertion); interposition.
intro-naménto, M.: stunning. ‖**-náre** [*in*, *trono*], TR.: stun (confound); INTR.: be stunned. **-náto**, PART.: stunned; deafened. **-natúra†**, F.: stunning; tingling noise.
intron-fiáre [*in*, *tronfio*], INTR.: swell with pride. **-fiáto**, PART.: haughty.
introniz-zá-re [*in*, *trono*], TR.: enthrone. **-túra**, F.: haughtiness. **-zióne**, F.: enthronization; installation.
in=trovábile, ADJ.: not findable.
intro-versióne†, F.: introversion (turning inward). **-vèrtere†**, TR.: introvert

(turn inward). **-vèrso**†, PART.: introverted.

intrúdere [L.], IRR.§; TR.: intrude (thrust in); introduce; REFL.: thrust one's self in.

§ Ind.: Pret. *intrú-si, -se; -sero.* Part. *intruso.*

intru-gliáre, TR.: mix with poor stuff; REFL.: soil (dirty). ‖**intrú-glio** [L. *trulla*, ladle, basin], M.: mixture; intrigue; confusion (perplexity). **=glióne**, M.: mixer.

intruon. .† = *intron.* .

intruppáre [*in*, *truppa*], REFL.: mix with inferior persons.

in-trusióne, F.: intrusion. ‖**-trúso**, PART. of *-trudere;* intruded (thrust in).

intufáre†, INTR.: have the smell of turf; have an earthy taste.

in=tuffáre, TR.: steep (soak, dip).

in-tuíre [L. *-tueri*, look in], TR.: know intuitively (know at a glance). **-tuitivaménte**, ADV.: intuitively. **-tuitívo**, ADJ.: intuitive. **-tuíto**, PART. of *-tuire.* **-túito**, M.: perception (intuition); glance; motive. **-tuizióne**, F.: intuition; (*theol.*) divine vision.

intumescènza [L. *-mescere*, begin to swell], F.: intumescence (swelling).

intumidíre [*in*, *tumido*], INTR.: become tumid (swell).

intuon. . = *inton.* .

inturgi-díre [*in*, *turgido*], INTR.: grow turgid (puff up). **-díto**, PART.: turgid (swollen).

intuzzáre†, TR.: blunt (dull); repel (resist).

inubbidi. . = *disubbidi.* .

inubbriacáre†, TR.: make drunk; INTR.: get drunk.

inudíto†, ADJ.: unheard.

inuggiolíre = *inuzzolire.*

inugual. . = *inegual.* .

inúlto [L. *-tus*], ADJ.: unavenged.

in-umanaménte, ADJ.: inhumanly (barbarously). **-umanità**, F.: inhumanity (cruelty). ‖**=umáno**, ADJ.: inhuman (barbarous, cruel).

inumá-re [*in*, *humare*], TR.: inhume (bury, inter). **-zióne**, F.: inhumation (burial).

inumi-díre [*in*, *umido*], TR.: wet (moisten); REFL.: get wet or damp. **-díto**, PART.: moistened (wet).

in=umiliábile, ADJ.: that cannot be humiliated.

inumiliáre†, TR.: humiliate; INTR.: humble.

inúngere†, IRR., TR.: anoint; = *ungere.*

inur-banaménte, ADV.: uncivilly (impolitely). **-banità**, F.: inurbanity (impoliteness). ‖**-báno** [*in-*, *u.* .], ADJ.: uncivil (unpolite).

inurbáre†, REFL.: enter a city.

inu-sáto [*in-*, *u.* .], ADJ.: obsolete (not in use). **-sitataménte**, ADV.: obsoletely; in an unusual manner. **-sitáto**, ADJ.: inusitate (out of use); unusual.

inúti-le [L. *-lis*], ADJ.: useless (inutile); unprofitable. **-lità**, F.: inutility (uselessness). **-lménte**, ADV.: uselessly (vainly).

inuzzolíre [*in*, *uzzolo*], TR.: excite a desire for.

invac-chiménto, M.: act of becoming useless. ‖**-chíre** [*in*, *vacca*], INTR.: become useless (become a drone).

invádere [L.], IRR.§; TR.: invade; attack (assail).

§ Ind.: Pret. *invá-si, -se; -sero.* Part. *invaso.*

inva-gáre† = *-ghire.* **-ghiacchiáre**†, REFL.: fall slightly in love (be smitten). **-ghiménto**, M: falling in love. ‖**-ghíre** [*in*, *vago*], TR.: inflame with love (charm); stimulate (urge); REFL.: be enamoured of; get fascinated. **-ghíto**, PART.: enamoured; fascinated.

inva-iáre† [*in*, *vaio*], INTR.: become spotted. **-ioláre**, INTR.: turn black.

in=valére, IRR.; INTR.: become valid (begin to have value); take footing.

invali-dábile, ADJ.: that can be invalidated. **-daménte**, ADV.: without validity. **-daménto**, M.: act of becoming invalid (annulling). **-dáre**, TR.: invalidate (render invalid). **-dazióne**, F.: invalidation. **-dità**, F.: invalidity; nullity. ‖**inváli-do** [L. *-dus*], ADJ.: invalid (infirm, weak); void (valueless); M.: disabled soldier.

invaligiáre [*in*, *valigia*], TR.: put in a valise (pack up).

invalláre [*in*, *valle*], REFL.: run (glide) between two valleys.

invaloríre†, TR.: strengthen (animate, encourage); INTR.: recover strength.

inva-niménto, M.: elation (pride). ‖**-níre** [*in*, *vano*], TR.: make vain or proud; render fruitless (frustrate); INTR., REFL.: become vain (grow proud); vanish (disappear)†. **-níto**, PART.: fruitless (vain); proud. **invá-no**, ADV.: vainly (uselessly).

invariá-bile [*in-*, *v.* .], ADJ.: invariable. **-bilità**, F.: invariability (immutability). **-bilménte**, ADV.: invariably. **invariáto**, ADJ.: unvaried (unchanged).

inva-saménto, M.: invasion (obsession). **-sáre** [L. *-so*], TR.: INVADE; seize; beset; (*fig.*†) ingulf (plunge); REFL.: be stupified or infatuated (be beset by something). **-sáto**, PART.: beset by devils; immersed (plunged)†; amazed†; stupified†. **-sazióne**†, F.: obsession; besetting. **-sióne**, F.: invasion. ‖**invá-so**, PART. of *vadere:* invaded; **-sóre**, M.: invader.

invec-chiaménto, M.: growing old; wasting away. ||**-chiáre** [*in, vecchio*], INTR.: grow old; TR.: make to appear old (cause to grow old). **-chiuzzíre,** TR.: waste; make worse; INTR.: decay (rot).
in=véce, ADV.: instead (in place of).
invecería, F.: foolishness (stupidity).
invedovíto [*in, vedova*], ADJ.: widowed.
inveggi.. = *invidi..*
inveíre [L. *in-vehere*], INTR.: inveigh.
invelenire [*in, veleno*], TR.: exasperate (provoke); INTR., REFL.: be irritated (become angry).
in=vendíbile, ADJ.: invendible (not salable).
in=vendicáto, ADJ.: unavenged (unpunished).
in=vendúto, ADJ.: unsold.
invenenáto†, ADJ.: poisoned (envenomed).
invènia [L. *in veniam* (-*nia*, grace)], F. (us'ly in pl.): caressing acts or words (insinuations).
invenire†, IRR.; TR.: find out (discover).
inven-táre, TR.: invent; devise (contrive); find out; compose: *non ha -tato la polvere*, he has not invented powder (he hasn't set the Thames on fire); — *delle cose false*, counterfeit (forge). **-tariáre,** TR.: make an inventory of; enter in an inventory. **-taríno,** *dim.* of *-tario.* **-tário** [L. *-tarium*], M.: inventory (list, catalogue). **-tatóre,** M.: inventor; contriver. **-tatorèllo,** *disp.* of *-tatore.* **-tíva,** F.: inventive faculty; invention. **-tívo,** ADJ.: inventive. ||**-to†** [*-tus* (*venire*, come)], ADJ.: invented. **-tóre,** M., **-tríce,** F.: inventor (deviser); inventress.
inventráre†, REFL.: penetrate deeply.
inventuráto†, ADJ.: fortunate (lucky).
inve-nustà [*in-, v..*], F.: inelegance. **-nustaménte,** ADV.: inelegantly. **-nústo,** ADJ.: inelegant; ungraceful; ugly.
inven-zioncèlla, -zioncína, *dim.* of *-zione.* ||**-zióne** [*-to*], F.: invention (contrivance); fiction; trick: *quadro d'* —, not copied.
invér† 1, PREP.: towards; against.
invér† 2 = *invero.*
inveráre†, REFL.: have the appearance of truth; partake of truth.
inverdíre [*in, verde*], INTR.: grow green; (*fig.*†) become young; gain strength or vigour.
invere-condaménte, ADV.: impudently (immodestly). **-cóndia,** F.: impudence. ||**-cóndo** [*in-, v..*], ADJ.: immodest (impudent, shameless).
invergognà-re [*in, v..*], TR.: dishonour (disgrace). **-taménte,** ADV.: disgracefully.
inverisimi-gliánte, ADJ.: improbable. **-gliánza,** F.: improbability (unlikelihood). **inverisimi-le** [*in-, v..*], ADJ.: improbable (unlikely). **-litúdine†,** F.: inverisimilitude. **-lménte,** ADV.: improbably.
invermigliáre [*in, vermiglio*], TR.: redden (vermillion); REFL.: become red.
invermi-naménto, M.: breeding of worms. **-náre,** ||**-nire** [*in, vermini*], INTR.: breed worms; become putrid. **-náto,** PART.: full of worms; corrupted.
inver-náccio, *disp.* of *-no.* **-nále,** ADJ.: invernal. **-náre,** REFL.: remain all winter; INTR.†: winter (pass the winter). **-náta,** F.: winter season (whole winter): *far l'* —, winter (take up winter quarters). **-natáccia, -natína,** *disp.* and *iron. dim.* of *-nata.*
inverni-cáre†, ||**-ciáre** [*in, vernice*], TR.: varnish; REFL.: paint one's face. **-ciáta,** F.: varnishing. **-ciáto,** PART.: varnished. **-ciatóre,** M.: varnisher. **-ciatúra,** F.: varnish; varnishing.
invèrno [L. *hibernus*], M.: winter.
in=véro, in véro, ADV.: in truth (truly, really).
inverosimi.. = *inverisimi..*
inver-saménte, ADV.: inversely. **-sáto,** ADJ.: opposed (contrary). **-sióne,** F.: inversion. ||**invèr-so** [*-tire*], ADJ.: inverse (inverted); reversed; opposed; upside down; relatively†; PREP.†: towards; in comparison; against.
in=vertebráto, ADJ., M.: invertebrate.
invèr-tere [L.], IRR.; TR.: invert; pervert. **-tíbile,** ADJ.: that can be inverted. **-timénto,** M.: inversion. **-tíre,** IRR.; TR.: invert (turn upside down); bend. **invèr-to,** PART.: inverted, etc.
inverzicáre†, INTR.: grow green.
inves-ca.., -chia.. = *invischia..*
investíbile [*-stire*], ADJ.: that can be invested.
investi-gábile, ADJ.: 1. investigable; 2. [*in-*, not], not to be investigated. **-gagióne†,** F., **-gaménto,** M.: investigation. ||**-gáre** [L.], TR.: investigate (search into). **-gatóre,** M., **-gatríce,** F.: investigator (ferreter). **-gazióne,** F.: investigation (examination, search).
inves-tigióne, F., **-timénto,** M.: investment (investing); encounter; investiture. ||**-tíre** [L. *in, vestire*, clothe], TR.: invest (clothe), put in possession; place, as money; (*mil.*) inclose (lay siege to); strike (hit); assault (attack); dress (clothe)†; covert†; inform†; REFL.: invest one's self; INTR.: become; fit. **-títa†,** F.: investment; purchase. **-títo†,** PART.: invested;

clothed (decked). **-titúra**, F.: investiture.

invete-ráre†, INTR.: grow old. ‖**-ráto** [L. *-ratus* (*veterus*, old)], ADJ.: inveterate (old).

inve-tráre† = *-triare*. **-triaménto**, M.: varnishing; vitrification (glazing). ‖**-triáre** [*in*, *vetro*], TR.: vitrify (glaze); varnish; reduce to the likeness of glass†. **-triáta**, F.: glass-window (sash-window); window glass. **-triáto**, PART.: vitrified; of glass; bold (brazen-faced); clear†; shining; smooth; M.†: the thing glazed; glazing; varnishing. **-triatúra**, F.: vitrification; varnishing; panes of a window†; kind of varnish or polish.

invet-tíva [Fr. *invective*], F.: invective (reproach). **-tivaménte**†, ADV.: invectively. **-tívo**†, ADJ.: invective (denunciatory).

invezzáre†, TR.: accustom (inure); REFL.: accustom one's self; indurate in vice.

in-viábile, ADJ.: that can be forwarded. **-viaménto**†, M.: forwarding (furthering); good beginning; means; instructions. ‖**-viáre** [L. (*via*, way)], TR.: forward (send, despatch); begin (commence)†; REFL.: put one's self on the way (set out). **-viáto**, PART.: forwarded (sent); M.: messenger; envoy. **-viatóre**, M.: instructor; director.

inví-dia [L.], F.: ENVY; grudge; hatred; desire; endive (succory)†. **-diábile**, ADJ.: enviable. **-diánte**, PART.: envious. **-diáre**, TR.: envy (grudge); deny; contest (dispute); hate†; take away†. **-diatóre**, M., **-diatríce**, F.: envier; maligner. **-diétta**, *dim.* of *-dia*. **-diosáccio**, *disp.* of *-dioso*. **-diosaménte**, ADV.: invidiously (enviously). **-diosèllo**, **-diosétto**, **-diosíno**, *dim.* of *-dioso*. **-dióso**, ADJ.: invidious (envious, jealous); odious (hateful)†; penurious (miserly)†; that excites or procures envy†; M.: envious person: *la raccolta è stata -diosa*, the crop has been envious (i.e., small to some and abundant to others). **-diúccia**, *dim.* of *-dia*. **invi-do**, ADJ.: envious.

invie-táre† = *-tire*. ‖**-tíre** [*in*, *vieto*], INTR.: become old, musty or rancid; lose freshness. **-títo**, PART.: musty, etc.

inviévole†, ADJ.: that can be sent or despatched.

invigi-lánte, ADJ.: vigilant (watchful). ‖**-láre** [L.], TR.: watch over; INTR.: be watchful (be vigilant).

inviglíacchíre [*in*, *vigliacco*], INTR.: become cowardly.

invigo-riménto, M.: strength (vigour). ‖**-ríre** [*in*, *vigore*], TR.: invigorate (strengthen); encourage; INTR., REFL.: become invigorated (gain strength).

invi-liménto, M.: act of making vile; loss of courage. ‖**-líre** [*in*, *vile*], TR.: render vile (invile); discourage (dishearten); vilify; INTR.: become vile; lose courage.

invilup-paménto, M.: involution; entanglement (embarrassment). ‖**-páre** [*in*, *viluppo*], TR.: envelop (wrap up); (*fig.*) confound (perplex); REFL.: wrap one's self up; entangle one's self; fill one's self†. **-páto**, PART.: enveloped; perplexed. **invilúp-po**, M.: packet (bundle); (*fig.*) embarrassment (confusion).

invincíbi-le [L. *-lis*], ADJ.: invincible (unconquerable). **-lità**, F.: invincibility. **-lménte**, ADV.: invincibly.

invincidíre [*in*, *vincido*], TR.: soften (make flabby); INTR.: grow soft or flabby.

invío [*inviare*], M.: forwarding; despatching; address (direction).

inviolá-bile [L. *-bilis*], ADJ.: inviolable. **-bilità**, F.: inviolability. **-bilménte**, ADV.: inviolably. **-taménte**, ADV.: inviolately. **inviolá-to**, ADJ.: inviolate (uncorrupted,); complete (entire).

inviolènto†, ADJ.: gentle (mild).

invipe-ráre† = *-rire*. ‖**-ríre** [*in*, *vipera*], INTR., REFL.: rage like a viper (get furious). **-ríto**, PART.: enraged (angered).

invironáre†, TR.: environ (surround, enclose).

inviscáre† = *invischiare*.

invisceráre [*in*, *viscere*], REFL.: penetrate deeply (go to the bottom); study thoroughly (know well); penetrate into the viscera or bowels.

invi-schiaménto, M.: allurement (enticement). ‖**-schiáre** [L. *-scare* (*viscus*, birdlime)], TR.: inviscate (daub with birdlime); REFL.: be caught or ensnared. **-schiatríce**, F.: allurer (enchantress).

invisci-diménto, M.: thickening. ‖**-díre** [*in*, *viscido*], INTR.: become viscid (condense). **-díto**, PART.: viscid (thickened).

invisíbi-le [L. *-lis*], ADJ.: invisible (imperceptible). **-lità**, F.: invisibility. **-lménte**, ADV.: invisibly.

inviso [L. *-sus* (*in-videre*, look askance at)], ADJ.: disliked (*a*, by).

invispíre [*in*, *vispo*], INTR.: become brisk or lively.

invi-tábile, ADJ.: that can be invited. **-taménto**, M.: invitation. **-tánte**, ADJ.: inviting (alluring); attractive (interesting). ‖**-táre**[1] [L.], TR.: invite; allure (entice); stake (at cards); propose; REFL.: invite one's self; offer one's services; toast each other: — *d'una cosa*, eat a thing.

invitáre[2] [*in*, *vite*], TR.: put on a screw; fasten with a screw (screw).

invi-táta†, F.: invitation. **-táto**, PART.: invited; M.: guest. **-tatóre**, M., **-tatríce**, F.: inviter (host or hostess). **-tatòrio**, ADJ.: inviting (attractive); M.: invitatory: *lettere d'* —, letters of invitation. **-tatúra**†, **-tazióne**†, F.: invitation. **-tévole**†, ADJ.: inviting (attractive). ||**invi-to** 1 [*-tare* 1], M.: invitation; game; bet (stake); health (toast)†: — *sacro*, ecclesiastical manifestation to the faithful.

invíto 2 [L. *in-vitus*], ADJ.: unwilling.

invítto [L. *in-victus*], ADJ.: unvanquished (invincible).

in=viziáre, TR.: vitiate (corrupt); REFL.: get spoiled (become corrupt).

invizzíre [*in, vizzo*], INTR.: fade away (wither, decay).

invo-cábile, ADJ.: that can be invoked. ||**-cáre** [L.], TR.: invoke (call upon). **-catívo**, ADJ.: fit for invoking. **-catóre**, M., **-catríce**, F.: invoker (suppliant). **-cazióne**, F.: invocation.

invò-glia†, F.: packing cloth; hide. **-gliaménto**, M.: desire (wish). ||**-gliáre** 1 [*in, voglia*], TR.: wish for (excite a longing for); REFL.: have a wish or desire.

in-vogliare† 2, TR.: wrap up. **-vòglio**†, M.: packing-cloth; packet. **-vogliúzzo**, M.: small parcel.

invo-laménto, M.: stealing (robbery). ||**-láre** [L.], TR.: steal; rape; surprise†; REFL.†: disappear (vanish). **-latóre**, M.: thief (robber).

invòl-gere [*in, v..*], IRR.; TR.: envelop (wrap around); involve (comprehend, contain). **-giménto**, M.: winding (intertwining); trick†; intricate discourse†.

involío†, M.: theft (robbery).

invólo†, ADV.: thievishly (stealthily).

involon-tariaménte, ADV.: involuntarily. ||**-tário** [*in-, v..*], ADJ.: involuntary; M.: involuntary action.

invol-páre [*in, volpe*], INTR.: get blighted. **-píre**, INTR.: become cunning (grow crafty).

invol-táre [*in, v..*], TR.: wrap up (envelop). **-táta**, F.: wrapping. **-tatína**, *dim.* of *-tata*. **-tíno**, *dim.* of *-to*. **invòl-to** [*-gere*], PART.: wrapped up (enveloped); M.: bundle (parcel). **-túra**†, F.: winding (intertwining); circuitous discourse; fraud.

invò-lucro, ||**-lúcro** [L. *-lucrum* (*-lvere*, wrap)], M.: capsule (seed-vessel).

invo-lutáre†, REFL.: roll (turn); be involved. ||**-lúto** [*-lgere*], PART.: enveloped (wrapped up); involved. **-luzióne**†, F.: wrapping up; involution: — *di parole*, beating about the bush. **invò-lvere**†, TR.: envelop (wrap up); involve (contain).

-lviménto†, M.: wrapping up; fraud (trick).

invulnerábi-le [L. *-lis*], ADJ.: invulnerable. **-lità**, F.: invulnerability. **-lménte**, ADV.: in an invulnerable manner.

inzacche-ráre [*in, zacchera*], TR.: splash with mud; REFL.: be covered with dirt; perplex one's self†. **-ráto**, PART.: covered with mud; confused (embroiled).

inza-fardáre [*in, z..*], TR.: soil with grease or dirt; defile. **-fardáto**, PART.: greasy; dirty.

inzampagliáto†, ADJ.: embarrassed (entangled); hampered.

inzampognáre†, TR.: make believe (deceive, impose upon).

inzavarda.. = *inzafarda..*

inzep-paménto, M.: heap (mass, pile). ||**-páre** [*in, zeppa*], TR.: wedge; heap up (gather up); fill (cram); drive in (thrust in).

inzibettáto†, ADJ.: perfumed with civet.

inziga..† = *istiga..*

inzipilláre [*in, zipillo*], TR.: instigate (incite, urge on); teach.

inzoccoláto†, ADJ.: wearing sandals or wooden shoes.

inzol-faménto, M.: daubing with sulphur or brimstone. ||**-fáre** [*in, z..*], TR.: daub with sulphur or brimstone. **-fatóio**, M.: place where sulphur is daubed; instrument for daubing sulphur on vines.

inzotichíre [*in, zotico*], TR.: make clumsy; INTR.: become awkward or coarse; grow worse.

inzozzáre [*in, zozza*], TR.: cause to drink liquor; REFL.: drink a kind of liquor.

inzucche-ráre [*in, zucchero*], TR.: sugar (sweeten with sugar); make sweet, gentle or pleasant. **-ráto**, PART.: sugared (sweet); loving. **-ráta**, F.: act of sweetening. **-ratúra**, F.: sweetening.

in=zufoláre, TR.: urge on (incite).

inzup-pábile, ADJ.: that can be soaked in or imbibed. **-paménto**, M.: act of imbibing or soaking in. ||**-páre** [*in, zuppa*], TR.: sop (soak in, suck in); REFL.: imbibe moisture. **-páto**, PART.: soaked (imbibed).

ío [L. *ego*], PRON.: I; M.: ego; egoism.

io-dáti, M. PL. of *-dio*; (*chem.*) iodate. **-dáto**, ADJ.: with iodine. **iò-dico**, ADJ.: iodic. ||**iò-dio** [Gr. *iódes*, violet], M.: iodine. **-dúro**, M.: ioduret.

iòide [Gr. *huoidés*], F.: hyoid bone.

ionadáttico [?], ADJ.: jargon-like.

iònico [Gr. *Ionikós*], ADJ.: Ionic.

iòsa [?]. ADV.: *a* —, in great quantity.

iòta [Gr.], M.: iota (tittle, jot).

ipállage [Gr. *hupallagé*, interchange], F.: (*gram.*) hypallage.

ipecacuána [*Brazil.*], F.: ipecac(uanha) root.

ipér- [Gr. *hupér*, OVER], PREP.: hyper-, over. **-bático**, ADJ.: hyperbatic (transposed). **-'bato** [Gr. *-baton*, transposed], M.: (*gram.*) hyperbaton. **ipèr-bola**, **-bole†** [Gr. *-bolé*, over-shooting], F.: (*math.*) hyperbola; (*gram.*) hyperbole. **-boleggiaménto**, M.: hyperbolical expression; exaggeration. **-boleggiáre**, INTR.: hyperbolise (exaggerate). **-bolicaménte**, ADV.: hyperbolically. **-bòlico**, ADJ.: hyperbolical (exaggerating); (*geom.*) hyperbolic. **-bolòide** [Gr. *-bolé*, *eidos*, form], F.: hyperboloid. **-bolóne†**, *aug.* of *-bole*. **-bòreo** [Gr. *-bóreos*, north wind], ADJ.: (*poet.*) hyperborean (northern); M.: hyperborean. **-dulía**, F.: hyperdulia. **-emía** [Gr. *haima*, blood], F.: overabundance of blood in any part of the body. **-trofía** [Gr. *-trophé*, nutrition], F.: hypertrophy. **-tròfico**, ADJ.: hypertrophic.

ipnò-tico [Gr. *hupnotikós* (*húpnos*, sleep)], ADJ.: hypnotic. **-tismo**, M.: hypnotism. **-tísta**, M.: hypnotist. **-tizzáre**, TR.: hypnotize.

ipo- [Gr. *hupó*, under], PREP.: hypo-; under. **-cáusto** [Gr. *-kaustón*, burning under], M.: hypocaust. **-condría**, F.: hypochondria. **-condríaco**, ADJ.: hypochondriacal; M.: hypochondriac. **-còndrio** [Gr. *-chóndrion*, under the breastbone], M.: (*anat.*) hypochondrium. **-còndro†** = *-condria*. **-crisía** [Gr. *-krisía*, simulation], F.: hypocrisy. **ipò-crita**, M.: hypocrite (dissembler). **-critáccio**, *disp.* of *-crita*. **-critaménte**, ADV.: hypocritically. **-critíno**, *dim.* of *-crito*. **ipò-crito**, M.: hypocrite; ADJ.: hypocritical. **-critóne**, *disp.* of *-crito*. **-dèrma**, M.: hypoderm (hypoblast). **-dèrmico**, ADJ.: hypodermic. **-gástrico**, ADJ.: hypogastric. **-gástrio** [Gr. *-gástrion* (*gastér*, stomach)], M.: hypogastrium. **-gèo** [Gr. *-geios* (*gé*, earth)], M.: hypogeum (cave); tomb (vault). **ipò-stasi** [Gr. *-stásis*, standing under, subsistence], F.: hypostasis (substance); (*theol.*) personality; hypostatic union; (*med.*) sediment. **-staticaménte**, ADV.: hypostatically. **-stático**, ADJ.: hypostatic. **-tèca** [Gr. *-théke* (root *the-*, put)], F.: hypotheca (mortgage); pledge (pawn). **-tecábile**, ADJ.: that can be mortgaged, etc. **-tecáre**, TR.: hypothecate (mortgage, pawn). **-tecariaménte**, ADV.: in a hypothecating manner. **-tecário**, ADJ.: belonging to a mortgage; M.: usurer. **-tenúsa** [Gr. *-teínousa*, SUB-TENDING], F.: (*math.*) hypotenuse. **ipò-tesi** [Gr. *-thesis*, SUP-position], F.: hypothesis (supposition). **-teticaménte**, ADV.: hypothetically. **-tètico**, ADJ.: hypothetical (conditional). **-trofía** [Gr. *-trophé*, under-nutrition], F.: (*med.*) insufficient nutrition.

ippágro [Gr. *híppos*, horse], M.: wild horse.

ippo- [Gr. *híppos*, horse]: **-cámpo** [Gr. *kámpein*, bend], M.: hippocamp (sea-horse). **-castáno**, M.: horse-CHESTNUT. **Ippò-crate**, PR. N.: Hippocrates: *scienza d'* —, science of medicine. **-crático**, ADJ.: Hippocratic: *faccia* —*a*, face of a sick person. **-cratísmo**, M.: Hippocratism. **-cratísta**, M.: follower or disciple of Hippocrates. **Ippo-crène** [Gr. *-kréne*, horse-fountain], PR. N.: Hippocrene (fountain sacred to the Muses); (*poet.*) poetry. **-crénidi**, F. PL.: Muses. **ippò-dromo** [Gr. *-dromos*, horse-course], M.: hippodrome (race-course). **-fagía** [Gr. *phagéin*, eat], F.: hippophagy. **-grífo** [Gr. *grifo*, griffin], M.: hippogriff (winged horse). **-pòtamo** [Gr. *-pótamos*, river-horse], M.: hippopotamus.

ipsilon(ne), **-lònne**, M.: ipsilon (Greek *υ*).

ipso iúre [L.], ADV.: by the law itself.

ira [L.], F.: anger (wrath); grave discord: *aver in* —, hate; *un'* — *di Dio*, a wicked person; *esser in* — *a uno*, be hated by one; *esser in* — *alla sorte*, be hated by fortune (be unfortunate); PL. *ire scatenate*, untamed shrews. **-condaménte**, ADV.: angrily (passionately). **-cóndia**, F.: habitual anger (wrath). **-condióso†**, **-cóndo**, ADJ.: irascible (choleric). **-cúndia†** = *-condia*. **-ménto**, M.: wrath (choler, anger).

iránico [fr. Pers.], ADJ.: Iranian.

irá-re†, REFL.: be angry (fume). **i-scíbile** [L. *-scibilis*], ADJ.: irascible (prone to anger). **-scibilità**, F.: irascibility. **-scibilménte**, **-taménte**, ADV.: irascibly (angrily). **irá-to**, ADJ.: irate (angry, enraged).

ircáno [*Ircanis*], ADJ.: Ircanian: *tigre* —*na*, Ircanian tiger (person hard of heart).

irco [L. *hircus*], M.: he-goat.

ire [L.], DEFECT.§; INTR.: go: — *per mala via*, go on badly; *se n' è ito*, he is gone (he is dead).

§ Ind. Pres.† *ite*. Impf.† *iva*, *ivi*, etc. Pret.† *isti*; *irono*. Part. *ito*.

i-reos [*Iris*], M.: iris (flag-flower). **-ridácee**, F. PL.: Iridaceæ. **i-ri†**, F.: iris (rainbow). **-ridáto**, ADJ.: variegated (many-coloured). **-ridáre**, TR.: give the colours of the rainbow. **Ii-ride** [L. *Iris*], F.: Iris, messenger of the gods; rainbow; iris of the eye; (*bot.*) iris order. **-ridescènte**, ADJ.: iridescent. **-ridescènza**, F.: iridescence. **-rídico**, PL. —*ci*, ADJ.: (*chem.*) iridic; M.: iridium (whitish metal).

i-ronía [L.], F.: irony. **-ronicaménte,** ADV.: ironically. **-rònico,** ADJ.: ironical. **-rosaménte,** ADV.: irefully (angrily). **-róso,** ADJ.: ireful (wrathful). **-rrabiosíto†,** ADJ.: enraged.

irraccontábile [*in-*, *r.*.], ADJ.: that cannot be related.

irra-diaménto, M.: irradiation. ‖**-diáre** [L.], TR.: irradiate (illuminate with rays); INTR.: shine. **-diáto,** PART.: radiant (shining).

irrafrenábile†, ADJ.: unrestrainable.

irrag-giaménto, M.: irradiation (emanation of rays). ‖**-giáre** [*irradiare*], TR.: irradiate (illuminate). **-giáto,** PART.: irradiated (illuminated). **-giatóre,** M.: enlightener (illuminator); instructor.

irragionévo-le [*in-*, *r.* .], ADJ.: unreasonable. **-lézza,** F.: unreasonableness. **-lménte,** ADV.: unreasonably.

irranci-diménto, M.: rancidness. ‖**-díre** [*in*, *rancido*], INTR.: become rancid.

irrappresentábile [*in-*, *r.* .], ADJ.: irrepresentable.

irrazio-nábile†, ADJ.: irrational (unreasonable). **-nabilità†,** F.: irrationalness. **-nabilménte†,** ADV.: irrationally. ‖**-nále** [L. *-nalis*], ADJ.: irrational (unreasonable). **-nalità,** F.: irrationality (unreasonableness). **-nalménte,** ADV.: irrationally (unreasonably).

irreconciliábi-le [*in-*, *r.* .], ADJ.: irreconcilable (implacable). **-lità,** F.: irreconcilableness. **-lménte,** ADV.: irreconcilably.

irrecuperábi-le [*in-*, *r.* .], ADJ.: irrecuperable (irrecoverable). **-lménte,** ADV.: irrecuperably.

irrecusábi-le [*in-*, *r.* .], ADJ.: irrecusable. **-lménte,** ADV.: irrecusably.

irreden-tísmo, M.: 'irredemption-ism' (political movement for unification in Italy). **-tísta,** M.: 'irredemptionist.' ‖**irredèn-to** [*in-*, *r.* .], ADJ.: unredeemed (lacking liberty).

irredimíbile [*in-*, *r.* .], ADJ.: irredeemable.

irrefragábi-le [L. *-lis*], ADJ.: irrefragable (unanswerable). **-lità,** F.: irrefragableness. **-lménte,** ADV.: irrefragably.

irrefrangíbile [*in-*, *r.* .], ADJ.: irrefrangible.

irrefrenábi-le [*in-*, *r.* .], ADJ.: unrestrainable. **-lménte,** ADV.: in an unrestrainable manner.

irrefutábile [L. *-lis*], ADJ.: irrefutable (undisputable).

irrego-láre [*in-*, *r.* .], ADJ.: irregular. **-larità,** F.: irregularity; incapacity of administering the sacrament. **-larménte,** ADV.: irregularly. **-lataménte†,** ADV.: in a disorderly manner. **-láto†,** ADJ.: irregular (disorderly).

irreli-gióne [L. *-gio*], F.: irreligion (impiety). **-giosaménte,** ADV.: irreligiously. **-giosità,** F.: irreligiousness. **-gióso,** ADJ.: irreligious.

irremeábile†, ADJ.: irremeable.

irreme-diábile [L. *-diabilis*], **-diévole,** ADJ.: irremediable. **-diabilménte,** ADV.: irremediably.

irremissíbi-le [L. *-lis*], ADJ.: irremissible (unpardonable). **-lménte,** ADV.: irremissibly.

irremovíbi-le [*in-*, *r.* .], ADJ.: irremovable; inflexible. **-lità,** F.: irremovability. **-lménte,** ADV.: irremovably.

irremune-rábile [L. *-rabilis*], ADJ.: irremunerable. **-ráto,** ADJ.: unrewarded.

irreparábi-le [L. *-lis*], ADJ.: irreparable. **-lménte,** ADV.: irreparably.

irreperíbile [*in-*, *r.* .], ADJ.: that cannot be found or met with.

irreprensíbi-le [L. *-lis*], ADJ.: irreprehensible (blameless, innocent). **-lità,** F.: irreprehensibility. **-lménte,** ADV.: irreprehensibly.

irreprobábile†, ADJ.: irreprovable (unblamable).

irrepugnábi-le [*in-*, *r.* .], ADJ.: unquestionable. **-lità,** F.: unquestionableness. **-lménte,** ADV.: unquestionably.

irre-quietaménte, ADV.: restlessly. **-quietézza,** F.: restlessness. ‖**-quièto** [L. *-quietus*], ADJ.: restless (unquiet, uneasy). **-quietúdine** = *-quietezza*.

irresipolíre [*in*, *resipola*], INTR., REFL.: take the erysipelas.

irresistíbi-le [L. *-lis*], ADJ.: irresistible. **-lità,** F.: irresistibleness. **-lménte,** ADV.: irresistibly.

irresolúbile†, ADJ.: irresoluble (insoluble); incorruptible.

irreso-lutaménte, ADV.: irresolutely. **-lutézza,** F.: irresoluteness. ‖**-lúto** [L. *-lutus*], ADJ.: irresolute; unsolved. **-luzióne,** F.: irresolution.

irrespirábile [*in-*, *r.* .], ADJ.: irrespirable.

irresponsábi-le [*in-*, *r.* .], ADJ.: irresponsible. **-lità,** F.: irresponsibility. **-lménte,** ADV.: irresponsibly.

irre-taménto†, M.: ensnaring. ‖**-tíre** [*in*, *rete*], TR.: catch in a snare or net; (*fig.*) ensnare.

irretrattábile = *irritrattabile*.

irreveren. . = *irriveren. .*

irrevo-cábile [L. *-cabilis*], ADJ.: irrevocable. **-cabilità,** F.: irrevocability. **-cabilménte,** ADV.: irrevocably (without recall). **-cáto,** ADJ.: not recalled (not revoked). **-chévole†** = *-cabile*.

irricchíre†, TR.: enrich; INTR.: become rich (thrive).

irriconoscíbi-le [*in-*, *r.* .], ADJ.: unrecognizable. **-lità,** F.: irrecognition.

irricordévole†, ADJ.: forgetful (unmindful).
irrídero [*in*, *r*. .], IRR.; TR.: deride (laugh at, mock).
irríducíbile [*in*-, *r*. .]. ADJ.: irreducible.
irriflos-sióne, F.: want of reflection (thoughtlessness). ‖**-sívo** [*in*-, *r*. .], ADJ.: thoughtless.
irri-gábile, ADJ.: easy to irrigate. ‖**-gáre** [L.], TR.: irrigate (water). **-gatóre**, M., **-gatríce**, F.: irrigator (moistener); machine for irrigating; (*med.*) injecting instrument. **-gatòrio**, ADJ.: that can irrigate. **-gazióne**, F.: irrigation.
irrigi-diménto, M.: stiffening (becoming rigid). ‖**-díre** [*in*, *rigido*], TR.: make rigid; INTR.: stiffen (become rigid).
irríguo [L. *-guus*, watering], ADJ.: watered (irrigated).
irrilevánte [*in*-, *r*. .], ADJ.: irrelevant.
irrimedi. .† = *irremedi*. .
irrimessi. .† = *irremissi*. .
irrimutábile [*in*-, *r*. .], ADJ.: immutable.
irri-sióne [L. *-sio*], F.: derision (scorn, mockery). **-sívo**, ADJ.: derisive (scornful). **irrí-so**, PART. of *-dere;* derided.
irrisolúto† = *irresoluto*.
irri-sóre [*-sione*], M.: mocker (derider). **-soriaménte**, ADV.: derisively (mockingly). **-sòrio**, ADJ.: derisory.
irri-tábile, ADJ.: irritable. **-tabilità**, F.: irritability. **-taménto**, M.: irritation (annoyance). ‖**-táre** [L.], TR.: irritate (exasperate); stimulate (urge on); REFL.: become angry. **-tatívo**, ADJ.: irritating (provoking). **-tatóre**, M., **-tatríce**, F.: provoker (exciter). **-tazioncèlla**, *dim.* of *-tazione*. **-tazióne**, F.: irritation (provocation).
írrito [L. *irritus* (*in*-, *ratus*, ratified)], ADJ.: vain (null, void).
irritrattábi-le [L. *ir-retractabilis*], ADJ.: that cannot be retracted or withdrawn. **-lità**, F.: state of not being retractable.
irritrosíre [*in*, *ritroso*], INTR.: become obstinate (grow stubborn).
irriuscíbi-le [*in*-, *r*. .], ADJ.: that cannot succeed. **-lità**, F.: unsuccessfulness.
irrivelábile [*in*-, *r*. .], ADJ.: irrevealable.
irrive-rènte [L. *irreverens*], ADJ.: irreverent (disrespectful). **-rentoménte**, ADV.: irreverently. **-rènza**, F.: irreverence (disrespect).
irrogá-re [L.], TR.: inflict (impose). **-zióne**, F.: infliction.
irrómpere [*in*-, *r*. .], IRR.; TR.: burst into (rush violently into).
irroráre [L.], TR.: bedew; wet (sprinkle).
irrubináre†, TR.: rubify (make red like the ruby).
irruènto [L. *ir-ruens* (*ruere*, rush)], ADJ.: rushing in (bursting in).
irruggini. . = *arruggini*. .
irrugiadáre†, TR.: cover with dew; sprinkle.
irruvidíre [*in*, *ruvido*], TR.: make harsh or rough; INTR., REFL.: become rough (grow rude).
irruzióne [*irrompere*], F.: irruption (sudden invasion, inroad).
ir-súto [L. *hirsutus*, rough, shaggy], ADJ.: hirsute (hairy). **-súzie**, F.: hirsuteness (hairiness). **ír-to** [L. *hirtus*], ADJ.: shaggy; rough.
isabèlla†, M.: Isabel colour (light bay).
isápo† = *isopo*.
isa-gòge [Gr. *eisagogé*], F.: isagoge (introduction). **-gògico**, ADJ.: isagogic.
isb. ., **isc**. . = *sb*. ., *sc*. .
is-chíade, F.: sciatica (hip-gout). **-chiádico**, **-chiático**, ADJ.: ischiadic. ‖**ís-chio** [Gr. *ischíon*], M.: (*anat.*) ischion; holm oak.
iscr. . = *inscr*. .
iscusáto [*scusare*], ADJ.: excused.
isd. . = *sd*. .
isg. . = *sg*. .
isl. . = *sl*. .
isla-mísmo [fr. Arab.], M.: Islamism. **-míta**, ADJ.: Mohammedan. **-mítico**, ADJ.: Islamitic.
ism. ., **isn**. . = *sm*. ., *sn*. .
is-o. . [Gr. *ísos*, equal]: **-ocronísmo**, M.: isochronism. **-òcrono** [Gr. *chrónos*, time], ADJ.: isochronal (uniform). **-ògono** [Gr. *gónos*, angle)], ADJ.: isogonic. **-ogòniche**, F. PL.: isogonic lines.
íso-la [L. *insula*], F.: island (isle); group of houses isolated from all others. **-lábile**, ADJ.: isolable. **-laménto**, M.: isolation. **-láno**, M.: islander. **-lánte**, ADJ.: insulating; M.: insulator. **-láre**, TR.: isolate; insulate; REFL.: separate one's self from society. **-lário**, M.: book which describes islands; number of islands. **-láto**, M.: isolated house (isolated quarter); PART.: isolated (solitary). **-latóre**, M., **-latríce**, F.: isolator; insulator (non-conducting stool). **-létta**, **-lína**, *dim*. of *-la*. **-lòtto**, M.: islet.
isònne (*a*) [?], ADV.: abundantly (in great quantity).
isòpo = *issopo*.
is-o. . [Gr. *ísos*, equal]: **-òscele** [*skélos*, leg], ADJ.: isosceles (with two equal sides). **-òtere** [Gr. *théros*, summer], ADJ.: isotheral. **-otèrmiche** [*thérmos*, heat], ADJ.: isothermal.
ispánico [L. *Hispania*, Spain], ADJ.: Spanish.
isp. ., cf. also *sp*. .
ispe-ttoráto, M.: inspector's office; room

or residence of the inspector. ||-ttóre [L. in-spector], M.: inspector (superintendent); (rail.) — dell' atrio, inspector of the railway station. -ttrice, F.: inspectress. -zionáre, TR.: inspect (examine). -zióne, F.: inspection; overseeing.

ispi-dézza, F.: roughness (ruggedness); hairiness. ||**ispi-do** [L. *hispidus*], ADJ.: rough (rugged); shaggy; thorny (bushy).

ispi-rábile, ADJ.: inspirable. ||**-ráre** [L. *in-spirare* (breathe)], TR.: inspire with (suggest, arouse); inspire (animate); induce (counsel); suggest; REFL.: get inspiration; breathe. **-ratóre**, M., **-ratrice**, F.: inspirer. **-razioneèlla**, *dim.* of *-razione*. **-razióne**, F.: inspiration.

isq. . = *sq.* .

israe-líta [*Israel*], M.: Israelite. **-lítico**, ADJ.: Israelitic.

issa†, ADV.: now (at this instant).

issáre [l. Ger. *hissen*], TR.: (*naut.*) hoist (lift up).

issofátto = *ipso facto*.

issòpo [L. *hyssopus*], M.: (*bot.*) hyssop.

ist. ., cf. also *st.* .

istan-taneaménte, ADV.: instantaneously. **-taneità**, F.: instantaneousness. **-táneo**, ADJ.: instantaneous. ||**istán-te** [L. *in-stans*], M.: instant (moment); ADJ.: instant (pressing, urgent); present†: *a ogni* —, frequent (often); *essere in* —†, be imminent. **-teménte**, ADV.: instantly. **istán-za**, F.: instance (solicitation); request; (*law*) judgment.

istáre = *instare*.

istáto = *stato*.

is-tèrico [L. *hystericus*, pertaining to the womb], ADJ.: hysteric (hysterical). **-terismo**, M.: hysteria.

is-tessaménte, ADV.: in the same manner. **-tésso** [*stesso*], ADJ.: same (self).

isti-gaménto, M.: instigation. ||**-gáre** [L. *instigare*], TR.: instigate (stimulate, incite). **-gatóre**, M., **-gatrice**, F.: instigator. **-gazióne**, F.: instigation.

istilláre = *instillare*.

istin-tivaménte†, ADV.: instinctively. **-tívo**, ADJ.: instinctive. ||**istín-to** [L. *instinctus*], M.: instinct (natural impulse).

isti-tuíre [L. *in-stituere*], TR.: institute (establish); instruct; undertake (begin). **-túto**, M.: institution; religious order; PART.† of *-tuire;* instituted. **-tutóre**, M., **-tutrice**, F.: institutor; preceptor or preceptress. **-tuzióne**, F.: institution; instruction; foundation; PL.: political organism; beginning of a science.

ist-mico, ADJ.: Isthmian. ||**ist-mo** [Gr. *isthmós*], M.: isthmus.

isto-logía [Gr. *histós*, tissue, *lógos*, treatise], F.: histology. **-lògico**, ADJ.: histological.

istò-ria [L. *historia*], F.: history (account, story). **-riále**†, ADJ.: historical. **-rialménte**†, ADV.: historically. **-riáre**, TR.: ornament (embellish). **-ricaménte**, ADV.: historically. **istò-rico**, ADJ.: historic; M.: historian. **-riétta**, F.: historiette (brief recital, tale). **-riògrafo**, M.: historiographer (historian); ADJ.†: historical.

istrad. . = *strad.* .

istràtto†, ADJ.: extracted; concave (hollow).

istrice [Gr. *hústrix*], M.: hedgehog (porcupine): *penna d'* —, porcupine quill; *pare un* —, he appears to be a porcupine (i.e., intractable).

istriodomía, F.: art of sailing.

istri-óne [L. *histrio*], M: histrion (actor, player). **-onésco**, ADJ.: histrionical. **-onicaménto**, ADV.: histrionically. **-ònico**, pl. *-onici* ADJ.: histrionic (theatrical).

istruíre [L. *in-struere*], IRR. (cf. *construire*); TR.: instruct (teach); inform; advise (counsel): — *un affare*, prosecute an affair.

istrumen-tále, ADJ.: instrumental. **-táre**, TR.: compose (operatic music); play upon an instrument. **-tário**, M.: case for musical instruments; maker of musical instruments†. **-tazióne**, F.: musical score. ||**istrumén-to** [L. *instrumentum*], M.: instrument (tool, implement); deed; PL.: arms.

istru-ttivaménte, ADV.: instructively. **-ttívo**, ADJ.: instructive. **-ttóre**, M.: instructor. **-ttòria**, F.: (*leg.*) instruction. **-ttòrio**, ADJ.: instructive. ||**-zióne** [*-ire*], F.: instruction (education); information; (*leg.*) acts necessary to prosecute a case.

istupi-díre [*stupido*], INTR.: become stupid; TR.: stupify (make stupid). **-díto**, PART.: stupified (senseless, dull).

isv. . = *sv.* .

ita-cismo [Gr. letter *eta*], M.: itacism (pronunciation of the Gr. η as *i*).

Itá-lia, F.: Italy. **-lianáccio**, *disp.* of *-liano*. **-lianaménte**, ADV.: after the Italian manner: *scrivere* —, write good Italian. **-lianáre**† = *-lianizzare*. **-lianeggiáre**, INTR.: speak in the Italian manner. **-lianismo**, M.: Italianism. **-lianità**, F.: Italian character. **-lianizzáre**, TR.: Italianize (render into Italian); affect (Italian manners). **-liáno**, ADJ., M.: Italian; ADV.: *all'* —*na*, in the Italian manner. **-licismo**, M.: Italicism. **itá-lico**, pl. —*ci*, ADJ.: Italic (Italian): *lingue -liche*, languages of ancient Italy. **itá-lo** = *-liano*.

item†, ADV.: item, also; likewise; again.

iterá-re [L. -re (*iter*, again)], TR.: iterate (repeat). **-taménte**, ADV.: repeatedly. **-zióne**† F.: reiteration (repetition).

itinerário [L. *itiner*, course], M.: itinerary (description of a journey); way.

ito, PART. of *ire*.

ittè-rico, pl. *-rici* [Gr. *ikteros*, yellow of the skin], ADJ.: icterical (jaundiced). **-rízia**, F.: jaundice.

ittiòfago, pl. *—gi* [Gr. *ichthuo-phágos*], ADJ.: fish eating; M.: fish-eater.

ittio-logía [Gr. *ichthuo-logía*, fish-treatise], F.: ichthyology. **-lògico**, ADJ.: ichthyological. **ittiò-logo**, pl. *—gi*, M.: ichthyologist.

iubilèo†, M.: jubilee.

iudicáre† *giudicare*.

iúgero [L. *-rum*], M.: fourth part of an acre (*juger*).

iúgo [L. *-gum*], M.: yoke; slavery.

iuguláre [L. *-laris*], ADJ.: jugular.

iunióre [L. *-nior*], M.: junior (younger).

iú-ra†, F.: conspiration (plot). ‖**iú-re** [L. *jus*], M.: law; right. **-rídico**, ADJ.: juridical (legal). **-ridizióne**, F.: jurisdiction.

iuspatronáto†, M.: patronage.

iusquiámo†, M.: (*bot.*) henbane.

iussióne [L. *-ssio*], F.: order (command); summons.

iust.. *giust..*

ivi [L. *ibi*], ADV.: there (in that place); there†: *entro*, within. **-rítta**†, ADV.: there (just there).

izza†, F.: anger (wrath).

izzappáre†, TR.: dig around or about; hoe.

K

k *cappa* or (*pop.*) *ca* [L., Gr.], M.: k (the letter). Used only in some foreign proper nouns.

L

L.], M.: l (the letter)
(before vowel or *h*), or *lo*.
illa], F., ART.: the; PR.: her, it;

labii, in a hymn], M.: (*mus.*) la.
se], ADV.: there; further on: --
thereabout, *più* , further that
fare in , go on or forwards;
crastinate), *entrar troppo in* ,
r; enlarge too much, *saper più*
better, be more cunning.
[*alabarda*], F.: HALBERD. **-dá-**
-low or thrust of a halberd.

lábaro [L. *-rum*], M.: labarum (Roman standard).

láb-bia†, F.: face, aspect (as pl. of *-bro*) lips. **-biále**, **-báto** = *labiale, labiato*.

lab-bráta, F.: slap on the mouth. **-bratóne**, *aug.* of *-brata*. **-brétto**, **-brettíno**, *car. dim.* of *-bro*. ‖**-bro**, pl. *-bri*, *-bra* [L. *-brum*], M.: LIP: (*fig.*) brim, edge. **-bróna**, F.: thick-lipped woman. **-bróne**, M.: *disp. aug.* of *-bro*; thick-lipped person. **-bráccio**, **-brúzzo**, *car. dim.* of *-bro*.

lá-be† [L. *-bes* (*labi*, fall)], F.: stain (spot). **-befatto** [L. *be-factus*], ADJ.: labefied (tottered, shaken, weakened).

laberínto [Gr. *-búrinthos*], M.: labyrinth.

la-biále [L. *-bium*, LIP], ADJ., M.: labial. **-biáto**, ADJ.: labiate.

lábi-le [L. *-lis* (*labi*, fall)], ADJ.: easily falling or sliding; slippery; transitory. **-lità**, F.: slipperiness; caducity.

labiodentále [L. *labium*, LIP, It. *dentale*], ADJ., M.: labiodental.

labirínto, pop. = *laberinto*.

labo-ratòrio, M.: laboratory. ‖**labò-re**† [L. *-r*], M.: labour (work, fatigue). **-riosaménte**, ADV.: laboriously. **-riosíssimo**, ADJ.: very (or most) laborious. **-riosità**, F.: laboriousness. **-rióso**, ADJ.: laborious.

lácca 1 [Pers. *lak* (red ink)], F.: lacquer; blow: *cera —*, sealing-wax.

lácca 2 [? Gr. *lakḗ*, ditch], F.: low place; bank; haunch.

laccétto, M.: *dim.* of *laccio*; esp. knotted strip (of ribbon or leather).

lac-chè [Fr. *laquais*], M.: lackey (footman). **-chezzíno**, *car. dim.* of *-chezzo*. **-chézzo**, [?], M.: dainty bit (tidbit); allurement (charm); smart saying (jest).

lacchétta† 1, *dim.* of *-ca* 2.

lacchétta† 2 [*racchetta*], F.: racket (battledore).

láccia†, F.: shadfish: *a prima —*, at the beginning of spring (the shad migrating then).

lac-ciáia, F.: large lasso. ‖**-cio** [L. *laqueus*, snare], M.: LASSO; gin (snare; deceit). **-cioletto**, **-ci(u)òlo**, *dim.* of *-cio*.

lace-rábile, ADJ.: lacerable (tearable). **-raménto**, M.: laceration (tearing); outrage (insult). ‖**-ráre** [L.], TR.: lacerate (tear, rend); outrage (slander). **-ratóre**, M., **-ratríce**, F.: lacerator; defamer. **-razióne**, F.: laceration (tearing); slander. **láce-ro**, ADJ.: lacerated (torn); defamed; M.: wear (decay).

lacèrt..† : *lucert..*

lacèrto [L. *-tus*], M.: lacertus (muscle of the upper arm).

láci†, ADV.: there (in that place).

láco† [L. *-cus*], M.: (*poet.*) lake.

laco-nicaménte, ADV.: laconically (concisely). ||**lacò-nico**, pl. *-ci* [*-nicus* (Gr. *lákon*, Laconian, Spartan)], ADJ.: laconic (concise, brief). **-nismo**, M.: laconism.

lácri-ma [L. *-ma*], F.: TEAR. **-mábile**†, ADJ.: lamentable (mournful, worthy of tears). **-mále**, ADJ.: lachrymal. **-mánte**, ADJ.: in tears (weeping). **-máre**, INTR.: shed tears (weep); deplore (bewail). **-máto**, ADJ.: bewailed (wept for, mourned for). **-matóio**, M.: tear-gland. **-crimatòrio**, ADJ.: lachrymatory. **-mazióne**, F.: lachrymation (weeping produced by disease of the eye). **-métta**, *car. dim.* of *-ma*. **-mévole**, ADJ.: lamentable (deplorable). **-mína**, **-míno**, *dim.* of *-ma*. **-mosaménte**, ADV.: with tears (mournfully). **-móso**, ADJ.: lacrimose (tearful, weeping); lamentable. **-múccia**, *dim.* of *-ma*.

lacú-na [L.], F.: lacuna (gap, space, defect); LAGOON†. **-nále**†, ADJ.: marshy. **-nóso**†, ADJ.: full of pools; full of gaps. **-náre**, M.: lacunæ (sunken panels in ceiling). **lacú-stre**, ADJ.: lacustral (found in lakes).

ladíno [*latino*], ADJ.: Ladinian; M.: Ladin (dialect in Tyrol, etc.).

laddó-ve [*là, dove*], ADV.: there where; while; on the contrary; CONJ.†: provided that. **-vúnque**, ADV.: everywhere.

ládo†, ADJ.: ugly; base (mean).

lá-dra, F.: thief; inside pocket. **-dracchièla**, **-dracchiòlo**, *dim.* of *-dro*. **-dráccio**, *disp.* of *-dro*. **-draménte**, ADV.: thievishly; rascally. **-drería**, F.: theft (stealing). **-dríno**, *dim.* of *-dro*. ||**-dro** [L. *-tro*], M.: thief (robber); candle-waster (broken wick wasting the candle); ADJ.: villainous; wretched; ugly (disagreeable): *al —*, thief! stop thief! **-drocínio**, M.: theft (robbery on a large scale). **-dronáia**, F.: thieving; cheating. **-dronáia**, F.: gang of thieves; robbery. **-dronáta**, F.: theft (thievish actions). **-droncèlla**, *dim.* of *-dra*. **-droncellería**, F.: petty theft; larceny. **-droncèllo**, *dim.* of *-dro*. **-dróne**, M.: *aug.* of *-dro*; highwayman (robber, bandit): *— di mare*, pirate. **-dronéccio**, **-dronéggio**, M.: thieving; cheating. **-droneggiáre**†, INTR.: thieve (rob). **-dronería**, F.: robbing (an employer, etc.), cheating, thievery. **-dronescaménte**, ADV.: thievishly; knavishly. **-dronésco**, ADJ.: thievish; knavish. **-drúccio**, *disp. dim.* of *-dro*. **-drúncolo**, *disp. dim.* of *-dro*.

lagèna [L.], F.: stone-jar (pitcher for wine, oil, etc.).

laggiù [*là, giù*], ADV.: there below (yonder); far off.

la-ghettíno, *dim.* of *-ghetto*. **-ghétto**, *car. dim.* of *lago*.

lá-gna†, F.: pain (anguish); affliction (trouble). **-gnaménto**†, M.: complaint (moan). **-gnánza**, F.: complaint; grief. ||**-gnáre** [L. *laniare*, rend], REFL.: grieve; complain (moan). **-gnévole**, ADJ.: plaintive; doleful. **-gno**, M.: grief; complaint (lamentation). **-gnosaménte**†, ADV.: mournfully. **-gnóso**†, ADJ.: mournful; plaintive.

lá-go [L. *-cus*], M.: fresh-water LAKE: *-ghi del cuore*, (*anat.*) ventricles. **-góne**, M.: *aug.* of *-go*; lagoon; pl. *-goni*, pools of boiling water on volcanic land.

lágrim.. = *lacrim..*

la-gúme†, F.: swamp (morass, marsh, fen). ||**-gúna** [L. *-cuna* (*lacus*, lake)], F.: lagoon; pool.

lái [Fr.], PL. M.: (*poet.*) plaint; lay (popular ballad).

lai-cále, ADJ.: laical (profane). **-ca(l)ménte**, ADJ.: laically (secular). **-cáto**, M.: laymen. **-cità**, F.: laity. **-cizzáre**, TR.: make laic. ||**lái-co**, pl. *-ci* [L. *-cus*], ADJ.: LAY (secular); ignorant†; M.: layman†: *frate —*, lay-brother.

lai-daménte, ADV.: uglily; indecently. **-dáre**†, TR.: soil (stain). **-dézza**, F.: ugliness; indecency. **-díre**† = *-dáre*. **-díssimo**, ADJ.: very (or most) ugly. **-dità**†, F.: ugliness; deformity. ||**lái-do** [Ger. *leid* (ak. to Eng. *loth*)], ADJ.: ugly (repulsive); indecent; M.: = *-dezza*. **-dúme**, M.: mass of ugly things (loathsome heap).

laldáre† = *laudare*.

láma 1 [L.], F.: swamp (bog, fen).

láma 2 [L. *-mina*], F.: sword-blade; plate†: *una buona —*, good swordsman.

láma 3, pl. *-mi* [fr. Thib.], M.: lama (chief priest of Thibetans).

láma 4 [Peruv.], M.: llama (South-Am. animal).

lamáccia, *disp.* of *lama* 2.

lambènte [L. *-bens*], ADJ.: lambent (licking); sliding.

lambic-caménto, M.: distillation; close examination (study). **-cáre**, TR.: distil†; examine closely; REFL.: examine one's self, puzzle: *-carsi il cervello*, puzzle one's brain. **-cáto**†, M.: distilled portion (extract). **-catóre**, M.: brain-puzzler (deep thinker). **-catúra**, F.: brain puzzling. ||**lambíc-co** [Ar. *al-anbiq*], M.: alembic (still).

lam-biménto†, M.: licking; lapping. ||**-bíre** [L. *-bere*], TR.: lick; LAP. **-bitívo**, M.: lambative.

lam-brúsca [L. *labrusca*], F.: wild grape. **-bruscáre**, REFL.: to grow wild. **-brúsco**, M.: wine of Bologna and Modena.

lamèl-la† [L.], F.: lamella (scale). **-lá-re**, ADJ.: lamellar (flat and thin).

lamen-tábile, ADJ.: lamentable. **-tabilménte**, ADV.: lamentably. **-taménto**†, M., **-tánza**, F.: lament (complaint). ‖**-táre** [L. *-tari*], TR.: lament (complain). **-táto**, ADJ.: lamented (complained). **-tatóre**, M.: lamenter (complainer). **-tatòrio**†, ADJ.: lamentable (plaintive, mournful). **-tatríce**, F.: lamenter. **-tazioncèlla**, *dim.* of *-tazione*. **-tazióne**, F.: lamentation; Lamentations (Old Testament). **-tévole**, ADJ.: lamentable (plaintive). **-tevolménte**, ADV.: lamentably. **-tío**, M.: prolonged lamentation. **lamé-nto**, M.: lament (wailing). **-tosaménte**, ADV.: lamentably. **-tóso**, ADJ.: lamentable (mournful).

lamét-ta, *dim.* of *lama* 2. **-tína**, *dim.* of *-ta*.

lámia†, F.: shark; also = *lammia*.

la-mièra, F.: metal plate; breastplate†. **-mieríno**, M.: thin metal plate. **-mieróne**, M.: heavy plate. ‖**lá-mina** [L.], F.: lamina (thin metal plate). **-mináre**, TR.: laminate (cover with plates). **-minatóio**, M.: machine for laminating. **-minatúra**, F.: lamination. **-mineria**, F.: laminating shop. **-minétta**, *dim.* of *-mina*. **-minóso**, ADJ.: laminated (plated).

lámmia† [L. *lamia*], F.: sorceress (witch); nymph; fabulous animal.

lám-pa† [L. *-pas*], F.: light; splendour.

lám-pada [L.], F.: lamp (light). **-padário**, M.: altar-lamp. **-padétta**, **-padína**, *dim.* of *-pada*. **lám-pana**, F.: church-lamp (light). **-panáio**, M.: lamp-maker; lamp-lighter. **-panétta**, *dim.* of *-pana*. **-panino**, M.: *dim.* of *-panetta*; (esp.) starlight. **-panéggio**†, M.: moonlight. **-pánte**, ADJ.: bright (clear, limpid). **-páre**† = *-peggiare*. **-peggiaménto**, M.: light (lustre, flash). **-peggiánte**, ADJ.: luminous (resplendant). **-peggiáre**, INTR.: lighten (shine, flash, glitter). **-péggio**†, M.: flash; lightning. **-pionàio**, M.: street-lamplighter. **-pioncíno**, *dim.* of *-pione*. **-pióne**, M.: street-lamp; carriage-lamp; porch-lamp. **lámpo**, M.: lightning; flash.

lampóne [?], M.: raspberry.

lamprè-da [L. *lampetra*], F.: lamprey. **-dòtto**, M.: *dim.* of *-da*; intestines of slaughtered animals.

lá-na [L.], F.: wool (fleece). **-nággio**, M.: raw wool. **-nai(u)òlo**, M.: worker in wools; wool-dealer. **-náto**†, ADJ.: woolly.

...n-ce† [L. *lanx*], F.: balance (scales). **...lla**, *dim.* of *-ce*. **...ceoláto**, ADJ.: lanceolate. **-cétta**, ...ancet; hand of a watch. **-cettáta**, F.: lance-thrust; lance-wound. **-cettína**, *dim.* of *-cetta*. ‖**lán-cia** [L. *-cea*], F.: lance (spear); lancer; long-boat. **-ciábile**, ADJ.: lanceable. **-ciáio**, M.: lance-maker. **-ciaménto**†, M.: lancing (thrusting, darting). **-ciáre**, TR.: lance (thrust, dart); REFL.: rush upon (fall upon). **-ciáta**, F.: lance-wound (thrust). **-ciatóia**, F.: bird-snare. **-ciatóre**, M., **-ciatríce**, F., **-cièro**, M.: lancer (knight). **-cièro**†, ADJ.: armed with a lance. **lán-cio**, M.: leap (bound). **-ciòla**†, *dim.* of *-cia*. **-cióne**, *aug.* of *-cia*. **-cionière**†, M.: lancer. **-ciottáre**†, TR.: wound with a lance. **-ciottáta**†, F.: lance-thrust. **-ciòtto**†, M.: short lance (javelin). **-ciuòla**† = *-ciola*.

lánda [Ger. *land*], F.: land; flat country.

lándra†, F.: prostitute.

landò [Ger. city *Landau*], M.: landau (coach, carriage).

landróne [*androne*], M.: corridor (hall, portal).

la-nería [*-na*], F.: large assortment of wool. **-nétta**, F.: *dim.* of *-na*; inferior wool.

lánfa [*nanfa*], ADJ.: flavoured with orange-flower extract.

langóre† = *-guore*.

lan-graviáto, M.: landgraviate (authority of landgrave). ‖**-grávio** [Ger. *landgraf*], M.: landgrave (German nobleman).

lan-gueggiáre† = *-guire*. **-guènte**, ADJ.: languid. **-guidaménte**, ADV.: languidly. **-guidétto**, *car. dim.* of *-guido*. **-guidézza**, F.: languidness (feebleness). **-guidíssimo**, ADJ.: very (most) languid. **lán-guido**, ADJ.: languid (weak, faint). **-guidóre**†, **-guiménto**, M.: languidness (weakness). ‖**-guíre** [L. *-guere*], INTR.: languish (grow weak, faint). **-guiscènte**†, ADJ.: languishing (weak, faint). **-guóre**, M., **-gúra**, F.: languor (weakness, faintness).

laniá-re† [L.], TR.: laniate (rend, tear). **-tóre**†, M.: killer of beasts.

lanière†, M.: lanneret (hawk).

la-nífero†, ADJ.: laniferous (bearing wool). **-nifíciò**†, ADJ.: woollen. **-nígero**, ADJ.: lanigerous (bearing wool). **-nína**, *dim.* of *-na*. **-níno**, M.: wool-worker; clothier. ‖**lá-no** [L. *-na*], ADJ.: woollen. **-nosità**, F.: woolliness. **-nóso**, ADJ.: woolly (hairy).

lantèr-na [L.], F.: lantern. **-náccia**, *disp.* of *-na*. **-nággio**, M.: lantern-duty. **-náio**†, M.: lantern-maker. **-nína**, **-nétta**, **-níno**, *dim.* of *-na*. **-nóne**, *aug.* of *-na*. **-núccia**, *disp. dim.* of *-na*. **-núto**†, ADJ.: lantern-like (thin, lean).

la-núgine [L. *-nugo* (*lana*, wool)], F.:

down (soft hair). **-nuginóso,** ADJ.: lanuginous (downy). **-núto,** ADJ.: woolly (downy). **-núzza†,** F.: fine wool; soft hair.

lan-zichenécco [Ger. *landsknecht*], M.: lansquenet (foot-soldier). **lán-zo,** M.: German foot-soldier.

laónde [*là, onde*], ADV.: therefore; wherefore; thus.

lapázio [L. *-pathum*], M.: sorrel (grass).

lápi-da [L. *-pis*], F.: stone. **-dábile,** ADJ.: worthy of being stoned. **-dáre,** TR.: stone. **-dária,** F.: lapidation; art of writing or interpreting inscriptions. **-dário,** ADJ.: lapidary; M.: lapidist (cutter of precious stones). **-datóre,** M., **-datríce,** F.: stone-thrower. **-dazióne,** F.: lapidation (stoning). **lápi-de,** F.: gravestone; precious stone. **-'deo,** ADJ.: stony. **-descènte,** ADJ.: lapidescent (petrifying). **-dificáre,** TR.: lapidify (make like stone). **-dificazióne,** F.: lapidification. **-difórme,** ADJ.: stone-like. **-dína,** *dim.* of *-de.* **-dóna,** *aug.* of *-de.* **-dóso†,** ADJ.: stony (full of stones). **-lláre†,** TR.: crystallize. **la-pí-llo,** M.: small stone; crystallized matter; broken pieces of lava. **-llóso,** ADJ.: crystalline. **lápi-s,** (*pop.*) **lá-pi-sse,** M.: leadpencil; lapis (stone); red chalk (hematite). **-slázzaro, -slázzoli, -slázzolo, -slázzuli,** M.: lapis lazuli (precious stone). **-sáccio,** *disp.* of *lapis.*

láppe láppe, or **láppi láppi** [echoic], M.: smacking (of the lips): *far — —,* have a longing, long.

láp-pola [L. *-pa*], F.: burdock. **-polétta, -polína,** *dim.* of *-pola.* **-polóna, -polóne,** *aug.* of *-pola.*

laqueáto†, ADJ.: vaulted.

lar-dáccio, *disp.* of *-do.* **-dáre** = *-dellare.* **-dáto†,** ADJ.: larded; greasy. **-datóio†,** M.: larding-pin. **-datúra,** F.: larding (stuffing with bacon or pork). **-delláre,** TR.: lard (stuff with bacon). **-delláto,** ADJ.: larded. **-dellatúra,** F.: larding. **-dellétto, -dellíno,** *dim.* of *-dello.* **-dèllo,** M.: piece of bacon or pork. **‖lár-do** [L. *-dum*], M.: lard (fat: Eng.† bacon, pork). **-dóne,** M.: salted pork.

lar-gáccio, *disp. aug.* of *-go.* **-gaménte,** ADV.: largely (widely, amply). **-gáre†,** TR.: enlarge (widen, expand). **-gheggiaménto,** M.: liberality. **-gheggiáre,** INTR.: be liberal; make largesses (presents). **-gheggiatóre,** M.: liberal man. **-ghétto,** ADJ.: *dim.* of *-go;* (*mus.*) slow. **-ghézza,** F.: width; liberality; abundance; permission†. **-ghíssimo,** ADJ.: very (most) large (wide). **-ghità†,** F.: largeness; liberality. **-giménto†,** M.: liberality. **-gíre,** TR.: give liberally (lavish); bestow (grant). **-gità,** F.: liberality (largess). **-gitóre,** M., **-gitríce,** F.: liberal giver; granter. **-gizióne,** F.: largition (gift). **‖lár-go** [L. *-gus*], ADJ.: large (wide, broad); liberal (generous, open-handed); ADV.: largely, broadly; M.: space; breadth (latitude). **-gòccio,** *aug.* of *-go.* **-goveggènte†,** ADJ.: far-sighted. **-gúra,** F.: space (wide extent).

lári [L. *-res*], M.: lares (household gods).

lári-ce [L. *-x*], F.: larch (tree). **-cíno†,** ADJ.: of the larch.

larín-ge [Gr. *lárunx*], F.: larynx. **larín-geo,** ADJ.: laryngeal. **-gíte,** F.: laryngitis. **-gotomía,** F.: laryngotomy.

lár-va [L.], F.: ghost (phantom); larva; mask†. **-vataménte,** ADV.: secretly. **-váto,** ADJ.: masked (hidden, concealed).

lasá-gna [L. *-num,* cooking vessel], F.: macaroni. **-gnáio†,** M.: macaroni-maker (seller). **-gníno,** ADJ.: with large leaves (of a cabbage). **-gnóne,** M.: simpleton (stupid fellow, ninny).

lá-sca [?], F.: roach (fish). **-schétta,** *dim.* of *-sca.*

la-schità, F.: idleness (laziness); vileness. **-sciaménto,** M.: leaving (abandoning); legacy. **-scia=passáre,** M.: written pass. **‖-sciáre** [L. *laxare*], TR.: abandon (leave, forsake); bequeath; allow (suffer, permit); REFL.: allow one's self; abandon one's self. **-sciáta,** F.: leaving (abandoning). **-scíbile,** ADJ.: dissolute (lax, debauched). **lá-scio,** M.: will (legacy); leash. **lá-scito,** M.: legacy. **-scíva†,** F.: wantonness. **-scivaménte,** ADV.: lasciviously (wantonly). **-scivánza** = *-scivia.* **-scívia,** F.: lasciviousness. **-sciváre†** = *-scivire.* **-scivíre†,** INTR.: become lascivious. **-scività,** F.: lasciviousness. **-scívo,** ADJ.: lascivious. **lá-sco†,** ADJ.: LAX (lazy, idle); weak (languid).

lás-sa†, F.: LEASH (for hounds). **-sáre** = *lasciare.* **-satívo,** ADJ.: laxative. **-sáto,** ADJ.: abandoned (left, forsaken); allow (permit); bequeath. **-sazióne†, -sézza,** F.: lassitude (languor, weakness). **-sísmo,** M.: laxity (slackness); religious belief. **lás-sito,** M.: legacy. **-situdine†,** F.: lassitude (weariness). **‖lás-so** [*laxus*], ADJ.: tired (fatigued, weary); unhappy.

las-sù [*là, su*], ADV.: there above. **-súso†** = *-sù.*

lá-stra [? ak. to Eng. *plaster*], F.: flat stone (for paving); slate; plate-glass. **-strai(u)òlo,** M.: paver. **-strétta, -strettína,** *dim.* of *-stra.* **-stricaménto,** M.: pavement. **-stricáre,** TR.:

pave. **-stricáto**, ADJ.: paved; M.: pavement. **-stricatóre**, M.: paver. **-stricatúra**, F.: paving; pavement. **lástrico**, pl. *—chi* or *—ci*, M.: pavement: *ridursi sul —*, bring one's self to beggary. **-stróne**, *aug.* of *-stra*. **-struccia**, *disp.* of *-stra*.

la-tèbra [L. (*-tere*, hide)], F.: hiding-place (dark recess, den); obscurity. **-tebróso†**, ADJ.: hidden (dark, concealed). **-tènte**, ADJ.: LATENT (hidden, concealed). **-tenteménte†**, ADV.: latently (secretly, furtively).

late-rále [L. *-ralis*], ADJ.: lateral. **-ralménte**, ADV.: laterally (sidewise).

làte-re† [L.], INTR.: lie hidden (concealed). **-rína†** = *latrina*.

laterízio [L. *-itius* (*later*, brick)], ADJ.: lateritious (like or of bricks).

latézza† [L. *-tus*], F.: latitude (width, extent).

latíbulo [L. *-bulum* (*latere*, hide)], M.: lurking place; secret (mystery).

laticlávio [L. *-vium*], M.: laticlave (Roman badge).

latifóndo [L. *-fundium*], M.: vast estate.

lati-naménte, ADV.: Eng.† latinly (in a Latin way); clearly†. **-neggiáre**, INTR.: latinise. **-nísmo**, M.: latinism. **-nísta**, pl. *—ti*, M.: latinist. **-nità**, F.: latinity. **-nizzaménto**, M.: latinization. **-nizzáre**, TR.: latinize. ‖**latí-no** [L. *-nus*], ADJ.: Latin; clear (plain, intelligible)†; comfortable (commodious)†; M.: Latin language; ADV.: in the Latin way, Latin. **-nòrum**, *disp.* of *-no*. **-núccio**, M.: *disp.* of *-no*; Latin exercise.

lati-tánte, ADJ.: latitant (hid, concealed, latent). ‖**-táre†** [L. *latere*, hide], INTR.: lie hidden.

la-titúdine, F.: latitude. ‖**lá-to** 1 [L. *-tus*], M.: side; place; part: *a —†*, beside; *da —*, aside (apart); *in ogni —*, on all sides. **lá-to** 2, ADJ.: wide (broad, large, extended).

latomía†, F.: marble quarry.

latóre [L. *-tor*], M.: bearer (porter).

la-trabilità, F.: barking quality. **-traménto**, M.: barking. ‖**-tráre** [L.], INTR.: bark (Eng.† latrate). **-tráto**, M.: bark. **-tratóre**, M.: barker.

latría [L.], F.: latria (worship of God as distinguished from worship of saints).

latríce [L. *latrix*], F.: bearer (porter).

latrína [L. (*latere*, hide)], F.: latrine, privy.

lá-tro [L.] M.: (*poet.*) thief (robber). **-trocínio**, M.: LARCENY (theft; Eng.† latrociny). **-trocíno**, ADJ.: villainous (wicked, abominable).

látta 1 [Ger. *latte*], F.: LATTEN (tin, sheet of iron).

látta 2 [?], F.: blow on the head (slap).

lat-táia, F.: milk. **-táio**, M.: milk-seller; ADJ.: abundant in milk. **-taiòlo**, M.: milk-tooth; ADJ.: pertaining to milk-tooth. **-taiuòla†**, F.: yellow succory (herb). **-taiuòlo**, M.: milk-tooth. **-tánte**, ADJ.: suckling (nursing, Eng.† lactant). **-táre**, TR.: give suck. **-táta**, F.: orgeat (flavouring extract). **-táto**, ADJ.: milky (Eng.† lactary); milk-white; M.: salt. **-tatríce**, F.: wet-nurse. ‖**látte** [L. *lac*], M.: milk (the drink; white juice, LATEX): *fiore di —*, cream; *fratello di —*, foster-brother. **-teggiánte**, ADJ.: milky; full of white juice. **-teggiáre**, INTR.: blend colours (painting). **-tènte†**, ADJ.: sucking (suckling). **látteo**, ADJ.: lacteous (milky): *via -tea*, milky way. **-tería**, F.: dairy. **-teruòlo†**, M.: curds and whey; curdled milk. **-ticínio**, M.: milk-food. **-ticinóso†**, ADJ.: milky; milk-white. **lát-tico**, ADJ.: lactic. **-tífero**, ADJ.: lactiferous (bearing milk). **-tificio**, M.: white juice of unripe figs. **-tifúgo**, M.: lactifuge (medicine). **-tigginóso**, ADJ.: milky. **-tíme**, M.: scab (of children). **-timóso**, ADJ.: scurfy (scurvy). **-tivéndolo**, M.: milk-seller.

lat-tonáre, TR.: strike (give blows). **-tonáta**, F.: blow. ‖**-tóne**, *aug.* of *-ta* 2.

lat-tónzo [*-te*], M.: sucking calf. **-tónzolo** = *-tonzo*. **-toscòpio**, M.: lactoscope.

lattováro [L. *electuarium*], M.: electuary (medicine).

lattu-cário, M.: lactucarium (thickened juice of lettuce). ‖**lattú-ga** [L. *lactuca*], F.: lettuce. **-gáccia**, *disp.* of *-ga*. **-gáccio**, M.: kind of flower. **-ghína**, *car. dim.* of *-ga*. **-góna**, **-góne**, *aug.* of *-ga*.

láu-da, (*poet.*) ‖**-de** [L. *laus*], F.: laud (praise, eulogy, worship). **-dábile**, ADJ.: laudable (praiseworthy, commendable).

láudano [Gr. *ládanon*], M.: laudanum.

lau-dáre, TR.: laud (praise, extol). **-dativaménte**, ADV.: laudably (commendably). **-datívo**, ADJ.: lauding (praising). **-datòrio**, ADJ.: laudatory (containing praise). **láu-de** (*poet.*) = *-da*. **-dèmio**, M.: fee for renewal of leasing contract. **-dése**, M.: chorister (hymn singer). **-dévole**, ADJ.: praiseworthy (commendable). **láu-di**, F. (PL.): lauds (Roman Catholic prayers). ‖**láu-do** [L. *-laus*], M.: praise; sentence (decision).

laúnque† [*là*, *unque*], ADV.: wherever.

láu-rea, F.: doctorship; wreath of laurel. **-reándo**, M.: candidate for doctorship; ADJ.: pertaining to candidate for doctorship. **-reáre**, TR.: laureate (crown with laurel); REFL.: take the laurel. **-reáto**, ADJ.: crowned with laurel; M.: laureate. **-reazióne†**, F.: laureation. **láu-reo**, ADJ.: (*poet.*) of laurel. **-rèola†**, F.: spurge-laurel (bay-tree). **-réto**, M.: laurel-grove. **-rína**, F.: laurine. **-ríno†**, ADJ.: of laurel. ||**láu-ro** [L. *-rus*], M.: laurel.

lau-taménte, ADV.: magnificently (grandly, sumptuously). **-tézza**, F.: magnificence (sumptuousness, splendour). **-tíssimo**, ADJ.: very (most) magnificent (splendid). ||**láu-to** [L. *-tus*], ADJ.: magnificent (splendid, sumptuous).

lá-va [L. *-vare*, wash], F.: lava. **-vábile**, ADJ.: washable. **-vábo**, M.: laver (washing-vessel, basin). **-vacápo**, M.: reprimand (rebuke, scolding). **-vacéci**, M.: dunce (stupid man, numskull); ADJ.: foolish (stupid). **-vácro**, M.: bath (washing-place).

lavágna [?], F.: schist (rock); slate (for writing, etc.).

lava=máno, —**i** [*-re mano*], M.: wash-basin-stand. **-ménto†**, M.: washing.

lavá-nda, F.: washing (bathing); lavender. **-ndáia**, F., **-ndáio**, M., **-ndára**, F., **-ndáro**, M.: clothes-washer (launderer). **-ndería**, F.: laundry. ||**lavá-re** [L.] TR.: LAVE (wash, cleanse; bathe); wash away; LAUNDER. **lavá-ta**, F.: washing (cleaning). **=piátti**, **=scodèlle**, M.: scullion (dish-washer). **-tína**, *dim.* of *-ta*. **-tívo**, M.: clyster (injection). **-tóio**, M.: wash-house (laundry). **-tóra**, F., **-tóre**, M.: washer; bleacher. **-túra**, F.: washing. **-zióne†**, F.: washing (wash).

lavéggio [?], M.: cooking-vessel (broth-pot).

lavo-rábile, ADJ.: workable. **-racchiáre**, INTR.: work little and slowly. **-ráccio**, *disp.* of *-ro*. **-ráre**, INTR.: labour (work, toil, strive); TR.: work (form, fabricate). **-ránte**, ADJ.: working; M.: workman. **-ratívo**, ADJ.: work (day); cultivable. **-ráto**, ADJ.: laboured (worked); ploughed (tilled); M.: ploughed land. **-ratévole†**, ADJ.: arable. **-ratóre**, M., **-ratríce**, F.: labourer (worker, tiller). **-ratúra**, F.: labour (work). **-razióne**, F.: labouring (working, fabricating); ploughing. **-réccio†**, M.: labour (work, toil). **-rería†**, F.: working place. **-rettíno**, **-rétto**, *dim.* of *-ro*. **-ricchiáre**, INTR.: work little and slowly. **-rièra†**, F.: working place. **-ríno**, *car. dim.* of *-ro*. **-río**, M.: intense labour (toil, exertion). ||**lavó-ro** [L. *labor*], M.: labour (work, toil). **-róne**, *aug.* of *-ro*. **-rucchiáre**, INTR.: labour little and slowly. **-rúccio**, *disp. dim.* of *-ro*.

lazzáre [*-zo*], INTR.: jest (joke, make fun).

lazza-rétto = *lazzeretto*. **-rísta**, M.: Lazarist (priest). ||**Lázza-ro** [*-rus*], M.: Lazarus; lazar (leper, diseased person). **-róne**, M.: lazzaroni (Neapolitan of the lowest class; vile, abject man).

lazza-ròla = *lazzerola*. **-ròlo**, ADJ.: pertaining to the apple-tree.

lazzeggiáre [*lazzo*], INTR.: jest (sport, make fun).

lazzerétto [*Lazzaro*], M.: lazaretto (pest-house, hospital).

lazze-ròla [Ar. *zazora*], F.: fruit of medlar-tree. **-ròlo**, **-ruòlo†**, M.: medlar-tree.

laz-zétto, *car.* of *-zo*. **-zézza†**, **-zità†**, F.: tartness (sharpness). ||**láz-zo** [?], M.: buffoonery (jesting); tartness (acidity); strange occurrence; ADJ.: jocose (comical, droll); tart (acid, sharp).

le, PL. of *la;* the; them; dat. of *ella*, to her; to you.

leá-le [L. *legalis*], ADJ.: LOYAL (leal, sincere, faithful). **-líssimo**, ADJ.: very (or most) loyal. **-lménte**, ADV.: loyally (faithfully, sincerely). **-ltà**, F.: loyalty (faithfulness, sincerity).

leándro [Gr. *rhododéndron*], M.: OLEANDER.

leárdo [OFr. *liart*], ADJ.: gray (dapple); Eng.† liard: — *pom(ell)ato*, dapple gray.

leático [?], M.: black grape.

léb-bra [L. *lepra*], F.: leprosy. **-bróso**, ADJ.: leprous; M.: leper.

lecca-ménto, M.: licking (lapping). **=pestèlli†**, **=piátti**, M.: glutton; parasite. **leccá-rda**, F.: dripping-pan. **leccá-rdo†**, ADJ.: greedy (gluttonous). ||**leccá-re** [OGer. *lecchôn*], TR.: LICK (lap); skim (graze); flatter (caress). **=scodèllo**, M.: glutton. **leccá-ta**, F.: licking. **-taménte**, ADV.: affectedly (with too much nicety, daintily). **-tína**, *dim.* of *-ta*. **leccá-to**, ADJ.: licked; affected. **-tóre**, M.: gourmand (glutton); parasite. **-túra**, F.: licking; slight wound.

lec-céta, F., ||**-céto** [*-cio*], M.: forest of holm-oaks; maze. **-cétto**, *dim.* of *-cio*.

lec-cheríа†, F.: greediness; dainties. ||**-chétto**, *dim.* of *-co*. **-chíno**, M.: vain young man (dandy).

léc-cia, F.: acorn. ||**léc-cio** [L. *ilex*], M.: ilex (holm-oak, evergreen oak); timber.

léc-co [*-care*], M.: daintiness; bribe; mark (aim, butt)†. **-concíno†**, *dim.* of *-cone*. **-cóne**, M.: gourmand. **-conería**, F.: greediness; dainty dish. **-conéssa†**, F.: woman fond of dainties. **-conía**, **-cornía†**, F.: daintiness. **-cucchiáre**, TR.: lick (lap). **-cúme**, M.: dainty bit (titbit); allurement (temptation).

leci-taménte, ADV.: licitly (lawfully, legitimately). **-tíssimo**, ADJ.: very (or most) lawful. ||**léci-to** [L. *licitus*], ADJ.: licit (lawful; legitimate).

lè-dere [L. *lædere*], DEFECT.§; TR.: offend (injure, hurt, damage). **-dènte**, ADJ.: offending; injuring.

§ Ind.: Pres. 3. *lède*. Impf. *ledéva*. Pret. *ledéi* or *lèsi*. Subj.: Impf. *ledésse*. Part. *lèso*.

leònа†, F.: lioness.

léga 1 [l. L. *liga* (L. *ligare*, bind)], F.: LEAGUE (alliance, compact); alLOY; ligature: *uomo di bassa* —, man of mean condition.

léga 2 [l. L. *leuca* (Celt.)], F.: LEAGUE (distance of about 3 Eng. miles).

le-gáccia† [L. *ligare*, bind], F., **-gáccio**, **-gaccidlo**, M.: tie (string, band); garter; chain. **-gággio**†, M.: list (note); invoice. **-gagióne**, F.: tying (binding).

legá-le [L. *-lis*], ADJ.: legal (lawful, legitimate). **-lità**, F.: legality (lawfulness). **-lizzáre**, TR.: legalize (make lawful). **-lizzazióne**, F.: legalization. **-lménte**, ADV.: legally (lawfully). **-lúccio**, *disp.* of *-le*.

legá-me, M.: ligature (bond, chain). **-ménto**, M.: ligament (binding, bond); ledgment. **legá-nza**†, F.: league (alliance, union). ||**legá-re** [L. *ligare*], TR.: tie (bind, unite); obLIGE (force, compel); bequeath; REFL.: bind one's self; make a league. **legá-ta**, F.: tying (binding, uniting). **-táccia**, *disp.* of *-ta*. **-tário**, M.: legatee. **-tína**, *dim.* of *-ta*. **-tíssimo**, ADJ.: very (or most) binding. **legáto**, ADJ.: tied (bound, united); obliged; M.: legate (ambassador, envoy); legacy. **-tóre**, M.: bookbinder. **-túra**, F.: ligature (band); bookbinding. **-turína**, *car. dim.* of *-tura*. **-túzzo**†, M.: trifling legacy. **-zióne**, F.: legation (embassy).

légge [L. *lex*], F.: law (statute, rule).

leg-gènda [L. *-enda*], F.: legend. **-gendáio**, M.: legend-seller. **-gendário**, ADJ.: legendary. **-gènte**, ADJ.: reading.

legge-raménte† [L. *-ro*], ADV.: lightly (inconsiderately). **-ránza**†, F.: lightness (nimbleness, fickleness, legerity)†.

lèggere [L. *legere*], IRR.§; TR.: read; instruct (teach); understand (divine).

§ Ind.: Pret. *lès-si*, *-se*; *-sero*. Part. *lètto*.

legge-rétto, *dim.* of *-ro*. **-rézza**, F.: lightness (nimbleness, fickleness). **-ríno**, *dim.* of *-ro*. **-rménte**, ADV.: lightly (nimbly, swiftly). ||**leggè-ro** [L. *levis*], ADJ.: light (slight; fickle; trifling).

leggiáccia, *disp.* of *legge*.

leggia-draménte, ADV.: gracefully (charmingly, gallantly). **-dría**, F.: grace (charm, gentility); elegance. ||**leggiádro** [L. *levis*], ADJ.: graceful (pretty, elegant, charming); M.†: lover (beau, gallant).

leggiaiòlo [*legge*], M.: ignorant advocate.

leg-gíbile [*-gere*], ADJ.: legible (readable). **-gicchiáre**, *disp. dim.* of *-gere*.

leg-gièro†, **-gièro**, ADJ.: light (nimble, swift).

leg-gío [*-gere*], M.: reading-desk. **-gitóre**, M., **-gitríce**, F.: reader (lecturer). **-giucchiáre**, *disp. dim.* of *-gere*.

leggiúccia, *disp.* of *legge*.

le-gionário, ADJ.: legionary. ||**-gióne** [L. *-gio*], F.: legion (military body).

legis-latívo [L. *lex*, law], ADJ.: legislative. **-latóre**, M., **-latríce**, F.: legislator (law-giver). **-latúra**, F.: legislature. **-lazióne**, F.: legislation. **legista**, M.: lawyer (jurisconsult).

legitti-ma, F.: lawful share of inheritance. **-maménte**, ADV.: legitimately (lawfully). **-máre**, TR.: legitimate (make lawful). **-mazióne**, F.: legitimation (making lawful). **-místa**, M.: legitimist (supporter of legitimate authority; of the Bourbon dynasty). **-mità**, F.: legitimacy (lawfulness). ||**legítti-mo** [L. *-gitimus*], ADJ.: legitimate (lawful, just, right).

legn-áccio, *disp.* of *legno*. **-áceo**, ADJ.: ligneous (woody, of wood). **-ággio**, M.: LINEAGE (race, progeny). **-áia**, F.: woodhouse; wood-pile: *mandare a* —, cudgel. **-aiòlo**, **-aiuòlo**†, **-amáre**†, M.: carpenter (joiner). **-áme**, M.: timber (wood for building). **-áre**, TR.: beat (cudgel); cut wood† (for fuel). **-áta**, F.: beating (cudgelling). **-ático**, pl.—*ci*, ADJ.: right of cutting wood. **-atína**, *dim.* of *-ata*. **-atúra**, F.: cudgelling; wood-cutting†. **-étta**, *dim.* of *legna*. **-ettíno**, **-étto**, *dim.* of *legno*. ||**légn-o**, pl. *-a* or *-e* [L. *lignum*], M.: wood (timber; fuel); ship; carriage: — *santo*, guaiacum (tree). **-osità**, F.: woodiness. **-óso**, ADJ.: ligneous (woody). **-úccio**, **-úzzo**†, *disp. dim.* of *legno*.

legorízia† [L. *liquiritia*], F.: licorice.

leguléio [L. *-eius*], M.: pettifogger.

legú-me [L. *-men*], M.: legume; pulse (pease, beans, etc.). **-minóso**, ADJ.: leguminous (pertaining to pulse).

lèi [L. *illæ*], PRON.: her; you; (*as subj.*) she; you.

lelláre†, INTR.: dally.

lémbo [L. *limbus*], M.: extremity, limit.

lèmma [Gr.], M.: lemma (preliminary proposition).

lèmme lèmme [?*lene*], ADV.: indifferently, leisurely.

lemòsina [Gr. *eleemosúne*], F.: charity (alms).

le-muráli, F. PL.: ghost-feast. ||**lèmure** [L. *-mur*], M.: lemur (ghost, spirit, spectre). **-mário**, M.: sacrifice (to spirits).

là-na or **lé-na** [L. *anelare*], F.: strength (force); breath†. **-náre**†, TR.: put in breath; strengthen (invigorate).
léndine [L. *lens*], F.: nit.
lendinèlla†, F.: kind of coarse cloth.
lendi-níno [-*ne*], *dim.* of -*ne*. **-nóso**, ADJ.: nitty.
lè-ne [L. -*nis*], ADJ.: (*poet.*) gentle (mild, humane). **-neménto**, ADV.: leniently (gently, mildly). **-niènte**†, ADJ.: lenient. **-nificaménto**†, M.: mitigation (softening). **-nificáre**†, TR.: lenify (mitigate, soften). **-nificatívo**†, ADJ.: lenitive (emollient, assuasive). **-niménto**, M.: liniment (softening, mitigating). **-níre**, TR.: lenify (soften, mitigate, assuage). **-nità**†, F.: lenity (gentleness, mildness). **-nitívo**, ADJ.: lenitive (assuasive, softening); M.: lenitive (palliative). **lè-no**†, ADJ.: weak (faint); flexible (supple, pliant). **-nocínio**, M.: decoying (enticing); charm (allurement). **-nóna**, F., **-nóne**, M.: pimp (pandèrer, procurer).
lèn-te [L. -*ticula*], F.: lentil; freckle. **-tággine**, F.: wild thyme.
len-taménte, ADV.: slowly; (*mus.*) lentiment. **-táre**, TR.: slacken (retard); REFL.: relent. ‖**lèn-te** [L. -*tus*], ADJ.: slack (loose); ADV.: slackly (loosely); slowly. **-teggiáre**, INTR.: be slack (loose). **-teménte**†, ADV.: slowly. **-tézza**, F.: slowness; slackness (looseness).
lèn-te 2 [L. *lens*], F.: lentil; lens (magnifying-glass). **-tícchia**, F.: lentil (pulse). **-ticoláre**, ADJ.: lenticular (like a lentil). **-tíggine**, F.: freckle (red spot). **-tigginóso**, ADJ.: freckled. **-tína**, *dim.* of -*te* 2. **-tíschio**, **-tíscot**, M.: lentisk.
len-tíssimo, ADJ.: very (or most) slow. ‖**lèn-to** [L. -*tus*], ADJ.: slow (sluggish, tardy); ADV.: slowly (sluggishly). **-tóre**†, M.: slowness; slackness (looseness).
lèn-za [L. *lintea*], F.: fish-line; linen bandage†. **-záre**†, TR.: bandage (bind). **-zoláccio**, **-zolúccio**, *disp.* of -*zolo*. **-zolétto**, **-zolíno**, pl. -*zoli* or -*zola*; M.: sheet.
leofán-te [L. *elephantus*], M.: elephant. **-téssa**†, F.: female elephant.
leo-ncèllo, **-ncíno**, *dim.* of -*ne*. ‖**leó-ne** [L. *leo*], M.: lion (the animal; *astr.* Leo); fashionable fellow (spark). **-nésco**, ADJ.: lion-like. **-néssa**, F.: lioness. **-níno**, ADJ.: leonine (like a lion). **-párdo**, M.: leopard.
lepi-daménte, ADV.: jocosely (cheerfully, pleasantly). **-dézza**, F.: jocoseness (cheerfulness, facetiousness). ‖**lèpi-do** [L. -*dus*], ADJ.: jocose (gay, pleasant, lepid).
lepidòtteri [Gr. *lepís*, scale, and *pterón*, wing], M. PL.: lepidoptera (order of insects).
lepo-ráio†, ‖**-rário**† [L. *lepus*], M.: warren.
lepóre†, M.: (*poet.*) gracefulness.
leporíno [L. -*pus*], ADJ.: leporine (like a hare).
leppáre†, TR.: take away (carry off); INTR.: run away.
léppo†, M.: strong odour of burning.
le-pracchiòtto, **-prátto**, M.: leveret (young hare). ‖**lè-pre** [L. -*pus*], F.: hare: *far da — vecchia*, be cautious. **-prétta**, **-prettína**, **-prettíno**, *car. dim.* of -*pre*. **-prieciuòla**†, *dim.* of -*pre*. **-príno**, ADJ.: leporine (hare-like). **-proncèllo**, **-proncíno**, *dim.* of -*prone*. **-próne**, *aug.* of -*pre*.
lepróso† [L. -*sus*], ADJ.: leprous.
le-prettíno, ‖**-pròtto** [L. -*pus*], *dim.* of -*pre*.
ler-ciáre†, TR.: sully (make dirty). ‖**lèr-cio**, pl. -*ce* and -*ci* [?], ADJ.: filthy (dirty, sullied). **-ciúme**, M.: dirty heap.
lèro [L. *ervum*], M.: bitter-vetch.
lési-na [OGer. *alasna*], F.: awl. **-náre**, TR.: economize. **-nería**, F.: economy. **-nína**, **-níno**, *dim.* of -*na*.
le-sióne [L. *læsio* (*lædere*, hurt)], F.: lesion (hurt, injury). **-sívo**, ADJ.: hurtful (injurious). **lè-so**, ADJ.: hurt (wronged, injured, damaged): *lesa maestà*, high treason.
les-sáccio, *disp.* of -*so*. ‖**-sáre** [L. *elixare*], TR.: cook in water (boil). **-sáto**, ADJ.: boiled. **-sáta**, **-satúra**†, F.: boiling.
lèssi, PRET. of *leggere*.
lèssi-co, pl. -*ci* [Gr. *lexikón*], M.: LEXICON (dictionary). **-cografía**, F.: lexicography. **-cográfico**, pl. —*ci*, ADJ.: lexicographical. **-cògrafo**, M.: lexicographer. **-grafía**, F.: lexigraphy. **-gráfico**, pl. —*ci*, ADJ.: lexigraphic.
lésso [L. *elixus*], ADJ.: boiled (cooked in water); M.: boiled meat.
les-taménte, ADV.: lightly (nimbly, quickly). **-tézza**, F.: nimbleness (lightness, quickness). **-tíno**, *dim.* of -*to*. **-tíssimo**, ADJ.: very nimble. ‖**lès-to** [?], ADJ.: nimble (agile, quick).
lesúra† [L. *læsio*], F.: injury (damage, hurt).
letále [L. -*lis*], ADJ.: (*poet.*) deadly (fatal, lethal).
leta-máio, M.: place for manure. **-maiuòlo**†, M.: street-sweeper (scavenger). **-máre**, TR.: manure. **-máto**, ADJ.: manured. ‖**letá-me** [L. *lætus*, glad; fertile], M.: manure (compost). **-minaménto**†, M.: manuring (improving). **-mináre**†, TR.: manure. **-minatúra**†, **-minazióne**†, F.: manuring.
letáne†, **letanie** [Gr. *litaneía*], F.: litany.

le-targía, F.: lethargy. **-tárgico**, pl. —*ci*, ADJ.: lethargic. **-tárgo**, M.: lethargy (deep, morbid sleep, drowsiness). ‖**Lè-te** [Gr. *Léthe*], M.: Lethe (river); oblivion.

leti-cáre [L. *litigare*], TR.: litigate (contest in law). **-chíno**, M.: one litigating frequently. **-chío**, M.: continued litigation. **-cóna**, F., **-cóne**, M.: wicked litigant.

le-tificáre, TR.: give joy (make glad). **-tificánte**, ADJ.: giving joy. **-tificáto**, ADJ.: gladdened. **-tízia**, F.: gladness (joy). **-tiziáre**, INTR., REFL.: be glad. (joyful). ‖**lé-to**† [L. *lætus*], ADJ.: glad.

lètta [*leggere*], F.: rapid reading (glance).

lètte-ra [L. *lit(t)era*], F.: letter (of alphabet); epistle; PL.: learning (erudition, knowledge): — *di cambo*, — *cambiale*, bill of exchange; *a tanto di -re*, frankly (freely). **-ráccia**, *disp.* of *-ra*. **-rále**, ADJ.: literal. **-ralménte**, ADV.: literally. **-rariaménte**, ADV.: in a literary manner. **-rário**, ADJ.: literary (pertaining to literature). **-ráta**, F.: learned woman. **-ratèllo**, **-ratíno**, *dim.* of *-rato*. **-ráto**, M.: learned man (literator). ADJ.: literate (learned). **-ratóne**, *aug.* of *-rato*. **-ratúccio**, **-ratúcolo**, *disp.* of *-rato*. **-ratúra**, F.: literature (learning, science, erudition). **-rína**, *car. dim.* *-ra*. **-ríno**, *dim.* of *-ra*. **-róna**, *aug.* of *-ra*. **-róne**, *disp. aug.* of *-ra*. **-rúccia**, *disp.* of *-ra*.

letti-ciuòlo, ‖**-cèllo** [*letto*], M.: small bed (couch).

lèttico, ADJ.: Lettic (language, etc.).

let-tièra, F.: bedstead; head-board. **-tíga**, F.: litter. **-tighétta**, **-tighína**, *dim.* of *-ga*. **-tighière**, **-tighièro**, M.: litter-bearer. **-tíno**, *dim.* of *-to*. ‖**lèt-to** 1 [L. *lectus*], M.: bed; bottom (of a river); layer (painting).

lètto 2 [*leggere*], PART.: read (perused).

lettóne [*-to*], M.: large bed.

let-toráto, M.: (*eccles.*) second of the four lower orders; lectureship. ‖**-tóre** [*leggere*], M.: reader; lecturer. **-tóra**, **-tríce**, F.: reader. **-toría**†, F.: degree of doctor; lectureship.

let-tucciáccio, *disp.* of *-tuccio*. ‖**-túccio** [*letto*], M.: wretched bed.

lettú-ra [L. *lectura*], F.: reading; lecture. **-rína**, *car. dim.* of *-ra*.

lemodio†, M.: clover-tree; stock-gilly-flower.

leúto† [?], M.: lute.

ˈè-va, F.: lever; levy (raising, collecting). **vábile**, ADJ.: raisable (movable, porta-). **-valdína**†, F.: theft. **-vamén-**†, M.: rising (elevation). **-vánte**, M.: ant (eastern country, *lit.* where the sun 'rises,' east), ADJ.†: levant (eastern, rising). **-vantína**, F., **-vantíno** [*-vante*], M.: Levantine (inhabitant of Levant); a kind of silk cloth. ‖**-váre** [L.], TR.: raise (lift up); levy (collect); deprive; prohibit; REFL.: rise; recover (from illness). **-váta**, F.: raising; getting up; levying†. **-vatáccia**, F.: getting up too soon. **-vatína**, *dim.* of *-vata*. **-váto**, ADJ.: raised (lifted). **-vatóio**, ADJ.: *ponte* —, drawbridge. **-vatóre**†, M.: raiser (lifter). **-vatríce**, F.: midwife. **-vatúra**, F.: understanding (intelligence, sense). **-vazióne**†, F.: rising (elevation).

lè-ve† [L. *-vis*], ADJ.: light. **-veménte**, ADV.: lightly. **-vézza**†, F.: lightness (levity).

levi-gáre [L.], TR.: make smooth (even); polish (levigate). **-gatézza**, F.: smoothness. **-gáto**, ADJ.: polished. **-gazióne**, F.: smoothing; polishing.

levístico† [L. *-cum*], M.: lovage (plant).

levíta, pl. —*ti* [L. *-tes*], M.: Levite (one of Jewish tribe).

levi-tà† [L. *-tas*], F.: levity (frivolity). **-táre**†, TR.: leaven (make light, ferment).

levítico, pl. —*ci* [*-ta*], M.: Leviticus (book of Bible); ADJ.: Levitical.

levri-èra, F.: greyhound. **-ère**, ‖**-èro** [L. *leporarius* (*lepus*, hare), hare-], M.: greyhound; ADJ. (*-ero*): like a greyhound. **-erína**, **-eríno**, *dim.* of *-ere*.

lèzia†, F., **lèzio** [L. *il-licium* (*lacere*, allure), allurement], M.: affectation (coquetry, affected tenderness).

lezion-áccia, *disp.* of *-e*. **-cèlla**, *dim.* of *-e*. **-cína**, *car. dim.* of *-e*. **-ciónа**, *aug.* of *-e*. ‖**lezión-e** [L. *lectio*], F.: LESSON; lecture (reproof, rebuke). **-úccia**, *disp.* of *-e*.

lezio-sággine, F.: affectation (tenderness, effeminacy). **-saménte**, ADV.: tenderly (effeminately). ‖**lezió-so** [*lezio*], ADJ.: affected (tender, effeminate, caressing).

lez-záre†, INTR.: emit an offensive smell. ‖**léz-zo** [*olezzo*], M.: offensive smell. **-zóna**, F., **-zóne**, M.: filthiness. **-zoneria**, F.: offensiveness. **-zóso**, ADJ.: strong-scented. **-zúme**, M.: offensive smell.

li [L. *illi*], ART. PL.: the; PRON.: them.

lì [L. *illic*], ADV.: there (that place, yonder).

lialtà†, F.: loyalty (devotion).

liáno [L. *planus*], M.: plain (level land).

li-bagióne [L. *-batio*], F.: libation. **-baménto**†, M.: drink-offering. **-báminа**†, F.: (*poet.*): perfumes.

libá-re [L.], TR.: make libations; taste

(try). **libá-to**, ADJ.: tasted. **-tório**, M.: libation cups. **-zióne**, F.: libation.
lib-bra [L. *libra*], F.: pound (weight). **-brétta**, **-brettína**, *dim.* of *-bra*. **-bróna**, *aug.* of *-bra*.
li-becciáta, F.: south-western gale. **||-béccio** [L. *-biticus*], M.: south-west ("Libyan") wind.
li-bellísta, M.: libeler. **||-bèllo** [L. *-bellus* (*liber*, book)], M.: libel (defamatory writing). **-bèllula**, F.: dragon-fly (libellula).
libènte†, ADJ.: willing.
libera-zióne†, F.: liberation (deliverance). **-láccio**, *disp.* of *-le*. **liberá-le**, ADJ.: liberal (free, generous, broad). **-lésco**, *disp.* of *-le*. **-lísmo**, M.: liberalism. **-lità**, F.: liberality (generosity). **-lménte**, ADV.: liberally (freely, generously). **-lóna**, **-lóne**, *aug.* of *-le*. **-ménte**, ADV.: liberally (freely, frankly). **-ménto†**, M., **liberá-nza**, F.: liberation (deliverance). **||liberá-re** [L. (*liber*, free)], TR.: liberate (set free, deLIVER); REFL.: free one's self. **liberá-to**, ADJ.: liberated (freed, delivered). **-tóre**, M., **-tríce**, F.: liberator (rescuer, deliverer). **-zióne**, F.: liberation (deliverance).
libèrcolo, *disp.* of *libro*.
liber-íssimo, ADJ.: very (or most) free (unrestrained). **||líber-o** [L. *liber*], ADJ.: free (unrestrained, sincere, open); ADV.: freely (frankly). **libèr-ta**, F.: freedwoman. **-tà** [L. *-tas*], F.: liberty (freedom, privilege, license). **-ticída**, F.: liberticide. **-tinággio**, M.: libertinism (licentiousness, libertinage). **-tíno**, M.: libertine; freedman; ADJ.: libertine (unrestrained, dissolute). **libèr-to**, M.: freedman; ADJ.: liberated (freed).
libídi-ne [L. *libido*], F.: libidinousness (wantonness, licentiousness). **-nosaménte**, ADV.: wantonly (libidinously). **-nóso**, ADJ.: wanton (libidinous).
libístico†, M.: lovage (plant).
líbito [L. *-ta*], M.: will (caprice, pleasure): *a* —, at will (pleasure).
líbra [L.], F.: balance; constellation: *tenere in* —, hold in suspense.
li-bráccio [*-bro*], *disp.* of *-bro*. **-braíne**, *dim.* of *-braio*. **-bráio**, M.: bookseller.
li-braménto, M.: balancing (libration). **||-bráre** [L.], TR.: balance (poise, librate, consider, judge); REFL.: balance one's self.
li-brário [*-bro*], ADJ.: pertaining to books. **-bráta**, F.: blow with a book.
li-brataménte, ADV.: in a balanced (poised) manner. **||-bráto** [*-brare*], ADJ.: balanced (weighed, considered). **-brazióne**, F.: balancing (poising, libration).
li-brería, F.: library. **-breriétta**, *dim.* of *-breria*. **-brerína**, *car. dim.* of *-breria*. **-brerióna**, *aug.* of *-breria*. **-breriúccia**, *disp.* of *-breria*. **-bréttine**, F. PL.: arithmetic. **-brettíno**, *dim.* of *libro*. **-brettísta**, M.: writer of a libretto. **-brétto**, M.: *car. dim.* of *libro*; libretto (words of an opera). **-brettúccio**, *disp.* of *-bretto*. **-briccíno**, *dim.* of *-bretto*. **-bricciòlo**, *dim.* of *-bro*. **-briciáttolo**, *disp.* of *-bro*. **-bríno**, *car. dim.* of *-bro*. **||lí-bro** [L. *liber*], M.: book; inner bark of tree: — *del quaranta*, pack of cards. **-bróne**, *aug.* of *-bro*. **-brucciáccio**, **-brúccio**, *disp. dim.* of *-bro*.
líccia†, F.: lists; palisades.
líccio [L. *licium*, thread of the web], M.: warp cord (cord serving to raise and lower the warp); hempen cord.
lice-ále [*liceo*], ADJ.: pertaining to a lyceum. **-ísta**, M.: student in a lyceum.
licèn-z(i)a [L. *-tia*], F.: licence (leave, permission): graduation: *prender* —, take one's leave. **-ziaménto**, M.: permission to leave (dismissal, disbanding). **-ziándo**, ADJ.: demanding permission, graduation; M.: one demanding permission. **-ziáre**, TR.: give permission (leave); dismiss (disband); REFL.: take leave (depart). **-ziáto**, ADJ.: licensed (permitted); M.: licentiate, graduate. **-ziatúra†**, F.: declaration of the licentiate. **-ziosaménte**, ADV.: licentiously. **-ziosità**, F.: licentiousness. **-zióso**, ADJ.: licentious (loose, dissolute).
licèo [L. *lyceum*], M.: lyceum (academy).
lícere†, INTR.: be lawful (allowed, permitted).
lichè-ne [Gr. *leichḗn*], M.: lichen (plant). **-nína**, F.: fecula (nutritious part of lichen, grains, etc.).
lici†, ADV.: there (in that place).
lici-taménte†, ADV.: lawfully (licitly). **-tézza†**, F.: lawfulness (right, licitness). **||líci-to†** [L. *-tus*], ADJ.: lawful (allowed, right).
licóre [L. *liquor*], M.: (*poet.*) liquor.
lído [L. *litus*], M.: shore (bank).
lìe, ADV.: (*pop.*) there.
Lièo [L. *Lyæus*], ADJ.: (*poet.*) Bacchian.
lie-taménte, ADV.: joyously (gladly, merrily). **-tézza†**, F.: joyousness (gladness). **-tíssimo**, ADJ.: very (or most) joyous. **-titúdine†**, F.: joyousness (gladness, mirth). **||liè-to** [L. *lætus*], ADJ.: joyous (glad, merry).
liè-va†, F.: importance, condition: — —, ADV.: away, away. **||-váre†** = *levare*.
liè-ve [L. *levis*], ADJ.: light (trifling); ADV.: lightly. **-veménte**, ADV.: lightly (easily, gently). **-vézza†**, **-vità**, F.:

lightness (easiness). **-vitáre,** TR.: leaven (ferment). **-vitáto,** ADJ.: leavened. **-vitatúra,** F.: leavening (fermenting).
liè-vito, M.: leaven, yeast (ferment); ADJ.: leavened (fermented).
lièvre†, F.: hare.
ligá-me†, F., **liga-ménto** [L. *-mentum*], M.: ligament (bandage, bond). **-mentóso,** ADJ.: binding (ligamentous). **ligáre,** TR.: bind.
ligiáre†, TR.: polish (make smooth).
ligio [L. *-gius*], ADJ.: liege (faithful, loyal).
ligistráre†, TR.: register.
ligíttimo†, ADJ.: legitimate.
lignággio [L. *linea*, line], M.: lineage (race, progeny).
lí-gneo, ADJ.: wooden (ligneous). **-gníte,** M.: lignite (coal). ||**lí-gno**† [L. *lignum*], M.: wood.
lí-gure [*Liguria*], **-gústico,** ADJ.: Ligurian. **-gúst(r)o,** M.: privet (plant).
lilla [Pers. *lilac*], F.: lilac.
lillipuziáno [Eng. *Liliput*], ADJ.: liliputian (dwarfed, diminutive), M.: Liliputian.
lí-ma [L.], F.: file; lime†; dab (fish)†: *far — —,* grumble (fret). **-mábile,** ADJ.: polishable.
limác-cio [*lima*], M.: mud (mire). **-ció-so,** ADJ.: muddy (miry).
líma-ménto, M.: filing (polishing). **li-má-re** [L. *lima*, file], TR.: file (polish, perfect). **-taménte,** ADV.: in a polished manner. **-tézza**†, F.: filing; polished condition. **limá-to,** ADJ.: filed (polished). **-tóre,** M., **-tríce,** F.: filer (polisher). **-túra,** F.: filing; file-dust.
limbèl-lo [*limbo*], M.: leather-cuttings. **-lúccio,** *disp.* of *-lo.*
lim-bicáre†, TR.: distil; examine too closely. **-bícco**†, M.: alembic (distilling vessel).
límbo [L. *-bus*, border], M.: limbo (place of judgment or misery).
limét-ta, ||**-tína** [L. *lima*], *dim.* of *lima.*
limi-tábile, ADJ.: limitable. **-táre,** TR.: limit (bound, restrain), M.: threshold. **-tataménte,** ADV.: within limits. **-tatézza,** F.: restrictiveness (limitedness). **-tativaménte,** ADV.: in a limiting (restrictive) manner. **-tatívo,** ADJ.: limiting (restricting, confining). **-táto,** ADJ.: limited (restricted). **-tatóre,** M., **-tatríce,** F.: limiter (restricter). **-tazióne,** F.: limitation (restriction). ||**límì-te** [L. *limes*], M.: limit (border, restraint). **-'trofo,** bordering upon.
...*us*], M.: mud (mire); (*poet.*) body.
..., M.: lemon-seller. **-náta,** ...le. **-ncèllo,** M.: *dim.* of *-ne;* ...**íno,** *dim.* of *-ne.* ||**limó-**...**ímû**], M.: lemon (fruit and ..., F.: lemonade.

limòsi-na [*elemosina*], F.: ALMS (charity). **-nánte,** ADJ.: begging (seeking alms). **-náre,** INTR.: ask alms; TR.: give alms. **-nário**†, M.: alms-giver. **-náta,** F.: alms-giving. **-náto,** ADJ.: given as alms. **-nière, -nièro,** M.: alms-giver (almoner). **-núccia,** *dim.* of *-na.*
li-mosità, F.: muddiness (mud). ||**-mó-so** [*-mo*], ADJ.: muddy.
limpi-daménte, ADV.: clearly (lucidly, purely). **-dézza,** F.: limpidness (clearness, brightness, transparency). **-díssimo,** ADJ.: very (or most) limpid. **-dità,** F.: limpidity (transparency). ||**límpi-do** [L. *-dus*], ADJ.: limpid (clear, transparent, pure).
límula†, F.: small file.
li-naiòlo [L. *linum*], M.: flax-seller. **-nária,** F.: toad-flax.
lin-ce [Gr. *lúnx*], F.: lynx. **lin-céo,** ADJ.: lynx-like.
línci†, ADV.: from there (from that place.)
lin-ciággio, M.: lynching. ||**-ciáre** [Am. (?)], TR.: lynch.
línda†, F.: sea-quadrant.
lin-daménte, ADV.: elegantly (in a finished manner). **-dézza,** F.: elegance (gracefulness, finish). **-díno,** *dim.* of *-do.* ||**lín-do** [*limpido*], ADJ.: elegant (polished, refined, graceful). **-dúra,** F.: elegance (refinement, gracefulness).
líne-a [L.], F.: line; lineage (family, progeny); infantry; equator. **-aménto,** M.: lineament (feature). **-áre,** ADJ.: linear, TR.: delineate (draw, sketch). **-arménte,** ADV.: lineally. **-áto,** ADJ.: delineated; striped†. **-atúra**†, **-aziónc**†, F.: lineament (feature). **-étta, -ettína, -ína,** *dim.* of *-a.*
lín-fa [L. *lympha*], F.: lymph. **-faticaménte,** ADV.: in the manner of a lymphatic. **-faticísmo,** M.: lymphatic condition. **-fático,** pl. *—ci,* ADJ.: lymphatic; weak.
lingería†, F.: linen-clothes.
lín-gua [L.], F.: tongue (speech, idiom): *dar —,* give intelligence. **-guáccia,** *disp.* of *-gua.* **-guacciúto,** ADJ.: prattling (slandering). **-guádro**†, M.: prattler (slanderer). **-guággio,** M.: language (speech, idiom). **-guáio,** M.: pedantic speaker. **-guále,** ADJ.: lingual (pertaining to the tongue). **-guáto**†, ADJ.: tongued; prattling (chattering). **-gueggiáre**†, INTR.: prattle (slander). **-guèlla**†, *dim.* of *-gua;* PL.: side strips of a glove-finger. **-guétta,** F.: *dim* of *-gua;* filter. **-guettáccia,** *disp.* of *-guetta.* **-guettáre**†, TR.: toil; stutter; filter. **-guettína,** *car. dim.* of *-guetta.* **-guína, -guíno,** *car. dim.* of *-gua.* **-guísta,** M.: linguist. **-guística,** F.: linguistics. **-guisticaménte,** ADV.:

in a linguistic manner. **-guístico**, pl. **—ci**, ADJ.: linguistic. **-guóso**†, **-gúto**†, ADJ.: long-tongued; prattling.
lín-o [L. -*num*], M.: flax; linen (cloth). **lin-teo**, ADJ.: linen, M.: linen-cloth. **-sémo**†, M.: linseed.
lintíggine†, F.: freckle (red spot).
liocórno [L. *unicornuus*], M.: unicorn (fabulous animal).
lion.. = *leon*..
líppa 1 [?], F.: tip-cat, cat (children's game).
líppa† 2, F.: a kind of darnel.
lippi-dóso†, ADJ.: blear-eyed (inflamed). **-túdine**†, F.: bleäredness (inflammation of the eyes).
li-quaménto†, M.: liquefaction (dissolving). **-quáre**†, TR.: clear (liquefy). **-quatívo**†, ADJ.: soluble (liquefiable). ||**-quefáre** [L. *lique-facere*], TR.: liquefy (melt, dissolve); REFL.: melt (dissolve). **-quefacènte**, ADJ.: liquefying (melting, dissolving). **-quefátto**, ADJ.: liquefied (melted, dissolved). **-quefazióne**, F.: liquefaction (melting, dissolving).
liqui-daménte, ADV.: smoothly (easily, liquidly); clearly. **-dáre**, TR.: pay (liquidate, settle). **-dáto**, ADJ.: paid (liquidated). **-datóre**, M., **-datríce**, F.: liquidator. **-dazióne**, F.: liquidation. **-dézza**, F.: liquidness (fluency). **-díre**, INTR.: become liquid (dissolve). **-dità**, F.: liquidity (smoothness, fluency). ||**líqui-do** [L. *-dus*], ADJ.: liquid (clear, smooth); M.: liquid substance.
liquirízia [Gr. *glukú-rrhiza*, 'sweet-root'], F.: licorice.
liquó-re [L. *liquor*], M.: liquor; liquid. **-rétto**, *car. dim.* of *-re*. **-rísta**, M.: liquor-dealer.
líra 1 [L. *líbra*, pound], F.: lira (coin = 20 cents).
lí-ra 2 [L. *lyra*], F.: lyre; lyric poetry (or style). **-résa**, F.: bad lyre. **lí-rica**, F.: lyric poetry. **-ricaménte**, ADV.: in a lyrical manner. **lí-rico**, ADJ.: lyric.
lís-ca [OGer.], F.: hurds of hemp; fish-bone. **-cáio**, M.: quantity of hemp-hurds.
li-sciézza [*liscio*], F.: smoothness (gloss).
lischino, *dim.* of *lisca*.
lí-scia†, F.: lye; rubber. **-sciaménte**, ADV.: smoothly (fluently); simply. **-sciaménto**, M.: smoothing (polishing); adulation. **-sciapiánte**, M.: shoemaker's rubber. **-sciárda**†, **-sciardièra**, F.: woman that uses rouge. **-sciáre**, TR.: smooth (polish); flatter (compliment); REFL.: smooth one's self. **-sciáta**, F.: smoothing. **-sciáto**, ADJ.: smoothed (polished); caressed (flattered). **-sciatóio**, M.: steel instrument for polishing. **-sciatóre**, M., **-sciatríce**, F.: polisher; flatterer. **-sciatúra**, F.: smoothing. ||**lí-scio** [Gr. *lissós*], ADJ.: smooth (polished, glossy); simple; M.. paint (rouge).
liscíva†, F.: lye.
liscóso [*lisca*], ADJ.: full of hurds; bony (of fishes).
lisirvíte†, F.: elixir (cordial).
lísma†, F.: ream of paper.
líso [?], ADJ.: wasted (worn out, consumed).
lís-ta [OGer.], F.: LIST (border, strip; roll, catalogue); stripe (line). **-táre**, TR.: fringe; stripe. **-tarèlla**, *dim.* of *-ta*. **-táto**, ADJ.: fringed; striped. **-tèllo**, M.: (*arch.*) listel; plinth. **-tína**, **-tíno**, *dim.* of *-ta*. **-tóna**, *aug.* of *-ta*. **lís-tra**†, F.: list (roll); strip; stripe.
litáme†, M.: manure.
litanía [Gr. *-neía*], F.: litany.
litáre†, TR.: make suitable sacrifice.
litarg..† = *letarg*..
líte [L. *lis*], F.: strife (contention, dispute, quarrel).
litíasi [Gr. *líthos*, stone], F.: lithiasis (formation of stone in body).
liti-cáre [L. *-gare*], TR.: dispute (quarrel, strive, litigate). **-gánte**, ADJ.: disputing (litigious); M.: pleader (litigant). **-gáre**, TR.: litigate.
litíggine†, F.: freckle (red spot).
lití-gio [L. *-gare*], M.: quarrel (contention, dispute). **-gióso**, ADJ.: contentious (quarrelsome, litigious).
líto [L. *-tus*], M.: (*poet.*) shore.
lito- [Gr. *líthos*, stone]: **-fiti**, M. PL.: lithophyte. **-genía**, F.: lithogenesy (science of origin of minerals). **-grafáre**, TR.: lithograph. **-grafía**, F.: lithography; lithograph. **-graficaménte**, ADV.: lithographically. **-gráfico**, pl. **—ci**, ADJ.: lithographic. **litò-grafo**, M.: lithographer. **-logía**, F.: lithology (science of rocks). **-lògico**, pl. **—ci**, ADJ.: lithological. **litò-logo**, M.: lithologist.
litorále [L. *-alis*], ADJ.: littoral (by the sea-shore).
lito-tomía [Gr. *líthos*, stone, *tómos*, cut], F.: lithotomy (surgical operation). **-tomísta**, **litò-tomo**, M.: lithotomist; ADJ.: lithotomic.
lítro [Gr. *-tra*], M.: liter (measure of capacity).
litto-rále [L. *litus*, shore], ADJ.: littoral (along the shore). **-ráno**, ADJ.: dwelling on shore.
littóre [L. *lictor*], M.: lictor (Roman official).
lituáno [*Lituania*], ADJ.: Lithuanian.
lítuo [L. *-tuus*], M.: augural staff; trumpet.
litúra†, F.: erasure; spot (blemish).
liturgí-a [Gr. *leit-ourgía*, 'public-work',

public service], F.: liturgy. **-caménte**, ADV.: in a liturgical manner. **litúrgi-co**, pl. *-ci*, ADJ.: liturgic.

liu-tàccia†, F.: bad lute. **-tísta**, M.: lute-player. ||**liú-to** [fr. Ar.], M.: lute.

livèl-la [L. *libra*, balance], F.: level (line, plane); a levelling instrument. **-laménto**, M.: levelling. **-láre**, TR.: level (make even).

livellário [*-llo* 2], ADJ.: having a lease; holder (tenant).

livella-tóio, M.: leveller (*instr.*). ||**-tóre** 1 [*-re*], M., **-tríce** 1, F.: leveller.

livella-tóre 2 [*livello* 2], M.: leaser (lord of manor). **-tríce**2, F.: leaser.

li-vellazióne, F.: levelling (equalization). ||**-vèllo** 1 [L. *libra*], M.: level (line, plane surface); levelling instrument.

livèllo2 [*libello*], M.: lease of lands; lands leased; rent.

liveráre†, TR.: deliver (give up); consume.

livi-daménte†, ADV.: in a livid manner. **-dástro**, ADJ.: somewhat livid. **-détto**, *dim.* of *-do*. **-dézza**, F.: lividity (lividness); rancour (hatred)†. **-díccio**, ADJ.: livid. **-díssimo**, ADJ.: very (or most) livid. ||**lívi-do** [L. *-dus*], ADJ.: livid (gray-blue, discoloured); M.: black and blue spot. **-dóre**, M.: lividity. **-dúra**, F.: bruise (livid spot).

livirítta†, ADV.: there (exactly in that place).

livó-re [L. *livor*], M.: hatred (spite, malice); lividness†. **-rosaménte†**, ADV.: maliciously (spitefully, enviously). **-róso†**, ADJ.: malicious (envious, spiteful).

lívra†, F.: livre (franc).

livráre†, TR.: finish (accomplish, complete).

livrè-a [Fr. *livrée*], F.: livery (servant's uniform); servants. **-ína**, *car. dim.* of *-a*.

lizza [?], F.: lists; palisades.

ló, pl. *gli* [L. *illo*], ART.: the; PRON.: him; it; so.

lo-báto, ADJ.: having lobes (lobate). ||**lò-bo** [Gr. *-bós*], M.: lobe. **-búlo**, M.: lobe of the ear.

locá-le [L. *-lis*], ADJ.: local. **-lità**, F.: locality (situation, place). **-lizzáre**, TR.: localize. **-lizzáto**, ADJ.: localized. **-lménte**, ADV.: locally. **locá-nda**, F.: inn (tavern, lodging-house). **-ndière**, M.: innkeeper. **locá-re**, TR.: locate (place, settle). **-tário**, M.: tenant (lodger). **-tívo**, ADJ.: locative. **-tóre**, M., **-tríce**, F.: letter (renter). **-zióne**, F.: letting (renting); location†.

lòco [L. *-cus*], M.: (*poet.*) place. **-mòbile**, M.: small locomotive. **-motíva**, ADJ.: locomotive; F.: locomotive-engine. **-motóre**, **-motríce**, ADJ.: locomotive. **-mozióne**, F.: locomotion. **-tenénte†**, M.: lieutenant.

locupletá-re [L. (*locus-ples*, 'land-rich')], TR.: make rich (enrich); REFL.: grow rich. **-zióne**, F.: wealth (gain, opulency).

locústa [L.], F.: locust; lobster†.

locuzióne [L. *locutio*], F.: locution (expression, phrase).

lò-da†, F.: praise (commendation, esteem). **-dábile**, ADJ.: laudable (praiseworthy). **-dabilità**, F.: laudableness (praiseworthiness). **-daménto†**, M.: praising (extolling). **-dáre**, TR.: praise (extol, commend, laud); REFL.: praise one's self; be pleased with. **-dataménte†**, ADV.: in a commendable manner. **-datívo**, ADJ.: praising (extolling). **-dáto**, ADJ.: praised (commended); M.: person praised. **-datóre**, M., **-datríce**, F.: praiser (commender). ||**lò-de** [L. *laus*], F.: praise (commendation). **-dévole**, ADJ.: praiseworthy (commendable). **-devolíssimo**, ADJ.: very (or most) praiseworthy. **-devolménte**, ADV.: commendably, laudably.

lodigiáno [*Lodi*], ADJ.: Lodian.

lòdo [L. *-de*], M.: sentence (of arbiter); praise†.

lòdo-la [L. *alauda*], F.: lark. **-lètta**, **-lína**, *dim.* of *-la*. **-líno**, M.: small lark.

lodrétto†, M.: pickled meat.

lòf-f(i)a [Eng. *loof*, wind], F.: wind (from the bowels). **lòf-fio**, ADJ.: flabby.

logáccio, *disp.* of *luogo*.

loga-èdi [Gr. *-oidikós*, 'prose-song'], ADJ.: logaœdic; M.: logaœdic meter. **-èdico**, pl. *—ci*, ADJ.: logaœdic.

loga-rítmico, **-rímmico**, pl. *—ci*, ADJ.: logarithmical. **-rítmo** [Gr. *lógos*, account, *arithmós*, number], M.: logarithm.

log-gétta, *dim* of *-gia*. **-gettína**, *dim.* of *-getta*. ||**lòg-gia** [OGer. *laubja* (= Ger. *laube*, arbour)], F.: open-columned structure; open gallery (archway; balcony); LODGE (Masons'); hall; room; palace; lodging†; lodge (hut)†; meeting†: — *da mercanzie*, luggage-room. **-giaménto**, M.: lodging. **-giáto**, M.: covered gallery. **-gióne**, M.: *aug.* of *-gia*; upper gallery of theatre.

lo-ghettíno, *car. dim.* of *-ghetto*. ||**-ghétto**, *car. dim.* of *luogo*. **-ghettúccio**, *disp. dim.* of *-ghetto*. **-ghicciòlo**, **-ghicciuòlo**, *dim.* of *luogo*.

lògi-ca [Gr. *-kós* (*lógos*, discourse)], F.: logic. **-cále†**, ADJ.: logical. **-caménte**, ADV.: logically. **-cáre†**, INTR.: reason (debate, argue). **-cáta**, F.: reasoning (argument). **-chétta**, *dim.* of *-cata*. **lògi-co**, pl. *-ci*, ADJ.: logical; M.: logician.

logí-stica, F.: logistics. **logí-stico**, pl. *-stici*, ADJ.: logistic.

lo-gliáto, ADJ.: with darnel (cockle-weed). ‖**ló-glio** [L. *-lium*], M.: darnel (cockle-weed). **-glióso**, ADJ.: full of darnel.
lògo [*luogo*], M.: place.
logo- [Gr. *lógos*, word]: **-grifo** [*gríphos*, riddle], M.: logogriph (kind of riddle). **-machía** [Gr. *máche*, battle], F.: logomachy (war of words).
logo-raménto, M.: wearing (consuming). ‖**-ráre** [?], TR.: wear (consume); REFL.: wear one's self out. **-ráto**, ADJ.: worn out (consumed). **-ratóre**, M., **-ratríce**, F.: wearer (consumer). **-río**, M.: excessive wearing.
logorízia†, F.: licorice.
lógoro 1 [*-rare*], ADJ.: worn out (consumed); M.: wearing away (consuming).
lógoro 2 [Ger. *luder*, LURE], M.: hunter's signal.
logote-nènte [*luogo, tenente*], M.: lieutenant. **-nènza**, F.: lieutenancy.
lográre† TR.: waste (consume, wear).
lòia [?], F.: filth (greasiness, dirtiness).
lòica†, F.: logic.
loiolésco [*Loiola*], ADJ.: Jesuit.
lòlla [?], F.: chaff; weak person.
lollígine†, F.: cuttlefish.
lom-bággine [*lombo*], F.: lumbago (rheumatism). **-bále**, ADJ.: lumbar (pertaining to loins).
lom-bárda†, F.: Lombard dance. **-bardésimo, -bardísmo**, M.: Lombard expression. ‖**-bárdo** [*Lombardia*], ADJ.: Lombard.
lom-báre, ADJ.: lumbar (of the loins). **-báta**, F.: loins. ‖**lóm-bo** [L. *lumbus*], M.: LOIN (hip, haunch).
lombri-cáio, M.: wormy place. **-cále**, ADJ.: like a worm (lumbrical). **-cáto**†, ADJ.: made of worms. **-chétto, -chíno**, *dim.* of *-co*. ‖**lombrí-co** [L. *lumbricus*], M.: earth-worm (lumbric). **-cóide**, M.: worm. **-cóne**, *aug.* of *-co*. **-cúzzo**, *dim.* of *-co*.
lóme†, M.: light.
lomía†, F.: sweet lemon.
longáni-me [L. *-mis*], ADJ.: patient (longsuffering). **-mità**, F.: patience (forbearance, Eng.† longanimity).
lon-gevità, F.: longevity. ‖**-gèvo** [L. *-gævus*], ADJ.: of great age (old).
longimetría [L. *longus*, long, Gr. *métron*, measure], F.: longimetry (measuring long distances).
lon-ginquità†, F.: great distance. ‖**-gínquo**†, ADJ.: remote (distant, very far off).
longi-tudinále, ADJ.: longitudinal. **-túdine** [L. *-tudo*], F.: longitude.
lonta-naménte, ADV.: distant (far off). **-nánza**, F.: distance (remoteness). **-náre**†, TR.: remove (send away). **-nétto**, *dim.* of *-no*. **-nézza**†, F.: distance (remoteness). **-níssimo**, ADJ.: very (or most) distant. ‖**lontá-no** [L. *longus*, long], ADJ.: distant (remote); ADV.: *di* —, far off. **-núccio**, *dim.* of *-no*. **-núcce**, F. PL.: short distance.
lóntra [L. *lutra*], F.: otter.
lónza [?], F.: panther.
lón-ze [OGer. *lúntussa*], F. PL.: fleshy parts. **lón-zo**, ADJ.: flabby.
lòp-pa [?], F.: chaff (husk). **lòp-pi**, M. PL.: dross (iron or coal waste). **-póso**, ADJ.: husky (full of chaff).
lo-quáce [L. *loquax*], ADJ.: talkative (loquacious). **-quacemènte**, ADV.: loquaciously. **-quacità**, F.: talkativeness (loquacity). **-quèla**, F.: speech (language).
lòrd [Eng.], M.: lord (title).
lor-dággine, F.: filthiness (dirtiness). **-daménte**, ADV.: filthily. **-dáre**, INTR.: make filthy (dirty). **-dézza**†, **-dízia**†, F.: filth. ‖**lór-do** [L. *luridus*], ADJ.: filthy (nasty, soiled). **-dúme**, M.: filthy heap. **-dúra**, F.: filthiness (foulness).
lorí-ca [L.], F.: cuirass. **-cáto**, ADJ.: armed with a cuirass (loricated); loricate (order of reptiles).
lóro [L. *illorum*, of them], PRON.: (to) them; they; you, to you; their(s): *il* —, theirs.
lósco [L. *luscus*], ADJ.: short-sighted.
lossúria†, F.: luxury.
lo-táre†, TR.: plaster with clay. ‖**lò-to** [L. *lutum*], M.: mud (mire, clay). **-tolènte**†, **-tóso**†, ADJ.: muddy (miry).
lò-to [Gr. *lotós*], M.: lotus (plant). **-tòfago**, ADJ.: lotus-eating.
lòt-ta [L. *lucta*], F.: struggle (striving, wrestling). **-táre**, TR.: struggle (strive, wrestle). **-tatóre**, M., **-tatríce**, F.: struggler (wrestler). **-teggiáre**†, TR.: struggle (wrestle).
lot-tería, F.: lottery. ‖**lòt-to** [Eng. *lot*], M.: lottery; lot (chance).
lubbióne [*loggione*], M.: gallery (theatre).
lubri-cánte†, ADJ.: lubricating, M.: lubricant. **-cáre**†, TR.: lubricate. **-cativo**†, ADJ.: making lubricant; laxative. **-chézza**†, F.: looseness (lubricity). **-cità**, F.: wantonness; lubricity. ‖**lúbri-co** [L. *-cus*], ADJ.: slippery (lubric); wanton.
lucaríno†, M.: canary-bird.
Lúc-ca, F.: city (of Lucca). **-chése**, ADJ.: Lucchese.
lucchesíno†, M.: scarlet (colour, cloth).
lucchétto [Fr. *loquet*], M.: padlock.
luc-cicánte, M.: eye†; ADJ.: gleaming (glittering). ‖**-cicáre** [*luce*], INTR.: gleam (glitter, twinkle). **-cichío**, F

flash (gleam, glitter). **-cicóne**, M.: big tears. **lúc-cio**, M.: pike (fish). **lúc-ciola**, F.: firefly. **-cioláio**, M.: great quantity of fireflies. **-ciolátо†**, M.: glow-worm. **-ciolétta**, *car. dim.* of *-ciola*. **-ciolóne**, M.: big tears.

lúcco [?], M.: robe (worn by Florentine magistrates).

lú-ce [L. *lux*], F.: light (brightness); eye: *dare alla —*, give birth; publish. **-cénte**, ADJ.: bright (shining). **-centeménte**, ADV.: brightly (splendidly, brilliantly). **-centézza**, F.: splendour (brilliance). **lú-cere†**, INTR.: shine (glitter). **-cèrna**, F.: lamp (light); cap (of marine officer). **-cernáccia**, *disp.* of *-cerna*. **-cerná-ta**, F.: lampful of oil; blow with a lamp. **-cernétta**, *car. dim.* of *-cerna*. **-cer-nière**, M.: lamp-stand. **-cernína**, *car. dim.* of *-cerna*. **-cernino**, *dim.* of *-cerno*. **-cernóne**, *aug.* of *-cerna*. **-cernúc-cia**, *disp.* of *-cerna*. **-cernúzza**, *disp.* of *-cerna*.

lu-cèrta† [L. *lacerta*], **-cèrtola**, F.: LIZARD. **-certolétta**, **-certolína**, *car. dim.* of *-certola*.

lucèrtolo [? *lacerto*], M.: meat (for boiling).

lucertolóne, *aug.* of *lucertola*.

luchè-rat, F.: look (regard). **-ráre†**, INTR.: scowl.

lucherino [L. *ligurinus* (*Liguria*)], M.: goldfinch.

lucia [*luce*], F.: small reptile; kermes insect (giving the cochineal).

luci damente, ADV.: brightly (clearly). **-damento**, M.: tracing. **-dáre**, TR.: counterdraw; trace. **-datóre**, M., **-da-trice**, F.: counter-drawer. **-dazióne**, F.: elucidation. **dézza**, F.: light (brightness, lucidity†). **dissimo**, ADJ.: very (or most) bright. **-dità**, F.: light (splendor, brightness). ||**lúci-do** [L. *-dus*], ADJ.: bright (clear, lucid). **lucí-fero**, M.: Lucifer (morning star). **-ficáre†**, TR.: light up (illuminate). **-gnoláto**, ADJ.: plaited (wicks). **-gnolétto**, **-gno-líno**, *dim.* of *gnolo*. **lucí gnolo**, M.: wick (of candle, lamp, etc.). **-gnolóne**, *aug.* of *gnolo*. **lina**, F.: combustible (of coal oil). **mento†**, M.: splendour (brightness).

[illegible]†, M.: wood (grove).

lucóre†, M.: light (splendor).

lu-crábile, ADJ.: gainable. **-craré**, [illegible] (gain). **-crativo**, ADJ.: lucrative (gainful). ||**lu-cro** [L. *-crum*], [illegible] (LUCRE). **-crosaménte**, [illegible] (with gain). **-cróso**, [illegible] (lucrative).

[illegible], ADJ.: shining (clear,

luculliáno [L. *Lucullus*, Roman consul], ADJ.: sumptuous (luxurious).

lú-dere†, IRR.; INTR.: sport (jest, play). ||**lú-di** [L. *-dus*], M. PL.: public games. **-díbrio**, M.: laughing-stock. **-dificá-re†**, TR.: jest (ridicule, quiz). **-dificazióne†**, F.: jesting (quizzing). **-dima-gístro**, M.: schoolmaster. **lú-do†**, M.: (*poet.*) game (sport, play).

lúe [L. *-s*], F.: plague (pestilence, lues).

lúffo†, M.: heap (mass).

luffomástro†, M.: steward.

lúgere†, INTR.: weep (bewail).

lúggiola†, F.: sorrel.

lu-gliático†, ADJ.: ripe (or flowering) in July. ||**lú-glio** [L. *Julius*], M.: July. **-gliòlo**, ADJ.: maturing in July.

lúgu-bre, **lugú-bre** (*poet.*) [L. *-bris*], ADJ.: mournful (sorrowful, lugubrious). **-breménte**, ADV.: mournfully (lugubriously).

lúi [L. *illum-hic*], PRON.: him; it.

luí [echoic], M.: wren.

luígi [Fr. *Louis*], M.: louis-d'or (money).

luíssimo†, PRON.: he himself.

lu-máca, ||**-máccia†** [L. *limax*], F.: snail: *scala a —*, winding staircase. **-machíno**, *dim.* of *-maca*. **-macóne**, *aug.* of *-maca*. **-macóso**, ADJ.: glossy.

lumáio [*lume*], M.: lamplighter; lamp-dealer.

lumbricále, ADJ.: lumbrical (muscle).

lú-me [L. *-men*], M.: light (lamp); knowledge. **-meggiaménto**, M.: lighting. **-meggiáre**, TR.: light up (illuminate). **-meggiánte**, ADJ.: illuminating. **-meg-giatúra**, F.: lighting. **lú-men Chri-sti**, M.: devotional candle. **-mettíno**, *car. dim.* of *-metto*. **-métto**, *car. dim.* of *-me*.

lumía†, F.: lime; lemon.

lumi-cíno [*lume*], *dim.* of *lume*. **-èra**, F.: chandelier. **-nára**, F.: public illumination. **-náre**, M.: luminary (star). **-na-tívo†**, ADJ.: illuminative. **-nazióne**, F.: illumination. **-nèllo**, M.: socket (of candlestick). **-nièra†**, F.: light (splendour); chandelier. **lumí-no**, *dim.* of *lume*. **-nosaménte**, ADV.: luminously. **-nosíssimo**, ADJ.: very (or most) luminous. **-nosità**, F.: brightness (luminousness). **-nóso**, ADJ.: luminous (bright, shining).

lumúccio, *disp. dim.* of *lume*.

lú-na [L.], F.: moon: *— scema*, wane of the moon. **-nagióne**, F.: lunation. **-náre**, ADJ.: lunar; M.: lunar course†. **-nariétto**, **-naríno**, *dim.* of *-nario*. **-nário**, M.: almanac (calendar). **-narí-sta**, M.: almanac maker (weather prophet). **-nariúccio**, *disp.* of *-nario*. **-náta**, F.: semi-circular corrosion (of rivers).

-naticheria, F.: lunacy (insanity). **-nático**, pl. *—ci*, ADJ.: lunatic (insane). **-náto**, ADJ.: lunate (crescent-shaped). **-nazióne**, F.: lunation (course of moon). **-ne=dì**, M.: Monday. **-nedìáre** [*-nedì*], INTR.: make (Monday) a holiday. **-nétta**, F.: lunette (*arch.*: wall between curves of a vault; semi-circular window; *fort.*: salient fieldwork; semi-circular object).

lun-gáccio, ADJ.: very slow (lazy). **-gággine**, F.: drawn-out thing or story, yarn. **-gágnola†**, F.: long net; tiresome story. **-gagnáta**, F.: wearisome discourse. **-gaménte**, ADV.: long (long time). **-ganimità†**, F.: patience (longanimity). **-gánimo†**, ADJ.: patient (forbearing). **-gáre†**, TR.: deviate (digress); REFL.: withdraw (go away). **-garnáta**, F.: walk (promenade). **-gárno**, M.: road (along the river Arno). **lún-ge**, ADV.: distant (far off). **-ghería**, F.: length. **-ghésso**, PREP.: along (by, near). **-ghétto**, *dim.* of *-go.* **-ghézza**, F.: length (duration). **-ghièra†**, F.: tedious discourse. **-ghissimaménte**, ADV.: lengthily. **-ghíssimo**, ADJ.: very (or most) long. **lún-gi**, ADV.: at a distance; PREP.: far. **-gitáno†**, ADJ.: distant (relation). **||lún-go** [L. *longus*], ADJ.: long (slow, tedious); ADV.: at length; PREP.: along (by); M.: length. **-gúra†**, F.: duration; longitude.

lunóna, *aug.* of *luna.*

luò-go [L. *locus*], M.: place (space, land): *aver* —, take place; *cedere il* —, give preference; *in* —, instead. **-gotenènte**, M.: lieutenant. **-gotenènza**, F.: lieutenancy.

lú-pa [*-po*], F.: she-wolf; strangle-weed; enticer†. **-pacchiótto**, **-pacchíno†**, *dim.* of *-po.* **-páccio**, *disp.* of *-po.* **-pája**, F.: wolf den. **-panáre**, M.: house of ill-fame. **-patèllo†**, **-pattíno**, *dim.* of *-po.* **-percáli**, F. PL.: Roman feast (for Pan). **-pèrci**, M. PL.: lupercal priests. **-pésco**, ADJ.: wolfish. **-pétto**, **-piccíno**, *car. dim.* of *-po.* **-pígno†**, ADJ.: wolfish. **-pináccio**, *disp.* of *-pino* 1. **-pinájo** [*-pino* 1], M.: seller of lupines; lupine field. **-pinèllo** [*-pino* 1], M.: wild lupine. **-píno** 1 [L. *-pinus*], M.: lupine (plant). **-píno** 2, ADJ.: wolfish (ravenous, lupine). **||lú-po** [L. *-pus*], M.: wolf: — *cerviero*, lynx.

luppo-lièra, F.: hop-field. **-lína**, F.: hop-powder (lupuline). **||lúppo-lo** [L. *lupulus*], M.: hops.

lúr-co [L.], ADJ.: greedy (voracious). **-cóne†**, *aug.* of *-co.*

luri-dézza, F.: ghastliness (dismalness). **||lúri-do** [L. *-dus*], ADJ.: lurid (ghastly, dismal).

lúsco [L. *-cus*], ADJ.: short-sighted.

lúsi†, PRET. of *ludere.*

lusignuòlo†, M.: nightingale.

lusín-ga [OFr. *losenge* (? L. *laus*, praise)], F.: flattery (adulation, allurement). **-gaménto**, M.: flattering. **-gáre**, TR.: flatter (wheedle, allure); REFL.: flatter one's self. **-gatóre**, M., **-gatríce**, F.: flatterer (wheedler, Eng.† LOSENGER). **-ghévole**, ADJ.: flattering, alluring. **-ghevolménte**, ADV.: flatteringly (alluringly). **-ghièro†**, **-ghièro**, ADJ.: flattering (alluring).

luso†, PART. of *ludere.*

lus-sáre [L. *luxare*], INTR.: dislocate (luxate). **-sazióne**, F.: dislocation (luxation).

lússi, PRET. of *lucere.*

lús-so [L. *luxus*], M.: LUXury (pomp; Eng.† LUXE). **-soriáre†**, INTR.: live luxuriously. **-sureggiánte**, ADJ.: luxuriant (exuberant). **-sureggiáre**, INTR.: live luxuriously (luxuriate); grow exuberantly. **-súria**, F.: luxury (voluptuousness). **-suriánte†**, ADJ.: luxurious (wanton). **-suriáre†**, INTR.: luxuriate (indulge to excess). **-surieggiáre†**, INTR.: live luxuriously; grow rank. **-suriosaménte**, ADV.: luxuriously (wantonly). **-surióso**, ADJ.: luxurious (voluptuous).

lú-stra [*-stro* 3], F.: den (hiding-place)†; deception.

lu-strále [*-stro* 2], ADJ.: lustral (purifying; quinquennial). **-straménto**, M.: polishing. **-stránte†**, ADJ.: brilliant (shining, bright). **-stra=piánte**, M.: shoe-polisher. **||-stráre** [L. (*lucere*, shine)], TR.: purify; give lustre to (polish, burnish); INTR.: shine (gleam, sparkle). **-stra=scárpe**, **-stra stiváli**, M.: bootblack; flatterer. **-stráta**, F.: quick polishing. **-stratína**, *dim.* of *-strata.* **-stráto**, ADJ.: polished (burnished). **-stratóre**, M.: polisher. **-stratúra**, F.: polishing (burnishing). **-strazióne**, F.: lustration (act or sacrifice of purification). **-stríno**, M.: lustring (silk cloth); tinsel; bootblack. **-stríssimo**, ADJ.: very (or most) illustrious. **lú-stro** 1, ADJ.: polished (smooth, shining); M.: lustre (gloss).

lústro 2 [L. *-strum* (*luere*, loose, pay)], M.: lustrum (Rom. ceremony of public purification every five years; space of five years).

lústro† 3 [L. *-strum* (*luere*, wash), bog; den], M.: den (hiding-place).

lustróre†, M.: splendour.

lu-táre† [*-to*], TR.: lute (seal with lute). **-tatúra†**, F.: luting.

lute-ranésimo, **-ranísmo**, M.: Lutheranism. **-ráno** [*Lutero*], ADJ.: Lutheran; M.: disciple of Luther.

lu-tifigolo†, M.: potter. ‖**lú-to** [L. *-tum*], M.: clay (mud, lute).

lút-ta†, F.: wrestling (striving).

lút-to [L. *luctus* (*lugere*, mourn)], M.: grief (mourning, lamentation); mourning-clothes. **-tóso**†, ADJ.: mournful (sorrowful). **-tuosaménte**, ADV.: mournfully (sorrowfully). **-tuóso**, ADJ.: mournful (sorrowful, sad).

lutulènto [*luto*], ADJ.: clayey (muddy, miry).

M

m *èmme* [L.], M., F.: m (the letter).

ma 1 [L. *magis*], CONJ.: but; even: — *che*, it is not so; is it possible? etc.; — *sì*, yes, indeed.

ma 2 [*madre*], F.: ma (for 'mamma').

má-cabra, ‖**-cábra** [?], ADJ., M.: *danza* —, dance of death.

máoca [OFr. *mache*, mass], F.: abundance; ADV.: *a* —, abundantly.

Maccabèi [*-beus*], M. PL.: Maccabees (apocryphal books of Old Testament).

maccatèl-la†, F.: minced meat (sausage); defect (blemish). **-lería**†, F.: exchanging (bartering).

maccheria†, F.: calm at sea.

macche-róne [?], M.: macaroni (food); stupid fellow; ADJ.: heavy. **-ronèa**, F.: medley (macaronic). **-ronésco**, **-rònico**, pl. *—ci*, ADJ.: burlesque (macaronic).

mác-chia [L. *macula*], F.: spot (stain, mark, blur, blemish); macula (sun-spot); rapid painting (sketch); painting broadly or in masses (sort of impressionist painting); thicket (copse, bush); ambush: *alla* —, in ambush; secretly (underhand); (*paint.*) in masses, broadly; *stare alla* —, lie in ambush; be a robber or assassin. **-chiáccia**, *disp.* of *-chia*. **-chiaiòlo**, M.: rapid sketcher (impressionist); woodman; dastard; ADJ.: of the woods, sylvan. **-chiáre**, TR.: spot (stain, blue); sketch; REFL.: stain one's self. **-chiáto**, ADJ.: spotted (stained). **-chiático**, pl. *—ci*, ADJ.: concerning fuel-gathering; M.: right of gathering fuel; tax (on fuel gathered). **-chierèlla**, *dim.* of *-chia*. **-chierellina**, *dim.* of *-chierella*. **-chiéto**, M.: woody place. **-chiétta**, *dim.* of *-chia*. **-chiettáre**, TR.: stain (spot). **-chiettáto**, ADJ.: covered with small stains. **-chiettina**, *dim.* of *-chia*.

mácchi-na [L. *machina*], F.: machine (engine); artifice (stratagem); large building; works (of a watch). **-náccia**, *disp.* of *-na*. **-nále**, ADJ.: mechanical. **-nalménte**, ADV.: mechanically. **-naménto**, M.: plot (scheme, machination). **-náre**, TR.: plot (scheme, machinate). **-náto**, ADJ.: plotted (contrived). **-natóre**, M., **-natrice**, F.: plotter (contriver, machinator). **-nazióne**, F.: plot (machination). **-nétta**, **-nína**, **-níno**, *dim.* of *-na*. **-nísmo**, M.: mechanism. **-nísta**, M.: engine-tender (engineer); machinist†. **-nóna**, **-nóne**, *aug.* of *-na*. **-nosaménte**, ADV.: powerfully (like machines). **-nóso**, ADJ.: powerful (strong).

mac-chiolina, *dim.* of *-chia*. **-chióne**, F.: filthiness. **-chióne**, M.: bushy place. **-chióso**, ADJ.: stained (spotted). **-chiúccia**, *dim.* of *-chia*. **-chiúzza**†, *dim.* of *-uccia*.

macciánghero†, ADJ.: coarse (awkward, stupid).

máoco [OFr. *mache*, mass], M.: bean-porridge; slaughter (butchery)†; ADV.†: *a* —, abundantly (plentifully).

macel-lábile, ADJ.: fit for slaughter. **-láio**, M.: butcher. **-laménto**, M.: slaughtering (butchering). **-lára**, F.: butcher's wife; meat-shop keeper. **-láre**1, TR.: butcher (slaughter, kill). **-láre**2, **-láro**1, ADJ.: grinding (teeth). **-láro**2, M.: butcher. **-láto**, ADJ.: slaughtered (killed). **-latóre**, M.: butcher (slaughterer). **-lazióne**, F.: butchering. **-lería**, F.: meat-shop; slaughter (carnage). ‖**macèl-lo** [L. *-lum*], M.: slaughter-house; slaughter.

mace-rábile, ADJ.: capable of maceration. **-raménto**†, M.: maceration. ‖**-ráre** [L.], TR.: soften (soak, steep, macerate); weaken†; REFL.: mortify; waste away. **-ratóio**, M.: steeping-trench (for flax). **-razióne**, F.: maceration. **-réto** [*-ria*], M.: heap of ruins. **-cèria**, F.: ruined wall. **máce-ro** [*-cerare*], ADJ.: steeped (macerated); exhausted; M.: maceration (steeping).

macceróne [?], M.: species of celery.

má-chia, F.: craft (duplicity). **-chiavellicaménte**, ADV.: craftily (cunningly). ‖**-chiavèllico**, pl. *—ci* [*Machiavelli*], ADJ.: Machiavelian (crafty, cunning). **-chióne**, ADJ.: very crafty.

macía [*-ceria*], F.: ruined wall.

mácie [L. *-cies*], F.: leanness (thinness).

macigno [*-cina*], M.: sort of granite, rock.

maci-lènte, ‖**-lènto** [L. *macies*], ADJ.: thin (lean, meagre). **-lènza**, F.: thinness (meagreness).

máci-na [L. *machina*, engine], F.: grindstone (millstone); oppressive weight (distress). **-naménto**†, M.: grinding (crushing, pulverizing). **-náre**, TR.: grind (crush, pulverise). **-náta**, F.: hopperful. **-náto**, M.: meal (flour); tax; ADJ.†: ruined. **-natóio**†, M.: oil-mill. **-nató-**

-re, M.: grinder. **-natúra**, **-nazióne**, F.: grinding (pulverizing). **máci-ne**, F.: grindstone (millstone); distress. **-nèlla†**, *dim.* of *-ne*. **-nèllo**, M.: colour-grinder. **-nétta**, *dim.* of *-na*. **-níno**, M.: grinder (for coffee, etc.).
maciúl-la [?], F.: hemp-brake (instrument). **-láre**, TR.: break (hemp, flax); chew†. **-láto**, ADJ.: broken (crushed).
mácco-la† [L. *macula*], F.: stain (spot, blemish). **-láre**, TR.: produce spots upon by beating or bruising (bruise); beat black and blue (thrash). **-láto**, ADJ.: bruised; thrashed. **-lazióne**, F.: bruising; thrashing. **mácco-lo**, ADJ.: bruised (thrashed).
mácero†, ADJ.: thin (lean); dry.
macú-ba [town, *M.*, W. Ind.], F.: snuff. **-bíno**, M.: kind of snuff.
mácu-la [L.], F.: stain (spot); sin†. **-láre**, TR.: = *macolare;* spot (stain, maculate). **-láto**, ADJ.: stained (impure, maculate). **-lazióne†**, F.: staining (maculating). **mácu-lo†**, ADJ.: stained (beaten, ill-used). **-lóso†**, ADJ.: full of spots (stains).
madá-ma [Fr. *-me*], F.: madam (mistress). **-migèlla**, F.: miss (young lady). **-mina**, *dim.* of *-ma*.
madernále†, ADJ.: maternal.
madesì†, ADV.: yes, indeed.
má-dia [L. *-gida*], F.: kneading-trough. **-diáta**, F.: troughful.
mádido [L. *-didus*], ADJ.: wet (damp, humid, madid).
madiè†, ADV.: yes, indeed.
ma-diétta, *dim.* of *-dia*. **-dióna**, *aug.* of *-dia*.
ma=dònna, F.: madame (my lady; dame); Madonna (Virgin Mary). **-donnétta**, *dim.* of *-donna*. **-donnína**, *car. dim.* of *-donna*. **-donníno**, M.: maiden-faced boy; money. **-donnóne**, M.: large figure of the Madonna. **-donnúccia**, *disp. dim.* of *-donna*.
madóre [L. *-dor*], M.: dampness (moisture, humidity).
madorná-le [*madrona*], ADJ.: maternal†; large (great); grave; extravagant; legitimate. **-lità**, F.: largeness; gravity.
mádre [L. *mater*], F.: mother; origin; mould (of statue, etc., form). **-ggiáre**, INTR.: be like the mother. **=pátria**, F.: mother country. **=pèrla**, F.: mother-of-pearl. **-perláceo**, ADJ.: like mother-of-pearl. **-'pora**, F.: madrepore (coral). **-pòrico**, pl. *—ci*, ADJ.: madreporite. **=sélva**, F.: woodbine; honeysuckle. **=víto**, M.: female screw.
madrigá-le [?], M.: madrigal (amourous lyric). **-leggiáre**, INTR.: compose madrigals. **-lésco**, ADJ.: resembling the madrigal. **-létto**, **-líno**, *dim.* of *-le*. **-lóne**, *aug.* of *-le*. **-lúccio**, *disp.* of *-le*.
ma-drína [*-dre*], F.: godmother; midwife†. **-dróna†**, F.: matron. **-dróne†**, M.: pain (in the side).
maes-tà [L. *majestas*], F.: majesty (grandeur). **-tèrio†**, **-tèro†**, M.: art (skilfulness); instruction. **-tévole†**, ADJ.: majestic (grand). **-tevolménte†**, **-tosaménte**, ADV.: majestically (with grandeur). **-tosíssimo**, ADJ.: very (or most) majestic. **-tosità**, F.: majesty. **-tóso**, ADJ.: majestic.
maè-stra, F.: school-mistress; mastery (skill). **-strále**, M.: northwest wind. **-straménto**, M.: conferring doctor's (or master's) degree. **-stránza**, F.: association of workmen. **-stráre†**, TR.: teach (instruct); confer doctor's degree on. **-stráto†**, ADJ.: taught; M.: magistrate. **-strèllo**, *dim.* of *-stro*. **-stréssa**, F.: school-mistress; mistress. **-strévole**, ADJ.: masterly (skilful). **-strevolménte**, ADV.: masterly (skilfully). **-stría**, F.: mastery (skill, dexterity). **-strína**, *dim.* of *-stra*. **-stríno**, *car. dim.* of *-stro*.
||**maè-stro** [L. *magister*], M.: MASTER (teacher, professor); head (principal); northwest wind; ADJ.: chief (principal): — *di campo*, field-marshal; — *di giustizia*, hangman; — *di casa*, steward. **-stróne**, *aug.* of *-stro*. **-strúccia**, **-strúccio**, **-strúcolo**, *disp. dim.* of *-stro*. **-strúzzo**, *disp.* of *-stro*.
mafátto†, ADJ.: ill-made (deformed); M.: misdeed.
máf-fia [OFr. *mafler*, devour], F.: Maffia (organization enforcing laws of its own, something between white-caps and labor union in Am.). **-fióso**, ADJ.: of the Maffia.
mága [L. *-gus*], F.: sorceress; hag.
magá-gna [OFr. *mehaing*], F.: defect (imperfection, blemish). **-gnaménto†**, M.: spoiling; defect. **-gnáre**, TR.: spoil (destroy, corrupt). **-gnáto**, ADJ.: spoiled (rotten). **-gnatúra†**, F.: defect (imperfection).
magá-ri, ||**-ra** [?], INTERJ.: yes, indeed! (certainly!).
magaz-zinággio, M.: storehouse dues. **-zinière**, M.: storehouse-keeper. ||**-zíno** [fr. Ar.], M.: magazine (storehouse).
magest. .† = *maest*. .
mag-gèngo, ADJ.: of May (month). **-gesáre**, TR.: plough (break up land). **-gesáto**, ADJ.: ploughed (broken up). **-gesatúra**, F.: ploughing (breaking up). **-géso**, ADJ.: of May; M.: fallow land. **-giaiòla**, F., **-giaiòlo**, M.: May-singer (boy or girl singing May carols); fever. **-giática**, F., **-giático**, M.: fallow ground.

‖**mág-gio** [L. *maius*], M.: May (month); song; festival; ADJ.†: greater; elder. **-gio-ciòndolo**†, M.: laburnum (ornamental tree). **-gioláta**, F.: May-song.

maggioràna [*amaraco*], F.: sweet MARJORAM (plant).

maggio-ránza, F.: majority. **-rásco**, M.: inheritance (of elder brother). **-rdòmo**, M.: major-domo. ‖**maggió-re** [L. *major*], ADJ.: major (greater, elder); M.: major (officer). **-rèllo**†, *dim.* of *-re*. **-rènne**, ADJ.: of age (of one just become major); M.: major. **-rènte**†, M.: magnate (chief man). **-rétto**†, *dim.* of *-re*. **-révole**†, ADJ.: chief (principal, senior). **-rézza**†, F.: greatness. **maggió-ri**, M. PL.: ancestors (forefathers). **-ría**†, F.: majority (superiority). **-ríngo**, M.: magnate (chief man). **-ríno**, *car. dim.* of *-re*. **-rità**, F.: major's office; majority† (of numbers). **-rménte**, ADV.: more (much more). **-rnáto**, M.: eldest born (son).

mághero = *magro*.

má-gi [L. *magus*], M.: magi (caste of Persian priests); ADJ.: of the three wise men (*Bibl.*). **-gía**, F.: magic (sorcery). **-gicále**†, ADJ.: magical. **-gicaménte**, ADV.: magically. **má-gico**, pl. —*ci*, ADJ.: magic.

maginá-re†, INTR.: imagine (think). **-zióne**†, F.: imagination.

ma-gioncèlla†, *dim.* of *-gione*. ‖**-gióne** [L. *mansio*], F.: MANSION (habitation). **-gionétta**†, *dim.* of *-gione*.

magiòstra†, F.: kind of strawberry.

magis-teriáto†, M.: magistracy. **-tèrio**†, ‖**-tèro** [L. *-terium*], M.: ability (MASTERY, skill); magistery (a precipitate); doctorship†; discipline†. **-trále**, ADJ.: magisterial (imperious). **-tralità**, F.: doctrine; science. **-tralménte**, ADV.: magisterially. **-tráto**, M.: magistrate. **-tratúra**, F.: magistracy. **-trévole**†, ADJ.: authoritative (magistral).

má-glia [L. *-cula*], F.: network; knitting; mail (coat of mail). **-gliáto**†, ADJ.: of mail. **-gliétta**, F.: small mesh; annulet. **-glína**, *dim.* of *-glietta*.

ma-gliétto, *dim.* of *-glio*. ‖**má-glio** [L. *malleus*], M.: forge-hammer; sledge-hammer; MALL (MALLET; beetle).

ma-gliolína, *dim.* of *-glia*.

magli-òlo, ‖**-uòlo**† [*-o*, like a hammer], M.: sprout (shoot).

magnaménte†, ADV.: grandly (nobly).

magnanáccio, *disp.* of *-gnano*.

magnani-maménte, ADV.: magnanimously (with dignity). **-mità**, F.: magnanimity. ‖**magnáni-mo** [L. *-mus*], ADJ.: magnanimous (high-souled, brave).

magnáno [OFr. *maignain*], M.: locksmith.

magnáre (*jest.*) = *mangiare*.

magná-te [L. *-tes*], M.: magnate; ADJ.: of high rank. **-tízio**, ADJ.: of note (distinction).

magnè-sia [city *M.*, Asia Min.], F.: magnesia (mineral). **-síaco**, pl. —*ci*, ADJ.: containing magnesia. **magnè-sio**, M.: magnesium. **-síte**, M.: magnesite.

magnè-te [L. *-s*], M.: magnet (loadstone). **-ticaménte**, ADV.: magnetically. **magnè-tico**, pl. —*ci*, ADJ.: magnetic. **-tísmo**, M.: magnetism. **-títe**, M.: magnetite. **-tizzáre**, TR.: magnetize. **-tizzáto**, ADJ.: magnetized. **-tizzatóre**, M., **-tizzatríce**, F.: magnetizer. **magnè-to-**, PREF.: magneto-. **-tòmetro**, M.: magnetometer (instrument).

magnífi-ca, F.: (*vulg.*) eating (grub); also = *-cat*. **-caménte**, ADV.: magnificently (grandly). **-caménto**, M.: magnifying (extolling). **-cáre**, TR.: magnify (extol, exalt). **magnífi-cat**, M.: Magnificat (song to Virgin Mary commencing with this word). **-cataménte**†, ADV.: magnificently. **-catóre**, M., **-catríce**, F.: magnifier. **-cènte**, ADJ.: magnificent (noble, splendid). **-centeménte**†, ADV.: magnificently. **-cènza**, **-cènzia**†, F.: magnificence (splendour). ‖**magnífi-co** [L. *-cus* (*magnus*, great)], ADJ.: magnificent (splendid, grand, noble).

magni-loquènte, ADJ.: magniloquent (bombastic). **-loquènza**, F.: magniloquence. ‖**-'loquo**† [L. *-loquus*], ADJ.: magniloquent. **-túdine**†, F.: magnitude.

mágno† [L. *-nus*], ADJ.: great (large, mighty).

magnòlia [botanist *Magnol*], F.: magnolia (plant).

mágo [L. *-gus*], M.: magician; ADJ.: magical.

magògano [Centr. Am. *mohagoni*], M.: mahogany.

magoláto†, M.: wide ridge (between furrows).

magó-na [?], F.: abundance (plenty); smithy (forge). **-ncína**, F.: shop (adjoined to smithy). **-nièro**, M.: founder (worker in smithy).

magraménte [*-gro*], ADV.: meagrely (poorly, stingily).

magrána†, F.: headache (megrim).

ma-grettíno, *car. dim.* of *-gretto*. **-grétto**, *dim.* of *-gro*. **-grézza**, F.: meagerness (leanness, poorness). **-gríno**, *dim.* of *-gro*. ‖**má-gro** [L. *-cer*], ADJ.: MEAGER (lean, scarce, arid). **-grógnolo**, *dim.* of *-gro*. **-gróne**, M.: lean hog; ADJ.: lean (of hogs).

mái [L. *magis*], ADV.: ever; never (with *non*): — *più*, nevermore; — *sì*, yes indeed; *sempre* —†, always (ever more).

maiá-la, F.: sow. **-láccio**, *disp.* of *-le.* **-láta**, F.: hog-like action. **-latúra**, F.: preparation (chopping, salting, etc.) of hog-meat. ||**maiá-le** [L. *-lis*], M.: hog. **-líno**, *car. dim.* of *-le.* **-lóna**, **-lóne**, *aug.* of *-la*, *-le.*

maiestà†, F.: majesty.

mainè†, ADV.: no (not at all).

máio†, M.: laburnum (tree).

maiòlica [isle *Majorca*], F.: potter's clay; majolica-ware.

maioràna†, F.: marjoram (plant).

maio-ránza†, F.: majority. **-rascáto**, M.: conditions (of inheritance). **-rásco**, M.: inheritance (of elder brother). **-rdòmo†**, M.: majordomo (steward). ||**maió-r-e†** [L. *-r*], M.: major; ADJ.: greater.

maiúsco-la, F.: capital letter. **-létto**, **-líno**, *dim.* of *-lo.* ||**maiúsco-lo** [L. *-ulus*], ADJ.: capital (great majuscule).

mal- [*-e*, *-o*, *-a*], *in composition:* mal-, bad(ly).

má-la, F. of *-lo;* in compound for *-la* or *-le.*

malabbiáto†, ADJ.: wicked (villainous). **-áccio**, M.: wickedness (great wrong); disease (of sheep). =**accòlto** [*mal*, *accolto*], ADJ.: ill-received. =**accóncio†**, ADJ.: unsuitable (improper). =**accortaménte**, ADV.: imprudently (uncautiously). =**accòrto**, ADJ.: imprudent (uncautious).

malachí-ta, ||**-te** [Gr. *-tes*], F.: malachite (mineral).

malacòtteri [Gr. *malakòs*, soft, *ptéron*, fin], M. PL.: malacopteri (order of fishes).

mala=creánza, F.: ill-breeding (rudeness, impoliteness). **-dettaménte**, ADV.: cursedly (detestably). **-détto**, ADJ.: cursed (detestable). **-dícere†**, ||**-díre** [*male*, *dire*], IRR.; TR.: curse (imprecate). **-díssi**, PRET. of *-dire.* **-dizióne**, F.: malediction (curse). **-fátta** [*male*, *fatta*], F.: mistake (in weaving); defect. =**féde**, F.: bad faith (deceit, treacherousness). **-ffètto†**, ADJ.: hateful (spiteful). =**fítta†**, F.: sinking (shrinking) earth.

málaga [*M.* in Spain], M., F.: Malaga wine.

mal=agévole, ADJ.: difficult (laborious, fatiguing); M.: difficulty. **-agevolézza**, F.: difficulty (laboriousness). **-agevolménte**, ADV.: laboriously (with difficulty). **-agiáto†**, ADJ.: uneasy; needy. **-a=grázia**, F.: bad grace (rudeness). =**auguráto**, ADJ.: ill-omened (unfortunate). **-agurióso†**, **-aguróso†**, ADJ.: ill-omened (unfortunate). **-aménte** [*male*], ADV.: badly (violently). **-andánza†**, F.: mischance (mishap). =**andáre†**, IRR.; INTR.: go badly (go to destruction). **-andáto**, ADJ.: broken down (ruined).

malándre†, F.: malanders (blisters on horses).

malan-drinésco, ADJ.: of highway robbers. **-drino**, M.: highway robber (thief, wicked man); ADJ.: roguish (malicious). ||**malán-dro†** [?], ADJ.: roguish (rascally).

mal=ánimo, M.: animosity (rancour). **-ánna**, F.: calamity (disaster). **-annággio**, INTERJ.: curse! (a curse upon!). =**ánno**, M.: illness; disaster (calamity, misfortune). **-a=paráta**, F.: trouble. **-ardíto†**, ADJ.: rash (foolhardy, daring). **-áre†**, INTR.: become sick. =**ária**, F.: malaria (bad air, fever). =**arnése**, M.: vagrant (rascal). =**arriváto†**, ADJ.: unfortunate (luckless, wretched). **-assètto†**, ADJ.: in disorder.

mala-tíccio, ADJ.: sickly. **-tíno**, *car. dim.* of *-to.* ||**malá-to** [*ammalato*], ADJ.: sick (ill, infirm). **mala-ttía** [*malato*], F.: sickness (disease, malady). **-ttiáccia**, *disp.* of *-ttia.* **-ttiúccia**, *disp. dim.* of *-ttia.* **-túccio**, *dim.* of *-to.*

mal-augurataménte, ADV.: unfortunately. **-auguráto**, ADJ.: ill-omened (unfortunate). =**augúrio**, M.: ill omen (misfortune). **-augurosaménte**, ADV.: unluckily (unfortunately). **-auguróso**, **-auróso†**, ADJ.: ill-omened (unfortunate). **-a=ventúra**, F.: mischance (misfortune). **-a=vòglia**, **-avogliènza†** [*voglia*], F.: malevolence. **-avvedutaménte**, ADV.: imprudently (incautiously). =**avvedúto**, ADJ.: imprudent (incautious). **-avventúra†**, F.: misfortune (disaster). **-avventuráto†**, ADJ.: unlucky (unfortunate). =**avvézzo**, ADJ.: ill-bred.

malazzáto [*malato*], ADJ.: sickly (weak).

mal=cadúco, M.: falling sickness (epilepsy). =**capitáto**, ADJ.: unlucky. **-cautaménte**, ADV.: incautiously (heedlessly). =**cáuto**, ADJ.: incautious (heedless). =**cèrto**, ADJ.: uncertain. =**collocáto**, ADJ.: badly-arranged. **-compostaménte†**, ADV.: disorderly (confusedly). =**compósto**, ADJ.: disarranged (disordered, confused). =**cóncio**, ADJ.: ill-treated. **-condescendènte†**, ADJ.: rude (impolite). =**condóttо†**, ADJ.: badly conducted. =**conoscènte†**, ADJ.: ungrateful. =**consigliáto**, ADJ.: ill-advised (incautious, imprudent). =**contènto**, ADJ.: discontented (dissatisfied); M.: discontent. =**copèrto**, ADJ.: scarcely covered (half bare). =**corrispondènte**, ADJ.: unsuitable (unbecoming). =**corrispósto**, ADJ.: unreturned. =**costumáto**, ADJ.: ill-bred (indecent, rude). =**creatèllo**, *dim.* of *-creato.* =**creáto**, ADJ.: ill-bred (rude). =**curánte†**, ADJ.: careless (negligent). =**dèstro**, ADJ.: without cunning or malice, innocent. =**détto**, ADJ.: badly said (rude, thoughtless). =**di=cápo**, M.: headache.

=**dicènte**, ADJ.: slandering; M.: slanderer (defamer). =**dicènza**, F.: slander (defamation). -**dicitóre**†, M.: slanderer. =**dispósto** [*male disposto*], ADJ.: ill-disposed (ill-intentioned). =**dòcchio** [*male di occhio*], M.: evil-eye. =**durévole**†, ADJ.: of short duration.

mále [L.], M.: evil (wrong, wickedness); hurt (damage); pain (sickness, infirmity), ADV.: illy (badly, rudely). =**bòlge**, F. PL.: eighth circle (in Dante's hell). =**dettaménte**, ADV.: in a cursed manner (miserably). -**détto**, ADJ.: cursed (execrated, detested); INTERJ.: a curse upon! damn! -**dicaménte**, ADV.: slanderously.

malè-dico, ADJ.: slanderous (malicious). ‖=**díre**, IRR.§; TR.: curse (imprecate). -**díssi**, PRET. of *-dire*. -**dizióne**, F.: curse (malediction, imprecation).

§ Like *dire*; but Impl. *male-dicéva* or *-diva*; Pret. *male-dissi* or *-dii*, *-disse* or *-dì*; *-dissero* or *-dirono*. — Pop. Pres. *male-disco*.

mal=educáto, ADJ.: uneducated (ignorant).

male=fátta, F.: mistake (in weaving); error (evil deed). -**ficaménte**, ADV.: wrongly (wickedly). -**ficènza**†, F.: wrong (evil, mischief). -**ficiáto**†, ADJ.: bewitched (fascinated). -**fício**, M.: evil deed; witchcraft (enchantment); malefice. -**ficóso**†, ‖**malè-fico** [L. *-ficus*], ADJ.: hurtful (pernicious, maleficent); M.†: magician. -**fízio**, M.: crime; enchantment.

malenconía†, F.: melancholy (sadness).

malèo†, ADJ.: sickly (weak).

malèscio [Fr. *mal-aisé*], ADJ.: sickly, (weak) uneatable.

mal=èssere, M.: bad feeling; straitened circumstances. -**estánte**†, ADJ.: poor (needy). -**estríno**, *dim.* of *-estro*. =**èstro**, M.: havoc (destruction).

malevo-gliènte†, ADJ.: malevolent (ill-disposed). -**gliènza**†, -**lènza**, F.: malevolence (ill-will). ‖**malèvo-lo** [L. *-lus*], ADJ.: malevolent (malicious, ill-disposed).

mal·facènte, ADJ.: hurtful (malefic). -**faciménto**†, M.: misdeed (crime). ‖-**fáre**, DEFECT. (only Inf. and Part.); INTR.: do wrong (evil, harm). -**fátto**, ADJ.: ill-made (ill-shaped, deformed); M.†: misdeed (crime). -**fattóra**, F., -**fattóre**, M.: evil-doer (malefactor). -**fattoría**†, F.: witchcraft (enchantment). -**féci**, PRET. of *fare*. =**férmo**, ADJ.: weak (unsteady, sick). =**fidáto**, ADJ.: untrustful; M.: [u]ntrustful person. =**fioríto**, ADJ.: with flowers (not flourishing). =**fondáto**, ill-founded (unsteady, weak). =**fran-**[…], M.: syphilis. =**gárbo**, M.: grace[…]ess. -**giudicáre**, INTR.: judge […]ly (misjudge). =**giudicáto**, ADJ.: […]ly judged (misjudged). =**govèrno**, M.: misgovernment. =**gradíto**, ADJ.: ill-received (unwelcome, disagreeable). =**grádo**, M.: displeasure (ill-will, spite); ADV.: in spite of (notwithstanding). =**graziosaménte**, ADV.: ungraciously (in a displeasing manner). =**grazióso**, ADJ.: ungracious (displeasing). =**guardáto**, ADJ.: ill-guarded. =**gústo**, M.: bad taste (sense).

malí-a [*malo*], F.: witchcraft (enchantment, charm). -**árda**, F., -**árdo**, M.: witch (wizard). -**fício**†, M.: witch (magician, sorcerer).

malígia†, F.: small red onion.

mali-gnaménte, ADV.: malignantly (maliciously). -**gnáre**, INTR.: show malice (injure, malign). -**gnétto**, *dim.* of *-gno*. -**gníssimo**, ADJ.: very (or most) malicious. -**gnità**, F.: malice (spite, malignity). ‖**malí-gno** [L. *-gnus*], ADJ.: malicious (spiteful, malignant); M.: hateful thing (demon). -**gnosaménte**†, ADV.: spitefully. -**gnóso**†, ADJ.: spiteful (malicious).

malí-na†, F.: evil (disease). -**nánza**†, F.: misfortune (disaster).

malinco-nía [Gr. *melan-cholía*, 'black-biled'], F.: melancholy. -**niáccia**, *disp.* of *-nia*. -**nicaménte**, ADV.: melancholically. **malincò-nico**, -**nióso**, -**nóso**†, ADJ.: melancholy (blue).

mal=in=còre, ADV.: sorrowfully (with grief). =**in=còrpo**, ADV.: unwillingly. =**in=cuòre** = *malincore*. =**intenzionáto**, ADJ.: ill-intentioned (with bad designs). =**intéso**, ADJ.: misunderstood (mistaken); unexperienced; M.: misunderstanding (disagreement). =**inventuráto**†, ADJ.: unfortunate (unlucky).

malióso†, ADJ.: using witchcraft (charms); M.: witch.

maliscálco†, M.: field-marshal; blacksmith.

malíssimo [*male*], ADJ.: very (or most) evil.

malíto†, ADJ.: sickly (infirm).

malí-zia [L. *-tia*], F.: malice (spite, ill-will); ADV.: *a* —, craftily. -**ziáccia**, *disp.* of *-zia*. -**ziáre**†, TR.: treat with malice (defame). -**ziataménte**†, ADV.: maliciously (with ill-will). -**ziétta**, -**zina**, *disp. dim.* of *-zia*. -**ziosáccio**, *disp.* of *-zioso*. -**ziosaménte**, ADV.: maliciously (spitefully). -**ziosétto**; -**ziosíno**, *car. dim.* of *-zioso*. -**zióso**, ADJ.: malicious (spiteful); M.: malicious (spiteful) person.

mal-leábile, ADJ.: MALLEABLE. -**leabilità**, F.: malleability. ‖-**leo**† [L. *-leus*], M.: hammer (MALLET). -**lèolo**, M.: ankle.

malle-vadóre, M.: surety (bondsman);

ADJ.: giving security. **-vadoría**, F.: promise. **-vadríce**, F. of *-vadore*. ‖**-váre†** [*mano, levare*, 'raise hand', in oath], INTR.: act as surety (give security). **-váto†**, ADJ.: bailed; M.: security. **-vería**, F.: security.

mállo [L.], M.: green shell (of nut).

mal=maritáta, ADJ.: badly married; F.: Institution (to recover runaway wives). **=menáre**, TR.: ill-use (abuse, harm). **-menáto**, ADJ.: abused (ill-used). **-menío** [*-menare*], M.: long abuse. **=mèrito†**, M.: bad service; ADJ.: ill-merited. **=méttere†**, IRR.; TR.: use badly; waste (dissipate, spend ill). **-mésso**, PART. of *-mettere*; unadapted (unsuitable). **-mísi**, PRET. of *-mettere*. **=náto**, ADJ.: ill-bred (rude); low born (ignoble, mean)†. **=naturáto**, ADJ.: thin (delicate, weak). **=nòto**, ADJ.: not well known.

málo [L. *-lus*], ADJ.: bad (ill, wrong).

mal=óra, F.: ruin (destruction, perdition). **-ordinatamènte**, ADV.: disorderly. ‖**=ordináto**, ADJ.: disordered (ill-arranged).

malóre [L. *-lus*], M.: sickness (illness, disease).

malòtico†, ADJ.: hurtful (malignant, pernicious).

mal-osserváto [*male osservato*], ADJ.: unobserved; poorly done. **=paráto†**, ADJ.: ill-prepared. **=persuáso**, ADJ.: unpersuaded. **=píglio**, M.: disdainful (angry) look. **=políto†**, **=prático**, pl. *—ci*, ADJ.: unpractised (inexperienced). **=preparáto**, ADJ.: ill-prepared. **=prò**, M.: injury (detriment, damage). **=procèdere**, M.: misbehaviour (rudeness). **=pròprio**, ADJ.: improper (unbecoming, unfit). **=provvedúto**, **=provvísto**, ADJ.: ill-provided. **=pulíto†** = *-polito*. **=rifátto**, ADJ.: poorly remade. **=saldáto**, ADJ.: poorly soldered. **-sanía**, F.: ill-health. **=sáno**, ADJ.: unhealthy; unhealthful. **=servíto**, ADJ.: poorly served. **=sicúro**, ADJ.: insecure (unsafe). **=sofferènte**, ADJ.: intolerent.

málta [Gr. *máltha*], F.: mortar; species of black bitumen; mud (slime).

mal=tagliáti, M. PL.: paste (for soup). **=talènto**, M.: grudge (ill-will). **=tèmpo**, M.: bad season (weather). **=tenúto**, ADJ.: poorly held.

maltése [*malta*], ADJ.: Maltese.

mal=tessúto, ADJ.: poorly woven. **=tínto**, ADJ.: poorly tinged (coloured). **=tollerábile**, ADJ.: intolerable (unendurable). **=tòlto**, M.: unjust appropriation; ADJ.: unjustly appropriated. **=tornito**, ADJ.: unpolished (rude, unrefined). **=trattamènto**, M.: bad treatment (ill-usage). **=trattáre**, TR.: abuse (maltreat). **-trattáto**, ADJ.: abused. **-trattatóre**, M.: abuser. **=trovamènto†**, M.: bad invention.

malúccio, *dim.* of *male*.

mal=umóre, M.: bad humour. **=usánza**, F.: misuse (abuse).

mál-va [L.], F.: mallows (plant). **-váceo**, ADJ.: pertaining to mallows (malvaceous).

malva-gía†, F.: wickedness. **-giamènte**, ADV.: wickedly. ‖**malvá-gio** [?], ADJ.: wicked (perfidious). **-gità**, F.: wickedness (perfidiousness). **-'go†**, ADJ.: undesirous.

malvasía [*M.*, in the Morea], F.: MALMSEY grape (or wine).

malvavíschio [L. *malva-ebiscum*], M.: marshmallows.

mal=vedére, IRR.; INTR.: look at with evil eye. **-vedúto**, ADJ.: hated. **=venúto**, ADJ.: unwelcome; M.: unwelcome person. **=vestíto**, ADJ.: poorly dressed (shabby). **-vídi**, PRET. of *-vedere*. **=vissúto**, ADJ.: of that which has lived badly (of evil life). **=vísto**, ADJ.: hated (despised). **=vivènte**, ADJ.: living wickedly (dissipated, dissolute); M.: dissipated person. **=vívo†**, ADJ.: half-dead (weak). **=vogliènte†** [*-volere*], ADJ.: ill-disposed (malevolent). **=volentièri**, ADV.: unwillingly. **=volére**, TR.: wish ill (be malicious); M.: ill-will (maliciousness). **=vòlto**, ADJ.: ill-formed; ill-disposed. **=volúto**, ADJ.: hated (abhorred).

mámma 1 [echoic], F.: mamma (mother, protectress).

mám-ma 2 [L.], F.: breast. **-máccia**, *disp.* of *mamma* 2.

mammalúcco [Ar. *mamluk*, slave], M.: mameluke; stupid fellow; ADJ.: stupid.

mamma=mía, M., F.: little hypocrite.

mammána†, F.: governess; midwife.

mam-mèlla [L. *-milla*], F.: breast (of woman). **-melláre**, ADJ.: mammillary. **-mellétta**, **-mellína**, *car. dim.* of *-mella*. **-mífero**, M.: mammifer. **-milláre**, ADJ.: mammillary.

mammína, *car. dim.* of *mamma* 1.

mámmo-la [L. *mammula* (dim. of *mamma* 2)], ADJ.: sweet violet. **-létta**, **-lína**, *car. dim.* of *-la*. **-líno†**, *dim.* of *-lo* 2. **mámmo-lo**, M.: 1. sort of grape-vine (also wine, grape); 2. little child†. **-lóne**, M.: kind of grape.

mammóne [L. *-mona*], M.: Mammon (god of riches).

mammóso†, ADJ.: mammiform.

má-na [L. *-nus*], F.: vulg. for *-no*. **-nále**, M.: glove (of shoemaker). **-náta**, F.: blow with the hand; handful; group: *a -nate*, by the handful. **-natèlla**, **-natína**, *car. dim.* of *-nata*.

mán-ca, F.: left hand; left side. **-ca-**

ménto, M.: defect (imperfection, want). **-cánte**, ADJ.: lacking (wanting, deficient). **-cánza**, F.: lack (want, deficiency, imperfection). ||**-cáre** [*-co*], INTR.: lack (want, need): — *a*, fail. **-cáto**, ADJ.: lost; dead. **-catóre**, M., **-catríce**, F.: one lacking (failing).

mancep-páre†, TR.: emancipate. **-pazióne**†, F.: emancipation.

manchévole [*mancare*], ADJ.: lacking (defective). **-volézza**, F.: deficiency (imperfection). **-volménte**, ADV.: imperfectly (faultily). **manchézza**, F.: lack (want, defect).

mán-cia [L. *-icia* (*-us*, hand), sleeve], F.: tip (gift of money). **-ciáta**, F.: great handful. **-ciatèlla**, **-ciatína**, *car. dim.* of *-cia*.

man-cína, ||**-cíno** [*-co*], ADJ.: left-handed; harsh (words); bad (wicked): *a* —, on the left hand.

mancípio [L. *-pium* (*manus*, hand, *capere*, take)], M.: slave.

mánco [L. *-cus*, maimed], ADJ.: left-handed; defective (imperfect)†; M.†: defect (imperfection).

man-daménto, M.: commission (order, mandate). **-dánte**, ADJ.: sending; M.: one sending. ||**-dáre** [L.], TR.: send (dispatch, give motion to); command (order, summon)†: — *a effetto*, accomplish; — *giù*, swallow; — *in lungo*, delay; — *a male*, waste.

manda-rináto, M.: task of mandarin. ||**-ríno** 1 [Chin.], M.: mandarin (Chinese official); mandarin orange; aromatic oil.

manda-ríno 2, M.: ball pitcher. **mandá-ta**, F.: sending; gang. **-tário**, M.: trustee (commissioned person, mandatary). **-tína**, *car. dim.* of *-ta*. **-tíno**, *dim.* of *-to*. ||**mandá-to** [*-re*], M.: mandate (order, command).

man-díbola, ||**-díbula** [L. *-dibula* (*-dere*, chew)], F.: mandible (lower jaw).

mándola† 1, F.: almond.

mandò-la 2 [L. *pandura*], F.: mandola. **-linísta**, pl. —*ti*, M., F.: mandolin-player. **-líno**, M.: mandolin.

mándor-la [l. L. *amandola*], F.: ALMOND; architectural ornament; small box (for perfume). **-láto**, M.: almond-paste. **-létta**, **-lína**, *car. dim.* of *-la*. **mándor-lo**, M.: almond-tree.

mán-dra [L.], F.: herd (flock); stall (stable, fold).

mandrácchia†, F.: prostitute.

mandrágola [Gr. *-góras*], F.: mandrake (plant).

mándri-a = *mandra*. **-álo**†, **-áno**, M.: herdsman (shepherd).

mandríllo [Sp. *-dril*], M.: mandrill (baboon).

mandrítta [*mano, ritta*], F.: right hand.

mándrola†, F.: almond.

manducáre [L.], TR.: (*jest.*) eat (masticate, manducate).

máne [L.], F.: morning.

maneg-gévole, **-giábile**, ADJ.: manageable (controllable). **-giaménto**†, M.: management (control, guidance). ||**-giá-re** [*mano*], TR.: manage (handle, guide, control). **-giáto**, ADJ.: managed (guided). **-giatóre**, M., **-giatríce**, F.: manager. **manég-gio**, M.: management (guidance, control); ability; intrigue.

manèlla†, F.: sheaf.

manére†, INTR.: remain (stay, reside).

manescálco = *maniscalco*.

ma-nescaménte, ADV.: readily (quickly, handily). ||**-nésco** [*mano*], ADJ.: handy, ready (quick). **-nétte**, F. PL.: manacles (handcuffs). **-névole**, ADJ.: manageable (tractable, flexible).

manfa-níle†, ||**mánfa-no** [?], M.: flail-handle.

manfòrte [*mano forte*], F.: firm hand (of one controlling).

manga-náre [*-no*], TR.: mangle (smooth linen). **-natúra**, F.: mangling, cost of mangling. **-neggiáre**†, TR.: mangle. **-nèlla**, F.: small cross-bow; balister; kind of lever; choir-seats.

manganése [?], M.: manganese (metal).

mánga-no [G. *-non*], M.: MANGONEL (balister); MANGLE (for smoothing linen).

man-geréccio, ADJ.: eatable, fit to eat. **-gería**, F.: extortion (exaction). **-giábile**, ADJ.: eatable. **-gia=cristiáni**, M.: fierce (impetuous) person. **-gia-fèrro**†, ADJ.: quarrelsome; M.: bully. **-giaménto**, M.: eating. **-gia=mòccoli**, M.: candle-stealing sacristan. **-gia=pagnòtte**, M.: lazy workman. **-gia=páne**, M.: worthless fellow. **-gia=pélo**†, M.: moth. **-gia=pére**, **-gia=pére**, M.: kind of grasshopper. **-gia=pòpoli**, M.: despot (tyrant). ||**-giáre** [L. *-ducare*, chew], TR.: eat (consume, destroy); make illicit gains; M.: food; eating: — *la foglia*, understand secret doings. **-giarétto**, *dim.* of *-giare*. **-giaríno**, *car. dim.* of *-giare*. **-giáta**, F.: satiety. **-giatáccia**, *disp.* of *-giata*. **-giatína**, *car. dim.* of *-giata*. **-giatívo**†, ADJ.: eatable. **-giatóia**, F.: manger. **-giatóna**, *aug.* of *-giata*. **-giatóra**, F., **-giatóre**, M.: eater (glutton). **-giatería**, F.: extortion. **-giatúra**, F.: traces of eating (left by insects). **-giatútti**, M.: very powerful person. **-giatútto**, M.: waster. **-giaúfo**, M.: lazy fellow. **-gíme**, M.: food (given to animals). **-gió-**

-**na**, F., -**gióne**, M.: gormand. -**giucchiáre**, TR.: eat little and fastidiously.
máni [L. -*nes*], M. PL.: ghosts (manes).
ma-nía [L.], F.: mania (madness). -**níaco**, pl. —*ci*, ADJ.: maniac (mad).
maniáto†, ADJ.: the very same.
máni-ca [L. (*manus*, hand)], F.: sleeve; handle; armour (for arm): *di — larga*, easy (in morals). -**cáccia**, *disp.* of -*ca*.
mani-caménto†, M.: eating. ||-**cáre**† [L. *manducare*, chew], TR.: (*poet.*) eat. -**carétto**, M.: appetizing food. -**catóre**, M.: eater (glutton).
mani-chétta, *dim.* of -*ca*. -**chétto**, *dim.* of -*co*. -**chíno**, M.: cuff. ||**mánico** [*mano*], M.: handle. -**cóna**, *aug.* of -*ca*. -**cóne**, *aug.* of -*co*.
manicòmio [Gr. *manía*, madness, *komeíon*, hospital], M.: insane hospital.
mani-còtto [-*ca*], M.: muff. -**còttolo**†, M.: hanging sleeve.
manièra [-*ro*], F.: manner (way, deportment, custom): *di — che*, so that. -**ráccia**, *disp.* of -*ra*. -**ráre**†, TR.: adorn (embellish). -**rataménte**, ADV.: in an affected manner. -**ratíssimo**, ADJ.: very (or most) affected in manners. -**ráto**, ADJ.: affected in manners. **manièro**† 1, ADJ.: obedient (docile).
manièro† 2, M.: manor (dwelling).
manie-rína, *car. dim.* of -*ra*. -**rísmo**, M.: mannerism. -**rísta**, pl. —*ti*, M.: mannerist. **manièro**†, ADJ.: tractable (docile). -**róna**, *disp. aug.* of -*ra*. -**róso**, ADJ.: over-affable (affected).
manifat-tóre [*mano, fattore*], M.: manufacturer. -**tríce**, F.: manufacturer (woman). -**túra**, F.: manufacture; manufactory. -**turière**, ADJ.: pertaining to manufactures.
manife-staménte, ADV.: manifestly (evidently). -**staménto**†, M.: manifestation. -**stáre**, TR.: reveal (make known, manifest); REFL.: make one's self known. -**statóre**, M., -**statríce**, F.: revealer (discloser). -**stazióne**, F.: manifestation (revelation). -**stíno**, *dim.* of -*sto*. ||**manifè-sto** [L. -*stus*], ADJ.: manifest (clear, evident); ADV.: manifestly (clearly); M.: manifesto (public declaration).
maní-glia [L. -*cula* (*manus*, hand)], F.: handle; bracelet†. -**gliétta**, -**glína**, *dim.* of -*glia*. **maní-glio**†, M.: bracelet. -**glióne**, M.: handle (on back of cannon).
mani-goldáccio, *disp.* of -*goldo*. ||-**góldo** [?], M.: rascal (rogue); hangman; great injury. -**goldóne**†, *aug.* of -*goldo*.
mani=lúvio [*mani, luvio* (*lavare*, wash)], M.: wash (for the hands).
mani-mésso, ADJ.: used. -**méttere** [*mano, mettere*], TR.: commence to use.
manimòrcia†, ADJ.: of a slovenly woman.
manína, *car. dim.* of *mano*.
manincon..† = *malincon..*
maníno, *dim.* of *mano*.
manipo-láre, TR.: manipulate (work with hands); adulterate (wine); M.†: soldier (maniple); ADJ.†: manipular. -**láto**, ADJ.: adulterated. -**latóre**, M., -**latríce**, F.: manipulator. -**lazióne**, F.: manipulation (work by hand). ||**manípo-lo** [L. *manus*, hand, *plere*, fill], M.: handful; scarf (worn by Catholic priests); maniple (cohort).
maniscálco [OGer. *mara*, horse, *scalc*, servant; ak. to Eng. *mar-shal*], M.: farrier (shoer of horses); veterinary†.
mánna 1 [L. (Heb.)], F.: manna (divine food; secretion of many trees).
mán-na 2 [l. L. *manua*, handful], F.: bundle (sheaf). -**náia**, F.: executioner's axe; crude guillotine; blade of the guillotine; hatchet; despotism. -**naiétta**, *dim.* of -*naia*. -**naióne**†, *aug.* of -*naia*. -**náro**, M.: sickness (form of insanity). -**nèllo**, M.: bundle (sheaf).
mannerino, M.: young wether.
máno [L. -*nus*], F.: hand; assistance (direction, work); side; faculty (power): *a — chiusa*, inconsiderately; *di — in —*, by degrees; *dar di —*, take up; *dar l' ultima —*, give last touches; *venire alle mani*, come to blows; *a — salva*, without risk. -**mésso**, ADJ.: handled (used).
manòmetro [Gr. *manós*, rare, *métron*, measure], M.: manometer (instr. to measure tension of gases).
mano méttere, IRR.; TR.: handle (use). -**mísi**, PRET. of -*mettere*. =**mòrta**, F.: untransferable property. **manó-na**, **manó-ne**, *aug.* of *mano*. **manò-pola**, F.: cuff; gauntlet. =**scrítto**, ADJ.: written; M.: manuscript. **manó-so**, ADJ.: pliant (to touch, soft). -**valdería**†, F.: guardianship. -**váldo**†, M.: guardian. -**vále** [L. *manualis*], ADJ.: manual. -**vèlla**, F., -**vèllo**†, M.: lever (for wine press, etc.).
manò-vra, F.: manœuvre (of a ship or army). -**vráre**, TR.: manœuvre.
man-rítta [*mano ritta*], F.: right hand. -**rítto**, ADJ.: right; ADV.: using right hand. -**rovèscio**, M.: back-stroke.
mansionário†, M.: chaplain.
mánso†, ADJ.: mild (gentle).
mansue-fáre, TR.: appease (calm, soften). -**fátto**, ADJ.: softened (appeased). -**féci**, PRET. of -*fare*. -**taménte**, ADV.: gently (mildly). ||**mansuè-to** [L. -*tus* (*manus-suescere*, accustom to the hand), tame], ADJ.: quiet (gentle, Eng.† mansuete). -**túdine**, F.: gentleness.
manta-cáre†, TR.: blow with bellows.

-**chétto**†, *dim.* of -*co.* ‖**mánta-co**†, M.: bellows; lungs. -**cúzzo**†, *dim.* of -*co.*
mantè-ca [Sp.], F.: ointment; butter; (*jest.*) pomade. -**cáre**, TR.: make into ointment (butter).
mantel-láre, TR.: cover with a mantle; excuse; REFL.: excuse one's self. -**láto**, ADJ.: coated (coloured). -**létta**, F.: small mantle. -**létto**, M.: *dim.* of -*lo;* movable parapet. -**lína**, F.: small mantle; cover (for sacred images). -**líno**, *dim.* of -*lo.* ‖**mantèl-lo** [L. -*lum*], M.: mantle (cloak); pretence (excuse, deceit). -**lóne**, *aug.* of -*lo.* -**luccíáccio**, *disp.* of -*luccio.* -**lúccio**, *disp.* of -*lo.*
mante-nénte†, ADV.: immediately (suddenly). ‖-**nére** [*mano, tenere*], IRR.; TR.: MAINTAIN (support, continue); REFL.: support one's self. -**níbile**, ADJ.: maintainable (sustainable). -**niménto**, M.: maintenance (support). -**nitóre**, M.: maintainer (sustainer). **manté-nni**, PRET. of -*tenere.* -**núta**, F.: wicked woman (mistress). -**núto**, ADJ.: maintained (supported, kept).
mánti-ce [L. -*ca* (*manus*, hand), bag], M.: bellows. -**cétto**, -**cino**, *dim.* of -*ce.* -**cióne**, *aug.* of -*ce.*
mantíglia [Sp. -*tilla* (cf. -*to*)], F.: mantilla.
mantíle†, M.: coarse table-cloth.
man-tíno, *dim.* of -*to;* silk lining (used by tailors). ‖**mán-to** 1 [L. -*tum*], M.: mantle: (*fig.*) *il tragico* —, tragedy.
mánto† 2, ADJ.: much.
mantru-giáre [?], TR.: handle (touch roughly). -**giáto**, ADJ.: rumpled.
manuá-le [L. -*lis*], ADJ.: manual (by hand); M.: handbook. -**létto**, -**líno**, *car. dim.* of -*le.* -**lménte**, ADV.: manually (by hand).
manúbrio [L. -*brium*], M.: handle (of rudder, etc.).
manucáre†, TR.: eat (gnaw).
manumissióne†, F.: manumission (liberation).
manuscritto = *manoscritto.*
manutèn-golo [*mano tenere*], M.: accomplice (of thieves, assassins, etc.). -**zióne**, F.: maintenance.
mán-za†, F.: heifer. ‖**mán-zo** [L. -*sus*, -*dere*, chew], M.: young steer. -**zòtta**†, F.: heifer.
maomet-táno [fr. Ar.], ADJ., M.: Mohammedan. -**tísmo**, M.: Mohammedism.
máppa [L.], F.: map. =**móndo**, M.: map of the world.
[m]**arabútto**†, M.: mainsail.
[m]**achèlla** [OFr. *marir*, destroy, con-...], F.: deceit (trick).
...**zo** [? -*re*], M.: crowd; refuse
marangóne [*mergo*], M.: diver (for wrecks, etc.); MERGUS (seafowl)†; joiner†.
marás-ca [*amarasca*], F.: sour cherry. -**chíno**, M.: maraschino (cherry spirit).
marásmo [Gr. *marásmos*, quench], M.: marasmus (wasting of flesh).
maravígli-a [L. *mirabilia*], F.: marvel (wonder): *a* —, marvellously (wonderfully). -**ábile**†, -**ábole**†, ADJ.: marvellous (wonderful). -**améntо**†, M.: wonder (surprise). -**ánte**, ADJ.: surprising. -**áre**, INTR.: marvel (wonder). -**áto**, ADJ.: struck with surprise. -**évole**†, ADJ.: marvellous. -**osaménte**, ADV.: marvellously (wonderfully). -**óso**, ADJ.: marvellous (wonderful).
márca 1 [OGer., confines], F.: MARCH (borderland).
már-ca 2 [OGer. *marc*], F.: MARK (stamp, money). -**cáre**, TR.: mark (stamp); set bounds†.
marcèllo [*M.*], M.: Venetian coin = 12 cents.
marcescíbile [L. -*lis*], ADJ.: corruptible (perishable, marcescible).
marchè-sa, F.: marchioness. -**sáccia**, *disp.* of -*se.* -**sána**†, F.: marchioness. -**sáto**, M.: marquisate. ‖**marchè-se** [*marca* 1, orig. protector of the marches], M.: marquis. -**sína**, *car. dim.* of -*sa.* -**síno**, *car. dim.* of -*se.* -**sóne**, *aug.* of -*se.*
marchi-áno, ADJ.: very great (marked; excessive; absurd). -**áre**, TR.: mark (stamp, brand). ‖**márchi-o** [L. *marculus*], M.: MARK (stamp, brand).
marchionále [L. *marchio*], ADJ.: of a marquis.
márcia 1 [-*cire*], F.: pus (discharge).
már-cia 2, F.: march (step; music). -**cia=piède**, M.: sidewalk (footpath). ‖-**ciáre** [Fr. -*cher*], TR.: march. -**ciáta**, F. march.
már-cido, ADJ.: decayed (putrified, MARCID). -**ciménto**, M.: putrefaction. -**cíno**, M.: wine (made from decaying grapes). **már-cio**, ADJ.: decayed (putrified, decomposed); M.: decayed spot (place). -**ciolíno**, M.: taste of wine (made from decaying grapes). -**ciscèllo**, *dim.* of -*cio.* -**cióso**, ADJ.: purulent. ‖-**círe** [L. -*cere*], INTR.: fester (become putrid, decomposed, MARCESCent); be distracted. -**cíta**, -**citéla**, F.: watered field (i.e., covered with running water in winter to protect grass). -**citíccio**, ADJ. of -*cita.* -**citúra**, F.: decaying (putrefaction). -**ciúme**, M.: heap of decayed things.
márco [L. -*cus*, hammer], M.: mark (sign, coin).
marcorèlla, F.: MERCURY (plant).

má-re [L.], M.: sea. **-ròa**, F.: tide (ebb and flow). **-reggiáre**, INTR.: roll (of the sea); M.: rolling (undulating). **-reggiáta**†, F.: tide. **-réggio**, M.: rolling (fluctuation). **-rémma** [L. *-ritima*], F.: swampy country (near the sea). **-remmáno**, ADJ.: of the low, marshy seashore; M.: inhabitant of the low, marshy seashore. **-re=mòto**, M.: sea-movement (produced by earthquakes).

marèna [*marasca*], F.: cherry drink.

marèngo [in memory of battle of *M.*], M.: gold coin (= $4).

mare-sciallàto, M.: marshalship. ‖**-sciállo** [Fr. *maréchal*], M.: marshal.

ma-résco†, ADJ.: marine. **-rése**†, M.: swamp (marsh).

ma-rétta [*mare*], F.: slight swell of the sea. **-rezzáre**, TR.: give a wavy appearance to (vein). **-rezzáto**, ADJ.: made wavy (veined). **-rezzatúra**, F.: waving (of wood vein). **-rézzo**, M.: waving (veining): *a* —, in waves (undulating).

márga [L.], F.: marl (earthy substance).

margá-rico [Gr. *márgaron*], ADJ.: margaric (of an acid). **-rína**, F.: margarine (substance extracted from vegetable oils, fats, etc.).

mar-garíta†, ‖**-gherita** [L. *-garita*], F.: pearl; daisy. **-gheritina**, M.: *car. dim.* of *-gherita;* daisy.

margigrána†, F.: kind of grape.

margi-nále, ADJ.: marginal. **-náre**, TR.: arrange with margins. **-náto**, ADJ.: with margins. **-natúra**, F.: margining. ‖**márgi-ne** [L. *margo*], M.: margin (border, brim); F.: scar. **-nétta**†, *dim.* of *-ne;* scar. **-nétto**, M.: *dim.* of *-ne;* (*typ.*) margin-piece.

margiòllo†, ADJ.: decayed (spoiled).

márgo†, M.: (*poet.*) margin (brim).

mar-gòtta†, F.: layer (offset, prostrate shoot). **-gottáre**, TR.: form shoots on. ‖**-gòtto** [Fr. *-cotte*], M.: layer (offset, shoot).

mar-graviáto, M.: margraviate (territory of margrave). ‖**-grávio** [Ger. *mark-graf* (cf. *-chese*)], M.: margrave (nobleman).

margútto†, ADJ.: ugly and malicious.

maricèllo†, M.: bitterness; bay.

marigiána†, F.: kind of duck.

marí-na [L. (*mare*, sea)], F.: surface of sea; sea-coast; marine (sea-soldier, navy): — —, along the coast. **-náio**, M.: mariner (seaman). **-nára**, F.: kind of coat. **-náre**, TR.: pickle; have in charge. **-narescaménte**, ADV.: seaman-like. **-narésco**, ADJ.: marine (of the sea). **-náro**, M.: seaman (mariner). **-nèlla**, F.: kind of cherry; ADJ.: of cherry. **-nería**, F.: seamanship; navy. **-nésco**†, ADJ.: of the sea. **-nière**†, **-nièro**†, M.: marine (seaman); ADJ.: marine (of the sea).

marí-no, ADJ.: marine (of the sea); M.: seaman.

mario-lárе†, TR.: cheat (swindle). **-lería**, F.: cheating (swindling). ‖**mariòlo** [?], M.: cheat (swindler, fraud).

marionét-ta [Fr. *-te*], F.: marionette (puppet). **-táta**, F.: performance of (or like) the marionette.

mariscálco†, M.: farrier (shoer of horses).

mari-táccio, *disp.* of *-to.* **-tággio**, M.: matrimony. **-tále**, ADJ.: marital (conjugal). **-talménte**, ADV.: conjugally. **-taménto**, M.: marriage. **-táre**, TR.: marry; REFL.: be married. **-táta**, F.: married woman. **-táto**, ADJ.: married; M.: married man. **-tazióne**, F.: marriage. **-tíno**, *car. dim.* of *-to.* ‖**marí-to** [L. *-tus*], M.: husband. **-'toto**†, M.: thy husband.

marittimo [L. *maritimus*], ADJ.: maritime (near the sea).

marizzáre†, TR.: wave (vein).

marmá-glia [OFr. *marme*], F.: rabble (mob). **-gliáccia**†, *disp.* of *-glia.*

mar-máre [L. *-mor*], TR.: make cool as marble. **-máto**, ADJ.: cold as marble.

marméggia [?], F.: maggot (worm).

marmelláta [Port. *-lada*], F.: marmalade (fruit preserve).

mar-mífero, ADJ.: abounding in marble. ‖**-míno** [*marmo*], M.: stone (used to keep doors open). **-místa**, M.: worker in marble.

marmít-ta [fr. Ar.], F.: soup-kettle. **-tína**, *dim.* of *-ta.* **-tóna**, **-tóne**, *aug.* of *-ta.*

mármo [L. *-mor*], M.: MARBLE (stone).

mar-mocchíno, *dim.* of *-mocchio.* ‖**-mòcchio** [OFr. *marme*], M.: little boy (child); childish man.

marmo-ráio† [*marmo*], M.: sculptor; statuary. **-ráre**†, TR.: marble (stain like marble). **-rária**†, F.: statuary (sculpture). **-rário**, M.: sculptor; statuary. **-réccio**, ADJ.: of marble. **marmòreo**, ADJ.: of (or like) marble. **-ríno**, M.: kind of cheese; ADJ.: of cheese. **-rizzáre**, TR.: marble (give appearance of marble). **-rizzáto**, ADJ.: marbled (made to look like marble).

marmòt-ta [OFr. *marmontain*], F.: marmot; lazy fellow. **-tína**, *car. dim.* of *-ta.* **-tíno**, *dim.* of *-ta.* **-tóna**, **-tóne**, *aug.* of *-ta.*

marocchíno = *marrochino.*

maroníta [*Maro*], ADJ.: Maronite (Christian sect).

maróso [*mare*], M.: surge (billow, wave).

már-ra [L.], F.: spade. **-raiuòlo**†, M.: digger (labourer).

marráno [Sp., pig], ADJ.: slovenly, rude; M.: sloven; boor (clown).
marreggiáre†, INTR.: dig.
mar-rétta, -rétto, *dim.* of *marra.*
marriménto†, M.: grief.
marrit-ta, -to = *manritta, -to.*
marròbbio†, M.: horehound (plant).
marrocchíno [*Marocco*], M.: Morocco leather.
marróne 1, *aug.* of *marra.*
marró-ne 2 [Fr. -*n*], M.: chestnut-tree; large chestnut (Eng.† marron); ADJ.: of the chestnut. **-néto**, M.: chestnut-grove.
marrovèscio [*mano, rovescio*], M.: backstroke.
marrú-ca [L. *-gina*], F.: buckthorn (plant). **-cáio, -chéto**, M.: place full of buckthorn bushes.
marruffíno†, M.: draper's man (clerk).
marsála, -sálla [*Marsala*], M.: Marsala wine.
marsigliése [Fr. *Marseilles*], F.: Marseillaise (hymn).
martagóne [Fr. *-gon*], M.: martagon (red lily).
Márte [L. *Mars*], M.: Mars (god of war); war. **marte=dì**, M.: Tuesday.
martel-láccio, *disp.* of *-lo.* **-laménto**, M.: hammering. **-láre** [*-lo*], TR.: hammer (beat, form). **-láta**, F.: blow with a hammer. **-latúra**, F.: hammering. **-létto**, *dim.* of *-lo.* **-lína**, F.: mason's hammer; hammer of arquebuse. **-líno**, *dim.* of *-lo.* **-lío**, M.: continued hammering. ||**martèl-lo** [L. *martulus*], M.: hammer; door-knocker; remorse†; affliction†: *sonare a* —, sound the alarm. **-lóne**, *aug.* of *-lo.*
martídio†, M.: martyrdom.
martinèlla [? *S. Martino*], F.: Florentine bell (rung in war-times).
marti-nèllo [ak. to *martello*], M.: crane (lever). **-nétto**, M.: windlass.
martingála [?], F.: flap on breeches (16th Cent.); martingale (strap).
martiníccà, M.: brake (of carts, etc.).
||**-tíno**† [*-tello*], M.: ram.
marti-ráre, TR.: put to torture; REFL.: be put to torture. ||**márti-re** [Gr. *mártur*, witness], M., F.: martyr; torture†.
martí-rio, M.: martyrdom (torture and death). **-rizzaménto**, M.: torture. **-rizzáre**, TR.: martyr (put to death, torture); REFL.: torment one's self. **-rizzáto**, ADJ.: martyred (tortured). **márti-ro**† = **-rològio**, M.: martyrology.
… [L. *martes*], F.: marten (animal,
… M.: countryman (clown).
… [ak. to *martire*], M.: MAR…
…**lo**†, *dim.* of *-re.* **-riaménture.** **-riáre**, TR.: torment; REFL.: be tormented. **-riatóre**, M., **-riatríce**, F.: tormenter. **martòrio**†, **martò-ro**, M.: martyrdom.
már-za [*-zo*], F.: graft. **-zaiuòlo**†, ADJ.: of March.
marzapáne [L. *maza*, frumenty, It. *pane*], M.: marchpane (sweet bread).
mar-zeggiáre [*-zo*], INTR.: be changeful (as the weather of March). **-ziále**, ADJ.: martial (military, warlike). **már-zio**, ADJ.: of Mars: *Campo* —, Campus Martius. ||**már-zo** [L. *Mars*, god of war], M.: March (month). **-zocchíno**, *dim.* of *-zocco.* **-zòcco**, M.: painted (or sculptured) lion; dunce (dolt). **-zolíno**, ADJ.: of March. **-zòlo**, ADJ.: of March; sown in March.
mascágnoʼ†, ADJ.: crafty (wily, sharp).
mascál-cia [*maniscalco*], F.: farrier's art. **-zóne**, M.: ruffian (brutal fellow, cutthroat†).
mascèl-la [L. *maxilla*], F.: jaw. **-láre**, ADJ.: maxillary (pertaining to the jaw). **-lína**, *dim.* of *-la.* **-lóna**, F., **-lóne**, M., *aug.* of *-la*; person with large jaws.
másche-ra [fr. Ar.], F.: mask (visor, cover, drama). **-ráccia**, *disp.* of *-ra.* **-ráio**†, M.: mask-seller. **-raménto**, M.: masking. **-ráre**, TR.: mask (cover, pretend); REFL.: put on a mask. **-ráta**, F.: masquerade (ball, disguise). **-rétta**, *dim.* of *-ra.* **-rína**, *car. dim.* of *-ra.* **-ríno**, *dim.* of *-ra.* **-rízzo**†, M.: livid spot. **-róne**, M.: *aug.* of *-ra*; ugly woman; bad portrait; stone or bronze figure (for a fountain).
mas-chiáccio, *disp.* of *-chio.* **-chiaménte**, ADV.: manfully. **-chiétto**, *car. dim.* of *-chio.* **-chiézza**, F.: manliness. **-chíle**, ADJ.: masculine (male). **-chil(e)ménte**, ADV.: manfully (masculinely). ||**más-chio** [L. *-culus*], ADJ.: MALE (manly, vigorous); M.: male; kind of fortification. **-chiòtto, -chiòtta**, *car. aug.* of *-chio.* **-colinità**, F.: manhood (masculinity). **-colíno**, ADJ.: masculine.
masná-da [L. *mansionata* (*mansio*, house)], F.: troop (company of armed men); mob (gang). **-dière**, M.: ruffian (assassin); soldier†.
más-sa [L.], F.: mass (heap, bulk): *a* —, in a mass. **-sáccia**, *disp.* of *-sa.*
mas-sacráre, TR.: massacre (butcher, slaughter). ||**-sácro** [Fr. *-sacre*], M.: massacre (butchery, carnage).
massággio [Ar. *mass*, touch], M.: massage (rubbing).
mas-sáia [L. *mansa*, part. of *manere*, remain], F.: housewife; manager. **-sáio, -sáro**†, M.: husband; house-steward.
massèllo [*massa*], M.: mass of raw iron; wood (for furniture).

masse-rízia [*massaia*], F.: household goods (furniture, provisions). **-riziuòla†**, *dim.* of *-rizia*.

massíc-cio [*massa*], ADJ.: massy; massive (solid). **-cióna, -cióne**, *aug.* of *-cio*.

mássi-ma, F.: maxim (adage). **-mamaménte, mássi-me**, ADV.: principally (chiefly, particularly). ‖**mássi-mo** [L. *maximus*], ADJ.: greatest (very great, supreme); M.: maximum.

másso [*-sa*], M.: rock; block of stone.

mas-sóne, M.: mason. ‖**-sonería** [Fr. *maçonnerie*], F.: masonry (society of Freemasons). **-sònico**, pl. *—ci*, ADJ.: masonic.

mastáccio†, ADJ.: strong (sturdy, stout).

mastèllo [?], M.: large bucket (tub).

másti-ca†, F.: resin (cement, mastic). **-cacchiáre**, TR.: chew (talk imperfectly). **-caménto**, M.: chewing (mastication). ‖**-cáre** [L.], TR.: chew (masticate; mumble words): — *veleno*, be very angry. **-catíccio†**, M.: mumbled speech. **-cáto**, ADJ.: chewed (masticated). **-catóre**, M.: chewer. **-catòrio**, ADJ.: chewing (masticatory). **-catúra**, F.: thing chewed (mumbled). **-cazióne**, F.: chewing (mastication).

másti-ce, ‖**-co†** [L. *-x*], M.: mastic (tree; putty; resin; cement).

mas-tiettáre, TR.: fit with hinges. **-tiettatúra**, F.: hinge-fitting; hinges. ‖**-tiétto** [*mastio*], M.: *dim.* of *-tio*; hinge.

mastíno [? **masnadino* (L. *mansio*), house-dog], M.: mastiff (watchdog).

mástio [*maschio*], M., ADJ.: male; M.: hinge; screw.

masto-dónto [Gr. *mastós*, breast, *odoús*, tooth], M.: mastodon. **-dòntico**, pl. *—ci*, ADJ.: mastodonic.

mastrevolménte†, ADV.: in a masterly way.

mástrice = *mastice*.

más-tro [*maestro*], ADJ.: chief: *libro* — or —, ledger.

matás-sa [L. *mataxa*], F.: skein; intrigue: *regger la* —, procure (pimp). **-sáccia**, *disp.* of *-sa*. **-sáta†**, F.: quantity of skeins. **-sétta, -sína, -síno**, *dim.* of *-sa*.

matemáti-ca [L. *mathematica*], F.: mathematics; divination†. **-cále†**, ADJ.: mathematical. **-caménte**, ADV.: mathematically (with precision). **matemáti-co**, pl. *—ci*, ADJ.: mathematic (accurate).

materás-sa [fr. Ar.], F.: mattress. **-sáio**, M.: mattress-maker, dealer, etc. **-sína, -síno**, *dim.* of *-sa*. **materás-so†**, M.: mattress. **-súccia, -súccio**, *disp. dim.* of *-sa*.

matèri-a [L.], F.: matter; material; cause†. **-áccia**, *disp.* of *-a*. **-aláccio**, *disp.* of *-ale*. **-ále**, ADJ.: material (physical); M.: material. **-alétto**, *dim.* of *-ale*. **-áli**, M. PL.: materials. **-alismo**, M.: materialism. **-alísta**, M.: materialist. **-alístico**, pl. *—ci*, ADJ.: materialistic. **-alità**, F.: materiality. **-alizzáre**, TR.: materialize. **-alménte**, ADV.: materially. **-alóne**, ADJ.: material (coarse, ordinary). **-áto†, -óso†**, ADJ.: material.

mater-nále, ADJ.: maternal (motherly). **-nalménte**, ADV.: maternally (in a motherly way). **-nità**, F.: maternity (motherhood). ‖**matèr-no** [L. *-nus*], ADJ.: maternal (mother, native). **máter-o**, M.: wicker (twig for basket-making).

matí-ta [Gr. *haimatítes*, blood-like], F.: hematite (an ore); pencil (crayon). **-tóio**, M.: pencil-holder.

matráccio†, M.: retort (vessel).

mátre†, F.: (*poet.*) mother.

matre=sélva†, F.: honeysuckle.

matri-cále, M.: species of camomile. **-cária**, F.: camomile. ‖**matrí-ce** [L. *-x* (*mater*, mother)], F.: matrix (womb; mould). **-cída**, M.: matricide; ADJ.: matricidal. **-cídio**, M.: matricide (murder of a mother). **-cína**, F.: sprouts (about a tree-stump). **-cíno**, ADJ.: of bearing sheep. **matrí-cola**, F.: register; certificate of matriculation; tax. **-coláre**, TR.: matriculate (register); REFL.: be matriculated. **-coláto**, ADJ.: matriculated (registered). **-colazióne**, F.: matriculation. **matrí-gna**, F.: stepmother (enemy, cruel mother). **-gnáre†, -gneggiáre†**, INTR.: act like a stepmother. **-gnescaménte**, ADV.: cruelly. **-gnésco**, ADJ.: cruel (as a stepmother). **-moniáccio**, *disp.* of *-monio*. **-moniále**, ADJ.: matrimonial (connubial). **-monialménte**, ADV.: matrimonially. **-mònio**, M.: matrimony (marriage). **-monióne**, M.: rich marriage. **matrí-na†**, F.: godmother. **-zzáre**, INTR.: resemble the mother.

matró-na [L. *mater*], F.: matron. **-nále**, ADJ.: matronly. **-nália**, F.: matronalia (festival celebrated by Roman women). **matró-ne†**, M.: pain (in the side). **-nímico**, pl. *—ci*, ADJ.: of one taking the mother's name.

mátta 1†, F.: mat (hassock).

mát-ta 2 [*-to*], F.: lamb's head; queen of hearts. **-tacchióne**, *aug.* of *-to*. **-taccíno**, ADJ., M.: mimic. **-táccio**, *disp.* of *-to*.

mattaióne [*malta*], M.: clay.

mat-taménte [*-to*], ADV.: madly (foolishly, rashly). **-tána**, F.: exasperation (irritability). **-táre**†, TR.: checkmate; punish. **-tarèllo**, *dim.* of *-to*, **-tàta**, F.: madness (foolish deed, irritable act). **-tèa**†, F.: *uccellare la* —, ridicule (quiz, sing). **-teggiáre**, INTR.: play the fool.

matterèllo [Gr. *máktron* (*máktra*, kneading-trough)], M.: rolling-pin.

mattería [*matto*], F.: madness (foolishness, insanity).

mátterò†, M.: cudgel (stick).

mat-teróne†, *disp.* of *-to*. **-terúgiolo**, **-terúgio**, ADJ.: of smaller species (of sparrows); M.: smaller species of sparrows; little fool. **-tésco**, ADJ.: mad (foolish). **-tézza**, F.: madness (insanity). **-tía**, F.: madness (folly).

mattí-na [L. *matutina*], F.: morning (Eng.† matin). **-náccia**, *disp.* of *-na*. **-náre**†, TR.: sing morning songs. **-náta**, F.: whole morning; morning song. **-natáccia**, *disp.* of *-na*. **-nièro**, ADJ.: morning-; early rising. **mattí-no**, M.: morning: *di buon* —, early; *mal* —, misfortune.

mat-tità, F.: madness. ‖**mát-to** [L. *-tus*, drunk], ADJ.: mad (insane, foolish); strange; M.: madman. **-tòide**, M.: madman.

mattolína†, F.: titlark.

matto-náia, F.: brick-yard. **-náio**, M.: brickmaker. **-náre**†, TR.: pave with bricks. **-náto**, M.: brick pavement. **-ncèllo**, *dim.* of *-ne*. **-ncíno**, M.: *dim.* of *-ne*; kind of paste (brick-shaped). ‖**mattó-ne** [?], M.: brick. **-nèlla**, F.: raised edge (of a billiard-table); ADV.: *di* —, indirectly. **mattó-ni**, F.: diamonds (suit at cards). **-nièro**†, M.: brickmaker.

mat-túgio, **-túgiolo** = *-terugio*.

mattu-tinále†, ADJ.: of the morning. **-tinánte**, ADJ.: of a priest who goes to morning-service; M.: priest who goes to morning-service. ‖**-tíno** [L. *matutinus*], ADJ.: morning (early, matutine); M.: morning; morning-service (matins).

matu-raménte, ADV.: maturely. **-ra-ménto**, M.: maturing (ripening). **-ráre**, INTR.: become mature (ripe); TR.: mature (ripen). **-ratívo**, ADJ.: maturative. **-ráto**, ADJ.: mature (ripe, due). **-razióne**, F.: ripeness (maturation). **-rézza**†, **-rità**, F.: maturity (ripeness, completeness). ‖**matú-ro** [L. *-rus*], ADJ.: mature (ripe). **-róne**, *aug.* of *-ro*.

máu [echoic], M.: mewing (of cat).

maúnque†, ADV.: never.

mauriziáno [*Maurizio*], ADJ.: of the Order of St. Maurice.

mausolèo [Gr. *-leion*], M.: mausoleum (magnificent tomb).

maví†, M.: bluish.

máximum [L.], M.: maximum.

mazúrca [Pol.], F.: mazurka (dance).

máz-za [L. °*matea*, fr. which *mateola*, mallet], F.: sprout (offshoot); stick (club, cane); staff (MACE); mallet: *menare alla* —†, betray; *menar la* — *tonda*†, treat without respect; *metter troppa* —†, speak too freely. **-zacavállo** [*-za*, *cavallo*], M.: sweep (of a well). **-záccherа**, F.: instrument for catching eels and frogs. **-záccia**, *disp.* of *-za*. **-za=frústo**†, M.: sling (ballister). **-za=gátti**, M.: kind of pistol. **-za=marróne**†, M.: blockhead (dunce). **-za=picchiáre**†, TR.: strike with a mallet. **-za=picchio**, M.: mallet: *dare del* — *in testa*, injure (defame). **-za=sètte**†, M.: bully (bravo). **-záta**, F.: blow with a club. **-zatèllo**†, M.: little bunch. **-zeránga**†, F.: rammer (heavy mallet). **-zerangáre**†, TR.: ram (beat with mallet). **-zeráre** [*mazzo*], TR.: drown in a sack with stones. **máz-zero**†, M.: club; unleavened bread. **-zétta**†, *car. dim.* of *-za*. **-zettína**, *car. dim.* of *-zetta*. **-zettíno**, *dim.* of *-zetto*. **-zétto**, *dim.* of *-zo*. **-zicáre**†, TR.: beat (pound, hammer). **-zicatóre**†, M.: beater; smith. **-zière**, M.: mace-bearer (procession-leader). **-zo** [ak. to *-za*], M.: bunch (bundle, pack; bouquet): *mettersi in* —, interfere; *in un* —, all at once. **-zocchiáia**†, F.: quantity of bunches (bundles). **-zòcchio**, ADJ.: of kind of wheat; M.: succory (endive); bunch (bundle)†. **-zocchiúto**†, ADJ.: with spikes (head of grain); knotty. **-zòla**, F.: mallet; punishment (striking with mallet); sprig (shoot, stick)†. **-zoláre**, TR.: embank; punish (with a mallet). **-zoláta**, F.: blow with a mallet. **-zolíno**, *dim.* of *-zo*. **-zòlo**, M.: stonecutter's hammer; embankment. **-zóne**, *aug.* of *-zo*. **-zòtto**, M.: beetle (heavy mallet). **-zuòla**, F.: mallet punishment (striking with mallet); twig (small stick)†. **-zuòlo**†, M.: owl-perch.

mé [L.], PRON.: me; I; (for *mi*) to me.

mé'†, ADV.: better.

meándro [L. *Meander*, winding river in Phrygia], M.: meander (maze, perplexity).

me-áre [L.], INTR.: pass, glide over. **-áto**, M.: passage (pore).

mècca [?], F.: kind of varnish.

meccá-nica [Gr. *mechanikḗ* (viz., *téchne*, art)], F.: mechanics (science). **-nica-ménte**, ADV.: mechanically. **meccá-nico**, pl. —*ci*, ADJ.: mechanical; M.: mechanic (artisan). **-nísmo**, M.: mechanism.

meccère†, M.: master.

mé-co [L. *-cum*], PRON.: with me.

mecònio [Gr. *-kónion* (*mékon*, poppy)], M.: meconium.

medá-glia [L. *metallea*, of metal], F.: medal (coin). **-glière**, M.: fine collection (of medals). **-gliétta**, **-glína**, *car. dim.* of *-glia*. **-glioncíno**, M.: *dim.* of *-glione;* watch-charm. **-glióne**, M.: medallion. **-glísta**†, M.: medalist. **-gliúccia**, *disp. dim.* of *-glia*.

medé-mo†, PRON.: same (self). **-simaménte**, ADV.: likewise (in the same manner, always). **-simáre**, REFL.: stand on same basis with some one. **-simézza**, **-simità**†, F.: sameness (identity). ‖**medé-simo** [OFr. *-sme* (L. *met-ipsimus*)], PRON.: same (self); M.: same person (or thing): *i tuoi —i*, your parents; *alle —e*, in the same way.

mèdi-a [L.], F.: middle (midst). **-áno**, ADJ.: middle (median); M.: middle. **-ánte**, PREP.: by means of (through). **-áre**†, INTR.: mediate (be in middle, interpose). **-ástino**, M.: mediastine (membrane separating the lungs). **-ataménte**, **-áte**, ADV.: mediately (by means). **-áto**, ADJ.: mediate (middle, interposed); fit (commodious)†. **-atóre**, M., **-atríce**, F.: mediator, -trix. **-azióne**, F.: mediation (intercession).

medi-cábile, ADJ.: curable (remediable). **-cáccio**, *disp.* of *-co*. **-cáme**†, **-caménto**, M.: curing; medicine (medicament). **-camentóso**, ADJ.: medicinal. **-cánte**†, M.: physician; surgeon. **-cáre**, TR.: cure (heal, medicate); REFL.: cure one's self. **-cástro**, *disp.* of *-co*. **-cáto**, ADJ.: cured (healed, medicated). **-catóre**, M., **-catríce**, F.: physician. **-catúra**, **-cazióne**, F.: medication (application of medicine, curing). **-chería**, F.: *disp.* of *-camento;* consultation room (in hospital). **-chéssa**, F.: woman physician. **-chettíno**, *car. dim.* of *-co*. **-chétto**, **-chévole**†, ADJ.: healing. **-cína**, F.: medicine (science, remedy, cure). **-cinále**, ADJ.: medicinal; M.: medicine (remedy). **-cinalménte**, ADV.: medicinally. **-cináre**†, TR.: cure (heal, medicate); REFL.: cure one's self. ‖**mèdi-co** [L. *-cus*], M.: physician (doctor); ADJ.: medical; medicinal. **-cóne**, *aug.* of *-co*. **-cónzolo**, **-cúccio**, *disp. dim.* of *-co*.

me-dietà†, F.: moiety (half). **-di=èvo**, M.: Middle Ages. **-dievále**, ADJ.: mediæval. ‖**mè-dío** [L. *-dius*], ADJ.: middle (average). **-diòcre**, ADJ.: mediocre (middling, medium). **-diocreménte**, ADV.: indifferently (passably, middlingly). **-diocríssimo**, ADJ.: very (or most) mediocre. **-diocrità**, F.: mediocrity: *aurea —*, golden mean. **-dioev.** = *-diev.*

meditá-bile, ADJ.: to be meditated upon. **-bóndo**, ADJ.: meditating. **-ménto**†, M.: meditation (reflection). ‖**meditá-re** [L. *-ri*], TR.: meditate (reflect, plan). **-taménte**, ADV.: deliberately (intentionally). **-tívo**, ADJ.: meditative. **meditá-to**, ADJ.: meditated (planned). **-zioncèlla**, *dim.* of *-zione*. **-zióne**, F.: meditation (reflection).

mediterráneo [*medio, terraneo*], ADJ.: mediterranean.

mée, *pop.* for *me*.

me-fíte [Gr. *-phitis*], F.: mephitis (offensive exhalations). **-fiticaménte**, ADV.: pestilently. **-fítico**, ADJ.: mephitic(al).

megaloma-nía [Gr. *mégas*, great, *mania*], F.: mania for greatness. **-níaco**, pl. *—ci*, ADJ., M.: megalomaniac (big head).

mè-glio [L. *melius*], ADJ.: better; ADV.: better; M.: best (thing); F.: best (proposition, condition): *aver la —*, overcome (outdo); *fare alla —*, adapt one's self. **-glioraménto**, M.: improvement (betterment). **-glioráre**, TR.: better (improve, meliorate).

mé-la [L. *malum*], F.: apple (fruit); round part of a cupola. **-lacchíno**†, ADJ.: honey-tasting. **-láccia**, *disp.* of *-la*. **-lacítola**†, F.: balm (mint). **-lacotógna** [*cotogno*], F.: quince. **-lagrána** [*-grano*], **-la=granáta**, F.: pomegranate. **-lagránela**†, F.: orange. **-la=gráno**, M.: pomegranate-tree.

melan-colía [Gr. *-cholía* (*mélas*, black, *cholé*, bile)], melancholy (dejection). **-còlico**, pl. *—ci*, ADJ.: melancholy (sad, gloomy). **-conía**, F.: melancholy; caprice. **-conicaménte**, ADV.: sadly (gloomily). **-cònico**, pl. *—ci*, ADJ.: melancholy; capricious.

melán-gola† [fr. Ar.], F.: melon; orange.

melán-golo†, M.: orange-tree; melon. **-sána**, F.: egg-plant.

melans.† = *melens.*

mel- [*-a*]: **=áppio**, M.: julep. **-aráncia**, F.: orange. **=aráncio**, M.: orange-tree. **-áre**, TR.: throw apples. **-ário**†, M.: bee-hive. **-a=rèsa**, F.: kind of apple.

melássa [*mele*], F.: molasses.

meláta 1 [*mela*], F.: blow with an apple; apple-marmalade†.

me-láta 2, F.: disease of plants. **-láto**, ADJ.: honied (sweet, mellifluent). ‖**mè-le** [L. *mel*], M.: honey.

me-lensággine, F.: stupidity (foolishness). ‖**-lènso** [?], ADJ.: stupid (foolish, insipid); M.: stupid fellow.

meléto [*melo*], M.: apple-orchard.

me-líaca, F.: apricot. ‖**-líaco**, pl. *—ci* [? *armeniaca*, Armenian], M.: apricot-tree.

mèlica†, F.: maize.

melichíno†, M.: hydromel (liquor).

mèlico, pl. *—ci* [Gr. *mélos*, song], ADJ.: melodious (musical); lyric.

melína, *car. dim.* of *mela*.

melinite [?], F.: melenite (explosive substance).

melissa [Gr.], F.: balm (plant).

mellét-ta [?], F.: mud (filth). **-tóne**, *aug.* of *-ta*.

mellí-fero [*mele*], ADJ.: melliferous. **-ficáre†**, INTR.: make honey. **-fluaménte**, ADV.: mellifluently. **mellí-fluo**, ADJ.: mellifluous.

mèlliga†, F.: maize.

mello-nággine, F.: stupidity (silliness, foolishness). **-náio†**, M.: watermelon patch. **-neèllo†**, *dim.* of *-ne*. ||**melló-ne†** [L. *melo*], M.: watermelon; stupid fellow.

mél-ma [OGer. *melm*, dust], F.: mud (mire). **-móso**, ADJ.: muddy (miry).

mé-lo [L. *malus*], M.: apple-tree. **-lo=cotógno†**, M.: quince-tree.

melò-de, F.: (*poet.*) melody. ||**-día** [Gr.], F.: melody. **-dicaménte**, ADV.: melodiously (musically). **melò-dico**, pl. *-dici*, ADJ.: melodic. **-diosaménte**, ADV.: melodiously. **-dióso**, ADJ.: melodious. **-drámma**, M.: melodrama. **-drammático**, pl. *—ci*, ADJ.: melodramatic.

melo=granáto, M.: pomegranate.

melóna, *aug.* of *mela*.

melopèa [Gr. *-poiía*, song-making], F.: melopœia (art of forming melody).

me-lúccia, *disp. dim.* of *-la*. **-lúggine†**, F.: wild apple-tree. **-lúzza†**. *disp. dim.* of *-la*. **-lúzzola†**, *dim.* of *-la*.

membrá-na [L.], F.: membrane. **-náceo**, **-nóso**, ADJ.: membranous.

mem-bránza†, F.: remembrance. **-bráre†**, TR.: (*poet.*) remember.

mem-bratúra, F.: symmetry (due proportion of the limbs). **-brettáro**, TR.: ornament (with frieze, cornice, moulding). **-brétto**, **-bricciuòlo†**, *dim.* of *-bro*. ||**mèm-bro**, pl. *-bri* or *-bra* [L. *-brum*], M.: member (limb, organ, person). **-brolíno†**, M.: particle. **-bróne†**, *aug.* of *-bro*. **-brúto**, ADJ.: large-limbed.

memèn-to [L.], M.: remember! personal prayer (part of mass). **-tòmo** [L. *memento homo!* 'remember, O man!'], M.: word pronounced by priest (on Ash-Wednesday).

mèm-ma†, F.: mud (mire). **-móso†**, ADJ.: muddy (miry).

memo-rábile, ADJ.: memorable (remarkable, famous). **-rabilménte**, ADV.: memorably. **-rándo**, ADJ.: worthy of being remembered. **-rándum**, M.: memorandum (note). **-ráre†**, TR., INTR.: remember (put in mind, memorate). **-ratíva†**, F.: faculty of remembering. **-ratívo†**, ADJ.: commemorative (memorative†).

||**mèmo-re** [L. *-r*], ADJ.: mindful (attentive, remembering). **-révole†**, ADJ.: memorable (remarkable, famous); mindful. **memò-ria**, F.: memory (remembrance, monumental record): *imparare a —*, learn by heart; *a —*, in the memory. **-riále**, M.: memorial (memorandum, petition). **-rialísta**, M.: memorialist. **-riétta**, *dim.* of *-ria*. **-rióna**, *aug.* of *-ria*. **-rióso†**, ADJ.: memorable. **-riúccia**, *disp. dim.* of *-ria*.

mèna†, F.: management; work; condition (state); affront; torment.

menadíto [*menare dito*]: *a —*, exactly (precisely, accurately).

menagería [Fr. *ménagerie*], F.: menagery.

menagióne†, F.: diarrhœa.

me-naménto†, M.: leading (conduct); agitation. ||**-náre** [L. *minare*], TR.: lead (conduct, guide); produce; manage†: *— buono*, allow; *— a effetto*, bring to pass; *— la vita*, spend one's life; *— per la lunga*, put off; *— la lingua*, slander; *— moglie†*, take a wife. **-narèla**, F.: kind of gimlet. **-náta†**, F.: conducting (leading); handful. **-natína†**, *dim.* of *-nata*. **-natóio†**, M.: stirrer (poker). **-natóre†**, M., **-natríce†**, F.: leader; manager. **-natúra†**, F.: leading (conducting); joint.

mén-cio [?], ADJ.: flabby (soft, flaccid). **-cióna**, F., **-cióne**, M.: flabby thing; ADJ.: *aug.* of *-cio*.

mènda [L.], F.: fault (mistake, sin); reparation†.

men-dáce [L. *-dax*], ADJ.: lying (false, mendacious). **-dácio**, M.: falsehood (lie).

mendáre†, TR.: make amends (repair).

mendi-cággine†, **-cagióne†**, F.: beggary. **-caménte**, ADV.: in a begging way. **-cánte**, ADJ.: begging (poor, mendicant); M.: beggar (mendicant). **-cánza†**, F.: beggary (mendicancy). **-cáre**, TR.: beg (mendicate); INTR.: ask alms (charity). **-cataménte†**, ADV.: in a begging way. **-cáto**, ADJ.: begged. **-catóre†**, M.: beggar (mendicant). **-catòrio†**, ADJ.: of begging (or beggars). **-cazióne†**, **-cità**, F.: beggary (mendicity). ||**mendi-co** [L. *-cus*], M.: poor man (beggar); ADJ.: poor (begging).

mèn-do [*-da*], M.: amends; fault (vice). **-dóso**, ADJ.: full of errors.

méne (*pop.*) = *me*.

mène [*mina* 2], F. PL.: plots.

menestrèllo [L. *ministrellus*], M.: minstrel (bard).

menim.. = *menom..*

menín-ge [Gr. *mêningx*, membrane], F.: meninges. **-gèo**, ADJ.: meningeal. **-gíto**, F.: meningitis (inflammation of meninges).

meni=possènte†, ADJ.: least powerful.
menippèa [*Menippo*], ADJ.: coarsely satirical; F.: malignant satire.
ménno [?], ADJ.: impotent; beardless; vain†; M.: eunuch.
mé-no [L. *minus*], ADV.: less: *venir* —, faint away; fail; be wanting; *senza* —, without fail; *a* — *che*, unless; ADJ.: less; M.: less. **-nomábile**†, ADJ.: diminishable. **-nomaménto**†, M.: diminution (decrease). **-nománza**†, F.: diminution; want (necessity). **-nomáre**, TR.: diminish (decrease, weaken, shorten); INTR.: fail. **-nomáto**, ADJ.: diminished (shortened). **-nomíssimo**, ADJ.: very least. **mè-nomo**, ADJ.: least (smallest). **-nomúccio**†, *dim.* of *-nomo*. **-nováie**, ADJ.: least. **-nováre**†, TR.: lessen (diminish).
mèn-sa [L.], F.: table; income (of bishop, archbishop). **-sétta**†, *dim.* of *-sa*.
mensí-le [L. *-s*, MONTH], ADJ.: monthly; M.: month's pay. **-lménte**, ADV.: by the month.
mènso-la [*mensa*], F.: bracket. **-láccia**, *disp.* of *-la*. **-létta**, **-lína**, *car. dim.* of *-la*. **-líno**, *dim.* of *-la*. **-lóne**, *aug.* of *-la*.
men-struále†, ADJ.: menstrual (monthly). ‖**-suále** [L. *-sis*, MONTH], ADJ.: monthly. **-sualménte**, ADV.: by the month.
mensuráre†, TR.: measure.
ménta [L. *-tha*], F.: mint (plant).
mentá-le [*mente*], ADJ.: mental (intellectual). **-lménte**, ADV.: mentally (intellectually).
ménte [L. *mens*], F.: MIND (intellect); memory: *saper a* —, know by heart. **=cattággine**, F.: stupidity (foolishness). **=cátto**, ADJ.: stupid (foolish, mad); M.: madman.
menti-èro†, M.: liar. **-ménto**†, M.: lying (falsehood).
mentína [*menta*], F.: pastil, lozenge of mint.
mentíno, *car. dim.* of *mento*.
mentí-re [L. *-ri*], INTR. (Pres. *-sco* or *mento*): lie (tell a falsehood); TR.: give the lie. **mentí-ta**, F.: accusation (of telling a falsehood). **-taménte**, ADV.: falsely. **mentí-to**, ADJ.: false (lying). **-tóre**, M., **-tríce**, F.: liar.
ménto [L. *-tum*], M.: chin.
mèntore [Gr. *Mêntor*], M.: mentor.
mentòsto†, ADV.: later (not so soon).
mento-váre [OFr. *menteroir*, have in MIND], TR.: mention (remind, name). **-váto**, ADJ.: mentioned.
méntre [L. *dum-interim*], ADV.: while (as long as); although.
men-zionáre, TR., INTR.: mention (speak of, remind). ‖**-zióne** [L. *-tio*], F.: mention (reference). **-zógna**, F.: falsehood (untruth). **-zognatóre**†, M.: liar. **-zogneraménte**†, ADV.: falsely (deceitfully). **-zognère**†, **-zognèro**, ADJ.: lying (deceitful); M.: liar. **-zonáre**†, TR.: mention.
meraménte [*mero*], ADV.: purely (simply, MERELY).
mera-víglia [L. *mirabilia*], F.: MARVEL (wonder). **-vigliosaménte**, ADV.: marvellously. **-viglióso**, ADJ.: marvellous.
mercan-táre, INTR.: traffic (trade, deal). ‖**mercán-te** [*mercare*], M.: merchant (dealer); ADJ.: merchant. **-teggiáre**, INTR.: traffic (trade, deal). **-tésco**, ADJ.: of a merchant; dealing. **-téssa**, F.: tradeswoman; wife of merchant. **-tévole**†, **-tíle**, ADJ.: mercantile (commercial). **-tilménte**, ADV.: commercially. **-tóne**, *aug.* of *-te*. **-túccio**, **-túzzo**†, *disp. dim.* of *-te*. **-zía**, F.: merchandise (goods). **-ziòla**, **-ziuòla**†, *dim.* of *-zia*.
mercá-re [L. *-ri* (*merx*, MERCHandise)], TR., INTR.: (*poet.*) traffic (deal in). **-tábile**†, ADJ.: salable. **-tále**†, M.: market. **-tant..**† = *-nt..* **-táre**†, INTR.: traffic; TR.: buy. **mercá-to**, ADJ.: traded (trafficked); M.: market (marketplace, price, quantity, bargaining): *a buon* —, cheap; *far* — *di una cosa*, abuse. **-túra**, F.: commerce (trading).
mèr-ce [L. *merx*], F.: merchandise (wares). **-cè**, F.: help; pity (MERCY); thanks: *gran* —, many thanks. **-céde**, F.: reward (recompense). **-cechè**†, CONJ.: since (because). **-cenáio**†, M.: mercenary (hireling). **-cenariaménte**, ADV.: mercenarily. **-cenário**, ADJ.: mercenary (hired); M.: mercenary (hireling). **-cenúme**†, M.: work for money. **-cería**, F.: mercery (trade, goods); shop (of mercer). **-ciáia**, F.: mercer's wife; tradeswoman. **-ciaíno**, *car. dim.* of *-ciaio*. **-ciáio**, M., **-ciai(u)òla**, F., **-ciaiuòlo**, M.: mercer (dealer in small wares). **-ciaiúccio**, *disp. dim.* of *-ciaio*. **-cimònio**, M.: illegal traffic (venal trade).
mer-coledì [*Mercurio*, Mercury; *dì*, day], M.: Wednesday. **-corèlla**, F.: mercury (plant). **-curiále**, ADJ.: mercurial (of mercury, lively)†. **-cúrio**, M.: mercury (quicksilver).
mèr-da [L.], F.: excrement (Eng.† merd). **-dáio**, M.: place full of excrement. **-daiòlo**, M.: street-cleaner. **-dòcco**, M.: depilatory. **-dosaménte**, ADV.: vilely (filthily). **-dóso**, ADJ.: vile (filthy).
merèn-da [L. (*merere*, MERIT)], F.: afternoon luncheon. **-dáccia**, *disp.* of *-da*. **-dáre**, INTR.: lunch. **-détta**, **-dína**, **-díno**, *dim.* of *-da*. **-dóna**, *aug.* of *-da*.

-**donáccio**, *disp.* of *-done.* -**dóne**, M.: *aug.* of *-da;* blockhead. -**dáccia**, -**dúzza**†, *disp. dim.* of *-da.*
mere-trice [L. *-trix* (*-re*, earn)], F.: prostitute. -**trício**, ADJ.: meretricious.
mèr-gere†, IRR.§; TR.: plunge (IMMERSE, merge). **mèr-go**†, M.: offshoot (sprout); plungeon (sea-fowl).
§ Pret. *mèr-si, -se; -sero.* Part. *mèrso.*
meri-diána, F.: sun-dial (instrument). -**diáno**, ADJ.: meridian; M.: meridian (midday, great circle). **merí-dio**†, ADJ.: meridian. -**dionále**, ADJ.: meridional; M.: southerner. -**dionalménte**, ADV.: meridionally. **mèri-e**, F. PL.: open air (out-of-doors). ‖**merí-ggie** [L. *meridies*, 'clear DAY'], **merí-ggia** (*poet.*) = *-ggio.* -**ggiána**, F.: midday: *far la* —, take a nap after dinner. -**ggiáno**†, ADJ.: meridian (of midday). -**ggiáre**, INTR.: rest in the noonshade. **merí-ggio**, M.: midday (noon); south; (noon-)shade; noon-rest; ADJ.: of noon. -**ggióne**†, ADJ.: lazy.
me-ríno [Sp. *-rinos*], ADJ.: merino (of a variety of sheep); M.: merino wool. -**ríni**, M. PL.: merino sheep.
meri-taménte, ADV.: with merit (deservedly). -**taménto**†, M.: merit (reward). -**táre**, TR.: merit (deserve, earn); INTR.: merit (acquire desert). -**taménte**, ADV.: by merit (meritedly). -**tatíssimo**, ADJ.: very (or most) merited. -**táto**, ADJ.: merited (deserved). -**tevolíssimo**, ADJ.: very (or most) deserving. -**tévole**, ADJ.: meriting (deserving). -**tevolménte**, ADV.: meritedly (deservedly). -**tíssimo**, ADJ.: very (or most) merited. ‖**mèri-to** [L. *-tus*], M.: merit (worth, praise, gratitude, retaliation, recompense†, fruit†); ADJ.†: merited. -**toriaménte**, ADV.: meritoriously. -**tòrio**, ADJ.: meritorious.
mèr-la, F.: merle (blackbird); battlement (merlon); sly person. -**láre**†, TR.: provide with battlements. -**láto**, ADJ.: battlemented. -**latúra**, F.: battlements. -**lettáre**, TR.: trim with lace. -**létto**, M.: lace. ‖**mèr-lo** [L. *-ulus*], M.: 1. merle (blackbird; simpleton; sly person); 2. [deriv. ?], merlon (battlement). -**lóne**†, M.: large blackbird; indentation (of battlement). -**lòtto**, M.: young blackbird; silly fellow.
merlúzzo [Fr. *-luche*], M.: codfish.
mèro [L. *-rus*], ADJ.: pure (genuine, MERE).
meróll-a†, F., -**o**†, M.: marrow (pitch).
mert. .† = *merit*. .
mèrulo†, F.: blackbird.
[m]**èr-si**†, PRET., -**so**†, PART. of *mergere.*
[me]**sá-ta** [*mese*], F.: entire month; month's [pay]. -**tína**, *dim.* of *-ta.*

mé-scere [L. *miscere*], TR. (part. *-sciuto*, or *misto*): pour out; MIX†; INTR.: become united. -**schiaménto**†, -**schiánza**†, M., F.: mixture. -**schiáre**†, TR.: mix.
meschi-náccio, *disp.* of *-no.* -**naménte**, ADV.: miserably (wretchedly). -**nèllo**, -**nétto**, *dim.* of *-no.* -**níssimo**, ADJ.: very (or most) miserable. -**nità**, F.: misery (wretchedness, meanness). ‖**meschí-no** [fr. Ar.], ADJ.: wretched (miserable, poor); M.: servant†. -**núccio**, *dim.* of *-no.*
méschio†, ADJ.: mixed (compounded, mixed).
meschíta†, F.: mosque.
me-sciácqua [*mescere acqua*], M.: water-pitcher. -**scíbile**, ADJ.: mixable. -**sci-ròba**, F.: ewer (pitcher). **mé-scita**, F.: retailment (of wine, etc.). -**scitóre**, M., -**scitríce**, F.: cup-bearer (butler). -**sciúto**, ADJ.: poured out; mixed†.
mesco-lábile, ADJ.: mixable. -**lamento**, M.: mixing (mixture, combining). -**lánza**, F.: mixture (combination, medley); salad. ‖-**láre** [*mescere*], TR.: MIX (blend, confuse, shuffle); REFL.: be mixed in. -**láta**, F.: mixing (shuffle). -**lataménte**, ADV.: confusedly (in a mixed manner). -**láto**†, ADJ.: mixed (confused); M.: mixture. -**latúra**†, F.: mixture (medley). **mesco-lío**, M.: mixing. **mèsco-lo**, PART. of *-lare;* M.: mixture.
mes-cug]iáre [*-colare*], TR.: make a bad MIXture. -**cúg]io**, M.: mixture (medley).
mescuráre†, TR.: pass over (neglect, omit).
mése [L. *mensis*], M.: MONTH; month's pay.
meşen-tèrico, ADJ.: mesenteric. ‖-**tèrio** [Gr. *mésos*, middle, *énteron*, intestine], M.: mesentery (abdominal membrane). -**teríte**, F.: mesenteritis (inflammation of mesentery).
mèşe-re, -**ro** [OFr. *mesre*], M.: long veil.
mesétto, *car. dim.* of *mese.*
meşme-ríşmo [*Mesmer*], M.: mesmerism. -**rizzáre**, TR.: mesmerize.
més-sa [L. *missus* (*mittere*, send; disMISS)], F.: stake (wager); offshoot (sprout); MASS (service); MESS (course)†; stock†; sending (mission)†. -**saggería**†, F.: embassy. -**saggèra**, F., -**saggèro**, M., -**saggièra**, F., -**saggière**, M.: messenger (envoy). -**sággio**, M.: message (communication); messenger. -**sále**, M.: missal (mass-book).
mèsse [L. *-ssis* (*metere*, MOW)], F.: harvest.
mes-serático†, M.: mastership (title of Sir). ‖-**sèr(e)** [*mio ser(e)*], M.: Sir (now chiefly to a Dr. of Law); master. -**serí-no**, *disp. dim.* of *-sere.*

messía [Heb. *mashiah*, anointed], M.: Messiah (Christ).
messidòro [L. *messis*, harvest, Gr. *dôron*, gift], M.: Messidor (June 19–July 18: calendar of the French Republic).
messióne†, F.: sending (mission).
messitíccio [*messa*], M.: sprout (of useless plant).
mésso [L. *missus*, sent], M.: MESSenger (envoy); message†; ADJ.: placed (assigned, set).
messóre†, M.: harvester.
mestaménte [*mesto*], ADV.: sadly (mournfully).
mes-taménto, M.: stirring (blending). ‖**-táre** [*misto*], TR.: stir (blend, mingle). **-tatóio**†, M.: stirrer (spoon, spatula). **-tatóre**, M., **-tatríce**, F.: stirrer (blender, mingler).
mèsti-ca [Fr. *mestèque*], F.: priming for canvas; mixed paints (on the pallet). **-cáre**, INTR.: mix paints. **-catóre**, M.: maker or seller of canvas-priming and oil-paints. **-cheria**, F.: art-store. **-chíno**, M.: spatula.
mesti-eránte, M.: business-man. ‖**-ère** [OFr. *-er* (L. *ministerium*)], M.: business (trade, occupation); need (necessity): *è -cri*, it is necessary. **-èro**, M.: business (trade); need. **-erúccio**, *disp.* of *-ere*.
me-stissimaménte, ADV.: very sadly. **-stíssimo**, ADJ.: very (or most) sad. **-stízia**, F.: sadness (gloom, sorrow). ‖**mè-sto** [L. *mæstus*], ADJ.: sad (sorrowful).
mésto-la [*mestare*], F.: ladle; trowel; battledore†; insipid person†. **-láia**, F., **-láio**, M.: seller of ladles (or trowels). **-láta**, F.: blow with ladle (or trowel); ladleful; trowelful. **-létta**, **-lína**, *car. dim.* of *-la*. **-líno**, *dim.* of *-lo*. **méstolo**, M.: ladle (large spoon). **-lóne**, M.: *aug.* of *-lo* or *-la*; great dunce. **mestó-na**, F., **mestó-ne**, M.: stirrer (wooden utensil).
mestru-ále, ADJ.: menstrual. **-áre**, INTR.: menstruate. **-áto**, ADJ.: Eng.† menstruate. **-azióne**, F.: menstruation. ‖**mèstru-o** [L. *menstruus* (*mensis*, MONTH)], M.: menses (Eng.† menstrue).
mestúra = *mistura*.
mèta 1 [L. conical post, end of Rom. circus], F.: (Eng.† mete); goal; aim.
méta 2, F.: dung.
metà [L. *medietas*], F.: half (moiety).
meta- [Gr. *metá*, between, MID-; after, beyond], in compounds.
meta=cárpo, M.: metacarpus (hand between wrist and fingers). **-croníşmo** [Gr. *chrónos*, time], M.: metachronism (error in chronology). **-fíşica** [Gr. *phúsis*, nature], F.: metaphysics (science). **-fişicále**†, ADJ.: metaphysical. **-fişicaménte**, ADV.: metaphysically. **-fişicáre**, INTR.: use metaphysics. **-fíşico**, pl. *—ci*, ADJ.: metaphysical; M.: metaphysician. **metá-fora** [Gr. *phérein*, BEAR], F.: metaphor (figure). **-foreggiáre**, INTR.: speak metaphorically. **-foricaménte**, ADV.: metaphorically. **-fòrico**, pl. *—ci*, ADJ.: metaphorical. **-forizzáre**, INTR.: speak metaphorically. **-foróna**, *aug.* of *-ra*. **metá-frași** [Gr. *phrázein*, speak], F.: metaphrase (verbal translation). **-fráste**, M.: metaphrast (translator). **-frástico**, pl. *—ci*, ADJ.: metaphrastic (literal). **-lèssi**, **-lèpsi** [Gr. *lêpsis*, taking], F.: (*rhet.*) metalepsis.
metál-lico, pl. *—ci*, ADJ.: metallic. **-lière**†, M.: metallist. **-lífero**, ADJ.: metalliferous (producing metals). **-líno**†, ADJ.: metalline. **-lizzaménto**, M.: metallization. **-lizzáre**, TR.: metallize. **-lizzazióne**, F.: metallization. ‖**metál-lo** [L. *-lum*], M.: metal. **-lografía**, F.: metallography. **-lòide**, F.: metalloid. **-lurgía**, F.: metallurgy. **-lúrgico**, pl. *—ci*, ADJ.: metallurgic. **-lúrgo**, pl. *—ghi* or *—gi*, M.: metallurgy.
meta- [Gr., cf. the word]: **-mòrfico**, pl. *—ci*, ADJ.: metamorphic. **-morfísti**, M. PL.: metamorphists. **-mòrfoși** [Gr. *morphé*, form], F.: metamorphosis (transformation). **-pláşmo** [Gr. *plássein*, mould], M.: metaplasm (change in a word). **-plástico**, pl. *—ci*, ADJ.: metaplastic. **metá=staşi** [Gr. *histánai*, place], F.: metastasis. **=társo**, M.: metatarsus (foot between toes and ankle). **metá-teşi** [Gr. *the-*, put], F.: metathesis (transposition).
metáto [?], M.: drying place (for chestnuts).
metempsicòși [Gr. *-psúchosis* (*metá*, beyond, *em-psuchoûn*, animate)], F.: metempsychosis (transmigration).
metèo-ra [Gr. *-ros*], F.: meteor. **meteò-rico**, ADJ.: meteoric. **-rografía**, F.: meteorography. **-rògrafo**, M.: meteorograph. **-rología**, F.: meteorology. **-rològico**, pl. *—ci*, ADJ.: of meteors (meteorological). **-ròlogo**, pl. *—gi*, M.: meteorology. **-roscòpio**, M.: meteoroscope.
metíccio [L. *mixtus*], ADJ.: of mixed blood; M.: MESTIZO.
metico-losaménte, ADV.: fastidiously. **-losità**, F.: fastidiousness. ‖**-lóso** [L. *-losus* (*metus*, fear)], ADJ.: fastidious (Eng.† meticulous).
met- [cf. *meta-*]: **-òdica**, F.: method. **-odicaménte**, ADV.: methodically. **-òdico**, pl. *—ci*, ADJ.: methodical; M.: ancient school of physicians. **-odíşmo**, M.: Methodism. **-odísta**, M.: Methodism. ‖**mè-**

t-odo [Gr. *hodós*, road], M.: method (order, manner, book). **-onimía** [Gr. *ónoma*, NAME], F.: metonymy (figure). **-onímico**, pl. —*ci*, ADJ.: metonymic. **mèt-opa** [Gr. *opé*, opening], F.: metope (space between triglyphs of Doric frieze). **-oposcopía**, F.: metoposcopy (study of physiognomy). **-opòscopo** [Gr. *skopein*, examine], M., F.: physiognomist (metoposcopist).

me-tricaménte, ADV.: metrically. **mètrico**, pl. —*ci*, ADJ.: metrical. ‖**mè-tro** [Gr. *-tron*, measure], M.: meter. **-trología**, F.: metrology (science). **-trològico**, pl. —*ci*, ADJ.: of metrology. **-trònomo**, M.: metronome.

metròpo-li [Gr. *-lis* (*méter*, mother, *pólis*, city)], F.: metropolis. **-líta**, M.: metropolitan (archbishop, bishop). **-litána**, F.: the Church. **-litáno**, ADJ.: metropolitan (of the Church).

mét-tere [L. *mittere*], IRR.§; TR.: put (place, assign, impose); suppose; admit; add; sprout (put forth); receive; translate; declare; commence; REFL.: begin (set about): — *addosso*, accuse; — *bottega*, set up shop; — *casa*, set up housekeeping; — *consiglio*, consider; — *in cuore*, put in one's mind; — *in novelle*, deride; — *paura*, frighten; — *ragione*, calculate; — *la tavola*, set the table; — *alla vela*, set sail; *-tersi in cuore*, make a resolution; *-tersi a tavola*, sit down at table. **-tíbile**, ADJ.: placeable. **-ti=bócca**, M., F.: meddler. **-ti=mále**, **-ti=scándoli**, M., F.: gossip (scandal-monger). **-titóra**, F., **-titóre**, M.: placer (putter.). **-titúra**, F.: placing (putting).

§ Pret. *misi* (so in comp.) or *méssi*, *mise* or *mésse*; *misero*, or *méssero*. Part.: Pr. *mettènte*, or, as noun, *mittènte*. Past. *mésso*.

méu†, M.: fennel (herb).

mèẓ-ẓa [-*zo*], F.: half-hour; half. **-ẓadría**, F.: partnership (in farming). **-ẓaiòla**, F., **-ẓai(u)òlo**, M.: partner (sharer). **-ẓa=lána**, F.: linsey-woolsey. **-ẓa=lúna**, F.: crescent (half moon, dagger). **-ẓána**, F.: kind of brick; mizzen (sail); middle string of violin, etc. **-ẓanaménte**, ADV.: middlingly. **-ẓaníno**, *dim.* of *-zano*, M.: mezzanine (entresol). **-ẓanità†**, F.: mediocrity. **-ẓáno**, ADJ.: middle (medium), M.: mediator (reconciler). **-ẓanóna**, **-ẓanóne**, *aug.* of *-zana*. **-ẓa=nòtte**, F.: midnight. **-ẓa=tèsta** [*mezza testa*], F.: head-armour. **-ẓa=tínta**, F.: half-tint. **-ẓatóre†**, M.: mediator. **-ẓèdima†**, F.: middle of the week. **-ẓería**, F.: partnership (in farming). **-ẓétta**, F.: small [w]ine-measure. **-ẓína** [?], F.: water-pitcher; [p]itcherful.

[mèẓ]**ẓo** I [L. *mitius* (*mitis*), ripe)], ADJ.: [over]-ripe; soaked; flabby.

mèẓ-ẓo 2 [L. *medius*], ADJ.: half; MIDDLE; MEDIUM, ADV.: half; almost (nearly); M.: half; middle; MEANS (aid; mediation); mediator: *per* —, by means of; *in questo* —, in the meantime; *esser di* —, intermeddle; *metter di* —, deceive; *produrre in* —, propose; *star di* —, be neutral. **-ẓo=bústo**, M.: bust. **-ẓo=cérchio**, M.: semi-circle. **-ẓo=colóre**, M.: pale colour. **-ẓo=dì**, M.: midday. **-ẓo=giórno**, M.: midday (noon); south. **-ẓo=gráppolo†**, M.: kind of wine. **-ẓolána†**, **-ẓolanità†**, F.: mediocrity. **-ẓoláno†**, ADJ.: mediocre (ordinary). **-ẓ=ómbra**, F.: light shade. **-ẓóne**, M.: kind of wine. **-ẓo=rilièvo**, M.: half-relief in figures (between high and low). **-ẓ=oscúro**, M.: half-tint. **-ẓo=sopráno**, M.: mezzo-soprano (medium soprano voice). **-ẓo=tèrmine**, M.: expedient (means). **-ẓúccio**, *disp.* of *-zo*. **-ẓúle**, M.: barrel-head.

mí [*me*], PRON.: me; to me.

mía [L. *mea*], PRON., F.: my, mine. **-fè†**, INTERJ.: by my faith!

míago-laménto, M.: mewing. **-lánte**, ADJ.: mewing. ‖**-láre** [*miau*], INTR.: mew (of a cat). **-láta**, F.: mewing. **-latóre**, M., **-latríce**, F.: mewer. **-lío**, M.: continued mewing. **miágo-lo**, M.: mew (of cat).

miagul. .† = *miagol.*.

miáo, **miáu** [echoic], M.: mew (of cat).

miás-ma [Gr.], M.: miasma (infection). **-mático**, pl. —*ci*, ADJ.: miasmatic.

míca I [L. *mica*, bit], ADV.: *non* . . . —, not . . . in the least (at all).

mí-ca 2 [L. *-care*, shine], F.: mica. **-cáceo**, ADJ.: micaceous (containing mica). **-cánte†**, ADJ.: shining. **-ca-schisto**, M.: mica-schist.

mícca†, F.: soup (porridge).

micchétto, *dim.* of *-cco*.

míccia I [*-cio*], F.: she-ass.

míccia 2 [l. L. *myxa*], F.: fuse.

miccianza†, F.: mixture; misfortune.

mic-cichíno†, M.: very little bit. **-cinino**, ADJ.: very little; M.: little bit. ‖**-cíno** [L. *mica*], ADJ.: little; *a* —, avariciously.

míccio [?], M.: ass.

mícco [?], M.: ape; burly pretender; fop.

michelétti [Sp. *miquelete*], M. PL.: Spanish milice.

mícia [*-cio*], F.: she-cat; pussy.

micid. .† = *omicid.*. **-diále**, ADJ.: murderous.

mi-cína, *dim.* of *-cia*. **-cíno**, *car. dim.* of *-cio*. ‖**mí-cio** [L. *musio*], M.: cat.

mico-lína [*mica* I], F., **-líno**, M.: tiny crumb.

micro- [Gr. *mikrós*, small]: **-`bio** [Gr. *bíos*, life], M.: microbe. **-cèfalo** [Gr.

kephalḗ, head], M.: small-headed animal; ADJ.: having a small head. **-còṣmo** [Gr. *kósmos*], M.: microcosm (little world). **micrò-fono** [Gr. *phonḗ*, sound], M.: microphone. **-grafía** [Gr. *gráphein*, write], F.: micrography. **micrò-grafo**, M.: micrographer. **-metría** [Gr. *métron*, measure], F.: micrometry. **micrò-metro**, M.: micrometer. **-scopía**, F.: microscopy. **-scòpico**, pl. —*ci*, ADJ.: microscopic (very small). **-scòpio** [Gr. *skopeîn*, examine], M.: microscope.

midól-la [L. *medulla*], F.: soft part of bread; marrow; pith. **-láre**, ADJ.: medullar. **-létta**, **-lína**, *car. dim.* of *-la*. **midól-lo**, M.: marrow; pith. **-lóne**, M.: *aug.* of *-lo*; kind-hearted fellow. **-lóso**, ADJ.: full of marrow (crumbs, pith).

mièle [L. *mel*], M.: honey.

miè-tere [L. *metere*], TR.: MOW (reap). **-titóre**, M., **-titríce**, F.: mower (reaper). **-titúra**, F.: reaping; harvest-time; harvest. **-túto**, ADJ.: reaped (gathered).

míga† = *mica* I.

mi-gliacciáre†, INTR.: eat millet-pudding. ‖**-gliáccio** [L. *miliaceum*], M.: millet-pudding; blood-pudding. **-gliacciòla**, F.: kind of fritter.

migliáio, pl. —*aia* [L. *mille*], M.: thousand.

migliáre [L. *milia*], F.: kind of fever.

migliarèllo, *iron. dim.* of *miglio* I.

mi-gliaríno, M.: chaffinch; small shot. **-gliaròla**, F.: small shot. ‖**mí-glio** I [L. *-lium*], M.: millet (plant).

míglio 2 [L. *millia*, 1000, viz. paces], M.: MILE.

míglio-raménto†, M.: best (flower); improvement. **-ránza**†, F.: improvement (amendment, melioration). **-ráre**, TR.: improve (make better, meliorate), blossom (as olive-trees). **-ratúra**, F.: blossoming (of olive-trees). ‖**miglió-re** [L. *melior*], ADJ.: better; right (hand); M.: best.

mignát-ta [?], F.: leech (blood-sucker); usurer; miser; bore. **-táio**, M.: one who sells or applies leeches. **-tína**, *car. dim.* of *-ta*. **-tóne**, *aug.* of *-ta*.

mígno-la, F.: olive-blossom. **-láre**, INTR.: blossom (of olives). ‖**mígno-lo** [? ak. to Fr. *-n*], M.: olive-blossom; kind of olive; little finger; ADJ.: olive; of the little finger.

mi-gnoncèllo†, *dim.* of *-gnone*. ‖**-gnóne** [Fr. *-gnonne*], M.: minion (small type; favorite†).

migrá-re [L.], INTR.: migrate (change residence or country). **-tóre**, M.: migrant. **-tòrio**, ADJ.: migratory. **-zióne**, F.: migration.

miíssimo, ADJ.: superl. of *mio*; my very self.

míla [L. *milia*], NUM. PL.: thousands.

milènso†, ADJ.: stupid (foolish).

miliárdo [L. *milia*], M.: milliard (thousand millions).

miliáre I [L. *-lium*, millet], ADJ.: miliary (fever).

miliáre 2 [L. *milia*], ADJ.: milliary (pertaining to a mile).

miliárico, pl. —*ci* [*miliare* 2], ADJ.: milliary.

mili-onário, ADJ.: millionary (consisting of millions). **-oncíno**, *car. dim.* of *-one*. ‖**-óne** [*mille*], M.: million. **-onèṣimo**, ADJ.: millionth.

mili-tánte, ADJ.: militant (combating). **-táre**, ADJ.: military (warlike); M.: soldier; INTR.: fight (be a soldier, militate). **-tarescaménte**, ADV.: in a military manner. **-tarésco**, ADJ.: military. **-taríṣmo**, M.: militarism. **-tariẓẓáre**, TR.: reduce to militarism. **-tarménte**, ADV.: in a military manner (as a soldier). **-tatóre**, M.: soldier. ‖**míli-te** [L. *miles*], M.: soldier (yeoman). **milí-zia**, F.: military profession; army (militia); host.

millán-ta [*mille*], F.: thousands. **-taménto**†, M.: boasting (vaunting). **-táre**, TR.: boast (exaggerate, brag); REFL.: boast. **-táto**, ADJ.: boasted (exaggerated). **-tatóre**, M., **-tatríce**, F.: boaster (braggart). **-tería**, F., **millán-to**†, M.: boasting (exaggeration, bragging).

míl-le [L.], ADJ., M.: thousand; ADV.: *a — a* · –, in great numbers. **-lècuplo**, ADJ.: thousand times more. **-le=fióri**, M.: all-flower water. **-le=fòglie**, M.: milfoil (herb). **-lenário**, ADJ.: millenary (consisting of a thousand); M. PL.: millenarists. **-lènne**, ADJ.: millennial. **-lènnio** [L. *annus*, year], M.: millennium (thousand years). **-le=pièdi**, M.: milliped (wood-louse). **-lèṣimo**, ADJ.: thousandth; M.: thousandth; millennium. **-liáre**, ADJ.: milliary (pertaining to a mile). **-li=grámma**, **-li=grámmo**, M.: milligramme (measure of weight). **-lí=litro**, M.: milliliter (measure of capacity). **-li=metro**, M.: millimeter (lineal measure). **-lionário**, M.: millionaire. **-lióne**, M.: million.

milvagíno [L. *-vago*], M.: flying-fish.

mílza [?], F.: spleen.

mílzo†, ADJ.: thin (poor).

mí-ma [*-mo*], F.: mimic (comedian, buffoon). **mí-mica**, F.: mimicry. **-micaménte**, ADV.: mimically. **mí-mico**, pl. —*ci*, ADJ.: mimic.

mím-ma [?], F.: baby (little girl, baby-faced woman). **mím-mo**, M.: baby (little boy).

mí-mo [L. *-mus*], M.: mimic (comedian, buffoon); mime (farce). **-mògrafo**, M.:

mimographer (writer of mimes). **-mósa**, F.: mimosa (genus of plants).

mína1 [Gr. *hemína*], F.: mina (Greek weight of about 15 ounces, Greek coin).

mí-na2 [l. L.], F.: mine. **-nábile**, ADJ.: minable.

minac-cévole, ADJ.: menacing (threatening). **-cevolménte**, ADV.: menacingly. ‖**minác-cia** [L. *-ia*], F.: MENACE (threat). **-ciábile**, ADJ.: worthy of being menaced. **-ciaménto**, M.: menacing (threatening). **-ciánte**, ADJ.: menacing. **-ciáre**, TR.: menace (threaten). **-ciáto**, ADJ.: menaced (threatened). **-ciatóre**, M., **-ciatríce**, F.: menacer (threatener). **-ciatúra**†, F.: menace (threat). **-ciosaménte**, ADV.: menacingly (threateningly). **-cióso**, ADJ.: menacing (threatening). **minác-e**†, ADJ.: (*poet.*) menacing.

mináre [L.], TR., INTR.: mine.

minaréto [fr. Ar.], M.: minaret.

minatóre [*minare*], M.: miner (digger of mines).

minatòrio [L. *minari*], ADJ.: menacing (threatening, minatory).

mín-chia† [L. *mentula*], F.: (*dial.*) male organ; odd thing; kind of fish. **-chiáte**, F. PL.: a game of cards.

minchio-náccio, *disp.* of *-ne*. **-náccia**, *disp.* of *-na*. **-náre**, TR.: jest (joke, banter). **-natóra**, F., **-natóre**, M.: jester (banterer). **-natòrio**, ADJ.: jesting (bantering). **-natúra**, F.: jesting (mockery, bantering). **-ncèllo**, *iron. dim.* of *-ne*. **-ncíno**, *iron.*, *car. dim.* of *-ne*. **-ncióne**, *aug.* of *-ne*. **minchió-na** [*minchia*], F., **-ne**, M.: simpleton; blockhead (fool). **-nería**, F.: jest (joke, trick); trifle (folly, error).

minerá-le [l. L. *-lis*], M.: mineral; ADJ.: mineral. **-lísta**, M.: mineralist. **-lizzáre**, TR.: mineralize; REFL.: become like mineral. **-lizzáto**, ADJ.: mineralized. **-lizzazióne**, F.: mineralization. **-logía**, F.: mineralogy. **-lògico**, pl. —*ci*, ADJ.: pertaining to mineralogy. **-logísta**, M.: mineralogist. **minerá-rio**, ADJ.: pertaining to mines.

minè-stra [*ministrare*], F.: soup. **-stráccia**, *disp.* of *-stra*. **-stráio**, ADJ.: fond of soup; M.: soup-maker. **-stráre**†, TR.: serve soup. **-strèlla**†, **-strína**, *car. dim.* of *-stra*. **-stróna**, F., **-stróne**, M.: *aug.* of *-stra*; mixture.

mingherlíno [?], ADJ.: slender (thin, lean).

-ínia [*minare*], F.: mine.

-ni-áre [L.], TR.: paint in miniature; -ribe minutely; REFL.†: paint one's **-áto**, ADJ.: miniatured. **-atóre**, miniature-painter. **-atúra**, F.: miniature-painting. **-aturína**, *car. dim.* of *-atura*.

minièra [L. *minera*], F.: mine (of minerals).

míni-ma, F.: minim (note in music). **-maménte**, ADV.: in the least. **-maménto**†, M.: diminution. **-máre**†, TR.: diminish (minimize). ‖**míni-mo** [L. *-mus*], ADJ.: least (smallest). **míni-mum**, M.: minimum.

mínio [L. *-nium*], M.: minium (red-lead); rouge; miniature†.

mini-steriále, ADJ.: ministerial (official). **-stèrio**†, **-stèro**, M.: ministry (government, office, residence). **miní-stra**, F.: minister (embassador, preacher). **-stráre**, TR.: administer (supply, furnish); INTR.: minister (officiate). **-stratóre**†, M.: administrator. **-strazióne**†, F.: ministration (ministry). **-strèllo**†, M.: *dim.* of *-stro*; minstrel. **-stréssa**, F.: wife of minister. **-strière**†, M.: minstrel. ‖**miní-stro** [L. *-ster*], M.: minister (embassador, priest, administrator).

mino-ránza, F.: minority. **-ráre**, TR.: diminish (lessen). **-rascáto**, M.: conditions of deed of trust. **-rásco**, M.: deed of trust. **-ratívo**, ADJ.: diminutive (lessening). **-razióne**, F.: diminution (lessening, minoration). ‖**minó-re** [L.], ADJ.: minor (less, younger). **-rènne**, ADJ., M.: minor (younger). **-rità**, F.: minority. **-rménte**†, ADV.: less.

minotáuro [L. *-rus*], M.: minotaur (fabled monster).

minu-ále†, ADJ.: of low birth. **-èndo** [*-ire*], M.: (*arith.*) minuend. **-ettína**†, *dim.* of *-etto*. ‖**-étto** [Fr. *menuet*], M.: minuet (dance).

minúgia [L. *minutia*], F.: guts†; strings (of an instrument).

mi-nuíre [L. *-nuere*], TR.: diMINish (lessen); INTR.: grow less. **-núscolo**, ADJ.: small; F. (*-la*): small letter.

minú-ta, F.: minute (first draught of writing, note). **-táglia**, F.: minutia (quantity of minute things). **-táme**, M.: heap of minute things. **-taménte**, ADV.: minutely (exactly). **-tánte**, ADJ.: noting down (minuting). **-táre**, TR.: make note of (minute, jot down). **-tería**, F.: trifles; goldsmith's trade. **-tézza**, F.: minuteness; trifle. **-tière**†, M.: goldsmith. **-tína**, F.: *dim.* of *-ta*; kind of salad. **-tíno**, *car. dim.* of *-to*. **-tíssimo**, ADJ.: very (or most) minute. ‖**minú-to** [L. *-tus*], ADJ.: minute (little, slender, detailed): of low birth (common); ADV.: minutely; M.: minute (sixtieth part of an hour or degree); herb-soup: *a* —, critically; *vendere a* —, sell by retail. **minú-zia**, F.: minutia (smallest detail). **-zióso**,

ADJ.: minute (detailed, exact). **-zzáme**, M.: heap of minute things. **-zzáre†**, TR.: mince (chop fine). **-zzáta**, F.: strewing (of leaves and flowers). **minú-zzo†**, **minú-zzolo**, M.: crumb (bit).

mío [L. *meus*], PRON.: my; mine.

mioeènico, pl. *—ci* [Gr. *meion*, less, *kainós*, recent], ADJ.: miocene (geological term).

miología [Gr. *mûs*, MUSCLE], F.: myology (study of muscles).

mío-pe [Gr. *-ps* (*múein*, close, *ôps*, EYE)], M.: myope (short-sighted person). **-pía**, F.: myopy (short-sightedness).

mí-ra [*-rare*], F.: aim (sight, intention, design). **-rábile**, ADJ.: admirable (wonderful). **-rabília**, F. PL.: wonderful things. **-rabilménte**, ADV.: admirably (wonderfully).

miráco-lo [L. *miraculum* (*mirari*, wonder)], M.: miracle (wonderful thing). **-lóne**, *aug.* of *-lo*. **-losaménte**, ADV.: miraculously. **-lóso**, ADJ.: miraculous (wonderful).

mi-radóre†, M.: admirer. ‖**-rágʟio** [*mirare*], M.: mirror (looking-glass).

mi=rallégro, M.: congratulation.

mirá-re [L. *-ri*], TR.: behold (look at); aim; INTR., REFL.: wonder (marvel). **-tóre**, M.: beholder; mirror.

miria- [Gr. *muriás*, myriad], M.: 10,000. **=grámma**, —o, M.: myriagram (about 22 pounds). **='litro**, M.: myrialiter (about 42 hogsheads). **='metro**, M.: myriameter (about 6 miles). **miría-de**, F.: myriad. **míriá=podi** [Gr. *poûs*, FOOT], M. PL.: myriapod (animal).

mi-ríca [Gr. *murikē*], F.: kind of tamarisk (plant). **-ríce†**, F.: tamarisk.

mi-rífico, pl. *—ci* [L. *-rificus*], ADJ.: magnificent (wonderful). **mí-ro†**, ADJ.: (*poet.*) wonderful (marvellous).

miróllа†, F.: marrow (pith); cream.

mír-ra [L. *myrrha*], F.: myrrh (gum-resin). **-ráre†**, TR.: perfume with myrrh. **mír-rico**, pl. *-rici*, ADJ.: myrrhic.

mír-teo†, ADJ.: of myrtle. **-této**, M.: myrtle-grove (plantation). **-tifórme**, ADJ.: myrtiform (resembling myrtle). **-tíllo†**, M.: myrtleberry. **-tíno†**, ADJ.: of myrtle. ‖**mír-to** [L. *-tus*], M.: myrtle (plant).

mis- [Ger. *miss-*], PREF.: mis-, wrong.

misál-ta†, F.: salted pork. **-táre†**, TR.: salt pork.

mi-ṣantropía, F.: misanthropy. **-ṣantròpico**, pl. *—ci*, ADJ.: misanthropic. ‖**-ṣántropo** [Gr. *miseîn*, hate, *ánthropos*, man], M.: misanthrope; ADJ.: misanthropic.

miṣ=avvedutaménte†, ADV.: without sagacity.

miṣ=avveniménto†, M.: misfortune (mischance, disaster). **=avveníre†**, IRR.; INTR.: happen ill. **=avventúra**, F.: misfortune (mishap). **-avvenúto†**, ADJ.: unfortunate.

mis=cadére†, IRR.; INTR.: happen ill.

mi-ṣcèa [L. *miscere*, mix], F.: trifle (bauble). **-ṣcèla**, F.: mixture (medley). **-ṣcellánea**, F.: miscellany (mixture). **-ṣcelláneo**, ADJ.: miscellaneous (mixed).

mísc*h*i-a, F.: quarrel (scuffle, conflict). **-ménto**, M.: mixing (shuffling, medley). **-ánza**, F.: mixture. ‖**-áre** [p. L. *misculare* (L. *miscere*)], TR.: mix (mingle); REFL.: intermeddle (interpose). **-áta†**, **-atúra**, F.: mixture (medley). **-ataménte**, ADV.: confusedly (indiscriminately). **mísc*h*i-o**, ADJ.: mixed (variegated).

miṣcíbile†, ADJ.: mixable (miscible).

miscognoṣc. † = *misconosc.*.

mis=conóṣcere, IRR.; TR.: fail to recognize; not care for. **-conoṣcènte**, ADJ.: ungrateful. **-conoṣciúto**, ADJ.: unrecognized.

mís=contènto†, ADJ.: discontented (unhappy).

mis-credènte, ADJ.: incredulous (sceptical); M.: unbeliever (infidel). **-credènza†**, F.: disbelief. **=crédere**, INTR.: misbelieve.

miscúgʟio [*mischiare*], M.: mixture (adulteration).

miṣ=díre†, IRR.; TR.: slander (speak ill, defame). **-détto†**, ADJ.: slandered.

miṣèllo (*jest.*) for *misero*.

miṣe-rábile, ADJ.: miserable (unfortunate, needy, unhappy). **-rabilíssimo**, ADJ.: very (or most) wretched. **-rabilità**, F.: misery (wretchedness, distress). **-rabilménte**, ADV.: miserably. **-raménte**, ADV.: miserably (poorly). **-rándo**, ADJ.: miserable (forlorn, pitiable). **-razióne†**, F.: mercy (compassion, pity). **-rèllo**, *dim.* of *-ro*. **-rère**, M.: miserere (Catholic psalm commencing thus); intestinal malady. **-révole**, ADJ.: miserable (pitiful). **-revolézza†**, F.: misery (pitifulness). **-revolménte**, ADV.: miserably (pitifully). **misè-ria**, F.: misery (wretchedness, extreme poverty, stinginess). **-ricòrde**, ADJ.: merciful (compassionate). **-ricordévole†**, ADJ.: worthy of pity. **-ricòrdia**, F.: mercy (pity, compassion). **-ricordiévole†**, ADJ.: pitiable (miserable). **-ricordievolménte†**, **-ricordiosaménte**, ADV.: mercifully (compassionately). **-ricordióso**, ADJ.: merciful (compassionate, humane). ‖**míṣe-ro** [L. *-r*], ADJ.: miserable (wretched, poor, unimportant, stingy, unhappy). **-róne**, *aug.* of *-ro*. **miṣè-rrimo**, ADJ.:

very (or most) miserable. **-rtà†**, F.: misery (poverty, want).

mis=fáre†, IRR.; INTR.: do wrong (do harm). **-fátto**, M.: misdeed (wrong. crime); ADJ.: wrongly done. **-fattóre†**, M.: malefactor (evil-doer).

mis=gradíto†, ADJ.: unwelcome (disagreeable).

mísi, PRET. of *mettere*.

misirízzi [*mi, si, rizzare*], M.: self-rising puppet (a toy).

misléa†, F.: fight (scuffle).

mis=leále, ADJ.: disloyal (perfidious); M.: disloyal person.

mis=pregiáre†, TR.: depreciate; despise.

mis = prèndere†, IRR.; TR.: mistake; INTR.: err (blunder). **-préisa†**, F.: mistake (error). **-préso†**, ADJ.: mistaken.

mis-sionário, M.: missionary. ‖**-sióne** [L. *-sio*], F.: mission (errand, commission). **-síva**, F.: missive. **mís-so†**, ADJ.: sent.

mistaménte [*misto*], ADV.: mixedly (confusedly).

miste-rialménte†, ADV.: mysteriously. **mistè-rio†**, M.: mystery (deep secret). **-riosaménte**, ADV.: mysteriously (secretly). **-rióso**, ADJ.: mysterious (secret, obscure). ‖**mistè-ro** [L. *mysterium*], M.: mystery (deep secret; sacred drama).

mís-tia†, F.: quarrel (scuffle). ‖**-tiáre** [*-chiare*], TR.: mix (mingle). **-tiánza†**, F.: mixture (medley).

místi-ca, F.: mystic (theology). **-caménte**, ADV.: mystically (obscurely). **-chità†**, F.: mysticalness. **-císmo**, M.: mysticism (doctrine of Mystics). **-cità**, F.: mysticalness. ‖**místi-co**, pl. *-ci* [L. *mysticus*], ADJ.: mystic (obscure); M. PL.: mystic (believer in mysticism).

mistière = *mestiere*.

mistificá-re [Fr. *mystifier*], TR.: mystify (deceive). **-zióne**, F.: mystification.

mi - stilínea [*linea*], F.: mixed line. **-stióne**, F.: mixture (mixtion). ‖**mí-sto** [L. *-xtus*], ADJ.: MIXED (mingled); M.: mixture (medley). **-stúra**, F.: mixture (medley, adulteration).

misú-ra [L. *mensura*], F.: measure (size; instrument; expedient; cadence): *a* —, proportionably; *a — che*, according as; *dar la* —, requite. **-rábile**, ADJ.: measurable. **-rabilità**, F.: measurableness. **-raménto†**, M.: measuring. **-ránza†**, measure (moderation). **-ráre**, TR.: [illegible]URE (estimate, value, adjust); REFL.: of one's self. **-ránte**, ADJ.: meas- **-rataménte**, ADV.: moderately [illegible]rately). **-ratézza†**, F.: measure [illegible]tion). **-ráto**, ADJ.: measured. [illegible]e, M., **-ratríce**, F.: measurer (land-surveyor, instrument). **-ratúra**, F.: measuring; expense of measuring. **-razióne**, F.: measuring. **-révole†**, ADJ.: measurable. **-ríno**, *dim.* of *-ra*.

mis-usáre†, TR.: misuse (abuse). **-úso†**, M.: misuse (abuse).

mis-veníre†, IRR.; INTR.: swoon; happen ill. **-ventúra†**, F.: misfortune. **-venúto†**, ADJ.: unfortunate.

mí-te [L. *-tis*], ADJ.: mild (clement, merciful, gentle). **-teménte**, ADV.: mildly (mercifully, gently).

míto-ra [*mitra*], F.: paper miter (worn at the pillory). **-ráre†**, TR.: put on the miter. **-ríno†**, ADJ.: deserving the miter (or pillory). **-róne**, *aug.* of *-ra*.

mitézza [*mite*], F.: mildness (gentleness).

míti-caménte, ADV.: mythically. ‖**míti-co**, pl. *-tici* [*mito*], ADJ.: mythical (fabulous).

mitídio [Gr. *mêtis*, sense], M.: common sense (judgment).

miti-gábile, ADJ.: calmable (mitigable). **-gaménto**, M.: mitigation (alleviation). ‖**-gáre** [L. (*mitis*, mild)], TR.: mitigate (soften); INTR.: lessen; REFL.: relent. **-gánte**, ADJ.: softening (mitigant). **-gatívo**, ADJ.: alleviating (mitigating). **-gatóre**, M., **-gatríce**, F.: mitigator. **-gazióne**, F.: mitigation (alleviation).

mí-to [Gr. *mûthos*], M.: myth (story). **-tología**, F.: mythology. **-tologicaménte**, ADV.: mythologically. **-tològico**, pl. *—ci*, ADJ.: mythological. **-tologísta**, **-tòlogo**, pl. *—gi*, M.: mythologist.

mítra [Gr.], F.: MITER (cap of high church dignitaries).

mitrá-glia [Fr. *-ille*], F.: grape-shot (mitraille). **-gliáre**, TR.: fire grape-shot (or canister-shot). **-gliáto**, ADJ.: fired at with grape-shot. **-gliatóre**, M., **-gliatríce**, F.: one firing with grape-shot; F.: mitrailleuse (kind of battery-gun).

mitráre, TR.: miter (crown with a miter). ‖**mí-tria** [*-tra*], F.: miter. **-triáre**, TR.: miter (crown with a miter). **-triáto**, ADJ.: mitered (crowned with a miter); M. PL.: the mitered (prelates).

mittènte [L. *mittere*], ADJ.: sending forth (Eng.† mittent); M.: sender (dispatcher).

mívolo†, M.: drinking glass.

mne-mònica [Gr. *-monikós*], F.: mnemonics (art of aiding the memory). **-mònico**, pl. *—ci*, ADJ.: mnemonic.

mò' [*modo*], M.: manner (way).

mò†, ADV.: now: — —, just now.

moarè [Fr. *moiré*], M.: moire (watered silk).

mòbi-le [L. *-lis*], ADJ.: mobile (MOVable, variable); M.: piece of furniture. **mo-**

bí-lia, F.: furniture. **-liáre**, TR.: furnish (a house). **-liáto**, ADJ.: furnished. **-líno**, *car. dim.* of *-le.* **-líssimo**, ADJ.: very (or most) movable). **-lità**, F.: activity (mobility). **-litáre**, TR.: mobilize (troops, wealth). **-litazióne**, F.: mobilization. **-lizzáre**, TR.: mobilize (troops). **-lménte**, ADV.: actively. **-lóne**, *aug.* of *-le.*

mobo-láto†, ADJ.: rich (wealthy). **mò-bo-le†**, M.: riches (wealth).

mòcca [Ar. harbour *Mokha*], M.: mocha (choice quality of coffee).

mocaiárdo†, M.: haircloth.

moccèca†, M.: ninny (stupid fellow).

moc-cicáglia, **-cicáia**, F.: mucus (of the nose). **-cicáre**, INTR.: snivel. **-ci-chíno**, M.: handkerchief. **-cicóne**, M.: great idiot. **-ciconeríat**, F.: stupidity. **-cicóso**, ADJ.: filthy (with mucus). ||**móc-cio** [L. *mucus*], M.: MUCUS (of the nose). **-cióne**, M.: great idiot. **-cióso**, ADJ.: filthy (with mucus). **-coláia**, F.: candle-snuff. **-colétto**, **-colíno**, *dim.* of *-colo.* **mòc-colo**, M.: piece of candle; tip of the nose†. **-colóne**, M.: great idiot.

mòco [Gr. *môkos*], M.: kind of pulse (for cattle).

mò-da, F.: mode (fashion; custom): *alla —*, fashionable. **-dáccia**, *disp.* of *-da.* **-dáccio**, *disp.* of *-do.* **-dále**, ADJ.: modal. **-dalità**, F.: modality. **-dana-túra**, F.: moulding. **-'dano**, M.: model (mould, pattern, module, measure); netting-mesh. **-dèlla**, F.: model (of an artist). **-dellábile**, ADJ.: modelable. **-della-ménto**, M.: modelling. **-delláre**, TR.: model (mould, fashion). **-delláto**, ADJ.: modeled (formed, fashioned). **-dellató-re**, M., **-dellatríce**, F.: modeller. **-del-latúra**, F.: modelling. **-dellétto**, **-del-líno**, *car. dim.* of *-dello.* **-dèllo**, M.: model (pattern, example). **-deraménto†**, M., **-derànza†**, F.: moderation. **-derá-re**, TR.: moderate (restrain, repress); REFL.: restrain one's self. **-deratamén-te**, ADV.: moderately. **-deratézza**, F.: moderateness (temperateness). **-de-ratívo**, ADJ.: moderating. **-deráto**, ADJ.: moderate (temperate, restrained). **-deratóre**, M., **-deratríce**, F.: moderator. **-derazióne**, F.: moderation (restraint, temperance). **-dernamén-te**, ADV.: recently (lately, Eng.† modernly). **-dernità**, F.: modernness (recentness, novelty). **-dèrno**, ADJ.: modern (recent, late). **-destaménte**, ADV.: modestly (discreetly). **-dèstia**, F.: modesty (discretion, bashfulness). **-destís-simo**, ADJ.: very (or most) modest. **-dèsto**, ADJ.: modest (discreet, unobtrusive). **-dicíssimo**, ADJ.: very (or most) small. **mò-dico**, pl. *—ci*, ADJ.: small (slight, moderate). **-dificábile**, ADJ.: modifiable. **-dificáre**, TR.: modify (vary, change). **-dificánte**, ADJ.: modifying; M.: modification. **-dificatívo**, ADJ.: modificative (qualifying). **-dificazióne**, F.: modification (variation, changing). **-diglioncíno**, *dim.* of *-diglione.* **-di-glióne**, M.: modillion (bracket under cornice of Corinth. entablature). **-diná-re**, TR.: model (shape). **-dinatúra**, F., **-'dine**, M.: model (mould, pattern, module). **-díno**, *car. dim.* of *-do.* **mò-dio†**, M.: bushel. **-dísta**, F.: modiste (milliner). ||**mò-do** [L. *-dus*], M.: mode (manner, means, custom): *a —*, nice; *a ogni —*, by all means; *in — che*, so that; *oltre —*, excessively; *far in —*, endeavour. **mò-dula**, F.: model (of writing). **-du-láre**, TR.: modulate (inflect). **-dulata-ménte**, ADV.: in a modulated manner. **-duláto**, ADJ.: modulated (inflected). **-dulatóre**, M., **-dulatríce**, F.: modulator. **-dulazióne**, F.: modulation. **mò-dulo**, M.: model (of writing); mould (frame); module (a measure).

moèrre = *moarè.*

mo-fèta [Fr. *-fette*], F.: mephitism (offensive exhalations). **-fètico**, pl. *—ci*, ADJ.: mephitic (poisonous).

mògano = *mogogano.*

mog-giáta, F.: Italian acre. ||**mòg-gio** [L. *modius*], M.: bushel.

mògio [?], ADJ.: stupid (sleepy, dull).

mó-gliama†, F.: my wife. **-'gliata†**, F.: thy wife. ||**mó-glie** [L. *mulier*], F.: wife. **-glièra†**, **-glière†**, F.: wife. **-gliésco**, ADJ.: like a wife. **-gliétta**, **-glína**, *car. dim.* of *-glie.*

mo-gògano, **-gògon** [S. Amer.], M.: MAHOGANY (wood).

moí-na [?], F.: caresses (flattery, cajolery). **-nière†**, M.: flatterer (cajoler).

mò-la [L.], F.: MILL-stone; mole (fleshy matter). **-láre**, ADJ.: molar (grinding); M.: molar (tooth).

mólcere [L. *mulcere*], DEFECT.§; TR.: soften (soothe, alleviate, moderate).

§ Pres. *mól-ci, -ce.* Impf. *-ceva*, (Subj. *-cesse*). Ger. *-cèndo.*

mò-le [L. *-les*, mass], F.: mass (pile); massive structure; mausoleum; size. **-lè-cola**, F.: molecule (invisible particle). **-lecolàre**, ADJ.: molecular.

molènda [L. *molere*, MILL], F.: miller's fee.

mole-staménte, ADV.: troublingly (annoyingly). **-staménto**, M.: molestation (annoyance). **-stáre**, TR.: molest (trouble, annoy). **-statóra**, F., **-statóre**, M., **-statríce**, F.: molester. **-stévole†**,

ADJ.: troublesome (molestful). **molè-stia**, F.: molestation (annoyance, vexation). ‖**molè-sto** [L. *-stus* (*moles*, mass)], ADJ.: molestful (troublesome, annoying).

mo-linèllo = *mulinello*. ‖**-líno** [L. *-lina*], M.: MILL.

mòl-la, F.: (elastic) spring; catch; PL.: fire-tongs. **-láccio**†, *disp.* of *-la*. **-láme**†, M.: soft flesh. **-láre**, TR.: slacken (loosen); INTR.: desist (cease). ‖**mòl-le** [L. *-lis*, soft], ADJ.: soaked; soft (tender; effeminate): *mettere in* —, soak. **-leggiaménto**, M.: pliancy. **-leggiáre**, INTR.: be pliant (flex). **-leménte**, ADV.: gently (softly); weakly. **-létta**, *dim.* of *-la;* PL.: pincers. **-lettína**, *car. dim.* of *-letta*. **-lézza**, F.: softness; delicacy; effeminacy. **mòl-li**†, F. PL.: fire-tongs. **-líca**, F.: crumb (of bread). **-líccio**, **-licèllo**, ADJ.: rather soft. **-lificaménto**, M.: mollifying. **-lificáre**, TR.: mollify (soften). **-lificatívo**, ADJ.: assuaging (mollient). **-lificazióne**, F.: mollification (softening). **-líre**†, TR.: mollify; enervate. **-litívo**†, ADJ.: assuaging (mollient). **-lízie**†, F.: softness; delicacy; effeminacy. **-lóre**†. **-lúme**, M.: dampness (from rain). **-lúsco**, M.: mollusk. **-luscòide**, M.: molluscoid (resembling the true mollusks).

mòlo [L. *-les*, mass], M.: MOLE (of a port; harbour).

molòsso [L. district *Molossus*], M.: mastiff (watchdog).

mòlsa†, F.: pith; marrow: crumb (of bread).

moltéplice [L. *multi-plex*], ADJ.: multiplex (manifold)

molti- = *molto*.

moltíccio†, M.: mud (mire).

molti=floríto, ADJ.: many-flowered (multiflorous). **=fórme**, ADJ.: multiform. **-látero**, ADJ.: many-sided (multi-lateral). **-lòquio**, M.: talkativeness (multiloquence).

moltí-paro†, ADJ.: multiparous (producing many). **-plicábile**, ADJ.: multipliable. **-plicamento**†, M.: multiplication. **-plicándo**, M.: (*arith.*) multiplicand. **=plicáre**, TR.: multiply (increase). **-plicánte**, ADJ.: multiplying. **-plicataménte**, ADV.: in various manners. **-plicatóre**, M.: multiplier. **-plicazióne**, F.: multiplication. **moltí-plice** [L. *multi-plex*], ADJ.: multiplex (numerous, various). **-pliceménte**, ADV.: in great quantity. **-plicità**, F.: multiplicity. **moltí-plico**†, M.: multiplication. **mól-tiplo**, M.: multiple. **=sonánte**, ADJ.: [illegible] of sound (multisonous). **-túdine** [*multitudo*], F.: multitude (numerous-throng).

[illegible] [L. *multus*], ADJ.: much (many, great); ADV.: much (greatly, very), M.: much (great quantity).

momen-táccio, *disp.* of *-to*. **-taneaménte**, ADV.: in a moment. **-táneo**, ADJ.: momentary (fleeting). **-tíno**, *car. dim.* of *-to*. ‖**momén-to** [L. *-tum*], M.: moment (instant, importance, motion).

mómmo [echoic], M.: (*child.*) drink.

mòna-ca, F.: nun; kind of plum. **-cále**, ADJ.: monastic (monachal). **-calménte**, ADV.: monastically. **-cánda**, F.: novice. **-cáre**†, TR.: make a nun; REFL.: become a nun. **-cáto**, M.: monastic life. **-cazióne**, F.: taking the veil. **-chétto**, M.: latch-catch: *dim.*† of *-co*. **-chíle**, ADJ.: monastic. **-chína**, *dim* of *-ca*. **-chíno**, M.: *dim.* of *-co;* man with thin voice; bulfinch. **-chísmo**, M.: monachism. **-cíle**†, ADJ.: monastic. ‖**mòna-co** [Gr. *-chos* (*mónos*, alone)], M.: MONK; bulfinch.

mònade [Gr. *monás*], F.: monad (indivisible thing).

monár-ca [Gr. *mónos*, alone, *árchein*, rule], M.: monarch. **-cále**†, ADJ.: monarchical. **-cáto**, M.: rank of a monarch. **-chía**, F.: monarchy (government, country). **-chicaménte**, ADV.: monarchically. **monár-chico**, pl. —*ci*, ADJ.: monarchical.

mo-nastèrio† [L. *-nasterium*], M.: monastery (cloister). **-nasticaménte**, ADV.: monastically. **-nástico**, pl. —*ci*, ADJ.: monastical.

mon-cheríno, M.: handless arm. **-chéz-za**, F.: maimedness (one-handedness). **-chíno**, M.: handless arm. ‖**món-co** [*manco*], ADJ.: one-handed (maimed); M.: one-handed person. **-cóne**†, M.: handless arm.

mon-dáccio, *disp.* of *-do*. **-daménte**, ADV.: cleanly (neatly). **-daménto**, M.: paring (peeling); polishing†; cleaning†. **-danaménte**, ADV: in a worldly manner (mundanely). **-daníssimo**, ADJ.: very (or most) worldly. **-danità**, F.: worldliness. **-dáno**, ADJ.: worldly (mundane); M.: worldly man. **-dáre**, TR.: pare (peel); skin; polish (mulberry leaves), sift; cleanse†. **-dáto**, ADJ.: pared; polished; clean, pure. **-datóre**, M., **-datríce**, F.: peeler; polisher; cleaner. **-datúra**, F.: peeling; cleaning (time and expense considered); peelings. **-dazióne**†, F.: peeling; sifting; cleaning. **-dézza**, F.: cleanness (purity). **-dezzáio**, M.: dumps. **-día**†, F.: cleanness (purity). **-diále**, ADJ.: worldly (mundane). **-dificaménto**, M.: cleansing (purifying). **-dificáre**†, TR., INTR.: cleanse (Eng.† mundify). **-dificatívo**†, ADJ.: cleansing (mundificative). **-dificazióne**†, F.: cleansing (mundification). **-díglia**, F.: parings; husks;

refuse. **-dína**, F.: chestnut (boiled without husk). **-dízia**, F.: cleanness (neatness, purity). ‖**món-do** [L. *mundus*], ADJ.: clean (neat, pure); polished; M.: world (universe, human race); great quantity.
monduáldo [Ger. *munt-walt*, 'guardian-power'], M.: guardian; permit for a woman to dispose of her dowry.
monel-loría, F.: roguery (mischievousness). **-lésco**, ADJ.: roguish. **-líno**, *dim.* of *-lo*. ‖**monèl-lo** [?], ADJ.: roguish (mischievous); M.: rogue; urchin (gamin). **-luccíáccio**, *disp.* of *-luccio*. **-lúccio**, *disp.* of *-lo*.
moné-ta [L.], F.: MONEY (coin): — *bianca*, silver money. **-táccia**, *disp.* of *-ta*. **-tággio**, M.: minting (coining). **-táre**, TR.: mint (coin). **-tário**, ADJ.: monetary; M.: coiner. **-táto**, ADJ.: minted (coined). **-tazióne**, F.: monetization. **-tière**, M.: coiner (minter). **-tína**, *car. dim.* of *-ta*.
mongána†, F.: milk-fed calf.
mongolfièra [inventor *Montgolfier*], F.: montgolfier (hot-air balloon).
moníle [L.], M.: necklace.
monimíento†, M.: monument (tomb).
monipòlio† = *monopolio*.
monistèrio† = *monastero*.
mòni-to [L. *-tum*], M.: admonition (reproof). **-tóre**, M.: monitor (name of some newspapers, adviser). **-toriále**, ADJ.: admonitory (reproving). **-tòrio**, M.: monitory letter (sent out by ecclesiastical judge). **-zióne**, F.: admonition (warning).
món-na [*madonna*], F.: dame†; ape†: (*fig.*) in *pigliar la* —, get drunk; *esser cotto com' una* —, be dead drunk. **-níno**†, *dim.* of *-na*. **-nóne**†, *aug.* of *-na*. **-nosíno**†, ADJ.: gracious; cheerful. **-núccia**, *dim.* of *-na*.
mono- [Gr. *mónos*, single]: -'**colo** = *-culo*. =**còrdo**, M.: monochord (musical instrument). **monò-culo** [L. *oculus*, EYE], ADJ.: one-eyed; M.: one-eyed person. **-día**, F.: monody (funeral song sung by one voice). **-gamía**, F.: monogamy. **monò-gamo**, M.: monogamist. **-grafía**, F.: monograph. **-gráfico**, pl. —*ci*, ADJ.: monographic. **-grafista**, M.: monographer. **-grámma**, M.: monogram. **-grammático**, pl. —*ci*, ADJ.: monogrammatic. **-líto**, M.: monolith (pillar, etc., of one stone). **monò-logo**, M.: monologue (soliloquy). **-manía**, F.: monomania (insanity). **-maníaco**, pl. —*ci*, ADJ.: monomaniac. **-metallismo**, M.: monometalism. **monò-metro**, ADJ.: monometric; M.: monometer. **monò-mio**, M.: monomial (algebraic expression). **-pòlio**, M.: monopoly. **-polista**, M.: monopolist. **-rímmo**, M.: monorhyme. **-sillábico**, pl. —*ci*, ADJ.: monosyllabic. =**síllabo**, M.: monosyllable. **-tonía**, F.: monotony. **monò=tono**, ADJ.: monotonous.
monsi-gnoráto, M.: dignity of a lord. ‖**-gnóre** [Fr. *mon seigneur*], M.: monsignore (prelate's title); my lord (title).
monsóni [Ar.], M. PL.: monsoon (winds).
món-ta [*-tare*], F.: mounting; elevation (rise); (of animals) covering (copulation); stud. **-tágna**, F.: mountain. **-tagnáccia**, *disp.* of *-tagna*. **-tagnétta**, *car. dim.* of *-tagna*. **-tagníno**†, ADJ.: mountainous. **-tagnòla**, *dim.* of *-tagna*. **-tagnòlo**, ADJ.: pertaining to a mountain. **-tagnóso**, ADJ.: mountainous. **-tagnuòla**, *dim.* of *-tagna*. **-tambánco**†, M.: mountebank. **-taménto**†, M.: mounting (ascending). **-tanáro**, M.: mountaineer; ADJ.: mountain. **-tanèllo**†, M.: tom-tit (bird). **-tanésco**†, ADJ.: of mountains. **-tanína**, F.: mountaineer. **-taníno**, ADJ.: of mountains; M.: mountaineer. **-táno**, ADJ.: (*poet.*) mountainous; of a mountain. **-tánza**†, F.: ascent; height; dignity. **-táre**, INTR.: mount (ascend); be of consequence; exalt†; TR.: increase (raise): — *in furore*, get angry. **-tánte**, ADJ.: amounting. **-táta**, F.: ascent (mounting). **-tatóio**, M.: mounting-block (or step). **-tatóre**, M.: mounter. **-tatúra**, F.: mounting (embellishment). ‖**món-te** [L. *mons*], M.: mountain; mass (heap, great quantity): — *di pietà*, pawnbroker's (loan office); *a -ti*, in great quantity. **-ticellíno**†, *dim.* of *-cello*. **-ticèllo**, *dim.* of *-te*. **-ticíno**, *car. dim.* of *-te*. **-tièra**†, F.: child's cap.
monton-cèllo, *dim.* of *-e*. **-cíno**, *car. dim.* of *-e*. ‖**montón-e** [?], M.: ram (wether); battering-ram; French coin; stupid man†.
mon-tuosità, F.: mountainousness. ‖**-tuóso** [*-te*], ADJ.: mountainous.
montúra [Fr. *-ture*], F.: mounting (equipment).
monu-mentále, ADJ.: monumental. ‖**-ménto** [L. *-mentum*], M.: monument (memorial).
monzicchio†, M.: small heap.
mòra 1 [L.], F.: delay (pause); mora (unit of length in prosody).
mòra 2 [?], F.: 'how many fingers do I hold up?' (a game).
mò-ra† 3 [*-ro* 2], F.: mulberry; blackberry; heap of stones. **-raiuòla**, F.: mulberry (fruit).
moraiòlo [*moro*], M.: kind of olive-tree.
morá-le [L. *-lis*], ADJ.: moral; M.: morals; F.: morality. **-lísta**, M.: moralist. **-lità**, F.: morality. **-lizzáre**, INTR.:

moralize; TR.: render moral. **-lizza-zióne**, F.: moralizing (moralization). **-lménte**, ADV.: morally.

moránza†, F.: delay (stay).

moráto [*mora* 3], ADJ.: of blackberry colour.

morbi-daménte, ADV.: delicately; weakly; effeminately. **-daménto**†, M.: softening; effeminacy. **-détto**, *car. dim.* of *-do*. **-dézza**, F.: delicacy; softness; effeminacy (wantonness). ‖**mòrbi-do** [L. *-dus*, sickly], ADJ.: delicate; soft (yielding, gentle); effeminate (wanton); sweet. **-dóne**, *aug.* of *-do*. **-dòtto**, *dim.* of *-do*.

mor-bífero, **-bífico**, pl. —*ci*, ADJ.: causing disease (morbific). **-bigliónе**†, M.: measles. **-bíllo**, M.: sickness (like measles). **-billóso**, ADJ.: resembling measles (morbillous). **-bíno**†, M.: wantonness. **-bisciáttо**†, ADJ.: sickly (weak). ‖**mòr-bo** [L. *-bus*], M.: disease (pestilence): — *sacro*, epilepsy; — *regio*, jaundice. **-bosaménte**, ADV.: by disease. **-bóso**, ADJ.: contagious; diseased (morbose).

mòr-chia [L. *amurca*], F.: dregs (of oil). **-chiáio**, ADJ.: containing dregs (of olive oil); M.: kind of olive. **-chióso**, ADJ.: full of dregs. **-chiáme**, M.: great quantity of dregs. **mòr-cia**†, F.: dregs (of oil).

mor-dácchia, F.: muzzle (noseband). **-dáce**, ADJ.: biting (sharp, sarcastic, mordaceous). **-daceménte**, ADV.: bitingly (mordaciously). **-dacétto**, *dim.* of *-dace*. **-dacità**, F.: sharpness (mordacity). **-dènte**, ADJ.: biting (sarcastic). ‖**mòr-dere** [L.], IRR.§; TR.: bite; censure (satirize). **-dicaménto**†, M.: biting (corroding). **-dicáre**†, TR.: corrode. **-dicatívo**†, ADJ.: corrosive. **-dicazióne**†, F.: biting (corrosion, mordication). **-digallína**†, F.: chickweed (weed). **-diménto**, M.: bite; censure (sarcasm). **-ditóre**, M., **-ditríce**, F.: biter; slanderer. **-ditúra**†, F.: slander. **-dúto**†, ADJ.: bitten.

§ Pret. *mòr-si*, *-se*; *sero*. Part. *mòr-so*.

morèlla† 1, F.: nightshade (morel).

morèlla† 2, F.: quoit.

mo-rellíno, *car. dim.* of *-rello*. ‖**-rèllo** [*moro*], ADJ.: black; M.: dark coat (of horses, mules, etc.).

morèna [?], F.: moraine (stones, etc., on the sides of glaciers).

mo-résca, F.: morris-dance. ‖**-résco** [*Moro*], ADJ.: Moorish. **-rétta**, *car. dim.* of *-ra*. **-rettína**, *car. dim.* of *-retta*. ...**to**, *dim.* of *-ro*.

...**a**†, F.: scurf; leprosy.

..., F.: mouth.

...**a** [L. *Morpheus*, god of sleep], F.: ...**o** (alkaloid of opium).

morfíre†, TR.: eat (devour).

morfo-logía [Gr. *morphé*, form], F.: morphology (science). **-lògico**, pl. —*ci*, ADJ.: morphological.

morga-náto†, ADJ.: noble (lordly); M.: lordship. ‖**-nático**, pl. —*ci* [? Ger. *morgen*, morn], ADJ.: morganatic (left-handed, viz. marriage).

morí-a [*morire*], F.: pestilence (deadly plague). **-bóndo**, ADJ.: dying (moribund); M.: dying person.

moríccia [?], F.: ruins.

mo-ríce† or **-ríci**, F. PL.: piles.

moricíno†, *dim.* of *moro*.

morige-ráre† [L. *-ror* (*mos*, manner)], TR.: tutor (bring up). **-ratézza**, F.: good manners. **-ráto**, ADJ.: well-bred.

morion-cèllo, **-cíno** *dim.* of *-e*. ‖**morión-e** [Sp. *morrión*], M.: morion (open helmet).

morí-re [L. *-ri*], IRR.§; INTR.: die (expire, go out). **-tóio**†, ADJ.: mortal. **-túro**, ADJ.: dying (about to die).

§ Ind.: Pres. *m(u)òio*, *m(u)òri*, *m(u)òre*; *moriámo* or *moiámo*, *moríte*, *m(u)òiono*. Fut. *morrò* (rarely *morirò*). Cond. *morrèi* (*morirèi*). Subj.: Pres. *m(u)òia*; *moriámo* or *moiámo*, *moriáte*, *m(u)òiano*. Part. *mòrto*.— Poet. forms: *mòro*, *-ri*, *-re*; *-ra*; *mòrano*.

mormo-racchiáre, INTR.: murmur a little. **-raménto**†, M.: murmur; buzzing. ‖**-ráre** [L. *murmurare*], INTR.: murmur (slander, grumble); TR.: murmur (say in a low voice). **-ránte**, ADJ.: murmuring. **-ráto**, ADJ.: murmured. **-ratóre**, M., **-ratríce**, F.: murmurer (grumbler). **-razióne**, F.: murmuring (slander). **-reggiáre**†, INTR.: murmur (grumble). **-révole**†, ADJ.: murmuring (slandering). **-río**, M.: murmur (whisper, complaint).

mòro 1 [L. *maurus*], M.: Moor.

mòro 2 [L. *-rum*], M.: mulberry tree.

moròi-de, **-di** = *emorroidi*.

mòrola†, F.: mulberry (fruit).

mo-rosaménte, ADV.: tardily (with delay). ‖**-róso** 1 [L. *mora*, delay], ADJ.: tardy (delaying, slow).

moróso 2 = *amoroso*.

mòr-sa, F.: screw-vise; muzzle; corner-stone (of a building). **-secchiáre**†, TR.: bite (nibble). **-secchiatúra**†, F.: biting; mark (of biting). **-seggiáre**†, TR., INTR.: nibble. **-sellétto**, *car. dim.* of *-sello*. **-sèllo**, *dim.* of *-so*. **-sétto**, *car. dim.* of *-so*. **mòr-si**, PRET. of *-dere*. **-sicáre**, TR.: bite (*dim.*: sting). **-sicáto**, ADJ.: bitten (nibbled); M.: thing bitten. **-sicatúra**, F.: biting; mark (of a bite). **-síno**, *dim.* of *-so*. ‖**mòr-so** [*mordere*], ADJ.: bitten; M.: bite (mouthful); mark (of a bite); curb (bit); grappling part (of pinchers); remorse†. **-súra**†, F.: bite; smart.

morta-dèlla, F., **-dèllo†**, M.: bologna-sausage. **-iétto**, *dim.* of *-io*. **-íno**, *car. dim.* of *-io*. ‖**mortá-io** [L. *-rium*], M.: MORTAR (vessel, piece of ordnance). **-ióne**, *aug.* of *-io*.
mortále [L. *-lis*], ADJ.: mortal (deadly); M.: mortal (human being).
mortalétto, *dim.* of *mortaio*.
mor-talità, F.: mortality. **-talménte**, ADV.: mortally (desperately). **-taménte**, ADV.: like a dead man. ‖**mòr-te** [L. *mors*], F.: death.
mortèl-la [Gr. *múrtos*], F.: myrtle. **-létta**, **-lína**, *dim.* of *-la*. **-lóne**, M.: myrtle (with large leaves).
mor-ticcio† [*-te*], ADJ.: half-dead. **-ticína**, **-ticíno**, *car. dim.* of *-to*. **-tiferaménte**, ADV.: in a deadly way. **-tífero**, ADJ.: deadly (fatal, mortiferous). **-tificaménto†**, M.: mortification. ‖**-tificáre** [L.], TR.: mortify (humble, vex, subdue); REFL.: be mortified (humble one's self). **-tificatívo†**, ADJ.: mortifying. **-tificáto**, ADJ.: with mortification†. **-tificazióne**, F.: mortification.
mor-tína†, **-tíne†**, F.: myrtle.
mòr-to [L. *-tuus*], ADJ.: dead (deceased); put out; miserable; M.: corpse (dead man): *acqua -ta*, stagnant water. **-tòrio**, M.: funeral (services). **-tuário**, ADJ.: mortuary (pertaining to burials); M.: pall-bearer.
morvid.. = *morbid..*
morviglióne [*morbillo*], M.: measles.
mo-saicísta, M.: worker in mosaic. ‖**-sáico**, pl. *—ci* [l. L. *-saicus*], M.: mosaic.
mósca [L. *musca*], F.: fly (insect); mole; goatee (imperial): — *cieca*, blindman's-buff; *saltar la —*, be offended; get angry; —*!* hush!
mosca-dáto†, ADJ.: musked. **-dèlla**, F.: muscadel (sweet wine-grapes). **-dellétto**, **-dellíno**, *dim.* of *-dello*. **-dèllo**, M.: muscadel (wine, grapes); ADJ.: muscadel. ‖**moscá-do** [l. L. *muschatus*], ADJ.: of musk; M.: kind of wine.
moscá-io [*mosca*], M.: great number of flies; wearisome thing. **-iòla**, F.: food-safe; fly-trap.
mo-scardíno [*muschio*], M.: dandy (fop). **-scatèllo**, M.: muscatel (wine, grapes). **-scáto** 1, ADJ.: *noce -scata*, nutmeg; muscat (wine); M.†: musk.
mo-scáto 2 [*mosca*], ADJ.: dapple-gray. **-sceríno**, M.: gnat (small fly).
moschè-a [fr. Ar.], F.: mosque (Mohammedan temple). **-áccia**, *disp.* of *-a*.
mosche-réccio, ADJ.: of flies. **-ríno**, M.: small fly. ‖**mosché-tta** [*mosca*], F.: *dim.* of *mosca*; dart (16th Cent.). **-ttáre**, TR.: shoot. **-ttáta**, F.: musket-blow. **-ttáto**, ADJ.: specked (spotted, dappled). **-ttatúra**, F.: dappledness. **-ttería**, F.: body of musketeers (Eng.† musketry). **-ttière**, M.: musketeer. **-ttína**, *dim.* of *mosca*. **mosché-tto**, M.: MUSKET (short fire-arm); arquebus. **-ttóne**, M.: blunderbuss; clasp (of watch-chain).
mo-schína, **-schíno†**, *dim.* of *-sca*.
mosciáme [*moscio*], M.: kind of sausage.
moscíno [*mosca*], M.: small fly.
móscio [? *mucido*], ADJ.: flabby (soft).
moscióne 1 [*mosca*], M.: small fly (inside casks, etc.); tippler (drunkard).
moscióne 2 [*moscio*], M.: old chestnut.
moscoleáto†, ADJ.: musked.
móscolo † = *muscolo* or *muschio*.
mosco-náccio, *disp.* of *-ne*. **-ncèllo**, **-ncíno**, *dim.* of *-ne*. ‖**moscó-ne**, M.: *aug.* of *mosca*; hornet.
mòs-sa, F.: movement (motion); gesture; act. **-sáccia**, *disp.* of *-sa*. **mòs-se**, F. PL.: starting-post (beginning). **-sétta**, *dim.* of *-sa*. **-settína**, *car. dim.* of *-setta*. **mòs-si**, PRET. of *movere*. ‖**mòsso**, PART. of *movere*: moved (stirred).
mossolína [city *Mosul*], F.: muslin (cloth).
mostác-chi, M. PL.: whiskers. **-ciáccio†**, *disp.* of *-cio*. **-ciáta†**, F.: blow on the face. **-císo**, *car. dim.* of *-cio*. ‖**mostác-cio** [Gr. *mústax*, mustache], M.: (*disp.* big, fat) face; snout; mustache†: *dirle sul —*, tell it frankly.
mostac-ciolétto, *dim.* of *-ciolo*. ‖**-ciòlo** [L. *mustaceus*], M.: cake (of spice and nuts).
mostaccióne, M.: *aug.* of *-ccio*; slap on the face.
mostacciuòlo† = *mostacciolo*.
mostacciúzzo†, *dim.* of *mostaccio*.
mos-táio, M.: grape (producing must); ADJ.: of the must-producing grape. **-tárda**, F.: mustard. **-tardièra**, F.: mustard-dish. **-tardína**, *car. dim.* of *-tarda*. ‖**mós-to** [L. *mustum*], M.: must (unfermented grape-juice). **-tóso**, ADJ.: of (or like) must.
mós-tra, F.: show (display, pretence); appearance; sample; show-window; dial-plate. **-trábile**, ADJ.: showable. **-traménto**, M.: showing (demonstration). **-tránza†**, F.: showing. ‖**-tráre** [L. *monstrare*], TR.: show (deMONSTRATE, reveal, teach); REFL.: appear (seem). **-tráto**, ADJ.: shown (demonstrated). **-tratóre**, M., **-tratríce**, F.: demonstrator. **-trazióne†**, F.: demonstration; display. **-treggiáto**, ADJ.: lapelled. **-treggiatúra**, F.: lapel. **-tricína**, *car. dim.* of *-tra*.
mó-stro [L. *monstrum* (*monere*, warn)], M.: monster (terrible creature, marvel). **-stróso†**, ADJ.: monstrous (strange). **-struosaménte**, ADV.: monstrously (

naturally). **-struosità**, F.: monstrosity. **-struóso**, ADJ.: monstrous (strange).

mò-ta [*malta*], F.: mud (mire). **-tác-cio**, M.: deep mud.

mo-terèllo, *dim.* of *moto*. **-tiva†**, F.: motive (cause). **-tiváre**, TR.: explain (declare, allege). **-tívo**, M.: motive (incentive, cause); ADJ.†: motive. ‖**mò-to** [*-vere*], M.: movement (motion); impulse: *di proprio* —, of one's own accord. **-to-pròprio**, M.: voluntary decree (of a prince). **-tóre**, M.: mover; promoter; ADJ.: moving.

motóso [*mota*], ADJ.: muddy.

motríce, F. of *-tore*.

mòtta†, F.: lump (of earth).

motteg-gévole, ADJ.: merry (jesting). **-gevolménte**, ADV.: merrily (jestingly). **-giaménto**, M.: jesting (raillery). ‖**-giá-re** [*motto*], INTR.: jest (joke); TR.: vex (with sharp words). **-giatóre**, M., **-gia-tríce**, F.: jester (banterer). **mottég-gio**, M.: jest (raillery). **-gióso†**, ADJ.: merry (jesting).

mot-tétto, M.: *dim.* of *-to;* motet (verse, vocal composition). ‖**mòt-to** [L. *muttum* (*mutire*, mutter)], M.: motto; jest (joke); word†; any kind of poetical composition. **-tázzo†**, *dim.* of *-to*.

motupròprio†, M.: voluntary decree.

mo-vènte, ADJ.: moving; M.: motive. **-vènza**, F.: graceful movement. ‖**mò-vere** [L.], IRR.§; TR.: move (remove, instigate, induce); INTR.: come forth (bud); depart; REFL.: be agitated; turn (revolve). **-vévole†**, **-víbile**, ADJ.: movable. **-vi-ménto**, M.: movement (agitation, manœuvre). **-vitíva†**, F.: cause. **-vití-vo†**, ADJ.: moving (unsteady); M.: cause. **-zióne**, F.: motion (movement, proposition); tumult (commotion)†.

§ Pop. *muòv-*; lit. *muòv-* (accented): Pres. *m(u)òvo*, *-vi*, *-ve*; *moviámo*, etc. Pret. *mòvvi*; or *móss-i*, *-e*; *-ero*. Part. *mòsso*.

moz-zaménte, ADV.: in a cutting (mutilating) manner. **-zaménto**, M.: cutting off (maiming). ‖**-záre** [? L. *mutilare*], TR.: cut off (mutilate, truncate, take away, abbreviate). **-záto**, ADJ.: cut off. **-zatú-ra**, F.: cuttings. **-zétta**, F.: cape. **-zi-códa†**, ADJ.: docked. **-zicóne**, M.: remainder (broken-off part). **-zína†**, ADJ.: cunning (sharp, crafty). **móz-zo¹**, ADJ.: cut off (mutilated).

[L. *mustus*, young], M.: stable-
-boy.
modius], M.: hub (of wheel).
[-*zare*], M.: end of a whip.
, M.: dog (or horse) with
: incompetent lawyer; rogue

milch-cow.

muccería†, F.: nonsense; insult.

múcchero†, M.: rose and violet water.

muc-chierèllo, *car. dim.* of *-chia*. **-chiettíno**, *car. dim.* of *-chietto*. **-chiét-to**, *dim.* of *-chio* ‖**múc-chio** [?], M.: heap (muss).

mucciáre†, TR.: mock (ridicule); avoid; INTR.: make faces.

múc-co [L. *-cus*], M.: mucus. **-cósa**, F.: mucous membrane. **-cosità**, F.: mucousness. **-cóso**, ADJ.: mucous.

mucellággine†, F.: mucilage.

mú-ci†, INTERJ.: puss! **mú-cia**, F.: puss (cat).

múcido [L. *-dus*], ADJ.: musty (mouldy); moist; silly†.

mucillággi-ne [L. *mucilago*], F.: mucilage. **-nóso**, ADJ.: mucilaginous (slimy, moist).

mucíno†, M.: little cat (kitten).

mu-cosità†, F.: sliminess (mucosity). ‖**-cóso†** [L. *-cosus*], ADJ.: mucous.

mú-da, F.: changing (moulting). **-da-gióne†**, F.: change. ‖**-dáre** [L. *-tare*, change], INTR.: moult (mew).

múf-fa [Ger. *muff*], F.: mould (mustiness). **-fáre**, INTR.: grow mouldy. **-faticcio†**, ADJ.: rather mouldy. **-fétto†**, M.: dandy (fop). **-fíre**, INTR.: grow mouldy. **múf-fo†**, ADJ.: mouldy (musty). **-fosità**, F.: mouldiness. **-fóso**, ADJ.: mouldy (musty).

muftì [Ar.], M.: mufti (high-priest of the Mohammedans).

mugávero†, M.: dart; pikeman.

mugellágine†, F.: mucilage.

mug-ghiaménto, M.: lowing (bellowing). ‖**-ghiáre** [*mugolare*], INTR.: low (bellow). **múg-ghio**, M.: lowing (bellowing).

múggine [L. *mugilis*], M.: mullet (fish).

mug-gioláre†, INTR.: bellow (howl). ‖**-gíre** [L. *mugire*], INTR.: low (bellow). **-gíto**, M.: lowing (bellowing).

mugherino, M.: kind of jessamine. ‖**-ghétto** [Fr. *muguet*], M.: lily of the valley.

mu-glioláre†, INTR.: bellow (howl). ‖**-gliáre** [*-golare*], INTR.: low (bellow, roar). **mú-glio**, M.: lowing (bellowing).

mu-gnáia, F.: miller's wife. **-gnaína**, **-gnaíno**, *car. dim.* of *-gnaia*, *-gnaio*. ‖**-gnáio** [L. *molinarius*], M.: MILLER; sea-gull; sea-mew; ADJ.†: of a mill.

mú-gnere†, IRR.; TR.: milk. **-gnitóre†**, M.: milker.

mu-goláre [L. *-gulare*], INTR.: whine; roar (howl); groan. **-golío**, M.: whining; howling; groaning.

múla [L.], F.: mule; slipper†.

mulác-chia†, F.: crow. **-chiáia**, F.: flight of crows; chattering.

mu-lattièra [*mula*], F.: for (or of)

mulea. **-lattière**, M.: mule-driver. **-látto** [cf. *-lo*], M.: mulatto. **-lésco**, ADJ.: mulish (stubborn). **-lètto**, *car. dim.* of *-lo*.

mulíaca†, F.: apricot (fruit).

muliebre [L. *-liebris* (*-lier*, woman)], ADJ.: womanish (of a woman).

muli-náre, INTR.: revolve in one's mind (contemplate). **-nèllo**, M.: windlass; mule (in spinning factories); whirlpool; whirlwind; 'wind-mill' (stick with a revolving card at the end; toy). **-nétto**, *dim.* of *-no*. ||**mulí-no** 1 [= *molino*], M.: mill.

mu-líno 2, ADJ.: of a mule. ||**mú-lo** [L. *-lus*], M.: mule; illegitimate offspring. **-lóna**, *aug.* of *-la*. **-lòtto**, *dim.* of *-lo*.

múlsa†, F.: hydromel (water and honey).

múl-ta [L.], F.: penalty (fine). **-táre**, TR.: fine.

múlti- [L., many]: =**colóre** [L. *color*], ADJ.: multicolour. =**fórme**, ADJ.: multiform. **-lòquio** [L. *loquus*], M.: talkative person. **multí-paro** [L. *parere*, breed], ADJ.: producing many (multiparous). **-plicáre**†, TR.: multiply. **multí-plice** [L. *-plex*,], ADJ.: multiplied. **múltiplo** [L. *-plus*], ADJ.: multiple (manifold); M.: multiple. **-túdine** [L. *-tudo*], F.: multitude (great number).

múmmi-a [fr. Pers.], F.: mummy. **-ficáre**, TR.: mummify (embalm). **-ficazióne**, F.: mummification.

mune-raménto†, M.: remuneration (reward). ||**-ráre**†, TR.: remunerate (reward).

mún-gere [L.], IRR.§; TR.: milk (extract); press. **-gitúra**, F.: milking; milk obtained.

§ Pret. *mún-si, -se; -sero.* Part. *múnto.*

muni-cipále, ADJ.: municipal. **-cipalità**, F.: municipality (district). ||**-cípio** [L. *-cipium*, town], M.: government (of a city); municipal residence; free town.

munifi-caménte, ADV.: munificently (liberally). **-cènte**, ADJ.: munificent (liberal). **-cènza**, **-cènzia**, F.: munificence (generosity, bounty). ||**muní-fico**, pl. *—ci* [L. *-ficus* (*munus*, gift, *facere*, make)], ADJ.: munificent (bounteous, liberal).

muniménto†, M.: monument.

mu-níre [L. (*mœnia*, wall)], TR.: provide; fortify (Eng.† munite). **-níto**, ADJ.: provided (fortified). **-nizióne**, F.: provision (ammunition). **-nizionière**, M.: furnisher; quartermaster.

múno†, M.: (*poet.*) gift (present).

mún-si, PRET. of *mungere*. **mún-to**, ADJ.: milked (extracted, drained).

munúscolo†, *dim.* of *muno*.

muòvere = *movere*.

mú-ra [*-ro*], F. PL.: walls (of city, house, fortress). **-racchiáre**, TR.: go on building a little. **-ráglia**, F.: long, high wall. **-raglióne**, *aug.* of *-raglia*. **-raiòlo**, ADJ.: of a wall. **-ràle**, ADJ.: mural (pertaining to a wall): *corona —*, mural crown (Roman military reward). **-raménto**, M.: walling (masonry). **-ráre**, TR.: wall (build, protect, enclose); REFL.: shut one's self in. **-rário**, ADJ.: pertaining to walling. **-ráta**†, F.: castle (fortress). **-ráte**, F. PL.: convent; prison (at Florence). **-ráto**, ADJ.: built (walled, enclosed). **-ratóre**, M.: wall-builder (mason). **-ratúra**, F.: wall-building (masonry). **-rázzi**, M. PL.: embankments (of Venetian lagoon).

murèna [L. *murœna*], F.: lamprey (eel-like fish).

mu-rétto [*muro*], *dim.* of *-ro*. **-ricèta**, F.: heap of stones (rude wall). **-ricciolétto**, **-riccíno**, *dim.* of *-ricciolo*. **-ricciòlo**, M.: low wall; stone bench. **-ricciolóne**, *aug.* of *-ricciolo*.

muriáti [L. *muria*, brine], M.: muriate (chemical compound).

múrice [L. *-rex*], F.: murex (genus of mollusks).

muri-cèllo, **-cíno**, *dim.* of *muro*.

murièlla [?], F.: quoit.

múrmure†, M.: murmur.

múro, pl. *-ri* or *-ra* [L. *-rus*], M.: wall (enclosure, Eng.† mure); hindrance (division): *stare a uscio e —*, be neighbours; *mettere i piedi al —*, be obstinate.

múr-ra [L. *-rha*], F.: murrha (costly ware). **-ríno**, ADJ., M.: murrhine.

mú-sa [L.], F.: muse; poetry; bagpipe; ADJ.: *mela —*, winter apple. **-sáccia**, *disp.* of *-sa*. **-sagète**, ADJ.: title of Apollo (leader of Muses). **-saic..** = *mosaic..*

musaròla [*muso*], F.: muzzle (for dogs).

mu-sárdo†, ADJ.: musing, loitering; M.: muser (loiterer). ||**-sáre**†, INTR.: muse; loiter; stare.

musáta [*muso*], F.: blow with the snout; grimace.

mus-cáto, **-chiáto**, ADJ.: musked (tasting of musk). **-chiétto**, M.: musk-pear. ||**mús-chio** [L. *-cus*], M.: musk-deer; musk; moss. **-chióso**, ADJ.: odorous with musk; mossy.

mú-scia†, F.: cat (puss). **-scína**†, F.: kitten.

músco [L. *-cus*], M.: moss.

musco-láre, ADJ.: muscular. **-latúra**, F.: muscular system. **-lazióne**, F.: study of muscular movements. **-leggiaménto**†, M.: muscular system. **-lína**, F.: musculine (organic principle of m cular tissue). **-líno**, *dim.* of *-lo*. ‖**mú-sco-lo** [L. *musculus*], M.: muscle. **-lo-sità**, F.: muscularity. **-lóso**, ADJ.: muscular. **-lúto**, ADJ.: of strong muscles.

muscóso [*musco*], ADJ.: mossy (full of moss).

museo [Gr. *mouseion*], M.: museum.

muso-rágnolo [*muso*, *ragnolo*], M.: shrew(-mouse). **-ròla** [*muso*], F.: muzzle (nose-band).

músi-ca [L.], F.: music; noise (tumult, uproar); musical company. **-cábile**, ADJ.: able to be sung or played. **-cáccia**, *disp.* of *-ca*. **-cále**, ADJ.: musical. **-cal-ménte**, ADV.: musically. **-cánte**, M.: musician. **-cáre**, TR.: put to music; INTR.: sing. **-cáto**, ADJ.: put to music; sung. **-chétto**, **-chíno**, *car. dim.* of *-co*. **-cí-sta**, M.: musician. **músi-co**, pl. —*ci*, M.: musician; ADJ.†: musical. **-cóne**, *aug.* of *-ca*.

mú-so [? L. *morsus*, bite], M.: MUZZLE (mouth, snout); grimace; anger; ADJ.†: musing (pouting). **-solièra**, F.: muzzle (nose-band). **-sóne**, M.: *aug.* of *-so*; pouter. **-sonería**, F.: sulkiness.

musso-lína [city *Mosul*], F.: muslin (cotton cloth). **-líno**†, M.: muslin.

mustác-chi [Gr. *mústax*], M. PL.: moustache. **-chióni**, *aug.* of *-chi*.

mustèla [L.], F.: weasel.

mustiáto [*muschiato*], ADJ.: muskod.

mústio [*muschio* (L. *muscus*)], M.: moss.

musulmáno [Ar. *moslem*], ADJ.: Mussulman (Mahommedan); M.: Mussulman.

mú-ta [*-tare*], F.: change (mutation). **-tá-bile**, ADJ.: changeable (unsteady, mutable). **-tabilità**, F.: change (mutability). **-tabilménte**, ADV.: changeably (mutably). **-taménto**, M.: change (mutation). **-tánde**, F. PL.: drawers. **-tandíne**, *dim.* of *-tande*. **-tánza**†, F.: change. ‖**-táre** [L.], TR.: change (alter, take off); REFL.: change (clothing). **-táto**, ADJ.: changed (altered); M.: thing changed. **-tatóre**, M.: changer. **-tatúra**, F.: changing (of clothes). **-tazioncèlla**, *car. dim.* of *-tazione*. **-tazióne**, F.: change (mutation, alteration). **-tévole**, ADJ.: changeable (mutable). **-tevol-ménte**, ADV.: changeably (mutably).

mutézza [*muto*], F.: muteness (dumbness).

muti-laménto, M.: mutilation. ‖**-láre** [L.], TR.: mutilate (maim). **-láto**, ADJ.: d. **-lataménte**, ADV.: in a nanner. **-latóre**, M., **-latrí-** tilator. **-lazióne**, F.: muti- **ti-lo**, ADJ.: mutilated (said etc.).

M.: muteness. ‖**mú-to** [L. mute (dumb, silent); F.: *let-tera -ta*, mute (letter); ADV.: *alla -ta*, silently. **-tolézza**†, F.: muteness. **-to-lína**, **-tolíno**, *car. dim.* of *-tolo*. **-mú-tolo**, ADJ.: mute (dumb, silent).

mútria [?], F.: grave face.

mu-tuaménte, ADV.: mutually. **-tuán-te**, ADJ.: lending; M.: lender. **-tuatário**, ADJ., M.: borrowing, mutuary (law term); borrower. **-tuazióne**, F.: exchange (Eng.† mutuation). ‖**mú-tuo** [L. *-tuus*], ADJ.: mutual (interchanged); M.: loan of money.

N

n *ènne* [L.], F., M.: n (the letter).

ná-bab or ‖**-bábbo** [Ar. *-báb*], M.: nabob (Indian prince); wealthy man.

na-bissáre†, TR.: swallow. **-bísso**†, M.: abyss.

ná-cchera [fr. Pers.], F.: castanet; nacre (mother-of-pearl). **-ccherétta**, *dim.* of *-cchera*. **-ccheríno**, *car. dim.* of *-cchera*. **-ccheróne**†, *aug.* of *-cchera*. **-cheríno**, M.: *dim.* of *-chero*; *car.* little boy. **ná-chero**, M.: dwarf; bow-legged person.

nácqui, PRET. of *nascere*.

nadír [Ar. *-thir*, opposite], M.: nadir (inferior pole of the horizon).

naffè†, INTERJ.: indeed.

náf-ta [L. *naphtha*], F.: naphtha (bituminous liquid). **-talína**, F.: naphthaline (substance distilled from coal tar).

náiade [L. *naias*], F.: naiad (water-nymph).

náib [Abyss.], M.: chief (prince).

ná-na [*-no*], F.: dwarf. **-nétto**, **-níno**, *dim.* of *-no*.

nánfa†, F.: orange-flower water.

nánna [echoic], F.: lullaby: *far la —*, lull to sleep.

ná-no [L. *-nus*], M.: dwarf. **-nússo**, *disp. dim.* of *-no*.

nánzi†, PREP.: before; in the presence of; ADV.: before (sooner).

na-pèa [Gr. *-paia*], F.: nymph; ADJ.: nymphal. **-pèllo**†, M.: wolf's-bane (poisonous plant).

nápo†, M.: turnip.

napoleóne [*Napoleone*], M.: napoleon (French gold coin worth $3.87).

náp-pa [*mappa*], F.: tassel (ornament): *— di cardinale*, kind of flower. **-pétta**, **-pína**, *car. dim.* of *-pa*.

náp-po [OGer. *hnap*], M.: pitcher; cup; goblet; basin†. **-póne**, *aug.* of *-po*.

narcíso [L. *-cissus*], M.: narcissus (daffodil, jonquil).

narcòtico, pl. —*ci* [Gr. *-ikós* (*nárke*, drowsiness)], ADJ.: narcotic (sleep-producing).

nar-díno, ADJ.: of spikenard. ||**nár-do** [L. *-dus*], M.: spikenard (aromatic plant).
ná-re† [L. *-ris*], F. PL.: nostrils. **ná-ri**, F. PL.: NOstrils. **-ríce**, F.: nostril.
narra-zióne†, F., **-ménto**, M.: narration. ||**narrá-re** [L.], TR.: narrate (relate, tell). **-tíva**, F.: narrative (account). **-tivaménto**, ADV.: narratively (by way of story). **-tívo**, ADJ.: narrative (story-telling). **-tóre**, M.: narrator (relater). **-tòrio†**, ADJ.: narrative. **-tríce**, F.: narrator (relater). **-zioncèlla**, **-zioncína**, *dim.* of *-zione*. **-zióne**, F.: narration (account, story).
narválo [Ger. *-wall* (OGer. *nar*, nose, *wall*, whale)], M.: narwhal (unicorn-whale).
na-sáccio, *disp.* of *-so*. **-sággine**, F.: great nose; person with a big nose. **-sále**, ADJ.: nasal. **-salménto**, ADV.: nasally. **-sáre†**, TR., INTR.: smell. **-sáta**, F.: blow with the nose; refusal (rebuff)†.
na-scènte, ADJ.: NASCENT (coming forth). **-scènza†**, F.: birth; tumour. ||**ná-scere** [L. *-sci*], IRR.§; INTR.: be born; come forth (bud, sprout); appear (show one's self). **-sciménto**, M.: birth (origin). **ná-scita**, F.: birth (race, extraction). **ná-scito†**, M.: birth. **-scitúro**, ADJ.: that will be born. **-sciúto**, ADJ.: (*poet.*): born.

§ Ind.: Pret. *nác-qui, -que; -quero.* Part. *náto.*

nas-cóndere [L. *in-abscondere*], IRR.§; TR.: hide (secrete, conceal). **-condévole†**, ADJ.: concealable. **-condíglio**, **-condígliolo**, **-condigliuòlo†**, M.: hiding-place. **-condiménto**, M.: hiding. **-conditóre**, M., **-conditríce**, F.: hider (concealer). **-cosaménte**, ADV.: secretly (stealthily). **-cósi**, PRET. of *-condere*. **-cóso**, ADJ.: hidden (secret, concealed). **-costaménte**, ADV.: secretly (stealthily). **-cósto**, ADJ.: hidden (concealed, secret).

§ Ind.: Pret. *nascó-si, -se; -sero.* Part. *nascósto*, rare *nascóso.*

na-sèllo, M.: bolt (catch); kind of fish. **-sétto**, *dim.* of *-so*. **-sièra**, F.: iron nose-band (for oxen). **-síno**, *car. dim.* of *-so*. ||**ná-so** [L. *-sus*], M.: nose. **-sóne**, M.: *aug.* of *-so*; man with large nose.
náspo [OGer. *haspa*], M.: reel (winder).
nássa [L.], F.: bow-net; phial.
násso†, M.: yew-tree.
na-stráia, F., **-stráio**, M.: ribbon-maker (or seller). **-strièra**, F.: knot of ribbons. **-stríno**, *car. dim.* of *-stro*; book-mark (of ribbon). ||**ná-stro** [OGer. *nèstila*], M.: ribbon (narrow strip).
nastúrzio [L. *nasturtium*], M.: nasturtium (water-cress).
nasúto [*naso*], ADJ.: big-nosed.

natá-le [L. *-lis*], ADJ.: natal (native); M.: birthday. **-lízio**, ADJ.: natal (pertaining to one's birth); M.: birthday.
natá-nte, ADJ.: swimming. ||**natá-re†** [L.], INTR.: swim (float). **-tóia**, F.: fin. **-tòria†**, F.: bathing-place. **-tòrio**, ADJ.: natatory (swimming).
náti-ca [L. *-s*], F.: nates (buttocks). **-cúto**, ADJ.: with large buttocks.
ná-tio, ADJ.: native (natal, natural). **-tivaménte**, ADV.: natively (naturally). **-tività**, F.: nativity (birth). **-tívo**, ADJ.: native (natal, natural); M.: native. ||**ná-to** [L. *-tus*], ADJ.: born; M.: (*poet.*) offspring (child).
natríce†, F.: water-snake.
nátta [?], F.: tumour (in the mouth); trick.
natú-ra [L.], F.: nature (universe); disposition (inclination); kind: *di sua —*, naturally. **-ráccia**, *disp.* of *-ra*. **-ràle**, ADJ.: natural (native, genuine, normal, unaffected); ADV.: naturally. **-ralézza**, F.: naturalness; nature†. **-ralísmo**, M.: naturalism (doctrine). **-ralísta**, M.: naturalist (student of natural sciences). **-ralístico**, pl. *—ci*, ADJ.: naturalistic. **-ralità**, F.: franchise (citizenship granted to some foreigner). **-ralizzáre**, TR.: naturalize (confer rights). **-ralizzáto**, ADJ.: naturalized. **-ralménte**, ADV.: naturally; of course. **-ránte**, ADJ.: producing. **-ráre†**, TR., INTR.: naturalize; REFL.: become accustomed to.
nau- [Gr. *nau-s*, L. *nav-is*, ship]: **-fragáre**, INTR.: shipwreck (be ruined). **-frágio**, M.: shipwreck (ruin). ||**náu-frago** [L. *-fragere*, BREAK], M.: shipwrecked person. **-fragóso†**, ADJ.: in danger of shipwreck. **náu-lo†**, M.: freight (Eng.† naulage). **-machía** [Gr. *máche*], F.: naval combat (naumachy). **náu-sea** [L.], F.: nausea (seasickness; loathing). **-seabóndo**, ADJ.: nauseating (disgusting). **-seaménto†**, M.: nausea. **-seánte**, ADJ.: nauseating. **-seáre**, TR.: nauseate (loathe); INTR.: feel disgust. **-seáto**, ADJ.: disgusted. **-seosaménte**, ADV.: in a nauseating manner. **-seóso**, ADJ.: disgusted; nauseating (loathsome). **-ta†** [L.], M.: (*poet.*) sailor (shipman). **náutica**, F.: science of navigation. **náutico**, pl. *—ci*, ADJ.: nautical (marine). **náu-tilo**, M: nautilus (mollusk).
na-válo, ADJ.: naval (marine); M.: dockyard. **-valèstro**, M.: ferry-boat; ferryman. **-váta**, F.: nave (of a church); ship's freight†. ||**ná-ve** [L. *-vis*], F.: ship (vessel); nave (of a church). **-veréccio†**, ADJ.: naval (maritime). **-vétta**, *dim.* of *-ve*. **-vicáre**, INTR.: navigate (sail); swim. **-vicèlla**, F.: *dim.* of *-e*

boat; vessel for incense. **-vicelláio**, M.: boatman; ferryman. **-vicelláta**, F.: boatful. **-vicèllo**, M.: small boat. **-vicellóne**, *aug.* of *-vicello*. **-vichièro†**, M.: boatman; ferryman. **-vigábile**, ADJ.: navigable. **-vigabilità**, F.: navigability. **-vigaménto†**, M.: navigation. **-vigánte**, M.: navigator (sailor). **-vigáre**, TR.: navigate (manage, direct); INTR.: navigate (sail). **-vigáto**, ADJ.: navigated. **-vigatóre**, M., **-vigatríce**, F.: navigator (seaman). **-vigatòrio**, ADJ.: of navigation. **-vigazióne**, F.: navigation (science, act). **-vígio†**, M.: ship (vessel). **-víglio**, M.: fleet; ship. **-víle†**, ADJ.: naval (marine); M.: fleet; ship. **-vílio**, M.: fleet; ship.

na-zionále, ADJ.: national (of the nation). ‖**-zióne** [L. *-tio*], F.: nation (people, race); extraction†.

né 1 [L. *inde*], PRON.: to us; us; some (of it, of them); with (him, her, it, them); ADV.: thence.

né 2, né' [*in i*], in the.

nè 3 [L. *nec*], CONJ.: neither; nor: — *anche*, — *anco*, not even.

néb-bia [L. *nebula*], F.: fog (mist, vapour): *incantare la* —, live well. **-biáccia**, *disp.* of *-bia*. **-biolína**, *car. dim.* of *-bia*. **-bióne**, *aug.* of *-bia*. **-biosità**, F.: fogginess (mistiness). **-bióso**, ADJ.: foggy (misty). **-'ula†**, F.: (*poet.*); fog (mist); cloud. **-ulóso**, ADJ.: foggy (nebulous); cloudy.

néccio [*castagneccio*], M.: kind of cake (made from chestnut flour).

nèce [L. *nex*], F.: (*poet.*) death.

neces-sariaménte, ADV.: necessarily (indispensably). ‖**-sário** [L. *-sarius*], ADJ.: necessary (essential); M.: necessary; closet. **necès-se†**, ADJ.: (*poet.*) necessary. **-sità**, F.: necessity (need, want). **-sitáre**, TR., INTR.: necessitate (make indispensable, compel). **-sitáto**, ADJ.: necessitated. **-sitóso**, ADJ.: necessitous (poor, needy).

necistà†, F.: necessity (need).

necro- [Gr. *nekrós*, dead person]: **-logía**, F.: necrology (speech in praise of one dead). **-lògico**, pl. —*ci*, ADJ.: necrological (relating to accounts of deaths). **-lògio**, M.: necrology (register of deaths). **-manzía†** [Gr. *mantéia*, divination], F.: necromancy (conjuration). **necrò-poli** [Gr. *pólis*, city], F.: necropolis (cemetery). **-scopía** [Gr. *skopein*, examine], F.: examination of dead bodies. **necrò-si**, F.: necrosis (mortification).

-fan-daménte, ADV.: wickedly (abominably). **-dézza**, **-dígia†**, **-dità**, F.: wickedness (atrociousness). ‖**nefán-do** [L. *-dus* (*ne*, not, *fari*, speak)], ADJ.: abominable (unfit to speak of, Eng.† nefandous).

ne-fariaménte, ADV.: wickedly (nefariously). ‖**-fário** [L. *-farius* (*ne-fas*, impious deed)], ADJ.: wicked (iniquitous, nefarious). **-fásto**, M.: unpropitious day; ADJ.†: wicked (execrable).

ne-fríte [Gr. *-phrítes* (*-phrós*, kidney)] F.: nephritis (inflammation); nephrite (mineral formerly worn for kidney disease). **-frítico**, pl. —*ci*, ADJ.: nephritic. **-frítide**, F.: nephritis.

negá-bile, ADJ.: deniable. **-bilità**, F.: falsehood (contradiction). **-ménto†**, M.: negation (denial). ‖**negá-re** [L.], TR.: deny (contradict, refute). **-tíva**, F.: negation (denial); negative (photography). **-tivaménte**, ADV.: negatively. **-tívo**, ADJ.: negative (denying, contrary). **negáto**, ADJ.: denied. **-tóre**, M., **-tríce**, F.: denier. **-zióne**, F.: negation (denying).

ne-gghiènte†, ADJ.: negligent (listless). **-gghiézza†**, F.: negligence (laziness). **-ghittosaménte**, ADV.: lazily (slothfully). **-ghittóso**, ADJ.: lazy (indolent). **-glèssi†**, PRET. of *-gligere*. **-glettaménte**, ADV.: neglectfully. ‖**-glètto** [*-gligere*], ADJ.: neglected (overlooked, despised). **-glezióne†**, F.: negligence (disregard).

négli [*in, gli*], in the.

negli-gentáccio, *disp.* of *-gente*. **-gentáre**, TR.: neglect (overlook). **-gènte**, ADJ.: negligent (careless, regardless); M.: negligent person. **-genteménte**, ADV.: negligently (carelessly). **-gentonáccio**, *disp.* of *-gentone*. **-gentóne**, *aug.* of *-gente*. **-gènza**, **-gènzia†**, F.: negligence (carelessness). ‖**neglí-gere** [L.], TR.: neglect (disregard, slight).

ne-gòssa†, F., **-gòsso†**, M.: sweep-net.

nego-ziábile, ADJ.: negotiable. **-ziáccio**, *disp.* of *-zio*. **-ziánte**, ADJ.: negotiating (transacting); M.: merchant (Eng.† negotiant). **-ziáre**, INTR.: negotiate (trade, transact); TR.: negotiate (arrange for). **-ziáto**, ADJ.: negotiated; M.: negotiation (treaty). **-ziatóre**, M., **-ziatríce**, F.: negotiator. **-ziazióne**, F.: negotiation. **-ziétto**, *dim.* of *-zio*. ‖**negò-zio** [L. *-tium*], M.: business; affair; trade; thing; club. **-zióne**, *aug.* of *-zio*. **-zióso†**, ADJ.: busy. **-ziúccio**, *disp. dim.* of *-zio*.

né-gra [*-gro*], F.: negress. **-greggiáre†**, INTR.: become black. **-grézza†**, F.: blackness.

negrigènte†, ADJ.: negligent (careless).

négro [L. *niger*], ADJ.: black; gloomy†; M.: negro.

negro-mánte [Gr. *ne-krós*, dead, *mántis*, diviner], M.: necromancer (one revealing the future by communication with the dead). **-mantéssa**, F.: necromancer (sorceress). **-mántico**, pl. *—ci*, ADJ.: necromantic. **-manzía**, F.: necromancy (art).

néi [*in*, *i*], in the.

n-él, **-élla**, ‖**-éllo** [*in il*, *la*, *lo*], in the. **-élle**, in them.

nem-bífero, ADJ.: bringing rainy clouds (nimbiferous). ‖**ném-bo** [L. *nimbus*], M.: tempest (storm). **-bóso**†, ADJ.: stormy (nimbose).

nemi-caménte, ADV: hostilely (inimically, unfriendly). **-cáre**, TR.: treat as an enemy (persecute). **-chévole**, ADJ.: cruel (fierce). **-chevolménte**, ADV.: cruelly (fiercely). **-cízia**, F.: enmity (hatred). ‖**nemí-co**, pl. *-ci* [L. *in-imicus*], ADJ.: hostile (inimical); M.: enemy (foe). **-stà**†, F.: enmity (hatred).

nemméno [*ne meno* (L. *nec minus*)], ADV.: not even (not so much as).

nènia [L.], F.: long, mournful wailing (lament); funeral song.

nénufar [Pers. *nilûfar*], M.: nenuphar (water-lily).

nèo [L. *nævus*], M.: mole (blemish); spot; patch.

nèo- [Gr. *néos*, new]: new. =**cattòlico**, pl. *—ci*, ADJ., M.: new Catholic. **neò-fito** [Gr. *phutós*, grown], M.: neophyte (proselyte). =**grèco**, ADJ.: Neo-Greek. =**latíno**, ADJ.: Neo-Latin (applied to Romance languages). **-lítico**, pl. *—ci* [Gr. *líthos*, stone], ADJ.: neolithic (pertaining to an era characterized by its remains in stone). **-logía** [Gr. *lógos*, discourse], F.: neology. **-lògico**, pl. *—ci*, ADJ.: neological. =**logíşmo**, M.: neologism. =**náto** [L. *natus*], ADJ., M.: new-born. =**platònico**, ADJ.: neoplatonic; M.: neoplatonist. =**platoníşmo**, M.: neoplatonism (school of philosophy).

nepènte [Gr. *-thes* (*ne*, not, *pénthos*, grief)], M.: nepenthes (plant).

nepitèlla [L. *nepita*], F.: catmint.

nepitèllo†, M.: rim of the eyelids.

nepó-te [L. *nepos*], M.: nephew; grandson; F.: niece; granddaughter. **-tíno**, *dim.* of *-te*. **-tíşmo**, M.: nepotism (favouritism for nephews shown by popes, etc.).

nèputa†, F.: catmint.

neppúre [*ne pure* (L. *nec pure*)], ADV.: not even (not so much as).

ne-quità†, **-quitánza**†, F.: wickedness (roguery). **-quitóso**†, ADJ.: wicked. ‖**-quízia** [L. *nequitia*], F.: badness (roguery).

ne-racchiòlo, ADJ.: dark (of skin). ‖**-rástro** [*nero*], ADJ.: rather black (dark).

ner-báre, TR.: beat. **-báta**, F.: blow with a tendon. **-batúra**, F.: beating; condition of the nerves. **-bicíno**, *dim.* of *-bo*. ‖**nèr-bo** [*nervo*], M.: nerve (fibre); sinew†; catgut. **-bolíno**, *dim.* of *-bo*. **-boráto**, **-bóso**, ADJ.: nervous (vigorous, strong).

nereg-giaménto, M.: blackening. **-giánte**, ADJ.: blackening. ‖**-giáre** [*nero*], INTR.: become black.

nerèide [L. *nereis*], F.: nereid (sea-nymph).

ne-rellíno, M.: *dim.* of *-ro*; small black spot. **-rettíno**, *dim.* of *-retto*. **-rétto**, *dim.* of *-ro*. **-rézza**, F.: blackness (swarthiness). **-ricánte**†, **-ríccio**, *dim.* of *-ro*; M.: rather dark person. **-ríno**, *car. dim.* of *-ro*. **-ríssimo**, ADJ.: very (or most) black. ‖**né-ro** [L. *niger*], ADJ.: black (dark, obscure, gloomy); M.: black (colour); negro: *veste di —*, mourning dress; *metter un po' di — sul bianco*, write a receipt. **-ro=fúmo**, M.: variety of black. **-rógnolo**, ADJ.: rather dark; M.: rather dark person. **-rúme**, M.: too black; quantity of black things.

ner-vále, ADJ.: of nerves. **-váta**†, F.: horsewhipping. **-vatúra**, F.: condition of the nerves. **nèr-veo**, ADJ.: nervous (of nerves). **-vettíno**, *dim.* of *-vetto*. **-vétto**, *dim.* of *-vo*. **-víno**, ADJ.: nervine (quieting the nerves). ‖**nèr-vo** [L. *-vus*], M.: nerve (fibre, sinew). **-volíno**, *dim.* of *-vo*. **-vosaménto**, ADV.: nervously. **-vosíssimo**, ADJ.: very (or most) nervous. **-vosità**, F.: nervousness (vigour). **-vóso**, **-váto**†, ADJ.: nervous (pertaining to the nerves, sinewy).

nè-sci [L. *ne-scire*, be ignorant], M.: *fare il —*, play possum. **-sciènte**, ADJ.: ignorant (unknowing). **-scienteménte**, ADV.: ignorantly. **-sciènza**, F.: ignorance (nescience). **nè-scio**†, ADJ.: (*poet.*) ignorant.

nèspo-la [L. *mespilum*], F.: medlar (fruit); blow (thrust). **nèspo-lo**, M.: medlar (tree).

nèsso [L. *nexus*], M.: NEXUS (conNEXion; bond); combination; syncopated writing (abbreviation).

nes-sunissimo, PRON.: not a single one. ‖**-súno** [L. *ne ipse unus*], PRON. (INDEF.): nobody (no one, not one); ADV.: no (not any).

nes-taiuòla†, F.: nursery-ground. **-táre**†, TR.: graft (implant). ‖**nès-to** [*innesto* (L. *insitus*)], M.: graft (shoot, scion).

netta=dènti, M.: tooth-polisher. **-ménte**, ADV.: cleanly (neatly, clearly). **-ménto**†, M.: cleaning (polishing). =**pánni** M.: clothes-cleaner. =**pénne**, M.: p[en-] wiper. =**pòrti**, M.: harbour-cleaner (

chine). ‖**nettá-re** 1 [L. *nitidare*], TR.: clean (scour, polish); INTR.†: decamp (go away).

nèt-tare 2 [L. *nectar*], M.: nectar (drink of the gods, delicious beverage). **-tá-reo,** ADJ.: nectareous (pertaining to nectar).

net-táto, ADJ.: cleaned (polished, scoured). **-tatóia,** F.: hod (for mortar). **-tatóio,** M.: cleaning cloth; broom. **-tatóre,** M., **-tatríce,** F.: cleaner. **-tatúra,** F.: cleaning; sweepings (dirt). **-tézza,** F.: cleanness (neatness); purity†; sincerity. ‖**nét-to** [L. *nitidus*], ADJ.: clean (neat); quick (ready); clear; net; ADV.: cleanly; clearly; honestly.

nettúnico, pl. —*ci* [*Nettuno*, Neptune], ADJ.: Neptunian (rocks).

neu-tránle, ADJ.: neutral (indifferent). **-tralità,** F.: neutrality. **-tralizzáre,** TR.: neutralize. **-tralizzazióne,** F.: neutralization. **-tralménte,** ADV.: neutrally (indifferently). ‖**nèu-tro** [L. *-ter*], ADJ.: neuter; neutral (indifferent); M.: neuter.

ne-váio, M.: great snowfall. **-váre†,** INTR., IMPERS.: snow. **-váta,** F.: snowfall. **-váto,** ADJ.: snowlike. ‖**né-ve** [L. *nix*], F.: snow. **-vicáre,** INTR., IMPERS.: snow. **-vicáta,** F.: snowfall. **-vicóso†,** ADJ.: snowy; full of snow. **-vischia†,** F., **-vischio, -vistio,** M.: sleet. **-vosità,** F.: snowiness (fall of snow). **-vóso,** ADJ.: snowy; white as snow†; M.: fourth month (of calendar of first French Republic).

nevr- [Gr. *neûron*, NERVE]: **-algía** [Gr. *álgos*, pain], F.: neuralgia. **-òsi,** F.: nervous sickness. **-òtico,** pl. —*ci*, ADJ.: neurotic (relating to the nervous system). **-oto-mía** [Gr. *tomé*, cut], F.: operation on a nerve.

nézza†, F.: niece.

níbbio [OFr. *nible*], M.: kite (bird of prey); blockhead†.

níc-chia [?], F.: sea-shell; niche (wall-cavity). **-chiaménto†,** M.: complaining. **-chiáre,** INTR.: complain (whine); be discontented and uncertain. **-chiét-ta, -chiettína,** *dim.* of *-chia*. **níc-** ... .: conch-shell; priest's cap; kind ... at. **-chiolíno,** *dim.* of *-chio*. ... *aug.* of *-chia*. **-chióne,** *aug.* ... *-chia*. **-chióso,** ADJ.: full of

... *cio*], M.: thin cake (of chest-

... †, F.: necessity.

... **-chèlio** [Sw. *nickel*], M.: nickel ... **-chelláre,** TR.: give the ap- ... of nickel.

... **smo,** M.: nihilism (Russian secret society). **-lísta,** pl. *-listi*, M.: nihilist. **-lità†,** F.: nothingness (nihility). ‖**ní-chi-lo†** [L. *nihil*], M.: nothing (naught).

nicotína [*Nicot*, introducer of tobacco in France], F.: nicotine (active principle of tobacco).

ni-dáta†, F.: nestful (brood). **-diáce,** ADJ.: fresh from the nest. **-diáta,** F.: nestful (brood). **-dificáre,** INTR.: make a nest. **-dificáto,** ADJ.: settled (in a nest). **ni-dio,** ‖**ní-do** [L. *-dus*], M.: nest; birds in a nest; bed.

niégo†, M.: refusal (denial).

niel-láre, INTR.: engrave (carve upon gold). **-láto,** ADJ.: engraved. ‖**niél-lo** [L. *nigellum* (*niger*, black), dark], M.: engraved work (on metal, the engraving often filled with a black substance).

nièn-te [OFr. *nient*], ADV.: nothing (not anything); M.: nothing. **-te=diméno, -te-méno,** ADV.: nevertheless (notwithstanding); just think! **-tíssimo,** ADV., M.: nothing at all.

nièvo†, M.: nephew.

níf-fa†, F., **-fo†, -folo†,** M.: snout (muzzle).

nigèlla [L. (*niger*, black)], F.: nigella (fennel-flower).

nighittóso†, ADJ.: idle (lazy).

nigrigènte†, ADJ.: negligent (careless).

nigro†, ADJ.: black.

nímbo [L. *-bus*], M.: storm (tempest).

nimi-cáre, TR.: treat as an enemy (persecute). **-cízia,** F.: enmity (hatred). ‖**nimí-co,** pl. *-ci* [L. *in-imicus*], ADJ.: hostile (unfriendly).

nímo† [L. *nemo*], PRON. (INDEF.): no one (nobody).

nín-fa [L. *nympha*], F.: nymph (goddess); chrysalis. **-fále,** ADJ.: nymphal (of a nymph); M.: head of a nymph (ornament). **-fèa,** F.: nymphæa (genus of aquatic plants, including the water-lily). **-fèo,** M.: temple (of the nymphs).

ninferm.. = *inferm..*

ninfétta, *car. dim.* of *ninfa*.

nín-na [echoic], F.: lullaby; baby-girl†. **-náre,** TR.: lull asleep; trifle (hesitate). **-náto,** ADJ.: lulled asleep. **-narèlla†,** *dim.* of *-na*. **-noláre,** TR.: amuse (with trifles); INTR.: trifle away one's time. **-nolétto, -nolíno,** *car. dim.* of *-nolo*. **nín-nolo,** M.: trifle (plaything). **-no-lóne,** M.: trifler (idler).

níno, M.: darling (dear).

nipitèlla [*nepitella*], F.: catmint.

nipó-te [L. *nepos*], M.: nephew; grandson; F.: niece; granddaughter. **-tíno,** *dim.* of *-te*. **-tísmo,** M.: nepotism (favoritism shown to nephews).

niquità†, F.: iniquity (wickedness).

nis-cond..., -ces.. = *nascond..., nasces..*

nissúno = *nessuno*.

niti-daménte, ADV.: clearly (brightly, splendidly). **-dézza**, F.: clearness (brightness). ||**níti-do** [L. *-dus*], ADJ.: clear (bright, neat, shining).

nitóre†, M.: clearness (brightness).

ni-tráto [*-tro*], M.: nitrate (salt). **ní-trico**, pl. —*ci*, ADJ.: nitric.

ni-tríre [L. *hinnire*], INTR.: neigh. **-trí-to**, M.: neighing.

ní-tro [L. *-trum*], M.: nitre (saltpetre). **-tro = glicerína**, F.: nitroglycerine. **-tróso**, ADJ.: nitrous.

ni-úno, -úna [L. *ne unus*], PRON.: nobody (no one, none).

níveo [L. *-veus*], ADJ.: snowy (niveous).

nizzárda [*Nizza*], F.: large, straw hat (worn by women).

nò [L. *non*], ADV.: no (not): *dico di* —, I say it is not.

no' [*noi* (L. *nos*)], PRON.: we; us.

nòbi-le [L. *-lis* (*noscere*, know)], ADJ.: noble (illustrious, worthy); M.: nobleman; coin (worth about $1.61). **-lèa**, F.: nobility (nobles). **-lésco**, ADJ.: noble. **-lézza**†, F.: nobility. **-líssimo**, ADJ.: very (or most) noble. **-litáre**, TR.: ennoble; REFL.: make one's self renowned. **-litáto**, ADJ.: ennobled. **-litatóre**†, M.: one conferring nobility. **-lménte**, ADV.: nobly (magnanimously). **-ltà**, F.: nobility (elevation, titled class). **-lúccio**, *disp. dim.* of *-le*. **-lúme**, M.: nobility (nobles).

nòcca [Ger. *knöchel*], F.: KNUCKLE (joint).

noc-chière, ||**-chièro** [L. *nau-clerus*], M.: pilot.

nocchie-róso, ||**-rúto** [*nocchio*], ADJ.: knotty (of wood).

nocchíno [*nocca*], M.: blow with the knuckles.

nòc-chio [*nucleo*], M.: knot (in trees); stone (in fruit); mineral fragments. **-chiolíno**, *dim.* of *-chio*. **-chióso**, ADJ.: knotty. **-chiúto**, ADJ.: full of knots.

noc-ciòla [*noce*], F.: hazel-nut; filbert. **-cioláio**, M.: nut-vender. **-ciolétta**, **-ciolína**, *dim.* of *-ciola*. **-ciolétto**, **-ciolíno**, *dim.* of *-ciolo*. **-ciòlo**, M.: nut-tree (hazel or filbert). **nòc-ciolo**, M.: stone (of fruit): *esser due anime in un* —, be near friends, be hand and glove. **-ciolúto**†, ADJ.: stony. **-ciuòla** = *-ciola*. **-ciuòlo**, M.: nut-tree (hazel or filbert)

nó-ce [L. *nux*], M.: walnut-tree; walnut wood; F.: walnut: — *moscada*, nutmeg. **-cèlla**, F.: joint of compasses, etc.; hazel-nut†.

no-cènte [*nocere*], ADJ.: hurtful (nocent). **-centíno** [*in-nocentino*], ADJ.: of a foundling; M.: foundling. **-cènza**†, F.: error (fault). ||**nò-cere** [L.], IRR.§; TR.: hurt (harm, prejudice).

§ Ind.: Pres.: 1. *n(u)òco* or *n(u)òccio*; 6. *n(u)òcono* or *n(u)òcciono*. Pret. *nòc-qui*, *-que*; *-quero*. Subj.: Pres. *n(u)òca* or *n(u)òccia*; *n(u)òcano* or *n(u)òcciano*.

nocéto [*noce*], M.: nut-grove.

nocévo-le [*nocere*], ADJ.: hurtful (injurious). **-lézza**, F.: hurtfulness. **-lménte**, ADV.: hurtfully.

nociménto†, M.: harm (injury).

no-cíno [*noce*], M.: kind of game (with nuts); ADJ.: of a nut: *lingua -cina*, slanderous tongue. **-cióna**, *aug.* of *-ce*.

no-ciúto, PART. of *-cere*. **-civaménte**, ADV.: hurtfully (perniciously). **-cívo**, **-citívo**†, ADJ.: hurtful (pernicious).

nó-cqui, PRET. of *-cere*. **-cuménto**, M.: harm (injury). **-cumentúccio**, *dim.* of *-cumento*.

no-dellétto, *car. dim.* of *-dello*. **-dèllo**, M.: joint (juncture); knot†. **-deróso**, **-derúto**†, ADJ.: knotty (knobby). ||**nò-do** [L. *-dus*], M.: KNOT; difficulty; joint (juncture): — *di vento*, whirlwind. **-doróso**†, ADJ.: knotty. **-dosaménte**, ADV.: in a knotted way. **-dosità**, F.: knottiness. **-dóso**, ADJ.: knotty.

no-dríce†, F.: nurse. ||**-dríre** [L. *nutrire*], TR.: (*poet.*) nourish (feed); educate.

noètico, pl. —*ci* [*Noè*, Noah], ADJ.: of Noah.

nói [L. *nos*], PRON., PERS.: we; us.

nò-ia [?], F.: weariness; annoyance (vexation, trouble). **-iáre**, TR.: weary; annoy (trouble); REFL.: trouble one's self. **-iáto**, ADJ.: wearied; vexed. **-iatóre**†, M.: bore. **-iévole**†, ADJ.: wearisome. **-iosaménte**, ADV.: wearisomely. **-iosità**, F.: tiresomeness. **-ióso**, ADJ.: wearisome (tiresome). **-iúccia**, *dim.* of *-ia*.

nòl [*non lo*], ADV.: not . . . it.

noleg-giaménto, M.: chartering; hiring; embarking. ||**-giáre** [*nolo*, freight], TR.: charter; hire; embark. **-giáto**, ADJ.: chartered; embarked. **-giatóre**, M.: charterer; freighter. **nolég-gio**, M.: freighting; hire.

nolènte [L. *nolens*], ADJ.: unwilling.

nòlo [Gr. *naûlon* (*naûs*, ship)], M.: freight; hire (rent).

nòmade [Gr. *nomádes*, shepherds], ADJ.: nomadic (wandering); M.: nomad (one of a wandering tribe).

nománza†, F.: reputation (name, renown).

nomár-ca [Gr. *-ches* (*nómos*, prefecture, *árchein*, command)], M.: nomarch. **-chía**, F.: nomarchy (prefecture).

no-máre, TR.: name (call, appoint). **-mataménte**†, ADJ.: namely. ||**nó-me** [L. *-men*], M.: name (title, renown, repute); watchword†. **-mèa**, F.: name (reputation). **-menclatóre**, M.: nomenclator (name-giver, dictionary). **-menclatúra**, F.: nomenclature. **-mígnolo**, M.: surname. **nó-mina**, F.: nomination; card of entrance (to some festival). **-minábile**, ADJ.: namable. **-minále**, ADJ.: nominal (pertaining to names). **-minália**, M. PL.: christening days (of children). **-minalísmo**, M.: nominalism. **-minalísta**, M.: nominalist. **-minánza†**, F.: name (reputation). **-mináre**, TR.: name (nominate, appoint). **-minataménte**, ADV.: by the name (namely). **-minatívo**, M.: nominative (case). **-mináto**, ADJ.: named. **-minatóre**, M.: namer (appointer). **-minazióne†**, F.: nomination (appointing, naming). **-míno**, *dim.* of *-me*.

nomísma†, M.: medal.

nón [L.], ADV.: not; no: — *che altro*, at least; — *pertanto*, nevertheless.

nòna [L.], F.: nones (ninth hour).

nona-genário [L. *-genarius*], ADJ.: ninety years old; M.: nonagenarian. **-gèsimo**, ADJ.: ninetieth.

noncovèlle†, M.: nothing (trifle).

non=curánte, ADJ.: careless (indifferent). **-curánza**, F.: carelessness (indifference).

non=di=máno, **=méno**, ADV.: nevertheless (however).

nòne [L. *nonæ*], F.: (*Rom. Calend.*) nones.

nònio [*Nonnius*], M.: nonius (short scale).

nòn-na, F.: grandmother. **-nína**, *car. dim.* of *-na*. ||**nòn-no** [L. *-nus*], M.: grandfather.

non=núlla, F.: trifle (thing of no importance).

nòno [*nove*], ADJ.: ninth.

non=ostánte, ADV.: notwithstanding (in spite of).

non=paríglia [Fr. *nonpareille*], F.: nonpareil (type).

non=pertánto, ADV.: notwithstanding.

norcíno [*Norcia*], M.: hog-butcher.

nòr-d, ||**nòr-do** [Ger. *nord*], M.: north; northern country. **nòr-dico**, pl. *—ci*, ADJ.: northern.

nòr-ma [L.], F.: norm (model, type); carpenter's square†. **-mále**, ADJ.: normal (ordinary). **-malità**, F.: normality. **-malménte**, ADV.: normally.

nòrt(e) [*nord*], M.: north; northern country.

nósco†, PRON.: with us.

nosocòmio [Gr. *nosokomeion*], M.: hospital.

-**talgía** [Gr. *nóstos*, return, *álgos*, ...], F.: homesickness (nostalgia).

...**rále**, ADJ.: of our own country.

...**lménte**, ADV.: as in our own country. **-tríssimo**, PRON. POSS.: our very own. ||**nòs-tro** [L. *noster*], PRON. POSS.: our; ours; of us.

nostròmo [*nostro, uomo*], M.: boatswain.

nò-ta [L.], F.: note (observation, mark, record, musical character). **-tábile**, ADJ.: notable (memorable); M.: notable (person of distinction); saying†. **-tabilità**, F.: notability. **-tabilménte**, ADV.: notably (remarkably). **-táio**, M.: notary. **-taiuòlo†**, *dim.* of *-taio*. **-tándo†**, ADJ.: notable. **-tanteménte†**, ADV.: notably. **-táre** 1, TR.: note (mark, observe); sing by note†.

notáre 2 [L. *natare*], INTR.: swim.

nota-résco, ADJ.: of (or like) a notary. **-ría†**, F.: notary; profession. **-riále**, ADJ.: notarial (of a notary). **-riáto**, M.: office or profession of a notary. **-ríle**, ADJ.: of a notary. ||**notá-ro** [L. *-rius* (*nota*, note)], M.: notary.

notáta [*notare* 2], F.: swim.

notataménte†, ADV.: notably (particularly).

nota-tóio†, M.: swim. ||**-tóre** 1 [*notare* 2], M., **-tríce**, F.: swimmer.

nota-tóre 2 [*notare* 1], M.: noter (observer). **-tríce**, F.: noter (observer).

notatúra†, F.: swimming.

no-tazióne [*nota*], F.: notation. **-terèlla**, *dim.* of *-ta*. **-tería†**, F.: notary's office. **-tévole**, ADJ.: notable (remarkable). **-tevolménte**, ADV.: notably (remarkably). **-tícina**, *car. dim.* of *-ta*. **-tificagióne†**, F., **-tificaménto**, M.: notification; notice. **-tificáre**, TR.: notify (make known). **-tificánte**, ADJ.: notifying; M.: notifier. **-tificáto**, ADJ.: notified; M.: person notified. **-tificatóre**, M., **-tificatríce**, F.: one notifying. **-tificazióne**, F.: notification (declaring). **-tíssimo**, ADJ.: best known. **-tízia**, F.: notice (information); news. **-tiziáccia**, *disp.* of *-tizia*. **-tiziário**, M.: note-book. **-tiziétta**, *dim.* of *-tizia*. **-tiziòla**, *disp. dim.* of *-tizia*.

nòto 1 [*notare* 2], M.: swimming.

nòto 2 [L. *-tus*], ADJ.: known.

noto-mía [*anatomia*], F.: anatomy: *far* —, examine closely. **-místa**, M.: anatomist. **-místico**, pl. *—ci*, ADJ.: anatomical. **-mizzáre**, TR.: anatomise (analyse). **-mizzáto**, ADJ.: anatomised.

no-toriaménte, ADV.: notoriously (openly). **-torietà**, F.: notoriety (publicity). ||**-tòrio** [L. *-torius*], ADJ.: notorious (publicly known).

notósco†, ADJ.: spotted (stained).

notricáre†, TR.: nourish (feed, raise).

nott-ambulísmo, M.: somnambulism. ||**-ámbulo** [*notte*, night, *ambulare*, walk], M.: somnambulist.

not-tánte, M., F.: night-watch (with

sick); night-nurse. **-táre†**, INTR.: grow dark. **-táta**, F.: whole night. **-tác-cia**, *disp.* of *-te.* ‖**nòt-te** [L. *nox*], F.: night: *di* —, by night. **-te=tèmpo**, **-te=tèmpore†**, ADV.: during the night. **-tí=vago**, ADJ.: noctivagant (wandering in the night). **nòt-tola**, F.: bat; door-latch. **-toláta†**, F.: whole night. **-to-lína†**, F., **-tolíno**, M.: small latch. **nòt-tolo†**, M.: bat. **-tolóne**, M.: large bat; night-walker†. **-túrno**, ADJ.: noc-turnal (by night); M.: nocturn (religious service).

nòva [*novo*], F.: news.

novále†, M.: fallow-ground.

novaménte [*novo*], ADV.: newly (again).

novan=sèi, ADJ.: ninety-six. **-sètte**, ADJ.: ninety-seven. ‖**nován-ta** [L. *nonaginta*], NUM. ADJ.: ninety. **-ta=nò-ve**, ADJ.: ninety-nine. **-téna†**, F.: ninety. **-tènne**, ADJ.: ninety years old. **-tèsimo**, ADJ.: ninetieth. **-tína**, F.: ninety. **-túno**, ADJ.: ninety-one.

nová-re† [*novo*], TR.: innovate. **-nová-stro†**, ADJ.: new (fresh). **-téra**, F., **-tóre**, M., **-tríce**, F.: innovator. **-zió-ne**, F.: innovation.

nò-ve [L. *-vem*], NUM. ADJ.: NINE. **-ve=cènto**, ADJ.: nine hundred.

novèl-la, F.: novel (tale); news. **-la-ménte**, ADV.: newly (recently). **-la-ménto†**, M.: story-telling. **-láre**, INTR.: tell stories; chatter; REFL.†: be renewed. **-láta**, F.: tale (ballad). **-latóre**, M.: story-teller. **-létta**, *car. dim.* of *-la.* **-lièra**, F., **-lière**, **-lièro†**, M.: story-teller (or writer); tale-bearer (telltale). **-lína**, *car. dim.* of *-la.* **-linità†**, F.: novelty (newness). **-líno**, *car. dim.* of *-lo.* **-lísta**, M.: novelist (story-writer). **-lízia†**, F.: first fruits. ‖**novèl-lo** [L. *-lus* (*novus*)], ADJ.: new (fresh, recent). **-lòzza†**, F.: laughable story. **-lúccia**, **-lúzza†**, *disp. dim.* of *-la.*

novèmbre [L. *-ber*], M.: November (month).

novè-na [L.], F.: novena (Roman Catholic devotion). **-nário**, ADJ.: novenary (pertaining to the number nine); M.: nine.

novendiále [L. *-dialis*], ADJ.: novendial (occurring on the ninth day).

no-vennále, ADJ.: novennial (recurring every ninth year). ‖**-vènne** [L. *-vennis*], ADJ.: (*poet.*) of nine years; nine years old. **-vènnio**, M.: space of nine years.

noverá-re [*novero*], TR.: number; count (compute). **noverá-to**, ADJ.: numbered. **-tóre†**, M., **-tríce†**, F.: numberer. **-zióne†**, F.: numbering; counting.

novèrca†, F.: (*poet.*) stepmother.

nòvero [*numero*], M.: number; multitude.

novèsimo, ADJ.: ninth.

no-vilúnio [L. *-vilunium*], M.: new moon. **-víssimo**, ADJ.: very (or most) new; most recent: *il — dì*, doomsday; M. PL.: four ends of man (death, judgment, hell, heaven). **-vità**, F.: novelty (newness). **-vízia**, F.: novice; young bride†. **-vizià-tico†**, **-viziáto**, M.: novitiate. **-vízio**, ADJ.: inexperienced (unskilled); M.: nov-ice. ‖**nò-vo** [L. *-vus*], ADJ.: NEW (fresh, recent, unaccustomed); M.: new things (state).

nozióne [L. *notio*], F.: notion (idea, conception).

nòz-ze [L. *nuptiæ*], F. PL.: NUPTIALS (marriage, wedding). **-zerésco†**, ADJ.: nuptial. **-zolíne†**, *dim.* of *-ze.*

nú-be [L. *-bes*], F.: (*poet.*) cloud. **-bífe-ro**, ADJ.: (*poet.*) surrounded by clouds (Eng.† nubiferous). **nú-bila†**, F.: cloud.

núbile [L. *-lis*], ADJ.: marriageable.

nubi-létta†, *dim.* of *-la.* **-lità**, F.: cloudiness (darkness). **núbi-lo†**, **-biló-so**, ADJ.: cloudy (dark).

núca [?], F.: nape (of the neck).

núcleo [L. *-cleus*], M.: nucleus (stone of fruit, nucleus).

nu-daménte, ADV.: nudely (nakedly). **-dáre**, TR.: strip (make naked); REFL.: strip one's self. **-dità**, F.: nudity (nakedness). ‖**nú-do** [L. *-dus*], ADJ.: nude (naked, bare); M.: nude figure.

nudríre [*nutrire*], TR.: nourish (feed, educate).

nuga-tòrio†, ADJ.: trifling (nugatory). **-zióne†**, F.: trifle.

núgola†, F.: cloud.

núl-la [L.], ADV.: nothing; M.: nothing: *metter al* —, destroy. **-ladiméno**, ADV.: nevertheless. **-lità**, F.: nullity (nothingness). **núl-lo**, ADJ.: no (none); void (useless); M.†: nobody.

núme [L. *-men*], M.: (*poet.*) deity (divinity).

nume-rábile, ADJ.: numerable (countable). **-rále**, ADJ., M.: numeral. **-ral-ménte**, ADV.: numerically. **-ráre**, TR.: enumerate (count). **-rário**, M.: metal money. **-rataménte**, ADV.: in a numbered way. **-ratívo**, ADJ.: counting. **-ratóre**, M., **-ratríce**, F.: counter; numerator. **-razióne**, F.: numeration; numbering. **-rétto**, *car. dim.* of *-ro.* **-ricaménte**, ADV.: numerically. **nu-mè-rico**, pl. *—ci*, ADJ.: numerical (denoting number). ‖**núme-ro** [L. *-rus*], M.: number (figure); multitude; rhythm. **-ró-ne**, *aug.* of *-ro.* **-rosaménte**, ADV.: numerously. **-rosíssimo**, ADJ.: very (or most) numerous. **-rosità**, F.: numerousness; harmony†. **-róso**, ADJ.: numerous; harmonious.

númine†, M.: deity (divinity).
nu-mismática, F.: numismatics (science of coins). **-mismático**, pl. —*ci*, ADJ.: numismatic; M.: numismatist. ‖**nú-mmo**†, [L. *-mmus*], M.: (*poet.*) money (coin).
nunc. . = *nunz.* .
nuncupa-tivaménte, ADV.: verbally (orally). ‖**-tívo** [L. *-tivus*], ADJ.: nuncupative (verbal, oral).
núndine [L. *-dinæ* (*novem*, nine, *dies*, day)], F. PL.: Roman fairs (held every nine days).
nun-ziáre, TR., INTR.: announce. **-ziatóre**, M.: messenger. **-ziatúra**, F.: Eng.† nunciature (office of a nuncio). ‖**nún-zio** [L. *-tius*], ADJ.: of a nuncio (ambassador); M.: nuncio (messenger, ambassador).
nuòcere = *nocere*.
nuòra [L. *nurus*], F.: daughter-in-law.
nuot. . = *not.* .
nuòv. . ('new,' etc.) = *nov.* ., etc.
nurághi [?], M.: nuraghe (ancient Sardinian monuments).
núro†, F.: daughter-in-law.
núto†, M.: nod (beck).
nutrí-bile†, ADJ.: that can be nourished. **-caménto**†, M.: nourishment. **-cáre**, TR.: nourish (feed, educate). **-catóre**†, M.: nourisher (sustainer). **nutrí-ce**, F.: wet-nurse; foster-mother. **-chévole**†, **-mentále**, ADJ.: nourishing (sustaining). **-ménto**, M.: nourishment. **-mentóso**†, ADJ.: nourishing. ‖**nutrí-re** [L.], IRR.§; TR.: nourish (feed, maintain, educate). **-ènte**, ADJ.: nourishing. **nutrí-to**, ADJ.: nourished. **-tívo**, ADJ.: nutritive (nourishing). **-tóre**, M.: nourisher (sustainer). **-túra**, F.: nutrition (food). **-zióne**, F.: nourishing.
§ Reg. or Ind.: Pres. *nú-tro, -tri, -tre; -trono.* Subj.: Pres. *nú-tra; -trano.*
núvo-la [L. *nubila* (*nubes*)], F.: cloud. **-láglia**, F., **-láto**†, M.: mass of clouds. **-létta**, *car. dim.* of *-la*. **-létto**, **-líno**, *dim.* of *-lo*. **núvo-lo**, M.: thick cloud; great quantity. **-lóne**, *aug.* of *-lo*. **-losità**, F.: cloudiness (darkness). **-lóso**, ADJ.: cloudy. **-lúzzo**, *disp. dim.* of *-lo*.
nuziál-e [L. *nuptialis*], ADJ.: nuptial (matrimonial). **-ménte**†, ADV.: in a nuptial manner.

O

ó 1, **ò** [L.], M., F.: o (the letter).
2 [L. *aut*], CONJ.: or; either: — . . . —, ...her . . . or.
...], INTERJ.: O! oh!
...Gr. *ôasis*], F.: oasis.
...ob], PREF.: ob-, to(ward); against.

obbe-diènte, ADJ.: obedient (dutiful). **-dienteménte**, ADV.: obediently. **-diènza**, F.: obedience. ‖**-díre** [L. *obedire*], TR.: OBEY (submit to). **-díto**, ADJ.: obeyed.
obbiett. .† = *obiett.* .
obbióso†, ADJ.: superstitious.
ob-blazióne† = *oblazione*.
ob-blío†, **-bliáre**† = *oblio*, *obliare*.
obbli-gagióne†, F., **-gaménto**†, M.: obligation. **-gánte**, ADJ.: obliging. **-gánza**†, F.: obligation (bond). ‖**-gáre** [L. *ob-ligare* (bind)], TR.: oblige (bind, compel, accommodate); REFL.: bind one's self. **-gataménte**, ADV.: in an obliging way. **-gatíssimo**, ADJ.: very much obliged. **-gáto**, ADJ.: obliged (bound, indebted). **-gatòrio**, ADJ.: obligatory (binding). **-gazióne**, F.: obligation (bond, promise). **òbbli-go**, M.: obligation (indebtedness).
ob-blío [L. *oblivium*], M.: forgetfulness (oblivion). **-blióso**†, ADJ.: forgetful (oblivious).
obbliqu. .† = *obliqu.* .
obbrig. .† = *obblig.* .
obbrò-brio [L. *opprobrium*], M.: opprobrium (shame, disgrace). **-briosaménte**, ADV.: opprobriously (shamefully). **-brióso**, ADJ.: opprobrious (shameful). **-briúzzo**†, *dim.* of *-brio*.
obedi. .† = *obbedi.* .
obelísco [Gr. *obeliskos*], M.: obelisk (pillar).
oberáto [L. *ob-æratus*], ADJ.: deeply in debt.
o-besità, F.: obesity (fleshiness). ‖**-béso** [L. *-besus* (*edere*, EAT)], ADJ.: obese (fleshy, fat).
ob-iettáre [L. *-jectare*], TR.: object (oppose). **-iettáto**, ADJ.: objected. **-iettívo**, ADJ.: objective. **-iètto**, M.: object (thing, aim). **-iezióne**, F.: objection (opposition).
objurgazióne†, F.: reproof (objurgation).
oblá-ta, F.: oblate (serving-sister, lay-sister). ‖**oblá-to** [L. *-tus*], ADJ.: offered up; M.: oblate (serving-brother, lay-brother). **-tóre**, M., **-tríce**, F.: offerer (bestower); out-bidder.
oblatratóre†, M.: barker; slanderer.
oblazióne [*oblato*], F.: oblation (offering, sacrifice).
ob-liáre, TR.: forget; REFL.: forget one's self. **-liáto**, ADJ.: forgotten. ‖**-lío** [L. *-livium*], M.: oblivion (forgetfulness).
obli-quaménte, ADV.: obliquely. **-quità**, F.: obliquity. ‖**oblí-quo** [L. *-quus*], ADJ.: oblique (indirect, slanting).
obliteráre [L. (*litera*, letter)], TR.: obliterate (cancel, efface).
oblivióne [L. *-vio*], F.: oblivion (forgetfulness.

oblóngo [L. *-gus*], ADJ.: oblong.
òboe, oboè [Fr. *haut-bois*], M.: hautboy (musical instrument).
òbolo [L. *-lus*], M.: obolus (Greek coin and weight).
obombr.. = *adombr..*
obrízzo†, M.: pure gold; ADJ.: of pure gold.
obrogá-re [L.], TR.: annul (Eng.† obrogate). **-zióne**, F.: annulment.
obtrettazióne†, F.: detraction (calumny, Eng.† obtrectation).
obumbr..† = *adombr..*
òc [L. *hoc*, this = 'yes'], in *lingua d'—*, langue d'oc (old South French).
oc- = *ob-*.
òca [L. L. *auca* (? L. *avis*, bird)], F.: goose; booby: *far il becco all' —*, put the finish to a work.
occáre†, TR.: harrow.
occasio-nále, ADJ.: occasional (casual, opportune). **-nalménte**, ADV.: occasionally. **-náre**, TR.: occasion (cause, produce). **-ncèlla**, *dim.* of *-ne*. ‖**occasió-ne** [L. *occasio*], F.: occasion (opportunity, occurrence).
occáso [L. *occasus*], M.: west; western country.
oc-chiáccio, *disp.* of *-chio*: *far gli —*, scowl. **-chiáia**, F.: hollow of the eye; dark rim under the eye. **-chialáccio**, M.: bad spectacles. **-chialáio**, M.: spectacle-maker (or seller). **-chiále**, ADJ.: of the eye: *dente —*, eye-tooth. **-chialétto**, M.: monocle. **-chiáli**, M. PL.: spectacles. **-chialíno**, *car.* of *-chialetto*. **-chialísta**, M.: optician. **-chialóne**†, *aug.* of *-chiale*. **-chiáre**, TR.: eye (ogle). **-chiáta**, F.: glance (look, ogle). **-chiatáccia**, *disp.* of *-chiata*. **-chiatèlla**†, **-chiatína**, *car. dim.* of *-chiata*. **-chiáto**†, ADJ.: full of eyes. **-chiatúra**†, F.: look (regard). **-chiceruleo**, ADJ.: blue-eyed. **-chibágliolo**†, M.: dizziness. **-chieggiáre**, TR., INTR.: eye (ogle, regard). **-chielláia**, F.: buttonhole maker. **-chiellatúra**, F.: buttonholes. **-chiellíno**, *dim.* of *-chiello*. **-chièllo**, M.: buttonhole. **-chiettáccio**, *disp. dim.* of *-chietto*. **-chiettíno**, *car. dim.* of *-chietto*. **-chiétto**, *car. dim.* of *-chio*. **-chíno**, *car. dim.* of *-chio*. ‖**òc-chio** [L. *oculus*], M.: eye (sight); bud; bull's eye (window); small circle (in handle of kitchen utensil, etc.): *a — e croce*, thereabout, without precision; *piangere a cald' —*, weep bitterly; *in un batter d' —*, in a trice; *avere buon —*, have a good appearance; *guardar sott' —*, look stealthily; *veder di buon —*, look kindly upon. **-chiolíno**, *car. dim.* of *-chio*. **-chióne**, *aug.* of *-chio*. **-chiúto**, ADJ.: full of eyes (or buds). **-chiúzzo**, *disp. dim.* of *-chio*.
oc-cidentále, ADJ.: occidental (western). **-cidènte**, M.: occident (west); western countries. ‖**-cídere**† [L. (*cadere*, fall)], INTR.: (set of the sun). **-cíduo**, ADJ.: western (occiduous).
occi-pitále, ADJ.: occipital. ‖**occí-pite** [L. *oc-ciput* (*caput*, head)], M.: occiput (back of head). **-pízio**, M.: nape (of the neck).
occisióne†, F.: killing (slaughter).
occitánico, pl. *—ci* [*oc*], ADJ.: of the langue d'oc.
occoltáre†, TR.: hide (conceal).
oc-corrènte, ADJ.: occurring (happening). **-corrènza**, F.: occurrence (circumstance); need (want). ‖**-córrere** [L. *-currere*, run to], IRR. (cf. *correre*); INTR.: OCCUR (happen); be needed (with dat. as subj.: need, want, wish); meet†: *Le -corre qualche cosa?* do you want (wish for) anything? *non mi -corre nulla*, I want nothing; *-corro?* anything you want? *non -corre*, (I want) nothing, thank you; *non -corr' altro*, I don't care for anything more; that's enough. **-corriménto**†, M.: meeting; recollection. **-córsi**, PRET. of *-correre*. **-córso**, PART. of *-correre*; ADJ.: needed; occurred; M.: meeting; happening.
occul-tábile, ADJ.: concealable. **-taménte**, ADV.: secretly (stealthily). **-taménto**, M.: concealment (hiding). ‖**-táre** [L.], TR.: conceal (hide). **-tatóre**, M., **-tatríce**, F.: concealer (hider). **-tazióne**, **-tézza**†, F.: hiding (of a heavenly body). **occúl-to**, ADJ.: occult (hidden, secret): *in —*, secretly.
occu-pábile, ADJ.: occupiable. **-paménto**†, M.: occupation (possession); ADJ.: occupying; M.: occupied land. ‖**-páre** [L.], TR.: occupy (possess, hold, use); REFL.: occupy one's self. **-páto**, ADJ.: occupied (busy). **-patíssimo**, ADJ.: very (or most) occupied. **-patóre**, M., **-patríce**, F.: occupier (usurper, possessor); ADJ.: occupying. **-pazioncèlla**, *dim.* of *-pazione*. **-pazióne**, F.: occupation (possession, employment, business).
o-ceánico, pl. *—ci*, ADJ.: oceanic. ‖**-ceáno** [L. *-ceanus*], M.: ocean.
ocò†, INTERJ.: hurrah! huzza!
ocóne†, *aug.* of *oca*.
ò-cra [L. *-chra*], F.: ochre (mineral). **-cráceo**, ADJ.: ochreous (Eng.† ochraceous). **ò-cria**, F.: ochre (mineral). **-cróso**, ADJ.: ochreous.
ocu-láre [L. *-laris*], ADJ.: ocular (of the eye); M.: eye-piece (of telescope or microscope): *testimone —*, eye-witness. **-lá-**

rìo, ADJ.: Eng.† oculary (ocular). **-larménte**, ADV.: ocularly. **-latamènte**, ADV.: cautiously (prudently). **-latézza**, F.: caution (prudence). **-làto**, ADJ.: cautious (prudent). **-lìsta**, M.: oculist. **-lìstico**, pl. —*ci*, ADJ.: oculist. **-lìstica**, F.: oculist's science.

òd [L. *aut*], CONJ.: or; either.

òda†, F.: ode (poem).

odalìsca [Turk. *odalik* (*oda*, room)], F.: slave (in a Turkish harem).

òde [Gr. *odḗ*], F.: ode (poem, song).

odèo [L. *odeum*], M.: odeon (Greek theatre).

o-diàbile, ADJ.: odious (hateful, detestable). **-diàle†**, ADJ.: hating. ‖**-diàre** [L. *odi*], TR.: hate (detest). **-diàto**, ADJ.: hated. **-diatóre**, M., **-diatrìce**, F.: hater. **-dìbile†**, ADJ.: odious (hateful).

o-diernamènte, ADV.: to-day (at present). ‖**-dièrno** [L. *hodiernus* (*ho-die*, to-day)], ADJ.: of to-day (of the present time).

odiévo-le†, ADJ.: odious (hateful, detestable). **-lézza†**, F.: hatefulness.

ò-dio [L. *-dium*], M.: odium (hatred, detestation). **-diosàggine†**, F.: hatred. **-diosamènte**, ADV.: odiously (hatefully). **-diosità**, F.: odiousness (hatefulness). **-dióso**, ADJ.: odious (hateful, abominable).

odìre†, TR.: hear; listen.

odissèa [Gr. *Odysseía*], F.: Odyssey.

odon-talgìa [Gr. (*odoús*, tooth, *álgos*, pain)], F.: odontalgia (toothache). **-tàlgico**, pl. —*ci*, ADJ.: odontalgic.

odo-ràbile, ADJ.: that can be smelled. **-racchiàre†**, INTR.: give a slight odour. **-ràccio**, *disp.* of *-re*. **-ramènto**, M.: odour (scent, smell). **-rànte†**, ADJ.: odorous (fragrant). **-ràre**, TR.: scent (smell, discover); INTR.: smell. **-ratìvo**, ADJ.: smelling. **-ràto**, M.: smell (the sense); ADJ.: odorous (fragrant). **-raziòne†**, F.: odour (scent, smell). ‖**odó-re** [L. *odor*], M.: odour (smell, scent). **-rétto**, *car. dim.* of *-re*. **-rettàccio**, *disp.* of *-retto*. **-rìfero**, ADJ.: odoriferous (fragrant). **-rìno**, *car. dim.* of *-re*. **-róne†**, M.: strong-scented flower. **-rosamènte**, ADV.: odorously (fragrantly). **-rosétto**, *car. dim.* of *-roso*. **-róso**, ADJ.: odorous (fragrant).

òf-fa [L.], F.: cake; biscuit. **-fèlla†**, *dim.* of *-fa*.

offèn-dere [L.], IRR. (cf. *difendere*); TR.: offend (affront); REFL.: feel offended. **-dévole†**, ADJ.: offensive (displeasing). **-dìbile**, ADJ.: easily offended. **-dicolo†**, M.: hindrance (difficulty). **-dimènto†**, M.: offence (affront). **-ditóre**, M., **-ditrìce**, F.: offender. **offèn-sa†**, **-sióne†**, F.: offence (injury). **-sivamènte**, ADV.: offensively (injuriously). **-sìvo**, ADJ.: offensive (hurtful, disagreeable). **offèn-so†**, ADJ.: offended. **-sóra**, F., **-sóre**, M.: offender.

offe-rènda†, F.: offer. **-rènte**, ADJ.: offering. ‖**-rìre**, or us'ly *offrire* [L. *offerre*], IRR. §; TR.: offer (present, propose, sacrifice); REFL.: present one's self. **-ritóre†**, M.: offerer. **offè-rta**, F.: offer (proposal, offering). **-rtàccia**, *disp.* of *-rta*. **offè-rto**, PART. of *-rire*. **-rtòrio**, M.: offertory.

§ Ind.: Pres. *offerisco* or *òffro*. Impf. *offeriva*. Pret. *offrìi* or *offerìi*, *offrì* or *offerse*; *offrirono*, *offersero*. Fut. *offrirò*. Cond. *offrirèi*. Part. *offèrto*.

of-fésa, F.: offence (injury, displeasure). **-fési**, PRET. of *-fendere*. ‖**-féso** [*-fendere*], PART.: offended (injured, displeased).

offi-ciàle, ADJ.: official; M.: officer. **-ciàre**, TR.: officiate. **-cìna**, F.: workshop (laboratory). **-cinàle**, ADJ.: officinal (medicine). ‖**offì-cio** [L. *-cium*], M.: office (place); duty. **-ciosamènte**, ADV.: officiously (kindly). **-ciosità**, F.: officiousness. **-cióso**, ADJ.: officious (kind); meddling.

offrìre = *offerire*.

offu-scamènto, M.: obfuscation (darkening). ‖**-scàre** [L.], TR.: obfuscate (darken, obscure). **-scatóre**, M., **-scatrìce**, F.: confuser. **-scazióne†**, F.: obfuscation (darkening).

ofi-ceria†, F.: office, church-service. ‖**-ciàle†**, M.: officer. **ofì-cio†**, M.: office; duty.

ofìte [Gr. *ophítes* (*óphis*, serpent)], F.: ophite (serpentine marble).

oftal-mìa [Gr. (*ophthalmós*, eye)], F.: ophthalmy (eye disease). **oftàl-mico**, pl. —*ci*, ADJ.: ophthalmic. **-mologìa**, F.: ophthalmology (treatise). **-moscopìa**, F.: ophthalmoscopy. **-moscòpio**, M.: ophthalmoscope (instrument).

ògà [Gog, people hostile to Israel], F.: distant land (ends of the earth; far away).

ogget-tivamènte, ADV.: objectively. **-tivàre**, TR.: objectize (make object of). **-tivìsta**, M.: objectist. **-tività**, F.: objectivity. **-tìvo**, ADJ.: objective. ‖**oggèt-to** [L. *objectus*], M.: object (thing; aim).

òg-gi [L. *hoc die*], ADV.: to-day; afternoon: — *a otto*, this day week. **-gi=dì**, **-gi=giórno**, ADV.: nowadays (at this time). **-gi=mài**, ADV.: now.

ogì-va [?], F.: ogive (Gothic vault). **-vàle**, ADJ.: ogival, pertaining to the ogive.

ó-gni [L. *omnis*], PRON.: every (all). **-gni=intèrno**, ADV.: from all sides (or places). **-gni=sánti**, M.: All Saints' day. **-gni=veggènte†**, ADJ.: all-seeing. **-gn=óra**, ADV.: always. **-gn=ora=chè -é**, ADV.: every time that. **-gn=úno**, PRON., INDEF: every one (everybody). **-gn=únque†**, PRON.: whoever; ADJ.: whatever.

ò-h [L. *o*], INTERJ.: oh! **ò-(h)i** [*oh*], INTERJ.: ah (alas)! **-(h)ibò** [? *bono*, viz., *Dio*], INTERJ.: shame! **-(h)i=mè**, INTERJ.: alas!

oídio [Gr. *oón*], M.: oidium (parasitic fungus).

òil [L. *hoc illud* (= Fr. *oui*)], in *lingua d'* —, langue d'oïl (old North French).

oitù†, INTERJ.: woe to thee!

o=là, INTERJ.: ho there! stop!

oláro†, M.: potter (earthenware dealer).

ò-lea [L.], F.: olea (olive). **-leáceo**, ADJ.: oleaginous (oily). **-leaginóso**, ADJ.: oleaginous (oily).

oleándro [Gr. *rhododéndron*], M.: oleander (rosebay).

oleástro†, M.: oleaster (wild olive-tree).

o-lèico, pl. *—ci* [L. *oleum*, oil], ADJ.: oleic (derived from oil). **-leífero**, ADJ.: oleiferous (producing oil). **-leificio**, M.: oil factory. **-leína**, F.: oleine.

olènte [L. *olens*], ADJ.: (*poet.*) fragrant (ODOROUS).

oleo-grafía [L. *oleum*, oil; Gr. *grápheín*, represent], F.: oleography. **-gráfico**, pl. *—ci*, ADJ.: oleographic. **=margarína**, F.: oleomargarine. **-sità**, F.: oiliness (Eng.† oleosity). **oleó-so**, ADJ.: oily (oleous, unctuous).

oles-zánte, ADJ.: fragrant (sweet-smelling). ‖**-záre** [L. *olere*], INTR.: smell sweet (be ODOROUS). **olés-zo**, M.: fragrance (odour).

ol-fáre† [L. *ol-facere*], INTR.: smell (scent). **-fátto**, M.: smell (sense). **-fattòrio†**, ADJ.: olfactory.

o-liándolo [*olio*], M.: oil-peddler. **-liáto**, ADJ.: seasoned with oil; oiled.

olíbano [?], M.: incense-tree; incense†.

olièra [*olio*], F.: cruet-stand.

oli-gárca, M.: oligarchist. ‖**-garchía** [Gr. (*olígos*, few, *árchein*, rule)], F.: oligarchy. **-gárchico**, pl. *—ci*, ADJ.: oligarchic.

olim-píaco, pl. *—ci*, ADJ.: of the Olympiads. ‖**-píade** [Gr. *olumpías*], F.: Olympiad (period of 4 years). **-picaménte**, ADV.: in an Olympic manner. **olím-pico**, pl. *—ci*, ADJ.: Olympic.

ò-lio [L. *oleum*], M.: oil (of olive, etc.): — *santo*, extreme unction. **-lióso†**, ADJ.: oily.

olíre†, INTR.: be fragrant.

olitòrio†, ADJ.: olitory (belonging to a kitchen-garden).

olí-va [L.], F.: olive (fruit or tree†). **-vástro**, ADJ.: olive-coloured; M.: wild olive tree. **-váto**, ADJ.: planted with olive trees. **-vèlla**, F., **-vèllo**, M.: privet (a shrub). **-véta**, F., **-véto**, M.: olive plantation. **-vetáno**, ADJ.: of Benedictine monks. **-vétta**, F.: olive-shaped ornament. **olí-vo**, M.: olive-tree.

òlla†, F.: earthen pot.

ol-máia, F.: row of elms. **-méto**, M.: elm grove. **-métto**, *dim.* of *-mo*. ‖**ól-mo** [L. *ulmus*], M.: elm-tree.

olocáusto [Gr. *holó-kaustos*, 'whole-burnt'], M.: holocaust (burnt-sacrifice).

ològrafo [Gr. *hólos*, whole, *grápheín*, write], ADJ.: holographic.

oloráre†, INTR.: smell (scent).

ól-tra† [L. *ultra*], PREP.: besides; beyond. **-traccið**, ADV.: moreover.

oltraco-tánte [*oltre cogitante*], ADJ.: arrogant. **-tánza**, F.: arrogance (insolence).

oltrag-giábile, ADJ.: that can be outraged. **-giaménto**, M.: outrage (insult). **-giáre**, TR.: OUTRAGE (abuse, insult). **-giatóre**, M., **-giatríce**, F.: outrager (abuser, insulter). ‖**oltrág-gio** [*oltre*], M.: OUTRAGE (abuse, affront): *a* —†, excessively. **-giosaménte**, ADV.: outrageously. **-gióso**, ADJ.: outrageous (violent).

oltra=montáno, ADJ.: ultramontane (beyond the mountains); M.: foreigner.

oltránza† [*oltre*], F.: outrage (insult): *a* —, excessively.

oltrárno [*oltre Arno*], M.: part of Florence (beyond the Arno).

óltre- [L. *ultra*], PREP.: besides (more than); beyond; ADV.: before; very far. **=máre**, ADV.: beyond the sea. **=marí-no**, ADJ.: ultramarine. **=misúra**, ADV.: excessively (beyond measure). **=mòdo**, ADV.: exceedingly. **=mónte**, **=mónti†**, ADV.: ultramontane (beyond the mountains). **=número†**, ADV.: innumerably. **=passáre**, TR.: go beyond (exceed).

omac-cíno, *car. dim.* of *-cio*. ‖**omác-cio** [*omo*], M.: bad man (rascal). **-cióne**, *aug.* of *-cio*.

omággio [l. L. *hominaticum* (*homo*, man, servant)], M.: homage (fealty, submission).

omái [*ormai*], ADV.: now; at length.

ombè†, ADV.: now then.

ombe-licále, ADJ.: umbilical. ‖**-lico** [L. *umbilicus*], M.: navel.

óm-bra [L. *umbra*], F.: shade (shadow, protection); pretext; spectre; trace (suspicion); umbrage. **-brácolo†**, **-bráculo†**, M.: bower (shady place); protection. **-bragióne†**, F.: shade. **-bra-ménto†**, M.: shadowing; shade. **-bra**

re, TR.: shade; INTR.: suspect; take umbrage. **-bráticо**†, **-brátile**†, ADJ.: suspicious. **-bráto**, ADJ.: shaded (protected). **-bratúra**, F.: shade (protection). **-brazióne**†, F.: shade. **-breggiaménto**, M.: shading; shadow. **-breggiáre**, TR.: shade (overshadow). **-breggiáto**, ADJ.: shaded. **-breggiatúra**, F.: shading; umbel (flower-cluster). **-brèlla**, F.: umbel (flower-cluster); umbrella†; slight shade†. **-brelláio**, M.: umbrella-maker (or seller). **-brelláta**, F.: blow with an umbrella. **-brellétta**, *dim.* of *-brella.* **-brellière**†, M.: umbrella-maker (or seller). **-brellífero**, M.: umbellifer (family of plants). **-brellíno**, M.: *dim.* of *-brello;* parasol. **-brèllo**, M.: umbrella. **-brévole**†, ADJ.: shady (dark). **-bría**†, F.: shade; ghost; protection. **-brína**, F.: umbrina (genus of fishes).

ombrèmetro [Gr. *ómbros*, rain, *métron*, measure], M.: rain-gauge (pluviometer).

ombro-saménte, ADV.: shadily. **-sétto**, **-síno**, *dim.* of *-so.* **-sità**, ADJ.: shadiness (obscurity); ignorance†. ‖**ombró-so** [*ombra*], ADJ.: shady (dark, obscure); shy.

omèga [Gr.], M.: omega (Ω, last letter of the Greek alphabet).

omèi†, M. PL.: groans (laments).

omelía [Gr. *homilia*], F.: homily (discourse).

omeo-patía [Gr. *hómoios*, like, *páthos*, sickness], F.: homeopathy. **-paticaménte**, ADV.: homeopathically. **-pático**, pl. *—ci*, ADJ.: homeopathic.

o-mericaménte, ADV.: in a Homeric manner. ‖**-mèrico**, pl. *—ci* [*Omero*], ADJ.: Homeric. **-merísta**, M.: student of Homer.

ómero [L. *humerus*], M.: shoulder.

o-mésso, PART. of *-mettere;* ADJ.: omitted. ‖**-méttere** [L. *-mittere*], IRR. (cf. *mettere*); TR.: omit (leave out).

o-mettíno [*omo*], *car. dim.* of *-mo.* **-métto**, *dim.* of *-mo.* **-micciòlo**, *disp. dim.* of *-mo.* **-miciatto**, **-miciáttolo**, *disp. dim.* of *-mo.*

omi-cída [L. *homi-cida*, man-slayer], M.: homicide (murderer); ADJ.: homicidal. **-cidiále**, ADJ.: homicidal (murderous). **-cídio**, M.: homicide (manslaughter).

omilía†, F.: homily.

omi-náccio, *disp.* of *omo.* **-níno**, *disp. dim.* of *-no.* ‖**omí-no** [*omo*], *dim.* of *omo.* **-nóne**, *aug.* of *-no.*

o-mísi, PRET. of *-mettere.* **-missióne**, F.: omission (leaving out). **-mméss...**† **-mmett...** = *-mess..*, *-mett..*.

òmni-bus [L., 'for all'], M.: omnibus. **-bussáio**, M.: driver (of an omnibus). *-bussáta*, *F.: omnibus load.*

òmo [L. *homo*], M.: man.

omo- [Gr. *homós*, SAME]: **-geneaménte**, ADV.: homogeneally. **-geneità**, F.: homogeneity. **-gèneo** [Gr. *génos*, kind], ADJ.: homogeneous (of same kind). **-logaménte**, ADV.: homologously. **-logáre**, TR.: ratify (confirm). **-logazióne**, F.: ratification. **-logía**, F.: homology. **-lògico**, pl. *—ci*, ADJ.: homological. **omòlogo** [Gr. *lógos*, speech], ADJ.: homologous (of same value). **-nimía**, F.: homonymy (ambiguity). **omò-nimo** [Gr. *ónoma* NAME], ADJ.: homonymous; M.: homonym.

omóre†, M.: humour (moisture; disposition).

onágro, **ònagro** [L. *onager*], M.: wild ass; kind of catapult.

óncia [L. *uncia*], F.: inch; ounce; ADV.: *a — a —*, little by little.

oncíno [L. *uncus*], M.: hook.

ón-da [L. *unda*], F.: wave; sea (billow): *a -de*, like waves; staggering. **-dánte**†, ADJ.: undulatory. **-dáta**, F.: wave dash.

ónde [L. *unde*], ADV.: whence; wherefore; in order to.

on-deggiaménto [*onda*], M.: undulation (vibration). **-deggiánto**, ADJ.: undulating. **-deggiáre**, INTR.: undulate (wave, vibrate); be agitated. **-deggiáto**, ADJ.: undulated. **-dicèlla**, *dim.* of *-da.* **-dosità**, F.: waviness. **-dóso**, ADJ.: wavy (full of waves). **-dulaménto**, M.: undulating. **-dulánto**, ADJ.: undulating. ‖**-duláre** [L. *undulare*], INTR.: undulate (wave). **-duláto**, ADJ.: undulated. **-dulatòrio**, ADJ.: undulatory. **-dulazióne**, F.: undulation (vibration).

ondúnque†, ADV.: wheresoever; on all sides.

one-ráre, TR.: oppress (burden, aggravate). **-rário**, ADJ.: having the care of: *navi -ri*, ships of burden. ‖**òno-re** [L. *onus*], M.: burden (load). **-róso**, ADJ.: onerous (burdensome).

one-stà, F.: honesty (virtue, decorum). **-staménte**, ADV.: honestly (decently). **-stáre**, TR.: make honest; veil; adorn†. **-steggiáre**†, TR.: act honestly. ‖**onèsto** [L. *honestus*], ADJ.: honest (virtuous, decent, just); ADV.: honestly; M.: honesty.

onfacíno†, ADJ.: of oil (made from unripe olives).

óniće† [Gr. *ónux*], F.: onyx (gem).

oníre†, TR.: shame.

ónni- [L. *omnis*, all]: **-naménte**, ADV.: entirely (wholly). =**possènte**, =**potènte**, ADJ.: omnipotent (all-powerful). **-potentemènte**, ADV.: omnipotently. =**potènza**, F.: omnipotence. =**presènza**, F.: omnipresence. =**sciènte**, ADJ.: omniscient (all-knowing). =**sciènza**, F.: omniscience. =**vedènte**†, =**veggènte**, ADJ.: all-seeing. =**veggènza**, F.: omniscience. **onni-voro** [L. *-vorus*], ADJ.: omnivorous (all-devouring).

onoma- [Gr., NAME]: **onomá-stico**, ADJ.: onomastic (pertaining to a name); M.: onomasticon (dictionary). **-topèa, -topèia** [Gr. *poieîn*, make], F.: onomatopœia. **-topèico**, pl. —*ci*, ADJ.: onomatopoetic.

ono-rábile, ADJ.: honourable (estimable). **-rabilità**, F.: honourableness. **-rabilménto**, ADV.: honourably. **-rándo**, ADJ.: worthy of honour (reverence). **-ránza**, F.: honour (respect). **-ránte**, ADJ.: honouring. **-ráre**, TR.: honour (esteem, revere). **-rário**, ADJ.: honorary; M.: fee (reward). **-rataménte**, ADV.: honourably (justly). **-ratézza**, F.: honourableness (probity). **-ráto**, ADJ.: honoured (respected). **-ratóre**, M., **-ratríce**, F.: honourer. ||**onóre** [L. *honor*], M.: honour (esteem, dignity, pomp). **-réttо**†, *dim.* of *-re*. **-révole**, ADJ.: honourable; splendid. **-revolézza**, F.: honour; splendour. **-revolíssimo**, ADJ.: very (or most) honourable. **-revolménte**, ADV.: honourably; splendidly. **-rificaménte**, ADV.: honourably. **-rificáre**†, TR.: honour (esteem). **-rificataménte**†, ADV.: honourably. **-rificènza**, F.: honour (glory). **-rífico**, pl. —*ci*, ADJ.: honourable.

ónta [Fr. *honte*], F.: shame (offence, disgrace): *ad — di*, in spite of (notwithstanding).

on-tanéto, M.: plantation (or grove) of elder-trees. ||**-táno** [?], M.: elder-tree (or alder).

on-tánza†, F.: shame (disgrace, offence). **-táre**†, **-tíre**, TR.: disgrace (dishonour).

onto-logía [Gr. *ón*, being, n. pl. *onta*, *lógos*, discourse], F.: cntology. **-lògico**, pl. —*ci*, ADJ.: ontological. **-logísmo**, M.: ontologism. **-logísta, ontò-logo**, M.: ontologist.

on-tosaménte, ADV.: shamefully (disgracefully). ||**-tóso** [*onta*], ADJ.: shameful (disgraceful).

onústo [L. *-stus* (*onus*, burden)], ADJ.: loaded (laden).

o-pacità, F.: opacity (opaqueness). ||**-páco** [L. *-pacus*], ADJ.: opaque.

opá-le [L. *opalus*], M.: opal (gem). **-lescènte**, ADJ.: opalescent. **-líno**, ADJ.: opaline.

opéfice†, M.: workman (artificer).

openióne†, F.: opinion (judgment).

òpe-ra [L.], F.: work (action, business); opera (musical composition). **-rábile**, ADJ.: practicable (Eng.† operable). **-ráccia**, *disp.* of *-ra*. **-rággio**†, M.: work (business). **-ragióne**†, F.: operation (action). **-ráio**, M.: workman. **-raménto**†, M.: operation (working). **-ránte**, ADJ.: operating; M.: operator. **-ráre**, INTR.: operate (act, work); TR.: do. **-rativaménte**, ADV.: operatively. **-ratívo**, ADJ.: operative (efficient). **-ráto**, ADJ.: operated (worked); M.: work (action). **-ratóre**, M., **-ratríce**, F.: operator (workman, cause). **-razioncèlla**, *disp. dim.* of *-razione*. **-razióne**, F.: operation (work, effect). **-rétta, -ricciòla**, *dim.* of *-ra*. **-rière**†, M.: workman. **-rína**, *car. dim.* of *-ra*. **-róna, -róne**, *aug.* of *-ra*. **-rosaménte**, ADV.: laboriously. **-rosità**, F.: laboriousness. **-róso**, ADJ.: laborious (busy, active; hard, Eng.† operose). **-rúccia**, *disp. dim.* of *-ra*.

opí-fice†, M.: workman. ||**-fício** [L. *-ficium*], M.: factory.

opímo [L. *opimus*], ADJ.: fat; fertile; abundant (rich).

opi-nábile, ADJ.: opinable (imaginable). **-nabilménte**, ADV.: by thought. **-nánte**, ADJ.: opining. ||**-náre** [L. *-nari*], INTR.: opine (think). **-natívo**, ADJ.: opining (thinking). **-natóre**, M., **-natríce**, F.: thinker (Eng.† opiner). **-nióne**, F.: opinion (judgment, mind).

oppiáre [*oppio*], TR.: opiate.

oppigno-raménto, M.: sequestration (separation). ||**-ráre** [L. (*pignus*, gage)], TR.: sequester (separate). **-razióne**, F.: sequestration (separation).

oppilá-re [L. (*pilare*, ram)], TR.: crowd together (Eng.† oppilate). **-tívo**, ADJ.: obstructive (Eng.† oppilative). **-zióne**, F.: obstruction (stoppage, Eng.† oppilation).

òppio 1 [L. *opium*], M.: opium.

òppio 2 [L. *opulus*], M.: white poplar.

op-ponènte, ADJ.: opposing; M.: opponent. **-poniménto**†, M.: opposition (resistance). ||**-pórre** [L. *-ponere*], IRR. (cf. *porre*); TR.: oppose (resist, withstand); REFL.: oppose.

opportu-naménte, ADV.: opportunely (seasonably). **-nísmo**, M.: opportunism. **-nísta**, M.: opportunist. **-nità**, F.: opportunity (occasion); need†. ||**opportúno** [L. *-nus*], ADJ.: opportune (timely).

oppó-si, PRET. of *-porre*. **-sit**. †= *-st*.. **-sitóre**, M.: opposer (adversary). **-sizioncèlla**, F.: *dim.* of *-sizione*; opposition (resistance). **-staménte**, ADV.: oppositely. **oppó-sto**, PART. of *opporre*; opposite (contrary).

op-premúto, ADJ.: oppressed. **-pressáre**, TR.: oppress (distress). **-pressióne**, F.: oppression (severity). **-pressivaménte**, ADV.: oppressively. **-pressívo**, ADJ.: oppressive (severe). **-prèsso**, ADJ.: oppressed. **-pressóre**, M.: oppressor. **-pressúra**†, F.: oppression.

-primènte, ADJ.: oppressing. ‖**-prímere** [L.], IRR. (cf. *comprimere*); TR.: oppress (overpower, burden).
oppu-gnábile, ADJ.: opposable; confutable. **-gnaménto**, M.: attack. ‖**-gnáre** [L.], TR.: combat (assault, Eng.† oppugn, resist); confute. **-gnatóre**, M., **-gnatríce**, F.: assailant. **-gnazióne**†, F.: attacking (assailing).
oppúre [*o pure*], CONJ.: or.
ò-pra [*opera*], F.: work (labour); pay. **-pránte**, M.: workman. **-práre**, INTR.: (*poet.*) work (labour).
opríre†, TR.: open (disclose).
optáre [L.], INTR.: choose (select).
opu-lènte†, ‖**-lènto** [L. *-lentus*], ADJ.: opulent (wealthy). **-lènza**, F.: opulence (wealth).
opusco-létto, **-líno**, *dim.* of *-lo*. ‖**opúsco-lo** [L. *-lum*], M.: opuscule (small work).
opzióne [L. *optio*], F.: option (choice).
óra 1 [L. *hora*], F.: hour; time: *che — è?* what time is it? *d' — in —*, from hour to hour; *a* (or *di*) *buon —*, early; ADV.: now; at present; *per —*, for the present; *— com' —*, for the present.
òra 2 [*aura*], F.: (*poet.*) air (breeze).
orácolo [L. *-culum*], M.: oracle (revelation, deity).
òrafo [L. *auri-fex*], M.: goldsmith.
orá-le [L. *os*, mouth], ADJ.: oral (spoken). **-lménte**, ADV.: orally.
ora-mái, ADV.: now (by this time); at length; after all.
orangután [Mal. *orang*, man, *utan*, forest], M.: orang-outang (monkey).
oráre [L. (*os*, mouth)], TR.: pray (beseech, entreat); harangue.
orário [*ora* 1], ADJ.: horary (indicating the hours); M.: register (of working hours), time-table.
oráta [L. *aurata*, gilded], F.: goldfish.
ora-tóre [L. *-tor*], M.: orator (haranguer); rhetorician; ambassador: *sacro —*, preacher; implorer†. **-tòria**, F.: oratory (eloquence). **-toriaménte**, ADV.: oratorically (eloquently). **-tòrio**, ADJ.: oratorical; M.: oratorio (place of worship; sacred musical composition). **-tríce**, F.: orator; worshipper. **-zioncèlla**, **-zioncína**, *dim.* of *-zione*. **-zióne**, F.: prayer (orison); oration (speech).
orbácca†, F.: berry.
or-bácelo, *disp.* of *-bo*. ‖**-báre** [*orbo*], TR.: (*poet.*) deprive (bereave). **-báto**, ADJ.: deprived; blinded†.
òrbe [L. *orbis*], M.: orb (sphere).
orbè [*ora bene*], ADV.: well and good (be it so).
orbézza†, F.: bereavement.
orbi-coláre†, **-coláto**†, ADJ.: orbicular (circular). **orbí-culo**, *dim.* of *orbe*. ‖**òrbi-ta** [L. (*orbis*)], F.: orbit (of a planet); cart-rut†; hollow of the eye.
or-bità†, F.: blindness. ‖**òr-bo** [L. *-bus*], ADJ.: bereft (deprived); blind.
òrca [L], F.: ork (sea-fish).
orcétto, *car. dim.* of *orcio*.
orchè-stra [Gr.], F.: orchestra; musicians, space in a theatre. **-strále**, ADJ.: orchestral. **-strazióne**, F.: orchestration.
órcia†, F.: mizzen-bowlines.
or-ciáccio, *disp.* of *-cio*. **-ciáia**, F.: room for (oil-)jars. **-ciáio**, M.: seller (or maker) of (oil-)jars. **-círo**, *dim.* of *-cio*. ‖**ór-cio** [L. *urceus* (ak. to *orca*)], M.: large oval jar or urn (esp. for holding oil; cf. Eng. URCEOLE). **-cioláio** = *-ciaio*. **-ciolétto**, **-ciolíno**, *dim.* of *-ciolo*. **-ciòlo**, **-ciuólo**†, M.: *dim.* of *-cio*; water-pitcher.
órco [L. *-cus*], M.: hobgoblin.
òrda [Mong. *ordoū*], F.: horde (tribe).
or-dégno†, ‖**-digno** [*-dire*], M.: machine (engine); instrument. **-diménto** [*-dire*], M.: warping.
ordi-nábile, ADJ.: that may be ordered. **-nále**, ADJ.: ordinal; ordinary (usual)†. **-nalménte**, ADV.: by (in) ordinals. **-naménto**, M.: ordering; arrangement. **-nándo**, ADJ.: of a candidate (for holy orders); M.: candidate (for holy orders). **-nánte**, ADJ.: ordering. **-nánza**, F.: order (of troops); ordinance (decree). **-náre**, TR.: order (arrange); command (conduct); ordain (confer holy orders); REFL.: prepare one's self. **-nariaménte**, ADV.: ordinarily (commonly). **-nário**, ADJ.: ordinary (usual, common); M.: ordinary: *d' —*, usually; *per l' —*, commonly (mostly). **-náta**, F.: ordinate; ADJ.: ordinate (regular). **-nataménte**, ADJ.: ordinately (methodically). **-natívo**, ADJ.: ordering; ordinal. **-náto**, ADJ.: ordered (regulated); ordained. **-natóre**, M., **-natríce**, F.: orderer (director); ordainer. **-nazióne**, F.: order (decree); ordination (to holy orders); medical prescription. ‖**órdi-ne** [L. *ordo*], M.: order (arrangement); file (line, series); command; commission; rank†: *in — a*, with regard to; *— di stanze*, suite of rooms; *mettere all' —*, prepare. **-nétto**†, *dim.* of *-ne*.
ordíngo = *ordigno*.
ordí-re [L. *-ri*], TR.: warp (lay the warp, begin a web); contrive (plot, machinate); plan; begin. **ordí-to**, ADJ.: woven; M.: warp (web, plot). **-tóio**, M.: loom. **-tóra**, F., **-tóre**, M.: warper (weaver, planner). **-túra**, F.: warping (weaving).
órdo†, ADJ.: filthy (foul).

orèade [L. *oreas*], F.: oread (mountain nymph).

orécchia, F.: ear; hearing (sense); fold. **-chiágnolo**, M.: ear-pull. **-chiánte**, ADJ.: learning (music) by ear. **-chiáre**, INTR.: listen. **-chiáta**, F.: box on the ear; pull of the ear. **-chíno**, M.: earring. ||**orécchio** [L. *auricola*], M.: EAR; hearing (sense); fold: *star cogli -chi tesi*, listen intently. **-chióne**, M.: *aug.* of *-chio;* orillon (tower). **-chióni**, M. PL.: mumps. **-chiúto**, ADJ.: long-eared.

oréfi-ce [L. *auri-fex*], M.: goldsmith. **-ceria**, F.: goldsmith's trade; goldsmith's shop.

orégliat†, F.: ear; hearing (sense); fold.

oreria [*oro*], F.: goldware.

oréz-za†, F., ||**-zo** [*aura*], M.: (*poet.*) gentle breeze.

òrfa-na, F.: orphan girl. **-nézza**†, F.: orphanage. ||**òrfa-no** [L. *orphanus*], ADJ., M.: orphan. **-notròfio**, M.: orphan asylum.

orga-nále†, ADJ.: organical. **-naménto**, M.: organization (organizing). **-náre**, TR.: organize. **-nétto**, *dim.* of *-no.* **-nicaménte**, ADV.: organically. **orgá-nico**, pl. —*ci*, ADJ.: organic. **-nísmo**, M.: accordion. **-nísmo**, M.: organism (structure). **-nísta**, M.: organist (organ-player). **-nizzaménto**, M.: organization (organizing). **-nizzáre**, TR., REFL.: organize. **-nizzáto**, ADJ.: organized. **-nizzatóre**, M., **-nizzatríce**, F.: organizer. **-nizzazióne**, F.: organization (organized condition). ||**órga-no** [L. *-num*], M.: organ (of the body); musical instrument. **-nografía**, F.: organography. **-nología**, F.: organology. **-noscopía**, F.: organoscopy. **-núto**†, ADJ.: harmonious (as an organ).

orgásmo [Gr. *-mós*], M.: orgasm (eager excitement).

òrgia [L.], F.: orgy (revel, carouse).

orgo-gliáre†, INTR.: grow proud. ||**orgó-glio** [OHG. *urguol*, superior], M.: pride (haughtiness). **-gliosaménte**, ADV.: proudly (haughtily). **-gliosétto**, *dim.* of *-glioso.* **-gliositá**†, F.: haughtiness. **-glióso**, ADJ.: proud (haughty, Eng.† orgillous). **-gliúzzo**, *disp. dim.* of *-glio.*

oriafiámma†, F.: oriflamme (banner).

oribándolo†, M.: kind of girdle.

oricálco [Gr. *orei-chalkón*, mountain-brass], M.: orichalcum (brass); brass kettle; trumpets.

oricánno†, M.: scent-bottle.

òrice [Gr. *óryx*], M.: oryx (S. Afr. antelope).

oricèllo [*orina*], M.: orchil (lichen furnishing a violet dye).

orichícco = *orochico.*

oricriníto [*oro, crinito*], ADJ.: golden-haired.

orien-tále, ADJ.: oriental (eastern). **-talísta**, M.: orientalist (student of oriental languages, etc.). **-talménte**, ADV.: in an oriental manner. **-táre**, REFL.: find out the east; find out one's position (get one's bearings). ||**oriën-te** [L. *oriens* (*orior*, rise)], ADJ.: orient (rising, eastern); M.: Orient (east).

orifiámma [L. *auri-flamma*, gold-flame], F.: oriflamme (ancient royal standard of France).

orificeria†, F.: goldsmith's trade; goldsmith's shop.

ori-ficio†, ||**-fízio** [L. *-ficium* (*os*, mouth, *facere*, make)], M.: orifice (mouth, aperture).

orígano [L. *-num*], M.: origanum (marjoram).

origi-nále, ADJ.: original (first); M.: original (first copy). **-nalitá**, F.: originality. **-nalménte**, ADV.: originally (primarily, at first). **-naménte**†, M.: origin (source, cause). **-náre**, TR.: originate (give origin to); INTR.: originate (have origin). **-nário**, ADJ.: original (Eng.† originary). **-natóre**, M., **-natríce**, F.: originator. ||**origi-ne** [L. *origo* (*orior*, rise)], F.: origin (rise, source, cause).

ori-gliáre [Fr. *oreiller* (*oreille*, EAR)], INTR.: stand listening (eavesdrop). **-glière**, M.: pillow (cushion).

orí-na [L. *urina*], F.: urine. **-naláta**, F.: blow with a chamber. **-nále**, M.: chamber(-pot); retort†. **-nalétto**, **-nalíno**, *dim.* of *-nale.* **-náre**, INTR.: urinate. **-nário**, ADJ.: urinary. **-natóio**, M.: urinal (closet).

orínci†, ADV.: very distant.

orinéso†, ADJ.: urinous.

ori-oláio, M.: watchmaker (or mender). ||**-òlo** [? *ora* I], M.: watch; clock.

ori=re† [L. *-ri*], INTR.: be born; rise. **-ándo**, ADJ.: original.

oriuòlo†, M.: watch; clock.

orizzon-tále, ADJ.: horizontal. **-talménte**, ADV.: horizontally. ||**orizzónte** [Gr. *horizónta* (*horízein*, limit)], M.: horizon.

or-láre, TR.: hem; border. **-láto**, ADJ.: hemmed; bordered. **-latóra**, F., **-latóre**, M., **-latríce**, F.: hemmer; borderer. **-latúra**, F.: hemming; border (edge). **-létto**, *dim.* of *-lo.* **-liccétto**, **-liccíno**, *dim.* of *-liccio.* **-líccio**, M.: end crust (of bread); rough edge. **-líno**, *car. dim.* of *-lo.* ||**ór-lo** [Fr. *-le* (L. *ora*, border); cf. Eng.† *-le*], M.: hem; border; edge (brim, rim).

órma [?], F.: footprint; trace (sign).

ormái = *oramai.*

ormá-re†, TR.: trace (follow up). **-tóre**†, M.: pursuer.
or-meggiáre, TR.: moor (anchor); REFL.: conduct one's self. ||**-méggio** [Gr. *hórmos*, link], M.: mooring; cable (of ship).
ormesíno†, M.: kind of silk.
orna-mentále, ADJ.: ornamental (embellishing). **-mentazióne**, F.: ornamentation. **-ménto**, M.: ornament (decoration); ornamenting. ||**orná-re** [L.], TR.: ornament (embellish, adorn). **-tamente**, ADV.: ornately (finely). **ornáto**, ADJ.: ornamented (ornate, adorned); honourable; M.: ornament. **-tóre**, M., **-tríce**, F.: ornamenter. **-túra**, F.: ornament (embellishment, finery).
ornèllo [*orno*], M.: kind of ash-tree.
orni-tología [Gr. *órnis*, bird, *lógos*, discourse], F.: ornithology. **-tològico**, pl. *—ci*, ADJ.: ornithological. **-tòlogo**, M.: ornithologist.
ornitoríneo [Gr. *órnis*, bird, *rhúncos*, beak], M.: ornithorhynchus (water-mole).
órno [L. *-nus*], M.: ash-tree.
òro [L. *aurum*], M.: gold (precious metal); money: *— filato*, gold wire; *star nell' —*, live at ease.
orobánche [Gr.], M.: orobanche (plant).
oro=chícco, M.: gum (from trees).
oro-grafía [Gr. *óros*, mountain, *gráphein*, describe], F.: orography. **-gráfico**, pl. *—ci*, ADJ.: orographic.
oro-logería, F.: horology. **-logiáio**, **-logière**†, M.: watchmaker (or mender). ||**-'logio** [L. *horo-logium*, 'HOUR-teller'], M.: timepiece (watch; clock, horologe): *— da sole*, sun-dial. **orò-scopo**, M.: horoscope.
orpel-láio†, M.: leather-gilder. **-laménto**, M.: tinselling; pretence. **-láre**, TR.: tinsel; disguise. ||**orpèl-lo** [l. L. *auripellum*, gold-flake], M.: tinsel; falsity (disguise).
orpiménto [L. *aurum*, gold, *pigmentum*, pigment], M.: orpiment (dye).
or-ránza†, F.: honour (respect). **-ráre**†, TR.: honour (respect).
or-rendaménte, ADV.: horribly (terribly). ||**-rèndo** [L. *horrendus*], ADJ.: horrible (terrible).
orret-tiziaménte, ADV.: surreptitiously (by stealth). ||**-tízio** [L. *ob-repticius* (*repere*, creep)], ADJ.: surreptitious (fraudulent); M.: surreption.
orrévol. . = *onorevol.* .
orrezióne†, F.: surreption (stealthy act).
orríbi-le [L. *horribilis*], ADJ.: horrible (frightful). **-lità**, F.: horribleness. **-lménte**, ADV.: horribly (frightfully).
orri-daménte, ADV.: horridly. **-dézza**, **-dità**†, F.: horridness. ||**òrri-do** [L. *horridus*], ADJ.: horrid (frightful, hideous).
orróre [L. *horror* (*horrere*, tremble)], M.: horror (fright, dread): *avere in —*, hate (detest).
ór-sa, F.: she-bear: *— maggiore*, great bear (constellation). **-sácchio**†, **-sacchíno**, **-sacchiòtta**, F., **-sacchiòtto**, M.: bear's cub. **-sáccio**, *disp.* of **-so**. **-sáta**†, F.: laments (groans). **-sátto**, **-sicèllo**, M.: bear's cub. **-síno**, ADJ.: of a bear; bear-like. ||**ór-so** [L. *ursus*], M.: bear; kind of shovel: *pigliar l' —*, get intoxicated.
orsóio [L. *-sus* (*-dire*, warp)], M.: silk-warp; web.
or=sù, INTERJ.: come on! courage!
or-táccio [*orto*, garden], *disp.* of *-to*. **-tággio**, M.: pot-herbs. **-táglia**, **-tále**†, M.: large kitchen-garden. **-tènse**, ADJ.: of a kitchen-garden (Eng.† hortensial).
ortí-ca [L. *urtica*], F.: nettle. **-cáio**, M.: place full of nettles. **-cária**, F.: urticaria (nettle-rash).
orticèllo, *dim.* of *orto*.
orti-cheggiáre†, TR.: sting with nettles. ||**-chéto** [-*ca*], M.: place full of nettles.
or-ticíno, *dim.* of *-to*. **-ticultóre**, M.: horticulturist. **-ticultúra**, F.: horticulture. **-tíno**, *dim.* of *-to*. **-tívo**, ADJ.: of kitchen-garden ground; ortive (rising). ||**òr-to** 1 [L. *hortus*], M.: kitchen-garden.
òrto 2 [L. *-tus* (*orior*, rise)], M.: Orient (east); birth†.
orto- [Gr. *orthós*, right]: **-dossaménte**, ADV.: orthodoxly. **-dossía**, F.: orthodoxy. **-dòsso** [Gr. *dóxa*, opinion], ADJ., M.: orthodox. **-epía** [Gr. *épos*, word], F.: orthoepy. **-fonía** [Gr. *phoné*, sound], F.: orthophony. **-grafía** [Gr. *gráphein*, write], F.: orthography. **-gráfico**, pl. *—ci*, ADJ.: orthographical. **-grafizzáre**†, INTR.: orthographize (spell correctly).
ortoláno [*orto* 1], ADJ.: of a gardener; M.: gardener; ortolan (singing-bird).
orto-logía [Gr. *orthós*, right, *lógos*, discourse], F.: orthology. **-pedía** [Gr. *pais*, child], F.: orthopedy. **-pèdico**, pl. *—ci*, ADJ.: orthopedical. **ortò-tteri** [Gr. *ptéron*, wing], M. PL.: orthoptera (order of insects).
orúccio, *disp. dim.* of *oro*.
or-vietáno, ||**-viéto** [*Orvieto*], M.: Orvieto wine; medicine.
òrza [?], F.: mizzen-bowline.
orzaiòlo [*orzo*], M.: pimple (on the eyelid).
orzáre [*orza*], INTR.: laveer (tack).
or-záta [*orzo*], F.: orgeat (beverage). **-záto**, ADJ.: made of barley.
orzéese†, M.: kind of wild vine.
òrzo [L. *ordeum*], M.: barley.

osán-na [fr. Heb.], M.: hosanna. **-náre†**, INTR.: sing hosannas.
osáre [L. *ausus*, part. of *audere*], TR., INTR.: dare.
osbèrgo† = *usbergo*.
osce-naménte, ADV.: obscenely. **-nità**, F.: obscenity. ‖**oscè-no** [L. *obscenus*], ADJ.: obscene (impure, foul).
oscil-láre [L.], INTR.: oscillate (vibrate). **-latòrio**, ADJ.: oscillatory. **-lazióne**, F.: oscillation (vibration).
oscitánza [L. *-tare*], F.: oscillation (uncertainty).
osculá-re [L. *-ri* (*os*, mouth)], TR.: osculate (kiss, touch). **-zióne**, F.: osculation.
oscu-rábile, ADJ.: that may be obscured. **-raménte**, ADV.: obscurely (darkly). **-raménto**, M.: obscuring (darkening); obscurity. **-ráre**, TR.: obscure (darken); REFL.: become dark. **-razióne**, F.: obscuring; eclipse. **-rétto**, *dim.* of *-ro*. **-rezza†**, F.: obscurity. **-ríccio†**, *dim.* of *-ro*. **-rità**, F.: obscurity (darkness, humility). ‖**oscú-ro** [L. *obscurus*], ADJ.: obscure (dark, humble); M.: dark (obscurity); ADV.: obscurely.
òsmio [Gr. *osmé*, odor], M.: osmium (metal).
òso†, ADJ.: (*poet.*) bold (audacious).
òs-pe†, M.: host; guest. **-pedále**, M.: hospital. **-pitábile†**, **-pitále**, ADJ.: hospitable. **-pitále**, M.: hospital. **-pitalière**, M.: hospitaller. **-pitalità**, F.: hospitality. **-pitalménte**, ADV.: hospitably. **-pitáre**, TR.: extend hospitality to. ‖**òs-pite** [L. *hospes*], M.: GUEST; HOST. **-piziáre†**, TR., INTR.: lodge. **-pízio**, M.: hospice (asylum, convent).
os-sáccio [*osso*], *disp.* of *-so*. **-sáio†**, M.: bone-worker. **-sáme**, M.: quantity of bones; pillars (columns, support). **-sário**, M.: ossuary (charnel-house). **-satúra**, F.: bony framework.
ossecrá-re†, INTR.: beseech (entreat). **-zióne†**, F.: entreaty.
òsseo [*osso*], ADJ.: osseous (bony, of bone).
osse-quènte, ADJ.: yielding (Eng.† obsequent). **-quiánte**, ADJ.: revering. **-quiáre**, TR.: revere (pay homage). **-quiáto**, ADJ.: revered. ‖**ossè-quio** [L. *obsequium*], M.: obsequiousness (reverence, homage). **-quiosaménte**, ADV.: obsequiously. **-quióso**, ADJ.: obsequious.
osserèllo, *dim.* of *osso*.
osser-vábile, ADJ.: observable (noticeable). **-vabilménte**, ADV.: observably. **-vaménto†**, M.: observation. **-vandíssimo**, ADJ.: most honoured. **-vánte**, ADJ.: observing; M.: observant (monk). **-vánza**, **-vánzia†**, F.: observance, homage. ‖**-váre** [L. *observare*], TR.: observe (notice, watch, obey, say, revere). **-vataménte†**, ADV.: observingly (attentively). **-vatívo**, ADJ.: observing (observative). **-váto**, ADJ.: observed. **-vatóre**, M., **-vatríce**, F.: observer. **-vatòrio**, M.: observatory. **-vazioncèlla**, **-vazioncína**, *dim.* of *-vazione*. **-vazióne**, F.: observing; observation (notice, comment); observance.
ossèsso [L. *ob-sessus*, be-SET], ADJ.: beset, possessed (by a demon).
ossétto, *dim.* of *osso*.
ossiacánta†, F.: barberry bush.
ossi-cèllo, -**cíno**, *dim.* of *osso*.
ossi-dáre [-*do*], TR.: oxydize; REFL.: become oxydized. **-dazióne**, F.: oxidation.
ossi-dionále, ADJ.: obsidional. ‖**-dióne†** [L. *ob-sidio*], F.: SIEGE.
oss-i. . [-*o*]: **-ífero**, ADJ.: ossiferous (containing bone). **-ificáre**, INTR.: ossify. **-ificazióne**, F.: ossification.
ossige-náre, TR.: oxygenate. **ossígeno**, ‖**ossíge-no** [Gr. *oxús*, acid, *gen-*, bring forth], M.: oxygen.
ossimèle†, M.: oxymel.
os-síno, *dim.* of *-so*. ‖**òs-so**, pl. *-si* or *-sa* [L. *os*], M.: bone; stone† (of fruit). **-sóso†**, **-súto**, ADJ.: bony.
òs-ta†, F.: hostess; landlady. ‖**-táccio**, *disp.* of *-te*.
ostácolo [L. *obstaculum*], M.: obstacle (obstruction).
ostággio [OFr. *ostage*], M.: hostage.
ostále†, M.: hospital.
os-tánte†, ADJ.: opposing; ADV.: notwithstanding. ‖**-táre** [L. *ob-*, *stare*], INTR.: oppose (withstand, hinder).
òs-te [L. *hospes*], M.: HOST (landlord, innkeeper); army†; GUEST†. **-teggiaménto†**, M.: encampment. **-teggiáre**, TR.: treat hostilely; attack†; INTR.: encamp. **-tellággio**, M.: inn (hostelry). **-tellá-no†**, M.: innkeeper. **-tellière†**, M.: inn. **-tèllo**, M.: (*poet.*) hospice (asylum).
osten-síbile [L. *-sus* (*os-tendere*, show)], ADJ.: ostensible (manifest). **-sívo**, ADJ.: ostensive (showing). **-sóre**, M.: shower (exhibitor). **-sòrio**, M.: ostensory. **-taménto**, M.: ostentation (boasting). **-táre**, TR.: boast (vaunt, ostentate). **-táto**, ADJ.: boasted. **-tatóre**, M., **-tatríce**, F.: boaster (Eng.† ostentator). **-tazióne**, F.: ostentation (vaunting).
osteología [Gr. *ostéon*, bone, *lógos*, discourse], F.: osteology.
oste-ría [OFr. *osterie*], F.: HOSTELRY (inn). **-riáccia**, *disp.* of *-ria*. **-riétta**, *dim.* of *-ria*. **-riúccia**, *disp. dim.* of *-ria*. **osté-ssa**, F.: landlady (hostess); innkeeper's wife.
ostè-trica, **-tríce†** [L. *obstetrix* (*ob-stare*, stand before)], F.: midwife. **-trí-**

cía, F.: obstetrics. **ostè-trico**, pl. —*ci*, ADJ.: obstetrician.

òstia [L. *hostia*], F.: victim; sacrifice; HOST (consecrated).

os-tiariáto, M.: office of a church-warden. ||**-tiário** [L. *-tiarius* (*-tium*, door)], M.: church-door keeper (church-warden, Eng.† ostiary).

osti-chézza†, F.: sharpness (harshness). ||**òsti-co**, pl. —*ci* [?], ADJ.: sharp (harsh, displeasing).

os-tière†, **-tièro†**, M.: innkeeper (landlord).

ostí-le [L. *hostilis*], ADJ.: hostile (unfriendly, warlike). **-lità**, F.: hostility. **-lménte**, ADV.: hostilely.

ostiná-re [L. (*ob-stinare*, per-SIST)], REFL.: be obstinate (stubborn). **-taménte**, ADV.: obstinately (stubbornly). **-tézza**, F.: obstinacy. **ostiná-to**, ADJ.: obstinate (pertinacious, stubborn). **-zióne**, F.: obstinacy (pertinacity).

os-tracíṣmo, M.: ostracism (expulsion). ||**òs-trica** [L. *ostrea*], F.: oyster (mollusk). **-tricáio**, M.: oyster-bed. **-trichétta**, **-trichína**, *dim.* of *-trica*.

òstro[1] [L. *ostrum*], M.: purple (colour, or cloth).

òstro[2] [L. *auster*], M.: south wind.

ostro=gòto, ADJ., M.: Ostrogoth.

ostru-ènte, ADJ.: obstructing. ||**-íre** [L. *ob-struere*], TR., INTR.: obstruct (impede, bar). **-ttívo**, ADJ.: obstructive (impeding). **-zioncèlla**, *dim.* of *-zione*. **-zióne**, F.: obstruction (check, bar).

ostupe-fáre†, IRR.; TR.: stupefy. **-fátto†**, PART. of *-fare*; ADJ.: stupefied. **-fazióne†**, F.: stupefaction. **-féci†**, PRET. of *-fare*.

otíte [Gr. *oûs*, ear], F.: otitis (inflammation of the ear).

ó-tre [L. *uter*], M.: leathern bottle. **-trèllo†**, *dim.* of *-tre*.

otriáca†, F.: treacle.

otri-cèllo, **-címo**, *dim.* of *otre*.

ótta†, F.: hour: *a — a —*, from time to time.

òtta- [L. *octo*, eight]: **=córdo**, M.: octachord (mus. instr.). **-èdrico**, ADJ.: octahedral. **-èdro** [Gr. *hédra*, base], M.: octahedron. **-gèsimo†**, ADJ.: eightieth. **-gonáto**, ADJ.: octagonal. **ottá-gono** [Gr. *gônos*, angle] M.: octagon.

ot-talmía [Gr. *ophthalmía* (*-mós*, eye)], F.: ophthalmia (eye disease). **-tálmico**, pl. —*ci*, ADJ.: ophthalmic.

ott-angoláre, ADJ.: octangular. ||**-ángolo** [*otto angolo*], M.: octagon.

ottan-sèi, NUM.: eighty-six. **-sètte**, NUM.: eighty-seven. ||**ottán-ta** [L. *octaginta*], NUM.: eighty. **-tèsimo**, ADJ.: eightieth. **-tína**, F.: about eighty. **-sèi**, **-sètte**, *pop.* = *-sei*, *-sette*.

ottárda†, F.: bustard (bird).

ottá-re [L. *optare*], TR.: (*polit.*) choose. **-tívo**, ADJ., M.: optative (grammar).

ottástilo [Gr. *oktástulos* (*októ*, eight, *stûlos*, pillar)), M.: octostyle (portico with eight pillars); ADJ.: octostyle.

ottá-va [*otto*], F.: octave (eight days, stanza, scale). **-vário**, M.: eight days of prayer (following a feast for a saint). **-verèlla**, *dim.* of *-va*. **-víno**, M.: kind of flute. **ottá-vo**, ADJ.: eighth; M.: octavo (book).

ottemperáre [L. *obtemperare*], INTR.: obey (submit, Eng.† obtemperate).

ottene-braménto, M.: darkening. ||**-bráre** [L. *obtenebrare*], TR.: darken (dim, obscure). **-brazióne**, F.: darkening [Eng.† obtenebration].

otte-nènte, ADJ.: obtaining. ||**-nère** [L. *ob-tinere*], IRR. (cf. *tenere*); TR.: OBTAIN (procure). **-níbile**, ADJ.: obtainable. **-niménto**, M.: obtainment (procuring).

ot-tènne [L. *octennis*], ADJ.: octennial (of eight years); eight years old; M.: octennial. **-tènnio**, M.: period of eight years.

òtti-ca [Gr. *optikós*], F.: optics; factory (of optical glass). **òtti-co**, pl. —*ci*, ADJ.: optical; M.: professor of optics; manufacturer (or seller) of optical glass.

otti-maménte, ADV.: in the best way. **-máte**, M.: optimate (noble, chief). **-míṣmo**, M.: optimism. **-místa**, M.: optimist. ||**òtti-mo** [L. *optimus*], ADJ.: best (very good); M.: best.

òtto [L. *octo*], NUM.: EIGHT. **-agèno†**, ADJ.: octogenarian. **-bráta**, F.: October excursion. **ottó-bre**, M.: October (month). **-bríno**, ADJ.: October (ripening in October). **-centèsimo**, ORD.: eight hundredth. **-cènto** [L. *-centum*], M.: eight hundred. **-genário†**, ADJ.: octogenarian (of eighty years of age).

ottomána [*ottomano*], F.: ottoman (Turkish couch).

otto=míla, NUM.: eight thousand.

otto-náio [*ottone*], M.: worker in brass (brasier). **-náme**, M.: brass work.

ottonário [L. *octonarius*], ADJ.: of eight (verse-syllables).

ottóne [*lattone* (aug. of *latta*)], M.: brass (alloy).

ottuagenário [L. *octo-generius*], ADJ., M.: octogenarian.

ottúndere [L. *ob-tundere*], TR.: blunt (dull, Eng.† obtund).

òttuplo [L. *octu-plus*], ADJ.: octuple (eightfold).

ottura-ménto, M.: obturation. ||**otturá-re** [L. *obturare*], TR.: stop up (close). **-tóre**, M.: obturator. **-tòrio**, ADJ.: stopping (closing). **-zióne**, F.: obturation.

ottu-samente, ADV.: obtusely (stupidly, bluntly). **-sezza**†, **-sione**†, **-sità**, F.: obtuseness (bluntness, dullness). **-sángolo**, ADJ.: obtusangular. ‖**ottú-so** [L. *ob-tusus*], ADJ.: obtuse (blunt, dull, stupid).

o-váia [*ovo*], F.: ovary (organ). **-váio**, ADJ.: egg-producing; M.: egg-seller. **-vaiòlo**, M.: egg-cup. **-vále**, ADJ.: oval (egg-shaped). **-valità**, F.: ovalness. **-vário**, M.: ovary. **-váto**†, ADJ.: oval. **ovát-ta**, F.: cotton-batting (glazed over with the white of 'egg'). **-vattáre**, TR.: line with cotton-batting.

ovazióne [L. *ovatio*], F.: ovation (applause).

óve [L. *ubi*], ADV.: where.

overáre†, TR.: do; INTR.: work.

òvest [Eng. *west*], M.: west.

ovi-cino, *dim.* of *ovo*. **-dótto**, M.: oviduct. **-fórme**, ADJ.: oviform (oval).

o-víle, M.: sheep-fold. **-vilúccio**, *dim.* of *-vile*. ‖**-víno** 1 [L. *-vis*], ADJ.: of a sheep.

o-víno 2, *dim.* of *-vo*. **-víparo**, ADJ., M.: oviparous. ‖**ò-vo**, pl. *-vi*, *-va* [L. *-vum*], M.: egg. **-voidále**, ADJ.: ovoidal (egg-shaped). **-vòide**, F.: ovoid. **-voláia**, F., **-voláio**, M.: nursery for olive plants. **-volazióne**, F.: ovulation. **ò-volo**, M.: (egg-like) mushroom; ovolo (moulding). **-vología**, F.: ovology. **-vos = mòlles**, M.: sort of ice-cream (with eggs). **-vúccio**, *disp. dim.* of *-vo*. **ò-vulo**, M.: ovule.

ò-vra†, F.: (*poet.*) work (action). **-vrággio**†, M.: manual labor. **-vráre**†, TR.: do (operate).

ovúnque [L. *ubi unquam*], ADV.: wherever.

ovvéro [*o vero*], CONJ.: either (or, or else).

ovvía [*o via*], INTERJ.: come on!

ov-viaménte, ADV.: obviously. **-viáre**, TR., INTR.: obviate (hinder). **-viatóre**†, M.: hinderer. **-viazióne**†, F.: obviating. ‖**òv-vio**, pl *-vi*, *-vii* [L. *obvius*], ADJ.: obvious (plain); trivial†.

oziaco†, ADJ.: unfortunate.

o-ziáre, **-zieggiáre**, INTR.: idle (pass time in leisure). ‖**ò-zio** [L. *-tium*], M.: idleness (leisure); PL.: time of repose (quiet). **-ziosággine**, F.: laziness (slothfulness). **-ziosaménte**, ADV.: lazily. (idly); uselessly. **-ziosétto**, *dim.* of *-zioso*. **-ziosità**, F.: idleness (laziness). **-zióso**, ADJ.: idle (lazy); useless.

o-zònico, pl. —*ci*, ADJ.: of ozone. ‖**-zòno** [Gr. *ózein*, smell], M.: ozone (oxygen). **-zonòmetro**, M.: ozonometer.

ozzi-máto†, ADJ.: full of sweet basil. **òzzi-mo**†, M.: (*bot.*) sweet basil.

P

p *pi* [L.], M.: p (the letter).

pacá-re† [L.], TR.: PACIFY (calm). **-taménte**, ADV.: quietly (placidly). **-tézza**, F.: quiet (calmness). **pacá-to**, ADJ.: quiet (calm, placid),

pácca [echoic], F.: slap.

pacchèo [?], M.: simpleton (ninny).

pacchétto, *dim.* of *-pacco*.

pác-chia [?], F.: feasting. **-chiaménto**, M.: feasting. **-chiáre**, INTR.: eat greedily. **-chiatóre**, M.: glutton. **-chierótto**, M.: fat boy.

pac-chína, F.: *dim.* of *-ca*; slap (on the head). **-chináre**, TR.: slap (strike).

pacchióne†, M.: glutton.

paccióme [?], M.: refuse of the woods.

pácco [l. L. *-cus*], M.: package (packet).

pá-ce [L. *pax*], F.: peace (calm, quiet); ease: *con buona* —, courteously; by leave; *in santa* —, quietly. **-cefficáre**†, TR.: pacify (quiet). **-cèra**, F., **-cère**, M.: peace-maker.

pachidèrmi [Gr. *pachús*, thick, *dérma*, skin], M. PL.: pachydermata (order of mammals).

pa-ciáro†, M.: peace-maker. **-cibilménte**†, ADV.: peaceably (quietly). **-ciènza**†, F.: patience. **-cièra**, F., ‖**-cière** [*pace*], M.: peace-maker. **-cifero**†, ADJ.: peace-bringing (peaceful).

pacifi-cábile, ADJ.: appeasable (placable). **-caménte**, ADV.: pacifically (peacefully). **-caménto**, M.: pacifying. **-cáre**, TR.: pacify (calm, appease). **-catóre**, M., **-catríce**, F.: peace-maker. **-cazióne**, F.: pacification. ‖**pacífi-co**, pl. —*ci* [L. *pacificus*], ADJ.: pacific (peace-making, appeasing).

pa-cioccóna, F., **-cioccóne**, M.: good-natured person. ‖**-cióne** [*pace*], ADJ.: pacific; M.: peaceful person.

padèl-la [L. *patella*], F.: frying-pan; knee-pan†. **-láio**, M.: maker (and seller) of frying-pans. **-láta**, F.: frying-panful. **-létta**, *dim.* of *-la*. **-lína**, F.: *dim.* of *-la*; small kettle; candle-safe (bobèche). **-líno**, *dim.* of *-la*. **-lóna**, **-lóne**, **-lòtto**†, *aug.* of *-la*.

padiglióne [L. *papilio*, butterfly], M.: PAVILION (tent); facet (of a diamond); auricle.

pá-dre [L. *-ter*], M.: father; church dignitary (priest). **-dreggiáre**, INTR.: resemble one's father. **pá-dria**† (*poet.*) fatherland. **-driciòllo**†, *d* *-dre*. **-drígno**, M.: stepfather. **no**, M.: *dim.* of *-dre*; godfather; (in a duel). **-dróna**, F.: mistress. **máccio**, *disp.* of *-drone*. **-dronág**

M.: ownership; possession. **-dronále,** ADJ.: of a master. **-dronánza,** F.: proprietorship (mastery, control). **-dronáto,** M.: estate (of a patron); possession; protection†. **-droncína,** *dim.* of *-drona.* **-droncíno,** *dim.* of *-drone.* **-dróne,** M.: patron (master); protector†. **-droneggiáre,** TR.: master (rule, govern). **-dronería†,** F.: ownership. **-dronésco,** ADJ.: master-like. **-dronéssa†,** F.: mistress. **-droníssimo,** M.: great master (patron).

padú-le [*palude*], M.: swamp (marsh). **-léscot,** ADJ.: swampy (marshy). **-létta, -létto,** *dim.* of *-le.*

pae-sáccio, *disp.* of *-se.* **-sággio,** M.: landscape. **-sáno,** ADJ.: native; M.: countryman. ‖**paé-se** [L. *pagensis* (*pagus,* land)], M.: country (land); territory (region); fatherland; village. **-sèllo, -sétto, -síno,** *dim.* of *-se.* **-sísta,** M.: painter of landscapes. **-sóne,** *aug.* of *-se.* **-súccio, -súcolo,** *disp. dim.* of *-se.*

paf-futèllo, *dim.* of *-futo.* ‖**-fúto** [*pappa*], ADJ.: plump. **-futóne,** *aug.* of *-futo.*

pá-ga [*-gare*], F.: pay (wages, salary). **-gábile,** ADJ.: payable. **-gáccia,** F.: bad payer. **-gaménto,** M.: paying; payment.

paga-naménte, ADV.: like a pagan. **-neggiáre,** INTR.: imitate (paganism). **-nésimo,** M.: paganism. **-nicaménte†,** ADV.: like a pagan (heathen). **-nísmo†,** M.: paganism. **-nizzáre†,** INTR.: paganize. ‖**pagá-no** [L. *-nus* (*pagus,* country)], ADJ.: pagan; M.: pagan (heathen).

pagá-nte, ADJ.: paying. ‖**pagá-re** [L. *pacare,* PACIFY], TR.: PAY (compensate); REFL.: pay one's self. **pagá-to,** ADJ.: paid. **-tóra,** F., **-tóre,** M., **-tríce,** F.: payer. **-torèllo,** M.: bad payer. **-túra†,** F.: payment.

pag-gería, F.: number of pages; college of pages; rank of a page. **-gétto, -gíno†,** *dim.* of *-gio.* ‖**pág-gio** [? Gr. *paidíon,* child], M.: PAGE (attendant, youth).

pagherò [fut. of *pagare*], M.: promissory note.

pági-na [L.], F.: page (of a book): *le sacre -ne,* the Bible. **-natúra,** F.: paging (of a book). **-nétta,** *dim.* of *-na.*

pá-glia [L. *-lea*], F.: straw. **-gliáccia,** *disp.* of *-glia.* **-gliacciáta,** F.: worthless play; clownishness. **-gliáccio,** M.: chopped straw; paillasse, pallet; mask; buffoon. **-gliaccióne,** *aug.* of *-gliaccio.* **-gliáio,** M.: straw-stack. **-gliaiòlo, -gliaiuòlo†,** M.: straw seller. **-gliaréscot,** ADJ.: made of straw. **-gliáto,** ADJ.: straw-coloured. **-gliericcio,** M.: paillasse, pallet; chopped straw. **-glieríno,** ADJ.: straw-coloured. **-gliettána,** F.: silver-eel. **-gliolája†,** F.: dewlap (of oxen). **-gliòlo,** M.: bottom (of a boat). **-gliéme,** M.: chopped straw. **-glióso,** ADJ.: full of straw; defective. **-gliúca†, -gliúcola,** F.: straw (fescue). **-gliúme†,** M.: heap of straws. **-gliuòlo†,** M.: bit of straw; pantry. **-gliúzza,** F.: straw (fescue).

pagnòt-ta [*pane*], F.: small loaf. **-tèlla, -tína,** F.: small loaf.

págo [*pagato*], ADJ.: satisfied (pleased); M.†: pay: *a —,* by pay.

pagòda [Pers.], F.: pagoda (temple); idol.

pagonázzo†, ADJ.: violet.

pagóne†, M.: peacock.

pai-áccio†, *disp.* of *-o.* **-étto,** *iron. dim.* of *-o.* ‖**pái-o,** pl. *-a* [*paro*], M.: PAIR (brace).

paio-láta, F.: potful. **-lína,** F.: kettle (with handles). **-líno,** M.: soft hat. ‖**paiò-lo** [?], M.: kettle (boiler, pot); potful.

paiuòl. .† = *paiol.*.

pála [L.], F.: shovel; ladle (of a water-mill); oar-blade.

pala-dína, F.: paladin; ADJ.: paladin. **-dinésco,** ADJ.: of a paladin. ‖**-díno** [L. *-tinus* (*-tium,* palace)], M.: paladin (knight).

palafít-ta [*palo fitto*], F.: embankment of piles. **-táre,** TR.: pile (strengthen with piles). **-táta,** F.: pile-work.

pala-frenière, -frenièro, M.: groom (stable-servant). ‖**-fréno** [l. L. *parafredus*], M.: PALFREY (saddle-horse).

palágio [L. *-latium*], M.: (*poet.*) palace.

paláia [*palo*], F.: heap of stakes (for vines).

palaménto [*pala,* oar-blade], M.: oaring (of a long-boat).

palamíta [Gr. *pelamús*], F.: pilchard (fish).

palán-ca [L. *planca*], F.: stake (stick); palisade (fence). **-cáto,** M.: enclosure (formed by a palisade). **-chíno,** M.: palanquin (sedan-chair). **palán-cola,** F.: plank (for crossing streams).

palán-dra [Fr. *balandran*], F.: great coat; bomb-ship. **-dràna, -dráno,** *disp.* of *-dra.* **-drèa†,** F.: kind of ship.

pa-láro [*-lo*], TR.: stake; drive stakes†; **-láta†1,** F.: palisade.

paláta2 [*pala*], F.: shovelful; simultaneous stroke (of oars)†.

palatále [*palato*], ADJ.: palatal.

palatína†, F.: fur-tippet.

pala-tináto, M.: palatinate (province or title). ‖**-tíno** [L. *-tinus* (*-tium,* ... ADJ.: palatine.

paláto [L. *-tum* ... ...

palatúra [*palare*], F.: staking (plants)
palaz-záccio, *disp.* of *-zo.* **-zétto, -zíno**, *car. dim.* of *-zo.* **-zína**, F.: beautiful little palace. ‖**paláz-zo** [L. *palatium*], M.: palace. **-zóno**, *aug.* of *-zo.* **-zótto**, M.: large palace; palace-like house.
pal-chétto, *dim.* of *-co;* shelf; small box (in a theatre). **-chista**, M.: owner of a theatre box. **-chistuòlo**†, M.: covering (roof). ‖**pál-co** [OGer. *balko*, beam, BALK], M.: joists (flooring); floor (story); scaffolding (BALcony); stage; (*theat.*) box; row-bench; bridge (of a ship); branching (of trees); horns (of a stag).
palèo [?], M.: top (child's toy).
paleo- [Gr. *palaiós*, ancient]: **-grafía** [Gr. *gráphein*, write], F.: paleography. **-gráfico**, pl. *—ci*, ADJ.: paleographical. **paleò-grafo**, M.: paleographer. **-lítico**, pl. *—ci* [Gr. *líthos*, stone], ADJ.: paleolithic (of the stone age). **-ntología** [Gr. *ónta*, beings, *lógos*, discourse], F.: paleontology. **-ntològico**, pl. *—ci*, ADJ.: paleontological. **-ntòlogo**, M.: paleontologist.
pale-ṣáre, TR.: disclose (reveal). **-ṣatívo**, ADJ.: disclosing (revealing). **-ṣatóre**, M.: discloser. ‖**palé-ṣe** [L. *palam*, openly], ADJ.: known (manifest, plain). **-ṣeménte**, ADV.: manifestly (plainly).
pa-lèstra [Gr. *-laístra*], F.: palestra (gymnastic, gymnasium). **-lèstrico**†, ADJ.: palestrical. **-lestríta**†, M.: wrestler.
palétta [*pala*], F.: fire-shovel; scapula (shoulder-blade).
palettáre [*-letto*], TR.: drive stakes into.
palet-táta [*paletta*], F.: fire-shovelful. **-tína**, *car. dim.* of *paletta.*
pa-létto, M.: *dim.* of *palo;* small bolt. **-liccetáta**†, F.: palisade. **-liccetuòlo**†, *dim.* of *-lo.* **-lificáre**†, INTR.: drive stakes (piles). ‖**-lína** [*palo*], F.: forest (for stake cutting).
palingènesi [Gr. *-sía* (*pálin*, again, *génesis*, birth)], F.: palingenesis (regeneration).
palinodía [Gr. (*pálin*, again, *odḗ*, song)], F.: palinode (recantation).
palinsèsto [Gr. *palímpsestos* (*pálin*, again, *psen-*, rub away)], M.: palimpsest (parchment used for two inscriptions, the first erased).
pá-lio, pl. *-lí* or *-lii* [L. *pallium*, cloak (prize at races)], M.: race (course); race-track; prize†; canopy†: *mandare al —*, set a-going; advertise; *portare al —*, see a thing through. **-liòtto**, M.: altar-cloth.
pali-scálmo†, ‖**-schérmo** [OFr. *palescrmel*], M.: small boat (*skiff*).
palissán-dro [Fr. *-dre*], M.: rosewood; violet-ebony (wood).
palizzáta, F.: palisade.
pálla 1 [OGer. *balla*], F.: ball: *avere* (or *balzar*) *la — in mano*, have the opportunity; *far alla — di*, toss about.
pálla 2 [L.], F.: pall (cloak, mantle); altar-cloth.
palla=còrda†, F.: tennis-court.
palládio [L. *-dium*], ADJ.: of Pallas; M.: palladium (statue of Pallas); protection.
pal-láio [*palla* 1], M.: ball-maker (or seller); score-keeper (at billiards). **-la=máglio**†, M.: PALL-MALL (game). **-lá-re**†, INTR.: play a ball-game; shake. **-láta**, F.: blow with a ball. **-láto**, ADJ.: spotted. **-leggiaménte**, M.: ball-throwing. **-leggiáre**, INTR.: play a ball-game; TR.: shake; tease. **-léggio**, M.: ball-throwing (playing); rebounding (of a ball); exchange.
pallènte†, ADJ.: pale (wan).
pallerino†, M.: ball-player.
pálleto = *palltò.*
pallétta, *dim.* of *palla.*
pal-liaménto, M.: palliation (hiding). ‖**-liáre** [L. (*pallium*, mantle)], TR.: palliate (cover, conceal). **-liatívo**, ADJ.: palliative (relieving). **-liáto**, ADJ.: palliated.
palli-daménte, ADV.: pallidly (wanly). **-détto, -díno**, *car. dim.* of *-do.* **-dézza**, F.: pallidness (paleness). **-díccio**, ADJ.: somewhat pale. **-dità**, F.: pallidness (paleness). ‖**pálli-do** [L. *-dus*], ADJ.: pallid (pale, wan). **-dóne**, *aug.* of *-do.* **-dóre**†, M.: pallor (paleness). **-dúccio**, *dim.* of *-do.* **-dúme**†, M.: paleness.
pal-lína, *dim.* of *-la.* **-líno**, M.: small shot; the small ball (in billiards, etc.).
pállio [L. *-ium*], M.: pallium (Grecian cloak); pall (church vestment).
pallo-náccio, *disp.* of *-ne.* **-náio**, M.: ball-maker; ball-tender. **-ncíno**, M.: *dim.* of *-ne;* small globes (used in illuminations). ‖**palló-ne** [*palla* 1], M.: large ball; balloon.
pallóre [L. *pallor*], M.: pallor (paleness).
pallòt-ta [*palla* 1], F.: small ball. **pal-lòt-tola**, F.: *dim.* of *palla;* bullet. **-to-láio**, M.: ball-ground. **-tolétta**, *dim.* of *-tola.* **-tolièra**†, F.: notch (in a crossbow). **-tolière**, M.: abacus (calculating-table). **-tolína**, *dim.* of *-tola.*
pál-ma [L.], F.: palm (of the hand); palm-tree (date-tree); symbol of victory. **-máre**, ADJ.: palmary (worthy of the palm, preëminent). **-máta**†, F.: slap (with the palm of the hand): *dar —*, shake hands. **-máto**, ADJ.: palmate.

palménto [?], M.: flour-receiver (*of* a mill); wine-press†; mill†: *macinare (mangiare) a due* —, eat a great deal; earn much.

pal-méto [*-ma*], M.: palm-tree plantation. **-mière†**, M.: palmer (pilgrim). **-mífero**, ADJ.: palmiferous (palm-bearing). **-mípede**, ADJ.: palmiped (web-footed). **-'mite†**, M.: branch (of a palm-tree). **-mízio**, M.: palm-branch (for Palm-Sunday); palm-tree†. **pál-mo**, M.: palm (of the hands); measure.

pálo [L. *-lus*], M.: stake (stay, pale): *saltar di — in frasca*, pass from one argument to another; — *di ferro*, fire-poker.

palombáro [L. *palumbarius*], M.: diver.

palómbo [L. *palumbes*], M.: kind of fish; wood-pigeon†.

pa-lóna, -lóne, *aug.* of *pala*.

palpá-bile, ADJ.: palpable (perceptible, plain). **-bilità**, F.: palpability. **-bilménte**, ADV.: palpably (plainly). **-ménto**, M.: palpation (touching). ‖**palpáre** [L.], TR.: feel (touch, handle); flatter†. **-tívo**, ADJ.: able to feel. **palpá-to**, ADJ.: felt (touched). **-tóre**, M., **-tríce**, F.: feeler; flatterer†.

pal-pèbra [L.], F.: eyelid. **-pebrále**, ADJ.: palpebral (pertaining to the eyelid). **-pèbre†**, M.: eyelid.

palpeg-giaménto, M.: feeling. ‖**-giáre** [*palpare*], TR.: feel (handle, touch repeatedly); flatter†.

palpévole†, ADJ.: palpable (perceptible).

palpi-taménto, M.: palpitation. **-tánte**, ADJ.: palpitating. ‖**-táre** [L.], INTR.: palpitate (throb). **-tazioncèlla**, *dim.* of *-tazione*. **-tazióne**, F.: palpitation.

pálpi-to, M.: (*poet.*) palpitation.

pal-tò, ‖**-'ton** [Fr. *-tot*], M.: paletot (loose overcoat). **-toncíno**, *dim.* of *-ton*.

paltó-ne†, M.: beggar (mendicant). **-neggiáre†**, INTR.: beg (ask alms). **-nería†**, F.: beggary. **-nière†**, M.: beggar.

palu-dále†, ADJ.: marshy (paludal).

palú-de [L. *palus*], M.: swamp (marsh). **-dèllo†**, *dim.* of *-de*. **-dóso**, ADJ.: swampy (marshy). **palú-stre**, ADJ.: of a swamp; swampy.

pal-váio, -vário, M.: soldier armed with a shield. **-váta**, F.: ordnance; testudo (cover with shields). ‖**-vése** [?], M.: large square shield; soldier (bearing a shield).

pám-pana†, F.: vine-foliage. **-panáio†**, ADJ.: producing vine-leaves. **-panáta**, F.: fumigation with vine-leaves. ‖**pámpano** [L. *-pinus*], M.: vine-foliage. **-panóso†**, **-panúto†**, ADJ.: full of vine-leaves. **-pinário**, ADJ.: of a vine-branch (with much foliage and little fruit). **-pínoo, -pinífero†**, ADJ.: bearing vine-leaves. **-pinifórme**, ADJ.: pampiniform (tendril-like). **pám-pino**, M.: vine-foliage. **-pinóso**, ADJ.: full of vine-leaves.

pan = *pane*.

panácela†, F.: wine-preservative.

panáccio, *disp.* of *pane*.

pána-ce†, ‖**-cèa** [Gr. *-keia* (*pân*, all, *ákos*, remedy)], F.: panacea (herb).

panággio†, M.: provision of bread.

panáma, pánama [*Panama*], M.: panama (kind of straw-hat).

pan-áre [*pane*], TR.: roll in crumbs. **-áta**, F.: blow (with a loaf of bread); panada†. **-atèllo**, *dim.* of *pane*. **-ática**, F.: provision of bread. **-attería**, F.: pantry. **-attièra†**, F.: bread-plate; shepherd's wallet. **-attière**, M.: bread-baker. =**bollíto**, M.: pap (soft food).

pán-ca [Ger. *bank*], F.: BENCH (seat). **-cáccia**, *disp.* of *-ca*. **-caccière†**, M.: lounger. **-cáccio**, M.: broad bench. **-cacciuòlo†**, M.: sword-grass. **-cále†**, M.: bench-cover. **-cáta**, F.: benchful; row of vines.

panceróne†, *aug.* of *-ciera*.

pancétta, *dim.* of *pancia*.

pan-chétta, -chettína, *dim.* of *-ca*, *-chetta*. **-chettíno**, *dim.* of *-chetto*. **-chétto**, M.: stool. **-chína**, *dim.* of *-ca*.

pán-cia [L. *-tex*], F.: PAUNCH (abdomen). **-cièra**, F.: cuirass. **-cína**, *car. dim.* of *-cia*. **-ciòlle**, ADV.: *stare in* —, be reclining (be comfortable). **-cióne**, *aug.* of *-cia*. **-ciòtto**, M.: under-waistcoat. **-ciúto**, ADJ.: with big paunch.

pan-concèllo, M.: *dim.* of *-cone*; lath. ‖**-cóne** [aug. of *panca*], M.: plank; carpenter's bench; land (for building). **-cóso**, ADJ.: of land (for building).

pan-còtto, M.: pap (soft food).

pán-crea, ‖**-creas** [Gr. (*pân*, all, *kréas*, flesh)], M.: pancreas (sweetbread). **-creático**, pl. —*ci*, ADJ.: pancreatic.

pandemònio [Gr. *pân*, all, It. *demonio*, demon], M.: pandemonium.

pándere†, TR.: publish (proclaim).

pandètte [L. *-decta* (Gr. *-déktes*, 'all-containing')], F. PL.: pandects (complete digest, esp. of old Rom. laws).

pandòra [L. *-dora*], F.: kind of lute.

páne [L. *panis*], M.: bread; loaf (cake); earth (about the roots of a plant): — *perduto*, good-for-nothing fellow; *esser come — e cacio*, be intimate friends; *mangiar il — a tradimento*, eat one's bread in idleness; *render — per focaccia*, give tit for tat.

pane-gírico, pl. —*ci* [Gr. *-guríkós* (*pân*, all, *ágoris*, assembly)], M.: panegyric (eulogy). **-girísta**, M.: panegyrist.

panellíno, *dim.* of *pane*.

panèllo†, M.: bonfire.

panerèccio [Gr. *pará*, near, *ónux*, nail], M.: whitlow (inflammation of the finger).

panet-tière†, M.: baker. ||**panét-to**, *dim.* of *pane*. **-toncíno**, *dim.* of *-tone*. **-tóne**, M.: kind of confection.

panfáno†, M.: galley-ship.

pan=fòrte, M.: kind of confection. **=grattáto**, M.: broth (made of crumbled bread).

pá-nia [?], F.: birdlime. **-niáccio**, M.: leather bag (for lime-twigs).

pani-cále [-*co*], M.: dry panicum (grass). **-castrèlla**, F.: kind of grass.

pa-níccia [?], F.: paste. **-níccio**†, M.: kneaded flour. **-niccinòlo**†, M.: small loaf.

pánico 1 [Gr. *-kós* (*Pán*, a god)], ADJ., M.: panic.

paníco 2 [L. *-cum*], M.: panicum (grass, millet).

pani-còcola [*pane cocere*], F.: baker. **-còcolo**, ADJ.: bread-baking; M.: baker.

panicoláio [-*co*], M.: place of disorder (confusion).

pa-nièra, F.: basket. **-nieráio**, M.: basket-maker. **-nieráta**, F.: basketful. ||**-nière** [L. *-narium* (*-nis*, bread), bread-basket], M.: basket (pannier). **-nierétta**, *dim.* of *-niera*. **-nierétto**, *dim.* of *-niere*. **-nieríma**, *dim.* of *-niera*. **-nieríno**, *dim.* of *-niere*. **-nieróna**, *aug.* of *-niera*. **-nieróne**, *aug.* of *-niere*. **-nificáre**†, TR., INTR.: make bread. **-nificazióne**, F.: bread-making. **-nifício**, M.: bread-making (kneading). **-níno**, *dim.* of *-ne*.

pa-nióne [aug. of *pania*], M.: lime-rod (for catching birds). **-niúzza**, F., **-niúzzo**, M.: lime-twig.

pánna [? *-nno*], F.: cream.

pannaiòlo [-*no*], M.: dry-goods merchant.

pan-náre [-*na*], INTR.: form cream. **-náto**, ADJ.: with cream.

pan-neggiaménto, M.: drapery. **-neggiáre** [-*no*], INTR.: drape (in painting). **-neggiáto**, ADJ.: draped. **-nèllo**, M.: bread-cloth; linen cloth (of medium coarseness); piece of cloth. **-nétto**, M.: small piece of cloth. **-nicèllo**, M.: little piece of cloth; inefficacious remedy. **-nicíno**, *dim.* of *-no*. **-nícolo**†, M.: little piece of cloth; diaphragm. **-nière**†, M.: dry-goods merchant. **-nilíno**, M.: linen cloth. **-nína**, F.: woollen cloth. ||**pán-no** [L. *-nus*], M.: cloth (stuff); sail-cloth; film, layer (on spoiled liquids, boiled milk, etc.); PL.: clothes (garments): *non potere star ne' -ni*, be unable to contain one's self.

pannòc-chia [L. *panucula*], F.: ear (of corn). **-chiétta**, **-chína**, *dim.* of *-chia*. **-chiúto**, ADJ.: with ears (of corn).

panno=láno, M.: woollen cloth. **=líno**, M.: linen cloth.

pan-òplia [Gr. *pân*, all, *ópla*, arms], F.: panoply. **-oráma**, PL. —*i*, M.: panorama.

pan=porcíno, M.: cyclamen plant (sow-bread). **=sánto**, M.: kind of fried bread.

panta-lonáta, F.: buffoonery. ||**-lóne** [*Pantalon*], M.: (Venetian) buffoon. **-lóni**, M. PL.: pantaloons.

pan-tanáccio, *disp.* of *-tano*. ||**-táno** [?], M.: mud-puddle; mire. **-tanóso**, ADJ.: miry (muddy).

pan-teísmo [Gr. *pántheos* (*pân*, all, *theós*, god)], M.: pantheism. **-teísta**, M.: pantheist. **-teístico**, pl. —*ci*, ADJ.: pantheistic.

pantelègrafo [Gr. *pân*, all, *téle*, afar off, *gráphein*, write], M.: pantelegraph.

pánteon [Gr. *pán-theion*, of 'all-gods'], M.: pantheon (temple for all gods).

pantèra [L. *-thera*], F.: panther.

panteránа†, F.: wood-lark.

pantòfola [?], F.: slipper.

pan-tògrafo [Gr. *pán*, all, *gráphein*, write], M.: pantograph. **-tòmetro** [Gr. *métron*, measure], M.: pantometer.

panto-míma, F.: pantomime. **-mímico**, ADJ.: pantomimic. ||**-míno** [L. *-mimus*], M.: pantomime actor.

pantráccola†, F.: story (fable).

pantúfola†, F.: slipper.

pan=únto, M.: bread (toasted and dipped in oil).

pánza†, F.: paunch.

panzá-na [?], F.: tale (story, fable). **-nèlla**, F.: bread dish (with onion basil).

pan-zeróne†, *aug.* of *-ziera*. **-zeruòla**†, *dim.* of *-ziera*. **-zétta**†, *dim.* of *-cia*. ||**-zièra** [-*cia*], F.: cuirass.

paolíno†, M.: young peacock.

páo-lo [pope, *P.* V.], M.: paolo (old coin, = about 11 cents; Rom. paolo less).

pa-onázzo, ADJ.: violet. ||**-óne** [-*vone*], M.: peacock.

pá-pa, pl. *-pi* [Gr. *-pás*, father], M.: pope. **-pábile**, ADJ.: able to become pope. **-páccio**, *disp.* of *-pa*. **-pále**, ADJ.: papal (of the pope). **-palína**, F.: kind of cap. **-palíno**, ADJ.: papal; M.: soldier (of the pope). **-pásso**†, M.: priest. **-páto**, M.: papacy.

papávero [L. *-ver*], M.: POPPY (plant); good-for-nothing fellow.

pápe-ra, F.: goose. **-rèllo**, M.: gosling; ADJ.: of a gosling. **-ína**†, F.: chickweed. **-ríno**, M.: gosling; ADJ.: of a gosling. ||**pápe-ro** [?], M.: young goose. **-ròtto**†, **-ròttolo**, *dim.* of *-ro*.

pa-pésco [-*pa*], ADJ.: popish. **-péssa**, F.: papess. **-pétto**, M.: silver coin.

papilióne [L. *-lio*], M.: papilio (genus of butterflies).

papíl-la [L.], F.: papilla (of the skin). **-láre**, **-lóso**, ADJ.: papillary.

papiro [L. *-pyrus*], M.: papyrus.

pa-pismo [*-pa*], M.: popery. **-pista**, M.: papist. **-pistico**, pl. *—ci*, ADJ.: papistic. **-pissáre**†, INTR.: be pope.

páp-pa [L. *papa*], F.: pap (soft food). **-paccéci**, M.: silly fellow; ADJ.: silly. **-pacchiónet**, M.: glutton.

pappafico†, M.: hood; main top-gallant mast.

pappa-gallésco, ADJ.: of a parrot. **-galléssa**†, F.: parrot. ‖**-gállo** [?], M.: parrot.

pappa=górgia, F.: double chin.

pappa=lárdo†, M.: hypocrite.

pappardèllo [*-ppare*], F. PL.: ribbon-vermicelli (with broth).

pappárdo†, M.: poppy (plant).

pap-páre [L. eat pap], TR.: gorge (eat greedily). **-páta**, F.: gorging. **-patáci**, M.: silent sufferer. **-patóra**, F., **-patóre**, M., **-patrice**, F.: glutton. **-patoría**, F.: gorging; extortion. **-pína**, *dim.* of *-pa*. **-píno**, M.: servant (in a hospital). **páp-po**, M.: bread. **-poláta**, F.: watery food; senseless talk. **-polóne**, M.: glutton; chatterer. **-póno**, M.: glutton; ADJ.: greedy.

pára†, F.: parrying (defence). **para-** 1 [*parare*], PREF.: para-, against; for.

para- 2 [Gr. *pará*, near, beside]: **-báse** [Gr. *-basis*, step], F.: parabasis (chief choral part in Greek comedy). **parábola** [Gr. *-bolé* (*bállein*, put)], F.: parable (allegory); parabola (curve). **-boláno**, M.: great talker (chatterer); ADJ.: talkative. **-bòlico**, pl. *—ci*, ADJ.: parabolic. **-boldide**, F., M.: paraboloid (geometric figure). **-bolóne**, M.: great talker. **-bolóso**, ADJ.: talkative.

para=cadúte [*para* 1], M.: parachute. **=cálci**, M.: bucking strap (to prevent horses from kicking). **camminétto**, **=cammíno**, M.: fireboard. **cárro**, M.: picket (on a road side, etc.). **cénere**, M.: fender (of a fireplace). **ci(e)lo**, M.: cover (for a bed, carriage, etc.).

pa-raclèto, ‖**-ráclito**† [Gr. (*pará*, beside, *kletós*, summoned)], M.: paraclete (Holy Spirit).

para córe, M.: lunge (of animals).

para-disiaco, pl. *—ci*, ADJ.: paradisaical. ‖**-diso** [L. *-disus*], M.: paradise (garden of Eden, place of bliss).

parados-sále, ADJ.: paradoxical. **-sáre**†, INTR.: talk in paradoxes. **-sista**, M.: speaker (of paradoxes. ‖**paradòsso** [Gr. *pará-doxos* (opinion)], M.: paradox; ADJ.: paradoxical.

para=fángo, M.: splasher (of a carriage).

parafèr-na [Gr. *pará-*, *pherné*, dowry], F.: paraphernalia (bride's belongings). **-nálo**, ADJ.: paraphernal.

para=fòco, M.: fireboard; screen.

para-frasáre, TR.: paraphrase (interpret). ‖**pará-frasi** [Gr. *-phrasis* (speaking)], F.: paraphrase (interpretation). **-fráste**, M.: paraphrast. **-frasticaménte**, ADV.: paraphrastically. **-frástico**, pl. *—ci*, ADJ.: paraphrastic.

para=fúlmine, M.: lightning-rod. **=fúmo**, M.: smoke-fender.

parággio†, M.: paragon (match, equal).

para-gòge [Gr. (*ágein*, put)], F.: paragoge (addition).

parago-nábile, ADJ.: comparable. **-nánza**†, F.: comparison. **-náre**, TR.: compare; INTR.: equal (be of same value); REFL.: be compared. ‖**para-góne** [?], M.: paragon (comparison; match; model): *oro di —*, pure gold; *a — di*, in comparison with.

pa-ragrafáre, TR.: paragraph (form into paragraphs). ‖**-rágrafo** [L. *-ragraphus*], M.: paragraph (division).

paraguánto†, M.: drink-money (tip).

paralásse†, F.: parallax (displacement).

paralèllo† = *parallelo*.

para=lipòmeni [Gr. *-léipein*, omit], M. PL.: paralipomenon (book of Chronicles).

pará-lisi, **-lisía** [Gr. *lúein*, loosen], F.: paralysis (palsy). **-lítico**, pl. *—ci*, ADJ.: paralytic. **-lissáro**, TR.: paralyze (palsy); neutralize.

parallásse [Gr. *allássein*, change], F.: parallax (angle).

parallè-la, F.: parallel (line); ADJ.: parallel. **-laménte**, ADV.: parallely. **-lepípedo**, ADJ.: parallelopiped (solid). **-lismo**, M.: parallelism. ‖**parallè-lo** [Gr. *-los*], ADJ.: parallel (equal). **-lográmmo**, M.: parallelogram (figure).

para=logismo [Gr. *logismós*, reasoning], M.: paralogism (kind of reasoning). **-logístico**, pl. *—ci*, ADJ.: paralogical. **-logissáre**, INTR.: paralogize (reason falsely).

para lúme, M.: shade (for the eyes). **-máno**, M.: sleeve cuff. **-ménto** [*-re*], M.: sacerdotal garment; PL.†: rich dress; caparison. **mósche**, M.: fly-flap.

parangóne [*paragone*], M.: (*typ.*) paragon (size of type).

para nínfo [Gr. *númphe*, bride], M.: paranymph (bride's man).

parán-za [?], F.: boat (with one mast). **-sèlla**, F.: large fishing boat.

para òcchi, M. PL.: blinds (for horses). **pètto**, M.: parapet (rampart). ‖**=píglia** [*pigliare*], F.: confusion.

paráre [L. *parare*], TR.: adorn (trim, deck); prevent (check, stop, PARRY); protect: offer (hold out), REFL.: robe one self; defend one's self, pre appear, meet: — dinanzi fore, meet

parasánga [Gr. *-ges*], F.: parasang (Persian measure of length, of nearly four English miles).
para=sártie, F. PL.: chain-wales (of a ship).
parasceve [Gr. *-skeué*, preparation], M.: parasceve (sixth day of the Jewish week).
para=síto [Gr. *-s* (*sítos*, food)], M.: parasite (hanger on, toady); parasitical plant.
para=sóle, M.: parasol (umbrella).
paras-síta [Gr. *pará-sitos* (*sítos*, food)], M.: parasite (sponger); parasitical plant. **-sitería**, F.: parasitism. **-sítico**, pl. **—ci**, ADJ.: parasitic. **-síto**, M.: parasite (sponger); parasitical plant. **-sitóne†**, *aug.* of *-sito*.
pará-ta [*-re*], F.: readiness (for defence); guard (defence); parrying (in fencing); parade (of soldiers); curvet (of a horse): *di* —, for parade, for special occasions; sumptuous, solemn; *veder la mala* —, see the poor chance; see the danger. **paratío†**, M.: parade; guard. **pará-to**, ADJ.: adorned (trimmed, decked out); ready (prepared); M.: drapery **-tóre**, M.: trimmer (ornamenter). **-túra**, F.: ornament (trimming). **=vènto**, M.: draft fender; screen.
parávola†, F.: word (term).
para=zònio [Gr. *zóne*, belt], M.: small sword.
par-caménte, ADV.: sparingly; discreetly. **pár-cere**, TR.: spare; pardon (forgive). **-chíssimo**, ADJ.: very (or most) sparing. **-cità†**, F.: parsimony (frugality). ‖**pár-co**1 [L. *-cus*], ADJ.: sparing (frugal); discreet.
párco2 [?], M.: park (deer-park; military park; military equipments).
par-díno†, ADJ.: of the leopard's skin. ‖**pár-do** [Gr. *-dos*], M.: leoPARD.
páre†, ADJ.: alike (equal).
parécchio [*pari*], ADJ.; M.: much; PL.: several (divers); ADV.: much.
pareg-giábile, ADJ.: comparable. **-giaménto**, M.: equalling; comparing. ‖**-giáre** [*pari*], TR.: equal (make equal, level); compare; settle (accounts); INTR.: become equal; REFL.: be compared; be levelled. **-giatúra†**, F.: levelness (evenness. **paréggio**, M.: settling (of accounts).
parèglio†, M.: parhelion (mock sun).
paregòrico†, M.: paregoric (anodyne).
parèlio [Gr. *-lios* (*para*, beside, *hélios*, sun)], M.: parhelion (mock sun).
parenchíma [Gr. *-chuma*], M.: parenchyma (mass of an organ).
paren-tádo, -tággio, M.: parentage (parents, extraction). **-tále†**, ADJ.: parental. **-táli**, M.: festivity (in celebration of some illustrious person). **-táto**, M.: parentage. ‖**parèn-te** [L. *parens*], M.: parent (relative, kindred). **-tèla**, F.: relationship (consanguinity); likeness. **-tésco†**, ADJ.: parental.
parèntesi [Gr. *-thesis*], F.: parenthesis (inserted word or sentence, sign).
paren-tévole†, ADJ.: affectionate. **-tevolménte**, ADV.: affectionately (kindly). **-tézza†**, F.: parentage.
pa-rènza†, F.: appearance. ‖**-rére** [L. *-rere*], IRR.§; INTR.: appear (seem); think (believe); REFL.: show one's self; M.: opinion (judgment); advice: *a — mio*, in my opinion.

§ Ind.: Pres. *páio, pári, páre; paiámo, paréte, páiono.* Pret. *párvi* or *pársi, párve* or *párse; párvero* or *pársero.* Fut. *parrò.* Cond. *parrèi.* Subj.: Pres. *páia.* I've wanting. Part. *párso* or *parúto.*

pare-táio, M.: place for setting bird-snares. ‖**paré-te** [L. *paries*], F.: wall (of a room); internal surface. **-tèlla†**, F.: folding-net. **-tèllo**, *dim.* of *-te.*
parévole†, ADJ.: appearing; visible.
pargo-larità†, F.: infancy. **-leggiáre**, INTR.: act as a child. **-létta**, F., **-létto**, M.: child. **-lézza†**, F.: childhood (infancy). ‖**párgo-lo** [L. *parvulus*], M.: (*poet.*) child (infant).
pá-ri [L. *-r*], ADJ.: equal (alike, like); ADV.: equally; M.: equal; peer (nobleman): *render — a —*, return like for like; *al —*, *del —*, equally (evenly). **-ría**1, F.: peerage.
pária2 [Ind.], M.: pariah (lowest class in India).
parie-tále, ADJ.: parietal (pertaining to the skull bones). **-tária**, F.: parietary (plants growing on old walls). ‖**paríete†** = *parete.*
parifi-caménto†, M.: equalling (levelling). ‖**-cáre** [*pari*], TR.: equal (level, make even).
pari=fórme†, ADJ.: of equal form.
parigi-na, F.: (*typ.*) pearl. ‖**-no** [*Parigi*, Paris], ADJ.: of a dandy; M.: dandy (fop); old French coin.
parí-glia [*pari*], F.: team (of horses); retaliation (retribution). **-glina**, *car. dim.* of *-glia.* **-ménte, -ménti**, ADV.: equally (alike); in the same time; in like manner.
pário [*Paros*, island in Ægean Sea], ADJ.: Parian (marble).
parità [*pari*], F.: parity (equality).
parlá-bile, ADJ.: speakable. **-dóre†**, M.: speaker (orator). **parlá-gio†**, M.: senate-house. **-gióne†**, F.: speaking. **-mentáre**, ADJ.: parliamentary (pertaining to parliament); TR.: speak (discuss); INTR.: parley (treat with); M.: parliamentarian. **-mentário**, ADJ.: parliamentary. **-mentarismo**, M.: par-

liamentarism. **-ménto**, M.: parley: parliament. **-ntína**, F.: loquacity (talkativeness). **-ntíno†**, ADJ.: talkative. **parlá-nza†**, F.: parlance (conversation). **-lánte**, PART.: speaking. ‖**parlá-re** [l. L. *parabolare* (cf. *parabola*)]: INTR.: speak (converse, discourse, harangue); TR.: speak (a language): tell; M.: speaking; speech. **parlá-ta**, F.: conversation; pronouncing. **parlá-to**, PART.: spoken. **-tóre**, M.: speaker (orator). **-tòrio†**, M.: parlour (of a convent). **-trí-ce**, F.: speaker. **-túra**, F.: speaking.

parlético, pl. **-ci** [*-ralitico*], M.: trembling (of an old or paralytic person); ADJ.: paralytic.

par-lévole†, ADJ.: speaking; speakable. **-lièro†**, M.: chatterer (idle talker). **-lottáre†**, INTR.: chatter (prate).

párma [L.], F.: light shield.

páro [L. *par*], M.: PAIR (couple).

paròcchi [*para occhi*], M.: blinders (of a horse).

pároco†, M.: rector (parson).

paro-día [Gr. *-día*], F.: parody (burlesque). **-diáre**, TR.: parody.

paròffia†, F.: parish church; parish.

paròla [*parabola*], F.: word (term); parole; permission†: *dar —*, promise; *dar parole*, coax (allure); *troncar* (or *rompere*) *le -le in bocca a uno*, interrupt. **-láccia**, *disp.* of *-la*. **-láio**, M.: chatterer (talkative person). **-létta**, **-lína**, *dim.* of *-la*. **-lóna**, *aug.* of *-la*. **-lóne**, *disp. aug.* of *-la*. **-lòzza†**, F.: coarse word. **-lúccia**, **-lúzza†**, *disp.* of *-la*.

paro-s(s)ìsmo† [Gr. *-xusmós*], M.: paroxysm.

parossítono [Gr. *-xú-tonos*], ADJ.: paroxytonic; M.: paroxytone.

paròtide [Gr. *-tís*], F.: parotid (salivary gland); ADJ.: parotid.

parpaglióne†, M.: kind of a sail.

parri-cída, pl. *—di* [L. (*pater*, father, *cædere*, kill)], M.: parricide (person). **-cídio**, M.: parricide (act).

parrocchétto [?], M.: foretop mast.

par-ròcchia [Gr. *par-oikía*, 'of same house'], F.: PARISH; parish church. **-rocchiále**, ADJ.: parochial (belonging to a parish). **-rocchialità**, F.: parochial rights (or duties). **-chialménte**, ADV.: parochially. **-rocchiáno**, M.: parishioner; rector†; ADJ.: parochial. **pàrroco**, pl. *—chi* or *—ci*, M.: rector (of a parish, parson).

parrúc-ca [Sp. *peluca* (L. *pilus*, hair)], F.: peruke (wig). **-chière**, M.: hairdresser. **-chíno**, M.: small peruke. **-cóne**, M.: *aug.* of *-ca*; serious old man.

parsimònia [L.], F.: parsimony (economy).

párso, PART. of *parere*.

par-táccia, F.: *disp.* of *-te*; sharp reproof. **-taccióne**, *aug.* of *-te*. ‖**párte** [L. *-s*], F.: part (portion, share); faction (party); office (duty); nature; place; side: *da — a —*, through and through; *dalla mia —*, for my part; *da — di tutti*, in the name of all.

partecí-pábile, ADJ.: sharable. **-pánte**, PART.: participating. ‖**-páre** [L. *parti-cipare*], INTR.: share in (participate in); TR.: impart (communicate). **-páto**, PART.: participated. **-patóre**, M., **-patríce**, F.: participator. **-pazióne**, F.: participation (sharing). **partécì-pe**, ADJ.: participant (sharing); M.: participant (sharer): *far —*, impart.

parteg-giaménto, M.: sharing. **-giánte**, PART.: siding with. ‖**-giáre** [*parte*], INTR.: side with (be with one party). **-giáto**, PART.: sided (taken side with).

parte-gnènza†, F.: appurtenance (adjunct). **-nére†**, INTR.: belong (concern).

partènza [*-tire*], F.: departure.

partèrre [Fr. *par*, on, *terre*, ground], M.: parterre (arrangement of flower-beds); (*theat.*) pit.

partévole†, ADJ.: divisible.

partí-bile, ADJ.: partible (divisible). **-cèlla**, F.: particle (atom; uninflected word). ‖**-cína** [*parte*], *dim.* of *parte*.

partici-pále, ADJ.: participant. **-paménto**, M.: participation. **-pánte**, ADJ.: participating. ‖**-páre** [L.], INTR.: participate (share); TR.: impart. **-patóre**, M.: participator. **-pazióne**, F.: participation (sharing). **partící-pio**, M.: participle (grammar).

partíco-la [L. *particula*], F.: host (consecrated bread); particle (atom). **-láre**, ADJ.: particular (especial, unusual); M.: particularity: *in —*, particularly. **-lareggiaménto**, M.: particularizing. **-lareggiáre**, TR.: particularize (specify in detail). **-lareggiáto**, PART.: particularized. **-larità**, F.: particularity (peculiarity, minute detail). **-larizzáre**, TR.: particularize (specify in detail). **-larizzazióne**, F.: particularization. **-larménte**, ADV.: particularly (especially).

particul. .† = *particol.*.

partigiá-na [? related to *-no*], F.: partisan (kind of halberd). **-naménte**, ADV.: like a partisan (party adherent). **-náta**, F.: thrust with a partisan. **-nèllo**, **-nétto**, *dim.* of *-no*. **-nería**, F.: partisanship. **partigiá-no**, M.: partisan (party adherent); ADJ.: partisan. **-nóne**, M.: large halberd.

par-tigióne†, F.: partition (division). **-timénto†**, M.: division; distribution. ‖**-tíre** [L.], IRR.; INTR.: PART (divide, apportion, share; separate†); REFL.: depart (go away). **-títa,** F.: quantity (of merchandise); entry (in a ledger); game; departure†; portion†; party†. **-titaménte,** ADV.: distinctly (singly). **-titánte,** ADJ.: supporter (defender). **-titína,** *car. dim.* of *-tita*. **-titívo,** ADJ.: partitive. **-títo,** ADJ.: divided (shared); departed; M.: agreement (contract); deliberation; judgment (decision); means; danger†; chance†: *mettere a —, far il —,* discuss; deliberate; *a — preso,* deliberately. **-titóre,** M.: divider; distributor. **-titúra,** F.: partition (score). **-titúzzo**†, M.: small means. **-tizióne,** F.: partition (division).

§ Ind.: Pres. *partisco,* I divide; *párto,* I depart.

pár-to [L. *-tus* (*parere,* bear)], M.: bearing (birth); offspring; production. **-toriènte,** ADJ.: parturient (bringing forth); confined woman. **-toríre,** TR.: bear (give birth, produce); INTR.: be delivered. **-toríto,** ADJ.: born (brought forth). **-toritríce,** F.: woman confined.

pa-rúta†, F.: appearance. ‖**-rúto** [*-rere*], PART.: appeared (seemed). **-rvènte,** ADJ.: apparent (visible). **-rvènza,** F.: appearance.

par-vificáre†, TR.: make small (lessen). **-vificazióne**†, F.: lessening. **-víflco**†, ADJ.: niggardly (stingy). **-vipèndere**†, TR., INTR.: undervalue. **-vità,** F.: smallness (Eng.† parvity). ‖**pár-vo** [L. *-vus*], ADJ.: small (little). **pár-volo,** M.: (*poet.*) child (infant).

parziá-le [L. *partialis*], ADJ.: partial. **-leggiáre**†, INTR.: show partiality. **-lità,** F.: partiality. **-lménte,** ADV.: partially (unjustly).

par-zionábile†, **-nále,** ADJ.: partial (unjust). **-zonière**†, ADJ.: participant (sharing).

pa-scènte, ADJ.: feeding. ‖**pá-scere** [L.], IRR.; TR.: feed (nourish, maintain); INTR.: graze; REFL.: feed one's self.

pa-scià [Turk. *pāsha*], M.: pasha (Turkish governor). **-scialáto,** M.: pasha-ship.

pa-scibiètola†, M.: simpleton (ninny). **-sciménto,** M.: grazing. **-scióna,** F.: rich pasture; land of abundance. ‖**-sciúto,** PART. of *-scere;* fed (nourished); grazed. **pá-sco**†, M.: (*poet.*) pasture. **-scolaménto,** M.: pasture; grazing. **-scoláre,** TR., INTR.: feed (nourish); pasture. **-scoláto,** PART.: pastured. **pá-scolo,** M.: pasture.

pásmo†, M.: spasm.

pás-qua [Heb. *pascha*], F.: Easter: *dar la mala —*†, afflict. **-quále,** ADJ.: paschal (of Easter). **-quáre**†, INTR.: observe Easter. **-quarèccio,** ADJ.: of Easter. **-quináta,** F, **-quíllo**†, M.: pasquinade (satirical writing). **-quíno,** M.: pasquin (mutilated statue at Rome).

pas-sábile [*-sare*], ADJ.: passable (bearable). **-sabilménte,** ADV.: passably. **-saggière**†, M.: passenger. **-sággio,** M.: passage (transit); way; passage-money; crossing: *esser di —,* be a passenger. **-samáno,** M.: ribbon (or lace) for trimming. **-samanteria,** F.: ribbon-factory. **-saménto**†, M.: passage. **-sánte,** ADJ.: passing; M.: leather-band. **-sa=pòrto,** M.: passport. ‖**-sáre** [*-so*], INTR.: pass (go through, proceed, traverse); lose (freshness); transmit; assign; end; transgress; TR.: pass (surpass); spend (time): *— bene,* succeed; REFL.: be contented with: *— di,* do without. **-sáta,** F.: passage; ridge (between furrows); omission: *far —,* consider a thing ended (finished). **-satèlla,** *dim.* of *-sata*. **-sa=tèmpo,** M.: pastime (diversion). **-satína,** *car. dim.* of *-sata*. **-sáto,** ADJ.: passed (ended); M.: past. **-satóia,** F.: kind of rug (to protect the carpet beneath). **-satóio,** M.: stepping-stone (crossing); ADJ.: easy to cross. **-satóra,** F., **-satóre,** M.: passer; passenger; transgressor. **-savía,** M.: passage-way (bridge). **-savogáre**†, INTR.: row amain. **-savolánte,** M.: small cannon; adventurer. **-seggiáre,** TR.: walk (promenade); inhabit (live in). **-seggiáta,** F.: walk (promenade); promenade (place): *fare una —,* take a walk. **-seggiatína,** *disp. dim.* of *-seggiata*. **-seggiáto,** PART.: walked. **-seggiatóre,** M.: walker (promenader). **-seggère, -seggèro, -seggière, -seggièro,** ADJ.: passing (fleeting); M.: passenger; toll-gatherer†. **-séggio,** M.: promenade (place); walking.

pásse-ra, F.: sparrow (bird). **-ráio,** M.: chirping (of sparrows). **pásse-re**†, M.: sparrow. **-rína,** *car. dim.* of *-ra*. **-ríno,** *car. dim.* of *-ro*. ‖**pásse-ro** [L. *-r*], M.: sparrow. **-ròtto,** M.: *dim.* of *-ro: fare un —,* act strangely.

passétto [dim. of *passo*], M.: yard (measure).

passíbi-le [L. *-lis* (*passus,* endured)], ADJ.: passible (susceptible of suffering). **-lità,** F.: passibility. **-lménte,** ADV.: passibly.

passimáta†, F.: hard cake.

passíno, M.: *car. dim.* of *-so;* width of the cloth (with loom-width as standard).

pás-sio [L. (*pati,* suffer)], M.: passion (account of the passion of Christ). **-sionále,** M.: Passional (title of a book). **-sionáre**†, TR.: torture (vex). **-sionáto,** ADJ.: tortured; passionate (vehement). **-sióne,** F.: suffering (of Christ); passion (ardent feeling, affection). **-sionísta,**

M.: Passionist (one of a religious order). **-sivaménte,** ADV.: passively (unresistingly). **-sività,** F.: passivity (passiveness); loss (detriment). **-sívo** [L. *-sivus*], ADJ.: passive (inactive). **pás-so** 1, ADJ.: withered (faded).

pásso 2 [L. *passus*], M.: PACE (step); walk (promenade); passage: *a un* —, near by; — —, *a* — *a* —, little by little; *uccello di* —, bird of passage.

pas-sonáta, F.: kind of palisade (fence). ‖**-sóne** 1 [L. *paxillus*], M.: large pale (stake).

passóne 2, *aug.* of *passo.*

passúro†, ADJ.: about to suffer.

pás-ta [L.], F.: paste (dough); confection (sweets): *di* — *grossa*, coarse-natured. **-táccia,** *disp.* of *-ta.* **-táccio**†, M.: stupid fellow. **-tadèlla**†, F.: fine paste. **-táia,** F., **-táio,** M.: seller of paste (for soup). **-teggiábile,** ADJ.: *vino* —, table wine. **-teggiáre,** TR.: drink (wine); feast; entertain†. **-tellétto,** *car. dim.* of *-tello.* **-tellière**†, M.: pastry-cook. **-tellíno,** *car. dim.* of *-tello.* **-tellísta,** M.: worker in pastel. **-tèllo,** M.: pastel (coloured crayon); blue colouring matter. **-tícca,** F.: pastil (lozenge). **-ticcèra,** F., **-ticcère,** M.: pastry-cook. **-ticcería,** F.: pastry shop (bakery). **-ticcière,** M.: pastry cook. **-ticcináio,** M.: maker (and seller) of tarts. **-ticcíno,** M.: tart. **-tíccio,** M.: pie; bad work; medley. **-ticcióna,** F., **-ticcióne,** M.: meddler (confuser). **-ticciòtto,** *dim.* of *-ticcio.* **-tícco**†, M., **-tíglia,** F., **-tíllo,** M.: pastel (lozenge).

pastináca [L.], F.: parsnip; kind of fish.

pa-stináre†, TR.: hoe (dig). **-stinazióne,** F.: hoeing (digging). **-stíno**†, M.: ploughed ground.

pásto [L. *-tus* (*pascere*, feed)], M.: meal (rePAST, food); eating; lungs (of animals): *a tutto* —, continually.

pastòc-chia [*pasta*], F.: foolish story (tale). **-chiáta**†, F.: nonsense.

pastofòrio†, M.: archives (of a church).

pastóia [*-to*], F.: PASTern (for PASTuring horses); tether (rope).

pastóne, M.: *aug.* of *-ta;* mass of dough.

pastó-ra, F.: shepherdess. **-ràle,** ADJ.: pastoral; M.: crosier (staff); F.: pastoral (poem). **-ralménte,** ADV.: pastorally. **-ráre**†, TR.: pasture. ‖**pastó-re** [L. *pastor*], M.: shepherd (herdsman); bishop. **-réccio,** ADJ.: (*disp.*) pastoral. **-rèlla,** F.: *car. dim.* of *-ra;* pastoral song. **-rèllo,** *car. dim.* of *-re.* **-rízia,** F.: pastoral occupation. **-rízio,** ADJ.: pastoral.

pas-tosità, F.: softness; mellowness. ‖**-tóso** [*-ta*], ADJ.: soft; mellow.

-strаnáio, M.: cloak checker (at a theatre). ‖**-stráno** [?], M.: kind of cloak.

pastricciáno [?], M.: parsnip; stupid fellow.

pas-túme [*-ta*], M.: paste (for soup).

pastú-ra [L.], F.: pasturage; pasture. **-rále**†, ADJ.: pastoral; M.: crosier (staff). **-ráre,** TR; INTR.: pasture (feed). **-révole**†, ADJ.: pasturable. **pastú-so**†, M.: pasturage; pasture.

patác-ca [?], F.: coin (of little value); stain. **-chína,** F.: Ligurian coin. **-cóna,** *aug.* of *-ca.* **-cóne,** M.: *aug.* of *-ca;* palisade; sluggish person.

patáffio†, M.: epitaph.

patáno [L. *-tere*, be open], ADJ.: large; clear and round.

patassío [Gr. *-tássein*, strike], M.: confusion (uproar).

patáta [N. Am.], F.: potato (vegetable).

patèlla†, F.: knee-pan.

patèma [Gr. *páthema*], M.: grief (affliction).

patèna [L., PAN], F.: paten (chalice cover).

paten-táto, ADJ.: patented. ‖**patènte** [L. *-s* (*patere*, be open)], ADJ.: clear (manifest); M.: letter-patent. **-temènte,** ADV.: clearly (plainly). **-tíno,** *dim.* of *-tente.*

pátera [L.], F.: patera (vessel).

pateràcchio [?], M.: agreement (contract); matrimony.

pateréccio = *panereccio.*

pateríno [?], M.: heretic; ADJ.: heretical.

pater-nále, F.: severe reproof; ADJ.†: paternal (fatherly). **-naménte,** ADV.: paternally. **-nità,** F.: paternity (fatherhood). ‖**patèr-no** [L. *-nus*], ADJ.: paternal (fatherly); hereditary. **-nòster,** **-nòstro,** M.: pater-noster (Lord's prayer).

pateti-caménte, ADV.: pathetically. **patèti-co,** pl. —*ci* [L. *patheticus*], ADJ.: pathetic (affecting, moving); M.: pathetic. **-cúme,** M.: (*disp.*) pathetic things.

pa-tiboláre, ADJ.: patibulary (pertaining to the gallows). ‖**-tíbolo** [L. *-tibulum* (*-tere*, be open)], M.: fork-shaped yoke; M.: instrument of death-punishment, gen'ly (gibbet, gallows, cross; orig'ly fork-shaped instrument to which the culprit was nailed or tied before going to his death); torment; place of execution.

pático†, ADJ.: hepatic (pertaining to the liver).

patiménto [*-tire*], M.: suffering (...

páti-na [L., PAN], F.: ... incrustation); ointm... **-re,** TR.: curr... curried. **-na...** **-tára,** F.: ...

patí-re [L... support): — with. **-tór...**

pato-logía [Gr. *páthos*, suffering, *lógos*, discourse], F.: pathology. **-lògico**, pl. *—ci*, ADJ.: pathologic. **-lòlogo**, M.: pathologist.

pá-tre† [L. *-ter*], M.: father. **pá-tria**, F.: fatherland (native land). **-triárca**, M.: patriarch. **-triarcále**, ADJ.: patriarchal. **-triarcalménte**, ADV.: in a patriarchal manner. **-triarcáto**, M., **-triarchía**, F.: patriarchate (dignity, residence of a patriarch). **-tríce**†, M.: patrician. **-tricíd.** . = *parricid.* . **-trício**, ADJ., M.: patrician. **-trígno**, M.: stepfather. **-trígnomo**†, M.: my stepfather. **-trimoniále**, ADJ.: patrimonial. **-trimoniétto**, **-trimoníno**, *dim.* of *-trimonio*. **-trimònio**, M.: patrimony (inheritance). **-trimonióne**, *aug.* of *-trimonio*. **-tríno**, M.: godfather; second (in a duel). **pá-trio**, ADJ.: native (of the fatherland); paternal. **-triòtta**, M.: patriot. **-triòttico**, pl. *—ci*, ADJ.: patriotic. **-triottísmo**, M.: patriotism. **-triòtto**, M.: patriot. **-trística**, F.: patristics. **-triziáto**, M.: patriciate (patrician class). **-trízio**, M., **-trízia**, F.: patrician (noble); ADJ.: patrician. **-trizzáre**, INTR.: resemble one's father. **-trocinánte**, ADJ.: defending. **-trocináre**, TR.: defend (sustain); plead. **-trocináto**, ADJ.: protected. **-trocinatóre**, M., **-trocinatríce**, F.: defender (advocate); patron. **-trocínio**, M.: protection (defence, patronage). **-tròna**, F.: protectress; patroness. **-tronále**, ADJ.: of a patron. **-tronáto**, M.: patronate (right or duty of a patron). **-tronéssa**, F.: patroness. **-tronímico**, ADJ.: patronymic; M.: patronymic (derived name). **-tròno**, M.: patron (saint, benefactor).

pát-ta [*-to*], F.: tie (in a game); epact (of the moon)†. **-táre**†, INTR.: equalize (make even). **-teggiaménto**, M.: agreement (compact). **-teggiáre**, TR., INTR.: agree (contract, stipulate); bargain. **-teggiáto**, ADJ.: agreed upon. **-teggiatóre**, M.: contractor; bargainer.

pat-tináre, INTR.: skate. **-tinatóre**, M., **-tinatríce**, F.: skater. **-tinatúra**, F.: skating. **pát-tino**, ‖**-tino** [Fr. *patin* (*patte*, paw)], M.: skate.

pátto [L. *pactum*], M.: PACT (agreement; compact): *di bel* —†, agreed; *con — che*, on condition that.

pattó-na [?], F.: polenta (made with chestnut flour). **-náio**, M.: seller of polenta.

pattovíre†, TR., INTR.: agree (stipulate).

pattú-glia [Fr. *patrouille*], F.: PATROL (guard). **-gliáre**, INTR.: patrol.

pat-tuíre [*-to*], TR., INTR.: agree (contract, stipulate). **-tuíto**, ADJ.: contracted.

pattúme [?], M.: sweepings (refuse, dirt); coarse straw.

patulláre [?], REFL.: amuse one's self idly (trifle).

pátulo†, ADJ.: open; ample (large).

pa-túrne, ‖**-túrnie** [L. *pati*, suffer], F. PL.: sadness (depression).

paú-ra [L. *pavor*], F.: fear (terror, fright): *aver* —, be afraid; *far* —, terrify. **-rétta**, *dim.* of *-ra*. **-révole**†, ADJ.: fearful (terrifying). **-ríccia**, F.: slight fear. **-rosaménte**, ADV.: fearfully (timidly). **-róso**, ADJ.: fearful (timid); frightful.

páu-sa [L.], F.: pause (rest); slowness. **-sáre**, INTR.: pause (stop, wait).

pá-ve [L. *-vet*], DEFECT.; INTR.: (*poet.*) he fears. **-vefátto**†, ADJ.: frightened. **-ventáre**, TR.: fear; INTR.: be afraid of. **-ventáto**†, ADJ.: afraid. **-ventévole**†, ADJ.: frightful (terrible). **-vènto**†, M.: fear (fright, dread). **-ventosaménte**†, ADV.: fearfully. **-ventóso**†, ADJ.: frightful (dreadful).

pa-vesáre, TR.: deck (trim); decorate a ship (with pennants). ‖**-vése** [=*palvese*], M.: large shield.

pavi-daménte, ADV.: fearfully (timidly). ‖**pávi-do** [L. *-dus*], ADJ.: fearful (timid); frightful.

pavi-mentáre, TR.: pave (floor). **-mentazióne**, F.: paving. ‖**-ménto** [L. *-mentum*], M.: pavement (floor).

pavó-na, F.: peahen; vain woman. **-nazzétto**, M.: kind of marble. **-názzo**, M.: violet (colour). **-ncèlla**, F.: lapwing (bird). **-ncèllo**, **-ncíno**, *dim.* of *-ne*. ‖**pavó-ne** [L. *pavo*], M.: peacock. **-neggiáre**, INTR., REFL.: strut (act as a peacock): — *di*, boast of. **-néssa**, F.: peahen.

pa-zientáre, INTR.: be patient. ‖**-ziènte** [L. *-tiens* (*patior*, endure)], ADJ.: patient (enduring, constant); M.: patient. **-zienteménte**, ADV.: patiently. **-ziènza**, **-ziènzia**†, F.: patience (endurance); friar's scapular.

paz-zacchióne, *aug.* of *-zo*. **-záccio**, *disp.* of *-zo*. **-zaménte**, ADV.: foolishly (madly). **-zarèllo**, *dim.* of *-zo*. **-zeggiáre**, INTR.: act the fool (be foolish). **-zerèlla**, **-zerèllo**, *car. dim.* of *-zo*. **-zerèlli**, M. PL.: inmates of an insane asylum. **-zerelláta**, F.: foolish actions. **-zerellíno**, *dim.* of *-zerello*. **-zerellóne**, *disp. aug.* of *-zerello*. **-zeréseo**†, ADJ.: mad (foolish). **-zería**, F.: ward for the insane (in a hospital). **-zeríccio**†, ADJ.: slightly foolish. **-zeróne**†,

M.: madman. -sescaménte, ADV.: madly (foolishly). -sésco, ADJ.: mad (foolish): *alla* —, madly (wildly). -sía, F.: madness (foolishness, strangeness). -siáre†, INTR.: act the fool (be foolish). -siccio†, ADJ.: slightly foolish. -siòla, -siuòla, *dim.* of *-sia.* ‖pás-so [?], ADJ.: mad (insane, foolish); strange (extravagant): *esser* — *di*, be very fond of; M.: insane person.

pé' for *per i*, for the.

pe-án(a), ‖**-áne**, pl. *-ana*, *-ani* [Gr. *paián*], M.: pæan (song of triumph); pæon (Greek foot).

pèc-ca, F.: fault (defect). **-cábile**, ADJ.: peccable (liable to sin). **-cabilità**, F.: peccability. **-cadígliot**†, *dim.* of *-cato.* **-caminóso**, ADJ.: sinful (bad). ‖**-cáre** [L.], INTR.: sin (transgress). **-catáccio**, *disp.* of *-cato.* **-cáto**, M.: sin (crime, error). **-catóre**, M., **-catríce**, F.: sinner. **-catúccio**, **-catúzzo**, *dim.* of *-cato.*

pécchero†, M.: large goblet.

péc-chia [L. *apicula* (dim. of *apis*)], F.: bee. **-chiáre**†, INTR.: drink (suck like a bee). **-chióne**†, *aug.* of *-chia.*

pèc-cia†, F.: paunch. **-ciáta**†, F.: blow in the stomach.

pé-ce [L. *pix*], F.: PITCH: — *greca*, resin. **-cétta**, F.: cerate. **-cióso**, ADJ.: smeared with pitch.

pèco-ra [L.], F.: sheep (ewe). **-ráccia**, *disp.* of *-ra.* **-ràggine**, F.: stupidity. **-rája**, F.: shepherdess. **-rájo**, M.: shepherd. **-rάme**, M.: flock of sheep (said of foolish people). **-ráro**, M.: shepherd. **-réccio**, M.: maze; confusion. **-rèlla**, F.: *dim.* of *-ra*; PL.: foam (of waves); white clouds. **-rescaménte**, ADV.: sheepishly. **-résco**, ADJ.: sheepish. **-rétta**, *dim.* of *-ra.* **-ríle**, M.: sheepfold; ADJ.: of a sheep; stupid. **-rína**, *car. dim.* of *-ra.* **-ríno**, ADJ.: of a sheep; M.: sheep-ordure; lamb. **pèco-ro**, M.: ram (wether). **-róne**, M.: *aug.* of *-ro*; blockhead.

pecúglio†, M.: flock; earnings.

peculáto [L. *-tus*], M.: peculation (embezzlement).

peculiá-re [L. *-ris*], ADJ.: peculiar (special). **-rità**, F.: peculiarity. **-rménte**, ADV.: peculiarly.

pecúlio [L. *-lium*], M.: earnings; property; flock†.

pecú-nia [L. *-s*, cattle], F.: money. **-niále**†, ADJ.: pecuniary. **-niariaménte**, ADV.: pecuniarily. **-niário**, ADJ.: pecuniary (relating to money). **-niósot**†, ADJ.: moneyed (wealthy).

pedág-gio [l. L. *pedaticum* (*pedes*, FOOT-traveller)], M.: toll. **-iáre**†, M.: toll-collector.

pedá-gna [L. *-nea* (*pes*, FOOT)], F.: footboard (of a boat). **-gnòlo**, M.: trunk (of a young tree); ADJ.: of the trunk.

pedago-ghería, F.: pedantry. **-ghéssa**, F.: pedant. **-gía**, F.: pedagogy.

pedagò-gico, pl. *—ci*, ADJ.: pedagogical. **-gísta**, M.: writer on (or teacher of) pedagogy. **-gizzáre**, INTR.: discourse on pedagogy. ‖**pedagò-go** [Gr. *paidagogós* 'child-leading'], M.: pedagogue (instructor).

pedágra† = *podagra.*

pedá-le [L. *-lis* (*pes*, FOOT)], M.: (of a tree); pedal; stirrup (of a **-leggiáre**, INTR.: use the pedals (of an instrument). **-lièra**, F.: pedals (of an instrument). **pedá-na**, F.: footboard (of a carriage); rug; lining. **pedá-neo**†, M.: tree-trunk; pedal; stirrup (of a shoe).

pedan-táccio, *disp.* of *-te.* **-tággine**, F.: pedantry. ‖**pedán-te** [Gr. *paideúein* (*pais*, boy) instruct], M.: pedagogue (instructor); pedant. **-teggiáre**, INTR.: pedantize (act the pedant). **-tèllo**, *dim.* of *-te.* **-tería**, F.: pedantry. **-tescaménte**, ADV.: pedantically. **-tésco**, ADJ.: pedantic. **-tíno**, ADJ.: pedantic; M.: pedant. **-tísmo**, M.: pedantism (pedantry). **-tóna**, **-tóne**, *aug.* of *-te.* **-túccio**, **-túcolo**, *dim.* of *-te.*

pe-d. . [L. *pes*, FOOT]: **-dáta**, F.: footprint (trace); footstep (sound); **-dèstre**, ADJ.: pedestrian; vulgar **-destreménte**, ADV.: on foot. **-dicciuòlo**†, M.: pedicel (flower-stalk). **coláre**, **-diculáre** [L. *-cularius* (*-culus*, louse)], F.: lice-bane; ADJ.: pedicular (lousy). **-dignóne** [?], M.: chilblain (on the foot). **-dilúvio**, M.: foot-bath. **-dína**, F.: pawn (at chess). **-dináre**, TR.: follow (spy). **-díno**, *dim.* of *piede.* **-dísequo**, ADJ.: following (on foot). **-'do**†, M.: staff (of a shepherd). **-dóna**, ADJ.: foot-; F.†: pawn (at chess): *strada* —, footpath; *alla* —, on foot. **-donággio**†, M., **-donáglia**†, F.: infantry (foot-soldiers). **-dóne** [*piede*], M.: foot-soldier; tree-trunk†. **-dòt(t)o**†, M., **-dòtta**†, F.: pilot (guide). **-dúccio**, M.: leg (of sheep, etc.); harefoot; console (bracket). **-dúle**, M.: foot (of a stocking).

pèg-gio [L. *pejor*], ADJ.: worse; M.: worst: *al* — *andare*, at the worst. **-gioraménto**, M.: growing worse. **-gioráre**, TR.: make worse; INTR.: grow worse. **-giorativaménte**, ADV.: in a worse way. **-giorativo**, ADJ.: making worse; growing worse; M.: growing worse. **-gioráto**, ADJ.: grown worse. **-gióre**, ADJ.: worse; M.: worst. **-gior-ménte**†, ADV.: in a worse way.

pégli [*per gli*], for the.

pé-gno [L. *pignus*], M.: pledge (security, token): pawn: *dar la fede in* —, pledge one's word; *metter* —, wager (bet). **-gnoráre**†, INTR.: seize (a pawn).

pégola†, F.: pitch.

pél [*per il*], for the, by the.

pela-cáne [*pelare, cane*], M.: currier (tanner). **-gátti**, M.: swindler (sharper).

pela-ghétto, *dim.* of *-go*. ‖**pèla-go** [L. *-gus*], M.: sea (ocean); confusion.

pela-grílli [*pelare, grillo*], M.: miser; ADJ.: avaricious (miserly). **-mantèlli**†, M.: knave (rascal).

pe-láme [*-lo*], M.: hair; same kind (nature). **-laménto**†, M.: pulling of the hair; plucking feathers. **-laníbbi**†, **-lapièdi**†, M.: exacter. **-lapèlli**, M.: plucker (of chickens); worthless fellow. **-láre**, TR.: strip the hair; pluck (of feathers); strip; skin; REFL.: despair. **-láta**, F.: plucking; skinning. **-latína**, F.: *dim.* of *-lata;* loss of hair†. **-láto**, ADJ.: plucked; picked; stripped. **-latóio**†, M.: flaying-place; flaying-knife. **-latúra**, F.: plucking (feathers); stripping; skinning. **-líno**, *car. dim.* of *-lo*.

pelliáccia, *disp.* of *pelle*.

pellá-gra [*pelle*, Gr. *ágra*], F.: pellagra (skin disease). **-gróso**, ADJ.: afflicted with pellagra. **-grosário**, M.: hospital.

pel-láio, M.: seller of lamb-skins. **-láme**, M.: skins (hides). ‖**pèl-le** 1 [L. *-lis*], F.: skin (hide); life, safety: *lasciar* (*scampare*) *la* —, lose (save) one's life; (*in*) — (*in*) —, superficially, lightly; *per la* —, to the core, through and through.

pèlle 2 [*per le*], for the.

pellegri-na, F.: pilgrim; cloak, cape. **-nággio**, M.: pilgrimage. **-náre**, INTR.: go on a pilgrimage. **-nazióne**†, F.: pilgrimage. **-nità**, F.: rarity (choice thing). ‖**pellegrí-no** [L. *peregrinus* (*per*, through, *ager*, country)], M.: pilgrim (wanderer); ADJ.: foreign (Eng.† peregrine); rare (exquisite).

pellicáno [L. *pelicanus*], M.: pelican (water-fowl).

pel-li. [L. *-lis*, skin]: **-licceria**, F.: fur store. **-líccia**, F.: pelisse (fur-coat); pelt; turf. **-licciáio**, **-licciaiuòlo**†, M.: furrier (fur-dealer). **-licciáre**†, TR.: fur (line, trim, etc., with fur). **-licciàro**†, M.: furrier. **-liccióne**, *aug.* of *-liccia*. **-licèlla**, F.: pellicle (film). **-licèllo**†, M.: finger-worm. **-líceo**†, ADJ.: of leather (hide); of fur. **-liciàttola**, *disp. dim.* of *-le*. **-licína**, *car. dim.* of *-le*. **-licino**†, M.: ear (of a sack); bottom (of a net). **-lícola**, F.: *dim.* of *-le;* pellicle. **-lolína**, *car. dim.* of *-le*.

pellúcido [L. *-dus*], ADJ.: pellucid (transparent, clear).

pé-lo [L. *pilus*], M.: hair; kind (nature, rank): *andare a* —, be acceptable; *vedere il* — *nell' uovo*, be very sharp-sighted; *a* —†, exactly; *a* — *d' acqua*, on the same level. **-lolíno**, *dim.* of *-lo*. **-losèlla**, F.: mouse-ear (plant). **-losína**, F.: first sleep (of silk-worms). **-losità**, F.: hairiness. **-lóso**, ADJ.: hairy.

pèl-ta [L.], F.: pelta (small shield). **-tásta**, M.: soldier (armed with a pelta). **-táto**, ADJ.: armed with a pelta; soldier.

pel-tráto†, ADJ.: tinned over. ‖**pél-tro** [OFr. *-tre*], M.: PEWTER.

pe-lúria, F.: down; soft hair. ‖**-lúzzo**, M.: *dim.* of *-lo; panno di* —, Florence plush.

pèlvi [L. *-s*], F.: pelvis.

pé-na [L. *pœna*], F.: punishment; PAIN (suffering); grief (affliction): *a* —, hardly (scarcely). **-náce**†, ADJ.: torturing; grieving. **-nále**, ADJ.: penal; F.: punishment. **-nalísta**, M.: criminalist. **-nalità**, F.: penalty (punishment). **-nalménte**, ADV.: penally. **-náre**, INTR.: suffer (endure); take pains (labour); delay; TR.†: pain (torture). **-narèlla**, *dim.* of *-na*.

penáti [L. *-tes*], M. PL.: Penates (household gods); ADJ.: of the house.

pen-coláre, INTR.: hang loosely; be insecure; be uncertain. **-dáglia**†, F., **-dáglio**, M.: belt; pendant (ear-ring). **-dènte**, ADJ.: pendent (hanging); inclining; depending†; M.: pendant (ear-ring): *in* —, in suspense. **-denteménte**†, ADV.: pendently (in a hanging way). **-dènza**, F.: Eng.† pendence (slope); undecided affair. ‖**pèn-dere** [L.], INTR.: hang (be suspended); slope (lean, incline); be undecided; TR.: hang; incline. **-dévole**†, ADJ.: hanging; inclining. **-díce**, F.: slope (declivity); outskirts. **-dío**, M.: slope (steepness). **pèn-dola**, F.: clock. **pèn-dolo**, ADJ.: pendulous (hanging); M.: pendulum. **-dolóne**†, ADV.: pendently. **-dóne**, M.: part of a curtain. **-dáto**, PART.: hung (suspen... in-clined.

pène [L. *-nis*], ...

penèlo [river ... *da pencia*, ln...

pènero [*pe*... woof).

pene-trábil... bilità, F.: ... F.: penetrat... tive; M.: ... a house). **-tránto**, ... F.: penetrat... trate (enter... penetrativ...

trative (piercing, discerning). **-tratóre,** M.: penetrator. **-trazióne,** F.: penetration (discernment). **-trévole†,** ADJ.: penetrative. **-trevolménte†,** ADV.: penetratingly.

penìso-la [L. *pen-insula*, 'almost island'], F.: peninsula. **-létta,** *dim.* of *-la.*

penitèn-te [L. *pœnitens*], ADJ.: penitent (repentant). **penitèn-za, penitèn-zia,** F.: penitence (contrition); penance. **-ziále,** ADJ.: penitential. **-ziáre†,** TR., INTR.: impose penance. **-ziário,** ADJ.: penitential; M.: penitentiary (house of correction). **-zière,** M.: penitentiary (confessor). **-zierìa,** F.: penitentiary's court. **-ziúccia†,** F.: slight penance.

pén-na [L.], F.: feather (plume); pen; writer; summit: *a   e a calamaio†*, precisely; *dar di   ,* sign; cancel; *lasciar nella   ,* omit; *temperare una   ,* make a pen. **nacchièra,** F.: helmet plumes. **-nacchiétto, nacchiettíno,** *dim.* of *-nacchio.* **-nácchio,** M.: crest (tuft of feathers). **-nacchiòlo,** *dim.* of *-nacchio.* **náccia,** *disp.* of *-na.* **-náio,** M.: feather dealer. **-naiòlo,** M.: pen-case; seller of pens†. **-náta,** F.: penful (of ink); pen-stroke; blow with a pen. **-náto,** ADJ.: feathered; M.: pruning-knife. **-necchíno,** *dim.* of *-necchio.* **-nécchio,** M.: distaff-ful. **-nelláre,** INTR.: paint. **-nelláta, -nellatúra†,** F.: brush-stroke. **-nelleggiáre,** INTR.: paint. **-nellétto, -nellettíno,** *dim.* of *-nello.* **-nèllo,** M.: pencil; paint-brush: *fatto a —,* very well made. **-nellóne,** *aug.* of *-nello.* **-nétta,** *dim.* of *-na.* **-nettína,** *dim.* of *-na.* **-níno,** M.: pen-point; aigrette. **-nolína,** *dim.* of *penna.* **-noncèllo,** M.: crest (tuft of feathers). **-nóne,** M.: pennon (flag, ensign). **-nonière,** M.: standard-bearer. **-nóso†,** ADJ.: feathery. **-núto,** ADJ.: feathered (covered with feathers); M. PL.: birds.

penómbra [L. *pæne*, almost, *umbra*, shadow], F.: penumbra (partial shadow).

pe-nosaménte, ADV.: painfully (with difficulty). ‖**-nóso** [*-na*], ADJ.: painful (distressing).

pen-sábile, ADJ.: capable of being thought. **-sagióne†,** F., **-saménto,** M.: thinking; thought. **-sánte,** ADJ.: thinking (pensive); M.: pensive person. ‖**-sáre** [L. (intens. of *pendere*, weigh)], INTR.: think (judge, reflect, imagine); believe; intend; M.: thinking. **-sáta†,** F.: thought. **-sataménte,** ADV.: on purpose. **-sáto,** PART.: thought; M.†: thought. **-satéio†,** M.: food for thought: *mettere nel —,* ... suspicion. **-satóre,** M., **-satríce,** thinker. **-sévole†,** ADJ.: considered. **-sieráccio,** *disp.* of *-siero.* **-sieróso†,** ADJ.: pensive (thoughtful). **-sière,** M.: thought; thinking; mind; care (attention). **-sierétto,** *dim.* of *-siero.* **-sierìno,** *car. dim.* of *-siero.* **-sièro,** M.: thinking; thought; mind; care (attention): *essere sopra —,* be preoccupied. **-sieróne,** *aug.* of *-siero.* **-sieróso,** ADJ.: thoughtful (pensive). **-sieruccio, -sierúzzo,** *dim.* of *-siero.*

pènsile [L. *-lis*], ADJ.: pensile (hanging).

pensio-náre, TR.: pension. **-nário†,** M.: pensioner (boarder). **-náto,** PART.: pensioned; M.: pensionary. **-ncèlla,** *dim.* of *-ne.* ‖**pensió-ne** [L. *pensio*, payment], F.: pension (stipend); French boarding-house.

pen-sívo†, -sóso [*-sare*], ADJ.: pensive (thoughtful).

pentácolo [L. *pendere*, hang], M.: amulet (talisman).

penta- [Gr. *pénte*, five]: **-còrdo** [Gr. *-chordos* (*chórde*, chord)], M.: pentachord (musical instrument). **-èdro** [Gr. *hédra*, base], M.: pentahedron (solid figure). **pentá-gono** [Gr. *gônos*, angle], M.: pentagon (plane figure). **pentá-metro** [Gr. *métron*, measure], M.: pentameter. **-pentá-poli** [Gr. *pólis*, city], F.: pentapolis. **-síllabo,** ADJ.: pentasyllabic. **-tèuco** [Gr. *teûchos*, book], M.: Pentateuch.

pentecòste [L., 50th], F.: Pentecost (festival).

pen-tére†, INTR.: repent (be contrite). **-tigióne†,** F., **-timénto,** M.: repentance. ‖**-tíre** [L. *pœnitere* (*pœna*, punishment)], REFL. (*mi pento*, etc.): REPENT (be sorry). **-títo,** ADJ.: repentant (sorry).

pénto-la [?], F.: earthen pot; mortar (piece of ordnance). **-láccia,** *disp.* of *-la.* **-láia,** F., **-láio, -láro,** M.: potter. **-láta,** F.: blow with a pot; potful. **-létta, -lína,** *dim.* of *-la.* **-líno,** *dim.* of *-lo.* **pénto-lo,** M.: small earthen pot. **-lóna,** *aug.* of *-la.* **-lóne,** *aug.* of *-la* or *-lo.*

pentúto†, ADJ.: repentant (sorry).

pènula [L. *pænula*], F.: kind of cloak (for rainy weather).

pe-nultimaménte, ADV.: penultimately. ‖**-núltimo** [L. *pæn-ultimus*], ADJ.: penultimate.

penú-ria [L.], F.: penury (want, poverty). **-riáre†,** INTR.: want (be in need). **-rióso†,** ADJ.: penurious (needy).

pen-zigliáro, -zoláre, INTR.: dangle (hang loosely). ‖**pèn-zolo** [L. *-silis*], M.: bunch of grapes; ADJ.†: hanging. **-zolóne†, -zolóni,** ADV.: in a dangling (hanging) way.

pèone [L. *pæon*], M.: pæon (Greek metre).

peònia [L. *paeonia*], F.: peony (plant).
peònico, pl. —*ci* [-*ne*], ADJ.: pæonic.
peòta [?], F.: kind of gondola.
pe-paiòla, F.: pepper-box. **-páto**, ADJ.: spiced: *pan -pato*, gingerbread. ‖**pé-pe** [L. *piper*], M.: pepper: *come di* —†, exactly, precisely. **-períno**, M.: peperine (volcanic rock). **-peroncíno**, *dim.* of *-perone*. **-peróne**, M.: Cayenne pepper. **-píno**, car. *dim.* of *-pe*.
pèplo [L. *peplum*], M.: woman's cloak (mantle).
pèplo†, M.: purslain (plant).
pepolíno [*pepe*], M.: thyme.
pepsína [Gr. *pépsis*, digestion], F.: pepsin.
pér [L.], PREP.: FOR; by; through; as; in; from: — *l'addietro*, heretofore; — *l'appunto*, precisely; — *l'innanzi*, heretofore; — *modo che*, so that; — *modo di parlare*, so to speak; — *tutto*, everywhere; — *parte di*, in the name of.
péra 1 [L. *pira*], F.: pear (fruit).
péra† 2, F.: pocket; wallet.
percállo [Fr. *-cale*], M.: percale (cloth).
percènto [*per cento*], M.: percentage.
per-cepíre [L. *-cipere*], TR., INTR.: PERCEIVE (discern). **-cepíto**, PART.: perceived. **-cettíbile**, ADJ.: perceptible (discernible). **-cettibilità**, F.: perceptibility. **-cettívo**, ADJ.: perceptive (perceiving). **-cètto**, PART.: perceived. **-cezióne**, F.: perception.
perchè *-é* [*per che*], ADV., CONJ.: why (for what reason)? why; because; so that: *dire il* —, tell the reason.
pèrchio†, M.: padlock.
perciò [*per ciò*], ADV.: therefore; for this reason: — *che*, in order that; since.
percípere†, TR.: perceive (discern).
per-córrere [L. *-currere*], IRR. (cf. *correre*); TR., INTR.: run through (over). **-córsi**, PRET. of *-correre*. **-córso**, PART.: passed over quickly.
per-còssa, F.: blow (thrust). **-cossióne**, F.: percussion (striking). **-còssi**, PRET. of *-cuotere*. **-còsso**, PART.: struck. **-cossúra**†, F.: striking. **-cotènte**, PART.: striking. ‖**-còtere** [L. ... IRR.§; TR.: strike (beat, hit ... ...); wound. **-cotiménto** ... ing (percussion). **-coti...** **trice**, F.: striki... striking, blow. ... **sáre**† = ... cussion (striki... ADJ.: perc... **sóre**, M.: ... striking.

§ Pret. ... *percòssi*, ...

loss; ruin. ‖**pèr-dere** [L.], IRR.§; TR.: lose (be deprived of, waste, forfeit): — *di vista*, lose sight of. **-dénza**†, F.: loss (destruction).

§ Ind.: Pret. *per-déi* or *-détti* or *pérsi*, etc. Part.: *perdúto* or *pérso*.

perdíce†, F.: partridge.
perdi-fiáto [*perdere*], ADV.: *a* —, breathlessly. **-gióne**†, F.: perdition (ruin). **-giórno**, M.: lazy fellow. **-ménto**, M.: losing; loss; waste. **pèrdi-ta**, F.: loss (injury); waste. **-tèmpo**, M.: wasted time. **-tóre**, M., **-trice**, F.: loser. **-zióne**†, F.: perdition (ruin).
perdo-nábile, ADJ.: pardonable. **-namènto**†, M.: pardon. ‖**-náre** [*per donare*], TR.: pardon (forgive, excuse); spare. **-náto**, PART.: forgiven. **-natóre**, M.: forgiver. **perdó-no**, M.: pardon (forgiveness).
per-dótto, PART.: conducted. ‖**-dúcere** [L.], IRR.; TR.: conduct (lead).
perduellióne [L. *-duellio*], F.: perduellion (treason).
perdu-rábile†, ADJ.: lasting (Eng.† perdurable). **-rabilità**†, F.: duration. **-rabilménte**†, ADV.: very durably. ‖**-ráre** [*per*, *d.*.], INTR.: endure (last, continue long). **-révole**, ADJ.: durable (lasting).
per-dúrre†, IRR. (cf. *addurre*); TR.: conduct (lead). **-dússi**†, PRET. of *-durre* (or *-ducere*).
per-dutaménte, ADV.: desperately (madly). ‖**-dúto** [*-dere*], ADJ.: lost (destroyed, wasted).
pere-grináre, INTR.: peregrinate (travel about). **-grinazióne**, F.: peregrination (travelling). ‖**-gríno** [L. *-grinus* (cf. *pellegrino*)], ADJ.: foreign (Eng.† peregrine); rare (exquisite).
perèn-ne [L. *-nis* (*per*, through, *annus*, year)], ADJ.: perennial (enduring). **-neménte**, ADV.: perennially (continually). **-nità**, F.: perennity (perpetuity).
peren-toriaménte, ADV.: peremptorily (positively). ‖**-tòrio** [L. *per-emptorius*], ADJ.: peremptory (decisive).
... **-equazióne** [L. *æquatio*], F.: equality ...
... [... *-ro*], M.: pear-tree orchard.
... **-aménte**, ADV.: perfectly (completely). **-fettíbile**, ADJ.: per... **-fettibilità**, F.: perfectibility. ... perfective (perfecting); ... **-fètto** [L. *-fectus*], ADJ.: per... ...; perfected†; M.†: ... **-bile**, ADJ.: capable ... **-fezionaménto**, ... improvement. ... complete, con-

-self. **-fezionatívo**, ADJ.: adapted to perfect. **-fezionatóre**, M., **-fezionatrice**, F.: perfecter. **-fezióne**, F.: perfection (completeness). **-ficere†**, TR.: perfect (complete). **-ficiènte†**, ADJ.: perfecting.

perfi-daménte, ADV.: perfidiously (treacherously). **-dézza, perfí-dia**, F.: perfidy (treachery, faithlessness). **-diáre**, INTR.: be obstinate. **-diosaménte**, ADV.: perfidiously; obstinately. **-dióso**, ADJ.: perfidious (faithless); obstinate (stubborn). ||**pèrfi-do** [L. *-dus*], ADJ.: perfidious (faithless, treacherous).

perfiguráre†, TR.: imagine (think).

perfíno [*per fine*], ADV.: *alla* —, finally.

perfo-rábile, ADJ.: that may be perforated. **-raménto**, M.: perforation (piercing); hole. **-ránte**, PART.: perforating. ||**-ráre** [L.], TR.: perforate (bore through, pierce). **-ráta**, F.: St. John's wort (herb). **-ratóre**, M., **-ratrice**, F.: perforator. **-razióne**, F.: perforation (piercing).

perfrequentáre†, TR.: frequent often.

perfuntoriaménte†, ADV.: perfunctorily (negligently).

perfusióne†, F.: perfusion (sprinkling).

pergamèna [L.], F.: PARCHMENT (vellum); lantern.

pèrgamo [L. *-mum*], M.: pulpit.

pergiuráre†, TR., INTR.: perjure (forswear).

pèrgo-la [L. *pergula*], F.: vine-trellis (bower): *esser* —, stand up like a post. **-láto**, M.: large trellis (bower). **-lése**, F.: large winter-grapes (kept on the vine-trellis); ADJ.: of winter-grapes. **-léto†**, M.: large vine-trellis. **pèrgo-lo†**, M.: stage; box (in a theatre).

pèri†, M. PL.: peers; paladins.

peri- [Gr., about]: **-cárdio** [Gr. *kardía*, heart], M.: pericardium. **-cardíte**, F.: pericarditis. **-cárpio** [Gr. *karpós*, fruit], M.: pericarp.

periclitáre†, INTR.: be in danger; run the risk.

pericco-laménto, M.: danger (peril, risk). **-lánte**, PART.: risking; running. **-láre**, INTR.: be in danger; run the risk; TR.: ruin (overthrow). **-latóre†**, M.: attorney. ||**perícco-lo** [L. *periculum*], M.: PERIL (danger, risk). **-losaménte**, ADV.: dangerously (perilously). **-lóso**, ADJ.: dangerous (perilous, hazardous).

peri- [Gr., about]: **-cránio** [Gr. *kraníon*, skull], M.: pericranium. **-èlio** [Gr. *hélios*, sun], M.: perihelion. **-fería** [Gr. *phéreín*, bear], F.: periphery (circumference of a circle, etc.). **-fèrico**, pl. —*ci*, ADJ.: peripheric. **-frasáre**, TR.: periphrase. ...rí-frasi [Gr. *-phrasis* (*phrázein*, ...ak)], F.: periphrase (circuit of words). **-frástico**, pl. —*ci*, ADJ.: periphrastic. **-gèo** [Gr. *gê*, earth], M.: perigee.

periglio.. (*poet.*) = *pericol*..

peri- [Gr., about]: **-metría**, F.: perimetry. **-mètrico**, pl. —*ci*, ADJ.: perimetric. ||**perí-metro** [Gr. *métron*, measure], M.: perimeter (circumference). **-nèo**, [Gr. *-'neos*], M.: perinæum.

perio-dáccio, *disp.* of *-do*. **-dáre**, INTR.: write (or speak) in periods. **-deggiáre**, INTR.: write (or speak) affectedly in periods. **-détto**, *car. dim.* of *-do*. **-dicaménte**, ADV.: periodically. **-dicità**, F.: periodicity. **periò-dico**, pl. —*ci*, ADJ.: periodical. **-díno**, *car. dim.* of *-do*. **perío-do** [L. *-dus*], M.: period (time, conclusion); sentence. **-dóne**, *aug.* of *-do*.

peri- [Gr., about]: **-òsteo, -òstio** [Gr. *ostéon*, bone], M.: periosteum. **-ostíte**, F.: periostitis. **-pateticaménte**, ADV.: peripatetically. **-pateticísmo**, M.: peripateticism. **-patètico**, pl. —*ci* [Gr. *patein*, walk], ADJ., M.: peripatetic. **-pezía** [Gr. *píttein*, fall], F.: sudden change (of fortune). **pèri-plo** [Gr. *plein*, sail], M.: circumnavigation (periplus). **-pneumonía** [Gr. *pneúmon*, lung], F.: peripneumony (inflammation of the lungs).

perire [L.], INTR.: perish (die, decay); languish; TR.: kill; ruin.

peri- [Gr., about]: **-spèrma** [Gr. *spérma*, seed], M.: perisperm (of a seed). **-stáltico** [Gr. *stéllein*, place], ADJ.: peristaltic. **-stílio** [Gr. *stúlos*, column], M.: peristyle.

peritaménte [*-to*], ADV.: skilfully (expertfully).

peri-tánza, F.: timidity (bashfulness). ||**-táre** [? L. *pigritari*, be sluggish], INTR.: be timid (bashful).

períto 1 [L. *-tus*], ADJ.: skilful (expert, dexterous); M.: appraiser.

períto 2 [*-rire*], ADJ.: perished (dead, decayed).

perito-nèo [Gr. *-naios* (*perí*, around, *teínein*, stretch)], M.: peritoneum (abdominal membrane). **-níte**, F.: peritonitis.

peritóso [*-tare*], ADJ.: timid (bashful).

peritúro [*perire*], ADJ.: perishing (short-lived, frail).

per-iúrio†, M.: perjury (false oath). **-iúro†**, M.: perjurer (forswearer).

perízia [L. *-ritia*], F.: skill (dexterity; adroitness, art); M.: valuation.

perizòma [Gr.], F.: cincture of mode...

pèr-la [?], F.: pearl. **-láceo**, ... pearly (perlacious). **-lagióne** ... dour of the pearl. **-l**... (pearl-coloured). **-létt**... **-la**. **-lismaltáto†**, ... with pearls.

perlustrá-re [L.], TR...

traverse). **-tóre,** M.: scourer. **-zióne,** F.: perlustration (examining).
permá-le [*per male*], ADV.: peevishly. **-losità,** F.: peevishness (captiousness). **-lóso,** ADJ.: touchy.
perma-nènte, ADJ.: permanent (durable, continuing). **-nentemènte,** ADV.: permanently. **-nènza,** F.: permanence (duration, fixedness); stay. ||**-nére†** [L.], IRR., (cf. *rimanere*); INTR.: be permanent (lasting, continuous). **-névole, -nsívo†,** ADJ.: permanent (lasting, fixed). **permá-si,** PRET., **permá-sto,** PART. of *-nere*.
permeá-bile [L. *-bilis*], ADJ.: permeable (penetrable). **-bilità,** F.: permeability. **-zióne,** F.: permeation.
per-messióne†, F.: permission (consent). **-messívo†,** ADJ.: permissive. **-mésso,** PART.: permitted (granted); M.: permission. **-mettènte,** PART.: permitting (allowing). ||**-méttere** [L. *-mittere*], IRR. (cf. *mettere*); TR.: permit (allow, consent to).
permis-chiáre† [*per mischiare*], TR.: mix (mingle, confuse). **-chiatamènte,** ADV.: in a mixed (confused) manner. **-chiataménto†,** M.: mixture (medley); scuffle (disturbance). **-chiáto,** ADJ.: mixed.
permis-síbile [*permettere*], ADJ.: permissible (allowable). **-sióne,** F.: permission (leave). **-sivaménte,** ADV.: permissively (by allowance). **-sívo,** ADJ.: permissive (allowing).
permistióne†, F.: permistion (mixing).
permoviménto†, M.: agitation (feeling).
pèrmu-ta, F.: permutation (exchange). **-tábile,** ADJ.: permutable (exchangeable). **-taménto,** M., **-tánza†,** F.: permutation (exchange, barter). ||**-táre** [L.], TR.: exchange (trade, barter; permute). **-tataménte†,** ADV.: by way of exchange. **-tatívo†,** ADJ.: exchanging (bartering). **-tazióne,** F.: permutation.
pernétto, *dim.* of *-no.*
perníce [L. *perdix*], F.: PARTRIDGE.
pernicció-sa, F.: kind of fever. **-saménte,** ADV.: perniciously (destructively). **-sità,** F.: perniciousness. ||**perniciósо** [L. *-sus* (*necare*, kill)], ADJ.: pernicious (destructive, hurtful).
pernicìòtto†, *dim.* of *-nice.*
pernicóne†, M.: kind of plum-tree (or the fruit).
pèr-nio, pèrno [Sp. -*nio*], M.: pivot ...): bolt.
... (pass-
...].

account); therefore; notwithstanding: — —, but. **=cchè** *-é*, CONJ.: because (since, for).
perondíno [?], M.: dandy (fop).
perorá-re [L.], TR.: plead (defend; discourse); INTR.: perorate (harangue). **-zióne,** F.: peroration.
peròssido [*per ossido*], M.: peroxide.
perpendico-láre, ADJ.: perpendicular (vertical). **-larità,** F.: perpendicularity. **-larménte,** ADV.: perpendicularly. ||**perpendíco-lo** [L. *per-pendiculum*], M.: plumb-line (plummet, perpendicle): *a* —, perpendicularly.
perpetrá-re [L.], TR.: perpetrate (do, commit). **-tóre,** M.: perpetrator. **-zióne,** F.: perpetration.
perpe-tuagióne†, F.: perpetuation (continuance). **-tuále†,** ADJ.: perpetual (constant). **-tualità†,** F.: perpetuity (continued existence). **-tualménte, -tuaménte,** ADV.: perpetually. **-tuánza†,** F.: perpetuity. **-tuáre,** TR.: perpetuate; REFL.: become perpetual. **-tuatóre,** M., **-tuatríce,** F.: one who perpetuates. **-tuazióne,** F.: perpetuation. **-tuità,** F.: perpetuity (continued existence). ||**perpè-tuo** [L. *-tuus*], ADJ.: perpetual (everlasting).
per-plessità, F.: perplexity (anxiety). ||**-plèsso** [L. *-plexus* (*plectere*, twist)], ADJ.: perplexed (bewildered).
perquisí-re [L. *per-quirere*], TR.: search diligently (pry). **-tívo†,** ADJ.: searching (prying). **perquisí-to,** PART. of *-re.* **-tóre,** M.: searcher (Eng.† perquisitor). **-zióne,** F.: perquisition (search, inquiry).
perrocchétto†, M.: fore-topmast.
perrúcca [Sp. *peluca*], F.: peruke (wig).
perscru-tábile, ADJ.: scrutable. ||**-táre** [L. *-tari*], TR.: scrutinize (search closely).
pèrsa†, F.: marjoram.
pèrsea [L.], F.: persea (genus of plants).
perse-cutóre, M., **-cutríce,** F.: persecutor. **-cuzioncèlla,** *dim.* of *-cuzione.* **-cuzióne,** F.: persecution (molestation). ||**-guíre** [L. *-qui*], TR. (Pres. *-guo*): persecute (harass, torment); pursue (continue). **-guitaménto†,** M.: persecution. **-guitáre,** TR.: persecute (harass); pursue. **-guitáto,** PART.: persecuted. **-guitazióne†,** F.: persecution (molestation). **-guito,** PART.: persecuted. **-guitóre†,** M.: persecutor.
perseve-ránte, ADJ.: persevering (steadfast). **-rantemènte,** ADV.: perseveringly. **-ránza,** F.: perseverance (persistance). ||**-ráre** [L.], INTR.: persevere (... continue). **-rataménte†,** ADV.: ...ingly. **-razióne†,** F.: persever-

persevráre†, INTR.: persevere (persist).

persiána [*Persia*], F.: Venetian blind.

pèrsi-ca [L.], F.: PEACH (fruit). **-cáta**†, F.: conserve of peaches. **pèrsi-co**, pl. *-ci*, ADJ.: Persian: *il pomo* —, peach-tree.

persíno [*per sino*], ADV.: until (as far as).

persis-tènza, F.: persistence (perseverance). **-tènte**, ADJ.: persistent (firm). ||**persís-tere** [L.], INTR. (part. *-tito*): persist (persevere). **-títo**, PART.: persisted.

pèrso 1 [*-dere*], PART.: lost (wasted, destroyed).

pèrso† 2, M.: reddish-black colour.

per=sòlvere†, IRR.; TR.: fulfil a duty. **-solúto**†, PART. of *-lvere*.

persó-na [L., mask, part], F.: person (man, form, body, life): *in — d'alcuno*, in a person's place. **-náccia**, *disp.* of *-na*. **-nággio**, M.: personage: *far un* —, play a part. **-nále**, ADJ.: personal; M.: personal form. **-nalità**, F.: personality. **-nalménte**, ADV.: personally (individually). **-ncína**, *car. dim.* of *-na*. **-ncíno**, *dim.* of *-na*. **-nificáre**, TR.: personify. **-nificáto**, PART.: personified. **-nificazióne**, F.: personification.

perspettíva†, F.: perspective.

perspi-cáce [L. *-cax*], ADJ.: perspicacious (keen). **-cacemènte**, ADV.: with perspicacity. **-cácia**, **-cacità**†, F.: perspicacity.

per-spicuità, F.: perspicuity (clearness). ||**-spícuo** [L. *-spicuus*], ADJ.: perspicuous (clear).

perspirazióne†, F.: perspiration.

persua-dènte, ADJ.: persuasive. ||**-dére** [L.], IRR.§; TR.: persuade (convince, satisfy); REFL.: persuade one's self. **-dévole**, **-díbile**, ADJ.: persuadable. **-síbile**, ADJ.: persuasible. **-sióne**, F.: persuasion (persuading); conviction. **persuá-si**, PRET. of *-dere*. **-síva**, F.: persuasiveness. **-sivaménte**, ADV.: persuasively. **-sívo**, ADJ.: persuasive. **persuá-so**, PART.: persuaded. **-sóre**, M.: persuader. **-sòrio**, ADJ.: persuasory (persuasive).

§ Pret. *persuá-si, -se; -sero.* Part. *persuáso.*

per=tánto, ADV.: however; therefore: *non* —, nevertheless.

per=tenére†, IRR.; INTR.: pertain (belong). **-ténni**†, PRET. of *-tenere*. **-tenúto**, PART.: pertained.

pèrti-ca [L.], F.: pole (long stick); kind of measure. **-cáre**†, TR.: beat down with a pole. **-cáta**, F.: blow with a pole. **-catóre**, M.: land-surveyor. **-chétta**, *car. dim.* of *-ca*. **-cóna**, **-cóne**, *aug.* of

perti-náce [L. *-nax*], ADJ.: pertinacious (stubborn, inflexible). **-nacemènte**, ADV.: pertinaciously. **-nácia**, F.: pertinacity (obstinacy).

pertinènza [L. *-nentia*], F.: appurtenance.

pertrattá-re [L. *per-tractare*], TR.: TREAT of (at length). **-zióne**, F.: treating (discoursing) at length; prolongation (delay)†.

per-tugiáre, TR.: pierce (bore, pertuse). ||**-túgio** [L. *-tusum* (*tundere*, strike)], M.: hole (aperture, Eng.† pertusion).

perturba-ménto, M.: perturbation (commotion). ||**perturbá-re** [*per turbare*], TR.: perturb (disturb, agitate). **-taménte**, ADV.: in a perturbed manner. **perturbá-to**, PART.: perturbed (disturbed). **-tóre**, M., **-tríce**, F.: perturber (disturber). **-zióne**, F.: perturbation (disturbance).

per-tusáre†, TR.: pertuse (pierce, bore). **-túso**†, M.: hole (aperture).

perúggine†, F.: wild pear-tree.

perugíno [*Perugia*], M.: kind of vine (and grape).

perve-niènte, ADJ.: coming to. **-niménto**†, M.: attaining (reaching). ||**-níre** [L.], IRR. (cf. *venire*); INTR.: come to (attain, reach). **pervé-nni**, PRET. of *-nire*. **-núto**, PART.: attained (reached).

perver-saménto, ADV.: perversely. **-sáre**†, INTR.: rage (storm); TR.: scold (abuse). **-sióne**†, F.: perversion (depravity). **-sità**, F.: perversity (wickedness, stubbornness). **pervèr-so**, ADJ.: perverse (wicked, stubborn). **-timénto**, M.: perversion (wickedness). ||**-tíre** [L. *-tere*], TR. (pres. *-to* or *-tisco*): pervert (corrupt, distort); REFL.: become perverted. **-titóre**, M., **-titríce**, F.: perverter (corrupter, distorter).

pervi-cáce [L. *-cax* (*-ncere*, conquer completely)], ADJ.: obstinate (Eng.† pervicacious). **-cácia**, F.: obstinacy (stubbornness, Eng.† pervicacity).

pervínca [L.], F.: periwinkle (plant).

pèrvio†, ADJ.: pervious (penetrable).

pé-sa†, F.: weight (load). **-sábile**, ADJ.: weighable. **-sa=lèttere**, M.: letter-weigher. **=liquòri**, M.: hydrometer. **-saménto**, M.: weighing. **-sa=móndi**†, M.: boaster (vaunter). **-sánte**, ADJ.: heavy; wearisome; important. **-santeménte**, ADV.: heavily; seriously. **-santézza**, **-sánza**†, F.: weight (heaviness); sorrow (trouble)†. ||**-sáre** [L. *pensare*], INTR.: weigh (be heavy); TR.: weigh; ponder (consider). **-sáta**, F.: weighing. **-sataménte**, ADV.: considerately (discreetly). **-satóre**, M., **-satríce**, F.: weigher. **-satúra**, F.: weighing.

pèsca 1 [*persica*], F.: PEACH (fruit); black and blue.

pé-sca 2, F.: fishing: *andare alla* —, go fishing. **-scadóre**†, M.: fisherman. **-scagióne**, F.: fishing. **-scáia**, F.: fish-bank; bank (embankment in a river). **-scaiòlo**, M.: ditch. **-scáre**, TR.: fish; search (hunt for); understand: — *a fondo*, examine thoroughly. **-scaréccio**, ADJ.: fishing; fishy. **-scáta**, F.: fishing; catch (of fish). **-scatèllo**, *dim.* of *-ce*. **-scatóre**, M.: fisherman (angler). **-scatòrio**, ADJ.: piscatory. **-scatríce**, F.: fisherwoman. ‖**pé-sce** [L. *piscis*], M.: fish: — *nuovo*†, simpleton; — *d' aprile*, April fool. **-sce=cáne**, M.: shark; dogfish. **-sce=dudva**†, F., **-dudvo**†, M.: omelet. **-scétto**, *dim.* of *-sce*. **-scheréccio**, ADJ.: of a fisherman; fishing. **-scheria**, F.: fish-market. **-schièra**†, F.: fish-pond (reservoir). **-sciáccio**, *disp. dim.* of *-sce*. **-sciuòla**, F.: fish-pot. **-sciaiòlo**, M.: fish-seller. **-sciarèllo**, **-sciatèllo**, *dim.* of *-sce*. **-scína**†, F.: fish-pond. **-scicoltúra**, F.: pisciculture. **pé-scio**, M.: fish. **-sciolíno**, *dim.* of *-sce*. **-scióne**, *aug.* of *-sce*. **-sciósо**†, ADJ.: fishy (full of fish). **-sciòtto**, *aug.* of *-sce*. **-sci=véndolo**, M.: fishmonger. **-sciuòlo**†, *dim.* of *-sce*.

pèsco 1 [*-ca* 1], M.: peach-tree.

pescóso [*-ce*], ADJ.: fishy (full of fish).

pe-sézza, F.: weightiness (heaviness). **-síno**, *dim.* of *-so*. ‖**pé-so** [L. *pensum* (*pendere*, weigh)], M.: weight (heaviness, load); anxiety; importance, charge: — *lordo*, gross weight; *far buon* —, give good weight; *a* —, by weight. **pè-solo**†, **-solóne**†, ADV.: in a hanging manner (dangling).

pessi-maménte, ADV.: very wickedly (miserably). **-mísmo**, M.: pessimism. **-míssimo**, ADJ.: very (or most) wicked. **-místa**, ADJ.: pessimistic; M.: pessimist. **-mità**†, F.: wickedness (great evil). ‖**pèssi-mo** [L. *-mus*], ADJ.: worst; most wicked (sinful).

pessína [*pepsina*], F.: pepsin.

pés-ta, F.: path; track; trail (trace, footstep); pounding†; crowd†. **-ta=colóri**, M.: paint-mill. **-taménto**, M.: pounding (stamping, bruising). **-ta=pépe**, M.: pepper-grinder; dunce (blockhead)†. ‖**-táre** [L.], TR.: pound (PESTLE, pulverise, bruise); trample. **-táta**, F.: pounding (bruising); beating. **-táto**, PART.: pounded (pulverised, bruised); trampled upon. **-tatéllo**†, M.: pestle. **-tatóre**, M.: pounder. **-tatúra**, F.: pounding; thing pounded.

pèste [L. *-tis*], F.: PEST (plague, pestilence).

pe-stellíno, *dim.* of *-stello*. ‖**-stèllo** [L. *pistillus*], M.: PESTLE.

pestí-fero [L. *-ferus* (*pestis*, pest, *ferre*, bring)], ADJ.: pestiferous (harmful, infectious). **-lènte**, ADJ.: pestilent (noxious, dangerous). **-lènza**, **-lènzia**†, F.: pestilence (plague). **-lenziále**, **-lenzióso**, ADJ.: pestilential (contagious, hurtful).

pe-stío, M.: pounding; stamping (trampling). ‖**pé-sto** [*-stare*], PART.: pounded (bruised); trampled upon. **-stóne**, M.: large pestle.

petacchína†, F.: kind of slipper.

petacciuòla†, F.: plantain.

pètalo [Gr. *-lon*], M.: petal (leaf).

pe-tardière, M.: petardeer. ‖**-tárdo** [*-to*], M.: petard.

pèta-so [L. *-sus*], M.: broad-brimmed hat. **-sétto**†, *dim.* of *-so*.

petéc-chia [L. *pestis*, pest], F.: purple spots (on the skin in fever). **-chiále**, ADJ.: petechial (with livid spots).

pe-tènte [L. *-tere*, seek], ADJ.: petitioning (seeking, asking). **-titóre**†, M.: petitioner. **-titòrio**, ADJ.: petitory (petitioning). **-tizióne**, F.: petition (request, entreaty).

péto [L. *peditum*], M.: fart.

petonciáno [fr. Ar.], M.: egg-plant.

pe-tráia [*pietra*], F.: mass of stones. **-trèlla**†, **-tricciuòla**†, *dim.* of *pietra*. **-trière**, **-trièro**, M.: swivel-gun (small cannon). **-trificáre**†, TR.: petrify. **-trificazióne**†, F.: petrifaction. **-trífico**†, ADJ.: petrific (changing to stone). **-trígno**†, ADJ.: stony. **-trína**, F.: small stone. **-tríno**†, ADJ.: stony (hard). **-trolière**, M.: user of petroleum (incendiary). **-tròlio** [*olio*, oil], M.: petroleum (rock-oil, kerosene).

petronciáno [*petonciano*], M.: pumpkin.

petróne†, *aug.* of *pietra*.

petro-sellíno†, **-sèllo**†, **-sémolo**†, **-síllo**†, M.: parsley.

pe-tróso [*pietroso*], ADJ.: (*poet.*) stony (hard). **-truzzuòla**†, *dim.* of *pietra*.

petta=bòtta, **=bbòtta**, F.: breastplate (cuirass). ‖**-ta** [*petto*], F.: blow upon the breast.

pettégo-la [?], F.: gossip (chattering) gossip. -lé...

pette...

petti...

petti...

petti...

Lie...

...

...

...

-na...

F.: combing; carding. ‖**pètti-ne** [L. *pecten*, comb, card], M.: comb; card; kind of shellfish. **-nèlla, -nína,** F.: comb (for the hair). **-nièra,** F.: comb-case.
pettiróseo [*petto rosso*], M.: robin redbreast.
pètto [L. *pectus*], M.: breast; thorax (heart, bosom); breast-strap: *a* —, in comparison; *avere a* —, have at heart; *stare a* —, face (cope with). **=biánco,** M.: partridge (with white breast).
pettò-ccio, *aug.* of *petto*. **-rále,** ADJ.: pectoral (pertaining to the breast); breast-strap (of a horse). **-ralménte†,** ADV.: pectorally. **-reggiáre†,** TR.: strike against breast of. **-rína,** F.: part of nursing-stays. **-rutaménte,** ADV.: haughtily (arrogantly). **-rúto,** ADJ.: high-breasted (haughty).
petu-lánte [L. *-lans*], ADJ.: petulant (peevish, arrogant). **-lanteménte,** ADV.: petulantly. **-lánza, -lánzia†,** F.: petulance (peevishness).
peucèdano [Gr. *peukédanon*], M.: hog-fennel (plant).
pévera [?], F.: large wooden funnel.
peveráda†, F.: broth (soup).
pévere†, M.: pepper.
peveríno†, *dim.* of *-ra*.
péverot, M.: ragout (stew).
pèza†, F.: net (for quails, fish, etc.).
peziènte†, M.: beggar.
peziòlo [L. *-tiolus*], M.: PETIOLE (leaf-stalk).
pèz-za F.: piece (strip, stripe, bit); silver coin: *uomo di* —, man of distinction; *buona* — *fa*, a good while ago; *a questa* —†, a little while ago. **-záccia,** *disp.* of *-za*. **-záccio,** *disp.* of *-zo*. **-zaláma,** F.: infant's napkin (diaper). **-záme,** M.: rubbish. **-záto,** ADJ.: spotted (speckled). **-zatúra,** F.: spottedness. **-zèndo†,** ADV.: *andar* —, go begging. **-zènte,** M.: beggar; ADJ.: begging. **-zétta,** F.: Spanish coin; small piece. **-zettína,** *dim.* of *-zetta*. **-zettíno,** *dim.* of *-zetto*. **-zétto, -zíno,** *dim.* of *-zo*. ‖**pèz-zo** [l. L. *petium*], M.: PIECE (bit, morsel): *un* — *fa*, some time ago; *esser d'un* —, be of one piece; be sincere. **-zòla,** F.: large handkerchief. **-zoláta,** F.: handkerchief-ful. **-zúccio,** *disp. dim.* of *-zo*. **-zuòla,** F.: large handkerchief; small piece. **-zuòlo†,** *dim* of *-zo*.
piaccian-tèo [? *piaccentare*], ADJ.: dull (slow, stupid); M.: stupid fellow.
piacci-chíccio [*spiaccicare*], M.: wet, slippery place. **-cóne,** ADJ.: slow (dull). **-cóso,** ADJ.: slimy; sticky. **-còtto,** M.: something badly done.
pia-centáre†, TR.: flatter (wheedle). **-cènte,** PART.: pleasing (gratifying). **-centeménte†,** ADV.: pleasantly (agreeably). **-centería,** F.: flattery (blandling). **-cent(i)ère†,** M.: flatterer. **-cènza†,** F.: pleasantness; grace (charm). ‖**-cére** [L. *placere*], IRR. §; INTR.: please (delight); REFL.: be pleased with; M.: pleasure (delight, favour, will): *mi piace*, I like it. **-cerétto,** *dim.* of *-cere*. **-ceríno,** *car.* of *-cere*. **-ceróne,** *aug.* of *-cere*. **-ceróso†,** ADJ.: courteous (ready to please). **-ceráccio, -ceruzzo†,** *disp. dim.* of *-cere*. **-cevolóccio,** *aug.* (and *disp.*) of *-cevole*. **-cevoláre†,** INTR.: joke (jest). **-cévole,** ADJ.: pleasing (agreeable, merry, jocose). **-cevoleggiáre,** INTR.: joke (be merry); be pleasing; TR.†: flatter (blandish). **-cevolétto†,** *dim.* of *-cevole*. **-cevolézza,** F.: pleasantness (affability, liveliness). **-cevolíno,** *dim.* of *-cevole*. **-cevolménte,** ADV.: pleasingly (courteously, merrily). **-cevolóne,** *aug.* of *-cevole*. **-ciménto,** M.: pleasing; pleasure (satisfaction, will). **-ciúto,** PART.: pleased (delighted, contented).

§ Ind.: Pres. *piáccio, piáci, piáce; piacciámo, piacéte, piácciono*. Pret. *piácqui, -que; -quero*. Subj.: Pres. *piáccia*.

piáculo [L. *-culum*], M.: piacle (crime).
piácqui, PRET. of *-cere*.
piá-ga [L. *plaga* (*plangere*, strike)], F.: PLAY (open sore); calamity. **-gáre,** TR.: make a sore in (wound); INTR.: ulcerate.
piagére†, INTR.: please (delight).
piag-gelláre, TR.: flatter over and over again; INTR.: idle away one's time. **-gellóna,** F., **-gellóne,** M.: idler (trifler). **-gerèlla,** *car. dim.* of *-gia*. **-gería,** F.: blandishing. **-gétta,** *dim.* of *-gia*. ‖**piág-gia** [L. *plaga*, region], F.: declivity (slope, hill-side); sea-shore (beach); country-side†; place†: *andar* — —, coast along. **-giaménto,** M.: flattery (blandishment). **-giáre,** TR.: coast along; flatter (coax, wheedle). **-giáto,** PART.: flattered (coaxed). **-giatóre,** M., **-giatríce,** F.: flatterer (coaxer). **-gióne,** *aug.* of *-gia*.
piaghétta, *dim.* of *-ga*.
pia-gne. = *piange.*. **-gnistèo,** M.: lamentation (weeping). **-gnóne,** M.: funeral attendant; followers of Savonarola. **-gnucolaménto,** M.: snivelling. **-gnucoláre,** INTR.: snivel. **-gnucolío,** M.: prolonged whining. **-gnucolóne,** M.: whiner, sniveller. **-gnucolóso,** ADJ.: snivelling.
pia-góso, ADJ.: full of open sores. ‖**-gáccia, -gúzza†,** *dim.* of *-ga*.
piál-la [L. *planula*], F.: carpenter's plane. **-láccio,** M.: board; shingle. **-láre,** TR.: plane. **-láta,** F.: stroke with the plane. **-latóre,** M.: planer.

-latúra, F.: chips. **-lettáre**, TR.: plane. **-létto**, *dim.* of *-la*. **-líno**, *dim.* of *-la*. **-lóne**, *aug.* of *-la*.

piaménte [*pio*], ADV.: piously (devoutly).

piá-na [*-no*], F.: rafter (joist); plank; square block (for jambs). **-naménte**, ADV.: softly (gently). **-náre†**, TR.: plane (make level). **-náto**, PART.: levelled. **-natóio**, M.: kind of chisel. **-natúra**, F.: planing. **-neggiáre**, INTR.: be level (plain). **-nèlla**, F.: slipper; brick. **-nelláio†**, M.: slipper-maker. **-nelláta**, F.: blow with a slipper. **-nellétta**, **-nellína**, *car. dim.* of *-nella*.

pia-nèra [*paniera*], F., **-nère**, M.: basket (hamper).

piane=ròtto† [*piano*], M.: little plain (level place). **-ròttolo**, M.: landing (of a stairway).

pianéta I [?], F.: priest's cope.

pianè-ta 2 [L. *planeta*], (*pop.*) **-to**, M.: planet (celestial body).

pia-nettaménte†, ADV.: very softly (gently). ‖**-nézza** [*-no*], F.: level (plainness, smoothness); clearness.

pian-gènte, PART.: weeping. ‖**piángere** [L. *plangere*, beat the breast, lament], IRR. §; INTR.: weep (shed tears, lament); grieve; weep (bemoan); miss sorely **-gévole†**, ADJ.: weeping; lamentable. **-gevolménte†**, ADV.: lamentably. **-giménto†**, M.: weeping (sorrowing). **-gitóra**, F., **-gitóre**, M., **-gitríce**, F.: weeper (sorrower). **-goláre**, INTR.: weep softly. **-golènto†**, ADJ.: weeping (sorrowing). **-golóso**, ADJ.: lamentable (sad).

§ Ind.: Pret. *piàn-si*, *-se*; *-sero*. Part. *piánto*. — Poet. forms: *piá-gni*, *-gne*; *-gna*; etc.

pia-nigiáno, ADJ.: of the plain; M.: lowlander. **-níno**, *dim.* of *-no*. **-nissimaménte**, ADV.: very softly. **-níssimo**, ADJ.: very (or most) soft. **-nísta**, M.: pianist. ‖**piá-no** [L. *planus*], ADJ.: PLAIN (level, smooth); clear (distinct); meek; ADV.: softly (quietly, gently); slowly; M.: plain (level country, surface); floor (story); piano: *andar per la -na*, take the easiest way; *di* —, plainly; easily; *pian* —, very softly (gently). **-no=fòrte**, M.: piano (musical instrument). **-nóne**, M.: large plank.

piánsi, PRET. of *-ngere*.

piàn-ta [L. *planta*], F.: PLANT; shoot (branch); race (extraction); plan (of a house); sole (of the foot): — *dell edifizio*, plan (of a building). **-tábile**, ADJ.: plantable. **-tadóso†**, ADJ.: full of plants. **-tággine**, F.: plantain. **-tagióne**, F., **-taménto†**, M.: planting. **-táre**, TR.: plant; place (set); propagate; build; camp (an army); REFL.: settle. **táta**, F.: plantation; planting. **-táto**, PART.: planted. **-tatóio**, M.: instrument for planting. **-tatóre**, M., **-tatríce**, F.: planter. **-tatúra**, F.: planting. **-tazióne†**, F.: plantation; planting. **-terèlla**, **-tétta**, **-tettína**, **-ticèlla**, **-ticellína**, **-ticína**, *dim.* of *-ta*. **-tími**, M. PL.: different kinds of planting. **-tína**, *dim.* of *-ta*.

piánto [*piangere*], PART. of *-piangere*; M.: weeping; plaint; PL.: tears (lamentation): *far il* — *di*, think no more of (consider it lost).

pianto-náia, F., **-náio**, M.: nursery. **-náre**, TR.: transplant. ‖**-ncèllo**, **-ncino** [*pianta*], M.: young plant. **pian-tó-ne**, M.: shoot (sucker); sapling; sentinel (guard).

pianúra [*-no*], F.: plain (flat country); (*poet.*) sea.

piáre [*pio* (echoic)], INTR.: chirp (twitter, sing).

piá-stra [l. L. *plastrum* (*emplastrum*)], F.: metal plate; armour; part of a door-lock; dollar; scale (dry scab)†. **-strèlla**, F.: kind of quoit. **-strèllo†**, M.: cloth (or leather) for plasters. **-strétta**, *dim.* of *-stra*. **-stríccio†**, M.: nonsense. **-stríngolo†**, M.: face-paint. **-stríno†**, M.: hauberk. **-stróne**, M.: *aug.* of *-stra*; plastron.

pia-teggiáre†, **-tíre**, INTR.: plead (go to law, contest); need: — *il pane*, die of hunger. **-titóre†**, M.: pleader. ‖**piáto** [L. *placitum*], M.: law-suit (PLEA, contention); affair†.

piát-ta†, F.: pontoon (flatboat). **-ta=fórma**, F.: PLATFORM; cannon-terrace; turn-table. **-táia**, F., **-táio**, M.: dealer in dishes. **-tellétto**, **-tellíno**, *dim.* of *-tello*. **-tèllo**, *dim.* of *-to*. **-tellóne**, *aug.* of *-tello*. **-tería**, F.: crockery-shop; dishes (plates). **-tíno**, *dim.* of *-to*.

piát-to [Gr. *platús*, spread], ADJ.: FLAT (plain); M.: dish (plate); meat (course).

piát-tola, F.: black beetle. **piát-tolo†**, M.: kind of fig. **-tolóne**, *aug.* of *-tola*. **-tolóso†**, ADJ.: full of lice. **-tonáre**, TR.: strike (with the flat of a sword, etc.). **-tonáta**, F.: blow with the flat of a sword. **-tóne**, M.: *aug.* of *-to*; crab-louse.

piáz-za [L. *platea*], F.: open PLACE (square); market-place; market; market-town; fortress: *far* —, make room; *far il bello in* —, lounge. **-zaioláta**, F.: vulgar actions. **-zaiòlo**, M.: vulgar, low fellow. **-zále**, M.: kind of place (square). **-záta**, F.: object of ridicule. **-zeggiáre†**, INTR.: lounge. **-zétta**, **-zòla**, *dim.* of *-za* **-zóne**, *aug.* of *-za*.

píca [L.], F.: magPIE.

píc-ca [? Celt. *pic*], F.: PIKE (spear); pique. **-cánte**, ADJ.: piquant (sharp). **-cáre**, REFL.: persist; pique one's self; TR.†: prick (pique, wound). **-cáro†**, M.: beggar (rogue). **-cáta**, F.: thrust with a pike. **-catíglio†**, M.: minced meat. **-cheggiáre**, TR.: tease; REFL.: tease each other. **-chettáre**, TR.: pink; dentelate; picket (set with stakes); INTR.: make staccatos. **-chettáto**, ADJ.: spotted (speckled). **-chétto**, M.: picket (guard); stake; piquet (game)†.
pic-chiaménto, M.: knocking; knock. **-chiánte†**, M.: ragout. **-chia=pètto**, M.: hypocrite; charm†. **-chiáre**, TR.: knock; beat (cudgel, strike); REFL.: strike one's self. **-chiáta**, F.: knock; blow; calamity (misfortune). **-chière†**, M.: pikeman. **-chierèlla†**, F.: knock (thump): *aver la* —, be very hungry. **-chierelláre**, TR., INTR.: strike with a bi-pointed hammer. **-chierèllo**, M.: small bi-pointed hammer (used by sculptors). **-chiettáre**, TR.: knock lightly; mark with spots. **-chiettáto**, ADJ.: spotted (speckled). **-chiettíno**, *dim.* of *-chietto*. **-chiétto**, *dim.* of *-chio*. ||**píc-chio** [L. *-ulus* (dim. of *-us*)], M.: wood-pecker; knocking; knock (blow, rap). **-chióne**, M.: knocker. **-chiottáre**, TR.: knock (with the door-knocker). **-chiòtto**, M.: door-knocker.
piccía [L. *picea* (*pix*, pitch)], F.: row of loaves stuck together, etc.
pic-cinácco†, **-cinácolo†**, M.: dwarf; ADJ.: small (dwarfed). **-cinería**, F.: little thing. **-ciníno**, *car. dim.* of *-cino*. **-cíno**, ADJ.: small (little, diminutive); M.: child. **-ciolánza†**, F.: smallness (littleness). **-ciolíno**, ADJ.: very small. ||**píc-ciolo** [*-colo*], ADJ.: small (diminutive); M.: small Florentine coin.
picciòlo [L. L. *petiolus*, a small foot], M.: petiole (stalk, stem).
picció-na, F.: pigeon. **-náia**, F.: pigeon-house; top-floor (of a house); top-gallery (of a theatre). **-ncèllo**, **-ncí-no**, *dim.* of *-ne*. ||**picció-ne** [L. *pipio*], M.: PIGEON; simpleton†.
picciuòlo† = *picciolo*.
pic-co [? Celt. *pic*], M.: peak (summit); ADJ.†: piqued (stung); *a* —, vertically. **-colaménte†**, ADV.: meanly (basely). **-colézza**, F.: smallness (littleness, meanness); frivolity. **-colíno**, *dim.* of *-colo*. **-colíssimo**, ADJ.: very small. **píc-colo**, ADJ.: small (little, short): *in* —, in small proportions; *da* —, from one's childhood. **-conáio**, M.: bailiff. **-cóne**, *aug.* of *-co*; pick-axe; kind of hammer. **-conière**, M.: picker. **-cosità**, F.: captiousness. **-cóso**, ADJ.: captious (peevish, touchy). **-cózza**, F.: hatchet. **-cozzíno**, M.: small hatchet.
pí-cea†, F.: pinaster (pine-tree). ||**pí-ceo** [L. *-ceus* (-*x*)], ADJ.: like pitch (pitch-black).
pícrico, pl. **—ci** [Gr. *-krós*, sharp], ADJ.: picric (acid).
pidoc-chiería, F.: stinginess (niggardliness); trifle†. **-chíno**, ADJ.: *dim.* of *-chio;* small (said of handwriting). **pi-dòc-chio** [L. *pediculus*], M.: louse. **-chióso**, ADJ.: lousy.
piè = *piede*, sing. or (*poet.*) pl.
pie-dáccio, *disp.* of *-de*. ||**piè-de** [L. *pes*], M.: foot (base, ground, support, measure); stalk: *a* —, on foot; *gente a* —, foot-soldiers; *a piè pari*, with ease; *ad ogni piè sostinto*, very often; *su due -di*, at once; *dar de' -di*, kick; *essere in* —, be alive; *farsi da -di*, recommence; *prender* —, get strength; *tenere il* — *in due staffe*, stand well with both sides. **-destállo†**, M.: pedestal (base).
piè-dica†, F.: snare (springe); trestle (saw-horse). **-díno** [*-de*], *car. dim.* of *-de*. **-distállo**, M.: pedestal (base). **-dóne**, *aug.* of *-de*.
piè-ga, F.: plait (fold); wrinkle; folding; (*fig.*) turn. **-gáccia**, *disp.* of *-ga*. **-gaménto**, M.: plaiting (folding); wrinkling. **-gánte**, PART.: folding. ||**-gáre** [L. *plicare*], TR.: PLAIT (fold); bend (overcome); incline; REFL.: yield (give in). **-gáta**, F.: folding. **-gatína**, *car. dim.* of *-gata*. **-gáto**, PART.: folded. **-gatóre**, M.: folder. **-gatúra**, F.: folding; plait (fold); inclination. **-gaturína**, *car. dim.* of *-gatura*. **-gheggiáre**, INTR.: paint the folds of drapery. **-ghétta**, **-ghettína**, *dim.* of *-ga*. **-ghettáre**, TR.: crease; wrinkle. **-ghétto**, *dim.* of *-go*. **-ghévole**, ADJ.: pliant (flexible); manageable. **-ghevolézza**, F.: pliantness (flexibility); docility. **-ghevolménte**, ADV.: pliantly (yieldingly).
piè-go, M.: packet (of letters, papers, etc.). **-golína**, *dim.* of *-ga*. **-golináre**, TR.: fold lightly (crease). **-góne**, *aug.* of *-ga*.
piè-na, F.: flood (overflow); crowd: (*fig.*) *andarsene colla* —, sail with the stream. **-naménte**, ADV.: fully (completely). **-nézza**, F.: fullness (entireness, [illegible] dance). **-níssimo**, ADJ.: very full. ||**pi**[illegible] *plenus*], (complete[illegible]le): (complet tirely (due. -
pierèt M.: cl
piè-ta

-tà [L. -tas], F.: PIETY (reverence); PITY (compassion, sympathy): monte di —, city pawnbroker. -tánza [?], F.: pittance (meat dish); pity†.

piètica [? L. pedica], F.: trestle (saw-horse).

pie-tísmo [-ta], M.: pietism. -tísta, M.: pietist. -tosaménte, ADV.: piteously. -tóso, ADJ.: piteous (sorrowful, compassionate).

piè-tra [L. petra], F.: stone; jewel: — di paragone, touchstone; — di scandalo, stumbling-block. -tráccia, disp. of -tra. -trámo, M.: mass of stones. -tráta, F.: blow with a stone. -trétta, dim. of -tra. -trièra, F.: kind of artillery. -trificáre, TR.: petrify. -trificáto, PART.: petrified. -trificazióne, F.: petrifaction. -trína, dim. of -tra. -tríno, ADJ.: stony (hard); M.: stone (to keep a door open). -trolína, dim. of -tra. -tróne, aug. of -tra. -trosità, F.: stoniness. -tróso, ADJ.: stony (full of stones); hard. -trúccola, -trúzza, -trúzzola†, disp. dim. of -tra.

pie-vanálo, ADJ.: of the parson. -vanía, F.: parsonage. -váno, M.: rector (of a parish, parson). ‖piè-ve [L. plebs], F.: parish-church; parish. -viále†, M.: cope.

pifanía†, F.: Epiphany.

pi-fera†, F.: fife. -(f)feráre†, INTR.: play the fife. -(f)feráta, F.: fife-playing. ‖pí-(f)fero [Ger. pfeifer], M.: fife; fifer. -(f)feróne, aug. of -ffero.

pígamo†, M.: bastard-rhubarb.

piggioráre†, TR.: make worse; INTR.: grow worse.

píghe-ro [L. piger], ADJ.: lazy (idle). -rtà†, F.: laziness (idleness).

pi-giaménto, M.: treading (pressing). ‖-giáre [L. *-nsiare (-nsere)], TR.: press (tread, crush); INTR.: press; be busy. -giáta, F.: pressing (treading). -giáto, PART.: pressed. -giatóre, M.: treader (grape-presser). -giatúra, F.: pressing (treading). pí-gio, M.: great crowd.

pigio-nále, ADJ.: lodging (renting); M.: lodger. -nánte, M.: lodger (tenant). ‖pigióne 1 [L. pensio], F.: lodgings; house-rent (pay): dare a —, let; prender a — una casa, rent a house; star a —, live in lodgings.

pigióne 2 [-giare], M.: chestnut-crusher.

pi-gliábile, ADJ.: takable. -gliaménto, M.: taking. ‖-gliáre [L. -lare, steal], TR.: take (select, seize, consider): pigliarla per uno, take one's part; pigliarsela con uno, be angry with some one; — fatica, take pains; — in fastidio, become disgusted with; — ad imprestito, borrow; — occhi, charm; — in ottimo, take at one's risk; — parola, get intelligence; — pruova, try; — querela, pick a quarrel; — terra, land. -gliévole†, ADJ.: takable. pí-glio, M.: taking; look†: dar di —, lay hold of; begin.

pigménto [L. -tum], M.: pigment.

pigmèo [L. pygmæus], M.: pygmy (dwarf).

pígna [L. pinna, feather], F.: massive top of a cupola; pump-borer (piercer); large pile (stake).

pignát-ta [L. pinea, PINE-cone], F.: broth-pot (earthen kettle). -táio, -táro, M.: potter.

pígnere†, IRR.; TR.: paint; push (thrust).

pi-gnéta†, F.: pine plantation. -gnòlo†, M.: kernel of pine-cone; kind of grape (and wine made from it).

pi-gnoncèllo, dim. of -gnone. ‖-gnóne [-gna], M.: dike.

pigno-raménto, M.: pledging; seizure. -ránte, M.: pledger. ‖-ráre [L. pignus, pledge], TR.: seize. -ratário, M.: seizer (of property). -ratívo, ADJ.: pignorative (pledging). -razióne, F.: pignoration (pledging, seizing).

pigo-laménto, M.: peeping; importuning. ‖-láre [L. pipilare], INTR.: peep; importune. -lío, M.: peeping; importuning. -lóne, M.: importuner; grumbler.

pi-graménte, ADV.: lazily (slowly, slothfully). -grézza, F.: laziness (sluggishness). -gríre†, INTR.: grow lazy. -grízia, F.: laziness (indolence). ‖pí-gro [L. -ger], ADJ.: lazy (indolent, sluggish).

píla 1 [L. (-lum, javelin)], F.: pillar; large pestle.

píla 2 [L. (pinsere)], F.: stone (or metal) vessel; pile (for electricity); olive press.

piláo [?], M.: boiled rice.

pila-stráta, F.: row of pilasters. -strèllo, -strétto, -stríno, dim. of -stro. ‖pilá-stro [pila 1], M.: pilaster (column). -stróne, aug. of -stro.

piláta [pila 2], F.: pressful of olives.

pileáto [L. -tus], ADJ.: wearing a skull-cap (ancient Roman hat).

piléggio†, M.: sea-journey.

píleo [L. -leus], M.: skull-cap (ancient Roman hat).

pilét-ta, -tína, dim. of pila.

pilière†, M.: pillar (column).

pilláccche-ra [pillola], F.: splash (of mud); fault (blemish); miser†. -róso, ADJ.: splashed (smeared).

pilláre†, TR.: pound (crush, grind).

pillicciáio†, M.: fur-dealer.

píllo [L. pilum (pinsere, crush)], M.: large pestle (pounder).

píllo-la [L. pilula, dim. of pila, ball], F.: pill (medicine). -létta, -lína, dim. of -la.

pillóne†, M.: beetle (mallet).

píl-lora [-lola], F.: pill. -loráta, F.

blow with a pill. **-lòtta†**, F.: ball; ball-game. **-lottáre†**, TR.: baste (meat); torment.

pí-lo [L. *-lum*], M.: javelin; pillar†. **-lóne**, M.: *aug.* of *-la*; pilaster; rammer.

pilòrcio†, ADJ.: stingy; M.: miser.

pi-lòrico, pl. *—ci*, ADJ.: pyloric. ‖**-lòro** [Gr. *pul-orós* (*púle*) gate-keeper], M.: pylorus.

pilóso†, ADJ.: PILOSE (hairy).

pi-lòta [?], M.: pilot (helmsman). **-lotággio**, M.: pilotage (Eng.† pilot's skill); pilot's fees. **-lòto**, M.: pilot (helmsman).

pilucc-áre [L. *pilare*], TR.: pluck grapes from (a bunch) one by one; eat up; seek (little earnings); REFL.: pull out one's hair. **-cóna**, F., **-cóne**, M.: pilferer (rascal).

pimác-cio†, M.: pillow (bolster, cushion). **-ciuòlo†**, *dim.* of *-cio*.

pimmèo [*pigmeo*], M.: pigmy (dwarf).

pimpinèlla†, F.: pimpernel (plant).

pína [L. *-nea*], F.: cone of the PINE-tree.

pinácolo†, M.: pinnacle (summit).

pinássa [L. *-nus*, pine-tree], F.: pinnace (vessel).

pínca†, F.: kind of long cucumber.

pínce [Eng. *pincher*], M.: kind of dog.

pincèrna†, M.: cup-bearer.

pincióne†, M.: chaffinch.

pínco [*-ca*], M.: dolt (stupid fellow).

pi-neále [L. *-nea*, PINE-cone], ADJ.: pineal. **-néta**, F., **-néto†**, M.: pine-grove.

píngere 1 [L.], IRR.§; TR.: (*poet.*) PAINT (represent).

§ Pret. *pín-si*, *-se*; *-sero*. Part. *pínto*.

píngere 2 [L. *pangere*], IRR. (cf. *-gere* 1); TR.: push (press, thrust); REFL.: advance.

pin-gue [L. *-guis*], ADJ.: fat (Eng.† pinguid). **-guèdine**, F.: fatness; fat.

pinífero [L. *-fer* (*pinus*, pine, *ferre*, bear)], ADJ.: pine-bearing.

pínna [L.], F.: FIN (of a fish).

pin-nacolétto, *dim.* of *-nacolo*. ‖**-nácolo** [L. *-naculum*], M.: pinnacle (summit).

pinnípedi [L. *-na*, fin, *pes*, foot], M. PL.: pinniped (class of crabs).

pí-no [L. *-nus*], M.: pine-tree; pine-wood; (*poet.*) ship. **-nocchiáta**, F., **-nocchiáto**, M.: sugared pine-seeds. **-nocchíno**, *car. dim.* of *-nocchio*. **-nòcchio**, M.: pine-seed.

pín-si, PRET. of *-gere*. **pín-ta** [*-gere* 1], F.: pint; [*-gere* 2] push (thrust, impulse)†. ‖**pín-to**, PART. of *-gere* 1, 2. **-tóre†**, M.: painter. **-tòrico†**, ADJ.: picturesque; of painting. **-túra†**, F.: picture.

pin-zácchio†, M.: weevil (insect). **-záre**, TR.: sting. **-záta**, F.: stinging. **-záto**, PART.: stung. **-zétte**, F. PL.: pincers. **-zimònio**, M.: celery dressing. ‖**pín-zo** 1 [?], M.: stinging; sting; mark (of a sting); motive.

pín-zo 2 [L. *-sus*, pounded], ADJ.: full (replete). **-zo** 3, M.: goatee (imperial).

pinzoche-ráto†, ADJ.: hypocritical. ‖**pinzòche-ro** [*bizzochero*], M.: devotee, hypocrite; ADJ.: hypocritical. **-róna**, **-róne**, *aug.* of *-ro*.

pinzúto [*-zo* 1], ADJ.: acute (sharp).

pío 1 [echoic], M.: peep (cry of chickens).

pío 2 [L. *-us*], ADJ.: PIOUS (devout, religious); compassionate.

piog-gerèlla, **-gétta**, *dim.* of *-gia*. ‖**piòg-gia** [L. *pluvia*], F.: rain; shower. **-giolína**, *car. dim.* of *-gia*. **-gióso**, ADJ.: rainy (PLUVIOUS).

piòlo [?], M.: round (of a ladder); planting-stick.

piom-bággine, F.: plumbago (black-lead). **-báre**, INTR.: be perpendicular; TR.: plumb (lead); hurl (cast); seal†. **-báta**, F.: leaden ball; leaded dart. **-báto**, ADJ.: plumbed (leaded); heavy. **-batóia**, F., **-batóio**, M.: hole in a parapet (for hurling down missiles). **-batúra**, F.: leading; leaden ball†; leaded dart†.

pióm-bico, pl. *—ci*, ADJ.: plumbic. **-bífero**, ADJ.: plumbiferous (lead-producing). **-bináre**, TR.: plumb (adjust by a plumb-line); empty. **-bíno**, ADJ.: plumbean (like lead); M.: plummet; black-lead; leadpencil. ‖**pióm-bo** [L. *plumbum*], M.: lead; PLUMMET; seal; bullet; *a —*, perpendicularly; *di —*, violently. **-bóso†**, ADJ.: leaden (heavy).

piop-páia, F.: poplar-grove. **-pétto**, *dim.* of *-po*. **-píno**, M.: kind of fungus.

piòppa†, F.: poplar-tree. ‖**piòp-po** [L. *populus*], M.: poplar-tree.

piórno†, ADJ.: watery.

piò-ta [?], F.: sole (of the foot); turf (sod). **-táre**, TR.: turf. **-táto**, ADJ.: turfed. **-tatúra**, F.: turfing. **-tétta**, *dim.* of *-ta*.

piòva [*pioggia*], F.: (*poet.*) rain.

piova-náto, M.: rectorship. **-nèllo**, **-níno**, *disp. dim.* of *-no*. ‖**piováno** 1 [*pievano*], M.: rector (parson).

piováno 2 [*-vere*], M.: rain; ADJ.: rainy: *acqua -vana*, rainwater.

piovanúccio, *disp. dim.* of *-no* 1.

pio-vigginàre†, INTR.: drizzle. **-vúto**, PART.: raining. ‖**piò-vere** [L. *pluere*], IRR.§; INTR.: rain; TR.: pour (shower). **-vévole†**, ADJ.: rainy (showering). **-vífero†**, ADJ.: bringing rain. **-viggináre**, INTR.: drizzle (rain lightly). **-vigginóso**, ADJ.: drizzling (misty). **-viscoláre**, INTR.: drizzle. **-vitúra†**, F.: heavy rain. **-vosità**, F.: raininess. **-vóso**, ADJ.: PLUVIOUS (rainy). **piòv-ve**, PRET. of *-vere*.

§ Ind.: Pret. *piòv-ve* (poet. *piòbbe*); *-vero* (*-bero*).

pí-pa, F.: pipe (for smoking). **-páccia**, *disp.* of *-pa*. ||**-páre** [L.], INTR.: smoke (a pipe). **-páta**, F.: pipe-smoking.
pipèrno [town *P.*], M.: piperno (kind of lava, porous rock).
pì pì [echoic], M.: peep. **pipiláre**, INTR.: peep (chirp).
pi-pína, **-píno**, *dim.* of *-pa*.
pipióna [?], F.: coarse Spanish wine.
pipistrèllo [L. *vespertilio* (*vesper*, evening)], M.: bat.
pipíta [l. L.], F.: hangnail; pip (disease of fowls); tendril.
píp-pio†, M.: spout (of a vessel). **-pionáta†**, F.: nonsense. **-pioncíno†**, *dim.* of *-pione*. **-pióne†**, M.: pigeon; blockhead.
píppolo [L. *papula*, pimple], M.: wart.
píra [L. *pyra*], F.: PYRE (funeral-pile).
pirami-dále, ADJ.: pyramidal. **-dalménte**, ADV.: pyramidally. ||**pirámide** [Gr. *puramís*], F.: pyramid; fusee (of a watch).
pi-ráta [?], M.: pirate. **-ratería**, F.: piracy (robbery). **-rático**, pl. —*ci*, ADJ.: piratical. **-ráto†**, M.: pirate (robber).
pí-rico, pl. —*ci* [Gr. *pûr*, FIRE], ADJ.: of fire, pyro-; pyrotechnic: *polvere -rica*, gunpowder. **-ríte**, F.: pirites.
piroètta [Fr. *pirouette*], F.: pirouette.
piròga [?], F.: pirogue (canoe).
pirolo [Nap.], M.: peg; round (of a ladder).
piro- [Gr. *pûr*, fire]: **-logía**, F.: pyrology (treatise on heat). **-mánte**, M.: pyromantic (diviner by fire). **-manzía** [Gr. *manteía*, divination], F.: pyromancy. **pirò-metro** [Gr. *métron*, measure], M.: pyrometer. **-'po** [Gr. *purōpós* (*pûr*, fire, *ṓps*, eye)], M.: ruby. **-'scafo** [Gr. *skáphe*, boat], M.: steamboat. **-tecnía**, **-tècnica** [Gr. *téchne*, art], F.: pyrotechnics (fireworks). **-tècnico**, **-tènnico**, pl. —*ci*, ADJ.: pyrotechnic.
pirrichio [Gr. *-rhíkios*], M.: pyrrhic (metrical foot).
pirro-nísmo [*Pyrrho*, a philosopher], M.: pyrrhonism (scepticism). **-nísta**, M.: pyrrhonist (sceptic).
piscatòrio [L. *-rius*], ADJ.: piscatory (relating to fishing).
pí-scia, F.: urine. **-sciacáne**, M.: chokeweed. **-sciácchera†**, F.: babe (child). **-sciáta**, F.: trifle. **-sciallètto**, M.: babe (child). **-sciáncio**, M.: kind of claret. ||**-sciáre** [echoic], INTR.: urinate. **-sciarèlla**, F., **-sciarèllo**, M.: kind of claret. **-sciáta**, F.: urination. **-sciatína**, *car. dim.* of *-sciata*. **-sciatóio**, M.: chamber; urinal. **-sciatóna**, *aug.* of *-sciata*.
pi-scicoltúra [L. *piscis*, FISH, culture], F.: pisciculture. **-scína**, F.: fishpond; pond (pool). **-scóso†**, ADJ.: full of fish.
pí-scio [*-sciare*], M.: urine. **-sciósò**, ADJ.: soiled with urine.
pisel-láio, M.: pea-field. **-láta**, F.: big meal of peas. **-létto**, **-líno**, *car. dim.* of *-lo*. ||**pisèl-lo** [L. *pisum*], M.: PEA (vegetable). **-lóne**, M.: *aug.* of *-lo*; blockhead.
piso-láre [L. *pensulare*], INTR.: nod; drowse. **-líno**, *dim.* of *-lo*. **piso-lo**, M.: doze (light sleep).
pis-pigliáre [L. *-pillare* (echoic)], INTR.: whisper. **-píglio**, M.: whisper. **-pillòria**, F.: noisy talk; whispering.
pis-pinèllo†, *dim.* of *-pino*. **-'pino†**, M.: waterspout (jet); fountain.
píspo-la [echoic], F.: meadow-lark. **-létta**, *car. dim.* of *-la*. **-láccia**, *disp. dim.* of *-la*.
píssi or **píssi píssi** [echoic], M.: imitative sound of whispering (chattering).
pissíde [Gr. *puxída*], F.: pyx (vase).
pis-tacchiáta, F.: confection of pistachio-nuts. ||**-tácchio** [L. *-tacium*], M.: pistachio-nut tree; pistachio-nut.
pistá-gna [?], F.: flounce. **-gnóna**, **-gnóne**, *aug.* of *-gna*.
pistilènzia†, F.: pestilence (plague).
pistíllo [L. *-llus*], M.: pistil (organ of a flower).
pístola† 1, F.: epistle (letter).
pistò-la 2 [town *Pistoia*], F.: pistol (firearm). **-lése**, M.: cutlass (sword).
pistolésса†, *disp.* of *-la* 2.
pisto-létta [*-la* 2], *car. dim.* of *-la*. **-lettáta**, F.: pistol-shot. **-lóne**, M.: kind of arquebuse.
pistolòtto [*pistola* 1], M.: brief composition.
pistóne [L. *pinsere*, pound], M.: piston; blunderbuss.
pistóre†, M.: baker.
pistrino†, M.: kind of mill.
pitáffio [*epitaffio*], M.: epitaph.
pitagòrico, pl. —*ci* [*Pitagora*, a philosopher], ADJ.: Pythagorean.
pitále [?], M.: chamber (vessel).
pitétto†, ADJ.: little (small).
pi-toccáre, INTR.: beg (ask alms). **-toccheria**, F.: sordidness (meanness). ||**-tòcco** [Gr. *ptochós*], M.: [illegible] dicant); ancient cloak
pi-tóne [L. *pytho*[illegible] slain by [illegible]
néssa [illegible]
nico. [illegible]
pitti[illegible]
epith[illegible]
pit-[illegible]
pict[illegible]
disp[illegible]

ADV.: picturesquely. **-toréseo**, ADJ.: picturesque. **-tòrico**, pl. *—ci*, ADJ.: of a painter. **-tríce**, F.: painter. **-túra**, F.: painting (the art); picture (description). **-turáccia**, *disp.* of *-tura*. **-turáre**, TR.: paint (in oils); describe. **-turétta**, **-turína**, *car. dim.* of *-tura*. **-turáto**, PART.: painted; described.

pitúi-ta [L.], F.: PITUITE (mucus). **-tário**, ADJ.: pituitary. **-tóso**, ADJ.: pituitous.

più, (*pop.*) **piúe** [L. *plus*], ADV.: more; above; many (divers); M.: majority (greater part): *al —*, at most; *assai —*, much more; *di —*, besides; *per lo —*, for the most part; *— tosto*, rather (sooner); *— volte*, several times; *— e — volte*, repeatedly.

piú-ma [L. *pluma*], F.: PLUME (feather); cushion; feather-bed; (*poet.*) pen. **-maccéttо†**, *dim.* of *-maccio*. **-máccio†**, M.: cushion; bolster. **-macciòlo**, M.: compress. **-macciuòlo†**, *dim.* of *-maccio*. **-mággio**, M.: PLUMAGE. **-máta†**, F.: small ball of feathers. **-máto**, ADJ.: feathery (covered with feathers, downy). **-míno**, M.: cushion; ostrich feather; aigrette. **-mosità**, F.: plumosity. **-móso**, ADJ.: plumose (feathery).

piuòlo† = *piolo*.

piuttòsto [*più tosto*], ADV.: rather (sooner, preferably).

piuvicáre†, TR.: publish (announce).

píva [*pipa*], F.: bagpipe.

pi-viále [L. *pluviale* (*pluvia*, rain-coat)], M.: sacerdotal coat. **-vière**, M.: plover (bird); jurisdiction of a parish†.

pívo†, M.: dandy (gallant).

pízza†, F.: kind of cake.

pizzi-cágnolo [*pinzo*, full], M.: delicatessen shopkeeper. **-caquestióni†**, M.: disputer (quarrelsome fellow). **-cáre**, TR.: pinch; pick; bite; prick (itch); INTR.: have a little dash of a thing. **-caruòlo†**, M.: pork-butcher. **-cáta** [*-care*], F.: pinch; touch; sugar-plum. **-cherìa**, F.: butcher-shop. **-chíno** [*-care*], M.: snuff. **pízzi-co**, M.: pinch (bit, little). **-córe**, M.: pricking (itching). **-coríno**, *dim.* of *-core*. **-cottáre**, TR.: pinch; pick. **-cottáta**, F.: pinching; pinch; picking (playing a stringed instrument). **-cótto**, M.: pinch (bit).

pízzo [*pinzo* 3], M.: goatee (imperial); fringe.

placá-bile, ADJ.: placable (appeasable). **-bilità**, F.: placability. **-bilménte**, ADV.: placidly (quietly). **-ménto**, M.: appeasing (pacification). ||**placá-re** [L.], TR.: placate (appease, pacify). **-tóre**, M., **-tríce**, F.: appeaser (pacifier). **-zióne†**, F.: appeasing (pacification).

plác-ca [?], F.: metallic plate. **-cáre**, TR.: plate (cover with metal).

placènta [L., cake], F.: placenta.

plá-cet, M.: permission. **-cidaménte**, ADV.: placidly (calmly). **-cidézza**, **-cidità**, F.: placidity (quietness; mildness). ||**plá-cido** [L. *-cidus* (*-cere*, please)], ADJ.: placid (serene, quiet, mild). **plá-cito**, M.: placit (decree); kindness.

plága [L.], F.: shore; region (tract).

pla-giário, M.: plagiarist (literary thief); ADJ.: plagiary. ||**plá-gio** [L. *-gium*], M.: plagiarism (literary theft).

planetário [L. *-rius*], ADJ.: planetary.

plani-metría [L. *planus*, plane, Gr. *métron*, measure], F.: planimetry. **planí-metro**, ADJ.: planimetric. **-sfèro** [L. *sphæra*], M.: planisphere.

plantário†, M.: plantation; plant.

plantigrádi [L. *planta*, sole of the foot, *gradi*, walk], M. PL.: plantigrade (animal).

plá-sma [Gr., formation], M.: plasma (of the blood); kind of quartz; clay figure. **-smáre**, TR.: form (shape, fashion). **-smatóre**, M.: former.

plásti-ca, F.: plastic art. **-caménte**, ADV.: in a plastic manner. **-cáre**, INTR.: make earthen figures. **-catóre**, M.: maker of earthen figures. **plásti-ce†**, F.: plastic art. ||**plásti-co**, pl. *-ci* [L. *-cus*], ADJ.: plastic (capable of being moulded).

plátano [L. *-nus*], M.: plane-tree.

pla-tèa [L.], F.: pit, orchestra (of a theatre); people (in the pit); area (of a building)†. **-teále**, ADJ.: common (trivial).

pláti-no [Sp. *plata*, silver], M.: platinum (metal). **-notipía**, F.: platinotype.

pla-tonicaménte, ADV.: platonically. ||**-tònico**, pl. *—ci* [*Plato*], ADJ.: Platonic. **-tonísmo**, M.: Platonism.

plau-dènte, PART.: applauding. ||**-díre** [L. *-dere*], TR. (pres. *-do* or *-disco*): (*poet.*) applaud. **-síbile**, ADJ.: plausible (worthy of praise); specious. **-sibilménte**, ADV.: plausibly. **-sibilità**, F.: plausibility. **pláu-so**, M.: applause.

pláustro [L. *-trum*], M.: chariot; Ursa Major (constellation).

ple-báccia, *disp.* of *-be*. **-bàglia**, *disp.* of *-be*. ||**plè-be** [L. *plebs*], F.: plebeian class (common people); populace (mob, Eng. † PLEBE); ADJ.: plebeian. **-beáccio**, *disp.* of *-beo*. **-beaménte**, **-beiaménte†**, ADV.: in a plebeian manner. **-beísmo**, M.: plebeian manner. **-bèo**, ADJ.: plebeian (vulgar, common); M.: plebeian. **-biscitário**, ADJ.: plebiscitary. **-biscito**, M.: plebiscitum, plebiscite.

plèiadi [Gr. *pleiádes* (*pleîn*, sail)], F.: Pleiades (constellation).

ple-nariaménte, ADV.: plenarily (fully). ‖**-nário** [L. *-narius* (*-nus*, full)], ADJ.: plenary (full).

pleni-lúnio [L. *-lunium* (*plenus*, full)], M.: full moon. **-potènza** [L. *-potentia*], F.: absolute power. **-potenziário**, M., ADJ.: plenipotentiary. **-túdine**†, F.: plenitude (completeness).

pleonásmo [L. *-nasmus*], M.: pleonasm. **-nasticaménte**, ADV.: pleonastically. **-nástico**, pl. —*ci*, ADJ.: pleonastic.

plèsso [L. *plexus*, intertwined], M.: plexus (network of vessels, fibres, etc.).

plè-tora [Gr. *-thóre*, fullness], F.: plethora (overfulness). **-tòrico**, pl. —*ci*, ADJ.: plethoric.

plèttro [L. *plectrum*], M.: plectrum.

plèu-ra [Gr. *-rá*, side], F.: pleura (serous membrane). **-risía**, **-ríte**, **-rítide**, F.: pleurisy. **-rítico**, pl. —*ci*, ADJ.: pleuritic.

plíade†, F. PL.: Pleiades (constellation).

plíco [L. *-care*, fold], M.: packet of letters.

plínto [Gr. *plínthos*], M.: PLINTH.

plòia†, F.: rain.

plo-ráre [L.], INTR.: weep (shed tears). **plò-ro**†, M.: weeping (tears).

plotóne [Fr. *peloton*], M.: platoon (military body).

plúmbeo [L. *-beus*], ADJ.: of lead (leaden); heavy.

pluré-le [L. *-lis* (*plus*)], ADJ.: plural; M.: plural number. **-lità**, F.: plurality. **-lizzáre**, TR.: pluralize. **-lménte**, ADV.: plurally (in the plural number).

plúteo [L. *-teus*], M.: pent-house (cover for besiegers); shelf of a book-case.

plutocrazía [L. *Plutus*, god of wealth], F.: plutocracy.

pluvi-ále [L. *-alis*], ADJ.: pluvial (rainy). **plúvi-o**, ADJ.: pluvious (rainy). **-òmetro**, M.: pluviometer (rain-gauge).

pneu-mático, pl. —*ci* [Gr. *-matikós* (*pneûma*, breath)], ADJ.: pneumatic. **-monía**, **-monìte**, F.: pneumonia.

po' = **poco**, ADJ.: little; few; M.: a few; little; ADV.: little (not much).

poána [?], F.: buzzard (bird of prey)

pocággine†, F.: littleness; scarcit[illegible]

pòc-cia [*poppa*], F.: breast [illegible] TR.: suck. **-ciósot**, ADJ. [illegible] (plump).

po-chettíno, dim. [illegible] dim. of *-co*. **-chézza** [illegible] (smallness); fewn[illegible] [L. *paucus*], ADJ. [illegible]

after (soon after). **-céllat**, F.: idle woman. **-colíno**, dim. of *-co*.

pòculo†, M.: (poet.) chalice (cup, bowl); draught.

po-dágra [Gr. (*poús*, foot; *ágra*, catching)], F.: gout. **-dágrico**, pl. —*ci*, **-dagróso**, ADJ.: gouty; M.: gouty person.

pode-rúccio, *disp.* of *-re*. **-rále**, ADJ.: of a farm. **-ránte**, M.: farm-owner; ADJ.: of a farm-owner. ‖**podé-re** [*potere*], M.: farm (manor); power†. **-rétto**, **-ríno**, *dim.* of *-re*. **-róne**, *aug.* of *-re*. **-rosaménte**, ADV.: powerfully (mightily). **-róso**, ADJ.: powerful (strong, vigorous). **-rúccio**, *disp. dim.* of *-re*. **-stà**, F.: power (authority); M.: magistrate (mayor). **-steria**, F.: jurisdiction (or palace) of a magistrate. **-stéssa**†, F.: magistrate's wife.

pòdio [L. *-dium*], M.: podium (open gallery).

poè-ma [Gr. *poíema* (*poiein*, create)] M.: poem. **-mótto**, *dim.* of *-ma*. **-móne**, *aug.* of *-ma*. **-sía**, F.: poesy (poetry).

poè-ta, M.: poet. **-tàccio**, *disp.* of *-ta*. **-tánat**, F.: poetess. **-tánte**, ADJ.: poetry-writing; M.: would-be poet. **-táre**, INTR.: write poetry; REFL.†: become laureate. **-tástro**, M.: poetaster (petty poet). **-teggiáre**, INTR.: poetize (compose verse). **-tésco**, ADJ.: poetical. **-téssa**, F.: poetess. **-tevolménte**†, ADV.: poetically. **poè-tica**, F.: poetics; poetry. **-ticaménte**, ADV.: poetically. **-ticáre**†, INTR.: write poetry. **-ticheria**†, F.: poetical style. **poè-tico**, pl. —*ci*, ADJ.: poetical; M.†: poet; professor of poetry. **-tíno**, *disp. dim.* of *-ta*. **-tíre**†, **-tizzáre**†, INTR.: poetize (compose verses). **-tóne**, *aug.* of *-ta*. **-tónzolo**, *disp. dim.* of *-ta*. **-tría**† F.: poetics; poetry. **-túccio**, **-túcolo**, **-túzzo**, *disp. dim.* of *-ta*.

poffáre [*pò* (*può*), *fare*], INTERJ.: wonderful! — *il cielo*, — *il mondo*, good Heavens!

pog-gerèllo, **-gettíno**, **-gétto**, *dim.* of *-gio*. **pòg-gia**, F.: starboard rope (of the mainsail); starboard-side. **-giáre**, [illegible] mount (ascend); INTR.: rise; steer [illegible] the wind; REFL.: lean upon. ‖**pòg-**[illegible]*-dium*], M.: hill (elevation). [illegible] dim. of *-giolo*. **-giòlo**, [illegible] **-giuòlo**†, M.: long bal-[illegible] (parapet).

[illegible] pooh!

[illegible] after; then; since†. [illegible] considering [illegible] since you will

polá-re [*polo*], ADJ.: polar. **-rità**, F.: polarity. **-rizzáre**, TR.: polarize. **-rizzazióne**, F.: polarization.

pòlca [Polish], F.: polka (dance or the dance-music).

po-ledríno, *dim.* of *-ledro*. ‖**-lédro** [*pollo*], M.: foal (young colt). **-ledrúccio**, *dim.* of *-ledro*.

poléggio†, M.: pennyroyal (plant).

polè-mica [Gr. *-mikós* (*pólemos*, war)], F.: polemics. **polè-mico**, pl. *—ci*, ADJ.: polemical. **-mista**, M.: polemist. **-mizzáre**, INTR.: hold a controversy (over religious subjects).

polemònia [Gr. *polemónion*], F.: valerian (plant).

polèn-da, **polèn-ta** [L.], F.: polenta (porridge, mush of Indian meal or of chestnut meal). **-dáio**, M.: porridge-maker. **-dína**, *car. dim.* of *-da*. **-dóne**, *aug.* of *-da*; ADJ., M.: sluggard.

pòli- [Gr. *polús*, many]: **-antèa** [Gr. *ánthos*, flower], F.: alphabetical collection of pieces. **-archía** [Gr. *archein*, rule], F.: polyarchy (joint government). **-árchico**, ADJ.: polyarchical. **-clínica**, F.: polyclinic (city hospital). **-clínico**, pl. *—ci*, ADJ.: of a polyclinic. **-cromía** [Gr. *chróma*, colour], F.: polychromy. **èdrico**, pl. *—ci*, ADJ.: polyhedral. **-èdro** [Gr. *hédra*, side], M.: polyhedron. **-fonía** [Gr. *phonē*, sound], F.: polyphony. **-gála** [Gr. *gála*, milk], F.: polygalaceæ (family of plants). **-gamía** [Gr. *gámos*, marriage], F.: polygamy. **-'gamo**, M.: polygamist; ADJ.: of a polygamist. **-glòtto** [Gr. *glôtta*, language], ADJ., M.: polyglot.

polí-gono [Gr. *gônos*, angle, M.: polygon; knot-grass (plant); ADJ.: polygonal. **-grafía** [Gr. *gráphein*, write], F.: polygraphy. **-gráfico**, pl. *—ci*, ADJ.: polygraphical. **polí-grafo**, M.: polygrapher.

polí-metro [Gr. *métron*, measure], M.: composition in various metres. **-nòmio** [Gr. *nómos*, term], M.: polynomial. **-pètalo** [Gr. *pétalon*], ADJ.: polypetalous. **pò-li-po** [Gr. *poûs*, foot], M.: polypus. **-pòdio†**, M.: polypody (plant). **-póso**, ADJ.: polypous.

políre†, TR.: polish; clean.

poli-sárcia [Gr. *polús*, much, many; *sarx*, flesh], F.: obesity. **-sènso**, ADJ.: of many senses. **-síllabo** [Gr. *sullabē*], ADJ.: polysyllabic; M.: polysyllable.

politaménte†, ADV.: politely (civilly); neatly.

poli-teáma [Gr. *polús*, much; *théama*, show], M.: kind of theatre. **-tècnico**, pl. *—ci* [Gr. *téchne*, art], ADJ.: polytechnic. **-teísmo** [Gr. *Théos*, God], M.: polytheism. **-teísta**, M.: polytheist. **-teístico**, pl. *—ci*, ADJ.: polytheistic.

politézza [*pulitezza*], F.: cleanliness (neatness); politeness.

polìti-ca, F.: politics; policy. **-caménte**, ADV.: politically. **-cánte**, M.: ignorant politician. **-cástro**, M.: politicaster. ‖**polìti-co** [L. *-cus*], ADJ.: political; M.: politician. **-cóne**, *aug.* of *-co*. **-cúccio**, **-cúzzo**, *disp. dim.* of *-co*.

polito†, ADJ.: polished (clean).

politrico†, M.: maidenhair (plant).

politropo†, ADJ.: versatile; astute.

poli-zía [L. *-tia*], F.: police. **-ziésco**, ADJ.: police-like. **-ziòtto**, *disp.* of *-zia*.

pòliz-za [?], F.: receipt; note (bill); lottery-ticket; POLICY: — *d' assicurazione*, insurance policy. **-zétta**, **-zína**, **-zíno**, *dim.* of *-za*. **-zòtto†**, *aug.* of *-za*.

pól-la [L. *pullus*, cf. *pollo*], F.: spring of water (well). **-láio**, M.: hen-roost; poultry-yard: *star bene a —*, be at one's ease; *andar a —*, go to sleep. **-laiòla**, F., **-laiòlo**, M.: poulterer. **-laióne†**, *aug.* of *-laio*. **-laiuòlo†**, M.: poulterer; ADJ.: poultry-. **-láme**, M.: poultry. **-lánca†**, F.: young turkey. **-láre**, INTR.: spring (flow forth). **-lário**, ADJ.: tender of fowls (for sacrifices). **-lástra**, F.: fat pullet. **-lastrèllo**, *dim.* of *-lastro*. **-lastrière**, M.: poulterer; ping. **-lastríno**, *dim.* of *-lastro*. **-lástro**, M.: young chicken. **-lastróna**, *aug.* of *-lastra*. **-lastróne**, *aug.* of *-lastro*. **-lastròtto**, M.: *aug.* of *-lastro*; simpleton. **-lèbro†**, M.: simpleton (good-for-nothing). **-lería**, F.: poultry-market (store). **-lézzola†**, F.: top of a bud (sprout).

pòllice [L. *-lex*], M.: thumb; great toe; inch (measure).

polli=coltúra, F.: poultry-raising. **-'na**, F.: hen-manure. **-máro†**, M.: poulterer.

pòlline [L. *-len*, fine flour], M.: pollen (of flowers).

pollíno1 [*-lo*], M.: hen-louse.

pollíno2 [*-la*], M.: marsh (near salt-water).

pól-lo [L. *pullus*, young, offspring], M.: fowl (chicken): — *d' India*, turkey. **-loncèllo**, *dim.* of *-lone*. **-lóne**, M.: sprout (offshoot). **-lonéto**, M.: nursery.

pollú-to [L. *-tus*], ADJ.: polluted (contaminated, unchaste). **-zióne**, F.: pollution (contamination).

polmentário†, M.: narrow-mouthed vase.

polmo-náre, ADJ.: pulmonary. **-nária**, F.: pulmonary (plant); ADJ.: pulmonary. ‖**polmó-ne** [L. *pulmo*], M.: lung. **-néa†**, F.: pulmonary consumption. **-nía**, F.: inflammation of the lungs.

pòlo [L. *-lus*], M.: pole (of an axis).

pól-pa [L. *pulpa*], F.: PULP; calf (of the leg). **-páccio**, M.: calf (of the leg);

fleshy end of the finger. **-pacciòlo**, M.: fleshy end of the finger. **-paccióno**, *disp.* of *-pa*. **-pacciúto**, ADJ.: pulpy (fleshy). **-pastrèllo**, M.: fleshy end of the finger. **-pétta**, F.: meat-ball; rebuke (reprimand). **-pettína**, *dim.* of *-petta*. **-pettóna**, F., **-pettóne**, *aug.* of *-petta*.

pèlpo [*polipo*], M.: polypus.

pol-póso, ‖**-púto** [*-pa*], ADJ.: pulpous (fleshy, brawny).

pol-seggiaménto, M.: pulsation. **-séttot**, M.: bracelet. **-síno**, M.: wristband (cuff). ‖**pól-so** [L. *pulsus*], M.: pulse: wrist; strength (force).

pòlta†, F.: porridge; mush (made with chestnut flour).

poltí-glia [L. *puls*], F.: mush (pudding); porridge; dough; mire (mud). **-glióso**, ADJ.: muddy (miry). **pol-tracchièllo**†, **-tracchíno**, *dim.* of *-tracchio*. ‖**-trácchio**, M.: colt (foal).

pol-tríre, INTR.: be lazy (slothful); lie abed. ‖**pól-tro**† [OGer. *polstar*, BOLSTER], ADJ.: lazy (sluggish, indolent). **-tróna**, F.: large armchair. **-tronáccio**, *disp.* of *-trone*. **-tronággine**, F.: laziness (sluggishness). **-troncèlla**, F.: *dim.* of *-trona* (lazy woman). **-troncèllo**, *dim.* of *-trone*. **-troncína**, *dim.* of *-trona* (armchair). **-troncióne**†, *aug.* of *-trone*. **-tróne**, M.: lazy fellow (sluggard); poltroon; ADJ.: lazy (sluggish). **-troneggiáre**, INTR.: live idly. **-tronería**, F.: laziness (sluggishness); cowardice. **-tronescaménte**, ADV.: lazily; cowardly. **-tronésco**, ADJ.: lazy (indolent); cowardly. **-tronía**†, F.: laziness. **-tronière**†, **-tronièro**†, M.: idle fellow (vagabond).

poltrúccio†, M.: foal (colt).

pól-ve, F.: (*poet.*) dust (powder). **-veráccio**, M.: cloud of dust; sheep manure. ‖**pól-vere** [L. *pulvis*], F.: dust (POWDER); gunpowder: *dar della — negli occhi a uno*, throw dust in some one's eyes. **-verezzáre**, TR.: pulverize. **-verièra**, F.: powder-mill (or magazine). **-verifício**, M.: powder-manufactory. **-veríno**, M.: powder-box; priming-powder; blotting sand. **-verío**, M.: cloud of dust. **-verísta**, M.: gunpowder maker. **-verizzábile**, ADJ.: pulverizable. **-verizzaménto**, M.: pulverizing; thing pulverized. **-verizzáre**, TR.: pulverize (reduce to powder). **-verizzáto**, PART.: pulverized. **-verizzatóre**, M.: pulverizer. **-verizzazióne**, F.: pulverization. **-verizzévole**†, ADJ.: pulverizable. **-veróne**, M.: cloud of dust. **-veróso**, ADJ.: dusty (covered with dust); dust-bringing. **-verúzza**, *dim. of -vere*. **-víglio** †, M.: fine dust. **-víscolo**, **-víschio**, M.: fine dust (powder); pollen.

polzèlla†, F.: maiden (young girl).

po-mário [L. *-marium*], M.: fruit-orchard; apple-orchard. **-máta**, F.: pomatum (unguent). **-máto**, ADJ.: full of apples (or apple-trees). **pó-mo**†, M.: apple (the fruit); apple-tree. **-melláto**, ADJ.: dappled (spotted); variegated. **-mèllo**†, *dim.* of *-mo*.

po-meridiáno [*post meridiano*], ADJ.: postmeridian (belonging to the afternoon). **-meríggio**, M.: afternoon.

pomèrio [L. *-rium*], M.: open space (within or without city walls).

pométo [*-mo*], M.: apple-orchard.

pomfolíge†, F.: kind of soot.

pómi-ce [L. *pumex*], F.: pumice-stone. **-ciáre**, TR.: rub with pumice-stone. **-cióso**, ADJ.: pumiceous.

po-mi=cultúra, F.: fruit-culture. **-midòro**, M.: love-apple (tomato). **-mière**†, M.: apple-orchard. **-mífero**, ADJ.: pomiferous (fruit-bearing). ‖**pó-mo**, pl. *-mi* or *-ma* [L. *-mum*], M.: apple (the fruit); apple-tree; pommel; hilt: — *cotogno*, quince. **-mo=dòro**, M.: love-apple (tomato). **-mo=granáto**, M.: pomegranate. **-mología**, F.: pomology. **-móso**†, ADJ.: full of apples.

pómpa 1 [L.], F.: pomp (display, ostentation).

póm-pa 2 [?], F.: pump. **-páre**, TR.: pump (water).

pompeggiáre [*-pa* 1], INTR.: parade (make a display, flaunt).

pompière [*-pa* 2], M.: fireman.

pompílo [L. *-lus*], M.: pilot-fish.

pom-posaménte, ADV.: pompously (ostentatiously). **-posità**, F.: pomposity. ‖**-póso** [*-pa* 1], ADJ.: pompous (showy, ostentatious).

pòn-ce [Pers.], M.: PUNCH (drink). **-cíno**, *car. dim.* of *-ce*.

póncio [Sp. *-cho*], M.: poncho (kind of cloak).

ponde-rábile, ADJ.: ponderable. **-rabilità**, F.: ponderability. ‖**-ráre** [L.], TR.: ponder (consider, muse); weigh†. **-rataménte**, ADV.: deliberately (with consideration). **-ratézza**, F.: pondering disposition (meditativeness). -
re, M., **-ratríce**, F.: ponder
zióne, F.: deliberation (cons
Eng.† ponderation). **-rosità**,
derosity (heaviness). **-róso**†,
derous (heavy, weighty, importa

pòn-di, M. PL.: bloody flux.
[L. *-dus*], M.: weight (burden)
ance.

po-nènte, M.: west (direction or
west-wind. ‖**pó-nere**† [L.],

put (place). **-niménto**, M.: putting (placing).

ponsò [Fr. *ponceau*], M.: poppy-colour.

póntat† = *punta*.

pontáio [*-te*], M.: frame-builder; bridge-guard.

pontáre = *puntare*.

pón-te [L. *-s*], M.: bridge; scaffolding (frame-work); deck; suspense: — *levatoio*, drawbridge; — *di sopra*, culvert. **-téfice**, M.: pontiff (high priest). **-ticèllo**, M.: *dim.* of *-te*; curve of a sword; bridge (of violin, etc.). **-ticíno**, *dim.* of *-te*.

ponti-cità†, F.: sharpness (acidity). **pònti-co**†, ADJ.: sharp (acid, tart).

pontière [*-te*], M.: bridge-building soldier.

pontifi-cále [*pontefice*], ADJ.: pontifical (pertaining to the high priest); M.: pontifical (ecclesiastical book, dress of a priest). **-calménte**, ADV.: pontifically. **-cáre**, INTR.: officiate as high-priest. **-cáto**, PART. of *-care;* M.: pontificate.

pontifí-cio, ADJ.: pontifical.

pònto [L. *-tus*], M.: (*poet.*) sea (ocean).

pon-tonáio†, M.: ferryman. ||**-tóne** [L. *-s*, bridge], M.: pontoon (ferryboat).

pontúra†, F.: puncture (prick).

pon-zaménto, M.: tenesmus. ||**-záre** [*-tare*], INTR.: make great efforts. **-zatúra**, F.: tenesmus.

popíllo†, M.: ward; pupil.

pòplite [L. *-les*], M.: hollow of the knee.

popo-láccio, M.: populace. **-láno**, M.: inhabitant (of a village); ADJ.: pertaining to a village inhabitant. **-láre**, ADJ.: popular (pleasing); low (inferior); TR.: people (populate); REFL.: become populated. **-larescaménte**, ADV.: vulgarly. **-laréseo**, ADJ.: popular (pertaining to the people). **-larità**, F.: popularity. **-larizzáre**, TR.: popularize. **-larménte**, ADV.: popularly. **-láto**, ADJ.: peopled (full of inhabitants). **-latóre**, M.: one who peoples. **-lazióne**, F.: population (inhabitants). **-lázzo**†, M.: populace. **-lésco**†, ADJ.: popular. **-lézza**†, F.: ignobleness (mean extraction). ||**pòpo-lo** [L. *populus*], M.: PEOPLE (nation); populace; multitude. **-lóso**, ADJ.: populous.

popo-náia, F.: melon-bed. **-náio**, M.: melon-seller; melon-bed†. **-neíno**, *dim.* of *-ne*. ||**popó-ne** [L. *pepo*], M.: melon (PEPO).

póppa 1 [L. *puppis*], F.: poop (deck).

póp-pa 2 [L. *puppa* (*pupa*, girl)], F.: breast (teat). **-páccia**, *disp.* of *-pa*. **-paióne**, M.: sucker (shoot of a plant). **-pánte**, PART.: sucking; M.: infant. **-páre**, TR., INTR.: suck (draw in, imbibe). **-páta**, F.: *sucking*. **-patóio**, M.: nipple-glass. **-pátola**, F.: puppet. **-patóra**, F., **-patóre**, M.: infant. **-pellína**†, *dim.* of *-pa*.

poppéso†, M.: shrouds (of a ship).

pop-pína, *car. dim.* of *-pa* 2. **-póna**, *aug.* of *-pa*. **-púto**, ADJ.: full-breasted.

populáto [*-polato*], ADJ.: populous.

popú-leo† [L. *-lus*, poplar], ADJ.: of the poplar. **-leóne**, M.: kind of unguent.

popul.. = *popol..*

poráre†, INTR.: pass through the pores.

pòrca 1 [L.], F.: ridge (between furrows).

pòr-ca 2, F.: sow. **-cáccio**, M.: sloven; ADJ.: slovenly. **-caccetèllo**, *disp. dim.* of *-caccio*. **-caccióne**, *aug.* of *-caccio*. **-cáio**, M.: hog-keeper. **-caménte**, ADV.: hoggishly. **-cáro**, M.: hog-keeper. **-cástro**, M.: young pig. **-cèlla**, F.: young sow. **-celláma** [orig. a kind of shell, "pork-shell"], F.: porcelain (ware); purslain (plant). **-cellétta**, F.: young sow. **-cellétto**, M.: young pig. **-cellíno**, *dim.* of *-cello*. **-cèllo**, *dim.* of *-co*. **-cellóne**, **-cellòtto**, *aug.* of *-cello*. **-cheggiáre**, INTR.: act like a hog. **-cheréccio**†, ADJ.: of (or for) hogs: *spiede* —, boar-spear. **-chería**, F.: nastiness (obscenity, filthiness). **-cheriòla**, *dim.* of *-cheria*. **-chétta**, F., **-chétto**, M.: little pig. **-cíle**, M.: pigsty; filthy place. **-cíno**, ADJ.: porcine (of a hog). ||**pòr-co** [L. *-cus*], M.: hog (pig, PORKER): — *spinoso*, porcupine; *far l' occhio del* —, cast a sheep's eye at one. **-cóna**, *aug.* of *-ca*. **-cóne**, *aug.* of *-co*. **-cúme**, M.: filthiness.

porétto, *dim.* of *-ro*.

pòr-fido, **-firo**† [Gr. *-phuroës*, purple-coloured], M.: porphyry (rock). **-fírico**, pl. —*ci*, ADJ.: porphyritic. **-firogènito**, ADJ.: born in purple (nobly born).

pòr-gere [L. *-rigere*], IRR.§; TR.: present (offer, hold out); give (bestow); promise; deliver; REFL.: present one's self: — *credenza*, give credit; — *orecchio*, listen. **-giménto**, M.: presenting (offering); giving. **-gitóre**, M., **-gitríce**, F.: presenter.

§ Ind.: Pret. *pòr-si*, *-se*; *-sero*. Part. *pòrto*.

pò-ro [L. *-rus*], M.: pore. **-rosíssimo**, ADJ.: very (or most) porous. **-rosità**, F.: porosity. **-róso**, ADJ.: porous.

pórpo-ra [L. *purpura*], F.: purple (colour or cloth); genus of mollusks. **-ráto**, ADJ.: clothed in purple; M.: cardinal. **-reggiáre**, INTR.: resemble purple. **-rína**, F.: bright red colour. **-ríno**, ADJ.: purple-coloured. **pórpo-ro**, M.: purple.

por-ráceo [*poro*], ADJ.: porraceous (greenish). **-ráio**, ADJ.: of a kind of onion. **-randèllo**, F.: wild leek. **-ráta**, F.: leek-soup.

pórre [L. *ponere*], IRR. § ; TR.: place (put); plant; assert; order (decree)†: — *cagione*, blame; — *il caso*, suppose; — *cura*, take care of; — *in effetto*, carry out (execute); — *fine*, finish; — *in luce*, publish; — *mente*, take heed; — *la mira*, aim at; — *in oblio*, forget; — *in opera*, set up; — *al sole*, destroy; — *studio*, take heed; — *in vendita*, expose for sale; — *in volta*, rout; REFL.: set one's self: — *con alcuno*, engage in any one's service; — *in cammino*, set out on a journey; — *in cuore*, resolve; — *a letto*, go to bed; — *a sedere*, sit down.

§ (Reg. tenses from *pónere*). Ind.: Pres. *póngo, póni, póne; poniámo* or *ponghiámo, ponéte, póngono*. Pret. *pó-si, -se; -sero*. Fut. *porrò*. Cond. *porrèi*. Subj.: Pres. *pónga; poniámo* or *ponghiámo*. I've *póni*. Part. *pósto*.

por-réttа†, F.: leek. **-rétto, -rína, -ríno**, *dim.* of *-ro*. ||**pòr-ro** [L. *-rum*], M.: leek; wart: *predicare a' -ri*, preach in vain. **-róso**, ADJ.: full of leeks; covered with warts.

pórsi, PRET. of *-gere*.

pòrta 1 [L.], F.: entrance (gateway, door, Eng.† PORT); (*nav.*) port(-hole): *vena* —, vein system.

pòr-ta 2, pl. *-ta* or *-ti* [*-tare*], M.: porter (bearer). **-ta=bacíno**, M.: basin-stand. **-tábile**, ADJ.: portable; supportable (endurable). **-ta=cáppe**†, M.: portmanteau. **-ta=cappèllo**, M.: hat-case.

portáccia, *disp.* of *porta* 1.

porta=bandièra, M.: standard-bearer. **=fiáschi**, M.: hamper (basket). **=fióri**, M.: flower-stand. **=fògli**, **=fòglio**, M.: portfolio (letter-case). **=gioièlli**, M.: jewel-box. **=lápis**, M.: pencil-holder. **=lèttero**, M.: letter-carrier. **=mantèllo**, M.: portmanteau (travelling-bag). **-ménto**, M.: deportment (demeanour, manner, mien). **=monéte**, M.: porte-monnaie (purse). **=mòrso**, M.: bit-strap. **portá-nte**, ADJ.: carrying; wearing; M.: amble (gait of a horse). **-ntína**, F.: sedan-chair. **-ntíno**, M.: chair-bearer. **=pénne**, M.: penholder; pen-case. ||**portá-re** [L.], TR.: carry (bear); transport (convey); delay (protract); induce; take away (steal); produce (bring forth); reduce; allege; excite; patronize; endure; REFL.: behave one's self; wear: — *bruno*, wear mourning; — *credenza*, believe; — *fuoco*, pick a quarrel; — *in pace*, bear patiently; — *pericolo*, hazard; — *la spesa*, be worth the trouble. **=ritrátti**, M.: picture-frame. **=sígari**, M.: cigar-case. **=spílli**, M.: pin-cushion. **=stánghe**, M.: shaft-loop (of harness); go-between. **=stécchi**, M.: toothpick-holder. **portá-ta**, F.: burden (of a ship); cannon range; calibre; revenue (income); quality (sort); ability; course (at table); list of taxable property: *fuori della* —, out of one's reach. **-tícсio**, ADJ.: by drift, drift. **portá-tile**, ADJ.: portable. **portá-to**, PART. of *-re*; M.: offspring (brood); production (work). **-tóre**, M., **-tríce**, F.: porter (carrier); bearer. **-túra**, F.: carrying; carriage (bearing); fashion; brood†. **-vènto**, M.: blasting-pipe. **=vivánde**, M.: tray. **=vóce**, M.: speaking-trumpet.

portèllo [*-ta* 1], M.: small door; aperture.

portèn-dere† [L.], IRR. (cf. *tendere*); TR.: portend (foreshow). **portèn-to**, M.: portent (omen). **-tosaménte**, ADV.: portentously (ominously). **-tóso**, ADJ.: portentous (ominous).

portería [*-ta*], F.: doorkeeper's lodge (at a convent).

por-tési, PRET. of *-tendere*. **-téso**, PART. of *-tendere*.

portévole†, ADJ.: tolerable (endurable).

por-ticciòla, *dim.* of *-ta* 1. **-ticciòlo**, *dim.* of *-to*. **-ticèlla**, *dim.* of *-ta* 1. **-tichétto**, *dim.* of *-tico*. **-ticína**, *dim.* of *-ta* 1. ||**pòr-tico** [L. *-ticus* (*-ta*, gate)], M.: portico (PORCH, colonnade). **-tièra** [*-ta* 1], F.: portière (door-curtain). **-tière**, M.: doorkeeper (usher). **-tína**†, F.: kind of black grape. **-tináia**, F., **-tináio, -tináro**†, M.: doorkeeper. **-tinería**, F.: doorkeeper's lodge.

port=inségna, M.: standard-bearer.

||**pòr-to** 1 [*-tare*], M.: carriage (bearing); (*pop.*) carrying: — *franco*, postage free (free of charge).

pòrto 2, PART. of *porgere*.

pòr-to [L. *-tus*], M.: port (harbour). **-toláno**†, M.: pilot; doorkeeper. **-tóne** [*-ta* 1], M.: great door (entrance); coach-gate. **-tuóso**, ADJ.: with a port or ports.

portuláca [L. *portare*, bear, *lac*, milk], F.: purslain.

por-zioncèlla, -zioncína, *dim.* of *-zione*. ||**-zióne** [L. *-tio*], F.: portion (part, share).

pò-sa, F.: repose (rest); pause (stop). **-saménto**, M.: reposing; rest. **-sánza**†, F.: repose (rest); pause (stop). **-sa=piáno**, M.: label (on boxes, etc., containing breakable material). **-sa=pièdi**, M.: footstool. ||**-sáre** [l. L. *pau*- pause], TR.: put down; rest (plac- tly); INTR.: repose (rest); REFL.: **-sáta**, F.: cover (knife, fork, etc. pause (stop); sediment (dregs) **ménte**, ADV.: quietly (gently **-satézza**, F.: calmness (tranqui posure). **-satína**, *dim.* of **-s** **to**, ADJ.: quiet (calm, tranqu-

-satóio, M.: perch (esp. of a cage). **-satúccia**, *disp.* of *-sata*. **-satúra**, F.: dregs (grounds).

pòscia [L. *postea*], ADV.: after (afterwards) or **-chè** *-é*, CONJ.: since; although.

pos-critto [L. *post scriptum*], M.: postscript. **-dománi**, M.: day after tomorrow.

posi, PRET. of *porre*.

posi-tivaménte, ADV.: positively. **-tivismo**, M.: positivism. **-tivista**, M.: positivist. ‖**-tivo** [L. *-tivus* (*ponere*, put)], ADJ.: positive (actual, certain). **-túra**, F.: posture (position). **-zióne**, F.: position (situation); proposition†.

pòso [*-sare*], M.: rest (repose, quiet).

pòso-la, F.: breeching (of a horse). **-latura**†, **-lièra**, F.: crupper. ‖**-líno** [L. *postilena*], M.: crupper-strap.

pospásto†, M.: dessert.

pos-pórre [*post*, *porre*], IRR.; TR.: postpone (defer); neglect (slight). **-posítivo**, ADJ.: post-positive (placed after); neglected. **-posizióne**, F.: postponing; delay. **-pósto**, PART. of *-porre*.

pòs-sa [L. *-se*, be able], F.: power (virtue). **-sánza**, F.: power (force).

pos-sedènte, PART.: possessing. ‖**-sedére** [L. *-sidere*], IRR. (cf. *sedere*); TR.: POSSESS (have, occupy). **-sediménto**, M.: possessing; possession (land); enjoyment. **-seditóre**, M., **-seditríce**, F.: possessor (holder). **-sedúto**, PART.: possessed (owned). **-sènte**, ADJ.: PUISSANT (powerful, mighty). **-sentemènte**, ADV.: powerfully. **-sessioncèlla**, *dim.* of *-sessione*. **-sessióne**, F.: possession (property). **-sessivaménte**, ADV.: possessively. **-sessívo**, ADJ.: possessive. **-sèsso**, M.: possession. **-sessóre**, M.: possessor (owner). **-sessòrio**, ADJ.: possessory.

possíbi-le [L. *-lis* (*posse*, be able)], ADJ.: possible. **-lità**, F.: possibility. **-lménte**, ADV.: possibly.

possi-dènte [*possedere*], M.: possessor (proprietor, owner); ADJ.: possessing. **-dentóne**, *aug.* of *-dente*. **-dentúccio**, **-dentúccolo**, *disp. dim.* of *-dente*. **-dènza**, F.: possession (ownership).

pòst- [L.], PREF.: post-, after.

pò-sta [L. *-sita*] F.: post (place, station); wait (ambush); rendezvous (meeting-place); messenger; hen-setting; stall (stable); post-office; opportunity†; footstep†; stake (wager)†; ambush†; situation†; posture†; plantation†: *cavallo di* —, post-horse; *naviglio di* —, packet-boat; *ufficio della* —, post-office; *a* —, on purpose; *di* —, directly; *di questa* —, at this rate; *da* (or *a*) *sua* —, of his own accord; *andar in* —, ride post; *far la* — *ad uno*, lie in wait. **-stále**, ADJ.: postal. **-stáre**, TR., REFL.: spy (watch for). **-starèlla**, *dim.* of *-sta*.

post=comúnio [L.], M.: after communion (part of the mass).

posteggiáre [*-ta*], TR.: lie in wait.

postè-ma [Gr. *apó-stema*], F.: aposteme (abscess). **-móso**, ADJ.: having abscesses.

postergáre [L. (*post-*, *tergum*, back)], TR.: throw behind; disdain (despise).

pòste-ri [L. (*post*)], M. PL.: descendants (offspring). **-rióre**, ADJ.: posterior (later); M.†: posteriors: *a -riori*, posteriorly. **-riorità**, F.: posteriority. **-riorménte**, ADV.: posteriorly (subsequently). **-rità**, F.: (*jest.*) posterity (offspring).

pòste-ro, M.: descendant.

postíccio [*appositizio*], ADJ.: put on (false, fictitious, counterfeit); provisional (temporary); M.: nursery-ground: *a* —, falsely. **-címo**, *car. dim.* of *-io*.

postici-páre [L. (*post*)], INTR.: delay (linger). **-páto**, PART.: delayed. **-pataménte**, ADV.: slowly (in a lingering manner). **-pazióne**, F.: delay.

postière† [*-ta*], M.: keeper of post-horses.

postièri†, M.: day before yesterday.

postièrla [L. *-terula*], F.: postern (small door).

postiglióne [*-ta*], M.: postilion.

postíl-la [L. *post illa* (sc. *verba*, 'after those words')], F.: postil (marginal note; short homily). **-láre**, TR.: postillate (make postils). **-láto**, PART.: with postils. **-latóre**, M.: postiller. **-latúra**, F.: notes.

pos-tíme, M.: plantation. **-tíno**, M.: postman (letter-carrier). ‖**-pós-to** [L. *-itus*], PART. of *porre*; ADJ.: placed (put); M.: post (place, country, station); office; space (room): — *che*, in case that.

postrèmo [L. *-mus*], ADJ.: last (final, rear).

postrí-bolo, ‖**-bulo**† [L. *prostibulum* (*pro-stare*, stand forth, be exposed for sale), PROSTITUTE], M.: house of prostitution (brothel).

postu-lánte, PART.: postulating; M.: postulant (candidate). ‖**-láre** [L.], TR.: postulate (ask, beseech). **-láto**, M.: postulate. **-latòrio**, ADJ.: petitionary. **-lazióne**, F.: postulation.

pòstumo [L. *-mus*], ADJ.: posthumous.

postúra [*-situra*], F.: posture; plot†.

postútto [*post tutto*], ADV.: *al* —, after all.

posvedére†, IRR.; TR.: see after.

potábile [L. *-lis*], ADJ.: drinkable (potable).

potággio†, M.: pottage (soup).

po-tagióne, F., **-taménto**, M.: pruning (trimming). ‖**-táre** [L. *putare* (*putus*, clean)], TR.: prune (trim).

po-tássa [Ger. *-tt-asche*], F.: potash. **-tássio**, M.: potassium.

pota-tóio [*-re*], M.: pruning-knife. **-tóre**, M., **-tríce**, F.: pruner. **-túra**, F.: pruning (trimming); branches. **-zióne**†, F.: pruning.

po-tentariaménte†, ADV.: like a prince. **-tentáto**, M.: potentate (prince). **-tènte**, ADJ.: potent (strong); M.: potentate (prince). **-tenteménte**, ADV.: potently (powerfully). **-tènza**, F.: potency (power): *in* —, virtually. **-tenziále**, ADJ.: potential. **-tenzialménte**, ADV.: potentially. **-tenziáto**, ADJ.: of a potential virtue. ‖**-tére** [L. *-sse*], IRR.§; INTR.: be able (have power, influence); M.: POWER (ability, strength); authority. **-testà**, F.: power (authority). **-testería**, F.: office (or jurisdiction) of a magistrate. **-tissimaménte**†, ADV.: principally. **-tíssimo**†, ADJ.: principal (most considerable, chief).

§ Ind.: Pres. *pòsso, puòi, può; possiámo, potéte, pòssono.* Fut. *potrò.* Cond. *potrèi.* Subj.: Pres. *pòssa.* I've lacking.
Poet. forms: Pres. 3. *puòte;* 6. *pònno.* Pret. 6. *potèro.* Cond. *porría.* Ger. *possèndo.*

pòto†, M.: (*poet.*) drink.

pottiníccio [?], M.: mud (mire); mixture (medley).

potúto, PART. of *potere.*

pove-ráccia, **-ráccio**, *disp.* of *-ro.* **-ráglia**, F.: lot of beggars. **-raménte**, ADV.: poorly. **-rèllo**, *dim.* of *-ro.* **-rettaménte**, ADV.: poorly (meanly). **-rétto**, *dim.* of *-ro.* **-rézza**†, F.: poverty (need, misery). **-ríno**, *dim.* of *-ro.* ‖**pòve-ro** [L. *pauper*], ADJ.: POOR (needy); sterile; M.: pauper; poverty (misery): — *in canna*, very poor; *alla -ra*, poorly. **-róne**, *disp. aug.* of *-ro.* **-rtà**, F.: poverty (need); scarcity; meanness. **-rúccio**, *car. dim.* of *-ro.*

pozióne [L. *potio*], F.: potion (drink).

pozió-re†, ADJ.: prior (former). **-rità**†, F.: priority (precedence).

póz-za, F.: pool. **-záccia**, *disp.* of *-za.* **-zánghera**, F.: puddle. **-zétta**, F.: *dim.* of *-za;* dimple. **-zettíno**, *dim.* of *-zetto.* **-zétto**, *dim.* of *-zo.* ‖**póz-zo** [L. *puteus*], M.: well (spring): — *di fuoco*, fire-pit; *mostrar la luna nel* —, make one believe the moon is made of green cheese.

pozzolána [*Pozzuoli*], F.: pozzolana (cement).

prammática [L. *pragmaticus*], F.: pragmatic sanction.

prán-dere†, IRR. (part. *-so*); INTR.: dine; eat. **prán-dio** [L. *-dium*], M.: (*poet.*) dinner. **-dípeta**, M., F.: sponger. **prán-so**, PART. of *-dere.* **-sáre**, INTR.: dine (banquet). **-satóre**, M.: diner. **-sétto**, *dim.* of *-zo.* ‖**prán-so** [L. *-dium* (*pra-*, early, *dies*, DAY)], M.: dinner (banquet).

prássino†, ADJ.: greenish.

prássio†, M.: horehound.

pra-taiòlo, ADJ.: of meadows; M.: meadow-mushroom. **-tellína**, F.: daisy. ‖**-tèllo** [*-to*], *dim.* of *-to.* **-tènse**, ADJ.: meadow (growing in meadows). **-tería**, F.: meadows; prairie.

práti-ca [*-co*], F.: practice (custom); action; plot; intercourse; experience; familiarity: *di* —, freely; *far* —, endeavour; *far le -che*, practice. **-cábile**, ADJ.: practicable (feasible). **-cabilità**, F.: practicability. **-cabilménte**, ADV.: practicably. **-cáccia**, *disp.* of *-ca.* **-caménte**, ADV.: by practice (use). **-cánte**, M.: practitioner. **-cáre**, TR.: practice (do, exercise); negotiate; frequent (visit); manage; INTR.: practice (exercise): — *bene*, live in good society. **-cáto**, PART. of *-care.*

praticèllo, *dim.* of *-to.*

prati-chétta, *dim.* of *-ca.* **-chézza**†, F.: practice (use); society; intimacy. ‖**práti-co** [L. *practicus*], F.: practical; practised (experienced); M.: practical. **-cóna**, *aug.* of *-ca.* **-conáccio**, *disp.* of *-cone.* **-cóne**, M.: great practitioner.

pra-tíle, M.: PRAirial (ninth month of the French Republican calendar). **-tívo**, ADJ.: meadow (of a meadow). ‖**prá-to**, pl. *-ti* or *-ta* [L. *-tum*], M.: meadow. **-tolína**, F.: kind of herb. **-tolíno**†, M.: field mushroom.

pra-vaménte, ADV.: wickedly (depravedly). **-vità**, F.: depravity (corruption). ‖**prá-vo** [L. *-vus*, distorted], ADJ.: depraved (wicked, corrupt).

pre- [L. *præ*, before): =**accennáre**, TR.: mention beforehand. =**accusáre**, TR.: accuse beforehand. =**allegáto**, ADJ.: before (above) alleged. =**amboláre**†, INTR.: preamble (introduce, preface). **-àmbolo** [*-ambulus*], M.: preamble. =**avvertíre**, TR.: advise beforehand.

prebèn-da [L. (*præbere*, offer)], F.: prebend (stipend). **-dário**, M.: prebendary. **-dático**†, M.: prebend. **-dáto**, M.: prebendaryship; ADJ.: possessing a prebend.

precá-re† [L. *-ri*], TR.: PRAY (entreat). **-riaménte**, ADV.: precariously. **-rietà**, F.: precariousness (uncertainty).

precá-rio, ADJ.: precarious (unsteady, doubtful).

pre=cauzióne, F.: precaution (care).

prèce [L. *prex*], F.: (*poet*) PRAYER (supplication).

prece-dènte, PART. of *-dere;* ADJ.: precedent (previous); M.: precedent (antecedent). **-denteménte**, ADV.: pre-

cedently (beforehand). **-dènza**, F.: precedence (antecedence, priority). ‖**precè-dere** [L. *præ-cedere*], REG. (or IRR., cf. *cedere*); TR.: precede (go before). **-dùto**, PART. of *-dere*.

precentóre [L. *canere*, sing], M.: precentor (choir-leader).

pre-cessióne, F.: precession. ‖**-cèsso**, PART. of *-cedere*. **-cessóre†**, M.: predecessor.

precet-tánto, PART.; M.: one summoned. ‖**-táre** [L. *præ-ceptare*], TR.: summon (call officially). **-táto**, PART. of *-tare*. **-tatóre†**, M.: preceptor (instructor). **-tísta**, M.: author of precepts. **-tística**, F.: book (or art) of precepts. **-tívo**, ADJ.: preceptive. **precèt-to**, M.: precept (injunction, maxim). **-toráto**, M.: office of a preceptor. **-tóre**, M.: preceptor (instructor). **-toría†**, F.: government.

precídere [L.], IRR.; TR.: cut off; impede.

precínto [L. *-cinctus* (*cingere*, gird)], ADJ.: encompassed; M.: precinct (district).

precipi tazménto†, M.: precipitation. **tánza†**, F.: headlong fall. ‖**-táre** [L. (*præ ceps*, headlong)], TR.: precipitate (throw headlong); hasten; INTR.: precipitate (sediment); REFL.: rush headlong. **-tataménte**, ADV.: precipitately. **-táto**, PART. of *-tare*; ADJ.: precipitate (headlong, hasty); M.: precipitate. **-tazióne**, F.: precipitation (great hurry); rashness. **precípi-te**, ADJ.: precipitate (headlong); precipitous (steep); rash. **-tévole**, ADJ.: precipitous. **-tevolissimevolménte** (*jest.*). **-tevolménte**, ADV.: precipitously. **-tosaménte**, ADV.: precipitously (with steep descent); precipitately (hastily). **-tóso**, ADJ.: precipitous (steep); hasty (rash). **-ziáre†**, INTR.: precipitate (hasten). **precipí-zio**, M.: precipice, headlong fall: *mandare in* [illegible], squander. [illegible], precipitously.

pre cipuaménte, ADV.: principally (chiefly). ‖**-cípuo** [L. *præcipuus* (*capere*, take)], ADJ.: principal (chief), only.

preci saménte, ADV.: precisely (accurately), briefly. **-sare**, TR.: tell with precision. **precí si**, PRET. of *-dere*. **-sióne**, F.: precision (accuracy, exactness). **-sívo†**, ADJ.: precise (exact). ‖**precí-so** [L. *præcisus*], ADJ.: precise (exact, accurate, strict); ADV.: precisely (exactly).

pre-citáto, ADJ.: cited beforehand.

pre-claraménte, ADV.: nobly (illustriously). ‖**-cláro** [L. *præ-clarus*], ADJ.: noble (illustrious, great).

pre-cludere, IRR.; TR.: preclude (prevent, deter). **-clúsi**, PRET. of *-cludere*. **-clúso**, PART. of *-cludere*.

precòce†, M.: prayer (supplication).

precò-ce [L. *præ-cox* (*coquere*, COOK)], ADJ.: precocious (premature). **-ceménte**, ADV.: precociously. **-cità**, F.: precocity (prematureness).

precogitáre†, INTR.: precogitate (consider beforehand).

pre-cognizióne, F.: precognition (foreknowledge). ‖**=cognóscere**, IRR.; TR.: know beforehand.

pre=concètto, ADJ.: preconceived; M.: preconception.

precò-nio†, M.: (*poet.*) praise (eulogy). ‖**-nizzáre** [L. *præco-nisare*], TR.: publish (proclaim, Eng.†, preconizate); extol†. **-nizzazióne**, F.: proclamation (Eng.† preconization).

preconó-bbi, PRET. of *-scere*. **-sciménto**, F.: precognition (foreknowledge). ‖**preconó-scere** [*pre*, *conoscere*], IRR.; TR.: know beforehand (foreknow). **-sciménto**, M.: foreknowledge. **-sciúto**, PART. of *-scere*.

pre-còrdi, **-còrdii** [L. *præcordia*], M. PL.: præcordia.

pre-corrènte, PART. of *-correre*. ‖**precórrere**, IRR.; INTR.: forerun (precede); forestall (prevent). **-corritóre**, M., **-corritríce**, F.: forerunner. **-córsi**, PRET. of *-correre*. **-córso**, PART. of *-correre*. **-corsóre**, M.: precursor (harbinger); messenger.

prè-da [L. *præda*], F.: PREY (spoil, plunder): *dare in —*, give up (expose). **-dáce**, ADJ.: predaceous (plundering). **-daménto**, M.: plundering; spoil (booty). **-dáre**, TR.: plunder (pillage). **-dáto**, PART. of *-dare*. **-datóra**, F., **-datóre**, M.: plunderer. **-datòrio†**, M.: predatory (pillaging). **-datríce**, F.: plunderer.

predecessóre [L. *prædecessor*], M.: predecessor; ancestor.

pre definíre, TR.: predetermine.

predèl-la [?], F.: platform of the altar; close-stool; foot-stool†; bridle-reins†. **-lína**, F., **-líno**, M.: small chair; high chair (for a child). **-lóne†**, M.: high stool. **-luccia**, F.: small chair (for a child).

predesti-náre [L.], TR.: predestine (foreordain). **-natívo**, ADJ.: predestinating. **-nazióne**, F.: predestination; predestinating. **predestí-no†**, M.: predestination.

pre determi-náre, TR.: predetermine. **-náto**, PART. of *-nare*. **-nazióne**, F.: predetermination.

predétto, PART. of *-dire*; ADJ.: foretold; M.: prediction (foretelling).

prediále [L. *prædium*, farm], ADJ.: predial (of land or farms).

prèdi-ca, F.: sermon; discourse (lecture). **-cábile**, ADJ.: predicable (assertable); M.: predicable (general attribute). **-caménto**, M.: predicament (condition); preaching†; sermon†. **-cánte**, M.: Protestant preacher: *frati -canti*, Dominican friars. **-cánza†**, F.: preaching; sermon. ‖**-cáre** [L. *præ-dicare*], TR.: PREACH; boast (vaunt); teach; lecture; exaggerate; affirm. **-cáto**, PART. of *-care;* M.: predicate. **-catóre**, M.: preacher. **-catorèllo**, *disp. dim.* of *-catore*. **-catoréssa**, **-catríce**, F.: chatterer. **-cazióne**, F.: preaching; sermon.

pre-dicènte, PART. of *-dicere* or *-dire*. ‖**-dícere** = *-dire*.

predi-chétta [*-ca*], *dim.* of *-ca*. **-chína**, **-chíno**, *dim.* of *-ca*.

predici-ménto [*predicere*], M.: prediction; foretelling. **-tóre**, M.: foreteller.

predicòzzo [*-care*], M.: long sermon.

predi-lètto, PART. of *-ligere;* M.: beloved; ADJ.: beloved. **-lezióne**, F.: predilection. ‖**-lígere** [L. *præ*, before, *diligere*, love], IRR.§; TR.: love with partiality.

§ Ind.: Pret. *predilès-si*, *-se*; *-sero*. Part. *predilètto*.

pre=dimostrazióne, F.: previous demonstration.

prèdio [L. *prædium*], M.: farm (estate); manor.

pre=díre, IRR.; TR.: predict (foretell, presage).

pre-disponènte, PART. of *-disporre*. ‖**=dispórre**, IRR.; TR.: predispose. **-dispósto**, PART. of *disporre*. **-disposizióne**, F.: predisposition.

predizióne [*-dire*], F.: prediction (foretelling).

predomi-nánte, PART. of *-nare*. **-nánza**, F.: predominance (prevalence). ‖**-náre** [*pre*, *dominare*], TR.: predominate (prevail, rule). **predomí-nio**, M.: predominancy (ascendancy).

predóne [*-dare*], M.: pillager (highway-robber).

pre=eccellènte, ADJ.: very excellent.

pre=elèggere, IRR.; TR.: preëlect (choose beforehand). **-elètto**, PART. of *-eleggere*.

pre=eminènz(i)a, F.: preëminence (superiority).

preesis-tènte, PART. of *-tere;* ADJ.: preëxistent. **-tènza**, F.: preëxistence. ‖**preesís-tere** [*pre*, *esistere*], IRR.; INTR.: preëxist. **-títo**, PART. of *-tere*.

pre-fáto [L. *præfatus* (*præ*, before, *fari*, speak)], ADJ.: aforesaid (cited). **-fázio**, M.: preface (prayer). **-fazióne**, F.: preface (introduction).

prefe-rènza, F.: preference (choice); precedence. **-ríbile**, ADJ.: preferable. **-ribilménte**, ADV.: preferably. **-riménto†**, M.: preference (choice). ‖**-ríre** [L. *præ-ferre*], TR.: prefer (choose, select). **-ríto**, PART. of *-rire*. **-ritóre**, M.: one preferring.

prefet-téssa, F.: wife of a prefect. **-tízio**, ADJ.: of a prefect. ‖**prefèt-to** [L. *præfectus*], M.: prefect (Roman officer); superintendent. **-túra**, F.: prefecture.

prèfica [L. *præ-fica* (*facere*, make)], F.: hired mourner (at funerals).

pre=fíggere†, IRR.; TR.: prefix (determine, settle); REFL.: take into one's head; resolve upon. **-figgiménto†**, M.: resolving; determination.

prefigu-raménto, M.: prefiguration. ‖**-ráre** [*pre*, *figurare*], TR.: prefigure. **-razióne**, F.: prefiguration.

pre=físsi, PRET., **-físso**, PART. of *-figgere*.

preformá-to [*pre*, *formato*], ADJ.: formed beforehand. **-zióne**, F.: preformation.

pre-gagióne†, F.: prayer (petition). ‖**-gáre** [L. *-cari*], TR.: PRAY (supplicate, entreat); wish. **-garía†**, F.: prayer. **-gáto**, PART. of *-gare*. **-gatóre**, M.: supplicator (implorer).

pregévo-le [*pregiare*], ADJ.: valuable (precious). **-lézza**, F.: value (worth).

pre-ghévole†, ADJ.: imploring (beseeching). ‖**-ghièra** [*-gare*], F.: prayer (petition).

pre-giábile, ADJ.: valuable (precious). **-giabilità**, F.: value (worth). **-giáre**, TR.: prize (value); esteem; estimate (value)†; REFL.: be proud of (boast of). **-giáto**, PART. of *-giare*. **-giatóre**, M.: appraiser; esteemer. ‖**prè-gio** [L. *-tium*], M.: value (worth, PRICE); esteem; reputation.

pregióne† = *prigione*.

pregióso†, ADJ.: precious (valuable).

pregiudi-cánte, ADJ.: harmful. ‖**-cáre** [L. *præ-judicare*], TR.: prejudge; prejudice (damage, hurt). **-catívo**, ADJ.: prejudicial (hurtful). **-cáto**, PART. of *-care*. **-cévole**, ADJ.: prejudicing (harming). **-ciále**, **-ziále**, ADJ.: prejudicial (hurtful, detrimental). **pregiudí-zio**, M.: prejudice (harm, damage). **-zióso†**, ADJ.: prejudicial (harmful).

pré-gna, ADJ.: pregnant. ‖**-gnánte** [L. *prægnans*], ADJ.: (*poet.*) pregnant; M.: one pregnant. **-gnanteménte†**, ADV.: pregnantly. **-gnézza**, F.: pregnancy. **-gno** = *-gna*.

prègo [*prece*], M.: prayer (supplication).

pregus-taménto, M.: tasting beforehand. ‖**-táre** [*pre*, *gustare*], TR.: taste beforehand (foretaste). **-tazióne**, F.: pregustation (foretaste).

pre=indicáto, ADJ.: indicated before.

pre=intèndere, IRR.; TR.: understand

before; hear before; INTR.: mean before. **-intéso**, PART. of *-intendere*.

pre-introdótto, PART. ‖**=introdúrre**, IRR.; TR.: introduce (bring in) before. **-introdússi**, PRET. of *-introdurre*.

pre=istòrico, pl. —*ci*, ADJ.: prehistoric.

prela-tízio, ADJ.: of (or from) a prelate. ‖**prelá-to** [L. *-tus* (*præ-ferre*, prefer)], M.: prelate. **-túra**, F.: prelacy; body of prelates. **-lazióne**, F.: prelation (preference); superiority†.

pre=leváre, TR.: take away. **-leváto**, PART. of *-levare*. **-levazióne**, F.: taking away. **-lezióne** [L. *lectio*], F.: beginning lecture (of a course). **-liáre**†, INTR.: fight. **=libáre** [L. *libit*], INTR.: taste (try) before. **-libáto**, PART. of *-libare;* ADJ.: excellent. **=liminare** [L. *limen*, threshold], ADJ.: preliminary (introductory); M.: preliminary (introduction). **=lodáto** [L. *laudatus*], ADJ.: praised before.

pre-lúdere [*præ-ludere* (play)], IRR. (cf. *alludere*); INTR.: prelude. **-lúdio** [L. *-ludium*], M.: prelude; forerunner. **-lúço**, PART., **-lússi**, PRET. of *-lucere*.

premáticа†, F.: pragmatic sanction.

prema-turaménte, ADV.: prematurely (too early). ‖**-túro** [L. *præmaturus*], ADJ.: premature (too early).

premedi-táre [L. *præmeditari*], TR.: premeditate. **-tataménte**, ADV.: premeditatedly. **-táto**, PART. of *-tare*. **-tazióne**, F.: premeditation.

premènte, PART. of *-mere;* ADJ.: pressing (squeezing).

pre=mentováto, ADJ.: mentioned before (or above).

prèmere [L.], TR. (pret. reg. or *pressi*†): press (squeeze); force out; crush (bruise); oppress; urge; INTR.: press; import.

pre-méssa, F.: premise (proposition). **-messióne**†, F.: preamble (preface). **-mésso**, PART. of *-mettere;* ADJ.: premised (set forth beforehand). ‖**=méttere**, IRR.; TR.: put before; explain beforehand; prefer (choose).

premiá-re [L. *præmiari* (*præmium*, premium, reward)], TR.: reward (repay). **-tívo**†, ADJ.: rewarding. **premiá-to**, PART. of *-re*. **-tóre**, M., **-tríce**, F.: rewarder (recompenser). **-zióne**, F.: reward (recompense).

premi-nènte [L. *præminens*], ADJ.: preeminent (excelling). **-nènza**, F.: preëminence (superiority).

prèmio [L. *præmium*], M.: PREMIUM (reward, prize).

premísi, PRET. of *-mettere*.

prèmi-to [*premere*], M.: pressing (pushing); tenesmus. **-tóre**†, M.: oppressor. **-túra**, F.: pressing (crushing); juice.

premízia†, F.: premices (first fruits).

premonizióne†, F.: premonition (fore-warning).

pre=morire, IRR.; INTR.: predecease (die sooner than). **-mòrto**, PART. of *-morire;* ADJ.: predeceased.

pre=munire, TR.: fortify beforehand; REFL.: be prepared. **-munizióne**, F.: premunition (preparation).

premú-ra [*premere*], F.: importance (weight); solicitude (concern); ardour. **-rosaménte**, ADV.: ardently (eagerly); urgently. **-róso**, ADJ.: pressing; ardent; important.

premutáre†, TR.: change the order of.

premúto, PART. of *-mere;* ADJ.: pressed (squeezed).

prenarrá-re†, TR.: tell beforehand. **-zióne**†, F.: previous narration.

prèn-ce [*principe*], M.: (*poet.*) prince. **-céssa**†, F.: (*poet.*) princess.

prèn-dere [L.], IRR.§; TR.: take (grasp, seize, accept); direct one's self; catch; surprise: — *in fallo*, surprise; — *fondo*, cast anchor; — *terra*, land; REFL.: be taken: — *dell' amore*†, fall in love with. **-díbile**, ADJ.: takable. **-diménto**†, M.: taking: *secondo il mio* —, as I take it. **-ditóre**, M., **-ditríce**, F.: taker. **-ditoría**, F.: lottery-bank.

§ Ind.: Pret. *prè-si, -se; -sero*. Part. *preso*.

prenó-me [L. *præ-nomen*], M.: Christian name. **-mináto**, ADJ.: before named.

preno-táre [L. *præ-notare*], TR.: note before. **-táto**, PART. of *-tare*. **-tazióne**, F.: prenotion (foreknowledge).

prenun-ziáre [L. *præ-nuntiare*], TR.: announce before (foretell). **-ziáto**, PART. of *-ziare*. **-ziatóre**, M., **-ziatríce**, F.: foreteller. **prenún-zio**, M.: announcing before (prenunciation).

pre=occupáre, TR.: preoccupy. **-occupáto**, PART. of *-occupare*. **-occupazióne**, F.: preoccupation.

pre=onoráto, ADJ.: honoured before.

pre=opinánte, M.: proponent.

preordi-náre [*pre, o.*], TR.: preordain (predetermine). **-náto**, PART. of *-nare*. **-nazióne**, F.: preordination.

prepara-ménto, M.: preparing; preparation. ‖**prepará-re** [L. *præ-parare*], TR.: prepare (make ready); adapt. **-tívo**, ADJ.: preparative. **-tóre**, M., **-tríce**, F.: preparer. **-tório**, ADJ.: preparatory. **-zióne**, F.: preparation.

preponde-ránte, PART. of *-rare;* ADJ.: preponderant. **-ránza**, F.: preponderance (outweighing). ‖**-ráre** [L.], INTR.: preponderate (outweigh); prevail. **-razióne**, F.: preponderance (outweighing).

pre=pórre, IRR.; TR.: put before (place above); prefer; promote (raise). **-pósi**,

PRET. of -porre. -poṣitívo, ADJ.: prepositive. -pòṣito, M.: provost. -poṣitúra, F.: prepositure (provostship). -poṣizióne, F.: placing before; preposition.
prepossènte [L. *præ-potens*], ADJ.: very powerful (superior).
pre-posteraménte†, ADV.: preposterously. ‖**-pòstero** [L. *præ-posterus*], ADJ.: preposterous (inverted, absurd).
pre=pósto, PART. of -porre; ADJ.: placed before; preferred (selected); advanced; M.: provost (dignitary).
prepotèn-te [L. *præ-potens*], ADJ.: very powerful; M.: tyrant. -**tèllo**, *dim.* of -*te*. -**teménte**, ADV.: tyrannically. -**tóne**, *aug.* of -*te*. **prepotèn-za**, F.: tyranny.
prepúzio [L. *præputium*], M.: prepuco.
prerogatí-va [L.], F.: prerogative (privilege). -**vaménte**, ADV.: prerogatively.
prerúttoo†, ADJ.: rugged (rough).
pré-sa [-*so*], F.: taking (capturing); grasp; prize (capture); prize-money; handle; dose (of medicine); pinch (small quantity); holder; (*agr.*) division of land: *dar* —, give occasion; *dar le -se*, give occasion; *venire alle -se*, come to blows; *di prima* —†, at first sight. -**sácchio**, M.: top of the handle (of a spade).
pre-ṣágio [L. *præ-sagium*], M.: presaging; presage (omen). -**ṣagíre**, TR.: presage (foretell); INTR.: presage. -**ṣágo**, M.: presager (foreteller).
presáme [-*so*], M.: rennet.
prèṣbi-ta†, ‖**prèṣbi-te** [Gr. -*bútes*, old], ADJ.: long-sighted; M.: long-sighted person. -**terále**, ADJ.: presbyterial (clerical). -**teráto**, M.: presbyterate (presbyteryship, priesthood). -**terianiṣmo**, M.: presbyterianism. -**teriáno**, ADJ., M.: presbyterian. -**tèrio**, M.: presbytery (body of elders); presbyterium.
pre=ṣcégliere, IRR.; TR.: choose before. -**ṣcélsi**, PRET. of -*scegliere*. -**ṣcélto**, PART. of -*scegliere*.
prèṣcia†, F.: haste (urgency).
pre=ṣciènte, ADJ.: prescient (foreknowing). =**ṣciènza**, F.: prescience (foresight).
pre=ṣcíndere, INTR.: prescind.
preṣcíto†, ADJ.: foreseen; damned.
preṣciútto [*prosciugare*], M.: ham.
prescri-ttíbile, ADJ.: prescriptible. -**ttívo**, ADJ.: prescriptive. **prescríssi**, PRET. of -*vere*. -**prescrí-tto**, PART. of -*vere*; ADJ.: prescribed (appointed); M.: prescript. ‖**prescrí-vere** [*pre-*, *s.* .], IRR.; TR.: prescribe (appoint, order); limit (fix); INTR.: prescribe (claim). -**viménto**, M.: order. -**zióne**, F.: prescription (recipe); claim.
pre=sedére, IRR.; INTR.: preside. -**sedúto**, PART. of -*dere*. -**seggènza**, F.: presidency.

preṣen-tábile, ADJ.: presentable. -**tagióne**†, F.: presentation. -**táneo**†, ADJ.: quick (Eng.† presentaneous). -**táre**, TR.: present (bestow, introduce, offer); REFL.: present one's self. -**táto**, PART. of -*tare*; M.: one presented (introduced). -**tazióne**, F.: presentation (offering, introduction). ‖**preṣèn-te** [L. *præsens*], ADJ.: present (existing, immediate); M.: present (time or person); present tense; gift: *al* —, at present; *di* —, presently. -**teménte**, ADV.: presently (at once); in person†.
presentiménto [-*sentire*], M.: presentiment (apprehension).
preṣentíno, M.: *dim.* of -*te*; small gift.
pre=sentíre, TR.: forebode (presage); INTR.: have a presentiment.
preṣentúccio, M.: *disp. dim.* of -*te*.
preṣèn-za, -**zia**† [-*te*], F.: presence; readiness (promptness); appearance (port): *di* —, in person. -**ziále**, ADJ.: present (Eng.† presential). -**zialménte**, ADV.: in presence (personally). -**ziáre**, INTR., TR.: be present.
pre-ṣèpe [L. *præ-sæpe* (*sæpes*, fence)], M.: (*poet.*) manger; stable. -**ṣèpio**, M.: manger (where Christ was born); stable.
preserèlla, *dim.* of *presa*.
preserva-ménto, M.: preservation. ‖**preservá-re** [L. *præservare*], TR.: preserve (keep, sustain); shield. -**tívo**, ADJ.: preservative. -**tóre**, -**tríce**, F.: preserver. -**zióne**, F.: preservation.
pré-si, PRET. of -*ndere*. -**siccio**, ADJ.: taken (caught); M.: captured bird.
prèsi-de [L. -*des* (*sedere*, SIT)], M.: president; rector. -**dènte**, ADJ.: presiding (ruling); M.: president. -**dentéssa**, F.: president. -**dènza**, F.: presidency (office or dignity); presidential residence. -**denziále**, ADJ.: presidential. -**diáre**, TR.: garrison (defend). -**diário**, ADJ.: presidiary (pertaining to a garrison). -**diáto**, PART. of -*diare*. **presí-dio**, M.: garrison; defence; protection; powerful remedy. -**èdere** (*pop.*) = *presedere*.
prèṣio†, M.: value (worth).
preṣistimazióne†, F.: great esteem (preference).
preṣmóne†, M.: must (from unpressed grapes).
préso, PART. of *prendere*.
preṣon-t. ., -**z**. . = *presun-t*. ., -*z*. .
preṣopop. . = *prosopop*. .
près-sa, F.: press (machine); crowd; eagerness (haste). -**sa=cárte**, M.: paper-weight. -**sánte**, PART. of -*sare*; ADJ.: pressing. -**sa=ppòco**, ADV.: nearly (almost). -**sáre**, TR.: press (squeeze); urge (solicit). -**satúra**, F.: press; en-

treaty†. **-sézza**†, F.: nearness. **-sióne**, F.: pression (pressing). ‖**près-so** [L. *-sus*], ADV., PREP.: near (close by); almost; about: — —†, near by; — *a poco*, nearly (almost); M. PL.: vicinity; ADJ.: near (close). **-so=chè** *-é*, ADV.: nearly. **-sóre**†, M.: presser. **-súra**, F.: pressure (crushing); oppression.

prèsta†, F.: lending; loan.

pre=stabilíre, TR.: preëstablish.

prestaménte†, ADV.: quickly.

prestaménto†, M.: lending; borrowing; loan.

pre-stánte, ADJ.: excellent (superior, rare). **-stanteménte**, ADV.: excellently. **-stánza**, F.: excellence (superiority, rarity); lending†; loan; tax (impost)†: *dare in* —, lend; *prendere in* —, borrow. **-stanziáre**†, TR.: tax. ‖**-stáre** [L. *præ-stare*, stand forth; offer], TR.: lend; give (grant): — *fede*, believe; — *giuramento*, give oath; — *orecchi*, listen. **-státo**, PART. of *-stare*. **-statóre**, M., **-statríce**, F.: usurer (lender). **-statúra**†, F.: lending; borrowing; loan. **-stazióne**, F.: revenue; loan†; tax†.

pre-stère†, M.: lightning. **-stévole**, ADJ.: ready (serviceable). ‖**-stézza** [*-sto*], F.: quickness (haste).

pre-stedigitazióne, F.: prestidigitation (juggling). **-stígia**†, F.: prestige (fascination, illusion). **-stigiáre**†, TR.: deceive (delude). **-stigiatóre**, M., **-stigiatríce**, F.: juggler (conjurer). ‖**-stígio** [L. *præstigium*], M.: prestige; juggling. **-stigióso**†, ADJ.: fascinating; deceitful.

prestíno, ADV.: rather quick.

prè-stita†, F., ‖**prè-stito** [*-stare*], M.: lending; borrowing; loan: *dare in* —, lend; *pigliare in* —, borrow. **prè-sto** 1, M.: loan; pawnbroker's shop.

prèsto 2 [L. *præstus*], ADJ.: ready (speedy, prompt); helpful; ADV.: readily (speedily, at once).

pre-sumènte, PART. of *-mere*. **-mènza**†, F.: presumption. ‖**-súmere** [L. *præsumere*], IRR.§; TR.: presume (take for granted); INTR.: presume (suppose, think). **-sumíbile**, ADJ.: presumable. **-sumibilménte**, ADV.: presumably. **-sumitóre**, M.: presumer (arrogant person). **-súnsi**, PRET. of *-sumere*. **-suntivaménte**, ADV.: presumptively. **-suntívo**, ADJ.: presumptive; apparent. **-súnto**, PART. of *-sumere*. **-suntuosággine**, F.: presumptuousness (arrogance). **-suntuosaménte**, ADV.: presumptuously (arrogantly). **-suntuosèllo**, **-suntuosétto**, *dim.* of *-suntuoso*. **-suntuosità**, F.: presumptuousness (arrogance). **-suntuóso**, ADJ.: presumptuous (arrogant). **-sunzióne**, F.: presumption (arrogance; probability; conjecture).

§ Pret. *pre-suméi* or *-súnsi*, *-súnse*; *-súnsero*. Part. *-súnto*.

presup-pórre [*pre*, *supporre*], IRR.; TR.: presuppose (take for granted). **-pósi**, PRET. of *-porre*. **-positívo**, ADJ.: serving for supposition. **-posizióne**, F.: presupposition. **-pósto**, PART. of *-porre*; ADJ.: presupposed; M.: presupposition (presumption).

presúra†, F.: taking (seizure, capture); rennet.

pre-tacchióne, *disp. aug.* of *-te*. **-táccio**, *disp.* of *-te*. **-táio**†, **-taiòlo**, ADJ.: fond of priests' company. **-taría**†, F.: number of priests. **-táticoo**†, **-táto**†, M.: priesthood. **-tazzuòlo**, *disp.* of *-te*. ‖**prè-te** [L. *-sbyter*, elder], M.: PRIEST (minister); bed-warming pan-holder.

pretèlle†, F. PL.: moulds (matrice).

preten-dènte, PART. of *-dere*; ADJ.: pretending; M.: pretender. ‖**pretèndere** [L. *præ-tendere*], IRR.; TR.: pretend (claim, assert); intend (propose); maintain. **-sióne**, F.: pretension (claim); pretext. **-sionóso**, ADJ.: pretentious (presuming). **-sóre**, M.: pretender. **-sionóso**, **-sióso**, ADJ.: pretentious (presuming).

preter- [L. *præter*, by, beyond], PREF.:

preter=íre, INTR.: fail of effect; TR.: omit; pass over. **-íto**, PART. of *-ire*; ADJ.: past. **pretèr-ito**, M.: preterite (past tense). **-izióne**, F.: preterition.

preter-mésso, PART. of *-mettere*; ADJ.: omitted. ‖**=méttere**, IRR.; TR.: pretermit (omit, pass over). **-missióne**, F.: omission.

preter=naturále, ADJ.: preternatural (strange). **-naturalménte**, ADV.: preternaturally (strangely).

pre-tésa, F.: pretence (pretext). ‖**-téso** [*-tendere*], PART. of *-tendere*: pretended.

pretésco [*prete*], ADJ.: priestly (clerical).

pre-tèsta [L. *prætexta* (*tegere*, weave)], F.: prætexta (Roman robe). **-testáto**, ADJ.: wearing the prætexta. **-tèsto**, M.: PRETEXT (pretence, show).

pre-tignuòlo, M.: poor priest. ‖**-tíno** [*-te*], ADJ.: of a priest (priest-); M.: *dim.* of *-te*. **-tísmo**, M.: priesthood. **-tóne**, *aug.* of *-te*. **-tònzolo**, *disp. dim.* of *-te*.

pretó-re [L. *prætor*], M.: pretor (Roman officer). **-ría**†, F.: pretorship. **-riáno**, ADJ.: pretorian. **pretò-rio**, ADJ.: pretorian; M.: pretorium (general's tent); residence (of a provincial governor).

pret-taménte, ADV.: plainly (honestly, sincerely). ‖**prèt-to** [*puretto*], ADJ.: pure (mere, unmixed).

pretúra [L. *pretura*], F.: pretorship.

pre-valénza, F.: prevalence (predominance). ‖**=valére**, IRR., INTR.: prevail (have the advantage over); REFL.: avail one's self of.

prevalie. .† = *prevaric*. .

pre-válso, **-valúto**, PART. of *-valere*; prevailed (predominant).

prevari-cáre [L. *præ-varicari*, walk crookedly], INTR.: prevaricate (turn from the right course, shuffle). **-cáto**, PART. of *-care*; ADJ.: prevaricated. **-catóre**, M., **-catrice**, F.: prevaricator. **-cazióne**, F.: prevarication (transgression, deceit).

pre-vedénza, F.: foresight (prudence). ‖**=vedére**, IRR., TR.: foresee; expect. **-vedíbile**, ADJ.: that may be foreseen. **-vedimento**, M.: prevision (foresight). **-vedúto**, PART. of *-vedere*.

pre-ven(i)ènte, ADJ.: preventing; preventive. **-veniménto**, M.: prevention; preoccupation. ‖**=veníre**, IRR., TR.: prevent (outstrip, anticipate); hinder (impede); prepossess. **-ventivaménte**, ADV.: previously. **-ventiváre**, TR.: prearrange (expenses). **-ventívo**, ADJ.: preventive. **-vènto**†, **-venúto**, PART. of *-venire*. **-venzióne**, F.: prevention; prepossession.

prevertíre†, TR.: pervert (seduce).

previdènza, F.: providence (foresight).

pre-viaménte, ADV.: previously. ‖**prèvio** [L. *præ-vius* (*via*, way)], ADJ.: previous (preceding).

pre-visióne [*-vedere*], F.: prevision (foresight). **-víso**†, **-vísto**, PART. of *-vedere*; ADJ.: foreseen.

prevòs-to [L. *præpositus*], M.: provost. **-túra**, F.: provostship.

pre-ziosaménte, ADV.: preciously. **-ziosità**, F.: preciousness. **-zióso**, ADJ.: precious (valuable). ‖**prè-zza**† [*-zzo*], F.: price (value); reward†. **-zzábile**, ADJ.: valuable (precious). **-zzáre**, TR.: prize (rate, set a price on); value (esteem). **-zzatóre**, M.: appraiser.

prezzémolo [Gr. *petrosélinon*], M.: PARSLEY.

pres-zévole†, ADJ.: precious (valuable). ‖**prèz-zo** [L. *pretium*], M.: PRICE (value); salary (pay); reward†: *a buon* —, cheap; *a caro* —, dear. **-zoláre**, TR.: bribe (corrupt). **-zoláto**, PART. of *-zolare*; ADJ.: bribed; hired.

pría [*prima*], ADV.: (*poet.*) before (first); rather (sooner).

pri-ègo†, F., ‖**-ègo** [*prego*], M.: (*poet.*) prayer (supplication).

prigió-na†, F.: prisoner. **-náre**†, TR.: imprison (captivate). **-nèlla**, *dim.* of *-na*. ‖**prigió-ne** [L. *prehensio*, seizing], F.: PRISON; M.: prisoner. **-nería**†, **-nía**, F.: imprisonment (confinement, captivity). **-nièra**, F., **-nière**, **-nièro**, M.: prisoner; jailer†.

prima [*-mus*], ADV.: before (first); sooner (rather: *come* —, as soon as; *da* —, in the beginning; *in* —, in the first place.

primáce. .† = *pinnace*. .

pri-máio†, ADJ.: first. **-maménte**, ADV.: first. **-mariaménte**, ADV.: primarily (in the first place). **-mário**, ADJ.: primary (first). **-másso**†, M.: chief man. **-máto**, M.: primate. **-matieciaménte**†, ADV.: early; first. **-matíccio**, ADJ.: early; first (primary)†. **-máto**, M.: highest place; ADJ.: first (chief). **-mavèra** [L. *ver*, spring], F.: spring. **-maveríle**, ADJ.: of spring. **-mazía**, F.: primacy. **-maziále**, ADJ.: primatical. **-meggiáre**, INTR.: excel (exceed). **-meggiáto**, PART. of *-meggiare*. **-meráno**†, ADJ.: first. **-miceriáto**, M.: deanship. **-micèrio**, M.: dean. **-mièra**, F.: primero (game at cards). **-mieraménte**, ADV.: first (in the first place). **-mierétta**, *car. dim.* of *-miera*. **-mieríno**, *dim.* of *-miera*. **-mièro**, ADJ.: first (former). **-migènio** [L. *-migenius* (*gignere*, beget)], ADJ.: primitive (first). **-mipiláre**, ADJ.: primipilar. **-mipílo** [L. *-mipilus* (*pilum*, javelin)], M.: first centurion. **-míssimo**, ADJ.: first. **-mitivaménte**, ADV.: primitively. **-mitívo**, ADJ.: primitive. **-mízia**, **-mízie**, F.: first fruits (Eng.† premices); new, delightful thing. ‖**prí-mo** [L. *-mus*], ADJ.: FIRST (foremost); primitive; chief; M.: first; forefather. **-mogènita**, F., **-mogènito**, M.: first-born (child). **-mogenitóre** [L. *genitor*, parent], M.: primogenitor (first father). **-mogenitríce**, F.: first mother. **-mogenitúra**, F.: primogeniture (birthright); seniority. **-mordiále** [L. *-mordialis* (*ordiri*, begin)], ADJ.: primordial (first in order).

prín-ce†, M.: prince (chief). **-cipále**, ADJ.: principal; M.: principal (chief). **-cipalità**, F.: principality (supreme power). **-cipalménte**, ADV.: principally. **-cipáre**†, TR.: domineer (govern). **-cipáto**, M.: principality; sovereignty. ‖**prín-cipe** [L. *-ceps* (*primus*, first, *caput*, head)], M.: PRINCE; CHIEF. **-cipescaménte**, ADV.: in a princely manner. **-cipésco**, ADJ.: princely. **-cipéssa**, princess. **-cipótto**, *dim.* of *-cipe*. **piaménto**†, M.: beginning. **-cipiánte**, ADJ.: beginning; M.: beginner (novice). **-cipiáre**, TR., INTR.: begin (commence). **-cipiáto**, PART. of *-cipiare*. **-cipiatívo**, ADJ.: serving to begin. **-cip**

dim. of *-cipe.* **-cìpio**, M.: principle; beginning; source: precepts. **-cipòtto**, *disp. dim.* of *-cipe.*

pri-óra, F.: prioress. **-orále**, ADJ.: of a prior. **-oráticо†**, **-oráto**, M.: priorship. ‖**-óre** [L. *-or*], M.: prior (priest below abbot). **-oría**, F.: priory; priorship. **-orísta**, M.: book (containing the names of the priors of a religious house). **-orità**, F.: priority. **-scaménte**, ADV.: formerly. **prí-sco**, ADJ.: former (ancient).

prìṣ-ma [Gr.], M.: prism. **-mático**, ADJ.: prismatic **-mètto**, **-mettíno**, *dim.* of *-ma.*

pristi-naménte, ADV.: formerly. ‖**prí-sti-no** [L. *-nus*], ADJ.: pristine (former).

priva-gióne†, F.: privation (lack). **-ménto**, M.: depriving. ‖**privá-re** [L.], TR.: deprive (take away from); REFL.: abstain from. **privá-ta†**, F.: sewer. **-taménte**, ADV.: privately. **-tiva-ménte**, ADV.: exclusively. **-tívo**, ADJ.: privative (depriving); exclusive. **privá-to**, PART. of *-re;* ADJ.: private; bereft; particular†; concealed†; M.†: privy. **-tó-re†**, M.: depriver. **-zióne**, F.: privation (need).

privìgno†, M.: stepson.

privi-legiáre, TR.: privilege (exempt). **-legiáto**, PART. of *-legiare;* ADJ.: privileged. ‖**-lègio** [L. *-legium* (*privus*, private; *lex*, law)], M.: privilege (right).

prìvo [L. *-vus*], ADJ.: deprived (*di*, lacking).

prizzáto†, ADJ.: spotted.

pro- [L.], PREF.: pro-, BEFORE. **prò** [L. *prodesse*], M.: good; advantage; ADJ.†: valiant (brave): *a che* —, of what use? *dare il buon* —, congratulate.

pro-áva, F.: great-grandmother. ‖**-ávo**, **-ávolo†**, M.: great-grandfather.

probábi-le [L. *-lis*], ADJ.: probable. **-lìṣmo**, M.: probabilism. **-lísta**, M.: probabilist. **-lità**, F.: probability. **-lménte**, ADV.: probably.

probaménte [*-bo*], ADV.: uprightly (honestly).

proba-tívo [L. *-tivus*], ADJ.: probative (proving). **-tòrio**, ADJ.: probatory. **-zióne†**, F.: proof; probation.

pròbbio†, M.: shame (infamy).

probità [*-bo*], F.: probity (integrity).

probivìri [L. *probi*, good, *viri*, men], M.: commissioners (commission).

problè-ma [Gr. *próblema*], M.: problem. **-maticaménte**, ADV.: problematically. **-maticità**, F.: quality of that which is problematic. **-mático**, pl. —*ci*, ADJ.: problematical. **-míno**, *dim.* of *-ma.* **-móne**, *aug.* of *-ma.*

pròbo [L. *-bus*], ADJ.: good (upright).

probòscide [Gr. *-boskís*], F.: proboscis.

proca-ccévole†, ADJ.: industrious. **procá-ccia**, pl. *-ccia* or *-cci*, M.: messenger. **-cciaménto**, M.: procuring. **-cciánte**, PART. of *-cciare;* ADJ.: diligent. **-cciá-re**, TR.: procure (get); endeavour; REFL.: procure one's self; strive†. **-cciáto**, PART. of *-cciare.* **-cciatóre**, M., **-cciatrice**, F.: industrious person. **procáccio**, M.: provision; letter-carrier. ‖**procá-ce** [L. *procax* (*procor*, ask)], ADJ.: bold (pert, saucy; wayward; Eng.† procacious). **-ceménte**, ADV.: saucily; petulantly. **procá-cia**, **-cità**, F.: impudence (Eng.† procacity).

procántо†, M.: preface (preamble).

proc-cianaménte†, ADV.: next. **-ciáno†**, ADJ.: near.

proccúr..† = *procur..*

proce-dènte, PART. of *-dere.* ‖**procè-dere** [L.], IRR. (cf. *concedere*); INTR.: proceed (advance); act; issue; conduct one's self. **-diménto**, M.: proceeding; progress. **-dúra**, F.: proceeding (transaction). **-dúto**, PART. of *-dere.*

procèl-la [L.], F.: storm; peril. **-lária**, F.: stormy-petrel (bird). **-lóso**, ADJ.: stormy (tempestuous).

proces-sánte, PART. of *-sare;* M.: prosecutor (plaintiff). ‖**-sáre** [*procedere*], TR.: sue (go to law). **-sáto**, PART. of *-sare.*

procès-si, PRET. of *procedere.* **-sional-ménte**, ADV.: in procession. **-sionáre**, INTR.: go in a procession. **-sióne**, F.: procession. **-sívo†**, ADJ.: proceeding (progressive). **procès-so**, M.: process (trial); progress: *far* — *ad uno*, sue one. **-suále**, ADJ.: of a process. **-súra†**, F.: proceeding(s); indictment; process.

pròci [L. *-cus*], M. PL.: suitors (of Penelope); fawner.

procínto [L. *-nctus*], M.: PRECINCT†; circuit†: in *essere* (or *mettersi*) *in* —, be on the point of.

procióne [Gr. *pro-kúon*, dog], M.: Procyon (star); glutton (an animal).

procissióne [*-cessione*], F.: procession.

proclá-ma, M.: proclamation. ‖**-máre** [L.], TR.: proclaim. **-mazióne**, F.: proclamation.

proclítico, pl. —*ci* [Gr. (*klínein*, lean)], ADJ., M.: proclitic.

proclí-ve [L. *-vis*], ADJ.: inclined (Eng.† proclive); M.†: propensity. **-vità**, F.: proclivity (inclination).

pròco†, pl. —*ci*, M.: suitor (lover).

procòio†, M.: herd of cattle.

pro-combènte, ADJ.: procumbent (prone). ‖**-cómbere** [L. *-cumbere*], INTR.: (poet.) fall forward.

pro-consoláre, ADJ.: proconsular. **-consoláto**, M.: proconsulship. ‖**-cònsolo**

[L. *-consul*], M.: proconsul. **-cònsolo,** M.: proconsul: *pescare per il* —, work in vain.

procrastiná-re [L. (*cras*, to-morrow)], INTR.: procrastinate (postpone, delay). **-tóre,** M.: procrastinator. **-zióne,** F.: procrastination (delay).

procrea-ménto, M.: procreating; generation. ‖**procreá-re** [L.], TR.: procreate (beget). **-tóre,** M., **-tríce,** F.: procreator.

procú-ra, F.: procuration (attorney's letter); attorney's office (or residence). ‖**-ráre** [L.], TR., INTR.: procure (obtain, attain); act as attorney†. **-ratía,** F.: office (or residence) of attorney. **-ratóre,** M.: procurer; attorney; procurator. **-razióne,** F.: procuration. **-rería**†, F.: attorney's office. **procú-ro**†, M.: procuration.

pròda [*prora*], F.: shore; edge; prow†.

prò-de [OFr.], ADJ.: valiant (brave, Eng.† PROW); M.†: profit. **-deménte,** ADV.: valiantly (bravely). **-dézza,** F.: prowess (valour, bravery).

pro-dicèlla, ‖**-dicína** [*-da*], *car. dim.* of *-da*. **-dière, -dièro,** M.: head-rower.

prodiga-líssimo, M.: very (or most) prodigal. **-lità,** F.: prodigality (extravagance). **-lizzáre,** TR.: squander (be prodigal). **-lménte, -ménte,** ADV.: prodigally (extravagantly). ‖**prodigá-re** [L. (*agere*, drive)], TR.: squander (be prodigal).

prodí-gio [L. *-gium*], M.: prodigy (wonder). **-giosaménte,** ADV.: prodigiously. **-giosità,** F.: prodigiousness. **-gióso,** ADJ.: prodigious.

pròdigo [L. *-gus*], ADJ.: prodigal (lavish); M.: prodigal.

prodíssimo [*-de*], ADJ.: very (or most) valiant.

prodi-tóre†, M.: traitor. **-toriaménte,** ADV.: traitorously. ‖**-tòrio** [L. *-tor*], ADJ.: traitorous (perfidious).

pro=dittatóre, M.: pro-dictator.

prodizióne†, F.: treachery.

prodótto, PART. of *-durre;* M.: product; fruit.

pròdromo [Gr. *pró-dromos*], M.: forerunner (Eng.† prodrome).

produ-cènte, PART. of *-rre;* ADJ.: producing. ‖**prodú-cere**† [L.], IRR. (cf. *-rre*); TR.: produce (bring forth); cause; lengthen†. **-cíbile,** ADJ.: producible. **-ciménto,** M.: producing; production. **-citóre,** M., **-citríce,** F.: producer.

produòmo†, M.: brave man.

pro-dúrre [L. *-ducere*], IRR. (cf. *addurre*); TR.: PRODUCE (bring forth); cause. **-dússi,** PRET. of *-durre.* **-duttíbile**†, ADJ.: producible. **-duttività,** F.: productiveness. **-duttívo,** ADJ.: productive. **-dútto**†, PART. of *-durre;* ADJ.: produced. **-duttóre,** M., **-duttríce,** F.: producer. **-duzióne,** F.: production.

proe-miále, ADJ.: prefatory (introductory). **-mialménte,** ADV.: by way of introduction. **-miáre,** TR.: preface. ‖**proè-mio** [L. *proœmium*], M.: preface (preamble, PROEM).

profa-naménte, ADV.: profanely. **-naménto,** M.: profanation. **-náre,** TR.: profane (desecrate, abuse). **-náto,** PART. of *-nare;* ADJ.: profaned. **-natóre,** M., **-natríce,** F.: profaner. **-nazióne,** F.: profanation. **-nità,** F.: profanity (irreverence). ‖**profá-no** [L. *-nus*], ADJ.: profane (irreverent, impious).

profèn-da [*prebenda*], F.: provender (feed). **-dáre**†, TR.: give provender to.

profe-rènte, PART. of *-rire.* **-ríbile,** ADJ.: utterable. **-riménto,** M.: uttering. ‖**-ríre** [L. *-rre*], TR.: utter (pronounce). **-ríto,** PART. of *-rire;* ADJ.: uttered. **-ritóre,** M.: utterer.

profes-sáre, TR.: profess (avow); exercise (a calling). **-sáto,** PART. of *-sare;* ADJ.: professed. **-satóre**†, M.: professor. **-sionále,** ADJ.: professional. **-sióne,** F.: profession (declaration); calling; religious order. **-sionísta,** M.: professional person. ‖**profès-so** [L. *-sus*], ADJ.: professed; M.: professed monk. **-sóra,** F.: professor. **-sorále,** ADJ.: professorial. **-sóre,** M.: professor. **-soriále,** ADJ.: professorial (belonging to a professor). **-soróne,** *aug.* of *-sore.*

profè-ta [L. *propheta*], M.: prophet. **-tále**†, ADJ.: prophetical. **-tánte,** PART. of *-tare.* **-táre,** TR.: prophesy (predict). **-teggiáre**†, TR.: prophesy (foretell). **-téssa,** F.: prophetess. **-tezzáre**†, TR.: prophesy (predict). **-ticaménte,** ADV.: prophetically. **profè-tico,** pl. *—ci,* ADJ.: prophetic. **-tizzáre,** TR.: prophesy (predict). **-zía,** F.: prophecy (prediction).

proffe-ráre†, TR.: utter (pronounce); proffer. **-rènza**†, F.: proffer (offering). **-rère**†, TR.: proffer (offer). **-ríbile,** ADJ.: that can be proffered. **-riménto,** M.: proffering. ‖**-ríre** [L. *proferre*], IRR. (cf. *offerire*); TR.: proffer (offer); show; REFL.: offer one's self. **-ríto** PART. of *-rire;* ADJ.: proffered. **proffè-rta,** F.: proffer (offering, propo... **proffè-rto,** PART. of *-rire;* ADJ.: ...fered; M.†: offer.

profiláre†, TR.: draw in profile.

proficiènte [L. *-ciens*], ADJ.: pro... (well-skilled).

pro-ficuaménte, ADV.: profitably. ...**cuo** [L. *-ficuus*], ADJ.: profitable (...

profiguráto†, ADJ.: compared.

profi-laménto, M.: profile drawing. ‖**-láre** [*-lo*], TR.: draw in profile.

profi-lássi [Gr. *phulássein*, guard], F.: prophylaxis. **-láttico**, pl. *—ci*, ADJ.: prophylactic.

pro-filáto, PART. of *-filare;* ADJ.: drawn in profile. **-filatúra**, F.: profile drawing; border. ‖**=fílo**, M.: profile; side-view.

profit-tábile†, ADJ.: profitable. **-táre**, INTR.: profit (make progress); be profitable; make profitable. **-tévole**, ADJ.: profitable. **-tevolménte**, ADV.: profitably. ‖**profít-to** [L. *profectus*], M.: profit (benefit).

profluvio [L. *-vius*], M.: overflowing (abundance).

profón-da†, F.: profundity. **-daménte**, ADV.: profoundly. **-daménto**, M.: sinking down. ‖**-dáre** [*-do*], INTR.: sink; perish; REFL.: sink; drown; TR.: sink (submerge); deepen. **-dataménte**†, ADV.: profoundly (very deeply). **-dáto**, PART. of *-dare;* ADJ.: sunk. **-dazióne**†, F.: digging.

pro=fóndere, IRR.; TR.: pour out abundantly; spend lavishly.

pro-fondità, F.: profundity (depth). ‖**-fóndo** [L. *-fundus*], ADJ.: profound (deep); ADV.: profoundly; M.: depth.

pròfugo [L. *-gus*], ADJ.: fugitive (wandering); M.: fugitive.

profu-maménto†, M.: perfuming; perfume. **-máre**, TR.: perfume. **-mataménte**, ADV.: delicately; finely. **-máto**, PART. of *-mare;* ADJ.: perfumed. **-matóre**, M., **-matríce**, F.: perfumer. **-matúzzo**†, M.: beau (fop). **-mería**, F.: perfumery (perfumer's shop or business). **profú-mico**†, M.: perfume. **-mièra**, F.: perfuming-vase. **-mière**, M.: perfumer. **-míno**†, M.: perfuming-pan. ‖**profú-mo** [*pro, fumo*], M.: perfume; flattery. **-móso**†, ADJ.: perfumed.

pro-fusaménte, ADV.: profusely. **-fúsi**, PRET. of *-fondere*. **-fusióne**, F.: profusion (abundance). ‖**-fúso**, PART. of *-fondere;* ADJ.: profuse (lavish).

progè-nie [L. *-nies*], F.: progeny (issue). **-nitóre**, M., **-nitríce**, F.: progenitor.

pro-gettáre, TR.: project (scheme). ‖**-gètto** [L. *-jectus*], M.: project (design).

progiudicáre = *pregiudicare*.

prò-gnosi [Gr. *prógnosis*], F.: prognosis. **-gnosticáre** = *-nosticare*, TR.: prognosticate (foreshow). **-gnòstico**, M.: prognostic.

prográmma [Gr.], M.: programme.

progre-diménto, M.: progression. **-díre** [L. *-di*], INTR.: proceed (advance). **-díto**, PART. of *-dire;* ADJ.: advanced. **-ssióne**, F.: progression (advance). **-ssionísta**, M.: progressionist. **-ssivaménte**, ADV.: progressively. **-ssívo**, ADJ.: progressive (advancing). **progrè-sso**, M.: progress (advance).

proibí-re [L. *prohibere* (*pro*, before, *habere*, have)], TR.: prohibit (interdict). **-tívo**, ADJ.: prohibitory. **proibí-to**, PART. of *-re;* ADJ.: prohibited. **-tóre**, M., **-tríce**, F.: prohibiter. **-zióne**, F.: prohibition.

pro-iciènte [L. *-icere*], ADJ.: projecting (throwing); M.: person (or thing) projecting. **-iettáre**, TR.: project (cast forward); devise. **-ièttile**, **-iètto**, M.: projectile. **-iettúra**†, F.: projection (jutting out). **-iezióne**, F.: projection (hurling); plan.

pro-lagáre†, INTR.: make a prologue. ‖**pròla-go** [*prologo*], M.: prologue.

prolásso [L. *-lapsus*], M.: prolapsus (falling down of a part of the body).

prolá-to†, ADJ.: uttered (spoken). **-tóre**†, M.: pronouncer. **-zióne**†, F.: pronunciation (prolation).

pròle [L. *-les*], F.: progeny (offspring).

prolegòmeni [Gr. *prolegómena* (*pro*, before, *légein*, say)], M. PL.: prolegomena (introductory discourse).

pro-lèpsi [Gr. *prolépsis*], **-lèssi**, F.: prolepsis (a rhetorical figure).

prole-tariáto, M.: proletariat. ‖**-tário** [L. *-tarius*], M.: proletary (base-born person).

pro-lificáre, TR.: generate. ‖**-lífico** [L. *proles*, offspring, *facere*, make], ADJ.: prolific (productive).

pro-lissaménte, ADV.: prolixly. **-lissità**, F.: prolixity (length). ‖**-lísso** [L. *-lixus*], ADJ.: prolix (long, diffuse).

prolo-gáre†, INTR.: make a prologue. **-gatóre**†, M.: maker (or speaker) of a prologue. **-ghétto**, **-ghíno**, dim. of *-go*. **-gizzáre**†, INTR.: make a prologue. ‖**pròlo-go** [L. *-gus*], M.: prologue; prologue-speaker.

prolúdere [L.], IRR. (cf. *alludere*; INTR.: prelude (begin, introduce).

prolungá-bile, ADJ.: prolongable. **-ménto**, M.: prolongation. ‖**prolungá-re** [L. *prolongare*], TR.: prolong (lengthen); defer. **-taménte**, ADV.: lengthily (diffusedly). **-tóre**, M., **-tríce**, F.: prolonger. **-zióne**, F.: prolongation (lengthening); delay.

pro-lusióne, F.: prelude (prolusion). ‖**-lúso**, PART. of *-ludere*.

pro=memòría, F.: memorandum.

pròmere†, TR.: disclose (tell).

pro-méssa, F.: promise; security†. **-messióne**†, F.: promise. **-mésso**, PART. of *-mettere;* ADJ.: promised. **-mettén-te**, PART. of *-mettere*. ‖**=méttere** [L.

-*méttere*], IRR.; TR.: promise (assure); REFL.: promise one's self. -**mettitóre**, M., -**mettitrice**, F.: promiser.
promi-nènte [L. -*nere*], ADJ.: prominent (jutting). -**nènza**, F.: prominence.
promis-cuaménte, ADV.: promiscuously. -**cuità**, F.: promiscuousness. ||**promí-s-cuo** [L. -*cuus*], ADJ.: promiscuous (mingled).
promís-i, PRET. of *promettere*. -**sióne**, F.: promise. -**sòrio**, ADJ.: promissory.
promontòrio [L. -*rium*], M.: promontory.
promò-ssi, PRET. of -*vere*. **promò-sso**, PART. of -*vere*. -**tóre**, M., -**trice**, F.: promoter. -**vènte**, ADJ.: promoting. ||**promò-vere** [*pro-*, *m*..], IRR.; TR.: promote (forward); elevate. -**viménto**, M.: promotion. -**vitóre**, M., -**vitrice**, F.: promoter. -**zióne**, F.: promotion.
promulgá-re [L.], TR.: promulgate (announce, publish). -**tívo**, ADJ.: that can be promulgated. -**tóre**, M., -**trice**, F.: promulgator. -**zióne**, F.: promulgation (declaration).
pro=muòvere = -*movere*.
promutáre†, TR.: exchange.
prònao [Gr. *pró-naos*, temple], M.: pronaos (vestibule of a temple).
pro-nepóte†, ||-**nipóte** [L. -*nepos*], M.: nephew's son; PL.: descendants.
próno [L. -*nus*], ADJ.: prone (inclined).
pronó-me [L. -*men*], M.: pronoun. -**minále**, ADJ.: pronominal. -**mináto**, ADJ.: renowned.
pronosti-caménto, M., -**cánza**†, F.: prognostication. -**cáre**, TR.: prognosticate (predict); INTR.: make a prediction. -**catóre**, M., -**catrice**, F.: prognosticator. -**cazióne**, F.: prognostication (predicting). ||**pronòsti-co**, pl. -*ci* [Gr. *pró-gnosis*], M.: prognostic (omen).
pron-taménte, ADV.: promptly (readily). -**táre**†, TR.: importune; INTR., REFL.: strive. -**tézza**, -**titúdine**†, F.: promptitude (readiness). **prón-to** [L. *promptus*], ADJ.: prompt (ready, quick); ADV.: promptly. -**tuário**, M.: promptuary (store-house).
prònu-ba [L.], F.: bridesmaid. **prònubo**, M.: bridesman.
pronúnz.. = *pronunz..*
pronún-zia, F.: pronunciation. -**ziábile**, ADJ.: pronounceable. -**ziaménto**, M.: pronunciation (utterance). ||-**ziáre** [L. -*ciare*], TR.: pronounce (utter); INTR.: speak; REFL.: declare one's self. -**ziatívo**, ADJ.: pronunciative. -**ziáto**, PART. of -*ziare*; ADJ.: pronounced. -**ziatóre**, M., -**ziatrice**, F.: pronouncer. -**ziazióne**†, F.: pronunciation.
propa-gábile, ADJ.: propagable. -**ga-ménto**, M.: propagation (increase). -**gánda**, F.: propaganda. -**gandísta**, M.: propagandist. -**gánte**, PART. of -*gare*. ||-**gáre** [L.], TR.: propagate (increase, spread); REFL.: be propagated. -**gáto**, PART. of -*gare*; ADJ.: propagated. -**gatóre**, M., -**gatrice**, F.: propagator. -**gazióne**, F.: propagation. -**gginaménto**, M.: propagation (by layers). -**gginare**, TR.: propagate (provine). -**ggináto**, PART. of -*gginare*; ADJ.: propagated (by layers). -**gginatóre**, M.: propagator. -**gginazióne**, F.: provining. **propá-ggine**, F.: vine-layer (or sucker).
propalá-re [L. (-*m*, openly)], TR.: divulge (publish). -**tóre**, M.: divulger. -**zióne**, F.: publication.
pro=parossítono, ADJ.: proparoxytone.
pròpe†, ADV.: near (at hand).
pro=pèndere, INTR.: propend (incline, be disposed to).
propensáre†, TR.: premeditate.
propensióne [-*pendere*], F.: propensity (disposition).
pro=perispòmeno, M.: properispome.
propilèo [Gr. *pro-púlaios* (*púle*, gate)], M.: propylæum (vestibule).
propí-na, F.: examiner's fee. ||-**náre** [L.], TR.: drink the health of (Eng.† propine).
pro-pinquaménte†, ADV.: near (hard by). -**pinquità**†, F.: propinquity. ||-**pínquo** [L. *pinquus*], ADJ.: near (nigh); related.
pròpio = *proprio*, ADJ.: proper (fit); own (peculiar); ADV.: properly; M.†: peculiar quality; ownership.
propi-ziáre, TR.: propitiate (conciliate). -**ziatóre**, M.: propitiator. -**ziatòrio**, ADJ.: propitiatory. -**ziazióne**, F.: propitiation. ||**propí-zio** [L. -*tius*], ADJ.: propitious (kind, favorable).
pròpoli [L. -*s*], F.: propolis.
propo-nènte, PART. of -*nere*; ADJ.: proposing. ||**propó-nere** [L.], IRR.; TR.: propose (set forth, declare). -**níbile**, ADJ.: that can be proposed. -**nimentáccio**, *disp.* of -*nimento*. -**niménto** purpose (intent); resolution. -**r** M.: proposer. **propó-rre**, IRR. *re*); TR.: propose (set fo
proporzio-nábile ble. -**nabilménte** ably. -**nále**, ADJ. **lità**, F.: proporti ADV.: proportional portion (adjust). proportionately. - ADJ.: proportioned proportions. ||**prop** *tio*], F.: proportio

vole, ADJ.: proportionable. **-nevolménte**, ADV.: proportionately.
propòscide = *proboscide*.
propó-si, PRET. of *-nere*. **-sitíssimo**, ADJ.: *a* —, very opportunely. **propòsito**, M.: purpose (design); cause; subject: *a* —, to the purpose (opportunely); *con* —, intentionally. **-sitúra**, F.: provostship. **-sizióne**, F.: proposition; proposal; maxim. **propó-sta**, F.: proposition. **-státo†**, M., **-stía†**, F.: provostship. **propó-sto**, PART. of *-nere* and *-rre*; ADJ.: proposed; M.: provost; purpose†.
propréso†, M.: enclosure (circumference).
propretóre [L. *-prætor*], M.: proprætor (Roman magistrate).
pro-priaménte, ADV.: properly; peculiarly. **-prietà**, F.: property (attribute); possession (ownership). **-prietário**, M.: proprietor. ‖**prò-prio** [L. *-prius*], ADJ.: proper (fit); own (peculiar); apt; ADV.: properly; M.†: peculiar quality; ownership: *amor* —, self-love.
propu-gnácolo, **-gnáculo†**, M.: fortress (rampart). ‖**-gnáre** [*pro-*, *p*. .], TR.: defend (resist; Eng.† propugn). **-gnatóre**, M., **-gnatrice**, F.: defender; supporter. **-gnazióne**, F.: defence.
propul-sáre [L.], TR.: repel (drive back). **-satóre**, M.: repeller. **-sióne**, F.: propulsion.
proquestóre, M.: proquæstor (Roman official).
proquóio†, M.: black cattle.
pròra [L.], F.: PROW (of a ship).
pròro-ga, F.: prorogation (lengthening). **-gábile**, ADJ.: that can be prorogued. ‖**-gáre** [L.], TR.: prorogue (prolong). **-gatíva†**, F.: prerogative; insolence. **-gazióne**, F.: prorogation (delay).
pro-rompènte, PART. of *-rompere*. ‖=**rómpere**, IRR.; INTR.: break forth (rush out). **-rompiménto**, M.: breaking forth. **-rótto**, PART. of *-rompere*. **-rúppi**, PRET. of *-rompere*.
prò-sa [L.], F.: prose. **-sáccia**, *disp.* of *-sa*. **-saicaménte**, ADV.: prosaically. **-sáico**, pl. —*ci*, ADJ.: prosaic. **-saísmo**, M.: prosaism.
prosápia [L.], F.: progeny (race, lineage).
prosá-re†, TR.: write (or speak) in prose; INTR.: joke. **-sticità**, F.: prosaic quality. ‖**prosá-stico** [*prosa*], ADJ.: prosaic. **-tóre**, M., **-tríce**, F.: prose-writer.
proscènio [L. *-nium* (*scena*, stage)], M.: proscenium.
prosciògliere IRR.; TR.: absolve (from a vow). **-sciogligióne†**, F., **-sciogliménto**, M.: absolution. **-sciòlsi**, PRET. of *-sciogliere*. **-sciòlto**, PART. of *-sciogliere*; ADJ.: absolved (freed). **-sciòrre** = *-sciogliere*; IRR.; TR.: absolve (from a vow).
prosciugáre, TR.: dry up. **-sciugáto**, PART. of *-sciugare*; ADJ.: dried. **-sciútto**, M.: gammon of bacon (ham).
pro-scrissi, PRET. of *-scrivere*. **-scrítto**, PART. of *-scrivere*; ADJ.: proscribed; M.: proscribed man. ‖=**scrívere**, IRR.; TR.: proscribe (banish). **-scrizióne**, F.: proscription.
prosecuzióne [L. *-cutio*], F.: prosecution (pursuit).
proseggiáre [*-sa*], INTR.: write in prose.
prose-guiménto, M.: prosecution (pursuit). ‖**-guíre** [L. *-qui*], TR.: prosecute (pursue, continue); go on. **-guitáre†**, TR.: pursue.
prose-litísmo, M.: proselytism. ‖**-lito** [L. *-litus*], M.: proselyte (disciple).
prosétta, *dim.* of *-sa*.
pro-sodía [L.], F.: prosody; treatise upon prosody. **-sòdico**, pl. —*ci*, **-sodíaco**, pl. —*ci*, ADJ.: prosodical.
prosóne†, M.: prosy fellow.
prosopo-pèa [L. *-peia*], F.: prosopopeia (rhetorical figure). **-pèico**, pl. —*ci*, ADJ.: pertaining to prosopopeia.
prospe-raménte, ADV.: prosperously. **-raménto**, M.: prospering. **-ráre**, INTR.: prosper (succeed); TR.: give success (favour). **-razióne†**, F.: prosperity. **-révole**, ADJ.: prosperous. **-revolménte**, ADV.: prosperously. **-rità**, F.: prosperity. ‖**pròspe-ro** [*-rus*], ADJ.: prosperous (thriving, fortunate). **-rosaménte**, ADV.: prosperously. **-róso**, ADJ.: prosperous (successful); stout.
pro-spettáre, TR.: see prospectively. **-spèttico**, pl. —*ci*, ADJ.: perspective. **-spettíva**, F.: perspective (art or painting). **-spettivísta**, M.: painter of perspective. **-spettívo†**, ADJ.: prospective. ‖**-spètto** [L. *-spectus* (*-spicere*, look forward)]; M.: prospect (view); design.
prossi-maménte, ADV.: next. **-mánо†**, ADJ.: near; kindred. **-mánza†**, F.: proximity. **-míssimo**, ADJ.: very (or most) near. **-mità**, F.: proximity; relationship. ‖**pròssi-mo** [L. *proximus*], ADJ.: near (next, neighbouring); related; M.: neighbour.
prò-stata [Gr. *-státes* (*statós*, placed)], F.: prostate. **-stático**, pl. —*ci*, ADJ.: prostate.
pro=stèndere, IRR.; TR.: prostrate (cast down); stretch; REFL.: prostrate one's self; stretch one's self.
proster-náre, TR.: throw down; REFL.: prostrate one's self. **-nazióne**, F.: prostration. ‖**prostèr-nere†** [L.], IRR.; TR.: prostrate (cast down); REFL.: prostrate one's self.

pròstesi [Gr. *prósthesis* (*pros*, before, *thésis*, putting)], F.: prosthesis (grammatical figure).

prostéso, PART. of *-stendere;* ADJ.: thrown down (prostrate); M.: prostrate person.

prosti-tuíre [L. *-tuere*], TR.: prostitute. **-túta**, F.: prostitute. **-tuzióne**, F.: prostitution.

pro-stramènto, M.: prostration. ‖**-stráre** [L. *-stratus*], TR.: prostrate (throw down); REFL.: prostrate one's self. **-stráto**, PART. of *-strare;* ADJ.: prostrated. **-strazióne**, F.: prostration.

prosùccia, *disp. dim.* of *-sa*.

prosum. . = *presum*. .

pro=suòcero, M.: father-in-law's father.

protagonísta [Gr. *protagonistés* (*prôtos*, first, *agonistés*, actor)], M.: protagonist.

pròtasi [Gr. *-s* (*tásis*, stretching)], F.: protasis (of a conditional sentence); prologue.

protèg-gere [L. *-ere*], IRR.§; TR.: protect (shield, defend). **-gitóre**, M., **-gitríce**, F.: protector.

§ Pret. *protès-si, -se; -sero.* Part. *protètto.*

proteifórme [*Proteo, forme*], ADJ.: protean (multiform).

pro=tèndere, IRR.; TR.: stretch out (hold forth); REFL.: stretch one's self.

pro-tervaménte, ADV.: arrogantly. **-tèrvia**, **-tervità**†, F.: arrogance (Eng.† protervity). ‖**-tèrvo** [L. *-tervus* (*-tere*, tread upon)], ADJ.: arrogant (insolent).

pròtesi 1 [Gr. *-sis* (*thésis*, placing)], F.: prosthesis.

pro-tési 2 [*-tendere*], PRET. of *-tendere*. **-téso**, PART. of *-tendere;* ADJ.: stretched out.

protèssi, PRET. of *-teggere*.

protès-ta, **-tagióne**†, F.: protestation. **-tánte**, ADJ., M.: Protestant. **-tantésimo**, **-tantísmo**, M.: Protestantism. ‖**-táre** [L. *-tari* (*pro*, openly, *testari*, bear witness)], TR.: protest (affirm). **-táto**, PART. of *-tare;* ADJ.: protested. **-tatóre**, M., **-tatríce**, F.: protester. **-tatòrio**, ADJ.: belonging to protestation. **-tazióne**, F.: protestation. **protès-to**, M.: protest (pretence).

prote-ttívo, ADJ.: protective (defending). ‖**protè-tto**, PART. of *-ggere;* ADJ.: protected. **-ttoráto**, M.: protectorate. **-ttóre**, M.: protector. **-ttríce**, F.: protectress. **-zióne**, F.: protection (shelter, defence). **-zionísmo**, M.: protectionism. **-zionísta**, ADJ., M.: protectionist.

pròto [cf. *proto-*], M.: (*typ.*) foreman.

pròto- [Gr. *prôtos*, first], M.: head (chief). **-còllo** [l. L. *-collum*], M.: protocol (registry-book). **=físico**, pl. *—ci*, M.: first physician. **=maèstro**, M.: first master. **=màrtire**, M.: protomartyr. **=mèdico**, M.: first physician. **-'neo**†, M.: empyreum. **=notariáto**, M.: prothonotaryship. **=notário**, M.: prothonotary (Roman church official). **-plásma** [Gr. *plásma*, formation], M.: protoplasm. **-plásto**, M.: first creator. **-plásto**, M.: protoplast (original). **-quámquam** [L. *quamquam*, although], M.: (*jest.*) master; wiseacre. **protò-ssido** [*ossido*], M.: protoxide. **protò=tipo**, M.: prototype; ADJ.: original. **-zòi** [Gr. *zôon*, animal], M. PL.: protozoa.

pro=tònico, pl. *—ci*, ADJ.: protonic.

pro-tráere†, ‖**=trárre**, IRR.; TR.: protract (extend; defer). **-trássi**, PRET. of *-trarre*. **-trátto**, PART. of *-trarre;* ADJ.: protracted. **-trazióne**, F.: protraction.

protuberánza [L. *-rare*], F.: protuberance (prominence).

pro=tutóre [L. *-tutor*], M.: pro-guardian.

prò-va [L. *-ba*], F.: proof (test); demonstration; witness; dispute: *in* —, on purpose; *a tutta* —, as much as possible; *far* —†, prove. **-vábile**, ADJ.: provable; probable†. **-vabilità**, F.: provableness. **-vagióne**†, F.: proving. **-vaménto**†, M.: proving; proof (trial). **-váno**†, ADJ.: obstinate. **-vánza**†, F.: proof (trial). **-váre**, TR.: prove (try); demonstrate; thrive; REFL.: prove one's self. **-vataménte**, ADV.: by proof. **-vatívo**†, ADJ.: proving. **-váto**, PART. of *-vare;* ADJ.: proved. **-vatóre**, M.: prover. **-vatúra**, F.: kind of buffalo cheese. **-vazióne**†, F.: proof (test); witness.

pro-vecciáre†, INTR.: make provision; REFL.: take advantage of. **-vèccio**†, M.: profit.

proved. . = *provved*. .

pro-veniènte, ADJ.: arising. **-veniènza**, F.: origin (rise). **-veniménto**†, M.: success, issue. ‖**=veníre**, IRR.; INTR.: arise (proceed, have origin). **-vénto**, M.: income; fee. **-venúto**, PART. of *-venire;* ADJ.: arisen.

provenzá-le [*Provenza*], ADJ.: Provençal. **-leggiáre**, INTR.: imitate the Provençal. **-lísmo**, M.: Provençal manner. **-lménte**, ADV.: in the Provençal manner.

prover-biále, ADJ.: proverbial. **-bialménte**, ADV.: proverbially. **-biáre**, TR.: ridicule; admonish (scold); INTR.: speak in proverbs. **-biatóre**, M.: ridiculer; admonisher. ‖**provèr-bio** [*-bium*], M.: proverb; offence†. **-biosaménte**†, ADV.: angrily. **-bióso**, ADJ.: full of proverbs; angry (scornful)†. **-bista**, M.: writer (or sayer) of proverbs.

provètto [L. *-vectus* (*pro*, forward, *vehere*, carry)], ADJ.: old (advanced in years); M.: old man.

provevolménte†, ADV.: probably.

proviánda [Fr. *-vende*], F.: provender (provisions).

pro-vicariáto, M.: provicariate. ‖**=vicário**, M.: pro-vicar (acting vicar).

provid.. = *provvid..*

províncat, F.: periwinkle.

provín-cia [L.], F.: province. **-cialáto**, M.: provincialship. **-ciále**, ADJ., M.: provincial. **-cialísmo**, M.: provincialism.

províno [*-vare*], M.: spirit-gauge.

provocá-bile, ADJ.: easily provoked. **-ménto**†, M.: provocation. **provocá-nte**, ADJ.: provoking. ‖**provocáre** [L. (*pro*, forth, *vocare*, call)], TR.: provoke (incite, call out). **-taménte**, ADV.: in an aroused way. **-tívo**, ADJ.: provocative. **provocá-to**, PART. of *-re*; ADJ.: provoked. **-tóre**, M., **-tríce**, F.: provoker. **-zióne**, F.: provocation.

prov-vedènte, PART. of *-vedere*, ADJ.: provident. **-vedènza**, F.: providence (foresight). ‖**=vedére**, IRR.; TR.: provide (prepare); procure†; recompense†. **-vediménto**, M.: foresight (care). **-veditoráto**, M.: office of purveyor. **-veditóre**, M.: purveyor (caterer). **-veditoría**, F.: office of purveyor. **-veditríce**, F.: purveyor. **-vedutaménte**, ADV.: providently (prudently). **-vedúto**, PART. of *-vedere*; ADJ.: provided; prudent. **-vidaménte**, ADV.: providently. **-vidènte**, PART. of *-vedere*; ADJ.: provident (prudent). **-vidènza**, F.: providence; forecast†. **-videnziále**, ADJ.: providential. **pròv-vido**, ADJ.: provident; cautious. **-vigióne**, F.: provision.

provvisáre†, TR.: improvisate (write extemporaneously).

provvi-sionále, ADJ.: provisional. **-sionalménte**, ADV.: provisionally. **-sionáre**, TR.: give a pension. **-sionáto**, PART. of *-sionare*; ADJ.: pensioner. **-sióne**, F.: provision; pension; commission: *per modo di* —, provisionally. **-sionière**, M.: purveyor; ADJ.: providing. ‖**provvíso**†, PART. of *provvedere*; M.: impromptu. **-sóre**†, M.: provider. **-soriaménte**, ADV.: conditionally. **-sòrio**, ADJ.: conditional (Eng.† provisory).

provví-sta, F.: provision. **provvísto**, PART. of *provvedere*.

pro=zía, F.: great-aunt. **=zío**, M.: granduncle.

prúa [*prora*], F.: (*poet.*) PROW.

prudèn-te [L. *-s* (*providens*)], ADJ.: prudent (careful, discreet). **-teménte**, ADV.: prudently. **-tóne**, *aug.* of *-te*. **prudèn-za**, F.: prudence. **-ziále**, ADJ.: prudential. **-zialménte**, ADV.: prudently.

prú-dere [L. *prurire*], INTR.: itch. **-dóre**, M., **-dúra**†, F.: pruriency (itching).

pru-eggiáre [*-a*], INTR.: turn the ship's head. **-éggio**, M.: steering (of the prow).

prú-gna [L. *-na* (pl. of *-num*)], F.: PLUM: *-gne secche*, PRUNES. **prú-gno**†, M.: plum-tree. **prú-gnola**, F.: sloe (wild plum). **-gnoláia**, F.: mushroom grounds. **-gnòlo**, M.: mushroom; wild plum-tree†.

pruí-na [L.], F.: (*poet.*) hoar-frost. **-nóso**, ADJ.: frosted (pruinose).

prú-na [pop. for *-gna*], F.: PLUM. **-náia**, F., **-náio**, M.: plum-tree orchard. **-náme**†, M.: place full of thorns (or briers). **-neggiuòlo**†, *dim.* of *-no*. **-nèta**, F.: thorn hedge. **-nèlla**, F.: wallwort (plant). **-nèllo**, M.: blackthorn. **-nèto**, M.: plum-orchard; thorny bush. **prú-no**, M.: thorn; bramble. **-nóso**†, ADJ.: thorny; full of brambles.

pruòva† [= *prova*], F.: proof (test).

pru-rígine [L. *-rigo*], F.: pruriency (itching). **-riginóso**, ADJ.: itching. **-ríre**†, INTR.: itch. **-ríto**, M.: itching. **prú-sa**†, F.: itching (smarting).

psèudo- [Gr. *pseûdos*, false]: **-`nimo** [Gr. *ónuma*, name], M.: pseudonym (author's assumed name); ADJ.: pseudonymous.

psi-chiátra [Gr. *psuché*, soul, *iatrós*, physician], M.: psychiater. **-chiatría**, F.: psychiatry. **-chiátrico**, pl. **—ci**, ADJ.: pertaining to psychiatry. **-cología** [Gr. *lógos*, discourse], F.: psychology. **-cologicaménte**, ADV.: psychologically. **-cològico**, pl. **—ci**, ADJ.: psychological. **-còlogo**, M: psychologist.

psíllio†, M.: fleabane (plant).

pubbli-cábile, ADJ.: fit to be published. **-caménte**, ADV.: publicly. **-caménto**†, M.: publication. **-cáno**, M.: publican. **-cáre**, TR.: publish. **-catóre**, M., **-catríce**, F.: publisher. **-cazióne**, F.: publishing; publication. **-císta**, M.: publicist (journalist). **-cità**, F.: publicity. ‖**púbbli-co**, pl. *-ci* [L. *-cus* (*populus*, people)], ADJ.: public (common, open); M.: public.

pú-be [L. *-bes*], M.: pubes. **pú-bere**, ADJ., M.: (of) one in puberty. **-bertà**, F.: puberty. **-bescènte**†, ADJ.: pubescent.

public..† = *pubblic..*

pu-dènda [L.], ADJ.: pudendal. **-dibóndo**, ADJ.: modest. **-dicaménte**, ADV.: chastely. **-dicízia**, F.: chastity (pudicity). ‖**-díco**, pl. **—ci** [L. *-dicus* (*pudere*, be ashamed)], ADJ.: chaste (virtuous). **-dóre**, M.: chastity (modesty).

puerí-le [L. *-lis* (*puer*, boy)], ADJ.: puerile (childish). **-lità**, F.: puerility. **-lménte**, ADV.: childishly. **puerí-zia**, F.: childishness.

puèr-pera [L. (*puer*, child, *parere*, bear)],

F.: confined woman. **-perále**, ADJ.: puerperal. **-pèrio**, M.: childbed.

pugi-láre, ADJ.: of boxing. ‖**-láto** [L. *-latus*], M.: boxing. **púgi-le**†, **-latóre**, M.: pugilist.

pugille†, M.: pinch (bit).

pú-gna [L.], F.: battle (combat). **-gnáce**, ADJ.: pugnacious. **-gnaceménte**†, ADV.: pugnaciously. **-gnaláre**, TR.: strike (with a dagger). **-gnaláta**, F.: thrust (with a dagger). **-gnále**, M.: dagger. **-gnalétto**, **-gnalíno**, *dim.* of *-gnale*. **-gnalóne**, *aug.* of *-gnale*. **-gnalòtto**, M.: dagger (of medium size). **-gnáre**, TR.: fight (combat). **-gnatóre**, M., **-gnatríce**, F.: fighter. **-gnazióne**†, F.: battle (fight). **-gnázzo**†, M.: skirmish.

pu-gnellétto, **-gnellettíno**, *dim.* of *-gnello*. ‖**-gnèllo** [*-gno*], M.: handful.

pú-gnere† = *pungere*. **-gneréccio**†, M.: pricking. **-gnétto**†, M.: sting.

pu-gnettíno, *dim.* of *-gno*. ‖**-gníno**, M.: *dim.* of *-gno*; child's fist.

pugni-tòccio†, M.: stimulus (incentive). ‖**-tòpo** [*pugnere, topo*], M.: small holly-oak. **-túra**†, F.: puncture, prick; pang.

pú-gno, pl. *-gni*, *-gna* [L. *-gnus*], M.: fist; cuff; handful; handwriting: *fare a' -gni*, *fare alle -gna*, box. **-gnolíno**, *dim.* of *-gno*. **-gnòlo**, **-gnòro**, M.: handful; ancient agrarian measure.

púh! **púhhh** [echoic], INTERJ.: pooh!

púla [?], F.: husks (chaff).

púlce [L. *-lex*], F.: FLEA.

pulcèl-la [l. L. *-licella*], F.: girl (virgin, Eng.† pucelle). **-lággio**†, M.: virginity. **-lèni**†, ADV.: unmarried.

pul-ceséccia [*pulce, s.*.], F.: flea-bite. **-ciáio**, M.: place full of fleas.

pulcí-na†, F.: PULLET. **-nèlla**, M.: punchinello (Neapolitan puppet). **-nelláta**, F.: play of punchinello. ‖**pulcí-no** [L. *pullicenus*], M.: chicken. **-cióso**, ADJ.: full of fleas.

púlcro†, ADJ.: (*poet.*) beautiful.

pulé-dra, F.: colt. **-dráccio**, **-drúccio**, *disp.* of *-dro*. **-dráia**, F.: stud (place for fine horses). **-drétto**, **-drína**, **-dríno**, *car. dim.* of *-dro*. ‖**pulé-dro** [*pollo* (L. *pullus*)], M.: colt (FOAL).

puléggia [ASax. *pullian*, draw], F.: pulley.

puléggio [L. *-legium*], M.: pennyroyal (plant): *dar* —, send away.

púli-ca, F.: air-bubble (in glass). **-cária**, F.: pulicaria (flea-bane). ‖**púli-ce**† = *pulce*. **púli-ga**, F.: air-bubble (in glass).

puli-mentáre, TR.: polish. **-ménto**, M.: polish. ‖**pulí-re** [L. *polire*], TR.: polish (clean); flatter†. **-sci=orrécchi**, M.: earpick. **-sci=pénne**, M.: penwiper. **-sci=piédi**, M.: door-mat. **pulí-ta**, F.: polishing. **-taménte**, ADV.: neatly; elegantly; smoothly. **-tézza**, F.: neatness; elegance; politeness. **pulí-to**, PART. of *-re*; ADJ.: polished (smooth, clean); elegant; polite. **-tóre**, M.: polisher. **-túra**, F.: polishing. **-zía**, F.: cleanliness.

pul-loláre† = *-lulare*; INTR.: germinate (bud). **-lulaménto**, M.: budding; multiplying. ‖**-luláre** [L. *-lulus* (*-lus*, young)], INTR.: germinate (bud, Eng.† pullulate); swarm. **-lulatívo**, ADJ.: germinating. **-lulazióne**, F.: germination.

pulmonário†, ADJ.: pulmonary.

pulpi-tíno, *dim.* of *-to*. ‖**púlpi-to** [L. *-tum*], M.: pulpit.

pul-sáre [L.], TR.: pulsate (beat, throb); M.: pulsation. **-sátile**, ADJ.: beating. **-sazióne**, F.: pulsation.

pulvíscolo [L. *-culus* (*pulvis*)], M.: dust (powder).

pulzèlla = *pulcella*.

púnga†, F.: fight (battle).

pun-gèllo†, M.: goad. **-genteménte**†, ADV.: pungently (sharply). **-gènte**, PART. of *-gere*; ADJ.: poignant. ‖**pún-gere** [L.], IRR.§; TR.: prick (stick, sting); vex. **-gétto**†, M.: goad. **-giglióne**, M.: sting (of insects); incentive; goad†. **-gigliósо**†, ADJ.: pungent; pointed. **-giménto**†, M.: pricking; compunction. **-gitívo**†, ADJ.: pungent; offensive. **-gitóio**†, M.: goad. **-gi=tòpo**, M.: small holly-oak. **-goláre**, TR.: goad. **pún-golo**, M.: goad.

§ Pret. *pún-si*, *-se*; *-sero*. Part. *púnto*.

puní-bile, ADJ.: punishable. **-bilità**, F.: punishableness. **-gióne**†, F., **-ménto**†, M.: punishment. ‖**puní-re** [L.], TR.: punish. **-tívo**, ADJ.: punishing (Eng.† punitive). **puní-to**, PART. of *-re*; ADJ.: punished. **-tóre**, M., **-tríce**, F.: punisher. **-zióne**, F.: punishment.

púnsi, PRET. of *-ngere*.

pún-ta, F.: point; sharp end (top); promontory; thrust; pleurisy: — *di soldati*, troop of soldiers; *di* —, roughly; *per* —, directly; *far — falsa*, make a feint; *pigliar la* —†, get sour (of wine). **-tagúto**†, ADJ.: sharp-pointed. **-tále**, M.: tag. **-talétto**, *dim.* of *-tale*. **-talménte**†, ADV.: minutely (exactly); jointly. **-taménto**, M.: pointing out. **-táre**, TR.: point (direct; aim); punctuate; mark; prick (goad, stimulate); sharpen†; INTR.: direct efforts to one point. make effort; thrust; REFL.: persis[t] ... **-ta**, F.: thrust with somethin[g] ... **-tataménte**†, ADV.: punctuall[y] ... PART. of *-tare*; ADJ.: urged ... sharpened. **-tatóre**, M.: urge[r] ... **-tatúra**, F.: censure (punishm[ent]) ... tuation†. **-tazióne**†, F.: ...

-tázza, F.: iron point (for stakes). **-tázzo†**, M.: headland. **-teggiaménto**, M.: punctuation. **-teggiáre**, TR.: point, punctuate. **-teggiatóre**, M.: pointer; punctuater. **-teggiatúra**, F.: punctuation. **-telláre**, TR.: prop (stay). **-telláto**, PART. of *-tellare;* ADJ.: propped. **-tellatúra**, F.: propping; props. **-tellétto**, **-tellíno**, *dim.* of *-tello.* **-tèllo**, M.: prop (support); help. **-terèlla**, *dim.* of *-ta.* **-terellína**, *dim.* of *-terella.* **-terèllo**, *dim.* of *-to.* **-tería**, F.: (*artil.*) pointing (aim). **-teròlo**, **-teruòlo**, M.: bodkin; weevil. **-tíglio**, M.: punctilio (nice point). **-tiglióso**, ADJ.: punctilious. **-tína**, *dim.* of *-ta.* **-tíno**, *dim.* of *-to.* ‖**pún-to**, PART. of *-ngere;* M.: point (mark); limit; condition; question; moment; stitch; ADV.†: at all; nothing at all: *a —*, exactly; *di —*, *in —*, *— per —*, distinctly; *a buon —*, by good luck; *essere in —*, be ready; *essere in buon —*, be in good health; *far —*, stop payment; *mettere in —*, set in order; *mettersi in —*, prepare one's self. **-tolína**, *car. dim.* of *-ta.* **-tolíno**, *dim.* of *-to.* **-toncèllo**, **-toncíno**, *dim.* of *-tone.* **-tóne**, M.: point; prop; ADV.†: with the point. **-tuále**, ADJ.: punctual; precise. **-tualíno**, *car. dim.* of *-tuale.* **-tualíssimo**, ADJ.: very (or most) punctual. **-tualità**, F.: punctuality. **-tualménte**, ADV.: punctually. **-tuazióne†**, F.: punctuation. **-túra**, F.: puncture (wound); hurt. **-turétta**, *dim.* of *-tura.* **-túto**, ADJ.: sharp-pointed. **-zecchiaménto**, M.: pricking. **-zecchiáre**, TR.: prick repeatedly; molest. **-zellaménto†**, M.: spurring. **-zelláre†**, TR.: spur (urge). **-zióne†**, F.: puncture. **-zóne**, M.: puncheon (stamping tool). **-zonétto**, **-zoncíno**, *dim.* of *-zone.*

pu-pílla¹ [*-pillo*], F.: pupil; ward. **-pílla**² [L.], F.: pupil (of the eye). **-pilláre**, ADJ.: pupillary. **-pillétta**, *dim.* of *-pilla.* **-pillína**, *dim.* of *-pilla.* **-pillíno**, *dim.* of *-pillo.* ‖**-píllo** [L. *-pillus*], M.: ward; pupil; simpleton. **-ppáttola**, F.: doll.

pu-raménte, ADV.: purely (only). **-rchè -***, CONJ.: provided that. ‖**pú-re** [L. (*-rus*)], ADV.: only; although; yet; nevertheless; however; moreover (besides); likewise (also): *lo so — troppo*, I know it but too well. **-rèllo†**, *dim.* of *-ro.* **-rézza**, F.: pureness.

púr-ga, F.: purging; purge. **-gábile**, ADJ.: that can be purged. **-gagióne**, F.: purging. **-gaménto**, M.: purging; **-gánte**, PART. of *-gare;* ADJ.: purgativo; M.: purge (cathartic); PL.: souls in purgatory. **-gantíno**, *dim.* of *-gante.* ‖**-gáre** [L.], TR.: purge (purify); clarify; REFL.: take a purge; clear one's self from accusation. **-gataménte**, ADV.: purely (correctly). **-gatézza**, F.: purity. **-gatína**, *dim.* of *-gata.* **-gatívo**, ADJ.: purgative. **-gáto**, PART. of *-gare;* ADJ.: purged; pure. **-gatóre**, M.: purger; cleaner. **-gatòrio**, ADJ.: purging (purgatory); M.: purgatory. **-gatríce**, F.: purger; cleanser. **-gatúra**, F.: refuse (sweepings). **-gazióne**, F.: purgation; cleansing. **-ghétta**, *dim.* of *-ga.* **púr-go**, M.: fulling-mill.

pu-rificaménto, M.: purifying. **-rificáre**, TR.: purify; REFL.: purify one's self. **-rificatívo**, ADJ.: purificative. **-rificatóio**, M.: purificatory. **-rificatóre**, M., **-rificatríce**, F.: purifier; ADJ.: purifying. **-rificazióne**, F.: purification. **-rísmo**, M.: purism. **-ríssimo**, ADJ.: very (or most) pure. **-rísta**, M.: purist. **-rità**, F.: purity (cleanness); chastity. **-ritanísmo**, M.: puritanism. **-ritáno**, M.: Puritano. ‖**pú-ro** [L. *-rus*], ADJ.: pure (clean); chaste; absolute; clear; sincere.

purpú-reo [L. *-reus*], ADJ.: purple. **-rína**, F.: purpurin.

pu-rulènto, ADJ.: purulent (putrid). **-rulènza**, F.: purulence. ‖**pú-s** [L.], M.: pus.

pu-signáre, INTR.: eat after supper. ‖**-sígno** [? L. *post-cœnium*], M.: after-supper lunch.

pusil-lanimeménte†, ADV.: in a pusillanimous manner. **-lánime**, ADJ.: pusillanimous (mean-spirited). **-lanimità**, F.: pusillanimity. **-lánime†**, ADJ.: pusillanimous (mean-spirited). **-lità†**, F.: meanness (cowardice). ‖**pusíl-lo** [L. *-lus* (*pusus*, boy)], ADJ.: humble; mean (petty, base); little†.

pús-tola [L. *-tula* (*pus*)], F.: pustule (pimple). **-tolétta**, **-tolettína**, *dim.* of *-tola.* **-tolóso**, ADJ.: pustulous. **pús-tula†**, F.: pustule (pimple). **-tulétta†**, *dim.* of *-tula.*

pú-ta [L., I've of *-tare*], M.: supposal. **-tativaménte**, ADV.: in a supposed manner. **-tatívo**, ADJ.: putative (supposed, reputed).

pu-tènte, ADJ.: offensive (vile-smelling; disgusting); fetid. **-tidóre†**, M.: stench; infection. **pú-tido**, ADJ.: foul (offensive). **-tifèrio**, M.: impropriety (offence, pest). **-tiglióso†**, ADJ.: offensive (in smell). ‖**-tíre** [L. *-tere*], INTR.: smell bad (stink). **-títo†**, PART. of *-tire;* ADJ.: offensive. **-tolènte†**, ADJ.: offensive (in smell).

pú-tre, ADJ.: (*poet.*) putrid (decomposed).

-trèdine, F.: putridness. **-tredinóso**, ADJ.: putrefied. **-tre=fáre**, IRR.; TR.: putrefy (cause to decay); INTR.: become putrid; REFL.: grow decayed. **-trefattévole†**, **-trefattíbile**, ADJ.: corruptible. **-trefattívo†**, ADJ.: putrefactive. **-trefátto**, PART. of *-trefare;* ADJ.: putrefied (decayed). **-trefazióne**, F.: putrefaction. **-trescènte**, ADJ.: putrescent (becoming putrid). **-trescènza†**, F.: putrescence. **-tridáme†**, M.: mass of putrid matter. **-tridíre†**, INTR.: putrefy (decay). **-tridità**, F.: putridity (corruption). **‖pú-trido** [L. *-tridus*], ADJ.: putrid (rotten, corrupted, decomposed). **-tridúme**, M.: mass of putrid matter.

pút-ta [L. *-a*], F.: (*poet.*) girl. **-tána**, F.: prostitute. **-taneggiáre**, INTR.: play the prostitute. **-tèlla†**, *dim.* of *-ta.* **-tèllo†**, *dim.* of *-to.* **-tína**, *dim.* of *-ta.* **-tíno**, *dim.* of *-to.* **pút-to**, M.: boy.

púz-za, F.: bad smell; pus†. **-zacchiáre**, *dim.* of *-zare.* **-záre**, INTR.: smell badly. **-zerèllo†**, *dim.* of *-zo.* **-zévole†**, ADJ.: offensive. **‖púz-zo** [L. *putidus*, PUTID], M.: stench; infection. **púz-zola**, F.: polecat; kind of ant; kind of fungus. **-zolènte**, ADJ.: offensive (bad smelling). **-zolenteménte**, ADV.: in an offensive manner. **-zóne**, ADJ.: offensive; M.: offensive thing. **-zóso†**, ADJ.: fetid. **-zúra†**, F.: stench; pus.

Q

q *cu* [L.], M.: q (the letter).

quà [L. *eccu hac*], ADV.: here (in this place): *di* —, this way; *da quel tempo in* —, since that time.

quàc-chero, **‖-quero** [Eng. *quaker*], M.: Quaker.

qua-derlétto, M.: gusset. **-dèrna**, F.: four joint numbers (in lottery). **-dernáccio**, *disp.* of *-derno.* **-dernále†**, M.: quatrain. **-dernário**, ADJ.: quaternary; M.: quatrain (stanza of four verses). **-dernáto**, ADJ.: divided in four. **-dernétto**, **-derníno**, *dim.* and *car.* of *-derno.* **-dèrno**, M.: copy (or writing)-book; quire (of paper); cater (at dice); square flower-bed: — *di cassa*, cash-book. **-dernúccio**, *disp. dim.* of *-derno.* **quá-dra**, F.: *dar la* —, quiz (banter); quadrant†. **-drábile**, ADJ.: reducible into a square; suitable. **-dragenário**, ADJ.: of forty; forty years old. **-dragèsima**, F.: Lent; forty days. **-dragesimále**, ADJ.: quadragesimal. **-dragèsimo**, ADJ.: fortieth. **-draménto**, M.: squaring; square. **-drangoláre**, ADJ.: quadrangular. **-drángolo**, M.: quadrangle (square). **-dránte**, M.: quadrant; ADJ.: suitable. **-dráre**, TR.: square; INTR.: please (suit). **-dráro**, M.: picture-seller. **-dratíno**, *dim.* of *-drato.* **-dratívo**, ADJ.: quadrative. **-dráto**, PART. of *-drare;* ADJ.: quadrate (square); well-made; M.: (*typ.*) quad(rat). **-dratóre**, M., **-dratríce**, F.: squarer. **-dratúra**, F.: quadrature (squaring); side of a square; quartile, aspect. **-drèlla**, F.: large four-sided file. **-drèllo**, M.: arrow (dart); any four-sided instrument; rule; square brick; packing-needle. **-drería**, F.: quantity of pictures. **-drettíno**, *dim.* of *-dretto.* **-drétto**, *dim.* of *-dro.* **-drettóne**, *aug.* of *-dretto.* **quá-dri**, F. PL.: diamond (of cards). **-drièннio**, M.: space of four years. **-drifido** [L. *fidus* (*fendere*, cleave)], ADJ.: quadrified (divided into four parts). **-drifogliáto** [*fogliato*], ADJ.: quadrifoliate. **-drifórme** [*forma*], ADJ.: square. **-drifrónte** [*fronte*], ADJ.: of four faces. **-dríga**, F.: (*poet.*) quadriga (chariot drawn by four horses). **-drigáto**, M.: ancient coin. **-dríglia**, F.: quadrille; troop of men. **-drigliáti**, M. PL., **-dríglio†**, M.: quadrille (game). **-drilátero** [L. *-drilaterus*], ADJ., M.: quadrilateral. **-drilúngo** [*lungo*], ADJ.: oblong square. **-drilústro** [L. *lustrum*], ADJ.: of four lustrums. **-drimèstre** [L. *mensis*, month], M.: space of four months; ADJ.: of a space of four months. **-drinòmio** [Gr. *nomé*, division], ADJ., M.: quadrinomial. **-dri=partíre†**, TR.: divide into four parts. **-dripartíto**, ADJ.: divided into four parts. **-dripartizióne**, F.: quadripartition. **-drirème** [L. *-driremis*], F.: quadrireme (galley); ADJ.: of a quadrireme. **-dri=síllabo**, ADJ.: having four syllables. **-drívio** [L. *-drivium* (*quatuor*, *via*, road)], M.: cross (where four roads meet). **quá-dro**, ADJ.: square; well-made; silly†; M.: square; picture; flower-bed; diam[illegible] (of cards). **-dróne**, M.: *aug.* of *-dro* [illegible] linen; stone-slab. **-dr**[illegible] brick; small picture. [illegible] ADJ.: [illegible] M.: [illegible] -dr [illegible] qu[illegible] qua[illegible] qua[illegible]

qua-glièro†, **-gliéri**†, M.: bird-call.
quál = *quale*, INTERJ.: what! ADJ.: some (any; one); whatever. =**che**, PRON.: some, any; what, whatsoever; whoever. **-che-dúno**, M.: somebody (some one, anybody). =**còsa**, F.: something (anything). **-cosel-lína**, *car. dim.* of *-cosa*. **-cosétta**, *dim.* of *-cosa*. **-cosína**, *car. dim.* of *-cosa*. **-cosúccia**, *disp. dim.* of *-cosa*. **-cú-no**, M.: somebody (some one, anybody). ‖**quál-e**, **-ésso**† [L. *-is*], PRON. REL.: who; which (that, what); whoever; whatever; such as.
qualí-fica, F.: qualification. **-ficánte**, PART. of *-ficare;* ADJ.: qualifying. ‖**-fi-cáre** [l. L. (*qualis*, of what sort, *facere*, do)], TR.: qualify (distinguish); INTR.: qualify (make one's self fitted for something). **-ficatívo**, ADJ.: qualifying. **-fi-cáto**, PART. of *-ficare;* ADJ.: qualified. **-ficatóre**, M.: qualifier. **-ficazióne**, F.: qualification. **-tà**, F.: quality (condition, kind); trait. **-tatívo**, ADJ.: qualitative.
qual-ménte [*-e*], ADV.: as (how). =**ó-ra**, ADV.: when (whenever, as often as). **-si=sía**, **-si=vòglia**, **-únche**†, **-ún-que**, PRON. INDEF.: whoever (who); whatever (what). =**vòlta**, ADV.: whenever.
quán-do [L.], ADV.: when (whenever); while; since: *a — a —*, now and then; *di — in —*, from time to time; *quand' anche*, even if; M.: time. **-docchè -é**, ADV.: whenever; if; even. **-dúnque**†, ADV.: whenever.
quanti-tà [L. *-tas* (*quantus*, how much)], F.: quantity (extent, amount); ADV.: *in —*, in abundance. **-tatívo**, ADJ.: quantitative.
quán-to [L. *-tus*], ADJ.: how much; how many; as many as; M.: quantity (number); ADV.: as far; how long; as for: *— mai*, extraordinarily; *— prima*, as soon as possible; *tanto o —*, a little; *a -ti siamo del mese?* what day of the month is it? **-tocchè -é**, CONJ.: although. **-túnque**, CONJ.: although; ADJ.: how much; how many; as much: *— volte*, whenever.
quarán-ta [L. *quadraginta*], ADJ.: FORTY. **-tána**†, **-tèna**, F.: forty days; quarantine. **-tèşimo**, ADJ.: fortieth.
quarantígia†, F.: guaranty.
quaran-tía, F.: Venetian tribunal (of forty men). ‖**-tína** [*-ta*], F.: about forty; quarantine. **-t' óre**, F. PL.: forty hours. **-tòtto**, ADJ.: forty-eight. **-sèi**, ADJ.: forty-six. **-sètte**, ADJ.: forty-seven.
quáre [L.], ADV.: why: *non sine —*, not without reason.
quarent. . = *quarant*. .
quarèşi-ma [*L. quadragesima*], F.: forty days (of Lent). **-mále**, ADJ.: quadragesimal; M.: book of sermons (for Lent).
quár-ta, F.: quarter; quart; quadrant. **-tabòno**, M.: wooden square rule. **-tá-le**, M.: quarter pay. **-tána**, F.: quartan ague; ADJ.: quartan (fourth day). **-tanáccia**, *disp.* of *-tana*. **-tanário**†, ADJ.: sick with quartan ague; M.: person sick with quartan ague. **-tanèlla**†, *dim.* of *-tana*. **-táto**, ADJ.: sturdy; quartered. **-terómo**†, M.: quarter (of the moon). **-teruòla**, F.: peck (measure). **-teruòlo**, M.: brass counter. **-tétto**, M.: quartette. **-tiáto**†, ADJ.: noble (in birth). **-ticèllo**, *dim.* of *-to*. **-tière**, **-tièri**†, M.: quarter (fourth part); military station; mercy; quarter (of a shield). **-tier=mástro**, M.: quartermaster. **-tí-na**, F.: (*poet.*) quatrain. **-tíno**, M.: small clarinet; quarter bottle. ‖**quár-to** [L. *-tus*], ADJ.: fourth; M.: quarter (fourth part); quarter (of a shield); peck (measure): *andare nel —*, bear no delay. **-todècimo**, ADJ.: fourteenth. **-to-gè-nito**, M.: fourth son; ADJ.: of the fourth. **-túccio**, M.: quarter of a peck. **-t=último**, M.: fourth from the last.
quár-zo [Ger. *-z* (? L. *quadratus*)], M.: quartz (mineral). **-zóso**, ADJ.: of quartz.
quá-şi [L.], ADV.: quasi (almost, as if, in a manner): *— —*, almost. **-şiménte**, ADV.: as if; almost.
quássia [*Quassy* (negro who used the bark as medicine)], F.: quassia (plant).
quas-sù, ‖**-súşo** [*qua su*], ADV.: here above.
quaternário [*-dernario*], M.: (*poet.*) quatrain.
quatríduáno [L. *-duanus*], M.: four days; ADJ.: of four days.
quat-taménte, ADV.: squatting (bending) ‖**quát-to** [L. *quactum*], ADJ.: squat; silent (still): *— —*, very silently (quietly). **-tóne**, *aug.* of *-to; andar —*, creep along.
quattordi-cènne, ADJ.: fourteen-year old. **-cèşimo**, ADJ.: fourteenth. ‖**quat-tórdi-ci** [L. *quatuordecim*], ADJ.: FOURTEEN.
quat-trináccio, *disp.* of *-trino*. **-tri-no**, **-trinálo**, M.: (*fam.*) money-maker. **-trináta**†, F.: farthing's worth. **-trí-no**, M.: farthing. **-trinúccio**, *disp. dim.* of *-trino*. ‖**quát-tro** [L. *-tuor*], M.: FOUR (the number): *a —*†, in plenty. **-tro=centèşimo**, ADJ.: four-hundredth. **-trocentísta**, M.: writer or artist of the 15th century. **-tro=cènto**, ADJ.: four hundred. **-tro=míla**, ADJ.: four thousand. **-tro=pièdi**, ADJ., M.: quadruped.
que' = *quegli*. **qué-gli**, PRON. DEM.,

M.: that person; PL.: they (them); those. **qué-i** = *-gli*. **qué-l** = *-llo*. **-lohessía**, PRON. INDEF.: whoever (or whatever) it may be. ‖**què-llo** [L. *eccu ille*], PRON. DEM.: he (that person); that: *in* —, at that moment; *quel tanto*, that quantity.

quèr-ce, F.: (*poet.*) oak(-tree). **-céta**, F., **-céto**, M.: oak-grove. ‖**quèr-cia** [L. *-cus*], F.: oak (wood or tree): *far* —†, stand upon one's head. **-cíno**, ADJ.: oaken. **-ciòla**, *dim.* of *-cia*: *far* —, stand upon one's head. **-ciolétto**, *dim.* of *-ciolo*. **-ciòlo**, M.: young oak. **-cióne**, *aug.* of *-cia*. **-ciuòlo†**, M.: young oak.

que-rèla [L.], F.: complaint (lament): *dar* (or *porre*) —, accuse one. **-relánte**, PART. of *-relare*; ADJ.: complaining; M.: accuser (complainer). **-reláre**, TR.: accuse; REFL.: lament (grieve). **-reláto**, PART. of *-relare*; ADJ.: accused; M.: accused person. **-relatóre**, M.: accuser (complainer). **-relatòrio**, ADJ.: complaining. **-relóso**, ADJ.: querulous (bewailing).

querènte†, ADJ.: demanding (seeking).

que-rimònia [L.], F.: lament (Eng.† querimony). **què-rulo**, **-rulóso†**, ADJ.: querulous (bewailing, mournful).

quesíto [L. *quæsitum*], M.: query (demand).

que-stésso†, PRON. DEM.: this one. ‖**quèsta** [*-sto*], **què-sti**, PRON. DEM.: this man (one, a thing); M. PL.: these.

questio-nábile, **-nále†**, ADJ.: questionable. **-nánte**, ADJ.: questioning; M.: quarrelsome person; litigator. **-náre**, TR.: question (interrogate); INTR.: ask questions; quarrel; REFL.: contend (dispute). **-nário**, M.: questionary. **-natóra**, F., **-natóre**, M., **-natríce**, F.: questioner. **-ncèlla**, **-ncína**, *dim.* of *-ne*. ‖**questió-ne** [L. *quæstio*], F.: question (query); strife (controversy); matter.

quésto [L. *eccu iste*, 'lo this'], PRON. DEM.: this: *con* —, nevertheless; *in* —, in the meantime.

ques-tóre [L. *quæstor*, (*quærere*, seek)], M.: questor (Roman officer). **-toría†**, F.: questorship. **-tòrio**, ADJ.: questorial.

què-stua, F.: begging; loan. **-tuánte**, PART. of *-tuare*; ADJ.: begging; M.: beggar. **-tuáre**, INTR.: beg (ask alms). **-tuóso†**, ADJ.: profitable (gainful). **-túra**, F.: questorship.

que-táre, TR.: quiet (appease); INTR.: be quiet; REFL.: rest one's self; be quiet. **-táto**, PART. of *-tare*; ADJ.: quieted. ‖**què-to** [*quieto*], ADJ.: quiet (at rest, calm): *di* —, quietly.

qui [L. *eccu hic*, 'lo here'], ADV.: here (in this place): *di* —, hence; *di* — *a pochi giorni*, in a few days.

quía [L.], ADV.: because; M.: reason: *stare al* —, stand to reason.

qui-ddità, ‖**-dità†** [l. L. *-ditas* (*quid*, what)], F.: quiddity (essence, nature). **-dditatívo**, ADJ.: essential.

quidsímile = *quissimile*.

quíe = *qui*, ADV.: (*poet.*) here (in this place).

quie-scènte, ADJ.: quiescent (still); M.: quiet person. **-scènza**, F.: quiescence. **quiè-scere†**, INTR.: repose (rest). **-tamènte**, ADV.: quietly. **-tánza**, F.: quittance (receipt). **-tanzáre**, TR.: receipt. **-táre**, TR.: quiet (calm, satisfy); discharge†; INTR.: be quiet (repose). **-tatívo†**, ADJ.: quieting. **-táto**, PART. of *-tare*; ADJ.: quieted. **-tazióne†**, F.: rest (repose). ‖**quiè-te** [L. *-s*], F.: quiet (tranquillity); rest. **-tézza†**, F.: quiet. **-tísmo**, M.: quietism. **-tísta**, M.: quietist. **-titúdine†**, F.: quietude. **quiè-to**, ADJ.: quiet (still, calm). **-túdine**, F.: quietude.

quílio [?], M.: *cantare in* —, sing in falsetto.

quinamònte†, ADV.: far away (yonder).

quinário [L. *-rius*], ADJ.: quinary (consisting of five); M.: quinary (verse of five syllables).

quinaválle†, ADV.: there below.

quín-ci [L. *eccu hinc*, 'lo hence'], ADV.: hence; here; afterwards: — *a poco*, a little after. **-ciòltre†**, ADV.: hereabout. **-daválle†**, ADV.: there below.

quindècimo [L. *-mus*], ADJ., M.: fifteen.

quindèna [L. *-deni*], F.: (space of) fifteen days.

quíndi [L. *eccu inde*, 'lo thence'], ADV.: thence (from that place); then; therefore: *da* — *innanzi*, hereafter; — *giù*, there below.

quíndi-cennále, ADJ.: occurring every fifteen years. **-cèsimo**, ADJ.: fifteenth. ‖**quíndi-ci** [L. *quindecim*], ADJ.: FIFTEEN. **-ci=míla**, M.: fifteen thousand. **-cína**, F.: about fifteen.

quíndòltre†, ADV.: thereabout.

quinqua-genário [L. (*-ginta*, fifty)], ADJ.: fifty years old; M.: man fifty years old. **-gèsima**, F.: PENTECOST. **-gèsimo**, ADJ.: fiftieth.

quin-quennále, ADJ.: quinquennial. **-quènne**, ADJ.: of five years. · **nio** [L. *-quennium*], M.: spac years. **-querème** [L. *-que* five-oared galley. **quín-ta**, quint. **-ta=dècima**, F.: full moon): *in* —, full moon. · quintain (tilting target); ga **máccio**, *disp.* of *-terno*. - **-termíno**, *dim.* of *-terno*.

M.: copy-book. **-tessènza** [L. *essentia*], F.: quintessence. **-tétto**, M.: quintette. **-tíle**, ADJ.: of the quintile; M.: quintile (fifth month of the Roman year). **-tína**, F.: five joint numbers (in lottery).
‖**quín-to** [L. *-tus*], ADJ.: FIFTH; M.: fifth part. **-to=dècimo**, ADJ.: fifteenth. **-to=gènito**, M.: fifth son. **-túltimo**, ADJ.: fifth from the last. **-tuplicáre**, TR.: quintuple (multiply by five). **-tuplicáto**, PART. of *-tuplicare;* ADJ.: quintupled. **-'tuplo** [L. *-tuplus*], ADJ.: quintuple.
quiríttа†, ADV.: just here.
quisíto = *quesito*.
quis-quígl̤ia, ‖**-quília** [L. *-quiliæ*], F.: trifles; nonsense; small fry.
quissímile [L. *quid simile*], M.: (*di*) somewhat like.
quistion. . = *question*. .
quita. . = *quieta*. .
quívi [L. *eccu ibi*], ADV.: there (in that place); then (at that time): — *medesimo*, just there; — *oltre*, — *vicino*, near there. **-ríttа**†, ADV.: just there.
quòcere† = *cocere*.
quòndam [L.], ADJ.: quondam (former); M.: quondam.
quò-ta [L. (*-tus*)], F.: quota (share, part). **-táre**, TR.: quote (set price on); dispose†.
quoti-dianaménte, ADV.: daily. **-dianeggiáre**†, INTR.: return daily (as a fever). ‖**-diáno** [L. *-dianus*], ADJ.: quotidian (daily).
quò-to, M.: order; proportionate part. ‖**-ziènte** [L. *-tiens*], M.: quotient.

R

r *èrre* [L.], M.: r (the letter): *perder l'erre*, become mad; be tipsy.
r- [for *ri-*, L. *re-*], PREF.: re-, again, back; (or simply emphatic or expletive).
ra- [*ri-* + *a* 2], PREF.: re-, again (or denoting application).
ra-bacchíno†, *dim.* of *-bacchio*. **-bácchio**†, M.: boy, lad.
rabárbaro [L. *rha-barbarum*, 'barbarian *rha*-plant'], M.: rhubarb.
rabattíno [*arrabattare*], ADJ.: toiling; M.: toiler.
r=aballináre = *abballinare*.
rabbass. . = *riabbass*. .
r=abbáttere, TR.: strike down, lower; half shut; flatten; beat back, refract; REFL.: meet again by chance. **=abbattúto**, PART.
r=abbatuf(f)oláre, TR.: throw in confusion (jumble together).
r=abbellíre = *abbellire*.
rabberciá-re [?], TR.: fix up bun[gle] (patch up, fix over, bungle). **-ticcio**, AD[J.] patching. **-tóre**, M.: patcher, bung[ler]. **-túra**, F.: patching, patchwork, bu[ng]ling.
rábbi [Heb. *rabb*, master], M.: rabbi.
ráb-bia [L. *rabies*], F.: rabies (hydropho[bia]); RAGE (fury); violent desire; pas[sion]. **-biétta**, *dim.* of *-bia*.
rab-bínico, ADJ.: rabbinical. **-bi[ni]smo**, M.: rabbinism. **-biníста**, pl. -[sti], M.: Rabbinist. ‖**-bíno** [*-bi*], M.: rabbi.
rab-biosáccio, *disp.* of *-bioso*. **-bios[a]ménte**, ADV.: rabidly, furiously, mad[ly]. **-biosèllo**, -**biosétto**, **-biosíno**, [&c.] *dim.* of *-bioso*. ‖**-bióso** [*-bia*], AD[J.] RABID (affected with rabies, mad; [en]raged, furious; violent; excessive; gree[dy]. **-biúccia**, **-biúzza**, *dim.* of *-bia*.
r=abboccáre, TR.: fill up again (to [the] 'mouth' or top); bite again. **-abbocc[a]túra**, F.: filling up; completion.
r=abbonacciáre, TR.: make calm (ca[lm]; pacify, appease); INTR.: grow calm, [...] REFL.: be pacified; be reconciled, be[come] friends again. **=abbonire**, TR.: pa[cify] (appease); REFL.: become appeased [or] reconciled).
r=abbordáre, TR.: board (a ship aga[in]).
r=abbracciáre†, TR.: embrace again.
r=abbrenciáre†, TR.: mend again.
r=abbreviáre†, TR.: abbreviate or shor[ten] again.
r=abbrividíre [*brivido*], INTR.: shi[ver] with cold, shudder.
rabbru-scaménto, M.: obscurity, clo[udi]ness; chilliness. ‖**-scáre** [*re-*, *brus*[*co*]], INTR., REFL.: get cloudy, grow rough, murky or chilly.
rabbuf-faménto, M.: confusion ([up]roar, disorder). ‖**-fáre** [? *buffare*], [TR.]: put in disorder, confuse; dishevel; [...] grow rough or murky or chilly (of wea[th]er). **rabbúf-fo** [ak. to Eng. *rebuff*], [M.]: rebuke (reprimand, scolding).
r=abbuiáre, INTR., REFL.: grow dark, cloudy (of the weather), grow murky.
rabes-cáme, M.: (mass of) arabesq[ues]. **-cáre**, TR.: ornament with arabesq[ues]. **-catúra**, F.: arabesque work. ‖[**-**]**bés-co** [*arabesco*], M.: arabesque. **-[co]ne**, *aug.* of *-co*.
rabicáno [*R.*, horse in Ariosto], M.: r[oan] horse; roan colour.
rábido†, etc. = *rabbioso*, etc.
rabín. . = *rabbin*. .
rábula [L.], M., F.: mean pettifogger.
raccapezzáre [*re-*, L. *capitium*, hea[d of] a skein], TR.: find out, find again; col[lect] (with diligence).
raccapigl. . = *riaccapigl*. .
raccapitoláre†, TR.: recapitulate.

raccappelláre† = *riacappellare*.
racca - priccíaménto, M.: horror. **-priccíánte**, ADJ.: horrifying. ‖**-priccíáre**, **-priccíre** [*ra-*, *capriccio*], INTR., REFL.: be horror-struck. **-priccío**, M.: horror, fright.
r=accartoccíáre, TR.: wrap or curl up (roll up); wrinkle; form in a cornet; REFL.: be formed in a cornet; be curled; be wrinkled.
raccattá-re [*r-*, *a..*], TR.: take or pick up again; recover; retrieve; redeem. **-tícío**, M.: picking up, gathering; recovery.
raccenciáre [*ra-*, *cencio*], TR.: patch up; piece; REFL.: patch or fix one's self up; resume one's rags; get reëstablished.
r=accèndere, IRR., TR.: rekindle; light up again; REFL.: be rekindled, break out anew; blush. **-accendiménto**, M.: rekindling; blushing anew.
r=accennáre† = *riaccennare*.
r=accerchiáre†, TR.: reëncircle, enclose; hoop again.
r=accertáre, TR.: reassert, reassure; REFL.: be reassured; cheer up again.
raccéso, PART. of *raccendere*.
r=accettáre (*pop.*) = *ricettare*. **-accètto** (*pop.*) = *ricetto*.
r=acchetáre, TR.: appease (hush, console); REFL.: cease weeping, be hushed or consoled.
racchétta [Ar. *raha*, palm], F.: RACKET (battledore).
r=acchioccioláre, REFL.: curl up (like a snail); squat.
r=acchiúdere, IRR.; TR.: enclose (include, contain). **-acchiúso**, PART. of *-acchiudere*.
r=acciabattáre, TR.: cobble, botch, patch.
r=accoccáre = *riaccoccare*.
racco-cogliènza, F.: reception; welcome. ‖**-còglíere** [*r-*, *ac-cogliere*], IRR.; TR.: take or pick up; recover; collect (gather; catch); pull in or draw (the reins, etc.); receive (lodge); comprise (comprehend; understand); infer; REFL.: gather, be enclosed; meet, take refuge; withdraw; collect one's thoughts; withdraw within one's self, be composed; resort to dignified silence; (*fenc.*) resort to the defensive. **-coglíménto**, M.: collection (gathering, heap); recollection; meditation; reception. **-coglíticcio**, ADJ.: picked up at random; M.: chance picking. **-coglítóre**, M., **-coglitríce**, F.: collector (gatherer, compiler); midwife. **-còlsi**, PRET. of *-cogliere*. **-còlta**, F.: collection (heap); harvest, crop; retreat: *suonare a* —, beat a retreat. **-coltaménto**, ADV.: collectedly. **-coltína**, car. dim. of *-colta*. **-còlto**, PART.: recovered; collected (gathered), etc.; contained; enounced with one breath (of diphthongs); M.: crop, harvest. **-coltóre**†, M.: collector, gather.
raccoman - dagíóne†, **-daménto**† = *-dazione*. ‖**-dáre** [*r-*, *accomandare*], TR.: recommend; commit to; REFL.: recommend one's self, entreat one's favour; present one's respects. **-datária**, F., **-datário**, M.: person to whom any one is recommended. **-datívo**†, ADJ.: recommendatory. **-datóre**, M., **-datríce**, F.: recommender. **-datòrio**†, ADJ.: recommendatory. **-dazióne**, **-dígia**†, F., **-'do**†, M.: recommendation; appeal.
r=accomiatáre†, TR.: dismiss.
raccomo-daménto, M.: repairing (mending). ‖**-dáre** [*r-*, *accomodare*], TR.: repair (fix over, amend). **-datóre**, M., **-datríce**, F.: repairer, mender. **-datúra**, F.: repairing.
r=accompagnáre, TR.: reconduct.
r=accomunáre, TR.: make common again.
raccon-ciaménto, M.: repairing, adjusting; reconcilement†. ‖**-ciáre** [*r-*, *acconciare*], TR.: fit together again, repair, mend; adorn; reconcile†. **-ciatóre**, M., **-ciatríce**, F.: repairer, mender. **-ciatúra**, F.: repair(ing). **raccón-cio**†, ADJ.: repaired, refitted; M.: repair(ing).
racconf..†, **racconos..**†, **raccons..** = *riconf..*, *riconos..*, *ricons..*
raccon-tábile, ADJ.: that may be related. **-taménto**†, M.: account; recital. ‖**-táre** [*r-*, *accontare*], TR.: recount (relate, narrate, recite). **-tatóre**, M., **-tatríce**, F.: relator (narrator). **-tíno**, *car. dim.* of *-to*. **raccón-to**, PART. (*pop.*) of *-tare*; M.: account (narration, story, report).
r=accoppiáre, TR.: combine.
raccor-ciaménto, M.: shortening (curtailing); contraction. ‖**-ciáre** [*r-*, *accorciare*], TR.: shorten (curtail, abridge); contract. **raccór-cio**, ADJ.: shortened, abridged. **-círe** = *-ciare*.
raccorda..† = *ricorda..*
raccòrgere†, REFL.: bethink one's self, repent.
raccòrre, pop. syncop. of *raccogliere*.
r=accortáre†, TR.: shorten, abridge.
r=accosciáre†, REFL.: squat, cower.
r=accostáre, TR.: accost, approach (again); REFL.: draw nearer.
raccoz-zaménto, M.: gathering; assembly. ‖**-záre** [*r-*, *accozzare*], TR.: throw or bring together, assemble; REFL.: gather, meet again.
raccré-scere†, IRR.: increase, grow. **-sciménto**, M.: increase.

r=acculáre† = *rinculare.*

r=accusáre† = *riaccusare.*

ra-cemífero†, ADJ.: bearing grapes. ‖**-cèmo**†, M.: grape. **-cemóso**†, ADJ.: full of clusters.

ra-chítico, pl. —*ci*, ADJ.: rickety. ‖**-chítide** [Gr. *rháchis,* spine], F.: RACHIS (rickets).

racimo-láre, TR.: pick by clusters, pluck, glean. **-latúra**, F.: picking clusters, plucking. **-létto**, *dim.* of *-lo.* ‖**racímo-lo** [L. *racemus,* bunch], M.: bunch or cluster of grapes; remainder. **-lúzzo**, *dim.* of *-lo.*

r=acquattáre, REFL.: squat, cower.

r=acquetáre, =**acquietáre**, TR.: quiet (calm, pacify).

racqui-stagióne†, F., **-staménto**, M.: regaining, recovery. ‖**-stáre** [*r-, acquistare*], TR.: regain, recover. **-statóre**, M.: regainer (recoverer). **-stazióne**†, F.: regaining (recovery). **-'sto**, M.: regaining, recovery.

ráda [? Scand.], F.: ROAD (roadsted, bay).

rada-ménte [*rado*], ADV.: rarely (seldom). **-túra**, F.: thinness, scarcity.

raddenzáre[*r-, a, denso*],TR.: recondense, thicken; REFL.: grow dense or thicker.

raddimandáre†, TR.: redemand.

raddiriz-zaménto, M.: straightening out (again); redress. ‖**-záre** [*r-, addirizzare*], TR.: straighten out again, set aright, correct, redress, rectify; direct†, instruct†: — *le gambe ai cani,* do a useless thing, waste the time.

raddol-cáre, INTR.: turn mild or nice (of weather); TR.†: soften, calm. **-ciménto**, M.: softening (tempering, mitigation). ‖**-círe** [*r-, addolcire*], TR.: soften (temper, modify, calm, pacify); sweeten.

raddomandáre† = *ridomandare.*

raddop-piaménto, M.: redoubling. ‖**-piáre** [*r-, addoppiare*], TR.: reduplicate, redouble; fold. **-piataménte**, ADV.: doubly. **radóp-pio**, M.: redoubling; rebound (of a ball).

r=addormentáre, TR.: put to sleep again; REFL.: fall asleep again.

r=addossáre, TR.: load upon one's back again, charge again: huddle up.

raddótto, PART. of *raddurre;* M.: resort; meeting-place.

raddrizz.. = *raddirizz..*

raddú-cere† = *raddurre.* **-citóre**†, M., **-citríce**†, F.: reducer. **raddú-rre**† = *ridurre.*

rádere [L.], IRR.§; TR.: shear, shave; ERASE, efface; graze (touch lightly, skim); scrape†; cancel†; weed†.

§ Pret. *rá-si, -se; -sero.* Part. *ráso.*

ra-détto, *dim.* of *-do.* **-dézza**, F.: thinness, scarcity.

ra-diále [*-dio*], ADJ.: radial. **-diánte**, ADJ.: radiant, beaming. **-diáre**, INTR.†: radiate, beam; TR.: cancel (for *radere*). **-diazióne**, F.: radiation, brilliancy.

rádi-ca, F.: rootlet (of certain plants); (*lit.*) root (gen'ly). **-cále**, ADJ.: radical; vital; M.: radical; extreme democrat. **-calménte**, ADV.: radically. **-caménto**, M.: radication. **-cáre**, INTR.: take root, strike root; be rooted. **-cáto**, PART.: rooted; inveterate. **-cazióne**, F.: taking root, radication. **radí-cchio**, M.: succory. **-cchióne**, M.: big lettuce. ‖**radí-ce** [L. *radix*], F: ROOT (radix; origin). **-cèlla**, **-cétta**, *dim.* of *-ce.* **-cína**, *car. dim.* of *-ce.* **-cióna**, F.: *aug.* of *-ce* (for eating). **-cóne**, *aug.* of *-ce.*

radificáre† = *rarefare.*

radimádia [*radere, madia*], F.: (*bak.*) trough-scraper.

rá-dio [L. *-dius*], M.: RAY†; radius (bone of the forearm). **-diosità**, F.: radiancy. **-dióso**, ADJ.: (*lit.*) radiant, beaming.

ra-dissimaménte, ADV.: very rarely. ‖**-díssimo** [*-do*], ADJ.: most (exceedingly, very) rare. **-dità** = *rarità.*

raditúra†, F.: erasure; scraping(s).

rá-do [dissim. of *raro*], ADJ.: rare (scarce, unfrequent); sheer (of fabrics); thin (sparse); ADV.: rarely, seldom; M.: scarcity: *di* —, rarely; *-de volte,* rarely, seldom. **-dóne**, ADV.: very sheer (of fabrics). **-dúme**, M.: scarcity, sparseness.

radu-naménto, M.: uniting, assembling; assembly. **-nánza**, F.: meeting (assemblage, congregation). ‖**-náre** [*r-, adunare*], TR.: bring together (assemble, convoke); REFL.: come together (assemble, meet). **-náta**, F.: reunion, assembly, meeting. **-natóre**, M., **-natríce**, F.: bringer together, convoker.

radúra [*rado*], F.: rarity.

ráfano [Gr. *ráphanos*], M.: horse-radish.

ráffa = *ruffa.*

raf-facciaménto, M.: reproach. ‖**-facciáre** [*r-, a, faccia*], TR.: ('throw into the face') reproach severely, blame for, taunt for. **-fáccio**, M.: reproach; taunt.

raffardelláre†, TR.: pack up, bundle up; carry off.

raffáre†, TR.: carry off, rob.

raffazzo-naménto, M.: retrimming. ‖**-náre** [*r-, affazzonare*], TR.: refashion, fit or trim up (again). **-natúra**, F.: refashioning, (re)trimming.

raffér-ma, F.: fixing firmer; confirmation; ratification. ‖**-máre** [*r-, affermare*], TR.: make firmer; reaffirm; confirm, ratify; settle; renew†. **-mazióne**, F.: confirmation. **raffér-mo**, ADJ.: confirmed; stale.

r=affibbiáre, TR.: buckle or button again; redouble, repeat.
ráffica [Ger. *raffen*, snatch], F.: sudden blow (of wind), squall.
r=affidáre, TR.: (*lit.*) inspire with confidence, encourage; REFL.: confide, trust. **-affidáto,** ADJ.: confident, trusty.
raffiétto, *dim.* of *raffio*.
raffigu-rábile, ADJ.: easily recognized. **-raménto,** M.: recognition. ‖**-ráre** [*r-, affigurare*], TR.: remember again (recognize).
raffi-láre [*r-, a, filo*], TR.: sharpen (whet, reset); cut (pare, clip). **-latóio,** M.: whetting-tool; cutting-tool. **-latúra,** F.: whetting; cutting; parings, shreds.
raffi-naménto, M.: refinement. ‖**-náre** [*affinare*], TR.: refine, purify; subtilize, sharpen. **-nataménto,** ADV.: in a refined manner. **-natézza,** F.: refinement. **-natóio,** M.: refining means, purifier. **-natóre,** M., **-natríce,** F.: refiner, purifier. **-natúra,** F.: refining, refinement. **-nería,** F.: refinery. **-niméntō†,** M.: refinement. **-níre†,** TR.: refine; INTR.: become refined.
ráffio [Ger. *raffen*, snatch], M. (us'ly in pl. *-ffi*): hook, grapple, harpoon: *tirar co' raffi*, get with great effort.
r=affittáre†, TR.: hire or lease again.
raffittíre [*fitto*], TR.: thicken; pack; INTR.: grow thicker.
raffondáre†, TR.: hollow out deeper.
raffor-zaménto, M.: reënforcing, reënforcement. ‖**-záre** [*forza*], TR.: reënforce (fortify, strengthen).
raffrancáre† = *rinfrancare*.
raffred-daménto, M.: refrigeration, cooling. ‖**-dáre** [*freddo*], TR.: cool, REFRIGERATE; INTR.: cool, grow cold; REFL.: grow cool; catch cold; grow indifferent. **-dáto,** PART.: cooled, grown cold; cool, indifferent. **-datóio,** M.: cooling-vessel. **-'do†,** ADJ.: cool; indifferent. **-dóre,** M.: bad cold, rheum.
raffre-nábile, ADJ.: refrainable. **-naménto,** M.: refraining (curbing, restraint). ‖**-náre** [*freno*], TR.: refrain (curb, restrain, check); REFL.: refrain (from), forbear. **-natívo,** ADJ.: refraining, etc.
raffre-scaménto, M.: refreshing, cooling; coolness. ‖**-scáre** [*fresco*], INTR.: grow fresh or cool. **-scáta,** F.: freshness, cooling (of the atmosphere).
raffriggeláto [*friggere*], M.: bad smell of frying.
raffron-taménto, M.: confrontation; meeting (encounter). ‖**-táre** [*fronte*], TR.: confront; compare; encounter; INTR.†: be confronted; agree. **-tatóre,** M., **-tatríce,** F.: confronter. **raffrón-to,** M.: confrontation; encounter.

raffuscáre†, INTR.: grow dim or dark.
raffusoláre†, TR.: trim, repair
rága-na† [? Gr. *drákaina*], F.: tree-frog; sea-dragon (fish). **-nèlla,** F.: tree-frog; rattle.
ragáz-za, F.: young girl, lass. **-záccia, -záccio,** *disp.* of *-za, -zo*. **-záglia,** F., **-záme,** M.: parcel of boys, (crowd of) noisy or naughty children. **-záta,** F.: childish prank (puerility, thoughtlessness). **-zétta,** *car. dim.* of *-za*. **-zétto,** *dim.* of *-zo*. **-zína,** F., **-zíno,** M., *car. dim.* of *-za, -zo;* waiter†. ‖**ragáz-zo** [?], M.: boy (lad); waiter; cabin-boy. **-zòla, -zòlo,** *dim.* of *-za, -zo*. **-zóna,** F., **-zóne,** M.: *aug.* of *-za, -zo;* large and robust boy, girl. **-zòtto,** *aug.* of *-zo;* very big boy. **-zúccia, -zúccio,** *disp. dim.* of *-za, -zo*. **-zuol.** = *-zol.*.
raggavignáre†, TR.: climb; REFL.: clamber up.
raggeláre [*ra-gelare*], TR.: congeal, freeze; REFL.: congeal.
raggentilíre [*gentile*], TR.: render genteel, polish.
raggèra [*raggio*], F.: sheaf of rays, radiation.
ragghiáre†, INTR.: bray.
ragghignáre†, INTR.: look sour or grim.
rágghio†, M.: braying.
rag-giaménto, M.: beaming, radiation. **-giánte,** ADJ.: radiant (beaming). **-giáre,** INTR.: radiate (beam). **-giáto,** PART.: radiated, reflected, beaming; F.† (*-giata*): thornback (fish). ‖**rág-gio,** pl. *-gi,* (*poet.*) *rai* [L. *radius*], M.: RAY (beam); radius; spoke (us'ly *razza*): *il nuovo —*, the morning.
r=aggiornáre, TR.: adjourn; INTR.: (*lit.*) return (of the day), grow light (again), dawn.
raggióso†, ADJ.: radiant (beaming).
raggi-raménto, M.: winding; cunning shift, subterfuge. ‖**-ráre** [*giro*], TR.: turn round (whirl)†; entice (lead) by the nose, trick; REFL.: gyrate (turn round)†, ramble; treat. **-ratóra,** F., **-ratóre,** M., **-ratríce,** F.: swindler, cheat. **-rétto,** *dim.* of *-ro*. **-révole†,** ADJ.: circuitous; tricky; shifty. **raggí-ro** M.: trick; subterfuge.
raggiugn†. = *raggiung.*.
raggiún-gere [*ra-, giungere*], IRR.; TR.: rejoin; overtake (catch up with); reach; REFL.: meet again. **-giménto†,** M.: rejoining, etc. **-'to,** PART. of *-gere*.
raggiuòlo, *dim.* of *-ggio*.
raggiu-staménto, M.: readjustment, mending. ‖**-stáre** [*r-, aggiustare*], TR.: readjust (refit, mend; reconcile, pacify); REFL.: be readjusted; be reconciled.
r=agglutináre, TR.: glue together ag

raggomicelláre†, TR.: agglomerate.

raggomito-laménto, M.: winding or coiling up again. ||**-láre** [*gomitolo*], TR.: wind upon a clue or ball, wind into a ball, coil up.

r=aggranchiáre, TR.: benumb with cold, freeze. **-aggranchíre**, INTR.: shrivel with cold.

r=aggrandíre, TR.: increase, enlarge.

raggranelláre [*granello*], TR.: gather (scattered grains, etc.), pick together (glean, collect).

r=aggraváre, TR.: overload; aggravate; INTR.: increase.

rag-gri(n)cchiáre†, **-gri(n)cciáre**, REFL.: shrivel up, shrink; cuddle up. **-grinzaménto**, M.: wrinkling; shrinking. **-grinzáre**, ||**-grinzíre** [*grinza*], TR.: wrinkle up, shrivel; REFL.: get wrinkled; shrink; lose courage.

r=aggrottáre, TR.: embank†; repair†: — *le ciglia*, knit the eyebrows, frown.

r=aggrovigliáre, TR.: curl up, twist up; entangle.

raggrup-paménto, M.: grouping, collection. ||**-páre** [*r- aggruppare*], TR.: group or heap up; make up in parcels, tie together; regroup; REFL.: be heaped up; curl up, twist. **-'po†**, M.: twisting up; complication.

raggruz-záre†, ||**-zoláre** [*gruzzolo*], TR.: scrape together, hoard up; REFL.: shrink, shrivel; squat.

raggua-gliaménte, ADV.: proportionally. **-gliaménto**, M., **-gliánza†**, F.: equalization, balancing; levelling; evenness. ||**-gliáre** [*r-, agguagliare*], TR.: equalize, even up, balance; compare; level; inform: — *le scritture* (*i conti*), balance or post up the books (the accounts). **-gliataménte**, ADV.: proportionately. **-gliatívo**, ADJ.: equalizing, balancing. **-gliatóre**, M.: equalizer; informer. **ragguá-glio**, M.: equalizing, balancing; equality, proportion; relation, account, notice: *a* —, *in* —, proportionately.

ragguar-dáre† [*guardare*], TR.: regard (look at, consider, examine; concern). **-datóre†**, M.: regarder, observer. **-dévole**, ADJ.: considerable (remarkable); clear (sharp). **-devolézza**, F.: considerableness. **-devolménte**, ADV.: considerably, remarkably.

ragguazzáre†, TR.: shake up, agitate; mix.

rágia [L. *rasis*], F.: resin; (*fig.*) catch, deceit, danger.

ragio-náccia, *disp.* of *-ne*. **-nále**, ADJ.: rational, reasonable. **-naménto**, M.: reasoning, discourse. **-náre**, INTR.: reason (discuss, discourse); compute; conclude; TR.: discuss; M.: reasoning (discourse, conversation). **-nánte**, ADJ.: reasoning; rational. **-nataménte**, ADV.: reasonably. **-natívo†**, ADJ.: reasonable, rational. **-náto**, PART.: reasoned, etc.; reasonable, judicious; rational; well explained, illustrated. **-natóre**, M.†, **-natríce**, F.: reasoner, talker. **-nélla**, *disp. dim.* of *-ne*. **-nína**, F.: *dim.* of *-ne*; (*iron.*) servant girl. ||**ragióne** [L. *ratio*], F.: REASON (sense, judgment; cause; argument, explanation); justice, right; law; account; ratio, rate, subject: *avere* —, be right, be in the right; *a* (or *in*) — *di*, at the rate of, in proportion to; *con* (or *di*) —, with good reason, justly; *chiedere* —, call to account; *creare una* —, form a company or partnership; *essere ben* —, be reasonable; *far* —, do justice; *far* — *nel bere*, pledge in drinking; *far la* —, make up accounts, compute; *mettere a* —, put to account; *render* —, give an account; *saldar la* —, close an account; *saper di* —, know bookkeeping; *tener* —, judge; *per* — *di mondo*, by natural law. **-nería**, F.: bookkeeping, account; accountant's office. **-nétta**, *dim.* of *-ne*. **-névole**, ADJ.: reasonable (rational; just, fair). **-nevolézza**, F.: reasonableness. **-nevolménte**, ADV.: reasonably (justly, fairly). **-nière**, M.: accountant, bookkeeper, auditor (of accounts).

ragióso [*ragia*], ADJ.: resinous.

ra-gliáre [?], INTR.: bray. **-gliáta**, F.: long braying. **rá-glio**, M.: braying.

rá-gna [L. *aranea*], F.: (*lit.*) spider's web; fowling-net, snare: *dare nella* —, fall into the snare. **-gnáia**, F.: place for laying bird-nets. **-gnáre**, INTR.: (become like a spider's web, hence) become thin or transparent, become threadbare, be worn out; (*lit.*) lay fowling-nets; fly into a net; be full of gossamers: TR.†: carry off. **-gna=téla†**, F., **-gna=téle**, M.: cobweb; (M.) spider†. **-gnateláccio**, **-gnatelúzzo**, *disp. dim.* of *-gnatelo*. **-gnatúra**, F.: threadbareness; gossamery condition (of the air). **rá-gno**, M.: spider; crabfish. **-'gnolo†**, M.: spider. **-gnuòla†**, *dim.* of *-gna*. **-gnuòlo†**, M.: spider.

ragu-naménto = *radunamento*. **-nánza** = *radunanza*. ||**-náre** [*radunare*], (*lit.*) = *radunare*; (*pop.*) recover. **-náta** = *radunata*. **-natíccio**, ADJ.: (*lit.*) collected, heaped together; M.: collection, heap.

rái = *raggi* (pl. of *raggio*).

raià [Sanskr. *rājā*], M., INVAR.: rajah (Hindoo king or ruler).

raiáre† = *raggiare*.

raitíre†, INTR. (imperf. *raitíeva*): scream.

ráitro [OGer. *raiter*, RIDER], M.: [illegible]

cavalryman, trooper: *alla* —, like a trooper.

rálla [? Lat. **radula* (*radere*, rub)], F.: wheel-grease.

r=allacciáre, TR.: lace, tie up; catch.

rallarga-ménto, M.: enlarging. ‖**r=allargá-re**, TR.: enlarge (widen, extend, dilate; REFL.: be enlarged or dilated; grow liberal. **-tóre**, M.: enlarger, dilator.

r=alleggiáre, TR.: relieve, comfort.

ralle-graménto, M., **-gránza†**, F.: rejoicing; joy, mirth. ‖**-gráre** [*r-*, *allegrare*], TR.: rejoice (gladden, amuse, cheer); REFL.: rejoice (be delighted); take pleasure. **-gráta**, F.: sportive leap, gambol. **-gratívo**, ADJ.: rejoicing, amusing; joyful. **-gratóre**, M., **-gratríce**, F.: rejoicer, cheerer. **-gratúra**, F.: joyfulness; joyful air or countenance; delight. **rallé-gro**, M.: joy; congratulation.

r=allenáre†, TR.: strengthen; REFL.: take breath.

rallenta-ménto, M.: slackening. ‖**r=allentá-re**, TR.: slacken (relax, abate); unbend; INTR.: slacken; relent.

r=alleváre, TR.: bring up (educate, rear).

r=allignáre, INTR.: take root again.

r=alluminare, TR.: illumine or enlighten (again); restore the sight of; REFL.: recover one's sight.

r=allungáre, TR.: lengthen out.

rá-ma [*-mo*], F.: branch, twig. **-máccia**, F.: *disp.* of *-ma;* broom.

ramái-o [*rame*], M.: coppersmith (brasier, kettlemaker. **-oláta**, F.: ladleful. **-(u)òlo**, M.: ladle.

raman-zína [*romanzina*], F.: reproval (reprimand, scolding). **-zière†**, **-'zo†** = *romanziere*, *-zo*.

ramárro [*rame*], M.: big lizard.

ramá-ta [*rame;* first made of copper thread], F.: bat (at bat-fowling): *a* —, abundantly. **-táre†**, TR.: knock down with a bat. **-táta**, F.: blow with a bat.

ra-matèlla†, *dim.* of *-ma*. **-matèllo†**, *dim.* of *-mo*. **-máto†** I, ADJ.: branchy, of branches; covered with branches.

ramá-to [*rame*], ADJ.: of copper, coppery. **-túra**, F.: copper covering.

ramázza = *ramaccia*; sled†.

ráme [L. *æramen*], M.: copper, brass; (object of copper, as) copper coin, copper tool; (*poet.*) copper vase; copper engraving; PL.: copper utensils.

ramerino = *rosmarino*.

ra-métta, **-métto**, *dim.* of *-ma*, *-mo*. **-micèlla**, F., **-micèllo**, M.: *dim.* of *-ma*, *-mo;* tender plant. **-mificáre**, INTR., REFL.: ramify. **-mificazióne**, F.: ramification.

ra-mífero [*rame*, L. *ferre*, BEAR], ADJ.: copper-bearing. **-mígno†**, ADJ.: of copper, coppery. **-mína**, F.: dross of copper.

ra-mingáre, INTR.: flutter from bough to bough†; flutter or wander about, roam. ‖**-míngo** [*-mo*], ADJ.: fluttering from bough to bough†; fluttering or wandering about, roaming, fugitive; homeless, alone.

ramíno [*rame*], M.: copper-boiler (brass-kettle).

rammantáre†, TR.: cover with a cloak, wrap.

rammanz. .† = *ramanz. .*

rammarc. .† = *rammaric. .*

rammarginare†, TR.: heal up.

rammari-caménto, M.: grief; complaint. ‖**-cáre** [*r-*, *amaricare*], TR.: afflict (grieve); INTR., REFL.: grieve; complain (lament); grumble. **-cáto**, ADJ.: afflicted, sad. **-catóre†**, M.: complainer, grumbler. **-cazioncèlla†**, *dim.* of *-cazione*. **-cazióne†**, F.: grief; complaint (lament). **-chévole†**, ADJ.: lamentable, doleful. **-chío**, M.: grief; complaint (lament). **ramári-co**, M.: grief; complaint, lament(ation). **-cóso**, ADJ.: complaining; grievous.

r=ammass. ., intens. of *ammass. .*

r=ammattonáre, TR.: repave with bricks.

rammembr. .† = *rimembr. .*

rammemo-rábile, ADJ.: that may be remembered. **-raménto**, M., **-ránza**, F.: remembrance. ‖**-ráre** [*memoria*], TR.: remind, record; REFL.: remind one's self, remember, recollect. **-razióne**, F.: remembrance, memory.

rammen-dáre [*r-*, *a. .*], TR.: mend (fix, correct, amend). **-datóre**, M., **-datríce**, F.: mender, amender, corrector. **-datúra**, F.: mending, correction. **rammén-do**, M.: mending, fixing, correction.

rammen-taménto†, M., **-tánza†**, F.: remembrance, recollection. ‖**-táre** [*r-*, *a mente*], TR.: remind; commemorate; REFL.: remember, recollect. **-tatóre**, M.: reminder, remembrancer. **-tío†**, M.: memorizing, repetition.

rammezzáre†, TR.: divide, cut in two.

rammol-láre† = *-lire*. **-liménto**, M.: mollifying, softening. ‖**-líre** [*molle*], TR.: mollify (soften, temper).

r=ammontáre, TR.: pile up, heap up.

rammor-bidáre†, TR.: soften; enervate. **-bidatívo†**, ADJ.: softening, emollient; enervating. **-bidíre** [*r-*, *ammorbidire*], **-vidáre†**, **-vidíre** = *-bidare*.

r=ammucchiáre, TR.: heap or pile u

rammuricáre†, TR.: heap together.

r=ammulináre, TR.: whirl.

rámno [L. *ramnus*], M.: buckthorn.

rámo [L. *-mus*], M.: branch, bou

shoot, rootlet; arm (of a river); PL.: branches; ramification: *avere un — di pazzia*, be rather extravagant, be somewhat out of one's head.
ramó-gna†, F.: journey. **-gnáre**†, INTR.: journey on happily.
ramoláccio [l. L. *armoracium*], M.: horse-radish.
ramo-ráto†, ADJ.: branchy, full of branches. **-scèllo**, *dim.* of *-mo*. **-sità**, F.: branchiness. ‖**-'so** [*ramo*], ADJ.: banchy, full of or covered with branches.
rám-pa, F.: (us'ly *her.*) paw, talon, claw, clutch. **-pánte**, ADJ.: (*her.*) rampant. ‖**-páre**† [Germ'c, ak. to Eng. *ramp*, leap], INTR.: climb; clutch; strike with the paw. **-páta** [*-pa*], F.: paw, claw; stroke of the paw, clawing; ascending street. **-picánte**, ADJ.: climbing. **-picáre**, INTR., REFL.: climb (clamber). **-picatóre**, M.: climber. **-pichíno**, M.: climber (small woodpecker). **-picóne**, M.: large harpoon, grappling iron. **-pináta**, F.: stroke of a harpoon; sting. **-píno**, M.: harpoon; grapple; prong (of a fork); sting (of an insect). **-po**†, M. = *-pino;* claw. **-pógna**, F., **-pognaménto**†, M.: (*poet.*) reproof (rebuke). **-pognáre**, TR.: (*lit.*) reprove (rebuke, scold); INTR., REFL.†: grumble; complain. **-pognatóre**†, M.: grumbler. **-pognévole**, ADJ.: rebuking, mordaceous. **-pognóso**†, ADJ.: rebuking, reproachful.
ram-pollaménto†, M.: source, spring. **-polláre**, INTR.: (*lit.*) sprout or shoot forth, issue, swarm; spring forth, gush out. ‖**-póllo** [? *ramopollo*, 'young branch'], M.: sprout (young shoot, offset of a tree); offspring; (*lit.*) jet of water (gush, spouting, spring).
rampó-ne, *aug.* of *rampino*. **-nière**, M.: harpooner (at whaling).
ra-muscèllo, **-múscolo**, *dim.* of *ramo*. **-musculóso**, ADJ.: branchy.
rána [L.], F.: frog.
ran-cáre [*-co*], INTR.: limp, hobble. **-cheggiáre**, **-chettáre**, INTR.: limp or hobble much.
ranciáto [*aranciato*], ADJ.: orange-coloured.
ránci-co, M.: rank smell or vapor. **-cóso**, ADJ.: rank, rancid; bad. **-daménto**, ADV.: rancidly. **-dézza**, **-dità**†, F.: rancidness, rancidity. ‖**ránci-do** [L. *-dus*], ADJ.: rancid (rank, musty). **-dúme**, M.: rancid or musty heap.
rán-cière, M.: distributer of rations. ‖**-cio** 1 [Sp. *-cho*, mess of persons], M.: ration (of soldiers), mess.
ráncio 2 [*arancio*], ADJ.: orange-coloured.
rán-cio† 3 ADJ.: rancid; stale, old, senile. **-cióso**, ADJ.: rancid, rank.
ránco [Ger. *rank*, crookedness], ADJ.: distorted (of legs, hence) lame, hobbling.
ran-córe [L. *-cor* (*-cere*, be rank)], M.: rancour (malignity, spite). **-cúra**†, F.: trouble (grief, affliction). **-curáre**†, TR.: trouble, grieve.
rán-da†, F.: edge; *a* —, on the point, near; exactly. **-dággine**†, F.: boldness: *andar* —, blunder on.
randágio [?], M.: rambler, wanderer.
ran-delláre, TR.: beat with a stick, cudgel. **-delláta**, F.: cudgelling. ‖**-dèllo** [?], M.: packing-stick; cudgel.
randióne†, M.: gerfalcon.
ranèlla†, F.: *dim.* of *rana;* abscess.
ránfia = *granfia*.
rángo [Fr. *rang*], M.: RANK (degree).
rángo-la†, F.: solicitude, anxiety. **-láre**†, INTR.: act with care; yawn; TR.: attend to with care, be solicitous about. **-lo**† = *-la*. **-lóso**†, ADJ.: solicitous, attentive; anxious.
raníno†, ADJ.: marshy, boggy.
rannáta [*ranno*], F.: buck, lye.
rannesta-ménto, M.: new graft(ing). ‖**r=annestá-re**, TR.: graft afresh.
rannicchiáre [*nicchia*], TR.: draw into a nook, retire; REFL.: withdraw, retire; shrink, shrivel; squat, crouch.
r=annid(i)áre, TR.: build (a nest†); harbour; REFL.: nestle, settle.
ran-nière†, M.: lye-tub. ‖**-no** [Gr. *rhámnos*], M.: buckthorn†; buck, lye.
rannobilíre [*nobile*], TR.: make noble.
rannoda-ménto, M.: tying again. ‖**r=annodá-re**, TR.: tie again, renew.
rannóso [*ranno*], ADJ.: lixivial.
rannuvola-ménto, M.: cloudiness. ‖**r=annuvolá-re**, INTR.: grow cloudy or gloomy; become clouded.
ranòc-chia [*rana*], F.: frog. **-chiésco**, ADJ.: (*jest.*) froggy. **-chiétto**, **-chína**, **-chíno**, *dim.* of *-chia*, *-chio*. **-chio**, M.: frog.
rán-to†, M.: rattling (in the throat). ‖**-toláre** [ak. to *rattle*], INTR.: rattle, give the death-rattle. **rán-tolo**, M.: rattling (in the throat), death-rattle. **-tolóso**, ADJ.: rattling, wheezing.
ranún-colo, ‖**-culo**† [L. *-culus* (*rana*, frog)], M.: ranunculus (crowfoot).
ranúzza†, *dim.* of *rana*.
rápa [L.], F.: turnip; radish.
rapá-ce [L. *rapax*], ADJ.: rapacious, greedy. **-ceménte**, ADV.: rapaciously, greedily. **-cità**, F.: rapacity, greed.
rapáio [*-pa*], M.: turnip-plot; vegetable-bed; (*fig.*) mish-mash (balderdash).
ra-páre [Sp. *-par*], TR.: clip close. **-páta**, F.: close clipping.
rapè [Fr. *-pé* (*râper*, RASP)], M.: rappee (snuff).

raperíno [*rapare*], M.: clipped head; greenfinch.

rape-rónzo†, ‖**-rónzolo** [*rapa*], M.: rampion (salad-root).

rapi-daménte, ADV.: rapidly. **-dità**, F.: rapidity, swiftness. ‖**rápi-do** [L. *-dus*], ADJ.: rapid (swift, quick).

rapi-ménto, M.: carrying off; rapture (ecstasy); rape. **rapí-na**, F.: rapine (prey); rapidity; violence. **-naménto**†, M.: snatching away, robbing. **-náre**†, TR.: snatch away, rob, plunder. **-natóre**†, M.: robber. **-nosaménte**†, ADV.: rapidly, violently. **-nóso**†, ADJ.: rapid, violent. ‖**rapí-re** [*rapere*], TR.: snatch away; RAVISH (RAPE; transport, charm). **-tóre**, M., **-tríce**, F.: ravisher; charmer.

rapónzolo = *raperonzolo*.

ráppa [Ger. *rappe*, bunch of grapes], F.: tassel; bunch of dry or artificial flowers; (*vet.*) chap.

rappa-ciáre [*r-*, *appaciare*], TR.: pacify (appease, calm). **-cificaménto**, M.: pacification. **-cificáre**, TR.: pacify (appease, calm). **-gáre**†, TR.: appease, satisfy.

r=appallottoláre, TR.: make up into balls or pills; REFL.: gather into knots, get curled up.

r=apparecchiáre†, TR.: set in order again, arrange again. **-appareggiáre**†, TR.: equalize; compare.

r=apparíre†, IRR.; INTR.: reappear.

rappattumáre [*pattume*], TR.: reconcile again, make up between; RECIPR.: become reconciled, make up (a quarrel).

r=appelláre, TR.: (*lit.*) recall; INTR.†: appeal.

rappez-zaménto, M.: piecing (patching, mending). ‖**-záre** [*pezzo*], TR.: piece (patch, mend). **-zatóre**, M., **-zatríce**, F.: patcher, mender. **-zatúra**, F.: piecing (patching, mending). **rappèz-zo**, M.: patch, mending; patched place; (*typ.*) sorts (additional type).

r=appianáre, TR.: plane off (smoothen, level).

r=appiastráre, TR.: replaster.

rappi-ccáre [*r-*, *appiccare*], TR.: attach again, hang up again; begin again. **-ccatúra**, F.: reattachment; reunion. **-cciccáre**, TR.: attach or stick again; RECIPR.: stick together. **-cciccottáre**, TR.: patch up.

r=appic-cinire, **-ciolíre**, TR.: make smaller (lessen, diminish).

rappi-gliaménto, M.: coagulation. ‖**-gliáre** [*r-*, *appigliare*], TR., INTR.: coagulate, curdle; REFL.: curdle; begin afresh.

rapporta-gióne†, **-taménto**†, M.: report(ing). ‖**-táre** [L. *re-portare*, 'bring back'], TR.: report; announce. **-tatóra**, F., **-tatóre**, M., **-tatríce**, F.: reporter; telltale. **-tazióne**†, F.: report(ing). **rappòr-to**, M.: report (statement, account; rumour); rapport (relation, connection, Eng.† report); ornament.

rap-prèndere [*r-*, *apprendere*], IRR.; INTR., REFL.: take back (recover)†; coagulate, curdle; stiffen (grow rigid; be benumbed); make reprisals†. **-preságlia**, F.: reprisals, retaliation. **-presagliáre**†, TR.: take as reprisals, seize, sequester.

rappresen-tábile, ADJ.: representable. **-taménto**†, M., **-tánza**, F.: representation; image (type). ‖**-táre** [*presentare*], TR.: represent (exhibit, signify; act, act as); REFL.: present one's self again; represent one's self (appear)†. **-tánte**, ADJ.: representing, etc.; M.: representative. **-tativaménte**, ADV.: representatively. **-tatívo**, ADJ.: representative. **-tatóre**, M., **-tatríce**, F.: representer, exhibitor. **-tazioncèlla**, **-tazioncína**, *dim.* of *-tazione*. **-tazióne**, F.: representation (representing; exhibit; acting, dramatic or theatrical performance, drama); (*leg.*) legal heirs. **-tévole**†, ADJ.: representable.

rappréso, PART. of *rapprendere*.

r=appressáre†, TR.: draw near again.

r=approfondáre†, TR.: deepen; go deep(er) into; examine thoroughly.

r=approssim..† = *approssim..*

r=appuntáre†, TR.: point again.

r=appuráre, TR.: purge (again).

raps-odía [Gr. *rhapsodía* (*rháptein*, sew, *odé*, song)], F.: rhapsody. **-odísta**, pl. *—ti*, M.: (*lit. disp.*) rhapsodist, big talker. **-òdo**, M.: (*lit.*) rhapsodist.

ra-raménte, ADV.: rarely, seldom. **-refaciènte**, ADJ.: rarefying. **-re=fáre**, IRR.; TR.: rarefy; dilate; REFL.: be rarefied or dilated. **-refattíbile**, **-refattívo**, ADJ.: rarefying. **-refátto**, PART. of *-refare*. **-refazióne**, F.: rarefaction. **-rétto**, *dim.* of *-ro*. **-rézza**, F.: rarity; thinness, scarcity. **-ríccio**†, ADJ.: very rare. **-rifica..**† = *-refa..* **-ríssimo**, ADJ.: most rare, very rare. **-rità**, F.: rarity, scarcity; curiosity. ‖**-ro** [L. *-rus*], ADJ.: rare (scarce; thin; choice); M.: rarity (rare thing; thinness); ADV.: rarely, seldom: *di —*, rarely. **-rúccio**†, *dim.* of *-ro*.

ra-sáre [*raso*], TR.: level off, even, strike (a measure of grain, etc.); clip, shave. **-sáto**, PART.: evened, etc.; even, smooth. **-satúra**, F.: shaving, scraping.

rá-schia†, F.: RASH (itch, scab). **-schiábile**, ADJ.: that may be scraped. **-schiaménto**, M.: scraping; erasure. ‖**-as**

re [p. L. ***-siculare** (cf. *-sare*)], TR.: scrape (rub, scratch, grate over; erase; abrade, remove by scraping). **-schiáta**, F.: scraping. **-schiatóio**, M.: scraper (instrument). **-schiatúra**, F.: scraping; (e)rasure. **-schiétto**, **-schíno**, M.: scraper. **-schío1**, M.: (continuous) scraping or rasping. **rá-schio2**, M.: rasping.

rá-scia [*R.*, place], F.: serge (woollen stuff). **-sciére**, M.: serge manufacturer.

rasciu-gaménto, M.: drying up, wiping off. ‖**-gáre** [*asciugare*], TR.: dry up, wipe (off); drink up; consume; outdo (get the better of, wipe out). **-gatúra**, F.: drying up, wiping off. **-gáto**, **rasciú-tto**, PART. of *-sciugare*.

ra-sentáre, TR.: graze (rub along the surface of, touch lightly; Eng.† RASE). **-sènte**, PREP.: grazing, close to, along. **-sétto**, *dim.* of *-so*. **-sièra**, F.: strickle (instrument for levelling a grain measure, strike); rasp†; trough-scraper†. **-sière†**, M.: shaver, barber. ‖**rá-so**, PART. of *-dere;* shorn, shaved; erased, etc.; even, open; M.: rasure†; satin. **-soiáccio**, *disp.* of *-soio*. **-sóio**, M.: RAZOR: *attaccarsi a' -soi*, be exceedingly captious.

rá-spa, F.: rasp. ‖**-spáre** [OGer. *raspōn*], TR.: rasp; scrape; scratch; paw; pluck; rob, pilfer. **-spatíccio**, M.: scratching; botch work, bungle. **-spatíno**, **-spáto**, M.: wine made of grape-stems (cf. *-spo*). **-spatúra**, F.: rasping, scraping. **-sperèlla†**, F.: wild broom. **-spíno**, *dim.* of *-spo*. **-spo**, M.: bunch of grape-stems (plucked bunch of grapes); bunch† of grapes; mange, itch. **-spolláre†**, TR.: glean (grapes). **-spéllo**, M.: small or thin bunch of grapes; cluster.

r=assaggiáre†, TR.: taste again.

r=assalíre†, TR.: assail again.

rassecur. . = *rassicur*. .

rasse-gáre [*r-*, *a*, *sego*], INTR., REFL.: change into fat (of gravy, soup, etc.), coagulate. **-gáto**, PART.: changed into fat, etc.; stiff, stale.

rassé-gna, F.: review (of troops), muster; registration (in a university). **-gnaménto**, M.: review(ing), muster. ‖**-gnáre** [L. *re-signare*], TR.: resign (renounce); consign (assign); restore; submit, return (thanks); pass (troops) in review, muster; write†, note†; pay tribute; REFL.: be resigned, submit; subscribe or sign one's self (at the end of letters); register. **-gnatamente**, ADV.: resignedly. **-gnáto**, PART.: resigned, etc. **-gnatóre**, M., **-gnatríce**, F.: resigner; consigner; inspector (of troops), mustering officer. **-gnazióne**, F.: resignation, submission.

rassembl. . = *rassembr*. .

rassem-braménto†, M., **-bránza†**, F.: resemblance. ‖**-bráre** [*r-*, *a*, *sembrare*], TR.: (*lit.*) resemble (be like); represent. **-'bro†**, M.: similarity.

rassere - naménto, M.: clearing up. ‖**-náre** [*r-*, *a*, *sereno*], TR.: render serene or clear, clear; exhilarate; REFL.: become serene, clear up. **-náto**, PART.: cleared up, serene; exhilarated.

rasset-taménto, M.: repairing, mending. ‖**-táre** [*r-*, *assettare*], TR.: repair (mend); arrange (adjust, settle)†; put together†; assemble†. **-tatóre**, M., **-tatríce**, F.: repairer (mender); adjuster†. **-tatúra**, F.: repairing; arrangement. **rassèt-to**, ADJ.: repaired; arranged.

rassicu-ránte, ADJ.: reassuring. ‖**-ráre** [*r-*, *assicurare*], TR.: reassure; REFL.: be reassured, take courage. **-razióne**, F.: reassurance.

rassoda-ménto, M.: consolidation. ‖**-'re** [*r-*, *assodare*], TR.: consolidate; strengthen.

rassodía = *rapsodia*.

rassomi-gliaménto†, M., **-gliánza**, F.: resemblance; comparison. ‖**-gliáre** [*r-*, *assomigliare*], TR.: resemble (be like, equal); compare. **-gliánte**, ADJ.: resembling, like. **-gliatívo**, ADJ.: resembling, like. **-gliatóre†**, M., **-gliatríce†**, F.: imitator.

r=assottigliáre, TR.: subtilize; render thin or pointed, lessen; REFL.: grow thin, taper off.

rastell. . (*pop.*) = *rastrell*. .

rasti. . (*pop.*) = *raschi*. .

ra-strelláre [*-strello*], TR.: rake; plane (metal); rob†. **-strelláta**, F.: rakeful. **-strellatúra**, F.: raking. **-strellièra**, F.: hayrack, rack; kitchen-shelf, dresser; stand for arms; row. **-strellíno**, *dim.* of *-strello*. **-strèllo**, M.: rake; railing; palisade (barrier); rack. ‖**-stro** [L. *-strum*], M.: (*poet.*) rake.

rasúra [*radere*], F.: (e)rasure, cancelling; scrapings†; tonsure†.

ráta [L., 'reckoned,' sc. *pars*], F.: rate (portion)†; portion due (for payment), payment, instalment; contribution.

ratafià [?], M.: ratafia (spirituous liquor).

ratifi-caménto, M.: ratification. ‖**-cáre** [L.], TR.: ratify. **-catóre**, M., **-catríce**, F.: ratifier. **-cazióne**, F.: ratification.

rátio†, ADV.: *andar —*, go searching (aimlessly).

ratíre†, INTR.: give the death-rattle, be in the pangs of death.

ráto [L. *-tus*, reckoned, fixed], ADJ.: RATIfied (confirmed).

r=attaccáre, TR.: reattack.

rattacco-naménto, M.: patching (shoes), mending. ‖**-náre** [*tacconi*], TR.: patch (shoes), botch.

rattaménte [*ratto*], ADV.: rapidly, swiftly; quickly.
rattarpáre† = *rattrappire*.
rattemperáre [*r-*, *a*, *temperare*], TR.: temper (moderate, repress); REFL.: restrain one's self, forbear.
ratte-nére [*r-*, *a*, *tenere*], IRR.; TR.: retain (keep back, check, restrain; detain); REFL.: contain one's self, pause; M.: retaining. **-niménto**, M.: retaining (retention, detention, checking). **-nitíva**, F.: retentiveness (of mind), memory. **-nitívo**†, M.: restraint; defence. **-núta**, F.: retention; (*agr.*) embankment. **-núto**, PART.: retained, etc.; restrained, cautious, discreet.
r=attestáre, TR.: join end to end; join again, reunite; RECIPR.: reunite, meet again, rally.
rattézza [*ratto*], F.: rapidity, swiftness.
rattiepe-dáre†, ||**-díre** [*tepido*], TR.: render tepid or lukewarm, cool.
rattívo†, ADJ.: rapacious, greedy.
r=attizzáre, TR.: stir (the fire) again; stir up again, rekindle.
rátto [L. *raptus*, snatched away], ADJ.: (*poet.*) snatched away; ravished; RAPID (swift); precipitous (steep); ADV.: suddenly, swiftly; M.: RAPINE (prey, robbery, RAPE); dash†; RAPTure (ecstasy).
rattop-paménto, M.: patching, mending. ||**-páre** [*r-*, *a*, *toppa*], TR.: patch (mend, botch). **-patóre**, M.: patcher. **-patúra**, F.: patching (mending).
r=attòrcere, IRR.: wring (twist).
rattóre† = *rapitore*.
r=attorniáre†, TR.: surround.
rattòrto, PART. of *rattorcere*.
rattrá-ere† = *rattrarre*. **-iménto**, M.: shrinking.
rattrappa..† = *rattrappi..*
rattrap-piménto, M.: contraction (of the nerves). ||**-píre** [Fr. *r-attraper*, catch back], INTR., REFL.: contract (of the nerves), shrink, be wrinkled; become paralyzed. **-pitúra**, F.: contraction (of the nerves), shrinking.
rattrárre [*trarre*], IRR.; INTR., REFL.: conTRACT, shrink.
r=attristáre, TR.: aggrieve, sadden; REFL.: grow sad. **-attristíre**, TR.: sadden, depress.
rattúra†, F.: RAPE, ravishment.
rau-caménte, ADV.: hoarsely. **-cèdine**, F.: hoarseness, ||**ráu-co** [*-cus*], ADJ.: hoarse (raucous); harsh, rough.
ra=umiliáre, TR.: humiliate; make humble, tame; calm.
rauna.. = *raduna..*
raugèo†, ADJ.: greedy; wicked.
raúno†, M.: reunion (assembly); heap (pile).
ravaglióne [metath. of *variolone* (cf. *vaiolo*)], M.: chicken-pox, measles.
rava-nèllo, ||**ráva-no**† [*rapa*], M.: radish.
raveggi(u)òlo [?], M.: cream-cheese (us'ly of goat's milk).
rave-rúschio, **-rústo** [*lambrusco*], M.: sort of wild vine or grape.
raviggiòlo 1 = *raveggiolo*.
ra-viggiólo 2, pl. *-violi* [?], M.: dumpling.
ravi(u)òli, pl. of *raviggiolo* 2.
r=avvaloráre, TR.: inspire with valour, encourage, fortify.
ravve-dére [*ra-*, *vedere*], IRR.; REFL.: recognize one's mistake (regret, repent); reform. **-diménto**, M.: repentance, amendment. **-dúto**, PART.
r=avversáre, TR.: turn back, set aright, arrange.
rav-viaménto, M.: setting aright; self-amendment. ||**-viáre** [*via*], TR.: set again in the right way, set aright, reform; rearrange, fix again; set on foot again; put together; REFL.: recommence one's journey. **-viáta**, F.: arranging (or fixing) the hair, toilet.
r=avvicináre, TR.: bring near again; approach; REFL.: approach (again); approach each other.
r=avvilíre†, TR.: make vile; terrify, dishearten.
ravvilup-paménto, M.: entanglement, confusion. ||**-páre** [*avviluppare*], TR.: envelop; involve, entangle, confound; REFL.: be involved or confounded; crowd together in the mind.
ravvíncere†, IRR.; TR.: tie around, fasten; surround again.
ravvincidíre†, INTR.: grow flabby or soft.
ravvínto†, PART. of *ravvincere*.
ravvi-sábile, ADJ.: recognizable. ||**-sáre** [*r-*, *a*, *viso*], TR.: recognize (by the 'face'); advise (inform)†; think†.
ravvísto, PART. of *ravvedere*.
ravvi-vaménto, M.: reviving, revival. ||**-váre** [*r-*, *avvivare*], TR.: revive, reanimate; resuscitate; REFL.: revive: *-varsi alla memoria*, return to the recollection. **-vatóre**, M.: reviver.
ravvòl-gere [*r-*, *a*, *volgere*], IRR.; TR.: involve; wrap (up), envelop; REFL.: be involved, be wrapped up; ramble about†; turn (of wine). **-giménto**, M., **-gitúra**†, F.: involving, inwrapping; winding about, turning. **-táre**†, TR.: wrap up. **ravvòl-to**, PART.: involved; wrapped (up), etc.; crooked; M.†: bundle. **-toláre**, TR.: go on involving; keep on wrapping.
razio-cinaménto†, M.: ratiocination. **-nánte**, M.: disputant. ||**-cináre**

ratiocinare (*ratio*, reason)], TR.: ratiocinate (REASON, argue). **-cinazióne**†, F., **-cínio**, M.: ratiocination (reasoning). **-nábile**, ADJ.: reasonable, rational. **-nabilità**, F.: reasonableness, reason. **-nabilménte**, ADV.: reasonably. **-nále**, ADJ.: rational, reasonable. **-nalísmo**, M.: rationalism. **-nalísta**, pl. *-nalisti*, M.: rationalist. **-nalità**, F.: rationality; power of reason. **-nalménte**, ADV.: rationally. ‖**razió-ne** [L. *ratio*], F.: RATION (daily portion); proportion, RATE.

rázza 1 [OHG. *reiza*, line], F.: RACE; lineage (family); breed (stock); kind; flock: *far — da sè*, live solitary, shun people.

rázza 2 [L. *raia*], F.: RAY (fish).

rázza 3 [L. *radius*, rod], F.: spoke (of a wheel).

razzáccia, *disp.* of *razza* 1.

raz-záre [-*zo*], TR.: lock (a wheel, *lit.* tie a 'spoke,' in steep descents), clog; illumine; touch† lightly (as with a 'rod'); INTR.: radiate; REFL.: spread in rays, be inflamed. **-zatúra**, F.: colouring like rays; rash. **-zeggiáre**, INTR.: radiate, shine. **-zènte**†, ADJ.: pungent, tart. **-zettíno**, **-zétto**, *dim.* of *-zo*.

razzería†, F.: tapestry.

razzièra [*razzo*], F.: rocket gun.

r=azzimáre†, TR.: adorn, deck.

razzína, *dim.* of *razza* 1.

rázzo [L. *radius*, rod, ray], M.: RAY (beam)†; rocket; spoke (of a wheel); sort of olive†. **-láre** [*razzare*, touch lightly], TR.: scratch (as a hen), scrape. **-láta**, F.: scratching. **-latóra**, F., **-latóre**, M.: scratcher, scraper. **-latúra**, F.: scratching. **-lío**, M.: continued scratching.

r=azzuffáre, REFL.: begin the battle anew, return to fight.

razzumáglia [*razzolare*], F.: scrapings (refuse); rabble (mob).

razzuòlo, *dim.* of *-zo*.

ré [L. *rex*], M.: king: — *d'armi*, herald; — *di siepe*, tomtit, wren.

re- [L.], PREF.: *re-*, again, back.

rè [L. *re-* of *resonare*, in a hymn], M.: (*mus.*) re.

re-agènte, ADJ.: reacting. **-agire** [L. *re-agere*], TR.: react.

reále 1 [L. *regalis* (*rex*, king)], ADJ.: ROYAL (kingly, regal): *alla* —, like a king.

reá-le 2 [L. *-lis* (*res*, thing)], ADJ.: real (true); loyal; frank. **-lísmo**, M.: realism. **-lísta**, pl. —*ti*, M.: realist.

rea-lità† [*-le* 1], F.: royalty. **-lménte** 1, ADV.: royally, regally.

eal-ménte 2 [*reale* 2], ADV.: really. **tà**, F.: reality.

ìme [*re*], M.: (*pop.*) REALM.

ménte [*reo*], ADV.: wickedly (crim-*lly*).

rèas†, M.: wild poppy.

re=assúmere, IRR.; TR.: take again (re-assume).

reatíno†, M.: wren.

reáto [*reo*], M.: crime, offence, infraction.

reattívo [*reagire*], ADJ.: reactive.

re-azionário, M.: reactionary. ‖**=azióne**, F.: reaction.

reb-biáre, TR.: strike with the prong of a fork, fork; thrash. **-biáta**, F.: blow with a fork; thrashing. ‖**rèb-bio** [?Ger. *riffel*, RIPPLE, flax-comb], M.: prong of a fork, etc.

rebell..† = *ribell..*

reboáto†, M.: loud voice.

rèbus [L., 'by things'], M.: rebus.

recadía†, F.: trouble, vexation.

recalcit.. = *ricalcit..*

recaménto† [*-care*], M.: bringing, fetching; producer, cause.

re=capitáre, TR.: have delivered; transmit, send; INTR.: arrive; suppurate. **-cápito**, M.: delivery; address (direction); introduction. **-capitol..** = *ricapitol..*

recá-re [OHG. *reichan*, REACH], TR.: bring (carry, fetch); acquire (gain); bring about (effect, cause); render (translate); attribute (ascribe, impute); reduce†; interpret (take)†; REFL.: bring (place); take; betake one's self; attribute to one's self (— *ad*, count, consider, take as): — *ad effetto*, bring into effect, effect; — *innanzi*, represent; — *d'una lingua in un' altra*, translate; — *a fine*, perfect; — *a volgare*, translate; — *a un dì*, squander; — *la cagione*, impute; — *a oro*, come to the point; — *a stretto*, unite; — *relazione*, give an account of; *-rsi adosso*, take upon one's self; *-rsi a mente*, remember; *-rsi a cuore*, take to heart; *-rsi ad onore*, consider as an honour; *-rsi ad ingiuria*, *-rsi a male*, take ill; *-rsi in braccio*, take into one's arms; *-rsi in collo*, take upon one's shoulders; *-rsi a noia*, begin to be tired; *-rsi le mani al petto*, examine one's conscience; *-rsi sopra di sè* (or *in sè stesso*), reflect within one's self; *-rsi in guardia*, put one's self on one's guard; — *a schifo*, loathe, abhor. **recá-ta**†, F.: bringing (fetching); list of immovables; sigh ('fetching' of the breath), rattle, plaint, lamentation: — *della morte*, death-rattle, last breath; *l' ultime -te*, the last breath or gasp. **-tóre**†, M., **-tríce**†, F.: bringer. **-túra**†, F.: bringing; carriage (porterage); bounty.

réc-chia† [*orecchia*], F.: ear. **-chiáta**†, F., **-chióne**†, M.: box on the ear.

recè-dere [L.], IRR., INTR.: recede (draw back, withdraw, retire). **-diménto**, M.: receding, withdrawal.

recen-sióne [L. *-sio* (*censere*, judge)], F.: recension. **-sóre**, M.: recensionist.
recèn-te [L. *-s*], ADJ.: recent, late: *di* —, recently, of late. **-teménte**, recently. **-tíssimo**, ADJ.: most (or very) recent.
recèpere† = *ricevere*.
rècere [L. *re-icere* (*jacere*, throw)], INTR.; throw up (vomit, spew); M.: disgusting thing: — *le budella*, laugh heartily; — *l' anima*, expire, die.
recèsso [*-cedere*], PART.: receded, etc.; M.: recess (retreat); (*med.*) retrogression.
recett.. = *ricett..*
re-cídere [L. (*cædere*, cut)], IRR., TR.: cut off, sever; RESCIND; REFL.: split, rip. **-cidiménto**†, M., **-cidítura**†, F.: incision (cut, notch).
reci-díva, F.: relapse. **-diváre**†, INTR.: relapse. ‖**-dívo** [L. *-divus* (*re-cadere*, fall back)], ADJ.: relapsing (backsliding; relapse).
re=cíngere, IRR.; TR.: gird; enclose. **-cínto**, PART.: girded; M.: enclosure; rampart.
rèci-pe [L. I've of *-pere*, take in], (on prescriptions:) 'take'; M.: recipe (prescription; receipt). **-piènte**, ADJ.: receiving†; capable, proper; agreeable; M.: recipient (receptacle, vase; bell-glass).
recipro-caménte, ADV.: reciprocally, mutually. **-caménto**, M.: reciprocation. **-cáre**, TR.: reciprocate, alternate; REFL.: be reciprocally proportionate. **-cazióne**, F.: reciprocation. **-cità**, F.: reciprocity. ‖**recípro-co**, pl. *-ci* or *-chi* [L. *-cus*], ADJ.: reciprocal, mutual.
re-císa, F.: cutting (off), severing; and cf. *-ciso*: *a* (or *alla*) —, the shortest way; briefly; inconsiderately. **-cisaménte**, ADV.: sharply; decisively; precisely. **-císi**, PRET. of *-cidere*. **-cisióne**, F.: cutting (off); recission; omission. ‖**-císo**, PART. of *-cidere*: cut, etc.; quick, sudden.
rèci-ta, F.: recitation, performance. **-tábile**, ADJ.: apt to be recited or represented. **-taménto**†, M.: recitation. **-tánte**, ADJ.: reciting; representing; M.: actor. ‖**-táre** [L.], TR.: recite; represent (act); pretend. **-tatívo**, M.: (*mus.*) recitative. **-tatóre**, M., **-tatríce**, F.: reciter; actor. **-tazióne**, F.: recitation, recital; representation.
re-citíccio, M.: vomits; refuse. ‖**-citúto**, PART. of *recere*.
re=clamáre, TR.: reclaim (claim back, redemand); INTR.: appeal, protest; complain; claim (demand). **-clamazióne**†, F., **-clámo**, M.: reclamation; appeal.
re-clináre [L.], INTR., TR.: recline, repose. **-clinatòrio**†, M.: resting-place; couch.

re-clusióne, F.: reclusion (seclusion). ‖**-clúso** [L. *-clusus* (*claudere*, close)] ADJ.: recluse (shut up). **-clusòrio**, M.: solitary confinement, cell.
reclú-ta [Fr. *recrue* (PART. of *re-croître*, increase)], F.: reënforcement; RECRUIT; collection†. **-táre**, TR.: recruit. **-tatóre**, M.: recruiter.
recogitáre†, TR.: think over.
recognizióne = *ricognizione*.
recolèndo†, ADJ.: reverend.
reconcil..† = *riconcil..*
recòndi-to [L. *-tus* (*con-dere*, put together)], ADJ.: recondite (hidden, abstruse). **-tòrio**, M.: altar shrine (for the relics of saints).
re-creáre†, **-criáre**† = *ricreare*.
recre-mentízio, ADJ.: (*med.*) recrementitious. ‖**-ménto** [L. *-mentum* (*re-, cernere*, sift)], M.: recrement (superfluous matter, dross).
recrimi-náre [L. *-nari* (*crimen*, crime)], TR.: recriminate. **-nazióne**, F.: recrimination.
recrudescènza [L. *re-crudescere*, become raw], F.: recrudescency (breaking out again, of sickness).
recuperá-re [L.], TR.: recuperate (RECOVER, regain). **-tòrio**, ADJ.: (*leg.*) recuperatory. **-zióne**, F.: recovery.
recurrènte†, ADJ.: recurrent.
recus.. = *ricus..*
rè-da† [*erede*], F.: heir; offspring; four-wheeled chariot. **-dággio**†, M.: inheritance. **-dáre**, TR.: inherit.
redar-guènte, ADJ.: reproving. ‖**-guíre** [L. *red-arguere*], TR.: reprove (rebuke, disprove). **-guizióne**†, F.: rebuking, rebuke.
reda-tóre†, M., **-tríce**†, F.: heir, heiress.
red-attóre [L. *-igere* (*agere*, act), redact], M.: editor (redacteur, redactor). **-azióne**, F.: redaction (editing); expounding.
rèd-dere† [L. (*dare*, give)], TR.: RENDER (restore, return). **-diménto**†, M.: rendition (reddition, restoration).
redd-íre = *redire*. **-íta**†, F.: return. **-íto**† 1, PART.: returned.
rèddito 2 [L. *-tus* (*dare*, give)], M.: revenue.
rède [*erede*], M.: (*vulg.*) heir.
redèn-to [*redimere*], PART.: redeemed, etc. **-tóre**, M.: redeemer (ransomer, saviour). **-tríce**, F.: redeemer. **-zióne**, F.: redemption; ransom; remedy†.
redificáre† = *riedificare*.
redígere [L. (*agere*, act)], DEFECT.; TR.: REDACT (digest and put in shape, edit); e[x]pound.
redí-mere [L. (*re, emere*, buy)], IR[R.], TR.: REDEEM (ransom; liberate, l[...]

-mibile, ADJ.: redeemable. **-mibilità**, F.: redeemableness.

§ Pret. *redèn-si, -se; -sero.* Part. *redènto.*

redimíre†, TR.: crown; decorate†.

rèdina, pl. *—ne* or *—ni* [? L. *retinere*, retain], F.: REIN.

red-íre [L.], INTR.: return (come back). **-íta**, F.: return.

redi-tà†, F., **-tággio**†, M.: heredity. **-tière**†, M.: heir.

redivívo [L. *-vivus* (alive)], ADJ.: returned to life.

redolíre†, INTR.: be redolent or fragrant.

rè-duce, M.: one who returned; ADJ.: returned. ||**-dúcere**† = *ridurre*. **-duci..** = *riduci..*

reduplicá-re†, TR.: reduplicate, redouble. **-tívo**†, ADJ.: reduplicative. **-zióne**, F.: reduplication.

redutt..† = *ridutt..*

reedific..† = *riedific..*

reézza†, F.: wickedness, crime.

re-faiuòlo†, M.: thread merchant. ||**ré-fe** [?], M.: thread, string; continuity: *cucire a — doppio*, deceive, trick; outdo; *cucirsi a suo —*, cheat one's self: — —, (*pop.*) just, precisely.

re-ferendário, M.: referendary, reporter; (*iron.*) spy. ||**-feríre** [*referre*], TR.: refer (relate, report, state; ascribe). **-fèrto**, M.: report; statement.

re-fettòrio [L. *-fectorius* (*-ficere*, restore)], M.: refectory. **-fezionáre**, TR.: give refection or refreshment to (refresh, Eng.† REFECT); INTR.: take refreshment, lunch. **-fezióne**, F.: refection (refreshment, repast); repair. **-ficáre**†, **-fiziáre**†, TR.: restore, repair. **-fiziatóre**†, **-fiziatríce**†, F.: restorer; comforter.

re-flessáre†, TR.: reflect. **-flessi..**† = *riflessi..* **-flèsso** = *riflesso*. **-flett..**† = *riflett..*

reflu.. = *riflu..*

refocill.. = *rifocill..*

rèfolo†, M.: squall.

re-frang.. = *rifrang..* **-frattário**, ADJ.: refractory, disobedient. **-frátto**†, **-frazióne** = *rifratto, rifrazione.*

refrenáre† = *raffrenare.*

refri-geránte, ADJ., M.: refrigerant. ||**-geráre** [L.], TR.: refrigerate (cool); alleviate (console). **-geratívo**†, **-geratòrio**†, ADJ.: refrigerative, cooling. **-gerazióne**, F.: refrigeration; cooling; refreshment. **-gèrio** [L. *-gerium*], M.: refreshment, relief, comfort.

refugi.., **refuggi..** = *rifugi.., rifuggi..*

re-fusáre, TR.: (*typ.*) set (type) wrongly, confuse. ||**-fúso** [L. *-fusus*], M.: (*typ.*) wrong type; PL.: (*typ.*) pi.

refut..† = *rifut..*

rega-lábile, ADJ.: presentable; remissible. ||**-láre** [?], TR.: present (make a present of, give away, bestow); remit (not exact, allow); waste (squander); regale (treat)†; garnish (adorn). **-láto**, PART.: presented (bestowed, etc.); unpaid; adorned, exquisite (delicious).

regá-le [L. *-lis* (*rex*, king)], ADJ.: regal, royal; M.: small organ, hand-organ. **-lía**, F.: regalia (royal prerogative).

regalíno, *car. dim.* of *-lo.*

rega-lísta†, pl. *—ti* [*-le*], M.: royalist. **-lménte**, ADV.: regally, royally. **-lità**, F.: royalty.

regá-lo [*-lare*], M.: present (gift, donation); (*fig.*) health; luck: *averlo per —*, have it for less than cost, have it cheap; *bel —*, (*iron.*) a nice thing! **-lúccio**, *disp. dim.* of *-lo.*

regáta [?], F.: regatta (boat-race).

rège [L. *rex*], M.: (*poet.*) king (= *re*).

regener.. = *rigener..*

règge†, F.: gate, entrance.

reg-gènte, ADJ.: ruling (governing, regent); M.: regent. **-gènza**, F.: regency. ||**règ-gere** [L. *regere*], IRR.§; TR.: rule (govern, master, manage); sustain (endure, bear); support (bear up, prop); resist (oppose); endure; defend, aid; INTR.: rule, prevail; endure (last, continue); subsist (live); REFL.: govern (check, stop) one's self, maintain one's self; adopt the proper means: — *alla fatica*, be able to bear fatigue; — *alle botte*, bear blows bravely; — *il tormento*, bear the rack without confessing; — *con uno*, agree to live in peace with one. **règ-gia** [L. *regia* (*rex*, king)], F.: royal palace; court. **-gíbile**, ADJ.: governable, manageable. **-giménto**, M.: government (rule, Eng.† regiment); support (help, assistance); regiment (of soldiers); procedure†; régime†; rudder†; military move†. **-gi-pància**, M.: girdle, truss, suspensory. **-gi-posáta**, M.: support for knife, fork and spoon (at table). **-gitóre**, M., **-gitríce**, F.: ruler (governor, RECTOR); support(er). **-ía**† = *-gia*. **-iaménte**, ADV.: royally. **-icída**, pl. *—di* [L. *rex*, king, *caedere*, kill], M.: regicide. **-icídio** [cf. *-icida*], M.: regicide. **-íme** [L.], M.: regimen, regime. **-ína** [L.], F.: queen. **règ-io**, ADJ.: royal (majestic, princely): *acqua -ia*, aqua regia. **-ionále**, ADJ.: regional (of a certain region), sectional. **-ionalísmo**, M.: sectionalism. **-ionalísta**, pl. *—ti*, M.: sectionalist. **-ionário**, M.: region or section superintendent, local chief. **-ióne** [L. *-io*], F.: region (district, province, section, country, part); ward.

§ *rès-si, -se; -sero.* Part. *rètto.*

regi-stráre, TR.: register. **-stratóre**, M.: registrar, recorder. **-stratúra**, **-strazióne**, F.: registration (registering; register). ‖**regí-stro** [L. *-strum* (*re-gerere*, bring back)], M.: register (record, book of records; *mus.*: compass of a voice or instrument; regulator): *mutar* —, change one's tone; *tassa di* —, registration fee.

re-gnáme†, M.: REALM, kingdom. **-gnánte**, ADJ.: reigning; M.: reigning prince, ruler, sovereign. **-gnáre** [L.], REIGN. **-gnatóre**, M., **-gnatríce**, F.: ruler, sovereign. **-gnícolo** [*colere*, inhabit], M.: inhabitant or native of a kingdom (as esp. of Naples), native citizen. ‖**ré-gno** [L. *-gnum* (*reg-*, rule)], M.: kingdom (realm; reign, dominion; Eng.† REIGN): *Regno*, kingdom of Naples; royal crown†; — *dei cieli*, paradise; *secondo* —, purgatory.

règo-la [L. *regula* (*reg-*, rule)], F.: RULE (law, ordination; order); model; (religious, monastic) order; convent†, monastery†; restraint (bridle); ruler (for drawing lines)†; PL.: menses: — *del tre*, (*math.*) Rule of Three; — *d'oro*, golden rule. **-laménto**, M.: regulation. **-láre** 1, ADJ.: regular (normal, orderly; exact; of a monastic order); M.: regular monk. **-láre** 2, TR.: regulate (order, arrange); rule. **-larità**, F.: regularity. **-larménte**, ADV.: regularly. **-lataménte**, ADV.: in a regular manner. **-latézza**, F.: regularity. **-láto**, PART.: regulated, etc.; regular (ordinary; of a monastic order). **-latóre**, M., **-latríce**, F.: regulator; director (*f.* directress); ADJ.: regulating. **-lazióne**, F.: regulation. **-létta**, *dim.* of *-la*. **-létto**, M.: *dim.* of *-lo*; (*arch.*) reglet, fillet; (*typ.*) reglet. **-lína**, *car. dim.* of *-la*. **-líno**, *dim.* of *-lo*.

regolízia [L. *liquiritia*], F.: licorice.

règo-lo 1 [*-la*], M.: ruler (for lining, rule); sliding ruler, computer; tailor's flat-iron (smoothing-iron); reglet (flat moulding, listel); line on a chess-board. **règo-lo** 2 [L. *-lus* (*rex*, king)], M.: petty king; prince of the royal blood; basilisk (sort of lizard; fabulous serpent, fr. Gr. *basileús*, 'king')†; wren, hedge-sparrow. **-lúccia**, **-lúzza**†, *disp. dim.* of *-la*. **-lúzzo**†, M.: *dim.* of *-lo* 2; petty prince.

regrèsso [*-ssus* (*gradi*, move)], M.: regress (retrogression, return); place of exit†.

regurg. . = *rigurg*. .

re-iètto [L. *-jectus*], ADJ.: rejected; spurned. **-iezióne**, F.: rejection.

reína [L. *regina*], F.: (*lit.*) queen; carp.

reinte-graménto, M.: reintegration. ‖**-gráre** [L. (*integer*, whole)], TR.: reintegrate (restore). **-gratívo**, ADJ.: serving to reintegrate, restorative. **-grazióne**, F.: reintegration.

reinvitáre†, TR.: invite again.

reità [*reo*], F.: guilt (culpability), crime.

re-iterábile, ADJ.: that may be reiterated. **-iteraménto**, M.: reiteration. ‖=**iteráre**, TR.: reiterate. **-iterataménte**, ADV.: reiteratedly, repeatedly. **-iterazióne**, F.: reiteration.

reiudicáta, **re iudicáta**, F.: cause already heard and decided.

relass. . = *rilass*. .

rela-tivaménte, ADV.: relatively; in respect (to). ‖**-tívo** [L. *-tivus*], ADJ.: relative. **-tóre**, M.: relater, reporter. **-zioncèlla**, *dim.* of *-zione*. **-zióne**, F.: relation (narration, report, account; connection, reference; analogy).

relegá-re, TR.: relegate (banish, confine). **-zióne**, F.: relegation.

reli-gionário, M.: confessor of some religion (religionist). ‖**-gióne** [L. *-gio*], F.: religion; religious order; cult; piety. **-giosaménte**, ADV.: religiously; piously. **-giosità**, F.: religiousness; piety. **-gióso**, ADJ.: religious; pious; scrupulous; monastic; M.: member of a religious order; monk, friar.

re-línquere† [L.], TR.: relinquish (LEAVE). **-líquia** [L.], F.: relic; relics. **-liquiário**, M.: reliquary (shrine). **-lítto**†, ADJ.: relinquished, left.

reluc. . = *riluc*. .

relutt. . = *rilutt*. .

rèma† = *reuma*.

remáio†, M.: oar-maker. **-mánte**, ADJ.: rowing; M.: rower. ‖**-máre** [*-mo*], TR.: row. **-máta**, F.: stroke of the oar.

remá-tico† = *reumatico* or *aromatico*. **-tísmo**† = *reumatismo*.

re-máto [*-mare*], PART.: rowed; ADJ.†: furnished with oars. **-matóre**, M.: rower. **-meggiáre**†, TR.: flap (the wings); row†. **-méggio**, M.: rowing; flapping (of the wings); (*coll.*) oars.

remènso†, ADJ.: measured, examined.

remi-gaménto, M.: rowing. **-gánte**, ADJ.: rowing; M.: rower. ‖**-gáre** [*r*- *mare*], TR.: row. **-gatóre**. **-gazióne**†, F.: rowing. rowing etc.; = *remeggi*

remini-scèns(i)a [*-sce* cence. **-scitíva**, F.: re of remembering).

remis-síbile, ADJ.: r able. **-sibilménte**, ‖**-sióne** [L. *-sio*], F.: abatement); respite†. in a remissive way, by vo, ADJ.: remissive (**-sòria**†, F.: certificat mission.

remit. . (*pop.*) = *eremit.* .

rèmo [L. *remus*], M.: oar; oar of a galley (= 'galley'): *remi da lancia* (or *accoppiati*), double set of oars; *remi di punta*, one set of oars; *dar de' remi* (*in acqua*), begin to row; *maltardato* —, indolence.

remoláre†, INTR.: delay, retard.

remo-líno, M.: whirlwind. ‖**rèmo-lo** [L. root, *mol-*, 'grind,' as in *mola*, MILLstone], M.: vortex, whirl, whirlpool.

rèmora [L. (*mora*, delay)], F.: obstacle, check (Eng.† remora); remora (sucking-fish).

re-mot. . = *rimot.* . **-movíbile**, (*pop.*) = *rimovibile.* **-mozióne** = *rimozione.*

remuner. . = *rimuner.* .

ré-na [*arena*], F.: sand. **-náccio**, M.: sandy ground. **-náio**, M.: sandy shore, sand-bank; sand-pit. **-naiòlo**, M.: sand-carrier.

renále [*rene*], ADJ.: renal (of the kidneys).

renáre [*rena*], TR.: polish (with sand).

rèn-dere [L. *red-dere* (*dare*, give)], IRR.§; TR.: render (restore, return; give up; make); produce (yield); bestow (give); emit; reduce; REFL.: render (or make) one's self; become (turn); betake one's self (repair, go); surrender (submit, yield)†: — *aria*, be like, resemble; — *avvertito*, advise, let know; — *l'anima*, give up the ghost; — *diletto*, please; — *fede*, assure, testify; — *grazia*, return thanks, thank. — *merito*, make amends; — *ragione*, administer justice; give reason, give an account; justify one's self; pay the penalty; *-dersi sicuro*, think one's self safe. **-dévole**†, ADJ.: yielding (pliant, supple). **-dévos**†, M.: rendez-vous. **-di=cónto**, M.: rendering account, declaration. **-diménto**, M.: rendition (reddition, returning, return, surrender). **rèn-dita**, F.: return (yield, RENT, revenue, interest). **-ditóre**, M.: restorer; bringer, giver. **-ditúccia**, **-ditúzza**†, *disp. dim.* of *-dita.* **-dúto**, PART. (*pop.*) of *-dere.*

§ Pret. *rési* (or *rendéi*, *rendètti*), *rése* (or *rendè*, *rendètte*), *résero*; 6. *rendérono* (or *rendèttero*). Part. *réso* or *rendúto.*

rène [L. *ren*], M.: kidney; pl. *rene* or *reni*, F.: loins (REINS): *dar*† *le reni*, take to one's heels, run away; *filo delle* —, spine (vertebral column).

re-nèlla [*rena*], F.: (*med.*) gravel; small sand†, sandy ground†. **-níccio**, M.: sand deposit, sand-bank. **-níschio**, **-nístio**†, M.: sandy ground.

reni-tènte [L. *-tens* (*niti*, strive)], ADJ.: renitent (reluctant, resistant, stubborn). **-tènza**, F.: renitency (reluctance, resistance).

rènna [Swed. *ren*], F.: REINdeer.

re-nóne, *aug.* of *-na.* **-nosità**, F.: sandiness. **-nóso**, ADJ.: sandy.

rèn-sa†, F., **-so**†, M.: lawn (fine linen).

renunz. . = *rinunz.* .

renúzza [*rena*], F.: small sand.

rèn-za†, **-zo**† = *-sa*, *-so.*

rèo [L. *reus* (*res*, thing, case)], ADJ.: accused; gen'ly criminal (guilty, iniquitous); wicked; wretched, bad; M.: criminal (guilty person, culprit); wretch; guilt.

reobárbaro (*pop.*) = *rabarbaro.*

rèom. . = *reum.* .

repara. . = *ripara.* .

re-part. .† = *ripart.* . **-párto**, M.: distribution.

repatr. .† = *rimpatr.* .

re-pellénte, ADJ.: repelling, repellent. ‖**-pèllere** [L.], IRR. (cf. *espellere*); TR.: repel, reject.

repen-táglio, M.: risk (peril, jeopardy). ‖**repèn-te** [L. *repens*], ADJ.: sudden (unexpected, violent; rapid); precipitous (steep)†: *di* —, suddenly. **-temente**†, **-tinaménte**, ADV.: suddenly. **-tíno**, ADJ.: sudden (unexpected).

rèpere†, INTR.: creep, crawl.

re-períbile, ADJ.: that may be found. ‖**-perire** [L. (*parere*, bring forth)], IRR.; TR.: find out (again), discover. **-períto**, **-pèrso**†, **-pèrto**†, PART. of *-perire.* **-pertòrio**, M.: repertory (répertoire; index).

repètere (*pop*). = *ripetere.*

repetío†, M.: dispute; complaint.

repetit. . = *ripetit.* .

re-plèto [L. *-pletus* (*plere*, FILL)], ADJ.: replete, full. **-plezióne**†, F.: repletion.

rèpli-ca, F.: repetition; REPLY (answer); knell† (of a bell). **-cábile**, ADJ.: answerable. **-caménto** = *-ca.* ‖**-cáre** [L. (*plicare*, FOLD)], TR.: repeat; REPLY (answer); contradict. **-cataménte**, ADV.: repeatedly. **-catívo**, ADJ.: proper to reply. **-cazióne**, F.: repetition; reply (Eng.† replication).

repò-sito† = *riposto.* **-sitòrio**, M.: repository. **-sizióne**†, F.: reposition.

reprens. . = *riprens.* .

re-pressióne, F.: repression. **-pressívo**, ADJ.: repressive. **-prèsso**, PART. of *-primere.* **-primènda**, F.: reprimand (severe reproof). **-priménto**† = *-primimento.* ‖**-prímere** [L. (*premere*, PRESS)], IRR. (cf. *comprimere*); TR.: REPRESS (restrain; check, quell); REFL.: restrain or check one's self, keep calm. **-primiménto**, M.: repressing, restraint. **-primúto**†, PART. of *-primere.*

re-prob. . = *riprov.* . **rè-probo** [L. *-probus*], ADJ.: reprobate (abandoned, depraved, vile); (*theol.*) condemned.

repromiss. . = *ripromiss.* .

reprov. . = *riprov.* .

repúbbli-ca [L. *res-publica*], F.: republic. **-caménte**, ADV.: in a republican way. **-caníşmo**, M.: republicanism. **-cáno**, ADJ., M.: republican. **-chétta**, *dim.* of **-ca**. **-cónet**, M.: busy-body.

repudi.. = *ripudi..*

repugn.. = *ripugn..*

repuls.. = *ripuls..*

repu-tánza†, F.: reputation. ‖**-táre** [L. (*pu'are*, deem)], TR.: repute (deem, esteem, think). **-tazióne**, F.: reputation.

re-quiáre [L. (*quies*, quiet)], INTR.: repose (one's self), rest. **rè-quie**, F.: repose, rest; quiet.

requi-şíre [L. *-rere* (*quærere*, seek)], TR.: require (exact). **-şíto**, PART.: required; exacted; requisite; M.: requisite (requirement, condition). **-şitòria**, F.: (*leg.*) public accusation, charge. **-şizióne**, F.: requisition, request; exaction.

résa [*rendere*], F.: (*mil.*) surrender.

re-şcíndere [L.], IRR.; TR.: rescind (rarely: cut again, cut off; us'ly: abrogate, annul, cancel). **-şcissióne**, F.: recission (annulling, abrogation). **-şcísso**, PART.: rescinded, etc. **-şcissòrio**, ADJ.: rescissory.

re-scrítto, PART.: copied, etc.; M.: rescript, decree. ‖**-scrívere**† [L. *-scribere*], TR.: rewrite, copy.

resecáre = *risecare*.

reserváre = *riservare*.

rési, PRET. of *rendere*.

reşía = *eresia*.

resi-dènte [L. *-dens* (*sedere*, SIT)], ADJ.: residing; M.: resident, minister. **-denteménte**, ADV.: as residing. **-dènza**, F.: residence (dwelling; dwelling-place); baldachin (over an altar); residuum (sediment). **-denziále**, ADJ.: residential. **-duáre**†, INTR.: form the residue. **re-sí-duo**, M.: residue, remainder.

réşi-na [L.], F.: resin, rosin. **-náceo**, ADJ.: resinous. **-nífero**, ADJ.: resiniferous. **-nóso**, ADJ.: resinous.

resipişcènza [L. *-scentia*], F.: resipiscence (repentance).

reşípola = *risipola*.

re-sistènte, ADJ.: resisting. **-sistènza**, F.: resistance. ‖**-sístere** [L. (*stare*, stand)], IRR. (cf. *assistere*); TR.: resist (withSTAND, oppose); endure (hold out). **-sistíto**, PART.: resisted, etc.

réso, PART. of *rendere*: rendered, etc. **-cónto**, M.: 'rendering account,' report.

resol.. = *risol..*

respet-tivaménte, ADV.: respectively. ‖**-tívo** [L. *re-spectus* (*specere*, look)], ADJ.: respective, relative; respectful.

rèspice [L.], F.: *no* —, nothing.

respíngere, IRR.; TR.: push or drive back, repel; reject. **-spínto**, PART.

respi-rábile, ADJ.: respirable (breathable). **-rabilità**, F.: respirableness, fitness for breathing. **-raménto**†, M.: respiration (breathing). ‖**-ráre** [L. (*spirare*, breathe)], INTR.: respire (breathe); breathe out; exhale; puff. **-ránte**, ADJ.: breathing. **-ratívo**†, ADJ.: respirative, respiratory; exhilarating. **-ratòrio**, ADJ.: respiratory. **-razióne**, F.: respiration (breath); pause. **respí-ro**, M.: breath (single breathing); breathing-time (pause, rest). **-róne**, *aug.* of **-ro**.

respítto = *rispitto*.

respón-dere† = *rispondere*. **-sábile**, ADJ.: responsible. **-sabilità**, F.: responsibility. **-sióne**†, F.: response (answer). **-sívo**, ADJ.: responsive. **respòn-so**, M.: response (answer, esp. of an oracle). **-sòrio**, M., **-súra**†, F.: response.

resquítto†, M.: repose, calm.

rèssa [*rissa*], F.: strife†; rashness, importunity.

rèsta 1 [? L. *restis*, rope], F.: beard (of corn); rope or string (of onions); fringe; string of figs†; sometimes used as an excuse for a thing that has to go on; prickles of a fish (? from L. *arista*).

rè-sta 2, F.: rest (for the butt of the lance); tumour (on a horse's foot). **-stánte**, PART.: resting (remaining); M.: remainder, residue. **-stánza**, F.: residue. ‖**-stáre** [L. (*stare*, stand)], INTR.: remain; be; REST (stay, abide; stop, cease, discontinue); omit; REFL.: stop; refresh one's self; give over. **-státa**†, F.: remainder; stop, end.

restau-ráre [L.], TR.: RESTORE. **-ratóre**, M., **-ratríce**, F.: restorer. **-razióne**, F.: restoration; recovery. **re-stáu-ro**, M.: restoration (repair); recompense†.

re-stiaménte†, ADV.: stubbornly, reluctantly. **-sticciòlo**, *dim.* of *resto*. ‖**-stío** [*-stare*], ADJ.: restive (stubborn, drawing back, fidgety); M.: restiveness.

resti-tuiménto†, M.: restitution. ‖**-tuíre** [L. *-tuere* (*statuere*, place)], TR.: restitute (restore; return, repay). **-tutóre**, M., **-tutríce**, F.: restorer. **-tuzióne**, F.: restitution (restoring, return; reintegration).

rèsto [*restare*], M.: rest (remainder, remnant, residue, surplus): *del* —, as for the rest; otherwise, but; moreover; *fare del* —, venture the rest (the last farthing), stake or venture one's all; *dare il* — *del carlino*, pay up in full, pay the remainder.

restóso [*resta* 2], ADJ.: bearded (of corn, tasselled); bony.

re-stringènte, ADJ.: restricting, restringent. ‖**-stríngere** [L.], IRR.; TR.: restrict (RESTRAIN, curb; confine, limit;

Eng.† restringe). **-strínto**, PART. of *-stringere*. **-stringiménto**, M.: restriction, restraint. **-stringitívo**, ADJ.: restrictive. **-strizióne**, F.: restriction (restraint; limitation, mental reservation).

resudáre†, TR.: SWEAT.

result. . = *risult*. .

resupíno [L. *-nus* (*supinus*, bent back)], ADJ.: (*lit.*) resupine (lying on the back, supine; indolent).

resur. . = *risor*. .

resusc. . = *risusc*. .

réta† = *rete*.

retà† = *reità*.

retággio [*ereditaggio*], M.: (*lit.*) HERITAGE, inheritance.

re-táre†, TR.: graticulate. **-táta**, F.: catch in a net, catch, haul. **ré-te** [L.], F.: net (fish-net, etc.; netting, network; rete; *fig.*: snare, plot).

reten. . = *riten*. .

reti-cèlla, F., **-cèllo**, M.: *car. dim.* of *rete*; lace-bonnet.

reticènza [L. *-centia* (*tacere*, be silent)], F.: reticence.

reticina, **-no**, *dim.* of *rete*.

rètico1 [*Rezia*], ADJ.: Rhetian.

rètico†2, ADJ.: HERETIC.

retí-cola, F.: little net. **-colaménto**, M.: reticulation. **-coláre**1, ADJ.: reticular. **-coláre**2, TR.: graticulate. ‖**-retí-colo** [L. *-colus*, little net], M.: reticule, reticle.

retific. .† = *ratific*. .

reti-fórme [L. *rete*, net], ADJ.: retiform.

retí-na, *dim.* of *rete*. **rèti-na**, F.: retina (of the eye).

reti-nènte† [L. *-nens*], ADJ.: reserved (cautious, wary). **-nènza**, F.: retentiveness.

retíno, *dim.* of *rete*.

rè-tore [L. *rhetor*], M.: rhetorician (Eng.† rhetor). **-toricástro**, M.: ignorant rhetorician, vaporous declaimer. **-tòrico**, ADJ.: rhetorical.

re-trárre, **-trátto** = *ritrarre*, *-tratto*.

retri-buiménto, M.: retribution. ‖**re-tri-buíre** [L. *re-tribuere* (bestow as tribute)], TR.: retribute (pay back, reward). **-buizióne** (*pop.*) = *-buzione*. **-buitóre**, TR.: retributor, requiter. **-buzióne**, F.: retribution.

retrívo [*retro*], ADJ.: backward (slow, tardy).

rètro [L.], ADV.: behind, backward; PREP.: retro-: *di* —, backward. **-attívo**, ADJ.: retroactive. **-azióne**, F.: retroaction. **-bottéga**, F.: back-shop, inner shop. **-cámera**, F.: back-room, inner room. **-camerino**, M.: little back-room. **-cárica**, F.: *breech-loading*, breech-loader. **-cèdere**, IRR.; INTR.: retrocede (move back); restore; (*leg.*) sell back again. **-cedimento**, M., **-cessióne**, F.: retrocession; restitution. **-cèsso**, PART. of *-cedere*. **-gradáre** [L. *gradi*, go], INTR.: retrograde. **-gradazióne**, F.: retrogradation. **-`grado**, ADJ.: retrograde, backward. **-gressióne**, F.: retrogression. **-guárdia**, F., **-guárdo**†, M.: rear-guard. **-guída**†, F.: leader of the rear-guard. **-pígnere** [cf. *spignere*], IRR.; TR.: push back. **-scrítto**, ADJ.: written back. **-`rso**†, ADV.: backward. **-spettívo**, ADJ.: retrospective. **-stánza**, F.: back-room, inner room. **-tráre**†, IRR.; TR.: pull back. **-trazióne**†, F.: pulling backward. **-véndita**, F.: selling back again (to first seller).

rètt-a1 [*-o*], F.: direct line (shortest line); cheap lodging, board. **rètt-a**2 [L. *erecta*, erect, sc. *auris*, ear], F.: attention (heed, ear); resistance†: *dar* —, lend an ear, give heed or attention; be persuaded, consent. **-aménte** [*-to*], ADV.: rightly, justly. **-angoláre**, ADJ.: rectangular. **-angolétto**, *dim.* of *-angolo*. **-ángolo**, ADJ.: rectangular; M.: rectangle.

rettáre†, TR.: creep, crawl.

rettézza†, F.: rectitude.

retti-fica, F.: rectification. **-ficaménto**, M.: rectification. ‖**-ficáre** [L. L. *recti-ficare*], TR.: rectify (set right; adjust, correct). **-ficatóre**, M., **-ficatríce**, F.: rectifier; regulator. **-ficazióne**, F.: rectification, adjusting.

rèttile [L. *reptilis* (*repere*, creep)], ADJ.†: reptile (creeping); M.: reptile.

ret-tilíneo, ADJ.: rectilinear. **-tíssimo**, ADJ.: very straight, most just. **-titúdine**, F.: rectitude. ‖**rèt-to** [part. of *reggere* = L. *rectus*], ADJ.: ruled (governed, directed); DIRECT, straight; right, upright, just; M.: (*anat.*) rectum. **-toráto**, M.: rectorate, rectorship. **-tóre**, M.: rector (director; prior). **-toría**, F.: rectory, rectorship.

rettòri-ca [L. *rhetorica*], F.: rhetoric. **-caménte**, ADV.: rhetorically. **rettò-ri-co**, pl. *-ci*, ADJ.: rhetorical; M.: rhetorician. **-cúccia**, *disp.* of *-ca*. **-cúccio**, *disp. dim.* of *-co*.

rettríce [*rettore*], F.: directress; ADJ.: directing; of the tail (said of feathers).

rèu-ma, pl. *-mi* [Gr. *rheûma* (*rhein*, flow)], M.: rheum (catarrh, cold). **-mático**, pl. —*ci*, ADJ.: rheumatic. **-matísmo**, M.: rheumatism. **-matizzáre**, TR.: affect with a rheum or rheumatism.

revela. . = *rivela*. .

re-vellènte, ADJ.: revulsive. ‖**-vèllere** [L. (*vellere*, pluck)], TR.: (*med.*) draw back (tumours), Eng.† revel.

reverber. . = *riverber*. .
reve-rendíssimo, ADJ.: most reverend (now of prelates and canons). **-rèndo**, ADJ.: reverend (of priests or monks); venerable. **-rènte**, ADJ.: reverent. **-renteménte**, ADV.: reverently. **-rènza**, **-rènzia†**, F.: reverence; respect; courtesy, bow: *far la* —, make a bow, salute. **-renziále**, ADJ.: reverential, respectful. ‖**-ríre** [L. *-vereri* (*vereri*, fear)], TR.: revere.
revi-sióne [L. *-sio*], F.: revision. **-sóre**, M.: reviser.
revocá-bile, ADJ.: revocable. **-bilità**, F.: revocability. **-ménto**, M.: revocation. ‖**revocá-re** [L.], TR.: revoke. **-zióne**, F.: revocation.
revoluz. . = *rivoluz*. .
revòlver [Eng.], M.: revolver.
revul-sióne [L. *-sio*], F.: revulsion. **-sívo**, ADJ.: revulsive.
rézza†, F.: sweep-net; blond-lace, caul.
rézzo [*orezzo*], M.: (*poet.*) shade; freshness; obscurity†.
ri- [L. *re-*], PREF.: re-, again (or emphatic).
ri=abbassáre, TR.: lower, etc., again.
ri=abbáttere, TR.: strike down, etc., again; half-shut.
ri=abbellíre, TR.: adorn anew.
ri=abbigliáre, TR.: dress or trim again.
ri=abboccáre, TR.: fill up, etc., again.
ri=abbottonáre, TR.: button up again.
ri=abbracciáre, TR.: embrace, etc., again.
ri=abilitáre, TR.: rehabilitate; reinstate; (*leg.*) restore to citizenship. **-abilitatóre**, M., **-abilitatrice**, F.: restorer. **-abilitazióne**, F.: rehabilitation.
ri=abitáre, TR.: inhabit, etc., again.
ri=accèndere, IRR.; TR.: rekindle. **-accendiménto**, M.: rekindling.
ri=accennáre, TR.: beckon, etc., again.
ri=accensióne, F.: rekindling, etc.
ri=accettáre, TR.: accept, etc., again.
ri=acciuffáre, TR.: catch (by the hair) again.
ri=accompagnáre, TR.: reconduct; see home.
ri=accostáre, TR.: accost, etc., again.
ri=accotonáre, TR.: card again.
ri-accozzaménto, M.: meeting again, reunion. ‖**=accozzáre**, TR.: reassemble.
ri=accreditáre, TR.: accredit again.
ri=accréscere, IRR.; TR.: augment (again), reincrease.
ri=acquistáre, TR.: acquire, etc., again, recover.
ri-adattaménto, M.: readaptation. ‖**=adattáre**, TR.: readapt.
ri=addomandáre, TR.: redemand.
ri=addormentáre, TR.: put to sleep again; REFL.: fall asleep again.
ri=addossáre, TR.: load, etc., again.
ri=adiráre, REFL.: be enraged, etc., again.
ri=adornáre, TR.: readorn.
ri=adottáre, TR.: readopt, adopt, etc., again.
ri=adunáre, TR.: reassemble.
ri=affermáre, TR.: reaffirm.
ri=afferráre, TR.: grasp, etc., again.
ri=affezionáre, REFL.: grow affectionate again.
ri=aggraváre, TR.: aggravate, etc., anew.
ri=aguzzáre, TR.: sharpen again.
riále†, M.: small rivulet, brook.
ri=allargáre, TR.: reënlarge.
ri=allogáre, TR.: replace.
ri=alteráre, TR.: alter, etc., again.
ri=álto, ADJ.†: elevated (high); M.: elevation (eminence, height). **-alzaménto**, M.: elevation. **-alzáre**, TR.: raise again; raise higher; REFL.: rise again. **-álzo**, M.: raise (of prices), rise.
ri=amáre, TR.: love in return.
ri=amicáre, TR.: make friends again, reconcile.
ri=ammaláre, REFL.: fall sick again.
ri=ammattonáre, TR.: repave.
ri-amméssо, PART.: readmitted. **=amméttere**, IRR.; TR.: readmit; receive again.
ri=ammogliáre, TR.: marry again.
ri=ammoníre, TR.: admonish or warn again.
ri-andaménto, M.: repassing; fresh inquiry. ‖**=andáre**, IRR.; TR.: repass; search again; reconsider.
ri=animáre, TR.: reanimate. **-animazióne**, F.: reanimation.
ri=annestáre, TR.: graft again.
ri=annodáre, TR.: tie, etc., again.
ri-apèrto [*-aprire*], ADJ.: opened again; reopened. **-apertúra**, F.: reopening.
ri=appariré, IRR.; INTR.: reappear. **-appárso**, PART.
ri=appigionáre, TR.: rent, etc., again.
ri=applicáre, TR.: apply, etc., again.
ri-apriménto, M.: reopening. ‖**=apríre**, IRR.; TR.: open again, reopen. **-aprítura†**, F.: reopening.
ri=aráre, TR.: plow, etc., again.
ri=árdere, IRR.; TR.: burn again; scorch, parch up; sear.
riargúto†, ADJ.: reprimanded.
ri-armaménto, M.: rearming. ‖**=armáre**, TR.: arm again.
ri=arrecáre, TR.: carry again.
ri=arricchíre, TR.: enrich again.
riárso, PART. of *riardere*.
ri=asciugáre, TR.: dry or wipe again.

ri=ascoltáre, TR.: hear again.
ri=assalíre, =assaltáre, TR.: assault, etc., again.
ri=assettáre, TR.: mend again, readjust.
ri=assicuráre, TR.: reassure; cheer; REFL.: be reassured, take courage again.
ri=assídere, REFL.: set down again. **-assíso,** PART.
ri-assorbiménto, M.: reabsorption. ‖**=assorbíre,** TR.: reabsorb.
ri=assúmere, IRR.; TR.: reassume (take up again); sum up. **-assuntívo,** ADJ.: reassuming; apt to be reassumed. **-assúnto,** PART.: reassumed; M.: reassumption.
ri=attaccáre, TR.: fasten or attach again, reattach; hitch up (horses) again; REFL.: attach one's self again, join or adhere again.
ri=attáre, TR.: readapt, order or arrange again.
ri=attèndere, IRR.; TR.: attend, wait.
ri=attizzáre, TR.: stir up again.
ri-aúto (*pop.*) = *riavuto.* ‖**=avére,** IRR.; TR.: have again; get again, regain, recover, resume; REFL.: recover one's strength.
riávolo [L. *rutabulum* (*ruere,* rush; rake up)], M.: oven-rake.
ri=avvertíre, TR.: advise, etc., again.
ri=avvezzáre, TR.: accustom, etc., again.
ri=avvicináre, TR.: bring nearer.
ri=avvoltáre, TR.: turn round, etc., again.
riavúto, PART. of *riavere.*
ri=baciáre, TR.: kiss again.
ri=badáre, REFL.: mind, observe.
riba-diménto, M.: riveting, clinching. ‖**-díre** [?], TR.: rivet, clinch. **-ditúra,** F.: riveting.
ri=bagnáre, TR: bathe or soak again.
ribal-dáccio, *disp.* of *-do.* **-dággine,** F.: rascality. **-dáglia,** F.: band of scoundrels. **-dáre**†, **-deggiáre,** INTR.: act the knave, play roguish tricks. **-dèlla,** F.: abandoned woman. **-dèllo,** *disp. dim.* of *-do.* **-dería,** F.: rascality, ribaldry (esp. in its arch. sense of 'low act'). ‖**ribál-do** [? Ger. *ribe,* prostitute], ADJ.: ribald (low, base, villainous); M.: ribald (low fellow, rascal; wretch); (*hist.*) sort of loose militia. **-donáccio, -dóne,** M.: great scoundrel.
ri=balláre, INTR.: dance again.
ribál-ta, F.: trap; trap-door, pitfall; movable top of a writing-desk; frame of footlights (for raising or lowering); (*nav.*) shipwright's scale. ‖**-táre** [*rivoltare*], TR.: overturn (trip up; capsize). **-tatúra,** F.: overturning.

ri-balzaménto, M.: rebound(ing). ‖**=balzáre,** INTR.: rebound. **-bálzo,** M.: rebound.
ri-bandiménto, M.: publishing again banns; exile again. ‖**=bandíre,** TR.: banish again; publish again banns.
ri=barbáre, TR.: take root again.
ri=bassáre, TR.: reduce (the price), abate. **-básso,** M.: falling or reduction (of price, abatement); rebate, discount.
ri=bastonáre, TR.: cudgel again.
ri=báttere, TR.: beat, etc., again; repeat; insist; combat (oppugn); beat back (repel, confute); reverberate, reflect; sharpen.
ri-battezzaménto, M.: rebaptizing. ‖**=battezzáre,** TR.: rebaptize.
ri-battiménto, M.: beating back; repercussion; reverberation; reflexion. **-battitóre,** M.: beater back; reverberator. **-battitúra,** F.: beating back; clinching. **-battúta,** F.: back-blow; whipping; (*hunt.*) chasing up. **-battutaménto,** ADV.: in a repellent manner. ‖**=battúto** [*-battere*], PART.: beaten back; reverberated, reflected; restamped.
ri-bèba†, ‖**-bèca** [OFr. *rebebe* (Ar. *rebeb*)], F.: rebec (mus. instrument).
ri=beccáre, TR.: peck again; recover; REFL.: pick together.
ribe-chíno, *dim.* of *-ca.* ‖**-chísta** [*-ca*], pl. *—ti,* M.: player on the rebec.
ri-bellagióne†, **-bellaménto**†, M.: rebellion. **-bellánte,** ADJ.: rebellious; M.: rebel. ‖**-belláre** [L. *re-bellare* (*bellum,* war), wage war again], TR.: make rebellious; REFL.: rebel; withdraw. **-bèlle** [L. *-bellis*], ADJ.: rebellious; M.: rebel. **-bellióne,** F.: rebellion, revolt. **-bèllo**†, M.: rebel; rebellion.
ri=benedíre, IRR.; TR.: bless again; reconsecrate. **-benedizióne,** F.: renewed blessing.
ri=beneficáre, TR.: return good for good.
ri=bére, IRR.; TR.: drink again.
ríbes [Ar. *ribas*], M.: ribes (shrub, including gooseberries, currants, etc.); gooseberry-bush.
ri=bévere = *ribere*
ribobe-létto, M.: little slang. **-lísta,** M.: one fond of vulgarities or slang. ‖**ribòbo-lo** [?], M.: vulgar word or phrase, slang; jest. **-lóne**†, M.: vulgar flatterer.
ri-boccáre [*bocca*], INTR.: be brimful, overflow; REFL.†: revolt. **-bócco**†, M.: superabundance: *a —,* in plenty.
ri-bolliménto, M.: ebullition. **-bollío**†, M.: boiling (boiling noise, ebullition). ‖**=bollíre,** INTR.: boil again, boil up; ferment, effervesce; be overheated. **-bollitíccio,** M.: fermented thing. **-bolli-**

-túra, F.: reboiling; fermenting; thing boiled again.
ribòtta [Fr. *-bote*], F.: merry feast, carousal, debauch.
ri=brezzáre [*brezza*], INTR.: feel chilly, shiver; REFL.: hide the defect of age. **-brézzo**, M.: shiver (shudder, fright).
ribruscoláre [*bruscolo*], TR.: glean, gather.
ri=bucáre, TR.: pierce anew.
ribúffo†, M.: rebuff; rebuke.
ri=burláre, TR.: return the joke.
ri-buttaménto, M.: rebuff, repulse. **-buttánte**, ADJ.: repulsive, repellent, disagreeable. ‖**=buttáre**, TR.: rebuff; repulse; reject, vomit; INTR.: be repugnant.
ri-cáccia, F., **-cacciaménto**, M.: expulsion. ‖**=cacciáre**, TR.: hunt or drive back, repulse; hunt for, hunt up, seek.
ri-cadènte, ADJ.: hanging down, pendent. ‖**=cadére**, IRR.; INTR.: fall again; fall back (relapse); be pendent (hang down); lie down (as corn); go (to, be inherited by); (*leg.* — *da*) lose, forfeit. **-cadía†**, F.: relapse; trouble. **-cadiménto**, M.: falling again; falling back, relapse. **-cadióso**, ADJ.: annoying, tiresome. **-cadúta**, F.: relapse; (and cf. next). **-cadúto**, PART. of *-cadere;* fallen back, relapsed, etc.; reduced to poverty; M., F.: person reduced to poverty; relapser (into sin); backslider. **-caggiménto†** = *-cadimento.*
ricagnáto = *rincagnato.*
ri=caláre, INTR.: come down again.
ri=calcáre, TR.: trample down again.
ri=calcináre, TR.: pulverize again.
ri-calcitraménto, M.: recalcitration (kicking back). **-calcitránte**, ADJ.: recalcitrant (kicking back, restive, refractory). ‖**-calcitráre** [L. (*calx*, heel)], INTR.: recalcitrate (kick back, be restive or refractory).
ri=calzáre, TR.: put on the shoes again.
ricama-ménto†, M.: embroidery, needlework. ‖**ricamá-re** [Ar. *raquama*], TR.: embroider. **-tóra**, F., **-tóre**, M., **-tríce**, F.: embroiderer. **-túra**, F.: embroidery.
ri=cambiáre, TR.: change, etc., again; exchange; requite (repay, return). **-cámbio**, M.: rechange; exchange; requital (return, recompense): *vele di* —, (*nav.*) spare-sails.
ricamétto, *dim.* of *-mo.*
ri=camminàre, INTR.: wander again; set out again.
ricámo [*-camare*], M.: embroidery.
ri=cancelláre, TR.: cancel again.
ri=cangiáre, TR.: repay, reward.
ri=cantáre, TR.: sing again. **-cantazióne**, F.: recantation (retraction).
ricapáre†, INTR.: choose the best.
ri=capitáre, **-cápito** = *recapitare, -capito.*
ri=capitoláre, TR.: recapitulate. **-capitolazióne**, F.: recapitulation.
ricápo†: *di* —, anew; again.
ricapoficcáre†, INTR.: fall head foremost.
ri=capruggináre, TR.: notch again.
ri=cardáre, TR.: card again.
ri=caricáre, TR.: load or charge again; heap again, add; REFL.: resume the charge.
ri=carmináre, TR.: card again; toss.
ri-cascánte, ADJ.: falling again or back; falling, pendent. **-cascaménto**, M.: falling again or back; relapse. ‖**=cascáre**, INTR.: fall again; relapse; fall back (be bent down, be pendent). **-cascáta**, F.: relapse. **-cascatézza**, F.: falling again, relapse; backsliding. **-cásco**, M.: pendant (of a vault).
ri=catenáre, TR.: fetter again.
ri-cattaménto, M.: recovery; rescue; revenge. ‖**-cattáre** [L. *re-captare* (*capere*, take)], TR.: take back (resume), recover; make up for; redeem; REFL.: vindicate one's self, be avenged; be requited. **-cattatóre**, M.: recoverer; redeemer; avenger; extortioner. **-cátto**, M.: recovery; redemption; vengeance; extortion: *bandiera* (or *pan*) *di* —, like for like.
ri=cavalcáre, INTR.: mount again.
ri=caváre, TR.: dig again, dig out; recover; gain; copy out (transcribe). **-cávo**, M.: thing dug out; recovery.
ric-cáccio, ADJ.: *disp.* of *ricco;* M.: rich curmudgeon. **-caménte**, ADV.: richly. **-chézza**, F.: richness (abundance; magnificence); PL.: riches.
ric-ciáia, F.: a place of chestnut burs; chestnut pile. ‖**-cio** [L. *ericius*], M.: URCHIN (hedge-hog); thistle; chestnut bur; frizzled hair; curl of hair, ringlet; curled part, scroll, twist; ADJ.: frizzled; curled, curly; shaggy. **-ciolíno**, *dim.* of *-ciolo.* **ríc-ciolo**, M.: curl, ringlet; frizzle. **-ciolóne**, *aug.* of *-ciolo.* **-ciolúto**, ADJ.: curled, curly; frizzled. **-ciutèllo**, *car.* of *-ciuto.* **-ciutíno**, *car. dim.* of *-ciuto.* **-ciúto**, ADJ.: curled, curly, in ringlets.
ric-co [OGer. *richi*], ADJ.: RICH. **-cóne**, M.: (*aug.*) very rich or wealthy man, opulent person. **-córe†**, M.: richness; PL.: riches.
ri=cèdere, IRR.; INTR.: yield again; recede.
ricènte = *recente.*
ri=centinàre, TR.: arch anew.
ricépere† = *ricevere.*
ri-cérca, F., **-cercaménto†**, M.: research; inquiry; search. ‖**=cercáre**, TR.: search again; search or seek out; rummage; RESEARCH (inquire into, ex-

amine); request, require, arrange; (*poet.*) touch (play an instrument); M.: (*mus.*) prelude ('seeking' the key or tune). **-cercáta**, PART., cf. —*to*; F.†: research, search; prelude. **-cercataménte**, ADV.: purposely, on purpose. **-cercatézza**, F.: unnaturalness. **-cercáto**, PART.: sought for; searched; in request; investigated; studied (exquisite; affected, unnatural). **-cercatóra**, F., **-cercatóre**, M., **-cercatríce**, F.: searcher, inquirer.

ri=cerchiáre, TR.: new-hoop.

ri=cèrnere†, TR.: sift, etc., anew.

ricessáre†, INTR.: stop, delay.

ricèsso† = *recesso*.

ricètta, F.: medical prescription (RECIPE, RECEIPT). **-táccolo**, **-táculo**†, M.: receptacle; asylum. **-taménto**, M.: reception. **-táre**, TR.: receive; receive and hide; lodge (shelter); write prescriptions (prescribe)†; REFL.: take refuge. **-tário**, M.: book of medical prescriptions (recipes), recipe-book. **-tatóre**, M., **-tatríce**, F.: receiver. **-tína**, *dim.* of *-ta*. **-tívo**, ADJ.: receptive. ‖**ricètto** [L. *re-ceptus*], ADJ.†: RECEIVED; M.: reception; lodging (shelter); asylum; private reception-room†, lobby†: *dar* —, lodge, shelter.

ricé-vere [L. *re-cipere* (*capere*, take)], TR.: receive (get, accept; admit; welcome); take in (lodge, shelter); sustain. **-vévole**†, ADJ.: receptive. **-viménto**, M.: receiving (reception); persons received (party). **-vitívo**†, ADJ.: receiving; receptive. **-vitóre**, M.: receiver. **-vitória**, F.: office; lottery-box. **-vitríce**, F.: receiver. **-vúta**, F.: receipt; reception†: *far la* —, (*vulg.*) vomit. **-vutína**, *dim.* of *-vuta*. **-zióne**†, F.: reception; admission.

richer. .† = *richied.* .

ri=chiamáre, TR.: call back (recall, RECLAIM)†; appeal; summon; sue; REFL.: appeal (refer to); complain†. **-chiamáta**, F.: recall, revocation. **-chiamatóre**, M., **-chiamatríce**, F.: recaller; reclaimer; summoner; appellant. **-chiámo**, M.: recall; calling back; note of recall; bird-call (decoy; allurement); appeal; good or striking advertisement (puff, send-off); catch-sign; complaint†.

ri=chièdere, IRR.; TR.: ask back (demand back); REQUIRE (demand); REQUEST (pray, entreat); summon (cite); desire (wish). **-chiediménto**†, M.: request (demand); summons. **-chieditóre**, M., **-chieditríce**, F.: demander. **-chièrere**† = *-chiedere*. **-chièsta**, F.: request (demand, petition); question; summons†; (and cf. *-chiesto*): *aver* —, be in demand. **-chièsto**, PART. of *-chiedere*.

ri=chináre, TR.: bend, etc., again; REFL.: humble one's self.

ri=chiúdere, IRR.; TR.: close again; close (close up, shut up); REFL.: close up; heal up. **-chiúso**, PART. of *-chiudere*. **-chiusúra**†, F.: small enclosure.

ri=ciarláre, INTR.: prattle again.

ricid. . = *recid.* .

ri=cígnere = *-cingere*. **-cigniménto**, M.: cincture, girdle.

ri=cimentáre, TR.: try anew; REFL.: try or venture anew.

ri=cíngere, IRR.; TR.: gird; enclose; beset.

ri=cinghiáre, TR.: gird, etc., anew.

ricíno [L. *ricinus*], M.: ricinus (castor-oil plant).

ricínto [*-cingere*], PART.: girt, enclosed; M.: enclosure.

ri=cioncáre, INTR.: drink again.

ricip. .† = *recip.* .

ri=circoláre, INTR.: circulate again; rove about. **-circolazióne**, F.: new circulation.

ri=circondáre, TR.: enclose again.

ricis. . = *recis.* .

riclam. . = *reclam.* .

ri=còcere, IRR.; TR.: cook again.

ri=còglière, IRR.; TR.: collect or gather (again); fetch; pick up; learn; take out of pawn; REFL.: get clear or rid (of). **-cogliménto**†, M.: gathering; crop; meditation. **-coglitóra**, F., **-coglitóre**, M., **-coglitríce**, F.: collector, gatherer; midwife†. **-coglitúra**, F.: gathering in or harvest (of chestnuts); chestnut season.

ri-cognizióne, F.: recognition, acknowledgment; reward; (*leg.*) recognizance; (*mil.*) reconnoitering (reconnoissance). **=cognóscere** = *-conoscere*.

ri=coláre, TR.: filter again; rebolt.

ri=colcáre, REFL.: lie down again; go down again.

ri=collegáre, TR.: bind, etc., again; REFL.: confederate again.

ri=collocáre, TR.: replace.

ri=colmáre, TR.: heap up again, etc. **-colmáto**, PART., **-cólmo**, ADJ.: heaped up; overwhelmed; abundant.

ri=coloráre, **=colorire**, TR.: colour again, recolour.

ri-còlta, F.: harvest (crop; usu'ly *raccolta*); harvest-time; retreat†. ‖**-còlto** [*-cogliere*], PART.: collected (gathered); M.: harvest (crop).

ri=combáttere, TR.: fight again.

ri=combináre, TR.: recombine.

ri-cominciaménto, M.: recommencement. ‖**=cominciáre**, TR.: begin again, recommence.

ri-comméssò, PART. of *-commettere*. ‖**=comméttere**, IRR.; TR.: recommit; relapse.

ri=comparíre, INTR.: appear again; reappear. **-compárso**, PART. of *-comparire*.

ri-compènsa, F., **-compensaméntо**†, M.: recompense, reward. ||**=compensáre**, TR.: recompense (reward, requite). **-compensazióne**†, F.: recompense. **-compènso**†, M.: compensation.

ricomper. .† = *ricompr.* .

ri=cómpiere, IRR.; TR.: fill again; fulfil; recompense†. **-compiménto**†, M.: fulfilment; compensation.

ri=compórre, IRR.; TR.: recompose; rearrange; compose (calm); reunite; reconcile. **-composizióne**, F.: recomposition.

ri-cómpra, **-compragióne**†, F., **-compraménto**, M.: buying again; ransom; recovery. ||**=compráre**, TR.: buy again; redeem (ransom). **-compratóre**, M., **-compratríce**, F.: repurchaser; redeemer. **-comprazióne**†, F.: rebuying; redeeming (ransom). **-comprévole**†, ADJ.: redeemable.

ri=comprováre, TR.: approve, etc., again.

ri-comúnica†, F.: absolution from excommunication. ||**=comunicáre**, TR.: communicate again; relieve from excommunication, absolve; bless again. **-comunicazióne**, F.: absolution from excommunication.

ri=concèdere, IRR.; TR.: grant again.

ri-concentraménto, M.: concentration. ||**=concentráre**, TR.: concentrate; REFL.: concentrate one's thoughts.

riconcèsso, PART. of *-concedere*.

ri=conchiúdere, TR.: conclude, etc., again.

ri=conciáre, TR.: trim again; prepare or trim, etc. (again); restore; reconcile; REFL.: grow fair again†.

ri-conciliábile, ADJ.: reconcilable. **-conciliagióne**†, F., **-conciliaménto**, M.: reconciliation, reconcilement. ||**=conciliáre**, TR.: reconcile; RECIPR.: be reconciled again; become friends again. **-conciliatóre**, M., **-conciliatríce**, F.: reconciler. **-conciliazióne**, F.: reconciliation, reconcilement.

ri=concimáre, TR.: manure again.

ricóncio [*riconciare*], ADJ.: trimmed again; prepared or fixed up (again), restored; seasoned again.

ri=condannáre, TR.: recondemn.

ri=condensáre, TR.: recondense.

ri=condíre, TR.: season again.

ricòndito† = *recondito*.

ri-condótta, F.: new conduct. **-condótto**, PART. of *-condurre*. ||**=condúrre**, IRR.; TR.: reconduct (bring back); reduce; lease or rent again†; REFL.: bring one's self back; get back, make one's tour back. **-conduttóre**, M., **-conduttríce**, F.: bringer back. **-conduzióne**†, F.: new lease.

ri-confèrma, F.: reconfirmation; renewed assurance. ||**=confermáre**, TR.: reconfirm, reassure. **-confermazióne** = *-conferma*.

ri=confessáre, TR.: confess again.

ri=conficcáre, TR.: nail or fix again.

ri=confidáre, INTR.: confide or trust again.

ri=confíggere, IRR.; TR.: nail or fix again. **-confítto**, PART. of *-configgere*.

ri=conformáre, TR.: conform again.

ri=confortáre, TR.: recomfort; comfort (fortify, encourage). **-confòrto**, M.: new comfort; comfort.

ri=confrontáre, TR.: confront again.

ri=congegnáre, TR.: reconnect.

ri=congiúngere, IRR.; TR.: reconjoin (join again, reunite); RECIPR.: become reunited. **-congiúnto**, PART. of *-congiungere*. **-congiunzióne**, F.: reuniting.

ri=coniáre, TR.: recoin, stamp anew.

ri=connèttere, IRR.; TR.: reconnect.

ri-conoscènte, ADJ.: recognizing; grateful (thankful). **-conoscènza**, F.: recognition (acknowledgment; reward); gratitude (thankfulness). ||**=conóscere**, IRR.; TR.: recognize (know again; acknowledge, avow; confess; reward); REFL.: acknowledge one's faults, confess. **-conoscíbile**, **-conoscitívo**, ADJ.: recognizable. **-conosciménto**, M.: recognition. **-conoscitóre**, M., **-conoscitóra**, F.: recognizer. **-conosciúto**, PART. of *-conoscere*.

ri-conquísta, F.: reconquest. ||**=conquistáre**, TR.: reconquer (recover).

ri=consacráre, TR.: reconsecrate.

ri-conségna, F.: consigning (or sending) back or again; return. ||**=consegnáre**, TR.: consign (or send) back or again, return, restore.

ri=consentíre, INTR.: consent again.

ri=consideráre, TR.: reconsider.

ri=consigliáre, TR.: counsel again; REFL.: come to a decision, determine.

ri-consolaménto†, M.: consolation. ||**=consoláre**, TR.: console again (Eng.† reconsolate). **-consolazióne**, F.: consolation.

ri=contáre, TR.: recount (count or reckon again); recount (tell over, repeat)†. **-cónto**†, M.: epilogue, summary.

ri=contradíre, IRR.; TR.: contradict again.

ri=convenire, IRR.; INTR.: reconvene; TR.: (*leg.*) sue (the plaintiff) in return, bring a counter-charge against; (*lit.*) correct, upbraid. **-convenúto**, PART. of

-convenire. **-convenzióne**, F.: reconvention (cross-demand).

ri=convertíre, TR.: reconvert.

ri=convíncere, IRR.; TR.: convince, etc., again; convince of error.

ri=convitáre, TR.: invite in return.

ri=coperchiáre†, TR.: cover again. **-copèrta**†, F.: covering; pretext, excuse; and cf. *-coperto*. **-copertaménte**†, ADV.: covertly, secretly. ‖**-copèrto**, PART. of *-coprire*. **-copertúra**, F.: covering again; covering up; pretext.

ri-còpia, F.: new copy. ‖**=copiáre**, TR.: copy again; imitate. **-copiatúra**, F.: (new) copy; imitation.

ri-copríbile, ADJ.: recoverable. **-copriménto**, M.: covering (up). ‖**=copríre**, IRR.; TR.: cover again (recover); cover (cover up; hide); mitigate (excuse); secure; REFL.: cover one's self; find excuse. **-copritóre**, M.: coverer.

ri=corcáre† = *-coricare*.

ricor-dábile, ADJ.: that may be (or to be) remembered; memorable. **-dabilménte**, ADV.: in a manner to be remembered. **-dagióne**†, F., **-daménto**†, M.: remembrance. **-dánza**, F.: remembrance; token of remembrance (keepsake, memorial). ‖**-dáre** [L. *re-cordari* (*cor*, HEART)], TR.: put in mind (remind); mention; REFL.: call to mind, remember (esp. with affection, stronger than *rammentare*). **-datívo**, ADJ.: worthy of remembrance). **-datóre**, M., **-datríce**, F.: rememberer. **-dazióne**†, F.: remembrance. **-dévole**, ADJ.: memorable. **-devolménte**, ADV.: memorably. **-díno**, *car. dim.* of *-do*. **ricòr-do**, M.: remembrance (memory); token of remembrance (memento, keepsake, remembrancer); sketch (general outlines, for remembering rough-draft); notice (warning); note (record).

ri=coricáre, TR.: lay down again; INTR., REFL.: lie down again; go down again; (*agr.*) breed.

ri=coronáre, TR.: crown again.

ricòrre = *ricogliere*.

ri=corrèggere, IRR.; TR.: correct again, revise.

ri-corrènte, ADJ.: recurrent; reflowing. **-corrènza**, F.: recurrence. ‖**=córrere**, IRR.; INTR.: run again; run back; RECUR (have recourse, resort; return); surround; TR.: run over again; review.

ricorrètto, PART. of *-correggere*.

ri-corriménto, M.: recourse, reflux. **-córsa**, F.: return; recourse. ‖**-córso** [*-correre*], PART.: run again, etc.; M.: running or flowing back (return, reflux; Eng.† recourse); recourse (resort, recurrence); *menstrual flow* (menses); (*hist.*) Florentine magistrate (as the court of appeal). **-corsóio**†: *bollire a —*, boil furiously.

ri=costeggiáre, TR.: coast along again.

ri=costituíre, TR.: reconstitute, reestablish. **-costituzióne**, F.: reëstablishment.

ri=costruíre, TR.: reconstruct, rebuild. **-costruttóre**, M.: reconstructor. **-costruzióne**, F.: reconstruction.

ri=cotonáre†, TR.: card again. **-cotonatúra**†, F.: recarding.

ri-còtta, F.: cheese of whey (sort of milk-food). **-cottáio**, M.: seller of whey-cheese. **-cottína**, **-cottóna**, **-cottóne**, *dim.* or *aug.* of *-cotta*. ‖**=còtto**, ADJ.: cooked or boiled again; well digested.

ri-coveraménto†, M.: recovering, recovery. ‖**-coveráre** [*ricuperare*], TR.: recover (gain or get back, retrieve); rescue (save); bring to; REFL.: have recourse to; take refuge (escape) to. **-coveratóre**, M., **-coveratríce**, F.: recoverer, restorer. **-cóvero**, M.: recovery†; place of refuge, retreat, refuge.

ri-creaménto, M.: recreation. ‖**=creáre**, TR.: recreate (create again; revive, refresh, divert, amuse); reëlect; REFL.: divert one's self. **-creatívo**, ADJ.: recreating (refreshing, diverting). **-creatóre**, M., **-creatríce**, F.: reviver, diverter. **-creatòrio**, M.: place (establishment) for recreation. **-creazióne**, F.: recreation, diversion.

ri-credènte, ADJ.: convinced, undeceived, disabused. ‖**=crédere**, TR.: believe again; convince, undeceive; REFL.: believe or trust again, change one's opinion or mind, undeceive one's self: *-credersi con*, open one's heart to. **-credúto**, PART. of *-credere*.

ri-crescènza, F.: excrescence. ‖**=créscere**, IRR.; INTR.: grow again; INCREASE (grow). **-cresciménto**, M.: increasing; increase, growth. **-créscita**, F.: increase.

ri-criáre†, **-crío**† = *ri-creare*, *-creamento*.

ri=crocifíggere, TR.: crucify **-crocifísso**, PART.

ri-cuciménto, M.: sewing again. **-cucíre**, TR.: sew again; sew up, repair; patch up. **-cucitóre**, M.: mender. **-cucitúra**, F.: sewing up; mending, patching.

ricunc. . = *ricoc.* .

ricupe-rábile, ADJ.: recoverable. ‖**-ráre** [L. *re-cuperare* (?)], TR.: recuperate (RECOVER, regain). **-ratóre**, M.: recoverer, redeemer; ADJ.: recuperating. **-razióne**, F.: recuperation, recovery.

ri=cúrvo, ADJ.: curved (bent round, crooked).

ricú-ṣa, F.: refusal, denial. ‖**-ṣáre** [L. *re-cusare* (*causa*, cause), reject], TR.: refuse (reject); renounce; Eng.† recuse (reject as a judge); REFL.: object. **-ṣánte**, ADJ.: refusing; M.: refuser. **-ṣazióne**, F.: refusal.

ridacchiáre [*ridere*], INTR.: smile, grin.

ridamáre† = *riamare*.

ridanciáno [*-dacchiare*], ADJ.: smiling, grinning.

ri=dáre, IRR.; TR.: give again; give back.

rid-da, F.: circular (village) dance; dizzy dance: *menar la* —, tread the dance. ‖**-dáre** [MHG. *riden*, turn], INTR.: dance in a ring; whirl around. **-dóne**†, M.: = *-da;* roundelay.

rídere [L.], IRR.§; INTR.: laugh, smile; grin; REFL.: (with *di*) laugh at, deRIDE, banter, mock.

§ Pret. *ri-si, -se; -sero.* Part. *riso.*

ri=destáre, TR.: awake again, rouse. **-destáto**, **-désto**, PART.: waked or stirred up, roused.

ri=détto, ADJ.: told again, repeated.

ridévol-e [*ridere*], ADJ.: laughable (ludicrous); smiling†. **-ménte**, ADV.: ludicrously.

ridi-cíbile [*-re*], ADJ.: that may be repeated. **-ciménto**†, M.: repetition. **-citóre**, M.: repeater; telltale.

ridico-lággine, F.: buffoonery. **-lézza**, F.: ridiculousness, nonsense. ‖**ridícolo** [L. *ridiculus* (*ridere*, laugh)], ADJ.: ridiculous (laughable); M.: ridicule; fun. **-losággine**†, F.: buffoonery. **-losaménte**†, ADV.: ridiculously. **-losità**†, F.: ridiculousness. **-lóso**, ADJ.: ridiculous.

ridicul. . = *ridicol.* .

ridific. . = *riedific.* .

ri=diminuíre, TR.: diminish again.

ri=dinternáre†, TR.: trace the contours of, outline again.

ri=dipíngere, IRR.; TR.: paint over again. **-dipínto**, PART.

ri=díre, IRR.; TR.: say or tell again (repeat); reply; continue; refer; reprehend (censure); REFL.: unsay, retract: *trovar a* —, find fault (with).

ri-diríttο†, ADJ.: set up straight again. ‖**=dirizzáre**, TR.: set up straight again; REDRESS.

ri=diṣciògliere, TR.: dissolve or untie again. **-diṣciòlto**, PART.

ri=discórrere, IRR.; INTR.: discourse or talk over again. **-discórso**, PART.

ri=disegnáre, TR.: sketch again.

ri=disputáre, TR.: discuss again.

ri=distaccáre, TR.: detach or separate again.

ri=distèndere, IRR.; TR.: stretch out again, redistend.

ri=distilláre, TR.: redistill.

ri=distínguere, IRR.; TR.: explain again or more clearly.

ri=distrúggere, TR.: destroy again.

ri=diveníre, IRR.; INTR.: become again.

ri=divídere, IRR.; TR.: divide again; subdivide.

ri=divincoláre, REFL.: twist again; twist about, wriggle; get out of the toils.

ri=dolére, IRR.; INTR.: feel pain again, suffer again; REFL.: complain again.

rídolo†, M.: trellis.

ri=domandáre, TR.: ask again.

ri=donáre, TR.: give back.

ridon-dánte, ADJ.: redundant (superfluous). **-dánza**, F.: redundancy. ‖**-dáre** [L. *re-d-undare* (*unda*, wave)], INTR.: redound (abound, overflow, be full); result.

ridóne [*ridere*], M.: laugher.

ri=dormíre, INTR.: sleep again.

ri=dòsso, M.: position above; (*nav.*) leeward side; concurrence: *a* —, behind; astraddle.

ri=dotáre, TR.: endow or bestow again.

ri-dottábile†, ADJ.: redoubtable. **-dottáre**†, TR.: dread (redoubt). **-dottévole**†, ADJ.: redoubtable.

ridótto, PART. of *-durre;* reduced; brought back, etc.; M.: resort (place of meeting; retreat, haunt); receptacle; (*fort.*) redoubt.

ri=dovére, IRR.; TR.: owe back or again.

ridrizzáre† = *ridirizzare.*

ri=dubitáre, INTR.: doubt again.

ri=dúcere† = *-durre.* **-ducíbile**, ADJ.: reducible. **-duciménto**, M.: reduction. **-ducitóre**, M.: reducer. **-dúrre** [*-ducere*], IRR. (cf. *addure*); TR.: reduce (bring back, force); REFL.: be reduced; assemble (meet); take refuge†; come or amount to†: *-dursi a mente*, recollect, call to mind. **-dútto**†, PART. of *-durre.* **-duttóre**, M.: reducer. **-duzióne**, F.: reduction.

ri=ècco, ADV.: here (or there) again! lo, again!

rièdere [L. *re-d-ire*, go back], DEFECT.; INTR.: come back (return).

ri=edificáre, TR.: rebuild; edify again. **-edificatóre**, M.: rebuilder. **-edificazióne**, F.: reëdification.

ri=elèggere, IRR.; TR.: reëlect. **-eleggíbile**, ADJ.: reëligible. **-eleggibilità**, F.: reëligibility. **-elezióne**, F.: reëlection.

ri=emendáre, TR.: emend (correct) again.

ri=émpiere, us'ly =**empíre**, TR.: fill up (again); overfill; delight. **-empiménto**, M.: filling up (again). **-empíre**, cf. above. **-empíta**, F.: filling up. **-em**

pitivaménte, ADV.: by filling up; superfluously. **-empitívo**, ADJ.: filling up; (*gram.*) EXPLETIVE; M.: filling; expletive. **-empitóre**, M.: filler. **-empitúra**, F.: filling up; filling (stuff); redundancy.

ri=enfiáre, INTR.: be inflated or swell again; puff up.

ri-entránte, ADJ.: reëntering, etc.; bending or turning back. **-entraménto**, M.: reëntering. ‖**=entráre**, INTR.: reënter; come in again (return); retire; shrink: — *in sè* (*stesso*), turn one's eyes inward, reflect, consider.

ri=epilogáre, INTR.: recapitulate. **-epílogo**, M.: recapitulation (summing up).

ri=èrgere, IRR.; TR.: erect or raise again.

ri=esamináre, TR.: reëxamine.

riesc. . = *riusc.* .

ri=fabbricáre, TR.: fabricate anew.

ri-facíbile, ADJ.: that may be remade or made again. **-faciménto**, M.: remaking; restoring; repolishing; indemnity. **-facitóre**, M., **-facitríce**, F.: restorer. ‖**=fáre**, IRR.; TR.: do or make again; restore (repair, mend; repolish; recast; reform); make up for; REFL.: be restored; recover; recuperate; reform; take some more (in eating or drinking); make up (with, for an offence, etc.): — *i danni*, make up for the loss, indemnify; *-farsi di checchessia*, be the better for a thing; *-farsi diritto*, draw one's self up, stand upright.

ri=fasciáre, TR.: bind again; wrap round. **-fáscio**: *a* —, ADV.: huddled together in confusion; confusedly.

ri-fattíbile, ADJ.: to be done again. ‖**-fátto**, PART. of *-fare*. **-fattúra**, F.: doing or making again; restoration.

ri=favoríre, TR.: favour again.

rifazióne† = *-facimento.*

ri=fecondáre, TR.: fecundate again.

rifedíre†, TR.: (*poet.*) wound again.

ri=fèndere, IRR.; TR.: split or cleave again.

ri-ferendário = *referendario*. **-feríbile**, ADJ.: referable. **-feriménto**, M.: referring (reference). ‖**-feríre** [L. *re-ferre*, bring back], TR.: refer (relate, state; ascribe); return; REFL.: refer or submit (to, appeal to): — *grazie*, return thanks.

ri-férma, F.: confirmation. ‖**=fermáre**, TR.: close again; confirm.

ri=ferráre, TR.: shoe again (a horse).

-ifèrto† = *riferito, referto.*

-esso, PART. of *-fendere.*

-steggiáre, TR.: feast again.

-ióne† = *refezione.*

[Bav. *riffen*], F.: private lottery; L.) authority; violence, imposition: *di* —, by violence, at all costs, whether or no. **-fusáccio**, *disp.* of *-foso*. **-fóso**, ADJ.: violent, overbearing.

ri=fiammeggiáre, INTR.: flame.

ri=fiancáre, TR.: flank, fortify. **-fiancheggiáre**†, TR.: strengthen the flanks of; succour.

ri-fiataménto, M.: respiration. ‖**-fiatáre**, INTR.: respire (breathe): *-fiata!* hush! **-fiatáta**, F.: breath. **-fiatatóna**, *aug.* of *-fiatata*.

ri=ficcáre, TR.: fix again; repeat (tell again).

rificolóna [for *fierucolona* (*fiera*)], F.: paper-lantern (carried on sticks in processions, etc.).

ri-fidáre, TR.: confide again; entrust.

ri=figgere, IRR.; TR.: refix.

ri=figliáre, TR., INTR.: produce little ones again; pullulate anew.

ri=figuráre, TR.: give a new shape to.

ri-finaménto†, M.: cessation. **-fináre**, INTR.: leave off, stop. **-finiménto**, M.: exhaustion; extenuation. ‖**=finíre**, TR.: finish (end, complete); use up (tire or wear out; reduce to misery). **-finitézza**, F.: exhaustion; emptiness. **-finitúra**, F., **-finitóre**, M.: finisher. **-finitúra**, **-finizióne**, F.: finishing off (finishing touch, finish).

ri-fioriménto, M.: flourishing anew. ‖**-fioríre**, INTR.: reflourish (flourish anew); TR.: adorn again. **-fioríta**, F.: reflourishing (once). **-fioritúra**, F.: reflourishing.

rifísso, **-fítto**, PART. of *-figgere*: *senza -fitto*, without delay or reply.

ri-fiutábile, ADJ.: refusable, deniable. **-fiutagióne**†, F., **-fiutaménto**†, M., **-fiutánza**, F.: refusal; denial; repudiation. ‖**-fiutáre** [L. *refutare*], TR.: REFUSE (deny); reject (renounce). **-fiutatóre**, M., **-fiutatríce**, F.: refuser (denier). **-fiúto**, M.: refusal (denial, rebuff); outcast (refuse, scum).

ri-flessaménte, ADV.: reflexively. **-flessíbile**, ADJ.: reflexible. **-flessáre**†, TR.: (*paint.*) reflect light upon (illumine). **-flessióne**, F.: reflection; consideration. **-flessivaménte**, ADV.: reflectively. **-flessívo**, ADJ.: reflective. **-flésso**, PART. of *-flettere*; reflected, etc.; M.: reflex; reflection; (*paint.*) lights. **-flessóre**, M.: reflector. ‖**=flèttere**, IRR. (part. *-flesso* or reg.); TR.: reflect (reverberate); INTR.: reflect (think: — *a, sopra*, consider).

ri=fluíre, INTR.: flow back. **-flússo**, PART.: flown back; M.: reflux; ebb-tide.

rifocil-laménto, M.: restoring, restoration. ‖**-láre** [L. (*focillo*, 'refresh' at the 'hearth,' *focus*)], TR.: restore (recreate, comfort, brace).

ri=fondáre, TR.: found again.

ri=féndere, IRR.; TR.: recast (melt again); reimburse. **-fondíbile**, ADJ.: that may be recast.

ri=forbíre, TR.: refurbish.

ri-fórma, F.: reform; reformation. **-formábile**, ADJ.: reformable. **-formagióne**, F., **-formaménto**, M.: reform(ation). ‖**=formáre**, TR.: reform; improve; remove from service (a soldier before he is pensioned); REFL.: become reformed; be one's self again. **-formatívo**, ADJ.: reformative. **-formatóre**, M., **-formatríce**, F.: reformer. **-formazióne**, F.: reform(ation).

ri=fornire, TR.: furnish again.

ri=fortificáre, TR.: fortify again; reenforce.

ri=frángere, IRR.; TR.: REFRACT. **-frangíbile**, ADJ.: refrangible. **-frangibilità**, F.: refrangibleness. **-frangiménto**, M.: refraction. **-fránto** = *-fratto*. **-frattívo**, ADJ.: refractive. **-frátto**, PART.: refracted. **-frazióne**, F.: refraction.

rifredd.. = *raffredd..*

rifren.. = *raffren..*

rifrig(g).. = *refrig..*

ri=fríggere, IRR.; TR.: fry again. **-frítto**, PART. of *-friggere*. **-frittúme**, M.: poor fried stuff (stale things fried up again). **-frittúra**, F.: fried dish (fry).

ri=frondíre†, INTR.: shoot new leaves.

ri=frucáre, **=frugáre**, TR.: grope or rummage again, ransack.

ri-frústa†, F.: rummaging (search). ‖**=frustáre**, TR.: rummage (search); knock (cane). **-frustatóre**, M., **-frustatríce**, F.: rummager (searcher).

ri=fruttáre, INTR.: bear fruit or produce again.

ri=fuggíre, INTR.: take refuge, fly. **-fuggíta**, F.: refuge. **-fuggíto**, PART.: taken refuge; run away; M.: refugee; runaway. **-fugiáre**, REFL.: seek refuge. **-fúgio**, M.: refuge (shelter).

ri-fulgènte, ADJ.: refulgent. ‖**-fúlgere** [L. *re-f..*], IRR. §; INTR.: be refulgent.

§ Pret. *rifúl-si, -se; -sero.* Part. lacking.

rifusáre†, TR.: refuse.

ri-fusióne, F.: refusion (melting again). ‖**-fúso**, PART. of *fondere*.

rifut.. = *rifiut..*

rí-ga [OGer.], F.: line (streak, stripe; row, file); ruler: *di prima* —, of the first order; *di bassa* —, low, mean; *andare per la* —, go on smoothly; *rimettere in* —, set straight again, force back to duty. **-gáglie**, F. PL.: internal parts (entrails, liver, etc., of fowl). **-gágno**†, **-gágnolo**, M.: streamlet; running ditch-water, gutter. **-gáre**, TR.: mark with lines (rule; stripe); rifle: — *diritto*, act straight, act honestly. **-gáta**, F.: blow with a ruler. **-gatíno**, M.: striped cloth.

rigattáto†, ADJ.: of bad life (rakish); M.: hang-rascal.

rigattière [OFr. *regratier*], M.: second-hand dealer (old-clothes man, huckster).

rigatúra [*-gare*], F.: lining (striping).

ri=generáre, TR.: regenerate. **-generatóre**, M., **-generatríce**, F.: regenerator. **-generazióne**, F.: regeneration.

rigentilíre†, TR.: make genteel or elegant, polish.

ri=germináre, **=germogliáre**, INTR.: germinate or sprout again.

ri-gettábile, ADJ.: rejectable. **-gettaménto**†, M.: rejection; vomiting. ‖**=gettáre**, TR.: reject (refuse); vomit (throw up). **-gettatóre**, M.: rejecter. **-gètto**, M.: rejection; thing rejected; refuse (outcast, sweepings).

righétta [*riga*], F.: small line.

ri=giacére, IRR.; INTR.: lie down again.

rigi-daménte, ADV.: rigidly. **-détto**, *dim.* of *-do*. **-dézza**, F.: rigour (stiffness; severity). **-dità**, F.: rigidity (rigidness; rigor). ‖**rígi-do** [L. *-dus*], ADJ.: rigid (stiff; severe); rigorous (of weather).

ri-giraménto, M.: turning about. ‖**=giráre**, INTR.: turn about (whirl); TR.: turn round; surround (environ); get around (deceive); REFL.: turn around or about. **-girazióne**†, F.: turning round. **=gíre**†, IRR.; INTR.: return. **-girévole**, ADJ.: easily turning. **-gírio**, M.: continual turning. **-gíro**, M.: turning round (turn, winding round); shifty trick (underhand dealing, intrigue).

ri=giuráre, INTR.: swear again.

rigiugn.. = *raggiung..*

ri-gnáre [*ringhiare*], INTR.: neigh. **rígno**†, M.: neighing.

rigo = *riga*.

ri=godére, INTR., TR.: enjoy again; rejoice.

rigó-glio [*orgoglio*], M.: vigour or rankness (in plants); sturdiness, boldness; arrogance†. **-gliosaménto**, ADV.: vigorously; rankly. **-glióso**, ADJ.: vigorous; rank; bold; arrogant†.

ri-gogolétto, *dim.* of *-gogolo*. ‖**-gògolo** [L. *auri-galgulus*], M.: yellow-hammer (bird).

rigolétto [*riga*], M.: round dance.

ri-gonfiaménto, M.: new swelling. ‖**=gonfiáre**, INTR.: swell (anew); swell up (puff up). **-gónfio**, ADJ.: swelled, puffed up.

rigó-re [L. *rigor*], M.: intense cold; chill; rigour (severity). **-rísmo**, M.: rigorism. **-rísta**, pl **-rísti**, M.: rigorist. **-ros**-

-ménte, ADV.: rigorously. -rosità, F.: rigorousness (severity). -róso, ADJ.: rigorous (severe).
rigóso†, ADJ.: watered; irrigated.
rigottáto†, ADJ.: crisped.
ri=governáre, TR.: strengthen (tone up); INTR., TR.: wash dishes, pans, etc., scour. -governáta, F.: (one) dish-washing. -governatúra, F.: dish-washing (scouring); dish-water.
ri=grattáre, TR.: scrape again.
rigrèsso† = *regresso*.
ri=gridáre, TR.: cry or call anew.
ri=guadagnáre, TR.: regain.
ri-guardaménto†, M.: regard (look). -guardánte, ADJ.: regarding (looking at or upon); facing; M.: looker-on (spectator). ‖=guardáre, TR.: regard (look at, view; concern); look upon or over (face); consider (mind); aim at; REFL.: take care of one's self: *la si -guardi*, take care of yourself, mind your health. -guardáto, PART.: regarded, etc.; circumspect. -guardatóre, M., -guardatríce, F.: looker-on (beholder); guardian. -guardévole†, ADJ.: remarkable, considerable. -guardevolézza†, F.: considerableness. -guardevolménte†, ADV.: considerably. -guárdo, M.: regard (look; consideration, respect); caution (circumspection, care); view (sight, aim)†; interest (on money)†: *a — a*, as regards, as to; *a — di*, in comparison with; *in — a*, as regards, as for, as to; *in — di*, on account of; *stare in —*, take care of one's self; *avuto —*, taking into consideration; *usar —*, be respectful. -guardosaménte, ADJ.: cautiously (circumspectly, carefully). -guardóso, ADJ.: cautious (circumspect, careful).
ri=guaríre, INTR.: be cured (get well again).
ri=guastáre, TR.: waste or spoil again.
ri=guiderdonáre†, TR.: remunerate.
ri-gurgitaménto, M.: regurgitation. ‖=gurgitáre, INTR.: regurgitate (overflow). -gúrgito, M.: gurgling up; overflow.
ri=gustáre, TR.: taste again.
ri=lasciáre, TR.: RELEASE (set free; pardon); yield, give. -láscio, M.: release (remission). -lassaménto, M.: relaxation; laxity. -lassánte, ADJ.: relaxing; laxative. -lassáre, TR.: relax (slacken; let go); REFL.: relax (give way). -lassatézza, F.: laxity (slackness). -lassazióne†, F.: relaxation. -lassatívo, ADJ.: (*med.*) laxative. -lásso†, ADJ.: lax (slack); wearied; lazy; ... : relay.
=laváre, TR.: wash again.
=lavoráre, TR.: work or plough again.

ri=leccáre, TR.: lick again.
ri-legaménto, M.: binding ag... -gáre, TR.: bind or tie ag... (books); also = *rilegare*. -l... M.: rebinder; binder (of books)... -túra, F.: rebinding; binding... -legaturína, *dim. of -legatur*...
ri=lèggere, IRR.; TR.: read ag...
ri-lentaménte†, ADV.: gentl... -lentaménto†, M.: relaxio... tion). ‖=lènto, -lènto, M.: ... tly (softly; cautiously).
ri-levaménto, M.: raising... (erection). ‖=leváre, TR.: ... again; raise (erect; enhance); ... educate; comfort; nurse (suckl... rise; be of importance (matte... rise up again; recover; be in re... out); be inferred, be clear: *poc*... matters little; *da queste notizi*... from these accounts we infer (... is clear). -levataménte, AD... lief; eminently. -levatíccio... upstart. -leváto, PART.: ... again), etc.; elevated (eminent); ... out in relief (projecting), swellin... up; M.: eminence (height); reli... ing. -levazióne, F.: elevat... tion); relief. -lèvo†, -lièvo... vation; relief; importance; ... (remark); leavings (of the t... mains).
ri=liberáre, TR.: free again.
ri=limáre, TR.: file or polish a...
ri=lodáre, TR.: laud or praise ...
ri=logáre† = *riallogare*.
ri=lucciciáre, INTR.: glitter... -lucènte, ADJ.: shining (bril... trous). -lucentézza, F.: ... ‖=lúcere, IRR.: shine (glitter... sy).
ri=lustráre, TR.: shine or ... (give a new lustre to).
ri=lutáre, TR.: lute or cement...
rilut-tánte [*luttare*], ADJ.: ... -tánza, F.: reluctance.
rí-ma [Germ'c *rîm*], F.: RHYME... *der per le -me*, answer frankly... ly). -máccia, *disp.* of -*ma*.
ri=macináre, TR.: grind agai...
ri=maledíre, TR.: curse anew.
ri=mandáre, TR.: send back... send again; dismiss. -mándo, ... ing or tossing back (return): ... return, at once, promptly; by... blow.
ri=maneggiáre, TR.: handle ... touch); repair.
ri-manènte, ADJ.: remaining... mainder (remnant). -manènza... mainder; permanence†; abode†. ...-nére, IRR.§; INTR.: remain (st...

(dwell); abstain (cease, give up): *-manerci*, die; *-manetevi con Dio!* God be with you; — *brutto*, be baffled; *non mi -marrò di*, I shall not cease to.

§ Ind.: Pres. *ri-mángo, -máni, -máne; -maniámo* or *-manghiámo, -manéte, mángono.* Pret. *rimá-si, -se; -sero.* Fut. *rimarrò.* Cond. *rimarrèi.* Subj.: Pres. *rimánga* (*rimágna*†). Part. *rimásto* (*-maso*†).

ri=mangiáre, TR.: eat again.

rimángo, PRES. of *-manere.*

rimánte [*-mare*], M.: rhymer.

ri=marcáre, TR.: mark again; remark (observe).

rimáre [*rima*], TR.: rhyme.

rimarginàre [*margine*], INTR.: heal up (cicatrise).

rimário [*-ma*], M.: rhyming dictionary.

ri=maritáre, TR.: marry again (to a second husband); reunite; INTR., REFL.: marry again.

ri-mása†, F.: stay; permanence. **-mási**, *pret.* of *-manere.* ‖**-máso**†, PART. of *-manere;* remained, etc.; left; M.: remnant (rest).

ri=masticáre, TR.: chew again; stutter.

rimásto, PART. of *rimanere;* remained, etc.; remaining.

rimasúglio [*rimanere*], M.: remains (bits, crumbs).

rima-tóre, M., **-tríce**, F.: rhymer (rhymster).

rimazióne†, F.: investigation.

r=imbaldanzíre, INTR.: embolden (take courage again); pick up courage. ‖**=imbaldíre**, INTR.: cheer up; rejoice.

rim-balzáre [*re, in, b..*], INTR.: rebound (bounce), hop; result. **-balzèllo**, M.: drakestone (ducks and drake, the play). **-balzíno**, M.: tossing coins (boys' game). **-bálzo**, M.: rebound; counterblow: *di* —, indirectly.

rim-bambiménto, M.: growing childish. ‖**-bamb(in)íre** [*bambino*], INTR.: grow childish, dote.

r=imbarbogíre, INTR.: grow childish, dote.

r=imbarcáre, INTR., REFL.: reëmbark; bend, warp (become bent or crooked).

r=imbastíre, TR.: baste, sew slightly.

r=imbeccáre, TR.: peck (with the bill); toss or fling back (fling in one's teeth); RECIPR.: bill (join bills). **-bécco**, M.: pecking; billing: *di* —, pertly, waspishly.

r=imbecillíre, INTR.: grow imbecile.

r=imbellíre, TR.: (re)embellish (make handsomer); REFL.: grow handsomer.

rimbore.. = *rabbere..*

r=imbiancáre, TR.: bleach (again), whiten.

r=imbiondíre, INTR.: grow blond (fair, light).

r=imboccáre, TR.: invert (turn upside down); overturn (upset); fold back. **-imbócco**, M.: inverting, upsetting; overflow†.

rim-bombaménto†, M.: resounding. **-bombáre**, TR.: resound (boom). **-bombévole**, ADJ.: resounding. **-bómbio**, M.: frequent resounding. ‖**-bómbo** [L. *bombus*], M.: resounding (booming, roar, report). **-bombóso**†, ADJ.: resounding.

r-imborsábile, ADJ.: that may be reimbursed. ‖**=imborsáre**, TR.: pocket again; reimburse (repay). **-imborsazióne**, F., **-imbórso**, M.: reimbursement.

r-imboscaménto, M.: hiding in the bush, skulking. ‖**=imboscáre**, TR.: hide in the bush; REFL.: hide one's self (skulk away). **-imboschiménto** = *-imboscamento.*

r=imbottáre, TR.: barrel up again.

r=imbrogliáre, TR.: perplex (confuse).

rim-brottáre [?], TR.: reprove (scold). **-bròtto**, M.: scolding.

r=imbruníre, TR.: burnish.

r=imbruttíre, INTR.: grow ugly.

r=imbucáre, INTR.: dodge into a hole.

r=imbuíre, INTR.: grow stupid.

rimbussoláre [*bossolo*], TR.: shake (a dice-box, etc.).

ri-mediábile, ADJ.: remediable. **-mediáre**, TR.: remedy (cure). **-mediatóre**, M.: repairer. ‖**-mèdio** [L. *remedium*], M.: remedy (cure; medicine). **-medíre**†, TR.: redeem; pick up.

ri=meditáre, INTR.: meditate again.

rimeggiáre [*rimare*], INTR.: make poor rhyme, rhyme.

ri=meglioráre, TR.: improve.

ri-membránte, ADJ.: remembering, mindful. **-membránza**, F.: remembrance (memory). **-membráre**, TR.: remember; remind; REFL.: call to mind (remember). ‖**=memoráre**†, TR.: remind.

ri=menáre, TR.: bring back; shake (stir). **-menáta**, F.: bringing back; shaking.

rimen-dáre [*ri-, emendare*], TR.: mend (repair, patch). **-datóra**, F., **-datóre**, M., **-datríce**, F.: mender (patcher). **-datúra**, F., **rimèn-do**, M.: mending (patching, *-do* esp. as done).

ri-ménio [*-menare*], M.: bringing back; shaking. **-méno**†, M.: return.

rimentíta, F.: new denial.

rimeri-tábile, ADJ.: that may be requited. **-taménto**, M.: recompense (reward). ‖**-táre** [*ri-, merito*], TR.: recompense (reward, requite).

ri=méscere, IRR.; TR.: pour again; remix; mix up. **-mescolaménto**, M.: mixing up; confusion. **-mescolánza**

F.: mixing up; mixture. ‖=**mescoláre**, TR.: mix up together (confound); stir; shuffle (cards); blend; REFL.: be mixed up; intermeddle; be troubled.
rimés-sa, F.: remittance (sending off or back; thing sent); storage; return; shoot (new sprout or growth); coach-house; cf. *-so*. **-samente**, ADV.: reservedly; submissively. **-síbile**†, ADJ.: remissible. **-sióne**, F.: remission. **-siticcio**, M.: new sprout. ‖**rimés-so**, PART. of *rimettere;* put back (replaced), etc.; subdued (dispirited); weak; M.: fold.
ri-mésta†, F.: mixture; reproof. ‖=**mestára**, TR.: mix (mingle); stir.
ri=méttere, IRR.; TR.: put or set back (replace, restore, return); remit (send; consign; pardon); repress (restrain); drive back (beat back); commit; INTR.: shoot afresh, recommence; REFL.: place one's self; refer (submit) to; be restored: — *il conto*, send in an account; — *il taglio a*, sharpen (set); — *in possesso*, put in possession; — *una cosa in uno*, refer a matter to some one; — *su*, bring up, bring into fashion; *-mettersi in carne*, get stout again. **-mettiménto**†, M.: setting back (replacing, return); remission. **-mettitíccio**, M.: scion (sucker). **-mettitéra**, F., **-mettitóre**, M.: replacer; remitter. **-mettitúra**, F.: replacing; remission.
ri=miráre, TR.: look at intently; consider. **-míro**†, M.: view; regard.
ri=mischiáre, TR.: mix again; disturb.
rimissióne = *remissione*.
ri=misuráre, TR.: measure again.
rimminchioníre [*ri-*, *im-*, *minchione*], INTR.: become silly, grow foolish.
r=immolláreI, TR.: wet, drench again.
ri=modelláre, TR.: remodel.
rimoder-naménto, M.: modernizing. ‖**-náre** [*moderno*], TR.: modernize.
rimolináre† = *rammulinare*.
ri-mondaménto†, M.: clean(s)ing. ‖=**mondáre**, TR.: clean (cleanse), purge; thin, prune; expiate. **-mondatúra**, M.: cleaning (cleansing); purging; pruning. **-móndo**, ADJ.: cleaned; pruned.
ri-mónta, F.: remounting (resetting); (*milit.*) remount. ‖=**montáre**, TR.: remount (go up, ascend; set up, fit up again, fix); go (pull, row, sail) up or against; wind up (a watch); (*milit.*) set up (equip). **-montatúra**, F.: remounting.
rimorbi-dáre†, **-díre**† = *rammorbidire*.
-morchiáre [L. *remulcare* (Gr. *rhúma*, -ne, *hélkein*, pull)], TR.: tow (haul); chide†. **-rchiatóre**, M.: tow-boat, tug. **-mòrchio**, M.: towing; tow-boat.
ri-mordènte, ADJ.: biting; pungent. ‖=**mòrdere**, IRR.; TR.: bite back or again; bite (sting); reproach bitterly†; INTR.: cause remorse. **-mordiménto**, M.: biting (back); sting (remorse, compunction).
rimóre† = *rumore*.
ri=moríre, IRR.; INTR.: die again; die out.
ri=mormoráre, INTR.: grumble again.
rimòrso, PART. of *-mordere;* M.: remorse.
riméso†, ADJ.: cracked (chinky).
rimòsso, PART. of *rimovere;* removed, etc.; remote (distant).
ri-mostránza, F.: remonstrance; representation. ‖=**mostráre**, TR.: show again; INTR.: remonstrate.
ri-motaménte, ADV.: remotely. **-móto** [L. *re-motus*], ADJ.: remote (distant). ‖=**mòvere**, IRR.; TR.: remove (take away); turn away (divert, dissuade); REFL.: retire (*di*, from: leave, quit). **-movíbile**, ADJ.: removable; changeable. **-moviménto**, M.: removal. **-movitóre**, M.: remover. **-mozióne**, F.: removal; change.
r=impadroníre, REFL.: take fresh possession of (seize on again).
rimpalmáre†, TR.: calk; tar.
r=impaludáre, TR.: grow marshy.
rimpannucciáre [*ri-*, *in-* *panno*], TR.: dress in better clothes; (us'ly fig. and) REFL.: improve one's conditions (retrieve one's self, recover).
r=imparáre, TR.: reacquire.
r=impastáre, TR.: knead again; retouch. **-impasticciáre**, TR.: jumble again: M.: medley.
r=impatriáre, INTR.: return to one's country. **-impátrio**, M.: return home.
r=impauráre†, =**impauríre**, INTR.: be terrified again.
r=impazzáre, INTR.: get ever madder, get worse and worse. **-impazzáta**: *alla* —, like a madman; extravagantly.
r=impeciáre, TR.: pitch (calk).
rimpeduláre [*pedulo*], TR.: sole; new-foot (stockings).
r=impegnáre, TR.: pledge again.
r=impennáre, TR.: feather anew.
rim-pettíre [*ri*, *im-*, *petto*], INTR., REFL.: walk high-breasted (strut). **-pètto**, ADV.: (us'ly *dirimpetto*) opposite (facing).
r=impiagáre, TR.: wound again.
rim=piángere, IRR.; TR.: regret; pity.
r=impiastráre, TR.: plaster up again.
rimpiat-táre [*ri-*, *im-*, *piatto*], TR.: hide (conceal); REFL.: hide; squat (cower). **-táto**, PART.: hidden; secret; squat. **-terèllo**, **-tíno**, M.: hide and seek (play).
rim-piazzáre† [Fr. *remplacer*], TR.: REPLACE. **-piázzo**†, M.: replacing.
r=impicciolíre, =**impiccolíre**, TR., INTR.: lessen.

r=impiegáre, TR.: reëmploy; use again.
r=impinguáre, TR.: fatten again.
r-impinzaménto, M.: cramming. ‖**=impinzáre**, TR.: cram (stuff, gorge).
rimpolpáre [*ri-, im-, polpa*], INTR.: grow plump or fleshy.
rimpolpettáre [*ri-, im-, polpetta*], INTR.: reprove (scold), insult; smooth over; answer back†.
r=impoltronire, TR.: make lazy.
r=impoverire, TR.: reimpoverish (make poor again).
r=impregnáre, INTR.: become pregnant again.
rim-proccévole†, ADJ.: reproaching. **-proccіaménto**†, M.: reproach. ‖**-proccіáre** [Fr. *reprocher*], TR.: REPROACH (blame). **-pròccio**, M.: reproach (blame): *per* —, disdainfully. **-proccióso**†, ADJ.: reproachful.
rim-promésso†, PART.: promised again. **-prométtere**†, IRR.; TR.: promise again.
rim-proverábile, ADJ.: blamable. **-proveraménto**†, M.: reproof. ‖**-proveráre** [Fr. *reprouver*], TR.: REPROVE (reproach); accuse; insult. **-proveratóre**, M.: reprimander. **-proverazióne**†, F., **-provério**†, **-pròvero**, M.: reproof (reproach, blame); insult.
rimpulizzire, TR.: repolish.
ri-mugghiáre, ‖**=muggire**, INTR.: bellow (roar) again.
rimuginárе [L. *muginari*, delay], TR.: search diligently, grope; dwell (on); weigh (consider) carefully, dwell.
rimune-raménto, M.: remuneration. ‖**-ráre** [L. *remunerari*], TR.: remunerate (reward). **-ratívo**, ADJ.: remunerative. **-ratóre**, M., **-ratríce**, F.: remunerator. **-razióne**, F.: remuneration.
rimuòvere = *rimovere*.
ri=muráre, TR.: wall up again (block up).
rimurch.. = *rimorch..*
ri-mutaménto, M., **-mutánza**†, F.: mutation (change, transformation). ‖**=mutáre**, TR.: change (alter, transmute, transform). **-mutazióne**†, F.: mutation (change, transformution).
rin- [*ri-, in-*], PREF.
r=inacerbire, TR.: exasperate (irritate).
ri=narráre, TR.: relate again.
ri-nascènte, ADJ.: renascent (reborn); M.: academician. **-nascènza**, F.: rebirth; regeneration. ‖**=náscere**, IRR.; INTR.: be born again (revive). **-nasciménto**, M.: rebirth (regeneration). **-náscita**, F.: rebirth (reproduction). **-náto**, PART. of *-nascere*.
r=inasprire, TR.: exasperate anew.
ri=navigáre, TR.: sail again.
r=incacciáre, TR.: drive or push back (repel).

rinca-gnáre [*ri-, in-, cane*], REFL.: (look like a dog, hence), look gruff, frown (scowl); esp. in **-gnáto**, PART.: *naso* —, flat nose, flat-nosed.
rincalciáre [*ri-, in-, calci*], TR.: kick back (push back, repel).
r=incalcináre†, TR.: whitewash again; plaster again.
r=incalorire, TR.: rekindle.
rin-calzaménto, M.: banking round (propping up). ‖**-calzáre** [*re-, in, c..*], TR.: bank round (prop up); mulch; tuck in (sheets and covers of a bed): *andare a — i caroli*, go to nourish the worms (die, kick the bucket). **-calzáta**, **-calzatúra**, F.: banking (support); mulching. **-cálzo**, M.: banking (support), prop; succour (aid); gain, fortune.
r=incamminárе, REFL.: set out again.
r=incantáre, TR.: reënchant; offer by auction again.
r=incantucciáre, TR.: drive into a corner, hide in a corner; REFL.: hide one's self in a corner.
r=incappáre, INTR.: be ensnared (caught) again.
rincappel-láre [*ri-, in-, cappello*], TR.: heap up; referment (old wine with new grapes); INTR.: fall sick again. **-lazióne**†, F.: reproof.
r=incaráre, **-incarire**†, TR.: raise the price of; INTR.: grow dearer: — *il fitto*, do one's worst.
r=incarnáre, TR.: turn into flesh; INTR.: grow fleshy again.
rincáro [*-carare*], M.: rise in price.
r=incartáre, TR.: wrap up again (in paper).
rincasáre [*ri-, in-, casa*], INTR., REFL.: (*fam.*) return home.
r=incattivire, INTR.: grow wicked (again).
rincavalláre†, TR.: set on a horse again; provide with another horse; REFL.: refit one's self.
r=incerconire, INTR.: grow sour (turn).
r=inchináre, INTR.: incline (bend).
r=inchiúdere, IRR.; TR.: enclose (shut in or up). **-inchiudiménto**†, M.: enclosing. **-inchiúso**, PART.: enclosed (shut in); M.: enclosure.
r=inciampáre, INTR.: stumble (again).
r=incingere†, IRR.; INTR.: be with child again.
r=inciprignire, INTR.: grow virulent (angry) again.
r=incivilire, INTR.: make civil or polite (again); polish.
r=incolláre, TR.: paste (glue) again.
rincòllo [*ri-, in-, collo*], M.: damming up
r=incolpáre, TR.: accuse (blame) again
r-incominciaménto, M.: recommence

ment. ‖=incominciáre, TR.: recommence (begin again).
r-incóntra†, PREP.: opposite, toward: *andare alla* —, go to meet. ‖=incontráre, TR.: meet (light on, find); REFL.: meet by chance. -incóntro, M.: rencounter (meeting); confronting: *a* —, *di* —, opposite.
r=incoraggíre, =incoraggiáre, TR.: reëncourage. -incoraménto, M.: encouragement. =incoráre, TR.: hearten (encourage, cheer); REFL.: take heart or courage.
rincordáre†, TR.: new-string.
r-incorporaménto, M.: reëmbodying. ‖=incorporáre, TR.: reincorporate (reëmbody).
rin=córrere [*re-*, *in-*, *c.*.], IRR.; TR.: run after (pursue). -córsa, F.: start (backstep before leaping, spring): *prendere la* —, take a start (before leaping). -córso, PART. of *-correre*.
rincrésc-ere [*re-*, *in-crescere*], IRR.; INTR.: ('grow in weight,' hence) become burdensome or wearisome; tire; annoy (vex, be disagreeable); be painful; REFL.: be annoyed, be sorry. -évole, ADJ.: tiresome (tedious, disagreeable). -evolézza, F.: tiresomeness (tediousness), disgust. -evolménte, ADV.: tediously (disagreeably). -iménto, M.: tiresomeness (tediousness). -ióso, ADJ.: annoying (wearisome).
r=increspáre, TR.: crisp again.
r=incrudelíre, -incrudíre, TR.: exasperate again.
rincu-láre [*ri-*, *in-*, *culo*], INTR.: RECOIL; retire (draw back). -láta†, F.: recoil; retrocession.
r=incurváre, -incurvíre, INTR.: be curved.
r=indolcíre, TR.: sweeten (again).
r=indossáre, TR.: reëndorse.
r=indugiáre, TR.: delay (put off) again.
ri=negáre, TR.: deny (again).
ri=nettáre, TR.: clean (again). -nettatúra, F.: cleaning again.
rinfac-ciaménto, M.: scolding (blame). ‖-ciáre [*ri-*, *in-*, *faccia*], TR.: reproach (censure, blame); taunt.
rinfalconáre†, REFL.: be overjoyed.
r=infanciullíre, INTR.: grow childish. -infantocciáre [*fantoccio*], TR.: dress like a puppet; grow childish†.
r=inferraioláre, TR.: cover with a cloak.
r=inferráre, TR.: fix anew with iron (as spades, etc.); REFL.: recover strength.
r=infervoráre, TR.: give renewed fervour to (invigorate).
r-infiammagióne†, F.: inflammation. ‖=infiammáre, TR.: inflame (anew), rekindle.
r-infiancaménto, M.: counterfort (buttress, prop). ‖=infiancáre, TR.: flank (buttress, prop), fortify. -infiánco, M.: flanking (buttressing).
rinfiochíre [*ri-*, *in-fioco*], INTR.: grow soft; wither.
rinfierire [*ri-*, *in-*, *fiero*], INTR.: grow more fierce; grow stronger; grow proud.
r=infiláre, TR.: thread or string again.
r=infioráre, TR.: adorn with flowers; adorn.
r=infittíre, TR.: refix; increase.
r=infocáre, TR.: rekindle, inflame. -infocoláre, TR.: feed the fire of (put fuel on, feed); stir up; rekindle.
rinfoderáre [*ri-*, *in-*, *fodero*], TR.: put back into the scabbard, sheathe; REFL.: draw in one's horns; shrink.
r=infornáre, TR.: put in the oven again.
r-inforzaménto, M.: reënforcement. ‖=inforzáre, TR.: reënforce (strengthen); REFL.: grow stronger. -inforzatá†, F.: reënforcement. -infórzo, M.: reënforcement; fresh supply.
rinfran-caménto, M.: strengthening. ‖-cáre [*ri-*, *in-*, *franco*], TR.: reinvigorate (strengthen, fortify); be strengthened; indemnify one's self. -cescáre, TR.: remind of. -chíre, REFL.: be strengthened. -'co, M.: fortification; aid; resource.
r=infrángere, IRR.; TR.: break (again). -infránto, PART.; M.: sort of patterned textile fabric (diaper).
rinfratelláre, REFL.: unite as brothers.
r=infrenáre, TR.: bridle again, curb.
rinfre-scaménto, M.: refreshing; refreshment. ‖-scáre [*ri-*, *in-*, *fresco*], TR.: refresh (cool; revive); REFL.: become cool, cool off; revive†. -scáta, F.: refreshing (cooling). -scatívo, ADJ.: refreshing (cooling). -scatúra, F.: refreshment. -scatóio†, M.: cooler, basin. rinfré-sco, M.: refreshment (cooling dish, etc.); sort of liquor.
rinfrigidáre†, REFL.: grow cold or frigid.
rinfrignáto, ADJ.: frowning.
rinfronzo-láre, ‖-líre [*re-*, *in-*, *fronzolo*], REFL.: deck one's self with ribbons, etc.
r=infurbíre, INTR.: grow knavish.
rin-fúsa: *alla* —, in confusion. -fusióne†, F.: reinfusion. ‖-fúso, PART. of *-fondere*; confused (mixed together), etc.; full.
r-ingagliardiménto, M.: strengthening. ‖=ingagliardíre, TR.: reinvigorate (strengthen); INTR.: grow strong (again).
ringalluzz-áre, ‖-íre [? *gallo*], REFL.: strut with elation.
ringambaláre, TR.: put on the last again (stretch).

r=ingangheráre, TR.: set on the hinges again.
r=ingarzullíre, REFL.: chuckle with joy.
ringavagnáre†, TR.: resume.
ringeneráre = *rigenerare*.
r=ingentilíre, TR.: make genteel (ennoble); embellish.
ringhiáre [L. *ringi*], INTR.: snarl (growl).
ringhièra [*aringhiera* (*-gare*)], F.: (*hist.*) platform (with railing, for addresses; tribune; rostrum; hustings); gallery; balcony.
rín-ghio [*-ghiare*], M.: snarling. **-ghióso**, ADJ.: snarling (snappish).
r=inghiottíre, TR.: swallow up again.
ringioíre†, INTR.: rejoice.
r=ingiovaníre, TR.: make young again (rejuvenate); INTR.: grow young again (be rejuvenated).
ringiovialíre [*re-*, *in-*, *gioviale*], TR.: render jovial.
ringiráre†, TR.: turn round.
r=ingoiáre, =**ingolláre**, TR.: swallow (engulf) again.
r-ingorgaménto, M.: gurgling up; boiling over. ‖=**ingorgáre**, INTR.: gurgle or swell up; boil over. **-górgo**, M.: overswelling.
ringranáre [*ri-*, *in-*, *grano*], TR.: sow with grain (corn) again.
r=ingrandíre, TR.: increase (enlarge).
r=ingrassáre, INTR.: grow fat again.
r-ingravidaménto, M.: fresh pregnancy. ‖=**ingravidáre**, TR., INTR.: make or become pregnant again.
ringra-ziábile, ADJ.: deserving thanks. **-ziaménto**, M.: (return of) thanks. ‖**-ziáre** [*ri-*, *in-*, *grazie*], TR.: return thanks to (render thanks, thank). **-ziazióne**, F.: (return of) thanks.
ringrinz.. = *raggrinz*..
r=ingrossáre, TR.: augment (enlarge). **-ingrossatúra**, F.: enlargement (swelling).
r=inguaináre, TR.: sheathe again.
ringurgitáre†, INTR.: regurgitate.
r=innalzáre, TR.: raise (elevate) again, raise higher; INTR.: be raised; increase.
r=innamoráre, TR.: enamour again; REFL.: be enamoured again.
rinne-gaménto, M.: abjuring (forswearing). ‖**-gáre** [*ri-*, *negare*], TR.: deny; abjure (forswear). **-gáto**, PART., M.: RENEGADE. **-gatóra**, F., **-gatóre**, M., **-gatríce**, F.: abjurer (forswearer), renegade. **-gazióne**, F.: negation; abjuring. **-ghería**†, F.: abjuring, apostasy.
r-innestaménto, M.: regraft(ing). ‖=**innestáre**, TR.: regraft.
rinnobilíre [*ri-*, *nobile*], TR.: render noble, ennoble.
rinnocáre [*ri-*, *in-*, *oca*], TR.: double (at the 'game of geese'); repeat (do again).
rinno-vábile, ADJ.: renewable. **-vaménto**, M., **-vánza**†, F.: renewing (renewal). ‖**-váre** [*ri-*, *in-*, *novo*], TR.: renew (renovate, restore); put on for the first time; REFL.: be renewed, be restored. **-vatívo**, ADJ.: renewing (renovating). **-vatóre**, M., **-vatríce**, F.: renewer. **-vazióne**, F., **-vellaménto**, M.: renewing (renewal). **-velláre**, TR.: renew; begin again; INTR.: be renewed.
rinnò-vo, M.: renewal.
rinocerónte [Gr. *rhino-kéros*, 'nose-horn'], M.: rhinoceros.
rino-mábile, ADJ.: renowned (famous). **-mánza**†, F.: renown (fame). ‖**-máre** [*ri-*, *nome*], TR.: make renowned or famous (celebrate). **-máta**†, F.: renown. **-máto**, PART.: renowned (famed, famous). **-mèa**†, **-minánza**†, F.: renown (fame). **-mináre**, TR.: renominate; commend.
rinò-mo†, M.: renown.
ri=notáre, TR.: note again.
rinov.. = *rinnov*..
rinquartáre [*ri-*, *in-*, *quattro*], TR.: quadruple; quarter; INTR.: (*billiard*) hit the four walls.
r-insaccaménto, M.: rebagging; jolting. ‖=**insaccáre**, TR.: bag (sack) again; overcome (vanquish); jolt or shake (in the saddle); INTR.: be jolted or shaken.
rinsal-daménto, M.: consolidation. ‖**-dáre** [*ri-*, *in*, *-saldare*], TR.: solder (heal) up; consolidate.
r=insalvatichíre, TR., INTR.: make or become savage again.
r-insanguáre [*sangue*], TR.: return blood to (strengthen); REFL.: get blood again, grow strong again. =**insanguináre**, TR.: make bloody (bleeding) again.
rinsa-nicaménto, M.: restoring to health (curing). **-nicáre**, **-nichíre**, TR.: restore to health (cure). ‖**-níre** [*ri-*, *in-*, *sano*], INTR.: grow sane or sound again; recover one's health.
rinsavíre [*ri-*, *in-*, *savio*], TR.: make wise or sensible (again), bring to senses.
r=insegnáre, TR.: inform again.
r=inselváre, REFL.: grow woody or wild again; hide in the woods (again).
rinseren-áre, **-íre** = *rasserenare*.
r=inserráre, TR.: shut up (lock up).
rinsignoríre [*ri-*, *in-*, *signore*], INTR.: become master again; take possession again.
r=intagliáre, TR.: engrave anew.
r-intanaménto, M.: hiding in a den. ‖=**intanáre**, TR.: drive into a den; REFL.: hide in a den, hide.
r=intasáre, TR.: refill with argol, sediment (mud, etc.); block (stop) up again.

r=intascáre, TR.: pocket again.

r=integráre, TR.: reintegrate (restore); INTR., REFL.: be reintegrated (restored). **-integratóre**, M., **-integratrice**, F.: reintegrator. **-integrazióne**, F.: reintegration.

r=intèndere, IRR.; INTR.: understand again; fix again.

r=intenerire, TR.: soften or move (again); REFL.: be softened, moved, touched (again).

rinteraménto†, M.: reintegration (restoring).

rinter-raménto, M.: filling (with earth). ‖**-ráre** [*ri-*, *in-*, *terra*], TR.: fill with earth (for sowing, etc.).

r=interrogáre, TR.: interrogate (ask) again.

rin-terzáre [*ri-*, *in-*, *terzo*], TR.: treble (triple); do a third time; (*agr.*) sow a third year; (*billiard*) make a double rebound and hit. **-terzatúra**, F.: trebling. **-tèrzo**, M.: (*billiard*) double rebound and hit.

r=intiepid-áre†, **-íre**, TR.: cool again; INTR.: grow cool again.

rin-toccáre [*ri-*, *in*, *t.* .], TR.: toll (a bell). **-tócco**, M.: tolling; striking (the hours).

r=intonacáre, TR.: roughcast (plaster) again.

r=intonáre, INTR.: resound.

r=intontíre, INTR.: become foolish or bewildered.

r-intoppaménto, M.: rencounter (meeting); shock. ‖**=intoppáre**, TR.: rencounter (meet unexpectedly, hit upon); botch (etc. = *rattoppare*)†; REFL.: meet (*con*, with), run against. **-intòppo**, M.: rencounter (meeting); shock: *di* —, by return (in return).

rintòrto† = *ritorto*.

rintrac-ciábile, ADJ.: traceable. **-ciaménto**, M.: tracing (investigation, inquiry). ‖**-ciáre** [*ri-*, *in-*, *traccio*], TR.: retrace; trace (investigate, search). **-ciatóre**, M.: tracer (searcher).

r=intrecciáre, TR.: interlace, entwine; REFL.: become entwined.

r-intronaménto, M.: resounding; stunning (roar). ‖**=intronáre**, TR., INTR.: resound (roar, peal); stun. **-intròno†**, M.: resounding.

rintuz-zaménto, M.: blunting; abatement. ‖**-záre** [? L. *in-tuditiare* (*tundere*, strike)], TR.: make obtuse (blunt); abate (repress); REFL.: grow blunted (dull).

-unci. . = *rinunzi. .*

-ún-zia, F.: renunciation. ‖**-ziáre** [*re-nuntiare*], TR.: renounce (reject; ...); denounce†; relate†. **-ziatário**, M.: person to whom a thing is renounced. **-ziatóre**, M.: renouncer; reporter†. **-ziazióne†**, F.: renunciation.

ri=nutríre, TR.: nourish again.

r=invalidáre, TR.: make valid again (reaffirm).

rinvangáre = *rivangare*.

r=invelenire, TR.: exasperate (again).

r-inveniménto, M.: finding out. ‖**=invenire**, IRR.; TR.: find again (recover); INTR.: soften; REFL.: recover one's senses, recover; be found; yield. **-invenúto**, PART. of *-invenire*.

rinvèrcio†, M.: reverse.

r=inverdíre, TR.: make green again; REFL.: grow green again.

rinvergáre†, TR.: find out (discover).

rinversáre†, TR.: overturn; overflow.

rinvertíre†, TR.: convert; exchange; INTR.: draw back; happen.

rin-verzáre [*ri-*, *in-*, (*s*)*verza*], TR.: stop up (with chips, wedge up). **-verzicáre**, **-verzicoláre**, **-verzíre**, INTR.: grow green (again); flourish.

r-investiménto, M.: reinvestment; investiture. ‖**=investíre**, TR.: reinvest; invest; convert (exchange); barter.

r=inviáre, TR.: send back (dismiss); defer.

r-invigoriménto, M.: renewal or recovery of strength. ‖**=invigoríre**, TR.: reinvigorate.

rin-viliáre [*ri-*, *in-*, *vile*], TR.: lower the price of (cheapen). **-vílio**, M.: lowering (cheapening). **-vilíre†**, TR.: make worse; vilify.

r=inviluppáre, TR.: wrap up (again); perplex.

rinvispíre [*ri-*, *in-*, *vispo*], TR.: enliven.

r=invitáre, TR.: reinvite; offer fresh stakes; REFL.: invite one another.

rinvivíre [*ri-*, *in-*, *vivo*], INTR.: revive.

rinvogliáre [*ri-*, *in-*, *voglio*], TR.: excite a desire for.

r=invòlgere, IRR.; TR.: envelop (wrap up; enclose); involve. **-invòlgolo†**, M.: little bundle. **-involtáre**, TR.: wrap up quickly. **-invòlto**, PART. of *-involgere*; M.: bundle (packet). **-involtúra**, F.: wrapping; trouble†.

rin=zaffáre, TR.: bung, wedge up (fill with tow, etc.). **-zaffatúra**, F., **-záffo**, M.: filling up; plastering.

r=inzeppáre, TR.: wedge, stop up. **-inzeppatúra**, F.: stopping (of chinks, etc.).

rio 1 (*poet.*) = *rivo*.

rio 2 (*poet.*) = *reo*.

ri-obbligáre TR.: oblige again.

ri=occupáre, TR.: reoccupy.

ri=offèndere, TR.: reoffend.

ri=offríre, TR.: offer again.

rióne [*regione*], M.: (*hist.*) ward (part of Rome).

ri=operáre, INTR.: operate (act) again.

ri-ordinaménto, M.: reordering ||**=ordináre**, TR.: reorder (set in order again, rearrange). **-ordinatóre**, M., **-ordinatríce**, F.: rearranger. **-ordinazióne**, F.: rearranging.

ri=ordíre, TR.: weave again.

ri=ornáre, TR.: ornament again.

riòt-ta† [Fr. *-e* (Eng. *riot*)], F.: quarrel (dispute). **-tosaménte**, ADV.: controversially. **-tóso**, ADJ.: quarrelsome (litigious, controversial, disputatious).

ri-òttolo†, **-òzzolo**†, M.: small rivulet.

rípa [L.], F.: bank; shore.

rí=pacificáre, TR.: pacify again.

ri=pagáre, TR.: repay.

ri-parábile, ADJ.: repairable. **-paraménto**, M.: repair. ||**=paráre**, TR.: repair (remedy, cure; restore); retrieve; make amends for; oppose (hinder); INTR.: take refuge; REFL.: frequent (haunt). **-paráta**, F.: rapid repair; goal†. **-paratóre**, M., **-paratríce**, F.: repairer. **-paratúra**†, **-parazióne**, F.: reparation (repair).

ripário [L. *-parius*], ADJ.: riparian (of a river-bank).

ri-parláre, INTR.: speak again.

ripáro [*riparare*], M.: remedy; expedient (resource); defence (protection; rampart); shelter (refuge); obstacle: *far* —, defend one's self.

ri-partigióne†, F., **-partiménto**, M.: division; portion. ||**=partíre**, TR.: divide (distribute; share); depart again. **-partitaménte**, ADV.: separately; on an average (roughly). **-partizióne**, F.: division (distribution). **-párto**, M.: division (apportionment).

ri=partoríre, TR.: bring forth again.

ri=páscere, TR.: feed again.

ri=passáre, TR.: repass (return across); go over again (revise; recount; retouch); run away: — *nella memoria*, recall to memory. **-passáta**, F.: repassing (crossing again); going over again (review); rebuff; *fare una* — *a*, reprehend, scold. **-passatína**, *car. dim.* of *-passata*. **=passeggiáre**, INTR.: walk again. **-pásso**, M.: repassing (return, esp. of birds of passage).

ri=patíre, INTR.: suffer again.

ri=peccáre, INTR.: sin again.

ri=peggioráre, TR., INTR.: make or become yet worse.

ri-pensaménto, M.: reconsideration. ||**=pensáre**, INTR.: think over again (reconsider); think over (revolve in one's mind; weigh); change one's mind†.

ri-pentiménto, M.: repentance. ||**=pentíre**, REFL.: repent. **-pentitóre**†, M.: repenter. **-pentúto**†, PART. of *-pentire*.

ri-percòssa, F.: repercussion. **-percòsso**, PART. of *-percotere*. **-percotiménto**, M.: repercussion (act of). ||**=perco(u)òtere**, IRR.; TR.: repercuss (beat back; send back). **-percussióne**, F.: repercussion (effect of; rebound; reflexion). **-percussívo**, ADJ.: repercussive.

ri=pèrdere, TR.: lose again. **-perdúto**, **-pèrso**, PART.

ri=pesáre, TR.: weigh again.

ri=pescáre, TR.: fish out again; fish up. **-pésco**, M.: (*pop.*) light love-affair.

ri=pestáre, TR.: pound again.

ri=pètere [L. *re-petere*], TR.: repeat (renew; rehearse); answer back; recall to memory†. **-petiménto**†, M.: repetition. **-petío**†, M.: dispute. **-petitóre**, **-petitríce**, F.: repeater; rehearser; private teacher. **-petitúra**†, F.: repetition. **-petizioncèlla**, *dim.* of *-petizione*. **-petizióne**, F.: repetition; burden (of a song): *oriolo a* — or —, repeater (watch).

ripétta, *dim.* of *ripa*.

ripetú-taménte, ADV.: repeatedly. ||**-to**, PART. of *ripetere*.

ripez-zaménto†, M.: mending. **-záre**†, TR.: mend (piece, patch). **-zatóre**†, M.: mender. **-zatúra**, F.: mending.

ripiaciménto†, M.: new pleasure.

ri=pialláre, TR.: plane again.

ri=pianáre, TR.: level down, smooth again.

ri=piángere, IRR.; INTR.: weep again; wail.

ri=piáno, M.: level or even part; landing (of a staircase).

ri=piantáre, TR.: replant.

ri=picchiáre, TR.: knock again. **-picchiáta**, **-picchiatúra**, F.: knocking again.

ripícco [*picca*], M.: retort (sharp answer); revenge.

ripi-daménte, ADV.: steeply. **-dézza**, F.: steepness (steep; declivity). **-díssimo**, ADJ.: most (or very) steep. ||**rípido** [L. *-dus*], ADJ.: steep (precipitous).

ri-piegaménto, M.: folding. ||**=piegáre**, TR.: fold (bend) again; fold up; plait; REFL.: fold (bend) back; give way (as troops); be reflected; be entangled. **-piegáta**, F.: folding (fold); bending. **-piegatúra**, F.: double fold (or plait); folding. **-pièga**, M.: expedient (resource, means).

ri-pienézza, F.: fulness (repletion); superabundance. ||**=pièno**, ADJ.: full (replete, abounding); M.: filling (filling up; stuffing; make-weight); woof; satisfaction†.

ri=pigiáre, TR.: press or stamp upon again.

ri-pigliaménto, M.: retaking; remorse; repetition†. ‖**=pigliáre**, TR.: retake (resume, recover); reprimand; reply (answer); REFL.: take back (repent); correct one's self. **-piglino**, M.: 'catch' (boys' game, throwing and catching nuts); cat's-cradle (game). **-píglio**†, M.: reprehension.

ri=píngere, IRR.; TR.: paint again. **-pínsi**, PRET., **-pínto**, PART.

ri=piombáre, INTR.: plunge down again.

ri=piòvere, IRR.; IMPERS.: rain again.

ripíre†, INTR.: climb.

ripitio†, M.: complaint; contrast.

riplacáre†, TR.: pacify again; REFL.: become appeased.

ri=pónere (*pop.*) = *-porre*. **-poniménto**, M.: replacing.

ri=popoláre, TR.: repopulate.

ri=pòrgere, IRR.; TR.: present or offer again.

ri=pórre, IRR.; TR.: replace (put back); place; restore (rebuild)†; depose (bury, hide)†; REFL.: put back (replace); seat one's self; set about (begin); hide one's self†: *andare a -porsi*, subside, submit, yield, give up.

ri-portaménto†, M.: report. ‖**=portáre**, TR.: carry (bring) back; carry over (a sum); gain (victories); bring (give); report (relate); translate (copy); REFL.: have recourse (to, refer, trust to). **-portatóre**, M., **-tatríce**, F.: who brings back; reporter. **-portatúra**, F.: bringing back; copying. **-pòrto**, M.: carrying back or over (esp. sum carried over); report; embroidery.

ri-posaménto†, M.: repose. ‖**=posáre** 1, TR.: put or place back (replace; lay to rest, depose); INTR.: repose (rest); pause (stop); REFL.: repose (be put to rest, be buried); die; be at rest (have no anxiety); discontinue: *andar a* —, go to bed; — *nel signore*, die; *-posarsi sopra*, rely upon, trust in. **-posáre** 2, M.: repose (rest); pause. **-posáta**, F.: repose (rest, stop); pause. **-posataménte**, ADV.: composedly (calmly). **-posatína**, *dim.* of *-posata*. **-posáto**, PART.: reposed, etc.; composed (calm, quiet). **-posatóre**†, M.: reposer; calmer. **-posévole**†, ADJ.: composed (calm). **-positório**†, M.: repository. **-pòso**, M.: repose (rest; calm).

ripos-taménte, ADV.: hiddenly, secretly. **-tíglio**, M.: little repository (recess, nook); lurking-place. ‖**ripós-to**, PART. of *riporre*; hidden: *tener* —, hide.

ri=potáre, TR.: prune again.

ri=pregáre, TR.: pray again.

ri=prèmere, TR.: press again; repress.

ri=prèndere, IRR.; TR.: retake (take again; recover); reprehend (reprimand, rebuke, scold); begin again; REFL.: correct one's self (amend); leave off. **-prendévole**†, ADJ.: reprehensible. **-prendevolménte**†, ADV.: reprehensibly. **-prendiménto**, M.: reprehension (rebuke). **-prenditóre**, M., **-prenditríce**, F.: reprehender (rebuker). **-prensíbile**, ADJ.: reprehensible. **-prensibilménte**, ADV.: reprehensibly. **-prensióne**, F.: reprehension (rebuke). **-prensívo**, ADJ.: reprehensive (reproving). **-prensóra**, F., **-prensóre**, M.: reprehender (censurer; fault-finder). **-prensòrio**, ADJ.: reprehensory (censuring). **-présa**, F.: resumption (renewal; repetition); revenue; resource; (*mus.*) sign of repetition; repetition; (*arch.*) reconstruction; turning-post (at races): *a -prese*, repeatedly, time and again.

ri=presentáre, TR.: represent.

ripréso, PART. of *riprendere*.

riprèsso†, PART. of *riprèmere*.

ri=prestáre, TR.: lend again.

ri=principiáre, TR.: begin again.

ripristiná-re [*pristino*], TR.: bring to a former condition, restore. **-tóre**, M.: restorer. **-zióne**, F.: restoration (to an earlier state).

ri-produciménto, M.: reproduction. ‖**=prodúrre**, IRR.; TR.: reproduce; cause. **-produttívo**, ADJ.: reproductive. **-produttóre**, M., **-produttríce**, F.: reproducer. **-produzióne**, F.: reproduction.

ri-prométto, PART. of *-promettere*. ‖**=prométtere**, IRR.; TR.: promise again; go security for; REFL.: hope. **-promissióne**, F.: new promise; hope.

ri=propórre, IRR.; TR.: repropose.

ri=pròva, F.: new proof (corroboration). **-provaménto**, M.: reproof. ‖**=prováre**, TR.: try again; reprobate (refute, confute; censure, disapprove); REFL.: make a new trial. **-provatíssimo**, ADJ.: most reprehensible. **-provàto**, PART. of *-provare*. **-provatóre**, M.: disapprover (censurer). **-provazióne**, F.: reprobation (rejection, censure).

ri=prov(v)edére, IRR.; TR.: reprovide; reëxamine.

ripruov..† = *riprov..*

ri-pudiábile, ADJ.: repudiable. **-pudiáre** [L. *re-pudiare*], TR.: repudiate. ‖**-púdio** [L. *re-pudium*], M.: repudiation.

ripug-gnánte, ADJ.: repugnant. **-gnanteménte**, ADV.: repugnantly. **-gnánza**, F.: repugnance. ‖**-gnáre** [L. *re-pugnare*], INTR.: be repugnant; resist. **-gnazióne**†, F.: repugnance.

ri-puliménto, M.: cleaning; repolish; polishing up. ‖**=pulíre**, TR.: clean; repolish; polish up (furbish); retouch (finish up); clean out; REFL.: fix one's self up (dress up). **-pulíta**, F.: cleaning, polish: *fare una* —, clean up. **-pulitúra**, F.: (re)polishing; cleaning up; retouch.

ri=pulluláre, INTR.: repullulate (bud forth again).

ripúl-sa [L. *re-pulsa*], F.: repulse, refusal. **-sáre**, TR.: refuse (reject). **-sióne**, F.: (*phys.*) repulsion. **-sívo**, ADJ.: repulsive (repellent).

ri=púngere, IRR.; TR.: sting again.

ri-púrga, F., **-purgaménto†**, M.: purgation; polishing; PL.: (monthly) courses. ‖**=purgáre**, TR.: purge again.

ripu-taménto†, M., **-tánza†**, F.: reputation. ‖**-táre** [L. *re-putare*], TR.: repute; attribute. **-táto**, PART.: reputed (renowned). **-tazióne**, F.: reputation.

riqua-draménto, M.: squaring. ‖**-dráre** [*quadro*], TR.: square; paint the borders of (a room); INTR.: be square. **-dratúra**, F.: squaring; quadrature.

riquiṣ. .† = *requis*. .

ri=rèndere, TR.: give back (return).

ri=rómpere, IRR.; TR.: break again.

rí-sa1, PL. of *-so* 2. **-sa†** 2 = *-sata*.

risagíre†, TR.: reinstate.

risáia [*riso*], F.: rice-field.

ri-saldaménto, M.: resoldering. ‖**=saldáre**, TR.: resolder. **-saldatúra**, F.: resoldering.

ri-saliménto, M.: reascension. ‖**=salíre**, INTR.: reascend (go up again). **-salíto**, PART.: reascended; ADJ., M.: upstart.

ri=saltáre, INTR.: leap again (rebound); jut out. **-sálto**, M.: rebound; jutting out (projection); relief (prominence): *dare* —, enhance.

ri=salutáre, TR.: salute again. **-salutazióne†**, M.: mutual salutation.

risaminàre† = *riesaminare*.

ri-sanábile, ADJ.: curable. **-sanaménto**, M.: cure (recovery). ‖**=sanáre**, TR.: cure (restore, heal); INTR.: be cured.

ri=sapére, IRR.; TR.: know again; come to know (be told).

ri=sarchiáre, TR.: weed again.

risar-cíbile, ADJ.: curable, mendable. **-ciménto**, M.: curing; mending (reparation). ‖**-círe** [Gr. *sárx*, flesh], TR.: heal up again; restore (repair, mend); make amends for.

risá-ta [*ridere*], F.: laughter (laugh). **-táccia**, *disp*. of *-ta*. **-tína**, *car*. or *iron*. *dim*. of *-ta*.

ri=sázio, ADJ.: (re)satiated.

ri-scaldaménto, M.: (re)heating; inflammation; pimple. ‖**=scaldáre**, TR.: heat (again), warm up; INTR.: warm up (grow warm); grow angry. **-scaldatívo**, ADJ.: heating. **-scaldáto**, PART.: heated, etc.; in passion. **-scaldatóre**, M., **-scaldatríce**, F.: heater (warmer). **-scaldatúra**, **-scaldazióne**, F.: heating (warming).

ri=scappáre, INTR.: escape again.

riscattá-re [for *ricattare*], TR.: redeem (from servitude), rescue; acquire†; REFL.: regain lost money (at play). **-tóra**, F., **-tóre**, M., **-tríce**, F.: redeemer, rescuer.

riscátto, M.: redemption; recovery.

ri=ṣcégliere, IRR.; TR.: select (choose) again.

ri=ṣcéndere, IRR.; INTR.: redescend.

riṣcérre† = *risceglìere*.

rischia-raménto, M.: clearing up. ‖**-ráre** [*chiaro*], TR.: clear up (illuminate; elucidate; grow clear); prune. **-ratóre**, M., **-ratríce**, F.: clearer up; illuminator.

ris-chiáre, TR., INTR.: risk. ‖**rís-chio** [*-co*], M.: risk. **-chióso**, ADJ.: risky.

ri-ṣciacquaménto, M.: rinsing. ‖**=ṣciacquáre**, TR.: rinse again; rinse (wash). **-ṣciacquáta**, F.: rinsing; scalding. **-ṣciacquatóio†**, M.: mill-dam. **-ṣciacquatúra**, F.: rinsing (washing); dish-water. **-ṣciácquo**, M.: side-ditch (sewer).

ri=ṣciògliere, IRR.; TR.: loosen again.

rísco† [p. L. **-sicus*], M.: risk.

ri=scontáre, TR.: discount again.

ri-scontrábile, ADJ.: that may be met with or found. **-scontraménto**, M.: meeting. ‖**=scontráre**, TR.: come upon (meet with, find); confront (compare, collate); verify; INTR.: meet; agree together (agree, tally); REFL.: come upon each other, meet by chance. **-scontráta**, F.: meeting; comparison, verification. **-scontratína**, *dim*. of *-scontrata*. **-scóntro**, M.: meeting; encounter; confronting (comparing, collation); evidence; obstacle; counterpart (example); opposite; garniture; suite (of rooms): *a* —, opposite, over against; *trovar* —, second.

ri=scoppiáre, INTR.: burst anew.

ri=scórrere, IRR.; TR., INTR.: run over (again), repeat; reconsider.

ri-scòssa, F.: recovery (RESCUE); support (of yielding troops); insurrection: *armata di* —, army of reserve; *stare alle -scosse*, answer exactly. **-scossióne**, F.: collection (receipt); exaction. **-scòsso**, PART. of *-scotere*. ‖**=scòtere**, IRR.; TR., INTR.: shake up, start up; exact (collect, get money due, etc.); get back; redeem; retaliate†; REFL.: be shaken up; start up; free one's self; be avenged†. **-scotiménto**, M.: exaction, receiving. **-scotitóre**, M., **-scotitríce**, F.: collector.

ri=scrívere, IRR.; TR.: rewrite.

riscuòtere = *riscotere*.

ri=seccáre, TR.: cut again. **-secazióne,** F.: recutting.
ri=seccáre, TR.: dry up; INTR.: grow dry. **-secchíre,** INTR.: grow dry. **-sécco,** ADJ.: dried up (arid).
ri-sedènte, ADJ.: residing; M.: resident. **-sedènza†,** F.: residence. ‖**=sedére,** IRR.; INTR.: reside (dwell). **-sèdio†, -sèggio†,** M.: residence.
ri-séga, F.: (*arch.*) jutting out (projection). ‖**=segáre,** TR.: saw again; cut off (retrench); divide. **-seghinétta,** F.: flesh-mark (from something tight).
ri-ségna†, F.: resignation. **-segnáre,** TR.: sign again; resign. **-segnazióne†,** F.: resignation.
ri=seguíre†, TR.: continue. **-seguitáre,** TR.: follow again.
risembráre†, TR.: resemble.
ri=semináre, TR.: sow again.
ri-sentiménto, M.: resentment (anger). ‖**=sentíre,** INTR.: feel (again); have a feeling (of); remind (of); hear again; REFL.: recover one's senses (recover, revive, grow well); awake; be angered; resent (be avenged). **-sentitaménte,** ADV.: resentingly. **-sentíto,** PART.: felt, etc.; resentful; roused (impassioned); contentious; energetic (strong); ADV.: resentfully.
ri-sèrba†, -serbagióne†, -serbánza† = *-serva*. ‖**=serbáre,** TR.: reserve; preserve; consider. **-serbat..** cf. also *-servat..* **-serbatézza,** F.: reserve; cautiousness. **-serbáto,** PART.: reserved; cautious. **-sèrbo,** M.: reservation; reserve; discretion (cautiousness).
ri-serraménto, M.: obstruction†. ‖**=serráre,** TR.: shut (close) again; rally; shut in.
risèr-va, F.: reservation; reserve. ‖**-váre** [L. *re-servare*], TR.: reserve. **-vataménte,** ADV.: reservedly; cautiously. **-vatézza,** F.: reservation; reserve. **-váto,** PART.: reserved; cautious. **-vatíssimo,** ADJ.: most reserved or cautious.
ri=servíre, TR.: serve again.
risèrvo [*-vare*], M.: reservation.
risettíno [*riso*], M.: smile (esp. ironical).
ri=sforzáre, TR.: force (again).
risguard.. = *riguard..*
rí-si, PRET. of *ridere*. **-síbile,** ADJ.: risible (laughable). **-sibilità,** F.: risibility.
risi-cáre, TR.: risk. ‖**rísi-co** [*risco*], M.: risk (hazard). **-cóso†,** ADJ.: risky.
risièdere = *risedere*.
risigállo†, M.: red arsenic.
risíno 1 [*riso 1*], M.: sweet smile.
risíno 2, *dim.* of *riso 3*.
·isipo-la [Gr. *erusi-pelas*, 'red-skin'], F.: (*med.*) erysipelas. **-lóso,** ADJ.: erysipe-

risist.. = *resist..*

ri-solúbile, ADJ.: resolvable. **-solutaménte,** ADV.: resolutely. **-solutézza,** F.: resoluteness. **-solutívo,** ADJ.: resolutive (dissolving). **-solúto,** PART. of *-solvere*; resolute (determined, bold). **-solutóre,** M., **-solutríce,** F.: resolver (resolvant). **-soluzióne,** F.: resolution; solution. ‖**=sòlvere,** IRR.; TR.: resolve (dissolve, melt; reduce; determine); solve. **-solvíbile,** ADJ.: resolvable. **-solviménto,** M.: resolution; (dis)solving. **-solvitóre,** M., **-solvitríce,** F.: resolver.
risomig]liáre† = *rassomigliare*.
ri=sommáre, TR.: sum up again.
ri=somméttere†, IRR.; TR.: resubmit.
ri=somministráre, TR.: provide again.
ri-sonánte, ADJ.: resonant (resounding). **-sonánza,** F.: resonance (resounding). ‖**=sonáre,** TR., INTR.: sound (ring) again; resound; publish loudly; signify.
risóne [*riso 3*], M.: grain of rice.
ri=sorbíre, TR.: swallow again, absorb.
ri-sorgènte, ADJ.: rising again. ‖**=sórgere,** INTR.: rise again (emerge); TR.: (*pop.*) yield (give). **-sorgiménto,** M.: rising again; resurrection. **-sorrèsse†** = *-surressi*. **-sórto,** PART.: risen again; resuscitated; M.: jurisdiction†.
ri=sospíngere, IRR.; TR.: beat back (repel). **-sospingiménto,** M.: fresh pulse or impulse. **-sospínto,** PART.
ri=sospiráre, INTR.: breathe again.
risòtto [*riso 3*], M.: rice-dish.
ri=sovveníre, IRR.; INTR., REFL.: have a remembrance (*di*, of: remember).
rispar-miaménto†, M.: thriftiness. **-miánte,** ADJ.: saving (thrifty). ‖**-miáre** [? ak. to Eng. *spare*], TR.: save (economize, hoard up; spare); INTR.: be thrifty; REFL.: take care of one's self. **-miatóra,** F., **-miatóre,** M.: saving (thrifty) person; manager. **-'mio,** M.: saving (thrift); thing saved (savings): *cassa di* —, savings-bank; *far — di*, use sparingly

or moderately; *a* —, moderately. **-miúc-cio**, *dim.* of *-mio.*
ri=spedíre, TR.: expedite (dispatch) again.
ri=spèndere, IRR.; TR.: spend again.
ri=spègnere, IRR.; TR.: reëxtinguish.
ri=spèrgere, IRR.; TR.: sprinkle again.
rispet-tábile, ADJ.: respectable. **-tán-te**, ADJ.: respectful. **-táre**, TR.: respect; honour. **-tévole†**, ADJ.: respectful. **-tivaménte**, ADV.: respectively. **-tívo**, ADJ.: respective; respectful. ‖**ri-spèt-to** [L. *re-spectus*], M.: respect (regard; reverence); favour (leave); sake (account); PL.: love ditties; PREP. (with *a*): relatively; for the sake of; in order that: *a* (or *in, per*) —, in comparison; as for, as to; for the sake of; *con — vostro*, with your leave; *per — di*, on account of; *per buon* —, with all due reference. **-tosaménte**, ADV.: respectfully. **-tó-so**, ADJ.: respectful. **-túccio**, *dim.* of *-to.*
ri=spianáre, TR.: smooth (even)
ri=spiáre, TR.: spy again.
rispiarm.. = *risparm..*
rispign.. = *risping..*
ri-spigolaménto, M.: fresh gleaning. ‖**=spigoláre**, TR.: glean (again), pick.
ri=spíngere, IRR.; TR.: drive back (repel). **-spínta**, F.: repulse. **-spínto**, PART. of *-spingere.*
rispir.., **rispitt..** = *respir..*, *rispett..*
ri-splendènte, ADJ.: resplendent. **-splendenteménte†**, ADV.: resplendently. **-splendènza†**, F.: resplendency. ‖**=splèndere**, INTR.: be resplendent, shine. **-splendévole†**, ADJ.: resplendent. **-splendiménto†**, **-splendóre†**, M.: splendour.
ri=spogliáre, TR.: strip again.
rispon-dènte, ADJ.: respondent (answering; suitable). **-dènza†**, F.: correspondence. ‖**rispón-dere** [L. *re-spondere*], IRR.§; (IN)TR.: respond (answer); correspond (agree, suit; be answerable, stand security); be situated opposite (face, look); yield. **-dévole†**, ADJ.: answerable; suitable. **-dièro**, ADJ.: answering back, impertinent (saucy); M.: saucy fellow. **-ditóre**, M.: responder; guarantor (bondsman). **-sábile**, ADJ.: responsible. **-sióne†**, F.: response. **-sívo** = *responsivo.*

§ Pret. *rispó-si, -se; -sero.* Part. *rispósto.*

ri=sposáre, TR.: marry again.
rispós-ta, F.: answer. **-táccia**, *disp.* of *-sposta.* **-tína**, *car.* or *iron. dim.* of *-ta.* ‖**rispós-to**, PART. of *rispondere.*
ri=sprangáre, TR.: bar again; rivet (mend).
risprèndere† = *risplendere.*
ri=spronáre, TR.: spur again.
ri=sputáre, TR.: spit again.
ris-sa [L. *rixa*], F.: quarrel (strife, dispute). **-sánte**, ADJ.: quarrelsome. **-sá-re**, INTR.: quarrel (wrangle); REFL.: quarrel (altercate). **-sóso**, ADJ.: quarrelsome.
ri-stabiliménto, M.: reëstablishment; repairing. ‖**=stabilíre**, TR.: reëstablish (restore).
ri=stacciáre, TR.: sift again; examine.
ri-stagnaménto, M.: staunching. ‖**=stagnáre**, TR.: solder with tin; staunch (stop); INTR.: stagnate. **-stagnatívo**, ADJ.: staunching. **-stagnatúra**, F.: staunching (stopping). **-stágno**, M.: staunching; stagnation.
ri-stámpa, F.: reimpression; new edition. ‖**=stampáre**, TR.: reprint: — *le orme di*, follow the footsteps of. **-stampatóre**, M.: reprinter.
ri-stánza†, F.: cessation. ‖**-stáre**, INTR.: cease (stop). **-státa†**, F.: stop.
ristaur.. = *restaur..*
ristecchíre†, INTR.: dry up.
ri=stilláre, TR.: redistill.
rístio† = *rischio.*
ri=stoppáre, TR.: stop with tow.
ri=stoppiáre, TR.: sow with grain (corn) again.
ristora-ménto, M.: refreshment; restoration; compensation. ‖**ristorá-re** [L. *re-staurare*], TR.: restore (return, repair); compensate (make up for; reward); REFL.: refresh one's self; recover one's self. **-tívo**, ADJ.: restorative. **-tóre**, M., **-tríce**, F.: restorer. **-zioncèlla**, *dim.* of *-zione.* **-zióne**, F.: restoration; compensation.
ri=stornáre, TR.: turn back. **-storní-no**, M.: 'rebound' (boy's game; throwing a coin, etc., rebounding against a wall). **-stórno**, M.: turning back.
ristòro [*-rare*], M.: restorative; comfort (relief); compensation.
ri-strettaménte, ADV.: narrowly; briefly (in short). **-strettézza**, F.: narrowness; restriction (restraint); straitened condition (want of means). **-strettíno**, *dim.* of *-stretto.* **-strettíre**, TR.: restrict (narrow). **-strettívo**, ADJ.: restrictive; astringent. **-strétto**, PART. of *-stringere*; restricted (limited, etc.); lowest; M.: restriction; abridgment (epitome); small group; lowest price: — *con*, confined with; *in* —, in short; summarily; *starsi* —, stand still; *il — del negozio*, the main part of a business. **-strign..** = *-string..* ‖**=stríngere**, IRR.; TR.: restrict (restrain; confine, limit); constrain (compress); tighten (as reins, etc.); bind (constipate); tie (unite); shut up; REFL.: be restricted (etc.); shrink (grow

narrow); become close (get intimate): *-stringersi con uno*, get intimate with one; *-stringersi nello spendere*, economize; *-stringersi nelle spalle*, shrug one's shoulders. **-stringiménto**, M.: restriction; constriction. **-stringitívo**, ADJ.: restrictive. **-strínto**, PART. of *-stringere*.
ri=strisciáre, INTR.: glide again.
ri-stuccaménto, M.: replastering. ‖**=stuccáre**, TR.: replaster; nauseate. **-stúcco**, ADJ.: surfeited (nauseated, weary; glutted).
ri=studiáre, TR.: study again.
risucit.. = *risuscit..*
ri=sudáre, INTR.: sweat again; evaporate.
ri=suggelláre, TR.: seal up again.
risul-taménto, M.: result. ‖**-táre** [L. *re-sultare*], INTR.: result (follow, arise). **-táto**, PART.; M.: result.
risupíno† = *resupino*.
ri-súrg.. (*lit.*) = *-sorg..* **-surrezióne**, F.: resurrection. **-súrto**, PART. of *-surgere*.
risuṣci-taménto, M.: resuscitation. ‖**-táre**, TR.: resuscitate; INTR.: be resuscitated.
ri-ṣvegliaménto, M.: (re)awakening; rousing. ‖**=ṣvegliáre**, TR.: (re)awaken, arouse; REFL.: wake up. **-ṣvegliatóre**, M., **-ṣvegliatríce**, F.: awakener, rouser. **-ṣvéglio**, M.: reawakening (revival).
ri=tagliáre, TR.: cut (again), slice (again); pare (clip). **-tagliatóre**, M.: cutter; RETAILER. **-tagliétto**, *car. dim.* of *-taglio*. **-táglio**, M.: piece of cloth cut out (cutting, shred); bit (— *di tempo*, odd or spare moment); RETAIL (in *a* —, by detail): *mercante a* —, retail-dealer.
ri-tardaménto, M., **-tardánza**, F.: retard (delay, stop). ‖**=tardáre**, TR.: retard (delay, stop). **-tardatívo**, ADJ.: retarding. **-tardatóre**, M.: retarder. **-tárdo**, M.: retard (delay): *in* —, behind time.
ritégno [*ri-tenere*], M.: restraint; reserve (self-possession; discretion); cessation; hindrance; retentiveness (memory)†.
ri=temperáre, TR.: temper (again).
ri-tenènza†, F.: retention; detention. ‖**=tenére**, IRR.; TR.: hold again; retain (hold back; stop; hinder; hold, keep); maintain; INTR., REFL.: restrain or contain one's self (forbear); close; reside†: — *una cosa*, keep a thing secret; — *il dono*, keep the present; *-tenersi con uno*, be friends with one. **-teniménto**, M.: retention; restraint (reserve). **-tenitíva**, F.: retentiveness (of memory). **-tenitóre**, M., **-tenitríce**, F.: retainer; stainer.
ri=tentáre, TR.: attempt again.
riten-tíva (*pop.*) = *ritenitiva*. **-úta**, F.: retention; restraint. **-utaménte**, ADV.: reservedly (cautiously). **-utézza**, F.: reserve (caution, moderation). **-zióne**, F.: retention (keeping); reserve.
ri=tèssere, TR.: weave again.
ri=tíngere, IRR.; TR.: dye again.
ri-tiraménto, M.: withdrawal; contraction; retreat. ‖**=tiráre**, TR.: draw again; draw back (RETIRE; withdraw; take back); shrink; fetch (get out); collect; INTR., REFL.: retire (withdraw, take refuge); retreat. **-tiráta**, F.: retreat (of troops; signal for retreat); withdrawal†; escape (evasion)†. **-tirataménte**, ADV.: retiredly; separately. **-tiratézza**, F.: retirement; seclusion. **-tiráto**, PART.: retired, etc.; solitary. **-tíro**, M.: retirement (withdrawal); retreat; seclusion.
rít-mica, F.: rhythmics. **-mico**, ADJ.: rhythmic(al). ‖**-mo** [L. *rhythmus*], M.: rhythm.
ríto [L. *-tus*], M.: rite (ceremony).
ri-toccaménto, M.: retouch(ing); rise† (in price). ‖**=toccáre**, TR.: retouch (touch again; fix up); touch upon or at again; trim; affect again; REFL.: fix one's self up; step with the hind-feet on the fore-feet (of horses). **-toccáta**, F.: retouch. **-toccatúra**, F.: retouching. **-tocchíno**, M.: slight luncheon (between meals). **-tócco**, ADJ.: retouched; M.: retouch(ing), correction.
ri=tògliere, IRR.; TR.: take back (retake, recover). **-togliménto**, M.: retaking. **-tòlto**, PART. of *-togliere*.
ritond.. = *rotond..*
ri=tòrcere, IRR.; TR.: wring or twist (again); turn back, RETORT; REFL.: turn aside. **-torcíbile**, ADJ.: that may be twisted or turned back. **-torciménto**, M., **-torcitúra**†, F.: twisting (winding, turning aside); retort.
ritor-nábile†, ADJ.: returnable. **-naménto**†, M.: return. ‖**-náre** [*tornare*], TR.: return; INTR.: return; become: — *in sè*, come to one's self again; — *il piede*, return back; — *sano*, get well again. **-náta**, F.: return; (*Rom. Cath.*) octave procession. **-nèllo**, M.: repetition; (*mus.*) ritornelle, -nello (burden of a song); sign of repetition. **ritór-no**, ADJ.: returned; M.: return: *di* —, returned, back (*esser di* —, return, be back).
ritòrre = *ritogliere*.
ri-tòrta = *-tortola*. ‖**-tòrto**, PART. of *-torcere*, twisted, etc.; tortuous. **-tòrtola**, F.: fagot-band, band: *aver più -tortole che fastella*, be ever ready with an answer; have a cure for every sore. **-tortúra**, F.: twist(ing).

ri=tosáre, TR.: shear again.
ri=tradúrre, IRR.; TR.: retranslate.
ritrá-ere, **-ggere** = *ritrarre.*
ri=trárre, IRR.; TR.: draw back; draw (move, direct); (re)trace (sketch, picture; delineate); reproduce; relate; take after (remind of); derive (deduce), infer; understand; retract; withdraw (remove); REFL.: retire (draw back, withdraw); take refuge; change one's mind (repent): — *da*, take after, be like; — *dall' impresa*, abandon the enterprise. **-trátta**†, F.: retreat. **-trattábile**, ADJ.: that may be retired or withdrawn. **-trattaménto**†, M.: retraction (disavowal). **=trattáre**, TR.: treat (handle, consider) again; retract (take back, disavow); portray (sketch); REFL.: retract; portray one's self; have one's portrait taken. **-trattazióne**, F.: retraction (disavowal). **-trattíno**, M.: *car. dim.* of *-tratto;* nice little portrait; miniature. **-trattísta**, M.: portrait-painter. **-trattívo**, ADJ.: retractive; portraying. **-trátto**, PART. of *-trarre;* M.: portrait (picture); result†.
ritrécine [?], M.: sink-net (fishing-net sunk by weights to the bottom); speeding contrivance (in water-mills): *a* —, confusedly; head over heels; ruinously; *andare a* —, go fast to ruins.
ri=trinceráre, **=trinciáre**, TR.: cut again; cut up.
ri=tritáre, TR.: bruise again.
ritrog. .† = *retrog*. .
ritrop. . (*pop.*) = *idrop*. .
ritró-sa, F.: bow-net; fowling-net; eddy in the hair. **-sáccio**, *disp.* of *-so*. **-sággine**, F.: contrariety (contrary or opposing spirit, stubbornness). **-saménte**, ADV.: adversely; stubbornly. **-sáre**†, INTR.: become contrary, grow crabbed. **-sèllo**, **-sétto**, *car. dim.* of *-so*. **-sía**, **-sità**, F.: adverseness; stubbornness. ‖**ritró-so** [L. *retrorsus* (*retro-versus*, 'back-turned')], ADJ.: adverse (opposed, contrary); stubborn; wayward (wrong-headed); backward†; M.: mouth of a net; trap; turning round (whirl)†: *a* —, in an opposite direction or sense; against the grain.
ri-trovábile, ADJ.: that may be found again (recoverable). **-trovaménto**, M.: finding again; discovery. ‖**=trováre**, TR.: find again (discover): find out; recognize; invent; REFL.: find one's self; be found (be); come; happen; find one's way: — *l' orme*, retrace one's steps. **-trováta**, F.: refinding; invention. **-trovatóre**, M.: **-trovatríce**, F.: finder; discoverer. **-trùvic**†, **-tròvo**, M.: reunion (meeting, society, circle).
rit-taménte†, ADV.: directly. ‖**-to** [*recto*], ADJ.: right (straight); upright (up; just); ADV.: directly; M.: right (side, etc.); straightening piece: *star* (*levarsi*) —, stand up; *andar* —, deal honestly; *per* —, perpendicularly; *avere due -ti*, or *non avere nè — nè rovescio*, be perfect from any side (or view). **-to=rovèscio**, ADV.: upside down.
rituá-le [L. *-lis*], ADJ., M.: ritual. **-lísta**, pl. —*ti*, M.: ritualist. **-lménte**, ADV.: by way of ritual.
ri=tuffáre, TR.: dip (plunge) again.
ri=turáre, TR.: shut (again), stop up.
ri=úngere, IRR.; TR.: grease or anoint again.
ri-uniménto†, M., **-unióne**, F.: reunion (assembly, meeting); heaping, uniting. ‖**=uníre**, TR.: reunite; unite (join); reconcile. **-unitívo**, ADJ.: capable of uniting.
ri=usáre, TR.: use again.
ri-uscíbile, ADJ.: that may succeed. **-uscibilità**, F.: possibility of success. ‖**=uscíre**, IRR. (pres. *-esc-*); INTR.: succeed (prosper); happen (turn out); come out (lead); conclude (end); finally become; dispatch: — *in* (or *a*), lead to; — *d' una cosa*, part with a thing; *-uscirsi d' una cosa*†, get rid of a thing. **-uscíta**, F.: issue (end); success; profit.
ríva [L. *ripa*], F.: bank; shore (coast); limit: — —, along the shore (or coast).
ri=vaccináre, TR.: revaccinate.
rivággio† = *riva*.
ri=vagheggiáre, TR.: court again.
rivá-le [L. *-lis*], M.: rival. **-leggiáre**, INTR.: be rivals (compete).
ri=valére, IRR.; REFL.: recover (grow strong again).
ri=valicáre, TR.: traverse again.
ri=validazióne, F.: rendering valid again; confirmation.
rivalità [*rivale*], F.: rivalry.
riválso, PART. of *rivalere*.
ri=vangáre, TR.: dig up (hoe) again; search into.
ri=varcáre, TR.: pass over (ford) again.
ri=vedére, IRR.; TR.: see again; review (revise); look over (again); examine; REFL.: see one another again (meet again): *a -vederci*, till we meet again, good-bye. **-vediménto**†, M.: revision. **-vedito-ráto**, M.: reviser's (reviewer's) office. **-veditóre**, M., **-veditríce**, F.: reviser, reviewer. **-vedúta**, F.: revision.
rive-lábile, ADJ.: revealable. **-laménto**†, M.: revealing. ‖**-láre** [L. *re-velare* (*velum*, veil)], TR.: reveal. **-latívo**, ADJ.: revealing. **-latóre**, M., **-latríce**, F.: revealer. **-lazióne**, F.: revelation.
rivellíno [?], M.: (*fort.*) RAVELIN (detached, salient work).

robínia [herbalist *Robin*], F.: (*bot.*) robinia.
robó-ne [*roba*], M.: official gown. **-nác-cia,** *disp. dim.* of *-ne.*
roboráre† = *corroborare.*
robu-staménte, ADV.: robustly (sturdily). **-stézza,** F.: robustness (sturdiness). **-stíssimo,** ADJ.: most vigorous. ||**ro-bú-sto** [L. *-stus*], ADJ.: robust (sturdy); vigorous.
rocággine [*raucedine*], F.: (*pop.*) hoarseness.
ròcca 1 [? Pers. *rukh*], F.: fort (mostly upon a rock, fortress, tower); (*poet.*) rock.
ròc-ca 2 [OGer. *-co*], F.: distaff. **-cáta,** F.: distaff-ful; blow with a distaff.
roccétto [Fr. *-chet* (OGer. *rok*, cloak)], M.: kind of surplice.
roc-chèlla, F.: bobbin. **-chétta,** *dim.* of *-ca* 1, *-ca* 2. **-chettíno,** *dim.* of *-chetto.* ||**-chétto** [*-ca* 2], M.: (*weav.*) bobbin (spool); quill (spindle); small cogwheel; rarely for *roccetto.*
ròcchio [*rocco* 1], M.: oblong roundish piece (of wood, stone, etc.; clump of wood); roller; piece of sausage; jet of water; PL.: curl: — *di voce*, strong voice.
ròc-cia [? Celt. *roc*], F.: rock (precipice); filth (dirt). **-cióso,** ADJ.: rocky; dirty.
ròcco† 1 [*-ca* 1], M.: ROOK (at chess).
ròcco† 2, M.: cane; crosier.
rococcò [Fr. *rococo*], M.: rococo (florid style in 18th Cent.).
ro-chézza, F.: hoarseness. ||**rò-co** [L. *raucus*], ADJ.: hoarse (raucous, harsh).
ro-dènto, ADJ.: gnawing (rodent, sharp). ||**ró-dere** [L.], IRR. §; TR.: gnaw (bite; corrode); REFL.: chafe with rage: — *il freno*, bite the bit; fret. **-diménto,** M.: gnawing; anguish. **-dío,** M.: constant gnawing. **-ditóre,** M., **-ditríce,** F.: gnawer. **-ditúra**†, F.: gnawing.
§ Pret. *ró-si, -se; -sero.* Part. *róso.*
rodomon-táta, F.: rodomontade (bluster). ||**Rodomón-te,** M.: Rodomonte (boasting hero in Orlando Furioso); rodomont (braggadocio). **-tésco,** ADJ.: rodomont (blustering).
róffia†, F.: dense fog.
rogá-re [L., ask], TR.: (*leg.*) draw up and sign as notary, execute. **-tóre,** M.: notary (attorney). **-tòrio,** ADJ.: rogatory. **-zióni,** F. PL.: rogation-week (2d before Whit-Sunday, when litanies were sung).
róggio†, ADJ.: reddish.
rògito [*rogare*], M.: (*leg.*) notarial execution (of a document; drawing up and signing it); PL.: rights of notarial execution.
ró-gna [OFr. *-gne* (L. *rubigo*, redness)], F.: scab (mange). **-gnétta,** *dim.* of *-gna.*
rognóne [Fr. *-gnon* (L. *ren*)], M.: kidney.
rognóso [*-gna*], ADJ.: scabby.
rògo 1 [L. *rogus*], M.: pyre (funeral pile).
rógo 2 [L. *rubus*], M.: blackthorn.
rogumáre†, TR.: ruminate.
romai-oláta, F.: ladleful. **-olíno,** *dim.* of *-olo.* ||**-òlo** [*ramaiolo*], M.: ladle.
roma-naménte, ADV.: in Roman fashion. **-'necio,** ADJ., M.: Rumansh (language). **-nésco,** ADJ.: Roman (esp. ref. to the mod. Roman dialect); M.: (*mod.*) Roman; (*mod.*) Roman dialect: *a la -nesca*, Roman fashion. **-nísmo,** M.: Romanism (expression of the Roman dialect). **-nísta,** pl. *—ti*, M.: 'Romanist' (one versed in old Roman law). ||**romá-no** 1 [L. *-nus*], ADJ., M.: Roman.
románo 2 [Ar. *rommana*], M.: weight of the steelyard.
roman-òlogo, ADJ.: versed in the Roman dialect or Romance languages. **-tica-ménte,** ADV.: romantically. **-tichería,** F.: romantic affectation. **-ticísmo,** M.: romanticism. **-'tico,** ADJ.: romantic; M.: Romanticist (adherent of the Romantic school). **-'za,** F.: romance; (*mus.*) romanza (air). **-záccio,** *disp.* of *-nzo.* **-zatóre**†, M.: romancer. **-zeggiáre,** INTR.: write romances. **-zéro,** M.: collection of romances. **-zésco,** ADJ.: romantic. **-zétto,** *car. dim.* of *-zo.* **-zièra,** F., **-zière,** M.: romancer (novel writer). ||**-'zó** [*-no*], ADJ.: Romance (ref. to language: *lingue -ze*, Romance languages); M.: romance (novel).
róm-ba [? echoic], F.: rumbling (roar). **-báre,** INTR.: rumble; hum. **-bázzo,** M.: rumbling (roar). **-'bo** 1, M.: rumbling (noise); humming (buzzing, whizz).
róm-bo 2 [L. *rhombus*], M.: rhomb. **-boi-dále,** ADJ.: rhomboidal. **-bòide,** M.: rhomboid.
rómbo-la†, F.: sling. **-láre**†, TR.: sling. **-latóre**†, M.: slinger.
ro-mèa, F. of *-meo.* **-meággio**†, M.: pilgrimage. ||**ro-mèo** [*Roma*, Rome], M.: pilgrim (orig'ly to Rome, then gen'ly).
rómice [L. *rumex*], M.: sorrel (the herb).
romíre†, INTR.: rumble.
romi-táccio, *disp.* of *-to.* **-tággio,** M.: hermitical life (seclusion); hermitage. **-táno,** ADJ.: solitary; M.: Augustine friar. **-tèllo,** *dim.* of *-to.* **-tésco**†, **-'tico**†, ADJ.: solitary. ||**romi-to** [*eremita*], ADJ.: eremitical, solitary (lonely); M.: hermit. **-tóne,** *aug.* of *-to.* **-tò-rio,** M.: hermitage.
romor.. = *rumor..*
róm-pere [L. *rumpere*], IRR. §; TR.: break; RUPTure; interRUPT (stop); ROUT; change; REFL.: break away: — *il capo a*, tease; — *la guerra*, make war; — *in*

mare, shipwreck; — *un pericolo*, turn aside a danger; — *la testa*, weary; *-persi ad ira*, fall into a passion; *-persi a ridere*, burst out laughing; *-persi di*, desist from; *-persi in parole*, begin speaking. **-pévole†**, ADJ.: fragile (brittle). **-pi=cápo**, M.: tiresome person or thing; bore. **-pi=còllo**, M.: dangerous person or thing; 'breakneck' (precipice); breakneck (rash) enterprise: *a* —, in a breakneck (ruinous) manner. **-piménto**, M.: breaking (fracture; breach). **-pi=scátole**, M., **-pi=stiváli**, F.: vexatious person (bore). **-pitóre**, M., **-pitríce**, F.: breaker. **-pitúra†**, F.: breaking.

§ Pret. *rúp-pi*, *-pe*; *-pero*; (rarely *róp-pi*, etc.). Part. *rótto*.

rón-ca [*-co*], F.: hedgebill, weeding-hook. **-cáre**, TR.: cut down (weed, clear). **-catúra**, F.: weeding.

rón-chio† [*rocchio*], M.: bunch; hump. **-chióne**, M.: large block (of wood or stone). **-chióso†**, ADJ.: rugged (rough).

ron-ciglláre†, TR.: catch with a hook. ‖**-cíglio** [*-co*], M.: hook; harpoon.

roncióne† = *ronzone*.

rón-co [L. *runcus*], M.: hedgebill†; blind alley. **-'cola**, F.: hedgebill. **-coláta**, F.: cut with hedgebill. **-'colo**, M.: curbed knife. **-cóne**, *aug.* of *-co*.

rónda [Fr. *ronde*], F.: round (patrol).

rón-dina†, ‖**-dine** [L. *hirundo*], F.: swallow. **-dinèlla**, **-dinétta**, F., **-diníno**, M.: *car. dim.* of *-dine* (esp. of the nest); early fig. **-dinòtto**, M.: young swallow. **-dóne**, M.: martin (swallow).

ron-fáre, ‖**-fiáre** [L. *re-in-flare* (blow)], INTR.: snore.

ron-zaménto, M.: humming (buzzing, rumble); ramble. ‖**-záre** [Ger. *runzen*], INTR.: hum (buzz), rumble; turn about, wander about (ramble).

ronzíno [OFr. *roncin* (?)], M.: driving-horse (pony).

ron-zío, ‖**rón-zo†** [*-zare*], M.: humming (buzz, rumble). **-zóne**, M.: large fly; stallion†.

ro-ráre†, TR.: bedew. **-rástro†**, M.: bryony. ‖**rò-rido** [L. *-ridus* (*ros*, dew)], ADJ.: (*poet.*) dewy.

rósa 1 [*-so* (*-dere*)], F.: itching; hollow (made by waters)†.

rò-sa 2 [L.], F.: rose; (*poet.*) virginity; rosette (badge); red spot; (— *de' venti*) compass-card; rose (opening in a guitar, etc.): — *canina*, dog-rose; *legno di* —, rosewood; *Pasqua di -se*, Pentecost; *far la* —, spread (of small shot). **-sáceo**, ADJ.: of rose-colour, rosy. **-saiétto**, *car. dim.* of *-saio*. **-saióne†**, *aug.* of *-saio*. **-sário**, M.: rosary. **-sáto**, ADJ.: rosy; made of roses: *acqua -sata*, rose-water; *giorni -sati*, white days, happy days; *Pasqua -sata* (us'ly *di rose*), Pentecost.

rosecch. . = *rosicch.* .

rosbiffe [Eng. *roast beef*], M.: roast beef.

ro-sellína [*-sa*], F.: damask-rose: *dar -selline*, flatter, court. **rò-seo**, ADJ.: rosy. **-séto**, M.: rose-plot, bed of roses. **-sétta**, *pop. dim.* of *-sa*; rosette; set of precious stones (in a ring, rose of diamonds); white spot (on horse's head).

rosi-cáre [*roso*], TR.: nibble; gnaw (eat). **-catúra**, F.: nibbling. **-cchiáre**, TR.: nibble.

rosicchièro†, M.: rose-coloured enamel.

rosícchiolo [*rosicchiare*], M.: dry piece of bread.

rosi-gnolétto, *car. dim.* of *-gnolo*. ‖**-gn(u)òlo** [p. L. **lusciniolus* (L. *luscinius*)], M.: nightingale.

rosmaríno [*-nus*], M.: rosemary.

róso, PART. of *rodere*.

roso-láccio [*rosa*], M.: wild poppy. **-láre**, TR.: roast; beat. **-lía**, F.: measles.

rosòlio [Fr. *rossolis* (L. *ros solis*, 'sun's dew')], M.: rosolis (kind of liquor).

ròsolo [*-lare*], M.: roasting.

rosóne [*rosa*], M.: rosette.

ros-páccio, M.: *disp.* of *-po*; clown; boor. **-pétto**, *dim.* of *-po*. ‖**ròs-po** [? L. *ruspari*, seek], M.: toad.

ros-sáccio, *disp.* of *-so*. **-sástro**, ADJ.: reddish. **-seggiánte**, ADJ.: tending to red (reddish). **-seggiáre**, INTR.: incline to red (be reddish). **-sellíno**, M.: sort of olive-tree. **-sèllo**, M.: red spot or scar. **-sétto**, ADJ.: reddish. **-sézza**, F.: redness. **-sicáre†**, INTR.: redden. **-síccio**, **-sígno**, ADJ.: reddish. ‖**rós-so** [L. *russus*], ADJ., M.: red: — *d' uovo*, yolk of an egg; *divenir* —, blush. **-'sola**, F.: red (eatable) mushroom. **-sóre**, M.: redness, blush. **-sorétto†**, *dim.* of *-sore*.

ròsta [Ger. *rost*, gridiron], F.: grated window over doors, etc. (fan-shaped door-window, transom); grating (of such window); big fan (leafy twig)†.

ros-ticcère [*arrostire*], M.: vender of roasted meat. **-ticcería**, F.: roast-meat shop. **-ticcio**, M.: dross (scoria), esp. in pl.; insignificant person (weakling). **ròs-to** = *arrosto*.

ro-stràle, ADJ.: rostral. **-stráto**, ADJ.: beaked. ‖**rò-stro** [L. *-strum*], M.: beak (of a bird; of a ship); proboscis†; rostrum.

ro-súme [*roso*], M.: gnawing. **-súra†**, F.: gnawing; erosion; PL.: crumbs.

rò-ta [L.], F.: wheel (circular-frame, circle, round; instrument of torture); tura:

— *con denti*, cog-wheel; — *di poppa*, (*nav.*) wheel of the stern-post; *le stellate -te*, the heavens; *andar a* —, wheel about. **-tábile**, ADJ.: practicable (fit to be travelled on).

rotacíṣmo [Gr. *rho*, 'r'], M.: rhotacism (change to r).

ro-táia [*rota*], F.: wheel-track (cart-rut); rail. **-taménto**, M.: rotation (rolling). **-táre**, INTR.: turn as a wheel (roll, wheel, ROTATE); TR.: break on the wheel (torture); REFL.: turn round (rotate). **-táto**, PART.: turned round, etc.; ADJ.: furnished with wheels. **-tatóre**, M., **-tatríce**, F.: rotator. **-tatòrio**, ADJ.: rotatory. **-tazióne**, F.: rotation. **-teaménto**, M.: rotation. **-teáre**, INTR.: rotate (go round, revolve). **-teazióne**, F.: rotation. **-tèlla**, F.: *dim.* of *-ta*; round shield (buckler); shield-like object; knee-pan. **-tellína**, *dim.* of *-tella*. **-tellóne**, *aug.* of *-tella*. **-tíno**, M.: *dim.* of *-ta*; front-wheel. **-tolaménto**, M.: rolling. **-toláre**, TR., INTR.: turn round (roll); roll down. **-tolétto**, *dim.* of *-tolo*. **rò-tolo**, M.: roll (scroll); roller. **-tolóne**, M.: big roll(ing): *a -toloni*, rolling; *andar* —, roll down.

rotón-da, F.: rotunda. **-daménte**, ADV.: circularly. **-dáre**, TR.: round (make round). **-deggiáre**, INTR.: become round (round). **-dézza**†, **-dità**, F.: rotundity (roundness). ‖**rotón-do** [L. *rotundus*], ADJ.: round (circular, rotund).

rotóne, *aug.* of *-ta*.

rót-ta, F.: rupture (breach); breaking down; rout (overthrow); confusion; wrath (anger): *mettere in* —, rout, defeat; *partire in* —, go away in anger; *partire a — di collo*, rush away in great hurry; *far la* —, open the way; *venire alle -te*, get angry, have a fall-out. **-táme**, M.: heap of broken things (fragments, crumbs). **-taménte**, ADV.: in a broken way; excessively†. **-tézza**, F.: rupture. ‖**rót-to**, PART. of *rompere*; broken (broken up; ruptured); routed; bruised; worn out; violent (boisterous); inclined; interrupted; M.: break (rupture, fracture); (*arith.*) fraction. **-tòrio**, M.: cautery. **-túra**, F.: break(ing), rupture (fracture; hernia); rent (cleft); breach: *venire a* —, have a fall-out.

ròtula [L. (cf. *rotella*)], F.: knee-pan.

rovaglióne† = *ravaglione*.

rovai-áccio†, *disp.* of *-o*. ‖**rovái-o** [?], M.: north-wind. **-onáccio**†, *disp.* of *-o*.

ro-vèlla†, F., **-vèllo**, M.: fury (madness). **-ventáre**, TR.: make red hot (inflame). ‖**-vènte** [L. *rubens*, REDdening], ADJ.: RED hot (burning; vehement); boiling†. **-ventézza**†, F.: burning heat. **-ventíno**, M.: black pudding (of hog's blood).

róvere [L. *robur*], M.: oak.

rovè-ṣcia, F.: lapel (facing, cuff). **-ṣciaménto**, M.: overturn; overthrow. **-ṣciáre**, TR.: overturn (invert; upset); overthrow (throw down); REFL.: be overturned (be upset, tip over); spill. **-ṣciatóre**, M.: overturner (upsetter). **-ṣciatúra**, F.: overturning; overthrowing. **-ṣcíno**, M.: knitting-loop (stitch). ‖**rovè-ṣcio** [L. *reversus*], ADJ.: REVERSE (opposite); M.: reverse (opposite) side; wrong side; reverse (opposite); part turned back (lapel, facing); inside (lining of a coat); sudden downpour (heavy shower); reprimand: *a* —, the wrong side outward (inside out); on the wrong side; quite contrary; the wrong way (wrongly); amiss; down on the back: *tenere uno a* —, keep one down on the back; — *di fortuna*, reverse of fortune. **-ṣcióne**, M.: *aug.* of *-scio*; great reverse; heavy downpour or shower; backstroke: *a* —, backward; upon one's back.

rovéto [*rovo*], M.: place full of briars.

roví-na [L. *ruina*], F.: RUIN (destruction); violence. **-naménto**†, M.: ruin. **-náre**, TR.: ruin (destroy); INTR.: fall into ruins; fall precipitously (from heaven). **-natíccio**†, ADJ.: somewhat ruined or dilapidated (falling into ruins). **-natóre**, M., **-natríce**, F.: ruiner (destroyer). **-névole**†, ADJ.: furious. **-nevolménte**†, ADV.: furiously. **-nío**, M.: falling into ruins; crash. **-nosaménto**, ADV.: ruinously; furiously. **-nóso**, ADJ.: ruinous (destructive); violent (furious).

rovi-stáre [? *revisitare*], TR.: rummage (ransack, search). **-statóre**, M.: rummager. **-stiáre**†, TR.: rummage; INTR., REFL.: wallow. **-stío**, M.: rummaging; confusion. **-stoláre**† = *-stare*.

róvo [L. *rubus*], M.: briar (bramble).

róẓẓa [? Ger. *ross*], F.: jade (sorry HORSE).

roẓ-ẓaménte, ADV.: roughly. **-ẓézza**, **-ẓità**†, F.: roughness. ‖**róẓ-ẓo** [L. *rudis*], ADJ.: rough (RUDE, rugged, harsh); raw: *seta -za*, raw silk. **-ẓóne**, *aug.* of *-zo*. **-ẓòtto**, ADJ.: rather rough (rude). **-ẓúme**†, M.: roughness (rudeness).

rúba [*-re*], F.: robbery (rapine); pillage: *mandar a* —, give up to pillage; *vendere a* —, sell rapidly. **-cchiaménto**, M.: petty theft (pilfering). **-cchiáre**, TR.: pilfer. =**c(u)òri**, M., F.: 'heart-robber' (charmer). **-gióne**†, F., **-ménto**, M.: robbery. =**mónte**, M.: a game of cards. ‖**rubá-re** [Ger. *rauben*], TR.: steal (ROB; take away; plagiarise): — *i cammini*, rob on the highroads. **-tóre**, M., **-tríce**, F.: thief (robber). **-túra**†, F.: robbery.

rúbbio [L. *rubidus* (divisions marked in 'red')], M.: sort of measure (about 3 hectolitres).

rubell. .† = *ribell*. .

rubería [-*bare*], F.: stealing (robbery).

rubest. .† = *robust*. .

rubicóndo [L. -*cundus*], ADJ.: rubicund (ruddy, red).

rubid. .† = *ruvid*. .

rubificá-re†, TR.: rubify (make red). **-tívo**†, ADJ.: making red.

rubíglia = *robiglia*.

ru-binéttо†, *dim.* of -*bino*. ‖**-bíno** [L. -*ber*, red], M.: RUBY. **-binésco**†, ADJ.: red as a ruby. **-biòla**†, F.: sort of grape. **-bísso, -bísso**, ADJ.: hale-looking (robust); of fresh colour (florid).

róbo† = *roro*.

rúblo [Russ. *rubl*], M.: ruble.

rúbri-ca 1 [L. *ruber*, red)], F.: red-chalk.

rubrí-ca 2, F.: rubric (title, once us'ly red; initial letters; lithurgic rules). **-cáre**, TR.: rubricate. **-cazióne**†, F.: redness. **-císta**, pl. —*ti*, M.: rubricist.

rúbro†, ADJ.: red.

rú-ca† [L .*eruca*], **-chétta**, F.: garden-rocket.

rúde [L. *rudis*], ADJ.: rude (rough).

rúderi [L. -*dera* (pl. of -*dus*)], M. PL.: rubbish (of old buildings).

rudi-mentále, ADJ.: rudimental. ‖**-ménto** [L. -*mentum*], M.: rudiment.

rúffa [OGer. (*h*)*ruf*, snatching], F.: scramble (for catching a thing thrown); wild rush; press (throng): *far la* —, start a scramble (by throwing coins, etc.); *far a ruffa*, make a scramble, catch what one can.

ruffiá-na, F.: procuress (pimp). **-náccia, -náccio**, *disp.* of -*na*, -*no*. **-naménto**†, M.: pimping. **-náre**†, **-neggiáre**, INTR.: pimp. **-nèlla**, *dim.* of -*na*. **-nería**, F.: pimping; artifice. **-nésco**, ADJ.: pimping. **-nésimo**, M.: pimping; artifice. ‖**ruffiá-no** [? L. *rufulus*, 'reddish' (ref. to dress or prostitutes' hats)], M.: procurer (pimp, go-between, Eng.† RUFFIAN).

rú(f)o-la [?], F.: palmer-worm. **-láre**, INTR.: grub; eat (said of beasts).

rúga [L.], F.: wrinkle; street†.

rúg-gere† = -*gire*. **-ghiaménto**†, M.: roar(ing). **-ghiáre**, INTR.: roar. **-'ghio**, M.: roar.

rúggi-ne [L. *aerugo*], F.: rust; mildew (blight); rancour. **-nènte**†, **-nóso**, ADJ.: rusty.

rúggio = *rugghio*.

ruggíre [L. *rugire*], INTR.: roar.

rugiá-da [Sp. *rociada* (L. *ros*, dew)], F.: dew. **-dóso**, ADJ.: dewy.

rugioléne†, M.: box (cuff).

rugitáre [*ruggire*], INTR.: growl; roar.

ru-gosità, F.: rugosity (wrinkled condition). ‖**-góso** [-*ga*], ADJ.: wrinkled (rugose).

rugum. .† = *rumin*. .

ruin. . (*poet.*) = *rovin*. .

ruíre†, INTR.: rush.

rul-láre [L. *rotolare*], TR.: roll; INTR.: roll (also of drums). **-lío**, M.: (continued) rolling **-lo**, M.: roller; casting; top.

rúm [Eng.], (*pop.*) **rúm-me**, M.: rum.

rumi-nánte, ADJ., M.: ruminant. ‖**-náre** [L.], INTR.: ruminate; (*fig.*) cogitate (ponder). **-natóre**, M., **-natríce**, F.: ruminator. **-nazióne**, F.: rumination.

rumó-re [L. -*r*], M.: indistinct noise (noise, rumbling, Eng.† RUMOR); uproar (tumult); rumor (report): *far* —, make a noise; be much talked about; burst out in anger. **-reggiaménto**†, M.: noise; uproar. **-reggiánte**, ADJ.: noisy. **-reggiáre**, INTR.: make a noise. **-ríccio**, *disp. dim.* of -*re*. **-ríno**, *dim.* of -*re*.

rumo-río, M.: (long) noise. **-rosaménte**, ADV.: noisily. **-róso**, ADJ.: noisy. **-rúccio**, *disp. dim.* of -*re*.

runcigl. .† = *roncigl*. .

ruòlo [Fr. *rôle*], M.: roll (register).

ruot. . = *rot*. .

rú-pe [L. -*pes*], F.: rock (cliff). **-picèlla**, *dim.* of -*pe*. **-pinóso**†, ADJ.: craggy, steep.

rurále [L. -*lis*], ADJ.: rural (rustic).

ru-scellétto, *car. dim.* of -*scello*. **-scellíno**, *poet. dim.* of -*scello*. ‖**-scèllo** [Fr. *ruisseau*], M.: RIVULET (brook).

rús-chia†, ‖**-co** [L. -*cus*], M.: butcher's broom.

rusignuòlo = *rosignolo*.

rú-spa, F.: scraping†; gathering; cart. ‖**-spáre** [L. -*spari*], INTR.: scrape†; gather chestnuts (olives); cart.

rú-spo [?], M.: sequin (Florentine coin); ADJ.: new-coined. **-spóne**, *aug.* of -*spo* (3 sequins).

rus-sáre, INTR.: snore. **-so**†, M.: snoring.

rusti-cággine, F.: rusticity. **-cále**, ADJ.: rustic (rural). **-ca(l)ménte**, ADV.: rustically. **-cáno**†, ADJ.: rustic. **-cáre**†, INTR.: rusticate (live in the country). **-chétto**, *dim.* of -*co*. **-chézza, -cità**, F.: rusticity. ‖**rústi-co** [L. -*cus* (*rus*, land)], ADJ.: rustic (rural; rude, coarse); M.: rustic (peasant). **-cóne**, *aug.* of -*co*.

rúta [L.], F.: rue (a plant).

ruticáre†, INTR.: budge.

ruti-lánte, ADJ.: resplendent. ‖**-láre**† [L.], INTR.: shine.

rut-táre, INTR.: eruct (belch). **-teggiáre**, INTR.: keep on belching. ‖**-to** [L. *ructus*], M.: (e)RUCTATION (belching, wind).

ruvi-daménte, ADJ.: roughly. **-détto**, *dim.* of *-do*. **-dézza**, **-dità**, F.: roughness. ||**rúvi-do** [L. *ruidus*], ADJ.: rough (uneven; harsh).
ruvistáre† = *rovistare*.
ruvístico [*ligustro*], M.: (*bot.*) privet (prim).
ruz-zaménto†, M.: sport (play). **-zánte**, ADJ.: sporting; sportful (playful). ||**-záre** [?], INTR.: sport (play). **-zo**, M.: sport; sportfulness; waggery; caprice (wantonness).
rúzzo-la [L. **roteola* (*rota*, wheel)], F.: peg-top (top). **-láre**, TR., INTR.: spin (a top, whirl; spin round); roll down; sink (of a ship). **-lóne**, *aug.* of *-la;* large rolling thing (as stone, etc.); large roll; sudden rolling down or fall: (*a*) *-loni*, rolling (down); *andare* (*a*) *-loni*, come rolling.

S

s *esse*, pl. *esse* or *essi* [L.], F., M.: s (the letter).
s-, **ş-**, **s=**, **ş=** [L. *ex-*, out of; or *dis-*, off]: privative or intensive prefix.
sabá-tico, ADJ.: Sabbatic. **-tína**, F.: Sabbath festivity. **-tíno**, ADJ.: of a Sabbath, Sabbath-. **-tişmo**, M.: observance of the Sabbath. ||**sába-to** [Heb. *shabath*, resting-day], M.: Sabbath: *far sera e* —, conclude in haste.
sabáudo [*Savoia*, Savoy], ADJ.: of Savoy.
sabba. .† = *saba*. .
sáb-bia [L. *-ula*, pl. of *-ulum*], F.: sand; gravel. **-biáre**†, TR.: fill or cover with sand. **-bioncèllo**, *dim.* of *-bione*. **-bióno**, M.: sandy soil. **-bioníccio**, *dim.* of *-bione*. **-bióso**, ADJ.: sandy.
sác-ca [L. *-cus*, SACK], F.: wallet (satchel); bag; also pl. of *-co*. **-cáccio**, *disp.* of *-co*. **-cáia**, F.: sack-rack (in a barn); knapsack†. **-ca=páne**, M.: breadbag. **-cardèllo**, *dim.* of *-cardo*. **-cárdo**†, M.: baggage master (of an army); soldier's scrub; rascal. **-carèllo**†, *dim.* of *-co*. **-cáta** [*-co*], F.: bagful (of clothes); piece of land (sowed by a sack of grain).
saccèn-te [*sapiente*], ADJ.: SAPIENT (pretentious of learning, pedantic); M.: wiseacre (witling, pedant). **-teménto**, ADV.: sapiently. **-tería**, F.: sapiency (pretence to learning, self-conceit). **-tíno**, *dim.* of *-te*. **-tóno**, *disp. aug.* of *-te*. **-túzzo** = *-tino*.
saccheg-giaménto, M.: sacking, pillaging. ||**-giáre** [*sacco*], TR.: SACK (a city). **-giatóre**, M., **-giatríce**, F.: pillager.
sacchég-gio, M.: sacking (pillaging).
sacchét-ta, *dim.* of *sacca*. **-táre**, TR.: beat with sand-bags. **-tína**, *dim.* of *-ta*. **-tíno**, *dim.* of *-to*. **-'to**, M.: small bag. **-tóne**, *aug.* of *-to*.
saccin-tèllo†, *dim.* of *-to*. **-tézza**, F.: pedantism, self-conceit. ||**-'to**† = *saccente*.
sác-co [L. *-cus*], pl. *-chi* or (esp. as full) *-ca*, M.: SACK (big bag); sackcloth; SACK (pillage); belly: *colmare il* —, pass the limits, overdo; *dare il* — *a*, pillage, plunder; *far* —, heap up; *vivere col capo nel* —, live thoughtlessly; *metter in* — *uno*, conquer one in debate; *sciorre il* —, let out the bag, slander; *tenere* (or *parare*) *il* —, be an accomplice; *a -chi* or *-ca*, in great quantity. **-coccia**, F.: pocket.
sác-colo†, M.: little sack. **-cománno**†, M.: sack (pillage); baggage-master; soldiers' scrub. **-co=méttere**†, TR.: give to plunder, sack. **-conáccio**, *disp.* of *-cone*. **-concèllo**, *dim.* of *-cone*. **-cóne**, M.: straw mattress.
saccu. .† = *sacco*. .
sacèllo [L. *-cellum* (dim. of *sacer*, SACRED)], M.: chapel, oratory.
sacer-dotále, ADJ.: sacerdotal (priestly). **-dotalménte**, ADV.: sacerdotally (in a priestly manner). **-dotático**†, M.: priesthood. ||**-dòte** [*-dos* (*sacer*, holy)], M.: priest. **-dotéssa**, F.: priestess. **-dòto**†, M.: priest. **-dòzio**, M.: priesthood, priestly function; ADJ.†: priestly.
sá-cra, F.: anniversary of consecration (of a church); holy-day†; dedication†. **-cramentále**, ADJ.: sacramental. **-cramentalménte**, ADV.: sacramentally. **-cramentáre**, TR.: administer the sacrament to; give the last sacrament, communicate; REFL.: receive communion. **-cramentário**, M.: sacramental rite. **-craménto**, M.: sacrament; blessed host; oath; divine revelation†; veil (of a nun)†. **-craré**, TR.: consecrate. **-crário**, M.: sacristy. **-cráto**, PART.: of *-crare*; M.: sacred ground (in front of a church). **-crestía**, F.: sacristy. **-crificaménto**, M.: sacrifice. **-crificánte**, PART. of *-crificare;* M.: sacrificer. **-crificáre**, TR.: sacrifice; consecrate. **-crificatóre**, M., **-crificatríce**, F.: sacrificer. **-crificazióne**, F.: sacrifice. **-crífico**†, ADJ.: sacrificial. **-crifício**, **-crifízio**, M.: sacrifice. **-crilegaménte**, ADV.: sacrilegiously. **-crilègio**, M.: sacrilege. **-crílego**, ADJ.: sacrilegious. **-cristáno**†, M.: sacristan (SEXTON). **-cristía**†, F.: sacristy. ||**-cro** [L. *-cer*, sacred], ADJ.: sacred: — *fuoco*†, St. Anthony's fire. **-cro=sánto**, ADJ.: sacred and holy.
sad(d)isfare† = *sodisfare*.
sa-eppoláre†, TR., INTR.: cut arrow-

shaped. ‖**-éppolo** [euph. fr. *-etta*], M.: vine-shoot; arrow†.

saét-ta, ‖**saèt-ta** [L. *sagitta*], F.: arrow (dart); flash of lightning; lively youth; passion†; lancet†; hand (of a dial)†: *far — a*, incite the anger of, provoke one; *una —*, the last thing (*non . . . una —*, nothing); *per —*, by necessity. **-táme**, M.: lot of arrows. **-taménto**, M.: darting; arrow. **-táre**, TR.: dart at. **-táta**†, F.: arrow-shot. **-tatóre**, M., **-tatríce**, F.: archer (bowman). **-tévole**†, ADJ.: of arrows, arrowy. **-tière**, M.: archer, bowman. **-toláre**, TR.: cut arrow-shaped. **saéttolo**†, M.: arrow; vine-shoot. **-tóne**, M.: acontias (serpent). **-túme**† = *-tame*. **-tuzza**†, F.: small arrow; lancet.

saffíro† = *zaffiro*, sapphire.

sá-ga†, F.: witch. ‖**-gáce** [L. *-gax*], ADJ.: sagacious (keen). **-gaceménte**, ADV.: sagaciously. **-gácia**, **-gacità**, F.: sagacity.

sagèna†, F.: trammel-net.

sag-gétte†, M.: test-tube. **-gézza**, F.: sagacity (wisdom). **-giaménte**, ADV.: testingly; wisely. ‖**-giáre** [*-gio*], TR.: assay (test), try; measure†. **-giatóre**, M.: assayer; test-balance. **-giatúra**, F.: assaying. **-gia=víno**, M.: wine-tester.

saggí-na [L. *sagina*, stuffing], F.: broom-corn. **-nále**, M.: broom-cornstalk. **-náre**†, TR.: fatten. **-náto**, ADJ.: of broom-corn. **-nèlla**, F.: broom-corn (for fodder).

ság-gio [L. *ex-agium*, weighing], M.: ASSAY (testing); proof; sample-flask. **-giòlo**, *dim.* of *-gio*.

saggitière†, M.: archer.

saggiuòlo† = *saggiolo*.

sa-gína†, F.: possession. **-gíre**†, TR.: put in possession.

sagittário [L. *-gitta*, arrow], M.: archer.

sagli. . = *sali. .*

ságo [L. *-gum*], M.: sagum (military cloak).

ságo-la [?], **-re**, TR.: (*nav.*) sounding-line. **-létta**, *dim.* of *-la*.

sá-goma [Gr. *-koma*], F.: moulding. **-gomáre**, TR.: provide with a moulding.

sá-gra [*-cro*], F.: anniversary of consecration; religious fair. **-gram. .** = *-cram. .* **-gratína**†, ADJ.: solemn. **-gráto**, M.: blasphemy; crypt. **-grestáno**, M.: sacristan (vestry-keeper). **-grestía**, F.: sacristy.

sagréto† = *secreto*.

ságri [Turk.], M.: SHAGREEN.

sa-grificáre = *-crificare*. **-grísta**, pl. *--ti*, M.: sacristan (dignitary of the Vatican). ‖**sá-gro** = *-cro*. **-grosánto** = *-crosanto*.

sái-a, F.: serge (woollen stuff). **-étta**, F.: light serge. ‖**sái-o** [L. *sagum*, cloak], M.: doublet, jerkin. **-órna**†, F.: long robe. **-òtto**†, M.: doublet, soldier's coat.

sal, abbr. of *salve*: *— mi sia!* God save me!

sála 1 [OGer. *sal*], F.: hall; drawing-room (SALon); ball-room; smoke-room; dining-room.

sála 2 [L. *axale* (*axis*)], F.: axle-tree.

sála 3 [?], F.: sword-grass.

salácca [L. *sala-caccabia*, SALTed food], F.: teleost (a thin bony fish); (*fig.*) lean fellow; wretched book; sword, wooden sword.

salá-ce [L. *-lax*], ADJ.: salacious (slippery). **-cità**, F.: salacity.

salamándra [L.], F.: salamander.

saláme [*sale*], M.: sausage.

salamalècche†, M.: SALAM (deep bow).

sala-místra†, F.: bluestocking. **-mistráre**†, INTR.: act the bluestocking. **-mistrería**†, F.: pretence to learning. **-místro**†, ADJ.: sapient.

salamòia [*sale*, *moia*], F.: brine, pickle.

salamó-na, F., ‖**-ne** [*Salomone*, Solomon], M.: wiseacre; bluestocking.

sa-láre [*-le*], TR.: SALT. **-láto**, ADJ.: salted; sharp; M.: salt meat or pork, ham: *costar —*, cost much; *pagarla* (*farla pagar*) *-lata*, pay dear. **-lariáre**, TR.: pay a salary. **-lário** [orig. 'SALT-money,' paid Rom. soldiers], M.: salary; hire.

sa-lassáre [*sangue-lassare*], TR.: (*med.*) bleed; extōrt money. **-lásso**, M.: bleeding.

salá-ta [*-re*], F.: salting. **-tóio**, M.: salting-room. **-túra**, F.: salting; salty taste.

sála-vo†, **-vóso**†, ADJ.: filthy (dirty).

sál-ce† [*-ice*], M.: willow. **-céto**, M.: willow plot; intricate affair. **-ciáia**, F.: repair by wickerwork. **-cígno**, ADJ.: gnarly (knotty); tough; ill-baked, sour (of bread). **sál-cio**, M.: willow.

salcráutte [Ger. *salz*, salt, *kraut*, herb], M.: sauerKRAUT (salted cabbage).

sál-da, F.: starch, paste; gum; SOLDER. **-daménte**, ADV.: firmly, strongly. **-daménto**, M.: soldering; settling (an account). **-dáre**, TR.: fasten (unite firmly); SOLDER; settle: *— un conto*, pay (settle) an account. **-datóio**, M.: soldering iron. **-datúra**, F.: soldering; seam. **-dézza**, F.: firmness, solidity. ‖**-do** [*solido*], ADJ.: SOLID (entire); staunch; firm; M.: settling (an account); balance.

sá-le [L. *sal*], M.: salt; pungency; boldness, impertinence; sea†: *— d' Inghilterra*, Epsom salt; *saper di —*, taste bitter; *apporre il —*, find fault. **-leggiáre**†, TR.: sprinkle with salt.

salènte†, ADJ.: ascending.

salétta† 1 [-*la* 1], F.: little parlour; little drawing-room.
sal-étta 2 [-*le*], F.: bad salt. **-gèmma**, F., **-gèmmo**, M.: mineral salt.
saliáre [L. -*ris* (*Salii*, priests of Mars)], ADJ.: Salian.
salíbile [-*lire*], ADJ.: ascendable.
salí-cále†, M.: willow plot. **-cástro**†, M.: wild-willow. ‖**sáli-ce** [L. -*x*], M.: willow (SALIX). **-céto**, M.: willow-plot.
sálico [L. *Salii*, Salian Franks], ADJ.: Salic (Salian).
salicóne [-*ce*], M.: tall white willow.
sa-lièra [-*le*], F.: salt-cellar; salt-pit†. **-lierétta**, **-lierína**, **-lieráccia**, *dim.* of -*liera*. **-lieróna**, *aug.* of -*liera*. **-lífero**, ADJ.: saliferous. **-lificáre**, TR.: (*chem.*) salify (reduce to salt). **-lígno**†, M.: marble.
salimbácca†, F.: mark (upon goods); seal (on patents, etc.); wooden vase.
saliménto [-*lire*], M.: mounting; ascent; pride.
salí-na [L. *sal*, salt], F.: salt-pit or -pond (salina); salt†, rocksalt†; salt-cellar†. **-náio**, **-natóre**, M.: salter. **-natúra**, **-nazióne**, F.: salt-mining.
salin-cèrbio, ‖**-cèrvo** [*salire in cerbio* or *cervo*], M.: leap-frog.
salíno [-*le*], ADJ.: saline, salty.
sa-líre [L., leap], IRR.§; TR., INTR.: ascend (climb, mount); amount; go out†; M.†: ascent; eminence. **-liscéndi**, M.: door-latch. **-líta**, F.: ascent, acclivity. **-litóio**†, M.: ladder. **-litóre**, M.: climber.

§ Ind.: Pres. *sálgo*, *-i*, *-e*; *-(gh)iámo*, *-íte*, *-gono*. Pret. *salìi* or *sálsi*, etc. Subj.: Pres. *sálga*, etc. — Poet. forms *sagl-*.

salí-va [L.], F.: SALIVA (spittle). **-vále**, ADJ.: salivary. **-váre**†, TR., INTR.: spit (expectorate). **-vatòrio**, ADJ.: salivatory. **-vazióne**, F.: salivation; expectoration.
sálma [Gr. *ságma*], F.: burden (load); corpse; body; punishment†; armour†.
sal-mástro [L. -*m-acidus*], ADJ.: saltish (briny). **-mastróso**, ADJ.: saltish.
salmeggia-ménto, M.: psalmody. ‖**-'re** [*salmo*], INTR.: read or sing psalms. **-tóre**, M., **-trice**, F.: psalm-singer.
salmería [*salma*], F.: baggage.
sal-místa, M.: psalmist. ‖**-mo** [L. *psalmus*], M.: psalm. **-modía**, F.: psalmody. **-modiáre**, INTR.: sing psalms (psalm).
salmóne [L. -*mo*], M.: salmon.
sal-nitráio, M.: maker of nitre. ‖**=nítro**, M.: nitric salt, saltpetre.
sa-lóne [-*la*], M.: large hall (salon). **-lottíno**, *dim.* of -*lotto*. **-lòtto**, *aug.* of -*la*.

salpáre [?], INTR.: (*nav.*) weigh anchor; separate; escape†.
sál-sa, F.: SAUCE; condiment, seasoning. **-saménto**†, M.: seasoning. **-sapariglia**, F.: sarsaparilla. **-sèdine**, F.: saltness. **-sedinóso**, **-sétto**†, ADJ.: saltish. **-sézza**†, F.: saltness. **-síccia**, F.: sausage. **-sicciáio**, M.: sausage-maker. **-sicciétte**, **-sicciòtto**, *aug.* of -*siccia*. **-sicciuòlo**, *dim.* of -*siccia*. **-sièra**, F.: sauce-dish. ‖**-so** [L. -*sus*], ADJ.: SALTY. **-súggine**, F.: saltness. **-sugginóso**, ADJ.: brackish. **-súmo**, M.: salt meat.
salta- [*saltare*]: **-bécca** [-*beccare*], F.: kind of locust. =**beccáre**, INTR.: frisk, gambol. =**fòssi**, M.: calash. =**martíno**, M.: short garment; jumping toy; light person, fop; small cannon. **-m=bárco**, M.: countryman's jerkin. **-mindòsso**†, M.: shabby dress. **-nséccia** [*salta in seccia*], F.: meadow-lark.
sal-táre [L.], TR., INTR.: leap (jump, skip); sport; dance: — *a fare*†, do a thing; — *in collera*, fly into a passion. **-tatóia**, F.: fish-net (stretched on the water surface for mullets to 'jump' into). **-tatóio**, M.: perch. **-tatóra**, F., **-tatóre**, M., **-tatrice**†, F.: jumper; dancer. **-tatòrio**, ADJ.: saltatorial. **-tazióne**†, F.: jumping; leap. **-teggiáre**, INTR.: skip in dancing. **-telláre**, *freq.* of -*tare*. **-tellíno**†, *dim.* of -*tello*. **-tèllo**, *dim.* of -*to*. **-tellóne**, *aug.* of -*tello*. **-torelláre**, INTR.: frisk, gambol. **-terèllo**, M.: *dim.* of -*to*; firecracker; key-hammer (in pianos, etc.); sort of combination of three notes; white grub; kind of dance.
saltèr(i)o [L. *psalterium*], M.: psaltery; psalm-book; horn-book; nun's veil†.
sal-tétto†, *dim.* of -*to*. **-tichiáre**, INTR.: skip; frisk; gambol. **-timbánco** [*salta-in-banca*], M.: mountebank (Eng.† saltimbanco). ‖**sál-to** [-*tare*], M.: leap; skip; bound; forest†: *a -ti*, by fits and starts.
salu-berrimaménte, ADV.: most wholesomely. ‖**salú-bre** [L. -*bris*], ADJ.: salubrious (sound). **-breménte**, ADV.: salubriously. **-brità**, F.: salubrity.
sa-lumáio, M.: seller of salted meat and pulse. ‖**-lúme** [-*le*], M.: salted meat. **-lumière** = -*lumaio*.
salu-táre 1, ADJ.: salutary. **-táre** 2, TR.: salute; greet; acclaim. **-táre**† 3, M.: saver. **-tatóia**, F., **-tatóre**, M.: saluter. **-tatòrio**, ADJ.: salutary. **-tatrice**, F.: saluter. **-tazióne**, F.: salutation. ‖**salú-te** [L. -*s*], F.: SAFETY; health; SALvation; F.: salute. **-tévole**, ADJ.: salutary. **-tevolménte**, ADV.: wholesomely. **-tífero**, ADJ.: salutiferous. **-to**, M.: salutation; bow.

sál-va [L. *-ve*], F.: volley (of guns, etc.; salute). ‖**-va=condótto** [*-vare*], M.: safe-conduct; passport. **-va=danáio, -va=danáro**, M.: child's money-box. **-vadóre†**, M.: saviour. **-fiáschi†**, M.: hamper; basket. **-va=gènte**, M.: life-preserver.

salvaggi.. = *selvaggi..*

sal-vagióne† = *-vazione*. **-va=guardáre**, TR.: place in safety, safeguard. **-va=guárdia**, F.: safeguard. **-vaménte**, ADV.: safely. **-vaménto**, M.: safety, preservation. **-vándo**, see *-vare*. **-vánza†**, F.: safety. ‖**-váre** [L.], TR.: SAVE; preserve; defend; spare: *-vando*, ellipt. for *-vando la grazia di Dio*, by the saving grace of God, God save me. **-va=ròba†**, M.: wardrobe.

salvati-caménte, ADV.: wildly; shyly. **-chèllo, -chétto**, *dim.* of *-co*. **-chézza**, F.: wildness; shyness. ‖**salváti-co** [L. *silvaticus*], ADJ.: wild; SAVAGE; rude, awkward. **-conáccio**, *disp.* of *-cone*. **-cóne**, *aug.* of *-co*. **-còtto†, -cúccio†**, ADJ.: rather shy. **-cúme**, M.: wildness; rusticity.

salva-tóra, F., ‖**-tóre** [*-re*], M., **-tríce**, F.: saviour; preserver. **-zióne**, F.: safety; salvation.

sál-ve [L. I've of *-vere*, be well], INTERJ.: hail! **-via** [L.], F.: (*bot.*) salvia (SAGE). **-viático†**, ADJ.: seasoned with sage.

sal-viétta [Fr. *ser-viette* (L. *-vire*, serve)], F.: napkin.

sal-vígia†, F.: safety. ‖**-vo** [L. *-vus*], ADJ.: SAFE; secure; ADV.: SAVE (except); M.: exception, reservations. **-vo=condòtto†** = *-vacondotto*.

sámbra†, F.: chamber.

sambúca [L.], F.: SAMBUKE (mus. instr.).

sam-buchèlla, F.: elder flower. **-buchíno†**, ADJ.: of elder tree. ‖**-búco** [L. *-bucus*], M.: elder tree.

sampog.. = *zampog..*

San for *santo* before consonant.

sa-nábile, ADJ.: curable. **-nabilità**, F.: sanableness. **-naménte**, ADV.: healthfully; soundly. ‖**-náre** [L.], TR.: cure (heal). **-nativo**, ADJ.: sanative. **-natóre**, M.: healer. **-natòrio†**, ADJ.: sanatory (healing). **-nazióne†**, F.: healing.

sancíre [L.], TR.: establish, decree.

sancta sanctòrum [L.], M.: holy of holies.

sán-dalo [L. *-dalium*, SANDAL], M.: sandal-wood; boat; sandal (slipper). **-dolíno**, M.: skiff.

sandrácca [Gr. *-drákē*], F.: orpiment.

sanèa†, F.: coast, seashore.

san-guáccio, *disp.* of *-gue*. ‖**-gue** [L. *-guis*], M.: blood; race (family); homicide; nature: *a — caldo*, in a fury. **-guífero**, ADJ.: sanguiferous. **-guificáre**, INTR.: produce blood. **-guificazióne**, F.: sanguification. **-guígna†**, F.: bloodstone, red lead. **-guígno**, ADJ.: bloody (of blood); sanguine, blood-coloured; of sanguine temperament; sanguinary†. **-guináccio**, M.: blood-pudding. **-guináre**, INTR.: make blood. **-guinária**, F.: bloodwort. **-guinário**, ADJ.: sanguinary, cruel. **-guíneo**, ADJ.: sanguine, bloody. **-guinità†**, F.: consanguinity, blood. **-guinolènte, -guinolènto**, ADJ.: bloody; sanguinary. **-guinolenteménte†**, ADV.: with much bloodshed. **-guinosaménte**, ADV.: sanguinarily. **-guinóso**, ADJ.: bloody; blood-stained. **-guisúga** [L. *sugere*, SUCK], F.: leech; blood-sucker.

sanicáre†, TR., INTR.: cure; recover.

sánie [L. *-nies* (*-nguis*, blood)], F.: SANIES (matter, pus).

sanificáre†, TR.: cure, heal.

sanióso†, ADJ.: full of pus.

sani-tà [L. *-tas*], F.: health (sanity). **-tário**, ADJ.: sanitary.

sán-na†, F.: tusk, fang.

sáno [L. *-nus*], ADJ.: healthy (sound); SANE; whole†.

sanrocchíno [*San Rocco*], M.: pilgrim's cloak.

sán-sa [L.], **-sèna**, F. PL.: olive-husks.

Sant' for *santo* before vowel.

santa=bárbara [*S..*, *B..*], F.: powder-room.

santágio†, ADJ.: slow, inactive.

santambárco†, M.: carter's frock.

san-taménte, ADV.: saintly, holily, devoutly. **-tarèllo, -terèllo**, M.: little saint. **-tése†**, M.: sexton, church warden. **-téssa†**, F.: hypocrite. **-tificaménto**, M.: sanctification. **-tificáre**, TR.: sanctify, canonize. **-tificatívo**, ADJ.: sanctifying. **-tificatóre**, M., **-tificatríce**, F.: sanctifier. **-tificazióne**, F.: sanctification. **-tífico†**, M.: holy man. **-timònia**, F.: holiness; sanctimony. **-tinfízza†**, M.: hypocrite. **-tíno**, M.: small image of a saint. **-tità**, F.: sanctity, holiness; his Holiness. ‖**-to** [L. *-ctus*], ADJ.: SAINTed, SACred, holy; blessed; M.: saint; sanctuary (church)†: *entrare in —*†, church. **-tocchiería**, F.: hypocrisy. **-tòcchio**, M.: bigot. **sán-tolo†**, M.: godfather. **-tóne**, M.: great saint, santon (Turk. saint); canting hypocrite.

santò-nico [*Santoni*, people of Aquitania], M.: wormwood. **-nína**, F.: (*chem.*) santonine.

santoréggia [L. *satureia*], F.: savory (plant).

san-tuário, M., **-tuária**, F.: sanctuary; temple. **-túria†**, F., PL. relics of saints.

sánna† = *zanna*.

sanzióne [L. *-nctio*], F.: sanction; judgment (law).
sápa [root of *-pere*], F.: mustard.
sa-pére [L. *sapere* (root *sap*, taste)], IRR.§; INTR.: know; understand; inform; learn; feel; taste; smell; displease. **-pévole**†, ADJ.: learned, informed. **-pevolménte**†, ADV.: learnedly. **-piènte**, ADJ.: learned; wise; piquant†. **-pienteménte**, ADV.: learnedly. **-piènz(i)a**, F.: learning; wisdom. **sá-pio**† = *-vio*.
§ Ind.: Pres. *sò, sái, sà; sappiámo, sapéte, sánno*. Pret. *sèp-pi, -pe; -pero*. Fut. *saprò*. Cond. *saprèi*. Subj.: Pres. *sáppia*, etc. I've *sáp-pi, -piáte*. Part.: Pres. *sapiènte*.
sapo-náceo, ADJ.: soapy, saponaceous. **-náia**†, F.: soapwort. **-náio**, M.: soap-boiler. **-nária**, F.: soapberry. **-náta**, F.: soap lather or froth. ||**sapé-ne** [L. *sapo*], M.: soap. **-nería**, F.: soap-boiling. **-nétta**, F.: cake of soap, wash-ball. **-nétto**†, M.: wash-ball. **-nificáre**, TR.: saponify. **-nificazióne**, F.: saponification.
sa-poráccio, *disp.* of *-pore*. **-poráre**†, TR., INTR.: savour; taste. ||**-póre** [L. *-por*], M.: SAVOUR, taste; relish†; pleasure. **-porétto**, *dim.* of *-pore*. **-poritaménte**, ADV.: relishingly. **-poritíno**, *dim.* of *-porito*. **-poríto**, ADJ.: savoury; delicious; pungent; sharp. **-porosaménte**, ADV.: savourily. **-porosità**†, F.: savouriness; flavour; relish. **-poróso**, ADJ.: savoury; tasty, relishing.
sa-púta [*-pere*], F.: knowledge; acquaintance. **-putèllo**, *dim.* of *-puto*. **-púto**† = *-puta*.
sára†, F.: saw-fish.
sara-céno, M.: = *-cino*; ADJ.: *grano* —, Indian corn (maize). **-cináre**†, INTR.: become black (as grapes). **-cinésca**, F.: portcullis. **-cinésco**, ADJ.: Saracen. ||**-címo** [fr. Ar.], M.: Saracen; tilting-post (in effigy of a Saracen). **-cini**, PL.: seeds of grapes becoming black.
sara-mentáre†, TR.: bind by an oath. ||**-ménto**†, M.: oath.
sar-cásmo [Gr. *-kasmós*], M.: sarcasm, taunt. **-casticaménte**, ADV.: sarcastically. **-cástico**, pl. *—ci*, ADJ.: sarcastic.
sar-chiagióne, F., **-chiaménto**, M.: weeding. **-chiáre**, TR.: weed. **-chiáta**, F.: weeding once. **-chiatóre**, M.: weeder. **-chiatúra**, F.: weeding. **-chièlla**, F.: weeding-hook. **-chielláre**, TR.: weed slightly. **-chièllo**, **-chiétto**, *dim.* of *-chio*. ||**sár-chio** [L. *-culum*], M.: weeding-hook. **-chiolíno**, **-chioncèllo**, *dim.* of *-chio*.
sárcina† [L.], F.: load (burden, weight).
sarcocòlla [L.], F.: balsam.
sarcòfago, pl. *—ghi*, *—gi* [Gr. *sárx*, flesh, *phágein*, eat], M.: sarcophagus (stone coffin).
sárd-a [L., Sardian stone], F.: sard (cornelian stone). **=ágata**, F.: sardachate.
sardanapalésco [L. *-licus* (*Sardanapalus*)], ADJ.: luxurious, effeminate.
sar-dèlla, ||**-dína** [L.], F.: sardine.
sar-do [Gr. *sárdios*], ADJ., M.: Sardian. **-dònico**, F.: sardonyx. **-dònico**, pl. *—ci*, ADJ.: sardonic (sneering).
sár-gano†, M., **-gína**†, F.: coarse woollen cloth. ||**sár-gia** [Fr. *-ge*, silky], F.: bed-coverlet; SERGE. **-giáio**, M.: painter of serge.
sárgo, pl. *—gi* [L. *-gus*], M.: sea-fish.
saríssa [L.], F.: Macedonian lance.
sarmén-to [L. *-tum*], M.: vine-brand; twig. **-tóso**, ADJ.: full of twigs.
sarnácchi-o†, M.: catarrhous spittle. **-óso**†, ADJ.: catarrhous.
sarpáre†, INTR.: weigh anchor.
sarrocchino = *sanrocchino*.
sárta, F. of *-to*.
sár-te, ||**-tie** [Gr. *ex-ártia*], F. PL.: (*nav.*) shrouds (stays). **-tiáme**, M.: cordage.
sár-ta, F.: mantua maker, seamstress. **-to** [L. *-tus* (*-cire*, mend)], M.: tailor. **-tóre**, M.: (*poet.*) tailor. **-toría**, F.: tailor-shop. **-túccio**, **-túcolo**, *disp.* of *-to*.
sas-safrásso [Eng. *-safras* (cf. *-sifraga*)], M.: SASSAFRAS. **-sáia**, F.: heap of stones; mound. **-saiòla**, F.: battle of stones. **-saiuòlo**†, M.: wood-pigeon. **-sáre**, TR.: stone. **-sáta**, F.: blow of a stone; rocky place; precipice. **-satèllo**, M.: *dim.* of *-so*; little stone. **-sèfrica** [L. *fricare*, 'rub'], F.: (*bot.*) goat's beard. **-sèllo**, M.: small stone or flint; kind of thrush.
sás-seo, ADJ.: stony. **-séto**, M.: stony place. **-settíno**, *dim.* of *-setto*. **-sétto**, *dim.* of *-so*. **-sificáre**†, TR.: petrify, turn into stone. **-sífraga** [L. *saxi-fraga* (*frangere*, break)], F.: (*bot.*) saxifrage. ||**sás-so** [L. *saxum*], M.: stone, rock; tomb. **-solinétto**, *dim.* of *-solino*. **-solíno**, *dim.* of *-so*. **-sóne**, *aug.* of *-so*. **-sóso**, ADJ.: stony, full of stones.
satá-n [Heb. *-n*, enemy], **sáta-na**, M.: Satan. **-násso**, M.: Satan; madman. **-nísmo**, M.: satanic action. **satá-nico**, pl. *—ci*, ADJ.: satanic, diabolical.
satèl-lite [L. *-les*, attendant], M.: satellite; bailiff; brigand. **-lízio**†, M.: duty of a satellite, set of satellites.
sáti-ra [L. *-ra*], F.: satire, lampoon. **-ráccia**, *disp.* of *-ra*.
satiráccio, *disp.* of *satiro* I.
satireggiáre [*satira*], TR.: satirize, lampoon, ridicule.
sati-rèllo, *dim.* of *-ro*. **-rescaménte**, ADV.: satirically. **-résco**, ADJ.: satirical (burlesque).

(clear). **-dáto†**, ADJ.: light blue; faded; pale (sickly): *cavallo* —, horse that has not had his oats. ‖**-díre** [*s-*, *biaro* or *biado*], INTR.: fade.

ṣbian-cáre [*s-*, *bianca*], INTR.: grow whitish (grow pale). **-cáto**, ADJ.: whitish (pale).

ṣbiaṣciatúra [*s-*, *biasciare*], F.: defect in shearing cloth.

ṣbiaváto = *sbiadato*.

ṣbicchio-ráre [*s-*, *bicchiere*], INTR.: sell wine or liquor by the glass (retail). **-ráta**, F.: selling (wine) by the glass (retailing).

ṣbie-caménte, ADV.: obliquely (slopingly, aslant, awry). **-cáre**, INTR.: slope (be awry); bias (swerve). ‖**ṣbiè-co** [*s-*, *bieco*], ADJ.: slant (crooked); M.: slant (bias): *fatto a* —, wrought in bias.

ṣbietoláre†, INTR.: weep for tenderness (be moved).

ṣbiettá-re [*s-*, *bietta*], TR.: pull the wedge from; twist; get away (pack off bag and baggage). **-túra**, F.: pulling out the wedge.

ṣbigot-timénto, M.: dismay (dread); amazement. ‖**-tíre** [?], TR.: terrify (awe); INTR., REFL.: be dismayed (become afraid, despond). **-titaménte†**, ADV.: tremblingly (with fear).

ṣbilan-ciaménto, M.: outweighing; bending downwards. ‖**-ciáre** [*s-*, *bilanciare*], TR.: unbalance (put out of equilibrium); INTR., REFL.: be unbalanced (lose the balance); outweigh. **ṣbilán-cio** = *-ciamento*. **-cióne**, M.: big leap; tumble.

ṣbilènco [?], ADJ.: bow-legged; knock-kneed; M., F. (*-ca*): bow-legged person.

ṣbir-báre [*s-*, *birba*], TR.: defraud (cheat). **-báto**, ADJ.: duped (swindled). **-bonáre**, TR.: go a-begging.

ṣbir-ciáre [*s-*, *bircio*], TR.: look narrowly at; leer (ogle). **-'cio**, ADJ.: short-sighted.

ṣbir-racchiòlo, ADJ.: pertaining to a bailiff. **-rágḷia**, F.: (*disp.*) lot of bailiffs or constables. **-racchiuòlo**, M.: under-bailiff. **-rería**, F.: = *-raglia*; office of bailiff. **-résco**, *disp.* of *-ro*. ‖**sbír-ro** [*s-*, *birro*], M.: policeman (bailiff, constable).

ṣbiṣacciáre†, TR.: draw out of the wallet.

ṣbiẓẓarríre [*s-*, *bizzarro*], TR.: cure of whims; disenchant.

[s]bocca-ménto, M.: disemboguing; mouth [(of] a stream). ‖**ṣboccá-re** [*s-*, *boccare*], [INTR.]: disemBOGUE, overflow; rush out; [break] the neck of a bottle. **-taménte**, [ADV.]: indecently, filthily. **ṣboccá-to**, [ADJ.: d]ischarged; foul-mouthed: *cavallo* —, hard-mouthed horse. **-túra**, F.: mouth (of a stream).

ṣboc-ciáre [*s-*, *boccia*], INTR.: open, expand (as flowers). **ṣbòc-cio**, M.: opening (blossoming): *donna di* —, vivacious woman.

ṣbócco = *sboccamento*.

ṣbocconcel-láre [*s-*, *bocconcello*], INTR.: nibble (eat slowly). **-láto**, ADJ.: cut in bits. **-latúra**, F.: nibbling.

ṣbogḷien-taménto†, M.: boiling; agitation. **-táre**, TR.: boil; disturb; INTR.: boil up (gurgle); become angry. ‖**ṣbollíre** [*s-*, *bollore*], INTR.: boil up.

ṣbolzonáre†, TR.: batter down (walls, etc.).

ṣbombardáre†, TR.: bombard.

ṣbombettáre†, INTR.: be always tippling.

ṣbontadiáto†, ADJ.: useless (vain, worthless).

ṣbonẓoláre [*s-*, *bonzola*], INTR.: be suspended; fall down; belly out; fall in ruins.

ṣborbottáre†, TR.: reproach (upbraid, scold, reprimand).

ṣborchiáre†, TR.: take off the studs, etc.

ṣbordel-laménto, M.: debauchery (riot). ‖**-láre** [*s-*, *bordello*], INTR.: riot (royster).

ṣbòr-nia [? *s-*, **ebronia* (*ebro*)], F.: drunkenness (inEBRIEty). **-niáre**, TR.: distinguish; attain; INTR.: succeed; REFL.: get drunk. **-niáto**, ADJ.: drunk(en).

ṣborráre [*s-*, *borra*], TR.: empty of stuffing (or filling); deprive of strength; blurt out; reduce to rubbish.

ṣbor-saménto, M.: disbursement, expenditure. ‖**-sáre** [*s-*, *borsa*], TR.: disburse, expend. **-satúra** = *-samento*. **ṣbórso**, M.: disbursement; sum paid.

ṣbos-caménto, M.: disforestation. ‖**-cáre** [*s-*, *bosco*], TR.: disforest.

ṣbotto-náre [*s-*, *bottone*], TR.: unbutton; (*fam.*) reveal; REFL.: open one's heart, speak out. **-natúra**, F.: unbuttoning. **-neggiáre**, TR.: *dim.* and *freq.* of *-nare*; satirize, ridicule.

ṣboẓẓacchíre [*s-*, *bozzacchio*], INTR.: revive; thrive, grow again.

ṣbozzá-re [*s-*, *bozza*], TR.: sketch; rough-draw (draw the outlines of); (*nav.*) take off the stoppers. **-tóre**, M.: sketcher; sculptor (copyist). **-túra**, F.: sketching.

ṣboẓẓimáre [*s-*, *bozzima*], TR.: wash off starch of.

ṣboz-zíno [*sbozzare*], M.: plane. **ṣbòz-zo**, M.: sketching, sketch.

ṣbozzolá-re [*s-*, *bozzolo*], TR.: take (silk-cocoons) from the branches; take the miller's fee†. **-túra**, F.: gathering of silk-cocoons; time of gathering cocoons.

ṣbra-cáre [*s-*, *bracare*], INTR.: gossip; be slovenly; REFL.†: take off one's small clothes; strain every nerve (strive, do one's best). **-catamente†**, ADV.: widely; excessively. **-cáto**, ADJ.: without one's small clothes; easy; delightful; happy.

ṣbrac-ciáre† [*s-*, *braccia*], TR.: take out of the arms; REFL.: uncover one's arms; use every effort or means. **-ciáto**, ADJ.: with sleeves tucked up. **ṣbrác-cio**, M.: elbow-room.

ṣbrá-cia†, M.: braggart (boaster). **-cia-ménto**, M.: stirring of the fire; boasting, bluster. ‖**-ciáre** [*s-*, *brace*], TR.: stir (the fire); lavish; boast. **-ciáta**, F., **-ciatóio**, **-cio**, M.: stirring of the fire; bragging. **-cióna**, F., **-cióne**, M.: boaster.

ṣbraculáto [*sbracare*], ADJ.: breechless.

ṣbrai-táre [OFr. *braire*, cry], INTR.: make a great uproar. **-tío**, M.: continuous uproar. **-tóne**, M.: shouter.

ṣbramáre [*s-*, *brama*], TR.: satisfy (content); gratify desire; REFL.: be content.

ṣbra-naménto, M.: tearing in pieces. ‖**-náre** [*s-*, *brano*], TR.: tear in pieces. **-natóre**, M.: tearer.

ṣbran-caménto, M.: separating from the flock. ‖**-cáre** [*s-*, *branco*], TR.: take from the flock; lop off, break; REFL.: separate; go astray.

ṣbrandelláre [*s-*, *brandello*], TR.: tear asunder.

ṣbráno [*sbranare*], M.: tearing, rending.

ṣbrattáre [*s-*, *bratta†*, dregs], TR.: clean, disencumber.

ṣbravaz-záre [*s-*, *bravazzone*], INTR.: bluster (bully). **-záta**, F.: bluster (swaggering). **-zóne**, M.: bully (swaggerer).

ṣbregáccia†, F.: tattling woman.

ṣbréndolo [*s-*, *brandello*], M.: dirty rags, tatters.

ṣbrícchi [?], M.: boy's game.

ṣbri-cconeggiáre [*s-*, *briccone*], INTR.: lead a dissolute life. **ṣbrí-cio†**, ADJ.: mean (vile).

ṣbricio-laménto, M.: crumbling, grinding. ‖**-láre** [*s-*, *briciolo*], TR.: crumble, grind (pulverize). **-latúra**, F.: pulverizing.

ṣbri-gaménto, M.: expedition, dispatch. ‖**-gáre** [*s-*, *briga*], TR.: expedite (despatch); REFL.: make haste: — *d' uno*, get rid of a person. **-gatívo**, ADJ.: expeditious, quick. **-gáto**, ADJ.: dispatched (done); quick (prompt); *la più -gata via*, the shortest cut.

ṣbri-gliáre [*s-*, *briglia*], TR.: unbridle. **-gliáta**, **-gliatúra**, F.: check with the reins; reproof (rebuke).

ṣbrindelláre [*s-*, *brindello*], TR.: tear.

ṣbrizzáre†, TR.: break into bits; splash, drop.

ṣbroc-cáre [*s-*, *brocco*], TR.: lop off, strip; smooth (silk). **-catúra**, F.: lopping, smoothing. **ṣbròc-co**, M.: smoothed silk; scion†.

ṣbroccoláre [*s-*, *broccolo*], TR.: strip the leaves from.

ṣbrodoláre [*s-*, *brodo*], TR.: grease, daub.

ṣbrogliáre [*s-*, *broglio*], TR.: disentangle (clear); REFL.: extricate or rid one's self.

ṣbronconáre [*s-*, *broncone*], TR.: clear of branches, etc.; rough-hew; clear (land).

ṣbrò-scia [*s-*, *broscia*], F.: weak, insipid drink. **-sciatúra**, F.: pelt-dye (dye used for pelts, already used for silks). **-sciúccia**, *dim.* of *-scia*.

ṣ=bruc áre, TR.: strip the leaves from.

ṣbruf-fáre [*s-*, ?*pro-flare*], INTR.: spirt out; besprinkle, bespit. **sbrúf-fo**, M.: besprinkling, besputtering; silence money.

ṣbucáre [*s-*, *buca*], INTR.: come out of a hole; TR.: draw out.

ṣbucchia..† = *sbuccia*..

ṣbuc-ciaménto, M.: barking, skinning. ‖**-ciáre** [*s-*, *buccia*], TR.: bark; peel (skin). **-ciatúra**, F.: barking (peeling). **-ciaturína**, *dim.* of *-ciatura*.

ṣbudel-laménto, M.: beating out of the bowels. ‖**-láre** [*s-*, *budello*], TR.: beat out the bowels of; thrash soundly.

ṣbuf-faménto, M.: fuming, panting. ‖**-fáre** [*s-*, *buffo*], INTR.: pant, fume (rage). **-fo**, M.: snorting, puffing.

ṣbufonchiáre [*s-*, *bofonchiare*], INTR.: mutter.

ṣbugiardáre [*s-*, *bugiardo*], TR.: give the lie to, convict of falsehood.

ṣburráre [*s-*, *burro*], TR.: remove the fat (buttery part) from.

ṣbuṣáre†, TR.: fleece (at cards), leave penniless (at play).

ṣbuzzáre [*s-*, *buzzo*], TR.: remove the abdomen of; strike severely in the abdomen; tap (a tumor).

scáb-bia [L. *scabies* (*scabo*, scratch)], F.: scab, itch. **-biáre†**, TR.: cure of the itch; polish, plane. **-bióṣa**, F.: scabwort, scabious. **-bióso**, ADJ.: scabby, rough, rugged, scaly.

scabèllo, M.: foot-stool.

scabíno [Ger. *schöppe*], M.: judge; sheriff (Eng.† ECHEVIN).

sca-brézza, F.: ruggedness, scragginess, roughness. ‖**scá-bro** [L. *-ber*], ADJ.: rugged (scraggy, rough, scabrous). **-brosità**, F.: ruggedness (roughness). **-bróso**, ADJ.: scabrous, rough, rugged, scraggy, hard.

scac-cáta† [*scacco*], F.: move at chess. **-cáto**, ADJ.: chequered. **-chi**, cf. *scacco*.

scacchiá-re [*s-*, *cacchio*], TR.: prune (trim). **-túra**, F.: pruning (trimming).

scacchiè-ra [*scacco*], F., **-re**, M.: chess-board, draught-board.

scac-ciagióne, F., **-ciaménto**, M.: chasing off, expulsion. **-ciamósche**, M.: fly-flap. **-ciapensièri**, M.: pastime, diversion; amusement; jew's-harp. ‖**-ciá-re** [*s-*, *cacciare*], TR.: drive away, expel; discharge (a servant). **-ciáta**, F.: driving away, expulsion. **-ciatóre**, M.: driver off, expeller. **-cíno**, M.: janitor, beadle (of a church).

scác-co [Pers. *shâh*, king (game against the king)], M.: square (in a chess-board); rout; pl. —*chi*, us'ly in: *gioco degli -chi*, game of chess; — *matto* (Pers. *shâh mât*, Shah is dead), check-mate; *dar lo* —, hurt, injure; *ricevere lo* —, receive injury; *vedere il sole a* —, be in prison; *a -chi*, chequered. **-co=mátto**, cf. *-co*.

sca-cciáto, PART.; as adv. with *bianco* = superl.: *bianco* — = *bianchissimo*. ‖**-ciáre**† [*scacciare*], TR.: drive away; exclude; balk.

sca-dènza, F.: fall, decay; expiration (of a bill of exchange), term of payment. ‖**-dére** [*s-*, *cadere*], IRR.; INTR.: DECAY, fall off; fall due; become due; devolve. **-diménto**, M.: decay, decline, ruin. **-dúto**, ADJ.: decayed, fallen; due.

scáfa†, F.: skiff, long boat, tender.

scafándro [Gr. *skáphe*, boat; *anḗr*, man], M.: diver's dress.

scaffále [? ak. to Eng. *scaffold*], M.: book-case (book-shelf).

scaffáre†, INTR.: make the game even; play odd and even; fall.

scáfo [? Gr. *-phos*, basin], M.: hulk (carcass of a ship).

scaggiále, M.: cincture, leather-belt.

s=cagionáre, TR.: exculpate.

scá-glia [L. *squamula*], F.: SCALE (of a fish or snake); chips of marble; PL.: sling. **-gliábile**, ADJ.: that may be scaled; darted. **-gliaménto**, M.: flinging, throw. **-gliáre**, TR.: scale; fling (hurl, dart); REFL.: struggle, be agitated: — *addosso ad alcuno*, pitch into a person. **-gliatóre**, M.: flinger. **-gliétta**, **-gliettína**, *dim.* of *-glia*. **-gliòla**, F.: little scale; little shell; gilder's plaster.

sca-glioncíno, *dim.* of *-glione*. ‖**-glióne** [*aug.* of *-la*], M.: step (esp. large, as of stone, artificial or natural); eye-tooth (of a horse).

sca-glióso [*-glia*], ADJ.: scaly (covered with scales). **-gliuòla** = *-gliola*.

-gnárdo†, ADJ.: dog-like, ugly, low, ...an. ‖**-gnáre** [*s-*, *cagna*], INTR.: bay ...dogs). **-gnío**, pl. —*ii*, M.: continuous ... **-gnòzzo**, ADJ.: miserable.

scá-la [L.], F.: staircase (stairs); step; scale; ladder; (for *-lo*) wharf†: — *a chiocciola*, winding-staircase; — *franca*, free ingress and egress. **-láccia**, *disp.* of *-la*. **-laménto**, M.: escalade, scaling a wall.

scalappiáre [*s-*, *calappio*], TR., INTR.: escape (from a snare).

sca-láre [*-la*], TR.: take by escalade, scale, storm. **-láta**, F.: escalade, storming. **-latóre**, M.: one who scales.

scalcagnáre [*s-*, *calcagno*], INTR.: tread on one's heels.

s=calcáre 1, TR.: tread upon, crush.

scal-cáre 2 [*-co*], TR.: carve (meat). **-catóre**, M., **-catríce**, F.: carver.

scalcheggiáre† = *scalciare*.

scalchería [*scalco*], F.: office of a carver.

scalciáre [*s-*, *calcio*], INTR.: kick.

scalciná-re [*s-*, *calcina*], TR.: unplaster (divest of plaster). **-túra**, F.: unplastering; unplastered place.

scálco [OGer. *scalc*, servant], M.: steward, carver (of meat).

scalda=lètto, M.: warming-pan. **=máni**, **-máno**, M.: hot cockles (boys' play). **-ménto**, M.: warming, heating. **=pánche**, M.: lounger (idle student). **=piátti**, M.: chafing-dish. **=pièdi**, M.: foot-warmer. ‖**scaldá-re** [*s-*, *caldo*], TR.: warm (heat); excite; REFL.: get warm; grow angry. **scaldá-ta**, F.: warming, heating. **-tína**, *car. dim.* of *-ta*. **-tóio**, M.: stove-room; warming-place. **-tóre**, M.: warmer. **=vivánde**, M.: chafing-dish.

scal-deggiáre [*-dare*], TR.: animate, spur on; excite. **-díno**, M.: a pot to warm hands.

scalèa [*scala*], F.: outside stone stairs.

scalèno [Gr. *-nós*], ADJ.: (*geom.*) scalene.

scalèlla†, F.: snare (gin, noose).

sca-lèo, M.: ladder. ‖**-létta**, F.: *dim.* of *-la*; little staircase, narrow stairs; flat tile. **-lettáto**, ADJ.: provided with stairs.

scal-fíre [L. *-pere*], TR.: cut (into or away); scratch. **-fítto**, PART.; M.†: scratch. **-fittúra**, F.: incision; scratch.

sca-lína, *car. dim.* of *-la*. **-lináta**, F.: flight of steps. **-líno**, M.: step (of stairs), stair.

scalmá-na [*scaldare*, *mano*], F.: chill. **-náre**, REFL.: get a chill.

scálmo [L. *-mus*], M.: thole (of a boat).

scálo [*scala*], M.: loading-place (wharf, quay); slope.

scalógno [L. *cæpa ascalonia*], M.: SCALLION (onion), shallot.

sca-lóna [*-la*], F., **-lóne**, M.: great staircase; = *-glione*.

scalorire† [*s*-, *calore*], TR.: draw out the heat of.

scalpel-láre, TR.: chisel. **-latóre**, M.: chiselling. **-latúra**, F.: chiselling. **-létto**, **-lettíno**, *dim.* of *-lo*. **-lináre**, TR., INTR.: work with small chisel. **-líno**, M.: chiseller. ||**scalpèl-lo** [L. *-lum*], M.: chisel (graver); (*fig.*) sculptor: *opera di* —, works of sculpture. **-lóne**, *aug.* of *-lo*.

scal-piecciaménto, M.: stamping or trampling under foot. **-piecciáre** [*-pitare*], INTR.: shuffle (scrape the feet along). **-píeccio**, M.: shuffle. **-pitaménto**, M.: stamping, trampling upon. ||**-pitáre** [? L. *-pere*, cut], TR.: stamp upon, paw; trample under foot. **-pitío**, M.: stamping, trampling. **-póre**, M.: loud resentment; angry tumult; uproar; grave effect.

scálpro† = *scalpello*.

scalter. .† = *scaltr*. .

scal-traménte, ADV.: cunningly, slyly. **-trézza**, F., **-triménto**, M.: cunning, craftiness, shrewdness, tact, address. ||**-tríre** [? L. *-pere*, cut], TR.: sharpen, teach wit; trick. **-tritaménte**, ADV.: cunningly, craftily. **-tríto**, **-tro**, ADJ.: sharp (cunning, crafty, shrewd).

scal-za=cáne, M.: ragamuffin, vagabond. **-za=gátto** = *-zacane*. **-zaménto**, M.: taking off one's shoes and stockings; hoeing up, digging, baring the roots. ||**-záre** [*s*-, *calzare*], TR.: strip of shoes and stockings; bare the roots of; strip; undermine; pump (a person). **-záto**, ADJ.: unshod, barefooted. **-zatóio**, M.: tooth-lancet. **-zatóre**, M.: remover of shoes and stockings; underminer. **-zatúra**, F.: removal of shoes and stockings; hoeing up; digging; marriage feast. **scál-zo**, ADJ.: unshod (bare, barefoot); miserable.

sca-matáre, TR.: beat (clothes, etc.). ||**-máto** [? Gr. *kámax*, pole], M.: rod.

scam-biaménto, M.: change, exchange; commutation; vicissitude. ||**-biáre** [*s*-, *cambio*], TR.: EXCHANGE; fill the place of†. **-biettáre**, INTR.: skip; change often†. **-biétto**, M.: skip; caper; frequent change†. **-biévole**, ADJ.: mutual; reciprocal. **-bievolézza**, F.: mutual change, reciprocity. **-bievolménte**, ADJ.: reciprocally, mutually, each other. **scámbio**, M.: change; exchange (barter); PREP.: instead (in place of): *togliere in iscambio*, mistake. **-bísta**, M.: barterer.

scameráre [*s*-, *camera*), TR.: take out of the treasury.

scamerita [?], F.: loin or fillet of pork.

scami-ciáre [*s*-, *camicia*], REFL.: remain in shirt-sleeves. **-ciáto**, ADJ.: in shirt-sleeves.

scamoiáre†, INTR.: scamper off.

sca-moşciáre [*s*-, *camoscio*], TR.: dress (shammy leather). **-moşciatóre**, M.: dresser of shammy leather. **-mòşcio**, ADJ.: of shammy.

scamoz-záre [*s*-, *capo*, *mozzare*], TR.: truncate, prune. **-zatúra**, F.: pruning.

scámpa† = *scampo*.

scampafórca [*scampare*, *forca*], M. INVAR.: scape-gallows (scapegrace).

scampagnáta [*s*-, *campagna*], F.: short country vacation.

scampaménto [*-po*], M.: escape, safety.

scampa-náre [*s*-, *campana*], INTR.: ring the chimes. **-náta**, F.: ringing the chimes, playing upon the bells. **-nelláre**, INTR.: ring the small bell. **-nelláta**, F., **-nellío**, M.: ringing of the small bells. **-nío**, M.: noisy ringing of the bells (chimes).

scam-páre [*s*-, *campo*], TR.: save (preserve, defend); INTR.: escape, get out of danger. **-patóre**, M.: rescuer, deliverer. **-po**, M.: safety; deliverance; escape, refuge; evasion: *non v' è* —, there's no remedy for it, no evading it. **-polétto**, **-políno**, *dim.* of *-polo*. **scám-polo**, M.: remnant, remainder.

scamúzzolo†, M.: bit, little bit.

scana-láre [*s*-, *canale*], TR.: channel (flute, chamfer); rifle; INTR.: slip out; depart from usual practice. **-latúra**, F.: channelling (fluting); channel.

scancel-lábile, ADJ.: that may be cancelled. **-laménto**, M.: cancelling, erasing. ||**-láre** [*s*-, *cancellare*], TR.: cancel (erase). **-latíccio**, M.: bad erasure. **-latúra**, **-lazióne**, F.: erasing.

scancèllo†, M.: book rack; pigeon-holes.

scan-cería†, F.: plate-shelf. **-cía**†, F.: book-shelf, book-case.

scancio [? Ger. *schwank*, curved], ADJ.: slanting (sloping); M.: crosscut.

scan-dagliáre, TR.: sound (examine carefully); explore. ||**-dáglio** [*scandere*], M.: plummet (sounding-line); examination.

scanda-leggiáre† = *-lizzare*. **-lizzánte**, ADJ.: scandalous. **-lizzáre**, TR.: scandalize (bring scandal upon); REFL.: be scandalized, take offence. **-lizzatóre**, M.: who causes scandal. ||**scándalo** [L. *-lum*], M.: scandal (offence; opprobrium, shame; calumny); bad example; discord (dissension): *pietra di* (or *dello*) —, rock (= cause) of offence or scandal. **-losaménte**, ADV.: scandalously. **-lóso**, ADJ.: scandalous (offensive, shameful).

scandèlla [L. *-dula*], F.: small brown wheat; rye.

scandèlle†, F. PL.: drops of oil floating on water.

scán-dere [L.], TR.: SCAN (verses);

INTR.†: ascend, climb. **-digliáre**†, TR.: sound, examine. **-díre** = *-dere*.
scandel. † = *scandal*.
scanfárdo†, ADJ.: dirty; scurvy.
scangèo†, M.: grosgrain shot-silk (stuff).
scangèo [? *cangiare*], M.: disaster (serious trouble); perplexity.
scanicáre†, TR., INTR.: beat down a wall; break the plastering.
scan-na-fòsso, M.: drain to a moat. ‖**-náre** [*s-*, *canna*], TR.: cut the throat of; ruin: *-nato*, wretched. **-natóio**, M.: cut-throat place; shambles. **-natóra**, F., **-natóre**, M., **-natríce**, F.: cut-throat. **-nellaménto**†, M.: fluting (chamfering). **-nelláre**, TR.: wind off; flute (chamfer); INTR.: gush out (spout). **-nellatúra** = *-alatura*. **-nèllo**, M.: kind of writing desk; scrutoire; small bench. **-nétto**†, M.: small stool (cricket).
scánno [L. *-nnum*], M.: seat (bench); sand-bank.
scannonezzáre†, TR.: cannonade; boast of.
s-canonizzáre, TR.: annul the canonization of.
scansa-fatíche, M., F.: shirk. **-ménto**, M.: avoiding (shunning). ‖**scansáre** [*s-*, L. *campsare*, turn], TR.: remove out of the way (displace); avoid (shun): — *un colpo*, dodge a blow; REFL.: withdraw (keep off). **-tóre**, M.: who shuns the danger; remover.
scansía [Ger. *schanz*], F.: book-case (*pl.* book shelves).
scansióne†, F.: SCANSION (of verses).
scánso [*-sare*], M.: avoiding (shunning).
scan-tonaménto, M.: breaking off the corners. ‖**-tonáre** [*s-*, *cantone*], TR.: knock the corners off; INTR.†: go away slyly (dodge, shun, elude). **-tonatúra**, F.: breaking off the corners. **-tuccettáre**, TR.: take away the corners.
sca-paccióne [*s-*, *capo*], M.: cuff or slap on the head: *passare a* —, pass on one's 'cheek.' **-páre**, TR.: remove the head from; REFL.: lose one's head; puzzle one's brains. **-patággine**, F.: heedlessness. **-páto**, ADJ.: heedless; M.: heedless person. **-patóne**, *aug.* of *-pato*.
sca-pecchiáre [*s-*, *capecchio*], TR.: dress or card (flax, hemp); REFL.: disentangle one's self. **-pecchiatóio**, M.: brake; flax-comb.
scape-stratággine, F.: heedlessness; licentiousness. ‖**-stráre**† [*s-*, *capestro*], TR.: take the halter from; debauch (pervert, corrupt); INTR., REFL.: slip one's head out of the halter; lead a dissolute life. **-strataménte**, ADV.: dissolutely (madly). **-stráto**, ADJ.: unbridled (unrestrained); licentious.
sca-pezzaménto, M.: pruning (lopping off). ‖**-pezzáre** [*s-*, *capo*], TR.: lop off; behead. **-pezzóne**, M.: slap on the head (cuff, rap).
sca-pigliáre [*s-*, *capello*], TR.: ruffle; rumple (one's) hair; INTR.†, REFL.: lead a dissolute life. **-pigliáto**, ADJ.: dishevelled; dissolute. **-pigliatúra**, F.: dissolute life (debauchery).
scapi-taménto†, M.: loss; detriment. ‖**-táre** [*s-*, *capitare*], INTR.: be a loser (lose, fall behind); deteriorate; TR.: lose: — *di*, lose. **scápi-to**, M.: loss: *dare* —, cause a loss; *dare a* —, sell at a loss.
scapitozzáre [*-pezzare*], TR.: lop (prune, head trees).
scápo [L. *-pus*], M.: SHAFT (of a column).
scá-pola [L. *-pula*], F.: scapula. **-poláre**, M.: cowl (scapulary).
scapo-láre [*s-*, ? L. *capulare*, catch], TR.: liberate (rescue, release); INTR.: escape (fly). **scápo-lo**, ADJ.: disengaged (free, unmarried, single); M.: bachelor.
scaponíre [*s-*, *capo*], TR.: overcome the obstinacy of (make less headstrong).
scap-paménto, M.: escaping (hurrying); escapement (of a watch). ‖**-páre** [*s-*, *cappa*, 'cloak' (*lit.* 'slip from the cloak')], INTR.: ESCAPE (hurry or run away); forget one's self. **-páta**, F.: escape (flight); sally; oversight (mistake); escapade. **-patèlla**, **-patína**†, F.: *dim.* of *-pata*; little escapade (little subterfuge). **-patóia**, F.: hole to escape through; evasion (subterfuge). **-pa-vía**, M.: = *-patoia*; corridor; outlet. **-pelláre**, TR.: unhood (a hawk); INTR., REFL.: take off one's hat (salute hat in hand). **-pelláta**, F.: salutation hat in hand. **-pelláto**, ADJ.: with one's hat off. **-pellatúra**, F.: a humble salutation. **-pellottáre**, TR.: slap or cuff on the head. **-pellòtto**, M.: blow on the head: *passare a* —, pass gratis, on one's 'cheek' or assurance.
scapperáccio†, M.: short cloak (with hood).
scap-pináre†, TR.: foot (stockings); put new soles to (shoes). **-pináto**†, ADJ.: new-soled. **-píno**†, M.: sock; foot of a stocking.
scapponáta [*s-*, *cappone*], F.: feast of capons; (*pop.*) feast for the first-born son.
scapponèo†, M.: reprimand (reproof).
scap-pucciáre [*s-*, *cappuccio*], INTR.: stumble (trip); fail; REFL.: take off one's hood. **-páccio**, M.: stumble; fault (blunder, oversight).
scaprestáre = *scapestrare*.
sca-pricciáre, ‖**-priccíre** [*s-*, *capriccio*], TR.: cure of whims; disenchant; INTR., REFL.: get cured of one's whims; satisfy one's self.

scápu-la†, F.: shoulder-blade. **-láre**†, M.: small hood (scapulary).
scara-báttola = *-battolo*. **-battolíno**, *dim.* of *-battolo*. ‖**-báttolo** [*s-*, *carabattola*], M.: show-case; show-window.
scara-bèo [Gr. *skarabaios*], M.: SCARABEE (black beetle). **-billáre**†, TR.: scrape (a violin). **-bocchiáre**, TR.: scribble (scrawl). **-bocchiatóre**, M.: scribbler (scrawler). **-bòcchio**, M.: scribbling (scrawl). **-bocchióna**, F., **-bocchióne**, M.: scribbler (scrawler). **-bóne**† = *-faggio*.
sca-racchiáre, INTR.: expectorate; TR.: despise (ridicule). ‖**-rácchio** [? echoic], M.: catarrhous spittle. **-racchióne**, M.: one who expectorates often (big spitter).
scara-faggéssa, F. of *-faggio*. ‖**-fággio** [variant of *-beo*], M.: scarab (beetle).
scarafaldóne†, M.: servants of the synagogue.
scaraffáre†, TR.: tear away by force.
scaramázzo†, ADJ.: not quite round (of pearls); uneven (unequal).
scara-múccia [*scherma*], F.: SKIRMISH. **-mucciáre**, INTR.: skirmish. **-múccio**† = *-muccia*.
scaraventáre [*s-*, *traventare* (L. *trans*, *ventus*, 'air')], TR.: hurl, throw with force.
scar-bonáre [*s-*, *carbone*], TR.: remove charcoal from. **-bonatúra**, F.: removing charcoal (from charcoal pit).
scarcáre, *poet.* for *-icare*.
scarcer-aménto, M.: release from prison (liberation). ‖**-áre** [*s-*, *carcere*], TR.: release from prison. **-azióne** = *-amento*.
scárco, *poet.* of *scarico*.
scar-dáre [*s-*, *cardo*], TR.: shell (chestnuts). **-dassáre**, TR.: card (wool); give a dressing down (scold). **-dassatóre**, M.: one who cards or combs (wool). **-dassatúra**, F.: carding (combing). **-dassière**, M.: carder (wool-comber). **-dásso**, M.: card (to comb wool, etc.).
scár-dine†, M., **-dova**, F.: sort of fresh water fish.
scarferóne†, M.: buskin (half-boot).
scári-ca, F.: unloading; landing; volley. **-ca=baríli**, M.: boy's play. **-cal=ásino** [*al*, *a*. .], M.: carrying on the shoulders (children's play); game at draughts†. **-ca=miràcoli**, M.: fibber; prater; quack. ‖**-cáre** [*s-*, *caricare*], TR.: unload (DISCHARGE); unbend; let fly; fire off (shoot); fulfil (satisfy): — *la coscienza*, ease one's conscience; — *il ventre*, unload one's stomach. **-catóio**, M.: landing-place (wharf); store-house; mart. **-catóre**, M.: unloader. **-catúra**, F.: unloading.
-cazióne†, F.: unloading (discharge).
scári-co, ADJ.: unloaded (discharged, eased); free; clear; serene (cheerful); M.: unloading, discharge; dump.
scarifi-cáre [L.], TR.: scarify. **-catóre**, M.: scarificator, scarifier. **-cazióne**, F.: scarification; incision.
scar-lattína, F.: scarlet-fever. **-lattíno**, ‖**-látto** [? Pers. *sakirlât*], M.: scarlet cloth; ADJ.: of scarlet-colour, scarlet.
scarmána† = *scalmana*.
scarmi-gliáre [? *s-*, *carminare*], TR.: rumple (ruffle, entangle); REFL.: struggle, take each other by the hair. **-gliatúra**, F.: rumpling (ruffling, entangling).
scármo†, M.: oar-peg (oar-pin).
scar-naménto, M.: scarification. ‖**-náre** [*s-*, *carne*], TR.: cut the flesh from the surface of; scarify; REFL.: lose one's flesh (grow lean). **-nasciaiáre**, INTR.: feast (banquet). **-natóio**, M.: flesh-scraper. **-natíno**, ADJ.: pink-coloured (flesh-coloured). **-natúra**, F.: scarification. **-nicciáre**, TR.: lance (scarify). **-nificáre**, TR.: cut the flesh off (divest of flesh); peel. **-níre**, TR.: cut the flesh off; INTR.: get lean. **-níto** = *-no*. **-nitúra**, F.: cutting off of flesh. **-no**, ADJ.: fleshless; emaciated (lean).
scarnovaláre [*s-*, *carnovale*], INTR.: enjoy the carnival.
scáro [Gr. *skáros*], M.: parrot-fish (scarus).
scarognáre [*s-*, *carogna*], INTR.: be untidy (slovenly).
scár-pa [Scand. *skarp*, SHARP], F.: (low) shoe; SCARP (slope of a ditch); brake (of a wheel): *a* —, sloping. **-páccia**, *disp.* of *-pa*. **-páre**, TR.: slope. **-páta**, F.: blow with a shoe.
scarpell. . = *scalpell*. .
scar-pétta, *dim.* of *-pa*. **-pettáccia**, *disp. dim.* of *-petta*. **-pettína**, **-pettíno**, *dim.* of *-petta*. **-pettóne**†, *aug.* of *-petto*. **-picciáre**, INTR.: shuffle, scrape the feet along. **-píccio**, pl. *—ii*, M.: continuous shuffling. **-pína**, **-píno**, *dim.* of *-pa*.
scarpióne [*scorpione*], M.: scorpion; SCULPIN.
scar-poncèllo, M.: low shoe. ‖**-póne**, *aug.* of *-pa*.
scar-rièra† [*s-*, *c*. .], F.: gang of vagabonds: *per* —, by good-luck. **-rieráre**, INTR.: change from one course to another.
scar-rozzáre [*s-*, *carrozza*], INTR.: ride in a coach. **-rozzáta**, F.: coach-ride. **-rozzío**, pl. *—ii*, M.: noisy, continuous coach-riding.
scarru-colaménto, M.: movement produced by pulleys. ‖**-coláre** [*s-*, *carrucola*], INTR.: run on the pulley; slip. **-coláto**, ADJ.: slipped; running; voluble

-colío, pl. —*ii*, M.: a continuous running of the pulley.

scarsaménte [-*so*], ADV.: scarcely (sparingly, poorly).

scarsapépe†, F.: wild marjoram (origan).

scarseggiáre [-*so*], INTR.: be short of (want); be stingy.

scar-sèlla [ak. to *sciarpa*], F.: pocket-purse. **-sellétta, -sellína**, F.: *dim.* of *-sella;* small pocket. **-sellóna**, F.: *aug.* of *-sella;* large pocket or purse.

scar-sétto, ADJ.: thin (slender, fine, delicate). **-sézza**, F.: scarcity; stinginess†. **-sità**, F.: scarcity; savingness (sparingness, penury). ||**scár-so** [l. L. *s-carpsus* (*carpere*, pluck)], ADJ.: SCARCE (stinted, stingy, niggardly); light; M.: scarcity (rarity, want): — *di danaro*, short of money.

scar-tabelláre, TR.: read carelessly, glance over. ||**-tabèllo**† [Sp. *carta-pel*, 'paper-of-skin' note; trashy notes], M.: worthless book.

scartafáccio [*carta, fascio*], M.: stitched book; quire.

scar-taménto, M.: discarding. ||**-táre** [*s-*, *carta*], TR.: take from the paper; disCARD (throw out of one's hand; cast off, reject). **-táta**, F.: discarding (refusal); refuse. **-to**, M.: discarding; refuse; rebuff; useless papers.

scar-toccciáre, TR.: take from the bag. ||**-tòccio** [= *cartoccio*], M.: paper cornet; lamp-chimney; (*arch.*) cone.

scárzo†, ADJ.: nimble (quick); slender.

scasáre [*s-*, *casa*], TR.: turn out of the house.

scáṣimo [?], M.: (*fam.*) endearments.

scas-sáre [*s-*, *cassa*], TR.: unpack, break open; grub up. **-sáta**, F.: breaking (ploughing). **-satína**, *dim.* of *-sata.* **-satúra**, F.: uncasing (taking out of a chest). **-sináre**, TR.: smash (shatter, ruin, destroy). **-so**, M.: breaking; grubbing up (tillage).

scastagnáre†, TR.: shuffle (evade); avoid (difficulties).

scatalúffo†, M.: rap (cuff).

scataròṣcio [?], M.: heavy shower of rain.

-tar-ráre [*s-*, *catarro*], INTR.: spit; [...]egm. **-ráta**, F.: spitting, spittle.

[...]árso = *catarzo.*

[...]lláto†, ADJ.: duped (laughed at).

[...]naménto, M.: unchaining. ||**-ná-** [...], *catena*], TR.: unchain (unfetter); [...]: burst one's chains (break loose, [...]out).

[...]la [?], F.: box: — *da tabacco*, [...]box; *dire a lettere di* —, speak [...] and freely. **-láio**, M.: box-mak[...]ller of boxes. **-létta**, *dim.* of *-la*.

-lièro† = *-laio*. **-líno** = *-letta*. **-ló-na, -lóne**, *aug.* of *-la*.

scat-táre [*s-*, L. *captare*, CATCH], INTR.: spring, snap; fly loose (get unbent; snap); run out; ESCAPE; lack. **-tatélo**†, M.: notch or nut of a bow.

scattiváre [*s-*, *cattivo*], TR.: remove the bad or spoiled portions of.

scátto [*-tare*], M.: flying loose (unbending); discrepance.

scaturiènte [*-turire*], ADJ.: spouting out.

scatu-rígine, F.: source (spring). **-riménto**, M.: spouting out, springing up. ||**-ríre** [L.], INTR.: spring, spout out; rise.

scáuro [L. *-rus*], M.: flamingo.

scaval-cáre [*s-*, *cavallo*], TR.: dismount, unhorse (a cavalier); supplant; INTR.: dismount (from a horse). **-catóre**, M.: who dismounts; supplanter. **-láre**, INTR.: trot or run about.

sca-vaménto, M.: excavation (digging). ||**-váre** [*s-*, *cavo*], TR.: excavate (dig). **-vatóre**, M.: digger (delver, miner). **-vatúra, -vazióne**, F.: excavation, digging.

scavez-zacòllo [*collo*], M.: breakneck fall (dangerous fall); jeopardy (peril); dissolute man: *a* —, rashly (precipitately, desperately). ||**-záre** [*scapezzare*], TR.: break; unhalter, overstrain. **-záto, -zo**, ADJ.: broken, overstrained; trifling.

scavitoláre† = *scavizzolare*.

scávo†, M.: cavity (hollow, ditch, pit).

scavizzoláre [?], INTR.: rummage (ransack, search); TR.: search out.

scazzáta [?], F.: (*pop.*) lucky hit.

scazzelláre†, INTR.: toy (frolic, play).

ṣcè-da [*scheda*], F.: raillery (joke, foolishness); PL.: minutes. **-dáto**, ADJ.: railing (satirical). **-deria**†, F.: nonsense (mockery).

ṣce-gliménto, M.: choice (selection; picking). ||**ṣcé-gliere** [L. *ex-eligere*], IRR. §; TR.: SELECT (choose); pitch upon; divide (separate). **-glitíccio**, M.: refuse (siftings, *pl.*). **-glitóre**, M., **-glitríce**, F.: chooser (picker).

§ Ind.: Pres. *scèlgo, scègli, scèglie; scegliámo, scegliéte, scèlgono.* Pret. *scèl-si, -se; -sero.* Fut. *sceglierò* (*scerrò*). Subj.: Pres. *scèlga.* I've *scègli.* Part. *scèlto.* — Poet. forms: Pres. *scè-glio, -gliono.* (Subj.) *scèglia.*

ṣcèicco [Ar. *scheikh*], M.: SHEIK.

ṣceler. .† = *sceller. .*

ṣcelle-rággine, -ratággine, F.: wickedness (villany). **-rataménte**, ADV.: wickedly (maliciously). **-ratézza**, F.: wickedness (villany). ||**-ráto** [L. *sceleratus*], ADJ.: criminal (wicked, villanous); M.: scoundrel (Eng.† SCELERAT). **-rità**† = *-ratezza*. **-róso**† = *-rato*.

ṣcellíno [Ger. *schilling*], M.: SHILLING.

scèlo† (*poet.*) = *scelleratezza.*
scél-si, PRET. of *scegliere.* **-ta**, F.: choice (selection); flower (best): *a sua* —, to one's mind; *far* —, choose (select). **-tézza**, F.: selectness (exquisiteness). ||**scél-to**, PART. of *scegliere;* SELECT (chosen, choice). **-túme**, M.: refuse (trash, cast-off).
sce-maménto, M.: diminution (reduction). **-máre**, TR.: diminish; cause to decay. **-matóre**, M.: diminisher (abater). ||**scé-mo** [L. *semus* (*semi-*, half)], ADJ.: diminished (decreased); wanting (deficient; not full); silly (foolish); M.: diminution (reduction, decrease): *luna -ma*, waning moon.
scem-piággine, F.: foolishness (stupidity). **-piáre**, TR.: 1. explain (make simple, unfold, interpret); 2. rack (torture)†. **-piatággine**, F.: foolishness (silliness). **-piataménte**, ADJ.: foolishly; confusedly. **-piáto**, ADJ.: unfolded; foolish. **-pietà**, **-piézza**, F.: folly, simplicity. ||**scém-pio** 1 [L. *simplus*], ADJ.: SIMPLE (not double); single; silly (imbecile); M.: fool (imbecile).
scémpio 2 [*esempio*], M.: torture (rack); slaughter.
scè-na [L.], F.: scene (stage, theatre); play†. **-náccia**, F.: *disp.* of *-na;* bad scene. **-nário**, M.: actor's guide (book); play-bill; side-scenes (decorations, *pl.*). **-náta**, F.: (violent) scene (curtain-lecture).
scén-dere [L. *descendere*], IRR. §; INTR.: descend (be descended); go down (lower in price). **-díbile**, ADJ.: easy to descend. **-diménto**, M.: descent; declivity.
§ Pret. *scé-si, -se; -sero.* Part. *scéso.*
sce-neggiaménto, M.: representing by scenery (representing upon the stage). **-neggiáre**, TR.: represent by scenery (represent upon the stage). **-neggiatúra**, F.: scenic effect. ||**-nétta**, F.: *dim.* of *-na;* little scene or play. **-nicaménto**, ADV.: in a theatrical manner. **scè-nico**, pl. —*ci*, ADJ.: scenic (theatrical). **-nografía** [*-na*, Gr. *gráphein*], F.: scenography. **-nográfico**, ADJ.: scenographic. **-nògrafo**, M.: scenograph.
scèntre†, M.: knowledge.
sceriffo [Eng. *sheriff*], M.: sheriff.
scèr-nere [L. *discernere*], IRR. §; TR.: discern (distinguish); choose (select). **-niménto**†, M.: discernment (selecting, pitching upon). **-níre**† = *-nere.*
§ Pret. *scèr-si, -se; -sero.* Part. lacking.
scer-páre, TR.: tear away (lacerate); REFL.: be broken (be lacerated). **-páto**, ADJ.: broken (lacerated).
scerpel-láto, ||**-líno** [*cerpellino* (*cispa*)], ADJ.: blear-eyed (bloodshot); distorted. **-lóne**, *M.: great blunder.*
scérre = *scegliere.*
scervel-láre [*s-*, *cervello*], TR.: rack the brains about. **-láto**, ADJ.: hare-brained (half-witted).
scé-sa [*scendere*], F.: descent (declivity); whim; flux of humours†; rheum (cold)†. **-si**, PRET. of *scendere.* **-so**, PART. of *scendere;* descended; issued.
scet-ticísmo, M.: scepticism. ||**scèt-tico** [Gr. *skeptikós*], ADJ.: sceptical; M.: sceptic.
scet-tráto, ADJ.: sceptred. ||**scèt-tro** [L. *sceptrum*], M.: sceptre.
sce-veraménto, M.: separating (separation). ||**-veráre** [*separare*], TR.: SEVER (separate); wean. **-veráta**†, F.: separating (severing). **-verataménte**, ADV.: separately (asunder). **-veratóio**, M.: separator works. **-veratóre**, M.: separator (divider). **scé-vero**† = *scevro.* **-vráre**† = *-verare.* **-vrataménte**† = *-veratamente.* **scé-vro**, ADJ.: severed; weaned; free from (lacking in).
schè-da [L. (Gr. *skízein*, split)], F.: bit of paper (serving as a note, etc.); note (billet); poll-ticket (ballot). **-dário**, M.: collection of notes or tickets. **schè-dula**†, F.: little note.
scheg-gétta, *dim.* of *-gia.* ||**schég-gia** [L. *schidia* (Gr. *skízein*, split)], F.: chip (splinter); crag; stem (of a tree)†. **-giále**†, M.: leather girdle. **-giáre**, TR.: make chips of; cleave (shatter, shiver); REFL.: burst in pieces (be shattered, be shivered). **-giaménto**, M.: cleaving (chipping, shattering). **-giatúra**, F.: chip; shatter (splinter). **schég-gio**†, M.: cliff (rock); splinter. **-giòla**, *dim.* of *-gia.* **-gióne**, M.: great reef; large splinter. **-gióso**, ADJ.: splintery (broken); craggy (rugged). **-giuòla**, **-giúzza**, F.: little splinter.
schele-tráme, M.: heap of skeletons. **-trizzáto**, ADJ.: worn to a skeleton. ||**schèle-tro** [Gr. *skeletón*], M.: skeleton.
schèma [Gr.], M.: scheme (plan, outline).
scheneíre†, TR., INTR.: go sloping; shrink; swerve.
scheráno [?], M.: assassin (brigand).
scheranzía† = *squinanzia*, F.: quinsy.
schèretro† = *scheletro.*
schericáto†, ADJ.: degraded (from priesthood).
schér-ma [OGer. *skerm*, 'shield'], F.: fencing: *maestro di* —, fencing-master. **-máglia**, F.: strife (quarrel, skirmish). **-máre** = *-mire.* **-migliáre**, TR.: rumple (the hair). **-míre**, INTR.: fence; REFL.: defend one's self (shield one's self). **-míta**†, F.: fencing. **-mitóre**, M.: fencing-master; swordsman. **schér-mo**, M.: defence; PL.: weapons.

schermágio†, M.: skirmish.
schér-na† = *-zo*. **-névole**, ADJ.: scornful (contemptuous). **-nevolménte**, ADV.: scornfully. **-niménto†**, M.: scorn (mockery). **-níre**, TR.: scorn (deride). **-nitívo†**, ADJ.: deriding (insulting). **-nitóre**, M., **-nitríce**, F.: scorner (scoffer). ||**schér-no** [OGer. *skern*], M.: SCORN (derision): *avere a —*, scorn; *prendere a —*, laugh at (deride).
scherzòla, F.: (*bot.*) skirret.
scher-záccio, M.: *disp.* of *-zo*, unpleasant joke. **-zaménto†**, M.: play (jest, pleasantry). **-zánte**, ADJ.: playful (jesting). **-záre**, INTR.: dally (play, sport); jest (joke, banter). **-zatóre**, M., **-zatríce**, F.: jester (banterer, wag). **-zétto**, M.: *dim.* of *-zo;* little jest (little sport). **-zévole**, ADJ.: pleasant (playful). **-zevolménte**, ADV.: in a playful manner (jestingly). ||**schér-zo** [Ger. *scherz*], M.: pleasantry (raillery, jest, sport): *da —*, in jest. **-zosaménte**, ADV.: facetiously (in jest). **-zosétto**, ADJ.: *dim.* of *-zoso;* a little playful. **-zóso**, ADJ.: playful (jocular, pleasant). **-zúccio**, M.: *dim.* of *-zo;* little joke.
schiác-cia, F.: brick trap (for birds, pitfall); wooden leg. **-ciaménto**, M.: crushing (squashing, contusion). **-cia=nóci**, M. INVAR.: nut-cracker. ||**-ciáre** [OGer. *klackjan*, break], TR.: crush (bruise, flatten); trample upon. **-ciáta**, F.: thin hard cake; scotch (thin oaten bread). **-ciatína**, F.: *dim.* of *-ciata;* small thin cake. **-ciáto**, ADJ.: crushed (bruised): *naso —*, flat nose. **-ciatúra**, F.: crushing (squashing). **-ciòla**, F.: fluting iron; crimping iron.
schi-affáre, TR.: cuff (slap), throw; push. **-affeggiáre**, TR.: give a slap on the face (cuff, box). ||**-áffo** [Ger. *schlappe*], M.: SLAP (box, cuff).
schia-mazzáre [freq. of L. *clamare*], INTR.: cackle; cry out (clamour). **-mazzatóre**, M.: brawler. **-mazzío**, **-mázzo**, M.: noise (brawling); bird-call; lure.
schian-cíana†, F.: diagonal line. **-'cio†**, M.: slope (oblique direction): *a —*, in bias (awry, athwart). **-círe†**, TR.: strike obliquely.
schian-taménto, M.: snapping off. ||**-táre** [?], TR.: snap off (burst, crack, split); brag. **-tatúra**, F.: snapping (break). **-tettíno**, M.: snap; fillip. **-to**, M.: snapping off (cracking, burst); crash (crack, peal); great noise.
schiánza†, F.: scab (scurf).
schiáp-pa†, F.: rolling-pin. **-páre†**, TR.: cleave, split (wood).
schia-ráre [*chiaro*], TR.: clear up (elucidate, explain); INTR.: become clear (clear up, brighten). **-ratóre**, M.: elucidator (explainer). **-rèa†**, F.: (*bot.*) clary (all-heal). **-riménto**, M.: clearing up (explaining). **-ríre**, TR.: clear up (illustrate, explain); INTR.: get clear; get thin; appear.
schiassáre [*s-*, *chiasso*], INTR.: be noisy (uproarious).
schiátta [OGer. *slahta* (= Ger. *geschlecht*)], F.: race (progeny).
schiat-táre [OGer. *skleizza*, SLIT], INTR.: burst. **-tíre** [?], INTR.: yelp (bark); squeak. **-tóna†**, F.: sturdy woman.
schiáva [*-vo*], F.: female slave.
schiavacciáre [*s-*, *chiavaccio*], TR.: unbolt (open); rattle the bolt.
schia-váccio, M.: (*pop.*) slave. **-vésco†**, ADJ.: of a slave (servile). **-vétta**, *dim.* of *-va*. **-vétto**, *dim.* of *-vo*. **-vína**, F.: slave's frock; pilgrim's robe. **-vitù**, **-vitúdine**, F.: slavery (servitude; bondage); bonds (chains, *pl.*).
schiá-vo [Ger. *sklave*], M.: SLAVE; captive; ADJ.: obliged (obsequious, most obedient): *venti -vi*, south-east winds. **-volíno†**, M.: *dim.* of *-vo*, little slave; young slave. **-vóne†**, M.: strong slave.
schiazzamáglia†, F.: rascality; rabble.
schicche-ra=cárte, M.: ignorant scribbler. **-raménto**, M.: daubing; scribbling; speaking openly; reporting. ||**-ráre** [?], TR.: daub; scribble; say openly; report. **-ratúra**, F.: daubing; scribbling; speaking openly; reporting. **-río**, M.: continuous scribbling, etc.
schi-dionáre, TR.: broach (spit meat). **-dionáta**, F.: spitful (as much as a spit will hold). ||**-dióne** [Gr. *-sion*], M.: spit (broach).
schiè-na [? OGer. *skina*, needle], F.: spine (backbone); croup; ridge. **-náccia**, *disp.* of *-na*. **-nále**, M.: back, croup.
schienanzía†, F.: quinsy.
schienèlla†, F.: wind-gall (a disease); trouble.
schie-nína, *dim.* of *-na*. **-núto**, ADJ.: strong-backed; sturdy.
schiè-ra [OGer. *scara*], F.: armed host (troop, band); body; herd; mass: *a —*, in troops, by bands; *— a —*, troop after troop; *far —*, set in array. **-raménto**, M.: arraying; battle-array. **-ráre**, TR.: draw up in line of battle.
schiericáre [*s-*, *chierico*], REFL.: cease being priest (doff the priestly habit).
schiet-taménte, ADV.: honestly; plainly (ingenuously, frankly, openly). **-tézza**, F.: uprightness; ingenuousness (frankness, sincerity). ||**schiét-to** [OGer. *sleht* (= Ger. *schlicht*)], ADJ.: plain (pure, unmixed); clean (neat); honest (sincere).

schi-falpòco, ADJ.: shy; prudish. **-fa-ménte**, ADV.: filthily (dirtily); timidly. **-faménto**†, M., **-fánza**†, F.: aversion; disdain (contempt). ||**-fáre** [*-fo* 2], TR.: shun (avoid, elude); refuse; loathe (abhor); REFL.: loathe; nauseate. **-fatóre**, M.: avoider; disapprover.

schifétto, *dim.* of *schifo* 1.

schi-févole† [*-fo* 2], ADJ.: despising (loathing); tired. **-fézza**, F.: nastiness; loathing (disgust); delicacy (daintiness)†; prudishness†. **-filtà**, F.: coyness (affected modesty, prudery); disgust (reluctance, aversion, loathing). **-filtóso**, ADJ.: shy (coy); difficult.

schífo 1 [Ger. *skif*], M.: SKIFF (small boat).

schí-fo 2 [Ger. *scheu*, SHY], ADJ.: repugnant (nauseous, disgusting, nasty); shy (coy, modest)†; over-nice†; discreet†: *prendere a* —, take a distaste for; *venire a* —, be disgusted with. **-fosaménte**, ADV.: nastily (disgustingly). **-fosità**, F.: nastiness; disagreeableness. **-fóso**, ADJ.: nasty (disgusting, nauseating, disagreeable).

schim-bèscore, ||**-bèscio** [*sghembo*], ADJ.: bandy-legged.

schinanzía†, F.: quinsy.

schinchimúrra†, F.: imaginary monster.

schínciot†, ADJ.: oblique (cross).

schinèlla†, F.: wind-gall.

schi-nièra† = *-niere*. ||**-nière** [OGer. *skina*, 'leg'], M.: greaves, leg-piece.

schiocc-cáre [*s-*, *chiocco*], TR.: crack; smack. **schiòc-co**, M.: crack (smack).

schioda=crísti, M.: hypocrite. ||**schio-dá-re** [*s-*, *chiodo*], TR.: unnail. **-túra**, F.: unnailing.

schiomáre [*s-*, *chioma*], TR.: disorder (the hair).

schiop-pettáta, F.: musket-shot. **-pet-tería**, F.: quantity of small guns. **-pet-tière**, M.: fusileer. **-pétto**, *dim.* of *-po*. ||**schiòp-po** [L. *stloppus*, 'slap'], M.: gun (musket): — *a capsola*, percussion-gun.

schippíre†, INTR.: slip away.

schiribìzzo = *ghiribizzo*.

schí-sa†, F.: *per* —, across (crossways). ||**-sáre** [Gr. *schízein*, 'divide'], TR.: reduce (to fractions). **-so**, M.: reduction to fractions; slant. **-sto**, M.: SCHIST. **-stóso**, ADJ.: schistose.

schitar-raménto, M.: guitar playing. ||**-ráre** [*s-*, *chitarra*], INTR.: drum on the guitar.

s=chiúdere, IRR.; TR.: disclose; open; INTR.: expand (as flowers, bloom).

schiú-ma [OGer. *scum*], F.: froth (SCUM, foam); dross. **-máre**, TR.: skim; INTR.: froth (foam). **-matóio**, M.: skimming ladle. **-móso**, ADJ.: frothy (foaming).

schiú-so, PART. of *-dere*; disclosed; opened.

schi-vábile, ADJ.: avoidable. **-váre**, TR.: avoid (shun). ||**schí-vo** [*-fo*], ADJ.: shy (retiring, bashful); reserved; modest; tiresome; gloomy.

schiz-zaménto†, M.: gushing out. ||**-zá-re** [?], TR.: SKETCH; INTR.: gush out; rush. **-záta**† F.: gush, dash. **-zatóio**, M.: syringe (squirt). **-zettáre**, TR.: syringe (squirt); inject. **-zettáta**, **-zet-tatúra**, F.: syringing (squirting); injection. **-zettíno**, *dim.* of *-zetto*. **-zétto**, M.: *dim.* of *-zo*; small syringe.

schizzi-nosaménte, ADV.: prudishly; disdainfully; harshly. **-gnóso**, ||**-nóso** [?], ADJ.: cynical; disdainful; contrary (indisposed, difficult).

schízzo [*-zzare*], M.: splash; sprinkling (mixture); dash (of the pen); rough sketch (outline).

scía 1 [Fr. *scie*, 'saw'], F.: ship's track.

scià 2 [Pers. *shâh*], M.: SHAH (Pers. king).

sciábica†, F.: fishing net.

sciá-bla = *-bola*. ||**sciá-bola** [Ger. *säbel*], F.: saber; scimitar. **-boláre**, TR.: saber. **-boláta**, F.: saber-blow.

sciabor-dáre [?], TR.: stir (a liquid); shake (roil, trouble). **-dío**, M.: roiling (shaking).

sciacállo [Turk. *schakal*], M.: JACKAL.

sciáccora†, F.: young woodcock.

sciacqua=bócca, F.: rinsing bowl. **=bu-dèlla**, M.: gulp: *bevere a* —, gulp. **=dènti**, M.: light breakfast with a glass of wine. ||**sciacquá-re** [*s-*, L. *aquare*], TR.: rinse (wash). **sciaquá-ta**, F.: quick rinse. **-tína**, *dim.* of *-ta*. **-túra**, F.: rinsing; dish-water.

sciaguat-taménto, M.: shaking (of fluids). ||**-táre** [? L. *suc-cutere*], TR.: shake (fluids); wash (lave).

sciagú-ra [*s-*, *auguria*], F.: misfortune (disaster). **-ránza**, F.: wickedness (baseness); wretchedness. **-ratáccio**, *disp.* of *-rato*. **-ratággine** = *-ranza*. **-ra-taménte**, ADV.: wretchedly (miserably); basely; unluckily. **-ratèllo**, ADJ.: *disp. dim.* of *-rato*; M.: little wretch. **-raté-za**, F.: rascality (wickedness); wretchedness. **-ráto**, ADJ.: wretched (miserable); base (wicked); pitiful (sorry); M.: wretched, etc., fellow. **-ratóne**, *aug.* of *-rato*.

scialac-quaménto, M.: prodigality (profusion). **-quánte**, ADJ.: lavish (prodigal); M.: spendthrift. ||**-quáre** [? *scialare*], TR.: lavish (squander). **-quata-ménte**, ADV.: profusely (lavishly). **-qua-tóre**, M.: prodigal (spendthrift, waster). **-quatúra**†, F.: prodigality (wasting).

scialac-quío, **scialác-quo**, M.: prfusion (waste). **-quóna**, F., **-quóne**, M.: prodigal (spendthrift).

şcialaménto [*-lare*], M.: pomp, display.

şcialándo†, M.: flat boat.

şcialáppa [Mex. *xalapa*], F.: JALAP (*med.* plant).

şcia-láre [L. *exhalare*], TR.: EXHALE†; evaporate; dissipate, have good time. **-latóre**, M.: exhaler; dissipator; feaster.

şcial-báre [L. *ex-albare*], TR.: whitewash; plaster (walls). **-batúra**, F.: whitewashing; plastering; rough-cast. **şciál-bo**, ADJ.: whitewashed; pale, wan.

şcialíva [L. *saliva*], F.: spittle (saliva).

şciál-le [Ar. *schâl*], M.: SHAWL. **-lettíno**, *dim.* of *-letto.* **-létto**, M.: *dim.* of *-le;* little shawl. **-lóne**, M.: *aug.* of *-le;* large shawl.

şciá-lo [*-lare*], M.: exhalation (vapour)†; display; extravagance (luxury). **-lóne**, M.: great spendthrift.

şcialúppa [Dutch *sloep*], F.: shallop: — *cannoniera*, gunboat.

şciaman-náre [*s-*, *manna*], TR.: be slovenly (disorderly). **-náto**, ADJ.: ill-built; awkward; slovenly: *alla -nata*, in a slovenly manner.

şcia-máre, INTR.: swarm. ||**şciá-me** [L. *examen* (*exagmen; ex-igo*, 'drive out')], M.: swarm (of bees); crowd.

şciámito [Gr. *hexá-mitos*, 'six-thread'], M.: kind of cloth; amaranth (flower).

şciámma [Ethiop.], M.: kind of large Abyssinian shawl.

şciámo = *-me.*

şciampágna [Fr. *Champagne*], F., M.: champagne (wine).

şciampiáre†, TR.: enlarge; widen.

şcian-cáre [*s-*, *ancare*], INTR.: be hip-shot. **-cáto**, ADJ.: hip-shot; lame. **-catamente**, ADV.: limpingly.

şciánto [?], M.: relaxation.

şciapi-díre†, INTR.: grow insipid or dull. **şciápi-do**†, ADJ.: insipid.

şciaráda [?], F.: CHARADE.

şciaráppa = *-lappa.*

şciáre [L. *secare*, cut], INTR.: cut or plough the wave.

şciár-pa [Ger. *schärpe*], F.: sash (official's scarf); lady's SCARF; PL.: tatters; gang†. **-pétta**, **-pettína**, *dim.* of *-pa.*

şciarpel-láre†, TR.: make blear-eyed. **-láto**†, ADJ.: blear-eyed. **-líno**†, ADJ.: blear-eyed.

şciár-ra†, F.: brawl (squabble). **-raménto**†, M.: routing (dispersing). **-ráre**†, TR.: rout (disperse). ||**-ráta** [?], F.: -uting (defeat); strife (quarrel).

-tica, F.: sciatica (hip-gout). ||**şciá-** [Gr. *ischion*, 'hip-joint'], ADJ.: sci- (having the hip-gout).

şciátta†, F.: ship's boat; small boat, canoe.

şciat-tággine, F.: unfitness. **-tamente**, ADV.: in a slovenly manner. **-táre**, TR.: ruin (spoil). **-tería**, **-tézza**, F.: slovenliness; misconduct (immodesty). ||**şciát-to** [? L. *exaptus*], ADJ.: slovenly; simple.

şciaur. .† = *sciagur. .*

şciávero [? *sciare*], M.: chip (trimming); remnant.

şcíbile [L. *scibilis* (*scire*, know)], ADJ.: knowable; M.: all that can be known.

şcièn-te [L. *-s* (*scire*, know)], ADJ.: knowing (learned). **-temente**, ADV.: learnedly (knowingly, wittingly). **-tificamente**, ADV.: scientifically. **-tífico**, ADJ.: scientific (learned, erudite). **-tremente**, ADV.: on purpose. **şcièn-za**, **şcièn-zia** [L. *scientia*], F.: science (knowledge, learning, erudition). **-ziataménte**, ADV.: in a scientific manner. **-ziáto**, ADJ.: learned (erudite); M.: man of science (scholar). **-ziuòla**, F.: little science (limited knowledge).

şcificáre†, TR.: foretell.

ş=cígnere†, IRR.; TR.: ungird; untie.

şcigrignáta†, F.: gash (slash).

şciléoca [?], F.: joke; trifle.

şcilin-guágnolo [**sub-linguaneus* (L. *lingua*, TONGUE)], M.: string or ligament of the tongue. **-guáre**, INTR.: stammer; lisp. **-guataménto**, ADV.: stammeringly; lispingly. **-guatèllo**, *irr.* *dim.* of *-gualo.* **-guáto**, ADJ.: stammering; lisping. **-guatóre**, M.: stammerer; lisper. **-guatúra**, F.: stammered word.

şcilíva [*scialiva*], F.: saliva.

şcíl-la [L.], F.: Scylla: *essere tra* — *Cariddi*, be between Scylla and Charybdis.

şcillòcco = *scirocco.*

şcillòma [?], F.: tedious speech (tiresome verbiage).

şci-loppáre, TR.: give syrup; coax (wheedle). **-loppáto**, ADJ.: fed with syrup; wheedled (cajoled). ||**-lòppo** [*-roppo*], M.: SYRUP.

şcímia†, etc. = *scimmia*, etc.

şcimitár-ra [fr. Pers.], F.: scimitar (sabre). **-ráta**, F.: sabre-stroke.

şcím-mia [L. *simia*, *simius*], F.: ape (monkey); PL.: apes (SIMIA). **-miático**†, ADJ.: apish, simious. **-mieggiáre**, INTR.: ape (mimic). **-miésco**, ADJ.: apelike, simious. **-miétta**, *dim.* of *-mia.* **-mióne**, *aug.* of *-mia.* **-miottáre** = *-mieggiare.* **-miòtto**, M.: *dim.* of *-mia:* *fare lo* —, ape, mimic.

şcimpanzé [Afric.], M.: chimpanzee.

şci-munitággine, F.: silliness (foolishness, imbecility). **-munitamente**, ADV.: sillily (foolishly). **-munitèllo**, ADJ.

dim. of *-munito;* somewhat silly; M.: little fool. ‖**-munito** [?], ADJ.: foolish (imbecile).

scindere [L.], IRR. §; TR.: divide (separate).

§ Pret. *scis-si, -se; -sero.* Part. *scisso.*

s=cingere, IRR.; TR.: ungird; untie.

scintil-la [L.], F.: spark (sparkle). **-láccia**, *disp.* of *-la.* **-laménto**, M.: sparkling (twinkling). **-láre**, INTR.: sparkle (twinkle). **-lazióne**, F.: scintillation, sparkling. **-létta**, F.: little spark; feeble light.

scinto, PART. of *-gere.*

sciò [? L. *ex hoc*], INTERJ.: shoo!

scioc-cáccio, M.: *disp.* of *-co;* great simpleton. **-cággine**, F.: foolishness, folly. **-caménte**, ADV.: foolishly, sillily. **-cheggiáre**†, INTR.: play the fool, act foolishly; talk foolish things. **-cherèllo**, ADJ.: *dim.* of *-co;* somewhat foolish; M.: little fool. **-chería, -chézza**, F.: foolishness (stupidity, silly thing, folly). **-chino**, ADJ.: *dim.* of *-co;* somewhat foolish. ‖**sciòc-co** [*s-*, L. *sucus*, 'juice'], ADJ.: insipid (silly, foolish); M.: silly fellow. **-conáccio**, ADJ.: *disp.* of *-cone;* very foolish. **-cóne**, M.: great fool (great booby).

scio-glíbile, ADJ.: capable of being untied, dissolved or accomplished. ‖**sciò-gliere** [*s-*, L. *solvere*], IRR. §; TR.: untie (loosen); dissolve; absolve; fulfil (accomplish); REFL.: free one's self from, get rid of: — *il ventre,* open the bowels; — *un voto,* pay a vow. **-gliménto**, M.: untying; explanation; dissoluteness (licence); diarrhœa; tumult (sedition, dissolution)†. **-glitóre**, M.: who unties; explainer.

§ Ind.: Pres. *sciòlgo, sciògli, sciòglie; scioglíámo, sciogliéte, sciòlgono.* Pret. *sciòl-si, -se; -sero.* Fut. reg. or *sciorrò.* Subj.: Pres. *sciòlga.* Part. *sciòlto.* — Poet. forms: *sciòglio,* etc.

scio-lézza, F.: superficial knowledge; pedantry. ‖**scío-lo** [L. *scire*], M.: sciolist.

sciòl-si, PRET. of *sciogliere.* **sciòl-ta**, F.: diarrhœa. **-taménte**, ADV.: freely (without impediment); nimbly; fluently. **-tézza**, F.: nimbleness (agility); freedom. ‖**sciòl-to**, PART. of *sciogliere;* untied, etc.; ungirt†; unshackled (free, independent); agile (nimble); easy; fluent; liquefied: *a briglia -ta,* with full speed; *libro —,* book in sheets; *versi -ti,* blank verse. **sciò-lvere**†, TR.: breakfast; M.: breakfast.

scio-náta†, F., **scio-ne**†, M.: squall.

sciope-rággine, F.: idleness (laziness, waste of time). **-ralibrái**, M.: sciolist; smatterer. **-raménte**†, M.: idleness (idle labour, loss of time). **-ránte**, M.: striker. ‖**-ráre** [L. *ex-operare*], TR.: keep from working; INTR., REFL.: leave off work (strike); idle. **-ratággine** = *-raggine.* **-rataménte**, ADV.: idly. **-ratézza**, F.: idleness. **-ratívo**†, **-ráto**, ADJ.: idle (unoccupied); sluggish. **-ratonáccio**, *disp.* of *-ratone.* **-ratóne**, M.: *aug.* of *-rato;* very idle fellow (lazy drone). **-río**, M.: idleness (slothfulness, losing time). **sciòpe-ro**, M.: strike (among workmen). **-róne**, M.: drone (stupid fellow).

sciopino†, M.: unhappy accident.

sciopr. .† = *scioper.* .

sciori-naménto, M.: airing (displaying). ‖**-náre** [*s-*, L. *aurare* (*aura*, air)], TR.: air (linen, etc.); display; disclose (divulge); turn over (the leaves of a book); REFL.: open one's clothes (undress); take a little relaxation (rest one's self).

sciòrre = *sciogliere.*

scipáre† = *sciupare.*

sci-pidézza†, F.: insipidity; silliness. **-pidíre**†, INTR.: grow insipid (grow stupid). ‖**scí-pido** [*s-*, *sipido* of *insipido*], ADJ.: INSIPID (tasteless, stupid). **-píre**† = *-pidire.* **-pitággine**, F.: insipidity (tiresomeness). **-pitaménte**, ADV.: insipidly (tastelessly, foolishly). **-pitèllo**, *dim.* of *-pito.* **-pitézza**, F.: insipidity. **-'pito** = *-pido.*

scirignáta†, F.: gash, slash.

sci-ringa†, F.: syringe. **-ringáre**†, TR.: syringe; inject.

sci-roccále, ADJ.: of the sirocco. ‖**-ròcco** [fr. Ar.], M.: sirocco (south-east wind).

sciròppo [Ar. *scharab*], M.: syrup.

scirpo†, M.: reed (rush); sedge.

scír-ro [Gr. *skirrhós*, 'hard'], M.: scirrhus (tumour). **-róso**, ADJ.: scirrhous.

scis-ma [Gr. *schisma* (*schid-*, split)], F.: schism (dissension). **-mático**, ADJ.: schismatic.

scís-si, PRET. of *scindere.* **scis-síle**, ADJ.: scissile (separable). **-sióne**, F.: scission (separation). ‖**scís-so**, PART. of *scindere.* **-súra**, F.: cleft (rent, chink); discord.

sciu-gáre [L. *ex-sucare* (*sucus*, moisture)], TR.: dry (wipe off). **-gatoíno**, *dim.* of *-gatoio.* **-gatóio**, M.: towel; napkin.

sciu-pacchiáre, TR.: waste but little; spoil or tear but little. ‖**-páre** [L. *dissipare* (*supare*, throw)], TR.: waste, (squander, DISSIPATE); spoil; tear; REFL.: waste (spoil, ruin). **-patóre**, M.: waster (spendthrift). **-pináre**, TR.: consume (wear out); destroy (spoil). **-pinío, -pío**, M.: wasting; consuming (wearing out); destruction. **-póne**, M.: squanderer (waster).

sciúttо†, ADJ.: dried (wiped off).

scivo-láre [?], INTR.: hiss; slide (skate). **-láta**, F.: slip (slide). **-létto**, *dim.* of *-lo*. **scívo-lo**, M.: (*mus.*) trill; passage.

sclamá-re [L. *ex-clamare*], INTR.: EXCLAIM (cry out). **-zióne**, F.: exclamation; outcry.

sclarèa [l. L.], F.: (*bot*). clary (all-heal).

scler-òsi [Gr. *sklerós*, hard], F.: sclerosis (induration). **-òtica**, F.: sclerotal.

scoccá-re [*s-*, *cocca*], TR.: let fly; shoot off; INTR.: escape; peep out. **-tóio**†, M.: notch (of a bow). **-tóre**, M., **-tríce**, F.: shooter with a bow (archer).

scoc-ciáre [*s-*, *coccio*], TR.: break (eggs, etc.). **-címo**, M.: egg-breaking (a game).

scóc-co, **-'co** [*-care*], M.: letting fly an arrow (shot); twang; striking (of the hour, stroke): — *dell'alba*, peep of day.

scoccobrínо†, M.: merry-andrew (buffoon).

scoccoláre [*s-*, *coccola*], TR.: pick (berries); scribble; report.

scoccolátо†, ADJ.: sifted; clear (distinct).

scoccoveggiáre†, TR., INTR.: flirt; banter.

scodáre [*s-*, *coda*], TR.: cut off the tail (dock); crop.

scodèl-la [L. *scutella*, salver], F.: soup-plate. **-delláre**, TR.: dish up (the soup); pour out. **-létta**, **-lína**, *dim.* of *-la*. **-líno**, M.: small soup-plate, saucer; powder-pan.

scodinzoláre [*s-*, *codinzolo*], INTR.: wag or shake the tail.

scofacciáre†, TR.: make flat.

scoffína†, F.: file; grater.

scògl̦ia†, F.: slough (cast skin of a serpent); PL.: old rags.

sco-gl̦iácciо, *disp.* of *-glio*. **-gl̦ièra**, F.: mass of naked rocks. **-gl̦iétto**, *dim.* of *-glio*. ‖**scò-gl̦io** [L. *scopulus*], M.: rock (reef); shelf (sand-bank); slough (husk, skin)†. **-gl̦ióso**, ADJ.: rocky (reefy). **-gl̦iúzzo** = *-glietto*.

scognoscènza = *sconoscenza*.

scoiáre [*s-*, *coio* (L. *corium*, skin)], TR.: flay (skin, gall).

scoiáttolo [Gr. *skíouros*], M.: SQUIRREL.

scoláio† = *-lare* 1.

scolaménto [*-lare* 2], M.: flowing (running out).

scò-la [L. *schola*], F.: = *scuola*, school (college); class. **-laráccio**, *disp.* of *-lare* 1. **-lára**, F., **-láre** 1, M.: scholar (learner, student, pupil); apprentice.

scoláre 2, INTR.: flow (run out); drop; drain; trickle.

sco-lareggiáre [*-la*], INTR.: act or play like a scholar. **-larésca**, F.: lot of schoolboys (students, *pl.*). **-larescaménte**, ADV.: scholarly. **-larésco**, ADJ.: of a scholar, of a schoolboy. **-larétta**, *dim.* of *-lara*. **-larétto**, *dim.* of *-lare* 1. **-larína**, *dim.* of *-lara*. **-laríno**, *dim.* of *-lare*. **-larménte**, ADV.: like a scholar. **-larúccio**, *disp.* of *-lare*. **-lástica**, F.: scholastic philosophy. **-lasticaménte**, ADV.: scholastically. **-lasticità**, F.: scholasticism. **-lástico**, ADV.: scholastic, of schools.

scolatívо†, ADJ.: causing to flow.

scola-tóio [*-lare* 2], M.: strainer; drain (sewer). **-túra**, F.: trickling; drained liquid.

scolétta [*-la*], *dim.* of *scuola*.

scoliáste [*-lio*], M.: scholiast (commentator).

scòlimo [L. *-lymos*], M.: thistle.

scòlio [Gr. *schólion*], M.: note (scholium, commentary).

scol-lacciáre [*s-*, *collo*], REFL.: uncover the neck too much. **-lacciáto**, ADJ.: décolleté (with uncovered neck). **-láre**, TR.: unglue (disjoin); uncover the neck. **-latúra** = *-lo*.

scolle-gaménto, M.: disjunction (breaking up). ‖**-gáre** [*s-*, *collegare*], TR.: separate; disunite.

scollináre [*s-*, *collina*], INTR.: go over hills and mountains.

scòllo [*s-*, *collo*], M.: neck-opening in a woman's clothing.

scolmáre [*s-*, *colmo*], TR.: take off the top (an over-full bushel, etc.).

scólo [*-lare* 2], M.: flowing off, running course; draining.

scolopèndra [L.], F.: scolopendra (milliped).

scolo-raménto, M.: loss of colour (paleness). ‖**-ráre** [*s-*, *colore*], TR.: discolour (tarnish); REFL.: lose colour (fade, get pale). **-riménto**, M.: loss of colour (paleness). **-ríre**, INTR., REFL.: grow pale (fade).

scol-paméntо†, M.: exculpation (justification). ‖**-páre** [*s-*, *colpa*], TR.: exculpate (justify). **-páto**, ADJ.: exculpated (justified).

scol-piménto, M.: engraving (carving). ‖**-píre** [L. *sculpere*], IRR. §; TR. (Pret. *-pii* or *sculsi*†): engrave (carve); articulate (pronounce) distinctly. **-pitaménte**, ADV.: distinctly (clearly). **-píto**, ADJ.: engraved (carved); pronounced distinctly. **-pitúra**†, F.: sculpture; impression.

§ Pret. *scolpii* or *scúlsi* (poet.). Part. *scolpito* or *scólto*; *scólto* (poet.)

scól-ta [*ascolta*], F.: sentinel (sentry, watch). **-táre**†, TR.: listen (hearken; attend.

scoltelláre [*s-*, *coltello*], TR.: cut out, weed out; RECIPR.: cut each other with knives.

scól-to [*-pire*], (*poet.*) for *-pito*. **-túra**, F.: sculpture.

scombavárе†, TR.: slaver over (slabber).

scomberèllo†, M.: holy-water sprinkler.

scombiccheráre [?], TR.: scribble.

scombi-náre [*s-*, *combinare*], TR.: discombine; discompose; disorder. **-nazióne**, F.: disorder (confusion).

scómbro [L. *-ber*], M.: mackerel.

scombú-glio, **-iaménto**, M.: confusion (disorder); dispersion; ruin. ‖**-iáre** [*s-*, *buio*], TR.: confuse (disarrange).

scombusso-laménto, M.: confusion. ‖**-láre** [*s-*, *bussola*], TR.: disturb (confuse) greatly, turn topsy-turvy. **-lío**, M.: continued confusion.

scom-méssa, F.: wager: *fare una* —, lay a wager. **-mésso**, PART. of *-mettere*. ‖**-méttere** [*s-*, *c.* .], IRR.; TR.: disjoin; bet (wager). **-mettitóre**, M.: bettor (wagerer); firebrand. **-mettitúra**, F.: wagering; disjuncture. **-mezzáre†**, TR.: divide in two parts.

scommiatáre†, TR.: dismiss; REFL.: take one's leave.

scommodáre = *scomodare*.

scom-mósso, PART. of *-movere*; moved, etc.; in commotion. ‖**-mòvere** [*s-*, *c.* .], IRR.; TR.: stir up; raise. **-moviménto**, M.: commotion (ferment). **-movitóre**, M.: disturber of the peace. **-movizióne†**, F.: revolt (rising). **-muòvere** = *-movere*.

scomo-daménte, ADV.: inconveniently (tiresomely). ‖**-dáre** [*s-*, *comodo*], TR.: discommode (trouble, disturb); tease: *non si -di*, don't trouble yourself. **-dáto**, ADJ.: disturbed (troubled); vexed; unwell. **-dézza†**, **-dità**, F.: inconvenience (trouble); disadvantage; indisposition.

scòmo-do, ADJ.: incommodious; inconvenient; tiresome; M.: inconvenience; pain.

scompagi-naménto, M.: disorder. ‖**-náre** [*s-*, *compagine*], TR.: disarrange (disorder); disjoint; unhinge. **-natúra**, **-nazióne**, F.: disorder; disjunction; disunion.

scom-pagnaménto, M.: disjunction (disunion). ‖**-pagnáre** [*s-*, *compagno*], TR.: disunite (separate, sever); INTR.: be separated from. **-pagnatúra**, F.: disunion.

scompannáre [*s-*, *panno*], TR.: toss the bedclothes from; REFL.: toss off the bedclothes; partially undress.

scom-paríre [*s-*, *comparire*], IRR.; INTR.: disappear; fade away; decline by comparison. **-pársa**, F.: disappearance; fading.

scompar-timénto, M.: partition; compartment. ‖**-tíre** [*s-*, *c.* .], TR.: divide into compartments; distribute.

scompia-cènte, ADJ.: discourteous (impolite). **-cènza**, F.: displacency; impoliteness. ‖**-cére** [*s-*, *com-piacere*], IRR.; TR.: displease; ignore; violate.

scompi-gliábile, ADJ.: that may be disordered; confused. **-gliaménto**, M.: disorder (confusion); rout. ‖**-gliáre** [*s-*, *compilare*], TR.: disorder (disturb), entangle, confuse; make uneasy. **-gliataménte**, ADV.: confusedly (in disorder).

scompí-glio, M.: confusion (disorder). **-gliúme**, M.: confused mass.

scompisciáre [*s-*, *piscio*], TR.: make water upon (wet).

scom-pletáre [*s-*, *completo*], TR.: complete. **-plèto**, ADJ.: incomplete.

scom-poniménto, M.: decomposing; disorder, confusion. ‖**-pórre** [*s-*, *com-porre*], IRR.; TR.: discompose (undo); disorder; decompose (analyze); confuse (abash); (*typ.*) distribute: *-porsi nel volto*, become abashed. **-pósi**, PRET. of *-porre*. **-positívo**, ADJ.: perturbing; disordering; decomposing. **-positóre**, M., **-positríce**, F.: decomposer; disorderer. **-posizióne**, F.: decomposition; perturbation; trouble. **-postaménte**, ADV.: in disorder; indecently. **-postézza**, F.: bad behaviour; disorder; immodesty. **-pósto**, PART. of *-porre*.

scompuzzáre†, TR.: fill with an offensive smell.

scomunáre†, TR.: divide; break up.

scomúni-ca, F.: excommunication. **-cagióne†**, F., **-caménto†**, M.: excommunication; curse. ‖**-cáre** [*s-*, *c.* .], TR.: excommunicate; curse. **-cáto**, ADJ.: excommunicated; cursed; villainous. **-catóre†**, M.: excommunicator. **-cazióne†**, F.: excommunication; curse.

scomúzzolo†, M.: none at all (not a bit of it).

sconcáre [*s-*, *conca*], TR.: take from the shell.

s=concatenáre, TR.: unchain (unjoin).

sconcennataménte†, ADV.: indecently.

sconcentráto [*s-*, *concentrare*], ADJ.: out of its centre.

sconcer-taménto, M.: disturbance; disagreement. ‖**-táre** [*s-*, *c.* .], TR.: disconcert (disturb); nauseate. **-tataménte**, ADV.: in a disorderly manner. **-tatóre**, M.: disturber. **sconcèr-to**, M.: disturbance; nausea; trouble.

scon-cézza, F.: loathesomeness; deformity; ugliness†; indecency†. **-ciaménte**, ADV.: indecently. **-ciaménto**, M.: spoiling; disarrangement. ‖**-ciáre** [*s-*, *c.* .], TR.: derange (spoil); confound (embroil);

REFL.: miscarry; be deranged, etc.; bring on a miscarriage. **-ciataménte†**, ADV.: in an unbecoming manner. **-ciatúra**, F.: miscarriage (abortion); dwarf. **scón-cio**, ADJ.: deformed (ugly; perverse); indecent; sprained; abortive.

sconclú-dere [*s-*, *c.* .], TR.: break off. **-sionáto**, ADJ.: inconclusive; ineffective.

sconcobríno†, M.: buffoon (merry-andrew).

scon-cordánte, ADJ.: discordant (dissonant). **-cordánza**, F.: false concord; irregularity. ‖**-cordáre** [*s-*, *c.* .], INTR.: be discordant (disagree). **-còrde**, ADJ.: discordant (dissonant). **-còrdia**, F.: discord; variance.

scóndere† = *nascondere*.

scodescen. .† = *scoscen. .*

sconditо†, ADJ.: unseasoned (insipid, tasteless, senseless).

sconfér-ma, F.: confirmation; evidence. ‖**-máre** [*s-*, *c.* .], TR.: disavow (disclaim).

sconfes-sáre [*s-*, *c.* .], TR.: disown (renounce, deny). **-sióne**, F.: disavowal (denial, disowning).

sconfic-cábile, ADJ.: removable. **-caménto**, M.: unfixing. ‖**-cáre** [*s-*, *c.* .], TR.: unfix (remove); unnail. **-catúra**, F.: unfixing.

sconfi-dánza†, F.: diffidence; mistrust (suspicion). ‖**-dáre** [*s-*, *c.* .], TR.: mistrust; INTR.: be diffident. **-dènza**, F.: diffidence, suspicion.

sconfíg-gere [*s-*, *c.* .], IRR.; TR.: unfix (free); discomfit (defeat, frustrate); bring to silence. **-giménto** = *sconfitta*. **-gitóre**, M., **-gitríce**, F.: who defeats.

sconfináre [*s-*, *confine*], INTR.: pass beyond the bounds or limits.

scon-fitta, F.: discomfiture (defeat, frustration. ‖**-fitto**, PART. of *-figgere*.

s confóndere, IRR.; TR.: confound; disturb; deter.

scon-fortaménto†, M.: dissuasion; discouragement. ‖**-fortáre** [*s-*, *c.* .], TR.: discourage; REFL.: be discomforted or discouraged (despond). **-fortévole**, ADJ.: discouraging. **scon-fòrto**, M.: discouragement; discomfort.

s congegnáre, TR.: disconnect (unjoin).

scon-giúgnere [*s-*, *c.* .], IRR.; TR.: disunite (unjoin). **-giugniménto**, M.: disjunction (disunion, parting). **-giuntúra†**, F.: disjunction (disunion, parting).

scongiu-raménto, M.: conjuration; entreaty. ‖**-ráre** [*s-*, *c.* .], TR.: conjure (entreat). **-ratóre**, M., **-ratríce**, F.: conjurer (exorcist). **-razióne**, F., **scongiú-ro**, M.: conjuration; supplication.

scon-nessaménte, ADV.: unconnectedly (disjointedly); discordantly. **-nessióne**, F.: want of connection (disunion). ‖**-nèttere** [*s-*, *c.* .], IRR.; TR.: disunite (sep rate); write unconnectedly; be discur (be rambling, incoherent, digress).

sconoc-chiáre [*s-*, *c.* .], TR.: spin off distaff-ful; draw out. **-chiatúra**, F spinning off a distaff-ful.

scono-scènte, ADJ.: ungrateful; u known; rash. **-scenteménte†**, ADV ungratefully; rashly. **-scènza**, F.: i gratitude (unthankfulness). **sconó-sce re** [*s-*, *c.* .], IRR.; TR., INTR.: not reco nise; be ungrateful; not know. **-sc ménto** = **-scenza**. **-sciutaménte** ADV.: without being known. **-sciú** ADJ.: unknown, obscure.

sconquas-saménto, M.: destructi crushing. ‖**-sáre** [*s-*, *c.* .], TR.: break pieces (destroy, squash, crush). **-satór** M.: destroyer (ravager). **sconquásso** M.: destruction (crush, ruin). **-sóne** M.: mass of destroyed things.

sconsa-craré [*s-*, *c.* .], **-gráre**, TR.: d ecrate (misuse).

sconsen-timénto, M.: disapprobati dissent. ‖**-tíre** [*s-*, *c.* .], INTR.: diss (disagree).

sconside-ránza†, F.: inconsideratene imprudence. **-rataménte**, ADV.: i considerately. **-ratézza** = **-ranza**. ‖**-ra to** [*s-*, *c.* .], ADJ.: inconsiderate; ra **-razióne**, F.: inconsideration; impr dence.

sconsi-gliáre [*s-*, *c.* .], TR.: dissua from (advise against). **-gliataménte** ADV.: unadvisedly (rashly). **-gliatéz** F.: inconsideration; imprudence.

sconso-laménto, M.: affliction (gri distress). ‖**-láre** [*s-*, *c.* .], TR.: dispi (sadden, grieve); REFL.: become disc solate. **-lataménte**, ADV.: discon lately. **-láto**, ADJ.: disconsolate. **-l zióne**, F.: affliction (grief).

scon-tábile, ADJ.: abatable (deductib reducible). ‖**-táre** [*s-*, *c.* .], TR.: d count (deduct, abate); compensate. **-t tóre**, M.: discounter.

scon-tentaménto, M.: discontent (d satisfaction). ‖**-tentáre** [*s-*, *c.* .], TI discontent (displease); disgust; griev vex; REFL.: vex one's self; be afflict **-tentézza**, F., **-tènto**[1], M.: disconte (displeasure); grief (sadness). **-tènto** ADJ.: discontented; sad.

scontessitúra [*s-*, *contessere*], F.: disc der (confusion).

s=continuáre, TR.: discontinue.

scon-tista, M.: discounter. ‖**scón-t** [*-tare*], M.: discount (abatement).

scon-torcènte, ADJ.: making contortio ‖**-tòrcere** [*s-*, *c.* .], IRR.; TR.: conto (twist, writhe about); REFL.: wri (twist, wriggle). **-torciménto**, M.: co

tortion (twisting). **-tòrto,** PART.: distorted; twisted.
s=contraffáre, TR.: counterfeit (imitate).
scon-tramento, M.: meeting (conflict, encounter). ‖**-tráre** [*s-*, *c.* .], TR.: encounter (meet with); check (an account); confront; REFL.: clash (meet). **-tráta,** F.: accidental meeting. **-trazzo**†, M.: rencounter. **-tríno,** M.: check. **scóntro,** M.: meeting (rencounter, meeting with) shock; fight; mark (token). **-trosággine,** F.: contrariety. **-tróso,** ADJ.: contrary (antagonistic, quarrelsome).
s=conturbáre, TR.: disturb (trouble); REFL.: be perturbed (be troubled). **-contúrbo,** M.: trouble; confusion.
sconve-nènza†, F.: inconvenience (unseasonableness, unseemliness). **-névole,** ADJ.: unbefitting (unseemly, indecent). **-nevolézza** = *-nenza*. **-nevolménte,** ADV.: unsuitably (unbecomingly). **sconvè-ngo,** PRES. of *-nire*. **-niènte,** ADJ.: unsuitable (unbecoming, indecent). **-nientemente,** ADV.: improperly (indecently). **-niènza,** F.: indiscretion (unsuitableness). ‖**-níre** [*s-*, *c.* .], IRR.; INTR.: misbecome (be unbecoming). **sconvé-nni,** PRET. of *-nire*. **-náto,** ADJ.: unbefitting (improper).
s=convertíre, TR.: reconvert (bring back again).
scon-vòlgere [*s-*, *c.* .], IRR.; TR.: turn upside down (overturn, upset); confound; dissuade. **-volgiménto,** M.: convulsion; disorder. **-volgitóre,** M.: disturber. **-vòlto,** PART. of *volgere;* overturned, etc.; sprained; crooked.
scó-pa [L.], F.: brush, furze; broom (shrub, besom); whipping (scourge); kind of game (with cards). **-paiòla,** F.: hedge-sparrow. **-pamestièri**†, M.: jack-of-all-trades. **-papollái,** M.: hen-roost cleaner; scullion. **-páre,** TR.: sweep; scourge (criminals). **-patóre,** M.: sweeper. **-patúra,** F.: sweeping; scourging (whipping); reprimand. **-pazzóne**†, M.: knock (slap, rap).
sco-perchiáre [*s-*, *c.* .], TR.: uncover (raise the lid of). **-perchiatúra,** F.: uncovering. **-pèrta,** F.: uncovering; discovery: *alla* —, openly (publicly). **-pertaménte,** ADV.: in an open manner. **-pèrto,** PART. of *-prire;* uncovered (open); bare (evident); M.: open place (clearing); open air. **-pertúra,** F.: opening (clearing, open place).
sco-petíno†, **-péto,** M.: field of brush. ‖**-pétta,** *dim.* of *-pa*. **-pettáre**†, TR.: brush (brush away, dust). **-pína,** ADJ.: shrubby (of heaths): *passero s* —, hedge-sparrow.

scòpo [Gr. *skopós*], M.: scope (mark, aim, intent, design).
scòpolo†, M.: high rock.
scoppettière† = *-piettiere*.
scop-piàbile, ADJ.: that may be cracked. **-piaménto,** M.: crash (crack). ‖**-piáre** 1 [*-pio*], INTR.: burst (crack, split, explode); pullulate; REFL.: burst; become cracked: — *dalle risa*, laugh heartily.
scop-piáre 2 [*s-*, *c.* .], TR.: uncouple (unjoin; despair).
scop-piáta [*-piare* 1], F.: burst (crack, explosion). **-piatúra,** F.: bursting (chink, rent, explosion). **-piettáre,** INTR.: crackle. **-piettáta**†, F.: gunshot; crack. **-piettería**†, F.: fusiliers; PL.: volley of small shot. **-piettière**†, M.: fusileer. **-piettío,** M.: crackling noise (crepitation). **-piétto**†, M.: slight cracking; light gun. ‖**scòp-pio** [metath. of *schioppo*], M.: crack (crash, explosion); light gun: *far* —, cut a dash.
sco-priménto, M.: discovery (disclosure). ‖**-príre** [*s-*, *c.* .], IRR.; TR.: uncover (disclose, open); discover; perceive (learn); REFL.: open (unbosom one's self): — *paese*, sound a person (feel his pulse). **-pritóre,** M., **-pritríce,** F.: discoverer. **-pritúra,** F.: discovery.
scò-pulo†, M.: rock (reef). **-lóso,** ADJ.: rocky.
scorag-giaménto, M.: discouragement. ‖**-giáre** [*s-*, *coraggio*], TR.: discourage (dishearten); REFL.: get discouraged (despond). **-giáto,** ADJ.: discouraged (disheartened, desponding). **-gíre,** TR.: discourage (dishearten); REFL.: get discouraged. **-gíto,** ADJ.: discouraged (disheartened).
sco-raménto, M.: discouragement (dejection). ‖**-ráre** [*s-*, *cuore*], TR.: dishearten (discourage).
scorbac-chiaménto, M.: defaming. ‖**-chiáre** [*s-*, *corbaccio*], TR.: expose to contempt (disgrace, traduce, defame). **-chiatúra,** F.: defaming.
scorbelláto [*s-*, *corbellare*], ADJ.: carping (scurrilous); M.: carper (taunter).
scòrbia = *sgorbia*.
scor-biáre, INTR.: make blots on paper. ‖**scòr-bio** [? *scorpio*], M.: blot (spot, defect).
scor-bútico, ADJ.: scorbutic (diseased with scurvy). ‖**scòr-buto** [Dutch *scheurbuk*], M.: (*med.*) SCURVY (Eng.† scorbute).
scorcáre†, INTR.: rise, get up (from bed).
scor-ciaménto, M.: shortening (curtailing, contraction). ‖**-ciáre** [*s-*, (*ac*)*corciare*], TR.: shorten (curtail, contract). **-ciatóia,** F.: cross-way (bypath). **scórcio,** M.: shortening (foreshortening); ...

(latter end): — *del giorno*, close of the day; *fare -ci*, paint the foreshortenings.

scor-daménto†, M.: forgetfulness (oblivion). **-dánza†**, F.: dissension (disagreement). ‖**-dáre** [*s-*, L. *cor*, heart], TR.: make discordant (put out of tune); INTR., REFL.: forget; be discordant (jar, disagree). **-dataménte**, ADV.: discordantly. **-dáto**, ADJ.: jarred; forgotten; out of tune (discordant).

scòrdeo† = *-dio*.

scordévole [*-dare*], ADJ.: forgetful (unmindful).

scòrdia = *discordia*.

scòrdio [Gr. *skórdion*], M.: (*bot.*) water-germander.

scorég-gia† [*s-*, *coreggia*], F.: leather-thong (strap); (*vulg.*) fart. **-giáre**, TR.: SCOURGE (flog, whip); (*vulg.*) fart. **-giáta†**, F.: cut with a whip (lash, flogging). **-giáto**, M.: flail.

scòr-gere [*s-*, L. *cor-rigere*, set RIGHT], IRR. (cf. *accorgere*); TR.: discern (perceive, distinguish); discover; guide (escort). **-gitóre**, M.: discerner; observer; guide.

scòria [Gr. *skória*], F.: scoria (dross, scum).

scoriáda [*s-*, L. *corium*, leather], F.: lash; SCOURGING.

sco-riazióne† [*-ria*], F.: scorification (reducing to scoria). **-rificatóio†**, M.: crucible; test.

scornac-chiaménto†, M.: disgrace (scorn). **-chiáre†**, TR.: ridicule (scorn). **-chiáta†** = *-nacchiamento*.

scor-náre [*s-*, *corno*], TR.: dishorn (deprive of horns); [? L. *cornix*, crow], disgrace (put to shame, mock, deride); REFL.: be disgraced; be ashamed (blush). **-náta**, F.: blow (thrust) of the horn. **-natúra**, F.: dishorning. **-neggiáre†**, TR.: butt (punch with the horns).

scorni-ciaménto, M.: cornicing. ‖**-ciáre** [*s-*, *cornice*], TR.: provide with cornices; deprive of cornices. **-ciatúra**, F.: cornice-work.

scòrno [*-nare*], M.: disgrace (shame, scorn).

scoronáre [*s-*, *corona*], TR.: discrown; remove the crown of (teeth); lop (a tree).

scor-pacciáta [*s-*, *corpaccio*], F.: hideful; bellyful, satiety. **-páre†**, TR.: eat a hideful (gorge).

scòr-pio† = *-pione*. **-pioncèllo**, *dim.* of *-pione*. ‖**-pióne** [L. *-pio*], M.: scorpion. **-pioncíno†**, *dim.* of *-pione*. **-pionísta†**, M.: two-faced rascal (double-dealer).

scorpo-ráre [*s-*, *corpo*], TR.: disembody; extract from the mass; take out of the capital stock. **-razióne**, F., **scòrpo-ro**, M.: disembodying; separating from the capital stock.

scorrazza-ménto, M.: skipping about. ‖**-záre** [*s-*, *correre*], INTR.: skip about, fidget.

s=corrèggere, IRR.; TR.: deteriorate (impair).

scor-rènte†, ADJ.: running (flowing). **-rènza†**, F.: flux (looseness). ‖**scórrere** [*s-*, *c.* .], IRR.; INTR.: run away (slip away); glide; TR.: run (pass) over; plunder: — *un libro*, run over a book; — *il ventre*, have a diarrhœa. **-rería**, F.: incursion (inroad).

scor-rettáccio, ADJ.: very incorrect. **-rettaménte**, ADV.: incorrectly; loosely. ‖**-rètto**, PART. of *-reggere*; incorrect (faulty).

scorrévo-le [*scorrere*], ADJ.: gliding (fluent); swift (transient). **-lézza**, F.: fluency.

scorrezióne [*-retto*], F.: typographical error; fault (mistake).

scorri-bánda, **-bándola†**, F.: little incursion. **-dóre**, M.: scout; military spy. ‖**-ménto** [*scorrere*], M.: inroad; flowing; flux. **-tóio†**, ADJ.: running; sliding: *nodo* —, running knot.

scor-rubbiáre†, REFL.: fall into a passion. **-rubbiáto†**, ADJ.: in a passion (angry). **-rubbióso†**, ADJ.: choleric (irascible). **-rucciáre** [*s-*, *c.* .], REFL.: become angry (fall into a passion). **-rúccio**, M.: anger (wrath); grief.

scórsa [*-rere*], F.: course (run): *dare una — ad un libro*, skim through a book.

scórsi 1, PRET. of *-gere*.

scór-si 2, PRET. of *-rere*. **-serèlla**, F.: little excursion (little run). **-sívo†**, ADJ.: that opens the bowels. **-scórso**, PART. of *-rere*; run out; past over (passed); spoiled; plundered; M.: oversight (mistake, irregularity, fault): *il mese* —, last month. **-sóio**, ADJ.: running; sliding (slipping).

scòr-ta [*-tare*], F.: escort (guide, convoy). **-taméntе†**, ADV.: prudently; warily.

scortaménto†, M.: contraction (abridgment).

scortáre 1 [*-gere*], TR.: escort (convoy).

scor-táre† 2, TR.: shorten (abridge). **-táto** 1, ADJ.: abridged.

scortáto 2 [*-tare* 1], ADJ.: escorted (guided).

scortec-ciaménto, M.: taking off the bark. ‖**-ciáre** [*s-*, *corteccia*], TR.: take off the bark (bark).

scorté-se [*s-*, *c.* .], ADJ.: discourteous (impolite). **-seménte**, ADV.: discourteously (disobligingly, uncivilly). **-sía**, F.: incivility (rudeness).

scorti-caménto, M.: excoriation (flaying). **-capidócchi†**, M.: skinflint. ‖**-cáre** [L. **ex-corticare* (*cortex*, bark)], TR.:

strip off the bark; skin (flay); fleece (extort). **-cáría**†, F.: seine (fishing-net). **-catóio**, M.: flaying knife; slaughter-house; excoriation. **-catóra**, F., **-catóre**, M., **-catríce**, F.: flayer; fleecer (extortioner). **-catúra**, **-cazióne**†, F.: scratch (excoriation); extortion. **-chíno**, M.: flaying-knife; flayer; usurer.

scortináre [*s-*, *cortina*], TR.: (*mil.*) batter down the curtain of (a fort).

scòrto, PART. of *-gere;* perceived, etc.; wary (clever, prudent); guided.

scórto† 2, ADJ.: shortened (abridged).

scòr-za [L. *cortex*], F.: bark; peel; shell; skin (hull); outside appearance. **-záre**, TR.: bark (peel); skin; divest; REFL.: cast off the skin (throw off the slough). **-zóne**, M.: unpolished person (boor, rustic). **-zonéra**, F.: (*bot.*) goat's-beard.

sco-scéndere [*s-*, *co-s. .*], IRR.; TR.: split (from the trunk); tear off; REFL.: burst asunder. **-scendiménto**, M.: rolling down, rushing down (of earth, etc.); burst (cleft); precipice. **-scéso**, PART. of *-scendere;* broken; steep (precipitous).

sco-sciáre [*s-*, *coscia*], TR.: sever (dislocate) the thighs of; REFL.: spread widely apart one's limbs; walk at big strides. **-sciáta**, F., **scò-scio**, M.: severing of the thighs; branching of the limbs; forking.

scòs-sa [*scuotere*, *scotere*], F.: shake (toss); leap; sudden shower. **-sáre**†, TR.: shake (jolt, toss). **-sétta**, **-settína**, F.: *dim.* of *-sa;* little shake (little shock). **scòs-si**, PRET. of *sc(u)otere*. **scòs-so**, PART. of *sc(u)otere*. **-sóne**, *aug.* of *-sa*.

scos-taménto, M.: keeping off (removing). ‖**-táre** [*s-*, (*ac*)*costare*], TR.: put away (remove, drive away); REFL.: go from (forsake). **-táto**, ADJ.: removed (distant).

scos-tumatamente, ADV.: indecently (rudely). **-tumatézza**, F.: impoliteness; indecency (libertinage). **-tumáto**, ADJ.: impolite (ill-bred, ungenteel). ‖**-túme**† [*s-*, *c. .*], M.: impoliteness; indecency.

scòtano [L. *rhus cotinus*], M.: (*bot.*) fustic.

scoten-náre [*s-*, *cotenna*], TR.: take off the sward of (bacon). **-náto**†, M.: hog's lard (grease).

scò-tere [L. *ex-cutere*], IRR.§; TR.: shake (stir; agitate, toss); shake or throw off; REFL.: start with fear (be startled); get rid of (leave off). **-timénto**, M.: shaking (shake, shock). **-titèrra**†, ADJ.: earth-shaking. **-titóio**, M.: salad-basket (strainer). **-titóre**, M.: shaker. **scò-tola**, F.: brake (to beat flax); scotching-handle. **-toláre**, TR.: beat flax; beat (cuff). **-tolatúra**, F.: flax-beating.

§ Pres. *sc(u)ò-*, accent.; *sco-*, unaccent. Pret. *scòs-si*, *-se*; *-sero*, Part. *scòsso*.

scoto-mático†, ADJ.: subject to dizziness (giddy). **-mía**†, F.: dizziness (vertigo).

scòtta 1 [? OGer. *schotte*], F.: whey.

scòtta 2 [Swed. *skot*], F.: (*nav.*) master-rope.

scot-taménto, M.: scalding (burning). ‖**-táre** [L. *ex*, *coquere*, COOK], TR.: scald (burn, scorch); sting (nettle); REFL.: burn one's self. **-tatúra**, F.: scalding (burning). **scòt-to** 1 †, M.: meal. **scòt-to** 2 [OGer. *skot*, SCOT], M.: bill: *pagare lo —*, pay the bill, pay dearly; *stare a —*, be a boarder.

scováre [*s-*, *covo*], TR.: drive out of the cave or den; dislodge; ferret out (discover).

scoverch. .† = *scoperch. .*

scovert. . = *scopert. .*

sco-víglia†, F.: sweepings, dirt. ‖**scó-volo** [L. *scopula*, little broom], M.: (*mil.*) scovel (malkin).

scovri. . = *scopri. .*

scòzia [L. *scotia*, darkness], F.: scotia (concave moulding).

scozzáre, TR.: shuffle (the cards).

scoz-zonáre [*s-*, *cozzone*], TR.: break (a horse); teach; teach sharpness (make witty). **-zonáto**, ADJ.: broken in; sharp. **-zonatóre**, M.: horse-breaker. **-zonatúra**, F.: horse-breaking. **-zóne**, M.: horse-breaker.

scramár. . = *sclamar. .*

scránna [OGer.], F.: chair.

screan-zatamente, ADV.: impolitely (rudely). ‖**-záto** [*s-*, *creanza*], ADJ.: ill-bred (rude, impolite).

screáto† = *scriato*.

scre-dènte†, ADJ.: disbelieving (incredulous); disobedient; stubborn. ‖**scré-dere** [*s-*, *c. .*], TR.: disbelieve.

scredi-táre [*s-*, *credito*], TR.: discredit (cry down). **-tévole**†, ADJ.: discreditable. **scrédi-to**, M.: discredit (disgrace).

screménto [*escremento*], M.: excrements.

scremenzía†, F.: quinsy.

scre-páre† [*s-*, *crepa*], **-poláre**, INTR.: crack (split, burst, chop). **-polatúra**, F., **scrè-polo**, M.: crevice (chink, chop, fissure, crack).

s=créscere†, IRR.; TR.: decrease (grow [less].

screspáre [*s-*, *crespa*], TR.: smooth.

scrè-zia† = *-zio*. **-ziáre**, TR.: variegate (speckle). **-ziatúra**, F.: variegation (speckling). ‖**scrè-zio** [? L. *dis-crepitus*], M.: quarrel (dispute); speckling.

scría [Tyrol. *cria* (L. *creare*, create)], F.: youngest of nestlings. ′**-to**, ADJ.: feeble, thin.

scrí-ba [L.], M.: scribe. **-bacchiáre**, TR.: scribble (scrawl). **-bacchíno**, M.: scribbler (scrawler).

scric-chiáre [*s-*, *cric*, echoic], **-chiolá-re**, INTR.: creak (rattle, crack). **-chio-láta**, F.: creaking (rustling). **-chiolío**, M.: continuous creaking.

scríc-ciolo†, ||**scríc-ciolo** [? ASax. *scric*, Gr. *kréx*], M.: wren.

scrí-gna† = *-gno*. **-gnétto**†, M.: small bunch; small casket. ||**scrí-gno** [L. *-nium*], M.: bunch; coffer (casket, strong box). **-gnúto**†, ADJ.: scraggy; crooked (hunchbacked).

scríma† = *scherma*.

scri-minatúra [L. *dis-criminare*, DIS-CERN, separate], F.: parting of the hair.

scrí-molo, M.: edge (brim, verge).

scrináre [*s-*, *crine*], TR.: clip the mane or tail of (crop).

scrío [?], ADJ.: that alone.

scríssi, PRET. of *scrivere*.

scrít-ta [*scrivere*], F.: writing (inscription); obligation (bond). **-táccio**, M.: bad writings (old papers). **-tarèllo**, *dim.* of *-to*. **scrít-to**, PART. of *scrivere*; M.: writing: — *fitto*, close writing. **-tóio**, M.: writing-desk; bureau; study. **-tóre**, M.: writer (author, copyist). **-torèllo**, M.: *disp.* of *-tore*; bad writer (scribbler). **-toría**†, F.: scrivener's office; bookkeeping. **-tríce**, F.: writer. **-túra**, F.: writing; Holy Scripture (Bible); document (bookkeeping). **-turábile**, ADJ.: that may be engaged. **-turáccia** = *-taccio*. **-turále**, ADJ.: of writing; scriptural; M.: scrivener (registrar, notary, copyist, clerk). **-turáre**, TR.: engage (by writing). **-turétta**, **-turína**, *dim.* of *-tura*. **-turísta**, pl. *—i*, M.: scripturist.

scri-vacchiáre, TR.: scribble. **-vane-ría**†, F.: scrivener's office. **-vanía**, F.: large writing-desk. **-váno**, M.: scrivener (writer). ||**scrí-vere** [L. *-bere*], IRR.§; TR.: write (compose); register; note. **-víbile**, ADJ.: writable. **-vicchiáre**, **-vucchiáre**, TR.: scribble.

§ Pret. *scris-si, -se; -sero.* Part. *scritto.*

scriziáto [*screzio*], ADJ.: speckled (spotted).

scrizióne [*scrivere*], F.: inscription; title; writing†.

scroc-cáre [? Fr. *croc*, hook], TR.: eat at the expense of others (sponge); enjoy (procure) fraudulently; REFL.: assume. **-catóre**, M.: sponger (sharper). **-chét-to**†, **-chettíno**, M.: little sponger. **scròc-chio**, M.: exorbitant profit (usury). **-chióne**†, M.: usurer. **scròc-co**, M.: sponging; cheating. **-cóne**, M.: sponger; sharper.

...**à-fa** [L.], F.: sow; king's evil†. **-fác-**... F.: *disp.* of *-fa*; big filthy sow; ... woman. **scrò-fola**, F.: scrofula ... *evil).* **-foláre**, ADJ.: scrofulous. **-folária**, F.: (*bot.*) blind-nettle (believed to cure scrofula). **-folóso**, ADJ.: scrofulous. **scrò-fula**† = *-fola*.

s=crogioláre, TR.: crunch.

scrol-laménto, M.: shaking (agitation). ||**-láre** [*s-*, *c.*.], TR.: shake (jog, toss, agitate); disturb. **-láta**, F.: shaking (jogging, tossing). **-latína**, *dim.* of *-lata*. **scròl-lo**, ADJ.: shaken; tired (fatigued); M.: shake (tossing, jog); vibration.

scrópo-lo†, M.: scruple. **-lóso**, ADJ.: (*poet.*) rugged (uneven).

scro-sciáre [ak. to *strosciare*], INTR.: patter; whiz (boil hard). **-sciáta**, F.: crackling (crash, rattling). **scrò-scio**, M.: bubbling or boiling violently; pattering: — *di risa*, loud burst of laughter.

scro-staménto, M.: taking off the crust; peeling off; clipping. ||**-stáre** [*s-*, *crosta*], TR.: take off the crust (peel); chip (bread). **-statúra**, F.: peeling; crust.

scròto [L. *-tum*], M.: scrotum.

scrudíre [*s-*, *crudo*], TR.: smooth; take the chill off.

scrunáre [*s-*, *cruna*], TR.: break the eye of (a needle).

scrupo-leggiáre, INTR.: scruple (be scrupulous). ||**scrúpo-lo** [L. *scrupulus*], M.: scruple (doubt); difficulty. **-losa-ménte**, ADV.: scrupulously. **-losità**, F.: scrupulousness (scruple). **-lóso**, ADJ.: scrupulous (over-nice); captious.

scrupul..† = *scrupol.*.

scru-tábile, ADJ.: scrutable (inquirable). ||**-táre** [L. *-tari* (*-ta*, SHRED), search even to the rags], TR.: scrutinize; search into (examine carefully). **-tatóre**, M., **-ta-tríce**, F.: searcher (scrutinizer, examiner, inquirer). **-tináre**, TR.: scrutinize; search into (examine). **-tinatóre**, M.: scrutinizer (examiner). **-tínio**, **-tíno**, M.: scrutiny (of votes); inquiry.

scucchiaiáre [*s-*, *cucchiaio*], INTR.: rattle (spoons, etc.).

s=cucíre, IRR.; TR.: unsew; undo. **-cu-citúra**, F.: unsewing; rip.

scu-dáio [*-do*], M.: buckler-maker; ADJ.†: armed with a shield. **-dáre**†, TR.: cover with a shield. **-deréseo**†, ADJ.: of a shield-bearer.

scudería [OFr. *escuerie* (OGer. *skura*, stall)], F.: stables (of a prince).

scu-détto, **-dice(u)òlo**, M.: *dim.* of *-do*; boss or stud (of a bridle, etc.). **-dière**, **-dièro**†, M.: ESQUIRE (knight's attendant).

scu-disciáre, TR.: beat with a switch (horsewhip). **-disciáta**, F.: horsewhipping. ||**-díscio** [L. *-tica*], M.: riding whip.

scú-do [L. *-tum*], M.: shield (buckler; SCUTcheon); defence (protection); crown (dollar). **-dóne**, *aug.* of *-do*.

scúf-fia [*s-, cuffia*], F.: woman's cap (coif, head-dress). **-fiára†**, F.: tire-woman, milliner. **-fiáre**, TR.: devour. **-fiétta, -fiettína**, *dim.* of *-fia*.
scuffi-na†, F.: file. **-náre†**, TR.: file.
scuf-fióne [*-fia*], *aug.* of *-fia*. **-fiòtto†**, M.: man's cap.
scu-lacciáre [*s-, culo*], TR.: spank. **-lacciáta**, F.: spanking. **-lacciatína**, *dim.* of *-lacciata*. **-lacciòne**, M.: *aug.* of *-lacciata*; severe spanking. **-lettáre**, INTR.: waddle, be off (run away). **-lmáto†**, ADJ.: lame (of horses).
scúl-si†, PRET. of *scolpire*. **-táre†**, TR.: carve (engrave). **-to†**, ADJ.: sculptured. ‖**-tóre** [*scolpire*], M.: sculptor. **-tòrio**, ADJ.: of sculpture. **-tríce** = *-tore*. **-túra**, F.: sculpture. **-turésco** = *-torio*.
scumarudòlo†, F.: skimmer (kitchen utensil).
scuoiáre†, TR.: flay, fleece.
scuò-la [= *scola*], F.: school (college); class. **-létta**, *dim.* of *-la*.
scuoráre† = *scorare*.
scuòt.. = *scot..*
scúra† = *scure*.
scu-raménte [*-ro*], ADV.: obscurely. **-raménto**, M.: darkening, dimming. **-ráre†**, TR.: cloud (darken, dim); REFL.: grow cloudy (grow gloomy). **-razióne†**, F.: darkening (dimming).
scúre [L. *securis* (*secare*, cut)], F.: axe: *darsi la — su' piedi*, hurt one's own case.
scu-rétto [*-ro*], ADJ.: darkish (rather dark). **-rézza**, F.: obscurity (darkness, gloom).
scuri-áda†, -áta†, F.: scourging; coachman's whip (lash).
scuríccio [*-ro*], ADJ.: darkish.
scuricèlla [*-re*], *dim.* of *-re*.
scuriosíre [*s-, curiosità*], TR.: satisfy the curiosity.
scuríre [*scuro*], TR.: darken (make obscure).
scurisciáre†, etc. = *scudisciare*, etc.
scu-rità†, F.: darkness (obscurity); difficulty; paleness; calamity. ‖**-ro** [*oscuro*], ADJ.: obscure (dark, gloomy); difficult; cruel (barbarous); M.: obscurity.
scurrí-le [L. *-lis* (*scurra*, buffoon)], ADJ.: scurrile (scurrilous; buffoon-like). **-lità**, F.: scurrility; buffoonery. **-lménte**, ADV.: scurrilously.
scú-sa, F.: excuse (pretext). **-sábile**, ADJ.: excusable (pardonable). **-sabilménte**, ADV.: in an excusable manner. **-saménto†**, M., **-sánza†**, F.: excuse (pretence, evasion). ‖**-sáre** [L. *ex-cusare*], TR.: excuse (justify, pardon); REFL.: excuse one's self. **-sáta†**, **-sazióne**, F.: excuse (justification). **-satóre**, M.: excuser (justifier). **-satòrio**, ADJ.: of an excuse (disculpating). **-satríce**, F.: excuser. **-serèlla**, F.: *dim.* of *-sa*; slight excuse. **-sévole†** = *-sabile*.
scós-si [*scuotere*], PRET. of *scuotere*. **-so**, PART. of *scuotere*; shaken etc.; stripped (naked, destitute); bereaved: *— di danaro*, penniless.
scútica†, F.: whip (lash).
scúto†, M.: small boat.
sdamáre [*s-, dama*], INTR.: vacate the king-row (at checkers).
sdá-re [*s-, dare*], REFL.: grow idle (grow sluggish). **sdá-to**, ADJ.: inattentive, sluggish.
sdebitáre [*s, debito*], REFL.: pay off one's debts; perform one's duty.
sde-gnaménto, M.: indignation (anger, passion). **-gnánte**, ADJ.: disdainful (angry). ‖**-gnáre** [*s-, d.*.], TR.: disdain (despise, scorn); REFL.: feel indignant; get angry; wither: *— lo stomaco*, have a distaste for. **-gnataménte†**, ADV.: indignantly (angrily). **-gnáto**, ADJ.: indignant (wrathful). **-gnatríce**, F.: scornful woman. **sdé-gno**, M.: indignation (wrath). **-gnosaménte**, ADV.: indignantly, scornfully. **-gnosétto**, *dim.* of *-gno*. **-gnosággine, -gnosità**, F.: disdain (indignation, wrath, anger). **-gnóso**, ADJ.: disdainful (scornful, angry). **-gnosúccio**, *disp.* of *-gnoso*. **-gnúzzo†**, M.: spite (malice).
sdelinquíre† = *sdilinquire*.
sden-táre [*s-, dente*], TR.: pull the teeth of. **-táto**, ADJ.: toothless.
sdétto, PART. of *sdire*.
s=diacciáre, TR.: melt.
s=dicévole, ADJ.: unbecoming.
sdíco, PRES. of *sdire*.
sdigiunáre [*s-, digiuno*], INTR.: break one's fast.
sdilacciáre†, TR.: unlace.
sdilin-quiménto, M.: swoon (fainting). ‖**-quíre** [*s-*, L. *de-liquere*, melt away], TR., INTR.: weaken; faint.
s=dimenticáre, etc. = *dimenticare*, etc.
s=dipíngere, IRR.; TR.: blot out a picture; erase (cancel).
s=díre, IRR.; TR.: deny; refuse; renounce; forbid; INTR.: misbecome (be unsuitable); REFL.: unsay (retract one's word).
sdiricciáre [*s-, di, riccio*], TR.: husk (chestnuts).
sdivezzáre [*s-, di, vezzo*], TR.: wean (disaccustom).
sdoganáre [*s-, dogana*], TR.: redeem from the custom-house (take out of bond).
sdo-gáre [*s-, doga*], TR.: strip of staves (unbind). **-gáto**, ADJ: without pipe-staves.
sdol-ciáto, ‖**-cináto** [*s-, dolce*], ADJ.

tasteless (insipid, mawkish). **-cinatúra,** F.: insipidity.

ṣdo-lenzíre, TR.: cure of numbness. ||**-lére†** [*s-*, *d.* .], INTR.: console one's self.

ṣdondoláre [*s-*, *d.* .], INTR.: swing; dally.

ṣdonnáre†, TR.: emancipate (set at liberty); REFL.: shake off the yoke (acquire one's freedom).

ṣdonneáre†, INTR.: cease loving.

ṣdonzelláre†, REFL.: play the fop; lounge about (trifle).

ṣ=doppiáre, TR.: undouble (unfold).

ṣ=doráre, TR.: remove the gilding from.

ṣdormen-táre [*s-*, *d.* .], TR.: awake (rouse); REFL.: awake. **-tíre†** = *-tare.*

ṣdossáre [*s-*, *dosso*], TR.: discharge a back-load; take off.

ṣdotto-ráre [*s-*, *dottore*], TR.: degrade, unrobe a doctor. **-reggiáre,** *freq.* of *-rare*

ṣdrai-áre [OGer. *straujan*, STREW], REFL.: stretch one's self (lie down). **ṣdrái-o,** M.: lying down. **-óne, -óni,** ADV.: in lying (at full length).

ṣdruccio-laménto, M.: slip (slide); false step. **-lánte,** ADJ.: slippery (sliding). ||**-láre** [? Ger. *straucheln*, stumble], INTR.: slip (trip, stumble). **-latívo, -lènte, -lévole,** ADJ.: slippery; easy; transitory (fleeting); perillous. **-levolménte,** ADV.: easily (readily). **ṣdrúcciolo-lo,** M.: slide; snare (treachery); stumbling-block; ADJ.: sliding (lubric); fleeting (transitory); accented on the antepenult (proparoxytone). **-lóne,** M.: slip (slide). **-lóso,** ADJ.: sliding (lubric); fleeting (transitory).

ṣdrú-cio, M.: unseaming (ripping); open seam; rent (cleft, crack). ||**-círe** [L. **diruscire* (*di-re-suere*, unsew)], TR. (Pres. *-cio* or *-cisco*): unstitch (unsew, rip); INTR.: get ripped; get leaky: — *un esercito*, break the ranks. **-cíto,** ADJ.: ripped (unseamed); rent; leaky. **-citúra,** F.: rip; rent; chink; leak. **-ṣcíre†** = *-cire.*

ṣ=duráre, TR.: soften (mollify).

se I [L. *si*], CONJ.: if; unless; thus: — *bene*, although; — *nonche*, unless, except; — *m' aiuti Dio!* so help me God!

se 2, **sè** *-é* (after prepos.) [L.], PRON.: one's self, himself, herself, itself, themselves: *lo fece da* (*per*) —, he did it by himself; *far sopra di* —, act for one's self; — *ne andò*, he went away.

sebá-ceo [L. *-ceus* (*sebum*, tallow)], ADJ.: sebaceous (fatty).

...**bbène** [*se* I, *bene*], CONJ.: although ...ugh).

...**nte,** F.: secant. ||**-cáre** [L], TR.:

...*-co*], F.: shallow (sand-bank, reef): *rimanere sulle -che*, be stranded. **-cábile,** ADJ.: subject to dry up. **-cággine,** F.: dryness (aridity, barrenness); tiresomeness (importunity); *dar* —, importune. **-cagginéso,** ADJ.: dry (withered, arid); tiresome (importunate). **-caggióne,** F.: withering. **-cágna†,** F.: shallows, shelves. **-cáia,** F.: withering. **-caíme,** M.: withered branch. **-caménte,** ADV.: dryly; abruptly (harshly). **-caménto,** M.: dryness (aridity). **-cáre,** TR.: dry up (drain); importune (weary, tease); REFL.: get dried up (grow arid). **-cáta,** F.: dry thing or story. **-catíccia,** F.: dead wood (small dry branches). **-catíccio,** ADJ.: almost dry (withered). **-catívo,** ADJ.: dessicative (drying). **-catóia,** F., **-catóio,** M.: drying-place. **-catóre,** M.: importunate fellow (prosy fellow); dun. **-catríce,** F.: tiresome woman. **-catúra,** F.: tiresomeness (importunity). **-cazióne†,** F.: drought (dryness). **-cheréccio,** ADJ.: half dry (withered); M.: = *-chezza.* **-cherèllo,** M.: small piece of dry bread. **-chézza,** F.: dryness (aridity); dry manner.

séc-chia [L. *situla*], F.: pail (bucket): *piovere a -chie*, rain cats and dogs. **-chiáta,** F.: bucketful; a blow with a bucket. **-chièllo,** M.: *dim.* of *-chio;* small pail (small bucket). **-chierèlla,** *dim.* of *-chia.* **-chíno,** *dim.* of *-chio.* **séc-chio,** M.: milk-pail. **-chiolína,** *dim.* of *-chia.* **-chiolíno,** *dim.* of *-chio.* **-chióne,** M.: *aug.* of *-chio;* large pail (large bucket).

secchità† [*-co*], F.: dryness (aridity); dry manner.

séccia [? **secca*], F.: stubble; stubble-field.

séc-co [L. *siccus*], ADJ.: dry (arid); meagre (thin); stingy (miserly); ADV.: dryly; harshly; stingily; M.: dryness (aridity): *rimanere in* —, be puzzled. **-córe,** M.: drought (dryness). **-cúme,** M.: dried leaves, branches or fruit.

se-centiṣmo, M.: (vitiated) style of the authors of the 17th century. ||**-cènto** [L. *sex-centi*], ADJ.: six hundred; M.: 17th century.

secèspita [L.], F.: sacrificial knife.

se-cessióne [L. *-cessio*], F.: secession (separation). **-cèsso,** M.: evacuation (stool); solitary place†.

secíspita = *-cespita.*

séco [L. *-cum*], PRON.: = *con sè;* with him (her, etc.): *con* —, along with him (etc.).

seco-láre, ADJ.: secular (worldly); M.: layman (worldly person). **-larescaménte,** ADV.: in a worldly manner. **-larésco,** ADJ.: secular (worldly, profane). **-larità†,** F.: secularity (worldliness). **-lariṣṣáre,** TR.: secularize. **-lariṣṣa-**

zióne, F.: secularization. **-létto**, M.: *disp.* of *-lo;* this miserable age (this wicked world). ||**sècо-lo** [L. *seculum*], M.: century (age): *ne' -li de' -li*, from age to age, forever and ever; — *d'oro*, golden age; *a' nostri -li*, in our times.

secón-da, F.: after-birth; aid; agreeableness: *andar a* —, follow the current; be prosperous; *andar a — ad uno*, humour a person; *a — di*, according to. **-daménte**, ADV.: secondly (in the second place). **-damentechè** *é*, CONJ.: according to (as). **-dáre**, TR.: second (assist, countenance, favour). **-dariaménte**, ADV.: in the second place. **-dário**, ADJ.: secondary (accessory); ADV.: in the second place. **-dína**†, F.: secundine (after-birth). **-díno**, M.: under-jailer. ||**secón-do** [L. *secundus*], ADJ.: second (inferior); propitious; ADV.: secondly (in the second place); PREP.: according to (after, pursuant to); M.: second (sixtieth part of a minute). **-do=chè** *-é*, CONJ.: according as. **-do=gènito**, M.: second-born (second son). **-dogenitúra**, F.: secundogeniture (right of inheritance of the second son).

secre-taménte†, ADV.: secretly (privately). **-táno**†, ADJ.: trusty (confidential, intimate). **-tário**†, M.: secretary; confidant. ||**secré-to** [L. *-tus*], M.: secret (secrecy). **-tòrio**, ADJ.: secretory. **-zióne**, F.: secretion.

sèculo† = *secolo*.

secu. .† = *sicu*. .

se-curità†, F.: security (assurance). ||**-cúro** [L. *-curus*], ADJ.: secure (safe, certain). **-curtà**, F.: security (assurance).

sèd† for *se*, if, before vowel.

sèdano [Gr. *sélinon*], M.: CELERY.

se-dánte, ADJ.: sedative (assuasive). ||**-dáre** [L. (*sedes*)], TR.: quiet (appease, compose). **-dataménte**†, ADV.: sedately (tranquilly, quietly). **-datívo**, ADJ.: sedative. **-datóre**, M., **-datríce**, F.: quieter.

sède [L. *sedes*], F.: SEAT: *la Santa* —, the Holy See.

sedècimo†, ADJ.: sixteenth.

se-déi, PRET. of *-dere*. **-dentário**, ADJ.: sedentary. **-dènte**, ADJ.: sitting; situated. ||**-dére** [L.], IRR.§; INTR.: sit down (be seated, be situated); M.: sitting down; seat (bottom): *-dete*, sit down (be seated); — *a mensa*, be at table. **-deríno**, M.: little seat (in a carriage).

sè-dia, F.: chair (seat); see. **-diário**, M.: one who brings chairs.

§ Pres. (Ind.) *siè-do* (or *sèggo*), *-di*, *-de* (or (*siède*); *sediámo*, *sedéte*, *siédono* (or *sèggono*). (Subj.) *siéda* or *sègga*; *siédano* or *sèggano*. —Poet. forms: *sèggio*; *-no*; *sèggia*. Ger. *seggèndo*.

se=dicènte, ADJ.: self-styled (pretended); so-called.

sedi-cèsimo, ADJ.: sixteenth. ||**sédi-ci** [L. *se-decim*], ADJ.: SIXTEEN; sixteenth.

sedi-le [L.], M.: SEAT (bench, coarse chair); stand for casks (gauntry). **-ménto** [L. *-mentum*], M.: sediment (dregs, lees). **-mentóso**, ADJ.: full of sediment (sedimentary). **sèdi-o** = *seggio*. **-òlo**, M.: light cart for one person. **-tóre**, M.: sitter (guest).

sedi-zióne [L. *-tio*], F.: sedition (tumult). **-ziosaménte**, ADV.: seditiously. **-zióso**, ADJ.: seditious (factious).

se-dótto, PART. of *-durre*. **-ducènte**, ADJ.: seducing (attractive). **-ducíbile**, ADJ.: seducible. **-duciménto**†, M.: seducing (corruption). ||**-dúcere**† = *-durre*.

sedu-lità, F.: sedulousness (assiduity). ||**sèdu-lo** [L. *-lus*], ADJ.: sedulous (assiduous).

se-dúrre [L. *-ducere*], IRR. (cf. *addurre*); TR.: SEDUCE (mislead; deceive). **-dússi**, PRET. of *-durre*.

se-dúta [*-de*], F.: sitting. **-dúto**, PART. of *-dere;* seated (sitting).

se-duttóre [*sedurre*], M., **-duttríce**, F.: seducer (corrupter). **-duzióne**, F.: seduction (corruption).

sé-ga [*-gare*], F.: saw: — *piccola*, hand-saw. **-gábile**, ADJ.: fit for sawing.

segáce†, etc. = *sagace*, etc.

séga-le [L. *secale*], F.: rye. **-lígno**, ADJ.: of the nature of rye; spare. **-líno**, ADJ.: of rye.

se-gaménto†, M.: sawing (section). **-gánte**, ADJ.: sawing (dividing). **-gantíno**, M.: sawyer. ||**-gáre** [L. *-care*], TR.: SAW, cut; mow; REFL.: (*geom.*) cross each other. **-gatíccio**, ADJ.: fit for sawing. **-gatóre**, M., **-gatríce**, F.: sawyer; mower. **-gatúra**, F.: sawing; sawdust; mowing; harvest (harvest-time). **-ga=véne**†, **-gavéni**†, M.: tyrant.

seg-gétta, F.: chair (close-stool). **-gettière**†, M.: chair-porter, chairman. **-gettína**, F.: small sedan (small close-stool). ||**sèg-gia**† [L. *sedia*], F., **-gio**, M.: chair (SEAT); SEE. **sèg-giola**, F.: chair. **-gioláccia**, *disp.* of *-giola*. **-gioláio**, M.: chairmaker, chair-seller. **-giolétta**, **-giolína**, **-giolíno**, *dim.* of *-giola*. **sèggiolo**, M.: side-seat (in a carriage). **-giolóna**, F., **-giolóne**, M.: *aug.* of *-giola;* large chair (armchair).

sèggo, PRES. of *sedere*.

se-ghería [*-gare*], F.: saw-mill. **-ghétta**, F.: *dim.* of *sega;* small saw (hand-saw); snaffle. **-gménto** [L. *-gmentum*], M.: segment.

se-gnacáso [*segnare*, *caso*], M.: preposition. ***-gnácolo*** [L. *signaculum*], M.: mark (sign); signet. ***-gnalánza***†, F.: distinction (preëminence). ***-gnaláre***, TR.: signalize; REFL.: distinguish one's self. ***-gnalataménte***, ADV.: principally (above all). ***-gnaláto***, ADJ.: signalized (famous). ***-gnále*** [L. *signalis* (*signum*)], M.: signal (sign, token); omen. ***-gnalétto***, ***-gnalúzzo***, M.: *dim.* of *-gnale;* little signal (little token). ***-gnáre***, TR.: mark (note, label); stamp; register; cross (make the sign of the cross upon); sign†; bleed†; REFL.: cross one's self. ***-gnataménte***, ADV.: particularly (expressly). ***-gnáto***, ADJ.: marked (noted); evident; engraved (imprinted); beaten (path); cited; M.: outside; appearance. ***-gnatóio***, M.: instrument for signalling. ***-gnatóre***, M., ***-gnatríce***, F.: marker. ***-gnatúra***, F.: mark; signature. ***-gnétto***, M.: *dim.* of *-gno;* little sign (little mark). ||**sé-*gno*** [L. *signum*], M.: sign (mark, token); wonder; ensign (standard); seal; trace (vestige); term: — *per* —, distinctively; precisely (exactly); *far stare a* —, make obey; keep in awe.

segnor. . = *signor*. .

seg*núzzo*, *dim.* of *segno.*

ségo [L. *sebum*], M.: SUET, tallow.

ségola† = *segale.*

sé-golo†, M.: hedging-bill; pruning knife. ||**-góne** [*-ga*], M.: large saw, hedging bill.

segóso [*sego*], ADJ.: of tallow (tallowy).

segregá-re [L. (*grex*, crowd)], TR.: segregate (separate, set apart). **-zióne**, F.: segregation.

segré-ta, F.: secret place; dungeon; helmet†; cap†. **-taménte**, ADV.: secretly (privately, stealthily). **-tariáto**, M.: secretaryship. **-tariésco**, ADJ.: of a secretary, confidant. **-tário**, M.: secretary; confidant; domestic†; portable desk†. **-táro**† = *-tario.* **-tería**, F.: secretariate; secretaryship. **-téssa**†, F.: female confidant. **-tézza**, F.: secrecy. **-tière**†, M.: secret person. **segré-to** [L. *secretus*], ADJ.: secret (hidden); unknown; ADV.: secretly (in secret); M.: secret (mystery); inmost soul; remedy; recipe; confidant†.

se-guáce [L. *-quax*], ADJ.: following; M.: follower. **-guèla**, F.: sequel; consequence. **-guènte**, ADJ.: following (succeeding). **-guenteménte**, ADV.: consequently (hence). **-guènza**, F.: sequence (continuity); series (suite; string, long row).

seguestr. . = *sequestr*. .

segúgio [?], M.: bloodhound.

seguiménto, M.: following, pursuit.

||**seguí-re** [L. *sequi*], TR.: follow (pursue); continue; accomplish; happen. **-tábile**, ADJ.: to be followed, imitable. **-taménte**, ADV.: consecutively (in order). **-taménto**, M.: following. **-tánte**, ADJ.: following; M.: follower (adherent). **-táre**, TR.: follow (pursue). **-tatóre**, M., **-tatríce**, F.: follower; imitator. **ségui-to**, M.: following (rest, continuation); SUITE (retinue, followers); issue; event; success. **seguí-to**, ADJ.: followed; happened; reputed (renowned). **-tóre**†, **-tríce**†, F.: follower.

sèi [L. *sex*], M., ADJ.: SIX. **-cènto**, M., ADJ.: six hundred. **seí-me**†, M.: two sixes (pair of sixes, at dice).

selbastrèlla = *selvastrella.*

sél-ce [L. *silex*], F.: flint-stone (silex); paving stone. **-ciáre**, TR.: pave (with round flints or pebbles). **-ciáta**†, F.: pavement (paving); stone-floor. **-ciáto**, M.: pavement. **-cióso**, ADJ.: flinty (stony).

sele-níte [Gr. *-nítes* (*-ne*, moon)], F.: selenite (mineral). **-nografía**, F.: selenography (description of the moon).

se-lètto [L. *-lectus*], ADJ.: selected. **-lezióne**, F.: selection.

sèl-la [L.], F.: SADDLE; SEAT†; throne†. **-láccia**, *disp.* of *-la.* **-láio**, M.: saddler (saddle-maker). **-láre**, TR.: saddle; burden. **-lería**, F.: saddler's shop. **-líno**, *dim.* of *-la.*

sél-va [L. *silva*], F.: wood (forest); grove; poetical miscellany. **-váccia**, *disp.* of *-va.* **-vaggiaménte**, ADV.: wildly; rudely. **-vaggína**, F.: venison, game. **-vággio**, ADJ.: wild (SAVAGE, desert, horrid); strange; raw; M.: savage. **-váno**† = *silvano.* **-varéccio**†, ADJ.: woody; wild; savage. **-vastrèlla**†, F.: (*bot.*) pimpernel. **-vático**, ADJ.: wild; savage. **-vétta**, **-vína**, F.: grove; boscage. **-vicoltúra**, F.: forestry. **-vóso**, ADJ.: woody (full of shrubbery).

semácco [Dutch *smak*], M.: SMACK.

se-mafòrico, pl. *—ci*, ADJ.: semaphoric (telegraphic). ||**-máforo** [Gr. *sêma*, sign, *phorós*, BEARing], M.: semaphore.

semáio [*-me*], M.: seed-seller.

sem-biábile†, ADJ.: resembling. **-biáglia** = *-braglia.* **-biánte**, ADJ.: resembling (similar); M.: countenance; look (air, mien); semblance (appearance); colour; show: *mostrar* —, make believe; *far strana* —, look strangely. **-biánza**, F.: face (countenance); appearance, resemblance; mark (token). **-biáre**†, INTR.: seem (appear). **-biévole**†, ADJ.: resembling. **-blábile**†, ADJ.: resembling. **-blánza**† = *-bianza.* ||**-bláre**† [L. *simulare* (*simul*, like)] = *-brare.* **-brábile**† = *-blabile.* **-brágliа**†, F.: troop of horsemen. **-bráre**, INTR.: seem (appear).

séme [L. *semen*], M.: seed (grain); semen; race; origin (cause, spring); one of the four suits of cards.

sè-mel, ‖**-méllo** [Ger. *semmel*], M.: sort of bun. **-melláio**, M.: bun-seller.

semén-ta [L.], F.: seed (sowing); cause; race (extraction). **-tábile**, ADJ.: that may be sown. **-táro**, TR.: sow (sow with corn). **-tatívo**, ADJ.: that may be sown. **-tatóre**, M.: sower. **semén-te** = *-ta*. **-tíno**, M.: Roman festival after sowing. **semèn-za**, F.: seed; sowed field; race (extraction); cause. **-záio**, M.: seed-plot (nursery). **-zína**, F.: (*bot.*) wormwood (semen sanctum). **-zíre**†, INTR.: run to seed.

se - mestrále, ADJ.: of six months. ‖**-mèstre** [L. *-mestris* (*sex*, *mensis*)], M.: semester (space of SIX MONTHS).

sémi- [L., half], PREF.

semi=brève, F.: (*mus.*) semibreve. **=cadènza**, F.: (*mus.*) semicadence. **=candíto**, ADJ.: almost white. **=cápro**, M.: half-goat (faun, sylvan). **=cavállo**, M.: half-horse (centaur). **=cérchio**, M.: semicircle. **=circoláre**, ADJ.: half round. **=círcolo**, M.: semicircle. **=còro**, M.: semichorus. **=cròma**, F.: (*mus.*) semiquaver. **-cúpio** [*cupo*], M.: half-bath. **=dèo**, M.: demi-god. **=diámetro**, M.: semidiameter (radius). **=dío**, M.: demi-god. **=dóppio**, M.: (*eccl.*) semidouble. **=dòtto**, ADJ.: half learned. **-gnoránte** [*ignorante*], ADJ.: almost ignorant (half taught).

semíla [*sei*, *mila*], ADJ.: six thousand.

semi=lunáre, ADJ.: semilunar. **=mòrto**, ADJ.: half dead. **=músico**, M.: ignorant musician.

semi-nábile, ADJ.: sowable. **-nagióne**, F.: sowing; sowing-time. **-nále**, ADJ.: fit for sowing. **-naménto**, M.: sowing (disseminating). ‖**-náre** [L. (*semen*)], TR.: sow (disseminate). **-nário**, M.: nursery (seed-plot); seminary (boarding-school). **-narísta**, M.: seminarist; boarder. **-natívo**, ADJ.: that may be sowed. **-náto**, ADJ.: sowed; dispersed; M.: place sowed (sown field); furrow (ridge): *uscir del* —, digress (be beside the question). **-natóio**, M.: sower. **-natóre**, M., **-natríce**, F.: sower (seedsman); disseminator; source (origin). **-natúra**, **-nazióne**, F.: sowing; seed-time. **-nío**, M.: long, continuous sowing. **-'no**, M.: *dim.* of *seme*; noodle (for soup).

semi=núdo [*semi*], ADJ.: half naked. **=poèta**, M.: poetaster. **=rètto**, ADJ.: half straight. **=rotóndo**, ADJ.: half round. **=spènto**, ADJ.: half extinguished.

sèmi-ta†, F.: footpath. **-tièro**†, M.: little footpath.

semi=tóndo [*semi*], ADJ.: half round. **=t(u)òno**, M.: (*mus.*) semitone. **=uòmo**, M.: shrimp of a man (little chap). **=vestíto**, ADJ.: half dressed. **=vívo**, ADJ.: half alive (half dead). **=vocále**, F.: semi-vowel; ADJ.: of a semivowel.

semmána† = *settimana*.

semménto [*segmento*], M.: segment; piece (shred).

sémo-la [L. *simila* (*si-*, sift)], F.: bran; freckle. **-líno**, M.: coarse flour. **-lóso**†, ADJ.: full of bran.

se=movènte, ADJ.: self-moving. **-movènza**, F.: self-moving.

sempiter-nále, ADJ.: sempiternal (everlasting). **-nalménte**, **-naménte**, ADV.: everlastingly. **-náre**, TR.: eternize (make eternal). ‖**sempitèr-no** [L. *-nus*], ADJ.: eternal (everlasting): **in** —, for ever and ever.

sémpli-ce [L. *simplex*], ADJ.: simple (single); pure (unmixed); bare (mere); plain (honest); weak (foolish). **-cèllo**†, ADJ.: somewhat simple. **-ceménte**, ADV.: simply; plainly (sincerely). **-cétto** = *-cello*. **-cézza**† = *-cità*. **sémpli-ci**, F. PL.: simples (medicinal herbs). **-ciáccio**†, M.: great simpleton. **-ciário**, M.: treatise on simples. **-ciòna**, F., **-cióne**, M.: simple-hearted (sincere) person. **-ciòtto**, ADJ.: simple; weak. **-císta**, M.: herbalist (botanist). **-cità**, F.: simplicity. **-ficáre**, TR.: simplify (make simple). **-ficazióne**, F.: simplification (simplifying).

sèmpre [L. *-per*], ADV.: always (ever): — *che*, provided; — *mai*, *mai* —, for ever (always). **=vérde**, M.: evergreen. **=víva**, F., **=vívo**, M.: house-leek (kind of plant).

sémprice† = *semplice*.

sèna 1 [L. *-ni* (*sex*)], F.: double SIX (in dice and dominoes).

sèna 2 [Ar. *sena*], F.: (*bot.*) senna.

sè-napa [L. *sinapi*], **sè-nape**, F.: mustard-seed; mustard. **-napísmo**, M.: cataplasm of mustard.

senário [L. *-rius*], ADJ.: senary (verse of SIX syllables).

sená-to [L. *-tus* (*senex*, old)], M.: senate, senate-house: *tenere il* —, convoke the senate. **-to=consúlto**, M.: senatus consultum. **-toráto**, M.: senatorship. **-tóre**, M.: senator. **-torèssa**, F.: wife of a senator. **-toría**, F.: senatorship. **-toriaménte**, ADV.: senatorially. **-tòrio**, ADJ.: senatorial. **-tríce**, F.: senator's wife.

senazióne†, F.: water-cresses.

séno 1 (pop.) = **sè**.

sè-no† 2 [L. *-nex*], ADJ.: old; M.: old man. **-nile** [L. *-nilis*], ADJ.: senile (decrepit).

sè-nio†, M.: old age (decrepitude). **-nió-re**, ADJ.: senior (older); M.: oldest man (senior).

seniscálco = *siniscalco.*

sen-níno, M.: *dim.* of *-no;* judicious youth. ‖**-no** [Ger. *sinn*, sense], M.: sense (judgment); knowledge (sentiment): *a mio* —, at my pleasure; *con* —, wisely; *da* —, seriously (in earnest); *uomo di* —, man of sense; *trarre del* —, drive one mad; *uscir di* —, lose one's senses (become deranged).

se=nnò or **se no**, CONJ.: otherwise.

sennáccio [*-nno*], M.: good sound sense.

séno [L. *sinus*], M.: bosom (breast, nipple); creek; little bay.

senòpia†, F.: sinoper (mineral).

sensá-le [Fr. *censal* (L. *censualis*, of the census)], M.: broker; agent; go-between. **-lúccio**, **-lúzzo†**, M.: *disp.* of *-le;* little broker; little agent.

sen-satamente, ADV.: sensibly (judiciously). **-satézza**, F.: good sense (wisdom, prudence). ‖**-sáto** [*-so*], ADJ.: sensible (judicious). **-sazióne**, F.: sensation (sense).

senserìa [*sensale*], F.: brokerage; agency.

sen-síbile [*-so*], ADJ.: sensible (perceptible, sensitive); sharp (pungent); affecting. **-sibilità**, F.: sensibility; tenderness. **-sibilménte**, ADV.: sensibly. **-sífero**, ADJ.: (*philos.*) ministering to the senses. **-sìsmo**, M.: (*philos.*) sensualism. **-sista**, M.: sensualist. **-sitíva**, F.: perceptive faculty; sensitive plant. **-sitivaménte**, ADV.: in a sensible manner. **-sitívo**, ADJ.: sensitive, ticklish, delicate, touchy. **-sivaménte**, ADV.: sensibly (sensitively). **-sívo**, ADJ.: sensible (sensitive). ‖**sèn-so** [L. *-sus*], M.: sense; sensuality; sentiment (feeling); meaning; understanding (judgment); direction. **-sòrium†**, M.: sensorium (seat of sense). **-suále**, ADJ.: sensual. **-sualísmo**, M.: sensualism. **-sualísta**, pl. **—ti**, M.: sensualist. **-sualità**, F.: sensuality; sense. **-sualménte**, ADV.: sensually; carnally. **-tácchio**, **-tacchióso**, ADJ.: quick of hearing. **-tènte**, ADJ.: sentient (feeling).

sentèn-za [L. *-tia*], F.: sentence (judgment; short saying, saw). **sentèn-zia†** = *-za.* **-ziáccia**, *disp.* of *-za.* **-ziále**, ADJ.: sentential. **-zialménte**, ADV.: sententiously. **-ziáre**, TR.: sentence. **-ziatóre**, M.: judge. **-zieggiáre**, INTR.: be pedantic, consequential. **-ziavolménte**, ADV.: by sentence (by decree). **-ziosaménte**, ADV.: sententiously, judiciously. **-zióso**, ADJ.: sententious; full of axioms.

sentiè-ro [L. *semitarius (semita, p...)], M.: path, byway. **-ruòlo**, M.: little narrow path.

senti-mentále, ADJ.: sentim... ‖**-ménto** [*-re*], M.: sentiment (... idea, esteem, opinion): *cavar*, *levar* ... stun. **-mentóne**, ADJ.: strong (... getic). **-mentúzzo**, M.: poor the...

sentína [L.], F.: hold (of a ship); s...

sentinèlla [?], F.: sentinel (guard); *fa...* *la* —, mount guard.

sen-tíre [L.], TR. (Pres. *-to*): feel, ... ceive, be sensible of); smell; ... judge (esteem); have: *ciò -te d'e...* that savours of heresy. **-títa**, F.: ... ing; tasting. **-titaménte**, ADV.: ... ciously (prudently). **-títo**, ADJ.: (perceived); heard; judicious†; cl... **-tóre**, M.: hint (advice, informa... smell (scent, odour)†; noise†: *aver* —, ... a hint.

sénza, **sànza** [L. *sine*], PREP.: wit... *senz' altro*, without fail (infallibly) ... *che*, besides; except; moreover; — ... uselessly (idly); — *più*, without any... else; simply (only); — *modo*, excess...

senziènte [L. *-tiens*], ADJ.: sentient...

sèpa† = *sepe.*

se-paiòla, F.: wren. ‖**-pále†** [*s...* M.: hedge.

sepa-rábile, ADJ.: separable. **-ra...** **tà**, F.: separableness. **-raménte...** separation (disjunction). **-rámento...** separation (parting). ‖**-ráre** [L.], ... separate (part); REFL.: separate ... self; depart; remove. **-rataménte**, ADV.: separately (apart). **-ratísta**, ... **—ti**, M.: separatist. **-ratívo**, ADJ.: ... arating (severing). **-ratóre**, M.: ... arator. **-ratòrio**, ADJ.: separ... **-ratrice**, F.: separator. **-razióne**, ... separation (setting apart).

sèpe†, F.: sort of lizard.

se-polcrále, ADJ.: sepulchral. ... **créto**, M.: place full of ancient t... **-polcríno**, M.: *dim.* of *-polcro;* ... sepulchre. **-pólcro** [L. *-pulcrum*], ... sepulchre (tomb); monument. **-p...** [L. *pultus*], ADJ.: buried; concealed. ... **túra**, F., **-ppelliménto**, M.: ... ulture (burial); tomb. ‖**-ppellíre** ... *sepelire*], TR. (Part. *reg.* or *-pólto*): ... (inter); hide. **-ppellitóre**, M.: bu...

sèp-pia [L. *sepia*], F.: cuttlefish. ... **re**, TR.: polish with cuttle-bone. **-pi...** **na**, *dim.* of *-pia.*

sètico†, ADJ.: septical (putrefactiv...

sepúlcr... † = *sepolcr...*

se-quèla [L.], F.: sequel (continuat... consequence; series. **-quènte**, ADJ.

lowing; consecutive. **-quèntia, -quènza,** F.: sequence (hymn introduced in mass).

seque-strábile, ADJ.: sequestrable. **-straménto** = *-strazione.* **-stráre,** TR.: sequester (set aside); seize; deprive of. **-stratário,** M.: sequestrator (one to whom the keeping of sequestered property is committed). **-strazióne,** F.: sequestration; seizure; setting apart; removal. ||**sequè-stro** [L. *-strum*], M.: sequestration (seizure).

sèr [*sire*], M.: sir; master.

séra [L. *-rus*, late], F.: evening.

será-fico, ADJ.: seraphic (angelical). ||**-fíno** [Heb. *-phim*], M.: seraph. **sèrafo†** = *-fino.*

se-rále [*-ra*], ADJ.: of the evening (evening). **-ralménte,** ADV.: every evening (nightly). **-ráta,** F.: evening (the whole evening). **-ratáccia,** *disp.* of *-rata.* **-ratína,** *dim.* of *-rata.*

ser-bábile, ADJ.: that can be kept, conservable. **-bánza†,** F.: keeping (preservation). ||**-báre** [L. *-vare*], TR.: keep (PRESERVE); reserve (hold back); put off (delay)†.

serbastrèlla†, F.: (*bot.*) pimpernel.

ser-batóio, ADJ.: conservable†; M.: conservatory (place for preserving); preserve (for birds, etc.); reservoir; coop. **-batóre,** M., **-batrice,** F.: keeper; depositary. **-bévole†,** ADJ.: that can be preserved or kept (conservable). ||**sèrbo** [*-bare*], M.: keeping (custody, deposit, charge): *dare in* —, entrust.

sère†, M.: Sir (my Lord, Master).

serèna† = *sirena.*

sere-naménte, ADV.: serenely (calmly). **-náre,** TR.: make clear (brighten up); appease (calm); console; INTR.: grow clear; be calm. **-náta,** F.: serenity (calmness)†; calm, cloudless weather†; (*mus.*) serenade. **-náto,** ADJ.: calmed, serene. **-natóre,** M.: calmer (soother). **-níssimo,** ADJ.: most serene (title of honour). **-nità,** F.: serenity (tranquillity, calm); brightness; serenity, Serene Highness (title). ||**seré-no** [L. *-nus*], ADJ.: serene (clear, calm, tranquil); joyful (happy); M.: clearness; open air; starry heavens; calm, cloudless weather: *al* —, in the open air.

serezzána†, F.: frosty breeze.

serfedòcco†, M.: simpleton.

ser-gènte [L. *-viens*, serving], M.: sergeant; constable†; servant†. **-gentína†,** F.: sergeant's pike (halberd). **-giére** = *-gente.*

sergenèllo†, M.: sorrel.

sergozzóne [*sor-gozzone*], M.: thump under the chin; (*arch.*)† modillion.

seriaménte [*serio*], ADV.: seriously.

sèri-co, pl. *-ci* [L. *-cus*], ADJ.: silken (silky). **-coltóre,** M.: silk-grower. **-coltúra,** F.: silk-husbandry.

sèrie [L. *-ries*], F.: series; succession, course.

se-rietà, F.: seriousness (gravity). ||**sèrio** [L. *-rius*], ADJ.: serious (grave); important; M.: seriousness (gravity): *sul* —, seriously. **-riogiocóso,** ADJ.: serio-comic; mock-heroic. **-riosaménte†,** ADV.: seriously (in earnest). **-rióso,** ADJ.: serious (grave); important.

ser-ménto = *-mento.* ||**-ménto** [*sarmento*], M.: vine-branch; tendril. **-mentóso,** ADJ.: full of sprigs.

sèr-mo† = *-mone.* **-mocináre†** = *-monare.* **-monáre,** INTR.: preach; harangue. **-monatóre,** M.: preacher; haranguer; proser. **-moncèllo, -moncíno,** M.: *dim.* of *-mone;* short sermon. ||**-móne** [L. *-mo*], M.: sermon (discourse); dialect; idiom.

sermóne 2 (*pop.*) = *salmone.*

sermoneggiáre [*sermone*], TR.: preach; harangue.

seròcchia† = *sirocchia.*

seros. .† = *sieros. .*

se-rotinaménte, ADV.: late (beyond the time). **-tíne†** = *-tino.* ||**-ròtino** [L. *-rotinus* (*-ro*, late)], ADJ.: late; late in the day or season; tardy.

ser-páio, M.: place full of snakes; wilderness. **-páto,** ADJ.: speckled like a snake.

sèr-pe, F.: serpent (snake). **-peggiaménto,** M.: winding (meander). **-peggiáre,** INTR.: wind (meander). **-peggiáto,** ADJ.: tortuous. **-pentáccio,** M.: *disp.* of *-pente;* large, ugly serpent. **-pentáre†,** TR.: importune (tease). **-pentária,** F.: dragon's-wort. **-pentário,** M.: (*astron.*) Serpentarius. **-pènte** [L. *-pentem*], M.: large serpent. **-pentèllo,** M.: *dim.* of *-pente;* young serpent; small snake. **-pentífero,** ADJ.: that produces serpents. **-pentíno,** ADJ.: serpentine (of a serpent); M.: serpentine stone. **-pentóne,** *aug.* of *-pente.* **-pentóso†,** ADJ.: full of serpents. ||**sèr-pere** [L.], INTR.: wind about; creep. **-pétta, -picèlla†,** F.: *dim.* of *-pe;* small serpent. **-picína,** F., **-picíno,** M.: *dim.* of *-pe;* young serpent (little serpent). **-pígine,** F.: ringworm; scab (scurf). **-píllo†, -pòllo†,** M.: (*bot.*) serpillum. **-polína,** *dim.* of *-pe.* **-póna, -póne,** *aug.* of *-pe.*

sér-qua [? L. *siliqua*], F.: dozen (of eggs, pears, etc.). **-quettína** = *-qua.*

sèrra 1 [L.], F.: saw†; defile (glen).

sèr-ra 2, F.: dam (bank); wall; (us'ly — —) crowd (throng, rush). **-rágl̥ia†** = *-raglio.* **-rágl̥io,** M.: harem (seraglio);

Sultan's palace; enclosure; park (menagerie). **-ráme**, M.: lock. **-raménto**, M.: locking-up (shutting-up). ||**-ráre** [L. *serare* (*sera*, bar)], TR.: lock up (shut close, shut up); conceal; keep in; wind up; bind; press; rush after (pursue closely): — *fuori*, shut out; — *il pugno*, clench one's fist; REFL.: unite closely; stand close; — *addosso a chechessia*, press upon anything. **-rataménte**, ADV.: closely; concisely; soundly. **-ra=tèste**, M.: close cap. **-ráto**, ADJ.: locked; shut; close (pressed together); thick: *panno* —, thick cloth. **-rátola**, F.: (*bot.*) sawwort. **-ratóre**, M.: shutter, locker-up. **-ratúra** F.: lock; closure (locking); lock.

sèrto [L. *-tum* (*sero*, weave)], M.: (*poet.*) garland (chaplet).

sèr-va, F.: servant-maid. **-vábile**†, ADJ.: that can be kept. **-váccio**, M.: very bad servant. **-vággio**, M.: servitude (slavery). **-vaménto**†, M.: keeping (preserving, maintaining). **-váre**†, TR.: keep (preserve, maintain); observe. **-vatóre**†, M., **-vatríce**, F.: keeper; preserver; observer. **-vènte**, ADJ.: serving (obedient, subservient); M.: servant; footman. **-ventése**, F., M.: kind of poetry of the troubadours. **-vétta**, F.: *dim.* of *-va;* little servant-maid. **-vicciòla**, F.: *dim.* of *-va;* little maid of all work (little scullion). **-vicèlla**†, **-vicína**†, F.: little maid-servant. **-vidorá-me**†, M.: crowd of men-servants. **-vidòre**† = *-vitore.* **-viènte** = *-vente.* **-vigétto**, M.: trifling service; kind office. **-vigiále**, M., F.: servant; serving brother or sister. **-vígio**, M.: service (employ); kind office (favour, pleasure); affair (matter). **-vigiúzzo**† = *-viziuccio.* **-víle**, ADJ.: servile (slavish); mean. **-vilità**, F.: servility. **-vilménte**, ADV.: servilely (slavishly); meanly. **-viménto**†, M.: service (servitude). **-víre**, TR. (Pres. = *-vo*): serve (wait on, help at table); do a service; assist one with money. **-víto**, ADJ.: served; helped; M.: service (at table); salary. **-vitóra**, F.: servant. **-vitoráccio**, M.: *disp.* of *-vo;* bad servant. **-vitoráme**, M.: (*disp.*) crowd of servants (menials); servile people. **-vitóre**, M.: servant; valet. **-vitorèllo**, **-vitorétto**, *dim.* of *-vitore.* **-vitorúme**, M.: (*disp.*) crowd of servants (menials). **-vitoríno**†, M.: little servant; lackey. **-vitríce**†, F.: waiting-maid; woman-servant. **-vitù**, F.: servitude; service (obligation); bond; ground-rent; servants. **-viziále**, M.: clyster, injection. **-viziáto**, ADJ.: serviceable; obliging. **-viziétto**, *dim.* of *-vizio.* **-vízio**, M.: service (employ); favour; affair. **-viziòlo**, *dim.* of *-vizio.* **-viziúccio**, M.: *disp.* of *-vizio;* little service; little kindness. ||**sèr-vo** [L. *-vus*], M.: serf (bondsman; slave); servant. **-vóne**, *aug.* of *-vo.*

sèsa-mo [L. *-mum*], M.: sesame (oily plant). **-mòide**, M.: (*anat.*) sesamoid bone; (*bot.*)† elecampane.

sescálco†, M.: seneschal; steward.

sesè-li, **-lio**, M.: (*bot.*) hartwort.

sesqui- [L.], PREF.: sesqui- (one and a half). **-áltero**, ADJ.: sesquialteral (once and a half more). **-pedále**, ADJ.: sesquipedal. **-tèrzo**, ADJ.: sesquitertian.

sessa- [L. *sexa-*], PREF.: sixty. **=genário** [L. *-genarius*], ADJ., M.: sexagenarian. **=gèsima** [L. *-gesimus*], F.: Sexagesima-Sunday. **-gèsimo**, ADJ.: sexagesimal (sixtieth). **sesságono**†, M.: (*geom.*) hexagon. ||**sessá-nta** [L. *-ginta*], NUM.: sixty. **-nta=míla**, NUM.: sixty thousand. **-nta=quattrèsimo**, ADJ.: sixty-fourth. **-ntèsimo**, ADJ.: sixtieth. **-ntína**, F.: full sixty (three-score).

sessènnio [L. *sexennium* (*sex*, six, *annus*, year)], M.: period of six years.

sès-sile [L. *-silis*, low (*sedere*, sit)], ADJ.: (*bot.*) sessile (without a petiole). **-sióne** [L. *-sio*], F.: session (sitting); act of sitting†.

sessitúra = *tessitura.*

sès-so [L. *sexus*], M.: sex; pudenda†; anus†. **-suále**, ADJ.: sexual. **-sualità**, F.: sexuality.

sèssola†, F.: (*nav.*) boat-scoop (laving-ladle).

sèsta 1 = *sesto.*

sèsta 2 [Gr. *xustón*, square], F.: pair of compasses: *colle* —, with much diligence; *le* —*te*, long legs; *a* —, exactly; *menar le* —*te*, run fast; *venir a* —, come to a resolution.

ses-tánte [L. *sextans*, sixth part], M.: sextant. **-tário** M.: sextary.

sèste = *sesta* 2.

sestèrzio [L. *-tertius*], M.: SESTERCE (Roman coin).

se-stière [*sei*], M.: division of a city; measure of two gallons. **-stíle**, M.: sixth part of a circle; (*astron.*) sestile: *di* —†, obliquely (askance). **-stína**, F.: stanza of six verses; sextain. ||**sè-sto** 1 [L. *sextus*], ADJ.: sixth; M.: sixth part; sext.

sèsto 2 [L. *sexus* (? *sectus*, cut)], M.: order (measure, rule); arch; form or size of a book; remedy†.

sest-odècimo = *sedicesimo.* **sèst-ula**†, F.: sixth part of an ounce. ||**-último** [*-to*, M. .], ADJ.: last but five. **sèst-uplo**, ADJ.: sextuple (sixfold).

sé-ta [L.], F.: silk; silk-stuff. **-táceo,** ADJ.: silky. **-taiòlo,** M.: silk-maker; silk-merchant.
setanásso† = *satanasso.*
se-tardònte, ADJ.: causing thirst. **-tá-ta**†, F.: great and continual thirst. ||**sé-te** 1 [L. *sitis*], F.: thirst; great desire: *aver* —, be thirsty.
séte† 2 = *siete* (cf. *essere*).
se-tería [*-ta*], F.: silk-mercery; all kinds of silk. **-tifícío,** M.: silk-manufacture. **-tíno,** M.: very fine silk; silk-drapery.
sé-tola 1, F.: hog's bristle; coarse hair; whisk.
séto-la 2 [L. *seclula* (*secare*, cut)], F.: cut (chap, cleft). **-láccia,** *disp.* of *-la.* **-lá-re,** TR.: brush (whisk, burnish). **-létta, -lína,** *dim.* of *-la.* **-léne,** M.: (*bot.*) horse-tail. **-léso,** ADJ.: full of cracks. **-lúto,** ADJ.: bristly (hairy). **setó-ne,** M.: (*med.*) seton (rowel). **setó-so**†, ADJ.: bristly.
sèt-ta [L. *secta* (*sequor*, follow)], F.: SECT (faction); conspiracy (cabal). **-táccia,** *disp.* of *-ta.*
set-tágono, M.: (*geom.*) heptagon. **-tan-golàre,** ADJ.: septangular. ||**-tángolo** [*sette, a.* .], ADJ.: heptagonal. **-tánta,** NUM.: SEVENTY. **-tantèsimo,** ADJ.: seventieth. **-tantòtto** [*-tanta, o.* .], NUM.: seventy-eight.
set-tário [*-ta*], ADJ.: sectarian; M.: sectary. **-tatóre,** M., **-tatrice,** F.: sectarian (follower).
sètte [L. *septem*], NUM.: SEVEN: — *suo,* so much the better for him; *tre* —, game of cards. **-cènto,** NUM.: seven hundred; *il* —, eighteenth century.
setteg-giánto, ADJ.: factious (seditious). ||**-giáre** [*setta*], INTR.: make a sect (form a party); enter a sect.
sette-, PREF.: = *sette.* **settè=mbre** [L. *septem-ber*], M.: September. **-mbréccia,** F.: autumn. **-mbríno,** ADJ.: of September; M.: turning sour (of wines). **set-tè-mplice,** ADJ.: of seven parts; having seven colours. **-nário,** ADJ., M.: septenary; (*metr.*) verse of seven syllables; space of seven years. **-nnále,** ADJ.: septennial. **settè-nnio** [*sette, anno*], M.: period of seven years. **-ntrionále,** ADJ.: northern. **-ntrióne** [L. *septentrio* (*septem, trio*, plough ox) seven stars of the Ursa major], M.: septentrion (north).
setti-, PREF.: = *sette.* **-clávio,** M.: (*mus.*) seven keys. **=fórme,** ADJ.: (*eccl.*) septiform. **-mána** [L. *septi-mana*, of the number seven], F.: week: — *mosaica,* space of seven years. **-manále,** ADJ., **-manalménte,** ADV.: weekly. **-máno** = *-mo.* **sèttimo,** ADJ.: seventh; ADV.: seventhly. **settí-na**†, F.: quantity or number of seven. **-zònio** [Gr. *zóne*, band, girdle], M.: (*arch.*) building surrounded by seven rows of columns; seven zones.
sèt-to [L. *sectum* (*secare*, cut)], M.: (*anat.*) separating membrane; diaphragm; ADJ.†: (*poet.*) divided (cut, separated). **-tóre,** M.: sector. **-to=trasvèrso,** M.: (*anat.*) diaphragm (midriff).
settua-genário [L. *septua-genarius*], M., ADJ.: septuagenarian. **-gèsima,** F.: Septuagesima Sunday. **-gèsimo** [L. *septuagesimus*], ADJ.: seventieth.
sèttuplo [L. *septuplus*], ADJ.: seven times greater.
severaménte [*severo*], ADV.: severely (roughly).
severáre†, TR.: sever (separate).
se-verità, F.: severity (rigour). ||**-vè-ro** [L. *-verus*], ADJ.: severe (rigorous); stern.
se-vízia, F.: cruelty (barbarity). ||**sè-vo**† 1 [*sævus*, cruel], ADJ.: cruel (inhuman).
sévo 2 [L. *sevum*], M.: tallow.
sevr. .† = *scevr.* .
se-zionáre, TR.: reduce into parts or sections. ||**-zióne** [L. *-ctio*], F.: section (division); (*med.*) dissection.
sez-záio†, **séz-zo**†, ADJ.: last: *al da* —, lastly; *da* —, at last.
sfaccen-dáre [*s-, faccenda*], TR.: do with ardour. **-dáto,** ADJ.: unoccupied (lazy); fruitless (vain).
sfaccettá-re [*f.* .], TR.: cut facet-wise. **-túra,** F.: cutting facet-wise.
sfacchináre [*s-, facchino*], INTR.: work like a porter.
sfaccia-ménto† = *-tezza.* **-táccio,** *disp.* of *-to.* **-tággine,** F.: boldness (impudence). **-taménte,** ADV.: impudently. **-tèllo,** *car. dim.* of *-to.* **-téz-za,** F.: effrontery (audacity). ||**sfacciá-to** [*s-, faccia*], ADJ.: impudent (bold); (of a horse) white-faced.
sfacèlo [Gr. *sphákelos*], M.: (*med.*) gangrene; ruin.
s=facimento, M.: ruin (destruction).
sfal-dáre [*s-, falda*], TR.: cut in slices; REFL.: fall into slips or splinters; exfoliate. **-datúra,** F.: exfoliation. **-dellá-re,** TR.: make lint; transform into lint.
sfal-láre† = *-lire.* **-lènte,** ADJ.: erring (mistaking); wandering. ||**-líre** [*s-, f.* .], INTR.: make a mistake (err, miss).
sfalsáre†, TR., INTR.: parry (ward off); elude.
sfa-máre [*s-, fame*], TR.: satiate (satisfy the hunger of); REFL.: eat one's fill. **-má-to,** PART.: satiated, etc. **-matúra,** F.: satisfying one's hunger.
sfangáre [*s-, fango*], INTR.: walk in the mud; get out of the mud; (*fig.*) get out of a mess.

sfáre = *disfare*.
sfarfal-láre [*s-*, *farfalla*], INTR.: become a butterfly; talk nonsense. **-latúra**, F.: becoming a butterfly. **-lóne**, M.: large butterfly; blunder.
sfari-nábile, ADJ.: that can be pulverized. **-nacciáre** = *-nare*. **-naménto**, M.: pulverization. ‖**-náre** [*s-*, *farina*], TR.: reduce to powder (pulverize); INTR.: get meally; become like flower or powder.
sfar-záccio, *aug.* of *-zo*. ‖**-zo** [Sp. *disfraz*, showy clothes], M.: pomp (ostentation). **-zosaménte**, ADV.: pompously. **-zosità**, F.: splendour (magnificence). **-zóso**, ADJ.: splendid (pompous).
sfa-sciaménto, M.: loosening (undoing); ruin. ‖**-sciáre** [*s-*, *f.* .], TR.: unswathe; ruin (cast down); REFL.: fall to ruins. **-sciatúra**, F.: sawings; sawdust. **-sciúme**, M.: ruins (rubbish).
s-fastidiáre†, TR.: divert (recreate, drive away ennui); REFL.: recover one's appetite.
sfatá-re [*s-*, *f.* .], TR.: lower in esteem. **-taménte**, ADV.: foolishly. **-'to**, ADJ.: foolish.
sfátto = *disfatto*.
sfavil-laménto, M.: brilliancy (sparkling). ‖**-láre** [*s-*, *favilla*], INTR.: sparkle (shine).
sfavo-révole, ADJ.: unfavourable. **-revolménte**, ADV.: unfavourably. ‖**-ríre** [*s-*, *f.* .], TR.: disserve; disoblige; prejudice.
sfederáre [*s-*, *inf.* .], TR.: pull off (the pillow-case).
sfega-táre [*s-*, *fegato*], REFL.: disturb the liver; (*fig.*) give one's self much trouble. **-táto**, PART.: much aroused; violently in love.
sfeláto†, ADJ.: tired; out of breath.
sfelíce† = *infelice*.
sfend. .† = *fend. .*
sfè-ra [L. *sphæra* (Gr. *sphaîra*)], F.: sphere (globe); science of the sphere (astronomy). **-ràle**†, ADJ.: spherical (round). **-rétta**, *dim.* of *-ra*. **-ricaménte**, ADV.: spherically. **-ricità**, F.: sphericity (roundness). **sfè-rico**, pl. *—ci*, ADJ.: spherical. **-ristério**, M.: tennis court (bowling-green). **-roidále**, ADJ.: spheroidal. **-ròide**, F.: spheroid. **-romachía** [Gr. *máche*, fight], F.: ancient game of tennis. **-róne**, M.: circular fishing-net.
sfèrra [*sferrare*], F.: old broken horseshoe; old clothes; base fellow.
sferraioláre [*s-*, *ferraiolo*], TR.: uncloak.
sferráre [*s-*, *ferro*], TR.: unshoe (remove the irons from); extract from a wound (a bit of iron, etc.); remove; REFL.: shake off a horseshoe, etc.
sferratóia†, F.: loop-hole (barbacan).
sfer-ratúra [*-rare*], F.: losing a shoe. **-ruzzáto**, ADJ.: of small pieces of chalkstone not well slackened.
sfervoráto [*s-*, *inf.* .], ADJ.: cooled; indifferent.
sfèr-za, F.: whip (scourge). ‖**-záre** [? L. *feritiare*, wound], TR.: chastise (whip). **-záta**, F.: lash; punishment. **-zatóre**, M.: whipper. **-zína**, F., **-zíno**, M.: cord of a net (whip-cord).
sfes-satúra†, F.: cleft (chink). **sfésso**†, PART. of *sfendere*; cleft, etc.
sfetteggiáre†, TR.: cut into slices.
sfiaccoláre [*s-*, *fiaccola*], INTR.: be very resplendent; be bright as a torch.
sfiaccoláto [dim. of *fiaccato*], ADJ.: fatigued (bending the head with fatigue).
sfian-caménto, M.: bursting of the sides. ‖**-cáre** [*s-*, *f.* .], INTR.: break in the lateral parts; get lean or thin-flanked; TR.: weaken; outflank. **-cáta**, F.: blow on the side; (*fig.*) impulsion. **-cáto**, PART.: thin-flanked (weakened).
sfiandronáta†, F.: rodomontade (brag).
sfia-taménto, M.: breathing; losing the breath. ‖**-táre** [*s-*, *f.* .], INTR.: breathe (respire); REFL.: lose one's breath. **-táto**, PART.: out of breath; exhausted. **-tatóio**, M.: vent (air-hole). **-tatúra** = *-tamento*. **sfiá-to**, M.: air-hole (spiracle).
sfibbiá-re [*s-*, *affibbiare*], TR.: unbuckle: — *il seno*, unlace the breast (begin to speak). **-túra**, F.: unbuckling.
sfi-braménto, M.: weakening the nerves. ‖**-bráre** [*s-*, *fibra*], TR.: unnerve; weaken (the nerves). **-brináre**, TR.: take away (the fibrin).
sfi-da, F., **-daménto**, M.: challenge (provocation to fight). **-dánza**†, F.: distrust (suspicion). ‖**-dáre** [*s-*, *diffidare*], TR.: defy (challenge); discourage†; mistrust (suspect)†; give over (a patient). **-dáto**, PART.: defied, etc. **-datóre**, M.: challenger (defier); one who distrusts. **-dúcia**, F.: distrust. **-duciáre**, TR.: distrust (suspect). **-duciáto**, ADJ.: mistrustful (suspicious, diffident).
sfienáre [*s-*, *fieno*], TR.: clean or select (sheafs of hay).
sfigu-ráre [*s-*, *f.* .], TR.: disfigure (deform). **-ráto**, ADJ.: disfigured.
sfi-lacciáre = *-lacciare*. **-lacciatúre**, F. PL.: unravellings. **-lacciáre**, INTR.: unweave (unravel). **-lacciatúra**, F.: unweaving. **-láccio**†, M.: thread (filament). ‖**-láre** [*s-*, *infilare*], TR.: unthread; unravel; INTR.: quit the ranks (disband); break one's back; go in file, file off. **-láta**, F.: rank (file). **-lataménte**, ADV.: in confusion. **-láto**†,

PART.: unstrung, etc.; wadding for guns: *alla -lata*, one after another.
sfilunguelláre [*s-*, *filunguello*], INTR.: be pedantic (prate in a learned manner).
sfingardággine = *infingardaggine*.
sfinge [Gr. *sphinx*], F.: sphinx.
sfi-niménto, M.: exhaustion, swoon (fainting fit). ||**-níre** [*s-*, *f.* .], INTR.: be exhausted; TR.†: finish (complete). **-ni-tézza**, F.: weakness; completion†.
sfintère [Gr. *sphinktếr* (*sphíngein*, strangle)], M.: sphincter (constrictory muscle).
sfioccáre [*s-*, *f.* .], TR., INTR.: unravel (unweave).
sfiocináre [*s-*, *fiocine*], TR.: take off (the peel of grapes).
sfiondá-re [*s-*, *fionda*], TR.: fling (cast, dart). **-túra**, F.: cast with a sling; gross falsehood†.
sfio-ráre [*sfiorire*], TR.: deflower; (*fig.*) dishonour; graze (touch, strike lightly against). **-rentináre** [*s-*, *fiorentino*], TR., REFL.: cause to lose, or lose, Florentine character. **-riménto**, M.: withering of flowers. ||**-ríre** [*s-*, *f.* .], TR.: deflower; INTR.: shed the blossoms; fade. **-ritúra**, F.: shedding the blossoms.
sfirèna [Gr. *sphúraina*], F.: large sea-pike.
s=fittáre [*s-*, *aff.* .], TR.: not to hire or let.
sfittonáre [*s-*, *fittone*], TR.: take up (the roots).
sflagelláre = *sfragellare*.
sfocáto†, ADJ.: cooled; abated (tempered).
sfoco-náre [*s-*, *focone*], TR.: stir (the fire); draw from the powder-pan; spoil the touch-hole of.
sfode-raménto, M.: unsheathing. ||**-rá-re** [*s-*, *f.* .], TR.: draw, unsheath; draw out (extract).
sfo-gaménto, M.: venting; letting out. ||**-gáre** [*sfocare*], TR.: vent; let out; breathe out; discharge: *luogo -gato*, open airy place; — *la collera*, vent one's anger; — *la vendetta*, wreak vengeance. **-gataménte**, ADV.: openly. **-gatóio**, M.: vent (air-hole).
sfog-giaménto = *-gio*. ||**-giáre** [*s-*, *foggiare*], TR.: dress sumptuously or magnificently, excel (surpass). **-giata-ménte**, ADV.: pompously; excessively. **-giatézza**, F.: splendor (pomp). **-giáto**, ADJ.: splendid (pompous); excessive; ADV.: immoderately. **sfòg-gio**, M.: splendour (sumptuousness).
sfò-glia [*s-*, *f.* .], F.: leaf; spangle (gold foil). **-gliáme**, M.: exfoliation (dross of metals). **-gliáre**, TR.: unleaf (strip the leaves off of); dry up† (consume); make thin†; scale†; REFL.: exfoliate (shell off). **-gliáta**, **-gliatúra**, F.: puff-paste (light pastry); unleafing, etc. **-gliáto**, PART.: stripped of leaves, etc. **-gliétta**, *dim.* of *-glia*.
s=fognáre, INTR.: open into a sewer; be born†.
sfógo [*sfogare*], M.: letting out; vent; summit of an arch.
sfolgo-raménto, M.: lightning; wasting. ||**-ráre** [*s-*, *folgore*], INTR.: shine (glitter, sparkle); TR.: hasten (expedite); ruin (destroy, waste). **-rataménte**, ADV.: resplendently; immoderately. **-rá-to**†, ADJ.: brilliant (shining); exorbitant (immoderate); unhappy (unfortunate). **-reggiánte**, ADJ.: resplendent (dazzling). **-reggiáre** = *-rare*. **-río**, M.: shining, glittering.
sfon-daménto, M.: knocking out or in the bottom; massacre (carnage)†. ||**-dá-re** [*s-*, *f.* .], TR.: knock out or in the bottom of; drive down (pull down); INTR.: sink (go to the bottom). **-dáto**, PART.: bottomless; destroyed (ruined); excessive; M. = *-do*: *ricco* —, exceedingly rich. **-datúra** = *-damento*. **-do**, M.: empty space in ceilings for paintings; paintings themselves. **-doláre** = *-dare*.
sforacchia. . = *foracchia.* .
sformá-re [*s-*, *f.* .], TR.: deform (disfigure); unmold; metamorphose; INTR.†: be vexed. **-taménte**, ADV.: formlessly; prodigiously; immoderately. **-túra**, **-zió-ne**, F.: deformity (ugliness).
sfor-naciáre, TR.: remove from the furnace. ||**-náre** [*s-*, *forno*], TR.: take out of the oven.
sfor-niménto, M.: unfurnishing; want (dearth). ||**-níre** [*s-*, *f.* .], TR.: unfurnish (deprive, strip).
sfortú-na [*s-*, *f.* .], F.: misfortune. **-na-ménto**, M.: misfortune (disaster; unhappiness). **-náre**†, TR.: render unfortunate (make unhappy). **-náto**, **-névo-le**, ADJ.: unfortunate (unhappy).
sfor-zaménto, M.: force (violence); effort (attempt). ||**-záre** [*s-*, *f.* .], TR.: force (compel); violate (ravish); debilitate (enervate); REFL.: endeavour (strive). **-za-taménte**, ADV.: with force (compulsively). **-zatíccio**, *dim.* of *-zato*. **-zá-to**, PART.: forced, etc.; ADJ.: immoderate (immense); overcharged. **-zatóre**, M.: forcer (compeller). **-zatúra** = *-za-mento*. **-zévole**, ADJ.: tyrannical (using violence). **-zevolménte**, ADV.: tyrannically (strenuously). **sfòr-zo**, M.: effort (endeavour, attempt).
sfos-sáre [*s-*, *fossa*], TR.: take out of the ditch. **-sáto**, PART., ADJ.: sunken (hollow).
sfracassáre = *fracassare*.

sfra-cellàre†, ‖**-gellàre** [*s-*, *flagellare*], TR.: ruin (break in pieces; split).

sfrangià-re [*s-*, *f.* .], TR.: unravel, fringe (unweave). **-túra**, F.: unravelling.

sfrascáre [*s-*, *frasca*], TR.: strip the leaves or branches off; reduce the swelling of.

sfratáre [*s-*, *frate*], TR.: unfrock (take from the cloister); REFL.: renounce the order.

sfrat-táre, TR.: dismiss (send away); INTR.: go away. ‖**-to** [? *fratta*], M.: flight (escape); expulsion: *dar lo —*, expel.

sfre-gacciáre, TR.: *freq.* of *-gare;* rub gently. **-gacciolàre** = *-gacciare*. **-gaménto**, M.: rubbing (friction). ‖**-gáre** [*s-*, *f.* .], TR.: rub. **-gatóio**, M.: rubber; brush.

sfre-giáre [*s-*, *f.* .], TR.: disadorn; gash in the face; defame (dishonour); REFL.: lose its brightness (get faded). **-gio**, M.: cut or gash in the face; scar; affront; disgrace.

sfrena-ménto, M.: impudence (insolence); licentiousness. ‖**sfrená-re** [*s-*, *f.* .], TR.: unbridle (let loose); REFL.: remove one's bridle (throw off all restraint). **-tággine** = *-tezza*. **-taménte**, ADV.: dissolutely. **-tézza**, F.: licentiousness (libertinism). **sfrená-to**, PART.: unbridled, etc.; ADJ.†: impetuous; excessive (immoderate). **-zióne**†, F.: impudence; licentiousness.

sfrí-ggere [*s-*, *f.* .], **-(g)goláre**, INTR.: make a noise like frying; TR.: fry. **-ggoláto** = *rifritto*. **-ggolío**, M.: continued frying noise.

sfringuelláre [*s-*, *fringuello*], INTR.: chirp (warble); gossip.

sfrizzáre† = *frizzare*.

sfrogiáto [*s-*, *froge*], ADJ.: flat or crushed (of the nose).

sfrombolàre, TR.: fling (cast with a sling).

sfron-daménto, M.: stripping off the leaves. ‖**-dáre** [*s-*, *fronda*], INTR.: strip off the leaves. **-dáto**, ADJ.: leafless. **-datóre**, M.: puller of leaves.

sfron-táre† [*s-*, *fronte*], INTR., REFL.: become bold (be shameless). **-tatággine** = *-tatezza*. **-tataménte**, ADV.: boldly (impudently). **-tatèllo**, *dim.* of *-tato*. **-tatézza**, F.: impudence (effrontery). **-táto**, ADJ.: bold (impudent, saucy).

sfronzáre [*s-*, *fronza*], INTR.: clip or plough (the edges of books); = *sfrondare*.

sfruttáre [*s-*, *f.* .], TR.: sterilize (impoverish).

sfucináta†, F.: great number (multitude).

sfug-gévole, ADJ.: fugitive (transitory); slippery. **-gevolézza**, F.: quickness (rapidity); slipperiness. **-giásco**, ADJ.: fugitive (wandering): *alla —sca*, in secret (by stealth). **-giménto**, M.: flight (running away). ‖**-gíre** [*s-*, *f.* .], TR.: avoid (shun, elude); flee from; INTR.: escape; run away. **-gíto**, PART.: avoided, etc.; ADJ.: fugitive: *alla -gita*, hurriedly.

sfulgóre†, M.: luxury (pomp).

sfu-maménto, M.: evaporation; appearance (sign). **-mánte**, ADJ.: evaporating (vanishing). ‖**-máre** [*s-*, *f.* .], INTR.: fume (exhale); evaporate (melt away); TR.: (*fig.*) shade or blend (colours); paint (the background). **-matézza**, F.: blending of colours. **-máto**, PART.: dying away. **-matúra**, F.: evaporation, etc.

sfu-riáre [*s-*, *furia*], INTR.: be very angry. **-riáta**, F.: anger (rage); abuse; great number. **-riatáccia**, *disp.* of *-riata*.

sgabbiáre [*s-*, *gabbia*], TR.: uncage (take out of the cage).

s=gabelláre, TR.: free from duty or tax; REFL.: get off (free one's self).

sgabel-létto, **-líno**, *dim.* of *-lo*. ‖**sgabèl-lo** [L. *scabellum* (dim. of *scamnum*)], M.: stool (joint-stool, desk-stool). **-lóne**, *aug.* of *-lo*.

sgabuzzíno [Eng. *caboose*], M.: retired room (secret closet).

sgagliardáre [*s-*, *gagliardo*], TR.: weaken (debilitate, enervate).

s=galánte†, ADJ.: ungallant (ungracious).

sgalláre [*s-*, *galla*], TR.: make a blister on.

sgallet-táre [*s-*, *galletto*], INTR.: (*fig.*) play the wit (try to be witty). **-tío**, M.: affecting wit.

sgallináre [*s-*, *gallina*], TR.: steal (chickens, etc.); INTR.: make merry (enjoy one's self).

sgam-báre, INTR.: stride; stem (remove the stems of); get tired. **-báto**, ADJ.: without stem; tired. **-bettáre**, INTR.: walk quickly (take short steps); run away; kick the legs about. **-bettáta** = *-betto*. ‖**-bétto** [*s-*, *g.* .], M.: scurvy trick; tripping up one's heels; (*fig.*) trap (stratagem). **-bucciáto**†, ADJ.: without stockings.

sga-nasciáre [*s-*, *ganascia*], TR.: dislocate (the jaws): *— dalle risa*, burst with laughter. **-nasciaménto**, M., **-nasciáta**, F.: immoderate laughter. **-nasciáre**, INTR.: laugh immoderately.

sganghe-raménto, M.: unhinging (taking off the hinges); disorder. ‖**-ráre** [*s-*, *g.* .], TR.: unhinge (take off the hinges); (*fig.*) disorder (derange); dislocate. **-ratáccio**, *disp.* of *-rato*. **-ratággine**, F.: awkwardness; confusion. **-rataménte**, ADV.: awkwardly; confusedly. **-rá-**

-to, PART.: off the hinges (disconnected); dislocated; awkward (rude); confused.

sganna. = *disinganna.*

sga-rére†, INTR.: carry off the prize (win); TR.: brave. **-ráto†,** PART.: come off victor, etc.

sgar-báccio, *disp.* of *-bo.* **-batággine** = *-batezza.* **-bataménte,** ADV.: impolitely (rudely). **-batézza,** F.: impoliteness (incivility). **-báto,** ADJ.: awkward (impolite, rude). ‖**sgár-bo** [*s-, g.* .], M.: rudeness; disagreeableness.

sgargarizz. = *gargarizz.*

sgargiánte [*squarciante*], ADJ.: stylish (well dressed).

sgarígliot†, M.: cutthroat.

sgaríre† = *sgarare.*

sgarráre [Fr. *égarer*, mislead], TR., INTR.: mistake (err).

sgarrettáre [*s-, garetto*], TR.: (*vet.*) hamstring (cut the ham or hough off).

sgattaioláre [*s-, gattaiola*], INTR.: get out of a difficulty.

sgattigliáre†, TR.: disburse.

sgavazzáre = *gavazzare.*

sghémbo [? OHG. *slimb*, oblique], ADJ.: crooked (awry); M.: obliquity (crookedness); awkwardness: *a —*, obliquely (on one side).

sghermí-re [*s-, g.* .], TR.: let go (let loose). **-tóre,** M.: one who lets loose.

sgheronáto [*s-, gherone*], ADJ.: cut aslant (in bias).

sgherráccio, *aug.* of *sgherro.*

sgherrettáre [*s-, garetto*], TR.: hamstring (hough); cf. *sgarrettare.*

sghèrro [?], M.: ruffian (cutthroat); (*fig.*) stylish man.

s=ghiacciáre, TR.: thaw (liquefy).

sghi-gnapáppole†, M.: hearty laugher. ‖**-gnáre** [*s-, gh.* .], TR.: laugh at (ridicule); INTR.: laugh contemptuously. **-gnáta†,** F., **-gnazzaménto,** M.: loud laughter. **-gnazzáre,** INTR.: burst out laughing (laugh immoderately). **-gnazzáta** = *-gnata.* **-gnazzío,** M.: continual loud laughter. **sghí-gno†,** M.: sneer. **-gnázzo,** *aug.* of *-gno.*

sghimbèscio [*sghembo*], M.: crooked line; ADJ.: bow-legged; ADV.: athwart (awry, aslant).

sgittaméntot†, M.: agitation.

s=gloriáto, ADJ.: unconcerned (careless, liberal).

sgob-báre [*s-, gobba*], INTR.: study hard. **sgòb-bo,** M.: working hard. **-bóne,** M.: very hard worker.

sgoccio-láre [*s-, g.* .], INTR.: drain (drop from); dry up (suck up); TR.: distil (drain out); empty: — *il barletto†*, tell all one knows. **-latóio,** M.: gutter (drain, eaves of a house). **-latúra,** F.: draining (dropping); eaves of a house. **-lío,** M.: continued dropping. **sgóccio-lo,** M.: rest (remainder); draining: *essere agli —*, be at the end.

sgo-láre [*s-, gola*], TR.: cut the throat of. **-láto,** PART., ADJ.: throatless; bare-necked; babbling (chattering).

sgom-boraménto, M.: removal (removing); removing from a dwelling. ‖**-boráre** [*s-, ingombrare*], TR.: remove from; carry away; drive off (separate); free (liberate); cleanse (purge); INTR.: remove (go away). **-boráto,** PART.: removed; disencumbered, etc. **-boratóre,** M.: remover. **-boratúra** = *-beramento.* **sgóm-bero,** PART.: removed, etc.; empty (unprovided); M.: removal; expulsion. **-bráre** = *-berare.* **-bratóre** = *-beratore.*

sgóm-bro 1 = *-bero.*

sgómbro 2 = *scombro.*

sgomen-taméntot†, M.: discouragement; astonishment; dismay. ‖**-táre** [?], TR.: frighten (dismay; discourage); REFL.: be terrified; lose courage. **-tévole†,** ADJ.: discouraging; alarming. **-tíre†** = *-tare.* **sgomén-to,** PART.: frightened, etc.; M.: fear (alarm).

sgomi-naménto, M.: disorder (confusion). ‖**-náre** [*s-*, L. *comminari*, threaten], TR.: put in confusion (disarrange, disorder). **-nío,** M.: continued disorder.

sgomitoláre [*s-, gomitolo*], TR.: unwind (untwist).

sgon-fiaménto, M.: lowering or lessening of a swelling. ‖**-fiáre** [*s-, g.* .], TR.: lower the swelling of; (*fig.*) humiliate (humble); kill†; REFL.: cease swelling. **-fiáto** = *-fio.* **sgón-fio,** ADJ.: unswollen (flabby); humbled. **-fiòtto,** *dim.* of *-fio.*

sgonnelláre [*s-, gonnella*], INTR.: take off the petticoats; seek a husband.

sgórbia [l. L. *gubia* (*gulbia*)], M.: COUGE.

sgor-biáre = *scorbiare.* **-bio** = *scorbio.* **-biolína,** *dim.* of *sgorbio.*

sgor-gaménto, M.: disgorging (overflowing). **-ganteménto,** ADV.: abundantly. ‖**-gáre** [*s-, gorgo*], INTR.: disgorge (overflow); (*fig.*) give to the winds (blab all one knows). **-gáta,** F.: quantity of air or water in a pump. **sgòr-go,** M.: overflowing; profusion; ADV.: abundantly (copiously).

s=governáre, TR.: govern ill (manage badly).

sgozzáre [*s-, gozzo*], TR.: cut the throat of; empty (the craw of poultry); swallow (an affront).

sgracimoláre = *racimolare.*

s=gradévole, ADJ.: disagreeable (displeasing). **-gradíre,** TR.: displease (disgust).

şgráf-fa, F.: (*typ.*) brace. ‖**-fiáre** [*s-*, *g..*], TR.: scratch; hatch (graze). **-fignáre**, TR.: steal (carry away). **şgráf-fio** 1, M.: scratch (tear). **-fióne**, *aug.* of *-fio*.
sgráf-fio 2, **-fito** = *graffito*.
şgrammaticáre [*s-*, *grammatica*], INTR.: make errors in grammar; TR.: explain grammatically.
şgramuffáre†, INTR.: (*iron.*) speak like a grammarian.
şgra-nábile, ADJ.: that can be shelled. **-naménto**, M.: shelling. ‖**-náre** [*s-*, *grano*], TR.: shell; burst open. **-natúra** = *-namento*.
şgran-chiáre, ‖**-chire** [*s-*, *aggranchiare*], TR.: stretch or extend (the limbs); arouse (quicken, stir up).
şgra-nellaménto, M.: stoning raisins. ‖**-nelláre** [*s-*, *granello*], TR.: stone (raisins, etc.). **-nellatúra** = *-nellamento*.
-nocchiáre, TR.: crunch (eat things that crackle).
şgra-vaménto, M.: ease (relief, comfort). ‖**-váre** [*s-*, *g..*], TR.: unload (disburden); relieve (alleviate); REFL.: lie in. **-vidánza**, F.: delivery (childbirth). **-vidáre**†, INTR.: lie in (be brought to bed). **-vio**, M.: unloading (discharge); ease (relief).
şgrá-zia† [*s-*, *g..*], F.: misfortune; disgrace. **-ziatáccio**, *disp.* of *-ziato*. **-ziatággine**, F.: awkwardness; ill grace. **-ziataménte**, ADV.: awkwardly; unfortunately. **-ziatèllo**, *dim.* of *-ziato*. **-ziáto**, ADJ.: awkward (ungraceful); unfortunate; wretched (miserable). **-ziatóne**, *aug.* of *-ziato*.
şgreto-laménto, M.: breaking (bruising). ‖**-láre** [? *gretola*], TR.: crunch; scatter (disunite); undo. **-lío**, M.: crunching; fermentation.
şgricchioláre† = *scricchiolare*.
şgriccíolo = *scricciolo*.
şgri-daménto, M.: scolding (reprimand; rebuke). ‖**-dáre** [*s-*, *g..*], TR.: rebuke (reprimand; scold). **-dáta**, F.: scolding; reprimand. **-datína**, *dim.* of *-data*. **-datóre**, M.: reprover (rebuker). **-do**† = *-damento*.
şgrigiáto†, ADJ.: of a grayish colour.
şgrigioláre†, INTR.: clank (clash).
şgrignáre†, INTR.: grin (laugh at).
şgrillettáre [*s-*, *grilletto*], TR.: pull (the trigger).
şgrondá-re [*s-*, *g..*], INTR.: fall in drops (drop). **-túra**, F.: dripping.
şgroppáre 1 = *sgruppare*.
[illegible]ppáre 2 [*s-*, *groppa*], TR.: spoil (the [illegible]r).
[illegible]ssaménto, M.: sketch (rough [illegible]). ‖**-sáre** [*s-*, *digrossare*], TR.: [illegible] (*rough-hew*).

şgrottá-re [*s-*, *grotta*], TR.: drain (vines). **-túra**, F.: draining (of vines).
şgru-gnáre [*s-*, *grugno*], INTR.: give a blow in the face. **-gnáta**, F., **-gno**, M.: blow in the face. **-gnóne**, *aug.* of *-gno*.
şgruppáre [*s-*, *gruppo*], TR.: untie or undo (a knot); separate.
şgua-gliánza, F.: inequality. ‖**-gliáre** [*s-*, *aggua..*], TR.: make unequal or uneven; disunite. **-glio**, M.: inequality; difference (disparity).
şguaia-tággine, F.: awkwardness. **-taménte**, ADV.: awkwardly. **-tèllo**, **-tíno**, *dim.* of *-to*. **-tóne**, *aug.* of *-to*. ‖**şguaiá-to** [Fr. *égayé*, happy], ADJ.: graceless (ill-mannered); stupid.
şguainàre [*s-*, *guaina*], TR.: unsheath (draw out).
şgualcíre [OHG. *walzjan*], TR.: rumple (crush).
şgualdrí-na [?], F.: prostitute (bad woman). **-nèlla**, *dim.* of *-na*.
şguán-cia [*s-*, *g..*], F.: check, strap (of a bridle). **-ciáre**, INTR.: strike (a glancing blow); break the check, strap (of a bridle)†. **-cio**†, M.: obliquity (slope); ADV.: awry (athwart).
şguar-aguardáre†, TR.: look at repeatedly or attentively. **-aguárdia**, F.: vanguard. **-daménto**†, M.: look (glance); view. ‖**-dáre**† [*s-*, *g..*], TR.: stare at (look at); explore; have a regard or respect for. **-dáta**, F.: glance; look (aspect). **-datáccia**, *disp.* of *-data*. **-datóre**, M.: looker on (beholder). **-datúra**, F.: mien (look, deportment). **-dévole**†, ADJ.: remarkable; respectable.
şguár-do, M.: look (glance); consideration (respect). **-dolíno**†, *dim.* of *-do*.
ş-guarníre, TR.: unfurnish; unprovide.
şguaz-záre [*s-*, *guazzo*], INTR.: ford; make merry; TR.: waste (dissipate). **-zatóre**, M.: feaster; lavisher. **-zugliáre**, INTR.: *freq.* of *-zare*.
şgúbbia = *sgorbia*.
şguerciatúra†, F.: contemptuous look (squint).
şguerguènza [?], F.: impolite act; something odd or reprehensible.
şguerníre = *sguarnire*.
şgu-fáre [*s-*, *gufo*], TR.: laugh at (ridicule, mock); slip. **-foneáre**, TR.: make fun of.
şguinzagliáre [*s-*, *guinzaglio*], TR.: uncouple (let loose).
şguisciáre [*s-*, OFr. *guenchir* (OGer. *wenkian*)], INTR.: skip (slide, frisk away); swim; bounce; escape.
şguittíre†, INTR.: yelp (squeak, howl).
ş-guizzáre, INTR.: = *sguisciare*: — *in piede*, start up.
şgu-sciáre [*s-*, *guscio*], TR.: shell (husk);

INTR. = *sguisciare*. **-sciáto**, PART.: shelled, etc.; M.: gouge (in wood, etc.). **-sciatúra**, F.: shelling; gouging, etc. **-scio**, M.: kind of gouge; hollow cavity.
si [L. *se*], PRON.: one, people, we, they; himself, herself, etc.
sì [L. *sic*], ADV.: yes, truly: — *bene*, yes indeed; — . . . — . . ., as well . . . as . . ., both . . . and . . .; — *veramente*, provided.
siaméșe, M.: siamese (coarse cotton cloth).
sibaríta [*Sibari* (in Lucania)], M.: sybarite.
sibi-láre [L. *-lo* (*-lus*, hissing)], INTR.: hiss (whistle). **-láto**, PART.: hissed; urged. **-latóre**, M.: whistler; scoffer. **-lío**, M.: prolonged hiss (hissing).
sibíl-la [L. *sibylla*, divine counsel (Gr. *siós*, God, *boulé*, counsel)], F.: sibyl (prophetess). **-líno**, ADJ.: sibylline (mysterious). **-lóne†**, M.: kind of riddle or enigma.
síbi-lo = *-lío*. **-lóso**, ADJ.: sibilant (hissing).
sicário [L. *-rius* (*sica*, knife)], M.: cutthroat (assassin).
síccera†, F.: cider.
sicchè -é [*sì, chè*], ADV.: thus; whence; therefore; cf. *sì*.
sícciolo = *cicciolo*.
siccità [L. *-tas*], F.: siccity (dryness, drought).
siccóme [*sì, come*], ADV.: as, so; as if; as soon as.
síclo [L. *siclus* (Heb. *shekel*)], M.: shekel.
sico-fánta, -fánte† [Gr. *suko-phántes*, fig-informer, slanderer], M.: sycophant; calumniator. **-mòro** [Gr. *sukó-moros*, fig-mulberry], M.: sycamore.
sicummèra†, F.: pomp (ceremony).
sicu-raménte, ADV.: certainly (surely). **-ránza†**, F.: security; assurance (boldness). **-ráre†** = *assicurare*. **-rézza**, **-rità** = *-rtà*. ||**sicú-ro** [*securo*], ADJ.: sure (secure); firm; certain (unquestionable); practised: *andar sul* —, go without fear (act confidently); *di* —, certainly (surely). **-rtà**, F.: security (safety); courage; assurance; faith (honesty); bail (security).
side-ràle [L. *-ralis*], ADJ.: sidereal. **-razióne**, F.: (*med.*) sideration (sudden mortification). **sidè-reo**, ADJ.: sidereal; celestial.
sidére† = *sedere*.
side-ríte [L. *-ritis*], F.: magnet; (*bot.*) ironwort. **-rúrgia**, F.: working in iron.
sído†, M.: excessive cold.
sídro [L. *sicera* (Gr. *síkera*)], M.: cider.
sièda = *sedia*.
sièffo†, M.: eye-salve (*collyrium*).

sie-páglia, *disp.* of *-pe*. **-páre†**, TR.: enclose (surround with hedges). ||**siè-pe** [L. *sæpes*], F.: hedge; enclosure: *tenere uno a* —, keep one in awe. **-póne**, *aug.* of *-pe*.
siè-ro, ||**-ro** [L. *serum*], M.: whey (buttermilk); serum (watery part of blood). **-rosità**, F.: serosity. **-róso**, ADJ.: serous.
siffátto [*sì, fatto*], ADJ.: such (exactly, the same).
sifi-líde [?], M.: syphilis. **-lítico**, ADJ.: syphilitic.
si-foncíno, *dim.* of *-fone*. ||**-fóne** [L. *sipho*], M.: syphon (pipe, tube; soda bottle).
siga-ráio, M.: cigar-maker. **-rétto**, **-ríno**, *dim.* of *-ro*. ||**síga-ro** [Sp. *cigarro* (*cigarar*, roll in paper)], M.: cigar.
sigil-láre, TR.: seal; confirm (fix); finish; stop. **-lataménte**, ADV.: exactly (distinctly). **-latóre**, M.: sealer. ||**sigíllo** [L. *-lum* (dim. of *signum*, figure)], M.: seal; stamp: *porre il* —, seal; — *di Ermete*, hermetical seal; — *di Salomone*, knot grass.
sígla [L.], F.: letter (cypher).
sigmòide [Gr. *-moeidés* (*sigma*, S, *eidos*, form)], F.: (*anat.*) sigmoidal valve.
si-gnatúra, F.: = *segnatura*; signature (tribunal at Rome). **-gnèra†**, F.: blood-letting (bleeding). **-gnífero†**, M.: standard-bearer (ensign); ADJ.: bearing the standard. **-gnificaménto**, M.: signification (meaning). **-gnificanteménte**, ADV.: significantly. **-gnificánza**, F.: sense (interpretation); sign. ||**-gnificáre** [L.], TR.: signify (mean); declare (express by signs); interest; inform. **-gnificataménte**, ADV.: in a signifying manner. **-gnificativaménte**, ADV.: expressively. **-gnificatívo**, ADJ.: expressive (that signifies); energetic. **-gnificáto**, M.: signification (meaning, sense). **-gnificazióne**, F.: = *-gnificato*; information; mark (sign).
signó-ra, F.: mistress, madam; Lady (a title); prostitute. **-rággio** = *-ria*. **-rázzo**, M.: great lord. ||**signó-re** [L. *senior*], M.: lord (nobleman); rich man; Lord; master; sir, gentleman: *il* — *Tale*, Mr. So-and-so. **-reggévole**, ADJ.: imperious (magisterial, stately). **-reggiaménto**, M.: sovereignty (empire); rule (power). **-reggiáre**, TR.: domineer (rule, govern). **-reggiatóre**, M.: dominator (ruler). **-rèllo**, *dim.* of *-re*. **-résco**, ADJ.: lordly (gentlemanly). **-réssa** = *-ra*. **-rétto**, *dim.* of *-re*. **-révole†**, ADJ.: imperious (magisterial); noble (genteel, agreeable). **-ría**, F.: dominion (lordship); supreme magistrate of a republic; jurisdiction; power (empire). **-rílo**, ADJ.: illustrious (lordly). **-rilità†**,

F.: nobility; stateliness. **-rilménte,** ADV.: nobly (illustriously). **-rína,** F.: *dim.* of *-ra;* young lady, miss. **-ríno,** *dim.* of *-re.* **signó-rmo†** [*-r, mio*], M.: my lord. **-rótto,** M.: country-squire (little lord). **signó-rso†** [*-r, suo*], M.: his lord. **signó-rto†** [*-r, tuo*], M.: thy lord or master.

signozzáre† = *singhiozzare.*

silèn-te [L. *-s*], ADJ.: silent; calm. **-ziário,** ADJ.: that imposes silence. **silènzio** [L. *-tium*], M.: silence; taciturnity; intermission (pause): *passar sotto —,* pass over in silence; *far —,* keep silence; *impor —,* command silence. **-zióso,** ADJ.: silent (still, taciturn).

sileos†, M.: heartwort.

silère†, INTR.: keep silent (be still).

silfide [*silfo*], F.: female sylph; graceful woman.

silfio†, M.: laserwort (laserpitium).

silfo [Gall.], M.: sylph.

sí-lice [L. *silex*], F.: flintstone (pebble); gun flint. **-líceo,** ADJ.: silicious (flinty).

silígine†, F.: siligo (fine wheat).

silio†, M.: spindle-tree.

siliqua† [L.], F.: siliqua (seed-vessel, husk); weight of four grains; siliqua (a coin).

síl-laba [L. *syllaba* (Gr. *sullabé*)], F.: syllable. **-labáre,** TR.: syllable (pronounce clearly); spell. **-labário,** M.: reading or spelling-book. **-labazióne,** F.: syllabification. **-lábico,** ADJ.: syllabical. **-labismo,** M.: syllabic writing.

síl-labo [l. L. *syllabus*], M.: index (catalogue, register).

sil-lèpsi [Gr. *súllepsis*], **-lèssi,** F.: (*gram.*) syllepsis.

sillo-gismo [L. *syllogismus*], M.: syllogism. **-gística,** F.: reasoning by syllogism. **-gisticaménte,** ADV.: syllogistically. **-gístico,** pl. *—ci,* ADJ.: syllogistic. **-gizzáre,** TR.: syllogize (reason).

silòcco†, M.: sirocco (south-east wind).

siloè [Gr. *xúleos*], M.: aloes (odoriferous wood).

silò-fago [Gr. *xulo-phágos* (*xúlon,* wood, *phagein,* eat)], M.: wood-eater. **-gráfia** [Gr. *gráphein,* write], F.: xylography (art of engraving wood). **-gráfico,** pl. *—ci,* ADJ.: xylographic(al).

silú-ro, ‖**-ri** [Gr. *sílouros*], M.: shad (a river-fish); torpedo (a fish).

sil-váno [*selva*], ADJ.: sylvan (rustic); ...ge); foreign. **-vèstre, -vè...**: woody; wild (rural). **-vóso,** ...y, etc.

...ziaménto, M.: symbolization. ..., TR.: symbolize (represent). ...*-lità.* **-licaménte,** ADV.: symbolically. **simbò-lico,** pl. *—ci,* ADJ.: symbolical. **-lità†,** F.: analogy (conformity); relation. **-lizzáre** = *-leggiare.*

‖**símbo-lo** [Gr. *súmbolon*], M.: symbol; image (allegory); creed.

si-metría [Gr. *simmetría* (*sun,* with, *métron,* measure)], F.: symmetry (proportion). **-mètrico** = *-mmetrico.*

símia† = *scimmia.*

simiáno†, M.: sort of plum-tree.

simigli. .† = *somigli. .*

simi-láre, ADJ.: similar (like). ‖**símile** [L. *-lis*], ADJ.: like (similar, even); equal; M.: like (fellow); fellow-creature; ADV.: in like manner. **-litudinariaménte†,** ADV.: comparatively. **-litudinário†,** ADJ.: similitudinary. **-litúdine,** F.: similitude (likeness); comparison; image (figure). **-lménte,** ADV.: likewise (also, too). **-lòro,** M.: pinchbeck.

simità†, F.: flatness of the nose.

sim-metría = *simetria.* **-mètrico,** ADJ.: symmetrical (proportionate). **-metrizzáre,** TR.: render symmetrical.

símo†, ADJ.: flat-nosed.

simo-neggiáre, INTR.: commit simony. ‖**-nía** [*Simon,* the magician, who wanted to buy eccl. offices of St. Peter], F.: simony (selling of ecclesiastical offices). **-niacaménte,** ADV.: by simony. **-níaco,** ADJ.: simoniacal (obtained by simony). **-nizzáre†** = *-neggiare.* **-nizzatóre,** M.: one guilty of simony.

sim-patía [Gr. *sumpátheia*], F.: sympathy. **-pático,** pl. *—ci,* ADJ.: sympathetic; homogeneous; attractive; congenial. **-patizzáre,** INTR.: sympathise.

simplic. .† = *semplic. .*

simplificá-re† [L.], REFL.: become simple; TR.: simplify. **-zióne,** F.: simplification.

sim-posíaco, ADJ.: of a feast or banquet. ‖**-pòsio** [Gr. *sum-pósion,* drinking together], M.: banquet (feast).

simu-lácro [L. *-lacrum*], M.: simulachre (image, statue). **-laménte†,** M.: simulation (pretence); deceit. **-lárdo,** ADJ.: deceitful; M.: dissembler. ‖**-láre** [L.], TR.: simulate (feign, pretend). **-lataménte,** ADV.: with pretence. **-latívo,** ADJ.: simulative (pretending). **-latóre,** M.: hypocrite (pretender). **-latòrio,** ADJ.: done with dissimulation. **-lazióne,** F.: dissimulation (disguise).

simul-taneità, F.: simultaneousness. ‖**-táneo** [l. L. *-taneus*], ADJ.: simultaneous.

sinagòga [Gr. *sun-agogé,* bringing together], F.: synagogue.

sinalèfe [Gr. *sun-aloiphé,* smearing together], F.: synalœpha.

sinapismo†, M.: mustard poultice.

sinattantochè *é* [*sin, tanto-chè*], CONJ.: till (until).

since-raménte, ADV.: sincerely; honestly. **-raménto**, M.: justification (exculpation). **-ráre**, TR.: make sincere; exculpate (justify); REFL.: justify one's self; ascertain. **-razióne**† = *-ramento*. **-rità**, F.: sincerity (candour); integrity; generosity. ||**sincè-ro** [L. *-rus*], ADJ.: sincere (true); genuine; loyal.

sinchè† *é*, CONJ., PREP.: until (till).

sínco-pa† = *-pe*. **-páro**, TR.: syncopate (elide). **-pataménte**, ADV.: in a syncopating manner. **-patúra**, F.: cutting off; contraction. ||**sínco-pe** [L. *syncope* (Gr. *sunkopé*)], F.: (*med.*) syncope (swooning); (*gram.*) elision. **-pizzáre**†, INTR.: faint or swoon away.

sin-croniśmo†, M.: synchronism. ||**sín-crono** [Gr. *sunchrónos*], ADJ.: synchronous.

sinda-cábile, ADJ.: that can be accounted for or criticized. **-caménto**, M.: account (explanation). **-cáre**, TR.: call to strict account; censure (blame, find fault with). **-cáto**, M.: account (strict account); comptrollership; permission; order: *tenere a —, stare a —*, call to an account. **-catúra**, F.: giving up of accounts. ||**sinda-co** [L. *syndicus*, city-advocate], M.: syndic (overseer, comptroller); mayor (city-magistrate); town-clerk.

sindèreśi [Gr. *suntéresis*, examination], F.: remorse of conscience.

sindi-cále, ADJ.: of a syndic. ||**-cáre** = *sindacare*. **-cáto**, M.: office of a syndic.

síndone [Gr. *sindón*, fine linen cloth], F.: sindon; the Saviour's shroud.

sinecúra [L.], F.: sinecure.

sinèddoche [Gr. *sun-ekdoché*, taking together], F.: (*gram.*) synecdoche.

sinèdrio [Gr. *sunédrion*, council], M.: sanhedrim.

sinèreśi [Gr. *sun-aíresis*, seizing together], F.: (*gram.*) syneresis.

sinèstro† = *sinistro*.

sinfonía [Gr. *sumphonía*], F.: symphony; concert.

sin-ghiottíre, **-ghiozzáre**, **-ghiozzíre**, INTR.: have the hiccups; sob (sigh). ||**-ghiózzo** [l. L. *suggultium* (L. *singultus*, sobbing)], M.: sob (sigh); hiccup. **-ghiozzóso**, ADJ.: sighing (sobbing).

singo-láre [L. *singularis*], ADJ.: singular; special (extraordinary, peculiar); excellent (rare); M.: singular number. **-lareggiáre**, INTR.: make singular; specialize. **-larità**, F.: singularity; excellency. **-larizzáre**, TR.: particularize (detail); REFL.: affect singularity. **-larménte**, ADV.: singularly (particularly). ||**síngo-lo** [L. *singulus*], ADJ.: single (each, every): *per —*, singly (individually); in particular.

sin-gozz.., **-gult..** = *singhiozz..*

singul..† = *singol..*

sinìbbio [?], M.: fine snow.

sini-scalcáto, M.: seneschal's office. **-scalchía**†, F.: seneschal's jurisdiction. ||**-scálco** [l. L. *senescalcus* (OGer. *sini*, old, *skalks*, servant)], M.: steward (major-domo); treasurer; officer in ancient armies.

siní-stra, F.: left hand: *a —*, on the left. **-straménte**, ADV.: sinistrously (ominously). **-stráre**†, INTR.: turn to the left; err; tergiversate; incommode one's self; REFL.: make a false step (slip). ||**siní-stro** [L. *-ster*], ADJ.: left; sinister (unfortunate); sad; M.: misfortune (mishap); disaster; failure.

sino 1 = *fino*.

síno 2 [*seno*], M.: (*math.*) sine; (*geog.*) gulf.

sinòco [Gr. *sunochós*, continuous], ADJ.: (*med.*) of or belonging to a continual fever.

sino-dále, ADJ.: synodal (of a synod). **-dalménte**, ADV.: synodically (by the synod). **sinó-dio**, M.: (*mus.*) duet. ||**si-no-do** [L. *synodus*, Gr. *súnodos* (*sun*, with, together, *hodós*, coming)], M.: synod.

sino-nimía, F.: synonymy. **-nímico**, pl. *—ci*, ADJ.: synonymal. **-nimizzáre**, INTR.: synonymize. ||**sinò-nimo** [Gr., *sunónumon* (*sun*, with, *ónoma*, name)], ADJ.: synonymous; M.: synonym.

si-nòpia [L. *-nopis* (earth of Sinope)], F.: sinoper (red ochre): *andar per il filo della —*, go straight to work (speak to the purpose). **-nòpico**, pl. *—ci*, ADJ.: of sinoper.

si-nòssi [Gr. *sún-opsis*, seeing together], F.: synopsis; abridgment (summary). **-nòttico**, pl. *—ci*, ADJ.: synoptical (brief).

sinò-via [Gr. *sun*, with, *oón*, egg (egg-like substance)], F.: synovia. **-viále**, ADJ.: synovial. **-vína** = *-via*.

sintáśsi [Gr. *sún-taxis* (*sun*, with, *táxis*, order), putting together in order], F.: syntax.

sin-teśi [Gr. *sún-thesis*, putting together], F.: synthesis. **-teticaménte**, ADV.: synthetically. **-tètico**, pl. *—ci*, ADJ.: synthetic; compounding.

sintílla† = *scintilla*.

sin-tòma†, M. = *-tomo*. **-tomático**, pl. *—ci*, ADJ.: symptomatic. ||**sin-tomo** [Gr. *súmptoma*], M.: symptom; accident.

sinuo-saménte, ADV.: sinuously. **-sità**, F.: sinuosity (crookedness). ||**sinuó-so** [L. *-sus*], ADJ.: sinuous (crooked).

sío†, M.: smallage (parsley).

siónet†, M.: whirlwind.
sipa†, ADV.: yes: *il popolo del* —, the people of Bologna.
sipário [L. *-rium*, little sail], M.: stage-curtain.
sire [cf. *signore*], M.: sire (lord).
sirèna [L. *sirena* (Gr. *seirén*)], F.: siren (mermaid).
siríṇ-ga [Gr. *suringa*], F.: syringe; Pan's pipe. **-gáre**, TR.: syringe. **-gatúra**, F.: act of syringing.
sírio [L. *-rius* (Gr. *seírios*, hot)], M.: Sirius (dog-star).
siròc-chia†, F.: sister. **siròc-chiama**†, F.: my sister. **-chiévole**†, ADJ.: sisterly (of a sister). **-chievolménte**†, ADV.: like a sister.
siròcco† = *scirocco*.
siròpp. . = *sciropp.* .
sírte [Gr. *surtis* (*surein*, move)], F.: syrtis (quicksand).
síşamo† = *sesamo*.
sişáro†, M.: skirret; yellow parsnip.
sisím-brio†, **-bro**†, M.: (*bot.*) water-cress.
síşma = *scisma*.
sís-mico, pl. —*ci* [Gr. *seismós*, shaking], ADJ.: of an earthquake. **-mògrafo**, M.: seismograph (instrument which indicates the intensity of an earthquake).
sistè-ma, pl. *-mi* [L. *systema*], M.: system. **-máre**, TR.: systematize. **-maticaménte**, ADV.: systematically. **-mático**, *pl.* —*ci*, ADJ.: systematical. **-matizzáre**, TR.: reduce to a system (systematise). **-mazióne**, F.: order (system).
sísto†, M.: ancient circus.
sístole [Gr. *sustolé*, contraction], F.: systole (contraction of the heart).
sístro [L. *-trum* (Gr. *seistron*)], M.: sistrum (cithern).
si-táre [*sito* 2], INTR.: emit a bad smell (stink). **-tarèllo**, **-terèllo**, *dim.* of *-to*.
sitibóndo [L. *-bundus*], ADJ.: very thirsty; greedy (covetous).
sí-tio = *sete*. **-tíre**†, INTR.: thirst (be dry); desire ardently.
síto 1 [L. *-tus*], ADJ.: placed; situated; M.: site (situation); habitation; position.
síto 2 [L. *-tus*, mustiness], M.: offensive odour (stench).
situa-zióne, F., **-ménto**†, M.: situation (site). ‖**situá-re** [*sito* 1], TR.: situate (seat); set up. **-zióne**, F.: situation (position); posture; condition.
si-ziènte†, ADJ.: thirsty (dry); desirous. ‖**sí-zio**, M.: = *-tio*; application.
síẓ-ẓa [?], F.: strong wind. **-ẓettína**, *dim.* of *-za*.
şlab-bráre [*s-*, *labbro*], INTR.: cut the lips; get out of order. **-bratúra**, F.: act of getting out of order, etc.
şlac-ciáre [*s-*, *all.* .], TR.: unlace (untie, loosen); REFL.: free one's self from annoyance. **-ciáto**, PART.: unlaced, etc.
şlan-ciaménto, M.: hurling (flinging). ‖**-ciáre** [*s-*, *l.* .], TR.: hurl (throw, fling); REFL.: rush or throw one's self upon. **şlán-cio**, M.: throwing (casting).
şlar-gaménto, M.: enlargement (widening). ‖**-gáre** [*s-*, *l.* .], TR.: enlarge (widen, extend); REFL.: become enlarged; expand (spread). **-gatúra** = *-gamento*.
şlásciot†, M.: remission (release): *a* —, hastily (impetuously).
şlatináre [*s-*, *latino*], INTR.: speak Latin pedantically or badly.
şlattáre [*s-*, *latte*], TR.: wean, separate.
şlavá-to [*s-*, *l.* .], ADJ.: washed away; faded. **-túra**, F.: washing away; fading.
şlaẓẓeráre†, TR.: take out; spend generously.
şleál-e [*s-*, *l.* .], ADJ.: disloyal (unfaithful). **-tà**, F.: disloyalty.
şle-gaménto, M.: separation (untying); dissolution. ‖**-gáre** [*s-*, *l.* .], TR.: loosen (untie, undo); REFL.: free or disentangle one's self.
şlentá-re [*s-*, *l.* .], TR.: slacken (relax). **-túra**, F.: relaxation (slackening).
şlít-ta [OFr. *eslider*, slip, trip (OHG. *slito*)], F.: sledge. **-táre**, INTR.: be carried on a sledge.
şlo-gaménto, M.: dislocation. ‖**-gáre** [*s-*, *luogo*], TR.: displace; dislocate (put out of joint). **-gatúra** = *-gamento*.
şloggiáre [*s-*, *loggia*], TR.: dislodge; INTR.: leave a place (decamp).
şlom-báre [*s-*, *lombo*], TR.: hurt the loins of; (*fig.*) weaken; REFL.: hurt one's self. **-báto**, PART.: crippled in the hip: *stile* —, slovenly, disjointed style.
şlon-tanaménto, **-tanaménto**, M.: removal (sending to a distance). ‖**-tanáre** [*s-*, *all.* .], TR.: remove (send to a distance); REFL.: withdraw. **-tanáto**, ADJ.: removed (distant).
şlungáre [*s-*, *lungo*], TR.: lengthen (stretch out); remove (put away); stretch; REFL.: become longer; remove or withdraw one's self.
şmac-cáre† [?], TR.: defame (slander); INTR.: become crushed; become insipid or flat. **-cáto**, ADJ.: flat (insipid): *rimanere* —, be insulted, look silly.
şmac-chiáre [*s-*, *macchia*], TR.: remove (stains); cut down or destroy (a forest); leave or abandon (one's abode). **-chiatóra**, F., **-chiatóre**, M.: one who removes (stains) or destroys a forest, etc. **-chiatúra**, F.: removing (stains); cutting a wood; abandoning one's home, etc.
şmácco [Ger. *schmach* (OHG. *smâhi*)], M.: affront (insult); abuse.
şma-gaménto†, M.: distraction; aston-

ishment. **-gáre†**, INTR.: be astonished or bewildered; lose courage; lose one's way; TR.: mislead (cause to lose one's way); mislay; squander.

smágio†, M.: affectation.

sma-gliánte, ADJ.: brilliant (bright). ‖**-gliáre** [*s-*, *maglia*], TR.: break the meshes of; excite (spur on); break; unpack; INTR.: sparkle; get confounded.

smágo†, M.: fright (terror, alarm).

sma-gra. .†, **-gri. .** = *dimagra. .*

smaliziáto†, ADJ.: cunning (crafty); mischievous.

smalláre [*s-*, *mallo*], TR.: shuck.

smal-taménto, M.: enamelling; enamel. **-táre**, TR.: enamel; cover with cement; cover (encrust); break the bottom of (rivers, etc.). **-tatúra** = *-tamento*. **-timénto**, M.: digestion (concoction); selling off (rapid sale). **-tíre**, TR.: digest; sell fast (dispose of); give exit to; get rid of; (*fig.*) bear (put up with, brook): — *il vino*, sleep one's self sober. **-tísta†** = *-titore*. **-títo**, PART.: digested; clear (easy); finished. **-titóio**, M.: sewer (sink). **-titóre†**, M.: enameller. ‖**smálto** [?], M.: cement (mortar); enamel (smalt); case (foundation); pavement; mosaic: *cuore di* —, heart of stone; *sommo*—, supreme or highest heaven; *pingere in ismalto*, enamel.

smam-moláre [*s-*, *mammolo* (pop. for *bambolo*)], INTR.: laugh heartily; be carried away by tenderness. **-máre†** = *-molare*.

smance-ría [?], F.: prudery (affectation, coyness). **-róso†**, ADJ.: affected (over-delicate, coy).

s=mangiáre, TR.: consume gradually (eat away).

smá-nia [*s-*, *m.* .], F.: agitation, restlessness; desire. **-niaménto†**, M.: having no rest. **-niáre**, INTR.: have no rest; long for; be mad for; go away. **-niatúra** = *-niamento*.

smanicáre [*s-*, *manico*], TR.: take away the handle of.

smaní-glia [*s-*, *m.* .], F., **-glio**, M.: bracelet.

smanióso [*smania*], ADJ.: desirous; affected.

smannáta [*s-*, *manna* 2], F.: crowd (assembly, troop).

smantel-laménto, M.: dismantling; destruction. ‖**-láre** [*s-*, *mantello*], TR.: dismantle (demolish).

sman-seróso†, ADJ.: coquettish (amourous); effeminate. **-sière†**, M.: beau (fop, dandy).

smar-giassáre, INTR.: bully (hector, boast). **-giassáta**, **-giasseria**, F.: boasting (bullying). ‖**-giásso** [Gr. *smaragizo*, make noise], M.: bully (braggadocio). **-giassóne**, *aug.* of *-giasso*.

smarginàre [*s-*, *margine*], TR.: cut off the margin of.

smargottáre [*s-*, *margotta*], TR.: replant (twigs, etc.).

smar-rigióne†, F., **-riménto**, M.: mislaying; mistake (error); fear; swoon. ‖**-ríre** [OFr. *esmarir* (OHG. *marjan*)], TR.: misplace (lose temporarily); mistake; confound (perplex); obscure†; lose sight of†; REFL.: be lost; be confounded or disheartened; become dazzled or blinded. **-ríto**, PART.: mislaid, etc.; abashed; discoloured.

smascel-laménto, M.: dislocation of the jaws; immoderate laughter. ‖**-láre** [*s-*, *mascella*], INTR.: dislocate one's jaws; burst with laughter. **-lataménte**, ADV.: rudely (coarsely).

smascheráre [*s-*, *maschera*], TR.: unmask (unveil); REFL.: take off the mask.

smaschiáto†, ADJ.: emasculated (castrated).

smáscio†, M.: superabundance of words.

smatassáre [*s-*, *matassa*], TR.: undo or unravel (the skein).

smattiáre [*s-*, *mattia*], INTR.: act very foolishly.

smattoná-re [*s-*, *amm.* .], TR.: unpave (take up the bricks, etc.). **-túra**, F.: unpaving, etc.

smelá-re [*s-*, *mele*], TR.: take out (the honey). **-tóre**, M.: one who gets the honey. **-túra**, F.: taking out honey.

smem-braménto, M.: dismembering. ‖**-bráre** [*s-*, *membro*], TR.: dismember; cut to pieces; part (divide); carve. **-bratúra** = *-bramento*.

smemo-rábile†, ADJ.: unworthy of memory. **-rággine** = *-rataggine*. **-raménto**, M.: forgetfulness; folly (stupidity). ‖**-ráre** [*s-*, *m.* .], INTR.: forget (lose one's memory); grow stupid. **-ratáccio**, *disp. aug.* of *-rato*. **-ratággine**, F.: forgetfulness; stupidity. **-rataménte**, ADV.: in a forgetful manner; stupidly. **-ratíno**, *dim.* of *-rato*. **-ráto**, PART.: forgotten, etc.; ADJ.: forgetful; rash (hair-brained); stupid. **-riát. .** = *-rat. .*

smenciáre [*s-*, *mencio*], TR.: cause to grow thin.

smenomáre†, TR.: lessen (diminish).

smensoláre [*s-*, *mensola*], TR.: work into the shape of a bracket or corbel.

smentáre†, TR.: chamfer (channel, flute).

smenti-cánza†, F.: forgetfulness. **-cáre†**, TR., INTR.: forget.

smen-timénto, M.: belying (giving the lie). ‖**-tíre** [*s-* *m.* .], TR.: give the lie (belie); contradict; REFL.: contradict one's self.

ṣme-raldíno, ADJ.: of emerald; of the colour of an emerald. ‖**-rálde** [L. *smaragdus*], M.: emerald.

ṣmeráre†, TR.: polish (clean, burnish); INTR.: become blind.

ṣmer-ciáre [*s-*, *merce*], TR.: sell (vend). **ṣmèr-cio**, M.: sale.

ṣmerdáre [*s-*, *merda*], TR.: befoul or soil with ordure.

ṣmèrgo [L. *mergus*], M.: diver (plungeon).

ṣme-rigliáre, TR.: polish with emery. ‖**-ríglio** 1 [?], M.: emery; small cannon.

ṣmerí-glio 2 [OFr. *esmeril*], M.: merlin (kind of hawk). **-glióne**, *aug.* of *-glio*.

ṣmérita. .† = *demerita*. .

ṣmer-láre [*s-*, *m.* .], TR.: embroider and cut the edge of (cloth, etc.), scallop. **-lettáre**, TR.: scallop. **-lòtto**, *dim.* of *-lo*. ‖**ṣmèr-lo** [*merlo*], M.: 1. hobby (kind of falcon); 2. (cf. *-lare*) scalloped work, scalloped edge.

ṣmé-sso, PART.: set aside (abandoned): *usanza -ssa*, obsolete usage. ‖**ṣmé-ttere** [*s-*, *m.* .], IRR.; TR.: set aside (throw off, abandon); give over.

ṣmez-zaménto, M.: sharing (dividing, division). ‖**-záre** [*s-*, *mezzo*], TR.: divide; share.

ṣmidol-láre [*s-*, *midolla*], TR.: take the pith or marrow out of; study or examine thoroughly; explain thoroughly; REFL.: rack one's brains; lose one's marrow. **-láto**, ADJ.: marrowless.

ṣmigliaceiáre [*s-*, *migliaccio*], TR.: eat much of (millet-pudding).

ṣmíla-ce [Gr. *smilax*], M.: (*bot.*) rose or bind-weed. **-cína**, F.: substance of sarsaparilla.

ṣmillán-ta†, **-tatóre**†, M.: boaster (braggadocio).

ṣmílzo [*s-*, *milza*], ADJ.: slender (thin, spare).

ṣmimoráto† = *smemorato*.

ṣminchionáre†, TR.: laugh at (jest).

ṣminu-iménto = *diminuimento*. **-íre** = *diminuire*. **-zzaménto**, M.: cutting or breaking into small pieces (mincing); detail. **-zzáre**, TR.: mince (cut into small pieces). **-zzatóre**, M.: that minces. **-zzatúra** = *-zzamento*. ‖**-zzoláre** [*s-*, *minuzzolo*], TR.: *freq.* of *-zzare*; mince; explain in detail; examine carefully.

ṣmiracchiáre† = *sbirciare*.

ṣmiracoláre [*s-*, *miracolo*], INTR.: perform miracles; compose a nenia or funeral dirge.

ṣmiráre†, TR.: look at; polish (burnish).

ṣmisu-rábile [*s-*, *m.* .], ADJ.: immeasurable (boundless). **-ránza**† = *-ratezza*. **-rataménto**, ADV.: immensely. **-ratézza**, F.: immensity (immensurability). **-ráto**, ADJ.: unmeasurable (boundless); numberless†; extraordinary†; intemperate†.

ṣmobiliáre [*s-*, *m.* .], TR.: take away the movables of (strip).

ṣmo-ccicaménto, M.: mucus (snot). ‖**-cciicáre** [*s-*, *m.* .], TR.: dirty with mucus; snivel. **-ccoláre**, TR.: snuff (a candle); behead; swear (blaspheme)†. **-ccolatóio**†, M., **-ccolatóie**, F. PL.: snuffers. **-ccolatúra**, F.: snuffing of a candle; candle-snuff. **-ccolatóre**, M.: candle-snuffer.

ṣmo-daménto, M.: excess (immoderation). ‖**-dáre**† [*s-*, *modi*], INTR.: become immoderate (grow excessive or intemperate). **-dataménte**, ADV.: immoderately. **-dáto**, ADJ.: immoderate (excessive). **-deraménte**†, **-deránza**† = *-deratezza*. **-derataménte**, ADV.: excessively (immoderately). **-deratézza**, F.: immoderateness; excess; intemperance. **-deráto**, ADJ.: immoderate (excessive).

ṣmo-gliáre† [*s-*, *moglie*], REFL.: desert one's wife; be without a wife. **-gliáto**†, PART.: unmarried; M.: bachelor.

ṣmolendáre [*s-*, *molenda*], TR.: take away (the miller's fee).

ṣmonacáre [*s-*, *monaca*], TR.: take away or abandon (the monastic state); REFL.: become a layman.

ṣmontáre [*s-*, *m.* .], INTR.: dismount; descend (alight from); become discoloured (fade); TR.: dismount.

ṣmorbáre [*s-*, *morbo*], TR.: cure; cleanse (purge).

ṣmòr-fia, ‖**-fiáta** [Gr. *morphé*, form, figure], F.: grimace (mocking look); affectation. **-fiétta**, *dim.* of *-fia*. **-fiettína**, *dim.* of *-fiella*. **-fiosétto**, *dim.* of *-fioso*. **-fióso**, ADJ.: full of grimaces (affected); disagreeable. **-fíre**, INTR.: make grimaces; be over-delicate.

ṣ=moríre†, TR.: turn pale.

ṣmorsáre†, TR.: unbridle; take away (the bit); INTR.: go away from.

ṣmor-tíccio, ADJ.: somewhat pale. **-tíre**, INTR.: become pale or wan. ‖**ṣmòrto**, PART. of *-tire*; pale as death; faded (withered); bleak. **-tóre**, M.: paleness. **-zaménto**, M.: act of extinguishing, etc. **-záre**, TR.: extinguish (put out); allay (calm); smother: — *la fama*, smother a report; — *la sete*, quench the thirst; — *la calcina*, slack lime; — *la polvere*, settle the dust. **-zatóre**, M.: extinguisher. **-zatúra** = *-zamento*.

ṣmòs-sa†, F.: movement (motion). ‖**ṣmòsso**, PART. of *smovere*; moved, etc.; affected.

smòt-ta [?], F.: land caved in. **-taménto**, M.: tumbling down or fall of earth, landslide. **-táre**, INTR.: roll down (cave in).

s=mòvere, IRR.; TR.: move with force or difficulty (shake); affect; stir up; entice (induce); dissuade: — *il corpo,* loosen the bowels. **-movitúra,** F.: movement; emotion.
smoz-záre [*s-, m.*.], TR.: lop off (shorten). **-zatúra,** F.: mutilation (cutting off); shortest way†. **-zicáre,** TR.: *freq.* of *-zare.* **-zicatúra,** F.: mutilation (maiming).
smuccicáre†, INTR.: slip (stumble); slip away.
smún-gere [*s-, m.*.], IRR.; TR.: milk dry; dry up; exhaust; REFL.: become dry; dissipate one's property. **-giménto,** M.: draining (squeezing out). **-gitóre,** M.: milker, etc.; tax-gatherer.
smunire†, TR.: reinstate; restore.
smúnto, PART. of *-gere;* consumed, etc.; meager (lean, thin); weakened.
smuòvere = *smovere.*
smuráre, TR.: unwall (dismantle).
smusá-ta [*s-, m.*.], **-túra,** F.: grimace (wry face).
smus-saménto, M.: act of removing the angles, etc. ||**-sáre** [Fr. *émousser,* blunt], TR.: remove the corners or angles of; blunt (render obtuse). **-sáto** = **-so.** **-so,** ADJ.: broken-cornered; truncated; M.: cutting off of a corner or angle.
snamoráre [*s-, inn.*.], TR.: cure of one's love; REFL.: cease loving.
sna-sáre [*s-, naso*], TR.: cut off the nose of. **-sáto,** PART.: noseless.
snatu-ráre [*s-, natura*], TR.: unnaturalize (change the nature of); REFL.: change one's nature. **-ráto,** PART.: unnatural (inhuman); cruel.
snebbiáre [*s-, ann.*.], TR.: dispel (the clouds); brighten.
snel-laménte, ADV.: nimbly (quickly). **-létto,** *dim.* of *-lo.* **-lézza, -lità†,** F.: agility (nimbleness, activity). **-líno,** *dim.* of *-lo.* ||**snèl-lo** [OFr. *esnel, isnel* (OHG. *snel,* Ger. *schnell*], ADJ.: agile (nimble); quick (swift); active.
sner-ba. = -v... **-vaménto,** M.: act of weakening or enervating. ||**-váre** [*s-, nervo*], TR.: unnerve; weaken (debilitate); REFL.: become enervated. **-vatèllo,** *dim.* of *-vato.* **-vatézza,** F.: weakness (debility).
snicchiáre†, REFL.: remove (from a niche); take out from the shell.
sni-dáre [*s-, nido*], TR.: take out of the nest; INTR., REFL.: fly out of the nest; quit one's home. **-dáto,** PART.: expelled from the nest, etc. **-diáre** = *-dare.*
snighittíre†, TR.: make careful or active; REFL.: grow active.
snocciolàre [*s-, nocciolo*], TR.: take out (the kernel); declare (explain); pay in cash; clear up. **-lataménte,** ADV.: carefully (clearly).
sno-daménto, M.: act of untying or undoing; solution. ||**-dáre** [*s-, ann.*.], TR.: untie (undo); disjoin (loosen): (*fig.*) — *la lingua,* begin to speak. **-datúra,** F.: untying, etc.; articulation of the joints. **-dévole,** ADJ.: that can be untied.
snomináre†, TR.: deprive of the name; misname.
snovizzáre†, TR.: sharpen (the wits); polish.
snudáre [*s-, nudo*], TR.: unsheath; strip naked.
soá-ve [L. *suavis*], ADJ.: SWEET (pleasant); ADV.: sweetly; slowly†; patiently†; quietly†. **-veménto,** ADV.: sweetly; patiently†. **-vézza†, -vità,** F.: suavity (sweetness); benignity; gentleness. **-vizzaménto†,** M.: sweetening (seasoning). **-vizzáre†,** TR.: sweeten; render mild.
sob- [L. *sub*], PREF.: under; below; beneath. **-bàggiolo** [L. *bajulus,* carrier], M.: folded cloth to level things. =**balzáre,** INTR.. jump up (leap up). **-barcáre** [L. *-brachiare,* put under the arm], TR.: put under (subject); REFL.: submit. **-bissáre†,** TR.: submerge. **-bolliménto,** M.: slight or slow boiling. =**bollíre,** INTR.: boil gently (parboil). =**bórgo,** M.: suburb. **-brevità†,** ADV.: briefly.
sobil-laménto†, M.: act of seducing or suborning. **-láre†,** TR.: draw aside; seduce (mislead).
sobissáre† = *sobbissare.*
sòbole†, F.: offspring (progeny).
sobranzáre†, TR.: surpass (excel).
so-briaménte, ADV.: soberly. **-brietà,** F.: sobriety (moderation). ||**sò-brio** [L. *-brius*], ADJ.: sober (temperate); calm.
sobúglio†, M.: sedition.
soccèdere = *succedere.*
soccenericcio†, ADJ.: baked under the ashes.
socchiamáre†, TR.: call in an undertone.
soc=chiúdere, IRR.; TR.: half-shut (leave ajar). **-chiúso,** PART.: half-shut (ajar).
sòc-cida, ||**-cio** [L. *socius,* companion], M.: hiring out of cattle; farmer of cattle.
sòcco [L. *soccus,* sock], M.: buskin; comedy or tragedy.
soccodágnolo†, M.: girth (band); crupper-strap.
soccómbere [L. *sub,* under, *cumbere,* lie], INTR.: succumb (yield, submit).
soc-corrènza†, F.: looseness (diarrhœa). ||=**córrere,** IRR.; TR.: SUCCOUR (aid, help); INTR.: run up (hasten); remember. **-corrévole,** ADJ.: auxiliary (helping). **-corriménto†,** M.: succour (help). -cor

ritóre, M., **-corritríce**, F.: helper; reliever. **-córso**, PART.: succoured, etc.; M.: aid (assistance): — *di Pisa*, tardy and useless assistance.

soccòscio [*soc-* (*sub*) *c*. .], M.: leg (of beef, etc.).

sò-cera, F.: mother-in-law; (*fig.*) learned or cunning woman. ‖**sò-cero** [L. *socer*], M.: father-in-law.

so-ciábile, ADJ.: sociable; amiable (affable). **-ciále**, ADJ.: social (loving society). **-cialísmo**, M.: socialism. **-cialísta**, pl. *—ti*, M.: socialist. **-cialità**, F.: sociability (socialness). **-cietà**, F.: society (human race); social intercourse (company); club; partnership: — *della strada ferrata*, railway company. **-ciévole**, ADJ.: loving society. **-cievolézza**, F.: society; socialness. ‖**sò-cio** [L. *-cius*], M.: companion; colleague; partner. **-ciología**, F.: sociology. **-ciòlogo**, pl. *—ghi*, *—gi*, ADJ.: sociologist.

socrático, ADJ.: Socratic.

sòda [?], F.: soda (alkali).

sodá-le†, M.: companion (comrade). ‖**-lízio** [L. *-litium* (*-lis*, comrade)], M.: society (company, fellowship).

so-daménte [*sodo*], ADV.: solidly; cautiously; stoutly. **-daméntо**†, M.: establishment (confirmation): security (bail). **-dáre**†, TR.: strengthen (consolidate); confirm; promise; give (bail or security).

sod-diaconáto, M.: subdeaconship (office of subdeacon). ‖**-diácono** [L. *sub-*, *d*. .], M.: subdeacon.

soddisfa. . = *sodisfa*. .

soddomía = *sodomia*.

soddu. . = *sedu*. .

so-détto, ADJ.: *dim.* of *-do*; somewhat firm, etc. ‖**-dézza** [*-do*], F.: solidity; stability (firmness); obstinacy; steadfastness.

sodis-facènte, PART.: satisfying. **-facenteménte**†, ADV.: satisfactorily. **-faciménto**, M.: satisfaction; atonement. ‖**-fáre** [L. *satis-facere*], IRR.; TR.: satisfy (please, content); pay (discharge a debt); fulfil: — *al suo obbligo*, discharge one's duty. **-fátto**, PART.: satisfied, etc. **-fattívo**, ADJ.: satisfactory. **-fattúra**, **-fazióne**, F.: satisfaction (reparation); contentment (pleasure).

sòdo [L. *solidus*, whole], ADJ.: hard; SOLID (stable); (*fig.*) firm; strong (vigorous); massy; M.: solid base (foundation); bail (security)†; ADV.: fast; hard; firmly; solidly: *star* —, remain firm; *fabbricare in sul* —, build upon a good foundation; *dire* or *favellare in sul* —, say or speak anything in earnest or seriously; *porre* or *mettere in* —, deliberate; resolve; *turar* —, stop or close fast.

sòdo-ma [*Sodom*], **-mía**, F.: sodomy. **-míta**, M.: sodomite. **-miticaménte**, ADV.: sodomitically. **-mítico**, pl. *—ci*, ADJ.: sodomitical. **-míto**, M.: Sodomite (inhabitant of Sodom).

sodu. . = *sedu*. .

sofà [Ar.], M.: sofa.

soffe-rènte, ADJ.: suffering (patient, enduring). **-rènza**, F.: sufferance (endurance); constancy. **-révole**, ADJ.: supportable (tolerable). **-ridóre** = *-ritore*. **-riménto**, M.: patience; toleration. ‖**-ríre**, us'ly *soffrire*, which see. **-ritóre**, M.: sufferer.

soffer-máre [L. *sub-*], TR.: stop a little; REFL.: pause for a moment. **-máta**, F.: pause (stop, suspension).

soffèrto, PART. of *sofferire*; suffered (endured); delivered.

sof-fiaménto, M.: breath (blowing, respiration); scandal (obloquy). ‖**-fiáre** [L. *sufflare*, BLOW out], TR.: blow; whisper; INTR.: blow; fume (rage); (*iron.*) spy; irritate (excite); prompt: *aprir la bocca e* —, speak inconsiderately. **-fiáta**, F.: act of blowing. **-fiatóre**, M.: blower; prompter. **-fiatúra**, F.: breath; blowing (puffing).

soffiocáre†, TR.: hide (conceal); INTR.: be hid; abscond.

sòffi-ce [L. *suffex* (*supplex*, kneeling down)], ADJ.: soft (easy, downy); elastic; M.†: square piece of iron. **-ceménte**, ADV.: softly; delicately.

soffiсen. . = *sufficien*. .

sof-fiettíno, *dim.* of *-fietto*. **-fiétto**, M.: *dim.* of *-fio*; pair of bellows: *lavorare di* —, act the spy. **-fíno**, M.: childish game. ‖**sóf-fio** [*-fiare*], M.: blowing (puff); breath: *in un* —, in an instant; — *di vento*, puff of wind. **sóf-fiola**†, F.: (*bot.*) melilot. **-fióne**, M.: blowing pipe (bellows); (*iron.*) spy (emissary); (*fig.*†) proud or haughty person. **-fionería**, F.: presumption (vainglory). **-fionétto**†, M.: *dim.* of *-fione*; little puff.

soffis. . = *sofis*. .

sof-fitta [L. *suffigere* (*sub*, beneath, *figere*, fasten)], F.: garret (attic); ceiling†; entresole†; (*arch.*†) entablature. **-fittáre**, TR.: ceil; build with entresoles. **-fitto**, M.: ceiling of a room; ADJ.: hidden (secret).

soffo-caménto, M.: suffocation (choking). ‖**-cáre** [L. *suffocare* (*sub*, under, *faux*, throat)], TR.: suffocate (choke, stifle); drown†. **-cáto**, PART.: suffocated, etc. **-cazióne**, F.: suffocation. **-ga**. . = *-ca*. .

soffoggiáta†, F.: bundle carried off slyly.

soffólto†, ADJ.: propped up (sustained).

soffornáto†, ADJ.: vaulted (arched).

soffragáneo†, ADJ.: suffragan.

soffrátta†, F.: penury (want).

sof-freddáre [*sob-*], TR.: cool. **-fréd-do**, ADJ.: rather cold.

soffre-gaménto, M.: rubbing (friction). ‖**-gáre** [*sob-*], TR.: rub lightly or gently, offer repeatedly†; REFL.: solicit.

sof-frènte† = *-ferente*. ‖**-fríbile** [*-frire*], ADJ.: sufferable (supportable).

soffríggere [*sob*, *f.* .], IRR. (cf. *friggere*); TR.: fry lightly.

soffrí-re [L. *sub-ferre*, 'BEAR up'], IRR. (cf. *offrire*); TR.: SUFFER (BEAR, endure); allow; INTR.: suffer; forbear. **-tóre**, M.: sufferer.

soffrítto, PART. of *soffriggere*.

soffumicáre [*sob-*, *f.* .], TR.: fumigate (smoke).

so-fígma [L. *sophisma*], M.: sophism. **-físta**, pl. *—ti*, M.: sophist. **-fisteria**† = *-fisticheria*. **-fística**, F.: sophistry; fallacious reasoning. **-fisticaménte**, ADV.: sophistically. **-fisticáre**, INTR.: sophisticate (cavil); falsify†; adulterate†. **-fisticheria**, F.: sophistry. **-fístico**, pl. *—ci*, *—chi*, ADJ.: sophistical; captious; M.: sophist.

sóga†, F.: leather-string (strap, girth).

sog-gettábile, ADJ.: that can be subjected (tamable). **-gettáccio**, *disp.* of *-getto*. **-gettaménte**, ADV.: in subjection. **-gettaménto**, M.: subjection (servitude). **-gettáre**, TR.: subject (subdue). **-gettatóre**, M.: conqueror (subduer). **-gettíno**, *car. dim.* of *-getto*. **-gettívo**, ADJ.: suggestive. ‖**-gètto** [L. *sub-jectus* (*jacere*, cast)], ADJ.: subjected (subdued); enslaved; placed beneath; M.: subject; substance. **-gezióne**, F.: subjection. **-gettitúdine**†, F.: subjection; suggestion (hint).

sog-ghignáre [*sub-*, *gh.* .], INTR.: grin (sneer). **-ghigno**, M.: grin (sneer).

soggia-cènte, ADJ.: lying under (subject). **-cére** [L. *sub-jacere*], IRR. (cf. *jacere*); INTR.: be subject or exposed to; be conquered. **-ciménto**, M.: subjection (submission); dependence. **-ciúto**, PART.: subjected (exposed); overcome.

soggiogáia†, F.: dewlap; kind of goitre.

soggio-gaménto, M.: subjugation. ‖**-gáre** [L. *sub-jugare* (*jugum*, YOKE)], TR.: subjugate (subdue, conquer). **-gatóre**, M.: subduer (conqueror). **-gazióne**, F.: subjugation (conquest).

soggiógo† = *soggiogaia*.

soggior-naménto, M.: sojourn (stay). ‖**-náre** [L. *sub-diurnare*, stay for awhile], INTR.: sojourn (abide); delay (put off)†; TR.†: take care of (watch): — *una stanza*, air or sun a room. **soggiór-no**, M.: sojourn (residence); delay; care (management).

sog-giúgnere†, ‖**-giúngere** [L. *sub-jungere*], IRR. (cf. *giungere*); TR.: subjoin (add); reply†; INTR.†: supervene (happen). **-giungiménto**, M.: subjunction (addition); reply. **-giuntívo**, ADJ., M.: subjunctive. **-giúnto**, PART.: subjoined; replied. **-giunzióne**† = *-giungimento*.

sóggo† = *solco*.

sog-golàre†, TR., INTR.: put on a wimple. ‖**-gólo** [L. *sub*, under, *gola*, throat], M.: tucker (wimple); throat-band; (*mil.*) helmet-tuft.

sog-guardáre [*sob-*], TR.: look at slyly (peep at).

sò-glia [L. L. *solium* (L. *solea*, sole of a shoe)], F., **-gliáre**†, M.: threshold; sole (a fish).

sòglio [L. *solium*, seat], M.: throne (royal seat).

sògliola [see *soglia*], F.: sole (kind of flat fish).

so-gnábile, ADJ.: that can be dreamed. **-gnáre**, INTR., REFL.: dream; fancy; build castles in the air; imagine. **-gnatóra**, F., **-gnatóre**, M.: dreamer; visionary. ‖**só-gno** [L. *somnium* (*somnus*, sleep)], M.: dream; revery; fiction: *mangiare dei -gni*, have nothing to eat.

sò-ia†, F.: silk; adulation (banter): *dar la* —, flatter. **-iáre**†, TR., INTR.: cajole (flatter).

sòl [L. *solve*, a word in a hymn], M.: (*mus.*) sol.

sóla†, F.: launch (skiff); shallop; sole (of a shoe).

soláio [L. *-larium* (*-l*, sun), place exposed to the sun], M.: floor (entresole, ceiling); attic.

solaménte [*solo*], ADJ.: solely (only).

soláno†, M.; nightshade (morel).

soláre† 1 = *solaio*.

so-láre 2 [L. *-laris* (*-l*, sun)], ADJ.: solar. **-láta**, F.: sunstroke. **-latío**, M.: sunny place; ADJ.: sunny (exposed to the sun): *a* —, to the south (southward).

solàto†, ADJ.: new-soled.

solátro† = *solano*.

solatúra [*sola*], F.: soles of shoes.

sol-cábile, ADJ.: that can be ploughed. **-caménto**, M.: making furrows; wake or track of a ship. ‖**-cáre** [*solco*], TR.: furrow; (*fig.*) plough the waves of. **-catúra**, F.: course of a furrow; ploughing. **-cherèllo**, **-chétto**, *dim.* of *-co*.

sólcio†, M.: pickled meat; pickle; preserve.

sólco [L. *sulcus*], M.: furrow; track; wrinkle: *andare per il* —, be upright.

soldá-na, F.: sultaness. **-náto**, M.: dignity or dominion of the Sultan. **-nía**, F.: country of a sultan. ‖**soldá-no** [*sultano*], M.: sultan.

sol-dáre†, TR.: enlist (recruit). **-da-rèllo**, *car. dim.* of *-do*. **-datáccio**, *disp.* of *-dato*. **-datáglia**, F.: bad, undisciplined troops. **-datèllo, -datíno**, *dim.* of *-dato*. **-datería**†, **-datésca**, F.: soldiery (troops, military). **-date-scaménte**, ADV.: soldierlike. **-daté-sco**, ADJ.: military (soldierly). **-dáto** [*assoldato*], M.: soldier; ADJ.: taken into pay (enlisted). **-datúccio, -datúzzo**, *disp.* of *-dato*. **-díno**, *car. dim.* of *-do*. ||**sòl-do** [L. *solidus*, money], M.: penny (small piece of money); pay (wages, salary. etc.); soldier's pay: *spendere il — per quattro quattrini*, spend money for useful purposes; *andare a -* , enlist one's self.

só-le [L. *sol*], M.: sun; (*fig.*) daylight (day); (*poet.*) day; eye: *fa* —, the sun shines; *avere* (*delle terre*) *al* —, possess some landed property; *andare al* —†, hide one's self because of inferiority; *render il - - di luglio*†, sell a worthless thing at a good price. **-lécchio**, M.: parasol (umbrella); shade.

solecísmo [L. *-læcismus*], M.: (*gram.*) solecism (incongruity of language).

soleg-giaménto, M.: exposing to the sun. ||**-giáre** [*sole*], TR.: sun (expose to the sun).

solèn-ne [L. *solemnis*], ADJ.: solemn; sumptuous (splendid); majestic; famous: *mangiatore* —, enormous feeder; *colpo* —, hard blow; *da* —, solemnly. **-neg-giáre**†, TR.: solemnize; INTR.: be solemnized. **-neménte**, ADV.: solemnly. **-nità**, F.: solemnity; splendour (pomp). **-nizzaménto**, M.: solemnization (celebration). **-nizzáre**, TR.: celebrate (solemnize). **-nizzazióne**† = *-nizzamento*.

solére [L.], IRR.§; INTR.: be accustomed (be wont); use; M.: custom (use).

§ Pres. (Ind.) *sòglio, suòli, suòle; sogliámo, soléte, sògliono.* (Subj.) *sòglia.*

solerétta [*solea*], F.: iron-sole.

so-lèrte [L. *-lers*, clever], ADJ.: diligent (attentive; careful). **-lèrzia**, F.: diligence (care; attention).

solét-ta [*solea*], F.: sole of a stocking. **-táre**, TR.: sole stockings or shoes. **-ta-túra**, F.: soling; materials for soling.

solétto [*solo*], ADJ.: alone (quite alone).

sòlfa [*sol, fa*], F.: (*mus.*) solfa (gamut).

sol-fanára†, **-fanária**†, F.: sulphur-mine. ||**-fanèllo** [*solfo*], M.: match. **-fá-re**, TR.: fumigate with sulphur. **-fáto**, ADJ.: sulphurated; sulphureous; M.: sulphate; sulphur (brimstone). **-fatára**, F.: sulphur-cave.

sol-feggiáre [*solfa*], TR., INTR.: (*mus.*) SOLFA (sing the gamut). **-féggio**, M.: (*mus.*) solfeggio.

sól-fo [L. *sulphur*], M.: sulphur. **-feráre**, TR.: fumigate with sulphur. **-feratóio**, M.: fumigating placc. **-feráio, -feráto**, ADJ.: sulphurous. **-fereggiáre**, INTR.: send forth sulphurous vapours. **-fèrico**, pl. *—ci*, ADJ.: sulphuric. **-fe-róso**, ADJ.: sulphurous.

sólgo† = *solco*.

solícchio† = *solecchio*.

soli-dále, ADJ.: (*leg.*) bound or made answerable for the whole. **-daménte**, ADV.: solidly; firmly. **-dáre**, TR.: render solid (consolidate, strengthen). **-da-rietà**, F.: act of being bound for the whole. **-dário** = *-dale*. **-dáto**, PART.: strengthened (consolidated). **-dézza, -di-tà**, F.: solidity (firmness); consistency; durability. ||**sòli-do** [L. *-dus*], ADJ.: solid; firm; consistent; well-connected; M.: solid; solidity; firmness: *in* —, for the whole, entirely.

solilòquio [L. *soliloquium*], M.: soliloquy.

solimáto† = *sublimato*.

so-lingaménte, ADV.: lonely. ||**-língo** [L. *solus*, alone], ADJ.: solitary (alone).

solí-no [?], M.: collar (neckband of a shirt). **-nóne**, *aug.* of *-no*.

sòlio† = *soglio*.

solíssimo, SUPERL. of *solo*: quite alone (by one's self).

solitaménto [*solito*], ADV.: in the usual way (customarily).

soli-tariaménte, ADV.: solitarily. **-ta-rietà**, F.: solitude. ||**-tário** [L. *-ta-rius*], ADJ.: solitary; retired; deserted (lonely); abandoned; M.: solitary (hermit); solitaire diamond: *passero* —, kind of sparrow.

sòlito, PART. of *solere*; accustomed (used, wont): *al* —, as usual; *è il suo* —, it is his way.

solitúdine [L. *-do*], F.: solitude; single life; retreat (hermitage).

solívago [L. *-gus* (*solus*, alone, *vagari*, wander)], ADJ.: fond of solitary walks; wandering alone.

sollalzáre†, TR.: lift up a little.

sollaz-zaménto = *sollazzo*. **-záre**, TR.: recreate (divert, please); REFL.: amuse one's self (tako pleasure in). **-zatóre**, M.: amusing fellow. **-zévole**, ADJ.: pleasant (agreeable); amusing. **-zevol-ménte**, ADV.: pleasantly (agreeably). ||**sollàz-zo** [L. *solatium*, SOLACE], M.: recreation (amusement, diversion); sport (jest)†. **-zóso**, ADJ.: pleasant (diverting).

solleccheráre†, INTR.: leap for joy.

solleci-taménte, ADV.: diligently (carefully). **-taménto**, M.: solicitation (instance). **-táre**, INTR.: hasten (be in haste); TR.: solicit (move, urge); annoy†. **-tatívo**, ADJ.: soliciting (pressing). **-ta-**

tóre, M.: solicitor; attorney. **-tatúra**†, F.: care (anxiety, solicitude). **-tazióne**, F.: solicitation (persuasion). ‖**sollécito** [L. *sollicitus*], ADJ.: quick (prompt); mindful (attentive); diligent. **-tóso**†, ADJ.: solicitous (anxious); diligent. **-túdine**, F.: solicitude; quickness (nimbleness); diligence (industry); charge (commission).

sollenáre†, INTR.: mitigate.

solleóne [L. *sub*, *leone*], M.: dog-days.

solleti-caménto, M.: tickling. ‖**-cáre** [?], TR.: tickle; flatter; please. **sollético**, M.: tickling; sport; pleasantry: *far il* —, tickle.

solle-vaménto, M.: lifting or heaving up; rising; insurrection (sedition); relief (comfort). ‖**-váre** [L. *sub-levare*, LIFT up], TR.: raise (lift, heave); stir up (a revolt); alLEVIATE (assuage); REFL.: rise or swell up; rise up in arms; amuse one's self. **-vatézza**, F.: sublimity. **-vatóre**, M.: riser; rebel. **-vazióne**, F.: elevation; rebellion (revolt).

sollicit. .† = *sollecit*. .

sollièvo [*sollevare*], M.: ease (relief).

sollióne = *solleone*.

sòllo†, ADJ.: soft (flabby); elastic.

solluche-raménto†, M.: tickling; sensibility; desire. ‖**-ráre**† [? L. *saliva*, saliva], TR.: tickle (cause desire); flatter. **sollúche-ro**, M.: yearning: *andare in* —, melt with joy.

sólo 1 [L. *-lus*], ADJ.: sole (only; single); alone (solitary); ADV.: only (but); solely; unless: *una sola volta*, a single time, once only; — *a* —, tête-à-tête (alone); — *che*, provided that.

sòlo 2, pl. *-li* or *-la* (soles) [L. *-lum*, bottom], M.: ground; pavement; SOLE (of a shoe); hoof: *a* — *a* —, one upon the other.

sol-stiziále [L. *-stitialis*], ADJ.: solstitial. ‖**-stízio** [L. *-stitium*], M.: solstice.

soltán-to [*solo*], ADV.: solely; but; only. **-to=chè** *è*, ADV.: provided that; such as.

sol-úbile, ADJ.: soluble. **-ubilità**, F.: solubility. **-utívo**, ADJ.: solutive (loosening). **-úto**, PART. of *-rere*. **-uzióne**, F.: solution; dissolution; explanation. ‖**sòl-vere** [L.], IRR.§; TR.: solve; loose (untie); dissolve; separate; exempt (absolve); pay (a debt): — *il desio*, gratify the desire; — *il ventre*, loosen the bowels; — *un voto*, pay a vow. **-víbile**, ADJ.: solvent (that can pay). **-vibilità**, F.: solvability. **-viménte**†, M.: untying; solution; explanation; liquefaction. **-vitóre**, M.: one who unties; explainer; solver.

sò-ma [l. L. *salma* (L., Gr. *ságma*)], F.: pack-saddle; burden (load, weight); aggravation (injury); tyranny: *a -me*, in great quantity, in lots; *pareggiar le -me*, act impartially; *porre la* —, punish; *levar le -me*, set off. **-máio**†, ADJ.: of burden; burdensome. **-mára**, F.: she-ass (donkey); beast of burden. **-maráccio**, **-marèllo**, **-marétto**, **-maríno**, *disp. dim.* of *-maro*. **-máro**, M.: beast of burden; ass. **-meggiáre**, TR., INTR.: carry a burden or load. **-mèlla**, **-merèlla**, **-métta**, **-mettína**, *dim.* of *-ma*. **-mería**†, F.: baggage (luggage); PL.: goods. **-mière**, **-mièro** = *-maro*.

somi-gliánte, ADJ.: like (resembling). **-glianteménte**, ADV.: likewise; in the same manner. **-gliánza**, F.: resemblance; portrait (likeness): *a* —†, likewise. ‖**-gliáre** [L. *similis*, like], INTR.: be like (reSEMBLE); imitate†; TR.: liken (compare); appear. **-gliévole**, ADJ.: resembling (like); conform.

sómma [L. *summa* (*-mus*, highest)], F.: SUM (amount); height; summary (compendium); result: *in* —, in short; *fare* —, multiply; *levar la* —, add up.

sommácco [Ar.], M.: sumach-tree.

som-maménte, ADV.: extremely. ‖**-máre** [*-ma*], TR.: sum up (add up); enumerate; amount to. **-marélla**, *dim.* of *-ma*. **-mariaménte**, ADV.: summarily (briefly). **-mário**, ADJ.: summary (short); chief (main)†; M.: summary (epitome); chief reason†. **-mataménte**, ADV.: summarily. **-máte**†, M.: optimate (grandee). **-máto**, M.: sum (total). **-matóre**, M.: calculator; compiler; editor.

sommèr-gere [L. *sub-mergere*], IRR. (cf. *emergere*); TR.: submerge (sink); destroy; REFL.: drown (sink down); get ruined. **-gíbile**, ADJ.: that can be submerged. **-giménto**, M.: act of submerging; drowning. **-gitóre**, M.: submerger or drowner. **-gitúra** = *-sione*. **-sáre**† = *-gere*. **-sióne**, F.: submersion; drowning. **sommèr-so**, PART.: submerged (sunk); M., PL.: damned spirits.

sommés-sa†, F.: underpart; right side (of cloth). **-saménte**, ADV.: softly; in a low voice. **-sévole**†, ADJ.: submissive (humble). **-sióne**†, F.: submission. **-sívo**, ADJ.: submissive. ‖**sommés-so** [*sommettere*], ADJ.: submissive (humble; subdued); low; M.: span (measure).

somméttа, *dim.* of *somma*.

somméttere [*sub-mittere*], IRR.; TR.: put under; submit; REFL.: submit (yield).

sommini-straménto, M.: act of providing or supplying. ‖**-stráre** [L. *sub-ministrare*], TR.: administer; furnish (supply). **-stratóre**, M.: provider. **-strazióne**, F.: providing (administering); provision (support).

soppestáre [*sub-*, *p.* .], TR.: bruise (pound, crush).

soppiánо†, ADV.: softly.

soppiantá-re [*sub-*, *p.* .], TR.: supplant (undermine); tread under foot†; cheat (deceive)†. **-tóre**, M.: supplanter; deceiver†.

soppiat-táre† [*sub-*, *appiattare*], TR.: hide (conceal). **-táto** = *-to*. **soppiátto**, ADJ.: secret; hidden; sly; ADV.: in a hidden manner (secretly, underhand). **-tonáccio**, *disp.* of *-tone*. **-tóne**, M.: two-faced person (dissembler).

soppiegáre†, TR.: bend (crook).

soppórre†, IRR. (cf. *porre*); TR.: place under or beneath; subject (submit): — *il parto*, falsify or substitute a child.

soppor-tábile, ADJ.: supportable. **-taménto**, M.: toleration (forbearance). ‖**-táre** [L. *sup-portare*, carry], TR.: support (bear); uphold (bear up): — *la spesa*, cover the expenses, be worth the while. **-tatóre**, M., **-tatríce**, F.: sufferer (bearer). **-tazióne** = *-tamento: con* —, with permission. **-tóvole**, ADJ.: tolerable. **-tevolménte**, ADV.: supportably (tolerably). **soppòr-to**, M.: tolerance (endurance).

soppositòrio†, M.: suppository.

soppósta = *soprapposta*.

soppósto, PART. of *sopporre;* placed under; submitted: *parto* —, supposititious child.

soppottière†, M.: meddler (busybody).

soppozzáre†, TR.: drown; sink (plunge).

sop-prèndere† = *sorprendere*. **-préso** = *sorpreso*.

sop-prèssa, F.: press; mangle. **-pressáre**, TR.: press (put in a press, calender); gloss (iron); torment (oppress)†. **-pressáto**, PART.: pressed, etc.; M.: kind of large sausage. **-pressióne**, F.: suppression (keeping down); oppression: — *del parto*, act of concealing the birth of a child. **-prèsso**, PART. of *-primere*. ‖**-prímere** [L. *sup-primere* (*premere*, press)], IRR. (cf. *opprimere*); TR.: SUPPRESS (repress); put down (tread under foot); oppress†.

soppriòre†, M.: sub-prior.

soppúnto [*sub-*, *p.* .], M.: running stitch (basting).

sópra [L. *supra*], PREP.: on (upon, over); above; beyond; about; towards; M.: upper part: — *mia fede*, upon my word; — *sera*, towards evening; — *sabato*, before Saturday; *esser* — *una cosa*, superintend a thing; *far disegno* — *una persona*, rely upon a person; *andar* — *sè*, walk upright: *lavorare* — *di sè*, work on one's own account; *morir* — *parto*, die in childbed.

sopra- [= *sopra*], PREF. (before vow. *sopr-*; initial simple cons't of next member doubled): =**bbenedíre**, IRR.; TR.: bless again. =**bbollíre**†, INTR.: boil too much. **-bbondánte** [*abbondante*], ADJ.: superabundant (excessive). **-bbondanteménte**, ADV.: superabundantly. **-bbondánza**, F.: superabundance (excess). **-bbondáre**, INTR.: superabound. **-bbondévole**, ADJ.: superabounding; superfluous. **-bbondevolézza** = *-bbondanza*. **-bbondevolménte**, ADV.: superabundantly. =**bbuòno**, ADJ.: over-good. **soprá-bito** [*abito*], M.: frock-coat (Prince-Albert coat); (less commonly) overcoat. **-bitóne**, *aug.* of *-bito*. =**ccálza**, F.: over-stocking. =**ccamiscia**, F.: overshirt. =**ccánto**†, M.: song. =**ccápo**, M.: troublesome or fastidious thought; superintendent (overseer)†. =**ccaricáre**, TR.: overload (overcharge). **-ccárico**†, M.: overburden (surcharge); aggravation; (*nav.*) supercargo. =**ccárta**, F.: address. =**ccássa**, F.: outside case of a watch. **-ccelèste**, ADJ.: supercelestial. **-ccennáre** [*accennare*], TR.: mention above. **-ccennáto**, PART.: above-mentioned. =**cchiamáre**, TR.: call in additional advice (consult). =**cchiáro**, ADJ.: very clear (most evident). =**cchièdere**†, IRR.; TR.: overcharge (ask too much). =**cchiúsa**, F.: addition (to a dam). =**ccièlo**, M.: tester, top, or canopy (of a bed or carriage). =**cciglio**, M.: eyebrow. =**ccínghia**, F.: surcingle (girth). **-ccínto**, ADJ.: girt above. **-cciò**, M.: highest person; pretended superior. =**ccitáre**, TR.: cite before. =**ccóda**, F.: tail-feather. =**ccòllo**, ADV.: in addition; moreover. =**ccòmito**, M.: chief officer of a galley. =**ccomperáre**†, TR.: buy dear (over-pay). =**ccònsolo**, M.: magistrate in the Venetian Republic. =**ccopèrta**, F.: counterpane (coverlet). =**ccórrere**, IRR.; INTR.: run upon; TR.: run over. =**ccréscere**, INTR.: grow still more. =**ccuòco**†, M.: head cook. **-ccúto**†, ADJ.: very sharp or acute. =**ddènte**, M.: double tooth. =**ddétto**, ADJ.: above-said. **-ddíre**†, TR.: add to what has been said; exaggerate; exceed; mention above. =**ddòta**†, F.: bride's clothes; paraphernalia. **-ddotále**, ADJ.: added to the dowry. **-ddotáre**, TR.: give above the marriage portion. **-ddòte** = *-ddota*. =**esaltáto**, ADJ.: greatly exalted. **-esaltazióne**, F.: great praise (high encomium). =**ffáccia**†, F.: surface; outside; pretext. =**ffaciménto**, M.: superfluity (excess). =**ffáre**, IRR.; TR.: overcharge; exceed; advance; tread upon†; overcome (surpass). =**ffátto**, PART.: overcharged, etc.; overdone; over-ripe: — *dall' affanno*, weighed down with grief. =**ffáscia**, F.: one band over another. =**ffinaménto**, M.: over-refinement. =**ffíne**, =**ffíno**, ADJ.: superfine (over-fine). =**fforíre**, INTR.: flourish (blossom again). =**ggiráre**†, INTR.: turn round again; turn over. =**ggítto**, M.: whip-stitch (hem-stitch). =**ggiudicáre**, TR.: command (rule); INTR.: be higher (be predominant). =**ggiúgnere**† = *-ggiungere*. =**ggiungènte**, ADJ.: happening. =**ggiúngere**, IRR.; INTR.: arrive unexpectedly (happen); TR.†: overtake; surprise. =**ggiungiménto**†, M.: unexpected event; overtaking. =**ggiúnta**, F.: unexpected circumstance. =**ggiúnto**, PART.: happened, etc. =**ggiuráre**†, INTR.: swear oath upon oath. =**ggrándo**, ADJ.: very great. =**ggraváre**, TR.: overload (surcharge). =**ggridáre**, INTR.: cry above or louder than another. =**gguárdia**†, F.: chief guard; guard (custody). =**impossíbile**, ADJ.: absolutely impossible. =**indoráre**, TR.: double-gild. =**indúrre**, TR.: superinduce; superadd. =**inségna**, F.: device (arms); mark (sign). =**intèndere**, TR.: superintend (direct). -**llegáre** [*allegare*], TR.: mention above (cite above). =**llodáre**, TR.: praise excessively (extol). -**llòde**†, F.: excessive praise. =**llunáre**, ADJ.: above the moon. -**lzáre** [*alzare*], TR.: raise up (elevate). -**mábile** [*amabile*], ADJ.: most amiable. =**mmániche**, F.: upper sleeves. =**mmáno**, ADV.: with an uplifted hand; haughtily; ADJ.†: extraordinary (excellent); M.: blow with an uplifted hand. =**mmaraviglióso**, ADJ.: most marvellous. =**mmattóne**, M.: single brick wall. =**mmentováto**, ADJ.: above-mentioned. =**mmercáto**, M.: surplus (above measure). =**mméttere**, TR.: place above. -**mmirábile**, ADJ.: very admirable. =**mmisúra**, ADV.: above measure (excessively). =**mmòdo**, ADV.: exceedingly (extremely). =**mmondáno**, ADJ.: ultramundane. =**mmontáre**, INTR.: superabound (increase). -**naménte**†, ADV.: wonderfully; excellently. **soprá-nimo** [*animo*], ADV.: with animosity (spitefully). -**níno**, *dim.* of -*no* -**nità**, F.: superiority (excellence). =**nnarráre**†, TR.: relate or tell before. =**nnáscere**, IRR.; INTR.: grow near or upon anything. =**nnáto**, ADJ.: grown upon; born after. =**nnaturále**, ADJ.: ...ernatural. =**nnaturalménte**, ADV.: ...naturally. =**nnestáre**, TR.: ingraft ... =**nníno**, *dim.* of -*nno*; ADJ.: ...y a year old. **soprá-nno** [*anno*], above a year old. =**nnomáre**, TR.: ...me (nickname). -**nnóme**, M.: sur... ; family name; nickname. -**nnomináre** = -*nnomare*. =**nnotáre**, INTR.: float above (be buoyant). =**nnumerário**, ADJ.: supernumerary. **sopráno**, M.: soprano (counter-tenor); highest key in music; sovereign (king)†; ADJ.†: superior (upper). -**nségna**† [*insegna*], F.: mark (sign); arms (device); PL.: uniform. -**ntendènte**, M.: superintendent (overseer). -**ntendènza**, F.: superintendence (direction); inspection. -**ntèndere** [*intendere*], IRR.; INTR.: superintend; surpass in knowledge. -**ntéso**, PART.: superintended, etc. =**ornáto**, M.: (*arch.*) architrave (entablature). =**ppagáre**†, TR.: overpay (pay too much). =**ppárto**, ADV.: in the act of lying-in. =**ppensièro**, ADJ.: very thoughtful. =**ppéso**, M.: additional weight (overweight). =**ppètto**, M.: coat of mail; waistcoat. =**ppiacènte**, ADJ.: very pleasing. =**ppiágnere**†, =**ppiángere**, IRR.; INTR.: weep bitterly. =**ppiéno**†, ADJ.: over-full; redundant. =**ppiglíáre**†, TR.: take more than is fit; seize upon; undertake. =**ppiù**, M.: overplus; addition; ADV.: moreover (besides); in addition. -**pponiménto**, M.: superposition; opposition. -**ppórre**, IRR.; TR.: put upon; add (join to)†; prefer to†; REFL.†: put one's self over or above. =**pportáre**, TR.: carry above or over. =**ppòrto**, M.: (*arch.*) ornament over the architrave of a door. =**pposizióne**, F.: placing over; opposition. =**ppósta**, F.: (*vet.*) hoof-disease; branched work†. =**ppósto**, ADJ.: set above (put over); added. =**pprèndere**†, IRR.; TR.: surprise; take more than necessary. -**pprendiménto**, M.: surprise; taking. -**ppréso**, PART.: surprised, etc. =**pprofóndo**†, ADJ.: very deep or profound. **soprá-re** = *superare*. =**rragionaménto**†, M.: epilogue. =**rragionáre**†, TR.: reason more than necessary. =**rrecáto**, ADJ.: mentioned above (aforenamed). -**rriváre** [*arrivare*], INTR.: supervene (happen). =**sbèrga**†, F.: soldier's coat; coat of mail. =**sbergáto**, ADJ.: wearing a soldier's coat. =**scapoláre**, ADJ.: (*anat.*) above the scapulary. =**schiéna**, F.: back-band (of harness). =**scrítta**, F.: inscription; superscription; address. -**scrítto**, ADJ.: above-written; addressed. -**scrívere**, IRR.; TR.: address (a letter). -**scrizióne**†, F.: superscription; title. =**sforzáto**†, ADJ.: very vehement. =**síndaco**, M.: chief-syndic (upper magistrate). =**smálto**, M.: highly polished enamel. =**smisuráto**†, ADJ.: unmeasurable (enormous). =**spárgere**†, IRR.; TR.: spread over (scatter over). =**spèndere**, IRR.; TR.: spend too much. =**speránza**†,

F.: certain hope. =**sperare**†, INTR.: have great hope; hope too much. =**spináto**, ADJ.: (*anat.*) placed above the spine. =**spirituále**, ADJ.: more than spiritual. =**ssagliènte**†, ADJ.: ascending. =**ssaláre**†, TR.: over-salt. =**ssalíre**†, IRR.; TR.: attack suddenly or unawares. =**ssálto**†, M.: relief; projection (jutting out); (*mil.*) sudden attack. =**ssapére**, IRR.; INTR.: know more than necessary. =**ssáta**, F.: kind of sausage. =**ssedènte**, ADJ.: sitting above. =**ssedére**, TR.: sit above or upon; defer (put off); supersede†; retard†. =**ssegnále**, M.: signal; label; mark. -**ssegnáre**†, TR.: mark (set a mark upon); REFL.: wear a mark or token. -**sségno**†, M.: mark (token, sign). =**ssèllo**, M.: surcharge; overplus (increase). -**sseminare**†, TR.: sow over again. =**ssénno**†, M.: great prudence (good sense). =**sservíre**, TR.: serve beyond what is required. -**ssèrvo**†, M.: worse than a slave. =**sséte**, F.: great thirst. =**ssíndaco** = -*sindaco*. =**ssòldo**, M.: increase of pay. =**ssòma**, F.: surcharge (additional load). =**ssottána**, F.: skirt. =**ssuòlo**, M.: surface (of earth, etc.). =**ssustánza**, F.: purified substance. =**staménto**, M.: superiority; delay; (*law*) demurrer. =**stánte**, ADJ.: eminent; high (lofty); superior; imminent; slow (dilatory); wavering; imperious; M.: officer (overseer, chief). -**stanteménte**, ADV.: eminently, etc. -**stánza**†, F.: superintendence; retard (delay); earnest entreaty. -**stáre**, IRR.; INTR.: stand above (be superior); delay; defer (put off); be imminent (impend); TR.: domineer (command)†; subdue (conquer)†; govern†; cease†. -**stévole**†, ADJ.: hindering (stopping); superintending. =**stizióne** = *superstizione*. **soprá-to**, PART. of -*re;* overcome (subdued). =**ttácco**, M.: upper heel (of a shoe). =**ttenére**, IRR.; TR.: detain (hold back); stop; arrest. -**ttenúto**, PART.: detained, etc. =**ttèrra**, ADV.: above the earth. =**ttétto**, ADV.: above the roof. =**ttièni** [*tenere*], M.: delay of payment (grace); respite; putting off. =**ttútto**, ADV.: above all; principally; especially. =**umáno**, ADJ.: superhuman. -**vanzaménto** = -*vanzo*. -**vanzáre** [*avanzare*], TR.: surpass; overcome (subdue); INTR.: jut out (project); advance; remain (be extant). -**vánzo**, M.: surpassing; overplus (remainder); remains. =**víncere** = -*vvincere*. =**vvanagloriòso**, ADJ.: very vainglorious. =**vvedére**, IRR.; TR.: provide; look at (observe carefully). -**vvedúto**, ADJ.: very cautious (very prudent). =**vvegghiáre**, INTR.: watch much; sit up many nights. =**vvegnènte**, ADJ.: supervening; happening; next (following). -**vvegnènza**, F.: happening; arrival. =**vvéndere**, TR.: sell too high; exact. =**vvenènte**†, -**vveniènte** = -*vvegnente*. =**vveniménto**, M.: unexpected event. =**vveníre**†, IRR.; TR.: surprise; INTR.: happen unexpectedly (come unlooked for). =**vvènto**, M.: advantage; command (authority); (*nav.*) favourable wind; ADV.†: unexpectedly: *stare* —, be to windward; *venir* —, surprise. =**vvenúta**, F.: unexpected event or arrival. =**vvenúto**, PART.: surprised, etc. =**vvèsta**, =**vvèste**, F.: overcoat; trooper's cloak; coat of mail; covering (veil, disguise). =**vvíncere**, IRR.; TR.: excel greatly (surpass). =**vvissúto**, PART.: having survived. =**vvivènte**, ADJ.: surviving (remaining). =**vvivènza**, F.: surviving (outliving); survivorship. =**vvívere**, IRR.; INTR.: survive (outlive). =**vvívolo**, M.: (*bot.*) house-leek.

sópr-e, PREP.: poet. for *sopra;* PREF. (*sopr-*): =**eccedènte**, ADJ.: excessive. =**eccedènza**, F.: excessive abundance. =**eccellènte**, ADJ.: superexcellent. =**edificáre**, TR.: build upon; (*fig.*) found (institute). =**eminènte**, ADJ.: supereminent (preëminent). =**eminènza**†, F.: super-eminence (highest place); supremacy. **sopr=ésso**†, ADV.: upon (upon it); besides. =**etórno**, ADJ.: more than eternal (everlasting). =**illústro**, ADJ.: most illustrious. =**innalzáre**, TR.: superexalt. =**intellettuále**, ADJ.: superintellectual. =**intendènte**, ADJ.: superintending; M.: superintendent. =**intendènza**, F.: superintendence. =**intèndere**, IRR.; TR.: superintend (have charge of, direct). =**invíto**, M.: (*gam.*) raise (higher bet). =**onoráte**, ADJ.: most honoured. =**ossicèllo**, *dim.* of -*osso*. =**òsso**, M.: exostosis (tumour); spavin (splint); inconvenience. =**ossúto**†, ADJ.: afflicted with exostosis; spavined. =**umáno**, ADJ.: superhuman (celestial). =**umerále**, M.: sacerdotal cloak. =**usáre**, TR.: misuse (abuse). =**úso**, M.: injury (abuse of power); arrogant act.

soq-quadráre, INTR.: throw into confusion; destroy (overthrow). -**quadrío**, *freq.* of -*quadro*. ‖-**quádro** [*sottosquadro*], M.: confusion (disorder); ruin (destruction): *metter a* —, turn topsy-turvy; *mandare a* —, pull or beat to pieces.

sòr 1 = *sopra*.

sór 2 (*fam.*) = *Signore* and *Signora*.

sòra [L. *soror*], F.: sister (nun).

soráre†, INTR.: soar (fly high).

sòr-ba [L., pl. of -*bum*], F.: sorb-apple

(service-berry); blow (cuff). **-báre**, TR.: give blows to (cuff).

sorbecchiáre = *sorbire*.

sorbet-táre, TR.: make ice-cream (or sherbet) of; freeze. **-táto**, PART.: frozen. **-tièra**, F.: ice-cream freezer. **-tière**, M.: ice-cream maker or seller. ‖**sorbétto** [Ar.], M.: SHERBET (ice-cream, ice).

sorbíno [*sorbo*], ADJ.: sour (bitter, sharp).

sorbíre [L. *-bere*], TR.: sup up (swallow down).

sòrbo [L. *-bus*], M.: service-tree (sorb-tree): *far il formicone di* —, play deaf.

sorbondáre† = *soprabbondare*.

sorbóne†, ADJ.: reserved (minding one's own interest); M.: sharp fellow.

sór-ce†, M.: rat; mouse. **-cfáia**†, F.: nest of mice.

sorcíglio† = *sopracciglio*.

sor-cíno, *dim.* of *-cio*. ‖**sór-cio** [L. *-ex*], M.: mouse; rat. **-cióne**, *aug.* of *-cio*.

sorcodánza†, F.: carelessness (heedlessness); arrogance.

sorco-létto†, *dim.* of *-lo*. **sórco-lo**†, M.: scion (graft).

sorcòtto†, M.: coat of mail.

sor-dacchióne [*-do*], M.: very deaf person. **-dággine**, F.: deafness. **-daménte**, ADV.: softly (gently); secretly (silently). **-daménto** = *-daggine*. **-dástro**, ADJ.: deafish (rather deaf).

sordétto†, ADJ.: above-said.

sordézza [*-do*], F.: deafness.

sordi-daménte, ADV.: sordidly; niggardly. **-dézza**, F.: sordidness (filthiness); niggardliness. ‖**sór-dido**, **sòr-dido** [L. *-didus*], ADJ.: sordid (filthy); stingy.

sor-dína, F.: *alla* —, stealthily. ‖**-díno** [*-do*], M.: (*mus.*) sordet (sordine): *sonare la* —, lend a deaf ear. **-dità**, F.: deafness.

sordízia† = *sordidezza*.

sór-do [L. *surdus*], ADJ.: deaf; dull; hard-hearted; M.: deaf man: *far il* —, play deaf; *guerra -da*, secret war; *lima -da*, fine file which makes no noise; cunning fellow (sharper); *ricco* —, miser; *lanterna -da*, dark lantern. **-do=muto**, M.: deaf and dumb person.

sorèl-la [dim. of *suora*], F.: sister; nun. **-lástra**, F.: half-sister. **-lévole**, ADJ.: sororal (of a sister). **-lína**, *dim.* of *-la*.

sor-gènte, F.: SOURCE (origin); spring (fountain). **sór-gere** [L. *surgere*, raise], IRR.§; INTR.: rise (come out, issue); ascend to; commence (arise from): arise. **-gévole**†, ADJ.: rising (coming from); ascending. **-giménto**, M.: act of rising. **-gitóre**, M.: port; mouth (of a river).

§ Pret. *sór-si, -se; -sero*. Part. *sórto*.

sorgiúgnere† = *sopraggiungere*.

sorgívo [*-gere*], ADJ.: sprouting up; F.: water issuing from a spring.

sórgo 1 [l. L. *surgum*], M.: sorghum.

sórgo† 2, M.: mouse; rat.

sorgoncèllo [*sorcolo*], M.: small graft or scion.

sorgozzóne [*sopra*, *gozzo*], M.: blow in the throat (cuff); stay (prop).

soriáno [*S.*, Syria], ADJ.: *gatto* —, Syrian cat (Maltese cat).

sorí-ce†, M.: field-mouse. **-cígno**†, ADJ.: mouse-coloured.

sorìte [Gr. *soreites* (*sorós*, mass)], F.: (*log.*) sorites.

sor=montáre, TR.: surmount (surpass); INTR.: increase (prosper); rise.

sor-nacáre†, **-nacchiáre**†, INTR.: expectorate (spit); snore. **-nácchio**†, M.: phlegm; severe catarrh.

sornió-ne, ‖**-na** [OFr. *sorne* (Fr. *sournois*, sly)], ADJ.: rude (uncivil); reserved; M.: impolite fellow; reserved man.

sòro† 1, ADJ.: not moulted (unmewed, sore); raw (inexperienced).

sòro† 2, ADJ.: sorrel (light bay).

soròre†, F.: sister.

sor-passánte, ADJ.: surpassing; incomparable. ‖**=passáre**, TR.: surpass (excel); exceed.

sor=più†, M.: overplus; ADV.: at the most.

sor=pósto = *soprapposto*.

sor-prendènte, ADJ.: surprising. ‖**=prèndere**, IRR.; TR.: surprise; amaze (astonish); deceive. **-présa**, F.: surprise (amazement); deceit. **-préso**, PART.: surprised, etc.

sor-quidánza†, F.: arrogance (presumption). **-quidáre**†, INTR., REFL.: become proud or arrogant; grow bold.

sórra [L. *sura*, pulp], F.: pickled tunny-fish.

sorrecchiáre†, INTR.: listen.

sor=règgere [*sub-*], IRR.; TR.: support (sustain); REFL.†: stop.

sorrèsso†, M.: resurrection.

sor-ridènte, ADJ.: smiling. **-ridentemente**, ADV.: smilingly (simperingly). ‖**-rídere** [L. *sub-ridere*], IRR. (cf. *ridere*); INTR.: laugh a little (smile). **-risétto**, **-risíno**, *car. dim.* of *-riso*. **-ríso**, M.: act of smiling, etc.; smile; PART.: smiled, etc.

sorsaltáre†, TR.: jump upon.

sor-sáre [*-so*], TR.: sip (drink by sips). **-sáta**, F.: sip; draught; rest. **-satína**, *dim.* of *-sata*. **-seggiáre**, TR., INTR.: sip frequently. **-sellíno**, *dim.* of *-sello*. **-sétto**, **-settíno**, **-síno**, *dim.* of *-so*.

sórsi, PRET. of *sorgere*.

sórso [L. *sorpsum*, part. of *sorbère*, sup up], M.: sip (draught); little comfort: *in un* —, at one gulp.

sòr-ta = *-te.* **-táccia,** F.: hazard (mere chance). ‖**sòr-te** [L. *sors,* lot], F.: sort (kind); condition; fate (fortune); chance; principal (capital)†; sorcery†: *di — che,* so that; *a —, per —,* by chance; *per mala —,* unfortunately; *tirar la —,* draw lots; *aver — —,* have a lot; *toccare in —,* fall by lot; *mettere alla —,* leave to chance (hazard); *pigliar —,* conjecture (surmise). **-teggiáre,** INTR.: allot; draw; leave to chance; TR.†: allot (distribute). **-téggio,** M.: augury (prophecy); allotment. **-teríа†,** F: lot (assortment); sorcery. **-tièra†,** F.: sorceress. **-tière†,** M.: sorcerer. **-tilègio,** M.: witchcraft (sorcery). **-tílego,** M.: wizard (necromancer). **-timénto†,** M.: sortment; selection (choice). **-tíre** [L. *-tiri,* draw lots], TR.: draw lots for; elect; INTR.: come out (of lots); acquire; come to; make a sortie (sally); go out; happen (befall)†. **-títa,** F.: sortie (sally); choice†; assortment†.

sórto, PART. of *sorgere.*

sortù†, M.: SURTOUT (great coat).

sorve-gliánza, F.: watch (vigilance). ‖**-gliáre** [*sor-, v.* .], TR.: watch carefully.

sor-vegnènte, ADJ.: happening (supervening). ‖**=veníre†,** IRR.; INTR.: happen unexpectedly.

sorvívere†, IRR.; INTR.: survive (outlive).

sorviziáto†, ADJ.: full of vices (very vicious).

sor=voláre, INTR.: fly over or above; surpass.

sos- = *sub-.*

soscri. . = *sottoscri. .*

sospeccia. .† = *sospetta. .*

sos=pèndere, IRR.; TR.: suspend (hang up); put off (defer); hinder (render doubtful); relieve†. **-pendíbile,** ADJ.: that can be suspended. **-pendiménto,** M., **-pensióne,** F.: act of suspending; suspending; suspension (cessation); hanging up (interruption). **-pensivaménte,** ADV.: in suspense. **-pensívo,** ADJ.: suspensive (that suspends). **-pensòrio,** M.: (*anat.*) suspensory; truss. **-pesaménte,** ADV.: dubiously; irresolutely. **-péso,** PART.: suspended (undecided); irresolute.

sos-pettábile, ADJ.: that excites suspicion. **-pettaménte,** ADV.: suspiciously. **-pettáre,** TR.: suspect; mistrust (doubt); suppose. **-pettévole,** ADJ.: suspicious; doubtful. **-pètto, -pettáto,** PART. of *-pettare.* ‖**-pètto** [L. *suspectus,* suspected], M.: suspicion (mistrust); fear. **-pettosaménte,** ADV.: suspiciously; doubtfully. **-pettóso,** ADJ.: suspicious (mistrustful); doubtful (uncertain). **-pezióne†,** F., **-picaménto†,** M.: suspicion (mistrust). **-picáre†, -picitáre†** = *-pettare.* **-piccinóso, -picióso** = *-pettoso.*

sospign. . = *sosping. .*

sos=píngere, IRR.; TR.: thrust (push with force); induce (persuade); force (compel)†. **-pingiménto,** M.: push (shove); impulse; instigation. **-pínta†,** F.: push (dash); instigation: *dare una —,* give a push or shove; *— mortale,* death. **-pínto,** PART.: pushed, etc. **-pinzióne†,** F.: shove; inducement; provocation.

sospi-ránte, ADJ.: sighing or longing for; M.: lover. ‖**-ráre** [L. *su-spirare*], INTR.: sigh; lament; TR.: long for (sigh for); wait for. **-ratóre,** M.: one who sighs often. **-rétto,** *car. dim.* of *-ro.* **-révole†,** ADJ.: full of sighs (doleful).

sospí-ro, M.: sigh; moan: *gittar un —,* fetch a sigh; *l' ultimo —,* last breath. **-róne,** *aug.* of *-ro.* **-rosaménte,** ADV.: plaintively (dolefully). **-róso,** ADJ.: sighing (plaintive).

sospizióne†, F.: suspicion (mistrust).

sossannáre†, TR.: laugh at (deride).

sossópra = *sottosopra.*

sòsta [*sostare*], F.: pause (stop, rest); intense desire†; truce (armistice)†; (*nav.*) master rope.

sostan-tivaménte, ADV.: substantively. **-tívo** [L. *substantivus*], M., ADJ.: substantive. ‖**sostán-za** [L. *sub-stantia*], M.: substance; body; patrimony (inheritance): *in —,* in sum. **-ziále,** ADJ.: substantial (real). **-zialità,** F.: substantiality; existence. **-zialménte,** ADV.: substantially. **-ziáre†,** INTR., REFL.: assume substance; exist. **-zièvole,** ADJ.: substantial; real; useful. **-ziosaménte,** ADV.: substantially (really). **-zióso,** ADJ.: substantial.

sostáre [L. *sub-stare,* stand firm], INTR.: stop (rest); suspend.

sosté-gno, M.: support (prop); assistance. **-nènte,** ADJ.: supporting; assisting. **-nènza†,** F.: tolerance (endurance); sustenance; stay (support). ‖**-nére** [*sos-, tenere*], IRR.; TR.: sustain (hold up); support (endure); defend; nourish (maintain); forbear†; grant†; delay†; guard†; REFL.: contain one's self (be grave and serious). **-níbile,** ADJ.: sustainable (bearable). **-niménto,** M.: food (maintenance); support; endurance; rest (respite). **-nitóre,** M., **-nitríce,** F.: maintainer; defender; preserver; sufferer. **-ntábile,** ADJ.: that can be supported. **-ntácolo†,** M.: support (stay); help; defence. **-ntaménto,** M.: prop; food (nourishment). **-ntáre** [L. *sus-tentare,* freq. of *sustinere*], TR.: nourish (feed, maintain); REFL.:

support one's self (nourish one's self). **-ntatívo**, ADJ.: supporting; nutritious. **-ntatóre**, M.: maintainer. **-ntazióne** = *-ntamento*. **-nutézza**, F.: gravity (stateliness). **-núto**, ADJ.: sustained (supported); elevated; grave (serious).

sosti-tuíre [L. *sub-stituere*], TR.: substitute; subrogate; entail. **-túto**, M.: substitute; surrogate. **-tutóre**, M., **-tutríce**, F.: one who substitutes. **-tuzióne**, F.: substitution; subrogation; entail.

sott-ácqua [*sotto, acqua*], ADV.: under water. **-ácqueo**, ADJ.: that is under water.

sotta-fittáre [*sotto, fittare*], TR.: rent from a tenant (under-lease). **-fittatóre**, M.: under-tenant. **-fítto**, M.: under-lease (under-letting).

sottá-na [l. L. *subtana* (*subtus*, beneath)], F.: petticoat; priest's cassock; (*mus.*)† octave (string of the lute or violin). **-nèlla**, *dim.* of *-na*.

sottangènte [*sotto, tangente*], F.: (*geom.*) subtangent.

sot-tanína, **-taníno**, *dim.* of *-tana*. **-tánot**†, ADJ.: inferior (under); M.: under-petticoat.

sottárco [*sotto, arco*], M.: under-part of the arch.

sottèc-che, **-chi**†, ‖**-co**† [*sotto, occhi*], ADV.: stealthily (secretly); askance.

sottèn-dere [*sotto, tendere*], INTR.: subtend (be extended under). **-traménto**, M.: slipping in (replacing). **-tráre**, INTR.: slip or creep under; succeed; happen (come to pass); fall. **-trazióne**† = *-tramento*.

sotterfúgio [L. *subter-fugium*], M.: subterfuge (evasion).

sottèr-ra [*sotto, terra*], ADV.: under ground. **-rábile**, ADJ.: that can be buried. **-raménto**, M.: inhumation (burial). **-ráneo**, ADJ.: subterraneous; M.: subterraneous place. **-ráre**, TR.: put under ground (inter); (*fig.*) survive; oppress (humble)†; drown†. **-ratóre**, M.: grave-digger (sexton). **-ratòrio**, M.: burying-place (sepulchre).

sot-tésa [*-tendere*], F.: (*geom.*) subtense. **-téso**, PART.: subtended.

sottésso [*sotto, esso*], ADV.: below (beneath).

sot-tigliaménto†, M., **-tigliánza**†, F.: subtilization (refinement); thinning (diminishing); whetting. **-tigliáre**†, TR.: sharpen (whet); make thin; subtilize (refine); REFL.: become thin or emaciated. **-tigliatívo**†, ADJ.: sharpening; thinning. **-tigliézza**, F.: subtility; sharpness; subtle-: want. **-tigliúme**, M.: thin food; cloth wants. ‖**-tíle** [L. *subtilis*, fine], ADJ.: (delicate, thin); sharp (brisk): subtle; witty; penurious; frugal; M.: delicate part; necessity (want); ADV.: subtilely; cunningly: *vino* —, thin wine; *mal* —, phthisis; *mensa* —, poor fare; *guardar nel* —, be over-particular (subtilize); *cavar* or *trarre il* — *del* —, make money on everything; *parlar* —, speak softly. **-tileménte**, ADV.: subtilely; slyly; sharply. **-tilétto**, **-tilíno**, *dim.* of *-tile*. **-tilità**, F.: subtility; thinness; craftiness (slyness)†; judgment†; dexterity†; perfection†. **-tilizzaménto**, M.: refinement; lessening (diminishing). **-tilizzáre**, INTR.: refine (subtilize); TR.: imagine (think). **-tilménte** = *-tilemente*.

sottin-tèndere [*sotto, intendere*], IRR.; TR.: understand (anything omitted). **-téso**, PART.: understood (left out).

sótto [L. *subtus*], PREP.: under (beneath); (*fig.*) hidden (secret); put down (conquered); during; imminent; M.: under part; ADV.: down (beneath); secretly: *avere* — *di sè*, have under one's command; — *voce*, low voice; — *brevità*, briefly; — *la sua parola*, upon his word; *dar* —, strike under; *andar* —, go down; *restar di* —, be worsted; be a loser; *tirar* —, continue. **-bóce** = *-voce*. **-cálza**, F.: under-stocking. =**calzóni**, M. PL.: drawers. =**cancellière**, M.: vice-chancellor. **-ccáre**†, TR.: touch very gently; prick slightly. **sottò-cchio** [*occhio*], ADV.: secretly; askance (under the eyes). =**códa**, M.: crupper-strap. =**copèrta**, F.: under-cover; under-deck. =**còppa**, M.: saucer (salver). =**cuòco**, M.: under-cook. =**divídere**, IRR.; TR.: subdivide. **-giacére**, IRR.; TR.: lie under; be subject or exposed to. =**góla**, M.: chin-strap; ADV.†: under the throat. =**grondále**, M.: (*arch.*) part of the cornice. =**intéso** = *sottinteso*. =**lineáre**, TR.: underline. =**lúme**, M.: light- (lamp-)mat. =**maèstro**, M.: under-master. =**mánica**, F.: undersleeve. =**máno**, ADV.: underhand (secretly); with the under part of the hand. =**máre**, M.: bottom of the sea. =**maríno**, ADJ.: submarine. **-messióne** [*-messo*], F.: submission (subjection). **-mésso**, PART. of *-mettere*. =**méttere**, IRR.; TR.: submit (subdue, subject); REFL.: submit (yield); acquiesce. =**moltíplice**, ADJ.: (*math.*) submultiple. =**mòrdere**†, IRR.; TR.: bite underneath. **-ntèndere**† = *sottintendere*. =**páncia**, M.: saddle-girth. **-poniménto** [*-porre*], M.: subjection (placing under). =**pórre**, IRR.; TR.: place under; subject (subdue). **-pósito** = *-posto*. **-posizióne** = *-ponimento*. **-pósto**, PART. of *-porre*; put under; subdued; ADJ.: supposititious; depending; feigned. =**prefètto**, M.: sub-prefect. =**prefettúra**, F.: sub-prefecture. =**prióre**, M.: sub-prior. =**provveditóre**, M.: under-purveyor. -**rdináto**† [*ordinato*], ADJ.. subordinate (subaltern). =**rídere**†, IRR.; INTR.: smile; flourish again. =**scála**, M.: space under a staircase. =**scrítta**, F.: signature (subscription). =**scrítto**, PART.: subscribed (signed); M.: subscriber. -**scrittóra**, F., -**scrittóre**, M., -**scrittríce**, F.: subscriber (underwriter). =**scrívere**, TR.: subscribe (underwrite). -**scrizióne**, F.: subscription. =**segretário**, M.: under-secretary. =**sópra**, ADV.: upside-down (topsy-turvy); in confusion; in haste: *metter* —, turn upside-down; *entrar* —†, come in in a rage. =**spiegáre**, TR.: show covertly (explain by halves). =**squádra**, F., =**squádro**, M.: hollow (cave, cavity); ADV.†: with hollows: *di* —, in a concave manner. =**stáre**, INTR.: be under; be subject. =**suòlo**, M.: lower strata of earth. =**tenènte**, M.: (*mil.*) sub-lieutenant. =**tíngere**, IRR.; TR.: give the first tint to. =**váso**, M.: under-pot (under-vase). =**vènto**, M.: (*nav.*) part to the leeward: *essere* —, be to leeward (have the wind against). =**vèste**, F.: under-vest or waistcoat. =**vóce**, ADV.: in a low voice.

sot-traiménto, M.: subtraction (deduction); privation. ‖-**trárre** [L. *sub-trahere*], IRR. (cf. *trarre*); TR.: take away (withdraw); subtract; entice (seduce)†; deprive†; REFL.: take one's self away (retire). -**trátto**, PART. of -*trarre*: subtracted, etc.; ADJ.: cunning; M.†: allurement; artifice. -**trattóre**†, M.: deceiver (seducer); (*math.*) subtractor. -**trattóso**†, ADJ.: cunning (artful). -**trazióne**, F.: withdrawal; privation; refusal; (*math.*) substraction.

sovátto†, M.: leather strap (thong).

sovèn-te [L. *sub-inde*, thereupon], ADV.: frequently. -**teménte**, ADV.: often (frequently). -'**ti**†, ADJ.: many.

sover-chiaménte, ADV.: excessively (too much). -**chiánza**†, F.: superabundance. -**chiáre**, TR.: surpass (excel); (*fig.*) overcome; INTR.: be overbearing; sink down (cave in)†; overflow†. -**chiatóre**, M.: overbearing fellow. -**chiería**, F.: overbearing act; fraud (trickery). -**chiévole**, ADV.: superfluous (useless). -**chiézza**†, F.: excess; villany†. ‖**sovèr-chio** [L. *superculus* (*super*, above)], ADJ.: excessive (SUPERabundant); M.: superabundance (superfluity); trickery†; ADV.: excessively (too much). -**chitá**†, F.: superabundance (excess).

sóvero†, M.: cork; cork-tree.

sóvra (*poet.*) = *sopra*.

sóvr-a. . [*sopra-*, *sopr*(*e*): cf. these for words not found here], PREF. (bef. vowel *sovr-*; initial simple cons't of next member doubled): =**abbondáre**, INTR.: superabound. =**accréscere**, IRR.; INTR.: grow over. -**a=illústre**, ADJ.: most illustrious. =**ammirábile**, ADJ.: most admirable. -**naménte**, ADV.: sovereignly (in a kingly manner). -**aneggiáre**, TR., INTR.: domineer (rule, be a sovereign). -**anità**, F.: sovereignty. -**áno** [l. L. *superanus* (L. *super*, above)], ADJ.: SOVEREIGN (superior); principal (chief); excellent; absolute; M.: sovereign; (*mus.*) soprano†. -**anzáre**†, TR., INTR.: surpass (exceed). -**a=ppórre**, IRR.; TR.: place or put upon; prefer. -**a=pposizióne**, F.: superposition. -**a=ppossènte**†, ADJ.: very powerful. -**a=stáre**, IRR.; INTR.: stand above or over; threaten (menace). =**eccellènte**†, ADJ.: most excellent. -**eggiáre**†, INTR.: be over or above (command); tarry (remain). =**eminènte**, ADJ.: supereminent. =**émpiere**†, IRR.; TR.: fill to the brim (overfill); load. =**ésso**, ADV.: upon (on). =**impósta**, F.: overtax. =**offésa**†, F.: very great offence. =**ossèquio**, M.: excessive veneration. =**umanità**, F.: supernatural existence. =**umáno**, ADJ.: superhuman (supernatural).

sovve-nènza†, F.: help (assistance). -**névole**†, ADJ.: helpful; beneficent. -**níbile**, ADJ.: that can be helped. -**niménto**, M.: assistance (aid, succour). -**nimentóso** = -*nevole*. ‖-**níre** [L. *subvenire*], IRR. (cf. *venire*); TR.: help (assist); relieve; INTR., REFL.: remember. -**nitóre**, -**ntóre**, M., -**nitríce**, F.: furnisher (provider); succourer (reliever). -**núto**, PART.: aided; remembered. -**nzióne**, F.: subsidy; aid; tax.

sovver-sióne, F.: subversion (ruin); rising in the stomach (vomit)†. **sovvèr-so**, PART. of -*tere*. -**sóre**, M.: destroyer (subverter); seducer. -'**tere**† = -*tire*. -**timénto** = -*sione*. ‖-**tíre** [L. *subvertere* (turn)], TR.: subvert (ruin, overthrow); pervert†; seduce†. -**titóre** = -*sore*.

sòzio†, M.: companion (partner).

soz-zaménte, ADV.: filthily (nastily); dishonestly. -**záre**†, TR.: soil (foul); corrupt. -**zézza**, -**zità**† = -*zura*. ‖**sóz-zo** [l. L. *sucius* (L. *sucidus*, juicy)], ADJ.: dirty (filthy); deformed†; wicked†; profligate†. -**zóre**†, -**zúme**, M., -**zúra**, F.: dirtiness (filthiness); deformity†.

spacca-légna, -**légne**, M. INVAR.: wood-splitter. -**ménto**, M.: cleaving (cutting). -**montágne**, -**mónti**, M.: boaster (braggart). -**piètre**, M.: rock-breaker. ‖**spaccá-re** [OGer. *spachen*

TR.: cleave (split); crack; REFL.: crack (burst). **-túra**, F.: cleft (crevice, chink).

spac-ciábile, ADJ.: vendable (salable). ‖**-ciáre** [*dispacciare*], TR.: sell (retail); EXPEDITE (DISPATCH); send out; declare ended (or incurable); make out to be (falsely); REFL.: explain one's self: — *per*, pretend to be; — *un luogo*†, clear a place; — *grosso*†, venture much: — *il terreno*†, walk fast. **-ciataménte**, ADV.: quickly (promptly); immediately. **-ciatívo**, ADJ.: quick (expeditious). **-ciáto**, ADJ.: sold; ruined; dispatched; finished: *essere* —, be past hopes of recovery; *sono* —, I am undone; *matto* —, stark mad. **-ciatóre**, M.: seller; destroyer; hastener. **spác-cio**, M.: sale; despatch (expedition)†; leave†; letter†.

spác-co [*-care*], M.: splitting; crack (split). **-conáta**, F.: braggardism. **-cóne**, M.: braggart (boaster).

spá-da [L. *spatha*], F.: sword; sabre (scimitar); punishment; (*fig.*) war; swordsman; spade (at cards): *metter a fil di* —, put to the sword; *andare come una* —, walk very erect; *pesce* —, sword-fish. **-dáccia**, F.: long sword. **-dacciátat**† = *-data*. **-daccíno** (*dim.*), M.: small sword; braggart (bully). **-daccinòla**†, F.: (*bot.*) sword-grass. **-dáio, -dáro**, M.: sword-cutter (sword-maker); sword-bearer. **-dáta**, F.: blow with the sword.

spadèrno [?], M.: bottom-fishing line.

spa-détta, -dína, *dim.* of *-da*.

spadíglia†, F.: ace of spades.

spa-dóna, -dóne, *aug.* of *-da*.

spadro-náre, *disp.* of *-neggiare*. ‖**-neggiáre** [*s-*, *p*. .], INTR.: act the master.

spadulárе†, TR.: drain fens or marshes.

spagáto†, ADJ.: discontented.

spaghéro†, M.: asparagus.

spaghétto, *dim.* of *spago*.

s-paginàre, TR.: undo the pages of.

spa-gliaménto, M.: act of winnowing. ‖**-gliáre** [*s-*, *paglia*], TR.: loosen or remove the straw of. **-gliatúra**, F.: removing the straw.

Spá-gna in der. *s-* [L. *Hispania*], F.: Spain: *cera di* —, sealing-wax; *pan di* —, kind of sweet bread. **-gnolággine**, **-gnoláta**, F.: exaggeration (boasting). **-gnoleggiáre**, INTR.: use Spanish words or customs. **-gnolescaménto**, ADV.: in a Spanish manner. **-gnolésco**, ADJ.: of or belonging to Spanish manners or customs. **-gnolétta**, F.: sash-window fastening; cigarette. **-gnolísmo**, M.: Spanish idiom or language. **-gn(u)òlo**, ADJ.: Spanish; M.: Spaniard.

spágo [?], M.: pack-thread (waxed-twine): *avere uno* —, have great fear.

spa-iaménto, M.: unmatching (unpairing). ‖**-iáre** [*s-*, *appaiare*], TR.: unmatch (unpair).

spalan-cáre [*s-*, *palanca*], TR.: open wide (throw open); tell openly†. **-cataménte**, ADV.: openly (freely); publicly†. **-catóre**, M.: opener. **-chío**, M.: keeping open; opening.

spaláre¹ [*s-*, *palo*], TR.: remove the props of.

spa-láre² [*s-*, *pala*], TR.: shovel off. **-láta, -latúra**, F.: shovelling away.

spalcáre [*s-*, *palco*], TR.: remove the ceiling of (unfloor); thin out (trees).

spáldo [?], M.: projecting gallery (balcony); bastion.

spaletáre†, TR.: drain off.

spál-la [L. *spatula*], F.: shoulder; (*fig.*) back: *alle -le*, at one's heels, behind; *di buone -le*, broad-shouldered, robust; *accarezzare le -le*, beat, cudgel; *buttarsi dietro le -le*, forsake, give up; *voltar, dare le -le*, run away (flee); *fare* —, assist (aid); *ristringersi nelle -le*, shrug one's shoulders. **-láccia**, F.: large, ugly shoulder; swelling on a horse's shoulder. **-láccio**, M.: shoulder-piece. **-láre**, TR.: sprain or dislocate (a horse's shoulder); REFL.: put one's shoulder out of joint. **-láto**, PART.: splayed (broken-shouldered); ruined. **-leggiaménto**, M.: (*mil.*) earthwork; support. **-leggiáre**, TR.: aid (uphold, assist); shoulder; INTR.: walk or go well (of horses). **-létta**, F.: parapet; epaulette†. **-lièra**, F.: back of a chair; ESPALIER; first bench of rowers in a galley. **-lière**, M.: head-rower (in a galley). **-lierétta**, *dim.* of *-liera*. **-lína**, F., **-líno**, M.: EPAULETTE. **-lóna**, *aug.* of *-la*. **-lúccia**, *disp. dim.* of *-la*: *far -lucce*, shrug one's shoulders. **-lucciáta**, F.: act of shrugging. **-lúto**†, ADJ.: large or broad-shouldered.

spal-máre [*s-*, *palma*], TR.: smear (tar, daub). **-máta**, F.: slap on the palm of the hand. **-matóre**, M.: dauber (smearer). **-matúra**, F.: act of daubing, etc.

spálto [*spaldo*], M.: (*mil.*) glacis (slope); pavement†.

spam-panaménto, M.: stripping the leaves (from a vine). ‖**-panáre** [*s-*, *pampano*], TR.: strip the leaves (from a vine); INTR.: burst forth (as buds); bloom. **-panáta**, F.: rhodomontade (boasting). **-panáto**, ADJ., PART.: without leaves, etc.: ridiculous (absurd). **-panatúra**, **-panazióne** = *-panamento*. **-pináre** = *-panare*.

spán-dere [L. *ex-pandere*, spread out], TR.: pour out; scatter (sow here and there); lavish (squander); manifest†; REFL., INTR.: overflow; spread abroad. **-diménto**, M.: effusion (shedding). **-di-**

tóio, M.: drying-room; PL.: drying-lines. **-ditóre**, M.: pourer; scatterer; divulger.
spaniáre [*s-*, *pania*], TR.: remove the lime-twigs from; disentangle (free).
spánna [OGer.], F.: SPAN (palm, hand).
spannáre [*s-*, *panna*], TR.: skim (milk); clean†.
spannòc-chia [*s-*, *p.*.], F.: ear of Indian corn. **-chiáre**, TR.: cut the ears of (corn).
span-táre†, INTR.: marvel at. **spán-to**†, PART. of *-dere;* ADJ.: pompous (ostentatious).
spappagalláre [*s-*, *pappagallo*], INTR.: act too much like a parrot.
spappoláre [*s-*, *pappa*], INTR.: dissolve; become pap.
sparabícco†, ADV.: *andare a —*, roam (rove).
spara-gèlla, **-ghèlla**, F.: kind of wild asparagus; sow-thistle. **-giáia**, F.: asparagus-bed. ||**spára-gio** [L. *asparagus*], M.: asparagus.
spa-raggiáre†, TR.: spare (save); pardon. **-rággo**†, M.: economy (frugality, husbandry).
sparalémbo†, M.: workman's apron.
sparaménto [*-rare*], M.: discharge of firearms.
sparapáne†, M.: devourer of bread; braggart.
spa-ráre [L. *ex-*, *parare*, prepare], TR.: embowel (gut); rip open; discharge (fire); unlearn; fling; kick: — *una lepre*, draw a hare; — *una casa*, unfurnish a house. **-ráta**, F.: vaunting (boasting); discharge (volley): *far una —*, make fine promises. **-ráto**, M.: opening of any garment (bosom of a shirt). **-ratóre**, M.: one who opens; boaster; shooter.
sparavière† = *sparviere*.
sparec-chiaménto, M.: act of clearing the table. ||**-chiáre** [*s-*, *app.*.], TR.: take away (clear the table); eat a great deal of. **-chiatóre**, M.: one who clears the table; great eater. **sparéc-chio**, M.: clearing the table.
sparéggio [*s-*, *p.*.], M.: disparity (inequality).
sparére† = *sparire*.
spár-gere [L.], IRR.§; TR.: scatter about (diffuse); divulge (publish); shed (spill); DISPERSE†; INTR.: expand. **-giménto**, M.: scattering; divulging; shedding (effusion); inattention. **-gitóre**, M., **-gitrí-ce**, F.: sower; publisher; shedder.

§ Pret. *spár-si*, *-se*; *-sero*. Part. *spár-so* or *-to*.

spa-riménto, M.: disappearing (vanishing). ||**-ríre** [*s-*, *app.*.], INTR.: disappear (vanish); go away; become nil; lose. **-rizióne**, F.: disappearance.
spar-laménto, M.: slander (calumny). ||**-láre** [*s-*, *p.*.], INTR.: speak ill of (slander). **-latóre**, M., **-latríce**, F.: calumniator (traducer).
sparmia.. = *risparmia*..
sparnas-saménto, M.: wasting (squandering). ||**-sáre** [ak. to *spargere*], INTR.: scatter; squander (waste). **-satóre**, M.: spendthrift (dissipator).
sparnic-ciaménto†, M.: scattering. **-ciáre**†, TR.: scatter (disperse).
spáro [*sparare*], M.: volley of firearms.
sparpa-gliaménto, M.: dispersion. ||**-gliáre** [? ak. to *spargere*], TR.: scatter here and there (disperse); squander; REFL.: spread abroad. **-gliataménte**, ADV.: dispersedly (in confusion). **-glío**, M.: continued scattering. **-glióne**, M.: person irregular in conduct or speech.
spar-saménte, ADV.: in a scattered manner. **spár-so**, ADJ.: scattered (dispersed); divulged; vanished; spotted. **-sióne** = *-gimento*. **-taménte**, **-tataménte**, ADV.: separately; privately. ||**-táto** [*-to*], ADJ.: separated (divided).
spar-tíbile, ADJ.: divisible (separable). **-tigióne**, F.: division of property. **-timénto**, M.: partition (sharing); lot (division); class†; grade†. ||**-tíre** [*s-*, *p.*.], TR.: divide (separate); share; allot. **-titaménte**, ADV.: separately (in detail). **-títo**, M.: (*mus.*) score; ADJ.: divided (separated). **-titúra**, F.: manner of dividing, etc. **-tizióne**, F.: partition or division of property.
spárto, PART. of *spartire* or *spargere*.
sparu-tèllo, **-tíno**, *dim.* of *-to*. **-téz-za**, F.: leanness (thinness). ||**sparú-to** [*sparito*], ADJ.: lean (thin, slender).
spar-vieráto†, ADJ.: swift (nimble); swift-sailing: *uomo —*, dashing, inconsiderate man. **-vieratóre**, M.: falconer. **-vière**, ||**-vièro** [OGer. *-wari*, SPARROW-hawk], M.: hawk (falcon).
spása†, F.: large flat basket.
spá-sima†, F.: spasm. **-simáre**, INTR.: have the spasms; be passionately in love; suffer; TR.†: covet (desire); consume (waste). **-simataménte**, ADV.: convulsively; passionately. **-simáto**†, PART.: enamoured (violently in love); in spasms. ||**spá-simo** [L. *-smus*], M.: convulsion (fit, spasm). **-simóso**†, ADJ.: subject to spasms. **-smòdico**, pl. *—ci*, ADJ.: spasmodic (convulsive).
spáso†, ADJ.: extended (flat).
spas-samentáre† = *-sare*. **-saménto**†, M.: pastime (diversion). ||**-sáre** [L. *expassare*, intens. of *expandere*, expand], TR.: divert (amuse); REFL.: amuse one's self. **-seggiaménto**, M.: walk. **-seg-giáre**, INTR.: walk (walk about). **-seg-**

giáta, F.: walk. **-séggio**, M.: walking (promenade). **-sévole**, ADJ.: amusing (diverting).

spassio-náre [*s-*, *passione*], REFL.: rid one's self of passion. **-nataménte**, ADV.: dispassionately. **-natézza**, F.: dispassion (indifference). **-náto**, PART.: dispassionate.

spásso [*spassare*], M.: amusement (pastime); recreation: *andar a* —, go and take a walk; *menare, portare a* —, put off (procrastinate); *dare* —, divert, amuse; *lavorante a* —, unoccupied labourer; *prendersi* — *d' uno*, ridicule a person.

spastáre [*s-*, *pasta*], TR.: unpaste; remove (take away); REFL.: free one's self from anything.

spastoiáre [*s-*, *pastoia*], TR.: take off (the shackles or fetters); REFL.: extricate one's self (get free).

s=paternostráre, INTR.: mumble paternosters.

spáto [Ger. *spath*], M.: spathum (spar).

spátola [L. *spatula*, flat blade], F.: spatula (spattle).

spatriáre [*s-*, *patria*], TR.: expatriate (banish); INTR., REFL.: leave one's country.

spau-racchiáre [*s-*, *paura*], TR.: frighten (scare). **-rácchio**, M.: bugbear (scarecrow). **-ráre†**, TR.: terrify (frighten). **-révole†**, ADJ.: frightful (fearful). **-riménto**, M.: fright (fear). **-ríre**, TR.: frighten (terrify); INTR., REFL.: be frightened or alarmed. **-róso**, ADJ.: fearful (timorous).

spa-valdería, F.: insolence (boldness). ‖**-váldo** [*s-*, L. *pavor*, fear], ADJ.: impudent (insolent, bold).

spavènio [?], M.: (*vet.*) spavin.

spaven-tácchio†, M.: scarecrow (bugbear). **-tággine†**, **-taménto** = *-to*. **-tánte**, ADJ.: frightful (terrifying). ‖**-táre** [*s-*, *p.* .], TR.: terrify (scare); INTR., REFL.: be frightened (be terrified). **-tataménte**, ADV.: in a frightened manner. **-tatíccio**, ADJ.: fearful (frightful). **-tatóre**, M.: one who frightens. **-tazióne** = *-to*. **-tévole**, ADJ.: frightful; strong (terrible); deformed (ugly). **-tevolézza** = *-to*. **-tevolménte**, ADV.: horribly (dreadfully); hugely; extremely. **spavèn-to**, M.: terror (fright, fear). **-tosaménte**, ADV.: fearfully. **-tosità**, F.: terror (fear). **-tóso**, ADJ.: dreadful (frightful).

spa-ziáre [*-zio*], INTR.: expatiate; wander about (rove). **-zieggiáre**, TR.: (*typ.*) space out.

spazientíre [*s-*, *pazienza*], REFL.: become impatient.

-ziétto, **-zíno**, *dim.* of *-zio*. ‖**spázio** [L. *-tium*], M.: space; distance; interval (of space or of time); (*typ.*) space. **-ziosaménte**, ADV.: spaciously. **-ziosità**, F.: spaciousness (space, extent). **-zióso**, ADJ.: spacious (extensive). **-zza=cammíno**, M.: chimney-sweeper. **-zza=campágna**, F.: blunderbuss; kind of horn. **-zza=contráde**, M.: idler (trifling fellow). **-zza=fórno**, M.: oven-rake (malkin, scovel). **-zzaménto**, M.: act of sweeping or mopping. **-zzáre** [L. *-tiari*, make spacious], TR.: sweep (mop); clear (empty). **-zzatóio**, M.: coal-rake (scovel). **-zzatúra**, F.: dirt (sweepings): *cassetta della* —, dust-hole. **-zzaturáio**, M.: scavenger (dustman). **-zzavènto†**, M.: very windy place. **-zzíno**, M.: sweeper; polisher. **spá-zzo**, M.: space; ground; pavement.

spázzo-la [L. *spatula*, flat blade], F.: clothes-brush; shoe-brush; whisk; scraper; shoot of wild asparagus. **-láre**, TR.: brush; whisk (dust). **-láta**, F.: brushing; dusting. **-létta**, **-lína**, *dim.* of *-la*. **-líno**, M.: small brush. **-lóne**, *aug.* of *-la*.

spec-chiáio†, M.: maker or seller of looking-glasses. **-chiaménto**, M.: act of looking in a glass. **-chiáre**, TR.†: gaze at, observe; REFL.: glass one's self; INTR.: be reflected. **-chiáto†**, PART.: clear; sound (valid): *persona* —*ta*, spotless person; *scrittura* —*ta*, valid document. **-chiatúra** = *-chiamento*. **-chiétto**, M.: *dim.* of *-chio*; small glass in the bottom of a jewel-casket; abridgment (summary): *fede di* —, certificate of good conduct; *a* —*ti*, bay speckled with white. ‖**spèc-chio** [L. *speculum*], M.: looking-glass (mirror); model: — *ardente* (or *ustorio*), burning glass; *pulito com' uno* —, most bright, free from any defect; — *d' asino*, kind of stone.

spècce = *specie*.

speciá-le [L. *-lis*], ADJ.: special (particular): — *mandato*, express command. **-lista**, pl. —*ti*, M.: specialist. **-lità**, F.: specialty (peculiarity). **-lizzáre**, TR., INTR.: specialize (particularize). **-lménte**, ADV.: specially (particularly).

spè-c(i)e [L. *-cies*, outward appearance], F.: species (kind); appearance; image; ADV.: specially: *far* —, make an impression; surprise. **-cífica**, F.: specified note. **-cificaménte**, ADV.: specifically (expressly). **-cificaménto**, M.: specification. **-cificáre**, TR., INTR.: specify (particularize). **-cificataménte**, ADV.: specifically (distinctly). **-cificatívo**, ADJ.: fit for specifying. **-cificazióne**, F.: specification (distinction). **-cífico**, pl. —*ci*, ADJ.: specific (particular); M.: (*med.*) specific. **-cíllo** [L. *-cillum*], M.:

probe. **-ciosità**, F.: extraordinary beauty (appearance). **-ciòso**, ADJ.: specious (seemingly true); beautiful (handsome); singular.

spèco [L. *-cus*], M.: cave (grotto).

spè-cola [L. *-cula*], F.: observatory (watchtower). **-colàre** = *-culare*. **spè-colo**, M.: (*med.*) speculum; observatory. **spè-cula** = *-cola*. **-culàbile**, ADJ.: fit to be looked at. **-culaménto**, M.: speculation; contemplation; meditation. ‖**-culàre** [L. *-culari*], TR.: look at (consider); INTR.: look from a watchtower; speculate (meditate, reflect, make an investment); ADJ.: specular (transparent). **-culataménte**, ADV.: designedly (purposely). **-culatíva** = *-culativo*. **-culativaménte**, ADV.: speculatively. **-culatívo**, ADJ.: speculative (contemplative). **-culatóra**, F., **-culatóre**, M., **-culatríce**, F.: speculator. **-culazióne**, F.: speculation (contemplation); theory. **spè-culo**, M.: looking-glass; [*-co*] cavern (den)†.

spedá-le [*ospedale*], M.: hospital. **-létto**, **-líno**, *dim.* of *-le*. **-lière**, M.: master of a hospital; Knight Hospitaller. **-língo**, M.: governor of a hospital. **-líno**, M.: student of medicine in a hospital. **-lità**, F.: *abstr.* of *-le*.

spedantíre [*s-*, *pedante*], TR., REFL.: free from pedantry.

spedá-re [*s-*, *piede*], TR.: spoil or hurt (the feet); weary; REFL.: get footsore. **-túra**, F.: weariness (lassitude).

spedicáre†, TR.: disengage (extricate); INTR.: get free.

spe-diènte, ADJ.: expedient (profitable, useful); M.: expedient (device); resource. ‖**-díre** [L. *ex-pedire* (*pes*, FOOT), free the feet], TR.: expedite (despatch, hasten); send; pronounce incurable; INTR., REFL.: make haste†; get disentangled. **-ditaménte**, ADV.: expeditiously (quickly); clearly. **-ditézza**, F.: quickness (promptitude). **-ditívo**, ADJ.: expeditive (quick). **-díto**, PART.: expedited; sent; concluded; freed; pronounced incurable; ADJ.: free; active (nimble); ADV.: readily (quickly). **-dizióne**, F.: expedition (dispatch); inroad; negotiation (commission); haste; order†: — *di mercanzie*, despatch of goods. **-dizionière**, M.: commissioner; shipper.

spèglio = *specchio*.

speggiáre [*s-*, *pegno*], TR.: redeem a pledge.

spèggere = *spengere*.

spelac-chiáre [*s-*, *pelo*], TR.: deprive of hair (make bald). **-chiáto**, PART.: bald; peeled; without a cent (broke).

spelagáre†, INTR.: raise or come out of the sea; get out of, be rid of.

spe-láre [*s-*, *pelo*], TR.: strip of the hair; make bald; REFL.: become bald. **-lazzáre**, TR.: pick wool; make bald†. **-lazzatúra**, F.: picking of wool. **-lazzíno**†, M.: wool-picker.

spèlda†, F.: spelt (small brown wheat).

spel-laménto, M.: excoriation. ‖**-láre** [*s-*, *pelle*], TR.: excoriate (tear the skin). **-latúra** = *-lamento*. **-licciáre**, TR.: tear off the skin; REFL.: bite or worry each other (as dogs). **-licciatúra**, F.: worrying (wrangling); dispute; reprimand.

spellicciósa†, F.: (*bot.*) wild thistle.

spelluzzicáre = *spilluzzicare*.

spelónca [L. *spelunca*], F.: cave (den, grotto); shelter (retreat).

spèlta† = *spelda*.

spelúnca† = *spelonca*.

spème [L. *spes*], F.: (*poet.*) hope.

spen-dènte, ADJ.: lavish (spending). ‖**spèn-dere** [L. *expendere*], IRR.§; TR.: spend (expend); consume; INTR.: buy provisions (cater). **-deréccio**, pl. —*ce*, ADJ.: fit to be spent; prodigal (wasteful). **-díbile**, ADJ.: that can be spent. **-dibilità**, F.: possibility of being spent. **-diménto**†, M.: act of spending. **spèndio**†, M.: expense. **-ditóre**, M., **-ditríce**, F.: purveyor (steward); spendthrift.

§ Pret. *spè-si*, *-se*; *-sero*. Part. *spéso*.

spène = *speme*.

spèn-gere [L. *ex-pingere* (PAINT)], IRR.§; TR.: extinguish (put out); quench; exterminate; annul; REFL.: be extinguished (go out; die). **-gíbile**, ADJ.: extinguishable. **-giménto**†, M.: extinguishing; extirpation; abolition. **-gitóio**, M.: extinguisher. **-gitúra**, F.: extinction; destruction.

§ Pret. *spèn-si*, *-se*; *-sero*. Part. *spènto*.

spen-nacchiáre, TR.: pluck off the feathers; pull one's hair; shame. **-nacchiáto**, PART.: unplumed; ill-dressed; astonished. **-nacchiétto**, *dim.* of *-nacchio*. ‖**-nácchio** [*s-*, *p.*.], M.: tuft of feathers (plume). **-náre**, TR.: pluck the feathers of; do injury to; REFL.: lose the feathers (moult). **-nataménto**, ADV.: without feathers. **-nelláta**, F.: heavy stroke of the brush.

spensaría†, F.: great expense.

spensie-ratággine, F.: thoughtlessness. **-rataménte**, ADV.: thoughtlessly (carelessly). **-ratézza**, F.: carelessness (negligence). ‖**-ráto** [*s-*, *pensiero*], ADJ.: thoughtless (heedless).

spènto†, ADJ.: spent; extinguished; dimmed; thin (spare).

spenzo-láre [*s-*, *p.*.], TR.: suspend (hang over); INTR., REFL.: hang (dangle). **-lóne**, **-lóni**, ADV.: hanging (dangling).

spèra [*spera*], F.: (*poet.*) sphere (globe); globe or shade of a lamp; mirror; (*fig.*) hope; (*nav.*) deal board.

spe-rábile, ADJ.: that may be hoped for. **-ránza**, F.: hope; expectation; confidence. **-ranzáre**, TR.: give hope to. **-ranzataménte**, ADV.: hopefully; confidently. **-ranzína**, *iron. dim.* of *-ranza*. **-ranzóso**, ADJ.: full of hope; confident. ‖**-ráre** 1 [L.], TR., INTR.: hope (expect); judge; fear†; await†.

speráre 2 [*spera*, mirror], TR.: look through; examine.

spèr-dere [*s-*, *p.*.], IRR.; TR.: lose; destroy (dissipate); REFL.: miscarry (fail); get lost. **-diménto**†, M.: miscarriage (abortion). **-ditóre**, M., **-ditríce**, F.: squanderer (prodigal). **-dúto**, PART.: lost, etc.

sperétta, *dim.* of *spera*.

spèr-gere [*dispergere*], IRR.§; TR.: sprinkle (scatter); dissipate (waste). **-gitóre**, M., **-gitríce**, F.: sprinkler; waster.

§ Pret. *spèr-si*, *-se*; *-sero*. Part. *spèrso*.

spergiu-raménto, M.: perjury. ‖**-ráre** [*s-*, *per*, *giurare*], INTR.: commit perjury (swear falsely). **-ráto**, PART.: forsworn (perjured); M.: perjurer. **-ratóre**, M., **-ratríce**, F.: perjurer. **-razióne**†, F.: forswearing (swearing falsely). **spergiú-ro**, ADJ.: perjured; M.: perjurer; false oath (perjury).

spèrico†, ADJ.: spherical.

sperico-láre [*s-*, *p.*.], REFL.: frighten one's self. **-láto**, PART.: alarmed; fearful.

speri-enz.., **-iment..** = *esperi-enz..*, *-iment..*

spèr-ma [Gr. *spérma*], M.: sperm (seed). **-mático**, pl. **—ci**, ADJ.: spermatic. **-macèti** [L. *cetus*, whale], M.: spermaceti.

speriment..† = *speriment..*

spèrnere [L.], TR.: disdain (despise).

speron.. = *spron..*

sperpe-raménto, M.: destruction; wasting. ‖**-ráre** [L. *perperus*, wrong], TR.: spoil (destroy, ruin); waste (squander). **-ratóre**, M.: spendthrift; ravager. **spèrpero** = *-ramento*.

sperpètua [L. *lux perpetua*, 'eternal light' (sung at funerals)], F.: great misfortune.

spèrso, PART. of *spergere*.

sperti-cáre [*s-*, *pertica*], INTR.: grow too high (of trees). **-cáto**, ADJ.: extremely tall; exaggerated; long-winded.

spèrto [*esperto*], ADJ.: expert.

spèrula†, F.: *dim.* of *spera*; small globe or sphere.

spervertíre† = *pervertere*.

spè-sa, F.: EXPENSE; cost; charges: *imparare a proprie -se*, learn at one's own cost; *questo non porta la —*, it is not worth while; *dare -se*†, occasion expense. **-sáccia**, *disp. aug.* of *-sa*. **-sáre**, TR.: bear one's charge (maintain). **-sária**†, **-séria**† = *-sa*. **-sarèlla**, **-serèlla**, **-sétta**, *dim.* of *-sa*. ‖**spé-so**†, PART. of *-ndere*; spent; consumed.

spes-saménte, ADV.: often (frequently); thickly. **-saménto**†, M.: thickening. **-sáre**†, TR.: make thick; repeat; INTR.: become thick. **-sazióne**†, F.: condensation; density. **-seggiaménto**, M.: reiteration (repetition); frequency. **-seggiáre**, TR.: reiterate (repeal); continue; INTR.: hasten. **-sézza**, F.: thickness (density); multitude (crowd). **-síre**†, INTR.: thicken. **-sità**†, **-situdine**† = *-sezza*. ‖**spés-so** [L. *spissus*, thick], ADJ.: thick (dense); compact; frequent (often); ADV.: frequently (very often); M.: thickness; size; depth: *-se volte*, many a time (frequently); — —, very often.

spetez-zaménto, M.: breaking of wind from behind. ‖**-záre** [*s-*, *pezzo*], INTR.: break wind from behind.

spetráre [*s-*, *petra*], TR.: soften (melt).

spettá-bile†, ADJ.: remarkable (notable). **spettá-colo** [L. *spectaculum*], M.: spectacle (public exhibition, show); grand sight; (*theat.*) play; audience†. **-colóne**, *aug.* of *-colo*. **-colóso**, ADJ.: spectacular. **-colosaménte**, ADV.: in a spectacular way. **-coláccio**, *disp.* of *-colo*. ‖**spettá-re** [L. *spectare*, look at], INTR.: (*pop.*) wait for; appertain (belong, — *a*, concern). **-tíva**, F.: hope (expectation). **-tóre**, M.: spectator. **-tríce**, F.: spectatress. **-zióne**, F.: expectation; prospect.

spettegoláre [*s-*, *pettegolo*], INTR.: gossip (tattle).

spettináre [*s-*, *p.*.], TR.: ruffle up.

spetto-ráre†, INTR., REFL.: uncover the breast; expectorate. **-rataménte**†, ADV.: with one's breast open. **-reggiáre**† = *-rare*.

spet-trále, ADJ.: spectral. ‖**spèt-tro** [L. *spectrum*], M.: spectre (ghost); spectrum.

spe-ziála, F.: lady druggist; druggist's wife. **-ziále**, M.: spice-dealer; apothecary (druggist); ADJ.: special (particular)†; ADV.: especially. ‖**spè-zie** [L. *-cies*], F. PL.: SPICES; drugs; F.† = *-cie*. **-zialità**† = *-cialità*. **-zierìa**, F.: apothecary's shop; PL.: spices (grocery wares); drugs. **-ziosaménte**†, ADV.: speciously; handsomely. **-ziosità**†, F.: great beauty. **-zióso**†, ADJ.: specious; handsome.

spez-zábile, ADJ.: frangible (easily broken). **-za-cuòri**, M., F.: coquette (heart-breaker). **-zaménto**, M.: act of breaking or fracturing. **-z-zanténne**, M.: yard-splitter (tempestuous wind). ||**-záre** [*s-*, *pezzo*], TR.: beat to pieces; vex (annoy); destroy; REFL.: — *il capo con alcuno*, come to loggerheads with a person. **-zataménte**, ADV.: by bits (by fits and starts). **-záto**, PART.: broken, etc.; ADJ.: incomplete; small (of money). **-zatóre**, M.: one who breaks or destroys. **-zatúra**, F.: breaking; fracture (break). **-zettáre**, *freq.* of *-zare*.

spí-a [*-are*], F.: spy; informer (talebearer). **-áccia**, *disp.* of *-a*.

spiaccicáre [*s-*, *piatto*], TR.: flatten (squash, crush).

spia-cènte, ADJ.: displeasing (unpleasant). **-cènza**†, F.: displeasure (discontent). ||**-cére** [*s-*, *p.*.], IRR.; INTR.: displease; vex (trouble): *mi -ce che*, I am sorry that. **-cévole**, ADJ.: disagreeable. **-cevolézza**, F.: disagreeableness. **-cevolménte**, ADV.: unpleasantly (disagreeably). **-ciménto**, M.: discontent (displeasure).

spiag-gétta, *dim.* of *-gia*. ||**spiág-gia** [*s-*, *p.*.], F.: sea-coast (strand); country (region). **-giáta**, F.: sea-coast; length of coasts. **-gióne**, *aug.* of *-gia*.

spiaménto [*spiare*], M.: spying (watching).

spia-naménto, M.: razing; levelling; exposition. ||**-náre** [*s-*, *piano*], TR.: make level (smooth); raze (pull down); EXPLAIN; INTR.: come to a level; extend: — *il pane*, roll out bread; — *le costure*, smooth down the seams. **-náta**, F., **-náto**, M.: level place; esplanade (glacis). **-natóio**, M.: rolling-pin; instrument for levelling or rolling. **-natóre**, M.: leveller; (*fig.*) great eater; pioneer. **-natúra**, **-nazióne**†, F.: levelling; smoothing; explanation. **spiá-no**, M.: (*rare*) = *-nato;* flattening: *a tutto* —, continuously.

spian-taménto, M.: destruction (ruin); uprooting. ||**-táre** [*s-*, *p.*.], TR.: destroy (ruin); uproot. **-táto**, PART.: destroyed, etc. **spián-to**, M.: ruin (destruction).

spiá-re [OGer. *spëhôn*], TR.: SPY (watch); investigate (seek out). **-tóre**, M., **-tríce**, F.: spy (emissary).

spiattel-láre [*s-*, *piatto*], TR.: speak plainly (speak out): *alla -lata*, openly (frankly). **-lataménte**, ADV.: plainly (openly).

spiaz-záta [*s-*, *piazza*], F.: empty space. **-'zo**, M.: space (extension).

spí-ca† [L.], F.: ear of corn (SPIKE). **-canárdi**, F.: spikenard. **-cáre**†, INTR.: grow into ears (ear).

spic-cágnolo, ADJ.: easily unhooked. **-caménto**, M.: act of detaching. **-cánte**, ADJ.: bright (shining); conspicuous. ||**-cáre** [*s-*, *appiccare*], TR.: detach (unhook); pull away; separate; INTR.: stand out (excel); REFL.†: leave (part from): — *salti*, leap (jump); — *le parole*, pronounce words distinctly. **-cataménte**, ADV.: brilliantly; conspicuously. **-cáto**, PART.: detached, etc.; ADJ.: conspicuous (clear); active (nimble). **-catúra**, F.: brightness (splendour). **-chiettíno**, **-chiétto**, *dim.* of *-chio*. **spíc-chio**, M.: clove of garlic; quarter of any fruit; small share (bit): — *di petto*, middle of the breast of animals; *a* —, like the clove of garlic; *a -chi*, quartered (in quarters). **-chiáto**†, ADJ.: divided into cloves, shives, leaves, etc.

spicciáre 1 [?], INTR.: gush forth (spout); unravel; despatch (hasten).

spicciá-re 2 [*s-*, *impicciare*], TR.: urge (excite); REFL.: make haste; be quick. **-tívo**, ADJ.: expeditive.

spicciáto†, M.: barrier (palisade, defence).

spíccio [*spicciare* 2], ADJ.: quick (expeditious).

spiccio-láme, M.: quantity of small things. ||**-láre** [*s-*, *picciolo*], TR.: change into small coin; pick (of grapes). **-lataménte**, ADV.: separately (little by little). **-láto**, PART.: changed, etc.: *fiori -lati*, flowers whose leaves have been plucked; *alla -lata*, singly (one by one). **spíc-ciolo**, ADJ.: *moneta -la*, small coin (cash).

spícco [*spiccare*], M.: brightness (lustre); appearance.

spicilègio [L. *-gium* (*spica*, ear, *legere*, collect)], M.: collection of literary scraps.

spicináre [?], TR.: make in small bits.

spi-culatóre†, M.: archer (bowman).

spí-culo†, M.: point of an arrow; arrow.

spidocchiáre [*s-*, *pidocchio*], TR.: free from lice.

spiè-de, (*pop.*) **-do** [OGer. *spiz*], M.: SPIT; boar-spear. **-dóne**, *aug.* of *-de*.

spie-gábile, ADJ.: explicable. **-gaménto**, M.: explanation; dilatation (widening). ||**-gáre** [L. *ex-plicare*], TR.: unfold (disPLAY); explain: — *le vele*, spread the sails. **-gataménte**, ADV.: openly (clearly). **-gatívo**, ADJ.: explanatory. **-gáto**, PART.: unfolded; explained; flying. **-gatúra**, **-gazióne**, F.: displaying; explanation (interpretation).

spiegazzáre†, TR.: rumple (crimple); rub down (a horse).

spieggiáre, *freq.* of *spiare*.

spieghévole [*spiegare*], ADJ.: explainable.

spie-tà† [*s-*, *p.*.], **-tánza**†, **-tatézza**

F.: cruelty (inhumanity). **-tataménte**, ADV.: unfeelingly (barbarously). **-táto**, ADJ.: pitiless (merciless, cruel); extraordinary; terrible; obstinate. **-tóso**† = *-tato*.

spietráre [*s-*, *impietrire*], TR.: soften.

spif-feráre, TR.: feel a draught; (*fig.*) say over again; speak frankly; improvize. ||**spíf-fero** [*s-*, *piffero*], M.: wind; draught.

spí-ga [L. *spica*], F.: ear of corn (SPIKE): *far la —*, form ears, ear. **-ganárdi**†, F.: spikenard. **-gáre**, INTR.: ear (put forth ears). **-gatúra**, F.: earing (growing into ears). **-ghétta**, **-ghína**, **-golína**, *dim.* of *-ga*.

spigio-náre [*s-*, *pigionale*], INTR.: be unoccupied. **-náto**, PART.: unoccupied.

spigli-taménte, ADV.: brilliantly; nimbly. **-tézza**, F.: brilliancy; dexterity. ||**spiglià-to** [*s-*, *impigliato*], ADJ.: brilliant; agile (nimble); free (easy).

spign. -† = *sping.*.

spí-go [*-ga*], M.: SPIKE-lavender (plant). **-goláre** [*-ga*], TR.: glean (gather). **-golatóre**, M., **-golatríce**, F.: gatherer (gleaner). **-golatúra**, F.: gleaning. **-golístro** [*-golo*, who stand at 'corners' in a church], M.: hypocrite; pedant; ADJ.†: false. **-'golo** [L. *spiculum*, arrow], M.: hard corner (angle). **-góso** [*-ga*], ADJ.: full of ears of corn.

spílla [L. *spinula*, small thorn], F.: pin (breast-pin, etc.).

spillaccheráre [*s-*, *pillacchera*], TR.: clean of mud.

spill-láncola†, F.: gudgeon (small prickly fish). **-láre**, TR.: tap (pierce, broach); spy (watch); INTR.†: distil. **-láticco**, pl. *—ci*, M.: allowance of pin-money. **-latúra**, F.: tapping (broaching); distilling†. **-lettáio**†, M.: maker or seller of pins. **-létto**, *dim.* of *-lo*. **-lettóne**, *aug.* of *-lo*. ||**spíl-lo** [*-la*], M.: pin; gimlet (drill); drill-hole; waterspout (jet); (*fig.*) stimulus. **-loncíno**, *dim.* of *-lo*. **-lóne**, *aug.* of *-lo*.

spilluzzi-caménto, M.: eating (little by little); tasting. ||**-cáre** [*spillare*], TR.: nibble off, eat (consume) little by little.

spillúzzi-co, ADV.: *a —*, little by little (bit by bit).

spilónca† = *spelonca*.

spi-lorcería, F.: stinginess (sordidness). ||**-lórcio** [*s-*, *pilorcio*], ADJ.: stingy (niggardly); M.: miser.

spilun-góna, ||**-góne** [*bis-lungone* (*-go*)], ADJ., M., F.: very tall (person).

spí-na [L.], F.: thorn; sting; stimulus (goad); fish-bone; awl; needle; pincers: *— alba*, white-thorn (hawthorn); *— cervina*, buckthorn (briar); *esser sulle -ne*, be upon thorns; *— ventosa*, internal caries in the bones; *— di fabbro*, punch (puncheon); *— giudaica*, sloe-shrub; *— magna*, wild plum-tree. **-náce**, **-nácio**, M.: spinach (spinage). **-naciéno**, M.: wild spinach. **-náio** = *-nelo*. **-nále**, ADJ.: spinal. **-na-pésce**, ADV.: in a wavy manner. **-náre**†, TR.: prick with thorns.

spin-cionáre, TR.: decoy the chaffinch; whistle (of a chaffinch). ||**-cióne** [? echoic], M.: chaffinch.

spi-nèlla [*-na*], F.: jardes (tumours in horses); spinel-ruby†. **-nèllo**, M.: spinel; dogfish. **-néto**, M.: place full of thorns and briars. **-nétta**, F.: *dim.* of *-na*; spinet (small harpsichord); kind of silk fringe†. **-nettáio**, M.: silk-lace maker; spinet-maker.

spingár-da [OGer. *springan*, fling], F.: kind of battering-ram; small piece of ordnance. **-dèlla**, F.: wall-gun (arquebuse).

spin-gáre†, INTR.: kick about; push. ||**spín-gere** [*s-*, *pingere*], IRR.; TR.: thrust (push, shove); incite (spur on); efface†. **-giménto**, M.: push (thrust); impulsion. **-gitóre**, M., **-gitríce**, F.: stimulator (exciter).

spí-no [*-na*], M.: briar (thorn); spinous herb; backbone†. **-nóla**†, *dim.* of *-na*. **-nóne**, M.: fine woollen cloth. **-nosità**, F.: spinosity; difficulty. **-nóso**, ADJ.: spinous (thorny); crabbed (ill-natured); difficult; M.: hedgehog.

spín-ta [*-gere*], F.: push (thrust); gust: *andare a —*, be thrust along. **-tóne**, *aug.* of *-ta*.

spinúzza, *dim.* of *spina*.

spiom-báre [*s-*, *piombo*], TR.: unlead (take lead from); INTR.: weigh heavily (weigh down). **-bináre**, TR.: plumb a line.

spio-náccio, *disp.* of *-ne*. **-nággio**, M.: system of spies. ||**spió-na**, F., **-ne**, M.: *aug.* of *spia*; great spy.

spiò-vere [*s-*, *piovere*], INTR.: cease raining; run over; run out (drop). **-viménto**, M.: ceasing of rain.

spípola†, F.: meadow-lark.

spippoláre [*s-*, *pippolo*, for *chicco*], TR.: pick out the grains or grapes of; speak out frankly.

spí-ra [L. *spira*, Gr. *speira*, coil, spire], F.: spiral curve or line.

spi-rábile [*-rare*], ADJ.: respirable. **-rácolo**†, **-ráglio**, M.: spiracle (breathing-hole); opening; gleam, glimpse†.

spirál-e [*spira*], ADJ.: spiral; twisted (wreathy); F.: spiral line or curve; spiral spring of a watch. **-ménte**, ADV.: in a spiral form.

spi-raménto, M.: breathing. ||**-ráre**

[L.], INTR.: breathe (blow gently); breathe forth (exhale); breathe out (EXPIRE); end; leak out; inspire; betray; TR.: long for†; spy†. **-ratóre,** M.: inspirer (suggester). **-razioncèlla,** *dim.* of *-razione*. **-razióne,** F.: respiration; inspiration; spiracle; light; (*theol.*) spiration.

spiri-táccio, *disp.* of *-rito*. **-tále,** ADJ.: spiritual; vital; religious. **-talménto,** ADV.: spiritually; devoutly. **-taménto,** M.: demoniacal frenzy. **-táre,** INTR.: be possessed of the devil; be frightened. **-tataménte,** ADV.: like a demoniac. **-tatíccio,** *dim.* of *-tato*. **-táto,** PART.: possessed by the devil; terrified; ADJ.: capricious. **-tèllo,** *car. dim.* of *-to*. **-téssa†,** F.: female spirit. **-tétto†** = *-tello*. **spirí-tico,** pl. *—ci*, ADJ.: spiritualistic. **-tismo,** M.: spiritism. **-tísta,** M.: spiritualist. **-tístico,** pl. *—ci*, ADJ.: spiritualistical. ||**spíri-to** [L. *-tus* (*spirare*, breathe)], M.: spirit; ghost; soul (mind); judgment; revelation; sentiment; breeze; vital spirits; spirits (liquor); way (motive); complexion of the body (constitution)†: *-ti forti*, freethinkers; *render la —*, expire (give up the ghost); *riconfortare gli -ti*, recover one's self; *uomo di —*, man of talent; *esser rapito in —*, be rapt in ecstasy; *di vero —*, heartily; *in —*, spiritually. **-tosággine,** F.: acts or words of pretended wit (silly witticism). **-tosaménto,** ADV.: in a witty manner (with spirit). **-tosità,** F.: quality of being witty. **-tóso,** ADJ.: lively (brisk); witty (ingenious); bright: *cavallo —*, mettlesome horse. **-to=sánto,** M.: Holy Ghost. **-tuále,** ADJ.: spiritual (incorporeal); devout; M.: spiritual jurisdiction: *padre —*, confessor. **-tualità,** F.: spirituality; devotion. **-tualizzaménto,** M.: spiritualization. **-tualizzáre,** TR.: spiritualize (make spiritual); REFL.: become spiritual. **-tualizzazióne†** = *-tualizzamento*. **-tualménte,** ADV.: spiritually; devoutly.

spí-ro†, M.: (*poet.*) respiration (breathing); spirit. **-rtále†,** *poet.* for *-rituale*. **-rto†,** *poet.* for *-rito*.

spittináre [? echoic], INTR.: sing (of a robin).

spiu-macciáre, TR.: air or shake up (a feather-bed). **-macciáta,** F.: act of beating or shaking a feather-bed. ||**-máre** [*piuma*], TR.: pick the feathers (strip); shake up (a feather-bed)†.

spizzi-cáre [*s-*, *p.* .], TR.: nibble off. **-catúra,** F.: (*typ.*) defect. **spízzi-ca, -co,** ADV. (*a —*): little by little (slowly).

splacáre†, TR.: squander (dissipate).

splebíre†, TR.: ennoble (raise up).

splen-dènte, ADJ.: splendid (bright, shining). **-dentemènte,** ADV.: splendidly. ||**splèn-dere** [L.], INTR.: be resplendent (shine). **-didaménte,** ADV.: splendidly (brilliantly). **-didèzza, -didità†,** F.: splendour (glitter); pomp (magnificence). **splèn-dido** [L. *-didus*], ADJ.: bright (glittering); splendid (magnificent). **-diménto†, -dóre,** M.: splendour (brightness); fame; pomp.

sple-nètico, pl. *—ci* [Gr. *splén*, spleen], ADJ.: splenetic (sick of the spleen). **splènico,** pl. *—ci*, ADJ.: splenic (of the spleen).

splènio [Gr. *splénion*, compress], M.: (*anat.*) splenius (muscle of the head).

sploratóre = *esploratore*.

spòc-chia [?], F.: haughtiness (pride). **-chióne, -chióso,** ADJ.: proud (haughty).

spodes-táre [*s-*, *p.* .], TR.: pluck the flower from; INTR.: lay down one's power (abdicate). **-táto,** PART.: powerless; violent (impetuous).

spódio†, M.: spodium (tutty).

spoe-táre [*s-*, *p.* .], TR.: deprive of the name of a poet; INTR.: give up being a poet. **-tizzáre,** TR.: take away the poetry of.

spò-glia [L., pl. *-lia*, what is stripped off], F.: SPOIL (booty); cast-off skin; carcass; cod (hull, husk); old clothes†; plaster (for a cast); PL.†: heap of fragments. **-gliagióne,** F., **-gliaménto,** M.: stripping; despoiling (robbing). **-gliáre,** TR.: undress (strip naked); despoil (rob); REFL.: pull off one's clothes (undress): *— le calze*, pull off one's stockings. **-gliatóio,** M.: dressing-room. **-gliatóra,** F., **-gliatóre,** M., **-gliatríce,** F.: spoiler (plunderer). **-gliatúra, -gliazióne,** F.: spoliation (stripping, divesting). **-gliázza†,** F.: whipping on the bare shoulders; spoil: *dar la — a una casa*, rob or ransack a house. **-gliazzáto†,** ADJ.: half undressed. **spò-glio,** M.: booty (spoil); act of despoiling; movables (goods); cast-off clothes.

spò-la [OFr. *espole* (OGer. *spuolo*, *spule*)], F.: weaver's shuttle. **-létta,** F.: *dim.* of *-la*; fuse of a bomb. **-létto,** M.: spindle or bobbin of the shuttle.

spoliticáre [*s-*, *p.* .], INTR.: prattle about politics.

spol-laiáre [*s-*, *app.* .], REFL.: (*disp.*) get out of bed. **-lináre,** TR.: clear away or pick (fleas, lice, etc.).

spollastráre [*s-*, *p.* .], INTR.: eat sumptuously.

spolmonáre [*s.*, *p.* .], TR.: despoil of lungs.

spol-paménto, M.: picking off the flesh. ||**-páre** [*s-*, *p.* .], TR.: pick the flesh off of; strip; make thin; REFL.: lose flesh (grow thin); deprive one's self; become weak. **-páto**, PART.: picked off, etc.

spól-po, ADJ.: lean (thin); weak.

spol-tráre†, **-tríre**, ‖**-troníre** [*s-*, *poltrone*], TR.: shake off (sloth or idleness); make energetic.

spolve-ramára†, M.: good-for-nothing fellow. ‖**-ráre** [*s-*, *polvere*], TR.: dust; pulverize (reduce to powder); rob; cover with dust†; INTR.: be a big eater; be pulverized. **-ráta**, F.: dusting. **-ratára**, F.: dusting (sweeping off the dust). **-rezzáre†** = *-rizzare*. **-ríma**, F.: travelling-coat. **-ríno** [*s-*, *p.* .], M.: powder-box; priming powder; coal dust. **-río**, M.: thick dust. **-rizzáre**, TR.: pulverize; sprinkle with powder or salt; trace (a drawing) with coal-dust. **-rízzo**, M.: act of pulverizing, etc.; pounce (charcoal-bag). **spólve-ro**, M.: dusting; dust; pricked design (coal-drawing).

spón-da [L., frame of a bed], F.: edge (extremity); side (bank, shore); parapet: — *di letto*, bedside; — *d' un pozzo*, curb-stone (brim of a well); — *di ponte*, rails on the outside of bridges. **-dággio**, M.: wharfage.

spon-dáico [L. *-daicus* (*-deus*)], ADJ.: spondaic. ‖**-dèo** [L. *-deus*], M.: spondee (— —).

sponderòla [*-da*], F.: kind of carpenter's plane.

spon-gáta†, F.: tart made of honey, nuts, etc. ‖**-gifórme** [L. *-gia*, *forma*], ADJ.: spongiform. **-gióso†**, ADJ.: spongy (fungous). **-gíte**, F.: spongy-stone.

sponi-ménto†, M.: explanation (exposition); interpretation. **-tóre†**, M.: expounder; interpreter.

sponsá-le [L. *-lis* (*sponsus*, bridegroom)], ADJ.: sponsal (relating to marriage). **-lízia†**, F., **-lízio**, M.: espousal (marriage); ADJ.: sponsal; cf. *sposalizio*.

spon-taneaménte, **-tanaménte**, ADV.: spontaneously. **-taneità**, F.: spontaneity (willingness). ‖**-táneo** [L. *-taneus* (*-te*, of free will)], **-tánot**, ADJ.: spontaneous (voluntary).

sponton. .† = *spunton*. .

spopolá-re [*s-*, *p.* .], TR.: depopulate; INTR.: become depopulated. **-zióne**, F.: depopulation (unpeopling).

spop-paménto, M.: act of weaning. ‖**-páre** [*s-*, *p.* .], TR.: wean. **-patúra**, F.: weaning.

spò-ra [Gr. *-rá*, seed sown], F.: seed. **-rádico**, pl. —*ci*, M.: sporadical.

spor-caménte, ADV.: nastily (filthily). **-cáre**, TR.: foul (dirty, soil). **-chería**, F.: nastiness (filth). **-chétto**, ADJ.: *dim. of -co;* somewhat dirty. **-chézza**, **-chígia**, **-cízia**, F.: foulness (dirtiness); obscenity. ‖**spòr-co** [L. *spurcus* (*spargere*, spatter)], ADJ.: dirty (filthy); impure (obscene).

spor-gènte, ADJ.: projecting. ‖**spòrgere** [*s-*, *porgere*], IRR.; TR.: stretch out (hold forth); bring; explain; INTR.: stand out (project); advance; REFL.: show one's self. **-giménto**, M.: jutting out (projection).

spórre = *esporre*.

spòrta [L.], F.: basket (hand-basket).

sportáre†, INTR.: project (stand out); TR.: transport.

sportèlla, *dim.* of *-ta*.

sportelláre†, TR.: open the postern-gate or wicket of.

sportellétta, *dim.* of *-tella*.

sportellétto, *dim.* of *-tello*.

sportellína, *dim.* of *-tella*.

spor-tellíno, *dim.* of *-tello*. ‖**-tèllo** [? *-to*], M.: wicket (postern-gate); coach-door; door of a cupboard; shop-door; panel: *a* —, half open.

sportic-ciòla, **-èlla**, **-ína**, *dim. of -ta*.

spòrto, PART. of *sporgere*; stretched-out, etc.; M.: (*arch.*) projection; buttress (projecture).

spor-tóna, *aug.* of *-ta*. ‖**spòr-tula** [L., little basket; gift], F.: fee (given to a judge).

spò-sa [L. *sponsa* (*spondere*, promise)], F.: bride; spouse (wife): *dare* —, give in marriage. **-salízia**, F., **-salízio**, M.: marriage ceremony; ADJ.: belonging to marriage. **-saménto**, M.: espousal (marriage). **-sáre**, TR.: espouse (marry); join in marriage; (*fig.*) join; REFL.: get married: — *una chiesa*, espouse a church (become pastor of it). **-sarécciο**, **-sarésco†**, ADJ.: conjugal (matrimonial). **-sétta**, **-sína**, *car. dim.* of *-sa*. **-síno**, *car. dim.* of *-so*.

sposi. . = *espos*. .

spò-so [cf. *-sa*], M.: bridegroom; husband (spouse). **-sóna**, **-sòtta**, *aug.* of *-sa*.

spos-sáre [*s-*, *possa*], TR.: take away the power or ability of (enervate, weaken); INTR.: grow weak from overwork; REFL.: ruin one's self. **-sataménte**, ADV.: powerlessly (without force). **-satézza**, F.: weakness (debility). **-sáto**, PART.: weakened, etc.

spossessáre [*s-*, *p.* .], TR.: dispossess (deprive of possession).

spos-taménto, M.: act of misplacing. ‖**-táre** [*s-*, *p.* .], TR.: misplace; REFL.: leave one's post. **-táto**, PART.: misplaced, etc.; M.: misdirected person: *ore -tate*, unseasonable hours. **-tatúra**, F.: misplacing; overturning; impolite act.

spotestáre = *spodestare*.

sprán-ga [OGer. *spanga*], F.: bar (cross-bar); holdfast; buckle (clasp)†. **-gáre**, TR.: bar (cross-bar); fasten with lattens. **-gatúra**, F.: barring, etc. **-ghétta**, F.: *dim.* of *-ga;* headache. **-ghettína**, *dim.* of *-ghetta.*

sprazzáre†, TR.: sprinkle (wet, asperse). ||**sprázzo** [OGer. *spratzen*], M.: sprinkling (aspersion); spot (in marble, etc.).

spre-caménto, M.: wasting (squandering). ||**-cáre** [?], TR.: dissipate (waste). **-catóre**, M., **-catríce**, F.: squanderer (dissipator). **-catúra**, F.: waste (dissipation). **-cóne**, M.: spendthrift (prodigal).

spre-gévole, ADJ.: despicable (vile). **-gevolménte**, ADV.: despicably. **-giaménto**, M.: contempt (scorn). **-giánte**, ADJ.: scornful (contemptuous). ||**-giáre** [*disp.* .], TR.: despise (scorn, contemn). **-giatóre**, M., **-giatríce**, F.: scorner (contemner). **-giévole** = *-gevole.* **sprègio**, M.: scorn (disdain).

spregiudicáto [*s-*, *p.* .], ADJ.: unprejudiced (impartial).

spregnáre [*pregna*], INTR.: lie in (be brought to bed); TR.: bring forth.

sprementáre† = *sperimentare.*

sprè-mere [*s-*, *p.* .], TR.: squeeze out (press out); express (declare)†. **-mitúra**, F.: squeezing or pressing out; matter extracted.

sprend. .† = *splend.* .

spress. . = *espress.* .

spretáre [*s-*, *prete*], REFL.: depose the clerical habit (quit the church).

spres-sábile, ADJ.: despicable (contemptible). **-zaménto**, M.: scorn (disdain). ||**-záre** [*s-*, *p.* .], TR.: despise (contemn): — *la fame*, ignore hunger. **-zataménte**, ADV.: scornfully (contemptuously). **-zatóre**, M.: despiser. **-zatúra**, F.: contempt (scorn). **-zevolménte**, ADV.: contemptuously. **sprèz-zo**, M.: act or effect of despising (scorn).

sprigio-naménto, M.: disincarceration. ||**-náre** [*s-*, *prigione*], TR.: release from prison (disincarcerate).

sprilláre†, TR.: squeeze (press out).

sprimac-ciáre [*spiumacciare*], TR.: shake up (a mattress). **-ciáta**, F.: shaking up (of a feather-bed).

sprime. . = *esprime.* .

springáre [Ger. *springen*], TR.: kick about.

sprizzáre [Ger. *spritzen*, spout], TR.: sprinkle; INTR.: spout or gush out (drip).

sproc-catúra, F.: prick or cut in the foot. **-chétto**, *dim.* of *-co.* ||**spròcco** [? *brocco*], M.: shoot (sprout, sucker); sharp stick; fagot-band (withe)†.

sprofon-daménto, M.: sinking; ruin. ||**-dáre** [*s-*, *p.* .], TR.: sink; INTR.: fall to the bottom (sink down).

sproldquio [L. *exproloquium*], M.: long, tedious discourse.

sprolungáre = *prolungare.*

spromèttere [*s-*, *p.* .], IRR.; TR.: retract (one's word or promise).

spro-náia, F.: wound made by a spur. **-náio**, M.: spur-maker (spurrier). **-náre**, TR.: spur; incite (urge on); INTR.†: hurry on. **-náta**, F.: spurring; prick of a spur; instigation. **-náto**, PART.: spurred, etc.: *cane, gallo* —, dog or cock that has spurs. **-natóre**, M.: spurrer; stimulator. ||**spró-ne** [OGer. *sporon*], M.: SPUR; cock-spur; beak of a ship; prop (support); shoot (sprig); (*fig.*) stimulus: *dar di* —, spur; *a -n battuto*, at full speed; — *di cavaliere*, larkspur. **-nèlla**, F.: rowel (of a spur).

spropia. . = *spropria.* .

sproporzio-nále, ADJ.: disproportioned (unequal). **-nalità**, F.: disproportion (inequality). **-nalménte**, ADV.: unequally. **-náre**, TR.: render unequal. **-náto**, PART.: disproportioned. ||**sproporzió-ne** [*s-*, *p.* .], F.: disproportion; inequality.

sproposi-táccio, *disp. dim.* of *-to.* **-táre**, INTR.: act foolishly (talk idly). **-tataménte**, ADV.: foolishly (ridiculously). **-táto**, ADJ.: foolish (absurd); excessive (extraordinary). ||**spropòsi-to** [*s-*, *p.* .], M.: absurdity (blunder); nonsense: *a* —, erroneously; *fare agli* —†, give out-of-the-way answers. **-tóne**, *aug.* of *-to.*

spro-priáre [*s*; *proprio*], TR.: dispossess; REFL.: divest one's self of one's property. **-priazióne** = *-prio.* **spròprio**, M.: expropriation; resignation.

sprotèttoi†, ADJ.: unprotected.

spro-vaménto†, M.: trial (experiment). **-váre†**, TR.: try (attempt); REFL.: exercise one's self.

sprov-vedére [*s-*, *p.* .], IRR.; TR.: leave unprovided for or in want. **-vedutaménte**, ADV.: rashly (inconsiderately). **-vedúto**, **-vísto**, PART.: unprovided; unprepared: *alla -vista*, unawares (unexpectedly). **-vistaménte**, ADV.: unexpectedly.

spruffáre† = *spruzzare.*

spru-náre†, TR.: lop off (prune). **-nèggio†**, M.: knee-holm or holly.

spruz-záglia, F.: things sprinkled; small, drizzling rain. **-zaménto**, M.: sprinkling (aspersion). ||**-záre** [Ger. *spritzen*], TR.: bathe lightly; sprinkle. **-zétto**, *dim.* of *-zo.* **sprúz-zo**, M.: act of sprinkling; that which is sprinkled. **-zoláre**, INTR.: drizzle (sprinkle); speckle. **spruzzoléo**, M.: slight sprinkling; fine rain.

spudoráto [*s-*, *pudore*], ADJ.: immodest.

spú-gna [L. *spongia*], F.: sponge; kind

of ornamental stone: *dar di* —, cancel (efface); *lasciar la* —, attempt impossibilities. **-gnáta**, F.: blow with a sponge. **-gnatúra**, F.: sponging. **-gnétta**, **-gnína**, *dim.* of *-gna*. **-gnitóso**, ADJ.: spongy (porous). **-gnóne**, M.: gypseous stone. **-gnosità**, F.: sponginess. **-gnóso**, ADJ.: spongy (spongious). **-gnúzza**, *dim.* of *-gna*.

spu-láre [*s-*, *pula*], TR.: winnow (part grain from chaff). **-latúra**, F.: winnowing.

spulcellàre†, TR.: depucelate.

spulciáre [*s-*, *pulce*], TR.: rid of fleas.

spu-leggiáre, ||**-lezzáre** [?], INTR.: flee (run away). **-lézzo**, M.: precipitate flight.

spu-líre [*s-*, *p.* .], TR.: take away the polish of (tarnish); polish. **-lizzíre**, TR.: polish.

spú-ma [L.], F.: spume (froth, foam). **-máre**, **-meggiáre**, INTR.: spume (foam). **spú-meo** = *-moso*. **-mífero**, ADJ.: foamy (frothy). **-mosità**, F.: frothiness. **-móso**, ADJ.: frothy (full of foam).

spuntá-re [*s-*, *p.* .], TR.: blunt (dull); efface; dissuade; conquer (overcome); turn aside; INTR.: sprout out (burst forth); peep (dawn); REFL.: become dull: — *la barba*, begin to have a beard; — *un sospiro*, fetch a sigh. **-túra**, F.: blunting; point blunted.

spuntel-láre [*s-*, *p.* .], TR.: remove the props from. **-láto**, PART.: unpropped.

spuntèrbo [*punta*], M.: toe-piece (of a shoe).

spuntíno [?], M.: little lunch.

spún-to [*punta*], M.: sour taste; discoloured (wan, sallow)†. **-tonáta**, F.: blow with a spontoon or halberd. **-toncèllo**, **-toncíno**, *dim.* of *-tone*. **-tóne**, M.: spontoon (halberd). **-zecchiáre**, TR.: spur on (stimulate). **-zonáta**, F.: blow with *-zone*. **-zóne**, M.: large pointed weapon.

spuòla†, F.: shuttle.

spuráre†, TR.: cleanse (purify).

spúrcido†, ADJ.: filthy (impure).

spur-gaménto, M.: purging (cleansing). ||**-gáre** [*s-*, *p.* .], TR.: spit out (expectorate); purge (cleanse); REFL.†: exculpate one's self. **-gazióne**, F.: purgation. **spúr-go**, M.: spitting; cleansing; thing cleansed.

spúrio [L. *-rius*], M.: illegitimate child.

spu-tacchiáre, INTR.: spit often: — *su altrui*, spit upon another for contempt. **-tacchièra**, F.: spittoon. **-tácchio**, M.: spit (spittle). **-tapépe**, F.: brisk, lively person. **-táre**, TR.: spit; fling: — *tondo*, assume a look of importance; — *bottoni*, ridicule (rail at): — *sur una cosa*, spit on a thing (despise a thing); — *senno*, affect learning. **-ta=sénno**, **-ta=sentènze**, M.: wiseacre. **-táto**, PART.: spit upon, etc. **-tatóndo**, M.: conceited man. ||**spú-to** [L. *-tum* (*-ere*, spit)], M.: spit; spitting.

spuzzáre† = *puzzare*.

squácchera†, F.: liquid fæces; looseness. ||**-cheráre†** [*cacchera*, laxative], TR.: do in a haste; INTR.: have a looseness. **-que..** = *-che..* **-querèlla**, F.: loose body.

squaderná-re [*s-*, *quaderno*], TR.: turn over (the leaves of a book); speak freely; show openly†; examine (consider)†. **-tóre**, M.: peruser; examiner.

squá-dra, F.: square; squadron; troop; angle†: *fuor di* —, out of place; *dar la* —, make one believe; *uscir di* —, diverge from a straight line. **-dráre**, TR.: square; consider attentively; measure accurately†; quarter†; level (a cannon). **-dratóre**, M.: squarer; stone-cutter; observer. **-dratúra**, F.: squaring (quadrature). **-dríglia**, F.: half a squadron. ||**-dro** [*s-*, *q.* .], M.: squaring; [L. *-tulus* (*-lus*), ak. to *quadro*], dogfish (skate). **-dronáre**, TR.: form into squadrons or squares; REFL.: be ranged in squadrons; perform military evolutions. **-droncèllo**, **-droncíno**, *dim.* of *-drone*. **-dróne**, M.: squadron; battalion; cavalryman's sabre.

squa-gliaménto, M.: liquefaction. ||**-gliáre** [*s-*, *ca.* .], TR.: melt (liquefy).

squal-lidézza, F.: squalor; paleness. **squál-lido** [L. *-idus* (*-ere*, be stiff with dirt)], ADJ.: squalid (nasty); dark; pale; gloomy (sad). **-lóre**, M.: squalor; deadly paleness.

squá-ma [L.], **-mma**, F.: scale (of a fish); coat of mail. **-(m)máre**, TR.: cause to lose (the scales). **-(m)móso**, ADJ.: squamous (scaly).

squar-cétto, *dim.* of *-cio*. **-cia=cuòri**, F.: coquette (heart-breaker). **-cia=góla** (*a*), ADV.: at the top of one's voice. **-ciaménto**, M.: tearing; rent. ||**-ciáre** [L. *ex-quartiare*], TR.: tear (rend). **-ciasácco†** (*a*), ADV.: scowlingly (with an evil eye). **-ciáta**, F.: cut (cutting blow). **-ciatóre**, M.: render (cutter). **-ciatúra**, F.: tearing (cutting); tear. **-cína**, F.: sabre (scimitar). **squár-cio**, M.: great or deep cut; passage; worthless book†. **-cióne**, M.: boaster (braggart).

squarquóio† [?], ADJ.: filthy (disgusting).

squar-taménto, M.: quartering. **-ta=píccioli**, M.: niggard (skinflint). ||**-táre** [L. *ex-*, *q.* .], TR.: quarter: — *lo sero*, split a hair (reckon with great care). **-tatóio**, M.: knife for quartering beasts.

-**tatóre**, M.: executioner; bully. **squárto**, M.: quartering.
squaçillo†, M.: great wonder; affectation.
squaçimodèo, M.: blockhead; INTERJ.†: upon my word (by my troth).
squas-saménto, M.: act of shaking or tossing. ‖-**sáre** [L. *quassare*], TR.: shake violently; brandish. **squás-so**, M.: violent shake (jog).
squattrináre [*s-*, *quattrino*], TR.: consider or weigh carefully.
squíl-la [OGer. *skilla*, *schelle*], F.: small bell; cow-bell; squill (sea-onion)†; shrimp†. -**lánte**, ADJ.: clear; resounding. -**lanteménte**, ADV.: with a clear sound. -**láre**, INTR.: ring (sound); TR.†: hurl (throw); ring. -**létto**, *dim.* of -*lo*. -**lítico**, ADJ.: of squills. **squíl-lo**, M.: sound (of a trumpet). -**lóne**, *aug.* of -*lo*.
squi-nantèo, F. PL.: order of bulrushes. ‖-**nánto** [Gr. *schoinos*, rush], M.: odoriferous bulrush.
squinanzía, F.: squinancy (quinsy).
squinternáre [*s-*, *quinterno*], TR.: disorder (the quire); glance over.
squiçi-taménte, ADV.: exquisitely. -**tézza**, F.: exquisiteness. ‖**squiçí-to** [L. *ex-quisitus*, carefully sought out], ADJ.: exquisite (excellent). -**túdine**, F.: excellence.
squit-tináre [fr. *scrutinare*], TR.: elect; INTR.: vote (poll). -**tinatóre**, M.: voter. -**tínio**, -**tíno**†, M.: poll (voting); scrutiny.
squittíre [Bav.], INTR.: yelp.
squociáre = *scoiare*.
squotoláre†, TR.: beat (flax); thresh; shake (beat).
çradi-caménto, M.: uprooting; eradication. ‖-**cáre** [*s-*, *r..*], TR.: uproot; extirpate (eradicate). -**catóre**, M.: extirpator (ruiner).
çragio-náre [*s-*, *r..*], INTR.: reason poorly. -**névole**, ADJ.: unreasonable.
çrego-laménto, M.: disorder (irregularity). -**lataménte**, ADV.: irregularly. -**latézza**, F.: irregularity. ‖-**láto** [*s-*, *r..*], ADJ.: irregular; excessive; disorderly.
çreve-rènte† [*s-*, *r..*], ADJ.: irreverent. -**renteménte**†, ADV.: irreverently. -**rènza**†, -**rènzia**, F.: irreverence (disrespect).
çrugginíre [*s-*, *ruggine*], TR.: clear the rust off of.
stá = *questa*.
stabaccáre [*s-*, *tabacco*], INTR.: take snuff often.
stab-biáre, TR.: manure. -**biatúra**, F.: manuring (dunging). ‖**stáb-bio** [L. -*ulum*, stall], M.: dung (manure). -**biòlo**, M.: *dim.* of -*bio*; small room.

stábi-le [L. -*lis* (*stare*, stand)], ADJ.: stable (firm); fixed (lasting), well done: *beni -li*, houses and lands. -**lézza** = -*lità*. -**liménto**, M.: establishment (foundation); stable condition†; solidity†. -**líre**, TR.: render stable or firm; establish (ordain); assign; plaster (walls, etc.); REFL.: place one's self; (of walls) settle. -**lità**, F.: stability (firmness). -**litóre**, M.: establisher. -**lménte**, ADV.: constantly (firmly).
stabu-láre†, INTR.: dwell in the stable; TR.: place in the stable. ‖-**lário** [L. -*larius* (-*lum*, stable)], M.: stable-boy (hostler).
stácca†, F.: iron hook (cramp-iron); staff.
stac-cábile, ADJ.: that can be detached. -**caménto**, M.: detaching; (*mil.*) detachment. ‖-**cáre** [*s-*, *att..*], TR.: detach (take off); remove; unhook; REFL.: — *da un amico*, get rid of a friend. -**catézza**, -**catúra**, F.: detachment (disjunction).
stac-cétto, *dim.* of -*cio*. -**ciáio**, M.: sieve-maker or seller. -**ciáre**, TR.: sift (bolt). -**ciáta**, F.: sieveful. -**ciatúra**, F.: sifting; bran (pollen). -**cíno**, *dim.* of -*cio*. ‖**stác-cio** [*setaccio* (*seta*)], M.: sieve (searce, bolter). -**ciuòlo**†, *dim.* of -*cio*.
stácco, M.: cloth for a coat.
stadè-ra [Gr. *statér*, weight], F.: steelyard (Roman balance). -**ráio**, M.: steelyard maker. -**rína**, *dim.* of -*ra*. -**róna**, -**róne**, *aug.* of -*ra*.
stádico† = *statico*.
stádio [L. -*dium* (Gr. -*dion*)], M.: stadium; furlong.
stáf-fa [OGer. *staph*, pace], F.: stirrup; cymbal; iron ring (mould): *tenere il piede in due -e*, (*fig.*) have two irons in the fire; *tirare alla* —, consent reluctantly. -**fáre**, -**feggiáre**, INTR.: lose one's stirrups. -**fétta**, F.: *dim.* of -*fa*; estifette (courier, express); cymbal: *a* —, by the post; quickly. -**fière**, M.: footman (groom). -**filaménto**, M.: lashing (whipping). -**filáre**, TR.: lash (whip, flog). -**filáta**, F.: blow with a stirrup-leather: whipping. -**filatóre**, M.: whi[illegible]
túra, -**filazióne**, F.: [illegible]
flogging. -**fíle**, M.: st[illegible]
stafiságra [illegible]
wild], F.: [illegible]
staggiár[illegible]
loaded w[illegible]
stag-gi[illegible]
fiscation)
gío [L[illegible]
crotche[illegible]
-**gíre**,
re, M.: [illegible]

stagio-náccia, *f.* [illegible] of -na. **-naménto**, M.: maturity (ripening). **-náre**, TR.: ripen; season. **-natamente**, ADV.: maturely [illegible]. **-natore**, M.: seasoner. **-natura**, F.: ripening (seasoning). ||**stagió-ne** [L. *statio*, station], F.: season; [illegible]; *la nuova* —, spring. **-névole**, ADJ.: maturative (seasonable).

sta-gliáre [*s-*, [illegible]], TR.: cut roughly (chop); [illegible] put an end to reckon in the gross. **-gliato**, [illegible]: hacked, etc.; [illegible] quickly (speedily); concisely. **stá-glio**, M.: rough computation; *a* —, by the lump (by the whole).

stagnaio [*stagno*²], M.: pewterer.

sta-gnamento, M.: stagnation. ||**-gná-re**¹ [*-gno*¹], INTR.: stagnate (be still); TR.: staunch (stop).

sta-gnare² [*-gno*²], TR.: tin over (pewter). **-gnata**, F.: can (pewter-pot); tinning. **-gnatura**, F.: covering with tin. **sta-gneo**, ADJ.: of pewter or tin. **-gnino**, M.: tinner (pewterer).

stagno¹ [L. *stagnum* (*stare*, stand)], M.: stagnant water (marsh); ADJ.: stagnated: *-gni salati*, salt water marshes.

sta-gno² [L. *stannum* (arch. *stagnum*)], M.: tin; pewter; PL.: pewter dishes, etc. **-gnóla**, F.: tin-foil. **-gnòlo**, **-gnuòlo**†, M.: pewter or counterfeit money; pewter vessel.

sta-io, **-ia** [L. *sextarius*, sixth part], M.: bushel. **-ioro**†, M.: ground covered by a bushel of seed. **-iuòlo**†, *dim.* of *-io*.

sta-lammite, ||**-lagmite** [Gr. *stálagma* (*stalássein*, drip), drop], F.: stalagmite. **-lammitico**, ADJ.: stalagmitical. **-lattite** [Gr. *-laktós*, drop], F.: stalactite. **-lattitico**, ADJ.: shaped like a stalactite.

stalentággine†, F.: awkwardness (incapacity).

stál-la [OGer. *stal* (STALL)], F.: stable: — *di buoi*, ox-stall: — *di pecore*, sheep-fold; — *di porci*, pigsty. **-láccia**, *disp.* of *-la*. **-lággio**, M.: money paid for stabling; stabling. **-láre**, INTR.: be in the stable; dung (stale)†. **-láta**, F.: stallful. **-látioo**, M. = *-laggio*. **-leggiáre**, INTR.: keep stables. **-létta**, **-lettína**, *dim.* of *-letta*. **-lía**†, F.: (*nar.*) time a ship remains in port. **-lière**, M.: stable-boy. **stal-lío**, **-lívo**, ADJ.: stable-fed; stalled. **stál-lo**, M.: bishop's chair; permanent place or situation; place of abode†. **-lóne**, M.: stallion; stable-boy (hostler).

stama-iòla [*stame*], F.: upper cross-pieces of the loom. **-iòlo**, M.: master-spinner.

sta-máne, ||**-máni** [L. *ista mane*], ADV.: this morning. **-mattína** = *-mane*.

stam-becchino, M.: archer (bowman); PL.: bows, arrows, etc.; ADJ.: of a wild goat. ||**-bécco** [Ger. *stein-bock*, goat of the rocks], M.: wild goat; (*nar.*) zebeck (kind of ship)†.

stam-bèrga [*stanza*, *albergo*], F.: dilapidated house. **-bergóne**, **-bergáccia**, *disp.* *aug.* of *-berga*. **-búgio** [*stanza*, *bugio*, hole], M.: miserable little room.

stambu-ráre [*s-*, *tamburo*], INTR.: drum (beat the drum). **-ráta**, F.: drumming.

stá-me [L. *-men* (Gr. *stémon*)], **-ménto**†, M.: yarn (thread, fine wool); (*bot.*) stamen. **-migna**, **-mína**, F.: bombasin; cloth for a sieve.

stám-pa, F.: press; impression (stamp); kind; form; printing; figure: *andare a* —, be published; *operare a* —, do a thing mechanically. **-pábile**, ADJ.: that can be stamped or printed. **-páccia**, *disp.* of *-pa*. **-panáre**†, TR.: rend (tear, lacerate). ||**-páre** [OGer. *-phon* (Ger. *-pfen*, tread upon)], TR.: stamp; imprint (print); engrave: — *nell'animo*, impress upon the mind. **-paría** = *-peria*. **-patèllo**, M.: stamp. **-patóre**, M., **-patríce**, F.: printer: — *in cotone*, calico-printer; — *di zecca*, coiner. **-patúra**, F.: printing.

stampèl-la [OGer. *staphon*, walk?], F.: crutch. **-lóne**, *aug.* of *-la*.

stam-pería, F.: printing-office. **-periúccia**, *disp.* of *-peria*. **-pétta**, *dim.* of *-pa*. **-píglia**, F.: sign-board. **-píne** = *bozze*. **-píno**, M.: (*typ.*) proof; stamp; stencil. **-píta**, F.: long discourse; sonata†; air (song). ||**stám-pe** [*-pare*], M.: press; stamp; punch. **-póne**, *aug.* of *-po*.

stanáre [*s-*, *tana*], TR.: force out of the hole or den.

stan-cábile, ADJ.: that can be tired or fatigued. **-caménto**, M.: weariness (lassitude). ||**-cáre** [?], TR.: tire (weary); INTR., REFL.: become tired; be exhausted (of land). **-cheggiáre**, TR.: annoy (tire). **-chétto**, *dim.* of *-co*. **-chévole**, ADJ.: wearisome. **-chézza**, F.: lassitude (fatigue). **-co**, ADJ.: tired; troubled; exhausted (of land).

stán-ga [OGer.], F.: bar (cross-bar); (*pop.*) misery; peg for clothes, etc.†; (*leg.*)† bar: — *di carretta*, cart-shaft; — *di* [*fi*]*nestra*, window-bar; *metter la* —, tightly. **-gáre**, TR.: bar. blow with a bar. with severity; put up bars. *dim.* of *-ga*; booting (kic *dim.* of (bronze b with a la

stanòtte (this nigh

stán-te, PART. of *stare;* M.: instant (moment); ADV., PREP.: since; after (afterwards): — *in piede*, on one's feet (upright); *male* —, in poor circumstances; *non molto* —, not long after; — *che*, inasmuch as, since. **-teménte**, ADV.: instantly. **-tío**, ADJ.: stale (old, withered); useless.

stantúffo [cf. *stampa*], M.: sucker (of a pump).

stán-za [l. L. *-tia* (*stare*, stand)], F.: room; house; strophe (stanza); stay (residence); instance†; moment (instant)†. **-záccia**, *disp.* of *-za*. **-zerèlla**, **-zétta**, **-zína**, *dim* of *-za*. **-zía**† = *-za, istanza*. **-ziále**, ADJ.: permanent (constant). **-zialménte**, ADV.: constantly. **-ziaménto**, M.: command (order). **-ziáre**, TR.: decree (order); establish; think (judge); place; INTR.: live (dwell); suppose. **-ziatóre**, M.: dweller; inhabitant. **-ziétta**, **-zína**, **-zíno**, *dim.* of *-za*. **-zinúccio**, *disp. dim.* of *-za*. **-zóne**, *aug.* of *-za*. **-zúccia**, *disp. dim.* of *-za*.

stappáre [*s-*, *t.* .], TR.: pull (the cork).

stáre [L.], IRR.§; INTR.: be; be placed; reside (dwell); remain; consent; cease; be on the point of; consist; refer to; delay (tarry); cost; stand security; recover; be open (of shops)†; continue†; M.: stay; delay; instant†; *come state?* how are you? *dove state di casa?* where do you live? *sto per dire*, I dare say; *lasciatemi* —, let me alone; *questo cappello vi sta*, that hat becomes you; — *dubbio*, doubt (suspect); — *a bottega*, keep shop; — *a diporto*, take one's pleasure; — *a filo*, be ready; — *mallevadore*, guarantee; — *a orecchio*, listen; — *alla prova*, stand trial; — *alla sentenza di uno*, leave it to one's judgment.

§ Ind.: Pres. *stò, stai, sta; stiámo, státe, stánno*. Impf. *stáva*, etc. Pret. *stètti* (pop. *stássi*), *stésti, stètte* or *stè; stémmo, stéste, stèttero*. Subj.: Pres. *sti-a, -a, -a; -ámo, -áte, -ano*. Impf. *stés-si, -si, -se; -simo, -ste, -sero*. I've *stá; státe*. So *ri-, sopra-stáre;* but reg. *re-, contra-, sovra-stare*.

stár-na [?], F.: gray partridge. **-náre**, TR.: take out the entrails of (the partridge). **-nazzáre**, INTR.: alight with a flutter; flutter (beat the wings). **-noncíno**, **-nòtto**, M.: young partridge.

starnu-taménto, M.: sternutation (sneezing). **-táre** = *-tire*. **-tatòrio**, M.: sternutatory (sneezing powder). **-tazióne** = *-tamento*. **-tíglia**, F.: snuff. **-tíre**, INTR.: sneeze. ||**starnú-to** [L. *sternutum* (*sternuere*) having sneezed], M.: sneezing.

starocсáre [*s-*, *tarocco*], INTR.: play the higher cards called tarocchi at the game tarocco.

staròsta†, M.: starost.

stasáre [*s-*, *taso*], TR.: free of tartar; open (unstop).

staséra [*questa, sera*], ADV.: this evening.

stásì†, F.: stasis (stagnation of the blood).

statáre [*state*], INTR.: pass the summer; allow the land to rest between ploughings.

statário [L. *-rius*, stationary (*stare*)], M.: Roman soldier; ADJ.: bloody.

stá-te [*estate*], F.: summer. **-teréccio**, ADJ.: estival (of summer).

stática [Gr. *-tikós*], F.: statics.

státicо†, M.: hostage.

sta-tísta, M.: statesman. **-tística**, F.: science of statistics. **-tístico**, ADJ.: statistical. ||**stá-to** 1 [L. *-tus* (*-re*, stand)], M.: state (condition); government; patrimony†; mode of living†; state of inertia†; dominion†; authority†: *un delitto di* —, state crime (as high treason); — *maggiore*, the staff.

státo 2, PART. of *essere*.

státo 3, PART. of *stare*.

stá-tua [L. (*-tuere*, set up)], F.: statue. **-tuáccia**, *disp.* of *-tua*. **-tuária**, F.: statuary. **-tuário**, ADJ.: statuary; M.: sculptor. **-tuétta**, **-tuína**, *dim.* of *-tua*. **-tuíre**, TR.: decree; deliberate (resolve). **-tumináre**†, TR.: strengthen; fortify. **-túra** [L.], F.: stature (size); height. **-tutále**, ADJ.: statutable. **-tutário**, ADJ.: lawgiver (legislator). **-túto**, M.: statute.

s=tavernáre†, INTR.: come out of a tavern.

stá-za†, F.: gauge. **-záre**†, TR.: gauge (measure). **-zatóre**†, M.: ganger. **-zatúra**†, F.: gauging.

stá-zio†, M.: chamber; dwelling. **-zionáre**, INTR.: dwell. **-zionário**, ADJ.: stationary. ||**-zióne** [L. *-tio* (*-re*, stand)], F.: STATION; church (for indulgences); delay†; residence (habitation)†.

stazzonáre†, TR.: handle (feel, touch).

steá-rico, pl. —*ci* [Gr. *stéar*], ADJ.: suet (tallow). **-rína**, F.: fat. **-títe**, F.: steatites.

stéc-ca, F.: paper-knife; shoemaker's cork; little stick; shoulder (of a spade); toothpick; (*bill.*) cue. **-cáccia**, *disp.* of *-ca*. **-ca=dènte**†, M.: toothpick. **-cáia**, F.: dam (breakwater); fold (palisade). **-cáre**, TR.: palisade (enclose); barricade. **-cáto**, M.: palisade; stockade; PL.: lists. **-cheggiáre**†, TR.: beat with a stake. **-chétto**, M.: *dim.* of *-co: stare a* —, keep one short of food. **-chína**, *dim.* of *-ca*. **-chíno**, M.: *dim.* of *-co;* toothpick; pencil. **-chíre**, INTR.: grow thin; dry up. **-chíto**, PART.: very thin; dried up. ||**stéc-co** [OGer. *-cho*], **-colo**, M.: dry twig (STICK); wood, etc., used in making clay figures: spontoon (halberd)†; toothpick. **-conáto**, M.: enclosure (palisade). **-cóne**, M.: *aug.* of *-co*: large stake.

stè-gola [L. *stipula*, stalk], F.: handle of a plough. **-golo**†, M.: arbour or shaft (of a mill): beam (spindle).

stél-la [L.], F.: star: constellation; (*poet.*) eye: destiny (fate): white spot in a horse's forehead; rowel (of a spur): — *dell' argano*, handle of a windlass; — *Diana*, morning star: *andare alla prima* —, get up early. **-lánte**, ADJ.: starry; bright (glittering). **-láre**, ADJ.: stellar (astral); TR.: fill with stars. **-lária**, F.: starwort (elecampane). **-láto**, PART.: starry: white-faced (of a horse). **-leggiáre**, TR.: cover with stars. **-lètta**, F.: *dim.* of *-la*; asterisk. **-lína**, F.: *dim.* of *-la*; kind of broth. **-líno**, M.: Tuscan coin.

stel-lionatário, M.: defrauder. **-lionáto**, M.: stellionate (cozenage). ‖**-lióne** [L. *-lio*], M.: stellion (newt); tarantula.

stel-lóne, M.: *aug.* of *-la*; sun. **-lúzza**, *dim.* of *-la*.

stèlo [L. *stilus*, stake], M.: stalk (stem); axis (pivot)†.

stèmma, pl. *-i* [Gr.], M.: coat of arms.

stempe-raménto, M.: dissolution; intemperance†; commotion†; excess†. **-ránza**†, F.: intemperance; inclemency. ‖**-ráre** [*s-*, *t...*], TR.: dissolve (dilute); lower the temperature of; soften (allay); REFL.†: corrupt (spoil); lose temperature: *-rarsi in lacrime*, melt into tears. **-rátaménte**, ADV.: intemperately. **-ratézza** *-ramento*. **-ráto**, PART.: diluted, etc.

stem-piáre† [*s-*, *tempia*], TR.: bare the temples of. **-piáto**, ADJ.: with bare temples; very great; absurd.

stempráre† = *stemperare*.

sten-dále† = *-dardo*. **-dardière**†, M.: standard-bearer. ‖**-dárdo** [*-dere*], M.: ecclesiastical banner; standard (banner).

stendáre†, INTR.: strike the tents (decamp).

stèn-dere [*s-*, *t...*], IRR. (cf. *tendere*); TR.: extend; stretch out; enlarge; REFL.: stretch one's self out; reach; divulge: — *un arco*, unbend a bow. **-diménto**, M.: extension (expansion). **-ditóio**, M.: drying-ground. **-ditóre**, M.: extender; enlarger; divulger.

stenebráre [*s-*, *tenebra*], TR.: light up.

steno-grafáre [Gr. *stenós*, narrow, *gráphein*, write], TR.: stenograph (write in shorthand). **-grafía**, F.: stenography. **-graficaménte**, ADV.: stenographically. **-gráfico**, pl. *-ci*, ADJ.: stenographical. **stenò-grafo**, M.: stenographer.

sten-sióne† = *-dimento*. **-sívo**, ADJ.: extensive (large); extensible.

sten-tacchiáre, *freq.* of *-tare*. ‖**-táre** [L. *abstentare* (*abs-tinere*, abstain)], INTR.: suffer want (be in want, be needy, be stinted); live by toil; labour (toil); be wearisome; TR.†: vex; put off (delay): *-ta a vivere*, he barely makes his living, he can hardly make both ends meet; *-to a crederlo*, I hardly believe it. **-tataménte**, ADV.: with difficulty (slowly). **-tatézza** = *-tatura*. **-táto**, PART.: laboured, etc.; thin (poor); painful; affected (overdone). **-tatúra**, F.: imperfect work. **-terèllo**, M.: Florentine mask; buffoon. **sténto**, M.: want (misery); drudgery: (*fig.*) *è uno — a vederla ballare*, it is a pity to see her dance; *a —*, hardly (with much difficulty). **-táme**, M.: slovenly work.

stenua. = *estenua*..

stèppa [Russ.], F.: steppe.

stèr-co [L. *-cus*], M.: dung (excrement). **-coráceo**, ADJ.: stercoraceous. **-corário**, ADJ.: of dung. **-corazióne**, F.: stercoration (manuring).

stereo- [Gr. *stereós*, solid], PREF.: **-grafía** [Gr. *gráphein*, write], F.: stereography. **-gráfico**, pl. *—ci*, ADJ.: stereographical. **stereò-metra**, M.: professor of stereometry. **-metría** [Gr. *métron*, measure], F.: stereometry. **-metricaménte**, ADV.: stereometrically. **-mètrico**, pl. *—ci*, ADJ.: stereometric. **-scòpio** [Gr. *skópein*, look at], M.: stereoscope. **-tipáre**, TR.: stereotype. **stereò-tipo**, M.: stereotype. **-tipía**, F.: art of stereotyping. **-tipísta**, M.: stereotypist, -per. **-tomía** [Gr. *tomé*, edge], F.: stereotomy.

stèri-le [L. *-lis*], ADJ.: sterile (barren). **-lézza** = *-lità*. **-líre**, TR.: make sterile; INTR.: become barren. **-lità**, F.: sterility. **-lménte**, ADV.: barrenly (unfruitfully).

ster-lína, ‖**-líno** [Eng. *sterling*], ADJ.: sterling; M.: sterling coin: *lira -ina*, pound sterling.

stermi-nábile, ADJ.: exterminable. **-naménto**, M.: extermination. ‖**-náre** [L. *ex-t...*], TR.: exterminate. **-nataménte**, ADV.: excessively. **-natézza**, F.: immense size. **-náto**, PART.: exterminated; extraordinary (enormous). **-natóre**, M., **-natríce**, F.: exterminator. **-nazióne**, F.: extermination; destruction. **stermi**-
nio = *esterminio*.

stèrnere†, TR.: stretch ...
(*fig.*) d...

stèrn...
(bres...

stern...

stèrn...
solid...

ster-p...

dry shoots. **-pagnòla**, F.: hedge-sparrow. **-pagnòlo**, ADJ.: of the nature of shoots; full of sprigs. **-páme** = *-paglia*. **-paménto**, M.: extirpation. **-páre**, TR.: root out (extirpate); pull the twigs off of. **stèr-pe** = *-po*. **-péto**, M.: place full of shoots. ||**stèr-po** [*stirpe*], M.: young dry shoot (sprig). **-póne**, *aug.* of *-po*. **-póso**, ADJ.: abounding with twigs or shoots.

sterquilín(i)o [L. *-linium*], M.: dung-hill.

ster-raménto, M.: digging. ||**-ráre** [*s-*, *terra*], TR.: take away (the earth); dig (the earth). **-ráto**, PART.: cleared away, etc.; M.: levelled place; ditch. **stèr-ro**, M.: clearing away; earth dug-out.

stertóre†, M.: wheezing (rattling).

sterzáre 1 [*terzo*], TR.: disTRIbute properly, arrange.

ster-záre 2, INTR.: turn (of carriages). ||**stèr-zo** [Ger. *sterz*], M.: turning-gear (of a waggon); cab (of 18th Cent.).

ste-saménte, ADV.: diffusely. ||**stè-so**† [*-sura*], ADJ.: diffused (scattered); ADV.: diffusely; M.: = *-sura*.

stessaménte = *medesimamente*.

s=tèssere, TR.: unweave (unravel).

stésso [L. *iste ipse*], ADJ.: same; self-same: *egli* —, he himself; *noi stessi*, we ourselves.

stesúra [*stendere*], F.: extension, etc.; diction (style).

stetoscópio [Gr. *stéthos*, breast, *skopein*, look], M.: stethoscope.

stía [OGer. *stiga*], F.: hencoop (aviary); den (prison).

stiacci.. = *schiacci..*

stiáffo = *schiaffo*.

stiamazzáre = *schiamazzare*.

stiant.. = *schiant..*

stianza = *schianza*.

stiapp.. = *schiapp..*

stiáre [*stia*], TR.: fatten (cram).

stiátta = *schiatta*.

stiávo = *schiavo*.

stidio..† = *schidio..*

stièna = *schiena*.

stiepidíre [*s-*, *t..*], TR.: make lukewarm.

stiètto = *schietto*.

stiga..† = *istiga..*

stígio [L. *Styx*], ADJ.: Stygian; infernal.

sti-gliaménto, M.: stripping flax. ||**-gliáre** [*s-*, *tiglio*], TR.: separate (the fibre from the flax).

stígma†, F.: stigma (mark).

stígnere = *stingere*.

sti-láre†, INTR.: be customary or usual. ||**stí-le** [L. *stylus*], M.: style (manner of writing; stylus); custom (style); knife; gnomon (pin of a sun-dial); haft (handle). **-lettáre**, TR.: wound with a dagger. **-lettáta**, F.: blow with a stiletto. **-létto**, M.: stiletto (poniard). **-li=fórme**, ADJ.: stiletto-shaped. **-lísta**, M.: user of a style. **-lística**, F.: rhetoric. **-lístico**, ADJ.: of a style-user.

stíl-la [L. *-la* (dim. of *stiria*)], F.: drop. **-laménto**, M.: distillation (dropping). **-láre**, TR.: distil; delay (put off); INTR.: drop down in drops; clarify (grow clear); REFL.: do one's best. **-láto**, PART.: distilled, etc.; M.: distilled drink; jelly-broth. **-latóre**, M.: distiller. **-lazióne**, F.: distillation; infusion. **-licídio** [L. *-licidium* (*stilla*, drop, *cadere*, fall)], M.: stillicide. **-líno**, M.: distiller. **-lo**, M.: vase of liquor or broth; carefully studied thing.

stílo = *stile*.

stí-ma, F.: estimation (value); regard (esteem); praise: *non fa — di nessuno*, he values nobody. **-mábile**, ADJ.: estimable. **-mabilità**, F.: estimableness (value). **-magióne**†, F., **-maménto**†, M.: estimation (valuation). ||**-máre** [L. *æsti..*], TR.: esteem (value); believe (judge).

stíma-te [Gr. *stigmata*, puncture (*stizein*, prick)], F. PL.: stigmata (marks, wounds). **-tína**, F., **-tíno**, M.: brother or sister of the stigmata (a religious company).

stima-tíva† [*-re*], F.: estimation; discerning faculty (judgment). **-tívo**, ADJ.: serving to estimate.

stímatiz-záre [Gr. *stigmatizein*], TR.: stigmatize. **-záto**, PART.: stigmatized.

sti-matóre†, M., **-matríce**, F.: estimator (appraiser). **-mazióne**, F.: estimation. ||**-mo** = *-ma*.

stí-mite†, **-mmáte** = *-mate*.

stimo-láre [L. *stimulare*, prick], TR.: prick with a goad; stimulate (spur on). **-latívo**, ADJ.: stimulative. **-latóre**, **-latríce**, F.: exciter (stimulator). **-lazióne**, F.: stimulation. ||**stímo-lo** [L. *stimulus*], M.: goad; spur (incentive); (*med.*) stimulant; anguish†. **-lóso**, ADJ.: sharp; vexing (exciting)†.

stínca†, F.: top or summit (of a mountain).

stincaiòlo [*-che*], M.: prisoner (for debt).

stincá-ta [*stinco*], F.: blow on the shin. **-túra**, F.: = *-ta*; mark of a kick.

stínche [fr. the name of a castle], F. PL.: debtors' prisons (in Florence).

stínco [OGer. *skinko*], M.: bone of the leg (shin); leg.

stinènzia† = *astinenza*.

stíngere [*s-*, *t..*], IRR.; TR.: take out the colour of (discolour); extinguish†; (*fig.*) darken (blacken); INTR., REFL.: fade; be extinguished.

stínguere† = *distinguere*.

stínto [*stingere*], PART.: discoloured, etc.; M.†: instinct.

stío†, ADJ.: of March flax.
stiòppo = *schioppo*.
stiòro, pl. —*ra*, —*ri* [*staioro* (dim. of *staio*)], M.: peck (quart measure).
stí-pa [L. *-pes*, trunk of a tree], F.: brushwood (twigs); stubble†; pig-sty†; heap (pile)†. **-pa-mácchie**, M.: one who clears away brushwood. **-páre**, TR.: clear away (brushwood, etc.); heap up; surround with twigs†. **-patóre** = *-pamacchie*. **-patúra**, F.: cleaning away (clearing).
stipen-diáre [L. *-diari*], TR.: recompense (pay a salary to); hire. **-diário**†, M.: pensioner (stipendiary); ADJ.: receiving pay. **-diáto**, PART.: paid with a stipend, etc. ‖**stipèn-dio** [L. *-dium*, tax (*stipipendium*; *stips*, money, *pendere*, pay)], M.: stipend (wages).
sti-pettáio, M.: cabinet-maker. ‖**-pét-to**, **-píno**, *dim.* of *-po*.
stipid.. = *stupid..*
stí-pite [L. *stipes*, log], M.: jamb (door-post); stalk (stem); stock; trunk. **-po**, M.: cabinet; = *-pite*†.
stípticо†, M.: (*med.*) styptic (astringent).
stípula†, F.: stubble.
stipulá-re [L. *-ri*], INTR.: stipulate (covenant). **-zióne**, F.: stipulation (agreement); bargain.
sti-racchiábile, ADJ.: subject to cavil. **-racchiaménto**, M.: overstretching; sophistry. **-racchiáre** [freq. of *-rare*], TR.: pull (stretch); overstrain; INTR.: cavil (sophisticate); cheapen (drive a hard bargain); toil†. **-racchiataménte**, ADV.: sophistically. **-racchiatézza**, F.: sophistry (cavilling). **-racchiatúra**, F.: captiousness (cavillation). **-raménto**, M.: stretching (straining); tension. ‖**-ráre** [*s-*, *t..*], TR.: iron; drag with violence; pull out (stretch). **-ratóra**, **-ratríce**, F.: ironer of linen. **-ratúra** = *-ramento*. **-rería**, F.: ironing establishment.
stir-páme, M.: quantity of briars, roots, etc. **-pa..** = *estirpa..* ‖**stír-pe** [L. *-ps*, stock], F.: race (family); progeny.
stiti-cággine, F.: = *-cheria*. **-caménte**, ADV.: stypticly. **-cáre**, INTR.: be costive. **-chería**, **-chézza**, **-citá**, F.: costiveness (constipation); close-fistedness; spleen. ‖**stíti-co** [L. *stypticus* (Gr. *stuptikós*)], ADJ.: styptic (costive); close-fisted; morose; insipid (dry). **-cúccio**, **-cúzzo**, *disp. dim.* of *-co*.
stituíre† = *istituire*.
stiuma.. = *schiuma..*
stíva = *stegola*.
[illegible] [L. *-va* (*stare*) standing thing], F.: [illegible] hold (bulkhead).
[illegible]*áccio*, *disp. aug.* of *-le*. **-láre**, INTR., REFL.: put on one's boots. **-láta**, F.: blow with a boot. **-láto**, PART.: booted. ‖**stivá-le** [Ger. *stiefel*], M.: boot; (*fig.*) stupid fellow: *ungere gli* —, flatter. **-lería**, F.: stupidity (simplicity). **-létto**, M.: half-boot (buskin). **-lóne**, *aug.* of *-le*.
sti-vaménto, M.: heap (hoard, pile); crowd. ‖**-váre** [*-pare*], TR.: fill (heap up); (*nav.*) stow away; REFL.: crowd together (assemble).
stivière†, M.: high shoe (buskin).
stíz-za [*tizzo*], F.: anger (wrath). **-záre**†, **-zíre**, TR.: make angry; REFL.: be angry (fall into a passion). **-zo**, M.: firebrand. **-zóne**, *aug.* of *-zo*. **-zosaménte**, ADV.: passionately (angrily). **-zosétto**, *dim.* of *-zoso*. **-zóso**, ADJ.: passionate (choleric).
stoccafísso [Ger. *stockfisch*], M.: stockfish.
stoc-cáta, F.: blow or thrust with a sword; (*fig.*) request for money; trouble (grief): *stare sulle* —*te*, be on one's guard. **-catèlla**, *dim.* of *-cata*. **-cheggiáre**, TR.: stab with sword (wound); (*fig.*) stand upon the defensive (be on one's guard). **-chétto**, *dim.* of *-co*. ‖**stòc-co** [Ger. *stock*, stick], M.: rapier (sword); sword-cane; pole† (of a hay-stack); stock (stump)†; race (family)†: *avere* —, have wit or understanding; *donna di* —, woman of honour.
stoccofisso = *-cafisso*.
stòf-fa [Ger. *stoff*], F.: cloth. **-`fo**†, M.: quantity of stuff or matter.
stòggio†, M.: ceremony; flattery.
stogli..† = *distogli..*
stò-ia [L. *storea*], F.: straw-mat (hassock). **-iáre**, TR.: supply with mats.
stoi-caménte, ADV.: stoically. **-cismo**, M.: stoicism. ‖**stòi-co**, pl. *-ci* [Gr. *-kós* (Gr. *stoá*, portico, where Zeno taught)], ADJ.: stoical.
stoíno, M.: *dim.* of *stoia*; door-mat.
stòla [L.], F.: stole; dress (robe).
stoli-daménte, ADV.: stolidly (foolishly). **-détto**, *dim.* of *-do*. **-dézza**, **-dità**, F.: stolidity (stupidity). ‖**stòli-do** [L. *-dus*], ADJ.: stolid (dull).
stóllo [?], M.: pole of a haystack; post.
stolóne [*stola*], M.: ornament of the priest's cape; (*agr.*) dog's grass.
stol-taménte, ADV.: foolishly. **-tézza**, F.: foolishness (stupidity). **-tilòquio**, M.: stultiloquy (foolish talk). **-tízia** = *-tezza*. ‖**stól-to** [L. *stultus*], ADJ.: simple (foolish); M.: fool.
stoma-cáccio, *disp.* of *-co*. **-cággine**†, F.: nausea (loathing). **-cále**, ADJ.: stomachic (cordial). **-cáre**, TR.: nauseate (turn the stomach); disgust; INTR.: have

one's stomach turn. **-cáto,** PART.: loathed, etc. **-cazióne†** = *-caggine*. **-chévole,** ADJ.: loathsome (disgusting). **-chevolménte,** ADV.: in a loathsome manner. **-chíno,** *dim.* of *-co*. ‖**stòma-co** [L. *-chus* (Gr. *-chos*)], M.: stomach; dislike; (*fig.*) anger (grudge): *contro* —, unwillingly; *buono* —, great eater. **-cóne,** *aug.* of *-co*. **-cosaménte,** ADV.: with disgust. **-cóso,** ADJ.: loathsome. **-cúzzo,** *disp.* of *-co*. **stomá-tico,** ADJ.: stomachic.

sto-nánte, ADJ.: discordant. ‖**-náre** [*s-, t.* .], INTR.: be out of tune; TR.: bewilder (confuse). **-natúra,** F.: getting out of tune.

stóp-pa [L. *stuppa*], F.: tow (hards of flax or hemp). **-páccio, -pácciolo†,** M.: wadding of a gun. **-páre,** TR.: stop with tow; stop (close); (*fig.*)† neglect.

stóppia [L. *stipula*], F.: stubble; stubble field.

stop-pináre [*-pina*], TR.: provide with a fuse; [*-pare*], stop or close up tightly. **-pinièra,** F.: lighter. ‖**-píno** [*-pa*], M.: wick; small taper; fuse.

stoppióne [*-pia*], M.: thistle.

stoppóso [*-pa*], ADJ.: flax-like (pulpy).

storáce [Gr. *stúrax*], M., F.: storax.

stòr-cere [*s-, torcere*], IRR.; TR.: twist (wrest, wring); untwist; dislocate; REFL.: writhe; oppose (resist)†: — *la bocca*, make wry faces. **-ci=léggi†,** M.: pettifogger (ignorant lawyer). **-ciménto,** M.: wringing (whirling); distortion.

stor-diménto, M.: stunning. ‖**-díre** [?], TR.: stun; confound; INTR.: be astonished. **-ditaménte,** ADV.: thoughtlessly. **-ditézza,** F.: heedlessness (giddiness). **-ditívo,** ADJ.: stunning (amazing).

stòri-a [L., Gr. *historía*], F.: history; tale (fable); poem (legend); historical picture; adventure. **-áccia,** *disp.* of *-a*. **-áio, -áro,** M.: seller of histories. **-ále†,** ADJ.: historical; M.: historian. **-alménte†,** ADV.: historically. **-áre,** TR.: write (histories, etc.); cf. *istoriare;* INTR.: linger (languish); lose time; make mad. **-caménte,** ADV.: historically. **stòrico,** ADJ.: historical; M.: historian. **-èlla, -étta,** *dim.* of *-ia*. **-évole,** ADJ.: historical. **-ografía,** F.: historical narration. **-ò-grafo,** M.: historiographer.

stori-oncèllo, *dim.* of *-one*. ‖**-óne** [L. *sturio*], M.: sturgeon.

stormeg-giáre†, INTR.: give the alarm; crowd (assemble). **-giáta,** F.: thundering noise (great uproar).

storménto† = *strumento*.

stor-míre, INTR.: rustle (make a noise).

‖**stór-mo** [Ger. *storm*, tempest], M.: throng (crowd, band); troop†; combat†: *sonare a* —, ring the alarm-bell.

stor-náre [*dis-, t.* .], TR.: push back; dissuade; INTR.: swerve (fall back). **-nèllo,** M.: *dim.* of *-no;* starling; small popular poem; peg-top (gig). **-noi,** M.: act of pushing back; lottery ticket.

stórno 2 [L. *sturnus*], M.: starling; of a white and black horse.

stor-piaménto, M.: maiming (mutilation). ‖**-piáre** [?], TR.: mutilate (cripple); (*fig.*) speak badly; hinder; violate. **-piataménte,** ADV.: in a mutilated manner. **-piáto,** PART.: mutilated, etc.; M.: cripple. **-piatóre,** M.: mutilator. **-piatúra,** F.: mutilation; bad pronunciation. **stòr-pio,** M.: maiming; hindrance (obstacle); cripple.

storráto†, ADJ.: dismantled (towerless).

stòrre† = *distogliere*.

storsióne = *estorsione*.

stòr-ta [*-cere*], F.: twisting (wresting); turn (winding); distiller's retort; scimitar. **-taménte,** ADV.: askance. **-tétta,** *dim.* of *-ta*. **-tézza** = *-ta*. **-tigliáto†,** M., **-tigliatúra†,** F., **-tiláto,** M.: (*vet.*) sprain. **-tína,** F.: *dim.* of *-ta;* (*mus.*) wind-instrument. **-'to,** PART. of *-cere;* perverse (wicked). **-túra,** F.: act of being twisted, etc.

sto-vígli† = *-viglie*. **-vigliáio,** M.: potter. ‖**-víglie** [?], F. PL.: earthenware vessels (pottery). **-vigliería,** F.: quality of earthenware.

stoz-záre, TR.: use the mandrel. ‖**stòzzo** [Ger. *stoss*, thrust], M.: mandrel (instrument for giving convexity to metal).

stra- [L. *extra*, out], PREP.: out of (without); besides; beyond; much; more than. **-balzaménto,** M.: tossing (throwing up). **=balzáre,** TR.: toss up and down. **=balzóni,** ADV.: in a tossing manner. **=báttere†,** TR.: trouble (vex, disturb). **=bèllo,** ADJ.: very beautiful. **=bène,** ADV.: very well. **=bére,** IRR.; TR.: drink immoderately. **-bevizióne,** F.: excessive drinking. **-biliáre, -bilíre†** [? L. *-bilicare*], INTR.: wonder (be amazed).

strabíșmo [Gr. *-bismós* (*-bós*, short-sighted)], M.: strabism (squinting).

straboc-caménto [*stra-, bocca*], M.: overflowing; excess (superfluity); precipitate fall. **-cáre,** INTR.: overflow; dash down exceed. **-cataménte,** ADV.[illegible] ly. **-cáto,** PART.: overflowe[illegible] siderate (heedless); preci[illegible] **vole,** ADJ.: immoderate [illegible] hasty; steep. **-cheval**[illegible] overflowingly; hastily (ra[illegible] **co,** M.: fall; ADJ.: pass[illegible]

stra=bondánza, F.: [illegible]

strábule†, F. PL.: bree[illegible]

stra=buòno, ADJ.: very good.

strabuzzáre†, TR.: stare (look askew).

stracanáre [*-ccare*], REFL.: fatigue one's self.

stra=cannáre [*canna*], TR.: transfer (the silk from one bobbin to another). **=cannatúra**, F.: transferring of silk. **=cantáre**, INTR.: sing too much or out of tune. **=cárico**, ADJ.: overloaded. **=cáro**, ADJ.: very dear.

strác-ca, F.: lassitude (weariness); girth: *a* —, by force of fatigue. **-cággine**, F.: languor. **-cále**, M.: strap (girth); tired person. **-caménto**, M.: weariness (fatigue). ||**-cáre** [OGer. *strecchan*], TR.: tire (fatigue); trouble; REFL.: get tired. **-catívo**, **-catóio**, ADJ.: tiresome (fatiguing). **-chézza**, F.: fatigue; annoyance. **-chíetto**, *dim.* of *-co*. **-chíno**, M.: Lombard cheese.

strac-ciábile, ADJ.: that can be torn. **-cia=fòglio**, M.: waste-book. **-ciaiòlo**, M.: silk-carder. **-ciaménto**, M.: tearing (rending); ruin (destruction)†. ||**-ciáre** [l. L. *extractiare* (L. *trahere*, DRAW)], TR.: tear (rend); break†; lacerate†; INTR.: leave the track. **-ciasácca**, **-ciasácco**, ADV.: askance (scowlingly). **-ciataménte**, ADV.: in pieces; in tatters. **-ciatóre**, M.: tearer; ruiner. **-ciatúra**, F.: tearing; destruction†.

straccicaláre†, INTR.: chatter intolerably (prattle).

strác-cio [*-ciare*], M.: piece (bit); rag (tatter); tear; PL.: coarse part of silk: *non ne sapere* —, know nothing of the matter; *fatto a* —†, bastard. **-cióne**, M.: ragged fellow; ADJ.: in tatters.

stràcco [*-ccare*], ADJ.: fatigued (tired); ruined; M.†: weariness; importunity: *terreno* —, barren ground.

stra=cocuranza†, F.: negligence (carelessness). **=cuòcere**, IRR.; TR.: overcook (overdo). **-colláre** [*collo*, top (of the foot)], REFL.: sprain one's self. **-collatúra**, F.: dislocation (luxation). **=consigliáre**, TR.: advise strongly; consult often. **=contènto**, ADJ.: very contented. **=córrere**, IRR.; INTR.: run very fast. **-corrévole**, ADJ.: fleet (fast). **-córso**, PART.: fled (passed away). **=cotánza†** = *tracotanza*. **=còtto**, PART. of *-cocere*; overdone.

strá-da [L. *-ta*], F.: STREET (road); career; (*mil.*) covered way: -- *laterale*, branch railroad; (*fig.*) *metter fuori di* —, lead into error; *andare alla* —, become highwayman; *trovarsi in una* —, be deprived everything. **-dáccia**, *disp.* of *-da*. **-le**, ADJ.: of a street or road. **-dato**, M.: act of showing the way; *ng the road*. **-dáre**, TR.: clear (the road); show the way; guide. **-dèlla**, **-dèllo**, **-détta**, **-dettína**, **-diccièla**, *dim.* of *-da*. **-dière**, M.: gabel-man (custom-officer). **-dína**, F.: street-walker (prostitute).

stradiòtto [Gr. *stratiótes*, soldier], M.: stradiot (Greek soldier).

stradóne, *aug.* of *strada*.

stra=dóppio, ADJ.: more than double.

stra-dúccia, **-dúzza**, **-dúcola**, *disp.* *dim.* of *-da*.

stráere† = *estrarre*.

stra=falciáre, TR.: mow carelessly (half mow)†; INTR.: act heedlessly; do carelessly or fitfully; (*fig.*) walk rapidly. **-falcióne**, M.: blunder (great error); extravagance. **=fáre**, IRR.; TR.: overdo. **-fátto**, PART.: overdone; over-ripe. **=feláre** [*fiele*], REFL.: be out of breath. **-ficáre†**, TR.: prune; disentangle; despatch (finish). **=figuríre**, TR.: transfigure (transform). **-figuríto**, **-figuráto**, PART.: transfigured. **=fíne**, ADJ.: superfine. **=foráre**, TR.: perforate (pierce through). **=formáre** = *trasformare*. **=fóro**, M.: act of boring through: *lavorare di* —, ornament with drillings, work underhandedly. **=fugáre** = *trafugare*.

strágе [L *-ges*, throwing down], F.: great slaughter; mortality; destruction; great abundance.

stra=giudiciále, **-giudiziále**, ADJ.: extrajudicial.

stráglio†, M.: (*nav.*) ship's stay.

stra=godére, INTR.: enjoy very much. **=gonfiáre**, TR.: overswell. **=gránde**, ADJ.: excessively great. **=gráve**, ADJ.: very grave.

strainárе† = *trainare*.

stral-ciáre, TR.: prune (nip off); (*fig.*) end (conclude). ||**strál-cio** [*s-*, *t.* .] M.: pruning; settlement.

strá-le [OGer. *-la* (Ger. *-hl*, flash)], M.: (*poet.*) arrow (dart). **-létto**, *dim.* of *-le*.

straligna. . = *traligna*. .

stra=lucènte, ADV.: very bright. **-lunaménto**, M.: rolling one's eyes. **=lunáre** [*luna*], TR.: roll (one's eyes); stare at. **-lunáto**, ADJ.: staring, etc. **=malvágio†**, ADJ.: very wicked. **=matúro**, ADJ.: over-ripe (too ripe).

stra=mazzáre, TR.: knock down; INTR.: fall down as dead. **-mazzáta**, F.: falling blow (floorer). **-mázzo†**, M.: stretching blow; violent fall; cf. *-punto*. **-mazzóne**, M.: violent fall; slash (cut).

strámba†, F.: rope of hay or broom.

strambasciáre† = *trambasciare*.

stram-belláre, TR.: cut or tear to pieces. **-bèllo**, M.: shred (bit); rag (tatter). ||**strám-bo** [L. *strabo* (Gr. *strabón*), squint-eyed], M., ADJ.: bandy-legged (bow-legged); M.†: = *-ba*. **-bòtto, -bòttolo,** M.: roundelay; blunder (insipidity).

strá-me [L. *-men* (*sternere*, strew) litter], M.: STRAW (hay, fodder); bed (litter). **-meggiáre†,** TR.: eat (hay, etc.).

stramenáre† = *straportare*.

stra=mezzáre = *tramezzare*. **=moggiáre,** INTR.: superabound (be very plentiful). **=mortíre,** INTR.: faint away (fall into a swoon).

strampa-latería, F.: extravagance (strangeness). ||**-láto** [*s-*, *trampalo* ?], ADJ.: extravagant (strange). **-latóne,** *aug.* of *-lato*. **-lería,** F.: strangeness.

stra-náccio, *aug.* of *-no*. **-naménte,** ADV.: strangely. **-náre,** TR.: maltreat (ill-use); alienate†; INTR.: act strangely; go away. **-naturáre†,** TR.: change the nature of. **-neáre†,** TR.: send away. **-nétto,** *dim.* of *-no*. **-nézza,** F.: strangeness; ill usage (abuse); whim (strange thing)†. **-ngio†** = *-no*.

stran-golaménto, M.: strangling. ||**-goláre** [L. *-gulare*], TR.: strangle (choke); REFL.: strangle one's self. **-golatóio,** ADJ.: strangling; dangerous. **-golatóre,** M.: strangler. **-golazióne,** F.: strangulation. **strán-golo†,** M.: choking (strangling). **-goscíáre†,** TR.: fatigue; INTR.: be choked with grief (grieve). **-gugl̤ióne,** M.: (*vet.*) quinsy; strangles.

strangú-ría [Gr. *strangouría*], F.: strangury. **-riáre,** INTR.: be afflicted with strangury.

stra-niánza† = *-nezza*. **-niáre,** TR.: alienate (send away); REFL.: part (go away); become a stranger. **-nière, -nièro,** ADJ.: strange (foreign); M.: stranger (alien). ||**strá-nio** [L. *extranius* (for *-neus*)], ADJ.: extraneous (alien, foreign); extraordinary (unusual); cf. Eng. EXTRANEOUS. **-no,** ADJ.: strange; unusual; rude (uncivil); ADV.†: rudely; proudly. **-núccio,** ADJ.: rather meagre; rather pale.

stra-nutèlla, F.: plant which causes sneezing. **-núto,** etc. = *starnuto*, etc.

straordi-nariaménte, ADV.: extraordinarily. **-narietà,** F.: extraordinariness. ||**-nário** [L. *extra-ordinarius*], ADJ.: extraordinary (unusual); M.: courier; mace-bearer (bailiff).

stra=pagáre, TR.: overpay.

strapanáto [*s-*, *t.* .], ADJ.: torn.

stra=parláre, INTR.: talk too much.

stra-passaménto, M.: ill-treatment; contempt. **-passáre,** TR.: ill-treat (abuse); disdain; slight; reprove; REFL.: tire one's self: — *un cavallo*, harass a horse; — *il mestiere*, slight a task. **-passáta,** F.: *reproof*. **-passataménte,** ADV.: carelessly. **-passatóre,** M.: abuser (insulter). ||**-pásso** [?], M.: abuso (ill-use); insult; excess; ADJ.: extravagant: *cavallo da* —, cab horse; *cosa da* —, thing for daily or common use; *abiti da* —, working clothes; *a* —, carelessly (negligently). **-passóso,** ADJ.: careless; superabundant.

stra-pèrdere, INTR.: lose a great deal. **=piacére,** TR.: please very much. **=piantáre,** TR.: transplant. **=pièno,** ADJ.: overfull. **-piombáre,** INTR.: be unvertical, out of plumb; (*fig.*) weigh too much. **=piómbo,** M.: being out of plumb; overweight. **=piòvere,** IRR.; INTR.: rain heavily. **=portáre,** TR.: transport; move (charm). **=potènte,** ADJ.: very powerful.

strap-paménto, M.: act of pulling away or tearing off. ||**-páre** [Ger. *-fen*], TR.: pull away (force away); grub up; lacerate (tear). **-páta,** F.: pulling out; strappado (kind of torture). **-patèlla,** *dim.* of *-pata*. **-patúra** = *-pamento*. **-po,** M.: tearing away; grubbing up; thing pulled up.

stra=pregáre, TR.: pray very earnestly.

stra-puntíno, *dim.* of *-punto*. ||**-púnto** [*s-*, *t.* .], M.: mattress.

stra=ríceo, ADJ.: very rich. **=ripévole†,** ADJ.: very steep (rugged).

strárre = *estrarre*.

stra=sapére, IRR.; INTR.: know too much. **-sapúto,** PART.: over-wise (very learned).

strasci-caménto, M.: act of drawing or dragging after. ||**-cáre** [*s-*, *trajicare* (*trahicare*)], TR.: drag (draw along); INTR.: go slowly (crawl). **strásci-co,** M.: drawing or dragging along; train of a gown; remnant (remainder): *favellar collo* —, drawl out one's words (speak very slowly). **-cóne,** M.: *aug.* of *-co*; one who drags himself along. **-cóni,** ADV.: drawlingly. **-naménto,** M.: drawing or dragging along. **-náre,** TR.: draw, drag or trail along. **-natúra** = *-namento*. **-nío,** M.: continued dragging along. **strásci-no1,** M.: dragging; bird or fish net. **strascí-no2,** M.: hawking butcher.

stra=secoláre [*secolo*], INTR.: wonder (be amazed); TR.: confound. **=servíto,** ADJ.: bountifully served. **-sordinário†** = *straordinario*. **-sportáre†** = *trasportare*.

stratagèmma† = *strattagemma*.

stratagl̤iáre†, TR.: cut (slash); INTR.: cut like a razor.

stra-tegía [Gr. *-tegía*, office of a general], F.: strategy (military tactics). **-tègico,** pl. *—ci*, ADJ.: strategic. ||**-tègo** [Gr. *-tegós*, general], M.: officer commanding a strategy (chief).

stra-tificáre [-*to*, *facere*], TR., INTR.: stratify (dispose in layers). **-tificazióne**, F.: stratification. **-tifórme** [-*ma*], ADJ.: stratiform. ‖**strá-to** [L. -*tum* (*sternere*, extend)], M.: stratum (layer); carpet; bed†.

strátta = *strappata*.

strattagèmma, pl. —*i* [*strategia*], M.: stratagem (trick).

strattóne, *aug.* of *stratta*.

stráttо†, ADJ.: strange (unusual); original; extracted; separated; inclined (disposed); M.: extract; abridgment (abstract).

stra=vacáto [L. *extra-vacuare*, make void or free], ADJ.: (of a page) loosened on account of poor binding. **-vagánte** [L. *extra-vagans*], ADJ.: extravagant; capricious (whimsical). **-vagantemé nte**, ADV.: extravagantly. **-vagantétto†**, *dim.* of *-vagante*. **-vagánza**, F.: extravagance (singularity): *far delle —ze*, do strange things. **-valicáre†**, TR.: pass over in haste. **-vaşaménto**, M.: (*med.*) extravasation. **-vaşáre**, INTR., REFL.: extravasate (be diffused). **=váşo**, M.: extravasating. **=vedére**, IRR.; TR., INTR.: see too much; see badly. **-venáre** [*vena*], INTR.: (*med.*) extravasate. **=véro**, ADJ.: very true (most true). **=vesti. .†** = *travesti. .* **=viáre**, TR.: take out of the road. **=víncere**, IRR.; TR., INTR.: win or gain too much. **=vişáre**, TR.: disguise (travesty); REFL.: disguise one's self. **=viziáre**, INTR.: banquet (feast); be dissolute. **=vízio**, M.: feasting (merry-making); excess (debauch). **-vizzáre†** = *-viziare*. **=vízzo**, M.: banquet of Florentine Academy of Letters; = *-vizio*. **=volére**, IRR.; TR.: desire or wish for too much; INTR.: wish too much or too often. **=vòlgere**, IRR.; TR.: twist around (wrest, writhe); REFL.: tumble down (fall over). **-volgiménto**, M.: contortion; revolution. **-voltaménte**, ADV.: in a twisted manner. **=voltáre**, TR.: twist; upset (throw into confusion). **-vòlto**, PART.: twisted, etc. **-voltúra**, F.: contortion (twisting); perverted interpretation.

stra-ziáre [*distractiare* (*distractus*, divided)], TR.: tear up; abuse (revile); deride; waste (spend); torment. **-ziataménte**, ADV.: in an outrageous manner. **-ziatóre**, M.: tormentor; insulter. **-zieggiáre†**, TR.: deride (mock, ridicule). **-zièvole†**, ADJ.: abusive (insulting). **strá-zio**, M.: torment (torture); tear; affront; prodigality. **-zioșaménte**, ADV.: shamefully (contumeliously).

strebbiáre†, TR.: polish (make clean); REFL.: fard (paint one's face).

streccíáre [*s-*, *treccia*], INTR.: loosen the tresses; TR.: unravel (undo).

strefoláre†, TR.: untwist (untwine).

stré-ga [L. *striga* (*strix*, screecher)], F.: witch (hag): *darsi alle -ghe*, get impatient (be vexed). **-gáccia**, *disp.* of *-ga*. **-gaménto**, M.: bewitching. **-gáre**, TR.: bewitch (charm, enchant). **-ghería**, F.: sorcery (witchcraft).

streg-gh. . = *stri-gl. .* **-ghiatóre**, M.: horse-currier; reprover. **-ghiatúra**, F.: currying; rebuke. **strég-lia** = *-ghia*.

strégola†, F.: slap (blow on the face).

stregó-ne, F.: = *strega*. **-náccia**, *disp.* of *-na*. **-náre** = *stregare*. **stregóne**, M.: wizard (sorcerer). **-náccio†**, M., **-nería**, F.: sorcery.

strégua [? *t.* .], F.: reckoning; measure.

stre-maménte, ADV.: extremely. **-máre**, TR.: diminish (lessen). **-menuáre†**, TR.: weaken (extenuate). **-mézza**, F.: extremity (want, necessity); extreme. **-mità**, F.: extremity (utmost part). ‖**strè-mo** [*estremo*], ADJ.: extreme (utmost); stingy; destitute; M.: extremity, necessity.

strènna [L. *strena*, omen], F.: drink-money; new-year's gift.

stre-nuaménte, ADV.: strenuously; valiantly. **-nuità**, F.: strenuousness; bravery. ‖**strè-nuo** [L. *-nuus*], ADJ.: strenuous (sturdy); valiant (bold).

strè-pere [L.], INTR.: make a noise. **-pidíre†**, **-píre†**, TR.: fill with noise; INTR.: be stunned with noise. **-pitaménto**, M.: act of making noise. **-pitánte**, ADJ.: noisy. **-pitáre** [L. intens. of *-pere*)], INTR.: make a great noise. **-piteggiáre†**, INTR.: make some noise. **strèpito** [L. *-pitus* (*-pere*) clashing, sound], M.: noise. **-pitosaménte**, ADV.: noisily (loudly). **-pitóso**, ADJ.: noisy (loud).

strét-ta, F.: squeezing (pressing); distress; quantity; strait (defile); want (penury)†: *dar l' ultima —*, kill; *esser alle -te*, be in straitened circumstances. **-taménte**, ADV.: closely; extremely; rigorously. **-terèlla**, *dim.* of *-ta*. **-tézza**, F.: narrowness (straitness); scarcity†: *— di cuore*, anxiety (trouble of mind). **-tíre**, TR.: diminish (make narrower). ‖**-to**, PART. of *stringere*; narrow (strait); intimate; private (secret); stingy; extreme; ADV.: close; meanly; M.: narrow place (defile); distress (trouble): *parente —*, near relative. **-tóia**, F.: band (bandage). **-toíno**, *dim.* of *-toio*. **-tóio**, M.: press (for wine, etc.); ligature (tight bandage).

strettuále†, ADJ.: of the same district.

strettúra [*-tto*], F.: tying tight; narrowness (straitness).

strí-a [L.], F.: (*arch.*) channelling (fluting). **-áre**, TR.: channel (chamfer). **-áto**, PART.: fluted, etc.

stribbiáre† = *strebbiare*.
stribui. .† = *distribui*. .
stric-nèe [L. *strychnus*], F. PL.: strychnus. **-nína**, F.: strychnine.
stri-dere [L.], INTR.: shriek (scream); creak. **-dèvole**†, ADJ.: sharp (shrill). **-dío**, M.: prolonged cry or shriek. **-díre**, INTR.: screech (cry). **strí-do**, M.: cry (shriek). **-dóre**, M.: = *-do*; excessive cold: — *di denti*, chattering (of the teeth). **strí-dulo**, ADJ.: shrill (shrieking); creaking.
stri-gáre [*s-*, *intr*. .], TR.: unravel (disentangle). **-gatóre**, M.: unraveller; explainer.
stríge [L. *strix*, screecher], F.: screech-owl.
strígilo [L. *-gilis*], M.: strigil (scraper).
strígio†, M.: (*bot.*) nightshade.
strí-glia [L. *-gilis*], F.: currycomb. **-gliáre**, TR.: curry.
strígnere = *stringere*.
stril-láre, INTR.: cry (shriek). ‖**-lo** [*stridulo*], M.: scream (cry).
strim-pellaménto, M.: scraping sound. ‖**-pelláre** [*t*. .], TR.: strum or scrape upon (an instrument). **-pelláta**, F.: strumming (scraping). **-pèllo**, M.: instrument scraped; harsh sound.
stri-náre [*ustr*. . (*urere*, burn)], TR.: singe. **-náto**, PART.: singed; very thin.
strín-ga = *aghetto*. **-gáio**, M.: maker or seller of tags and laces.
strin-gáre, TR.: restrain (restrict). **-gáto**, PART.: restrained; concise. ‖**strín-gere** [OGer. *string-*, bind], IRR.§; TR.: bind fast (tie tight); close; press; force (compel); urge; grasp; REFL.: meet together: — *uno tra l' uscio e il muro*, drive one up in a corner (reduce one to straits); — *il sangue*, staunch the blood; — *amicizia*, form a friendship; — *i panni addosso a uno*, force one to a conclusion; *-gersi nelle spalle*, shrug one's shoulders. **-ghétta**, *dim.* of *-ga*. **-giménto**, M.: binding fast. **-gitóre**, M.: one who binds or ties. **-gitúra**, F.: tying. **strín-ta**, **-to** = *strét-ta*, *-to*.

§ Pret. *strín-si*, *-se*; *-sero*. Part. *strétto* (or *strinto*).

strióne†, M.: actor.
strip-páre [*s-*, *trippa*], INTR.: cram or stuff one's belly. **-páta**, F.: cramming (stuffing).
strí-scétta, *dim.* of *-scia*. ‖**strí-scia** [? OFr. *estrece*, narrow thing], F.: band (strip); PL.: kind of macaroni; (*mil.*) long two-edged sword (scimitar); serpent; beam of light: *fucile a* —, rifle-barrelled gun. **-sciaménto**, M.: slipping (gliding). **-sciáre**, TR.: slip (slide); INTR., REFL.: crawl (glide); shave (*graze*). **-sciáta**, F.: slipping; narrow country. **-sciataménte**, ADV.: in a sliding manner. **-scio**, M.: sliding. **-sciòla**, *dim.* of *-scia*. **-sciolína**, *dim.* of *-sciola*. **-scióne**, M.: slider (glider). **-scióni**, ADV.: *camminar* —, shuffle along (crawl).
strito-lábile, ADJ.: friable (brittle). **-laménto**, M.: grinding (pulverization). ‖**-láre** [*s-*, *tritolo*], TR.: crumble (triturate); break; REFL.: be ground; long for. **-latúra**, F.: act of crumbling, etc.
striz-za=limóni, M.: lemon-squeezer. ‖**-záre** [*strictiare* (*strictus*, drawn together)], TR.: squeeze out (express): — *l' occhio*, tip the wink. **-záta**, F.: squeezing. **-zatína**, *dim.* of *-zata*. **-zóne**, M.: strong squeeze.
stròfa [Gr. *-phé*], F.: strophe (stanza). **-fáccia**, **-fétta**, **-fettína**, *disp.* and *dim.* of *-fa*. **-fe** = *-fa*.
strofi-cciáccio†, **-náccio**, **-náceiolo**, M.: dish-clout (dusting-clout). **-naménto**, M.: rubbing (polishing). ‖**-náre** [?], TR.: scour (rub, polish). **-náta**, F.: rubbing (polishing). **-natína**, *dim.* of *-nata*. **-nío**, M.: continual rubbing.
strofúccia, *disp.* of *-fa*.
strogoláre [*s-*, *trogolo*], INTR.: soil one's self while eating.
stro-lag. ., **-log**. . = *astrolog*. .
strom-báre†, TR.: expand (widen, open). **-batúra**†, F.: widening.
strom-bazzáre, TR.: trumpet (announce). **-bazzáta**, F.: sound of a trumpet; signal for battle. ‖**-bettáre** [*s-*, *t*. .], TR.: sound (a trumpet); proclaim or publish with sound of trumpet. **-bettáta**, F.: sound of a trumpet; noise (rumour); complaint. **-bettière**, M.: trumpeter. **-bottío**, M.: trumpeting.
stroménto = *strumento*.
stron-caménto, M.: retrenching (cutting off). ‖**-cáre** [*s-*, *tr*. .], TR.: retrench (cut off, shorten). **-catúra**, F.: retrenchment (cutting off). **-co**, ADJ.: cut off.
stronfiáre [*s-*, *tr*. .], INTR.: rage (grumble, fume).
stronomía = *astronomia*.
strón-zo, ‖**strón-zolo** [OGer. *strunzan*], M.: excrement (dung).
stropic-ciaménto, M.: rubbing (friction). ‖**-ciáre** [?], TR.: rub together; vex (trouble)†; strike against†. **-ciáta**, F.: friction (rubbing). **-ciatèlla**, *dim.* of *-ciata*. **-ciatúra**, F.: rubbing; trouble (fatigue). **stropíc-cio**, **-cío**, M.: continual rubbing. **-cióna**, F., **-cióne**, M.: bigot (hypocrite).
stroppi. . = *storpi*. .
stroppelatúra†, F.: block (strop).
stròscia [*s-*, *t*. .], F.: splash; roar; stream. **-sciáre**, INTR.: splash down;

roar. **strò-scio**, M.: splash; falling noise.
stròz-za [OGer. *drozâ*], F.: throat (gullet). **-zaménto**, M.: strangling (suffocation). **-záre**, TR.: strangle (choke). **-záto**, PART.: choked, etc.; M.: narrow-necked vase (demijohn). **-zatóio**, ADJ.: choking; with a narrow neck†. **-zatúra**, F.: strangling; narrowness. **-zière**†, M.: falconer. **-zíno**, M.: kind of a trap; (*fig.*) usurer.
strub-biáre [cf. *trebbiare*], TR.: consume (devour). **strúb-bio**, M.: consumption. **-bióne**, M.: big eater.
strúcio = *trucio*.
strúf-fo†, **-folo**†, M.: heap of shreds.
strúg-gere [L. *destruere*, destroy], IRR.§; TR.: dissolve (melt); consume; have a great desire for; destroy†; REFL.: waste (pine) away. **-gibúco**, M.: tedious affair. **-gi-cuòre**, M.: melting of the heart. **-giménto**, M.: dissolving (melting); destruction; disquiet; passion (desire). **-gitóre**, M., **-gitríce**, F.: destroyer; consumer.

§ Pret. *strús-si*, *-se*; *-sero*. Part. *strútto*.

struíre = *istruire*.
strúma†, F.: scrofula (king's evil).
strumen-táccio, *disp.* of *-to*. **-táio**†, M.: musical-instrument maker. **-tále**, ADJ.: instrumental. **-talménte**, ADV.: instrumentally. **-táre**, TR.: compose (the instrumental music of an opera, etc.). **-tíno**, *dim.* of *-to*. ||**strumén-to** [*istr*..], M.: instrument; implement (tool); musical instrument; deed; (*fig.*) wretched subject.
strupáre = *stuprare*.
struscíáre [? *strisciare*], TR.: consume (spoil; damage); (*fig.*) = *strisciare*.
strút-ta [*struggere*], F.: melting (liquefaction). **-to**, PART.: melted; M.: lard.
struttúra [L. *structura* (*struere*, build)], F.: structure; construction.
struzióne, F.: destruction.
strúz-zo [Gr. *strouthíon*, young sparrow], **-zolo**†, M.: OSTRICH; (*fig.*) great feeder.
stuc-caménto, M.: covering with stucco. ||**-cáre** [*-co*], TR.: stop or do over with stucco; surfeit (disgust). **-catóre**, M.: plasterer. **-catúra**, F.: plastering. **-chènte** = *-chevole*. **-chevolággine**, F.: tediousness; disgust. **-chevoláre**†, TR.: annoy; disgust; tire. **-chévolo**, ADJ.: tedious (tiresome); loathsome. **-chevolézza**, F.: tediousness; disgust; surfeit. **-chevolménte**, ADV.: tediously; disgustingly; tiresomely. **-chináio**, M.: maker or seller of stucco figures. **-chíno**, M.: small stucco figure.
stúccio†, M.: small case (sheath).
stúc-co [OGer. *-chi*, crust], M.: stucco; grumbler; ADJ.: surfeited (satiated); tired. **-cóso**, ADJ.: very tiresome; distasteful.
stu-dènte, PART.: studious; student. **-diábile**, ADJ.: fit to be studied. **-diacchiáre**, INTR.: study unwillingly. **-diaménto**, M.: study; care (diligence). ||**-diáre** [L. *-dere*, strive], TR.: study; attend to (reflect upon); hasten; urge†; cultivate (till)†; REFL.: endeavour (strive). **-diáto**, PART.: studied, etc.; M.: composition; lucubration. **-diatóre**, M.: student. **-dievolménte**, ADV.: on purpose (precisely). **stú-dio**, M.: study; industry (diligence); painting (model); study-hall; office; university (school): *a bello* —, on purpose (wilfully). **-diolíno**, *dim.* of *-diolo*. **-diòlo**, *dim.* of *-dio*. **-diosaménte**, ADV.: studiously (diligently). **-dióso**, ADJ.: studious (industrious); quick (swift)†; careful†.
stuel-láre, TR.: stop with tow. ||**stuèllo** [?], M.: dossil (pledget, lint).
stú-fa [? OGer. *-pâ*], F.: stove; a heated room; (*chem.*) stove; fomentation†; hot-bath†. **-faiòlo**†, M.: master or keeper of a bath; maker or seller of stoves. **-fáre**, TR.: stew slowly; annoy (weary); INTR.: take a hot-bath†. **-fáto**, PART.: stewed; annoyed, etc.; M.: stewed meat (ragout). **-fatúra**, F.: stewing (steaming). **-fo**, ADJ.: wearied; disgusted.
stultízia = *stoltizia*.
stummi.., **stumi**.. = *schism*..
stuoi.. = *stoi*..
stuòlo [Gr. *stólos*, expedition], M.: troop (company, band); quantity.
stuo-nánte†, ADJ.: out of tune (dissonant). **-náre**†, INTR.: be or sing out of tune.
stu-pefáre [L. *-pe-facere*], TR.: stupefy (amaze); INTR.: become stupid; be surprised at. **-pefattívo**, ADJ.: stupefactive. **-pefátto**, PART.: stupefied, etc. **-pefazióne**, F.: stupefaction. **-pendaménte**, ADV.: stupendously. **-pèndo**, ADJ.: prodigious (wonderful); excellent (exquisite). **-pidáccio**, ADJ.: *disp.* of *-pido*; M.: very stupid fellow. **-pidézza**, F.: stupidity (folly). **-pidíre**, TR.: amaze (astonish); INTR.: grow stupid; be astonished. **-pidità**, F.: stupidity. **stú-pido**, ADJ.: amazed; dull (stupid); benumbed. **-píre**, INTR.: be astonished or amazed. **-póre**, M.: stupor.
stu-práre, TR.: stuprate (depucelate). **-pratóre**, M.: ravisher (violator). ||**stúpro** [L. *-prum*, defilement], M.: depucelation (rape).
stú-ra, F.: act of uncorking; waste. ||**-ráre** [*s-*, *t*..], TR.: uncork (unstop).
stur-baménto, M., **-bánza**, F.: disturbance (disorder, trouble). **-báre**, TR.:

disturb, vex. **-batóre**, M.: troubler. **-bazióne**†, F., **-bo**, M.: trouble (annoyance).
stutáre†, TR.: deaden (extinguish).
stúzia = *astuzia*.
stúzio†, M.: wild cabbage.
stuzzi-ca=dènti, M.: toothpick. **-caménto**, M.: stirring; irritation. ‖**-cáre** [?], TR.: stir a little (move); stir up (incite): — *i denti*, pick the teeth; (*fig.*) eat something to arouse the appetite. **-catóio**, M.: prick (goad); poker. **-catóre**, **-chíno**, M.: instigator; stirrer. **-corécchi** [*-co-orecchi*], M.: ear-pick.
su [L. *sub*], PREP.: on (upon); about; towards; near; ADV.: up; above; before; very far: — *e giù*, up and down; *venir* —, come up (thrive); — —, cheer up!
sua-dére†, TR.: persuade. **-dévole**†, ADJ.: persuasive. **-do**†, ADJ.: persuasory.
su=accennáto, ADJ.: above-mentioned.
sua-síbile† [*-dere*], ADJ.: persuasible. **-sióne**†, F.: persuasion. **-sívo**†, ADJ.: persuasive. **-so**†, PART.: (*poet.*) persuaded.
suav.. = *soav*..
sub- [L., under], PREP.: **-ácido**, ADJ.: subacid (slightly sour). **-álbido**†, ADJ.: whitish. **-alternáre**†, TR.: make subordinate. **-alternatívo**†, ADJ.: that may be subordinate. **-alternáto**†, **-altèrno**†, ADJ.: subaltern (subordinate). **-astáre**†, TR.: sell by auction. **-astazióne**†, F.: selling by auction. **-avvisáre**†, TR.: advise secretly.
súb-bia [L. *-ula*, awl], F.: chisel. **-biáre**, TR.: carve (chisel). **-biétta**, *dim.* of *-bia*.
subbiètto [L. *-jectus*], M.: subject; object.
subbilláre = *sobillare*.
súbbio [L. *subulum*], M.: weaver's beam; tree-trunk.
subbiss.. = *subiss*..
sub- [L., under]: =**bollíre**†, TR.: parboil (boil slowly). **-búglio** [*-bollire*], M.: confusion (of persons). =**cutáneo**, ADJ.: subcutaneous. **súb=dolo** [L. *-dolus*], ADJ.: deceitful (somewhat crafty). **súb=duplo** = *sud-duplo*. **-entráre**, TR.: succeed (come after). **-iètto** = *-bietto*. **-illaménto**†, M.: act of instigating; subornation. **-illáre**†, TR.: draw aside; suborn. **-intèndere** = *sottintendere*. =**íre**, TR.: bear (support); meet with. **-issáre**, TR.: overthrow; destroy; INTR.: fall down; perish. **-isso** [*sub-*, *abisso*], M.: ruin (destruction); great quantity; prodigy. **-itaménte**, **-itaneaménte**, ADV.: suddenly. **-itaneità**, F.: promptitude (quickness). **-itáneo**, **-itáno**†, ADJ.: sudden (subitaneous). **-itánza**†, **-itézza**†, F.: suddenness; quickness. **súbito** [L. *-itus* (*-ire*, go beneath = steal on)], ADJ.: sudden; hasty (irritable); ADV.: suddenly. **-itosaménte**, ADV.: suddenly (unawares). **-iugáre**† = *soggiogare*. **-iuntívo**, M.: subjunctive (mood). **-limaménto**, M.: sublimation (promotion). **-limáre** [L.], TR.: exalt (advance, raise); sublimate; praise†. **-limatòrio**, ADJ.: of a vase used in sublimation. **-limazióne**, F.: sublimation; preferment (advancement). **-líme** [L. *-limis*], ADJ.: sublime (lofty, high). **-limeménte**, ADV.: sublimely; nobly. **-limità**, F.: sublimity (loftiness). **-límo**† = *-lime*. **-linguále**†, ADJ.: sublingual. =**lunáre**, ADJ.: sublunary. =**odoráre** [*odore*], TR.: smell out (learn craftily); INTR.: smell slightly. **-ordinaménto**, M.: subordination. =**ordináre**, TR.: subordinate; INTR.: be subordinate or dependent upon. **-ordinataménte**, ADV.: subordinately. **-ordináto**, ADJ.: subordinate. **-ordinazióne**, F.: subordination (dependence). **-ornáre** [L.], TR.: suborn (instigate, bribe). **-ornatóre**, M.: suborner (inducer). **-ornazióne**, F.: subornation; corruption. **-úglio** = *-buglio*. **-urbáno** [L. *-urbanus*], ADJ.: suburban. **-urbicário**, ADJ.: suburbicarian. =**úrbio** [L. *-urbium* (*urbs*, city)], M.: suburb.
suc- [L. for *sub*, 'under,' bef. *c*], PREP.:
succe-dáneo [L. *-daneus*], ADJ.: succedaneous; M.: equivalent. **-dènte**, PART.: subsequent (succeeding). ‖**succè-dere** [L. (*sub*, *cedere*, go)], IRR. (cf. *concedere*); INTR.: succeed (follow); inherit; happen (come to pass). **-dévole**, ADJ.: succeeding (subsequent). **-devolménte**, ADV.: successively. **-diménto**, M.: success; issue; adventure. **-ditóre**, M., **-ditríce**, F.: succeeder; successor. **-dúto**, PART.: succeeded, etc.
succenerìccio†, ADJ.: baked under the ashes.
succes-sióne [L. *-sio*], F.: succession (event, issue); inheritance. **-sivaménte**, ADV.: successively. **-sívo**, ADJ.: successive (subsequent); ADV.: successively. **succès-so**, M.: success (event, issue). **-sòra**, F., **-sóre**, M.: successor. **-sòrio**, ADJ.: successory.
suc-chiaménto, M.: sucking (attraction). ‖**-chiáre** [L. *-ulare*], TR.: suck; bore with a gimlet (pierce). **-chiatóio**, M.: bee's sucker. **-chiellaménto**, M.: act of boring or piercing. **-chielláre**, TR.: bore with a wimble: — *le carte*, unfold maps slowly. **-chiellétto**, *dim.* of *-chiello*. **-chiellináio**, M.: maker or seller of gimlets, wimbles, etc. **-chiellináre**, TR.: bore often (pierce frequently). **-chièllo**, M.: wimble (small gimlet

or augur). **súc-chio**, M.: sap (juice); augur (gimlet): (*fig.*) *mettere uno in* —, cause one to desire something. **-chióne**, M.: bud; young shoot. **-ciabeóne†**, M.: drunkard. **-cia=méle**, M.: honeysuckle. **-ciaménto**, M.: sucking (suction). **-cia=minèstre**, M.: worthless fellow. **-ciáre**, TR.: suck; imbibe; swallow (pocket). **-cia=sángue**, M.: blood-sucker (leech). **-ciatóre**, M., **-ciatríce**, F.: sucker.

succídere [L.], TR.: cut from below; cut off (lop off)†.

suc=cígnere†, **=cíngere**, IRR.; TR.: tuck up (gird up).

súccino [L. *-cinum*], M.: amber.

suc-cintaménte, ADV.: succinctly. **-cintézza**, F.: succinctness. ‖**-cínto** [L. *-cinctus* (*cingere*, gird)], ADJ.: tucked up; succinct (short).

súc-cio [*-chiare*], M.: sucking (draught); red spot (left by a kiss): *in un* —, in a moment. **-ciòla**, F.: boiled chestnut: *andarsene in broda di* —, be overcome with joy. **-cióne**, M.: young shoot (bud).

succíso, PART. of *-cidere;* cut under; lopped off; taken away.

succo. . = *sugo. .*

súccubo [L. *-bare* (lie)], M.: succubus (a demon; nightmare).

succulènto [L. *-tus*], ADJ.: succulent.

succursále [L. *-cursus* (*-currere*, run under, relieve)], ADJ.: aiding (assisting); succursal; F.: chapel of ease; (*com.*) branch.

suc=cutáneo, ADJ.: subcutaneous.

sucid. . = *sudic. .*

súco† = *sugo.*

sud [OGer.], M.: south.

sudacchiáre, *dim.* of *sudare.*

su-dámini, M., PL.: blotches or breakings out (from heat). ‖**-dáre** [L.], INTR.: SWEAT (perspire); TR.: gain with sweat. **-dário**, M.: holy handkerchief; towel†. **-dáta**, F.: sweating. **-dáto**, PART.: perspired; done. **-datíccio**, *dim.* of *-dato.* **-datína**, *dim.* of *-data.* **-datòrio**, ADJ.: sudorific; M.: sudatorium (sweating-room); sweating-bath.

sud- = *sub-:* **-decanáto**, M.: subdiaconate. **=decáno**, M.: subdeacon (subdean). **=delegáre**, TR.: subdelegate. **-delegazióne**, F.: subdelegation. **=détto**, ADJ.: above-said (afore-mentioned). **-diaconáto**, M.: order of sub-deacon. **=diácono**, M.: sub-deacon. **=distínguere**, IRR.; TR.: subdistinguish. **-distinzióne**, F.: subdistinction. **=ditánza**, F.: subjection (submission). **=dito** [L. *subditus* (*dare*, put)], ADJ.: subject (bound, liable); M.: vassal. **=dividere** [*subd. .*], IRR.; TR.: subdivide. **-divisíbile**, ADJ.: that can be subdivided. **-divisióne**, F.: subdivision. **-divíso**, PART.: subdivided. **-'duplo**, ADJ.: subduplicate.

su-diceria, F.: filthiness (dirtiness). **-diciaménte**, ADV.: nastily. **-díccio**, ADJ.: somewhat dirty. **sú-dicio** [mutil. for L. *sucidus*, juicy], ADJ.: nasty (filthy, greasy). **-dicióne**, *aug.* of *-dicio.* **-diciòtto**, ADJ.: rather dirty. **-diciúme**, M.: nastiness (filthiness).

sudó-re [L. *-r*], M.: sweat; labour (toil); reward. **-rétto**, *dim.* of *-re.* **-rífero**, ADJ.: sudorific. **-rífico**, pl. **—ci** = *-rifero.* **-ríno**, *dim.* of *-re.*

suf- [L., for *sub*, 'under,' bef. *f*]: **-fétto** [L. *-fectus*], ADJ.: substituted. **-fic(i)ènte** [L. *-ficiens*], ADJ.: sufficient; capable (qualified for). **-fic(i)entemènte**, ADV.: sufficiently. **-ficientézza†**, **-fic(i)ènza**, F.: sufficiency; ability (capacity); plenty. **=físso** [*-fixus* (*-figere*, fix on)], M.: suffix. **-fizien. .†** = *-ficien. .* **-foca. .†** = *soffoca. .* **-fólcere†**, **-fólgere†**, IRR.; TR.: sustain (prop up); put upon. **-fólto†**, PART.: sustained, etc. **=formatívo**, ADJ.: subordinately formative. **-fragáneo**, ADJ.: suffragan. **-fragáre** [L. *-fragari*], INTR.: be useful to; TR.: help; vote for. **-frágio** [L. *-fragium* (*frangere*, BREAK)], M.: suffrage (vote); relief. **=frútice**, M.: shrub. **-fumicaménto** = *-fumicazione.* **=fumicáre**, TR.: suffumigate. **-fumicazióne**, F.: suffumigation. **-fumigáre** = *-fumicare.* **-fumígio**, M.: suffumigation. **-fusióne**, F.: suffusion; cataract. **=fúso**, ADJ.: sprinkled (suffused).

sufola. . = *zufola. .*

sugáre [*-go*], TR.: suck up (absorb); (*agr.*) manure; blot: *carta sugante*, blotting paper.

sugátto [L. *subactum*], M.: soft leather (for straps, etc.).

sug-gellaménto, M.: sealing (wafering). ‖**-gelláre** [L. *-gillare*], TR.: seal; stop; imprint; mark with a hot iron†. **-gèllo**, M.: seal; print (mark).

súggere = *succhiare.*

sugge-riménto, M.: suggestion. ‖**-geríre** [L. *-gerere* (*sub*, under, *gerere*, carry)], TR.: suggest (insinuate). **-geritóra**, F., **-geritóre**, M., **-geritríce**, F.: suggester; (*theat.*) prompter. **-gestióne**, F.: suggestion; prompting. **-gestivaménte**, ADV.: suggestively (artfully). **-gestívo**, ADJ.: suggestive (insidious).

sug-gett. . = *soggett. .* **-gez. .** = *soggez. .*

suggiugáre = *soggiogare.*

súghe-ra, F.: cf. *-ro.* **-ráre**, TR.: streak (with cork). **-ráto**, PART.: corked

(furnished with cork); made of cork. **-rèlla**, F.: (*bot.*) kind of false cork. **-réta**, F., **-réto**, M.: wood of cork-tree. ‖**súghe-ro** [L. *suber*], M.: cork; cork-tree.
súgli = *su gli*.
sugliárdo†, ADJ.: dirty (filthy).
sú-gna [L. *axungia*, stuff for anointing], F.: swine's grease (lard). **-gnáccia**, *disp.* of *-gna*. **-gnóso**, ADJ.: fat (greasy).
sú-go [L. *-cus*], M.: sap (juice); gravy; manure; substance (quintessence). **-gosaménte**, ADV.: in a juicy manner. **-gosità**, F.: moisture (juice). **-góso**, ADJ.: juicy (full of juice).
sugumèra†, F.: ceremony (ostentation).
súi = *su i*.
sui-cída [L. *-cidium* (*cædere*) killing of one's self], M.: self-murderer (suicide). **-cídio**, M.: suicide (self-murder).
suíno [L. *-nus* (*sus*, hog)], ADJ.: swinish.
sul = *su il*.
sulfúreo [L. *-phureus*], ADJ.: sulphureous.
súlla = *su la*.
súllo = *su lo*.
sul-logáre [*sub-*, *luogo*], TR.: underlease. **-lunáre**†, ADJ.: sublunary.
sul-tána, F.: sultaness. **-taníno**, M.: sultanine (Turkish coin). ‖**-táno** [l. L. *-tanus*], M.: sultan.
sumministra. . = *somministra*. .
summómolo†, M.: blow under the chin.
summormoráre†, TR.: murmur low (hum).
sún-to [L. *sumptum* (*sumere*, take up)], M.: abridgment (abstract, epitome). **-tuária** [L. *sumptuaria*], ADJ.: sumptuary. **-tuóso** = *sontuoso*.
súo (pl. *suoi*, *sue*), poet. *sui* [L. *suus*], PRON. POSS.: his, her, its; M.: his property; PL.: his or her relations or friends; misfortunes: *far delle sue*, play tricks, play the fool.
suòcer-a, **-o** = *socer-a*, *-o*.
suòlo = *solo*.
suo-náre = *sonare*. ‖**suò-no** [L. *sonus*], M.: sound (noise); instrument to play upon; music (tune)†; fame (renown)†.
suòra [L. *soror*, sister], F.: nun; sister†.
super- [L.], PREF.: over; above; upon; beyond. **-ábile**, ADJ.: superable; surmountable. **-abilità**, F.: surmounting. **-aménto**, M.: victory (conquest). **-áre** [L. *-are* (*super*, above), be above], TR.: surmount (overcome); surpass. **-atóre**†, M.: conqueror (subduer). **-báccio**, *disp.* of *-bo*. **-baménte**, ADV.: haughtily (proudly); nobly. **-bétto**, *dim.* of *-bo*. **supèr-bia** [L.], F.: pride (arrogance). **-biaménte**† = *-bamente*. **-biáre**† = *-bire*. **-biènte**†, ADJ.: haughty (proud). **-biosaménte**, ADV.: haughtily. **superbio**†, **-bióso** = *-bo*. **-bíre**, INTR.: grow proud or haughty. **-biúzza**, F.: pride. **supèr-bo** [L. *-bus*], ADJ.: arrogant (proud); magnificent (sumptuous); (*poet.*) rough: *muscolo* —, superciliary muscle. **-bóne**, *aug.* of *-bo*. **-búzzo**, *dim.* of *-bo*. **-chi**. . = *soperchi*. . **-cíglio**†, M.: eye-brow. **-eminènte**†, ADJ.: supereminent. **-erogazióne**†, F.: supererogation (overdoing). **-fetazióne** [L. *-fetare* (f(o)etus)], F.: superfetation. **-fície** = *-ficie*. **-ficétta**, *dim.* of *-fice*. **-ficiále**, ADJ.: superficial (slight); imperfect. **-ficialità**, F.: superficiality. **-ficialménte**, ADV.: superficially; outwardly. **-fície** [L. *-ficies*], F.: superficies (surface). **-fluaménte**, ADV.: superfluously. **-fluità**, F.: superfluity (profusion). **supèr-fluo** [L. *-fluus* (*-fluere*, run over)], ADJ.: superfluous; M.: that which is superfluous.
súper-i, M. PL.: supernal gods. **-infúso**†, PART.: poured or infused upon. **-ióra**, F.: superior; mother-superior. **-ioráto**, M.: office and grade of a superior. **-ióre** [L. *-ior*], ADJ.: superior (upper); preceding†; M.: better (conqueror); upper part (of a country); chief. **-iorità**, F.: superiority (preëminence). **-iorménte**, ADV.: in a superior manner. **-lativaménte**, ADV.: superlatively. **-latívo** [L. *-lativus*], ADJ.: superlative (highest); M.: superlative. **-lazióne**, F.: exaggeration (amplification); hyperbole†. **-nále**†, ADJ.: supernal; divine. **-nalménte**†, ADV.: supernally; divinely. **supèr-no** [L. *-nus*], ADJ.: supernal (superior); divine. **súper-o**, ADJ.: (*poet.*) upper (higher); celestial. **supèr-stite** [L. *-stes*], ADJ.: surviving (outliving). **-stizióne** [L. *-stitio*], F.: superstition. **-stiziosaménte**, ADV.: superstitiously. **-stiziosità**, F.: superstitiousness. **-stizióso**, ADJ.: superstitious; overnice. **-umerále** [L. *humerale*], M.: kind of sacerdotal cloak. **-vacáneo**†, ADJ.: superfluous (useless).
supi-naménte, ADV.: supinely. **-náre**†, REFL.: lie on one's back. **-nazióne**, F.: supination. ‖**supí-no** [L. *-nus*], ADJ.: supine (on one's back); idle (negligent); ADV.: upside down; M.: (*gram.*) supine.
suppállido†, ADJ.: palish (somewhat pale).
suppedáneo [L. *-neum*], M.: footstool.
suppellèttile [L. *-llectilis*], F.: household goods (furniture); stores.
supplantáre [L.], see *soppiantare*.
sup-pleménto [L. *-plementum*], M.: supplement. **-plènza**, F.: supplying. **-pletívo**, **-pletòrio**, ADJ.: suppletory (supplementary).
súppli-ca, F.: petition (memorial). **-cábile**, ADJ.: worthy of being supplicated.

-cánte, ADJ.: supplicating; M.: supplicant (petitioner). **-canteménte**, ADV.: with supplication. ‖**-cáre** [L.], TR.: supplicate (entreat). **-catóre**, M., **-catríce**, F.: supplicant (prayer). **-catòrio**, ADJ.: supplicatory. **-cazióne**, F.: supplication (petition). **súppli-ce** [L. *-plex* (*sub, plicare*), bending down], ADJ.: supplicant (entreating). **-ceménte**, ADV.: humbly (with entreaty). **-chévole**, ADJ.: supplicant. **-chevolménte**, ADV.: in an entreating way.

supplícto†, M.: punishment; torment.

sup-pliménto = *-plemento*. ‖**-plíre** [L. *-plere*, fill up], TR.: supply; substitute: — *a un ufficio*, fill an office.

supplízio [L. *-plicium*, bending down], M.: punishment; penalty; torment (torture).

sup-poníbile, ADJ.: supposable (imaginable). ‖**-pórre** [L. *-ponere*, place beneath], IRR.; TR.: suppose; substitute; place under†. **-positivaménte**, ADV.: supposedly. **-positívo**, ADJ.: suppositive (supposed). **-positiziaménte**, ADV.: supposititiously. **-positízio**, ADJ.: supposititious. **-pòsito**† = *-posto*. **-positòrio** = *-posta*. **-posizióne**, F.: supposition. **-pósta**, F.: (*med.*) suppository. **-pósto**, PART.: supposed; M.: supposition.

suppregáre†, TR.: supplicate.

sup-press. . = *soppress*. . **-prímere** = *sopprimere*.

suppu-rábile, ADJ.: suppurative. **-raménto** = *-razione*. ‖**-ráre** [L. *-rare* (*sub, pus*)], INTR.: suppurate. **-ratívo**, ADJ.: suppurative. **-razióne**, F.: suppuration.

supputá-re†, TR.: suppute (calculate). **-zióne**†, F.: supputation (reckoning).

supre-maménte, ADV.: supremely. **-mazía**, F.: supremacy. **-mità**, F.: superiority (supreme authority). ‖**suprè-mo** [L. *-mus*], ADJ.: supreme (highest); extreme (last).

suprestiz. . = *superstiz*. .

sur = *su*.

surále†, ADJ.: sural.

surerogazióne†, F.: supererogation.

surg. . † = *sorg*. .

surressióne†, F.: resurrection.

surre-tiziaménte, ADV.: surreptitiously (fraudulently). ‖**-tízio** [L. *-reptitius* (*sub-repere*, creep along)], ADJ.: surreptitious. **-zióne**†, F.: resurrection.

surro-gábile, ADJ.: that can be surrogated. **-gaménto** = *-gazione*. ‖**-gáre** [L.], TR.: surrogate (depute, substitute). **-gazióne**, F.: surrogation (substitution).

súrto†, PART. of *surgere*; see *sorgere*.

su-scettíbile [L. *-sceptibilis*], ADJ.: susceptible; irascible. **-scettibilità**, F.: susceptibility. **-scettívo**, ADJ.: susceptive. **-scezióne**†, F.: susception (act of taking).

susci-taménto, M.: suscitation; insurrection. ‖**-táre** [L. *-tare*, lift or stir up], TR.: (*poet.*) resuscitate (revive); excite (stir up); REFL.: return to life. **-tatóre**, M.: resuscitator (reviver); instigator.

susí-na [?], F.: plum. **-nétta**, **-nína**, *dim.* of *-na*. **susí-no**, M.: plum-tree.

súso† = *su*, *sopra*.

su-sorniáre†, INTR.: make a noise; whisper (murmur). **-sornióne**†, M.: sullen or reserved man. **-sórno**†, M.: suffumigation; knock on the head.

sus-pens. . † = *sospens*. . **-pes**. . = *sospes*. .

sus-picáre†, TR.: suspect (mistrust). **-pizióne**†, F.: suspicion (doubt).

susse-cutivaménte, ADV.: subsequently. ‖**-cutívo** [L. *sub-secutus* (*-sequi*)], ADJ.: subsequent (following). **-guènte**, **-quènte**, ADJ.: subsequent (consecutive). **-quenteménte**, ADV.: subsequently; in train. **-quènza**, F.: subsequence (consequence); issue.

sússi† [?], M.: sort of game.

sussi-dènza†, F.: subsidence; sediment (dregs); deposition of pus in a bag. **-diáre**, TR.: give help to (assist). **-diariaménte**, ADV.: subsidiarily. **-diário**, ADJ.: subsidiary. **-diatóre**, M.: auxiliary (helper). ‖**sussí-dio** [L. *subsidium*, auxiliary corps; (*fig.*) aid], M.: subsidy (assistance, help); (*mil.*) reserve; suggestion (insinuation)†.

sussiègo [Sp. *sosiego*], M.: gravity (seriousness).

sus-sistènte, ADJ.: subsistent; stable; self-existent. **-sistènza**, F.: subsistence; sustenance; essence (nature). ‖**-sístere** [L. *subs*. .], IRR. (cf. *assistere*); INTR.: subsist; exist (sustain one's self).

sussoláno†, M.: east wind.

sus-sultáre [L.], INTR.: give a start or jump. **-súlto**, M.: start (jump); (*med.*) palpitation. **-sultòrio**, ADJ.: starting; palpitating.

sussur-ráre [L. *susurro*, low gentle noise], TR., INTR.: whisper (murmur). **-ráto**, PART.: whispered, etc.; M.: murmur; slander. **-razióne**†, F.: susurration (whispering). **-río**, M.: prolonged whisper; confused noise. **-róne**, M.: grumbler; backbiter (slanderer).

sústa [?], F.: spring; packing cord†: *esser, entrar in* —, be in, or commence, motion.

sus-tánte† (*in*), ADV.: on foot (standing). **-tan**. . † = *sostan*. . **-ten**. . † = *sosten*. . **-titu**. . † = *sostitu*. .

susurr.. = *susurr..*
sutter-fúgere [L. *subter..*], INTR.: avoid (shun). **-fúgio,** M.: subterfuge (evasion).
suttrárre† = *sottrarre.*
sutúra [L.], F.: suture; seam.
suver..† = *sugher..*
suv-vers† = *sovvers..* **-vert..†** = *sovvert..*
sú=vvi, ADV.: above it (there above); cf. *su, sopra.*
sus-sácchera, F.: oxycrate (composition of sour milk, sugar, etc.)†; jujube. **-şaménto,** M.: drying (airing); absorbing. ‖**-şáre** [*succiare*], TR, INTR.: dry up; absorb. **-şáto,** PART.: dried up, etc. **-şatóre,** M.: drier. **-şo** = *-zato.*
şva-gaménto, M.: distraction (diversion). ‖**-gáre** [*s-, v..*], TR.: divert from (distract); interrupt; REFL.: unbend one's mind (rest); amuse one's self. **-gatézza,** F.: distraction. **-gatívo,** ADJ.: serving to recreate, etc. **-go,** M.: act of distracting. **-goláre,** TR.: *dim. freq.* of *-gare;* go wandering about.
şvali-giaménto, M.: act of unpacking. ‖**-giáre** [*s-, valigia*], TR.: take out of a valise (unpack); rob (steal).
şvalo-ríre†, INTR.: lose courage; grow weak. **-ríto†,** PART.: weak.
şvampáre [*s-, vampa*], INTR.: go out (be extinguished); end in nothing.
şvanáre†, TR.: pluck or cleanse (felt).
şva-niménto, M.: fading away; staleness. **-níre,** INTR.: disappear (vanish); come to nothing; grow vain; fade away; become vapid; REFL.: humble or debase one's self. **-nizióne†,** F.: act of disappearing, etc. ‖**şvá-no** [*s-, v..*], M.: void, hollow room.
şvantág-gio [*s-, v..*], M.: disadvantage (loss). **-giosaménte,** ADV.: disadvantageously. **-gióso,** ADJ.: disadvantageous.
şvapo-rábile, ADJ.: evaporable. **-raménto,** M.: evaporation. ‖**-ráre** [*s-, v..*], INTR.: evaporate (send forth vapours); vent one's passion; dry up; vanish. **-razióne,** F., **şvapó-re†,** M.: evaporation.
şva-riaménto, M.: diversity (variety); frenzy (wrath, dotage)†. **-riáre,** TR.: vary (change); distract; INTR.†: dissent (disagree). **-riataménte,** ADV.: differently (separately). **-riáto,** PART.: variegated (diversified): — *di mente†,* mad (distracted). ‖**şvá-rio** [*s-, v..*], M.: diversity (difference, variance); ADJ.: variegated; different. **-rióne,** M.: great blunder.
şvec-chiáre [*s-, vecchio*], TR.: renew (refresh, reform). **-chiatúra,** F.: renewing, etc.

şve-gghi.. = *svegli..* **-glia,** F.: alarm; alarm-clock; kind of pipe (to play upon); wooden-horse (for torture). **-gliaménto,** M.: awaking. ‖**-gliáre** [*s-, v..*], TR.: awake (rouse up); excite (encourage); begin to play upon (a mus. instrument); REFL.: awake; become attentive. **-gliaríno,** M.: thing that reminds one of a duty; = *-glia.* **-gliáta,** F.: act of awaking, etc. **-gliatézza,** F.: sagacity (vivacity). **-gliáto,** PART.: awaked, etc.; lively (sprightly); clever. **-gliatóio,** M.: something able to awake. **-gliatóre,** M.: awaker (arouser); boots.
şvègliere = *svellere.*
şvegliévole†, ADJ.: easily awaked.
şvegliménto† = *svellimento.*
şve-laménto, M.: unveiling (revealing). ‖**-láre** [*s-, v..*], TR.: unveil (reveal); REFL.: make one's self known; open one's mind to. **-lataménte,** ADV.: openly.
şvele-náre†, TR.: take away the poison from; REFL.: vent one's spite. ‖**-níre** [*s-, inv..*], TR.: appease (allay, mitigate).
şvèl-lere [*s-, L. v..*], **-gere†,** IRR.§; TR.: tear up (uproot). **-liménto†,** M.: tearing up. **-tézza,** F.: dexterity (nimbleness). **-tíre,** TR.: make lithe or agile; REFL.: be nimble. **şvèl-to,** PART.: uprooted, etc.; easy; slender; nimble (active, agile); ready; quick; sharp.

§ Ind.: Pres. *svèl-go, -gi* (or *-li*), *-ge* (or *-le*); *-giámo, -gite, -gono.* Pret. *svèl-si, -se; -sero.* Part. *svèlto.*

şve-naménto, M.: cutting or rupture of a vein. ‖**-náre** [*s-, vena*], TR.: cut or open (a vein); chisel (metal statues). **-natóio,** M.: fine chisel. **-natúra,** F.: small nitch in the edge of a knife.
şvenenáre† = *svelenare.*
şve-nevolággine = *-nevolezza.* **-névole,** ADJ.: affected. **-nevolézza,** F.: affectation. **-nevolménte,** ADV.: affectedly. **-nevolóne,** *aug.* of *-nevole.*
şvè-nia, F.: caresses (flatteries). **-niménto,** M.: fainting-fit (swoon). ‖**-níre** [*s-, vanire,* by false etym. from *venire*], IRR. (cf. *venire*); INTR.: faint (swoon away).
şven-táre [*s-, avventare*], TR.: counteract the explosion of (frustrate, baffle); blow out; = †*-tolare:* — *una mina,* countermine; — *un disegno,* baffle a design; — *grano,* winnow corn; — *una vena,* open a vein (let blood). **-táto,** PART.: vent, etc.; rash (foolish, lightheaded). **-tatézza,** F.: vent. **-tolaménto,** M.: fanning; flapping. **-toláre,** TR.: spread forth (give to the gale); winnow (fan); flout (flap); INTR.: blow; flutter; REFL.: fan one's self; flap in the

air. **-tolío**, M.: continual blowing, winnowing, flapping, etc.

ṣven-tráre [*s-*, *ventre*], TR.: disembowel (gut); run through the belly; INTR.†: eat and drink too much. **-tráta**, F.: disembowelling; bellyful. **-tráto**, PART.: disembowelled, etc.; insatiable. **-trató-re**, M.: disemboweller.

ṣventú-ra [*s-*, *v.* .], F.: ill-fortune (bad luck). **-rataménte**, ADV.: unfortunately. **-ráto**, ADJ.: unfortunate (unhappy). **-róso**, ADJ.: unlucky (wretched).

ṣvenúto, PART. of *svenire*; fainted.

ṣverdíre [*s-*, *verde*], INTR.: lose its green colour (dry up).

ṣverghеggiáre†, TR.: whip (lash).

ṣvergi-naménto, M.: defloration. ‖**-náre** [*s-*, *vergine*], TR.: deflower (depucelate); begin to use. **-natóre**, M.: ravisher.

ṣvergo-gnaménto, M., **-gnánza**, F.: impudence (shamelessness). ‖**-gnáre** [*s-*, *v.* .], TR.: dishonour (shame); deflower†; INTR.†: be ashamed. **-gnatággine** = *-gnatezza*. **-gnataménte**, ADV.: impudently (shamelessly). **-gnatézza**, F.: effrontery (insolence). **-gnáto**, PART.: dishonoured, etc.; impudent.

ṣver-naménto, M.: wintering; chirping†. ‖**-náre** [*s-*, *v.* .], INTR.: winter (pass the winter); be past winter; chirp (warble)†: — *alle murate*, go to prison.

ṣvèrre† = *svellere*.

ṣversáto [*s-*, *verso*], ADJ.: impolite (rude).

ṣvertáre†, TR.: empty (the nets); speak openly.

ṣvèr-za [*s-*, *v.* . (L. *viridia*, green plants)], F.: chips (shavings); cabbage (greens)†. **-záre**, TR.: chip (cut to chips); stop with chips; INTR.: be shattered (split). **-zétta**, **-zettína**, *dim.* of *-za*. **-zíno**, M.: twine on the end of a whip.

ṣvesciáre [*s-*, *vescia*], TR., INTR.: blab (divulge, reveal).

ṣvescicáre [*s-*, *vescica*], TR.: remove the bladder.

ṣvesció-na, F., ‖**-ne** [*svesciare*], M.: divulger (tattler).

ṣvestíre [*s-*, *v.* .], TR.: undress; REFL.: undress one's self.

ṣvet-taménto, M.: act of cutting off the tops, etc. ‖**-táre** [*s-*, *vetta*], TR.: cut off the tops of (trees, plants, etc.); vibrate; undulate. **-tatúra** = *-tamento*. **-taturína**, *dim.* of *-tatura*.

ṣvezzáre = *divezzare*.

ṣvi-aménto, M.: wandering (deviation); error. ‖**-áre** [*s-*, *via*], TR.: put out of the way (divert, misguide); REFL.: go astray; forsake: — *un colpo*, ward off a blow. **-atóre**, M.: misguider; seducer.

ṣvignáre [OGer. *swinan*, vanish], INTR.: run off (slip away).

ṣvigoríre [*s-*, *vigore*], TR.: take away the vigour of; REFL.: lose one's strength.

ṣvi-liménto, M.: abasement (contempt). ‖**-líre** [*s-*, *avvi.* .], TR.: abase (disgrace). **-litaménte**, ADV.: in a contemptible manner.

ṣvillaneg-giaménto, M.: abuse (insulting language). **-giánte**, ADJ.: abusive. ‖**-giáre** [*s-*, *v.* .], TR.: abuse (revile, vilify); REFL.: abuse one another. **-giatóre**, M.: blackguard (insulter).

ṣvilleggiáre [*s-*, *v.* .], INTR.: finish country diversions (leave the villa).

ṣvilup-paménto, M.: unfolding (development). **-páre**, TR.: unravel (unfold); develop; make manifest (clear); REFL.: disentangle or extricate one's self. **-páta**, F.: (*geom.*) evolute (original curve). ‖**ṣvilúp-po** [*s-*, *v.* .], M.: development; explication.

ṣvi-náre [*s-*, *vino*], TR.: draw off (new wine). **-natúra**, F.: drawing off the new wine.

ṣvinciglіáre†, TR.: beat with a switch.

ṣviṣáre [*s-*, *viso*], TR.: disfigure (scratch one's face); alter (change).

ṣvisce-raménto, M.: disembowelling (gutting). ‖**-ráre** [*s-*, *viscera*], TR.: eviscerate (disembowel); treat profoundly; put in evidence. **-rataménte**, ADV.: lovingly (passionately). **-ratézza**, F.: violent love (affection). **-ráto**, PART.: eviscerated, etc.; tenderest (most sincere): *amico* —, bosom friend. **-ratóre**, M.: eventerator.

ṣvísta [*s-*, *v.* .], F.: oversight (error).

ṣvi-táre [*s-*, *vite*], TR.: unscrew; disinvite. **-tatúra**, F.: unscrewing, etc. **-ticchiáre** [*s-*, *avvi.* .], TR.: disentwine (disentangle); tear off; REFL.: disentangle one's self.

ṣvituperáre†, TR.: vituperate; dishonour.

ṣviva-gnatáccio†, *disp.* of *-gnato*. **-gnáto†**, ADJ.: unravelled; awkward (foolish).

ṣviziáre†, TR.: cure of vice.

ṣvízzero [lit. 'Swiss'], M.: hunter (kind of servant).

ṣvocicchiáre†, TR.: decry (defame).

ṣvo-gliaménto, M.: beginning of disgust. ‖**-gliáre** [*s-*, *invo.* .], TR.: take away the desire for; REFL.: grow weary (become disgusted); grow out of conceit. **-gliatággine**, F.: satiety (disgust); weariness. **-gliataménte**, ADV.: fastidiously; carelessly. **-gliatèllo**, *car.* *dim.* of *-gliato*. **-gliatézza** = *-gliataggine*. **-glíáto**, PART.: disgusted, unwilling, etc.

ṣvo-laménto†, M.: act of flying (flight). **-láre†**, INTR.: fly (soar). **-lazzaménto**, M.: fluttering or flying about. ‖**-laz-**

=záre [freq. of *-volare*], TR.: flutter (the wings); INTR.: flutter; fly gently about. **-lazzatóio,** ADJ.: flying; ruffled (mussed). **-lazzétto,** *dim.* of *-lazzo*. **-lazzío,** M.: continued flying or fluttering. **-lázzo,** M.: fluttering or flying about; flourishes (of the pen).

s=voléret, IRR.; TR.: not to will (refuse to will).

ṣvòl-gere [*s-, avvolgere*], TR.: unfold (display); (*poet.*) untie; exhaust (treat exhaustively); dissuade; REFL.: get out of joint (twist). **-gimènto,** M.: opening (unfolding). **ṣvòl-ta,** F.: turn (of a road, etc.). **-taménto,** M.: turning (bending); winding. ‖**-táre** [*s-, v.* .], TR.: unwind (unfold); bend (turn); deviate. **-tatóre,** M.: unwinder; deviator. **-tatúra,** F.: turning; turn; fold (pleat)†; sprain†. **-ticchiáre,** TR.: resume the journey; REFL.: writhe. **-tolaménto,** M.: rolling (wallowing). **-toláre,** TR., INTR.: turn or roll over (tumble, toss). **-tolóne,** M.: turning over (revolution, somerset). **-túra†,** F.: turning about; fold; dislocation. **ṣvòl-vere,** IRR.; TR.: unfold; dissuade (remove).

T

t *ti* [L.], M., F.: t (the letter).

tabac-cáia, F., **-cáio,** M.: tobaccoseller. **-chièra,** F.: snuff-box. **-chísta†,** M.: snuff-taker. ‖**tabác-co** [Sp. *tabaco* (Carib.)], M.: tobacco; snuff. **-cóna,** F., **-cóne,** M.: excessive user of tobacco. **-cóso,** ADJ.: full of (smeared with) tobacco.

tabállo† = *timballo*.

tabáno [L. *-nus*, gadfly, tabanus], ADJ.: back-biting (slanderous); satirical.

tabar-ráccio, *disp.* of *-ro*. **-rétto,** **-ríno,** *dim.* of *-ro*. ‖**tabár-ro** [?], M.: winter cloak, coarse cloak. **-róne,** *aug.* of *-ro*.

tábe [L. *tabes*], F.: (*med.*) tabes (wasting away); putrefaction. **=fátto†,** ADJ.: tabefied (emaciated); putrid.

tabèl-la [L. (*tabula*, table)], F.: table (tabulated statement, compendium); clapperboard (thin board with wooden clapper rung by boys during holy week); votive tablet. **-lário,** M.: letter-carrier; messenger. **-lióne,** M.: scribe, notary.

taber-nacolétto, -nacolíno, *dim.* of *-nacolo*. ‖**-nácolo** [L. *-naculum* (*-na*, hut)], M.: tabernacle, chapel.

tá-bido†, ADJ.: (*med.*) tabid (affected with tabes; emaciating). **-bífico†,** ADJ.: wasting, putrefying.

tácca [?], F.: notch (cut); notched stick; injury†, blemish (spot)†; condition.

tac-cagnería, *disp.* of *-cagno*. ‖**-cágno** [Sp. *-año*], ADJ.: niggard, covetous, sordid.

taccherèlla, *dim.* of *-ca*.

tac-chína, F.: turkey-hen. ‖**-chíno** [?], M.: turkey-cock.

tác-cia [*-ca*], F.: stain (spot, blemish); imputation. **-ciáre,** TR.: blot; blame; impute.

táccto [*tacere*], in: *fare* (or *dare*) *un* —, transact; make an end (cut short).

tác-co [*-ca*], M.: heel (of a shoe): *batter il* —, take to the heels. **tác-cola,** F.: trifle; defect (blemish); crow†; romp.† **-coláre†,** INTR.: chatter. **tác-colo,** M.: small deficit or debt; romp†; diversion†; confusion†. **-conáre,** TR.: double-sole. **-cóne,** *aug.* of *-co*: *batter il* —, take to the heels.

taccuíno [fr. Ar.], M.: note-book; calendar.

ta-cènte, ADJ.: tacit (silent, quiet). ‖**-cé-re** [L.], IRR.§; INTR.: be silent (be quiet); M.: silence. **-cévole†,** ADJ.: tacit (silent). **-ciménto†,** M.: silence. **-citaménte,** ADV.: tacitly (silently). **tá-cito,** ADJ.: tacit (silent; secret). **-citurnaménte,** ADV.: taciturnly. **-citurnità,** F.: taciturnity. **-citúrno,** ADJ.: taciturn. **-ciúto,** PART. of *-cere*; kept silent or secret. **tá-cqui,** PRET. of *-cere*.

§ Ind. Pres. *táccio, táci, táce; taciámo, tacéte, tácciono.* Pret. *tácqui, tácque; tácquero;* (pop. *tacéi*, etc.). I've *táci*. — Poet. forms: Pret. *tacètt-i, -e; -ero*.

ta-fanário, M.: (*vulg.*) backside (buttocks). ‖**-fáno** [L. *-banus*], M.: tabanus (gadfly, horsefly).

taffería [? Ar.], F.: wooden bowl.

tafferúglio [?], M.: quarrel (brawl, uproar).

taffettà [fr. Pers.], M.: taffeta.

taffiáre [Ger. *tafel*, TABLE], INTR.: eat voraciously; gormandize.

tá-glia, F.: cutting; slaughter; cut (form); stature (size); TALLY (orig'ly piece of wood with notches); TAILLE (tax, impost); price; reward (to slayers of assassins, etc.): *di mezza* —, middle-sized. **-gliá-bile,** ADJ.: that may be cut, scissible. **-glia=bórse,** M.: cutpurse (pickpocket). **-glia=cantóni†,** M.: ruffian **-glia=fèrro,** M.: fine scalpel. **légna,** M. INVAR.: **máre,** M.: (*nav.*) **to,** M.: cutting; **tre,** M.: stonec *lea*, stick], TR.: fell; adulterate *a uno*, slander — *le capriole*, **-gliáta,** F.: **-gliatèlli,**

-gliatíni, *dim.* of *-gliatelli*. **-gliáto**, PART. of *-gliare*: *ben* —, well formed, shapely. **-gliatóra**, F., **-gliatóre**, M., **-gliatríce**, F.: cutter. **-gliatúra**, F.: cutting; slash; incision; scar. **-glieggiáre**, TR.: assess (tax); set a price on the head of. **-gliènte**, ADJ.: cutting (sharp, keen); abrupt. **-glienteménte**, ADV.: cuttingly; abruptly. **-glière**, M.: chopping block (wooden board or block for kitchen use); trencher (plate): *giubba a* —, waistcoat with flaps (like a *-gliere*); *esser a* — *con*†, eat together with. **-glierétto**, **-glieríno**, **-glierúccio**, *dim.* *dim.* of *-gliere*. **-gliettíno**, *dim.* of *-glietto*. **-gliétto**, *dim.* of *-glio*. **táglio**, M.: cut; slash (wound); slice (piece); shape (figure); edge; opportunity; adulteration; possibility†: *a* —, by the slice, in slices or pieces; — *d'abito*, piece of cloth for a suit; — *morto* (or *ottuso*), dull edge; *metter al* — (*della spada*), put to the sword; *cadere* (or *venire*) *in* —, come opportunely, suit one's purpose. **-gliòla**, F.: steel-trap. **-glioliní**, M. PL.: kind of vermicelli. **-gliòlo**, *dim.* of *-glio*. **-glióne**, M.: retaliation (like for like). **-gliuòla**, **-gliuòlo** = *-gliola*, *-gliolo*. **-gliuzzaménto**, M.: mincing (hashing). **-gliuzzáre**, TR.: cut to pieces (mince, hash).

talaccimánno [fr. Ar.], M.: (Ar.) temple-summoner.

tálamo [Gr. *thálamos*], M.: nuptial-bed; bed†.

talá-re [L. *-ris* (*talus*, heel)], ADJ.: reaching to the ankles, long (of priestly robes). **-'ri**, M. PL.: talaria (winged sandals of Mercury).

tal = *tale*.

tal=chè *-é*, CONJ.: so that.

tál-co [Sp.], M.: talc, mica. **-cóso**, ADJ.: of talc.

tále [L. *-lis*], PRON.: such (like); some one; such a one: —*che*, so that, insomuch that; *il Signor* —, Mr. Such-a-one (So-and-so); *a* —, to such a point.

talèa†, F.: stock; graft.

talen-táccio, M.: wonderful talent. **-táre**, INTR.: be genial, please. ‖**talèn-to** [L. *-tum*], M.: talent (certain weight of money; ability, skill); inclination, wish: *di buon* —†, willingly; *mal* —, dislike; *a mal* — *di*†, in spite of.

talio. † = *taglio*.

talismáno [fr. Ar.], M.: talisman.

tállero [Ger. *thaler*], M.: thaler (Ger. coin = 85 cents).

tal-lettíno, **-létto**, **-líno**, *dim.* of *-lo*. **-líre**, INTR.: run to seed. ‖**tál-lo** [Gr. *allós*], M.: shoot (sprout); stalk: *rimetter un* — *sul vecchio*, rejuvenate.

tallóne [L. *talus*, ankle], M.: heel; heel-bone.

tallónzolo, *dim.* of *tallo*.

talménte [*tale*], ADV.: in such a manner (so); so much.

talmú-dico [*Talmud*], ADJ.: Talmudic. **-dísta**, pl. —*ti*, M.: Talmudist.

tal=óra, **-òtta**†, ADV.: sometimes (now and then).

tál-pa [L.], **-pe**†, F.: mole.

tal=úno, PRON.: some one, some. **=vòlta**, ADV.: sometimes (now and then).

tamánto†, ADJ.: so large (so great).

tamarigi [L. *-rice*], M.: tamarisk.

tamaríndo [fr. Ar.], M.: tamarind.

tamarísco = *-rigi*.

tambellóne [*tabella*], M.: large brick; dolt, fool.

tambène†, ADV.: as well as.

tambu-ráccio, M.: *disp. aug.* of *-ro*. **-ragióne**† = *-razione*. **-ráio**, M.: drum-maker. **-ráre**, TR.: beat (drub); accuse (by anonymous letter placed in a so-called *-ro*), impeach. **-razióne** [cf. *-rare*], F.: accusation (impeachment). **-rèllo**, M.: *dim.* of *-ro*; battledoor. **-rétto**, M.: *dim.* of *-ro*; tambourine. **-ríno**, M.: *dim.* of *-ro*; tambourine; rattle-box, booby; drummer (drummer-boy). **-rlanétto**, *dim.* of *-rlano*. **-rláno**, M.: drying-vat; (*chem.*) receiver. ‖**tambú-ro** [fr. Pers.], M.: drum; barrel (of a watch); vault-support. **-ssáre**†, TR.: beat, thump.

ta-migiáre†, TR.: bolt, sift. **-migio**†, M.: bolter, sieve.

tampòco†, ADV.: no more, not even, neither.

tána [?], F.: den (cave, hole).

tanacéto†, M.: tansy.

tanà-glia, us'ly in pl. ‖**-glie** [L. *tenacula* (*tenere*, hold)], F.: pincers. **-gliáre**, TR.: tear with pincers; torment. **-gliétta**, *dim.* of *-glia*. **-glióne**, *aug.* of *-glia*.

tanè [Fr. *tanné*], M.: TAN-colour.

tanfanáre†, TR.: beat; torment.

tan-fétto, *dim.* of *-fo*. ‖**-fo** [OGer. *tamf*, DAMP], M.: mouldy smell or taste.

tan-gènte, ADJ.†: touching; M.: tangent. **-gènza**†, F.: touch. ‖**tán-gere** [L.], TR.: touch.

tanghe-rèllo, *dim.* of *-ro*. ‖**tánghera** [OGer. *-r*, rough], F., **-ro**, M.: rude or clownish person (boor).

tangíbi-le [L. *-lis*], ADJ.: tangible. **-lità**, F.: tangibility.

tangòccio†, ADJ.: clumsy.

tanníno [?], M.: (*chem.*) tannin.

tantafè-ra [?], **-ráta**, F.: tedious talk (galimatias).

tan-tinétto, *dim.* of *-tino*. **-tíno**, ADJ.:

dim. of *-to*; very little; M.: little bit, ever so little; moment. ‖**-to** [L. *-tus*], ADJ., ADV.: so (as) much, so (as) many, enough; a little; in order; such a: *due volte* —, twice as much (as many); — *o quanto*, so and so; but little: *tant' è*, just as well; *a* (or *di*) —, so, to such a degree; *di* — *in* —, from time to time; *in* —, in the mean time; *non* —, not only, notwithstanding; *per* —, however, nevertheless; *a* — *per* —, at this rate; — *per uno*, so much a piece; *ogni* —, every now and then; — *più che*, the more so as. **-to-chè** *-è*, CONJ.: insomuch; as long as, until, so that. **-tolíno**, M.: very little thing or piece. **-tòsto†**, ADV.: suddenly, immediately.

ta-pinaménte, ADV.: wretchedly. **-pi-náre**, INTR.: live a wretched life; drudge; REFL.: worry. **-pinèllo**, *dim.* of *-pino*. ‖**-píno** [Gr. *-peinós*], ADJ.: mean (wretched, miserable); M. (f. *-pina*): wretch (poor creature).

tapiòca [Braz.], F.: tapioca.

táppa [Ger. *stapel*, STAPLE], F.: STAGE (on a journey or march).

tappáre [*tappo*], TR.: close with a bung or stopper (bung, plug, cork).

tappé-to [L. *tapete*], M.: carpet: TAPESTRY carpet; cover: *mettere sul* —, introduce, broach, propose. **-túccio**, *disp.* *dim.* of *-to*. **-zzáre**, TR.: hang with tapestry or paper, paper. **-zzería**, F.: tapestry (hanging); wall-paper. **-zzière**, M.: upholsterer; paper-hanger.

tap-píno, *dim.* of *-po*. ‖**-po** [l. Ger. *tap*, stop], M.: stopper (bung; cork); (*nav.*) shot-plug.

tára [l. L. (Ar. *terha*, loss)], F.: TARE, waste (of goods); discount; (*fig.*) censure.

tarabarálla [echoic], ADV.: about (nearly, almost).

tarabáso [Fr. *tarabuster*, plague], M.: bittern.

taradóre†, M.: vine-fretter.

tarándo†, M.: reindeer.

taran-tèlla, F.: tarantella (dance, supposed to cure the bite of the tarantula); nervous disease (supposed to be due to a bite of the tarantula). ‖**tarán-tola** [*Taranto*, in south of Italy], F.: tarantula. **-toláto†**, ADJ.: bit by a tarantula. **-tolétta**, *dim.* of *-tola*. **-tolismo**, M.: tarantism (disease, cf. *-tella*).

tará-re [*tara*], TR.: deduct the tare from: discount (abate). **-tóre**, M ...

tarchi-atèllo, *dim.* of *-ato* ... *gu*], ADJ.: square-built (robust ... *dim.* of *-tto*.

tar-damènte, ADV.: tardily ... **-damentot†**, M.: delay. **-dan** ... ADV.: lingeringly (slowly) ...

tardiness (delay); stay. **-dáre**, TR.: retard (delay); INTR.: be late; seem late. **-détto**, **-dettíno**, *dim.* of *-do* or *-di*. **-dézza**, F.: tardiness; slowness (dilatoriness). **-di**, ADV.: tardily (slowly); late; sluggishly: *al più* —, at the latest; *tosto o* —, sooner or later; *si fa* —, it is getting late. **-dità**, F.: tardiness; slowness, indolence. **-dívo**, ADJ.: tardy (late; slow). ‖**-do** [L. *-dus*], ADJ.: tardy, late; slow; dull; ADV.: late: *occhi -di*, serious countenance.

tár-ga [Germ'c *targe*], F.: TARGET (shield, buckler). **-gáta**, F.: blow with a target (shield). **-ghétta**, **-ghettína**, *dim.* of *-ga*. **-góne**, *aug.* of *-ga*.

tariffa [Ar. *ta-rif*, information], F.: tariff (price-list); price.

taríscat†, F.: social repast (feast).

tar-láre, INTR.: get worm-eaten. **-latúra**, F.: worm-eating, worm-holes. ‖**-lo** [*-ma*], M.: wood-worm, wood-louse: *avere il* — *con uno*, have a rancour against one; *l' amor del* —, self-seeking.

tár-ma [L. *-mes* (*tero*, bore)], F.: moth. **-máre**, INTR.: be worm-eaten. **-máto**, ADJ.: worm-eaten; (*jest.*) pock-marked.

taroccáre [L. *altercare*, wrangle], INTR.: bluster, rage, grumble.

taròcco [?], M.: card in the play 'at checkered cards'; PL.: the play itself: *essere come il matto fra* —*chi*, be here and there, and everywhere.

tarpáno [Ger. *tölpel*], ADJ.: rude (clownish); M.: rude fellow (clown).

tarpáre [?], TR.: clip the wings of, clip; (*fig.*) render powerless; deduct from.

tarpína, F.: monk's-rhubarb.

tar-sía, F.: tarsia (kind of mosaic in woodwork, checkered work); provision†. ‖**-so** [Gr. *-sós*, hurdlework; flat surface, sole], M.: tarsus (hind part of the foot).

társo† 2, M.: (Tuscan) white marble.

tarta-gliáre [echoic], TR., INTR.: stammer (stutter). **-gliéna**, F., **-glióne**, M.: stammerer (stutterer).

tartá-na [fr. Ar.], F.: tartane (fishing vessel). **-nèlla**, *dim.* of *-na*. **-nóne**, M.: kind of net.

tártara†, F.: sort of ... -pudding.

tartá-reo, ADJ.: ... -ish. **-ris-gáro** ... **-ta-ro** [L. *-rus*] ... hell.

tárt ... ADJ.: ...

tart ... TOR- ...

wallet (satchel)†. -cábile, ADJ.: pocketable. -cáccia, disp. of -ca. -cáta, F.: pocketful; pouchful. -chétta, -chettína, -chína, -chíno, -cóccia, dim. of -ca. -cóna, -cóne, aug. of -ca.

táso [Fr. tas, heap], M.: tartar (salt).

tás-sa, F.: tax (impost, duty, assessment). -sábile, ADJ.: taxable. -sagióne† = -sazione. ‖-sáre [L. taxare], TR.: TAX (assess rate; fig.: accuse, blame). -sativaménte, ADV.: precisely. -sativo, ADJ.: determining (settling); precise. -sazióne, F.: taxation.

tas-selláre, TR.: piece; sample; tesselate. -sellatúra, F.: piecing -sellétto, -sellíno, dim. of -sello. ‖-sèllo [L. taxillus (dim. of talus, die)], M.: small piece (for joining or filling); collar piece (cape)†. -settíno, dim. of -setto. -sétto, M.: little anvil.

tásso¹ [? Ger. dachs], M.: badger.

tásso² [L. taxus], M.: yew-tree. =barbásso, M.: mullein.

tásta [?], F.: dossil (lint to keep wounds open); tent; testing-stick (for grain); (fig.)† annoyance.

tas-táme†, M.: keys (of an organ, etc.). -taménto, M.: touching; examining; touch. ‖-táre [L. *taxitare (taxare, freq. of tangere, touch)], TR.: touch (frequently and with skill), handle; feel and examine (examine, probe; try); TASTE. -táta, F.: touching; examining, touch. -tatína, F.: slight touch; small trial. -tatóre, M.: toucher. -tatúra†, F.: key-bord, keys. -teggiaménto, M.: touching; feeling.

tastétta, dim. of tasta.

tas-tièra, F.: keyboard. ‖-to [-tare], M.: touch, feeling; TACT; key (of a piano, etc.): andare a —, 'go by touch,' feel one's way, grope along, move at haphazard; toccare un —, touch lightly upon, examine; toccare un — buono, touch the right chord, make a happy hit.

tastolína†, F.: small lint (or dossil: cf. tasta).

tastó-ne [tasto], -ni, a —, ADV.: by touch, gropingly: andar a —, grope along.

tá-ta, F., ‖-to [L.], M.: child's name for one dear (sister, brother, friend, dear).

tattamèl-la†, F.: tittle-tattle, chat (pers.). -láre†, INTR.: prattle.

táttera†, F.: spot (blemish, defect); bagatelle (trifle); disease.

tátti-ca [Gr. taktikḗ], F.: tactics. -co, ADJ.: tactical; M.: tactician. -cóna, F., -cóne, M.: great tactician.

tát-tile, ADJ.: tactile. ‖-to [L. tactus (tangere, touch)], M.: touch (sense of feeling); TACT.

[Gr. tauto-logia, 'same-

(pub-

lic house; saloon, grog-shop). -náio†, M.: tavern-keeper; tavern-frequenter. -nèlla, dim. of -na. -nière† = -naio.

távo-la [L. tabula], F.: board (plank); table (board; table of contents, index; chess-board, etc.); square canvas (for painting); altar-piece; tablet; front; drawn game: di poche -le, of little significance or value; è in —, dinner is on the table; levare la —, take away, clear the table; mettere la —, lay the cloth; portare in —, bring (dinner, etc.) on the table, serve up; — dipinta, painting, picture; — rotonda, table d'hôte. -laccetáio, M.: target-maker. -laccíno, M.: bailiff (of a Florentine magistrate). -láccio, M.: bench (bunk); wooden target. -láta, F.: guest table. -láto, ADJ.: wainscotted; M.: wainscot (panelling), floor; partition-wall. -leggiáre, INTR.: attend at table. -leggiánte, M.: waiter. -lèlla, F.: small checker-board; (painter's) pallet. -lèllo†, M.: office. -létta, dim. of -la. -lière, -lièri†, M.: checker-board: esser sul —†, be in danger; metter sul —, risk. -lína, F.: dim. of -la: small table or picture. -linoíno, -linétto, -liníno, dim. of -lino. -líno, M.: dim. of -lo: guerra di —, politics; poeta di —, improviser; — da notte, night-stand; bureau. -linúccio, disp. dim. of -lino. -lito† = -lo. -lóne, aug. of -la. -lòtto, dim. of -la. -lòzza, F.: (painter's) palette. -lúccia, disp. dim. of -la.

táz-za [Ar. thaça], F.: (big) cup; flat tumbler; basin (of a fountain). -zúccia, disp. dim. of -za. -zétta, -zína, -zíno, dim. of -za. -zóne, aug. of -za.

té [L.], PRON.: thee; thou.

tè [Chin. tcha], M.: tea.

te'†, for tieni (cf. tenere).

tea-tràle, ADJ.: theatrical. -tralità, F.: theatricality (theatrical nature). -tralménte, ADV.: theatrically. -trína, dim. of -tro. ‖teá-tro [L. theatrum (Gr. thea-, show)], M.: theatre.

Tebáide [Tebe, Thebes], F.: solitary place.

técca [= tacca], F.: small spot; little defect; dot†, bit†.

tecchíre†, INTR.: thrive; shoot up.

técco-la, dim. of tecca. -lína, dim. -la.

tec-nicaménte, ADV.: technically. **-nicismo**, M.: technics. ‖**tèc-nico**, pl. *-ci* [Gr. *-nikós* (*-ne*, art)], ADJ.: technic(al). **-nologìa**, F.: technology. **-nològico**, ADJ.: technological.
tèco [L. *te-cum*], PRON.: with thee. **-mé-co†** [L. *me-cum*], M.: backbiter.
tèda [L. *tæda*], F.: larch-tree; nuptial torch; (*fig.*) nuptials.
ted(d)èo†, M.: Te Deum.
te-diáre†, TR.: tire, annoy. ‖**tè-dio** [L. *tædium*], M.: tedium (tediousness, irksomeness, wearisomeness). **-diosaménte**, ADV.: tediously. **-diosità**, F.: tediousness. **-dióso**, ADJ.: tedious (tiresome, irksome).
tega-máta, F.: potful; blow with a pan. ‖**tegá-me** [L. *tegere*, cover], M.: crock, pot. **-míno**, *dim.* of *-me*. **-móne**, *aug.* of *-me*.
tégghia† = *teglia*.
té-glia [L. *tegula*, TILE], F.: baking-pan, pie-dish. **-gliáta**, F.: panful. **-glióne**, M.: *aug.* of *-glia*; big hat.
tegnèn-te [*tenere*], ADJ.: (*agr.*) tenacious (sticky, tough); viscous; mean†; sordid†. **-za†**, F.: tenaciousness.
tégo-la [L. *tegula* (*teg-*, lover)], F.: TILE. **-láta**, F.: blow of a tile. **-létta**, **-létto**, **-lína**, **-líno**, *dim.* of *-la*. **tégo-lo**, M.: tile.
teguménto [L. *-mentum* (*teg-*, cover)], M.: tegument.
te-ismo [Gr. *theós*, god], M.: theism. **-ísta**, pl. *—i*, M.: theist.
té-la [L. *tela* (*tec-*, weave)], F.: TEXtile fabric (cloth, linen, canvas); picture: — *d'oro*, gold braid; tinsel; — *di ragno*, spider's web (cobweb). **-lággio**, M.: weaving; (quality of) texture. **-laiétte**, **-laíno**, *dim.* of *-laio*. **-láio**, M.: loom; frame (weaver's, painter's, carpenter's, etc.); painter's chase†. **-larétto†**, *dim.* of *-laio*. **-láro†** = *-laio*.
tele- [Gr. *tēle*, far]: **-fonáre**, TR.: telephone. **-fonía**, F.: telephony. **-fònico**, ADJ.: telephonic. **-foníeta**, pl. *—i*, M.: telephoner. **telè-fono** [Gr. *phoné*, sound], M.: telephone. **-grafía**, F.: telegraphy. **-gráfico**, ADJ.: telegraphic(al). **-grafísta**, pl. *—i*, M.: telegraphist, -pher. **telè-grafo** [Gr. *gráphein*, write], M.: telegraph. **-grámma**, M.: telegram.
telería [*tela*], F.: linen-drapery.
tele-scòpico, ADJ.: telescopic. ‖**-scòpio** [Gr. *tēle*, far, *skopein*, view], M.: telescope.
telét-ta, **-tína**, F.: *dim.* of *-la*; light cloth; tinsel.
tellína [Gr. *-ne*], F.: cockle-shell: *far ridere le -ne*, do ridiculous things.
tellúr(i)o [L. *tellus*, earth], M.: tellurium (metallic element).
tèlo 1 [*-lum*], M.: (*poet.*) missile (dart, arrow).
té-lo 2 [*-la*], M.: width of cloth. **-lóna**, *aug.* of *-la*. **-lóne**, M.: curtain.
telònio [Gr. *-neion* (*télos*, toll)], M.: tax-gatherer's desk or office; broker's counter.
telúccia [*tela*], F.: bit of cloth or linen; rag.
téma 1 [*-mere*], F.: fear, alarm.
tè-ma 2, pl. *—i* [Gr. *théma* (*the-*, put)], M.: theme (topic; stem of a word). **-mático**, ADJ.: thematic.
te-mènte [*-mere*], ADJ.: fearing. **-mènza**, F.: fear, apprehension.
teme-rariaménte, ADJ.: with temerity. ‖**-rário** [L. *-rarius* (*-re*, by chance)], ADJ.: temerarious (heedless, audacious).
temére [L. *timere*], TR.: fear (dread; apprehend); feel keenly.
temerità [L. *-ritas* (*-re*, by chance)], F.: temerity (rashness; audacity).
temí-bile [*temere*], ADJ.: fearful (timorous). **-ménto†**, M.: fear.
tèmo [L.], M.: (*poet.*) rudder, helm.
tèmolo [L. *thyminus*], M.: river-trout.
temon. .† = *timon*. .
tempáccio, *disp.* of *tempo*.
tempaiòlo [? *-po*], M.: sucking-pig.
tempel-laménto†, M.: shake, stroke; hesitation. **-láre†**, TR.: shake, toss, strike; INTR.: vacillate, waver. **-láta†**, F.: tinkling, chime. **tempèl-lo†**, M.: tinkling, chime, wavering. **-lóne†**, M.: blockhead; time-server.
tèmpe-ra, F.: temper (hardness of metal); (*fig.*, us'ly *tempra*) water-colour; (*mus.*) quality of sound (tone, timbre); temper† (temperament, disposition; kind): *dipingere a* —, paint in water-colours. **-raménto**, M.: tempering (adjustment, modification, Eng.† temperament); temperament (constitution); government†, measure†. **-ránte**, ADJ.: temperate, sober. **-ránza**, F.: temperance (moderation, sobriety). ‖**-ráre** [L. (*tempus*, time)], TR.: temper (iron, etc., i.e., 'season'; adjust; modify, assuage); harmonize†; prepare†; regulate†: — *una penna*, make a quill-pen. **-rataménte**, ADV.: temperately. **-ratézza**, F.: temperance. **-ratívo**, ADJ.: tempering (modifying, allaying). **-ráto**, ADJ.: tempered; temperate. **-ratóio†**, M.: penknife. **-ratóre**, M.: moderator; regulator. **-ratúra**, F.: temperature; making a quill-pen. **-razióne†**, F.: temperance. **tempè-rie**, F.: temperateness, mildness. **-rináta**, F.: cut with a penknife. **-ríno**, M.: penknife.
tempè-sta [L. *-stas* (*tempus*, time)], F.:

tempest. **-stánte,** ADJ.: tempestuous. **-stánza†,** F.: tempest. **-stáre,** INTR.: be tempestuous (Eng.† tempest), storm; rage; TR.: harass, afflict; annoy†; overturn. **-stivaménte,** ADV.: opportunely. **-stívo,** ADJ.: timely (seasonable, opportune, suitable). **-stosaménte,** ADV.: tempestuously. **-stóso,** ADJ.: tempestuous, stormy.

tempétto, *dim.* of *-po.*

tèm-pia, pl. *-pie,* (*poet.*) *-pia* [L. *-pora* (*-pus,* time)], F.: TEMPLE (of the head). **-piále,** M.: TEMPLE (of a loom; of the head†).

tem-pière, M.: temple-guardian; templar. **-pierèllo†, -piétto,** *dim.* of *-pio.* ||**tèm-pio** [L. *-plum* (*tem,* cut: place marked off)], M.: TEMPLE (of worship).

tempióne [*-pia*], M.: blow on the temples; dullard.

tempíssimo [superl. of *-po*], ADJ.: most (very) timely or opportune.

tem-pláre, M.: knight (Templar). ||**tèm-plo** [cf. *-pio*], M.: (*poet.*) temple.

tèm-po [L. *-pus*], M.: time (period; occasion); weather: *a* —, in (good) time; *a -pi,* timely, opportunely; in the nick of time; *col* —, in time; *di* — *in* —, now and then; *per* —, betimes, early; *uomo di* —, aged man; *già* —, a long while ago, long since; *avanzar* —, anticipate; *dar* —, delay, defer; *darsi buon* —, live merrily. **-póne,** M.: long time; feasting. **-'pora,** F. PL.: ember time; M. PL.†: time. **-poràle,** ADJ.: temporal (transitory; of the temples); M.: pope's territory; tempest (foul weather, squall); time†, season†. **-poralità,** F.: temporariness, transitoriness; worldliness†. **-poralménte,** ADV.: temporarily. **-poraneità,** F.: temporariness. **-poráneo,** ADJ.: temporary (Eng.† temporaneous). **-'pore,** in *ex* — (Lat.), ADV.: extempore. **-poreggiaménto,** M.: temporizing, delay. **-poreggiáre,** INTR.: temporize (delay, put off). **-'pra,** F.: temper, quality. **-práre,** TR.: temper (metals); moderate. **-púccio,** *dim.* of *-po.*

temúto, PART. of *temere.*

tená-ce [L. *-x* (*tenere,* hold)], ADJ.: tenacious (reTENtive; persevering; viscous); close-fisted (greedy)†. **-ceménte,** ADV.: tenaciously. **-cétto,** *dim.* of *-ce.* **-cità,** F.: tenacity; avarice†.

tenáglia = *tanaglia.*

tencion. .† = *tenzon.* .

tèn-da, F.: ('stretched-out cloth'), awning; hangings, curtain; TENT: *al tirare delle -de,* at the last. **-dále,** *aug.* of *tende.* **-daròla,** *dim.* of *-da.* **-dáto,** *M.: encampment* (assemblage of tents).

-dènte, ADJ.: tending, aiming. **-dènza,** F.: tendency (propensity; direction). ||**tèn-dere** [L.], IRR.§; TR.: extend (stretch); direct (the glance, etc.); bend (a bow); lay or set (a snare); tend. **-détta, -dina,** *dim.* of *-da.* **-'dine,** F.: tendon. **-dineo,** ADJ.: tendinous (of a tendon). **-dinétto,** *dim.* of *-dine.* **-dinóso,** ADJ.: tendinous, sinewy. **-ditóre,** M.: extender; setter (of snares). **-dóne,** M.: *aug.* of *-da;* theatre-curtain.

§ Pret. *tè-si, -se; -sero.* Part. *téso.*

tène-bra, rarely **tenè-bra,** F.: poet. for *-bre.* **-bráre†,** INTR.: darken; grow gloomy. ||**tène-bre** [L. *-bræ*], F. PL.: obscurity (darkness); ignorance; (*Rom. Cath.*) Thursday, Friday, and Saturday matins sung in the afternoon of the preceding day in Passion week (tenebræ). **-bría,** F.: darkness. **-bróne,** M.: blusterer, grumbler. **-brosità,** F.: tenebrosity (darkness, gloom). **-bróso,** ADJ.: tenebrous (dark, gloomy).

tenènte [*tenere*], ADJ.: holding; M.: lieuTENANT.

teneraménte [*-ro*], ADV.: tenderly.

tenére [L.], IRR.§; TR.: hold (keep, have; remain; contain; maintain, believe); hold on to (follow), take; reach, arrive at; INTR.: dwell (live); be firm; set off; REFL.: hold or think one's self; hold out; defend; restrain (forbear): — *a dozzina,* take boarders; — *duro,* hold firm, hold out, resist; — *fronte,* withstand, bid defiance; — *mano,* assist; — *mente,* be attentive; mind; — *occhio,* look well; — *in piè,* keep on foot, maintain; — *di patti,* consent, agree; — *via,* have the means.

§ Ind.: Pres. *tèngo, tièni, tiène; teniámo* or *tenghiámo, tenéte, tèngono.* Pret. *ténni, -e; -ero.* Fut. *terrò.* Cond. *terrèi.* Subj.: Pres. *tènga; -ghiámo,* etc. I've *tièni.* — Poet. forms *tegn-* for *teng-.*

tene-rèllo, -rétto, *dim.* of *-ro.* **-rézza,** F.: tenderness (softness; affection; youth). **-ríno,** *car. dim.* of *-ro.* ||**tè-ne-ro** [L. *tener*], ADJ.: tender (soft, delicate; youthful; sensitive); ticklish, captious. **-róne,** *disp. aug.* of *-ro.* **-rètto, -rúccio,** *dim.* of *-ro.* **-rúme,** M.: cartilages; tendrils. **-rúzzo†** = *-ruccio.*

tèngo, Pres. Ind. of *tenere.*

tènia [L. *tænia* (Gr. *tainía,* band)], F.: tænia (tape-worm).

tenière†, M.: stock (of a cross-bow).

te-niménto, M.: holding; territory; stay (prop, support)†; property†; obligation†. **-nitóio†,** M.: handle. **-nitóre†,** M.: holder. **-nitòrio†, -nitòro†,** M.: territory; possession. **-nitúra†,** F.: holding; property. ||**tén-ni,** PRET. of *-nere.* **-nóre** [L. *-nor*], M.: tenor (mode, drift,

intent, stamp; *mus.*: tenor, tenor-singer). **-noreggiáre**, INTR.: have a tenor voice.
ten-síle [L. *-sus*, tense], ADJ.: tensile. **-sióne**, F.: tension.
tèn-ta, F.: probe; attempt†; experiment†. **-tábile**, ADJ.: attemptable. **-tácolo**, M.: tentacle (feeler, antenna). **-taménto**†, M.: attempt, trial; temptation. ‖**-táre** [L.], TR.: attempt (try); test (examine, probe); touch lightly; tempt (instigate). **-tativo**, M.: attempt; trial, experiment. **-tatóre**, M., **-tatríce**, F.: attempter. **-tazioncèlla**, *dim.* of *-tazione*. **-tazióne**, F.: temptation (allurement): *persona contro le -tazioni*, very ugly person.
tentelláre†, TR.: tingle, tinkle.
tentén-na, M., F.: irresolute or restless person. **-naménto**, M.: wavering, tossing; vacillation. ‖**-náre** [L., jingle], INTR.: tremble, shake; waver, vacillate; toss; rap; tinkle†; TR.: shake, toss. **-náta**, F.: shaking; wavering; agitation; knock. **-natóre**, M., **-natríce**, F.: shaker, stirrer, mover. **-nèlla**, F.: cog; hopper. **-níno**, M.: *dim.* of *-na*; restless fellow; devil†. **-nío**†, M.: continued shaking or agitation; wavering. **-nóne**, *aug.* of *-na*. **-nóni**, ADV.: in shaking; waveringly.
tentó-ne [*tentare*], or **-ni**, ADV.: feeling one's way, groping: *andar —*, grope along.
tè-nue [L. *-nuis*], ADJ.: THIN (slender); slight (poor, insignificant). **-nueménte**, ADV.: slenderly, poorly. **-nuità**, F.: thinness, tenuity; scantiness; insignificance.
te-núta, PART., cf. *-nuto*; F.: content; possession (estate); capacity. **-nutário**, M.: possessor; tenant. **-nutèlla**, *dim.* of *-nuta*. ‖**-núto**, PART. of *-nere*.
tèn-za†, **-zióna**, **-zióne**† = *-zone*. **-zonaménto**, M.: contest, fight. **-zonáre**, INTR.: conTENd (contest, combat, dispute). ‖**-zóne** [L. *-sum*, ger. of *-dere*, stretch], F.: conTENTION (contest, dispute); fight.
teo- [Gr. *theós*, God]: **-craticaménte**, ADJ.: theocratically. **-crático**, ADJ.: theocratic(al). **-crazía** [Gr. *theo-kratía*, 'God-rule'], F.: theocracy. **-día** [Gr. *odé*, song], F.: canticle, anthem. **-gonía** [Gr. *gónos*, birth], F.: theogony. **-logále** [Gr. *lógos*, doctrine], ADJ.: theological. **-logánte**, M.: theologian, divine. **-logáre**, INTR.: theologize. **-logástro**, *disp.* of *-logo*. **-logía**, F.: theology. **-logicaménte**, ADV.: theologically. **-lògico**, ADJ.: theological. **-logizzáre**, INTR.: theologize. **teò-logo**, M.: theologian, divine. **-logóne**, *aug.* of *-logo*.
teo-rèma [Gr. *theórema* (*-rein*, view)], M.: theorem. **-remático**, ADJ.: theorematic(al). **-rètico**, ADJ.: theoretic(al). **-ría** [Gr.]. **teò-rica**, F.: theory (Eng.† theoric). **-ricaménte**, ADV.: theoretically, speculatively. **teò-rico**, ADJ.: theoretical (Eng.† theorical), speculative; M.: theorist.
teo-sofía [Gr. *theós*, god, *sophía*, wisdom], F.: theosophy. **teò-sofo**, M.: theosoph, theosophist.
te-pefáre†, TR.: make tepid. ‖**tè-pere** [L. *-pere*], INTR.: (*poet.*) be tepid or lukewarm. **-pidaménto**, ADJ.: in a lukewarm manner, rather coldly, indifferently. **-pidário**, M.: tepidarium (warming-room). **-pidétto**, *dim.* of *-pido*. **-pidézza**, **-pidità**, F.: tepidity, lukewarmness; indifference. **tè-pido** [L. *-pidus*], ADJ.: tepid, lukewarm; indifferent. **-pificáre**, TR.: make tepid, warm a little. **-póre**, M.: lukewarmness.
tera-pèutica [Gr. *therapeutiké* (*-peúein*, serve)], F.: therapeutics. **-pèutico**, ADJ.: therapeutic(al).
tèrchio†, ADJ.: rude, rough.
tere-bentína = *trementina*. ‖**-bínto** [l. L. *-binthus*], M.: terebinth (turpentine-tree).
terèdine [L. *terere*, rub], F.: wood-louse, milleped.
tergèmino [L. *-nus*], ADJ.: tergeminous (threefold).
tèrgere [L.], IRR.§; TR.: scour, polish, clean; wipe dry.

§ Pret. *tèr-si*, *-se*; *-sero*. Part. *tèrso*.

tergi- [L. *tergum*, back], **-duttóre**, M.: commander of the rear-guard. **-versáre** [L. *vertere*, turn], INTR.: tergiversate (shift, shuffle). **-versazióne**, F.: tergiversation (shift, subterfuge). **-vèrso**†, ADJ.: shifting.
tèrgo [L. *-gum*], M.: back: *a —*, behind.
teriáca [= *triaca*], F.: treacle.
tèr-ma [Gr. *thérme*, heat], us'ly in pl. *-me*, which see. **-mále**, ADJ.: thermal. **-'me**, F. PL. of *-ma*; thermes (thermæ, hot baths).
termi-nábile, ADJ.: terminable, limitable. **-nále**, ADJ.: terminal. **-naménto**†, M.: limit(ing), term; termination. **-náre**, TR.: limit (bound); terminate (conclude, close); INTR.: terminate (end, be finished); border. **-nataménte**, ADV.: definitely (precisely; expressly). **-natézza**†, F.: boundary, limit; end. **-natívo**, ADJ.: terminative (terminating, definitive). **-natóre**, M., **-natríce**, F.: terminator. **-nazióne**, F.: termination (end, term; (*gram.*) ending). ‖**tèrmine**† [L. *-nus*], **-no**, M.: term (limit, bound); word, expression; part of a syllogism; boundary sign; (*poet.*) confine;

PL.: condition (state): — *di una corsa*, goal or winning post of a race-course: *uscir dei -mini*, become unreasonable, bolt.
termòmetro [Gr. *thermós*, hot, *métron*, measure], M.: thermometer.
ter-nário, **-nárе†**, ADJ.: triple, threefold. ‖**tèr-no** [L. *-nus* (*ter*, THREE)], M.: three (at dice); tern (at lottery).
tèr-ra [L.], F.: earth (our globe or world; land; region, soil, ground); land (landed property, estate, farm): — *di pentolaio*, potter's clay; *rasellame di* —, earthenware; — *marina*, seaport town; *andare* — —, sail along the shore; *pigliar* —, touch shore, cast anchor. **-ráccia**, *disp.* of *-ra*. **-ra=còtta**, F.: terra-cotta (terra-cotta work). **-racrèpolo**, M.: sort of sow-thistle. **-ra=férma**, F.: terra firma, land. **-ra=finárе†**, TR.: banish. **-rafíne†**, **-rafíno†**, M.: banishment. **-rág̃lia**, us'ly pl. **-rág̃lie**, F.: earthenware, pottery. **-rág̃lio†**, M.: terrace, level ground. **-rágno†**, **-rágnolo**, **-raiòlo**, ADJ.: earth-; low; creeping. **-rapienáre**, TR.: (*fort.*) provide with a terreplein; platform. **-ra=piè-no**, M.: (*fort.*) terreplein (platform of rampart for the cannon); platform, terrace. **-ráqueo**, ADJ.: terraqueous. **-rático**, M.: renting of land; land-rent. **-ráto†**, M.: rampart. **-rázza**, F.: upper terrace (of a building), flat roof. **-razzáno**, M.: (*lit.*) countryman (compatriot); highlander; peasant†. **-razzíno**, *dim.* of *-razzo*. **-rázzo**, M.: balcony, belvedere; terrace (of a house). **-razzóne**, *aug.* of *-razza*, *-razzo*. **-re=mòto**, M.: earthquake. **-renaménte**, ADV.: in a worldly manner. **-renèllo**, *dim.* of *-reno*. **-réno**, ADJ.: earthly; ground-; M.: land (ground; territory†, district); ground-floor; vestibule: *pian* —, ground-floor, basement; *mancare il* —, fear, be afraid. **tèr-reo**, ADJ.: earthy. **-rèstre**, ADJ.: earthly, terrestrial. **-restreità†**, F.: earthliness.
terrí-bile [L. *-bilis*], ADJ.: terrible. **-bilità**, F.: terribleness. **-bilménte**, ADV.: terribly.
ter-ríccio [*-ra*], M.: mould (decayed matter, rich soil), decayed manure, compost. **-ricci(u)òla**, F.: agricultural land; village. **-rière**, M.: countryman (peasant).
terrífico†, ADJ.: terrific, terrible.
ter-rígeno†, ADJ.: earth-born, earthly. ‖**-rígno** [*-ra*], ADJ.: of the earth, earthen. **-ritoriále**, ADJ.: territorial. **-ritòrio**, M.: territory. **-rolína**, F.: soft earth (mould).
terró-re [L. *-r*], M.: terror, dread. **-rí-smo**, M.: terrorism. **-rísta**, pl. **—i**, M.: terrorist.
terróso [*terra*], ADJ.: earthy, terreous.
ter-saménte, ADV.: tersely (neatly, elegantly). **-sézza**, F.: terseness (neatness, elegance). **-'si**, PRET. of *-gere*; PL. of *-so*. ‖**tèr-so**, PART. of *-gere*; scoured (polished; terse (neat, elegant).
ter-zána, F.: tertian fever; ADJ.: tertian. **-zanèlla**, F.: tertian fever. **-zárе†**, TR.: plough the third time. **-z=ávo**, **-z=ávolo**, M.: great-great grandfather. **-zería†**, F.: third, third part. **-zeruòlo**, M.: (*nav.*) stay-sail; holster-pistol. **-zétta**, F.: pocket-pistol. **-zettáta**, F.: hit from a *-zetta*. **-zétto** (*lit.*) = *-zina*. **-ziaménte**, ADV.: thirdly. **-ziário**, ADJ.: of the third order; tertiary. **-zíg̃lio**, **-zílio**, M.: game of cards (also called *calabresella*). **-zína**, F.: terzina (triplet, strophe of three lines). **-zíno**, M.: small bottle (third of a large); third of a bottle (measure, nearly a pint). ‖**tèr-zo** [L. *-tius* (*ter*, THREE)], ADJ.: third; M.: third; third part; company of soldiers. **-zo=dècimo**, ADJ.: thirteenth. **-zo=gènito**, **-zo=náto**, ADJ.: third born. **-zóne**, M.: packing-cloth, canvas. **-zuò-lo†**, M.: t(i)ercel (male hawk).
tésa [*-so*], F.: tension, stretching; place where snares are laid; brim (of a hat).
tesaur. . .† = *tesor*. .
tes-chiétto, *disp. dim.* of *-chio*. ‖**tè-schio** [L. *-tula* (*-ta*, head)], M.: skull; head (cut off).
tèsi [Gr. *thésis*, putting], M.: thesis.
téso, PART. of *tendere*; stretched, distended; intent.
teso-reggiáre, TR.: treasure up, hoard. **-rería**, F.: treasury. **-rièra**, F.: treasurer's wife. **-rière**, M.: treasurer. **-riz-záre**, TR.: treasure up, hoard. ‖**tesò-ro** [Gr. *thesaurós* (*the-*, put)], M.: treasure.
tèssera [L., die; ticket], F.: ticket (sign, mark, tally); PL. (Rom.) the four dies of a game: —*i militari*, patrol sign.
tes-serándolo†, M.: weaver; contriver. ‖**tès-sere** [L. *texere*], TR.: weave; †TEXTURE, interweave; plot (contrive). **-síle**, ADJ.: textile. **-siménto**, M.: weaving, texture. **-sitóra**, F., **-sitóre**, M., **-sitríce**, F.: weaver. **-sitúra**, F.: weaving (web, texture), framework. **-súto**, PART.: woven; M.: TISSUE, texture; framework.
tèsta [L., vase], F.: head (of an organic or unorganic body; mind; chief; extremity, top; front, etc.); obstinacy†; terracotta vase†: *non aver* —, have no mind; *esser* —† (or *di* —), be obstinate; *far* — *a*, oppose, resist, stem; *darsi su per la* —,

come to blows; *darsi la — contra*, dash one's head against.
testábile, ADJ.: subject to testamentary disposition, that may be left by will.
te-stácea, *disp.* of *-sta*. **-stáceo**, ADJ.: testaceous, crustaceous.
testa-mentáre†, INTR.: make one's testament or will. **-mentário**, ADJ.: testamentary. ‖**-ménto** [L. *-mentum* (cf. *-re*)], M.: testament (will; Testament).
testárdo [*testa*], ADJ.: headstrong (wilful, obstinate, Eng.† testif).
testáre [L. *-tari* (*-tis*, witness)], INTR.: make one's will or testament (Eng.† test); TR.†: attest.
te-státa [*-sta*], F.: head or end (of a beam, etc., extremity, top). **-stático**, M.: poll-tax (taxation by head).
te-statóre [*-stare*], M., **-statrice**, F.: testator, testatrix. ‖**tè-ste** [L. *-stis*], M.: witness.
testè *-é* [= *te-steso* (L. *ante ist' ipsum*)], ADV.: just now, but a short while ago.
testerèccio [*testa*], ADJ.: headstrong.
testéso†, cf. *testè*.
testicci(u)òla [*testa*], F.: lamb's head.
te-sticoláre, ADJ.: testicular. ‖**-stícolo** [L. *-sticulus*], M.: testicle.
testièra [*testa*], F.: head-stall (of a bridle); head-gear; milliner's head.
testi-ficánza†, F.: testimony. ‖**-ficáre** [L. *-ficari* (*testis*, witness)], TR.: testify (attest, witness). **-ficatívo**†, ADJ.: testifying. **-ficazióne**†, F.: testifying; testimony. **-mòne** [L. *-monium*, -mony], M.: witness (testifier). **-mònia**†, F.: testimony. **-moniále**, ADJ.: testimonial. **-moniánza**, F.: testimony (evidence, proof). **-moniáre**, TR.: testify (give evidence). **-mònio**, M.: (*pop.*) = *-mone;* also testimony†.
te-stína, *car.* or *disp. dim.* of *testa*. **-stíno**, M.: (*typ.*) brevier; † = *-stina*.
tèsto 1 [L. *textus* (*-xere*, weave)], M.: TEXT: *far* —, be authority or standard.
tè-sto 2 [L. *-sta*, vase], M.: earthen pot-lid; baking pan; flower-pot†. **-stolína**, *car.* or *iron. dim.* of *-sta*. **-stóna**, F., **-stóne**, M.: *aug.* of *-sta;* (*fig.*) thick-head, headstrong person.
te-stóre†, M.: = *-ssitore;* author. ‖**-stuále** [*-sto* 1], ADJ.: textual. **-stualménte**, ADV.: textually.
te-stúdo†, **-stúdine** = *testuggine*. **-studíneo**†, ADJ.: tortoise-like. ‖**-stúggine** [L. *testudo*], F.: tortoise; testudo (war-engine).
testúra [L. *textura*], F.: (*poet.*) texture (tissue, weaving).
tètano [Gr. *-nos* (*teínein*, stretch)], M.: tetanus (cramp).
tetra- [Gr., FOUR]: **-còrdo**, M.: tetrachord. **-èdro** [Gr. *hédra*, SEAT, base], M.: tetrahedron.
tetrággine [*tetro*], F.: gloom (obscurity, dreariness).
tetr- [Gr. *tétra*, FOUR]: **-ágono** [Gr. *gónos*, angle], M.: tetragon. **-alogía**, F.: tetralogy. **-ámetro** [Gr. *métron*, measure], M.: tetrameter. **-árca**, pl. *-archi* [Gr. *árchos*, ruler], M.: tetrarch. **-arcáto**, M., **-archía**, F.: tetrarchate. **-ástico**, pl. —*ci* [Gr. *stíchos*, line], M.: tetrastich (stanza of four lines).
te-tricità, F.: (*lit.*) gloominess (gloom, dreariness). **tè-trico**†, ‖**tè-tro** [L. *teter*, horrid], ADJ.: gloomy (obscure, sad, dark; dismal, melancholy; morose, Eng.† tetric).
tétta [ak. to Eng. *teat*], F.: teat (nipple, breast).
tettaiòlo [*tetto*], M.: garret mouse; ADJ.: like a garret mouse: *un topo* —, a recluse, closet cynic.
tettáre [*tetta*], TR.: suck.
tettarèllo, *dim.* of *tetto*.
tètte [echoic], M.: (child's name for) dog.
tet-tíno, *dim.* of *-to*. ‖**tét-to** [L. *tectum*], M.: roof; house: *a* —, at or on the roof; *camera* (or *stanza*) *a* —, garret, attic. **-tóia**, F.: shed, pent-house; cart-house. **-túccio**, *dim.* of *-to*.
te-urgía [Gr. *theourgía* (*theós*, god, *érgon*, work)], F.: theurgy (miracle, sorcery). **-úrgico**, ADJ.: theurgic(al). **-úrgo**, M.: theurgist.
thè = *tè*.
ti [L. *te*], PRON.: THEE; to thee; REFL.: thyself, to thyself.
tiára [Gr. (Pers.)], F.: tiara, mitre.
tí-bia [L.], F.: tibia (shin-bone; flute, flageolet). **-bicine**, M.: flute-player. **-'bio**, ADJ.: tibial.
ticchio [? OGer. *ziki*, kid], M.: caprice, (whim, odd habit).
tientamménte†, M.: nudge, cuff.
tiepid. . = *tepid.* .
tí-fo [Gr. *tû-phos*, mist], M.: typhus. **-fòide**, **-foidèo**, ADJ., M.: typhoid.
tífolo†, M.: cry, squeak.
ti-fóne [Gr. *tuphôn* (*-phos*, cloud)], M.: typhoon (whirlwind). **-fònico**, ADJ.: typhoon (of a whirlwind).
tí-glia† [L. *-lia*], F.: linden-tree; chestnut. **-gliáta**, F.: boiled, pealed chestnut. **tí-glio**, M.: linden(-tree); linden wood; inner bark of the linden, fibre of plants generally; vein (in stones). **-glióso**, ADJ.: fibrous, tough.
tigna [L. *tinea*], F.: scurf; miser.
tignere = *tingere*.
tign-òla [*-a*], F.: weevil, moth. **-óso**, ADJ.: scurfy, scabby.
tí-gra, F.: tigress. **-gránet**, **-gráto**, ADJ.: of tiger-colour, brindled, flecked.

‖**tí-gre** [L. *-gris*], M.: tiger. **-grétto†**, **-gríno†**, *dim.* of *-gre.* **-gro†** = *-gre.* **-gròtto**, M.: young tiger.
timbállo [fr. Ar.], M.: tymbal (kettle-drum).
tim-bra†, F., **-bro**, M.: (*bot.*) savory.
tími-daménte, ADV.: timidly. **-détto**, *dim.* of *-do.* **-dézza**, **-dità**, F.: timidity. ‖**tími-do** [L. *-dus*], ADJ.: timid, fearful.
tímo [Gr. *thumós*], M.: thyme.
timó-ne [L. *temo*, pole], M.: rudder (helm); carriage-pole, waggon-tongue; guide; regulator. **-neggiáre**, TR.: steer; rule. **-nèlla**, F.: little carriage. **-niè-re**, **-nísta†**, pl. *—i*, M.: steersman, pilot.
timo-ráto, ADJ.: God-fearing, pious. ‖**timó-re** [L. *timor*], M.: fear (fright, apprehension, alarm). **-rosaménte**, ADV.: timorously. **-rosétto**, *dim.* of *-roso.* **-rosità†**, F.: timidity. **-róso**, ADJ.: timorous (fearful). **-morúccio†**, M.: slight fear..
timpa-neggiáre, TR.: beat the drum. **-nèllo**, M.: (*typ.*) small tympan. **-nét-to**, M.: small kettle-drum. **-nísta**, pl. *—i*, M.: player on the timbrel, etc. **-níte**, **-nítide**, M.: (*med.*) timpany. ‖**tímpa-no** [L. *tympanum* (Gr. *túptein*, beat)], M.: tympano (kettle-drum, TIMBREL, tabour); tympanum (ear-drum; air-sack; drum-shaped wheel).
tí-na† [L. *-na*, wine-vessel], F.: small vat, tub. **-náia**, F.: stand for vats or casks.
tín-ca [L.], F.: TENCH (a fish). **-chétta**, F.: small tench. **-cóne**, M.: bubo (swelling in the groin).
tinèl-la [*tina*] = *-lo.* **-létto**, **-lét-ta**, **-líno**, **-lína**, *dim.* of *-lo.* **tinèl-lo**, M.: small vat or tub; servants' hall.
tín-gere [L.], IRR.§; TR.: tinge (dye, stain). **-gitúra**, F.: tinging, tinge.

§ Pret. *tín-si, -se; -sero.* Part. *tinto.*

tí-no [L. *-na;* cf. *-na*], M.: large vat (wine-cask); dyeing tub; bathing tub. **-nózza**, F.: large tub, recipient; washing tub; bathing tub.
tín-si, PRET. of *-tingere.* **-ta** [*-to*], F.: tint, colour; superficial notice; dye-house†. **-ti(l)láno†**, M.: fine cloth dyed in grain.
tin-tín [echoic], M.: tinkle. **-tinnábu-lo†**, M.: small bell. **-tinnaménto**, M.: tinkling, tinkle. **-tinnáre**, INTR.: (*lit.*) tinkle, resound. **-tinnío**, M.: tinkle. **-tinníre** = *-tinnare.* **-tínno**, M.: tinkling, tinkle. **-tintò**, M.: dingdong (of a bell).
tín-to, PART. of *-gere;* M.†: tincture, dye, colour. **-tóre**, M.: dyer. **-toría**, F.: dye-house. **-tòrio**, ADJ.: dyeing; of dye-stuffs. **-túra**, F.: dyeing; dye, *tint; tincture;* extract.
tiòrba [fr. name of inventor], F.: theorbo (sort of large lute).
tí-pico, ADJ.: typical. ‖**-'po** [Gr. *túpos* (*tup-*, beat)], M.: type; model. **-pogra-fía**, F.: typography. **-pográfico**, ADJ.: typographical. **-pògrafo**, M.: typographer, printer.
tipóre† = *tepore.*
tíra [*tirare*], F.: drawing, draft; strife (dispute, scramble). **=línee**, M. INVAR.: ruler; drawing-pen. **=lòro**, M.: gold-washer. **-ménto**, M.: drawing, pulling.
tirán-na, F.: tyrannical woman. **-nác-cio**, M.: cruel tyrant. **-náre†**, **-neg-giáre**, TR.: tyrannize. **-nèllo**, *dim.* of *-no.* **-nería†** = *-nia.* **-nescamén-te**, ADV.: in a very cruel manner. **-né-sco**, ADJ.: very cruel or tyrannous. **-nía**, F.: tyranny. **-nicaménte**, ADV.: tyrannically. **-nicída**, pl. *—i*, M.: tyrannicide. **tirán-nico**, ADJ.: tyrannical. **tirán-nide**, F.: tyranny; absolute government. **-'nio†** = *-nico.* **-nizzáre†** = *-neggiare.* ‖**tirán-no** [L. *tyrannus*], M.: tyrant.
ti-ránte, ADJ.: drawing (pulling); tough; tending to; M.: horse-collar; boot-strap; boot-hook; puller: *far da —*, help in a dishonest work. ‖**-ráre** [Germ'c, ak. to Eng. *tear*], TR.: draw (pull, drag; attract, allure; infer; draw lots; pull out); draw out (extend); (pull the trigger; hence, fire off; shoot, let fly); lounge out, kick; (*typ.*) pull, strike off: *— calci*, kick; *— in lungo*, prolong, protract; *— per avan-ti*, go on; *— via*, be off; *— sopra*, shoot at; *— al*, incline to; *— da*, resemble; *— per sorte*, draw lots; *-rarsi addosso*, bring upon one's self. **-ra=stiváli**, M.: boot-jack. **-ráta**, F.: drawing; draught; way. **-ra=táppi**, M.: tap or cork-puller. **-ráto**, PART.: drawn, etc.; close-fisted. **-ratí-na**, *dim.* of *-rata.* **-ratóio**, M.: stretching place (for woollen stuffs); drawer. **-ratóre**, M.: drawer; shooter: *è gran —*, he is an excellent shot. **-ratúra**, F.: drawing (pulling, etc.); printing off.
tir-chiería, F.: niggardliness. ‖**-'chio** [?], ADJ.: niggardly, sordid.
tirèlla [*-rare*], F.: traces (of a harness).
tiriáca† = *triaca.*
tiritèra [ak. to *tirare*], F.: drawn out or tedious discourse.
tíro [*-rare*], M.: drawing (pull); firing off (shot), throw; shot's distance (reach); line; draught; yoke; gibe, trick; viper†: *a — di moschetto*, within the reach of shot; *a — di sasso*, at a stone's throw; *essere a —*, be closing with each other in a bargain; *— a sei*, coach and six; *— a due, a quattro*, match, pair; set of coach horses; pair of oxen.

ti-rocínio, M.: noviciate. ‖**-róne**† [L. *-ro*, recruit], M.: recruit; tyro, novice.

tirói-de [Gr. *turo-eidés*, 'cheese-form'], F.: thyroid cartilage (Adam's apple). **-dèo,** ADJ.: thyroid.

tírso [Gr. *thúrsos*], M.: thyrsus (Bacchus' staff).

tisána [Gr. *ptisáne*], F.: ptisan (barley decoction).

tí-si [Gr. *phthísis*], **-si,** F.: phthisis (consumption). **-sichézza,** F.: consumptiveness. **tí-sico,** ADJ.: phthisical (consumptive). **-sicúme,** M.: consumption; lean body.

titil-laménto, M.: titillation, tickling. ‖**-láre** [L.], TR.: titillate (tickle; please). **-lazióne,** F.: titillation (tickling).

tito-láccio, *disp.* of *-lo*. **-láre** 1, ADJ.: titular. **-láre** 2, TR.: title, call. **-lário**†, M.: book of titles, peerage book. **-láto,** PART.†: titled; M.: titled person. ‖**títo-lo** [L. *titulus*], M.: title (name; dignity; renown; plea; title-page). **-lóne,** *aug.* of *-lo*.

titu-baménto, M.: hesitation. ‖**-báre** [L.], INTR.: waver (hesitate, vacillate; cf. Eng.† titubate). **-bazióne,** F.: wavering (hesitation).

tízzo [L. *titio*], M.: firebrand, brand.

tò' [*togliere*], for *togli*.

tòcca 1 [cf. *-cco* 2], F.: cloth of silk and gold; gauze.

tóc-ca 2, F.: pavement crack or hole. **-cábile,** ADJ.: touchable, tangible. **-ca=lápis,** M.: sliding pencil (pencil case). **-caménto,** M.: touching; contact. **-cánte,** ADJ.: touching, etc.; concerning. ‖**-cáre** [OGer. *zuchon*, ak. to Eng. *tuck*, *tug*], TR.: TOUCH (have contact with; handle; feel; concern, affect; impress, move; play upon); beat (strike); offend; M.: touch(ing), feeling; handling: — *la mano*, give a tip; *-ca a voi di*, it's your turn to; — *delle busse*, be beaten; — *la fregola*, have a burning wish; — *sul vivo*, touch to the quick; — *un tasto* (or *cantino*), strike a delicate chord; hit in the sore place. **-cáta,** cf. *-cato;* F.: prelude. **-catína,** *dim.* of *-cata*. **-catívo,** ADJ.: touching (affecting, affective). **-cáto,** PART.: touched, etc.; M.: touch, feeling. **-catóre,** M.: toucher; tipstaff. **-cheggiáre,** INTR.: toll. **-chétto,** *dim.* of *-co*1 or *-co*2. **tóc-co**1, PART. (*pop.*) of *-care;* M.: touching, touch; stroke (of a clock, etc., blow): *al — della campana*, at the stroke of the bell; *al —*, at one o'clock; *fare al —*, draw.

tòcco 2 [fr. Celt.], M.: large piece (judge's) cap or bonnet, skull-cap.

tò-ga [L. (*tegere*, cover)], F.: (Rom.) toga; robe. **-gáto,** ADJ.: togated, robed.

tò-gliere [L. *tollere*], IRR. §; TR.: take away (remove, carry off; snatch, take off); seize; undertake (try); dissuade; deliver: — *di mira*, aim at; — *ad interesse*, borrow on interest; *vi — la volta*, be beforehand; *tolga Iddio!* God forbid! **-glimento,** M.: taking away, etc.; theft. **-glitóre,** M.: remover; thief.

§ Ind.: Pres. *tòlgo, tògli, tòglie; togliámo, togliéte, tòlgono*. Pret. *tòl-si, -se; -sero*. Fut. *torrò* or *toglierò*. Cond. *torrèi* or *toglierèi*. Subj.: Pres. *tòlga*. Ive *tògli*. Part. *tòlto*. — Poet. forms. *togl-* for *tolg-*. Pret. *tòlli*, etc

tòlda [fr. Scand.], F.: deck (of a ship).

toléttа†, F.: toilet, dressing-table.

tòlgo, PRES. of *togliere*.

tolle-rábile, ADJ.: tolerable. **-rabilménte,** ADV.: tolerably. **-ránte,** ADJ.: tolerant (long-suffering; liberal). **-ránza,** F.: tolerance, toleration. ‖**-ráre** [L.], TR.: tolerate (support, bear with, endure). **-ratóre,** M.: who tolerates.

tòllere† = *togliere*.

Tolommèa [*Tolomeo*, Heb. traitor and murderer], ADJ.: (*lit.*) of a traitor's place (in Dante's Inferno).

tòl-si, PRET. of *togliere*. **-'to,** PART. of *togliere;* F.: taking away; bargain.

tolù [*T.*, in Granada], M.: tolu (plant; balm).

tomáio [? Russ. *towár*, skin], M.: upper leather, vamp.

tomáre†, INTR.: tumble; roll.

tómba [L. *tumba*], F.: tomb; villa†; granary†.

tómbola [?], F.: tombola (kind of lottery).

tombo-láre [ak. to *tumble*], TR.: make tumble, overthrow. **-láta,** F.: tumble, overthrow. **-létto, -líno,** M.: little fat fellow; ADJ.: roly-poly. **tómbo-lo,** M.: tumble; cylindrical cushion (sofa cushion); embroidery cushion, lace pillow (for lace-making). **-lòtto,** M.: short fat person, roly-poly.

tomísta, pl. —*i* [*Thomas*], M.: follower of St. Thomas.

tòmo 1 [Gr. *-mos*, cut, section], M.: tome (volume).

tómo† 2 [*-mare*], M.: tumble.

tòna-ca [L. *tunica*], F.: tunic, robe; monk, priest. **-cáccia,** *disp.* of *-ca*. **-chèlla, -chétta, -chína,** *dim.* of *-ca*. **-chíno,** *jest. dim.* of *-ca*.

to-nalità [*tono*], F.: tonality. ‖**-náre** [L.], IRR. §; INTR.: THUNder, roar. **-natóre,** M.: thunderer.

§ *t(u)òn-* accented, *ton-* unaccented.

ton-chiáre, INTR.: be eaten by weevils. ‖**tón-chio** [?], M.: weevil, mite. **-chióso,** ADJ.: full of weevils.

ton-daménto†, M.: rounding, chipping. ‖**-dáre** [-do], TR.: round, prune. **-da-**

tára, F.: rounding; chipping. **-deggiaménto**, M.: rounding out, embossment. **-deggiáre**, TR.: round out; emboss; INTR.: be roundish. **-dellíno**, *dim.* of *-do*. **-dèllo**, M.: round of beef, etc.

tòndere [L.], TR.: shear, shave, clip.

ton-derèllo, **-dettíno**, **-détto**, ADJ.: *dim.* of *-do;* roundish. **-dézza**, F.: roundness (rotundity). **-díno**, M.: (round) plate, breakfast plate.

tonditúra† [*-dere*], F.: shearing, clipping; clippings.

tón-do [*rotondo*], ADJ.: ROUND (circular, ROTUND; entire); in relief; stupid, coarse; M.: sphere (globe); plate; stupid fellow, bumpkin, fool: *alla* (or *in*) —, round about; by repetition; *cifra -da*, number ending with a zero; *sputar* —, play the wiseacre, act big. **-dóne**, ADJ.: *aug.* of *-do;* M.: large fritter.

tondúto†, PART. of *tondere*.

tón-fano, **-'fano**, M.: deep part (of a river), gulf. **-fáre**, INTR.: make a splash or noise. ‖**tón-fo** [variant of *tuffo*], M.: plunge, fall; splash, noise. **-foláre†** = *-fare*.

tónica† I (*vulg.*) = *tonaca*.

tòni-ca 2 [*tono*], F.: tonic (key-tone). **-co**, ADJ.: tonic.

ton-nára, F.: tunny-place. **-naròtto**, M.: tunny-fisher. **-neggiáre**, INTR.: haul with a cable. **-néggio**, M.: hauling. **-nína**, F.: pickled tunny. ‖**tón-no** [L. *thunnus*], M.: tunny (fish).

tò-no I [*-nare*], M.: thunder; roar, rumbling; rumour†. **tò-no** 2 [L. *-nus*], M.: tone.

ton-sílla [L. *-silis*], F.: tonsil. **-silláre**, ADJ.: tonsilar.

tòn-so [*-dere*], ADJ.: shorn. **-súra**, F.: tonsure. **-suráre**, TR.: give the tonsure. **-suráto**, ADJ.: tonsured.

tontína [*Tonti*, originator], F.: tontine (sort of insurance).

tónto [for *tonito* (*attonito*)], ADJ.: silly, foolish, stupid; M.: blockhead.

tò-pa [*talpa*], F.: (*jest.*) mouse; rat. **-pác-cio**, *disp.* of *-po*. **-páia**, F., **-páio†**, M.: rat's nest; (*fig.*) wretched place, hole.

topázio [Gr. *-zion*], M.: topaz.

to-pésco, ADJ.: (*jest.*) rat-like; full of rats, rat-. ‖**-pétto**, *dim.* of *-po*.

tòpi-ca, F.: topic. ‖**-co**, pl. *-ci* [Gr. *-kós* (*tópos*, place)], ADJ.: topical, local.

to-pináia, F.: mice-nest; mole-hill; (*fig.*) wretched place, hole. **-pinára†**, F.: mote. **-píno**, M.: *dim.* of *-po;* sort of olive. ‖**tò-po** [*talpa*], M.: mouse; rat; sort of olive; — *campagnuolo*, field-mouse; *-pi matti*, fireworks.

topo-grafía [Gr. *tópos*, land, *grápheïn*, write], F.: topography. **-gráf-** —*ci*, ADJ.: topographic(al). **top-** **fo**, M.: topographer.

topolíno, *dim.* of *topo*.

tòp-pa, F.: patch; temporary door-lock; key-hole; breech flap; at hazard (with three cards). **-p** *disp.* of *-pa*. **-paiuòlo†**, **-pai-** **vo†**, M.: locksmith. **-páre†**, TR. consent. **-páto**, ADJ.: stained wi- **-pétto**, *dim.* of *-po*. ‖**tòp-po** Eng. *top*], M.: log, piece of wood wedge. **-póne**, M.: patchwork q placing under children or sick per

to-ráce [Gr. *thórax*], M.: thora- **cico**, ADJ.: thoracic.

tórba I [Germ'c *torf*], F.: TURF;

tór-ba† 2, F.: turbid or muddy **-báre†**, TR.: make turbid, trouble **cio**, ADJ.: somewhat turbid or **-bidaménte**, ADV.: turbidly. **to**, **-bidíno**, *dim.* of *-bido*. **-bi** F.: turbidness, muddiness. **-bid** ADJ.: rather turbid or muddy. ‖ **do**, ADJ.: turbid (muddy, trouble bulent. **tór-bo**, ADJ.: turbid muddy).

tòr-cere [L. *torquere*], IRR. §; TR (wring, writhe, wrest); REFL.: tw self about: — *il muso* (or *la bocca* a wry face, grin. **-cettíno**, *-cetto*. **-cétto**, M.: *dim.* of *-c* taper (of four long candles co **-chiáccio**, *disp.* of *-chia*. **-c** TR.: press. **-chiatúra**, F.: p

tòr-chio [L. *-culum*], M.: press;

tòr-cia, F.: TORCH; wax tape *-cetto*, which see). **-ciáre†**, TR. tie together. **-ci=còllo**, M.: rhe in the neck; (*fig.*) devotee, big wing. **-c(i)ère**, M.: big candlest the *-cia*). **-ci-fèccio†**, **-ci-fè** [*feccia*], M.: straining bag, filte **gliáre†**, TR.: twist, twine.

§ Pret. *tòr-si*, *-se*; *-sero*. Part. *t*

torcimánno [Ar. *tergeman*], M.: man (interpreter).

tor-ciménto [*-cere*], M.: twisting **tóio**, M.: twisting instrument, silk twisting-wheel. **-citúra**, F. ing, twist. **-coláre†** [*-chio*], M. **-colétto**, *dim.* of *-colo*. **-coliè** press worker. **tòr-colo†** [cf. *-c* press.

tor-dáio†, M.: thrush coop. **-d** large thrush. ‖**tór-do** [L. *turd* THRUSH. **-dáccio**, *dim.* of *-do*.

to-rèllo, **-rétto**, *dim.* of *toro*.

toríccia [?], F.: young she-goat,

tórlo [L. *torulus* (*-rus*, bulge), part], M.: yolk (of the egg); (*fi* thing.

tórma [L. *turma*], F.: (*lit.*) flock, troop; (Rom.) troop of 32 cavalrymen.
tormén-ta, F.: fierce Alpine storm. **-tagióne†**, **-taménto†**, M.: torment. **-táre**, TR.: torment. **-tatóra**, F., **-tatóre**, M., **-tatríce**, F.: tormenter, -tor, tormentress. **-tílla**, F.: tormentil (plant).
‖**tormén-to** [L. *-tum* (*torquere*, twist)], M.: torment (torture; vexation). **-tosaménte**, ADV.: tormentingly, cruelly. **-tóso**, ADJ.: tormenting. **-túzzo**, *dim.* of *-to*.
torna=cónto, M.: profitable thing, profitableness. **=gústo**, M.: appetizer, enticing thing. **=lètto**, M.: valance (drapery round a bed). ‖**torná-re** [L., turn in a lathe], INTR.: reTURN (turn back); begin again; turn out, happen; turn; revolve; become: — *bene*, fit, become, be profitable; — *conto*, be of use, profit; *-rne*, aid; profit; — *a mano*, be handy. **=sóle**, M.: heliotrope†, sunflower. **torná-ta**, F.: return(ing); weaning; meeting, assembly; last strophe.
tor-neaménto, M.: tournament. **-neatóre**, M.: combatant in a tournament. ‖**-nèo** [*-nare*], M.: tourney (tournament, joust, tilt); turn†.
tornése [*Tours*], M.: coin (of varied value, first struck at T.).
tor-n(i)áio, M.: turner (on the lathe). ‖**tór-nio** [L. *-nus*, lathe], M.: turner's wheel, lathe. **-níre**, TR.: turn (in a lathe); turn out. **-nitóre**, M.: turner. **-nitúra**, F.: turning (in the lathe); chips (from turning).
tórno [*-nare*], M.: turn, revolution; twist†; return†; ADV.: (= *intorno*) about, nearly: — —, round about; *a* —, round about; *in quel* —, at about.
tò-ro [L. *taurus*], M.: bull; (*astr.*) Taurus; nuptial bed (for — *maritale*); big moulding (at the base of a column). **-róso**, M.: (*lit.*) robust, stout.
tor-pèdine [L. *-pedo*], F.: torpedo (fish; explosive engine); torpor, sluggishness. **-pedinièra** [*-pedine*], F.: torpedo-boat. **-pènte**, ADJ.: benumbed, lazy. **-pidézza**, F.: torpidness. ‖**tór-pido** [L. *-pidus* (*-pere*, be numb)], ADJ.: torpid (numb, dull, sluggish). **-póre**, M.: torpor, sluggishness.
tor-ráccia, **-ráccio**, *disp.* of *-re*. **-raiòlo**, ADJ.: of the stock-dove (cf. *terraiuolo*).
tòrre 1, syncop. form of *togliere*.
tór-re 2 [L. *turris*], F.: TOWER; castle (at chess). **-reggiáre**, INTR.: tower, rise up.
tor-rentáccio, *disp.* of *-rente*. ‖**-rènte** [L. *-rens* (*-rere*, burn, boil)], M.: torrent. **-rentèllo**, *disp. dim.* of *-rente*. **-renziále**, ADJ.: torrential.
tor-rétta, **-ricciòla**, **-ricèlla**, F.: *dim.* of *-re;* turret.
tòrrido [L. *-dus*], ADJ.: torrid.
tor-rière [*-re*], M.: (*lit.*) keeper of a tower, warden. **-rigiáno†**, M.: tower guard. **-rioncèllo**, **-rioncíno**, *dim.* of *-rione*. **-rióne**, M.: old big tower.
torróne [?], M.: almond cake.
torsióne [*torcere*], F.: torsion; colic.
tor-sèllo†, M.: small bale of goods; pincushion; roll. ‖**tór-so** [? L. *thyrsus*, stem], M.: torso, bust; stalk; core. **-soláta**, F.: blow with a stalk, core. **tórsolo**, M.: stalk (of cabbage, etc.), stem; core (of fruit).
tòr-ta 1, F.: twist(ing). **tór-ta** 2 [L.], F.: TART: *mangiar la* — *in capo a*, be taller than, surpass. **-taménte**, ADV.: in a twisted manner, crookedly; in a wrong sense. **-tèlla**, *dim.* of *-ta* 2. **-telláio**, M.: tart-seller, confectioner. **-tellétta**, *dim.* of *-tella*. **-tèllo**, M.: little pie or bun. **-tevolménte**, ADV.: wrongfully. **-tézza**, F.: (*lit.*) twisted shape, crookedness. **-tiglióne**, M.: barrel (of a gun); gun; ADV.†: tortuously. **-tiglióso†**, ADJ.: tortuous, twisted, winding. **-tína**, **-tino**, *dim.* of *-ta* 2. **-tíre†**, INTR.: twist; wrap. **-titúdine†**, F.: tortuousness, crookedness. ‖**tòr-to**, PART. of *torcere;* twisted, etc.; wrong; unjust; M.: wrong; injury; insult: *avere* —, be wrong; *dar* — *a uno*, declare one to be wrong, decide against one, side against one, contradict one; *a* —, wrongly, unjustly.
tortol. .† = *tortor*. .
tortóne [*torta* 2], M.: big tart.
tórto-ra, F., ‖**-re†** 1 [L. *turtur*], M.: turtle-dove.
tortóre† 2, M.: torturer.
torto-rèlla, **-rétta**, *dim.* of *-ra*.
tor-tóso†, ADJ.: wrongful, unjust. **-tuosaménte**, ADV.: tortuously. **-tuosità**, F.: tortuosity. ‖**-tuóso** [*-to*], ADJ.: tortuous, winding. **-túra**, F.: torture (torment); tortuousness (twistedness)†; injustice†. **-turáre**, TR.: torture, torment.
tor-vaménte, ADV.: scowlingly, with a surly look. **-vità†**, F.: surliness, sternness. ‖**tór-vo** [L. *-vus*, staring, stern], ADJ.: looking black; scowling.
torzióne†, F.: contortion; extortion.
tor-zoncèllo, *dim.* of *-zone*. ‖**-zóne** [?], M.: serving lay-friar.
tósa†, F.: girl, lass.
to-saménto, M.: shearing, clipping. ‖**-sáre** [L. *tonsus*, PART. of *tondere*, crop], TR.: shear (crop, clip, shave). **-sáto**, PART.: sheared, cropped. **-satóre**, M.: shearer, clipper. **-satúra**, F.: shearing, clipping; clippings.

tosca-naménte, ADV.: in the Tuscan manner. **-neggiáre**, INTR.: affect Tuscan ways. **-nería**, F.: affected Tuscan style or phrase. **-néşimo**, **-nişmo**, M.: Tuscan expression, Tuscanism. **-nità**, F.: Tuscanism. **-nizzáre**, TR.: Tuscanize. ||**toscá-no** or (*lit.*) **tósco** 1 [L. *tuscus*], ADJ.: Tuscan.

tòsco 2 [abbr. of *tossico*], M.: (*poet.*) poison, venom.

toşétta†, *dim.* of *-sa.*

tó-şo [L. *tonsus*], PART. (*vulg.*) of *-sare;* shorn, etc. **-şoláre**, TR.: shear, clip. **-şóne** [L. *tonsio*], M.: golden fleece (order of chivalry, est. 1450); (*myth.*) ram with the golden fleece.

tós-sa†, ||**-se** [L. *tussis*], F.: cough. **-serèlla**, **-serellína**, *dim.* of *-sa.* **-settáccia**, **-settína**, *disp.* and *dim.* of *-sa.* **-sicchiáre**, INTR.: cough slightly.

tòssico, pl. *—ci* [Gr. *toxikón*], M.: poison, venom. **-logía**, F.: toxicology. **-lògico**, pl. *—ci*, ADJ. toxicological.

tossicóne, *aug.* of *tosse.*

tossicóso† [*-co*], ADJ.: poisonous.

tos-siménto†, M.: cough(ing). ||**-síre** [*-se*], INTR. (Pres. *tosso*): cough.

to-staménte [*tosto* 2], **-stanaménte**†, ADV.: (*lit.*) quickly (speedily, promptly). **-stanézza**†, F.: quickness, promptness. **-stáno**†, ADJ.: quick, prompt. **-stánza**, speed, velocity.

to-stáre [L. *-stus*, part. of *torrere*, parch], TR.: toast (roast). **-statúra**, F.: roasting. **-stíno**, M.: roaster, roasting-pan.

tòsto 1, ADJ.: roasted, hard; impudent, bold.

tòsto 2 [? L. *tot-cito*, 'as soon'], ADJ.: quick, sudden; ADV.: soon: — *che*, as soon as.

totá-le [L. *-lis*], ADJ.: total (entire, complete); M.: entirety, sum. **-lità**, F.: totality. **-lménte**, ADV.: totally, entirely,

tòtano [L. *tutilus*], M.: cuttlefish.

tótto [cf. *tette*], INTERJ.: don't touch! (to children).

tová-glia [ak. to Eng. *towel*], F.: tablecloth. **-gliáccia**, *disp.* of *-glia*. **-gliétta**, **-glína**, *dim.* of *-glia*. **-gliolíno**, *dim.* of *-gliolo*. **-gliòlo**, M.: napkin. **-glióna**, **-glióne**, **-gliúccia**, *disp. aug.* of *-glia.* **-gliuòla**†, *dim.* of *-glia.*

toz-zétto, *dim.* of *-zo.* ||**tòz-zo** [?], ADJ.: squat, short and thick, stubby; morsel of dry, hard bread, morsel, bit. **-zoláre**†, INTR.: go seeking bits of bread, go begging. **-zòtto**, *aug.* of *-zo.*

tra 1 [L. *intra*], PREP.: within (in; in the course of); among, between; on: — *pochi giorni*, in a few days; — *via*, on the way; — *tutto*, on the whole.

tra 2 [L. *ultra*], PREP.: beyond, besides, moreover. **=antíco**, ADJ.: very old or antique. **=aváro**, ADJ.: very greedy.

trabác-ca†, F., **-co**†, M.: pavillion, booth. **-chétta**†, *dim.* of *-ca.*

trabáccolo [L. *-culum* (*trabes*, beam)], M.: merchant vessel with two masts.

trabal-dáre†, TR.: steal; defraud. **-dería**, F.: stealing, cheating.

tra=balláre, INTR.: stagger, vacillate. **-ballío**, M.: staggering, vacillation. **-ballóne**, M.: big totter. **=balzáre**, TR.: toss up and down.

trabálzo†, M.: usury, illegal profit.

trabánte [Ger. *-bant* (*-ben*, trot)], M.: yeoman of the guard, trooper.

trá-bea [L.], F.: (Rom.) trabea (short toga). **-beáto** 1, ADJ.: dressed in a trabea.

tra=beáto† 2, ADJ.: most happy. **=bèllo**†, ADJ.: very beautiful. **=bène**†, ADV.: excellently, extremely well. **=bére**†: IRR.; TR., INTR.: drink excessively.

trabíccolo [variant of *-baccolo*], M.: sort of warming-pan; implement; rickety thing.

traboc-caménto, M.: overflow; downfall. **-canteménte**, ADV.: precipitously. ||**-cáre** [*tra*, *bocca*], INTR.: overflow, boil over; superabound; exceed; (*lit.*) fall flat, tumble; TR.†: inundate; throw down, precipitate, hurl; batter down. **-chèllo**†, **-chétto** [*-co*], M.: pitfall, trap-door, man-trap. **-chévole**†, ADJ.: overflowing, excessive, immense, huge. **-chevolménte**†, ADV.: excessively. **trabóc-co**, M.: overflow, flow; downfall†; pitfall†; balista.

trabendáre†, INTR.: superabound, overflow.

trabuc. .† = *traboc.* .

tra=buòno†, ADJ.: exceedingly good. **-cannáre** [*canna*], INTR., REFL.: drink hard. **-cannatóre**, M.: drunkard. **=capáce**†, ADJ.: very capable. **=cáro**†, ADJ.: extremely dear. **-cattívo**†, ADJ.: exceedingly wicked.

tracchéggiáre [Sp. *traquear*, move to and fro], TR.: waver and delay (procrastinate, defer).

trác-cia [l. L. **tractiare* (L. *trahere*, draw)], F.: TRACE (track, vestige, footstep; mark); troop (band)†; treatise†: *andare in* —, run after, hunt after. **-ciaménto**, M.: tracing; snare. **-ciáre**, TR.: trace (track); contrive. **-ciatóre**, M.: tracer.

tra-chèa [Gr. *-cheia*, rough], F.: trachea (windpipe). **-cheále**, ADJ.: tracheal.

tra=chiáro†, ADJ.: most clear. **=codárdo**†, ADJ.: very cowardly. **-còlla** [*collo*], F.: shoulder-belt. **-collaménte**

[*-collare*], M.: tumble. **-colláre** [*collo*], INTR.: fall headlong, tumble; threaten to fall; impend. **=còllo**, M.: tumble, downfall; ruin. **=confortáre†**, TR.: comfort. **=convenévole†**, ADJ.: exceedingly convenient. **=cordáre**, INTR., REFL.: agree well. **=corrènte**, ADJ.: running swiftly. **=córrere†**, IRR.; INTR.: run swiftly. **=córso†**, ADJ.: passed, elapsed. **=cortése†**, ADJ.: exceedingly polite. **=cotánto**, ADJ.: (*lit.*) haughty, overbearing. **=cotánza**, F.: (*lit.*) haughtiness. **=cotáre**, INTR.: behave insolently, grow bold. **=còtto**, ADJ.: too much cooked or baked, overdone. **=cruccióso†**, ADJ.: extremely irritated. **=curággine†**, **=curánza†**, **=cutággine†**, F.: negligence. **=cutáto**, ADJ.: negligent. **-dere†**, INTR.: inform; betray. **-digióne†**, F., **-diménto** [*-dire*], M.: treason, perfidy: *a* —, unexpectedly; deceitfully. **-diritto†**, ADJ.: very straight.

tra-díre [L. *tra-dere* (*dare*, give)], TR.: BETRAY. **-ditévole†**, ADJ.: traitorous. **-ditevolménte**, ADV.: treacherously. **-díto**, PART. of *-dire*. **-ditóra**, F.: traitress. **-ditoráccio**, M.: infamous traitor. **-ditóre**, M.: traitor. **-ditorèllo**, *dim.* of *-ditore*. **-ditorescaménte**, ADV.: treacherously. **-ditorésco**, ADJ.: treacherous. **-ditríce**, F.: traitress. **-dizionále**, ADJ.: traditional. **-dizióne**, F.: tradition.

tra=dólce, ADJ.: very sweet.

tra-dótto, PART. of *-durre;* translated; transferred†. **-ducíbile**, ADJ.: translatable. **-dúco**, PRES. of *-durre*. ‖**-dúrre** [L. *-ducere*], IRR. (cf. *addurre*); TR.: translate; transfer†. **-duttóre**, M.: translator. **-duzioncèlla**, *dim.* of *-duzione*. **-duzióne**, F.: translation, version.

tra-ènte, ADJ.: drawing, attractive; M.: drawer (of a bill of exchange). **-ènza†**, F.: attraction. ‖**trá-ere†** = *trarre*.

trafe-laménto, M.: exhaustion. ‖**-láre** [? Ger. *träufeln*, 'drip' with sweat], TR., INTR.: pant with exhaustion, be tired out. **-láto**, ADJ.: exhausted.

tra-feríre†, TR.: strike. **-fésso†**, ADJ.: cleft, split.

traffi-cábile, ADJ.: trafficable, practicable. **-cánte**, ADJ.: trading. ‖**-cáre** [?], TR., INTR.: traffic (trade); be busy†; manage†. **-catóre**, M.: trader, merchant. **tráffi-co**, M.: traffic (trade, commerce).

traffière†, M.: dagger.

tra=fíggere, IRR.; TR.: transfix (transpierce, run through, pierce). **-figgiménto**, M.: transfixing, piercing; wound. **-figgitóre**, M., **-figgitríce**, F.: transfixer, piercer. **-figgitúra†**, F.: piercing; wound.

tra-fíla [*filo*], F.: wire-drawing plate. **-filáre**, TR.: wire-draw.

tra-físso†, PART.: pierced. **-fítta**, F.: piercing; wound; puncture. **-fittívo†**, ADJ.: piercing. ‖**-fítto**, PART. of *-figgere*. **-fittúra**, F.: piercing; wound.

trafòglio† = *trifoglio*.

tra=foráre, TR.: bore or pierce through; INTR.: cut fancy-work. **-forazióne**, F.: boring or piercing through. **-fóro**, M.: piercing; openwork lace; hole, hiding-place.

tra=fréddo, ADJ.: extremely cold.

tra-fugaménto, M.: carrying away by stealth. ‖**=fugáre**, TR.: carry away by stealth, run away with; REFL.: run or steal away. **-fúgo**: *di* —, by stealth, secretly. **-fuggíre†**, INTR.: run away.

tra-furellería†, F.: deceit, roguery. **-furèllo†**, **-furellíno†**, M.: little thief, little knave.

trafúso-la [*fuso*], F.: skein of silk. **-lo†**, M.: shin-bone.

tragè-dia [L. *tragœdia* (Gr. *trágos*, goat, *oidè*, song)], F.: tragedy. **-diánte**, M.: tragedian. **-dieggiáre**, TR.: turn into a tragedy. **-diògrafo**, M.: tragedian (writer of tragedies). **-diúccia**, *dim.* of *-dia*. **tragè-do†**, ADJ.: tragic(al); M.: tragedian (writer or actor).

tragett.. = *tragitt..*

trág-gere (*poet.*) = *trarre*. **-gitóre**, M., **-gitríce**, F.: dragger, drawer. **trág-go**, PRES. of *trarre*.

traghett.. = *tragitt..*

tragi-caménte, ADV.: tragically. ‖**trá-gi-co**, pl. —*ci* [Gr. *-kós*], ADJ.: tragic(al); M.: tragedian (writer of tragics). **=còmico**, ADJ.: tragi-comic. **=commèdia**, F.: tragi-comedy.

tra=giovánte, ADJ.: extremely helpful.

tra=gittáre, TR.: pass or bring over (a stream, etc.); toss†, shake†; INTR.: pass over; perform legerdemain. **-gitto**, M.: passing over, passage (across), transportation; road across, passage; crossway†.

tra=giústo†, ADJ.: very just or fair. **=glorióso†**, ADJ.: most glorious. **=gránde†**, ADJ.: extremely great. **=guárdo**, M.: level (instrument).

trágula [L.], F.: javelin, dart.

trai, cf. *trarre*.

tra=iettárre, TR.: pass across.

trai-ménto†, M.: drawing. **-náre**, TR.: drag along, haul; trail along. ‖**trái-no** [L. *trahere*, draw], M.: DRAY; carriage; TRAIN, railway-train; TRAIL (of a gown, etc.); waggon-load, baggage; raft†; train (attendance)†.

tra-íre†, **-itóre†** = tra-dire, -ditore.

quillize, calm, quiet. ||**tranquíl-lo** [L. *-lus* (*trans*, *quies*, quiet)], ADJ.: tranquil (quiet, calm); M.†: tranquillity (quiet, calm).

trans- [L.], PREF.: trans-, beyond. **=alpíno**, ADJ.: transalpine. **=animazióne**†, F.: transmigration (of souls). **=átto**, **=azióne**, F.: contract (agreement, transaction); compromise; transfer. **-céndere**† (*tran*, *scendere*), IRR.; TR.: transcend. **tráns-eat** [L.], M.: let it pass, all right. **-égna**†, F.: cloak; coat of mail. **-ígere** [L. *agere*, act], TR.: come to terms, compound; transfer. **-itáre**, INTR.: make a transit, pass by. **-íre**† [L.], INTR.: pass; die. **-itivaménte**, ADV.: transitively, in a transitive manner. **-itívo**, ADJ.: transitive. **tráns-ito** [L. *-itus* (*i-*, go)]; M.: passage, passing, transit; cross-road, crossing; PART.†: passed. **-itoriaménte**, ADV.: transitorily. **-itòrio**, ADJ.: transitory, transient. **-izióne**, F.: transition. **-la**.. = *trasla*.. **=lúcido**, ADJ.: translucid, -lucent. **-padáno** [L. *Padus*, Po], ADJ.: (*lit.*) transpadane (of beyond the Po, from Rome, i.e., north). **-port**.. = *trasport*..

transustan-ziáre [L. *trans-substantiare*], TR.: transubstantiate. **-ziazióne**, F.: transubstantiation.

tranvái [Eng. *tramway*], M.: tramway, street-car.

trapa-naménto, M.: boring, trepanning. **-náre**, TR.: bore, trepan. **-nazióne**, F.: boring, trepanning. ||**trápa-no** [l. L. *-num* (Gr. *trupân*, bore)], M.: bore, auger; trepan.

tra-passábile, ADJ.: passable; transient†. **-passaménto**, M.: passing over or across; transgression†, death†; lapse of time†. ||**=passáre**, INTR.: pass over or across (Eng.† transpass), cross over, cross; TR.: pass (of time); outrun; exceed (of number, etc.), surpass; pass beyond (die); transgress (TRESPASS against); omit†. **-passáto**, PART.: passed over, etc.; elapsed, past; M.: deceased person. **-passatóre**†, M.: trespasser, transgressor. **-pásso**, M.: passing over or across, passage; amble; crossing-place†; trespass†; decease.

tra-peláre [*tra*, *pelo*], INTR.: drop, leak, ooze out; TR.: understand from the slightest hint. **-pélo**, M.: extra draught-horse, etc. (for steep hills).

tra=pensáre†, INTR.: think seriously; muse.

trapè-zio [Gr. *-za* (for *tetrá-peza*, four-footed), table], M.: trapeze (trapezium). **-zòide**, M.: trapezoid.

tra-piantaménto, M.: transplantation. ||**=piantáre**, TR.: transplant. **-piantatóio**, M.: transplanting implement. **-piantazióne**, F.: transplanting.

tra=píccolo, ADJ.: exceedingly small.

tra=pórre, IRR.; TR.: put between (interpose; insert); transplace (transfer).

traport..† = *trasport*..

trapossènte†, ADJ.: very powerful.

trapósto, PART. of *traporre*.

trappísta [*Trappe*, monastery in Normandy], M.: Trappist (Cisternian monk).

tráppo-la [l. L. *trappa* (fr. Ger.)], F.: TRAP (snare; artifice). **-láre**, TR.: entrap, ensnare; dupe. **-latóre**, M.: (en)-trapper. **-lería**, F.: entrapping, ensnaring; cheating. **-lière**†, M.: entrapper. **-létta**, *dim.* of *-la*. **-líno**, M.: harlequin. **-lóne**, M.: entrapper, cheat; meddler.

trap-pórre†, **-pósto**† = *traporre*, *-posto*.

tra-puntáre, TR.: embroider, quilt. ||**=púnto**, M.: embroidery, quilting; ADJ.: embroidered; extenuated (thin)†; aggrieved†.

tra=reverèndo†, ADJ.: very reverend. **=ríсco**†, ADJ.: exceedingly rich.

tra-ripaménto†, M.: overflowing; passing across. ||**-ripáre**† [*ripa*], TR.: overflow; INTR.: tumble into a ravine; pass across (from bank to bank); overflow.

tra=rómpere, IRR.; TR.: (*pop.*) break in two, break; interrupt; change. **-rótto**†, PART.

tra=róşşo†, ADJ.: exceedingly red.

trárre [L. *trahere*], IRR.§; TR.: draw (pull); pluck (take out); reap; (*lit.*) move.

§ Ind.: Pres. *trággo*, *trái*, *tráe*; *tragghiámo*, *traéte*, *trággono*. Pret. *trássi*, *traésti*, *trásse*; *traémmo*, *traéste*, *trássero*. Fut. *trarrò*. Cond. *trarrèi*. Subj.: *trágga*; *tragghiámo*, *trággano*. I've *trái*. Part. *trátto*. Other forms from *tráere*.—Poet. forms.: Inf. *trággere*. Pres. (I.) *trággio*, *tróggi*, *trágge*; *trag(g)iámo* (S.) *trággia*.

tra-rupáre†, INTR.: hurl from a rock, precipitate. **-rupáto**†, PART.: precipitated; precipitous, steep.

tras- [L. *trans*]: PREF.: trans-, beyond, exceedingly, very.

tra=salíre, INTR.: leap or start back, be startled. **-saltáre**†, INTR.: make a big leap.

traşamáre†, INTR.: love passionately.

traş-andaménto, M.: passing over, negligence; omission. ||**=andáre**, TR.: pass over, neglect; surpass†; INTR.†: pass beyond; not abide by terms; be without effect. **-andatúra**†, F.: passing over; negligence; omission.

tra=sapére†, INTR.: know a great deal.

traş attáre†, REFL.: appropriate, usurp.

tra=sávio†, ADJ.: very wise or learned.

traş=bòno†, ADJ.: exceedingly good.

trascannáre†, TR.: wind upon another skein.

tra=sçégliere, IRR.; TR.: select (choose, pick). **-sceglimento**, M., **-scélta**, F.: selection, choice. **-scélto**, PART. of *-scegliere.*

tra-scendentále, ADJ.: transcendental. **-scendentalménte**, ADV.: transcendentally. **-scendènte**, ADJ.: transcendent. **-scendènza**, F.: transcendency. ‖**-scéndere** [L. *transcendere* (*trans*, *scandere*, climb)], IRR.; TR.: transcend (surpass, exceed, excel). **-scendiménto**, M.: transcending.

trascérre, abbrev. of *trascegliere.*

trascináre [? *trainare*], TR.: drag along, move.

tra-sciòcco†, ADJ.: very foolish.

trascoláre†, INTR.: trickle through, leak.

tras-coloráre, TR., REFL.: change colour.

trascorporazióne†, F.: transmigration.

tras=córrere, IRR.; TR.: run or pass over; omit; INTR.: pass (of time). **-corrévole**, ADJ.: running over. **-correvolménte**, ADV.: transiently, by the way. **-corriménto**, M.: running or passing over; passage; lapse. **-córsa**†, cf. *-corso.* **-corsivaménte**†, ADV.: by the way. **-córso**, PART. of *-correre;* run or passed over; past; omitted; M.: oversight; mistake: *in —*, by the way.

tra-scrítto, PART. of *-scrivere.* ‖**=scrívere**, IRR.; TR.: transcribe, copy. **-scrizióne**, F.: transcription, copy.

tras-curággine, F.: carelessness, negligence. **-curánte**, ADJ.: careless, negligent. **-curánza**, F.: carelessness, negligence. ‖**=curáre**, TR.: treat carelessly, neglect; pass over. **-curatáccio**, *disp.* of *-curato.* **-curatággine**, F.: carelessness, negligence. **-curataménte**, ADV.: carelessly, negligently. **-curatézza**, F.: carelessness, neglect. **-curáto**, PART.: neglected; careless, negligent. **-curatóre**, M.: neglecter.

tra=secoláre [*secolo*, as if issuing from another century], INTR.: be amazed, marvel; TR.†: confound.

tra-sentíre†, TR., INTR: hear wrong.

tras-feríbile, ADJ.: transferable. **-feriménto**, M.: transfer(ring). ‖**-feríre** [L. *trans-ferre* (BEAR)], TR.: TRANSFER (convey, remove); REFL.: repair to, go or move to.

tras-figuraménto, rare for *-figurazione.* ‖**=figuráre**, TR.: transfigure (transform, change). **-figurazióne**, F.: transfiguration (transformation, change).

tras=fóndere, TR.: TRANSFUSE, pour over.

tras-formábile, ADJ.: transformable. **-formaménto**†, M., **-formánza**†, F.: transformation. ‖**=formáre**, TR.: transform. **-formatívo**, ADJ.: transformative. **-formazióne**, F.: transformation.

trasfug.. = *trafug..*

tras-fusióne, F.: transfusion. ‖**-fúso**, PART. of *-fondere.*

traș-grediménto, M.: transgression. ‖**-gredíre** [L. *trans-gredi* (*gradior*, walk)], TR., INTR.: TRANSGRESS, trespass. **-greditóre**†, M.: transgressor. **-gressioncèlla**, *dim.* of *-gressione.* **-gressióne**, F.: transgression, trespass; digression†. **-gressóre**, M.: transgressor, trespasser.

trasì†, ADV.: so, thus; as much.

tra-sicuraménte, ADV.: very securely.

traș-lataménte, ADV.: metaphorically. **-latáre**, TR.: translate (transfer, render)†. **-latívo**, ADJ.: (*lit.*) transferable; metaphorical. ‖**-láto** [L. *translatus*, transferred], ADJ.†: translated (transferred); M.: metaphor. **-lazióne**, F.: translation (transference; rendering).

traș-locaménto, M.: translocation. ‖**=locáre**, TR.: transfer, remove.

traș=maríno, ADJ.: transmarine.

traș-mésso, PART. of *-mettere.* ‖**=méttere**, IRR.; TR.: transmit (send over; communicate); (*fig.*) send back. **-mettitóre**, M.: transmitter.

traș-migraménto, M.: transmigrating, transmigration. ‖**=migráre**, INTR.: transmigrate. **-migrazióne**, F.: transmigration.

traș-missíbile [L. *trans-missus*, transmitted], ADJ.: transmissible. **-missióne**, F.: transmission.

traș-modaménto, M.: excess. ‖**-modáre** [*modo*], INTR.: (*lit.*) be out of measure, exceed. **-modataménte**, ADV.: exceedingly. **-modáto**, ADJ.: excessive.

traș-mutábile, ADJ.: transmutable. **-mutaménto**†, M., **-mutánza**†, F.: transmutation. ‖**=mutáre**, TR.: transmute (transform, change). **-mutazióne**, F.: transmutation.

trașnaturáre†, INTR., REFL.: become unnatural.

trașnèllo†, ADJ.: very nimble.

trasoáve†, ADJ.: exceedingly gentle.

tra-sognaménto, M.: astonishment. ‖**=sognáre**, INTR.: astonish. **-sognáto**, ADJ.: astonished, dumbfounded.

trasollecitaménte†, ADV.: very earnestly.

traș-ordináre†, TR.: disorder; INTR.: lead a disorderly life. **-ordinário**†, ADJ.: disordinate, extraordinary. **-órdine**†, M.: disorder, excess.

trașorière = *tesoriere.*

traspadáno = *transpadano.*

tras-par(i)ènte, ADJ.: transparent; M.: painted window screen; illumined festoon,

etc. -**parènza**, F.: transparency. ‖-**parire** [*trans, apparire*], INTR.: be transparent.
tras-piantaménto†, M.: transplantation. =**piantáre**†, TR.: transplant.
tra-spirábile, ADJ.: transpirable. ‖=**spiráre**, INTR.: transpire; perspire; trickle through (leak out). -**spirazióne**, F.: transpiration; perspiration.
tras=pónere†, =**pórre**, IRR.; TR.: transpose (transplace, move), transport; translate†.
tras-portábile, ADJ.: transportable. -**portaménto**, M.: transport. ‖=**portáre**, TR.: transport. -**portatóre**, M.: transporter. -**portazióne**, F., -**pòrto**, M.: transportation; transport (transportation; carriage, vehement emotion, passion): *carro di* —, (*rail.*) truck, box-car.
trans-posizioncèlla, *dim.* of -*posizione*. -**posizióne**, F.: transposition. ‖-**pósto**, PART. of -*porre*.
trasricchíre†, INTR.: grow exceedingly rich.
trássi, PRET. of *trarre*.
trassináre [variant of *trascinare*], TR.: shake, molest, abuse; touch (handle, manage)†.
trastornáre†, TR.: divert from, hinder.
trastul-láre, TR.: divert, amuse; REFL.: divert one's self, play. -**latóre**, M.: amuser, wag. -**létto**, *dim.* of -*lo*. -**lévole**, ADJ.: diverting, amusing. -**líno**, *dim.* of -*lo*. ‖**trastúl-lo** [? OGer. *stulla*, time], M.: pastime (diversion, amusement): *compagno di* —, playfellow.
tra-sudaménto, M.: perspiration. ‖=**sudáre**, INTR.: transude (perspire freely, produce moisture). -**sudazióne**, F.: transudation.
tras=umanáre, INTR.: become transhuman or superhuman. -**umanazióne**, F.: becoming superhuman, assuming divine nature.
tras-versále, ADJ.: transversal (transverse, oblique). -**versalménte**, ADV.: transversally. ‖-**vèrso**† [L. -*versus*], ADJ.: transverse (oblique); perverse.
trasvi. = *travi*..
tras=voláre, TR.: pass rapidly over; fly rapidly; treat lightly.
tras=vòlgere†, IRR.; TR.: sweep off, disorder, overturn. -**vòlto**†, PART.
trát-ta [-*to*], F.: drawing (pull, pulling out, drawing of lots or votes); election; TRAIN (troop, crowd); course, draft (bill); traffic; heaving (a sigh)†; withdrawing; shot (of a bow, etc.)†; space (distance)†; handle (of certain mus. instruments); licence; concourse. -**tábile**, tractable, flexible. -**tabilíssimo**, ADJ.: most tractable. -**tabilità**, F.: tractability (tractableness, docility). -**tabilménte**, ADV.: tractably. -**taménto**, M.: treatment. -**táre**, TR.: TREAT (manage; discuss); touch†; REFL.: be treated, be prepared; be under treatment, be in question; cause to be an advocate or lawyer: *si* -*ta di*, it is the question of, the question is; *si* -*ta della vita*, life is at stake; — *con uno*, have a conversation, intercourse with one. -**tatèllo**, *dim.* of -*tato*. -**tatísta**, pl. —*i*, M.: writer of treatises; tract writer. -**tatíva**, F.: treaty. -**táto**, M.: TREATise (dissertation; tractate; TRACT); treaty; conspiracy†, machination†. -**tatóre**†, M.: negociator; plotter; interpreter. -**tazióne**, F.: treatment. -**teggiaménto**, M.: drawing (lines), outlining. -**teggiáre**, TR.: draw (lines, contours, etc.), depict; etch. -**teggiatúra**, F.: drawing, sketching, depicting.
trat=tenére, IRR.; TR.: hold back (reTAIN, check, keep waiting); entertain†; REFL.: stay, delay. -**teniménto**, M.: holding back, checking; staying; entertainment. -**tenitóre**, M., -**tenitríce**, F.: retainer; entertainer. -**tenúto**, PART. of -*tenere*.
trattévole†, ADJ.: tractable.
trát-to [*trarre*], PART.: drawn, etc.; M.: drawing (pull, draft); stroke (of the pen); space, moment; TRAIT (lineament, feature); mode (manner); trick†; motto†, bon mot†; opportunity†: *a*(*d*) *un* —, at once, suddenly; *ad ogni* —, every moment; *di primo* —, at first; *di* — *a* —, or — —, from time to time; *dare i* -*ti*, expire; *un bel* —, a fine move, a good manner or stroke; *innanzi* —, beforehand, first of all. -**tóre**, M.: drawer†; silk spinner; restaurant-keeper, innkeeper. -**toría**, F.: restaurant, eating-house (finer than *osteria*, less fine than *locanda*). -**tóso**†, ADJ.: affable, pleasing. -**túra**, F.: drawing, pulling.
travá-glia†, -**gliaménto**, M.: toil, work. -**gliánte**, ADJ.: laborious. -**gliáre**, INTR.: toil, work; torment; TR.: give work to; REFL.: vex or torment one's self; intermeddle†; get angry†. -**gliataménte**, ADV.: laboriously, painfully. -**gliatóre**, M., -**gliatríce**, F.: toiler; vexer; cheat. ‖**travá-glio** [Fr. *travail*], M.: TRAVE (brake for refractory horses); toil; work (labour; piece of work); distress (pain, travail). -**gliosaménto**, ADV.: laboriously; painfully. -**glióso**, ADJ.: laborious; painful.
travalc.. (*poet.*) = *travalic*..
tra=valènte†, ADJ.: exceedingly clever.
tra-valicaménto, M.: passing across, crossing; transgression†. ‖=**valicáre**,

pass over or across, cross; transgress†. **-valicatóre**, M.: crosser.

travaménto [*trave*], M.: beams (collectively); beam work.

tra-vasaménto, M.: transfusion, decanting. ‖**-vasáre** [*vaso*], TR.: pour from one vessel into another, decant, transfuse. **-váso**, M.: decanting.

tra-váta, F.: beams or rafters (collectively), beam or frame-work; (*fort.*) pole-work. **-váto**, ADJ.: of beams. **-vatúra**, F.: rafters (of a roof), rafter-work. ‖**trá-ve** [L. *trabes*], F., M.: beam; roof-beam, rafter.

tra=vecchiézza†, F.: decrepitude.

tra=vedére, IRR.; INTR: see one thing for another, see double; see indistinctly. **-vedimento**, M.: hallucination; dimness of sight. **-véggole**, F. PL.: distorted or double sight, dimness of sight.

tra-vèrsa, F.: (anything crossing, as) cross-piece, bar; traverse (barrier; (*fort.*) obstructing work; cross-accident)†; cross-road; (*rail.*) sleeper: *alla* —, across; crosswise. **-versále**, ADJ.: transversal (crossing, cross). **-versalménte**, ADV.: transversely, crosswise. **-versaménto**, M.: crossing. **-versáre**, TR.: traverse (cross, pass over or through); INTR.†: — *con*, meddle. **-versáta**, F.: crossing. **-versía**, F.: tempest (squall); cross-accident (contrariety, adversity). **-versíno**, M.: cross-piece, brace, transverse-beam. ‖**-vèrso** [L. *trans-versus* (*vertere*, turn)], ADJ.: transverse (crossing, crosswise, oblique); wrong; adverse (contrary, untoward); broad; sturdy (strong); M.: width: *a* —, across, athwart; adversely, badly; although; *di* —, by width, wide; bad; distorted; *in* —, obliquely; askance; *per* —, transversely, across, from side to side. **-versóne**, M.: cross-piece; (*nav.*) north-eastern; slant-stroke.

travertíno [*Tiburtino* (*Tibur* = Tivoli)], M.: Travertine marble.

tra-vestiménto, M.: disguise. ‖**=vestíre**, TR.: disguise.

trávet [*Travet*, a comedy], M.: poor employee.

travétta, *dim.* of *trave*.

tra-viaménto, M.: leading astray. ‖**-viáre** [*via*], TR.: lead from the right way, lead astray; INTR., REFL.: go astray; deviate†. **-viatóra**, F., **-viatóre**, M., **-viatríce**, F.: misleader; ADJ.: leading astray, misguiding, corrupting.

travicèllo [*trave*], M.: small beam, joist.

tra-visaménto, M.: disguise. ‖**-visáre** [*viso*], TR.: mask, disguise; counterfeit, deceive. **-víso**†, M.: mask, disguise; deceit.

tra=vàlgere, IRR.; TR.: sweep off, overturn; confuse. **-vòlto**, PART.

travóne, *aug.* of *-ve*.

travvéggole† = *traveggole*.

trazióne [L. *tractio*], F.: traction, drawing.

tré [L. *tres*], ADJ.: three.

trébbia [*tribbio*], F.: flail; thrashing†.

trebbiáno [fr. name of place], M.: sort of white grape or wine.

trebbiá-re [*trebbia*], TR.: thrash. **-túra**, F.: thrashing.

trébbio†, M.: place where three roads meet; diversion, fun.

tréc-ca†, F.: huckster, fruit-woman. **-cáre**†, TR.: huckster, retail; trick. **-cheria**†, F.: huckstering, fruit-selling; trickery. **-chièro**†, M.: huckstering: tricking.

tréc-cia [? Gr. *tricha*, THREEfold], F.: TRESS (plait, braid, curl). **-ciáia**, F., **-ciáio**, M., **-ciaiòla**, F., **-ciaiòlo**, M.: hair-dresser. **-ciáre**†, TR.: tress, braid. **-cièra**†, F.: topknot, ornament. **-ciuòla**†, F.: little tress or curl.

treccóne†, M.: huckster, green grocer.

tre=centèsimo, ADJ.: three hundredth. **-centísta** [*-cento*], pl. *—i*, M.: writer or person of the 14th century. **=cènto**, ADJ.: three hundred; M.: 14th century (for *mil trecento*). **=dècimo**†, **-dicèsimo**, ADJ.: thirteenth. **tré-dici**, ADJ.: THIRTEEN; thirteenth. **=fòglio**†, M.: trefoil. **tré-folo**†, M.: twist; strand (of a rope).

tregènda [L. *tre-centa*, 300; = great number], F.: troop of devils, wicked band.

treggèa†, F.: (she) confectioner.

trég-gia [?], F.: (wheel-less) sledge. **-giáta**, F.: sledge-load. **-giatóre**, M.: sledge-driver. **-gióne**, M.: big sledge.

trégua [OGer. *triwa*, troth], F.: TRUCE (armistice); rest.

tre-macuòre [*core*], M.: tremor of the heart, palpitation. **-maménto**, M.: trembling. **-mánte**, ADJ.: trembling, quivering. ‖**-máre** [L. *-mere*], INTR.: TREMBLE (shiver, quiver). **-marèlla**, F.: tremor, slight fear. **-mebóndo**, ADJ.: trembling. **-mefátto**, ADJ.: (*lit.*) terrified. **-mendaménte**, ADV.: tremendously. **-mèndo**, ADJ.: tremendous, immense.

trementína [*terebinto*], F.: turpentine.

tremerèlla [*-mare*], F.: tremor, slight fear.

tre=míla, ADJ.: three thousand.

trè-mito [*-mare*], M.: trembling (tremor, shiver). **trè-mola**, F.: torpedo. **-moláre**, INTR.: tremble (quiver, shiver). **-molánte**, ADJ.: trembling, quivering; **-molánti**, M. PL.: plumage (in ladies' hats). **-molío**, M.: trembling. **trè-**

melo = *-mulo*. **-moléso** = *-moroso*. **-móre**, M.: tremor. **-moréso**†, ADJ.: tremulous.
tremòto [pop. for *terre-moto*, as if from *tremare*], M.: earthquake; stirring thing or person: *dar le mosse a' —ti*, bluster, swagger; *è un —*, he is a fierce fellow.
trèmu-la†, F.: aspen-tree. ‖**-láre** = *tremolare*. **trèmu-lo**, ADJ.: tremulous, quivering: M.: (*mus.*) trill.
trèno 1 [Fr. *train*], M.: TRAIN (suit; railway-train): — *di persone*, passenger-train; — *di vagoni*, — *di vetture*, freight-train.
trèno 2 [Gr. *thrênos*], M.: lament(ation).
trén-ta [L. *tri-ginta*], ADJ.: THIRty. **-ta=mìle**, ADJ.: thirty thousand. **-tancánna**†, **-tavècchia**†, F.: monster, goblin. **-tèsimo**, ADJ.: thirtieth. **-tína**, F.: about thirty, some thirty. **-t=úno**, ADJ.: thirty-one.
trepestío [*pestare*], M.: great stamping or beating.
trepi-dáre, INTR.: tremble (quake, shake with fear). **-dánte**, ADJ.: trembling, trepid. **-dánza**, **-dazióne**, (*lit.*) **-dézza**, F.: trepidation, trembling. ‖**trèpido** [L. *-dus*], ADJ.: (*lit.*) trepid (trembling, tremulous).
treppèllo†, M.: troop, band.
tre=piède, **-pièdi**, M. INVAR.: tripod.
tré-sca, F.: rustic dance, romping party; amorous and immoral relation. **-scaménto**, M.: rustic or romping performance. ‖**-scáre** [ak. to Eng. *thresh*], INTR.: romp (dance or play rudely, sport); have an immoral relation; practise; touch (handle)†. **-scherèlla**, *dim.* of *-sca*. **-scóne**, M.: sort of rustic dance (by fours).
trés-pide† [*tre, piedi*], **très-polo**, M.: scaffolding (with three legs trestle, support).
tressètti [*tre, sette*], M.: sort of game (at cards).
trézza† = *treccia*.
tri- [L.], PREF.: tri-, THREE-.
triáca [Gr. *theriakḗ* (*thḗr*, beast)], F.: treacle (medicine against wild or venomous beasts), electuary; remedy†.
tríade [Gr. *triás*], F.: triad.
tri-angoláre, ADJ.: triangular. **-angolarità**, F.: triangularity. **-angolazióne**, F.: triangulation. **-angolétto**, **-angolíno**, *dim.* of *-angolo*. ‖**=ángolo**, M.: triangle.
tribaldáre†, TR.: steal, carry off.
trib-biáre [L. *-ulare*], TR.: thrash; break. **-biatúra**, F.: thrashing, breaking. ‖**tríbbio** [L. *tribulum*], M.: thrashing sledge.
tríbo† = *tribù*.
tribo-láre [L. *tribulare* (cf. *tribbio*)], TR.: afflict (torment, trouble). **-latóra**, F., **-latóre**, M., **-latríce**, F.: tormenter. **-lazióne**, F.: tribulation. **tríbolo**, M.: (*fig.*) tribulation (trouble); bramble (thistle); caltrop (iron shard to check cavalry). **-lóso**†, ADJ.: afflicting, vexatious.
tribórdo [Icel. *styri-bord*, steer board], M.: (*nav.*) STARBOARD.
tribrá-chio, ‖**-co** [Gr. *tri-brachus*, three-short, viz., syllables], M.: tribrach (⏑⏑⏑).
tribù [L. *-bus*], M.: tribe.
tribul. .† = *tribol*. .
tribú-na, F.: tribune (platform, pulpit). **-nále**, M.: tribunal (court of justice). **-nalménte**, ADV.: by or in the tribunal. **-náto**, M.: tribuneship. **-nésco**, ADJ. of *-na*. **-nízio**, ADJ.: tribunary, tribunitial. ‖**tribú-no** [L. *-nus*, orig. 'head of a tribe'], M.: tribune (people's officer).
tribu-táre, TR.: pay as tribute, pay. **-tário**, M.: tributary. ‖**tribú-to** [L. *-tum*], M.: tribute.
tri=cíclo, M.: tricycle. **-clínio** [L. *-clinium* (Gr. *klíne*, couch)], M.: triclinium (Rom. couch for reclining at meals, round three sides of the table). **=colóre**, ADJ.: three-coloured. **=còrde**, ADJ.: three-stringed. **=còrno**, M.: cockle (shell). **=corpòreo**, ADJ.: tricorporal. **-cuspidále**, ADJ.: tricuspidate, three-pointed. **=cúspide**, ADJ.: tricuspid. **-dentáto**, ADJ.: tridentate. **=dènte**, M.: trident. **-duáno** [*-duo*], ADJ.: triduan (of three days). **trí-duo** [L. *-duus* (*dies*, day)], M.: period of three days. **-ennále**, **-ènne**, ADJ.: triennial. **-ènnio** [L. *-ennium* (*annus*, year)], M.: triennium. **-fáuce** [L. *-faux*], ADJ.: three-jawed. **-'fido** [L. *-fidus* (*findere*, split)], ADJ.: trifid. **-fogliáto**, ADJ.: trifoliate. **=fòglio**, M.: trefoil. **=forcáto**, **=forcúto**, ADJ.: three-forked. **=fórme**, ADJ.: three-formed. **-gèsimo**, ADJ.: (*lit.*) thirtieth.
tríglia [Gr. *tríglē*], F.: mullet (fish).
tríglifo [Gr. *-gluphos* (*glúphein*, carve)], M.: triglyph.
triglína, *dim.* of *triglia*.
tri-gono [Gr. *-gonos* (*gonía*, angle)], triangle. **-gonometría**, F.: trigonometry. **-gonomètrico**, pl. *—ci*, ADJ.: trigonometrical. **-laterále**, **-látero** [L. *latus*, side], ADJ.: trilateral. **-líneo**, ADJ.: trilinear. **-língue**, ADJ.: trilingual.
tril-láre [echoic], INTR.: trill, quaver. **-lettíno**, *dim.* of *-lo*.
trillióne [after *milione*], M.: trillion.
trillo [*-llare*], M.: trill, quaver.
tri=lobáto [*lobo*], ADJ.: trilobate. **-logía** [Gr. (*lógos*, discourse)], F.: trilogy. **-mèmbre**, ADJ.: three-membered. **-mèstre** [L. *mestris* (*mens*, month)], ADJ.: trimestrial. **trí-metro** [Gr. *-metros*], M.: trimeter; ADJ.: trimetric.

trimpel-láre [? *trampolo*], INTR.: shake, (wag, totter, flicker); reel along; loiter, act slowly. **-líno**, M.: shaking, etc.; loitering. **-lío**, M.: violent shaking.

trí-na [-*no*], F.: open-work lace or trimming. **-náia**, F.: lace-maker. **-náre**, TR.: trim with lace. **-náto**, PART.

trín-ca, M.: drinker (tippler, toper). ‖**-cáre** [Ger. *trinken*], TR.: drink greedily (tope, tipple). **-cáta**, F.: drinking, carousal. **-cáto**, PART.: drunk (tippled); thorough, cunning (*furbo* —, arrant knave); M.: knave. **-catóre**, M.: toper.

trin-cèa [-*ciare*], **-cèra**, F.: TRENCH; entrenchment; (*rail.*) cut. **-ceraménto**, M.: entrenchment. **-ceráre**, TR.: entrench. **-ceráto**, M.: entrenchment. **-cétto**, M.: shoemaker's knife.

trin-chétta [? L. *tri-*, three: 'triangular'], F.: forestay sail. **-chettína**, F.: topsail. **-chétto**, M.: foremast; foremast pennon; forestay sail.

trin-ciánte, ADJ.: cutting (sharp, trenchant); M.: carver; braggadocio. **-cia=páglia**, F.: scythe. ‖**-ciáre** [OFr. *trenchier* (L. *truncare*)], TR.: cut up (in pieces), carve, pink; devour, eat; affect; REFL.: be cut, break: — *capriole*, cut capers. **-ciáta**, **-ciatúra**, F.: cutting, cut. **-cier.** . = *-cer.* . **-cio†**, M.: cutting; open-work.

trincóne [-*care*], M.: hard drinker, toper.

tri-nità [L. *-nitas* (*tri*, three)], F.: Trinity; Trinity Sunday or Feast. **-nitário**, ADJ., M.: Trinitarian. **-no** [L. *-nus*], ADJ.: (*lit.*) of three. **-nòmio**, M.: trinomial. **-o**, M.: trio; glee. **-òcco** [? der.], M.: boisterous company.

trion-fále, ADJ.: triumphal. **-falménte**, ADV.: triumphantly. **-fáre**, INTR.: triumph; (*card-pl.*) trump. **-fánte**, ADJ.: triumphant. **-fatóre**, M., **-fatríce**, F.: triumpher. ‖**trión-fo** [L. *triumphus* (?)], M.: triumph; (*card-pl.*) TRUMP.

tri=partíre, TR.: (*lit.*) divide into three. **-partíto**, ADJ.: tripartite. **-partizióne**, F.: tripartition.

tri pètalo, ADJ.: tripetalous.

tri-plicáre, TR.: triple, treble. **-plicataménte**, ADV.: triply, trebly. **-plicazióne**, F.: triplication. ‖**trí-plice** [L. *-plex*], ADJ.: triple (threefold). **-pliceménte**, ADJ.: in threefold manner, triply. **-plicità**, F.: triplicity. **-plo** [L. *-plus*], ADJ.: triple (threefold).

[t]rí-podo [L. *-pus* (*pes*, FOOT)], M.: tripod, trivet. **-podía**, F.: tripody.

[tr]ípolo [*Tripoli*], M.: tripoli (polishing substance).

[tri]p-pa [Fr. *tripe* (?)], F.: tripe; belly. **[-pá]ccia**, F.: *disp.* of *-pa*; big belly or paunch. **-páio**, M.: tripe-hawker. **-paiuòla**, F.: tripe-woman. **-páre**, TR.: cook like tripes. **-píno**, *car. dim.* of *-pa*.

tri-pudiaménto, M.: feasting for joy. **-pudiáre** [L.], INTR.: leap or dance for joy, caper, tripudiate. **-pudiatóre**, M., **-pudiatríce**, F.: joyous dancer. ‖**-púdio** [-*pudium* (*pu-*, stamp)], M.: leaping or dancing for joy.

tri=régno, M.: (Pope's) triple crown.

trirème [L. *-mis* (*remus*, oar)], M.: trireme (Rom. galley with three banks).

trisàgio†, ADJ.: most holy.

trisávolo [L. *tres*, three, *avus*, grandfather], M.: great-great-grandfather.

tri=sillábico, ADJ., M.: trisyllabic(al).

tri-stáccio, *disp.* of *-sto*. **-stággine†** = *-stezza*. **-staménte**, ADV.: sadly. **-stánza†** = *-stezza*. **-stanzuòlo†**, ADJ.: *dim.* of *-sto*; wretched; weakly†, spare, thin. **-starèllo**, *dim.* of *-sto*. **-stáre†**, INTR.; REFL.: grow sad. ‖**-sto** [L. *-stis*], ADJ.: (*lit.*) sad (melancholy; sorrowful; Eng.† trist); wretched. **-sterellíno**, *dim.* of *-starello*. **-stézza**, **-stízia** (*lit.*), F.: sadness (melancholy, grief); wretchedness. **-sto**, ADJ.: sad (melancholy, sorrowful); wretched; miserable (depraved; cunning, wicked); ADV.: woe! **-stóre**, F.: sadness, grief. **-stósot**, ADJ.: sad; wretched. **-stúccio**, *dim.* of *-sto*.

trisúlco [L. *-cus*, three-cleft], ADJ.: with three points.

tríta† 1, F.: felucca (small vessel).

tríta 2, F.: thrashing, grinding. **-taménte**, ADV.: in small bits; distinctly. **-táre**, TR.: grind, pound. **-tatúra**, F.: grinding, pounding. **-tèllo**, M.: fine bran. **-tícco†**, ADJ.: grain. **trí-tico†**, M.: grain, wheat. **-tíno**, *dim.* of *-to*. ‖**-to** [L. *-tus* (*terere*, grind)], ADJ.: ground, pounded, minced; TRITE (worn, hackneyed). **-toláre†**, INTR.: triturate, grind; REFL.: be agitated. **trí-tolo**, M.: fragment, bit.

tritóne [L. *-ton*], M.: triton.

trí=tono, M.: (*mus.*) tritone.

trittòngo [Gr. *tri-phthongos*, 'three-sound'], M.: triphthong.

tritú-me, M.: fragments. **-'ra†**, F.: grinding, pounding. **-rábile**, ADJ.: triturable. **-raménto**, M.: grinding, pounding. ‖**-ráre** [L.], TR.: triturate (grind, bruise). **-razióne**, F.: trituration.

trium-viráto, M.: triumvirate. ‖**triúmviro** [L. *-vir*], M.: triumvir.

triunvir. . = *triumvir*.

tri-vèlla [*terebella*, dim. of L. *terebra*, bore], F.: auger. **-velláre**, TR.: bore through. **-vellatúra**, F.: boring. **-vèllo**, M.: auger.

tri-viále [L. *-vialis*, 'of the crossroads

or public places'], ADJ.: trivial (commonplace, vulgar). **-vialità**, F.: triviality. **-vialménte**, ADV.: trivially. ‖**trí-vio** [L. *-vium*], M.: place where three streets meet, crossroad.

tro-cáico, ADJ.: trochaic(al). ‖**-chèo** [Gr. *-chaîos* (*tréchein*, run)], M.: trochee (— ⌣)

tro-chísco†, **-císco** [Gr. *-chískos*, little wheel], M.: trochiscus (*med.*, lozenge). ‖**trò-co** [Gr. *-chós*, wheel], M.: sort of mollusk.

tròclea†, F.: pulley.

tro-fealménte, ADV.: as a trophy. ‖**-fèo** [L. *-phæum* (Gr. *-pé*, turn, viz., of the enemy)], M.: trophy; trophies.

tr-ogliáre†, INTR.: stammer. **-ògliot**†, M.: stammering.

troglodíta, pl. *—ti* [Gr. *-dútes* (*trógle*, cavern, *dúein*, enter)], M.: troglodite.

tr-ogolétto, *dim.* of *-ogolo.* ‖**-ògolo** [Ger. *trog*, TROUGH], M.: trough.

trò-ia [l. L. *troga* (? Celt.)], F.: sow; shameful woman; sort of catapult. **-iáccia**, *disp.* of *-a.* **-iáio**, M.: gang or den of highwaymen (cf. *-ata*).

troiáno [*Troia*], ADJ., M.: Trojan.

troiáta [*troia*], F.: (*vulg.*) filthy act or thing; gang of highwaymen†.

tróm-ba 1 [?], F.: TRUMP(ET), TROMP; water-pump, siphon; leg (of a boot); ear-trumpet; water-spout; (*jest.*) trunk (of elephants, gnats, etc., proboscis); public auction; forepart of a mortar: *-be*, high card (representing Fame with her trumpets). **-ba** 2, pl. *-bi*, **-badóre**†, M.: trumpeter. **-báio**, M.: maker of water-pipes, siphons, etc. **-báre**, INTR.†: sound the trumpet; TR.: decant (wine, etc.) by a siphon or pump; sell at auction. **-beggiáre**†, INTR.: sound the trumpet. **-bétta**, F.: small trumpet; trumpeter. **-bettáre**†, TR.: trumpet, proclaim. **-bettatóre**†, **-bettière**, M.: trumpeter. **-bettína**, *dim.* of *-betta.* **-bettíno**†, **-bétto**, M.: trumpeter. **-bóna**, *aug.* of *-ba.* **-bonáta**, F.: blow of a trumpet or musket. **-bóne**, M.: trombone, sackbut.

tron-cábile, ADJ.: that may be cut off. **-caménte**, ADV.: interruptedly. **-caménto**, M.: truncating (cutting off); suppression. **-cáre**, TR.: truncate (cut off, break off); cut short; suppress; kill†. **-cataménte**, ADJ.: in a truncated or shortened manner; by snatches, fitfully. **-catívo**, ADJ.: subject to be cut off or broken; brittle. **-catúra**, F.: truncation; cutting off; suppression. **-chétto**, M.: low shoe. ‖**trón-co** [L. *truncus*], ADJ.: cut off; docked; M.: trunk (stem; body apart from head and limbs, main body, torso); shoe; lineage (race). **-concèllo**, *dim.* of *-cone.* **-cóne**, M.: *aug.* of *-co;* large trunk; trunk; stump.

tron-fiáre [? L. *trans*, *inflare*, inflate], INTR.: be puffed up, grow haughty, strut proudly. **-fiézza**, F.: haughtiness. **trón-fio**, ADJ.: puffed up, haughty; angry.

tro-mièra, F.: loop-hole, embrasure. ‖**trò-no**† 1 [*tono*], M.: thunder.

tròno 2 [L. *thronus*], M.: throne.

tro-picále, ADJ.: tropical. ‖**trò-pico**, pl. *—ci* [Gr. *-pikós* (*trépein*, turn)], M.: tropic. **trò-po** [Gr. *-pos*], M.: trope (figure of speech). **-pología**, F.: tropology.

tròppo [l. L. *troppus*, troop, crowd], ADJ., ADV.: too much, too many; excessive; excessively; M.: over-much, excess.

tròscia [Goth. *ga-drausian*, fall down], F.: tanner's vat; furrow†.

tròta [L. *tructa* (Gr. *trógein*, eat)], F.: TROUT.

trot-táre [? Germ'c], INTR.: trot; walk fast. **-táta**, F.: trot. **-tatóra**, F., **-tatóre**, M., **-tatríce**, F.: trotter. **-terelláre**, INTR.: keep trotting. **tròt-to**, M.: trot. **tròt-tola**, F.: peg-top, whirligig. **-toláre**, INTR.: whirl like a top, spin. **-tolíno**, M.: little whirligig; (*fig.*) little romping boy. **-tolóne**, *aug.* of *-tola.* **-tóne**†, M.: *aug.* of *-to;* ADV.: at a trot: *andare* —, trot along.

tro-vábile, ADJ.: that may be found. **-vaménto**, M.: finding, discovery. ‖**-vá-re** [? L. *turbare*, 'disturb,' so 'rummage'], TR.: find; discover, invent; observe; REFL.: find one's self, be found; be. **-váta**, F.: finding, discovery; invention; device. **-vatèlla**, F., **-vatèllo**, M.: foundling. **-váto**, PART.: found, etc.; M.: discovery; invention, device. **-vatóre**, M.: troubadour (poet of Provence, XI–XIII Cent.); poet (XIV Cent.); finder (inventor)†. **-v(i)èro**, M.: trouvère (poet of north. France, XI–XIV Cent.).

tròzzo†, M.: crowd of armed men, rabble.

truc-cáre [*-co*], TR.: disguise; cheat; hit (the ball, at billiards). ‖**-co** [? Ger. *druck*, pressure], M.: sort of billiards. **-cóne**, M.: swindler, meddler.

trú-ce [L. *trux*], ADJ.: cruel, ferocious, sanguinary. **trú-cia**, F.: misery, poverty, raggedness. **-cidaménto**, M.: slaughter. **-cidáre** [L.], TR.: massacre, murder, butcher. **-cidatóre**, M.: assassin, murderer. **trú-cio**, M.: wretch, ragamuffin.

tru-cioláre [? l. L. **tortiolare* (L. *torquere*, twist)], TR.: cut into shavings. **trú-ciolo**, M.: shaving.

truculènto [L. *-culentus* (*trux*, fierce)], ADJ.: truculent (ferocious, cruel).

trúf-fa [?], F.: deceit, knavery, fraud

-**faldíno**, M.: buffoon. -**fáre**, TR.: cheat, defraud; mock†. -**fatívo**†, ADJ.: deceitful. -**fatóre**, M., -**fatríce**, F.: cheat, swindler, knave. -**fería**, F.: piece of roguery, fraud. -**fière**, M.: cheat, swindler.

trugioláre† = *truciolare.*

trunca. .† = *tronca*. .

trùgo†, -**golo**† = *trogolo.*

truòno† = *trono* 1.

trúppa [Fr. *troupe*], F.: TROOP.

trutiláre†, INTR.: whistle (like the thrush).

tu [L.], PRON.: THOU: *dare del — a*, say 'thou' to, thee and thou.

tú-ba [L.], F.: tuba (ancient trumpet). -**báre**, INTR.: coo.

tuberco-láre, ADJ.: tubercular. -**létto**, -**líno**, *dim.* of *-lo.* ||**tubèrco-lo** [L. *tuberculum* (*tuber*, swelling)], M.: tubercle; pimple. -**lóso**, ADJ.: tuberculous. -**lúto**, ADJ.: full of tubercles.

túbe-ro [L. *tuber*, swelling], M.: tuber; small medlar-tree†. -**rosità**, F.: tuberosity. -**róso**, ADJ.: tuberous; M.: tuberose.

tú-bo [L. *-bus*], M.: tube, pipe; socket. **tú-bulo**, *dim.*

tuòllo [?], M.: (*vet.*) coffin-bone.

tufáceo [*-fo*], ADJ.: tufaceous.

tu-fáre [Span. *tufo* (Gr. *tûphos*), vapour], REFL.: crouch down; be low and oppressive. -**fáto**, ADJ.: musty.

tuf-faménto, M.: plunging, immersion. ||-**fáre** [OGer. *toufan* (= Ger. *taufen*), DIP], TR.: plunge (into the water), immerse; REFL.: plunge, rush into, be lost. -**fatóre**, M.: plunger. -**fe-táffe** [imitation of blows], INTERJ.: thump! **túf-fete**, M.: sudden blow. -**fo**, M.: plunging; ruin. **túf-folo**, M.: plungeon (bird).

túfo [L. *tofus*], M.: tufa (soft stone).

tu-guriétto, M.: *dim.* of *-gurio.* ||-**gú-rio** [L. *tegurium* (*tegere*, cover)], M.: lowly or squalid house, hut.

tulí-pa, F., ||-**páno** [Turk. *tulbend*, turban], M.: tulip.

tu-mefáre [L. *-me-facere*], TR., INTR.: tumefy. -**mefátto**, ADJ.: tumefied. -**mefazióne**, F.: tumefaction. -**mideggiáre**†, INTR.: grow tumid, swell up; swell with pride. -**midétto**, *dim.* of *-mido.* ||**tú-mido** [L. *-midus* (*-mere*, swell)], ADJ.: tumid (swelling, puffy, inflated). -**móre** [L. *-mor*], M.: tumour, swelling. -**morétto**, *dim.* of *-more.* -**moróso**†, ADJ.: tumorous. -**muláre** [*-mulo*], TR.: (*lit.*) bury, inter. **tú-mulo** [L.], M.: (*lit.*) tumulus; tomb, grave.

tumúl-to [L. *-tus* (? *tu-*, swell)], M.: tumult, uproar. -**tuánte**, ADJ.: tumultuous. -**tuáre**, INTR.: make a tumult, be tumultuous. -**tuariaménte**, ADV.: tumultuously. -**tuário**, ADJ.: tumul-

túni-ca [L.], F.: tunic (under-garment; membrane). -**cáto**, ADJ.: dressed in a tunic; tunicated. -**chétta**, -**chína**,

il —,

; *della*

one of

ciolo. -**ráccolo**, M.: stopper (cork, bung). -**rággio**†, -**rámo**†, M.: stopper; stopple. -**raménto**, M.: stopping up (corking). ||-**ráre** [abbr. of *ot-turare*], TR.: stop up (cork, bung, close).

túr-ba [L., cf. *-bare*], F.: crowd, mob. -**bábile**, ADJ.: easily disturbed, prone to trouble. -**baménto**, M.: disturbance, confusion; commotion. -**bánte** 1, ADJ.: disturbing.

turbánte 2 [Turk. *tulbend*], M.: turban; light muslin.

tur-bánza†, F.: disturbance. ||-**báre** [L. (*-ba*, turmoil)], TR.: DISTURB (perturb, TROUBLE, molest); REFL.: be disturbed, be disconcerted; grow angry; grow cloudy. -**bataménte**, ADV.: in a perturbed manner. -**batíva**, F.: (*leg.*) complaint. -**batívo**, ADJ.: disturbing, molesting. -**batóre**, M., -**batríce**, F.: disturber. -**bazioncèlla**, *dim.* of *-bazione.* -**bazióne**, F.: disturbance (disorder, trouble). -**bináre** [*-bine*], INTR.: whirl. **túr-bine** [L. *-bo*], M.: whirlwind; screw-shell. -**binío**, M.: whirling, tumult. -**binóso**, ADJ.: whirling, tempestuous. -**bo** (*poet.*) = *-bine.* -**bolentaménte**, ADV.: turbulently. -**bolènto**, ADJ.: ... **lènza**, F.: turbulence.

turcásso [fr. Pers.], M.: ...

tur-chésco, *disp.* of *-co.* ...

M.: turquoise (bluish gem ...

sort of dove. -**chína**, F.: turquoise (gem). -**chinétto**, M.: turquoise colour, azure. -**chiníccio**, *dim.* of *-chino.* -**chíno**, ADJ., M.: azure, sky-blue.

turcimánno [Arab. *terjeman*], M.: (*lit.*, *jest.*) dragoman (interpreter).

túrco [Tartar orig.], M.: Turk; ADJ.: Turkish.

tur-gènza†, F.: turgescence, swelling. ||**túr-gere**† [L. *-gere*], INTR.: swell out, become turgid. -**gidétto**, *dim.* of *-gido.* -**gidézza**, F.: turgidity, swelling. **túr-gido**, ADJ.: turgid (swollen, bombastic).

turí-bolo†, ||**-'bolo** [L. *t(h)uribulum* (*thus*, incense)], M.: censer, perfuming-pan. **-ferário**, M.: censer-bearer. **-ficáre**, TR.: incense, perfume. **-ficazióne**, F.: incensation, perfuming.

túrma = *torma*.

túrno [variant of *torno*], M.: turn (regular succession).

túr-pe [L. *-pis*], ADJ.: shameful (infamous, vile, nasty). **-peménte**, ADV.: shamefully, basely. **-pézza**, F.: turpitude, infamy. **-pi=lòquio**, M.: vile or low talk. **-pissimaménte**, ADV.: most shamefully, most infamously. **-pità†**, **-pitúdine**, F.: turpitude (infamy, baseness). **-po†** = *-pe*.

turri(b). . = *turi(b)*. .

turrito [L. *-tus* (*turris*, tower)], ADJ.: guarded with towers.

turtumáglio† = *tutumaglio*.

tusántí†, F.: All(-)Saints; All-Saints day.

tu-tèla [L. (*-eri*, protect)], F.: tutelage (guardianship). **-teláre**, ADJ.: tutelar, guardian. **-tóre** [L. *-tor*], M.: tutor (guardian, keeper). **-toría†**, F.: guardianship. **-tríce**, F.: tutoress (guardian).

tut-t', *abbrev.* of *-to*. **-tafiáta†**, ADV.: continually. **-ta=vía**, **-ta=vòlta†**, ADV.: always (incessantly); as often as (whenever); however (nevertheless). **-te=sálle** [*le sa*], M.: omniscient pretender, wiseacre. **-tíssimo**, ADJ.: (*jest.*) all and all, most entire. ||**tút-to** [L. *totus*], ADJ.: all (whole, entire); PL.: all, every; ADV.: wholly (entirely, quite); very: *-ti quanti*, every one; *-ti dì*, *-ti i tempi*, every day, all the time, continually; *al* —, *del* —, entirely, quite; *per* —, everywhere; *in* — *e per* —, entirely, thoroughly; throughout; — *che*, although; almost; — *a un tempo*, all at once, all of a sudden; *con* — (*ciò*), for all that, nevertheless; *-t' uno*, all one, quite the same; — *d' un pezzo*, all of a piece, thoroughly honest. **-to=dì**, ADV.: every day, ever. **-t=óra**, **-t' óra**, ADV.: always, ever, continually; nevertheless†.

tutumáglio†, M.: milk-thistle.

túzia [fr. Arab.], F.: tutty (chem. substance).

tuziorísmo [L. *tutior*, safer], M.: (*phil.*) principle of following the safest opinion or law, safe side (principle).

U

u [L.], M. (F.): u (the letter).

ub-bía [?], F.: superstition; ill omen. **-biáccia**, *disp.* of *-bia*.

ubbidíre = *obbedire*.

ubbióso [*-bia*], ADJ.: superstitious; ominous.

ubbli. .†, **ubblig. .†** = *obli. .*, *obblig. .*

ubbriac. .† = *ubriac. .*

ube-ríforo†, ADJ.: having paps (mamillary); copious (abundant). ||**úbe-ro†** [L. *uber*], M.: breast (teat); pap. **-rtà** [L. *-rtas*], F.: fertility (abundance). **-rtóso**, ADJ.: fertile (abundant).

úbi [L.], ADV.: where. **-cazióne**, F.: location (whereabouts). **-quità**, F.: ubiquity.

ubíno†, M.: Shetland pony; nag; small donkey.

ubria-cáccio, M.: great drunkard. **-chèllo**, M.: little drunkard. **-chézza**, F.: drunkenness. ||**ubriá-co** [L. *ebriacus* (*ebrius*, full)], ADJ.: drunk. **-cóne**, M.: great drunkard.

uccèl-la† [*-lo*], F.: she-bird. **-lábile**, ADJ.: that may be caught (cf. *-lare*), gullible, simple. **-láccio**, M.: *disp.* of *-lo*; voracious bird; gull (simpleton). **-lagióne**, F.: fowling; fowling-place. **-láia†**, F.: aviary; flock of birds; illicit relation; deceit. **-láme**, M.: quantity of birds; fowl killed (game). **-laménto**, M.: bird-catching; raillery (ridicule). **-lánte**, M.: fowler. **-láre**, INTR.: go bird-catching (fowl); gull (banter, rail); M.: place for bird-catching: — *a†*, try to gain. **-latóio**, M.: place for bird-catching. **-latóre**, M.: bird-catcher (fowler); banterer (quiz). **-latúra**, F.: fowling; fowling-season. **-lettíno**, *dim.* of *-letto*. **-létto**, *dim.* of *-lo*. **-lièra**, F.: aviary. **-líno**, M.: *car. dim.* of *-lo*: *pigliar gli -lini*, play the fool. ||**uccèl-lo** [L. *avicella* (*avis*, bird)], M.: bird; simpleton†: *essere* (*star*) *come l'* — *sulla frasca*, lead an uncertain or trying life. **-lóne**, *disp. aug.* of *-lo*. **-lúzzo**, *dim.* of *-lo*.

ucchièllo = *occhiello*.

ucci-dere [L. *oc-cidere* (*cædere*, cut)], IRR.§; TR.: kill (murder). **-diménto†**, M.: killing (murder). **-ditóre**, M.: killer (slayer). **-'si**, PRET. of *-dere*. **-sióne**, F.: killing (slaying, slaughter). **-'so**, PART. of *-dere*. **-sóra**, F., **-sóre**, M.: killer (slayer, murderer).

§ Pret. *ucci-si, -se; -sero*. Part. *ucciso*.

udí-bile, ADJ.: audible. **-ènte**, ADJ.: hearing. **-ènza**, **-ènzia†**, F.: audience (hearing); auditory: *sala d'* —, audience-room. **-ménto†**, M.: hearing. ||**udí-re** [L. *audire*], IRR.§; TR.: hear; listen to. **-'ta**, F.: hearing: *per* —, by hearsay. **-tívo**, ADJ.: auditory. **-'to**, ADJ.: heard; M.†: hearing; sense of hearing. **-toráto**, M.: auditor's office. **-tóre**, M.: hearer (listener); auditor. **-tório**, M.:

auditory; audience. **-tríce**, F.: hearer (listener). **-zióne**, F.: hearing.

§ Ind.: Pres. *ódo, ódi, óde; udiámo, udíte, ódono.* Fut. *ud(i)rò.* Cond. *ud(i)rèi.* Subj.: Pres. *óda; udiámo, udiáte, ódano.*

uffi-cèllo, *dim.* of *-cio.* **-ciále**, ADJ.: official; officiating; M.: functionary; officer. **-cialménte**, ADV.: officially. **-ciáre** = *ufiziare.* ||**uffí-cio** [L. *officium*], M.: office; duty; and cf. *-zio.* **-cióso**, ADJ.: officious; complaisant; busy†. **-ciuòlo**, *dim.* of *-cio.* **-ziáre**, TR., INTR.: officiate. **-ziatúra**, F.: officiating; church-service; benefice. **uffí-zio**, M.: office (function; office-room); DAILY prayers of the priests (except at Mass): *Sant'* —, Holy Office (tribunal of inquisition at Rome). **-ziòlo**, M.: morning worship (to the Virgin); prayer-book. **-zióso** = *-cioso.*

úfo [?], M.: *a* —, at others' expense; without profit.

úggia [?], F.: darkness (gloom); annoyance; shade†; omen†: *aver (prender) in* —, have (conceive) an aversion for; *essere* (for *trovarsi*) *in* —, be hated, be disliked.

uggio-láre [L. *ejulare* (*hei!* excl.)], INTR.: wail. **-lío**, M.: continued wail.

ug-giosaménte, ADJ.: darkly (gloomily); annoyingly. **-gióso**, ADJ.: dark (gloomy, shady); annoying. **-gíre**, TR.: darken (render gloomy); annoy (tire).

úgioli [?], M.: *tra — e barugioli,* altogether.

ú-gna [L. *ungula* (*unguis*, nail)], F.: NAIL, claw. **-gnáre**, TR.: cut obliquely. **-gnáta**, F.: cut by a nail; notch in a knife blade. **-gnatúra**, F.: oblique cut, paring. **-gnèlla**, F.: wart on a horse's hoof. **-gnèllo**, *dim.* of *-gna.*

úgnere = *ungere.*

ugnétto [*ugna*], M.: graver; puncheon.

ugniménto = *ungimento.*

u-gnòlo, *dim.* of *-gna.* **-gnóne**, *aug.* of *-gna.*

úgola [L. *urula* (*uva*, grape)], F.: uvula.

ugonòtto [?], M.: Huguenot, Calvinist.

ugua-gliaménto, M.: equalizing. **-gliánza**, F.: equality. **-gliáre**, TR.: equalize. **-gliatóre**, M.: equalizer. **-láre** = *-gliare.* ||**uguá-le** [L. *æqualis*], ADJ.: EQUAL. **-lità**, F.: equality. **-lménte**, ADV.: equally (alike).

uguánno†, ADV.: this year.

uh [echoic], INTERJ.: ah! oh!

uláno [Ger. *uhlan* (Turk.)], M.: uhlan.

úlce-ra, ||**-re** [L. *ulcer*], F.: ulcer. **-ragióne**†, F., **-raménto**, M.: ulceration. **-ráre**, TR.: ulcerate. **-razióne**, F.: ulceration. **-rétta**, *dim.* of *-ra.* **-ro** = *-ra.* **-róso**, ADJ.: ulcerous.

ulígi-ne [L. *uligo*], F.: moistness. **-nóso**, ADJ.: moist (damp).

ulíre† = *olire.*

ulí-va [L. *oliva*], F.: olive. **-vále**, **-váre**†, ADJ.: olive-like. **-vástro**, etc. = *olivastro*, etc.

úlna [L.], F.: forearm.

ul-terióre [L. *-terior* (*-tra*, beyond)], ADJ.: ulterior (further). **-teriorménte**, ADV.: furthermore (moreover). **-timaménte**, ADV.: ultimately (lastly). **-timáre**, TR.: bring to an end (complete). **-timátum**, M.: ultimatum. **-timazióne**, F.: ending (completing). **-timíssimo**, **úl-timo**, ADJ.: last, utmost: *all'* —, lastly. **-timo-gènito**, ADJ., M.: last born.

úl-to [L. *-tus* (*-cisci*, avenge)], ADJ.: avenged. **-tóre**, M., **-tríce**, F.: avenger.

ultra- [L.], ultra-, exceedingly.

úlu-la† [L.], F.: OWL. **-láre**, INTR.: howl (screech). **-láto**, PART.: howled; M.: howling. **úlu-lo**, M.: howl.

uma-naménte, ADJ.: humanely (kindly). **-nárे**, REFL.: become man or incarnate; be humanized. **-nésimo**, M.: Renaissance (cf. next). **-nísta**, pl. *—ti*, M.: humanist (scholar of the Renaissance period; professor or student of the humanities). **-nità**, F.: humanity (human nature); humaneness (kindness); PL.: humanities (polite learning). **-nitário**, ADJ.: humanitarian. ||**umá-no** [*humanus* (*homo*, man)], ADJ.: human; humane (kind); M.: man; PL.: human beings: *lettere -ne*, polite literature (belles-lettres).

umbè†, INTERJ.: ah well!

umbèlla† = *ombrella.*

um-bilicále, ADJ.: umbilical. **-bilicáto**, ADJ.: umbilicate(d). ||**-bilíco** [L. *-bilicus*], M.: umbilicus (NAVEL).

umbrat..† = *ombrat..*

ume-rále, M.: shoulder-tippet (worn by priests). ||**úme-ro**† = *omero.*

umet-tábile, ADJ.: that may be moistened. **-taménto**, M.: humectation (moistening). ||**-táre**, TR.: moisten (wet, Eng.† humect). **-tatívo**, ADJ.: moistening. **-tazióne**, F.: humectation. **-tóso**†, ADJ.: humid (moist).

umi-détto, ADJ.: somewhat humid or moist. **-dézza**, F.: humidity (dampness). **-díccio**, *disp. dim.* of *-do.* **-díno**, *dim.* of *-do.* **-díre**†, TR.: moisten. **-dità**, F.: humidity. ||**úmi-do** [L. *humidus*], ADJ.: humid (moist); M.: humidity (moisture); stew. **-dóre**†, M.: humidity. **-dóso**†, ADJ.: humid.

úmi-le, (*poet.*) **umí-le** [L. *-lis* (*humus*, earth)], ADJ.: humble (modest; low). **-leménte** (*poet.*) = *-lmente.* **-liaménto**, M.: humiliation. **-liánza**†, F.: humility. **-liáre**, TR.: humiliate (humble; lower). **-liatívo**, ADJ.: humiliating. **-líssimo**, ADJ.: most humble. **-lità**† = *-ltà.* **-lli-**

mo† = *-lissimo*. **-lménte**, ADV.: humbly. **-ltà**, F.: humility (humbleness).

umo-ráccio, *disp.* of *-re*. **-rále**, ADJ.: humoral. ‖**umó-re** [L. (*h*)*umor*], M.: humor (animal moisture or fluid); disposition (temper). **-rótto**, *dim.* of *-re*. **-rismo**, M.: humourism (humorousness). **-rísta**, pl. *—ti*, M.: humourist; ADJ.: humouristic. **-rístico**, ADJ.: humouristic (humourous). **-rositá†**, F.: fullness of humours. **-róso**, ADJ.: full of humours (plethoric).

un for *uno*. ‖**-a**, F. of *-o;* ADV.†: together. **-animaménte†**, ADV.: unanimously. **-ánimine** [L. *animus*, soul], ADJ.: unanimous. **-animità**, F.: unanimity (accord).

uncio..† = *uncin..*

unci-náre, TR.: hook; snatch. **-náto**, ADJ.: hooked (taken by or made like a hook). **-nèllo**, **-nétto**, *dim.* of *-no*. ‖**uncí-no** [L. *uncus*], M.: hook; grappling-iron. **-núto**, ADJ.: hooked; rapacious†.

un-dècimo, **-dicèsimo**, ADJ.: eleventh. ‖**ún-dici** [L. *-decim* (*unus*, ONE, *decem*, TEN)], NUM.: eleven. **-dici=míla**, NUM.: eleven thousand.

undúnque†, ADV.: whatsoever.

ún-gere [L.], IRR.§; TR.: anOINT, grease: — *le mani ad uno*, bribe one.

§ Pret. *ún-si*, *-se*; *-sero*. Part. *únto*.

unghe-rése, ADJ.: Hungarian. **úngheró**, M.: Hungarian; ducat.

ún-ghia [L. *unguis*], F.: NAIL; claw (talon); hoof: *dar nelle -ghie*, fall into the clutches. **-ghiáccia**, *dim.* of *-ghia*. **-ghiáta**, F.: clawing (scratch with a claw or nail). **-ghiáto**, ADJ.: provided with claws or nails. **-ghièlla**, F.: hoof wart. **-ghióne**, *aug.* of *-ghia*.

ungiménto†, M.: anointing (unction).

unguánno†, M.: this year.

unguen-táre, TR.: anoint. **-tário**, ADJ.: unguentary; M.†: perfumer. **-tière**, M.: perfumer. **-tífero**, ADJ.: unguiferous (producing unguent). ‖**unguèn-to** [L. *-tum*], M.: unguent, OINTment.

uni- [L. *unus*, ONE]: **uní-bile**, ADJ.: that may be united or joined; compatible. **-caménte**, ADV.: uniquely (only); exclusively. **-cità**, F.: uniqueness; singularity (peculiarity). **ún-ico**, ADJ.: unique (sole, only; singular, peculiar). **-córno** [L. *cornu*, HORN], M.: unicorn. **-ficáre**, TR.: unify (unite, join). **-ficazióne**, F.: unification. **-formáre**, TR.: render uniform, conform. **-fórme**, ADJ.: uniform. **-formeménte**, ADV.: uniformly. **-formità**, F.: uniformity. **-gènito**, ADJ.: only-begotten; M.: only son (Christ). **-ménto†**, M.: uniting; union. **-óne**, F.: union; concord. **uní-paro** [L. *parere*, breed], ADJ.: uniparous. **uníre**, TR.: unite, join. **-sillábico**, ADJ.: monosyllabic. **uní-sono**, M.: unison. **-taménte**, ADV.: unitedly (jointly). **-tà**, F.: unity (union; concord). **-tário**, ADJ.: unitary; unitarian. **-tézza**, F.: unity. **-tívo**, ADJ.: unitive, uniting. **-'to**, ADJ.: united (joined). **-válve**, **-válvo**, ADJ.: univalve. **-versále**, ADJ.: universal; M.: universal; bulk. **-versalità**, F.: universality. **-versalizzáre**, TR.: universalize (generalize). **-versa(l)ménte**, ADV.: universally (generally). **-versità**, F.: university; universality. **-versitário**, ADJ.: of a university. **-vèrso**, M.: universe; ADJ.: universal (whole, general). **-vocaménte**, ADJ.: univocally. **uní-voco** [L. *vox*, voice], ADJ.: univocal (of one meaning).

úno, *un*, *f. una*, *un'* [L. *unus*], NUM.: ONE; ART.: a, an: — *ad* —, one by one; *in* —, together; *ad un' ora*, at the same time; — *tanto per* —, so much a person.

ún-qua†, **-quánche†**, **-que†**, ADV.: never; in no degree. **-quemái†**, ADV.: never.

un-táre, TR.: anOINT; grease. **-táta**, F.: anointing. **-tatúra**, F.: anointing; flattery (adulation). **-tíccio**, *dim.* of *-to*. ‖**ún-to** [part. of *-gere*], ADJ.: anointed; greasy (fat); M.: ointment; grease (fat). **-tóre**, M.: anointer. **-tòrio†**, M.: ointment. **-tosità** = *-tuosità*. **-túme**, M.: lot of grease (dirt). **-tuosità**, F.: unctuosity, greasiness. **-tuóso**, ADJ.: unctuous (oily); greasy. **-zioncèlla**, *dim.* of *-zione*. **-zióne**, F.: unction (ointment); disposition†.

uom.. = *om..*

uòpo [L. *opus*], M.: need (necessity); advantage, account, pro: *aver* (or *esser* or *far*) *d'* —, be necessary; *a mio* —, for me.

uòse [OGer. *hosa*, HOSE], F. PL.: gaiters, spatterdasher.

uòv.. = *ov..*

upíglio†, M.: white garlic.

úpupa [L.], F.: lapwing; tuft.

ura-cáno†, ‖**-gáno** [Carib. *Huracan*, god of the tempest], M.: hurricane.

urángo = *orangutan*.

ur-banaménte, ADV.: urbanely (politely). **-banità**, F.: urbanity. ‖**-báno** [L. *-banus* (*urbs*, city)], ADJ.: urbane (courteous).

úrea [l. L.], F.: urea.

ur-èdine [L. *-edo*], F.: uredo (rust). **-ènte** [*-ere*, burn], ADJ.: burning.

úre-tra [ak. to *urine*], F.: urethra. **-trále**, ADJ.: urethral.

ur-gènte, ADJ.: urgent. **-gentemènte**,

ADV.: urgently. **-ġènza**, F.: urgency. ‖**úr-gere** [*urgere*], TR.: urge.

urín. .† = *orin.* .

ur-laménto†, M.: howling. ‖**-láre** [L. *ululare*], INTR.: howl (shriek). **-latóre**, M.: howler. **-lío**, M.: continued howl. **-lo**, pl. *-li*, *-la*, M.: howl (loud shriek). **-lóna**, F., **-lóne**, M.: loud, shrieking debater.

úr-na [L.], F.: urn (vase); ballot-box. **-nétta**, **-nettína**, *dim.* of *-na.*

úro [L. *urus*], M.: wild ox.

ur-taménto, M.: shock, knock. ‖**-táre** [?], TR.: push against, run against, offend, HURT. **-táta**, F.: a push; hurt. **-tatóre**, M.: pusher. **-tatúra**, F.: pushing against. **-to**, ADJ.: pushed, run against; M.: hit (encounter, hurt). **-tóne**, *aug.* of *-to.*

ú-ṣa†, F.: copulation. **-ṣábile**, ADJ.: usable. **-ṣággio**†, **-ṣaménto**†, M.: usage (custom; practice). **-ṣánza**, F.: use (custom, fashion; practice, habit, manner); intercourse: *aver — con*, be familiar with. ‖**-ṣáre** [*-so*], TR.: use (make use of); frequent†; converse†; exercise†, hold (office)†; INTR.: use (be used or wont); be familiar: *— con*, have to do with. **-ṣáta**†, F.: use, custom. **-ṣataménte**, ADV.: usually (generally). **-ṣatívo**†, ADJ.: fit for use (employable). **-ṣáto**, ADJ.: used (accustomed; practised); beaten; worn out (old); frequented†; M.: usage, custom. **-ṣatóre**†, M.: user; frequenter.

uṣát-to [dim. of *uosa*], M.: boot. **-tíno**, M.: half-boots, buskins.

uṣbèrgo [OGer. *hals-berc*, 'neck-guard'], M.: HAUBERK (coat of mail; breastplate).

uṣcènte [*uscire*], ADJ.: going out; issuing.

u-ṣcétto, *dim.* of *-scio.* **-ṣciále**, M.: glass-door; folding screen. **-ṣciáta**, F.: slam(ming) of the door. **-ṣcièra**, F., **-ṣcière**, M.: doorkeeper (usher).

uṣciménto [*uscire*], M.: going out; issue.

ú-ṣcio [L. *ostium* (*os*, mouth)], M.: door (smaller than *porta*), entrance; passage: *— di casa*, house door, entrance; *— di camera*, door of a room; *esser a — e bottega*, be a close neighbour; *trovarsi tra l'— e il muro*, be between two fires. **-ṣcioletto**, **-ṣciolíno**, **-ṣciòlo**, *dim.* of *-scio.*

u-ṣcíre [for *escire* (L. *ex-ire*, go out), but assimil. to *uscio*], IRR.§; INTR.: go or come out, ISSUE; proceed; escape; open towards (open into); sprout: *far —*, drive or squeeze out; urge, press: *— alla luce*, be published; *— a riva*, come ashore: *— di sè*, get beyond one's self; get deranged; *— di cervello*, become mad; *— di mente*, forget; *— di bando*, be recalled from

-ṣcíto, PART. of *-scire*; M.: evacuation,

; uscidamo, uscite,
escono. Subj. *esca*, etc. I've *esci; uscite.*

: as usual; com-

; M.: use, usage; custom, habit; rule, direction; coition†;

: hussar.

ústa† [Germ'c *nüstern*, NOSTRIL ?], F.: scent of wild animals.

ustióne [L. *ustio* (*urere*, burn)], F.: burning, combustion.

ustoláre [*usta*], INTR.: yelp (of dogs on the scent); pant or burn with desire (yearn).

ustòrio [L. root *us-*, burn], ADJ.: burning.

uṣu-ále [*uso*], ADJ.: usual. **-alità**, F.: usualness. **-alménte**, ADV.: usually. **-capióne**, F.: usucaption (property by long possession). **-capíre** [L. *capere*, take], TR.: hold by usucaption (by long possession). **-cátto**, PART. of *capire*. **-fruttáre**, TR.: have the usufruct of. **-frútto**, M.: usufruct (profit, use). **-fruttuária**, F., **-fruttuário**, M.: usufructuary. **uṣú-ra**, F.: usury. **-ráio**, **-rário**†, ADJ.: usurious; M.: usurer. **-rière**, M.: usurer. **-rpaménto**, M.: usurpation. **-rpáre** [L.], TR.: usurp. **-rpativaménte**, ADV.: by usurpation. **-rpatóre**, M., **-rpatríce**, **-rpazióne**, F.: usurpation.

utèllo†, M.: cruet.

utensíle [L. *-lis* (*uti*, use)], M.: utensil.

ute-ríno, ADJ.: uterine. *-rus*], M.: uterus (womb).

úti-le [L. *-lis* (*uti*, use)], ADJ.: useful. **-lità**, F.: utility. **-litáre**†, INTR.: profit. **-litário**, ADJ., M.: utilitarian. **-litarismo**, M.: utilitarianism. **-lizzáre**, TR.: utilize (derive profit from). **-lménte**, ADV.: usefully (advantageously).

utim. .† = *ultim.* .

uto-pía [Gr. *ou*, not, *tópos*, place], F:

Utopia. **-písta**, pl. *—ti*, M.: Utopist (Utopian).
útre† = *otre*.
utriáca = *triaca*.
ú-va [L.], F.: grape: — *secca*, raisin; — *de' frati*, currant; — *spina*, gooseberry; *corre* (*cogliere*) *-ve*, gather grapes; (*fig.*) mock, quiz. **-váceo**, ADJ.: of grapes (grape-). **-'vea**, F.: second tunicle of the eye. **-'veo**, ADJ.: of grapes (grape-). **-'vero**†, M.: nipple (breast). **-vízzolo**†, M.: wild vine.
uz-záto, ADJ.: bulged, rotund. ||**-zo** [?], M.: bulge (of a barrel); paunch.
úzzolo [? L. root *us-*, burn], M.: burning or intense desire; pruriency.

V

v *vu* [L.], M.: v (the letter).
va, 3 Pres. Ind., or 2 (also *va'*) I've of *andare*.
va-cánte, ADJ.: vacant (VOID, empty); wanting. **-cantería**†, F.: superfluity; vanity. **-cánza**, F.: vacancy; vacation (school-holidays, short or long). ||**-cáre** [L., be empty], INTR.: be vacant, be free; cease (end)†; be wanting†; repose†; be superfluous†; (*leg.*) adjourn. **-cáto**, PART.: vacant, empty; ceased†, etc. **-cazióne**†, F.: vacancy; vacation; repose; failure; want.
vá-cca [L.], F.: cow; bad woman; idle silkworm; cowhide†: *lingua di* —, sort of anvil. **-ccáio**, M.: cowherd, cowkeeper. **-ccarèlla** = *-ccherella*. **-ccáro** = *-ccaio*. **-ccherèlla**, F.: young cow (heifer). **-cchétta**, F.: little cow†; cowhide, neat's leather: account-book (us'ly leather-bound); parish-book. **-ccina**, F.: beef (bovine animal). **-ccinábile**, ADJ.: capable of vaccination. **-ccináre** [*-ccino*], TR.: vaccinate. **-ccinazióne**, F.: vaccination. **-ccíno**, ADJ.: of cows (bovine); vaccine; M.: vaccine; vaccinia (cowpox).
vácelo†, ADJ.: active; ADV.: soon.
vacil-laménto, M., **-lánza**†, F.: vacillation (wavering, irresolution). ||**-láre** [L.], INTR.: vacillate (waver, reel; hesitate); fancy†. **-lazióne**, F.: vacillation (wavering, hesitancy). **-lità**†, F.: doubtfulness; ambiguity.
va-cuáre†, TR.: evacuate (empty). **-cuazióne**†, F.: evacuation, emptying. **-cuità**, F.: vacuity, emptiness. ||**vá-cuo** [L. *-cuus*], ADJ.: vacuous (empty, VOID, vacant); free; unprovided†; M.: vacuity (void, emptiness), vacuum.
váda, Pres. Subj. of *andare*.
vádo† = *guado*.
váfro†, M.: crafty, cunning.
vaga-bondággine, F.: vagabondage, -dry. **-bondággio**, M.: vagabondage (rambling). **-bondáre**, INTR.: vagabond (ramble, stroll, wander like a vagabond). **-bondità**†, F.: vagabondage (rambling). **-bóndo**, ADJ.: vagabond (vagrant, rambling); M.: vagabond (tramp). **-bund**. .†, etc. = *-bond*. ., etc. **-ménte** [*vago*], ADV.: vaguely; charmingly (gracefully, handsomely). **-ménto**†, M.: rambling (wandering). ||**vagá-re** [L. *-ri* (*vagus*, roving)], INTR.: rove (ramble, wander). **-tóre**, M.: rambler. **-zióne**†, F.: roving (wandering).
vagelláio [*-llo*], M.: dyer; potter†.
vagel-laménto, M.: raving. ||**-láre** [*vacillare*], INTR.: wander†; rave.
vagèl-lo [*vasello*], M.: dyer's vat; large boiler†. **-lóne**†, M.: large vessel or vat.
va-gheggería†, F., **-gheggiaménto**, M.: ogling (a lady), courting. ||**-gheggiáre** [*vago*], TR.: cast amourous glances upon (ogle); court (woo); REFL.: regard one's self complacently (admire one's self). **-gheggiatóre**, M.: **-gheggiatríce**, F.: admirer, lover. **-gheggína**, F., **-gheggíno**, M.: flirt; (M.) beau (lady's man); gallant (dandy). **-ghétto**† [*-go*], ADJ.: genteel, pretty. **-ghézza** [*-go*], F.: lively desire (eagerness); delight; loveliness (gracefulness); charming thing.
vagill. .† = *vacill*. .
vagiménto† = *vagito*.
vagí-na [L. (*vas*, vessel)], F.: sheath (scabbard); (*anat.*) vagina. **-nále**, ADJ.: vaginal.
va-gíre [L.], INTR.: cry (as a baby). **-gíto**, M.: baby-cry.
vágl̦ia [*valere*], F.: worth (ability, power); validity: — *postale*, post-order.
va-gl̦iáio, M.: sieve-maker. **-gl̦iáre**, TR.: sift (riddle), cull (select). **-gl̦iáta**, F.: sifting. **-gl̦iatóre**, M.: sifter; picker. **-gl̦iatúra**, F.: sifting, picking. **-gl̦iétto**, *dim.* of *-glio*. ||**vá-gl̦io** [**vanlus*, L. *vannus*, VAN], M.: corn-sieve (riddle): *far* (*portar*) *l' acqua col* —, do useless things.
vá-go [L. *-gus* (cf. *-gare*)], ADJ.: vague (rambling; undefined); eager (greedy; fond, glad); attractive (graceful, lovely, fascinating); fond lover†, admirer: *sarei — di sapere*, I should be glad to know. **-goláre** [freq. of *-gare*], INTR.: ramble, wander about.
vái, 2 Pres. Ind. or I've† of *andare*.
vaiáio†, M.: furrier.
vaiáno [*vaio*], M.: black grape; wine (of it).
vainíglia [Sp. *-nilla*], F.: vanilla.

vá-io [*vario*], ADJ.: spotted†, blackish (of fruit, etc.; esp. in pl.); M.: gray miniver (kind of ermine); (*her.*) vary. **-ioláre,** INTR.: change colour (of grapes). **-iòlo,** M.: variola (smallpox). **-iolóso,** ADJ.: (of the) smallpox. **-iuol**†. . = *-iol.* .

valánga [Fr. *avalanche* (*à val*, 'to the valley')], F.: avalanche (snow-slip).

válco† = *valico.*

vá-le [L.], INTERJ., M.: vale, farewell. **-léggio**†, M.: power. **-lènte,** ADJ.: valid; able (skilful, clever); valiant (strong)†. **-lenteménte,** ADV.: ably (skilfully); valiantly (strongly). **-lentería**†, **-lentía, -lentígia**†, F.: ability (skill, merit); valour (bravery). **-lent=uòmo, -lent' uòmo,** M.: man of merit, excellent man. ||**-lére** [L.], IRR.§; INTR.: have worth, be valid; be able; prevail; TR.: be worth (cost; be equal to; deserve, merit); signify; M.†: value (worth, price); valour, force; REFL.: avail one's self, profit: — *meglio*, be better; — *di meglio*, turn to a better account; *-le a dire*, that is to say; *non — niente*, be worth nothing; *non — la pena*, not be worth the trouble; *sapere farsi* —, know how to make one's self respected.

§ Ind.: Pres. *válgo, váli, vále; valghiámo, valète, válgono.* Pret. *vál-si, -se; -sero.* Fut. *varrò* Cond. *varrèi.* Subj.: Pres. *válga; valghiámo, valghiáte, válgano.* Part. *válso* or *valúto.* — Rare forms: Pres. *váglio.* (Subj.) *váglia.*

valeriána [*Valeriano*], F.: (*bot.*) valerian.

va-lète [L. (cf. *-le*)], INTERJ.: farewell (ye)! **-letudinário,** ADJ., M.: valetudinarian. **-letúdine,** F.: health, healthiness. **-lévole,** ADJ.: valid: useful (profitable). **-levolménte,** ADV.: usefully (profitably).

vali-cábile, ADJ.: that can be crossed. ||**-cáre** [cf. *varcare*], TR.: pass beyond (cross); break†; transgress†. **-catóre,** M., **-catríce,** F.: passer (beyond); transgressor†. **váli-co,** M.: passage (pass, entry; ford); spinning wheel.

vali-daménte, ADV.: in a valid manner. **-dáre**†, TR.: render valid; ratify (confirm). **-dità,** F.: validity, strength. ||**váli-do** [L. *-dus*], ADJ.: valid (legal); vigorous (powerful); able. **-dóre**† = *valore.*

vali-gería, F.: trunk store. ||**valígia** [l. L. **-sia* (? L. *vidulus*, wallet)], F.: VALISE (portmanteau; carpet-bag): *entrare* (*essere*) *in* —, get angry. **-giáccia,** *disp.* of *-gia.* **-giáio,** M.: valise-maker or seller, trunk-maker or seller. **-gína, -gióna,** *disp. dim.* of *-gia.* **-giòtto,** *aug.* of *-gio.*

vali-ménto†, M.: value, worth. **-túdine**†, F.: health.

vallámo†, M.: space (between valleys).

vallá-re 1 [L. *-ris* (*vallus*, wall)], ADJ.: mural: *corona* —, mural crown (bestowed on the Rom. soldier who first mounted a wall). **-re** 2, TR.: (*poet.*) surround with a wall or trenches. **-'ta**† 1, F.: circumvallation.

val-láta† 2, F.: space of a valley, valley. ||**vál-le** [L. *-les*], F.: valley (vale, dale). **-lèa,** F.: (*poet.*) valley (vale). **-létta, -lettína,** *dim.* of *-le.*

vallétto [dim. of l. L. *vass(all)us*], M.: valet (gentleman's servant).

valli-cèlla [*valle*], F.: small or narrow valley. **-cóso**†, ADJ.: full of valleys. **-giáno,** M.: valley-dweller (inhabitant of a valley).

vállo [L. *-llum*], M.: palisade, intrenchment; fence.

val-lonáccio, M.: gloomy valley or glen. **-lonáta,** F.: large valley. **-loncèllo,** M.: little valley, glen. ||**-lóne** [*aug.* of *valle*], M.: wide, deep valley.

vallonèa [*Vallona*, in Albania], F.: nutgall.

va-loráre†, TR.: reinvigorate. ||**-lóre** [L. *-lor* (*-lere*, be worth)], M.: value (worth, price); valour (bravery, courage); signification; consideration. **-lorosaménte,** ADV.: valorously (valiantly, bravely). **-lorόso,** ADJ.: valorous (valiant, brave). **-lsènte,** M.: value (amount); faculty. **-lsi,** etc., PRET. of *-lere.* **-lso** (= *-luto*), PART. of *-lere.* **-lúra**†, F.: value. **-lúta,** F.: value (worth, price; amount); money; power†, faculty†: *a* —, according to (or at) its value. **-lutábile,** ADJ.: valuable; estimable. **-lutáre,** TR.: value, estimate. **-lutazióne,** F.: valuation (appraisement).

válva [L.], F.: valve (of a shell).

valvas-sóre, ||**-sòro** [l. L. *vavassor* (*vassus*)], M.: vavasor (vassal under a baron).

válvola [L. *-vula* (cf. *-va*)], F.: (*mech., anat.*) valve: — *di sicurtà*, safety-valve.

válzer [Ger. *walzer*], M.: waltz.

vám-pa [*-po*], F.: blast of hot air; ardour (passion). **-páccia,** *disp.* of *-pa.* **-peggiánte,** ADJ.: glowing. **-peggiáre,** INTR.: burn fiercely.

vampíro [Ger. *-pyr* (Serv.)], M.: vampire.

vám-po [L. *vapor*, heat], M.: puff of heat; flame (flare, flash); ardour (passion): *menar* —, be kindled or infuriated; be proud, boast. **-póre**† = *-po.*

vana-glòria [L.], F.: vainglory. **-gloriáre,** INTR., (us'ly) REFL.: be vainglorious, pride one's self. **-gloriosaménte,** ADV.: vaingloriously. **-glorióso,** ADJ.: vainglorious. **-ménte** [*vano*], ADV.: vainly. **-'re**† = *vaneggiare.*

vándalo [L. *Vandalus*], ADJ., M.: Vandal.

va-neggiaménto, M.: empty or wild dreaming (roving fancy); raving; nonsense (dotage). ‖**-neggiáre** [-*no*], INTR.: indulge in empty dreams (imagine wildly), rave; talk incoherently, talk nonsense; TR.†: render vain. **-neggiatóre,** M., **-neggiatríce,** F.: day-dreamer; raver. **-nerèllo,** *dim.* of *-no;* ADJ.: rather vain or conceited; M.: fop (would-be dandy). **-negiáta,** F.: act of vanity. **-nèsio,** ADJ.: vain (conceited); M.: conceited person. **-nézza,** F.: vanity.

ván-ga [OGer. *wanka* (= Ger. *-ge*)], F.: spade; mattock. **-gáccia,** *disp.* of *-ga.* **-gaiòla,** F.: small fishing net. **-gáre,** TR.: spade, dig. **-gáta,** F.: stroke with a spade; spading (digging, spading work). **-gatóre,** M.: digger. **-gatúra,** F.: spading, digging; digging-time.

van-gèle† = *-geli.* **-gèlico**†, ADJ.: evangelical. **-gèlio**† = *-gelo.* **-gelista,** M.: evangelist. **-gelizzáre,** TR.: evangelize. ‖**-gèlo** [= *evangelo*], M.: Gospel.

van-ghéggia, -ghéggiola [*-ga*], F.: blade of a spade; ploughshare (coulter). **-gíle,** M.: shoulder (of a spade, foot-hold).

vanguárdia [*avanti, guardia*], F.: vanguard, van.

vá-nia† = *-nità.* **-niáre** = *-neggiare.* **-nilòquio,** M.: vain discourse. **-níre,** INTR.: (*poet.*) = *svanire,* disappear. ‖**-nità** [L. *-nitas* (*-nus,* vain)], F.: vanity. **-nitóso,** ADJ.: vain (conceited); M.: conceited person (vain fool).

vánni [L. *-nnus,* van, FAN], M. PL.: (*poet.*) pinions (wings).

vánno, 3 Pl. Pres. of *andare.*

váno [L. *-nus*], ADJ.: vain; M.: void (emptiness, empty space); inanity, inutility: *in —,* in vain, vainly; *sparir nel —,* vanish in empty space; melt away in thin air; *pelo —,* down of the face.

van-taggétto, *dim.* of *-taggio.* **-taggiáre,** TR.: gain the advantage over; surpass (excel, exceed); advance or further the interest of (favour); INTR., REFL.: profit, gain, acquire. **-taggiataménte,** ADV.: advantageously. **-taggiáto,** PART.: surpassed, etc. (cf. *-taggiare*); ADJ.: abundant; easy and comfortable; full. **-taggíno,** M.: extra weight or measure, overweight, addition. ‖**-tággio** [*avanti*], M.: advantage (superiority, profit, benefit); good fortune: *da —,* moreover, besides; more; *dar —,* give an advantage; give the overweight; *giuocator di —,* swindler, sharper, blackleg; *star a —,* be above or superior; *di gran —,* remarkably well. **-taggiosaménte,** ADV.: advantageously. **-taggióso,** ADJ.: advantageous, superior; useful; looking out for his advantage, selfish. **-taggiúzzo,** *dim.* of *-taggio.*

van-taménto, M.: vaunting, boasting, vainglory. ‖**-táre** [*vano*], TR.: VAUNT (praise, extol, boast); INTR., REFL.: boast (brag, pretend). **-tatóra,** F., **-tatóre,** M., **-tatríce,** F.: boaster, braggart. **-tazióne, -tería,** F.: vaunting (boasting, vainglory). **-tévole**†, ADJ.: vain (proud). **-to,** M.: vaunt (boast, boasting); praise (glory); advantage (superiority, preference): *dar il —,* give the preference; *darsi —,* boast, pretend. **-áme,** M.: mass of vanities, nonsense. **-'vera,** M.: *a —,* at random, heedlessly.

vapo-rábile, ADJ.: evaporable. **-rabilità,** F.: vaporability. **-ráccio,** *disp.* of *-re.* **-rále**†, ADJ.: vaperous. **-ráre,** TR.: evaporate (exhale); REFL.: evaporate (fume off). **-rativo,** ADJ.: evaporable. **-razióne,** F.: evaporation, exhalation. ‖**vapó-re** [L. *vapor*], M.: vapour (steam); steam-engine; train; fine stuff: *a —,* steam- (as *battello a —,* steamboat, etc.). **-rétto, -ríno,** M.: small steamer; steam-tug. **-révole**†, ADJ.: vaporable. **-rièra,** F.: locomotive. **-rosità,** F.: vaporousness; exhalation. **-róso,** ADJ.: vaporous (vapory), steaming.

vapulazióne†, F.: chastisement.

varáno† = *vaiano.*

varáre [L. *vara,* trestle], TR.: launch (a vessel); approach (the shore)†.

var-cábile, ADJ.: that may be passed over or crossed. ‖**-cáre** [L. *varicare* (*vara,* forked pole), straddle], TR.: pass across (cross, traverse); issue. **-co,** M.: crossing (border-line, passage); gap; issue.

vari-ábile, ADJ.: variable. **-abilità,** F.: variableness. **-aménte,** ADV.: variously, differently. **-aménto,** M.: variation. **-ánte,** ADJ.: varying (different). **-anteménte**†, ADV.: differently. **-ánza**†, F.: variance (diversity). ‖**-áre** [L.], TR.: vary (diversify; differ). **-ataménte,** ADV.: variously (differently). **-áto,** ADJ.: varied (different). **-azióne,** F.: variation (difference).

varíce [L. *-rix*], F.: varicose (dilated) vein.

varicèlla [L. *-riola*], F.: spurious small-pox.

vari-cocèle [L. *varix,* dilated vein, Gr. *kéle,* tumour], M.: varicocele. **-cóso,** ADJ.: varicose.

va-rieggiáre [freq. of *-riare*], INTR.: vary (change frequently, change). **-rietà,** F.: variety (diversity). ‖**vá-rio** [L. *-rius*], ADJ.: various (different; unlike; diverse; several); M.: variety. **-riopínto** [*pinto*], ADJ.: many-coloured (variegated, speckled). **-ro**† = *-rio.*

va-rrò, FUT., **-rrèi**, COND. of *valere*.
varròcchio [?], M.: crane (windlass).
varvas-sóre†, M.: man of merit. **-sò-ro**† = *valvassore*.
va-sáio [-*so*], M.: potter, china-ware maker. **-sca**, F.: basin, reservoir. **-scellétto**, *dim*. of *-scello*. **-scèllo**, M.: VESSEL (ship). **-'scolo**, M.: small vase or vessel. **-scoláre**, ADJ.: vascular. **-scolóso**, ADJ.: vascular. **-so**† = *-so*. **-sellággio**†, M.: dishes. **-selláio**†, M.: potter. **-sellá-me**, **-sellaménto**†, pl. —*a*, M.: (collection of) vases, dishes, plates, earthenware. **-sellettièra**†, F.: cupboard. **-sellettíno**, M.: small vase. **-sellétto**, *dim*. of *-sello*. **-sellière**†, M.: potter. **-sèllo**, pl. (*poet.*) —*a*, M.: small vase; vessel (ship)†. ||**-'so** [L. *vas*], M.: vase (cup, pot, vessel); (blood-)vessel; receptacle; capacity (of a theatre, church, etc.). **-sòtto**, *aug*. of *-so*.
vas-sallággio, M.: vassalage. ||**-sállo** [l. L. *vass(all)us* (Celt.)], M.: vassal; dependent (servant).
vas-sèllo†, etc. = *vascello*, etc. **-soiétto**, *dim*. of *-soio*. ||**-sóio** [L. *-sorium* (*vas*, vase)], M.: tray, platter.
va-staménte, ADV.: vastly (extensively). **-tézza**, **-stità**, F.: vastness (great extent). ||**-'sto** [L. *-stus*], ADJ.: vast (extensive, ample); M.: (*poet.*) ocean (main).
vá-te [L. *-tes*], M.: (*poet.*) bard, poet. **-ticináre**, TR.: vaticinate (prophesy, foretell). **-ticinatóre**, M.: vaticinator (prophet). **-ticinazióne**, F., **-ticínio**, M.: vaticination (prophecy, prediction).
vattel'a pésca [*va te lo*], INTERJ.: "go fishing for it!" find it out if you can!
ve, **ve-**, for *vi* before another pronoun.
ve', contraction of *vedi*: see! lo!
vèc-chia, ADJ.: cf. *-chio*; F.: old woman. **-chiáccia**, **-chiáccio**, *disp*. of *-chia*, *-chio*. **-chiáia**, F.: old age. **-chiárdo**†, M.: old man. **-chiarèllo**, *dim*. of *-chio*. **-chiécio**†, ADJ.: rather old. **-chierellino**, **-chierèllo**, *dim*. of *-chio*. **-chiétto**, *dim*. or *car*. of *-chio*. **-chiézza**, F.: old age. **-chiníccio**, ADJ.: rather old. **-chína**, **-chíno**, ADJ., F., M.: *car. dim*. of *-chia*, *-chio* (nice little old person). ||**vèc-chio** [L. *vetulus* (*dim*. of *vetus*, old)], ADJ.: old (aged; ancient); senior; M.: old man; forefather. **-chióna**, **-chióne**, ADJ.: *aug*. of *-chio*; F., M.: hale or venerable old person; chestnut dried in the shell. **-chiòtto**, ADJ.: rather old; M.: rather old man, strong old man. **-chitúdine**†, F.: old age. **-chiúccio**, ADJ.: weak old man. **-chiúme**, M.: heap of old things (old rubbish, old rags or clothes); old branches; oldness, antiquity.
vèc-cia [L. *vicia*], F.: vetch. **-ciáto**, ADJ.: mixed with vetch; vetchy. **-cióne**, M.: wild vetch; buckshot. **-ciòso**, ADJ.: mixed with vetch; vetchy.
véce [L. *vic-em* (acc.), change, VICISSItude], F.: change; substitute (place, stead); portion; prefix for *vice-*†: *a* (*or in*) — *di*, instead of, in the place of; *adempiere* (or *far*, *sostenere*) *la* — (*or le* —*i*) *d'uno*, fill one's position, substitute or surrogate one. **-cancellière**†, M.: vice-chancellor. **-cónte**†, M.: viscount.
ve-dére [*videre*], INTR.§; TR.: see (perceive, observe, notice); M.: sight (appearance): — *il bello*, look out for the opportunity; — *in viso*, distinguish clearly; — *torto*, see wrong; judge wrongly, mistake; — *volontieri*, see willingly; receive cordially; *dare a* —, show; demonstrate, make one believe; *fare* —, show; inform; *al* —, apparently; *dal* — *al non* —, in the twinkling of an eye. **-détta**, F.: vedette (outpost, sentinel): *star alle -dette*, be on the lookout, beware. **-diménto**†, M.: sight, view. **-ditóre**, M.: spectator (beholder, observer); sentinel†.

§ Ind.: Pres. *védo* or *véggo*, *védi*, *véde*; *vediámo*, *vedéte*, *véggono* or *védono*. Pret. *vidi*, *-de*; *-dero*. Fut. *vedrò*. Cond. *vedréi*. Subj. *véda* or *végga*; *vediámo*, *vediáte*, *védano* or *véggano*. Impv. *védi*; *vedéte*. Part.: Pres. *vedénte* or *veggénte*. Past *vísto* or *vedúto*. — Poet. forms: Pres. *véggio*; *veggiámo*, *véggiono*, (S.) *véggia*. Pop. forms: Pret. *véddi* or *víddi*, etc.

védo-va [L. *vidua*, cf. *-vo*], ADJ.: cf. *-vo*; F.: WIDOW. **-vággio**†, M.: widowhood. **-vále**† = *-vile*. **-vánza**, F.: widowhood. **-váre**, TR.: widow, bereave. **-vático**†, widowhood; mourning garment. **-vèlla**, *car. dim*. of *-va*. **-vétta**, *dim*. of *-va*. **-vézza**†, F.: widowhood. **-víle**, ADJ.: of a widow or widower (a widow's, a widower's); M.: widow's portion (jointure); widowhood†. **-vína**, F.: *car. dim*. of *-va*. **-vità**†, F.: widowhood. ||**védo-vo** [L. *viduus*, bereft], ADJ.: widowed; bereft; M.: widower. **-vóna**, **-vòtta**, F.: *aug*. of *-va*; buxom widow; old widow.
ve-drò, FUT., **-drèi**, COND. of *vedere*.
veduità†, F.: widowhood.
vedú-ta, F. of *-to*; F.: sight (view, prospect); point of vision; show: *far* —, make a show, feign, pretend; *far la* —, examine (at the custom-house), search; *testimonio di* —, eye-witness; *di* —, by sight. **-taménte**, ADV.: visible, evidently (clearly). ||**vedú-to** [part. of *vedere*], PART.: seen, etc.; M.: thing seen.
vee-ménte [L. *vehemens*], ADJ.: vehement (violent, energetic, forcible). **-menteménte**†, ADV.: vehemently. **-ménza**, F.: vehemence.
vege-tábile, ADJ.: vegetable, vegetative;

M. PL.: vegetables. **-tabilità**, F.: vegetable quality (Eng.† vegetability). **-tále**, ADJ.: vegetal; vegetable; M.: vegetable. **-táre** [L.], INTR.: vegetate. **-tatívo**, ADJ.: vegetative. **-tazióne**, F.: vegetation (growth). **-tévole**†, ADJ.: vegetable. ‖**vège-to** [L. *-tus* (*vegeo*, move, stir)], ADJ.: vigorous; prosperous (flourishing).

veggènte [*vedere*], ADJ.: seeing; M.: seeing (sight): *a mio* —, in my sight, before my eyes; *chiaro* —, clear-sighted. **-ménte**†, ADV.: visibly (openly).

vegghi. .† = *vegli*. .

véggia†, F.: cask; sledge.

veg-gino, *dim.* of *-gio*. ‖**vég-gio** [*laveggio*], M.: earthenware pot for keeping hands and feet warm (used in Italy; warming-pan).

veggiòlo†, M.: bitter vetch.

véggo, PRES. (*pop.*) of *vedere*.

véglia [L. *vigilia*], F.: WAKing (VIGIL, WATCHing, watch); evening (passed in conversation); evening call; evening party, ball; sentinel: *frutti delle -glie*, products of midnight toil; *cose da dire a* —, nonsensical stories.

vegliárdo [Fr. *vieillard* (cf. *vecchio*)], M.: old man.

ve-gliáre [L. *vigilare*], INTR.: keep AWAKE; watch, sit up; be VIGILant (be on the alert); be in force†; TR.: watch over (guard). **-gliánte**, PART.: watching; watchful. **-gliatóre**, M., **-gliatríce**, F.: watcher (sitter up). **-gliévole**†, ADJ.: vigilant (watchful).

vèglio 1 [cf. *vecchio*], ADJ.†: old (ancient); M.: (*poet.*) old man.

vèglio† 2, M.: fleece.

ve-glióne [*-glia*], M.: opera ball or masquerade. **-gliúccia**, F.: short watch; small evening party.

vegnènte† = *veniente*.

vègno, PRES. (*poet.*) of *venire*.

véi† = *vedi*, from *vedere*.

veícolo [L. *vehiculum* (*veh-*, bear)], M.: vehicle.

vé-la [L. (pl. of *-lum*, sail; VEIL, cf. *-lo*)], F.: sail; PL.: sails, vessels: — *majore* (or *maestra*), mainsail; *far* —, set sail; *essere alla* —, be under sail. **-lábile** [*-lare*], ADJ.: that may be veiled. **-láme**, M.: lot or stock of veils; veiling, veil; covering, pellicle. **-laménto**, M.: veiling, covering; veil. **-láre**, TR.: veil (cover with a veil, conceal); REFL : take the veil; be covered with thin ice: — *l' occhio*, fall into a slight slumber. **-lário**, M.: (*arch.*) awning (cover). **-láta**, *f.* of *-lato*; F.: sailing (sail, run). **-lataménte**, ADV.: in a veiled or secret manner (secretly). **-láto**, PART.: veiled; furnished with sails. **-latóro**, M., **-latríce**, F.: veiler. **-latúra**, F.: veiling; providing with sails; sails. **-leggiáre**, INTR.: sail (navigate); REFL.: be sailed. **-leggiáta**, F.: sailing (sail, run); course. **-leggiatóre**, M.: sailer (sailing-ship).

vele-náre†, TR.: poison. **-nífero**, ADJ.: venomous (poisonous). ‖**velé-no** [L. *venenum*], M.: poison (VENOM; spite). **-nosaménte**, ADV.: venomously. **-nosétto**, *dim.* of *-noso*. **-nosità**, F.: poisonousness (venomousness, poison, venom). **-nóso**, ADJ.: poisonous, venomous.

velétta [for *vedetta*], F.: vedette (sentry)†; PL.: *in stare alle* —*e*, (*nav.*) be on the lookout; be on picket duty.

vèlia [L. *avicula* (*avis*, bird)], F.: seagull.

ve-lièra [*vela*], **-lière**, ADJ.: fast sailing. **-lificáre**†, INTR.: sail; set sail. **-líno**, ADJ.: white (as a sail): *-lina carta*, paper fine as a veil.

vèliti [L. *-tes*], M. PL.: velites (Roman light soldiers).

vèl-le [L.], M.: WILL. **-leità**, F.: velleity (feeble will or wish).

vèl-lere† = *svellere*. **-licaménto**, M.: pricking; titillation. **-licáre** [L., pluck], TR.: twitch, prick; tickle, titillate. **-licazióne**, F.: twitching; tickling.

vèllo 1, for *ve' lo* (*vedi lo*): see him! there he is!

vèl-lo 2 [L. *villus*], M.: fleece; wool; tuft. **-lóso**, ADJ.: woolly (shaggy). **-lutáto**, ADJ.: of or like velvet (velvet-, velvety). **-lutíno**, *car. dim.* of *-luto*. **-lúto**, M.: VELVET: — *liscio*, shorn velvet; — *fino di cotone*, velveteen.

vélo [L. *-lum*, sail, veil], M.: VEIL (crape; *fig.*, cover, pretext); thin ice; scum.

veló-ce [L. *velox*], ADJ.: swift (rapid, quick). **-ceménte**, ADV.: swiftly. **-cípede**, M.: velocipede, bicycle. **-cipedísta**, pl. —*i*, M.: velocipedist, bicycler. **-cità**, F.: velocity (swiftness). **-citáre**†, TR.: impart velocity to, hasten. **-citazióne**, F.: increase of velocity.

velóna [*vela*], F.: large sail.

vèl-tro [l. L. *-trum*], M., **-tra**, F.: greyhound.

velúzzo [*-lo*], M.: little veil.

véna [L.], F.: VEIN; disposition; grain (in wood): *aver* — *d' una cosa*, have a natural bent for a thing; — *di pazzo*, dash of madness.

venagióne†, F.: chase.

vená-le [L. *-lis* (*venus*, sale)], ADJ.: venal (mercenary, vendible). **-lità**, F.: venality.

venardì† = *venerdì*.

venáto [*vena*], ADJ.: veined, striated.

vena-tóre [L. *-tor*], M.: hunter.

rio, ADJ.: of the chase, hunting (Eng.† venatorial, venatic). **-tríce**, F.: huntress.

venatúra [*-nato*], F.: veinous condition; veining (veins).

vendém-mia [L. *vin-demia* (*de- emere*, take), 'grape-gathering'], F.: VINTAGE; vintage-time. **-miáio**, M.: vendémiaire (1st month of the French republ. calendar: Sept. 21–Oct. 20). **-miále**, ADJ.: of September. **-miaménto**, M.: vintage. **-miánte**, M.: vintager. **-miáre**, TR.: gather (the vintage); harvest, hoard up. **-miatóre**, M., **-miatríce**, F.: vintager.

vénde-re [L.], TR.: sell (VEND): — *pei tempi*, sell on credit. **-réccio**, ADJ.: venal (mercenary).

vendét-ta [L. *vindicta* (*vindicare*, avenge)], F.: vengeance (revenge, redress; vendetta); amends†: *far* —†, make amends; (*jest.*) sell. **-táccia**, **-túccia**, *disp. dim.* of *vendetta*.

ven-dévole†, ‖**-díbile** [*-dere*], ADJ.: salable (vendable).

vendi-cábile, ADJ.: that may be avenged. **-caménto**†, M., **-cánza**†, F.: vengeance (revenge). ‖**-cáre** [L. *vindicare*], TR.: AVENGE (revenge; vindicate); REFL.: avenge one's self (retaliate); be revenged; pay†. **-cativaménte**, ADV.: vindictively. **-cativo**, ADJ.: revengeful (vindictive). **-catóra**, F., **-catóre**, M., **-catríce**, F.: avenger. **-chévole**†, ADJ.: revengeful (vindictive). **véndi-co**† for *-cato*, ADJ.: avenged.

vendi-fròttole [*vendere*, *frottola*], M.: intriguer (meddler); worthless fellow. =**fúmo**, M.: 'seller of smoke,' idle talker, worthless fellow. **-ménto**, M.: selling.

véndi-ta, F.: sale; auction. **-tóra**, F., **-tóre**, M., **-tríce**, F.: seller (vender). **-toruccio**, *disp. dim.* of *-tore*.

vendúto [*-dere*], PART.: sold.

ve-nefício, M.: poisonment (poisoning). **-nèfico**, ADJ.: poisonous (venomous); preparer of poisons†; sorcerer†. ‖**-néno** [L. *-nenum*], M.: (*poet.*) poison, venom (= *veleno*). **-nenóso**†, ADJ.: poisonous, venomous.

vene-rábile, ADV.: venerable. **-rabilità**, F.: venerableness. **-rándo**, ADJ.: venerable. **-ránza**†, F.: veneration (reverence). ‖**-ráre**, TR.: venerate (reverence, revere). **-ráto**, ADJ.: venerated (revered, reverend). **-ratóre**, M., **-ratríce**, F.: reverer (worshipper). **-razióne**, F.: veneration (reverence).

-dì [L. *dies*, DAY], M.: Friday: — Good Friday. ‖**Vèner-e** [L. *Venus* (desire)], F.: Venus (goddess of beauty; sensuality); grace. **-ea-** [*-eo*], ADV.: lasciviously.

venerèlla [*vena*], F.: little vein.

venèreo [*Venere*], ADJ.: of Venus; (us'ly) venereal.

venerévol. .† = *venerabil*. .

venerína [*Venere*], F.: little Venus (painted or sculptured).

venétta [*vena*], F.: little vein.

vengia. .† = *vendica*. .

vèngo, PRES. of *venire*.

vè-nia [L.], F.: indulgence (grace, remission, pardon). **-niále**, ADJ.: venial (pardonable). **-nialménte**, ADV.: in a venial manner.

ve-niménto†, M.: coming (arrival); event. **-niénte**, ADJ.: coming. ‖**-níre** [L.], IRR.§; INTR.: come (arrive; be derived, descend; happen); come to be, appear; become, be; come out (develop, grow): — *appresso*, come after, follow; — *a battaglia*, fight; — *a capo*, bring about, end; — *a grado*, please, be to one's mind; — *alle mani*, come to blows, fight; — *a mano*, be handy; — *meno*, faint, swoon; fail, be wanting; — *voglia* (*talento*), have a mind, fancy; — *bene* (or *innanzi*), thrive, shoot up; — *in luce*, appear, be published; — *incontro*, present itself; meet with; — *ai ferri*, come to close quarters; come to a conclusion; — *fatto*, succeed; — *trovato*, find, light on, meet with. **vé-nni**, PRET. of *-nire*.

§ Ind.: Pres. *vèngo*, *vièni*, *viène*; *veniámo* or *venghiámo*, *venite*, *vèngono*. Pret. *vén-ni*, *-ne*; *-nero*. Fut. *verrò*. Cond. *verrèi*. Subj.: Pres. *vènga*, etc. I've *vièni*; *venite*. Part.: Pres. *veniènte* or *vegnènte*. Past *venúto*.— Poetic forms: Pres. *vègno*; *vègnono*. (S.) *vègna*.

ve-nolína [*-na*], F.: little vein. **-nóso**, ADJ.: veinous (veined, streaked).

ven-táccio, *disp.* of *-to*. **-táglia**, F.: ventail (air-hole in the visor of a helmet). **-tagliáio**, M.: fan maker or seller. **-tá-glio**, M.: fan. **-táre**, INTR.: (*poet.*) blow; breathe; TR.†: blow or dash against. **-taròla**, F.: bandrol; vane (weathercock); fire-fan. **-táta**, F.: blow of gust of wind. **-távolo**†, M.: north-wind. **-teggiáre**†, INTR.: be windy (blow). **-terèllo**, M.: gentle breeze.

ven-tèsimo, ADJ.: twentieth; M.: twentieth part. ‖**vén-ti** [L. *viginti*], ADJ.: twenty.

venticèllo [*vento*], M.: pleasant wind, zephyr.

venti=cinque, ADJ.: twenty-five. =**cinquína**, F.: about twenty-five. **-ti=dúe**, ADJ.: twenty-two.

ven-tièra [*-to*], F.: (*mil.*) screen; ventilator (fan)†. **-tilábro**, M.: winnowing shovel. **-tilaménto**, M.: ventilating (ventilation, fanning). ‖**-tiláre** [L. (*-tus*, wind)], TR.: ventilate (air; winnow, fan;

sift, discuss). **-tilatóre**, M.: ventilator. **-tilazióne**, F.: ventilation, etc. (cf. *-lare*).
ventína [*-ti*], F.: score, about twenty.
ventipiòvolo†, M.: rainy wind, south-wind.
venti=quáttro, ADJ.: twenty-four: *le* —, the last hour of the day, sunset. **=sèi**, ADJ.: twenty-six. **=sètte**, ADJ.: twenty-seven. **=trè**, ADJ.: twenty-three: *le* —, the hour before sunset.
vèn-to [L. *-tus*], M.: WIND; (*fig.*) hint; vanity: — *fresco*, stiff breeze (gale); *aver il — in poppa*, have the wind aft, sail before the wind; prosper; *sotto il* —, leeward; *dar calci al* —, dance upon nothing, be hanged; *far* —, be windy, blow. **vèntola**, F.: fan (fire-fan; winnowing fan†); screen (shade); chandelier: *muro a* —, partition, wall. **-toláccio**, M.: (sifted) chestnut-shell. **-toláre**, TR.: winnow (as grain; sift chestnuts)†. **-tolíno**, *dim.* of *-to*. **-tósa**, F.: cupping-glass. **-tosaménte**, ADV.: vainly. **-tosáre**†, TR.: apply the cupping-glass to, vaccinate. **-tosità**, F.: ventosity (windiness). **-tóso**, ADJ.: ventose (windy; flatulent); exposed to the wind; apt to produce flatulency; inflated (vain, conceited); swift†.
vent=òtto, ADJ.: twenty-eight.
ven-tráccio, *aug.* of *-tre*. **-tráia**, F.: *disp.* of *-tre;* paunch. **-traiuòla**†, F.: tripe-woman. ‖**vèn-tre** [L. *-ter*], M.: belly (paunch; stomach). **-trésca**, F.: paunch; stuffing. **-trícchio**†, M.: gizzard, stomach (of a fowl). **-tricíno**, M.: *dim.* of *-tre;* (*fig.*) pluck. **-tríccolo**, M.: ventricle; stomach. **-trièra**, F.: waist-belt (for money). **-tríglio**† = *-tricchio*. **-trilòquio**, M.: ventriloquism. **-tríloquo**, ADJ.: ventriloquous.
ventúccio [*-to*], ADJ.: light breeze.
vent-unèsimo, ADJ.: twenty-first. ‖**=úno**, ADJ.: twenty-one.
ven-túra [L. (pl. of *-turus*, about to come)], F.: fate (fortune, chance, luck, venture); adventure: *a* (*per*) —, by chance; *alla* —, at a venture, at random; *mettersi alla* —, trust to chance or good luck; *far la* —, tell fortunes; *compagnie di* —, bands of fortune, mercenary troops. **-turière**, M.: soldier of fortune, volunteer; adventurer; ADJ.: adventurous. **-turína**, F.: imitation-jewelry. **-túro**, ADJ.: come (future, next). **-turosaménto**, ADV.: fortunately, luckily. **-turóso**, ADJ.: fortunate (lucky, favourable).
ve-nustà, F.: loveliness (comeliness, grace). ‖**-nústo** [L. *venus*, grace], ADJ.: lovely (graceful, charming, comely, beautiful).

venú-ta, F.: arrival; access†. ‖**-'to**, PART. of *venire*.
venúzza [*-na*], F.: small vein.
venzèi, *vulg.* for *ventisei*.
ve-práio, M.: brambly place. ‖**vè-pre** [L. *-pres*], M.: bramble, brier.
ver'; poet. for *verso*.
verá-ce [L. *verax*], ADJ.: true; sincere; veracious. **-ceménte**, ADV.: truly; really. **-cità**, F.: veracity, truth. **-ménte**, ADV.: truly; indeed.
veránda [Pers.], F.: veranda.
verátro [L. *-trum*], M.: (*bot.*) veratrum (hellebore).
ver-bále [*-bo*], ADJ.: verbal (literal); M.: verbal report. **-balménte**, ADV.: verbally; word by word.
verbèna [L.], F.: verbena (vervain).
ver-bigrátia, **-bigrázia** [L. *-bi gratia*], ADV.: for example, for instance. ‖**vèr-bo** [L. *-bum*], M.: WORD (Eng.† VERB); verb: (*a*) — *a* —, word for word. **-bosità**, F.: verbosity, verbiage. **-bóso**, ADJ.: verbose (wordy; talkative).
ver-dácchio, ADJ.: greenish. **-dáccio**, ADJ.: *disp. aug.* of *-de;* M.: (*paint.*) verditure. **-dástro**, ADJ.: greenish. **-dazzúrro**, **d' azzúrro** [*azzurro*], ADJ.: greenish blue, sea-green. ‖**vér-de** [L. *viridis*], ADJ.: green (of a green colour; fresh; young, unripe); M.: green (verdure); youth, vigor: *esser al* —, be at one's last shift, be without means; — *antico*, sort of marble. **-dèa**, F.: sort of white grape; wine made from it. **-de=chiáro**, **-de=cúpo**, ADJ., M.: light green. **-deggiaménto**, M.: becoming green; verdure. **-deggiánte**, ADJ.: becoming green; verdant (flourishing). **-deggiáre**, INTR.: become green; be verdant. **-de=giállo**, ADJ., M.: apple-green. **-de=márco**, M.: (*bot.*) wild rue. **-de=máre**, ADJ., M.: sea-green. **-de=mèzzo**†, ADJ.: half green (of fruit, etc.); half raw (of meat). **-de=ráme**, M.: verdigris. **-de=rógnolo**†, ADJ.: greenish. **-de=sécco**†, ADJ.: half-dry. **-détto** 1, ADJ.: greenish; sourish; M.: green colour (German green).
verdétto 2 [L. *vere dictum*, 'truly said'], M.: verdict.
ver-dézza [*-de*], F.: verdure (greenness); tartness. **-dicáre**† = *-deggiare*. **-díccio**, **-dígno**, ADJ.: greenish. **-díno**, M.: sort of fig-tree. **-dòccio**, ADJ.: faintly green. **-dógnolo**, ADJ.: greenish. **-dóne**, M.: green-finch. **-dóre**†, M.: verdure. **-dúco** [Sp. *-dugo* (? L. *viridis*), shoot; narrow sword], M.: rapier. **-dúme**, M.: greenness. **-dúra**, F.: verdure, greenness; PL.: greens, vegetables.
vere-condaménte, ADV.: bashfully

modestly. **-cóndia**, F.: bashfulness: modesty. ||**-cóndo** [L. *-cundus* (-or, reVERE, fear)], ADJ.: bashful (modest); respectful; chaste. **-cúndia**† = *-condia*.

vér-ga [L. *virga*, twig], F.: rod (switch; wand); sceptre; bar (stripe); yard; virile member: — *d'oro*, bar of gold, ingot. **-gáio** = *-garo*. **-gáre** 1, TR.: beat with a rod, whip; streak, stripe, trace, write.

vergáre 2 [L. *variegare*], INTR., REFL.: turn colour, turn black (of chestnuts).

ver-gáta [*-ga*], F.: blow with a rod, stroke. **-gataménte**, ADV.: with stripes. **-gatíno**, M.: striped cloth. **-gáto** [*-gare*], ADJ.: whipped; striped; striped cloth†; medley†. **-gèlla**, F.: small rod, switch. **-gèllo**, M.: lime-twig.

vèrgere†, INTR.: turn, twist.

ver-gheggiáre, TR.: whip (scourge, switch); dust (clothes). ||**-ghétta** [*-ga*]. **-ghettína**, F.: little rod (switch). **-ghettáto**, ADJ.: (*her.*) striped. **-gíllo**, M.: lime-rod.

vergi-nále, ADJ.: virginal (maidenly). ||**vérgi-ne** [L. *virgo*], F.: virgin (maid; Virgin). **-nèlla**, F.: *dim.* of *-ne*; image of the Virgin. **-'neo**†, ADJ.: virginal. **-nétto**, ADJ.: virginal, of a little maid; F.: = *-nella*. **-níssimo**, ADJ.: most (very) virginal. **-nità**, F.: virginity (maidenhood).

vergó-gna [L. *verecundia* (*vereor*, fear)], F.: shame (expression of shame or guilt), bashfulness; dishonour; PL.: pudenda: *aver* —, be ashamed. **-gnáccia**, F.: great outrage. **-gnáre**, TR.†: shame; REFL.: be ashamed. **-gnáto**, ADJ.: ashamed (abashed). **-gnèvole**†, ADJ.: shameful (bashful). **-gnósa**, cf. *-gnoso*; F.: mimosa (sensitive plant). **-gnosaménte**, ADV.: shamefully; modestly. **-gnosétto**, *dim.* of *-gnoso*. **-gnóso**, ADJ.: shameful (abashed, bashful); modest: *le parti -gnose*, pudenda.

vérgola 1 [*-gere*], F.: sort of silk.

vér-gola 2 [*-ga*, rod, etc.], *dim.* of *-ga*. **-golaménto**†, M.: striping, streaks. **-goláre**†, TR.: stripe (streak); underline. **-góne**, M.: *aug.* of *-ga*; lime-twig. **-gúccia**, *dim.* of *-ga*.

veri-dicaménte, ADV.: truly. **-dicità**, F.: veracity (truthfulness). **verídico**, ADJ.: veracious (truthful, veridical, sincere). **-ficábile**, ADJ.: verifiable. **-ficáre**, TR.: verify (ascertain, examine). **-ficatóra**, F., **-ficatóre**, M., **-ficatríce**, F.: verifier (examiner). **-ficazióne**, F.: verification. **-lòquio**†, M.: true account or story. **-simigliánte**, ADJ.: verisimilar (probably, likely). **-simigliánza**, F.: verisimilitude (probability, likelihood). **-símile**, ADJ.: verisimilar (probable, likely); M.: probability. **-similitúdine**†, F.: verisimilitude. **-similménte**, ADV.: probably. ||**-tà** [L. *-tas* (*verus*, true)], F.: truth, verity: *di* (*in*, *per*) —, in truth, truly; indeed. **-tábile**†, ADJ.: truthful. **-tévole**†, **-tièro**†, **-tièro**, ADJ.: truthful (true, sincere).

vèrlia† = *velia*.

vèrme [L. *-mis*], M.: WORM.

ver-mèna [L. *verbena*], F.: twig, shoot. **-menèlla**†, F.: small twig.

ver-métto [dim. of *-me*], **-micciòla**, F.: small worm, maggot. **-micellàio**, M.: vermicelli-maker. **-micellétto**, *dim.* of *-micello*. **-micèllo**, M.: *dim.* of *-me*; small worm, maggot; PL.: vermicelli (thin macaroni). **-micoláre**, ADJ.: vermicular (worm-like). **-micolária**, F.: knotgrass. **-micolóso**†, ADJ.: wormy (full of worms, maggoty). **-mifórme**, ADJ.: vermiform. **-mífugo**, ADJ.: vermifuge. **-míglia**, ADJ.: *f.* of *-miglio*; F.: sort of precious red stone. **-migliáre**†, TR.: vermillion (colour with vermillion). **-migliétto**, *dim.* of *-miglio*. **-migliézza**, F.: vermillion colour. **-míglio** [L. *-miculus*, little worm; red dye once obtained from the kermes insect], M.: vermillion; ADJ.: of vermillion colour; lively red. **-miglióne**†, M.: vermillion pigment. **-minára**†, F.: gray lizard. **vèr-mine**, M.: (*vulg.*) worm; vermin. **-minétto**, *dim.* of *-mine*. **-minóso**, ADJ.: wormy; verminous. **-mívoro**, ADJ.: vermivorous.

vèr-mo (*poet.*) = *-me*.

vermút(te) [Ger. *wermuth*, wormwood], M.: vermuth (a drink).

vernáccia [?], F.: sort of white wine.

vernáccio, *disp.* of *verno*.

vernácolo [L. *-culus* (*verna*, house-servant)], ADJ., M.: vernacular.

vernále†, ADJ.: vernal.

ver-náre [*-no*], INTR.: winter (pass the winter). **-náta**, F.: (*vulg.*) winter season. **-neréccio**, ADJ.: winter, winterly (hibernal).

ver-nicáre†, TR.: varnish. ||**-níce** [l. L. *-nicium* (L. *vitrum*, glass)], M.: VARNISH; paint (rouge); lustre. **-niciáre**, TR.: varnish. **-niciatúra**, F.: varnishing (varnish).

ver-níno, ADJ.: winterly, hibernal. ||**vèrno**, M.: (*pop.*) = *inverno*, winter.

véro [L. *-rus*], ADJ.: true (correct, certain; real; right, legitimate); M.: truth (verity): *da* (or *in*) —, in truth, truly; in earnest; *nel* —, indeed, truly; *è ben* — *che*, true, however, nevertheless; *un* — *scioceo*, a regular fool.

veron-cèllo, **-cino**, *dim.* of *-e*. ||**verón-e** [for *virone* (L. *vir*, man): cf. *androne*], M.: terrace, open gallery.

verosímile = *verisimile*.
vèrre [L. *-rres*], M.: male swine (boar).
verrét-ta [?], F.: dart (small arrow). **-táta**, F.: stroke of a dart.
ver-ricèllo, M.: sort of capstan, jack-screw. ‖**-rína** [L. *-unia* (*-u*, spit)], F.: wimble (borer). **-rináre**, TR.: bore (pierce).
verrò 1, FUT. of *venire*.
vèrro 2 = *verre*.
verrú-ca [L.], F.: wart. **-cária**, F.: wartwort.
verrúto†, M.: pike; dart.
ver-sáccio, *disp.* of *-so*. **-saménto**, M.: effusion (pouring out, spilling). **-sáre** [L. *-sus* (*-tere*, turn)], TR.: overturn; pour out (spill, shed); diffuse; INTR.: run over (overflow); REFL.: overflow; turn, consist. **-sátile**, ADJ.: versatile. **-sáto**, PART.: poured, etc.; ADJ.: versed (expert). **-satilità**, F.: versatility (skill). **-satóre**, M.: pourer. **-seggiáre**, TR.: versify; INTR.: make verses. **-seggiatóre**, M., **-seggiatríce**, F.: versifier. **-seggiatúra**, F.: versification (versifying). **-sétto**, *dim.* of *-so*. **-sicciòlo**, *dim.* of *-so*. **-sièra** [L.*adversaria* (*ad-versus*, against)], F.: (*vulg.*) the devil's wife (to scare children), goblin (bugaboo). **-sificáre** = *-seggiare*. **-sificatóre**, **-sificatòrio**, M.: versifier. **-sificatorèllo**, M.: poetaster. **-sificatríce**, F.: poetess. **-sificazióne**, F.: versification. **-síno**, *dim.* of *-so*. **-sióne**, F.: version (translation). **-sipèlle**, ADJ.: shrewd (crafty). ‖**vèr-so** [*-sus* (*-tere*, turn)], M.: verse (poetry); melody (tune); mode (manner); direction, way; part; ADV.: towards, in the direction of; about: *trovar il — di*, find the way (or time) to; *mutar —*, change one's tune; *pigliar una cosa pel suo —*, take the right way of doing a thing; *andar a —* (or *a -si*) *d' alcuna* or *a alcuno*, meet any one's wishes, give into or humour or please any one; go to one's mind. **-solíno**, *dim.* of *-so*. **-súcolo**, *disp. dim.* of *-so*. **-súto**†, ADJ.: shifty, cunning.
vertà = *verità*.
vèr-ta†, F.: pouch (bottom of a fishing-net). **vèr-tebra**, F.: vertebra. **-tebrále**, ADJ.: vertebral. **-tebráto**, ADJ.: vertebrate. **-tènte**†, ADJ.: current (present). **-tènza**†, F.: affair, subject. ‖**vèrtere** [L.], IMPERS.: turn or depend (upon), be question (of); import. **-ticále**, ADJ.: vertical. **-ticalità**, F.: verticalness. **-ticalménte**, ADV.: vertically. **vèrtice**, M.: vertex (summit, top). **-ticilláto** [*-ticillo*], ADJ.: verticillate(d). **-ticíllo**, M.: verticil. **-tígine**, F.: vertigo (dizziness). **-tiginóso**, ADJ.: vertiginous (whirling; dizzy).
vertù† = *virtù*.
verúno [L. *vel*, even, *unus*, one], PRON.: not (even) one, no one, nobody, not any.
verzi-cánte, ADJ.: verdant (flourishing). ‖**-cáre** [*verde*], INTR.: be or grow green; be verdant (flourish).
verzícola [? L. *versus*, line], F.: sequence (at cards).
verzière [L. *viridarium* (*-dis*, green)], M.: garden.
verzíno [? *Brasile*], M.: brazil-wood.
ver-zíre† = *-zicare*. **-zòtto**, M.: colewort, cabbage. **-zúme**†, M.: greenness. **-zúra**, F.: verdure; green plants; grass-plot.
véschio† = *vischio*.
véscia [Germ'c *fise* ?], F.: toadstool, puff-ball; idle story (yarn, nonsense).
vescí-ca [L. *vesica*], F.: vesicle (bladder, blister); bubble; alembic. **-cánte**, **-catòrio**, M.: vesicant, vesicatory. **-chétta**, **-'cola**, *dim.* of *-ca*. **-coláre**, ADJ.: vesical (of the bladder). **-cóne**, *aug.* of *-ca* **-cóso**, ADJ.: vesicular. **-cúzza**, *dim.* of *-ca*.
vé-sco† = *-scovo*. **-scovádo**, M.: episcopacy (dignity, office of bishop); bishopric (house, district). **-scovále**† = *-scovile*. **-scováto** = *-scovado* (esp. referring to the charge, time of office, district). **-scovíle**, ADJ.: episcopal. **-scovilménte**, ADV.: episcopally. ‖**vé-scovo** [Gr. *epí-scopos*, 'over-seer'], M.: BISHOP.
vè-spa [L.], F.: WASP. **-spáio**, M.: wasp's nest; sort of ornament; bed of pebbles (under a house to prevent dampness). **-spaióso**†, ADJ.: spongy. **-spéto**†, M.: wasp's nest.
vè-spero [L. *-sperum* (*-sper*, evening)], M.: (*poet.*) evening; vespers; vesper (evening star, Venus). **-spertílio**, **-spertíllo**, M.: bat. **-spertíno**, ADJ.: vespertine (of the evening). **-spistrèllo**†, M.: bat.
vespóna, *aug.* of *vespa*.
vèspro [cf. *-pero*], M.: evening-hour (of the Rom. Cath. Breviary); vespers (evening service); (*poet.*) evening.
vessa-ménto = *-zione*. ‖**vessá-re** [L. *vexare*], TR.: vex (molest, harass, torment). **-tóre**, M., **-tríce**, F.: vexer, tormentor. **-zióne**, F.: vexation (harassing; annoyance).
vessica.. (*vulg.*) = *vescic*..
vessil-lário, M.: vexillary (standard-bearer). **-lazióne**, F.: vexillation (company under one flag). **-lífero**, M.: vexillary (standard-bearer). ‖**vessíl-lo** [L. *vexillum*], M.: vexillum (Rom. standard); banner (sign).
vèsta (*pop.*) = *veste*.
Vès-ta [L.], F.: Vesta (goddess of the hearth). **-tále**, ADJ., F.: vestal.

vè-ste [L. *-stis*], F.: woman's attire (dress, garment, VESTment); robe (gown). **-stét-ta**, *dim.* of *-ste*. **-stiário**†, M.: vestry (dressing-room).

vestí-bolo, ‖**-'bulo** [L. *-bulum* (?)], M.: vestibule (hall).

vesticciòla, *dim.* of *-te*.

vestí-gia, F., ‖**-gio** [L. *-gium*], M.: vestige (trace).

ve-stimènta, F. = *-ste*. **-stiménto**, pl. *—i*, *—a*, M.: vestiary; dressing as a nun (taking the veil). **-stína**, *dim.* of *-ste*. ‖**-stíre** [L.], TR.: dress (VEST, attire, clothe); dress up; put on; REFL.: dress (put on one's clothes). **-stitáccio**, **-sti-tèllo**, **-stitíno**, *disp. dim.* of *-stito*. **-stíto**, PART.: dressed, etc.; having more than one stanza; M.: dress (any dress of man or woman, garment, clothes; coat): *essere nato* —, be born to luck. **-stitúc-cio**, *disp. dim.* of *-stito*. **-stitúra**, F.: vesture, dress. **-stizióne**, F.: taking the religious or knightly vestment. **-stó-na**, F., **-stóne**, M.: *aug.* of *-ste;* wide, stately robe. **-stúra**† = *-stitura*.

veteráno [L. *-nus* (*vetus*, old)], ADJ., M.: veteran.

veteri-nária, F.: veterinary art. ‖**-ná-rio** [L. *-narius* (?)], M., ADJ.: veterinary.

vétero† = *vetusto*.

vèto [L.], M.: veto.

ve-tráia [*-tro*], F.: glass manufactory. **-tráio**, M.: glass seller; glazier. **-trá-me**, M.: glass-ware; glass-beads, etc. **-trário**, ADJ.: glass, vitreous. **-tráta**, F.: large glass window or door, pane. **-triáta**, F.: = *-trata;* glazing.

vétri-ce [L. *vitex* (*vi-*, bind)], F. (M.): osier (WITHE). **-ciáio**, M.: plantation of osiers. **-cióne**, M.: *aug.* of *-ce;* salix alba.

ve-trièra, F.: glass-door (of coloured glass), glass-pane. **-trificábile**, ADJ.: vitrifiable. **-trificáre**, TR.: vitrify. **-trificazióne**, F.: vitrification. **-trí-na**, F.: glazing (glass-like covering, enamel); glass-case (show-case); glass cupboard; ADJ.: cf. *-trino;* brittle (as glass); of a light gray colour (said of the iris): *bar-ba -trina*, beard tender to shaving; *occhio* —, wall-eye. **-trièla**, ADJ.: *erba* —, sort of herb for polishing glass. **-triòlo**, M.: vitriol. **-triuol**. . = *-triol*. . ‖**vé-tro** [L. *vitrum*], M.: glass (the substance; *poet.:* drinking-glass, glassware); PL.: glassware (glasses, bottles, etc.).

vét-ta [? L. *vitta*, fillet], F.: summit (top, apex, top bow); crop (of a flail); fillet†; twig†; pole†. **-taiòlo**, ADJ.: growing in the top (said of fruit); trashy. **-ta-rèlla**, *dim.* of *-ta*. **vèt-te**†, M.: lever. **-ticciòla**, **-ticína**, ADJ.: of the top-most twig; mountain top. **-tína**†, F.: amphora. **-tolína**, F.: *dim.* of *-ta;* cruet†. **-tóne**, M.: sucker (sprig, shoot).

vettóre [?], M.: radius.

vettòria† = *vittoria*.

vettová-glia [L. *victualia* (*vivere*, live)], F.: victuals (provisions). **-gliaménto**, M.: victualling. **-gliáre**, TR.: victual (supply with provisions).

vettúccia [*vetta*], F.: top twig.

vettú-ra [L. *vectura* (*vehere*, carry)], F.: conVEYance (transportation); burden; heavy VEHicle (hackney-coach, carriage); coach-hire, fare: *bestie da* —, beasts of burden; *far* —, enter (board) carriage; *fare una* —, drive a carriage, be a driver; *fare* (*dare*, *prestare*) *a* —, let out; *prendere a* —, take on hire, hire; — *a vapore*, steam-carriage. **-rále**, M.: driver (of a *vet-tura*), hackney-coachman, carrier. **-reg-giáre**, TR.: convey, carry, transport. **-ríno**, M.: hackney-coach driver, driver, hackman.

vettuv. . = *vettov*. .

ve-tustà, F.: (*poet.*) antiquity (ancient-ness). ‖**-tústo** [L. *-tustus* (*-tus*)], ADJ.: (*poet.*) ancient (old, Eng.† vetust).

vez-zataménto†, ADV.: caressingly, graciously. **-záto**†, ADJ.: gracious, flattering; crafty. **-zeggiaménto**, M.: caressing; flattering. **-zeggiáre**, TR.: caress (fondle); flatter; INTR.: be caressing, etc.; REFL.: pamper one's self. **-zeggiatívo**, ADJ.: caressing; flattering. ‖**véz-zo** [variant of *vizio:* orig. bad habit, spoiling by caress], M.: caress (fondling); grace (fondling) habit; necklace (of pearls, etc.); sport (amusement, play)†. **-zosaménte**, ADV.: caressingly; gracefully (agreeably). **-zosèllo**, **-zosétto**, *car. dim.* of *-zoso*. **-zóso**, ADJ.: caressing; graceful (pleasing, agreeable); delicate (nice); flattering†.

vi [L. *ibi*], ADV.: there; PRON.: (*conjunct.*) you; to you; (to) yourself, -lves.

ví-a [L.], F.: way (road; street; course; manner, means); ADV.: way, away, off; by way of, by; times (= multiplied by); (*exhort. particle*) come (come on, now)! off! fy (for shame): — *di mezzo*, middle way or course, golden mean; *mettersi in* —, set out; *mettersi la — tra le gambe*, take to one's heels; — *ferrata*, railway; — *di diramazione*, branch railway; — *più* (*meno*), much more (less); *andate* —, go away, be off; — —, directly, at once; pretty well, so so; *via* —, immediately; *tre — quattro*, three times four; *e — discorrendo*, and so forth; —, *andia-mo!* come, let us be off! —, *briccone*, off, you rascal! *va —!* fy (upon it)! for shame! **-abilità**, F.: suitableness for a common road or street. -a=dótto, M.: viaduct. -aggétto, *dim.* of *-aggio*. -aggiánte, ADJ.: travelling (journeying); M.: traveller. -aggiáre, TR.: travel (journey). -aggiatóre, M., -aggiatríce, F.: traveller (passenger). -ággio, M.: journey (VOYAGE, travel): *far un — e due servizi*, kill two birds with one stone; *mandare pel mal —*, waste, destroy; *buon —*, pleasant journey. -ále, M.: shaded road or alley, avenue; ADJ.†: of the road; placed on the road. -alétto, -alíno, *dim.* of *-ale*. -andánte [*andare*], ADJ.: wayfaring (travelling); wayfarer (traveller). -arécciot, ADJ.: (for) travelling. -ático, M.: viaticum ('journey-provision': communion to a person about to die). -atóre, M., -atríce, F.: traveller (passenger). -atòrio, ADJ.: of a journey (journey); transitory. -avái [*va-*, go], M.: coming and going.

vibrá-nte, ADJ.: vibrating. ‖**vibrá-re** [L.], TR., INTR.: vibrate; shake; hurl. -tézza; F.: vibration; force. -tòrio, ADJ.: vibratory (quivering). -zioncèlla, *dim.* of *-zione*. -zióne, F.: vibration (quiver).

vibúrno [L. *-num*], M.: viburnum (wild vine).

vicá-ría 1, F.: vicar's wife. -ría 2, F.: vicarship (office); subsidiary troops; supreme court at Naples. -riáto, M.: vicarage (ref. to district, tenure). ‖**vicário** [L. *-rius* (*vicis*, turn)], M.: vicar (curate); magistrate ad interim; governor; substitute; ADJ.†: substitute.

více [L. *-cem*, turn], F.: (*poet.*) = *vece*; PREF.: vice-. =amirágl̦io, M.: vice-admiral, rear-admiral. =cancellière, M.: vice-chancellor. =dòmino, M.: under-governor; magistrate. =gerènte, M.: vice-gerent. =legáto, M.: deputy-legate, etc.

vicèn-da [*vice*], F.: turn; VICissitude (change, succession, alternation); return (requital); affair (business); turn (place, stead): *a —*, in turn, each in (his, etc.) turn; one another; *ognuno a —*, each in his turn. -dévole, ADJ.: alternate, successive; mutual, reciprocal. -devolézza, F.: vicissitude (alternation, interchange); reciprocity. -devolménte, ADV.: alternately (by turns); reciprocally.

vicennále [L. *viceni*, twenty each], ADJ.: of (every) twenty years.

vice=patriárca, M.: vice-patriarch. =rè, M.: viceroy. =reggènte, M.: vice-regent. =segretário, M.: vice-secretary. -vèrsa [L.], ADV.: vice-versa.

vicheria† = *vicaria* 2.

vice=imperatóre, M.: vice-emperor.

vici-nále, ADJ.: neighbouring (contiguous, vicinal, near): *strada —*, road connecting neighbouring districts, parish-road. -náme, *disp.* of *-nato*. -naménte, ADV.: near, nearly. -nánte, ADJ.: neighbouring; M.: neighbour. -nánza, F.: vicinage (neighbourhood, nearness); neighbours. -náre†, INTR., REFL.: be near, border (upon). -náta†, F.: vicinity. ‖**vicí-no** [L. *-nus* (*vicus*, village)], ADJ.: neighbouring (contiguous, near, adjacent, VICINE); M.: neighbour; citizen; PREP. (*a*): near, near by, close to, about to; ADV.: near: *vicin —*, very near; *da —*, near, from a short distance; *— a morire*, near dying, about to die; *sta —*, he stands near (near by); stand near!

vicissitúdine [L. *-tudo* (*vicis*, turn)], F.: vicissitude (change).

vicitáre† = *visitare*.

ví-co† [L. *-cus*], M.: borough; narrow street (lane). -colétto, -colíno, *dim.* of *-lo*. **ví-colo**, M.: narrow street (lane, passage).

vi-dènte, M.: seer, prophet. ‖-'di, PRET. of *vedere*.

vidu. .† = *vedov. .*

vie [? *via*], ADV.: much (very, far); (*sometimes affixed*): *— più* or *viepiù*, much more; *— via* or *vivvia*, immediately.

vièlla†, *dim.* of *via*.

vièra† = *ghiera*.

vie-tábile, ADJ.: that may be forbidden. -taménto, M.: prohibition, prevention. ‖-táre [L. *vetare*], TR.: forbid (prohibit); prevent. -tatívo, ADJ.: forbidding, prohibitory. -tatóre, M.: forbidder.

vièto [L. *-tus*, withered], ADJ.: rancid (musty); stale (obsolete); sallow, yellow (of complexion).

viétta, *dim.* of *via*.

vietúme [*-to*], M.: rancid (musty) stuff.

vievía for *vie via*, ADV.: immediately (instantly).

vígere [L.], DEFECT. INTR.: be strong or vigorous; flourish; (*leg.*) be in force.

vigèsimo [L. *-mus*], ADJ.: twentieth.

vigi-lánte, ADJ.: vigilant. -lanteménte, ADV.: vigilantly. -lánza, F.: vigilance. -láre, INTR.: be vigilant, watch; TR.: watch, observe. -lazióne, F.: watching. ‖**vígi-le** [L. *-l*], ADJ.: vigilant; M.: fireman. **vigí-lia**, F.: watching, sitting up; vigil (praying and fasting on the eve of a feast; day and night preceding a feast), watch; eve; watch over a dead body†: *— di Natale*, Christmas eve; *digiunare la — di Santa Caterina*, have good luck in marrying.

vigl̦iac-cáccio, *disp.* of *-co*. -caménte, ADJ.: cowardly (like a coward or poltroon). -chería, F.: cowardliness (poltroonery).

vin-chétto [-*co*], M.: osier plot or plantation. ‖**-'chio**† [L. -*clum*, tie, fetter], M.: osier (withe).

vincibòsco [*avvincere, bosco*], M.: honeysuckle (woodbine).

vincido [? *viscido*], ADJ.: flaccid (flabby).

vin-cíglia†, F., ‖**-cíglio** [*vinco*], M.: osier twig (withe); band.

vincimènto† [-*cere*], M.: vanquishing; conquest.

vincíre†, TR.: bind round (tie, fetter).

vín-cita [*vincere*], F.: gain (winning; winnings, sum won). **-citóra**, F., **-citóre**, M., **-citríce**, F.: victor (conqueror, gainer). **-citúto**†, PART. of -*cere*.

vinco 1 = *vincido*.

vinco 2 [for *vincio*], M.: osier (withe): us'ly *vetrice*. **-láre**, TR.: fetter (bind); fix. ‖**vínco-lo** [L. *vinculum* (*vincire*, bind)], M.: bond (fetter, tie).

víndice [L. -*dex*], ADJ.: avenging; M., F.: avenger.

vi-nèllo, M.: thin wine. **-nettíno**, **-nétto**, *dim.* of -*no*. **-nífero**, ADJ.: wine-producing. ‖**ví-no** [L. -*num*], M.: wine: — *nero*, red wine; *bere il — in agresto*, spend one's money before getting it; *diciotto di —*, being bent on something regardless of consequences; stubborn; *dare* (or *mescere*) *del —*, pour out wine, fill one's glass. **-nolènte**, ADJ.: addicted to wine. **-nolènza**, F.: fondness of wine (drink), drunkenness. **-nosità**†, F.: vinosity (vinous quality). **-nóso**, ADJ.: vinous (of wine; juicy); addicted to wine.

vín-si, PRET. of -*cere*. **-ta**, **-to**, PART. of -*cere*; vanquished, etc.; F.†, M.†: victory: *darla -ta*, yield, give in, cede, agree to; *darle -te*, humour, connive at; *darsi —* (or *per —*), confess one's self vanquished.

vinúccio [*vino*], M.: wretched wine.

viòla 1 [L.], F.: (*bot.*) viola (violet).

viòla 2 [l. L. *vitula* (?)], F.: (*mus.*) viola, viol.

violábile [-*lare*], ADJ.: violable.

vio-lácea [-*la* 1], F.: violet. **-láceo**, ADJ.: of violet colour. **-láio**, M.: violet-plot.

vio-laménto, M.: violation; rape. ‖**-láre** [L.], TR.: violate (ravish; break); profane; corrupt. **-láto** 1, PART.: violated, etc.

violáto† 2 [-*la* 1], ADJ.: of violet colour, violet.

vio-latóre [-*lare*], M., **-latríce**, F.: violator (ravisher; infringer, etc.). **-lazióne**, F.: violation (rape; infringement, breach). **-lentaménto**, M.: violence. **-lentáre**, TR.: do violence to; force (constrain). **-lentatóre**, M.: compeller. **-lènte**†, ADJ.: violent (impetuous). **-lenteménte**, ADV.: violently (impetuously). **-lènto**, ADJ.: violent (impetuous, forcible). **-lènza**, F.: violence.

vio-létta, *car. dim.* of -*la* 1. **-létto**, ADJ.: violet (of violet colour). **-lína** = -*letta*.

vio-linísta, pl. —*i*, M.: violinist. ‖**-líno** [-*la* 2], M.: violin, fiddle.

viòlo [-*la* 1], M.: violet-plant.

violon-cellísta, pl. —*ti*, M.: violoncellist. **-cèllo**, M.: violoncello. ‖**violóne** [*viola* 2], M.: bass-viol.

vi-òttola [dim. of *via*], F.: narrow way, path, garden-walk; lane. **-ottolína**, *dim.* of -*ottola*. **-òttolo** = -*ottola*.

vípe-ra [L.], F.: viper. **-ráio**, M.: vipernest (place full of vipers); viper-catcher. **-ráto**, ADJ.: fed with vipers; (*med.*) with viper-infusion. **vipè-reo**, ADV.: viperine, of a viper. **-rétta**, *dim.* of -*ra*. **-ríno**, ADJ.: viperine (of or resembling a viper); M.: young viper.

vipistrèllo† = *pipistrello*.

vi-rágine, ‖**-rágo** [L. (*vir*, man)], F.: virago (strong, mannish woman).

viráre, TR.: (*nav.*) VEER.

virènte†, ADJ.: verdant (flourishing).

virgapastòris [L. *virga pastoris*, 'pastor's rod'], M.: wild thistle.

virgin.. = *vergin*..

vírgo† = *vergine*.

vír-gola [L. *virgula* (*virga*, rod)], F.: comma (Eng.† virgule). **-goláre**, **-goleggiáre** (less common), TR.: punctuate. **-golétta**, **-golína**, *dim.* of -*gola*. **-gúlto**, M.: slender rod; young shoot.

viri-dário†, M.: (*poet.*) garden. **víride**, etc. = *verde*, etc.

vi-ríle, ADJ.: virile (manly). **-rilità**, F.: virility (manhood). **-rilménte**, ADV.: manfully (like a man). ‖**-'ro** [L. *vir*], M.: man. **-róne**†, M.: man.

viróla†, F.: plate of a watch.

vir-tù [L. -*tus* (*vir*, man)], F.: virtue. **-tuále**, ADJ.: virtual (effectual). **-tualità**, F.: virtuality (efficacy). **-tualménte**, ADV.: virtually. **-tuosaménte**, ADV.: virtuously. **-tuóso**, ADJ.: virtuous (pure, chaste); efficacious; M.: virtuoso.

viru-lènto, ADJ.: virulent (malignant). **-lènza**, F.: virulence. ‖**víru-s** [L.], M.: virus.

vi-sáccio† [-*so*], M.: ugly face. **-sággio**, M.: visage (face).

visce-rále, ADJ.: visceral. ‖**vísce-re** [L. -*ra*], M. (pl. -*ri*, or f. pl. -*re*): viscera (entrails, bowels).

ví-schio [L. -*sum*], M.: mistletoe; birdlime. **-schióso**, ADJ.: viscous, sticky. **-scidità**, F.: viscidity, stickiness. **víscido**, ADJ.: viscous (viscid, sticky, clammy).

viscìol. . = *bisciol.* .

vìsco = *vischio.*

vis-contàdo, M.: viscountship. ‖**-cónte** [*vice conte*], M.: viscount. **-contèa**, F.: viscounty. **-contéssa**, F.: viscountess.

vis-cosétto, *dim.* of *-coso*. **-cosità**, F.: viscosity. ‖**-cóso** [*-co*], ADJ.: viscous (viscid, sticky, clammy).

viș-dominàto, M.: vicarship, vicarage (for administration). **-dòmine**, ‖**-dòmino** = *vicedomino.*

vi-șìbile [L. *-sus* (*-dere*, see), seen], ADJ.: visible; M.: the visible. **-șibìlio** [for *in-visibilio*, pop. *in visibilio*], M.: infinite multitude: *andare in* —, be enraptured (be entranced). **-șibilità**, F.: visibility. **-șibilménte**, ADV.: visibly. **-șièra**, F.: vizor; mask†. **-șionàrio**, ADJ.: visionary. **-șióne**, F.: vision (apparition; spectre); revelation.

vișìr [Ar. *ouazir*], **-e**, M.: vizier. **-àto**, M.: vizierate.

vì-șita, F.: visit. **-șitaménto**, M.: visiting, visit. **-șitàre**, TR.: visit (go and see); examine. **-șitatóre**, M., **-șitatrìce**, F.: visitor; examiner. **-șitazióne**, F.: visitation. **-șivaménte**, ADV.: visibly. **-șìvo**, ADJ.: visible, visual. ‖**vì-șo** [L. *-sus* (*-dere*, see), seen], M.: VISage (face, countenance): sight†; view (opinion)†: *a — aperto*, with open face; boldly; *mostrar il* —, show a bold face, stand up boldly; *mutar* —, change colour; *far buon — a*, look favourably upon, welcome; *dar nel* —, display too much boldness; *dir sul* —, say to one's face; *a — a* —, tête-à-tête. **-șóne**, *aug.* of *-so*. **-șòrio**, ADJ.: visual.

vi-spézza, F.: briskness, vivacity. ‖**-'spo** [? *-sto*], ADJ.: brisk (quick, lively, nimble, sharp).

vìs-si, PRET., **-so**†, **-sùto**, PART. of *vivere*.

vìs-ta, PART. (cf. *-to*); F.: sight (eyesight; view, prospect; appearance; show); window†: *a* —, at sight; within sight; *di* —, by sight; *perder di* —, lose sight of, forget; *far le -te di*, pretend not to; *bastar la* —, have the courage. **-taménte**†, ADV.: quickly, rapidly. ‖**-'to**, PART. of *vedere*; seen, etc.; brisk†, quick, sprightly. **-tosaménte**, ADV.: showily, strikingly. **-tosétto**, *dim.* of *-toso*. **-tosità**, F.: showiness, strikingness. **-tóso**, ADJ.: showy (striking, sightly). **viș-uàle**, ADJ.: visual (visible).

vì-ta [L.], F.: life; bust (upper part of the body, waist): *a* —, for life; *viva la* —, life is at stake; *far buona* —, live well; *far mala* —, have a hard life; *donna di bella* —, woman with well-made figure; *andar in sulla* —, walk in a stately manner. **-tàccia**, *disp.* of *-ta*.

vitàlba [L. *vitis alba*, white vine], F.: briony.

vità-le [L. *-lis*], ADJ.: vital. **-lità**, F.: vitality. **-lizzàre**, TR.: vitalize. **-lìzio**, M.: life annuity. **-lménte**, ADV.: vitally.

vitàme [*vite*], M.: vine plantation, vineyard.

vitàre† = *evitare*.

vìte [L. *vitis*, vine], F.: vine; screw; vice: *a* —, like a screw, spiral. **=biànca**, F.: briony.

vitèl-la, F.: heifer. **-létta**, F.: young heifer. **-létto**, M.: young calf. **-lìna**, F.: young heifer. **-lìno**, M.: young calf; ADJ.†: of a calf, yellow. ‖**vitèl-lo** [L. *vitulus*], M.: calf; VEAL: — *arrosto*, roast veal.

vi-tìcchio† [*-te*], M.: convolvulus. **-tìccio**, M.: vine-sucker; tendril; sconce. **-ticèlla**, F.: young vine. **-ticoltóre**, M.: viticulturist (vine-dresser). **-ticoltùra**, F.: viticulture (grape-growing). **-ticult** = *-ticolt.* . **-tìfero**, ADJ.: vine-bearing. **-tìgno**, M.: wild vine. **-tóne**, M.: big screw or vice.

vitìna [*vita*], F.: short bust.

vitip. .†, **vìtop.** .† = *vitup.* .

vì-treo [L. *-treus*], ADJ.: vitreous (glassy). **-trif.** . = *vetrif.* . **-tri(u)òlo**, M.: vitriol. **-tri(u)olàre**, TR.: steep or sprinkle with vitriol.

vìtta†, F.: fillet, band.

vìttima [L. *victima*], F.: victim.

vìtto 1 [L. *victus* (*vivere*, live)], M.: victuals, food.

vìt-to† 2, PART. of *vincere*. **-tòria**, F.: victory. **-torìale**†, ADJ.: of victory, triumphant. **-toriàre**†, INTR.: gain the victory (conquer). **-toriosaménte**, ADV.: victoriously. **-torióso**, ADJ.: victorious. **-trìce**, F.: victress (vanquisher).

vittuà-glia†, **-rìa**†, F.: victuals (provisions).

vìtu-la†, **-lo** = *vitella*, *-llo*.

vituper-àbile, ADJ.: vituperable. ‖**-àre** [L. (*vitium*, fault, *par-*, breed)], TR.: vituperate (revile, abuse). **-atìvo**, ADJ.: vituperative (reviling, abusive). **-atóre**, M., **-atrìce**, F.: vituperator (reviler). **-azióne**, F.: vituperation (reviling, abuse). **-évole**, ADJ.: vituperable (shameful). **-evolménte**, ADJ.: blamably; shamefully. **vitupèr-(i)o**, M.: disgrace (dishonour, infamy). **-osaménte**, ADV.: shamefully. **-óso**, ADJ.: disgraceful (infamous, shameful).

viùz-za [*via*], F., **-zo**, M.: narrow path, lane. **-'zola**, **-zolìna**, *dim.* of *-za*.

vì-va [I've of *-vere*], INTERJ.: vivat! long live! hurray! **-vacchiàre**, INTR.: manage to live (get along). **-vàce**, ADJ.: lively (gay, vivacious). **-vaceménte**,

ADV.: lively (vivaciously). **-vacézza**†, **-vacità**, F.: vivacity (liveliness, briskness). **-vágno** [der. ?], M.: selvage (of cloth); edge, bank. **-vaiétto**, *dim.* of *-vaio*. **-váio**, M.: fish-pond. **-vaménte**, ADV.: vividly (lively, briskly; sharply). **-vánda**, F.: victuals (food, eatables); pittance. **-vandáre**†, INTR.: live well (fare daintily). **-vandétta**†, F.: savory dish. **-vandièra**, F.: vivandière (female sutler). **-vandière**, M.: sutler; caterer. **-vattáre**†, INTR.: fare poorly. **-vènte**†, ADJ.: living (alive); M.: living person: — *il padre*, during the father's life. ‖**vívere** [L.], IRR.§; INTR.: live (be alive; live on; subsist, etc.); M.: living; PL.: victuals (food, provisions): — *dì per dì*, live from hand to mouth; — *del suo*, live on one's income; — *tra due*, live in uncertainty or suspense. **-vévole**†, ADJ.: lively; sharp. **-vézza**, F.: vivacity (liveliness). **vívido**, ADJ.: vivid (active, brisk; vigorous). **-vificaménto**, M.: vivification. **-vificáre**, TR.: vivify. **-vificatívo**, ADJ.: vivifying. **-vificatóre**, M., **-vificatríce**, F.: vivifier (enlivener). **-vificazióne**, F.: vivification. **-vífico**, ADJ.: vivific (reviving, vivifying). **-víparo** [*par-*, breed], ADJ.: viviparous. **-victoria**, ADJ.: most lively (very vivid). **-vo** [L. *-vus*], ADJ.: alive (lively, live); vivid (lively, spirited, brisk, strong); effective†; hard; M.: life, quick (cf. *al* —); mercury; burning coal: *al* (or *nel*, *sul*) —, to the quick; *toccare nel* (*sul*) —, touch to the quick, offend deeply; *argento* —, quicksilver, mercury; *carbone* —, burning coal; *calcina -va*, quicklime; *carne -va*, quick; *di -va voce*, by word of mouth; *acqua -va*, living water, spring water; *per -va forza*, by main force.

§ Pret. *vís-si*, *-se*; *-sero*. Fut. *vivrò*. Cond. *vivrèi*. Part. *vissúto* or (rarely) *vivúto*, *visso*†.

vivòla† = *viola* I, 2.
vivole [? *vivo*], F. PL.: (*vet.*) vives.
vivacchiáre [*vivere*], INTR.: live poorly; barely get along.
vivuò-la, **-lo** = *viola* I, 2, *violo*.
vi-ziáccio, *disp.* of *-zio*. **-ziáre**, TR.: VITIATE (corrupt, defile). **-ziataménte**, ADV.: malignantly; fraudulently. **-ziáto**, PART.: vitiated, etc.; vicious (malicious). **-ziatóre**, M., **-ziatríce**, F.: vitiator, defiler, depraver. ‖**ví-zio** [L. *-tium*], M.: vice (bad habit; imperfection, defect). **-ziosaménte**, ADV.: viciously. **-ziosità**, F.: viciousness: defectiveness. **-zióso**, ADJ.: vicious (wicked; defective).
vízzo [? L. *victus*], ADJ.: flaccid; withered.
vó, PRES. of *andare*.
vo' (*poet.*) = *voglio*.
vo-cabolário, M.: vocabulary. **-cabolarísta**, M.: vocabulist, lexicographer. **-cábolo**, M.: vocable (word, term). **-cále**, ADJ.: vocal; M.: vowel. **-calizzáre**, TR.: use many vowels in; (*mus.*) vocalize. **-calménte**, ADV.: vocally. **-cáre**†, TR.: call, name. **-catívo**, ADJ.: vocative; M.: vocative (case). **-cazióne**, F.: vocation, calling. ‖**vó-ce** [L. *vox*], F.: VOICE (sound of mouth, utterance; expression; vocable, word; counsel; influence); vote (suffrage); fame†: *a* —, *a viva* —, by word of mouth; *ad una* —, unanimously; *ad alta* —, aloud; *sotto* —, in a low voice, softly; *corre* —, it is reported; *dar* —, spread about, report; *dar una* — *ad uno*, give one a call; *dar la* —, give one's vote, vote; *far* —, speak; *dare in sulla* —, contradict; *far* —, keep or be silent. **-cerèlla**, **-cerellína**, **-cerétta**, *dim.* of *-ce*. **-ciáccia**, *disp.* of *-ce*. **-ciáre**, INTR.: cry loud (bawl). **-ciatóre**, M., **-ciatríce**, F.: loud crier (shouter, bawler). **-ciferánte**, ADJ.: vociferous (loud). **-ciferáre**, TR.: vociferate, talk loud and long; INTR.: spread a report, rumour. **-ciferazióne**, F.: vociferation (clamour); report. **-cína**, F., **-cíno**, M.: *dim.* of *-ce*; soft, low or thin voice. **-ciòna**, F., **-cióne**, M.: *aug.* of *-ce*; strong (manly) voice. **-cionáccio**, ADJ.: loud crying (bawling); M., F.: loud crier (bawler). **-citáre**†, TR.: clamour; call.
vòcolo†, ADJ.: blind.
vó-ga, F.: rowing, course; vogue (fashion); impetus (ardour): *essere in* —, be in fashion. **-gánte**, ADJ.: rowing; M.: rower. ‖**-gáre** [OGer. *wogôn*, move], TR.: row (impel by oars). **-gáta**, F.: rowing; speed (imparted by oars). **-gatóre**, M.: rower. **-g=avánti**, M.: head-rower (in a galley).
vò-glia [*volere*], F.: will (wish, desire, fancy, appetite); mother's mark (congenital mark upon the body, pop. believed to come from an unfulfilled wish; mole, spot): *di* —, willingly; *di mala* —, unwillingly; *dar* —, excite, provoke; *morirsi di* —, be dying for, desire eagerly; *sputare la* —, surrender one's desire, give up. **-gliènte**, ADJ.: willing (wishing). **-gliènza**†, F.: will (wish, mind). **-glierèlla**, **-gliétta**, *dim.* of *-glia*. **-gliévole**†, ADJ.: wishing, desirous. **-'glio**, PRES. of *-lere*. **-gliolína**, *dim.* of *-glia*. **-gliosaménte**, ADV.: willingly. **-glióso**, ADJ.: willing (desirous, eager). **-gliúzza**, F.: *disp. dim.* of *-glia*: whim, light fancy.
vói [L. *vos*], PRON.: you (pl.; sing. to God, sovereigns, or in informal or literary style): *dar del* —, use voi to (in addressing).

vo-laménto†, M.: flying; flight. **-lán-da**, F.: fly-wheel. **-landolíno**†, M.: small fly-wheel; voluble person. **-láno**, M.: shuttlecock. **-lánte**, ADJ.: flying; fickle (light); M.: fly-sheet; shuttlecock. ‖**-láre** [L.], INTR.: fly; M.: flying (flight, rapid course). **-láta**, F.: flight; high note; high-flying ball; fore-part of a gun: *tirare di* —, fire with a high elevation (or aim); fire instantly†. **-lática**, F.: (*med.*) ringworm. **-lático**†, ADJ.: flying. **-lá-tile**, ADJ.: volatile (Eng.† capable of flying; evaporable); M. PL.: birds of the air. **-latilità**, F.: volatility. **-lati-lizzáre**, TR.: volatilize. **-latilizzazió-ne**, F.: volatilization. **-latína**, *dim.* of *-lata*. **-láto**, ADJ.: flown; fled; passed swiftly; M.: flight (rapid course; lapse). **-latóre**, M.: flyer.

voloant†.. = *vulcan*..

vo-lènte, ADJ.: willing: *non* —, unwilling. **-lentièri**, **-lentierménte**†, ADV.: willingly, gladly. **-lentièro**†, ADJ.: willing. **-lentieróso**, ADJ.: willing; desirous. **-lènza**†, F.: will, wish. ‖**-lére** [p. L., for L. *velle*], IRR.§; TR., INTR.: WILL (wish, desire; command; be about to); like; require (need, want); will; pleasure: *Iddio voglia*, may it please God; — *dire*, mean (e.g., *ciò vuol dire*, that means, that signifies, that is); — *bene*, love; — *male*, bear an ill-will, hate; *-lerla con alcuno*, have a design upon one; *vuol piovere*, it is going to rain; *di buon* —, willingly.

§ Ind.: Pres. *vòglio* or *vò'*, *vuòi* or *vuò'*, *vuòle; vogliámo, voléte, vògliono*. Pret. *vòl-li, -le; -lero*. Fut. *vorrò*. Cond. *vorrèi*. Subj.: Pres. *vòglia*, etc. I've: *vògli; vogliá-te*. Part. *volúto*. — Poet. forms: Pres. 2. *vò-gli*; 6. *vònno*. Pret. *vòl-si, -se; -sero*.

volgá-re [L. *vulgaris*], ADJ.: vulgar; M.: vulgar tongue or dialect. **-reménte**† = *-rmente*. **-réşimo**† = *-rismo*. **-rità**, F.: vulgarity. **-rizzaménto**, M.: translation (version). **-rizzáre**, TR.: translate (from Latin or Greek), render; render common or public. **-rizzazióne**, F.: translation (version). **-rménte**, ADV.: vulgarly; in the vulgar tongue. **volgá-ta**, F.: Vulgate. **volgá-to**, ADJ.: common; published (divulged).

vol-gènte, ADJ.: revolving (turning). **vòl-gere** [L. *-vere*], IRR.§; TR.: turn (REVOLVE, roll: esp. in intellect. sense; turn aside, change; persuade; bend): direct; INTR.: revolve (turn round), twist; REFL.: turn (change; turn sour): — *le spalle*, turn one's back, run away; — *al*, incline to; — *un ponte*, form the arches of a bridge; *-gersi ad uno*, side with one. **-gíbile**, ADJ.: that may turn; changeable. **-gimènto**, M.: turning, whirl; change (vicissitude). **-gitáio**†, ADJ.: turning; M.: wrapper. **-gitóre**, M., **-gi-trice**, F.: turner (turning agent), changer.

§ Pret. *vòl-si, -se; -sero*. Part. *vòlto*.

vólgo [L. *vulgus*], M.: lower mass (multitude, mob); low, ignorant person (Eng.† vulgar).

vòlgolo [*volvere*], M.: bundle, pack(age).

vo-licchiáre, ‖**-litáre** [L. (*-lare*, fly)], INTR.: fly to and fro, flutter about.

vo-litívo, ADJ.: volitive; commanding. **-lizióne**, F.: volition, will. **-lièn-za**†, F.: will; wish. ‖**vòl-li**, PRET. of *-lere*.

vólo [*-lare*], M.: flight: *di* —, very quickly, in passing, by the way; *dare il* —, abandon; *levarsi a* —, take one's flight; *veduta a — d'uccello*, bird's-eye view.

volon-tà [L. *voluntas*], F.: will (faculty of willing; free will; testament); desire (wish): *di* —, willingly, spontaneously. **-tariaménte**, ADV.: voluntarily. **-tá-rio**, ADJ.: voluntary, spontaneous; M.: volunteer. **-tar(i)ésco**† = *-teroso*. **-te-rosaménte**, ADV.: willingly, eagerly. **-teróso**, ADJ.: willing (desirous, eager). **-tièra**†, **-tièri**†, **-t(i)èro**†, ADV.: = *volentieri*, willingly.

vol-pacchiòtta, F., **-pacchiòtto**, M.: young fox. **-páccia**, *disp.* of *-pe*. **-pája**†, F.: fox-hole. **-páre**, INTR.: take the blight, be blighted: *grano -pato*, blighted grain. ‖**vól-pe** [L. *vulpes*], F.: fox; crafty person; blight (mildew). **-peg-giáre**, INTR.: play the fox, be crafty. **-pétta**, **-picélla**, **-picína**, **-picíno**, **-pína**, **-píno** 1, *dim.* of *-pe*. **-píno** 2, ADJ.: of a fox, fox-; foxy, crafty. **-pó-na**, **-póne**, *aug.* of *-pe*.

vòlsi † 1, PRET. of *volere*.

vòlsi 2, PRET. of *volgere*.

volsúto†, PART. of *volere*.

vòl-ta [*-vere*], F.: turn (turning, revolving; whirl; winding; new direction; stroll); time; (*man.*) VOLT; VAULT; lapse: *alcune -te, alle -te*, sometimes; *alla* —, towards; *altre -te*, formerly; *andare alla — di*, go towards; *andare in -te*, go rambling about, rove: *dar* —, wheel round, run away; *dare* (or *pigliare*) *una* —, take a turn (little walk); *dare la* —, overturn; be on the wane, go down; stumble, fall; get sour; *dare di* —, come back; *due -te*, twice; *dopo una* —, too late; *finite una* —, have done at length, I say; *per* —, by turns, alternately; *più -te*, frequently; *il più delle -te*, for the most part, mostly; *stare sulle -te*, be on the look-out; (*nav.*) beat, tack; — *del tempo*, lapse of time. **-tábile**, ADJ.: easy to turn; inconstant (changeable). **-ta=fáccia**, M.: (*ideal.*) turncoat (weathercock); revolution. **-ta-**

ménto, M.: turning, change. **-táre**, TR.: turn (turn aside or round, change; roll); turn away (dismiss); convert; translate; transfer (an account, etc.); INTR.: turn; wane (decrease); REFL.: turn; change one's mind; be transformed. **-táta**, F.: turn(ing), change. **-tátile**†, ADJ.: easily turned (changeable). **-tatína**, *dim.* of *-tata*. **-tazióne**†, F.: turn(ing); changing, change. **-teggiaménto**, M.: whirling or fluttering about; vaulting. **-teggiáre** [freq. of *-tare*], TR., INTR.: whirl or flutter about, tumble about, fly about; vault; shuffle. **-teggiatóre**, M.: vaulter, tumbler; rope-dancer; light-infantryman. **-ticèlla**, **-ticína**, *dim.* of *-ta*. **-vòlto** 1, PART. of *-gere*; turned, etc.; deep red; M.: vault.

vólto 2 [L. *vultus*], M.: face (visage: more choice than *viso*): *avere il — da*, have the boldness to; *gettare al — a*, reproach, throw in the teeth of; *mostrare il —*, show one's teeth, show one's self resolute.

vol-tóio [*-tare*], M.: snaffle (bridle-bit). **-tolaménto**, M.: rolling; wallowing. **-toláre**, TR.: roll (turn around; wallow); REFL.: roll one's self (wallow, welter). **-tolóne**, **-tolóni**, ADV.: in rolling. **-tóne**, M.: *aug.* of *-ta*; lofty vault. **-túra**, F.: turning over, transfer; revolution†; translation†.

volú-bile [L. *-bilis* (*volvere*, roll)], ADJ.: voluble (easily rolling; flippant; variable); M.: blindweed. **-bilità**, F.: volubility; fickleness. **-bilménte**, ADV.: volubly; flippantly. **volú-me** [L. *-men* (orig. 'roll')], M.: volume (book; mass). **-métto**, *dim.* of *-me*. **-minóso**, ADJ.: voluminous (copious, bulky). **volú-ta**, F.: folding; volute, scroll; revolution.

volúto, PART. of *volere*.

volut-tà [L. *voluptas* (*vol-*, WILL)], F.: voluptuousness. **-t(u)ário**†, ADJ.: voluptuous; M.: voluptuary. **-tuosaménte**, ADV.: voluptuously. **-tuóso**, ADJ.: voluptuous; lascivious.

vòl-vere (*poet.*) = *-gere*. **-'volo**, M.: volvulus (severe colic).

vòme-re 1 [L. *vomer*], (*poet.*) **-ro**, M.: coulter (ploughshare).

vò-mere 2 [L.], (*poet.*, *fig.*) = *vomitare*, TR.: vomit. **vò-mico**, ADJ.: vomitive. **-mitaménto**, M.: vomiting. **-mitáre** [L.], TR.: vomit, throw up. **-mitatívo**, ADJ.: vomitive. **-mitatòrio**, M.: vomitive (emetic). **-mitívo**, ADJ.: vomitive. **vòmito**, M.: vomiting; vomit. **-mitòrio**, M.: vomitory (principal door of an ancient theatre, etc.; emetic).

vo-ráce [L. *-rax*], ADJ.: voracious. **-racemónte**, ADV.: voraciously. **-racità**, F.: voracity (greed). **-rágine** [L. *-rago*], M.: gulf (abyss, gap). **-raginóso**, ADJ.: voraginous (of a gulf, engulfing). **-ráre**† [L.], TR.: devour. **-ratóre**, M., **-ratríce**, F.: devourer. **-ratúra**, F.: devouring.

vor-rò, FUT., **-rèi**, COND. of *volere*.

vòrti-ce [L. *vortex*], M.: vortex (whirlpool). **-cosaménte**, ADV.: like a whirlpool. **-cóso**, ADJ.: vorticose (vortical, whirling); full of whirlpools.

vòsco [for *con voi*], with you.

vosignoría, **voss.**.† [*vostra signoria*], F.: 'your Lordship,' sir; you, sir.

vo-stríssimo, SUPERL. of *-stro*: your Worship, your Honour. ‖**vò-stro** [L. *-ster*], PRON.: you, yours; M.: yours, your estate or property. **-sustríssima**, F.: (*jest.* or *iron.*) your most illustrious Worship.

vota=bórse, ADJ.: expensive (costly); M.: costly thing. **=cáse**, ADJ.: consuming; M.: spendthrift (prodigal). **=cèssi**, M.: cleaner of CESSpools. **-ménto**, M.: emptying; evacuation. **=pózzi**, M.: cleaner of wells or cesspools. ‖**votá-re** 1 [*v(u)oto*, void], IRR.§; TR.: VOID (empty, clear).
§ *V(u)o-*, accented; *vo-*, unaccented.

votá-re 2 [*voto*, vote], TR.: vote; vow; dedicate. **-tóre** 1, M.: voter; dedicator.

vota-tóre 2 [*-re* 1], M.: emptier. **-túra** 1, F.: voiding (emptying).

votatúra 2 [*votare* 2], F.: voting.

votazióne 1 [*-tare*, vote], F.: voting.

vo-tazióne 2 [*-tare*, void], F.: voiding, emptying. **-tázza**, F.: scoop; ladle.

vo-tívo, ADJ.: votive. ‖**vó-to** 1 [L. *-tum* (*-vere*, VOW)], M.: vow; wish; vote (suffrage).

vòto 2 [? p. L. *vituitus* (L. *viduus*, bereft)], ADJ.: VOID (empty); deprived; inane; M.: void (vacuum, empty space): *sparare a —*, fire with blank cartridges; fire at random; *a —*, in vain, vainly; *bestia —a*, beast without a burden.

vul-cánico, **-cánio**, ADJ.: volcanic. **-caníste**, M.: vulcanist. ‖**-cáno** [L. *-canus*], M.: Vulcan; volcano.

vulg.. = *volg*..

vulne-rábile, ADJ.: vulnerable. ‖**-ráre** [L.], TR.: wound. **-rária**, F.: kidneywort. **-rário**, ADJ.: vulnerary (good for healing wounds).

vúl-va [L.], F.: vulva (womb). **-vário**, ADJ.: of the vulva.

vuò' (*poet.*) = *vuole*.

vuot.. = *vot*..

W

w *vu dòppio* [Germ'c], M.: **w** (only in purely foreign words or names).

X

x, *iccase*, (*math.*) *iks* or *is* [L.], M.: x (only in purely foreign words, being ordinarily supplanted in Italian by *ss*, *s*, or *z*).

Xánto, M.: Xanto (river), Scamander.

Xères [Sp. *Xeres*, name of a town], M.: SHERRY.

Y

y *ípsilon* or *i grèco* [L.], M.: y (only in foreign words or names).

yagáro [Ger. *jäger*], M.: yager (light-infantryman).

Z

z *zéta* [L.], z (the letter).

ẓa [echoic], INTERJ.: whizz! slash! here†.

ẓabaióne [Illyr. *sabaia*, kind of drink], M.: sort of light drink (of Marsala wine and eggs, etc.).

zabattièro†, M.: cobbler (shoemaker).

zaccagnáre†, INTR.: busy one's self (fuss).

zaccarále†, M.: press (for wine, etc.).

zác-caro†, M., ‖**-chera** [? OGer. *zahar*], F.: splash of mud (on clothes, etc.); trifle (bagatelle, trash)†; worthless person†; perplexity†; trick†. **-cherèlla**, *dim.* of *-chera*. **-cheróna**, *aug.* of *-chera*. **-cheróne**, ADV.: with a big splash of mud. **-cherósо**†, ADJ.: splashed. **-cherúzza**†, *disp. dim.* of *-chera*.

zafard.. = *inzafard..*

zaffaménto [*-ffare*], M.: stopping.

zaffard.. = *inzafard..*

zaffá-re [*zaffo*], TR.: stop (with a bung), bung; dam up. **zaffá-ta** [infl. by *zampata*], F.: jet or squirting (of liquor, outburst on uncorking); scolding, upbraiding. **-táccia**, *disp.* of *-ta*. **-túra**, F.: stopping (up).

ẓáffera†, F.: azure.

ẓaffe-ranáto, ADJ.: saffroned. ‖**-ráno** [Ar. *za farân*], M.: saffron.

ẓaf-firíno, ADJ.: saphirine. ‖**-fíro** [L. *sapphirus* (Orient.)], M.: sapphire.

záffo [OGer. *zapfo*], M.: bung (stopper, TAP); tipstaff (constable, beadle)†.

ẓaffróne [*-fferano*], M.: bastard-saffron.

ẓagá-glia [Fr. *zagaie*], F.: short javelin. **-gliáta**, F.: javelin thrust. **-gliétta**, *dim.* of *-glia*.

ẓai-nétto, *dim.* of *-zo*. ‖**ẓái-no** [variant of *zana*], M.: pouch (of skin), knapsack; bay or black coat of a horse.

ẓa-becchíno†, **-bécco**†, M.: sort of ship or boat.

zamberlúcco [? *zambra*, *lucco*], M.: Turkish gown.

zámbra†, F.: chamber; water-closet.

zám-pa [OGer. *tappe*], F.: claw (esp. of a beast); paw, foot. **-páre**, TR.: strike with the claws or paw, scratch, paw. **-páta**, F.: kick; stroke with the paw, clawing; slap. **-peggiáre**, TR.: kick; claw, paw furiously. **-pétta**, *dim.* of *-pa*. **-pettáre**, INTR.: move the paws; begin to walk (of children). **-pétto**, *dim.* of *-pa*.

zampil-laménto, M.: spouting or gushing out. **-lánte**, ADJ.: spouting forth, gushing. **-láre**, INTR.: spout out (gush out). **-létto**, *dim.* of *-lo*. **-lío**, M.: spouting, (gushing). ‖**zampíl-lo** [dim. of *zaffo*], M.: fine jet or spout; fountain.

zam-pína, **-píno**, *dim.* of *-pa*.

zampó-gna [L. *symphonia*], F.: (shepherd's) pipe, reed; (*south It.*) bagpipe. **-gnáre**, INTR.: play upon the pipe, pipe; shriek†. **-gnatóre**, M.: piper. **-gnétta**, F., **-gníno**†, *dim.* of *-gna*.

zampóne [*-pa*], M.: big claw or paw; ragout of pig's feet (pig's feet with spiced meat).

zá-na [OGer. *zainâ*], F.: basket; cradle; (*arch.*) niche; drain (of a road, etc.); basket-woman (who brings vegetables, etc.)†; cheat. **-naiuòlo**†, M.: basket-man (who brings vegetables, etc.). **-náta**, F.: basketful. **-nèlla**, *dim.* of *-na*.

zángola [? *zana*], F.: charm.

zán-na [? Ger. *zahn*, TOOTH], F.: long tooth, fang, tusk: *dar di* — = *-nare*. **-náre**, TR.: polish (gold or silver) with a tooth. **-náta** 1, F.: cut with a tooth, bite.

ẓan-náta 2, F.: buffoonery (harlequinade). **-nésco**, ADJ.: buffoon-like (scurrilous). **-nétto**, *dim.* of *-ni*. ‖**ẓán-ni** [= pr. name *Gianni*], M.: merry-andrew (buffoon).

zannúto [*-nna*], ADJ.: with fangs, tusked.

ẓanẓá-ra [echoic], F.: gnat (midge). **-rétta**, **-rettína**, *dim.* of *-ra*. **-rière**, M.: gnat or mosquito-net.

zanzaveráta†, F.: sauce, relish.

záp-pa [L. *sap(p)a*], F.: hoe, mattock. **-patóre**† = *-patore*. **-paménto**, M.: hoeing, digging. **-páre**, TR.: hoe, dig; sap. **-páta**, F.: stroke of the hoe; hoeing. **-pa=tèrra**, M.: clodhopper, boor. **-patóre**, M.: digger; delver. **-paterèllo**, M.: young digger. **-patúra**, F.: hoeing, digging; hoed ground. **-pétta**, *dim.* of *-pa*. **-pettáre**, TR.: hoe or dig lightly, scratch, scrape. **-pettína**, **-pettíno**, **-pétto**, *dim.* of *-pa*. **-ponáre**, TR.: dig, hoe; sap. **-poncèllo**, *dim.* of *-pone*. **-póna**, F., **-póne**, M.: *aug.* of *-pa*; mattock.

ẓá-ra, ‖**-ro**† [Ar. *zar*, die], F.: sort of play with dice; risk. **-róso**, ADJ.: hazardous.
zát-ta [*chiatta*], F.: raft; sort of melon.
zát-tera, F.: raft; float (of timber).
ẓavadáre†, TR.: daub.
ẓavòr-ra [L. *saburra* (*sabulum*, sand)], F.: ballast. **-ránte**, M.: (*nav.*) lighterman. **-ráre**, TR.: ballast.
ẓázze-ra [OGer. *zatâ*], F.: long hanging hair. **-ráccia**, *disp.* of *-ra*. **-rétta**, **-ríma**, F.: *car. dim.* of *-ra*; nice little head of hair, nice-haired fellow. **-róne**, M.: long-haired fellow. **-ráto**, ADJ.: long-haired; M.: long-haired fellow.
ẓèba†, F.: she-goat.
ẓèbra [Afric.], F.: zebra.
ẓebù [?], M.: zebu (bovine mammal).
zécca 1 [Ger. *zecke*], F.: (*ent.*) TICK.
zéc-ca 2 [Ar. *sekkah*, balance], F.: mint: *nuovo di* —, brand-new. **-chière**†, **-chièro**†, M.: director of the mint. **-chinétta**, F.: sort of play. **-chíno**, M.: sequin (a coin).
zéccola [*zecca*], F.: burdock.
ẓedoária†, F.: wild ginger.
zè-firo, ‖**ẓè-firo**† [L. *zephirus*], M.: zephyr.
ẓelamína†, F.: zinc.
ẓe-lánte, ADJ.: zealous (fervent). **-lanteménte**, ADV.: zealously. **-láre**, INTR.: be zealous (be devoted). **-láto**, ADJ.: zealous (fervent). **-latóre**, M., **-latríce**, F.: zealous person (zealot); partisan. ‖**ẓè-lo** [L. *-lus*], M.: zeal (ardour, fervour). **-los..**† = *gelos..*
ẓendá-do, ‖**-'lo** [*sindone*], M.: cloth; taffeta.
ẓèndo, M.: Zend (Avestan dialect).
ẓènit(to) [Ar. *semt*, vertical point], M.: zenith.
ẓenẓánia† = *zizzania*.
ẓenẓára† = *zanzara*.
ẓèn-ẓero [L. *zinziber*], **-ẓávero**, M.: GINGER. **-ẓeveráta**†, F.: (*med.*) compound; medley.
zép-pa [OGer. *zepfe*], F.: wedge; puncheon; basil (angle of a cutting edge, edge): *mettere -pe*, cause discord or dissension. **-paménto**, M.: cramming. **-páre**, TR.: stamp down; cram (stuff). **-patóre**, M.: crammer. **-patúra**, F.: cramming (stuffing). **-'po**, ADJ.: crammed (full to overflowing, crowded); M.†: (*nav.*) wedge. **-polína**, *dim.* of *-pa*. **-políno**, M.: sort of black grape.
ẓer-binería, F.: dandyism, affectation in dress. ‖**-bíno** [*Zerbino*, character in Orlando Furioso], M.: dandy (exquisite, fop, lion). **-binòtto**, *dim.* of *-bino*.
ẓèro 1 [Ar. *cifron*], M.: zero (cipher; nothing).
ẓèro 2 [?], M.: kind of fish (like sardines).

ẓèta, F.: name of the letter *z*; zeta.
ẓetètico [Gr. *-kós* (*zetein*, seek)], ADJ.: zetetic.
zéẓẓo† = *sezzo*.
zézzolo†, M.: nipple (teat).
zi, INTERJ.: pst! hush!
zía [cf. *zio*], F.: aunt.
ẓibal-donáccio, *disp.* of *-done*. ‖**-dóne** [?], M.: mixture (medley).
ẓibellíno [l. L. *sabellum*, marten], M.: SABLE; fur of the sable; ADJ.: of sable.
ẓibétto [Orient.], M.: zibet(h).
ẓibíbbo [Ar. *sibîb*], M.: red raisin.
zíe=mo†, M.: my uncle.
ẓiènda†, F.: affair (business).
ẓígolo [? echoic], M.: greenfinch.
ẓígoma [Gr. *zúgoma* (*-goûn*, YOKE)], F.: zygoma (cheekbone).
ẓigríno [Turk. *saghri*, back of a horse], M.: shagreen.
ẓígẓag [Fr.], M.: zigzag.
ẓimár†, M.: verdigris.
ẓimár-ra [Sp. *zamarra*, sheepskin dress], F.: priest's cassock, wide robe (worn by men of prominence and by women). **-ráccia**, *disp.* of *-ra*. **-rétta**, **-rína**, *dim.* of *-ra*. **-róne**, *aug.* of *-ra*.
zimbel-láre, TR.: allure with a decoy-bird; allure (entice); strike with a satchel; INTR.†: sport (jest, banter). **-láta**, F.: bird-call (note of); blow with a play-bag†; banter†. **-latóre**, M., **-latríce**, F.: bird-caller; allurer. **-latúra**, F.: calling of birds. **-lièra**, F.: twig, etc., to which the decoy-bird is tied. ‖**zimbèl-lo** [L. *cymbellum* (dim. of *cymbalum*, cymbal)], M.: decoy-bird, bird-call; decoy (lure, bait, allurement); play-bag† (stuffed bag, tied to a string with which children beat one another in playing): *essere lo* (or *servire di*) —, be the jest or laughing-stock.
ẓimíno [?], M.: vegetable stew (used with fish on fast-days).
ziná-le†, M.: apron. **-líno**†, M.: small apron.
ẓínco or **z-** [Ger. *zink*], M.: zinc.
zincóne = *zingone*.
ẓinépro = *ginepro*.
zinfonía = *sinfonia*.
zingan.. (*pop.*) = *zingar..* **-áre**†, INTR.: wander as gipsies (vagabond).
zínga-ra, F.: gipsy. **-rèlla**, *dim.* of *-ra*. **-rèllo**, *dim.* of *-ro*. **-résca**, F.: gipsy song (Bohemian song). **-résco**, ADJ.: gipsy- (Bohemian). ‖**zínga-ro** [*tzengaris*, their own name], M.: gipsy.
zinghináia†, F.: habitual ill-health.
zín-na†, F.: nipple (breast); bottle. **-náccia**, *disp.* of *-na*. **-nále**, M.: breast-cloth. **-náre**, TR.: suck.
ẓinẓan..† = zizzan..

ẓin-ẓibo†, **-ẓibio** = *zenzero.*

zin-zin(n)áre†, INTR.: sip; tipple. **-zin(n)atóre**†, M., **-zin(n)atrice**†, F.: tippler. ‖**-zíno** [?], M.: sip; little drop (smallest bit).

zío [L. L. *thius* (Gr. *theios*)], M.: uncle.

zipo-láre, TR.: stop with a peg, plug. **-létto**, *dim.* of *-lo*. ‖**zípo-lo** [Ger. *zipfel*, top], M.: plug; spigot; peg.

zir-laménto, M.: whistling (of thrushes, etc.). ‖**-láre** [L. *zinzilulare* (echoic)], INTR.: whistle (of thrushes, etc.), pipe. **-létto**, *dim.* of *-lo*. **zír-lo**, M.: whistling (of thrushes, etc.); (caged) singing thrush.

zíro†!, M.: oil pot (jar).

ẓíro ẓíro, ẓíru ẓíru [echoic], M.: denoting sounds produced by friction or fiddling.

ẓiẓ-ca†, **-ga**, F.: sort of grape.

zit, INTERJ.: tst! hush!

zit. .† = *zitt. .*

zít-ta† [*citta*], F.: lass (young girl). **-tèlla**, F.: lass (girl, maid); (*leg.*) spinster: *vecchia* —, old maid. **-tèllo**†, M.: lad, boy. **-tellóna**, F.: old maid. **-tellóne**, M.: spruce old fellow.

zit-tíno, ADJ.: silent, hushed. ‖**-tíre** [*zit*], INTR.: make a slight noise (*zi*), esp. of discontent, hiss slightly; breathe. **-'to**, ADJ.: silent, hushed; M., INTERJ.: silence, hush: *state* —, keep silence! be still!

ẓivolo = *zigolo.*

zizza†, F.: breast (teat).

ẓiẓẓá-nia [Gr. *zizánion*, weed], F.: tares; rabble, mob; discord. **-nióso**, ADJ.: sowing discord (turbulent).

zíẓ-ẓiba†, **-ẓifa**†, F.: jujube. **-ẓibo**†, ‖**-'ẓifo**† [Gr. *zízuphon*], M.: jujube-tree. **-ẓola**, F.: jujube. **-ẓolo**, M.: jujube-tree.

zocco-láio, M.: wooden-shoe maker or seller. **-lánte**, ADJ.: clattering about with wooden shoes; M.: stupid fellow; Franciscan friar. **-láre**, INTR.: go clattering along with wooden shoes. **-láta**, F.: kick or blow with a wooden shoe. **-létto**, **-líno**, *dim.* of *-lo*. ‖**zòcco-lo** [L. *soccolus* (dim. of *soccus*, SOCK, low shoe)], M.: wooden shoe or sandal (i.e., with wooden sole); slipper; plinth (SOCLE, subbase, block); clod; ninny (clown, fool): *dire -li*, say wonders; *frittata con gli -li*, ham omelet. **-lóne**, *aug.* of *-lo*.

ẓo-diacále, ADJ.: zodiacal. ‖**-díaco** [L. *-diacus* (Gr. *zōon*, animal)], M.: Zodiac.

ẓòforo†, M.: (*arch.*) frieze.

ẓolf. . = *solf. .*

ẓòl-la or **z-** [OGer. *skolla* (= Ger. *scholle*)], F.: clod (lump of clay). **-láta**, F.: stroke with a lump of clay. **-létta**, *dim.* of *-la*. **-lóne**, *aug.* of *-la*. **-lóso**, ADJ.: of clods, clodded (lumpy).

ẓom-bamento, M.: banging. ‖**-báre** [echoic], TR.: thump (bang). **-báta**, F.: (one) thump, bang. **-batóre**, M.: thumper (banger). **-batúra**, F.: thumping (banging). **-bol. .** = **-bo. .**

ẓòna [Gr. *zōne*], F.: zone (girdle, cincture).

ẓónzo [?], M.: *andar a* —, ramble about.

ẓoo- [Gr. *zōon*, animal]: **-fíto** [Gr. *phutón*, plant], M.: zoöphyte. **-líto** [Gr. *líthos*, stone], M.: zoölite. **-logía** [Gr. *lógos*, discourse], F.: zoölogy. **-lògico**, ADJ.: zoölogical. **-tomía** [Gr. *tomé*, cut], F.: zoötomy, etc.

zop-páccio, dim. of *-po*. **-pággine**, F.: lameness. **-peggiáre**, INTR.: limp badly (be very lame). **-pétto**, *dim.* of *-po*. **-picaménto**, M.: limping. **-picáre**, INTR.: go lame, limp, hobble. **-picánte**, ADJ.: limping. **-picatúra**, F.: limping (lameness). **-picóne**, **-picóni**, ADV.: limpingly (lamely, in hobbling). ‖**zóp-po** [Ger. *schupfen*, push], M.: limping (lame); defective.

ẓoti-cáccio, *disp.* of *-co*. **-cággine**, F.: rudeness (clownishness). **-caménte**, ADV.: rudely (clownishly). **-chétto**, *dim.* of *-co*. **-chézza**, F.: rudeness, clownishness. ‖**ẓòti-co** [?], ADJ.: rough (coarse, boorish, clownish); intractable; M.: rough fellow. **-conáccio**, *disp.* of *-cone*. **-cóne**, *disp.* of *-co*.

ẓòẓ-ẓa [?], F.: dram (mixture of drinks, used by the people). **-ẓáio**, M.: dram-seller; drinker.

ẓuávo [Ar. *zouaoua*, tribe of Cabyles], M.: Zouave.

zúc-ca [? *cucuzza*], F.: gourd (pumpkin); (*jest.*) noddle, (pate, head); blockhead: *in* —, bareheaded; — *vuota al vento*, light-headed person; *avere poco sale in* —, be a witless fellow, be a man without brains. **-cáccia**, *disp.* of *-ca*. **-cáio**, M.: bed of gourds, pumpkin field; ADJ.: of a sort of cherry or grape. **-caiu(o)la**, F.: (*ent.*) mole-cricket. **-áta**, F.: blow of a gourd.

zucche-ráio, M.: sugar-dealer. **-ráre**, TR.: sugar. **-ráto**, ADJ.: sugared. **-rièra**, F.: sugar-bowl; sugar-box. **-ríno**, ADJ.: of sugar; sugary; saccharine; M.: sweetmeat. ‖**zúcche-ro** [Ar. *sokkar*], M.: SUGAR: — *bianco*, refined sugar; — *d'orzo*, barley-sugar; — *in pani*, loaf-sugar; — *rosato*, conserve of roses; — *rosso*, raw sugar; *un pane di* —, a loaf of sugar; *parere uno* —, look overjoyed. **-róso**, ADJ.: sugary (saccharine, sweet).

zuc-chétta [dim. of *-ca*], F.: small gourd or pumpkin, etc.; kind of sausage. **-chettína**, *dim.* of *-chetta*. **-chettíno**, *dim.* of *-chetto*. **-chétto**, M.: *dim.*; small gourd or pumpkin, etc.; cap, bonnet.

-chettóne, *aug.* of *-chetto.* **-chino,** *dim.* of *-ca.* **-'colo†,** M.: crown of the head, pate. **-conaménto,** M.: shaving of the head. **-conáre,** TR.: shave the head of, shear. **-conatóre,** M.: hair-cutter. **-cóne,** M.: big gourd or pumpkin; big head; blockhead. **-còtto** = *-chetto.*

zúffa 1 [ak. to *zuppa*], F.: mess of pudding.

zúf-fa 2 [Ger. *zupfen*, pull, pluck], M.: (*mil.*) hand-to-hand fight (mêlée); fray (wrangle, altercation). **-fétta,** *dim.* of *-fa.* **-fettina,** *dim.* of *-fetta.*

zufo-laménto, M.: whistling, whizzing. ‖**-láre** [old *sifilare* (*sibilo*)], INTR.: whizzle; flute; whiz (hiss). **-latóre,** M., **-latríce,** F.: whistler; whisperer. **-létto,** *dim.* of *-lo.* **zúfo-lo,** M.: whistle; flageolet; whistle†, hiss†; spy†. **-lóne,** *aug.* of *-lo.*

zu-ghétto†, *dim.* of *-go.* **-go†,** M.: kind of fritters; insipid fellow, ninny. **-golíno†,** *dim.* of *-go.*

zulfúreo [*zolfo*], ADJ.: sulphuric.

zúp-pa [Ger. *suppe*], F.: broth on toast (sop; soup); toast in wine; mixture (confusion): *far la — nel paniere*, pour water into a sieve; *mangiar la — coi ciechi*, have to do with ignorance. **-páre,** TR.: soak. **-pétta,** *dim.* of *-pa.* **-pièra,** F.: soup-bowl. **-po,** ADJ.: soaked, saturated. **-póna, -póne,** *aug.* of *-pa.*

zur-láre†, INTR.: sport (joke). **-lo†,** M.: merriment (mirth): *andare in —*, be merry; *mettere in —*, divert; awake a desire in. **-ro†,** M.: gaiety (mirth); eagerness.

GEOGRAPHICAL NAMES

A

Abissínia, Abyssinia.
Abissíno, Abyssinian.
Abuchíro, Abukir.
Acáia, Achaia.
Adriático, Adriatic.
Adrianòpoli, Adrianople.
Áia, the Hague.
Albanése, Albanian.
Albióne, Albion.
Alemágna, Germany.
Alessándria, Alexandria.
Algárvia, Algarve.
Algèri, Algiers.
Algeríno, Algerine.
Álpi, Alps.
Alsázia, Alsace.
Alvèrnia, Auvergne.
Ambúrgo, Hamburg.
Amèrica, America.
Americáno, American.
Amsterdámo, Amsterdam.
Ánau, Hanau.
Ánde, Andes.
Angiò, Anjou.
Annónia, Hainault.
Annòver, Hanover.
Antíbo, Antibes.
Antílle, Antilles, Caribee Islands.
Antiòchia, Antioch.
Anvèrsa, Antwerp.
Apponníni, Apennines.
Aragóna, Arragon.
Arcángelo, Archangel.
Argentína (Repúbblica), Argentine Republic.
Ássia, Hesse.
Assíria, Assyria.
Ástracan, Astrachan.
Atène, Athens.
Atenése, Ateniénse, Athenian.
Atlánte, Atlas.
Atlántico, Atlantic.
Avána, Havana.
Augústa, Augsburg.
Avignóne, Avignon.
Azzòrre, Azores.

B

Babilònia, Babylon.
Báden, Baden.
Balcáno, Balcan.
Baleári, Baleares.
Báttria, Bactria.
Bavarése, Bávaro, Bavarian.
Bavièra, Bavaria.
Bèlgico, Bèlgio, Belgian.
Bèlgio, Belgium.
Bengáia, Bengal.
Berlinése, Berlinian.
Berlíno, Berlin.
Bermúde, Bermudas.
Bèrna, Bern.
Besanzóne, Besançon.
Bettlèmme, Bethlehem.
Biscáglia, Biscáia, Biscay.
Bitínia, Bithynia.
Boèmia, Bohemia.
Boèmo, Bohemian.
Bordò, Bordeaux.
Borgógna, Burgundy.
Bòsforo, Bosphorus.
Brabanzése, Brabantine.
Brasíle, Brazil.
Brèma, Bremen.
Breslávia, Breslaw.
Bretágna, Brittany. Great Britain.
Británnico, Briton.
Brunsvígo, Brunswick.
Brussèlles, Brussels.
Bucaréstа, Bucharest.
Burgògna, Burgundy.

C

Cádice, Cadiz.
Cáffro, Caffre.
Caiènna, Cayenna.
Calmúcco, Calmuc.
Cambrígge, Cambridge.
Campágna, Campania.
Canárie (Ísole), Canary Islands.
Canníbali, *Isole de'* —, Caribbee Islands.
Cantorberè, Canterbury.
Cápo, Cape: — *di Buona Speranza*, Cape of Good Hope; — *del Nord*, North Cape; — *San Vincenzo*, Cape St. Vincent.
Caríddi, Charybdis.
Carmèlo, Carmel.
Cartagèna, Carthagena.
Cartágine, Carthage.
Cassèlla, Cassel.
Castíglia, Castile.
Cáucaso, Caucasus.
Célibi, Celebes.
Chilónia, Kiel.
China, China.
Cicládi, Cyclades.
Cípro, Cyprus.
Coblènts, Coblentz.
Cològna, Colònia, Cologne.

Copená-ghen or **-ga**, Copenhagen.
Cordiglière, Cordilleras.
Corintiáno, Corinthian.
Corínto, Corinth.
Cornovágl̥ia, Cornwall.
Corsicáno, Corsican.
Cosśacco, Cossack.
Costantinòpoli, Constantinople.
Costánza, Constance.
Cracòvia, Cracow.
Crèta, Crete.
Croázia, Croatia.
Curassáo, Curaçoa.

D

Dalmázia, Dalmatia.
Damásco, Damascus.
Danése, Dane.
Danimárca, Denmark.
Danúbio, Danube.
Dánzica, Dantsick.
Dardanèlli, Dardanells.
Delfináto, Dauphiny.
Drèşda, Dresden.
Dublíno, Dublin.
Duína, Dwina.
Dunchèrche, Dunkirk.

E

Edimbúrgo, Edinburgh.
Efeşíno, Ephesian.
Èfeşo, Ephesus.
Égra, Eger.
Eşítto, Egypt.
Eşízio, Egyptian.
Eidelbèrga, Heidelberg.
Èno, Inn.
Ercoláno, Herculaneum.
Esquiméşi, Esquimaux.
Estònia, Esthonia.
Etiòpia, Ethiopia.
Eufráto, Euphrates.
Euròpa, *Europe.*

F

Faènza, Fayance.
Fenícia, Phœnicia.
Fiándra, Flanders.
Filadèlfia, Philadelphia.
Filippíne (Íşole), Philippine Islands.
Finlandése, Finlander.
Finlándia, Finland.
Fiorentíno, Florentine.
Firènze, Florence.
Francéşe, French.
Fráncia, France.
Francofòrte, Frankfort.
Francònia, Franconia.
Franconiáno, Franconian.
Fríşia, Friesland.

G

Galázia, Galatia.
Galilèa, Galilee.
Galízia, Galicia.
Gálles, Wales.
Gángo, Ganges.
Garònna, Garonne.
Gascógna, Gascony.
Gascóne, Gascon.
Ģeniśèa, Jenisea.
Ģènova, Genoa.
Ģermánia, Germany.
Ģerśèi, Jersey.
Ģerusalèmme, Jerusalem.
Ģiamáica, Jamaica.
Ģiappóne, Japan.
Ģiapponése, Japanese.
Ģiáva, Java.
Ģibiltèrra, Gibraltar.
Ģinèvra, Geneva.
Ģiordáno, Jordan.
Ģiudèa, Judea.
Ģiulièri, Juliers.
Glaşgòvia, Glasgow.
Gottárdo (Monte San), St. Gothard.
Gòzia, Gothia.
Grecia, Greece.
Grenvíco, Greenwich.
Grigióni, Grisons.
Groenlandése, Greenlander.
Groenlándia, Greenland.
Guiènna, Guienne.

I

Ibèrnia, Hibernia.
Illíria, **Illírico**, Illyricum.
Índo, Indus.
Inghiltèrra, England.
Inglése, English; Englishman.
Iórca, York.
Ípra, Ypres.
Irlánda, Ireland.
Irlandése, Irishman.
Irócco, Iroquois.
Íschia, Ischia.
Işlánda, Iceland.
Işlandése, Icelander.
Íspaan, Ispahan.
Işraelíta, Israelite.
Ítaca, Ithaca.
Itália, Italy.
Italiáno, Italian.

L

Lancástro, Lancaster.
Lappóno, **Lapponése**, Laplander.
Lappònia, Lapland.
Latíno, Latin.
Lázio, Latium.
Lemáno, Lake Leman.
Lènno(s), Lemnos.
Lèşbo, Lesbos.
Líbano, Lebanon.
Liégi, Liege.
Lióne, Lyons.
Lípsia, Leipsic.

Lisbóna, Lisbon.
Lisbonése, Lisbonian.
Lituánia, Lithuania.
Liverpúla, Liverpool.
Livórno, Leghorn.
Lòfodi, Lofods.
Loíra, Loire.
Lombárdia, Lombardy.
Lóndra, London.
Loréna, Lorrain.
Losánna, Lausanne.
Lubècca, Lubec.
Lucembúrgo, Luxemburg.
Lucèrna, Lucern.
Luigiána, Louisiana.
Lúnda, Lund.
Lusáto, Lusatian.
Lusaziáno, Lusatian.
Lussembúrgo, Luxemburg.

M

Maddebúrgo, Magdeburg, Maidenburgh.
Mánica (la), British Channel.
Mántoa, Mántova, Mantua.
Mantoáno, Mantováno, Mantuan.
Mároa, Márchia, March.
Márna, Marne.
Marratóna, Marathon.
Marsíglia, Marseilles.
Martiníca, Martinique.
Maurízio (San), St. Maurice.
Médo, Mede.
Mènfi, Memphis.
Messicáno, Mexican.
Mèssico, Mexico.
Miláno, Milan.
Milèto, Miletus.
Mitávia, Mitau.
Móldo, Moldau.
Molúcche (Ísole), Molucca Islands.
Mònaco, Munich.
Montebiánco, Mont Blanc.
Monferráto, Montferrat.
Montalbáno, Montauban.
Montbegliárdo, Montbelliard.
Montereále, Montreal.
Montgòmmeri, Montgomery.
Moráto, Morat.
Mòro, Moor.
Mósa, Meuse.
Mósca, Moscow.
Moscovíta, Moscovite.
Mozambíco, Mozambique.

N

Nancì, Nancy.
Nápoli, Naples.
Napolitáno, Neapolitan.
Nanchíno, Nankin.
Narbóna, Narbonne.
Násso, Naxus.
Nassóvia, Nassau.
Názaret, Nazareth.
Neubúrgo, Newborough.
Nicòpoli, Nicopolis.
Niéper, Dnieper.
Nílo, Nile.
Nínive, Nineveh.
Nízza, Nice.
Norimbèrga, Nuremberg.
Normándia, Normandy.
Normáno, Norman.
Nortámton, Northampton.
Nortúmbria, Northumberland.
Norvègia, Norway.
Nottingámo, Nottingham.
Numantíno, Numantian.

O

Òdera, Oder.
Oíse, Oise.
Olánda, Holland.
Olandése, Hollander, Dutchman.
Oldembúrgo, Oldenberg.
Olmúzza, Olmutz.
Olsázia, Holstein.
Olsaziése, Holstenian.
Opórto, Porto.
Orcádi (Ísole), Orkneys.
Òreb, Horeb.
Orleáns, Orleans.
Osfórdia, Oxford.
Òsimo, Osimum.
Osnabrúga, Osnaberg.
Ostènda, Ostend.
Otaíti, Otahaiti.
Otentòtti, Hottentots.
Ottomána (La Porta), the Ottoman Port.

P

Pádoa, Pádova, Padua.
Paési Bássi, Low Countries, Netherlands.
Palatináto, Palatinate.
Palatíno, Palatinian.
Palestína, Palestine.
Pamplóna, Pampeluna.
Panfília, Pamphylia.
Parígi, Paris.
Parigíno, Parisian.
Pártia, Parthia.
Pártico, Parthian.
Passávia, Passau.
Pásso di Calè, the Straits of Dover.
Pátmo, Patmos.
Patrásso, Patros.
Pechíno, Peking.
Pelèvio, Pelew Isles.
Peloponnéso, Peloponnesus.
Pembròche, Pembroke.
Pèrgamo, Pergamus.
Perpignáno, Perpignan.
Perúgia, Perugia.
Perugíno, Perugian.

Pèsto, Pesth.
Piacènza, Piacenza.
Piccárdia, Picardy.
Piemónte, Piedmont.
Pietrobúrgo, Petersburg.
Píndo, Pindus.
Pirenèi, Pyrenees.
Pirmónti, Pyrmont.
Plimúto, Plymouth.
Pològna, Poland.
Polonéṣe, Pole.
Pònto, Pontus.
Portogállo, Portugal.
Portoghéṣe, Portuguese.
Portsmúto, Portsmouth.
Potsdámo, Potsdam.
Prága, Prague.
Presbúrgo, Pressburg.
Propòntide, Propontis.
Provènza, Provence.
Púglia, Apulia.

Q

Quebècco, Quebec.
Quedlimbúrgo, Quedlinburg.
Querfúrto, Querfurt.

R

Radzivílla, Radzevil.
Ratisbóna, Ratisbon.
Reíms, Rheims.
Rèno, Rhine.
Rèzie = *Alpe*.
Roáno, Rouen.
Roccèlla, Rochelle.
Ròdano, Rhone.
Ródi, Rhodes.
Róma, Rome.
Romanésco, Romanian.
Románo, Roman.
Rosbúrgo, Roxburgh.
Rossiglióne, Roussillon.
Roterdámo, Rotterdam.
Rubicóne, Rubicon.
Rutlándia, *Rutland*.

S

Sabíno, Sabine.
Sagúnto, Saguntum.
Sáhara, Sahara.
Salamína, Salamis.
Salisbúrgo, Salzberg.
Salisburì, Salisbury.
Saloníchi, Thessalonica.
Samoiáde, Samoide.
Samotrácia, Samothrace.
Sanníta, Samnite.
Santógna, Saintonge.
Sáona, Saône.
Saracíno, Saracen.
Sardégna, Sardinia.
Sárdo, Sardinian.
Sarmáto, Sarmatian.
Sarmázia, Sarmatia.
Sássone, Saxon.
Sassònia, Saxony.
Sáva, Save.
Savòia, Savoy.
Savoiárdo, Savoyard.
Sciaffúsa, Schaffhausen.
Scarbúrgo, Scarborough.
Ṣcèlda, Scheld.
Schiavònia, Sclavonia.
Ṣcílla, Scylla.
Scòtto = *Scozzese*.
Scòzia, Scotland.
Scozzése, Scotch, Scotchman.
Selándia, Zealand.
Sempióne, Simplon.
Senegállo, Senegal.
Sènna, Seine.
Sevèrna, Severn.
Sicília, Sicily.
Sidóne, Sidon.
Sinigáglia, Senegallia.
Siracúsa, Syracuse.
Síria, Syria.
Sírio, Syrian.
Sivíglia, Seville.
Ṣlèṣia, Silesia.
Smírna, Smyrna.
Smolènsco, Smolensk.
Soláro, **Solúra**, Soleure.
Spágna, Spain.
Spagnuòlo, Spaniard.
Spíra, Spire.
Spitzbèrgo, Spitzbergen.
Staffòrdo, Stafford.
Státi Uníti, United States.
Stettíno, Stettin.
Stíria, Styria.
Stoccólma, Stockholm.
Stralsúnda, Stralsund.
Strasbúrgo, Strasburg.
Stutgárdia, Stutgart.
Suèvia, Suabia.
Suèvo, Suabian.
Ṣvedése, Swede.
Ṣvèzia, Sweden.
Ṣvízzera, Switzerland.
Ṣvízzero, Swiss.
Súnd, The Sound.
Sundgóvia, Sundgaw.
Suráto, Surat.
Surinámo, Surinam.
Suterlándia, Sutherland.

T

Tágo, Tagus.
Tamígi, Thames.
Tartária, Tartary.
Tártaro, Tartar, Tartarian.
Tebáno, Theban.
Tèbe, Thebes.
Termòpili, Thermopylæ.
Terran(u)òva, Newfoundland.
Tesságlia, Thessaly.
Tessaliáno, Thessalonian.
Tévere, Tiber.
Tígri, Tigris.
Tíro, Tyre.
Tiròlo, Tyrol.
Tóbol, **Tobólsca**, Tobolsk.
Tolóṣa, Toulouse.
Toríno, Turin.
Toscána, Tuscany.

Toscáno, Tuscan.
Trácia, Thrace.
Trebisónda, Trebizond.
Trentíno, Trentine.
Trènto, Trent.
Trèveri, Treves.
Trièsto, Triest.
Tròia, Troy.
Tulóno, Toulon.
Tunchíno, Tonquin.
Túnisi, Tunis.
Turchía, Turkey.
Túrco, Turk.
Turíngia, Thuringia.
Túsculo, Tusculum.

U

Ucránia, Ukraine.
Úlma, Ulm.
Ungheria, Hungary.
Unghéro, Hungarian.
Upsála, Upsal.

V

Valacchía, Wallachia.
Valácco, Wallachian.
Valènza, Valence, Valencia.
Valèsia, Valais.
Valchiúsa, Vaucluse.
Valláno, Wallonian.
Vallèsia, Vaud.
Varságlia, Versailles.
Varsávia, Varsóvia, Warsaw.
Vendèa, Vendee.
Vèneto = *Veneziano*.
Venèzia, Venice.
Veneziáno, Venetian.
Venósa, Venusium.
Veracróce, Vera Cruz.
Verdúno, Verdun.
Verságli , Versailles.
Vesália, Wesel.
Vèsera, Weser.
Vestfália, Westphalia.
Vesúvio, Vesuvius.
Villafránca, Villefranche.
Vílna, Wilna.
Virtembèrga, Wurtemberg.
Vístola, Vistula.
Vitèrbo, Viterbum.
Vivèrse, Viviers.
Volínnia, Volhynia.
Vórmes, Worms.
Vósghi, Volges.
Vurtsbúrgo, Wurtzburg.

Z

Záara, Sahara.
Zelánda, Zealand.
Zèlla, Zell.
Zém(b)la (Nuòva), Nova Zembla.
Zurígo, Zurich.
Zuydersèo, Zuyder-Zee.

PERSONAL NAMES

A

Abelárdo, Abelard.
Abèle, Abel.
Abrámo, Abraham.
Adeláide, Alice.
Adòlfo, Adolphus.
Agnèse, Agnes.
Agostína, Austina.
Agostíno, Austin.
Alárico, Alaric.
Albáno, Alban.
Albèrto, Albert.
Albíno, Albin.
Alessándro, Alexander.
Alèssio, Alexis.
Alfònso, Alphonsus.
Alvíno, Alvin.
Anastásio, Anastasius.
Andrèa, Andrew.
Annína, Nanny.
Ansèlmo, Anselm.
Antònio, Anthony, Tony.
Armándo, Armand.
Arnòldo, Arnold.
Arrígo, Henry.
Augústo, Augustus.
Aurèlio, Aurelius.

B

Baltassárre, Balthasar.
Bárnaba, Barnaby.
Bartolommèo, Bartholomew, Bat.
Basílio, Basil.
Batílde, Bathilda.
Battísta, Baptist.
Benedètta, Benedicta.
Benedètto, Benedict, *Bennet.*
Beniamíno, Benjamin, Ben.
Bernárdo, Bernard.
Bèrta, Bertha.
Bortrándo, Bertram.
Biánca, Blanche.
Biágio, Blase.
Bonifázio, Boniface.
Brígida, Bridget, Biddy.
Brunóne, Bruno.

C

Camíllo, Camillus.
Cárlo, Charles.
Carlomágno, Charlemagne.
Carlòtta, Charlotte.
Carolína, Caroline.
Casimíro, Casimir.
Caterína, Catharine, Catherine, Kate.
Celestíno, Celestine.
Cèlso, Celsus.
Cèsare, Cæsar.
Chiára, Clare, Clair.
Cipriáno, Cyprian.
Cirillo, Cyril.
Círo, Cyrus.
Clemènte, Clement.
Cornèlio, Cornelius.
Corrádo, Conrad.
Còsimo, Cosmus.
Costantíno, Constantine.
Costánza, Constance.
Crisóstomo, Chrysostom.
Crispíno, Crispin.
Cristiáno, Christian.
Cristína, Christina.
Cristòforo, Christopher.
Cunigónda, Cunigunda.

D

Dagobèrto, Dagobert.
Damiáno, Damian.
Danièle, Daniel.
Davídde, David.
Dècio, Decius.
Desidèrio, Desiderius.
Diodáto, Deodatus.
Dionígi, Dionysius.
Dionísio, Dionysius.
Diteríco, Derric.
Doménico, Dominic.
Donáto, Donatus.
Dorotèa, Dorothy.

E

Edmóndo, Edmund.
Edítta, Edith.
Edovíno, Edwin.
Eduárdo, Edward, Ned.
Eduíge, Hedwige.
Èlena, Helen.
Eleonòra, Eleanor.
Elisabètta, Elizabeth, Bet, Betty, Bess.
Emanuèle, Immanuel.
Emílio, Emelius, Emilius.
Enrichétta, Harriet.
Enríco, Henry.
Erásmo, Erasmus.
Eríco, Eric.
Ermínio, Herminius.
Ernèsto, Ernest.
Everárdo, Everard.
Eugènio, Eugenius, Eugene.
Eusèbio, Eusebius.
Eustáchio, Eustachius, Eustathius.

F

Fabiáno, Fabian.
Fabrízio, Fabricius.
Fáusto, Faustus.
Federíco, Frederick.
Federíga, Frederica.
Felíce, Felix.
Felícia, Felicia.
Ferdinándo, Ferdinand.
Filibèrta, Philiberta.
Filibèrto, Philibert.
Filippína, Philippa.
Fiorentína, Florentina.
Fiorentíno, Florentine.
Francésca, **Francescʰína**, Frances, Fanny.
Francésco, Francis, Frank.

G

Gabrièle, Gabriel.
Gaetáno, Cajetan.
Gásparo, **Gásparo**, Gaspar.
Gastóne, Gaston.
Genevièffa, Genevieve.
Gertrúda, Gertrude.
Geremía, Jeremiah.
Gerónimo, Jerome.
Giacomína, Janet.
Giácomo, James.
Giannétta, **Giannína**, Janet.
Gioacchíno, Joachim.
Giòbbe, Job.
Giocónda, Jocunda.
Giorgína, Georgiana.
Giórgio, George.
Giosuè, Joshua.
Giovánna, Jane.
Giovánni, John, Jack.
Giovannína, Jenny.
Girolámo, Jerome.
Giudítta, Judith.
Giúlia, Julia.
Giuliána, Juliana.
Giuliáno, Julian.
Giúlio, Julius.
Giusèppe, Joseph.
Giuseppína, Josephine.
Goffrédo, Jeffrey.
Graziáno, Gratian.
Gualtièro, Walter.
Guglielmína, Wilhelmina.
Guglièlmo, William.
Guído, Guy.
Guillibáldo, Willibald.
Gustávo, Gustavus.

I

Ignázio Ignatius.
Ilário, Hilary.
Isácco, Isaac.

L

Lambèrto, Lambert.
Lattánzio, Lactantius.
Lázzaro, Lazarus.
Leándro, Leander.
Leonárdo, Leonard, Len.
Leóne, Leo.
Leopóldo, Leopold.
Lívio, Livy.
Lorènzo, Lawrence.
Lúca, Luke.
Lúcia, Lucy.
Luciáno, Lucian.
Lúcio, Lucius.
Ludòlfo, Ludolphus.
Luígi, Lewis.

M

Maddaléna, Magdalen, Madeline.
Marcèllo, Marcellus.
Márco, Marcus, Mark.
Margaríta, **Margheríta**, Margaret, Margery, Mag, Peg, Polly.
María, Mary.
Mariánna, Marian.
Mariétta, **Mariúccia**, Molly, Moll.
Martíno, Martin.
Massimiliáno, Maximilian.
Mássimo, Maximus.
Mattèo, Matthew.
Mattía, Matthias.
Maurízio, Maurice.
Medárdo, Medard.
Melchiòrre, Melchior.
Michaélo, **Michéle**, Michael, Mike.
Mosè, Moses.

N

Napoleóne, Napoleon.
Neemía, Nehemiah.
Neróne, Nero.
Nicándro, Nicander.
Nicodèmo, Nicodemus.
Nicoláo, **Nicolò**, Nic(h)olas.
Noà, **Noè**, Noah.
Núccia, Jenny.
Núccio, Johnny.

O

Olivièro, Oliver.
Orlándo, Rowland.
Órsola, Ursula.
Ortènsia, Hortense.
Ottóne, Otho.

P

Páola, **Paolína**, Paulina.
Paolíno, Paulinus.
Páolo, Paul.
Patrízio, Patrick.
Petrònio, Petronius.
Piètro, Peter.
Pío, Pius.
Pompèo, Pompey.

R

Rachèle, Rachel.
Raffaèle, Raphael.
Raimóndo, Raymund.
Randòlfo, Randolph.
Remígio, Remy.
Riccárdo, Richard.
Rinàldo, Reynold.
Robèrto, Robert, Robin, Rob.
Roderíco, Roderick.
Rodòlfo, Rudolphus, Ralph.
Rosalía, Rosalie.
Rufíno, Rufus.
Ruggèro, Roger.
Rupèrto, Rupert, Robin.

S

Salomóne, Solomon.
Samuèle, Samuel.
Sansóne, Samson.
Savèrio, Xaverius.
Scipióne, Scipio.
Sebastiáno, Sebastian, Sib.
Semirámide, Semiramis.
Semprònio, Sempronius.
Serafíno, Seraphinus.
Sibílla, Sibyl.
Sigefrédo, Siegfried.
Sigismónda, Sigismunda.
Sigismóndo, Sigismund.
Silváno, Sylvanus.
Silvèstro, Sylvester.
Simeóne, Simeon.
Simóne, Simon, Sim.
Sísto, Sixtus.
Sofía, Sophia, Sophy.
Stanisláo, Stanislaus.
Stéfano, Stephen.
Susánna, Susan.

T

Tácito, Tacitus.
Taddèo, Thaddeus.
Tancrédi, Tancred.
Teobáldo, Theobald.
Teodòra, Theodora.
Teodòro, Theodore.
Teodòsio, Theodosius.
Teòfilo, Theophilus.
Tibèrio, Tiberius.
Timòteo, Timothy, Tim.
Tiziáno, Titian.
Tobía, Tobias, Toby.
Tommáso, Thomas, Tommy, Tom.

U

Ubáldo, Hubaldus.
Úgo, Hugh.
Udalríca, Ulrica.
Udalríco, Ulric.

V

Valeriáno, Valerian.
Valèrio, Valerius.
Vencesláo, Wenceslaus.
Vincènzo, Vincent.
Vitále, Vitellius.

Z

Zacchèo, Zaccheus.

ENGLISH–ITALIAN

GEOGRAPHICAL NAMES

A

Abissínia, Abyssinia.
Abissíno, Abyssinian.
Abuchíro, Abukir.
Acáia, Achaia.
Adriático, Adriatic.
Adrianòpoli, Adrianople.
Áia, the Hague.
Albanése, Albanian.
Albióne, Albion.
Alemágna, Germany.
Alessándria, Alexandria.
Algárvia, Algarve.
Algèri, Algiers.
Algeríno, Algerine.
Álpi, Alps.
Alsázia, Alsace.
Alvèrnia, Auvergne.
Ambúrgo, Hamburg.
Amèrica, America.
Americáno, American.
Amsterdámo, Amsterdam.
Ánau, Hanau.
Ánde, Andes.
Angiò, Anjou.
Annónia, Hainault.
Annòver, Hanover.
Antíbo, Antibes.
Antílle, Antilles, Caribee Islands.
Antiòchia, Antioch.
Anvèrsa, Antwerp.
Appennini, Apennines.
Aragóna, Arragon.
Arcángelo, Archangel.
Argentína (Repúbblica), Argentine Republic.
Ássia, Hesse.
Assíria, Assyria.
Ástracan, Astrachan.
Atène, Athens.
Atenése, **Ateniénse**, Athenian.
Atlánte, Atlas.
Atlántico, Atlantic.
Avána, Havana.
Augústa, Augsburg.
Avignóne, Avignon.
Azzòrre, Azores.

B

Babilònia, Babylon.
Báden, Baden.
Balcáno, Balcan.
Baleári, Baleares.
Báttria, Bactria.
Bavarése, **Bávaro**, Bavarian.
Bavièra, Bavaria.
Bèlgico, **Bèlgio**, Belgian.
Bèlgio, Belgium.
Bengála, Bengal.
Berlinése, Berlinian.
Berlíno, Berlin.
Bermúde, Bermudas.
Bèrna, Bern.
Besanzóne, Besançon.
Bettlèmme, Bethlehem.
Biscáglia, **Biscáia**, Biscay.
Bitínia, Bithynia.
Boèmia, Bohemia.
Boèmo, Bohemian.
Bordò, Bordeaux.
Borgógna, Burgundy.
Bòsforo, Bosphorus.
Brabanzése, Brabantine.
Brasíle, Brazil.
Brèma, Bremen.
Breslávia, Breslaw.
Bretágna, Brittany. Great Britain.
Británnico, Briton.
Brunsvígo, Brunswick.
Brussèlles, Brussels.
Bucaréstа, Bucharest.
Burgògna, Burgundy.

C

Cádice, Cadiz.
Cáffro, Caffre.
Caiènna, Cayenna.
Calmúcco, Calmuc.
Cambrígge, Cambridge.
Campágna, Campania.
Canárie (Ísole), Canary Islands.
Cannibali, *Isole de' —*, Caribbee Islands.
Cantorberì, Canterbury.
Cápo, Cape: *— di Buona Speranza*, Cape of Good Hope; *— del Nord*, North Cape; *— San Vincenzo*, Cape St. Vincent.
Caríddi, Charybdis.
Carmèlo, Carmel.
Cartagèna, Carthagena.
Cartágine, Carthage.
Cassèlla, Cassel.
Castíglia, Castile.
Cáucaso, Caucasus.
Célibi, Celebes.
Chilónia, Kiel.
China, China.
Cicládi, Cyclades.
Cipro, Cyprus.
Coblènte, Coblentz.
Cològna, **Colònia**, Cologne.

Copená-ghen or **-ga**, Copenhagen.
Cordiglière, Cordilleras.
Corintiáno, Corinthian.
Corínto, Corinth.
Cornovágḷia, Cornwall.
Corsicáno, Corsican.
Cossácco, Cossack.
Costantinòpoli, Constantinople.
Costánza, Constance.
Cracòvia, Cracow.
Crèta, Crete.
Croázia, Croatia.
Curazzáo, Curaçoa.

D

Dalmázia, Dalmatia.
Damásco, Damascus.
Danése, Dane.
Danimárca, Denmark.
Danúbio, Danube.
Dánzica, Dantsick.
Dardanèlli, Dardanells.
Delfináto, Dauphiny.
Drèṣda, Dresden.
Dublíno, Dublin.
Duína, Dwina.
Dunchèrche, Dunkirk.

E

Edimbúrgo, Edinburgh.
Efeṣíno, Ephesian.
Èfeṣo, Ephesus.
Égra, Eger.
Egítto, Egypt.
Egízio, Egyptian.
Eidelbèrga, Heidelberg.
Èno, Inn.
Ercoláno, Herculaneum.
Esquiméṣi, Esquimaux.
Estònia, Esthonia.
Etiòpia, Ethiopia.
Eufráte, Euphrates.
Euròpa, Europe.

F

Faènza, Fayance.
Fenícia, Phœnicia.
Fiándra, Flanders.
Filadèlfia, Philadelphia.
Filippíne (Íṣole), Philippine Islands.
Finlandése, Finlander.
Finlándia, Finland.
Fiorentíno, Florentine.
Firènze, Florence.
Franceṣe, French.
Fráncia, France.
Francofòrte, Frankfort.
Franconia, Franconia.
Franconiáno, Franconian.
Fríṣia, Friesland.

G

Galázia, Galatia.
Galilèa, Galilee.
Galízia, Galicia.
Gálles, Wales.
Gánge, Ganges.
Garònna, Garonne.
Guascógna, Gascony.
Gascóne, Gascon.
G̣eniṣèa, Jenisea.
G̣ènova, Genoa.
G̣ermánia, Germany.
G̣ersèi, Jersey.
G̣erusalèmme, Jerusalem.
G̣iamáica, Jamaica.
G̣iappóne, Japan.
G̣iapponése, Japanese.
G̣iáva, Java.
G̣ibiltèrra, Gibraltar.
G̣inèvra, Geneva.
G̣iordáno, Jordan.
G̣iudèa, Judea.
G̣iulièri, Juliers.
Glaṣgòvia, Glasgow.
Gottárdo (Monte San), St. Gothard.
Gòzia, Gothia.
Grècia, Greece.
Grenvíco, Greenwich.
Grig̣ióni, Grisons.
Groenlandése, Greenlander.
Groenlándia, Greenland.
Guièmna, Guienne.

I

Ibèrnia, Hibernia.
Illíria, **Illírico**, Illyricum.
Índo, Indus.
Inghiltèrra, England.
Inglése, English; Englishman.
Iórca, York.
Ípra, Ypres.
Irlánda, Ireland.
Irlandése, Irishman.
Irócco, Iroquois.
Íschia, Ischia.
Iṣlánda, Iceland.
Iṣlandése, Icelander.
Íspaan, Ispahan.
Iṣraelíta, Israelite.
Ítaca, Ithaca.
Itália, Italy.
Italiáno, Italian.

L

Lancástro, Lancaster.
Lappóne, **Lapponése**, Laplander.
Lappònia, Lapland.
Latíno, Latin.
Lázio, Latium.
Lemáno, Lake Leman.
Lèmno(s), Lemnos.
Lèṣbo, Lesbos.
Líbano, Lebanon.
Liég̣i, Liege.
Lióne, Lyons.
Lípsia, Leipsic.

Lisbóna, Lisbon.
Lisbonése, Lisbonian.
Lituánia, Lithuania.
Liverpúla, Liverpool.
Livórno, Leghorn.
Lòfodi, Lofods.
Loíra, Loire.
Lombárdia, Lombardy.
Lóndra, London.
Lorèna, Lorrain.
Losánna, Lausanne.
Lubècca, Lubec.
Lucembúrgo, Luxemburg.
Lucèrna, Lucern.
Luigiána, Louisiana.
Lúnda, Lund.
Lusáto, Lusatian.
Lusaziáno, Lusatian.
Lussembúrgo, Luxemburg.

M

Maddebúrgo, Magdeburg, Maidenburgh.
Mánica (la), British Channel.
Mántoa, Mántova, Mantua.
Mantoáno, Mantováno, Mantuan.
Márca, Márchia, March.
Márna, Marne.
Marratóna, Marathon.
Marsíglia, Marseilles.
Martiníca, Martinique.
Maurízio (San), St. Maurice.
Médo, Mede.
Mènfi, Memphis.
Messicáno, Mexican.
Mèssico, Mexico.
Miláno, Milan.
Milèto, Miletus.
Mitávia, Mitau.
Móldo, Moldau.
Molúcche (Ísole), Molucca Islands.
Mònaco, Munich.
Montebiánco, Mont Blanc.
Monferráto, Montferrat.
Montalbáno, Montauban.
Montbegliárdo, Montbelliard.
Montereále, Montreal.
Montgòmmeri, Montgomery.
Moráto, Morat.
Mòro, Moor.
Mósa, Meuse.
Mósca, Moscow.
Moscovíta, Moscovite.
Mozambíco, Mozambique.

N

Nancì, Nancy.
Nápoli, Naples.
Napolitáno, Neapolitan.
Nanchíno, Nankin.
Narbóna, Narbonne.
Násso, Naxus.
Nassóvia, Nassau.
Názaret, Nazareth.
Neubúrgo, Newborough.
Nicòpoli, Nicopolis.
Niéper, Dnieper.
Nílo, Nile.
Nínive, Nineveh.
Nízza, Nice.
Norimbèrga, Nuremberg.
Normándia, Normandy.
Normáno, Norman.
Nortámton, Northampton.
Nortúmbria, Northumberland.
Norvègia, Norway.
Nottingámo, Nottingham.
Numantíno, Numantian.

O

Òdera, Oder.
Oíse, Oise.
Olánda, Holland.
Olandése, Hollander, Dutchman.
Oldembúrgo, Oldenberg.
Olmúzza, Olmutz.
Olsázia, Holstein.
Olsaziése, Holstenian.
Opórto, Porto.
Orcádi (Ísole), Orkneys.
Òreb, Horeb.
Orleáns, Orleans.
Osfórdia, Oxford.
Òsimo, Osimum.
Osnabrúga, Osnaberg.
Ostènda, Ostend.
Otaíti, Otahaiti.
Otentòtti, Hottentots.
Ottomána (La Porta), the Ottoman Port.

P

Pádoa, Pádova, Padua.
Paési Bássi, Low Countries, Netherlands.
Palatináto, Palatinate.
Palatíno, Palatinian.
Palestína, Palestine.
Pamplóna, Pampeluna.
Panfília, Pamphylia.
Parígi, Paris.
Parigíno, Parisian.
Pártia, Parthia.
Pártico, Parthian.
Passávia, Passau.
Pásso di Calè, the Straits of Dover.
Pátmo, Patmos.
Patrásso, Patros.
Pechíno, Peking.
Polèvio, Pelew Isles.
Peloponnéso, Peloponnesus.
Pembròche, Pembroke.
Pèrgamo, Pergamus.
Perpignáno, Perpignan.
Perúgia, Perugia.
Perugíno, Perugian.

Pèste, Pesth.
Piacènza, Piacenza.
Piccárdia, Picardy.
Piemónte, Piedmont.
Pietroburgo, Petersburg.
Píndo, Pindus.
Pirenèi, Pyrenees.
Pirménti, Pyrmont.
Plimúte, Plymouth.
Pològna, Poland.
Polenése, Pole.
Pònto, Pontus.
Portogállo, Portugal.
Portoghése, Portuguese.
Portsmúte, Portsmouth.
Potsdámo, Potsdam.
Prága, Prague.
Presbúrgo, Presburg.
Propòntide, Propontis.
Provènza, Provence.
Pùglia, Apulia.

Q

Quebècco, Quebec.
Quedlimbúrgo, Quedlinburg.
Querfúrto, Querfurt.

R

Radzivílla, Radzevil.
Ratisbóna, Ratisbon.
Reims, Rheims.
Rèno, Rhine.
Rèzie = *Alpe*.
Roáno, Rouen.
Roccèlla, Rochelle.
Ròdano, Rhone.
Ródi, Rhodes.
Róma, Rome.
Romanésco, Romanian.
Románo, Roman.
Rosbúrgo, Roxburgh.
Rossiglióne, Roussillon.
[Rotter]dámo, Rotterdam.
[Rubic]óne, Rubicon.
[Rutl]ándia, Rutland.

S

Sabína, Sabina.
Sagúnto, Saguntum.
Sáhara, Sahara.
Salamína, Salamis.
Salisbúrgo, Salzburg.
Salisburì, Salisbury.
Salonícchi, Thessalonica.
Samoiádo, Samoide.
Samotrácia, Samothrace.
Sannita, Samnite.
Santógna, Saintonge.
Sáona, Saône.
Saracíno, Saracen.
Sardégna, Sardinia.
Sárdo, Sardinian.
Sarmáto, Sarmatian.
Sarmázia, Sarmatia.
Sássone, Saxon.
Sassònia, Saxony.
Sáva, Save.
Savòia, Savoy.
Savoiárdo, Savoyard.
Sciaffúsa, Schaffhausen.
Scarbúrgo, Scarborough.
Scèlda, Scheld.
Schiavònia, Sclavonia.
Scilla, Scylla.
Scòtto = *Scozzese*.
Scòzia, Scotland.
Scozzése, Scotch, Scotchman.
Selándia, Zealand.
Sempióne, Simplon.
Senegállo, Senegal.
Sènna, Seine.
Sevèrna, Severn.
Sicília, Sicily.
Sidóne, Sidon.
Sinigáglia, Senegallia.
Siracúsa, Syracuse.
Síria, Syria.
Sírio, Syrian.
Sivíglia, Seville.
Slèsia, Silesia.
Smírna, Smyrna.
Smolènsco, Smolensk.
Soláro, **Solára**, Soleure.
Spágna, Spain.
Spagnuòlo, Spaniard.
Spíra, Spira.
Spitzbèrga, Spitzbergen.
Staffórdia, Stafford.
Státi Uníti, United States.
Stettíno, Stettin.
Stíria, Styria.
Stoccólma, Stockholm.
Stralsúnda, Stralsund.
Strasbúrgo, Strasburg.
Stutgárdia, Stutgart.
Suèvia, Suabia.
Suèvo, Suabian.
Svedése, Swede.
Svèzia, Sweden.
Svízzera, Switzerland.
Svízzero, Swiss.
Súnd, The Sound.
Sundgóvia, Sundgaw.
Suráte, Surat.
Surináme, Surinam.
Suterlándia, Sutherland.

T

Tágo, Tagus.
Tamígi, Thames.
Tartária, Tartary.
Tártaro, Tartar, Tartarian.
Tebáno, Theban.
Tèbe, Thebes.
Termòpili, Thermopylæ.
Terran(u)òva, Newfoundland.
Tesságlia, Thessaly.
Tessaloniáno, Thessalonian.
Tévere, Tiber.
Tígri, Tigris.
Tíro, Tyre.
Tiròlo, Tyrol.
Tóbol, **Tobólsco**, Tobolsk.
Tolósa, Toulouse.
Toríno, Turin.
Toscána, Tuscany.

Toscáno, Tuscan.
Trácia, Thrace.
Trebisónda, Trebizond.
Trentíno, Trentine.
Trènto, Trent.
Trèveri, Treves.
Trièste, Triest.
Tròia, Troy.
Tulóne, Toulon.
Tunchíno, Tonquin.
Túnisi, Tunis.
Turchía, Turkey.
Túrco, Turk.
Turíngia, Thuringia.
Túsculo, Tusculum.

U

Ucránia, Ukraine.
Úlma, Ulm.
Unghería, Hungary.
Unghéro, Hungarian.
Upsála, Upsal.

V

Valacchía, Wallachia.
Valácco, Wallachian.
Valènza, Valence, Valencia.
Valèsia, Valais.
Valchiúsa, Vaucluse.
Valláno, Wallonian.
Vallèsia, Vaud.
Varságla, Versailles.
Varsávia, **Varsóvia**, Warsaw.
Vendèa, Vendee.
Vèneto = *Veneziano*.
Venèzia, Venice.
Veneziáno, Venetian.
Venósa, Venusium.
Veracróce, Vera Cruz.
Verdúno, Verdun.
Verságlia, Versailles.
Vesália, Wesel.
Vèsera, Weser.
Vestfália, Westphalia.
Vesúvio, Vesuvius.
Villafránca, Villefranche.
Vílna, Wilna.
Virtembèrga, Wurtemberg.
Vístola, Vistula.
Vitèrbo, Viterbum.
Vivèrse, Viviers.
Volínnia, Volhynia.
Vórmes, Worms.
Vóseghi, Volges.
Vurtsbúrgo, Wurtzburg.

Z

Záara, Sahara.
Zelánda, Zealand.
Zèlla, Zell.
Zém(b)la (Nuòva), Nova Zembla.
Zurígo, Zurich.
Zuydersèe, Zuyder-Zee.

PERSONAL NAMES

A

Abelárdo, Abelard.
Abèle, Abel.
Abrámo, Abraham.
Adeláide, Alice.
Adòlfo, Adolphus.
Agnèse, Agnes.
Agostína, Austina.
Agostíno, Austin.
Alárico, Alaric.
Albáno, Alban.
Albèrto, Albert.
Albíno, Albin.
Alessándro, Alexander.
Alèssio, Alexis.
Alfònso, Alphonsus.
Alvíno, Alvin.
Anastásio, Anastasius.
Andrèa, Andrew.
Annína, Nanny.
Ansèlmo, Anselm.
Antònio, Anthony, Tony.
Armándo, Armand.
Arnòldo, Arnold.
Arrígo, Henry.
Augústo, Augustus.
Aurèlio, Aurelius.

B

Baltassárre, Balthasar.
Bárnaba, Barnaby.
Bartolommèo, Bartholomew, Bat.
Basílio, Basil.
Batílde, Bathilda.
Battísta, Baptist.
Benedètta, Benedicta.
lètto, Benedict,
Beniamíno, Benjamin, Ben.
Bernárdo, Bernard.
Bèrta, Bertha.
Bertrándo, Bertram.
Biánca, Blanche.
Biásio, Blase.
Bonifázio, Boniface.
Brígida, Bridget, Biddy.
Brunóne, Bruno.

C

Camíllo, Camillus.
Cárlo, Charles.
Carlomágno, Charlemagne.
Carlòtta, Charlotte.
Carolína, Caroline.
Casimíro, Casimir.
Caterína, Catharine, Catherine, Kate.
Celestíno, Celestine.
Cèlso, Celsus.
Césare, Cæsar.
Chiára, Clare, Clair.
Cipriáno, Cyprian.
Ciríllo, Cyril.
Círo, Cyrus.
Clemènte, Clement.
Cornèlio, Cornelius.
Corrádo, Conrad.
Còsimo, Cosmus.
Costantíno, Constantine.
Costánza, Constance.
Crisóstomo, Chrysostom.
Crispíno, Crispin.
Cristiáno, Christian.
Cristína, Christina.
Cristòforo, Christopher.
Cunigónda, Cunigunda.

D

Dagobèrto, Dagobert.
Damiáno, Damian.
Danièle, Daniel.
Davídde, David.
Dècio, Decius.
Desidèrio, Desiderius.
Diodáto, Deodatus.
Dionígi, Dionysius.
Dionísio, Dionysius.
Ditorico, Derric.
Doménico, Dominic.
Donáto, Donatus.
Dorotèa, Dorothy.

E

Edmóndo, Edmund.
Edítta, Edith.
Edovíno, Edwin.
Eduárdo, Edward, Ned.
Eduíge, Hedwige.
Èlena, Helen.
Eleonòra, Eleanor.
Elisabètta, Elizabeth, Bet, Betty, Bess.
Emanuèle, Immanuel.
Emílio, Emelius, Emilius.
Enrichétta, Harriet.
Enríco, Henry.
Erásmo, Erasmus.
Eríco, Eric.
Ermínio, Herminius.
Ernèsto, Ernest.
Everárdo, Everard.
Eugènio, Eugenius, Eugene.
Eusèbio, Eusebius.
Eustáchio, Eustachius, Eustathius.

F

Fabiáno, Fabian.
Fabrízio, Fabricius.
Fáusto, Faustus.
Federico, Frederick.
Federíga, Frederica.
Felíce, Felix.
Felícia, Felicia.
Ferdinándo, Ferdinand.
Filibèrta, Philiberta.
Filibèrto, Philibert.
Filippína, Philippa.
Fiorentína, Florentina.
Fiorentíno, Florentine.
Francésca, **Franceschína**, Frances, Fanny.
Francésco, Francis, Frank.

G

Gabrièle, Gabriel.
Gaetáno, Cajetan.
Gáspare, **Gásparo**, Gaspar.
Gastóne, Gaston.
Genevièffa, Genevieve.
Gertrúda, Gertrude.
Geremía, Jeremiah.
Gerónimo, Jerome.
Giacomína, Janet.
Giácomo, James.
Giannétta, **Giannína**, Janet.
Gioacchíno, Joachim.
Giòbbe, Job.
Giocónda, Jocunda.
Giorgína, Georgiana.
Giórgio, George.
Giosuè, Joshua.
Giovánna, Jane.
Giovánni, John, Jack.
Giovannína, Jenny.
Girolámo, Jerome.
Giudítta, Judith.
Giúlia, Julia.
Giuliána, Juliana.
Giuliáno, Julian.
Giúlio, Julius.
Giusèppe, Joseph.
Giuseppína, Josephine.
Goffrédo, Jeffrey.
Graziáno, Gratian.
Gualtièro, Walter.
Guglielmína, Wilhelmina.
Guglièlmo, William.
Guído, Guy.
Guillibáldo, Willibald.
Gustávo, Gustavus.

I

Ignázio Ignatius.
Ilário, Hilary.
Isácco, Isaac.

L

Lambèrto, Lambert.
Lattánzio, Lactantius.
Lázzaro, Lazarus.
Leándro, Leander.
Leonárdo, Leonard, Len.
Leóne, Leo.
Leopóldo, Leopold.
Lívio, Livy.
Lorènzo, Lawrence.
Lúca, Luke.
Lúcia, Lucy.
Luciáno, Lucian.
Lúcio, Lucius.
Ludòlfo, Ludolphus.
Luígi, Lewis.

M

Maddaléna, Magdalen, Madeline.
Marcèllo, Marcellus.
Márco, Marcus, Mark.
Margaríta, **Margheríta**, Margaret, Margery, Mag, Peg, Polly.
María, Mary.
Mariánna, Marian.
Mariétta, **Mariúccia**, Molly, Moll.
Martíno, Martin.
Massimiliáno, Maximilian.
Mássimo, Maximus.
Mattèo, Matthew.
Mattía, Matthias.
Maurízio, Maurice.
Medárdo, Medard.
Melchiòrre, Melchior.
Michaéle, **Michéle**, Michael, Mike.
Mosè, Moses.

N

Napoleóne, Napoleon.
Neemía, Nehemiah.
Neróne, Nero.
Nicándro, Nicander.
Nicodèmo, Nicodemus.
Nicoláo, **Nicolò**, Nic(h)olas.
Noà, **Noè**, Noah.
Núccia, Jenny.
Núccio, Johnny.

O

Olivièro, Oliver.
Orlándo, Rowland.
Órsola, Ursula.
Ortènsia, Hortense.
Ottóne, Otho.

P

Páola, **Paolína**, Paulina.
Paolíno, Paulinus.
Páolo, Paul.
Patrízio, Patrick.
Petrònio, Petronius.
Piètro, Peter.
Pío, Pius.
Pompèo, Pompey.

R

Rachèle, Rachel.
Raffaèle, Raphael.
Raimóndo, Raymund.
Randòlfo, Randolph.
Remígio, Remy.
Riccárdo, Richard.
Rináldo, Reynold.
Robèrto, Robert, Robin, Rob.
Roderíco, Roderick.
Rodòlfo, Rudolphus, Ralph.
Rosalía, Rosalie.
Rufíno, Rufus.
Ruggèro, Roger.
Rupèrto, Rupert, Robin.

S

Salomóne, Solomon.
Samuèle, Samuel.
Sansóne, Samson.
Savèrio, Xaverius.
Scipióne, Scipio.
Sebastiáno, Sebastian, Sib.
Semirámide, Semiramis.
Semprònio, Sempronius.
Serafíno, Seraphinus.
Sibílla, Sibyl.
Sigefrédo, Siegfried.
Sigismónda, Sigismunda.
Sigismóndo, Sigismund.
Silváno, Sylvanus.
Silvèstro, Sylvester.
Simeóne, Simeon.
Simóne, Simon, Sim.
Sísto, Sixtus.
Sofía, Sophia, Sophy.
Stanisláo, Stanislaus.
Stéfano, Stephen.
Susánna, Susan.

T

Tácito, Tacitus.
Taddèo, Thaddeus.
Tancrédi, Tancred.
Teobáldo, Theobald.
Teodòra, Theodora.
Teodòro, Theodore.
Teodòsio, Theodosius.
Teòfilo, Theophilus.
Tibèrio, Tiberius.
Timòteo, Timothy, Tim.
Tiziáno, Titian.
Tobía, Tobias, Toby.
Tommáso, Thomas, Tommy, Tom.

U

Ubáldo, Hubaldus.
Úgo, Hugh.
Udalríca, Ulrica.
Udalríco, Ulric.

V

Valeriáno, Valerian.
Valèrio, Valerius.
Venceslào, Wenceslaus.
Vincènzo, Vincent.
Vitále, Vitellius.

Z

Zacchèo, Zaccheus.

ENGLISH–ITALIAN

sudden, subitamente; — *over*, da per tutto; *not at* —, no certo; — *the better*, tanto meglio; *nowhere at* —, in nessun luogo; *'tis — one*, è tutt' uno; *by — means*, onninamente, certamente, in ogni modo; ADV.: in tutto, intieramente.

allāy 1, S.: lega, misura, *f.* **allay** 2, TR.: allegare, mescolare. **-er**, S.: alleggiatore; mitigatore, *m.* **-ment†**, S.: alleggiamento; comforto, *m.*

ăll-cheering, ADJ.: rallegrante. **-conquering**, ADJ.: invincibile.

allegātion, S.: allegazione; dichiarazione, *f.*

allĕg-e, TR.: allegare; dichiarare. **-eable**, ADJ.: che può allegarsi. **-ement**, S.: allegamento, *m.*; difesa, *f.* **er**, S.: allegatore, dichiaratore, *m.*

allēgian-ce, S.: lealtà, fedeltà, *f.*: *oath of* —, giuramento di fedeltà. **-t**, ADJ.: leale, fedele.

alle-gŏric(al), ADJ.: allegorico. **-gŏrically**, ADV.: allegoricamente. **ălle-gorise**, TR.: allegorizzare. **-gory**, S.: allegoria, *f.*

allĕgro, S.: allegro, *m.*

allēvia-te, TR.: alleviare; mitigare. **-ation**, S.: alleviamento; comforto, *m.*

ălley, S.: viale di giardino; chiassolino, chiasso, *m.*: *blind* —, angiporto.

all-hăllowtide, S.: primo di novembre, *m.*

alli-ance, S.: alleanza; affinità, *f.* **-ed**, ADJ.: alleato, confederato, *m. pl.*

ălligate, TR.: collegare.

ălligator, S.: alligatore, *m.*

alliterātion, S.: alliterazione; ripetizione, *f.*

ăll-knowing, ADJ.: onnisciente.

allocūtion, S.: allocuzione, *f.*

allōdium, S.: (*jur.*) allodio, *m.*

allŏt, TR.: assegnare; aggiudicare. **-ment**, S.: assegnazione; distribuzione, *f.*

allŏw, TR.: accordare, concedere; permettere; dedurre: — *me to tell you*, permettete che io vi dica. **-able**, ADJ.: ammissibile; permesso, giusto. **-ableness**, S.: legittimità; proprietà; giustezza, *f.* **-ance**, S.: mantenimento, *m.*; concessione; razione, *f.*; *make* —, essere indulgente; *a yearly* —, un assegno annuo.

ăll-sŏulsdāy, S.: festa di tutti i Santi, *f.*

allūde, INTR.: alludere, sottintendere.

allūr-e, TR.: adescare, allettare. **-ement**, S.: adescamento, allettamento, *m.* **-er**, S.: adescatore, allettattore, *m.* **-ing**, ADJ.: lusinghevole; fallace; S.: allettamento, *m.* **-ingly**, ADV.: lusinghevolmente. **-ingness**, S.: allettanza; lusinghieria, *f.*

[allusion], *S.*: allusione, *f.* **-sive**, ADJ.: allusivo. **-sively**, ADV.: in modo allusivo. **-siveness**, S.: allusione, *f.*

allūvion, S.: alluvione, *f.*

ăll-wise, ADJ.: onnisciente.

allȳ 1, S.: alleato; parente, *m.* **ally** 2, TR.: associare; legare.

ălmanac, S.: almanacco, *m.*

almighty-tiness, S.: onnipotenza, *f.* **-ty**, ADJ.: onnipotente.

ālmond, S.: mandorla, *f.*: — *tree*, S.: mandorlo. **-s**, PL.: glandule, *f. pl.*; orrecchioni, *m. pl.*

ălmoner, S.: elemosiniere; capellano, *m.* **-monry**, S.: ufficio dell' elemosiniere, *m.*

ălmost, ADV.: quasi; pressochè.

ālms, S. PL.: limosina, *f.* **-basket**, S.: paniere da limosine, *m.* **-deed**, S.: dono caritatevole, *m.* **-giver**, S.: limosiniere, *m.* **-house**, S.: spedale, *m.* **-man**, S.: limosinante, mendicante, *m.*

ălnight†, S.: candela di cera; lumicina, *f.*

ăloes, S.: aloè, *m.*

alŏft, ADJ.: alto, elevato, pomposo. **aloft**, ADV., PREP.: su; in alto.

alōne, ADJ., ADV.: solo, solitario: *all* (*or quite*) —, solo soletto; *let* —, lasciare stare, abbandonare; *let him — for that*, lasciate, fare a lui.

alŏng, ADV., PREP.: pur via; alla lunga, lungo; accosto; appresso: *come* —, avanti; venite pur via; — *with*, unitamente a, in compagnia di. **-side**, PREP.: lungo di bordo, accosto, lungo la banda.

alōof, ADV.: di lungi; da lontano; (*nav.*) al vento.

alŏud, ADV.: ad alta voce; forte.

ălpha-bet, S.: alfabeto, *m.* **-bĕtical**, ADJ.: alfabetico. **-bĕtically**, ADV.: alfabeticamente.

alrĕady, ADV.: già, di già, innanzi.

ălso, CONJ.: anche, ancora; oltre.

ăltar, S.: altare, *m.*

altar-piece, S.: quadro d' altare, pallio.

ăl-ter, TR.: alterare; cangiare; rifare; INTR.: cambiare, variare; corrompersi. **-terable**, ADJ.: alterabile. **-terableness**, S.: attezza ad alterarsi, *f.* **-terably**, ADV.: in modo alterabile. **-terant**, ADJ.: alterante. **-terātion**, S.: alterazione, *f.* **-tercātion**, S.: altercazione; contesa, *f.* **-tĕrnacy**, S.: alternazione, *f.* **-tĕrnate** 1, ADJ.: alternativo, reciproco. **-tĕrnāte** 2, TR.: alternare; avvicendare. **-tĕrnately**, ADV.: a vicenda. **-tĕrnateness**, S.: vicendevolezza, scambievolezza, *f.* **-ternātion**, S.: alternazione, *f.* **-tĕrnative**, ADJ.: alternativo; S.: alternativa, *f.* **-tĕrnatively**, ADV.: alternativamente.

althŏugh, CONJ.: benchè, ancorchè, sebbene.

ăltitude, S.: altitudine, altezza, *f.*

altogĕther, ADV.: affatto, interamente.
ăl-um, S.: allume, *m.* **-lūminous**, ADJ.: alluminoso.
ălways, ADV.: sempre, continuamente.
ăm, PRES. di *be*.
amability, S.: amabilità; piacevolezza, *f.*
amāin, ADV.: vigorosamente; (*nav.*) a tutta forza.
amălga-mate, TR.: amalgamare. **-mā-tion**, S.: amalgamazione, *f.*
amanuĕnsis, S.: amanuense, copista, segretario, *m.*
ămaranth, S.: amaranto, *m.*
amáss, TR.: ammassare, accumulare. **-ment**, S.: ammassamento, *m.*
amatēur, S.: amatore, dilettante, *m.*
ămatory, ADJ.: amatorio.
amāz-e 1, S.: stupore, *m.*, sorpresa, *f.* **-e** 2, TR.: stordire; sorprendere. **-edly**, ADV.: in modo sorprendente. **-edness**, **-ement**, S.: sorpresa, *f.*, stupore, *m.* **-ing**, ADJ.: stupendo, maraviglioso. **-ingly**, ADV.: maravigliosamente.
ămazon, S.: amazzone, *f.*
ambass. = *embass*.
ămber, S.: ambra, *f.*; ADJ.: ambrato, d'ambra. **-coloured**, S.: color d'ambra, *m.* **-gris**, S.: ambracane, *m.*
ambi-dĕxter, S.: ambidestro; furbo, *m.* **-dextĕrity**, S.: dissimulazione, *f.*, furberia. **-dĕxtrous**, ADJ.: ambidestro, doppio.
ămbient, ADJ.: ambiente.
am-bigūity, S.: ambiguità; dubbiezza, *f.* **-biguous**, ADJ.: ambiguo, equivoco. **-biguously**, ADV.: ambiguamente, equivocamente. **-biguousness**, S.: ambiguità, *f.*
ămbit, S.: circuito, *m.*, circonferenza, *f.*
ambi-tion, S.: ambizione, *f.* **-tious**, ADJ.: ambizioso. **-tiously**, ADV.: ambiziosamente. **-tiousness**, S.: ambizione, *f.*
ămbl-e 1, S.: ambio, *m.* **-e** 2, INTR.: andar l'ambio. **-er**, S.: cavallo ambiante, *m.* **-ing**, ADJ.: ambiante: — *pace*, pace, ambio portante. **-ingly**, ADV.: col passo dell'ambio.
ambrō-sia, S.: ambrosia, *f.* **-sial**, ADJ.: d'ambrosia; ambrosio.
ămbsace, S.: ambassi, *m. pl.*
ămbu-late, INTR.: ambulare. **-lātion**, S.: andamento, passeggio lento, *m.* **-latory**, ADJ.: ambulatorio.
am-buscāde, **ăm-bush**, S.: imboscata, *f.*, agguato, inganno, *m.*: *lay in* —, tender un agguato; *lie in* —, stare in agguato, imboscarsi. **-bushed**, ADJ.: imboscato; in agguato.
amēlio-rate, TR.: migliorare. **-rātion**, S.: miglioramento, *m.*
amĕn, ADV.: amen, così sia.
amēnable, ADJ.: risponsabile; tenuto.
amĕnd, TR.: ammendare, correggere, purgare; INTR.: ammendarsi; correggersi, migliorarsi. **-er**, S.: ammendatore, correttore, *m.* **-ment**, S.: ammendamento, *m.*; riforma, *f.* **-s**, S.: ammenda; ricompensa, *f.*: *make* —, ricompensare, rimunerare, risarcire.
amĕnity, S.: amenità; piacevolezza, *f.*
amērce, TR.: imporre una multa. **-able**, ADJ.: soggetto all'ammenda. **-ment**, S.: ammenda, multa, *f.*
ăme-thyst, S.: amatista, *f.* **-thўstine**, ADJ.: dell'amatista.
ămiabl-e, ADJ.: affezionato, affabile, avvenente. **-eness**, S.: affabilità, grazia; benignità, *f.* **-y**, ADV.: amabilmente, benignamente.
ămicabl-e, ADJ.: amichevole, piacevole. **-eness**, S.: benevolenza; cordialità, *f.* **-y**, ADV.: amichevolmente.
ămice, S.: ammitto, *m.*
amid, **-st**, PREP.: fra; nel mezzo.
amiss, ADV.: male; a male, in mala parte: *take* —, aver a male, prendere in mala parte.
amission, S.: perdita, *f.*
ămity, S.: amicizia; concordia, *f.*
ammunition, S.: munizione, *f.* **-bread**, S.: pane di munizione, *m.*
ămnesty, S.: amnistia, *f.*, perdono generale, *m.*
amōmum†, S.: amomo, *m.*
among, **-gst**, PREP.: fra, tra, infra.
ămo-rist, S.: amante, innamorato, *m.* **-rous**, ADJ.: amoroso. **-rously**, ADV.: amorosamente, con amore. **-rousness**, S.: amorevolezza, affezione, *f.*
amŏrphous, ADJ.: amorfo.
amôrt, ADJ.: ammortito, malinconico. **-izātion**, S.: (*law*) estinzione, *f.* **-ize**, TR.: amortizzare, estinguere.
amōtion, S.: rimovimento, *m.*
amount 1, S.: montante, *m.*; somma totale, *f.*: *to the* — *of*, fino alla concorrenza di. **amount** 2, INTR.: montare; arrivare; ascendere; valere.
amōur, S.: intrigo amoroso, *m.*
amōve, TR.: rimuovere.
amphibious, ADJ.: anfibio.
amphibŏlogy, S.: anfibologia, *f*
ămphibrach, S.: anfibraco.
amphictyŏnic, ADJ.: anfizionico. **Amphictyons**, S. PL.: Anfizioni.
amphithē-atre, S.: anfiteatro, *m.* **-ă-trical**, ADJ.: anfiteatrale.
ăm-ple, ADJ.: ampio, largo. **-pleness**, S.: ampiezza; grandezza, *f.* **-plificate**, TR.: amplificare. **-plificātion**, S.: amplificazione, *f.* **-plifier**, S.: amplificatore, *m.* **-plify**, TR.: amplificare; esagerare; INTR.: diffondersi; distendersi

-plitude, S.: amplitudine; ampiezza, *f.* **-ply**, ADV.: ampiamente, largamente, copiosamente.
ămpu-tate, TR.: amputare; troncare. **-tātion**, S.: (*surg.*) amputazione, *f.*; troncamento, *m.*
ămulet, S.: amuleto, *m.*
amūs-e, TR.: trattenere, tenere a bada. **-ement**, S.: trattenimento; passatempo, *m.* **-er**, S.: trastullatore, *m.* **-ive**, ADJ.: dilettevole, sollazzevole.
ăn, ART. = a.
anabáptist, S.: anabattista, *m.*
anăchronism, S.: anacronismo, *m.*
ăna-gram, S.: anagramma, *m.* **-grăm-matist**, S.: anagrammatista, *m.* **-grăm-matize**, INTR.: anagrammatizzare.
ănalects, S. PL.: analetti, *m. pl.*
an-alŏgical, ADJ.: analogico. **-alŏg-ically**, ADV.: analogicamente, per analogia. **-ălogize**, TR.: spiegare per analogia. **-ălogous**, ADJ.: analogo, simile. **-ălogy**, S.: analogia, conformità, *f.*
ăn-alyze = *-yze*. **-ălysis**, S.: analisi, *f.* **-alўtical**, ADJ.: analitico. **-alўt-ically**, ADV.: per via d'analisi. **-alyze**, TR.: analizzare. **-alyzer**, S.: analista; notomista, *m.*
anănas, S.: ananasso, *m.*
ăn-arch, S.: anarchista, *m.* **-ărchi-c(al)**, ADJ.: anarchico, d'anarchia. **-ar-chist**, S.: anarchista, *m.* **-archy**, S.: anarchia, *f.*
anăthe-ma, S.: anatema; scomunica, *f.* **-mătical**, ADJ.: d'anatema. **-mătic-ally**, ADV.: per via d'anatema. **-ma-tize**, TR.: anatemizzare, scomunicare.
an-atŏmical, ADJ.: anatomico. **-atŏm-ically**, ADV.: anatomicamente. **-ăto-mist**, S.: anatomista, notomista, *m.* **-ătomize**, TR.: notomizzare. **-ătomy**, S.: anatomia, notomia.
ănces-tor, S.: antenato; predecessore, *m.* **-tral**, ADJ.: d'antenati, ereditario. **-try**, S.: schiatta; razza, *f.*
ănchor, S.: ancora, *f.*: *cast* —, gettar l'ancora; *lie, ride at* —, essere all'ancora; *weigh* —, sciogliер l'ancora. **an-chor**, INTR.: gettar l'ancora, ancorare. **-age**, S.: ancoramento, *m.*
ănchorite, S.: anacoreta, eremita, *m.*
anchŏvy, S.: acciuga, *f.*
ăncient 1, ADJ.: antico, vecchio: *grow* —, invecchiare. **ancient** 2, S.: bandiera, *f.*; pennoncello, *m.* **-bearer**, S.: portastandardo, *m.* **-ly**, ADV.: anticamente; a' tempi andati. **-ness**, S.: antichità, anzianità, *f.* **-ry**, S.: anzianità, *f.*
ănd, CONJ.: e, ed.
ăndiron, S.: alare, *m.*
ăndrogyne, S.: androgino, ermafrodito, *m.*

ănecdote, S.: aneddoto, *m.*

anew, ADV.: di nuovo, ancora, *m.*
ăngel, S.: angelo, angiolo, *m.*: *guardian* —, angelo custode.

S.: (*bot.*)

ADV.: adiratamente, stizzosamente.
ăn-gle 1, S.: amo (da pigliar pesci): (*geom.*) angolo, *m.* **-gle** 2, TR.: pescare coll'amo; allettare. **-gler**, S.: pescatore coll'amo, *m.* **-rod**, S.: canna da

ăngling, S.: pescare coll'amo, *m.*
ăn-grily, ADV.: con collera, iratamente. **-gry**, ADJ.: irato, collerico: *be* —, essere in collera: *make* —, far adirare; *get* —, adirarsi; — *with*, adirato contro.
ănguish, S.: angoscia, *f.*, affanno, dolore, *m.* **-ed**, ADJ.: angosciato.
ăngu-lar, ADJ.: angolare, angoloso. **-larly**, ADV.: con angoli. **-larness**, S.: forma angolare, *f.* **-lated**, ADJ.: angolato.
angŭst†, ADJ.: angusto, stretto.
anhelātion, S.: anelito, *m.*
anights†, ADV.: di notte, in tempo di notte.
ăn-ileness†, **-ility**, S.: vecchiezza (d'una donna), *f.*
animadvĕr-sion, S.: osservazione, *f.* **-sive**, ADJ.: censurante, critico. **-t**, TR.: osservare, considerare; notare. **-ter**, S.: censore, critico, *m.*
ăni-mal 1, S.: animale, *m.* **-mal** 2, ADJ.: animale. **-mălcule**, S.: animaletto, *m.* **-mălity**, S.: qualità d'un animale, *f.*
ăni-mate, TR.: animare; incoraggiare. **-mate(d)**, ADJ.: animato, brioso. **-mate-ness**, **-mation**, S.: animazione; vivacità, *f.* **-mative**, ADJ.: vivificante. **-mator** S.: animatore, *m.*
ăni-mose, ADJ.: animoso. **-mŏsity**, S.: animosità, *f.*; rancore, *m.*
ănise, S.: anice, *m.*
ănkle, **-bone**, S.: caviglia
ăn-nalist, S.: analista, *m.*
annali, *m. pl.*
annēal, TR.: temperare (il vetro).
an-nĕx, TR.: giungere, unire. **-nexā-tion**, S.: aggiunzione, *f.* **-nexion**, S.: aggiungimento, *m.*; aggiunta, *f.*
annihi-lable, ADJ.: che può annichilarsi. **-late**, TR.: annichilare. **-lātion**, S.: annichilazione; distruzione, *f.*

anniversary, ADJ.: annuale; S.: anniversario, *m*.
ănno-tate, TR.: annotare. **-tātion**, S.: annotazione; osservazione, *f*. **-tātor**, S.: annotatore, *m*.
annŏunce, TR.: annunziare; pubblicare. **-er**, S.: annunziatore, *m*.
annŏy, TR.: annoiare, molestare; infastidire. **-ance**, S.: annoiamento, *m*. **-er**, S.: importuno, *m*.
ănnual, ADJ.: annuale, annuario. **-ly**, ADV.: annualmente, d' anno in anno.
annū-itant, S.: pensionario, *m*. **-ity**, S.: annualità; rendita annuale, *f*.: *settle an — upon any one*, costituire ad alcuno un annuo assegno.
annŭl, TR.: annullare, estinguere.
ănnular, ADJ.: annullare; annulario.
annŭlling, S.: annullazione, *f*.
annūmerate†, TR.: annoverare.
annŭn-ciate†, TR.: annunziare. **-ciātion**, **-ciation-day**, S.: annunziazione, *f*.
ănodyne, ADJ.: (*med*.) anodino.
anŏint, TR.: ungere, unguentare. **-er**, S.: che fa l' unzione. **-ment**, S.: unzione, *f*.
anŏma-lous, ADJ.: anomalo, irregolare. **-lously**, ADV.: irregolarmente. **-ly**, S.: anomalia, irregolarità, *f*.
anŏn, ADV.: adesso adesso, fra poco; subito: *ever and —*, ogni tanto, ad ogni momento.
anŏnymous, ADJ.: anonimo. **-ly**, ADV.: anonimamente.
anŏther, ADJ.: (un) altro; differente: *one —*, l' un l' altro; *one after —*, un dopo l' altro.
ănswer 1, S.: risposta, replica, *f*.: *give —s*, rimbeccare ogni parola. **answer** 2, INTR.: rispondere, replicare; corrispondere; essere mallevadore; (*com*.) soddisfare; — *a question* (*letter*), rispondere ad una domanda (lettera); *I will — for him*, io gli starò mallevadore. **-able**, ADJ.: risponsabile; conforme. **-ableness**, S.: convenenza; conformità, *f*. **-er**, S.: risponditore, *m*.
ănt, S.: formica, *f*.
antăgo-nist, S.: antagonista; rivale, *m*. **-nize**, INTR.: contendere.
antărctic, ADJ.: antartico.
antecē-de, INTR.: andare innanzi. **-dence**, S.: precedenza, priorità, *f*. **-dent**, S.: antecedente, *m*. **-dently**, ADV.: antecedentemente, innanzi.
antecĕssor, S.: antecessore, *m*.
antechămber, S.: anticamera, *f*.
ăntedate, TR.: antidatare.
antedilūvian, ADJ.: antediluviano.
ăntelope, S.: antilope, *f*.
antemeridian, ADJ.: antemeridiano.
antepēnult, S.: antepenultima, *f*.
antēri-or, ADJ.: anteriore, precedente. **-ŏrity**, S.: anteriorità, priorità, *f*.
ănthem, S.: antifona, *f*.; inno, *m*.
ănt-hill, S.: formicaio, *m*.
anthŏlogy, S.: antologia, *f*.
Ănthony's fire, S.: risipola, *f*.
anthropŏlogy, S.: antropologia, *f*.
ăntic 1, ADJ.: lepido; grottesco. **antic** 2, S.: buffone, *m*.
antichristian, ADJ.: anticristiano.
antici-pate, TR.: anticipare, prevenire. **-pātion**, S.: anticipazione, prevenzione, *f*.
ănticly, ADV.: in modo faceto.
ăntidate = *antedate*.
ăntidōte, S.: antidoto, *m*.
antipathy, S.: antipatia, avversione, *f*.
antipodes, S.: antipodi, *m. pl*.
ăn-tiquary, S.: antiquario, *m*. **-tiquate**, TR.: invecchiare, abolire, annullare. **-tique**, S.: anticaglia, *f*. **-tiquity**, S.: antichità, *f*.
antithesis, S.: antitesi, *f*.
ăntitype, S.: figura, *f*., simbolo, *m*.
ăntler, S.: pugnale delle corna del cervo, *m*.
ănvil, S.: incude, incudine, *f*.
anxiety, S.: ansietà, *f*.; affanno, *m*.
ănxious, ADJ.: ansioso. **-ly**, ADV.: ansiosamente, con ansietà. **-ness**, S.: ansietà, sollecitudine, *f*.
ăny, ADJ., PRON.: ogni, ognuno, chiunque; qualunque; del (dello, della, etc., *as a partitive*: e. g. *have you — paper?* avete della carta? *as partitive also untranslated*); ne (e. g. *has he —?* ne ha?): *in — place*, ovunque si sia; — *farther*, più oltre; — *longer*, più lungo tiempo; — *more*, più. **-body**, PRON.: chiunque, ciascuno, qualcuno. **-how**, ADV.: come si voglia; in qualunque modo; tuttavia, nondimeno. **-one**, PRON.: ciascheduno, ognuno; qualcuno. **-thing**, PRON.: qualche cosa; qualunque cosa, ogni cosa. **-way(s)**, ADV.: in qualunque modo. **-where**, ADV.: dovunque: — *else*, altrove. **-whither†**, ADV.: dovunque. **-wise**, ADV.: in qualsiasi (*or* qualunque) modo.
apāce, ADV.: presto, prestamente; forte.
apărt, ADV.: da parte, da canto.
apărtment, S.: appartamento, *m*.
ăpathy, S.: apatia; indolenza, *f*.
āpe 1, S.: scimmia, *f*.: babbuino, *m*. **ape** 2, TR.: scimmiottare, contraffare, imitare.
apēak, **apēek**, ADV.: a picco; perpendicolarmente.
a-pērient, **-pēritive**, ADJ.: (*med*.) aperiente, aperitivo. **-pērt**, ADJ.: aperto. **-pērtly**, ADV.: apertamente. **ă-perture**, S.: apertura, *f*.
apĕtalous, (bot.) apetalo.

ăpex, S.: colmo, *m.*, sommità; cima, *f.*
ăphọ-rĭsm, S.: aforismo, *m.;* massima, *f.* **-rĭstical**, ADJ.: aforistico.
āpiary, S.: arnia, *f.;* alveare, *m.*
apiece, ADV.: a testa, a ciascuno.
āpish, ADJ.: di scimmia; giullaresco: — *trick*, giulleria, *f.* **-ly**, ADV.: da scimmia; buffonescamente. **-ness**, S.: buffoneria; giulleria, *f.*
apŏca-lypse, S.: apocalisse, *f.* **-lўptic(al)**, ADJ.: apocalittico.
apŏcriphal, ADJ.: apocrifo, non autentico.
apọdictic, -al, ADJ.: apodittico.
ăpọgee, S.: apogeo, *m.*
apolọgĕtical, ADJ.: apologetico.
apŏ-lọgist, S.: apologista; difensore. **-lọgise**, INTR.: fare un' apologia, chiedere scusa, scolparsi.
ăpọ-logue, S.: apologo, *m.;* favola morale, *f.* **-lọgy**, S.: apologia, difesa, *f.*
ăpọphthegm, S.: apotegma, *m.*
apọ-plĕctical, ADJ.: apopletico. **ăpọplexy**, S.: apoplessia, *f.*
apŏs-tasy, S.: apostasia, *f.*, rinnegamento, *m.* **-tạte**, S.: apostata, rinnegato, *m.* **-tatise**, INTR.: apostatare.
apŏs-tẹmate, INTR.: impostemire. **ăpos-tẹme**, S.: apostema, postema, *f.*
apŏs-tle, S. appostolo, apostolo, *m.* **-tleship**, S.: appostolato, *m.* **-tŏlical**, ADJ.: appostolico. **-tŏlically**, ADV.: appostolicamente.
apŏs-trọphẹ, S.: apostrofo, *m.;* apostrofe, *f.* **-trọphise**, TR.: apostrofare; indirizzare la parola ad altra persona.
ăpostụme, S.: (*surg.*) apostema, *f.*
apŏthẹcạry, S.: farmacista, speziale, *m.*: —'*s shop*, farmacia, spezeria.
appăll, TR.: stupefare; atterrire; spaventare. **-ment**, S.: stupore; spavento, *m.*
ăppanạge, S.: appanaggio, *m.*
apparātus, S.: apparato; apparecchio, *m.*
appărel 1, S.: addobbamento; vestimento, vestito, *m.* **apparel** 2, TR.: addobbare; vestire.
appărent, ADJ.: apparente, evidente; verosimile, presuntivo: *heir* —, erede presuntivo. **-ly**, ADV.: apparentemente, chiaramente. **-ness**, S.: evidenza, chiarezza, *f.*
ap-parĭtion, S.: apparizione, visione, *f.* **-părĭtọr**, S.: cursore; bidello, *m.*
appēal 1, S.: appellazione; accusa, *f.;* *court of* —, corte d' appello; *lodge an* —, interporre appello. **appeal** 2, INTR.: appellare; accusare. **-ant**†, S.: appellante, *m.*
appēar, INTR.: apparire; comparire; farsi vedere: *it* —*s*, pare, è manifesto; *make* —, far vedere, dimostrare. **-ance**, S.: apparenza; probabilità, *f.*: *at first* —, a prima vista; *personal* —, comparsa personale, *f.*
appēa-sable, ADJ.: placabile. **-sableness**, S.: placabilità; riconciliazione, *f.* **-se**, TR.: pacificare, placare; quietare; mitigare. **-sement**, S.: placamento, *m.* **-sẹr**, S.: pacificatore, intercessore, *m.*
appĕl-lant, S.: appellante, *m.* **-lātion**, S.: appellazione, *f.* **-lative**, S.: (*gram.*) appellativo, *m.* **-latively**, ADV.: a modo d' appellativo. **-lēe**, S.: (*jur.*) accusato, *m.*
appĕnd, TR.: appendere, sospendere. **-age**, **-ant**, S.: accessorio, *m.* **-ix**, S.: appendice; dipendenza, *f.*
appẹrtāin, INTR.: appartenere; convenirsi. **-ment**, S.: privilegio, *m.*
ăppẹ-tence, **-tency**, S.: appetenza; brama, *f.* **-tible**, ADJ.: appetibile, desiderabile. **-tite**, S.: appetito, *m.;* avidità, *f.* **-tition**, S.: appetizione, *f.*
applău-d, TR.: applaudire, approvare. **-der**, S.: applauditore, acclamante, *m.* **-se**, S.: applauso, acclamazione, *f.*
ăpple, S.: pomo, *m.;* mela, *f.*: *the* — *of the eye*, la pupilla dell' occhio; *crab*—, mela selvatica. **-cart**, S.: carretta di pomi, *f.* **-dumpling**, S.: torta di mela, *f.* **-grove**, S.: pometo, *m.* **-harvest**, S.: raccolta delle mele, *f.* **-monger**, S.: venditore di mele, *m.* **-parings**, S. PL.: scorze di mela, *f. pl.* **-sauce**, S.: conserva di pomi, *f.* **-tree**, S.: melo, *m.* **-woman**, S.: donna che vende mele, *f.* **-yard**, S.: pometo, *m.*
appli-able, ADJ.: convenevole, conforme. **-ance**, S.: adattamento, *m.*
ăppli-cable, ADJ.: applicabile; convenevole. **-cableness**, S.: conformità, *f.* **-cably**, ADV.: convenevolmente. **-cātion**, S.: applicazione, *f.*, applicare, *m.;* assiduità, *f.;* ricorso, rifugio, *m.*: *make* — *to one*, aver ricorso ad uno. **-cạtive**, ADJ.: applicabile.
applȳ, TR.: applicare, adattare; ricorrere, rifuggire; REFL.: applicarsi; impiegarsi: (*rail.*) — *the brake*, frenare; — *one's mind to*, applicarsi a.
appŏĭnt, TR.: ordinare; regolare; destinare, assegnare, fissare: — *a day*, fissare un giorno. **-ẹr**, S.: ordinatore, *m.* **-ment**, S.: decreto, mandato; assegnamento; impiego, *m.*: *seek an* —, chiedere un impiego.
appŏrtion, TR.: proporzionare. **-ment**, S.: uguale distribuzione, *f.*
ăppọ-site, ADJ.: adatto, proprio, congruo. **-sitely**, ADV.: propriamente, convenevolmente. **-siteness**, S.: proprietà; acconcezza; convenienza, *f.* **-sĭtion**, S.: apposizione, *f.*

appräi-se, TR.: apprezzare, stimare. **-sement**, S.: estimazione, *f.* **-ser**, S.: apprezzatore, estimatore, *m.* **-sing**, S.: estimazione, *f.*

appré-ciable, ADJ.: apprezzabile, estimabile. **-ciate**, TR.: stimare, valutare, pregiare. **-ciátion**, S.: apprezzamento, *m.*

appre-hénd, TR.: prendere, catturare; intendere, conoscere; temere. **-hénder**, S.: sergente; intenditore, *m.* **-hénsible**, ADJ.: apprensibile; comprensibile. **-hénsion**, S.: cattura; concezione; comprendimento, intelletto, *m.*; paura, *f.*, timore, *m.*: *in my* —, a parer mio; *dull of* —, d'ingegno ottuso. **-hénsive**, ADJ.: apprensivo; pauroso.

appréntice 1, S.: apprendente, fattorino, *m.* **apprentice** 2, TR.: prendere per fattorino. **-ship**, S.: noviziato, tirocinio, garzonaggio, *m.*: *serve one's* —, fare il tironcinio.

apprise, TR.: informare.

appróach 1, S.: avvicinamento; accesso, *m.*; (*mil.*) PL.: approcci. **approach** 2, TR.: avvicinare; approssimare; INTR.: avvicinarsi, accostarsi, approssimarsi. **-able**, ADJ.: accessibile. **-ing**, ADJ.: approssimante, vicino. **-ment**, S.: avvicinamento, accostamento, *m.*

approbátion, S.: approbazione, *f.*

appròpri-ate 1, TR.: appropriare: — *to one's self*, appropriarsi. **appropri-ate** 2, ADJ.: appropriato; convenevole, idoneo. **-átion**, S.: appropriazione, *f.*

appró-vable, ADJ.: approvabile: lodevole. **-val**, S.: approbazione, *f.* **-ve**, TR.: approvare; avere per buono; accettare, ricevere: *I cannot* — *of it*, non posso approvar ciò. **-vement**, S.: approbazione, *f.*; miglioramento, *m.* **-ver**, S.: approvatore, *m.*

appròxi-mate 1, INTR.: approssimarsi, accostarsi. **-mate** 2, ADJ.: prossimo, vicino. **-mátion**, S.: avvicinazione, *f.* **-mative**, ADJ.: approssimativo.

appúrtenance, S.: appartenenza, attenenza, *f.*

ápricot, S.: albicocca, *f.*

April *ā*-, S.: aprile, *m.*: — *fool*, pesce d'aprile, corbellatura.

ápron *or* *purn*, S.: grembiule, *m.*

àpropos, ADV.: a proposito.

àpsis, S.: apside, *f.*

àpt, ADJ.: atto, idoneo, acconcio: *be* — *to learn*, imparare facilmente; *he is* — *to make such mistakes*, egli è molto soggetto a fare simili errori. **-ate**, TR.: adattare. **-itude**, S.: attezza, naturale disposizione, *f.* **-ly**, ADV.: attamente, acconciamente; a proposito. **-ness**, S.: attezza, convenienza; conformità, *f.*

āqua-fortis, S.: acquaforte, *f.* **-vitæ**, S.: acquavite, *f.*

aquàtic, ADJ.: acquatico.

àqueduct, S.: acquidotto; canale, *m.*

āqueous, ADJ.: acquoso.

àquiline, ADJ.: aquilino, d'aquila.

A-rab *ā*-, S.: arabo, *m.* **-rábian**, ADJ.: arabo, di Arabia; S.: arabo, *m.*

àr-able, ADJ.: arabile. **-átion**, S.: aratura, *f.*, aramento, *m.*

àrbalist, S.: balestra, *f.* **-er**, S.: balestriere, *m.*

àr-biter, S.: arbitro; arbitratore, *m.* **-bitrable**, ADJ.: arbitrario. **-bitrage**, **-bitrament**, S.: arbitrio, *m.*; scelta, *f.* **-bitrarily**, ADV.: arbitrariamente. **-bitrariness**, S.: autorità assoluta, *f.* **-bitrary**, ADJ.: arbitrario, assoluto; despotico. **-bitrate**, TR.: arbitrare; giudicare. **-bitrátion**, S.: arbitrato, *m.* **-bitrator**, S.: arbitratore, arbitro, *m.* **-bitrement**, S.: arbitrato; compromesso, *m.* **-bitress**, S.: arbitra, *f.*

àrbour, S.: pergola, *f.*, pergolato, *m.*

àrc, S.: arco; segmento (d'un cerchio), *m.*

arcánum, S.: arcano, segreto, *m.*

àrch 1, S.: volta, *f.*, arco, *m.*; capo, *m.*: *triumphal* —, arco trionfale, *m.* **arch** 2, ADJ.: astuto, mascagno; arci: *look* —, inarcare le ciglia. **arch** 3, TR.: archeggiare.

arch-ángel, S.: arcangelo, *m.* **-bishop**, S.: arcivescovo, *m.* **-bishopric**, S.: arcivescovado, *m.* **-déacon**, S.: arcidiacono, *m.* **-déaconry**, S.: arcidiaconato, *m.* **-dúchess**, S.: arciduchessa, *f.* **-dúke**, S.: arciduca, *m.* **-dúkedom**, S.: arciducato, *m.*

àrched, ADJ.: arcato, curvo.

archeòlogy, S.: archeologia, *f.*

àrcher, S.: arciere, tiratore d'arco, *m.* **-y**, S.: arte di tirare l'arco, *m.*

àrche-type, S.: archetipo, originale, *m.* **-týpal**, ADJ.: d'archetipo.

archiepiscopal, ADJ.: d'arcivescovo.

àrchi-tect, S.: architetto, *m.* **-tectónic**, ADJ.: architettonico. **-téctural**, ADJ.: d'architettura. **-técture**, S.: architettura, *f.*

àrchitrave, S.: (*arch.*) architrave, *m.*

àrchives, S. PL.: archivio, *m.*

àrchly, ADV.: giocosamente.

àrchpriest, S.: arciprete, *m.*

àrchtraitor, S.: gran traditore, traditoraccio, *m.*

àrchwise, ADJ.: in forma d'arco.

Arctic *ărc*-, ADJ.: artico, settentrionale.

àrcu-ate, ADJ.: piegato in arco. **-átion**, S.: curvità, *f.*

àr-dency, S.: ardore; fervore, *m.*; passione, *f.* **-dent**, ADJ.: ardente; appassionato. **-dently**, ADV.: ardentemente;

con passione. **-dentness**, S.: ardore, *m.*; violenza, *f.* **-dour**, S.: ardore; desiderio intenso, *m.* **-duous**, ADJ.: arduo; difficile. **-duousness**, S.: arduità; difficoltà, *f.*
área, S.: area, *f.*; spazio, *m.*
arenáceous, ADJ.: sabbioso.
areómeter, S.: areometro, *m.*
árgil, S.: argilla, argiglia, *f.* **-áceous**, **-lous**, ADJ.: argiglioso.
árgu-e, INTR.: arguire; disputare, contestare; accusare. **-er**, S.: argomentatore, disputatore, *m.* **-ment**, S.: argomento; indizio, *m.*; controversia, *f.* **-mentátion**, S.: argomentazione, *f.* **-méntative**, ADJ.: argomentativo.
argúte†, ADJ.: arguto, pronto; vivace.
ár-id, ADJ.: arido, secco; sterile. **-ídity**, S.: aridezza, aridità, *f.*
áries, S.: (*astr.*) ariete, *m.*
ariétta, S.: arietta; canzonetta, *f.*
aríght, ADV.: dirittamente; precisamente; sanamente: *set* —, aggiustare.
a-ríse, IRR.; INTR.: levarsi; venire, derivare, procedere. **-rísen**, part. del v. *arise*.
aristócracy, S.: aristocrazia, *f.* **arístocrat**, S.: aristocratico, *m.* **-crátical**, ADJ.: aristocratico. **-crátically**, ADV.: in modo aristocratico.
aríth-metic, S.: aritmetica, arimmetica, *f.* **-métical**, ADJ.: arimmetico, d'arimmetica. **-métically**, ADV.: aritmeticamente. **-metícian**, S.: aritmetico, arimmetico, *m.*
árk, S.: arca, *f.*
árm 1, S.: braccio; ramo; potere, *m.* **arm** 2, arme, arma, *f.*: *small* —, bracciolino; *big* —, braccione; *coat of* —*s*, arme; *by force of* —*s*, a forza d'arme; *take up* —*s*, prender l'armi; *lay down* —*s*, metter giù l'armi. **arm** 3, TR.: armare; munire; guernire; INTR.: armarsi; munirsi. **-áda**, S.: armata, *f.* **-ament**, S.: armamento, *m.* **-ature**, S.: armatura, armadura, *f.* **-ed**, ADJ.: armato: dalle braccia. **-chair**, S.: sedia a bracciuoli, *f.* **-ful**, S.: bracciata, *f.*: *by* —*s*, a bracciate. **-hole**, S.: ascella, *f.* **-illary**, ADJ.: (*astr.*) armillare. **-ístice**, S.: armistizio, *m.* **-let**, S.: bracciolino, bracciale, *m.* **-orer**, S.: armaiuolo, *m.* **-our**, S.: armatura, *f.*; armi, *f. pl.* **-pit**, S.: ascella, *f.* **-y**, S.: esercito, *m.*; armata, *f.*: *standing* —, armata permanente.
aró-ma, S.: aroma, *m.* **-mátic(al)**, ADJ.: aromatico, di buon odore. **-mátics**, S. PL.: spezie, *f.*; aromi, *m. pl.* **-matizátion**, S.: aromatizzare, *m.* **-matize**, TR.: aromatizzare; profumare.
aróund, ADV., PREP.: intorno, all' intorno (di).

aróuse, TR.: svegliare; stimolar[e] ...tare.
arów, ADV.: in fila, in ordine.
árque-buse, S.: archibuso, arcob[...] **-busáde**, **-busier**, S.; archibusie[...]
arráign, TR.: assettare; citare [...] dizio, accusare. **-ment**, S.: acc[...] processo, *m.*
arránge, TR.: porre in ordine; [...] stare, assettare. **-ment**, S.: a[...] mento, ordine; assettamento, *m.*
árrant, ADJ.: mero, vero, di prim[...] — *knave*, furbaccio, *m.* **-ly**, ADV[...] versamente, corrottamente.
árras, S.: arrazzo, *m.*
arráy 1, S.: vestito, abito, *m.*; schi[...] *in battle* —, schierato. **array**[...] vestire, abbigliare; schierare.
arréar, S.: debito, *m.*; retrog[...] (d' un esercito), *f.*: *be in* —*s*, resta[...] tore. **-age**, S.: arretrato, *m.*
arrést 1, S.: arresto, *m.*, cattura, *f.* [...] rest 2, TR.: arrestare, catturar[e] *under* —, mettere agli arresti.
arríde, TR.: arridere; ridersi di u[...]
arriere-guard, S.: retroguardia, [...]
arrí-val, S.: arrivo, *m.*, venuta, *f.* [...] INTR.: arrivare; venire; accedere.
árro-gance, **-gancy**, S.: arr[...] presunzione; temerità, *f.* **-gant**, [...] arrogante, presuntuoso. **-gantly**[...] arrogantemente, orgogliosamente. [...] INTR.: presumere; arrogarsi. **-g**[...] S.: pretensione, *f.*
árrow, S.: saetta, freccia, *f.*; da[...] **-shaped**, ADJ.: sagittato. **-y**, A[...] freccia.
árse, S.: culo, deretano, *m.*
ársenal, S.: arsenale, *m.*
ár-senic, S.: arsenico, *m.* **-séni**[...] ADJ.: d' arsenico.
árson, S.: arsione, *f.*; delitto d' i[...] rio, *m.*
árt, S.: arte; professione; indust[...] *the fine* —*s*, le belle arti: *the liber*[...] le arti liberali; *black* —, arte mag[...] *master of* —*s*, maestro d'arti, *m.*
artérial, ADJ.: arteriale, arterios[...]
ártery, S.: arteria, *f.*
ártful, ADJ.: artificioso; abile. [...] ADV.: con arte, maestramente. **-n**[...] maestria, destrezza; astuzia, *f.*
ar-thrític, **-thrítical**, ADJ.: a[...] **-thrítis**, S.: artetica, *f.*
ártichoke, S.: carciofo, *m.*
ár-ticle 1, S.: articolo, *m.*: *defin*[...] articolo determinante; *leading* — [...] colo di fondo. **-ticle** 2, INTR.: sti[...] patteggiare. **-tícular**, ADJ.: arti[...] **-tículate** 1, ADJ.: articolato, di[...] **-ticulate** 2, TR.: articolare; pron[...] distintamente. **-ticulately**, ADV[...]

tintamente. **-ticulātion**, S.: articolazione; giuntura, *f.*
ār-tifice, S.: artificio; astuzia, *f.* **-tificer**, S.: artefice, artista; artigiano, *m.* **-tificial**, ADJ.: artificiale, artificioso. **-tificially**, ADV.: artificialmente, con artificio. **-tificialness**, S.: destrezza, sottigliezza; astuzia, *f.*
artillery, S.: artiglieria, *f.: heavy* —, artiglieria grossa. **-man**, S.: artigliere, *m.*
ār-tisan, S.: artigiano, artefice, *m.* **-tist**, S.: artista, artefice, *m.* **-tistic(al)**, ADJ.: artistico.
ārtless, ADJ.: senz' arte, semplice. **-lessly**, ADV.: senz' arte, naturalmente.
ăs, ADV., CONJ.: mentre, come; così; quale; pressochè; perchè, poichè: — *for*, come per; — *for to*, in quanto a; — *it were*, per così dire; — *often* —, ogni volta che; — *much* —, tanto quanto; — *many* —, tanti quanti, altrettanti; — *much* —, per quanto; — *soon* —, subito che, quanto prima; — *well* —, così, tanto bene che; — *rich* —, così ricco come; — *though*, benchè; sebbene; — *you love me*, se m' amate.
asbĕs-tine, ADJ.: incombustibile. **-tos**, S.: amianto, *m.*
ascĕn-d, IN(TR.): ascendere, montare. **-dant**, ADJ.: superiore, predominante; —, S.: ascendente, *m.;* superiorità, *f.* **-dency**, S.: influenza, *f.*, potere, *m.*, facoltà, *f.* **-sion**, S.: ascensione, *f.*, ascendimento, *m.* **-t**, S.: salita, montata; eminenza; (*rail.*) salita, acclività, *f.: steep* —, salita ripida.
ascertāin, TR.: accertare; verificare; fissare; tassare, apprezzare. **-ment**, S.: accertamento; modello, *m.*
ascĕt-ic, S.: asceta, *m.* **-icism**, S.: asceticismo.
ascribe, TR.: ascrivere, attribuire, imputare.
ăsh, S.: frassino, *m.*
ashāmed, ADJ.: vergognoso, confuso: *be* —, aver vergogna.
ăsh-coloured, ADJ.: cenericcio. **-es**, S. PL.: cenere, *f.*, ceneri, *f. pl.: be reduced to* —, ridursi (andare) in cenere.
ashōre, ADV.: a terra, a riva.
Ash-Wednesday, S.: mercoledì delle ceneri, *m.* **ăshy**, ADJ.: ceneroso; sparso di cenere.
aside, ADV.: a parte, da banda: *go* —, andare in disparte; *take one* —, prendere uno a parte; *lay* —, metter da parte; *stand* —, starsi in disparte.
āsk, TR.: domandare; chiedere: — *advice*, domandar consiglio; — *again*, ridimandare; — *pardon*, domandar perdono.
a-skānce, **-skānt**. ADV.: a traverso; biecamente.
āsker, S.: dimandatore, domandante, *m.*
askēw, ADV.: biecamente, stortamente.
āsking, S.: domanda, *f.*
aslănt, ADV.: obliquamente.
aslēep, ADJ.: addormito, sonnoglioso: *be* —, dormire; *fall* —, addormentarsi.
aslōpe, ADV.: a sghembo, a traverso.
ăsp, S.: tremula, *f.;* aspide, *m.*
aspăragus, S.: asparago, sparagio, *m.*
ăspect, S.: aspetto, *m.;* vista, *f.;* aria; apparenza, presenza, *f.*
ăspen, ADJ.: di tremula; S.: tremula, *f.*
ăs-perate, TR.: render aspro. **-pĕrity**, S.: asprezza, ruvidezza; severità, *f.* **-perous**, ADJ.: aspro; difficile.
aspĕr-se, TR.: aspergere; (*fig.*) diffamare. **-sion**, S.: aspersione; (*fig.*) calunnia, diffamazione, *f.*
ăs-phalt, TR.: asfaltare. **-phăltic**, ADJ.: d' asfalto, bituminoso. **-phăltos**, S.: asfalto, *m.*
ăsphodel, S.: asfodillo, *m.*
ăspic, S.: aspe, aspide, *m.*
ăs-pirate, TR.: aspirare, pronunziare con aspirazione. **-pirātion**, S.: aspirazione; brama, *f.* **-pire**, INTR.: aspirare; bramare. **-pirer**, S.: aspirante, candidato, *m.*
asportātion, S.: asportazione, *f.*
asquint, ADV.: biecamente, di traverso: *look* —, guardar losco.
ăss, S.: asino; minchione, *m.: she*—, asina, *f.;* — *driver*, asinaio, *m.*
assāil, TR.: assalire, attaccare. **-ant**, **-er**, S.: assalitore, aggressore, *m.*
assăssin, S.: assassino, *m.* **-ate**, TR.: assassinare. **-ātion**, S.: assassinamento, *m.* **-ator†**, S.: assassino, *m.*
assāult 1, S.: assalto, *m.;* ingiuria, *f.:* — *and battery*, minaccia e vie di fatto; *take by* —, prender d' assalto. **assault** 2, TR.: assaltare, attaccare. **-er**, S.: assalitore, aggressore, *m.*
assāy 1, S.: prova, *f.;* sperimento, *m.* **assay** 2, TR.: provare; assaggiare; INTR.: tentare; provarsi. **-er**, S.: saggiatore, *m.* **-ing**, S.: saggio, sperimento, *m.*
assectātion, S.: accompagnamento, corteggio, *m.*
assĕm-blage, S.: adunamento; concorso, *m.* **-ble**, TR.: adunare, riunire; INTR.: adunarsi; unirsi. **-bly**, S.: assemblea; adunanza, *f.*
assĕnt 1, S.: assenso; consenso, *m.* **assent** 2, INTR.: assentire, consentire. **-ātion**, S.: compiacenza, adulazione, *f.* **-ator**, S.: assentatore, adulatore, *m.* **-er**, S.: consentore, *m.* **-ment**, S.: assentimento, *m.*
assĕr-t, TR.: asserire; mantenere, sostenere. **-tion**, S.: asserzione, *f.* **-tive**, ADJ.: assertivo, affermativo. **-tor**, S.: assertore; protettore, *m.*

assĕss, TR.: tassare. **-ment**, S.: tassare, *m.*; tassa; tassazione, *f.* **-or**, S.: assessore; tassatore, *m.*

assĕts, S. PL.: (*jur.*) beni sufficienti, *m. pl.*

asseverātion, S.: asseveranza; affermazione, *f.*

as-sidūity, S.: assiduità, diligenza, *f.* **-sĭduous**, ADJ.: assiduo, diligente. **-sĭduously**, ADV.: assiduamente; continuamente. **-sĭduousness**, S.: assiduità, *f.*

assiege, TR.: assediare.

as-sign, TR.: assegnare, commettere, delegare; addurre: — *a reason*, addurre una ragione. **-signable**, ADJ.: che può assegnarsi. **-signātion**, S.: assegnazione, *f.*; appuntamento, *m.* **-signēe**, S.: deputato; sostituto, *m.* **-signer**, S.: costituitore, *m.* **-signment**, S.: consegnazione; cessione, *f.*; deposito, *m.* **-signs**, S. PL.: esecutori testamentari, *m. pl.*

assimil-ate, TR.: assimigliare; comparare. **-ātion**, S.: assimigliamento, paragone, *m.*

assist, TR.: assistere, soccorrere, aiutare. **-ance**, S.: assistenza, *f.*; soccorso, aiuto, *m.*: *signal for* —, segnale d'angustia. **-ant**, S.: assistente, aiutatore, *m.*

assize 1, S.: sessione di giudici; assisa; tariffa, *f.*: *court of* —, corte d'assise.

assize 2, TR.: tassare; regolare.

assō-ciate 1, S.: associato; compagno, *m.* **-ciate** 2, TR.: associare; accompagnare; praticare. **-ciātion**, S.: associazione, unione; società; taglia, *f.*

assöil†, TR.: assolvere; perdonare.

ăssonance, S.: assonanza, *f.*

assôrt, TR.: assortire; classare. **-ment**, S.: assortimento, sortimento, *m.*

as-suāge, TR.: alleviare; mitigare; placare, pacificare; INTR.: alleviarsi, mitigarsi. **-suāgement**, S.: addolcimento; conforto, *m.* **-suāger**, S.: mitigatore, pacificatore, *m.* **-suāsive**, ADJ.: mitigativo, lenitivo. **-suefăction**, S.: assuefazione, accostumanza, *f.*

assūm-e, TR.: assumere, prendere; presumere, arrogarsi. **-er**, S.: arrogante, *m.* **-ing**, ADJ.: presuntuoso.

assŭmp-sit, S.: (*leg.*) promessa verbale, *f.* **-tion**, S.: assunzione, arroganza, *f.* **-tive**, ADJ.: che può assumersi. **-tively**, ADV.: assuntivamente.

as-sūrance, S.: assicurazione; sicurezza; fidanza; costanza, *f.* **-sūre**, TR.: assicurare; asserire, affermare. **-sūred**, ADJ.: sicuro, certo: *rest* —, esser sicuro. **-sūredly**, ADV.: sicuramente, certamente. **-sūrer**, S.: assicuratore; mallevadore, *m.*

ăster-isk, S.: asterisco, *m.* **-ism**, S.: (*astr.*) costellazione, *f.*

astĕrn, ADV.: per la poppa, in poppa.

ăsth-ma, S.: asma, asima, *f.* **-mătic**, ADJ.: asmatico.

as-tŏnish, TR.: stupire; stordire. **-tŏnishment**, S.: stupore, *m.*, sopresa, *f.*: *strike with* —, far stupore; *fill with* —, colmare di stupore. **-tŏund**, TR.: costernare, stordire.

astrăddle, ADV.: a cavalcioni.

ăstral, ADJ.: astrale, degli astri.

astrāy, ADV.: fuor di via: *go* —, smarrirsi; errare; *lead* —, sviare, deviare.

astric-t, TR.: contrarre; ristringere. **-tion**, S.: astringimento, *m.* **-tive**, ADJ.: astringente, costrettivo.

astrīde, ADV.: a cavalcioni.

astring-e, TR.: astringere; contrarre. **-ency**, S.: astringenza. **-ent**, ADJ.: astringente.

as-trŏloger, S.: astrologo, *m.* **-trolŏgical**, ADJ.: astrologico. **-trŏlogy**, S.: astrologia, *f.* **-trŏnomer**, S.: astronomo, *m.* **-tronŏmical**, ADJ.: astronomico. **-tronŏmically**, ADV.: in modo astronomico, da astronomo. **-trŏnomy**, S.: astronomia, *f.*

astŭn, TR.: stordire, stupefare.

asŭnder, ADV.: separatamente; in due parti: *cut* —, tagliar per mezzo; *put* —, dividere, separare.

asȳlum, S.: asilo; rifugio, *m.*

ăt, PREP.: a, ad; da; in; per; al, alla, agli, alle: — *first*, alla prima; — *hand*, vicino, appresso; — *home*, a casa; — *last*, in fine, finalmente; — *least*, per lo meno, almeno; — *leisure*, a bell'agio; — *most*, al più; — *once*, subito, alla prima; — *odds*, male insieme; — *least*, almeno; — *peace*, in pace; — *present*, per adesso; — *sea*, sul mare, per mare; — *school*, alla scuola; — *the*, al, ecc.; — *a word*, in una parola.

ā-theism, S.: ateismo, *m.* **-theist**, S.: ateista, ateo, *m.* **-theistical**, ADJ.: ateistico.

athirst, ADJ.: assetato, sitibondo; ADV.: sitibondamente.

ăth-lete, S.: atleta, *m.* **-lĕtic**, ADJ.: atletico, vigoroso.

athwârt, ADV., PREP.: a traverso, a sghembo.

atilt, ADV.: con botta.

ătlas, S.: atlante, *m.*

ătmos-phere, S.: atmosfera, *f.* **-phĕrical**, ADJ.: dell'atmosfera.

ăt-om, S.: atomo, *m.* **-ŏmical**, ADJ.: consistente d'atomi.

atōne, TR.: espiare; purgare; INTR.: convenire; concordare. **-ment**, S.: espiazione, *f.*; placamento, *m.*

ătony, s.: (*med.*) atonia, *f.*
atŏp, ADV.: in alto; sulla sommità.
atrabilărian, ADJ.: atrabiliare, malinconico.
atrōcious, ADJ.: atroce, orribile, enorme. **-ly**, ADV.: atrocemente; fieramente. **-ness**, **atrŏcity**, s.: atrocità; enormità; scelleratezza, *f.*
ătrophy, s.: atrofia, consunzione, *f.*
attăch, TR.: arrestare, catturare; guadagnare, sequestrare; affezionare: *he is —ed to you*, vi è affezionato. **-ment**, s.: aderenza, *f.*, affetto; sequestro, *m.*
attăck 1, s.: attacco, assalimento, *m.*
attack 2, TR.: attaccare, assalire. **-er**, s.: assalitore, assaltatore, *m.*
attāin, TR.: ottenere, conseguire, acquistare; INTR.: arrivare; pervenire: *— to honours*, pervenire agli onori. **-able**, ADJ.: acquistabile. **-der**, s.: convinzione, *f.* **-ment**, s.: acquisto, acquistamento, *m.* **-t**, TR.: macchiare; corrompere; disonorare; infettare; accusare. **-ted**, ADJ.: corrotto; disonorato; accusato. **-ture**, s.: imputazione, *f.*
attĕmper, TR.: temperare; calmare.
attĕmpt 1, s.: tentativa, *f.*; sperimento, *m.* **attempt** 2, TR.: tentare; provare, esperimentare; intraprendere. **-able**, ADJ.: che può tentarsi. **-er**, s.: tentatore; sperimentatore, *m.*
attĕnd, TR.: accompagnare; essere presente; INTR.: stare attento, attendere; osservare; badare: *— a business*, dar opera ad un affare; *— a patient*, aver cura di un malato. **-ance**, s.: servizio; assiduità; cura, *f.*; corteggio, *m.*: *dance —*, fare spalliera; *be in —*, essere di servizio. **-ant**, s.: servidore; seguace, *m.* **-er**, s.: compagno, socio, *m.*
attĕntate, s.: tentativa, *f.*
attĕntion, s.: attenzione, *f.*: *give —, pay —*, far attenzione; *pay —s to*, usare attenzioni a. **-tive**, ADJ.: attento, ufficioso. **-tively**, ADV.: attentamente, con cura. **-tiveness**, s.: attendimento assiduo, *m.*
attĕnu-ant, ADJ.: attenuante. **-ate** 1, TR.: attenuare, affievolire; diminuire. **-ate** 2, ADJ.: attenuato, affievolito. **-ăting**, ADJ.: attenuante. **-ātion**, s.: attenuazione; diminuzione, *f.*
attĕst, TR.: attestare, certificare. **-ātion**, s.: attestazione, testimonianza, *f.*
At-ticism *ăt-*, s.: atticismo, *m.*; eleganza, *f.* **-tic**, ADJ.: elegante; delicato.
attīre 1, s.: abbigliamento, *m.*; corna del cervo, *f. pl.* **attire** 2, TR.: abbigliare, acconciare; abbellire, ornare.
ăttitude, s.: attitudine, *f.*
attŏrn-ey, s.: notaio, procuratore, *m.*: *— general*, procuratore generale; *— at law*, causidico, patrocinatore, *m.* **-eyship**, s.: ufficio di procuratore, *m.* **-ment**, s.: cessione, cedizione, *f.*
attrăc-t, TR.: attrarre; allettare. **-tion**, s.: attrazione, *f.*; allettamento, *m.* **-tive**, ADJ.: attrattivo. **-tively**, ADV.: per attrazione. **-tiveness**, s.: attraimento, *m.* **-tor**, s.: agente, *m.*; forza attrattiva, *f.*
ăt-tribute 1, s.: attributo, *m.*; proprietà, *f.* **-tribute**, TR.: attribuire, imputare, ascrivere. **-tribūtion**, s.: attribuzione; commendazione, *f.*
attrition, s.: attrizione, *f.*; tritamento, *m.*
attūne, TR.: render armonioso, accordare.
atwēen† = *between*.
atwixt† = *betwixt*.
ăuburn, ADJ.: bruno.
ăuction, s.: incanto, *m.*: *sale at —*, vendita all'incanto (*or* all'asta). **-eer**, s.: venditore all'incanto, *m.*
audācious, ADJ.: audace, temerario; presuntuoso. **-ly**, ADV.: audacemente; arditamente. **-ness**, **audăcity**, s.: audacia; baldanza, arditezza, *f.*
ăudibl-e, ADJ.: udibile; alto, sonoro. **-y**, ADV.: ad alta voce.
ăudience, s.: udienza, *f.*; uditorio, *m.*; *— chamber*, camera d'udienza, *f.*
ăudit 1, s.: esame d'un conto, *m.*
audit 2, TR.: esaminare conti. **-or**, s.: uditore, *m.* **-ory**, ADJ.: auditorio; acustico (*nerve, etc.*); s.: uditorio, auditorio, *m.*; udienza, *f.*
ăuger, s.: succhiello, *m.*
ăught, PRON.: checchessia, qualche cosa: *for — I know*, per quanto io sappia.
aug-mĕnt, TR.: aumentare; accrescere; INTR.: aumentarsi. **-'ment**, **-mentā-tion**, s.: aumento, incremento; accrescimento, *m.* **-mĕntative**, ADJ.: aumentativo.
ău-gur 1, s.: auguratore, *m.* **-gur** 2, **-gurate**, INTR.: augurare; conghietturare. **-gurātion**, s.: augurio, *m.*; conghiettura, *f.* **-gūrial**, ADJ.: augurale. **-gurize**, TR.: indovinare. **-gurous**, ADJ.: auguroso, profetante. **-gury**, s.: augurio, presagio, *m.*
Au-gust *ā'-*, s.: (*month*) agosto, *m.* **-gŭst**, ADJ.: augusto, nobile. **-gŭstan**, ADJ.: d'Augusto: *the — age*, il secolo d'Augusto. **-gŭstness**, s.: maestà, dignità, *f.*
ăulic, ADJ.: aulico.
ăunt, s.: zia, *f.*
aurēlia, s.: aurelia; crisalide, *f.*
ău-ricle, s.: auricola; orecchietta, *f.* **-ricula**, s.: cortusa; orecchia d'orso, *f.* **-ricular**, ADJ.: auricolare. **-ricularly**, ADV.: all'orecchio, segretamente.

aurĭferous, ADJ.: che produce oro.
aurōra, S.: aurora, *f.*: — *borealis*, aurora boreale, *f.*
auscultātion, S.: auscultazione, *f.*
âu-spice, S.: auspicio, *m.*; grazia, *f.* **-picious**, ADJ.: favorevole; fausto. **-piciously**, ADV.: favorevolmente. **-piciousness**, S.: prosperità; buona fortuna, felicità, *f.*
aus-tēre, ADJ.: austero, rigido; severo. **-tērely**, ADV.: austeramente; severamente. **-tēreness**, S.: asprezza, *f.*, rigore, *m.*, severità, *f.* **-tĕrity**, S.: austerità; mortificazione, *f.*
Austin-friar â-, S.: Agostiniano frate, *m.* **-nun**, S.: Agostiniana monaca, sorore, *f.*
âustral, ADJ.: australe, meridionale.
authĕn-tic(al), ADJ.: autentico, valido. **-tically**, ADV.: autenticamente. **-ticate**, TR.: autenticare; convalidare. **-ticity**, **-ticness**, S.: autenticità, *f.*
âuthor, S.: autore; inventore, *m.* **-thŏritative**, ADJ.: autorevole, d'autorità. **-thŏritatively**, ADV.: in maniera autorevole, con autorità. **-thŏrity**, S.: autorità; stima, *f.*; credito, *m.*: *established* —, autorità constituite; *be an* —, fare autorità; *have* —, esser autorizzato, aver autorità; *have from good* —, aver da buona fonte. **-thorization**, S.: autorizzazione, *f.* **-thorize**, TR.: autorizzare, dare autorità. **-thorless**, ADJ.: senza autore. **-thorship**, S.: qualità d'esser autore, *f.*
âu-tograph, S.: autografo, *m.* **-tŏgraphy**, S.: autografia, *f.* **-tŏmaton**, S.: automato, *m.* **-tomŏbile**, S.: automobile, *m.*
âu-tumn, S.: autunno, *m.* **-tŭmnal**, ADJ.: autunnale, d'autunno.
auxiliar(y), ADJ.: ausiliario.
avāil, S.: profitto, avantaggio, *m.* **avail**, TR., INTR.: giovare; valere; servire; esser profittevole: *what —s it?* a che serve? — *one's self of the opportunity*, valgersi (*or* profitare), dell' occasione. **-able**, ADJ.: utile; giovevole. **-ableness**, S.: vantaggio, *m.* **-ment**, S.: utilità, *f.*; profitto, giovamento, *m.*
avāle, INTR.: scendere abbasso.
avânt-guârd, S.: vanguardia, *f.*
ăva-rice, S.: avarizia, cupidità, *f.*: *from* —, per avarizia. **-ricious**, ADJ.: avaro, cupido. **-riciously**, ADV.: avaramente, cupidamente. **-riciousness**, S.: avarizia, spilorceria, *f.*
avâst, INTERJ.: basta! fermate!
avâunt, INTERJ.: via! indietro!
avĕng-e, TR.: vendicare. **-er**, S.: vendicatore, *m.* **-eress**, S.: vendicatrice, *f.* **-ing**, ADJ.: vendicatore, ultore; S.: vendetta, vendicanza, *f.*

ăvenue, S.: passaggio; viale d' alberi, *m.*
avēr, TR.: avverare, verificare.
ăverage, S.: averia; tributo; ragguaglio, *m.*; ADJ.: medio: *the — price*, il prezzo medio.
avērment, S.: avveramento, certificamento, *m.*
averrŭnc-ate†, TR.: sradicare, estirpare. **-ātion†**, S.: sradicamento, *m.*
avĕr-se, ADJ.: repugnante; contrario: *be* —, aborrire. **-sely**, ADV.: repugnantemente, malvolentieri. **-seness**, **-sion**, S.: avversione, repugnanza; antipatia, *f.* **-t**, TR.: avvertere; allontanare.
āviary, S.: uccelliera; gabbia, *f.*
avidity, S.: avidità; cupidigia, *f.*
ăvoc-ate, TR.: chiamare fuori. **-ātion**, S.: impiego, *m.*; faccenda, *f.*
avŏid, TR.: evitare, schivare; sfuggire, INTR.: essere vacante. **-able**, ADJ.: evitabile. **-ance**, S.: evitazione; vacanza, *f.*; scampo, *m.* **-er**, S.: evitatore, *m.* **-less**, ADJ.: inevitabile.
avoirdupŏis, S.: peso di sedici once per libbra, *m.*
avolātion†, S.: volata, *f.*; volo, *m.*
avŏuch, TR.: affermare; mantenere; asseverare. **-able**, ADJ.: che può affermarsi. **-er**, S.: affermatore, *m.* **-ment**, S.: dichiarazione, *f.*
avŏw, TR.: confessare. **-able**, ADJ.: che può confessarsi. **-al**, S.: confessione, dichiarazione; giustificazione, *f.* **-ed**, ADJ.: manifesto, pubblico. **-edly**, ADV.: apertamente, schiettamente. **-ée**, S.: padrone, *m.* **-er**, S.: millantatore; difenditore, *m.* **-ry**, S.: giustificazione; difesa, *f.* **-sal**, S.: confessione; dichiarazione; affermazione, *f.*
awāit, S.: aguato, *m.*; insidia, *f.* **await**, TR.: aspettare.
awāke 1, IRR.; TR.: svegliare; ravvivare; —, INTR.: svegliarsi, destarsi. **awake** 2, ADJ.: svegliato, destato. **-n**, INTR.: svegliarsi, riscuotersi dalla letargia.
awârd 1, S.: giudicio, *m.*; sentenza, *f.* **award** 2, TR.: aggiudicare, sentenziare; determinare.
awâre 1, ADJ.: avveduto, avvertito: *be* —, presentire; *I am — of it*, ne sono avvertito; lo so; *be — of one*, guardarsi da uno; *be — of a thing*, andar cauto; *before he (she, they) was* —, all' improvvista. **aware** 2, INTR.: guardarsi, essere avveduto.
awāy, ADV.: via: *go* —, andar via; *run* —, fuggirsene; *send* —, mandar via; *get away!* andate via! via!
âwe 1, S.: tema; riverenza, *f.*, rispetto, *m.*: *keep in* —, tenere a segno; *stand in* —, paventare, rispettare. **awe** 2, TR.: tenere in timore, inspirare tema.

a-wĕathẹr, ADV.: (*nav.*) al vento.
âwful, ADJ.: terribile; maestoso. **-ly,** ADV.: in modo terribile. **-ness,** S.: terribilità; grandezza, *f.*
awhile, ADV.: qualche tempo, alquanto: — *ago*, qualche tempo fù.
âwkwẹrd, ADJ.: goffo, sgraziato. **-ly,** ADV.: goffamente, sgraziatamente. **-ness,** S.: goffaggine, sgraziataggine, *f.*
âwl, S.: lesina, *f.*
âwless, ADJ.: sfrontato; senza rispetto.
âwl-maker, S.: facitore di lesine, *m.*
âwning, S.: tenda, *f.*; padiglione, *m.*
a-wõrk(ing), ADV.: in opera, in azione.
awrỹ, ADJ.: storto, sconvolto, distorto; ADV.: di traverso, obliquamente: *go* —, camminare storto.
âxe, S.: accetta, scure, *f.*
axillary, ADJ.: dell' ascella.
âxiọm, S.: assioma, *m.*; sentenza, *f.*
âxis, S.: asse, *f.*
âxlepin, S.: caviglia della ruota, *f.* **-tree,** S.: asse, sala, *f.*
ây, ADV.: sì; INTERJ.: ohimè! infelice me! **ây**(*e*), ADV.: sì.
âye, ADV.: sempre, per sempre.
âyry†, S.: nido d' aquila, *m.*
âzimuth, S.: azzimutto, *m.*
âzụre, S.: azzurro, *m.*; ADJ.: azzurro, turchino.

B

b *bē* (*the letter*), S.: b, *m.*
bâa, S.: belar, belato, *m.* **baa,** INTR.: belare (come una pecora).
băb-ble 1, S.: ciarla, cicaleria, *f.*, cicalamento, *m.* **-ble** 2, INTR.: ciarlare, cicalare, parlar troppo. **-blement,** S.: parole vane, *f. pl.* **-blẹr,** S.: ciarlone, cicalone, *m.*; cicaliera, berlinghiera, *f.* **-bling,** S.: ciarla, *f.*, cicalamento, cicaleccio, *m.*
bâb-e, S.: bambino, bambolino, *m.* **-ish,** ADJ.: bambinesco, di bambino.
babŏon, S.: babbuino, *m.*
bâby, S.: bambino, fantolino, fantoccio, *m.*: — *things*, bambocceria, fantocceria, baggatella, *f.*
băccạted, ADJ.: bacchifero; ornato di perle.
bac-chanălian, S.: briacone; bevone, *m.* **băc-chanalṣ,** S. PL.: baccanali, *f. pl.*
baccifẹrous, ADJ.: baccifero.
băchẹlọr, S.: baccelliere; celibe, *m.* **-ship,** S.: baccelleria, *f.*; celibato, *m.*
băck 1, ADV.: dietro, indietro; di nuovo: *go* —, andare in dietro; *keep* —, ritenere; *send* —, rimandare; *I shall be — directly*, valo e vengo; *a few years* —, alcuni anni fa. **back** 2, S.: *dorso, dosso, m.*; schiena, *f.*: *break one's* —, romper la schiena ad uno, spiantar uno; *turn one's* —, prender la fuga, fuggire; *turn one's — on one*, volger le spalle ad uno. **back** 3, TR.: montare (a cavallo); secondare: (*nav.*) — *the sails*, metter le vele al vento. **-bite,** TR.: calunniare, diffamare. **-biter,** S.: calunniatore, maledicente, *m.* **-blow,** S.: rovescione, *m.* **-board,** S.: dossiere d' una lancia, *m.* **-bone,** S.: spina, *f.*: *to the* —, fino al midollo delle ossa. **-door,** S.: porta di dietro, *f.*; sotterfugio, *m.* **-friend,** S.: amico falso, *m.*, amica falsa, *f.* **-gămmọn,** S.: tavoliere, *m.* **-house,** S.: parte deretana d' una casa; ritirata, *f.*; luogo commodo, *m.* **-room,** S.: camera di dietro, *f.* **-shop,** S.: bottega di dietro, *f.* **-side,** S.: deretano; riverso, *m.* **-slide,** INTR.: tergiversare. **-slider,** S.: apostata, *m.* **-sliding,** S.: tergiversazione, *f.* **-stairs,** S.: scala segreta, *f.* **-sword,** S.: sciabla, sciabola, *f.* **-wẹrd,** ADJ.: addietro, rimasto, restio, tardivo, tardo; ADV.: indietro, di dietro, addietro; *go* —, indietreggiare, rinculare. **-wẹrdly,** ADV.: con repugnanza, mal volentieri. **-wẹrdness,** S.: tardità, tardezza, repugnanza, *f.* **-wẹrdṣ,** ADV.: di dietro, indietro. **-yard,** S.: cortile di dietro, *m.*
bâcon, S.: lardone, lardo, *m.*: *ham of* —, giambone; *save one's* —, uscire salvo d' un affare.
băd, ADJ.: cattivo, vizioso, dannoso; male (*sick*).
bădge 1, S.: segno; indizio, *m.*; divisa; scialuppa, *f.* **badge** 2, TR.: segnare, marcare, mettere un segno.
bădgẹr, S.: tasso; incettatore; rivenditore, *m.*
băd-ly, ADV.: male, malamente. **-ness,** S.: cattiva qualità, *f.*; difetto, *m.*
băf-fle 1, S.: inganno, *m.*; frode, *f.* **-fle** 2, TR.: eludere; frustrare, schernire; rovinare. **-flẹr,** S.: ingannatore, furbo, *m.*
băg 1, S.: sacco, sacchetto, *m.*; borsa, *f.*: *truss up — and baggage*, levar le tende. **bag** 2, TR.: insaccare, mettere in sacco. **-atĕlle,** S.: bagattella; chiappola, *f.* **-gạge,** S.: bagaglio, *m.*; bagascia, *f.*; (*rail.*) roba di passaggiere, *f.*
băgnio, S.: bagno, *m.*; stufa, *f.*; bordello, *m.* **-keeper,** S.: stufaiuolo, *m.*
băgpi-pe, S.: cornamusa; piva, *f.* **-pẹr,** S.: suonatore di cornamusa, *m.*
bāil 1, S.: sicurtà, *f.*; mallevad- *give* —, dar mallevadoria; *be* stare mallevadore. **bail** 2, TR vare; dare sicurtà. **-able,** AD può mallevare. **-ee,** S.: colui fidate delle merci. **-iff,** S.: be gente; fattore, *m.*: —'*s fellows*.

(d' un messo), *m.* **-iwick**, S.: baliaggio; giuridizione d' un podestà, *f.*
bâit 1, S.: esca, *f.*; inganno, allettamento, *m.* **bait** 2, TR.: adescare, allettare, lusingare; INTR.: battere le ali: — *a hook*, adescare, mettere l' esca all' amo. **-ing**, S.: esca, *f.* **-place**, S.: osteria, *f.*, albergo, *m.*: *bull* —, combattimento di tori, *m.*
bā-ke, IRR.; TR.: cuocere al forno; fare il pane; INTR.: cuocersi. **-ke-house**, S.: bottega di fornaio, *f.* **-ker**, S.: fornaio, panattiere, *m.*: *—'s trade*, mestiere del fornaio, *m.* **-ery**, S.: panatteria; bottega di fornaio, *m.* **-king**, S.: cocitura; fornata, *f.* **-pan**, S.: tegghia, teglia, *f.*
bálan-ce 1, S.: bilancia, *f.*; contrappeso; bilancio; equilibrio: — *of an account*, bilancio d' un conto; *strike a* —, stabilire un bilancio, bilanciare; *turn the* —, dare il tracollo alla bilancia. **-ce** 2, TR.: bilanciare; contrappesare, aggiustare; esaminare; INTR.: esitare, fluttuare. **-cer**, S.: quello che pesa. **-beam**, S.: bilanciere, *m.* **-sheet**, S.: bilancio, *m.*
bálcony, S.: balcone, *m.*; (*nav.*) galleria, *f.*
bâld, ADJ.: calvo; spelato; usato.
báldachin, S.: baldacchino, *m.*
bâlderdash 1, S.: mescuglio; anfanamento, cialeccio, *m.* **balderdash** 2, TR.: mescolare, adulterare.
bâldly, ADV.: nudamente; senz' ornamento.
bâldmony, S.: (*bot.*) genziana, *f.*
bâld-ness, S.: calvezza, calvizie, *f.* **-pated**, ADJ.: calvo. **-rib**, S.: costa di porco, *f.*
bâldric, S.: cintura, *f.*, pendaglio: zodiaco, *m.*
bâle 1, S.: balla, *f.*; fascio; mazzo, *m.*: *make up into a* —, imballare. **bale** 2, TR.: imballare. **-ful**, ADJ.: triste, lamentevole; infausto. **-fully**, ADV.: in modo lamentevole; infaustamente.
bâlk 1, S.: trave, *f.*; solco; contrattempo, *m.*; mancanza, *f.*; danno, pregiudizio, *m.* **balk** 2, TR.: tralasciare, omettere; frustrare; mancare di parola.
bâll 1, S.: palla, *f.*; globo, *m.*; (*bill.*) biglia, *f.* **ball** 2, (*danc.*) ballo, *m.*
bâllad, S.: ballata: canzone, *f.* **-singer**, S.: cantatore di canzoni, *m.*
bâllast 1, S.: (*nav.*) zavorra, savorra, stiva, *f.* **ballast** 2, TR.: (*nav.*) zavorrare, stivare.
bâllet, S.: balletto, *m.*
ballōon, S.: pallone, *m.*
bâllot, S.: voto, suffragio, *m.* **ballot**, INTR.: ballottare; dare la sua voce. **-box**, S.: urna dello squittinio, bossolo dello scrutinio. **-ing**, S.: ballottare, *m.*, ballottazione, *f.*
bâlm, S.: balsamo (*fig.*) addolcimento, *m.* **balm**, TR.: imbalsamare, (*fig.*) addolcire. **-tree**, S.: balsamino, *m.* **-y**, ADJ.: balsamico; lenitivo.
bâlneary, S.: luogo da bagnarsi, *m.*
bâl-sam, S.: balsamo, balsimo, *m.* **-sâmic**, **-sâmical**, ADJ.: balsamico; lenitivo.
bálustrade, S.: balaustrata; colonnata, *f.*
bambōo, S.: canna nodosa (d' India), *f.*
bambōo-zle, TR.: minchionare, ingannare. **-zler**, S.: ingannatore, *m.*
băn, S.: bando, *m.*, proclama; scomunica, *f.*; *put under the* —, mettere al bando. **ban**, TR.: maledire; scommunicare.
bănd, S.: vincolo; legame, *m.*; banda, compagnia, truppa, *f.*; *by* —*s*, in truppa. **band**, TR.: legare; fasciare; radunare. **-age**, S.: fascia, *f.*; vincolo; legame, legaccio, *m.*; *head* —, frontale. **-box**, S.: scatola per biancherie, *f.* **-elet**, S.: (*arch.*) listello, *m.*
băndit, **banditto**, S.: bandito; proscritto, ladrone, *m.*
băndog, S.: mastino, *m.*
bandolēer, S.: bandoliera, *f.*; cartoccio, *m.*
băndrol, S.: banderuola, *f.*
băndy 1, S.: mestola, *f.*; bastone curvo, *m.* **bandy** 2, ADJ.: torto, storto, curvo. **bandy** 3, TR.: ballottare; palleggiare; scuotere; discutere; trattare; cospirare. **-legged**, ADJ.: dalle gambe torte.
băne 1, S.: veleno, *m.*; rovina, *f.*: *rat's* —, arsenico, *m.* **bane** 2, TR.: avvelenare; corrompere. **-ful**, ADJ.: velenoso; pernizioso, destruttivo. **-wort**, S.: solano, *m.*
băng 1, S.: colpo, *m.*; percossa, *f.* **bang** 2, TR.: battere, tambussare.
bănian, S.: vesta da camera, *f.*
bănish, TR.: bandire, esiliare; discacciare. **-er**, S.: che manda in esilio, *m.* **-ment**, S.: esilio; sbandimento, *m.*
bănk 1, S.: sponda, riva, *f.*; lido; scoglio; *m.*; (*com.*) banco *or* (*on a larger scale*) banca: — *of England*, banca d' Inghilterra; *national* —, banca nazionale; *joint-stock* —, banca per azioni, *f.*; *keep the* —, far banco. **bank** 2, TR.: arginare; danari nel banco. **-bill**, S.: banco, *m.* **-er**, S.: banchiere, *m.* **-ing**, S: occupazione di *f.* **-ing-house**, S.: casa b **-ing-company**, S.: società **-note** = *bankbill*. **-rupt**, S. fallito, *m.*; *be a* —, *turn* —, fallimento. **-ruptcy**, S.: falli
bănner, S.: bandiera, *f.*, sten **-et**, S.: cavaliere banderese, *m.*
bănnian, S.: vesta di camera, *f.*

bănnock, S.: focaccia d' avena, schiacciata, *f.*
bănquet 1, S.: banchetto; convito, *m.* **banquet** 2, INTR.: banchettare, fare banchetti. **-er**, S.: che banchetta, convitatore, *m.* **-hall**, S.: aula del banchetto, *f.* **-ing-house**, S.: casa da banchettare, *f.*
bănter 1, S.: burla, beffa, *f.*, scherno, *m.* **banter** 2, TR.: burlare, beffare, soiare. **-er**, S.: beffatore, schernitore, *m.*
băntling, S.: bambino, bambolino, *m.*
băp-tism, S.: battesimo, *m.* **-tismal**, ADJ.: battesimale, di battesimo. **-tist**, S.: battezzatore, battezziere, *m.* **-tist(e)ry**, S.: battistero, fonte battesimale, *m.* **-tise**, TR.: battezzare. **-tiser**, S.: battezzatore, *m.*
băr 1, S.: barra, sbarra, stanga, *f.*; ostacolo, impedimento; foro, *m.*; (*mus.*) battuta, *f.*; (*nav.*) secca, *f.* **bar** 2, TR.: sbarrare, stangare; escludere; interdire.
bârb 1, S.: barba, *f.* **barb** 2, S.: cavallo barbero. **barb** 3, S.: corridore, *m.* **barb** 4, TR.: fare la barba; intagliare.
bârbacan, S.: barbacane; canale, *m.*
bar-bârian, S.: barbaro, villano, *m.* **-bărio**, ADJ.: barbaresco, strano. **-barism**, S.: barbarismo, *m.* **-bărity**, S.: barbarie; inumanità, *f.* **-barous**, ADJ.: barbaro, inumano. **-barously**, ADV.: barbaramente; crudelmente. **-barousness**, S.: crudeltà; rozzezza, ignoranza, *f.*
bârbecue, S.: bue o porco cotto intero, *m.*
bârbed, ADJ.: barbato; pennuto.
bârbel, S.: barbio, *m.* (pesce).
bârber, S.: barbiere, *m.*
bârberry, S.: berbero, frutto del berbero, *m.*
bârd, S.: bardo, vate, poeta, *m.*
bâre 1, ADJ.: nudo, ignudo, raso, scoperto; puro, mero; privo: *lay* —, mettere a nudo, denudare. **bare** 2, TR.: nudare, scoprire; privare. **-bone**, S.: magro, scheletro, *m.* **-faced**, ADJ.: sfacciato; aperto, **-fâcedly**, ADV.: sfacciatamente. **-facedness**, S.: sfacciatezza, impudenza, *f.* **-foot(ed)**, ADJ.: a piedi nudi, scalzo. **-headed**, ADJ.: colla testa scoperta. **-ly**, ADV.: solamente; poveramente. **-ness**, S.: nudità; povertà, *f.*
bârgain, S.: patto, accordo; mercato; *a* — *is a* —, *'tis a* —, quel che è fatto è fatto; *I give you this into the* —, vi do questo di soprappiù; *buy a* —, far un accordo; *strike a* —, patteggiare. **bargain**, INTR.: patteggiare, pattuire. **-er**, S.: patteggiatore, *m.*
bârge, S.: barca, barchetta, *f.* **-man**, S.: barcaruolo; nocchiere, *m.*
bârk 1, S.: scorza, corteccia. **bark** 2, S.: barca, *f.* **bark** 3, TR.: scorzare, scortecciare. **bark** 4, INTR.: abbaiare; sgridare: - - *at the moon*, abbaiare alla luna. **-er**, S.: abbaiatore, *m.* **-ing** 1, S.: abbaiamento, *m.* **-ing** 2, S.: scorzare, *m.*; ingiuria, *f.* **-y**, ADJ.: di scorza.
bârley, S.: orzo, *m.*: — *bread*, pane d' orzo, *m.*; — *corn*, grano d' orzo, *m.*; — *meal*, farina d' orzo; — *sugar*, zuccherino, *m.*; — *water*, acqua d' orzo, *f.*
bârm, S.: fermento, lievito, *m.* **-y**, ADJ.: che contiene del lievito.
bârn, S.: capanna, *f.* **-floor**, S.: aia, *f.*
bârnacle, S.: barnacla; oca di Scozia, *f.*
barŏmeter, S.: barometro, *m.* **-mĕtrical**, ADJ.: di barometro.
băron, S.: barone; giudice, *m.* **-age**, S.: baronia, *f.* **-ess**, S.: baronessa, *f.* **-et**, S.: baronetto, *m.* **-y**, S.: baronia, *f.*
băroscope, S.: baroscopio, *m.*
bărracan, S.: barracane, *m.*
bărrack, S.: baracca, *f.* **-s**, S.: caserma, *f.*
bărra-tor, S.: cavillatore, beccalite; brigante, *m.* **-try**, S.: baratteria, truffa, *f.*; inganno, *m.*
bărrel 1, S.: barile; cilindro, *m.*; canna, *f.*: — *of a gun*, canna di fucile; *little* —, bariletto, *m.* **barrel** 2, TR.: imbottare.
bărren, ADJ.: sterile, infruttuoso; arido, magro. **-ly**, ADV.: sterilmente; aridamente. **-ness**, S.: sterilità; aridità, *f.*
bârrful, ADJ.: pieno d' ostacoli.
barricâde 1, S.: barricata, *f.*; ostacolo, *m.* **barricade** 2, TR.: barricare, fortificare con barricate, sbarrare.
bărrier, S.: barriera, *f.*; ostacolo, *m.*
bărrister, S.: avvocato patrocinante, *m.*
bâr-room, S.: taverna, *f.*, buffetto, *m.*
bărrow, S.: barella, *f.*: *wheel*—, carriuola, *f.*; — *grease*, grasso di porco, *m.*; — *hog*, porco castrato, *m.*
bâr-shot, S.: palle ramate, *f. pl.*
bârter 1, S.: baratto, cambio, *m.* **barter** 2, TR.: barattare, cambiare. **-er**, S.: barattatore, cambiatore, *m.* **-ing**, S.: baratto, *m.* **-y**, S.: barattare, *m.*
bârtram, S.: (*bot.*) parietaria, *f.*
bărytone, S.: baritono, *m.*
basăl-t, S.: basalte, *m.* **-tic**, ADJ.: di basaltite.
bâse 1, S.: base, basa, *f.*; piedestallo; basso, *m.*: — *coin*, moneta di bassa lega. **base** 2, ADJ.: vile, basso, abietto. **-born**, ADJ.: vilmente nato, bastardo. **-court**, S.: bassa corte, *f.* **-minded**, ADJ.: servile, sordido. **-ly**, ADV.: bassamente, abiettamente, vilmente. **-ness**, S.: bassezza, viltà; indegnità; pusillanimità, *f.* **-viol**, S.: viola, *f.*
băsh, INTR.: vergognarsi
bashâw, S.: bascia, bassà, *m.*

băsh-fụl, ADJ.: timido, vergognoso. **-fụl-ly**, ADV.: timidamente, vergognosamente; modestamente. **-fụlness**, S.: timidità, vergogna, modestia, *f.*
bāsic, ADJ.: a base di.
băsil, S.: (*bot.*) basilico, *m.*
băṣilisk, S.: basilisco; pezzo d'artiglieria, *m.*
bāsin, S.: bacino, bacile, *m.*
bāsis, S.: basa, *f.*, fondamento; sostegno, *m.*
băsk, INTR.: scaldarsi al sole.
băsket, S.: canestra, *f.*, canestro, *m.*, paniera, *f.*: *hand* —, sporta, sportella, *f.*; *wicker* —, cestella, zana, *f.*, *little* —, canestrino, canestrello, *m.* **-maker**, S.: panieraio, cestaiuolo, *m.* **-woman**, S.: zanaiuola, *f.* **-work**, S.: mestiere del panieraio, *m.*
bāss 1, S.: basso, contrabbasso, *m.* **băss** 2, S.: pesce persico, *m.* **băss** 3, S.: tiglio, *m.*; stoia, *f.*
băsset, bassetta, *f.* (giuoco di carte).
bassōon, S.: bassone, *m.*
băss(ọ)-relīēf, S.: bassorilievo, *m.*
băstạrd 1, S.: bastardo, *m.*; bastarda, *f.*
băstard 2, ADJ.: bastardo, illegittimo. **-īze**, imbastardire; falsificare. **-ly**, ADV.: in modo di bastardo, bastardamente. **-y**, S.: bastardigia, *f.*
bāste, TR.: bastonare; imbastire; spruzzare.
bastinā-de 1, **-dọ**, S.: bastonata, *f.* **-de** 2, **-do**, TR.: bastonare, *f.*
bạsting 1, S.: colpi di bastoni, *m. pl.* **basting** 2, S.: (*cook.*) pillottare.
băstiọn, S.: bastione; riparo, *m.*
băt 1, S.: (*club*) mazza, *f.* **bat** 2, S.: (*zoöl.*) pipistrello, *m.*
bātable†, ADJ.: contestabile, disputabile.
bătch, S.: fornata di pane, *f.*
bāte, TR.: sbattere; diminuire, difalcare. **-ment**, S.: ribasso, *m.*; diminuzione, *f.*
băth, S.: bagno, *m.*; stufa, *f.* **bāth-e**, TR.: bagnare; innaffiare; INTR.: bagnarsi. **-ing**, S.: bagnare, *m.*; — *place*, S.: bagno, *m.* **-ing-establishment**, S.: stabilimento di bagni. **-house**, **-place**, **-room**, **-tub**, S.: bagno, *m.* **-keeper**, S.: stufaiuolo, *m.*
bāting, PREP.: eccetto che; salvo.
bătlet†, S.: pilo, pestone, *m.*
batōon, S.: bastone, *m.*, mazza, *f.*
bat-tālia, S.: ordine di battaglia, *m.*; battaglia, *f.* **-tālion**, S.: battaglione, *m.*
bătten, TR.: ingrassare; INTR.: ingrassarsi, impinguarsi.
băttẹr 1, S.: farinatta; fritella, *f.* **batter** 2, TR.: battere; demolire, rovinare. **-ẹr**, S.: battitore, *m.* **-ing**, S.: battimento, *m.*; — *ram*, S.: ariete, *f.* **-y**, S.: batteria, *f.*; battimento, *m.*

băttle 1, S.: battaglia, *f.*; combattimento, *m.*: — *array*, schiera; — *field*, campo di battaglia; *pitch* —, battaglia campale; *sham* —, battaglia finta; *join* —, appiccar battaglia; *in* — *array*, schierato. **battle** 2, TR.: combattere, pugnare. **-ax**, S.: azza, *f.* **-door**, S.: racchetta, *f.* **-field**, S.: campo di battaglia, *m.* **-ment**, S.: (*fort.*) merlo, *m.* **-mented**, ADJ.: merlato.
bătty, ADJ.: di pipistrello.
băvin, S.: stecco, fascetto, fastello, *m.*
bău-ble, S.: bagattella, cosa da nulla. **-bling**, ADJ.: vile, da nulla.
băwd 1, S.: ruffiana, mezzana, *f.* **bawd** 2, INTR.: far il ruffiano, ruffianare; sviare. **-ily**, ADV.: oscenamente, sporcamente. **-iness**, S.: oscenità, *f.*
băwdric, S.: pendaglio, *m.*
băw-dry, S.: ruffianeria, *f.*, ruffianesimo, *m.* **-dy**, ADJ.: osceno, disonesto: — *house*, S.: bordello, *m.*
băwl, INTR.: gridare; strillare; proclamare ad alta voce. **-ẹr**, S.: gridatore, *m.* **-ing**, S.: gridio, *m.*, gridata, *f.*, schiamazzo, *m.*
bāy 1, S.: baia, *f.*; golfo. **bay** 2, S.: alloro. **bay** 3, S.: belamento, *m.*: *keep at* —, tener a bada. **bay** 4, ADJ.: baio, castagnino. **bay** 5, INTR.: abbaiare, belare. **-tree**, S.: lauro, alloro, *m.* **-salt**, S.: sale nero, sale marino, *m.* **-window**, S.: finestra tonda, *f.*
bāyọnnet, S.: baionetta, *f.*
bē, IRR.; INTR.: essere, esistere; trovarsi; stare: *I have been*, sono stato; — *hungry* (*thirsty*, *warm*, *cold*), aver fame (sete, caldo, freddo); *how are you to-day?* come state quest'oggi? *I am better*, sto meglio; *it is fine weather to-day*, oggi fa bello; *there he is*, eccolo; *there are*, ve ne sono; *what's the matter?* che c'è?
bēach, S.: lito, *m.*, riva; sponda, *f.* **-y**, ADJ.: maritimo, littorale.
bēacon, S.: faro, fanale, *m.*; lanterna, *f.*
bēad, S.: pallottolina; perla, *f.* **-ṣ**, PL.: rosario, *m.*
bēadle, S.: bidello, sergento, *m.*
bēagle, S.: bracco, *m.*
bēak, S.: becco, rostro; sprone, *m.* **-ed**, ADJ.: in forma di becco. **-ẹr**, S.: tazza, ciotola, *f.*
bēam 1, S.: trave, *f.*; timone; stilo; raggio, *m.* **beam** 2, INTR.: raggiare. **-y**, ADJ.: radiante, raggiante; fulgido.
bēan, S.: fava, *f.*: *kidney* —*s*, *French* —*s*, fagiuoli, *m. pl.*; — *stalk*, fusto, gambo di fave; *shell* —*s*, agusciare fave.
beâr 1, S.: orso, *m.*; (*astr.*) orsa, *f.*: **-'s-ear**, S.: sanicula, *f.* **-driver**, S.: menatore d'orso, *m.* **-hunt**, S.: caccia d'orsi, *f.*

bear 2, IRR.; TR.: portare; generare, produrre; INTR.: sofferire; comportarsi: — *against*, resistere, opporsi; — *arms against one*, prendere le armi contro ad uno; — *company*, accompagnare; — *down*, abbattere, abbassare, — *a grudge*, voler male, odiare; — *witness*, far testimonianza, testificare; affermare; — *off*, portare via per forza; — *out*, proteggere; difendere; — *through*, condurre; maneggiare; — *up*, appoggiari; — *with*, sopportare, compatire.

beard 1, S.: barba, *f.* **beard** 2, TR.: strappare la barba; affrontare. **-ed**, ADJ.: barbato, penuto. **-less**, ADJ.: sbarbato, imberbe.

bear-er, S.: portatore, *m.*; portatrice, *f.* **-ing**, S.: portamento, *m.*; situazione, *f.*; patimento, *m.*, afflizione, *f.*, dolore, *m.*

beast, S.: bestia, *f.*, bruto, *m.* **-liness**, S.: brutezza, brutalità, *f.* **-ly**, ADJ.: bestiale, brutale.

beat 1, S.: colpo, *m.*; percossa, *f.* **beat** 2, IRR.; TR.: battere; percuotere; INTR.: palpitare, pulsare: — *against*, dar contro, urtarsi; — *back*, rispingere, ributtare; — *down*, abbattere; demolire; rincarare (il prezzo); — *in*, cacciare, ficcare con forza; — *into*, inculcare, imprimere; — *off*, scacciare; — *out*, cavare; trarre; espellere; — *upon*, battere. **-en**, ADJ.: battuto, trito; vinto (cf. *beat*). **-er**, S.: battore; pestello, *m.*; berta, *f.*

be-atific(al), ADJ.: beatifico. **-atification**, S.: beatificazione, *f.* **-ătify**, TR.: beatificare.

beating, S.: battimento; palpitamento, *m.*; correzione, *f.*

beătitude, S.: beatitudine, felicità. *f.*

beau *bō*, S.: zerbinotto, parigino, *m.*

beaū-teous, ADJ.: bello, vago. **-teously**, ADV.: bellamente. **-teousness**, S.: bellezza, *f.* **-tiful**, ADJ.: bello, leggiadro, vago. **-tifully**, ADV.: bellamente, vezzosamente. **-tifulness**, S.: bellezza, vaghezza, *f.* **-tify**, TR.: ornare, abbellire; REFL.: ornarsi, abbellirsi. **-ty**, S.: bellezza, beltà; vaghezza, *f.* **-spot**, S.: mosca, *f.*

beaver, S.: castoro; capello di castoro.

becafico, S.: beccafico, *m.*

becâlm, TR.: calmare; moderare; (*nav.*) togliere il vento.

becâuse, CONJ.: perchè, perciocchè.

bĕck, S.: segno; cenno, *m.* **-on**, TR.: invitare col dito; far cenno a; INTR.: fare cenno, accennare; assentire.

becŏm-e, IRR.; INTR.: convenire; stare bene; divenire, diventare: *what will — of me?* che sarà mai di me? *this dress —s you*, questa veste vi sta bene; *it ill —s him*, gli sta male. **-ing**, ADJ.: convenevole, decente; decoroso. **-ingly**, ADV.: convenevolmente. **-ingness**, S.: convenevolezza, convenenza; proprietà, *f.*

bĕd, S.: letto; matrimonio; quadro, *m.*: *go to —*, andare a letto; *be brought to —*, partorire; *folding —*, letto a cinghie, portatile; *sick —*, letto di dolore. **-chamber**, S.: camera da letto, *f.* **-clothes**, S. PL.: coperte del letto, *f. pl.* **-curtain**, S.: cortina da letto, *f.* **-fellow**, S.: compagno di letto, *m.* **-maker**, S.: servitore (nelle università), *m.* **-mate**, S.: compagno di letto, *m.* **-post**, S.: colonna di letto, *f.* **-presser**, S.: dormitore, *m.* **-room** = *bed-chamber*. **-side**, S.: sponda del letto, *f.* **-stead**, S.: legname del letto, *m.*; lettiera, *f.* **-straw**, S.: pagliariccio, *m.* **-tick**, S.: fodera d' un guanciale, *f.* **-time**, S.: ora d' andare a letto. **bed**, TR.: mettere in letto; stendere; colcare.

bedăbble, TR.: umettare, spruzzare; bagnare.

bedăggle, TR.: sporcare, imbrattare.

bedăsh, TR.: spruzzare, imbrattare.

bedăub, TR.: macchiare, bruttare, scarabocchiare.

bedăzzle, TR.: abbagliare, abbacinare; appannar la vista.

bĕdding, S.: apparecchio compiuto del letto, *m.*, biancheria da letto, *f.*

bedĕck, TR.: abbellire, addobbare.

bĕdehōuse†, S.: spedale, *m.*

bedew, TR.: umettare, innaffiare.

bedight, TR.: ornare, abbellire.

bedim, TR.: oscurare, offuscare.

bedizen, TR.: ornare; decorare.

Bĕdlam, S.: pazzarelli, *m. pl.*; pazzo, *m.* **-ite**, S.: pazzo, forsennato, *m.*

bedrăggle, TR.: imbrattare; INTR.: infangarsi.

bedrĕnch, TR.: adacquare, umettare; abbeverare.

bĕdrid(den), ADJ.: obbligato a letto.

bedrŏp, TR.: gocciolare, aspergere.

bedŭst, TR.: impolverare, gettar della polvere.

bedwărf, TR.: render piccolo, sminuire.

bēe, S.: ape; pecchia, *f.* **-garden**, S.: luogo da tenervi le pecchie, *m.* **-hive**, S.: alveare, alveario, *m.*, arnia, *f.* **-master**, S.: che tiene pecchie.

bēech, S.: faggio, *m.* **-en**, ADJ.: di faggio. **-tree**, S.: faggio, *m.*

bēef, S.: vaccina; carne di bue, *f.*: *boiled —*, manzo lesso, *m.*; *powdered —*, manzo salato, *m.* **-steak**, S.: bistecca, carbonata di vaccina, *f.*

bēer, S.: birra, *f.*: *small —*, birra leggiera, *f.*; *strong —*, birra forte, *f.*, birrone *m.* **-cask**, S.: botte da birra, *f.* **-cellar**, S.: canova di birra, *f.* **-glass**, S

bicchiere da birra, *m.* **-jug**, S.: brocca da birra, *f.* **-house, -shop**, S.: taverna da birra, birreria, *f.* **-soup**, S.: zuppa di birra, *f.*
bēestings, S.: primo latte d' una vacca, *m.*
bēet, S.: bietola, bieta, *f.*
bēetle, S.: scarafaggio; maglio, *m.* **-browed**, ADJ.: dispettoso, arcigno; **-headed**, ADJ.: sciocco, ottuso.
bēetradish, S.: barbabietola, *f.*
bēeves, S. PL.: buoi, *m. pl.*
befăll, IRR.; TR.: accadere, avvenire.
befit, TR.: convenire, essere convenevole.
befōol, TR.: infatuare.
befōre, ADV., PREP.: avanti, prima, innanzi; primieramente: — *dinner*, prima di pranzo; *as I said* —, come dissi dianzi; *go* —, precedere, andare avanti; — *I set out*, prima di partire. **-hand**, ADV.: avanti tratto, anticipatamente, in avanzo: *pay* —, pagare anticipatamente. **-mentioned**, ADJ.: suddetto. **-time**, ADV.: anticamente, altre volte; un tempo.
befōul, TR.: sporcare, imbrattare.
befriĕnd, TR.: favorire, proteggere.
befringe, TR.: ornare di frange.
bĕg, TR.: domandare; pregare; chiedere; INTR.: mendicare, chiedere limosina: *I — your pardon*, vi domando perdono; *I — to inform you*, ho l' onore d' informarvi.
begĕt (*begot, begotten*), IRR.; TR.: generare; produrre. **-ter**, S.: genitore, generatore, *m.*
bĕg-gar 1, S.: mendicante, pezzente, *m.* **-woman**, S.: mendica, *f.* **-gar** 2, TR.: impoverire; spogliare. **-garliness**, S.: mendicità, povertà; miseria, *f.* **-garly** 1, ADJ.: povero; miserabile. **-garly** 2, ADV.: poveramente, meschinamente. **-gary**, S.: mendicità; miseria, indigenza, *f.* **-ging**, S.: mendicare, *m.*: *go a-begging*, andar mendicando. **-gingly**, ADV.: da mendicante.
begin, IRR.; TR.: cominciare, principiare: — *again* (*afresh*), ricominciare; — *the world*, entrar nel mondo. **-ner**, S.: principiante; novizio, *m.* **-ning**, S.: principio, *m.*; origine, *f.*: *make a* —, comminciare.
begird, IRR.; TR., INTR.: cingere, circondare.
begnăw, TR.: andar rodendo.
begōne! INTERJ.: vanne via! vattene!
begŏtten, PART.: generato, nato: *first* —, primogenito; *only* —, unigenito, unico.
begrēase, TR.: sporcare.
begrime, TR.: annerare.
begui-le, TR.: ingannare, truffare. **-ler**, S.: ingannatore, truffatore, *m.* **-ling**, S.: inganno, *m.*, truffa, *f.*
behălf, S.: favore, *m.*, causa; difesa, *f.*: *in — of*, in favore di; *in your* —, in vostro favore.
behāve, INTR.: comportarsi, condursi.
behāvio(u)r, S.: portamento; condotto, *m.*
behĕad, TR.: decapitare, decollare. **-ing**, S.: decapitazione, *f.*
behĕst, S.: comando, ordine, *m.*; promessa, *f.*
behind, ADV., PREP.: dietro, indietro, addietro, di dietro: *come* —, tener dietro; *stay* —, restare indietro; *leave* —, lasciare addietro. **-hand**, ADV.: indietro; in cattivo stato.
behōld 1, IRR.; TR.: riguardare; osservare; vedere. **behold!** 2 INTERJ.: ecco! **-en**, ADJ.: obbligato; debitore. **-er**, S.: spettatore, *m.* **-ing**, ADJ.: riguardante; riconoscente; grato. **-ingness**, S.: obbligazione, *f.*
behōof, S.: profitto; comodo, *m.*; utilità, *f.*
behōove, INTR.: convenire; bisognare; essere proprio. **-ful†**, ADJ.: profittevole, utile. **-fully†**, ADV.: profittevolmente, utilmente.
behōwl†, TR.: ululare, urlare.
bēing 1, S.: essere, ente, *m.*; esistenza, *f.*: *the Supreme* —, l'Ente supremo; *call into* —, chiamare all' esistenza; *for the time* —, pel tempo attuale. **being** 2, CONJ.: posto che, poichè, giacchè.
belābo(u)r, TR.: bastonare, battere.
belāce, TR.: attaccare; guarnire di merletti.
belamōur†, S.: galante, amante, *m.*
bĕlamy†, S.: amico intimo, *m.*
belāted, ADJ.: attardato, ritardato; sorpreso dalla notte.
belāy†, TR.: impedire; insidiare.
bĕlch 1, S.: rutto, *m.*, eruttazione, *f.* **belch** 2, INTR.: ruttare, eruttare.
bĕldam, S.: vecchiaccia, *f.*
belēaguer, TR.: assediare, bloccare. **-er**, S.: assediatore, assediante, *m.*
bĕlfry, S.: campanile, *m.*
belie, TR.: smentire; dimentire, imitare; calunniare.
belie-f, S.: fede, fidanza; credenza; opinione, *f.*: *light* (*ready*) —, credulo, credenzone; *slow of* —, incredulo; *to the best of my* —, per quanto consta a me. **-vable**, ADJ.: credibile; degno di fede. **-ve**, TR.: credere; prestar fede: INTR.: pensare; immaginarsi; darsi a credere: *I — so*, credo di sì; *I — not*, credo di no; *make one* —, dare a credere. **-ver**, S.: credente; fedele; cristiano, *m.* **-vingly**, ADV.: in modo credibile.
belike†, ADV.: verisimilmente, probabilmente.

belive, ADV.: prontamente, adesso adesso.
bëll, S.: campana, *f.*: *little* —, campanella, *f.*; *ring the* —, suonar la campana; —*clapper*, battaglio, *m.* **-flower**, S.: (*bot.*) campanella, *f.*; —*founder*, fonditore di campane, *m.* **-man**, S.: banditore, campanaro, *m.* **-metal**, S.: bronzo, *m.* **-wether**, S.: montone che porta il campanaccio, *m.*
bëlle, S.: vaga donna, *f.*
belles-lëttres, S. PL.: belle lettere, *f. pl.*
belligerent, **-rous**, ADJ.: belligerante, guerreggiante.
bëllow, INTR.: mugghiare, mugire.
bëllows, S. PL.: soffietto, *m.*
bëlly, S.: ventre, *m.*; pancia, *f.* **-ache**, S.: mal di ventre, *m.* **-band**, S.: panciera, *f.* **-bound**, ADJ.: stitico, costipato. **-ful**, S.: corpacciata; sazietà, *f.*
belöng, INTR.: appartenere; aspettarsi. **-ing**, S.: che appartiene; qualità, *f.*
belöved, ADJ.: amato, diletto.
belöw, ADV., PREP.: sotto; giù; a basso; quaggiù: *here* —, quaggiù; *he is* —, egli è basso, giù.
bëlt, S.: budriere, pendaglio, *m.*: *shoulder*—, ciarpa, *f.*
bemire, TR.: infangare, sporcare, imbrattare.
bemöan, TR.: compiangere, deplorare. **-er**, S.: compiangitore, *m.* **-ing**, S.: compianto, lamento, *m.*
bënch, S.: scanno, banco, sedile, *m.*; corte, *f.*: *joiner's* —, panca di falegname; *judge's* —, scranna del giudice. **-er**, S.: assessore, giurisconsulto, *m.*
bënd 1, S.: piegatura, curvità, *f.*; costole (di nave), *f. pl.* **bend** 2, IRR; TR.: tendere; curvare, piegare; (*nav.*) dar volta: — *a bow*, tendere un arco; — *one's mind*, volger l'animo; INTR.: curvarsi, piegarsi, sommettersi: — *forwards*, inchinare; — *under a burden*, incurvarsi sotto un peso. **-able**, ADJ.: pieghevole, flessibile. **-er**, S.: piegatore; strumento da piegare, *m.* **-ing**, S.: piegamento, *m.*, piegatura, curvità, *f.*
beneath, ADV., PREP.: sotto, di sotto; giù; a basso.
benediction, S.: benedizione; grazia, *f.*
benefäc-tion, S.: benefizio; favore, *m.* **-tor**, S.: benefattore, *m.* **-tress**, S.: benefattrice, *f.*
bënefice, S.: beneficio, *m.*; parrocchia, *f.* **-ed**, ADJ.: beneficiato.
benëf-icence, S.: beneficenza, liberalità, *f.* **-icent**, ADJ.: beneficente, liberale.
bene-ficial, ADJ.: profittevole, vantaggioso, utile. **-ficially**, ADV.: profittevolmente, utilmente. **-ficialness**, S.: profitto, *m.*, utilità, *f.* **-ficiary**, S.: beneficiato, beneficiario, *m.*

bënefit 1, S.: benefizio; profitto, vantaggio, *m.*: — *of clergy*, privilegio del clero, *m.* **benefit** 2, TR.: beneficare; giovare, vantaggiare; INTR.: profittare; avanzarsi.
benëvo-lence, S.: benevolenza; liberalità, *f.* **-lent**, ADJ.: benevolo, benefìcente. **-lently**, ADV.: con benevolenza.
benight, TR.: oscurare; ditenere infino alla notte. **-ed**, ADJ.: sorpreso dalla notte.
be-nign, ADJ.: benigno, favorevole, liberale. **-nignity**, S.: benignità, bontà; affabilità, *f.* **-nignly**, ADV.: benignamente; dolcemente.
bënison, S.: benedizione, *f.*
bënt, ADJ.: piegato, inclinato; propenso; piega; inclinazione, *f.*: *be* — *upon*, esser risoluto di far.
benümb, TR.: intirizzire, agghiacciare, stupefare. **-edness**, S.: intirizzamento, *m.*; torpidezza, *f.*
bën-zine, S.: benzina, *f.* **-zöin**, S.: benzoino, belzuino, *m.*
bepäint, TR.: coprire di colore, colorire.
bepinch, TR.: pizzicare.
bepräise, TR.: lodare.
be-quëath, TR.: legare, lasciare in testamento. **-quëather**, S.: testatore, *m.* **-quëathment**, **-quëst**, S.: legato, lascito.
bërberry, S.: coccola acre, *f.*
be-rëave, IRR.; TR. (*bereaved*, *bereft*; *bereft*); privare; spogliare. **-rëft**, ADJ.: privato, spogliato.
bërgamot, S.: pera bergamotta, *f.*; bergamotto, *m.*
berhyme, TR.: celebrare in versi.
berlin, S.: berlina, *f.* (carrozza).
bërry 1, S.: bacca, baia, coccola, *f.* **berry** 2, TR.: produrre bacche.
bëryl, S.: berillo, *m.*
bescrëen, TR.: velare; proteggere.
beseech, IRR.; TR.: supplicare; scongiurare. **-er**, S.: pregatore, supplicante, *m.*
beseem, INTR.: convenire, essere proprio. **-ing**, ADJ.: convenevole, dicevole; S.: decenza, leggiadria, *f.*
besët, IRR.; TR.: assediare; circondare, angustiare.
be-shrew *-shrü*, INTR.: maledire.
beside(s) PREP.: accanto, accosto, presso; fuorchè; oltre; ADV.: inoltre d'altronde: *be* — *one's self*, esser fuor di senno).
besië-ger, TR.: assediare, blocca... S.: assediatore: assediante, ... S.: assediamento. *m.*
beslübber, TR.: imbrattare, sporcare.
be-smëar, **-smirch**, TR.: sporcare, lordare.
besmöke, TR.: affumicare.

assĕss, TR.: tassare. **-ment**, S.: tassare, *m.*; tassa; tassazione, *f.* **-or**, S.: assessore; tassatore, *m.*
assĕts, S. PL.: (*jur.*) beni sufficienti, *m. pl.*
asseveràtion, S.: asseveranza; affermazione, *f.*
as-sidūity, S.: assiduità, diligenza, *f.* **-sidūous**, ADJ.: assiduo, diligente. **-siduously**, ADV.: assiduamente; continuamente. **-siduousness**, S.: assiduità, *f.*
assiege, TR.: assediare.
as-sign, TR.: assegnare, commettere, delegare; addurre: — *a reason*, addurre una ragione. **-signable**, ADJ.: che può assegnarsi. **-signàtion**, S.: assegnazione, *f.*; appuntamento, *m.* **-signēe**, S.: deputato; sostituto, *m.* **-signer**, S.: costituitore, *m.* **-signment**, S.: consegnazione; cessione, *f.*; deposito, *m.* **-signs**, S. PL.: esecutori testamentari, *m. pl.*
assimil-ate, TR.: assimigliare; comparare. **-àtion**, S.: assimigliamento, paragone, *m.*
assist, TR.: assistere, soccorrere, aiutare. **-ance**, S.: assistenza, *f.*; soccorso, aiuto, *m.*: *signal for* —, segnale d'angustia. **-ant**, S.: assistente, aiutatore, *m.*
assize 1, S.: sessione di giudici; assisa; tariffa, *f.*: *court of* —, corte d'assise.
assize 2, TR.: tassare; regolare.
assō-ciate 1, S.: associato; compagno, *m.* **-ciate** 2, TR.: associare; accompagnare; praticare. **-ciàtion**, S.: associazione, unione; società; taglia, *f.*
assōil†, TR.: assolvere; perdonare.
ăssonance, S.: assonanza, *f.*
assôrt, TR.: assortire; classare. **-ment**, S.: assortimento, sortimento, *m.*
as-suāge, TR.: alleviare; mitigare; placare, pacificare; INTR.: alleviarsi, mitigarsi. **-suāgement**, S.: addolcimento; conforto, *m.* **-suāger**, S.: mitigatore, pacificatore, *m.* **-suāsive**, ADJ.: mitigativo, lenitivo. **-suefàction**, S.: assuefazione, accostumanza, *f.*
assūm-e, TR.: assumere, prendere; presumere, arrogarsi. **-er**, S.: arrogante, *m.* **-ing**, ADJ.: presuntuoso.
assŭmp-sit, S.: (*leg.*) promessa verbale, *f.* **-tion**, S.: assunzione, arroganza, *f.* **-tive**, ADJ.: che può assumersi. **-tively**, ADV.: assuntivamente.
as-sūrance, S.: assicurazione; sicurezza; fidanza; costanza, *f.* **-sūre**, TR.: assicurare; asserire, affermare. **-sūred**, ADJ.: sicuro, certo: *rest* —, esser sicuro. **-sūredly**, ADV.: sicuramente, certamente. **-sūrer**, S.: assicuratore; mallevadore, *m.*

ăster-isk, S.: asterisco, *m.* **-ism**, S.: (*astr.*) costellazione, *f.*
astĕrn, ADV.: per la poppa, in poppa.
ăsth-ma, S.: asma, asima, *f.* **-mătic**, ADJ.: asmatico.
as-tŏnish, TR.: stupire; stordire. **-tŏnishment**, S.: stupore, *m.*, sopresa, *f.*: *strike with* —, far stupore; *fill with* —, colmare di stupore. **-tŏund**, TR.: costernare, stordire.
astrăddle, ADV.: a cavalcioni.
ăstral, ADJ.: astrale, degli astri.
astrāy, ADV.: fuor di via: *go* —, smarrirsi; errare; *lead* —, sviare, deviare.
astric-t, TR.: contrarre; ristringere. **-tion**, S.: astringimento, *m.* **-tive**, ADJ.: astringente, costrettivo.
astride, ADV.: a cavalcioni.
astring-e, TR.: astringere; contrarre. **-ency**, S.: astringenza. **-ent**, ADJ.: astringente.
as-trŏloger, S.: astrologo, *m.* **-trolŏgical**, ADJ.: astrologico. **-trŏlogy**, S.: astrologia, *f.* **-trŏnomer**, S.: astronomo, *m.* **-tronŏmical**, ADJ.: astronomico. **-tronŏmically**, ADV.: in modo astronomico, da astronomo. **-trŏnomy**, S.: astronomia, *f.*
astŭn, TR.: stordire, stupefare.
asŭnder, ADV.: separatamente; in due parti: *cut* —, tagliar per mezzo; *put* —, dividere, separare.
asȳlum, S.: asilo; rifugio, *m.*
ăt, PREP.: a, ad; da; in; per; al, alla, agli, alle: — *first*, alla prima; — *hand*, vicino, appresso; — *home*, a casa; — *last*, in fine, finalmente; — *least*, per lo meno, almeno; — *leisure*, a bell'agio; — *most*, al più; — *once*, subito, alla prima; — *odds*, male insieme; — *least*, almeno; — *peace*, in pace; — *present*, per adesso; — *sea*, sul mare, per mare; — *school*, alla scuola; — *the*, al, ecc.; — *a word*, in una parola.
ā-theism, S.: ateismo, *m.* **-theist**, S.: ateista, ateo, *m.* **-theistical**, ADJ.: ateistico.
athirst, ADJ.: assetato, sitibondo; ADV.: sitibondamente.
ăth-lete, S.: atleta, *m.* **-lĕtic**, ADJ.: atletico, vigoroso.
athwârt, ADV., PREP.: a traverso, a sghembo.
atilt, ADV.: con botta.
ătlas, S.: atlante, *m.*
ătmos-phere, S.: atmosfera, *f.* **-phĕrical**, ADJ.: dell'atmosfera.
ăt-om, S.: atomo, *m.* **-ŏmical**, ADJ.: consistente d'atomi.
atōne, TR.: espiare; purgare; INTR.: convenire; concordare. **-ment**, S.: espiazione, *f.*; placamento, *m.*

ătony, S.: (*med.*) atonia, *f.*
atŏp, ADV.: in alto; sulla sommità.
atrabilărian, ADJ.: atrabiliare, malinconico.
atrōcious, ADJ.: atroce, orribile, enorme. **-ly**, ADV.: atrocemente; fieramente. **-ness**, **atrŏcity**, S.: atrocità; enormità; scelleratezza, *f.*
ătrophy, S.: atrofia, consunzione, *f.*
attăch, TR.: arrestare, catturare; guadagnare, sequestrare; affezionare: *he is —ed to you*, vi è affezionato. **-ment**, S.: aderenza, *f.*, affetto; sequestro, *m.*
attăck 1, S.: attacco, assalimento, *m.* **attack** 2, TR.: attaccare, assalire. **-er**, S.: assalitore, assaltatore, *m.*
attāin, TR.: ottenere, conseguire, acquistare; INTR.: arrivare; pervenire: — *to honours*, pervenire agli onori. **-able**, ADJ.: acquistabile. **-der**, S.: convinzione, *f.* **-ment**, S.: acquisto, acquistamento, *m.* **-t**, TR.: macchiare; corrompere; disonorare; infettare; accusare. **-ted**, ADJ.: corrotto; disonorato; accusato. **-ture**, S.: imputazione, *f.*
attĕmper, TR.: temperare; calmare.
attĕmpt 1, S.: tentativa, *f.*; sperimento, *m.* **attempt** 2, TR.: tentare; provare, esperimentare; intraprendere. **-able**, ADJ.: che può tentarsi. **-er**, S.: tentatore; sperimentatore, *m.*
attĕnd, TR.: accompagnare; essere presente; INTR.: stare attento, attendere; osservare; badare: — *a business*, dar opera ad un affare; — *a patient*, aver cura di un malato. **-ance**, S.: servizio; assiduità; cura, *f.*; corteggio, *m.*: *dance* —, fare spalliera; *be in* —, essere di servizio. **-ant**, S.: servidore; seguace, *m.* **-er**, S.: compagno, socio, *m.*
attĕntate, S.: tentativa, *f.*
attĕntion, S.: attenzione, *f.*: *give* —, *pay* —, far attenzione; *pay —s to*, usare attenzioni a. **-tive**, ADJ.: attento, ufficioso. **-tively**, ADV.: attentamente, con cura. **-tiveness**, S.: attendimento assiduo, *m.*
attĕnu-ant, ADJ.: attenuante. **-ate** 1, TR.: attenuare, affievolire; diminuire. **-ate** 2, ADJ.: attenuato, affievolito. **-ăting**, ADJ.: attenuante. **-ātion**, S.: attenuazione; diminuzione, *f.*
attĕst, TR.: attestare, certificare. **-ātion**, S.: attestazione, testimonianza, *f.*
At-ticism *ăt-*, S.: atticismo, *m.*; eleganza, *f.* **-tic**, ADJ.: elegante; delicato.
attīre 1, S.: abbigliamento, *m.*; corna del cervo, *f. pl.* **attire** 2, TR.: abbigliare, acconciare; abbellire, ornare.
ăttitude, S.: attitudine, *f.*
attŏrn-ey, S.: notaio, procuratore, *m.*: — *general*, procuratore generale; — *at law*, causidico, patrocinatore, *m.* **-eyship**, S.: ufficio di procuratore, *m.* **-ment**, S.: cessione, cedizione, *f.*
attrăc-t, TR.: attrarre; allettare. **-tion**, S.: attrazione, *f.*; allettamento, *m.* **-tive**, ADJ.: attrattivo. **-tively**, ADV.: per attrazione. **-tiveness**, S.: attraimento, *m.* **-tor**, S.: agente, *m.*; forza attrattiva, *f.*
ăt-tribute 1, S.: attributo, *m.*; proprietà, *f.* **-tribute**, TR.: attribuire, imputare, ascrivere. **-tribūtion**, S.: attribuzione; commendazione, *f.*
attrition, S.: attrizione, *f.*; tritamento, *m.*
attūne, TR.: render armonioso, accordare.
atwēen† = *between*.
atwixt† = *betwixt*.
ăuburn, ADJ.: bruno.
ăuction, S.: incanto, *m.*: *sale at* —, vendita all' incanto (*or* all' asta). **-ĕer**, S.: venditore all' incanto, *m.*
audācious, ADJ.: audace, temerario; presuntuoso. **-ly**, ADV.: audacemente; arditamente. **-ness**, **audăcity**, S.: audacia; baldanza, arditezza, *f.*
ăudibl-e, ADJ.: udibile; alto, sonoro. **-y**, ADV.: ad alta voce.
ăudience, S.: udienza, *f.*; uditorio, *m.*; — *chamber*, camera d' udienza, *f.*
ăudit 1, S.: esame d' un conto, *m.* **audit** 2, TR.: esaminare conti. **-or**, S.: uditore, *m.* **-ory**, ADJ.: auditorio; acustico (*nerve*, *etc.*); S.: uditorio, auditorio, *m.*; udienza, *f.*
ăuger, S.: succhiello, *m.*
ăught, PRON.: checchessia, qualche cosa: *for — I know*, per quanto io sappia.
aug-mĕnt, TR.: aumentare; accrescere; INTR.: aumentarsi. **-'ment**, **-mentā-tion**, S.: aumento, incremento; accrescimento, *m.* **-mĕntative**, ADJ.: aumentativo.
ău-gur 1, S.: auguratore, *m.* **-gur** 2, **-gurate**, INTR.: augurare; conghietturare. **-gurātion**, S.: augurio, *m.*; conghiettura, *f.* **-gūrial**, ADJ.: augurale. **-gurize**, TR.. indovinare. **-gurous**, ADJ.: auguroso, profetante. **-gury**, S.: augurio, presagio, *m.*
Au-gust *ă'-*, S.: (*month*) agosto, *m.* **-gŭst**, ADJ.: augusto, nobile. **-gŭstan**, ADJ.: d' Augusto: *the — age*, il secolo d' Augusto. **-gŭstness**, S.: maestà, dignità, *f.*
ăulic, ADJ.: aulico.
âunt, S.: zia, *f.*
aurēlia, S.: aurelia; crisalide, *f.*
ău-ricle, S.: auricola; orecchietta, *f.* **-ricula**, S.: cortusa; orecchia d' orso, *f.* **-ricular**, ADJ.: auricolare. **-ricularly**, ADV.: all' orecchio, segretamente.

luogo, posto, *m.*: *new* —, rigenerazione; *give* — *to*, far nascere, produrre. **-day**, s.: giorno di nascita, natale, *m.* **-place**, s.: luogo natale, *m.* **-right**, s.: primogenitura, *f.*

biscuit, s.: biscotto, biscottino, *m.*

bisĕct, INTR.: dividere in due parti. **-tion**, s.: bissezione, divisione in due, *f.*

bishop, s.: vescovo, *m.* **-ric**, s.: vescovado, *m.*

bisk, s.: zuppa, *f.*; brodo, *m.*

bismuth, s.: bismutte, *m.*

bissĕxtile, ADJ.: bisestile.

bistoury, s.: (*surg.*) bistorì, *m.*

bisŭlcous, ADJ.: bisulco.

bit 1, s.: pezzo; boccone; freno, morso, *m.*: *not a* —, *never a* —, niente affatto; *a* — *of bread*, un tozzo di pane; *not a* — *of it*, niente affatto; nulla di tutto ciò; *by* —*s*, in pezzi; — *of a key*, buco della chiave, *m.* **bit** 2, TR.: imboccare, imbrigliare (un cavallo).

bitch, s.: cagna, *f.*

bi-te 1, s.: morso, *m.*; morsura, *f.* **bite** 2, IRR.; TR.: mordere, morsicare; pizzicare; ingannare, trappolare: — *off*, portar via il pezzo mordendo. **-ter**, s.: morditore; furbone, *m.* **-ting**, ADJ.: mordente; pungente.

bitter, ADJ.: amaro, aspro; piccante; crudele. **-ish**, ADJ.: amaragnolo. **-ly**, ADV.: amaramente; acutamente, severamente.

bittern, s.: tarabuso, *m.*

bitter-ness, s.: amarezza, *f.*; rancore, *m.*; afflizione, *f.*, cordoglio, *m.* **-sweet**, s.: dulcamara, *f.* **-wort**, s.: genziana gialla.

bitū-men, s.: bitume, *m.* **-minous**, ADJ.: bituminoso.

bival-ve, **-vular**, ADJ.: bivalve.

bivious, ADJ.: bivio.

blăb 1, s.: ciarlatore, ciarlone, *m.* **blab** 2, TR.: ciarlare, chiacchierare, calunniare. **-ber**, s.: ciarlatore, chiacchierone, *m.* **-berlipped**, ADJ.: che ha le labbra grosse, labbrato.

blăck, ADJ.: nero; funesto, triste; cattivo; s.: nero, color nero; lutto; negro, *m.*: — *and blue*, livido; *put on* —, vestirsi di nero; — *art*, arte magica, *f.* **-amoor**, s.: negro, *m.* **-berry**, s.: mora di rovo, *f.* **-bird**, s.: merlo, *m.* **-en**, TR.: annerare, far nero; INTR.: divenir nero. **-eyed**, ADJ.: che ha gli occhi neri. **-faced**, ADJ.: brunetto, negretto. **-friar**, s.: frate Domenicano, *m.* **-guard** *blă'gârd*, s.: birbone, briccone, *m.* **-ish**, ADJ.: nericcio, neretto. **-lead**, s.: piombaggine, *f.* **-letter**, s.: lettera gotica, *f.* **-moor**, s.: moro, negro, *m.*, negra, *f.* **-ness**, s.: nerezza; atrocità, *f.* **-pudding**, s.: sanguinaccio, *m.* **-smith**, s.: fabbro, *m.* **-thorn**, s.: prugno salvatico, *m.*; susina salvatica, *f.*

blădder, s.: vescica, *f.*: *little* —, vescichetta, vescicola.

blăd-e, s.: lama, *f.*; fusto; stelo; bracciuolo, *m.*; (*nav.*) palma del remo, *f.* **-ebones**, s.: osso della spalla, *m.* **-ed**, ADJ.: gambuto.

blăin, s.: ciccione, tumore, *m.*

blām-able, ADJ.: biasimevole; colpevole. **-ableness**, s.: colpa, *f.*; mancamento, *m.* **-ably**, ADV.: biasimevolmente. **-e**, s.: biasimo; obbrobrio, *m.*; colpa, *f.*: *lay the* — *upon*, incolpare. **-e**, TR.: biasimare, censurare; condannare. **-eable** = *blamable*. **-eful**, ADJ.: biasimevole; colpevole, colpabile. **-eless**, ADJ.: incolpabile, innocente. **-elessly**, ADV.: innocentemente. **-elessness**, s.: innocenza, *f.* **-er**, s.: biasimatore, incolpatore **-eworthiness**, s.: biasimevolezza, *f.* **-eworthy**, ADJ.: biasimevole.

blânch, TR.: bianchire; far impallidire; mondare; dissimulare.

blănd, ADJ.: dolce; blando; piacevole, placido. **-iloquence**, s.: blandimento, *m.*, carezze, *f. pl.* **-ish**, TR.: blandire, accarezzare. **-ishment**, s.: blandimento, *m.*, carezza, lusinga, *f.* **-ness**, s.: natura (condotta) blanda.

blănk, ADJ.: bianco; pallido; confuso; sciolto; s.: spazio vuoto; bianco; bersaglio, *m.*; — *verse*, versi sciolti; *left* —, lasciato in bianco.

blănket 1, s.: coperto da letto (*or* di lana). **blanket** 2, TR.: coprire con una coperta di lana; trabalzare in una coperta.

blănk-ly, ADV.: nettamente; confusamente. **-ness**, s.: pallidezza; confusione, *f.*

blăre, INTR.: muggire; liquefarsi.

blăsh, TR.: imbrattare, sporcare.

blas-phēme, TR.: bestemmiare. **-phēmer**, s.: bestemmiatore, *m.* **blăs-phemous**, ADJ.: esecrabile, empio. **-'phemously**, ADV.: esecrabilmente, in modo empio. **-'phemy**, s.: bestemmia, *f.*

blâst 1, s.: soffio di vento, *m.*; bruma; golpe, *f.*: — *furnace*, fornace. **blast** 2, TR.: annebbiare; ingiuriare; — *some one's reputation*, intaccare l'altrui riputazione. **-ment**, s.: infezione; contagione, *f.*

blātant, ADJ.: mugghiante; ciarliero.

blătter, INTR.: muggire, far gran rumore.

blăy, s.: argetino, *m.* (pesce).

blāz-e 1, s.: fiamma, vampa, *f.* **-e** 2, TR.: allumare; pubblicare, divolgare; INTR.: scintillare; splendere. **-er**, s.: divolgatore, *m.* **-on**, TR.: blasonare; divisare; divolgare. **-onry**, s.: blasone araldica, *f.*

blĕach, TR.: imbiancare al sole; INTR.: bianchire. **-ing**, S.: bianchire, bianchimento, *m.*
blĕak 1, ADJ.: pallido; smorto; aspro, freddo. **bleak** 2, S.: argentino, *m.* (pesce). **-ness**, S.: pallidezza; freddura, *f.*, freddo, *m.* **-y**, ADJ.: freddo; smorto.
blĕar 1, ADJ.: oscuro; cisposo. **blear** 2, TR.: offuscare; intorpidare la vista. **-edness**, S.: cispa, *f.* **-eyed**, ADJ.: cisposo, lippo.
blĕat 1, S.: belamento, belato, *m.* **bleat** 2, INTR.: belare.
blĕb, S.: pustula; bolla, *f.*
blĕed, IRR.; TR.: cavare sangue; INTR.: gettare sangue: — *at the nose*, gettar sangue dal noso. **-er**, S.: che cava sangue. **-ing**, S.: cavata di sangue, *f.*
blĕmish 1, S.: macchia, *f.*; disonore, *m.*, infamia, *f.* **blemish** 2, TR.: macchiare; annerire, diffamare. **-less**, ADJ.: senza macchia. **-ment**, S.: macchia, *f.*; disonore, *m.*
blĕnch, TR.: impedire, porre ostacolo; INTR.: tremare di paura; rannicchiarsi.
blĕnd, TR.: mescolare, mischiare; bruttare.
blĕss, TR.: benedire; glorificare: *God — you!* Dio vi benedica! — *my heart!* per Bacco! **-ed**, ADJ.: felice, beato; santo: *the* —, i beati. **-edly**, ADV.: felicemente, beatamente. **-edness**, S.: beatitudine, felicità, *f.* **-er**, S.: che benedice. **-ing**, S.: benedizione; grazia di Dio, *f.* **-t**, ADJ.: beato, benedetto.
blight 1, S.: nebbia; golpe, *f.* **blight** 2, TR.: annebbiare; guastare. **-ed**, **-y**, ADJ.: annebbiato; guasto, corrotto.
blind 1, ADJ.: cieco; nascoso, oscuro; S.: gelosia, persiana, *f.*; sotterfugio, *m.*: — *man*, cieco; — *woman*, cieca. **blind** 2, TR.: acciecare; ingannare. **-fold** 1, ADJ.: cogli occhi bendati. **-fold** 2, TR.: bendare gli occhi a; acciecare. **-ly**, ADV.: ciecamente, alla cieca. **-man's buff**, S.: giuoco della cieca, *m.* **-ness**, S.: cecità, *f.*; accecamento, *m.* **-side**, S.: debolezza, *f.*; difetto, *m.* **-worm**, S.: cicigna, *f.*
blink 1, S.: occhiata, *f.* **blink** 2, INTR.: ammiccare, accennar cogli occhi. **-ard**, S.: guercio, losco, *m.* **-ers**, S. PL.: paraocchi, *m. pl.*
bliss, S.: felicità, beatitudine, *f.* **-ful**, ADJ.: felice, beato. **-fully**, ADV.: felicemente, beatamente. **-fulness**, S.: felicità, beatitudine, *f.* **-less**, ADJ.: infelice.
blister 1, S.: vescica; bolla, *f.*; vescicante, *m.* **blister** 2, TR.: applicare un vescicante; INTR.: formarsi in vesciche. **-ing-fly**, S.: cantaride, *f.*
blithe, ADJ.: gioioso, giocondo, lieto. **-ly**, ADV.: giocondamente, lietamente. **-ness**, S.: giocondità, allegrezza, *f.* **-some**, ADJ.: giocoso, lieto. **-someness** = *blitheness.*
blōach, S.: pustula, *f.*
blōat 1, ADJ.: enfiata, gonfio. **-bloat** 2, TR.: enfiare; gonfiare; INTR.: gonfiarsi. **-edness**, S.: enfiagione, gonfiezza, *f.*
blŏbber, S.: bubbola, bollicina, *f.* **-lip**, S.: labbro troppo grosso, *m.* **-lipped**, ADJ.: labbruto.
blŏck 1, S.: ceppo, *m.*; forma; testa di moro, *f.*; ostacolo, intoppo, *m.* **block** 2, TR.: bloccare, assediare: — *up*, fermare, chiudere. **-āde**, S.: bloccatura, *f.*; blocco, *m.* **-ade**, TR.: bloccare, assediare. **-head**, S.: babbaccione, sciocco, *m.* **-headed**, ADJ.: stupido, balordo, gaglioffo. **-house**, S.: fortezza, *f.* **-ishly**, ADV.: scioccamente, goffamente. **-ishness**, S.: sciocchezza, balordaggine, *f.* **-tin**, S.: stagno puro, *m.*
blŏmary, S.: fornace da fondare il ferro, *f.*
blŏnd-lace, S.: merletto di seta, *m.*
blóod 1, S.: sangue, *m.*; famiglia; stirpe; ira, collera, *f.*: *let* —, cavar sangue. **blood** 2, TR.: insanguinare; esasperare. **-guiltiness**, S.: omicidio, assassinamento, *m.* **-hound**, S.: limiero, *m.* **-ily**, ADV.: sanguinosamente; crudelmente. **-iness**, S.: crudeltà, inumanità, *f.* **-less**, ADJ.: esangue; morto. **-let**, TR.: cavar sangue. **-letting**, S.: cavata di sangue, *f.* **-shed**, S.: spargimento di sangue, *m.* **-shedder**, S.: assassino, micidiale, *m.* **-shot**, ADJ.: stravasato. **-stone**, S.: sanguigna, *f.* **-sucker**, ADJ.: sanguisuga. **-thirstiness**, S.: sete di sangue, *f.* **-thirsty**, ADJ.: sanguinolente. **-vessel**, S.: vaso sanguigno, *m.* **-wort**, S.: sanguinaria, *f.* **-y**, sanguinoso, sanguinario; crudele: — *flux*, flusso di sangue, *m.*
blòom 1, S.: fiore, *m.* **bloom** 2, INTR.: fiorire; germogliare. **-y**, ADJ.: fiorito, pieno di fiori.
blōre†, S.: soffio, *m.*
blŏssom = *bloom.*
blŏt 1, S.: macchia; cancellatura; infamia, *f.* **blot** 2, TR.: macchiare; cassare, scancellare; disonorare: *this paper —s*, questa carta spande l' inchiostro.
blŏtch, S.: pustula; macchia, *f.*
blōte, TR.: affumicare, seccare al fumo; INTR.: gonfiarsi. **-ed**, ADJ.: affumicato; gonfio.
blŏtting-paper, S.: carta sugante; straccia, *f.*
blōw 1, S.: colpo, *m.*, botta, *f.*; disastro *m.*: *slanting* —, rovescione, *m.*; coma

—*s*, venire alle mani. **blow** 2, IRR.; TR.: soffiare; suonare; INTR.: alenare, ansare; aprirsi, dilatarsi; — *away*, dissipare; — *down*, rovinare, rovesciare; mandare giù; — *in*, fare entrare soffiando; penetrare; — *one's nose*, soffiarsi il naso; — *off*, dissipare soffiando, dispergere; — *out*, estinguere; smorzare; — *up*, far saltar in aria, pubblicare; *I'll — him up*, gli darò una buona lavata di capo. **-er**, S.: soffiatore, *m.* **-ing**, S.: soffiamento, soffiare, *m.* **-pipe**, S.: canna da soffiare, *f.*

blōwz-e, S.: dondolona, paffuta, *f.* **-y**, ADJ.: abbronzato, rosso.

blŭbber 1, S.: polmone marino, *m.*; untuosa parte della balena, *f.* **blubber** 2, INTR.: gonfiarsi le guance.

blŭdgeon, S.: bastone, bastonaccio, *m.*

blūe 1, ADJ.: turchino, azzurro. **blue** 2, TR.: tingere di turchino. **-bell**, S.: baccara, *m.* **-bird**, S.: cutrettola, *f.* **-bottle**, S.: fioraliso, *m.* **-ly**, ADJ.: di color turchino, azzurrino.

blŭff, ADJ.: rustico, grossolano. **-ness**, S.: rustichezza, *f.*

blūish, ADJ.: azzurrino.

blŭnder 1, S.: errore; fallo, marrone, *m.*: *make a —*, pigliar un granchio. **blunder** 2, TR.: confondere; imbrogliare; INTR.: sbagliare, ingannarsi. **-buss**, S.: moschettone, *m.* **-er**, S.: sciocco, balordo, *m.* **-head**, S.: pecorone, babbaccione, *m.* **-ingly**, ADV.: stupidamente.

blŭnt 1, ADJ.: ottuso, grossolano, rozzo. **blunt** 2, TR.: spuntare; reprimere. **-ish**, ADJ.: alquanto spuntato. **-ly**, ADV.: bruscamente, rozzamente. **-ness**, S.: ottusità *f.* rozzezza, *f.*

blŭr 1, S.: macchia, *f.*; disonore, *m.* **blur** 2, TR.: macchiare; disonorare.

blŭrt, TR.: sbalestrare, strafalciare.

blŭsh 1, S.: rossore, *m.*; vergogna, *f.*: *put to the —*, far arrossire; *at first —*, a prima vista. **blush** 2, INTR.: arrossire; essere confuso. **-ful**, ADJ.: vergognoso. **-less**, ADJ.: senza rossore; impudente. **-y**, ADJ.: vermiglio; vergognoso.

blŭs-ter 1, S.: fracasso, *m.*; millanteria, *f.* **-ter** 2, INTR.: strepitare; tempestare. **-terer**, S.: bravaccione, rodomonte, *m.* **-tering**, ADJ.: tempestoso; pomposo. **-t(e)rous**, ADJ.: tumultuoso, turbulento.

bōar, S.: verro, *m.*: *wild —*, cignale, cinghiale, *m.*

bōard 1, S.: asse; tavola; sala del consiglio, *f.*; bordo, *m.*: *on — a ship*, a bordo di un bastimento; *deal above —*, trattare aperto (*or* con ischiettezza). **board** 2, TR.: intavolare; abbordare; INTR.: tenere a dozzina; stare a dozzina: *I — at Mr. A.*, sto a dozzina dal signor A. **-er**, S.: pensionario, dozzinante, *m.* **-ing**, S.: abbordaggio; arrembaggio, *m.* **-ing-school**, S.: pensione, *f.*, convitto, *m.* **-wages**, S. PL.: salario di vitto, *m.*

bōarish, ADJ.: di cinghiale; rozzo.

bōast 1, S.: jattanza, millanteria, *f.*: *make a —*, vantarsi, gloriarsi. **boast** 2, TR.: vantare; esaltare; INTR.: vantarsi, millantarsi. **-er**, S.: millantatore, vantatore, *m.* **-ful**, ADJ.: vanagloriosо. **-ing**, S.: millanteria, ostentazione, *f.* **-ingly**, ADV.: in modo vantevole, da millantatore.

bōat 1, S.: battello, *m.*, barca, *f.*: *little —*, barchetta; *ship's —*, schifo. **boat** 2, TR.: trasportare in barca; INTR.: andare in barca. **-builder**, S.: costruttore di battelli, *m.* **-hook**, S.: gancio di lancia, *m.* **-man**, S.: barcaiuolo, barcaruolo, *m.* **-swain** coll. *bō's'n*, S.: bosman, *m.*

bŏb 1, S.: oggetto pendente; ciondolo; sughero (d'una lenza) tirico, *m.*; botta, *f.* **bŏb** 2, TR.: battere; ingannare; INTR.: ciondolare; **-bin**, S.: cannello, *m.* **-cherry**, S.: giuoco della ciriegia, *m.* **-tail**, S.: coda corta, *f.* **-tailed**, ADJ.: scodato, senza coda. **-wig**, S.: parrucca corta, *f.*

bōde, TR.: presagire, pronosticare. **-ment**, S.: presagio, pronostico, *m.*

bŏdge, INTR.: esitare.

bŏdi-ce, S.: busto; corsaletto; giubbettino, *m.* **-less**, ADJ.: incorporeo. **-ly**, ADJ.: corporeo; ADV.: corporeamente.

bōding, S.: presagio, pronostico, *m.*

bŏdkin, S.: punteruolo; stiletto, *m.*

bŏdy, S.: corpo; guscio (d'una carrozza); sostanza; società, *f.*: *any—*, *every—*, ognuno, chiunque; *little —*, corpicciuolo, corpicello; — *politic*, corpo politico; *busy—*, faccendone, broglione. **-guard**, S.: guardie del corpo, *f. pl.*

bŏg, S.: palude, pantano, *m.*

bŏggl-e, INTR.: esitare, bilanciare. **-er**, S.: uomo dubitativo, uomo timido, *m.* **-ing**, S.: esitazione, irresoluzione, *f.*

bŏggy, ADJ.: paludoso, pantanoso.

bŏil 1, S.: fignolo; ciccione, *m.*, ulcera, *f.* **boil** 2, TR.: lessare, bollire; cuocere; INTR.: bollire; ondeggiare: *—ed meat*, lesso, *m.*, carne lessa, *f.* **-er**, S.: caldaja, *f.*; (*loc.*) calderone a vapore, *m.* **-ing**, S.: bollimento, *m.*

bŏisterous, ADJ.: furioso, tempestoso, violento. **-ly**, ADV.: furiosamente, violentemente. **-ness**, S.: impetuosità, turbolenza; violenza, *f.*

bōld, ADJ.: ardito, bravo, coraggioso; impudente: *make —*, prendersi la libertà, osare. **-en**, TR.: incoraggiare. **-face**, S.: sfacciatezza, impudenza, *f.* **-faced**, ADJ.: sfacciato, sfrontato, impudente. **-ly**, ADV.: arditamente, con bravura

-ness, S.: arditezza, intrepidità, temerità, *f.*; coraggio, *m.*
bōle, S.: tronco; bolo, *m.*; sei moggi, *m. pl.*
bōll, S.: stelo; gambo, *m.*
bōlster 1, S.: primaccio, piumaccio, *m.* **bolster** 2, TR.: appoggiare; avvolgere con banda: — *up*, farsi fautore di. **-er**, S.: protettore, fautore, *m.* **-ing**, S.: sostegno, *m.*; protezione, *f.*
bōlt 1, S.: freccia, *f.*; dardo; catenaccio, *m.* **bolt** 2, TR.: incatenacciare; abburattare; crivellare; INTR.: uscire subitaneamente. **-er**, S.: burattello, buratto, *m.* **-ing-house**, S.: buratteria, *f.* **-ing-hutch**, S.: buratto, frullone, *m.*
bōlus, S.: bolo, *m.*; pillola, *f.*
bŏm-b, S.: bomba, *f.* **-bârd**, TR.: bombardare. **-bardier**, S.: bombardiere, *m.* **-bârdment**, S.: bombardamento, *m.*
bombaçin, S.: bambagino, *m.*
bŏm-bast, S.: ampollosità, *f.*, anfanamento, *m.* **-băst(ic)**, ADJ.: ampolloso, gonfio.
bombilătion, S.: strepito, *m.*
bŏmbshell, S.: bomba, *f.*
bŏnd, S.: nodo, legame, *m.*; obbligazione, promessa, *f.*: — *of friendship*, legami d' amicizia. **-age**, S.: schiavitù; servitù, *f.* **-maid**, S.: schiava, *f.* **-man**, **-servant**, S.: schiavo, *m.* **-service**, S.: schiavitù, servitù, *f.* **-slave**, S.: schiavo, *m.* **-sman**, S.: mallevadore, *m.*; sicurtà, *f.* **-woman**, S.: schiava, *f.*
bōne 1, S.: osso, *m.*: *make no —s*, non farsi scrupolo; *pick a* —, rosicchiare un osso. **bone** 2, TR.: disossare. **-less**, ADJ.: senza ossa, disossato. **-setter**, S.: chirurgo che rimette le ossa dislogate, *m.*
bŏnfire, S.: fuoco d' allegrezza, *m.*
bŏnnet, S.: berretta, cappellina, *f.*
bŏn-nily, ADV.: graziosamente, aggradevolmente. **-ny**, ADJ.: leggiadro; grazioso.
bŏnnyclabber, S.: siero di latte, *m.*
bōny, ADJ.: ossuto, ossoso.
bōoby, S.: balordo, sciocco, *m.*
bŏok 1, S.: libro; tomo, *m.*: *bound* —, libro legato; *stitched* —, libro in brosciura; — *in boards*, libro cartonato; *without* —, a mente; *keep —s*, tenere i libri. **book** 2, TR.: allibrare, scrivere nel libro. **-binder**, S.: legatore di libri, *m.* **-case**, S.: libreria, scandia, *f.*; armadio, *m.* **-ful**, ADJ.: pieno di nozioni indigeste. **-ish**, ADJ.: studioso. **-ishness**, S.: amor eccessivo dello studio, *m.*; bibliomania, *f.* **-keeper**, S.: ragioniere, contabile, *m.* **-keeping**, S.: tenere i libri, *m.* **-learned**, ADJ.: versato nei libri, erudito. **-learning**, S.: erudizione, *f.* **-man**, S.: uomo studioso, *m.* **-mate**, S.: compagno in istudio, *m.* **-seller**, S.: libraio, *m.* **-selling**, S.: commercio di libri, *m.* **-shop**, S.: bottega del libraio; libreria, *f.* **-stall**, S.: banchino di libri usati. **-stand**, S.: leggio, *m.* **-store**, S.: libreria, *f.* **-trade** = *bookselling*. **-worm**, S.: tignola, *f.*; uomo troppo studioso, *m.*
bōom 1, S.: (*nav.*) boma, *f.*, polo (di vela), *m.* **boom** 2, INTR.: sbalzare; lanciarsi. **-ing**, S.: rimbombo, *m.*
bōon 1, S.: dono; favore, *m.*, grazia, *f.* **boon** 2, ADJ.: buono; lieto, gioviale.
bōor, S.: rustico, villano, *m.* **-ish**, ADJ.: rustico, villano, rozzo. **-ishly**, ADV.: rusticamente, rozzamente. **-ishness**, S.: rustichezza; zotichezza, *f.*
bōose, S.: stalla pel bue, *f.*
bōot 1, S.: stivale, *m.*: *put on one's —s*, stivalarsi, calzar gli stivali; *in —s*, stivalato. **boot** 2, S.: profitto guadagno, *m.*: *to* —, per soprappiù. **boot** 3, TR.: profittare; inricchire; INTR.: mettersi gli stivali. **-black**, S.: lustrascarpe, lustrastivali, *m.* **-ed**, ADJ.: stivalato.
bōoth, S.: capanna, *f.*
bōot-hose, S.: calzetta grossa, *f.* **boot-jack**, S.: cavastivali, *m.* **-last** = *boot-tree*.
bootless, ADJ.: inutile, svantaggioso.
boot-tree, S.: forma da stivali, *f.* **-s**, S.: = *bootblack*.
bōoty, S.: bottino; predamento, *m.*, preda, *f.*
bopēep, INTR.: *play* —, far capolino, guardar sott' occhi.
borăchio†, S.: imbriacone, trincone, *m.*
bōrable, ADJ.: che può forarsi.
bòrage, S.: boraggine, borrana, *f.*
bōrax, S.: borrace, *m.*
bôrder 1, S.: orlo, lembo, *m.*; estremità, *f.* **border** 2, TR.: orlare; confinare; INTR.: essere contiguo. **-er**, S.: confinante, *m.* **-ing**, ADJ.: contiguo, limitrofo.
bōre 1, S.: bocca (d' un arme), *f.*, calibro; succhiello, *m.* **bore** 2, TR.: forare, bucare, pertugiare; annoiare, tediare.
bōrea-l, ADJ.: boreale, settentrionale. **Bōrea-s**, S.: borea, aquilone, *m.*
bōrer, S.: foratoio; succhiello, *m.*
bōrn, ADJ.: nato; destinato: *be* —, nascere; *where were you —?* dove siete nato?
bórough, S.: borgo; villaggio, *m.*
bŏrrel, ADJ.: ruvido.
bŏrrow, TR.: pigliare in prestito, *m.* **-er**, S.: prenditore in prestito, *m.* **-ing**, S.: prestito, *m.*, prestanza, *f.*
bŏs-cage, S.: boschetto, *m.* **-ky**, ADJ.: boscoso, selvoso.
bóșom 1, S.: seno, grembo; cuore; desiderio; golfo, *m.*: — *of a shirt*, sparato (d' una camicia), *m.* **bosom** 2, TR.: chiu

dere in seno, insenare: —*friend*, amico intimo, *m*.
bŏss 1, S.: gobba. **boss** 2, S.: borchia; figura (di rilievo), *f*. **-age**, S.: bozzo, *m*.
bot-ănical, ADJ.: botanico. **bŏt-anist**, S.: botanico, *m*. **bŏt-any**, S.: botanica, *f*.
bŏtch 1, S.: enfiato, *m*., pustula, *f*. **botch** 2, TR.: rappezzare, rattoppare, ciarpare. **-er**, S.: rappezzatore, *m*. **-ery**, S.: rappezzare, *m*. **-ingly**, ADV.: alla grossolana, malamente. **-y**, ADJ.: rappezzato; malfatto.
bōth 1, ADJ.: ambo, ambe; l'uno e l'altro, ambidue: — *hands*, ambo le mani; — *of them*, ambedue; *on* — *sides*, da tutte le parti. **both** 2, CONJ.: egualmente che: *both* . . . *and*, e . . . e; si . . . che; così bene . . . come.
bŏther 1, TR.: imbarrazzare, confondere; annoiare, importunare. **bother** 2, S.: annoiamento; annoiatore, *m*.
bŏttle 1, S.: bottiglia, *f*.; fiasco; fastello (di fieno), *m*.: *big* —, fiascone, *m*.; *cork a* —, turare una bottiglia. **bottle** 2, TR.: infiascare; affastellare, imbottigliare. **-brush**, S.: spazzola, *f*. **-screw**, S.: cavasughero, *m*.
bŏttom 1, S.: fondo, fondamento, *m*.; valle; fine, *f*.; vascello, *m*.: — *of the heart*, imo del cuore; — *of the stairs*, fondo della scala; *stand upon a good* —, esser bene in gamba; *go to the* —, andare a fondo; *sink to the* —, mandare al fondo, sprofondare; *at* —, a fondo, in sostanza. **bottom** 2, TR.: fondare, fare fondo. **-ed**, ADJ.: fondato, inaspato. **-less**, ADJ.: senza fondo. **-ry**, S.: prestito alla grossa avventura; cambio marittimo, *m*.
bōuge †, INTR.: enfiarsi, gonfiarsi.
bŏugh, S.: ramo, *m*.
bought 1 *bāt*, pret. di *buy*.
bŏught † 2, S.: curvatura, *f*.
bŏunce 1, S.: strepito, fracasso, *m*; bravata, *f*. **bounce** 2, INTR.: strepitare, stricchiolare; vantarsi. **-er**, S.: millantatore, *m*. **-ingly**, ADV.: con strepito.
bŏund 1, S.: limite. **bound** 2, S.: salto, sbalzo, *m*. **bound** 3, TR.: limitare, terminare; destinare, obbligare; reprimere. **bound** 4, INTR.: sbalzare. **bound** 5, PART. (di *bind*): *the ship is* — *for L.*, il bastimento è caricato per L. **-ary**, S.: termine; confine, *m*. **-en**, ADJ.: obbligato, tenuto. **-ing**, ADJ.: balzante, saltante. **-less**, ADJ.: immenso, infinito. **-lessness**, S.: immensità, infinità, *f*. **-stone**, S.: termine, *m*.
bŏunteous, ADJ.: buono, benigno; liberale. **-ly**, ADV.: benignamente, liberalmente. **-ness**, S.: munificenza, liberalità, *f*.
bŏuntiful, ADJ.: generoso, liberale. **-ly**, ADV.: benignamente, generosamente. **-ness**, S.: benignità, generosità, *f*.

bŏunty, S.: bontà; liberalità, *f*.
bōurd † 1, S.: scherzo, *m*. **bourd** † 2, INTR.: scherzare.
boūrgeon, INTR.: germogliare.
bōurn 1, S.: limite. **bourn** 2, S.: rivoletto, *m*.
bōuse, INTR.: trincare, sbevazzare. **-y**, ADJ.: imbriaco, inebbriato.
bŏut, S.: volta, fiata, *f*.; tratto, *m*.: *for this* —, per questa volta; *drinking* —, bevuta, *f*.
boutāde, S.: bizzarria, *f*.
bōw 1, S.: arco, archetto; inchino, *m*. **bōw** 2, S.: riverenza, *f*.: *draw the long* —, lanciar campanili, spacciare a credenza. **bōw** 3, TR.: curvare, piegare; deprimere; INTR.: inchinarsi; — *down*, prostrarsi. **-bent**, ADJ.: arcato, arcuato, curvo.
bŏwel, TR.: sventrare. **-s**, S. PL.: viscere, budella, *f. pl.*; compassione, tenerezza, *f*.
bŏwer 1, S.: pergola, *f*., pergolato, ombroso recesso, *m*.; ancora di posta, *f*. **bower** 2, INTR.: alloggiare. **-y**, ADJ.: pieno di pergole; ombroso, frondoso.
bŏwge, TR.: (*nav.*) foracchiare.
bōwl 1, S.: tazzone; bacino, *m*. **bowl** 2, S.: boccia, pallottola, *f*. **bowl** 3, TR.: giuocar alle boccie.
bōwlder, **-stone**, S.: ciotto, ciottolo; (*geol.*) masso erratico, *m*.
bōw-legged, ADJ.: sbilenco.
bōwler, S.: giuocatore di boccie, *m*.
bōwless, ADJ.: senz' arco.
bōwline, S.: (*nav.*) bolina, *f*.
bōwling(-green), S.: giuoco di boccie, *m*.
bōwman, S.: arciere, arcatore; (*nav.*) brigadiere, *m*.
bŏwse, TR.: (*nav.*) tirare (una corda).
bōw-shot, S.: tiro d'arco, *m*.
bōwsprit, S.: (*nav. arch.*) bompresso, *m*.
bōw-string, S.: corda dell'arco, *f*. **-window**, S.: finestra ovale, *f*. **-yer**, S.: arciere, *m*.
bŏx 1, S.: (*shrub*) bossolo, *m*.; (*case*) scatola, cassetta, *f*.; bosso; palco (in teatro), *m*.: *little* —, cassettina; — *on the ear*, schiaffo, *m*.; — *of a wheel*, mozzo di ruota; *be in the wrong* —, trovarsi in cattivi panni. **box** 2, TR.: chiudere in una scatola; INTR.: battersi a pugni: (*nav.*) — *a ship*, mettere una nave in panna. **-en**, ADJ.: fatto di bosso.
bŏx-er, S.: pugilatore, *m*. **-ing**, S.: il far a pugni. **-match**, S.: pugilato, *m*.
bŏy, S.: giovanetto, ragazzo; servo, *m*.: *be past a* —, esser uomo fatto; —*'s trick*, ragazzata, *f*. **-hood**, S.: puerizia, infanzia, *f*. **-ish**, ADJ.: puerile, fanciullesco. **-ishly**, ADV.: fanciullescamente. **-ishness**, **-ism**, S.: puerilità, fanciullaggine, *f*.

brăbbl-e 1, s.: querela, disputa, *f.* **brabble** 2, INTR.: rissare strepitosamente, disputare. **-er**, s.: contenditore, gridatore, *m.*
brăc-e 1, s.: coppia, *f.*, pajo, *m.*; cintura, *f.*, cignone; (*nav.*) cordame, *m.*: — *of pistols*, pajo di pistole; — *of grayhounds*, coppia di levrieri. **brace** 2, TR.: legare, bendare; ristringere; (*nav.*) bracciare. **-elet**, s.: braccialetto, *m.* **-er**, s.: cintura, fascia, *f.*
brăch, s.: bracco, *m.*
brăchial, ADJ.: del braccio.
brachўgraphy, s.: tachigrafia, stenografia, *f.*
brăck, s.: breccia; rottura, *f.*; sale, *m.*
brăcket, s.: beccatello, *m.* **-s**, s. PL.: parentesi, *m.*; clausole, *f.*; (*nav.*) candelieri, *m. pl.*
brăckish, ADJ.: salmastro. **-ness**, s.: salsezza, salsaggine, *f.*
brăg 1, s.: vantamento, *m.*, millanteria, *f.* **brag** 2, INTR.: vantarsi, iattarsi; millantarsi. **-gadōcio**, **-gart**, **-ger**, s.: bravaccio, vantatore, millantatore, *m.*
brăid 1, s.: tessitura, *f.*; intrecciamento, *m.* **braid** 2, TR.: intrecciare.
brăils, s. PL.: cordicelle, *f. pl.*
brăin 1, s.: cervello; giudizio, senno, *m.*: *little* —, cervelletto; cerebello: *congestion of the* —, congestione cerebrale; *blow out one's* —*s*, bruciarsi il cervello; *rack one's* —*s*, stillarsi il cervello, lambiccarsi il cervello; *beat one's* —*s*, lambiccarsi il cervello, sottilizzare; *break one's* —*s*, rompersi la testa. **brain** 2, TR.: ammazzare; discervellare. **-less**, ADJ.: scervellato, sciocco. **-pan**, s.: cranio, *m.* **-sick**, ADJ.: sciocco, frenetico. **-sickness**, s.: freneticheżza; stolidezza, *f.*
brăk-e, s.: maciulla, *f.*; briglione, *m.*, morsa; madia, *f.*; spine, *f. pl.*; (*rail.*) freno, *m.*: *apply the* —, frenare. **-y**, ADJ.: spinoso.
brămble, s.: rovo; crespino, *m.*
brăn, s.: crusca, *f.*
brănch 1, s.: ramo, *m.*; progenie, *f.* **branch** 2, TR.: ramificare; dividere, separare; INTR.: spargersi in rami. **-ed**, ADJ.: ramoso, pieno di rami; diviso. **-iness**, s.: ramificazione, *f.* **-less**, ADJ.: senza rami, diramato. **-line**, s.: (*rail.*) strada laterale, *f.* **-railway**, s.: (*rail.*) strada (ferrata) laterale, *f.* **-y**, ADJ.: ramoso, ramoruto.
brănd 1, s.: tizzone, brando; fulmine, *m.* **brand** 2, TR.: suggellare con ferro infocato; diffamare, macchiare. **-iron**, s.: ferro da bollare. **-ish**, TR.: brandire; vibrare.
brăndy, s.: acquavite, *f.*
brăngl-e 1, s.: querela, rissa, *f.* **-e** 2, INTR.: contendere, disputare, rissare. **-er**, s.: contenditore, riottoso, *m.* **-ing**, s.: contendimento, *m.*, querela, rissa, *f.*
brănk, s.: grano Saraceno, *m.*
brănny, ADJ.: cruscoso; simigliante alla crusca.
brăntgoose = *brandgoose.*
brășier, s.: calderaio, *m.*; stufa, *f.*: —*'s ware*, lavori del calderaio, *m. pl.*
brăss, s.: rame, bronzo, *m.*; sfacciatezza, *f.*: *yellow* —, ottone, *m.*; *have* —, aver faccia tosta, essere sfrontato *or* impudente. **-foundry**, s.: fonderia d'ottone, *f.* **-iness**, s.: somiglianza di rame, *f.* **-y**, ADJ.: di rame; impudente.
brăt, s.: bambino, babbuino, *m.*
bravădo, s.: bravata, millanteria, *f.*
brăv-e 1, ADJ.: bravo, coraggioso; nobile; s.: bravaccio, millantatore, *m.* **-e** 2, TR.: bravare, insultare. **-ely**, ADV.: coraggiosamente. **-ery**, s.: bravura, *f.*, coraggio, *m.*; magnificenza, *f.*
brăvo, s.: assassino prezzolato, *m.*
brăwl 1, s.: querela, rissa, *f.*; contrasto, *m.* **brawl** 2, INTR.: rissare; contendere. **-er**, s.: sgridatore; litigatore, *m.*
brăwn, s.: polpa; forza; carne di verro, *f.* **-iness**, s.: parte carnosa; forza, *f.*; vigore, *m.* **-y**, ADJ.: carnoso; robusto, forte.
brăy 1, s.: ragghio, ragghiare; strepito, *m.* **bray** 2, TR.: pestare, macinare; INTR.: ragliare, ragghiare. **-er**, s.: macina, *f.* **-ing**, s.: pestamento, macinamento; rumore, *m.*
brăze, TR.: coprire di rame; saldare; bravare. **-n**, ADJ.: di rame, di bronzo; impudente. **-n**, INTR.: essere impudente. **-nface**, s.: impudente, sfacciato, *m.* **-faced**, ADJ.: sfrontato, impudente.
brăzier = *brasier.*
Brăzil-wood, s.: legno del Brasile, *m.*
brĕach, s.: breccia; apertura; mancanza; violazione, *f.*
brĕad 1, s.: pane, *m.*; sussistenza, *f.*: *brown* —, pane bruno, *m.*; *stale* —, pane assettato; *a loaf of* —, un pane; *be out of* —, essere fuor d'impiego; *get one's* —, guadagnare la sua vita. **bread** 2, TR.: tagliare del pane per la zuppa. **-basket**, s.: pancia, *f.*, canestro da pane, *m.* **-chipper**, s.: garzone del fornajo, *m.* **-corn**, s.: frumento, *m.* **-room**, s.: pagliuolo, *m.*
brĕadth, s.: larghezza, ampiezza, *f.*
brĕăk 1, s.: rompimento; (*rail.*) freno, *m.*: — *of day*, spuntar del giorno, *m.* **break** 2, IRR.; TR.: rompere; spezzare; fracassare, rovinare; debilitare; violare; vincere, sottomettere; proporre, offerire; INTR.: rompersi; spezzarsi, spaccarsi; fallire: — *the back*, slombare; dilombar-

si; — *ground*, aprire una trincea, zappare; — *the heart*, spezzare il cuore; — *a horse*, scozzonare un cavallo; — *into laughter*, sganasciarsi dalle risa; — *a jest*, burlare, schernire; — *the neck*, rompersi il collo; — *in pieces*, mettere in pezzi; — *silence*, rompere il silenzio; — *one's word*, mancare di parola; — *off one's work*, tralasciare il lavoro; — *asunder*, rompere per metà; — *down*, abbattere, distruggere; —*forth*, sorgere; spuntare; —*from*, separare, disunire; — *in*, entrare impetuosamente; — *into*, sforzare; — *into a house*, sfondare una porta; — *off*, rompere, spezzare; lasciare; — *open*, aprire a forza; — *out*, inondare, zampillare; — *over*, spandersi; traboccare; — *through*, passare a traverso; — *up*, separare; stendare; — *wind*, tirare coreggie; — *with*, cessare d' esser amico. **-age**, S.: frattura, *f.* **-er**, S.: rompitore, *m.* **-fast** 1 *brĕkfest*, S.: colazione, *f.*, asciolvere, *m.* **-fast** 2, INTR.: far colazione, asciolvere. **-ing**, S.: rompimento, *m.*; frattura, crepatura, *f.*; — *up*, vacanze, *f. pl.* **-neck**, S.: precipizio; rompicollo, *m.* **-promise**, S.: mancatore di parola, *m.* **-man**, S.: (*rail.*) frenaio, *m.*

brēam 1, S.: reina, *f.* (pesce). **bream** 2, TR.: (*nav.*) spalmare, dar il fuoco.

brĕast, S.: seno, petto, *m.*; coscienza *f.*; (*nav.*) fianco, *m.* **-bone**, S.: (*anat.*) sterno, *m.* **-high**, ADJ.: dell' altezza di parapetto. **-knot**, S.: fiocco di nastri, *m.* **-plate**, S.: pettabotta, corazza, *f.* **-work**, S.: parapetto, *m.*; sponda, *f.*

brĕath, S.: lena, *f.*, fiato, respiro; soffio, *m.*: *in a* —, tutt' ad un tratto, affatto; *to the last* —, fin' all' ultimo sospiro; *shortness of* —, asma, ambascia, *f.*; *draw* (*take*) —, respirare, alenare; *gasp for* —, boccheggiare; *run one's self out of* —, correre fin che si perda il fiato.

brēath-able, ADJ.: respirabile.

brēath-e, TR.: respirare; esalare; INTR.: respirare, anelare; prender ristoro: — *vengeance*, agognare la vendetta: — *one's last*, spirare; — *after*, aspirare; bramare; — *into*, ispirare; — *on*, soffiare; spirare; — *out*, esalare; — *out one's last*, spirare; morire. **-ing**, S.: ansamento, respiro; riposo, *m.* **-ing-hole**, S.: spiraglio, spiracolo, *m.* **-ing-time**, S.: tempo di riposo, *m.*

brĕathless, ADJ.: anelante; trafelato.

brĕd, ADJ.: allevato, nutrito: *well* —, costumato, ben educato, gentile; *ill* —, malcreato.

brēe, S.: tafano, *m.*

brēech 1, S.: diretano, *m.*: — *of a gun*, culatta di cannone, *f.* **breech** 2, TR.: mettere i calzoni ad un ragazzo. **-es**, S. PL.: calzoni, *m. pl.*, bracche, *f. pl.*

brēed 1, S.: razza; ventrata, *f.* **breed** 2, IRR.: TR.: produrre, generare; allevare; INTR.: generarsi; partorire: — *teeth*, mettere i denti; — *youth*, educare giovani. **-ing**, S.: educazione; (buona) creanza; civiltà, *f.*: *good* (*bad*) —, buona (mala) creanza.

brēez-e, S.: aura, *f.*, venticello; tafano, *m.* **-y**, ADJ.: rinfrescante, refrigerante.

brĕt, S.: lima, *f.*

brĕthren, S. PL.: fratelli, *m. pl.*

brē-ve, S.: breve, *f.* **-viary**, S.: breviario, *m.* **-viate**, S.: compendio; estratto, *m.* **-viature**, S.: abbreviazione, *f.*

brevier, S.: (*typ.*) testino, *m.*

brĕvity, S.: brevità; precisione, *f.*

brew *brū*, TR.: mescolare; tramare, INTR.: far la birra o cervogia: *be* —*ing*, mescolarsi. **-age**, S.: mistura, *f.* **-er**, S.: birraio, *m.* **-ery**, **-house**, S.: birreria, *f.* **-ing**, S.: fare la birra, *m.* **-is**, S.: fetta di pane intinta nel brodo, *f.*

briar = *brier*.

brib-e 1, S.: donativo per corrompere, *m.*: *take a* —, lasciarsi corrompere co' regali. **-e** 2, TR.: subornare, corrompere, comprare. **-er**, S.: corruttore, subornatore, *m.* **-ery**, S.: corrompimento, subornamento, *m.*

brick, S.: mattone; pane, *m.* **-bat**, S.: pezzo di mattone, *m.* **-kiln**, S.: fornace da mattoni, *f.* **-layer**, S.: muratore, *m.* **-maker**, S.: mattoniero; fornaciaio, *m.* **-wall**, S.: muro di mattoni, *m.* **-work**, S.: mattonato, *m.*

bridal, ADJ.: nuziale, sposereccio; S.: sposalizio, *m.*

bride, S.: sposa, *f.* **-bed**, S.: letto sposereccio, *m.* **-cake**, S.: chicca, focaccia di nozze, *f.* **-groom**, S.: sposo, *m.* **-maid**, S.: fanciulla che accompagna per onore la sposa, *f.* **-man**, S.: giovanotto che accompagna per onore lo sposo, *m.* **-room**, S.: camera nuziale, *f.*

Bridewell, S.: casa di correzione (in Londra), *f.*

bridge, S.: ponte; rialto (del naso), *m.*: — *of a violin*, ponte d' un violino; — *of the nose*, rialto del naso, *m.*

bridle 1, S.: briglia, *f.*, freno, *m.*: —*s of the bowline*, patte della bolina, *f. pl.*

bridle 2, TR.: imbrigliare; raffrenare, ristringere; INTR.: gonfiarsi, ingalluzzarsi. **-hand**, S.: mano con cui si tiene la briglia, *f.*

brīēf, ADJ.: breve; succinto, conciso; S.: breve; compendio; brevetto, *m.*: *in* —, alle corte. **-ly**, ADV.: brevemente, in poche parole. **-ness**, S.: brevità; precisione, *f.*

brier, S.: rovo, pruno, *m.*; spine, *f. pl.* **-y**, ADJ.: pieno di pruni, spinoso.
bri-gāde, S.: brigata, *f.* **-gadiēr**, S.: brigadiere, *m.*
brigan-d, S.: brigante, ladrone, masnadiere, *m.* **-dage**, S.: brigantaggio, *m.*; ruberia, *f.* **-dine**, **-tine**, S.: brigantino, *m.* **-dish**, ADJ.: brigantesco.
bright, ADJ.: lucido; brillante: *it is* —, il giorno comincia a spuntare. **-en**, TR.: lustrare, illustrare; pulire; INTR.: diventare lucido. **-ish**, ADJ.: alquanto lucente. **-ly**, ADV.: splendidamente, chiaramente. **-ness**, S.: splendore, lustro, *m.*; chiarezza; acutezza, *f.*
brigōse†, ADJ.: litigioso. **brigue**, S.: briga, trama; contesa, *f.*
brillian-cy, S.: lucidezza, *f.*; splendore, *m.* **-t**, ADJ.: brillante; risplendente; S.: brillante; diamante, *m.* **-tly**, ADV.: splendidamente. **-tness**, S.: lucidezza; chiarezza, *f.*
brills, S. PL.: peli sopra i cigli del cavallo, *m. pl.*
brim 1, S.: orlo, *m.*; margine; stremità, *f.*: *to the* —, fino all' orlo; — *of a hat*, falda d' un cappello, *f.* **brim** 2, TR.: empiere fino all' orlo; INTR.: esser pieno. **-ful**, ADJ.: colmo, pieno fino all' orlo. **-fulness**, S.: pienezza fino all' orlo, *f.* **-mer**, S.: bicchiere traboccante, *m.* **-stone**, S.: solfo, zolfo, *m.*: — *match*, zolfanello, *m.*; — *mine*, zolfanaia, *f.* **-stony**, ADJ.: sulfureo, pieno di solfo.
brindl-e, S.: macchia, punzecchiatura, *f.* **-ed**, ADJ.: punzecchiato.
brine, S.: salamoia, *f.*; (*fig.*) lagrime, *f. pl.* **-pit**, S.: pozzo d' acqua salata, *m.*
bring, IRR.; TR.: portare, recare; trasferire; menare; condurre; ridurre: — *close*, avvicinare; accostare; — *about*, effettuare; riuscire; — *away*, portare via; — *back*, riportare, ricondurre; restituire; — *down*, abbassare; umiliare; — *forth*, produrre; partorire; — *forward*, avanzare; — *in*, fare entrare; produrre; — *off*, dissuadere; liberare; — *on*, impegnare, intrigare; — *out*, far vedere, mostrare; — *under*, soggiogare, sottomettere; — *up*, allevare; insegnare; costumare; — *upon*, attrarre; meritare; — *to*, indurre; attrarre; — *together*, mettere d' accordo; — *ill luck*, portare mal augurio; — *low*, umiliare, abbattere; — *into favour*, mettere in grazia; — *to pass*, effettuare, eseguire; — *to perfection*, perfezionare; — — *to do*, indurre, persuadere; — *to know*, fare sapere; — *word*, informare. **-er**, S.: portatore, *m.*: — *up*, insegnatore; allevatore, *m.*
brinish, ADJ.: salmastro, salso. **-ness**, S.: salsezza; salamoia, *f.*
brink, S.: orlo, lembo, *m.*; ripa, *f.*
briny, ADJ.: salino, salso.
brisk 1, ADJ.: vivace, lieto, giocoso, spiritoso. **brisk** 2 (— *up*), INTR.: avanzarsi; rallegrarsi.
brisket, S.: petto d' un animale, *m.*
brisk-ly, ADV.: vigorosamente; lietamente, giovialmente. **-ness**, S.: vivacità, allegria, *f.*; vigore, *m.*
bristl-e 1, S.: setola, *f.* **-e** 2, INTR.: arricciarsi; star a un punta. **-y**, ADV.: setoso; arricciato.
brittl-e, ADJ.: fragile, frale, fievole. **-eness**, S.: fragilità, fralezza, *f.* **-y**, ADV.: fragilmente.
brize, S.: tafano, *m.*
brōach 1, S.: spiedo, schidione, *m.* **broach** 2, TR.: infilzare nello stidione; spillare; divulgare, pubblicare. **-er**, S.: spiedo, inventore, *m.*
broād, ADJ.: largo, esteso; aperto, osceno: — *daylight*, giorno chiaro, *m.*; *at* — *noon*, in sul mezzo giorno; *grow* —, allargarsi, slargarsi. **-cloth**, S.: panno largo, *m.* **-en**, TR.: allargare; INTR.: allargarsi, estendersi. **-eyed**, ADJ.: cogli occhi aperti. **-faced**, ADJ.: che ha una gran faccia. **-leaved**, ADJ: che ha le foglie larghe. **-ly**, ADV.: largamente; ampiamente. **-ness**, S.: larghezza, ampiezza; rozzezza, *f.* **-shouldered**, ADJ.: che ha le spalle larghe. **-side**, S.: sparo, *m.*, bordata, *f.* **-sword**, S.: spada tagliente, *f.* **-ways**, **-wise**, ADV.: secondo la larghezza.
brocād-e, S.: broccato, *m.* **-ed**, ADJ.: vestito di broccato.
brōcage, S.: guadagno del sensale; mestier del rigattiere, *m.*
brōccoli, S.: broccoli, *m. pl.*
brōck, S.: tasso, *m.*
brōcket, S.: cerviatto; cervo giovine, *m.*
brōdekin†, S.: stivaletto, *m.*
brōggle, TR.: (*prov.*) pescare per anguille.
brōgue, S.: scarpa di legno, *f.*; cattivo dialetto, parlar corrotto, *m.*
brōider, TR.: ricamare. **-y**, S.: ricamo, *m.*
brōil 1, S.: rissa; disputa, *f.*; rumore, *m.* **broil** 2, TR.: arrostire; INTR.: ardere: —*ed meat*, braciuola.
brōkage = *brocage*.
brōk-e, INTR.: contrattar negozi per altri, negoziare (cf. *break*). **-en**, ADJ.: rotto, spezzato; lacero; avvilito: — *language*, lingua corrotta, *f.*; *speak* — *English*, parlar inglese scorrettamente (alla forastiera); — *meat*, minuzzoli; bricioli (di carne), *m. pl.*; — *sleep*, sonno interrotto, *m.*; — *voice*, voce indebolita, . **-en-hearted**, ADJ.: squarciato, oppresso di dolore; cuore spezzato (with ave.

-**enly**, ADV.: interrottamente. -**enness**, S.: afflizione, contrizione, *f.* -**er**, S.: sensale; rigattiere: *exchange* —, agente di cambio; *pawn*—, usuraio, *m.* -**erage**, S.: senseria, *f.*

brŏnchial, ADJ.: bronchiale.

brŏnze, S.: bronzo, *m.*; medaglia, *f.*

brōōch 1, S.: spillo da petto; gioiello; ornamento di gioielli, *m.* **brooch** 2, TR.: adornare di gioie.

brōod 1, S.: covata; razza; schiatta, *f.* **brood** 2, (IN)TR.: covare, maturare.

bróok 1, S.: ruscello, *m.* **brook** 2, (IN)TR.: sofferire, tollerare.

bróom, S.: ginestra, scopa di ginestra. -**staff**, -**stick**, S.: manico della scopa, *m.* -**y**, ADJ.: pieno di ginestre.

brŏth, S.: brodo, *m.*

brŏthel, S.: bordello; lupanare, *m.*

brother, S.: fratello, *m.*: *elder* —, fratello maggiore; *younger* —, fratello minore; *lay* —, frate laico; — *in arms*, camerata; commilitone. -**hood**, S.: fratellanza, fraternità, *f.* -**in-law**, S.: cognato, *m.* -**ly**, ADJ.: fraterno; ADV.: fraternamente; da fraterno.

brŏw, S.: ciglio, *m.*; fronte; sommità, cima (d' un monte), *f.*: *knit the* —, increspar la fronte. -**beat**, TR.: guardare con cipiglio.

brŏwn, ADJ.: bruno, nero; nereggiante: *make* —, *grow* —, imbrunire; — *bread*, pane nero, *m.*; — *man*, bruno, brunetto, *m.*; — *paper*, carta straccia *or* brunella; — *sugar*, zucchero rottame, *m.*; — *woman*, bruna, brunetta, *f.* -**ish**, ADJ.: brunazzo, brunetto. -**ness**, S.: brunezza, *f.*

brŏwse 1, S.: messa, *f.*; pollone, *m.* -**e** 2, INTR.: mangiare foglie. -**ing**, S.: pascolo, pascimento, *m.*

brŭise 1, S.: ammaccamento, *m.*; schiacciatura; contusione, *f.* -**e** 2, TR.: ammaccare; schiacciare; rompere, pestare. -**er**, S.: pugilatore.

brŭit 1, S.: rumore, *m.*; fama, *f.* **bruit** 2, dar voce, rapporture.

brŭmal, ADJ.: brumale.

brunĕtte, S.: brunetta, *f.*

brŭnt, S.: urto; impeto; disastro, *m.*

brŭsh 1, S.: spazzola; granata, *f.*; impeto, incontro, *m.* **brush** 2, TR.: spazzolare; toccare leggermente; INTR.: muoversi o passare in fretta: — *away*, calcagnare; fuggire; — *off*, portare via. -**maker**, S.: che fa le spazzole, *m.* -**wood**, S.: bosco basso, *or* ceduo, *m.*; boscaglia, *f.* -**y**, ADJ.: setoloso, peloso.

brŭstle, INTR.: scoppiettare.

brŭ-tal, ADJ.: brutale; crudele. -**táli-** S.: brutalità, rustichezza; crudeltà, *f.* -**ize**, TR.: rendere brutale, rendere *tico*; INTR.: diventare brutale. -**tal-ly**, ADV.: brutalmente; crudelmente. -**te** 1, ADJ.: bruto, feroce; bestiale, rozzo. -**te** 2, S.: bruto, *m.*, bestia, *f.* -**teness**, S.: brutalità, *f.* -**tify**, TR.: rendere brutale. -**tish**, ADJ.: brutale, bestiale; feroce. -**tishly**, ADJ.: brutalmente, bestialmente, ferocemente. -**tishness**, S.: brutalità, bestialità salvatichezza, *f.*

bryony, S.: brionia, *f.*

bŭbbl-e 1, S.: bubbola, bolla; bagattella, *f.*; sciocco, goffo, *m.* -**e** 2, INTR.: bollire; ingannare. -**er**, S.: ingannatore, truffatore, *m.* -**ing**, S.: bollimento; garrito, *m.*

buccanéer, -**nier**, S.: buccaniere, filibustiere, pirato, ladrone di mare, *m.*

bŭck 1, S.: daino maschio; bucato, *m.* **buck** 2, TR.: fare il bucato; far razza dei daini. -**basket**, S.: paniere da portar il bucato, *m.*

bŭcket, S.: secchia, *f.*; (*nav.*) bugliolo, *m.*

bŭcking, S.: fare il bucato, *m.* -**cloth**, S.: ceneracciolo, *m.* -**tub**, S.: tinozza da farvi il bucato, *f.*

bŭckl-e 1, S.: fibbia, *f.*, fermaglio; riccio, *m.* -**e** 2, TR.: affibbiare; chiudere; manellare; INTR.: piegare; applicarsi: — *with*, essere alle mani. -**er** 1, S.: scudo, clipeo, *m.* -**er** 2, TR.: fare scudo; proteggere.

bŭckmast, S.: faggiuola, *f.*

bŭckram, S.: bugrane, *f.*

bŭck's-horn, S.: gramigna, *f.*

bŭck-thorn, S.: spinamagna, *f.* -**wheat**, S.: grano saraceno; miglio, *m.*

bucŏlic, ADJ.: buccolico, pastorale.

bŭd 1, S.: bottone, germoglio, *m.* **bud** 2, TR.: innestare; inserire; INTR.: germinare; pullulare.

bŭdge 1, S.: pelle d' agnello, *f.* **budge** 2, ADJ.: affettato, intirizzato. **budge** 3, INTR.: muoversi, cangiare sito.

bŭdget, S.: valiggia; provvisione, *f.*: *the year's* —, il bilancio annuale.

bŭff, S.: cuoio di bufalo, *m.* -**ale**, S.: bufalo, bufolo, *m.*

bŭffer(-head), S.: (*rail.*) cuscino da urto, *m.*

bŭffet 1, S.: schiaffo, *m.*; guanciata, *f.* **buffet** 2, TR.: schiaffeggiare: INTR.: giuocare alle pugna. -**er**, S.: pugilatore, *m.*

bŭffle†, S.: bufalo, *m.* -**headed**†, ADJ.: stupido.

buffōon, S.: buffone, zanni, *m.*: *play the* —, buffoneggiare. -**ery**, S.: buffoneria, zannata, *f.*

bŭg, S.: cimice, *m.* -**bear** 1, S.: spaventacchio, *m.* -**bear** 2, TR.: spaventare.

bŭggy, ADJ.: pieno di cimici.

bŭgle, S.: bugola, *f.* (-**horn**), S.: corno da caccia, *m.*

bŭgloss, s.: buglossa, *f.*
build, IRR.; TR.: edificare; costruire; INTR.: fidarsi, confidarsi: — *castles in the air*, fare castelli in aria. **-er**, s.: edificatore; fabbricatore, *m.* **-ing**, s.: edificio, *m.*; fabbrica; costruzione, *f.*
bŭlb, s.: bulbo, *m.*; cipolla, *f.* **-āceous**, **-ous**, ADJ.: bulboso.
bŭlge 1, s.: parte gonfiante della botte; protuberanza, *f.*, gonfiamento; convesso, *m.* **bulge** 2, INTR.: gonfiarsi, spingere in fuori; (*nav.*) fare acqua; affondarsi.
bŭlimy, s.: bulimia, fame canina, *f.*
bŭlk 1, s.: massa; grossezza, *f.*; grosso; tronco, busto; (*nav.*) scaffo, *m.*: *in* —, alla rinfusa; *by the* —, all' ingrosso. **bulk** 2, INTR.: piegare innanzi. **-head**, s.: (*nav. arch.*) spartimento, *m.*, separazione, *f.* **-iness**, s.: grossezza; larghezza, *f.* **-y**, ADJ.: grosso, massiccio.
bull 1, s.: toro; sbaglio, *m.*; assurdità, *f.*: *John Bull*, Giovanni Toro. **bull** 2, s.: bolla, *f.*: *papal* —, bolla pontifica, *f.*
bŭllace, s.: prugnola, *f.* **-tree**, s.: prugnolo, *m.*
bŭll-baiting, s.: combattimento di cani con tori, *m.* **-beef**, s.: carne di toro, *f.* **-beggar**, s.: spaventacchio, *m.* **-calf**, s.: vitello maschio; minchione, *m.* **-dog**, s.: alano, *m.*
bŭllet, s.: palla (di moschetto o di cannone), *f.*
bŭlletin, s.: bulletino, *m.*
bŭllet-shot, s.: cannonata, *f.*
bŭll-fight, s.: combattimento di tori, *m.* **-finch**, s.: fringuello marino, *m.* **-fly**, s.: tafano, *m.* **-head**, s.: ghiozzo; goffo, *m.* **-headed**, ADJ.: ostinato, ritroso.
bŭllion, s.: verga d' oro o d' argento, *f.*
bŭllock, s.: torello, bue giovine, *m.*
bŭlly 1, s.: bravo, sgherro, *m.* **bully** 2, INTR.: fare il bravaccio.
bŭlrush, s.: giunco, *m.*
bŭlwark 1, s.: baluardo, bastione, *m.* **bulwark** 2, TR.: fortificare.
bŭm, s.: diretano, *m.*
bŭm-bailiff, s.: sbirro, sergente, *m.*
bŭm-boat, s.: battello da provvisioni, *m.*
bŭmp 1, s.: tumore, *m.*; protuberanza, *f.*; colpo, *m.* **bump** 2, TR.: strepitare.
bŭmper, s.: bicchiere traboccante, *m.*
bŭmpkin, s.: contadinaccio, *m.*
bŭnch, s.: gobba, *f.*; tumore; fascio; nodo, *m.*: — *of feathers*, pennacchio; — *of grapes*, grappolo d' uva, *m.*; — *of keys*, mazzo di chiavi, *m.* **-backed**, ADJ.: gobbo. **-y**, ADJ.: crescente in grappoli; gobbo, gibboso.
bŭndle 1, s.: fardello, fagotto, *m.* **bundle** 2, TR.: affastellare, affardellare, impacchettare, fare un fardello.
bŭng 1, s.: turacciolo, cocchiume, *m.*
bung 2, TR.: turare, stoppare. **-hole**, s.: buca della botte, *f.*
bŭngl-e 1, s.: sbaglio, marrone, *m.* **-e** 2, TR.: acciarpare, acciabattare. **-er**, s.: ciarpone, ciarpiere, *m.* **-ingly**, ADV.: sciocamente, grossolanamente.
bŭnn, s.: schiacciatina, *f.*
bŭnt, s.: cavità, *f.*; gonfiamento, *m.*
bŭnter, s.: cenciaiuola, *f.*
bŭnting, s.: calandra, *f.*
buōy 1, s.: (*nav.*) gavitello; segnale dell' ancora, *m.* **buoy** 2, TR.: galleggiare; nuotare: — *up by hope*, animare dalla speranza. **-ancy**, s.: leggerezza, elasticità, *f.* **-ant**, ADJ.: galleggiante; leggiere.
bŭr, s.: lappola maggiore, *f.*
bŭrbot, s.: morena, *f.* (pesce).
burdelāis, s.: sorta d' uva, *f.*
bŭrden 1, s.: soma, *f.*, carico, peso; ritornello, *m.*: *beast of* —, bestia da soma, *f.*
burden 2, TR.: caricare; imbarazzare. **-er**, s.: caricatore, *m.* **-some**, ADJ.: grave; oppressivo; molesto. **-someness**, s.: peso, *m.*, gravezza, *f.*; incomodo, *m.*
bŭrdock, s.: lappola, *f.*
bŭreau *-rō*, s.: segreteria, *f.*, scrittoio, armario, *m.*
bŭrgamot, s.: bergamotta, *f.*
bŭrganot, s.: borgognotta, *f.*
burgeois *-zwa*, **bŭrgess**, s.: borghese, cittadino, *m.*
bŭrgh, s.: borgo, castello, *m.* **-er**, s.: borghese, *m.* **-ership**, s.: borghesia, cittadinanza, *f.*
bŭrghmote, s.: baliaggio, *m.*
bŭrglar, s.: ladro domestico o notturno, rubatore per rottura, *m.* **-y**, s.: rubare per rottura, *m.*
bŭrgomaster, s.: burgomastro, *m.*
buri-al *bĕri-*, s.: sepoltura, *f.*; funerali, *m. pl.* **-al-ground**, **-place**, s.: cimiterio, *m.* **-er**, s.: beccamorto, becchino, *m.*
bŭrin, s.: bulino, *m.*
burlésque 1, ADJ.: burlesco; faceto; s.: discorso burlesco, *m.* **burlesque** 2, TR.: burlare, beffare.
bŭr-liness, s.: grossezza, grandezza, *f.* **-ly**, ADJ.: grosso, corpacciuto.
bŭrn 1, s.: scottatura, *f.*, abbruciamento, *m.* **burn** 2, IRR.; TR.: abbruciare, bruciare; INTR.: ardere: — *away*, bruciarsi; consumarsi; — *up*, bruciare affatto; — *to ashes*, ridurre in cenere; — *one's fingers*, scottarsi le dita; — *one's self*, abbrucciarsi. **-er**, s.: incendiario; bocciuolo; becco di gas.
bŭrnet, s.: pimpinella, *f.*
bŭrning, ADJ.: abbruciante; caldo; s. fuoco; incendio, *m.* **-glass**, s.: vetro ardente, *m.*

bŭrnish, TR.: brunire; dare il lustro; INTR.: diventare lucido. **-er**, S.: brunitore, brunitoio, *m.* **-ing**, S.: brunitura, *f.*

bŭrnt, ADJ.: abbruciato, scottato (ecc., *cf. burn*).

bŭrr, S.: oreglia, *f.*: timpano dell' orecchio, *m.*

bŭrrel, S.: sorta di pera, *f.* **-fly**, S.: tafano, *m.*

bŭrrow 1, S.: borgo, *m.*; tana di coniglio, *f.* **burrow** 2, INTR.: nascondersi.

bŭr-sar, S.: tesoriere, *m.* **-se**, S.: borsa, *f.*; banco, *m.*

bŭrst 1, S.: crepatura, rottura, *f.*; fracasso, *m.* **burst** 2, IRR.; TR.: crepare; scoppiare; INTR.: creparsi; aprirsi: — *from*, scappare; fuggire; — *into tears*, pianger dirottamente; — *out*, spaccarsi; uscire; — *with laughi...*, morire dalle risa; smascellare dalle risa.

bŭrt, S.: lima, *f.* (pesce).

bŭrthen† = *burden.*

bury 1 *bĕri*, S.: borgo, *m.*; abitazione, *f.*
bury 2, TR.: sotterrare, seppellire. **-ing**, S.: seppellimento, *m.* **-ing-ground**, S.: cimiterio, *m.* **-ing-place**, S.: sepolcro, *m.*; sepoltura, *f.*

bŭsh, S.: cespuglio, *m.*; frasca; coda di volpe, *f.*: *go about the* —, menar il can per l' aia.

bŭshel, S.: staio, *m.*

bŭsh-iness, S.: foltezza, *f.* **-ment**†, S.: macchia, *f.*, boschetto, *m.*, siepaglia, *f.* **-y**, ADJ.: cespuglioso.

busi-less *bĭ-*, ADJ.: sfaccendato, scioperato. **-ly**, ADV.: attivamente; diligentemente; arditamente. **-ness**, S.: affare, negozio, *m.*, facenda, bisogna, *f.*: *full of* —, affacendato; *do one's* —, andar del ventre; *come into* —, avere degli affari; essere in voga; *mind your own* —, badate a' fatti vostri; *settle a* —, aggiustare una faccenda; *how is* —? come vanno gli affari? *transact a* —, condurre un negozio.

bŭsk, S.: stecca, *f.*; cespuglio, *m.*

bŭskin, S.: borsacchino; stivaletto, *m.* **-ed**, ADJ.: calzato di stivaletti.

bŭsky, ADJ.: selvoso.

bŭss 1, S.: bacio, *m.*; barca da pescare, *f.*
buss 2, TR.: baciare.

bŭst, S.: busto, *m.*

bŭstard, S.: ostardo, *m.*

bŭstl-e 1, S.: tumulto; rumore, *m.* **-e** 2, INTR.: far strepito, affrettarsi. **-er**, S.: uomo attivo, affannone, *m.*

busy 1 *bĭ-*, ADJ.: affaccendato, occupato.
busy 2, TR.: occupare; INTR. (REFL.): occuparsi; intromettersi; pigliar briga. **-body**, S.: faccendone, *m.*, -na, *f.*; affannone, *m.*, -na, *f.*

but 1, CONJ.: ma, però; fuorchè, eccetto; ADV.: solamente: — *one*, uno soltanto; non . . . che uno; *nothing* —, non . . . che; *the last* — *one*, il penultimo; — *for you*, senza di voi, se non foste voi. **but** 2 = *butt.*

bŭtcher 1, S.: macellaio, beccaio, *m.*: —*'s meat*, carne di beccheria, *f.*; —*'s shop*, beccheria, *f.*, macello, *m.* **butcher** 2, TR.: macellare; assassinare, uccidere. **-ly**, ADJ.: crudele, sanguinario. **-y**, S.: beccheria; macello, *m.*

bŭtler, S.: dispensiere, canovaio, *m.* **-ship**, S.: uffizio del dispensiere, *m.*

bŭtment, S.: (*arch.*) commesso, *m.*

bŭtshaft†, S.: freccia, *f.*

bŭtt 1, S.: fine, limite, *m.*, estremità, *f.*; scopo, *m.*; mira, *f.*; segno, *m.*; botta, *f.* **butt** 2, TR.: cozzare; urtare: — *one another*, percuotersi colle corna. **-end**, S.: punta grossa; estremità, *f.*; calcio (d'un fucile), *m.*

bŭtter 1, S.: burro, (*rare*) butirro, *m.*: *melted* —, salsa di butirro; *slice of bread and* —, fetta di pane unto con burro, *f.*
butter 2, TR.: condire con burro, ungere con burro; truffare: — *bread*, ungere il pane con burro. **-y**, ADJ.: burroso: —, dispensa, *f.* **-flower**, S.: fioretto giallo, *m.* **-fly**, S.: farfalla, *f.*, parpaglione, *m.* **-milk**, S.: siero di latte; latte di burro, *m.* **-wife**, **-woman**, S.: donna che vende burro, *f.*

bŭttock, S.: chiappa, natica, *f.*: — *of beef*, coscia di manzo, *f.*; —*s of a horse*, groppa d'un cavallo, *f.*

bŭtton 1, S.: bottone, *m.*; boccia, *f.* **button** 2, TR.: abbottonare. **-hole**, S.: asolo, occhiello, *m.* **-maker**, S.: bottonaio, *m.* **-ware**, S.: assortimento di bottoni, *m.*

bŭttress 1, S.: barbacane; sostegno, *m.*
buttress 2, TR.: far un barbacane; sostenere, appoggiare.

bŭttshaft = *butshaft.*

bŭtyrous, ADJ.: burroso.

bŭxom, ADJ.: obbediente; allegro, giocondo, lieto. **-ly**, ADV.: amorosamente; lietamente. **-ness**, S.: trattabilità, benignità; allegria, ilarità, *f.*

bŭy, IRR.; TR.: comp(e)rare: — *dear* (*cheap*), comprare caro (a buon patto); — *for cash*, comprare a contanti; — *on credit*, comprare a credito; — *up*, far acquisto di; — *and sell*, trafficare, negoziare; — *one off*, corrompere alcuno. **-er**, S.: compratore, *m.* **-ing**, S.: comperamento, *m.*, compra, *f.*

bŭzz 1, S.: ronzo, susurro, *m.* **buzz** 2, INTR.: ronzare, susurrare.

bŭzzard, S.: bozzago, *m.*

bŭzzing, S.: ronzo, mormorio, *m.*

bȳ, PREP., ADV.: per; da; al; vicino; appresso: — *everybody*, da tutti; — *the post*, per la posta; — *sea*, per mare; —

trade, di mestiere; — *day*, di giorno; — *much* (*far*), di molto, di gran lunga; — *degrees*, gradamente, poco a poco; — *this time*, a questa ora; — *and* —, adesso adesso; — *the bye*, di volo; *one* — *one*, uno ad uno; *year* — *year*, d'anno in anno; *hard* —, qui vicino; — *chance*, a caso; *I will stand* — *you*, vi spalleggerò. **-end**, S.: vantaggio particolare, *m.* **-gone**, ADJ.: passato: — *ages*, età trascorse. **-lane**, S.: vico; vicolo, *m.* **-law**, S.: statuto, *m.* **-lander**, S.: balandra, *f.* **-name**, S.: soprannome, *m.* **-path**, S.: strada poco frequentata, *f.* **-profits**, S. PL.: casuale, *m.* **-road**, S.: sentiero discosto, *m.* **-room**, S.: gabinetto, spogliatoio, *m.* **-stander**, S.: spettatore, *m.* **-street**, S.: strada fuor di mano, *f.* **-view**, S.: disegno particolare, *m.* **-walk**, S.: viale, *m.* **-way**, S.: traversa, *f.* **-word**, S.: proverbio, *m.*; massima, *f.*

Byzantine, ADJ.: bisantino.

C

c *sī* (*the letter*), S.: c, *m.*

căb, S.: carrozza d'affitto, *f.*; calesso, *m.*

ca-băl 1, S.: cabala: trama, cospirazione, *f.* **-bal** 2, INTR.: tramare, cospirare. **că-balist**, S.: cabalista, *m.* **-balistic(al)**, ADJ.: cabalistico. **-băller**, S.: macchinatore, *m.*

căbaret, S.: taverna, osteria, *f.*

căbbage 1, S.: cavolo, *m.* **cabbage** 2, TR.: rubare irritagli, cestire. **-head**, S.: cesto di cavolo, *m.* **-lettuce**, S.: lattuga cappuccia, *f.* **-tree**, S.: spezie di palma, *f.*

căbin 1, S.: camerino; gabinetto, *m.* **cabin** 2, TR.: chiudere in un luogo ristretto; INTR.: vivere in un luogo ristretto. **-boy**, S.: mozzo, camerotto, *m.*

căbinet, S.: gabinetto; armadio, *m.*; TR.: rinchiudere. **-council**, S.: gabinetto della corte, *m.* **-maker**, S.: ebanista, *m.* **-making**, S.: ebanisteria, *f.* **-work**, S.: lavoro d'ebanista, *m.*

căbl-e, S.: (*nav.*) gomena, *f.*, canapo, *m.*: —'*s length*, lunghezza di gomena, *f.*; *bit the* —, abbittare la gomena; *splice a* —, impiombare. **-et**, S.: (*nav.*) gomenetta, *f.* **-ish**, S.: boscaglie, *f. pl.*

căbman, S.: brumisto, fiaccheraio, *m.*

cabŏose, S.: cucina di nave, *f.*

cabriolĕt, S.: birroccio, birroccino, *m.*

cacāo, S.: cacao, *m.*

cachĕctic(al), ADJ.: cachettico.

cachinātion, S.: riso smoderato, *m.*

cackl-e 1, S.: croccio, chiocciare (dell'oca), *m.* **-e** 2, INTR.: crocciare, chiacciare. **-er**, S.: chioccia, *f.*; chiacchierone, *m.* **-ing**, S.: chiacciare, *m.*

căcochymy, S.: cacochimia, *f.*

cacodēmon, S.: maligno spirito, *m.*

cacŏphony, S.: cacofonia: discordanza, *f.*

cacūminate, TR.: rendere acuto, appuntare.

cadăverous, ADJ.: cadaveroso.

căddis, S.: cadi, *m.*

căde 1, S.: barile, *m.* **cade** 2, ADJ.: domestico, addimesticato.

căden-ce, **-cy**, S.: cadenza, *f.* **-t**, ADJ.: cadente; debile.

cadĕt, S.: cadetta; volontario, *m.*

cădg-e, TR.: portare una soma. **-er**, S.: pollaiuolo, *m.*

cădi, S.: cadi, *m.*

cadū-ceus, S.: caduceo, *m.* **-city**, S.: caducità; fragilità, *f.*

cæsūra *se-*, S.: (*pros.*) cesura, *f.*

căg, S.: carratello, *m.*

căge 1, S.: gabbia; prigione, *f.* **cage** 2, INTR.: chiudere in gabbia; prigionare.

căic, S.: caicco, *m.*

căitiff, S.: furfante; barattiere, *m.*

cajōl-e, TR.: lusingare, vezzeggiare; adulare. **-er**, S.: lusinghiere; adulatore, *m.* **-ery**, S.: lusingheria, adulazione, carezza, *f.* **-ing**, S.: lusingamento, *m.*, carezza, *f.*

căk-e 1, S.: focaccia, sfogliata, *f.* **-e** 2, INTR.: rappigliarsi, incrostarsi. **-ed**, ADJ.: rappigliato, rappreso. **-e-woman**, S.: offellara, *f.*

călabash, S.: zucca, *f.*

calamănco, S.: durante, *m.* (sorta di panno).

călamine, S.: giallamina, *f.*

călamint, S.: calaminta, nepitella, *f.*

calămi-tous, ADJ.: calamitoso. **-ity**, S.: calamità; infortunio, *m.*, miseria, *f.*

călamus, S.: calamo, *m.*

calăsh, S.: calesso, *m.*

calcāreous, ADJ.: calcareo, di calcina.

calcĕdony, S.: calcedonia, *f.* (pietra).

căl-cinate, TR.: calcinare. **-cinātion**, S.: calcinazione, calcinatura, *f.* **-cinatory**, ADJ.: calcinatorio. **-cine** = *calcinate*.

călcu-late, TR.: calcolare, computare. **-lating**, **-lātion**, S.: calculazione, *f.*, computo, *m.* **-lator**, S.: calculatore, computista. **-latory**, ADJ.: di calculazione. **-le**, S.: calcolo; computo, *m.* **-lose**, **-lous**, ADJ.: calcoloso.

căldron, S.: caldaia, *f.*, caldaio; paiuolo, *m.*

cale-făction, S.: calefazione, *f.* **-făctive**, ADJ.: calefattivo, riscaldativo. **căle-fy**, INTR.: riscaldarsi.

călendar, S.: calendario, almanacco, *m.*

călender 1, S.: mangano, *m.* **calen**

der 2, TR.: manganare. **-er**, S.: che mangana; lustratore, *m.*

călends, S.: calende, *f. pl.*

călenture, S.: febbre maligna, febbre ardente, *f.*

călf (pl. *calves*), S.: vitello, *m.*, vitella, *f.*; polpa delle gambe, *f.*: —*'s leather*, pelle di vitella, *f.*

căliber, S.: calibro, *m.*

călice, S.: calice, *m.*, coppa, *f.*

călico, S.: sorta di tela di cotone, *f.*

că-lid†, ADJ.: caldo, calido. **-lidity**†, S.: calidità, caldezza, *f.*

călif, S.: califfo, *m.* **-ate**, S.: califato, *m.*

ca-ligātion, S.: oscuramento; abbagliamento, *m.* **-liginous**, ADJ.: caliginoso, oscuro. **-liginousness**, S.: caligine, oscurità, *f.*

caligraphy, S.: calligrafia, *f.*

căliver†, S.: fucile, schioppo, *m.*

călix, S.: (*bot.*) calice, *m.*

călk, TR.: calafatare, calefatare. **-er**, S.: calafao, calfato, *m.* **-ing**, S.: calafatare; riparo (d' una nave), *m.* **-ing-iron**, ferro da calafato, *m.*

căll 1, S.: chiamata, *f.*, chiamamento, *m.*; vocazione, *f.*; invito; (*nav.*) fischio, *m.*; *at* —, in ordine, apparecchiata; *I will give you* —, passerò da voi. **call** 2, TR.: chiamare; appellare; nominare; convocare, radunare; ordinare, comandare: *he is called A.*, si chiama A.; *how do you — that?* come chiamate questa cosa? *I'll — on you*, passerò da voi; — *by name*, chiamare per nome; — *names*, ingiuriare, svillaneggiare; — *up spirits*, scongiurare i demoni; — *in question*, mettere in dubbio; — *after*, chiamare ad alta voce; — *again*, richiamare; ritornare; — *aloud*, gridare ad alta voce; — *aside*, prendere da parte; — *at*, andare a casa di; — *away*, chiamare fuori; dire d' uscire; — *back*, richiamare; far ritornare; — *down*, chiamare giù; far scendere; — *for*, domandare, cercare; — *forth*, chiamare fuori; far uscire; — *in*, chiamare dentro; dire d' entrare; — *off*, dissuadere; — *on*, esortare, incitare; — *out*, chiamare fuori; — — *together*, convocare, adunare; — *up*, svegliare; dire di salire; — *upon*, invocare; ricorrere ad; — *upon one*, andare a vedere, visitare alcuno.

callidity, S.: astuzia, sagacità, *f.*

călling, S.: vocazione, *f.*; mestiere, uffizio, impiego, *m.*

călliperş, S. PL.: (*nav.*) seste da calibrare, *f. pl.*

'lŏsity, S.: callosità, *f.*

lous, ADJ.: calloso; insensibile. **-ness**, callosità; insensibilità; durezza, *f.*

ow, ADJ.: spiumato, nudo; S.: ragaz-, ragazza, *f.*

căllus, S.: callo, *m.*; durezza, *f.*

călm 1, ADJ.: calmo, tranquillo, quieto; S.: calma; tranquillità, *f.* **calm** 2, TR.: calmare, placare; abonacciare; quietare. **-ly**, ADV.: tranquillamente, quietamente, placabilmente. **-ness**, S.: calma, tranquillità, *f.* **-y**, ADJ.: calmo, calmato.

călomel, S.: mercurio dolce, *m.*

ca-lŏric, ADJ.: calorico. **-lorific**, ADJ.: calorifico.

calŏtte, S.: berretta, *f.*; berettino, *m.*

căltrop, S.: tribolo; cardo, *m.*

calŭm-niate, TR.: calunniare, diffamare. **-niātion**, S.: diffamazione, *f.* **-niator**, S.: calunniatore, *m.* **-nious**, ADJ.: calunnioso, diffamatorio. **călum-ny**, S.: calunnia, diffamazione, *f.*

călve, INTR.: fare un vitello; figliare.

Călvi-nism, S.: calvinismo, *m.* **-nist**, S.: calvinista, *m.* **-nistic**, ADJ.: calvinistico.

cālx, S.: calce, calcina, *f.*

cămbered, ADJ.: (*arch.*) arcuato.

cāmbric, S.: cambraia, *f.*

cămel, S.: cammello, *m.* **-driver**, S.: cammeliere, *m.* **-hair**, S.: pelo di cammello, *m.*

camēleon† = *chameleon*.

camēlopard, S.: cammello pardalo, *m.*

cămelot, S.: cambellotto, *m.*

cămer-ated, ADJ.: arcato, incurvato. **-ātion**, S.: (*arch.*) arcatura, *f.*

cămis†, S.: veste leggiera. **-ade**, S.: (*mil.*) camicia sopra l' arme, *f.*; assalto di notte, *m.* **-ated**, ADJ.: colla camicia sopra l' arme.

cămomile, S.: camomilla, *f.*

cămp 1, S.: campo, *m.* **camp** 2, TR.: accampare; INTR.: accamparsi, porsi a campo. **-aign**, S.: campagna, *f.*

campăniform, ADJ.: (*bot.*) campaniforme.

campănulate, ADJ.: campanulato.

campēstral, ADJ.: campestre, rurale.

căm-phor, S.: canfora, *f.* **-phorate**, ADJ.: canforato.

cămping, S.: accampamento; campare, *m.*

cămpion, S.: anemone, *f.*

căn 1, S.: boccale, *m.*; pippa, *f.*, vaso, *m.*

can 2, IRR.; INTR.: potere; sapere: *if I could*, se potessi; *that — not be*, ciò non può essere; *I — not tell*, non so; *how — you tell?* come lo sapete?

canāille, S.: canaglia, *f.*

canăl, S.: canale, condotto, *m.*

canāry, S.: vino di Canaria, *m.* **-bird**, S.: canarino, *m.*

căncel, TR.: cancellare, annullare. **-lated**, ADJ.: cancellato, intraversato. **-ling**, **-lātion**, S.: cancellamento, *m.*, cancellazione, *f.*

căn-cer, S.: granchio; (*surg.*) canchero, *m.* **-cerate**, INTR.: incancherirsi. **-ceration**, S.: divenir canchero, *m.* **-cerous**, ADJ.: cancheroso.
căn-dent†, ADJ.: candente; infocato. **-did**, ADJ.: candido, ingenuo, sincero. **-didate**, S.: candidato; competitore, *m.* **-didly**, ADV.: candidamente; sinceramente. **-didness**, S.: candidezza; ingenuità, *f.*
căndied, ADJ.: candito, confetto.
căndify†, TR.: rendere candido.
căndle, S.: candela, *f.*; luminario, *m.*: *tallow* —, candela di sevo, *f.*; *rush* —, candela di giunco, *f.*; *wax* —, candela di cera, *f.* **-light**, S.: lume di candela, *m.*: *by* —, alla candela; al lume di candela. **-mas**, S.: candellaio, *f.* **-snuffer**, S.: smoccolatoio, *m.* **-stick**, S.: candeliere, *m.*: *branched* —, candelabro, *m.* **-stuff**, S.: sevo; grasso, *m.* **-waster**, S.: prodigo, dissipatore, spendereccio, *m.*
căndour, S.: candore, *m.*; ingenuità; sincerità, *f.*
căndy 1, TR.: candire, confettare; INTR.: diventare candito; congelare. **candy** 2, ADJ.: candito: *sugar* —, zucchero candito, *m.*
căne 1, S.: canna, *f.*; bastone, *m.*: *sugar* —, cannamele, *f.*; *head of a* —, pomo d' un bastone. **cane** 2, TR.: bastonare.
canicular, ADJ.: canicolare.
canine, ADJ.: canino: — *hunger*, fame canina, *f.*
căning, S.: colpi di canna, bastonata: *get a* —, ricevere una buona bastonatura.
cănister, S.: scatola da tè; panierina, *f.*
cănker 1, S.: canchero, *m.* **canker** 2, TR.: corrompere, corrodere; INTR.: corrompersi. **-bit**, ADJ.: morso da dente avvelenato, *m.* **-worm**, S.: bruco, *m.* **-ous**, ADJ.: cancheroso.
cănnabine, ADJ.: di canapa.
cănnibal, S.: cannibale, *m.* **-ly**, ADV.: a modo di cannibale.
cănnipers = *callipers*.
cănnon, S.: cannone, *m.*: *fire a* —, sparare un cannone; — *shot*, tiro di cannone. **-ball**, S.: palla di cannone, *f.* **-ăde** 1, S.: cannonata, *f.* **-ade** 2, TR.: cannoneggiare, cannonare. **-ăding**, S.: cannonata, *f.* **-iēr**, S.: cannoniere, bombardiere, *m.*
canōe, S.: sciatta, barchetta, *f.*
că-non, S.: canone (legge ecclesiastica), *m.*; regola, *f.*: — *law*, legge canonica, *f.* **-noness**, S.: canonichessa, *f.* **-nŏnical**, ADJ.: canonicale, canonico: — *hours*, ore canoniche, *f. pl.* **-nŏnically**, ADV.: canonicamente, regolarmente. **-nonist**, S.: dottore in legge canonica, *m.* **-nonizātion**, S.: canonizzazione, *f.* **-nonize**, TR.: canonizzare, dichiarare santo. **-nonry**, **-nonship**, S.: canonicato, *m.*
căn-opied, ADJ.: coprito con baldacchino. **-opy** 1, S.: baldacchino, *m.* **-opy** 2, TR.: coprire con baldacchino.
canōrous, ADJ.: canoro, armonioso.
cănt 1, S.: gergo, *m.*; vendita, *f.* **cant** 2, TR.: gettare via, rigettare; INTR.: parlar in gergo; ribaltare.
cantâta, S.: (*mus.*) cantata, *f.*
cantēen, S.: cantinella di transporto; canova.
cănter 1, S.: galloppo piccolo; ipocrito, *m.*: *take a* —, levare il galoppo. **canter** 2, INTR.: andar l' ambio galoppare.
canthărides, S. PL.: canterelle, cantaridi, *f. pl.*
căntiole, S.: cantica, *f.*
cănting, S.: gergo, *m.*
căntle 1, S.: pezzo, tozzo, *m.* **cantle** 2, TR.: tagliare in pezzi, smembrare.
căntō, S.: canto, *m.*
cănton 1, S.: cantone, *m.* **canton** 2, **-ize**, TR.: dividere in cantoni. **-ment**, S.: alloggiamento militare, *m.*
cănvas, S.: canavaccio, *m.*
cănvass, TR.: esaminare, consultare; INTR.: brigare, sollecitare. **-er**, S.: sollecitatore, *m.* **-ing**, S.: esame; sollecitamento, *m.*
cănzonet, S.: canzonetta, *f.*
căp 1, S.: berretta, *f.*, cappello, *m.*; testa, *f.*, capo; saluto, *m.*: *night* —, berretta da notte; *cardinal's* —, cappello di cardinale; *doff one's* — *to*, sberrettarsi a. **cap** 2, TR.: sberrettare.
capability, S.: capacità, attezza, *f.*
cāpable, ADJ.: capace; atto, idoneo. **-ness**, S.: capacità, abilità, *f.*; sapere, *m.*
capācious, ADJ.: capace, ampio, spasioso. **-ness**, S.: capacità; ampiezza, larghezza, *f.*
capăci-tate, TR.: rendere capace. **-ty**, S.: capacità; abilità; disposizione, *f.*
cap-a-piē, ADV.: da capo a piedi.
capărison 1, S.: copertina, gualdrappa, *f.* **caparison** 2, TR.: porre la copertina (ad un cavallo), guarnire.
cāpe, S.: capo, promontorio; collare, *m.*
cāper 1, S.: capriola, *f.*; 2 (*spice*), cappero, *m.*: *cut* —, fare (delle) capriuole. **caper** 3, INTR.: capriolare. **-bush**, S.: cappero, *m.* **-er**, S.: che fa capriole; saltatore, ballerino, *m.* **-sauce**, S.: capperottato, *m.*
căpillary, ADJ.: capillare.
capillament, S.: capillamento, *m.*
căpital, ADJ.: capitale; principale; [illegible] timo; S.: fondo, *m.*; capitale, metro[illegible] *f.*; (*arch.*) capitello, *m.* **-ly**, ADV.: [illegible] talmente, mortalmente.

capitātion, s.: capitazione, tassa per testa, *f.*
cápitol, s.: campidoglio, *m.*
capit-ular, ADJ.: capitolare, di capitolo; s.: membro d' un capitolo, *m.* **-ulate**, INTR.: capitolare, fare convenzioni. **-ulātion**, s.: capitolazione, convenzione, *f.*
cápmaker, s.: berrettaio, *m.*
cápon 1, s.: cappone, *m.* **capon** 2, TR.: capponare.
capót 1, s.: capotto, *m.* **capot** 2, TR.: fare capotto.
capó(u)ch, s.: capuccio, *m.*
cápper, s.: berrettaio, *m.*
cáppy, s.: (*mil.*) cappi, *m.*
ca-príce, s.: capriccio, *m.*, fantasia, *f.* **-prícious**, ADJ.: capriccioso, fantastico. **-príciously**, ADV.: capricciosamente. **-príciousness**, s.: capricciosità, fantasia, *f.*
Cápricorn, s.: (*astr.*) capricorno, *m.*
cápriole, s.: capriola, cavriuola, *f.*
cápstan, s.: (*nav.*) argano di vascello, *m.*
cápsular(y), ADJ.: cassulare.
cáptain, s.: capitano; capo, *m.*: — *of foot*, capitano d' infanteria; — *of horse*, capitano di cavalleria; *sea* —, capitano di bastimento. **-ry**, s.: capitananza, capitaneria, *f.* **-ship**, s.: grado, ufficio di capitano, *m.*
captātion, s.: corteggiamento, *m.*
cáp-tion, s.: cattura, *f.*, arresto, *m.* **-tious**, ADJ.: cavilloso, insidioso; critico, sofistico. **-tiously**, ADV.: cavillosamente; criticamente. **-tiousness**, s.: cavillazione, furberia, *f.*
cáp-tivate, TR.: cattivare; soggiogare. **-tivāting**, ADJ.: incantevole, ammaliante. **-tivātion**, s.: l'atto del cattivare. **-tive** 1, s.: cattivo, schiavo, *m.*, -va, *f.* **-tive** 2, TR.: fare prigione. **-tivity**, s.: cattività, schiavitù, *f.* **-tor**, s.: che fa una preda. **-ture** 1, s.: cattura, presura, *f.* **-ture** 2, TR.: catturare, cattivare.
cápuchin, s.: cappuccia (da donna), *m.*
cár, s.: carretta, *f.*, carro, *m.*
cára-bine, s.: carabina, *f.* **-binier**, s.: carabiniere, *m.*
cárack, s.: carracca, *f.*
cáracole 1, s.: caracollo, volteggiamento, *m.* **caracole** 2, INTR.: (*mar.*) caracollare, volteggiare.
cárat, s.: carato, *m.*
cára-van, s.: carovana, *f.* **-vánsary**, s.: albergo delle carovane, *m.*
cárbine = *carabine*.
cár-bon, s.: carbonio, *m.* **-bonáceous**, ADJ.: carbonico. **-bonáde** 1, s.: carbonata, *f.* **-bonade** 2, TR.: tagliare in fette. **-bonize**, TR.: carbonizzare.
cár-buncle, s.: carboncello, carbonchio, *m.* **-buncled**, ADJ.: fregiato di carbonchi. **-búncular**, ADJ.: rosso come un carbonchio.
cárcanet, s.: collana, *f.*
cárcass, s.: carcame, *m.*; carcassa, *f.*
cárcelage †, s.: spese del carceriere, *f. pl.*
cárd 1, s.: cartina: carta (da giuoco), *f.*; biglietto, *m.*: *post(al)* —, cartolina postale, *f.*: *mariner's* —, rosa di venti, *f.*; *visiting* —, biglietto di visita, *m.*; *pack of* —*s*, mazzo di carte, *m.* **card** 2, *m.*: carda. **card** 3, TR.: cardare, cardeggiare.
cárdamom, s.: cardamomo, *m.*
cárd-case, s.: portabiglietti, *m.*
cárder, s.: cardatore, *m.*
cardiac(al), ADJ.: cardiaco, cordiale.
cárdialgy, s.: mal di cuore, *m.*
cárdinal, ADJ.: cardinale, principale; s.: cardinale, *m.* **-ate**, **-ship**, s.: cardinalato, *m.*
cárd-maker, s.: cartaio, cartaro, *m.* **-match**, s.: zolfanello di carta, *m.*
cardóon, s.: (*bot.*) cardone, *m.*
cárd-paper, s.: cartosino, *m.* **-table**, s.: tavoliere, *m.*
cáre 1, s.: cura; sollecitudine: *take* —, *have a* —, badare, prender guardia; *take* — *of yourself*, la si conservi (*or* riguardi). **care** 2, INTR.: curare, aver cura; apprezzare, stimare: *what do I* —*?* che importa a me? *I do not* —, non me ne curo; *I don't* — *a fig for it* (*him*, ecc.), non me ne curo (*or* calo) un fico. **-crazed**, ADJ.: caricato di cure, inquieto.
carēen 1, (*nav.*) carena, *f.* **careen** 2, TR.: carenare.
carēer 1, s.: carriera, *f.*; corso, *m.* **career** 2, correre con velocità, andar prestamente.
cáre-ful, ADJ.: sollecito, accurato, diligente, cauto. **-fully**, ADV.: cautamente, accuratamente. **-fulness**, s.: cura; attenzione; cautela, prudenza, *f.* **-less**, ADJ.: negligente, trascurato. **-lessly**, ADV.: senza cura, negligentemente. **-lessness**, s.: negligenza, trascuranza, *f.*
carēss 1, s.: carezza, amorevolezza, *f.* **caress** 2, TR.: accarezzare, vezzeggiare.
cárgo, s.: carico, *m.*
cáricatur-e, s.: caricatura, *f.* **-e**, TR.: mettere in ridicolo. **-ist**, s.: che fa caricature.
cá-ries, s: carie; putrefazione, *f.* **-riŏsity**, s.: putrefazione; putridezza, *f.* **-rious**, ADJ.: carioso.
cárk, s.: cura, ansietà, *f.*
cárl, s.: rustico, contadino, *m.* **-ish-ness**, s.: ruvidezza, *f.* **-ot**, s.: rustico, zotico, *m.*
cárman, s.: carrettiere, carrettaio, *m.*
Cârmelite, s.: carmelitano, *m.*
carminative, s.: carminativo.
cármine, s.: carminio, *m.*

càr-nage, S.: macello, *m.*; strage, *f.* **-nal**, ADJ.: carnale, sensuale. **-nălity**, S.: sensualità, incontinenza, *f.* **-nally**, ADV.: carnalmente, sensualmente. **-nā-tion**, S.: carnagione, *f.*; garofano, *m.*: — *colour*, colore incarnato. **-naval** = *carnival*. **-nēlian**, S.: corniola, *f.* **-neous**, ADJ.: di carne, carnoso. **-nify**, TR.: fare carne; INTR.: incarnarsi. **-ni-val**, S.: carnasciale, carnovale, *m.* **-niv-orous**, ADJ.: carnivoro, vorace. **-nŏs-ity**, S.: carnosità, *f.*

càrol 1, S.: carola, *f.*, canto divoto; canto d' allegrezza, *m.*: *Christmas* —, cantico del Natale. **carol** 2, TR.: carolare; celebrare.

caröuse-al, S.: gozzoviglia, crapula, *f.* **-e** 1, S.: gozzoviglia; ubbriachezza, *f.* **-e** 2, INTR.: gozzovigliare, bere di molto. **-er**, S.: trincone, beone, *m.*

càrp 1, S.: carpione, *m.*: *young* —, carpioncino, *m.* **carp** 2 (*at*), TR.: criticare, censurare.

càrpen-ter, S.: legnaiuolo, falegname; (*nav.*) carpentiere, *m.* **-try**, S.: arte del legnaiuolo, *f.*; legname, *m.*

càrper, S.: cavillatore, biasimatore, censore, *m.*

càrpet 1, S.: tappeto, *m.*: *to be on* (*upon*) *the* —, essere sul tappeto. **carpet** 2, TR.: coprire d' un tappeto.

càrping, ADJ.: critico, litigioso. **-ly**, ADV.: criticamente.

càrriage, S.: porto; carriaggio, *m.*, vettura; carrozza, carretta, *f.*; portamento, *m.*: *one-horse* —, carozza a un sol cavallo; *of a good* —, di bella portatura; *beast of* —, bestia da soma, *f.* **-house**, S.: (*rail.*) loggia da vagoni, alla da vagoni, *f.*

càrrier, S.: vetturino; portatore, *m.*

càrrion, S.: carogna, *f.*

carronāde, S.: (*nav.*) carronata, *f.*

càrrot, S.: carota, *f.* **-iness**, S.: pelo rosso, *m.* **-y**, ADJ.: rosso, rossigno.

càrry, TR.: portare; condurre; guadagnare; INTR.: comportarsi; procedere: — *the day*, ottenere la vittoria; — *it cunningly*, usare furberia; — *it high*, procedere con alterigia; — *it fair with*, trattare bene; — *about*, portare addosso; — *away*, portar via, rapire; — *back*, riportare, rimenare; — *down*, portare giù, abbassare; — *forth*, avanzare; mantenere; — *from*, trasportare; — *in*, portare entro; — *off*, portare via; ammazzare; — *on*, continuare; proseguire; — *out*, portare fuor; — *one's self*, comportarsi; — *over*, trasferire, trasportare; — *through*, condurre a termine, effectuare; — *up*, portare su; esaltare, alzare. **-ing**, S.: trasporto, trasportamento, *m.* **-tale**, S.: rapportatore, ciarlone, *m.*, spia, *f.*

càrt 1, S.: carretta, *f.*, carro, *m.*: *put the — before the horse*, mettere il carro innanzi a' buoi; *child's* —, *go*- —, carruccio, *m.*; *dung*- —, carro da letame, *m.* **cart** 2, TR.; INTR.: esporre sur un carro; condurre col carro.

càrteblanche, S.: carta bianca, *f.*

cartĕl, S.: cartello, *m.*, disfida, *f.*

càrt-er, S.: carrettiere, carrettaio, *m.* **-horse**, S.: cavallo di caretta, *m.*

Carthūsian, S.: frate Certosino, *m.*

càrti-lage, S.: cartilagine, *f.* **-lăgi-nous**, ADJ.: cartilagineo, cartilaginoso.

càrt-load, S.: carrettata, carrata, *f.*

cartōon, S.: cartone, *m.*

car-tōuch, S.: cartoccio, *m.*: — *box*, giberna, tasca di cartocci, *f.* **càr-trage**, **-tridge**, S.: carica di munizione, *f.*, cartoccio, *m.*

càrt-rut, S.: rotaia, *f.* **-shed**, S.: rimessa, *f.* **-way**, S.: via del carro, *f.* **-wheel**, S.: ruota di carro, *f.* **-wright**, S.: carradore, carraio, *m.*

càruncle, S.: (*surg*) caruncola, *f.*

càr-ve, TR.: tagliare, scolpire: trinciare; INTR.: intagliare. **-ver**, S.: scultore, intagliatore; trinciante, *m.* **-ving**, S.: scultura, *f.*, scolpire, *m.*

caryătid, pl. -(e)s, S.: (*arch.*) cariatide, *f.*

cascāde, S.: cascata, cateratta, *f.*

cāse 1, S.: caso; stato, *m.*, condizione; scatola; guaina, *f.*, astuccio, *m.*: — *of books*, cassa di libri; *a plain* —, una cosa chiara; *a strange* —, un caso strano; *in such a* —, in tal caso; *in a sad* —, in cattivo stato: *if you were in my* —, se voi foste nel luogo mio (ne' miei panni); *that's another* —, quello è un altro affare; *it is all a* —, è tutt' uno; *put the* —, dare il caso, supporre una cosa. **case** 2, TR.: incassare, mettere in una cassa, serrare. **-harden**, TR.: indurare. **-knife**, S.: astuccio per le coltella, *m.*

cāsemate, S.: casamatta, *f.*

cāsement, S.: finestra, *f.*

căsh, S.: danaro contante, *m.*, cassa, *f.*: *keep the* —, tener la cassa. **-box**, S.: cassa, *f.* **-iēr** 1, S.: cassiere, banchiere, *m.* **-ier** 2, TR.: cassare; congedare. **-keeper**, S.: cassiere, banchiere, *m.*

cashōo, S.: cassiù, *m.* (gomma).

cāsing, S.: astuccio, fodero, *m.*

căs-k, S.: botte, *f.*, barile, *m.* **-ket** 1, S.: cassetta, *f.* **-ket** 2, TR.: riporre nella cassetta. **-que**, S.: caschetto, elmo, *m.*

căs-sate, TR.: cassare, cancellare. **-sā-tion**, S.: cassamento, *m.*, cassagione, *f.*

căssava, S.: cassava, *f.*

căssia, S.: (*med.*) cassia, *f.*

căssock, S.: sottana, *f.*

că-ssowary, S.: casuare, *m.*

căst 1, s.: tiro; colpo, *m.*; tirata, *f.*, getto; aspetto, *m.*; forma; estremità; maniera, *f.*: — *of the eyes*, occhiata, *f.* **cast** 2, IRR.; TR.: (*cast; cast*) gettare, lanciare; guadagnare; condannare; INTR.: ruminare; pensare, considerare; piegarsi; — *an account*, fare un conto; — *anchor*, gettar l' ancora, dar fondo; — *feathers*, mutar le penne; — *forth beams*, scintillare; — *lots*, tirar le sorti; — *a smell*, avere odore; — *about*, spargere per ogni parte; — *against*, rimproverare; *to — aside*, rigettare, ributtare; — *away*, gettare via, abbandonare; — *down*, deprimere; affliggere; — *down one's eyes*, abbassare (*or* chinare) gli occhi; — *forth*, mandare fuora; esalare; — *off all shame*, bandire ogni vergogna; — *off*, gettare via; lasciare; — *out*, mandare fuora; scacciare; — *out devils*, scacciare i diavoli; — *up*, calcolare, computare; — *upon*, avere ricorso a.
căstanet, s.: castagnetta, *f.*
căstaway, s.: reprobo, malvagio.
căstellan, s.: castellano, *m.* **-y**, s.: castellania, castellaneria, *f.*
căster, s.: gettatore; calcolatore, *m.*
căsti-gate, TR.: gastigare, punire. **-gātion**, s.: gastigamento, *m.*, punizione, *f.* **-gatory**, ADJ.: gastigante.
căsting, s.: (il) gettare, *m.* **-house**, s.: fonderia, *f.* **-net**, s.: ritrecine, *f.* (rete). **-vote**, s.: voto decisivo, *m.*
căstle 1, s.: castello, *m.*, fortezza, *f.*: *build —s in the air*, fare castelli in aria. **castle** 2, INTR.: roccare, fare rocco. **-d**, ADJ.: munito di castelli.
căstor, s.: castoro; cappello, *m.*
castrametātion, s.: accampamento, *m.*
cās-trate, TR.: castrare; mutilare. **-trātion**, s.: castrazione, castratura, *f.*, castrare, *m.* **-trāto**, s.: castrato, *m.*
căsual, ADJ.: casuale, fortuito. **-ly**, ADV.: casualmente, fortuitamente. **-ness**, s.: casualità, avventura, *f.* **-ty**, s.: caso fortuito, caso, accidente, *m.*
căs-uist, s.: casuista, *m.* **-uistical**, ADJ.: casuistico. **-uistry**, s.: scienza del casuista, *f.*
căt, s.: gatto, *m.*, gatta, *f.*: *—'s paw*, zampa del gatto; zimbello d' un furbo.
catachrēsis, s.: (*rhet.*) catacresi, *f.*
cătaclysm, s.: cataclisma, (*pop.*) -mo, *m.*
cătacombs, s. PL.: catacombe, *f. pl.*
cătalogue, s.: catalogo, registro, *m.*
cătaplasm, s.: cataplasma, *m.*
cătapult, s.: catapulta, *f.*
cătaract, s.: cateratta; cascata, *f.*
catărrh, catarro, *m.* **-al**, **-ous**, ADJ.: catarroso.
catăstrophe, s.: catastrofe, *f.*
cătcall, s.: fischio; zufolo, *m.*
cătch 1, s.: presa, cattura, *f.*; bottino, profitto; ritornello; annello, *m.*: *be upon the —*, tendere insidie. **catch** 2, IRR.; TR.: prendere; chiappare, pigliare; rapire; INTR.: attacarsi; essere contagioso; comunicarsi; arrivare: — *cold*, infredarsi; raffreddarsi; — *a fall*, cascare; — *fire*, accendersi; infocarsi; — *hold of*, impegnare, afferraro; — *at*, acchiappare; — *up*, prendere, impugnare. **-bit**, s.: scroccone, ghiottone, *m.* **-er**, s.: pigliatore, ingannatore, *m.* **-ing** 1, s.: presa, cattura, *f.* **-ing** 2, ADJ.: contagioso. **-păll**, s.: sbirro, zaffo, *m.* **-word**, s.: rimando, *m.*
catechĕtical, ADJ.: catechistico. **-ly**, ADV.: in forma catechistica.
căte-chise, TR.: catechizzare; interrogare. **-chism**, s.: catechismo, *m.* **-chist**, s.: catechista, *m.*
catechūmen, s.: catecumeno, *m.*
categŏrical, ADJ.: categorico. **-ly**, ADV.: categoricamente.
cătegory, s.: categoria, *f.*
căte-nate, TR.: catenare, incatenare, legare, connettere. **-nātion**, s.: concatenazione; connessione, *f.*
cāter, INTR.: provvedere, far le provvisioni; procacciare. **-er**, s.: provveditore, *m.* **-ess**, s.: provveditrice, *f.*
căterpillar, s.: bruco, *m.*
căterwaul, INTR.: miagolare, gnaulare.
cātes, s. PL.: vivande squisite, *f. pl.*; cibo, *m.*
căt-fish, s.: gatto marino, *m.* **-gut**, s.: corda di minugia, *f.*
cathărtic(al), ADJ.: catartico, purgativo.
cathēdral, s.: cattedrale, *f.*
căthetor, s.: (*surg.*) catetero, *m.*
Că-tholic, ADJ.: cattolico; s.: cattolico, *m.* **-thŏlicism**, s.: religione cattolica, *f.*
cătkin, s.: (*bot.*) fiocchi, *m. pl.*
căt's-eye, s.: (*min.*) bellochio, *m.* **-foot**, s.: edera terrestre, *f.* **-tail**, s.: fiacco, *m.*
căttle, s.: bestiame, *m.*, pecore, *f. pl.*: *black —*, bestie bovine, *f. pl.* **-shed**, s.: stalla del bestiame, *f.* **-trade**, s.: commercio del bestiame, *m.*
căudle, s.: bevanda composta d' orzo e di vino, *f.*
căuf, s.: pescaia, *f.*; serbatoio, *m.*
căul, s.: cuffia, *f.*; integumento, *m.*
căuldron, s.: calderone, *m.*, caldaia, *f.*
căuliflower, s.: cavolfiore, *m.*
căulk = *calk*.
cău-sal, ADJ.: causale, causativo. **-săl-ity**, s.: causalità, *f.* **-sally**, ADV.: casualmente, con cagione. **-sative**, ADJ.: causativo. **-sāter**, s.: causatore, autore, *m.* **-se** 1, s.: causa; cagione; ragione, motivo; luogo; processo, *m.*, lite, *f.*: *give —*, dar luogo; *plead a —*, difendere una

lite; *stand for the* —, seguitare il buon partito. **-se** 2, TR.: causare, cagionare; eccitare; — *sorrow*, dar dispiacere; — *a thing to be done*, procurare che una cosa si faccia. **-seless**, ADJ.: senza causa; ingiusto. **-selessly**, ADV.: senza causa. **-ser**, S.: causatore, autore, agente, *m*.
càu-seway, **-sey**, S.: marciapiedi, *m*.
càustical, ADJ.: caustico, corrosivo.
càu-tel †, S.: cautela, *f*., scrupolo, *m*. **-telous**†, ADJ.: circospetto, astuto. **-telously** †, ADV.: cautamente.
cau-terizàtion, S.: cauterizzare, *m*. **-terize**, TR.: cauterizzare. **-tery**, S.: cauterio, *m*.
càution 1, S.: prudenza; circospezione, sagacità, *f*.; avvertimento, avviso, *m*. **caution** 2, TR.: avvertire, ammonire. **-ary**, ADJ.: d' ostagio.
càutious, ADJ.: prudente, acorto. **-ly**, ADV.: accortamente; sagacemente. **-ness**, S.: prudenza, accortezza, circospezione, *f*.
càval-cade, S.: cavalcata, *f*. **-ièr**, S.: cavaliere, *m*. **-ièrlike**, ADV.: cavallerescamente. **-ièrly**, ADV.: da cavaliere. **-ry**, S.: cavalleria, *f*.
cà-vate, TR.: cavare, scavare. **-vàtion**, S.: cavamento, *m*., cavatura, *f*.
càve 1, S.: cava, spelonca, *f*., antro, *m*. **cave** 2, INTR.: dimorare in una spelonca.
càveat, S.: avvertenza; ammonizione, *f*., avviso, *m*.
càvern, S.: caverna; spelonca, *f*. **-ous**, ADJ.: cavernoso, cavo.
càvesson, S.: cavezzone, *m*.
càviar, **caviare**, S.: caviale, *m*.
càvil 1, S.: cavillazione, *f*., sofisma, *m*. **cavil** 2, TR.: cavillare; criticare. **-ler**, S.: cavillatore, *m*., sofista, *m*. **-lingly**, ADV.: cavillosamente. **-lous**, ADJ.: cavilloso, sofistico.
càvity, S.: cavità, *f*.; buco, *m*.
càw, INTR.: crocitare; gracchiare.
cèa-se, TR.: cessare; discontinuare, finire. **-seless**, ADJ.: incessante, continuo. **-selessly**, ADV.: incessantemente, continuamente. **-sing**, S.: cessazione, *f*.: *without* —, incessantemente.
cècity, S.: cecità, *f*.
cecùtiency, S.: offuscazione della vista, *f*.
cèdar, S.: cedro, *m*.
cède, TR.: cedere; abbandonare; INTR.: cedero; darsi per vinto.
cèdrine, ADJ.: cedrino, di cedro.
cèdule, S.: cedola, *f*.
cèil, TR.: soffitare. **-ing**, S.: soffitta, *f*., soffitto, *m*.
cèlandine, S.: celidonia, *f*.
cèlature, S.: intaglio, *m*.
cèl-ebrate, TR.: celebrare; esaltare. **-ebrated**, ADJ.: celebrato, esaltato. **-ebràtion**, S.: celebramento, *m*.; lode, *f*. **-ebrater**, S.: lodatore, panegirista, *m*. **-èbrious**†, ADJ.: celebre, rinomato. **-èbriously**†, ADV.: con celebrità. **-èbriousness**, S.: celebrità, riputazione; gloria, *f*. **-èbrity**, S.: celebrità; fama, *f*.
celèriac, S.: appio navone, *m*.
celèrity, S.: celerità, prestezza, *f*.
cèlery, S.: appio, *m*.: *head of* —, piede di sedano, *m*.
celèstial, ADJ.: celestiale, celeste; S.: celestiale, beato, *m*. **-ly**, ADV.: celestialmente.
cèliac, ADJ.: (*med.*) celiaco.
celi-bacy, **cèli-bate**, **-bateship**, S.: celibato, *m*.
cèll, S.: cella, cellula, *f*. **-ar**, S.: cantina, canova, *f*. **-arage**, S.: cantine, *f*. *pl*. **-arist**, S.: celleraio, canovaio, *m*. **-ular**, ADJ.: cellulare. **-ule**, S.: cellula, *f*.
cèlsitude†, S.: celsitudine; altezza, *f*.
cemènt 1, S.: cimento, smalto, *m*. **cement** 2, TR.: assodare, saldare; INTR.: affermarsi, unirsi. **-àtion**, S.: cementazione, *f*.
cèmetery, S.: cimitero, cimiterio, *m*.
cenobitical, ADJ.: cenobitico.
cènotaph, S.: cenotafio, *m*.
cen-se 1, S.: censo, *m*., imposta, *f*., tributo, *m*. **-se** 2, TR.: incensare, profumare. **-ser**, S.: incensiere, turibile, *m*.
cèn-sor, S.: censore, critico, *m*. **-sòrious**, ADJ.: censorio, severo. **-sòriously**, ADV.: da censore; in modo severo. **-sòriousness**, S.: censura; severità, *f*. **-sorlike**, ADV.: da censore. **-sorship**, S.: dignità di censore, *f*., censorato, *m*. **-surable**, ADJ.: censurabile; biasimevole. **-sure** 1, S.: censura; riprensione, *f*.: *vote of* —, voto di biasimo. **-sure** 2, TR.: censurare, criticare; biasimare. **-surer**, S.: riprenditore, biasimatore, *m*.
cènsus, S.: censo, *m*.
cènt, S.: cento, *m*.: *five per* —, cinque per cento; *discount of ten per* —, sconto di dieci per cento.
cèntaur, S.: (*astron.*) centauro, *m*. **-y**, S.: centaurea, *f*.
cèn-tenary, ADJ.: centenario, di cento anni; S.: centinaio, *m*. **-tèsimal**, ADJ.: centesimo. **-tifòlious**, ADJ.: centifoglio. **-tiped**, S.: centupede, *m*.
cèn-tral, ADJ.: centrale, centrico. **-trally**, ADV.: centralmente, nel mezzo. **-tre** 1, S.: centro; cuore, *m*. **-tre** 2, TR.: concentrare, centreggiare; INTR.: concentrarsi. **-tric**, **-trical**, ADJ.: centrico, centrale. **-trifugal**, ADJ.: centrifugo. **-tripetal**, ADJ.: centripeta.
cèn-tuple, ADJ.: centuplo. **-tùplicate**, TR.: centuplicare.
centù-riate, TR.: dividere in centinai. **-rion**, S.: centurione, *m*.

cěntury, S.: centuria, *f.*; secolo, *m.*: *the last* —, lo scorso secolo.
cěph-alalgy, S.: (*med.*) cefalalgia, *f.* **-ălic**, ADJ.: (*med.*) cefalico.
cē-rate, S.: (*phar.*) cerotto, *m.* **-rated**, ADJ.: incerato. **-re**, TR.: incerare, coprire di cera.
cěrebel, S.: cerebello, *m.*
cērecloth, S.: incerato, *m.*, tela incerata, *f.*
ceremō-nial, ADJ.: ceremoniale; S.: ceremoniale; rito, *m.* **-nious**, ADJ.: ceremonioso. **-niously**, ADV.: ceremoniosamente, con cerimonia. **-niousness**, S.: vaghezza di ceremonie; maniera formale, *f.* **cěremo-ny**, S.: cerimonia, formalità, *f.*; complimento, *m.*: *without* —, senza cerimonie (*or* soggezione).
cērtain, ADJ.: certo, sicuro, fisso; evidente: *for* —, di certo, per certo; *a* — *person*, una certa persona, un tale, il tale. **-ly**, ADV.: certamente, senza dubbio. **-ty**, S.: certezza, sicurezza, *f.*
cer-tificate, S.: certificato, *m.*, attestazione, *f.* **-tify**, TR.: certificare, render certo; confermare: *the undersigned certifies, etc.*, il sottoscritto certifica, ecc. **-titude**, S.: certezza; sicurezza, *f.*
cerū-lean, **-leous**, ADJ.: ceruleo, turchino.
cerūmen, S.: cerume, *m.*
Cesārian, ADJ.: cesareo.
cess-ātion, S.: cessazione, *f.*, cessamento; tralasciamento, *m.*: — *of arms*, sospensione d'armi, *f.* **-ible**, ADJ.: atto a cedersi.
cession, S.: cessione; rassegnazione, *f.* **-ary**, ADJ.: cessionario.
cessment†, S.: tassa, imposizione, *f.*
cěstus, S.: cesto, *m.*
cesūra, S.: (*pros.*) cesura, *f.*
cetāceous, ADJ.: cetaceo.
chāfe 1, S.: ardore, furore, *m.*, rabbia, *f.*; fremito, fremere, *m.* **-e** 2, TR.: scaldare; irritare, stizzire, mettere in collera; INTR.: fremere; adirarsi, incollerirsi. **-er**, S.: colui che (si) irrita; (*zoöl.*) scarafaggio, *m.*
chāff, S.: lolla, loppa, *f.*
chăffer 1, S.: mercanzia, *f.* **chaffer** 2, INTR.: trafficare, stiracchiare; trattare. **-er**, S.: comperatore, mercante, *m.*
chăffern†, S.: caldaia, *f.*
chăffinch, S.: fringuello, pincione, *m.*
chăff-less, ADJ.: senza lolla. **-y**, ADJ.: paglioso.
chāfing-dish, S.: scaldaviveane, *m.*
chagrin 1, S.: affanno, *m.*, stizza, *f.* **chagrin** 2, TR.: affannare, adirare.
chāin 1, S.: catena; concatenamento, *m.*, serie, *f.*; S. PL.: catene, *f. pl.*; schiavitù, *f.*: *little* —, catenella, catenuzza. **chain** 2, TR.: incatenare, mettere alla catena, legare con catena. **-ing**, S.: incatenamento, *m.* **-pump**, S.: tromba grande e doppia, *f.* **-shot**, S.: palle incatenate, *f. pl.*
chāir, S.: sedia; sedia portatile, *f.*; cattedra, *f.*; seggio (presidenziale), *m.*: *fill the* —, tenere la presidenza; *found a* —, fondare una cattedra. **-man**, S.: presidente, *m.*
chāise, S.: calesso, biroccio, *m.*
chalcŏgra-pher, S.: calcografo, *m.* **-phy**, S.: intagliare in rame, *m.*
chāldron, S.: 36 moggi di carbone, *m. pl.*
chălice, S.: calice, *m.*, coppa, *f.*
châlk 1, S.: creta, *f.*, gesso, *m.*, marna, *f.* **chalk** 2, segnare col gesso; schizzare: — *out*, segnare; mostrare. **-cutter**, S.: che scava la marna. **-pit**, S.: cava di marna, *f.* **-y**, ADJ.: cretoso.
chăllen-ge 1, S.: disfida; pretensione, *f.*; rigettamento, rifiuto, *m.* **-ge** 2, (IN)TR.: sfidare; recusare; chiamare a battaglia; rifiutare. **-ger**, S.: sfidatore, *m.*
chamāde, S.: chiamata, battuta di tamburo, *f.*
chāmber 1, S.: camera; stanza, *f.*: — *of a cannon*, camera di cannone; *dark* —, camera oscura. **chamber** 2, TR.: intrigarsi. **-fellow**, S.: camerata, *m.* **-lain**, S.: camerlingo, cameriere, *m.*: *Lord High* —, Gran Ciamberlano. **-lainship**, S.: uffizio del camerlingo. **-maid**, S.: cameriera, *f.* **-pot**, S.: orinale, *m.*
chāmbrel, S.: garretta, *f.*
chamēleon, S.: camaleonte, *m.*
chămfer 1, S.: scanalatura, *f.* **chamfer** 2, TR.: scanalare.
chămois, S.: camoscio, *m.*
chămomile, S.: camomilla, *f.*
chămp, TR.; INTR.: masticare, rodere.
champāign†, S.: campagna, *f.*, paese aperto, *m.*
champāgne, S.: (vino di) Sciampagna, *m.*: *iced* —, sciampagna al ghiaccio; *sparkling* —, sciampagna spumante.
champignon *-pinyon*, S.: fungo, *m.*
chămpion 1, S.: campione, eroe, *m.* **champion** 2, TR.: sfidare a singolar certame.
chānce 1, S.: azzardo, *m.*, ventura, *f.*, caso, *m.*, sorte, *f.*: *take one's* —, arrischiare; *good* (*lucky*) —, buona ventura; *try the* — *of war*, tentare la fortuna della guerra; *meet by* —, incontrare a caso; — *customer*, avventore, compratore casuale; *take one's* —, correre il rischio, arrischiarsi. **chance** 2, INTR.: accadere, avvenire, occorrere. **-able†**, ADJ.: accidentale, casuale. **-guest**, S.: sopravvegnente, inaspettato, *m.*
chān-cel, S.: santuario, *m.* **-cellor**, S.:

cancelliere, *m.*; *Lord High* —, gran cancelliere (d' Inghilterra), *m.* **-cellorship**, S.: cancelleria, *f.* **-cery**, S.: cancelleria, *f.*
chăn-cre, S.: (*surg.*) canchero, cancro, *m.* **-crous**, ADJ.: cancheroso, ulceroso.
chandelier, S.: candelabro, *m.*; lumiera, *f.*
chândler, S.: candelaio venditor a minuto, *m.*
chānge 1, S.: cambiamento, *m.*; mutazione, vicenda; alterazione; varietà; moneta, *f.* **-e** 2, TR.: cambiare; mutare, alterare; INTR.: cangiarsi; mutarsi; — *place*, cambiar di luogo; — *colour*, cambiare di colore; cambiarsi nel viso, arrossire; — *one's opinion*, mutare pensiero, **-eable**, ADJ.: cambiabile, cangiabile; variabile, incostante. **-eableness**, S.: incostanza, mutabilità, *f.* **-eably**, ADV.: incostantemente. **-eful**, ADJ.: incostante, instabile. **-eless**, invariabile, costante. **-eling**, S.: parto supposto, sciocco. **-er**, S.: cambiatore, banchiere, *m.* **-ing**, S.: cambiamento, *m.*
chănnel 1, S.: canale; letto (d' un fiume), *m.*; scanalatura, *f.*: *the Channel*, il canale della Manica; *little* —, canaletto, *m.* **channel** 2, TR.: scanalare.
chânt 1, S.: canto, *m.* **chant** 2, TR.: cantare; celebrare. **-er**, S.: cantatore, cantore, *m.* **-icleer**, S.: gallo, *m.* **-ress**, S.: cantatrice, *f.* **-ry**, S.: dignità del cantore, *f.*
chā-os, S.: caos, *m.*; confusione, *f.* **-ŏtic**, ADJ.: confuso.
chăp 1, S.: fessura; crepatura, *f.*, fesso, *m.* **chap** 2, INTR.: crepare; spaccarsi, fendersi.
chāpe, S.: puntale; rampone, fermaglio, *m.*
chăpel, S.: cappella, chiesetta, *f.* **-ry**, S.: cappellania, *f.*
chăperon, S.: cappuccio, *m.*
chăpiter, S.: (*arch.*) capitello, *m.*
chăplain, S.: cappellano; limosiniere, *m.* **-ship**, S.: carica di cappellano, *f.*
chăpless, ADJ.: magro, smunto.
chăplet, S.: corona, *f.*; rosario, *m.*
chăpman, S.: compratore; mercante, *m.*
chăps = *chops*.
chăpt, ADJ.: fesso, spaccato.
chăpter, S.: capitolo; capo, *m.* **-house**, S.: capitolo, *m.*
châr 1, S.: giornata, *f.* **char** 2, TR.: ridurre in carbone, bruciacchiare; INTR.: lavorare alla giornata.
chăracter 1, S.: carattere; segno, *m.*; lettera; descrizione; dignità, *f.*: *an odd* —, un uomo strambo; *he is quite a* —, egli è un originale; *take away one's* —, diffamare uno. **character** 2, TR.: intagliare; inscrivere. **-istic**, S.: caratteristica, *f.* **-istic(al)**, ADJ.: caratteristico. **-isticalness**, S.: qualità propria, caratteristica, *f.* **-ize**, TR.: caratterizzare. **-less**, ADJ.: senza carattere. **-y**, S.: impressione, *f.*
chârcoal, S.: carbone di legna, *m.*
chârd, S.: cardo; cardone, *m.*
chârge 1, S.: carico, *m.*, carica, soma, *f.*, peso, *m.*; cura, incombenza, *f.*; uffizio, impiego, *m.*; accusa, imputazione, *f.*; deposito, *m.*; spesa, *f.*; assalto, *m.*: *heavy* —, peso gravoso; *customary* —, solito prezzo; —*s included*, comprese le spese; *lay to one's* —, incolpare alcuno; *take the* — *of something*, pigliarsi l' incombenza di qualche cosa. **-e** 2, TR.: caricare; comandare, imporre; accusare, incolpare; — *with*, commettere alla cura. **-eable**, ADJ.: imputabile, dispendioso. **-eably**, ADV.: con dispendio. **-er**, S.: cavallo da guerra; gran piatto, *m.*
châr-ily, ADV.: frugalmente. **-iness**, S.: prudenza; cautela, *f.*
chăriot 1, S.: carro, *m.*, carrozza, *f.* **chariot** 2, INTR.: condurre in carrozza. **-eer**, S.: cocchiere, conduttor del carro, *m.* **-race**, S.: corsa di carri, *f.*
chări-table, ADJ.: caritatevole, benefacente. **-tableness**, S.: beneficenza, *f.* **-tably**, ADV.: caritatevolmente. **-ty**, S.: carità; beneficenza, limosina, *f.*: *beg* —, domandar la limosina; *for* —*'s sake*, per l' amor di Dio; — *begins at home*, la prima carità è l' aver cura. **-ty-school**, S.: scuola gratuita, *f.*
chârla-tan, S.: ciarlatano, cantambanco, *m.* **-tănical**, ADJ.: ciarlatanesco. **-tanry**, S.: ciarlataneria, *f.*
Chârles'-wāin -*zez*-, S.: (*astr.*) orsa maggiore. *f.*
chârlock, S.: loglio, *m.*, zizzania, *f.*
chârm 1, S.: incanto; allettamento, *m.* **charm** 2, TR.: incantare, ammaliare, allettare, rapire: — *away*, scongiurare. **-er**, S.: incantatore, *m.*, incantatrice, *f.* **-ing**, ADJ.: vezzoso, vago; S.: incantamento, *m.* **-ingly**, ADV.: vagamente, piacevolmente. **-ingness**, S.: attrativa; bellezza, *f.*
chârnel-house, S.: carnaio, *m.*
chârt, S.: carta di navigare, *f.*
chârter, S.: patente; privilegio; statuto; carta constituzionale. **-party**, S.: (*nav.*) contratto di noleggio, *m.* **-ed**, ADJ.: privilegiata, immune, esente.
chârwoman, S.: donna lavorante alla giornata, *f.*
chāry, ADJ.: accorto, prudente.
chās-e 1, S.: caccia; foresta, *f.* **-e** 2, TR.: cacciare; mandar via. **-er**, S.: cacciatore, perseguitore, *m.*
chăsm, S.: fessura; apertura; lacuna, vacuo, *m.*

chās-te, ADJ.: casto, pudico; onesto; puro: *have — ears*, aver buon orecchio. **-tely**, ADV.: castamente; pudicamente. **-ten**, TR.: castigare, punire; correggere. **-teness**, S.: castità, pudicizia; modestia, *f.*

chastis-e, TR.: castigare, punire. **-ement**, S.: castigo, *m.*; punizione, *f.* **-er**, S.: gastigatore, punitore, *m.*

chăstity, S.: castità; purità, *f.*

chăsuble, S.: pianeta di prete, *f.*

chăt 1, S.: ciarla, *f.*; cicaleccio, *m.*: *little* —, chiacchierata, *f.* **chat** 2, INTR.: ciarlare; cornacchiare.

chătellany, S.: castellania, castellaneria, *f.*

chăttel, S.: mobile, *m.*

chăt-ter 1, S.: ciarla, *f.*, cicalare, *m.* **-ter** 2, INTR.: ciarlare, cornacchiare; tremare, battere i denti. **-terer**, S.: ciarliero, ciarlatore, *m.* **-tering**, S.: cicaleria, *f.*; battimento di denti, *m.* **-ting**, S.: ciarla, *f.*, cicalamento, *m.* **-ty**, ADJ.: loquace, ciarlone.

chătwood, S.: legna per il fuoco, *f. pl.*

chăwe, TR.: masticare; ruminare.

chăwdron, S.: viscere, interiora, *f. pl.*

chēap, ADJ.: a buon mercato. **-en**, TR.: prezzolare, mercatare. **-ener**, S.: prezzolatore, *m.* **-ly**, ADV.: a buon mercato, per poco. **-ness**, S.: buon mercato, vil prezzo, *m.*

chēat 1, S.: frode, furberia, *f.*, inganno; furbo; barattiere; giuntatore, *m.* **cheat** 2, TR.: far fraude a, ingannare, truffare; giuntare: — *at cards (play)*, truffare al giuoco. **-er**, S.: ingannatore, truffatore, *m.* **-ingly**, ADV.: ingannevolmente, con frode.

chĕck 1, S.: scacco; ostacolo, impedimento; rimprovero, *m.*, riprensione, *f.*: *give one a* —, fare una riprensione ad uno; *take a — at*, offendersi di; *keep a — upon one*, tenere uno in freno; — *to the king*, scacco al re. **check** 2, TR.: frenare, reprimere; riprendere; INTR.: fermarsi; opporsi: — *one's anger*, rattenere la collera; — *an account*, riscontrare (*or* verificare) un conto; — *one's self*, fermarsi, raffrenarsi.

chĕcker, TR.: fare a scacchi; intarsiare; screziare. **-wise**, ADJ.: a scacchi. **-work**, S.: tarsia, *f.*; screzio *m.*

chĕck-less, ADJ.: irresistibile. **-mate**, S.: scaccomatto, *m.* **-y**, ADJ.: intarsiato; mischiato.

chēek, S.: guancia; gota, *f.*: *chubby —s*, guance paffute; — *by jowl*, testa a testa. **-bone**, S.: mascella, *f.* **-tooth**, S.: dente mascellare, *m.* **-y**, ADJ.: sfacciato, ardito.

cheer 1, S.: pasto; banchetto, *m.*; allegrezza, *f.*, umore, coraggio; volto, *m.*: *good* —, mangiare e bere bene; *loud —s*, strepitosi applausi. **cheer** 2, TR.: rallegrare; animare; INTR.: rallegrarsi, incoraggiarsi, farsi animo: — *up*, farsi animo, rasserenarsi; — *up!* animo! coraggio! **-ful**, ADJ.: gaio, allegro, lieto, gioioso. **-fully**, ADV.: allegramente, lietamente. **-fulness**, **-ishness**, S.: gioia, allegrezza, *f.*; contento, *m.* **-ity**, ADV.: allegramente. **-less**, ADJ.: tristo, malinconoso. **-ly** †, **-y**, ADJ.: gaio, gioioso, lieto, allegro.

chēese, S.: formaggio, cacio, *m.* **-cake**, S.: tortelletta di cacio, *f.* **-curds**, S. PL.: latte rappreso, *m.* **-monger**, S.: formaggiaio; pizzicagnolo, *m.* **-press**, **cheese-vat**, S.: graticcio, *m.* **-y**, ADJ.: caseoso, cacioso.

chĕmical, ADJ.: chimico. **-ly**, ADV.: chimicamente.

che-mise, S.: camicia da donna, *f.* **chemisĕtte**, S.: camicetta, *f.*, camicino, *m.*

chĕmist, S.: chimico, *m.*: — *and druggist*, farmacista, speziale, *m.* **-ry**, chimica, *f.*

chĕrish, TR.: amare teneramente; mantenere; allevare: *he —ed the hope*, egli nutriva la speranza. **-er**, S.: amatore; mantenitore, protettore, *m.* **-ment**, S.: incoraggiamento; sostegno, *m.*

chĕrry 1, S.: ciriegia, *f.*: *wild* —, agriotta, *f.* **cherry** 2, ADJ.: rosso, vermiglio: — *cheeks*, guance vermiglie, *f. pl.* **-orchard**, S.: ciriegeto, *m.* **-pit**, S.: fossetta; buca, *f.* **-stone**, S.: nocciolo di ciriegia, *m.* **-tree**, S.: ciriegio, ciliegio, *m.*

chĕr-ub, S.: cherubino, *m.* **-ŭbic(al)**, ADJ.: cherubico.

chĕrvil, S.: cerfoglio, *m.*

chĕsnut = *chestnut.*

chĕss, S.: scacchi, *m. pl.*: *game of* —, giuoco degli scacchi, partita di scacchi; *play at* —, giuocare agli scacchi. **-board**, S.: scacchiere tavoliere, *m.* **-man**, S.: pedina, *f.*; scacco, *m.* **-player**, S.: giuocatore di scacchi, *m.*

chĕst, S.: cassa, *f.*; casso, cassero (del corpo); (*nav.*) forziere, *m.*: — *of drawers*, stipo, armadio, *m.* **-ed**, ADJ.: di petto. **-foundered**, ADJ.: bolso. **-foundering**, S.: bolsaggine, *f.*

chĕstnut, S.: castagna, *f.*; ADJ.: castagnino, castagno. **-colour**, ADJ.: castagnino. **-plot**, S.: castagneto, *m.* **-tree**, S.: castagno, *m.*

che-valiēr, S.: cavaliere, *m.* **-vaux-de-frise** -vō-, S.: (*mil.*) cavalli di frisa, *m. pl.*

chĕven, S.: ghiozzo, *m.* (pesce).

chĕveril †, S.: pelle di capretto, *f.*

chĕvisance †, S.: mercato ingiusto, *m.* intrapresa, *f.*

chĕvron, S.: travicello; (*her.*) caprone, *m.*
chew *chū*, TR.: masticare; ruminare; considerare, meditare: — *the cud*, ruminare; — *tobacco*, masticare tabacco.
chică-ne, S.: cavillo, inganno, rigiro, *m.* **-ne**, INTR.: cavillare; sofisticare. **-ner**, S.: cavillatore, *m.* **-nery**, S.: cavillo, *m.*; sofisticheria, *f.*
chick, **chick-en**, S.: pollastro, *m.* **-en-hearted**, ADJ.: timido, pauroso. **-en-pox**, S.: morviglione, *m.* **-peas**, S. PL.: cece, *m.* **-weed**, S.: centocchio, *m.*
chid, impf. e part. del v. *chide*.
chi-de, IRR.; TR. (*chid; chid, chidden*): biasimare; riprendere; INTR.: disputare, querelare, schiamazzare. **-der**, S.: riprenditore, *m.* **-ding**, S.: riprensione, *f.* **-dingly**, ADV.: in modo di riprensione.
chief, ADJ.: primo, principale; S.: capo, comandante; direttore, socio principale, *m.*: *in* —, in capo; *Lord — Justice*, primo giudice (in Inghilterra), *m.* **-dom**, S.: sovranità, *f.* **-less**, ADJ.: senza capo. **-ly**, ADV.: principalmente. **-tain**, S.: comandante; capitano, *m.* **-tainry**, **-tainship**, S.: capitanato, *m.*
chilblain, S.: (*med.*) pedignone, *m.*
child, S.: fanciullo; figlio, figliuolo; bambino, ragazzo, infante, *m.*: *little* —, bimbo, bambinello; *adopted* —, figlio addottivo; *natural* —, figlio naturale (illegitimo); *naughty* —, ragazzaccio; *stillborn* —, nato morto; *foster* —, figlio (-lia) di latte; *from a* —, dall' infanzia, dalla culla; *bring forth a* —, partorire; *be past a* —, aver passato l' infanzia; *be with* —, essere incinta. **-bearing**, S.: pregnezza, gravidanza, *f.* **-bed**, S.: letto della partoriente; tempo del parto, *m.* **-birth**, S.: parto; partorire, *m.* **-hood**, S.: infanzia; fanciullezza, *f.* **-ish**, ADJ.: bambinesco, fanciullesco. **-ishly**, ADV.: a modo di fanciullo. **-ishness**, S.: bambinaggine, infanzia, puerilità, *f.* **-less**, ADJ.: senza figliuoli. **-like**, ADJ.: fanciullesco, bambinesco.
children, PL. di *child*.
chiliad, S.: migliaio, *m.*
chill 1, ADJ.: freddo, freddoloso; S.: freddo, *m.*, freddura, *f.*: *cold* —*s*, brividi, ribrezzi di febbre. **chill** 2, TR.: freddare; gelare. **-iness**, S.: freddura, *f.*; brivido, *m.* **-y**, ADJ.: alquanto freddo, freddotto; freddoso, freddoloso.
chime 1, S.: scampanata, *f.*; accordo, *m.*, armonia, *f.*: —*s*, armonia di campane. **chime** 2, INTR.: scampanare; accordarsi, unirsi: — *in*, consonare, essere d' accordo.
chi-mēra, S.: chimera, *f.* **-mĕrical**, ADJ.: chimerico. **-mĕrically**, ADV.: chimericamente.
chimney, S.: cammino, focolare, *m.* **-corner**, S.: luogo de' ciarloni, *m.* **-piece**, S.: cornice del cammino, *f.* **-sweeper**, S.: spazzacammino, *m.*
chin, S.: mento, *m.*
china, S.: porcellana; majolica, *f.* **-man**, S.: mercante di porcellana, *m.* **-orange**, S.: melarancia dolce, *f.* **-root**, S.: cina, *f.*
chin-cloth, S.: bavaglio, *m.* **-cough**, S.: tossa violenta, *f.*
chine 1, S.: schiena; spina, *f.* **chine** 2, TR.: sfilare.
Chinēse, ADJ.: chinese; S.: Chinese, *m.*
chink 1, S.: fessura, crepatura, *f.* **chink** 2, TR., INTR.: tintinnare; spaccarsi. **-y**, ADJ.: screpolato, fesso.
chinse, TR.: (*nav.*) calafatare.
chints, S.: indiana, *f.* (tela dipinta).
chip 1, S.: scheggia, *f.*; bruciolo, *m.*: —*s of bread*, croste di pane, *f. pl.*; *he is a — of the old block*, quale padre tale figlio; a' segni si conoscono le balle. **chip** 2, TR.: truciolare, sbriciolare, sminuzzare.
chirăgrical, ADJ.: chiragrico.
chirŏgrapher, S.: chirografario, *m.*
chiro-mancer, S.: chiromante, *m.* **-mancy**, S.: chiromanzia, *f.*
chirp 1, S.: garrito; pigolare, *m.* **chirp** 2, TR.: garrire; pigolare, piare. **-er**, S.: gridatore, *m.* **-ing**, S.: garrito; canto (d' uccelli), *m.*
chisel 1, S.: scalpello, *m.* **chisel** 2, TR.: scarpellare, intagliare. **-work**, S.: lavoro di scultura, *m.*
chit 1, S.: bambino; stipite, *m.* **chit** 2, INTR.: germinare, germogliare.
chitchat, S.: ciarla, ciarleria, *f.*
chitterlings, S. PL.: budella, minugia, *f. pl.*
chival-rous, ADJ.: cavalleresco. **-ry**, S.: dignità di cavaliere, cavalleria, *f.*
chives, S. PL.: costole di fiori, *f. pl.*; cipolletta, *f.*
chŏck, S.: sorgozzone; attacco, *m.*
chŏcolate, S.: cioccolato, *m.* **-pot**, S.: cioccolattiera, *f.* **-dealer**, S.: cioccolatiere, *m.*
chŏice 1, S.: scelta, elezione, eletta; varietà, *f.*: *make* —, scegliere. **choice** 2, ADJ.: scelto, squisito, raro. **-less**, ADJ.: senza il potere di scegliere, indifferente. **-ly**, ADV.: caramente. **-ness**, S.: rarità; delicatezza, *f.*
choir *kwīr*, S.: coro (d' una chiesa), *m.*
chŏk-e 1, S.: fieno del carciofo, *m.* **-e** 2, TR.: suffocare, strangolare; turare, stoppare; INTR.: soffocarsi, affogarsi: — *up*, ingorgare. **-e-pear**, S.: pera strozzatoia, *f.* **-ing**, S.: suffocamento, *m.* **-y**, ADJ.: suffocante, strozzatoio.
chŏlagogues, S.: (med.) colagogo, *m.*

ciliary, ADJ.: ciliare.
cimeter, S.: scimitarra, sciabla corta, *f.*
cincture, S.: cintura, fascia, *f.*
cinder, S.: cenere, *f.* **-wench**, **-woman**, S.: cenciaiuola, *f.*
cineritious, ADJ.: cenericcio.
cingle, S.: cinghia, *f.*
cinnabar, S.: cinabro, vermiglione, *m.*
cinnamon, S.: cinnamomo, *m.*, cannella, *f.* **-tree**, S.: albero della cannella, *m.*
cinque, S.: cinque, *m.* **-foil**, S.: cinquefoglie, *f.*
cipher 1, S.: cifra, cifera, *f.*: *a mere* —, un nulla, uno zero. **cipher** 2, TR., INTR.: calcolare, computare. **-ing**, S.: calcolo, computo, *m.*
circinate, TR.: delineare un circolo.
cir-cle 1, S.: circolo, cerchio, *m.*; società, *f.*: *little* —, circoletto, cerchietto. **-cle** 2, TR.: cerchiare; limitare, cingere; INTR.: muovere in giro, girare. **-cled**, ADJ.: circulato, tondo; circolare. **-clet**, S.: cerchietto, cerchiello, *m.* **-cling**, ADJ.: circolare, rotondo.
circuit 1, S.: circuito; contorno, *m.* **circuit** 2, INTR.: circuire, andare attorno.
cir-cuition, S.: circuimento, *m.* **-cuitous**, ADJ.: circolare. **-cuitously**, ADV.: circolarmente.
circu-lar, ADJ.: circolare, rotondo. **-lărity**, S.: circolarità, rotondezza, *f.* **-larly**, ADV.: circolarmente, in cerchio. **-lāte**, INTR.: circolare; girare attorno, volgersi intorno: *the blood* —*s*, il sangue circola; *the money* —, il danaro corre. **-lating**, ADJ.: circolante; — *library*, libreria circolare, *f.* **-lātion**, S.: circulazione, *f.* **-latory**, ADJ.: circolatorio, circolare; circolatojo, *m.*
circum-ămbient, ADJ.: circumambiente. **-ămbulate**, INTR.: passeggiare attorno. **-ambulātion**, S.: passeggiata attorno, *f.* **-cise**, TR.: circoncidere. **-ciser**, S.: che fa la circoncisione, circoncisore, *m.* **-cision**, S.: circoncisione, *f.* **-ference** *-cŭm-*, S.: circonferenza, *f.*; circuito, *m.* **-ferĕntor**, S.: (*math.*) doppio grafometro, *m.* **-flex**, S.: accento circonflesso, *m.* **-fluent**, **-fluous** *-cŭm-*, ADJ.: scorrente intorno. **-fūse**, TR.: circonfondere. **-jăcent**, ADJ.: contiguo, circonvicino. **-locūtion**, S.: circonlocuzione, *f.* **-lŏcutory**, ADJ.: perifrastico. **-năvigable**, ADJ.: navigable intorno. **-năvigate**, INTR.: navigare intorno. **-navigātion**, S.: circonnavigazione, *f.* **-pōlar**, ADJ.: circonpolare. **-rotātion**, S.: rotazione, *f.* **-scribe**, TR.: circoscrivere; limitare. **-scription**, S.: circoscrizione, *f.* **-scriptive**, ADJ.: limitativo. **-spect**, ADJ.: circospetto, considerato, cauto; prudente. **-spĕction**, S.: circospezione; prudenza, *f.* **-spĕctive**, ADJ.: accorto, cauto, considerato. **-spĕctively**, **-spectly**, ADV.: accortamente, consideratamente, prudentemente. **-spĕctness**, S.: accortezza, prudenza, *f.* **-stance** 1, S.: circostanza, *f.*; evento, *m.*; condizione, *f.*, stato, *m.*: *according to* —*s*, secondo le occorrenze; *in easy* —*s*, agiato, comodo; *mitigating* —, circostanza attenuante. **-stance** 2, TR.: circostanziare, specificare. **-stanced**, ADJ.: posto: *being thus* —, trovandomi in tale stato. **-stant**, ADJ.: circostante. **-stăntial**, ADJ.: accidentale, casuale; minuto. **-stăntially**, ADV.: secondo le circostanze, casualmente. **-vāllate**, TR.: circonvallare, fortificare. **-vallātion**, S.: circonvallazione, *f.* **-vĕnt**, TR.: circonvenire, ingannare, insidiare. **-vĕntion**, S.: circonvenzione, *f.*, inganno, *m.*; insidia, *f.* **-vĕntive**, ADJ.: ingannevole. **-volūtion**, S.: avvolgimento, *m.* **-vŏlve**, TR.: avvolgere.
circus, S.: circo, *m.*
cist, S.: integumento, *m.*; cuticola, *f.*
cistern, S.: cisterna, *f.*
cit, S.: cittadino, cittadinello, *m.*
citadel, S.: cittadella, fortezza, *f.*
ci-tātion, S.: citazione; allegazione, *f.*
ci-tatory, ADJ.: citatorio. **-te**, TR.: citare, assegnare; allegare. **-ter**, S.: citatore, accusatore, *m.*
cithern, S.: sistro, *m.*
citizen, S.: borghese, cittadino, *m.*: *fellow* —, concittadino, *m.* **-like**, ADV.: da cittadino, cittadinesco. **-ship**, S.: cittadinanza, *f.*
citrine, ADJ.: citrino.
citron, S.: cedro, *m.* **-tree**, S.: cederno, cedro, *m.* **-water**, S.: acqua cedrata, *f.*
citrul, S.: zucca, *f.*
city, S.: città, *f.*: *mother*-—, città vecchia, *f.*; *freedom of a* —, cittadinanza, *f.*; — *court*, consiglio municipale, *m.*
cives, S. PL.: porri, *m. pl.*
civet, S.: zibetto, *m.* **-cat**, S.: zibetto, *m.* (animale).
civic, ADJ.: civico, da cittadino.
civ-il, ADJ.: civile; politico; cortese: — *law*, S.: legge civile, *f.*; — *list*, lista civile, *f.*; — *war*, guerra civile, *f.* **-ilian**, **-ilist**, S.: giureconsulto, *m.* **-ility**, S.: civiltà; urbanità, cortesia, *f.* **-ilization**, S.: civilizzazione, *f.*, stato civilizzato, *m.* **-ilize**, TR.: civilizzare, coltivare, dirozzare. **-illy**, ADV.: civilmente, cortesemente.
clăck 1, S.: strepito; nottolino di molino, *m.* **clack** 2, INTR.: strepitare; scoppiare. **-ing**, S.: strepito, romore, schiamazzo, *m.*

clăd, ADJ.: vestito, coperto (cf. *clothe*).

clāim 1, S.: diritto, *m.*; pretensione: *lay — to a thing*, pretendre, aver diritto a qualche cosa. **claim** 2, TR.: richiamare; pretendere; arrogarsi: — *a privilege*, domandare (pretendere a) un previlegio; — *the first place*, arrogarsi il primo posto; — *as one's own*, appropriarsi. **-able**, ADJ.: che può richiamarsi. **-ant**, S.: pretendente, *m.*

clămber, INTR.: rampicarsi.

clāimer = *claimant*.

clăm 1, S.: sorta di pettine, mollusco bivalve americano, *m.* **clam** 2, TR.: invescare, impeciare. **-miness**, S.: viscosità; tenacità, *f.* **-my**, ADJ.: viscoso; tenace.

clămor 1, S.: clamore; strepito; grido, *m.* **clamor** 2, INTR.: strepitare; gridare: — *against*, richiamarsi contro; — *for*, domandare tumultuariamente. **-ous**, ADJ.: strepitoso, tumultuoso. **-ously**, ADV.: strepitosamente.

clămp 1, S.: mezza puleggia, *f.*; incastro, *m.* **clamp** 2, TR.: incastrare.

clăn, S.: famiglia, razza; tribù, *f.*

clăncular†, ADJ.: segreto, privato.

clandĕs-tine, ADJ.: clandestino. **-tinely**, ADV.: in modo clandestino.

clăn-g 1, S.: suono acuto; romore, *m.* **-g** 2, INTR.: strepitare; suonare. **-gor**, S.: strombettata, *f.* **-gorous**, ADJ.: strepitoso.

clănk 1, S.: suono acuto, strepito. **clank** 2, TR.: suonare, tintinnire; strepitare.

clăp 1, S.: strepito; colpo; fracasso, *m.*: — *of thunder*, scoppio di tuono, colpo di fulmine; *at one* —, in un colpo, alla prima. **clap** 2, TR.: battere; applaudire; applicare: — *the door*, chiudere la porta; — *hands*, picchiar le mani, applaudire; — *spurs to a horse*, dar di sprone ad un cavallo; — *in*, ficcare; avvanzarsi; — *up a bargain*, fare un accordo. **-board**, S.: doga, *f.* **-per**, S.: applauditore, approvatore; battaglio (di campana); martello (d' una porta); battente (di molino), *m.*: — *of rabbits*, conigliera, *f.* **-perclaw**, TR.: rabbuffare; rampognare. **-ping**, S.: battimento, plauso, *m.* **-trap**, S.: calappio, inganno, colpo teatrale, *m.*; ADJ.: frodoloso, insidioso.

clāre-obscure, S.: chiaroscuro, *m.*

clăret, S.: claretto, *m.*

clărichord, S.: clavicembalo, *m.*

clari-ficātion, S.: chiarificazione, *f.* **-fy**, TR.: chiarificare, chiarire; conciare [illegible]on colla (il vino); INTR.: chiarirsi.

[illegible]**inet**, S.: chiarina, *f.*

[illegible]**n**, S.: clarino, *m.*, chiarina, *f.*

[illegible]**y**, S: chiarezza, *f.*, splendore, *m.*

[illegible] S.: (*bot.*) schiarea, *f.*

clăsh 1, S.: urto; fracasso; contrasto, *m.*, differenza, contesa, *f.* **clash** 2, INTR.: urtarsi; scontrarsi, dibattersi, disputare: — *with*, essere opposto a. **-ing**, S.: urto; contrasto, *m.*; opposizione, *f.*

clăsp 1, S.: fermaglio; ganghero; abbracciamento, amplesso, *m.* **clasp** 2, TR.: affibbiare; abbracciare: *with —ed hands*, a mani giunte. **-knife**, S.: coltello da tasca, *m.* **-nail**, S.: chiodo senza testa, *m.*

clăss 1, S.: classe, *f*; ordine, *m.*: *the middle —es*, il ceto medio; *the lower —es*, la classe dei poveri; *attend a* —, frequentare un corso. **class** 2, TR.: classificare; ordinare.

clăss-ic, S.: autore classico, *m.* **-ic(al)**, ADJ.: classico. **-ificātion**, S.: classificazione, *f.*

clăssis†, S.: ordine, *m.*; spezie, *f.*

clăss-room, S.: classe, scuola, aula scolastica, *f.*

clătter 1, S.: strepito, fracasso, *m.* **clatter** 2, IN(TR).: strepitare; cicalare. **-coat**, S.: ciarlone, *m.* **-ing**, ADJ.: strepitoso; S.: schiamazzo, strepito, *m.*

clăudi-cate†, INTR.: zoppicare. **-cation**, S.: zoppicamento, *m.*

clăuse, S.: clausola, *f.*; articolo, *m.*; stipolazione, condizione, *f.*

clăustral, ADJ.: claustrale.

clăusure, S.: clausura, *f.*

clăvicle, S.: clavicola, *f.*

clăw 1, S.: artiglio, *m.*; branca; rampa, *f.* **claw** 2, TR.: graffiare, sgraffiare; adulare, lusingare. **-back**, S.: adulatore, lusingatore, *m.* **-footed**, ADJ.: piè di grifone.

clăy 1, S.: creta; argilla, argiglia, *f.* **clay** 2, TR.: coprire d' argilla. **-cold**, ADJ.: inanimato, morto. **-ey**, **-ish**, ADJ.: argilloso. **-land**, S.: terra argillosa, *f.* **-pit**, S.: cava d' argilla, *f.*

clĕan 1, ADJ., ADV.: netto, puro, bianco; affatto, intieramente. **clean** 2, TR.: nettare; lavare, pulire: — *the boots*, pulire gli stivali. **-er**, S.: (*rail.*) nettatore della macchina (locomotiva), *m.* **-lily** *klĕn-*, ADV.: nettamente, pulitamente. **-liness** *klĕn-*, S.: nettezza; pulitezza; purità, *f.* **-ly** *klĕn-*, ADJ., ADV.: puro, netto, pulito; elegante; pulitamente; elegantemente. **-ness**, S.: nettezza; purità, *f.*

clĕan-se, TR.: purgare, purificare. **-ser**, S: purgatore, *m.* **-sing**, S.: nettamento, pulimento, *m.*

clĕar 1, ADJ.: chiaro, puro; innocente; evidente; ADV.: affatto, intieramente: — *conscience*, coscienza netta; — *gain*, netto guadagno; *get — of*, uscire di; *keep — of*, evitare. **clear** 2, TR.: chiarire; purgare; giustificare, assolvere; INTR.:

divenire chiaro: — *accounts*, liquidare conti; — *a passage*, spacciare un passagio; — *a cape*, oltrepassare un capo; — *one's debts*, pagare i suoi debiti; — *a difficulty*, sciogliere una difficoltà; — *the table*, sparecchiare la tavola; — *up*, chiarirsi, rasserenarsi. **-ance**, S.: bulletta di passaporto, *f.*, certificato, *m.*; (*nav.*) spedizioni di dogana, *f. pl.* **-headed**, ADJ.: sagacio, giudizioso. **-ing**, S.: terreno disboscato, *m.*; (*com.*) giramento, *m.* **-ing-house**, S.: uffizio di liquidazione, *m.* **-ly**, ADV.: chiaramente, evidentemente. **-ness**, S.: chiarezza, *f.*, splendore, *m.*; nettezza; purità; innocenza, *f.* **-sighted**, ADJ.: perspicace, giudizioso. **-sightedness**, S.: perspicacità, intelligenza, *f.* **-starch**, TR.: inamidare. **-starcher**, S.: che inamida.

clĕav-e, IRR.; TR.: fendere; spaccare; INTR.: fendersi; dividersi, spaccarsi; attaccarsi: — *to*, attaccarsi (*or* appiccarsi), a. **-er**, S.: coltellaccio da beccaio, *m.*

clĕf, S.: chiave, *f.*

clĕft, ADJ.: fesso; spaccato (cf. *cleave*); S.: fessura; apertura, *f.*

clĕmen-cy, S.: clemenza; benignità, *f.* **-t**, ADJ.: clemente, benigno.

clĕrgy, S.: clero, *m.*, ecclesiastici, *m. pl.* **-man**, S: ecclesiastico, prete, *m.*

clĕrical, ADJ.: chericale.

clĕrk, S.: cherico, chierico; commesso; sagristano; scrivano; segretario, *m.*: *head* —, primo commesso, capo d' uffizio; (*leg.*) primo scritturale. **-like**, ADJ.: da cherico. **-ship**, S.: chericato, *m.*; carica di scrivano; dottrina, *f.*

clĕver, ADJ.: abile, destro; svelto. **-ly**, ADV.: abilmente, destramente. **-ness**, abilità, destrezza, *f.*

clew, S.: gomitolo, *m.*; guida, *f.*

click 1, S.: saliscendo, *m.* **click** 2, INTR.: tintinnare; scricchiolare.

clicket, S.: campanella, *f.*; martello di porta, *m.*

client, S.: cliente, *m.* **-ed**, ADJ.: che ha de' clienti. **-ship**, S.: clientela, *f.*

cliff, **-t**, S.: rupe, *f.*, luogo scosceso, *m.* **-ty**, ADJ.: dirupato.

climactĕric(al), ADJ.: climaterico.

climate, S.: clima, *m.*; regione, *f.*

climax, S.: gradazione, *f.*

climb, IRR.; TR.: rampicare; montare, scalare; INTR.: arrampicarsi; salire. **-er**, S.: che rampica, salitore, *m.*

clime = *climate*.

clinch 1, S.: bisticcio; equivoco, *m.*; (*nav.*) maglia, *f.* **clinch** 2, TR.: impugnare; serrare; ribadire; (*nav.*) magliettare: — *a nail*, ribadire un chiodo. **-er**, S.: rampone; rampicone, *m.*

cling, IRR.; INTR.: appiccarsi; appassarsi; aggrapparsi: — *together*, unirsi, attacarsi insieme. **-y**, ADJ.: viscoso, tenace.

clinic(al), ADJ.: clinico.

clink 1, S.: tintinno, tintinnio, *m.* **clink** 2, TR.: fare suonare; INTR.: tintinnire; risuonare.

clinquant†, ADJ.: sfavillante; S.: cantùtiglia, *f.*

clip 1, S.: colpo; abbracciamento, *m.* **clip** 2, TR.: tosare, tondere; tarpare; abbracciare: — *the wings off*, tarpare le ali a. **-per**, S.: tosatore; cimatore, *m.* **-ping**, S.: il tossare, *m.*; S. PL.: tosatura, tonditura, *f.*

clister = *clyster*.

cliver, S.: meliloto, *m.*, soffiola, *f.*

clōak 1, S.: mantello; pretesto, *m.* **cloak** 2, TR.: mantellare; palliare; nascondere. **-bag**, S.: valigia, *f.*, baule, *m.*, borsa, *f.* **-room**, S.: camera da mantelli, *f.*

clŏck, S.: orologio, oriuolo, *m.*; pendula, *f.*: *what o'— is it?* che ora è? *it is one o'—*, è una ora, è la una; *it is two o'—*, son le due; *it is a quarter* (*ten minutes*) *past two*, sono le due ed un quarto (e dieci). **-maker**, S.: oriuolaio, orologiaio, *m.* **-making**, S.: arte dell' orologiaio, *f.* **-work**, S.: struttura d' un oriuolo, *f.*

clŏd 1, S.: zolla (di terra), *f.*; sciocco, babbuasso, *m.* **clod** 2, TR.: erpicare; INTR.: rappigliarsi; coagularsi. **-dy**, ADJ.: zolloso, grumoso. **-pate**, S.: goffo, *m.*; testaccia, *f.* **-pated**, ADJ.: sciocco, grosso.

clŏg 1, S.: ostacolo; zoccolo, *m.*: *be a — upon*, essere d' ingombo a. **clog** 2, TR.: imbarazzare; caricare; INTR.: coagularsi; unirsi. **-ged**, ADJ.: imbarazzato; caricato. **-giness**, S.: imbarazzo, *m.*; confusione, *f.* **-gy**, ADJ.: imbarazzante, incomodo, pesante.

clŏister 1, S.: chiostro, monastero, *m.* **cloister** 2, TR.: rinchiudere in un convento. **-al**, ADJ.: claustrale. **-ed**, ADJ.: rinchiuso in un chiostro. **-ess**, S.: monaca, *f.*

clŏmb†, impf. e part. del v. *climb*.

clōs-e 1, ADJ., ADV.: serrato, stretto; contiguo, vicino; conciso; celato, segreto; riserbato; fosco, oscuro; appresso; S.: conclusione, chiusura, *f.*; fine, *m.*: — *by*, molto vicino, di presso; — *to*, rasente; *sit —*, *follow —*, incalzare; *keep —*, stare quatto quatto; *shut —*, chiudere bene; *stand —*, stringersi insieme; *study —*, applicarsi allo studio; *write —*, scrivere stretto; — *fight*, zuffa rabbiosa; — *room*, camerina; — *weather*, tempo fosco.

clōs-e 2, TR.: serrare; chiudere; terminare; INTR.: chiudersi, scaldarsi; riunirsi; accordarsi: — *an account*, saldare un conto; — *in*, rinchiudere, rinserrare; — *up*, consolidare; appiccare; — *upon*,

căst 1, s.: tiro; colpo, *m.*; tirata, *f.*, getto; aspetto, *m.*; forma; estremità; maniera, *f.*: — *of the eyes*, occhiata, *f.* **cast** 2, IRR.; TR.: (*cast; cast*) gettare, lanciare; guadagnare; condannare; INTR.: ruminare; pensare, considerare; piegarsi; — *an account*, fare un conto; — *anchor*, gettar l' ancora, dar fondo; — *feathers*, mutar le penne; — *forth beams*, scintillare; — *lots*, tirar le sorti; — *a smell*, avere odore; — *about*, spargere per ogni parte; — *against*, rimproverare; *to* — *aside*, rigettare, ributtare; — *away*, gettare via, abbandonare; — *down*, deprimere; affliggere; — *down one's eyes*, abbassare (*or* chinare) gli occhi; — *forth*, mandare fuora; esalare; — *off all shame*, bandire ogni vergogna; — *off*, gettare via; lasciare; — *out*, mandare fuora; scacciare; — *out devils*, scacciare i diavoli; — *up*, calcolare, computare; — *upon*, avere ricorso a.

căstanet, s.: castagnetta, *f.*

căstaway, s.: reprobo, malvagio.

căstellan, s.: castellano, *m.* **-y**, s.: castellania, castellaneria, *f.*

căster, s.: gettatore; calcolatore, *m.*

căsti-gate, TR.: gastigare, punire. **-gātion**, s.: gastigamento, *m.*, punizione, *f.* **-gatory**, ADJ.: gastigante.

căsting, s.: (il) gettare, *m.* **-house**, s.: fonderia, *f.* **-net**, s.: ritrecine, *f.* (rete). **-vote**, s.: voto decisivo, *m.*

căstle 1, s.: castello, *m.*, fortezza, *f.*: *build* —*s in the air*, fare castelli in aria. **castle** 2, INTR.: roccare, fare rocco. **-d**, ADJ.: munito di castelli.

căstor, s.: castoro; cappello, *m.*

castrametātion, s.: accampamento, *m.*

căs-trate, TR.: castrare; mutilare. **-trātion**, s.: castrazione, castratura, *f.*, castrare, *m.* **-trāto**, s.: castrato, *m.*

căsual, ADJ.: casuale, fortuito. **-ly**, ADV.: casualmente, fortuitamente. **-ness**, s.: casualità, avventura, *f.* **-ty**, s.: caso fortuito, caso, accidente, *m.*

căsu-ist, s.: casuista, *m.* **-istical**, ADJ.: casuistico. **-istry**, s.: scienza del casuista, *f.*

căt, s.: gatto, *m.*, gatta, *f.*: —*'s paw*, zampa del gatto; zimbello d' un furbo.

catachrēsis, s.: (*rhet.*) catacresi, *f.*

cătaclysm, s.: cataclisma, (*pop.*) -mo, *m.*

cătacombs, s. PL.: catacombe, *f. pl.*

cătalogue, s.: catalogo, registro, *m.*

cătaplasm, s.: cataplasma, *m.*

cătapult, s.: catapulta, *f.*

cătaract, s.: cateratta; cascata, *f.*

catărrh, catarro, *m.* **-al**, **-ous**, ADJ.: catarroso.

catăstrophe, s.: catastrofe, *f.*

cătcall, s.: fischio; zufolo, *m.*

cătch 1, s.: presa, cattura, *f.*; bottino, profitto; ritornello; annello, *m.*: *be upon the* —, tendere insidie. **catch** 2, IRR.; TR.: prendere; chiappare, pigliare; rapire; INTR.: attacarsi; essere contagioso; comunicarsi; arrivare: — *cold*, infredarsi; raffreddarsi; — *a fall*, cascare; — *fire*, accendersi; infocarsi; — *hold of*, impegnare, afferraro; — *at*, acchiappare; — *up*, prendere, impugnare. **-bit**, s.: scroccone, ghiottone, *m.* **-er**, s.: pigliatore, ingannatore, *m.* **-ing** 1, s.: presa, cattura, *f.* **-ing** 2, ADJ.: contagioso. **-păll**, s.: sbirro, zaffo, *m.* **-word**, s.: rimando, *m.*

catechĕtical, ADJ.: catechistico. **-ly**, ADV.: in forma catechistica.

căte-chise, TR.: catechizzare; interrogare. **-chism**, s.: catechismo, *m.* **-chist**, s.: catechista, *m.*

catechūmen, s.: catecumeno, *m.*

categŏrical, ADJ.: categorico. **-ly**, ADV.: categoricamente.

căteg ory, s.: categoria, *f.*

căte-nate, TR.: catenare, incatenare, legare, connettere. **-nation**, s.: concatenazione; connessione, *f.*

căter, INTR.: provvedere, far le provvisioni; procacciare. **-er**, s.: provveditore, *m.* **-ess**, s.: provveditrice, *f.*

căterpillar, s.: bruco, *m.*

căterwaul, INTR.: miagolare, gnaulare.

cătes, s. PL.: vivande squisite, *f. pl.*; cibo, *m.*

căt-fish, s.: gatto marino, *m.* **-gut**, s.: corda di minugia, *f.*

cathărtic(al), ADJ.: catartico, purgativo.

cathēdral, s.: cattedrale, *f.*

cătheter, s.: (*surg.*) catetero, *m.*

Că-tholic, ADJ.: cattolico; s.: cattolico, *m.* **-thŏlicism**, s.: religione cattolica, *f.*

cătkin, s.: (*bot.*) fiocchi, *m. pl.*

căt's-eye, s.: (*min.*) bellochio, *m.* **-foot**, s.: edera terrestre, *f.* **-tail**, s.: fiacco, *m.*

căttle, s.: bestiame, *m.*, pecore, *f. pl.*: *black* —, bestie bovine, *f. pl.* **-shed**, s.: stalla del bestiame, *f.* **-trade**, s.: commercio del bestiame, *m.*

căudle, s.: bevanda composta d' orzo e di vino, *f.*

căuf, s.: pescaia, *f.*; serbatoio, *m.*

căul, s.: cuffia, *f.*; integumento, *m.*

căuldron, s.: calderone, *m.*, caldaia, *f.*

căuliflower, s.: cavolfiore, *m.*

căulk = *calk*.

cău-sal, ADJ.: causale, causativo. **-săllity**, s.: causalità, *f.* **-sally**, ADV.: casualmente, con cagione. **-sative**, ADJ.: causativo. **-sāter**, s.: causatore, autore, *m.* **-se** 1, s.: causa; cagione; ragione, motivo; luogo; processo, *m.*, lite, *f.*: *give* —, dar luogo; *plead a* —, difendere una lite; *stand for the* —, seguitare il buon partito. **-se** 2, TR.: causare, cagionare; eccitare; — *sorrow*, dar dispiacere; — *a thing to be done*, procurare che una cosa si faccia. **-seless**, ADJ.: senza causa; ingiusto. **-selessly**, ADV.: senza causa. **-ser**, S.: causatore, autore, agente, *m.*

cău-seway, -sey, S.: marciapiedi, *m.*

căustical, ADJ.: caustico, corrosivo.

cău-tel †, S.: cautela, *f.*, scrupolo, *m.* **-telous**†, ADJ.: circospetto, astuto. **-telously** †, ADV.: cautamente.

cau-terizătion, S.: cauterizzare, *m.* **-terize**, TR.: cauterizzare. **-tery**, S.: cauterio, *m.*

căution 1, S.: prudenza; circospezione, sagacità, *f.*; avvertimento, avviso, *m.* **caution** 2, TR.: avvertire, ammonire. **-ary**, ADJ.: d' ostagio.

căutious, ADJ.: prudente, acorto. **-ly**, ADV.: accortamente; sagacemente. **-ness**, S.: prudenza, accortezza, circospezione, *f.*

căval-cade, S.: cavalcata, *f.* **-iër**, S.: cavaliere, *m.* **-iërlike**, ADV.: cavallerescamente. **-iërly**, ADV.: da cavaliere. **-ry**, S.: cavalleria, *f.*

că-vate, TR.: cavare, scavare. **-vătion**, S.: cavamento, *m.*, cavatura, *f.*

căve 1, S.: cava, spelonca, *f.*, antro, *m.* **cave** 2, INTR.: dimorare in una spelonca.

căveat, S.: avvertenza; ammonizione, *f.*, avviso, *m.*

căvern, S.: caverna; spelonca, *f.* **-ous**, ADJ.: cavernoso, cavo.

căvesson, S.: cavezzone, *m.*

căviar, caviare, S.: caviale, *m.*

căvil 1, S.: cavillazione, *f.*, sofisma, *m.* **cavil** 2, TR.: cavillare; criticare. **-ler**, S.: cavillatore, *m.*, sofista, *m.* **-lingly**, ADV.: cavillosamente. **-lous**, ADJ.: cavilloso, sofistico.

căvity, S.: cavità, *f.*; buco, *m.*

căw, INTR.: crocitare; gracchiare.

cēa-se, TR.: cessare; discontinuare, finire. **-seless**, ADJ.: incessante, continuo. **-selessly**, ADV.: incessantemente, continuamente. **-sing**, S.: cessazione, *f.*: *without* —, incessantemente.

cēcity, S.: cecità, *f.*

cecūtiency, S.: offuscazione della vista, *f.*

cēdar, S.: cedro, *m.*

cēde, TR.: cedere; abbandonare; INTR.: cedere; darsi per vinto.

cēdrine, ADJ.: cedrino, di cedro.

cēdule, S.: cedola, *f.*

cēil, TR.: soffitare. **-ing**, S.: soffitta, *f.*, soffitto, *m.*

cĕlandine, S.: celidonia, *f.*

cĕlature, S.: intaglio, *m.*

cĕl-ebrate, TR.: celebrare; esaltare. **-ebrated**, ADJ.: celebrato, esaltato. **-ebrătion**, S.: *celebramento, m.*; lode, *f.* **-ebrater**, S.: lodatore, panegirista, *m.* **-ĕbrious**†, ADJ.: celebre, rinomato. **-ĕbriously**†, ADV.: con celebrità. **-ĕbriousness**, S.: celebrità, riputazione; gloria, *f.* **-ĕbrity**, S.: celebrità; fama, *f.*

celĕriac, S.: appio navone, *m.*

celĕrity, S.: celerità, prestezza, *f.*

cĕlery, S.: appio, *m.*: *head of* —, piede di sedano, *m.*

celĕstial, ADJ.: celestiale, celeste; S.: celestiale, beato, *m.* **-ly**, ADV.: celestialmente.

cēliac, ADJ.: (*med.*) celiaco.

celi-bacy, cĕli-bate, -bateship, S.: celibato, *m.*

cĕll, S.: cella, cellula, *f.* **-ar**, S.: cantina, canova, *f.* **-arage**, S.: cantine, *f. pl.* **-arist**, S.: celleraio, canovaio, *m.* **-ular**, ADJ.: cellulare. **-ule**, S.: cellula, *f.*

cĕlsitude†, S.: celsitudine; altezza, *f.*

cemĕnt 1, S.: cimento, smalto, *m.* **cement** 2, TR.: assodare, saldare; INTR.: affermarsi, unirsi. **-ătion**, S.: cementazione, *f.*

cĕmetery, S.: cimitero, cimiterio, *m.*

cenobitical, ADJ.: cenobitico.

cĕnotaph, S.: cenotafio, *m.*

cen-se 1, S.: censo, *m.*, imposta, *f.*, tributo, *m.* **-se** 2, TR.: incensare, profumare. **-ser**, S.: incensiere, turibile, *m.*

cĕn-sor, S.: censore, critico, *m.* **-sōrious**, ADJ.: censorio, severo. **-sōriously**, ADV.: da censore; in modo severo. **-sōriousness**, S.: censura; severità, *f.* **-sorlike**, ADV.: da censore. **-sorship**, S.: dignità di censore, *f.*, censorato, *m.* **-surable**, ADJ.: censurabile; biasimevole. **-sure** 1, S.: censura; riprensione, *f.*: *vote of* —, voto di biasimo. **-sure** 2, TR.: censurare, criticare; biasimare. **-surer**, S.: riprenditore, biasimatore, *m.*

cĕnsus, S.: censo, *m.*

cĕnt, S.: cento, *m.*: *five per* —, cinque per cento; *discount of ten per* —, sconto di dieci per cento.

cĕntaur, S.: (*astron.*) centauro, *m.* **-y**, S.: centaurea, *f.*

cĕn-tenary, ADJ.: centenario, di cento anni; S.: centinaio, *m.* **-tĕsimal**, ADJ.: centesimo. **-tifōlious**, ADJ.: centifoglio. **-tiped**, S.: centupede, *m.*

cĕn-tral, ADJ.: centrale, centrico. **-trally**, ADV.: centralmente, nel mezzo. **-tre** 1, S.: centro; cuore, *m.* **-tre** 2, TR.: centrare, centreggiare; INTR.: trarsi. **-tric, -trical**, ADJ.: centrale. **-trifugal**, ADJ.: **-tripetal**, ADJ.: centripeta.

cĕn-tuple, ADJ.: centuplo. **-t** TR.: centuplicare.

centū-riate, TR.: dividere in **-rion**, S.: centurione, *m.*

céntury, S.: centuria, *f.*; secolo, *m.*: *the last* —, lo scorso secolo.
céph-alalgy, S.: (*med.*) cefalalgia, *f.* **-álic**, ADJ.: (*med.*) cefalico.
cé-rate, S.: (*phar.*) cerotto, *m.* **-rated**, ADJ.: incerato. **-re**, TR.: incerare, coprire di cera.
cérebel, S.: cerebello, *m.*
cérecloth, S.: incerato, *m.*, tela incerata, *f.*
ceremó-nial, ADJ.: ceremoniale: S.: ceremoniale; rito, *m.* **-nious**, ADJ.: ceremonioso. **-niously**, ADV.: ceremoniosamente, con cerimonia. **-niousness**, S.: vaghezza di ceremonie; maniera formale, *f.* **cèremo-ny**, S.: cerimonia, formalità, *f.*; complimento, *m.*: *without* —, senza cerimonie (o soggezione).
cèrtain, ADJ.: certo, sicuro, fisso; evidente: *for* —, di certo, per certo; *a — person*, una certa persona, un tale, il tale. **-ly**, ADV.: certamente, senza dubbio. **-ty**, S.: certezza, sicurezza, *f.*
cer-tificate, S.: certificato, *m.*, attestazione, *f.* **-tify**, TR.: certificare, render certo: confermare: *the undersigned certifies, etc.*, il sottoscritto certifica, ecc. **-titude**, S.: certezza: sicurezza, *f.*
cerú-lean, **-leous**, ADJ.: ceruleo, turchino.
cerúmen, S.: cerume, *m.*
Cesárian, ADJ.: cesareo.
cess-átion, S.: cessazione, *f.*, cessamento; tralasciamento, *m.*: — *of arms*, sospensione d'armi, *f.* **-ible**, ADJ.: atto a cedersi.
cession, S.: cessione; rassegnazione, *f.* **-ary**, ADJ.: cessionario.
cessment†, S.: tassa, imposizione, *f.*
céstus, S.: cesto, *m.*
cesúra, S.: (*pros.*) cesura, *f.*
cetáceous, ADJ.: cetaceo.
cháfe 1, S.: ardore, furore, *m.*, rabbia, *f.*; fremito, fremere, *m.* **-e** 2, TR.: scaldare; irritare, stizzire, mettere in collera: INTR.: fremere; adirarsi, incollerirsi. **-er**, S.: colui che (si) irrita: (*zoöl.*) scarafaggio, *m.*
cháff, S.: lolla, loppa, *f.*
cháffer 1, S.: mercanzia, *f.* **chaffer** 2, INTR.: trafficare, stiracchiare; trattare. **-er**, S.: comperatore, mercante, *m.*
cháffern†, S.: caldaia, *f.*
cháffinch, S.: fringuello, pincione, *m.*
cháff-less, ADJ.: senza lolla. **-y**, ADJ.: paglioso.
cháfing-dish, S.: scaldaviveane, *m.*
chagrin 1, S.: affanno, *m.*, stizza, *f.* **chagrin** 2, TR.: affannare, adirare.
chain 1, S.: catena; concatenamento, *m.*, *f.*; S. PL.: catene, *f. pl.*; schiavitù, *little* —, catenella, catenuzza. **chain** 2, incatenare, mettere alla catena, legare con catena. **-ing**, S.: incatenamento, *m.* **-pump**, S.: tromba grande e doppia, *f.* **-shot**, S.: palle incatenate, *f. pl.*
cháir, S.: sedia; sedia portatile, *f.*; cattedra, *f.*; seggio (presidenziale), *m.*: *fill the* —, tenere la presidenza; *found a* —, fondare una cattedra. **-man**, S.: presidente, *m.*
cháise, S.: calesso, biroccio, *m.*
chalcógra-pher, S.: calcografo, *m.* **-phy**, S.: intagliare in rame, *m.*
cháldron, S.: 36 moggi di carbone, *m. pl.*
chálice, S.: calice, *m.*, coppa, *f.*
chálk 1, S.: creta, *f.*, gesso, *m.*, marna, *f.* **chalk** 2, segnare col gesso; schizzare: — *out*, segnare; mostrare. **-cutter**, S.: che scava la marna. **-pit**, S.: cava di marna, *f.* **-y**, ADJ.: cretoso.
chállen-ge 1, S.: disfida; pretensione, *f.*; rigettamento, rifiuto, *m.* **-ge** 2, (IN)TR.: sfidare; recusare; chiamare a battaglia; rifiutare. **-ger**, S.: sfidatore, *m.*
chamáde, S.: chiamata, battuta di tamburo, *f.*
chámber 1, S.: camera; stanza, *f.*: — *of a cannon*, camera di cannone; *dark* —, camera oscura. **chamber** 2, TR.: intrigarsi. **-fellow**, S.: camerata, *m.* **-lain**, S.: camerlingo, cameriere, *m.*: *Lord High* —, Gran Ciamberlano. **-lainship**, S.: uffizio del camerlingo. **-maid**, S.: cameriera, *f.* **-pot**, S.: orinale, *m.*
chámbrel, S.: garretta, *f.*
chaméleon, S.: camaleonte, *m.*
chámfer 1, S.: scanalatura, *f.* **chamfer** 2, TR.: scanalare.
chámois, S.: camoscio, *m.*
chámomile, S.: camomilla, *f.*
chámp, TR.; INTR.: masticare, rodere.
champáign†, S.: campagna, *f.*, paese aperto, *m.*
champágne, S.: (vino di) Sciampagna, *m.*: *iced* —, sciampagna al ghiaccio; *sparkling* —, sciampagna spumante.
champignon *-pinyon*, S.: fungo, *m.*
chámpion 1, S.: campione, eroe, *m.* **champion** 2, TR.: sfidare a singolar certame.
cháner 1, S.: azzardo, *m.*, ventura, *f.*, caso, *m.*, sorte, *f.*: *take one's* —, arrischiare; *good* (*lucky*) —, buona ventura; *try the — of war*, tentare la fortuna della guerra; *meet by* —, incontrare a caso; — *customer*, avventore, compratore causale; *take one's* —, correre il rischio, arrischiarsi. **chance** 2, INTR.: accadere, avvenire, occorrere. **-able**†, ADJ.: accidentale, casuale. **-guest**, S.: sopravvegnente inaspettato, *m.*
chán-cel, S.: santuario, *m.* **-celler**, S.:

cancelliere, *m.; Lord High* —, gran cancelliere (d' Inghilterra), *m.* **-cellorship**, s.: cancelleria, *f.* **-cery**, s.: cancelleria, *f.*
chăn-cre, s.: (*surg.*) canchero, cancro, *m.* **-crous**, ADJ.: cancheroso, ulceroso.
chandelier, s.: candelabro, *m.;* lumiera, *f.*
chândler, s.: candelaio venditor a minuto, *m.*
chānge 1, s.: cambiamento, *m.;* mutazione, vicenda; alterazione; varietà; moneta, *f.* **-e** 2, TR.: cambiare; mutare, alterare; INTR.: cangiarsi; mutarsi; — *place*, cambiar di luogo; — *colour*, cambiare di colore; cambiarsi nel viso, arrossire; — *one's opinion*, mutare pensiero, **-eable**, ADJ.: cambiabile, cangiabile; variabile, incostante. **-eableness**, s.: incostanza, mutabilità, *f.* **-eably**, ADV.: incostantemente. **-eful**, ADJ.: incostante, instabile. **-eless**, invariabile, costante. **-eling**, s.: parto supposto, sciocco. **-er**, s.: cambiatore, banchiere, *m.* **-ing**, s.: cambiamento, *m.*
chănnel 1, s.: canale; letto (d' un fiume), *m.;* scanalatura, *f.: the Channel*, il canale della Manica; *little* —, canaletto, *m.* **channel** 2, TR.: scanalare.
chânt 1, s.: canto, *m.* **chant** 2, TR.: cantare; celebrare. **-er**, s.: cantatore, cantore, *m.* **-icleer**, s.: gallo, *m.* **-ress**, s.: cantatrice, *f.* **-ry**, s.: dignità del cantore, *f.*
chā-os, s.: caos, *m.;* confusione, *f.* **-ŏtic**, ADJ.: confuso.
chăp 1, s.: fessura; crepatura, *f.*, fesso, *m.* **chap** 2, INTR.: crepare; spaccarsi, fendersi.
chāpe, s.: puntale; rampone, fermaglio, *m.*
chăpel, s.: cappella, chiesetta, *f.* **-ry**, s.: cappellania, *f.*
chăperon, s.: cappuccio, *m.*
chăpiter, s.: (*arch.*) capitello, *m.*
chăplain, s.: cappellano; limosiniere, *m.* **-ship**, s.: carica di cappellano, *f.*
chăpless, ADJ.: magro, smunto.
chăplet, s.: corona, *f.;* rosario, *m.*
chăpman, s.: compratore; mercante, *m.*
chăps = *chops.*
chăpt, ADJ.: fesso, spaccato.
chăpter, s.: capitolo; capo, *m.* **-house**, s.: capitolo, *m.*
châr 1, s.: giornata, *f.* **char** 2, TR.: ridurre in carbone, bruciacchiare; INTR.: lavorare alla giornata.
chăracter 1, s.: carattere; segno, *m.;* lettera; descrizione; dignità, *f.: an odd* —, un uomo strambo; *he is quite a* —, egli è un originale; *take away one's* —, diffamare uno. **character** 2, TR.: intagliare; inscrivere. **-istic**, s.: caratteristica, *f.* **-istic(al)**, ADJ.: caratteristico. **-isticalness**, s.: qualità propria, caratteristica, *f.* **-ize**, TR.: caratterizzare. **-less**, ADJ.: senza carattere. **-y**, s.: impressione, *f.*
chârcoal, s.: carbone di legna, *m.*
chârd, s.: cardo; cardone, *m.*
chârge 1, s.: carico, *m.*, carica, soma, *f.*, peso, *m.;* cura, incombenza, *f.;* uffizio, impiego, *m.;* accusa, imputazione, *f.;* deposito, *m.;* spesa, *f.;* assalto, *m.: heavy* —, peso gravoso; *customary* —, solito prezzo; —*s included*, comprese le spese; *lay to one's* —, incolpare alcuno; *take the* — *of something*, pigliarsi l' incombenza di qualche cosa. **-e** 2, TR.: caricare; comandare, imporre; accusare, incolpare; — *with*, commettere alla cura. **-eable**, ADJ.: imputabile, dispendioso. **-eably**, ADV.: con dispendio. **-er**, s.: cavallo da guerra; gran piatto, *m.*
châr-ily, ADV.: frugalmente. **-iness**, s.: prudenza; cautela, *f.*
chăriot 1, s.: carro, *m.*, carrozza, *f.* **chariot** 2, INTR.: condurre in carrozza. **-eer**, s.: cocchiere, conduttor del carro, *m.* **-race**, s.: corsa di carri, *f.*
chări-table, ADJ.: caritatevole, benefacente. **-tableness**, s.: beneficenza, *f.* **-tably**, ADV.: caritatevolmente. **-ty**, s.: carità; beneficenza, limosina, *f.: beg* —, domandar la limosina; *for* —*'s sake*, per l' amor di Dio; — *begins at home*, la prima carità è l' aver cura. **-ty-school**, s.: scuola gratuita, *f.*
chârla-tan, s.: ciarlatano, cantambanco, *m.* **-tănical**, ADJ.: ciarlatanesco. **-tanry**, s.: ciarlataneria, *f.*
Chârles'-wāin *-zez-*, s.: (*astr.*) orsa maggiore. *f.*
chârlock, s.: loglio, *m.*, zizzania, *f.*
chârm 1, s.: incanto; allettamento, *m.* **charm** 2, TR.: incantare, ammaliare, allettare, rapire: — *away*, scongiurare. **-er**, s.: incantatore, *m.*, incantatrice, *f.* **-ing**, ADJ.: vezzoso, vago; s.: incantamento, *m.* **-ingly**, ADV.: vagamente, piacevolmente. **-ingness**, s.: attrativa; bellezza, *f.*
chârnel-house, s.: carnaio, *m.*
chârt, s.: carta di navigare, *f.*
chârter, s.: patente; privilegio; statuto; carta constituzionale. **-party**, s.: (*nav.*) contratto di noleggio, *m.* **-ed**, ADJ.: privilegiata, immune, esente.
chârwoman, s.: donna lavorante alla giornata, *f.*
chāry, ADJ.: accorto, prudente.
chās-e 1, s.: caccia; foresta, *f.* **-e** 2, TR.: cacciare; mandar via. **-er**, s.: cacciatore, perseguitore, *m.*
chăsm, s.: fessura; apertura; læcu vacuo, *m.*

chās-te, ADJ.: casto, pudico; onesto; puro: *have — ears*, aver buon orecchio. **-tely**, ADV.: castamente; pudicamente. **-ten**, TR.: castigare, punire; correggere. **-teness**, S.: castità, pudicizia; modestia, *f.*
chastis-e, TR.: castigare, punire. **-ement**, S.: castigo, *m.;* punizione, *f.* **-er**, S.: gastigatore, punitore, *m.*
chăstity, S.: castità; purità, *f.*
chăsuble, S.: pianeta di prete, *f.*
chăt 1, S.: ciarla, *f.;* cicaleccio, *m.: little —*, chiacchierata, *f.* **chat** 2, INTR.: ciarlare; cornacchiare.
chătellany, S.: castellania, castellaneria, *f.*
chăttel, S.: mobile, *m.*
chăt-ter 1, S.: ciarla, *f.*, cicalare, *m.* **-ter** 2, INTR.: ciarlare, cornacchiare; tremare, battere i denti. **-terer**, S.: ciarliero, ciarlatore, *m.* **-tering**, S.: cicaleria, *f.;* battimento di denti, *m.* **-ting**, S.: ciarla, *f.*, cicalamento, *m.* **-ty**, ADJ.: loquace, ciarlone.
chătwood, S.: legna per il fuoco, *f. pl.*
chăw, TR.: masticare; ruminare.
chăwdron, S.: viscere, interiora, *f. pl.*
chēap, ADJ.: a buon mercato. **-en**, TR.: prezzolare, mercatare. **-ener**, S.: prezzolatore, *m.* **-ly**, ADV.: a buon mercato, per poco. **-ness**, S.: buon mercato, vil prezzo, *m.*
chēat 1, S.: frode, furberia, *f.*, inganno; furbo; barattiere; giuntatore, *m.* **cheat** 2, TR.: far fraude a, ingannare, truffare; giuntare: *— at cards (play)*, truffare al giuoco. **-er**, S.: ingannatore, truffatore, *m.* **-ingly**, ADV.: ingannevolmente, con frode.
chĕck 1, S.: scacco; ostacolo, impedimento; rimprovero, *m.*, riprensione, *f.: give one a —*, fare una riprensione ad uno; *take a — at*, offendersi di; *keep a — upon one*, tenere uno in freno; *— to the king*, scacco al re. **check** 2, TR.: frenare, reprimere; riprendere; INTR.: fermarsi; opporsi: *— one's anger*, rattenere la collera; *— an account*, riscontrare (*or* verificare) un conto; *— one's self*, fermarsi, raffrenarsi.
chĕcker, TR.: fare a scacchi; intarsiare; screziare. **-wise**, ADJ.: a scacchi. **-work**, S.: tarsia, *f.;* screzio *m.*
chĕck-less, ADJ.: irresistibile. **-mate**, S.: scaccomatto, *m.* **-y**, ADJ.: intarsiato; mischiato.
chēek, S.: guancia; gota, *f.: chubby —s*, guance paffute; *— by jowl*, testa a testa. **-bone**, S.: mascella, *f.* **-tooth**, S.: dente mascellare, *m.* **-y**, ADJ.: sfacciato, ardito.
cheer 1, S.: pasto; banchetto, *m.;* allegrezza, *f.*, umore, coraggio; volto, *m.: good —*, mangiare e bere bene; *loud —s*, strepitosi applausi. **cheer** 2, TR.: rallegrare; animare; INTR.: rallegrarsi, incoraggiarsi, farsi animo: *— up*, farsi animo, rasserenarsi; *— up!* animo! coraggio! **-ful**, ADJ.: gaio, allegro, lieto, gioioso. **-fully**, ADV.: allegramente, lietamente. **-fulness**, **-ishness**, S.: gioia, allegrezza, *f.;* contento, *m.* **-ily**, ADV.: allegramente. **-less**, ADJ.: tristo, malinconoso. **-ly** †, **-y**, ADJ.: gaio, gioioso, lieto, allegro.
chēese, S.: formaggio, cacio, *m.* **-cake**, S.: tortelletta di cacio, *f.* **-curds**, S. PL.: latte rappreso, *m.* **-monger**, S.: formaggiaio; pizzicagnolo, *m.* **-press**, **cheese-vat**, S.: graticcio, *m.* **-y**, ADJ.: caseoso, cacioso.
chĕmical, ADJ.: chimico. **-ly**, ADV.: chimicamente.
che-mise, S.: camicia da donna, *f.* **chemisĕtte**, S.: camicetta, *f.*, camicino, *m.*
chĕmist, S.: chimico, *m.: — and druggist*, farmacista, speziale, *m.* **-ry**, chimica, *f.*
chĕrish, TR.: amare teneramente; mantenere; allevare: *he —ed the hope*, egli nutriva la speranza. **-er**, S.: amatore; mantenitore, protettore, *m.* **-ment**, S.: incoraggiamento; sostegno, *m.*
chĕrry 1, S.: ciriegia, *f.: wild —*, agriotta, *f.* **cherry** 2, ADJ.: rosso, vermiglio: *— cheeks*, guance vermiglie, *f. pl.* **-orchard**, S.: ciriegeto, *m.* **-pit**, S.: fossetta; buca, *f.* **-stone**, S.: nocciolo di ciriegia, *m.* **-tree**, S.: ciriegio, ciliegio, *m.*
chĕr-ub, S.: cherubino, *m.* **-ŭbic(al)**, ADJ.: cherubico.
chĕrvil, S.: cerfoglio, *m.*
chĕsnut = *chestnut.*
chĕss, S.: scacchi, *m. pl.: game of —*, giuoco degli scacchi, partita di scacchi; *play at —*, giuocare agli scacchi. **-board**, S.: scacchiere tavoliere, *m.* **-man**, S.: pedina, *f.;* scacco, *m.* **-player**, S.: giuocatore di scacchi, *m.*
chĕst, S.: cassa, *f.;* casso, cassero (del corpo); (*nav.*) forziere, *m.: — of drawers*, stipo, armadio, *m.* **-ed**, ADJ.: di petto. **-foundered**, ADJ.: bolso. **-foundering**, S.: bolsaggine, *f.*
chĕstnut, S.: castagna, *f.;* ADJ.: castagnino, castagno. **-colour**, ADJ.: castagnino. **-plot**, S.: castagneto, *m.* **-tree**, S.: castagno, *m.*
che-valiĕr, S.: cavaliere, *m.* **-vaux-de-frise** *-vō-*, S.: (*mil.*) cavalli di frisa, *m. pl.*
chēven, S.: ghiozzo, *m.* (pesce).
chĕveril †, S.: pelle di capretto, *f.*
chĕvisance †, S.: mercato ingiusto, *m.* intrapresa, *f.*

chĕvron, S.: travicello; (*her.*) caprone, *m.*
chew *chū*, TR.: masticare; ruminare; considerare, meditare: — *the cud*, ruminare; — *tobacco*, masticare tabacco.
chicā-ne, S.: cavillo, inganno, rigiro, *m.* **-ne**, INTR.: cavillare; sofisticare. **-ner**, S.: cavillatore, *m.* **-nery**, S.: cavillo, *m.*; sofisticheria, *f.*
chick, chick-en, S.: pollastro, *m.* **-en-hearted**, ADJ.: timido, pauroso. **-en-pox**, S.: morviglione, *m.* **-peas**, S. PL.: cece, *m.* **-weed**, S.: centocchio, *m.*
chid, impf. e part. del v. *chide.*
chi-de, IRR.; TR. (*chid; chid, chidden*): biasimare; riprendere; INTR.: disputare, querelare, schiamazzare. **-der**, S.: riprenditore, *m.* **-ding**, S.: riprensione, *f.* **-dingly**, ADV.: in modo di riprensione.
chief, ADJ.: primo, principale; S.: capo, comandante; direttore, socio principale, *m.*: *in* —, in capo; *Lord — Justice*, primo giudice (in Inghilterra), *m.* **-dom**, S.: sovranità, *f.* **-less**, ADJ.: senza capo. **-ly**, ADV.: principalmente. **-tain**, S.: comandante; capitano, *m.* **-tainry, -tainship**, S.: capitanato, *m.*
chilblain, S.: (*med.*) pedignone, *m.*
child, S.: fanciullo; figlio, figliuolo; bambino, ragazzo, infante, *m.*: *little* —, bimbo, bambinello; *adopted* —, figlio addottivo; *natural* —, figlio naturale (illegitimo); *naughty* —, ragazzaccio; *still-born* —, nato morto; *foster* —, figlio (-lia) di latte; *from a* —, dall' infanzia, dalla culla; *bring forth a* —, partorire; *be past a* —, aver passato l' infanzia; *be with* —, essere incinta. **-bearing**, S.: pregnezza, gravidanza, *f.* **-bed**, S.: letto della partoriente; tempo del parto, *m.* **-birth**, S.: parto; partorire, *m.* **-hood**, S.: infanzia; fanciullezza, *f.* **-ish**, ADJ.: bambinesco, fanciullesco. **-ishly**, ADV.: a modo di fanciullo. **-ishness**, S.: bambinaggine, infanzia, puerilità, *f.* **-less**, ADJ.: senza figliuoli. **-like**, ADJ.: fanciullesco, bambinesco.
children, PL. di *child.*
chiliad, S.: migliaio, *m.*
chill I, ADJ.: freddo, freddoloso; S.: freddo, *m.*, freddura, *f.*: *cold* —*s*, brividi, ribrezzi di febbre. **chill** 2, TR.: freddare; gelare. **-iness**, S.: freddura, *f.*; brivido, *m.* **-y**, ADJ.: alquanto freddo, freddotto; freddoso, freddoloso.
chime I, S.: scampanata, *f.*; accordo, *m.*, armonia, *f.*: —*s*, armonia di campane. **chime** 2, INTR.: scampanare; accordarsi, unirsi: — *in*, consonare, essere d' accordo.
chi-mēra, S.: chimera, *f.* **-mĕrical**, ADJ.: chimerico. **-mĕrically**, ADV.: chimericamente.
chimney, S.: cammino, focolare, *m.* **-corner**, S.: luogo de' ciarloni, *m.* **-piece**, S.: cornice del cammino, *f.* **-sweeper**, S.: spazzacammino, *m.*
chin, S.: mento, *m.*
china, S.: porcellana; majolica, *f.* **-man**, S.: mercante di porcellana, *m.* **-orange**, S.: melarancia dolce, *f.* **-root**, S.: cina, *f.*
chin-cloth, S.: bavaglio, *m.* **-cough**, S.: tossa violenta, *f.*
chine I, S.: schiena; spina, *f.* **chine** 2, TR.: sfilare.
Chinēse, ADJ.: chinese; S.: Chinese, *m.*
chink I, S.: fessura, crepatura, *f.* **chink** 2, TR., INTR.: tintinnare; spaccarsi. **-y**, ADJ.: screpolato, fesso.
chinse, TR.: (*nav.*) calafatare.
chints, S.: indiana, *f.* (tela dipinta).
chip I, S.: scheggia, *f.*; bruciolo, *m.*: —*s of bread*, croste di pane, *f. pl.*; *he is a — of the old block*, quale padre tale figlio; a' segni si conoscono le balle. **chip** 2, TR.: truciolare, sbriciolare, sminuzzare.
chirāgrical, ADJ.: chiragrico.
chirŏgrapher, S.: chirografario, *m.*
chiro-mancer, S.: chiromante, *m.* **-mancy**, S.: chiromanzia, *f.*
chirp I, S.: garrito; pigolare, *m.* **chirp** 2, TR.: garrire; pigolare, piare. **-er**, S.: gridatore, *m.* **-ing**, S.: garrito; canto (d' uccelli), *m.*
chisel I, S.: scalpello, *m.* **chisel** 2, TR.: scarpellare, intagliare. **-work**, S.: lavoro di scultura, *m.*
chit I, S.: bambino; stipite, *m.* **chit** 2, INTR.: germinare, germogliare.
chitchat, S.: ciarla, ciarleria, *f.*
chitterlings, S. PL.: budella, minugia, *f. pl.*
chival-rous, ADJ.: cavalleresco. **-ry**, S.: dignità di cavaliere, cavalleria, *f.*
chives, S. PL.: costole di fiori, *f. pl.*; cipolletta, *f.*
chŏck, S.: sorgozzone; attacco, *m.*
chŏcolate, S.: cioccolato, *m.* **-pot**, S.: cioccolattiera, *f.* **-dealer**, S.: cioccolatiere, *m.*
chŏice I, S.: scelta, elezione, eletta; varietà, *f.*: *make* —, scegliere. **choice** 2, ADJ.: scelto, squisito, raro. **-less**, ADJ.: senza il potere di scegliere, indifferente. **-ly**, ADV.: caramente. **-ness**, S.: rarità; delicatezza, *f.*
choir *kwīr*, S.: coro (d' una chiesa), *m.*
chōk-e I, S.: fieno del carciofo, *m.* **-e** 2, TR.: suffocare, strangolare; turare, stoppare; INTR.: soffocarsi, affogarsi: — *up*, ingorgare. **-e-pear**, S.: pera strozzatoia, *f.* **-ing**, S.: suffocamento, *m.* **-y**, ADJ.: suffocante, strozzatoio.
chŏlagogues, S.: (med.) colagogo, *m.*

-bly, ADV.: a comparazione; a petto. **-părative**, ADJ.: comparativo; S.: (*gram.*) comparativo, *m.* **-părativsly**, ADV.: a comparazione, rispetivamente. **-pàre** 1, S.: comparazione, *f.*; agguaglio, *m.*, somiglianza, *f.* **-pare** 2, TR.: comparare, paragonare; assimigliare, agguagliare; *—d to*, paragonato a, a petto di, a confronto di. **-părison**, S.: comparazione; analogia, *f.*: *in — with*, in paragone di; *beyond —*, senza comparazione, senza paragone.

compârt, TR.: compartire, dividere. **-ment**, S.: compartimento, *m.* **-ition†**, S.: scompartimento, *m.*, divisione, *f.*

cómpass 1, S.: circuito; giro; spazio, *m.*; bussola, *f.*, compasso, *m.*: *a pair of —es*, un compasso; un paio di seste; *mariner's —*, bussola; *of great —*, di grande estensione; *keep within —*, contenersi, regolarsi. **compass** 2, TR.: circondare; cingere; INTR.: venire a capo, ottenere; riuscire. **-es**, S. PL.: compasso, *m.*

compăssion, S.: compassione, pietà, *f.* **-able**, ADJ.: compassionevole. **-ate**, TR.: commiserare, compatire. **-ately**, ADV.: con compassione.

com-patibility, S.: compatibilità, convenanza, attezza, *f.* **-pătible**, ADJ.: compatibile, convenevole. **-pătibleness**, S.: convenenza, conformità, *f.* **-pătibly**, ADV.: conformemente, attamente.

compătriot, S.: compatriota, *m.*

compēer 1, S.: campagno, collega, *m.* **compeer** 2, TR.: andar del pari, agguagliare, adeguare.

compĕl, TR.: costringere, forzare, obbligare. **-lable**, ADJ.: che può essere costretto, forzato. **-lātion**, S.: nome, titolo, *m.* **-ler**, S.: forzatore, *m.*

cŏm-pend, S.: compendio, abbreviamento, *m.* **-pendiŏsity**, S.: brevità, concisione, *f.* **-pĕndious**, ADJ.: compendioso, succinto, conciso. **-pĕndiously**, ADV.: in compendio. **-pĕndiousness**, S.: brevità, concisione, cortezza, *f.* **-pĕndium**, S.: compendio, sommario, *m.*

compĕnsable, ADJ.: compensabile.

cŏm-pensate, TR.: compensare; rimunerare. **-pensātion**, S.: compensazione, *f.*, compensamento, *m.*: *as a — for*, in compenso di; *by way of —*, per compenso. **-pĕnsative**, **-pĕnsatory**, ADJ.: compensabile, equivalente. **-pĕnse†**, TR.: compensare; rimunerare.

compe̦rĕndi-nate†, TR.: procrastinare, differire.

compe̦ten-ce, **-cy**, S.: competenza, sufficienza, *f.*: *have a —*, aver il bisognevole, aver comodo. **-t**, ADJ.: competente, bastevole. **-tly**, ADV.: competentemente.

-pĕtible†, ADJ.: convenevole, conforme. **-petition**, S.: competenza, concorrenza, *f.* **-pĕtitor**, S.: competitore, concorrente, *m.*

com-pilātion, S.: compilazione, collezione, *f.* **-pile**, TR.: compilare; ordinare; comporre. **-pilement**, S.: compilazione, *f.*, compilamento, *m.*; collezione, *f.* **-piler**, S.: compilatore, *m.*

complăcen-ce, **-cy**, S.: compiacenza, piacevolezza, *f.* **-t**, ADJ.: compiacente; civile.

complăin, TR.: deplorare; INTR.: compiangere, lamentarsi. **-ant**, S.: querelante, attore, *m.* **-er**, S.: compiangitore, *m.* **-t**, S.: doglianza, querela, *f.*; lamento; affanno, *m.*: *prefer a — against*, accusare querelarsi di.

cŏmplaisan-ce, S.: compiacenza, cortesia, *f.* **-t**, ADJ.: cortese, civile. **-tly**, ADV.: cortesemente, con civiltà. **-tness**, S.: affabilità, civiltà, *f.*

cŏmple-ment, S.: compimento, *m.* **-mĕntal**, ADJ.: aggiunto.

complē-te 1, ADJ.: compiuto, completo, perfetto. **-te** 2, TR.: compire; finire. **-tely**, ADV.: compiutamente; perfettamente. **-teness**, S.: compimento, *m.*, perfezione, *f.* **-tion**, S.: adempimento; colmo, *m.* **-tive**, ADJ.: che compisce.

cŏm-plex, ADJ.: complesso, composto; S.: complesso, *m.*, complicazione; unione, *f.* **-plĕxed**, ADJ.: composto. **-plĕxedness**, S.: complesso; adunamento, *m.* **-plĕxion**, S.: carnagione, *f.*, colore, *m.*; complessione, costituzione, *f.*, stato del corpo, *m.* **-plĕxional**, ADJ.: che viene da costituzione. **-plĕxionally**, ADV.: da costituzione. **-plĕxioned**, ADJ.: complesso. **-plĕxity**, S.: complicazione, *f.* **-plĕxly**, ADV.: in modo complesso, unitamente. **-plĕxness**, S.: complicazione, *f.*

compli-able, ADJ.: compiacente. **-ance**, S.: compiacenza, *f.*; consenso, *m.*: *in — with*, conforme a. **-ant**, ADJ.: condiscendente.

cŏmpli-cate, TR.: imbrogliare, intrecciare. **-cate(d)**, ADJ.: complicato; composto, imbrogliato: *get —*, complicarsi. **-cateness**, S.: involvimento, imbroglio, *m.* **-cātion**, S.: complicazione, unione; aggregazione, *f.*

cŏmplice, S.: complice, confederato, *m.*

complier, S.: che compiace facilmente.

cŏmpli-ment 1, S.: complimento, *m.*: *pay a —*, far un complimento. **-ment** 2, TR.: complimentare, far cerimonie. **-mĕntal**, ADJ.: cerimonioso. **-mĕntally**, ADV.: cortesemente. **-menter**, S.: che fa complimenti, adulatore, *m.*

cŏm-plot, S.: cospirazione, congiura, *f.* **-plŏt**, TR.: cospirare, congiurare. **-plŏtter**, S.: cospiratore, congiuratore, *m.*

complȳ, INTR.: conformarsi, adattarsi; acconsentire; condiscendere: — *with*, acconsentire a; conformarsi a. **-ing**, S.: condiscendenza, *f*.
compōnent, ADJ.: componente, costituente.
cŏm-port 1, S.: portamento; modo, *m*. **-pōrt** 2, TR.: sofferire; INTR.: convenire; comportarsi, accomodarsi: — *one's self*, comportarsi, procedere. **-pōrtable**, ADJ.: convenevole. **-pōrtment**, S.: portamento, *m*.
com-pōse, TR.: comporre; ordinare, regolare; accomodare: — *one's self*, tranquillarsi, mettersi sul serio; — *a difference*, decidere una differenza. **-pōsed**, ADJ.: composto, quieto; grave. **-pōsedly**, ADV.: compostamente, seriamente. **-pōsedness**, S.: compostezza; tranquillità, *f*. **-pōser**, S.: componitore, compositore; autore, *m*. **-pōsing-stick**, S.: compositoio, *m*. **-pŏsite**, S.: composto. **-position**, S.: composizione, *f*.; composto, *m*. **-pŏsitive**, ADJ.: componente. **-pŏsitor**, S.: compositore, stampatore, *m*.
cŏmpost 1, S.: letame, concime, *m*. **compost** 2, TR.: letamare, concimare.
compōsure, S.: compositura; quiete, tranquillità, *f*.
compotātion, S.: compotazione, gozzoviglia, *f*.
cŏmpound 1, ADJ.: composto; mescolato; S.: composto; componimento, *m*.: — *interest*, interessi composti. **-pŏund** 2, TR.: comporre, combinare; INTR.: aggiustarsi; accordarsi, convenire. **-pŏundable**, ADJ.: che può essere composto. **-pŏunder**, S.: mediatore, *m*.
comprehĕn-d, comprendere, intendere; contenere. **-sible**, ADJ.: comprensibile, intelligibile. **-sibly**, ADV.: in modo comprensibile. **-sion**, S.: comprensione; intelligenza, *f*. **-sive**, ADJ.: che comprende molto; succinto. **-sively**, ADV.: comprensivamente. **-siveness**, S.: precisione, *f*.
cŏm-press, S.: (*surg.*) piumacciuolo, *m*. **-prĕss**, TR.: comprimere, ristringere. **-pressibility**, S.: attezza ad essere compresso, *f*. **-prĕssible**, ADJ.: che può essere compresso. **-prĕssion**, **-prĕssure**, S.: compressione, *f*.
compri-sal, S.: comprendimento, *m*. **-se**, TR.: comprendere, contenere.
cŏmpro-bate†, TR.: comprovare. **-bātion**†, S.: approvazione, *f*.
cŏmpro-mise 1, S.: (*jur.*) compromesso, *m*. **-mise** 2, TR.: compromettere; INTR.: venir ad un accomodamento; aggiustarsi. **-missōrial**, ADJ.: di compromesso. **-mit**, TR.: compromettere.
comptrŏll. = *controll*..

compŭl-satory, ADJ.: coercitivo, coattivo. **-sion**, S.: costringimento, *m*.; violenza, forza, *f*. **-sive**, ADJ.: coercitivo. **-sively**, ADV.: forzatamente, per forza. **-siveness**, S.: costringimento, *m*., forza, *f*. **-sorily**, ADV.: in modo coercitivo. **-sory**, ADJ.: coercitivo, compellente.
compŭnction, S.: compunzione, *f*.; rimorso, pentimento, *m*.
compurgātion, S.: giustificazione, *f*.
compŭt-able, ADJ.: che si può computare. **-ātion**, S.: computo, calcolo, *m*. **-e** 1, S.: computo, conto, *m*. **-e** 2, TR.: computare; calcolare. **-er**, S.: computista, *m*.
cŏmrade, S.: camerata, compagno, sozio, *m*.
cŏn 1, ADV.: contra: *pro and* —, pro e contra. **con** 2, TR.: studiare; sapere.
concăt-enate, TR.: concatenare, collegare; unire insieme. **-enātion**, S.: concatenazione; seguenza, serie, *f*.
cŏn-cave, ADJ.: concavo. **-căvity**, S.: concavità, *f*. **-cāvous**, ADJ.: concavo, concavato. **-cāvously**, ADV.: in forma concava.
concēal, TR.: celare, nascondere. **-able**, ADJ.: che si può celare. **-edness**, S.: nascondimento, *m*. **-er**, S.: nasconditore, occultatore, *m*. **-ment**, S.: celamento; nascondimento, *m*.
concēde, TR.: concedere, permettere; acconsentire.
concēit 1, S.: concetto, pensiero, *m*.; fantasia; voglia, *f*.: *idle* —*s*, ghiribizzi, *m. pl.* **conceit** 2, INTR.: immaginarsi, pensare, credere. **-ed**, ADJ.: affettato, vano, vanitoso, gonfio, presuntuoso. **-edly**, ADV.: in modo affettato, fantasticamente; vanamente. **-edness**, S.: affettazione, presunzione; vanagloria, *f*. **-less**, ADJ.: inconsiderato, stupido.
concēiv-able, ADJ.: concepibile, che può concepirsi, intelligibile. **-ableness**, S.: concepimento, *m*. **-ably**, ADV.: in modo comprensibile. **-e**, TR.: concepire, comprendere; INTR.: pensare, figurarsi, immaginarsi: — *of things clearly*, concepir le cose chiaramente. **-er**, S.: comprenditore, *m*. **-ing**, S.: concepimento, *m*.
concĕlebrate†, TR.: celebrare.
concĕnt†, S.: concento, *m*.; armonia, *f*.
concĕn-ter, **-trate**, TR.: concentrare; INTR.: concentrarsi. **-trātion**, S.: concentrazione, *f*. **-tric(al)**, ADJ.: concentrico.
concĕntual†, ADJ.: armonioso.
cŏn-cept, S.: concetto, *m*.; formula, *f*. **-cĕptible**, ADJ.: comprensibile, intelligibile. **-cĕption**, S.: concezione, *f*.; concepimento; pensiero, *m*. **-cĕptive**, ADJ.: atto a concepire.

concern 1, S.: affare; negozio; interesse, *m.*; importanza, conseguenza, *f.*: *mind your own —s*, badate ai fatti vostri. **concern** 2, TR.: concernere; appartenere; riguardare; importare: — *one's self*, ingerirsi, impacciarsi; tormentarsi; *that does not — me*, ciò non mi riguarda; *when a thing is —ed*, quando si tratta d'una cosa. **-ed**, ADJ.: interessato; afflitto, inquieto: *the parties —*, le parti interessate; *he is not at all — about it*, egli non se ne cura punto. **-ing**, PREP.: concernente, intorno. **-ment**, S.: affare, *m.*; importanza, *f.*

cŏn-çert 1, concerto; accordo, *m.* **-çĕrt** 2, TR.: concertare; deliberare. **-çertā-tion**†, S.: querela, contesa, *f.* **-çerta-tive**†, ADJ.: contenzioso, rissoso.

con-cĕssion, S.: concessione, *f.*, concedimento, *m.* **-cĕssionary**, ADJ.: conceduto. **-cĕssive**, ADJ.: concesso. **-cĕs-sively**, ADV.: per concessione.

cŏnch, S.: conca, *f.*

concil-iate, TR.: conciliare; unire, accordare. **-iātion**, S.: conciliazione, *f.* **-iator**, S.: conciliatore, mediatore, *m.* **-iatory**, ADJ.: conciliatorio, che concilia.

concin-nity, S.: concinnità; decenza, eleganza, *f.* **-nous**, ADJ.: decente; piacevole.

con-cise, ADJ.: conciso, succinto. **-cise-ly**, ADV.: concisamente, con brevità. **-ciseness**, S.: brevità; precisione, *f.* **-cision**, S.: concisione, *f.*

concitātion†, S.: concitamento, *m.*, agitazione, commozione, *f.*

cŏnclave, S.: conclave, *m.*

conclū-de, TR.: conchiudere; terminare; risolvere, decidere: *to —*, in conclusione, per finirla. **-dency**†, S.: conchiusione, conseguenza, *f.* **-dent**†, ADJ.: concludente; decisivo. **-sion**, S.: conchiusione, *f.*; fine, *m.*; decisione, *f.*: *bring to a —*, condurre a termine. **-sive**, ADJ.: conclusivo, decisivo. **-sively**, ADV.: conclusivamente. **-siveness**, S.: conclusione; conseguenza, *f.*

concŏc-t, TR.: concuocere; digerire, digestire. **-ted**, ADJ.: concotto, digesto. **-tion**, S.: concozione; digestione, *f.*

concŏmitan-ce, **-cy**, S.: concomitanza; compagnia, *f.* **-t**, ADJ.: concomitante; S.: concomitante, compagnone, *m.* **-tly**, ADV.: in compagnia.

cŏn-cord, S.: concordia; armonia, *f.* **-cŏrdance**, S.: concordanza, *f.*; accordo, *m.* **-cŏrdant**, ADJ.: concordante; conforme. **-cŏrdat**, S.: concordato, *m.*, convenzione, *f.*

concŏrpo-rate†, TR.: incorporare. **-rā-tion**, S.: incorporamento, *m.*

cŏncourse, S.: concorso, *m.*; moltitudine, *f.*

cŏncrement†, S.: concrezione, *f.*

cŏn-crete 1, ADJ.: concreto, spessato; S.: concreto; attaccamento, *m.* **-crēte** 2, TR.: congelare, coagulare; INTR.: congelarsi, coagularsi. **-crētely**, ADV.: in modo concreto. **-crēteness**, S.: congelazione, *f.* **-crētion**, S.: concrezione; coalescenza, *f.* **-crētive**, ADJ.: coagulativo.

concrew† *-crū*, INTR.: crescere insieme; mescolarsi.

concūbinage, S.: concubinato, *m.* **cŏn-cubine**, S.: concubina, *f.*

concūlcate†, TR.: conculcare; calpestare, rintuzzare.

concūpis-cence, S.: concupiscenza, *f.* **-cent**, ADJ.: libidinoso. **-cible**, ADJ.: concupiscibile.

concŭr, INTR.: concorrere; cooperare; convenire. **-rence**, **-rency**, S.: concorrenza; unione; assistenza, *f.* **-rent**, ADJ.: concorrente; S.: competitore, *m.*

concŭssion, S.: concussione, *f.*

cŏnd, TR.: governare un vascello.

condĕm-n, TR.: condannare; disapprovare, biasimare. **-nable**, ADJ.: condannabile; biasimevole. **-nātion**, S.: condanna, *f.*; gastigo, *m.* **-natory**, ADJ.: condannatorio. **-ner**, S.: biasimatore, riprenditore, *m.*

condĕn-sable, ADJ.: condensabile. **-sate** 1, ADJ.: condensato, spessito. **-sate** 2, TR.: condensare, spessire; INTR.: condensarsi, spessirsi. **-sātion**, S.: condensamento, *m.* **-se**, TR.: condensare, spessire; INTR.: condensarsi. **-ser**, S.: condensatore, *m.* **-sity**, S.: densità; spessezza, *f.*

condescĕn-d, INTR.: condiscendere; acconsentire. **-dence**, S.: condiscendenza, *f.* **-dingly**, ADV.: in modo condiscendente, obbligantemente. **-sion**, S.: condiscendimento, *m.* **-sive**, ADJ.: condescensivo; cortese.

con-dign, ADJ.: condegno, meritato. **-dignity**, S.: condegnità, *f.* **-dignly**, ADV.: condegnamente; meritevolmente. **-dignness** = *condignity*.

cŏndiment, S.: condimento, *m.*; salsa, *f.*

condisciple, S.: condiscepolo, *m.*

condite†, TR.: condire, marinare.

condition 1, S.: condizione, *f.*; patto; stato; grado; umore, *m.*, tempra, *f.*: *upon — that*, a condizione che, con patto che.

condition 2, TR.: stipulare, fare contratto. **-al**, ADJ.: condizionale. **-ality**, S.: stipulazione, *f.* **-ally**, ADV.: condizionalmente, con patto. **-ary**, ADJ.: stipulato. **-ate**, ADJ.: condizionato, stipulato. **-ed**, ADJ.: condizionato, di quali-

zione: *well* —, ben condizionato, in buono stato.
condŏl-atory, ADJ.: di condoglienza. **-e**, TR.: lamentare; INTR.: condolersi. **-ement**, S.: afflizione, *f.*; dolore, *m.* **-ence**, S.: condoglienza, *f.*
condonātion, S.: perdono, *m.*
condū-ce, TR.: condurre; guidare; INTR.: contribuire, servire, esser utile; aiutare. **-cible**, ADJ.: che contribuisce, utile, favorevole. **-cibleness**, S.: utilità, *f.* **-cive**, ADJ.: acconcio, conducevole: *be — to*, contribuire a, tendere a. **-civeness**, S.: acconcezza; attezza, *f.*
cŏn-duct 1, S.: condotta; scorta; direzione, *f.*: *safe* —, salvo condotto. **-dŭct** 2, TR.: condurre, guidare. **-dŭctor**, S.: conduttore; direttore; (*rail.*) conduttore, *m.* **-dŭctress**, S.: conduttrice; direttrice, *f.* **-duit**, S.: condotto; acquidotto, *m.*
cōne, S.: (*geom.*) cono, *m.*
confăb-ulate, INTR.: confabulare, discorrere insieme. **-ulātion**, S.: confabulazione, *f.*, discorso, *m.*
cŏn-fect 1, S.: confetto, *m.* **-fĕct** 2, TR.: confettare, far confezione. **-fĕction**, S.: confezione; confettura, *f.* **-fĕctionary**, S.: bottega di confettiere, *f.* **-fĕctioner**, S.: confettiere, *m.*
confĕd-eracy, S.: confederazione, lega, *f.* **-erate**, ADJ.: confederato, in lega; S.: confederato, *m.* **-erate**, INTR.: confederarsi, collegarsi. **-erātion**, S.: confederazione, *f.*: *enter into a* —, formare una confederazione, confederarsi.
con-fĕr, TR.: comparare; accordare; INTR.: conferire; discorrere. **cŏn-ference**, S.: conferenza, *f.* **-fĕrrer**, S.: presentatore, donatore, *m.*
con-fĕss, TR.: confessare; concedere; INTR.: confessarsi. **-fĕssedly**, ADV.: per confessione di tutti, manifestamente. **-fĕssion**, S.: confessione, affermazione, *f.*: *auricular* —, confessione auricolare, *f.*; *dying* —, confessione in extremis. **-fĕssional**, **-fĕssionary**, ADJ.: confessionale. **-fĕssor**, S.: confessore, *m.* **-fĕst**, ADJ.: confessato; aperto, chiaro. **-fĕstly**, ADV.: certamente, evidentemente.
con-fidănt(*e*), S., *m.* (*f.*): confidente; familiare, *m.*, *f.* **-fide**, INTR.: confidare; confidarsi: *don't — in him*, non vi fidate di lui.
cŏnfi-dence, S.: confidanza, fiducia, *f.*: *inspire one with* —, inspirar fiducia ad uno. **-dent**, ADJ.: sicuro; sfacciato, temerario; S.: confidente; amico, *m.*: *feel — that*, nutrir fiducia che. **-dĕntial**, ADJ.: confidenziale, di confidenza. **-dently**, ADV.: confidentemente; certamente. **-dentness**, S.: fiducia, fidanza, *f.*

con-figurātion, S.: configurazione; (*astr.*) costellazione, *f.* **-figure**, TR.: configurare; conformare.
cŏn-fine 1, S.: confine, limite, *m.* **-fine** 2, TR.: limitare; imprigionare; INTR.: confinare, essere contiguo. **-fined**, ADJ.: limitato, ristretto, rinchiuso: — *to one's bed*, obbligato a letto. **-fineless**, ADJ.: senza confini; illimitato, immenso. **-finement**, S.: costringimento, *m.*; prigione, *f.*: *solitary* —, reclusione cellulare; *strict* —, stretta custodia, rigorosa prigionia. **-finer**, S.: confinante, limitrofo; vicino, *m.* **-finity**, S.: prossimità, vicinanza, *f.*
confirm, TR.: confermare; ratificare. **-able**, ADJ.: che si può confermare. **-ātion**, S.: confermazione; ratificazione; prova, *f.* **-ator cŏn-**, S.: confermatore, *m.* **-atory**, ADJ.: confermativo. **-er**, S.: affermatore, *m.*
confiscable, ADJ.: confiscabile.
cŏn-fiscate, TR.: confiscare. **-fiscated**, ADJ.: confiscato. **-fiscātion**, S.: confiscazione, *f.* **-fiscator**, S.: confiscatore, *m.*
cŏnfit, S.: confetto, *m.*
cŏnfitent†, S.: confitente, confessante, *m.*
cŏnfiture, S.: confettura, *f.*
con-fix, TR.: conficcare, attaccare. **-fixure**, S.: conficcamento, *m.*
cŏnflict 1, S.: conflitto, combattimento, *m.*
conflict 2, INTR.: contendere; combattere; trovarsi in contraddizione.
cŏn-fluence, S.: confluenza, *f.*; concorso, *m.* **-fluent**, ADJ.: confluente; concorrente. **-flux**, S.: concorso, *m.*; calca, *f.*
confŏrm 1, ADJ.: conforme; simile. **conform** 2, TR.: conformare; concordare; INTR.: conformarsi. **-able**, ADJ.: conformevole, conforme; conseguente. **-ableness**, S.: conformità, *f.* **-ably**, ADV.: in conformità. **-ātion**, S.: conformazione, *f.* **-ist**, S.: conformista, *m.* **-ity**, S.: conformità, simiglianza, *f.*: *in — with*, conforme a.
confortātion†, S.: confortamento, *m.*, corroborazione, *f.*
confŏund, TR.: confondere; scompigliare; imbrogliare; distruggere. **-ed**, ADJ.: confuso; cattivo, maledetto. **-edly**, ADV.: cattivamente; orribilmente. **-er**, S.: confonditore, *m.*
confratĕrnity, S.: confraternità; società, *f.*
confricātion†, S.: fregamento, *m.*
confrŏnt, TR.: confrontare; comparare, paragonare. **-ātion**, S.: confrontazione, *f.*; riscontro, *m.*
confū-se, TR.: confondere, disordinare. **-sed**, ADJ.: confuso, imbrogliato, perplesso. **-sedly**, ADV.: confusamente. **-sion**, S.: confusione, disordine, *f.*; perturbamento, *m.*, distruzione, *f.*

[illegible]

-tutional. ADJ.: costituzionale. [illegible] **-tutive.** ADJ.: costitutivo.

constrain. TR.: costringere, forzare, [illegible] **-able.** ADJ.: [illegible] **-edly.** ADV.: [illegible] **-er.** S.: [illegible] **-t.** S.: costringimento, m. [illegible]

con-stríct. TR.: [illegible] **-striction.** S.: costringimento, [illegible] **-strictor.** S.: [illegible] **-stringe.** TR.: costringere [illegible] **-stringent.** ADJ.: [illegible]

con-strúct. TR.: costruire, fabbricare. **-struction.** S.: costruzione, costruttura; [illegible] **-structive.** ADJ.: [illegible] **-strúe.** TR.: [illegible]

constu-prate. TR.: [illegible] **-pration.** S.: [illegible]

consubstan-tial. ADJ.: [illegible] **-tiality.** S.: [illegible] **-tiate.** TR.: [illegible] **-tiation.** S.: [illegible]

consul. S.: console, m. [illegible] **-ar.** ADJ.: [illegible] **-ate.** [illegible] **-ship.** S.: [illegible]

consult. TR.: consultare; INTR.: [illegible] **-ation.** S.: [illegible] **-er.** S.: [illegible]

consú-mable. ADJ.: consumabile. **-me.** TR.: consumare, [illegible] **-mer.** S.: [illegible] **-ming.** ADJ.: [illegible]

consum-mate ADJ.: [illegible] **consum-mate 2.** TR.: [illegible] **-mately.** ADV.: [illegible] **-mation.** S.: compimento, m. [illegible]

consump-tion. S.: consumazione, f. [illegible] **-tive.** ADJ.: consuntivo, [illegible] **-tiveness.** S.: [illegible]

cóntact. S.: contatto, toccamento, m.: come into —, incontrarsi, imbattersi.

contá-gion. S.: contagione, peste, f.: catch the —, contrarre il contagio. **-gious.** ADJ.: contagioso, pestilenziale. **-giousness.** S.: qualità contagiosa, f.

contáin. TR.: contenere, comprendere; raffrenare, reprimere; temperare: — one's self, contenersi. **-able.** ADJ.: che può contenersi.

contámi-nate 1. ADJ.: contaminato; corrotto. **-nate** 2. TR.: contaminare; corrompere. **-nation.** S.: contaminazione; bruttura, f.

contém-n. TR.: contennere, sdegnare, disprezzare. **-ner.** S.: disprezzatore, m.

cón-template. TR.: contemplare, considerare. **-templation.** S.: contemplazione, f.: have in —, intendere, progettare. **-templative.** ADJ.: contemplativo. **-templatively.** ADV.: per contemplazione. **-templator.** S.: contemplatore, m.

con-temporaneous. **-témporary.** ADJ.: contemporaneo.

contémpt. S.: dispregio, sprezzo: bring into —, mettere in discredito; hold in —, avere tenere a vile; scherno, m.; — of court, contumacia, f. **-ible.** ADJ.: disprezzevole, spregevole. make —, avvilire. **-ibleness.** S.: disprezzamento, disprezzo, m. **-ibly.** ADV.: disprezzevolmente. **-uous.** ADJ.: sprezzante; sdegnoso. **-uously.** ADV.: fieramente, sdegnosamente. **-uousness.** S.: insolenza, arroganza, f.

contend. TR.: contendere, contrastare; INTR.: contrastare, sforzarsi: I — that, mantengo pretendo che. **-ent, -er.** S.: antagonista, oppugnante, m. **-ing.** S.: contendimento, m.

contént 1. ADJ.: contento, soddisfatto; S.: contento, m.: soddisfazione, f.: —s, contenuto, contenimento, m.: table of —s, indice, m. **content** 2. TR.: contentare, soddisfare, piacere. — one's self, contentarsi. **-ation.** S.: contentamento, m. **-ed.** ADJ.: contentato, soddisfatto: — with, contento soddisfatto di: easily —, di facile contentatura. **-edly.** ADV.: contentamente, lietamente. **-edness.** S.: contentezza, soddisfazione, f.

conten-tion. S.: contenzione, disputa, f.: bone of —, pomo di discordia. **-tious.** ADJ.: contenzioso, litigioso, cavilloso, litigante. **-tiously.** ADV.: contenziosamente, litigiosamente. **-tiousness.** S.: disposizione a disputare, f.

contént-less. ADJ.: scontento. **-ment.** S.: contentamento, contento, m., soddisfazione, f., piacere, m.

contérminous. ADJ.: confinante, limitrofo.

contést 1. TR.: contestare, questionare; disputare. **cóntest** 2. S.: contesa, lite; disputa, questione, f. **-able.** ADJ.: contestabile, disputabile. **-ation.** S.: contesa, disputa, f.

cón-text. S.: tessitura, f.; contesto, m.

-tĕxt† 2, ADJ.: contesto, unito insieme. **-tĕxt** † 3, contessere, intrecciare. **-tĕx-ture**, S.: tessitura, *f.*, tessuto, *m.*

con-tigūity, S.: contiguità, vicinanza, *f.* **-tiguous**, ADJ.: contiguo, vicino. **-tiguously**, ADV.: vicinamente, prossimamente. **-tiguousness**, S.: vicinità; prossimità, *f.*

cŏnti-nence, **-nency**, S.: continenza; castità, *f.* **-nent**, ADJ.: continente; casto; S.: continente, *m.*, terra ferma, *f.* **-nĕntal**, ADJ.: continentale. **-nently**, ADV.: continentemente.

contin-gençe, **-gency**, S.: contingenza, *f.*, accidente, *m.* **-gent**, ADJ.: contingente, casuale; S.: contingente, *m.*, parte, porzione, *f.* **-gently**, ADV.: casualmente.

contin-ual, ADJ.: continuo, perpetuo. **-ually**, ADV.: continuamente, di continuo, sempre. **-uance**, S.: continuanza; durazione, permanenza, *f.*: *in — of time*, in progresso di tempo, alla lunga. **-uate**, ADJ.: continuato. **-uātion**, S.: continuazione; serie; sequela, *f.* **-uative**, S.: durata, durazione continua, *f.* **-uator**, S.: continuatore, *m.* **-ue**, TR.: continuare, seguitare, proseguire; INTR.: perseverare, persistere, durare; dimorare. **-ued**, ADJ.: continuo. **-uedly**, ADV.: continuamente, senza interruzione. **-ūity**, S.: continuità; serie, *f.* **-uous**, ADJ.: continuo, unito insieme.

contôr-t, TR.: contorcere; attorcigliare. **-tion**, S.: contorsione, *f.*

contōur, S.: contorno; circonferenza, *f.*; delineamento, *m.*

cŏntra, PREP.: contro, contra. **-band** 1, ADJ.: di contrabbando; proibito, illegale. **-band** 2, TR.: fare il contrabbando. **-bandist**, S.: contrabbandiere, *m.*

contrăc-t 1, TR.: contrattare; contrarre; ritirare; INTR.: contrarsi, ristringersi. **cŏntrac-t** 2, S.: contratto, accordo, *m.*: *draw up —*, redigere un contratto; *enforce —*, fare eseguire un contratto; *enter into —*, addivenire ad un contratto. **-ted**, ADJ.: contratto, raggricchiato, negoziato; angusto, ristretto: *— for*, patteggiato, comprato. **-tedness**, S.: raggrinzamento, *m.* **-tibility**, S.: attezza a contrarsi, *f.* **-tible**, ADJ.: che può contrarsi. **-tile**, ADJ.: contrattile. **-tion**, S.: contrazione, *f.*; raccorciamento, *m.*; abbreviatura, *f.* **-tor**, S.: contrattante; contraente, *m.*

contradic-t, TR.: contraddire. **-ter**, S.: contraddittore, opponente, *m.* **-tion**, S.: contraddizione, opposizione, *f.*; ostacolo, *m.* **-tious**, ADJ.: contraddicente; inconsistente. **-tiousness**, S.: contraddizione; insussistenza, *f.* **-torily**, ADV.: contraddittoriamente. **-toriness**, S.: contraddizione, *f.* **-tory**, ADJ.: contraddittorio; S.: contraddicimento, *m.*

contradis-tinction, S.: proposizione opposta, *f.*: *in —*, in opposizione. **-tinguish**, TR.: contraddistinguere; contrassegnare.

contranitency, S.: contrannitenza, resistenza, *f.*

contraposition, S.: opposizione, *f.*

con-trăriant, ADJ.: contrariante, contrario. **-trariety**, S.: contrarietà; opposizione, *f.* **cŏn-trarily**, ADV.: contrariamente. **-trărious**, ADJ.: contrario, opposto. **-trăriously**, ADV.: contrariamente. **cŏn-trariwise**, ADV.: in modo contrario, al contrario. **cŏn-trary** 1, ADJ.: contrario, opposto; S.: contrario, *m.*, contrarietà, *f.*: *on the —*, al contrario. **-trary** 2, TR.: contrariare, contraddire, opporsi.

cŏn-trast 1, S.: contrasto, *m.*; opposizione, *f.* **-trâst** 2, TR.: fare un contrasto; porre all' incontro.

contravallātion, S.: (*fort.*) fosso con parapetto, *m.*

contra-vēne, TR.: contravvenire, disubbidire. **-vēner**, S.: contravventore, disubbidiente, *m.* **-vĕntion**, S.: contravvenzione, *f.*

contrib-utary, ADJ.: tributario, contribuente. **-ute**, TR.: contribuire. **-ūtion**, S.: contribuzione, *f.*: *lay under —*, mettere a contribuzione; *levy a —*, imporre una contribuzione. **-utive**, ADJ.: che può contribuire. **-utor**, S.: contribuente, *m.* **-utory**, ADJ.: contribuente.

contris-tate†, TR.: contristare, affligere. **-tātion**†, S.: afflizione, *f.*, cordoglio, *m.*

cŏn-trite, ADJ.: contrito, compunto. **-tritely**, ADV.: con contrizione. **-triteness**, **-trition**, S.: contrizione, *f.*; pentimento, *m.*

contri-vable, ADJ.: che può inventarsi. **-vance**, S.: invenzione, *f.*; progetto, *m.*; pratiche segrete, *f. pl.* **-ve**, TR.: inventare, trovare; concertare; tramare, macchinare, s'ingegnere. **-vement**, S.: invenzione, arte, *f.* **-ver**, S.: inventore; artefice, autore; macchinatore, *m.*

contrōl 1, S.: registro; ristringimento, *m.*; autorità, *f.* **control** 2, TR.: controllare; raffrenare; ristringere; governare; verificare. **-ler**, S.: registratore, controllore, *m.* **-lership**, S.: uffizio del controllore, *m.* **-ment**, S.: soprintendenza; opposizione; refutazione, *f.*

contro-vĕrsal†, **-vĕrsary**†, ADJ.: di controversia.

cŏntro-verse 1, S.: controversia, disputa, *f.* **-verse** 2, TR.: disputare. **-vĕrser**, S.: controversista, m. **-vĕrsial**, ADJ.: di controversia. **-versy**, S.: c troversia: contesa, disputa, *f.* **-vert**, TR.: controvertere, contendere, disputare. **-vĕrtible**, ADJ.: controvertibile, disputabile. **-vertist**, S.: controversista, *m.*

contumācious, ADJ.: contumace, ostinato, caparbio. **-ly**, ADV.: contumacemente, ostinatamente. **-ness**, S.: ostinazione, caparbietà, *f.*

cŏntumacy, S.: contumacia; ostinazione, *f.*

contumē-lious, ADJ.: contumelioso, ingiurioso. **-liously**, ADV.: contumeliosamente, ingiuriosamente. **-liousness**,

cŏntumely, S.: contumelia, ingiuria, *f.*

contū-se, TR.: ammacare. **-sion**, S.: contusione, *f.*, ammaccamento, *m.*

conŭndrum, S.: facezia plebea, *f.*, bisticcio, *m.*

convalĕscen-ce, **-cy**, S.: convalescenza, *f.*; ADJ.: convalescente.

convē-nable, ADJ.: convenevole, conveniente. **-ne**, TR.: convocare; adunare; INTR.: adunarsi, ragunarsi. **-ner**, S.: convocatore, *m.*

convēnien-ce, **-cy**, S.: convenienza, comodità; proporzione, *f.*: *at your* —, a vostro comodo, a vostro bell' agio. **-t**, ADJ.: conveniente, convenevole, comodo, atto; ragionevole. **-tly**, convenientemente, comodamente.

cŏnvent 1, S.: convento; monastero, *m.*

convĕnt 2, TR.: citare in giudizio, chiamare alla ragione.

convĕnticl-e, S.: conventicolo, conciliabolo, *m.* **-er**, S.: membro d' un conventicolo, *m.*

convĕntion, S.: convenzione, *f.*; patto, accordo, *m.* **-al**, ADJ.: convenzionale. **-ally**, ADV.: convenzionalmente, per patto. **-ary**, ADJ.: convenzionale, stipulato per patto. **-er**, S.: membro d' un assemblea, *m.*

convĕntual, ADJ.: conventuale; S.: conventuale, religioso, *m.*

convĕr-ge, INTR.: tendere al medesimo punto. **-gence**, S.: convergenza, *f.* **-gent**, ADJ.: convergente.

convĕr-sable, ADJ.: conversabile, sociabile. **-sableness**, S.: sociabilità, *f.* **-sably**, ADV.: in modo conversabile. **-sant**, ADJ.: conversante; versato, pratico, esperto. **-sātion**, S.: conversazione; familiarità, *f.*; commercio: *private* —, testa a testa, *f.* **-sative**, ADJ.: sociabile; affabile; pratico. **cŏnver-se** 1, S.: società; familiarità, *f.*; commercio, *m.*; pratica, *f.* **-se**, INTR.: conversare, praticare; bazzicare.

convĕrsely, ADV.: reciprocamente, a vicenda.

convĕr-sion, S.: conversione, *f.*; rivolgimento, *m.* **-sive**, ADJ.: sociabile.

cŏn-vert 1, S.: convertito, *m.*: *make a* — *of*, convertire. **-vĕrt** 2, TR.: convertire, trasmutare; INTR.: convertirsi; — *sinners*, convertire i peccatori. **-vĕrter**, S.: convertitore, *m.* **-vĕrted**, ADJ.: convertito, cambiato, tramutato. **-vĕrtible**, ADJ.: convertibile. **-vĕrtibly**, ADV.: reciprocamente.

cŏn-vex, **-vĕxed**, ADJ.: convesso. **-vĕxedly**, ADV.: in forma convessa. **-vĕxity**, **-vĕxness**, S.: convessità, *f.* **-vĕxo-concave**, ADJ.: convesso-concavo.

convēy, TR.: trasferire, trasportare, trasmettere; condurre; comunicare; mandare: — *away*, portare via; — *in*, introdurre; — *off*, portar via; — *by water* (*by steam*), mandare per acqua (col vapore); — *intelligence*, comunicare notizie. **-ance**, S.: trasporto; mezzo di trasporto, veicolo, *m.*, vettura; occasione, *f.*: — *by water*, trasporto per mare, *m.*; *by private* —, per occasione. **-ancer**, S.: notaio, notaro, *m.* **-er**, S.: vetturino, *m.*

cŏn-vict 1, S.: bandito; fuoruscito, *m.* **-vict**† 2, ADJ.: convinto, criminale. **-vict** 3, TR.: convincere, provare reo. **-victed**, ADJ.: convinto. **-viction**, S.: convinzione; refutazione; condannazione, *f.* **-victive**, ADJ.: convincente. **-victiveness**, S.: evidenza, prova, dimostrazione, *f.*

convin-ce, TR.: convincere; provare. **-ced**, ADJ.: convinto, persuaso. **-cement**, S.: convincimento, *m.*, persuasione, *f.* **-cible**, ADJ.: atto a convincere, convincente. **-cingly**, ADV.: in modo convincente, evidentemente. **-cingness**, S.: convinzione; prova, evidenza, *f.*

con-vival† = *-vivial.* **-vive**†, TR.: convitare; festeggiare. **-vivial**, ADJ.: festivo; sociabile.

cŏn-vocate, TR.: convocare; adunare, ragunare. **-vocātion**, S.: convocazione; assemblea, *f.* **-vōke**, TR.: convocare; adunare.

con-volūtion, S.: avvolgimento; viluppo, *m.* **-vŏlve**, TR.: avvolgere.

cŏn-voy 1, S.: convoglio, *m.*, scorta, accompagnatura, *f.* **-vŏy** 2, TR.: convogliare, accompagnare. **-vŏy-ship**, S.: bastimento di scorta.

convŭl-se, TR.: cagionare convulsioni, rendere convulso, agitare con violenza, scuotere; *be* —*d*, spasimare. **-sion**, S.: convulsione; commozione; turbolenza, *f.*: *slight* —, convulsioncella, *f.*; *be taken with* —*s*, esser preso da convulsioni. **-sive**, ADJ.: convulsivo. **-sively**, ADV.: in modo convulsivo.

cōny, S.: coniglio, *m.* **-burrow**, S.: conigliera, *f.* **-catch**, TR.: ingannare

con furberia. **-catcher**, S.: furbo, furfante, *m.* **-warren**, S.: conigliera, *f.*
cōo, INTR.: susurrare; gemere. **-ing**, S.: mormorio de' colombi, *m.*
cóok 1, S.: cuoco, cuciniere, *m.*; cuoca, *f.* **cook** 2, TR.: fare la cucina, cucinare. **-ery**, S.: arte del cuoco, cucina, *f.* **-maid**, S.: cuoca, cuciniera, *f.* **-room**, S.: (*nav.*) cucina, *f.* **-shop**, S.: bettola, trattoria, *f.*
cōol 1, ADJ.: fresco, freddo; S.: fresco, freddo, *m.*: *it is* —, fa fresco; *it is getting* —, comincia a far fresco. **-cool** 2, TR.: rinfrescare, raffreddare: moderare, sminuire; INTR.: rinfrescarsi, raffreddarsi. **-er**, S.: refrigerativo, refrigerante, *m.* **-ing**, ADJ.: refrigerativo; S.: rinfrescamento, *m.* **-ish**, ADJ.: freschetto. **-ly**, ADJ.: freddamente; indifferentemente. **-ness**, S.: freschezza, freddura, *f.*, freddo, *m.*
cōop 1, S.: stia, *f.*; barile, *m.* **coop** 2, INTR.: rinchiudere; ingabbiare: —*ed up*, in gabbia, in prigione. **-er**, S.: bottaio, *m.* **-erage**, S.: lavoro del bottaio, *m.*, mestiere del bottaio, *m.*
co-öperate, TR.: cooperare, concorrere. **-operātion**, S.: cooperazione; concorrenza, *f.* **-öperative**, ADJ.: cooperativo, cooperante. **-öperater**, S.: cooperatore, *m.*
cóopery †, S.: arte di bottaio, *m.*
cooptātion, S.: assunzione, *f.*
coördi-nate 1, ADJ.: coordinato. **-nate** 2, TR.: coordinare. **-nately**, ADV.: nel medesimo ordine. **-nateness**, **-nātion**, S.: coordinazione; ugualità, *f.*
cōot, S. smergo, *m.*
cŏp, S.: cima, sommità, *f.*; capo, *m.*
copáiba, S.: copaiba, *f.*
cōpal, S.: coppale, *f.*
copár-cener, S.: coerede; compagno, *m.* **-ceny**, S.: porzione uguale dell'eredità, *f.*
copártment †, S.: compartimento, *m.*
copártner, S.: socio, compagno, *m.* **-ship**, S.: società, compagnia, *f.*
cōpe 1, S.: pianeta di prete, *f.* **cope** 2, TR.: barattare; INTR.: — *with*, contendere; far testa a, rivaleggiare.
cōpesmate †, S.: compagno; commensale, *m.*
cōpier, S.: copista, copiatore, *m.*
cōping, S.: comignolo; colmo, *m.*, cima, *f.*
cōpious, ADJ.: copioso, abbondevole. **-ly**, ADV.: copiosamente; abbondantemente, largamente. **-ness**, S.: abbondanza, ricchezza, dovizia, *f.*
cōpist, S.: copista, copiatore, scriba, *m.*
cōpland †, S.: pezzo di terreno con un angolo, *m.*
cōpped, ADJ.: crestuto, puntuto.
cŏppel, S.: copella, *f.*
cŏpper 1, S.: rame (*metal*); calderone (*kettle*, ecc.), *m.* **copper** 2, TR.: foderare di rame. **-as**, S.: vitriuolo, *m.* **-coloured**, ADJ.: colore di rame, bronzato. **-money**, S.: moneta di rame, *f.* **-nose**, S.: naso rosso, *m.* **-plate**, S.: stampa di rame, lastra di rame, *f.* **-smith**, S.: calderaio, *m.* **-wire**, S.: filo di rame, *m.* **-work**, S.: manifattura di rame, fucina del rame, *f.* **-y**, ADJ.: che contiene del rame.
cŏppice, S.: macchia, macchietta, *f.*; bosco ceduo, *m.*
cŏppled, ADJ.: conico.
cŏpse 1, S.: macchia, macchietta, *f.* **copse** 2, TR.: conservare i boschi tagliati bassi.
Cŏptic, ADJ., S.: copto.
cŏp-ula, S.: copula, *f.* **-ulate**, TR.: copulare; unire; INTR.: accoppiarsi; congiungersi. **-ulātion**, S.: congiungimento, *m.* **-ulative**, ADJ.: (*gram.*) copulativo.
cŏpy 1, S.: copia, *f.*; manoscritto; esemplare, originale, *m.* **copy** 2, TR.: copiare; trascrivere; imitare: — *out*, fare una copia di, trascrivere. **-book**, S.: quaderno, quinterno, *m.* **-er** = *copyist*. **-hold**, S.: podere d'un feudo, *m.* **-holder**, S.: censuario, *m.* **-ing-machine**, S.: copialettere; pantografo, *m.* **-ist**, S.: copista, *m.* **-right**, S.: diritto di proprietà letteraria; manoscritto, *m.*
coquĕt, TR.: trattare con finta tenerezza; INTR.: civettare. **-ry**, S.: civetteria, *f.* **-te**, S.: civetta, *f.* **-tish**, ADJ.: da civetta.
córacle, S.: barchetta da pescatori, *f.*
cŏral, S.: corallo, *m.* **-diver**, **-fisher**, S.: pescatore di coralli, *m.* **-fishery**, S.: spesca de' coralli, *f.* **-line**, ADJ.: corallino, di corallo; S.: coralina, *f.* **-reef**, S.: banco di corallo, *m.* **-tree**, S.: albero del corallo, *m.*
co-rănt, **-rāto**, S.: (*danc.*) corrante, *f.*
córban, S.: cassetta della limosina, *f.*
córbel, S.: canestro, *m.*; nicchia, *f.*
córd 1, S.: corda; tendine, *f.*: — *of wood*, S.: catasta, misura di legna, *f.* **cord** 2, TR.: legare con corde. **-age**, S.: cordame; sartiame, *m.* **-ed**, ADJ.: legato con corde; infunato. **-elier**, S.: Francescano, *m.*
córdi-al 1 *-jal*, S.: cordiale, *m.* (brodo da bere). **-al** 2, ADJ.: cordiale; affettuoso. **-ălity**, S.: cordialità, *f.*; affetto cordiale, *m.*, svisceratezza, *f.* **-ally**, ADV.: cordialmente.
córd-maker, S.: funaiuolo, funaio, *m.* **-on**, S.: cordone; ordine, *m.*
córdovan, S.: cordovano, *m.*

côre, S.: torso; interiore; marciume, *m.*
coregent, S.: coreggente, *m.*
coriàceous, ADJ.: di cuojo; duro.
coriànder, S.: coriandro, *m.*
còrinth† = *currant*. **Corinthian**, ADJ.: di Corinto, corintio, dissoluto†.
còrk 1, S.: sughero, turacciolo, *m.* **cork** 2, TR.: turare. **-screw**, S.: cavaturacciuoli, *m.* **-tree**, S.: quercia del sughero. **-y**, ADJ.: di sughero.
còrmorant, S.: cormorante (uccello acquatico); ghiottone, *m.*
côrn 1, S.: frumento; grano, *m.*: (*Am.*, '*Indian* —') mais, granturco, frumentone: — *of salt*, granello di sale, *m.* **corn** 2, S.: callo, *m.* **corn** 3, TR.: insaleggiare, saleggiare; macinare in polverei: —*ed beef*, manzo salato. **-age**, S.: dazio sopra il grano, *m.* **-chandler**, S.: venditore di grano, *m.* **-cutter**, S.: tagliatore di calli, *m.* **-dealer**, S.: mercante di grano, *m.*
côr-nel, S.: corniola, *f.*; corniolo, cornio, *m.* **-nēlian**, S.: cornalina, *f.* **-nemuse**, S.: cornamusa, piva, *f.* **-neous**, ADJ.: corneo, calloso.
côrner, S.: angolo; canto, cantone, *m.*; cantonata; estremità, *f.* **-house**, S.: S.: casa della cantonata, *f.* **-stone**, S.: pietra angolare, *f.* **-wise**, ADV.: diagonalmente, ad angoli.
côrnet, S.: cornetta, *m.*, *f.*; corno, *m.* **-cy**, S.: grado di cornetta, *m.* **-ter**, S.: suonatore della cornetta, *m.*
côrn-factor, S.: mercante di grano, *m.* **-field**, S.: seminato, *m.* **-floor**, S.: granaio, *m.*, aia, *f.* **-flower**, S.: fioraliso, *m.*, battisegola, *f.*
côrnice, S.: (*arch.*) cornice, *f.*
côr-nicle, S.: picciol corno, cornetto, *m.* **-nigerous**, ADJ.: cornuto.
côrn-land, S.: terreno frumentario, *m.* **-loft**, S.: granaio, *m.* **-merchant**, S.: mercante di grano, *m.* **-mill**, S.: mulino da macinare le biade, *m.* **-rose**, S.: nigella, *f.* **-salad**, S.: valeriana domestica, *f.* **-trade**, S.: traffico di biade, *m.*
cornucôpia, S.: cornucopia; (*fig.*) abbondanza, *f.*
cornûte, ADJ.: cornuto.
côrny, ADJ.: corneo; producente grano.
còrollary, S.: corollario, *m.*
còro-nal, ADJ.: (*anat.*) coronale; S.: corona di fiori, ghirlando, *f.* **-nary**, ADJ.: coronario. **-nātion**, S.: coronamento, *m.* **-ner**, S.: ufficiale che esamina un corpo morto, *m.* **-net**, S.: coronetta.
côr-poral, ADJ.: corporale, materiale; S.: caporale; corporale, *m.* **-porālity**, S.: sustanza corporea, *f.* **-porally**, ADV.: corporalmente. **-porate**, ADJ.: unito in un corpo: — *body*, comunità.

corradiātion, S.: punto de' raggi, *m.*
corrèc-t 1, ADJ.: corretto, esatto. **-t** 2, TR.: correggere; punire, castigare; temperare, moderare. **-tion**, S.: correzione; emendazione, *f.*; castigo, *m.*; riprensione, *f.*: *under* —, con rispetto; *house of* —, casa di correzione. **-tive**, ADJ.: correttivo; S.: correttivo, *m.*; restrizione, *f.* **-tly**, ADV.: correttamente, esattamente. **-tness**, S.: accuratezza, esattezza, *f.* **-tor**, S.: correttore; revisore, *m.*: — *of the press*, correttore di stampa, *m.*
cor-relāte, INTR.: avere correlazione. **-rèlative**, ADJ.: correlativo, reciproco. **-rèlativeness**, S.: relazione reciproca, *f.*
corrèption†, S.: riprensione, *f.*, rimprovero, *m.*
correspòn-d, INTR.: corrispondere, aver proporzione, confarsi; far commercio. **-dence**, **-dency**, S.: corrispondenza; intelligenza, *f.*: *keep up a — with*, avere corrispondenza con, carteggiare con. **-dent**, ADJ.: corrispondente; conforme, proporzionato; S.: corrispondente, *m.* **-sive**, ADJ.: congruente.
còrridor, S.: corridoio, *m.*, galleria, *f.*
còrrigible, ADJ.: corrigibile.
corròbo-rant, ADJ.: corroborante, corroborativo. **-rate**, TR.: corroborare, confermare, fortificare. **-rātion**, S.: corroborazione, *f.* **-rative**, ADJ.: corroborativo.
corrô-de, TR.: corrodere; consumare a poco a poco. **-ding**, ADJ.: che corrode: — *cares*, cure edaci. **-dent**, ADJ.: corrodente. **-dible**, ADJ.: che può corrodersi. **-sion**, S.: corrosione, *f.*, corrodimento, *m.* **-sive**, S.: (*med.*) corrosivo, *m.* **-sively**, ADV.: in modo corrosivo. **-siveness**, S.: qualità corrosiva, *f.*
còrru-gate, TR.: increspare, aggrinzare; INTR.: incresparsi, corrugarsi. **-gātion**, S.: increspamento, *m.*
corrùp-t 1, ADJ.: corrotto, guasto, depravato; cattivo. **-t** 2, TR.: corrompere, guastare, depravare; INTR.: corrompersi; guastarsi. **-ter**, S.: corrompitore, corruttore, *m.* **-tibility**, S.: corruttibilità, *f.* **-tible**, ADJ.: corruttibile. **-tible-**

ness, S.: attezza ad essere corrotto, corruttibilità; corruzione, *f.* **-tibly**, ADV.: in maniera corruttibile. **-tion**, S.: corruzione; depravazione, *f.* **-tive**, ADJ.: corruttivo. **-tless**, ADJ.: incorruttibile. **-tly**, ADV.: corrottamente. **-tness**, S.: corruzione, corruttela; putrescenza, *f.* **-tress**, S.: corrompitrice, *f.*

côrsair, S.: corsale, corsaro, ladrone di mare, *m.*

côr-set, S.: corsè, corsetto; busto (da donna). **-slet**, S.: corsaletto, *m.*

côr-tex, S.: corteccia, *f.* **-tical**, ADJ.: di corteccia, di scorza.

corŭscant, ADJ.: brillante, resplendente. **-cātion**, S.: balenamento, lampeggiamento, *m.*

côrvet, S.: sorta di naviglio, *f.*

corўmbus, S.: (*bot.*) corimbo, *m.*

cosĕcant, S.: (*geom.*) cosecante, *m.*

cōsine, S.: (*geom.*) cosseno, *m.*

cosmĕtic, ADJ.: cosmetico; S.: cosmetico; abbellimento, *m.*

cŏsmical, ADJ.: cosmico. **-ly**, ADV.: (*astr.*) cosmicamente, col sole.

cosmŏ-gony, S.: cosmogonia, *f.* **-grapher**, S.: cosmografo, *m.* **-grăphic-(al) -c-**, ADJ.: cosmografico. **-graphy**, S.: cosmografia, *f.* **-pŏlitan -c-**, S.: cosmopolita, abitante del mondo, *m.*

cŏsset, S.: agnello allevato senza la madre, *m.*

cŏst 1, S.: spesa, *f.*; costo; prezzo, valore, *m.*: *net* —, costo di fabbrica prima; *free of* —, gratis; *to my* —, alle mie spese. **cost** 2, IRR.; (IN)TR.: costare: — *what it will*, costi ciò che vuole.

cŏs-tal, ADJ.: costale. **-tard**, S.: testa; mela tonda e grossa, *f.*

cŏstive, ADJ.: costipativo. **-ness**, S.: costipamento, riserramento, *m.*

cŏst-liness, S.: suntuosità; spesa grande, *f.* **-ly**, ADJ.: caro, suntuoso, dispendioso; splendido.

cŏstume, S.: costume, *m.*

cŏt 1, S.: capanna, *f.*: *sheep* —, ovile, *m.* **cot** 2, INTR.: impacciarsi.

cotăngent, S.: (*geom.*) cotangente, *m.*

cotĕmporary, ADJ.: contemporaneo, coetaneo.

coterie, S.: società, brigata, *f.*

cŏttage, S.: capanna, *f.*, tugurio, *m.*; villa, *f.* **-er**, S.: che abita in una capanna.

cŏtton 1, S.: cotone, *m.*, bambagia, *f.*: *gun* — (Amer.), *explosive* — (Eng.), fulmicotone, *m.* **cotton** 2, INTR.: accotonarsi, adattarsi; convenire. **-factory**, S.: filatoio di cotone, *m.*, filanda, *f.* **-mill**, S.: cotonificio, *m.* **-thread**, **-yarn**, S.: filo di cotone, *m.* **-tree**, S.: albero che produce il cotone, *m.*

cŏuch 1, S.: lettuccio, lettucciuolo, *m.* **couch** 2, TR.: coricare; stendere; INTR.: coricarsi; distendersi: — *in writing*, mettere in iscritto; — *the lance*, mettere la lancia in resta. **-ant**, ADJ.: giacente. **-ĕe**, S.: giacimento, *m.* **-er**, S.: oculista che leva la cattaratta; registratore, *m.* **-fellow**, S.: compagno di letto, *m.* **-grass**, S.: gramigna, *f.*

cough 1 *kăf*, S.: tossa, tosse, *f.*: *have a* —, aver la tosse; *whooping* —, mal di castrone, *m.* **cough** 2, INTR.: tossire: — *out* (*up*), espettorare, espurgare. **-er**, S.: che ha la tosse. **-ing**, S.: tossire, tossimento, *m.*

cŏulter, S.: coltro, vomero, *m.*

cŏuncil, S.: concilio, consiglio; avvocato, *m.*: *privy* —, consiglio di Stato, *m.*; *common* —, consiglio della città, *m.*; — *of war*, consiglio di guerra, *m.* **-board**, S.: tavola del consiglio, *f.* **-chamber**, S.: camera del consiglio, *f.* **-lor**, S.: consigliere; membro del consiglio, *m.*

counite †, TR.: unire.

cŏunsel 1, S.: consiglio; avviso; avvocato, *m.*: *ask* — *of one*, dimandar il consiglio d' alcuno; *give one* —, consigliare uno; *keep* —, esser segreto. **counsel** 2, TR.: consigliare, dare consiglio: — *against*, sconsigliare, dissuadere. **-able**, ADJ.: che può esser consigliato. **-lor**, S.: consigliere; avvocato, *m.*: *privy* —, consigliere di Stato, *m.*; — *at law*, avvocato, *m.* **-lorship**, S.: dignità (ufficio) di consigliere, *f.*

cŏunt 1, S.: numero; conto, computo. **count** 2, S.: conte, *m.* **count** 3, TR.: contare, computare, calcolare; stimare: — *upon*, fondarsi. **-able**, ADJ.: che si può contare. **-book**, S.: libro di conti, *m.*

cŏuntenance 1, S.: aria, *f.*; viso, volto; aspetto; favore, *m.*, protezione, *f.*; aiuto, *m.*: *pleasing* —, viso piacevole; *put one out of* —, far arrossire (*or* sconcertare, confondere), alcuno; *give* — *to*, far buon viso a, favoreggiare, appoggiare; *be in* —, esser favorito; *give* —, favorire. **-e** 2, TR.: favorire, favoreggiare; proteggere, caldeggiare. **-er**, S.: fautore, protettore, *m.*

cŏunter 1, ADV.: contro; a rimpetto: *run* —, opporsi, contrariare. **counter** 2, S.: banco; gettone, *m.* **-ăct**, TR.: attraversare, contrariare. **-ăction**, S.: opposizione, *f.* **-bălance** 1, S.: contrappeso, *m.* **-balance** 2, TR.: contrappesare; adequare, aggiustare. **-bass**, S.: contrabasso, *m.* **-băttery**, S.: contrabbatteria, *f.* **-bŭff** 1, S.: ripercotimento, ripicchio, *m.* **-buff** 2, TR.: rispingere ripercuotere. **-chănge** 1, S.: contracambio, *m.* **-change** 2, TR.: contracc biare. **-chărm** 1, S.: contramalia, *f.* **-charm** 2, TR.: impedire l' incanto. **-chĕck** 1, S.: opposizione, resistenza; censura reciproca, *f.* **-check** 2, TR.: opporre. **-cunning**, S.: astuzia contro la parte avversa, *f.* **-distinction**, S.: contradistinzione; opposizione, *f.* **-drâw**, IRR.; TR.: retare (un disegno). **-evidence**, S.: testimonio contrario, *m.* **-feit** 1, ADJ.: contraffatto, imitato, falso; supposto; S.: falsificazione, *f.*; impostore, ingannatore, *m.* **-feit** 2, TR.: contraffare; imitare; falsificare; falsare: — *a will*, falsare un testamento; — *the coin*, fare moneta falsa. **-feiter**, S.: contraffacitore, falsario, *m.*: — *of coin*, monetario falso, *m.* **-feiting**, S.: contraffacimento, *m.*; imitazione, *f.* **-feitly**, ADV.: fintamente, falsamente. **-foil**, S.: contrataglia, *f.* **-forts**, S. PL.: (*fort.*) contrafforti, *m. pl.* **-guard**, S.: contragguardia, *f.* **-lath** 1, S.: panconcello, *m.* **-lath** 2, TR.: impalcare i panconcelli. **-light**, S.: contrallume, *m.* **-mând** 1, S.: contrammandato, *m.* **-mand** 2, TR.: contrammanare. **-mârch** 1, S.: contrammarcia, *f.* **-march** 2, INTR.: far contrammarcia. **-mârk** 1, S.: contrammarca, *f.*, contrassegno, *m.* **-mark** 2, TR.: mettere una seconda marca, contrassegnare. **-mine** 1, S.: contrammina, *f.* **-mine** 2, TR.: contramminare. **-motion**, S.: moto contrario, *m.* **-mure**, S.: muro di rinforzo, antimuro, *m.* **-natural**, ADJ.: contrannaturale. **-ôrder**, S.: contr' ordine, *m.* **-pace**, S.: misura contraria, *f.* **-pâne**, S.: coltre; coperta da letto, *f.* **-part**, S.: copia; (*mus.*) parte opposta, *f.* **-plĕa**, S.: replica, *f.* **-plŏt** 1, S.: artifizio opposto ad artifizio, *m.* **-plot** 2, TR.: opporre artifizio ad artifizio. **-pŏint**, S.: contrappunto, *m.* **-pŏise** 1, S.: contrappeso, *m.* **-poise** 2, TR.: contrappesare. **-poison**, S.: contravveleno, *m.* **-pressure**, S.: forza opposta, *f.* **-project**, S.: corrispondente progetto, *m.* **-proof**, S.: prova del contrario, *f.* **-revolution**, S.: rivoluzione opposta, *f.* **-scarp** 1, S.: (*fort.*) contrascarpa, *f.* **-scarp** 2, TR.: (*fort.*) fare una contrascarpa. **-sĕal**, TR.: contrasigillare. **-security**, S.: seconda mallevadoria, *f.* **-sign**, TR.: contrassegnare. **-signal**, S.: (*nav.*) contrassegnale, *m.* **-tenor**, S.: contralto, *m.* **-tide**, S.: marca di rovescio, *f.* **-time**, S.: contrattempo, *m.*; opposizione, *f.* **-turn**, S.: catastrofe, *f.* **-vail** 1, S.: equivalenza, equiponderanza, *f.* **-vâil†** 2, INTR.: valere altrettanto, equivalere. **-view**, S.: opposizione, *f.*; contrasto, *m.* **-wôrk**, IRR.; *TR.: contramminare.*

cŏuntess, S.: contessa, *f.*

cŏunt-ing-house, S.: banco (*de' mercanti*), *m.*; fattoria, *f.* **-less**, ADJ.: innumerabile.

coŭntry 1, S.: contrada, *f.*; paese, *m.*; campagna; provincia, *f.*; patria, *f.*: *my* (*own*) —, il mio paese natio, la mia patria; *a fertile* —, un paese fertile; *we go into the* —, andiamo in campagna (*or* in villa). **country** 2, ADJ.: rustico, campestre. **-ballad**, S.: canzonetta, frottola, *f.* **-dance**, S.: contraddanza, *f.* **-house**, S.: villa, casa di campagna, *f.* **-life**, S.: vita campestre, *f.* **-man**, S.: contadino, paesano; villano; compaesano, compatriota, *m.*: *fellow* —, compatriota. **-parson**, S.: curato di villaggio, *m.* **-put**, S.: ignorante, minchione, *m.* **-seat** = *country-house.* **-squire**, S.: gentiluomo di provincia, *m.* **-woman**, S.: contadina, *f.* **-word**, S.: parola volgare, *f.*

cŏunty, S.: contea; provincia, *f.*

coupée, S.: (*danz.*) fioretto, *m.*

coŭp-le 1, S.: coppia, *f.*; paio, *m.* **-le** 2, TR.: accoppiare; maritare; INTR.: accoppiarsi, copularsi, congiungersi. **-let**, S.: paio; (*pros.*) distico, *m.* **-ling**, S.: accoppiamento, congiungimento, *m.*

coŭrage, S.: coraggio; animo, *m.*; bravura, *f.*: *pick up* —, farsi animo; —! animo! coraggio! **-râgeous**, ADJ.: coraggioso, bravo. **-râgeously**, ADV.: coraggiosamente. **-râgeousness**, S.: coraggio; valore, *m.*

cŏurier, S.: corriere, messaggiere, *m.*

cŏur-se 1, S.: corso, *m.*; carriera, *f.*; ordine; viaggio; cammino; metodo, *m.*, maniera; usanza, *f.*, rito; servizio (di tavola), *m.*: —*s*, mestrui, mesi, *m. pl.*; *of* —, naturalmente, necessariamente; *thing of* —, cosa naturale; *words of* —, complimenti, *m. pl.*; *take your* —, fate quel che volete; *take a wise* —, pigliar buone misure; *follow the* — *of time*, navigare secondo il vento; *let things take their* —, lasciare andar l' acqua alla china. **-se** 2, TR.: cacciare, dare la caccia; INTR.: vagare. **-ser**, S.: corsiere; destriere, *m.*

cŏurt 1, S.: corte, *f.*; cortile; tribunale, *m.*; giudici, *m. pl.*: *go to* —, andare alla corte. **court** 2, TR.: corteggiare; brigare; sollecitare: — *a young lady*, corteggiare una damigella. **-baron**, S.: corte del padrone del fondo, *f.* **-card**, S.: carta figurata, *f.* **-chaplain**, S.: cappellano di corte, *m.* **-day**, S.: giorno curiale, *m.* **coŭrt-eous**, ADJ.: cortese, gentile; grazioso, benevole. **coŭrt-eously**, ADV.: cortesemente; gentilmente. **coŭrt-eousness**, S.: cortesia; gentilezza; benevolenza, *f.* **-esan**, S.: cortigiana, *f.*

cou̇rt-ęsy 1, s.: civiltà, pulitezza, *f.*; (*cŭrt'sy*) riverenza (di donna). **-esy** 2, INTR.: fare la riverenza. **-ier**, s.: cortigiano; uomo cortese, *m.* **-ing**, s.: corteggiare, *m.* **-lady**, s.: dama di corte, *f.* **-like**, ADJ.: cortigianesco, civile, elegante. **-liness**, s.: affabilità, compiacenza; eleganza, *f.* **-ly** 1, ADV.: cortigianamente, civilmente, elegantemente. **-ly** 2, ADJ.: civile; grazioso. **-martial**, s.: corte marziale, *f.*, consiglio di guerra, *m.* **-minion**, s.: mignone, favorito, *m.* **-plaster**, s.: taffeta inglese, *m.* **-promises**, s. PL.: belle parole senza fatti, *f. pl.* **-ship**, s.: civiltà, compiacenza, pulitezza; galanteria, *f.* **-visit**, s.: visita di corte; visita breve, *f.* **-yard**, s.: anticorte, *f.*

cóuṣin, s.: cugino, *m.*, cugina, *f.*

cōve, s.: cala piccola, *f.*; rifugio, *m.*

cóvęnant 1, s.: patto, contratto, *m.* **covenant** 2, INTR.: pattuire, trattare: — *of grace*, alleanza di grazia. **-ēe**, s.: contrattante, contraente, *m.* **-ęr**, s.: confederato, *m.*

cóvęr 1, s.: coperchio; rifugio; pretesto, *m.*, scusa, *f.*: *table* —, tappeto da tavola, *m.* **cover** 2, TR.: coprire; celare, palliare: — *up*, coprire affatto; *be —d!* copritevi! **-ing**, s.: coprimento; vestimento, *m.* **-let**, s.: copertura, coperta, *f.* **-t**, ADJ.: coperto, nascosto, segreto; s.: luogo coperto, nascondiglio; rifugio, *m.* **-tly**, ADV.: copertamente, segretamente, di nascosto. **-tness**, s.: segretezza; ritiratezza, *f.* **-ture**, s.: copertura; protezione; condizione di donna maritata, *f.* **-t-way**, s.: (*fort.*) strada coperta, *f.*

cóvet, TR.: bramare, desiderare. **-able**, ADJ.: desiderabile, appetibile. **-ed**, ADJ.: bramato, desiderato; ambito. **-ous**, ADJ.: avido, avaro; sordido. **-ously**, ADV.: avaramente; sordidamente. **-ousness**, s.: avarizia; cupidità, *f.*

cóvey, s.: covata; nidiata, *f.*

cŏw 1, s.: vacca, *f.*: *little* —, vacchetta, *f.*; *milch* —, vacca da latte, *f.* **cow** 2, TR.: intimorire, spaventare.

cŏwąrd, s.: codardo; poltrone, vigliacco, *m.* **-ice**, s.: codardia, vigliaccheria, *f.* **-liness**, s.: timidezza, pusillanimità, codardia, *f.* **-ly**, ADJ.: codardo, vigliacco, pusillanimo; ADV.: poltronescamente, vigliaccamente; vilmente. **-ship** † = *cowardliness*.

cŏwęr, INTR.: appiattarsi; chinarsi.

cŏw-hęrd, s.: vaccaro, *m.* **-house**, s.: stalla da vacche, *f.* **-keeper**, s.: vaccaro, *m.*

cŏwl, s.: cappuccio, *m.*: *take the* —, farsi frate.

cŏw-leech, s.: medico alle vacche, manescalco, *m.* **-pox**, s.: vaccina, *f.*

cǫwŏrkęr, s.: cooperatore, collaboratore, *m.*

cŏwslip, s.: tassobarbasso, *m.*, primavera, *f.*

cŏx-cǫmb, s.: cresta d'un gallo, *f.*; sciocco, farfallino, *m.* **-cŏm(b)ical**, ADJ.: da sciocco, affettato. **-cǫmbry**, s.: fatuità, sciocchezza, babbuassaggine, *f.*

cŏy 1, ADJ.: schifo; modesto, riserbato. **coy** 2, INTR.: comportarsi con riserva; farsi pregare. **-ish**, ADJ.: contegnoso; timido. **-ly**, ADV.: contegnosamente. **-ness**, s.: contegno, *m.*; ritrosia, modestia affettata, *f.*

cózen, TR.: ingannare, truffare. **-age**, s.: truffa, *f.*, inganno, *m.* **-ęr**, s.: ingannatore, giuntatore, *m.*

cráb, s.: granchio; cancro, *m.*; mela salvatica, *f.* **-bed**, ADJ.: aspro; arcigno. **-bedly**, ADV.: aspramente; arcignamente. **-bedness**, s.: asprezza; arcignezza, *f.*; viso arcigno, *m.*; difficoltà, *f.* **-by**, ADJ.: ruvido; difficile. **-fish**, s.: granchio, *m.* **-tree**, s.: melo salvatico, *m.*

cräck 1, s.: crepatura, fessura; scoppiata, *f.*, fracasso; millantatore, *m.* **crack** 2, TR.: crepare, fendere; schiacciare; rompere; INTR.: fendersi, scoppiare; vantarsi, millantarsi: — *out*, intimorire; — *nuts*, rompere le nocciuole; — *a joke*, fare uno scherzo; — *the fingers*, farsi scricchiolare le dita. **-brained**, ADJ.: scervellato. **-ęr**, s.: salterello; millantatore; biscottino, *m.* **-le**, INTR.: scoppiettare, scricchiolare. **-ling**, s.: scoppiettata, *f.* **-nel**, s.: ciambella, *f.*

crädle 1, s.: culla, cuna; infanzia, *f.*; letto per varare un vascello, *m.* **cradle** 2, TR.: cullare.

cräft, s.: mestiere, *m.*, professione; astuzia, *f.*, artificio, *m.*; barca, *f.*, battello, *m.*, chiatta, *f.* **-ily**, ADV.: astutamente, con astuzia. **-iness**, s.: astuzia; stratagemma, *f.* **-sman**, s.: artigiano, artefice, *m.* **-smaster**, s.: artefice esperto, *m.* **-y**, ADJ.: astuto, scaltro, volpino.

cräg, s.: rupe, balza (*rock*); collottola (*neck piece*), *f.* **-ged**, ADJ.: aspro, erto, scosceso, pieno di balze. **-gedness**, **-giness**, s.: asprezza; ertezza, *f.* **-gy** = *cragged*.

crăm, TR.: impinzare; ficcare; stivare; INTR.: impinzarsi (di carne, ecc.): — *turkeys*, ingrassare i polli d' India; — *in*, ficcar dentro con isforzo.

crămbę, s.: giuoco di rima, *m.*

crămp 1, ADJ.: difficile; intrigato; s.: granchio; ritiramento di muscoli; ostacolo, *m.* **cramp** 2, uncinare; costrignere. **-ed**, ADJ.: affettato, intirizzato

-fish, s.: torpedine, *f.* -iron, s.: rampicone; graffio, *m.*

crampōon, s.: rampicone; fermaglio, *m.*

cránberry, s.: mora di prunaio, *f.*

cráne 1, s.: grù, grue, *f.*; argano; sifone, *m.* **crane** 2 (*up*), TR.: tirare su per mezzo d' un argano. -'s-bill, s.: geranio, *m.*; pinzette, *f. pl.*

crani-ŏlogy, s.: craniologia, *f.* -um, s.: cranio, *m.*

cránk 1, s.: manovella, lieva; sinuosità, *f.*; ghiribizzo; uomo ghiribizzoso (eccentrico, scervellato), visionario, pazzo, *m.* **crank** 2, ADJ.: gagliardo; (*nav.*) tentennante.

cránkle, INTR.: serpeggiare. -s, s. PL.: serpeggiamenti, *m. pl.*

cránkness, s.: sanità, *f.*; vigore, *m.*

cránky, ADJ.: visionario, pazzo.

crán-nied, ADJ.: crepato, crepolato. -ny, s.: crepatura, fessura, *f.*

crápe, s.: velo, *m.*

crásh 1, s.: fracasso, strepito, *m.* **crash** 2, TR.: fracassare; rompere; INTR.: strepitare. -ing, s.: conquassamento, *m.*

crásis, s.: temperamento, *m.*; (*pros.*) crasi, *f.*

cráss, ADJ.: crasso; grosso, grande. -itude, s.: crassezza; grossezza, *f.*

crastinátion†, s.: dilazione, *f.*, ritardo, *m.*

crátch†, s.: rastrelliera, greppia, mangiatoia, *f.*

cráter, s.: cratere, *m.*

cráunch, TR.: schiacciare in bocca, agretolare.

cravát, s.: cravatta, *f.*

cráve, TR.: pregare, implorare.

cráven 1, s.: gallo scorato; codardo, *m.* **craven** 2, TR.: intimidire; scoraggiare.

crá-ver, s.: domandatore, *m.* -ving, ADJ.: insaziabile; avido. -vingness, s.: insaziabilità, *f.*

cráw, s.: gozzo, *m.*

cráwfish, s.: granchio, gambero, *m.*

crawl 1, s.: vivaio, *m.* **crawl** 2, INTR.: strascinare, rampicare; umiliarsi: *make one's flesh* —, fare accaponar la vita. -er, s.: rettile, *m.*

cráyon 1, s.: pastello, *m.* **crayon** 2, TR.: disegnare col pastello.

cráz-e, TR.: fracassare, rompere; dimentare. -ed, ADJ.: rotto, scemo, forsennato: — *with grief*, pazzo dal dolore. -edness, s.: decrepità, vecchiezza estrema, *f.* -iness, s.: infermità, imbecillità, *f.* -y, ADJ.: decrepito; debile, malsano.

créak, INTR.: scricchiolare; cigolare. -ing, s.: scricchiolata, *f.*

créam 1, s.: crema, fiore di latte, *m.*: *whipped* —, capo di latte. **cream** 2, TR.: schiumare; INTR.: rappigliarsi. -coloured, ADJ.: colore di crema. -faced, ADJ.: pallido. -y, ADJ.: pieno di crema.

créance†, s.: credenza, *f.*

créase 1, s.: piega, crespa, riga, *f.* **crease** 2, TR.: piegare, increspare.

cre-á-te, TR.: creare, causare; suscitare. -tion, s.: creazione; elezione, *f.* -tive, ADJ.: creativo, generativo. -tor, s.: creatore, *m.* -ture *krī-*, s.: creatura, *f.*; ente, animale, *m.*: *our fellow* —s, i nostri simili; *there is not a living* —, non vi è anima viva.

créb-ritude†, s.: frequenza, *f.* -rous†, ADJ.: frequente.

cré-dence, s.: credenza; fede; fama, *f.* -dénda, s.: articoli di fede, *m. pl.* -dent, ADJ.: credente; accreditato. -déntials, s. PL.: lettere credenziali, *f. pl.*

credibility, s.: credibilità, probabilità, *f.*

créd-ible, ADJ.: credibile, degno di fede. -ibleness, s.: probabilità, verisimilitudine; credenza, *f.* -ibly, ADV.: credibilmente. -it 1, s.: credito, *m.*; fede; riputazione, fama, stima; autorità, *f.*: *letter of* —, lettera di credito, *f.*; *give* — *to*, dar credito (prestar fede) a; *debit and* —, dare ed avere, debito e credito. -it 2, TR.: credere, prestar fede; far onore; fidarsi. -itable, ADJ.: onorevole; stimabile. -itableness, s.: onorevolezza; riputazione, *f.* -itably, ADV.: con credito, onorevolmente. -itor, s.: creditore, *m.* -itrix, s.: creditrice, *f.* -úlity, s.: credulità, *f.* -ulous, ADJ.: credulo, agevole al credere. -ulously, ADV.: da credulo. -ulousness, s.: facilità a credere, *f.*

créed, s.: credo, *m.*; confessione di fede, *f.*

créek 1, s.: cala, calanca, *f.*, seno di mare, *m.* **creek** 2, INTR.: scricchiolare. -y, ADJ.: pieno di cale.

créep, IRR.; INTR.: rampicare, strisciare, serpeggiare; abbassarsi, umiliarsi: — *in, into*, ficcarsi; insinuarsi; — *into one's favour*, insinuarsi nell' altrui favore; — *on*, accostarsi insensibilmente; — *out*, andare via sottilmente; — *up*, arrampicarsi. -er, s.: pianta strisciante (*or* rampicante), *f.*; alare del fuoco, *m.* -hole, s.: buco per scampare; pretesto, *m.* -ing, ADJ.: strisciante, serpeggiante; s.: bassezza, viltà, *f.*: — *thing*, rettile, *m.* -ingly, ADV.: a modo de' rettili.

cré-mate, TR.: cremare. -mátion, s.: cremazione, *f.* -matory, s.: crematoio, *m.*

crémor, s.: cremore, *m.*

crénated, ADJ.: merlato.

crépi-tate, INTR.: scoppiettare. -tátion, s.: scoppiettio, crepito, *m.*

crepuscu-le, S.: crepuscolo; bruzzolo, *m.* **-lous**, ADJ.: tra 'l dì e la notte.
crĕscent, ADJ.: crescente; S.: luna crescente, *f.*
crĕss, S.: crescione, *m.*
crĕsset, S.: fanale, faro, *m.*
crĕst, S.: cresta, *f.;* pennacchio; orgoglio; animo, *m.* **-ed**, ADJ.: crestuto. **-fallen**, ADJ.: sgomentato, sbigottito. **-less**, ADJ.: senza cresta; senza insegna.
cretāceous, ADJ.: cretaceo.
crĕvice 1, S.: crepatura, fessura, *f.* **crevice** 2, TR.: spaccare, fendere.
crew *krū*, S.: banda; torma; mano, *f.;* (*nav.*) equipaggio, *m.*, chiurma, *f.*
crewel *krū-*, S.: lana filata, *f.*
crib 1, S.: mangiatoia; capanna, *f.* **crib** 2, TR.: ingabbiare; rubare. **-bage**, S.: spezie di giuoco di carte (in Inghilterra), *f.* **-biter**, S.: cavallo ch' appoggia i denti alla mangiatoia, *m.*
cribble, S.: crivello, cribro, *m.*
cribrātion, S.: cribrazione, *f.*
crick†, S.: scricchiolata, *f.*
cricket 1, S.: grillo. **cricket** 2, S.: sgabello; giuoco alla palla, *m.*
crier, S.: banditore, *m.*
crime, S.: delitto, crimine, *m.;* colpa, *f.* **-ful†**, ADJ.: scellerato, malvagio; colpevole. **-less**, ADJ.: incolpevole, innocente.
crim-inal, ADJ.: criminale; colpevole; S.: delinquente, malfattore, *m.* **-inălity**, ADV.: criminalità, *f.* **-inally**, ADV.: criminalmente. **-inalness**, S.: criminalità, *f.;* delitto, *m.* **-inate**, TR.: incolpare. **-inātion**, S.: incolpamento, *m.*, accusa, *f.* **-inatory**, ADJ.: incolpante, accusante. **-inous**, ADJ.: criminoso, colpevole, iniquo. **-inously**, ADV.: colpabilmente. **-inousness**, S.: malvagità, *f.;* crime, *m.*
crimp 1, ADJ.: fragile. **crimp** 2, TR.: arricciare i capelli. **-le**, TR.: increspare, grinzare; INTR.: raggrinzarsi, ritirarsi.
crimson 1, ADJ.: chermisino; S.: chermisì, *m.* **crimson** 2, TR.: tingere in chermisì.
crincum, S.: capriccio, *m.*, fantasia, *f.*
cring-e 1, S.: ossequio servile, *m.* **-e** 2, TR.: contrarre, increspare; INTR.: adulare vilmente, far il lusinghiere. **-ing**, ADJ.: abietto, servile, basso; S.: sommessione bassa; adulazione, *f.*
crinigerous, ADJ.: pieno di capelli, peloso, capelluto.
crinkle 1, S.: piega, grinza; sinuosità, *f.* **crinkle** 2, INTR.: serpeggiare, volteggiare.
crinōse, ADJ.: crinuto, pieno di capelli.
cripple 1, ADJ.: zoppo, mutilato. **cripple** 2, TR.: storpiare, mutilare; (*nav.*) disarmare, disfare. **-ness**, S.: storpiatura, mutilazione, *f.*

crisis, S.: crisi, *f.;* periodo decisivo, *m.*
crisp 1, ADJ.: crespo. **crisp** 2, TR.: increspare; inanellare, arricciare. **-ātion**, S.: raggrinzamento, arricciamento, *m.;* crespezza, *f.* **-ing-iron**, S.: calamistro, *m.* **-ness**, S.: increspatura, *f.* **-y**, ADJ.: crespo, increspato, arricciato.
criss-cross-row, S.: alfabeto, *m.*
critērion, S.: criterio; indizio, *m.*
criti-c, ADJ.: critico; S.: critico; censore, *m.* **-cal**, ADJ.: critico; esatto, accurato. **-cally**, ADV.: criticamente, da critico; esattamente. **-calness**, S.: esattezza, accuratezza, *f.* **-cise**, TR.: criticare, censurare. **-cism**, S.: criticismo, *m.;* critica, *f.*
crōak, INTR.: gracidare, crocitare. **-ing**, S.: gracchiamento, *m.*
crōceous, ADJ.: croceo.
crŏck 1, S.: pignatta, *f.* **crock** 2, TR.: annerare. **-butter**, S.: burro salato, *m.* **-ery**, S.: stoviglie, *f. pl.;* maiolica, *f.* **-ery-ware**, S.: maiolica, *f.*
crŏcodile, S.: coccodrillo, *m.*
crōcus, S.: croco, *m.*
crŏft, S.: chiuso piccolo, *m.*
croïs-ā'de†, **-ādo†**, S.: crociata, *f.* **-es†**, S. PL.: crociati, *m. pl.*
crōn-e, S.: pecora vecchia, vecchiaccia, *f.* **-y**, S.: amico vecchio, *m.*, conoscenza vecchia, *f.*
crŏok 1, S.: uncino; crocco; rocco, *m.:* *by hook or by* —, per ruffa e raffa. **crook** 2, TR.: incurvare; piegare; INTR.: piegarsi. **-back**, S.: gobbo; scrignuto, *m.* **-backed**, ADJ.: gobbo, scrignuto. **-ed**, ADJ.: piegato, adunco; perverso. **-edly**, ADV.: tortamente; mal volontieri. **-edness**, S.: curvatura, piegatura, sinuosità, *f.* **-legged**, ADJ.: storto di gambe.
crōon, INTR.: tubare, gemicare.
crŏp 1, S.: gozzo (d'uccello), *m.;* ricolta, raccolta, *f.;* cavallo scodato, *m.:* — *of wheat*, ricolta da frumento. **crop** 2, TR.: scortare; tosare; INTR.: fare la raccolta; mietere. **-ful**, ADJ.: sazio, satollo. **-sick**, ADJ.: impinzato.
crōsier, S.: pastorale, bastone vescovile, *m.*
crŏslet, S.: frostale, *m.*, crocetta, *f.*
crŏss 1, S.: croce; afflizione, pena, *f.*, tormento; infortunio, *m.:* *the holy* —, la santa croce; *the sign of the* —, il segno della croce. **cross** 2, ADJ.: traverso, contrario, opposto; perverso. **cross** 3, TR.: attraversare; impedire; INTR.: opporsi: — *out*, cancellare; — *over*, varcare; passare; — *one's legs*, incrocicchiare le gambe; — *one's self*, far il segno della croce; — *over the street*, attraversare la strada. **-bar**, S.: sbarra, *f.* **-bar-shot**, S.: palla di canone ramata

m. **-tū́tional**, ADJ.: costituzionale; legale. **-tutive**, ADJ.: costitutivo.

constrā́in, TR.: costringere; sforzare; arrestare; astringere; frenare, tener a freno. **-able**, ADJ.: che si può costringere. **-edly**, ADV.: per forza. **-er**, S.: che costringe; sforzatore, *m.* **-t**, S.: costringimento, *m.*, forza, violenza, *f.*: *by* —, colla forza; *without* —, senza soggezione, liberamente; *under* —, impacciato.

con-strict, TR.: contrarre; condensare. **-striction**, S.: costringimento, condensamento, *m.* **-strictor**, S.: costrittore, *m.* **-stringe**, TR.: costringere; comprimere; condensare. **-stringent**, ADJ.: costringente.

con-strŭct, TR.: costruire; fabbricare. **-strŭction**, S.: costruzione, costruttura; fabbricazione; interpretazione, *f.*: *put a good — on*, interpretare favorevolmente. **-strŭctive**, ADJ.: costruttivo. **-strŭcture**†, S.: costruttura; fabbrica, *f.* **-strŭe**, TR.: costruire; ordinare; interpretare; tradurre.

cŏnstu-prate, TR.: stuprare; sforzare. **-prā́tion**, S.: stupro, *m.*, violazione, *f.*

consubstăn-tial, ADJ.: (*theol.*) consustanziale. **-tiắlity**, S.: (*theol.*) consustanzialità, *f.* **-tiate**, TR.: unire nella sostanza, incorporare. **-tiā́tion**, S.: consustanziazione, *f.*

cŏnsul, S.: consolo, console, *m.*: — *general*, console generale. **-ar**, ADJ.: consolare. **-ate**, **-ship**, S.: consolato, *m.*, dignità di consolo, *f.*

consŭlt, TR.: esaminare; mirare; INTR.: consultare, deliberare. **-ā́tion**, S.: consultazione, consulta, *f.*; consiglio, *m.* **-er**, S.: consultore, *m.*

consū́-mable, ADJ.: consumabile. **-me**, TR.: consumare; spendere; INTR.: consumarsi. **-mer**, S.: consumatore, guastatore, *m.* **-ming**, ADJ.: consumante.

consŭm-mate[1], ADJ.: perfezionato, finito, perfetto: — *villain*, uomo scelleratissimo, *m.* **cŏnsum-mate**[2], TR.: perfezionare; terminare, finire. **-mately**, ADV.: compiutamente, perfettamente. **-mā́tion**, S.: compimento, *m.*; perfezione, *f.*

consŭmp-tion, S.: consumazione, *f.*; sciupio, consumo, consumamento, *m.*; (*med.*) consunzione; atrofia, etisia, *f.*: *pulmonary* —, etisia *f.*; tisi polmonare, *m.* **-tive**, ADJ.: consuntivo, etico, tisico. **-tiveness**, S.: tisichezza, *f.*; smagramento, *m.*

cŏntact, S.: contatto, toccamento, *m.*: *come into* —, incontrarsi, combaciarsi.

contā́-gion, S.: contagione; peste, *f.*: *catch the* —, contrarre il contagio. **-gious**, ADJ.: contagioso, pestilenziale. **-giousness**, S.: qualità contagiosa, *f.*

contā́in, TR.: contenere; comprendere; raffrenare, reprimere; temperare: — *one's self*, contenersi. **-able**, ADJ.: che può contenersi.

contăm-inate[1], ADJ.: contaminato; corrotto. **-inate**[2], TR.: contaminare; corrompere. **-inā́tion**, S.: contaminazione; bruttura, *f.*

contĕm-n, TR.: contennere, sdegnare, disprezzare. **-ner**, S.: disprezzatore, *m.*

cŏn-template, TR.: contemplare, considerare. **-templā́tion**, S.: contemplazione, *f.*: *have in* —, intendere, progettare. **-tĕmplative**, ADJ.: contemplativo. **-tĕmplatively**, ADV.: per contemplazione. **-templator**, S.: contemplatore, *m.*

con-temporā́neous, **-tĕmporary**, ADJ.: contemporaneo.

contĕmpt, S.: dispregio, sprezzo: *bring into* —, mettere in discredito; *hold in* —, avere (tenere) a vile; scherno, *m.*; — *of court*, contumacia, *f.* **-ible**, ADJ.: disprezzevole, spregevole: *make* —, avvilire. **-ibleness**, S.: disprezzamento, dispregio, *m.* **-ibly**, ADV.: disprezzevolmente. **-uous**, ADJ.: sprezzante; sdegnoso. **-uously**, ADV.: fieramente, sdegnosamente. **-uousness**, S.: insolenza, arroganza, *f.*

contĕnd, TR.: contendere, contestare; INTR.: contrastare; sforzarsi: *I — that*, mantengo (pretendo) che. **-ent**, **-er**, S.: cambattitore, opponente, *m.* **-ing**, S.: contendimento, *m.*

contĕnt[1], ADJ.: contento, soddisfatto; S.: contento, *m.*; soddisfazione, *f.*: **—s**, contenuto, contenimento, *m.*: *table of —s*, indice, *m.* **contĕnt**[2], TR.: contenare; soddisfare; piacere; — *one's self*, contentarsi. **-ā́tion**†, S.: contentezza, *f.* **-ed**, ADJ.: contentato, soddisfatto: — *with*, contento (soddisfatto) di; *easily* —, di facile contentatura. **-edly**, ADV.: contentamente; lietamente. **-edness**, S.: contentezza; soddisfazione, *f.*

contĕn-tion, S.: contenzione; disputa, *f.*: *bone of* —, pomo di discordia. **-tious**, ADJ.: contenzioso, litigioso, cavilloso, bisbetico. **-tiously**, ADV.: contenziosamente, litigiosamente. **-tiousness**, S.: disposizione a disputare, *f.*

contĕnt-less, ADJ.: scontento. **-ment**, S.: contentamento, contento, *m.*; soddisfazione, *f.*; piacere, *m.*

contĕrminous, ADJ.: confinante, limitrofo.

contĕst[1], TR.: contestare, quistionare; disputare. **cŏntest**[2], S.: contesa, rissa; disputa, quistione, *f.* **-able**, ADJ.: contestabile, disputabile. **-ā́tion**, S.: contesa; disputa, *f.*

cŏn-text[1], S.: tessitura, *f.*; contesto, *m.*

-tĕxt † 2, ADJ.: contesto, unito insieme. **-tĕxt** † 3, contessere, intrecciare. **-tĕxture**, S.: tessitura, *f.*, tessuto, *m.*

con-tigŭity, S.: contiguità, vicinanza, *f.* **-tiguous**, ADJ.: contiguo, vicino. **-tiguously**, ADV.: vicinamente, prossimamente. **-tiguousness**, S.: vicinità; prossimità, *f.*

cŏnti-nence, **-nency**, S.: continenza; castità, *f.* **-nent**, ADJ.: continente; casto; S.: continente, *m.*, terra ferma, *f.* **-nĕntal**, ADJ.: continentale. **-nently**, ADV.: continentemente.

contin-gence, **-gency**, S.: contingenza, *f.*, accidente, *m.* **-gent**, ADJ.: contingente, casuale; S.: contingente, *m.*, parte, porzione, *f.* **-gently**, ADV.: casualmente.

contin-ual, ADJ.: continuo, perpetuo. **-ually**, ADV.: continuamente, di continuo, sempre. **-uance**, S.: continuanza; durazione, permanenza, *f.*: *in — of time*, in progresso di tempo, alla lunga. **-uate**, ADJ.: continuato. **-uâtion**, S.: continuazione; serie; sequela, *f.* **-uative**, S.: durata, durazione continua, *f.* **-uator**, S.: continuatore, *m.* **-ue**, TR.: continuare, seguitare, proseguire; INTR.: perseverare, persistere, durare; dimorare. **-ued**, ADJ.: continuo. **-uedly**, ADV.: continuamente, senza interruzione. **-ŭity**, S.: continuità; serie, *f.* **-uous**, ADJ.: continuo, unito insieme.

contôr-t, TR.: contorcere; attorcigliare. **-tion**, S.: contorsione, *f.*

contŏur, S.: contorno; circonferenza, *f.*; delineamento, *m.*

cŏntra, PREP.: contro, contra. **-band** 1, ADJ.: di contrabbando; proibito, illegale. **-band** 2, TR.: fare il contrabbando. **-bandist**, S.: contrabbandiere, *m.*

contrăc-t 1, TR.: contrattare; contrarre; ritirare; INTR.: contrarsi, ristringersi. **cŏntrac-t** 2, S.: contratto, accordo, *m.*: *draw up —*, redigere un contratto; *enforce —*, fare eseguire un contratto; *enter into —*, addivenire ad un contratto. **-ted**, ADJ.: contratto, raggricchiato, negoziato; angusto, ristretto: *— for*, patteggiato, comprato. **-tedness**, S.: raggrinzamento, *m.* **-tibility**, S.: attezza a contrarsi, *f.* **-tible**, ADJ.: che può contrarsi. **-tile**, ADJ.: contrattile. **-tion**, S.: contrazione, *f.*; raccorciamento, *m.*; abbreviatura, *f.* **-tor**, S.: contrattante; contraente, *m.*

contradic-t, TR.: contraddire. **-ter**, S.: contraddittore, opponente, *m.* **-tion**, S.: contraddizione, opposizione, *f.*; ostacolo, *m.* **-tious**, ADJ.: contraddicente; inconsistente. **-tiousness**, S.: contraddizione; insussistenza, *f.* **-torily**, ADV.: contraddittoriamente. **-toriness**, S.: contraddizione, *f.* **-tory**, ADJ.: contraddittorio; S.: contraddicimento, *m.*

contradis-tinction, S.: proposizione opposta, *f.*: *in —*, in opposizione. **-tinguish**, TR.: contraddistinguere; contrassegnare.

contranitency, S.: contrannitenza, resistenza, *f.*

contraposition, S.: opposizione, *f.*

con-trăriant, ADJ.: contrariante, contrario. **-trariety**, S.: contrarietà; opposizione, *f.* **cŏn-trarily**, ADV.: contrariamente. **-trărious**, ADJ.: contrario, opposto. **-trăriously**, ADV.: contrariamente. **cŏn-trariwise**, ADV.: in modo contrario, al contrario. **cŏn-trary** 1, ADJ.: contrario, opposto; S.: contrario, *m.*, contrarietà, *f.*: *on the —*, al contrario. **-trary** 2, TR.: contrariare, contraddire, opporsi.

cŏn-trast 1, S.: contrasto, *m.*; opposizione, *f.* **-trâst** 2, TR.: fare un contrasto; porre all' incontro.

contravallâtion, S.: (*fort.*) fosso con parapetto, *m.*

contra-vĕne, TR.: contravvenire, disubbidire. **-vĕner**, S.: contravventore, disubbidiente, *m.* **-vĕntion**, S.: contravvenzione, *f.*

contrib-utory, ADJ.: tributario, contribuente. **-ute**, TR.: contribuire. **-ŭtion**, S.: contribuzione, *f.*: *lay under —*, mettere a contribuzione; *levy a —*, imporre una contribuzione. **-utive**, ADJ.: che può contribuire. **-utor**, S.: contribuente, *m.* **-utory**, ADJ.: contribuente.

contris-tate†, TR.: contristare, affligere. **-tâtion**†, S.: affizione, *f.*, cordoglio, *m.*

cŏn-trite, ADJ.: contrito, compunto. **-tritely**, ADV.: con contrizione. **-triteness**, **-trition**, S.: contrizione, *f.*; pentimento, *m.*

contri-vable, ADJ.: che può inventarsi. **-vance**, S.: invenzione, *f.*; progetto, *m.*; pratiche segrete, *f. pl.* **-ve**, TR.: inventare, trovare; concertare; tramare, macchinare, s'ingegnere. **-vement**, S.: invenzione, arte, *f.* **-ver**, S.: inventore; artefice, autore; macchinatore, *m.*

contrŏl 1, S.: registro; ristringimento, *m.*; autorità, *f.* **control** 2, TR.: controllare; raffrenare; ristringere; governare; verificare. **-ler**, S.: registratore, controllore, *m.* **-lership**, S.: uffizio del controllore, *m.* **-ment**, S.: soprintendenza; opposizione; refutazione, *f.*

contro-vĕrsal †, **-vĕrsary** †, ADJ.: di controversia.

cŏntro-verse 1, S.: controversia, disputa, *f.* **-verse** 2, TR.: disputare. **-vĕrser**, S.: controversista, m. **-vĕrsial**, ADJ.: di controversia. **-versy**, S.:

troversia; contesa, disputa, *f.* **-vert**, TR.: controvertere, contendere, disputare. **-vĕrtible**, ADJ.: controvertibile, disputabile **-vertist**, S.: controversista, *m.*

contumăcious, ADJ.: contumace, ostinato, caparbio. **-ly**, ADV.: contumacemente, ostinatamente. **-ness**, S.: ostinazione, caparbietà, *f.*

cŏntumacy, S.: contumacia; ostinazione, *f.*

contumē-lious, ADJ.: contumelioso, ingiurioso. **-liously**, ADV.: contumeliosamente, ingiuriosamente. **-liousness**, **cŏntume-ly**, S.: contumelia, ingiuria, *f.*

contū-se, TR.: ammacare. **-sion**, S.: contusione, *f.*, ammaccamento, *m.*

conŭndrum, S.: facezia plebea, *f.*, bisticcio, *m.*

convalĕscen-ce, **-cy**, S.: convalescenza, *f.*; ADJ.: convalescente.

convē-nable, ADJ.: convenevole, conveniente. **-ne**, TR.: convocare; adunare; INTR.: adunarsi, ragunarsi. **-ner**, S.: convocatore, *m.*

convēnien-ce, **-cy**, S.: convenienza, comodità; proporzione, *f.*: *at your* —, a vostro comodo, a vostro bell' agio. **-t**, ADJ.: conveniente, convenevole, comodo, atto; ragionevole. **-tly**, convenientemente, comodamente.

cŏnvent 1, S.: convento; monastero, *m.*

convĕnt 2, TR.: citare in giudizio, chiamare alla ragione.

convĕnticl-e, S.: conventicolo, conciliabolo, *m.* **-er**, S.: membro d' un conventicolo, *m.*

convĕntion, S.: convenzione, *f.*; patto, accordo, *m.* **-al**, ADJ.: convenzionale. **-ally**, ADV.: convenzionalmente, per patto. **-ary**, ADJ.: convenzionale, stipulato per patto. **-er**, S.: membro d' un assemblea, *m.*

convĕntual, ADJ.: conventuale; S.: conventuale, religioso, *m.*

convĕr-ge, INTR.: tendere al medesimo punto. **-gence**, S.: convergenza, *f.* **-gent**, ADJ.: convergente.

convĕr-sable, ADJ.: conversabile, sociabile. **-sableness**, S.: sociabilità, *f.* **-sably**, ADV.: in modo conversabile. **-sant**, ADJ.: conversante; versato, pratico, esperto. **-sātion**, S.: conversazione; familiarità, *f.*; commercio: *private* —, testa a testa, *f.* **-sative**, ADJ.: sociabile; affabile; pratico. **cŏnverse** 1, S.: società; familiarità, *f.*; commercio, *m.*; pratica, *f.* **-se**, INTR.: conversare, praticare; bazzicare.

convĕrsely, ADV.: reciprocamente, a vicenda.

convĕr-sion, S.: conversione, *f.*; rivolgimento, *m.* **-sive**, ADJ.: sociabile.

cŏn-vert 1, S.: convertito, *m.*: *make a — of*, convertire. **-vĕrt** 2, TR.: convertire, trasmutare; INTR.: convertirsi; — *sinners*, convertire i peccatori. **-vĕrter**, S.: convertitore, *m.* **-vĕrted**, ADJ.: convertito, cambiato, tramutato. **-vĕrtible**, ADJ.: convertibile. **-vĕrtibly**, ADV.: reciprocamente.

cŏn-vex, **-vĕxed**, ADJ.: convesso. **-vĕxedly**, ADV.: in forma convessa. **-vĕxity**, **-vĕxness**, S.: convessità, *f.* **-vĕxo-concave**, ADJ.: convesso-concavo.

convêy, TR.: trasferire, trasportare, trasmettere; condurre; comunicare; mandare: — *away*, portare via; — *in*, introdurre; — *off*, portar via; — *by water* (*by steam*), mandare per acqua (col vapore); — *intelligence*, comunicare notizie. **-ance**, S.: trasporto; mezzo di trasporto, veiculo, *m.*, vettura; cessione, *f.*: — *by water*, trasporto per mare, *m.*; *by private* —, per occasione. **-ancer**, S.: notaio, notaro, *m.* **-er**, S.: vetturino, *m.*

cŏn-vict 1, S.: bandito; fuoruscito, *m.* **-vict**† 2, ADJ.: convinto, criminale. **-vict** 3, TR.: convincere, provare reo. **-victed**, ADJ.: convinto. **-viction**, S.: convinzione; refutazione; condannazione, *f.* **-victive**, ADJ.: convincente. **-victiveness**, S.: evidenza, prova, dimostrazione, *f.*

convĭn-ce, TR.: convincere; provare. **-ced**, ADJ.: convinto, persuaso. **-cement**, S.: convincimento, *m.*, persuasione, *f.* **-cible**, ADJ.: atto a convincere, convincente. **-cingly**, ADV.: in modo convincente, evidentemente. **-cingness**, S.: convinzione; prova, evidenza, *f.*

con-vīval† = *-vivial*. **-vīve**†, TR.: convitare; festeggiare. **-vĭvial**, ADJ.: festivo; sociabile.

cŏn-vocate, TR.: convocare; adunare, ragunare. **-vocātion**, S.: convocazione; assemblea, *f.* **-vōke**, TR.: convocare; adunare.

con-volūtion, S.: avvolgimento; viluppo, *m.* **-vŏlve**, TR.: avvolgere.

cŏn-voy 1, S.: convoglio, *m.*, scorta, accompagnatura, *f.* **-vŏy** 2, TR.: convogliare, accompagnare. **-vŏy-ship**, S.: bastimento di scorta.

convŭl-se, TR.: cagionare convulsioni, rendere convulso, agitare con violenza, scuotere; *be* —*d*, spasimare. **-sion**, S.: convulsione; commozione; turbolenza, *f.*: *slight* —, convulsioncella, *f.*; *be taken with* —*s*, esser preso da convulsioni. **-sive**, ADJ.: convulsivo. **-sively**, ADV.: in modo convulsivo.

cŏny, S.: coniglio, *m.* **-burrow**, S.: conigliera, *f.* **-catch**, TR.: ingannare

con furberia. **-catcher**, S.: furbo, furfante, *m.* **-warren**, S.: conigliera, *f.*
cōo, INTR.: susurrare; gemere. **-ing**, S.: mormorio de' colombi, *m.*
cōok 1, S.: cuoco, cuciniere, *m.*; cuoca, *f.* **cook** 2, TR.: *fare* la cucina, cucinare. **-ery**, S.: arte del cuoco, cucina, *f.* **-maid**, S.: cuoca, cuciniera, *f.* **-room**, S.: (*nav.*) cucina, *f.* **-shop**, S.: bettola, trattoria, *f.*
cōol 1, ADJ.: fresco, freddo; S.: fresco, freddo, *m.*: *it is* —, fa fresco; *it is getting* —, comincia a far fresco. **-cool** 2, TR.: rinfrescare, raffreddare: moderare, sminuire; INTR.: rinfrescarsi, raffreddarsi. **-er**, S.: refrigerativo, refrigerante, *m.* **-ing**, ADJ.: refrigerativo; S.: rinfrescamento, *m.* **-ish**, ADJ.: freschetto. **-ly**, ADJ.: freddamente; indifferentemente. **-ness**, S.: freschezza, freddura, *f.*, freddo, *m.*
cōop 1, S.: stia, *f.*; barile, *m.* **coop** 2, INTR.: rinchiudere; ingabbiare: —*ed up*, in gabbia, in prigione. **-er**, S.: bottaio, *m.* **-erage**, S.: lavoro del bottaio, *m.*, mestiere del bottaio, *m.*
co-ŏperate, TR.: cooperare, concorrere. **-operātion**, S.: cooperazione; concorrenza, *f.* **-ŏperative**, ADJ.: cooperativo, cooperante. **-ŏperator**, S.: cooperatore, *m.*
cōopery †, S.: arte di bottaio, *m.*
coöptātion, S.: assunzione, *f.*
coôrdi-nate 1, ADJ.: coordinato. **-nate** 2, TR.: coordinare. **-nately**, ADV.: nel medesimo ordine. **-nateness**, **-nātion**, S.: coordinazione; ugualità, *f.*
cōot, S. smergo, *m.*
cŏp, S.: cima, sommità, *f.*; capo, *m.*
copāiba, S.: copaiba, *f.*
cōpal, S.: coppale, *f.*
copâr-cener, S.: coerede; compagno, *m.* **-ceny**, S.: porzione uguale dell'eredità, *f.*
copârtment †, S.: compartimento, *m.*
copârtner, S.: socio, compagno, *m.* **-ship**, S.: società, compagnia, *f.*
cōpe 1, S.: pianeta di prete, *f.* **cope** 2, TR.: barattare; INTR.: — *with*, contendere; far testa a, rivaleggiare.
cōpesmate †, S.: compagno; commensale, *m.*
cōpier, S.: copista, copiatore, *m.*
cōping, S.: comignolo; colmo, *m.*, cima, *f.*
cōpious, ADJ.: copioso, abbondevole. **-ly**, ADV.: copiosamente; abbondantemente, largamente. **-ness**, S.: abbondanza, ricchezza, dovizia, *f.*
cōpist, S.: copista, copiatore, scriba, *m.*
cōpland †, S.: pezzo di terreno con un angolo, *m.*
cŏpped, ADJ.: crestuto, puntuto.
cŏppel, S.: copella, *f.*
cŏpper 1, S.: rame (*metal*); calderone (*kettle*, ecc.), *m.* **copper** 2, TR.: foderare di rame. **-as**, S.: vitriuolo, *m.* **-coloured**, ADJ.: colore di rame, bronzato. **-money**, S.: moneta di rame, *f.* **-nose**, S.: naso rosso, *m.* **-plate**, S.: stampa di rame, lastra di rame, *f.* **-smith**, S.: calderaio, *m.* **-wire**, S.: filo di rame, *m.* **-work**, S.: manifattura di rame, fucina del rame, *f.* **-y**, ADJ.: che contiene del rame.
cŏppice, S.: macchia, macchietta, *f.*; bosco ceduo, *m.*
cŏppled, ADJ.: conico.
cŏpse 1, S.: macchia, macchietta, *f.* **copse** 2, TR.: conservare i boschi tagliati bassi.
Cŏptic, ADJ., S.: copto.
cŏp-ula, S.: copula, *f.* **-ulate**, TR.: copulare; unire; INTR.: accoppiarsi; congiungersi. **-ulātion**, S.: congiungimento, *m.* **-ulative**, ADJ.: (*gram.*) copulativo.
cŏpy 1, S.: copia, *f.*; manoscritto; esemplare, originale, *m.* **copy** 2, TR.: copiare; trascrivere; imitare: — *out*, fare una copia di, trascrivere. **-book**, S.: quaderno, quinterno, *m.* **-er** = *copyist*. **-hold**, S.: podere d'un feudo, *m.* **-holder**, S.: censuario, *m.* **-ing-machine**, S.: copialettere; pantografo, *m.* **-ist**, S.: copista, *m.* **-right**, S.: diritto di proprietà letteraria; manoscritto, *m.*
coquĕt, TR.: trattare con finta tenerezza; INTR.: civettare. **-ry**, S.: civetteria, *f.* **-te**, S.: civetta, *f.* **-tish**, ADJ.: da civetta.
cŏracle, S.: barchetta da pescatori, *f.*
cŏral, S.: corallo, *m.* **-diver**, **-fisher**, S.: pescatore di coralli, *m.* **-fishery**, S.: spesca de' coralli, *f.* **-line**, ADJ.: corallino, di corallo; S.: coralina, *f.* **-reef**, S.: banco di corallo, *m.* **-tree**, S.: albero del corallo, *m.*
co-rānt, **-rāto**, S.: (*danc.*) corrante, *f.*
côrban, S.: cassetta della limosina, *f.*
côrbel, S.: canestro, *m.*; nicchia, *f.*
côrd 1, S.: corda; tendine, *f.*: — *of wood*, S.: catasta, misura di legna, *f.* **cord** 2, TR.: legare con corde. **-age**, S.: cordame; sartiame, *m.* **-ed**, ADJ.: legato con corde; infunato. **-elier**, S.: Francescano, *m.*
côrdi-al 1 *-jal*, S.: cordiale, *m.* (brodo da bere). **-al** 2, ADJ.: cordiale; affettuoso. **-ălity**, S.: cordialità, *f.*; affetto cordiale, *m.*, svisceratezza, *f.* **-ally**, ADV.: cordialmente.
côrd-maker, S.: funaiuolo, funaio, *m.* **-on**, S.: cordone; ordine, *m.*
côrdovan, S.: cordovano, *m.*

dămsel, S.: damigella, zitella, *f.*
dămson, S.: pruna di Damasco, *f.*
dânc-e 1, S.: ballo, *m.*, danza, *f.* **-e** 2, TR.: fare ballare; INTR.: ballare, danzare, riddare: — *attendance*, aspettar lungo tempo invano, fare spalliera; — *in*, entrare danzando; — *out*, uscire danzando. **-er**, S.: ballerino, ballatore, *m.* **-ing**, S.: ballare, danzare; ballo, *m.*: — *master*, maestro di ballo, *m.*; — *room*, salla da ballo, *f.*; — *school*, scuola da ballo, *f.*
dăndelion, S.: macerone, *m.*
dăndiprat, S.: nano, *m.*
dăndl-e, TR.: dondolare; accarezzare; ritardare, procrastinare. **-er**, S.: accarezzatore, *m.* **-ing**, S.: carezza, *f.*, vezzeggiamento, *m.*
dăndruff, S.: forfora, forforaggine, *f.*
dăndy, S.: dandy, damerino, *m.*
dânewort, S.: ebbio, ebulo, *m.*
dânger 1, S.: periglio, pericolo; rischio, *m.*: *be in* —, pericolare; *run a* —, correr pericolo. **danger** 2, TR.: arrischiare. **-less**, ADJ.: senza pericolo, sicuro. **-ous**, ADJ.: periglioso, rischioso. **-ously**, ADV.: perigliosamente. **-ousness**, S.: pericolo; azzardo, *m.*
dăngl-e, INTR.: pendere, dondolare; corteggiare vilmente. **-er**, S.: galante; innamorato, *m.*
dănk, ADJ.: umido, molle. **-ish**, ADJ.: umidiccio, umidetto. **-ishness**, S.: umidità, *f.*
dăp, INTR.: lasciar cadere pianamente nell' acqua.
dăpper, ADJ.: lesto, attivo, vivace. **-ling**, S.: nano, omiciattolo, *m.*
dăpple 1, ADJ.: pezzato, pomato. **dapple** 2, TR.: variar le strisce, strisciare. **-grey**, ADJ.: leardo pomato.
dâr-e 1, S.: disfida; provocazione, *f.* **-e** 2, IRR.; TR.: sfidare; provocare; INTR.: ardire, osare, arrischiarsi: *do it if you* —, fatelo se vi basta l' animo. **-eful**, ADJ.: baldo, burbero. **-ing**, ADJ.: ardito; audace. **-ingly**, ADV.: arditamente; coraggiosamente. **-ingness**, S.: ardimento, *m.*; audacia, *f.*
dârk, ADJ.: oscuro, fosco; ignorante; S.: oscurita, *f.*; buio, *m.*; tenebre, *f. pl.*; ignoranza, *f.*: — *lantern*, lanterna sorda, *f.*; — *saying*, detto oscuro, *m.*; *it is getting* —, si fa scuro. **-en**, TR.: oscurare; intenebrare; offuscare; imbarazzare; INTR.: oscurarsi. **-ening**, S.: oscuramento, *m.* **-ish**, ADJ.: oscuretto, alquanto buio. **-ling**, ADJ.: offuscato; ignorante, cieco. **-ly**, ADV.: oscuratamente; ciecamente. **-ness**, S.: oscurità, *f.*, tenebre, *f. pl.* **-some**, ADJ.: oscuro, fosco, nero.
dârling, ADJ.: favorito, diletto, caro; S.: favorito, caro, prediletto, *m.*; cara, prediletta, *f.*
dârn 1, S.: cucitura, *f.* **darn** 2, TR.: rassettare, cucire; unire.
dârnel, S.: loglio, *m.*, zizzania, *f.*
dâr-ner, S.: racconciatore, rimendatore, *m.* **-ning**, S.: cucitura di due pezzi, *f.*
dărrei(g)n†, TR.: disporre per la battaglia; battagliare.
dârt 1, S.: dardo, *m.* **dart** 2, TR.: dardeggiare; lanciare; INTR.: andar velocemente.
dăsh 1, S.: collisione, *f.*; tratto; colpo, *m.*: *at one* —, ad un tratto, subito; — *of the pen*, pennata, *f.* **dash** 2, TR.: colpire; urtare; spruzzare; percuotere; fracassare; cancellare; confondere; INTR.: lanciarsi; sgorgare: — *one's hopes*, frustrare le speranze d' alcuno; — *in pieces*, mettere in pezzi, spezzare; — *down*, precipitare; — *forward*, precipitarsi, affeltarsi; — *out*, uscire di slancio.
dăstard, S.: codardo, poltrone, *m.* **-ize**, TR.: intimidire, spaventare; render vigliacco. **-liness**, S.: codardia, *f.* **-ly**, ADJ.: codardo, poltronesco. **-y**, S.: codardia, poltroneria, *f.*
dâte 1, S.: data; conclusione, *f.*; dattero, *m.*: *out of* —, fuor d' uso, vecchio; *under* — *of*, in data di. **date** 2, TR.: mettere la data, datare; notare. **-book**, S.: giornale, *m.* **-less**, ADJ.: senza data.
dâte-tree, S.: palma, *f.*
dătive, ADJ.: dativo: — *case*, dativo, *m.*; — *guardian*, tutela, *f.*
dâub 1, S.: pitturaccia, *f.* **daub** 2, TR.: imbrattare; schiccherare; piaggiare; INTR.: far l' ipocrita. **-er**, S.: pittoraccio, *m.* **-ery**, S.: artificio, *m.* **-y**, ADJ.: viscoso, glutinoso.
dâughter, S.: figlia; figliuola, *f.* **-in-law**, S.: figliastra, *f.*: *grand*—, nipote, *f.*
dâunt, TR.: intimidire; spaventare, sgomentare. **-less**, ADJ.: intrepido, coraggioso. **-lessness**, S.: intrepidezza, *f.*
dâuphin, S.: delfino, *m.* **-ess**, S.: moglie del delfino, *f.*
dăvit, S.: (*nav.*) arganello, *m.*
dâw, S.: gracchia, cornacchia, *f.*
dâwdl-e, INTR.: indugiare. **-er**, S.: indugiatore, *m.*
dâwk†, S.: buco, *m.*, incisione, *f.*
dâwn 1, S.: alba, *f.*, spuntare del giorno; cominciamento, *m.* **dawn** 2, INTR.: spuntare; cominciare a nascere, apparire.
dây, S.: giorno; dì; lume, *m.*; giornata, *f.*: *by* —, di giorno; *a (whole)* —, giornata; *it is broad* —, fa giorno; *the next* —, l' indomani; — *by* —, ogni mano; — *before yesterday*, avantieri; *every other* —, ogni secondo giorno; *from* — *to* —, di giorno in giorno; *from this* —, d' ora innanzi; *in the* —*s of old*, anticamente; *this* — *sennight*, oggi a otto;

this many a —, molti giorni sono; *to this* —, fin al giorno d' oggi; *this* —, oggi, oggidì; *this — week*, oggi a otto; *in his* —*s*, nel suo tempo; *gain the* —, guadagnar la battaglia. **-bed**, S.: lettuccio; seggiolone, *m.* **-book**, S.: giornale, diario, *m.* **-break**, S.: spuntare del giorno, *m.* **-fly**, S.: mosca effimera, *f.* **-labor**, S.: giornata, *f.* **-laborer**, S.: operaio alla giornata, *m.* **-light**, S.: giorno chiaro, *m.*; luce, *f.*: *in plain* —, di giorno chiaro. **-lily**, S.: asfodillo, *m.* **-peep**, S.: alba, *f.*, spuntare del sole, *m.* **-scholar**, S.: scolare esterno, *m.* **-school**, S.: scuola diurna, scuola di esterni, *f.* **-spring**, S.: alba, *f.*, spuntare del giorno, *m.* **-star**, S.: stella del mattino, *f.* **-time**, S.: giorno, *m.*; chiarezza del sole, *f.* **-work**, S.: lavoro d' un giorno, *m.*

dāisied, ADJ.: pieno di margheritine.

dāzzl-e, TR.: abbagliare, offuscare; INTR.: esser abbagliato. **-ing**, S.: abbaglio, offuscamento, *m.*

dēacon, S.: diacono, *m.* **-ess**, S.: diaconessa, *f.* **-ry**, **-ship**, S.: diaconato, *m.*

dĕad 1, ADJ.: morto; stupefatto: *half* —, mezzo morto; *he is just* —, è morto or ora; *fall* —, cascar morto; — *calm*, gran calma, bonaccia, *f.*; — *coal*, carbone estinto, *m.*; — *drink*, bevanda svaporata, *f.*; — *drunk*, ebbrissimo; — *place*, luogo solitario, deserto, *m.*; — *sleep*, letargia, *f.*; — *water*, acqua stagnante; (*nav.*) stella, *f.*; — *weight*, peso morto, *m.*; — *winter*, verno tristo, *m.* **dead** 2, S.: silenzio profondo, *m.*: — *of night*, silenzio della notte, *m.*; *the* —, i morti. **dead** 3, ADV.: grandemente, affatto. **-en**, TR.: rallentare; addormentare. **-lift**, S.: condizione disperata, *f.* **-liness**, S.: mortalità, *f.* **-ly**, ADJ.: mortale, periglioso, fatale; violento; implacabile; ADV.: mortalmente; estremamente. **-ness**, S.: addormentamento, *m.*; scipitezza, *f.*

dĕaf, ADJ.: sordo; insensibile: — *and dumb*, sordomuto; *lend a — ear*, far il sordo. **-en**, TR.: assordare; produrre sordità. **-ish**, ADJ.: alquanto sordo. **-ly**, ADV.: sordamente; chetamente. **-ness**, S.: sordità, sordaggine, *f.*

dēal 1, S.: quantità, abbondanza, *f.*; abete, *m.*: *a great* —, *a good* —, molto, assai; — *at cards*, fare le carte, *m.*; mano, *f.*; *it is your* —, tocca a voi a dare le carte. **deal** 2, IRR.; TR.: distribuire; dare; INTR.: negoziare, trafficare: — *at cards*, fare le carte; — *by*, comportarsi; trattare; — *in*, avere da fare con; occuparsi; — *out*, ripartire, dare; — *with*, combattere, contendere, trattare (bene, male). **-bord**, S.: pancone d' abete, *m.*

deăl-bate†, TR.: imbiancare. **-bātion**, S.: imbiancatura, *f.*

dēal-er, S.: mercante, trafficatore, *m.*; colui che distribuisce le carte: *double* —, uomo di cattiva fede, furfante, *m.*; *plain* —, uomo di buona fede, *m.* **-ing**, S.: traffico, negozio, commercio, *m*; affari, *m. pl.*: *fair* —, probità, *f.*; *I have no* —*s with him*, non ho che fare coi fatti suoi.

deămbu-late†, INTR.: spasseggiare. **-lātion**†, S.: passeggiata, *f.*

dēan, S.: decano, *m.* **-ery**, **-ship**, S.: decanato; grado del decano, *m.*

dēar, ADJ.: diletto, caro, amato, favorito; ADV.: caramente; caro: — *bought*, comprato a gran prezzo; *my* —, mia cara; *my — friend* (*fellow*), mio caro; *it will cost you* —, vi costerà caro. **-ling**†, S.: favorito, cucco, *m.* **-ly**, ADV.: caramente; teneramente.

dēarn†, ADJ.: triste, malincolico.

dēarness, S.: amore, *m.*; scarsità, carestia, *f.*

dēarth, S.: scarsezza, carestia, *f.*; mancamento, *m.*

deărticulate, TR.: dislogare.

dĕath, S.: morte, *f.*; trapasso, *m.*: *at the point of* —, nel punto della morte; *die an honourable* —, fare morte onorevole; *sentence to* —, giudicare a morte; *die a natural* —, morire di sua morte; *suffer* —, sostener la morte; *upon pain of* —, sotto pena della vita; *put to* —, far morire. **-bed**, S.: agonia, *f.* **-bell**, S.: campana da morte, *f.* **-blow**, S.: colpo mortale, colpo di grazia, *m.* **-less**, ADJ.: immortale; eterno. **-like**, ADJ.: inanimato; letargico. **-rattle**, S.: rantolo della morte, *m.* **-struggle(s)**, S.: agonia, *f.* **-warrant**, S.: ordine d' esecuzione, *m.* **-watch**, S.: grillo, *m.* **-wound**, S.: piaga mortale, *f.*

debâr, TR.: escludere; proibire, prevenire.

debârb, TR.: radere; fare la barba.

debârk, TR.: sbarcare. **-ātion**, S.: sbarcare, *m.*

debās-e, TR.: avvilire; disprezzare; falsificare. **-ement**, S.: abbassamento, avvilimento; dispregio, *m.* **-er**, S.: dispregiatore; falsificatore, *m.*

debā-table, ADJ.: contestabile, disputabile. **-te** 1, S.: contesa; disputa, discussione, *f.* **-te** 2, TR.: discutere; esaminare; INTR.: deliberare, meditare; contendere, disputare. **-teful**, ADJ.: contenzioso, litigioso. **-tement**, S.: contesa; disputa; controversia, quistione, *f.* **-ter**, S.: disputatore, *m.*: *ready* —, oratore pronto (nei dibattimenti).

debāuch 1, S.: gozzoviglia, crapula, dissolutezza, *f.* **debauch** 2, TR.: corrom pere; sedurre; frastornare. **-edness**, s.: sfrenatezza, *f.* **-ée**, s.: dissoluto, discolo, *m.* **-er**, s.: corrompitore, seduttore, *m.* **-ery**, s.: dissolutezza, sfrenatezza, *f.* **-ment**, s.: corruzione, *f.*

debénture, s.: restante d' un debito, obbligo, *m.*

débile, ADJ.: debile, debole; languido.

debíli-tate, TR.: debilitare, affievolire. **-tátion**, s.: debilitazione, *f.* **-ty**, s.: debilità, debolezza, *f.*

débit, s.: debito, *m.*

debonáir, ADJ.: cortese, affabile, gentile, civile. **-ly**, ADV.: cortesemente, civilmente, affabilmente. **-ness**, s.: cortesia, affabilità, *f.*

débt, s.: debito, obbligo, *m.*: *small* —, debituzzo, *m.*; *be in* —, essere indebitato; *contract* —*s*, *run into* —*s*, contrarre debiti, indebitarsi. **-ed**, ADJ.: indebitato, obbligato. **-less**, ADJ.: senza debito. **-or**, s.: debitore, *m.*

décade, s.: decade, decina, *f.*

decádency, s.: decadenza; ruina, *f.*

déca-gon, s.: (*geom.*) decagono, *m.* **-logue**, s.: decalogo, *m.*

decámp, INTR.: levare il campo; fuggire. **-ment**, s.: decampamento, *m.*

decánt, TR.: decantare, travasare. **-átion**, s.: decantazione, *f.*; travasamento, *m.* **-er**, s.: guastada, caraffa.

decápi-tate, TR.: decapitare. **-tátion**, s.: decapitazione, decollazione, *f.*

decáy [1], s.: decadenza, *f.*, decadimento, declino, *m.*, rovina, *f.*: *go to* —, andare in rovina. **decay** [2], TR.: consumare; rovinare; INTR.: consumarsi; decadere; declinare; diminuire, appassarsi.

decéase [1], s.: morte, *f.*, trapasso, *m.* **decease** [2], INTR.: morire, trapassare.

decéit, s.: inganno, *m.*; fraude; furberia, baratteria, *f.* **-ful**, ADJ.: ingannevole, fraudolento, fallace. **-fully**, ADV.: ingannevolmente, fraudolentemente, falsamente. **-fulness**, s.: inganno, *m.*; furberia, *f.* **-less**, ADJ.: senza inganno, sincero.

decéi-vable, ADJ.: facile ad esser ingannato, *f.* **-vableness**, s.: facilità ad esser ingannato, *f.* **-ve**, TR.: ingannare; gabbare; truffare: *be* —*d*, ingannarsi; *I may be* —*d*, forse m' inganno; — *with fair words*, infinocchiare. **-ver**, s.: ingannatore, *m.*

Decémber, s.: decembre, *m.*

decém-pedal, ADJ.: lungo dieci piedi. **-vir**, s.: decenviro, *m.* **-virate**, s.: decenvirato, *m.*

décency, s.: decenza, modestia, *f.*

decénnial, ADJ.: decennale, di dieci anni.

décent, ADJ.: decente, decoroso, dicevole; convenevole. **-ly**, ADJ.: [...]mente, con decenza.

de-ceptibílity, s.: attezza a[...] gannato, *f.* **-céptible**, ADJ.: [...] esser ingannato. **-céption**, s.[...] *f.*; inganno, *m.*: *liable to* —, s[...] esser ingannato. **-céptious**, -[...] ADJ.: ingannevole; falso, fallac[...]

decérp-t†, ADJ.: mozzo. **-tion**[...] zamento, *m.*, diminuzione, *f.*

decertátion, s.: contesa, *f.*

dechárm, TR.: disfare l' incant[...]

decíd-e, TR.: decidere, risolve[...] dere un partito; determinare, [...] **-ed**, ADJ.: deciso, fermo; [...] **-edly**, ADV.: decisivamente.

décidence, s.: caduta, *f.*; cad[...]

decíder, s.: arbitratore, giudi[...]

decíduous, ADJ.: cadente; cad[...]

déci-mal, ADJ.: decimale. **-m**[...] decimare, levare la decima. -[...] s.: decimazione, *f.*

decípher, TR.: decifrare. **-e**[...] ciferatore; espositore, *m.*

de-císion, s.: decisione; determ[...] *f.*: *come to a* —, applicarsi a[...] tito. **-císive**, ADJ.: decisiv[...] **-císively**, ADV.: decisivament[...] mente. **-císiveness**, s.: dete[...] ne, *f.* **-císory** = *decisive*.

déck [1], s.: bordo, *m.*, coperta, [...] (di nave), *m.* **deck** [2], TR.: [...] adornare, addobbare, acconciare [...] *self out*, mettersi in gala, ac[...] attillarsi. **-er** [1], s.: adornatore, [...] —, vascello a due ponti, *m.* -[...] ornamento, *m.*, gala, *f.*

de-cláim, INTR.: declamare; [...] **-cláimer**, s.: declamatore; arr[...] *m.* **-clamátion**, s.: declamaz[...] ringheria, *f.* **-clamator dé-**, [...] tore; arringatore, *m.* **-clám**[...] ADJ.: declamatorio.

de-clárable, ADJ.: dichiarabile. [...] **átion**, s.: dichiarazione, *f.*, [...] mento, *m.* **-clárative**, ADJ.: [...] tivo. **-cláratorily**, ADV.: in [...] claratorio. **-cláratory**, ADJ.: [...] torio. **-cláre**, TR.: dichiarare; [...] re, manifestare; INTR.: dichiara[...] nifestarsi: — *war*, intimar la [...] **-cláred**, ADJ.: dichiarato; ap[...] lese. **-clárement**, s.: dichiar[...] **-clárer**, s.: dichiaratore, espos[...] **-cláring**, s.: dichiaramento, *m.*

de-clénsion, s.: declinazione, *f.* [...] **able**, ADJ.: declinabile. **-cli**[...] s.: declinazione, *f.*, declinament[...] mamento, *m.* **-clinatory**, A[...] clinatorio. **-clíne** [1], s.: decl[...] *f.*, scadimento, *m.*; decadenza, [...] *f.*: *in the* —, in decadenza. -[...]

TR.: declinare; evitare, scansare; cludere; INTR.: decadere, calare; abbassarsi: — *an honour*, declinare un honore. **-clining**, S.: declinante, scadimento, *m.*: — *age*, declinante età.
de-clivity, S.: declività, *f.*; pendio, *m.*; (*rail.*) discesa, *f.* **-clivous**, ADJ.: declivo, a pendio; declinante.
decoc-t, TR.: bollire; digerire. **-tible**, ADJ.: atto ad essere decotto. **-tion**, S.: decozione, *f.*; decotto, *m.*
decol-late, TR.: decollare. **-lation**, S.: decollazione, decapitazione, *f.*
decoloration, S.: scoloramento, *m.*
decom-pose, TR.: scomporre; analizzare. **-posite**, ADJ.: ricomposto. **-position**, S.: disciogliimento, *m.*; analisi, *f.* **-pound**, comporre di composti, scomporre.
deco-rate, TR.: decorare, ornare. **-ration**, S.: decorazione, *f.*, ornamento; abbellimento, *m.* **-rator**, S.: adornatore, *m.*
decorous, ADJ.: decoroso; decente. **-ly**, ADV.: decorosamente; convenevolmente.
decorti-cate, TR.: scorticare, sbucciare. **-cation**, S.: scorticamento, *m.*
decorum, S.: decoro, *m.*; decenza, *f.*: *observe* —, mantenere il decoro, osservare le convenienze soziali; *offend against* —, offendere il decoro, mancare alle convenienze sociali.
decoy 1, S.: allettamento, zimbello, *m.*; seduzione, *f.* **decoy** 2, TR.: allettare, zimbellare; sedurre. **-bird**, **-duck**, S.: allettaiuolo; anatra di zimbello, *f.*
decrease 1, S.: decrescimento; scemamento, *m.*, diminuzione, *f.* **decrease** 2, TR.: diminuire; INTR.: sminuire, scemare; calare; declinare.
decree 1, S.: decreto; statuto, *m.* **-decree** 2, TR.: decretare; statuire, ordinare.
decrement, S.: decrescimento; scemamento, *m.*
decrepit, ADJ.: decrepito. **-ation**, S.: decrepitazione, *f.* **-ate**, TR.: decrepitare. **-ness**, **-ude**, S.: decrepità, *f.*
decrescent, ADJ.: decrescente; in decadenza.
decretal, ADJ.: decretale.
decretory, ADJ.: decretorio, decisivo.
de-crial, S.: censura strepitosa, *f.* **-cry**, TR.: screditare; biasimare.
decumben-ce, **-cy**, S.: giacimento, *m.*
decuple, ADJ.: decuplo.
decurion, S.: decurione; caporale, *m.*
decus-sate, TR.: decussare. **-sation**, S.: decussazione, *f.*
dedeco-rate†, TR.: disonorare, disgraziare. **-ration**†, S.: disonoramento, *m.* **-rous**, ADJ.: disonorevole.
dedentition, S.: perdita de' denti, *f.*
dedi-cate 1, ADJ.: dedicato; consecrato. **-cate** 2, TR.: dedicare; consecrare. **-cation**, S.: dedicazione, *f.*, dedicamento, *m.* **-cator**, S.: che dedica (un libro, ecc.). **-catory**, ADJ.: dedicatorio: — *epistle*, dedica, *f.*
dedu-ce, TR.: dedurre; inferire; conchiudere. **-cement**, S.: deduzione; conseguenza, *f.* **-cible**, ADJ.: deducibile.
deduc-t, TR.: dedurre; sottrarre. **-tion**, S.: sottraimento, *m.*; deduzione, conseguenza, *f.*: *logical* —, conclusione logica, *f.* **-tively**, ADV.: conseguentemente.
deed, S.: fatto, atto, *m.*; azione, *f.*; contratto; (*leg.*) strumento notarile, atto, rogito, *m.*: *good* —, opera buona; buona azione; *splendid* —*s*, gloriose gesta; *draw up a* —, redigere un atto; *execute a* —, completare un atto; *witness a* —, sottoscrivere un atto come testimonio; *in the very* —, sul fatto. **-less**, ADJ.: scioperato, indolente.
deem 1, S.: opinione, *f.* **deem** 2, IRR.; INTR.: giudicare; pensare.
deep 1, ADJ.: profondo; alto, sommo; grave; sagace; segreto, nascosto; astuto, fino: *be — in debt*, esser pieno di debiti; — *blue*, turchino scuro, *m.*; — *fetches*, pratiche segrete, *f. pl.*; — *mourning*, gran bruno, *m.*; — *notion*, concetto oscuro, *m.*; — *sleep*, sonno profondo, alto sonno, *m.*; — *water*, acqua profonda (*or* alta). **deep** 2, ADV.: profondamente. **deep** 3, S.: abisso; mare; silenzio oscuro, *m.* **-en**, TR.: affondare; cavare; oscurare. **-ening**, S.: profondamento, *m.* **-ly**, ADV.: profondamente; seriosamente, gravemente; tristamente. **-musing**, ADJ.: contemplativo, meditativo. **-ness**, S.: profondità, *f.*, profondo, *m.*
deer, S.: cervo; daino, *m.*
defac-e, TR.: disfigurare, distruggere; guastare, rovinare; scancellare. **-ement**, S.: disfiguramento; guastamento, *m.*, distruzione; rovina; ingiuria, *f.* **-er**, S.: rovinatore, *m.*
defailance†, S.: mancamento, *m.*, mancanza, *f.*
defal-cate, TR.: difalcare; sottrarre. **-cation**, S.: difalcazione, *f.*, diffalco; scemamento, *m.*
de-famation, S.: diffamazione, calunnia, *f.* **-famatory**, ADJ.: diffamatorio, calunnioso. **-fame**, TR.: diffamare, calunniare. **-famer**, S.: diffamatore, calunniatore, *m.* **de-famous**†, ADJ.: calunnioso.
defat-igable, ADJ.: fatichevole. **-igate**, TR.: faticare; straccare. **-igation**, S.: stanchezza, lassezza, lassitudine, *f.*
default 1, S.: diffalta; mancanza; colpa, *f.*, vizio, *m.*: *in — whereof*, in diffalta

difetto) di che. **default** 2, TR.: diffaltare; scemare. **-er**, S.: reo di peculato; concussionario, *m.*

defĕa-sance, S.: annullamento, cancellamento, *m.* **-sible**, ADJ.: che si può annullare. **-t** 1, S.: sconfitta; rotta, *f.* **-t** 2, TR.: sconfiggere; frustrare, deludere.

dĕfe-cate 1, ADJ.: chiarificato, raffinato. **-cate** 2, TR.: defecare; chiarificare, raffinare. **-cātion**, S.: purgazione, *f.*, raffinamento, *m.*

defĕc-t, S.: difetto; mancamento, *m.*; colpa, *f.*, vizio, *m.* **-tibility**, S.: imperfezione, *f.*, difetto, *m.* **-tible**, ADJ.: difettoso. **-tion**, S.: rivolta, rivoluzione, apostasia, *f.* **-tive**, ADJ.: difettivo, imperfetto. **-tively**, ADV.: imperfettamente. **-tiveness**, S.: difettuosità; imperfezione, *f.* **-tuous**, ADJ.: difettoso. **-tuousness**, S.: difettuosità, *f.*

defĕn-ce, S.: difesa; protezione, *f.*, scudo, *m.*; bastioni, *m. pl.* **-celess**, ADJ.: senza difesa, senza guardia; impotente. **-celessness**, S.: stato senza difesa, *m.*; debolezza, *f.* **-d**, TR.: difendere; proteggere; conservare: — *one's self*, difendersi. **-dable**, ADJ.: difendevole. **-dant**, ADJ.: difensivo; S.: che si difende. **-der**, S.: difensore, difenditore, protettore, *m.* **-sative**, S.: difesa; guardia, *f.*; legame, *m.* **-sible**, ADJ.: che può essere difeso. **-sive**, ADJ.: difensivo; S.: difesa; guardia; salvaguardia, *f.*: *stand on the* —, mettersi in atto (*or* istato) di difesa. **-sively**, ADV.: sulla difesa.

defĕr 1, TR.: differire; prolungare; INTR.: indugiare. **defer** 2, TR.: deferire.

dĕference, S.: rispetto, riguardo, *m.*; considerazione, *f.*: *out of* — *to*, per deferenza a.

defĕr-ment, S.: prolungamento, *m.* **-ring**, S.: ritardo; indugio, *m.*

defiance, S.: disfida; chiamata, *f.*: *bid* —, fare una disfida; *in* — *of*, ad onta di, a dispetto di.

deficien-ce, -cy, S.: diffalta, *f.*; mancamento, difetto, *m.* **-t**, ADJ.: deficiente; difettivo, imperfetto: *be* — *in*, mancare di.

defier, S.: sfidatore, sprezzatore, *m.*

defigurātion, S.: difformità, *f.*

defī-le 1, S.: passaggio stretto, *m.* **-le** 2, TR.: macchiare; contaminare; lordare; violare, deflorare; INTR.: marciare alla sfilata. **-lēe**, S.: passaggio stretto, *m.* **-lement**, S.: macchia, *f.*; imbrattamento, *m.* **-ler**, S.: imbrattatore, corruttore, *m.*

[illegible]-nable, ADJ.: che si può definire. [illegible] TR.: definire, diffinire; limitare; determinare; decidere. **-ner**, S.: [illegible]re, *m.*

dĕf-inite, ADJ.: diffinito, determinato; esatto, preciso. **-initeness**, S.: determinazione, limitazione, certezza, *f.* **-inition**, S.: diffinizione, *f.* **-initive**, ADJ.: diffinitivo, positivo. **-initively**, ADV.: diffinitamente, precisamente. **-initiveness**, S.: decisione, *f.*

de-flagrability, S.: combustibilità, *f.* **-flāgrable**, ADJ.: combustibile. **-flagrātion**, S.: abbruciamento; incendio, *m.*

deflĕc-t, INTR.: deviare; uscire della via. **-tion**, S.: deviazione, *f.*, deviamento, *m.*

de-florātion, S.: disfioramento, *m.* **-flōur**, TR.: deflorare.

dĕf-luous†, ADJ.: fluente. **-lŭxion**, S.: flussione, *f.*; flusso, *m.*

defôrm 1, ADJ.: deforme, sfigurato. **deform** 2, TR.: sformare, disfigurare. **-ātion**, S.: deformazione, *f.* **-ed**, ADJ.: sformato, deforme, difforme. **-edly**, ADV.: deformemente. **-ity**, S.: deformità, difformità; bruttezza, *f.*

defrăud, TR.: defraudare; truffare. **-ātion**, S.: defraudazione, trufferia, *f.* **-er**, S.: defraudatore, truffatore, *m.* **-ment** = *defraudation.*

defrāy, TR.: spesare, dare la spesa; pagare: — *the expenses*, pagare le spese. **-er**, S.: che paga le spese. **-ment**, S.: pagamento delle spese, *m.*

dĕft, ADJ.: vago, vezzoso; destro, agile, pronto. **-ly**, ADV.: pulitamente; destramente, accortamente. **-ness**, S.: pulitezza; destrezza, *f.*

defŭnc-t, ADJ.: defunto, morto; S.: defunto, *m.* **-tion**, S.: morte, *f.*; morire, *m.*

defȳ 1, S.: sfidamento, *m.*, disfida, *f.* **defy** 2, TR.: sfidare; sdegnare, bravare. **-er**, S.: sfidatore; provocatore, *m.*

degĕner-acy, S.: degenerazione, depravazione; bassezza, *f.* **-ate** 1, ADJ.: degenerato, abietto. **-ate** 2, INTR.: degenerare, corrompersi, tralignare. **-ateness**, **-ātion**, S.: depravazione; corruzione, *f.* **-ous**†, ADJ.: degenerato, vile, basso, abietto. **-ously**†, ADV.: in modo degenerato.

deglŭ-tinate, TR.: scollare. **-tition**, S.: deglutizione, *f.*, inghiottimento, *m.*

de-gradātion, S.: degradazione, *f.*, degradamento, *m.* **-grāde**, TR.: degradare; avvilire; REFL.: degradarsi, abbassarsi.

degrēe, S.: grado; ordine, *m.*; condizione, *f.*: *by* —*s*, a grado a grado, successivamente; *admit to* — *of doctor*, addottorare.

degŭst†, TR.: gustare. **-ātion**, S.: gustamento, *m.*

dehôrt†, TR.: dissuadere, sconsigliare. **-ātion**, S.: dissuasione, *f.* **-atory**, ADJ.: deortatorio; dissuasorio.

dē̆i-cīde, s.: deicidio, *m.* **-ficātion**, s.: deificazione, apoteosi, *f.* **-form**, ADJ.: deiforme. **-fy**, TR.: deificare; divinizzare.
dēign, TR.: accordare; concedere; INTR.: degnarsi.
deintegrate†, TR.: sminuire.
dē-ism, s.: deismo, *m.* **-ist**, s.: deista, *m.* **-istic(al)**, ADJ.: del deismo. **-ity**, s.: deità, divinità, *f.*
dejĕc-t 1, ADJ.: afflitto, tristo. **-t** 2, TR.: abbattere, sgomentare; affliggere. **-tedly**, ADV.: afflittamente, tristamente. **-tedness**, s.: abbattimento, *m.*; deiezione; pusillanimità, *f.* **-tion**, s.: afflizione, tristezza, malinconia, *f.* **-ture**, s.: egestione, *f.*; (*med.*) escrementi, *m. pl.*
delaceration, s.: laceramento, *m.*
delactātion, s.: spoppamento, *m.*
delāpsed†, ADJ.: ruinoso.
delā-te†, TR.: trasportare; accusare. **-tion†**, s.: delazione, accusa, *f.* **-tor**, s.: delatore, accusatore, *m.*
delāy 1, s.: ritardo, indugio, *m.* **delay** 2, TR.: ritardare, indugiare, differire; INTR.: arrestarsi; tardare. **-er**, s.: indugiatore, *m.* **-ment**, s.: tardamento, indugiamento, *m.*
delĕc-table, ADJ.: dilettabile; grato. **-tableness**, s.: dilettabilità, *f.*; diletto, *m.* **-tably**, ADV.: dilettevolmente, piacevolmente. **-tātion**, s.: dilettamento; piacere, *m.*
dĕle-gacy = *delegation.* **-gate** 1, ADJ.: delegato, deputato; s.: delegato, commessario, *m.* **-gate** 2, TR.: delegare, deputare. **-gātion**, s.: delegazione; commissione, *f.*
delē-te, TR.: cancellare; radere. **deletērious**, ADJ.: distruttivo. **-tion**, s.: cancellatura; rasura, *f.* **dĕle-tery†** = *deleterious.*
dĕlf†, s.: miniera; maiolica, *f.*
delibātion, s.: assaggiamento, *m.*
deliber-ate 1, ADJ.: ponderato, cauto, accorto, maturo. **-ate** 2, TR.: deliberare, ponderare, considerare. **-ated**, ADJ.: deliberato, consultato, risoluto. **-ately**, ADV.: deliberatamente, ponderatamente, cautamente. **-ateness**, s.: circospezione, prudenza, *f.* **-ātion**, s.: deliberazione, *f.* **-ative**, ADJ.: deliberativo, deliberato; s.: consultazione, *f.* **-atively**, ADV.: in modo deliberativo, deliberatamente.
dĕli-cacy, s.: delicatezza; squisitezza; mollezza, *f.* **-cate**, ADJ.: delicato, squisito; gentile, gracile; ameno, grato; effeminato, molle. **-cately**, ADV.: delicatamente, amenamente; debolmente. **-cateness**, s.: delicatezza, *f.* **-cates**, s. PL.: ghiottornie, leccornie, *f. pl.*

delicious, ADJ.: delizioso, squisito. **-ly**, ADV.: deliziosamente, amenamente, gratamente. **-ness**, s.: deliziosità, squisitezza, *f.*; diletto, piacere, *m.*
delight 1, s.: diletto, piacere, *m.*; delizia, *f.*; passatempo, divertimento, *m.*: *take — in*, prender (*or* aver) diletto in, dilettarsi di.
delight 2, TR.: dilettare, ricreare; contentare; INTR.: dilettarsi, avere diletto. **-ed**, ADJ.: allietato, dilettato, contentissimo, rapito: *I should be —*, sarei pur lieto; *I was — with it*, mi piacque tanto. **-ful**, ADJ.: dilettevole, delizioso. **-fully**, ADV.: dilettevolmente, deliziosamente. **-fulness**, s.: delizia, *f.*, piacere, *m.* **-some**, ADJ.: dilettevole, grato. **-somely**, ADV.: dilettevolmente, dilettosamente. **-someness**, s.: dilettamento, *m.*, delizia, *f.*, piacere, *m.*
delin-eate, TR.: delineare; disegnare. **-eātion**, s.: delineazione, *f.*, delineamento; schizzo, *m.*
delinquen-cy, s.: delitto; misfatto, *m.*; colpa, *f.* **-t**, s.: delinquente, malfattore, *m.*
dĕli-quate†, INTR.: liquefarsi, fondersi. **-quātion†**, s.: liquefazione, *f.*
de-lirament†, s.: delirio, *m.* **-lirate**, INTR.: delirare, *m.* **-lirious**, ADJ.: delirante, in delirio: *be —*, delirare; *become —*, cadere in delirio, cominciare a farneticare. **-liriousness**, s.: delirio, *m.*, pazzia, *f.* **-lirium**, s.: delirio, *m.*: *— tremens*, delirio tremulo, *m.*
deliver, TR.: dare, rimettere, commettere; presentare; liberare; restituire; assistere nel parto: *— a speech*, far un discorso; *— in trust*, affidare; *— over*, trasmettere; rimettere; *— up*, restituire; abbandonare. **-ance**, s.: liberazione, *f.* **-er**, s.: liberatore, *m.* **-y**, s.: liberamento; parto, *m.*
dĕll, s.: cavo; fosso, *m.*; valle, *f.*
delū-dable, ADJ.: atto ad essere deluso. **-de**, TR.: deludere; ingannare, truffare, beffare. **-der**, s.: ingannatore, truffatore, *m.*
dĕluge 1, s.: diluvio, *m.*, inondazione, *f.* **deluge** 2, TR.: diluviare, inondare.
delū-sion, s.: delusione, *f.*, inganno, *m.* **-sive**, **-sory**, ADJ.: ingannevole, fraudolento, fallace.
dĕlv-e 1, s.: cava, *f.*, fosso; antro, *m.* **-e** 2, TR.: scavare; zappare. **-er**, s.: zappatore, *m.*
dĕmagog(ue), s.: demagogo, capo di fazione popolare, *m.*
demând 1, s.: domanda; richiesta; quistione; vendita, *f.*: *be in —*, aver richiesta; *in full of all —s*, in saldo. **demand** 2, TR.: domandare; esigere; questionare; fare istanza. **-able**, ADJ.

esigibile; riscuotibile. **-ant**, S.: domandante, *m.* **-er**, S.: domandatore, petitore, *m.*

demarcâtion, S.: demarcazione, *f.*

deméan 1, S.: condotta, *f.*: **—s**, dominio, patrimonio, *m.* **demean** 2, TR.: avvilire, umiliare: — *one's self*, comportarsi. **-or**, S.: portamento, *m.*; condotta, *f.*

demént, **-ate**, TR.: dementare, far impazzire. **-âtion**, S.: pazzia, *f.* **-ted**, ADJ.: demente, insano.

demérit, S.: demerito; fallo, *m.*

demér-sed, ADJ.: demerso. **-sion**, S.: demersione, *f.*

deméane, S.: dominio, patrimonio, *m.*

dĕmi-, ADJ.: mezzo, semi-. **-god**, S.: semideo, *m.*

dĕmi-grate†, TR.: migrare. **-grâtion†**, S.: migrazione; partenza, *f.*

dĕmi-john, S.: damigiana, *f.*, fiascone, *m.* **-lune**, S.: (*fort.*) mezzaluna, *f.*

de-mise 1, S.: trapasso, *m.*, morte, *f.* **-mise** 2, TR.: lasciare in testamento, legare; affittare. **-miss†**, ADJ.: umile. **-mission**, S.: demissione; digradazione, *f.*

dĕmi-tone, S.: semitono, *m.*

demŏcracy, S.: governo popolare, *m.*, democrazia, *f.*

dĕm-ocrat, S.: democratico, *m.* **-ocrât-ical**, ADJ.: democratico.

de-mŏlish, TR.: demolire; abbattere, distruggere. **-mŏlisher**, S.: distruttore, rovinatore, *m.* **-molition**, S.: demolizione, distruzione, rovina, *f.*

dē-mon, S.: demonio, *m.* **-mōniac**, S.: demoniaco, *m.* **-moniacal**, ADJ.: diabolico.

demŏn-strable, ADJ.: dimostrabile, ostensibile. **-strably**, ADV.: dimostrativamente; evidentemente. **dĕmon-strate**, TR.: dimostrare; provare. **-strâtion**, S.: dimostrazione, *f.*, pruova evidente; dimostramento, *m.*: *make a* —, far una dimostrazione. **-strative**, ADJ.: dimostrativo. **-stratively**, ADV.: dimostrativamente, visibilmente.

dĕmonstrator, S.: dimostratore, *m.*

de-moralizâtion, S.: demoralizzazione, *f.* **-mŏralize**, TR.: distruggere la morale, demoralizzare. **-mŏralized**, ADJ.: demoralizzato; sfiducciato.

demŭl-ce, TR.: addolcire, mitigare. **-cent**, ADJ.: emolliente, mitigativo.

demŭr 1, S.: dubitazione, incertezza, *f.* **demur** 2, TR.: sospettare; dubitare; INTR.: differire; esitare.

demûre, ADJ.: ritroso; serioso, grave; decente. **-ly**, ADV.: ritrosamente; gravemente, modestamente. **-ness**, S.: contegno, *m.*; discrezione; gravità, serietà, *f.*

demŭrrer, S.: (*leg.*) dilazione, sospensione, *f.*

dĕn, S.: caverna, spelonca, *f.*

denâtionalize, TR.: levar via i diritti nazionali.

denây†, S.: rifiuto, *m.*, ripulsa, negativa, *f.*

dendrŏlogy, S.: storia naturale degli alberi, *f.*

dĕnegate, TR.: negare.

de-niable, ADJ.: negabile; recusabile. **-nial**, S.: diniego, negamento, rinnegamento, rifiuto, *m.* **-nier**, S.: rifiutatore, *m.*

dĕni-grate, TR.: annerare; diffamare. **-grâtion**, S.: denigrazione, *f.*

dĕn-izen = *denizen*. **-izâtion**, S.: privilegio di franchigia, *m.* **-izen** 1, S.: forestiere matricolato, *m.* **-izen** 2, TR.: francheggiare.

denŏmi-nate, TR.: denominare, nominare. **-nâtion**, S.: denominazione, *f.* **-native**, ADJ.: denominativo. **-nator**, S.: (*arith.*) denominatore, *m.*

denō-table, ADJ.: notabile. **-tâtion**, S.: denotazione; nota, *f.* **-te**, TR.: denotare, indicare. **-tement**, S.: denotazione, *f.*

denouement -*mâng*, S.: scioglimento del intreccio, *m.*

denŏun-ce, TR.: denunziare, notificare; dichiarare. **-cement**, S.: denunzia, accusa, *f.* **-cer**, S.: accusatore, *m.*

dĕn-se, ADJ.: denso, condensato; spesso, compatto: — *cloud*, nuvolo denso. **-seness**, **-sity**, S.: densità; spessezza, *f.*

dĕnt 1, S.: dente, *m.*, tacca, *f.* **dent** 2, TR.: dentare.

dĕnt-al, ADJ.: dentale. **-icles**, S. PL.: (*arch.*) modiglioni, *f. pl.* **-iculated**, ADJ.: dentellato. **-iculâtion**, S.: dentello, *m.* **-ifrice**, S.: polvere da nettare i denti, *f.* **-ist**, S.: dentista, cavadenti, *m.* **-ition**, S.: dentizione, *f.*

denū-date = *denude*. **-dâtion**, S.: spogliamento, *m.* **-de**, TR.: denudare, nudare, render nudo, spogliare.

denŭn-ciate, TR.: denunziare. **-ciâtion**, S.: denunziamento, *m.*; minaccia, *f.* **-ciator**, S.: denunziatore, accusatore, *m.*

denȳ, TR.: negare; rinnegare; rifiutare, ricusare, rinunziare; INTR.: dir di no: *I — it*, lo nego; — *one's self*, astenersi; smentirsi, rinnegarsi.

de-obstrŭct, TR.: deostruere, aprire. **-ŏbstruent**, S.: (*med.*) deostruente, aperiente, *m.*

dēodand, S.: deodandum, *m.*

deŏppi-late, INTR.: (*med.*) disturare. **-lâtion**, S.: scioglimento d' ostruzioni, *m.* **-lative**, ADJ.: (*med.*) deostruente.

depâint, TR.: dipingere; rappresentare.

depârt 1, S.: partenza; morte, *f.* **depart** 2, TR.: separare; dividere; INTR.;

partire; morire: — *from*, sviarsi, allontanarsi; — *this life*, morire, passare a miglior vita. **-er**, s.: affinatore, *m.* **-ment**, s.: dipartimento, spartimento, *m.* **-ure**, s.: partenza, *f.*; abbandono, *m.*: *take one's* —, partire.

depásture, TR.: pasturare, pascere, pascolare.

depăuperate, TR.: impoverire.

depěctible†, ADJ.: tenace, vischioso.

depeculățion†, s.: peculato, *m.*

depěnd, INTR.: dipendere; essere dipendente: — *of*, consistere; — *on*, *upon*, confidarsi, aver confidenza; — *upon it!* siate securo! *it will* — *upon circumstances*, ciò sarà secondo le occorrenze. **-ance**, **-ancy**, **-ant** = *dependence*, *etc.* **-ence**, **-ency**, s.: dipendenza, fidanza, *f.*; dipendimento, *m.*; paese dipendente; — *on*, confidenza, fiducia. **-ent**, ADJ.: dipendente, che dipende, soggetto; s.: dipendente, *m.*: *be* — *on*, dipendere di *or* da.

deperdițion†, s.: deperdimento, *m.*, perdita, *f.*

depict, TR.: dipingere; descrivere.

dě-pilate, TR.: dipelare, far cadere i peli. **-pilățion**, s.: depilazione, *f.* **-pilatory**, s.: depilatorio, *m.* **-pilous**, ADJ.: dipelato, senza capelli.

deplěțion, s.: vuotamento, *m.*

deplō-rable, ADJ.: deplorabile, lamentabile. **-rableness**, s.: stato deplorabile, *m.*, miseria, *f.* **-rably**, ADV.: in modo lamentevole. **-rate**, ADJ.: deplorabile, lamentevole; disperato. **-rățion**, s.: lamentazione, *f.*, compianto, *m.* **-re**, TR.: compiangere, lamentare. **-redly**, ADV.: lamentevolmente. **-rer**, s.: che lamenta.

deplöy, TR.: sviluppare.

de-plumățion, s.: spiumare, *m.* **-plūme**, TR.: spiumare, spennare.

de-pōne, TR.: deporre; impegnare. **-pōnent**, s.: testimonio, teste; (*gram.*) deponente, *m.*

depŏpu-late, TR.: spopolare; devastare. **-lățion**, s.: spopolazione, *f.*; devastamento, desolamento, *m.* **-lator**, s.: devastatore, distruttore, *m.*

depōrt 1, s.: portamento, *m.*, condotta, *f.* **deport** 2, TR.: — *one's self*, comportarsi, portarsi. **-ățion**, s.: deportazione, *f.*; esilio, *m.* **-ment**, s.: portamento, *m.*; condotta, *f.*

de-pōșal, s.: deposizione, *f.* **-pōșe**, TR.: deporre; testificare, attestare, privare. **-pŏșit** 1, s.: deposito; pegno, *m.* **-posit** 2, TR.: depositare; impegnare. **-pŏșitary**, s.: depositario, *m.* **-poșițion**, s.: deposizione; testimonianza, *f.* **-pŏșitory**, s.: deposito, *m.*; depositeria, *f.*

de-pravățion, s.: depravazione, corruzione, *f.* **-prāve**, TR.: depravare, corrompere. **-prāved**, ADJ.: depravato, corrotto: *become* —, depravarsi, corrompersi, pervertirsi. **-prāvedness**, **-prāvement**, s.: depravazione, corrutela, *f.* **-prāver**, s.: depravatore, corruttore, *m.* **-prăvity**, s.: stato depravato, *m.*; depravazione, corruttela, *f.*

děpre-cate, TR.: divertirsi pregando un male; supplicare. **-cățion**, s.: deprecazione. **-cative**, **-catory**, ADJ.: deprecativo, supplichevole.

deprē-ciate, TR.: dispregiare, abbassare il prezzo, avvilire. **-ciățion**, s.: abbassamento di prezzo, svilimento, *m.*

děpre-date, TR.: depredare, saccheggiare, guastare. **-dățion**, s.: depredamento, saccheggio, *m.* **-dator**, s.: depredatore, rubatore, *m.*

deprehěn-d, TR.: sorprendere, chiappar sul fatto; scoprire. **-sible**, ADJ.: comprensibile. **-sion**, s.: sorpresa; scoperta, *f.*

de-prěss, TR.: deprimere; abbassare, avvilire. **-prěșșion**, s.: depressione, *f.*; avvilimento, *m.* **-prěssor**, s.: depressore; oppressore, *m.*

de-privățion, s.: privazione; (*law*) deposizione, *f.* **-prive**, TR.: privare; deporre. **-privement**, s.: privazione, *f.* **-priver**, s.: colui che priva.

děpth, s.: profondità, *f.*; fondo; abisso, *m.*; oscurità, *f.*; mezzo, *m.*: *in the* — *of the sea*, al fondo del mare; *in the* — *of winter*, nel cuor del verno. **-en**, TR.: cavare; affondare.

depūcelate†, TR.: deflorare.

depŭl-șion, s.: espulsione, *f.* **-sory**, ADJ.: espellente.

děpu-rate 1, ADJ: depurato, purgato. **-rate** 2, TR.: depurare, purgare. **-rățion**, s.: depurazione; chiarificazione, *f.*

de-putățion, s.: deputazione, *f.* **-pūte**, TR.: deputare, delegare.

děputy, s.: deputato, delegato, commessario, *m.*: *Lord* —, vicerè, *m.*

derăcinate, TR.: sradicare; sbarbare.

de-rāi(g)n†, TR.: provare, giustificare. **-rāi(g)nment**†, s.: prova, giustificazione, *f.*

derānge, TR.: disordinare, sconcertare; **-d**, ADJ.: disordinato, sconcertato, scompigliato: *be* — (*out of mind*), aver perduto il cervello; mezzo pazzo; esser demente. **-ment**, s.: disordinanza, *f.*

derāy†, s.: tumulto, strepito, *m.*

děre-lict, ADJ.: abbandonato. **-lictțion**, s.: abbandonamento, abbandono, *m.*

de-ride, TR.: deridere; beffare. **-rider**, s.: deriditore; beffatore, *m.* **-rișion**, s.: derisione, *f.*; scherno, *m.* **-risive**, **-risory**, ADJ.: derisorio,

formare; adattare; inventare; sorpassare; — *up*, trinciare; notomizzare.
cutāneous, ADJ.: cutaneo.
cū-ticle, S.: cuticola, pellicola, *f.* **-tic-ular** = *cutaneous*.
cŭt-lass, S.: scimitarra, *f.* **-ler**, S.: coltellinaio, *m.* **-lery**, S.: arte del coltellinaio, *f.*
cŭtlet, S.: costoletta, braciuola, *f.*
cŭt-pŭrse, S.: tagliaborse; borsaiuolo, *m.* **-ter**, S.: tagliatore; cottero, *m.*, scialuppa, *f.*: *stone* —, tagliapietre, *m.* **-throat**, ADJ.: barbaro, crudele; S.: assassino, tagliacantone; luogo periglioso, *m.* **-ting**, ADJ.: pungente; satirico; S.: ritaglio, *m.*, tagliata, *f.*: *open* —, (*rail.*) intaglio, *m.*, trincea, *f.*; —*s*, ritagli.
cŭttle, S.: seppia, *f.* (pesce); maldicente, *m.*
cŭt-water, S.: (*nav.*) tagliamare, *m.*
cȳ-cle, S.: ciclo; corso, *m.* **-cloid**, S.: (*geom.*) cicloide, *f.*
cyclopædia *-pē-*, S.: enciclopedia, *f.*
cȳgnet, S.: cigno giovine, *m.*
cȳl-inder, S.: cilindro, *m.* **-lindric(al)**, ADJ.: cilindrico.
cymâr, S.: zimarra, *f.*
cȳmbal, S.: cemballo, *m.*
cynănthropy, S.: frenesia canina, *f.*
cynegĕtics, S. PL.: arte della caccia, *f.*
cȳnic, S.: cinico, *m.* **-al**, ADJ.: cinico; brutale.
cȳnosure, S.: cinosura; (*astr.*) orsa minore; mira, guida, *f.*
cȳpress, **-tree**, S.: cipresso, *m.*; *grove of* —*es*, cipresseto, *m.* **-wood**, S.: cipresso, *m.*
cȳprus, S.: velo, *m.*
cȳst, S.: cisti, *f.*, tumore, *m.* **-ic**, ADJ.: cistico, tumoroso. **-ŏtomy**, S.: estrazione della cisti, *f.*
czâr, S.: czar, imperatore della Russia, *m.* **-ina**, S.: imperatrice della Russia, *f.*

D

d *dē* (*the letter*), S.: d, *f.*
dăb 1, S.: pezzo, piccolo sciaffo, *m.*: — *of dirt*, zacchera, *f.* **dab** 2, TR.: percuotere leggermente. **-ble**, TR.: imbrattare; schiccherare; INTR.: imbrattarsi, sporcarsi, impacciarsi: — *in politics*, immischiarsi negli affari politici. **-bler**, S.: guastamestiere, *m.*
dāce, S.: spezie di lasca, *f.*
dăctyle, S.: (*pros.*) datillo, *m.*
dăd, S.: babbo, padre, *m.*
dăddle, INTR.: camminare vacillando.
dăddy = *dad*.
dăffo-dil, **-dilly**, S.: asfodillo, *m.*
dăft, TR.: rigettare; sdegnare.
dăg†, S.: daga, *f.*, stiletto, scoppietto, *m.*
dăgger, S.: pugnale, *m.*, daga, *f.*: *look* —*s*, fare el viso dell' armi; *speak* —*s*, dire parole di fuoco. **-s-drawing**, S.: baruffa; lite, *f.*: *be at* —, venire a' coltelli.
dăggle, TR.: imbrattare, sporcare; INTR.: imbrattarsi. **-tail**, ADJ.: imbrattato, infangato.
daguĕrreotyp-e 1, S.: dagherreotipia, *f.* **-e** 2, TR.: dagherreotipare. **-ist**, S.: dagherreotipista, *m.* **-y**, S.: dagherreotipia, *f.*
dāily, ADJ.: quotidiano, diurno; ADV.: giornalmente, ogni giorno: — *bread*, pane quotidiano, *m.*; — *news*, cronaca giornaliere, *f.*
dāin-tily, ADV.: delicatamente, deliziosamente: elegantemente. **-tiness**, S.: delicatezza; squisitezza, leccornia, *f.* **-ty**, ADJ.: delicato, squisito; spregioso, elegante; S.: delicatezza, *f.*
dāiry, **-house**, cascina, *f.*; latticini, *m. pl.* **-maid**, S.: lattaia, *f.* **-woman**, S.: lattivendola, *f.*
dāisy, S.: margheritina, *f.*
dāle, S.: valle, valletta, *f.*
dăl-liance, S.: amorevolezza, *f.*, trastullo, *m.*; ritardanza, *f.* **-lier**, S.: accarezzatore, burlatore, scherzatore, *m.* **-ly**, INTR.: scherzare; accarezzare; dimorare, indulgiare.
dalmătic, S.: tonicella; dalmatica, *f.*
dăm 1, S.: madre (delle bestie), *f.*; molo, *m.*, cateratta, *f.* **dam** 2, TR.: stoppare, turare; murare: — *in*, chiudere con diga.
dămage, S.: danno, detrimento, *m.*; *cost and* —*s*, spese e indennizzazione. **damage**, TR.: danneggiare; INTR.: ingiuriarsi. **-able**, ADJ.: dannoso, pernizioso.
dămascene, S.: pruna di Damasco, *f.*
dămask 1, S.: dammasco, *m.* **damask** 2, ADJ.: dammaschino, di damasco: — *linen*, biancherie dammaschinate, *f. pl.* **damask** 3, TR.: dammascare. **-rose**, S.: rosa dammaschina, *f.*
dāme, S.: dama, signora, *f.*
dăm-n, TR.: dannare, condannare; fischiare. **-nable**, ADJ.: dannabile. **-nably**, ADV.: dannabilmente; orribilmente. **-nātion**, S.: dannazione, *f.* **-natory**, ADJ.: dannante. **-ned**, ADJ.: dannato, abbominevole. **-nific**, ADJ.: dannoso, nocivo. **-nify**, TR.: danneggiare, dannificare; nuocere. **-ningness**, S.: tendenza alla dannazione, *f.*
dămp 1, ADJ.: umido; depresso, tristo; S.: umidatà; afflizione, *f.*: *rather* —, umidetto. **damp** 2, TR.: inumidire; s-mentare, discoraggiare. **-ish**, ADJ.: r-diccio. **-ishness**, S.: umidità le-nebbia leggera, *f.* **-ness**, S.: umi-umidità, *f.* **-y†**, ADJ.: tristo, malinc-

detrūde, TR.: cacciare in giù.

detrŭn-cate, TR.: scappezzare, mozzare, troncare. **-cātion**, S.: mozzamento, m.

detrūsion, S.: atterramento, m.

deūce, S.: due, m. (al giuoco di carte).

deūce, S.: diavolo, m.

deuter-ŏgamy, S.: matrimonio secondo, m. **-ŏnomy**, S.: deuteronomio, m.

dévas-tate, TR.: devastare, desolare. **-tātion**, S.: devastazione, f., desolamento, m.

devélop, INTR.: sviluppare. **-ment**, S.: sviluppamento, m.

devĕrgence†, S.: divergenza.

devĕst, TR.: privare, spogliare.

devĕxity†, S.: declività, f.

dēvi-ate, INTR.: deviare, sviarsi. **-ātion**, S.: deviamento, m.

device, S.: invenzione; spediente, mezzo, m.; divisa, emblema, f.

dĕvil, S.: diavolo, demonio, m.: *great* —, diavolone, m.; *little* —, diavoletto, m.; *give the* — *his due*, non fate il diavolo più nero che non è; *a* — *of a fellow*, un vero demonio. **-ish**, ADJ.: diabolico. **-ishly**, ADV.: diabolicamente. **-ishness**, S.: natura diabolica, f. **-kin**, S.: diavoletto, m.

dēvious, ADJ.: deviato, errante.

devī-se 1, S.: legato; lascito; spediente; disegno, m. **-se** 2, TR.: immaginare; formare; INTR.: consultare, legare, lasciare. **-sēe**, S.: legatario, m. **-ser**, S.: inventore, autore, m. **-sor**, S.: (*leg.*) testatore, m.

dĕvi-table†, ADJ.: evitabile. **-tātion†**, S.: evitazione, f.

devŏid, ADJ.: vuoto, vacuo; destituto.

devoir *-vwŏr*, S.: dovere; ossequio, m.

de-volūtion, S.: devoluzione, f.; rivolgimento, scadimento, m. **-vŏlve**, TR.: devolvere; ricadere, scadere. **-vŏlved**, ADJ.: devoluto; ricaduto.

devorātion†, S.: divoramento, m.

devō-te, TR.: votare, dedicare; dare; consegnare: — *one's self to*, dedicarsi a, darsi a. **-ted**, ADJ.: dedito, dedicato. **-tedness**, S.: divozione, f. **-tēe**, S.: bacchettone, ipocrita, m. **-tion**, S.: divozione; disposizione, f. **-tional**, ADJ.: pio, divoto. **-tionalist**, S.: zelatore; ipocrita, m.

devŏur, TR.: divorare; inghiottire; — *with one's eyes*, cacciare (*or* ficcare) gli occhi addosso a. **-er**, S.: divoratore, m. **-ingly**, ADV.: ingordamente, avidamente, golosamente.

devōut, ADJ.: divoto, religioso, pio. **-ly**, ADV.: divotamente. **-ness**, S.: divozione; [illegible], f.

dew 1, S.: rugiada, f. **dew** 2, TR.: in[illegible]; aspergere. **-berry**, S.: moro di rove, m. **-besprĕnt**, ADJ.: sparso di rugiada. **-drop**, S.: goccia di rugiada, f. **-lap**, S.: giogaia, pappagorgia, f. **-lapt**, ADJ.: fornito di giogaia. **-worm**, S.: verme di rugiada, m. **-y**, ADJ.: rugiadoso.

dĕx-ter, ADJ.: destro, a man destra. **-tĕrity**, S.: destrezza; abilità, f. **-terous**, ADJ.: destro, accorto. **-terously**, ADV.: destramente, accortamente. **-terousness** = *dexterity*. **-tral**, ADJ.: dritto, diritto. **-trous** = *dexterous*.

diabētes, S.: (*med.*) diabete, f.

diabŏlic(al), ADJ.: diabolico, infernale. **-ally**, ADV.: diabolicamente. **-alness**, S.: diavoleria, f.

diadem, S.: diadema, m.; corona, f. **-ed**, ADJ.: cinto d' un diadema.

diaĕresis, S.: dieresi, f.

diagnŏstic, S.: indizio, sintomo, m.

diăgonal, ADJ.: diagonale; S.: diagonale, f. **-ly**, ADV.: diagonalmente.

diagram, S.: diagramma, m.; descrizione, f.

dial, S.: oriuolo a sole, m.; mostra d' orologio, f.

dia-lect, S.: dialetto; stilo, m. **-lĕctic**, S.: dialettica, logica, f. **-lĕctical**, ADJ.: dialettico, logicale. **-lĕctically**, ADV.: in maniera dialettica.

dial-ing, S.: gnomonica, f. **-ist**, S.: fabbricatore d' orologi solari, m.

di-alŏgical, ADJ.: dialogico. **-ălogist**, S.: dialogista, m. **-alogistically**, ADV.: in modo dialogico. **-ălogize**, TR.: dialogizzare. **di-alogue** 1, S.: dialogo, m. **-alogue** 2, INTR.: dialogizzare; discorrere.

dial-plate, S.: mostra d' orologio, f.

diălysis, S.: (*gram.*) sillaba divisa in due, f.

diăm-eter, S.: diametro, m. **-etral**, **-ĕtrical**, ADJ.: diametrale. **-ĕtrically**, ADV.: per diametro.

diamond, S.: diamante, m. **-cutter**, S.: gioielliere, m.

diapāson, S.: (*mus.*) ottava, f.

diaper 1, S.: biancheria tessuta a figura, f. **diaper** 2, TR.: damascare.

di-aphanĕity, S.: diafanità, trasparenza, f. **-aphănic**, **-ăphanous**, ADJ.: diafano.

diaphorĕtic, ADJ.: (*med.*) diaforetico, sudorifico.

diaphragm, S.: (*anat.*) diaframma, m.

diar-rhēa, **-rhœa**, S.: diarrea, f. **-rhĕtic**, ADJ.: purgativo.

diary, S.: diario, giornale, m.

diăstole, S.: (*anat.*) diastole, f.

diatĕssaron, S.: (*mus.*) diatessaron, m.

diatŏnic, ADJ.: (*mus.*) diatonico.

dibble, S.: piuolo da piantare, m.

this many a —, molti giorni sono; *to this* —, fin al giorno d' oggi; *this* —, oggi, oggidì; *this — week*, oggi a otto; *in his —s*, nel suo tempo; *gain the* —, guadagnar la battaglia. **-bed**, S.: lettuccio; seggiolone, *m.* **-book**, S.: giornale, diario, *m.* **-break**, S.: spuntare del giorno, *m.* **-fly**, S.: mosca effimera, *f.* **-labor**, S.: giornata, *f.* **-laborer**, S.: operaio alla giornata, *m.* **-light**, S.: giorno chiaro, *m.*; luce, *f.*: *in plain* —, di giorno chiaro. **-lily**, S.: asfodillo, *m.* **-peep**, S.: alba, *f.*, spuntare del sole, *m.* **-scholar**, S.: scolare esterno, *m.* **-school**, S.: scuola diurna, scuola di esterni, *f.* **-spring**, S.: alba, *f.*, spuntare del giorno, *m.* **-star**, S.: stella del mattino, *f.* **-time**, S.: giorno, *m.*; chiarezza del sole, *f.* **-work**, S.: lavoro d' un giorno, *m.*

dāzied, ADJ.: pieno di margheritine.

dăzzl-e, TR.: abbagliare, offuscare; INTR.: esser abbagliato. **-ing**, S.: abbaglio, offuscamento, *m.*

dēacon, S.: diacono, *m.* **-ess**, S.: diaconessa, *f.* **-ry**, **-ship**, S.: diaconato, *m.*

dĕad 1, ADJ.: morto; stupefatto: *half* —, mezzo morto; *he is just* —, è morto or ora; *fall* —, cascar morto; — *calm*, gran calma, bonaccia, *f.*; — *coal*, carbone estinto, *m.*; — *drink*, bevanda svaporata, *f.*; — *drunk*, ebbrissimo; — *place*, luogo solitario, deserto, *m.*; — *sleep*, letargia, *f.*; — *water*, acqua stagnante; (*nav.*) stella, *f.*; — *weight*, peso morto, *m.*; — *winter*, verno tristo, *m.* **dead** 2, S.: silenzio profondo, *m.*: — *of night*, silenzio della notte, *m.*; *the* —, i morti. **dead** 3, ADV.: grandemente, affatto. **-en**, TR.: rallentare; addormentare. **-lift**, S.: condizione disperata, *f.* **-liness**, S.: mortalità, *f.* **-ly**, ADJ.: mortale, periglioso, fatale; violento; implacabile; ADV.: mortalmente; estremamente. **-ness**, S.: addormentamento, *m.*; scipitezza, *f.*

dĕaf, ADJ.: sordo; insensibile: — *and dumb*, sordomuto; *lend a — ear*, far il sordo. **-en**, TR.: assordare; produrre sordità. **-ish**, ADJ.: alquanto sordo. **-ly**, ADV.: sordamente; chetamente. **-ness**, S.: sordità, sordaggine, *f.*

dēal 1, S.: quantità, abbondanza, *f.*; abete, *m.*: *a great* —, *a good* —, molto, assai; — *at cards*, fare le carte, *m.*; mano, *f.*; *it is your* —, tocca a voi a dare le carte. **deal** 2, IRR.; TR.: distribuire; dare; INTR.: negoziare, trafficare: — *at cards*, fare le carte; — *by*, comportarsi; trattare; — *in*, avere da fare con; occuparsi; — *out*, ripartire, dare; — *with*, combattere, contendere, trattare (bene, male). **-bord**, S.: pancone d' abete, *m.*

deăl-bate†, TR.: imbiancare. **-bātion**, S.: imbiancatura, *f.*

dēal-er, S.: mercante, trafficatore, *m.*; colui che distribuisce le carte: *double* —, uomo di cattiva fede, furfante, *m.*; *plain* —, uomo di buona fede, *m.* **-ing**, S.: traffico, negozio, commercio, *m*; affari, *m. pl.*: *fair* —, probità, *f.*; *I have no —s with him*, non ho che fare coi fatti suoi.

deămbu-late†, INTR.: spasseggiare. **-lātion**†, S.: passeggiata, *f.*

dēan, S.: decano, *m.* **-ery**, **-ship**, S.: decanato; grado del decano, *m.*

dēar, ADJ.: diletto, caro, amato, favorito; ADV.: caramente; caro: — *bought*, comprato a gran prezzo; *my* —, mia cara; *my — friend* (*fellow*), mio caro; *it will cost you* —, vi costerà caro. **-ling**†, S.: favorito, cucco, *m.* **-ly**, ADV.: caramente; teneramente.

dēarn†, ADJ.: triste, malincolico.

dēarness, S.: amore, *m.*; scarsità, carestia, *f.*

dēarth, S.: scarsezza, carestia, *f.*; mancamento, *m.*

deărticulate, TR.: dislogare.

dĕath, S.: morte, *f.*; trapasso, *m.*: *at the point of* —, nel punto della morte; *die an honourable* —, fare morte onorevole; *sentence to* —, giudicare a morte; *die a natural* —, morire di sua morte; *suffer* —, sostener la morte; *upon pain of* —, sotto pena della vita; *put to* —, far morire. **-bed**, S.: agonia, *f.* **-bell**, S.: campana da morte, *f.* **-blow**, S.: colpo mortale, colpo di grazia, *m.* **-less**, ADJ.: immortale; eterno. **-like**, ADJ.: inanimato; letargico. **-rattle**, S.: rantolo della morte, *m.* **-struggle(s)**, S.: agonia, *f.* **-warrant**, S.: ordine d' esecuzione, *m.* **-watch**, S.: grillo, *m.* **-wound**, S.: piaga mortale, *f.*

debâr, TR.: escludere; proibire, prevenire.

debârb, TR.: radere; fare la barba.

debârk, TR.: sbarcare. **-ātion**, S.: sbarcare, *m.*

debās-e, TR.: avvilire; disprezzare; falsificare. **-ement**, S.: abbassamento, avvilimento; dispregio, *m.* **-er**, S.: dispregiatore; falsificatore, *m.*

debā-table, ADJ.: contestabile, disputabile. **-te** 1, S.: contesa; disputa, discussione, *f.* **-te** 2, TR.: discutere; esaminare; INTR.: deliberare, meditare; contendere, disputare. **-teful**, ADJ.: contenzioso, litigioso. **-tement**, S.: contesa; disputa; controversia, quistione, *f.* **-ter**, S.: disputatore, *m.*: *ready* —, oratore pronto (nei dibattimenti).

debāuch 1, S.: gozzoviglia, crapula, solutezza, *f.* **debauch** 2, TR.: cor bare; sedurre; sfastoriare. **-edness**, s.: sfrenatezza, f. **-ee**, s.: dissoluto, libertino, m. **-er**, s.: corruttore, seduttore, m. **-ery**, s.: dissolutezza, sfrenatezza, f. **-ment**, s.: corruzione, f.

debénture, s.: restante f. di debito, bonigo, m.

débile, ADJ.: debile, debole, languido.

debíli-tate, TR.: debilitare, affievolire. **-tátion**, s.: debilitazione, f. **-ty**, s.: debilità, debolezza, f.

débit, s.: debito, m.

debonáir, ADJ.: cortese, affabile, gentile, civile. **-ly**, ADV.: cortesemente, civilmente, affabilmente. **-ness**, s.: cortesia, affabilità, f.

débt, s.: debito, obbligo, m.: *small* —, debituzzo, m.: *be in* —, essere indebitato: *run into* —*s*, *run into* —*s*, contrarre debiti, indebitarsi. **-ed**, ADJ.: indebitato, obbligato. **-less**, ADJ.: senza debito. **-or**, s.: debitore, m.

décade, s.: decade, decina, f.

decádency, s.: decadenza, rovina, f.

déca-gon, s.: *geom.* decagono, m. **-logue**, s.: decalogo, m.

decámp, INTR.: levare il campo, fuggire. **-ment**, s.: decampamento, m.

decánt, TR.: decantare, travasare. **-átion**, s.: decantazione, f.: travasamento, m. **-er**, s.: guastada, caraffa.

decápi-tate, TR.: decapitare. **-tátion**, s.: decapitazione, decollazione, f.

decáy 1, s.: decadenza, f., decadimento, declino, m., rovina, f.: *go to* —, andare in rovina. **decay** 2, TR.: consumare; rovinare; INTR.: consumarsi; decadere; declinare; diminuire, appassarsi.

decéase 1, s.: morte, f., trapasso, m. **decease** 2, INTR.: morire, trapassare.

decéit, s.: inganno, m.: frode; furberia, baratteria, f. **-ful**, ADJ.: ingannevole, fraudolento, fallace. **-fully**, ADV.: ingannevolmente, fraudolentemente, falsamente. **-fulness**, s.: inganno, m.: furberia, f. **-less**, ADJ.: senza inganno, sincero.

decéi-vable, ADJ.: facile ad esser ingannato, f. **-vableness**, s.: facilità ad esser ingannato, f. **-ve**, TR.: ingannare; gabbare; truffare; *be* —*d*, ingannarsi; *I* ... —*d*, forse m'inganno; — *with* ... infinocchiare. **-ver**, s.: in-
... m.
... s.: decembre, m.
...l, ADJ.: lungo dieci piedi.
...mviro, m. **-virate**, s.: de-
...

...ecenza, modestia, f.
...J.: decennale, di dieci
...

...ecente, decoroso, dicevo-

le, convenevole. **-ly**, ADV.: decentemente, con decenza.

decep-tibílity, s.: attezza ad esser ingannato, f. **-céptible**, ADJ.: atto ad esser ingannato. **-céption**, s.: frode, f.: inganno, m.: *liable to* —, soggetto ad esser ingannato. **-céptious**, **-céptive**, ADJ.: ingannevole; falso, fallace.

decérp-t, ADJ.: mozzo. **-tion**, s.: mozzamento, m., diminuzione, f.

decertátion, s.: contesa, f.

decharm, TR.: disfare l'incantesimo.

decíd-e, TR.: decidere, risolvere; prendere un partito; determinare, risolvere. **-ed**, ADJ.: deciso, fermo; deliberato. **-edly**, ADV.: decisivamente.

décidence, s.: caduta, f.; cadimento, m.

decíder, s.: arbitratore, giudice, m.

decíduous, ADJ.: cadente; caduca.

déci-mal, ADJ.: decimale. **-mate**, TR.: decimare, levare la decima. **-mátion**, s.: decimazione, f.

decípher, TR.: decifrare. **-er**, s.: deciferatore; espositore, m.

decísion, s.: decisione; determinazione, f.: *come to a* —, applicarsi ad un partito. **-císive**, ADJ.: decisivo, ultimo. **-císively**, ADV.: decisivamente, ultimamente. **-císiveness**, s.: determinazione, f. **-císory** = *decisive*.

déck 1, s.: bordo, m., coperta, f.; ponte di navi, m. **deck** 2, TR.: coprire; adornare, addobbare, acconciare: — *one's self out*, mettersi in gala, acconciarsi, attillarsi. **-er** 1, s.: adornatore, m.: *two* —, vascello a due ponti, m. **-ing**, s.: ornamento, m., gala, f.

de-cláim, INTR.: declamare; arringare. **-cláimer**, s.: declamatore; arringatore, m. **-clamátion**, s.: declamazione; arringheria, f. **-clamator** *de-*, declamatore; arringatore, m. **-clámatory**, ADJ.: declamatorio.

de-clárable, ADJ.: dichiarabile. **-clarátion**, s.: dichiarazione, f., dichiaramento, m. **-clárative**, ADJ.: dichiarativo. **-cláratorily**, ADV.: in modo declaratorio. **-cláratory**, ADJ.: declaratorio. **-cláre**, TR.: dichiarare; mostrare, manifestare; INTR.: dichiararsi; manifestarsi: — *war*, intimar la guerra. **-cláred**, ADJ.: dichiarato; aperto, palese. **-clárement**, s.: dichiarazione, f. **-clárer**, s.: dichiaratore, espositore, m. **-cláring**, s.: dichiaramento, m.

de-clénsion, s.: declinazione, f. **-clínable**, ADJ.: declinabile. **-clinátion**, s.: declinazione, f., declinamento; scemamento, m. **-clínatory**, ADJ.: declinatorio. **-clíne** 1, s.: declinazione, f., scadimento, m.; decadenza, rovina, f.: *in the* —, in decadenza. **-cline** 2,

TR.: declinare; evitare, scansare; chiudere; INTR.: decadere, calare; abbassarsi: — *an honour*, declinare un honore. **-clining**, S.: declinante, scadimento, *m.*: — *age*, declinante età.
de-clivity, S.: declività, *f.*; pendio, *m.*; (*rail.*) discesa, *f.* **-clivous**, ADJ.: declivo, a pendio; declinante.
decoc-t, TR.: bollire; digerire. **-tible**, ADJ.: atto ad essere decotto. **-tion**, S.: decozione, *f.*; decotto, *m.*
decol-late, TR.: decollare. **-lation**, S.: decollazione, decapitazione, *f.*
decoloration, S.: scoloramento, *m.*
decom-pose, TR.: scomporre; analizzare. **-posite**, ADJ.: ricomposto. **-position**, S.: discioglimento, *m.*; analisi, *f.* **-pound**, comporre di composti, scomporre.
deco-rate, TR.: decorare, ornare. **-ration**, S.: decorazione, *f.*, ornamento; abbellimento, *m.* **-rator**, S.: adornatore, *m.*
decorous, ADJ.: decoroso; decente. **-ly**, ADV.: decorosamente; convenevolmente.
decorti-cate, TR.: scorticare, sbucciare. **-cation**, S.: scorticamento, *m.*
decorum, S.: decoro, *m.*; decenza, *f.*: *observe* —, mantenere il decoro, osservare le convenienze soziali; *offend against* —, offendere il decoro, mancare alle convevenienze sociali.
decoy 1, S.: allettamento, zimbello, *m.*; seduzione, *f.* **decoy** 2, TR.: allettare, zimbellare; sedurre. **-bird**, **-duck**, S.: allettaiuolo; anatra di zimbello, *f.*
decrease 1, S.: decrescimento; scemamento, *m.*, diminuzione, *f.* **decrease** 2, TR.: diminuire; INTR.: sminuire, scemare; calare; declinare.
decree 1, S.: decreto; statuto, *m.* **decree** 2, TR.: decretare; statuire, ordinare.
decrement, S.: decrescimento; scemamento, *m.*
decrepit, ADJ.: decrepito. **-ation**, S.: decrepitazione, *f.* **-ate**, TR.: decrepitare. **-ness**, **-ude**, S.: decrepità, *f.*
decrescent, ADJ.: decrescente; in decadenza.
decretal, ADJ.: decretale.
decretory, ADJ.: decretorio, decisivo.
de-crial, S.: censura strepitosa, *f.* **-cry**, TR.: screditare; biasimare.
decumben-ce, **-cy**, S.: giacimento, *m.*
decuple, ADJ.: decuplo.
decurion, S.: decurione; caporale, *m.*
decus-sate, TR.: decussare. **-sation**, S.: decussazione, *f.*
dedeco-rate†, TR.: disonorare, disgraziare. **-ration**†, S.: disonoramento, *m.* **-rous**, ADJ.: disonorevole.
dedentition, S.: perdita de' denti, *f.*
dedi-cate 1, ADJ.: dedicato; consecrato. **-cate** 2, TR.: dedicare; consecrarc. **-cation**, S.: dedicazione, *f.*, dedicamento, *m.* **-cator**, S.: che dedica (un libro, ecc.). **-catory**, ADJ.: dedicatorio: — *epistle*, dedica, *f.*
dedu-ce, TR.: dedurre; inferire; conchiudere. **-cement**, S.: deduzione; conseguenza, *f.* **-cible**, ADJ.: deducibile.
deduc-t, TR.: dedurre; sottrarre. **-tion**, S.: sottraimento, *m.*; deduzione, conseguenza, *f.*: *logical* —, conclusione logica, *f.* **-tively**, ADV.: conseguentemente.
deed, S.: fatto, atto, *m.*; azione, *f.*; contratto; (*leg.*) strumento notarile, atto, rogito, *m.*: *good* —, opera buona; buona azione; *splendid* —*s*, gloriose gesta; *draw up a* —, redigere un atto; *execute a* —, completare un atto; *witness a* —, sottoscrivere un atto come testimonio; *in the very* —, sul fatto. **-less**, ADJ.: scioperato, indolente.
deem 1, S.: opinione, *f.* **deem** 2, IRR.; INTR.: giudicare; pensare.
deep 1, ADJ.: profondo; alto, sommo; grave; sagace; segreto, nascosto; astuto, fino: *be — in debt*, esser pieno di debiti; — *blue*, turchino scuro, *m.*; — *fetches*, pratiche segrete, *f. pl.*; — *mourning*, gran bruno, *m.*; — *notion*, concetto oscuro, *m.*; — *sleep*, sonno profondo, alto sonno, *m.*; — *water*, acqua profonda (*or* alta). **deep** 2, ADV.: profondamente.
deep 3, S.: abisso; mare; silenzio oscuro, *m.* **-en**, TR.: affondare; cavare; oscurare. **-ening**, S.: profondamento, *m.* **-ly**, ADV.: profondamente; seriosamente, gravemente; tristamente. **-musing**, ADJ.: contemplativo, meditativo. **-ness**, S.: profondità, *f.*, profondo, *m.*
deer, S.: cervo; daino, *m.*
deface-e, TR.: disfigurare, distruggere; guastare, rovinare; scancellare. **-ement**, S.: disfiguramento; guastamento, *m.*, distruzione; rovina; ingiuria, *f.* **-er**, S.: rovinatore, *m.*
defailance†, S.: mancamento, *m.*, mancanza, *f.*
defal-cate, TR.: difalcare; sottrarre. **-cation**, S.: difalcazione, *f.*, diffalco; scemamento, *m.*
de-famation, S.: diffamazione, calunnia, *f.* **-famatory**, ADJ.: diffamatorio, calunnioso. **-fame**, TR.: diffamare, calunniare. **-famer**, S.: diffamatore, calunniatore, *m.* **de-famous**†, ADJ.: calunnioso.
defat-igable, ADJ.: fatichevole. **-igate**, TR.: faticare; straccare. **-igation**, S.: stanchezza, lassezza, lassitudine, *f.*
default 1, S.: diffalta; mancanza; colpa *f.*, vizio, *m.*: in — whereof, in diffalta (

difetto di che. **default** 2, TR.: diffaltare; scemare. **-er**, S.: reo di peculato; concussionario, *m*.

defēa sance, S.: annullamento, cancellamento, *m*. **-sible**, ADJ.: che si può annullare. **-t** 1, S.: sconfitta; rotta, *f*. **-t** 2, TR.: sconfiggere; frustrare, deludere.

dĕfe-cate 1, ADJ.: chiarificato, raffinato. **-cate** 2, TR.: defecare; chiarificare, raffinare. **-cātion**, S.: purgazione, *f*., raffinamento, *m*.

defĕc t, S.: difetto; mancamento, *m*.: colpa, *f*., vizio, *m*. **-tibility**, S.: imperfezione, *f*., difetto, *m*. **-tible**, ADJ.: difettoso. **-tion**, S.: rivolta, rivoluzione, apostasia, *f*. **-tive**, ADJ.: difettivo, imperfetto. **-tively**, ADV.: imperfettamente. **-tiveness**, S.: difettuosità; imperfezione, *f*. **-tuous**, ADJ.: difettoso. **-tuousness**, S.: difettuosità, *f*.

defen ce, S.: difesa; protezione, *f*., scudo, *m*., bastioni, *m. pl*. **-celess**, ADJ.: senza difesa, senza guardia; impotente. **-celessness**, S.: stato senza difesa, *m*.; debolezza, *f*. **-d**, TR.: difendere; proteggere, conservare: — *one's self*, difendersi. **-dable**, ADJ.: difendevole. **-dant**, ADJ.: difensivo; S.: che si difende. **-der**, S.: difensore, difenditore, protettore, *m*. **-sative**, S.: difesa; guardia, *f*.; legame, *m*. **-sible**, ADJ.: che può essere difeso. **-sive**, ADJ.: difensivo; S.: difesa; guardia, salvaguardia, *f*.: *stand on the* —, mettersi in atto (*or* istato) di difesa. **-sively**, ADV.: sulla difesa.

defer 1, TR.: differire; prolungare; INTR.: indugiare. **defer** 2, TR.: deferire.

déference, S.: rispetto, riguardo, *m*.; considerazione, *f*.: *out of* — *to*, per deferenza a.

defer ment, S.: prolungamento, *m*. **-ring**, S.: ritardo; indugio, *m*.

defiance, S.: disfida; chiamata, *f*.: *bid* —, fare una disfida; *in* — *of*, ad onta di, a dispetto di.

deficien ce, **-cy**, S.: diffalta, *f*.: mancamento, difetto, *m*. **-t**, ADJ.: deficiente; difettivo, imperfetto: *be* — *in*, mancare di.

defier, S.: sfidatore, sprezzatore, *m*.

defigurātion, S.: difformità, *f*.

defi le 1, S.: passaggio stretto, *m*. **-le** 2, TR.: macchiare; contaminare; lordare; violare, deflorare; INTR.: marciare alla sfilata. **-lēe**, S.: passaggio stretto, *m*. **-lement**, S.: macchia, *f*., imbrattamento, *m*. **-ler**, S.: imbrattatore, corruttore, *m*.

defi-nable, ADJ.: che si può definire. **-ne**, TR.: definire, diffinire: limitare; INTR.: determinare; decidere. **-ner**, S.: definitore, *m*.

déf-inite, ADJ.: diffinito, determinato; esatto, preciso. **-initeness**, S.: determinazione, limitazione, certezza, *f*. **-inition**, S.: diffinizione, *f*. **-initive**, ADJ.: diffinitivo, positivo. **-initively**, ADV.: diffinitamente, precisamente. **-initiveness**, S.: decisione, *f*.

de-flagrability, S.: combustibilità, *f*. **-flagrable**, ADJ.: combustibile. **-flagrātion**, S.: abbruciamento; incendio, *m*.

deflĕc-t, INTR.: deviare; uscire della via. **-tion**, S.: deviazione, *f*., deviamento, *m*.

de-florātion, S.: disfioramento, *m*. **-flōur**, TR.: deflorare.

déf-luous†, ADJ.: fluente. **-lūxion**, S.: flussione, *f*.; flusso, *m*.

defōrm 1, ADJ.: deforme, sfigurato. **deform** 2, TR.: sformare, disfigurare. **-ātion**, S.: deformazione, *f*. **-ed**, ADJ.: sformato, deforme, difforme. **-edly**, ADV.: deformemente. **-ity**, S.: deformità, difformità; bruttezza, *f*.

defrāud, TR.: defraudare; truffare. **-ātion**, S.: defraudazione, trufferia, *f*. **-er**, S.: defraudatore, truffatore, *m*. **-ment** = *defraudation*.

defrāy, TR.: spesare, dare la spesa; pagare: — *the expenses*, pagare le spese. **-er**, S.: che paga le spese. **-ment**, S.: pagamento delle spese, *m*.

dĕft, ADJ.: vago, vezzoso; destro, agile, pronto. **-ly**, ADV.: pulitamente; destramente, accortamente. **-ness**, S.: pulitezza; destrezza, *f*.

defūnc-t, ADJ.: defunto, morto; S.: defunto, *m*. **-tion**, S.: morte, *f*.: morire, *m*.

defȳ 1, S.: sfidamento, *m*., disfida, *f*. **defy** 2, TR.: sfidare; sdegnare, bravare. **-er**, S.: sfidatore; provocatore, *m*.

degĕner-acy, S.: degenerazione, depravazione; bassezza, *f*. **-ate** 1, ADJ.: degenerato, abietto. **-ate** 2, INTR.: degenerare, corrompersi, tralignare. **-ateness**, **-ātion**, S.: depravazione; corruzione, *f*. **-ous** †, ADJ.: degenerato, vile, basso, abietto. **-ously** †, ADV.: in modo degenerato.

deglū-tinate, TR.: scollare. **-tītion**, S.: deglutizione, *f*., inghiottimento, *m*.

de-gradātion, S.: degradazione, *f*., degradamento, *m*. **-grāde**, TR.: degradare; avvilire; REFL.: degradarsi, abbassarsi.

degrēe, S.: grado; ordine, *m*.; condizione, *f*.: *by* —*s*, a grado a grado, successivamente; *admit to* — *of doctor*, addottorare.

degūst †, TR.: gustare. **-ātion**, S.: gustamento, *m*.

dehōrt †, TR.: dissuadere, sconsigliare. **-ātion**, S.: dissuasione, *f*. **-atory**, ADJ.: dehortatorio; dissuasorio.

dēi-cīde, S.: deicidio, *m.* **-ficātion**, S.: deificazione, apoteosi, *f.* **-form**, ADJ.: deiforme. **-fy**, TR.: deificare; divinizzare.
dēign, TR.: accordare; concedere; INTR.: degnarsi.
deintegrate†, TR.: sminuire.
dē-ism, S.: deismo, *m.* **-ist**, S.: deista, *m.* **-istic(al)**, ADJ.: del deismo. **-ity**, S.: deità, divinità, *f.*
dejěc-t 1, ADJ.: afflitto, tristo. **-t** 2, TR.: abbattere, sgomentare; affliggere. **-tedly**, ADV.: afflittamente, tristamente. **-tedness**, S.: abbattimento, *m.*; deiezione; pusillanimità, *f.* **-tion**, S.: afflizione, tristezza, malinconia, *f.* **-ture**, S.: egestione, *f.*; (*med.*) escrementi, *m. pl.*
delaceration, S.: laceramento, *m.*
delactātion, S.: spoppamento, *m.*
delăpsed†, ADJ.: ruinoso.
delā-te†, TR.: trasportare; accusare. **-tion**†, S.: delazione, accusa, *f.* **-tor**, S.: delatore, accusatore, *m.*
delāy 1, S.: ritardo, indugio, *m.* **delay** 2, TR.: ritardare, indugiare, differire; INTR.: arrestarsi; tardare. **-er**, S.: indugiatore, *m.* **-ment**, S.: tardamento, indugiamento, *m.*
delěc-table, ADJ.: dilettabile; grato. **-tableness**, S.: dilettabilità, *f.*; diletto, *m.* **-tably**, ADV.: dilettevolmente, piacevolmente. **-tātion**, S.: dilettamento; piacere, *m.*
děle-gacy = *delegation*. **-gate** 1, ADJ.: delegato, deputato; S.: delegato, commessario, *m.* **-gate** 2, TR.: delegare, deputare. **-gātion**, S.: delegazione; commissione, *f.*
delē-te, TR.: cancellare; radere. **deletērious**, ADJ.: distruttivo. **-tion**, S.: cancellatura; rasura, *f.* **děle-tory**† = *deleterious*.
dělf†, S.: miniera; maiolica, *f.*
delibātion, S.: assaggiamento, *m.*
deliber-ate 1, ADJ.: ponderato, cauto, accorto, maturo. **-ate** 2, TR.: deliberare, ponderare, considerare. **-ated**, ADJ.: deliberato, consultato, risoluto. **-ately**, ADV.: deliberatamente, ponderatamente, cautamente. **-ateness**, S.: circospezione, prudenza, *f.* **-ātion**, S.: deliberazione, *f.* **-ative**, ADJ.: deliberativo, deliberato; S.: consultazione, *f.* **-atively**, ADV.: in modo deliberativo, deliberatamente.
děli-cacy, S.: delicatezza; squisitezza; mollezza, *f.* **-cate**, ADJ.: delicato, squisito; gentile, gracile; ameno, grato; effeminato, molle. **-cately**, ADV.: delicatamente, amenamente; debolmente. **-cateness**, S.: delicatezza, *f.* **-cates**, S. PL.: ghiottornie, leccornie, *f. pl.*

delicious, ADJ.: delizioso, squisito. **-ly**, ADV.: deliziosamente, amenamente, gratamente. **-ness**, S.: deliziosità, squisitezza, *f.*; diletto, piacere, *m.*
delight 1, S.: diletto, piacere, *m.*; delizia, *f.*; passatempo, divertimento, *m.*: *take — in*, prender (*or* aver) diletto in, dilettarsi di.
delight 2, TR.: dilettare, ricreare; contentare; INTR.: dilettarsi, avere diletto. **-ed**, ADJ.: allietato, dilettato, contentissimo, rapito: *I should be —*, sarei pur lieto; *I was — with it*, mi piacque tanto. **-ful**, ADJ.: dilettevole, delizioso. **-fully**, ADV.: dilettevolmente, deliziosamente. **-fulness**, S.: delizia, *f.*, piacere, *m.* **-some**, ADJ.: dilettevole, grato. **-somely**, ADV.: dilettevolmente, dilettosamente. **-someness**, S.: dilettamento, *m.*, delizia, *f.*, piacere, *m.*
delin-eate, TR.: delineare; disegnare. **-eātion**, S.: delineazione, *f.*, delineamento; schizzo, *m.*
delinquen-cy, S.: delitto; misfatto, *m.*; colpa, *f.* **-t**, S.: delinquente, malfattore, *m.*
děli-quate†, INTR.: liquefarsi, fondersi. **-quātion**†, S.: liquefazione, *f.*
de-lirament†, S.: delirio, *m.* **-lirate**, INTR.: delirare, *m.* **-lirious**, ADJ.: delirante, in delirio: *be —*, delirare; *become —*, cadere in delirio, cominciare a farneticare. **-liriousness**, S.: delirio, *m.*, pazzia, *f.* **-lirium**, S.: delirio, *m.*: *— tremens*, delirio tremulo, *m.*
deliver, TR.: dare, rimettere, commettere; presentare; liberare; restituire; assistere nel parto: *— a speech*, far un discorso; *— in trust*, affidare; *— over*, trasmettere; rimettere; *— up*, restituire; abbandonare. **-ance**, S.: liberazione, *f.* **-er**, S.: liberatore, *m.* **-y**, S.: liberamento; parto, *m.*
děll, S.: cavo; fosso, *m.*; valle, *f.*
delū-dable, ADJ.: atto ad essere deluso. **-de**, TR.: deludere; ingannare, truffare, beffare. **-der**, S.: ingannatore, truffatore, *m.*
děluge 1, S.: diluvio, *m.*, inondazione, *f.* **deluge** 2, TR.: diluviare, inondare.
delū-sion, S.: delusione, *f.*, inganno, *m.* **-sive**, **-sory**, ADJ.: ingannevole, fraudolento, fallace.
dělv-e 1, S.: cava, *f.*, fosso; antro, *m.* **-e** 2, TR.: scavare; zappare. **-er**, S.: zappatore, *m.*
děmagog(ue), S.: demagogo, capo di fazione popolare, *m.*
demănd 1, S.: domanda; richiesta; quistione; vendita, *f.*: *be in —*, aver richiesta; *in full of all —s*, in saldo. **demand** 2, TR.: domandare; esigere; quistionare; fare istanza. **-able**, ADJ.

disintĕr, TR.: disseppellire.
disinterest, S.: disinteresse, *m.* **-ed**, disinteressato. **-edly**, ADV.: disinteressatamente. **-edness**, S.: disinteressatezza, *f.*
disintĕrment, S.: disotterramento, *m.*
disintricate, TR.: sviluppare, strigare.
disinûre, TR.: svezzare.
disjöin, TR.: disgiungere, separare.
disjöint, TR.: slogare; smembrare; INTR.: disgiungersi. **-ed**, ADJ.: slogato, smembrato; slombato. **-(ed)ly**, ADV.: separatamente.
disjŭnc-t, ADJ.: disgiunto, separato. **-tion**, S.: disgiunzione, *f.*; separamento, *m.* **-tive**, ADJ.: disgiuntivo. **-tively**, ADV.: disgiuntivamente.
disk, S.: disco, *m.*
diskindness†, S.: mancanza d' affetto, *f.*; pregiudizio, *m.*
dislik-e 1, S.: disgusto, *m.*; avversione, *f.*: *give a — to*, disgustare di; *have a — for*, provare antipatia per, sentire avversione (*or* ripugnanza) per. **-e** 2, TR.: disapprovare, dispiacere, disamare. **-eful†**, ADJ.: maligno. **-ent†**, TR.: differenziare. **-eness**, S.: dissomiglianza, differenza, *f.* **-er**, S.: disapprovatore, *m.* **-ing**, S.: disgusto, *m.*; ripugnanza, *f.*
dislimb†, TR.: membrare.
dislimn†, TR.: cancellare (una pittura).
dislocate, TR.: slogare, dislogare. **-cation**, S.: slogamento, *m.*; scommettitura, *f.*
dislŏdge, TR.: disloggiare, scacciare; INTR.: mutar casa.
dislöyal, ADJ.: disleale, infedele; perfido. **-ly**, ADV.: dislealmente, infidamente. **-ness**, **-ty**, S.: dislealtà, infedeltà; perfidia, *f.*
dismal, ADJ.: tristo, misero, funesto; orribile. **-ly**, ADV.: tristamente; orribilmente. **-ness**, S.: affanno; cordoglio, *m.*
dismăntle, TR.: smantellare; spogliare.
dismăsk, TR.: smascherare.
dismăst, TR.: disalberare.
dismāy 1, S.: smarrimento d' animo; terrore, *m.* **dismay** 2, TR.: spaventare, scoraggiare, stupefare. **-ed**, ADJ.: sgomentato, esterrefatto, stupefatto: *look —*, parer costernato (preso da sgomento). **-edness**, S.: spaventamento, *m.*
disme, S.: decima, *f.*
dismĕmber, TR.: smembrare, sbranare, dilaniare. **-ment**, S.: smembramento, *m.*
dis-miss, TR.: congedare, licenziare; ripudiare. **-mission**, TR.: licenziamento, congedo, *m.*
...ismôrtgage†, TR.: redimere un pegno, ...icomprare.
...smŏunt, TR.: scavalcare, smontare, scavallare; imboccare; INTR.: dismontare; scendere.
dis-năturalise, TR.: privare del privilegio di naturalità. **-nătured**, ADJ.: disnaturato.
dis-obĕdience, S.: disubbidienza, *f.* **-obĕdient**, ADJ.: disubbidiente. **-obĕdiently**, ADV.: disubbidientemente, con disubbidienza. **-obêy**, TR.: disubbidire; trasgredire.
dis-obligătion, S.: disobbligazione, *f.*; dispiacere, *m.*, offesa, *f.* **-oblige**, TR.: disobbligare, dispiacere; offendere. **-obliging**, ADJ.: scortese, incivile. **-obligingly**, ADV.: scortesemente, incivilmente. **-obligingness**, S.: scortesia, inciviltà, *f.*
disôrbed, ADJ.: fuor della propria orbita.
disôrder 1, S.: disordine, *m.*, irregolarità, *f.*; turbamento, *m.*, confusione; commozione; indisposizione, *f.*: *throw in —*, scampigliare, gettare in confusione. **disorder** 2, TR.: disordinare, mettere in disordine; perturbare, sconcertare. **-ed**, ADJ.: disordinato, scompigliato. **-edness**, S.: disordine, disordinazione, *f.* **-ly**, ADJ.: confuso, tumultuoso; ADV.: senza ordine, confusamente; viziosamente.
disôrdinate, ADJ.: disordinato, sregolato. **-ly**, ADV.: disordinatamente.
dis-organisătion, S.: disorganizzazione, *f.* **-ôrganise**, TR.: disorganizzare.
disōwn, TR.: non confessare, negare; rinunziare.
dispăce†, INTR.: spaziarsi.
dispăn-d†, TR.: spandere, dilatare. **-sion†**, S.: spandimento, *m.*, dilatazione, *f.*
dispărag-e, TR.: sprezzare; avvilire; far poco conto di, detrarre da. **-ement**, S.: sprezzamento, scherno, disonore, *m.* **-er**, S.: dispregiatore, *m.*
dis-parate, ADJ.: dissimile; separato. **-părity**, S.: disparità; disuguaglianza; differenza, *f.*
dispârk, TR.: rompere i palizzati d' un parco.
dispârt†, TR.: spartire; rompere.
dispăssion, S.: tranquillità di mente; insensibilità, *f.* **-ate**, ADJ.: spassionato, quieto.
dispătch = *despatch*.
dispĕl, TR.: espellere; scacciare.
dispĕn-d†, TR.: spendere. **-sable**, ADJ.: dispensabile. **-sary**, S.: fondaco di medicinali, *m.*; spezieria, *f.* **-sătion**, S.: dispensa, distribuzione, *f.* **dispen-sator**, S.: dispensatore, *m.* **-satory**, S.: ricettario, *m.*, farmacopea, *f.* **-se** 1, S.: dispensa; esenzione, *f.*; privilegio, *m.* **-se** 2, TR.: dispensare; distribuire; esentare:

— *with*, far senza, scusare, esentare; —*ing power*, diritto di grazia. **-er**, s.: dispensatore, distributore, *m*.

dispéopl-e, TR.: spopolare; distruggere, desolare. **-er**, s.: desolatore, *m*.

dispèrge, TR.: inaffiare, spruzzare.

dispèr-se, TR.: dispergere; sparpagliare. **-sedly**, ADV.: sparsamente. **-sedness**, s.: dispersione, *f*. **-ser**, s.: spargitore, *m*. **-sion**, s.: dispersione, *f*., dispergimento, *m*.

dispirit, TR.: scoraggiare, sgomentare. **-edness**, s.: avvilimento d'animo, *m*.

displâce, TR.: dislogare; rimuovere; disordinare; scavallare. **-ment**, s.: slogamento, rimovimiento, *m*.; quantità (d'acqua, ecc.) slogata.

displâcency†, s.: dispiacenza; incivilità, *f*.

displâcing, s.: rimovimento, *m*.

displánt, TR.: spiantare; sradicare. **-átion**, s.: spiantamento, sbarbicamento, *m*.

displáy 1, s.: esposizione, mostra, *f*., sviluppo, sviluppamento, *m*.; pompa, *f*.: *make — of one's eloquence*, far sfoggio della sua eloquenza. **display** 2, TR.: esporre; spiegare; far mostra.

dis-pléasant†, ADJ.: spiacevole; molesto, offensivo. **-pléase**, TR.: dispiacere; offendere: *that —s me*, ciò mi dispiace (*or* contraria); *I am —d at it*, me ne dispiace. **-pléased**, ADJ.: dispiaciuto. **-pléasedness**, **-pléasingness**, *f*., dispiacere, *m*. **-pléasure**, s.: dispiacere; disgusto; scontento, *m*.; noia, *f*.

displô-det, TR.: scoppiare; spaccarsi. **-sion**, s.: scoppiettata, *f*.

dispórt 1, s.: diporto; passatempo, *m*.; ricreazione, *f*. **disport** 2, TR.: divertire; ricreare; dar sollazzo; INTR.: diportarsi, divertirsi, ricrearsi.

dispó-sable, ADJ. ... disposizione, ba... your —, è a... TR.: disper... ... :; ...l- ...-s, —d ...aa. *ill-* *to be* ...legro. ...n, s.: ...ne; ta- ...tive†, prepara-

dispósuret, s.: disposizione, *f*.; maneggio, *m*.; volontà, *f*.

disprái-se 1, s.: biasimo, rimprovero, *m*. **-se** 2, TR.: biasimare; criticare, censurare. **-ser**, s.: biasimatore, critico, censore, *m*. **-singly**, ADV.: biasimevolmente.

dispréad, TR.: spandere, sparpagliare; INTR.: spandersi.

disprise, TR.: dispregiare.

disprófit† 1, s.: svantaggio, pregiudizio; detrimento, danno, *m*. **disprofit**† 2, INTR.: pregiudicare, nuocere.

dispróof, s.: confutazione, *f*.

dispropórtion 1, s.: disproporzione, inegualità; disparità, *f*. **disproportion** 2, TR.: sproporzionare. **-able**, ADJ.: sproporzionato. **-ableness**, s.: sproporzionalità, *f*. **-ably**, ADV.: sproporzionatamente. **-al**, **-ate**, ADJ.: sproporzionale, sproporzionato; ineguale; dissimile. **-ateness**, s.: disproporzione, *f*. **-ed** = *disproportional*.

disprôv-e, TR.: disapprovare, rimproverare, confutare; convincere. **-er**, s.: confutatore; contradditore, *m*.

dis-pútable, ADJ.: disputabile. **-putant**, ADJ.: disputante; s.: disputatore; controversista, *m*. **-putátion**, s.: disputazione; controversia, *f*.: *hold a —*, mantenere una disputa. **-putátious**, **-pútative**, ADJ.: disputativo, contenzioso. **-púte** 1, s.: disputa, contesa, controversia, *f*.: *beyond —*, senza contraddizione; *admit of —*, ammetter discussione; esser discutibile. **-pute** 2, (IN)TR.: disputare, dibattere; contrastare: *— about trifles*, disputare dell' ombra dell' asino. **-púteless**, ADJ.: incontestabile. **-púter**, s.: disputatore; controversista, *m*.

dis-qualificátion, s.: inettitudine, inabilità, *f*. **-quálify**, TR.: rendere inetto.

disquiet 1, s.: inquietudine, tribolazione, *f*.; travaglio, *m*. **disquiet** 2, TR.: inquietare, tribolare; travagliare. **-er**, s.: perturbatore, disturbatore; tormentatore, *m*. **-ly**, ADV.: inquietamente; senza riposo. **-ness**, **-ude**, s.: inquietudine, tribolazione, anzietà, *f*.

disquisition, s.: disquisizione, *f*.; esame, *m*.

disránk, TR.: degradare†; disordinare, metter in disordine.

disregárd 1, s.: trascuraggine, indifferenza; negligenza, *f*. **disregard** 2, TR.: trascurare; disprezzare; vilificare. **-ful**, ADJ.: trascurante, negligente; disprezzante. **-fully**, ADV.: dispregevolmente.

disrélish 1, s.: cattivo gusto, disgusto, *m*.

disrelish 2, TR.: disapprovare, non ap-

f. **-ấte**, S.: cattiva riputazione, *f.*, discredito, *m.*: *bring into* —, mettere in discredito.

disrespéct 1, S.: mancanza di rispetto, irriverenza, *f.*: *hold in* —, sprezzare, rispettare poco. **disrespect** 2, TR.: disprezzare; insultare. **-ful**, ADJ.: irriverente; incivile. **-fully**, ADV.: senza rispetto. **-fulness**, S.: mancanza di rispetto, *f.*

disrṓbe, TR.: svestire; spogliare.

disrŭp-t, TR.: dirompere. **-țion**, S.: dirompimento, *m.*, rottura; crepatura, *f.* **-ture** = *-tion.*

dis-satisfắcțion, S.: scontento, malcontento; disgusto, dispiacere, *m.* **-satisfắctory**, ADJ.: spiacevole; molesto. **-sắtisfied**, ADJ.: malcontento, scontento; disgustato. **-sắtisfy**, TR.: scontentare; dispiacere.

dissée-t, TR.: notomizzare. **-țion**, S.: dissezione; analisi; notomia, *f.* **-tor**, S.: dissettore; anatomista, notomista, *m.*

disséis-e, TR.: (*leg.*) dispossessare. **-in**, S.: (*leg.*) spogliamento de' beni, dispossessato, *m.*

dissém-blance, S.: dissomigliansa, *f.* **-ble**, TR.: dissimulare, simulare; fingere; palliare, coprire; INTR.: fare l' ipocrita. **-bler**, S.: dissimulatore; ipocrita, *m.* **-bling**, ADJ.: dissimulato, finto, artificioso; S.: dissimulazione, finzione, *f.* **-blingly**, ADV.: dissimulatamente, artificiosamente.

dissém-inate, TR.: disseminare; spargere; propagare. **-inắțion**, S.: disseminazione, *f.* **-inator**, S.: disseminatore; propagatore, *m.*

dissén-șion, S.: dissensione; discordia, *f.* **-șious**, ADJ.: litigioso, contenzioso. **-t** 1, S.: sentimento contrario, *m.*, opinione contraria, *f.* **-t** 2, INTR.: dissentire, differire; discordare. **-tắneous**, ADJ.: discordante, differente; contrario. **-ter**, S.: nonconformista; discordante, *m.* **-țient**, ADJ.: discordante.

dissertắțion, S.: dissertazione, *f.*; discorso, *m.*

dissér-ve, TR.: disservire, pregiudicare, nuocere. **-vice**, S.: disservigio; torto, danno, *m.* **-viceable**, ADJ.: pregiudiziale, nocevole. **-viceableness**, S.: pregiudizio, nocimento; danno, *m.*

dissḗttle†, TR.: disordinare, sregolare; scomporre.

dissḗver, TR.: sceverare; separare. **-ance**, S.: separazione, *f.*

dissiden-ce, S.: dissensione, discordia, *f.* **-t**, S.: dissidente, *m.*

dissim-ilar, ADJ.: dissimile; diverso. **-ilarity**, **-ilitude**, S.: dissomiglianza, differenza; disparità, *f.* **-ulate**, INTR.: dissimulare. **-lắțion**, S.: dissimulazione; finzione, *f.*

dissi-pable, ADJ.: dissipabile; consumabile. **-pate**, TR.: dissipare; distruggere; consumare; traviar (la mente). **-pated**, ADJ.: dissipato, distrutto; consumato; disattento. **-pắțion**, S.: dissipamento, *m.*, distruzione, *f.*

dissṓ-ciate, TR.: disunire, separare. **-ciắțion**, S.: disunione, *f.*

dis-soluble, ADJ.: dissolubile. **-solute**, ADJ.: dissoluto, scapestrato, licenzioso. **-solutely**, ADV.: dissolutamente. **-soluteness**, S.: dissolutezza; licenza, sfrenatezza, *f.* **-solûțion**, S.: dissoluzione; liquefazione; licenza, *f.* **-sŏlvable**, ADJ.: dissolubile. **-sŏlve**, TR.: dissolvere, fondere; disfare, disunire; INTR.: disciogliersi; dissiparsi, separarsi. **-sŏlvent**, ADJ.: dissolvente; dissolutivo. **-sŏlver**, S.: dissolvente, dissolutivo, *m.*

dissonan-ce, S.: dissonanza, discordanza, *f.* **-t**, ADJ.: dissonante; dissimile, differente.

dissuấ-de, TR.: dissuadere; sconsigliare. **-der**, S.: che dissuade. **-șion**, S.: dissuasione, *f.* **-sive**, ADJ.: dissuasivo, dissuadente; S.: argomento dissuasorio, *m.*

dis-syllắbic, ADJ.: disillabo. **-syllable**, S.: disillabo, *m.*

distaff, S.: conocchia, rocca, *f.*

distấin, TR.: macchiare; lordare.

dis-tance 1, S.: distanza, *f.*, intervallo; decoro; rispetto, *m.*: *at a* (*in the*) —, in lontananza; *at a great* —, in gran distanza; *out of* —, a perdita di vista; *keep one's* —, portar rispetto; *keep one at a* —, guardar il suo decoro. **-tance** 2, TR.: discostare; lasciare indietro. **-tant**, ADJ.: distante, discosto: *be* —, distare; *six miles* —, distante sei miglia.

distấste 1, S.: disgusto; dispiacere; tedio, *m.*: *take a* — *for*, aver a fastidio, fastidire. **distaste** 2, TR.: dispiacere; fastidire; avere in fastidio. **-ful**, ADJ.: fastidioso, tedioso; ingrato; offensivo. **-fulness**, S.: disgusto, *m.*, avversione, *f.*

distémper 1, S.: malattia, *f.*, morbo; disordine, imbroglio, *m.* **distemper** 2, TR.: disordinare; disturbare. **-ate**, ADJ.: immoderato, eccessivo. **-ature**, S.: intemperatura; indisposizione, *f.* **-ed**, ADJ.: indisposto, ammalato.

distĕn-d, TR.: stendere; allargare. **-șion**, S.: distendimento, *m.*, estensione, *f.* **-t**, S.: distesa; estensione; ampiezza, *f.*

distich, S.: distico, *m.*

distil, TR.: stillare, distillare, gocciolare. **-lable**, ADJ.: che si può distillare. **-lắțion**, S.: distillazione, *f.* **-latory**, ADJ.: distillatorio. **-ler**, S.: distillatore, *m.* **-ling**, ADJ.: distillante; S.: distillamento, *m.*, distillazione, *f.*

distinc-t, ADJ.: distinto, chiaro; separato; dissimile, differente. **-tion**, S.: distinzione; differenza, diversità, *f.*: *make a — between*, fare una distinzione (differenza) fra; *persons of —*, persone distinte, nomini insigni; donne di condizione. **-tive**, ADJ.: distintivo. **-tively**, ADV.: in modo distintivo, per distinzione. **-ly**, ADV.: distintamente; chiaramente. **-ness**, S.: chiarezza, lucidezza, *f.*
distinguish, TR.: distinguere; separare; notare: *— one's self*, distinguersi, segnalarsi. **-able**, ADJ.: che si può distinguere. **-ableness**, S.: differenza, *f.* **-ed**, ADJ.: distinto, eminente, insigne; elegante. **-er**, S.: distinguitore, osservatore giudizioso, *m.* **-ingly**, ADV.: con distinzione, onorevolmente. **-ment**, S.: distinzione; osservazione, *f.*; giudizio, *m.*
distòr-t, TR.: contorcere; rivolgere; stralunare. **-tion**, S.: contorsione, *f.*, storcimento, *m.*
distràc-t, IRR.; TR.: distrarre; separare; impazzire; molestare: *— the mind from*, svagare la mente da. **-ted**, ADJ.: distratto, diviso; forsennato, pazzo: *run —*, smaniare, infuriare; *drive one —*, far impazzire uno; *become —*, distrarsi, svagarsi, smanire, impazzire. **-tedly**, ADV.: forsennatamente. **-tedness**, S.: smania, *f.* **-tion**, S.: distrazione; angoscia, *f.*
distràin, TR.: staggire; sequestrare, confiscare. **-er**, S.: staggitore, *m.* **-t**, S.: staggimento, sequestramento, sequestro, *m.*
distràught = *distracted*.
distrèss 1, S.: staggina; calamità, miseria, estremità, *f.*: *pecuniary —*, scarsezza del numerario, angustia; *— of mind*, affanno, afflizione. **distress** 2, TR.: staggire; angustiare, tribolare, vessare. **-ed**, ADJ.: misero, affannato, tribolato; bisognoso. **-edness**, S.: calamità, miseria, *f.* **-ful**, ADJ.: affannoso, misero. **-fully**, ADV.: miseramente.
distrib-ute, TR.: distribuire, dividere: *distributing regulator*, timone, regolatore, *m.* **-utor**, S.: distributore, *m.* **-ùtion**, S.: distribuzione, *f.* **-utive**, ADJ.: distributivo. **-utively**, ADV.: distributivamente.
district, S.: distretto, *m.*; regione; giurisdizione, *f.*
distrùst 1, S.: sfidanza, *f.*; sospetto, *m.* **distrust** 2, TR.: diffidare di; non fidarsi di, sospettare: *they — me*, diffidano di mi. **-ful**, ADJ.: diffidente; sospettoso. **-fully**, ADV.: sospettosamente. **-fulness**, S.: diffidenza, *f.*; sospetto, *m.* **-less**, ADJ.: senza diffidenza.
distùrb, TR.: disturbare; inquietare; impedire, molestare; dispiacere: *I am sorry to — you*, mi rincresce d' incomodarvi. **-ance**, S.: disturbanza; confusione; alterazione, *f.*; tumulto, *m.*: *make a —*, produrre disordine (scompiglio). **-er**, S.: perturbatore, sturbatore, *m.*
distùrn†, TR.: mandar via, scacciare.
disù-nion, S.: disunione; dissensione; controversia, *f.* **-nite**, TR.: disunire, disgiungere; separare; INTR.: disunirsi, disgiungersi; separarsi. **-nity**, S.: disunione, separazione, *m.*
disùse 1, S.: disuso, *m.*; disusanza, *f.*: *fall into —*, cadere in disuetudine. **disùse** 2, INTR.: disusarsi, lasciar l' uso.
dis-valuàtion, S.: dispregiamento, dispregio; disonore, *m.* **-vàlue**, TR.: disprezzare, avvilire.
disvèlop†, TR.: sviluppare, scoprire.
disvòuch†, TR.: discreditare; contraddire, opporsi.
diswònt†, TR.: disavvezzare.
ditch 1, S.: fosso, *m.*, fossa, *f.* **ditch** 2, TR.: fare un fosso, affossare. **-er**, S.: che affossa; zappatore, *m.*
dithyràmbic, ADJ.: ditirambico; S.: ditirambo, *m.*
dittany, S.: dittamo, *m.*
dittied, ADJ.: accoppiato con musica.
ditto, S.: medesimo, sopradetto, *m.*
ditty, S.: canzone, *f.*
diurètic, ADJ.: (*med.*) diuretico, aperitivo.
diùrnal, ADJ.: diurno, giornale; S.: giornale, *m.* **-ly**, ADV.: ogni giorno, giornalmente.
diutùrnity, S.: diuturnità, *f.*
divàn, S.: divano, *m.*
divàri-cate, TR.: dividere in due; INTR.: dividersi in due parti. **-càtion**, S.: divisione in due parti, *f.*
div-e, TR.: tuffare, immergere; esplorare; INTR.: tuffarsi; penetrare. **-er**, S.: tuffatore; investigatore; marangone, palombaro, *m.*
divèr-ge, INTR.: divergere; essere divergente. **-gence**, **-gency**, S.: divergenza, *f.* **-gent**, ADJ.: divergente.
di-vers, ADJ.: diverso; diversi; parecchi. **-verse**, ADJ.: diverso, differente, vario; ADV.: diversamente. **-vèrsely**, ADV.: diversamente, differentemente, variamente. **-versification**, S.: diversificazione; varietà, *f.* **-vèrsify**, TR.: diversificare; differenziare, variare. **-vèrsion**, S.: diversione, *f.*; passatempo, *m.*, ricreazione, *f.* **-vèrsity**, S.: diversità, differenza, *f.*
divèrt, TR.: divertire, distornare; stornare, distrarre; INTR.: far diversione. **-er**, S.: alleggerimento, *m.* **-ing**, ADJ.: sollazzevole; ricreativo; grato. **-ingness**, S.: divertimento, trattenimento, *m.* **-ise**†, TR.: ricreare, sollazzare, r

detrūde, TR.: cacciare in giù.

detrŭn-cate, TR.: scappezzare, mozzare, troncare. **-cātion**, S.: mozzamento, *m.*

detrūsion, S.: atterramento, *m.*

deūce, S.: due, *m.* (al giuoco di carte).

deūce, S.: diavolo, *m.*

deuter-ŏgamy, S.: matrimonio secondo, *m.* **-ŏnomy**, S.: deuteronomio, *m.*

dĕvas-tate, TR.: devastare, desolare. **-tātion**, S.: devastazione, *f.*, desolamento, *m.*

devĕlop, INTR.: sviluppare. **-ment**, S.: sviluppamento, *m.*

devĕrgence†, S.: divergenza.

devĕst, TR.: privare, spogliare.

devĕxity†, S.: declività, *f.*

dēvi-ate, INTR.: deviare, sviarsi. **-ātion**, S.: deviamento, *m.*

devīce, S.: invenzione; spediente, mezzo, *m.*; divisa, emblema, *f.*

dĕvil, S.: diavolo, demonio, *m.*: *great* —, diavolone, *m.*; *little* —, diavoletto, *m.*; *give the — his due*, non fate il diavolo più nero che non è; *a — of a fellow*, un vero demonio. **-ish**, ADJ.: diabolico. **-ishly**, ADV.: diabolicamente. **-ishness**, S.: natura diabolica, *f.* **-kin**, S.: diavoletto, *m.*

dēvious, ADJ.: deviato, errante.

devī-se[1], S.: legato; lascito; espediente; disegno, *m.* **-se**[2], TR.: immaginare; formare; INTR.: consultare, legare, lasciare. **-sēe**, S.: legatario, *m.* **-ser**, S.: inventore, autore, *m.* **-sor**, S.: (*leg.*) testatore, *m.*

dēvi-table†, ADJ.: evitabile. **-tātion**†, S.: evitazione, *f.*

devŏid, ADJ.: vuoto, vacuo; destituto.

devoir *-vwŏr*, S.: dovere; ossequio, *m.*

de-volūtion, S.: devoluzione, *f.*; rivolgimento, scadimento, *m.* **-vŏlve**, TR.: devolvere; ricadere, scadere. **-vŏlved**, ADJ.: devoluto; ricaduto.

devorātion†, S.: divoramento, *m.*

devō-te, TR.: votare, dedicare; dare; consegnare: — *one's self to*, dedicarsi a, darsi a. **-ted**, ADJ.: dedito, dedicato. **-tedness**, S.: divozione, *f.* **-tēe**, S.: bacchettone, ipocrita, *m.* **-tion**, S.: divozione; disposizione, *f.* **-tional**, ADJ.: pio, divoto. **-tionalist**, S.: zelatore; ipocrita, *m.*

devŏur, TR.: divorare; inghiottire: — *with one's eyes*, cacciare (*or* ficcare) gli occhi addosso a. **-er**, S.: divoratore, *m.* **-ingly**, ADV.: ingordamente, avidamente, golosamente.

devŏut, ADJ.: divoto, religioso, pio. **-ly**, ADV.: divotamente. **-ness**, S.: divozione; pietà, *f.*

dew[1], S.: rugiada, *f.* **dew**[2], TR.: innaffiare; aspergere. **-berry**, S.: moro di rovo, *m.* **-besprent**, ADJ.: asperso di rugiada. **-drop**, S.: goccia di rugiada, *f.* **-lap**, S.: giogaia, pagliolaia, *f.* **-lapt**, ADJ.: fornito di giogaia. **-worm**, S.: verme di rugiada, *m.* **-y**, ADJ.: rugiadoso.

dĕx-ter, ADJ.: destro, a man destra. **-tĕrity**, S.: destrezza; abilità, *f.* **-terous**, ADJ.: destro, accorto. **-terously**, ADV.: destramente, accortamente. **-terousness** = *dexterity*. **-tral**, ADJ.: dritto, diritto. **-trous** = *dexterous*.

diabētes, S.: (*med.*) diabete, *f.*

diabŏlic(al), ADJ.: diabolico, infernale. **-ally**, ADV.: diabolicamente. **-alness**, S.: diavoleria, *f.*

diadem, S.: diadema, *m.*; corona, *f.* **-ed**, ADJ.: cinto d' un diadema.

diærĕsis, S.: dieresi, *f.*

diagnŏstic, S.: indizio, sintomo, *m.*

diăgonal, ADJ.: diagonale; S.: diagonale, *f.* **-ly**, ADV.: diagonalmente.

diagram, S.: diagramma, *m.*; descrizione, *f.*

dial, S.: oriuolo a sole, *m.*; mostra d' orologio, *f.*

dia-lect, S.: dialetto; stilo, *m.* **-lĕctic**, S.: dialettica, logica, *f.* **-lĕctical**, ADJ.: dialettico, logicale. **-lĕctically**, ADV.: in maniera dialettica.

dial-ing, S.: gnomonica, *f.* **-ist**, S.: fabbricatore d' orologi solari, *m.*

di-alŏgical, ADJ.: dialogico. **-ălogist**, S.: dialogista, *m.* **-alogistically**, ADV.: in modo dialogico. **-ălogise**, TR.: dialogizzare. **di-alogue**[1], S.: dialogo, *m.* **-alogue**[2], INTR.: dialogizzare; discorrere.

dial-plate, S.: mostra d' orologio, *f.*

diălysis, S.: (*gram.*) sillaba divisa in due, *f.*

diăm-eter, S.: diametro, *m.* **-etral**, **-ĕtrical**, ADJ.: diametrale. **-ĕtrically**, ADV.: per diametro.

diamond, S.: diamante, *m.* **-cutter**, S.: gioielliere, *m.*

diapāson, S.: (*mus.*) ottava, *f.*

diaper[1], S.: biancheria tessuta a figura, *f.* **diaper**[2], TR.: damascare.

di-aphanĕity, S.: diafanità, trasparenza, *f.* **-aphănic**, **-ăphanous**, ADJ.: diafano.

diaphorĕtic, ADJ.: (*med.*) diaforetico, sudorifico.

diaphragm, S.: (*anat.*) diaframma, *m.*

diar-rhœa, **-rhea**, S.: diarrea, *f.* **-rhœtic**, **-rhetic**, ADJ.: purgativo.

diary, S.: diario, giornale, *m.*

diăstole, S.: (*anat.*) diastole, *f.*

diatessaron, S.: (*mus.*) diatessaron, *m.*

diatŏnic, ADJ.: (*mus.*) diatonico.

dibble, S.: piuolo da piantare, *m.*

dibstone, s.: sassolino, *m*.
dicacity†, s.: ciarleria, *f*.
dic-e 1, s. pl.: dadi, *m. pl.*: *cog the* —, mettere dadi falsi; *set the — upon*, truffare, ingannare. **-e** 2, intr.: giuocare a' dadi. **-e-box**, s.: bossolo, *m*. **-er**, **-e-player**, s.: giuocatore di dadi, *m*.
dichŏt-omize, tr.: spartire in due. **-omy**, s.: dicotomia, *f*.
dicing, s.: giuoco di dadi, *m*.
dicker, s.: diecina di cuoia, *f*.
dic-tate 1, s.: regola, *f.*; precetto, *m*. **-tate** 2, tr.: dettare; prescrivere. **-tā-tion**, s.: dettatura, *f*. **-tātor**, s.: dittatore, *m*. **-tatŏrial**, adj.: dittatorio, autorevole, assoluto. **-tātorship**, **-tature**, s.: dittatura, *f*.
diction, s.: dizione, *f.*; stile, *m*. **-ary**, s.: dizionario, vocabolario, *m*.
did, impf. del v. *do*.
didăctic(al), adj.: istruttivo.
didapper, s.: mergo, *m*.
diddle, intr.: vacillare.
die 1 (pl. *dice*), s.: dado, *m*. **die** 2 (pl. *dies*), s.: conio, *m.*; tintura; tinta, *f*., colore, *m*. **die** 3, intr.: morire; sventare, svaporare: — *a natural death*, morire di morte naturale; *he was near dying*, egli fu per morire; — *off* (*away*), cessar a poco, spegnersi.
di-et†, **-er**† = *dy-e*, *-er*.
diesis, s.: (*mus.*) diesi, *f*.
diet 1, s.: nutrimento, *m.*; dieta; assemblea, *f.*; *put upon* —, tenere alla dieta. **diet** 2, tr.: dietare; nutrire; intr.: nutrirsi, fare dieta, mangiare. **-drink**, s.: tisana, *f*. **dietic(al)**, adj.: dietetico.
differ, intr.: differire, esser dissimile, variare. **-ence** 1, s.: differenza: disparità; diversità; disputa, dissenzione, *f.*: *that makes no* —, ciò non fa niente. **-ence** 2, tr.: differenziare; distinguere. **-ent**, adj.: differente; dissimile. **-ĕntial**, s.: (*alg.*) differenziale. **-ently**, adv.: differentemente; variamente. **-ing**, adj.: differente.
diffi-cile, adj.: difficile; malagevole; scrupoloso. **-cileness**, s.: difficoltà, *f*. **-cult**, adj.: difficile; faticoso. **-cultly**, adv.: difficilmente, con difficoltà. **-culty**, s.: difficoltà, perplessità, *f*., dubbio; ostacolo, *m.*; *serious* —, difficoltà grave; *be in* —, essere in angustia, patir disagio: *labor under a* —, lottare contro una difficoltà; *with great* —, a mala pena.
diffiden-ce, s.: diffidenza, *f*., sospetto, *m*. **-t**, adj.: diffidente, sospettoso. **-tly**, adv.: con diffidenza, sospettosamente.
diffluen-ce, **-cy**, s.: fluidità, fluidezza, *f*. **-t**, adj.: fluido, diffuso.
dif-form, adj.: difforme; irregolare. **-fŏrmity**, s.: difformità; irregolarità, *f*.
diffū-se 1, tr.: diffundere; spargere: — *knowledge*, diffondere le cognizioni, spargere l'istruzione. **-se** 2, **-sed**, adj.: diffuso, sparso, prolisso. **-sedly**, adv.: diffusamente; copiosamente. **-sedness**, **-sion**, s.: diffusione; spargimento, *m.*; copiosità, *f*. **-sive**, adj.: diffusivo, prolisso. **-sively**, adv.: diffusamente. **-siveness**, s.: distesa, estensione; prolissità, *f*.
dig, irr.; tr.: zappare, vangare; scavare: — *deep*, affondare; — *out*, sterrare, cavare della terra.
digerent, adj.: (*med.*) digerente, digestivo.
digĕs-t 1, tr.: digerire; smaltire, far la digestione di; fare un digesto; disporre. intr.: suppurare, venire a suppurazione. **diges-t** 2, s.: digesto, *m*., pandette, *f. pl.* **-ter**, s.: digestore; digestivo, *m*. **-tible**, adj.: digestibile. **-tion**, s.: digestione, *f.*; suppuramento, *m*. **-tive**, adj.: digestivo, suppurativo; s.: rimedio digestivo, *m*.
digger, s.: zappatore, vangatore, *m*.
dight, tr.: ornare; addobbare.
digit, s.: dito, digito, *m*. (misura). **-ated**, adj.: (*bot.*) digitato.
digladiātion†, s.: azzuffamento, *m*.
dignificātion, s.: esaltamento, *m*.
digni-fied, adj.: investito di dignità; dignitoso; elevato, esaltato: *a — bearing*, un far dignitoso. **-fy**, tr.: elevare; esaltare. **-tary**, s.: prelato, *m*. **-ty**, s.: dignità, *f.*; grado d'onore, *m.*; importanza, *f.*: *air of* —, aria autorevole (nobile), portamento distinto; *rise to* —, innalzarsi, distinguersi.
di-grĕss, intr.: fare digressione. **-grĕssion**, s.: digressione, *f*., sviamento, *m*.
dijūdi-cate†, tr.: giudicare, decidere; distinguere. **-cātion**†, s.: distinzione giuridica, *f*.
dike, s.: fosso; canale; vallo, *m*.
dilăcer-ate, tr.: dilacerare, stracciare. **-ātion**, s.: lacerazione, *f*., stracciamento, *m*.
dilăni-ate, tr.: dilaniare; sbranare. **-ātion**, s.: sbranamento, *m*.
dilăpi-date, tr.: dilapidare. **-dātion**, s.: dilapidamento, *m.*; rovina, *f*.
di-latability, s.: dilatabilità; estensione, *f*. **-lātable**, adj.: dilatabile. **-latātion**, s.: dilatazione, *f*. **-lāte**, tr.: dilatare; stendere; intr.: dilatarsi, distendersi; diffondersi. **-lātor**, s.: (*surg.*) dilatatore, *m*. **di-latoriness**, s.: lentezza; infingardia, *f*. **di-latory**, adj.: dilatorio, tardo: *be* —, procrastinare in lungo.
dilĕction†, s.: dilezione, *f*.
dilĕmma, s.: dilemma, *f*.,

dilig-en-ce, s.: diligenza, assiduità, sedulità, cura, prontezza; diligenza, vettura, *f.* **-t**, ADJ.: diligente; assiduo. **-tly**, ADV.: diligentemente.
dill, s.: aneto, *m.*
dilū-cid†, ADJ.: lucido, chiaro. **-cidate**†, TR.: dilucidare, far chiaro, spiegare. **-cidātion**†, s.: dilucidazione, spiegazione, *f.*
di-luent, ADJ.: diluente, dissolvente, *m.*; s.: diluente, *m.* **-lūte**, TR.: stemperare; mescolare. **-lūter**, s.: dissolvente, *m.* **-lūtion**, s.: stemperamento, *m.*
dilūvian, ADJ.: diluviano.
dim 1, ADJ.: oscuro, fosco, annebbiato; chiaroscuro, stupido. **dim** 2, TR.: oscurare; offuscare.
dimĕnsion, s.: dimensione, estensione, *f.* **-less**, s.: infinito; immenso.
dimin-ish, TR.: diminuire; INTR.: diminuirsi; decrescere. **-ishing**, s.: diminuimento, *m.* **-ishingly**, ADV.: diminutivamente; in modo vilipeso. **-ūtion**, s.: diminuzione, *f.*; discredito, *m.* **-utive**, ADJ.: diminutivo, piccolo; s.: diminutivo, *m.* **-utively**, ADV.: in modo diminutivo. **-utiveness**, s.: piccolezza, *f.*
dimish, ADJ.: alquanto oscuro.
di-mission†, s.: congedo, *m.* **-missory**, ADJ.: dimissoriale.
dimity, s.: dimito, *m.*
dim-ly, ADV.: oscuramente. **-ness**, s.: oscuramento, *m.*; stupidità, *f.*
dimpl-e 1, s.: pozzetta, piccola fossetta, *f.* **-e** 2, INTR.: formare delle pozzette. **-ed**, ADJ.: adornato di pozzette. **-y**, ADJ.: pieno di pozzette.
dim-sighted, ADJ.: che ha la vista offuscata.
din 1, s.: strepito, fracasso, *m.* **din** 2, TR.: stordire; schiamazzare.
dine, TR.: invitare a desinare; INTR.: desinare; pranzare: *come and — with me*, venite a pranzo con me; *— out*, pranzare fuori di casa; *have you —d?* avete desinato?
ding†, TR.: sbattere, spezzare; infrangere; INTR.: schiamazzare, vantarsi; tintinnire. **-dong**, s.: tintinnio delle campane, *m.*
dingle, s.: valle; valletta, *f.*
dingy, ADJ.: oscuro; bruno.
dining-room, s.: sala da mangiare, *f.*
dinner, s.: desinare; pranzo, *m.*: *poor —*, tristo desinare; *sumptuous —*, pranzo lautissimo; *ask to —*, convitare. **-bell**, s.: campana (dell' ora) del pranzo. **-party**, s.. pranzo con inviti, convito, *m.*: *dull —*, desinare tristo. **-time**, s.: ora di pranzo, *f.*
dint 1, s.: impressione, *f.*, vestigio; segno; colpo; forza, *f.* **dint** 2, TR.: fare una bozza su.
diō-cesan, s.: diocesano, *m.* **dio-cese**, s.: diocesi, *f.*
diŏptric, **-al**, ADJ.: diottrica. **-s**, S. PL.: diottrica, *f.*
diorâma, s.: diorama, *m.*
dip, IRR.; TR.: intingere, immollare; INTR.: immergersi; penetrare.
dipĕtalous, ADJ.: bipetale, di due corolle.
diphthong, s.: dittongo, *m.*
diplō-ma, s.: diploma, *m.*, lettera patente, *f.* **-macy**, s.: diplomazia, *f.* **-mătic**, ADJ.: diplomatico. **-mătics**, S. PL.: arte diplomatica, *f.*
dip-per, s.: che immerge nell' acqua; mestola, *f.* **-ping**, s.: immersione, *f.* **-ping-needle**, s.: ago calamitato, *m.*
dire, ADJ.: diro, orrendo.
dirĕc-t 1, ADJ.: retto, diretto; chiaro. **-t** 2, TR.: dirigere; indirizzare; regolare, ordinare: *— a letter to*, indirizzare (*or* mandare) una lettera a. **-ter**, s.: direttore, *m.*; squadra, *f.* **-tion**, s.: direzione; soprascritta, *f.*, indirizzo, *m.*, incombenza, *f.*; ordine, *m.*: *go in the — of*, andare alla volta di; *write the — on a letter*, scrivere l'indirizzo sopra una lettera. **-tive**, ADJ.: directivo. **-tly**, ADV.: direttamente; immediate: *— against*, dirimpetto. **-tness**, s.: dirittura; rettitudine, *f.* **-tor**, s.: direttore, *m.* **-tory**, s.: direttorio, *m.* **-tress**, s.: direttrice, *f.*
dire-ful, ADJ.: diro, terribile. **-fulness**, **-ness**, s.: orrore, terrore, *m.*; enormità, *f.*
dirĕption, s.: rapina, *f.*; sacco, *m.*
dirge, s.: canzone funebre, *f.*
dirk 1, s.: pugnale, *m.*, daga, *f.* **dirk** 2, TR.: stilettare.
dirt 1, s.: fango; loto, *m.*; immondizia; bassezza, *f.* **dirt** 2, TR.: sporcare; infangare. **-ily**, ADV.: sporcamente, sordidamente; vilmente. **-iness**, s.: sporcheria; bassezza, *f.* **-y** 1, ADJ.: sporco, sucido, fangoso, sordido; vile, infame. **-y** 2, TR.: sporcare; lordare; disonorare: *— trick*, brutto scherzo; *— fellow*, sudicione, sciattone, *m.*
dirŭption, s.: dirupamento, *m.*
dis-ability, s.: incapacità, inabilità; impotenza, *f.* **-āble**, TR.: rendere incapace; (*mar.*) mettere fuor di servizio, disarmare. **-āblement**, s.: inabilità; impotenza, *f.*
disabūse, TR.: disingannare, sgannare.
disaccŏmmo-date, TR.: incomodare. **-dātion**, s.: incomodezza, incomodità, *f.*
disaccŭstom, TR.: disusare, divezzare.
disacknŏwledge, TR.: negare; disapprovare.
disadvân-tage 1, s.: disavvantaggio, pregiudizio, danno, *m.* **-tage** 2, TR.: di-

savvantaggiare, pregiudicare; nuocere. **-tágeous**, ADJ.: svantaggioso. **-tágeously**, ADJ.: con isvantaggio. **-tágeousness**, S.: svantaggio, *m.*

disadvén-ture, S.: disavventura, disgrazia, *f.* **-turous**, ADJ.: sfortunato.

disafféc-t, TR.: alienare; scontentare; odiare. **-ted**, ADJ.: disaffezionato, malcontento. **-tedly**, ADV.: in modo scontentato. **-tedness**, S.: scontentezza, *f.* **-tion**, S.: malevolenza, *f.* **-tionáte**, ADJ.: disaffezionato, malcontento.

disaffírm, TR.: contraddire, negare. **-ance**, S.: contraddizione, *f.*

disagrée, INTR.: discrepare, differire; discordare: — *with*, far male a; incommodare. **-able**, ADJ.: sgradevole, spiacevole, contrario, disdicevole, discaro. **-ableness**, S.: contrarietà, spiacevolezza, *f.*; disgusto, *m.* **-ably**, ADV.: spiacevolmente. **-ment**, S.: differenza; discordanza, *f.*

disallów, TR.: disapprovare; biasimare; INTR.: non permettere; rifiutare. **-able**, ADJ.: inammissibile. **-ance**, S.: proibizione, *f.*; divieto, *m.*

disánchor, TR.: salpare l' ancora.

disáni-mate, TR.: disanimare; scoraggiare. **-mátion**, S.: privazione di vita, *f.*

disannúl, TR.: annullare; cassare. **-ment**, S.: annullamento, *m.*

disappéar, TR.: sparire, svanire. **-ance**, S.: svanimento, *m.*

disappóint 1, TR.: deludere l' aspettativa di; mancar di parola, frustrare, deludere, sconcertare: — *one's friends*, mancare agli amici. **-ment**, S.: delusione, speranza delusa, *f.*; mancamento di parola, *m.*; traversia, *f.*

disap-probátion, S.: censura, *f.*; biasimo, *m.*, riprovazione, *f.* **-próve**, TR.: disapprovare, censurare.

disárm, TR.: disarmare. **-ing**, S.: disarmamento, *m.*

disarránge, TR.: disordinare. **-ment**, S.: disordinanza, *f.*

disarráy 1, S.: disordine, *m.*; confusione, *f.* **disarray** 2, TR.: divestire; spogliare.

disás-ter 1, S.: disastro; infortunio, *m.* **-ter** 2, TR.: affliggere. **-trous**, ADJ.: disastroso, calamitoso, funesto. **-trously**, ADV.: sventuratamente, funestamente. **-trousness**, S.: infortunio, *m.*

disáuthorize, TR.: privare d' autorità.

disavóuch, TR.: disapprovare, negare.

disavów, TR.: negare; disdire. **-al**, S.: disapprovazione, *f.*, negamento, *m.*

disbánd, TR.: sbandare; congediare; INTR.: sbandarsi; disperdersi.

disbárk, TR.: sbarcare.

disbelíé-f, S.: incredulità, *f.* **-ve**, TR.: scredere; miscredere; diffidare; dubitare. **-ver**, S.: scredente, incredulo; miscredente, *m.*

disbówel, TR.: sviscerare.

disbránch, TR.: diramare; spiccare.

disbúd, TR.: spampanare.

disbúrden, TR.: scaricare; agravare.

disbúr-se, TR.: sborsare; spendere. **-sement**, S.: sborsamento; pagamento, *m.* **-ser**, S.: che sborsa, pagatore, *m.*

discál-ceated†, ADJ.: scalzo, scalzato. **-ceátion**†, S.: scalzamento, *m.*

discándy†, TR.: dissolvere, liquefare.

discárd, TR.: scartare; licenziare. **-ure**†, S.: scartamento; congedo, *m.*

discáse, TR.: svestire, spogliare.

disceptátion†, S.: disputa, contesa, *f.*

discérn, TR.: discernere; differenziare; distinguere. **-er**, S.: discernitore, *m.* **-ible**, ADJ.: discernevole, percettibile; apparente. **-ibleness**, S.: visibilità, apparenza; percezione, *f.* **-ibly**, ADV.: visibilmente. **-ing**, ADJ.: giudizioso; perspicace; S.: discernimento, *m.* **-ingly**, ADV.: giudiziosamente. **-ment**, S.: discernimento; giudizio, *m.*

discérp, TR.: lacerare, dilaniare. **-tibility**, S.: frangibilità, *f.* **-tible**, ADJ.: frangibile; separabile. **-tion**, S.: laceramento, strazzio, *m.*

dischárg-e 1, S.: scaricamento, scarico; sparo, *m.*; liberazione; licenza, libertà; quittanza, ricevuta; discolpa; assoluzione, *f.*; sbocco, *m.*, uscita, *f.* **-e** 2, TR.: scaricare; liberare, licenziare; sprigionare; assolvere; adempire; INTR.: scaricarsi; dissiparsi: — *one's duty*, fare il suo debito; — *one's promise*, tener la promessa; — *a business*, spedire un affare; — *one's debts*, pagare i suoi debiti; — *a soldier*, cassare un soldato; — *an officer*, dimettere un ufficiale; — *a prisoner*, liberare un prigioniero. **-er**, S.: che libera, che scarica.

discínd†, TR.: discindere, tagliare; spiccare.

discíple 1, S.: discepolo, scolare, *m.* **disciple** 2, TR.: istruire; dar disciplina. **-ship**, S.: discepolato, *m.*

disciplin-able, ADJ.: disciplinabile; docile. **-ableness**, S.: docilità, *f.* **-árian**, ADJ.: di disciplina; S.: presbiteriano, puritano, *m.* **-ary**, ADJ.: disciplinale, di disciplina. **discipli-ne** 1, S.: disciplina, *f.*; insegnamento, *m.*; educazione; sommissione, *f.* **-e** 2, TR.: disciplinare; insegnare; regolare. **-ed**, ADJ.: disciplinato.

disclaím, TR.: rifiutare, negare; rinunziare. **-er**, S.: rifiutatore, *m.* **-ing**, S.: rinunziamento, *m.*; negazione, *f.*

disclóse, TR.: scoprire, palesare: — *secret*, palesare un secreto. **-ser**, scopritore, palesatore, *m.* **-ṣure**, S.: scoperta, *f.;* rivelamento, *m.*

dis-cọlorā̤tiọn, S.: discolorazione, *f.*, scoloramento, *m.* **-còlọur**, TR.: discolorare; INTR.: perder il colore.

discòm-fit 1, TR.: disfare; sconfiggere; vincere. **-fit** 2, **-fiture**, S.: sconfitta; strage, *f.*

discòmfọrt 1, S.: sconforto, *m.;* afflizione, *f.* **discomfort** 2, TR.: sconfortare; affliggere. **-able**, ADJ.: sconfortante; affiittivo.

discommĕnd, TR.: biasimare, censurare, condannare. **-able**, ADJ.: biasimevole. **-ableness**, S.: biasimo, *m.* **-ā̤tiọn**, S.: biasimo, *m.;* censura; vergogna, *f.* **-ẹr**, S.: biasimatore; censore, *m.*

discom-mōde, TR.: incomodare, importunare, disagiare. **-mōdious**, ADJ.: incomodo, molesto. **-mŏdity**, S.: incomodità, *f.;* disagio, *m.*

discompō-ṣe, TR.: scomporre; sconcertare, disordinare, disturbare, confondere. **-ṣedness**, S.: disordine, confusione, *f.* **-ṣure**, S.: disordine, perturbamento; travaglio, *m.*

disconcĕrt, TR.: sconcertare, disordinare; confondere.

discon-fôrmity, **-grŭity**, S.: disconvenienza, incongruità, *f.*

discon-nĕct, TR.: disunire. **-nĕxiọn**, S.: disunione, *f.*

discŏnsọlate, ADJ.: sconsolato, inconsolabile. **-ly**, ADV.: sconsolatamente. **-ness**, S.: sconsolamento, *m.*, sconsolazione, *f.*, dolore, *m.*

discontĕnt 1, ADJ.: scontento, mal contento, dispiaciuto; S.: scontento; *m.;* scontentezza, *f.* **discontent** 2, TR.: scontentare. **-ed**, ADJ.: scontento, dispiaciuto. **-edly**, ADV.: con iscontento, noiosamente. **-edness**, **-ment**, S.: scontentamento, scontento, *m.*

discontin-ụance, **-ụā̤tiọn**, S.: discontinuazione, intermissione, interruzione; cessazione, *f.* **-ụe**, TR.: discontinuare, interrompere; cessare. **-ŭity**, S.: disunione, *f.* **-ụous**, ADJ.: esteso, aperto.

disconvēnien-ce, S.: disconvenienza, *f.* **-t**, ADJ.: disconveniente.

discôrd 1, INTR.: discordare; disconvenire. **discọrd** 2, S.: discordia; dissonanza, *f.: apple of* —, pomo di discordia. **-ance**, **-ancy**, S.: discordanza; discordia, dissensione. **-ant**, ADJ.: discordante. **-antly**, ADV.: con discordanza.

discŏụnsel, TR.: sconsigliare, dissuadere.

dĭ'scŏụnt 1, S.: sconto, *m.;* sottrazione, *f.: at a* —, in disfavore; *at a — of 2%*, collo sconto del due per cento. **discount** 2, TR.: scontare; dedurre: — *a bill*, scontare una cambiale.

discŏụntẹnan-ce 1, S.: freddezza; indifferenza, *f.* **-ce** 2, TR.: turbare; raffrenare; scoraggiare; disapprovare. **-cẹr**, S.: che scoraggia.

discŏụrạg-e, TR.: scoraggiare; dissuadere. **-ement**, S.: sgomentamento, sgomento, *m.* **-ẹr**, S.: che scoraggia. **-ing**,

discŏụrs-e 1, S.: discorso; ragionamento; trattato, *m.* **-e** 2, TR.: discorrere; ragionare; discutere; esaminare. **-ẹr**, S.: ragionatore; oratore, *m.* **-ive**, ADJ.: discorsivo.

discŏụr-tẹous, ADJ.: scortese, incivile. **-tẹously**, ADV.: scortesemente. **-tẹsy**, S.: scortesia, inciviltà, *f.*

discous, ADJ.: in forma di disco, ampia, piatto.

discŏvẹr, TR.: scoprire; rivelare; manifestare; trovare. **-able**, ADJ.: che si può scoprire. **-ẹr**, S.: scopritore; esploratore, *m.* **-y**, S.: scoperta, *f.*, scoprimento, *m.*

discrĕdit 1, S.: discredito; disonore, *m.: bring into* —, far cadere in discredito; *do — to*, far disonore; *throw — on*, gettare discredito su di. **discredit** 2, TR.: discreditare; disonorare.

discrĕet, ADJ.: discreto, circospetto; giudizioso, prudente, savio. **-ly**, ADV.: discretamente; prudentemente, saviamente. **-ness**, S.: discrezione, discretezza; prudenza, *f.*

discrĕpan-ce, S.: differenza; contrarietà, *f.* **-t**, ADJ.: discrepante, differente; contrario.

dis-crēte, ADJ.: distinto. **-crĕtiọn**, S.: discrezione, prudenza; giudizio; volontà, libertà, *f.: I leave it to your* —, lo rimetto alla vostra discrezione. **-crĕtiọnary**,

discrim-inable, ADJ.: distinguibile; caratteristico. **-ināte**, TR.: distinguere; separare. **-inạtely**, ADV.: distintamente. **-inạteness**, S.: differenza; specificazione, *f.* **-inā̤tiọn**, S.: differenza; distinzione, *f.* **-inative**, ADJ.: distintivo; caratteristico. **-inous†**, ADJ.: periglioso, azzardoso.

discŭlpạte†, TR.: scusare.

discŭmbency, S.: star appoggiato a tavola, *m.*

discŭmbẹr, TR.: sgombrare, disimpegnare; spacciare.

discŭr-sive, ADJ.: vagante, discorsivo. **-sively**, ADV.: in modo discorsivo. **-sory**, ADJ.: discorsivo.

discus, S.: disco, *m.*

dis-cŭss, TR.: discutere, esaminare, sciogliere: — *a question*, discutere una questione. **-cŭssẹr**, S.: esaminatore, *m.* **-cŭssiọn**, S.: discussione; disquisizione, *f.*: *give rise to* —, provocare la discussione. **-cŭssive**, ADJ.: (*med.*) risolutivo, risolvente. **-cŭtient**, S.: rimedio risolutivo, *m.*

disdāin, S.: spregio, disdegno, sprezzo, scorno, *m.*: *hold one in* —, sdegnare, disprezzare uno. **disdain** 2, TR.: disdegnare, disprezzare, aver a sdegno. **-ful**, ADJ.: sdegnoso. **-fully**, ADV.: sdegnosamente. **-fulness**, S.: dispregiamento, disprezzo, sdegno, *m.*

diseāse 1, S.: malattia, *f.*, morbo, *m.* **-se** 2, TR.: ammalare, incomodare, cagionare malattia; infestare. **-sed**, ADJ.: ammalato; indisposto, incomodato; ammorbato. **-sedness**, S.: indisposizione, malattia. **-sement**†, S.: incomodo, *m.*; indisposizione, *f.*

disĕdge, TR.: spuntare, rendere ottuso.

disembârk, (IN)TR.: sbarcare **-ātion**, **-ing**, S.: sbarco, sbarcare, *m.*

disembărrass, TR.: sbarazzare. **-ment**, S.: sgombramento, *m.*

disembitter, TR.: addolcire.

disembŏgue, INTR.: sboccare.

disembŏwel, TR.: eviscerare.

disembröil, TR.: sbrogliare; sviluppare.

disenāble, TR.: rendere incapace.

disenchânt, TR.: levare l' incanto.

disencŭm-ber, TR.: sbrogliare, sbarazzare, sgombrare. **-brance**, S.: sgombramento, sbarazzare, *m.*

disengāge, TR.: liberare, separare, disimpegnare; INTR.: liberarsi; sbrigarsi. **-d**, ADJ.: disoccupato, disimpegnato, libero: *shall you be — this evening?* sarete in libertà stasera? **-ment**, S.: disimpegno, *m.*; disoccupazione; libertà, *f.*

disentăngle, TR.: sviluppare, disimpegnare; separare: — *one's self*, stricarsi, uscir d' impaccio.

disentĕr = *disinter.*

disenthrāl, TR.: liberare.

disenthrōne, TR.: detronizzare.

disespŏuse, TR.: annullare il matrimonio.

disestēem 1, S.: dispregio, disprezzo, *m.* **disesteem** 2, TR.: dispregiare, sprezzare, vilipendere,

disfāvour 1, S.: disfavore, *m.*, disgrazia, *f.*; disgusto, *m.* **disfavour** 2, TR.: disfavorire.

dis-figurātion, S.: difformità, bruttezza, *f.* **-figure**, TR.: disfigurare, difformare. **-figurement**, S.: difformità, bruttezza, *f.*

disfrânchise, TR.: privare della franchigia. **-ment**, S.: privazione della franchigia, *f.*

disfŭrnish, TR.: sfornire; spogliare.

disgârnish, TR.: sguernire.

disglōrify, TR.: privare di gloria.

disgôrge, TR.: vomitare; recere.

disgrā-ce 1, S.: disonore; disgrazia, disfavore, *m.*; ignominia, *f.*: *be a — to one's family*, esser la vergogna della sua famiglia. **-ce** 2, TR: disonorare, svergognare, disgraziare. **-ceful**, ADJ.: disonorevole, ignominioso. **-cefully**, ADV.: ignominiosamente, disonorevolmente. **-cefulness**, S.: disonore, *m.*, infamia; ignominia, *f.* **-cer**, S.: che disonora. **-cious**, ADJ.: spiacevole, scortese; disfavorevole.

disguī-se 1, S.: travestimento, *m.*; maschera, *f.* **-se** 2, TR.: travestire, mascherare; fingere; dissimulare: — *one's self*, mascherarsi, travestirsi. **-sement**, S.: travestimento, *m.*; maschera, *f.* **-ser**, S.: che s' immaschera.

disgŭst 1, S.: disgusto; fastidio, *m.* **disgust** 2, TR.: disgustare, prender disgusto; dispiacere; *be —ed with*, disgustarsi di. **-ful**, ADJ.: disgustoso.

dish 1, S.: piatto, *m.*; vivanda, scodella, *f.*: *wash —es*, lavar scodelle. **dish** 2, TR.: mettere nel piatto; minestrare.

dishabille, S.: abito di camera, *m.*

dishârmony, S.: discordanza, *f.*

dish-clout, S.: strofinaccio, *m.*

dis-heârten, TR.: scoraggiare, disanimare; sgomentare, intimorire. **-heârtened**, ADJ.: scorato, perso di animo. **-heartening**, ADJ.: scoraggiante, desolante.

dis-hĕrison, S.: diseredazione, *f.* **-hĕrit**, TR.: diseredare.

dishĕvel, TR.: scapigliare.

dish-meat, S.: minestra, *f.*

dishŏnest, ADJ.: disonesto, ignominioso, infame. **-ly**, ADV.: disonestamente, impudicamente. **-y**, S.: disonestà; impudicizia, *f.*

dishŏnour 1, S.: disonore, *m.*; infamia, *f.*: *hold it a — to*, tenersi disonorato di. **dishonour** 2, TR.: disonorare; svergognare. **-able**, ADJ.: disonorevole. **-ably**, ADV.: disonorevolmente. **-er**, S.: insultatore; rapitore, seduttore, *m.*

dishôrn, TR.: privare di corna.

dishŭmour, S.: cattivo umore, *m.*

dish-wash, **-water**, S.: lavatura di scodelle, *f.*

disimprŏvement, S.: peggioramento, *m.*

disincârcerate, TR.: scarcerare.

disin-clinātion, S.: indifferenza, *f.*; disgusto; disprezzo, *m.* **-cline**, TR.: produrre disgusto, disgustare.

disincôrporate, TR.: separare.

disinfĕct, TR.: torre l' infezione.

disin-genŭity, S.: dissimulazione; doppiezza, *f.* **-gĕnuous**, ADJ.: simulato, finto, artificioso. **-gĕnuously**, ADV.: simulatamente, artificiosamente. **-gĕnuousness**, S.: dissimulazione, *f.*, artificio, *m.*

disinhăbited, ADJ.: inabitato.

disinhĕr-ison, S.: diseredazione, *f.* -

TR.: diseredare, disereditare.

disintèr, TR.: dissotterrare.
disinterest, s.: disinteresse, m. **-ed**, ADJ.: disinteressato. **-edly**, ADV.: disinteressatamente. **-edness**, s.: disinteressamento.
disintèrment, s.: dissotterramento, m.
disintricate, TR.: sviluppare, sbrigare.
disinvite, TR.: [illegible].
disjoin, TR.: disgiungere, separare.
disjoint, TR.: slogare, smembrare; INTR.: disgiungersi. **-ed**, ADJ.: slogato, smembrato, disunito. **-edly**, ADV.: separatamente.
disjunc-t, ADJ.: disgiunto, separato. **-tion**, s.: disgiunzione, f., separamento, m. **-tive**, ADJ.: disgiuntivo. **-tively**, ADV.: disgiuntivamente.
disk, s.: disco, m.
diskindness, s.: mancanza d'affetto, f., pregiudizio, m.
dislik-e 1, s.: disgusto, m., avversione, f.: give a — to, disgustare di: have a — for, provare antipatia per, sentire avversione o ripugnanza per. **-e** 2, TR.: disapprovare, dispiacere, biasimare. **-eful**†, ADJ.: maligno. **-en**, TR.: differenziare. **-eness**, s.: dissomiglianza, differenza, f. **-er**, s.: disapprovatore, m. **-ing**, s.: disgusto, m., ripugnanza, f.
dislimb†, TR.: membrare.
dislimn†, TR.: cancellare (una pittura).
dislo-cate, TR.: slogare, dislogare. **-cátion**, s.: slogamento, m.; scommettitura, f.
dislódge, TR.: disloggiare, scacciare; INTR.: mutar casa.
dislóyal, ADJ.: disleale, infedele; perfido. **-ly**, ADV.: deslealmente, infidamente. **-ness**, **-ty**, s.: dislealtà, infedeltà; perfidia, f.
dismal, ADJ.: tristo, misero, funesto; orribile. **-ly**, ADV.: tristamente; orribilmente. **-ness**, s.: affanno; cordoglio, m.
dismántle, TR.: smantellare; spogliare.
dismásk, TR.: smascherare.
dismást, TR.: disalberare.
dismáy 1, s.: smarrimento d' animo; terrore, m. **dismay** 2, TR.: spaventare, scoraggiare, stupefare. **-ed**, ADJ.: sgomentato, esterrefatto, stupefatto: *look* —, parer costernato (preso da sgomento). **-edness**, s.: spaventamento, m.
disme, s.: decima, f.
dismémber, TR.: smembrare, sbranare, dilaniare. **-ment**, s.: smembramento, m.
dis-miss, TR.: congedare, licenziare; ripudiare. **-mission**, TR.: licenziamento, congedo, m.
dismórtgage†, TR.: redimere un pegno, ricomprare.
dismóunt, TR.: scavalcare, smontare, scavallare: imbeccare; INTR.: dismontare: scendere.
dis-náturalize, TR.: privare del privilegio di naturalità. **-nátured**, ADJ.: disnaturato.
dis-obédience, s.: disubbidienza, f. **-obédient**, ADJ.: disubbidiente. **-obédiently**, ADV.: disubbidientemente, con disubbidienza. **-obéy**, TR.: disubbidire; trasgredire.
dis-obligátion, s.: disobbligazione, f.; dispiacere, m., offesa, f. **-oblige**, TR.: disobbligare, dispiacere; offendere. **-obliging**, ADJ.: scortese, incivile. **-obligingly**, ADV.: scortesemente, incivilmente. **-obligingness**, s.: scortesia, inciviltà, f.
disórbed, ADJ.: fuor della propria orbita.
disórder 1, s.: disordine, m., irregolarità, f.: turbamento, m., confusione; commozione: indisposizione, f.: *throw in* —, scompigliare, gettare in confusione. **disorder** 2, TR.: disordinare, mettere in disordine: perturbare, sconcertare. **-ed**, ADJ.: disordinato, scompigliato. **-edness**, s.: disordine, disordinazione, f. **-ly**, ADJ.: confuso, tumultuoso; ADV.: senza ordine, confusamente; viziosamente.
disórdinate, ADJ.: disordinato, sregolato. **-ly**, ADV.: disordinatamente.
dis-organizátion, s.: disorganizzazione, f. **-órganize**, TR.: disorganizzare.
disówn, TR.: non confessare, negare; rinunziare.
dispáce†, INTR.: spaziarsi.
dispán-d†, TR.: spandere, dilatare. **-sion**†, s.: spandimento, m., dilatazione, f.
dispárag-e, TR.: sprezzare; avvilire; far poco conto di, detrarre da. **-ement**, s.: sprezzamento, scherno, disonore, m. **-er**, s.: dispregiatore, m.
dis-parate, ADJ.: dissimile; separato. **-párity**, s.: disparità; disuguaglianza; differenza, f.
dispárk, TR.: rompere i palizzati d'un parco.
dispárt†, TR.: spartire; rompere.
dispássion, s.: tranquillità di mente; insensibilità, f. **-ate**, ADJ.: spassionato, quieto.
dispátch = *despatch*.
dispél, TR.: espellere; scacciare.
dispén-d†, TR.: spendere. **-sable**, ADJ.: dispensabile. **-sary**, s.: fondaco di medicinali, m.; spezieria, f. **-sátion**, s.: dispensa, distribuzione, f. **dispen-sator**, s.: dispensatore, m. **-satory**, s.: ricettario, m., farmacopea, f. **-se** 1, s.: dispensa; esenzione, f.; privilegio, m. **-se** 2, TR.: dispensare; distribuire; esentare;

— *with*, far senza, scusare, esentare; —*sing power*, diritto di grazia. **-ser**, s.: dispensatore, distributore, *m*.

dispéopl-e, TR.: spopolare; distruggere, desolare. **-er**, s.: desolatore, *m*.

dispĕrge, TR.: inaffiare, spruzzare.

dispĕr-se, TR.: dispergere; sparpagliare. **-sedly**, ADV.: sparsamente. **-sedness**, s.: dispersione, *f*. **-ser**, s.: spargitore, *m*. **-sion**, s.: dispersione, *f*., dispergimento, *m*.

dispirit, TR.: scoraggiare, sgomentare. **-edness**, s.: avvilimento d' animo, *m*.

displāce, TR.: dislogare; rimuovere; disordinare; scavallare. **-ment**, s.: slogamento, rimovimiento, *m*.; quantità (d'acqua, ecc.) slogata.

displācency†, s.: dispiacenza; incivil-tà, *f*.

displācing, s.: rimovimento, *m*.

displănt, TR.: spiantare; sradicare. **-ātion**, s.: spiantamento, sbarbicamento, *m*.

displāy 1, s.: esposizione, mostra, *f*., sviluppo, sviluppamento, *m*.; pompa, *f*.: *make — of one's eloquence*, far sfoggio della sua eloquenza. **display** 2, TR.: esporre; spiegare; far mostra.

dis-plĕasant†, ADJ.: spiacevole; molesto, offensivo. **-plĕase**, TR.: dispiacere; offendere: *that —s me*, ciò mi dispiace (*or* contraria); *I am —d at it*, me ne dispiace. **-plĕased**, ADJ.: dispiaciuto. **-plĕasedness**, **-plĕasingness**, *f*., dispiacere, *m*. **-plĕasure**, s.: dispiacere; disgusto; scontento, *m*.; noia, *f*.

displō-de†, TR.: scoppiare; spaccarsi. **-sion**, s.: scoppiettata, *f*.

dispōrt 1, s.: diporto; passatempo, *m*.; ricreazione, *f*. **disport** 2, TR.: divertire; ricreare; dar sollazzo; INTR.: diportarsi, divertirsi, ricrearsi.

dispō-sable, ADJ.: disponibile. **-sal**, s.: disposizione, balia, *f*.; potere, *m*.: *it is at your —*, è alla vostra disposizione. **-se**, TR.: disporre, aggiustare; preparare; dare; assettare; INTR.: prevalersi; disfarsi; contrattare: — *of*, disporre, alienare; — *of another man's money*, servirsi dell' altrui danaro; *man proposes and God —s*, l' uomo propone e Dio dispone; *I have —d of my house*, ho venduto la mia casa. **-sed**, ADJ.: disposto, inclinato: *be ill- — towards*, essere indisposto a; — *to be merry*, disposto alla gioia, d' umor allegro. **-ser**, s.: dispensatore, *m*. **-sition**, s.: disposizione, inclinazione, *f*.; ordine; talento; carattere, *m*. **dispō-sitive†**, INTR.: dispositivo; preparativo, preparatorio. **-sitively†**, ADV.: dispositivamente.

dispossĕss, TR.: dispossessare; spogliare.

dispōsure†, s.: disposizione, *f*.; maneggio, *m*.; volontà, *f*.

disprāi-se 1, s.: biasimo, rimprovero, *m*. **-se** 2, TR.: biasimare; criticare, censurare. **-ser**, s.: biasimatore, critico, censore, *m*. **-singly**, ADV.: biasimevolmente.

disprĕad, TR.: spandere, sparpagliare; INTR.: spandersi.

disprize, TR.: dispregiare.

disprŏfit† 1, s.: svantaggio, pregiudizio; detrimento, danno, *m*. **disprofit†** 2, INTR.: pregiudicare, nuocere.

disprōof, s.: confutazione, *f*.

disprŏpōrtion 1, s.: disproporzione, ineguālità; disparità, *f*. **disproportion** 2, TR.: sproporzionare. **-able**, ADJ.: sproporzionato. **-ableness**, s.: sproporzionalità, *f*. **-ably**, ADV.: sproporzionatamente. **-al**, **-ate**, ADJ.: sproporzionale, sproporzionato; ineguale; dissimile. **-ateness**, s.: disproporzione, *f*. **-ed** = *disproportional*.

disprōv-e, TR.: disapprovare, rimproverare, confutare; convincere. **-er**, s.: confutatore; contradditore, *m*.

dis-pŭtable, ADJ.: disputabile. **-pŭtant**, ADJ.: disputante; s.: disputatore; controversista, *m*. **-pŭtātion**, s.: disputazione; controversia, *f*.: *hold a —*, mantenere una disputa. **-pŭtātious**, **-pūtative**, ADJ.: disputativo, contenzioso. **-pūte** 1, s.: disputa, contesa, controversia, *f*.: *beyond —*, senza contraddizione; *admit of —*, ammetter discussione; esser discutibile. **-pute** 2, (IN)TR.: disputare, dibattere; contrastare: — *about trifles*, disputare dell' ombra dell' asino. **-pūteless**, ADJ.: incontestabile. **-pūter**, s.: disputatore; controversista, *m*.

dis-quălificātion, s.: inettitudine, inabilità, *f*. **-quălify**, TR.: rendere inetto.

disquiet 1, s.: inquietudine, tribolazione, *f*.; travaglio, *m*. **disquiet** 2, TR.: inquietare, tribolare; travagliare. **-er**, s.: perturbatore, disturbatore; tormentatore, *m*. **-ly**, ADV.: inquietamente; senza riposo. **-ness**, **-ude**, s.: inquietudine, tribolazione, anzietà, *f*.

disquisition, s.: disquisizione, *f*.; esame, *m*.

disrănk, TR.: degradare†; disordinare, metter in disordine.

disregărd 1, s.: trascuraggine, indifferenza; negligenza, *f*. **disregard** 2, TR.: trascurare; disprezzare; vilificare. **-ful**, ADJ.: trascurante, negligente; disprezzante. **-fully**, ADV.: dispregevolmente.

disrĕlish 1, s.: cattivo gusto, disgusto, *m*. **disrelish** 2, TR.: disapprovare, non approvare, guastare.

disrĕp-ŭtable, ADJ.: vergognoso. **-ŭtātion**, s.: disonore, discredito; disgrazia, *f.* **-âte**, s.: cattiva riputazione, *f.*, discredito, *m.*: *bring into* —, mettere in discredito.

disrespĕct 1, s.: mancanza di rispetto, irriverenza, *f.*: *hold in* —, sprezzare, rispettare poco. **disrespect** 2, TR.: disprezzare; insultare. **-ful**, ADJ.: irriverente; incivile. **-fully**, ADV.: senza rispetto. **-fulness**, s.: mancanza di rispetto, *f.*

disrōbe, TR.: svestire; spogliare.

disrŭp-t, TR.: dirompere. **-tion**, s.: dirompimento, *m.*, rottura; crepatura, *f.* **-ture** = *-tion.*

dis-satisfăction, s.: scontento, malcontento; disgusto, dispiacere, *m.* **-satisfăctory**, ADJ.: spiacevole; molesto. **-săt-isfied**, ADJ.: malcontento, scontento; disgustato. **-sătisfy**, TR.: scontentare; dispiacere.

dissĕc-t, TR.: notomizzare. **-tion**, s.: dissezione; analisi; notomia, *f.* **-tor**, s.: dissettore; anatomista, notomista, *m.*

dissēis-e, TR.: (*leg.*) dispossessare. **-in**, s.: (*leg.*) spogliamento de' beni, dispossessato, *m.*

dissĕm-blance, s.: dissomiglianza, *f.* **-ble**, TR.: dissimulare, simulare; fingere; palliare, coprire; INTR.: fare l' ipocrita. **-bler**, s.: dissimulatore; ipocrita, *m.* **-bling**, ADJ.: dissimulato, finto, artificioso; s.: dissimulazione, finzione, *f.* **-blingly**, ADV.: dissimulatamente, artificiosamente.

dissĕm-inate, TR.: disseminare; spargere; propagare. **-inâtion**, s.: disseminazione, *f.* **-inator**, s.: disseminatore; propagatore, *m.*

dissĕn-sion, s.: dissensione; discordia, *f.* **-sious**, ADJ.: litigioso, contenzioso. **-t** 1, s.: sentimento contrario, *m.*, opinione contraria, *f.* **-t** 2, INTR.: dissentire, differire; discordare. **-tâneous**, ADJ.: discordante, differente; contrario. **-ter**, s.: nonconformista; discordante, *m.* **-tient**, ADJ.: discordante.

dissertâtion, s.: dissertazione, *f.*; discorso, *m.*

dissĕr-ve, TR.: disservire, pregiudicare, nuocere. **-vice**, s.: disservigio; torto, danno, *m.* **-viceable**, ADJ.: pregiudiziale, nocevole. **-viceableness**, s.: pregiudizio, nocimento; danno, *m.*

dissĕttle, TR.: disordinare, sregolare; scomporre.

dissĕver, TR.: sceverare; separare. **-ance**, s.: separazione, *f.*

dissiden-ce, s.: dissensione, discordia, *f.* [illegible] s.: dissidente, *m.*

[illegible] **-im-ilar**, ADJ.: dissimile; diverso. [illegible] **-ity**, **-ilitude**, s.: dissomiglianza, [illegible]; disparità, *f.* **-ulate**, INTR.: dissimulare. **-lâtion**, s.: dissimulazione; finzione, *f.*

dissi-pable, ADJ.: dissipabile; consumabile. **-pate**, TR.: dissipare; distruggere; consumare; traviar (la mente). **-pated**, ADJ.: dissipato, distrutto; consumato; disattento. **-pâtion**, s.: dissipamento, *m.*; distruzione, *f.*

dissō-ciate, TR.: disunire, separare. **-ciâtion**, s.: disunione, *f.*

dis-soluble, ADJ.: dissolubile. **-solute**, ADJ.: dissoluto, scapestrato, licenzioso. **-solutely**, ADV.: dissolutamente. **-soluteness**, s.: dissolutezza; licenza, sfrenatezza, *f.* **-solûtion**, s.: dissoluzione; liquefazione; licenza, *f.* **-sŏlvable**, ADJ.: dissolubile. **-sŏlve**, TR.: dissolvere, fondere; disfare, disunire; INTR.: disciogliersi; dissiparsi, separarsi. **-sŏlvent**, ADJ.: dissolvente; dissolutivo. **-sŏlver**, s.: dissolvente, dissolutivo, *m.*

dissonan-ce, s.: dissonanza, discordanza, *f.* **-t**, ADJ.: dissonante; dissimile, differente.

dissuâ-de, TR.: dissuadere; sconsigliare. **-der**, s.: che dissuade. **-sion**, s.: dissuasione, *f.* **-sive**, ADJ.: dissuasivo, dissuadente; s.: argomento dissuasivo, *m.*

dis-syllăbic, ADJ.: dissillabo. **-syllable**, s.: dissillabo, *m.*

distaff, s.: canocchia, rocca, *f.*

distâin, TR.: macchiare; lordare.

dis-tance 1, s.: distanza, *f.*, intervallo; decoro; rispetto, *m.*: *at a* (*in the*) —, in lontananza; *at a great* —, in gran distanza; *out of* —, a perdita di vista; *keep one's* —, portar rispetto; *keep one at a* —, guardar il suo decoro. **-tance** 2, TR.: discostare; lasciare indietro. **-tant**, ADJ.: distante, discosto: *be* —, distare; *six miles* —, distante sei miglia.

distâste 1, s.: disgusto; dispiacere; tedio, *m.*: *take a* — *for*, aver a fastidio, fastidire. **distaste** 2, TR.: dispiacere; fastidire; avere in fastidio. **-ful**, ADJ.: fastidioso, tedioso; ingrato; offensivo. **-fulness**, s.: disgusto, *m.*, avversione, *f.*

distĕmper 1, s.: malattia, *f.*, morbo; disordine, imbroglio, *m.* **distemper** 2, TR.: disordinare; disturbare. **-ate**, ADJ.: immoderato, eccessivo. **-ature**, s.: intemperatura; indisposizione, *f.* **-ed**, ADJ.: indisposto, ammalato.

distĕn-d, TR.: stendere; allargare. **-sion**, s.: distendimento, *m.*, estensione, *f.* **-t**, s.: distesa; estensione; ampiezza, *f.*

distich, s.: distico, *m.*

distil, TR.: stillare, distillare, pocciolare. **-lable**, ADJ.: che si può distillare. **-lâtion**, s.: distillazione, *f.* **-latory**, ADJ.: distillatorio. **-ler**, s.: distillatore, *m.* **-ling**, ADJ.: distillante; s.: distillamento, *m.*, distillazione, *f.*

distinc-t, ADJ.: distinto, chiaro; separato; dissimile, differente. **-tion**, S.: distinzione; differenza, diversità, *f.*: *make a — between*, fare una distinzione (differenza) fra; *persons of —*, persone distinte, nomini insigni; donne di condizione. **-tive**, ADJ.: distintivo. **-tively**, ADV.: in modo distintivo, per distinzione. **-ly**, ADV.: distintamente; chiaramente. **-ness**, S.: chiarezza, lucidezza, *f.*
distinguish, TR.: distinguere; separare; notare: *— one's self*, distinguersi, segnalarsi. **-able**, ADJ.: che si può distinguere. **-ableness**, S.: differenza, *f.* **-ed**, ADJ.: distinto, eminente, insigne; elegante. **-er**, S.: distinguitore, osservatore giudizioso, *m.* **-ingly**, ADV.: con distinzione, onorevolmente. **-ment**, S.: distinzione; osservazione, *f.*; giudizio, *m.*
distôr-t, TR.: contorcere; rivolgere; stralunare. **-tion**, S.: contorsione, *f.*, storcimento, *m.*
distrâc-t, IRR.; TR.: distrarre; separare; impazzire; molestare: *— the mind from*, svagare la mente da. **-ted**, ADJ.: distratto, diviso; forsennato, pazzo: *run —*, smaniare, infuriare; *drive one —*, far impazzire uno; *become —*, distrarsi, svagarsi, smanire, impazzire. **-tedly**, ADV.: forsennatamente. **-tedness**, S.: smania, *f.* **-tion**, S.: distrazione; angoscia, *f.*
distrâin, TR.: staggire; sequestrare, confiscare. **-er**, S.: staggitore, *m.* **-t**, S.: staggimento, sequestramento, sequestro, *m.*
distrâught = *distracted.*
distrěss 1, S.: staggina; calamità, miseria, estremità, *f.*: *pecuniary —*, scarsezza del numerario, angustia; *— of mind*, affanno, afflizione. **distress** 2, TR.: staggire; angustiare, tribolare, vessare. **-ed**, ADJ.: misero, affannato, tribolato; bisognoso. **-edness**, S.: calamità, miseria, *f.* **-ful**, ADJ.: affannoso, misero. **-fully**, ADV.: miseramente.
distrib-ute, TR.: distribuire, dividere: *distributing regulator*, timone, regolatore, *m.* **-utor**, S.: distributore, *m.* **-ûtion**, S.: distribuzione, *f.* **-utive**, ADJ.: distributivo. **-utively**, ADV.: distributivamente.
district, S.: distretto, *m.*; regione; giurisdizione, *f.*
distrŭst 1, S.: sfidanza, *f.*; sospetto, *m.* **distrust** 2, TR.: diffidare di; non fidarsi di, sospettare: *they — me*, diffidano di mi. **-ful**, ADJ.: diffidente; sospettoso. **-fully**, ADV.: sospettosamente. **-fulness**, S.: diffidenza, *f.*; sospetto, *m.* **-less**, ADJ.: senza diffidenza.
distŭrb, TR.: disturbare; inquietare; impedire, molestare; dispiacere: *I am sorry to — you*, mi rincresce d' incomodarvi. **-ance**, S.: disturbanza; confusione; alterazione, *f.*; tumulto, *m.*: *make a —*, produrre disordine (scompiglio). **-er**, S.: perturbatore, sturbatore, *m.*
distŭrn†, TR.: mandar via, scacciare.
disû-nion, S.: disunione; dissensione; controversia, *f.* **-nite**, TR.: disunire, disgiungere; separare; INTR.: disunirsi, disgiungersi; separarsi. **-nity**, S.: disunione, separazione, *m.*
disûse 1, S.: disuso, *m.*; disusanza, *f.*: *fall into —*, cadere in disuetudine. **disûse** 2, INTR.: disusarsi, lasciar l' uso.
dis-valuâtion, S.: dispregiamento, dispregio; disonore, *m.* **-vălue**, TR.: disprezzare, avvilire.
disvĕlop†, TR.: sviluppare, scoprire.
disvŏuch†, TR.: discreditare; contraddire, opporsi.
diswŏnt†, TR.: disavvezzare.
ditch 1, S.: fosso, *m.*, fossa, *f.* **ditch** 2, TR.: fare un fosso, affossare. **-er**, S.: che affossa; zappatore, *m.*
dithyrămbic, ADJ.: ditirambico; S.: ditirambo, *m.*
dittany, S.: dittamo, *m.*
dittied, ADJ.: accoppiato con musica.
ditto, S.: medesimo, sopradetto, *m.*
ditty, S.: canzone, *f.*
diurĕtic, ADJ.: (*med.*) diuretico, aperitivo.
diŭrnal, ADJ.: diurno, giornale; S.: giornale, *m.* **-ly**, ADV.: ogni giorno, giornalmente.
diutŭrnity, S.: diuturnità, *f.*
divăn, S.: divano, *m.*
divări-cate, TR.: dividere in due; INTR.: dividersi in due parti. **-câtion**, S.: divisione in due parti, *f.*
div-e, TR.: tuffare, immergere; esplorare; INTR.: tuffarsi; penetrare. **-er**, S.: tuffatore; investigatore; marangone, palombaro, *m.*
divĕr-ge, INTR.: divergere; essere divergente. **-gence**, **-gency**, S.: divergenza, *f.* **-gent**, ADJ.: divergente.
di-vers, ADJ.: diverso; diversi; parecchi. **-verse**, ADJ.: diverso, differente, vario; ADV.: diversamente. **-vĕrsely**, ADV.: diversamente, differentemente, variamente. **-versificâtion**, S.: diversificazione; varietà, *f.* **-vĕrsify**, TR.: diversificare; differenziare, variare. **-vĕrsion**, S.: diversione, *f.*; passatempo, *m.*, ricreazione, *f.* **-vĕrsity**, S.: diversità, differenza, *f.*
divĕrt, TR.: divertire, distornare; stornare, distrarre; INTR.: far diversione. **-er**, S.: alleggerimento, *m.* **-ing**, ADJ.: sollazzevole; ricreativo; grato. **-ingness**, S.: divertimento, trattenimento, *m.* **-ise**†, TR.: ricreare, sollazzare,

grare. **-isement**†, s.: divertimento; piacere, *m.* **-ive**, ADJ.: ricreativo; piacevole.
divĕst, TR.: divestire; spogliare, privare: — *one's self*, svestirsi, spogliarsi. **-ure**, s.: spogliamento, *m.*; rinunzia; cessione, *f.*
divi-dable, ADJ.: divisibile. **-de**, TR.: dividere, spartire, disunire; distribuire; INTR.: dividersi; disunirsi, separarsi. **-dedly**, ADV.: separatamente. **dividend**, s.: (*arith.*) dividendo; (*com.*) dividendo, usufrutto, interesse, *m.* **-der**, s.: dividitore, distributore, *m.*
div-ination, s.: divinazione, *f.*, indovinamento, *m.* **div-inator**, s.: divinatore, *m.* **-inatory**, ADJ.: divinatorio. **-ine** 1, ADJ.: divino; eccelente; s.: ecclesiastico; teologo, *m.* **-ine** 2, TR.: indovinare; presagire; INTR.: congetturare, presentire. **-ined**, ADJ.: indovinato, predetto. **-inely**, ADV.: divinamente; eccellentemente. **-ineness**, s.: divinità, *f.* **-iner**, s.: divinatore, indovino, *m.* **-ineress**, s.: divinatrice, indovina, *m.*
diving, s.: immersione, *f.* **-bell**, s.: campana di marangone, *f.*
divinity, s.: divinità; teologia, *f.*: *doctor of* —, dottore in teologia.
div-isibility, s.: divisibilità, *f.* **-isible**, ADJ.: divisibile; partibile. **-isibleness** = *divisibility*. **-ision**, s.: divisione, *f.*, spartimento, *m.*; scissione, scissura, *f.* **-isional**, ADJ.: di divisione, divisionario. **-isor**, s.: divisore, *m.*
divŏr-ce 1, s.: divorzio, *m.*; separazione, *f.* **-ce** 2, TR.: far divorzio; ripudiare; separare. **-cement**, s.: divorzio, ripudio, *m.* **-cer**, s.: che fa divorzio. **-cing**, s.: divorzio, ripudio, *m.*
divŭl-ge, TR.: divulgare, pubblicare. **-ger**, s.: che divulga, divulgatore, *m.* **-sion**, s.: divellimento, staccamento, *m.*; separazione, *f.*
dizen, TR.: adornare, abbellire.
dizzard†, s.: scioccone, balordo, *m.*
diz-ziness, s.: vertigine, *f.*, capogiro, *m.* **-zy** 1, ADJ.: vertiginoso, sventato. **-zy** 2, TR.: stordire.
dō 1, IRR.; TR.: fare; operare, effettuare, finire; cuocere; cucinare; INTR.: stare, portarsi: *have to — with*, aver che fare con; *pray*, —, ve ne prego; *how — you —?* come state? come sta? *that won't* —, questo non basta; *that won't — for me*, ciò non fa per me; — *in Rome as Rome —es*, vivi in Roma alla romana; — *a business*, spe-[illegible]are un negozio; — *good*, beneficare; [illegible]re; — *like for like*, render la pari-[illegible] *have to — with one*, aver da fare [illegible]; *I have nothing to — with it*, non mi riguarda; — *again*, rifare; [illegible]s, far male; — *away*, levare; — [illegible]re; levare via; — *on*, porre; mettere; — *over*, — *up*, piegare; imballare.
do 2, s.: fracasso, strepito, chiasso, *m.*
dŏc-ible, ADJ.: docile; trattabile. **-ibleness**, s.: docilità; trattabilità, *f.* **-ile**, ADJ.: docile; disciplinabile. **-ility**, s.: docilità, *f.*
dŏck 1, s.: darsena, *f.*, bacino, cantiere, *m.*
dock 2, s.: coda troncata, *f.*; lapazio, *m.*
dock 3, TR.: scodare. **dock** 4, TR.: scolare, racconciare. **dock** 5, TR.: rimpalmare (un vascello). **-et** 1, s.: direzione, cedola, *f.*; estratto, sommario, *m.* **-et** 2, TR.: notare, segnare. **-yard**, s.: cantiere, *m.*
dŏctor 1, s.: dottore; medico, *m.*: *poor* —, dottoraccio, dottorello, dottoricchio, *m.*: — *of divinity*, dottore di teologia; *take the degrees of* —, prender la laurea.
doctor 2, TR.: medicare, dare medicine. **-al**, ADJ.: dottorale, di dottore. **-ally**, ADV.: in modo dottorale, da dottore. **-ate**, TR.: dottorare. **-ess**, s.: dottoressa, *f.* **-ship**, s.: dottorato, *m.*, dignità del dottore, *f.*
dŏc-trinal, ADJ.: dottrinale, istruttivo. **-trinally**, ADV.: dottrinalmente, positivamente. **-trine**, s.: dottrina, scienza; istruzione, *f.*
dŏcument 1, s.: documento; precetto, *m.* **document** 2, **-ize**, TR.: provare con documenti; insegnare, istruire.
dŏdder, s.: (*bot.*) epitimo, *m.*
dodĕcagon, s.: dodecagono, *m.*
dŏd-ge, INTR.: acquattarsi; appiattarsi, sfuggire, schivare; operare con astuzia: — *a blow*, schivare un colpo; — *a person*, pedinare (*or* codiare) uno. **-ger**, s.: intrigante, *m.* **-gery**, s.: cavillazione, *f.*
dōe, s.: daina, capriola, *f.*
dōer, s.: facitore, fattore, *m.*
dŏff, TR.: svestire, spogliare; differire, ritardare.
dŏg 1, s.: cane; (*astr.*) sirio, *m.*: *big* —, cagnone, cane grosso; *little* —, cagnetto; *nice little* —, cagnolino; *be treated like a* —, esser trattato da cane. **dog** 2, TR.: codiare; spiare. **-berry**, s.: corniuola, *f.* **-brier**, s.: rosa canina, rosa salvatica, *f.* **-cheap**, ADJ.: a buon mercato, a vil prezzo. **-days**, s. PL.: canicola, *f.*, giorni canicolari, *m. pl.*
dōge, s.: doge, *m.*
dŏg-fish, s.: cane di mare, *m.* (pesce). **-ged**, ADJ.: cagnesco; arcigno, burbero, aspro. **-gedly**, ADV.: d' un' aria arcigna. **-gedness**, s.: umore arcigno, ghiribizzo, capriccio, *m.*
dŏgger, s.: bastimento olandese, *m.*
dŏggerel, s.: cattiva poesia, *f.*; cattivi versi, *m. pl.*
dŏg-gish, ADJ.: cagnesco; brutale **-grass**, s.: gramigna, *f.*

dŏggrel = *doggerel.*
dŏg-hearted, ADJ.: crudele, inumano. **-kennel**, S.: canile, *m.* **-louse**, S.: zecca, *f.*
dŏg-ma, S.: dogma, domma, *m.* **mătic(al)**, ADJ.: dogmatico. **-mătically**, ADV.: in maniera dogmatica. **-măticalness**, S.: stile dogmatico, *m.* **-matist**, S.: che dogmatizza. **-matize**, TR.: dogmatizzare; insegnare.
dŏg-sleep, S.: sonno finto, *m.* **-meat**, S.: cibo da cani, *m.;* cosa vile, *f.* **-star**, S.: canicola, *f.;* sirio, *m.* **-tooth**, S.: gramigna, *f.* **-trick**, S.: furberia, *f.* **-trot**, S.: trotto di cane, *m.* **-weary**, ADJ.: stracco come un cane, stanchissimo.
dŏily, S.: tovaglietta picciola†; salvietta, *f.*
dŏing, PART.: facendo; S.: fatto, *m.*, azione, *f.;* PL.: fatti, evento, *m. pl.: it is a—*, si sta facendo; *what are you —?* che fate? *keep one —*, dar dell' impiego ad alcuno.
dŏit, S.: bezzo, quattrino, *m.*
dōle 1, S.: distribuzione; porzione; elemosina, *f.;* affanno, *m.* **dole** 2, TR.: distribuire; dare: — *out*, spartire, scompartire. **-ful**, ADJ.: tristo, doloroso, mesto, lugubre. **-fully**, ADV.: tristamente, lamentevolmente, dolentemente. **-fulness**, S.: tristezza; doglia, afflizione, *f.;* dolore, *m.* **-some**, ADJ.: doglioso, affannoso, **-someness**, S.: malinconia, tristezza, tristizia, *f.*
dŏll, S.: bambola, *f.*, fantoccio; bamboccio, *m.*
dŏllar, S.: dollaro (*in Am. freq.* scudo), *m.*
dolorif-erous, **-ic**, ADJ.: dolorifico, che reca dolore.
dōlor, S.: dolore, *m.;* afflizione, *f.* **-ous**, ADJ.: doloroso; tristo, lugubre. **-ousness**, S.: dolore, *m.*, doglia, *f.*
dŏlphin, S.: delfino, *m.*
dōlt, S.: minchione, balordo, *m.* **-ish**, ADJ.: sciocco, stupido. **-ishly**, ADV.: scioccamente, stupidamente. **-ishness**, S.: scempitaggine, stupidità, *f.*
domāin, S.: dominio, *m.;* sovranità; possessione, *f.*
dōme, S.: cupola, volta, *f.*, duomo, *m.*
domĕs-tic, S.: domestico; servo, *m.* **-tic(al)**, ADJ.: domestico, dimestico, familiare, dimesticare. **-ticate**, TR.: domesticare, dimesticare.
dŏm-icile, S.: domicilio; albergo, *m.* **-icillary**, ADJ.: domiciliario.
dŏm-inant, ADJ.: dominante. **-inate**, TR.: dominare, prevalere. **-ination**, S.: dominio, imperio, *m.*, signoria, *f.* **-inator**, S.: dominatore, *m.* **-inēer**, TR.: dominare; signoreggiare. **-inēering**, ADJ.: dominante; imperioso, insolente, altiero.

domĭnical, ADJ.: dominicale, del Signore.
Domĭnican, S.: domenicano, *m.*
domĭnion, S.: dominio; territorio, *m.;* giurisdizione, *f.*
dŏn 1, S.: don, signore, *m.* **don** 2, TR.: metter su.
dōnary, S.: offerta, obblazione, *f.*
don-ātion, S.: donazione, *f.*, dono, donamento, *m.* **dŏn-ative**, S.: dono, presente, *m.*
dōne, ADJ.: fatto; conchiuso; cotto: —! fatto! accettato! vada!
do-nēe, S.: (*leg.*) donatario, *m.* **dō-nor**, S.: donatore, *m.*
dōodle, S.: scioperone, ozioso, sfaccendato, *m.*
dōom 1, S.: sentenza; condannazione, *f.* **doom** 2, TR.: sentenziare; condannare. **-ful**, ADJ.: funesto. **-sday**, S.: giudizio universale, *m.* **-sday-book**, S.: catastro, *m.*
dōor, S.: porta; entrata, *f.;* uscio, *m.: back —*, porta di dietro; *carriage —*, sportello, *m.;* — *posts*, imposte, *f. pl.; next —*, la prima porta, la casa attigua; *folding —*, porta a due imposte, *f.; within —*, in casa; *out—s*, fuor di casa; *keep within —s*, non uscire, rimanere in casa; *knock at the —*, picchiare alla porta; *turn out of —s*, scacciar fuor di casa, mettere alla porta. **-bar**, S.: sbarra di porta, *f.* **-case**, S.: impostatura di porta, *f.* **-handle**, S.: manubrio dell' uscio, *m.* **-keeper**, S.: portinaio; carceriere, *m.* **-knob**, S.: bottone dell' uscio, *m.* **-post**, S.: imposta della porta, *f.* **-way**, S.: usciale, *m.*
Dŏric, ADJ.: dorico.
dôr-mant, ADJ.: dormiente; segreto. **-mer-window**, S.: spiraglio, abbaino, *m.* **-mitory**, S.: dormitorio, *m.* **-mouse**, S.: ghiro, *m.*
dôrp†, S.: villagio, *m.*
dôrr, S.: pecchione; calabrone, *m.*
dôr-sel, **-ser**, S.: cesta, paniera, *f.*
dōse 1, S.: dosa, dose; presa, *f.* **dose** 2, TR.: (*med.*) dosare.
dŏssil, S.: (*surg.*) piumacciuolo, *m.*
dŏt 1, S.: punto, *m.* **dot** 2, INTR.: puntare; porre i punti.
dōtage, S.: perdita d' intelletto; imbecillità, *f.;* vaneggiamento, *m.*
dōtal, ADJ.: dotale, di dote.
dōtard, S.: vecchio rimbambito, *m.* **-ly**, ADV.: imbecille.
dotātion, S.: dotazione, *f.*
dō-te, INTR.: vaneggiare, bamboleggiare, amare soverchiamente: — *upon*, essere inamoratissimo di, amare perdutamente. **-ter**, S.: che ama soverchiamente. **-tingly**, ADV.: con soverchio amore, appassionatamente. **-tish**, ADJ.: imbecille

dŏttard, s.: albero nano, *m.*

dŏub-le 1, ADJ.: doppio; simulato; s.: doppio; artificio; inganno, *m.*: *see things* —, vedere gli oggetti raddoppiati. **-le** 2, TR.: doppiare, raddoppiare; dissimulare; piegare; (*nav.*) trapassare. **-le-barrelled**, ADJ.: a due canne. **-le-buttoned**, ADJ.: a due ordini di bottoni. **-le-chin**, s.: doppio mento, *m.* **-le-dealer**, s.: furfante, furbo, *m.* **-le-dealing**, s.: furberia, trufferia, *f.*; inganno, *m.* **-le-dye**, TR.: tingere in grana. **-le-edged**, ADJ.: a due tagli. **-le-handed**, ADJ.: ambidestro, ingannatore. **-le-headed**, ADJ.: a due teste. **-le-lock**, TR.: serrare a doppia chiave. **-le-meaning**, s.: ambiguità, *f.* **-le-minded**, ADJ.: falso, furbo. **-leness**, s.: doppiezza, *f.*; raddoppiamento, *m.* **-ler**, s.: che raddoppia; filatore, *m.* **-let**, s.: giubbone; paio, *m.* **-le-tongued**, ADJ.: furbo, ingannoso, insidioso. **-ling**, s.: raddoppiamento; artificio, *m.* **-lōon**, s.: dobblone, doppione, *m.* (moneta). **-ly**, ADV.: doppiamente, a doppio.

dŏubt 1, s.: dubbio, *m.*, incertezza; difficoltà, *f.*: *without* —, senza dubbio; *I have no* — *about it*, non ne dubito. **doubt** 2, TR.: sospettare; esitare; INTR.: dubitare, stare (essere, trovarsi) in dubbio: *I* — *it*, ne dubito; *I* — *whether*, dubito se. **-er**, s.: che dubita. **-ful**, ADJ.: dubbioso, incerto; dubbio: *man of* — *character*, uomo dubbio (sospetto); *of* — *virtue*, di dubbia virtù. **-fully**, ADV.: dubbiosamente. **-fulness**, s.: dubbio, *m.*; incertezza; ambiguità, *f.* **-ingly**, ADV.: dubbiosamente, in modo dubbioso. **-less**, ADJ.: indubitabile, sicuro, certo; ADV.: indubitabilmente, senza dubbio, sicuramente, certamente.

dŏucets, s. PL.: testicoli di cervo, *m. pl.*

dŏugh, s.: pasta, *f.* **-baked**, ADJ.: mezzo cotto.

dŏughty, ADJ.: valoroso, coraggioso.

dŏughy, ADJ.: pastoso.

dŏuse, TR.: immergere all' improvviso; INTR.: cascare nell' acqua improvvisamente.

dŏut†, TR.: estinguere. **-er**, s.: spegnitoio, *m.*

dŏve, s.: colomba, *f.* **-cot**, **-house**, s.: colombaia, *f.* **-like**, ADJ.: simile ad una colomba. **-tail** 1, s.: (*join.*) coda di rondine; incastratura, *f.* **-tail** 2, TR.: incastrare, intagliare. **-tailed**, ADJ.: incastrato.

dŏwager, s.: vedova, *f.*

dŏwdy, s.: donnaccia, *f.*

dŏwer, s.: dote, dota, pensione, *f.* **-ed**, ADJ.: dotato. **-less**, ADJ.: senza dote, *non dotato*; povero. **-y** = *dower*.

dŏwlas, s.: sorta di tela grossolana, *f.*

dŏwn 1, s.: penna matta; lanugine, *f.*

down 2, PREP., ADV.: giù: a basso, abbasso; a secondo: — *the stream*, a seconda la corrente; *up and* —, su e giù; qua e là; *upside* —, sossopra: *farther* —, più abbasso; — *stairs*, abbasso; *bring* —, portar giù, calare; *fall* —, cascare; *lie* —, giacere; coricarsi, sdraiarsi; *look* —, abbassare gli occhi; *pay money* —, pagar danari contanti; *set* —, adagiare; mettere in iscritto, registrare; *sit* —, sederai; *turn upside* —, rovesciare, mettere a rovescio. **down** 3, TR.: abbattere, soverchiare, vincere. **-cast**, ADJ.: abbattuto; dimesso; modesto: *with* — *eyes*, cogli occhi bassi. **-fall**, s.: traboccamento, *m.*; rovina, *f.* **-fallen**, ADJ.: rovinato. **-hearted**, ADJ.: abbattuto, scoraggiato. **-hill**, s.: discesa, *f.*; declivio, *m.* **-looked**, ADJ.: tristo, malinconico. **-right**, ADJ.: evidente; franco; ADV.: giù a piombo. **-rightness**, s.: franchigia; sincerità, *f.* **-sitting**, s.: riposo, *m.*; quiete, *f.* **-ward**, ADJ.: declive; abbattuto, dimesso, afflitto. **-ward(s)**, ADV.: giù, abbasso.

dŏwny, ADJ.: lanuginoso; molle.

dŏw-re, **-ry**, s.: dote, dota, *f.*

dŏwse 1, s.: schiaffo, *m.* **dowse** 2, TR.: schiaffeggiare.

dŏxy, s.: donna di mala vita, *f.*

dōse, TR.: addormentare; rendere stupido; INTR.: essere sonnoglioso.

dŏzen, s.: dozzina, *f.*: *by* —*s*, a dozzine.

dō-ziness, s.: sonnolenza, *f.*; addormentamento, *m.* **-zy**, ADJ.: sonnoglioso, addormentato.

drăchm, s.: dramma, *f.*

drăff, s.: feccia, *f.*; beverone, *m.* **-y**, ADJ.: feccioso; sudicio.

drăft, s.: tratto, *m.*, strappata; corrente d' aria, *f.*; tiro d' acqua (di una nave); piano (d' un edifizio), *m.*, pianta, *f.*; abbozo, schizzo, disegno; prima copia (d' uno scritto), stracciafoglio, *m.*; tratta, cambiale, *f.*, mandato; (*mil.*) straccamento, *m.*, leva, *f.*: *I enclose you my* — *for* 100 *frs.*, vi acchiudo la mia tratta per 100 fr.; *play at* —*s*, giuocare allo tavole (alle dame); *at a* —, ad un sorso. **-board**, s.: tavoliere, scacchiere, *m.* **-horse**, s.: cavallo da tiro, *m.*

drăg 1, s.: uncino; gancio; tramaglio, *m.* **drag** 2, (IN)TR.: tirare per forza; strascinare: — *in* (*out*), strascinare dentro (fuori). **-chain**, s.: catena da frenare, *f.*

drăggle, TR.: infangare, imbrattare; INTR.: infangarsi, imbrattarsi. **-tail**, s.: zitella sporca, *f.*

drăg-net, s.: tramaglio, *m.*

drăgoman, S.: dragomanno, *m.*

drăgon, S.: dragone, *m.* **-et**, S.: dragoncello, *m.* **-fly**, S.: libellula, *f.* **-ish**, ADJ.: dragoniforme. **-like**, ADJ.: furioso, feroce. **-'s-blood**, S.: sangue di dragone, *m.*

dragōon 1, S.: dragone, *m.* **dragoon** 2, TR.: saccheggiare; sottomettere.

drāin 1, S.: fogna, *f.*, condotto sotterraneo, *m.* **drain** 2, TR.: seccare; fognare. **-able**, ADJ.: che si può seccare. **-er**, S.: sgocciolatoio, *m.*

drāke, S.: anitra, *f.*; cannoncino, *m.*

drăm 1, S.: dramma, *f.*; sorso (di qualche liquore), *m.* **dram** 2, INTR.: bere liquori distillati.

drâ-ma, S.: dramma, *m.* **-mátic(al)**, ADJ.: drammatico. **-máticálly**, ADV.: a modo di dramma. **-matist**, S.: autore drammatico, *m.*

drăm-drinker, S.: bevitore di liquori distillati, *m.*

drāper, S.: mercante di panni; pannaiuolo, *m.*: *linen* —, mercante di tele, *m.* **-y**, S.: drapperia; manifattura di panni, *f.*

drăstic, ADJ.: drastico, vigoroso.

draugh *drâf*, S.: feccia, *f.*; beverone, *m.*

draught *drâft* (cf. *draft*), S.: sorso; piano; disegno, *m.*; copia; tratta, *f.*; tiro (d' acqua); biglietto; sommario, *m.*: *at one* —, ad un sorso; — *of horses*, tirella, *f.*; tiramento, *m.*; — *of soldiers*, distaccamento, *m.*; *ship of small* —, nave che pesca poco. **-board**, S.: tavoliere; scacchiere, *m.* **-horse**, S.: cavallo da tiro, *m.* **-house**, S.: cloaca, *f.* **-ox**, S.: bove da tiro, *m.* **-s**, S. PL.: giuoco delle tavole, o delle dame: *play at* —, giuocare alle tavole, o alle dame. **-s'man**, S.: disegnatore; copista, *m.*

drâw, IRR.; TR.: tirare, trarre, trainare; attrarre, allettare; disegnare; strascinare, dedurre; INTR.: accorciarsi, ristringersi; ritirarsi: — *blood*, salassare; — *breath*, respirare; — *lots*, tirar a sorte; — *to a head*, far capo; — *out a party*, fare un distaccamento; — *a picture*, fare un ritratto; — *a pond*, pescare un vivaio; — *out a tooth*, cavar un dente; — *again*, disegnare di nuovo; ritirare; — *along*, strascinare; — *aside*, menar a banda; — *asunder*, separare; dividere; — *away*, portare via; [illegible]; — *back*, tirarsi indietro; — [illegible] *[illegible]ward*; — *for-* [illegible] durre; [illegible]-

mento, pregiudizio, svantaggio, *m.* **-bar**, S.: (*rail.*) sbarra di congiungitura, *f.* **-beam**, S.: argano, *m.* **-bridge**, S.: ponte levatoio, *m.* **-er**, S.: tiratore; disegnatore; tiratoio, *m.* **-ers**, S. PL.: sottocalzoni, *m. pl.*; mutande, *f. pl.*: *a pair of* —, un paio di mutande. **-ing**, S.: delineamento, disegno, *m.* **-ing-board**, S.: tavola da disegnare, *f.* **-ing-master**, S.: maestro di disegno, *m.* **-ing-paper**, S.: carta da disegnare, *f.* **-ing-room**, S.: salotto, salone, *m.*; anticamera; assemblea, *f.*

drâwl 1, S.: voce languida, *f.* **drawl** 2, INTR.: strascinare (le parole): — *out*, proferire collo strascico.

drâw-latch, S.: saliscendo, *m.* **-n**, ADJ.: tirato, tratto; cavato: — *battle*, S.: battaglia indecisa, *f.*; — *sword*, S.: spada nuda, *f.* **-well**, S.: pozzo profondo, *m.*

drāy-cart, S.: carro, *m.*; slitta, treggia, *f.* **-horse**, S.: cavallo da traino, *m.* **-man**, S.: carrettiere, *m.*

drĕad 1, ADJ.: terribile, formidabile, orribile; S.: spavento; terrore, *m.*, paura, *f.* **dread** 2, IRR.; TR.: temere, paventare. **-er**, S.: che teme. **-ful**, ADJ.: terribile, spaventevole. **-fully**, ADV.: terribilmente, spaventevolmente. **-fulness**, S.: orrore, terrore, spavento, *m.* **-less**, ADJ.: intrepido; forte. **-lessness**, S.: intrepidezza, *f.*

drēam 1, S.: sogno, *m.*; stravaganza, *f.* **dream** 2, IRR.; TR.: vedere in sogno; IRR.: sognare; immaginare; immaginarsi. **-er**, S.: sognatore; pensieroso; infingardo, *m.* **-ing**, ADJ.: sognante; lento, **-ingly**, ADV.: con lentezza. **-less**, ADJ.: senza sogni.

drēar, ADJ.: terribile; tristo, deserto. **-ily**, ADV.: orribilmente; tristamente. **-iness**, S.: orrore, terrore, *m.* **-y**, ADJ.: orribile, lugubre; tristo, penoso; deserto.

drĕd-ge 1, S.: tramaglio, *m.* **-ge** 2, TR.: raccogliere con un tramaglio; insaleggiare. **-ger** 2, S.: pescatore con un tramaglio, *m.* **-ging-machine**, S.: cavafango, *m.*

drĕg-gish, **-gy**, ADJ.: feccioso, pieno di feccia; impuro. **-s**, S. PL.: feccia, *f.*, sedimento, *m.*: — *of the people*, feccia del popolo; canaglia.

drĕnch 1, S.: beveraggio, *m.* (medicina d' animale). **drench** 2, TR.: abbeverare; bagnare; innaffiare, umettare.

drĕss 1, S.: abito, vestimento; addobbamento, ornamento, *m.*; cuffia, *f.*: *full* —, abito di gran gala. **dress** 2, TR.: vestire; addobbare, adornare; acconciare; cucinare; cuocere; INTR.: aggiustarsi; acconciarsi; REFL.: vertirsi: — *flax*, scotere il lino; — *a garden*, coltivare un [illegible]ino; — *the hair*, acconciare i capelli; — *leather*, conciare della pelle; — *a ship*, pavesare una nave; — *a tree*, dibruscare, rimondare; — *a vine*, potare una vigna; — *a wound*, medicare una ferita; *right —!* a destra riga! **-ed**, ADJ.: vestito, *etc.*, cf. *dress: well —*, ben vestito; *ill —*, male in ornese. **-er**, S.: acconciatore; cuoco, *m.;* tavola di cucina, *f.* **-ing**, S.: vestire; vestimento; addobbamento; apparato; medicamento, *m.;* fascia, *f.* **-ing-case**, S.: necessario, *n.* **-ing-cloth**, S.: mantellina; toeletta, *f.* **-ing-gown**, S.: veste di camera, zimarra, *f.* **-ing-room**, S.: camera da vestirsi, *f.* **-ing-table**, S.: toeletta, *f.*

drib 1, S.: goccia, stilla, *f.* **drib** 2, TR.: tagliare via; scemare. **-ble**, TR.: stillare; INTR: cascare giù, gocciolare; fare bava.

driblet, S.: piccol debito, *m.*

drier, S.: (*med.*) disseccativo, *m.*

drift 1, S.: impulso; corso; oggetto; maneggio, *m.: — of ice*, pezzo di ghiaccio, *m.; — of sand*, alzamento di rena mobile, *m.; — of snow*, caduta di neve, *f. pl.*, falde di neve. **drift** 2, TR.: spingere; cacciare; accumulare; INTR.: accumularsi.

drill 1, S.: succhiello, spillo; babbuino; (*mil.*) exercizio, *m.* **drill** 2, TR.: forare; disciplinare. **-bow**, S.: archetto, *m.*

drink 1, S.: bevanda, *f.*, beveraggio, *m.: give me some —*, datemi a bere. **drink** 2, IRR.; TR.: bere, bevere; assorbire; tracannare; INTR.: imbriacarsi, inebriarsi: — *to*, far brindisi; *I — your health*, bevo alla vostra salute; — *coffee*, bere il caffè; — *in*, imbevere; succiare; — *out*, vuotare (a forza di bere); — *up*, bevere tutto. **-able**, ADJ.: potabile. **-er**, S.: bevitore; beone, *m.* **-ing**, S.: bere; bevimento, *m.* **-ing-bout**, S.: beveria, *f.* **-ing-companion**, S.: compagno in beveria, *m.* **-ing-cup**, S.: tazza, coppa, *f.* **-ing-glass**, S.: bicchiere, *m.* **-ing-house**, S.: bettola, *f.* **-ing-song**, S.: canzone gioviale, *f.* **-money**, S.: mancia, *f.;* paraguanto, *m.*

drip 1, S.: goccia, gocciola, *f.* **drip** 2, (IN)TR.: spruzzare, gocciolare, stillare. **-ping**, S.: (il) gocciolare, (lo) stillare; unto, *m.* **-ping-pan**, S.: ghiotta, leccarda, *f.*

drive 1, IRR.; TR.: condurre, guidare, menare; cacciare; spingere, impellere, forzare; INTR.: aver in mira, tendere; avanzare: — *a carriage*, guidare una carrozza; — *a nail*, ficcare un chiodo; — *stakes*, ficcare pali; — *off time*, procrastinare, indugiare; — *along*, proseguire, continuare; — *away*, scacciare; — back, rispingere; ributtare; — *in*, *into*, fare entrare; cacciare; — *on*, impellere; spingere; andare avanti; avanzare; — *out*, scacciare; fare uscire; andare fuori in carozza; *can you —?* sapete guidare? **drive** 2, S.: scarrozzata, passeggiata in carrozza, *f.*

drivel 1, S.: bava, saliva, *f.;* pazzo, sciocone, *m.* **drivel** 2, INTR.: bavare; esser bavoso. **-er**, S.: goffone, idiota, minchione, *m.*

dri-ver, S.: conduttore, *m.;* zeppa, *f.* **-ving**, S.: condotta, *f.;* carriaggio, *m.* **-ving-box**, S.: sedile del cocchiere, *m.*

driz-zle, (IN)TR.: spruzzolare, gocciolare: *drizzling rain*, spruzzaglia, *f.* **-zly**, ADJ.: piovigginoso, umido.

dröil† 1, S.: infingardo, fuggifatica, *m.* **droil** 2, INTR.: lavorar con fatiga, tentennare.

dröll 1, ADJ.: comico, burlevole; S.: buffone; schernitore, *m.* **droll** 2, INTR.: buffoneggiare, beffare. **-ery**, S.: buffoneria, facezia; farsa, *f.* **-ingly**, ADV.: buffonescamente. **-ish**, ADJ.: buffonesco.

drómedary, S.: dromedario, *m.*

drōn-e 1, S.: pecchione; infingardaccio, *m.* **-e** 2, INTR.: ronzare; tentennare, cincischiare. **-ish**, ADJ.: lento, ozioso, inerte. **-ishness**, S.: poltroneria, *f.*

drōop, INTR.: languire; infiebolire; affliggersi, esser tristo. **-ing**, ADJ.: languido; afflitto, tristo; S.: abbattimento; languore, *m.* **-ingly**, ADV.: languidamente; debolmente.

drŏp 1, S.: goccia, *f.*, gocciolo; orecchino, *m.: little —*, gocciolina; *a few —s*, poche gocciole; — *by —*, a goccia a goccia; *by —s*, a goccia a goccia. **drop** 2, TR.: lasciare cascare (*or* cadere); abbandonare; cessare; metter da bando; INTR.: gocciolare; cascare; svenire, sparire; morire: —*s*, goccie medicinali; — *anchor*, ancorarsi; — *a design*, desistere da un disegno; — *a word*, lasciar scappare una parola; *the curtain —s*, cade il sipario; — *with sweat*, gocciolare di sudore; — *in*, introdurre; entrare; venire improvviso; — *off*, scadere; venire in decadenza; — *out*, sparire, dissiparsi. **-ping**, S.: goccia, gocciola, *f.: — of the nose*, gocciola al naso, *f.* **-let**, S.: piccola goccia, gocciolina, *f.* **-pingly**, ADV.: a goccia a goccia. **-serene**, S.: gotta serena, *f.*

drŏpsical, ADJ.: idropico.

drŏp-stone, S.: marcassita, *f.*

drŏpsy, S.: idropisia, *f.*

drŏpwort, S.: (*bot.*) filipendula, *f.*

drŏss, S.: scoria; feccia, *f.;* rifiuto, *m.* **-iness**, S.: spuma; sporcizia, *f.* **-y**, ADJ.: pieno di scoria; feccioso; sporco.

dröught, s.: secchezza, siccità; sete, *f.* **-iness**, s.: aridità, siccità, *f.* **-y**, ADJ.: secco, arido; assetato, sitibondo.

dröv-e 1, impf. del v. *drive*, **-e** 2, s.: branco, *m.*; gregge; folla, *f.* **-er**, s.: bifolco, *m.*

dröwn, TR.: annegare; immergere; INTR.: annegarsi; immergersi, affogarsi: — *one's self*, annegarsi, gettarsi nell' acqua; *be —ed*, annegare, essere annegato.

dröw-ṣe, TR.: addormentare, render sonnacchioso; INTR.: dormire. **-ṣily**, ADV.: sonnacchioni; lentamente. **-ṣiness**, s.: sonnolenza; indolenza; pigrizia, *f.* **-ṣy**, ADJ.: sonnolento, sonnacchioso; stupido: *grow* —, addormentarsi. **-ṣy-head**, s.: sopore, *m.* **-ṣy-headed**, ADJ.: sonnolento, sopito.

drŭb 1, s.: colpo, *m.*; botta, *f.* **drub** 2, TR.: battere, bastonare; percuotere. **-bing**, s.: bastonata, bastonatura, *f.*: *give one a sound* —, dare ad uno un buon carpiccio.

drŭd-ge 1, s.: facchino, *m.* **-ge** 2, INTR.: affaticarsi; stentare. **-ger**, s.: facchino; bossoletto, *m.* **-gery**, s.: servigio vile, *m.* **-ging-box**, s.: bossoletto da infarinare; polverino, *m.* **-gingly**, ADV.: con pena, con molto affaticamento.

drŭg 1, s.: droga, *f.*; rifiuto, *m.* **drug** 2, TR.: mescolare con ingredienti medicinali. **-get**, s.: droghetta, *m.* **-gist**, s.: droghiere, droghiero, farmacista, *m.*

drŭid, s.: druido, *m.*

drŭm 1, s.: tamburo; timpano; tamburino, *m.*: *beat the* —, battere il tamburo; — *of the ear*, timpano dell' orecchio. **drum** 2, INTR.: battere il tamburo.

drŭmble†, INTR.: poltroneggiare, tentennare, cincischiare.

drŭm-major, s.: tamburino maggiore, *m.* **-maker**, s.: fabbricante di tamburi, *m.* **-mer**, s.: tamburino, *m.* **-ming**, s.: battimento del tamburo, *m.* **-stick**, s.: bacchetta di tamburo, *f.*

drŭnk, ADJ.: ebrio, ubriaco: *make* —, imbriacare; *get* —, imbriacarsi, ubriacarsi; *dead* —, ubriacaccio. **-ard**, s.: imbriacone, trincone, *m.* **-en**, ADJ.: imbriaco, inebbriato. **-enly**, ADV.: da imbriaco. **-enness**, s.: imbriachezza, ubriachezza, *f.*

drȳ 1, ADJ.: secco, arido, asciutto; sitibondo, assetato; insipido; ... — ..., assecchire, diventar ... *terra ferma*, *f.*, continen... TR.: seccare, inaridire; ... seccarsi, inaridirsi.

drȳad, s.: driada, *f.*

dry-ṣe, s.: (*med.*) diu... ADJ.: ... *lagrima* ... *di ...*, di ... *ects, di* ...

cate, *f. pl.* **-ly**, ADV.: senza umidità, aridamente; freddamente; poveramente. **-ness**, s.: siccità; freddezza; insipidezza, *f.* **-nurse** 1, s.: nutrice non lattante, *f.* **-nurse** 2, TR.: allevare senza lattare. **-shod**, ADJ.: a secco; a piè secco.

dū-al, ADJ.: duale; da due. **-ăl'ity**, s.: dualità, *f.*

dŭb 1, s.: colpo, *m.*, percossa, *f.* **dub** 2, TR.: fare; creare; armare (un cavaliere).

dubiŏsity, s.: dubbiezza, *f.*

dū̆b-ious, ADJ.: dubbioso, incerto, indeciso. **-iously**, ADV.: dubbiosamente, con dubbio. **-iousness**, s.: dubbiezza, *f.*, dubbio, *m.*, incertezza, *f.* **-itable**, ADJ.: dubitevole, dubbioso, incerto. **-itably**, ADV.: in modo dubbioso. **-itātion**, s.: dubitazione; dubitanza, *f.*

dūcal, ADJ.: ducale, di duca, da duca.

dŭcat, s.: ducato, *m.* (moneta).

dŭch-ess, s.: duchessa, *f.* **-y**, s.: ducato, *m.*

dŭck 1, s.: anatra; inchinata, riverenza, *f.*: *my* —! mio caro! mia cara! **duck** 2, TR.: tuffare, immergere; INTR.: tuffarsi. **-er**, s.: marangone, parasito, *m.* **-ing**, s.: (*nav.*) cala, *f.*, tuffo, battesimo del tropico, *m.*: *give one a* —, tuffare uno, dargli un tuffo. **-legged**, ADJ.: che ha gambe corte. **-ling**, s.: anatrina, *f.* **-meat**, s.: lente palustre, *f.* **-afoot**, s.: serpentaria, *f.* **-weed** = *duck-meat*.

dŭct, s.: guida, *f.*; passaggio; canale, *m.* **-ile**, ADJ.: duttile; flessibile; trattevole. **-ileness**, **-ility**, s.: duttilità; flessibilità; docilità, *f.*

dŭdc, s.: damerino, elegante, *m.*

dŭdgeon, s.: daga piccola; mala parte, *f.*: *take in* —, sdegnarsi, dar nel cencio.

dūe 1, ADJ.: debito, dovuto: *in — time*, opportunamente; s.: debito; tributo, *m.*; imposta, *f.* **due** 2, ADV.: debitamente; esattamente: *your bill falls* —, la vostra cambiale scade. **-fŭl†**, ADJ.: convenevole, conveniente.

dūel 1, s.: duello, *m.*: *fight a* —, battersi in duello. **duel** 2, INTR.: duellare, fare duello. **-ler**, ... duellista, *m.* **-ling**, s.: duel... **-list**, s.: duellista ... *f.* ... *f.* ... capezzolo, ... *m* ...; ottu-...

— *sight*, vista fosca, *f.*; — *wit*, ingegno ottuso, *m.* **dull** 2, TR.: stupidire; render ottuso; offuscare; INTR.: intormentirsi. **-ard**, S.: babbuasso, *m.* **-brained**, ADJ.: stupido, scempiato, capocchio. **-head**, S.: minchione, balocco, *m.* **-ness**, S.: stupidezza, balordaggine, pigrizia, lentezza; sonnolenza, *f.* **-pated**, ADJ.: stupido, insensato. **-witted**, ADJ.: stordito, balordo. **-y**, ADV.: stupidamente; lentemente.

dŭly, ADV.: debitamente, convenevolmente; esattamente, precisamente.

dŭl-cet, ADJ.: dolce (al gusto), dolcigno; armonioso. **-cificātion**, S.: (*chem.*) dolcificare, *m.* **-cify**, TR.: dolcificare; raddolcire, mitigare. **-cimer**, S.: salterio, saltero, *m.* **-corate**, TR.: addolcire, rendere dolce. **-corātion**, S.: addolcimento, *m.*, dolcificazione, *f.*

dŭmb, ADJ.: muto, taciturno: *strike* —, far ammutire. **-bells**, PL.: pesi ginnastici, *m. pl.* **-found**, TR.: render muto; confondere. **-ly**, ADV.: in silenzio, senza parlare. **-ness**, S.: mutezza, *f.*; silenzio, *m.* **-waiter**, S.: calapranzi, *m.*

dŭmp 1, S.: cordoglio, *m.* **dump** 2, S.: tristezza, malinconia, *f.* **-ish**, ADJ.: tristo, mesto. **-ishly**, ADV.: tristamente. **-ishness**, S.: tristezza, malinconia, *f.*

dŭmp-ling, S.: podingo, *m.* **-y**, ADJ.: corto e grosso.

dŭn 1, ADJ.: bruno, fosco; tanè. **dun** 2, S.: creditore importuno, *m.* **dun** 3, TR.: importunare, molestare. **-bee**, S.: tafano, *m.*

dŭn-ce, S.: goffo, babbuasso, *m.* **-cery**, S.: goffaggine, balordaggine, *f.* **-cical**, ADJ.: sciocco, balordo.

dŭng 1, impf. e part. del v. *ding.* **dung** 2, S.: concime, letame; sterco, *m.* **dung** 3, TR.: concimare, letamare. **-cart**, S.: carretta da trasporre il letame, *f.*

dŭngeon, S.: prigione sotterranea, *f.*

dŭng-fork, S.: forcone del letame, *m.* **-hill**, ADJ.: nato nel letame; vile, abbietto; S.: concime; letamaio, *m.* **-y**, ADJ.: pieno di letame; abbietto. **-yard**, S.: luogo da riporvi il letame, cortile, *m.*

dŭnnage, S.: (*nav.*) pagliuolo, *m.*

dŭnner, S.: riscuotitore, esattore, *m.*

dŭnnish, ADJ.: brunotto.

dŭnny, ADJ.: sordo.

dūo, S.: (*mus.*) duetto, *m.* **-decimo**, S.: in dodici; libro in duodecimo, *m.*

dūpe 1, S.: merlotto, gonzo, ingannato, *m.* **dupe** 2, TR.: ingannare, truffare.

dū-plicate 1, S.: duplicato, *m.*, copia, *f.* **-plicate** 2, TR.: raddoppiare; piegare. **-plicātion**, S.: duplicazione, *f.*, raddoppiamento, *m.* **-plicity**, S.: duplicità; doppiezza, *f.*

durability, S.: durabilità, *f.*

dū-rable, ADJ.: durabile; solido. **-rableness**, S.: durabilità, *f.* **-rably**, ADV.: durabilmente, durevolmente. **-rance**, S.: incarcerazione, prigionia, *f.* **-rātion**, S.: durazione, durata, *f.* **-re†**, INTR.: durare; perseverare. **-reful†**, ADJ.: durevole; stabile; permanente. **-reless†**, ADJ.: transitorio, cadevole. **-ress**, S.: incarcerazione, prigionia, *f.* **-ring**, PREP., CONJ.: per, durante. **-rity**, S.: durezza; fermezza, solidezza, *f.*

dŭsk 1, ADJ.: oscuro, fosco, bruno, bujo; S.: crepuscolo, bruzzo, bruzzolo, *m.*: *in the — of the evening*, in sul far bruzzo; al far della notte. **dusk** 2, TR.: oscurare; INTR.: oscurarsi; imbrunire, divenire bruno. **-ily**, ADV.: oscuramente, foscamente. **-(i)ness**, S.: oscurità, *f.*; buio, *m.* **-y**, ADJ.: alquanto scuro, fosco, oscuretto.

dŭst 1, S.: polvere; povertà, *f.*: *the rain has laid the* —, la pioggia ha ammorzato la polvere; *trample in the* —, calpestare. **dust** 2, TR.: coprire di polvere; — *off*, nettare da polvere, spazzare. **-box**, S.: polverino, *m.* **-er**, S.: strofinaccio, *m.* **-iness**, S.: polverio, *m.* **-man**, S.: paladino, *m.* **-y**, ADJ.: polveroso, coperto di polvere.

Dŭtch, ADJ., S.: olandese. **-man**, S.: olandese, *m.*

dū-teous, **-tiful**, ADJ.: ubbidiente, ossequioso; rispettoso. **-tifully**, ADV.: ossequiosamente, sommessamente. **-tifulness**, S.: ubbidienza; sommessione, *f.* **-ty**, S.: dovere, debito, *m.*; funzione, *f.*; uffizio, *m.*; tassa; dogana, gabella, *f.*: *on* —, *upon* —, di servizio, in funzione; *pay one's* —, render rispetto; *present one's* —, riverire, salutare.

duŭmvirate, S.: duumvirato, *m.*

dwärf 1, S.: nano; caramogio, *m.* **dwarf** 2, TR.: impedire dal crescere. **-elder**, S.: ebbio, *m.* **-ish**, ADJ.: piccoletto, piccino. **-ishly**, ADV.: in modo piccino. **-ishness**, S.: picciolezza, *f.* **-tree**, S.: albero nano, *m.*

dwĕll, IRR.; INTR.: abitare, dimorare; stare; dilatarsi, allargarsi. **-er**, S.: abitatore, abitante, *m.* **-ing**, S.: abitazione, dimora, *f.* **-ing-house**, S.: casa; abitazione, *f.*

dwindle, INTR.: impiccolire, diminuire; consumarsi; peggiorare.

dȳ-e 1, S.: tinta, tintura, *f.*, colore, *m.*: — *stuff*, materia tintoria, *f.* **-e** 2, TR.: tingere, colorare: — *black* (*blue*, etc.), tingere in nero (turchino, ecc.); — *in grain*, tingere in lana. **-eing**, S.: tintura; il tingere. **-er**, S.: tintore, *m.* **-e-house**, S.: tintoria, *f.* **-e-works**, S.: tintoria, *f.*

dȳing, ADJ.: moriente; moribondo; S.: morte, *f.*

dȳnast, S.: dinasta, *m.* **-y**, S.: dinastia; sovranità, *f.*

dȳs-crasy, S.: (*med.*) discrasia, *f.*, stemperamento d'umori, *m.* **-entery**, S.: (*med.*) dissenteria, *f.* **-pĕpsy**, S.: (*med.*) dispepsia, *f.* **-ury**, S.: disuria, stranguria, *f.*

E

ē (*the letter*), S.: e, *m.*

ēach, PRON.: ciascheduno, ciascuno: *on — side*, dalle due bande; *— other*, l'un l'altro.

ēager, ADJ.: desideroso, bramoso, fervente, ardente; veemente. **-ly**, ADV.: ferventemente, ardentemente; veementemente. **-ness**, S.: premura, *f.*, fervore, ardore, *m.*; passione; veemenza, violenza, *f.*

ēagl-e, S.: aquila, *f.*: *great —*, aquilotto. **-e-eyed**, ADJ.: con occhi d'aquila; di vista acuta. **-e-stone**, S.: pietra aquilina, etite, *f.* **-et**, S.: aquila piccola, *f.*

ēagre, S.: (*nav.*) marea di rovesci, *f.*

ēar 1, S.: orecchio, *m.*; orecchia; spiga, *f.*: *deaf in one —*, sordo d'un orecchio; *box on the —*, schiaffo, *m.*; *sing by the —*, cantare a orecchio; *the —s of a pot*, i manichi d'un vaso; *— of corn*, spiga; *— of Indian corn*, panocchia di granoturco; *be in debt over head and —s*, esser pieno di debiti; *give —*, prestare orecchio, ascoltare attentamente; *turn a deaf —*, far orecchi di mercante. **ear** 2, TR.: lavorar la terra; INTR.: spigare, fare la spiga. **-ache**, S.: male all'orecchio, *m.* **-drops**, S. PL.: orecchini, *m. pl.* **-drum**, S.: timpano, *m.* **-ed**, ADJ.: che ha degli orecchi; spigato.

ēarl, S.: conte, *m.*

ēar-lap, S.: oreglia, *f.*

ēarldom, S.: contea, *f.*

ēarless, ADJ.: senza orecchi; senza spighe.

ēar-liness, S.: prontezza, fretta; diligenza, *f.* **-ly**, ADJ.: mattutino; pronto; mattiniero; primaticcio, prematuro: ADV.: di buon'ora, a buon'ora, per tempo: *— fruits*, frutti primatici; *— to rise*, alzarsi di buon'ora; *very —*, per tempissimo; *— in the morning*, al far del giorno; *— in the spring*, al principio della primavera.

ēarn, TR.: guadagnare; meritare, lucrare, acquistare.

ēarnest, ADJ.: ardente; zelo[illegible] S.: serio, *m.*; caparra, *f.*, pegno, [illegible] *business*, negozio d'importanza. [illegible] *entreaty*, istanza, domanda f[illegible] *—, in good —*, sul serio, serio[illegible] vero. **-ly**, ADV.: strettamente, premurosamente, seriosamente; istantemente; zelantemente; fissamente. **-money**, S.: caparra, *f.* **-ness**, S.: ardore, *m.*, premura, veemenza; diligenza, *f.*

ēar-pick, S.: stuzzicorecchi, *m.* **-piercing**, ADJ.: penetrante. **-ring**, S.: orecchino, ciondolino, *m.* **-shot**, S.: portata dell'orecchio (dell'udito), *f.*

ēarth 1, S.: terra, *f.*; suolo, mondo, *m.*: *potter's —*, argilla, *f.* **earth** 2, TR.: coprire di terra; INTR.: nascondersi sotto terra. **-born**, ADJ.: terrestre; di vil nascita. **-bound**, ADJ.: appiccato della terra. **-en**, ADJ.: di terra; argilloso: *— pan*, piattello di terra, *m.*, terrina, *f.*; *— ware*, vasellame, *m.* **-flax**, S.: asbesto, *m.* **-iness**, S.: qualità terrestre. **-liness**, S.: mondanità, *f.*; carattere mondano, *m.* **-ling**, S.: abitatore di questo mondo, *m.* **-ly**, ADJ.: terrestre, del mondo, corporale. **-ly-minded**, ADJ.: dedito alle cose del mondo. **-quake**, S.: terremoto, tremoto, *m.* **-worm**, S.: lombrico, *m.* **-y**, ADJ.: di terra, terrestre, terreno; grossolano.

ēar-trumpet, S.: cerbottana, *f.* **-wax**, S.: cerume, *m.* **-wig**, S.: formicola pinzaiuola, *f.* **-witness**, S.: testimonio auriculare, *m.*

ēase 1, S.: agio; comodo, alleggiamento; conforto; riposo, *m.*; tranquillità; facilità, *f.*; *at heart's —*, a seconda; *at your —*, a bell'agio; *be at —*, essere tranquillo; star comodo; *take one's —*, prender agio; *do a thing at one's —*, far una cosa a bell'agio; *live at —*, vivere comodamente; *love one's —*, amare i suoi piaceri. **ease** 2, TR.: alleviare; mitigare, addolcire; (*nav.*) alleggerire; *— one's self*, andar del ventre; *— the helm!* poggia! vele piene! **-ful**, ADJ.: tranquillo, quieto.

ēasel, S.: telaio, *m.*

ēa-sement, S.: sollievo; aiuto; conforto, ristoro, *m.*: *—s*, cesso, *m. pl.* **-sily**, ADV.: agevolmente; facilmente. **-siness**, S.: agevolezza; facilità; condiscendenza, *f.*; riposo, *m.*: *— of belief*, credulità, *f.*

ēast, S.: levante, oriente, *m.*

Easter ē-, S.: [illegible] *f.* **-day**, S.: giorno di [illegible] -e, S.: vigilia di pasqua, *f.* [illegible]

ēast-erly [illegible] ale, orientale, [illegible] : verso l'or[illegible] : vento d'o[illegible]

[illegible]

quillare; *in — circumstances*, benestante, comodo.

ĕat, IRR.; TR.: mangiare; consumare; rodere; INTR.: fare un pasto; pascolare: — *well*, avere buon gusto; far buona tavola; — *a good meal*, far un buon pasto; — *one's words*, disdirsi; — *away*, rodere, consumare; — *into*, penetrare rodendo; — *up*, divorare; rovinare. **-able**, ADJ.: da mangiare. **-ables**, S. PL.: vivande, *f. pl.*, viveri, *m. pl.* **-er**, S.: mangiatore, corrosivo, *m.* **-ing**, S.: mangiare; vivere bene, *m.* **-ing-house**, S.: trattoria, osteria; taverna, *f.*

ĕaves, S.: gronda, grondaia, *f.* **-drop**, INTR.: ascoltare presso la finestra. **-dropper**, S.: ascoltatore, *m.*

ĕbb 1, S.: riflusso, *m.*, bassa marea, *f.*; scemamento, *m.*: *at a low* —, in basso stato. **ebb** 2, INTR.: rifluire; calare; decrescere, scemare. **-ing**, S.: riflusso, *m.*

ĕbon-ist, S.: ebanista, *m.* **-y**, S.: ebano, *m.*

e-briety, S.: ebbrezza, ubbriachezza, *f.* **-briŏsity**, S.: ebbrietà, ubbriachezza, *f.*

ebŭl-liency, S.: ebullizione, *f.* **-lient**, ADJ.: ebulliente. **-lition**, S.: ebollimento, *m.*; effervescenza, *f.*

eccĕn-tric(al), ADJ.: eccentrico. **-tricity**, S.: eccentricità, *f.*

ecclesiăstic, ADJ.: ecclesiastico; S.: ecclesiastico, chierico, *m.* **-al**, ADJ.: ecclesiastico.

echinus, S.: echino, *m.*

ĕcho 1, S.: eco, *m.* **echo** 2, TR.: echeggiare, risuonare per eco, rimbombare.

eclâircissement, S.: schiarimento, *m.*

eclât, S.: splendore, *m.*; gloria; pompa, *f.*

eclĕctic, ADJ.: scelto.

eclip-se 1, S.: eclisse, ecliasi, *f.* **-se** 2, TR.: eclissare; oscurare; *fig.*, sormontare; disgraziare; INTR.: oscurarsi **-tic**, S.: eclittica, *f.*

ĕclogue, S.: egloga, poesia pastorale, *f.*

e-conŏmic(al), ADJ.: economico; frugale. **-cŏnomist**, S.: economo, *m.* **-cŏnomy**, S.: economia; frugalità, *f.*

ĕcs-tasied, ADJ.: estatico, in estasi. **-tasy**, S.: estasi, *f.*; rapimento, *m.* **-tătic(al)**, ADJ.: estatico, in estasi; — *fit*, estasi, *f.*

ĕcty-pal, ADJ.: preso dall' originale, copiato, imitato. **-pe**, S.: copia, imitazione, *f.*

e-dācious, ADJ.: edace, vorace; ghiotto, goloso. **-dăcity**, S.: edacità, voracità; ghiottornia, *f.*

ĕddish, S.: guaime, *m.*

[illegible]y 1, S.: gorgo; riflusso impetuoso, *m.*

[illegible]y 2, *INTR.*: *girare, aggirarsi.*

[illegible]atose, *ADJ.*: edematoso.

edĕntated, ADJ.: sdentato.

ĕdge 1, S.: orlo, margine; taglio; filo; sponda, spiaggia; *fig.*, estremità; sagacità, *f.*: — *of a book*, taglio d' un libro, *m.*; — *of the sword*, filo della spada, *m.*; — *of a tool*, filo, taglio d' uno strumento, *m.*; *give an* — *to*, affilare, aguzzare, rendere tagliente; *set an* —, affilare, aguzzare; *set the teeth on* —, allegare i denti; *take off the* —, rintuzzare. **-e** 2, TR.: affilare, aguzzare; orlare; eccitare, irritare; INTR.: opporsi: — *away*, allontanarsi; — *forwards*, avanzare, promuovere; — *towards*, avvicinarsi, venir addosso; — *in*, fare entrare. **-ed**, ADJ.: aguzzato, tagliato. **-eless**, ADJ.: sfilato, ottuso. **-e-tool**, S.: strumento tagliente, *m.* **-ewise**, ADV.: col taglio volto; da canto; a sghembo, sull' orlo. **-ing**, S.: orlo, *m.*, frangia, *f.*

ĕdible, ADJ.: commestibile, mangereccio.

ĕdict, S.: editto, bando, *m.*

ĕdi-ficant, ADJ.: edificante. **-fication**, S.: edificazione, *f.*; edificamento, *m.* **-ficatory**, ADJ.: edificatorio. **-fice**, S.: edifizio, *m.*; fabbrica, *f.* **-fier**, S.: istruttore, precettore, *m.* **-fy**, TR.: edificare; fabbricare; istruire. **-fying**, ADJ.: edificante, edificatorio; S.: edificamento, *m.*

ĕdile, S.: edile, *m.*

ĕd-it, TR.: preparare un' edizione, pubblicare; compilare. **-ition**, S.: edizione; pubblicazione; stampa, *f.* **-itor**, S.: editore, redattore, pubblicatore, *m.*

ĕdu-cate, TR.: educare; istruire. **-cation**, S.: educazione; istruzione, *f.* **-cator**, S.: educatore, *m.*

e-dūce, TR.: estrarre; cavare. **-dŭction**, S.: estrazione; esposizione, *f.*; producimento, *m.*

ĕeke† = *eke*.

ĕel, S.: anguilla, *f.* **-pie**, S.: pasticcio d' anguilla, *m.* **-spear**, S.: fiocina, *f.*

e'en, **e'er** = *even*, *ever*.

ĕffable, ADJ.: che può esprimersi con parole.

effāce, TR.: scancellare; cassare. **-ment**, S.: cancellatura, *f.*

effĕct 1, S.: effetto; successo, *m.*; realità, *f.*: *to take* —, aver effetto, riuscire; —*s*, effetti; beni, *m. pl.*; —*s of passengers*, roba di passaggiere, *f.*; *carry into* —, effettuare. **effect** 2, TR.: effettuare, eseguire. **-ible**, ADJ.: fattibile, fattevole; eseguibile, possibile. **-ive**, ADJ.: effettivo; attivo. **-ively**, ADV.: effettivamente, con effetto. **-less**, ADJ.: inefficace; impotente. **-or**, S.: facitore, autore, *m.* **-ual**, ADJ.: effettuale, effettivo. **-ually**, ADV.: effettualmente, con effetto. **-ualness**, S.: efficacità, *f.* **-uate**, TR.: effettuare, eseguire.

effĕm-inacy, S.: effeminatezza; mollezza,

f. **-inate**, ADJ.: effeminato, morbido; delicato. **-inate**, TR.: effeminare; ammollare; INTR.: effeminarsi, devenire effeminato. **-inately**, ADV.: effeminatamente, mollemente. **-inateness**, S.: effeminatezza, *f.* **-ination**, S.: effeminamento, *m.*; mollezza, *f.*

effervĕsce, INTR.: essere in effervescenza, bollire. **-cence**, S.: effervescenza, *f.*; fervore, *m.*

effēte, ADJ.: sterile, infecondo; frusto.

efficācious, ADJ.: efficace, efficiente. **-ly**, ADV.: efficacemente.

ĕfficacy, S.: efficacia; forza; virtù, *f.*

efficien-ce, -cy, S.: virtù; potenza, *f.* **-t**, ADJ.: efficiente, efficace.

effĭ-giate, TR.: formar l' effigie; rappresentare. **ĕffi-gy**, S.: effigie; immagine, *f.*, ritratto, *m.*

efflorĕscen-ce, -cy, S.: fiorire, *m.*; fiori, *m. pl.*; eruzione, *f.* **-t**, ADJ.: in forma di fiori; vescicoso.

ĕffluence, S.: effusione, *f.*, effondimento, *m.*

efflŭvia, S.: effluvio, *m.*; evaporazione, *f.*

ĕf-flux, S.: effusione, *f.*; flusso, *m.* **-flŭx**, INTR.: dileguarsi, diffondersi, spargersi. **-flŭxion**, S.: emanazione, *f.*; effondimento, *m.*

effŏrce†, TR.: sforzare.

effŏrm†, TR.: formare. **-ātion†**, S.: formazione, *f.*

ĕffort, S.: sforzo, *m.*

effrāy, TR.: spaventare.

effrŏntery, S.: sfacciatezza, impudenza, *f.*

effŭl-gence, S.: splendore, *m.*; lucidezza, *f.* **-gent**, ADJ.: rifulgente, splendente.

effū-se, TR.: diffondere; spandere. **-sion**, S.: effusione, *f.*, versamento; spargimento, *m.* **-sive**, ADJ.: diffusivo.

e.g., per essempio.

egĕs-t, TR.: evacuare; mandare fuori. **-tion**, S.: egestione, evacuazione, *f.*

ĕgg 1, S.: uovo, *m.*: *poached —s*, uova affogate, *f. pl.*; *new laid —*, uovo fresco; *soft boiled —s*, uova al latte; *white of an —*, albume, chiaro dell' uovo; *sit on —s*, covare delle uova. **egg** 2, TR.: incitare, stimolare. **-cup**, S.: portauovo, *m.*, tazza da uovo, *f.* **-shell**, S.: guscio dell' uovo, *m.*

ĕglantine, S.: rosa salvatica, *f.*

ĕgo-tism, S.: egoismo, egotismo, *m.* **-tist**, S.: egoista, egotista. **-tistical**, ADJ.: da egoista. **-tize**, INTR.: egotizzare.

egrēgious, ADJ.: egregio, eccellente, insigne: *— fool*, scioccone di prima classe, *m.* **-ly**, ADV.: egregiamente, eccellentemente.

ē-gress, -grĕssion, S.: esito, *m.*, uscita, sortita, *f.*

ēgret, S.: garza bianca (aghirone), *f.*; piumino, *m.*

ēgriot, S.: amarasca, *f.* (ciriegia).

ēigh-t, ADJ.: otto. **-teen**, ADJ.: diciotto. **-teenth**, ADJ.: diciottesimo. **-tfold**, ADJ.: otto volte. **-th**, ADJ.: ottavo. **-thly**, ADV.: in ottavo luogo. **-tieth**, ADJ.: ottantesimo. **-tscore**, ADJ.: otto ventine, cento sessanta. **-ty**, ADJ.: ottanta.

ēigne, ADJ.: primogenito.

ēither, PRON.: l' uno o l' altro, ciascuno, qualunque; CONJ.: sia, sia che; ovvero che; o: *— . . . or*, o . . . o; *on — side*, dalle due bande; *I will take —*, prenderò l' uno o l' altro; *I will not take —*, non voglio ne l' uno ne l' altro.

ejăcu-late, TR.: lanciare, gettare. **-lātion**, S.: corta e fervente preghiera, eiaculazione, *f.*; sbalzo, *m.* **-latory**, ADJ.: eiaculatorio, subito.

ejĕc-t, TR.: gettare; mandare fuora. **-tion**, S.: espulsione; (*med.*) evacuazione; egestione, *f.* **-tment**, S.: spogliamento del possesso, *m.*, espropriazione, *f.*

ejulātion†, S.: lamento, compianto, *m.*

ĕke† 1, ADV.: anche, ancora; parimente. **eke** 2, TR.: slargare, allungare; dilatare, aumentare, accrescere: *— out*, accrescere, prolungare; appena far. **eke** 3, S.: aumentazione, *f.*

elăbo-rate, ADJ.: elaborato, perfetto. **-rate**, TR.: elaborare; limare, perfezionare, finire. **-rately**, ADV.: laboriosamente, con diligenza, accuratamente, con esattezza. **-rateness**, S.: elaboratezza, *f.* **-ration**, S.: squisita diligenza, *f.*, perfezionamento, *m.*

elānce†, TR.: lanciare, gettare.

elăpse, INTR.: scorrer via, svanire, passare.

elăs-tical, ADJ.: elastico. **-ticity**, S.: elasticità; molla, *f.*

elā-te 1, ADJ.: elato, innalzato, orgoglioso, altiero. **-te**, TR.: insuperbire; esalt... innalzare. **-ted**, ADJ.: elato, innal... *be (feel) —*, ringalluzzarsi, sentirsi ri... zullire. **-tedly**, ADV.: orgogliosa... **-tion**, S.: elazione, *f* ... perbia, *f.*

ĕlbow 1, S.: gomito ... *be at the —* ... —, appo... TR.: dare ... INTR.: f... dia d' a... spazio, ... **ĕld†**, S.: ... —, altre... maggiora...

grare. **-isement**†, s.: divertimento; piacere, *m.* **-ive**, ADJ.: ricreativo; piacevole.
divĕst, TR.: divestire; spogliare, privare: — *one's self*, svestirsi, spogliarsi. **-ure**, s.: spogliamento, *m.*; rinunzia; cessione, *f.*
divi-dable, ADJ.: divisibile. **-de**, TR.: dividere, spartire, disunire; distribuire; INTR.: dividersi; disunirsi, separarsi. **-dedly**, ADV.: separatamente. **dividend**, s.: (*arith.*) dividendo; (*com.*) dividendo, usufrutto, interesse, *m.* **-der**, s.: dividitore, distributore, *m.*
div-ination, s.: divinazione, *f.*, indovinamento, *m.* **div-inator**, s.: divinatore, *m.* **-inatory**, ADJ.: divinatorio. **-ine** 1, ADJ.: divino; eccelente; s.: ecclesiastico; teologo, *m.* **-ine** 2, TR.: indovinare; presagire; INTR.: congetturare, presentire. **-ined**, ADJ.: indovinato, predetto. **-inely**, ADV.: divinamente; eccellentemente. **-ineness**, s.: divinità, *f.* **-iner**, s.: divinatore, indovino, *m.* **-ineress**, s.: divinatrice, indovina, *m.*
diving, s.: immersione, *f.* **-bell**, s.: campana di marangone, *f.*
divinity, s.: divinità; teologia, *f.*: *doctor of* —, dottore in teologia.
div-isibility, s.: divisibilità, *f.* **-isible**, ADJ.: divisibile; partibile. **-isibleness** = *divisibility*. **-ision**, s.: divisione, *f.*, spartimento, *m.*; scissione, scissura, *f.* **-isional**, ADJ.: di divisione, divisionario. **-isor**, s.: divisore, *m.*
divŏr-ce 1, s.: divorzio, *m.*; separazione, *f.* **-ce** 2, TR.: far divorzio; ripudiare; separare. **-cement**, s.: divorzio, ripudio, *m.* **-cer**, s.: che fa divorzio. **-cing**, s.: divorzio, ripudio, *m.*
divŭl-ge, TR.: divulgare, pubblicare. **-ger**, s.: che divulga, divulgatore, *m.* **-sion**, s.: divellimento, staccamento, *m.*; separazione, *f.*
dizen, TR.: adornare, abbellire.
dizzard†, s.: scioccone, balordo, *m.*
diz-ziness, s.: vertigine, *f.*, capogiro, *m.* **-zy** 1, ADJ.: vertiginoso, sventato. **-zy** 2, TR.: stordire.
dō 1, IRR.; TR.: fare; operare, effettuare, finire; cuocere; cucinare; INTR.: stare, portarsi: *have to — with*, aver che fare con; *pray*, —, ve ne prego; *how — you —?* come state? come sta? *that won't* —, questo non basta; *that won't — for me*, ciò non fa per me; — *in Rome as Rome —es*, vivi in Roma alla romana; — *a business*, spedire, fare un negozio; — *good*, beneficare; assistere; — *like for like*, render la pariglia; *have to — with one*, aver da fare con uno; *I have nothing to — with it*, questo non mi riguarda; — *again*, rifare; — *amiss*, far male; — *away*, levare; — *off*, difare; levare via; — *on*, porre; mettere; — *over*, — *up*, piegare; imballare.
do 2, s.: fracasso, strepito, chiasso, *m.*
dŏc-ible, ADJ.: docile; trattabile. **-ibleness**, s.: docilità; trattabilità, *f.* **-ile**, ADJ.: docile; disciplinabile. **-ility**, s.: docilità, *f.*
dŏck 1, s.: darsena, *f.*, bacino, cantiere, *m.*
dock 2, s.: coda troncata, *f.*; lapazio, *m.*
dock 3, TR.: scodare. **dock** 4, TR.: scolare, racconciare. **dock** 5, TR.: rimpalmare (un vascello). **-et** 1, s.: direzione, cedola, *f.*; estratto, sommario, *m.* **-et** 2, TR.: notare, segnare. **-yard**, s.: cantiere, *m.*
dŏctor 1, s.: dottore; medico, *m.*: *poor* —, dottoraccio, dottorello, dottoricchio, *m.*: — *of divinity*, dottore di teologia; *take the degrees of* —, prender la laurea.
doctor 2, TR.: medicare, dare medicine. **-al**, ADJ.: dottorale, di dottore. **-ally**, ADV.: in modo dottorale, da dottore. **-ate**, TR.: dottorare. **-ess**, s.: dottoressa, *f.* **-ship**, s.: dottorato, *m.*, dignità del dottore, *f.*
dŏc-trinal, ADJ.: dottrinale, istruttivo. **-trinally**, ADV.: dottrinalmente, positivamente. **-trine**, s.: dottrina, scienza; istruzione, *f.*
dŏcument 1, s.: documento; precetto, *m.* **document** 2, **-ise**, TR.: provare con documenti; insegnare, istruire.
dŏdder, s.: (*bot.*) epitimo, *m.*
dodĕcagon, s.: dodecagono, *m.*
dŏd-ge, INTR.: acquattarsi; appiattarsi, sfuggire, schivare; operare con astuzia: — *a blow*, schivare un colpo; — *a person*, pedinare (*or* codiare) uno. **-ger**, s.: intrigante, *m.* **-gery**, s.: cavillazione, *f.*
dōe, s.: daina, capriola, *f.*
dōer, s.: facitore, fattore, *m.*
dŏff, TR.: svestire, spogliare; differire, ritardare.
dŏg 1, s.: cane; (*astr.*) sirio, *m.*: *big* —, cagnone, cane grosso; *little* —, cagnetto; *nice little* —, cagnolino; *be treated like a* —, esser trattato da cane. **dog** 2, TR.: codiare; spiare. **-berry**, s.: corniuola, *f.* **-brier**, s.: rosa canina, rosa salvatica, *f.* **-cheap**, ADJ.: a buon mercato, a vil prezzo. **-days**, s. PL.: canicola, *f.*, giorni canicolari, *m. pl.*
dōge, s.: doge, *m.*
dŏg-fish, s.: cane di mare, *m.* (pesce). **-ged**, ADJ.: cagnesco; arcigno, burbero, aspro. **-gedly**, ADV.: d' un' aria arcigna. **-gedness**, s.: umore arcigno, ghiribizzo, capriccio, *m.*
dŏgger, s.: bastimento olandese, *m.*
dŏggerel, s.: cattiva poesia, *f.*; cattivi versi, *m. pl.*
dŏg-gish, ADJ.: cagnesco; brutale **-grass**, s.: gramigna, *f.*

dŏggrel = *doggerel.*
dŏg-hearted, ADJ.: crudele, inumano. **-kennel**, S.: canile, *m.* **-louse**, S.: zecca, *f.*
dŏg-ma, S.: dogma, domma, *m.* **mătic(al)**, ADJ.: dogmatico. **-măticaIly**, ADV.: in maniera dogmatica. **-măticalness**, S.: stile dogmatico, *m.* **-matist**, S.: che dogmatizza. **-matize**, TR.: dogmatizzare; insegnare.
dŏg-sleep, S.: sonno finto, *m.* **-meat**, S.: cibo da cani, *m.*; cosa vile, *f.* **-star**, S.: canicola, *f.*; sirio, *m.* **-tooth**, S.: gramigna, *f.* **-trick**, S.: furberia, *f.* **-trot**, S.: trotto di cane, *m.* **-weary**, ADJ.: stracco come un cane, stanchissimo.
dŏily, S.: tovaglietta piccola†; salvietta, *f.*
dŏing, PART.: facendo; S.: fatto, *m.*, azione, *f.*; PL.: fatti, evento, *m. pl.*: *it is a—*, si sta facendo; *what are you —?* che fate? *keep one —*, dar dell' impiego ad alcuno.
dŏit, S.: bezzo, quattrino, *m.*
dōle 1, S.: distribuzione; porzione; elemosina, *f.*; affanno, *m.* **dole** 2, TR.: distribuire; dare: *— out*, spartire, scompartire. **-ful**, ADJ.: tristo, doloroso, mesto, lugubre. **-fully**, ADV.: tristamente, lamentevolmente, dolentemente. **-fulness**, S.: tristezza; doglia, afflizione, *f.*; dolore, *m.* **-some**, ADJ.: doglioso, affannoso, **-someness**, S.: malinconia, tristezza, tristizia, *f.*
dŏll, S.: bambola, *f.*, fantoccio; bamboccio, *m.*
dŏllar, S.: dollaro (*in Am. freq.* scudo), *m.*
dolorif-erous, -ic, ADJ.: dolorifico, che reca dolore.
dōlor, S.: dolore, *m.*; afflizione, *f.* **-ous**, ADJ.: doloroso; tristo, lugubre. **-ousness**, S.: dolore, *m.*, doglia, *f.*
dŏlphin, S.: delfino, *m.*
dōlt, S.: minchione, balordo, *m.* **-ish**, ADJ.: sciocco, stupido. **-ishly**, ADV.: scioccamente, stupidamente. **-ishness**, S.: scempitaggine, stupidità, *f.*
domāin, S.: dominio, *m.*; sovranità; possessione, *f.*
dōme, S.: cupola, volta, *f.*, duomo, *m.*
domĕs-tic, S.: domestico; servo, *m.* **-tic(al)**, ADJ.: domestico, dimestico, familiare, dimesticare. **-ticate**, TR.: domesticare, dimesticare.
dŏm-icile, S.: domicilio; albergo, *m.* **-iciliary**, ADJ.: domiciliario.
dŏm-inant, ADJ.: dominante. **-inate**, TR.: dominare, prevalere. **-ination**, S.: dominio, imperio, *m.*, signoria, *f.* **-inator**, S.: dominatore, *m.* **-ineer**, TR.: dominare; signoreggiare. **-ineering**, ADJ.: dominante; imperioso, insolente, altiero.
domĭnical, ADJ.: dominicale, del Signore.
Domĭnican, S.: domenicano, *m.*
domĭnion, S.: dominio; territorio, *m.*; giurisdizione, *f.*
dŏn 1, S.: don, signore, *m.* **don** 2, TR.: metter su.
dōnary, S.: offerta, obblazione, *f.*
donā-tion, S.: donazione, *f.*, dono, donamento, *m.* **dŏn-ative**, S.: dono, presente, *m.*
dōne, ADJ.: fatto; conchiuso; cotto: *—!* fatto! accettato! vada!
do-nēe, S.: (*leg.*) donatario, *m.* **dō-nor**, S.: donatore, *m.*
dōodle, S.: scioperone, ozioso, sfaccendato, *m.*
dōom 1, S.: sentenza; condannazione, *f.*
doom 2, TR.: sentenziare; condannare. **-ful**, ADJ.: funesto. **-sday**, S.: giudizio universale, *m.* **-sday-book**, S.: catastro, *m.*
dōor, S.: porta; entrata, *f.*; uscio, *m.*: *back —*, porta di dietro; *carriage —*, sportello, *m.*; *— posts*, imposte, *f. pl.*; *next —*, la prima porta, la casa attigua; *folding —*, porta a due imposte, *f.*; *within —*, in casa; *out—s*, fuor di casa; *keep within —s*, non uscire, rimanere in casa; *knock at the —*, picchiare alla porta; *turn out of —s*, scacciar fuor di casa, mettere alla porta. **-bar**, S.: sbarra di porta, *f.* **-case**, S.: impostatura di porta, *f.* **-handle**, S.: manubrio dell' uscio, *m.* **-keeper**, S.: portinaio; carceriere, *m.* **-knob**, S.: bottone dell' uscio, *m.* **-post**, S.: imposta della porta, *f.* **-way**, S.: usciale, *m.*
Dŏric, ADJ.: dorico.
dôr-mant, ADJ.: dormiente; segreto. **-mer-window**, S.: spiraglio, abbaino, *m.* **-mitory**, S.: dormitorio, *m.* **-mōuse**, S.: ghiro, *m.*
dôrp†, S.: villagio, *m.*
dôrr, S.: pecchione; calabrone, *m.*
dôr-sel, **-ser**, S.: cesta, paniera, *f.*
dōse 1, S.: dosa, dose; presa, *f.* **dose** 2, TR.: (*med.*) dosare.
dŏssil, S.: (*surg.*) piumacciuolo, *m.*
dŏt 1, S.: punto, *m.* **dot** 2, INTR.: puntare; porre i punti.
dōtage, S.: perdita d' intelletto; imbecillità, *f.*; vaneggiamento, *m.*
dōtal, ADJ.: dotale, di dote.
dōtard, S.: vecchio rimbambito, *m.* **-ly**, ADV.: imbecille.
dotā-tion, S.: dotazione, *f.*
dō-te, INTR.: vaneggiare, bam[illegible] amare soverchiamente: — [illegible] inamoratissimo di, amare pe[illegible] **-ter**, S.: che ama soverchiame[illegible] **ly**, ADV.: con soverchio am[illegible] sionatamente. **-tish**, ADJ.: [illegible]

dŏttard, S.: albero nano, *m.*

dŏub-le 1, ADJ.: doppio; simulato; S.: doppio; artificio; inganno, *m.*: *see things* —, vedere gli oggetti raddoppiati. **-le** 2, TR.: doppiare, raddoppiare; dissimulare; piegare; (*nav.*) trapassare. **-le-barrelled**, ADJ.: a due canne. **-le-buttoned**, ADJ.: a due ordini di bottoni. **-le-chin**, S.: doppio mento, *m.* **-le-dealer**, S.: furfante, furbo, *m.* **-le-dealing**, S.: furberia, trufferia, *f.*; inganno, *m.* **-le-dye**, TR.: tingere in grana. **-le-edged**, ADJ.: a due tagli. **-le-handed**, ADJ.: ambidestro, ingannatore. **-le-headed**, ADJ.: a due teste. **-le-lock**, TR.: serrare a doppia chiave. **-le-meaning**, S.: ambiguità, *f.* **-le-minded**, ADJ.: falso, furbo. **-leness**, S.: doppiezza, *f.*; raddoppiamento, *m.* **-ler**, S.: che raddoppia; filatore, *m.* **-let**, S.: giubbone; paio, *m.* **-le-tongued**, ADJ.: furbo, ingannoso, insidioso. **-ling**, S.: raddoppiamento; artificio, *m.* **-lōon**, S.: dobblone, doppione, *m.* (moneta). **-ly**, ADV.: doppiamente, a doppio.

dŏubt 1, S.: dubbio, *m.*, incertezza; difficoltà, *f.*: *without* —, senza dubbio; *I have no — about it*, non ne dubito. **doubt** 2, TR.: sospettare; esitare; INTR.: dubitare, stare (essere, trovarsi) in dubbio: *I — it*, ne dubito; *I — whether*, dubito se. **-er**, S.: che dubita. **-ful**, ADJ.: dubbioso, incerto; dubbio: *man of — character*, uomo dubbio (sospetto); *of — virtue*, di dubbia virtù. **-fully**, ADV.: dubbiosamente. **-fulness**, S.: dubbio, *m.*; incertezza; ambiguità, *f.* **-ingly**, ADV.: dubbiosamente, in modo dubbioso. **-less**, ADJ.: indubitabile, sicuro, certo; ADV.: indubitabilmente, senza dubbio, sicuramente, certamente.

dŏucets, S. PL.: testicoli di cervo, *m. pl.*

dŏugh, S.: pasta, *f.* **-baked**, ADJ.: mezzo cotto.

dŏughty, ADJ.: valoroso, coraggioso.

dŏughy, ADJ.: pastoso.

dŏuse, TR.: immergere all' improvviso; INTR.: cascare nell' acqua improvvisamente.

dŏut, TR.: estinguere. **-er**, S.: spegnitoio, *m.*

dŏve, S.: colomba, *f.* **-cot**, **-house**, S.: colombaia, *f.* **-like**, ADJ.: simile ad una colomba. **-tail** 1, S.: (*join.*) coda di rondine; incastratura, *f.* **-tail** 2, TR.: incastrare, intagliare. **-tailed**, ADJ.: incastrato.

dŏwager, S.: vedova, *f.*

dŏwdy, S.: donnaccia, *f.*

dŏwer, S.: dote, dota, pensione, *f.* **-ed**, ADJ.: *dotato.* **-less**, ADJ.: senza dote, non dotato; povero. **-y** = *dower.*

dŏwlas, S.: sorta di tela grossolana, *f.*

dŏwn 1, S.: penna matta; lanugine, *f.*

down 2, PREP., ADV.: giù; a basso, abbasso; a secondo: — *the stream*, a seconda la corrente; *up and* —, su e giù; qua e là; *upside* —, sossopra; *further* —, più abbasso; — *stairs*, abbasso; *bring* —, portar giù, calare; *fall* —, cascare; *lie* —, giacere; coricarsi, sdraiarsi; *look* —, abbassare gli occhi; *pay money* —, pagar danari contanti; *set* —, adagiare; mettere in iscritto, registrare; *sit* —, sedersi; *turn upside* —, rovesciare, mettere a rovescio. **down** 3, TR.: abbattere, soverchiare, vincere. **-cast**, ADJ.: abbattuto; dimesso; modesto: *with — eyes*, cogli occhi bassi. **-fall**, S.: trabuccamento, *m.*; rovina, *f.* **-fallen**, ADJ.: rovinato. **-hearted**, ADJ.: abbattuto, scoraggiato. **-hill**, S.: discesa, *f.*; declivio, *m.* **-looked**, ADJ.: tristo, malinconico. **-right**, ADJ.: evidente; franco; ADV.: giù a piombo. **-rightness**, S.: franchigia; sincerità, *f.* **-sitting**, S.: riposo, *m.*; quiete, *f.* **-ward**, ADJ.: declive; abbattuto, dimesso, afflitto. **-ward(s)**, ADV.: giù, abbasso.

dŏwny, ADJ.: lanuginoso; molle.

dŏw-re, **-ry**, S.: dote, dota, *f.*

dŏwse 1, S.: schiaffo, *m.* **dowse** 2, TR.: schiaffeggiare.

dŏxy, S.: donna di mala vita, *f.*

dōze, TR.: addormentare; rendere stupido; INTR.: essere sonnoglioso.

dŏzen, S.: dozzina, *f.*: *by* —*s*, a dozzine.

dō-ziness, S.: sonnolenza, *f.*; addormentamento, *m.* **-zy**, ADJ.: sonnoglioso, addormentato.

drăchm, S.: dramma, *f.*

drăff, S.: feccia, *f.*; beverone, *m.* **-y**, ADJ.: feccioso; sudicio.

drăft, S.: tratto, *m.*, strappata; corrente d' aria, *f.*; tiro d' acqua (di una nave); piano (d' un edifizio), *m.*, pianta, *f.*; abbozo, schizzo, disegno; prima copia (d' uno scritto), stracciafoglio, *m.*; tratta, cambiale, *f.*, mandato; (*mil.*) straccamento, *m.*, leva, *f.*: *I enclose you my — for* 100 *frs.*, vi acchiudo la mia tratta per 100 fr.; *play at* —*s*, giuocare alle tavole (alle dame); *at a* —, ad un sorso. **-board**, S.: tavoliere, scacchiere, *m.* **-horse**, S.: cavallo da tiro, *m.*

drăg 1, S.: uncino; gancio; tramaglio, *m.* **drag** 2, (IN)TR.: tirare per forza: strascinare: — *in* (*out*), strascinare dentro (fuori). **-chain**, S.: catena [illegible] re, *f.*

drăggle, TR.: infangare, im[illegible]; INTR.: infangarsi, imbrattarsi. [illegible] S.: zitella sporca, *f.*

drăg-net, S.: tramaglio, *m.*

enamour, TR.: innamorare; accender d'amore. **-ed**, ADJ.: innamorato: *become* —, invaghirsi, affezionarsi.
enarrātion, S.: narrazione; spiegazione, *f.*
enarthrōsis, S.: (*anat.*) enartrosi, *f.*
encāge, TR.: ingabbiare; rinchiudere; imprigionare.
encámp, INTR.: accamparsi. **-ment**, S.: accampamento, campo, *m.*
encāse, TR.: incassare.
encāve, TR.: mettere in cantina, incavernare.
encâustic, ADJ.: encaustico.
enchāfe†, TR.: irritare; provocare.
enchāin, TR.: incatenare; legare.
enchânt, TR.: incantare; dilettare in sommo grado. **-er**, S.: incantatore, *m.* **-ingly**, ADV.: in modo incantevole. **-ment**, S.: incanto, *m.* **-ress**, S.: incantatrice, ammaliatrice, *f.*
enchârge, TR.: incaricare, commettere; confidare.
enchā-se, TR.: incastrare, incassare. **-sing**, S.: incastratura, *f.*
encir-cle, TR.: incerchiare, circondare, cingere. **-clet**†, S.: cerchio; anello, *m.*
enclitic, S.: (*gram.*) enclitica, *f.*
enclōister, TR.: chiudere in un chiostro.
enclō-se, TR.: chiudere, inchiudere; comprendere; circondare: *I — you my acceptance*, vi acchiudo la mia accettazzione. **-sure**, S.: ricinto; circuito; chiuso, *m.*
encō-miast, S.: encomiaste, panegirista, *m.* **-miástic(al)**, ADJ.: lodativo. **-mium**, S.: encomio, elogio, *m.*
encómpass, TR.: circondare; attorniare. **-ment**, S.: circonlocuzione, *f.*
encōr-e 1 **-an-**, ADV.: ancora, di nuovo. **encore** 2, (IN)TR.: domandare la ripetizione (d'una canzone, ecc.).
encŏun-ter, S.: incontro, conflitto, duello, *m.*, scaramuccia, *f.* **-ter** 2, TR.: incontrare; assaltare; INTR.: incontrarsi, azzuffarsi; combattere. **-terer**, S.: antagonista, avversario, *m.*
encoŭrag-e, TR.: incoraggiare, animare. **-ement**, S.: incoraggiamento, *m.* **-er**, S.: protettore, fautore, *m.* **-ingly**, ADV.: in modo incoraggiante.
encrōach, INTR.: impadronirsi poco a poco, usurpare poco a poco; estendersi (sopra): — *upon*, intaccare, usurpare. **-er**, S.: che s' impadronisce poco a poco. **-ingly**, ADV.: usurpativamente. **-ment**, S.: usurpare poco a poco, *m.*
encrŭst, TR.: incrostare.
encŭm-ber, TR.: imbarazzare, impedire; caricare. **-brance**, S.: imbarazzo; impedimento; intrigo, *m.*; ipoteca, *f.*
encyclical, ADJ.: enciclico, circolare.
encyclopē-dia, S.: *enciclopedia, f.* **-dian**, ADJ.: enciclopedico. **-dist**, S.: enciclopedista, *m.*
ĕnd 1, S.: fine, *m.*; estremità, *f.*, termine, capo; disegno; avvenimento, evento, *m.*: *at the — of this street*, in capo di questa via; *at the — of this year*, alla fine dell' anno; *to no —*, in vano, inutilmente; *to the — that*, affinchè, perchè, acciocchè; *make an — of one*, spacciare, spedire uno; *make an — with one*, accordarsi con uno; *be at one's wit's —*, non saper che fare, stillarsi il cervello; *have at one's fingers' —s*, aver su per le dita; *without —*, in sempiterno. **end** 2, TR.: finire, terminare; INTR.: venire a fine; cessare.
endāmage, TR.: danneggiare, guastare. **-ment**, S.: danno, detrimento, *m.*, perdita, *f.*
endānger, TR.: esporre a pericolo, arrischiare.
endēar, TR.: rendere caro. **-ment**, S.: tenerezza; affezione, *f.*, amore, *m.*
endĕavour 1, S.: sforzo, sforzamento, *m.* **endeavour** 2, TR.: tentare; INTR.: sforzarsi, affaticarsi. **-er**, S.: che si sforza.
endĕcagon, S.: endecagono, *m.*
en dēmial, **-dĕmic(al)**, ADJ.: endemio.
endict, TR.: accusare, denunziare. **-ment**, S.: accusa, denunziazione, *f.*
ĕnding, S.: fine, conclusione; decisione, *f.*
ĕndive, S.: indivia, endivia, *f.*
ĕnd-less, ADJ.: infinito, perpetuo. **-lessly**, ADV.: senza fine, perpetuamente. **-lessness**, S.: perpetuità, infinità, *f.* **-long**†, ADV.: in linea retta, drittamente. **-most**, ADJ.: remotissimo, lontanissimo.
endôrs-e, TR.: indossare. **-ement**, S.: girata, *f.* **-er**, S.: giratario, *m.*
endŏw, TR.: dotare; arricchire. **-er**, S.: dotatore, fondatore, *m.* **-ment**, S.: dote, *f.*; dono, *m.*, fondazione, *f.*
endūe, TR.: dotare; rivestire; adornare.
endū-rable, ADJ.: sopportevole, soffribile. **-rance**, S.: durazione; pazienza, sofferenza, *f.* **-re**, TR.: sopportare, soffrire; INTR.: durare. **-rer**, S.: tolleratore, *m.* **-ing**, ADJ.: durabile, durevole; tollerante, paziente.
ĕndwise, ADV.: a perpendicolo, in punta; capo a capo.
ĕnecate†, TR.: ammazzare.
ĕnemy, S.: nemico, inimico, avversario, *m.*: *make an — of one*, inimicarsi alcuno.
en-ergĕtic, ADJ.: energico, vigoroso; efficace. **ĕn-ergy**, S.: energia; efficacia, *f.*
enĕr-vate, TR.: snervare, spossare, debilitare. **-vātion**, S.: snervamento, indebolimento, *m.* **-ve**† = *enervate.*
enfāmish, TR.: affamare.
enfēeble, TR.: indebolire, debilitare. **-ment**, S.: debilitamento, *m.*; debolezza, *f.*

pelli. — [illegible] [illegible] della pelle. — [illegible] [illegible] una nave. — [illegible] [illegible] [illegible] [illegible]. — [illegible] [illegible] [illegible] una [illegible]. — [illegible] [illegible], medicare una ferita [illegible]. — [illegible] [illegible] [illegible]. -ed, ADJ. [illegible] [illegible] [illegible] [illegible]. [illegible] — [illegible] [illegible] [illegible] — [illegible] [illegible] [illegible]. -er, s.: [illegible] [illegible], m.; tavola di cucina, f. -ing, s.: vestire, vestimento; [illegible] [illegible] medicamento, m.; [illegible], f. -ing-case, s.: necessario, m. -ing-cloth, s.: mantellina; [illegible], f. -ing-gown, s.: veste di camera, zimarra, f. -ing-room, s.: camera da vestire, f. -ing-table, s.: toeletta, f.

drib 1, s.: goccia, stilla, f. **drib** 2, TR.: tagliare [illegible] scemare. -ble, TR.: [illegible]; INTR.: cascare giù, gocciolare: fare bava.

driblet, s.: [illegible] [illegible], m.

drier, s.: [illegible] disseccante, m.

drift 1, s.: impulso, corso, oggetto, [illegible], m.; — of ice, pezzo di ghiaccio, m.; — of sand, ammasso di rena mobile, m.; — of snow, massa di neve, f.; [illegible] di neve. **drift** 2, TR.: spingere; cacciare, accumulare; INTR.: accumularsi.

drill 1, s.: succhiello, spillo; babbuino; mil. esercizio, m. **drill** 2, TR.: forare; [illegible]. -bow, s.: archetto, m.

drink 1, s.: bevanda, f., beveraggio, m.: give me some —, datemi a bere. **drink** 2, IRR.; TR.: bere, bevere; assorbire; tracannare; INTR.: imbriacarsi, inebriarsi: — to, far brindisi: I — your health, bevo alla vostra salute; — coffee, bere il caffè; — in, imbevere; succiare; — out, vuotare (a forza di bere); — up, bevere tutto. -able, ADJ.: potabile. -er, s.: bevitore; beone, m. -ing, s.: bere; bevimento, m. -ing-bout, s.: beveria, f. -ing-companion, s.: compagno in beveria, m. -ing-cup, s.: tazza, coppa, f. -ing-glass, s.: bicchiere, m. -ing-house, s.: bettola, f. -ing-song, s.: canzone gioviale, f. -money, s.: mancia, f.; paraguanto, m.

drip 1, s.: goccia, gocciola, f. **drip** 2, (IN)TR.: spruzzare, gocciolare, stillare. -ping, s.: (il) gocciolare, (lo) stillare; unto, m. -ping-pan, s.: ghiotta, leccarda, f.

drive 1, IRR.; TR.: condurre, guidare, menare; cacciare; spingere, impellere, forzare; INTR.: aver in mira, tendere; avanzare: — a carriage, guidare una carrozza; — a nail, ficcare un chiodo; — stakes, ficcare pali; — off time, procrastinare, indugiare; — along, proseguire, continuare; — away, scacciare; — back, risospingere; ributtare; — in, into, fare entrare; cacciare; — on, impellere; spingere, andare avanti; avanzare; — out, scacciare; fare uscire; andare fuori in carrozza: can you —? sapete guidare? **drive** 2, s.: scarrozzata, passeggiata in carrozza, f.

drivel 1, s.: bava, saliva, f.; pazzo, sciocco, m. **drivel** 2, INTR.: bavare; esser insano. -er, s.: goffone, idiota, minchione, m.

dri-ver, s.: conduttore, m.; zeppa, f. -ving, s.: condotta, f.; carriaggio, m. -ving-box, s.: sedile del cocchiere, m.

driz-zle, (IN)TR.: spruzzolare, gocciolare: drizzling rain, spruzzaglia, f. -zly, ADJ.: piovigginoso, umido.

drōil 1, s.: infingardo, faggifatica, m. **droil** 2, INTR.: lavorar con fatiga, tentennare.

drōll 1, ADJ.: comico, burlevole; s.: buffone; scherzatore, m. **droll** 2, INTR.: buffoneggiare, beffare. -ery, s.: buffoneria, facezia; farsa, f. -ingly, ADV.: buffonescamente. -ish, ADJ.: buffonesco.

drŏmedary, s.: dromedario, m.

drōne 1, s.: pecchione; infingardaccio, m. -e 2, INTR.: ronzare; tentennare, cincischiare. -ish, ADJ.: lento, ozioso, inerte. -ishness, s.: poltroneria, f.

drōop, INTR.: languire; infiebolire; affliggersi, esser tristo. -ing, ADJ.: languido; afflitto, tristo; s.: abbattimento; languore, m. -ingly, ADV.: languidamente; debolmente.

drŏp 1, s.: goccia, f., gocciolo; orecchino, m.: little —, gocciolina; a few —s, poche gocciole; — by —, a goccia a goccia; by —s, a goccia a goccia. **drop** 2, TR.: lasciare cascare (or cadere); abbandonare; cessare; metter da bando; INTR.: gocciolare; cascare; svenire, sparire; morire: —s, goccie medicinali; — anchor, ancorarsi; — a design, desistere da un disegno; — a word, lasciar scappare una parola; the curtain —s, cade il sipario; — with sweat, gocciolare di sudore; — in, introdurre; entrare; venire improvviso; — off, scadere; venire in decadenza; — out, sparire, dissiparsi. -ping, s.: goccia, gocciola, f.: — of the nose, gocciola al naso, f. -let, s.: piccola goccia, gocciolina, f. -pingly, ADV.: a goccia. -serene, s.: gotta [illegible]

drŏpsical, ADJ.: idropico.

drŏp-stone, s.: marcassi[illegible]

drŏpsy, s.: idropisia [illegible]

drŏpwort, s.: [illegible]

drŏss, s.: scoria [illegible] -iness, s.: [illegible] ADJ.: pieno di [illegible] sporco.

drought, S.: secchezza, siccità; sete, *f.* **-iness**, S.: aridità, siccità, *f.* **-y**, ADJ.: secco, arido; assetato, sitibondo.

dröv-e 1, impf. del v. *drive*, **-e** 2, S.: branco, *m.*; gregge; folla, *f.* **-er**, S.: bifolco, *m.*

drŏwn, TR.: annegare; immergere; INTR.: annegarsi; immergersi, affogarsi: — *one's self*, annegarsi, gettarsi nell' acqua; *be —ed*, annegare, essere annegato.

drŏw-se, TR.: addormentare, render sonnacchioso; INTR.: dormire. **-sily**, ADV.: sonnacchioni; lentamente. **-siness**, S.: sonnolenza; indolenza; pigrizia, *f.* **-sy**, ADJ.: sonnolento, sonnacchioso; stupido: *grow* —, addormentarsi. **-sy-head**, S.: sopore, *m.* **-sy-headed**, ADJ.: sonnolento, sopito.

drŭb 1, S.: colpo, *m.*; botta, *f.* **drub** 2, TR.: battere, bastonare; percuotere. **-bing**, S.: bastonata, bastonatura, *f.*: *give one a sound* —, dare ad uno un buon carpiccio.

drŭd-ge 1, S.: facchino, *m.* **-ge** 2, INTR.: affaticarsi; stentare. **-ger**, S.: facchino; bossoletto, *m.* **-gery**, S.: servigio vile, *m.* **-ging-box**, S.: bossoletto da infarinare; polverino, *m.* **-gingly**, ADV.: con pena, con molto affaticamento.

drŭg 1, S.: droga, *f.*; rifiuto, *m.* **drug** 2, TR.: mescolare con ingredienti medicinali. **-get**, S.: droghetta, *m.* **-gist**, S.: droghiere, droghiero, farmacista, *m.*

drŭid, S.: druido, *m.*

drŭm 1, S.: tamburo; timpano; tamburino, *m.*: *beat the* —, battere il tamburo; — *of the ear*, timpano dell' orecchio. **drum** 2, INTR.: battere il tamburo.

drŭmble†, INTR.: poltroneggiare, tentennare, cincischiare.

drŭm-major, S.: tamburino maggiore, *m.* **-maker**, S.: fabbricante di tamburi, *m.* **-mer**, S.: tamburino, *m.* **-ming**, S.: battimento del tamburo, *m.* **-stick**, S.: bacchetta di tamburo, *f.*

drŭnk, ADJ.: ebrio, ubriaco: *make* —, imbriacare; *get* —, imbriacarsi, ubriacarsi; *dead* —, ubriacaccio. **-ard**, S.: imbriacone, trincone, *m.* **-en**, ADJ.: imbriaco, inebbriato. **-enly**, ADV.: da imbriaco. **-enness**, S.: imbriachezza, ubriachezza, *f.*

[illegible] ADJ.: secco, arido, asciutto; siti- [illegible]to; insipido; meschino: *get* [illegible] diventar secco; — *land*, [illegible]ente, *m.* **dry** 2, [illegible]cingare; INTR.

[illegible]

cate, *f. pl.* **-ly**, ADV.: senza umidità, aridamente; freddamente; poveramente. **-ness**, S.: siccità; freddezza; insipidezza, *f.* **-nurse** 1, S.: nutrice non lattante, *f.* **-nurse** 2, TR.: allevare senza lattare. **-shod**, ADJ.: a secco; a piè secco.

dū-al, ADJ.: duale; da due. **-ălity**, S.: dualità, *f.*

dŭb 1, S.: colpo, *m.*, percossa, *f.* **dub** 2, TR.: fare; creare; armare (un cavaliere).

dubiŏsity, S.: dubbiezza, *f.*

dŭb-ious, ADJ.: dubbioso, incerto, indeciso. **-iously**, ADV.: dubbiosamente, con dubbio. **-iousness**, S.: dubbiezza, *f.*, dubbio, *m.*, incertezza, *f.* **-itable**, ADJ.: dubitevole, dubbioso, incerto. **-itably**, ADV.: in modo dubbioso. **-itâtion**, S.: dubitazione; dubitanza, *f.*

dŭcal, ADJ.: ducale, di duca, da duca.

dŭcat, S.: ducato, *m.* (moneta).

dŭch-ess, S.: duchessa, *f.* **-y**, S.: ducato, *m.*

dŭck 1, S.: anatra; inchinata, riverenza, *f.*: *my* —! mio caro! mia cara! **duck** 2, TR.: tuffare, immergere; INTR.: tuffarsi. **-er**, S.: marangone, parasito, *m.* **-ing**, S.: (*nav.*) cala, *f.*, tuffo, battesimo del tropico, *m.*: *give one a* —, tuffare uno, dargli un tuffo. **-legged**, ADJ.: che ha gambe corte. **-ling**, S.: anatrina, *f.* **-meat**, S.: lente palustre, *f.* **-sfoot**, S.: serpentaria, *f.* **-weed** = *duck-meat.*

dŭct, S.: guida, *f.*; passaggio; canale, *m.* **-ile**, ADJ.: duttile; flessibile; trattevole. **-ileness**, **-ility**, S.: duttilità; flessibilità; docilità, *f.*

dŭde, S.: damerino, elegante, *m.*

dŭdgeon, S.: daga piccola; mala parte, *f.*: *take in* —, sdegnarsi, dar nel cencio.

dūe 1, ADJ.: debito, dovuto: *in* — *time*, opportunamente; S.: debito; tributo, *m.*; imposta, *f.* **due** 2, ADV.: debitamente; esattamente: *your bill falls* —, la vostra cambiale scade. **-ful†**, ADJ.: convenevole, conveniente.

dūel 1, S.: duello, *m.*: *fight a* —, battersi in duello. **duel** 2, INTR.: duellare, fare duello. **-ler**, S.: duellante, *m.* **-ling**, S.: duellare, duello, *m.* **-list**, S.: duellista, duellante, *m.*

dūeness, S.: convenevolezza, *f.*

duénna, S.: donna attempata, *f.*

duét, S.: duetto, duo, *m.*

dŭg 1, S.: tetta, mammella, *f.*, capezzolo, *m.* **dug** 2, impf. e part. del v. *dig.*

dūke, S.: duca, *m.* **-dom**, S.: ducato, *m.*

dŭll 1, ADJ.: fosco, scuro, uggioso; ottuso, stupido, goffo, tristo, mesto; tedioso: [illegible] *of hearing*, duro d' orecchio; *get* [illegible], perdere il filo, attondarsi; [illegible] *colour*, colore smorto, *m.*; [illegible] *hearing*, udito duro, [illegible] noise, mormorio, bisbiglio, *m.*;

— *sight*, vista fosca, *f.*; — *wit*, ingegno ottuso, *m.* **dull** 2, TR.: stupidire; render ottuso; offuscare; INTR.: intormentirsi. **-ard**, S.: babbuasso, *m.* **-brained**, ADJ.: stupido, scempiato, capocchio. **-head**, S.: minchione, balocco, *m.* **-ness**, S.: stupidezza, balordaggine, pigrizia, lentezza; sonnolenza, *f.* **-pated**, ADJ.: stupido, insensato. **-witted**, ADJ.: stordito, balordo. **-y**, ADV.: stupidamente; lentemente.

dūly, ADV.: debitamente, convenevolmente; esattamente, precisamente.

dŭl-cet, ADJ.: dolce (al gusto), dolcigno; armonioso. **-cificātion**, S.: (*chem.*) dolcificare, *m.* **-cify**, TR.: dolcificare; raddolcire, mitigare. **-cimer**, S.: salterio, saltero, *m.* **-corate**, TR.: addolcire, rendere dolce. **-corātion**, S.: addolcimento, *m.*, dolcificazione, *f.*

dŭmb, ADJ.: muto, taciturno: *strike* —, far ammutire. **-bells**, PL.: pesi ginnastici, *m. pl.* **-found**, TR.: render muto; confondere. **-ly**, ADV.: in silenzio, senza parlare. **-ness**, S.: mutezza, *f.*; silenzio, *m.* **-waiter**, S.: calapranzi, *m.*

dŭmp 1, S.: cordoglio, *m.* **dump** 2, S.: tristezza, malinconia, *f.* **-ish**, ADJ.: tristo, mesto. **-ishly**, ADV.: tristamente. **-ishness**, S.: tristezza, malinconia, *f.*

dŭmp-ling, S.: podingo, *m.* **-y**, ADJ.: corto e grosso.

dŭn 1, ADJ.: bruno, fosco; tanè. **dun** 2, S.: creditore importuno, *m.* **dun** 3, TR.: importunare, molestare. **-bee**, S.: tafano, *m.*

dŭn-ce, S.: goffo, babbuasso, *m.* **-cery**, S.: goffaggine, balordaggine, *f.* **-cical**, ADJ.: sciocco, balordo.

dŭng 1, impf. e part. del v. *ding*. **dung** 2, S.: concime, letame; sterco, *m.* **dung** 3, TR.: concimare, letamare. **-cart**, S.: carretta da trasporre il letame, *f.*

dŭngeon, S.: prigione sotterranea, *f.*

dŭng-fork, S.: forcone del letame, *m.* **-hill**, ADJ.: nato nel letame; vile, abbietto; S.: concime; letamaio, *m.* **-y**, ADJ.: pieno di letame; abbietto. **-yard**, S.: luogo da riporvi il letame, cortile, *m.*

dŭnnage, S.: (*nav.*) pagliuolo, *m.*

dŭnner, S.: riscuotitore, esattore, *m.*

dŭnnish, ADJ.: brunotto.

dŭnny, ADJ.: sordo.

dūo, S.: (*mus.*) duetto, *m.* **-dĕcimo**, S.: in dodici; libro in duodecimo, *m.*

dūpe 1, S.: merlotto, gonzo, ingannato, *m.* **dupe** 2, TR.: ingannare, truffare.

dū-plicate 1, S.: duplicato, *m.*, copia, *f.* **-plicate** 2, TR.: raddoppiare; piegare. **-plicātion**, S.: duplicazione, *f.*, raddoppiamento, *m.* **-plicity**, S.: duplicità; doppiezza, *f.*

bleness, S.: durabilità, *f.* **-rably**, ADV.: durabilmente, durevolmente. **-rance**, S.:

-ress, S.: incar-

f. **-ring**, PREP.,

-rity, S.: durezza;

dŭsk 1, ADJ.: oscuro, fosco, bruno, buio: S.: crepuscolo, bruzzo, brunolo, *m.*: *in the — of the evening*, in sul far bruzzo; al far della notte. **dusk** 2, TR.: oscurare; INTR.: oscurarsi; imbrunire, divenire bruno. **-ily**, ADV.: oscuramente, foscamente. **-(i)ness**, S.: oscurità, *f.*; buio, *m.* **-y**, ADJ.: alquanto scuro, fosco, oscuretto.

dŭst 1, S.: polvere; poverìa, *f.*: *the rain has laid the* —, la pioggia ha ammorzato la polvere; *trample in the* —, calpestare. **dust** 2, TR.: coprire di polvere; — *off*, nettare da polvere, spazzare. **-box**, S.: polverino, *m.* **-er**, S.: strofinaccio, *m.* **-iness**, S.: polverio, *m.* **-man**, S.: paladino, *m.* **-y**, ADJ.: polveroso, coperto di polvere.

Dŭtch, ADJ., S.: holandese. **-man**, S.: holandese, *m.*

dū-teous, **-tiful**, ADJ.: ubbidiente, ossequioso; rispettoso. **-tifully**, ADV.: ossequiosamente, sommessamente. **-tifulness**, S.: ubbidienza; sommessione, *f.* **-ty**, S.: dovere, debito, *m.*; funzione, *f.*; uffizio, *m.*; tassa; dogana, gabella, *f.*: *on* —, *upon* —, di servizio, in funzione; *pay one's* —, render rispetto; *present one's* —, riverire, salutare.

duŭmvirate, S.: duumvirato, *m.*

dwârf 1, S.: nano; caramogio, *m.* **dwarf** 2, TR.: impedire dal crescere. **-elder**, S.: ebbio, *m.* **-ish**, ADJ.: piccoletto, piccino. **-ishly**, ADV.: in modo piccino. **-ishness**, S.: picciolezza, *f.* **-tree**, S.: albero nano, *m.*

dwĕll, IRR.; INTR.: abitare, dimorare; stare; dilatarsi, allargarsi. **-er**, S.: abitatore, abitante, *m.* **-ing**, S.: abitazione, dimora, *f.* **-ing-house**, S.: casa; abitazione, *f.*

dwindle, INTR.: impiccolire, diminuire; consumarsi; peggiorare.

dȳ-e 1, S.: tinta, tintura, *f.*, colore, *m.*: — *stuff*, materia tintoria, *f.* **-e** 2, TR.: tingere, colorare: — *black* (*blue*, *etc.*, tingere in nero (turchino, ecc.); — *in grain*, tingere in lana. **-eing**, S.: tintura; (il) tingere. **-er**, S.: tintore, *m.* **-e-house**, S.: tintoria, *f.* **-e-works**, S.: tintoria, *f.*

-distantly, ADV.: in modo equidistante. **-lăteral**, ADJ.: (*geom.*) equilatero. **-librate**, TR.: equilibrare, pesare ugualmente, contrappesare. **-librātion**, S.: equilibrio, contrappesamento, *m.* **-librium**, S.: equilibrio, *m.* **-nĕcessary**, ADJ.: ugualmente necessario. **-nŏctial**, ADJ.: equinoziale, di equinozio; S.: equinoziale; equatore, *m.* **ĕqui-nox**, S.: equinozio, *m.*

equip, TR.: fornire; allestire, preparare, apparecchiare; (*nav.*) equipaggiare.

ĕquip-age, S.: fornimento, apparecchio; equipaggio; arnese; vassoio, *m.*

equipĕndency, S.: equilibrio, *m.*

equipment, S.: armamento; acconciamento; equipaggiamento, *m.*

ĕquipŏise 1, S.: equilibrio, contrappesamento, *m.* **equipoise** 2, TR.: equilibrare, contrappesare.

equipŏllen-ce, S.: equipollenza, equivalenza, *f.* **-t**, ADJ.: equipollente, equivalente.

equipŏnder-ance, -ancy, S.: equiponderanza, *f.* **-ant**, ADJ.: equiponderante, d' uguale peso. **-ate**, INTR.: equiponderare, contrappesare.

ĕquitabl-e, ADJ.: equo, ragionevole. **-eness**, S.: equità, imparzialità, *f.* **-y**, ADV.: con equità, giustamente.

equitātion, S.: equitazione, *f.*

ĕquity, S.: equità, imparzialità, giustizia, *f.*

equivalen-ce, -cy, S.: equivalenza, *f.*, equivalere, *m.* **-t**, ADJ.: equivalente, di valore uguale: *be* —, equivalere; S.: equivalente, *m.*

equivo-cal, ADJ.: equivoco, ambiguo; dubbio. **-cally**, ADV.: equivocamente; dubbiamente. **-calness**, S.: equivocamento, *m.*, ambiguità, *f.* **-cate**, TR.: equivocare. **-cātion**, S.: equivocazione, *f.* **-cator**, S.: equivocante, *m.*

ēra, S.: era, epoca, *f.*

erădi-ate, TR.: irradiare, irraggiare. **-ātion**, S.: irradiazione, *f.*; splendore, *m.*, lucentezza, *f.*

erădi-cate, TR.: eradicare, estirpare; sbarbare. **-cātion**, S.: eradicare; estirpamento, *m.* **-cative**, ADJ.: (*med.*) eradicativo.

erās-e, TR.: raschiare, scancellare; distruggere, devastare. **-er**, S.: gomma da radere, *f.*, raschino, *m.* **-ment**, S.: scancellatura, *f.*; distruggimento, *m.*, distruzione, *f.*

ēre, ADV.: prima, prima che, più tosto, anzichè: — *long*, fra breve, fra non molto, frappoco.

erĕc-t 1, ADJ.: eretto, innalzato; dritto: *walk* —, andare in sulla *persona.* **-t** 2, TR.: *ergere, innalzare; rizzare*; incoraggiare; INTR.: levarsi, alzarsi, rizzarsi. **-tion**, S.: stabilimento, *m.*; struttura, *f.* **-tness**, S.: diritezza, *f.*; stare ritto in piedi, *m.*

ĕre-mite, S.: eremita, romito, *m.* **-mitical**, ADJ.: eremitico, di romito.

erĕption, S.: rapimento, arrappare, *m.*

erewhile† *-hwīl*, ADV.: fra breve; qualche tempo fa, poco fa, non ha guari.

ĕrgot, S.: sprone, sperone, *m.*

eringo, S.: eringio, *m.*, eringe, *f.* (erba).

eristic(al)†, ADJ.: eristico.

ĕrmine, S.: ermellino, *m.* **-d**, ADJ.: foderato d' ermellino.

ĕrn(*e*), S.: aia, *f.*

erō-de, TR.: rodere, corrodere; distruggere. **-sion**, S.: erosione, *f.*, corrodimento, *m.*

erŏtic, ADJ.: erotico, amoroso.

ĕrr, INTR.: errare, sbagliare, traviare; ingannarsi. **-able**, ADJ.: soggetto ad errare. **-ableness**, S.: attezza ad ingannarsi, *f.*

ĕrrand, S.: messaggio, *m.*; ambasciata, *f.*: *go to an* —, fare un messaggio; *fool's* —, messaggio impertinente. **-boy**, S.: servitorino, servitorello, *m.* **-man**, S.: messaggiere, messo, *m.*

ĕrrant, ADJ.: errante; vagabondo. **-ry**, S.: vagamento, vagare, *m.*

errāta, S. PL.: errori (di stampa), *m. pl.*

errătic, ADJ.: erratico, errante; irregolare. **-ally**, ADV.: in modo erratico.

errātum (pl. *errata*), S.: errore (di stampa), *m.*

ĕrring, S.: traviamento, *m.*

errōneous, ADJ.: erroneo, falso. **-ly**, ADV.: erroneamente, con errore. **-ness**, S.: errore, *m.*, falsità, *f.*

ĕrror, S.: errore, traviamento; sbaglio; mancamento, *m.*: *gross* —, errore madornale; *lead into* —, indurre in errore.

ĕrst, -while†, ADV.: altre volte, anticamente, un tempo.

erubĕscen-ce, -cy, S.: rossore; pudore, *m.* **-t**, ADJ.: rossiccio.

erŭct, INTR.: eruttare, ruttare. **-ātion**, S.: eruttazione, *f.*

ĕru-dite, ADJ.: erudito, istrutto. **-dition**, S.: erudizione, *f.*, ammaestramento, *m.*; dottrina, *f.*

erūginous, ADJ.: rugginoso.

erŭp-tion, S.: eruzione; sortita impetuosa, impetuosità, *f.* **-tive**, ADJ.: prorompente con isforzo.

erysipelas, S.: (*med.*) risipola, *f.*

escalāde, S.: (*fort.*) scalata, *f.*

escāpe 1, S.: fuga, *f.*, scampo; errore, sbaglio, *m.*: *make an* —, fuggire, prender la fuga; *have a narrow* —, scappare con difficoltà. **escape** 2, TR.: evitare; schivare; INTR.: scampare, fuggire: — *narrowly*, scapparla bella; *it* —*d me that* mi sfuggì detto che.

eschalŏt, S.: cipollina, *f.*

eschéat 1, S.: profitto casuale; diritto, *m.* **escheat** 2, INTR.: scadere in diritto. **-ẹr**, S.: esattore di beni confiscati, *m.*

eschéw, TR.: evitare; sfuggire.

ĕs-cọrt 1, S.: scorta, guida, *f.*, convoglio, *m.* **-cŏrt** 2, TR.: scortare, accompagnare, convoiare.

escóụt, S.: spia, *f.*, spiatore, esploratore, *m.*

escritoir *-twâr*, S.: scrittoio, calamaio, *m.*

ĕscụlent, ADJ.: esculento, edulo; S.: alimento, *m.*

escŭtcheọn, S.: scudo, *m.*; arme, insegne, *f. pl.*

espălịẹr, S.: spalliera, *f.*

espârcet, S.: spezie di trifoglio, *f.*

espĕçịal, ADJ.: speciale, singolare, particolare. **-ly**, ADV.: specialmente; principalmente. **-ness**, S.: particolarità, singolarità, *f.*

espíal, S.: spione; esploratore†, *m.* **ĕspịọnage**, S.: spiare, *m.*

esplanáde, S.: (*fort.*) spianata, *f.*, spianato, *m.*

espóụ-ṣal, ADJ.: di matrimonio, nuziale. **-ṣals**, S. PL.: sponsalizia, *f.*, sposamento, *m.* **-ṣe**, TR.: sposare; difendere: — *one's cause*, pigliare la difesa d' uno. **-ṣẹr**, S.: difensore, *m.*

espý, TR.: spiare; osservare, scoprire.

esquíre 1, S.: scudiere, *m.* **esquíre** 2, TR.: servire come scudiere; signore: *B. Macauly, Esq.*, al Signore, il Signor B. M.

ĕssay 1, S.: sperimento, saggio, *m.*, prova, *f.*: *make an* —, fare un saggio. **essáy** 2, TR.: tentare, assaggiare, sforzarsi. **-ist**, S.: saggiatore, sperimentatore, *m.*

ĕs-sence 1, S.: essenza, *f.*; profumo, *m.* **-sence** 2, TR.: profumare, odorare. **-sĕnṭịal**, ADJ.: essenziale, principale; S.: essenziale, *m.* **-sĕnṭịălity**, S.: essenzialità; essenza, *f.* **-sĕnṭịally**, ADV.: essenzialmente.

essóịn 1, S.: (*leg.*) esenzione, scusa legale, *f.* **essoin** 2, TR.: (*leg.*) scusare una persona che non comparisce in giustizia.

estăblish, TR.: stabilire, firmare, fissare; fondare. **-ẹr**, S.: fondatore, *m.* **-ment**, S.: stabilimento, fondamento, instituto, *m.*; approvazione, *f.*; modello, *m.*

estafĕt, S.: staffetta, *f.*

estáte 1, S.: stato, *m.*; condizione; fortuna, *f.*, beni, *m. pl.*; terra, *f.*; corpo politico, ordine, *m.*: *real and personal* —, beni mobili ed immobili; *small* —, piccola terra; *man's* —, età virile, *f.* **estate** 2, TR.: dotare.

estéem 1, S.: stima, considerazione, *f.*;

estéem 2, TR.: stimare, apprezzare; pesare. **-ẹr**, S.: stimatore, apprezzatore, *m.*

ĕsti-mable, ADJ.: stimabile, apprezzabile. **-mableness**, S.: qualità estimabile, *f.* **-mate** 1, S.: estimazione, *f.*, prezzo; computamento, conto, *m.*: *rough* —, stima approssimativa. **-mate** 2, TR.: stimare, apprezzare; valutare. **-máṭịọn**, S.: estimazione, stima; opinione, *f.*; conto, *m.* **-mative**, ADJ.: estimativo. **-mátọr**, S.: stimatore, apprezzatore, *m.*

ĕstival, ADJ.: estivale, estivo.

estŏppel, S.: (*jur.*) ostacolo, *m.*, opposizione, *f.*

ẹstráde, S.: estrada, *f.*, palchetto a rigoglio, *m.*

estrān-ge, TR.: alienare; allontanare; separare; rimuovere; dissuadere. **-gement**, S.: alienazione; separazione; distanza, *f.* **-gẹr**, S.: straniere, *m.*

estrapáde, S.: strapata, *f.*

estráy, TR.: sviarsi, smarrirsi.

estréat, S.: copia, *f.*

estrĕpement, S.: guasto; danno, *m.*

ĕstụ-ance, S.: calore, *m.* **-ary**, S.: estuario, braccio (di mare), *m.*, bocca, *f.* **-ate**, TR.: bollire, fervere. **-áṭịọn**, S.: estuazione, *f.*, bollimento, *m.*

ẹsū-rient, ADJ.: affamato, vorace.

ĕtch, TR.: scolpire con acqua forte; intagliare. **-ing**, S.: intaglio (con acqua forte), *m.*; incisione all' acqua forte, *f.*

ẹtẽr-nal, ADJ.: eterno, perpetuo. **-nalize**, eternare; immortalare. **-nally**, ADV.: eternamente, in eterno. **-nity**, S.: eternità, perpetuità, *f.* **-nize**, TR.: eternare.

ēth-ẹr, S.: aria, *f.*; cielo, etere; (*chem.*) etere, *m.* **-ẽrẹal**, **-ẽrẹous**, ADJ.: etereo, dell' etere, celeste.

ĕthic(al), ADJ.: etico, morale. **-ally**, ADV.: eticamente, moralmente. **-s**, S. PL.: etica, morale, *f.*

ĕthnic, ADJ.: etnico, pagano, gentile. **-s**, S. PL.: pagani, gentili, *m. pl.*

eth-ọlŏgical, ADJ.: morale. **-ŏlogy**, S.: etologia, *f.*

ẹtiŏlogy, S.: etiologia, *f.*

ĕtiquette, S.: etichetta, *f.*

ẹtụí, S.: astucchio, *m.*, guaina, *f.*

ety-mọlŏgical, ADJ.: etimologico. **-mŏlọgist**, S.: etimologista, *m.* **-mŏlogy**, S.: etimologia, *f.*

ĕtymon, S.: parola primitiva; origine, *f.*

eūcha-rist, S.: eucharistia, comunione, *f.* **-ristical**, ADJ.: eucaristico.

euchŏlogy, S.: eucologio, *m.*

eūlọ-gize, TR.: lodare, encomiare. **-gy**, S.: elogio, *m.*, lode, *f.*

eūnuch, S.: eunuco, *m.*

Eūrus, S.: euro, *m*.
eūrythmy, S.: euritmia, *f*.
eu-thanāsia, -thānasy, S.: morte placida, *f*.
evācate†, TR.: votare, cavare.
evāc-uant, ADJ.: (*med*.) evacuante. **uate**, TR.: evacuare; mandare fuori. **-uātion**, S.: evacuazione, *f*., evacuamento, *m*. **-uative**, ADJ.: (*med*.) evacuativo.
evāde, TR.: scampare, scappare; scappolare; INTR.: evadere; fuggire.
evagātion, S.: evagazione, *f*., svagamento, *m*.
evanēscen-ce, S.: svanire, *m*., svanizione, *f*. **-t**, ADJ.: che svanisce, fugitivo.
evangēlical, ADJ.: evangelico. **-ly**, ADV.: evangelicamente.
evānge-lism, S.: promulgare del vangelo, *m*. **-list**, S.: evangelista, *m*. **-lize**, TR.: evangelizzare, predicare il vangelo. **-ly**, S.: vangelo, m.
evān-id†, ADJ.: che svanisce; debole; fugitivo. **-ish**, INTR.: svanire; evadere, fuggire.
evāpo-rable, ADJ.: evaporabile, evaporante. **-rate**, TR.: svaporare; dissipare; INTR.: evaporare; dissiparsi. **-rātion**, S.: evaporazione, *f*., evaporamento, *m*.
evā-sion, S.: scappata, *f*.; sotterfugio, pretesto, *m*. **-sive**, ADJ.: evasivo, sofistico. **-sively**, ADV.: sofisticamente.
ēve 1, S.: vigilia, *f*. **eve** 2, **-n** 1, S.: sera, *f*.: *at* —, sulla sera. **-n** 2, ADJ.: uguale, pari, simile; piano, unito, uniforme: *make* —, spianare; *be* — *with*, rendere la pariglia a. **-n** 3, ADV.: anche, anzi, ancora; quasi; fino, infino; — *as*, come, come se; — *down*, diritto giù; — *now*, or' ora; — *on*, dirittamente, a dirittura; — *so*, appunto così, giusto così. **-n**, TR.: appianare, agguagliare. **-n-handed**, ADJ.: imparziale; equo.
ēvening, S.: sera, serata, *f*.: — *tide*, sera, *f*.; — *party*, serata, conversazione; — *star*, stella della sera.
ēven-ly†, ADV.: ugualmente, uniformemente. **-ness**, S.: ugualità, uniformità; imparzialità, *f*.; livello, *m*.
evĕnt, S.: evento, avvenimente, esito, *m*.
evĕnterate, TR.: sventrare, sviscerare.
evĕntful, ADJ.: pieno d' avvenimenti.
ēventide, S.: sera, serata: *at* —, alla sera.
evĕnti-late†, TR.: ventolare; discutere; esaminare. **-lātion**†, S.: ventilazione; discussione, *f*.
evĕn-tual, ADJ.: eventuale, casuale, fortuito. **-tuālity**, S.: eventualità, *f*. **-tually**, ADV.: eventualmente, a caso, fortuitamente. **-tuate**, INTR.: terminare.
ĕver, ADV.: *siempre, sempremai,* maisempre, mai, tuttavia: *for* —, *for* — *and* —, per sempre, eternamente; in sempiterno, ne' secoli de' secoli; — *and anon*, di quando in quando; — *before*, da ogni tempo; *as much as* —, quanto mai; *as soon as* —, quanto prima; — *since*, da quel tempo in qua, dipoi, dopo; — *and anon*, ogni tanto, ogni poco, di quando in quando. **-dūring**, ADJ.: eterno, perpetuo. **-green**, ADJ.: sempre verde; S.: sempreviva, barba di Giove, *f*. **-lāsting**, ADJ.: eterno, perpetuo; S.: eternità, perpetuità, *f*. **-lāstingly**, ADV.: eternamente, perpetuamente, senza fine. **-lāstingness**, S.: eternità, perpetuità, *f*. **-living**, ADJ.: semprevivo, immortale. **-mōre**, ADV.: sempremai; eternamente.
evĕr-sion, S.: sovvertimento, sconvolgimento, rovinamento, *m*. **-t**, TR.: sconvolgere, rovinare, distruggere.
ĕvery, PRON.: ogni, ciascuno, ciascheduno: — *other day*, un giorno sì un giorno no; — *whit*, ogni cosa, tutto; affatto. **-body**, PR.: ognuno, ciascuno. **-day**, ADV.: di ogni giorno. **-one** = *everybody*. **-thing**, PR.: ogni cosa. **-way**, ADV.: da ogni banda. **-where**, ADV.: da per tutto, ovunque.
ēvesdropper, S.: ascoltatore; spione, *m*.
evic-t, TR.: evincere, convincere; provare. **-tion**, S.: evizione; evidenza, *f*.
ĕviden-ce 1, S.: evidenza; prova, *f*., testimonio, *m*. **-ce** 2, TR.: provare, mostrare. **-t**, ADJ.: evidente, apparente, manifesto, chiaro. **-tly**, ADV.: evidentemente, chiaramente. **-tness**, S.: evidenza; prova, *f*.
ēvil 1, ADJ.: cattivo, malo, perverso; S.: male, *m*.; malvagità; calamità, *f*.; *the* — *one*, il maligno (Satana). **evil** 2, ADV.: male, malemente. **-affected**, ADJ.: malvagio, malevolo. **-doer**, S.: malfattore; furfante, *m*. **-favoured**, ADJ.: brutto, deforme. **-favouredness**, S.: bruttezza, laidezza, difformità, *f*. **-ly**, ADV.: male, malamente. **-minded**, ADJ.: maldisposto, malevolo, malizioso, maligno. **-ness**, S.: malvagità, malizia; perversità, *f*. **-speaking**, S.: maldicenza, calunnia, *f*. **-wishing**, ADJ.: malevolo, maligno. **-worker**, S.: malfattore, *m*.
evin-ce, TR.: evincere, convincere; provare; dimostrare. **-cible**, ADJ.: dimostrabile; provabile. **-cibly**, ADV.: dimostrativamente, chiaramente.
ēvirate†, TR.: castrare.
eviscerate, TR.: sviscerare, sventrare.
ĕvi-table, ADJ.: evitabile. **-tate**, TR.: evitare, scappare, sfuggire. **-tātion**, S.: evitazione; scappata, fuga, *f*.
ĕvo-cāte, TR.: evocare. **-cātion**, S. invocare, congiuramento, *m*.

evolūtion, s.: sviluppo; rivolgimento, *m.*; (*mil.*) evoluzione, *f.*

evŏlve, TR.: sviluppare; stendere; INTR.: svolgersi, svilupparsi; stendersi: *be(come)* —*d*, svolgersi.

evŭl-gate, TR.: divolgare, pubblicare. **-gātion**, s.: pubblicazione, *f.*

evŭlsion, s.: divellimento, *m.*

ēwe 1, s.: pecora, *f.* **ewe** 2, INTR.: figliare (delle pecore). **-lamb**, s.: mannerino, *m.*, pecorella, *f.*

ēwer, s.: mesciroba; acquareccia, *f.* **-y**, s.: uffizio del vasellame reale, *m.*

ex-, ex: —*-king*, l' ex-re, ecc.

exăcer-bate, TR.: esacerbare, inasprire. **-bātion**, s.: esacerbazione, *f.*, esasperamento, provocamento, irritamento, *m.*

exăc-t 1, ADJ.: esatto, puntuale; diligente; giusto. **-t** 2, TR.: esigere; domandare; strappare. **-ter**, s.: esattore, *m.* **-tion**, s.: esazione, estorsione, *f.* **-titude**, s.: esattezza, *f.* **-tly**, ADV.: esattamente, accuratamente, diligentemente. **-tness**, s.: esattezza; puntualità, *f.* **-tor** = *exacter.*

exăggerate, TR.: esagerare, amplificare. **-ātion**, s.: esagerazione, amplificazione, *f.*

exăgi-tate, TR.: esagitare, agitare; tormentare. **-tātion**, s.: agitazione, *f.*; scuotimento, *m.*

exălt, TR.: esaltare, innalzare; alzare; estollere, lodare, vantare. **-ātion**, s.: esaltazione, *f.*, esaltamento; elevamento, *m.* **-ed**, ADJ.: alzato, elevato, sublime; lodato.

ex-aminātion, s.: esame, esaminamento; (*leg.*) interrogatorio: *a strict* —, un esame rigoroso; *post mortem* —, autopsia (del cadavere); *undergo an* —, subire (passare) un esame. **-āminator**, s.: esaminatore; inquisitore, *m.* **-āmine**, TR.: esaminare, interrogare; pesare, considerare; discutere. **-āminer**, s.: esaminatore, interrogatore, investigatore, *m.*; esaminatrice, ecc., *f.* **-āmining**, s.: inquisizione, investigazione, *f.*

ĕx-amplary†, ADJ.: esemplare. **-ămple** 1, s.: esempio; esemplare; modello, *m.*: *for* —, per esempio; *give* (*set*) *an* —, dar esempio; *make one an* —, punir alcuno esemplarmente. **-ample** 2, TR.: dar esempio; esemplificare.

exănguious, ADJ.: esangue, senza sangue.

exăni-mate, ADJ.: esanimato; scorato, scoraggiato. **-mātion**, s.: disanimare, *m.*, privazione della vita, *f.* **-mous**, ADJ.: esanimo, morto.

xan-thēma (pl. *exanthemata*), s.: (*med.*) *uzione; efflorescenza, f.* **-thēmatous**, *a.: (med.) pieno di bollicelle.*

exarticulātion, s.: dislogamento, *m.*, lussazione, *f.*

exăsper-ate, TR.: esasperare; inacerbare, irritare, provocare. **-ātion**, s.: esasperamento; irritamento, *m.* **-ater**, s.: irritatore, provocatore, *m.*

excandĕscen-ce, **-cy**, s.: escandescenza, *f.*

excărnate, TR.: divestire della carne, scarnare.

excarnificātion, s.: divestimento della carne, *m.*

ĕxca-vate, TR.: scavare, cavare. **-vātion**, s.: scavamento, *m.*; cavità, *f.*; (*rail.*) intaglio, *m.*, trincea, *f.* **-vater**, s.: scavatore, *m.*

excēed, TR.: eccedere; trapassare, superare; INTR.: passare oltre, oltrepassare; uscir del convenevole. **-ing**, ADJ.: eccedente, eccessivo. **-ingly**, ADV.: eccessivamente; perfettamente.

excĕl, TR.: eccellere, sorpassare; INTR.: superare; essere eminente.

ĕxcellen-ce, **-cy**, s.: eccellenza, eccellenzia, preeminenza, superiorità, *f.* **-t**, ADJ.: eccellente, eminente. **-tly**, ADV.: eccellentemente.

excĕp-t 1, TR.: eccettuare, escludere; INTR.: obbiettare, ricusare; opporsi: — *against*, allegare. **-t** 2, CONJ.: a meno che, eccettochè. **-t** 3, **-ting**, PREP.: eccetto, fuorche, a meno che. **-tion**, s.: eccezione, eccettuazione; esclusione, *f.*: *take — to*, trovar a redire, aver a male; offendersi. **-tionable**, ADJ.: che si può obbiettare; ricusabile. **-tious**, ADJ.: stizzoso, uggioso, delicato. **-tive**, ADJ.: eccetuativo. **-tless**, ADJ.: senza eccezione. **-tor**, s.: che fa delle obbiezioni; censore, *m.*

excern†, TR.: rigettare, ributtare; ventolare; separare; purgare, nettare.

excĕrp, TR.: scegliere; spigolare; estrarre. **-tion**, s.: sceglimento; spigolare; estratto, *m.* **-tor**, s.: raccoglitore, *m.* **-ts**, s. PL.: estratti, *m. pl.*

excĕss, s.: eccesso, trapassamento; disordine, *m.*; intemperanza, *f.* **-ive**, ADJ.: eccessivo, soverchio. **-ively**, ADV.: eccessivamente, fuor di modo. **-iveness**, s.: eccesso, *m.*, soprabbondanza, *f.*

exchānge 1, s.: cambio, *m.*; permuta, *f.*, baratto, *m.*; borsa, *f.*: *bill of* —, lettera di cambio, *f.*; *course of* —, corso dei cambi; listino della borsa; *the stock* —, la Borsa. **-e** 2, TR.: cambiare, barattare; permutare. **-eable**, ADJ.: che si può cambiare. **-e-broker**, s.: sensale di cambio, *m.* **-er**, s.: cambiatore, *m.* **-e-office**, s.: ufficio di cambio, cambiavalute, *m.*

exchĕquer, s.: erario, tesoro regio; scacchiere, *m.*

ex-ciṣable, ADJ.: gabellabile, che paga la tassa. **-ciṣe** 1, S.: assisa, tassa; imposizione, imposta, *f.* **-cise** 2, TR.: levare un' imposta, tassare. **-ciṣeman**, S.: ufficiale dell' assisa, gabelliere, *m.* **-ciṣe-office**, S.: uffizio dell' assisa, *m.*, gabella, dogana, *f.* **-ciṣion**, S.: estirpamento, *m.*; distruzione, *f.*
ex-citability, S.: capacità d' esser eccitato, irritabilità, *f.* **-citable**, ADJ.: facile ad esser eccitato, irritabile. **-citate**, TR.: eccitare, irritare. **-citātion**, S.: eccitamento, *m.*, provocazione, *f.* **-cite**, TR.: eccitare, stimolare, incoraggiare. **-citement**, S.: eccitamento, aizzamento, stimolo, *m.* **-citer**, S.: eccitatore, istigatore, provocatore, *m.*
ex-clāim, INTR.: sclamare; gridare ad alta voce. **-clamātion**, S.: esclamazione, *f.*, sclamare, *m.*: — *point*, punto d' esclamazione. **-clămatory**, ADJ.: esclamativo, di esclamazione.
exclū-de, TR.: escludere; eccettuare. **-sion**, S.: esclusione, esclusiva; eccezione, *f.* **-sive**, ADJ.: esclusivo, escludente. **-sively**, ADV.: esclusivamente. **-sory**, ADJ.: esclusivo.
excŏct†, TR.: fare bollire, lessare.
excŏg-itate, TR.: pensare, inventare, immaginare. **-itātion**, S.: invenzione, *f.*
excommūni-cate, TR.: scomunicare. **-cātion**, S.: scomunicazione, *f.*
excŏri-ate, TR.: scorticare, torre via la pelle. **-ātion**, S.: scorticamento, *m.*
excorticātion, S.: dibuccio, *m.*
ĕxcre-ate†, TR.: sputare. **-ātion†**, S.: escreato, *m.*
ĕxcre-ment, S.: escremento, *m.* **-mĕntal**, **-mentitious**, ADJ.: escrementoso.
excrĕscen-ce, **-cy**, S.: escrescenza, *f.*; tumore, *m.*
excrē-tion, S.: separazione d' umori, *f.* **-tive**, **-tory**, ADJ.: (*med.*) escretorio.
excrū-ciable, ADJ.: atto a tormentare. **-ciate**, TR.: tormentare. **-ciating**, ADJ.: atroce, dolorisissimo. **-ciātion**, S.: tormento, *m.*; afflizione, *f.*
excŭl-pate, TR.: scolpare, scusare, giustificare. **-pātion**, S.: scolpamento, *m.*, giustificazione, *f.* **-patory**, ADJ.: scusante, giustificante.
excŭr-sion, S.: sviamento, *m.*; escursione; digressione, *f.* **-sive**, ADJ.: digressivo; errante, deviante. **-siveness**, S.: traviamento, *m.*
excū-sable, ADJ.: scusabile, perdonabile. **-sableness**, S.: scusa, scusazione, *f.* **-sātion†**, S.: discolpa, scusa, *f.* **-satory**, ADJ.: apologetico, giustificativo. **-se** 1, S.: scusa, discolpa; giustificazione; apologia, *f.* **-se** 2, TR.: scusare, scolpare, giustificare; *esentare; perdonare.* **-seless**, ADJ.: inescusabile. **-ser**, S.: scusatore, perdonatore, *m.*
ex-cŭss, TR.: staggire; sequestrare. **-cŭssion**, S.: staggimento; sequestro, *m.*
ĕxe-crable, ADJ.: esecrabile, detestabile. **-crableness**, S.: azione esecrabile, *f.*; orrore, *m.* **-crably**, ADV.: esecrabilmente. **-crate**, TR.: esecrare, detestare. **-crātion**, S.: esecrazione, detestazione, imprecazione, maledizione, *f.* **-cratory**, ADJ.: esecratorio.
ĕxe-cute, TR.: eseguire, adempire, effettuare; esercitare; giustiziare (un malfattore): — *a deed*, validare un atto. **-cuter**, S.: esecutore, ministro, *m.* **-cūtion**, S.: esecuzione, *f.*, esequimento, compimento; sequestrazione, *f.*, staggimento, *m.*: *place of* —, luogo del supplicio, *m.*; *writ of* —, mandato, *m.* **-cūtioner**, S.: boia, carnefice, *m.*
exĕcu-tive, ADJ.: esecutivo. **-tor**, S.: esecutore testamentario, *m.* **-torship**, S.: uffizio d' un esecutore, *m.* **-tory**, ADJ.: esecutorio. **-trix**, S.: esecutrice testamentaria, *f.*
exe-gēsis, S.: esegesi, *f.* **-gĕtical**, ADJ.: esegetico.
exĕmplar, S.: esemplare, modello, *m.*; copia, *f.*
ĕxem-plarily, ADJ.: esemplarmente. **-plariness**, S.: esemplarità, *f.* **-plary**, ADJ.: esemplare.
ex-emplificātion, S.: esemplificazione; prova; copia, *f.* **-ĕmplify**, TR.: esemplificare; provare con esempli; copiare.
exĕmp-t 1, ADJ.: esente, privilegiato. **-t** 2, TR.: esentare, privilegiare. **-tion**, S.: esenzione, *f.*; privilegio, *m.* **-titious**, ADJ.: separabile.
exĕnter-ate, TR.: sviscerare, sventrare. **-ātion**, S.: svisceramento, sviscerare, *m.*
exĕquial, ADJ.: esequiale, d' esequie.
ĕxequies, S. PL.: esequie, *f. pl.*, funerale, *m.*
ĕxerci-se 1, S.: esercitamento; esercizio; travaglio, lavoro; tema, *m.*: *take* —, far del moto, passeggiare. **-se** 2, TR.: esercitare; addestrare; praticare; INTR.: esercitarsi; applicarsi. **-ser**, S.: esercitatore, *m.*
exercitātion, S.: esercizio, *m.*; pratica, *f.*
exĕr-t, TR.: adoprare, impiegare; mettere in uso; compire; mostrare, dimostrare: — *one's self*, adoprarsi, sforzarsi. **-tion**, S.: adoperamento; sforzo; potere, *m.*
exfō-liate, INTR.: sfaldarsi. **-liātion**, S.: sfaldatura, *f.* **-liative**, ADJ.: atto a sfaldarsi.
ex-hālable, ADJ.: esalabile, vaporabile. **-halātion**, S.: esalazione, *f.*, evaporamento; vapore, *m.* **-hāle**, TR.: esalare

evaporare. **-hâlement**, S.: esalazione, evaporazione, *f.*

exhâus-t, TR.: esaurire; rasciugare. **-tible**, ADJ.: esauríbile. **-tion**, S.: disseccamento, *m.* **-tless**, ADJ.: inesauribile, inesausto.

exhêre-dàte, TR.: diseredare, esereditare. **-dâtion**, S.: diseredazione, *f.*, eseredare, *m.*

exhib-it 1, S.: esibizione, *f.*; documento, *m.* **-it** 2, TR.: esibire; mostrare, produrre. **-iter**, S.: esibitore, *m.* **-ition** *exhib-*, S.: esibizione; presentazione; borsa, *f.* **-itioner**, S.: borsaio, *m.* **-itive**, ADJ.: rappresentativo.

exhila-rate, TR.: rallegrare; divertire. **-ration**, S.: gioia, allegrezza, giocondità, *f.*; piacere, *m.*

exhôrt, TR.: esortare; incitare, animare, incoraggiare. **-âtion**, S.: esortazione, *f.* **-ative**, **-atory**, ADJ.: esortatorio, esortativo. **-er**, S.: esortatore, *m.*

exiccate = *exsiccate.*

èxigen-ce, **-cy**, S.: esigenza, necessità, *f.*, bisogno; affanno, *m.*, afflizione, *f.* **-t**, ADJ.: esigente, urgente; premuroso; S.: necessità urgente, *f.*; bisogno, *m.*

ex-igûity, S.: minutezza, piccolezza, sottigliezza, *f.* **-iguous**, ADJ.: esiguo, piccolo, sottile, minuto. **-iguousness**, S.: piccolezza; minutezza, *f.*

exile 1, ADJ.: esile, tenue; sottile, magro.

exile 2, S.: esilio, sbandeggiamento, *m.*

exile 3, TR.: esiliare, mandare in esilio, sbandeggiare. **-ment**, S.: esilio, bando, sbandimento, *m.*

exillition†, S.: esplosione, *f.*

exility, S.: piccolezza, sottigliezza, *f.*

eximious†, ADJ.: esimio, eccellente, illustre.

exist, INTR.: esistere, essere. **-ence**, **-ency**, S.: esistenza, *f.*: *call into* —, chiamare all' esistenza. **-ent**, ADJ.: esistente. **-ible**, ADJ.: che può esistere.

ex-it, S.: esito, *m.*, uscita; partita, *f.*: *make one's* —, uscir di vita, morire. **-itíal†**, **-itious†**, ADJ.: esiziale; fatale, funesto, pernicioso.

èxod-us, **-dy†**, S.: esodo, *m.*

exolûtion, S.: (*med.*) rilassazione (dei nervi), *f.*

exôlve†, TR.: assolvere, slacciare.

exômphalos, S.: (*med.*) esonfalo, *m.*

exôner-ate, TR.: esonerare, sgravare, discaricare, alleggerire, alleviare; liberare. **-âtion**, S.: scaricamento, *m.*

èxorable, ADJ.: esorabile, compassionevole.

exôrbitan-ce, **-cy**, S.: esorbitanza, enormità, *f.* **-t**, ADJ.: esorbitante, eccessivo. **-tly**, ADV.: esorbitantemente.

èxor-cise, TR.: esorcizzare, scongiurare. **-cism**, S.: esorcismo, scongiuramento, *m.* **-cist**, S.: esorcista, *m.*

exôrdium, S.: esordio; prologo, *m.*

exornâtion, S.: ornamento, abbellimento, *m.*

exôtic, ADJ.: esotico, straniero; S.: pianta esotica, *f.*

expân-d, TR.: spandere, dilatare; INTR.: spandersi, dilatarsi; palesarsi. **-se**, S.: espansione, estensione, *f.*: — *of water*, specchio di acqua; *the broad* —, l'alto mare. **-sibility**, S.: facoltà di dilatarsi. **-sible**, ADJ.: espansivo. **-sion**, S.: espansione, dilatazione, *f.*, dilatamento, *m.* **-sive**, ADJ.: espansivo.

expâtiate, INTR.: distendersi.

expêct, TR.: aspettare, attendere; sperare; aspettarsi: *I did not* — *it*, non me l'aspettava; *what can you* —? che potete aspettarvi? *as was to be* —*ed*, come era d'aspettarsi. **-ance**, **-ancy**, S.: aspettazione; speranza, *f.* **-ant**, ADJ.: aspettante; S.: aspettante, aspettatore, *m.* **-âtion**, S.: aspettazione, aspettativa, speranza, *f.*: *sanguine* —, viva speranza (fiducia); *beyond my* —*s*, al di là delle mie speranze; *contrary to* —, contro ogni aspettativa; *be in* —, esser nell' aspettazione. **-er**, S.: aspettante, *m.*

expêct-orant, S.: medicina espettorante, *f.* **-orate**, TR.: espettorare, espurgare. **-orâtion**, S.: espettorazione, *f.* **-orative**, ADJ.: (*med.*) espettorante.

expédien-ce, **-cy**, S.: convenevolezza, convenienza; utilità; proprietà; spedizione, *f.* **-t**, ADJ.: convenevole; utile; S.: espediente; mezzo, *m.*: *it is* —, conviene. **-tly**, ADV.: convenevolmente.

èxpe-dite 1, ADJ.: spedito, pronto; agile. **-dite** 2, TR.: spedire, abbreviare, dispacciare; accelerare. **-ditely**, ADV.: speditamente, prontamente, agilmente. **-dition**, S.: spedizione; prestezza, celerità, fretta, *f.* **-ditious**, ADJ.: speditivo, pronto. **-ditiously**, ADV.: affrettatamente, prontamente.

expél, TR.: espellere, scacciare. **-ler**, S.: espulsore, scacciatore, *m.* **-ling**, S.: espulsione, *f.*

expén-d, TR.: spendere, sborsare. **-diture**, S.: spesa, *f.*, costo; sacrificio, *m.* **-se**, S.: spesa, *f.*; sborso, sborsamento, *m.*: *free of* —, senza spesa; franco; *trifling* —, tenue spesa; *defray one's* —*s*, spesare uno; *learn at one's* —, imparare alle proprie spese. **-seful**, ADJ.: dispendioso. **-seless**, ADJ.: senza spesa, senza costo. **-sive**, ADJ.: dispendioso, spendereccio; prodigo. **-sively**, ADV.: dispendiosamente, con grande spesa. **-siveness**, S.: dispendio, *m.*; stravaganza; prodigalità, *f.*

expĕrien-ce 1, s.: sperienza; cognizione; pratica, usanza, *f.*: *know by* —, sapere per esperienza. **-ce** 2, TR.: sperimentare, provare. **-cer**, s.: sperimentatore, *m.*
expĕri-ment 1, s.: sperimento, *m.*, prova, *f.* **-ment** 2, TR.: sperimentare, provare. **-mĕntal**, ADJ.: sperimentale. **-mĕntalist**, s.: sperimentatore, *m.* **-mĕntally**, ADV.: esperimentalmente. **-menter**, s.: sperimentatore, provatore, *m.*
expĕrt, ADJ.: esperto, sperimentato, versato, pratico. **-ly**, ADV.: espertamente. **-ness**, s.: abilità, destrezza, *f.*
ĕxpi-able, ADJ.: che si può espiare. **-ate**, TR.: espiare; reparare. **-ātion**, s.: espiazione; reparazione, *f.*: *as an — for*, in espiazione di. **-atory**, ADJ.: espiatorio.
expilātion, s.: (*leg.*) espilazione, *f.*
ex-pirātion, s.: espirazione, esalazione; respirazione; morte, *f.* **-pire**, TR.: spirare, esalare, finire, terminare; INTR.: morire.
ex-plāin, TR.: esplicare, spiegare; interpretare: *hard to* —, difficile a spiegarsi; — *away a difficulty*, far dileguare una difficoltà a forza di spiegazioni. **-plāinable**, ADJ.: esplicabile, spiegabile. **-plāiner**, s.: esplicatore, dichiaratore; interprete, *m.* **-planātion**, s.: esplicazione, interpretazione, *f.*, spiegamento, *m.* **-plānatory**, ADJ.: esplicativo, espositivo.
ĕxpletive, ADJ.: espletivo, riempitivo.
ĕxpli-cable, ADJ.: esplicabile, spiegabile. **-cate**, TR.: spiegare, dichiarare, dilucidare. **-cātion**, s.: esplicazione, spiegazione, *f.* **-cative**, ADJ.: esplicativo, espositivo. **-cator**, s.: espositore; comentatore, interprete, *m.*
explicit, ADJ.: espresso, distinto, chiaro, manifesto. **-ly**, ADV.: espressamente, direttamente, formalmente. **-ness**, s.: chiarezza; evidenza, *f.*
explŏd-e, INTR.: esplodere, far esplosione, scoppiare; TR.: far scoppiare (saltare in aria); rigettare, disapprovare, condannare; fischiare. **-er**, s.: fischiatore, *m.*
explŏit 1, TR.: eseguire un gran fatto. **exploit** 2, s.: fatto d' arme, fatto illustre, *m.*: *great* —*s*, gloriose gesta.
explŏ-rate, TR.: esplorare, esaminare, investigare. **-rātion**, s.: investigazione; ricerca, *f.* **-rator ĕx-**, s.: esploratore, investigatore, *m.* **-ratory**, ADJ.: esplorante. **-re**, TR.: esplorare, investigare, ricercare; esaminare. **-rement**, s.: investigamento, *m.*, ricerca, *f.*
explŏ-sion, s.: esplosione, *f.*; scoppio, scoppiamento, *m.* **-sive**, ADJ.: esplodente, che scoppia: — *cotton*, cotone esplosivo, fulmicotone, *m.*

expŏlish†, TR.: pulire, lisciare; perfezionare.
expŏ-nent, s.: (*algeb.*) esponente, *m.* **-nĕntial**, ADJ.: (*algeb.*) esponenziale.
expŏrt 1, TR.: esportare, trasportare. **ĕxport** 2, **-ātion**, s.: trasporto, trasportamento, *m.*: — *duty*, dazio d' uscita. **-er**, s.: esportatore.
ex-pŏse, TR.: esporre; mostrare; scoprire; abbandonare; REFL.: esporsi; pericolarsi: —*ed to*, esposto a, sottoposto a. **-position**, s.: esposizione, *f.*; spiegamento, *m.*; interpretazione, *f.* **-pŏsitive**, ADJ.: espositivo, esplicativo. **-pŏsitor**, s.: espositore; comentatore, interprete, *m.* **-pŏsitory**, ADJ.: espositivo, esplicativo.
expŏstu-late, TR.: questionare, contendere, disputare; INTR.: lamentarsi, querelarsi: — *with*, lagnarsi con. **-lātion**, s.: discussione, disputa, *f.* **-lator**, s.: rimostrante, *m.* **-latory**, ADJ.: rimostrante.
expŏsure, s.: esposizione; situazione, *f.*; pericolo, *m.*
expŏund, TR.: spiegare, spianare, interpretare. **-er**, s.: comentatore, interprete, *m.* **-ing**, s.: esposizione, interpretazione, *f.*, schiarimento, *m.*
ex-prĕss 1, ADJ.: espresso, preciso, distinto; simile, apparente; s.: espresso, corriere mandato, *m.*: — *train*, treno diretto; *by* —, per espresso; con istaffetta. **-press** 2, TR.: esprimere; spiegare, manifestare, mostrare; rappresentare. **-prĕssible**, ADJ.: che può esprimersi; effabile. **-prĕssion** s.: espressione; locuzione; rappresentazione, *f.* **-prĕssive**, ADJ.: espressivo. **-pressively**, ADV.: con modo espressivo. **-prĕssiveness**, s.: forza d' espressione, energia, *f.* **-prĕssly**, ADV.: espressamente, direttamente. **-prĕssure**†, s.: espressione; impressione, *f.*
ĕxpro-brate†, TR.: biasimare, rimproverare. **-brātion**†, s.: rimprovero, biasimo, rinfacciamento, *m.*
exprŏpri-ate, TR.: espropriare. **-ātion**, s.: espropriazione, *f.*
ex-pūgn, TR.: espugnare, vincere per forza. **-pugnātion**, s.: espugnazione, *f.*
expŭl-se†, TR.: espellere, scacciare. **-sion**, s.: espulsione, *f.*, scacciamento, *m.* **-sive**, ADJ.: espulsivo.
expŭn-ction, s.: cancellazione, cancellatura, *f.* **-ge**, TR.: espungere, cancellare.
ĕx-purgate, TR.: (e)spurgare. **-purgātion**, s.: purgazione, *f.* **-pŭrgatory**, ADJ.: espurgatorio, purgativo. **-pŭrge** = *expurgate*.
ĕxquisite, ADJ.: squisito, eccellente, perfetto. **-ly**, ADV.: esquisitamente, ottimamente

enféoff, TR.: infeudare, dare in feudo. **-ment**, S.: infeudamento, *m.*, infeudazione, *f.*
enfétter, TR.: incatenare.
enfilàde1, S.: (*mil.*) passaggio stretto, *m.*
enfilade2, TR.: (*mil.*) infilare, traversare.
enfór-ce, TR.: assodare; fortificare; invigorare, forzare; imporre, obbligare; INTR.: provare. **-cedly**, ADV.: sforzevolmente, per forza. **-cement**, S.: costringimento, *m.*, violenza; approvagione, sanzione, *f.* **-cer**, S.: che costringe, sforzatore, *m.*
enfránchise, TR.: porre in libertà, affrancare; naturalizzare. **-ment**, S.: privilegio di naturalità; liberamento, *m.*
engág-e, TR.: impegnare, obbligare; attaccare; indurre; INTR.: impegnarsi; combattere: — *the affections*, cattivarsi l' affetto. **-ed**, ADJ.: impegnato, occupato; promesso; invitato. **-ement**, S.: impegno; obbligo, *m.*; occupazione, *f.*; conflitto, combattimento, *m.* **-ing**, ADJ.: attrattivo, grato. **-ingly**, ADV.: in modo attrattivo.
engáol†, TR.: imprigionare, incarcerare.
engárrison, TR.: presidiare.
engénder, TR.: generare, formare, produrre; INTR.: prodursi, formarsi.
éngine, S.: macchina, *f.*; ingegno; artificio, stratagemma, *m.*: *take an — to pieces*, smontare una macchina. **-builder**, S.: costruttore di macchine, *m.* **-cleaner**, S.: (*rail.*) nettatore della macchina (locomotiva), *m.* **-driver**, **-man**, S.: (*rail.*) conduttore di locomotiva, macchinista, *m.* **-room**, S.: stanza della macchina a vapore. **-ér**, S.: ingegnere; (*rail.*) macchinista, *m.* **-ry**, S.: artiglieria, *f.*
engird, IRR.; TR.: cingere, circondare.
English *ing-*, ADJ., S.: inglese: *the — language*, la lingua inglese; *a young — lady*, una damigella inglese, una inglesina.
englút, TR.: inghiottire, trangugiare, satollare.
engórge, INTR.: ingorgare, inghiottire, divorare.
engráft, TR.: innestare. **-ment**, S.: innestamento, *m.*
engráin, TR.: tingere in grana.
engrápple, INTR.: venire alle prese, lottare.
engrásp, TR.: afferrare.
engráv-e, IRR.; TR.: intagliare, scolpire; seppellire. **-er**, S.: intagliatore, scultore, *m.* **-ing**, S.: intaglio, intagliamento, *m.*, intagliatura, *f.*
engriéve, TR.: affannare.
engróss, TR.: ingrassare, spessare; incettare. **-er**, S.: incettatore, monopolista, *m.* **-ment**, S.: incetta, *f.*, monopolio, *m.*

enguárd, TR.: proteggere; difendere.
enhán-ce, TR.: alzare il prezzo, incarare; aumentare; aggravare; encomiare, lodare. **-cer**, S.: esaltatore, laudatore, *m.* **-cement**, S.: aumento in valore, *m.*; aumentazione, *f.*
enhárden, TR.: avvalorare, incoraggiare.
enharmónic, ADJ.: enarmonico.
enig-ma, S.: enimma, enigma (*-gm-* also *in deriv.*), *m.* **-mátic(al)**, ADJ.: enimmatico; allegorico. **-máticallly**, ADV.: enimmaticamente, in modo enimmatico. **-matist**, S.: che enimmatichizza. **-matize**, INTR.: enimmatichizzare.
enjóin, TR.: ingiungere; ordinare, prescrivere. **-ment**†, S.: ordine; comando, *m.*
enjóy, TR.: godere, sentir piacere; possedere; INTR.: gioire, rallegrarsi; REFL.: divertirsi, sollazzarsi, godersela, darsi buon tempo. **-er**, S.: che si rallegra; goditore; possessore, *m.* **-ing**, S.: piacere, *m.*; felicità, *f.* **-ment**, S.: godimento, *m.*, gioia, *f.*; possesso, *m.*
enkindle, TR.: accendere, infiammare; INTR.: accendersi; infiammarsi.
enlárge, TR.: distendere, dilatare; aggrandire; liberare; INTR.: distendersi, dilatarsi: — *upon*, distendersi sopra, parlare (*or* scrivere) alla distesa di. **-ment**, S.: ampliazione, aumentazione, *f.*, aumento; aggrandimento; liberamento, *m.*
enlíght, TR.: illuminare. **-en**, TR.: schiarare; istruire, insegnare: — *the mind*, illuminare lo spirito. **-ener**, S.: illuminatore; insegnatore, *m.*
enlínk, TR.: incatenare; attaccare.
enlíst, TR.: arrolare; INTR.: arrolarsi per soldato: — *the sympathies*, cattivarsi le simpatie. **-ing**, **-ment**, S.: arrolamento, *m.*
enliven, TR.: animare, avvivare; esilarare. **-er**, S.: che anima, che invigorisce.
enmésh, TR.: intralciare.
énmity, S.: inimicizia, *f.*; odio, *m.*
ennóble, TR.: annobilire, nobilitare. **-ment**, S.: nobilitare, *m.*
ennui *an-nwi*, S.: noia, *f.*, fastidio, *m.*
enodátion, S.: scioglimento, solvimento, *m.*
enór-mity, S.: enormità; atrocità, *f.* **-mous**, ADJ.: enorme, eccessivo; atroce. **-mously**, ADV.: enormemente, eccessivamente. **-mousness**, S.: enormità, *f.*
enough1 *enúf*, ADV.: abbastanza, a sufficienza, assai: *well —*, bastantemente bene; *it is —*, basta. **enough**2, S.: sufficienza, bastevolezza, *f.*: — *is as good as a feast*, chi ha il bastevole è ricco.
enóunce, TR.: pronunziare, dichiarare.
enów† = *enough*.
enquire, TR.: domandare; INTR.: informarsi.

enráge, TR.: fare arrabbiare; irritare.
enránge, TR.: ordinare; disporre.
enránk, TR.: collocare in ordine, schierare
en-rápt, ADJ.: rapito, in estaso. **-ráptụre**, **-rávish**, TR.: ravire, incantare. **-ravishing**, ADJ.: incantevole, dilettevole. **-ravishment**, S.: ratto, rapimento, *m.*; estasi, *f.*
enrích, TR.: arricchire; ornare, abbellire; fertilizzare. **-ment**, S.: arricchimento; abbelimento, *m.*
enrídge, TR.: solcare, fare delle cime.
enríng, TR.: accerchiare, circondare.
enrípen†, TR.: maturare.
enríve†, IRR.: TR.: fendere, spaccare.
enróbe, TR.: mettere i vestimenti [illegible]
enróll, TR.: arrolare, registrare. **-er**, S.: registratore, *m.* **-ment**, [illegible] mento, registramento *m.*
enróot, TR. radicare piantare
ensámpler, S. modello esemplare, esempio, *m.*, mostra *f.*
ensánguine, TR. insanguinare
ensčónce, TR. difendere [illegible] assicurare
enséam, TR. [illegible]
enséar TR. cauterizzare
enshíeld, TR. [illegible] teggere
enshríne, TR. [illegible]
énsign, S. insegna [illegible] S.: bagno alfiere *m.* **-bearer** alfiere insegna *m.* **-cy** [illegible]
enslávé, TR. [illegible] sottomettere **-ment** [illegible] **-er** [illegible]
ensúe, [illegible]
ensúre [illegible]
en-tábláture **-tábletnent** [illegible]
entáil [illegible] **entail** [illegible]
entángle [illegible] **-glement** [illegible] **-gler** [illegible]
énter, [illegible] **-ing** [illegible]
enterláce [illegible]

enterólogy, [illegible]
enterpárlance, [illegible] conferenza *f.*
énterprise, [illegible] mento, *m.* **-er** [illegible] **-ing** [illegible]
entertáin, [illegible] **-ment** [illegible]
entháral [illegible]
enthúsiasm [illegible] **-ástic** [illegible] **-astically** [illegible]
entíce, [illegible] **-ment**, [illegible] **-ing** [illegible] **-ly** [illegible]
en-tíre [illegible] **-tirely** [illegible] **-tireness** [illegible] **-tirety** [illegible]
entítle, [illegible]
éntity, [illegible]
entóil [illegible]
entómb, [illegible] **-ment**, [illegible]
entomólogy [illegible]
entráil, [illegible]
entrámmel, [illegible]
entrance [illegible] **entránce**, [illegible] **-money**, [illegible]
entráp, [illegible]
entréat, [illegible] supplicare [illegible] **-ance** [illegible] **-er**, [illegible] **-y**, [illegible]

entremêts *en-*, S. PL.: tramesso, *m.*
entrŭst = *intrust*.
ĕntry, S.: entrata, *f.*, ingresso: passaggio; introito; accesso (al possesso), *m.*; registratura, *f.*: *book of entries*, libro d'iscrizioni, *m.*; *by double —*, in partita doppia.
entūne, TR.: intonare.
en-twīne, **-twist**, TR.: intrecciare, avviluppare.
enūbilate, TR.: disnebbiar.
enūcleate, TR.: spiegare, dichiarare. **-cleātion**, S.: spiegamento, *m.*, dichiarazione, *f.*
enūmer-ate, TR.: enumerare, annoverare. **-ātion**, S.: enumerazione, *f.*, annovero, *m.*
enŭn-ciate, TR.: enunciare; dichiarare. **-ciātion**, S.: enunciazione, *f.* **-ciative**, ADJ.: enunciativo, espressivo. **-ciatively**, ADV.: in modo declaratorio, dichiaratamente.
envĕlop 1, TR.: inviluppare, involgere. **envelop** 2, **ĕnvelope**, S.: involto, *m.*, coperta, *f.* **-ment**, S.: inviluppamento, avvolgimento, *m.*
envĕnom, TR.: avvelenare, intossicare.
ĕn-viable, ADJ.: invidiabile. **-vied**, ADJ.: invidiato. **-vier**, S.: invidiatore, *m.* **-vious**, ADJ.: invidioso, astioso. **-viously**, ADV.: con invidia. **-viousness**, S.: invidia, *f.*
envīron, TR.: circondare, intornare; assediare. **-s**, S. PL.: contorni, *m. pl.*, vicinanze, *f. pl.*
ĕ'nvöy, S.: inviato, delegato, *m.*
ĕnvy 1, S.: invidia; rivalità, *f.*: *out of —*, per invidia. **envy** 2, TR.: invidiare, portar invidia.
enwiden†, TR.: allargare.
enwŏmb, TR.: ingravidare†; nascondere, celare.
eōlian, ADJ.: eolico: *— harp*, arpa d'Eolo, *f.*
ĕpact, S.: epatta, *f.*
ĕp-aulet, S.: spalletta, *f.* **-păulement**, S.: (*fort.*) gabbionata, fascinata, *f.*
ephĕm-era, S.: effimero, *m.* **-eral**, **-eric**, ADJ.: effimero, d'un giorno. **-eris**, S.: effemeride, *f.*; calendario, *m.* **-erist**, S.: astrologo, *m.*
Ephēsian *e-*, ADJ.: d'Efeso, *m.*; efesio.
ĕphod, S.: efod, *m.*
ĕpic, ADJ.: epico, eroico.
epicēdium, S.: epicedio, *m.*
ĕpicene, ADJ.: epiceno.
ĕpics, S. PL.: poesia epica, *f.*
ĕpicu-re, S.: epicureo, *m.* **-rēan**, ADJ.: epicureo, lussurioso. **-rism**, S.: epicureismo, *m.*; sensualità, lussuria, *f.*
icycle, S.: epiciclo, *m.*
idĕmic(al), ADJ.: epidemico.

epidĕrmis, S.: (*anat.*) epidermide, *f.*
ĕpi-gram, S.: epigramma, *m.* **-grammătic(al)**, ADJ.: epigrammatico. **-grămmatist**, S.: epigrammatista, *m.*
ĕpigraph, S.: epigrafe, iscrizione, *f.*
ĕpi-lepsy, S.: epilessia, *f.*, malcaduco, *m.* **-lĕptic**, ADJ.: epiletico.
ĕpilogue, S.: epilogo, *m.*
epiphany, S.: epifania, *f.*
epiphysis, S.: (*surg.*) epifisi, *f.*
epis-copacy, S.: episcopato, vescovado, *m.* **-copal**, ADJ.: episcopale. **-copălians**, S. PL.: episcopali, *m. pl.* **-copate**, S.: episcopato; vescovado, *m.* **-copy**, S.: inspezione, intendenza, *f.*
ĕpi-sode, S.: episodio, *m.* **-sŏdic(al)**, ADJ.: episodico, digressivo.
epispăstic, ADJ.: (*med.*) epispastico.
epis-tle, S.: epistola, lettera, *f.* **-tler**, S.: cattivo scrittore di lettere, scrittoruccio, *m.* **-tolar(y)**, ADJ.: epistolare.
ĕpistyle, S.: (*arch.*) architrave, *m.*
ĕpitaph, S.: epitaffio, *m.*
epithalămium, S.: epitalamio, *m.*
ĕpi-them, S.: (*pharm.*) epittema, *f.* **-thet**, S.: epiteto, *m.*
epit-ome, S.: epitome; sommario, *m.* **-omist**, S.: abbreviatore, *m.* **-omize**, TR.: epitomare, abbreviare, sommare. **-omizer**, S.: abbreviatore, *m.*
ĕpoch, S.: epoca, era, *f.*
ĕpode, S.: (*poes.*) epodo, *m.*
ĕpopee, S.: (*poes.*) epopeia, *f.*
ĕpu-lary, ADJ.: epulonesco; festevole, lieto. **-lătion**, S.: banchetto; festino, *m.* **-lŏtic**, ADJ.: epulotico; cicatrizzante.
equability, S.: equabilità; uniformità, *f.*
ĕqu-able, ADJ.: equabile, uguale. **-ably**, ADV.: equabilmente, ugualmente, con equalità; uniformemente **-al** 1, ADJ.: uguale, pari; uniforme; simile, simigliante; imparziale; S.: uguale; simigliante; compagno, *m.* **-al** 2, TR.: agguagliare; compensare, pareggiare; corrispondere. **-alize**, TR.: agguagliare, far uguale; aggiustare. **-ality**, S.: equalità, parità; uniformità, *f.* **-ally**, ADV.: ugualmente, a un pari; senza parzialità. **-alness**, S.: equalità, uniformità, *f.* **-ăngular**, ADJ.: equiangolo. **-animity**, S.: equanimità, tranquillità di mente; moderazione, *f.* **-ănimous**, ADJ.: equanimo; moderato. **-ātion**, S.: equazione, *f.*; aggiustamento, pareggiamento, *m.*: *simple —*, equazione di primo grado. **-ātor**, S.: equatore, *m.* **-atŏrial**, ADJ.: dell'equatore.
ĕquer(r)y, S.: scudiere d'un principe, *m.*
equĕstrian, ADJ.: equestre, di cavaliere; S.: cavalcatore, *m.*
equi-bălance, S.: equilibrio, *m.* **-crūral**, ADJ.: equicrure, di due lati uguali. **-distant**, ADJ.: (*geom.*) equidistante.

-distantly, ADV.: in modo equidistante. **-lăteral**, ADJ.: (*geom.*) equilatero. **-librate**, TR.: equilibrare, pesare ugualmente, contrappesare. **-librătion**, S.: equilibrio, contrappesamento, *m.* **-librium**, S.: equilibrio, *m.* **-něcessary**, ADJ.: ugualmente necessario. **-nŏctial**, ADJ.: equinoziale, di equinozio; S.: equinoziale; equatore, *m.* **ĕqui-nox**, S.: equinozio, *m.*

equip, TR.: fornire; allestire, preparare, apparecchiare; (*nav.*) equipaggiare. **ĕquip-age**, S.: fornimento, apparecchio; equipaggio; arnese; vassoio, *m.*

equipĕndency, S.: equilibrio, *m.*

equipment, S.: armamento; acconciamento; equipaggiamento, *m.*

ĕquipŏise 1, S.: equilibrio, contrappesamento, *m.* **equipoise** 2, TR.: equilibrare, contrappesare.

equipŏllen-ce, S.: equipollenza, equivalenza, *f.* **-t**, ADJ.: equipollente, equivalente.

equipŏnder-ance, **-ancy**, S.: equiponderanza, *f.* **-ant**, ADJ.: equiponderante, d' uguale peso. **-ate**, INTR.: equiponderare, contrappesare.

ĕquitabl-e, ADJ.: equo, ragionevole. **-eness**, S.: equità, imparzialità, *f.* **-y**, ADV.: con equità, giustamente.

equitătion, S.: equitazione, *f.*

ĕquity, S.: equità, imparzialità, giustizia, *f.*

equivalen-ce, **-cy**, S.: equivalenza, *f.*, equivalere, *m.* **-t**, ADJ.: equivalente, di valore uguale: *be* —, equivalere; S.: equivalente, *m.*

equivo-cal, ADJ.: equivoco, ambiguo; dubbio. **-cally**, ADV.: equivocamente; dubbiamente. **-calness**, S.: equivocamento, *m.*, ambiguità, *f.* **-cate**, TR.: equivocare. **-cătion**, S.: equivocazione, *f.* **-cator**, S.: equivocante, *m.*

ēra, S.: era, epoca, *f.*

erădi-ate, TR.: irradiare, irraggiare. **-ătion**, S.: irradiazione, *f.*; splendore, *m.*, lucentezza, *f.*

erădi-cate, TR.: eradicare, estirpare; sbarbare. **-cătion**, S.: eradicare; estirpamento, *m.* **-cative**, ADJ.: (*med.*) eradicativo.

erās-e, TR.: raschiare, scancellare; distruggere, devastare. **-er**, S.: gomma da radere, *f.*, raschino, *m.* **-ment**, S.: scancellatura, *f.*; distruggimento, *m.*, distruzione, *f.*

ēre, ADV.: prima, prima che, più tosto, anzichè: — *long*, fra breve, fra non molto, frappoco.

erĕc-t 1, ADJ.: eretto, innalzato; dritto: *walk* —, andare in sulla persona. **-t** 2, TR.: ergere, innalzare; *rizzare; incoraggiare*; INTR.: levarsi, alzarsi, rizzarsi. **-tion**, S.: stabilimento, *m.*; struttura, *f.* **-tness**, S.: diritezza, *f.*; stare ritto in piedi, *m.*

ĕre-mite, S.: eremita, romito, *m.* **-mitical**, ADJ.: eremitico, di romito.

erĕption, S.: rapimento, arrappare, *m.*

erewhile† *-hwil*, ADV.: fra breve; qualche tempo fa, poco fa, non ha guari.

ĕrgot, S.: sprone, sperone, *m.*

eringo, S.: eringio, *m.*, eringe, *f.* (erba).

eristic(al)†, ADJ.: eristico.

ĕrmine, S.: ermellino, *m.* **-d**, ADJ.: foderato d' ermellino.

ĕrn(e), S.: aia, *f.*

erō-de, TR.: rodere, corrodere; distruggere. **-sion**, S.: erosione, *f.*, corrodimento, *m.*

erŏtic, ADJ.: erotico, amoroso.

ĕrr, INTR.: errare, sbagliare, traviare; ingannarsi. **-able**, ADJ.: soggetto ad errare. **-ableness**, S.: attezza ad ingannarsi, *f.*

ĕrrand, S.: messaggio, *m.*; ambasciata, *f.*: *go to an* —, fare un messaggio; *fool's* —, messaggio impertinente. **-boy**, S.: servitorino, servitorello, *m.* **-man**, S.: messaggiere, messo, *m.*

ĕrrant, ADJ.: errante; vagabondo. **-ry**, S.: vagamento, vagare, *m.*

errāta, S. PL.: errori (di stampa), *m. pl.*

errătic, ADJ.: erratico, errante; irregolare. **-ally**, ADV.: in modo erratico.

errātum (pl. *errata*), S.: errore (di stampa), *m.*

ĕrring, S.: traviamento, *m.*

errōneous, ADJ.: erroneo, falso. **-ly**, ADV.: erroneamente, con errore. **-ness**, S.: errore, *m.*, falsità, *f.*

ĕrror, S.: errore, traviamento; sbaglio; mancamento, *m.*: *gross* —, errore madornale; *lead into* —, indurre in errore.

ērst, **-while**†, ADV.: altre volte, anticamente, un tempo.

erubĕscen-ce, **-cy**, S.: rossore; pudore, *m.* **-t**, ADJ.: rossiccio.

erŭct, INTR.: eruttare, ruttare. **-ātion**, S.: eruttazione, *f.*

ĕru-dite, ADJ.: erudito, istrutto. **-dition**, S.: erudizione, *f.*, ammaestramento, *m.*; dottrina, *f.*

erūginous, ADJ.: rugginoso.

erŭp-tion, S.: eruzione; sortita impetuosa, impetuosità, *f.* **-tive**, ADJ.: prorompente con isforzo.

erysipelas, S.: (*med.*) risipola, *f.*

escalāde, S.: (*fort.*) scalata, *f.*

escāpe 1, S.: fuga, *f.*, scampo; errore, sbaglio, *m.*: *make an* —, fuggire, prender la fuga; *have a narrow* —, scappare con difficoltà. **escape** 2, TR.: evitare; schivare; INTR.: scampare, fuggire: — *narrowly*, scapparla bella; *it* —*d me that*, mi sfuggì detto che.

eschalŏt, s.: cipollina, *f.*
eschēat 1, s.: profitto casuale; diritto, *m.* **escheat** 2, INTR.: scadere in diritto. **-er**, s.: esattore di beni confiscati, *m.*
eschēw, TR.: evitare; sfuggire.
ĕs-cort 1, s.: scorta, guida, *f.*, convoglio, *m.* **-cŏrt** 2, TR.: scortare, accompagnare, convoiare.
escōut, s.: spia, *f.*, spiatore, esploratore, *m.*
escritoir *-twŏr*, s.: scrittoio, calamaio, *m.*
ĕsculent, ADJ.: esculento, edulo; s.: alimento, *m.*
escŭtcheon, s.: scudo, *m.*; arme, insegne, *f. pl.*
espălier, s.: spalliera, *f.*
espărcet, s.: spezie di trifoglio, *f.*
espĕcial, ADJ.: speciale, singolare, particolare. **-ly**, ADV.: specialmente; principalmente. **-ness**, s.: particolarità, singolarità, *f.*
espial, s.: spione; esploratore†, *m.* **ĕspionage**, s.: spiare, *m.*
esplanāde, s.: (*fort.*) spianata, *f.*, spianato, *m.*
espōu-sal, ADJ.: di matrimonio, nuziale. **-sals**, s. PL.: sposalizia, *f.*, sposamento, *m.* **-se**, TR.: sposare; difendere: — *one's cause*, pigliare la difesa d' uno. **-ser**, s.: difensore, *m.*
espȳ, TR.: spiare; osservare, scoprire.
esquire 1, s.: scudiere, *m.* **esquire** 2, TR.: servire come scudiere; signore: *B. Macauly, Esq.*, al Signore, il Signor B. M.
ĕssay 1, s.: sperimento, saggio, *m.*, prova, *f.*: *make an* —, fare un saggio. **essāy** 2, TR.: tentare, assaggiare, sforzarsi. **-ist**, s.: saggiatore, sperimentatore, *m.*
ĕs-sence 1, s.: essenza, *f.*; profumo, *m.* **-sence** 2, TR.: profumare, odorare. **-sĕntial**, ADJ.: essenziale, principale; s.: essenziale, *m.* **-sĕntiălity**, s.: essenzialità; essenza, *f.* **-sĕntially**, ADV.: essenzialmente.
essōin 1, s.: (*leg.*) esenzione, scusa legale, *f.* **essoin** 2, TR.: (*leg.*) scusare una persona che non comparisce in giustizia.
estăblish, TR.: stabilire, firmare, fissare; fondare. **-er**, s.: fondatore, *m.* **-ment**, s.: stabilimento, fondamento, instituto, *m.*; approvazione, *f.*; modello, *m.*
estafĕt, s.: staffetta, *f.*
estāte 1, s.: stato, *m.*; condizione; fortuna, *f.*, beni, *m. pl.*; terra, *f.*; corpo politico, ordine, *m.*: *real and personal* —, beni mobili ed immobili; *small* —, piccola terra; *man's* —, età virile, *f.* **estate** 2, TR.: dotare.
estēem 1, s.: stima, considerazione, *f.*; conto, *m.*: *in high* —, molto stimato; *hold one in* —, aver della stima per uno.
esteem 2, TR.: stimare, apprezzare; pensare. **-er**, s.: stimatore, apprezzatore, *m.*
ĕsti-mable, ADJ.: stimabile, apprezzabile. **-mableness**, s.: qualità estimabile, *f.* **-mate** 1, s.: estimazione, *f.*, prezzo; computamento, conto, *m.*: *rough* —, stima approssimativa. **-mate** 2, TR.: stimare, apprezzare; valutare. **-mātion**, s.: estimazione, stima; opinione, *f.*; conto, *m.* **-mative**, ADJ.: estimativo. **-mator**, s.: stimatore, apprezzatore, *m.*
ĕstival, ADJ.: estivale, estivo.
estŏppel, s.: (*jur.*) ostacolo, *m.*, opposizione, *f.*
estrāde, s.: estrada, *f.*, palchetto a rigoglio, *m.*
estrān-ge, TR.: alienare; allontanare; separare; rimuovere; dissuadere. **-gement**, s.: alienazione; separazione; distanza, *f.* **-ger**, s.: straniere, *m.*
estrapāde, s.: strapata, *f.*
estrāy, TR.: sviarsi, smarrirsi.
estrēat, s.: copia, *f.*
estrēpement, s.: guasto; danno, *m.*
ĕstu-ance, s.: calore, *m.* **-ary**, s.: estuario, braccio (di mare), *m.*, bocca, *f.* **-ate**, TR.: bollire, fervere. **-ātion**, s.: estuazione, *f.*, bollimento, *m.*
esū-rient, ADJ.: affamato, vorace.
ĕtch, TR.: scolpire con acqua forte; intagliare. **-ing**, s.: intaglio (con acqua forte), *m.*; incisione all' acqua forte, *f.*
etĕr-nal, ADJ.: eterno, perpetuo. **-nalize**, eternare; immortalare. **-nally**, ADV.: eternamente, in eterno. **-nity**, s.: eternità, perpetuità, *f.* **-nize**, TR.: eternare.
ĕth-er, s.: aria, *f.*; cielo, etere; (*chem.*) etere, *m.* **-ĕreal**, **-ĕreous**, ADJ.: etereo, dell' etere, celeste.
ĕthic(al), ADJ.: etico, morale. **-ally**, ADV.: eticamente, moralmente. **-s**, s. PL.: etica, morale, *f.*
ĕthnic, ADJ.: etnico, pagano, gentile. **-s**, s. PL.: pagani, gentili, *m. pl.*
eth-olŏgical, ADJ.: morale. **-ŏlogy**, s.: etología, *f.*
etiŏlogy, s.: etiologia, *f.*
ĕtiquette, s.: etichetta, *f.*
etui, s.: astucchio, *m.*, guaina, *f.*
ety-molŏgical, ADJ.: etimologico. **-mŏlogist**, s.: etimologista, *m.* **-mŏlogy**, s.: etimologia, *f.*
ĕtymon, s.: parola primitiva; origine, *f.*
eūcha-rist, s.: eucaristia, comunione, *f.* **-ristical**, ADJ.: eucaristico.
euchŏlogy, s.: eucologio, *m.*
eūlo-gize, TR.: lodare, encomiare. **-gy**, s.: elogio, *m.*, lode, *f.*
eūnuch, s.: eunuco, *m.*
eu-phŏnical, ADJ.: eufonico, armonico.
eū-phony, s.: eufonia, *f.*

Eurus, s.: euro, *m.*
eurythmy, s.: euritmia, *f.*
eu-thanasia, **-thanasy**, s.: morte placida, *f.*
evacate†, TR.: votare, cavare.
evac-uant, ADJ.: (*med.*) evacuante. **-uate**, TR.: evacuare; mandare fuori. **-uation**, s.: evacuazione, *f.*, evacuamento, *m.* **-uative**, ADJ.: (*med.*) evacuativo.
evade, TR.: scampare, scappare; scappolare; INTR.: evadere; fuggire.
evagation, s.: evagazione, *f.*, svagamento, *m.*
evanescen-ce, s.: svanire, *m.*, svanizione, *f.* **-t**, ADJ.: che svanisce, fugitivo.
evangelical, ADJ.: evangelico. **-ly**, ADV.: evangelicamente.
evange-lism, s.: promulgare del vangelo, *m.* **-list**, s.: evangelista, *m.* **-lize**, TR.: evangelizzare, predicare il vangelo. **-ly**, s.: vangelo, m.
evan-id†, ADJ.: che svanisce; debole; fugitivo. **-ish**, INTR.: svanire; evadere, fuggire.
evapo-rable, ADJ.: evaporabile, evaporante. **-rate**, TR.: svaporare; dissipare; INTR.: evaporare; dissiparsi. **-ration**, s.: evaporazione, *f.*, evaporamento, *m.*
eva-sion, s.: scappata, *f.;* sotterfugio, pretesto, *m.* **-sive**, ADJ.: evasivo, sofistico. **-sively**, ADV.: sofisticamente.
eve 1, s.: vigilia, *f.* **eve** 2, **-n** 1, s.: sera, *f.: at* —, sulla sera. **-n** 2, ADJ.: uguale, pari, simile; piano, unito, uniforme: *make* —, spianare; *be* — *with*, rendere la pariglia a. **-n** 3, ADV.: anche, anzi, ancora; quasi; fino, infino; — *as*, come, come se; — *down*, diritto giù; — *now*, or' ora; — *on*, dirittamente, a dirittura; — *so*, appunto così, giusto così. **-n**, TR.: appianare, agguagliare. **-n-handed**, ADJ.: imparziale; equo.
evening, s.: sera, serata, *f.:* — *tide*, sera, *f.;* — *party*, serata, conversazione; — *star*, stella della sera.
even-ly†, ADV.: ugualmente, uniformemente. **-ness**, s.: ugualità, uniformità; imparzialità, *f.;* livello, *m.*
event, s.: evento, avvenimente, esito, *m.*
eventerate, TR.: sventrare, sviscerare.
eventful, ADJ.: pieno d' avvenimenti.
eventide, s.: sera, serata: *at* —, alla sera.
eventi-late†, TR.: ventolare; discutere; esaminare. **-lation**†, s.: ventilazione; discussione, *f.*
even-tual, ADJ.: eventuale, casuale, fortuito. **-tuality**, s.: eventualità, *f.* **-tually**, ADV.: eventualmente, a caso, fortuitamente. **-tuate**, INTR.: terminare.
ever, ADV.: siempre, sempremai, mai, sempre, mai, tuttavia: *for* —, *for* — *and* —, per sempre, eternamente; in sempiterno, ne' secoli de' secoli; — *and anon*, di quando in quando; — *before*, da ogni tempo; *as much as* —, quanto mai; *as soon as* —, quanto prima; — *since*, da quel tempo in qua, dipoi, dopo; — *and anon*, ogni tanto, ogni poco, di quando in quando. **-during**, ADJ.: eterno, perpetuo. **-green**, ADJ.: sempre verde; s.: sempreviva, barba di Giove, *f.* **-lasting**, ADJ.: eterno, perpetuo; s.: eternità, perpetuità, *f.* **-lastingly**, ADV.: eternamente, perpetuamente, senza fine. **-lastingness**, s.: eternità, perpetuità, *f.* **-living**, ADJ.: semprevivo, immortale. **-more**, ADV.: sempremai; eternamente.
ever-sion, s.: sovvertimento, sconvolgimento, rovinamento, *m.* **-t**, TR.: sconvolgere, rovinare, distruggere.
every, PRON.: ogni, ciascuno, ciascheduno: — *other day*, un giorno sì un giorno no; — *whit*, ogni cosa, tutto; affatto. **-body**, PR.: ognuno, ciascuno. **-day**, ADV.: di ogni giorno. **-one** = *everybody*. **-thing**, PR.: ogni cosa. **-way**, ADV.: da ogni banda. **-where**, ADV.: da per tutto, ovunque.
evesdropper, s.: ascoltatore; spione, *m.*
evic-t, TR.: evincere, convincere; provare. **-tion**, s.: evizione; evidenza, *f.*
eviden-ce 1, s.: evidenza; prova, *f.*, testimonio, *m.* **-ce** 2, TR.: provare, mostrare. **-t**, ADJ.: evidente, apparente, manifesto, chiaro. **-tly**, ADV.: evidentemente, chiaramente. **-tness**, s.: evidenza; prova, *f.*
evil 1, ADJ.: cattivo, malo, perverso; s.: male, *m.;* malvagità; calamità, *f.; the* — *one*, il maligno (Satana). **evil** 2, ADV.: male, malemente. **-affected**, ADJ.: malvagio, malevolo. **-doer**, s.: malfattore; furfante, *m.* **-favoured**, ADJ.: brutto, deforme. **-favouredness**, s.: bruttezza, laidezza, difformità, *f.* **-ly**, ADV.: male, malamente. **-minded**, ADJ.: maldisposto, malevolo, malizioso, maligno. **-ness**, s.: malvagità, malizia; perversità, *f.* **-speaking**, s.: maldicenza, calunnia, *f.* **-wishing**, ADJ.: malevolo, maligno. **-worker**, s.: malfattore, *m.*
evin-ce, TR.: evincere, convincere; provare; dimostrare. **-cible**, ADJ.: dimostrabile; provabile. **-cibly**, ADV.: dimostrativamente, chiaramente.
evirate†, TR.: castrare.
eviscerate, TR.: sviscerare, sventrare.
evi-table, ADJ.: evitabile. **-tate**, TR.: evitare, scappare, sfuggire. **-tation**, s.: evitazione; scappata, fuga, *f.*
evo-cate, TR.: evocare. **-cation**, s. invocare, congiuramento, *m.*

evolūtion, s.: sviluppo; rivolgimento, *m.*; (*mil.*) evoluzione, *f.*

evŏlve, TR.: sviluppare; stendere; INTR.: svolgersi, svilupparsi; stendersi: *be(come) —d*, svolgersi.

evŭl-gate, TR.: divolgare, pubblicare. **-gātion**, s.: pubblicazione, *f.*

evŭlsion, s.: divellimento, *m.*

ewe 1, s.: pecora, *f.* **ewe** 2, INTR.: figliare (delle pecore). **-lamb**, s.: mannerino, *m.*, pecorella, *f.*

ewer, s.: mesciroba; acquareccia, *f.* **-y**, s.: uffizio del vasellame reale, *m.*

ex-, ex: *—-king*, l' ex-re, ecc.

exăcer-bate, TR.: esacerbare, inasprire. **-bātion**, s.: esacerbazione, *f.*, esasperamento, provocamento, irritamento, *m.*

exăc-t 1, ADJ.: esatto, puntuale; diligente; giusto. **-t** 2, TR.: esigere; domandare; strappare. **-tor**, s.: esattore, *m.* **-tion**, s.: esazione, estorsione, *f.* **-titude**, s.: esattezza, *f.* **-tly**, ADV.: esattamente, accuratamente, diligentemente. **-tness**, s.: esattezza; puntualità, *f.* **-tor** = *exacter*.

exăggerate, TR.: esagerare, amplificare. **-ātion**, s.: esagerazione, amplificazione, *f.*

exăgi-tate, TR.: esagitare, agitare; tormentare. **-tātion**, s.: agitazione, *f.*; scuotimento, *m.*

exălt, TR.: esaltare, innalzare; alzare; estollere, lodare, vantare. **-ātion**, s.: esaltazione, *f.*, esaltamento; elevamento, *m.* **-ed**, ADJ.: alzato, elevato, sublime; lodato.

ex-aminātion, s.: esame, esaminamento; (*leg.*) interrogatorio: *a strict —*, un esame rigoroso; *post mortem —*, autopsia (del cadavere); *undergo an —*, subire (passare) un esame. **-āminator**, s.: esaminatore; inquisitore, *m.* **-āmine**, TR.: esaminare, interrogare; pesare, considerare; discutere. **-āminer**, s.: esaminatore, interrogatore, investigatore, *m.*; esaminatrice, ecc., *f.* **-āmining**, s.: inquisizione, investigazione, *f.*

ĕx-amplary†, ADJ.: esemplare. **-ămple** 1, s.: esempio; esemplare; modello, *m.*: *for —*, per esempio; *give (set) an —*, dar esempio; *make one an —*, punir alcuno esemplarmente. **-ample** 2, TR.: dar esempio; esemplificare.

exănguious, ADJ.: esangue, senza sangue.

exăni-mate, ADJ.: esanimato; scorato, scoraggiato. **-mātion**, s.: disanimare, *m.*, privazione della vita, *f.* **-mous**, ADJ.: esanimo, morto.

exan-thēma (pl. *exanthemata*), s.: (*med.*) rŭzione; efflorescenza, *f.* **-thēmatous**, ADJ.: (*med.*) pieno di bollicelle.

exarticulātion, s.: dislogamento, *m.*, lussazione, *f.*

exăsper-ate, TR.: esasperare; inacerbare, irritare, provocare. **-ātion**, s.: esasperamento; irritamento, *m.* **-ator**, s.: irritatore, provocatore, *m.*

excandĕscen-ce, **-cy**, s.: escandescenza, *f.*

excărnate, TR.: divestire della carne, scarnare.

excarnificātion, s.: divestimento della carne, *m.*

ĕxca-vate, TR.: scavare, cavare. **-vātion**, s.: scavamento, *m.*; cavità, *f.*; (*rail.*) intaglio, *m.*, trincea, *f.* **-vator**, s.: scavatore, *m.*

excēed, TR.: eccedere; trapassare, superare; INTR.: passare oltre, oltrepassare; uscir del convenevole. **-ing**, ADJ.: eccedente, eccessivo. **-ingly**, ADV.: eccessivamente; perfettamente.

excĕl, TR.: eccellere, sorpassare; INTR.: superare; essere eminente.

ĕxcellen-ce, **-cy**, s.: eccellenza, eccellenzia, preeminenza, superiorità, *f.* **-t**, ADJ.: eccellente, eminente, **-tly**, ADV.: eccellentemente.

excĕp-t 1, TR.: eccettuare, escludere; INTR.: obbiettare, ricusare; opporsi: *— against*, allegare. **-t** 2, CONJ.: a meno che, eccettochè. **-t** 3, **-ting**, PREP.: eccetto, fuorche, a meno che. **-tion**, s.: eccezione, eccettuazione; esclusione, *f.*: *take — to*, trovar a redire, aver a male; offendersi. **-tionable**, ADJ.: che si può obbiettare; ricusabile. **-tious**, ADJ.: stizzoso, uggioso, delicato. **-tive**, ADJ.: eccetuativo. **-tless**, ADJ.: senza eccezione. **-tor**, s.: che fa delle obbiezioni; censore, *m.*

excern†, TR.: rigettare, ributtare; ventolare; separare; purgare, nettare.

excĕrp, TR.: scegliere; spigolare; estrarre. **-tion**, s.: sceglimento; spigolare; estratto, *m.* **-tor**, s.: raccoglitore, *m.* **-ts**, s. PL.: estratti, *m. pl.*

excĕss, s.: eccesso, trapassamento; disordine, *m.*; intemperanza, *f.* **-ive**, ADJ.: eccessivo, soverchio. **-ively**, ADV.: eccessivamente, fuor di modo. **-iveness**, s.: eccesso, *m.*, soprabbondanza, *f.*

exchāng-e 1, s.: cambio, *m.*; permuta, *f.*, baratto, *m.*; borsa, *f.*: *bill of —*, lettera di cambio, *f.*; *course of —*, corso dei cambi; listino della borsa; *the stock —*, la Borsa. **-e** 2, TR.: cambiare, barattare; permutare. **-eable**, ADJ.: che si può cambiare. **-e-broker**, s.: sensale di cambio, *m.* **-er**, s.: cambiatore, *m.* **-e-office**, s.: ufficio di cambio, cambiavalute, *m.*

exchĕquer, s.: erario, tesoro regio; scacchiere, *m.*

ex-cisable, ADJ.: gabellabile, che paga la tassa. **-cise** 1, S.: assisa, tassa; imposizione, imposta, *f.* **-cise** 2, TR.: levare un' imposta, tassare. **-ciseman**, S.: ufficiale dell' assisa, gabelliere, *m.* **-cise-office**, S.: uffizio dell' assisa, *m.*, gabella, dogana, *f.* **-cision**, S.: estirpamento, *m.*; distruzione, *f.*

ex-citability, S.: capacità d' esser eccitato, irritabilità, *f.* **-citable**, ADJ.: facile ad esser eccitato, irritabile. **-citate**, TR.: eccitare, irritare. **-citation**, S.: eccitamento, *m.*, provocazione, *f.* **-cite**, TR.: eccitare, stimolare, incoraggiare. **-citement**, S.: eccitamento, aizzamento, stimolo, *m.* **-citer**, S.: eccitatore, istigatore, provocatore, *m.*

ex-claim, INTR.: sclamare; gridare ad alta voce. **-clamation**, S.: esclamazione, *f.*, sclamare, *m.*: — *point*, punto d' esclamazione. **-clamatory**, ADJ.: esclamativo, di esclamazione.

exclū-de, TR.: escludere; eccettuare. **-sion**, S.: esclusione, esclusiva; eccezione, *f.* **-sive**, ADJ.: esclusivo, escludente. **-sively**, ADV.: esclusivamente. **-sory**, ADJ.: esclusivo.

excŏct†, TR.: fare bollire, lessare.

excŏg-itate, TR.: pensare, inventare, immaginare. **-itation**, S.: invenzione, *f.*

excommūni-cate, TR.: scomunicare. **-cation**, S.: scomunicazione, *f.*

escōri-ate, TR.: scorticare, torre via la pelle. **-ation**, S.: scorticamento, *m.*

excorticātion, S.: dibuccio, *m.*

ĕxcre-ate†, TR.: sputare. **-ation**†, S.: escreato, *m.*

ĕxcre-ment, S.: escremento, *m.* **-mĕntal**, -**mentitious**, ADJ.: escrementoso.

excrĕscen-ce, **-cy**, S.: escrescenza, *f.*; tumore, *m.*

excrē-tion, S.: separazione d' umori, *f.* **-tive**, **-tory**, ADJ.: (*med.*) escretorio.

excrū-ciable, ADJ.: atto a tormentare. **-ciate**, TR.: tormentare. **-ciating**, ADJ.: atroce, dolorisissimo. **-ciation**, S.: tormento, *m.*; afflizione, *f.*

excŭl-pate, TR.: scolpare, scusare, giustificare. **-pation**, S.: scolpamento, *m.*, giustificazione, *f.* **-patory**, ADJ.: scusante, giustificante.

excūr-sion, S.: sviamento, *m.*; escursione; digressione, *f.* **-sive**, ADJ.: digressivo; errante, deviante. **-siveness**, S.: traviamento, *m.*

excū-sable, ADJ.: scusabile, perdonabile. **-sableness**, S.: scusa, scusazione, *f.* **-sation**†, S.: discolpa, scusa, *f.* **-satory**, ADJ.: apologetico, giustificativo. **-se** 1, S.: scusa, discolpa; giustificazione; apologia, *f.* **-se** 2, TR.: scusare, scolpare, giustificare; esentare; perdonare. **-seless**, ADJ.: inescusabile. **-ser**, S.: scusatore, perdonatore, *m.*

ex-cūss, TR.: staggire; sequestrare. **-cŭssion**, S.: staggimento; sequestro, *m.*

ĕxe-crable, ADJ.: esecrabile, detestabile. **-crableness**, S.: azione esecrabile, *f.*; orrore, *m.* **-crably**, ADV.: esecrabilmente. **-crate**, TR.: esecrare, detestare. **-cration**, S.: esecrazione, detestazione, imprecazione, maledizione, *f.* **-cratory**, ADJ.: esecratorio.

ĕxe-cute, TR.: eseguire, adempire, effettuare; esercitare; giustiziare (un malfattore): — *a deed*, validare un atto. **-cuter**, S.: esecutore, ministro, *m.* **-cūtion**, S.: esecuzione, *f.*, esequimento, compimento; sequestrazione, *f.*, staggimento, *m.*: *place of* —, luogo del supplicio, *m.*; *writ of* —, mandato, *m.* **-cūtioner**, S.: boia, carnefice, *m.*

exĕcu-tive, ADJ.: esecutivo. **-tor**, S.: esecutore testamentario, *m.* **-torship**, S.: uffizio d' un esecutore, *m.* **-tory**, ADJ.: esecutorio. **-trix**, S.: esecutrice testamentaria, *f.*

exe-gēsis, S.: esegesi, *f.* **-gĕtical**, ADJ.: esegetico.

exĕmplar, S.: esemplare, modello, *m.*; copia, *f.*

ĕxem-plarily, ADJ.: esemplarmente. **-plariness**, S.: esemplarità, *f.* **-plary**, ADJ.: esemplare.

ex-emplificātion, S.: esemplificazione; prova; copia, *f.* **-ĕmplify**, TR.: esemplificare; provare con esempli; copiare.

exĕmp-t 1, ADJ.: esente, privilegiato. **-t** 2, TR.: esentare, privilegiare. **-tion**, S.: esenzione, *f.*; privilegio, *m.* **-titious**, ADJ.: separabile.

exĕnter-ate, TR.: sviscerare, sventrare. **-ation**, S.: svisceramento, sviscerare, *m.*

exēquial, ADJ.: esequiale, d' esequie.

ĕxequies, S. PL.: esequie, *f. pl.*, funerale, *m.*

ĕxercis-e 1, S.: esercitamento; esercizio; travaglio, lavoro; tema, *m.*: *take* —, far del moto, passeggiare. **-e** 2, TR.: esercitare; addestrare; praticare; INTR.: esercitarsi; applicarsi. **-er**, S.: esercitatore, *m.*

exercitātion, S.: esercizio, *m.*; pratica, *f.*

exĕr-t, TR.: adoprare, impiegare; mettere in uso; compire; mostrare, dimostrare: — *one's self*, adoprarsi, sforzarsi. **-tion**, S.: adoperamento; sforzo; potere, *m.*

exfō-liate, INTR.: sfaldarsi. **-liation**, S.: sfaldatura, *f.* **-liative**, ADJ.: atto a sfaldarsi.

ex-hālable, ADJ.: esalabile, vaporabile. **-halātion**, S.: esalazione, *f.*, evaporamento; vapore, *m.* **-hāle**, TR.: esalare svaporare. **-hâlement**, S.: esalazione, evaporazione, *f.*

exhâus-t, TR.: esaurire; rasciugare. **-tible**, ADJ.: esauribile. **-tion**, S.: disseccamento, *m.* **-tless**, ADJ.: inesauribile, inesausto.

exhère-date, TR.: diseredare, eseredi-tare. **-dâtion**, S.: diseredazione, *f.*, eseredare, *m.*

exhib-it 1, S.: esibizione, *f.*; documento, *m.* **-it** 2, TR.: esibire; mostrare, produrre. **-iter**, S.: esibitore, *m.* **-ition** *ex-hib-*, S.: esibizione; presentazione; borsa, *f.* **-itioner**, S.: borsaio, *m.* **-itive**, ADJ.: rappresentativo.

exhila-rate, TR.: rallegrare; divertire. **-ration**, S.: gioia, allegrezza, giocondità, *f.*; piacere, *m.*

exhôrt, TR.: esortare; incitare, animare, incoraggiare. **-âtion**, S.: esortazione, *f.* **-ative**, **-atory**, ADJ.: esortatorio, esortativo. **-er**, S.: esortatore, *m.*

exiccate = *exsiccate.*

èxigen-ce, **-cy**, S.: esigenza, necessità, *f.*, bisogno; affanno, *m.*, afflizione, *f.* **-t**, ADJ.: esigente, urgente; premuroso; S.: necessità urgente, *f.*; bisogno, *m.*

ex-igûity, S.: minutezza, piccolezza, sottigliezza, *f.* **-iguous**, ADJ.: esiguo, piccolo, sottile, minuto. **-iguousness**, S.: piccolezza; minutezza, *f.*

exile 1, ADJ.: esile, tenue; sottile, magro. **exile** 2, S.: esilio, sbandeggiamento, *m.* **exile** 3, TR.: esiliare, mandare in esilio, sbandeggiare. **-ment**, S.: esilio, bando, sbandimento, *m.*

exilition†, S.: esplosione, *f.*

exility, S.: piccolezza, sottigliezza, *f.*

eximious†, ADJ.: esimio, eccellente, illustre.

exist, INTR.: esistere, essere. **-ence**, **-ency**, S.: esistenza, *f.*: *call into* —, chiamare all' esistenza. **-ent**, ADJ.: esistente. **-ible**, ADJ.: che può esistere.

ex-it, S.: esito, *m.*, uscita; partita, *f.*: *make one's* —, uscir di vita, morire. **-itial**†, **-itious**†, ADJ.: esiziale; fatale, funesto, pernicioso.

èxod-us, **-dy**†, S.: esodo, *m.*

exolûtion, S.: (*med.*) rilassazione (dei nervi), *f.*

exôlve†, TR.: assolvere, slacciare.

exômphalos, S.: (*med.*) esonfalo, *m.*

exôner-ate, TR.: esonerare, sgravare, discaricare, alleggerire, alleviare; liberare. **-âtion**, S.: scaricamento, *m.*

èxorable, ADJ.: esorabile, compassionevole.

exôrbitan-ce, **-cy**, S.: esorbitanza, enormità, *f.* **-t**, ADJ.: esorbitante, eccessivo. **-tly**, ADV.: esorbitantemente.

[illegible]

-cism, S.: esorcismo, scongiuramento, *m.* **-cist**, S.: esorcista, *m.*

exôrdium, S.: esordio; prologo, *m.*

exornâtion, S.: ornamento, abbellimento, *m.*

exôtic, ADJ.: esotico, straniero; S.: pianta esotica, *f.*

expân-d, TR.: spandere, dilatare; INTR.: spandersi, dilatarsi; palesarsi. **-se**, S.: espansione, estensione, *f.*: — *of water*, specchio di acqua; *the broad* —, l'alto mare. **-sibility**, S.: facoltà di dilatarsi. **-sible**, ADJ.: espansivo. **-sion**, S.: espansione, dilatazione, *f.*, dilatamento, *m.* **-sive**, ADJ.: espansivo.

expâtiate, INTR.: distendersi.

expèct, TR.: aspettare, attendere; sperare; aspettarsi: *I did not* — *it*, non me l'aspettava; *what can you* —? che potete aspettarvi? *as was to be* —*ed*, come era d'aspettarsi. **-ance**, **-ancy**, S.: aspettazione; speranza, *f.* **-ant**, ADJ.: aspettante; S.: aspettante, aspettatore, *m.* **-âtion**, S.: aspettazione, aspettativa, speranza, *f.*: *sanguine* —, viva speranza (fiducia); *beyond my* —*s*, al di là delle mie speranze; *contrary to* —, contro ogni aspettativa; *be in* —, esser nell' aspettazione. **-er**, S.: aspettante, *m.*

expèct-orant, S.: medicina espettorante, *f.* **-orate**, TR.: espettorare, espurgare. **-orâtion**, S.: espettorazione, *f.* **-orative**, ADJ.: (*med.*) espettorante.

expèdien-ce, **-cy**, S.: convenevolezza, convenienza; utilità; proprietà; spedizione, *f.* **-t**, ADJ.: convenevole; utile; S.: espediente; mezzo, *m.*: *it is* —, conviene. **-tly**, ADV.: convenevolmente.

èxpe-dite 1, ADJ.: spedito, pronto; agile. **-dite** 2, TR.: spedire, sbrigare, dispacciare; accelerare. **-ditely**, ADV.: speditamente, prontamente, agilmente. **-dition**, S.: spedizione; prontezza, celerità, fretta, *f.* **-ditious**, ADJ.: speditivo, pronto. **-ditiously**, ADV.: speditamente, prontamente.

expèl, TR.: espellere, scacciare. **-ler**, S.: espulsore, scacciatore, *m.* **-ling**, S.: espulsione, *f.*

expèn-d, TR.: spendere, sborsare. **-diture**, S.: spesa, *f.*, costo; sacrificio, *m.* **-se**, S.: spesa, *f.*; sborso, sborsamento, *m.*: *free of* —, senza spesa; franco; *trifling* —, tenue spesa; *defray one's* —*s*, spesare uno; *learn at one's* —, imparare alle proprie spese. **-seful**, ADJ.: dispendioso. **-seless**, ADJ.: senza spesa, senza costo. **-sive**, ADJ.: dispendioso, spendereccio; prodigo. **-sively**, ADV.: dispendiosamente, con grande spesa. **-siveness**, S.: dispendio, *m.*; stravaganza; prodigalità, *f.*

expĕrien-ce 1, S.: sperienza; cognizione; pratica, usanza, *f.*: *know by* —, sapere per esperienza. **-ce** 2, TR.: sperimentare, provare. **-cer**, S.: sperimentatore, *m.*

expĕri-ment 1, S.: sperimento, *m.*, prova, *f.* **-ment** 2, TR.: sperimentare, provare. **-mĕntal**, ADJ.: sperimentale. **-mĕntalist**, S.: sperimentatore, *m.* **-mĕntally**, ADV.: esperimentalmente. **-menter**, S.: sperimentatore, provatore, *m.*

expĕrt, ADJ.: esperto, sperimentato, versato, pratico. **-ly**, ADV.: espertamente. **-ness**, S.: abilità, destrezza, *f.*

ĕxpi-able, ADJ.: che si può espiare. **-ate**, TR.: espiare; reparare. **-ātion**, S.: espiazione; reparazione, *f.*: *as an — for*, in espiazione di. **-atory**, ADJ.: espiatorio.

expilātion, S.: (*leg.*) espilazione, *f.*

ex-pirātion, S.: espirazione, esalazione; respirazione; morte, *f.* **-pire**, TR.: spirare, esalare, finire, terminare; INTR.: morire.

ex-plāin, TR.: esplicare, spiegare; interpretare: *hard to* —, difficile a spiegarsi; — *away a difficulty*, far dileguare una difficoltà a forza di spiegazioni. **-plāinable**, ADJ.: esplicabile, spiegabile. **-plāiner**, S.: esplicatore, dichiaratore; interprete, *m.* **-planātion**, S.: esplicazione, interpretazione, *f.*, spiegamento, *m.* **-plānatory**, ADJ.: esplicativo, espositivo.

ĕxpletive, ADJ.: espletivo, riempitivo.

ĕxpli-cable, ADJ.: esplicabile, spiegabile. **-cate**, TR.: spiegare, dichiarare, dilucidare. **-cātion**, S.: esplicazione, spiegazione, *f.* **-cative**, ADJ.: esplicativo, espositivo. **-cator**, S.: espositore; comentatore, interprete, *m.*

explicit, ADJ.: espresso, distinto, chiaro, manifesto. **-ly**, ADV.: espressamente, direttamente, formalmente. **-ness**, S.: chiarezza; evidenza, *f.*

explōd-e, INTR.: esplodere, far esplosione, scoppiare; TR.: far scoppiare (saltare in aria); rigettare, disapprovare, condannare; fischiare. **-er**, S.: fischiatore, *m.*

explŏit 1, TR.: eseguire un gran fatto. **exploit** 2, S.: fatto d' arme, fatto illustre, *m.*: *great —s*, gloriose gesta.

explō-rate, TR.: esplorare, esaminare, investigare. **-rātion**, S.: investigazione; ricerca, *f.* **-rator** *ĕx-*, S.: esploratore, investigatore, *m.* **-ratory**, ADJ.: esplorante. **-re**, TR.: esplorare, investigare, ricercare; esaminare. **-rement**, S.: investigamento, *m.*, ricerca, *f.*

explō-sion, S.: esplosione, *f.*; scoppio, scoppiamento, *m.* **-sive**, ADJ.: esplodente, che scoppia: — *cotton*, cotone esplosivo, *fulmicotone*, *m.*

expŏlish†, TR.: pulire, lisciare; perfezionare.

expō-nent, S.: (*algeb.*) esponente, *m.* **-nĕntial**, ADJ.: (*algeb.*) esponenziale.

expōrt 1, TR.: esportare, trasportare. **ĕxport** 2, **-ātion**, S.: trasporto, trasportamento, *m.*: — *duty*, dazio d' uscita. **-er**, S.: esportatore.

ex-pōse, TR.: esporre; mostrare; scoprire; abbandonare; REFL.: esporsi; pericolarsi: —*ed to*, esposto a, sottoposto a. **-position**, S.: esposizione, *f.*; spiegamento, *m.*; interpretazione, *f.* **-pŏsitive**, ADJ.: espositivo, esplicativo. **-pŏsitor**, S.: espositore; comentatore, interprete, *m.* **-pŏsitory**, ADJ.: espositivo, esplicativo.

expŏstu-late, TR.: questionare, contendere, disputare; INTR.: lamentarsi, querelarsi: — *with*, lagnarsi con. **-lātion**, S.: discussione, disputa, *f.* **-lator**, S.: rimostrante, *m.* **-latory**, ADJ.: rimostrante.

expōsure, S.: esposizione; situazione, *f.*; pericolo, *m.*

expŏund, TR.: spiegare, spianare, interpretare. **-er**, S.: comentatore, interprete, *m.* **-ing**, S.: esposizione, interpretazione, *f.*, schiarimento, *m.*

ex-prĕss 1, ADJ.: espresso, preciso, distinto; simile, apparente; S.: espresso, corriere mandato, *m.*: — *train*, treno diretto; *by* —, per espresso; con istaffetta. **-press** 2, TR.: esprimere; spiegare, manifestare, mostrare; rappresentare. **-prĕssible**, ADJ.: che può esprimersi; effabile. **-prĕssion** S.: espressione; locuzione; rappresentazione, *f.* **-prĕssive**, ADJ.: espressivo. **-pressively**, ADV.: con modo espressivo. **-prĕssiveness**, S.: forza d' espressione, energia, *f.* **-prĕssly**, ADV.: espressamente, direttamente. **-prĕssure**†, S.: espressione; impressione, *f.*

ĕxpro-brate†, TR.: biasimare, rimproverare. **-brātion**†, S.: rimprovero, biasimo, rinfacciamento, *m.*

exprōpri-ate, TR.: espropriare. **-ātion**, S.: espropriazione, *f.*

ex-pūgn, TR.: espugnare, vincere per forza. **-pugnātion**, S.: espugnazione, *f.*

expŭl-se†, TR.: espellere, scacciare. **-sion**, S.: espulsione, *f.*, scacciamento, *m.* **-sive**, ADJ.: espulsivo.

expŭn-ction, S.: cancellazione, cancellatura, *f.* **-ge**, TR.: espungere, cancellare.

ĕx-purgate, TR.: (e)spurgare. **-purgātion**, S.: purgazione, *f.* **-pŭrgatory**, ADJ.: espurgatorio, purgativo. **-pŭrge** = *expurgate*.

ĕxquisite, ADJ.: squisito, eccellente, perfetto. **-ly**, ADV.: esquisitamente, ottima

mente. -**ness**, s.: squisitezza; perfezione, *f.*
exscind, TR.: scindere.
exsic-cant, ADJ.: essiccante, disseccativo. -**cate** TR.: disseccare, seccare. -**cā-tion**, s.: essiccazione, *f.*, disseccamento, *m.* -**cative**, ADJ.: disseccativo.
exsūction, s.: succhiamento, *m.*
ex-sudātion, s.: traspirazione, *f.*, sudore, *m.* -**sūde**, INTR.: sudare, traspirare.
exsŭfflolate, TR.: bisbigliare, parlare all' orecchio; parlottare.
exsŭscitate†, TR.: svegliare; ravvivare.
ĕxtacy = *ecstasy*.
ĕxtan-cy, s.: proietto, *m.*, proiettura, *f.* -**t**, ADJ.: esistente, sussistente.
extĕmpo-ral, ADJ.: improvviso, subito. -**rally**, ADV.: improvvisamente. -**rāne-ous**, ADJ.: estemporaneo: — *speaker*, improvvisatore. -**rary**, ADJ.: estemporale; improvviso. -**re**, ADV.: all' improvviso: *deliver* —, improvisare; *speak* —, parlare all' improvviso. -**riness**, s.: improvvisazione, *f.* -**rize**, INTR.: improvvisare.
extĕn-d, TR.: stendere; dilatare, allargare; (*leg.*) valutare; INTR.: stendersi, distendersi. -**der**, s.: stenditore, *m.* -**dible**, ADJ.: estendibile. -**sibility**, s.: facoltà di stendersi, capacità d' essere esteso, *f.* -**sible**, ADJ.: estensibile, estendibile; dilatabile. -**sion**, s.: estensione, *f.*; distendimento, allungamento, *m.* -**sive**, ADJ.: estensivo, largo. -**sively**, ADV.: estensivamente, largamente, ampiamente. -**siveness**, s.: estensione, larghezza, *f.* -**sor**, s.: (*anat.*) estensore, *m.* -**t**, s.: estensione, ampiezza, larghezza, *f.*; allargamento, *m.*; comunicazione; staggina, *f.*, sequestro, *m.*: *to the full* —, in tutta la sua estensione.
extĕnu-ate, TR.: attenuare, diminuire, mitigare; estenuare. -**ātion**, s.: estenuazione; mitigazione; magrezza, *f.*: *in* — *of*, per mitigare.
extē-rior, ADJ.: esteriore, esterno; s.: esteriore, il di fuori, *m.*: *of pleasing* —, di bella presenza. -**riŏrity**, s.: esteriorità, *f.* -**riorly**, ADV.: esteriormente.
extĕrmi-nate, TR.: sterminare, stirpare, distruggere, rovinare. -**nātion**, s.: esterminazione, *f.*, distruggimento, *m.*, rovina, *f.* -**nator**, s.: sterminatore, *m.* -**ne**, TR.: esterminare, distruggere.
extĕr-n(al), ADJ.: esterno, esteriore; visibile. -**nally**, ADV.: esternamente, nell' esterno.
extimu-late†, TR.: stimolare, eccitare. -**lātion**†, s.: stimolazione, *f.*
extin-ct, ADJ.: estinto; abolito; morto: *become* —, estinguersi. -**ction**, s.: estinzione; abolizione, *f.*; distruggimento, *m.* -**guish**, TR.: estinguere; spegnere, smorzare. -**guishable**, ADJ.: estinguibile. -**guisher**, s.: spegnitoio, *m.* -**guishment**, s.: estinguimento, spegnimento, *m.*
extir-pate, TR.: estirpare, distruggere, sradicare; svellere. -**pātion**, s.: estirpazione, *f.*, estirpamento, *m.*; distruzione, *f.* -**pator**, s.: estirpatore, distruttore, *m.*
extŏl, TR.: estollere, esaltare, lodare. -**ler**, s.: esaltatore, lodatore, *m.*
extŏr-sive, ADJ.: forzante, violento; iniquo. -**sively**, ADV.: per estorsione iniqua, violentemente. -**t**, TR.: estorquere; pigliar per violenza, torre per forza; INTR.: usare violenza, fare angheria. -**ter**, s.: esattore; oppressore, *m.* -**tion**, s.: estorsione; esazione violenta, *f.* -**tioner**, s.: esattore; oppressore, *m.*
ĕxtra, ADV.: di più, di giunta, in oltre: *the* — *amount*, il di più, l' eccedenza.
ĕx-tract, s.: estratto; sommario, *m.* -**trăct**, TR.: estrarre; cavare; scegliere; separare. -**trăction**, s.: estrazione; nascita, discendenza, schiatta, *f.*: *of noble* —, di alto lignaggio; *of low* —, di bassa mano. -**trăctive**, ADJ.: estrattivo. -**trăctor**, s.: che estrae, estrattore, *m.*
extradition, s.: estradizione, *f.*
extrajudicial, ADJ.: estragiudiziale. -**ly**, ADV.: estragiudicialmente.
extramission, s.: emissione, *f.*
extramŭndane, ADJ.: oltremondano.
extrāneous, ADJ.: estraneo, forestiero.
extraordinar-ies, s. PL.: spese straordinarie, *f. pl.* -**ily**, ADV.: straordinariamente. -**iness**, s.: occasione straordinaria; singolarità, *f.* -**y**, ADJ.: straordinario, raro.
extraparŏchial, ADJ.: di nessuna parrocchia.
extrăvagan-ce, -**cy**, s.: stravaganza; prodigalità, profusione; bizzarria, *f.*; ghiribizzo, *m.* -**t**, ADJ.: stravagante, eccessivo, esorbitante; prodigo; fantastico, bizarro; s.: spendereccio, prodigo, *m.* -**tly**, ADV.: stravagantemente. -**ness**, s.: stravaganza, *f.*; eccesso, *m.*
extrăva-gate, INTR.: vaneggiare, farneticare; bolleggiare; farneticare; delirare. -**gation**, s.: stravaganza, *f.*
extrăva-sated, ADJ.: stravasato. -**sation**, s.: estravasazione, *f.*, stravasamento, *m.*
ex-trēme, ADJ.: estremo, ultimo; grandissimo; s.: estremo, *m.*, estremità, *f.*: *go from one* — *to another*, passare d' un estremo all' otro; *run into* —*s*, trascorrere agli estremi; —*s meet*, gli estremi si toccano. -**trēmely**, ADV.: estremamente, in estremo; sommamente. -**tremity**, s.: estremità, estrema parte; [illegible]; miseria, calamità, *f.*

ĕxtri-cable, ADJ.: che si può sviluppare. **-cate**, TR.: distrigare, sviluppare. **-cātion**, S.: scioglimento, sviluppamento, *m.*
extrinsic(al), ADJ.: estrinseco, esterno. **-ally**, ADV.: estrinsecamente, esteriormente.
extrū-de, TR.: estrudere, cacciare con violenza. **-sion**, S.: espulsione, *f.*, scacciamento, *m.*
extūberance, S.: tumore, *m.*, gonfiezza, *f.*
extumĕscence, S.: enfiato, tumore, *m.*
exūber-ance, S.: esuberanza, soprabbondanza, *f.* **-ant**, ADJ.: esuberante, soprabbondante. **-antly**, ADV.: esuberantemente, soprabbondevolmente. **-ate**, INTR.: soprabbondare, ridondare.
exudātion, S.: traspirazione, *f.*
ex-ūde, INTR.: sudare, traspirare.
exūlcer-ate, TR.: esulcerare, ulcerare. **-ātion**, S.: esulceramento, *m.*, ulcerazione, *f.* **-atory**, ADJ.: esulcerativo.
exŭlt, INTR.: esultare. **-ance**, **-ātion**, S.: esultazione; allegrezza, gioia, *f.*
exŭn-date, INTR.: inondare, soprabbondare. **-dātion**, S.: inondazione, *f.*
exūper-ance†, S.: esuperanza, *f.* **-ate**†, TR.: sorpassare, sormontare; eccellere.
exŭscitate†, TR.: svegliare; eccitare.
exūs-t, TR.: bruciare. **-tion**, S.: ustione, *f.*, abbruciamento, *m.*
exūviae, S.: spoglia; scoglia, *f.*
eyas, S.: falcone giovine, falconetto, *m.*
eye 1, S.: occhio, *m.*; vista, *f.*; rampollo, *m.*, gemma, *f.*, bottone; viso, aspetto, *m.*: *large* —, occhione, *m.*; *small* —, occhietto, occhiuzzo, *m.*; *blue* —*s*, occhi azzurri; *glass* —, occhio di cristallo; *in the twinkling of an* —, in un batter d' occhio; — *of a plant*, occhio (nesto, gemma) di pianta; — *of a needle*, foro dell' ago, *m.*; *cast of the* —, occhiata, *f.*; *have an* — *upon one*, osservare alcuno; *keep a strict* — *upon one*, aver l' occhio sopra alcuno; *shut one's* —*s*, chiudere gli occhi. **eye** 2, TR.: considerare, guardare; osservare; INTR.: parere, mostrarsi: *have sore* —*s*, aver male agli occhi; *cast a sheep's* — *at*, (ad)occhiare, vagheggiare; *keep an* — *upon him*, tenetelo d' occhio. **-ball**, S.: pupilla dell' occhio, *f.* **-bright**, S.: eufragia, *f.* **-brow**, S.: ciglio, *m.* **-drop**, S.: lagrima; stilla, *f.* **-glance**, S.: occhiata, *f.*, sguardo, *m.* **-glass**, S.: occhiale, binoculo, oculare, *m.* **-lash**, S.: pelo della palpebra, *m.* **-less**, ADJ.: senz' occhi, cieco. **-let**, S.: occhiello, *m.* **-lid**, S.: palpebra, *f.* **-salve**, S.: collirio, *m.* **-servant**, S.: servente cattivo, *m.* **-shot**, S.: occhiata, *f.* **-sight**, S.: vista, *f.*; *occhi, m. pl.* **-sore**, S.: fastidio, *m.* **-string**, S.: nervo dell' occhio, *m.* **-tooth**, S.: dente occhiale, *m.* **-water**, S.: acqua buona per gli occhi, *f.* **-wink**, S.: segno dell' occhio, *m.*; occhiata, *f.* **-witness**, S.: testimonio oculare, *m.*
ēyre, S.: corte de' giudici ambulanti, *f.*
ēyry, S.: nido d' uccello di rapina, *m.*

F

f *eff* (*the letter*), S.: f, *m.* or *f.*
fâ, S.: (*mus.*) fa, *m.*
fabāceous, ADJ.: della natura di fave.
făbl-e 1, S.: favola; finzione, *f.* **-e**, TR.: favoleggiare, raccontare favole; INTR.: dire bugie. **-ed**, ADJ.: celebre. **-er**, S.: favolatore, *m.*
făbric 1, S.: fabbrica, *f.*; edifizio, *m.*
fabric 2, TR.: fabbricare, costruire, formare. **-ate**, TR.: fabbricare; edificare; immaginare, inventare. **-ātion**, S.: fabbricazione, *f.*, fabbricamento; facimento, *m.* **-ator**, S.: fabbricatore, *m.*
făbu-list, S.: scrittore di favole, *m.* **-lous**, ADJ.: favoloso, controvato. **-lously**, ADV.: favolosamente.
façâde, S.: facciata, *f.*
fāce 1, S.: faccia, *f.*; viso, volto, fronte; *m.*; ciera; aria, *f.*; prospetto, aspetto, *m.*; facciata; superfizie; apparenza, *f.*, esteriore; stato, *m.*; confidenza; assicuranza, *f.*: *handsome* —, bella faccia; — *to* —, faccia a faccia; *before my* —, in presenza mia; *before the* — *of God*, in faccia a Dio; *in the* — *of heaven*, a faccia del cielo; *look one in the* —, guardare alcuno nel viso; *make* —*s*, far delle smorfie; *put on a new* —, cangiarsi il viso; *have a* — *of religion*, aver qualche apparenza di religione; *carry two* —*s*, avere due visi; *have a brazen* —, essere sfacciato. **face** 2, TR.: guardare nel viso; voltare (una carta); INTR.: fare faccia, fare fronte; far delle smorfie; affrontare, bravare; — *the enemy*, far faccia al (affrontare il) nemico; — *out a lie*, mantenere una bugia; — *sleeves*, mettere le mostre; — *about*, fare fronte, voltarsi; — *out*, mantenere; opporsi; — *with*, coprire. **-d**, ADJ.: dalla faccia, che ha la faccia, di viso. **-less**, ADJ.: senza faccia; impudente. **-painter**, S.: pittore di ritratti, *m.* **-painting**, S.: arte del fare ritratti, *f.*
făcet, S.: faccetta, *f.*
facētious, ADJ.: faceto, giocoso, burlesco; piacevole. **-ly**, ADV.: facetamente, giocosamente, burlescamente; piacevolmente. **-ness**, S.: facezia; piacevolezza, *f.*
fācial, ADJ.: faciale, della faccia.

fă-cile, ADJ.: facile; agevole; trattabile; pieghevole. **-cilitate**, TR.: facilitare, rendere facile. **-cilitation**, S.: facilitare, *m.* **-cility**, S.: facilità; agevolezza, destrezza; affabilità, *f.*

fāeing, S.: fronte, *m.*; facciata; mostra; guernitura, *f.*

facinorous†, ADJ.: facinoroso, scellerato. **-ness†**, S.: scelleratezza, iniquità, *f.*

facsimile, S.: copia esatta, *f.*, facsimile, *m.*

făct, S.: fatto; atto, *m.*: *in* —, effettivamente; in fatto; *matter of* —, cosa di fatto, *f.*; *matter of* — *man*, uomo pratico (*or* positivo); *the* — *is*, il fatto si è.

făc-tion, S.: fazione; discordia, *f.* **-tionary**, **-tioner**, S.: fazioso, *m.* **-tious**, ADJ.: fazioso, fazionario, sedizioso. **-tiously**, ADV.: in modo sedizioso. **-tiousness**, S.: spirito di fazione, *m.* **-titious**, ADJ.: fattizio, artifiziale. **-titiousness**, S.: artifizio, *m.*, accortezza, *f.*

făctor, S.: fattore; agente, *m.* **-ship**, S.: fattoria, *f.* **-y**, S.: fabbrica, fattoria; società (di mercanti), *f.*

factōtum, S.: faccendiere, faccendone, *m.*

făcture, S.: fattura, *f.*; facimento, *m.*

făculty, S.: facoltà, potenza; podestà, *f.*; privilegio, *m.*

făc-und†, ADJ.: facondioso, eloquente. **-ŭndity†**, S.: facondia, eloquenza, *f.*

făddle, TR.: badaluccare; vezzeggiare.

fāde, TR.: appassare; seccare; INTR.: sfiorire; languire. **-less**, ADJ.: che non può appassirsi.

fădge, INTR.: convenire; accordarsi.

fāding, ADJ.: languido; S.: debolezza, *f.*

fæces *fē-*, S.: feccia, *f.*; sedimento, *m.*

făg1, S.: galuppo, schiavo; groppo (di panno), *m.* **fag**2, INTR.: affaticarsi; dimenarsi. **-end**, S.: estremità, punta, *f.*

făgot1, S.: fagotto, fastello, fascio, *m.* **fagot**2, TR.: affastellare, affasciare. **-band**, S.: ritorta, *f.*; vinciglio, *m.*

fāil1, S.: fallo; errore; mancamento, *m.*, omissione, *f.*: *without* —, senza fallo. **fail**2, TR.: abbandonare, cessare; omettere, negligere; INTR.: fallare, errare; mancare; perire, morire: — *in one's duty*, mancare al suo dovere; *he has* —*ed*, è fallito. **-ance**, S.: fallo, *m.* **-ing**, S.: fallo, errore, *m.*; colpa; mancanza, *f.* **-ure**, S.: deficienza; mancanza, *f.*; fallimento, *m.*: *it was a complete* —, è stato un fiasco completo.

fāin1, ADJ.: obbligato, sforzato, costretto. **fain**2, ADV.: benvolentieri, pure: *he would* — *persuade me*, egli vuole in ogni modo persuadermi. **fain**3, INTR.: desiderare, bramare.

fāint1, ADJ.: languido, debole, fiacco; ti-

venir meno. **faint**2, TR.: d
abbattere, indebolire; INTR.: div
guido; svenire; tramortire: (
away, ella svenne. **-hearted**,
mido, pusillanime, codardo. **-h**
ly, ADV.: timidamente, pusillani
-heartedness, S.: timidezza,
mità, *f.* **-ing**, ADJ.: languente;
quio, svenimento, *m.* **-ing-fit**,
quio, svenimento, *m.*: *to fall in*
cadere in deliquio. **-ish**, ADJ.
detto, debole, fiacco. **-ishness**
guidezza, debolezza, fiacchezza, *f.*
ADJ.: timoroso. **-ly**, ADV.: de
languidamente. **-ness**, S.: debo
volezza, fiacchezza, *f.*; languore,
ADJ.: debole; languido, fiacco.

fāir1, ADJ.: bello, vezzoso, buon
sereno; sincero, candido, franco;
favorevole; biondo: — *sex*, bel s
— *proposal*, proposizione ragion
— *woman*, donna bionda, *f.*; *be*
way, esser bene incamminato;
giuocar senza inganno; *use* —
trattar con piacevolezza. **fair**
pian piano; civilmente: — *e*
ly, adagio; — *and square*, co
rità. **fair**3, S.: bella, bella d
bel sesso, *m.* **fair**4, S.: fiera, *f*
to pubblico, *m.*: *come a day afte*
venire troppo tardi. **-complex**
ADJ.: biondo. **-day**, S.: giorno
m. **-dealing**, S.: buona fede;
f. **-faced**, ADJ.: di bel viso, be
-ing, S.: donativo di fiera, *m.*,
-ish, ADJ.: assai bello. **-ly**
vagamente; bene, di buona fede,
mente; piacevolmente. **-ness**, S
probità, onestà, *f.*; candore, *m.*
en, ADJ.: affabile, elegante;
-time, S.: tempo di fiera, *m.*

fāiry1, S.: fata, maga, *f.* **fairy**
di fate, incantevole.

fāith, S.: fede; credenza; lealt
rità, veracità, *f.*: *by my* —, affè
of —, violazione di fede. **-b**
-break, S.: perfidia, *f.* **-ful**,
dele; onesto, candido; S.: fed
stiano, *m.* **-fully**, ADV.: fed
sinceramente; esattamente. **-f**
S.: fedeltà; buona fede; lealtà;
-less, ADJ.: perfido, infido; i
-lessness, S.: perfidia; incredul

falcāde, S.: curvetta, *f.*

fălcated, ADJ.: falcato, curvat
-tion, S.: curvatura, *f.*

fălchion, S.: falcione, *m.*, scimit

fălcon, S.: falcone, *m.* **-er**, f
niere, *m.* **-et**, S.: falconetto,
S.: falconeria; caccia del falcone

făldstool, S.: sgabello del co

fall 1, S.: caduta; decadenza; cascata; (*rail.*) discesa, *f.*: *get a* —, cadere; cascare; *give a* —, fare cascare. **fall** 2, IRR.; INTR.: cadere, cascare; declinare; abbassarsi; perire; TR.: abbassare, abbattere: — *again*, ricadere, ricascare; — *all along*, cadere tutto disteso; — *asleep*, — *into a sleep*, addormentarsi; — *a-crying*, mettersi a piangere, darsi a piangere; — *a-fighting*, cominciare a battersi; — *headlong*, cimbottolare; — *in love*, innamorarsi; — *in with one*, prender la parte d'uno, associarsi; — *in with the enemy*, incontrare il nemico; — *into a passion*, mettersi in collera, stizzarsi; — *to pieces*, cascare a pezzi; partorire; — *short*, non venire a fine, mancare; — *sick*, ammalarsi; — *into a swoon*, svenire, tramortire; ricascare; — *away*, smagrire; — *back*, rinculare; ritrattarsi; — *backward*, cadere disteso; — *down*, cascare; prostrarsi; smottare; — *forward*, cadere boccone; — *from*, abbandonare; rinunziare; — *in*, coincidare, concorrere; cedere; — *into*, cascare; entrare; mettersi in; — *off*, cascare da; disdirsi; separarsi; apostatare; — *out*, accadere; avvenire, succedere; venire a parole (*or* alle mani); — *over*, rivoltarsi; — *to*, cominciare; — *under*, cadere sotto; presentarsi; — *upon*, avventarsi; lanciarsi, attaccare; — *upon one's knees*, inginocchiarsi.

fallácious, ADJ.: fallace, falso. **-ly**, ADV.: fallacemente, falsamente. **-ness**, S.: inganno, *m.*, frode; falsità, *f.*

fállacy, S.: fallacia, *f.*, sofismo, *m.*, falsità, *f.*

fállen, part. del v. *fall*.

fal-libílity, S.: fallibilità, attezza ad errare, *f.* **-lible**, ADJ.: fallibile.

fálling, ADJ.: cadente, cascante; S.: cadimento, *m.*, caduta; decadenza, *f.*; (*nav.*) — *off*, abbrivo, *m.*; — *away*, smagrimento, scemamento, *m.*; — *in*, incontro, *m.*; rottura, *f.*; — *out*, dissensione; disputa, *f.* **-sickness**, S.: mal caduco, *m.*, epilessia, *f.*

fállow, ADJ.: rossigno; incolto, negletto: — *deer*, cervo, *m.*; — *field*, maggese, *m.* **fallow** 2, TR.: dare la prima aratura, rompere il terreno, dissodare. **-ground**, S.: terreno incolto, *m.* **-ness**, S.: (*agr.*) maggese, campo sodo, *m.*; sterilità, *f.*

fáls-e, ADJ.: falso, menzognero; finto, contraffatto, perfido; ADV.: falsamente: — *curls*, ricci posticci; — *teeth*, denti finti. **-ehearted**, ADJ.: ingannevole; perfido. **-eheartedness**, S.: perfidia, *f.* **-ehood**, S.: falsità; perfidia, *f.* **-ely**, ADV.: falsamente; perfidamente. **-eness**, S.: falsità, *f.* **-étto**, S.: (*mus.*) falsetto, *m.* **-ifiable**, ADJ.: *che si può falsificare.* **-ification**, S.: falsificazione, *f*, falsificamento, *m.* **-ifier**, S.: falsificatore, falsatore, *m.* **-ify**, TR.: falsificare; contraffare; INTR.: mentire, dire menzogne, dire bugie. **-ity**, S.: falsità, falsezza, *f.*; errore, *m.*

fálter, INTR.: balbettare, esitare; mancare, fallire. **-ing**, S.: balbuzie, esitazione, *f.* **-ingly**, ADV.: con esitazione, con difficoltà.

fámble†, INTR.: balbettare.

fáme 1, S.: fama; rinomanza, *f.*; rumore, *m.* **fame** 2, INTR.: far famoso. **-d**, ADJ.: rinomato, famoso, celebre. **-less**, ADJ.: senza fama; ignobile.

famil-iar, ADJ.: famigliare, domestico; ordinario, comune; S.: famigliare, intimo amico, *m.*: — *with*, pratico di; *render one's self* — *with*, rendersi famigliare di, impratichiarsi di. **-iárity**, S.: famigliarità, dimestichezza, *f.* **-iarize**, INTR.: render famigliare, dimesticare; abituare; impratichiarsi. **-iarly**, ADV.: famigliarmente.

fámily, S.: famiglia; schiatta; spezie, *f.*: *in the* — *way*, incinta; — *tree*, albero genealogico, *m.*

fám-ine, S.: carestia, penuria di viveri; fame, *f.* **-ish**, TR.: affamare; INTR.: essere affamato, avere fame. **-ished**, ADJ.: affamato, famelico. **-ishment**, S.: fame; penuria, carestia, *f.*

famósity† = *famousness*.

fámous, ADJ.: famoso, rinomato. **-ly**, ADV.: famosamente; celebremente. **-ness**, S.: rinomanza; celebrità, *f.*

fámulate, TR.: servire.

fán 1, S.: ventaglio; vaglio, *m.*: *pretty* —, ventaglino, *m.* **fan** 2, TR.: ventilare; vagliare.

fanát-ic, ADJ.: fanatico; S.: fanatico, entusiasta, *m.* **-ically**, ADV.: da fanatico. **-icism**, S.: fanatismo; entusiasmo, *m.*

fán-ciful, ADJ.: fantastico, bizzarro, capriccioso. **-cifully**, ADV.: fantasticamente, capricciosamente. **-cifulness**, fantasticaggine, fantasia, *f.* **-cy** 1, S.: fantasia, immaginazione; visione; idea, *f.*, gusto; capriccio, *m.*, voglia, *f.*: *whimsical fancies*, bizzarre fantasie; *it is my* —, così mi piace; *I had a* —, mi venne voglia; *take a* — *to a thing*, pigliar amore ad una cosa. **-cy** 2, TR.; INTR.: amare; figurarsi, immaginarsi; pensare, credere. **-cy-monger**, S.: visionario, *m.* **-cy-sick**, ADJ.: languente d' amore.

fáne, S.: tempio, *m.*, chiesa, *f.*

fánfaron, S.: millantatore, vantatore, *m.* **-áde**, S.: bravata, millanteria, burbanza, *f.*

fáng 1, S.: zanna, branca, *f.*; artiglio,

dente, *m.* **fang** 2, TR.: afferrare colle ugne, abbrancare; aggrappare. **-ed,** ADJ.: fornito di zanne.

făngle, S.: invenzione, *f.*, capriccio, *m.*

făngless, ADJ.: senza zanne, senza branche; sdentato.

făn-like, ADJ.: a foggia di ventaglio.

fănnel, S.: manipolo, *m.* (ciarpa).

fănner, S.: vagliatore, *m.*

făn-tasied†, ADJ.: ghiribizzoso, bizzarro; capriccioso. **-tasm,** S.: fantasima; chimera, *f.* **-tăstic(al),** ADJ.: fantastico, stravagante, bizzarro, bisbetico. **-tăstically,** ADV.: fantasticamente, capricciosamente. **-tăsticalness, -tăsticness,** S.: fantasticaggine, *f.* **-tasy,** S.: fantasia, immaginazione, *f.*

fâr 1, ADJ.: lontano, remoto, distante; alieno: *it is — in the day*, è tardi. **far** 2, ADV.: lontano; lunge; di gran lunga, di molto; bene: *by* —, di molto; — *from*, lungi da, lontano da; — *otherwise*, tutto 'l contrario; — *and near*, — *and wide*, per ogni lato; dappertutto; — *better*, molto migliore, nel miglior modo; molto meglio; *as — as I see*, per quanto posso vedere; — *be it from me*, Dio me ne guardi; *how —?* fin dove? *how — is it thither?* quanto è lontano di qui? *is it — from here?* v' è molto di qui?

fâr-ce 1, S.: farsa, *f.*; ripieno, *m.* **-ce** 2, TR.: (*cook.*) empire di condimento, far un ripieno. **-cical,** ADJ.: comico, burlesco. **-cing,** S.: ripieno, *m.*

fârcy, S.: scabbia; rogna de' cavalli, *f.*

fârd, TR.: imbellettare.

fârdel, S.: fardello, fascio; mazzo, *m.*

fâre 1, S.: cera, *f.*, mangiare, *m.*, viveri, *m. pl.*; nolo, passaggio; prezzo, *m.*: *bill of* —, lista; nota della spesa, carta, *f.* **fare** 2, INTR.: andare, stare; mangiare; vivere: — *you well*, conservatevi; addio; — *like a prince*, vivere da principe; *they — well*, si trattano bene. **-well,** ADV.: addio, vale; conservatevi; S.: addio, congedo, *m.*: *bid* —, dire addio; partire.

fâr-fetch†, S.: astuzia, *f.* **-fetched,** ADJ.: affettato, studiato.

farināceous, ADJ.: farinaceo.

fârm 1, S.: affitto; allogamento, *m.*, villa, *f.*: *small* —, poderetto, *m.*; *model* —, fattoria modello, *m.*; *rent a* —, prendere in affitto un podere. **farm** 2, TR.: affittare, prendere a fitto: — *out*, dare in affitto, appaltare. **-er,** S.: affittaiuolo, appaltatore, castaldo, *m.*: *gentleman* —, proprietario coltivatore, agricoltore, *m.* **-house,** S.: casa del podere, cascina, *f.*; cascino, *m.* **-ing,** S.: affitto a censo, *m.*

fâr-most, ADJ.: più remoto, lontanissimo. **-ness,** S.: allontanamento, *m.*, distanza, *f.*

far-răginous, ADJ.: farragginoso. **-răgo,** S.: farraggine, *f.*

fărrier, S.: maniscalco, maliscalco, *m.*

fărrow 1, S.: porcello, porchetto, *m.* **farrow** 2, TR.: fare i porcelli.

fâr-shooting, ADJ.: disteso, esteso.

fâr-ther 1, ADJ.: ulteriore, più lontano. **-ther** 2, ADV.: avanti, innanzi, oltre. **-ther** 3, TR.: avanzare; aiutare; facilitare. **-therance,** S.: aiuto, *m.*, assistenza, *f.* **-thermore,** ADV.: di più, inoltre. **-thest** 1, ADJ.: remotissimo, lontanissimo. **-thest** 2 ADV.: al più distante; al più tardi.

fârthing, S.: fardino, *m.*

fârthingale, S.: piccola faldiglia, *f.*

fârthingsworth, S.: valsente d' un fardino, *m.*, valuta, *f.*; prezzo, *m.*

făsces, S. PL.: fasci, *m. pl.*

făs-cia, S.: fascia, banda, *f.* **-ciated,** ADJ.: fasciato. **-ciātion,** S.: fasciatura, *f.*

făsci-nate, TR.: affascinare; ammaliare; abbagliare. **-nating,** ADJ.: affascinante, ammaliante: — *lady*, affascinatrice, donna ammaliante. **-nātion,** S.: fascino, ammaliamento, *m.*

fascine, S.: fascina, *f.*, fagotto, *m.*

făshion 1, S.: maniera, guisa, forma; usanza, voga, moda; condizione; guisa, sorte; aria, apparenza, *f.*: *people of* —, gente distinta, nobiltà, *f.*; *after the* —, alla moda; *in* —, alla moda; *bring into* —, mettere in voga, introdurre la moda; *out of* —, fuor di moda. **fashion** 2, TR.: affazzonare; formare. **-able,** ADJ.: alla moda; elegante: — *lady*, signora elegante, dama distinta. **-ableness,** S.: eleganza; moda; usanza, *f.* **-ably,** ADV.: alla moda; elegantemente. **-er,** S.: affazzonatore, formatore, *m.*, -trice, *f.* **-ist,** S.: seguitatore delle mode; modista, *m.* **-monger,** S.: vagheggino, attillatuzzo, *m.*

făst 1, ADJ.: fermo, saldo, stretto; stabile, fisso: — *sleep*, sonno profondo, *m.*; *make* —, serrare. **fast** 2, ADV.: fermamente; fermo, stretto; saldamente; subitamente, subito: *be — asleep*, dormire profondamente; *go* —, andare a gran passi; *stand* —, star saldo, star fermo; tener duro; *stick* —, appiccarsi tenacemente. **fast** 3, S.: digiuno, *m.*, astinenza da cibi, *f.*: *break one's* —, rompere il digiuno; far colazione; *keep a* —, osservare il digiuno. **fast** 4, INTR.: digiunare. **-day,** S.: giorno magro, *m.*

făsten, TR.: legare; attaccare, fissare, serrare, fermare; INTR.: appiccarsi; attaccarsi: — *one's eyes upon a thing*, fissare gli occhi sopra qualche cosa; — *upon a thing*, afferrare una cosa; — *a crime*

upon one, imputare un delitto ad uno. **-er**, s.: che lega, legatore; serratore, *m.*
fāster, s.: digiunatore, *m.*
fāsthanded, ADJ.: avaro, spilorcio.
fas-tidiŏsity† = *-tidiousness*. **-tidious**, ADJ.: fastidioso, sdegnoso. **-tidiously**, ADV.: fastidiosamente. **-tidiousness**, s.: fastidiosità, *f.*, sdegno, disprezzo, *m.*, noia, *f.*
fāsting 1, ADV.: a digiuno, senza aver mangiato. **fasting** 2, s.: digiunare, *m.*: — *day*, giorno di digiuno, giorno magro, *m.*
fāstness, s.: fermezza, *f.*; forte, luogo forte, *m.*
fāstuous†, ADJ.: fastoso, vanaglorioso, superbo.
făt 1, ADJ.: grasso, carnoso, pingue, obeso; untuoso; s.: grosso, *m.*; sugna, pinguedine, *f.*: *grow* —, divenir grasso, ingrassare; *make* —, ingrassare. **fat** 2, TR.: ingrassare; impinguare; INTR.: divenire grasso, ingrassare.
fā-tal, ADJ.: fatale; funesto. **-talism**, s.: fatalismo, *m.* **-talist**, s.: fatalista, *m.* **-tālity**, s.: fatalità; predestinazione, *f.* **-tally**, ADV.: fatalmente, funestamente. **-talness**, s.: fatalità, *f.*, destino inevitabile, *m.* **-te**, s.: fato, destino, *m.* **-s**, s. PL.: parche, *f. pl.* **-ted**, ADJ.: fatato, decreto.
fāther 1, s.: padre; genitore, *m.* **father** 2, TR.: adottare: — *upon*, attribuire, imputare. **-hood**, s.: paternità, *f.* **-in-law**, s.: suocero, *m.* **-less**, ADJ.: senza padre, orfano. **-liness**, s.: amor paterno, *m.*, cura paterna, *f.* **-ly** 1, ADJ.: paternale, paterno. **-ly** 2, ADV.: da padre; a modo di padre.
făthom 1, s.: braccio, *m.* (misura); acutezza, *f.* **fathom** 2, TR.: scandagliare, affondare; penetrare. **-less**, ADJ.: non misurabile, immenso; impenetrabile.
fa-tidical, ADJ.: fatidico, indovino. **-tiferous**†, ADJ.: fatale, mortale, esiziale.
făt-igable, ADJ.: faticabile; penoso. **-igate**, TR.: fatigare, travagliare, affannare; straccare. **-igue**, s.: fatica, pena, *f.*; affanno, *m.*: *be worn out with* —, essere affranto dalla fatica; *man capable of resisting* —, uomo da fatica. **-igue** 2, TR.: affaticare, travagliare; stancare.
făt-ling, s.: bestia grassa, *f.* **-ness**, s.: grassezza; untuosità, *f.* **-ted**, ADJ.: ingrassato, grasso. **-ten**, TR.: ingrassare; INTR.: divenire grasso, ingrassare. **-tening**, s.: ingrassamento, *m.* **-tish**, ADJ.: grassetto. **-ty**, ADJ.: grasso; untuoso, olioso.
fatū-ity, s.: fatuità, stupidezza, *f.* **fătuous**, ADJ.: fatuo, stolto, stupido.
fătwitted, *ADJ.: stupido, sciocco.*
fāucet, s.: zaffo, *m.*; canella, *f.*
faugh, INTERJ.: eh via!
fāulchion, s.: falcione, *m.*, scimitarra, *f.*
fāulcon = *falcon.*
fāult 1, s.: fallo, difetto, errore, *m.*; colpa; offesa, *f.*: *whose* — *is it?* di chi è la colpa? — *of the printer*, errore di stampa, *m.*; *find* — *with*, trovar da dire, riprendere, vituperare. **fault** 2, TR.: riprendere, criticare; INTR.: errare. **-er** = *falter*. **-finder**, s.: censore, critico, *m.* **-ful**, ADJ.: colpevole. **-ily**, ADV.: impropriamente. **-iness**, s.: difetto; delitto, *m.* **-less**, ADJ.: senza errori; perfetto, eccellente. **-lessness**, s.: perfezione, *f.* **-y**, ADJ.: colpevole; difettoso.
fāun, s.: (*myth.*) fauno, *m.*
fāutor†, s.: fautore, favoreggiatore, *m.*
fāvor 1, s.: favore; grazia; cortesia, *f.*; servizio; credito, *m.*; ciera, aria, *f.*; fiocco di nastri, *m.*: *with your* —, con vostra licenza; *be in* —, esser in grazia; *curry* —, corteggiare, ingraziarsi; *do one a* —, fare un favore ad uno, servire alcuno; *do me the* —, fatemi la grazia; *do me the* — *to pass the book*, mi favorisca il libro. **favor** 2, TR.: favorire, esser favorevole; vantaggiare; appoggiare; approvare; aiutare; somigliare. **-able**, ADJ.: favorevole; propizio. **-ableness**, s.: favore, *m.*, bontà; benignità; grazia, *f.* **-ably**, ADV.: favorevolmente. **-ed**, ADJ.: favorito, appoggiato: *ill*-—, malfatto, brutto, sgraziato; *well*-—, ben fatto, vago. **-edly**, ADV.: favorevolmente. **-edness**, s.: apparenza, *f.* **-er**, s.: fautore, protettore, *m.* **-ite**, s.: favorito, *m.* **-less**, ADJ.: senza protezione, sfavorevole, infausto.
fāwn 1, s.: cervetto, daino giovine, *m.* **fawn** 2, TR.: figliare; corteggiare servilmente; lusingare, adulare. **-er**, s.: adulatore; lusinghiero, *m.* **-ing**, s.: adulazione, *f.*; carezzine, *f. pl.* **-ingly**, ADV.: lusinghevolmente, servilmente.
fāy 1, s.: fata, maga, incantatrice; fede†, *f.*: *by my* —, alla fè. **fay** 2, INTR.: conguagliare, aggiustare.
fēalty, s.: fedeltà, lealtà, fedelità, *f.*
fēar 1, s.: timore, *m.*, paura, tema, *f.*: *for* —, per tema, per timore; *be in* —, *stand in* —, temere; *put in* —, atterrire, spaventare; *there's no* —, non v' è pericolo; *vain* —*s*, ubbie. **fear** 2, TR.: temere, paventare; INTR.: avere paura; dubitare, esitare. **-ful**, ADJ.: timido, timoroso; orribile. **-fully**, ADV.: timidamente; terribilmente. **-fulness**, s.: timidità, paura, *f.*, timore, *m.* **-less**, ADJ.: intrepido, ardito, bravo, coraggioso. **-lessly**, ADV.: senza timore, intrepidamente. **-lessness**, s.: intrepidezza, *f.*; ardimento, *m.*, baldanza, *f.*

svaporare. **-hâlement**, s.: esalazione, evaporazione, *f.*
exhâus-t, TR.: esaurire; rasciugare. **-tible**, ADJ.: esauribile. **-tion**, s.: disseccamento, *m.* **-tless**, ADJ.: inesauribile, inesausto.
exhĕre-date, TR.: diseredare, esereditare. **-dâtion**, s.: diseredazione, *f.*, eseredare, *m.*
exhib-it 1, s.: esibizione, *f.*; documento, *m.* **-it** 2, TR.: esibire; mostrare, produrre. **-iter**, s.: esibitore, *m.* **-ition** *exhib-*, s.: esibizione; presentazione; borsa, *f.* **-itioner**, s.: borsaio, *m.* **-itive**, ADJ.: rappresentativo.
exhila-rate, TR.: rallegrare; divertire. **-ration**, s.: gioia, allegrezza, giocondità, *f.*; piacere, *m.*
exhôrt, TR.: esortare; incitare, animare, incoraggiare. **-âtion**, s.: esortazione, *f.* **-ative**, **-atory**, ADJ.: esortatorio, esortativo. **-er**, s.: esortatore, *m.*
exiccate = *exsiccate.*
ĕxigen-ce, **-cy**, s.: esigenza, necessità, *f.*, bisogno; affanno, *m.*, afflizione, *f.* **-t**, ADJ.: esigente, urgente; premuroso; s.: necessità urgente, *f.*; bisogno, *m.*
ex-iguity, s.: minutezza, piccolezza, sottigliezza, *f.* **-iguous**, ADJ.: esiguo, piccolo, sottile, minuto. **-iguousness**, s.: piccolezza; minutezza, *f.*
exile 1, ADJ.: esile, tenue; sottile, magro.
exile 2, s.: esilio, sbandeggiamento, *m.*
exile 3, TR.: esiliare, mandare in esilio, sbandeggiare. **-ment**, s.: esilio, bando, sbandimento, *m.*
exilition†, s.: esplosione, *f.*
exility, s.: piccolezza, sottigliezza, *f.*
eximious†, ADJ.: esimio, eccellente, illustre.
exist, INTR.: esistere, essere. **-ence**, **-ency**, s.: esistenza, *f.*: *call into* —, chiamare all'esistenza. **-ent**, ADJ.: esistente. **-ible**, ADJ.: che può esistere.
ex-it, s.: esito, *m.*, uscita; partita, *f.*: *make one's* —, uscir di vita, morire. **-itial**†, **-itious**†, ADJ.: esiziale; fatale, funesto, pernicioso.
ĕxod-us, **-dy**†, s.: esodo, *m.*
exolûtion, s.: (*med.*) rilassazione (dei nervi), *f.*
exŏlve†, TR.: assolvere, slacciare.
exŏmphalos, s.: (*med.*) esonfalo, *m.*
exŏner-ate, TR.: esonerare, sgravare, discaricare, alleggerire, alleviare; liberare. **-âtion**, s.: scaricamento, *m.*
ĕxorable, ADJ.: esorabile, compassionevole.
exŏrbitan-ce, **-cy**, s.: esorbitanza, enormità, *f.* **-t**, ADJ.: esorbitante, eccessivo. **-tly**, ADV.: esorbitantemente.
ĕxor-cise, TR.: esorcizzare, scongiurare. **-cism**, s.: esorcismo, scongiuramento, *m.* **-cist**, s.: esorcista, *m.*
exôrdium, s.: esordio; prologo, *m.*
exornâtion, s.: ornamento, abbellimento, *m.*
exôtic, ADJ.: esotico, straniero; s.: pianta esotica, *f.*
expăn-d, TR.: spandere, dilatare; INTR.: spandersi, dilatarsi; palesarsi. **-se**, s.: espansione, estensione, *f.*: — *of water*, specchio di acqua; *the broad* —, l'alto mare. **-sibility**, s.: facoltà di dilatarsi. **-sible**, ADJ.: espansivo. **-sion**, s.: espansione, dilatazione, *f.*, dilatamento, *m.* **-sivé**, ADJ.: espansivo.
expâtiate, INTR.: distendersi.
expĕct, TR.: aspettare, attendere; sperare; aspettarsi: *I did not* — *it*, non me l'aspettava; *what can you* —? che potete aspettarvi? *as was to be* —*ed*, come era d'aspettarsi. **-ance**, **-ancy**, s.: aspettazione; speranza, *f.* **-ant**, ADJ.: aspettante; s.: aspettante, aspettatore, *m.* **-âtion**, s.: aspettazione, aspettativa, speranza, *f.*: *sanguine* —, viva speranza (fiducia); *beyond my* —*s*, al di là delle mie speranze; *contrary to* —, contro ogni aspettativa; *be in* —, esser nell'aspettazione. **-er**, s.: aspettante, *m.*
expĕct-orant, s.: medicina espettorante, *f.* **-orate**, TR.: espettorare, espurgare. **-orâtion**, s.: espettorazione, *f.* **-orative**, ADJ.: (*med.*) espettorante.
expĕdien-ce, **-cy**, s.: convenevolezza, convenienza; utilità; proprietà; spedizione, *f.* **-t**, ADJ.: convenevole; utile; s.: espediente; mezzo, *m.*: *it is* —, conviene. **-tly**, ADV.: convenevolmente.
ĕxpe-dite 1, ADJ.: spedito, pronto; agile. **-dite** 2, TR.: spedire, sbrigare, dispacciare; accelerare. **-ditely**, ADV.: speditamente, prontamente, agilmente. **-dition**, s.: spedizione; prestezza, celerità, fretta, *f.* **-ditious**, ADJ.: speditivo, pronto. **-ditiously**, ADV.: sollecitamente, prontamente.
expĕl, TR.: espellere, scacciare. **-ler**, s.: espulsore, scacciatore, *m.* **-ling**, s.: espulsione, *f.*
expĕn-d, TR.: spendere, sborsare. **-diture**, s.: spesa, *f.*, costo; sacrificio, *m.* **-se**, s.: spesa, *f.*; sborso, sborsamento, *m.*: *free of* —, senza spesa; franco; *trifling* —, tenue spesa; *defray one's* —*s*, spesare uno; *learn at one's* —, imparare alle proprie spese. **-seful**, ADJ.: dispendioso. **-seless**, ADJ.: senza spesa, senza costo. **-sive**, ADJ.: dispendioso, spendereccio; prodigo. **-sively**, ADV.: dispendiosamente, con grande spesa. **-siveness**, s.: dispendio, *m.*; stravaganza; prodigalità, *f.*

expĕrien-ce 1, s.: sperienza; cognizione; pratica, usanza, *f.: know by* —, sapere per esperienza. **-ce** 2, TR.: sperimentare, provare. **-cer**, s.: sperimentatore, *m.*
expĕri-ment 1, s.: sperimento, *m.*, prova, *f.* **-ment** 2, TR.: sperimentare, provare. **-mĕntal**, ADJ.: sperimentale. **-mĕntalist**, s.: sperimentatore, *m.* **-mĕntally**, ADV.: esperimentalmente. **-menter**, s.: sperimentatore, provatore, *m.*
expĕrt, ADJ.: esperto, sperimentato, versato, pratico. **-ly**, ADV.: espertamente. **-ness**, s.: abilità, destrezza, *f.*
ĕxpi-able, ADJ.: che si può espiare. **-ate**, TR.: espiare; reparare. **-ātion**, s.: espiazione; reparazione, *f.: as an — for*, in espiazione di. **-atory**, ADJ.: espiatorio.
expilātion, s.: (*leg.*) espilazione, *f.*
ex-pirātion, s.: espirazione, esalazione; respirazione; morte, *f.* **-pire**, TR.: spirare, esalare, finire, terminare; INTR.: morire.
ex-plāin, TR.: esplicare, spiegare; interpretare: *hard to* —, difficile a spiegarsi; — *away a difficulty*, far dileguare una difficoltà a forza di spiegazioni. **-plāinable**, ADJ.: esplicabile, spiegabile. **-plāiner**, s.: esplicatore, dichiaratore; interprete, *m.* **-planātion**, s.: esplicazione, interpretazione, *f.*, spiegamento, *m.* **-plănatory**, ADJ.: esplicativo, espositivo.
ĕxpletive, ADJ.: espletivo, riempitivo.
ĕxpli-cable, ADJ.: esplicabile, spiegabile. **-cate**, TR.: spiegare, dichiarare, dilucidare. **-cātion**, s.: esplicazione, spiegazione, *f.* **-cative**, ADJ.: esplicativo, espositivo. **-cator**, s.: espositore; comentatore, interprete, *m.*
explicit, ADJ.: espresso, distinto, chiaro, manifesto. **-ly**, ADV.: espressamente, direttamente, formalmente. **-ness**, s.: chiarezza; evidenza, *f.*
explōd-e, INTR.: esplodere, far esplosione, scoppiare; TR.: far scoppiare (saltare in aria); rigettare, disapprovare, condannare; fischiare. **-er**, s.: fischiatore, *m.*
explŏit 1, TR.: eseguire un gran fatto. **exploit** 2, s.: fatto d'arme, fatto illustre, *m.: great —s*, gloriose gesta.
explō-rate, TR.: esplorare, esaminare, investigare. **-rātion**, s.: investigazione; ricerca, *f.* **-rator** ĕx-, s.: esploratore, investigatore, *m.* **-ratory**, ADJ.: esplorante. **-re**, TR.: esplorare, investigare, ricercare; esaminare. **-rement**, s.: investigamento, *m.*, ricerca, *f.*
explō-sion, s.: esplosione, *f.;* scoppio, scoppiamento, *m.* **-sive**, ADJ.: esplodente, che scoppia: — *cotton*, cotone esplosivo, fulmicotone, *m.*
expŏlish†, TR.: pulire, lisciare; perfezionare.
expō-nent, s.: (*algeb.*) esponente, *m.* **-nĕntial**, ADJ.: (*algeb.*) esponenziale.
expōrt 1, TR.: esportare, trasportare. **ĕxport** 2, **-ātion**, s.: trasporto, trasportamento, *m.: — duty*, dazio d'uscita. **-er**, s.: esportatore.
ex-pōse, TR.: esporre; mostrare; scoprire; abbandonare; REFL.: esporsi; pericolarsi: *—ed to*, esposto a, sottoposto a. **-position**, s.: esposizione, *f.;* spiegamento, *m.;* interpretazione, *f.* **-pŏsitive**, ADJ.: espositivo, esplicativo. **-pŏsitor**, s.: espositore; comentatore, interprete, *m.* **-pŏsitory**, ADJ.: espositivo, esplicativo.
expŏstu-late, TR.: questionare, contendere, disputare; INTR.: lamentarsi, querelarsi: — *with*, lagnarsi con. **-lātion**, s.: discussione, disputa, *f.* **-lator**, s.: rimostrante, *m.* **-latory**, ADJ.: rimostrante.
expōsure, s.: esposizione; situazione, *f.;* pericolo, *m.*
expŏund, TR.: spiegare, spianare, interpretare. **-er**, s.: comentatore, interprete, *m.* **-ing**, s.: esposizione, interpretazione, *f.*, schiarimento, *m.*
ex-prĕss 1, ADJ.: espresso, preciso, distinto; simile, apparente; s.: espresso, corriere mandato, *m.: — train*, treno diretto; *by* —, per espresso; con istaffetta. **-press** 2, TR.: esprimere; spiegare, manifestare, mostrare; rappresentare. **-prĕssible**, ADJ.: che può esprimersi; effabile. **-prĕssion** s.: espressione; locuzione; rappresentazione, *f.* **-prĕssive**, ADJ.: espressivo. **-pressively**, ADV.: con modo espressivo. **-prĕssiveness**, s.: forza d'espressione, energia, *f.* **-prĕssly**, ADV.: espressamente, direttamente. **-prĕssure**†, s.: espressione; impressione, *f.*
ĕxpro-brate†, TR.: biasimare, rimproverare. **-brātion**†, s.: rimprovero, biasimo, rinfacciamento, *m.*
exprōpri-ate, TR.: espropriare. **-ātion**, s.: espropriazione, *f.*
ex-pūgn, TR.: espugnare, vincere per forza. **-pugnātion**, s.: espugnazione, *f.*
expŭl-se†, TR.: espellere, scacciare. **-sion**, s.: espulsione, *f.*, scacciamento, *m.* **-sive**, ADJ.: espulsivo.
expŭn-ction, s.: cancellazione, cancellatura, *f.* **-ge**, TR.: espungere, cancellare.
ĕx-purgate, TR.: (e)spurgare. **-purgātion**, s.: purgazione, *f.* **-pŭrgatory**, ADJ.: espurgatorio, purgativo. **-pŭrge** = *expurgate*.
ĕxquisite, ADJ.: squisito, eccellente, perfetto. **-ly**, ADV.: esquisitamente, ottimamente

fess [illegible] s.: [illegible] fascia, *f.*
festal, [illegible]: festivo, allegro.
fester, [illegible]: suppurare, impostemire. **-ing**, s.: suppurazione, *m.*
festi-nate, [illegible]: frettoloso, spedito. **-nately**, [illegible] in fretta, speditamente. **-nation**, s.: [illegible] fretta, sollecitudine, *f.*
fes-tival, [illegible]: festivo, festevole; s.: giorno festivo, *m.*, festa, *f.*, anniversario, *m.* **-tive**, ADJ.: festivo, festevole; lieto, allegro. **-tivity**, s.: allegrezza, *f.*, [illegible] giorno festivo, *m.* **-tivous**, ADJ.: festivo, festoso, giocondo, lieto.
festoon, s.: festone, *m.*
fet[illegible], s.: pezzo, straccio, *m.*
fetch 1, s.: artificio, *m.*, astuzia, *f.*; pretesto, raggiro, *m.* **fetch** 2, TR.: andare a cercare, recare; portare, produrre; — a blow, colpire; — one's breath, prender respiro, respirare; — a leap, fare un salto, saltare; — a sigh, trar un [illegible] gettare, cavare un sospiro, sospirare; — a walk, fare una passeggiata; — away, portare via, strappare; — down, portare giù; abbattere, [illegible]; — in, portare dentro, introdurre; — off, levare via, [illegible]; — out, portare fuora; — over, attrappare, truffare; — up, portare su; [illegible] **-ed**, ADJ.: cercato. **-er**, s.: [illegible] a cercare.
fete [illegible], s.: festa, *f.*
fet-ich (or **-ish**), s.: feticcio, *m.* **-ich-ism**, **-ishism**, s.: feticismo, *m.*
fetid, ADJ.: fetido, puzzolente, rancido, [illegible]. **-ness**, s.: fetore, puzzo, *m.*
fetlock, s.: barbetta (della pastoia), *f.*
fetter, TR.: mettere in catena. **-s**, S. PL.: catene, *f. pl.*; ferri, ceppi, *m. pl.*
fettle, TR.: (*prov.*) badaluccare.
fetus, s.: feto, embrione, *m.*
feud, s.: feudo, *m.*; contesa, altercazione, rissa, *f.* **-al**, ADJ.: feudale, di feudo; s.: feudo, *m.* **-atory**, s.: feudatario, *m.* **-ist**, s.: feudista, *m.*
fever 1, s.: febbre, *f.*: *be in a —*, *have a —*, aver la febbre, febbricitare; *strong —*, febbrone, *m.*; *slight —*, febbretta, febbricetta, *f.*; *acute —*, febbre acuta; *intermittent —*, febbre intermittente; *child-bed —*, febbre puerperale; *fit of —*, accesso di febbre. **fever** 2, TR.: dar la febbre, cagionare la febbre. **-et**, s.: febbretta, *f.* **-few**, s.: matricale, camamilla, *f.* **-ish**, ADJ.: febbricoso, febbroso. **-ishness**, s.: febbricità, *f.* **-ous**, **-y**, ADJ.: febbroso, febbricoso, febbrifero.
few, ADJ.: pochi (*f.* -che), piccolo numero [illegible], alcuni pochi: *very —*, assai [illegible] *in (a) — words*, in poche parole, [illegible] parola, in breve.
[illegible] = *fuel*.
few-er, ADJ.: meno, non tanto. **-ness**, s.: pochezza, *f.*, poco numero, *m.*
fey, TR.: purgare un fosso.
fiance, TR.: fidanzare.
fiants, S. PL.: sterco di volpe, *m.*
fiat, s.: decreto, ordine, *m.*
fib 1, s.: bugia, menzogna, *f.* **fib** 2, INTR.: dire bugie, mentire. **-ber**, s.: bugiardo, mentitore, *m.*
fi-bre, s.: fibra, *f.*, filamento, *m.* **-bril**, s.: fibretta, fibrilla, *f.* **-brous**, ADJ.: fibroso.
fibula, s.: fermaglio, *m.*; (*anat.*) fibula, *f.*
fickl-e, ADJ.: mutabile, incostante. **-eness**, s.: mutabilità, instanza, *f.* **-y**, ADV.: incostantemente.
fic-tile, ADJ.: fittile. **-tion**, s.: finzione; invenzione, *f.* **-tious**, **-titious**, ADJ.: fittizio, finto. **-titiously**, ADV.: fintamente. **-titiousness**, s.: finzione, invenzione, *f.* **-tive**, ADJ.: finto, fittizio, inventato.
fiddl-e 1, s.: violino, *m.*: *play on the —*, suonare il violino; *play (the) second —*, fare la parte secondaria. **fiddle** 2, TR.: suonare il violino. **-e-bridge**, s.: ponticello di violino, *m.* **-e-faddle**, s.: balocccheria, bagatella, *f.* **-er**, s.: suonatore di violino, violinista, *m.* **-e-stick**, s.: archetto di violino, *m.*: *—s!* oibò! trottole! **-e-string**, s.: corda da violino, *f.* **-ing**, ADJ.: frivolo, vano: — *business*, faccenda di poca importanza, *f.*
fidelity, s.: fedeltà, lealtà, onestà, *f.*
fidg-et 1, **-et** 1, INTR.: agitarsi, dimenarsi. **-et** 2, s.: agitazione, inquietezza, impazienza, *f.* **-ety**, ADJ.: inquieto, impaziente.
fidu-cial, ADJ.: fiduciale, affidato. **-cially**, ADV.: fiducialmente. **-ciary**, ADJ.: fiduciario, fiduciale; s.: fiduciario, depositario, fedecommissario, *m.*
fief, s.: feudo, *m.*
field, s.: campo, *m.*; campagna, *f.*; spazio, *m.*: — *of battle*, campo di battaglia, *m.*; *take the —*, uscire in campagna. **-battle**, s.: campo di battaglia, *m.*, giornata, *f.* **-bed**, s.: letto da campo; lettuccio, *m.* **-day**, s.: rassegna, *f.*, giorno di rivista, mostra, *f.* **-ed**, ADJ.: schierato, in ordinanza. **-fight**, s.: battaglia campale, *f.* **-marshal**, s.: maresciallo di campo, *m.* **-mouse**, s.: sorcio di campo, *m.* **-officer**, s.: ufficiale dello stato maggiore, *m.* **-piece**, s.: pezzo d'artiglieria, *m.* **-preacher**, s.: cappellano d'un reggimento, *m.* **-sports**, S. PL.: caccia, *f.* **-works**, S. PL.: opere, *f. pl.*, lavori, *m. pl.*
fiend, s.: nemico; demonio, spirito maligno, *m.* **-like**, ADJ.: diavolesco; ADV.: da nemico.

fierce, ADJ.: fiero, furioso; feroce; crudele; impetuoso, terribile. **-ly**, ADV.: fieramente, furiosamente; crudelmente. **-ness**, S.: fierezza, ferocità; violenza; crudeltà, *f.*
fier-iness, S.: ardore, fervore; impeto, *m.* **-y**, ADJ.: igneo; collerico, impetuoso, furioso, focoso.
fif-e 1, S.: piffero, *m.* **fif-e** 2, INTR.: fischiare. **-er**, S.: piffero, suonatore di piffero, *m.*
fif-teen, ADJ.: quindici. **-teenth**, ADJ.: quindecimo. **-th**, ADJ.: quinto: *four (etc.) —s*, quattro (ecc.) quinti. **-tieth**, ADJ.: cinquantesimo. **-thly**, ADV.: in quinto luogo. **-ty**, ADJ.: cinquanta.
fig 1, S.: fico, *m.*; bagattella, *f.*: *I care not a — for him*, mi rido di lui. **fig** 2, TR.: beffare, berteggiare.
figary†, S.: capriccio, *m.*, fantasia, *f.*
fight 1, S.: combattimento, *m.*, battaglia, *f.*; conflitto, *m.*, zuffa, mischia, *f.*: *cock-—*, combattimento di galli, *m.*; *sea-—*, combattimento navale, *m.* **fight** 2, IRR.; TR.: pugnare, contrastare; IRR.; INTR.: combattere, far battaglia: *— a duel*, duellare, fare duello; *— hand to hand*, battersi corpo a corpo; *— hard*, battersi gagliardamente; *— it out*, decidere colle armi; *— one's way*, farsi strada; *— a duel*, battersi in duello, duellare. **-er**, S.: combattitore; duellante, *m.* **-ing**, ADJ.: combattente; guerriero, bellico; S.: combattimento, *m.* **-ing-field**, S.: campo di battaglia, *m.* **-ing-man**, S.: combattente, *m.*
fig-leaf, S.: foglia di fico, *f.*
figment, S.: finzione; invenzione, *f.*
fig-pecker, S.: beccafico, *m.* **-tree**, S.: fico (albero), *m.*
figur-able, ADJ.: figurabile. **-ate**, ADJ.: figurato. **-ation**, S.: figuramento, figurare, *m.*; immaginazione, *f.* **-ative**, ADJ.: figurativo, allegorico. **-atively**, ADV.: figurativamente, figuratamente. **-e** 1, S.: figura, forma; immagine, *f.*; aspetto, *m.*; apparenza; eminenza, *f.*: *make some — in the world*, far figura nel mondo; *cut a pretty —*, far bella figura; *wax —*, figura di cera. **-e** 2, TR.: figurare; rappresentare: *— one's self*, figurarsi, immaginarsi. **-e-head**, S.: (*nav.*) pulena, *f.*, tagliamare, *m.*; (un) nulla, (uno) zero, *m.*
figwort, S.: scrofolaria, *f.*
filāceous, ADJ.: filamentoso, fibroso.
fila-ment, S.: filamento, *m.*, fibra, *f.* **-mĕntous**, ADJ.: filamentoso.
filanders, S. PL.: filandre (del falcone), *f. pl.*
filbert, S.: nocciuola, avellana, *f.* **-tree**, S.: nocciuolo, *m.*
filch, TR.: truffare, ingannare, fraudare. **-er**, S.: truffatore, giuntatore, furbo, *m.* **-ing**, S.: truffa, furberia, *f.*
file 1, S.: filo, *m.*; fila; lista, linea, *f.*; ordine, *m.*; lima, *f.*: *— of papers*, fascetto, mazzo (di scritti), *m.*; *— of pearls*, filo di perle, vezzo, *m.*; *— after —*, alla sfilata.
file 2, TR.: infilare; limare; pulire: *— off*, sfilare; marciare alla sfilata. **-cutter**, S.: fabbro di lime, *m.* **-dust**, S.: limatura, *f.*
filemot, S.: colore di foglia morta, *m.*
filer, S.: limatore, *m.*
fil-ial, ADJ.: filiale, di figliuolo. **-ially**, ADV.: in modo filiale. **-iātion**, S.: filiazione; discendenza, *f.*
fili-granet†, **-grēe**, S.: filigrana, *f.*
filing, S.: (il) limare; **-s**, PL.: limatura, *f.*; (*leg.*) deposito, *m.*; presentazione d' una domanda, *f.*
fill 1, S.: sufficienza, abbondanza, *f.*: *eat one's —*, mangiare a crepapelle, satollarsi. **fill** 2, TR.: empiere, empire; saziare; versare; INTR.: empiersi, riempirsi: *— up*, compire; colmare; rimpiazzare; *— to overflowing*, colmare; *— a place*, coprire una carica; *— a glass*, empire un bicchiere. **-er**, S.: ingombro; caricatore, *m.*
fillet 1, S.: banda; striscia, *f.*; (*arch.*) astragalo; *— of veal*, filetto, lombo di vitello, *m.*, coscia di vitello, *f.* **fillet** 2, TR.: bendare; ornare d' un tondino.
fillibeg, S.: spezie di gonnella, *f.*
filling, ADJ.: che sazia, che satolla, saziévole; S.: empiere, *m.*
fillip 1, S.: buffetto, biscottino, *m.* **fillip** 2, TR.: dare un biscottino.
filly, S.: cavalla giovane, cavallina, *f.*, puledra, *f.*
film 1, S.: membrana, pellicina, pellicola, buccia, *f.* **film** 2, TR.: coprire d' una pellicola. **-y**, ADJ.: membranoso.
filter 1, S.: filtro, colatoio, *m.* **filter** 2, TR.: colare, filtrare; purificare. **-ing**, ADJ.: filtrante, trapelante. **-stone**, S.: pietra da filtrare, *f.* **-paper**, S.: linguetta, *f.*
filth, S.: sporcizia, schifezza; spazzatura; corruzione, *f.* **-ily**, ADV.: sporcamente, schifamente, rozzamente. **-iness**, S.: sporcheria, schifezza, bruttura, lordura, *f.* **-y**, ADJ.: sporco, sucido, sordido.
fil-trate, TR.: filtrare, feltrare, colare. **-trātion**, S.: filtrazione, *f.*, colamento, *m*
fimbriate, TR.: orlare, fregiare.
fin, S.: ala; pinna (de' pesci), *f.*
finable, ADJ.: soggetto ad ammenda, degno di multa.
final, ADJ.: finale, ultimo, estremo. **-ly**, ADV.: finalmente, ultimamente.
finăn-ce, S.: finanza, rendita, entrata, *f.* **-cial**, ADJ.: relativo alle finanze. **-cier**, S.: finanziere, uffiziale delle finanze, *m.*

finary, S.: fucina, ferriera, *f.*
finch, S.: fringuello, *m.*
find, IRR.: TR.: trovare; scoprire, rinvenire; fornire, provvedere; INTR.: avvedersi, accorgersi: — *one's self*, trovarsi, sentirsi; — *fault with*, trovar a ridire a; riprendere, biasimare, criticare; — *one's way*, introdursi; — *out*, trovare, inventare, spiegare, scoprire. **-er**, S.: trovatore, scopritore, *m.* **-fault**, S.: censore, critico, *m.*
fine 1, ADJ.: fino, sottile; pulito; bello; elegante; puro; lucido, chiaro; acuto, affilato; squisito, eccellente; pomposo, grazioso; destro, abile, svelto; scaltrito, artificioso: — *young fellow*, bel giovinotto. **fine** 2, S.: multa, ammenda; conclusione, *f.*: *in* —, finalmente, in somma. **fine** 3, TR.: affinare; chiarare; purgare; condannare all' ammenda; INTR.: pagare l' ammenda. **-draw**, TR.: cucire, risarcire. **-drawer**, S.: cucitore, risarcitore, racconciatore, *m.* **-drawing**, S.: cucitura, *f.*, risarcimento, racconciamento, *m.* **-fingered**, ADJ.: abile, destro. **-ly**, ADV.: finamente, pulitamente; elegantemente; vagamente. **-ness**, S.: finezza; delicatezza; bellezza, *f.* **-er**, S.: affinatore, raffinatore, *m.* **fine-ry**, S.: ornamento; aggiustamento, *m.* **-spoken**, ADJ.: affettatamente civile. **-spun**, ADJ.: sottile.
finèsse, S.: artificio, *m.*, stratagemma, *f.*
finger 1, S.: dito, *m.*: *have a thing at one's —'s end*, saper una cosa su per le dita; *have a — in the pie*, esser complice nella cosa. **finger** 2, TR.: maneggiare, toccare. **-board**, S.: (*instr.*) tastatura, *f.* **-ed**, ADJ.: che ha le dita, dalle dita. **-ing**, S.: maneggiamento, toccamento, *m.* **-stall**, S.: fasciatura d' un dito, *m.*
fingle-fangle, S.: bagattella, chiappoleria, *f.*
finical, ADJ.: affettato, ritroso, schifo, studiato. **-ly**, ADV.: con affettazione. **-ness**, S.: affettazione; schifiltà; ritrosia, *f.*
fining, S.: multare; chiarificare, *m.*, purificazione, *f.*
finish 1, S.: fine; compimento, *m.* **finish** 2, TR.: finire, terminare; compire: — *off*, ultimare, dare gli ultimi tocchi a. **-ed**, ADJ.: finito, perfetto; compito; terminato. **-er**, S.: finitore, compitore; giustiziere, boia, *m.* **-ing**, ADJ.: che finisce, che mette fine a: — *blow*, colpo di grazia.
finite, ADJ.: limitato, determinato. **-less**, ADJ.: immenso, illimitato. **-ly**, ADV.: finitamente, con limitazione. **-ness**, S.: limitazione, *f.*, limiti, *f. pl.*
fin-less, ADJ.: senza pinne. **-like**, ADJ.: fatto a modo di pinna. **-ny**, ADJ.: fornito di pinne. **-toed**, ADJ.: di piè membranoso, palmipede.
fipple, S.: zaffo (d' un flauto), *m.*
fir, S.: abete, *m.* **-cone**, S.: pigna, *f.*
fire 1, S.: fuoco; incendio; abbruciamento, *m.*: *St. Anthony's* —, risipola, *f.*: *make a* —, far fuoco; *take* —, pigliar fuoco, cominciare ad ardere. **fire** 2, TR.: mettere il fuoco; infiammare; INTR.: tirare; dar fuoco. **-arms**, S. PL.: armi da fuoco, *f. pl.* **-ball**, S.: granata, bomba; meteora, *f.* **-brand**, S.: tizzone, *m.* **-brush**, S.: piccola scopa da fuoco, *f.* **-company**, S.: compagnia di pompieri, *f.* **-drake**, S.: dragone volante, *m.* **-engine**, S.: tromba, pompa da fuoco, *f.* **-fan**, S.: parafuoco, *m.* **-fork**, S.: forcone, attizzatoio, *m.* **-grate**, S.: grata del focolare, *f.* **-kiln**, S.: fornello, *m.*, fornace (da fondere), *f.* **-lock**, S.: archibuso, schioppo, *m.* **-man**, S.: pompiere; (*rail.*) fuochista, *m.* **-new**, ADJ.: giusto uscito del fuoco; nuovo. **-ordeal**, S.: prova del fuoco, *f.* **-pan**, S.: focone dell' armi, *m.* **-place**, S.: focolare, *m.* **-proof**, ADJ.: a pruova di fuoco. **fire-r**, S.: incendiario, *m.* **-room**, S.: camera con un cammino, *f.* **-screen**, S.: parafuoco, *m.* **-ship**, S.: brulotto, *m.* **-shovel**, S.: paletta da fuoco, *f.* **-side**, S.: focolare; cammino, *m.* **-stick**, S.: tizzone, tizzo, *m.* **-stone**, S.: focolare, *m.*, pirite, *f.* **-tongs**, S. PL.: mollette, *f. pl.* **-wood**, S.: legna, *f. pl.* **-work**, S.: fuoco artifiziale, *m.* **-worker**, S.: facitore di fuochi artifiziali; ingegnere, *m.*
firing, S.: scarica, *f.*; legna†, *f. pl.*
firk†, TR.: battere, sferzare, frustare.
firkin, S.: quarteruola, *f.* (misura).
firm 1, ADJ.: fermo, fisso, stabile, costante: *the — land*, il continente. **firm** 2, S.: associazione (di mercanti), firma, *f.* **firm** 3, TR.: fermare, fissare; confermare; stabilire.
firma-ment, S.: firmamento, cielo, *m.* **-mĕntal**, ADJ.: del firmamento, celeste.
firm-ly, ADV.: fermamente; con istabilità. **-ness**, S.: fermezza; costanza, *f.*
first, ADJ.: primo; principale; ADV.: primieramente, in primo luogo: *in the — place*, in primo luogo, primieramente; *at — sight*, a prima vista, subito; — *or last*, presto o tardi; *at* —, alla prima; *at — blush*, sul primo. **-born**, S.: primogenito, *m.* **-cousin**, S.: cugino germano, *m.* **-fruits**, S. PL.: frutti primaticci, *m. pl.*, primizie, *f. pl.* **-ling**, S.: primo nato, *m.*
fir-tree, S.: abete, *m.*
fisc, S.: fisco, *m.* **-al**, ADJ.: fiscale.
fish 1, S.: pesce, *m.*; (*nav.*) lapazza, *f.*

fish 2, TR.: pescare; (*nav.*) traversare, capponare (l' ancora): — *a mast*, lapazzare un pennone. **-bone**, S.: spina di pesce, *f.* **-day**, S.: giorno magro, *m.* **-er**, **-erman**, S.: pescatore, *m.* **-er-woman**, S.: pescivendola, *f.* **-ery**, S.: pesca, *f.*; pescare, *m.* **-ful**, ADJ.: pieno di pesci. **-gig**, S.: (*nav.*) fiocina, *f.* **-hook**, S.: amo, *m.* **-ing**, S.: pesca, pescagione, *f.* **-ing-boat**, S.: barca di pescatore, *f.* **-ing-gear**, S.: attrezzi pescherecci, *m. pl.* **-ing-line**, S.: lenza, *f.* **-ing-place**, S.: pescheria, *f.* **-ing-rod**, S.: canna da pescare, verga dell' amo, *f.* **-ing-spear**, S.: rampone, *m.* **-kettle**, S.: navicella da pesce, *f.* **-market**, S.: pescheria, *f.* **-meal**, S.: dieta di pesce; cattiva cera, *f.* **-monger**, S.: pescivendolo, *m.* **-pond**, S.: vivaio, *m.*, peschiera, *f.* **-wife**, **-woman**, S.: pescivendola, *f.* **-y**, ADJ.: abbondante di pesci.

fisk†, INTR.: correre qua e là; sfuggire la scuola.

fi-ssile, ADJ.: fissile; che può spaccarsi. **-ssion**, S.: spacamento, *m.* **-ssure**, S.: fessura, spaccatura, crepatura, *f.*

fist, S.: pugno, *m.* **-icuffs**, S. PL.: percosse col pugno, pugna, *f. pl.*: *go to* —, fare alle pugna.

fistu-la, S.: fistola, *f.* **-lar**, ADJ.: fistolare. **-lous**, ADJ.: fistoloso.

fit 1, ADJ.: idoneo, atto, capace; convenevole, giusto, proporzionato; apparecchiato, pronto: *make one's self — for*, prepararsi; *be — to*, esser in istato di. **fit** 2, S.: accesso, attacco, parossismo; capriccio, *m.*, fantasia, *f.*, ghiribizzo, *m.*: *ague*, — accesso di febbre terzana, *m.*; — *of gout*, attacco di podagra, *m.*; — *of love*, trasporto d' amore, *m.*; — *of madness*, pazzia; frenesia, *f.*; *by —s*, a scosse; qualche volta, di tempo in tempo; *by —s and starts*, a stento, a spilluzzico. **fit** 3, TR.: aggiustare, adattare, accomodare; preparare; assortire; INTR.: accomodarsi; convenire: — *out*, provvedere, fornire; armare; — *up*, addobbare, guarnire.

fitch, S.: veccia, *f.*: *wild* —, veccia salvatica, *f.* **-'ew**, S.: puzzola, *f.*

fitful, ADJ.: variabile; irregolare; incerto.

fit-ly, ADV.: convenevolmente, giustamente, attamente. **-ment**, S.: adattamento, *m.*; conformità; convenienza, *f.* **-ness**, S.: convenienza; attitudine, proporzione, *f.* **-table**†, ADJ.: convenevole. **-tedness**, S.: attitudine, convenienza, *f.* **-ter**, S.: che adatta; fetta, *f.* **-ting**, ADJ.: convenevole; giusto, idoneo; S.: attezza; convenevolezza, *f.*: — *out*, allestire, equipaggiare, armamento, *m.*

five, ADJ.: cinque: — *hundred*, cinquecento; — *thousand*, cinquemila. **-fold**, ADJ.: quintuplo. **-leaved**, ADJ.: cinquefoglio. **-s**, S. PL.: vivole, *f. pl.*

fix, TR.: fissare, affissare, piantare; stabilire; INTR.: fissarsi; coagularsi; determinarsi, risolvere; stabilire la sua dimora: — *a business*, terminare un negozio; — *a day*, appuntare un giorno, convenire del giorno; — *upon*, scegliere, eleggere; — *the eyes upon one*, fissare gli occhi in alcuno. **-ation**, S.: fissazione, *f.*; stabilimento, *m.* **-ed**, ADJ.: fisso, affissato; destinato, determinato. **-edly**, ADV.: fissamente; certamente. **-edness**, S.: stabilità; attenzione, applicazione, *f.* **-ity**, S.: fissezza, *f.* **-ture**, S.: fermezza, *f.*; mobile, *m.*

fizgig, S.: rampone, *m.*; fiocina, *f.*

flabby, ADJ.: floscio, vizzo, moscio.

flac-cid, ADJ.: flaccido, moscio. **-cidity**, **-cidness**, S.: flaccidità; fiacchezza, rilassazione, *f.*

flacker, INTR.: (*prov.*) sfavillare.

flag 1, S.: bandiera, *f.*; stendardo; ghiaggiulo, *m.*: *union* —, bandiera dell' unione; — *of truce*, bandiera bianca; *haul down the* —, ammaniare (abbassare) la bandiera; *hoist the* —, issare la bandiera. **flag** 2, TR.: lasciare cadere; lastricare; INTR.: cadere; sgomentarsi; avvilirsi; languidire. **-broom**, S.: scopa di giunchi, *f.*

flagel-late, TR.: flagellare. **-lation**, S.: flagellazione, *f.*

flageolet, S.: zufolo, *m.*

flag-giness, S.: allentamento; rilassamento, *m.*; debolezza, *f.* **-gy**, ADJ.: fiacco, floscio, molle; insipido.

flagitious, ADJ.: flagizioso, scellerato. **-ness**, S.: scelleratezza, ribalderia, malvagità, *f.*

flag-officer, S.: caposquadra, *m.*

flagon, S.: fiasco, *m.*, boccetta, *f.*

flagran-ce, **-cy**, S.: ardore, fervore, fuoco, *m.* **-t**, ADJ.: ardente, fervente, focoso; famoso, notorio. **-tly**, ADV.: ardentemente; notoriamente.

flagship, S.: ammiraglio, *m.* (nave).

flail, S.: coreggiato, *m.*

flak-e 1, fiocco, *m.*; scintilla; lamina, *f.*: — *of ice*, ghiacciuolo, *m.*; — *of wool*, fiocco di lana. **-e** 2, INTR.: rompersi in lamine, spelarsi. **-y**, ADJ.: fioccoso, laminoso.

flam 1, S.: menzogna, bugia, favola, ciarla, carota, *f.* **flam** 2, TR.: ingannare con una bugia, deludere.

flambeau -bo, S.: face, fiaccola, *f.*; torchio, *m.*

flame 1, S.: fiamma, *f.*; fervore; amo[r] *m.*: *little* —, fiammata; *be in a* —, fi[am]meggiare; *set all in* —, mett[ere] ...

fuoco e fiamma. **flame** 2, INTR.: fiammeggiare; ardere. **-coloured**, ADJ.: di color di fiamma.

flāmen, S.: (*myth.*) flamine, *m.*

flāming, ADJ.: fiammeggiante, ardente.

flamingo, S.: fenicottero, *m.*

flăm-mable†, ADJ.: infiammabile, accendibile. **-meous**†, ADJ.: fiammesco, di fiamma. **-mivomous**, ADJ.: vomitante fiamme. **-y**, ADJ.: fiammante; ardente.

flanconāde, S.: fiancata, *f.*

flănk 1, S.: fianco, lato, *m.*: *in the* —, nel fianco. **flank** 2, TR.: fiancheggiare, fiancare. **-er**, S.: (*fort.*) fianco, *m.* **-ed**, ADJ.: fiancuto.

flănnel, S.: flanella, *f.*: — *shirt*, camiciuola, *f.*; corpetto di flanella, *m.*

flăp 1, S.: lembo, *m.*; botta, percossa, *f.*, colpo, *m.*: — *of a coat*, falda d' un vestito, *f.*; — *of the ear*, oreglia, *f.*; orecchio esteriore, *m.*; — *of a shoe*, orecchio d' una scarpa, *m.* **flap** 2, TR.: battere, percuotere: — *the wings*, battere le ale; — *down*, abbassarsi. **-dish**, S.: tavola da ripiegarsi, *f.* **-jack**, S.: torta di mele, *f.*

flăr-e, INTR.: splendere con luce transitoria; consumarsi, struggersi. **-ing**, ADJ.: abbagliante, splendente.

flăsh 1, S.: fiamma subita; vampa, *f.*; baleno; lampo, *m.*: — *of the eye*, occhiata, *f.*, sguardo, *m.*; — *of fire*, vampa, *f.*; — *of lightning*, baleno, lampo, *m.*; — *of mirth*, effusione di gioia, *f.*; — *of wit*, arguzia, *f.*; concetto spiritoso, *m.* **flash** 2, TR.: schizzare, zaccherare; spruzzare; INTR.: risplendere, lampeggiare, scintillare. **-er**, S.: uomo superficiale, *m.* **-ily**, ADV.: di poca cognizione. **-ing**, S.: vivezza subita di lume, *f.*; splendore; spruzzo (d' acqua), *m.* **-y**, ADJ.: frivolo, insipido; pomposo.

flăsk, S.: fiasco, *m.*, fiaschetta, *f.* **-et**, S.: paniera, cesta, *f.*; canestro, *m.*

flăt 1, ADJ.: piatto, spianato; sventato, insipido; franco, *f.*; S.: pianura, *f.*; paese piano; (*nav.*) basso fondo, *m.*, secca, *f.*; (*mus.*) bimmolle, *m.*: — *discourse*, discorso insipido, *m.*; — *drink*, bevanda sventata, *f.*; — *lie*, bugia manifesta, *f.*; — *nose*, naso schiacciato, *m.*; — *side*, piatto (d' una spada), *m.*; — *voice*, voce di basso, *f.*; *give a — denial*, ricusare nettamente; *grow* —, indebolirsi; *lay* —, appianare; demolire; *lie — upon the ground*, stendersi per terra. **flat** 2, TR.: spianare, appianare; sventare; INTR.: appianarsi; insipidire. **-bottomed**, ADJ.: (*nav.*) col fondo piano. **-nosed**, ADJ.: camuso. **-ly**, ADV.: in no, sulla terra; schiettamente. **-ness**, pianezza; insipidezza; debolezza, *f.* **ed**, ADJ.: camuso, rincagnato. **-ted**, ADJ.: spianato, appianato. **-ten**, TR.: appianare; abbattere; INTR.: appianarsi; insipidire. **-tening**, S.: stiacciatura, *f.*

flătter 1, S.: martello, martellino, *m.* **flatter** 2, TR.: adulare, lusingare. **-er**, S.: adulatore, lusingatore, *m.* **-ing**, ADJ.: lusinghevole; piacevole. **-ingly**, ADV.: piacevolmente, dolcemente. **-y**, S.: adulazione, lusinga, *f.*, lusingamento, *m.*

flăttish, ADJ.: alquanto piatto; insipido.

flăt-ulency, S.: flatuoistà, *f.* **-ulent**, ADJ.: flatuoso, ventoso; frivolo. **-uŏsity**, S.: flatuosità, ventosità, *f.* **-uous**, ADJ.: flatuoso, ventoso.

flătwise, ADV.: in piano, di piatto, sulla terra.

flăunt 1, S.: pompa, *f.* **flaunt** 2, INTR.: pompeggiare, pavoneggiarsi. **-ing**, ADJ.: attillato, acconcio, albagioso, pomposo.

flăvour 1, S.: sapore gustoso, gusto gradevole, odore, *m.* **flavour** 2, TR.: dare un gusto aromatico, dar fragranza, render saporito. **-ous**, ADJ.: odorante, saporito. **-less**, ADJ.: senza aroma (*or* profumo), insipido.

flăw 1, S.: fessura, crepatura, *f.*; difetto, errore, *m.*; invalidità; commozione, *f.*, tumulto, *m.*: *find a — in*, trovar un diletto in; — *of wind*, soffio, *m.*; folata di vento, sbuffo di vento, *m.* **flaw** 2, TR.: rompere, crepare, spezzare; danneggiare, violare. **-less**, ADJ.: senza fessure; senza difetto, perfetto. **-y**, ADJ.: crepato, fesso; defettuoso, imperfetto.

flăx 1, S.: lino, *m.*: *dress* —, scotolare il lino. **-comb**, S.: scotola, *f.* **-dresser**, S.: che scotola il lino, ecc. **-en**, ADJ.: di lino; biondo. **-field**, S.: lineto, *m.* **-finch**, S.: fanello, *m.* **-seed**, S.: linseme, *m.* **-y** = *flaxen*.

flāy, TR.: scorticare. **-er**, S.: scorticatore, *m.* **-ing**, S.: scorticamento, scorticare, *m.*

flēa 1, S.: pulce, *f.* **flea** 2, TR.: torre le pulci, spulciare. **-bane**, S.: pulicaria, *f.* **-bite**, **-biting**, S.: morsicatura di pulce, *f.* **-bitten**, ADJ.: morsicato da pulci.

flēak† 1, S.: fiocco, *m.*; ciocca, *f.*

flēam, S.: lancetta, *f.*

flĕcker, TR.: macchiare; pezzare.

flĕction = *flexion*.

flĕdge 1, ADJ.: piumato, coperto di piume. **fledge** 2, TR.: coprire di piume; dar delle ale; INTR.: cominciare a metter le piume.

flēe, IRR.; INTR.: fuggire; voltare le calcagna; — *from*, scappare da.

flēece-e 1, S.: tosone, vello, *m.* **-e** 2, TR.: tondere; pelare; scorticare. **-er**, S.: tosatore; scorticatore, *m.* **-y**, ADJ.: lanuto, lanoso.

flēer 1, S.: derisione, beffa, *f.* **fleer** 2, INTR.: deridere; schernire, beffeggiare, beffare. **-er**, S.: deriditore, beffatore, *m.* **-ing**, ADJ.: sfacciato; S.: viso arcigno, *m.*

flēet 1, ADJ.: presto, veloce; spedito; leggiero. **fleet** 2, flotta; armata di mare, *f.*; golfo, *m.*, baia, *f.* **fleet** 3, IRR.; TR.: passare leggiermente; toccare; INTR.: scorrere; svanire: — *milk*, levar il fior del latte. **-ing**, ADJ.: transitorio, passeggiero. **-ly**, ADV.: con velocità, agilmente, leggiermente. **-ness**, S.: celerità, velocità, prestezza, *f.*

flĕsh 1, S.: carne; polpa; (*fig.*) carnalità, *f.*: *gather* —, ingrassare; *go the way of all* —, morire; *take* —, incarnarsi. **flesh** 2, indurire; animare, incoraggiare; saziare. **-broth**, S.: brodo di carne, *m.* **-colour**, S.: colore di carne, *m.*; carnagione, *f.* **-coloured**, ADJ.: colore di carne, incarnato. **-day**, S.: giorno grasso, *m.* **-diet**, S.: cibo di carne, *m.* **-ful**, ADJ.: carnoso, carnuto. **-hook**, S.: forcina, forchetta, *f.* **-iness**, S.: carnosità; pinguedine, *f.* **-less**, ADJ.: magro, macilento, smunto. **-liness**, S.: carnalità; sensualità, *f.* **-ly**, ADJ.: carnale; sensuale, animale. **-meat**, S.: carne (da mangiare), *f.* **-pot**, S.: ramino, *m.*, pentola, *f.* **-quake**†, S.: tremito del corpo, *m.* **-y**, ADJ.: carnoso; polposo.

fle-x, TR.: flettere†, piegare. **-xibility**, S.: flessibilità, arrendevolezza; compiacenza, *f.* **-xible**, ADJ.: flessibile, pieghevole, arrendevole; cortese. **-xibleness** = *flexibility*. **-xion**, S.: flessione; piegatura, *f.* **-xor**, S.: (*anat.*) flessore, *m.* **-xuous**, ADJ.: flessuoso, pieghevole; variabile. **-xure**, S.: flessura; curvatura, *f.*

flicker, INTR.: svolazzare, dimenarsi.

flier, S.: bilanciere; fuggitore, fuggitivo, *m.*

flight, S.: fuga; volata, *f.*, stormo, *m.*: — *of arrows*, tirata di frecce, *f.*; — *of birds*, stormo d' uccelli, *m.*; — *of folly*, stravaganza, sciocchezza, *f.*: — *of genius*, concetto spiritoso, *m.*; — *of steps*, terrazzo, *m.*; loggia, *f.*; *take* —, spiccar il volo; *take to* (*the*) —, fuggirsene, scappare. **-iness**, S.: leggerezza; irregolarità, *f.* **-shot**, S.: frecciata, *f.* **-y**, ADJ.: fuggitivo, veloce; fantastico.

flimflam†, S.: baloccheria, frascheria, bagattella, *f.*

flim-siness, S.: fiacchezza; leggerezza, trivialità, *f.* **-sy**, ADJ.: fiacco, moscio, floscio; triviale: — *stuff*, stoffa floscia.

flinch, INTR.: sbigottirsi; ritirarsi; tralasciare, desistere; abbandonare. **-er**, S.: codardo, pusillanimo, *m.*

flinder, S.: scheggia, *f.*; frammento, *m.* **-mouse** †, S.: pipistrello, *m.*

fling 1, S.: colpo, *m.*, botta; beffa, burla, *f.* **fling** 2 (*flung*; *flung*), IRR.; TR.: gettare, buttare; vibrare; lanciare; spandere; INTR.: calcitrare: — *at*, lanciare; avventarsi; — *away*, ributtare; dissipare; involarsi; — *down*, buttar giù, atterrare; rovinare, disfare; — *off*, schivare; cacciare; — *out*, buttare fuori; ostinarsi; — *up*, abbandonare; ritirarsi. **-er**, S.: gettatore; beffatore, *m.*

flint, S.: pietra focaia, selce, *f.*; ciottolo, *m.* **-glass**, S.: vetro di rocca, *m.* **-hearted**, ADJ.: spietato, crudele. **-stone**, S.: selce, *f.* **-y**, ADJ.: selcioso; spietato, inesorabile.

flip, S.: bevanda cordiale, *f.*

flippan-cy, S.: ciarla, ciarleria, *f.* **-t**, ADJ.: vivace, allegro; svegliato, ciarliero: — *discourse*, discorso vano, *m.*; — *person*, persona linguacciuta, *f.*; — *tongue*, lingua sciolta, *f.* **-tly**, ADV.: spensieratamente.

flirt 1, S.: moto celere ed elastico, *m.*; civetta, sfacciatella, *f.* **flirt** 2, TR.: lanciare, gettare; far muovere; INTR.: muoversi; beffeggiare; civettare. **-ation**, S.: civetteria, f.

flit, INTR.: svolazzare, fuggire; esser instabile.

flitch, S.: lardone; costereccio di porco, *m.*

flitter, S.: cencio; straccio; brandello, *m.* **-mouse**, S.: pipistrello, vipistrello, *m.*, nottola, *f.*

flit-tiness†, S.: leggerezza, instabilità, *f.* **-ting**, S.: offesa; colpa; fuggita, *f.* **-ty**†, ADJ.: instabile, variabile.

flōat 1, S.: traino, fodero di legname, *m.*; zatta, *f.*; sughero, *m.* **float** 2, TR.: immergere, inondare; INTR.: fiottare, galleggiare, ondeggiare; star sospeso. **-boat**, S.: zatta, zattera, chiatta, *f.* **-board**, S.: pala (di ruota di mulino), *f.* **-ing-bridge**, S.: ponte di barche, pontone, *m.* **-y**, ADJ.: galleggiante, a galla.

flŏck 1, S.: banda, truppa; turba: gregge, mandra, *f.*; fiocco, *m.*: — *of wool*, bioccolo di lana, *m.* **flock** 2, INTR.: affollarsi, adunarsi attorno. **-bed**, S.: letto di borra, *m* **-ing**, S.: folla di popolo, concorso, *m.*

flŏg, TR.: frustrare, sferzare. **-ging**, S.: fustigazione, flagellamento, *m.*, bastonata, *f.*

flŏod 1, S.: inondazione, *f.*, diluvio; flusso. torrente, *m.*: — *of tears*, torrente di lagrime, *m.* **flood** 2, TR.: inondare; sommergere. **-gate**, S.: cateratta; imposta, *f.*

flŏŏk, S.: uncino, raffio dell' ancora, *m.*, patta, *f.*

fea-sibility, S.: agevolezza a farsi, possibilità, *f.* **-sible**, ADJ.: fattevole, fattibile, agevole a farsi. **-sibleness** = *feasibility*. **-sibly**, ADV.: praticabilmente, in modo possibile.

fēast 1, S.: festino, banchetto, *m.*; festa, festività, *f.* **feast** 2, TR.: regalare; INTR.: festeggiare, banchettare. **-er**, S.: che banchetta, festeggiante, *m.* **-ful**, ADJ.: festoso, delizioso, grato. **-ing**, S.: festini, *m. pl.*

fēat 1, S.: fatto, atto, *m.*, azione, *f.* **feat** 2, ADJ.: destro, svelto. **-eous†**, ADJ.: pulito; destro, accorto. **-eously†**, ADV.: pulitamente; destramente.

fĕather 1, S.: piuma, penna, *f.*; ornamento, *m.*; bagatella, *f.*: *birds of a — flock together*, ogni simile ama il suo simile; *shed its —s*, mutar le penne; *show the white —*, mostrarsi vigliacco. **feather** 2, TR.: coprire di piume; abbellire, ornare; INTR.: camminare come un gallo: — *one's nest*, arricchirsi. **-bed**, S.: letto di piume, *m.*, coltrice, *f.* **-broom**, S.: mazzo di piume, *m.* **-ed**, ADJ.: guernito di piume. **-footed**, ADJ.: co' piedi alati, piumate. **-less**, ADJ.: senza piume, spiumato. **-seller**, S.: mercante di piume, *m.* **-y**, ADJ.: coprito di piume, vestito di piume.

fēat-ly†, ADJ.: agilmente, destramente, gentilmente. **-ness†**, S.: agilità, destrezza; pulitezza, gentilezza, *f.*

fēature 1, S.: lineamento, *m.*; fattezza, faccia, *f.* **feature** 2, INTR.: aver somiglianza nelle fattezze. **-d**, ADJ.: dalle fattezza, che ha il viso, dalla faccia.

fēaze, TR.: storcere, svolgere.

fĕbri-fuge, S.: febbrifugo, *m.* **-le**, ADJ.: febbrile, di febbre.

Fĕbruary, S.: febbraio, *m.*

fē-ces, S. PL.: feccia, *f.*; escrementi, *m. pl.*

fĕcu-lence, **-lency**, S.: torbidezza, *f.* **-lent**, ADJ.: feccioso.

fĕc-und, ADJ.: fecondo, fertile. **-undā-tion**, S.: fecondazione, *f.*, fecondare, *m.* **-ŭndify**, TR.: fecondare, fertilizzare. **-ŭndity**, S.: fecondità, fertilità; copia, *f.*

fĕdary†, S.: associato, confederato, compagno, *m.*

fĕder-al, ADJ.: alleato, federativo. **-alism**, S.: federalismo, *m.* **-alist**, S.: federalista, *m.* **-ary**, S.: confederato, alleato; complice, *m.* **-ate**, ADJ.: confederato, collegato. **-ātion**, S.: confederazione, *f.* **-ative**, ADJ.: federativo; confederato.

fēe 1, S.: feudo, *m.*; ricompenza, sportula; mercede, paga, *f.*, onorario, salario, *m.*: *—s*, guadagno casuale, *m.*, sportule, *f. pl.*; — *simple*, franco allodio, feudo assoluto. **fee** 2, TR.: pagare, rimunerare; corrompere.

fēebl-e 1, ADJ.: debole, infermo, fiacco: *grow —*, divenire debole, affievolirsi. **-e** 2, TR.: indebolire, affievolire. **-minded**, ADJ.: debole di mente, imbecille. **-eness**, S.: debolezza, infermità, *f.* **-y**, ADV.: debolmente, fievolmente.

fēed 1, ADJ.: pagato, remunerato; corrotto. **feed** 2, S.: nutrimento, *m.*; pastura, *f.* **feed** 3 (*fed*; *fed*), INTR.; TR.: nutrire, pascere; alimentare; conservare; dilettare; INTR.: nutrirsi; pascersi; divenir grasso, ingrassare: — *upon*, nutrirsi di; — *the fire*, conservare il fuoco. **-er**, S.: nutritore, mangiatore; ghiottone; fautore, *m.* **-ing**, S.: nutrimento; pascolo, *m.*: *high —*, buona cera, buona tavola, *f.*

fēe-farm, S.: censo enfiteutico, *m.*

fēel 1, S.: tatto, tocco, *m.* **feel** 2, INTR.; TR.: essere sensibile, essere sensitivo; — *cold*, essere freddo; — *the pulse*, toccare (tastare) il polso; — *soft*, esser morbido al tatto; — *one's way*, andare a tastoni; essere circospetto; — *for*, compiangere. **-er**, S.: toccatore, tastatore, *m.*; (*ent.*) antenna, *f.*; tentacolo, *m.* **-ing**, ADJ.: sensibile; sensitivo; S.: tatto; sentimento, *m.* **-ingly**, ADV.: sensibilmente; vivamente.

fēe-simple, S.: feudo assoluto, *m.*

fēetless, ADJ.: senza piedi.

fēign, TR.: fingere, simulare; inventare; INTR.: infingersi, immaginarsi, rappresentarsi; esitare, dubitare. **-ed**, ADJ.: finto, simulato, dissimulato; inventato: — *story*, finzione; favola, *f.*; — *treble*, (*mus.*) falsetto; soprano, *m.* **-edly**, ADV.: fintamente, falsamente. **-edness**, S.: finzione; falsezza, *f.*, inganno, *m.* **-er**, S.: simulatore; inventore, *m.* **-ing**, S.: fingimento; travestimento, *m.* **-ingly**, ADV.: fintamente.

fēint, S.: finzione; (*fenc.*) finta, *f.*

felici-tate, TR.: felicitare; congratularsi. **-tātion**, S.: congratulazione, *f.* **-tous**, ADJ.: felice, fortunato; pellegrino, squisito. **-tously**, ADV.: felicemente, prosperamente. **-ty**, S.: felicità, prosperità, *f.*

fēline, ADJ.: felino, di gatto.

fĕll 1, ADJ.: barbaro, inumano, fiero. **fell** 2, S.: pelle, pelliccia, *f.*; cuoio, *m.* **fell** 3, TR.: atterrare: abbattere; tagliare. **-able**, ADJ.: buono a tagliare (alberi). **-er**, S.: falegname; taglialegna, *m.* **-ing**, S.: taglio, tagliamento, atterramento, *m.*

bia, *f.*

fĕllọe = *felly* 1.

fĕllọw 1, s.: compagno, compagnone; socio, camerata, collega; membro (d' un collegio), uomo, individuo; gaglioffo, *m.*: *base* —, furfante, scellerato, *m.*; *gay* —, giovialone; *good* —, buon diavolo; *old* —, vecchiardo, vecchiaccio, *m.*; *queer* —, goffo, sguaiato; *saucy* —, impertinente; *stupid* —, stupidaccio; *my dear* —, mio caro; *young* —, giovane, giovanaccio, *m.* **fellow** 2, TR.: appaiare, assortire; accoppiare. **-citizen**, s.: concittadino, *m.* **-commoner**, s.: compagno di tavola, *m.* **-creature**, s.: simile, *m.* **-feeling**, s.: simpatia, *f.* **-heir**, s.: coerede, *m.* **-helper**, s.: coadiutore, *m.* **-labourer**, s.: collaboratore, cooperatore, *m.* **-like**, ADJ.: da socio. **-prisoner**, s.: compagno della prigione, *m.* **-servant**, s.: compagno nel servire, *m.* **-ship**, s.: compagnia, società; intimità, *f.* **-soldier**, s.: compagno in guerra, compagno d' armi, *m.* **-student**, s: condiscepolo, *m.* **-sufferer**, s.: compagno in miseria, *m.* **-traveller**, s.: compagno di viaggio, *m.* **-wọrt**, s.: (*bot.*) genziana, *f.*

fĕlly 1, s.: razzo (circulo) di ruota, *m.*

felly 2, ADV.: crudelmente, barbaramente.

fĕlọ-dẹ-sẹ, s.: uccisore di sè stesso, *m.*

fĕl-ọn, s.: fellone, malfattore; (*med.*) panereccio, *m.* **-ōnious**, ADJ.: fellonesco, crudele, inumano. **-ōniously**, ADV.: fellonescamente, da fellone. **-ọny**, s.: fellonia; scelleratezza, *f.*

fĕlt 1, s.: feltro, *m.*; borra; tosatura, *f.* **felt** 2, TR.: feltrare. **-ẹr**, TR.: imbrogliare, sconciare. **-ing**, s.: feltrare, *m.* **-maker**, s.: feltraiuolo, *m.*

fẹlŭcca, s.: felucca, *f.*

fēmạle, ADJ.: femmineo, femminino, di femmina; s.: femmina, *f.*

fem-inălity, s.: femminilità, *f.*

fĕminine, ADJ.: femminino, femminesco.

fĕmọral, ADJ.: femorale.

fĕn, s.: palude, pantano, *m.*, maremma, *f.*

fĕnce 1, s.: siepe, chiusura; difesa, *f.*, riparo; schermo, *m.*: — *of pales*, palificata, palizzata, *f.* **-e** 2, TR.: chiudere; palificare; difendere, proteggere; INTR.: schermire. **-eless**, ADJ.: senza chiusura, aperto. **-ẹr**, s.: schermitore, *m.* **-ible**, ADJ.: difendevole. **-ing**, s.: scherma, arte della scherma, *f.* **-ing-master**, s.: maestro di scherma, *m.* **-ing-school**, s.: scuola di scherma, *f.*

fĕn-cress, s.: crescione di paludi, *m.* **-cricket**, s.: grillotalpa, *f.*

fĕnd, TR.: parare, schivare, scansare; sfuggire; INTR.: difendersi; disputare; ragionare; altercare. **-ẹr**, s.: gardata, *f.*: **—s**, (*nav.*) pagliette, *f. pl.*

fĕn-duck†, s.: anatra salvatica, *f.*

fĕnẹrạte, INTR.: usureggiare.

fĕn-fowl, s.: pollo di paludi, *m.* **-land**, s.: terreno paludoso, *m.*

fĕnnel, s.: finocchio, *m.*

fĕnny, ADJ.: paludoso, pantanoso.

feod *fūd*, s.: feudo, *m.* **-al**, ADJ.: feudale, di feudo. **-ary**, **-atọry**, s.: feudatario, *m.*

fĕoff, TR.: infeudare. **-ēe**, s.: donatario, *m.* **-ẹr**, s: donatore, *m.* **-ment**, s.: infeudazione, *f.*: — *in trust*, fedecommesso, *m.*

fẹ-rāciọus†, ADJ.: fertile. **-răcity**†, s.: fertilità; fecondità, *f.*

fēral, ADJ.: tristo, funebre.

fērial, ADJ.: feriale.

fērịne, ADJ.: salvatico; feroce.

fĕrment 1, s.: fermento, lievito, *m.* **fẹrmĕnt** 2, (IN)TR.: fermentare, lievitare. **-mĕntable**, ADJ.: disposto a fermentare. **-mĕntal**, ADJ.: fermentativo. **-mentāțiọn**, s.: fermentazione, *f.* **-mĕntative**, ADJ.: fermentativo.

fĕrmillet†, s.: fermaglio, *m.*, fibbia, *f.*

fĕrn, s.: felce, *f.* **-y**, ADJ.: pieno di felce.

fẹr-ōciọus, ADJ.: feroce, fiero, crudele. **-ōciously**, ADJ.: ferocemente. **-ōciousness**, **-ŏcity**, s.: ferocità, fierezza, ferocia, *f.*

fĕrrẹous, ADJ.: ferreo, di ferro.

fĕrret 1, s.: furetto; floretto, *m.* **ferret** 2, TR.: cacciare col furetto, ricercare, investigare. **-ẹr**, s.: cacciatore col furetto; investigatore, *m.*

fĕrriage, s.: passaggio, *m.*

ferrŭginous, ADJ.: ferruginoso, ferrigno.

fĕrrụle, s.: ghiera, viera, *f.*

fĕrry 1, s.: chiatta, *f.*; passaggio, *m.* **ferry** 2, TR.: passare col barchetto: — *over*, traghettare nel barchetto, passare col navalestro. **-boat**, s.: chiatta, *f.*, barchetto, *m.* **-man**, s.: barcaiuolo, navicellaio, *m.*

fĕr-tile, ADJ.: fertile, fecondo, fruttuoso. **-tileness**, **-tility**, s.: fertilità; fecondità, *f.* **-tilịze**, TR.: fertilizzare; fecondare. **-ti(le)ly**, ADV.: fertilmente.

fĕrụle 1, s.: ferza, sferza, *f.* **ferule** 2, TR.: sferzare.

fĕr-vency, s.: fervore; zelo, affetto, *m.* **-vent**, ADJ.: fervente, fervido, ardente. **-vently**, ADV.: con f[illegible] ardentemente. **-vid**, ADJ.: [illegible] **-vidity**, **-vidness**, [illegible] zelo, *m.* **-vọr**, s.: [illegible] fetto, *m.*

fĕscụe, s.: fuscello, *m.* [illegible] ta, *f.*, ecc., per indicare [illegible] tere); (*bot.*) festuca, *f.*

fĕss(*e*), S.: (*her.*) fascia, *f.*

fĕstal, ADJ.: festevole; allegro.

fĕster, INTR.: suppurare, impostemire. **-ing**, S.: suppuramento, *m.*

fĕsti-nate†. ADJ.: frettoloso, spedito. **-nately**†, ADV.: in fretta, speditamente. **-nātion**†, S.: festinazione; fretta; sollecitudine, *f.*

fĕs-tival, ADJ.: festivo, festevole; S.: giorno festivo, *m.*, festa, *f.*; anniversario, *m.* **-tive**, ADJ.: festivo, festevole; lieto, allegro. **-tivity**, S.: allegrezza, *f.*, giubilo; giorno festivo, *m.* **-tivous**, ADJ.: festivo, festoso; giocoso, lieto.

festōon, S.: festone, *m.*

fĕt†, S.: pezzo, straccio, *m.*

fĕtch 1, S.: artificio, *m.*, astuzia, *f.*; pretesto, rigiro, *m.* **fetch** 2, TR.: andare a cercare; recare; portare; produrre: — *a blow*, colpire; — *one's breath*, prender respiro, respirare; — *a leap*, fare un salto, saltare; — *a sigh*, trar (*or* gettare, cavare) un sospiro, sospirare; — *a walk*, fare una passeggiata; — *away*, portare via; straportare; — *down*, portare giù; affievolire; abbattere; — *in*, portare dentro, introdurre; — *off*, levare via, torre; — *out*, portare fuora; — *over*, attrappare; truffare; — *up*, portare sù; condurre. **-ed**, ADJ.: cercato. **-er**, S.: che anda a cercare.

fête (*ê Engl. acc.*), S.: festa, *f.*

fĕt-ich *or* **-ish**, S.: feticcio, *m.* **-ichism**, **-ishism**, S.: feticismo, *m.*

fĕtid, ADJ.: fetido, puzzolente, rancido, nauseoso. **-ness**, S.: fetore, puzzo, *m.*

fĕtlock, S.: barbetta (della pastoia), *f.*

fĕtter, TR.: mettere in catena. **-s**, S. PL.: catene, *f. pl.*; ferri, ceppi, *m. pl.*

fĕttle, TR.: (*prov.*) badaluccare.

fētus, S.: feto, embrione, *m.*

feūd, S.: feudo, *m.*; contesa, altercazione, rissa, *f.* **-al**, ADJ.: feudale, di feudo; S.: feudo, *m.* **-atory**, S.: feudatario, *m.* **-ist**, S.: feudista, *m.*

fēver 1, S.: febbre, *f.*: *be in a* —, *have a* —, aver la febbre, febbricitare; *strong* —, febbrone, *m.*; *slight* —, febbretta, febbricetta, *f.*; *acute* —, febbre acuta; *intermittent* —, febbre intermittente; *child-bed* —, febbre puerperale; *fit of* —, accesso di febbre. **fever** 2, TR.: dar la febbre, cagionare la febbre. **-et**, S.: febbretta, *f.* **-few**, S.: matricale, camamilla, *f.* **-ish**, ADJ.: febbricoso, febbroso. **-ishness**, S.: febbricità, *f.* **-ous**, **-y**, ADJ.: febbroso, febbricoso, febbrifero.

fēw, ADJ.: pochi (*f.* -che), piccolo numero di: *a* —, alcuni pochi; *very* —, assai pochi; *in* (*a*) — *words*, in poche parole, in una parola, in breve.

fewel† = *fuel*.

fēw-er, ADJ.: meno, non tanto. **-ness**, S.: pochezza, *f.*, poco numero, *m.*

fēy†, TR.: purgare un fosso.

fiance, TR.: fidanzare.

fiants, S. PL.: sterco di volpe, *m.*

fiat, S.: decreto, ordine, *m.*

fib 1, S.: bugia, menzogna, *f.* **fib** 2, INTR.: dire bugie, mentire. **-ber**, S.: bugiardo, mentitore, *m.*

fi-bre, S.: fibra, *f.*, filamento, *m.* **-bril**, S.: fibretta, fibrilla, *f.* **-brous**, ADJ.: fibroso.

fibula, S.: fermaglio, *m.*; (*anat.*) fibula, *f.*

fickl-e, ADJ.: mutabile, incostante. **-eness**, S.: mutabilità, instanza, *f.* **-y**, ADV.: incostantemente.

fic-tile, ADJ.: fittile. **-tion**, S.: finzione; invenzione, *f.* **-tious**, **-titious**, ADJ.: fittizio, finto. **-titiously**, ADV.: fintamente. **-titiousness**, S.: finzione, invenzione, *f.* **-tive**, ADJ.: finto, fittizio, inventato.

fiddl-e 1, S.: violino, *m.*: *play on the* —, suonare il violino; *play* (*the*) *second* —, fare la parte secondaria. **fiddle** 2, TR.: suonare il violino. **-e-bridge**, S.: ponticello di violino, *m.* **-e-faddle**, S.: baloccheria, bagatella, *f.* **-er**, S.: suonatore di violino, violinista, *m.* **-e-stick**, S.: archetto di violino, *m.*: —*s!* oibò! trottole! **-e-string**, S.: corda da violino, *f.* **-ing**, ADJ.: frivolo, vano: — *business*, faccenda di poca importanza, *f.*

fidĕlity, S.: fedeltà, lealtà, onestà, *f.*

fidg-et†, **-et** 1, INTR.: agitarsi, dimenarsi. **-et** 2, S.: agitazione, inquietezza, impazienza, *f.* **-ety**, ADJ.: inquieto, impaziente.

fidū-cial, ADJ.: fiduciale, affidato. **-cially**, ADV.: fiducialmente. **-ciary**, ADJ.: fiduciario, fiduciale; S.: fiduciario, depositario, fedecommissario, *m.*

fief, S.: feudo, *m.*

field, S.: campo, *m.*; campagna, *f.*; spazio, *m.*: — *of battle*, campo di battaglia, *m.*; *take the* —, uscire in campagna. **-battle**, S.: campo di battaglia, *m.*, giornata, *f.* **-bed**, S.: letto da campo; lettuccio, *m.* **-day**, S.: rassegna, *f.*, giorno di rivista, mostra, *f.* **-ed**, ADJ.: schierato, in ordinanza. **-fight**, S.: battaglia campale, *f.* **-marshal**, S.: maresciallo di campo, *m.* **-mouse**, S.: sorcio di campo, *m.* **-officer**, S.: ufficiale dello stato maggiore, *m.* **-piece**, S.: pezzo d'artiglieria, *m.* **-preacher**, S.: cappellano d'un reggimento, *m.* **-sports**, S. PL.: caccia, *f.* **-works**, [illegible] *f. pl.*, lavori *m. pl.*

fiend. [illegible] gno, da [illegible]

fierce, ADJ.: fiero, furioso; feroce; crudele; impetuoso, terribile. **-ly**, ADV.: fieramente, furiosamente; crudelmente. **-ness**, S.: fierezza, ferocità; violenza; crudeltà, *f.*

fier-iness, S.: ardore, fervore; impeto, *m.* **-y**, ADJ.: igneo; collerico, impetuoso, furioso, focoso.

fif-e 1, S.: piffero, *m.* **fif-e** 2, INTR.: fischiare. **-er**, S.: piffero, suonatore di piffero, *m.*

fif-teen, ADJ.: quindici. **-teenth**, ADJ.: quindecimo. **-th**, ADJ.: quinto: *four (etc.) —s*, quattro (ecc.) quinti. **-tieth**, ADJ.: cinquantesimo. **-thly**, ADV.: in quinto luogo. **-ty**, ADJ.: cinquanta.

fig 1, S.: fico, *m.*; bagattella, *f.*: *I care not a — for him*, mi rido di lui. **fig** 2, TR.: beffare, berteggiare.

figary†, S.: capriccio, *m.*, fantasia, *f.*

fight 1, S.: combattimento, *m.*, battaglia, *f.*; conflitto, *m.*, zuffa, mischia, *f.*: *cock-—*, combattimento di galli, *m.*; *sea-—*, combattimento navale, *m.* **fight** 2, IRR.; TR.: pugnare, contrastare; IRR.; INTR.: combattere, far battaglia: — *a duel*, duellare, fare duello; — *hand to hand*, battersi corpo a corpo; — *hard*, battersi gagliardamente; — *it out*, decidere colle armi; — *one's way*, farsi strada; — *a duel*, battersi in duello, duellare. **-er**, S.: combattitore; duellante, *m.* **-ing**, ADJ.: combattente; guerriero, bellico; S.: combattimento, *m.* **-ing-field**, S.: campo di battaglia, *m.* **-ing-man**, S.: combattente, *m.*

fig-leaf, S.: foglia di fico, *f.*

figment, S.: finzione; invenzione, *f.*

fig-pecker, S.: beccafico, *m.* **-tree**, S.: fico (albero), *m.*

figur-able, ADJ.: figurabile. **-ate**, ADJ.: figurato. **-ation**, S.: figuramento, figurare, *m.*; immaginazione, *f.* **-ative**, ADJ.: figurativo, allegorico. **-atively**, ADV.: figurativamente, figuratamente. **-e** 1, S.: figura, forma; immagine, *f.*; aspetto, *m.*; apparenza; eminenza, *f.*: *make some — in the world*, far figura nel mondo; *cut a pretty —*, far bella figura; *wax —*, figura di cera. **-e** 2, TR.: figurare; rappresentare: — *one's self*, figurarsi, immaginarsi. **-e-head**, S.: (*nav.*) pulena, *f.*, tagliamare, *m.*; (un) nulla, (uno) zero, *m.*

figwort, S.: scrofolaria, *f.*

filáceous, ADJ.: filamentoso, fibroso.

fila-ment, S.: filamento, *m.*, fibra, *f.* **-méntous**, ADJ.: filamentoso.

[f]landers, S. PL.: filandre (del falcone), [illegible]

[illegible] S.: nocciuola, avellana, *f.* **-tree**, [illegible]olo, *m.*

filch, TR.: truffare, ingannare, fraudare. **-er**, S.: truffatore, giuntatore, furbo, *m.* **-ing**, S.: truffa, furberia, *f.*

file 1, S.: filo, *m.*; fila; lista, linea, *f.*; ordine, *m.*; lima, *f.*: — *of papers*, fascetto, mazzo (di scritti), *m.*; — *of pearls*, filo di perle, vezzo, *m.*; — *after —*, alla sfilata. **file** 2, TR.: infilare; limare; pulire: — *off*, sfilare; marciare alla sfilata. **-cutter**, S.: fabbro di lime, *m.* **-dust**, S.: limatura, *f.*

filemot, S.: colore di foglia morta, *m.*

filer, S.: limatore, *m.*

fil-ial, ADJ.: filiale, di figliuolo. **-ially**, ADV.: in modo filiale. **-iation**, S.: filiazione; discendenza, *f.*

fili-granet, **-grée**, S.: filigrana, *f.*

filing, S.: (il) limare; **-s**, PL.: limatura, *f.*; (*leg.*) deposito, *m.*; presentazione d'una domanda, *f.*

fill 1, S.: sufficienza, abbondanza, *f.*: *eat one's —*, mangiare a crepapelle, satollarsi. **fill** 2, TR.: empiere, empire; saziare; versare; INTR.: empiersi, riempirsi: — *up*, compire; colmare; rimpiazzare; — *to overflowing*, colmare; — *a place*, coprire una carica; — *a glass*, empire un bicchiere. **-er**, S.: ingombro; caricatore, *m.*

fillet 1, S.: banda; striscia, *f.*; (*arch.*) astragalo; — *of veal*, filetto, lombo di vitello, *m.*, coscia di vitello, *f.* **fillet** 2, TR.: bendare; ornare d'un tondino.

fillibeg, S.: spezie di gonnella, *f.*

filling, ADJ.: che sazia, che satolla, saziévole; S.: empiere, *m.*

fillip 1, S.: buffetto, biscottino, *m.* **fillip** 2, TR.: dare un biscottino.

filly, S.: cavalla giovane, cavallina, *f.*, puledra, *f.*

film 1, S.: membrana, pellicina, pellicola, buccia, *f.* **film** 2, TR.: coprire d'una pellicola. **-y**, ADJ.: membranoso.

filter 1, S.: filtro, colatoio, *m.* **filter** 2, TR.: colare, filtrare; purificare. **-ing**, ADJ.: filtrante, trapelante. **-stone**, S.: pietra da filtrare, *f.* **-paper**, S.: linguetta, *f.*

filth, S.: sporcizia, schifezza; spazzatura; corruzione, *f.* **-ily**, ADV.: sporcamente, schifamente, rozzamente. **-iness**, S.: sporcheria, schifezza, bruttura, lordura, *f.* **-y**, ADJ.: sporco, sucido, sordido.

fil-trate, TR.: filtrare, feltrare, colare. **-tration**, S.: filtrazione, *f.*, colamento, *m.*

fimbriate, TR.: orlare, fregiare.

fin, S.: ala; pinna (de' pesci), *f.*

finable, ADJ.: soggetto ad ammenda, degno di multa.

final, ADJ.: finale, ultimo, estremo. **-ly**, ADV.: finalmente, ultimamente.

finán-ce, S.: finanza, rendita, entrata, *f.* **-cial**, ADJ.: relativo alle finanze. **-cier**, S.: finanziere, ufficiale delle finanze, *m.*

finary, S.: fucina, ferriera, *f.*
finch, S.: fringuello, *m.*
find, IRR.; TR.: trovare; scoprire, rinvenire; fornire, provvedere; INTR.: avvedersi, accorgersi: — *one's self*, trovarsi, sentirsi; — *fault with*, trovar a ridire a; riprendere, biasimare, criticare; — *one's way*, introdursi; — *out*, trovare, inventare, spiegare, scoprire. **-er**, S.: trovatore, scopritore, *m.* **-fault**, S.: censore, critico, *m.*
fine[1], ADJ.: fino, sottile; pulito; bello; elegante; puro; lucido, chiaro; acuto, affilato; squisito, eccellente; pomposo, grazioso; destro, abile, svelto; scaltrito, artificioso: — *young fellow*, bel giovinotto. **fine**[2], S.: multa, ammenda; conclusione, *f.*: *in* —, finalmente, in somma. **fine**[3], TR.: affinare; chiarare; purgare; condannare all' ammenda; INTR.: pagare l' ammenda. **-draw**, TR.: cucire, risarcire. **-drawer**, S.: cucitore, risarcitore, racconciatore, *m.* **-drawing**, S.: cucitura, *f.*, risarcimento, racconciamento, *m.* **-fingered**, ADJ.: abile, destro. **-ly**, ADV.: finamente, pulitamente; elegantemente; vagamente. **-ness**, S.: finezza; delicatezza; bellezza, *f.* **-er**, S.: affinatore, raffinatore, *m.* **fine-ry**, S.: ornamento; aggiustamento, *m.* **-spoken**, ADJ.: affettatamente civile. **-spun**, ADJ.: sottile.
finësse, S.: artificio, *m.*, stratagemma, *f.*
finger[1], S.: dito, *m.*: *have a thing at one's —'s end*, saper una cosa su per le dita; *have a — in the pie*, esser complice nella cosa. **finger**[2], TR.: maneggiare, toccare. **-board**, S.: (*instr.*) tastatura, *f.* **-ed**, ADJ.: che ha le dita, dalle dita. **-ing**, S.: maneggiamento, toccamento, *m.* **-stall**, S.: fasciatura d' un dito, *m.*
fingle-fangle, S.: bagattella, chiappoleria, *f.*
finical, ADJ.: affettato, ritroso, schifo, studiato. **-ly**, ADV.: con affettazione. **-ness**, S.: affettazione; schifiltà; ritrosia, *f.*
fining, S.: multare; chiarificare, *m.*, purificazione, *f.*
finish[1], S.: fine; compimento, *m.* **finish**[2], TR.: finire, terminare; compire: — *off*, ultimare, daro gli ultimi tocchi a. **-ed**, ADJ.: finito, perfetto; compito; terminato. **-er**, S.: finitore, compitore; giustiziere, boia, *m.* **-ing**, ADJ.: che finisce, che mette fine a: — *blow*, colpo di grazia.
finite, ADJ.: limitato, determinato. **-less**, ADJ.: immenso, illimitato. **-ly**, ADV.: finitamente, con limitazione. **-ness**, S.: limitazione, *f.*, limiti, *f. pl.*
fin-less, ADJ.: senza pinne. **-like**, ADJ.: fatto a modo di pinna. **-ny**, ADJ.: fornito di pinne. **-toed**, ADJ.: di piè membranoso, palmipede.
fipple, S.: zaffo (d' un flauto), *m.*
fir, S.: abete, *m.* **-cone**, S.: pigna, *f.*
fire[1], S.: fuoco; incendio; abbruciamento, *m.*: *St. Anthony's* —, risipola, *f.*; *make a* —, far fuoco; *take* —, pigliar fuoco, cominciare ad ardere. **fire**[2], TR.: mettere il fuoco; infiammare; INTR.: tirare; dar fuoco. **-arms**, S. PL.: armi da fuoco, *f. pl.* **-ball**, S.: granata, bomba; meteora, *f.* **-brand**, S.: tizzone, *m.* **-brush**, S.: piccola scoppa da fuoco, *f.* **-company**, S.: compagnia di pompieri, *f.* **-drake**, S.: dragone volante, *m.* **-engine**, S.: tromba, pompa da fuoco, *f.* **-fan**, S.: parafuoco, *m.* **-fork**, S.: forcone, attizzatoio, *m.*

f. **-lock**, S.: archibuso, schioppo, *m.* **-man**, S.: pompiere; (*rail.*) fuochista, *m.* **-new**, ADJ.: giusto uscito del fuoco; nuovo. **-ordeal**, S.: prova del fuoco, *f.* **-pan**, S.: focone dell' armi, *m.* **-place**, S.: focolare, *m.* **-proof**, ADJ.: a pruova di fuoco. **fire-r**, S.: incendiario, *m.* **-room**, S.: camera con un cammino, *f.* **-screen**, S.: parafuoco, *m.* **-ship**, S.: brulotto, *m.* **-shovel**, S.: paletta da fuoco, *f.* **-side**, S.: focolare; cammino, *m.* **-stick**, S.: tizzone, tizzo, *m.* **-stone**, S.: focolare, *m.*, pirite, *f.* **-tongs**, S. PL.: mollette, *f. pl.* **-wood**, S.: legna, *f. pl.* **-work**, S.: fuoco artifiziale, *m.* **-worker**, S.: facitore di fuochi artifiziali; ingegnere, *m.*
firing, S.: scarica, *f.*; legna†, *f. pl.*
firk†, TR.: battere, sferzare, frustare.
firkin, S.: quarteruola, *f.* (misura).

te: *the — land*, il continente. **firm**[2], S.: associazione (di mercanti), firma, *f.* **firm**[3], TR.: fermare, fissare; confermare; stabilire.

: primo no-

to, *m.*
fir-tree, S.: abete, *m.*
fisc, S.: fisco, *m.* **-al**, ADJ.:
fish[1], S.: pesce, *m.*; (*nav.*)

fish 2, TR.: pescare; (*nav.*) traversare, capponare (l' ancora): — *a mast*, lapazzare un pennone. **-bone**, S.: spina di pesce, *f.* **-day**, S.: giorno magro, *m.* **-er**, **-erman**, S.: pescatore, *m.* **-er-woman**, S.: pescivendola, *f.* **-ery**, S.: pesca, *f.*; pescare, *m.* **-ful**, ADJ.: pieno di pesci. **-gig**, S.: (*nav.*) fiocina, *f.* **-hook**, S.: amo, *m.* **-ing**, S.: pesca, pescagione, *f.* **-ing-boat**, S.: barca di pescatore, *f.* **-ing-gear**, S.: attrezzi pescherecci, *m. pl.* **-ing-line**, S.: lenza, *f.* **-ing-place**, S.: pescheria, *f.* **-ing-rod**, S.: canna da pescare, verga dell' amo, *f.* **-ing-spear**, S.: rampone, *m.* **-kettle**, S.: navicella da pesce, *f.* **-market**, S.: pescheria, *f.* **-meal**, S.: dieta di pesce; cattiva cera, *f.* **-monger**, S.: pescivendolo, *m.* **-pond**, S.: vivaio, *m.*, peschiera, *f.* **-wife**, **-woman**, S.: pescivendola, *f.* **-y**, ADJ.: abbondante di pesci.

fisk†, INTR.: correre qua e là; *sfuggire* la scuola.

fis-sile, ADJ.: fissile; che può spaccarsi. **-sion**, S.: spacamento, *m.* **-sure**, S.: fessura, spaccatura, crepatura, *f.*

fist, S.: pugno, *m.* **-icuffs**, S. PL.: percosse col pugno, pugna, *f. pl.*: *go to* —, fare alle pugna.

fistu-la, S.: fistola, *f.* **-lar**, ADJ.: fistolare. **-lous**, ADJ.: fistoloso.

fit 1, ADJ.: idoneo, atto, capace; convenevole, giusto, proporzionato; apparecchiato, pronto: *make one's self* — *for*, prepararsi; *be* — *to*, esser in istato di. **fit** 2, S.: accesso, attacco, parossismo; capriccio, *m.*, *fantasia*, *f.*, ghiribizzo, *m.*: *ague*, — accesso di febbre terzana, *m.*; — *of gout*, attacco di podagra, *m.*; — *of love*, trasporto d' amore, *m.*; — *of madness*, pazzia; frenesia, *f.*; *by* —*s*, a scosse; qualche volta, di tempo in tempo; *by* —*s and starts*, a stento, a spilluzzico. **fit** 3, TR.: aggiustare, adattare, accomodare; preparare; assortire; INTR.: accomodarsi; convenire: — *out*, provvedere, fornire; armare; — *up*, addobbare, guarnire.

fitch, S.: veccia, *f.*: *wild* —, veccia salvatica, *f.* **-ew**, S.: puzzola, *f.*

fitful, ADJ.: variabile; irregolare; incerto.

fit-ly, ADV.: convenevolmente, giustamente, attamente. **-ment**, [illegible] mento, *m.*; conformità; [illegible] **-ness**, S.: convenienza; [illegible] porzione, *f.* **-table**†, ADJ. [illegible] **-tedness**, S.: attitudine, [illegible] **-ter**, S.: che adatta; [illegible] ADJ.: convenevole; giusto, [illegible] tezza; convenevolezza, *f.* [illegible] re, equipaggiare, armamento, [illegible]

five, ADJ.: cinque: — *hun*[illegible] cento; — *thousand*, cinquemila. **-fold**, ADJ.: quintuplo. **-leaved**, ADJ.: cinquefoglio. **-s**, S. PL.: vivole, *f. pl.*

fix, TR.: fissare, affissare, piantare; stabilire; INTR.: fissarsi; coagularsi; determinarsi, risolvere; stabilire la sua dimora: — *a business*, terminare un negozio; — *a day*, appuntare un giorno, convenire del giorno; — *upon*, scegliere, eleggere; — *the eyes upon one*, fissare gli occhi in alcuno. **-ation**, S.: fissazione, *f.*; stabilimento, *m.* **-ed**, ADJ.: fisso, affissato; destinato, determinato. **-edly**, ADV.: fissamente; certamente. **-edness**, S.: stabilità; attenzione, applicazione, *f.* **-ity**, S.: fissezza, *f.* **-ture**, S.: fermezza, *f.*; mobile, *m.*

fizgig, S.: rampone, *m.*; fiocina, *f.*

flabby, ADJ.: floscio, vizzo, moscio.

flac-cid, ADJ.: flaccido, moscio. **-cidity**, **-cidness**, S.: flaccidità; fiacchezza, rilassazione, *f.*

flacker, INTR.: (*prov.*) sfavillare.

flag 1, S.: bandiera, *f.*; *stendardo*; ghiaggiulo, *m.*: *union* —, bandiera dell' unione; — *of truce*, bandiera bianca; *haul down the* —, ammaniare (abbassare) la bandiera; *hoist the* —, issare la bandiera. **flag** 2, TR.: lasciare cadere; lastricare; INTR.: cadere; sgomentarsi; avvilirsi; languidire. **-broom**, S.: scopa di giunchi, *f.*

flagel-late, TR.: flagellare. **-lation**, S.: flagellazione, *f.*

flageolet, S.: zufolo, *m.*

flag-giness, S.: allentamento; rilassamento, *m.*; debolezza, *f.* **-gy**, ADJ.: fiacco, floscio, molle; insipido.

flagitious, ADJ.: flagizioso, scellerato. **-ness**, S.: scelleratezza, ribalderia, malvagità, *f.*

flag-officer, S.: caposquadra, *m.*

flagon, S.: fiasco, *m.*, boccetta, *f.*

flagran-ce, **-cy**, S.: ardore, fervore, fuoco, *m.* **-t**, ADJ.: ardente, fervente, focoso; famoso, notorio. **-tly**, ADV.: ardentemente; notoriamente.

flagship, [illegible] (nave).

flail, [illegible]

flak[illegible] : lamina, *f.*: [illegible] — *of wool*, [illegible] rompersi in [illegible] fioccoso, la- [illegible] la, clar- [illegible] nare con

fuoco e fiamma. **flame** 2, INTR.: fiammeggiare; ardere. **-coloured**, ADJ.: di color di fiamma.
flāmen, S.: (*myth.*) flamine, *m.*
flāming, ADJ.: fiammeggiante, ardente.
flamingo, S.: fenicottero, *m.*
flăm-mablet†, ADJ.: infiammabile, accendibile. **-meous**†, ADJ.: fiammesco, di fiamma. **-mivomous**, ADJ.: vomitante fiamme. **-y**, ADJ.: fiammante; ardente.
flancgnāde, S.: fiancata, *f.*
flănk 1, S.: fianco, lato, *m.*: *in the* —, nel fianco. **flank** 2, TR.: fiancheggiare, fiancare. **-er**, S.: (*fort.*) fianco, *m.* **-ed**, ADJ.: fiancuto.
flănnel, S.: flanella, *f.*: — *shirt*, camiciuola, *f.*; corpetto di flanella, *m.*
flăp 1, S.: lembo, *m.*; botta, percossa, *f.*, colpo, *m.*: — *of a coat*, falda d' un vestito, *f.*; — *of the ear*, oreglia, *f.*; orecchio esteriore, *m.*; — *of a shoe*, orecchio d' una scarpa, *m.* **flap** 2, TR.: battere, percuotere: — *the wings*, battere le ale; — *down*, abbassarsi. **-dish**, S.: tavola da ripiegarsi, *f.* **-jack**, S.: torta di mele, *f.*
flār-e, INTR.: splendere con luce transitoria; consumarsi, struggersi. **-ing**, ADJ.: abbagliante, splendente.
flăsh 1, S.: fiamma subita; vampa, *f.*; baleno; lampo, *m.*: — *of the eye*, occhiata, *f.*, sguardo, *m.*; — *of fire*, vampa, *f.*; — *of lightning*, baleno, lampo, *m.*; — *of mirth*, effusione di gioia, *f.*; — *of wit*, arguzia, *f.*; concetto spiritoso, *m.* **flash** 2, TR.: schizzare, zaccherare; spruzzare; INTR.: risplendere, lampeggiare, scintillare. **-er**, S.: uomo superficiale, *m.* **-ily**, ADV.: di poca cognizione. **-ing**, S.: vivezza subita di lume, *f.*; splendore; spruzzo (d' acqua), *m.* **-y**, ADJ.: frivolo, insipido; pomposo.
flăsk, S.: fiasco, *m.*, fiaschetta, *f.* **-et**, S.: paniera, cesta, *f.*; canestro, *m.*
flăt 1, ADJ.: piatto, spianato; sventato, insipido; franco, *f.*; S.: pianura, *f.*; paese piano; (*nav.*) basso fondo, *m.*, secca, *f.*; (*mus.*) bimmolle, *m.*: — *discourse*, discorso insipido, *m.*; — *drink*, bevanda sventata, *f.*; - - *lie*, bugia manifesta, *f.*; — *nose*, naso schiacciato, *m.*; — *side*, piatto (d' una spada), *m.*; — *voice*, voce di basso, *f.*; *give a* — *denial*, ricusare nettamente; *grow* —, indebolirsi; *lay* —, appianare; demolire; *lie* — ... *ground*, stendersi per terra. ... : spianare, appianare; sven- ... appianarsi; insipidire. **-bot-** ... : (*nav.*) col fondo piano. ... : camuso. **-ly**, ADV.: in ... ; schiettamente. **-ness**, ... insipidezza; debolezza, *f.* ... camuso, rincagnato. **-ted**, ADJ.: spianato, appianato. **-ten**, TR.: appianare; abbattere; INTR.: appianarsi; insipidire. **-tening**, S.: stiacciatura, *f.*
flătter 1, S.: martello, martellino, *m.*
flatter 2, TR.: adulare, lusingare. **-er**, S.: adulatore, lusingatore, *m.* **-ing**, ADJ.: lusinghevole; piacevole. **-ingly**, ADV.: piacevolmente, dolcemente. **-y**, S.: adulazione, lusinga, *f.*, lusingamento, *m.*
flăttish, ADJ.: alquanto piatto; insipido.
flăt-ulency, S.: flatuosità, *f.* **-ulent**, ADJ.: flatuoso, ventoso; frivolo. **-uosity**, S.: flatuosità, ventosità, *f.* **-uous**, ADJ.: flatuoso, ventoso.
flătwise, ADV.: in piano, di piatto, sulla terra.
flăunt 1, S.: pompa, *f.* **flaunt** 2, INTR.: pompeggiare, pavoneggiarsi. **-ing**, ADJ.: attillato, acconcio, albagioso, pomposo.
flāvour 1, S.: sapore gustoso, gusto gradevole, odore, *m.* **flavour** 2, TR.: dare un gusto aromatico, dar fragranza, render saporito. **-ous**, ADJ.: odorante, saporito. **-less**, ADJ.: senza aroma (*or* profumo), insipido.
flăw 1, S.: fessura, crepatura, *f.*; difetto, errore, *m.*; invalidità; commozione, *f.*, tumulto, *m.*: *find a* — *in*, trovar un diletto in; — *of wind*, soffio, *m.*; folata di vento, sbuffo di vento, *m.* **flaw** 2, TR.: rompere, crepare, spezzare; danneggiare, violare. **-less**, ADJ.: senza fessure; senza difetto, perfetto. **-y**, ADJ.: crepato, fesso; defettuoso, imperfetto.
flăx 1, S.: lino, *m.*: *dress* —, scotolare il lino. **-comb**, S.: scotola, *f.* **-dresser**, S.: che scotola il lino, ecc. **-en**, ADJ.: di lino; biondo. **-field**, S.: lineto, *m.* **-finch**, S.: fanello, *m.* **-seed**, S.: linseme, *m.* **-y** = *flaxen*.
flāy, TR.: scorticare. **-er**, S.: scorticatore, *m.* **-ing**, S.: scorticamento, scorticare, *m.*
flēa 1, S.: pulce, *f.* **flea** 2, TR.: torre le pulci, spulciare. **-bane**, S.: pulicaria, *f.* **-bite**, **-biting**, S.: morsicatura di pulce, *f.* **-bitten**, ADJ.: morsicato da pulci.
flēak† 1, S.: fiocco, *m.*; ciocca, *f.*
flēam, S.: lancetta, *f.*
flĕcker, TR.: macchiare; pezzare.
flĕction = *flexion*.
flĕdge 1, ADJ.: piumato, coperto di piume.
fledge 2, TR.: coprire di piume; dar delle ale; INTR.: cominciare a metter le piume.
flēe, IRR.; INTR.: fuggire; voltare le calcagna; — *from*, scappare da.
flēec-e 1, S.: tosone, vello, *m.* **-e** 2, TR.: tondere; pelare; scorticare. **-er**, S.: tosatore; scorticatore, *m.* **-y**, ADJ.: lanuto, lanoso.

fléer 1, s.: derisione, beffa, *f.* **fleer** 2, INTR.: deridere; schernire, beffeggiare, beffare. **-er**, s.: deriditore, beffatore, *m.* **-ing**, ADJ.: sfacciato; s.: viso arcigno, *m.*

fléet 1, ADJ.: presto, veloce; spedito; leggiero. **fleet** 2, flotta; armata di mare, *f.*; golfo, *m.*, baia, *f.* **fleet** 3, IRR.; TR.: passare leggiermente; toccare; INTR.: scorrere; svanire: — *milk*, levar il fior del latte. **-ing**, ADJ.: transitorio, passeggiero. **-ly**, ADV.: con velocità, agilmente, leggiermente. **-ness**, s.: celerità, velocità, prestezza, *f.*

flésh 1, s.: carne; polpa; (*fig.*) carnalità, *f.*: *gather* —, ingrassare; *go the way of all* —, morire; *take* —, incarnarsi. **flesh** 2, indurire; animare, incoraggiare; saziare. **-broth**, s.: brodo di carne, *m.* **-colour**, s.: colore di carne, *m.*; carnagione, *f.* **-coloured**, ADJ.: colore di carne, incarnato. **-day**, s.: giorno grasso, *m.* **-diet**, s.: cibo di carne, *m.* **-ful**, ADJ.: carnoso, carnuto. **-hook**, s.: forcina, forchetta, *f.* **-iness**, s.: carnosità; pinguedine, *f.* **-less**, ADJ.: magro, macilento, smunto. **-liness**, s.: carnalità; sensualità, *f.* **-ly**, ADJ.: carnale; sensuale, animale. **-meat**, s.: carne (da mangiare), *f.* **-pot**, s.: ramino, *m.*, pentola, *f.* **-quake**†, s.: tremito del corpo, *m.* **-y**, ADJ.: carnoso; polposo.

fle-x, TR.: flettere†, piegare. **-xibility**, s.: flessibilità, arrendevolezza; compiacenza, *f.* **-xible**, ADJ.: flessibile, pieghevole, arrendevole; cortese. **-xibleness** = *flexibility*. **-xion**, s.: flessione; piegatura, *f.* **-xor**, s.: (*anat.*) flessore, *m.* **-xuous**, ADJ.: flessuoso, pieghevole; variabile. **-xure**, s.: flessura; curvatura, *f.*

flicker, INTR.: svolazzare, dimenarsi.

flier, s.: bilanciere; fuggitore, fuggitivo, *m.*

flight, s.: fuga; volata, *f.*, stormo, *m.*: — *of arrows*, tirata di frecce, *f.*; — *of birds*, stormo d' uccelli, *m.*; — *of folly*, stravaganza, sciocchezza, *f.*: — *of genius*, concetto spiritoso, *m.*; — *of steps*, terrazzo, *m.*; loggia, *f.*; *take* —, spiccar il volo; *take to* (*the*) —, fuggirsene, scappare. **-iness**, s.: leggerezza; irregolarità, *f.* **-shot**, s.: frecciata, *f.* **-y**, ADJ.: fuggitivo, veloce; fantastico.

flimflam†, s.: baloccheria, frascheria, bagattella, *f.*

flim-siness, s.: fiacchezza; leggerezza, trivialità, *f.* **-sy**, ADJ.: fiacco, moscio, floscio; triviale: — *stuff*, stoffa floscia.

flinch, INTR.: sbigottirsi; ritirarsi; tralasciare, desistere; abbandonare. **-er**, s.: codardo, pusillanimo, *m.*

flinder, s.: scheggia, *f.*; frammento, *m.* **-mouse**†, s.: pipistrello, *m.*

fling 1, s.: colpo, *m.*, botta; beffa, burla, *f.* **fling** 2 (*flung*; *flung*), IRR.; TR.: gettare, buttare; vibrare; lanciare; spandere; INTR.: calcitrare: — *at*, lanciare; avventarsi; — *away*, ributtare; dissipare; involarsi; — *down*, buttar giù, atterrare; rovinare, disfare; — *off*, schivare; cacciare; — *out*, buttare fuori; ostinarsi; — *up*, abbandonare; ritirarsi. **-er**, s.: gettatore; beffatore, *m.*

flint, s.: pietra focaia, selce, *f.*; ciottolo, *m.* **-glass**, s.: vetro di rocca, *m.* **-hearted**, ADJ.: spietato, crudele. **-stone**, s.: selce, *f.* **-y**, ADJ.: selcioso; spietato, inesorabile.

flip, s.: bevanda cordiale, *f.*

flippan-cy, s.: ciarla, ciarleria, *f.* **-t**, ADJ.: vivace, allegro; svegliato, ciarliero: — *discourse*, discorso vano, *m.*; — *person*, persona linguacciuta, *f.*; — *tongue*, lingua sciolta, *f.* **-tly**, ADV.: spensieratamente.

flirt 1, s.: moto celere ed elastico, *m.*; civetta, sfacciatella, *f.* **flirt** 2, TR.: lanciare, gettare; far muovere; INTR.: muoversi; beffeggiare; civettare. **-ation**, s.: civetteria, f.

flit, INTR.: svolazzare, fuggire; esser instabile.

flitch, s.: lardone; costereccio di porco, *m.*

flitter, s.: cencio; straccio; brandello, *m.* **-mouse**, s.: pipistrello, vipistrello, *m.*, nottola, *f.*

flit-tiness†, s.: leggerezza, instabilità, *f.* **-ting**, s.: offesa; colpa; fuggita, *f.* **-ty**†, ADJ.: instabile, variabile.

flóat 1, s.: traino, fodero di legname, *m.*; zatta, *f.*; sughero, *m.* **float** 2, TR.: immergere, inondare; INTR.: fiottare, galleggiare, ondeggiare; star sospeso. **-boat**, s.: zatta, zattera, chiatta, *f.* **-board**, s.: pala (di ruota di mulino), *f.* **-ing-bridge**, s.: ponte di barche, pontone, *m.* **-y**, ADJ.: galleggiante, a galla.

flóck 1, s.: banda, truppa; turba: gregge, mandra, *f.*; fiocco, *m.*: — *of wool*, bioccolo di lana, *m.* **flock** 2, INTR.: affollarsi, adunarsi attorno. **-bed**, s.: letto di borra, *m* **-ing**, s.: folla di popolo, concorso, *m.*

flóg, TR.: frustrare, sferzare. **-ging**, s.: fustigazione, flagellamento, *m.*, bastonata, *f.*

flóod 1, s.: inondazione, *f.*, diluvio; flusso. torrente, *m.*: — *of tears*, torrente di lagrime, *m.* **flood** 2, TR.: inondare; sommergere. **-gate**, s.: cateratta; imposta, *f.*

flóok, s.: uncino, raffio dell' ancora, *m.*, patta, *f.*

flōor 1, s.: palco; pavimento, suolo; piano, appartamento; (*nav.*) fondo, taglio, *m.*: *brick* (*tile*) —, ammattonato, *m.*; *ground* —, pian terreno, *m.*; *second* —, secondo piano; *on a* —, di fuga. **floor** 2, TR.: intavolare, coprir di tavole, impalcare con tavole: — *one*, stramazzare uno. **-ing**, s.: impalcamento, *m.*

flŏp, TR.: battere le ale, scoppiare.

flōral, ADJ.: florale.

flŏrence, s.: panno di Firenze, *m.*

flŏret, s.: fioretto, *m.*

flŏr-id, ADJ.: florido, vago, adornato. **-idity**, **-idness**, s.: floridezza, freschezza di colore, *f.*, colorito delle guance **-iferous**, ADJ.: pieno di fiori.

flŏrin, s.: fiorino, *m.*

flŏrist, s.: fiorista, dilettante di fiori, *m.*

flŏrulent†, ADJ.: fiorente, in fiori.

flŏsculous, ADJ.: (*bot.*) flosculoso.

flŏss, s.: borra, *f.*; rifiuto, *m.*: — *silk*, borra di seta, *f.*

flŏt-sam, **-son**, s.: merci (di naufragio), che il mare getta sulla spiaggia.

flŏunce 1, s.: guarnizione, balzana, *f.* **flounce** 2, TR.: guarnire di balzane; INTR.: tuffarsi; dimenarsi, dibattersi: — *about*, sbuffare di sdegno.

flŏunder 1, s.: sogliola, pesce passera, lima, *f.* **flounder** 2, INTR.: dibattersi; agitarsi, dimenarsi.

flŏur, s.: farina, *f.*; fiore del grano, *m.*

flŏur-ish 1, s.: fiorita, *f.*; ornamento; tratto di penna, ghirigoro, *m.*; (*arch.*) fiorone, rosone, *m.*; (*mus.*) preludio, *m.*: — *in discourse*, fiore di parlare, *m.*; — *of a trumpet*, trombata, *f.*; — *of words*, spampanata, millanteria, burbanza, *f.* **-ish** 2, TR.: ornare di fiori; ornare, adornare, abbellire; INTR.: essere in fiore, fiorire; prosperare; gloriarsi, vantarsi; (*mus.*) preludiare, suonare un preludio: — *with a pen*, intrecciare linee; — *a trumpet*, suonare di trombe; — *a sword*, brandire la spada. **-ishing**, ADJ.: fiorente, florido; prospero; pomposo; s.: ampolosità, *f.*; vanto, *m.* **-ishingly**, ADV.: pomposamente.

flŏut 1, s.: scherzo, *m.*, beffa, burla, *f.* **flout** 2, INTR.: schernire, beffare, burlare. **-er**, s.: beffatore, burlone, *m.*

flōw 1, s.: flusso, *m.*; abbondanza, copia, *f.* **flow** 2, TR.: inondare, diluviare; INTR.: colare; provenire: — *in*, affluire; — *over*, traboccare; inondare, allagare.

flŏwer 1, s.: fiore; ornamento, *m.*: *small* —, fiorellino, *m.*; *artificial* —*s*, fiori finti; *in the — of age*, nel fiore dell' età. **flower** 2, TR.: ornare di fiori, ricamare; INTR.: fiorire; spumare, fermentare. **-bud**, s.: bottone, *m.* **-dust**, s.: polline, *m.* **-ed**, ADJ.: fiorito, guernito di fiori. **-de-luce**, s.: fiordaliso, *m.* **-et**, s.: fioretto, fiorellino, *m.* **-garden**, s.: giardino da fiori, *m.* **-iness**, s.: abbondanza di fiori; *fig.*, floridezza, *f.* **-less**, ADJ.: senza fiori. **-pot**, s.: testo (per i fiori), *m.* **-stalk**, s.: peduncolo, *m.* **-stand**, s.: canestra da fiori, *f.* **-work**, s.: ricamo, *m.* **-y**, ADJ.: pieno di fiori, in fiori.

flōwing, ADJ.: fluido; scorrente, sorgente; volubile; s.: colamento; flusso, *m.*: *ebbing and* —, flusso e riflusso. **-ly**, ADV.: lindamente, con facilità. **-ness**, s.: volubilità (della lingua), *f.*

flōwn, ADJ.: fuggito; enfiato (*cf. fly*): *high* —, altiero, superbo.

flŭctu-ancy, s.: fluttuazione, *f.*, vacillamento, *m.*; irresoluzione, *f.* **-ant**, ADJ.: fluttuante; irresoluto, incerto. **-ate**, INTR.: fluttuare; bilanciare; esitare. **-ating**, ADJ.: fluttuante, ondeggiante; irresoluto. **-ātion**, s.: fluttuamento, ondeggiamento, *m.*; irresoluzione, incertezza, *f.*

flūe, s.: tubo, *m.*; calugine, *f.*

fluĕllin, s.: veronica, *f.*, abrotano, *m.*

flūen-cy, s.: fluidità, volubilità; abbondanza, *f.*: *speak with* —, parlare speditamente. **-t**, ADJ.: fluente; copioso, abbondante; volubile; eloquente; s.: corrente, canale d' acqua, *m.*: — *speaker*, oratore facondo. **-tly**, ADV.: lindamente con facilità, con grazia.

flū-id, ADJ.: fluido, liquido; corrente; s.: fluido, liquore, *m.* **-idity**, **-idness**, s.: fluidezza, liquidità, *f.*

flūke, s.: marra, *f.*, raffio dell' ancora, *m.*

flŭmmery, s.: coagulamento d' avena cotta, *m.*, sciocchezze, *f. pl.*

flŭor, s.: fluore; flusso, *m.*

flŭrry 1, s.: colpo di vento, burrasca; agitazione, fretta, *f.*: *in a* —, in trambusto, in confusione. **flurry** 2, TR.: agitare; spaventare.

flŭsh 1, ADJ.: fresco, vigoroso; elato; s.: affluenza subita, *f.*; flusso, *m.*: — *of joy*, trasporto di gioia. **flush** 2, TR.: animare, incoraggiare; alzare; INTR.: arrossire; scorrere con impeto. **-ed**, ADJ.: rosso; pieno inebbriato; esaltato. **-er**, s.: laniere, *m.* **-ing**, s.: rossore, *m.*, rossezza (nel viso), *f.* **-ness**, s.: freschezza, *f.*; vigore, *m.*

flŭster 1, s.: collera, *f.* **fluster** 2, TR.: inebriare; turbare.

flūt-e 1, s.: flauto, *m.*; (*arch.*) scanalatura: *play upon the* —, suonar il flauto. **-e** 2, TR.: scanalare, accanalare. **-e-player**, s.: suonatore di flauto, *m.* **-e-stop**, s.: registro del flauto, *m.* **-ing**, s.: scanalatura, *f.*

flŭtter 1, s.: ondulazione, *f.*; dimenamen-

to, *m.;* confusione, *f.* **flutter** 2, TR.: sconcertare; disordinare, turbare; INTR.: svolazzare; agitarsi, dimenarsi.
fluviătio, ADJ.: fluviale.
flŭ-x 1, S.: flusso; concorso, *m.;* disenteria, *f.* **-x** 2, TR.: dissolvere. **-xibility,** S.: flussibilità, *f.* **-xible,** ADJ.: flussibile. **-xility,** S.: fusibilità, *f.* **-xing,** S.: flusso di bocca, *m.;* salivazione, *f.* **-xion,** S.: flussione, *f.;* flusso, *m.* **-xure,** S.: fluidità, *f.*
flȳ 1, S.: mosca; ala, volante; (*watch.*) bilanciere, *m.:* *Spanish* —, cantaride, cantarella, *f.* **fly** 2, IRR.; INTR.: volare; involarsi; fuggirsene, fuggire; TR.: schivare, scansare; sfuggire: *let* —, tirare; sparare; — *in battle,* volgere (le spalle); — *into a passion,* montare in collera; andare sulle furie; — *in pieces,* saltare in pezzi; scoppiare; — *about,* spandersi, dilatarsi; — *at,* lanciarsi; avventarsi; — *away,* scappare via, fuggire; — *back,* rinculare, arretrarsi; — *from,* sottrarsi; — *off,* sollevarsi; ribellarsi; — *open,* aprirsi; — *out,* rompersi; fuggire prestamente; incollerirsi; — *to,* andare via; migrare; — *upon,* salire; montare. **-blow** 1, S.: cacatura di mosche, *f.* **-blow** 2, TR.: guastare (con cacchioni); corrompere. **-boat,** S.: brigantino, *m.* **-catcher,** S.: cacciatore di mosche, *m.* **-er,** S.: fuggitore; bilanciere; volante, *m.* **-fish,** TR.: pescare a lenza. **-flap,** S.: cacciamosche, paramosche, *m.* **-ing,** ADJ.: volante; fuggitivo: — *camp,* campo volante, *m.;* — *coach,* carrozza di posta, *f.;* — *colours,* bandiere spiegate, *f. pl.* **-ing-fish,** S.: pesce volante, *m.* **-paper,** S.: carta moschicida, *f.* **-trap,** S.: cacciamosche, *m.* **-wheel,** S: bilanciere, *m.*
fōal 1, S.: puledro, *m.;* cavallina, *f.:* — *of an ass,* puledro asinino, *m.* **foal** 2, INTR.: fare un puledro, figliare.
fōam 1, S.: spuma, schiuma, *f.* **foam** 2, INTR.: spumare, schiumare. **-y,** ADJ.: spumante, spumoso.
fŏb 1, S.: borsellino, *m.,* borsa, *f.;* gonzo, *m.* **fob** † 2, TR.: ingannare; truffare: — *off,* giuntare, beffare; disfarsi.
fōcal, ADJ.: del fuoco, centrico.
fociilātion †, S.: consolazione, *f.,* sostegno, *m.*
fōcus, S.: fuoco; centro, *m.*
fŏdder 1, S.: foraggio, *m.,* vettovaglia, *f.* **fodder** 2, TR.: pasturare con cibo secco, vettovagliare. **-er,** S.: foraggiere, *m.*
fōe, S.: nemico, avversario, *m.* **-like,** ADJ.: da nemico. **-man,** S.: nemico in guerra, *m.*
foētus, S.: feto, embrione, *m.*
fŏg, S.: nebbia, nebula, *f.* **-giness,** S.: aria nebulosa, *f.* **-gy,** ADJ.: nebuloso, nebbioso.
fŏh! INTERJ.: oibò!
fŏible, ADJ.: debole; S.: debolezza, *f.*
fŏil 1, S.: fioretto, *m.;* disfatta; foglia; ripulsa, *f.:* *give a* —, ripulsare. **foil** 2, TR.: superare; vincere.
fŏint † 1, S.: botta, *f.,* colpo, *m.* **foint** † 2, INTR.: dare una botta, dare un colpo.
fŏison †, S.: abbondanza, copia, *f.*
fŏist, TR.: inserire; alterare; falsificare, falsare. **-er,** S.: falsario, *m.*
foist-iness †, S.: fetore, *m.* **-y** †, ADJ.: mucido.
fōld 1, S.: ovile, *m.;* gregge; piega, crespa, *f.;* limite, *m.;* complicazione, *f.* **fold** 2, (IR)R.; TR.: chiudere nell' ovile; piegare; INTR.: piegarsi. **-ing,** S.: piegatura, *f.,* piegamento, *m.;* doppiatura, *f.* **-ing-chair,** S.: ciscranna, *f.* **-ing-door,** S.: porta a due battenti, *f.* **-ing-screen,** S.: paravento, *m.* **-ing-stick,** S.: stecca da piegare, *f.*
foliāceous, ADJ.: fogliaceo.
fōli-age, S.: fogliame, *m.;* frondi, *f. pl.* **-ate,** TR.: ridurre in lamine. **-ātion,** S.: fogliame, *m.*
fōlio, S.: libro in foglio, *m.*
fōlk, S.: gente, popolo, *m.:* *the* —*s say,* si dice.
fŏllicle, S.: (*bot.*) follicola, *f.;* guscio, *m.*
fŏllow, TR.: seguire; tener dietro a; accompagnare; imitare; INTR.: seguire, provenire, procedere: — *one's books,* applicarsi allo studio; — *one's business,* badare ai fatti suoi; — *one's example,* seguire l' altrui esempio; — *the law,* studiare la legge; — *a trade,* attendere a qualche mestiere. **-er,** S.: seguace; aderente; imitatore; settatore, *m.* **-ing,** ADJ.: seguente; seguace.
fŏlly, S.: pazzia; stravaganza, *f.*
fomĕnt, TR.: fomentare; incoraggiare. **-ātion,** S.: fomentazione, *f.;* fomento, *m.* **-er,** S.: fomentatore; fautore, *m.*
fŏnd 1, ADJ.: appassionato, indulgente, benigno; frivolo: *be* — *of,* essere invaghito (*or* tenero) di; amare con passione; *get* — *of,* affezionarsi a; *be passionately* — *of,* amar perdutamente. **-le,** TR.: accarezzare, vezzeggiare. **-ler,** S.: che carezza, accarezzatore, *m.* **-ling,** S.: mignone, favorito, *m.* **-ly,** ADV.: teneramente, appassionatamente. **-ness,** S.: tenerezza, indulgenza; debolezza, *f.;* affetto, amore, *m.*
fŏnt, S.: fonte battesimale, *m.* **-anel,** S.: fontanella, *f.,* cauterio, *m.*
fōod, S.: cibo, pasto, nutrimento, *m.;* esca, *f.* **-ful,** ADJ.: nutritivo; fertile. **-less,** ADJ.: sterile. **-y,** ADJ.: nutritivo.
fōol 1, S.: sciocco, pazzo; matto; buffone,

m.: *play the* —, fare il pazzo; burlare, scherzare; *make a* — *of*, farsi beffa di; —'*s cap*, beretta da pazzo. **fool** 2, TR.: frustrare; ingannare; INTR.: fare il pazzo, pazzeggiare; scherzare, ruzzare. **-born**, ADJ.: pazzo nato. **-ery**, S.: pazzia, follia; impertinenza; bagattella, *f.* **-hardiness**, S.: arditezza, temerità, *f.* **-hardy**, ADJ.: ardito, temerario. **-ish**, ADJ.: pazzo, stolto, sciocco; indiscreto, impertinente. **-ishly**, ADV.: follemente, stoltamente; imprudentemente. **-ishness**, S.: pazzia; imprudenza, *f.* **-trap**, S.: trappola, *f.*

fŏot 1 (pl. *feet*), S.: piede; passo, *m.*; base; fanteria, *f.*: — *by* —, poco a poco; *go on* —, andare a piedi; *be on the same* — *with another*, essere del pari con alcuno; *set on* —, mettere in piedi, cominciare; *tread under* —, calpestare; *have a sore* —, aver male al piede; *fore feet*, zampe (piedi) davanti; *hind* —, zampe (piedi) di dietro; *six feet high*, alto sei piedi. **foot** 2, TR.: calcitrare; calpestare; INTR.: andar a piedi; camminare; ballare, saltellare. **-ball**, S.: pallone, *m.* **-board**, S.: predella, *f.*, sgabello, *m.* **-boy**, S.: lacchè, *m.* **-bridge**, S.: piccol ponte di legno, ponticello, *m.* **-company**, S.: compagnia d'infanteria, *f.* **-ed**, ADJ.: rimpedulato; che ha il piè (i piedi) . . .; -pede. **-fight**, S.: combattimento d'infanteria, *m.* **-hold**, S.: pedata, *f.* **-ing**, S.: pedata, traccia, *f.*; passo; sentiero; ballo, *m.*; base, *f.*, fondamento; cominciamento, principio; stato, *m.*, condizione, *f.*: *get a* — *in a place*, fermare il piede in un luogo; stabilirsi in un luogo. **-licker**, S.: adulatore, *m.* **-man**, S.: staffiere; fantaccino, *m.* **-pace**, S.: passo lento; pianerottolo, *m.* **-pad**, S.: ladro a piedi, *m.* **-passenger**, S.: pedone, *m.* **-path**, S.: sentiero; marciapiede, *m.* **-post**, S.: corriere a piedi, *m.* **-stall**, S.: base, *f.*; piedestallo, *m.* **-step**, S.: vestigio, *m.*, traccia, *f.* **-stool**, S.: predella, *f.*, sgabello, marciapiede, *m.* **-stove**, S.: caldanino, *m.* **-warmer**, S.: caldanino, *m.* **-way**, S.: sentiero, *m.*

fŏp, S.: zerbino, damerino, parisino, sciocco, *m.* **-doodle**, S.: minchione, sciocco, *m.* **-ling**, S.: sciocchereIlo, *m.* **-pery**, S.: impertinenza; affettazione, *f.* **-pish**, ADJ.: attillato, affettato, sciocco. **-pishly**, ADV.: in modo affettato, con vanità, boriosamente. **-pishness**, S.: affettazione, ostentazione; vanità, *f.*

fŏr, PREP., CONJ.: per, in luogo di, perchè, perciocchè; a causa, a cagione che: — *my part, as* — *me*, per me, in quanto a me; — *example*, per esempio; — *my sake*, per l'amor mio; — *how much*, per quanto; — *ever and ever*, per sempre; — *as much as*, perciocchè, avvegnachè, a cagione che; *but* — *you*, senza di voi; — *what?* perchè? *I start* — *Genoa*, parto per Genova.

fŏrag-e 1, S.: foraggio, *m.*, vettovaglia, *f.* **-e** 2, TR.: foraggiare, saccheggiare. **-er**, S.: foraggiere, *m.*

forăminous, ADJ.: foraminoso, pieno di buchi.

forbeăr (*forbore, forborn*), IRR.; TR.: evitare; interrompere; risparmiare; sopportare, tollerare; INTR.: cessare; astenersi, raffrenarsi; tralasciare; fuggire: *I could hardly* — *weeping*, a gran pena ritenni le lagrime. **-ance**, S.: intermissione; pazienza, indulgenza, *f.*

forbĭd, IRR.; TR.: proibire; impedire; difendere; vietare, divietare; *God* (*Heaven*) —, Iddio non voglia. **-dance**, S.: proibizione, *f.*; divieto, *m.* **-denly**, ADV.: in modo illecito. **-der**, S.: proibitore, vietatore, *m.* **-ding**, ADJ.: spiacevole, austero; S.: proibizione, *f.*, vieto, vietamento, *m.*

fōrce 1, S.: forza; violenza, *f.*; potere, *m.*; necessità, *f.*; —*s*, forze, truppe, *f. pl.*; milizia, *f.*: *by* —, a (*or* per) forza; *by main* —, a viva forza; *a law in* —, un legge in vigore. **force** 2, TR.: forzare, sforzare; violentare; obbligare; costringere; superare, vincere; violare, stuprare; INTR.: sforzarsi; insistere; chiedere instantemente: — *back*, rispingere; rincacciare; — *in*, conficcare, fare entrare; — *out*, fare uscire per forza; — *out from*, svellere; rapire; — *upon*, imporre. **-d**, ADJ.: forzato; non naturale, affettato. **-dly** *-ed-*, ADV.: per forza, violentemente. **-ful**, ADJ.: poderoso, energico, vigoroso. **-fully**, ADV.: forzatamente, violentemente, impetuosamente. **-less**, ADJ.: senza forza, impotente, debole.

fōrceps, S.: forcipe, *m.*, tanaglia, *f.*

fōrcibl-e, ADJ.: forte; potente, vigoroso; efficace; prevalente. **-eness**, S.: forza; violenza, *f.* **-y**, ADV.: per forza fortemente, efficacemente.

fōrd 1, S.: guado, vado, guazzo, *m.* **ford** 2, TR.: guadare; passare a cavallo, passare a piedi. **-able**, ADJ.: che si può guadare, guadoso. **-age**, S.: nolo, *m.*

fōre 1, ADJ.: anteriore, antecedente, precedente. **fore** 2, ADV.: anteriormente, innanzi: (*nav.*) — *and aft*, per poppa e prua. **-advise**, TR.: prevenire, avvisare. **-appoint**, TR.: determinare innanzi. **-arm**, S.: cubito, *m.* **-ărm**, TR.: armare avanti, premunire. **-bōde**, TR.: presagire, pronosticare. **-bōdement**, S.: presagio, indovinamento, *m.* **-bōder**, s.: indovinatore, *m.* **-bȳ**, PREP.: presso, appresso. **-cast**, s.: prevedimento, *m.*, preconoscenza, *f.* **-cást**, IRR.; INTR.: prevedere, considerare innanzi, concertare. **-cáster**, s.: che prevede. **-castle**, s.: (*nav.*) castello di prua, *m.* **-chōsen**, ADJ.: preeletto, predestinato. **-cited**, ADJ.: suddetto, soprammentovato. **-clōse**, TR.: (*jur.*) escludere. **-deck**, s.: prua, *f.* **-dēem**, TR.: indovinare, conghietturare. **-design**, TR.: progettare, delineare anticipatamente; concertare. **-determine**, TR.: determinare innanzi. **-dō**, IRR.; TR.: rovinare; vessare; derogare. **-dōing**, s.: derogazione, *f.* **-dōom**, TR.: predestinare. **-door**, s.: porta d' avanti, *f.* **-end**, s.: parte d' avanti, *f.* **-fathers**, s. PL.: antenato, progenitore, predecessore, *m.* **-fēnd**, TR.: proibire, impedire, avertere; difendere. **-finger**, s.: indice, dito indice, *m.* **-flap**, s.: falda d' avanti, *f.* **-foot**, s.: piede d' avanti, *m.* **-gō**, IRR.; TR.: precedere; cedere; abbandonare. **-gōer**, s.: antecessore, *m.* **-gōing**, ADJ.: precedente, antecedente. **-ground**, s.: parte inferiore d' una pittura, *f.* **-hand**, ADJ.: anticipato, prematuro; s.: parte anteriore, *f.* **-handed**, ADJ.: fatto a tempo, opportuno. **-head** *fŏred*, s.: fronte; impudenza, sfacciatezza, *f.* **-hōlding**, s.: predicimento, *m.* **-horse**, s.: cavallo che va avanti, *m.*

fŏreign, ADJ.: forestiere, straniero; estero, estraneo, alieno: — *country*, paese estero; — *rule*, tirannia straniera; — *wares*, merci straniere; *secretary for — affairs*, segretario al dicastero degli affari esteri. **-er**, s.: forestiere, straniero, *m.* **-ness**, s.: allontanamento, *m.*

fore-imágine, TR.: immaginare innanzi, conghietturare. **-jŭdge**, TR.: giudicare innanzi; prevedere. **-knōw**, IRR.; TR.: preconoscere; sapere avante; prevedere. **knōwable**, ADJ.: che si può preconoscere. **-knōwledge**, s.: preconoscenza, prescienza. **-land**, s.: capo, promontorio, *m.* **-lāy**, IRR.; TR.: tendere insidie, mettere in aguato. **-lock**, s.: capelli d' avanti, *m. pl.*, ciuffo, *m.*; (*nav.*) chiavetta, *f.* **-man**, s.: capo, condottiere; capo de' giurati; (*print.*) proto, *m.* **-mast**, s.: albero di trinchetto, *m.* **-mentioned**, ADJ.: soprammentovato, predetto. **-most**, ADJ.: primo in ordine; primiero: *I went* —, io camminava primo. **-named**, ADJ.: prenominato. **-noon**, s.: mattina, *f.* **-notice**, s.: avviso anticipato, *m.*

forĕnsic, ADJ.: forense.

fore-ordáin, TR.: ordinare avanti, preordinare, predestinare. **-part**, s.: parte d' avanti, parte anteriore, *f.* **-past**, ADJ.: passato avanti, precedente. **-possĕssed**, ADJ.: preoccupato. **-rank**, s.: primo ordine, *m.*; fronte, *f.* **-recited**, ADJ.: soprammentovato. **-rŭn**, IRR.; TR.: precorrere; precedere. **-rŭnner**, s.: precursore; foriere, *m.* **-said**, ADJ.: sopraddetto. **-sail**, s.: mezzana, *f.* **-sāy**, IRR.; TR.: predire; profetizzare. **-sēe**, IRR.; TR.: prevedere, antivedere, presentire. **-sēeing**, s.: preconoscenza, *f.* **-sēen**, ADJ.: preveduto, antivisto. **-ship**, s.: (*nav.*) prua, *f.* **-shôrten**, TR.: raccorciare. **-shôrtening**, s.: raccorciamento, *m.* **-shōw**, IRR.; TR.: premostrare; predire, pronosticare. **-sight**, s.: prevedimento, *m.*; prescienza, *f.* **-sightful**, ADJ.: provvido, presciente. **-skin**, s.: prepuzio, *m.* **-speech**, s.: prologo, *m.* **spĕnt**†, ADJ.: guastato, stanco, lasso. **-spŭrrer**, s.: postiglione; corriere, corriero, *m.*

fŏrest, s.: foresta, selva, *f.*

fōre-staff, s.: (*nav.*) balestra, *f.*; astrolabio, *m.* **-stăll**, TR.: anticipare, preoccupare; incettare. **-stăller**, s.: incettatore, monopolista, *m.* **-stălling**, s.: incetta, preferenza nella compra, *f.*; monopolio, *m.*

fŏrest-born, ADJ.: nato in una foresta. **-er**, s.: guardaboschi, uffiziale de' boschi, *m.*

fōre-taste, s.: saggio, assaggiamento, *m.* **-tāste**, TR.: pregustare, assaggiare. **-tĕll**, IRR.; TR.: predire; presagire; profetizzare. **-tĕller**, s.: pronosticatore, profeta, *m.* **-tĕlling**, s.: predizione, *f.*; pronosticamento, *m.* **-thought**, s.: premeditazione, *f.* **-token**, s.: pronostico, augurio, presagio, *m.* **-tōken**, TR.: presagire, pronosticare. **-tōld**, ADJ.: predetto, pronosticato. **-tooth**, s.: dente d' avanti, incisore, *m.* **-top**, s.: cuffio, *m.*; (*nav.*) coffa di parrocchetto, *f.*: — *mast*, albero di parrocchetto, *m.*; — *sail*, vela di parrocchetto, *f.* **-vŏuched**, ADJ.: affermato anticipatamente. **-ward**, s.: avanguardia; fronte, *f.* **-wărn**, TR.: avvertire avanti, dar avvisi. **-wărning**, s.: avvertimento, *m.* **-wheel**, s.: ruota d' avanti, *f.* **-wind**, s.: vento in poppa, *m.* **-wish**, TR.: desiderare avanti, bramare avanti. **-wōrn**, ADJ.: usato, guastato del tempo, logorato.

fŏrfeit I, ADJ.: confiscato, sequestrato; s.: ammenda; transgressione, *f.*; misfatto, delitto, *m.* **forfeit** I, TR.: perdere per sequestrazione: — *one's word*, mancare di parola; — *one's life*, perder la vita; — *one's confidence*, demeritare la fiducia di. **-able**, ADJ.: confiscabile. **-ure**, s.: confiscazione; multa, pena, *f.*

forfĕnd, TR.: prevenire; preservare.
fōr-ge 1, S.: fucina, ferriera; fabbrica, *f.* **-ge** 2, TR.: fabbricare; contraffare; macchinare, inventare: — *a will*, falsificare un testamento. **-ger**, S.: fabbro; inventore, macchinatore; falsario, *m.* **-gery**, S.: lavoro di fabbro; falsificamento, *m.*; falsità, *f.*
forgĕt, IRR.; TR.: dimenticare, scordare; obbliare; disimparare; negligere. **-ful**, ADJ.: dimentichevole, obblioso; negligente. **-fulness**, S.: dimenticamento, obblio, *m.*; negligenza, *f.* **-ter**, S.: che dimentica, obbliatore, *m.*
forgiv-e, IRR.; TR.: perdonare; rimettere. **-eness**, S.: perdono, *m.*; remissione, *f.* **-er**, S.: perdonatore, *m.* **-ing**, S.: perdono, *m.*, remissione, *f.*
forinsecal†, ADJ.: estraneo, forestiero.
fōrk 1, S.: forca, forchetta, *f.* **fork** 2, INTR.: biforcarsi; spartirsi. **-ed**, ADJ.: forcuto. **-edly**, ADV.: in forma di forca. **-edness**, S.: forcatura, *f.* **-et**, S.: forchetta, *f.* **-head**, S.: punta di freccia, *f.* **-y**, ADJ.: forcuto, biforcato.
forlōrn, ADJ.: abbandonato, derelitto: — *hope*, soldati esposti in un assalto, *m. pl.* **-ness**, S.: abbandono, *m.*; solitudine; miseria, *f.*
fōrm 1, S.: forma, figura; foggia; maniera; moda; formalità, cerimonia; panca, *f.*; banco; covo, *m.*: *human* —, corpo umano; *in due* —, nelle forme, in forma; *for —'s sake*, per formalità; (*print.*) *take off a* —, levare una forma. **form** 2, TR.: formare; concertare; ordinare, comporre; istruire, informare. **-al**, ADJ.: formale; affettato. **-alist**, S.: formalista; uomo preciso, *m.* **-ălity**, S.: formalità; forma; cerimonia, *f.*; *formalities*, veste solenni, *f. pl.*: *matter of mere* —, affare di pura forma. **-alize**, TR.: modellare, modificare; trattare con troppa affettazione. **-ally**, ADV.: formalmente. **-ātion**, S.: formazione, *f.* **-ative**, ADJ.: formativo, plastico. **-er** 1, S.: formatore, inventore *m.*
fōrmer 2, ADJ.: primiero, passato; quegli. **-ly**, ADV.: tempo fà, altre volte, nel tempo passato.
formicātion, S.: formicolio, *m.*
fōrmidabl-e, ADJ.: formidabile, terribile. **-eness**, S.: qualità formidabile, *f.*, orrore, terrore, *m.* **-y**, ADV.: spaventevolmente, orribilmente.
fōrmless, ADJ.: informe, sformato.
fōrmu-la, S.: formula, *f.* **-lary**, S.: formolario, *m.* **-le**, S.: formula, formola, *f.*
fōrni-cate, INTR.: fornicare; adulterare. **-cātion**, S.: fornicazione, *f.*; adulterio, *m.* **-cator**, S.: fornicatore, *m.* **-catress**, S.: fornicatrice, *f.*

fōrray 1, S.: depredazione, *f.* **forray** 2, TR.: depredare.
forsāk-e, IRR.; TR.: (*forsook*; *forsaken*) lasciare, abbandonare. **-er**, S.: abbandonatore, *m.* **-ing**, S.: abbandonamento, *m.*
forsāy†, IRR.; TR.: proibire, difendere.
forsōoth, ADV.: in verità, veramente.
forswēar, IRR.; TR.: spergiurare, rinunziare con giuramento: — *one's self*, rendersi spergiuro, spergiurare. **-er**, S.: spergiuro, spergiuratore, *m.* **-ing**, S.: spergiuro, spergiuramento, *m.*
fōrt, S.: forte, *m.* **-ed**, ADJ.: fortificato, munito.
fōrth, ADJ.; ADV.: innanzi, avanti; fuor, fuori; affatto: *and so* —, eccetera; e così; via via; e così di; mano in mano; *go* —, uscire; *come* —, venire fuori, uscire; *set* —, partire, derivare; presentare; *set — a book*, pubblicare un libro. **-coming**, ADJ.: sul punto d'apparire; S.: comparigione, *f.* **-with**, ADV.: incontinente, subito.
fōrtieth, ADJ.: quarantesimo.
fōrti-fiable, ADJ.: che si può fortificar. **-ficātion**, S.: fortificazione; cittadella, *f.* **-fier**, S.: fortificatore, *m.* **-fy**, TR.: fortificare; munire. **-tude**, S.: fortezza, *f.*, coraggio, *m.*
fōrtlet, S.: fortino, *m.*
fōrtnight, S.: quindici giorni, *m. pl.*: *in a* —, di qui a quindici giorni; *to-morrow* —, domani a quindici.
fōrtress, S.: fortezza; bastita, *f.*
fortūitous, ADJ.: fortuito, casuale, inaspettato. **-ly**, ADV.: fortuitamente, accidentalmente, per caso. **-ness**, S.: caso, accidente, evento, *m.*
fōrtunate, ADJ.: fortunato, avventuroso. **-ly**, ADV.: fortunatamente. **-ness**, S.: buona fortuna, *f.*, successo, *m.*; prosperità, *f.*
fōrtune 1, S.: fortuna, *f.*; sorte; caso, avvenimento, evento, stato, *m.*, condizione, *f.*; beni, *m. pl.*; ricchezze, *f. pl.*; ricco partito, *m.*: *good* —, buona fortuna; *ill* —, mala fortuna, disgrazia, *f.*; *make one's* —, far fortuna, arricchirsi; *have a large* —, avere una grossa dota; *marry a* —, sposare una donna ricca; *risk one's* —, rimettersi alla fortuna. **fortune** 2, INTR.: accadere, avvenire. **-book**, S.: libro di magia, *m.* **-d**, ADJ.: fortunato. **-hunter**, S.: che va a caccia di donne ricche. **-teller**, S.: indovino, *m.*, -a, *f.*; (*by cards*) cartomante, *m.*, *f.* **-telling**, S.: indovinamento, *m.*; cartomanzia, *f.*
fōrty, ADJ.: quaranta.
fōrum, S.: foro, *m.*
fōrward 1, ADV.: avanti, innanzi; *go* —, *set* —, avanzare, avanzarsi; *go on* —! fatevi avanti, innoltratevi! *push* — [illegible]

carsi avanti. **forward**, ADJ.: anticipato, avanzato, presto; attivo; ardito; presuntuoso; pronto, disposto: *—fruit*, frutto primaticcio, *m*. **forward** 3, TR.: avanzare, promuovere, accelerare, affrettare; favorire; spedire: *— goods*, spedire merci. **-er**, S.: affrettatore, promotore, fautore, *m*. **-ing**, S.: (lo) spedire, innoltro, *m*. **-ly**, ADV.: frettolosamente, in fretta. **-ness**, S.: prontezza; premura, *f*., ardore; progresso, *m*.; sollecitudine, *f*. **-s**, ADV.: avanti (cf. *forward*).

fosse, S.: fosso, *m*.; gran fossa, *f*. **-way**, S.: ghiaiata, *f*.

fossil, ADJ.: fossile; S.: fossile, *m*.

foster 1, ADJ.: nutritivo. **foster** 2, TR.: nutrire; allevare; governare; educare. **-age**, S.: cura di nutrire, *f*. **-brother**, S.: fratello di latte, *m*. **-child**, S.: allievo, *m*. **-dam**, S.: nutrice, lattatrice, *f*. **-earth**, S.: terra nutritiva, *f*. **-er**, S.: nutricatore, *m*. **-ess**, S.: nutrice, *f*. **-father**, S.: balio, *m*. **-ling**, S.: allievo, *m*. **-mother**, S.: balia; nutrice, *f*. **-nurse**, S.: nutrice, balia, *f*. **-ship**, S.: foresta soggetta a un boscaiuolo, *m*. **-sister**, S.: sorella di latte, *f*. **-son**, S.: allievo, *m*.

fother, TR.: (*nav*.) stagnare.

foul 1, ADJ.: sozzo, sporco, impuro; cattivo; indegno, vergognoso; S.: (*boat race*) collisione, *f*.; urto, *m*.; (*baseball*) palla perduta: *— breath*, cattivo fiato; *— copy*, quadernaccio, stracciafoglio, *m*.; *— dealing*, fraude, *f*., inganno, *m*.; *— weather*, tempo burrascoso, *m*., tempesta, *f*.; *— work*, fracasso, romore, *m*.; *play —*, truffare nel giuoco; *run — of*, urtarsi contro. **foul** 2, TR.: sporcare, lordare, imbrattare; intorbidare. **-ly**, ADV.: bruttamente, bassamente, vergognosamente. **-mouthed**, ADJ.: maledico, indecente. **-ness**, S.: sporcizia, bruttezza, deformità, *f*.

found, TR.: fondare; stabilire, edificare.

foun-dā'tion, S.: fondamento, *m*., base, *f*.: *from the —*, di pianta; *lay the —*, gettare le fondamenta: *lay the — stone*, porre la prima pietra. **foun der** 1, S.: fondatore; fonditore, *m*. **-der** 2, TR.: strapazzare, affaticare; stroppiare; INTR.: affondare, andar a fondo.

foundery = *foundry*.

foundling, S.: bambino, fanciullo esposto, *m*.: *— house*, spedale de' fanciulli esposti, *m*.

foun-dress, S.: fondatrice, *f*. **-dry**, S.: fonderia, *f*.

foun-t(ain), S.: fonte, *m*., fontana, *f*. **-tain-head**, S.: scaturigine, fonte, *f*. **-tful**, ADJ.: pieno di sorgenti d' acqua.

four, ADJ.: quattro: *walk on all —s*, andar carpone.

fourb(e)†, S.: furbo; truffatore, *m*.

four-cornered, ADJ.: quadrangolare. **-fold**, ADJ.: quattro volte tanto, quadruplo. **-footed**, ADJ.: quadrupede. **-score**, ADJ.: ottanta. **-square**, ADJ.: quadrato. **-teen**, ADJ.: quattordici. **-teenth**, S.: quartodecimo, quattordicesimo, *m*. **-th**, ADJ.: quarto. **-thly**, ADV.: in quarto luogo. **-wheeled**, ADJ.: con quattro ruote.

fowl 1, S.: uccello; pollame, *m*. **fowl** 2, INTR.: uccellare, andare a caccia d' uccelli. **-er**, S.: uccellatore, *m*. **-ing-piece**, S.: scoppietto da uccellare, *m*.

fox, S.: volpe, *f*.; (*fig*.) uomo astuto, volpone, *m*.: *—'s cub*, volpicino, *m*.; *—'s kennel*, tana delle volpi, *f*.; *she —*, volpe femmina, *f*. **-bane**, S.: aconito, *m*. **-brush**, S.: coda di volpe, *f*. **-case**, S.: pelle di volpe, *f*. **-chase**, S.: caccia delle volpi, *f*. **-glove**, S.: (*bot*.) bacchera, *f*. **-hunter**, S.: cacciatore delle volpi, *m*. **-ish**†, ADJ.: astuto, accorto. **-ship**, S.: astuzia; malizia, *f*. **-tail**, S.: coda di volpe, *f*. **-trap**, S.: trappola da volpi, *f*. **-y**, ADJ.: astuto, scaltro.

frac-t, TR.: rompere; violare. **-tion**, S.: frangimento, rompimento, *m*.; frazione, *f*.: *simple —*, frazione ordinaria. **-tional**, ADJ.: (*arith*.) frazionario; rotto: *— parts*, frazioni, *f*. *pl*. **-tious**, ADJ.: perverso; litigioso, stizzoso, rissoso. **-tiously**, ADV.: stizzosamente; fastidiosamente. **-tiousness**, S.: vaghezza d' altercare, *f*. **-ture** 1, S.: frattura, *f*.; rompimento, *m*. **-ture** 2, TR.: rompere con violenza, frangero, fracassare.

frá-gile, ADJ.: fragile, frale; caduco, debole. **-gility**, S.: fragilità; fralezza, debolezza, *f*. **-gment**, S.: frammento, *m*.: *—s of meat*, rimasugli di carne, *m*. *pl*. **-gmentary**, ADJ.: composto di frammenti.

frágran-ce, **-cy**, S.: fragranza, *f*., odor soave, *m*. **-t**, ADJ.: odoroso, odorifero. **-tly**, ADV.: odorosamente, soavemente.

frail 1, ADJ.: frale, fragile; fievole. **frail** 2, S.: paniera; sporta, *f*.; cesto, *m*. **-ness**, **-ty**, S.: fragilità, fralezza, debolezza; instabilità; incostanza, *f*.

främ-e 2, S.: armatura di legname struttura; fabbrica, *f*.; quadro, telaio, *m*.; impannata; cassa; disposizione, *f*.: *be in a right —*, esser ben disposto; *be out of —*, essere indisposto. **-e** 2, TR.: formare adattare; comporre; costruire, fabbricare; controvare, inventare. **-er**, S.: formatore, facitore; inventore, *m*. **-ework**, S.: intelaiatura, armadura, *f*.; carcame, *m*.

främ-pel†, **-pold**†, ADJ.: arcigno.

fräno, S.: franco, *m*.

frănchişe, s.: franchigia, *f.*; privilegio, *m.* **franchise** 2, TR.: esentare; fare franco, francare. **-ment**, s.: liberazione, *f.*
Franciscan, s.: Francescano, *m.*
fran-gibility, s.: fragilità, *f.* **-gible**, ADJ.: fragile.
frănk 1, ADJ.: franco, libero; sincero, generoso, liberale. **frank** 2, s.: porcile; franco, *m.* **frank** 3, TR.: ingrassare; francare, privilegiare (lettere). **-chase**, s.: libertà da cacciare, *f.* **-fee**, s.: feudo libero, *m.* **-incense**, s.: incenso, *m.* **-ly**, ADV.: francamente; schiettamente. **-ness**, s.: franchezza; sincerità; ingenuità, *f.*
frăntic, **-al**, ADJ.: frenetico, furioso. **-ally**, ADV.: da frenetico. **-ness**, s.: pazzia, *f.*
fratĕr-nal, ADJ.: fraterno. **-nally**, ADV.: fraternamente, da fratello. **-nity**, s.: fraternità, fratellanza; compagnia, *f.* **-nizātion**, s.: fratellanza, *f.*
frătęr-nīze, TR.: fraternizzare.
frătricīde, s.: fraticidio; fraticida, *m.*
frăud, s.: fraude, frode; trufferia, *f.*; inganno, *m.* **-ful**, ADJ.: fraudevole, ingannevole. **-fully**, ADV.: con fraude. **-dulence**, **-ulency**, s.: fraudolenza; frode, *f.* **-ulent**, ADJ.: fraudolente. **-ulently**, ADV.: fraudolentemente.
frăught, PART.: caricato, noleggiato; empiuto, fornito: — *with*, pieno di, ricco di, zeppo di. **-age**†, s.: carico (d' un vascello), *m.*
frăy 1, s.: rissa, contesa; zuffa, *f.* **fray** 2, TR.: fregare, usare; spaventare, intimorire; INTR.: usarsi.
frēak 1, s.: ghiribizzo, capriocio, *m.*; fantasia, *f.* **freak** 2, TR.: picchiettare, divisare a più colori. **-ish**, ADJ.: fantastico, capriccioso. **-ishly**, ADV.: capricciosamente, a capriccio; di fantasia. **-ishness**, s.: bizzarria, *f.*
frĕck-le, s.: lentiggine; macchia rossa, *f.* **-led**, **-ly**, ADJ.: lentigginoso.
frēe 1, ADJ.: libero, franco; liberale; immune; ingenuo, sincero; naturale; volontario: — *trade*, libero scambio; — *will*, libero arbitrio; — *from care*, sciolto da cure; *make too* —, arrogarsi troppa licenza; — *of postage*, franco di porto; *be* — *from business*, esser disoccupato; *be too* —, arrogarsi troppa licenza; (*nav.*) *go* —, navigare contro vento; *set* —, francare, affrancare. **free** 2, TR.: liberare, essentare; francare. **-booter**, s.: rubatore, scorridore, *m.* **-booting**, s.: bottino; predamento, *m.* **-born**, ADJ.: nato libero. **-chapel**, s.: cappella pubblica, *f.* **-cost**†, ADJ.: gratuito, senza spesa. **-d**, ADJ.: liberato; francato. **-dman**, s.: schiavo fatto libero, liberta, *m.* **-dom**, s.: libertà; franchigia, *f.*; privilegio, *m.*, immunità; facilità, *f.* **-hearted**, ADJ.: liberale, generoso. **-heartedness**, s.: liberalità, generosità, *f.* **-hold**, s.: feudo, *m.* **-holder**, s.: franco livellario, *m.* **-ly**, ADV.: liberamente, volentieri. **-man**, s.: uomo libero, borghese, *m.* **-mason**, s.: framassone, *m.* **-masonry**, s.: framassoneria, *f.* **-minded**, ADJ.: libero, ingenuo. **-ness**, s.: libertà; liberalità; sincerità, *f.* **-school**, s.: scuola pubblica, *f.* **-spoken**, ADJ.: franco, candido, ingenuo. **-stone**, s.: pietra macigna, *f.*, macigno, *m.* **-thinker**, s.: libero pensatore, *m.* **-thinking**, **-thought**, s.: libero pensiero, *m.* **-will**, s.: libero arbitrio, *m.* **-woman**, s.: donna libera, *f.*
frēeze, IRR.; TR.: gelare, congelare, agghiacciare; INTR.: gelare, congelarsi, agghiacciarsi: — *to death*, assiderare; far morire di freddo.
frēight 1, s.: nolo, noleggio, *m.*, carica, *f.* **freight** 2, (IR)R.; TR.: noleggiare; caricare. **-er**, s.: noleggiatore, *m.* **-ing**, s.: nolo, *m.*
Frĕnch, ADJ., s.: francese, di Francia: — *bean*, fagi(u)olo, *m.*; — *language*, lingua francese; — *woman*, francese, *f.* **-ify**, TR.: infrancesare, dare le maniere francesi, far divenir francese. **-man**, s.: francese, *m.*
frenĕtic, ADJ.: frenetico, insano, furioso.
frĕnzy, s.: frenesia, pazzia, *f.*, furore, *m.*
frē-quence, **-quency**, s.: frequenza; moltitudine, *f.*, concorso, *m.* **-quent** 1, ADJ.: frequente; frequentato. **-quĕnt** 2, TR.: frequentare; spesseggiare. **-quĕntable**, ADJ.: accessibile, conversabile. **-quĕntative**, ADJ.: frequentativo. **-quĕnter**, s.: frequentatore, *m.* **-quĕnting**, s.: frequentazione, *f.* **-quently**, ADV.: frequentemente, spesso. **-quentness**, s.: frequenza, *f.*
frĕsco, s.: pittura a fresco, *f.*
frĕsh, ADJ.: fresco, nuovo, recente: — *water*, acqua dolce, *f.*; s.: (*nav.*) corrente d' acqua dolce, *m.* **-en**, TR.: rinfrescare, dissalare; INTR.: rinfrescarsi. **-et**, s.: laghetto d'acqua dolce, *m.* **-ly**, ADV.: frescamente; recentemente, novellamente. **-ness**, s.: freschezza, *f.*, fresco, *m.*
frĕt 1, s.: fermentazione; agitazione; cruccio; tasto; stretto, *m.*: *be in a* —, crucciarsi, corrucciarsi, stizzarsi. **fret** 2, TR.: fregare; vessare, irritare, stizzare, cruciare; INTR.: agitarsi, inquietarsi, alterarsi, adirarsi. **-ful**, ADJ.: stizzoso, cruccioso. **-fully**, ADV.: in modo stizzoso. **-fulness**, s.: umore stizzoso, *m.*,

iracondia, fantasticaggine, *f.;* capriccio, *m.* **-saw**, s.: piccola sega, *f.* **-ting**, s.: agitazione, *f.* **-ty**, ADJ.: intagliato. **-work**, s.: intaglio: lavoro di rilievo, *m.*

fri-ability, s.: friabilità, *f.* **-able**, ADJ.: friabile, polverizzabile.

friar, s.: frate, monaco, religioso, *m.* **-like**, **-ly**, ADJ.: da frate, fratesco. **-y**, s.: monasterio, convento, *m.*

frib-ble, INTR.: baloccare. **-bler**, s.: babbaccio; damerino, *m.*

fricassée, s.: (*cook.*) fricassea, *f.*

fricātion, **friction**, s.: fregamento, *m.*

Friday, s.: venerdì, *m.*: *good* —, venerdì santo, *m.*

fridge, INTR.: saltellare.

fridstoll†, s.: rifugio, asilo, *m.*

friĕnd 1, s.: amico, *m.;* amica, *f.;* confidente; compagno, *m.*: —*s*, parenti, congiunti, *m. pl.* **friend** 2, TR.: favorire, proteggere. **-less**, ADJ.: senza amici. **-like**, ADJ.: da amico, benevolente. **-liness**, s.: amicizia, benevolenza, *f.* **-ly**, ADJ.: amichevole, benevolo; ADV.: amichevolmente, da amico. **-ship**, s.: amicizia, *f.*

frieze, s.: fregio, *m.*

frigate, s.: fregata, *f.*

fright, s.: timore, *m.*, paura, *f.*, spavento, terrore, *m.*: *put in* —, intimorire, spaventare; *take* —, spaventarsi, impaurire; (*of horses*) ombrare. **-en**, TR.: intimorire, impaurire, spaventare, sbigottire: — *one out of his wits*, atterrire (sbalordire) uno. **-ful**, ADJ.: spaventevole, terribile. **-fully**, ADV.: spaventevolmente. **-fulness**, s.: orrore, terrore, *m.*

frig-id, s.: frigido, freddo, *m.* **-idity**, s.: frigidità, freddezza; impotenza, *f.* **-idly**, ADV.: freddamente. **-idness**, s.: frigidità, *f.*

frigorific, ADJ.: frigorifico, frigorifero.

frill, INTR.: tremare di freddo.

fringe 1, s.: frangia, *f.;* cerro, *m.* **fringe** 2, TR.: frangiare, guarnire di frange.

frip-per(er), s.: rigattiere, *m.* **-pery**, s.: strada de' rigattieri, *f.;* ciarpe, *f. pl.*

frisqur, s.: acconciatore dei capelli, parrucchiere, *m.*

frisk 1, ADJ.: gioioso, allegro; s.: salto, *m.;* gaiezza, allegria, *f.* **frisk** 2, INTR.: salterellare; scambiettare. **-er**, s.: saltatore, *m.* **-iness**, s.: allegrezza, vivacità, gaiezza, *f.* **-y**, ADJ.: gaio, allegro, vivace, svelto: *he is getting* —, egli comincia a fare il libertino.

frith, s.: stretto, braccio di mare, *m.*

fritillary, s.: (*bot.*) fritillaria, *f.*

fritter 1, s.: frittella, *f.* **fritter** 2, TR.: tritare, sminuzzare; consumare.

frivŏlity, s.: frivolezza, *f.*

frivolous, ADJ.: frivolo, vano. **-ly**, ADV.: frivolmente; di poca importanza. **-ness**, s.: frivolezza, *f.*

friz-zle, TR.: arricciare, inanellare. **-zler**, s.: acconciatore de' capelli, *m.*

frō, ADV.: qua e là; indietro: *go to and* —, andare qua e là, andare e venire.

frŏck, s.: abito, vestimento, *m.*

frŏg, s.: rannochia, rana, *f.;* (*vet.*) fettone, *m.;* spaccatura, *f.*

frŏlic 1, ADJ.: ghiribizzoso, fantastico, gaio, lieto; s.: ghiribizzo, *m.*, fantasia, *f.* **frolic** 2, INTR.: ghiribizzare, burlare, beffare. **-ly**, ADV.: gaiamente, allegramente. **-some**, ADJ.: scherzoso, gaio. **-somely**, ADV.: scherzosamente. **-someness**, s.: scherzo, *m.;* beffe, *f. pl.*

frŏm, PREP.: da, dal (dallo, dalla) di: — *abroad*, di fuori; — *that moment*, da quel momento; — *time to* —, di quando in quando; — *henceforth*, da qui innanzi: — *whence?* di dove? donde? — *my youth*, — *my childhood*, dalla mia fanciullezza; — *top to toe*, da capo a piedi; *tell him* — *me*, ditegli da parte mia; — *what I see*, per quel che vedo. **-ward**, ADV.: dalla parte opposta.

frondiferous, ADJ.: frondifero.

frŏnt 1, s.: fronte, *f.;* frontispizio, *m.;* vanguardia; impudenza, *f.* **front** 2, TR.: fronteggiare; INTR.: stare a fronte. **-al**, s.: frontale, *m.;* benda, striscia, *f.* **-box**, s.: mezzo palchetto, *m.* **-ier**, ADJ.: limitrofo; confinante; s.: frontiera, limite, *f.* **-ispiece**, s.: frontispizio, *m.;* facciata, *f.* **-less**, ADJ.: sfacciato, impudente. **-let**, s.: frontale, *m.*, benda, *f.* **-ōon**, s.: frontone, frontispizio, *m.* **-room**, s.: camera di dinanzi, *f.*

frŏppish†, ADJ.: stizzoso, malinconico.

frŏry†, ADJ.: agghiacciato, gelato.

frŏst, s.: gelata, *f.;* ghiaccio, *m.*: *hard* —, gran gelata; *hoar* —, brina(ta), *f.* **-bitten**, ADJ.: attaccato dal ghiaccio, gelato. **-ed**, ADJ.: agghiacciato, diacciato. **-ily**, ADV.: con freddo eccessivo. **-iness**, s.: freddo acuto, *m.* **-nail**, s.: chiodo a ghiaccio, *m.* **-y**, ADJ.: ghiacciato, gelato.

frŏth 1, s.: schiuma, spuma, *f.* **froth** 2, INTR.: schiumare, spumare. **-y**, ADJ.: spumoso; frivolo, vano.

frŏunce, TR.: arricciare i capelli.

frŏusy, ADJ.: nebbioso; fosco; mucido, fetido.

frŏward, ADJ.: stizzoso, arcigno, bizzarro, fantastico; ostinato, perverso. **-ly**, ADV.: ostinatamente, perversamente. **-ness**, s.: cattivo umore, *m.;* ostinazione, perversità, *f.*

frŏwn 1, s.: raggrinzamento (della fronte); sdegno, disprezzo, *m.* **frown** 2

INTR.: ringhiare; increspare le ciglia: — *back*, respingere con uno sguardo; — *down*, atterrire. **-ing**, ADJ.: arcigno, burbero, torvo. **-ingly**, ADV.: con viso arcigno, stortamente.

fröze, impf. del v. *freeze*. **-n**, ADJ.: gelato, agghiacciato (cf. *freeze*).

fructif-erous, ADJ.: fruttifero, fruttuoso. **-icâtion**, S.: fruttificazione, *f.* **-y**, TR.: rendere fertile, fertilizzare, fecondare; INTR.: fruttare, fare frutto.

fructu-ôsity, S.: fertilità, *f.* **-ous**, ADJ.: fruttuoso, fruttifero, fecondo; utile.

frü-gal, ADJ.: frugale; parco, economo; moderato, sobrio. **-gâlity**, S.: frugalità; moderanza, *f.* **-gally**, ADV.: frugalmente; parcamente. **-giferous**, ADJ.: frugifero, fruttifero.

frûit, S.: frutto; profitto, *m.*, rendita, entrata, *f.*: *first* —*s*, premizie, *f. pl.* **-age**, S.: frutta, *f. pl.* **-basket**, S.: paniere delle frutta, *m.* **-bearer**, S.: albero fruttifero, *m.* **-bearing**, ADJ.: fruttifero. **-erer**, S.: fruttaiolo, fruttaiuolo, *m.* **-ery**, S.: dispensa delle frutta, *f.*; frutta, *f. pl.* **-ful**, ADJ.: fertile; fecondo; profittabile, utile. **-fully**, ADV.: fertilmente. **-fulness**, S.: fertilità, fecondità; abbondanza, *f.* **-grove**, S.: verziere, *m.* **-house**, S.: dispensa delle frutta, *f.* **fruition**, S.: fruizione, *f.*; godimento, *m.* **-less**, ADJ.: infruttuoso, sterile; inutile. **-lessly**, ADV.: inutilmente; vanamente. **-lessness**, S.: sterilità; inutilità, *f.* **-loft**, S.: dispensa delle frutta, *f.* **-seller**, S.: fruttaiuolo, *m.* **-time**, S.: stagione de' frutti, *f.* **-trade**, S.: commercio delle frutta, *m.* **-tree**, S.: albero fruttifero, *m.*

frumentâceous, ADJ.: frumentaceo.

frûmenty, S.: farinata fatta con latte, *f.*

frûmp† 1, S.: burla, beffa, *f.* **frump**† 2, TR.: burlare, beffare; schernire.

frûs-trate 1, ADJ.: vano; inutile; inefficace. **-trate** 2, TR.: frustrare; annullare; deludere. **-trâtion**, S.: delusione, *f.*; disfacimento, *m.* **-trative**†, **-tratory**†, ADJ.: frustraneo, vano.

frûstum, S.: frusto, pezzuolo, frammento, *m.*

frŷ 1, S.: fregola, *f.*, pesciolini, *m. pl.*; sciame di bambini, *m.*; frittura, *f.* **fry** 2, TR.: friggere. **-ing-pan**, S.: padella, *f.*

fûage, S.: tassa de' fuochi, *f.*

fûb† 1, S.: fanciullo grassotto e paffuto, *m.* **fub**† 2, TR.: differire, mandare in lungo.

fû-cated, ADJ.: fucato, orpellato. **-cus**, S.: belletto; liscio, *m.*

fûddl-e, TR.: ubbriacare, imbriacare; INTR.: imbriacarsi. **-ed**, ADJ.: briaco, imbriaco. **-er**, S.: imbriaco, *m.* **-ing**, S.: imbriacamento, *m.*

fûdge, INTERJ.: minchionerie! son frottole!

fûel, S.: provvisione di legna, carboni, ecc., *f.*: *add — to flame*, aggiunger legna al fuoco.

fu-gâcious, ADJ.: fugace; transitorio. **-gâciousness**, **-gâcity**, S.: fugacità; fuga, *f.*

fûgh, INTERJ.: oibò!

fûgitive, ADJ.: fuggitivo; volatile; S.: fuggitivo, fuggitore, *m.* **-ness**, S.: instabilità, volatilità; incertezza, *f.*

fûgue, S.: (mus.) fuga, *f.*

fulfil, TR.: adempire, compire; satisfare; effettuare. **-ler**, S.: adempitore, *m.* **-ling**, **-ment**, S.: adempimento, compimento, *m.*

fûl-gency, S.: fulgidezza, *f.*; splendore; fulgore, *m.* **-gent**, ADJ.: fulgente. **-gid**, ADJ.: fulgido, lucido. **-gidity**, **-gor**, S.: fulgidezza, *f.*; fulgore, *m.* **-gurate**, INTR.: folgorare. **-gurâtion**, S.: folgorare; folgore, baleno, *m.*

fuliginous, ADJ.: fuligginoso, fumoso.

fûll 1, ADJ.: pieno, ripieno, colmo, compito; intero, totale; S.: compimento; tutto, totale, *m.*: — *face*, viso pienotto, *m.*; — *moon*, plenilunio, *m.*; — *power*, pieno potere, *m.*; — *sea*, alto mare, *m.*; *of — age*, adulto; *to the* —, interamente, affatto, del tutto, appieno; *the moon is in the* —, la luna è piena. **full** 2, ADV.: pienamente, interamente, affatto; esattamente; bene. **full** 3, TR.: sodare; follare, calpestare. **-age**, S.: pagamento del sodare i panni, *m.* **-bodied**, ADJ.: grosso, corpacciuto. **-eared**, ADJ.: pieno di spighe. **-face**, S.: viso pienotto, *m.* **-faced**, ADJ.: pienotto, paffuto.

fûller, S.: follone; purgatore, *m.*: —*'s earth*, creta da sodare i panni, *f.*; —*'s weed*, cardo da cardare i panni, *m.* **-y**, S.: gualchiera, *f.*

fûll-eyed, ADJ.: che ha occhi grandi. **-fed**, ADJ.: grosso, corpulento. **-grown**, ADJ.: di pieno crescimento, grosso.

fûlling-mill, S.: mulino da sodare i panni, *m.*; gualchiera, *f.*

fûll-laden, ADJ.: affatto caricato, pieno. **-moon**, S.: luna piena, *f.* **-orbed**, ADJ.: intieramente illuminato. **-y**, ADV.: interamente, pienamente, ampiamente.

fûlmi-nant, ADJ.: fulminante. **-nate**, (IN)TR.: fulminare. **-nâtion**, S.: fulminazione, *f.* **-natory**, ADJ.: fulmineo, fulminante.

fûlness, S.: ripienezza; abbondanza, *f.*

fûlsome, ADJ.: dispiacevole, nauseoso, fastidioso; osceno. **-ly**, ADV.: fastidiosamente. **-ness**, S.: nausea, *f.*, fastidio, disgusto, *m.*; oscenità, *f.*

fûl-vid, **-vous**, ADJ.: fulvo.

fumādo, S.: pesce affumicato, *m.*
fūmatory, S.: fumosterno, *m.*
fŭmbl-e, INTR.: maneggiare con mala grazia, malmenare; balbettare. **-er**, S.: bietolone, scempiato; sciocco, *m.* **-ingly**, ADV.: goffamente, in modo malaccorto.
fū-me 1, S.: fumo, vapore, *m.;* esalazione; vanità, chimera, *f.* **-me** 2, TR.: seccare al fumo, fumicare; esalare; INTR.: fumare; svaporarsi; adirarsi. **-met** 1, S.: sterco di cervo, *m.* **-met** 2, **-mĕtte**, S.: odore (della carne), *m.* **-mid**, ADJ.: fumoso. **-midity**, S.: fumosità, *f.* **-migate**, TR.: suffumicare, fumicare. **-migation**, S.: fumigazione, *f.*, suffumicamento, *m.* **-mingly**, ADV.: adiratamente, collericamente. **-mish**, ADJ.: fumoso; collerico. **-mitory**, S.: fumosterno, *m.* **-mous**, **-my**, ADJ.: fumoso, vaporoso.
fŭn, S.: divertimento, passatempo, *m.;* baia, burla, *f.: make — of*, farsi beffa di.
funămbulist, S.: funambolo, *m.*
fŭnction, S.: funzione, *f.;* impiego, *m.;* facoltà, *f.* **-ary**, S.: impiegato, *m.*
fŭnd 1, S.: fondo; capitale; banco, *m.: sinking —*, cassa di ammortizzazione; *the —s are up*, i fondi sono in rialzo. **fund** 2, TR.: collocare i denari. **-ament**, S.: fondamento, *m.* **-amĕntal**, ADJ.: fondamentale, principale; S.: fondamento, *m.;* base, *f.* **-amĕntally**, ADV.: fondamentalmente. **-ed**, ADJ.: (impiegato) nei fondi publici; (investito) in rendita dello stato: *— debt*, debito consolidato.
fū-neral, ADJ.: funerale, funebre; S.: funerale; mortorio, *m.;* esequie, *f. pl.: attend the —*, assistere alle esequie; *— expenses*, spese funerarie; *— pile*, rogo; pira funerea; *— procession*, comitiva (accompagnamento) funebre; *— service*, mortorio; ufficio dei morti; *— song*, canto funebre. **-nerary**, ADJ.: funereo, funebre; lugubre. **-nerātion**, S.: esequie, *f. pl.* **-nĕreal** = *funerary*.
fun-gŏsity, S.: escrescenza carnosa, *f.* **-gous**, ADJ.: fungoso, spugnoso. **-gus**, S.: fungo, *m.;* escrescenza di carne, *f.*
fū-nicle, S.: funicella, *f.*, funicello, *m.* **-nicular**, ADJ.: funicolare.
fŭnk, S.: (*low*) fetore; tanfo, *m.*
fŭnnel, S.: imbuto, *m.*, pevera, *f.*
fŭnny, ADJ.: buffonesco, giocoso; strano.
fŭr 1, S.: pelliccia, pelle, *f.* **fur** 2, TR.: foderare; impellicare.
fu-rācious, ADJ.: furace, inclinato a rubare. **-rāciousness**, **-răcity**, S.: inclinazione a rubare, *f.*
fŭrbelow, S.: falbala; guarnizione, *f.* **furbelow** 2, TR.: guarnire di falbale.
fŭrbish, TR.: forbire, pulire. **-er**, S.: forbitore, spadaio, *m.*
furcātion, S.: forcatura, forcata, *f.*
fŭrfur, S.: forfora, tigna, scabbia, *f.* **-āceous**, ADJ.: forforaceo.
fūrious, ADJ.: furioso, frenetico. **-ly**, ADV.: furiosamente, con furia. **-ness**, S.: furia, frenesia, pazzia, *f.*
fŭrl, TR.: (*nav.*) ammainare, serrare (le vele); piegare. **-ing-line**, S.: (*nav.*) matafione, *m.*
fŭrlong, S.: ottava parte d' un miglio, *f.;* stadio, *m.*
fŭrlough 1, S.: permissione d' assenza; licenza, *f.: in —*, in congedio. **furlough** 2, TR.: licenziare, congedare.
fŭrmenty, S.: farinata, *f.*
fŭrnace, S.: fornace, *f.*, forno grande, *m.: blasting —*, forno alto; *melting —*, forno, fornello di fusione, *m.*
fŭr-nish, TR.: fornire; provvedere; addobare, mobiliare (*a house*). **-nished**, ADJ.: provveduto; addobuto, mobiliato; munito: *— rooms*, stanze mobiliate. **-nisher**, S.: che fornisce, provveditore, *m.* **-niture**, S.: guarnitura, *f.;* fornimento, *m.;* addobbi, mobili, *m. pl.: piece of —*, mobile, *m.*
fŭrrier, S.: pellicciaio, pellicciere, *m.*
fŭrrow 1, S.: solco; fosso, fossatello, *m.* **furrow** 2, TR.: solcare, assolcare; rugare.
fŭrry, ADJ.: coprito di pelliccia.
fŭrther 1, ADJ.: ulteriore; più rimoto; novello; ADV.: più in là, più oltre; di più, più avanti, più innanzi, ancora: *a little —*, un po' più in là; *I cannot go —*, non posso andar più oltre. **further** 2, TR.: avanzare, assistere, aiutare; promuovere. **-ance**, S.: aiuto, *m.*, assistenza, *f.;* avanzamento, progresso, *m.* **-er**, S.: promotore; protettore, *m.* **-more**, ADV.: di più, oltre; oltre a ciò. **-most**, ADJ.: il più lontano, lontanissimo, rimotissimo: *at —*, al più tardi.
fŭrtive, ADJ.: furtivo, di furto; segreto. **-ly**, ADV.: furtivamente; segretamente.
fūruncle, S.: furuncolo, ciccione, *m.*
fūry, S.: furia, frenesia; ira, stizza, *f.;* impeto, furore, *m.: break into a fit of —*, entrare in furia; dar nelle furie; *rouse to —*, far salire in furia. **-like**, ADJ.: come una furia, arrabbiato.
fūrz-e, S.: (*bot.*) erica, *f.* **-y**, ADJ.: pieno d' eriche.
fus-cātion, S.: oscurità, *f.;* oscuramento, *m.* **-cous**, ADJ.: fosco, oscuro.
fūse 1, TR.: fondere; INTR.: liquefarsi, struggersi; dilatarsi. **fuse** 2, S.: tubo a combustibili.
fusēe, S.: fuso, *m.;* (*watch.*) piramide, *f.*
fusibility, S.: fusibilità, *f.* **fūsible**, ADJ.: fusibile, fusile.
fūsil, S.: fucile, focile; schioppo, *m.*

-ier, S.: archibusiere, schioppettiere, fusiliere, *m.*
fūsion, S.: fusione, liquefazione, *f.*
fŭss, S.: fracasso, strepito, *m.*: *make a* —, menar scalpore; affaccendarsi.
fŭst, S.: fusto, *m.*; odore muffato, *m.*
fŭstian, ADJ.: di frustagno; ampolloso; S.: frustagno; anfanamento, *m.*, ampollosità, *f.*
fŭsti-gāte, TR.: frustrare, sferzare. **-gātion**, S.: sferzata, bastonatura, *f.*
fustilārian†, S.: briccone, furfante, *m.*
fŭs-tiness, S.: mucidezza, muffa, *f.*; tanfo, *m.* **-ty**, ADJ.: mucido, muffato.
fū-tile, ADJ.: futile, frivolo. **-tility**, S.: leggerezza; vanità; garrulità, *f.* **-tilous**, ADJ.: futile, di niun valore.
fŭttocks, S. PL.: (*nav.*) bracciuoli, *m. pl.*
fū-ture, ADJ.: futuro, che viene; S.: futuro, avvenire, *m.*: *for the* —, nell' avvenire. **-tureless**, ADJ.: senza futuro. **-turely**†, ADV.: in futuro, per l' avvenire. **-tūrity**, S.: tempo futuro, avvenire, *m.*
fŭzz, S.: pezzo, *m.*; inezia, *f.* **-ball**, S.: veccia, *f.* (fungo).
fȳ, INTERJ.: oibò! — *for shame!* deh vergognatevi!

G

g gē (*the letter*), S.: g, *m.*
găb 1, S.: muso, ceffo; cicalio, *m.*: *have the gift of* —, avere una buona parlantina. **gab** 2, INTR.: cicalare.
gabardine, S.: palandrano, gabbano, *m.*
găbbl-e 1, S.: chiacchieria, ciarla, *f.*, garrimento, *m.* **-e** 2, INTR.: cicalare, barbugliare. **-er**, S.: ciarlone, ciarliero, *m.* **-ing**, S.: cicalamento, cicalio; susurro, *m.*
gābel, S.: gabella; tassa, imposizione, *f.* **-er**, S.: gabelliere, *m.*
gābion, S.: (*mil.*) gabbione, *m.* **-āde**, S.: (*mil.*) gabbionata, *f.*
gāble, **-end**, S.: gronda, *f.*
găd 1, S.: pezzo d' acciaio; bulino, *m.* **gad** 2, INTR.: andare qua e là; girare: — *abroad*, — *about*, vagabondare, vagare; — *up and down*, andare ramingo. **-about**, S.: donna che va vagando, *f.* **-der**, S.: vagabondo; perdigiorno, *m.* **-ding**, S.: vagare, vagamento, *m.* **-dingly**, ADV.: in modo vagabondo. **-fly**, S.: tafano, *m.*
găff, S.: uncino, graffio, m.
găffer, S.: buon compagno; compadre, *m.* **-ăffles**, S. PL.: sproni d' acciaio per i galli, *m. pl.*; chiave da tendere la balestra, *f.*
g 1, S.: sbarra, *f.*; impedimento, *m.* **g** 2, TR.: porre in bocca una sbarra.
găg-e 1, S.: pegno, *m.*; sicurtà; stazza, *f.* **-e** 2, TR.: impegnare; dare in pegno, stazare. **-er**, S.: misuratore, *m.*
găggl-e, INTR.: gridare, gracidare. **-ing**, S.: grido (d' oca), *m.*
gāi-ety, S.: gioia, gaiezza; letizia, *f.* **-ly**, ADV.: gioiosamente, gaiamente; allegramente.
gāin 1, S.: guadagno, lucro, profitto, *m.*: *clear* —, guadagno netto. **gain** 2, TR.: guadagnare; acquistare, far acquisto, meritare; ottenere; INTR.: avvanzarsi; impadronirsi; aggrandirsi: — *the day* (*victory*), guadagnar (riportar) la battaglia; — *one's end*, ottenere il suo intento, riuscire; venire a capo; — *ground*, avere l' avvantaggio; — *over*, persuadere; convertire. **-able**, ADJ.: ottenibile, impetrabile. **-er**, S.: guadagnatore, *m.* **-ful**, ADJ.: lucrativo, vantaggioso, profittevole, fruttuoso; utile. **-fully**, ADV.: profittevolmente, vantaggiosamente; utilmente. **-fulness**, S.: guadagno, profitto, lucro, vantaggio, *m.* **-giving**, S.: presentimento, *m.* **-less**, ADJ.: disavvantaggioso, inutile. **-lessness**, S.: inutilità, *f.*
gāinly†, ADV.: destramente, prontamente, facilmente.
gainsāy, TR.: contraddire; opporsi, contrariare, contrastare. **-er**, S.: contraddicitore; oppositore, *m.* **-ing**, S.: contraddizione, *f.*
'gāinst = *against*.
gāin-stand†, **-strive**†, TR.: resistere, opporsi.
gāirish, ADJ.: fastoso, pomposo, splendido, sfoggiato. **-ness**, S.: fasto, sfoggio, *m.*; stravaganza, *f.*
gāit, S.: andamento, portamento, *m.*; aria, *f.*
gāiters, S. PL.: ghette, *f. pl.*
gāla, S.: gala, *f.*; banchetto, *m.*: — *day*, giorno di gala.
gălaxy, S.: (*astr.*) galassia, via lattea, *f.*
gălbanum, S.: galbano, *m.*
gāle 1, S.: vento fresco, colpo di vento, *m.* **gale** 2, TR.: cantare (uccelli).
găleas, S.: galeazza, *f.*
găliot, S.: galeotta, *f.*
gâll 1, S.: fiele; (*fig.*) odio; rancore, *m.* **gall** 2, TR.: scorticare; tormentare, molestare, infastidire; offendere; INTR.: tormentarsi; affligersi.
găllant, ADJ.: galante; attillato, elegante; gentile, onesto; bravo, vigoroso: — *man*, galantuomo, *m.* **gallănt**, S.: zerbino; innamorato, amante, *m.* **-ly**, ADV.: galantemente, cortesemente; gagliardamente, bravamente. **-ness**, S.: galanteria, garbatezza, *f.* **-ry**, S.: galanteria, *f.*; coraggio, *m.*, bravura, *f.*, valore, *m.*
gâll-bladder, S.: vescica del fiele, *f.*

găllęọn, s.: galeone, *m.*
găllęry, s.: galleria; loggia, *f.*; andito, *m.*: *open* —, loggia; *covered* —, androne, *m.*
găllęy, s.: galea, galera, *f.* **-slave**, s.: galeotto, forzato, *m.*
găllįard, s.: gagliardo, *m.*; gagliarda, *f.* **-įze†**, s.: allegria, gaiezza, gioia, *f.*
găllicįsm, s.: gallicismo, *m.*
galligăskins, s. pl.: calzoni grandi, *m. pl.*
gallimăufry, s.: cibreo, manicaretto di più vivande riscaldate, *m.*
gălliot = *galiot*.
găllipot, s.: alberello, *m.*
găll-nut, s.: noce di galla; galluzza, *f.*
găllọn, s.: misura di quattro boccali, *f.*
gallōon, s.: gallone, *m.*; guarnizione, *f.*
găllọp 1, s.: galoppo; galoppare, *m.*: *go a* —, galoppare; *at full* —, a briglia sciolta (*or* a carriera). **gallop** 2, INTR.: galloppare; correre. **-pẹr**, s.: galoppatore, *m.* **-ping**, s.: galoppare, *m.*; galoppata, *f.*
găllọw†, TR.: spaventare, atterrire.
găllọwęy, s.: piccolo cavallo inglese, ronzino, *m.*
găllọwș (pl. —, *or* -ęș), s.: forca, *f.*, patibolo, *m.* **-bird**, s.: capestro, *m.* **-tree** = *gallows*.
galōsh, s.: galoscia, soprascarpa, *f.*
galvănic, ADJ.: galvanico: — *battery*, pila voltaica, *f.*
găl-vanįșm, s.: galvanismo, *m.* **-vanįze**, TR.: galvanizzare.
gambā-do, **-dọ**, s.: uosa, *f.*; stivaletto, *m.*
găm-ble, INTR.: giuocare; barare, mariolare. **-blẹr**, s.: giuocatorone; scroccone, *m.* **-bling-house**, s.: casino da giuocare, *m.*, bisca, biscazza, *f.*
gambōge, s.: gommagutte, *f.*
găm̆bol 1, s.: salto, scambietto, *m.*; capriola, *f.* **gambol** 2, INTR.: salterellare.
găm̆brel, s.: gamba deretana (d' un cavallo), *f.*
gāme 1, s.: giuoco; scherzo, passatempo, *m.*; caccia, salvaggina, *f.*: *play a* —, fare (*or* giocare) una partita; *make* — *of*, beffare, farsi giuoco di. **game** 2, INTR.: giuocare; biscazzare; scherzare. **-bag**, s.: carniera, *f.*, carniere, *m.* **-cock**, s.: gallo di combattimento, *m.* **-keeper**, s.: guardiano di caccia, *m.* **-sọme**, ADJ.: giocoso, allegro, giocondo. **-sọmely**, ADV.: giocosamente, scherzevolmente. **-sọmeness**, s.: scherzo, trastullo, *m.*; baia, *f.* **-stẹr**, s.: giuocatore; biscazziere, *m.*
gāming, s.: giuoco, giuocare, biscazzare, *m.* **-house**, s.: biscazza, bisca, *f.* **-table**, s.: tavola da giuoco, *f.*
găm̆mọn, s.: presciutto; sbaraglino, *m.*
gămut, s.: (*mus.*) solfa, zolfa, *f.*
găndẹr, s.: maschio dell' oca, *m.*
găng 1, s.: truppa, banda; società, *f.* **gang** 2, INTR.: andare, camminare. **-board**, s.: (*nav.*) tavola da sparco, *f.*
gănglion, s.: (*anat.*) ganglio, *m.*
găngrę-ne 1, s.: (*med.*) cangrena, *f.* **-ne** 2, INTR.: incancherire, incangrenarsi. **-nous**, ADJ.: cangrenoso.
găng-way, s.: passavanti d' una nave da guerra, corridore, *m.* **-week**, s.: settimana delle Rogazioni, *f.*
gănt-let 1, s.: (*mil.*) bacchette, *f. pl.*; (*nav.*) bolina, *f.*: *run the* —, passar per le bacchette, correre la bolina. **-let** 2 = *gauntlet*. **-lope** = *-let*.
gănza, s.: oca salvatica, *f.*
gāol, s.: prigione, *f.*, carcere, *m.* **-ẹr**, s.: guardiano delle prigioni, carceriere, *m.*
găp, s.: apertura, crepatura; lacuna; breccia; deficienza, *f.*
găp-e, INTR.: sbadigliare; creparsi, spaccarsi, aprirsi: — *after*, desiderare; aspirare; — *at*, guardare colla bocca aperta; desiderare; — *for*, desiderare con avidità, bramare con ansietà. **-ẹr**, s.: che spadiglia; che brama con ansietà. **-ing**, s.: spadigliamento, *m.*; fessura, crepatura, *f.*: *stand* —, baloccare; fraschеggiare.
găp-toothed, ADJ.: sdentato.
gârb, s.: vestimento, abito, *m.*; aria; maniera, *f.*, portamento, *m.*
gârbąge, s.: trippe, *f. pl.*; rifiuto, *m.*, spazzatura, *f.*
gâr-ble, TR.: scegliere; scernere, separare. **-blẹr**, s.: sceglitore, *m.* **-bleș**, s. pl.: mondiglie, vagliature (di droghe, ecc.), *f. pl.*
gârboįl, s.: disordine, confusione; tumulto, romore, *m.*
gârden 1, s.: giardino, *m.*: *little* —, giardinetto, *m.*; — *plot*, parterre, *m.*; — *walks*, viali, andari, *m. pl.* **garden** 2, INTR.: far il giardiniere. **-ẹr**, s.: giardiniere, *m.*; giardiniera, *f.* **-ing**, s.: coltivare un giardino, giardinaggio, *m.*, erbaggi, *m. pl.* **-mold, mould**, s.: terra vegetabile, *f.* **-plot**, s.: spartimento d' un giardino, *m.* **-stuff, -ware**, s.: erbaggio, *m.*
gāre, s.: lana piena di zacchere, *f.*
gârgarįșm, s.: gargarismo, *m.*
gârgle 1, s.: gargarismo, *m.* **gargle** 2, TR.: gargarizzare.
gârgọl, s.: lebbra de' porci, *f. pl.*
gârish, ADJ.: splendido, pomposo. **-ness**, s.: pompositá, *f.*
gârland, s.: ghirlanda, *f.*
gârlic, s.: aglio, *m.* **-eater**, s.: guidone, uomo basso, *m.* **-sauce**, s.: agliata, *f.*
gârment, s.: abito, vestito, vestimento,

gârner 1, s.: granaio, magazzino del grano, *m.* **garner** 2, TR.: accumulare, ammassare.
gârnet, s.: granato, *m.*; (*nav.*) carrucola, *f.*
gâr-nish 1, s.: ornamento, *m.*; (*fig.*) catene, *f. pl.* **-nish** 2, TR.: guarnire, ornare, abbellire; catenare. **-nishment**, s.: ornamento; abbellimento, *m.*; (*leg.*) citazione, *f.* **-niture**, s.: guarnitura, *f.*; fornimento, *m.*; addobbi, *m. pl.*
gárran, s.: cavallo montagnuolo, cavallino, *m.*
gárret, s.: solaio; soffitta, stanza a tetto, *f.* **-ĕer**, s.: abitatore d' una soffitta, *m.*
gárrison 1, s.: guarnigione, *f.*; soldati, *m. pl.* **garrison** 2, TR.: mettere guarnigione, presidiare; munire.
gar-rŭlity, s.: garrulità, loquacità, ciarleria, *f.* **-rulous**, ADJ.: garrulo, loquace; ciarliero. **-rulousness** = *garrulity*.
gárter 1, s.: legaccio, *m.*, giarrettiera, giartera, *f.*: *knight of the* —, cavaliere della giartera, *m.* **garter** 2, TR.: legare con un legaccio, legarsi i legacciuoli.
gárth, s.: cortile; ricinto, *m.*; grossezza del corpo, *f.*
gás, s.: gas, gaz, *m.*: *jet of* —, getto di gaz: *light with* —, illuminare a gaz; *turn off the* —, chiudere la chiavetta del gaz; *turn on the* —, aprire la chiavetta del gaz. **-burner**, s.: becco del gaz, *m.*
gasconāde 1, s.: guasconata, *f.*, vanto, *m.* **gasconade** 2, INTR.: millantarsi, vantarsi.
gáseous, ADJ.: gasoso, gazoso.
gásh 1, s.: sfregio, taglio, *m.*; cicatrice, *f.* **gash** 2, TR.: sfregiare, tagliare.
gáskins, S. PL.: calzoni grandi, *m. pl.*, brache grandi, *f. pl.*
gás-lamp, s.: lampada di gas, *f.* **-lantern**, s.: lanterna di gas, *f.* **-light**, s.: lume di gas, *m.* **-lighting**, s.: illuminazione di gas, *f.* **-ŏmeter**, s.: gasometro, *m.*
gásp 1, s.: anelito, respiro, ansamento, *m.*: *to the last* —, fin' all' ultimo respiro. **gasp** 2, INTR.: anelare, respirare con affanno: — *after*, desiderare, bramare; — *for breath*, far degli sforzi per respirare; — *for life*, essere al punto di morte, essere agli estremi. **-ing**, s.: respiro con affanno, *m.*, respirazione, *f.*
gás-pipe, s.: tubo, *m.*
gást†, TR.: spaventare, impaurire, atterrire. **-ly**† = *ghastly*.
gás-tric, ADJ.: gastrico. **-triloquist**, s.: ventriloquo, *m.* **-trŏtomy**, s.: (*surg.*) gastrotomia, *f.*
gáte, s.: porta, *f.*: portone; portamento, *m.*: *field*-—, cancello, *m.*; *flood*-—, cateratta, *f.* **-keeper**, s.: guardaporte, portinaio, *m.* **-vein**, s.: (*anat.*) vena porta, *f.* **-way**, s.: portone, passaggio, *m.*
gáther 1, s.: crespa, riga; piega, *f.* **gather** 2, TR.: cogliere, raccogliere; adunare, ramassare; riacrespare, piegare; conchiudere, inferire; INTR.: accumularsi; assembrarsi, adunarsi; condensarsi: — *breath*, respirare; — *the corn*, mietere il grano; — *dust*, impolverarsi; — *the grapes*, vendemmiare; — *riches*, accumulare dovizie; — *rust*, irrugginirsi; — *strength*, rinvigorirsi; — *together*, accozzare, radunare; REFL.: accumularsi, addensarsi; — *up*, raccogliere; — *wealth*, accumulare ricchezze; — *up*, ammassare; rilevare. **-er**, s.: ricoglitore, raccoglitore, *m.*: — *of corn*, mietitore, *m.*; — *of grapes*, vendemmiatore, *m.*; — *of taxes*, collettore di tasse, *m.* **-ing**, s.: collezione, *f.*, coglimento, *m.*: *make a* —, fare una collezione.
gâud 1, s.: ornamento, abbigliamento, *m.* **gaud** 2, TR.: rallegrarsi; divertirsi. **-ery**, s.: vestire pomposo, fasto, *m.* **-ily**, ADV.: fastosamente; sfoggiatamente. **-iness**, s.: sfoggio, fasto, *m.*; ostentazione, *f.* **-y**, ADJ.: pomposo, fastoso; s.: festa, *f.*; festeggiamento, *m.*
gâu-ge 1, s.: staza, *f.*: *narrow* — *railway*, ferrovia a rotaie strette. **-ge** 2, TR.: stazare; misurare. **-ger**, s.: stazatore, misuratore di liquidi, *m.* **-ging**, s.: stazatura, *f.*, stazare, *m.*
gâunt, ADJ.: magro, affilato, smunto.
gâunt-let 1, s.: guanto di ferro, manopolo, *f.* **-let** 2 = *gantlet*.
gâunt-ly, ADV.: magramente; sottilmente. **-ness**, s.: magrezza, *f.*
gâuze, s.: velo, *m.*; tocca, *f.*
gável, s.: terreno, suolo, *m.*; dogana, tassa, *f.* **-kind**, s.: spartimento uguale, *m.* **-man**, s.: vassallo, *m.*
gávelock†, s.: dardo, *m.*
gável-work, s.: servitù, *f.*
gávot, s.: gavotta, *f.* (sorta di ballo).
gâwk, s.: cucco; sciocco, minchione, *m.* **-y**, ADJ.: sciocco, balocco.
gáy, ADJ.: gaio, gioioso, lieto: — *colours*, colori vivaci; — *dress*, veste gaia. **-ety**, s.: gioia, gaiezza; allegrezza, *f.* **-ly**, ADV.: gaiamente, gioiosamente, allegramente. **-ness**, s.: giocondità, gioia, *f.* **-some**, ADJ.: gaio, gioioso, allegro.
gáze 1, s.: sguardo fisso, *m.*; sorpresa, *f.* **gaze** 2, INTR.: guardare fissamente. **-ful**, ADJ.: riguardante fissamente; sorpreso. **-hound**, s.: levriere, *m.*
gazél(le), s.: gazzella, *f.*
gáze-ment†, s.: sguardo fi[illegible]
s.: spettato[illegible] [illegible]
gazétt-e, s[illegible] -[illegible]
zettiere; s[illegible]

gázing-stock, S.: obbietto di sprezzo; spettacolo, *m.*
gazōn, S.: erbuccia; zolla di terra, *f.*
gêar 1, S.: vestimenti; mobili, *m. pl.*; roba, *f.*: *in* —, in movimiento, in azione; *out of* —, fermato, in riposto; *head* —, cuffia, *f.* **gear** 2, TR.: vestire; aggiogare.
gĕck, S.: goffo, balordo, sciocco, *m.*
gêese, PL. di *goose*.
gĕl atine, -átinous, ADJ.: gelatinoso.
gĕld, TR.: castrare; scemare; troncare. **-er**, S.: castraporcelli, castraporci, *m.* **-ing**, S.: cavallo castrato, *m.*
gĕl-id, ADJ.: gelido, gelato, freddo. **-id-ity**, S.: freddo eccessivo, gelo, *m.* **-ly**, S.: gelatina, *f.*; brodo rappreso, *m.*: *beat to a* —, spuppolare, stritolar le ossa di.
gĕlt†, S.: canutiglia, *f.*
gĕm 1, S.: gemma, *f.* **gem** 2, TR.: adornare di gemme; INTR.: germogliare.
gĕmi-nate, TR.: geminare; raddoppiare. **-nátion**, S.: geminazione, *f.*; raddoppiamento, *m.* **-ni**, S.: (*astr.*) gemini, *m. pl.* **-nous**, ADJ.: gemino. **-ny**†, S.: gemelli, *m. pl.*; paio, *m.*, coppia, *f.*
gĕm-meous, -my, ADJ.: gemmeo.
gĕnder 1, S.: genere, *m.* **gender** 2, TR.: generare; INTR.: ingenerarsi, accoppiarsi.
gene-alŏgical, ADJ.: genealogico. **-ălogist**, S.: genealogista, *m.* **-ălogy**, S.: genealogia, *f.*
gĕnerable, ADJ.: generabile.
gĕner-al 1, ADJ.: generale, universale; comune; S.: maggior parte, *f.*; tutto, *m.*: *in* —, in generale, generalmente. **-al** 2, S.: generale, *m.* **-alissimo**, S.: generalissimo, *m.* **-ălity**, S.: generalità; maggior parte, *f.* **-alizátion**, S.: riducimento ad un genere, *m.* **-alize**, TR.: generalizzare. **-ally**, ADV.: generalmente, universalmente. **-alness**, S.: generalità, *f.* **-alship**, S.: generalato, m. **-alty**, S.: generalità; totalità, *f.*
gĕner-ant, S.: principio generativo, *m.* **-áte**, TR.: generare; produrre; cagionare. **-átion**, S.: generazione; produzione; razza, *f.* **-ative**, ADJ.: generativo, generante. **-ator**, S.: generatore, creatore; principio, *m.*
genĕric(al), ADJ.: generico. **-ly**, ADV.: in modo generico.
gen-erŏsity, S.: generosità; liberalità, *f.* **-erous**, ADJ.: generoso, magnanimo; liberale. **-erously**, ADV.: generosamente, nobilmente, liberalmente. **-erousness**, S.: generosità, *f.*
...sis, S.: genesi, *f.*
..., S.: ginnetto, *m.*
... = *gin*.
...: geniale; naturale; giocon-
... — *air*, aria d' incontro. **-ly**, ADV.: genialmente, in modo geniale; naturalmente.
geniculated, ADJ.: genicolato, nodoso.
gĕni-tal, ADJ.: genitale; naturale. **-s**, S. PL.: parti genitali, *f. pl.* **-tive**, S.: (*gram.*) genitivo, *m.* **-tor**, S.: genitore, padre, *m.*
gĕnius, S.: genio; spirito; talento; carattere, *m.*: *man of* —, uomo d' ingegno, genio.
gentēel, ADJ.: gentile, grazioso, elegante; cortese: — *society*, ceto elegante. **-ly**, ADV.: gentilmente, graziosamente, elegantemente; cortesemente. **-ness**, S.: gentilezza; bella maniera, cortesia, *f.*
gĕntian, S.: (*bot.*) genziana, *f.*
gĕn-tile, S.: gentile; pagano, *m.* **-tilism**, S.: gentilesimo, paganismo, *m.*
gen-tilitious†, ADJ.: gentilizio. **-tility**, S.: gentilità; gentilezza; nobilità, *f.*
gĕntle 1, ADJ.: dolce; piacevole; benigno; domestico, mansueto. **-gentle** 2, TR.: render mansueto, addomesticare. **-folk**, S.: gente nobile, nobilità, *f.* **-man**, S.: gentiluomo; signore, *m.*: *young* —, giovine signore; *perfect* —, signore compito; *play the* —, far il gran signore, far-la da grande; *you are no* —, voi non siete un gentiluomo. **-manlike, -manly**, ADJ.: da gentiluomo. **-ness**, S.: gentilezza, cortesia; dolcezza, amorevolezza, bontà, *f.* **-ship**†, S.: cortesia; grazia, affabilità, *f.* **-woman**, S.: gentildonna; damigella, *f.*
gĕntly ADV.: dolcemente; gentilmente; benignamente.
gĕntry, S.: gentiluomini, *m. pl.*; secondo ordine, *m.*
genuflĕxion, S.: genuflessione, *f.*
gĕnuine, ADJ.: genuino, vero, naturale; proprio. **-ly**, ADV.: veramente; naturalmente. **-ness**, S.: purità; realità; autenticità, *f.*
geo-cĕntric, ADJ.: geocentrico. **-dĕtic(al)**, ADJ.: geodetico.
geŏ-grapher, S.: geografo, *m.* **-grăphical**, ADJ.: geografico. **-grăphically**, ADV.: in modo geografico. **geŏgraphy**, S.: geografia, *f.* **-lŏgical**, ADJ.: geologico. **-logy**, S.: geologica, *f.* **-meter**, S.: geometro, geometra, *m.* **-metral**, ADJ.: geometrico. **-mĕtrical**, ADJ.: geometrico, di geometria. **-mĕtrically**, ADV.: geometricamente. **-metrician**, S.: geometra, *m.* **-metrize**, INTR.: geometrizzare, fare da geometra. **-metry**, S.: geometria, *f.*
geôrg-e, S.: *brown* —, pane bigia, *m.* **-ic**, ADJ.: georgico, rurale.
gerănium, S.: geranio, *m.*
gĕrfalcon, S.: girfalco, *m.*
gĕrm, S.: germe, germoglio, *m.*

Gĕrman 1, ADJ. *or* S.: tedesco, *m.*, -ca, *f.*; lingua tedesca, *f.* **german** 2, ADJ.: germano (parente): *cousin* —, cugino germano, *m.*, cugina germana, *f.*

germănder, S.: (*bot.*) camedrio, *m.*, querciuola, *f.*

Gĕrmanism, S.: germanismo, *m.*

germāne, ADJ.: parente, affine, appropriato.

gĕrmin, **-al**, ADJ.: germinale. **-ate**, INTR.: germogliare. **-ātion**, S.: germinazione, *f.*

gĕrund, S.: gerundio, *m.*

gĕst, S.: gesto; fatto glorioso, *m.*; pompa, *f.*

gestātion, S.: gestazione; gravidanza, pregnezza, *f.*

gesticu-late, INTR.: gesteggiare, far troppi gesti. **-lātion**, S.: gesticulazione, *f.*, gesteggiare, *m.*

gĕsture, S.: gesto, atto delle membra, *m.*; positura, *f.*

gĕt 1, IRR.; TR.: guadagnare; procurare, acquistare; impetrare, ricevere; meritare; impadronirsi, prendere, pigliare, impegnare; INTR.: venire; arrivare; aver ricorso: — *angry*, adirarsi; — *fat*, ingrassire; — *thin*, ammagrire, dimagrire; — *drunk*, ubbriacarsi; — *the better*, aver la superiorità, aver vantaggio; — *children*, generar figliuoli; — *clear*, sbrigarsi, liberarsi; — *a cold*, pigliare un' infreddatura; — *a footing*, stabilirsi; — *friends*, farsi amici; — *a habit*, prendere un usanza; — *an ill habit*, prendere un cattivo abito; — *by heart*, imparare a mente; — *home*, arrivare a casa; — *one's lesson*, imparare la sua lezione; — *money*, guadagnar danari; — *money of one*, ricevere danari da uno; — *a name*, acquistar fama, mettersi in credito; — *a place*, trovare un impiego; — *ready*, apparecchiare, preparare; — *one's self ready*, apparecchiarsi; — *riches*, acquistare ricchezze; — *rid of*, disfarsi, distrigarsi; — *a thing done*, far fare una cosa; — *well again*, ristabilirsi; — *a wife*, prender moglie, sposare; — *above*, superare, vincere; — *away*, andare via, ritirarsi; — *away!* levati di costà! va via! — *before*, prevenire, precedere; — *down*, scendere, tragugiare; — *from*, andare via; cavare da; — *in*, entrare; fare entrare; — *into*, entrare; insinuarsi; seguire; — *off*, scappare, fuggire; — *off from*, smontare da; — *on*, montare, mettere; — *out*, uscire, fare uscire, cavare; — *over*, sormontare, superare; passare avanti, avanzare; vincere; — *through*, traversare; investigare; — *together*, metter insieme; adunare, radunare, accozzare; radunarsi; unirsi; — *up*, levare, alzare; levarsi; — *up again*, rifarsi; ripigliar le forze; — *up to*, avanzare; — *upon*, montare. **-ter**, S.: guadagnatore; acquistatore, *m.* **-ting**, S.: acquistamento; lucro, *m.*

gĕwgaw, S.: bubbola, *f.*; cose da nulla, *f. pl.*

ghāst†, TR.: spaventare. **-ful**†, ADJ.: tristo, malinconico; spaventevole, orribile. **-liness**, S.: viso spaventoso, *m.*; squallidezza, vista orrenda, *f.* **-ly**, ADJ.: squallido, orrendo.

ghĕrkin, S.: cetriuolo confettato con aceto, *m.*

ghōst, S.: spirito, *m.*; anima de' morti, ombra, *f.*: *holy* —, Spirito Santo; *give up the* —, render l' anima; *conjure up a* —, evocare uno spirito (spettro). **-liness**, S.: tendenza spirituale, *f.* **-ly**, ADJ.: spirituale.

ghoūl, S.: spirito maligno che ruba e divora cadaveri, *m.* **-ish**, ADJ.: diabolico, infernale; antropofago.

giant, S.: gigante, *m.*; ADJ.: gigantesco: *with* — *steps*, a passi di gigante. **-ess**, S.: gigantessa, *f.* **-like**, **-ly**, ADJ.: gigantesco, giganteo. **-ship**, S.: forma eccessiva, *f.*

gib†, S.: gatto vecchio, *m.*

gibber, INTR.: parlare confusamente, barbugliare, borbottare. **-ish**, S.: gergo, *m.*, gramuffa *f.*: *talk* —, parlare in gergo.

gibbet 1. S.: forca, *f.*; giubetto, *m.* **gibbet** 2, TR.: impiccare, appiccare; appendere.

gibble-gabble, S.: cicalamento, *m.*

gib-bŏsity, S.: scrigno, *m.*; gobba; curvità, *f.* **-bous**, ADJ.: gibboso, gibbuto; scrignuto, curvo. **-bousness**, S.: convessità; prominenza, gobba, *f.*

gib-cat†, S.: gatto vecchio, *m.*

gib-e 1, S.: beffa, burla, *f.*; scherno, disprezzo, *m.* **-e** 2, TR., INTR.: beffare, burlare; schernire. **-er**, S.: beffatore, burlattore: schernitore, *m.* **-ingly**, ADV.: sprezzevolmente, con dispresso; ironicamente.

giblets, S. PL.: frattaglie (dell' oca, ecc.), *f. pl.*

gid-dily, ADV.: inconsideratamente, negligentemente, trascuratamente. **-diness**, S.: capogiro, *m.*, vertigine; incostanza, *f.* **-dy**, ADJ.: vertiginoso; incostante. **-dy-brained**, **-dy-headed**, ADJ.: scervellato; leggiero, incostante. **-dy-paced**, ADJ.: inconsiderato, imprudente. **-dy-pate**, S.: minchione, sciocco, *m.*

gift, S.: dono; talento, *m.*; facoltà, *f.*: *new year's* —, strenna, *f.*, capo d' anno, *m.*; *free* —, dono gratuito; —,

fardello da nozze. **-ed**, ADJ.: donato, dottato; *highly* —, di gran ingegno.
gig, S.: ruzzola, trottola, *f.*, paleo; biroccio, *m.*
gi-gantēan, **-găntic**, ADJ.: gigantesco, di gigante.
giggl-e, INTR.: ghignare, sogghignare, sghignazzare. **-er**, S.: ghignatore, *m.* **-ing**, S.: ghignetto, sghignazzamento, ghigno, *m.*
gig-mill, S.: gualchiera, *f.*
gigot, S.: coscia; gamba, *f.*
gild, (IRR.); TR.: dorare, indorare. **-er**, S.: doratura, *f.*, indoramento, *m.*
gill 1, S.: quarto d' una foglietta (misura).
gill 2, S.: edera; bevanda di birra e d' edera, *f.* **-s**, PL.: branchie (di pesci), *f. pl.*
gillyflower, S.: leucoio, *m.*
gilt 1, S.: doratura, *f.*, indoramento, *m.*
gilt 2, ADJ.: dorato, indorato, cf. *gild*. **-edged**, ADJ.: dorato sul taglio. **-head**, S.: dorado, *m.*, orata, *f.* (pesce).
gim, ADJ.: (*prov.*) galante; pulito, bello.
gimblet, S.: succhio, succhiello, punteruolo, *m.*
gimcrack, S.: meccanismo volgare, *m.*; chiappola, bazzecola, *f.*
gimlet = *gimblet*.
gimp, S.: merletto, *m.*
gin, S.: trappola; stiaccia, *f.*; ginepro, liquore, *m.*
ginger, S.: zenzero, zenzevero, gengiovo, *m.* **-bread**, S.: bericuocolo, confortino, *m.* **-breadbaker**, **-breadmaker**, S.: bericuocolaio, confortinaio, *m.* **-ly**, ADV.: dolcemente; pian piano. **-ness**, S.: delicatezza; tenerezza, *f.*
gingle = *jingle*.
ginnet, S.: bidetto, ronzino, *m.*
gin-shop, S.: bottega di liquorista, *f.*
gipsy = *gypsy*.
girasol, S.: girasole†; opale, *m.*
gird 1, S.: beffa, burla, *f.*, scherno, *m.*: *by —s and snatches*, alla sfuggita. **gird** 2, (IRR.); TR.: cingere, circondare; beffare, burlare. **-er**, S.: trave maestra, *f.* **-le** 1, S.: cintura, chiusura; zona, *f.* **-le** 2, TR.: cingere, circondare, rinchiudere; attorniare. **-le-belt**, S.: cinturino, cintolo, *m.* **-ler**, S.: facitore di cinture; venditore di cinture, *m.*
girl, S.: fanciulla, ragazza, zittella, donzella, *f.*: *little* —, ragazzina; *pretty little* —, bella ragazzina; *servant* —, serva, *f.* **-hood**, S.: giovinezza (di donzella). **-ish**, ADV.: di ragazza, donzellesco, fanciullesco; vivace. **-ishly**, ADV.: da ragazza, donzellescamente, a modo di zitella.
girt 1, **girth**, S.: cinghia, cintura, *f.*
girt 2, **girth**, TR.: cinghiare, cingere; legare. **-leather**, S.: sopraccinghia, sopraccigna, *f.*
giv-e, IRR.; TR.: dare; donare; conferire; rimettere; cedere, rilassarci, piegarsi; ammollirsi; IRR.; INTR.: — *alms*, fare limosine; — *an account of*, rendere conto di; — *back*, restituire; — *battle*, dare la battaglia, presentare la battaglia; — *a call*, chiamare; invitare; visitare; — *in charge*, incaricare; commettere, ordinare; — *credit*, prestar fede, fare credito, credere; — *a description*, descrivere, dipingere; — *ear*, dare orecchio, ascoltare; — *evidence*, render testimonianza; — *a fall*, fare cascare, abbattere; — *fire*, tirare, sparare; — *ground*, rinculare; ritirarsi, fuggire; — *hearing*, dare udienza; — *heed*, badare; stare attento; — *hopes*, promettere; — *joy*, felicitare, congratularsi; — *judgment*, pronunziare la sentenza; — *leave*, dare licenza, permettere; — *like for like*, render la pariglia; — *a look*, dare un' occhiata; osservare; mirare; esaminare; — *one's mind*, applicarsi; affezionarsi; — *notice*, avvertire; fare sapere; — *oath*, proporre il giuramento; — *over*, desistere, cessare; — *place*, dare luogo; cedere; — *a push*, dare una spinta; spingere; — *the slip*, scappare; salvarsi; — *suck*, allattare; — *thanks*, render grazie, ringraziare; risalutare; — *trouble*, impacciare, incomodare, molestare; — *in one's verdict*, dar la sua voce, dar il suo suffragio; — *a visit*, fare visita, visitare; — *warning*, avvertire, far sapere; — *way*, cedere, abbandonarsi; — *again*, rendere, restituire; — *away*, rimettere; cedere; concedere; — *back*, rendere, restituire; — *forth*, pubblicare, promulgare, divolgare; — *one's self for*, passarsi, riputarsi; — *in*, cedere; ridursi; — *into*, entrare; consentire; adottare; — *off*, discontinuare, desistere; — *out*, distribuire, dare; pubblicare, divolgare; — *over*, tralasciare, lasciare, desistere; finire; — *one's self to*, applicarsi, attaccarsi; — *up*, cedere; abbandonare; rendere. **-en**, ADJ.: dato, ecc. (cf. *give*); *at a — time*, ad un tempo dato (*or* convenuto). **-er**, S.: donatore, distributore, *m.* **-ing**, S.: donazione, *f.*, dono, *m.*
gizzard, S.: ventriglio, *m.*
glăb-rity, S.: liscezza; calvezza, *f.* **-rous**, ADJ.: liscio.
glā-cial, ADJ.: glaciale; gelato, ghiacciato. **-ciate**, INTR.: agghiacciare, congelare. **-ciătion**, S.: agghiacciamento, *m.*, congelazione, *f.* **-cier**, S.: ghiacciaio, *m.*
glădis, S.: spalto; (*fort.*) pendio, *m.*
glăd, ADJ.: contento, lieto, allegro: *make* —, rallegrare; *I am — of it*, me ne allegro; *I am — to see you*, mi rallegro di vedervi; *make* —, rallegrare, allietare;

very —, contentissimo. **-den**, TR.: rallegrare.

glāde, S.: viale d'alberi, entrata, f.

glădful, ADJ.: gioioso, lieto. **-ness**, S.: gioia, allegrezza, letizia, f.

glădiator, S.: gladiatore, m.

glăd-ly, ADV.: di buon grado, con piacere, volentieri. **-ness**, S.: gioia, giubilo, f. **-some**, ADJ.: gioioso, giocondo, allegro. **-somely**, ADV.: gioiosamente. **-someness**, S.: allegria, f., piacere, m.; allegrezza, f.

glāire 1, S.: albume, m.: chiara d'uovo, f. **glaire** 2, TR.: impiastricciare con l'albume d'uovo.

glănce 1, S.: occhiata, f.: raggio di luce; baleno, m.: *at the first* —, a prima vista. **-ce** 2, INTR.: raggiare: dar un'occhiata, occhiare; scalfire: — *upon*, scorrere; *I'll take a — at it*, gli darò un'occhiata. **-cingly**, ADV.: leggiermente, alla sfuggita.

glănd, S.: glandula, ghiandola, f. **-ers**, S. PL.: stranguglioni (de' cavalli), m. pl. **-iferous**, ADJ.: ghiandifero. **-ule**, S.: glanduletta, f. **-ulōsity**, S.: collezione di glandule, f. **-ulous**, ADJ.: glanduloso.

glār-e 1, S.: luce soverchia; occhiata che penetra, occhiata feroce, f. **-e** 2, INTR.: splendere; fiammeggiare; abbagliare; occhiare: — *at*, guardar con occhio bieco (*or* feroce). **-eous**, ADJ.: viscido, mucilaginoso. **-ing**, ADJ.: manifesto, evidente: *a — error*, un errore che salta agli occhi. **-ingly**, ADV.: evidentemente.

glāsier = *glazier*.

glăss 1, S.: vetro; bicchiere; specchio, m.; ADJ.: di vetro, invetriato. **glass** 2, TR.: invetriare; incassare in vetro; inverniciare. **-beads**, S.: margheritine, f. pl. **-blower**, S.: vetraio, m. **-blowing**, S.: soffiatura del vetro, f. **-bottle**, S.: fiasco di vetro, m., bottiglia, f. **-bowl**, S.: tazza di cristallo, f. **-case**, S.: custodia di vetro (*or* campana) di vetro, mostra, f. **-door**, S.: porta a invetriate, f. **-furnace**, S.: fornace da vetraia, f. **-grinder**, S.: lisciatore di vetri, m. **-house**, S.: vetraia, fabbrica de' vetri, f. **-maker**, S.: vetraio, bicchieraio, m. **-making**, S.: arte vetraria, f. **-man**, S.: venditore di vetraia, m. **-metal**, S.: vetro in fusione, m. **-shop**, S.: bottega di vetraio, f. **-trade**, S.: commercio vetrario, m. **-ware**, S.: vetreria, f., cristalli, m. pl.: *small* —, vetrame, m. **-window**, S.: vetriera, f. **-work**, S.: vetraia; fabbrica di vetro, f. **-y**, ADJ.: vitreo, cristallino; invetriato; fragile.

glaucōma, S.: (*med.*) glaucoma, m., cateratta, f.

glāver, S.: spuma, f.; mibalascia(?), m.

glăver, TR.: adulare, accarezzare; lusingare. **-er**, S.: adulatore, m.

glāze, TR.: invetriare; verniciare, inverniciare, smaltare; lustrare. **-ed**, PART.: invetriato: — *frost*, brina, f. **-zier**, S.: vetraio, m. **-zing**, S.: invetriamento, m.

glēde, S.: nibbio, m.

glēam 1, S.: raggio; lampo; barlume, m. **gleam** 2, INTR.: risplendere, scintillare, sfavillare. **-y**, ADJ.: scintillante, sfavillante.

glēan 1, S.: spigolatura; raccolta laboriosa, f. **glean** 2, TR.: spigolare; raccogliere; racc. raspollare. **-er**, S.: spigolatore, raccoglitore, m. **-ing**, S.: spigolatura, f., spigolare, m.: *literary* —s, squarci scelti.

glēbe, S.: zolla, gleba, f.; terreno, suolo, m.

glēde, S.: nibbio, m.

glēe, S.: gioia, gaiezza, f.; giubilo, m.

glēed†, S.: carbone acceso, m.

glēe-ful, ADJ.: gioioso, gaio, allegro. **-fulness**, S.: allegrezza, gioia, f. **-man**, S.: musico, m.

glēen†, INTR.: risplendere.

glēesome, ADJ.: gioioso, allegro, lieto.

glēet 1, S.: puzza, f.; marciume, m. **gleet** 2, INTR.: docciare, colare; suppurare. **-y**, ADJ.: icoroso, sieroso.

glĕn, S.: valle, vallata, f.

glĭb 1, ADJ.: liscio (lubrico)†; volubile, loquace. **glib** 2, TR.: castrare; lisciare. **-ly**, ADV.: correntemente; con facilità; volubilmente. **-ness**, S.: volubilità, facilità, loquacità, f.

glīde, INTR.: scorrere; passare leggiermente.

glĭm, S.: candela, f.

glĭmmer 1, S.: luce debole, f.; splendore debole, m.; (*min.*) mica, f. **glimmer** 2, INTR.: tralucere, trasparire.

glĭmpse, S.: barlume, balenamento, m.: *catch a — of*, vedere alla sfuggita.

glĭsten, INTR.: splendere, scintillare; brillare.

glĭtter 1, S.: splendore; lustro, m. **glitter** 2, INTR.: rilucere; brillare. **-ing**, ADJ.: lucente, risplendente, scintillante. **-ingly**, ADV.: splendidamente, con i splendore.

glōar†, INTR.: guardare biecamente, far il viso arcigno.

glōat, INTR.: guardar sottocchi.

glō-bated, ADJ.: globos[illegible] rotondo. **-be**, S.: globo, [illegible] —, globetto, m. [illegible] sferico. **-bōsity**, [illegible] tà, f. **-bous**, ADJ. [illegible] tondo.

glŏb-ular = *glob*[illegible]

bulo, piccol globo, *m.* -**ulous**, ADJ.: globuloso.
glŏmer-ate, INTR.: aggomitolare, accumulare. -**ātion**, S.: aggomitolare, *m.*, accumulazione, *f.* -**ous**, ADJ.: aggomitolato, conglomerato.
glōom 1, S.: oscurità; tristezza, *f.*
gloom 2, INTR.: divenir oscuro; essere tristo. -**ily**, ADV.: oscuramente; tristamente. -**iness**, S.: oscurità; tristezza, malinconia, *f.* -**y**, ADJ.: oscuro, nuvoloso, fosco; tristo, malinconico.
glō-ried, ADJ.: illustre, celebre. -**rifi-cātion**, S.: glorificazione, *f.*, glorificamento, *m.* -**rify**, TR.: glorificare; celebrare: — *one's self*, glorificarsi, vantarsi. -**rious**, ADJ.: glorioso, nobile; famoso, illustre. -**riously**, ADV.: gloriosamente, nobilmente, illustremente. -**ry** 1, S.: gloria; fama, rinominanza, celebrità; aureola, *f.*: *vain* —, vana gloria; *halo of* —, aureola di gloria, corona; *thirst after* —, anellare alla gloria. -**ry** 2, INTR.: gloriarsi, vantarsi; lodarsi.
glōse = *gloze.*
glŏss 1, S.: lustro, liscio, *m.* **gloss** 2, TR.: lustrare, pulire. **gloss** 3, S.: glosa, *f.*; commento. **gloss** 4, TR.: glosare, far glose. -**ary**, S.: glossario, *m.* -**er**, S.: glosatore; interprete, *m.*
glŏssiness, S.: pulimento, *m.*, pulitura, *f.*
glossŏgra-pher, S.: glossografo, glosatore, *m.* -**phy**, S.: glossografia, *f.*
glŏssy, ADJ.: liscio, pulito, lucido.
glŏttis, S.: (*anat.*) glottide, glotta, *f.*
glŏut†, INTR.: fare un mal viso, mostrar mal umore; ringhiare.
glŏv-e 1, S.: guanto, *m.*: *excuse my* —, amore passa il guanto; *throw down the* —, gettar il guanto; sfidare; *take up the* —, raccogliere il guanto; *be hand and* — *with one*, essere amicissimi. -**e** 2, TR.: mettere i guanti. -**e-money**, S.: buona mano, mancia, *f.* -**er**, S.: guantaio, *m.*
glōw 1, S.: ardore; splendore, *m.*; vivezza, *f.*: — *of youth*, ardore giovantile.
glow 2, INTR.: rosseggiare; esser infuocato, esser infiammato. -**ing**, ADJ.: rosseggiante, ardente, infuocato; S.: roventezza, *f.*; ardore, fuoco, *m.* -**ingly**, ADV.: ardentemente; splendidamente. -**worm**, S.: lucciola, *f.*
glōz-e 1, S.: adulazione; lusinga, *f.* -**e** 2, TR.: adulare, carezzare; lusingare. -**er**, S.: adulatore, *m.* -**ing**, S.: adulazione, *f.*, lusingheria, *f.*
glū-e 1, S.: colla, *f.*, cemento, *m.* -**e** 2, TR.: incollare, appiccare con colla; unire. -**e-boiler**, S.: fabbricatore di colla, *m.* -**er**, S.: che incolla. -**ey**, -**ish**, ADJ.: tenace, viscoso, glutinoso.
-**m**, ADJ.: arcigno, ritroso, cagnesco; grave. -**my**†, ADJ.: torbido, brusco, oscuro.
glŭt 1, S.: satollezza; abbondanza, *f.*
glut 2, TR.: inghiottire; satollare, saziare: — *one's self with*, satollarsi; impinzarsi; — *the market*, far rigurgitare la piazza.
glūti-nate, TR: incollare. -**nātion**, S.: incollamento, *m.* -**nŏsity**, S.: glutinosità, viscosità, *f.* -**nous**, ADJ.: glutinoso, viscoso; tenace. -**nousness**, S.: viscosità, *f.*
glŭtton, S.: ghiotto, ghiottone, goloso, mangione, *m.* -**ize**, TR.: mangiare assai. -**ous**, ADJ.: ghiotto, ingordo, goloso. -**ously**, ADV.: ghiottamente, golosamente, avidamente. -**y**, S.: ghiottornia, ingordezza, ingordigia, *f.*
glўcerine, S.: glicerina, *f.*
glўn†, S.: valle, vallea, *f.*
glyp-tographic, ADJ.: glittografico. -**tŏgraphy**, S.: glittografia, *f.*
gnârl, INTR.: borbottare, mormoreggiare. -**ed**, ADJ.: nodoso.
gnăsh, (IN)TR.: digrignare i denti, stridere, ringhiare. -**ing**, S.: stridore de' denti, *m.*
gnăt, S.: zanzara, *f.*; moscherino, *m.* -**snapper**, S.: monachino, *m.* (uccello).
gnâw, (IN)TR.: rodere, rosicchiare: —*ing cares*, cure mordaci. -**er**, S.: roditore, che rosicchia, *m.* -**ing**, S.: rodimento, *m.*, roditura, *f.*
gnō-me, S.: gnome, *m.* -**mon**, S.: gnomone, *m.* -**mŏnics**, S. PL.: gnonomica, *f.*
gō 1, IRR.; INTR.: andare, camminare; marciare; passare; andarsene; partirsi: — *a-foot*, andare o camminare a piedi; — *ashore*, approdare, sbarcare; — *about the bush*, andar per ambage; — *with child*, essere incinta; — *halves with one*, andare di meta con uno, spartire con uno; — *near*, avvicinarsi; — *shares*, spartire, dividere; — *about a thing*, mettersi a fare qualche cosa; — *about*, fare il giro di; mettersi a fare; intraprendere, tentare; intrigarsi; — *abroad*, uscire; divenir pubblico; — *against*, opporsi; — *along*, andare via; avanzare; — *along!* va (*or* andate) via! — *along with*, andar con, accompagnare; — *aside*, andare a parte; ritirarsi; — *astray*, uscire di via, sviarsi; — *asunder*, separarsi, spartirsi; — *away*, andare via; partirsi; — *away with*, portare via; togliere; — *back*, rinculare; ritirarsi; — *backward*, andare a ritrorso; — *before*, andare avanti; precedere; — *behind*, andare dietro; seguitare; — *between*, interporre, accomodare; conciliare; — *beyond*, trapassare; surpassare; — *by*, passare vicino; scorrere; regolarsi; — *down*, scendere; piacere;

approvare; — *for*, andare a cercare; passare per; — *forth*, uscire; mostrarsi; — *forward*, avanzare; fare progressi; — *from*, lasciare; disdirsi; — *in*, entrare; — *in and out*, aver l'entrata; — *off*, lasciare; scoppiare; vendersi, smaltire; uscire di vita, morire; — *on*, avanzare; continuare; attaccare; — *on with*, proseguire; — *on a journey*, fare un viaggio; — *out*, uscire; spegnersi; — *over*, traversare, attraversare; — *round*, andare in ronda; circolare; — *to*, arrivare, montare; impegnarsi; — *to!* animo! coraggio! — *through*, passare per; — *together*, andare in compagnia; — *under*, sopportare; perire; — *up*, scendere; alzarsi; — *up and down*, andare qua e là; — *upon*, fondare, stabilire; intraprendere; — *with*, accompagnare; — *without*, soddisfarsi, contentarsi. **go**², s.: andazzo, *m.*, voga, *f.*: *it was all the* —, era l'andazzo, era in voga.

gōad¹, s.: pungiglione; stimolo, *m.*

goad², TR.: punzecchiare, pungere, stimolare, eccitare.

gōal, s.: termine, *m.*, meta, *f.*; segno; intento; carcere, *m.*

gōar = *gore*.

gōat, s.: capra, *f.*: *he*-—, becco, *m.*; *she*-—, capra, *f.*; *young* —, capretto, cavretto, *m.*; —*'s-beard*, barba caprina, *f.* **-beard**, s.: caprifoglio, *m.*, madreselva, *f.* **-ēe**, mosca, *f*, pizzo (sul mento). **-herd**, s.: capraio, *m.* **-ish**, ADJ.: di becco; lascivo. **-skin**, s.: pelle caprina, *f.* **-'s-milk**, s.: latte di capra, *m.* **-'s-rue**, s.: capraria, capraggine, *f.*

gŏb, **-bet**, s.: boccone, pezzo, *m.* **-bet**, TR.: inghiottire a grossi bocconi.

gŏbbl-e, TR.: ingozzare, ingorgiare. **-er**, s.: ghiottone, mangione, *m.*

gō-between, s.: mezzano, *m.*, -na, *f.*; ruffiano, *m.*, -na, *f.*

gŏblet, s.: ciotola, tazza, *f*, bicchiere, *m.*

gŏblin, s.: larva; ombra, *f.*, spirito, fantasma, *m.*

gō-by, s.: sotterfugio; artifizio, *m.*, astuzia, *f.* **-cart**, s.: carruccio, corico, carrettino di bimbo, *m.*

Gŏd, s.: Dio, Iddio, *m.*: — *be thanked*, grazie a Dio; — *be with you*, andate con Dio; — *forbid!* tolga Iddio; — *bless you!* Iddio vi benedica; — *help me*, così Iddio mi aiuti. **-child**, s.: figlioccio, *m.*, figlioccia, *f.* **-daughter**, s.: figlioccia, *f.* **-dess**, s.: dea, *f.* **-dess-like**, ADJ.: come una dea. **-father**, s.: patrino, compare, *m.*: *stand* — *to*, tenere a battesimo. **-head**, s.: divinità, *f.* Dio, *m.* **-less**, ADJ.: ateo, empio. **-lessness**, s.: empietà, *f.* **-like**, ADJ.: divino, celeste. **-lily**†, ADV.: religiosamente, piamente. **-liness**, s.: divozione; pietà, *f.* **-ling**, s.: divinità piccola; innamorata, *f.* **-ly**¹, ADJ.: divoto, pio, religioso. **-ly**², ADV: divotamente, piamente, religiosamente. **-mother**, s.: matrina; santola, *f.*: *be* —, tenere un fanciullo a battesimo. **-ship**, s.: essenza di Dio; divinità, *f.* **-son**, s.: figlioccio, *m.* **-wit**, s.: francolino, *m.* (uccello).

gōer, s.: ambulante, camminatore, *m.*: —*s and comers*, quelli che vanno e vengono.

gŏff, s.: mucchio di fieno; goffo, balordo, *m.* **-ish**, ADJ.: goffo, sciocco.

gŏg†, s.: fretta, *f.*: *be a* — *for*, aver gran voglia di, desiderare ardentemente.

gŏggl-e, INTR.: guardare di traverso, guardare biecamente. **-eyed**, ADJ.: guercio; bieco, stralunato.

gōing, PART.: andante; andando; s.: andare, *m.*, andatura, *f.*; passo, *m.*: *the* — *down of the sun*, il declinare (*or* tramontare) del sole.

gōitre, s.: gozzo, *m.*

gōld, s.: oro, *m.*; moneta, *f.* **-beater**, s.: battiloro, *m.* **-bound**, ADJ.: fregiato d'oro. **-coin**, s.: moneta d'oro, *f.* **-dust**, s.: polvere d'oro, *f.* **-en**, ADJ.: d'oro; eccellente, *f* **-fields**, s: campi auriferi, *m. pl.* **-finch**, s.: calderino, cardellino, *m.* **-finder**, s.: votacesso, *m.* **-finer**, s.: affinatore d'oro, *m.* **-fish**, s.: orata, *f.* **-flower**, s.: tornasole, eliotropio, *m.* **-hammer**, s.: rigogolo, *m.* **-mine**, s.: miniera d'oro, *f.* **-paper**, s.: carta indorata, *f.* **-sand**, s.: sabbia d'oro, *f.* **-smith**, s.: orefice, *m.* **-weight**, s.: peso d'oro, *m.* **-wire**, s: fil d'oro, *m.*

gŏn-dola, s.: gondola, *f.* **-dolier**, s.: gondoliere, barcaiuolo, *m.*

gŏne, PART.: andato, ecc. (cf. *go*): *far* — *in years*, avanzato in età, attempato: *I must be* —, bisogna che me ne vada; *get you* —, andatevene.

gŏnfa-lon, **-non**, s.: gonfalone, *m.*, bandiera, *f.*

gŏng, s.: campana piatta, *f.*

gonorrhoēa, s.: gonorrea, *f.*

gŏod¹, ADJ.: buono; dabbene; benigno; virtuoso; favorabile; convenevole; s.: bene, vantaggio, profitto, *m.* **-s**, PL.: beni, effetti, merci, *m. pl.*; mercanzie, *f. pl.*: — *man*, uomo dabbene; — *turn*, servizio, favore, *m.*; *all in* — *time*, ogni cosa a suo tempo; *in* — *earnest*, in sul serio; *a* — *deal*, molto; *a* — *while*, un pezzo, tempo lungo; *a* — *while ago*, già da gran tempo; *as* — *as*, tanto quanto; come; — *breeding*, civiltà, educazione

ne, *f.*; — *luck*, prosperità, buona ventura, *f.*; — *will*, buona volontà, benevolenza, *f.*; *I have a — mind to do it*, ho voglia di farlo
good, ADV.: bene; giustamente: *make* —, compensare; rimunerare; provare; giustificare; *think* —, approvare, acconsentire. **-bye**, S.: addio. **-conditioned**, ADJ.: ben condizionato. **-Friday**, S.: venerdì santo, *m.* **-hūmored**, ADJ.: gioioso, allegro, lieto. **-liking**, S.: approvazione, *f.*, assenso, *m.* **-liness**, S.: bellezza; eleganza, *f.* **-ly**, ADJ.: bello, vago; splendido. **-man**, S.: buon uomo; padrone, *m.* **-nāture**, S.: bontà; umanità, *f.* **-nātured**, ADJ.: di buon cuore, benigno. **-ness**, S.: bontà, benignità; affabilità, *f.* **-now**, ADV.: a tempo, opportunamente. **-wife**, S.: padrona di casa, *f.* **-will**, S.: benevolenza, bontà, *f.* **-y**, S.: buona donna, madonna, *f.*
gōose (pl. *geese*), S.: oca, *f.*; (*tail*) quadrello, *m.*: *green* —, papero, *m.* **-berry**, S.: uva spina, *f.* **-berry-bush**, S.: pianta dell' uva spina, *f.* **-cap**, S.: balordo, minchione, *m.* **-flesh**, S.: pelle d'oca, *f.* **-foot**, S.: belladonna, *f.* **-giblets**, S. PL.: regali d'oca, *m. pl.* **-grass**, S.: meliloto, tribolo, *m.* **-pen**, S.: stalla delle oche, *f.* **-quill**, S.: cannone della penna, *m.*
Gôrdian knot, S.: nodo gordiano, *m.*
gorbĕl-lied†, ADJ.: grasso, panciuto. **-ly**†, S.: grossa pancia, *f.*
gôr-cock, S.: (*prov.*) gallo di montagna, *m.* **-crow**, S.: (*prov.*) cornacchia, *f.*
gōre 1, S.: sangue; sangue guagliato, *m.*; punta di camicia da donna, *f.* **gore** 2, TR.: punzecchiare; stilettare; trafiggere.
gôr-ge 1, S.: gola, *f.*; gozzo; sorso, *m.* **-ge** 2, TR.: satollare, ingorgare, impinzare; saziare: — *one's self*, empirsi la pancia, satollarsi. **-geous**, ADJ.: fastoso, magnifico, pomposo. **-geously**, ADV.: fastosamente; suntuosamente. **-geousness**, S.: magnificenza; pompa, *f.*, splendore, fasto, *m.* **-get**, S.: gorgiera, gorgierina, *f.*
gôrgon, S.: (*myth*) gorgone, *f.*
gorilla, S.: gorilla, *m.*
gôrmand, S.: ghiottone, mangione, *m.* **-ize**, INTR.: mangiare avidamente; esser dedito alla gola. **-izer**, S.: ghiotto, ghiottone, mangione, *m.* **-izing**, S.: ghiottoneria, ghiottornia, golosità, *f.*
gôrse, S.: erica, *f.*
gōry, ADJ.: coperto di sangue.
gōs-hawk, S.: avoltoio, *m.* **-ling**, S.: papero, *m.*
gŏspel, S.: vangelo, evangelo, *m.* **-ize**, TR.: evangelizzare, predicare il vangelo. **-ler**, S.: che predica il vangelo.
gŏssamer, S.: filamenti di S. Maria, *m. pl.*
gŏssip 1, S.: compare, *m.*; comare, *f.*
gossip 2, INTR: ciarlare, cicalare, tracannare. **-ping**, S.: cicalamento, *m.*, ciarleria, *f.*
Gŏthic, ADJ.: gotico; S.: lingua gotica, *f.*
gŏuge, S.: scarpello a doccia, *m.*
gōurd, S.: zucca, *f.* **-iness**, S.: enfiato ne' piedi de' cavalli, *m.* **-y**, ADJ.: enfiato; grosso.
gŏut, S.: gotta; podagra, *f.*: — *in the hips*, sciatica, *f.* **-y**, ADJ.: gottoso, podagroso.
gōve†, S.: mucchio (di fieno), *m.*; bica, *f.*
gŏvern, (IN)TR.: governare; regolare; reggere. **-able**, ADJ.: docile, trattabile. **-ance**, S.: governamento, *m.*; condotta, *f.* **-ante**, S.: governatrice, tutrice, *f.* **-ess**, S.: direttrice, insegnatrice, *f.* **-ment**, S.: governo, reggiamento, *m*; amministrazione, *f.*; maneggio, *m.*, direzione, *f.*: *military* —, governo militare; *petticoat* —, reggime della gonnella, governo donnesco. **-or**, S.: governatore, direttore, *m.* **-orship**, S.: carica di governatore, *f.*
gŏwn, S.: veste, roba, gonna; toga, *f.*: *morning* —, veste da camera, zimarra, guarnacca, *f.*; *wedding* —, veste da nozze. **-ed**, ADJ.: vestito di toga, togato. **-man**, S.: uomo togato, *m.*, persona di toga, *f.*
grăbble, TR.: palpare, palpeggiare; INTR.: giacere disteso.
grāce 1, S.: grazia; bontà, *f.*; favore, *m.*, avvenanza, *f.*; perdono, *m.*; eleganza; leggiadra, *f.*: — *at meals*, ringraziamento, *m.*; *act of* —, decreto d'amnistia, *m.*; *by the* — *of God*, per la grazia di Dio; *the three* —*s*, le tre Grazie; *with a good* —, garbatamente; *days of* —, giorni di grazia, *m. pl.*; *say* —, benedire la tavola.
grace 2, TR.: abbellire, ornare; favorire. **-d**, ADJ.: bello, vago; virtuoso. **-ful**, ADJ.: grazioso, leggiadro, elegante; amabile. **-fully**, ADV.: con grazia, elegantemente, gentilmente, garbatamente. **-fulness**, S.: gentilezza; leggiadria, venustà, eleganza, *f.* **-less**, ADJ.: sgraziato; sfacciato; empio, scellerato. **-lessness**, S.: empietà; scelleratezza, *f.* **-s**, S. PL.: grazie, *f. pl.*
grăc-ile†, ADJ.: gracile, sottile; debole. **-ilent**†, ADJ.: magro, macilente, smunto. **-ility**, S.: gracilità, sottigliezza; debolezza, *f.*
grācious, ADJ.: grazioso, benevolo, favorabile, favorevole. **-ly**, ADV.: graziosamente, benevolmente, favorevolmente. **-ness**, S.: amorevolezza, affabilità, cortesia; benignità, *f.*
gradātion, S.: gradazione, *f.*
grādient, S.: (*rail.*) salita, salita o discesa, *f.*

gráđ-ual, ADJ.: graduale: progressivo; s. graduale, m. **-uăl-ity**, s. gradazione, f., progresso regolare, m. **-ually**, ADV.: gradualmente, per gradi. **-uate**, s.: graduato, m. **-uate**, TR.: conferire un grado a, addottorare, innalzare; INTR.: prendere un grado, divenire dottore. **-uā-tion**, s.: graduazione, f.

gráff, s.: fosso, m., fossa, f.

gráft 1, s.: innesto, m. **graft** 2, TR.: innestare, innestare. **-er**, s.: innestatore, m. **-ing**, s.: innestatura, f., innestamento, m. **-ing-knife**, s.: coltello da innesto, m.

gráin, s.: grano, granello, seme, m., semenza, f.; frumento: umore, m., disposizione, f.: —s, cereali: — *of salt*, grano di sale; — *of mustard seed*, granello di senape: — *of allowance*, indulgenza, f.: *against the* —, a contracuore, mal volentieri; *dyed in* —, tinto in grana; *rogue in* —, furbo in chermisi, gran furfante, m. **-ed**, ADJ.: granato, granoso, granito. **-y**, ADJ.: pieno di granelli.

gramércy†, INTERJ.: vi ringrazio.

gramin-eous, ADJ.: erboso, coperto d'erba. **-ivorous**, ADJ.: che mangia l'erba, che si pasce d'erba.

grám-mar, s.: grammatica, f.: *little* —, grammatichetta, f. **-márian**, s.: grammatico, m. **-mar-school**, s.: scuola di grammatica, f.; ginnasio, m. **-máti-cal**, ADJ.: grammaticale. **-mátically**, ADV.: grammaticalmente.

granád-e, -o = *grenade*.

gránary, s.: granaio, granaro, m.

gránate, s.: granato, m.: — *marble*, granito, m.

gránd, ADJ.: grande; nobile, illustre. **-am**, s.: ava, avola, f. **-child**, s.: nipote, nipotino, m.; nipotina, f. **-daughter**, s.: figlia della figlia, nipotina, f.: *great* —, pronipote, f. **-ée**, s.: grande, nobile di Spagna, m. **-éeship**, s.: grandezza, f. **-eur**, s.: grandezza; magnificenza, f. **-father**, s.: avolo, avo, m.: *great* —, bisavo, m. **-iloquence**, s.: grandiloquenza, vanteria, f. **-iloquous**, ADJ.: grandiloquo, pomposo. **-mother**, s.: ava, avola, f.: *great*—, bisava, f. **-ness** = *grandeur*. **-sire**, s.: avo; avolo, m. **-son**, s.: figlio del figlio o della figlia, nipotino, m.: *great* —, pronipote, m.

gránge, s.: masseria, casa del massaio, m.

gránite, s.: granito, m.

granivorous, ADJ.: granivoro.

gránnam, s.: (*colloq.*) ava, avola, f.

gránt 1, s.: dono, m.; permissione, concessione, f., privilegio, m.: *make a — of*, far concessione di. **grant** 2, TR.: concedere, permettere, accordare, dare: — *a privilege*, dare (accordare) un privilegio; *I take it for —ed*, presuppongo: — *it (to) be so*, supposto che sia come dite; —*ed!* d'accordo! **-able**, ADJ.: concessibile, accordevole. **-ée**, s.: donatario, m. **-er**, s.: donatore, m.; che fa una concessione.

gránu-lar, **-lary**, ADJ.: granulare; sodo, massiccio. **-late**, TR.: granulare; granire: fare il granello. **-lation**, s.: granulazione, f. **-le**, s.: granello, m. **-lous**, ADJ.: pieno di granelli.

grápe, s.: uva, f.: *bunch of* —*s*, grappolo d'uva, m.: *glean* —*s*, raspollare; *gather* —*s*, vendemmiare. **-gathering**, s.: vendemmia, f. **-gleaner**, s.: raspollatore, vendemmiatore, m. **-less**, ADJ.: sciapito. **-shot**, s.: mitraglia, f. **-stone**, s.: granello dell'uva, m., acino, m.

gráph-ic-al, ADJ.: grafico, delineato; esatto, perfetto. **-ically**, ADV.: in modo grafico. **-ómeter**, s.: grafometro, m.

gráp-nel, s.: ancora di galea, ancoretta, f.: grappino, m. **-ple** 1, s.: grappino, m. **-ple** 2, TR.: afferrare, afferrare, aggrappare; INTR.: aggrapparsi, azzuffarsi, attaccarsi: — *with*, venire alle prese con. **-plement**, s.: venire alle prese, m., contesa, f. **-pling-iron**, s.: grappino, m.

grázier, s.: ingrassatore di bestiame, m.

grásp 1, s.: impugnatura: manata, brancata, f.: — *of the hand*, stretta di mano; *within* —, in propria balia. **grasp** 2, TR.: impugnare, aggrappare, abbracciare, abbrancare: acciuffare; INTR.: sforzarsi di prendere: tentare: — *at*, tentare di afferrare.

gráss 1, s.: erba: gramigna: pastura, f.: — *of the second crop*, guaime, m. **grass** 2, INTR.: produrre erba. **-green**, ADJ.: verde d'erba: verdeggiante. **-hopper**, s.: cavalletta: locusta, f. **-iness**, s.: abbondanza d'erba, f.: verdume, m. **-plot**, s.: terra coperta d'erba, f. **-week**, s.: Rogazioni, f. pl. **-widow**, s.: donna separata dal marito, f. **-y**, ADJ.: erboso, coperto d'erba.

gráte 1, s.: graticola, gratella; ferrata; gelosia, f. **grate** 2, TR.: grattugiare: fregare: offendere: — *the teeth*, digrignare i denti; — *up*, mettere una grata; — *upon*, urtare. **-ful**, ADJ.: grato, riconoscente. **-fully**, ADV.: gratamente, con gratitudine. **-fulness**, s.: gratitudine, riconoscenza.

gráter, s.: grattugia, raspa, f.

grati-ficátion, s.: gratificazione, f.; riconoscimento; piacere, m.; ricompensa, f.

gráti-fy, TR.: gratificare, compensare: compiacere, piacere [illegible] **-fy**[illegible] ADJ.: gradevol[illegible]

gráting, ADJ[illegible] s.: cancello, [illegible] pl. **-ly**, ADV[illegible]

grā́tis, ADV.: gratis, gratuitamente, per nulla.
grā́titūde, S.: gratitudine, *f.*; riconoscimento, *m.*: *out of* —, per riconoscenza.
gratū́i-tous, ADJ.: gratuito, volontario. **-tously**, ADV.: gratuitamente, per grazia. **-ty**, S.: dono, presente gratuito, *m.*; liberalità, buona mano, mancia, *f.*
grā́tu-lāte, TR.: congratularsi; rallegrarsi. **-lā́tion**, S.: congratulazione, *f.*, gratularsi, *m.* **-latory**, ADJ.: di congratulazione.
grā́ve 1, ADJ.: grave, serio, composto; solenne: — *look*, aria grave e composta. **grave** 2, S.: sepolcro, *m.*; fossa, tomba, *f.* **grave** 3, IRR.; TR.: intagliare; scolpire; (*nav.*) spalmare. **-clothes**, S. PL.: vestimento de' morti, *m.* **-digger**, S.: beccamorti, *m.*
grā́vel 1, S.: ghiaia; rena; (*med.*) renella, *f.* **gravel** 2, TR.: coprire di ghiaia; imbarazzare.
grā́veless, ADJ.: senza sepoltura, insepolto.
grā́vel-ly, ADJ.: sabbionoso, ghiaioso, renoso. **-pit**, S.: renaio, *m.*; cava di sabbione, *f.* **-walk**, S.: viale ghiaiato, *m.*
grā́vely, ADV.: gravemente, con gravità, seriamente.
grā́ve-maker, S.: beccamorti, *m.*
grā́ven, ADJ.: intagliato, scolpito.
grā́veness, S.: serietà, gravità, solennità, *f.*
gravéolent, ADJ.: fetido, puzzolente.
grā́ver, S.: intagliatore, scultore; bulino, *m.*
grā́ve-stone, S.: lapida; tomba, *f.*; tumulo, *m.* **-yard**, S.: sepolcreto, campo santo, cimiterio, *m.*
gravidity, S.: gravidanza, pregnezza, *f.*
grā́ving, S.: intaglio, intagliamento, *m.* **-tool**, S.: bulino, *m.*
grā́vi-tāte, INTR.: gravitare, pesare: aggravare. **-tā́tion**, S.: gravitazione, *f.*, peso, *m.* **-ty**, S.: gravità, serietà; importanza, *f.*
grā́vy, S.: sugo, succo (della carne), *m.*
grā́y 1, ADJ.: bigio, grigio, cenerino; canuto: — *horse*, cavallo leardo, *m.*; *get* —, divenire grigio; incanutire. **gray** 2, S.: tasso porco, *m.* **-beard**, S.: barbabianca, vecchio, vecchione, *m.* **-eyed**, ADJ.: che ha gli occhi grigi. **-haired**, ADJ.: canuto, incanutito. **-ish**, ADJ.: alquanto bigio, bigiccio. **-ling**, S.: ombrina, *f.* (pesce). **-ness**, S.: colore bigio, grigio, *m.*
grā́-ze, (IN)TR.: pascere, pascolare; rasentare. **-zier**, S.: ingrassatore di bestiame, *m.*
-ze 1, S.: grasso; untume, sucidume, *m.* **-se** 2, TR.: ungere; macchiare; subornare. **-sily**, ADV.: sucidamente, sporcamente. **-siness**, S.: grassume, untume, sudiciume, *m.* **-sy**, ADJ.: grasso, untuoso; sudicio, sporcato, macchiato.
grêat, ADJ.: grande; illustre, nobile, generoso; S.: grosso; maggior numero, *m.*: *a — deal*, molto, gran quantità, *f.*; *a — many*, molti, *m. pl.*, molte persone, *f. pl.*; *a — while*, lungo tempo; — *grandfather*, bisavolo, *m.*; — *grandson*, pronipote, *m.*; *by the* —, all' ingrosso. **-bellied**, ADJ.: panciuto. **-en**, TR.: aggrandire; INTR.: aggrandirsi; accrescere. **-hearted**, ADJ.: magnanimo, generoso, nobile. **-horse**, S.: cavallo di maneggio, cavallo addestrato, *m.* **-ly**, ADV.: molto; grandemente, estremamente; nobilmente. **-ness**, S.: grandezza; dignità, *f.*; potere, *m.*; magnificenza, eccellenza, *f.*
grēaves, S. PL.: gamberuoli, *m. pl.*, gambiere, *f. pl.*
Grēcian, ADJ.: greco. **-cism**, S.: grecismo, ellenismo, *m.* **-cize**, INTR.: grecizzare, grecchizzare.
grēet, S.: benevolenza, *f.*; grado, *m.*, dignità, *f.*
grēed-ily, ADV.: golosamente; avidamente. **-iness**, S.: ghiottoneria, golosità; avidità, *f.* **-y**, ADJ.: goloso, ghiotto, vorace; avido; desideroso, bramoso: — *after gain*, ingordo di danaro; — *of honours*, ambizioso, vago d' onori; — *of money*, avaro, spilorcio. **-y-gut**, S.: ghiottone, mangione, *m.*
Grēek, ADJ.: greco; S.: Grec-o, *m.*, -a, *f.*; lingua greca, *f.*
grēen 1, ADJ.: verde; fresco; immaturo; nuovo; giovane; S.: color verde; verdume, *m.*; verdura, *f.*: — *fruit*, frutta verde (*or* non matura); — *old age*, vecchiezza vegeta e prosperosa. **grēen** 2, TR.: tingere di verde. **-cloth**, S.: consiglio regio, *m.* **-corn**, S.: grano in erba, *m.* **-finch**, S.: verdone, *m.* **-fish**, S.: merluzzo fresco, *m.* **-gage**, S.: susina di color verde, *f.* **-goose**, S.: papero, *m.* **-grocer**, S.: fruttaiuolo, *m.* **-hood**, S.: verdura, *f.*, verdume, *m.* **-horn**, S.: minchione, *m.* **-house**, S.: stufa (per le piante), *f.* **-ish**, ADJ.: verdiccio, glauco. **-ly**, ADV.: frescamente, immaturamente; timorosamente. **-ness**, S.: verdura, *f.*, verdume, *m.*; immaturità, *f.*; vigore, *m.* **-s**, S. PL.: erbaggio, *m.*; legumi, *m. pl.* **-sickness**, S.: malore donzellesco, *m.*, clorosi, *f.* **-sward**, S.: erbuccia; pianura verde, *f.* **-woman**, S.: fruttaiuola, *f.* **-yard**, S.: legnaia, *f.*
grēet, TR.: salutare; felicitare. **-er**, S.: colui che saluta. **-ing**, S.: saluto; complimento, *m.*

grēçe†, s.: scaglione, grado (d' una scala), m.
gregārious, ADJ.: gregario, di gregge.
Gregōrian, ADJ.: gregoriano.
gre-nāde, s.: (mil.) granata, f. **-nadier**, s.: granatiere, m.
grèy 1 = *gray*. **grey** 2, s.: bigio; colore bigio, grigio, m. **-hound**, s.: levriere, m.
griddle, s.: tegghia, f.
gridelin, s.: gridellino, m.
gridīron, s.: graticola, f.
grie-f, s.: cordoglio; rammarico, m.; afflizione, f., affanno, m.; angoscia, f. **-vance**, s.: gravamento, gravame, m., querela, f.; torto, m.: *redress —s*, togliere (*or* riformare) gli abusi. **-ve**, TR.: attristare; affannare, affliggere; INTR.: attristarsi, affannarsi, affliggersi: *be —ed at*, dolersi di. **-vingly**, ADV.: cordogliosamente, con doglia, affannosamente. **-vous**, ADJ.: cordoglioso, affannoso; grave, enorme, orribile. **-vously**, ADV.: gravemente; dolorosamente; rigorosamente, atrocemente, crudelmente. **-vousness**, s.: cordoglio, m.; afflizione; calamità; enormità, f.
grif-fin, **-fon**, s.: griffo, grifone, m.
grig, s.: (*prov.*) anguilla piccola, f.; buon compagno, m.
grill, TR.: arrostire sulla gratella; bruciare. **-ade**, s.: carbonata; braciuola arrostita, f.
grim, ADJ.: orrido, austero, rigido; arcigno.
grimace, s.: smorfia, contorsione (di bocca); dissimulazione, affettazione, f.
grimālkin, s.: gatta vecchia, f.
grime 1, s.: sporcizia, sporchezza, sporcheria, f.; sucidume, m. **grime** 2, s.: sporcare, lordare.
grim-faced, **-looking**, ADJ.: arcigno, torvo. **-ly**, ADV.: orridamente; austeramente, arcignamente. **-ness**, s.: orrore; viso torvo, m.; severità, austerità, f.
grin 1, s.: morfia, f.; stridore de' denti, m.
grin 2, INTR.: fare morfie; digrignare i denti.
grind, IRR.; TR.: macinare, tritare; masticare; opprimere: — *a knife*, affilare (arrotare) un coltello; — *wheat*, macinare il formento; — *the teeth*, digrignare i denti; — *down*, ridurre in polvere. **-er**, s.: arrotino; mulino, m.; denti mascellari, m. pl. **-ing**, s.: macinamento, m.; estorsione, f. **-ing-mill**, s.: mulino da grano, m. **-stone**, s.: macina, mola, f.
grin-ner, s.: ghignatore; smorfioso, m. **-ningly**, ADV.: ghignantemente.
grip, s.: stretta, f., piglio, m.
grip-e 1, s.: pugnello, m.; manata; presa; oppressione; afflizione, f. **-e** 2, TR.: impugnare; aggrappare, abbrancare; premere; INTR.: causare dolori colici. **-er**, s.: avaro, spilorcio, taccagno, m. **-es**, s. PL.: colica, f., dolori colici, m. pl. **-ing**, s.: aggrappare, m., presa; colica, f., dolori colici, m. pl. **-ingly**, ADV.: con dolori colici.
grip-pe, s.: influenza, f. **-ple**†, s.: avaro, spilorcio, m.
grisètte, s.: grisetta, donnicciola, f.
grisly, ADJ.: orribile, terribile.
grist, s.: macinamento, m.; farina, f.; provvedimento, m.
gris-tle, s.: cartilagine, f. **-tly**, ADJ.: cartilagineo, cartilaginoso.
grist-mill, s.: molino, m.
grit, s.: crusca; sabbia; limatura (di metallo), f.; fossile, m. **-tiness**, s.: qualità sabbionosa, f. **-ty**, ADJ.: calcoloso, arenoso, sabbionoso.
grizelin, ADJ.: grigio.
griz-zle, s.: color grigio, m.; canutezza, f. **-zle(d)**, ADJ.: di color bigio, canuto. **-zly**, ADJ.: alquanto grigio, bigiccio: — *bear*, orso grigio americano.
grōan 1, s.: gemito; sospiro, m.; doglia, f. **groan** 2, INTR.: gemere; sospirare, piangere, dolersi. **-ful**, ADJ.: tristo, mesto; dolente. **-ing**, s.: gemito, m.
groāt, s.: quattro soldi, m. pl.
groāts, s.: farina d' avena, f.
grōcer, s.: droghiere, m.: —'*s shop*, bottega di droghiere, m. **-ies**, s.: spezierie, f. pl. **-y**, s.: drogheria, f., droghe, f. pl.
gròggy, ADJ.: ebbro, ubbriaco.
gròg-ram, **-ran**, s.: grossa grana, f.
grōin, s.: anguinaia.
grōom, s.: palafreniere, mozzo di stalla; servo, fante; nuovamente unito, sposo, m.: — *of the chamber*, cameriere, m.
grōove 1, s.: antro profondo, m.; scanalatura, f. **groove** 2, TR.: scanalare.
grōp-e, TR.: palpare, palpeggiare, toccare, tastare; cercare: — *about*, andare tastoni, brancolare. **-er**, s.: toccatore, m. **-ing**, ADV.: tastone, tentone: *go* —, andare tastoni.
grōss, ADJ.: grosso, spesso; rozzo, basso; stolto, ignorante; s.: grosso, m.; parte maggiore, f.: *the — amount*, l' ammontare, la somma totale; — *language*, villanie, f. pl. **-ly**, ADV.: in grosso; rozzamente, zoticamente; di molto. **-ness**, s.: grossezza; rozzezza, f.
grō-t, s.: grotta, caverna, f. **gro-tèsque**, ADJ.: grottesco. **-to**, s.: grotta, f.
grōund 1, impf. e part. del v. *grind*.
ground 2, s.: suolo, m.; terra, f.; terreno; paese, campo; fondamento; soggetto, m.; ragione, f. **-s**, PL.: feccia, f.; residuo, m.; principi, m. pl.: *be above* —, essere in vita; *gain* —, avanzare; *give* —, dar luogo, cedere; *keep one's* —, stare fermo;

tener duro; *lose* —, rinculare, tirarsi indietro; *quit one's* —, ritirarsi; partirsi; *without* —*s*, senza motivo. **ground** 3, TR.: stabilire, fondare; (*nav.*) mettere a secco. **-age**, S.: (*nav.*) ancoraggio, *m.* **-bait**, S.: esca fatta d'orzo, *f.* **-edly**, ADV.: fondatamente; certamente. **-floor**, S.: quartiere a terreno, *m.* **-ivy**, S.: edera terrestre, *f.* **-less**, ADJ.: malfondato; senza ragione. **-lessly**, ADV.: senza fondamento, senza ragione. **-lessness**, S.: mancanza di fondamento, *m.* **-ling**, S.: gobbione, *m.* (pesce). **-ly**, ADV.: fondatamente; solidamente. **-plot**, S.: base, *f.*, fondamento, principio, *m.* **-rent**, S.: terratico, *m.* **-room**, S.: camera terrena, *f.* **-sel**, S.: soglia, *f.*; crescione, *m.* **-tackle**, S.: (*nav.*) guarnitura delle ancore, *f.* **-work**, S.: fondo, fondamento, *m.*

group 1, S.: gruppo, groppo, *m*; folla, *f.* **group** 2, TR.: aggroppare, formare in groppo.

grouse, S.: francolino, *m.*

grout, S.: crusca, farina d'avena, *f.*; sedimento, *m.*

grove, S.: boschetto; viale d'alberi, *m.*, selvetta, *f.*

grovel, INTR.: rampicare; abbassare, avvilirsi.

grow, IRR.; TR.: coltivare; far crescere, farsi (*obj. as subj.*); INTR.: crescere; divenir grande, ingrandire, divenir, farsi; pervenire; arrivare; (*nav.*) chiamare: — *apace*, crescere ad occhio veggente; — *better*, migliorarsi, ammendarsi; correggersi; — *big*, divenir grosso, ingrossare; — *dear*, divenir caro, incarire; — *fat*, divenir grasso, impinguarsi; — *handsome*, divenir bello; — *heavy*, divenir pesante, aggravarsi; — *into favour*, essere favorito; — *late*, farsi tardi; — *lean*, divenir magro, smagrire; — *less*, decrescere, diminuire; — *light*, divenir chiaro, schiarare; — *little*, impiccolirsi, diminuire; — *old*, invecchiare; farsi vecchio; — *poor*, divenir povero, impoverire; — *proud*, divenir superbo, insuperbirsi; — *rich*, divenir ricco, arricchirsi; — *sleepy*, addormentarsi; — *strong*, divenir forte, invigorirsi; — *tame*, addimesticarsi, ammansarsi; — *thick*, divenir denso, spessare; — *ugly*, divenir brutto, imbruttire; — *out of use*, divenir fuor d'uso; passare; — *up*, venir su, farsi grande; — *weary*, faticarsi; infastidire, tediarsi; — *well*, ristabilirsi; riaversi; — *worse*, diventare peggiore; — *young*, ringiovanire, rinnovarsi; — *again*, rigermogliare; — *into*, passare in; — *near*, avvicinarsi; — — *on*, avanzarsi; — *out*, allargarsi, distendersi; — *together*, crescere insieme, unirsi; — *up*, crescere; alzarsi; sorgere; — *up again*, rinascere; rivenire; *begin to* —, germogliare; *they* — *potatoes in that ground*, in quel terreno si fanno le patate. **-er**, S.: aumentatore; coltivatore, *m.* **-ing**, ADJ.: crescente; nascente.

growl 1, S.: borbottamento, *m.* **growl** 2, INTR.: grugnare, borbottare. **-er**, S.: brontolone, *m.*

growth, S.: crescimento; aggrandimento, *m.*; sviluppa; origine, *f.*: *this wine is of my own* —, questo vino è del mio proprio terreno; *of English* —, d'origine inglese.

grub 1, S.: lombrico; nano; caramogio, *m.* **grub** 2, TR.: sradicare, svellere; dissodare; sarchiare.

grubble†, INTR.: andare tentone.

grudge 1, S.: odio, rancore, *m.*; ira, *f.* **-ge** 2, TR.: portare invidia, invidiare; rimproverare; confutare; INTR.: dolersi, lamentarsi. **-ging**, S.: invidia, *f.*, rancore, *m.*, gelosia, *f.* **-gingly**, ADV.: a contracuore.

gruel, S.: polenta, *f.*

gruesome, ADJ.: raccapricciante, spaventoso, orrendo.

gruff, ADJ.: arcigno, burbero, aspro, rozzo. **-ly**, ADV.: arcignamente; aspramente. **-ness**, S.: arcignezza, asprezza, *f.*

grum, ADJ.: stizzoso, dispettoso, ritroso.

grumble, INTR.: borbottare, brontolare, mormorare. **-bler**, S.: borbottatore, brontolone, *m.* **-bling**, S.: borbottamento, mormoramento, *m.*

grume, S.: grumo; quagliamento, *m.*

grumly, ADV.: con viso arcigno.

grumous, ADJ.: grumoso, quagliato. **-ness**, S.: coagulamento, *m.*, coagulazione, *f.*

grunt, INTR.: grugnire, grugnare. **-er**, S.: borbottone, sgridatore, *m.* **-ing**, S.: grugnito, borbottamento, *m.* **-le** = *grunt*. **-ling**, S.: porcello, porchetto, *m.*

guano, S.: guano, *m.*

gua-rantee, S.: sicurtà, *f.*; mallevadore, *m.* **guá-ranty**, TR.: mallevare; guarantire.

guard 1, S.: guardia, custodia; difesa; (*fenc.*) elsa, *f.*; (*rail.*) conduttore, *m.*: *be on* —, essere di guardia; stare all'erta; *be on your* —, state all'erta; *come off from* —, smontar di guardia; *stand* —, stare in sentinella, fare la guardia. **guard** 2, TR.: guardare, custodire, difendere; proteggere; INTR.: stare in guardia; preservarsi. **-age**, S.: carica del curatore, *f.* **-edly**, ADV.: cautamente. **-edness**, S.: cauzione, precauzione, prudenza, *f.* **-er**, S.: custode; protettore, *m.*

-**ful**, ADJ.: cauto, prudente. -**house**, S.: corpo di guardia, *m.* -**ian**, ADJ.: guardiano; tutelare; S.: guardiano; curatore, protettore, *m.* -**ianship**, S.: carica del guardiano, *f.* -**less**, ADJ.: senza guardia, senza protezione. -**room**, S.: corpo di guardia, *m.* -**ship**, S.: cura; protezione, *f.*; (*nav.*) guardacoste, *m.*

gûber-natet†, TR.: governare. -**natô-rial**, ADJ.: governatorio, di governatore.

gûdgeon, S.: ghiozzo (pesce); affronto, *m.*

guèrdon, S.: guiderdono, *m.*, ricompensa, *f.*, premio, *m.*

guerilla, S.: guerilla: — *warfare*, guerra alla spicciolata, *f.*

guéss 1, S.: conghiettura; supposizione, *f.* **guess** 2, TR.: conghietturare; indovinare; apporsi: *if I — right*, s' io m' appongo. -**er**, S.: conghietturatore; indovinatore, *m.* -**ing**, ADJ.: conghietturale, congetturale. -**ingly**, ADV.: in modo congetturale.

guést, S.: convivato; forestiere; ladro (della candela), *m.* -**chamber**, S.: stanza de' forestieri, *f.*

gŭggle = *gurgle*.

gui-dage, S.: salario del condottore, *m.* -**dance**, S.: guida, scorta, condotta, *f.* -**de** 1, S.: guida; scorta, *f.*; condottore, cicerone, *m.* -**de** 2, TR.: guidare; dirigere; accompagnare. -**deless**, ADJ.: senza guida. -**de-post**, S.: colonna migliaria, *f.* -**der**, S.: guida; direttore, *m.* -**don**, S.: stendardo, *m.*

guild, S.: società, fraternità; compagnia, *f.*

guilder, S.: fiorino, *m.*

guildhall, S.: casa della città, *f.*

guile, S.: inganno, *m.*; furberia, *f.* -**ful**, ADJ.: ingannoso, furbo. -**fully**, ADV.: ingannevolmente; da traditore. -**fulness**, S.: frode; furberia, impostura, *f.*, inganno, *m.* -**less**, ADJ.: senza frode, senza inganno. -**lessness**, S.: sincerità, innocenza, *f.* -**er**, S.: truffatore, giuntatore, *m.*

guil-lotine, S.: ghigliottina, *f.* -**lotine**, TR.: ghigliottinare.

guilt, S.: delitto, misfatto, *m.*; colpa; colpabilità, *f.* -**ily**, ADV.: criminalmente. -**iness**, S.: delitto, *m.*; colpa, scelleratezza, *f.* -**less**, ADJ.: netto di colpa, innocente. -**lessly**, ADV.: innocentemente. -**lessness**, S.: innocenza, *f.* -**y**, ADJ.: colpevole, reo, criminoso; scellerato: *not* —, innocente; *verdict of* —, giudizio di colpevole; *plead* —, dichiararsi colpevole, confessarsi reo; *plead not* —, dichiararsi innocente.

guinea, S.: ghinea, *f.* -**dropper**, S.: [illegible], *m.* -**hen**, S.: gallina di faraone, *f.* -**pepper**, S.: pepe d' India, *m.* -**pig**, S.: porcello d' India, *m.*

guise, S.: guisa, foggia; maniera, *f.*, modo; costume; talento, *m.*

guitâr, S.: chitarra, *f.*: *play upon the* —, suonar la chitarra.

gûlch, S.: ghiottoncello, *m.*

gŭlf, S.: golfo; seno di mare; abbisso, *m.* -**y**, ADJ.: pieno di golfi.

gŭll 1, S.: gabbiano; furbo; balordo, *m.* **gull** 2, TR.: ingannare, truffare. -**catcher**, -**er**, S.: ingannatore, furbo, *m.* -**ery**, S.: inganno, *m.*, furberia, beffa, *f.*

gŭllet, S.: gola, strozza, *f.*; collo, *m.*

gull-ibility, S.: credulità, *f.* -**ible**, ADJ.: credulo.

gŭllish†, ADJ.: imbecille, stupido.

gŭlly, S.: borro, *m.* -**gut**†, S.: ghiotto, *m.* -**hole**, S.: chiavica, *f.*, smaltitoio, *m.*

gulôsity, S.: golosità; ghiottorneria, *f.*

gŭlp 1, S.: gorgo; sorso, tratto, *m.* **gulp** 2, TR.: ingozzare; inghiottire, trangugiare; palpitare.

gŭm 1, S.: gomma: — *arabic*, gomma arabica. **gum** 2, S.: gengiva, *f.*: — *of the eyes*, cispa, *f.* **gum** 3, TR.: ingommare, impiastrare con gomma. -**miness**, -**môsity**, S.: viscosità, *f.* -**mous**, ADJ.: gommoso, gommifero. -**my**, ADJ.: pieno di gomma; gommoso, viscoso.

gŭmption, S.: desterità; intelligenza, *f.*

gŭm-tree, S.: albero gommifero, *m.*

gŭn, S.: schioppo, moschetto, fucile; archibuso, *m.*: *great* —, cannone, *m.*; *heavy* —*s*, artiglieria di piazza. -**barrel**, S.: canna da schioppo, *f.* -**boat**, S.: scialuppa cannoniera, *f.* -**carriage**, S.: (*art.*) affusto, *m.* -**cotton**, S.: fulmicotone. -**deck**, S.: batteria, *f.* -**nel**, S.: (*nav.*) parapetto, orlo, *m.* -**ner**, S.: cannoniere, artigliere, *m.* -**nery**, S.: arte di sparare il cannone, arte del cannoniere, *f.* -**port**, S.: cannoniera, *f.* -**powder**, S.: polvere da cannone, *f.* -**room**, S.: (*nav.*) Santa Barbara, *f.* -**shot**, S.: tiro di moschetto, tiro di cannone, *m.*; portata, *f.* -**smith**, S.: armaiuolo, fabbricatore d'armi, *m.* -**stick**, S.: bacchetta dello schioppo, *f.* -**stock**, S.: cassa d' uno schioppo, *f.*

gŭrge, S.: golfo; abbisso, *m.*

gŭrgl-e, INTR.: gorgogliare. -**ing**, S.: gorgogliamento, *m.*

gŭsh 1, S.: sgorgamento; trabocco, *m.* **gush** 2, INTR.: sgorgare, sboccare.

gŭsset, S.: gherone, *m.*

gŭst 1, S.: colpo di vento, *m.* **gust** 2, S.: gusto; desiderio. **gust** 3, TR.: gustare, assaggiare. -**able**, ADJ.: gustevole, gustoso. -**ation**, S.: gustamento, gustare, *m.* -**ful**, ADJ.: gustevole; piacevole al gusto. -**less**, ADJ.: senza gusto, insipido.

-o, S.: gusto; discernimento; piacere, *m.* **-y**, ADJ.: tempestoso, procelloso.
gŭt 1, S.: budello, intestino, *m.*; ghiottornia, *f.*: *greedy* —, ghiottone, leccone, *m.* **gut** 2, TR.: sviscerare, sventrare, sbudellare. **-string**, S.: corda di minugia, minugia, *f.*
gŭtter 1, S.: gronda, grondaia, *f.*, ruscelletto, *m.* **gutter** 2, TR.: scanalare; INTR.: scolare. **-stone**, S.: pietra della gronda, *f.* **-tile**, S.: tegola, *f.*
gŭttural, ADJ.: gutturale. **-ness**, S.: pronunzia gutturale, *f.*
gŭzzl-e, INTR.: gozzovigliare, crapulare, impinzarsi. **-er**, S.: ghiottone, mangione; crapulone, *m.*
guy 1, S.: corda da sostegno (da guida), *f.* **guy** 2, TR.: dirigere. **guy** 3, S.: figura grottesca. **guy** 4, TR.: beffare; ingannare.
gȳbe = *jibe.*
gym-nasium, S.: ginnasio, *m.* **-nastic**, ADJ.: ginnastico. **-nastically**, ADV.: in modo ginnastico; da atleta. **-nastics**, S. PL.: ginnastica, *f.* **-nic**, S.: ginnastico, *m.*
gyp-seous, ADJ.: gessoso. **-sum**, S.: gesso, *m.*
gypsy, S.: zingaro, *m.*, zingara, *f.*; lingua degli zingari, *f.* **-like**, ADJ.: da zingaro.
gyration, S.: giramento, *m.*
gyre, S.: giro, cerchio; rivolgimento, *m.*
gyve, TR.: incatenare, porre in ceppi. **-s**, S. PL.: catene, *f. pl.*; ceppi, ferri, *m. pl.*

H

h *ăch* (*the letter*), S.: h, *f.*
hâ! INTERJ.: ah! ahi!
hâbeas côrpus, S.: habeas corpus, *m.*
hăberdasher, S.: merciaio, merciaiuolo, *m.* **-y**, S.: merceria, *f.*
hăberdine, S.: merluzzo salato, *m.*
habērgeon, S.: piastrone, giaco; corsaletto, *m.*
habiliment, S.: abbigliamento, abito; vestito, *m.*
habili-tate, TR.: abilitare. **-tation**, S.: abilitazione; qualificazione, *f.* **-ty**, S.: abilità, facoltà, *f.*, potere, *m.*
hăb-it 1, S.: abitudine, consuetudine, *f.*; costume, uso; abito, vestimento, vestito, *m.*; complessione, disposizione (del corpo), *f.*: *by* —, per abito; *get into a* —, prendere costume, abituarsi; *sedentary* —*s*, abitudini sedentarie. **-it** 2, TR.: provvedere d' abiti, vestire; INTR.: vestirsi. **-itable**, ADJ.: abitabile, abitevole. **-itableness**, S.: stato d' una casa abitabile, *m.* **-itant**, S.: abitante, abitatore, *m.* **-itation**, S.: abitazione; casa, *f.* **-itator**, S.: abitatore, *m.* **-itual**, ADJ.: abituale; consueto; ordinario. **-itually**, ADV.: abitualmente, per abito. **-ituate**, TR.: abituare; accostumare: — *one's self*, abituarsi, accostumarsi; assuefarsi; solere. **-itude**, S.: abitudine; costume, *f.*; uso, *m.*; disposizione, *f.*
hăbnab†, ADV.: a caso, alla ventura.
hăck 1, S.: marra, zappa, *f.* **hack** 2, S.: cavallo d' affitto, *m.* **hack** 3, TR.: sminuzzare, tritare; stroppiare (una lingua).
hăckle 1, S.: seta cruda, *f.* **hackle** 2, TR.: tagliuzzare, sminuzzare.
hăckney 1, S.: cavallo d' affitto, *m.*; rozza, carogna, *f.* **hackney** 2, ADJ.: d' affitto, mercenario. **hackney** 3, TR.: esercitare, accostumare, avvezzare. **-ed**, ADJ.: trito, troppo usato. **-coach**, S.: carrozza d' affitto, carrozza a nolo, *f.*
hăddock, S.: baccalà, *f.* (pesce).
hâft 1, S.: manico, *m.* **haft** 2, TR.: mettere il manico.
hăg 1, S.: strega, maga; vecchiaccia, *f.* **hag** 2, TR.: tormentare, vessare.
hăggard, ADJ.: selvaggio; ruvido, fiero, intrattabile. **-ly**, ADV.: ruvidamente.
hăg-ged†, ADJ.: da strega; logorato; magro, macilento. **-gish**, ADJ.: di strega; deforme; orrido.
hăggl-e, TR.: taggliuzzare; mutilare; INTR.: stiracchiare nel prezzo, indugiare; badare. **-er**, S.: che stiracchia il prezzo; irresoluto, *m.*
hagiŏgrapher, S.: scrittore sacro, *m.*
hâh! INTERJ.: ah!
hāil 1, S.: grandine, gragnuola, *f.* **hail** 2, TR.: salutare; implorare; IMP.: grandinare. **hail!** 3, INTERJ.: Iddio vi salvi! ave! **-shot**, S.: migliarola, *f.*; pallino, *m.* **-stone**, S.: grano di gragnuola, *m.* **-storm**, S.: temporale con grandine, *m.*; grandinata, *f.* **-y**, ADJ.: grandinoso.
hāir, S.: capello; pelo; crino (d' un cavallo), *m.*; cosa minuta, *f.*: *false* —, capelli posticci; *a fine head of* —, una bella capigliatura; *within a* —*'s breadth*, poco manca, vicino; *against the* —, a contrappelo; mal volentieri; *to a* —, per l' appunto, esattamente. **-bell**, S.: giacinto, *m.* **-brained**, ADJ.: scervellato. **-breadth**, S.: (*fig.*) poca distanza, *f.* **-broom**, S.: scopa di setole di porco, *f.* **-brush**, S.: spazzola pei capelli, *f.* **-button**, S.: bottone di pelo, *m.* **-cloth**, S.: cilicio, *m.* **-dresser**, S.: perrucchiere, acconciatore, *m.* **-dye**, S.: tintura pei capelli, *f.* **-ed**, ADJ.: capelluto. **-iness**, S.: capellamento, *m.*, quantità di capelli, *f.*, peli, *m. pl.* **-lace**, S.: intrecciatoio, *m.* **-less**, ADJ.: senza capelli, calvo. **-needle**, S.: forcella, *f.* **-pin**,

s.: treccia finta in capelli, f. **-powder**, s.: cipria, f. **-sieve**, s.: staccio, m. **-splitting**, ADJ.: sottile, sottilizzante; s.: sottigliezza, f. **-y**, ADJ.: capelluto, peloso, irsuto.
hálberd, s.: alabarda, f. **-ier**, s.: alabardiere, m.
hálcyon, s.: alcione, m. **halcyon** 2, ADJ.: quieto, tranquillo.
hále 1, ADJ.: sano, vigoroso; forte; gagliardo. **hale** 2, TR.: tirare; strascinare; (mar.) rimorchiare. **-er**, s.: alzaio; che tira a tracolla; (mar.) che rimorchia.
hálf 1, ADJ.: mezzo. **half** 2, ADV.: a metà, per metà; in parte; a parte. **half** 3, pl. halves, s.: metà, f.: by halves, per metà, negligentemente. **-blood**, s.: fratello da un lato, m., sorella da un lato, f. **-blooded**, ADJ.: degenerato. **-brother**, s.: fratello da un lato, fratello uterino, m. **-moon**, s.: mezza luna, f. **-penny**, s.: mezzo soldo, m. **-pike**, s.: mezza picca, f. **-pint**, s.: mezza foglietta, f. **-sister**, s.: sorella da un lato, sorella uterina, f. **-sphere**, s.: emisfero, m. **-strained**, ADJ.: imperfetto. **-tone**, ADJ.: a mezza tinta; s.: fotoincisione, incisione a mezza tinta, f. **-way**, ADV.: nel mezzo della strada, a mezza strada. **-wit**, s.: sciocco, balordo, m. **-witted**, ADJ.: sciocco, stolto.
hálibut, s.: passere, m. (pesce).
háll, s.: sala, f., palazzo; vestibulo, m.
hallelújah -jah, s.: alleluia, m.
hallóo, TR.: incoraggiare (i cani); chiamare.
hállow, TR.: santificare, consacrare.
hallúci-nate, INTR.: ingannarsi, sbagliare. **-nátion**, s.: allucinazione, f.; abbaglio, errore, m.
hálm = *haulm*.
hálo, s.: aureola, f.
hálser = *hawser*.
hált 1, ADJ.: zoppo, azzoppato; s.: posa, fermata, f.; (*mil.*) alto, m. **halt** 2, INTR.: fare alto, fermarsi; zoppicare; (*fig.*), stare in dubbio, dubitare.
hálter 1, s.: zoppo; capestro, m.; cavezza; corda, fune, f. **halter** 2, TR.: incapestrare; legare con una corda.
hálting, s.: zoppicare, m. **-ly**, ADV.: in modo zoppicante.
hálve, TR.: dividere in due, dimezzare.
hályards, s. PL.: (*nav.*) drizze, f. pl.
hám, s.: garretto; prosciutto, presciutto, m.
hámlet, s.: borghetto, casale, m.
hámmer 1, s.: martello, m. **hammer** 2, TR.: martellare; inventare, immaginare: — *out*, stendere col martello; indagare. **-er**, s.: che lavora col martello. **-ing**, s.: *martellare*, m.
hámmock, s.: amaca, branda, f.
hámper 1, s.: paniere; cesto grande, m. **hámper** 2, TR.: imbarazzare, imbrogliare, confondere: *be —ed*, stare alle strette, essere impastoiato (*or* impedito).
hámstring 1, s.: tendine del garretto, m. **hamstring** 2, TR.: tagliare i tendini del garretto.
hánaper, s.: tesoreria, f., erario; tesoro, m.
hánd 1, s.: mano; palma; scrittura, soscrizione, f.; lato; ago (d'un oriuolo); (*mar.*) marinaio, m.: *in* —, fra le mani; in avanza; *at the first* —, di prima mano; *near at* —, qui vicino; — *in* —, insieme, di concerto; *on the one* —, da una parte; *on the other* —, dall' altra parte; *under* —, sotto mano; segretamente; *out of* —, presto, speditamente; — *over head*, inconsideratamente, temerariamente; *keep your —s off!* non lo toccate! *fall into one's —s*, dar nelle mani; *fight — to* —, venire alle prese; *go — in* —, tenersi per la mano; *have a — in a business*, aver parte in un negozio; *live from — to mouth*, vivere alla giornata; *take in* —, intraprendere; *shake —s*, stringersi la mano; *write a good* —, avere una bella scrittura. **hand** 2, TR.: dar la mano; dare di mano in mano; menare: — *round*, far passare (in giro); — *down to posterity*, tramandare ai posteri. **-barrow**, s.: barella, f. **-basket**, s.: sporta, f.; paniere con manico, m. **-bell**, s.: campanello, m. **-bill**, s.: biglietto, m. **-breadth**, s.: larghezza della mano, f., palmo, m.; spanna, f. **-cloth**, s.: fazzoletto, m. **-cuff**, s.: manette, f. pl. **-cuff**, TR.: mettere le manette. **-ed**, ADJ.: dato di mano in mano; dalle mani. **-er**, s.: trasmettitore, m. **-fast**, s.: presa, cattura, f., arresto, m., prigione, f. **-fetters**, s. PL.: manette, f. pl. **-ful**, s.: pugno, m.; manata, f. **-gallop**, s.: piccolo galloppo, m. **-gearing**, s.: (*loc.*) governo, regolatore, m. **-gearing-rod**, s.: (*loc.*) sbarra di governo, f. **-gun**, s.: schioppo, fucile, m. **-icap** 1, s.: impiccio, ostacolo. **-icap** 2, TR.: ostacolare, impicciare, imbarazzare. **-icraft**, s.: mestiere, m., professione, f. **-icraftsman**, s.: artigiano; artefice, m. **-ily**, ADV.: destramente, con destrezza, con abilità. **-iness**, s.: destrezza, abilità, f. **-iwork**, s.: opera manuale; manifattura, f. **-kerchief**, s.: fazzoletto, moccichino, m. **-le** 1, s.: manico; orecchio, m.; impugnatura, f. **-le** 2, TR.: maneggiare; trattare. **-less**, ADJ.: monco, manco. **-ling**, s.: maneggiamento, toccamento, m. **-maid** [illegible] ancella, f. **-mill**, s.: m[illegible]

-sails, S. PL.: vele maneggiate colle mani, *f. pl.* **-saw**, S.: seghetta, sega piccola, *f.* **-sel**, S.: primo uso, *m.*; prima vendita, *f.* **-sel**, TR.: far uso per la prima volta; fare per la prima volta. **-some**, ADJ.: bello, avvenevole, elegante. **-somely**, ADV.: bellamente, elegantemente; piacevolmente. **-someness**, S.: bellezza; grazia, eleganzia, *f.* **-spike**, S.: (*nav.*) manovella, *f.* **-vice**, S.: morsa, *f.* **-worm**, S.: pellicello, *m.* **-writing**, S.: manoscritto, *m.*, scrittura; mano, *f.* **-y**, ADJ.: destro, abile; convenevole. **-y-blow**, S.: colpo di mano, *m.* **-y-dandy**, S.: giuoco da battersi sulle mani, *m.*

hăng, (IR)R.; TR.: appendere, appiccare; piegare; sospendere, collocare; INTR.: pendere; stare sospeso; contrappesare: — *loose*, star penzolone; — *a robber*, impiccare un ladro; — *a room*, tappezzare una camera; — *the rudder*, montare il timone; — *about*, stare pendente, penzolare; — *back*, eludere; schivare; — *by*, appendere, appiccare; — *down*, pendere; abbassare; chinare; — *on*, appendere; attaccarsi, aggrapparsi; — *out* (*nav.*), inalberare; — *together*, accordarsi; — *up*, sospendere, appendere. **-er**, S.: scimitarra, *f.*; coltellaccio, *m.* **-er-on**, S.: parassito, scroccone, *m.* **-ing**, ADJ.: pendente, sospeso; degno di forca; S.: impiccagione, *f.*: — *garden*, giardino pensile; —*s*, tappezzerie, *f. pl.*, cortinaggio, *m.* **-lock**, S.: lucchetto, *m.* **-man**, S.: carnefice, boia, giustiziere, *m.*

hănk, S.: matassa, *f.*; gomitolo, *m.*; propensione, inclinazione, *f.*

hănker, INTR.: desiderare ardentemente. **-ing**, ADJ.: bramoso; S.: inclinazione, *f.*, desiderio, *m.*

Hanseătic, ADJ.: anseatico.

hănsel = *handsel.*

Hănse-town, S.: città anseatica, *f.*

hăp 1, S.: caso, accidente, *m.*; sorte, *f.* **hap** 2, INTR.: accadere, avvenire, succedere. **-hazard**, S.: accidente, avvenimento, evento casuale, *m.* **-less**, ADJ.: sfortunato, sventurato, disgraziato. **-ly**, ADV.: forse; per accidente, a caso. **-pen**, INTR.: accadere, avvenire; darsi: *I —ed to mention it*, mi accadde di farne menzione; — *what will*, avvenga quel che può avvenire; *what has —ed to you?* che vi è seguito? *as it —s*, ad ogni modo. **-pily**, ADV.: fortunatamente, per sorte. **-piness**, S.: felicità; buona ventura, fortuna, sorte, *f.* **-py**, ADJ.: felice, fortunato, prospero: *make* —, render felice, felicitare; *I am — to hear it*, son pur lieto di sentirlo.

harăn-gue 1, S.: aringa, *f.* **-gue** 2, TR.: aringare; perorare. **-guer**, S.: aringatore, oratore, *m.*

hărass 1, S.: guasto, discrtamento, *m.* **harass** 2, TR.: stancare, allassare, faticare; distruggere, rovinare. **-er**, S.: guastatore, rovinatore, *m.*

hârbinger, S.: foriere; precursore, *m.*

hârbour 1, S.: alloggio; rifugio, ricovero, riparo; porto, *m.* **harbour** 2, TR.: alloggiare, albergare; INTR.: soggiornare, dimorare. **-age**, S.: accoglimento, ricovero; rifugio, asilo, *m.* **-er**, S.: ospite; protettore, *m.* **-less**, ADJ.: senza porto; senza rifugio. **-master**, S.: capitano del porto, *m.*

hârd 1, ADJ.: duro; fermo, sodo; severo, aspro, rigoroso; faticoso, molesto; difficile; oneroso: — *wood*, legno duro; — *heart*, cuore duro; — *task*, compito difficile; — *drinking*, eccesso nel bere; — *winter*, inverno rigoroso; — *words*, parole dure; — *of belief*, incredulo; — *to get*, raro; — *of hearing*, sordastro, quasi sordo; — *to be understood*, inintelligibile. **hard** 2, ADV.: presso a poco; forte, fortemente; difficilmente: — *by*, qui vicino, presso; *it freezes* —, gela forte; *it rains very* —, piove dirottamente; *the wind blows* —, fa gran vento; *drink* —, bere eccessivamente; *follow one* —, seguitare alcuno d'appresso. **-bound**, ADJ.: stitico, costipato. **-en**, TR.: indurare, indurire; INTR.: divenire duro. **-ening**, S.: induramento, *m.* **-favoured**, ADJ.: laido, deforme. **-favouredness**, S.: laidura, bruttezza, *f.* **-featured**, ADJ.: dalle fattezze dure. **-fought**, ADJ.: ostinato. **-gotten**, ADJ.: ottenuto a stento. **-handed**, ADJ.: ruvido. **-hearted**, ADJ.: crudele, inumano. **-heartedness**, S.: crudeltà, inumanità, *f.* **-ihead**, **-ihood**, S.: intrepidità, bravura, *f.* **-ily**, ADV.: coraggiosamente, animosamente, arditamente. **-iness**, S.: pena, difficoltà; arditezza, *f.* **-ly**, ADV.: appena, difficilmente, severamente, rigorosamente. **-mouthed**, ADJ.: duro di bocca; restio, caparbio. **-ness**, S.: durezza; difficoltà; asprezza, *f.*: — *of the winter*, severità del verno, *f.* **-nibbed**, ADJ.: di punta dura.

hârds, S.: stoppa, *f.*

hârd-ship, S.: durezza; difficoltà, fatica, *f.*, travaglio, *m.*: *life of* —, vita stentata. **-ware**, S.: chincaglia, *f.* **-wareman**, S.: chincagliere, *m.* **-witted**, ADJ.: goffo, stupido. **-y**, ADJ.: ardito, coraggioso, bravo, robusto, forte.

hâre 1, S.: lepre, *f.*: *young* —, lepretto, *m.* **hare** 2, TR.: spaventare. **-bell**, S.: convolvolo, *m.* **-brained**, ADJ.: scervellato, pazzesco. **-foot**, S.: piè di lepre, *m.* (erba). **-hearted**, ADJ.: timoroso, timido, pauroso. **-hunting**, S.: caccia di lepri, *f.* **-lip**, S.: labbro fesso, *m.* **-lipped**, ADJ.: dal labbro leporino (*or* fesso). **-ragout**, S.: frattaglie delle lepri, *f. pl.*

hārem, S.: arem, *m.*

hāricot, S.: fagiuolo, *m.*

hārk 1, INTERJ.: odi! sta attento! **hark** 2, TR.: ascoltare, stare attento.

hārl, S.: fibre della canapa, *f. pl.*

hārlequin, S.: arlecchino, *m.* **-āde**, S.: arlecchineria, *f.*

hārlot, S.: cortigiana, prostituta, zambracca, *f.*; ADJ.: impudico, lascivo.

hārm 1, S.: male; danno, pregiudizio; delitto, *m.*: *keep out of —'s way*, porsi in sicuro, evitare il pericolo. **harm** 2, TR.: nuocere; far torto, pregiudiziare. **-ful**, ADJ.: nocevole, dannoso. **-fully**, ADV.: nocevolmente. **-fulness**, S.: nocimento, male, *m.* **-less**, ADJ.: innocente. **-lessly**, ADV.: innocentemente. **-lessness**, S.: innocenza, *f.*

har-mŏnic(al), ADJ.: armonico, melodioso. **-mōnious**, ADJ.: armonioso. **-mōniously**, ADV.: con armonia; dolcemente. **-mōniousness**, S.: armonia, consonanza; proporzione, *f.* **hār-monise**, TR.: armonizzare; aggiustare; proporzionare; INTR.: esser d'accordo: *the facts —*, i fatti s'accordano fra loro.

hār-mony, S.: armonia; melodia, *f.*

hārness 1, S.: arnese, *m.*; armatura compita, *f.* **harness** 2, TR.: mettere in arnese; arredare. **-maker**, S.: valigiaio, sellaio, *m.*

hārp 1, S.: arpa, *f.*: *play* (*upon*) *the —*, suonare dell' arpa, suonar l' arpa. **harp** 2, INTR.: arpeggiare, suonare l' arpa: *— upon a subject*, ripetere frequentemente, parlare d' una cosa fino a dar noia. **-er**, S.: arpista, suonatore d' arpa, *m.*

harpōon, S.: fiocina da punta, *f.*, arpone, *m.* **-er**, S.: fiociniere, *m.*

hārpsichord, S.: gravicembalo, buonaccordo, *m.*

hārpy, S.: arpia, *f.*

hārqueb.. = *arqueb..*

hārridan, S.: rozza, *f.*

hārrier, S.: levriere, *m.*

hārrow 1, S.: erpice, *f.* **harrow** 2, TR.: erpicare. **-er**, S.: che erpica; spezie di falcone, *f.* **-ing**, S.: erpicare, *m.*

hārry, TR.: tormentare; rubare.

hārsh, ADJ.: aspro, austero, afro, amaro, rigido, duro; severo. **-ly**, ADV.: aspramente, rigidamente; severamente, rigorosamente. **-ness**, S.: asprezza, rigidezza, durezza; severità, *f.*

hārslet, S.: frattaglie di porco, *f. pl.*

hārt, S.: cervo; daino, *m.* **-s-horn**, S.: corno di cervo, *m.*; (*bot.*) aristologia, *f.* **-s-tongue**, S.: scolopendria, *f.*

hārvest 1, S.: messe, raccolta; mietitura, *f.*: *make* (*get in*) *—*, far la raccolta, mietere; *reap the —*, mietere. **harvest** 2, TR.: mietere; raccogliere. **-home**, S.: festino della mietitura, *m.* **-lord**, S.: capo de' mietitori, *m.* **-er**, **-man**, S.: mietitore, segatore, *m.* **-time**, S.: tempo di mietere, *m.*, mietitura, *f.*

hāsh 1, S.: ammorsellato, *m.* **hash** 2, TR.: sminuzzare, tritare.

hāslet = *harslet.*

hāsp 1, S.: aspo, fermaglio, fibbiaglio, *m.* **hasp** 2, TR.: affibbiare con fermaglio, annaspare.

hāssock, S.: inginocchiatoio, cuscino, *m.*

hās-te, S.: fretta, prestezza, *f.*: impeto, *m.*: *in —*, in fretta, in furia; *make —*, affrettarsi; spicciarsi. **-te**, **-ten**, TR.: affrettare; sollecitare; INTR.: affrettarsi, spacciarsi: *— back*, ritornare presto. **-tener**, S.: affrettatore, *m.* **-tily**, ADV.: in fretta, frettolosamente; iratamente, stizzosamente. **-tiness**, S.: fretta, prestezza; diligenza; stizza, collera, *f.* **-tings**, S. PL.: piselli primaticci, *m. pl.* **-ty**, ADJ.: presto, pronto, stizzoso, prematuro: *— decision*, giudizio avventato. **-ty-pudding**, S.: pappa, *f.*

hāt, S.: cappello, *m.*: *—s off!* giù col cappello! *take off one's —*, levarsi il cappello. **-band**, S.: cordone di cappello, *m.* **-box**, **-case**, S.: cappelliera, *f.*

hātch 1, S.: covata; scoperta, *f.*; (*nav.*) boccaporto, *m.* **hatch** 2, TR.: covare; tramare, far pratiche; tratteggiare.

hātchel 1, S.: pettine, scardasso, *m.* **hatchel** 2, INTR.: pettinare, scardassare. **-ler**, S.: pettinatore (di lino, ecc.), *m.*

hātches, S. PL.: (*nav.*) boccaporto, *m.*

hātchet, S.: azza, scure, *f.*; segolo, *m.* **-face**, S.: viso sfregiato, *m.*

hātchment, S.: scudo, *m.*; arme della famiglia, *f. pl.*

hātch-way, S.: boccaporto, *m.*

hāt-e 1, S.: odio, rancore, *m.* **-e** 2, TR.: odiare, aver in odio; detestare: *they — each other*, si detestano l'un l'altro. **-eful**, ADJ.: odioso, odievole; noioso. **-efully**, ADV.: odiosamente. **-efulness**, S.: qualità odiosa, odiosità; malevoglienza, *f.* **-er**, S.: odiatore; nemico, *m.* **-red**, S.: odio; abborrimento, *m.*

hātter 1, S.: cappellaio, *m.* **hatter** 2, TR.: stancare, noiare; tormentare.

hāuberk, S.: usbergo, *m.*

hāught†, ADJ.: altiero, orgoglioso, superbo. **-ily**, ADV.: fieramente, orgogliosamente. **-iness**, S.: superbia, alterigia, *f.*, orgoglio, *m.* **-y**, ADJ.: orgoglioso, superbo.

hăul 1, s.: tiramento; strascinamento, *m.* **haul** 2, TR.: tirare a braccia, strascinare. **-ing**, s.: tiramento, strascinamento, *m.*
hău(l)m, s.: stoppia; paglia, *f.*
hâunch, s.: anca, coscia, *f.*
hâunt 1, s.: covile; ricovero, *m.*; pratica, *f.* **haunt** 2, TR.: frequentare, bazzicare; molestare, noiare: *a house —ed by spirits*, una casa infestata dagli spiriti. **-er**, s.: frequentatore, *m.* **-ing**, s.: frequentazione; usanza, *f.*
hautböy *hō-*, s.: oboè, *m.*
hauteur *hō-*, s.: orgoglio, *m.*; arroganza, *f.*
hăve, IRR.; TR.: avere; possedere; tenere; fare. — *by heart*, sapere a mente; — *rather*, voler più tosto; amar meglio; — *from good authority*, sapere da buona fonte.
hăven, s.: porto, *m.*; ricovero, asilo, *m.* **-er**, s.: ispettore d' un porto di mare, *m.*
hăver, s.: che possiede.
hăversack, s.: bisaccia, *f.*
hâving, s.: possesso, *m.*: beni, *m. pl.*; ricchezze, *f. pl.*, fortuna, *f.*
hăvoc 1, s.: rovina, *f.*; guasto, desolamento, saccheggiamento, *m.*: *make* —, fare strage, distruggere, dissipare. **havoc** 2, TR.: devastare, rovinare, distruggere.
hăw 1, s.: moro di spinalba, siepe; maglia (negli occhi), *f.* **haw** 2, INTR.: parlare con esitazione; star dubbioso. **-finch**, s.: frisone, *m.*
hăwk 1, s.: falcone, *m.* **hawk** 2, TR.: falconare. **hawk** 3, s.: rivendere. **-ed**, ADJ.: curvato, aquilino. **-er**, s.: merciaiuolo, *m.* **-ing**, s.: caccia col falcone, falconeria, *f.*
hăw-ṣe, s.: (*nav.*) cubia, *f.* **-ṣer**, s.: (*nav.*) gherlino, *m.*
hăwthorn, s.: spinalba, *f.*
hāy, s.: fieno, *m.*: *make* —, far fieno. **-cock**, s.: bica di fieno, *f.* **-harvest**, s.: raccolta di fieno, *f.* **-loft**, s.: fienile, *m.* **-maker**, s.: segatore di fieno, *m.* **-market**, s.: mercato di fieno, *m.* **-rick**, s.: mucchio di fieno, *m.* **-seed**, s.: seme di fieno, *m.* **-stack** = *hay-rick*. **-time** = *hay-harvest*.
hăzard 1, s.: rischio; pericolo; accidente; sorte, *m.*; fortuna, *f.*: *run a* —, arrischiare. **hazard** 2, TR.: arrischiare, avventurare. **-able**, ADJ.: rischioso, pericoloso. **-er**, s.: che arrischia. **-ous**, ADJ.: arrischievole, pericoloso; dubbioso: *rather* —, rischiosetto. **-ously**, ADV.: pericolosamente. **-ousness**, s.: azzardo, *m.* **-ry**, s.: temerità, baldanza, *f.*
hāze 1, s.: nebbia, *f.*, vapore denso, *m.* **haze** 2, TR.: spaventare; INTR.: piovigginare.
hāzel, s.: nocciuolo, *m.* **-ly**, ADJ.: del colore delle nocciuole. **-nut**, s.: nocciuola, *f.* **-tree**, s.: nocciuolo, *m.*
hā-ziness, s.: tempo nebbioso, *m.* **-zy**, ADJ.: nebbioso, fosco, oscuro.
hē, PRON.: egli, esso, colui.
hĕad 1, s.: testa, *f.*; capo; punto principale; teschio (d'un cinghiale), *m.*; cima, sommità, *f.*: titolo, frontispizio; intelletto, *m.*: — *of hair*, capigliatura, *f.*; — *of a cane*, pomo d' una canna, *m.*; — *of a cask*, fondo d' un barile, *m.*; — *of a door*, listello d' una porta, *m.*; — *of a river*, sorgente d' un fiume, *f.*; — *of a ship*, prua d' un naviglio, *f.*; — *and ears*, interamente, estremamente; *from — to foot*, da capo a piedi; *so much a* —, tanto per testa; — *to* —, a quattr' occhi; *bring to a* —, terminare, conchiudere; *make — against*, far fronte a, resistere, opporsi; *put a thing into one's* —, mettersi una cosa in testa. **head** 2, TR.: guidare, comandare; condurre; decapitare; dicimare; levare la cima, spuntare. **-ache**, s.: mal di capo, *m.* **-band**, s.: benda; striscia, *f.* **-dress**, s.: acconciatura (di capo), cuffia, *f.* **-ily**, ADV.: inconsideratamente, follemente. **-iness**, s.: pertinacia, temerità, *f.* **-land**, s.: promontorio, *m.*, punta di terra, *f.* **-less**, ADJ.: senza capo; scervellato. **-long**, ADJ.: temerario, inconsiderato; ADV.: all' impazzata, inconsideratamente; temerariamente. **-money**, s.: capitazione, *f.*, testatico, *m.* **-piece**, s.: caschetto; intelletto, *m.* **-quarters**, s. PL.: quartiere del generale, *m.* **-ship**, s.: primo luogo, primato, *m.*; autorità, *f.* **-sman**, s.: boia; giustiziere, *m.* **-stall**, s.: testiera (d' una briglia), *f.* **-stone**, s.: pietra angolare, *f.*; cantone, *m.* **-strong**, ADJ.: ostinato, caparbio, protervo. **-way**, s.: avanzo, progresso, *m.* **-workman**, s.: primo operaio, *m.* **-y**, ADJ.: ostinato, temerario; violento.
hēal, (IN)TR.: guarire, sanare; rimarginare; (*fig.*) riconciliare: — *a sore*, cicatrizzare; saldare una piaga. **-able**, ADJ.: guaribile, sanabile. **-ing**, ADJ.: consolidativo; s.: guarimento, *m.*
hĕalth, s.: salute; sanità; prosperità, *f.*: *how is your* —, come va la salute; *take care of your* —, la si riguardi; *in good* —, in buona salute; *bill of* —, patente di sanità, *m.*; *drink to one's* —, bere alla salute di qualcheduno. **-ful**, ADJ.: sano; salutifero, salubre. **-fully**, ADV.: in buona salute; salutevolmente, sanamente. **-fulness**, s.: salute; salubrità, *f.* **-ily**, ADV.: vigorosamente. **-iness**, s.: stato di salute, *m.* **-less**, ADJ.: malaticcio, ammalato; debole, infermo.

-some, ADJ.: salubre; salutifero. **-y**, ADJ.: sano, vigoroso; salubre; salutare: — *body*, corpo sano; — *climate*, clima salubre; — *exercise*, esercizio buono (salutare).

hēam, S.: secondina delle bestie, *f.*

hēap 1, S.: mucchio, cumulo, *m.*; bica; massa, *f.*: *by* —*s*, in folla, in abbondanza, in copia. — *of gold*, mucchio d'oro; — *of grain*, monte di grano. **heap** 2, TR.: accumulare, ammontare, ammassare: — *up*, ammucchiare. **-er**, S.: accumulatore, ammassatore, *m.* **-y**, ADJ.: accumulato, ammassato.

hēar, IRR., TR.: intendere, stare attento, ascoltare; INTR.: IRR.: udire; essere informato, imparare: — *ill*, esser in cattiva riputazione: *I have* —*d from your brother*, ho ricevuto una lettera di vostro fratello; *I* — *you are going to be married*, sento che siete per ammogliarvi. **-er**, S.: uditore, ascoltatore, *m.* **-ing**, S.: udito, udire, *m.*; udienza, *f.*: *be hard of* —, essere quasi sordo; *in the* — *of all*, in udienza di tutti.

heárken, INTR.: ascoltare, dare orecchio, stare ad udire. **-er**, ascoltatore, uditore, *m.*

hēarsay, S.: fama, *f.*, romore, *m.*: *by* —, per udita.

hēarse 1, S.: carro funebre; catafalco, *m.* **hearse** 2, TR.: mettere in sulla bare. **-cloth**, S.: panno funebre, *m.*

heárt, S.: cuore; coraggio; vigore; centro; mezzo; amore, *m.*: *by* —, a mente, a memoria; *with all my* —, di tutto cuore; *give* —, incoraggiare; *put out of* —, scoraggiare; *take to* —, prendere a cuore; *die of a broken* —, morire di crepacuore; *have you the* — *to?* vi da il cuore di? **-ache**, S.: cordoglio, affanno; dolore, *m.* **-break**, **-breaking**, S.: crepacuore, *m.* **-breaking**, ADJ.: affittivo, desolante. **-broken**, ADJ.: afflitto, che muore di crepacuore. **-burn**, S.: cardialgia, *f.*; anticuore, *m.*; acredine nello stomaco, *f.* **-burning**, S.: crudezze, *f. pl.*; odio segreto, *m.*, affizione, *f.* **-dear**, ADJ.: dilettisimo. **-ease**, S.: quiete; tranquillità d'animo; consolazione, *f.*, conforto, *m.* **-easing**, ADJ.: consolatorio, confortativo. **-en**, TR.: incoraggiare, animare; eccitare; fortificare. **-ening**, ADJ.: incoraggiante; nutritivo. **-felt**, ADJ.: sensitivo, sensibile.

heárth, S.: focolare, cammino, *m.*

heár-tily, ADV.: cordialmente, sinceramente; diligentemente. **-tiness**, S.: cordialità, sincerità; diligenza, *f.* **-tless**, ADJ.: senza cuore; spietato, inumano, crudele; scoraggiato, timido. **-tlessly**, ADV.: spietatamente, crudelmente; senza coraggio, timidamente. **-tlessness**, S.: inumanità, crudeltà, *f.*; mancanza di cuore, poltroneria, *f.* **-t's-ease**, S.: viola, *f.* **-t-sick**, ADJ.: pieno d'affizione. **-t-sickening**, S.: che abbatte il cuore, angoscioso, desolante. **-t-string**, S.: fibra del cuore, *f.* **-t-struck**, ADJ.: impresso nella mente. **-whole**, ADJ.: spassionato. **-wounded**, ADJ.: pieno d'amore. **-wringing**, S.: che strazia il cuore, angoscioso. **-ty**, ADJ.: sincero; sano, vigoroso.

hēat 1, S.: calore, caldo, *m.*; vivacità, animosità, *f.*, ardore, zelo, fervore; corso, *m.*; corsa, *f.*: *sultry* —, caldo, affannosa; *in the* — *of*, nell' ardenza di; — *of youth*, bollori della gioventù, *m. pl.*; *be in a great* —, esser molto adirato. **heat** 2, REG. *or* IRREG.: TR.: scaldare, riscaldare; infiammare. **-er**, S.: ferro da distendere (i panni), *m.*

hēath, S.: landa; scopa; macchia, *f.* **-cock**, S.: francolino, *m.*

hēathen, ADJ.: pagano, idolatro; S.: pagano, *m.*; idolatra, *f.* **-ish**, ADJ.: pagano, salvaggio. **-ishly**, ADV.: paganamente, da pagano. **-ism**, S.: paganesimo, *m.*

hēathy, ADJ.: coperto d'eriche, pieno di scope.

hēatless, ADJ.: senza calore, freddo.

hēave 1, S.: alzata con forza, *f.*; sforzo; sollevamento, *m.* **heave** 2, REG. *or* IRREG.; TR.: alzare, sollevare; elevare; (*nav.*) virare; INTR.: sollevarsi; enfiarsi; palpitare; respirare; nauseare: — *overboard*, gettare in mare; — *a sigh*, gettare un sospiro; — *to* (*nav.*), bracciare in panno.

hēaven, S.: cielo; firmamento, *m.*: *thanks to* —, grazie a Dio; *would to* —, voglia Iddio. **-born**, ADJ.: divino, celestiale. **-ly** 1, ADJ.: celeste; divino. **-ly** 2, ADV.: divinamente. **-ward**, ADV.: verso il cielo, in alto.

hēav-e-offering, S.: primizie, *f. pl.* **-er**, S.: manovella, *f.*

hēav-ily, ADV.: pesantemente, gravemente; grandemente; affannosamente. **-iness**, S.: gravezza; sonnolenza; depressione, *f.*

hēaving, S.: alzamento, *m.*; palpitazione, *f.*

hēavy, ADJ.: grave; pesante; tristo, affiittivo; balocco, insensato.

hēb-domad, S.: settimana, *f.* **-dŏmadal**, **-dŏmadary**, ADJ.: d'una settimana.

hēbe-tate, TR.: stupefare, rendere stupido. **-tātion**, S.: stupefazione, stupidezza, *f.*

Hē-braism, S.: ebraismo, *m.* **-braist**, S.: dotto nell' ebraico, *m.* **-brew** rā-, ADJ.: ebreo, ebraico; S.: ebreo, giudeo, *m.*

hĕcatomb, s.: ecatombe, *f.*
hĕck, s.: rastrelliera, *f.*
hĕc-tic 1, s.: febbre etica, *f.* **-tic(al)** 2, ADJ.: etico, tisico.
hĕctolitre, s.: ettolitro, *m.*
hĕctor 1, s.: ammazzasette, bravo, *m.* **hector** 2, TR.: braveggiare, millantarsi, bravare.
hederāceous, ADJ.: ederaceo.
hĕdg-e 1, s.: siepe, siepaglia, *f.* **-e** 2, TR.: siepare, cinger di siepe. **-e-alehouse**, s.: bettola, *f.* **-e-bird**, s.: perdigiorno, *m.* **-e-born**, ADJ.: vilmente nato, vile. **-e-creeper**, s.: vagabondo, *m.* **-ehog**, s.: riccio; spinoso, *m.* (animale). **-e-marriage**, s.: matrimonio clandestino, *m.* **-epig**, s.: riccio giovane, *m.* **-er**, s.: facitore di siepi, *m.* **-e-row**, s.: filare d' alberi, *m.* **-e-sparrow**, s.: verdino, *m.* **-ing-bill**, s.: rancone, *m.*
hēed 1, s.: cura, guardia; osservazione; attenzione, *f.*: *give* —, attendere; *take* —, aver cura di. **heed** 2, TR.: attendere, badare; osservare; notare. **-ful**, ADJ.: attento, circospetto; prudente. **-fully**, ADV.: cautamente, prudentemente. **-fulness**, s.: attenzione; prudenza, *f.* **-ily†**, ADV.: cautamente, accortamente. **-iness**, s.: attenzione, *f.* **-less**, ADJ.: disattento, trascurato. **-lessly**, ADV.: senza cura, trascuratamente. **-lessness**, s.: trascuraggine, negligenza, *f.*
hēel 1, s.: calcagno, tallone, *m.*: *take to one's —s, betake one's self to one's —s*, fuggire, calcagnare. **heel** 2, INTR.: ballare; pendere; (*shoe.*) rattacconare. **-maker**, s.: facitore di calcagni di legno, *m.* **-piece**, s.: taccone di scarpe, *m.* **-piece**, TR.: mettere un taccone, rattacconare.
hĕft, s.: peso; sforzo; manico, *m.*
hegira, s.: egira, *f.*
hĕifer, s.: giovenca, *f.*
heigh-ho, INTERJ.: oimè! olà!
height, s.: altezza; elevazione; sommità; grandezza, eminenza, *f.*: — *of ignorance*, colmo dell' ignoranza. **-en**, TR.: alzare; accrescere, aumentare; migliorare.
hĕinous, ADJ.: odioso; atroce, abbominevole. **-ly**, ADV.: odiosamente; atrocemente. **-ness**, s.: atrocità; enormità, *f.*
hĕir, s.: erede, *m.* **-apparent**, s.: erede presuntivo, *m.* **-ess**, s.: erede, ereda, *f.* **-less**, ADJ.: senza erede. **-loom**, s.: (*jur.*) mobili non alienabili, *m. pl.* **-ship**, s.: diritto d' erede, *m.*
hĕld, impf. e part. del v. *hold.*
heliacal, ADJ.: (*astr.*) eliaco.
hĕlical, ADJ.: spirale.
helio-cĕntric, ADJ.: (*astr.*) eliocentrico. **heliŏ-meter**, s.: eliometro, *m.* **-scope**, s.: (*astr.*) elioscopio, *m.* **-trope**, s.: elitropia, *f.*; girasole, eliotropio, *m.*
hĕlix, s.: linea spirale, elica, *f.*
hē'll = *he will.*
hĕll, s.: inferno, *m.*
hĕllebore, s.: (*phar.*) ellebro, *m.*
hĕllen-ism, s.: ellenismo, *m.* **-ist**, s.: ellenista, *m.*
hĕll-fire, s.: fuoco dell' inferno, *m.* **-hound**, s.: cane d' inferno, *m.* **-ish**, ADJ.: d' inferno; infernale, diabolico. **-ishly**, ADV.: in maniera infernale, diabolicamente. **-ishness**, s.: infernalità, nequizia infernale, *f.* **-ward**, ADV.: verso l' inferno; a basso.
hĕlm 1, s.: elmo; timone, gubernacolo; (*fig.*) governo, *m.* **helm** 2, TR.: condurre, dirigere; governare.
hĕlmet, s.: elmo, casco, *m.*
hĕlmsman, s.: timoniere, *m.*
hĕlp 1, s.: aiuto, soccorso; appoggio; rimedio, domestico, servitore, *m.*: *bring* —, dar soccorso; *call for* —, gridar accor' uomo. **help** 2, REG. *or* IRREG.; TR.: aiutare, assistere, sovvenire; servire (a tavola): *I cannot — it*, non è mia colpa; — *one another*, aiutarsi l' un l' altro; — *down*, aiutare a scendere; — *forward*, avanzare; promuovere; — *in*, far entrare; — *out*, aiutare ad uscire, fare uscire; — *up*, aiutare a salire. **-er**, s.: aiutatore, *m.* **-ful**, ADJ.: utile; salutevole. **-fulness**, s.: aiuto, soccorso, *m.* **-less**, ADJ.: senza soccorso; che non può aiutarsi, impotente; inutile. **-lessly**, ADV.: senza aiuto. **-lessness**, s.: mancanza di soccorso, *f.*; abbandono, *m.*: *utter* —, colmo della miseria. **-mate**, s.: compagno, *m.*, -gna, *f.*; consorte, *m., f.*
hĕlter-skĕlter, ADV.: in gran fretta, scompigliatamente.
hĕlve 1, s.: manico (di coltello, ecc.), *m.* **helve** 2, TR.: porre il manico.
hĕm 1, s.: orlo, *m.* **hem** 2, TR.: orlare, fregiare; circondare, cingere; INTR.: spurgarsi: — *in*, cingere, circondare. **hem!** 3, INTERJ.: ehi! vedi!
hĕmi-crany, s.: emicrania, *f.* **-cycle**, s.: semiciclo, *m.* **-plegy**, s.: (*med.*) emiplegia, *f.* **-sphere**, s.: emisfero, emispero, *m.* **-sphĕrical**, ADJ.: emisferico. **-stichs**, s.: (*poet.*) emistichio, *m.*
hĕmlock, s.: cicuta, *f.*
hĕmo-rrhage, s.: profluvio di sangue, *m.* **-rrhŏidal**, ADJ.: emorroidale. **-rrhŏids**, s. PL.: emorroide, morici, *f. pl.*
hĕmp, s.: canapa, *f.*, canape, *m.* **-en**, ADJ.: di canapa. **-field**, s.: canapaia, *f.* **-seed**, s.: canapuccia, *f.* **-stalk**, s.: fusto del canape, *m.*
hĕn, s.: gallina; femmina (degli uccelli), *f.*: — *sparrow*, passera, *f.*; *Turkey* —,

gallina d' India, *f.* **-bane**, S.: giusquiamo, *m.*

hence 1, ADV.: da qui; perciò, dunque. **hence** 2, TR.: mandar via. **-forth**, **-forward**, ADV.: di qui innanzi, per innanzi, all' avvenire; in appresso.

hénchman, S.: staffiere, paggio, *m.*

hendécagon, S.: endecagono, *m.*

hen-hearted, ADJ.: pusillanimo. **-house**, S.: gallinaio, pollaio, *m.* **-pecked**, ADJ.: governato dalla moglie; menato pel naso: *he is* —, sua moglie porta i calzoni. **-roost**, S.: gallinaio, *m.*

hepátic(al), ADJ.: epatico, del fegato.

héptachord, S.: (*mus.*) ettacordo, *m.*

hép-tagon, S.: ettagono, *m.* **-tágonal**, ADJ.: di sette angoli.

héptarchy, S.: governo condotto da sette duci, *m.*

hér, PRON.: lei, la, le; il suo, la sua, i suoi, le sue; il (la, i) di lei: —*s*, suo (ecc.), di lei.

hér-ald 1, S.: araldo, *m.* **-ald** 2, TR.: nunziare; introdurre. **-áldic**, ADJ.: araldico. **-aldry**, S.: araldica, *f.*, blasone, *m.* **-aldship**, S.: ufficio d' araldo, *m.*

herb, S.: erba, *f.* **-áceous**, ADJ.: erbaceo, erboso. **-age**, S.: erbaggio, *m.*, erba da pascolo; pastura, *f.* **-al**, S.: erbolaio; erbario, *m.* **-alist**, **-arist**, S.: raccoglitore d' erbe, botanico, *m.* **-elet**, S.: erbetta, *f.* **-ous**, ADJ.: erboso, coperto d' erba. **-woman**, S.: rivendugliola d' erbe, erbolaia, *f.* **-y**, ADJ.: erboso.

hercúlean, ADJ.: erculeo: — *labour*, fatica erculea.

hérd 1, S.: branco; armento, *m.*; mandra, gregge; turba, *f.*, volgo, *m.*: — *of cattle*, armento, *m.* **herd** 2, INTR.: andare in truppa; associarsi. **-sman**, S.: pastore, *m.*

hére 1, ADV.: qui, in questo luogo: — *is*, — *are*, ecco qui, ecco; — *and there*, qua e là; — *below*, quaggiù, qua sotto; *come* —, venite qua; — *she comes*, eccola che viene; —*'s to you!* alla vostra salute! **-abouts**, ADV.: qui vicino; qui all' intorno. **-áfter**, ADV.: da qui innanzi, da qui avanti, all' avvenire. **-ăt**, ADV.: a questo, a ciò; in questo mentre. **-by**, ADV.: per questo mezzo; per questo; col presente; così.

heréd-itable, ADJ.: che si può avere per eredità. **-itament**, S.: eredità, successione, *f.* **-itarily**, ADV.: a modo d' eredità. **-itary**, ADJ.: ereditario, d' eredità.

here-fróm, ADV.: da qui. **-in**, **-intŏ**, ADV.: in questo mentre, in ciò.

heremit. = *hermit*.

here-ŏf, ADV.: di questo, di quello. **-ŏn**, ADV.: *su questo*. **-ŏut**, ADV.: fuor di qui.

hér-esiarch, S.: eresiarca, *m.* **-esy**, S.: eresia, *f.* **-etic**, S.: eretico, *m.* **-étic(al)**, ADJ.: eretico. **-étically**, ADV.: ereticamente, da eretico.

here-tŏ, ADV.: a ciò, a questo. **-tofóre**, ADV.: altre volte, un tempo; a' tempi andati, per lo passato. **-untŏ**, ADV.: a questo, a ciò. **-upŏn**, ADV.: in questo mezzo (*or* mentre), in quella. **-with**, ADV.: con ciò; per questo mezzo; in questo; *I — enclose you*, colla presente vi compiego (*or* accludo).

héri-table, ADJ.: che si può ereditare. **-itage**, S.: eredità, successione, *f.*

hermáphrodite, S.: ermafrodito, *m.*

hermĕtic(al), ADJ.: ermetico. **-ally**, ADV.: ermeticamente.

hér-mit, S.: eremita, romito, solitario, *m.* **-mitage**, S.: eremitaggio, eremo, *m.* **-mitical**, ADJ.: ermitico.

hérn, S.: aghirone, airone, *m.*

hérnia, S.: ernia, rottura, *f.*

hé-ro, S.: eroe, *m.* **-róic(al)**, ADJ.: eroico, illustre. **-róically**, ADV.: eroicamente, da eroe. **-roine** *hé-*, S.: eroina, *f.* **-roism**, S.: eroismo, *m.*

héron, S.: aghirone, airone, *m.* **-ry**, **-shaw**, S.: uccelliera d' aironi, *f.*

hér-pes, S.: (*med.*) erpete, *m.* **-pétic**, ADJ.: (*med.*) erpetico.

hĕrring, S.: aringa, *f.*: *red* —, aringa affumata, *f.*; *salt* —, aringa salata, *f.* **-time** (*-season*), S.: pesca dell' aringhe, *f.* **-woman**, S.: pescivendola, *f.*

hérs, PRON.: suo, sua; suoi, sue.

hérse, S.: saracinesca (con puntali), *f.*

hersélf, PRON.: se stessa, essa stessa.

hés-itancy, S.: incertezza; dubbiezza, irresoluzione, *f.*, dubbio, *m.* **-itate**, INTR.: esitare, star dubbioso, essere incerto. **-itátion**, S.: esitazione; incertezza, dubitazione, *f.*

hést, S.: comando; precetto, ordine, *m.*

hétero-clite, S.: (*gram.*) eteroclito, *m.* **-clitical**, ADJ.: (*gram.*) irregolare. **-dox**, ADJ.: eterodosso. **-doxy**, S.: eterodossia, *f.* **-géneal** = **-geneous**. **-genéity**, S.: eterogeneità, diversità di genere, *f.* **-géneous**, ADJ.: eterogeneo, di genere diverso.

héw, IRR.; TR.: sminuzzare; tagliare; formare: — *down*, abbattere. **-er**, S.: tagliatore di legne; abbattitore.

héx-achord, S.: (*mus.*) esacordo, *m.* **-agon**, S.: esagono, *m.* **-ágonal**, ADJ.: di sei lati. **-ámeter**, S.: (*pros.*) esametro, *m.* **-amétric**, ADJ.: esametrico.

héy, INTERJ.: ah! olà! **-dáy** 1, INTERJ.: ohi! **-day** 2, S.: allegrezza, gaiezza, *f.*

hiátus, S.: apertura, lacuna, *f.*

hibérnal, ADJ.: iemale, vernale.

hic-cough 1 **-kŭp**, S.: singhiozzo, singulto, *m.* **-cough** 2, **-cup**, INTR.: singhiozzare.

hiddenly, ADV.: nascosamente.

hide 1, S.: pelle, *f.*, cuoio, *m.*: — *of land*, iugero, *m.* **hide** 2, IRR.; TR.: nascondere, celare; INTR.: nascondersi: — *one's self*, nascondersi; *play — and seek*, giuocare a capo nascondere.

hidebound, ADJ.: intrattabile; spilorcio, misero.

hideous, ADJ.: orrido, orribile, spaventevole. **-ly**, ADV.: orridamente, orribilmente. **-ness**, S.: orrore, *m.*, terribilità, *f.*

hi-der, S.: nasconditore, occultatore, *m.* **-ding-place**, S.: nascondimento, nascondiglio, *m.*

hie, INTR.: affrettarsi.

hier-arch, S.: gerarca, *m.* **-ârchical**, ADJ.: gerarchico. **-archy**, S.: gerarchia, *f.*

hiero-glyph, S.: geroglifico, *m.* **-glyphic(al)**, ADJ.: geroglifico, mistico. **-glyphically**, ADV.: in modo geroglifico.

hierŏgraphy, S.: scrittura sacra, *f.*

higgle, INTR.: rivendere.

higgledy-piggledy, ADV.: confusamente, alla rinfusa.

higgler, S.: rivenditore, *m.*

high 1, ADJ.: alto, elevato; eminente; eccelso, sublime; eccessivo, esorbitante; altiero, arrogante; nobile, illustre; tempestoso, violento: *rise* —, elevarsi, innalzarsi; essere violento; *at — noon*, di mezzo dì; *'tis — time*, è gia tempo; — *day*, gran festa, *f.*; — *mass*, messa cantata, *f.*; — *treason*, delitto di lesa maestà, *m.*; — *wind*, gran vento, vento tempestoso; *High Church*, chiesa dell' Alta Gerarchia; — *life*, mondo elegante, *m.* **high** 2, ADV.: alto: *play* —, giuocare gran giuoco. **high** 3, S.: alto; sommo; colmo, *m.*; cima, *f.*: *from* —, *on* —, da alto, in alto, in su. **-altar**, S.: altare maggiore, *m.* **-aimed**, ADJ.: ambizioso, altiero. **-blest**, ADJ.: supremamente felice. **-blown**, ADJ.: molto gonfiato. **-born**, ADJ.: d' alta nascita, bennato. **-coloured**, ADJ.: di colore vivido. **-flier**, S.: uomo fantastico, stravagante, *m.* **-flown**, ADJ.: orgoglioso, fiero, superbo. **-land**, S.: paese montagnoso, *m.* **-lander**, S.: montanaro, *m.* **-ly**, ADV.: in alto; molto, grandemente; altieramente. **-mettled**, ADJ.: focoso, ardente. **-minded**, ADJ.: ambizioso, fiero, arrogante. **-most**, ADJ.: altissimo, supremo. **-ness**, S.: altezza; grandezza, *f.* **-priest**, S.: sommo sacerdote, *m.* **-red**, ADJ.: di colore rosso oscuro. **-road**, S.: strada maestra, *f.*, stradone, *m.* **-seasoned**, ADJ.: savore piccante. **-sounding**, ADJ.: [illegible]sante. **-spirited**, ADJ.: ardito, orgoglioso, fiero; insolente; feroce, crudele. **-stomached**†, ADJ.: ostinato, superbo.

hight 1 = *height*. **hight**† 2, (IN)TR.: chiamarsi, esser nominato.

high-water, S.: marea alta, *f.*, acque piene, *f. pl.* **-way**, S.: strada maestra, *f.* **wayman**, S.: malandrino, rubatore, *m.* **-wrought**, ADJ.: ben lavorato, ben finito, di squisito lavoro.

hi-lârity, S.: ilarità, allegrezza, giocondità; gaiezza. **-lârious**, ADJ.: ilare.

hilding†, S.: uomo vile, codardo, *m.*

hill, S.: colle, *m.*, collina, *f.*: *little* —, collina. **-iness**, S.: natura montuosa, *f.* **-ock**, S.: collinetta, *f.*, monticello, *m.* **-y**, ADJ.: montagnoso; pieno di colli lo colline.

hilt, S.: guardia, elsa, manica (della spada), *f.*

him, PRON.: lui, lo. **-sĕlf**, PRON.: sè stesso, egli stesso; si.

hind 1, S.: cerva, damma, *f.*; rustico, *m.* **hind** 2, **-er**, ADJ.: posteriore; deretano.

hinder, TR.: impedire, interrompere; imbarazzare; guastare; ostruire; stornare. **-ance**, S.: impedimento, ostacolo, *m.*; ostruzione, *f.*

hinder-castle, S.: (*nav.*) castello di poppa, *m.*

hinderer, S.: impeditore, *m.*

hind-erling†, S.: animale degenerato, *m.* **-ermost**, ADJ.: ultimo, più indietro. **-leg**, S.: piede di dietrò, *m.* **-most** = *hindermost*. **-part**, S.: parte deretana, *f.* **-quarter**, S.: quarto di dietro, *m.*

hinge 1, S.: arpione, cardine; punto principale, *m.*: *be off the —s*, esser fuor di sè. **hinge** 2, TR.: gangherare.

hint 1, S.: indizio, avviso, sentore; cenno; barlume, *m.*: *give one a* —, dare cenno ad uno; *take the* —, intendere l' avviso (*or* il cenno). **hint** 2, TR.: intimare; insinuare, dare un indizio, accennare; suggerire; alludere.

hip 1, S.: anca, *f.*: *have on the* —, avere vantaggio sopra. **hip** 2, TR.: guastare l' anca. **-gout**, S.: sciatica, *f.*

hippish, ADJ.: ipocondriaco, fantastico.

hippo-griff, S.: ippogrifo, *m.* **-pŏtamus**, S.: ippopotamo, *m.*

hĭpshot, ADJ.: sciancato, zoppo.

hir-e 1, S.: affitto, *m.*, pigione, *f.*, nolo; salario, stipendio, *m.*: *for* —, da affittare. **-e** 2, TR.: affittare, appigionare, pigliare a fitto; allogare: — *out*, dare a nolo, allogare; — *one's self out*, andare a padrone. **-eling**, ADJ.: venale; S.: mercenario, mercenaio, *m.* **-er**, S.: affittatore, allogatore, *m.*

hirsûte, ADJ.: irsuto, ruvido. **-ness**, S.: irsuzia, *f.*

his, PRON.: suo, sua; suoi, sue; di lui.

hiss 1, S.: fischio, sibilo, *m.* **hiss** 2, TR.: fischiare; INTR.: sibilare; scoppiare. **-ing**, S.: fischiata, *f.*, fischiare, *m.*
hist, INTERJ.: silenzio! zitto!
his-tōrian, S.: istorico, storico, scrittore di storia, *m.* **-tŏric(al)**, ADJ.: istorico, storico, istoriale. **-tŏrically**, ADV.: istoricamente, storicamente. **-tŏrify**, TR.: istoriare, narrare; far storia. **-toriŏgrapher**, S.: istoriografo, istorico, *m.* **-toriŏgraphy**, S.: arte di fare storia, *f.* **-'tory**, S.: storia, istoria, *f.* **-'tory-painter**, S.: pittore d' istorie, *m.* **-'tory-piece**, S.: pittura istorica, *f.*
histriŏnic(al), ADJ.: d' istrione, di commediante; teatrale.
hit 1, S.: colpo, *m.*, percossa, botta, *f.*; azzardo, *m.*: *lucky* —, colpo fortunato; — *or miss*, a tutto rischio. **hit** 2, IRR.; TR.: battere, bastonare, percuotere; INTR.: pervenire; incontrare; urtarsi: — *home*, ributtare; — *the mark*, dar nel segno; — *the nail on the head*, colpire nel brocco, imberciare; — *him!* dagli! — *against*, dar contro, urtarsi; — *off*, riuscire; accadere felicemente; — *together*, incontrarsi; abbattersi; — *upon*, abbattersi; — *upon by chance*, trovare per caso.
hitch 1, S.: (*nav.*) nodo, groppo, *m.* **hitch** 2, INTR.: dimenarsi; muoversi, agitarsi; (*nav.*) annodare.
hither 1, ADJ.: citeriore, di qua. **hither** 2, ADV.: qui, qua; a questo fine. **-most**, ADJ.: il più vicino. **-to**, ADV.: fin' adesso, fin qui, fino a quest' ora. **-ward(s)**, ADV.: da questa banda.
hiv-e 1, S.: arnia, *f.*, alveare, *m.* **-e** 2, TR.: fare entrare nell' arnia; dar ricetto; INTR.: raccogliersi; rifugiarsi. **-er**, S.: colui che ha cura delle pecchie.
hō! hōa! INTERJ.: oh! ahì!
hōar 1, ADJ.: bianco, canuto. **hoar** 2, INTR.: muffare, muffarsi.
hōard 1, S.: mucchio segreto; tesoro, *m.* **hoard** 2, TR.: ammassare, accumulare: — *up money*, accumular danari. **-er**, S.: accumulatore (di danari), *m.*
hōarfrost, S.: brina, pruina, *f.*
hōariness, S.: bianchezza; canutezza; mucidezza, muffa, *f.*
hōarse, ADJ.: rauco, affiocato: *grow* —, divenir rauco, affiocare. **-ly**, ADV.: con voce rauca. **-ness**, S.: raucedine, fiocchezza di voce, affìcatura, *f.*
hōary, ADJ.: bianco, bigio, canuto; mucido: *grow* —, muffarsi; incanutire; *grow* — *with age*, incanutire.
hōax 1, S.: frode per ischerzo, *f.*, inganno, *m.* **hoax** 2, TR.: coccare, ingannare (per burla).
hŏb, S.: villano, rustico, *m.*
hŏbbl-e 1, S.: zoppicamento, andar zoppiconi, *m.* **-e** 2, INTR.: zoppicare; mancare. **-ingly**, ADV.: in modo zoppo; con mala grazia, rozzamente.
hŏbby, S.: cavallino; sciocco, *m.* **-horse**, S.: ghiribizzo, *m.*; pazzia, follia, *f.*
hŏbgoblin, S.: folletto; fantasma, *m.*
hŏb-like, ADJ.: rustico, villano. **-nail**, S.: chiodo da ferrare un cavallo, *m.*
hŏck 1, S.: garretto; vecchio vino del Reno, *m.* **hock** 2, TR.: guastare i tendini delle gambe. **-herb**, S.: malva, *f.*
hŏckle, TR.: tagliare i tendini delle gambe.
hōcus-pōcus, S.: gherminella; trompería, *f.*
hŏd, S.: vassoia, truogolo, *m.*
hŏdgepodge, S.: manicaretto; ammorsellato, *m.*
hŏdman, S.: manovale, operario, *m.*
hōe 1, S.: zappa, marra, *f.* **hoe** 2, TR.: zappare; scavare.
hŏg, S.: porco, *m.* **-cote**, S.: porcile, *m.* **-gerel**, S.: pecora di due anni, *f.* **-gish**, ADJ.: porcino, di porco; ingordo. **-gishly**, ADV.: da porco; ingordamente. **-gishness**, S.: porcheria; sudiceria; golosità, *f.* **-herd**, S.: porcaio, *m.* **-shead**, S.: botte, *f.*, barile, *m.* **-sty**, S.: porcile, *m.* **-wash**, S.: lavatura, *f.*
hŏiden† 1, S.: ragazza grossolana, *f.* **-hoiden**† 2, INTR.: saltare grossolanamente.
hŏist, TR.: alzare, inalberare; issare, spiegare (le vele).
hŏity-tŏity, ADJ.: insolente, sollazzevole; ADV.: insolentemente.
hōld 1, S.: presa, cattura; prigione; fortezza, *f.*; influsso, *m.*, influenza; (*nav.*) stiva, *f.*; fondo, *m.*: *lay* — *on*, *take* — *of*, prendere, pigliare. **hold** 2, INTERJ.: olà! fermate! **hold** 3, IRR.; TR.: tenere; pigliare, prendere; contenere; ritenere; possedere, fruire; convocare; celebrare; INTR.: continuare, durare; credere, pensare: attaccarsi, rappigliarsi; fermarsi: — *one's breath*, ritenere il fiato; — *a consultation*, tener consulta; — *in contempt*, dispregiare; — *in hand*, tenere a bada; trattenere; — *one's tongue*, tacersi; trattenere la lingua; — *true*, trovarsi vero; — *back*, ritenere, ricusare; tener per sè; — *forth*, offerire; proporre; aringare, predicare; — *in*, ristringere, governare; ritenersi; — *off*, scostare; ributtare, ritardare, differire; — *on*, continuare; protrarre; procedere; — *out*, stendere; offerire; sussistere; resistere, durare, mantenersi; — *over*, ditenere; — *together*, stare unito; — *up*, alzare, levare; appoggiare; sostenersi; fermarsi per rubare; — *with one*, abbracciare il

partito d' alcuno, tener per uno. **-er**, s.: tenitore; vassallo, *m.*: *—forth*, s.: aringatore, predicatore, *m.*; *— of bonds*, detentore di boni. **-fast**, s.: rampone; annello; meschino, spilorcio, *m.* **-ing**, s.: feudo; affitto, *m.*

hōle 1, s.: buco, pertugio, forame, *m.*; caverna, *f.*: *full of —s*, bucato; *make a — in*, bucare, far buco in. **hole** 2 TR.: *bucare.*

hŏliday, s.: giorno di festa (*sp.* secolare), *m.*; vacanza, *f.*

hōli-ly, ADV.: santamente, inviolabilmente. **-ness**, s.: santità; pietà, *f.*

hŏllo, INTERJ.: ola! ehi! oh!

hŏllands, s.: ginepro, *m.*

hŏllow 1, ADJ.: cavo, vuoto; vacuo, finto, doppio, perfido: *— eyes*, occhi cavi; *— cheeks*, guancie infossate; *— voice*, voce rauca; *— noise*, rumore sordo. **hollow** 2, s.: cavo, *m.*; cavità; fossa, *f.*, canale, *m.*; tana, *f.* **hollow** 3, TR.: cavare, scavare; vuotare; INTR.: gridare; acclamare. **-ly**, ADV.: con delle cavità; senza sincerità, disonestamente. **-ness**, s.: cavità; dissimulazione, *f.*

hŏlly, s.: agrifoglio, *m.* **-hock**, s.: alcea, bismalva, *f.*

hōlm, s.: elce, *f.*; leccio, *m.*

hŏlocaust, s.: olocausto, *m.*

hōlster, s.: fodera della pistola, *f.* **-cap**, s.: fonda della pistola, *f.*

hōlt, s.: boschetto, *m.*

hōly, ADJ.: santo, sacrato, pio, religioso, casto: *make —*, santificare; *the — one*, Iddio Santissimo; *— Ghost*, Spirito Santo; *— water*, acqua santa; *— writ*, Sacre Scritture. **-day**, s.: giorno di festa; (*sp.* religiosa), *m.* **-Thursday**, s.: giorno dell' ascensione, *m.* **-watersprinkle**, s.: aspersorio, *m.* **-week**, s.: settimana santa, *f.*

hŏmag-e 1, s.: omaggio; rispetto, *m.*, riverenza, *f.*; tributo, *m.* **-e** 2, TR.: render omaggio, rispettare, riverire. **-er**, s.: vassallo, *m.*

hōme 1, s.: casa; dimora, *f.*; domicilio, *m.*; stanza; patria, *f.*: *charity begins at —*, il primo prossimo è sè medesimo. **home** 2, ADV.: in casa, in patria sua: *speak —*, parlare a proposito. **-born**, ADJ.: nativo, naturale; domestico. **-bound**, ADJ.: di ritorno. **-bred**, ADJ.: del paese, nostrale, nativo; grossolano, rozzo. **-felt**, ADJ.: interno, interiore; segreto. **-less**, ADJ.: senza tetto, senza ricovero. **-lily**, ADV.: grossolanamente, rozzamente. **-liness**, s.: rustichezza, rozzezza, grossezza, *f.* **-ly**, ADJ.: casalingo; semplice; rozzo, grossolano, incolto. **-made**, ADJ.: casalingo, fatto nella casa.

homeopăthical, ADJ.: omeopatico. **-ŏpathist**, s.: medico omeopatico, *m.* **-ŏpathy**, s.: omeopatia, *f.*

hōme-sick, ADJ.: nostalgico, preso da nostalgia. **-sickness**, s.: nostalgia, *f.* **-spun**, ADJ.: casereccio, casalingo. **-ward(s)**, ADV.: verso casa: *— bound ship*, bastimento di ritorno.

homicidal, ADJ.: micidiale; cruento.

hŏmicide, s.: omicido; omicida, *m.*

homilĕtic(al), ADJ.: omiletico; conversevole.

hŏm-ilist, s.: autore d' omilie, *m.* **-ily**, s.: omilia, *f.*

homogē-neal = *-neous*. **-nealness**, **-neity** = *-neousness*. **-neous**, ADJ.: omogeneo, della stessa natura. **-neousness**, s.: omogeneità, *f.*

homŏl-ogate, TR.: omologare; ratificare. **-ogous**, ADJ.: omologo; corrispondente.

homŏn-ymous, ADJ.: omonimo, equivoco. **-ymy**, s.: omonimia; ambiguità, *f.*

hōne 1, s.: cote, *f.* **hone** 2, TR.: affilare, aguzzare; INTR.: bramare, languire.

hŏnest 1, ADJ.: onesto, probo, integro, giusto, sincero; casto. **honest** 2, TR.: onestare; abbellire. **-ly**, ADV.: onestamente, giustamente. **-y**, s.: onestà; sincerità, verità; virtù, *f.*: *— is the best policy*, l' onestà è la miglior politica.

hŏney 1, s.: m(i)ele, *m.* **honey** 2, TR.: addolcire; INTR.: adulare, careggiare. **-bag**, s.: stomago della pecchia, *m.* **-comb**, s.: favo, fiale, *m.* **-dew**, s.: manna; rugiada dolce, *f.* **-ed**, ADJ.: melato, condito di mele; dolce. **-moon**, s.: luna di mele, *f.* **-suckle**, s.: caprifoglio, *m.* **-wort**, s.: cerinta, *f.*

hŏnied = *honeyed.*

hŏnour 1, s.: onore; rispetto, *m.*; stima; fama; figura, testa, *f.*: *upon my —*, sul mio onore, parola d' onore; *point of —*, punto d' onore, *m.*; *word of —*, parola d' onore, *f.*; *man of —*, uomo di onore; *do the —s of the house*, far gli onori di casa. **honour** 2, TR.: onorare, riverire, rispettare: *— a bill of exchange*, fare onore ad (accettare) una lettera di cambio. **-able**, ADJ.: onorevole, illustre. **-ableness**, s.: generosità; magnificenza, *f.* **-ably**, ADV.: onorevolmente, nobilmente. **-ary**, ADJ.: onorario, d' onore; s.: onorario, salario, *m.* **-er**, s.: onoratore, veneratore, *m.* **-less**, ADJ.: senza onore, disonorato.

hōod 1, s.: cappuccio, capperone, *m.*; cuffia, *f.* **hood** 2, TR.: incappucciare; coprire. **-man-blind**, s.: mosca cieca, *f.* (giuoco). **-wink**, TR.: bendare gli occhi; acciecare; truffare, ingannare.

hōof, s.: unghia, *f.* **-bound**, ADJ.: incastellato.

s.: forcella, forcina da capelli, *f.* **-powder**, s.: cipria, *f.* **-sieve**, s.: setaccio, *m.* **-splitting**, ADJ.: sottile, sottilizzante; s.: sottigliezza, *f.* **-y**, ADJ.: capelluto, peloso, crinuto.
hălberd, s.: alabarda, *f.* **-ier**, s.: alabardiere, lanzo, *m.*
hálcyon 1, s.: alcione, *m.* **halcyon** 2, ADJ.: quieto, tranquillo.
hāle 1, ADJ.: sano, vigoroso; forte; gagliardo. **hal-e** 2, TR.: tirare; strascinare; (*nav.*) rimurchiare. **-er**, s.: alzaio; che tira a braccia; (*nav.*) che rimurchia.
hâlf 1, ADJ.: mezzo. **half** 2, ADV.: a metà, per metà, di pari; in parte. **half** 3 (pl. *halves*), s.: metà, *f.*: *in halves*, per metà; negligentemente. **-blood**, s.: fratello da un lato, *m.*; sorella da un lato, *f.* **-blooded**, ADJ.: degenerato. **-brother**, s.: fratello da un lato, fratello uterino, *m.* **-moon**, s.: mezza luna, *f.* **-penny**, s.: mezzo soldo, *m.* **-pike**, s.: mezza picca, *f.* **-pint**, s.: mezza foglietta, *f.* **-sister**, s.: sorella da un lato, sorella uterina, *f.* **-sphere**, s.: emisfero, *m.* **-strained**, ADJ.: imperfetto. **-tone**, ADJ.: a mezza tinta; s.: fotoincisione, incisione a mezza tinta, *f.* **-way**, ADJ.: nel mezzo della strada, a mezza strada. **-wit**, s.: sciocco, balordo, *m.* **-witted**, ADJ.: sciocco, stolto.
hălibut, s.: passere, *m.* (pesce).
hâll, s.: sala, *f.*, palazzo; vestibulo, *m.*
hallelūjah *-ya*, s.: alleluia, *m.*
hallōo, TR.: incoraggiare (i cani); chiamare.
hăllow, TR.: santificare, consacrare.
hallūci-nate, INTR.: ingannarsi, sbagliare. **-nātion**, s.: allucinazione, *f.*; abbaglio, errore, *m.*
hâlm = *haulm.*
hālo, s.: aureola, *f.*
hâlser = *hawser.*
hâlt 1, ADJ.: zoppo, azzoppato; s.: posa, fermata, *f.*; (*mil.*) alto, *m.* **halt** 2, INTR.: fare alto, fermarsi; zoppicare; (*fig.*), stare in dubbio, dubitare.
hâlter 1, s.: zoppo; capestro, *m.*; cavezza; corda, fune, *f.* **halter** 2, TR.: incapestrare; legare con una corda.
hâlting, s.: zoppicare, *m.* **-ly**, ADV.: in modo zoppicante.
hâlve, TR.: dividere in due, dimezzare.
hălyards, s. PL.: (*nav.*) drizze, *f. pl.*
hăm, s.: garretto; prosciutto, presciutto, *m.*
hămlet, s.: borghetto, casale, *m.*
hămmer 1, s.: martello, *m.* **hammer** 2, TR.: martellare; inventare, immaginare: — *out*, stendere col martello; indagare. **-er**, s.: che lavora col martello. **-ing**, s.: martellare, *m.*

hămmock, s.: amaca, branda, *f.*
hămper 1, s.: paniere; cesto grande, *m.* **hamper** 2, TR.: imbarazzare, imbrogliare, confondere: *be —ed*, stare alle strette, essere impastoiato (*or* impedito).
hămstring 1, s.: tendine del garretto, *m.* **hamstring** 2, TR.: tagliare i tendini del garretto.
hănaper, s.: tesoreria, *f.*, erario; tesoro, *m.*
hănd 1, s.: mano; palma; scrittura, soscrizione, *f.*; lato; ago (d' un oriuolo); (*nav.*) marinaio, *m.*: *in* —, fra le mani; in avanza; *at the first* —, di prima mano; *near at* —, qui vicino; — *in* —, insieme, di concerto; *on the one* —, da una parte; *on the other* —, dall' altra parte; *under* —, sotto mano; segretamente; *out of* —, presto, speditamente; — *over head*, inconsideratamente, temerariamente; *keep your* —*s off!* non lo toccate! *fall into one's* —*s*, dar nelle mani; *fight* — *to* —, venire alle prese; *go* — *in* —, tenersi per la mano; *have a* — *in a business*, aver parte in un negozio; *live from* — *to mouth*, vivere alla giornata; *take in* —, intraprendere; *shake* —*s*, stringersi la mano; *write a good* —, avere una bella scrittura. **hand** 2, TR.: dar la mano; dare di mano in mano; menare: — *round*, far passare (in giro); — *down to posterity*, tramandare ai posteri. **-barrow**, s.: barella, *f.* **-basket**, s.: sporta, *f.*; paniere con manico, *m.* **-bell**, s.: campanello, *m.* **-bill**, s.: biglietto, *m.* **-breadth**, s.: larghezza della mano, *f.*, palmo, *m.*; spanna, *f.* **-cloth**, s.: fazzoletto, *m.* **-cuff**, s.: manette, *f. pl.* **-cuff**, TR.: mettere le manette. **-ed**, ADJ.: dato di mano in mano; dalle mani. **-er**, s.: trasmettitore, *m.* **-fast**, s.: presa, cattura, *f.*, arresto, *m.*, prigione, *f.* **-fetters**, s. PL.: manette, *s. pl.* **-ful**, s.: pugno, *m.*; manata, *f.* **-gallop**, s.: piccolo galloppo, *m.* **-gearing**, s.: (*loc.*) governo, regolatore, *m.* **-gearing-rod**, s.: (*loc.*) sbarra di governo, *f.* **-gun**, s.: schioppo, fucile, *m.* **-icap** 1, s.: impiccio, ostacolo. **-icap** 2, TR.: ostacolare, impicciare, imbarazzare. **-icraft**, s.: mestiere, *m.*, professione, *f.* **-icraftsman**, s.: artigiano; artefice, *m.* **-ily**, ADV.: destramente, con destrezza, con abilità. **-iness**, s.: destrezza, abilità, *f.* **-iwork**, s.: opera manuale; manifattura, *f.* **-kerchief**, s.: fazzoletto, moccichino, *m.* **-le** 1, s.: manico; orecchio, *m.*; impugnatura, *f.* **-le** 2, TR.: maneggiare; trattare. **-less**, ADJ.: monco, manco. **-ling**, s.: maneggiamento, toccamento, *m.* **-maid**, s.: serva, ancella, *f.* **-mill**, s.: mulinello, molinello, *m.*

-sails, s. pl.: vele maneggiate colle mani, *f. pl.* **-saw**, s.: seghetta, sega piccola, *f.* **-sel**, s.: primo uso, *m.*; prima vendita, *f.* **-sel**, tr.: far uso per la prima volta; fare per la prima volta. **-some**, adj.: bello, avvenevole, elegante. **-somely**, adv.: bellamente, elegantemente; piacevolmente. **-someness**, s.: bellezza; grazia, eleganzia, *f.* **-spike**, s.: (*nav.*) manovella, *f.* **-vice**, s.: morsa, *f.* **-worm**, s.: pellicello, *m.* **-writing**, s.: manoscritto, *m.*, scrittura; mano, *f.* **-y**, adj.: destro, abile; convenevole. **-y-blow**, s.: colpo di mano, *m.* **-y-dandy**, s.: giuoco da battersi sulle mani, *m.*

hăng, (ir)r.; tr.: appendere, appiccare; piegare; sospendere, collocare; intr.: pendere; stare sospeso; contrappesare: — *loose*, star penzolone; — *a robber*, impiccare un ladro; — *a room*, tappezzare una camera; — *the rudder*, montare il timone; — *about*, stare pendente, penzolare; — *back*, eludere; schivare; — *by*, appendere, appiccare; — *down*, pendere; abbassare; chinare; — *on*, appendere; attaccarsi, aggrapparsi; — *out* (*nav.*), inalberare; — *together*, accordarsi; — *up*, sospendere, appendere. **-er**, s.: scimitarra, *f.*; coltellaccio, *m.* **-er-on**, s.: parassito, scroccone, *m.* **-ing**, adj.: pendente, sospeso; degno di forca; s.: impiccagione, *f.*: — *garden*, giardino pensile; —*s*, tappezzerie, *f. pl.*, cortinaggio, *m.* **-lock**, s.: lucchetto, *m.* **-man**, s.: carnefice, boia, giustiziere, *m.*

hănk, s.: matassa, *f.*; gomitolo, *m.*; propensione, inclinazione, *f.*

hănker, intr.: desiderare ardentemente. **-ing**, adj.: bramoso; s.: inclinazione, *f.*, desiderio, *m.*

Hanseătic, adj.: anseatico.

hănsel = *handsel.*

Hănse-town, s.: città anseatica, *f.*

hăp 1, s.: caso, accidente, *m.*; sorte, *f.* **hap** 2, intr.: accadere, avvenire, succedere. **-hazard**, s.: accidente, avvenimento, evento casuale, *m.* **-less**, adj.: sfortunato, sventurato, disgraziato. **-ly**, adv.: forse; per accidente, a caso. **-pen**, intr.: accadere, avvenire; darsi: *I —ed to mention it*, mi accadde di farne menzione; — *what will*, avvenga quel che può avvenire; *what has —ed to you?* che vi è seguito? *as it —s*, ad ogni modo. **-pily**, adv.: fortunatamente, per sorte. **-piness**, s.: felicità; buona ventura, fortuna, sorte, *f.* **-py**, adj.: felice, fortunato, prospero: *make* —, render felice, felicitare; *I am — to hear it*, son pur lieto di sentirlo.

harăn-gue *1, s.: aringa, f.* **-gue** 2, tr.: aringare; perorare. **-guer**, s.: aringatore, oratore, *m.*

hărass 1, s.: guasto, disertamento, *m.* **harass** 2, tr.: stancare, allassare, faticare; distruggere, rovinare. **-er**, s.: guastatore, rovinatore, *m.*

hârbinger, s.: foriere; precursore, *m.*

hârbour 1, s.: alloggio; rifugio, ricovero, riparo; porto, *m.* **harbour** 2, tr.: alloggiare, albergare; intr.: soggiornare, dimorare. **-age**, s.: accoglimento, ricovero; rifugio, asilo, *m.* **-er**, s.: ospite; protettore, *m.* **-less**, adj.: senza porto; senza rifugio. **-master**, s.: capitano del porto, *m.*

hârd 1, adj.: duro; fermo, sodo; severo, aspro, rigoroso; faticoso, molesto; difficile; oneroso: — *wood*, legno duro; — *heart*, cuore duro; — *task*, compito difficile; — *drinking*, eccesso nel bere; — *winter*, inverno rigoroso; — *words*, parole dure; — *of belief*, incredulo; — *to get*, raro; — *of hearing*, sordastro, quasi sordo; — *to be understood*, inintelligibile. **hard** 2, adv.: presso a poco; forte, fortemente; difficilmente: — *by*, qui vicino, presso; *it freezes* —, gela forte; *it rains very* —, piove dirottamente; *the wind blows* —, fa gran vento; *drink* —, bere eccessivamente; *follow one* —, seguitare alcuno d'appresso. **-bound**, adj.: stitico, costipato. **-en**, tr.: indurare, indurire; intr.: divenire duro. **-ening**, s.: induramento, *m.* **-favoured**, adj.: laido, deforme. **-favouredness**, s.: laidura, bruttezza, *f.* **-featured**, adj.: dalle fattezze dure. **-fought**, adj.: ostinato. **-gotten**, adj.: ottenuto a stento. **-handed**, adj.: ruvido. **-hearted**, adj.: crudele, inumano. **-heartedness**, s.: crudeltà, inumanità, *f.* **-ihead**, **-ihood**, s.: intrepidità, bravura, *f.* **-ily**, adv.: coraggiosamente, animosamente, arditamente. **-iness**, s.: pena, difficoltà; arditezza, *f.* **-ly**, adv.: appena, difficilmente, severamente, rigorosamente. **-mouthed**, adj.: duro di bocca; restio, caparbio. **-ness**, s.: durezza; difficoltà; asprezza, *f.*: — *of the winter*, severità del verno, *f.* **-nibbed**, adj.: di punta dura.

hârds, s.: stoppa, *f.*

hârd-ship, s.: durezza; difficoltà. fatica, *f.*, travaglio, *m.*: *life of* —, vi

-ware, s.: chincaglia, *f.*

s.: chincagliere, *m.* **-v**

goffo, stupido. **-y**, adj.: gioso, bravo, robusto, forte

hāre 1, s.: lepre, *f.*: *youn*

m. **hare** 2, tr.: spaven

s.: convolvolo, *m.* **-br**

scervellato, pazzesco. **-fo**

make a — and cry after one, perseguitar alcuno con grida.

hŭff 1, S.: impeto di collera, *m.*: *be in a* —, essere in collera, incollerirsi. **huff** 2, TR.: soffiare; insultare; bravare; INTR.: strepitare. **-er**, S.: millantatore, bravo, *m.* **-ing**, S.: bravata, *f.* **-ish**, ADJ.: insolente, arrogante; petulante. **-ishly**, ADV.: insolentemente, imperiosamente, alteramente. **-ishness**, S.: insolenza, arroganza; petulanza, *f.*

hŭg 1, S.: abbracciata, *f.*, abbracciamento, *m.* **hug** 2, TR.: abbracciare; careggiare: (*nav.*) — *the wind*, serrare il vento.

hūge, ADJ.: vasto, smisurato, enorme. **-ly**, ADV.: vastamente, smisuratamente. **-ness**, S.: vastità, smisuratezza; grandezza, *f.*

hŭgger-mugger†, S.: nascondiglio, *m.*

hŭgging, S.: abbracciata, *f.*, abbracciamento, *m.*

Hūguenot, S.: ugonotto, *m.*

hŭlk 1, S.: carena (d' un naviglio); massa, *f.* **hulk** 2, TR.: sviscerare.

hŭll 1, S.: baccello; guscio, *m.*; pelle, *f.* **hull** 2, TR.: sgranare (fave); INTR.: galleggiare. **-y**, ADJ.: pieno di baccelli.

hŭm 1, S.: rombo; ronzamento, mormorio; applauso, *m.* **hum** 2, INTR.: rombare, ronzare, mormoreggiare; borbogliare: — *a tune*, cantellare un' aria.

hūman, ADJ.: umano; mortale. **-māne**, ADJ.: umano; affabile, cortese, benigno: — *learning*, belle lettere, *f. pl.* **-mānely**, ADV.: umanamente, benignamente, cortesemente. **-manist**, S.: umanista: filologo, *m.* **-mănity**, S.: umanità; benignità, cortesia; tenerezza, *f.* **-manize**, TR.: umanizzare, render umano. **-mankind**, S.: genere umano, *m.* **-manly**, ADV.: benignamente, affabilmente.

hŭm-bird = *humming-bird.*

hŭmble 1, ADJ.: umile; modesto; vile. **humble** 2, TR.: umiliare, abbassare; mortificare: — *one's self*, umiliarsi.

hŭmble-bee, S.: peccione; calabrone, *m.*

hŭmbl-eness, S.: umiltà, sommessione; modestia, *f.* **-er**, S.: che umilia, che mortifica.

hŭmbles, S. PL.: interiora del cavriolo, *m. pl*

hŭm-bling, S.: umiliazione, *f.* **-bly**, ADV.: umilmente.

hŭmbug 1, S.: ciarlataneria, trappola, *f.*; ciarlatano, *m.* **humbug** 2, TR.: trappolare; corbellare.

hŭmdrum, ADJ.: stolto, sciocco, infingardo: — *fellow*, addormentatore, *m.*

hūméc-t(ate), TR.: umettare, immolare; bagnare. **-tātion**, S.: umettazione, *f.*, immollamento, *m.*

hūmeral, ADJ.: (*anat.*) omerale, delle spalle.

hū-mid, ADJ.: umido, umidito. **-midity**, **-midness**, S.: umidità, umidezza, *f.*

humil-iate, TR.: umiliare, mortificare. **-iātion**, S.: umiliazione, sommessione; mortificazione, *f.* **-ity**, S.: umiltà, sommessione, *f.*

hŭm-mer, S.: che ronza; applauditore, *m.* **-ming**, S.: rombo, ronzo, ronzamento; mormorio, susurro, bisbiglio, *m.* **-ming-bird**, S.: colibri, *m.*

hūmo(u)r 1, S.: umore, *m.*, disposizione dell' animo, indole; capriccio, *m.*; fantasia, *f.*: *in good* —, di buon umore, faceto, allegro, gioviale; *in ill* —, *out of* —, di cattivo umore, capriccioso, bizzarro. **humo(u)r** 2, TR.: gratificare; contentare, compiacere, piacere: *you — him to much*, avete troppa condiscendenza per lui. **-al**, ADJ.: umorale. **-ist**, S.: uomo fantastico, *m.* **-ous**, ADJ.: fantastico, capriccioso, faceto. **-ously**, ADV.: fantasticamente, capricciosamente. **-ousness**, S.: capriccio, *m.*; incostanza, leggerezza, *f.* **-some**, ADJ.: fantastico, bisbetico. **-somely**, ADV.: fantasticamente. **-someness**, S.: capriccio; umore, *m.*

hŭmp, S.: gobba, *f.*; scrigno, *m.* **-back**, S.: gobbo, scrignuto, *m.* **-backed**, ADJ.: gobbo, scrignuto.

hŭnch 1, S.: gomitata, *f.* **hunch** 2, TR.: dare gomitate. **-back**, S.: gobbo, *m.*, gobba, *f.* **-backed**, ADJ.: gobbo, scrignuto.

hŭndred, ADJ: cento; S.: centinaio, *m.* **-fold**, ADJ.: centuplo: *a* —, a canto doppio. **-th**, ADJ.: centesimo. **-weight**, S.: cantaro, quintale, *m.*

hŭn-ger 1, S.: fame, *f.*; appetito; (*fig.*) desiderio grande, *m.* **-ger** 2, INTR.: avere fame; (*fig.*) bramare. **-ger-bit(ten)**, ADJ.: debole per fame. **-gerly** 1, ADJ.: affamato. **-gerly** 2, ADV.: con appetito grande, avidamente, ingordamente. **-ger-starved**, ADJ.: moriente di fame. **-gered** = *hungry*. **-grily**, ADV.: con gran fame, con appetito grande **-gry**, ADJ.: affamato; magro, sterile: *be* (*feel*) —, avere fame, avere appetito; *be very* —, aver gran fame.

hŭnks, S.: avaro, spilorcio, misero, *m.*

hŭnt 1, S.: caccia; muta di cani, *f.* **hunt** 2, TR.: cacciare; perseguitare; INTR.: proseguire, seguire: — *after*, andare a traccia di; cercare premurosamente; — *out*, scoprire; trovare; — *up and down*, cercare dappertutto. **-er**, S.: cacciatore; cavallo di caccia; cane da caccia, bracco, *m.* **-ing**, S.: caccia, *f.*: *go a*-—, andare alla caccia. **-ing-bag**, S.: carniere, *m.* **-ing-coat**, S.: [illegible] caccia, *m.* **-ing-dog**, S.: cane di caccia, *m.* **-ing-horn**, S.: corno di caccia, *m.* **-ing-nag**, S.: cavallo da caccia, *m.* **-ing-piece**, S.: archibugio da caccia, *m.* **-ing-sport**, S.: divertimento della caccia, *m.* **-ress**, S.: cacciatrice, *f.* **-sman**, S.: cacciatore; capocaccia, *m.* **-smanship**, S.: arte di cacciare, venagione, *f.*

hŭrdle 1, S.: graticcio, caniccio, *m.* **hurdle** 2, TR.: circondare di graticci.

hŭrds, S. PL.: stoppa, *f.*

hŭrdy-gurdy, S.: viola da orbo, *f.*

hŭrl 1, S.: tumulto, *m.;* riotta, *f.*, sollevamento, *m.*, commozione, *f.* **hurl** 2, TR.: lanciare; scagliare. **-bat**, S.: clava, massa ferrata, *f.* **-wind**, S.: turbine, *m.*

hŭrly-burly, S.: tumulto, garbuglio, *m.*, calca, *f.*

hurrâh! INTERJ.: urra! evviva!

hŭrricane, S.: uracano, *m.*, burrasca, *f.*

hŭrry 1, S.: precipitazione, fretta, *f.;* tumulto, *m.;* confusione, *f.:* *in a —*, in fretta. **hurry** 2, TR.: affrettare; precipitare; INTR.: affrettarsi, correre quanto si può; fare diligenza: *— away*, strascinare, strascicare; condurre seco; *— on*, affrettare, sollecitare, spronare; *— out*, scacciare; *— one out*, cacciar (strascinar) fuori alcuno.

hŭrt 1, S.: ferita, *f.;* detrimento, danno, pregiudizio; sconcio, *m.* **hurt** 2, IRR.; TR.: ferire; fare male; danneggiare: *— one's reputation*, staccare la reputazione di uno. **-ful**, ADJ.: nocivo, dannoso, pernizioso. **-fully**, ADV.: in modo nocivo, perniziosamente. **-fulness**, S.: nocimento; detrimento, *m.*

hŭrtle, TR.: urtare; giostrare; INTR.: scaramucciare; incontrarsi.

hŭrtleberry, S.: uva orsina, *f.*

hŭrtless, ADJ.: che non fa male; innocente. **-ly**, ADV.: senza fare niuno male.

hŭsband 1, S.: marito, sposo; massaio; agricola, *m.* **husband** 2, TR.: maritare; coltivare, usar economia di, spender bene. **-less**, ADJ.: senza marito. **-ly**, ADJ.: frugale; economo, parco; moderato. **-man**, S.: agricoltore; bifolco, *m.* **-ry**, S.: agricoltura; economia, *f.;* risparmio, *m.;* coltura, *f.*

hŭsh! 1, INTERJ.: silenzio! zitto! **hush** 2, TR.: imporre silenzio; calmare; placare; INTR.: star zitto, tacere. **-money**, S.: subornamento, guadagno illecito, *m.*

hŭsk 1, S.: baccello; guscio, [illegible] pelle, *f.* **husk** 2, TR.: [illegible] ADJ.: coperto d'un [illegible] raucedine, *f.* **-y**, ADJ.: [illegible]

hussâr, S.: ussaro, [illegible]

Hŭssite, S.: ussita, [illegible]

hŭssy, S.: donnaccia, buona roba, *f.*

hŭstings, S. PL.: luogo da eleggere; consiglio, *m.*

hŭstle, TR.: agitare insieme; INTR.: stringere le spalle.

hŭswif-e 1, S.: massaia; economa, *f.* **-e** 2, TR.: maneggiare gli affari domestici; usare con economia. **-ery**, S.: economia, *f.;* governo domestico, *m.*

hŭt 1, S.: capanna, baracca, *f.* **hut** 2, TR.: baraccare.

hŭtch, S.: madia; cassa; arca, *f.*

hŭzz, INTR.: ronzare; bisbigliare, susurrare, mormoreggiare.

huzzâ 1, S.: viva, *m.;* acclamazione, *f.* **huzza** 2, TR.: ricevere con acclamazioni; INTR.: gridare i viva; acclamare, applaudire.

hȳacinth, S.: giacinto, *m.*

hȳbrid, **-ous**, ADJ.: ibrido.

hȳdr-a, S.: idra, *f.* **-âulic(al)**, ADJ.: idraulico. **-âulics**, S. PL.: idraulica, *f.* **-ogen**, S.: idrogeno, *m.* **-ŏgrapher**, S.: idrografo, *m.* **-ográphical**, ADJ.: idrografico. **-ŏgraphy**, S.: idrografia, *f.* **-ŏlogy**, S.: idrologia, *f.* **-omel**, S.: idromele, *m.* **-ŏmeter**, S.: idrometro, *m.* **-ŏmetry**, S.: idrometria, *f.* **-ŏpathy**, S.: idropatia, *f.* **-ophŏbia**, S.: idrofobia, *f.* **-ŏpic(al)**, ADJ.: idropico. **-ostátical**, ADJ.: idrostatico. **-ostátically**, ADV.: secondo l'idrostatica. **-ostátics**, S. PL.: idrostatica, *f.*

hyēmal, ADJ.: iemale, vernale; del verno.

hyēna, S.: iena, *f.*

hȳgi-ene, S.: igiene, *f.* **-ĕnic**, ADJ.: igienico.

hȳmen, S.: imeneo; matrimonio; imene, *m.* **-ēal**, ADJ.: nuziale; maritale; S.: epitalamio, *m.*

hȳmn 1, S.: inno; cantico, *m.* **hymn** 2, TR.: adorare con inni, laudare.

hypĕr-bole, S.: iperbola; esagerazione, *f.* **-bŏlic(al)**, ADJ.: iperbolico. **-bŏlically**, ADV.: iperbolicamente. **-bolize**, TR.: iperboleggiare; aggrandire (con parole). **-bŏrean**, ADJ.: iperboreo; settentrionale. **-critic**, S.: critico severo, *m.*

hȳphen, S.: divisione, *f.;* tratto d'unione, *m.*

hyp-nŏtic, S.: ipnotico. **-notism**, S.: [illegible] **-notist**, S.: ipnotista, ipno- [illegible] **-tize**, TR.: ipnotizzare. [illegible] **-ca**, S. PL.: ipocondria, *f.* [illegible]ondrico; S.: ipocon- [illegible] ipocrisia, *f.* **hȳpo-** [illegible] ipocrita, *m.* **-crit-** [illegible]; finto. **-critic-** [illegible] [illegible]rmico.

hypo-gástric, ADJ.: ipogastrico; dell' ipogastrio. **-gástrium**, S.: ipogastrio, *m.*
hypŏ-stasis, S.: ipostasi; personalità, *f.* **-státical**, ADJ.: ipostatico; di personalità. **-tenuse**, S.: ipotenusa, *f.* **-thĕca**, S.: ipoteca, *f.* **-thecate**, TR.: ipotecare. **-thesis**, S.: ipotesi, *f.* **-thĕtic(al)**, ADJ.: ipotetico, supositivo. **-thĕtically**, ADV.: per ipotesi.
hŷssop, S.: isopo, issopo, m.
hys-téria, S.: isterismo, *m.* **-tĕric(al)**, ADJ.: isterico, uterino. **-tĕrics**, S. PL.: (*med.*) isteralgia, *f.*; dolori isterici, *m. pl.*

i (*the letter*), S.: i, *m. or f.*
I i, PRON.: io.
iámbic, ADJ.: iambico.
ibis, S.: ibi, *m.*
ice¹, S.: ghiaccio, (*pop.*) diaccio; sorbetto: *break the* —, rompere il ghiaccio; *take an* —, prendere un sorbetto. **ice**², TR.: ghiacciare; congelare. **-bound**, ADJ.: serrato di ghiaccio. **-cellar**, **-house**, S.: ghiacciaia, diacciaia, *f.* **-cream**, S.: crema ghiacciata, crema al ghiaccio, *f.*; sorbetto, *m.* **-d**, ADJ.: ghiacciato, al ghiaccio.
ichneúmon, S.: icneumone, *m.*
ichnográphical, ADJ.: ignografico. **-nŏgraphy**, S.: icnografia, *f.*
ichor, S.: icore, *m.* **-ous**, ADJ.: icoroso, sieroso.
ichthyŏlogy, S.: ictiologia, *f.*
icicle, S.: ghiacciuolo, *m.*
i-con, S.: immagine; pittura, *f.*; ritratto, *m.* **-cŏnoclast**, S.: iconoclasta, rompitore d' immagini, *m.* **-conŏlogy**, S.: iconologia, *f.*
ictĕric(al), ADJ.: itterico.
icy, ADJ.: agghiacciato; frigido: — *cold*, freddo come il ghiaccio.
idé-a, S.: idea; immaginazione, *f.* **-al**, ADJ.: ideale; intellettuale. **-alize**, TR.: ideare. **-ally**, ADV.: idealmente.
idén-tic(al), ADJ.: identico, medesimo. **-tify**, TR.: identificare; riconoscere, verificare. **-tity**, S.: identità, medesimezza, *f.*: *prove one's* —, provare (constatare) l' identità di alcuno.
ides, S. PL.: idi, *m. pl.*
idiocy, S.: imbecillità, debolezza di mente, *f.*
idi-om, S.: idioma, *m.*: favella, *f.*; idiotismo, frase, *m.* **-omátic(al)**, ADJ.: *idiomatico.*
idiŏpathy, S.: (*med.*) idiopatia, *f.*
idiot, S.: idiota, ignorante, sciocco, *m.* **-ism**, S.: imbecillità, *f.*
idl-e¹, ADJ.: pigro, ozioso; inutile, frivolo, vano: *be* —, star ozioso; — *fellow*, scioperato, infingardo, *m.*; — *question*, questione oziosa (*or* vana). **-e**², INTR.: poltroneggiare, consumare il tempo in vano: — *away one's time*, sprecare il tempo. **-e-headed**, ADJ.: stolto, stupido, irragionevole. **-eness**, S.: ozio, *m.*, infingardaggine, dappocaggine; negligenza, *f.* **-er**, S.: poltrone; infingardo; scioperato, sfaccendato, *m.* **-y**, ADV.: oziosamente, in ozio; vanamente: *talk* —, vaneggiare.
idol, S.: idolo, *m.*, immagine, *f.*: — *worship*, idolatria, *f.*
idŏl-ater, S.: idolatra, idolatre, *m.* **-atrize**, TR.: idolatrare, adorare gli idoli. **-atrous**, ADJ.: idolatrico, idolatro. **-atrously**, ADV.: da idolatra. **-atry**, S.: idolatria, *f.*
idol-ist, S.: idolatra, adoratore d' idoli, *m.* **-ize**, TR.: idolatrare, amare pazzamente.
idyl, S.: idillio, *m.*
if, CONJ.: se; purchè, benchè.
ig-neous, ADJ.: igneo. **-nis-fátuus**, S.: fuoco fatuo, *m.* **-nite**, TR.: accendere, infiammare. **-nition**, S.: infocamento, accendimento, *m.*
ignŏbl-e, ADJ.: ignobile; basso. **-eness**, S.: ignobilità; viltà, *f.* **-y**, ADV.: ignobilmente; bassamente.
ignomin-ious, ADJ.: ignominioso, infamante. **-iously**, ADV.: ignominiosamente. **ignomin-y**, S.: ignominia, infamia, *f.*
ignorámus, S.: ignorante, sciocco, *m.*
ig-norance, S.: ignoranza, *f.* **-norant**, ADJ.: ignorante; illetterato: — *fellow*, ignorante, *m.*; *be* — *of*, non sapere, ignorare. **-norantly**, ADV.: ignorantemente, per ignoranza, rozzamente. **-nore**, TR.: ignorare, non sapere; non riconoscere, sconoscere. **-nóscible**†, ADJ.: perdonabile, scusabile.
ile, S.: nave, navata (d' una chiesa), *f.*
ilex, S.: elce, *f.*
iliac, ADJ.: iliaco: — *passion*, passione iliaca, *f.*
Iliad, S.: Iliade, *f.*
ill¹, ADJ.: malo, cattivo; ammalato: — *luck*, infortunio, *m.*, disgrazia, *f.*; — *news*, cattive novelle, *f. pl.* **ill**², ADV.: male, malamente: *a little* —, un poco indisposto; *fall* —, cadere ammalato, ammalare; *take* —, prendere in mala parte, avere a male; *think* — *of one*, avere cattiva opinione di qualcheduno; *do not take it* —, non l' abbiate a male. **ill**³, S.: male, infortunio, *m.*, disgrazia, miseria, *f.*; dolore, *m.*
illápse, S.: illapso, attacco subito, *m.*

illăque-ate, TR.: illaqueare, illacciare. **-ātion**, S.: laccio, tranello, inganno, *m.*
illātion, S.: illazione, inferenza, conclusione, conseguenza, *f.*
illative, ADJ.: illativo.
illău-dable, ADJ.: indegno di lode. **-dably†**, ADV.: indegnamente.
ill-bōding, ADJ.: sinistro, funesto. **-bred**, ADJ.: grossolano, rustico, rozzo. **-conditioned**, ADJ.: mal condizionato.
illē-gal, ADJ.: illegale, illecito. **-găllity**, S.: cosa illegale; ingiustizia, *f.* **-gally**, ADV.: illecitamente; ingiustamente.
illĕgible, ADJ.: che non si può leggere.
illegit-imacy, S.: illegittimità, *f.* **-imate**, ADJ.: illegittimo, bastardo. **-imately**, ADV.: illegittimamente. **-imātion†**, S.: illegittimità; bastardigia, *f.*
ill-fāted, ADJ.: sfortunato, sventurato. **-făvoured**, ADJ.: sgraziato, deforme. **-făvouredly**, ADJ.: sgraziatamente. **-făvouredness**, S.: bruttezza, difformità, *f.* **-gröunded**, ADJ.: mal fondato.
illiber-al, ADJ.: illiberale; sordido. **-ălity**, S.: spilorceria, sordidezza, *f.* **-ally**, ADV.: in modo illiberale; sordidamente, vilmente.
illicit, ADJ.: illecito, proibito. **-ness**, S.: illegalità, *f.*
illimited, ADJ.: illimitato, senza limiti. **-ness**, S.: illimitazione; immensità, *f.*
illiter-ate, ADJ.: illetterato; ignorante. **-ateness**, **-ature†**, S.: ignoranza, *f.*
ill-minded, ADJ.: mal intenzionato. **-nāture**, S.: cattivo umore, *m.* **-nātured**, ADJ.: di cattivo umore, maligno, malizioso. **-nāturedness**, S.: malignità, malevolenza, *f.* **-ness**, S.: malattia; indisposizione, *f.*
illŏgical, ADJ.: senza ragionamento.
ill-shāped, ADJ.: mal fatto, deforme.
illūde, TR.: illudere; ingannare.
illū-me, **-minate**, TR.: illuminare. **-minātion**, S.: illuminazione, *f.*, illuminamento; splendore, *m.* **-minative**, ADJ.: illuminativo. **-minator**, S.: illuminatore, *m.* **-mine**, TR.: illuminare.
illū-sion, S.: illusione, *f.*, errore; inganno, *m.* **-sive**, **-sory**, ADJ.: illusorio.
illŭs-trate, TR.: illustrare; dilucidare, schiarire. **-trātion**, S.: illustrazione, *f.*, illustramento, *m.*, dichiarazione, *f.*, spiegamento, *m.* **-trative**, ADJ.: illustrante. **-tratively**, ADV.: in un modo espositivo. **-trator**, S.: illustratore, interprete, *m.* **-trious**, ADJ.: illustre, celebre; nobile. **-triously**, ADV.: illustremente; nobilmente. **-triousness**, S.: celebrità; nobilità, *f.*
ill-will, *S.: malevolenza, f.*
image 1, *S.: immagine; statua, f.* **im-age** 2, TR.: immaginare, figurare; rappresentarsi. **-ry**, S.: immagini; idee chimeriche, *f. pl.*
imăg-inable, ADJ.: immaginabile; concepibile. **-inary**, ADJ.: immaginario, chimerico. **-inātion**, S.: immaginazione; idea, *f.* **-inative**, ADJ.: immaginativo, visionario: —*faculty*, immaginativa, *f.* **-ine**, TR.: immaginare; inventare, disegnare; INTR.: imaginarsi, figurarsi. **-iner**, S.: immaginatore, inventore, *m.*
imba. . = *emba*. .
imbe-cile, ADJ.: imbecille; sciocco. **-cility**, S.: imbecillità; debolezza, *f.*
imbib-e, TR.: imbevere; succiare. **-er**, S.: che imbeve; succiatore, *m.* **-ition**, S.: succiamento, *m.*
imbitter, TR.: amareggiare; addolorare; inasprire, provocare.
imbo. . = *embo*. .
imbröwn, TR.: imbrunire; oscurare.
imbrūe, TR.: immollare; inzuppare.
imbrūte, TR.: rendere stupido; avvilire; INTR.: istupidire, divenir insensato; avvilirsi.
imbūe, TR.: imbevere; infondere, inspirare.
imbūrse, TR.: imborsare, mettere nella borsa.
imitability, S.: qualità imitativa, *f.*
imi-table, ADJ.: imitabile. **-tate**, TR.: imitare, copiare, contraffare. **-tātion**, S.: imitazione, copia, *f.* **-tative**, ADJ.: imitativo, imitante. **-tator**, S.: imitatore, *m.*
immăculate, ADJ.: immaculato, puro. **-ness**, S.: purità, *f.*
immănacle, TR.: ammanettare.
immanent, ADJ.: intrinsico, interno.
immănity, S.: crudeltà, ferocità, *f.*
immăsk, TR.: mascherare; coprire; velare.
immatēri-al, ADJ.: immateriale; incorporale: *it is* —, poco importa. **-ălity**, S.: immaterialità, *f.* **-ally**, ADV.: immaterialmente.
immatūr-e, ADJ.: immaturo, prematuro. **-ely**, ADV.: immaturamente, prematuramente. **-eness**, **-ity**, S.: immaturità, *f.*
immĕasur-able, ADJ.: immensurabile, immenso. **-ably**, ADV.: immensamente, smisuratamente.
immēdiate, ADJ.: immediato. **-ly**, ADV.: immediatamente, immediate; instantemente, subitamente. **-ness**, S.: momento presente, *m.*
immĕdicable, ADJ.: immedicabile, incurabile.
immĕmorable, ADJ.: immemorabile.
immemōrial, ADJ.: immemorabile.
immĕns-e, ADJ.: immenso, vasto. **-ely** ADV.: immensamente. **-sity**, S.:

hiss 1, S.: fischio, sibilo, *m.* **hiss** 2, TR.: fischiare; INTR.: sibilare; scoppiare. **-ing**, S.: fischiata, *f.*, fischiare, *m.*

hist, INTERJ.: silenzio! zitto!

his-tŏrian, S.: istorico, storico, scrittore di storia, *m.* **-tŏric(al)**, ADJ.: istorico, storico, istoriale. **-tŏrically**, ADV.: istoricamente, storicamente. **-tŏrify**, TR.: istoriare, narrare; far storia. **-toriŏgrapher**, S.: istoriografo, istorico, *m.* **-toriŏgraphy**, S.: arte di fare storia, *f.* **-'tory**, S.: storia, istoria, *f.* **-'tory-painter**, S.: pittore d' istorie, *m.* **-'tory-piece**, S.: pittura istorica, *f.*

histriŏnic(al), ADJ.: d' istrione, di commediante; teatrale.

hit 1, S.: colpo, *m.*, percossa, botta, *f.; azzardo, *m.*: *lucky* —, colpo fortunato; — *or miss*, a tutto rischio. **hit** 2, IRR.; TR.: battere, bastonare, percuotere; INTR.: pervenire; incontrare; urtarsi: — *home*, ributtare; — *the mark*, dar nel segno; — *the nail on the head*, colpire nel brocco, imberciare; — *him!* dagli! — *against*, dar contro, urtarsi; — *off*, riuscire; accadere felicemente; — *together*, incontrarsi; abbattersi; — *upon*, abbattersi; — *upon by chance*, trovare per caso.

hitch 1, S.: (*nav.*) nodo, groppo, *m.* **hitch** 2, INTR.: dimenarsi; muoversi, agitarsi; (*nav.*) annodare.

hither 1, ADJ.: citeriore, di qua. **hither** 2, ADV.: qui, qua; a questo fine. **-most**, ADJ.: il più vicino. **-to**, ADV.: fin' adesso, fin qui, fino a quest' ora. **-ward(s)**, ADV.: da questa banda.

hiv-e 1, S.: arnia, *f.*, alveare, *m.* **-e** 2, TR.: fare entrare nell' arnia; dar ricetto; INTR.: raccogliersi; rifugiarsi. **-er**, S.: colui che ha cura delle pecchie.

hō! hōa! INTERJ.: oh! ahi!

hōar 1, ADJ.: bianco, canuto. **hoar** 2, INTR.: muffare, muffarsi.

hōard 1, S.: mucchio segreto; tesoro, *m.* **hoard** 2, TR.: ammassare, accumulare: — *up money*, accumular danari. **-er**, S.: accumulatore (di danari), *m.*

hōarfrost, S.: brina, pruina, *f.*

hōariness, S.: bianchezza; canutezza; mucidezza, muffa, *f.*

hōarse, ADJ.: rauco, affiocato: *grow* —, divenir rauco, affiocare. **-ly**, ADV.: con voce rauca. **-ness**, S.: raucedine, fiocchezza di voce, afficatura, *f.*

hōary, ADJ.: bianco, bigio, canuto; mucido: *grow* —, muffarsi; incanutire; *grow* — *with age*, incanutire.

hōax 1, *S.*: *frode per ischerzo*, *f.*, *inganno*, *m.* **hoax** 2, TR.: coccare, ingannare (*per burla*).

ŏb, *S.*: *villano*, *rustico*, *m.*

hŏbbl-e 1, S.: zoppicamento, andar zoppiconi, *m.* **-e** 2, INTR.: zoppicare; mancare. **-ingly**, ADV.: in modo zoppo; con mala grazia, rozzamente.

hŏbby, S.: cavallino; sciocco, *m.* **-horse**, S.: ghiribizzo, *m.*; pazzia, follia, *f.*

hŏbgoblin, S.: folletto; fantasma, *m.*

hŏb-like, ADJ.: rustico, villano. **-nail**, S.: chiodo da ferrare un cavallo, *m.*

hŏck 1, S.: garretto; vecchio vino del Reno, *m.* **hock** 2, TR.: guastare i tendini delle gambe. **-herb**, S.: malva, *f.*

hŏckle, TR.: tagliare i tendini delle gambe.

hōcus-pōcus, S.: gherminella; trompería, *f.*

hŏd, S.: vassoia, truogolo, *m.*

hŏdgepodge, S.: manicaretto; ammorsellato, *m.*

hŏdman, S.: manovale, operario, *m.*

hōe 1, S.: zappa, marra, *f.* **hoe** 2, TR.: zappare; scavare.

hŏg, S.: porco, *m.* **-cote**, S.: porcile, *m.* **-gerel**, S.: pecora di due anni, *f.* **-gish**, ADJ.: porcino, di porco; ingordo. **-gishly**, ADV.: da porco; ingordamente. **-gishness**, S.: porcheria; sudiceria; golosità, *f.* **-herd**, S.: porcaio, *m.* **-shead**, S.: botte, *f.*, barile, *m.* **-sty**, S.: porcile, *m.* **-wash**, S.: lavatura, *f.*

hoiden†1, S.: ragazza grossolana, *f.* **-hoiden**†2, INTR.: saltare grossolanamente.

hoist, TR.: alzare, inalberare; issare, spiegare (le vele).

hoity-toity, ADJ.: insolente, sollazzevole; ADV.: insolentemente.

hōld 1, S.: presa, cattura; prigione; fortezza, *f.*; influsso, *m.*, influenza; (*nav.*) stiva, *f.*; fondo, *m.*: *lay* — *on*, *take* — *of*, prendere, pigliare. **hold** 2, INTERJ.: olà! fermate! **hold** 3, IRR.; TR.: tenere; pigliare, prendere; contenere; ritenere; possedere, fruire; convocare; celebrare; INTR.: continuare, durare; credere, pensare: attaccarsi, rappigliarsi; fermarsi: — *one's breath*, ritenere il fiato; — *a consultation*, tener consulta; — *in contempt*, dispregiare; — *in hand*, tenere a bada; trattenere; — *one's tongue*, tacersi; trattenere la lingua; — *true*, trovarsi vero; — *back*, ritenere, ricusare; tener per sè; — *forth*, offerire; proporre; aringare, predicare; — *in*, ristringere, governare; ritenersi; — *off*, scostare; ributtare, ritardare, differire; — *on*, continuare; protrarre; procedere; — *out*, stendere; offerire; sussistere; resistere, durare, mantenersi; — *over*, ditenere; — *together*, stare unito; — *up*, alzare, levare; appoggiare; sostenersi; fermarsi per rubare; — *with one*, abbracciare il partito d' alcuno, tener per uno. **-er**, s.: tenitore; vassallo, *m.*: *—forth*, s.: aringatore, predicatore, *m.*; *— of bonds*, detentore di boñi. **-fast**, s.: rampone; anello; meschino, spilorcio, *m.* **-ing**, s.: feudo; affitto, *m.*

hōle 1, s.: buco, pertugio, forame, *m.*; caverna, *f.*: *full of —s*, bucato; *make a — in*, bucare, far buco in. **hole** 2 TR.: *bucare.*

hŏliday, s.: giorno di festa (*sp.* secolare), *m.*; vacanza, *f.*

hōli-ly, ADV.: santamente, inviolabilmente. **-ness**, s.: santità; pietà, *f.*

hŏllo, INTERJ.: ola! ehi! oh!

hŏllands, s.: ginepro, *m.*

hŏllow 1, ADJ.: cavo, vuoto; vacuo, finto, doppio, perfido: *— eyes*, occhi cavi; *— cheeks*, guancie infossate; *— voice*, voce rauca; *— noise*, rumore sordo. **hollow** 2, s.: cavo, *m.*; cavità; fossa, *f.*, canale, *m.*; tana, *f.* **hollow** 3, TR.: cavare, scavare; vuotare; INTR.: gridare; acclamare. **-ly**, ADV.: con delle cavità; senza sincerità, disonestamente. **-ness**, s.: cavità; dissimulazione, *f.*

hŏlly, s.: agrifoglio, *m.* **-hook**, s.: alcea, bismalva, *f.*

hŏlm, s.: elce, *f.*; leccio, *m.*

hŏlocaust, s.: olocausto, *m.*

hōlster, s.: fodera della pistola, *f.* **-cap**, s.: fonda della pistola, *f.*

hōlt, s.: boschetto, *m.*

hōly, ADJ.: santo, sacrato, pio, religioso, casto: *make —*, santificare; *the — one*, Iddio Santissimo; *— Ghost*, Spirito Santo; *— water*, acqua santa; *— writ*, Sacre Scritture. **-day**, s.: giorno di festa; (*sp.* religiosa), *m.* **-Thursday**, s.: giorno dell' ascensione, *m.* **-watersprinkle**, s.: aspersorio, *m.* **-week**, s.: settimana santa, *f.*

hŏmage 1, s.: omaggio; rispetto, *m.*, riverenza, *f.*; tributo, *m.* **-e** 2, TR.: render omaggio, rispettare, riverire. **-er**, s.: vassallo, *m.*

hōme 1, s.: casa; dimora, *f.*; domicilio, *m.*; stanza; patria, *f.*: *charity begins at —*, il primo prossimo è sè medesimo. **home** 2, ADV.: in casa, in patria sua: *speak —*, parlare a proposito. **-born**, ADJ.: nativo, naturale; domestico. **-bound**, ADJ.: di ritorno. **-bred**, ADJ.: del paese, nostrale, nativo; grossolano, rozzo. **-felt**, ADJ.: interno, interiore; segreto. **-less**, ADJ.: senza tetto, senza ricovero. **-lily**, ADV.: grossolanamente, rozzamente. **-liness**, s.: rustichezza, rozzezza, grossezza, *f.* **-ly**, ADJ.: casalingo; semplice; rozzo, grossolano, incolto. **-made**, ADJ.: casalingo, fatto nella casa.

home-opăthical, ADJ.: omeopatico. **-ŏpathist**, s.: medico omeopatico, *m.* **-ŏpathy**, s.: omeopatia, *f.*

hōme-sick, ADJ.: nostalgico, preso da nostalgia. **-sickness**, s.: nostalgia, *f.* **-spun**, ADJ.: casereccio, casalingo. **-ward(s)**, ADV.: verso casa: *— bound ship*, bastimento di ritorno.

homicidal, ADJ.: micidiale; cruento.

hŏmicide, s.: omicido; omicida, *m.*

homilĕtic(al), ADJ.: omiletico; conversevole.

hŏm-ilist, s.: autore d' omilie, *m.* **-ily**, s.: omilia, *f.*

homogé-neal = *-neous.* **-nealness**, **-neity** = *-neousness.* **-neous**, ADJ.: omogeneo, della stessa natura. **-neousness**, s.: omogeneità, *f.*

homŏl-ogate, TR.: omologare; ratificare. **-ogous**, ADJ.: omologo; corrispondente.

homŏn-ymous, ADJ.: omonimo, equivoco. **-ymy**, s.: omonimia; ambiguità, *f.*

hōne 1, s.: cote, *f.* **hone** 2, TR.: affilare, aguzzare; INTR.: bramare, languire.

hŏnest 1, ADJ.: onesto, probo, integro, giusto, sincero; casto. **honest** 2, TR.: onestare; abbellire. **-ly**, ADV.: onestamente, giustamente. **-y**, s.: onestà; sincerità, verità; virtù, *f.*: *— is the best policy*, l' onestà è la miglior politica.

hóney 1, s.: m(i)ele, *m.* **honey** 2, TR.: addolcire; INTR.: adulare, careggiare. **-bag**, s.: stomago della pecchia, *m.* **-comb**, s.: favo, fiale, *m.* **-dew**, s.: manna; rugiada dolce, *f.* **-ed**, ADJ.: melato, condito di mele; dolce. **-moon**, s.: luna di mele, *f.* **-suckle**, s.: caprifoglio, *m.* **-wort**, s.: cerinta, *f.*

hónied = *honeyed.*

hŏnour 1, s.: onore; rispetto, *m.*; stima; fama; figura, testa, *f.*: *upon my —*, sul mio onore, parola d' onore; *point of —*, punto d' onore, *m.*; *word of —*, parola d' onore, *f.*; *man of —*, uomo di onore; *do the —s of the house*, far gli onori di casa. **honour** 2, TR.: onorare, riverire, rispettare: *— a bill of exchange*, fare onore ad (accettare) una lettera di cambio. **-able**, ADJ.: onorevole, illustre. **-ableness**, s.: generosità; magnificenza, *f.* **-ably**, ADV.: onorevolmente, nobilmente. **-ary**, ADJ.: onorario, d' onore; s.: onorario, salario, *m.* **-er**, s.: onoratore, veneratore, *m.* **-less**, ADJ.: senza onore, disonorato.

hóod 1, s.: cappuccio, capperone, *m.*; cuffia, *f.* **hood** 2, TR.: incappucciare; coprire. **-man-blind**, s.: mosca cieca, *f.* (giuoco). **-wink**, TR.: bendar gli occhi; acciecare; truffare, ingannare.

hōof, s.: unghia, *f.* **-bound**, ADJ.: castellato.

impŏwer = *empower*.

im-practicability = *impracticableness*. **-prăcticable**, ADJ.: impraticabile; impossibile. **-prăcticableness**, S.: qualità di ciò che è impraticabile; impossibilità, *f*.

imprecate, TR.: imprecare, maledire. **-cātion**, S.: imprecazione, maledizione, *f*. **-catory**, ADJ.: imprecativo.

imprĕgn†, TR.: impregnare; riempire.

imprĕg-nable, ADJ.: inespugnabile. **-nate¹**, ADJ.: impregnato. **-nate²**, TR.: impregnare; satollare; INTR.: impregnarsi; imbevere, riempirsi. **-nātion**, S.: impregnamento, *m*.; pregnezza, *f*.

impresário, S.: impresario, *m*.

imprescriptible, ADJ.: (*leg.*) imprescrittibile.

im-press¹, S.: impressione; impronta; sentenza, *f*, motto, *m*. **-prĕss²**, TR.: imprimere, improntare; levar gente per forza: — *on the mind*, scolpire nella mente; —*ed with the idea*, compenetrato dell' idea. **-prĕssion**, S.: impressione; stampa; edizione, *f*. **-prĕssive**, ADJ.: imprimente; espressivo, energico, impetuoso. **-prĕssively**, ADV.: energicamente. **-prĕssure**, S.: impressione; impronta, *f*.

imprīmis, ADV.: primieramente.

imprint¹, TR.: imprimere; stampare.

imprint², S.: impronta, *f*.; luogo di stampa, *m*.

imprison, TR.: imprigionare. **-ment**, S.: imprigionamento, *m*.

im-probability, S.: improbabilità, *f*. **-prŏbable**, ADJ.: improbabile, inverosimile. **-prŏbably**, ADV.: improbabilmente.

impro-bate, TR.: disapprovare, riprovare, rigettare, condannare. **-bātion**, S.: riprovazione, *f*., rigettamento, *m*.

imprŏbity, S.: improbità; disonestà; malignità, *f*.

imprŏmptu, S.: improvvisata, *f*.

imprŏper, ADJ.: improprio, disadatto; indecente. **-ly**, ADV.: impropriamente.

impropŏrtion-able, **-ate**, ADJ.: improporzionale.

imprŏpriate†, TR.: appropriarsi; arrogarsi.

impropriety, S.: improprietà; sconvenevolezza, *f*.

imprŏsperous, ADJ.: sfortunato, sventurato, infelice. **-ly**, ADV.: sfortunatamente, infelicemente.

im-provability = *improvableness*. **-prŏvable**, ADJ.: che si può migliorare. **-prŏvableness**, S.: capacità di miglioramento, *f*. **-prŏve**, TR.: migliorare; perfezionare; INTR.: profittare; far pro- [illegible] migliorar sorte; — *one's mind*, addottrinarsi; *to greatly —d*, aver fatto grandi progressi. **-prŏvement**, S.: miglioramento; avanzamento, progresso, *m*.; coltivazione, *f*. **-prŏver**, S.: che migliora; che profitta, che avanza.

im-provided†, ADJ.: improvviso, inaspettato. **-prŏvidence**, S.: improvidenza, imprudenza, *f*. **-prŏvident**, ADJ.: improvido, inconsiderato. **-prŏvidently**, ADV.: improvidamente.

imprŏvisator, S.: improvvisatore, improvisante, *m*.

improvision, S.: improvidenza, *f*.

imprūden-ce, S.: imprudenza; indiscrezione, *f*. **-t**, ADJ.: imprudente; indiscreto. **-tly**, ADV.: imprudentemente.

impuden-ce, **-cy**, S.: impudenza, sfacciataggine, *f*. **-t**, ADJ.: impudente, sfacciato, sfrontato. **-tly**, ADV.: impudentemente, sfrontatamente.

impudicity, S.: impudicizia, *f*.

impūgn, TR.: impugnare, oppugnare; assaltare, assalire. **-er**, S.: impugnatore; assaltatore, *m*.

impūissance, S.: impotenza; debolezza, *f*.

im-pulse, **-pŭlsion**, S.: impulso, incitamento, *m*. **-pŭlsive**, ADJ.: impulsivo, incitativo.

impū-nely, ADV.: impunemente. **-nity**, S.: impunità, *f*.

impūr-e, ADJ.: impuro, immondo; disonesto; impudico. **-ely**, ADV.: impuramente. **-ity**, S.: impurità, immondizia; oscenità, *f*.

impŭrple, TR.: tingere di color di porpora, imporporare. **-d**, ADJ.: porporato, purpureo.

impū-table, ADJ.: imputabile. **-tableness**, S.: qualità d' esser imputabile, *f*.; imputamento, *m*. **-tātion**, S.: imputazione, *f*. **-tative**, ADJ.: imputativo, incolpante. **-te**, TR.: imputare, attribuire la colpa. **-ter**, S.: imputatore, accusatore, *f*.

impu-trescibility, S.: incorruttibilità, *f*. **-trĕscible**, ADJ.: immarcescibile, incorruttibile.

in, PREP.: in; entro, dentro; fra: — *the*, nel (nello, nella, nei, negli, nelle); — *as much as* = *inasmuch as*; — *the city*, nella città; — *comparison*, a paragone; — *contempt*, per disprezzo; — *the daytime*, di giorno; — [illegible] rare; — *order*, [illegible] affine di, per; [illegible] — *respect to*, [illegible] somma, finalm[illegible] per lo passato [illegible] be — *for it*, [illegible]

inability, S.: inabilità, incapacità, *f.*
inábstinence†, S.: intemperanza, immoderanza, *f.*
inac-cessibility, S.: inaccessibilità, impossibilità d' approcciare, *f.* **-céssible**, ADJ.: inaccessibile. **-céssibleness** = *inaccessibility.*
ináccu-racy, S.: inesattezza, trascuranza, negligenza, *f.* **-rate**, ADJ.: poco esatto, trascurato, negligente. **-rately**, ADV.: senza esattezza, incorrettamente.
inác-tion, S.: inazione; disoccupazione, *f.* **-tive**, ADJ.: non attivo, ozioso, pigro. **-tively**, ADV.: senza attività; pigramente. **-tivity**, S.: inerzia, trascuraggine, *f.*
inádequate, ADJ.: inadeguato, sproporzionato, difettoso, imperfetto, incompleto. **-ly**, ADV.: imperfettamente. **-ness**, S.: sproporzione; insufficienza, *f.*
inadmissible, ADJ.: inammissibile.
inadvérten-ce, **-cy**, S.: inavvertenza, *f.*, trascuraggine, *f.*: *through* —, per inavvertenza. **-t**, ADJ.: disattento, trascurato. **-tly**, ADV.: inadvertentemente, trascuratamente.
in-affability, S.: incompatibilità, scortesia, *f.* **-áffable**, ADJ.: incompatibile, scortese.
inaffectátion, S.: sincerità, *f.*
inálienable, ADJ.: inalienabile. **-ness**, S.: inalienabilità, *f.*
inálterable, ADJ.: inalterabile.
inadmissible, ADJ.: inamissibile.
inámour, TR.: innamorare.
ináne, ADJ.: vuoto, vano; inefficace.
ináni-mate, **-mated**, ADJ.: inanimato.
in-anítion, S.: inedia; mancanza di forza, debolezza, *f.* **-ánity**, S.: inanità; vacuità; inutilità, *f.*
ináppetency, S.: inappetenza, *f.*; disgusto, m.
inápplicable, ADJ.: non applicabile. **-cátion**, S.: trascurataggine, negligenza, incuria, *f.*
inapprehénsive, ADJ.: trascurante.
ináptitude, S.: disadattaggine; inabilità, *f.*
inárable, ADJ.: inetto ad essere arato.
inárch, TR.: (*gard.*) innestare.
inarticulate, ADJ.: inarticolato, indistinto. **-ly**, ADV.: indistintamente. **-ness**, S.: pronunzia inarticolata, *f.*
inartificial, ADJ.: senza arte; naturale, puro. **-y**, ADV.: naturalmente.
inasmúch, ADV.: — *as*, in quanto chè, perchè, poichè, giacchè.
…ttén-tion, S.: inattenzione; trascu…a, *f.* **-tive**, ADJ.: disattento, tras-
…ADJ.: inaudibile.
…TR.: *inaugurare, investire*
…razione, investitura, f.

inauspícious, ADJ.: malauguroso, infausto. **-ly**, ADV.: infaustamente, infelicemente.
inbéing, S.: inerenza, *f.*
inborn, ADJ.: innato; ingenito; naturale.
inbréathed, ADJ.: inspirato.
inbred, ADJ.: prodotto dentro; del paese.
incáge, TR.: ingabbiare; imprigionare.
incálculable, ADJ.: fuor di calcolo, innumerabile.
incandéscen-ce, S.: incandescenza, *f.* **-t**, ADJ.: incandescente.
in-cantátion, S.: incantamento; incantesimo, *m.* **-cántatory**, ADJ.: incantevole, magico.
incánton, TR.: unire ad un cantone, *f.*
in-capability, S.: incapacità, *f.* **-cápable**, ADJ.: incapace; inabile. **-cápableness** = *incapability.*
incapácious, ADJ.: incapace; stretto, angusto. **-ness**, S.: strettezza, *f.*
incapác-itate, TR.: rendere incapace. **-ity**, S.: incapacità, inabilità, *f.*
incárcer-ate, TR.: incarcerare, imprigionare. **-átion**, S.: incarcerazione, *f.*
incár-nadine†, ADJ.: incarnatino, incarnato. **-nate**, ADJ.: incarnato. **-nate**, TR.: incarnare. **-nátion**, S.: incarnazione, *f.* **-native**, ADJ.: (*med.*) incarnativo.
incáse, TR.: incassare; serrare, rinchiudere; coprire.
incásk, TR.: imbottare.
incáutious, ADJ.: incauto; trascurato. **-ly**, ADV.: incautamente; imprudentemente. **-ness**, S.: mancanza di cautela, imprudenza, *f.*
incén-diary, S.: incendiario; sedizioso, capo di parti, *m.* **-dious**, ADJ.: sedizioso.
in-cénse, TR.: inasprire, irritare; provocare: *be* (*become*) —*d*, adirarsi, sdegnarsi, inasprirsi. **in-cense**, S.: incenso, *m.* **-cénsement**†, S.: collera; furia, *f.*, furore, *m.* **-cénsion**†, S.: abbruciamento, *m.* **-cénsive**, ADJ.: incensivo, infiammante. **-cénsor**, S.: aizzatore, *m.* **-cénsory**, S.: incensiere, turibile, *m.* **-céntive**, ADJ.: incitativo, impulsivo; S.: incentivo, motivo; incoraggiamento, *m.*
incép-tion, S.: cominciamento, principio, *m.* **-tive**, ADJ.: cominciante, elementale. **-tor**, S.: cominciante, principiante, *m.*
incér-tainty†, **-titude**, S.: incertezza; dubbiezza, *f.*
incéssant, ADJ.: incessantemente, continuamente; sempre.
in-cest, S.: incesto, *m.* **-céstuous**, ADJ.: incestuoso.
inch I, S.: dito, pollice (duodecima

d' un piede), *m.*: — *by* —, poco a poco, a goccia a goccia, poco per volta. **inch** 2, TR.: misurare a dita; INTR.: avanzarsi a piccioli gradi.

inchĕst, TR.: incassare.

inchmeal, S.: pezzo lungo d' un dito, *m.*

in-chọạte, TR.: principiare, cominciare. **-chọā̦tiọn**, S.: principio, cominciamento, *m.* **-chŏative**, ADJ.: incoativo.

inci-dence, **-dency**, S.: (*geom.*) incidenza, *f.*; (*fig.*) caso, accidente, *m.* **-dent**, ADJ.: incidente; casuale, fortuito; inseparabile; S.: accidente, caso, *m.* **-dĕnt-al**, ADJ.: accidentale, fortuito. **-dĕnt-ally**, ADV.: incidentemente.

incinerā̦tiọn, S.: incinerazione, *f.*

incipiency, S.: cominciamento, *m.*

incircumspĕctiọn, S.: mancanza di cautela, negligenza, *f.*

in-ciṣe, TR.: incidere, tagliare. **-ciṣiọn**, S.: incisione, *f.*; taglio, *m.* **-cisive**, ADJ.: incisivo. **-ciṣọr**, S.: incisore; dente incisivo, *m.*

in-citā̦tiọn, S.: incitamento, *m.* **-cite**, TR.: incitare, eccitare; instigare; sollecitare; indurre. **-citement**, S.: incitamento, stimolo, *m.* **-citing**, ADJ.: incitativo; S.: incitamento, eccitamento, *m.*

inciv-il, ADJ.: incivile, scortese; grossolano. **-ility**, S.: inciviltà, scortesia; rustichezza, rozzezza, *f.* **-illy**, ADV.: incivilmente; rusticamente.

inclăsp, TR.: tener fermo.

inclĕmen-cy, S.: inclemenza; severità, *f.*, rigore, *m.* **-t**, ADJ.: inclemente, rigoroso, severo.

in-clinable, ADJ.: inclinabile, inclinevole; prono. **-clinā̦tiọn**, S.: inclinazione; propensione; tendenza, *f.*; pendio, *m.* **-cline**, (IN)TR.: inclinare, inchinare; incurvare; tendere. **-clining**, ADJ.: inclinante; S.: inclinamento, *m.*; propensione, *f.*

inclip†, TR.: abbracciare; circondare, cingere.

inclöistẹr = *encloister*.

inclō-ṣe, TR.: rinchiudere; includere (una lettera): *the* —*d*, l' inclusa. **-ṣụre**, S.: ricinto; orto assiepato, *m.*

inclŏụd, TR.: annuvolare; offuscare.

inclū-de, TR.: inchiudere; comprendere, contenere: *not* —*d*, non compreso. **-sive**, ADJ.: inclusivo, che comprende. **-sively**, ADV.: inclusivamente.

incŏg = *incognito*.

incŏg-itable, ADJ.: incogitabile. **-itancy**, S.: inconsiderazione, inconsideratezza, *f.* **-itant**, **-itạtive**, ADJ.: sconsiderato; imprudente.

incŏgnitọ, ADJ.: incognito; ADV.: incognitamente.

incọhēren-ce, **-cy**, S.: incoerenza, discrepanza, *f.* **-t**, ADJ.: incoerente, discrepante. **-tly**, ADV.: in modo incoerente.

incom-bustibility, S.: incombustibilità, *f.* **-bŭstible**, ADJ.: incombustibile. **-bŭstibleness** = *incombustibility*.

incọme, S.: rendita, entrata, *f.* **-tax**, S.: imposta sulla rendita, *f.*

incom-menṣụrability, S.: incommensurabilità, *f.* **-mĕnṣụrable**, **-mĕnṣụrạte**, ADJ.: incommensurabile.

incŏm-mọdạte†, **-mōde**, TR.: incomodare, scomodare. **-mōdious**, ADJ.: incomodo, inconveniente, importuno. **-mōdiously**, ADV.: incomodamente. **-mōdiousness**, **-mŏdity**, S.: incomodità, *f.*, incomodo, *m.*

incom-mụnicability, S.: incomunicabilità, *f.* **-mūnicable**, ADJ.: incomunicabile. **-mūnicably**, ADV.: in modo incomunicabile. **-mūnicạting**, ADJ.: senza comunicazione.

incom-mụtability, S.: incommutabilità, *f.* **-mūtable**, ADJ.: incommutabile.

incompăct(ed), ADJ.: disgiunto, disunito, incoerente; vago.

incŏmparabl-e, ADJ.: incomparabile; eccellente. **-eness**, S.: eccellenza, *f.* **-y**, ADV.: incomparabilmente.

incompăṣṣiọnạte, ADJ.: senza compassione; duro, crudele.

incom-patibility, S.: incompatibilità, *f.* **-pătible**, ADJ.: incompatibile; contrario, opposto. **-pătibly**, ADV.: in modo incompatibile.

incŏmpẹten-cy, S.: incompetenza; incapacità, *f.* **-t**, ADJ.: incompetente; incapace. **-tly**, ADV.: incompetentemente.

incomplēte, ADJ.: incompleto, incompiuto, difettoso, imperfetto. **-ness**, S.: imperfezione, *f.*

incompliance, S.: poca compiacenza, ritrosia, *f.*

incompō-ṣed†, ADJ.: incomposto, disordinato. **-ṣedness**, S.: disordine, *m.*

incomprẹ-hensibility, S.: incomprensibilità, *f.* **-hĕnsible**, ADJ.: incomprensibile. **-hĕnsibly**, ADV.: incomprensibilmente.

incom-pressibility, S.: incapacità d' esser compresso, *f.* **-prĕssible**, ADJ.: che non può esser compresso.

inconcĕalable, ADJ.: che non si può celare.

inconcĕiva-ble, ADJ.: inconcepibile, incomprensibile. **-bly**, ADV.: in modo inconcepibile.

inconcinnity, S.: disproporzione, *f.*

inconclūsive, ADJ.: inconcludente. **-ly**, ADV.: senza evidenza. **-ness**, S.: mancanza d' evidenza, *f.*

inconcoc-t(ed), ADJ.: indigesto. **-tiọn**, S.: indigestione, crudità, *f.*

incondĕnsable, ADJ.: non condensabile.
inconfŏrmity, S.: mancanza di conformità, *f.*
incŏn-gruence, **-grŭity**, S.: incongruenza, incongruità; inconsistenza; assurdità, *f.* **-gruous**, ADJ.: incongruo, improprio. **-gruously**, ADV.: incongruentemente, impropriamente.
incŏnscionable, ADJ.: senza coscienza, irragionevole.
incŏnse-quence, S.: inconseguenza, *f.* **-quent**, **-quĕntial**, ADJ.: irregolare, fondato, mal falso.
inconsider-able, ADJ.: inconsiderabile; di poco momento. **-ableness**, S.: poca importanza, *f.* **-ate**, ADJ.: inconsiderato. **-ately**, ADV.: inconsideratamente. **-ateness**, **-ātion**, S.: inconsiderazione, negligenza, incuria, *f.*
inconsisten-ce, **-cy**, S.: inconsistenza, incoerenza, incompatibilità, incongruità, *f.* **-t**, ADJ.: inconsistente; incoerente, non consentaneo: — *with*, non consentaneo a, disdicevole a. **-tly**, ADV.: incongruentemente; assurdamente.
inconsōlable, ADJ.: inconsolabile.
incŏnsonancy, S.: dissonanza, *f.*
inconspicuous, ADJ.: incospicuo.
incŏnstan-cy, S.: incostanza, leggerezza, *f.* **-t**, ADJ.: incostante; instabile. **-tly**, ADV.: incostantemente, instabilmente.
incon-sūmable, **-sŭmptible†**, ADJ.: inconsumabile.
incontĕsta-ble, ADJ.: incontestabile. **-bly**, ADV.: incontestabilmente.
incontiguous, ADJ.: non contiguo.
incŏntinen-ce, **-cy**, S.: incontinenza, *f.* **-t**, ADJ.: incontinente; sfrenato; impudico. **-tly**, ADV.: incontinentemente; subitamente, prestamente; impudicamente.
incontrovĕrtibl-e, ADJ.: incontrovertibile, indisputabile. **-y**, ADV.: certamente.
inconvēnien-ce, **-cy**, S.: inconvenienza, *f.* **-t**, ADJ.: inconveniente, incomodo, sconveniente. **-tly**, ADV.: inconvenientemente.
inconvĕrsable, ADJ.: insociabile.
inconvĕrtible, ADV.: che non si può convertire, inalterabile.
inconvincible, ADJ.: inconvincibile.
incôr-poral, ADJ.: incorporale; immateriale. **-porălity**, S.: incorporalità; immaterialità, *f.* **-porally**, ADV.: incorporalmente. **-porate**, ADJ.: incorporato. **-porate**, TR.: incorporare; unire; associare; INTR.: incorporarsi; associarsi. **-porātion**, S.: incorporazione, *f.*, incorporamento, *m.* **-pōreal**, ADJ.: incorporeo; spirituale. **-pōreally**, ADV.: incorporalmente, immaterialmente. **-poreity**, S.: immaterialità, *f.*
incôrpse, TR.: incorporare; unire insieme.
incorrĕct, ADJ.: incorretto, scorretto, difettoso. **-ly**, ADV.: scorrettamente. **-ness**, S.: scorrezione, mancanza d' esattezza, *f.*
incŏrrigibl-e, ADJ.: incorrigibile; inemendabile. **-eness**, S.: incorrigibilità, *f.* **-y**, ADV.: incorrigibilmente.
incorrŭp-t, **-ted**, ADJ.: incorrotto. **-tibility**, S.: incorruttibilità, *f.* **-tible**, ADJ.: incorruttibile, durabile. **-tibleness** = *incorruptibility*. **-tibly**, ADV.: incorruttibilmente. **-tion**, S.: incorruzione; durabilità, *f.* **-tness**, S.: purità; integrità, *f.*
incrăs-sate, TR.: ingrossare; spessare, condensare. **-sātion**, S.: ingrossamento; condensamento, *m.* **-sative**, ADJ.: incrassante.
in-crease 1, S.: accrescimento, aumento, *m.*, aumentazione, *f.* **-crēase** 2, TR.: aumentare, ingrandire; INTR.: crescere, aumentarsi, aggrandirsi. **-crēaser**, S.: aumentatore, *m.*
in-credibility, S.: incredibilità, *f.* **-crĕdible**, ADJ.: incredibile. **-crĕdibleness** = *incredibility*. **-crĕdibly**, ADV.: incredibilmente. **-credūlity**, S.: incredulità, miscredenza, *f.* **-crĕdulous**, ADJ.: incredulo, miscredente. **-crĕdulousness** = *incredibility*.
incrēmable, ADJ.: incombustibile.
increment, S.: incremento, accrescimento, *m.*
incriminate, TR.: incolpare, accusare.
incrŭs-t, **-tate**, TR.: incrostare, intonacare. **-tātion**, S.: incrostatura, *f.*
incu-bate, INTR.: covare. **-bātion**, S.: covatura, *f.*, covare, *m.* **-bus**, S.: incubo, *m.*
incŭl-cate, TR.: inculcare; imprimere: — *a thing upon*, inculcare una cosa a. **-cātion**, S.: inculcazione, *f.*
incŭlpa-ble, ADJ.: incolpabile, incolpevole, non biasimevole; innocente. **-bly**, ADV.: incolpabilmente; innocentemente.
incŭlt, ADJ.: incolto.
incŭm-bency, S.: incombenza, *f.*, possesso d' un beneficio, *m.* **-bent**, ADJ.: appoggiato; S.: beneficiato, *m.*
incŭm-ber, TR.: ingombrare; impedire. **-brance**, S.: ingombro, *m.*
incŭr, TR.: incorrere in, esporsi a, attirarsi addosso: — *one's displeasure*, attirarsi addosso lo scontento (la dispiacenza) di alcuno; — *a penalty*, esporsi ad una multa.
in-curability, S.: stato incurabile, *m.* **-cūrable**, ADJ.: incurabile, irre

bile. **-cūrableness** = *incurability*. **-cū-rably**, ADV.: da non potersi curare.
in-curiósity, S.: trascuraggine, negligenza; disavvertenza, *f.* **-cūrious**, ADJ.: negligente, trascurato; disattento. **-cū-riously**, ADV.: negligentemente. **-cū-riousness** = *incuriosity*.
incūrsion, S.: incursione, invasione, *f.*
incūr-vate, TR.: incurvare; piegare. **-vātion**, S.: incurvazione; piegatura, *f.* **-vity**, S.: curvatura; flessione, *f.*
inda-gate, TR.: indagare, investigare; ricercare; esaminare. **-gātion**, S.: indagazione, investigazione; ricerca, *f.* **-ga-tor**, S.: indagatore, investigatore; esaminatore, *m.*
indârt†, S.: lanciare dentro, dardeggiare.
indĕbt, TR.: indebitare, obbligare. **-ed**, ADJ.: indebitato, obbligato, tenuto: *be — to one for a thing*, esser obbligato ad uno per checchessia; *I am — to you for my happiness*, vi sono debitore della mia felicità.
indĕcen-cy, S.: indecenza, sconvenevolezza, *f.* **-t**, ADJ.: indecente, sconvenevole. **-tly**, ADV.: indecentemente.
indeciduous, ADJ.: durabile, stabile.
inde-cision, S.: irresoluzione; incertezza, *f.* **-cisive**, ADJ.: indeciso, irresoluto; incerto.
indeclinable, ADJ.: indeclinabile.
indecŏ-rous, ADJ.: indecoro, indecente. **-rously**, ADV.: indecentemente, sconvenevolmente. **-rum**, S.: sconvenevolezza, indecenza, *f.*
indĕed, ADV.: in verità, in vero, da vero (davvero), in fatto: *no —*, no davvero.
indefátigabl-e, ADJ.: indefaticabile, indefesso. **-eness**, S.: indefaticabilità, *f.* **-y**, ADV.: indefaticabilmente, indefessamente.
indefĕasible, ADJ.: irrevocabile; insolubile.
inde-fectibility, S.: indefettibilità, *f.* **-fĕctible**, ADJ.: indefettibile.
indefen-sible, **-sive**, ADJ.: da non potersi difendere.
indefi-ciency, S.: indeficienza, perfezione, *f.* **-cient**, ADJ.: indeficiente; inalterabile.
indefinable, ADJ.: indefinibile.
indĕfinite, ADJ.: indefinito, indeterminato. **-ly**, ADV.: indefinitamente.
indelĭberat-e, **-ed**, ADJ.: indeliberato, inconsiderato. **-ely**, ADV.: inconsideratamente.
indĕlible, ADJ.: indelibile.
indĕl-icacy, S.: mancanza di delicatezza, *grossezza*, *f.* **-icate**, ADJ.: grossolano; *indecente*. **-icately**, ADV.: indecente*mente*.
in-demnificātion, S.: indennizzazione, **-nity**, S.: indennità, *f.*
indĕnt[1], S.: incisione, *f.*; taglio, *m.* **in-dent**[2], TR.: intaccare, intagliare; INTR.: contrattare, fare contratto. **-ātion**, S.: intagliamento, *m.*, intaccatura, *f.* **-ure**, S.: contratto; accordo, *m.*

: inesorabile.
.: indescrivibile, in-

gersi.

minarsi. **-nate**, ADJ.: indeterminato, indeciso. **-nately**, ADV.: indeterminatamente. **-nātion**, S.: irresoluzione, dubbiezza; perplessità, *f.* **-ned** = *indeterminate*.
indevōtion, S.: indevozione, irreligione, *f.*
indevōut, ADJ.: indivoto.
index[1], S.: indice, *m.*; tavola, rubrica, lista, *f.*; sommario, *m.* **index**[2], TR.: provvedere d' un indice (sommario); INTR.: mettere un indice.
indextĕrity, S.: mancanza di destrità, goffaggine, *f.*
India-ink, S.: inchiostro della Cina, *f.* **-n**, ADJ.: indiano. **-rubber**, S.: gomma elastica, *f.*
in-dicant, ADJ.: indicante. **-dicate**, TR.: indicare; accennare, mostrare; accusare. **-dicātion**, S.: indicazione, *f.*; segno; sintomo, *m.* **-dicative**, ADJ.: indicativo: *— mood*, indicativo, *m.* **-dicator**, S.: indicatore, *m.* **-dicatory**, ADJ.: indicativo.
in-dict, TR.: dinunziare, accusare: *stand —ed*, essere accusato. **-diction**, S.: dichiarazione, *f.* **-dictment**, S.: (*jur.*) accusa, *f.*: *prefer an —*, intentare un processo.
indifferen-ce, **-cy**, S.: indifferenza; imparzialità, *f.* **-t**, ADJ.: indifferente, poco curante; imparziale; mediocre. **-tly**, ADV.: indifferentemente.
indigen-ce, **-cy**, S.: indigenza; povertà, *f.*
indigenous, ADJ.: indigeno, nativo d' un paese.
indigent, ADJ.: indigente; povero.
indigĕs-t(ed), ADJ.: indigesto. **-tible**, ADJ.: indigestibile. **-tibleness**, S.: indigestibilità; indigestione, *f.* **-tion**, S.: indigestione; crudità, *f.*
indign, ADJ.: indegno, immeritevole.

indig-nant, ADJ.: indegnato, sdegnato. **-nátion**, S.: indegnazione, *f.*, sdegno, *m.* **-nity**, S.: indegnità, *f.*; oltraggio, affronto, *m.*
indigo, S.: indaco, *m.*
indirĕc-t, ADJ.: indiretto; curvo; disleale, disonesto. **-tion**, S.: mezzo indiretto, *m.* **-tly**, ADV.: indirettamente. **-tness**, S.: obbliquità; dislealtà, disonestà, *f.*
indiscĕrnibl-e, ADJ.: impercettibile. **-eness**, S.: impercettibilità, *f.* **-y**, ADV.: impercettibilmente.
indisciplinable, ADJ.: indisciplinabile, intrattabile.
indis-crĕet, ADJ.: indiscreto, imprudente, sconsiderato. **-crĕetly**, ADV.: indiscretamente. **-crĕtion**, S.: indiscrezione; imprudenza, *f.*
indiscriminate, ADJ.: indistinto. **-ly**, ADV.: senza distinzione.
indispĕnsa-ble, ADJ.: indispensabile. **-bleness**, S.: indispensabilità; necessità, *f.*, bisogno, *m.* **-bly**, ADV.: indispensabilmente, necessariamente.
indispŏ-se, TR.: rendere incapace, rendere avverso. **-sed**, ADJ.: indisposto, ammalato. **-sedness**, S.: ripugnanza, avversione, *f.* **-sition**, S.: indisposizione, *f.*: *slight* —, indisposizioncella, *f.*
indisputa-ble, ADJ.: incontestabile, incontrastabile; certo. **-bleness**, S.: incontestabilità; certezza, evidenza, *f.* **-bly**, ADV.: indisputabilmente.
in-dissolubility, S.: indissolubilità; stabilità, fermezza, *f.* **-dissoluble**, ADJ.: indissolubile. **-dissoluble**, ADJ.: indissolubile. **-dissolubleness**, S.: indissolubilità; costanza, *f.* **-dissolubly**, ADV.: indissolubilmente. **-dissŏlvable**, ADJ.: indissolubile.
indistinc-t, ADJ.: indistinto, disordinato, confuso. **-tion**, **-tness**, S.: confusione, *f.* **-ly**, ADV.: indistintamente.
indistŭrbance, S.: tranquillità, quiete, *f.*
indite = *indict.* **-ment** = *indictment.*
individu-al, ADJ.: individuale; individuo; S.: individuo, *m.* **-ăllty**, S.: individualità, *f.* **-ally**, ADV.: individualmente. **-ate**, TR.: individuare, singolarizzare; distinguere.
indi-visibility, S.: indivisibilità, *f.* **-visible**, ADJ.: indivisibile. **-visibly**, ADV.: indivisibilmente.
indŏ-cible, **-cile**, ADJ.: indocile; caparbio, restio. **-cility**, S.: indocilità; caparbietà, *f.*
indŏctri-nate, TR.: addottrinare, insegnare, istruire, ammaestrare. **-nātion**, S.: istruzione, *f.*
indolen-ce, **-cy**, *S.*: *indolenza, trascuraggine, pigrizia, f.* **-t**, ADJ.: indolente; infingardo, pigro. **-tly**, ADV.: indolentemente, negligentemente, senza cura.
indŏmitable, ADJ.: indomabile.
indôr-se, TR.: indossare, girare. **-sement**, S.: indossamento, *m.* **-ser**, S.: indossante, *m.*
indrĕnch†, TR.: ammollare, inzuppare, sommergere.
indū-bious, ADJ.: senza dubbio, certo. **-bitable**, ADJ.: indubitabile; certo. **-bitably**, ADV.: indubitabilmente. **-bitate**, ADJ.: indubitato.
indū-ce, TR.: indurre; persuadere: *be —d*, indursi. **-cement**, S.: inducimento, incitamento, motivo, *m.* **-cer**, S.: inducitore, instigatore, *m.* **-cing**, ADJ.: induttivo.
indŭc-t, TR.: introdurre. **-tion**, S: introduzione, induzione; entrata, *f.* **-tive**, ADJ.: inducente, induttivo; persuasivo. **-tively**, ADV.: per conseguenza. **-tor**, S.: beneficiario, *m.*
indūe, TR.: investire; provvedere.
indŭl-ge, TR.: favorire; careggiare; concedere, dare: — *in*, abbandonarsi; applicarsi; *like to — one's self*, amare i propri comodi, accarezzarsi; — *children too much*, essere troppo indulgente verso i figliuoli. **-gence**, **-gency**, S.: indulgenza, *f.* **-gent**, ADJ.: indulgente; facile. **-gently**, ADV.: con indulgenza.
indŭlt(o), S.: indulto, privilegio, *m.*, esenzione, *f.*
indu-rate, TR.: indurare, divenir duro. **-rātion**, S.: induramento, *m.*
indŭs-trious, ADJ.: industrioso, laborioso; diligente. **-triously**, ADV.: industriosamente. **industry**, S.: industria; diligenza, assiduità, *f.*
indwelling, ADJ.: immanente; interno.
inēbri-ate, TR.: inebbriare, ubbriacare. **-ātion**, S.: inebbriazione, ubbriachezza, *f.*
inĕdited, ADJ.: inedito.
in-effability, S.: ineffabilità, *f.* **-ĕffable**, ADJ.: ineffabile, indicibile. **-ĕffableness** = *ineffability.* **-ĕffably**, ADV.: ineffabilmente.
ineffĕc-tive, **-tual**, ADJ.: inefficace; inutile. **-tually**, ADV.: senza effetto, inutilmente, in vano. **-tualness**, S.: inefficacia, *f.*
in-efficācious, ADJ.: inefficace. **-efficāciousness**, **-ĕfficacy**, S.: inefficacia, *f.*
inefficien-cy, S.: inefficacia; debolezza, *f.* **-t**, ADJ.: inefficace; insufficiente, debole.
inĕlegan-ce, **-cy**, S.: mancanza di grazia, inciviltà, *f.*; ADJ.: inelegante; incolto. **-t**, ADJ.: inelegante.
inĕloquent, ADJ.: senza eloquenza.
inĕpt, ADJ.: inetto, disadatto, goffo. **-ly**, ADV.: inettamente, disadattamente. **-ness**, **-itude**, S.: inettudine, incapacità, *f.*

inequálity, S.: inegualità, differenza, *f.*
in-errability, S.: infallibilità, *f.* **-érrable**, ADJ.: infallibile. **-érrableness** = inerrability. **-érrably**, ADV.: infallibilmente, senza errore. **-érrant**, ADJ.: infallibile. **-érringly**, ADV.: senza errore, certamente.
inért, ADJ.: inerte, infingardo, pigro. **-ly**, ADV.: con inerzia, pigramente. **-ness**, S.: inerzia, infingardaggine, *f.*
inéstimabl-e, ADJ.: inestimabile, imprezzabile. **-y**, ADV.: inestimabilmente.
inévident, ADJ.: non evidente, oscuro.
in-evitability, S.: impossibilità d' evitare; certezza, *f.* **-évitable**, ADJ.: inevitabile, da non evitarsi. **-évitably**, ADV.: inevitabilmente, infallibilmente.
inexáct, ADJ.: non esatto; scorretto, difettoso. **-ness**, S.: mancanza d' esattezza, *f.*
inexcúsabl-e, ADJ.: inescusabile. **-y**, ADV.: inescusabilmente.
inexháus-ted, ADJ.: inesausto; indeficiente. **-tible**, ADJ.: inesauribile.
inexisten-ce, S.: insussistenza, non-esistenza, *f.* **-t**, ADJ.: che non esiste.
in-exorability, S.: inesorabilità, *f.* **-éxorable**, ADJ.: inesorabile; implacabile.
inexpédien-ce, **-cy**, S.: sconvenevolezza, *f.* **-t**, ADJ.: sconvenevole.
inex-périence, S.: inesperienza, imperizia, *f.* **-périenced**, **-pért**, ADJ.: inesperto; senza pratica, poco pratico.
inéxpia-ble, ADJ.: inespiabile; inappurabile. **-bly**, ADV.: inespiabilmente, da non potersi espiare.
in-expláinable, **-éxplicable**, ADJ.: inesplicabile.
inexprés-sible, ADJ.: inesprimibile, ineffabile, indicibile. **-sibleness**, S.: ineffabilità, *f.* **-sibly**, ADV.: ineffabilmente.
inexpúgnable, ADJ.: inespugnabile, invincibile.
inextinguishable, ADJ.: inestinguibile.
inextirpable, ADJ.: inestirpabile.
inéxtric-able, ADJ.: inestricabile, insolubile. **-ably**, ADV.: in modo inestricabile.
ineye, TR.: inocchiare, innestare.
in-fallibility, S.: infallibilità, *f.* **-fál-lible**, ADJ.: infallibile; certo. **-fálli-bleness** = *infallibility*. **-fállibly**, ADV.: infallibilmente.
infáme†, TR.: infamare, diffamare.
infam-ous, ADJ.: infame. **-ously**, ADV.: infamemente, con infamia. **-ousness**, **-y**, S.: infamia, *f.*
in-fancy, S.: infanzia, infantilità, *f.* **-fant**, *S.: infante*; bambino, *m.* **-fánta**, *S.: infanta, f.* **-fánticide**, S.: *infanticidio, m.* **-fantile**, **-fantine**, ADJ.: *infantile, d' infante*; puerile. **-fantry**, S.: fanteria, *f.*: *light* —, fanteria leggiera; *heavy* —, fanteria di linea.
infárction, S.: costipazione, *f.*
infátigable, ADJ.: infaticabile.
infát-uate, TR.: infatuare; ammaliare. **-uátion**, S.: ammaliamento, impazzamento, *m.*
in-féasibility, S.: impraticabilità, impossibilità, *f.* **-féasible**, ADJ.: che non si può fare. **-féasibleness** = *infeasibility*.
inféc-t, TR.: infettare; corrompere. **-tion**, S.: infezione; contagione, *f.* **-tious**, ADJ.: infetto, contagioso: — *disease*, malattia appiccaticia. **-tiously**, ADV.: in modo contagioso. **-tiousness**, S.: qualità contagiosa; contagione, infezione, *f.* **-tive**, ADJ.: infettivo, contagioso.
inféc-und, ADJ.: infecondo, sterile. **-úndity**, S.: infecondità, sterilità, *f.*
infélici-ty, S.: infelicità, miseria, calamità, *f.* **-tous**, ADJ.: infelice; inetto.
infér, TR.: inferire, dedurre; conchiudere. **-able**, ADJ.: che si può inferire.
inference, S.: inferenza, induzione; conseguenza, conclusione, *f.*: *draw an* —, trarre (dedurre) conseguenza; arguire.
inféri-or, ADJ.: inferiore; subordinato: — *officer*, uffiziale subalterno, *m.*; *he is* — *to none*, egli non la cede a nessuno. **-órity**, S.: inferiorità, *f.*, grado inferiore, *m.*
inférnal, ADJ.: infernale, d' inferno: — *stone*, pietra infernale.
infér-tile, ADJ.: infertile, infecondo. **-tility**, S.: infecondità, sterilità, *f.*
infést, TR.: infestare, importunare, noiare, molestare. **-átion**, S.: infestazione, *f.* **-ive**, ADJ.: privo di gioia, tristo. **-ivity**, S.: mancanza d' allegria, tristezza, *f.* **-uous**, ADJ.: infesto; importuno; pericoloso.
infeudátion, S.: infeudazione, *f.*
infi-del, S.: infedele; miscredente, *m.* **-délity**, S.: infedeltà; perfidia, *f.*; inganno, *m.*
infiltrate, TR.: infiltrare.
in-finite, ADJ.: infinito, illimitato, immesto. **-finitely**, ADV.: infinitamente. **-finiteness**, S.: infinità, illimitazione, immensità, *f.* **-finitésimal**, ADJ.: infinitesimale. **-finitive**, S.: (*gram.*) infinitivo, *m.* **-finitude**, **-finity**, S.: infinità, *f.*; gran numero, *m.*
infirm, ADJ.: infermo, debole. **-ary**, S.: infermeria, *f.* **-ity**, S.: infermità; fralezza, *f.* **-ness**, S.: debolezza; fiacchezza, *f.*
infix, TR.: figgere dentro; scolpire nella mente, imprimere.
in-fláme, TR.: infiammare, accendere;

INTR.: infiammarsi, accendersi. **-flāmer**, S.: accenditore; istigatore, *m.* **-flammability**, S.: infiammabilità, *f.* **-flammable**, ADJ.: infiammabile, accendibile. **-flammableness** = *inflammability*. **-flammātion**, S.: infiammazione, *f.* **-flămmatory**, ADJ.: infiammatorio.

inflā-te, TR.: enfiare, gonfiare; ispirare. **-ted**, ADJ.: enfiato, gonfio; tronfio, turgido. **-tion**, S.: enfiature, *f.*; gonfiamento, *m.*

inflĕc-t, TR.: inflettere, piegare; (*gram.*) dare le desinenze a; coniugare. **-tion**, S.: inflessione; variazione; (*mus.*) modulazione di voce, *f.*; (*gram.*) declinazione; coniugazione, *f.* **-tive**, ADJ.: flessibile; pieghevole.

in-flexibility, S.: inflessibilità; pertinacia, ostinazione, *f.* **-flĕxible**, ADJ.: inflessibile; inalterabile; ostinato. **-flexibleness**=*inflexibility*. **-flĕxibly**, ADV.: inflessibilmente; ostinatamente. **-flĕxion** = *inflection*.

inflic-t, TR.: infliggere; condannare. **-ter**, S.: punitore, condannatore, *m.* **-tion**, S.: punimento, *m.*, condannazione, *f.* **-tive**, ADJ.: stabilito in pena, condannatorio.

in-fluence 1, S.: influenza, *f.*; ascendente, *m.*, autorità, *f.* **-fluence** 2, TR.: influire, causare. **-fluent**, ADJ.: influente. **-fluĕntial**, ADJ.: che influisce. **-flux**, S.: influsso; affluenza, *f.*; sboccamento (d' un fiume), *m.*; infusione, *f.* **-flŭxive**, ADJ.: influente. **-fluĕnza**, S.: influenza (malattia), *f.*

infōld, TR.: involvere; inviluppare.

infōliate, TR.: coprire di foglie.

infōrm, TR.: informare, dar notizia, insegnare; notificare: — *against one*, accusare alcuno; — *one of*, ragguagliare uno di. **-al**, ADJ.: irregolare. **-ălity**, S.: irregolarità, *f.* **-ant**, S.: che informa; denunzistore, accusatore, *m.* **-ātion**, S.: informazione; instruzione, *f.* **-ed**, ADJ.: istrutto: *well* —, dottrinato, erudito. **-er**, S.: accusatore, delatore, *m.*

infōrmidable†, ADJ.: non formidabile.

infōr-mity, S.: informità, difformità, bruttezza, *f.* **-mous**, ADJ.: informe, sformato.

infōrtunate†, ADJ.: infortunato, infelice.

infrăc-t, TR.: infrangere, rompere. **-tion**, S.: infrangimento; trasgredimento, *m.* **-tor**, S.: trasgreditore.

infrăngible, ADJ.: infrangibile.

infrĕquen-ce, **-cy**, S.: infrequenza, rarità, *f.* **-t**, ADJ.: infrequente, raro.

infring-e, TR.: trasgredire; violare. **-ement**, S.: *trasgressione, infrazione, violazione, f.* **-er**, *S.: trasgreditore*, violatore, *m.*

infū-riate, ADJ.: arrabbiato, furioso. **-riate**, TR.: render furioso.

infŭscate, TR.: annerare; oscurare.

infū-se, TR.: infondare; ispirare. **-sible**, ADJ.: infusibile. **-sion**, S.: infusione, *f.*, infondimento, *m.* **-sive**, ADJ.: atto ad essere infuso. **-sōria**, S.: (*zoöl.*) infusori, *m. pl.*

ingăthering, S.: raccolta, *f.*

ingĕmi-nate 1, ADJ.: geminato, raddoppiato. **-nate** 2, TR.: geminare, raddoppiare. **-nātion**, S.: geminazione, *f.*, raddoppiamento, *m.*; ripetizione, *f.*

ingĕner-able, ADJ.: ingenerabile. **-at(ed)**, ADJ.: ingenito, innato.

ingĕnious, ADJ.: ingegnoso, inventivo. **-ly**, ADV.: ingegnosamente, con ingegno. **-ness**, S.: ingegno, genio, *m.*; acutezza, *f.*

in-genuity, S.: ingenuità, franchezza, sincerità; destrezza, abilità, *f.*; genio, *m.* **-gĕnuous**, ADJ.: ingenuo, sincero, franco. **-gĕnuously**, ADV.: ingenuamente; francamente. **-gĕnuousness**, S.: ingenuità; sincerità, *f.*, candore, *m.*

inglōrious, ADJ.: inglorioso, disonorevole, disonorato. **-ly**, ADV.: disonorevolmente. **-ness**, S.: poca gloria; disonestà, *f.*

ingot, S.: verga (d' oro o d' argento), *f.*

ingrâft, TR.: innestare, inocchiare. **-ment**, S.: innestamento, *m.*

ingrain 1, S.: sorta di tappeto, *m.* **ingrāin** 2, TR.: tingere in lana.

ingrāte(ful), ADJ.: ingrato; nauseoso; vile. **-fulness**, S.: ingratitudine, *f.*

ingrātiate, INTR.: entrare in grazia, ingraziarsi: — *one's self with*, insinuarsi nelle buone grazie di.

ingrătitude, S.: ingratitudine, *f.*

ingrăvidate, TR.: ingravidare.

ingrēdient, S.: ingrediente, *m.*

in-gress, **-grĕssion**, S.: ingresso, *m.*, entrata, *f.*

inguinal, ADJ.: inguinale.

ingŭlf, TR.: inghiottire, ingoiare avidamente; divorare.

ingŭrgi-tate, INTR.: ingurgitare, divorare. **-tātion**, S.: ingorgamento, *m.*, ghiottoneria, voracità, *f.*

inhăb-ile†, ADJ.: inabile, disadatto, incapace. **-ility**†, S.: inabilità, *f.*

inhăbit, TR.: abitare, dimorare; vivere. **-able**, ADJ.: abitabile. **-ance**, S.: dimoranza, *f.*; domicilio, *m.*, residenza, *f.* **-ant**, S.: abitante, abitatore, *m.* **-ātion**, S.: abitazione, dimora, *f.* **-er**, S.: abitante, abitatore, *m.*

inhāle, TR.: spirare, respirare.

inhar-mōnic(al), **-mōnious**, ADJ.: senza armonia, discordante.

inhēr-e, INTR.: essere inerente. **-ence**

-ency, S.: inerenza, *f.* **-ent**, ADJ.: inerente; inseparable.

inhĕrit, TR.: ereditare. **-able**, ADJ.: che si può ereditare, ereditario. **-ance**, S.: eredità, *f.*, ereditaggio, *m.* **-or**, S.: erede, *m.*; ereda, *f.* **-ress**, **-rix**, S.: ereda, ereditiera, *f.*

inhēsion, S.: inerenza, *f.*; attaccamento, *m.*

inhib-it, TR.: inibire, proibire; vietare. **-ition**, S.: inibizione, proibizione, *f.*

inhŏspit-able, ADJ.: inospitale; duro. **-ably**, ADV.: in modo inospitale. **-ableness**, **-ălity**, S.: inospitalità, *f.*

inhū-man, ADJ.: inumano, barbaro, crudele. **-mănity**, S.: inumanità, crudeltà, *f.* **-manly**, ADV.: inumanamente, crudelmente.

inhū-mate, TR.: interrare, sotterrare, seppellire. **-mātion**, S.: sepoltura, *f.* **-me** = *inhumate*.

inimăginable, ADJ.: inconcepibile.

inimical, ADJ.: inimichevole; ostile: *be — to*, osteggiare.

in-imitability, S.: incapacità d'imitazione, *f.* **-ĭmitable**, ADJ.: inimitabile. **-imitably**, ADV.: inimitabilmente.

iniqui-tous, ADJ.: iniquitoso, iniquo, ingiusto; cattivo. **-tousness**, **-ty**, S.: iniquità; ingiustizia, *f.*

ini-tial, ADJ.: iniziale; cominciante: — *letter*, lettera maiuscola, *f.* **-tiate**, TR.: iniziare; dare le prime lezioni; INTR.: iniziarsi. **-tiātion**, S.: iniziazione, *f.*; cominciamento, *m.* **-tiatory**, ADJ.: iniziale, iniziativo. **-tion**, S.: inizio, *m.*

injĕc-t, TR.: fare un'iniezione, schizzettare. **-tion**, S.: iniezione, *f.*

injudicious, ADJ.: poco giudizioso. **-ly**, ADV.: senza giudizio. **-ness**, S.: mancanza di giudizio, mancanza di considerazione, *f.*

injŭnction, S.: comando, ordine, *m.*

in-jure, TR.: ingiuriare, far ingiuria *or* torto a; offendere, nuocere (a): — *a good cause*, nuocere ad una buona causa. **-jurer**, S.: ingiuriatore, offenditore, *m.* **-jūrious**, ADJ.: ingiurioso, ingiusto, oltraggioso. **-jūriously**, ADV.: ingiuriosamente. **-jūriousness**, S.: qualità ingiuriosa, prontezza ad ingiuriare, *f.* **-jury**, S.: ingiuria; offesa, *f.*, oltraggio; danno, *m.*

injŭstice, S.: ingiustizia: iniquità, *f.*, torto, *m.*

ink 1, S.: inchiostro, *m.*: *daub with —*, schiccherare. **ink** 2, TR.: imbrattare con inchiostro. **-blot**, S.: sgorbio, *m.* **-horn**, *S.*: *calamaio*, *m.*

inkle, S.: passamano stretto. **-weaver**, *S.*: *passamanaro*, *m.*

inkling, S.: avviso; vento, sentore, *m.*

ink-maker, S.: facitore d'inchiostro, *m.* **-stand**, S.: calamaio, *m.* **-y**, ADJ.: macchiato d'inchiostro; nero come inchiostro.

inlāid, ADJ.: intarsiato: — *work*, tarsia, intarsiatura, *f.*

inland, ADJ.: interiore, interno; S.: interiore d'un paese, *m.* **-er**, S.: abitante [illegible]

inlăpidate, TR.: petrificare.

in-lay†, S.: intarsiatura, *f.*, lavoro a tarsia, *m.* **-lāy**†, IRR.; TR.: intarsiare rieggiare.

inlet, S.: passaggio, *m.*, entrata, *f.*

inlist, TR.: mettere in lista.

inlŏok, TR.: rinchiudere, serrare.

inly, ADJ.: interiore, interno; ADV. teriormente, internamente.

inmate, S.: pigionale, *m.*

inmost, ADJ.: interiore; profondissimo; recondito, segreto: — *recess*, l'imo.

inn 1, S.: osteria, *f.*, albergo, ostello; taverna, *f.*: *landlord, lady of an —*, albergatore, -trice; *stop (put up) at an —*, smontare ad un albergo; *keep an —*, tenere osteria. **inn** 2, TR.: albergare, al-

innate, **-d**, ADJ.: innato, naturale. **-ness**,

inn-holder, **-keeper**, S.: oste, albergatore, locandiere, *m.*

innocen-ce, **-cy**, S.: innocenza, *f.* **-t**, ADJ.: innocente; puro; S.: innocente; idiota, *m.* **-tly**, ADV.: innocentemente.

innŏcuous, ADJ.: innocuo, non nocivo. **-ly**, ADV.: innocuamente. **-ness**, S.: qualità innocua; innocenza, *f.*

innŏminate, ADJ.: innominato.

inno-vate, TR.: innovare, innovellare.

innŏxious, ADJ.: che non nuoce, non nocivo, innocente. **-ly**, ADV.: non nocivamente. **-ness**, S.: qualità innocente, *f.*

innuĕndo, S.: avviso indiretto; sentore, *m.*

innūmer-able, ADJ.: innumerabile. **-ableness**, S.: quantità innumerabile, infinità, *f.* **-ably**, ADV.: innumerabilmente. **-ous** = *innumerable*.

inobēdien-ce†, S.: inobbedienza, *f.* **-t**,

inobsĕr-vable, ADJ.: inosservabile; impercettibile. **-vance**, S.: mancanza d'obbedienza, negligenza, *f.*

inŏcu-late, TR.: inocchiare, inoculare, innestare. **-lātion**, S.: [illegible], *f.*, innesto, *m.* **-lator**, S.: [illegible], nestatore, *m.*

inòdorous, ADJ.: inodorabile, senza odore.
inoffènsive, ADJ.: inoffensivo; innocente. **-ly**, ADV.: innocentemente. **-ness**, S.: innocenza, *f.*
inofficious, ADJ.: incivile, scortese. **-ness**, S.: scortesia, *f.*
inòpinate†, ADJ.: inopinato, improvviso, subito. **-ly†**, ADV.: improvvisamente, subitamente.
inopportùne, ADJ.: inopportuno, intempestivo. **-ly**, ADV.: inopportunamente.
inôrdi-nacy, S.: sregolatezza, *f.; eccesso, m.* **-nate**, ADJ.: inordinato, irregolare. **-nately**, ADV.: inordinatamente. **-nateness**, **-nàtion**, S.: inordinatezza, *f.*
inorgànical, ADJ.: senza organi.
inòsculate, INTR.: (*anat.*) combaciarsi, esser congiunto.
inquest, S.: inchiesta, ricerca, *f.*, ricercamento, *m.*, investigazione, *f.: coroner's* —, inchiesta del 'coroner.'
inquietude, S.: inquietudine; agitazione, *f.*
inqui-nate†, TR.: imbrattare, contaminare, macchiare; lordare. **-nàtion**, S.: imbrattamente, contaminamento, *m.;* macchia, *f.*
inqui-rable, ADJ.: che può essere ricercato. **-re**, TR.: ricercare; esaminare; INTR.: informarsi: — *into*, investigare; — *at Mr. B.'s*, s' indirizzarsi dal sig. B. **-rer**, S.: inquisitore, ricercatore, *m.* **-ry**, S.: inchiesta, ricerca; esaminazione, *f.*
in-quisìtion, S.: inquisizione; ricerca, *f.* **-quisitive**, ADJ.: curioso, bramoso di sapere; investigatore. **-quisitively**, ADV.: con curiosità, curiosamente. **-quisitiveness**, S.: curiosità; ricerca, *f.* **-quisitor**, S.: inquisitore, ricercatore; giudice del santo ufficio, *m.*
inràil, TR.: chiudere con cancelli o balustri.
inroad, S.: incursione, invasione, *f.*
inròll, TR.: arrolare. **-ment**, S.: arrolamento, registratamento, *m.*
insalù-brious, ADJ.: insalubre, malsano. **-brity**, S.: insalubrità, *f.*
insànable, ADJ.: insanabile, incurabile.
in-sàne, ADJ.: insano, pazzo, demente; stolto. **-sànely**, ADV.: insanamente, pazzamente. **-sànity**, S.: insania, pazzia, *f.*
insà-tiable, ADJ.: insaziabile; smoderato. **-tiableness**, S.: insaziabilità, *f.* **-tiably**, ADV.: insaziabilmente. **-tiety**, S.: insazietà, insaziabilità, *f.*
insàturable, ADJ.: insaziabile.
in-scribe, TR.: iscrivere, porre iscrizione; indirizzare; (*geom.*) disegnare: — *a poem to*, dedicare *un poema a.* **-scription**, *S.: iscrizione; soprascritta, f.*

in-scrutability, S.: inscrutabilità, *f.* **-scrùtable**, ADJ.: inscrutabile, investigabile.
insculpt†, TR.: scolpire, intagliare. **-ture**, S.: scolpitura, *f.*, intaglio, *m.*
inseam, TR.: cicatrizzare.
insect, S.: insetto, *m.* **-ivorous**, ADJ.: insettivoro. **-powder**, S.: polvere insetticida, *f.*
insectà-tion†, S.: persecuzione, *f.* **-tor†**, S.: perseguitatore, persecutore, *m.*
insecù-re, ADJ.: non sicuro, rischioso, pericoloso; incerto. **-rity**, S.: rischio, pericolo, *m.;* incertezza, *f.*
insènsate, ADJ.: insensato, stupido.
in-sensibility, S.: insensibilità; stupidezza, *f.* **-sènsible**, ADJ.: insensibile; impercettibile. **-sènsibleness** = *insensibility.* **-sènsibly**, ADV.: insensibilmente.
in-separability, S.: indivisibilità, *f.* **-sèparable**, ADJ.: inseparabile, indivisibile. **-sèparableness** = *inseparability.* **-sèparably**, ADV.: inseparabilmente.
in-sèrt, TR.: inserire, intercalare; aggiungere; far l' inserzione: — *this advertisement*, fate l' inserzione di questo annunzio. **-sèrtion**, S.: inserzione, intercalazione, *f.*
inship†, TR.: imbarcare.
inshrine = *enshrine.*
inside, S.: interiore, interno, *m.*, parte interna, *f.*, fondo, *m.;* ADJ.: dell' interiore, dell' interno: *the* — *of an edifice*, il di dentro di un edifizio.
insid-iate†, TR.: insidiare. **-ious**, ADJ.: insidioso. **-iousness**, S.: insidia, *f.* **-iously**, ADV.: insidiosamente, con insidia.
insight, S.: inspezione; conoscenza intima, notizia, *f.;* indizio, *m.*
insignia, S. PL.: insegne, *f. pl.*
insignifican-ce, **-cy**, S.: cosa vana, cosa inutile, *f.* **-t**, ADJ.: insignificante. **-tly**, ADV.: in modo insignificante.
insin-cère, ADJ.: non sincero, falso, perfido; guasto, corrotto. **-cèrely**, ADV.: in modo poco sincero, dissimulatamente, falsamente. **-cèrity**, S.: mancanza di sincerità, dissimulazione, falsità, *f.*
insi'new†, TR.: fortificare, corroborare.
insin-uant, ADJ.: insinuante. **-uate**, TR.: insinuare, intimare; introdurre; INTR.: insinuarsi; introdursi. **-uàtion**, S.: insinuazione, *f.;* introducimento, *m.* **-uative**, ADJ.: insinuante.
insip-id, ADJ.: insipido, scipito, sciocco. **-idity**, S.: insipidezza, *f.* **-idly**, ADV.: insipidamente, scipitamente. **-idness**, S.: insipidezza, *f.* **-ience**, S.: insipienza, sciocchezza, *f.*
insist, INTR.: insistere, persistere.
insìtion, S.: innestamento, *m.*

impŏwer = *empower*.
im-practicabĭlity = *impracticableness*. **-prăcticable**, ADJ.: impraticabile; impossibile. **-prăcticableness**, S.: qualità di ciò che è impraticabile; impossibilità, *f.*
imprecate, TR.: imprecare, maledire. **-cātion**, S.: imprecazione, maledizione, *f.* **-catory**, ADJ.: imprecativo.
imprĕgn†, TR.: impregnare; riempire.
imprĕg-nable, ADJ.: inespugnabile. **-nate**[1], ADJ.: impregnato. **-nate**[2], TR.: impregnare; satollare; INTR.: impregnarsi; imbevere, riempirsi. **-nātion**, S.: impregnamento, *m.*; pregnezza, *f.*
impresārio, S.: impresario, *m.*
imprescriptible, ADJ.: (*leg.*) imprescrittibile.
im-press[1], S.: impressione; impronta; sentenza, *f*, motto, *m.* **-prĕss**[2], TR.: imprimere, improntare; levar gente per forza: — *on the mind*, scolpire nella mente; —*ed with the idea*, compenetrato dell' idea. **-prĕssion**, S.: impressione; stampa; edizione, *f.* **-prĕssive**, ADJ.: imprimente; espressivo, energico, impetuoso. **-prĕssively**, ADV.: energicamente. **-prĕssure**, S.: impressione; impronta, *f.*
imprimis, ADV.: primieramente.
imprint[1], TR.: imprimere; stampare.
imprint[2], S.: impronta, *f.*; luogo di stampa, *m.*
imprison, TR.: imprigionare. **-ment**, S.: imprigionamento, *m.*
im-probability, S.: improbabilità, *f.* **-prŏbable**, ADJ.: improbabile, inverosimile. **-prŏbably**, ADV.: improbabilmente.
improbate, TR.: disapprovare, riprovare, rigettare, condannare. **-bātion**, S.: riprovazione, *f.*, rigettamento, *m.*
imprŏbity, S.: improbità; disonestà; malignità, *f.*
imprŏmptu, S.: improvvisata, *f.*
imprŏper, ADJ.: improprio, disadatto; indecente. **-ly**, ADV.: impropriamente.
improportion-able, **-ate**, ADJ.: improporzionale.
imprŏpriate†, TR.: appropriarsi; arrogarsi.
impropriety, S.: improprietà; sconvenevolezza, *f.*
imprŏsperous, ADJ.: sfortunato, sventurato, infelice. **-ly**, ADV.: sfortunatamente, infelicemente.
im-provability = *improvableness*. **-prŏvable**, ADJ.: che si può migliorare. **-prŏvableness**, S.: capacità di miglioramento, *f.* **-prŏve**, TR.: migliorare; perfezionare; INTR.: profittare; far progressi; ammendarsi: — *one's condition*, migliorar sorte; — *one's mind*, addottrinarsi; *be greatly* —*d*, aver fatto grandi progressi. **-prŏvement**, S.: miglioramento; avanzamento, progresso, *m.*; coltivazione, *f.* **-prŏver**, S.: che migliora; che profitta, che avanza.
im-provided†, ADJ.: improvviso, inaspettato. **-prŏvidence**, S.: improvidenza, imprudenza, *f.* **-prŏvident**, ADJ.: improvido, inconsiderato. **-prŏvidently**, ADV.: improvidamente.
imprŏvisator, S.: improvvisatore, improvvisante, *m.*
improvision, S.: improvidenza, *f.*
imprŭden-ce, S.: imprudenza; indiscrezione, *f.* **-t**, ADJ.: imprudente; indiscreto. **-tly**, ADV.: imprudentamente.
impuden-ce, **-cy**, S.: impudenza, sfacciataggine, *f.* **-t**, ADJ.: impudente, sfacciato, sfrontato. **-tly**, ADV.: impudentemente, sfrontatamente.
impudicity, S.: impudicizia, *f.*
impūgn, TR.: impugnare, oppugnare; assaltare, assalire. **-er**, S.: impugnatore; assaltatore, *m.*
impūissance, S.: impotenza; debolezza, *f.*
im-pulse, **-pŭlsion**, S.: impulso, incitamento, *m.* **-pŭlsive**, ADJ.: impulsivo, incitativo.
impū-nely, ADV.: impunemente. **-nity**, S.: impunità, *f.*
impūr-e, ADJ.: impuro, immondo; disonesto; impudico. **-ely**, ADV.: impuramente. **-ity**, S.: impurità, immondizia; oscenità, *f.*
impŭrple, TR.: tingere di color di porpora, imporporare. **-d**, ADJ.: porporato, purpureo.
impū-table, ADJ.: imputabile. **-tableness**, S.: qualità d' esser imputabile, *f.*; imputamento, *m.* **-tātion**, S.: imputazione, *f.* **-tative**, ADJ.: imputativo, incolpante. **-te**, TR.: imputare, attribuire la colpa. **-ter**, S.: imputatore, accusatore, *f.*
impu-trescibility, S.: incorruttibilità, *f.* **-trĕscible**, ADJ.: immarcescibile, incorruttibile.
in, PREP.: in; entro, dentro; fra: — *the*, nel (nello, nella, nei, negli, nelle); — *as much as* = *inasmuch as*; — *the city*, nella città; — *comparison*, a paragone; — *contempt*, per disprezzo; — *the daytime*, di giorno; — *my opinion*, a mio parere; — *order*, per ordine; — *order to*, affine di, per; ad effetto, per cagione di; — *respect to*, per rispetto a; — *short*, in somma, finalmente; — *the times past*, per lo passato; *be* —, essere impegnato; *be* — *for it*, esser in mal punto; *go* —, entrare.

inability, s.: inabilità, incapacità, *f.*
inăbstinenee†, s.: intemperanza, immoderanza, *f.*
inac-cessibility, s.: inaccessibilità, impossibilità d' approcciare, *f.* **-cĕssible**, ADJ.: inaccessibile. **-cĕssibleness** = *inaccessibility*.
inăccu-racy, s.: inesattezza, trascuranza, negligenza, *f.* **-rate**, ADJ.: poco esatto, trascurato, negligente. **-rately**, ADV.: senza esattezza, incorrettamente.
inăc-tion, s.: inazione; disoccupazione, *f.* **-tive**, ADJ.: non attivo, ozioso, pigro. **-tively**, ADV.: senza attività; pigramente. **-tivity**, s.: inerzia, trascuraggine, *f.*
inădequate, ADJ.: inadeguato, sproporzionato, difettoso, imperfetto, incompleto. **-ly**, ADV.: imperfettamente. **-ness**, s.: sproporzione; insufficienza, *f.*
inadmissible, ADJ.: inammissibile.
inadvĕrten-ce, **-cy**, s.: inavvertenza, *f.*, trascuraggine, *f.*: *through* —, per inavvertenza. **-t**, ADJ.: disattento, trascurato. **-tly**, ADV.: inadvertentemente, trascuratamente.
in-affability, s.: incompatibilità, scortesia, *f.* **-ăffable**, ADJ.: incompatibile, scortese.
inaffectātion, s.: sincerità, *f.*
inălienable, ADJ.: inalienabile. **-ness**, s.: inalienabilità, *f.*
inălterable, ADJ.: inalterabile.
inadmissible, ADJ.: inamissibile.
inămour, TR.: innamorare.
ināne, ADJ.: vuoto, vano; inefficace.
inăni-mate, **-mated**, ADJ.: inanimato.
in-anition, s.: inedia; mancanza di forza, debolezza, *f.* **-ănity**, s.: inanità; vacuità; inutilità, *f.*
inăppetency, s.: inappetenza, *f.*; disgusto, m.
inăppli-cable, ADJ.: non applicabile. **-cātion**, s.: trascurataggine, negligenza, incuria, *f.*
inapprehĕnsive, ADJ.: trascurante.
inăptitude, s.: disadattaggine; inabilità, *f.*
inărable, ADJ.: inetto ad essere arato.
inărch, TR.: (*gard.*) innestare.
inarticulate, ADJ.: inarticolato, indistinto. **-ly**, ADV.: indistintamente. **-ness**, s.: pronunzia inarticolata, *f.*
inartificial, ADJ.: senza arte; naturale, puro. **-y**, ADV.: naturalmente.
inasmŭch, ADV.: — *as*, in quanto chè, perchè, poichè, giacchè.
inattĕn-tion, s.: inattenzione; trascuranza, *f.* **-tive**, ADJ.: disattento, trascurato.
inaudible, ADJ.: inaudibile.
inăugu-rate, TR.: *inaugurare*, investire *-rātions*, s.: *inaugurazione*, investitura, *f.*

inauspicious, ADJ.: malauguroso, infausto. **-ly**, ADV.: infaustamente, infelicemente.
inbēing, s.: inerenza, *f.*
inborn, ADJ.: innato; ingenito; naturale.
inbrēathed, ADJ.: inspirato.
inbred, ADJ.: prodotto dentro; del paese.
incāge, TR.: ingabbiare; imprigionare.
incălculable, ADJ.: fuor di calcolo, innumerabile.
incandĕscen-ce, s.: incandescenza, *f.* **-t**, ADJ.: incandescente.
in-cantātion, s.: incantamento; incantesimo, *m.* **-căntatory**, ADJ.: incantevole, magico.
incăntoṇ, TR.: unire ad un cantone, *f.*
in-capability, s.: incapacità, *f.* **-cāpable**, ADJ.: incapace; inabile. **-cāpableness** = *incapability*.
incapācious, ADJ.: incapace; stretto, angusto. **-ness**, s.: strettezza, *f.*
incapăc-itate, TR.: rendere incapace. **-ity**, s.: incapacità, inabilità, *f.*
incărcer-ate, TR.: incarcerare, imprigionare. **-ātion**, s.: incarcerazione, *f.*
incăr-nadine†, ADJ.: incarnatino, incarnato. **-nate**, ADJ.: incarnato. **-nate**, TR.: incarnare. **-nātion**, s.: incarnazione, *f.* **-native**, ADJ.: (*med.*) incarnativo.
incāse, TR.: incassare; serrare, rinchiudere; coprire.
incăsk, TR.: imbottare.
incăutious, ADJ.: incauto; trascurato. **-ly**, ADV.: incautamente; imprudentemente. **-ness**, s.: mancanza di cautela, imprudenza, *f.*
incĕn-diary, s.: incendiario; sedizioso, capo di parti, *m.* **-dious**, ADJ.: sedizioso.
in-cĕnse, TR.: inasprire, irritare; provocare: *be* (*become*) —*d*, adirarsi, sdegnarsi, inasprirsi. **ĭn-cense**, s.: incenso, *m.* **-cĕnsement†**, s.: collera; furia, *f.*, furore, *m.* **-cĕnsion†**, s.: abbruciamento, *m.* **-cĕnsive**, ADJ.: incensivo, infiammante. **-cĕnsor**, s.: aizzatore, *m.* **-cĕnsory**, s.: incensiere, turibile, *m.* **-cĕntive**, ADJ.: incitativo, impulsivo; s.: incentivo, motivo; incoraggiamento, *m.*
incĕp-tion, s.: cominciamento, principio, *m.* **-tive**, ADJ.: cominciante, elementale. **-tor**, s.: cominciante, principiante, *m.*
incĕr-tainty†, **-titude**, s.: incertezza· dubbiezza, *f.*
incĕssant, ADJ.: incessantemente, tinuamente; sempre.
in-cest, s.: incesto, *m.* -[illegible] ADJ.: incestuoso.
ĭnch 1, s.: dito, pollice (duodecima

d' un piede), *m.*: — *by* —, poco a poco, a goccia a goccia, poco per volta. **inch** 2, TR.: misurare a dita; INTR.: avanzarsi a piccioli gradi.
inchêst, TR.: incassare.
inchmeal, s.: pezzo lungo d' un dito, *m.*
in-chọạte, TR.: principiare, cominciare. **-chọạ̄tion**, s.: principio, cominciamento, *m.* **-chōative**, ADJ.: incoativo.
inci-dence, **-dency**, s.: (*geom.*) incidenza, *f.*; (*fig.*) caso, accidente, *m.* **-dent**, ADJ.: incidente; casuale, fortuito; inseparabile; s.: accidente, caso, *m.* **-dĕntal**, ADJ.: accidentale, fortuito. **-dĕntally**, ADV.: incidentemente.
incinerā̤tion, s.: incinerazione, *f.*
incipiency, s.: cominciamento, *m.*
incircumspĕction, s.: mancanza di cautela, negligenza, *f.*
in-cise, TR.: incidere, tagliare. **-cision**, s.: incisione, *f.*; taglio, *m.* **-cisive**, ADJ.: incisivo. **-cisor**, s.: incisore; dente incisivo, *m.*
in-citā̤tion, s.: incitamento, *m.* **-cite**, TR.: incitare, eccitare; instigare; sollecitare; indurre. **-citement**, s.: incitamento, stimolo, *m.* **-citing**, ADJ.: incitativo; s.: incitamento, eccitamento, *m.*
inciv-il, ADJ.: incivile, scortese; grossolano. **-ility**, s.: inciviltà, scortesia; rustichezza, rozzezza, *f.* **-illy**, ADV.: incivilmente; rusticamente.
inclâsp, TR.: tener fermo.
inclĕmen-cy, s.: inclemenza; severità, *f.*, rigore, *m.* **-t**, ADJ.: inclemente, rigoroso, severo.
in-clinable, ADJ.: inclinabile, inclinevole; prono. **-clinā̤tion**, s.: inclinazione; propensione; tendenza, *f.*; pendio, *m.* **-cline**, (IN)TR.: inclinare, inchinare; incurvare; tendere. **-clining**, ADJ.: inclinante; s.: inclinamento, *m.*; propensione, *f.*
inclip†, TR.: abbracciare; circondare, cingere.
inclöịster = *encloister*.
inclō-se, TR.: rinchiudere; includere (una lettera): *the* —*d*, l' inclusa. **-sure**, s.: ricinto; orto assiepato, *m.*
inclọ̈ud, TR.: annuvolare; offuscare.
inclū-de, TR.: inchiudere; comprendere, contenere: *not* —*d*, non compreso. **-sive**, ADJ.: inclusivo, che comprende. **-sively**, ADV.: inclusivamente.
incŏg = *incognito*.
incŏg-itable, ADJ.: incogitabile. **-itancy**, s.: inconsiderazione, inconsideratezza, *f.* **-itant**, **-itative**, ADJ.: sconsiderato; imprudente.
incŏgnito, ADJ.: incognito; ADV.: incognitamente.
incohĕren-ce, **-cy**, s.: incoerenza, discrepanza, *f.* **-t**, ADJ.: incoerente, discrepante. **-tly**, ADV.: in modo incoerente.
incom-bustibility, s.: incombustibilità, *f.* **-bŭstible**, ADJ.: incombustibile. **-bŭstibleness** = *incombustibility*.
income, s.: rendita, entrata, *f.* **-tax**, s.: imposta sulla rendita, *f.*
incom-mensurability, s.: incommensurabilità, *f.* **-mĕnsurable**, **-mĕnsurate**, ADJ.: incommensurabile.
incŏm-modate†, **-mōde**, TR.: incomodare, scomodare. **-mōdious**, ADJ.: incomodo, inconveniente, importuno. **-mōdiously**, ADV.: incomodamente. **-mōdiousness**, **-mŏdity**, s.: incomodità, *f.*, incomodo, *m.*
incom-municability, s.: incomunicabilità, *f.* **-mūnicable**, ADJ.: incomunicabile. **-mūnicably**, ADV.: in modo incomunicabile. **-mūnicating**, ADJ.: senza comunicazione.
incom-mutability, s.: incommutabilità, *f.* **-mūtable**, ADJ.: incommutabile.
incompăct(ed), ADJ.: disgiunto, disunito, incoerente; vago.
incŏmparabl-e, ADJ.: incomparabile; eccellente. **-eness**, s.: eccellenza, *f.* **-y**, ADV.: incomparabilmente.
incompăssionate, ADJ.: senza compassione; duro, crudele.
incom-patibility, s.: incompatibilità, *f.* **-pătible**, ADJ.: incompatibile; contrario, opposto. **-pătibly**, ADV.: in modo incompatibile.
incŏmpeten-cy, s.: incompetenza; incapacità, *f.* **-t**, ADJ.: incompetente; incapace. **-tly**, ADV.: incompetentemente.
incomplēte, ADJ.: incompleto, incompiuto, difettoso, imperfetto. **-ness**, s.: imperfezione, *f.*
incompliance, s.: poca compiacenza, ritrosia, *f.*
incompō-sed†, ADJ.: incomposto, disordinato. **-sedness**, s.: disordine, *m.*
incompre-hensibility, s.: incomprensibilità, *f.* **-hĕnsible**, ADJ.: incomprensibile. **-hĕnsibly**, ADV.: incomprensibilmente.
incom - pressibility, s.: incapacità d' esser compresso, *f.* **-prĕssible**, ADJ.: che non può esser compresso.
inconcĕalable, ADJ.: che non si può celare.
inconcēiva-ble, ADJ.: inconcepibile, incomprensibile. **-bly**, ADV.: in modo inconcepibile.
inconcinnity, s.: disproporzione, *f.*
inconclūsive, ADJ.: inconcludente. **-ly**, ADV.: senza evidenza. **-ness**, s.: mancanza d' evidenza, *f.*
inconcŏc-t(ed), ADJ.: indigesto. **-tion**, s.: indigestione, crudità, *f.*

incondĕnsable, ADJ.: non condensabile.
inconfŏrmity, S.: mancanza di conformità, *f.*
incŏn-gruence, **-grūity**, S.: incongruenza, incongruità; inconsistenza; assurdità, *f.* **-gruous**, ADJ.: incongruo, improprio. **-gruously**, ADV.: incongruentemente, impropriamente.
incŏnsciọnable, ADJ.: senza coscienza, irragionevole.
incŏnsẹ-quence, S.: inconseguenza, *f.* **-quent**, **-quĕntial**, ADJ.: irregolare, fondato, mal falso.
inconsidẹr-able, ADJ.: inconsiderabile; di poco momento. **-ableness**, S.: poca importanza, *f.* **-ạte**, ADJ.: inconsiderato. **-ạtely**, ADV.: inconsideratamente. **-ạteness**, **-ātiọn**, S.: inconsiderazione, negligenza, incuria, *f.*
inconsĭsten-ce, **-cy**, S.: inconsistenza, incoerenza, incompatibilità, incongruità, *f.* **-t**, ADJ.: inconsistente; incoerente, non consentaneo: — *with*, non consentaneo a, disdicevole a. **-tly**, ADV.: incongruentemente; assurdamente.
inconsōlable, ADJ.: inconsolabile.
incŏnsọnancy, S.: dissonanza, *f.*
inconspĭcuous, ADJ.: incospicuo.
incŏnstan-cy, S.: incostanza, leggerezza, *f.* **-t**, ADJ.: incostante; instabile. **-tly**, ADV.: incostantemente, instabilmente.
incon-sūmable, **-sŭmptible**†, ADJ.: inconsumabile.
incontĕsta-ble, ADJ.: incontestabile. **-bly**, ADV.: incontestabilmente.
incontĭguous, ADJ.: non contiguo.
incŏntinen-ce, **-cy**, S.: incontinenza, *f.* **-t**, ADJ.: incontinente; sfrenato; impudico. **-tly**, ADV.: incontinentemente; subitamente, prestamente; impudicamente.
incontrọvĕrtibl-e, ADJ.: incontrovertibile, indisputabile. **-y**, ADV.: certamente.
inconvēnịen-ce, **-cy**, S.: inconvenienza, *f.* **-t**, ADJ.: inconveniente, incomodo, sconveniente. **-tly**, ADV.: inconvenientemente.
inconvĕrsable, ADJ.: insociabile.
inconvĕrtible, ADV.: che non si può convertire, inalterabile.
inconvĭncible, ADJ.: inconvincibile.
incôr-pọral, ADJ.: incorporale; immateriale. **-pọrălity**, S.: incorporalità; immaterialità, *f.* **-pọrally**, ADV.: incorporalmente. **-pọrạte**, ADJ.: incorporato. **-pọrạte**, TR.: incorporare; unire; associare; INTR.: incorporarsi; associarsi. **-pọrātiọn**, S.: incorporazione, *f.*, incorporamento, *m.* **-pōrẹal**, ADJ.: incorporeo; spirituale. **-pōrẹally**, ADV.: incorporalmente, immaterialmente. **-pọrēity**, S.: immaterialità, *f.*
incôrpse, TR.: incorporare; unire insieme.
incorrĕct, ADJ.: incorretto, scorretto, difettoso. **-ly**, ADV.: scorrettamente. **-ness**, S.: scorrezione, mancanza d' esattezza, *f.*
incŏrrigibl-e, ADJ.: incorrigibile; inemendabile. **-eness**, S.: incorrigibilità, *f.* **-y**, ADV.: incorrigibilmente.
incorrŭp-t, **-ted**, ADJ.: incorrotto. **-tibility**, S.: incorruttibilità, *f.* **-tible**, ADJ.: incorruttibile, durabile. **-tibleness** = *incorruptibility*. **-tibly**, ADV.: incorruttibilmente. **-tiọn**, S.: incorruzione; durabilità, *f.* **-tness**, S.: purità; integrità, *f.*
incrăs-sạte, TR.: ingrossare; spessare, condensare. **-sātiọn**, S.: ingrossamento; condensamento, *m.* **-sative**, ADJ.: incrassante.
in-crẹase 1, S.: accrescimento, aumento, *m.*, aumentazione, *f.* **-crēase** 2, TR.: aumentare, ingrandire; INTR.: crescere, aumentarsi, aggrandirsi. **-crēasẹr**, S.: aumentatore, *m.*
in-credibility, S.: incredibilità, *f.* **-crĕdible**, ADJ.: incredibile. **-crĕdibleness** = *incredibility*. **-crĕdibly**, ADV.: incredibilmente. **-crẹdūlity**, S.: incredulità, miscredenza, *f.* **-crĕdụlous**, ADJ.: incredulo, miscredente. **-crĕdụlousness** = *incredibility*.
incrĕmable, ADJ.: incombustibile.
increment, S.: incremento, accrescimento, *m.*
incrĭminạte, TR.: incolpare, accusare.
incrŭs-t, **-tạte**, TR.: incrostare, intonacare. **-tātiọn**, S.: incrostatura, *f.*
incụ-bạte, INTR.: covare. **-bātiọn**, S.: covatura, *f.*, covare, *m.* **-bus**, S.: incubo, *m.*
incŭl-cạte, TR.: inculcare; imprimere: — *a thing upon*, inculcare una cosa a. **-cātiọn**, S.: inculcazione, *f.*
incŭlpa-ble, ADJ.: incolpabile, incolpevole, non biasimevole; innocente. **-bly**, ADV.: incolpabilmente; innocentemente.
incŭlt, ADJ.: incolto.
incŭm-bency, S.: incombenza, *f.*, possesso d' un beneficio, *m.* **-bent**, ADJ.: appoggiato; S.: beneficiato, *m.*
incŭm-bẹr, TR.: ingombrare; impedire. **-brance**, S.: ingombro, *m.*
incŭr, TR.: incorrere in, esporsi a, attirarsi addosso: — *one's displeasure*, attirarsi addosso lo scontento (la dispiacenza) di alcuno; — *a penalty*, esporsi ad una multa.
in-cụrability, S.: stato incurabile, *m.* **-cūrable**, ADJ.: incurabile, irremedia-

in-tuiţion, S.: intuizione, *f.* **-tūitive**, ADJ.: intuitivo. **-tūitively**, ADV.: intuitivamente.

intumĕscen-ce, **-cy**, S.: intumescenza, *f.*, gonfiamento, *m.*

inturgĕscence, S.: turgenza, *f.*, gonfiamento, *m.*

intwine, TR.: intrecciare, attorcigliare, intessere.

inŭmbrate, TR.: adombrare, ombreggiare.

inŭncţion, S.: ungimento, *m.*, unzione, *f.*

inŭn-date, TR.: inondare. **-dāţion**, S.: inondazione, *f.;* diluvio, *m.*

inūre, TR.: accostumare, assuefare, avvezzare. **-ment**, S.: abitudine, *f.*, abito; uso, costume, *m.*

inūrn, TR.: metter nell' urna, seppellire,

inū-tile†, ADJ.: inutile, vano. **-tility**, S.: inutilità, *f.*

inŭtterable, ADJ.: inesprimibile, indicibile.

invā-de, TR.: invadere, assaltare; usurpare; violentare. **-der**, S.: invasore, assalitore; usurpatore, *m.*

invăl-id, ADJ.: invalido, infermo, debole; S.: invalido, *m.: be an* —, essere invalido (ammalato). **-idate**, TR.: invalidare, fare invalido. **-idity**, S.: invalidità; debolezza, *f.* **-uable**, ADJ.: inestimabile, imprezzabile.

invāriabl-e, ADJ.: invariabile, immutabile. **-eness**, S.: invariabilità, immutazione, permanenza, *f.* **-y**, ADV.: invariabilmente.

invā-ţion, S.: invasione, incursione; usurpazione, *f.* **-sive**, ADJ.: d' invasione; d' usurpazione.

invĕctive, ADJ.: invettivo, abusivo; satirico; S.: invettiva; bravata, *f.* **-ly**, ADV.: invettivamente; satiricamente.

invĕigh, INTR.: censurare, rimproverare, biasimare; ingiurare, calunniare. **-er**, S.: biasimatore, *m.*

invĕigl-e, TR.: attrarre, allettare, indurre; ingannare. **-er**, S.: allettatore; ingannatore, *m.*

invĕn-t, TR.: inventare; imaginare; macchinare. **-ter**, S.: inventore; autore; macchinatore, *m.* **-ţion**, S.: invenzione; finzione, furberia, *f.*, inganno, *m.* **-tive**, ADJ.: inventivo, ingegnoso. **-tor** = *inventer*. **inven-tory**, S.: inventario, *m.* **-tress**, S.: inventrice; autrice, *f.*

invĕr-se, ADJ.: inverso, trasposto. **-sion**, S.: inversione, trasposizione, *f.* **-t**, TR.: invertere, trasporre; rivoltare, arrovesciare. **-tedly**, ADV.: inversamente, in ordine inverso. **-tebrate**, ADJ.: invertebrato.

invĕst, TR.: investire; rivestire, installare; collocare: — *with*, investire (rivestire) di; — *a place*, (*mil.*) investire (assediare) una piazza; — *a sum of money*, collocare una somma di dinaro.

invĕsti-gable, ADJ.: investigabile, che può essere scoprito. **-gate**, TR.: investigare, diligentemente cercare; esaminare. **-gāţion**, S.: investigazione; ricerca, *f.* **-gator**, S.: investigatore, *m.*

invĕst-iture, S.: investitura, *f.* **-ment**, S.: l' atto dell' investire; investimento; vestimento, abito, *m.;* (*mil.*) l' investire; (*com.*) il collocare (mettere): *make an* — *in the funds*, collocare una somma nei fondi pubblici.

invĕter-acy, S.: continuazione inveterata, *f.* **-ate**[1], ADJ.: inveterato, invecchiato. **-ate**[2], TR.: inveterare, invecchiare; INTR.: indurarsi. **-ateness**, S.: abitudine inveterata, *f.*

invĭdious, ADJ.: invidio, invidioso. **-ly**, ADV.: invidiosamente, con invidia; malignamente. **-ness**, S.: invidia; malignità, *f.*

invĭgor-ate, TR.: invigorire; inanimire. **-āţion**, S.: rinvigorimento; vigore, forza, *f*

in-vincibility, S.: qualità invincibile, invincibilità, *f.* **-vincible**, ADJ.: invincibile; insuperabile. **-vincibleness** = *invincibility*. **-vincibly**, ADV.: invincibilmente.

in-violability, S.: inviolabilità, *f.* **-violable**, ADJ.: inviolabile. **-violableness** = *inviolability*. **-violably**, ADV.: inviolabilmente. **-violate**, ADJ.: inviolato, non corrotto.

in-visibility, S.: invisibilità, *f.* **-visible**, ADJ.: invisibile; impercettibile. **-visibleness** = *invisibility*. **-visibly**, ADV.: invisibilmente.

in-vitāţion, S.: invitamento, invito, *m.: decline an* —, ricusare un invito. **-vitatory**, ADJ.: invitante. **-vite**, TR.: invitare; incitare. **-viter**, S.: invitatore, *m.* **-viting**, ADJ.: invitante; attrattivo; S.: invitamento, *m.* **-vitingly**, ADV.: in modo allettativo, con occhio attrattivo.

invo-cate, TR.: invocare; supplicare. **-cāţion**, S.: invocazione, *f.*

invoice, S.: polizza di carico, fattura, *f.;* TR.: fare una fattura.

invōke, TR.: invocare.

invŏlun-tarily, ADV.: involontariamente. **-tary**, ADJ.: involontario, sforzato.

in-volūţion, S.: involuzione, *f.*, involvimento, *m.* **-vŏlve**, TR.: involgere, inviluppare, avviluppare; impacciare, imbrigare.

in-vulnerability, S.: invulnerabilità, *f.* **-vŭlnerable**, ADJ.: invulnerabile. **-vulnerableness** = *invulnerability*.

inwall, TR.: cingere con muro.
inward, ADJ.: interno, interiore; intimo. **-ly**, ADV.: interiormente, internamente, addentro. **-ness**, S.: intima unione, intrinsichezza, familiarità, *f.* **-s** 1, ADV.: interiormente, al di dentro. **-s** 2, S. PL.: interiora, viscere, *f. pl.*
inweave, IRR.; TR.: intrecciare, intessere.
inwrap, TR.: involgere, inviluppare; imbrogliare.
inwreathe, IRR.; TR.: cingere, circondare; inghirlandare.
inwrought *rât*, ADJ.: ornato con lavori.
iodine, S.: iodio, *m.*
iota, S.: iota, *f.*
ipecacuanha, S.: (*phar.*) ipecaquana, *f.*
ir-ascibility, S.: irascibilità, *f.* **-ascible**, ADJ.: irascibile, collerico, stizzoso.
ire, S.: ira, collera, stizza, *f.* **-ful**, ADJ.: irato, adirato, stizzoso. **-fully**, ADV.: iratamente, con ira, collericamente.
iris, S.: iri, iride, *f.*; arcobaleno, *m.* **iridescent**, ADJ.: tinto come l' arcobaleno.
Irish, ADJ. *or* S.: irlandese, *m., f.* **-man**, S.: irlandese.
irk, TR.: dispiacere; rincrescere. **-some**, ADJ.: tedioso, noioso, increscevole, affannoso. **-somely**, ADV.: increscevolmente, con tedio. **-someness**, S.: rincrescimento; tedio, *m.*, noia, *f.*
iron 1 *ī'ūrn*, S.: ferro, *m.*; S.: catene, *f. pl.*; ceppi, *m. pl.* **iron** 2, ADJ.: di ferro; (*fig.*) severo, rigido: *old* —, ferri vecchi, *m. pl.*; sferre, *f. pl.* **iron** 3, TR.: ripassare con ferro caldo, appianare, lisciare; catenare. **-clad**, ADJ.: corazzato; S.: (*nav.*) corazzata, *f.*
ironical, ADJ.: ironico. **-ly**, ADV.: ironicamente, con ironia.
iron-mill, S.: ferriera, *f.* **-mine**, S.: miniera di ferro, *f.* **-monger**, S.: ferraio, fabbro ferraio, *m.* **-railroad**, S.: strada ferrata, *f.* **-tool**, S.: strumento di ferro, *m.* **-ware**, S.: mercanziuole di ferro, *f. pl.* **-wire**, S.: filo di ferro, ferro filato, *m.* **-wood**, S.: legno duro come il ferro, *m.* **-work**, S.: ferri, *m. pl.*, ferratura, *f.*; S.: ferriera, *f.* **-wort**, S.: siderite, *f.*
irony 1, S.: ironia; derisione, *f.*
irony 2, ADJ.: ferrigno, ferruginoso.
irradi-ance, **-ancy**, S.: irradiazione, *f.*, splendore; lustro, *m.* **-ate**, TR.: irradiare, raggiare, scintillare, brillare. **-ation**, S.: irradiazione, *f.*
irration-al, ADJ.: irrazionale, irragionevole. **-ality**, S.: irrazionalità, *f.* **-ally**, ADV.: irragionevolmente.
irreclaimabl-e, ADJ.: che non può riformarsi, irreparabile, incorrigibile. **-y**, ADV.: irreparabilmente.
irrecon-cilable, ADJ.: irreconciliabile, implacabile. **-cilably**, ADV.: irreconciliabilmente. **-cilement**, **-ciliation**, S.: incompatibilità, *f.*; rancore, *m.*
irrecóvera-ble, ADJ.: irrecuperabile; irreparabile. **-bly**, ADV.: irreparabilmente.
irreducible, ADJ.: irreduttibile.
ir-refragability, S.: irrefragabilità, *f.* **-refragable**, ADJ.: irrefragabile. **-refragableness** = *irrefragability*. **-refragably**, ADV.: in modo irrefragabile.
irrefutable, ADJ.: incontestabile.
irregu-lar, ADJ.: irregolare, sregolato. **-larity**, S.: irregolarità, sregolatezza, *f.* **-larly**, ADV.: irregolarmente. **-late**†, TR.: render irregolare, disordinare, confondere.
irrelative, ADJ.: disunito, disgiunto, non connesso. **-ly**, ADV.: disgiuntamente.
irrelevant, ADJ.: irrilevante.
irrelievable, ADJ.: irremediabile.
irreligion, S.: irreligione, empietà, *f.* **-gious**, ADJ.: irreligioso, empio. **-giously**, ADV.: irreligiosamente. **-giousness** = *irreligion*.
irremeable†, ADJ.: senza ritorno.
irremé-diable, ADJ.: irremediabile, incurabile. **-diably**, ADV.: irremediabilmente.
irremissi-ble, ADJ.: irremissibile, imperdonabile. **-bleness**, S.: atto irremissibile, *m.* **-bly**, ADV.: irremissibilmente.
irremovable, ADJ.: immutabile; costante.
irremunerable, ADJ.: irremunerabile.
irrenowned, ADJ.: senza onore.
irrepara-ble, ADJ.: irreparabile, senza riparo. **-bly**, ADV.: irreparabilmente.
irreprehen-sible, ADJ.: irreprensibile. **-sibly**, ADV.: irreprensibilmente.
irreproacha-ble, ADJ.: irreprobabile; integro, innocente. **-bleness**, S.: integrità; innocenza, *f.* **-bly**, ADV.: irreprobabilmente.
irreprovable, ADJ.: irreprensibile.
irre-sistibility, S.: irresistibilità, potenza irresistibile, *f.* **-sistible**, ADJ.: irresistibile. **-sistibleness** = *irresistibility*. **-sistibly**, ADV.: irresistibilmente.
irresoluble, ADJ.: indissolubile, insolubile.
irreso-lute, ADJ.: irresoluto, dubbioso, incerto. **-lutely**, ADV.: dubbiosamente. **-lution**, S.: irresoluzione; incertezza, *f.*
irresolvedly, ADV.: senza determinazione.
irrespective, ADJ.: indipendente: — of, senza badare a. **-ly**, ADV.: assolutamente.

irrespónsible, ADJ.: non risponsabile, inescusabile.

irretrieva-ble, ADJ.: irreparabile. **-bleness**, S.: irreparibilità, irremediabilità. **-bly**, ADV.: irreparabilmente.

irréveren-ce, S.: irreverenza, irriverenza, *f.* **-t**, ADJ.: irreverente, senza reverenza. **-tly**, ADV.: irreverentemente.

irrevérsi-ble, ADJ.: irretrattabile; irrevocabile. **-bly**, ADV.: da non retrattarsi, immutabilmente.

irre-vocability, S.: irrevocabilità, *f.* **-vócable**, ADJ.: irrevocabile, immutabile. **-vócableness** = *irrevocability*. **-vócably**, ADV.: irrevocabilmente.

ir-rigate, TR.: irrigare, innaffiare, bagnare. **-rigátion**, S.: irrigamento, bagnamento, *m.* **-riguous†**, ADJ.: irriguo, irrigato, innaffiato.

irrision, S.: irrisione, derisione, *f.*

irritability, S.: irritabilità, *f.*

irri-table, ADJ.: irritabile; irascibile, iracondo. **-tant**, ADJ.: irritante, *m.* **-tate**, TR.: irritare, adizzare, provocare. **-tátion**, S.: irritazione, *f.*, irritamento, *m.* **-tative**, **-tatory**, ADJ.: irritative, irritante.

irrúption, S.: irruzione, incursione, *f.*

ischury, S.: iscuria, dissuria, *f.*

isicle† = *icicle*.

isinglass, S.: colla di pesce, *f.*

is-land, S.: isola, *f.* **-lander**, S.: abitatore d' isola; isolano, *m.* **-le**, S.: isola; nave (di chiesa), *f.* **-let**, S.: isoletta, *f.*

isóchro-nal, **-nous**, ADJ.: isocrono.

isolated, ADJ.: isolato, separato.

isósceles, ADJ.: isoscele.

issue 1, S.: uscita, *f.*, esito; evento; termine, fine; successo, *m.*; progenie, prole, *f.*; cauterio, *m.*, fontanella, *f.* **issue** 2, TR.: promulgare, pubblicare; mandare, comandare; INTR.: uscire; provenire, emanare, discendere. **-less**, ADJ.: senza prole.

isthmus, S.: istmo, *m.*

it, PRON.: il, lo, la; egli, esso.

Itá-lian, ADJ., S.: italiano, lingua italiana, *f.*; italiano, *m.* **-lic**, ADJ.: italico; S.: (*typ.*) carattere corsivo, *m.* **-licize**, TR.: stampare in carattere corsivo.

itch 1, S.: rogna, sabbia, *f.*; prurito, *m.*, prurigine, *f.*, pizzicore, *m.* **itch** 2, INTR.: pizzicare; aver la voglia di. **-ing**, S.: prurito, pizzicore, *m.* **-y**, ADJ.: rognoso, scabbioso, pruriginoso.

item 1, ADV.: di più, inoltre, parimente. **item** 2, S.: articolo; avviso; cenno, *m.*

iter-ate, TR.: iterare, ripetere. **-átion**, S.: iterazione; ripetizione, *f.* **-ative**, ADJ.: iterante.

itiner-ant, ADJ.: ambulante; errante. **-ary**, S.: itinerario, *m.*

its, PRON.: suo, sua, suoi, sue. **-self**, PRON.: sè stesso.

ivied, ADJ.: coperto d' edera (d' ellera).

ivory, S.: avorio, *m.*

ivy, S.: edera, ellera, *f.* **-mantled**, ADJ.: coperto d' edera.

J

j jā (*the letter*), S.: j, i lungo, *m.*

jábber 1, S.: ciarla, ciarleria, *f.*, cicalamento, *m.* **jabber** 2, INTR.: cicalare, borbottare. **-er**, S.: barbottone, ciarlone, *m.* **-ing**, S.: ciarla, ciancia, *f.*

jácent, ADJ.: giacente; disteso.

jácinth, S.: giacinto, *m.*

jáck, S.: girarrosto, menarrosto; grillo, *m.*; brocca, *f.*, otre, otre; cavalletto; salterello; cavastivali; giaco; luccio; bersaglio; maschio (d' alcuni animali); giannotto, *m.*; (*nav.*) bandiera di prua, *f.*: — *tar*, mozzo marinaio; *be — of all sides*, voltarsi ad ogni bandiera; *be — of all trades*, fare ogni mestiere.

jáckal, S.: sciacallo, *m.*

jáck-a-lent, S.: semplicietto, *m.* **-a-dandy**, S.: ciondolone, balordo, *m.* **-anapes**, S.: scimia, *f.*; sciocco, babbuino, *m.* **-ass**, S.: asino; goffone, *m.* **-boots**, S. PL.: stivali grossi, *m. pl.* **-daw**, S.: cornacchia, gracchia, *f.*

jácket, S.: giacchetto, saione, *m.*, casacca, *f.*

jáck-pudding, S.: buffone, zanni, *m.* **-sprat**, S.: sciocherello, *m.*

Jáco-bin, S.: domenicano, *m.* **-bine**, S.: piccione con un ciuffo sul capo, *m.* **-bites**, S. PL.: giacobite, *m. pl.*

jác-tancy, S.: iattanza, ostentazione, *f.* **-(ti)tátion**, S.: agitazione, inquietudine, impazienza, *f.*

jácu-late, TR.: scagliare. **-latory**, ADJ.: iaculatorio.

jád-e 1, S.: rozza, carogna: sgualdrina, donnaccia, *f.* **-e** 2, TR.: allassare, affaticare, straccare, stancare; infastidire, annoiare; INTR.: stancarsi; tediarsi. **-ish**, ADJ.: vizioso, cattivo; licenzioso, impudico.

jág 1, S.: dentello, *m.*, tacca, intaccatura, *f.* **jag** 2, TR.: intaccare. **-gedness**, S.: dentello; intagliamento, *m.*

jáguar, S.: giaguaro, *m.*, onza, *f.*

jággy, ADJ.: dentellato, intaccato.

jáil, S.: prigione, *f.*, carcere, *m.* **-bird**, S.: che è stato in prigione, uccello di prigione, prigioniere, *m.*

jákes, S.: privato, cesso, *m.*

jálap, S.: gialapa, *f.*

jám 1, S.: conserva, confettura, *f.* **jam** 2, TR.: serrare insieme; (*nav.*) legare, puntellare.

jámb, S.: imposta, *f.*, stipite, *m.*

jăn-gle, INTR.: contendere, disputare, contrastare; rissare. **-gler**, S.: contenditore, garritore, *m.* **-gling**, S.: contesa, disputa, *f.*
jănitor, S.: portinaio, *m.*
jănizary, S.: giannizzero, *m.*
jănnock, S.: pane di vena, *m*,
Jănse-nism, S.: giansenismo, *m.* **-nist**, S.: giansenista, *m.*
jânt = *jaunt.*
jan-tiness, S.: leggierezza, *f.* **-ty**, S.: accoccio, belloccio, leggiadro.
Jănuary, S.: gennaio, *m.*
japăn I, S.: lavoro verniciato, *m.* **japan** 2, TR.: verniciare. **-ner**, S.: inverniciatore; forbitore di scarpe, *m.* **-work**, S.: lavoro inverniciato, *m.*
jăpe I, S.: novella, farsa, *f.* **jape** 2, INTR.: contar delle novelle; scherzare, burlare.
jâr I, S.: discordia, discrepanza, contesa. **jar** 2, INTR.: dissonare, discordare; disputare, contendere. **jar** 3, S.: (*pot*) giara, *f.*: *Leyden* —, bottiglia di Leyden; *leave a door on a* —, socchiudere (accostare) una porta.
jârgon, S.: gergo, *m.*
jârring, ADJ.: dissonante; discordante; S.: dissonanza; contesa, disputa, *f.*
jăshawk, S.: falcone soro, *m.*
jăsmine, S.: gelsomino, *m.*
jăsper, S.: diaspro, iaspide, *m.*
jâundice, S.: itterizia, *f.* **-d**, ADJ.: itterico.
jâunt I, S.: scorsa; girata, *f.* **jaunt** 2, INTR.: andare qua e là, andare vagando, scorrere. **-iness**, S.: vivacità; bellezza, *f.*
jăvelin, S.: giavellotto, *m.*, chiaverina, *f.*
jâw, S.: mascella, ganascia; bocca, *f.* **-teeth**, S. PL.: macellari, *m. pl.*
jāy, S.: ghiandaia, gazza, *f.* (*pop.*) scioccone.
jĕalous, ADJ.: geloso, sospettoso: *grow* —, divenir geloso, ingelosire; *make* —, ingelosire. **-ly**, ADV.: gelosamente, con gelosia. **-ness**, **-y**, S.: gelosia, invidia, sospezione; vigilanza, *f.*, timore, *m.*: *from* (*out of*) —, per gelosia.
jēer I, S.: burla, beffa, baia, *f.*, scherzo, *m.* **jeer** 2, (IN)TR.: burlare, beffare, dar la baia, buffonare. **-er**, S.: burlatore, beffatore, baione, *m.* **-ing**, S.: burla, beffa, *f.*, scherzo, *m.* **-ingly**, ADV.: scherzevolmente.
jejūne, ADJ.: magro, arido; insipido; incolto, sterile. **-ness**, S.: scarsezza; sterilità; povertà, *f.*
jĕl-lied, ADJ.: glutinoso, viscoso. **-ly**, S.: gelatina, *f.*; sugo premuto, *m.* **-ly-broth**, S.: consumato, *m.*
jĕnnet, *S.: giannetto, m.* (cavallo).
jĕopard, **-ize**, *TR.: arrischiare, avventurare*; sperimentare. **-ous**, ADJ.: rischioso, pericoloso. **-y**, S.: azzardo, rischio; pericolo, *m.*
jĕrk I, S.: sferzata, frustata, sbrigliata; spinta, scossa, *f.*; balzo, urto, *m.*: *at one* —, in un tratto, in un subito; *by* —*s*, a sbalzi; *give a* —, balzare. **jerk** 2, TR.: sferzare, frustare; INTR.: calcitrare.
jĕrkin, S.: giaco, *m.*, casacca, *f.*; falcone, *m.*
jĕrsey, S.: fina lana, filata, *f.*
jĕss, S.: (*falc.*) geto, *m.*
jĕssamine, S.: gelsomino, *m.*
jĕsse, S.: lustro, candelabro, *m.*
jĕst I, S.: burla, beffa, *f.*, scherzo, *m.*: *in* —, da burla, per ischerzo; *biting* —, motto pungente; *make a* —, burlare, motteggiare, scherzare. **jest** 2, INTR.: burlare, beffare, motteggiare. **-er**, S.: beffatore, beffardo, burlone, *m.* **-ing** I, ADJ.: burlevole, scherzevole, scherzoso. **-ing** 2, S.: beffa, burla, *f.*; scherno, *m.* **-ingly**, ADV.: scherzosamente, in modo scherzevole. **-ing-stock**, S.: bersaglio delle minchionature, *m.*
Jĕsuit, S.: gesuita, *m.* **Jesuit-ic(al)**, ADJ.: gesuitico. **-ism**, S.: gesuitismo, *m.* **-'s-bark**, S.: chinachina, *f.*
Jēsus, S.: Gesù.
jĕt I, S.: lustrino, zampillo; getto, *m.*: — *of gas*, getto di gaz. **jet** 2, INTR.: sporgere; intrudere; paoneggiarsi. **-sam**, **-som**, S.: (*nav.*) gettito, *m.* **-ty**, ADJ.: fatto di lustrino; nero.
Jēw, S.: giudeo, ebreo, *m.*
jēwel, S.: gioia, pietra preziosa, *f.* **-box**, S.: scrigno, *m.* **-led**, ADJ.: ornato di gioie. **-ler**, S.: gioielliere, *m.* **-ry**, S.: traffico di gioie, *m.*
Jēw-ess, S.: giudea, ebrea, *f.* **-ish**, ADJ.: giudaico, ebraico. **-ry**, S.: ghetto, *m.* **-'s-harp**, S.: scacciapensieri, *m.*
jĭb, S.: (*nav.*) flocco, *m.*
jībe, INTR.: accordare.
jĭg I, S.: giga, *f.* (ballo). **jig** 2, INTR.: ballare; battere la giga.
jĭgot, S.: lacchetta; coscia, *f.*
jĭll = *gill.*
jĭlt I, S.: civetta, civettina, *f.* **jilt** 2, TR.: civettare.
jĭngle I, S.: tintinno, tintinnio, *m.* **jingle** 2, INTR.: tintinnire, risonare.
jŏb I, S.: lavoro; affare, taccio, *m.*; bisogna, *f.*; colpo (di pugnale), *m.*: *undertake a* —, pigliare a taccio; *work by the* —, lavorare a pezzo, a cottimo; *a pretty* —, un bell' affare. **job** 2, TR.: trafiggere subitamente; INTR.: fare il sensale; fare un traffico usuraio. **-ber**, S.: artigiano a taccio; sensale; negoziante all' ingrosso; speculatore nei fondi pubblici, *m.*
jŏckey I, S.: mezzano, fantino, jock

s.: che si nasconde, che sta in agguato. **-ing-place**, s.: nascondiglio, ripostiglio, agguato, m.
lŭscious, ADJ.: melato, dolce; piacevole. **-ly**, ADV.: in modo sdolcinato, dolcemente. **-ness**, s.: dolcezza smoderata, *f.*
lŭserne, s.: cedrangola, *f.*, trifoglio, *m.*
lŭsh, ADJ.: di buon colore; fresco; s.: (*pop.*) ubbriaccone.
lŭsk†1, ADJ.: pigro, neghittoso. **lusk**†2, INTR.: poltroneggiare, star ozioso. **-ish**†, ADJ.: infingardo. **-iness**†, s.: infingardia, pigrizia; lentezza, *f.*
lusōrious†, **lŭsory**†, ADJ.: giocoso, scherzevole.
lŭst 1, s.: concupiscenza, *f.*, senso, *m.*, sensualità; incontinenza, *f.* **lust** 2, TR.: concupiscere; desiderare. **-er**, s.: uomo cupido (*or* lascivo), *m.* **-er** 2 = *lustre.* **-ful**, ADJ.: sensuale, libidinoso, lascivo. **-fully**, ADV.: sensualmente, libidinosamente. **-fulness**, s.: concupiscenza; sensualità; libidine, voluttà; lascivia, *f.* **-ihead**, **-ihood**, s.: vigore, *m.* **-ily**, ADV.: vigorosamente; con forza. **-iness**, s.: vigore, *m.*, forza di corpo, robustezza, *f.* **-less**†, ADJ.: debole.
lŭs-tral, ADJ.: lustrale; purificativo. **-trate**, TR.: lustrare; purificare. **-trā-tion**, s.: lustrazione; purificazione, *f.* **-tre**, s.: lustro, splendore, *m.* **-tring**, s.: lustrino, *m.* (drappo). **-trous**, ADJ.: lucido, luminoso. **-trum**, s.: lustro, *m.*
lŭsty, ADJ.: vigoroso, gagliardo, forte.
lūtanist, s.: suonatore di liuto, *m.*
lūte 1, s.: loto, *m.* **lute** 2, s.: leuto, liuto. **lute** 3, INTR.: lutare, impiastrar di luto. **-maker**, s.: facitore di liuti, *m.* **-player**, s.: suonatore di liuto, *m.* **-string**, s.: corda di liuto, *f.*
Lūtheran, s.: luterano, *m.* **-ism**, s.: luteranismo, *m.*
lūtist = *lute-player.*
lūtulent†, ADJ.: lutulento, lotoso, fangoso.
lŭx-(ate), TR.: (*surg.*) lussare, dislogare. **-ātion**, s.: lussazione, *f.*, slogamento, *m.*
lŭxe, s.: lusso, *m.*, lussuria, *m.*
luxū-riance, **-riancy**, s.: abbondanza; copia, *f.* **-riant**, ADJ.: soprabbondante, superfluo. **-riantly**, ADV.: abbondantemente. **-riate**, TR.: esser troppo abbondante, crescere con esuberanza. **-rious**, ADJ.: lassurioso, voluttuoso. **-riously**, ADV.: voluttuosamente. **-riousness**, **lŭxu-ry**, s.: lussuria; esuberanza; voluttà, *f.*
lycēum, s.: liceo, *m.*; scuola, *f.*
***lȳe**, s.: ranno, bucato, m.*, lisciva, *f.*
***lȳing**, s.: partorire, puerperio, m.*; menzogna; bugia, *f.*
lȳmph, s.: linfa, *f.* **-ătic**, ADJ.: linfatico, di linfa.
lȳnx, s.: lince, *m.*
lȳ-re, s.: lira, *f.* (strumento musicale). **lȳ-ric(al)**, ADJ.: lirico. **lȳ-rist**, s.: suonatore di lira, *m.*

M

m ĕm (*the letter*), s.: m, *f.*
Măb, s.: regina delle fate; donna sudicia, *f.*
macădamize, TR.: macadamizzare.
macarōni, s.: maccherone, *m.*, paste, *f. pl.*
maca-rŏnic, ADJ.: maccheronico. **-rōon**, s.: maccherone, biscottino; villano, *m.*
macāw, s.: specie di pappagallo d'India, *m.* **-tree**, s.: sorta di palma, *f.*
măce, s.: mazza, massa; mace, *f.* **-bearer**, s.: mazziere, bidello, *m.*
măcer-ate, TR.: macerare, inzuppare; affievolire, mortificare. **-ātion**, s.: macerazione, *f.*, macerare, *m.*; mortificazione, *f.*
machīnal, ADJ.: macchinale, di macchina.
măchi-nate, TR.: macchinare, apparecchiare, ordinare; tramare. **-nātion**, s.: macchinamento; artifizio, *m.*; trama, *f.* **-nator**, s.: macchinatore, inventore, *m.*
ma-chine, s.: macchina, *f.*; strumento, *m.* **-chinery**, s.: ordinanza, disposizione, *f.*; meccanismo, *m.*; arte, *f.* **-chinist**, s.: macchinista, *m.*
măc(k)intosh, s.: impermeabile, *m.*
măckerel, s.: sgombro, *m.* (pesce). **-boat**, s.: battello da pesca, *m.*
măcrocosm, s.: macrocosmo, *m.*
măcu-la, s.: macchia, macola, *f.* **-lāte**, TR.: macchiare, macolare, imbrattare, bruttare. **-lātion**, s.: macchiare, *m.*; macchia; sporcizia, *f.* **-latures**, s. PL.: cartacce, *f.* **-le**, s.: macola, macchia, *f.*
măd 1, ADJ.: pazzo, matto, forsennato, arrabbiato, appassionato: *stark* —, pazzo da catena; — *dog*, cane idrofobo; — *fit*, capriccio, *m.*, fantasia, *f.*; *drive* —, far impazzire, far arrabbiare. **mad** 2, TR.: fare arrabbiare, fare smaniare; INTR.: impazzire.
mădam, s.: madama, signora, *f.*
măd-brain(ed), ADJ.: matto, insensato. **-cap**, s.: pazzo, scervellato, *m.* **-den**, TR.: far arrabbiare, impazzare.
mădder, s.: robbia, *f.* (erba).
măd-ding, ADJ.: arrabbiato, furioso, forsennato. **-dish**, ADJ.: pazzarello; scherzevole.

jūlep, S.: giulebbo, giulebbe, *m.*: *mint* —, bevanda spiritosa americana che contiene foglie di mento, *f.*
July, S.: luglio, *m.*
jūmart, S.: animale nato di toro e cavalla, *m.*
jŭm-ble 1, S.: mescuglio confuso, *m.* **-ble** 2, TR.: confondere; mescolare; INTR.: mescolarsi; esser agitato; sollevarsi: — *together*, gettare insieme alla rinfusa. **-blement**, **-bling**, S.: mescolamento, *m.* **-bler**, S.: imbroglione, *m.*
jŭmp 1, ADV.: esattamente. **jump** 2, S.: salto; giustacorpo; caso di fortuna, sorte felice, *m.* **jump** 3, INTR.: saltare; incontrarsi; accordarsi: — *about*, spiccar salti; — *over*, scavalcare; — *up*, saltar su. **-er**, S.: saltatore, *m.*
jŭnc-tion, S.: congiunzione, unione, *f.* **-ture**, S.: congiuntura, giuntura; circostanza, *f.*, stato, *m.*
Jūne, S.: giugno, *m.*
jŭngle, S.: macchia folta (nell' Africa), *f.*
jūnior, ADJ.: più giovine; iuniore, minore: *the — brothers*, i fratelli minori; *Mr. A.* —, signor A. iuniore; *your —s*, le persone più giovani di voi.
jūniper, S.: ginepro, *m.* **-berry**, S.: coccola del ginepro, *f.* **-lecture**, S.: rimprovero, rabbuffo, *m.* **-tree**, S.: ginepro, ginepraio, *m.*
jŭnk, S.: giunca, *f.*
jŭnket 1, S.: tortelletta, confettura, *f.*; festino, *m.* **junket** 2, INTR.: gozzovigliare, banchettare. **-ing**, S.: gozzoviglia, *f.*
jŭn-ta, **-to**, S.: assemblea, radunanza, cabala, *f.*
juppŏn†, S.: giubbone, *m.*
jū-rat, S.: giurato, *m.* **-ratory**, ADJ.: giuratorio.
jurídical, ADJ.: giuridico. **-ly**, ADV.: giuridicamente.
juris-cŏnsult, S.: giurisconsulto, legista, *m.* **-diction**, S.: giurisdizione, *f.* **-dictional**, ADJ.: giurisdizionale; legale. **-prūdence**, S.: giurisprudenza, *f*
jū-rist, S.: giurista, giureconsulto, *m.* **-ror**, S.: giurato, *m.* **-ry**, S.: giurì, *m.*; giurati, *m. pl.*: *grand* —, giurì d' accusa; *common* (*petty*) —, piccolo giurì; *trial by* —, giudizio per giurati; *be on the* —, essere membro di un giurì; *challenge a* —, ricusare un giurì; *pack a* —, scegliere giurati corrotti; *foreman of a* —, capo (*or* primo) dei giurati; *verdict of the* —, verdetto dei giurati. **-ryman**, S.: giurato, *m.* **-rymast**, S.: (*nav.*) albero temporale, albero di ricambio, *m.*
jŭst 1, S.: torniamento, *m.*, giostra, *f.* **just** 2, INTR.: giostrare. **just** 3, ADJ.: giusto, onesto, virtuoso, probo; esatto.
just 4, ADV.: giustamente, esattamente, precisamente, appunto: — *as if*, come se; — *now*, or' ora, in questo punto, testè; — *so*, appunto così; — *tell me*, ora ditemi. **-ice** 1, S.: giustizia, *f.*; giudice, *m.*: — *of the peace*, giudice di pace, *m.*; *do* —, render giustizia, amministrar giustizia. **-ice** 2, TR.: render giustizia. **-iceable†**, ADJ.: soggetto alla giustizia. **-icement†**, S.: ordine giudiziario, *m.* **-icer†**, S.: giustiziere, *m* **-iceship**, S.: uffizio di giudice, *m.* **-iciable†** = *justiceable*. **-iciary**, S.: giustiziere, carnefice, *m.* **-ifiable**, ADJ.: giustificabile. **-ifiableness**, ADJ.: rettitudine; difesa, *f.* **-ifiably**, ADV.: giustificatamente. **-ificātion**, S.: giustificazione, scusa, difesa, *f.* **-ificative**, ADJ.: giustificativo. **-ificātor**, **-ifier**, S.: giustificatore, *m.* **-ify**, TR.: giustificare; provare; aggiustare.
jŭstle, TR.: urtare; incontrare; INTR.: urtarsi; incontrarsi.
jŭst-ly, ADV.: giustamente; esattamente. **-ness**, S.: giustizia; equità; giustezza, esattezza, *f.*
jŭt 1, **-ty**, S.: risalto, sporto, *m.* **jut** 2, **-ty**, INTR.: sporgere; uscire di linea. **-window**, S.: finestra che sporge in fuora, *f.*; sporto, balcone, *m.*
jūve-nĕscent, ADJ.: che ringiovanisce. **-nile**, ADJ.: giovanile. **-nility**, S.: giovanezza, gioventù, *f.*
juxtaposition, S.: apposizione, *f.*: — *of parts*, contiguità delle parti, *f.*

K

k *kā* (*the letter*), S.: k, *m.*
kāle, S.: cavolo riccio, *m.*
kaleidoscope, S.: caleidoscopio, *m.*
kălendar, S.: calendario, *m.*
kāli, S.: cali, *m.*
kămt†, ADJ.: torto, curvo; gobbo.
kangarōo, S.: canguro, *m.*
kātydid, S.: specie di grillo americano, *m.*
kāw 1, S.: crocito del corvo, crocitare, *m.* **kaw** 2, INTR.: crocitare, cornacchiare, gracchiare.
kāyles, S.: sbrigli birilli, *m. pl.* (giuoco).
keck 1, S.: nausea, *f.* **keck** 2, INTR.: sforzarsi di vomitare.
kĕck-le, TR.: (*nav.*) vestire una gomena di corde. **-ling**, S.: (*nav.*) fasciame, *m.*
kĕck-sy, S.: cicuta, *f.* **-y**, ADJ.: frascato, ramoso.
kĕdg-e 1, ADJ.: allegro, vivace. **-e** 2, TR.: (*nav.*) ammainare. **-er**, S.: ancorotta, ancora piccola, *f.*

insnâr-e, TR.: inlacciare, accalappiare: — *one's self*, cader nel laccio, inlacciarsi; intrigarsi. **-er**, S.: insidiatore, ingannatore, *m*.

insobriety, S.: ubbriachezza, intemperanza, *f*.

insôciable, ADJ.: insociabile, non compagnevole; fastidioso. **-ness**, S.: umore poco sociabile, *m*., disposizione insociabile, *f*.

inso-late, TR.: soleggiare, esporre al sole. **-lâtion**, S.: insolazione; esposizione al sole, *f*.

insolen-ce, **-cy**, S.: insolenza, arroganza, *f*. **-t**, ADJ.: insolente, arrogante; orgoglioso. **-tly**, ADV.: insolentemente, arrogantemente, altieramente.

insolidity, S.: mancanza di solidità; debolezza, *f*.

insŏl-uble, ADJ.: insolubile, indissolubile. **-vable**, ADJ.: *(com)* insolvibile. **-vency**, S.: incapacità di pagare, *f*. **-vent**, ADJ.: che non può pagare.

insomŭch, CONJ.: di modo che, talmente che

inspĕc-t, TR.: i(n)spezionare, vegliare; osservare; esaminare. **-tion**, S.: ispezione; cura, *f*.; visitamento, *m* **-tor**, S.: ispettore, soprantendente; visitatore, *m*.: *(rail.)* — *of the railway-station*, ispettore dell' atrio, ispettore della stazione, *m*. **-torship**, S.: ispettorato, *m*., soprantendenza, *f*.

in-spirable, ADJ.: inspirabile, spirabile; respirabile. **-spirâtion**, S.: inspirazione, spirazione, *f*. **-spire**, TR.: inspirare, spirare, infondere: — *with*, infondere. **-spirer**, S.: inspiratore, *m*. **-spirit**, TR.: animare; incoraggiare.

inspis-sate, TR.: spessare, condensare. **-sâtion**, S.: condensamento, spessire, *m*.

in-stability, S.: instabilità, incostanza, mutabilità, *f*. **-stâble**, ADJ.: instabile, incostante; mutabile. **-stâbleness** = *instability*.

in-stâll, TR.: installare, stabilire, mettere in possesso. **-stallâtion**, S.: stabilimento in possesso, *m*.; promozione, *f*. **-stâlment**, S.: installazione, promozione, *f*.; pagamento fisso, *m*., rata, *f*.

ĭnstan-ce 1, S.: istanza, istanzia; sollecitazione; prova, *f*., esempio, *m*.: *for* —, per esempio; *in several* —*s*, a diversi casi. **-ce** 2, TR.: citare, addurre esempi, produrre l' autorità. **-cy** = *instance*. **-t**, ADJ.: pressante, urgente, premuroso; S.: istante, momento; presente, *m*.: *at this very* —, in questo punto. **-tâneous**, ADJ.: istantaneo, momentaneo. **-tâneously**, ADV.: istantaneamente. **-tly**, ADV.: istantemente, in un istante, adesso.

ĭnstâte, TR.: stabilire; investire, mettere in possesso.

in-stauration, S.: ristorazione; rinnovazione, *f*. **instaurator**, S.: ristoratore, *m*.

instĕad, ADV.: in (suo, *etc*.) luogo, in vece. **instead of**, PREP.: in luogo di, in vece di.

instēep, TR.: infondere; macerare.

ĭnstep, S.: collo del piede, *m*.

ĭnsti-gate, TR.: instigare, stimolare, incitare, eccitare. **-gâtion**, S.: instigazione, *f*., incitamento, provocamento, *m*. **-gator**, S.: instigatore, incitatore, *m*.

instĭll, TR.: instillare, infondere. **-âtion**, S.: istillazione, infusione, *f*.

in-stinct 1, S.: istinto, *m*.: *by* —, per istinto. **-stinct** 2, ADJ.: animato (*with*, di), pieno. **-stinctive**, ADJ.: fatto per istinto; naturale. **-stinctively**, ADV.: per istinto; naturalmente.

ĭnsti-tute 1, S.: instituto; precetto, *m*. **-tute** 2, TR.: instituire, stabilire; cominciare; ordinare; formare. **-tûtion**, S.: instituzione, *f*.; stabilimento, *m*.; istruzione, *f*. **-tutionary**, ADJ.: elementario. **-tutor**, S.: istitutore; insegnatore; fondatore, *m*.

instrŭc-t, TR.: istruire, ammaestrare, insegnare, informare. **-ter** = *-tor*. **-tion**, S.: insegnamento, *m*.; dottrina, *f*. **-tive**, ADJ.: istruttivo. **-tor**, S.: istruttore, insegnatore, *m*

ĭnstru-ment, S.: istrumento, strumento; ordigno; *(jur.)* contratto, *m*. **-mĕntal**, ADJ.: instrumentale; organico. **-mĕntally**, ADV.: strumentalmente. **-mĕntalness**, S.: mezzo; espediente, *m*.

insubôrdi-nate, ADJ.: insubordinato. **-nâtion**, S.: insubordinazione, disubbidienza, *f*.

insŭffera-ble, ADJ.: insoffribile, intollerabile. **-bly**, ADV.: insoffribilmente.

insufficien-ce, **-cy**, S.: insufficienza; incapacità, *f*. **-t**, ADJ.: insufficiente; incapace. **-tly**, ADV.: insufficientemente.

ĭnsu-lar(y), ADJ.: isolano, d' isola. **-lated**, ADJ.: isolato, solitario. **-lator**, S.: isolatore, *m*.

insŭlse†, ADJ.: insulso; sciocco, stupido.

ĭn-sult 1, S.: insulto, *m*.; ingiuria, *f*.; oltraggio, *m*. **-sŭlt** 2, TR.: insultare; oltraggiare, bravare, beffeggiare. **-sultâtion**, S.: insulto, *m*. **-sŭlter**, S.: insultatore, *m*. **-sŭltingly**, ADV.: d' una maniera insultante, in modo oltraggioso.

in-sûperable, ADJ.: insuperabile, invincibile. **-sûperableness**, S.: forza insuperabile, *f*. **-sûperably**, ADV.: in maniera insuperabile, invincibilmente.

insuppôrta-ble, ADJ.: insopportabile. **-bly**, ADV.: insopportabilmente.

insû-rable, ADJ.: che può esser assicurato. **-rance**, S.: assicurazione, [illegible]

curanza, *f.*: — *company*, compagnia di assicurazione; *life* —, assicurazione sulla vita; *fire* —, assicurazione contro gl' incendi. **-re**, TR.: assicurare, guarentire. **-rer**, S.: assicuratore, *m.*
insŭrgent, S.: insurgente, ribello, *m.*
insurmŏuntab-le, ADJ.: insormontabile. **-ly**, ADV.: insuperabilmente.
insurrĕction, S.: insurrezione, sedizione, sollevazione, rivolta, *f.* **-al**, **-ary**, ADJ.: sedizioso, ribellante.
intăctible, ADJ.: intangibile, intoccabile.
intăglio, S.: intaglio, *m.*, scultura, *f.*
intăngible, ADJ.: intangibile.
intăstable, ADJ.: senza gusto, insipido
in-teger, S.: integrità, totalità, *f.* **-tegral**, ADJ.: integrale, intero, compiuto; S.: integrale, *m.* **-tegrant**, ADJ.: integrante, integrate. **-tĕgrity**, S.: integrità, totalità; probità, onestà, *f.*
intĕgument, S.: integumento, *m.*; cute, *f.*
intel-lect, S.: intelletto, *m.*; intelligenza, *f.* **-lĕction**, S.: intelligenza, *f.*; intendimento, *m.* **-lĕctive**, ADJ.: intellettivo. **-lĕctual**, ADJ.: intellettuale; ingegnoso
intĕlli-gence, **-gency**, S.: intelligenza, intelligenzia; novella, *f.*, avviso, *m.*; corrispondenza, *f.*: *foreign* —, notizie estere; *latest* —, ultimi avvisi; — *office*, agenzia d' impieghi; ufficio d' avvisi; *give* —, avvertire, avvisare. **-gencer**, S.: novellista, gazzettiere, *m.*; gazzetta, *f.* **-gent**, ADJ.: intelligente; penetrativo; erudito. **-gĕntial**, ADJ.: intellettuale, spirituale; perspicace. **-gibility**, S.: intelligibilità; perspicacità, *f.* **-gible**, ADJ.: intelligibile, concepibile; chiaro. **-gibleness** = *intelligibility*. **-gibly**, ADV.: intelligibilmente.
intĕmerate†, ADJ.: intemerato, incontaminato.
intĕmper-ament, S.: complessione cattiva, *f.* **-ance**, S.: intemperanza, *f.*; disordine, eccesso, *m.* **-ate**, ADJ.: intemperato, moderato. **-ately**, ADV.: intemperatamente. **-ateness**, **-ature**, S.: intemperanza; intemperatura; intemperie, *f.*; eccesso, *m.*
intempĕstive, ADJ.: intempestivo, fuor di tempo. **-ly**, ADV.: intempestivamente.
intĕnd, TR.: intendere, avere intenzione, avere in pensiero, proporsi; disegnare.
intĕndan-cy, S.: sovrintendenza; podesteria, *f.* **-t**, S.: intendente; governatore, *m.*
intĕnd-ed, ADJ.: disegnato, progettato, proposto: *your* —, il vostro pretendente, il vostro promesso sposo, *m.*; la vostra promessa sposa, *f.* **-ment**†, S.: intento, disegno, *m.*

intĕner-ate, TR.: intenerire; ammollire. **-ātion**, S.: tenerezza; compassione, *f.*
intĕn-se, ADJ.: intenso; veemente, eccessivo. **-sely**, ADV.: intensamente; veementemente **-seness**, **-sion**, S.: intensione; energia; violenza, *f.* **-sity**, S.: eccesso; ardore, *m.* **-sive**, ADJ.: intensivo, intento; eccessivo. **-sively**, ADV.: intensivamente; eccessivamente.
intĕn-t, ADJ.: intento, attento, assiduo; S.: intento, disegno, proponimento, *m.*: *be* —, affissarsi; *with the* — *to*, col disegno di; *to all* —*s and purposes*, in tutte le maniere, in ogni qualunque modo, del tutto, affatto. **-tion**, S.: intento; disegno; proponimento, *m.* **-tional**, ADJ.: intenzionale. **-tionally**, ADV.: intenzionalmente, con intenzione, a posta. **-tioned**, ADJ.: intenzionato. **-tive**, ADJ.: intentivo, attento, fisso. **-tively**, **-tly**, ADV.: intentivamente; con attenzione. **-tness**, S.: applicazione, attenzione; preoccupazione, *f.*
intĕr, TR.: sotterare, seppellire.
intĕrca-lar, **-lary**, ADJ.: intercalare. **-late**, TR.: intercalare, inserire. **-lātion**, S.: intercalazione, *f.*
intercē-de, TR.: intercedere; essere mediatore. **-der**, S.: interceditore, intercessore, *m.* **-ding**, S.: intercessione, *f.*
intercĕp-t, TR.: intercettare; arrestare. **-tion**, S.: intercezione, *f.*; ostacolo, impedimento, *m.*; ostruzione, *f.*
inter-cĕssion, S.: intercessione, mediazione, *f.* **-cĕssor**, S.: intercessore, mediatore, *m.*
inter-change 1, S.: cambio, barattamento, *m.* **-chānge** 2, TR.: cambiare, cangiare, permutare. **-chāngeable**, ADJ.: scambievole; mutuo. **-chāngeableness**, S.: scambievolezza; permutazione, *f.* **-chāngeably**, ADV.: scambievolmente, vicendevolmente. **-chāngement**, S.: cambio, barattamento, *m.*
intercipient, ADJ.: intercettante; S: intercezione, *f.*
intercision, S.: intercisione, *f.*; interrompimento, *m.*
inter-clūde, INTR.: interchiudere; impedire. **-clūsion**, S.: ostruzione; interruzione, *f.*; impedimento, ostacolo, *m.*
intercommūnity, S.: comunicazione mutua, *f.*
intercŏstal, ADJ.: intercost-
intercourse, S.: commer-
municazione, corrispondenza
intercŭrren-ce, S.: pass-
zo, *m.* **-t**, ADJ.: corrente
inter-dict, S.: interdetto,
ne, *f.* **-dict**, TR.: inter-
vietare. **-diction**, S.: inte-
bizione, *f.*

sione, *f.* **-pan**, S.: patella del ginocchio, *f.* **-tribute**, S.: genuflessione, *f.*

knĕll, S.: suono della campana funebre, *m.*, *f.*, suono funebre, *m.*

knife, S.: coltello, *m.*: *carving* —, coltello da trinciare; *pruning* —, roncone, falcetto, *m.*; *table* —, coltello da tavola; *sharpen a* —, arrotare (affilare) un coltello.

knight 1, S.: cavaliere, *m.*: — *of the garter*, cavaliere della giarrettiera. **knight** 2, TR.: creare cavaliere. **-errant**, S.: cavaliere errante, *m.* **-ĕrrantry**, S.: cavalleria errante, *f.* **-hood**, S.: dignità di cavaliere, *f.*; ordine di cavalleria, *m.* **-ly**, ADJ.: cavalleresco, di cavaliere. **-marshal**, S.: maresciallo di corte, *m.* **-service**, S.: servizio di cavaliere, *m.* **-templar**, S.: templario, tempiere, *m.*

knit 1, S.: lendine, *f.* **knit** 2, S.: lavoro a maglie, *m.* **knit** 3, (IR)R.; TR.: legare, annodare; unire; INTR.: lavorare all' ago: — *the brows*, increspar la fronte; — *stockings*, far (lavorar) calze; — *a net*, fare un rete, intrecciare. **-ter**, S.: lavoratore a maglie, lavoratore all' ago, *m.* **-ting-needle**, S.: gucchia, *f.*, ago da lavorare a maglie, *m.* **-ting-sheath**, S.: cannello per le gucchie, *m.* **-ting-yarn**, S.: filo da fare calzette, *m.* **-tle**, S.: cordicella, *f.*, cordoncino (di borsa), *m.* **-work**, S.: lavoro a maglie, *m.*

knŏb, S.: tumore; nodo, *m.*; bozza, *f.* **-bed**, ADJ.: nodoso, nocchioso. **-biness**, S.: nodosità; callosità, *f.* **-by**, ADJ.: nodoso, nocchioso; calloso.

knŏck 1, S.: colpo, *m.*, percossa, botta, *f.*; picchio (alla porta), *m.* **knock** 2, TR.: battere; colpire, picchiare; urtare, bussare; INTR.: urtarsi: — *away*, seguitar a picchiare; — *down*, atterrare; ammazzare; — *in*, ficcare dentro per forza; — *off*, rompere; far saltare; cessare di lavorare; — *out*, cacciare fuori per forza; — *under*, arrendersi, sommettersi; cedere; — *up*, risvegliare; straccare; *I am —ed up*, sono stracco. **-er**, S.: martello (di porta), *m.* **-ing**, S.: picchio; strepito, fracasso, romore, *m.*

knōll, TR.: sonare (la campana); sonare a morto.

knŏt 1, S.: nodo; nocchio; gruppo, *m.*; banda, brigata, *f.*; stormo; intrigo, imbroglio, *m.*, difficoltà, *f.*: *Gordian* —, nodo gordiano; *run nine —s an hour*, fare nove nodi per ora. **knot** 2, TR.: annodare; imbrogliare, intrigare; INTR.: annodarsi; germogliare; spuntare. **-grass**, S.: sanguinaria, *f.* **-ted**, ADJ.: annodato; nodoso, nocchioso. **-tiness**, S.: nodosità; difficoltà, *f.*, imbroglio, intrigo, *m.* **-y**, ADJ.: nodoso, nocchiuto; difficile, intricato: — *question*, quistione intralciata.

knŏut, S.: frusta russa (per punire), *f.*

knōw, IRR.; TR.: sapere, conoscere; INTR.: essere informato; sapere: — *one's self*, conoscersi; *let* —, far sapere, dar avviso, avvisare; — *by experience*, saper per prova; — *by sight*, conoscere di vista; — *thoroughly*, sapere a fondo; *that I* —, che io sappia. **-able**, ADJ.: conoscibile; che si può sapere. **-er**, S.: conoscitore, sapiente, *m.* **-ing** 1, ADJ.: sapevole, saputo, intelligente, accorto. **-ing** 2, S.: sapere, *m.*, notizia, scienza, *f.* **-ingly**, ADV.: sapevolmente, a bello studio. **knowledge**, S.: conoscenza; scienza; notizia; abilità, *f.*: *to my* —, a mia saputa; *without my* —, senza la mia saputa; *get* — *of*, informarsi. **-n**, ADJ.: cognito, conosciuto, saputo: *well* —, conosciutissimo.

knŭb, **-ble**, TR.: battere, schiaffeggiare.

knŭckle 1, S.: congiuntura, *f.*; garretto di vitella, *m.* **knuckle** 2, TR.: battere; INTR.: arrendersi, sommettersi. **-d**, ADJ.: nocchiuto, nocchieruto.

knur = *knar*. **-ry**, ADJ.: nodoso.

kōdak, S.: macchina fotografica per dilettanti, *f.*

kōran, S.: alcorano, *m.*

L

l *ell* (*the letter*), S.: l, *m.* *or f.*

lā†, INTERJ.: là: ecco! vedi! guarda!

lăbdanum, S.: ladano, laudano, *m.*

lab-efăction, S.: debilitamente, *m.* **-efy**, TR.: indebolire.

lābel 1, S.: cartello, *m.*; inscrizione, etichetta, *f.* **label** 2, TR.: notare, segnare.

lā-bial, ADJ.: labiale; di viva voce. **-biated**, ADJ.: (*bot.*) labbiato.

lābor = *labour*.

lăboratory, S.: laboratorio, *m.*; fonderia, *f.*

labōrious, ADJ.: laborioso, faticoso, difficile; assiduo. **-ly**, ADV.: laboriosamente, con fatica. **-ness**, S.: fatica; difficoltà; diligenza, assiduità, *f.*

lābour 1, S.: lavoro, travaglio, *m.*; fatica, pena, opera, *f.*: *be in* —, aver le doglie. **labour** 2, TR.: lavorare; affaticare, tormentare; affliggere; battere; INTR.: affaticarsi, impiegarsi; esercitarsi: — *with child*, aver le doglie; — *for an office*, cercare una carica; — *under a mistake*, sbagliarsi; — *under many difficulties*, aver molte difficoltà a vincere. **-er**, S.: lavorante; operaio, *m.* **-less**, ADJ.: senza fatica. **-some**, ADJ.: laborioso, faticoso, difficile, arduo.

lăbyrinth, s.: laberinto, *m.*
lăc, s.: lacca, *f.*
lăce 1, s.: stringa, *f.*; merletto; nastro, *m.* **lace** 2, tr.: allacciare; gallonare, guarnire di merletto; bastonare. **-maker**, s.: facitore di merletto, *m.* **-man**, s.: che fa i passamani, fabbricatore di merletti, *m.* **-merchant**, s.: mercante di merletti, *m.* **-pillow**, s.: tombolo, *m.*
lăcer-able, adj.: lacerabile, che può lacerarsi. **-ate**, tr.: lacerare; stracciare. **-ātion**, s.: lacerazione, *f.*, laceramento; stracciamento, *m.*
lăce-woman, s.: donna che fa merletti con piombini, *f.* **-work**, s.: passamano, merletto, *m.*
lăch-rymal, adj.: lagrimale, lacrimale. **-rymātion**, s.: lagrimazione, *f.* **-rymatory**, s.: lacrimatoio, *m.*
lăck 1, s.: mancanza, *f.*, bisogno, *m.*: *be in — of*, mancare di, di fettare. **lack** 2, tr.: mancare, avere bisogno. **-a-day!** interj.: cappita! capperi! **-brain**, s.: scioccone, minchione, *m.*
lăcker 1, s.: vernice della Cina, lacca, *f.* **lacker** 2, tr.: vernicare, verniciare, inverniciare.
lăckey 1, s.: lacchè, staffiere, *m.* **lackey** 2, intr.: servire vilmente.
lăck-lustre, adj.: senza splendore.
lacŏnic(al), adj.: laconico, conciso. **-ally**, adv.: laconicamente, strettamente, brevemente.
lăconism, s.: laconismo, *m.*
lăc-tary 1, adj.: latteo, lattifero. **-tary** 2, s.: cascina, *f.*; latticini, *m. pl.* **-tātion**, s.: allattamento, *m.* **-teal**, adj.: latteo, lattifero, latticinoso: *— veins*, vene lattee, *f. pl.* **-teous**, adj.: latteo, chiloso. **-tĕscence**, s.: formazione del latte, *f.* **-tĕscent**, adj.: latteggiante, chilificante. **-tiferous**, adj.: (*anat.*) lattifero, latteo.
lacūna, s.: lacuna, *f.*, vuoto in un manoscritto, *m.*
lăd, s.: giovanetto, adolescente; garzone, *m.*
lădanum = *labdanum.*
lădder, s.: scala a piuoli; gradazione, *f.*, digradamento, *m.* **-rope**, s.: (*nav.*) guardamano, *m.* **-stop**, s.: piuolo, *m.*
lăd-e 1, s.: bocca; imboccatura d' un fiume, *f.* **-e** 2, (ir)r.; tr.: caricare; colmare. **-en**, adj.: carico, aggravato, oppresso. **-ing**, s.: caricamento, caricare; noleggio, *m.*: *bill of —*, polizza di carico, *f.*
lădle, s.: cucchiaione, *m.*, mestola, *f.*; romaiuolo, *m.* **-ful**, s.: cucchiaiata, *f.*
lădy, s.: dama, signora, *f.*; padrona di casa; donna nobile (contessa, ecc.): *Our —*, nostra Signora, la Madonna; *young —*, damigella; *young married —*, giovine signora. **-bird**, **-cow**, s.: coccinella, *f.* (insetto). **-day**, s.: annunziazione, *f.* **-like**, adj.: donnesco; gentile, elegante. **-ship**, s.: qualità di donna; Signoria, Eccellenza, *f.*
lăg 1, adj.: ultimo; tardo, pigro; negligente. **lag** 2, s.: ultimo, *m.*; ultima classe, *f.*; rifiuto, *m.* **lag** 3, intr.: restare dietro; muoversi pigramente; tentennare: *— behind*, star indietro, indugiare. **-gard**, **-ger**, s.: infingardo, pigro; tentennone; indugiatore, *m.*
lăger, **-beer**, s.: birra fermentata alla tedesca, *f.*
la-gōon, **-gūne**, s.: laguna, palude, *f.*
lăic(al), adj.: laico, secolare.
lāid, part.: messo, posto; ordinato (cf. *lay*).
lāin, part.: stato, giacciuto (cf. *lie*).
lāir, s.: ricettacolo; covile, *m.*; tana, *f.*
lāird, s.: signore d' un feudo, *m.*
lāity, s.: laici, secolari, *m. pl.*
lāke, s.: lago, *m.*; lacca, *f.*
lăm, tr.: bastonare, battere.
lămb 1, s.: agnello, *m.* **lamb** 2, intr.: far un agnello.
lăm-bative, s.: (*med.*) lambitivo, *m.* **-bent**, adj.: lambente, leccante; leggiere
lămb-kin, s.: agnellino, agnelletto, *m.* **-'s-wool**, s.: lana d' agnello; sorta di birra, *f.*
lāme 1, adj.: zoppo, storpiato; imperfetto: *— of one leg*, storpiato d' una gamba; *go —*, zoppicare. **lame** 2, tr.: storpiare, stroppiare; troncare, guastare.
lămellated, adj.: lamellato.
lāme-ly, adv.: stortamente; imperfettamente; contra voglia. **-ness**, s.: storpiatura; imperfezione, *f*
lamĕnt 1, s.: lamento, *m.*, lamentazione, *f.*, compianto; gemito, *m.* **lament** 2, tr.: deplorare, compiangere; intr.: lamentarsi, dolersi. **-able**, adj.: lamentevole, lamentabile, compassionevole, deplorabile. **-ably**, adv.: lamentevolmente. **-ātion**, s.: lamentazione, *f.*, lamento, pianto, *m.* **-er**, s.: che si lamenta, che si deplora, lamentatore, *m.* **-ing**, s.: lamento, *m.*
lămi-na, s.: lamina, lama; piastra di metallo, *f.* **-nated**, adj.: ridotto in lamine, laminoso.
lămm = *lam.*
lămmas, s.: primo giorno d' agosto, *m.*
lămp, s.: lampada, lampana, lucerna, *f.*: *little —*, lampionino, lampioncino; *street —*, lampione, *m* **-black**, s.: nero di fummo, *m.*
lămpern, s.: lampreda, *f.*, lampredotto, *m.*
lămp-maker, s.: lampanaio, *m.*

mistura, *f.* **mash** 2, TR.: mescolare, mischiare; pestare. **-er**, S.: pestatore; zerbino, giovane elegante, *m.*

măsk I, S.: maschera; mascherata, *f.;* colore, pretesto, *m.: take off the* —, cavarsi la maschera. **mask** 2, TR.: mascherare; velare; INTR.: mascherarsi. **-er**, S.: che porta la maschera, maschera, *f.*

māson, S.: muratore; fabbricatore; ciabattino; framassone, *m.* **-ry**, S.: fabbrica; struttura, *f.*

masquerāde I, S.: mascherata, *f.;* travestimento, *m.* **-e** 2, INTR.: andare in maschera. **-er**, S.: che va in maschera, maschera, *f.*

măss I, S.: massa, gran quantità, *f.;* pezzo; tutto, *m.* **mass** 2, S.: messa, *f.: high* —, messa solenne (*or* maggiore); *say* —, dire la messa.

măssacre I, S.: macello, *m.;* strage, uccisione, *f.* **massacre** 2, TR.: macellare, fare strage, trucidare.

măssage *or -ā'ge*, S.: massaggio, *m.*

măss-book, S.: messale, *m.*

măs-siness, S.: gravezza, *f.*, peso, *m.* **-sive**, ADJ.: massiccio, solido. **-siveness** = *massiness.* **-sy** = *massive.*

măst I, S.: albero (di nave), *m.;* ghianda; faggiuola, *f.:* (*nav.*) *fore*—, albero di trinchetto, *m.; main*—, albero maestro, *m.; mizzen*—, albero di mezzana, *m.; mizzen-top*—, albero di contramezzana, *m.* **mast** 2, TR.: metter gli alberi, alberare (un bastimento). **-ed**, ADJ.: alberato, corredato d' alberi.

măster I, S.: padrone; maestro; signore; (*nav.*) capitano, comandante, *m.:* — *at arms*, capitano di armi, *m.;* — *of arts*, maestro delle arti, dottore, *m.;* — *of the horse*, cavallerizzo, *m.;* — *mason*, maestro muratore, architetto, *m.; dancing* —, ballerino, *m.; school*—, maestro di scuola, *m.; be* — *of*, possedere; esser perfetto. **master** 2, TR.: sormontare; dominare, governare; rintuzzare, raffrenare. **-builder**, S.: architetto, *m.* **-dom**, S.: dominio, *m.*, sovranità, *f.* **-hand**, S.: mano di maestro, *f.* **-key**, S.: chiave maestra, *f.* **-less**, ADJ.: senza maestro; intrattabile. **-like**, ADJ.: da maestro, magistralmente. **-ly**, ADJ.: da maestro; fatto con arte; ADV.: da maestro: *in a* — *manner*, maestrevolmente. **-piece**, S.: capo d' opera, *m.* **-ship**, S.: maestria; eccellenza, *f.* **-spring**, S.: molla maestra, *f.* **-string**, S.: corda maestra, *f.* **-stroke**, S.: colpo di maestro, *m.* **-teeth**, S. PL.: mascellari, *m. pl.* **-y**, *S.: padronanza*, signoria; autorità; superiorità, *f.: great* — *of language*, grande *padronanza* di lingua.

măstful, ADJ.: pieno di ghiande.

mas-ticātion, S.: masticamento, masticare, *m.* **-ticatory**, ADJ.: masticatorio. **-tic(h)**, S.: mastice, mastrice, *f.*

măstiff, S.: mastino, cane di pastore, *m.*

măstless, ADJ.: senza albero (di nave); senza ghiande.

măstlin, S.: mistura di grani, *f.*

măstodon, S.: mastodonte, *m.*

masturbātion, S.: masturbazione, *f.*

măt I, S.: stuoia, stoia; materassa, *f.* **mat** 2, TR.: coprire di stuoie; intrecciare. **-maker**, S.: facitore di stuoie, *m.*

mătadore, S.: mattadore, *m.*

mătch I, S.: zolfanello, fiammifero, *m.;* miccia, *f.* **match** 2, S.: partito; matrimonio, *m.;* partita, *f.: he is not your* —, egli non è della vostra taglia; *the* — *is broken off*, il matrimonio è andato a monte; *make a* —, maritare. **match** 3, TR.: assortire; pareggiare, uguagliare; maritare; INTR.: unirsi; esser conforme. **-able**, ADJ.: che si può agguagliare; convenevole; conforme. **-box**, S.: scatola da zolfanelli, *f.* **-less**, ADJ.: impareggiabile, senza pari. **-lessly**, ADV.: in modo impareggiabile, incomparabilmente. **-lessness**, S.: esser impareggiabile, stato incomparabile, *m.* **-lock**, S.: fucile a miccia, *m.* **-maker**, S.: mezzano di matrimoni, *m.* **-making**, S.: il fare trattati di matrimonio, *m.*

māte I, S.: consorte, compagno, *m.*, compagna, *f.;* assistente; sottopadrone (d' un vascello), piloto, *m.* **mate** 2, TR.: pareggiare, uguagliare, aggiustare; sposare; mortificare.

matēri-al, S.: materiale, *m.;* materia prima, *f.;* ADJ.: materiale, essenziale; importante: *raw* —, materia greggia; *it is not* —, poco importa. **-alism**, S.: materialismo, *m.* **-alist**, S.: materialista, *m.* **-ălity**, S.: materialità; corporeità, *f.* **-alize**, TR.: rendere materiale. **-ally**, ADV.: materialmente, essenzialmente; di momento. **-alness**, S.: essenziale, *m.;* importanza, *f.* **-als**, S. PL.: materiali, *m. pl.* **-ate**†, **-ated**†, ADJ.: materiale, composto di materia.

matēr-nal, ADJ.: maternale, materno. **-nity**, S.: maternità, *f.*, essere di madre, *m.*

măth† = *aftermath.*

mathemăt-ic(al), ADJ.: matematico: — *instrument*, strumento di matematica, *m.* **-ically**, ADV.: matematicamente. **-ician**, S.: matematico, *m.* **-ics**, S. PL.: matematica, *f.*

mathēsis, S.: scienza della matematica, *f.*

mătin, ADJ.: mattutinale, mattutino. **-s**, S. PL.: mattina, *f.*, orazioni del mattutino, *f. pl.*

lard 2, TR.: lardare, lardellare, ingrassare. **-er**, S.: dispensa; guardavivande, *f.* **-ing-pin**, S.: (*cook.*) lardatoio, *m.*
lârdon, S.: lardello, lardellino, *m.*
lâr-ge, ADJ.: largo, grosso, grande, ampio, spazioso, vasto; liberale: — *dog*, grosso cane; — *field*, campo spazioso; — *city*, città grande; — *man*, omone; *at* —, ampiamente; *set at* —, liberare. **-gely**, ADV.: largamente; copiosamente, abbondantemente; diffusamente. **-geness**, S.: larghezza, grandezza, ampiezza, *f.* **-gess**, S.: largità, liberalità; larghezza, *f.* **-gition**†, S.: dono, donativo, *m.*
lârk, S.: allodola, lodola, *f.*: *have a* —, fare un tiro da biricchino. **-er**, S.: uccellatore d' allodole, *m.* **-spur**, S.: (*bot.*) consolida reale, *f.*
lărum, S.: allarme, *m.*; campana a stormo, *f.*
lâr-va, S.: larva, *f.*, spettro, *m.* **-vated**, ADJ.: larvato, mascherato.
lărynx, S.: laringe, *f.*
lasciv-iency† = *lasciviousness*. **-ious**, ADJ.: lascivo, lussurioso; impudico. **-iously**, ADV.: lascivamente; impudicamente. **-iousness**, S.: lascivia, lascività, impudicità, *f.*
lăsh 1, S.: sferzata, frustata; cinghia, *f.*; (*fig.*) motto pungente; ciglio, *m.* **lash** 2, TR.: sferzare, frustare; cinghiare; (*fig.*) censurare aspramente. **-er**, S.: sferzatore, frustatore, *m.* **-ing**, S.: (*nav.*) aghetto, *m.*
lâss, S.: zitella, fanciulla, ragazza, *f.*
lăssitude, S.: lassezza, stanchezza; fatica, *f.*
lâsslorn, ADJ.: abbandonato dalla sua ragazza.
lăsso, S.: laccio, *m.*
lâst 1, ADJ.: ultimo; passato; ADV.: ultima volta, finalmente: — *night*, iersera; — *week*, settimana passata; *at* —, in fine; finalmente; *to the* —, sino alla fine; — *but one* (*two*), penultimo, antepenultimo; *the* — *time*, l' ultima volta, finalmente. **last** 2, S.: fine, estremità. **last** 3, S.: (*shoe*) forma, *f.* **last** 4, S.: (*nav.*) lasto, *m.* **last** 5, INTR.: durare, continuare; sussistere.
lâstage, S.: lassa sopra le mercanzie; (*nav.*) zavorra, *f.*
lâst-ing, ADJ.: durevole, duraturo, permanente. **-ingly**, ADV.: durevolmente, perpetuamente. **-ingness**, S.: durevolezza; continuazione, *f.* **-ly**, ADV.: in fine, alla fine, finalmente; in somma.
lătch 1, S.: saliscendo, *m.* **latch** 2, TR.: chiudere con saliscendo. **-et**, S.: correggia; cintura, *f.*
lāt-e, ADJ., ADV.: lento, tardo; ultimo: *of* —, ultimamente, non ha guari; *of* — *years*, da qualche anno, in questi ultimi anni; *the* — *king*, il re defunto; *the* — *minister*, l' ex-ministro. **-ed**†, ADJ.: sorpreso dalla notte.
latēen, ADJ.: (*nav.*) latino: — *sail*, vela latina, *f.*
lātely, ADV.: ultimamente, poco fa; non è gran tempo; poco stante.
lātency, S.: oscurità, *f.*, nascondimento, *m.*
lāteness, S.: tempo più tardo, *m.*; tardezza, *f.*; indugio, *m.*
lātent, ADJ.: latente, segreto, occulto.
lāter, ADJ.: posteriore; susseguente; ADV.: più tardi; dopo.
lăteral, ADJ.: laterale, da' fianchi. **-ly**, ADV.: lateralmente, da' fianchi.
lā-test, ADJ.: ultimo, più tardo. **-teward**†, ADV.: alquanto tardo.
lăth 1, S.: panconcello, *m.*, assicella, *f.*
lăth 2, TR.: inchiodare i panconcelli, coprire di assicelle.
lāthe, S.: tornio, *m.*
lăther 1, S.: saponata, schiuma di sapone, *f.* **lather** 2, TR.: insaponare; INTR.: schiumare, spumare.
Lăt-in, S.: lingua latina, *f.* **-inism**, S.: latinismo, *m.* **-inist**, S.: latinista, *m.* **-inity**, S.: latinità, lingua latina, *f.* **-inize**, TR.: latinizzare; dire in latino.
lātish, ADJ.: alquanto tardo, tardetto, tardivo.
lătitant†, ADJ.: nascosto, celato.
lătitud-e, S.: latitudine; larghezza, *f.*; spazio, *m.* **-inārian**, ADJ.: latitudinario; non limitato; S.: libertino, *m.*
lătten 1, S.: ottone, *m.*; latta, *f.* **latten** 2, ADJ.: d' ottone: — *wire*, fil d' ottone, *m.*
lătter, ADJ.: ultimo; recente; moderno; questi. **-ly**, ADV.: ultimamente, finalmente, poco fa, non è gran tempo.
lăttice 1, S.: graticciata, *f.*, graticcio, *m.*
lattice 2, TR.: ingraticciare, ingraticolare; cancellare. **-d**, ADJ.: ingraticciato, chiuso con graticcio. **-window**, S.: inferriata, gelosia, *f.* **-work**, S.: inferriata, *f.*
lâud 1, S.: lode, laude; commendazione, *f.* **-laud** 2, TR.: lodare; commendare; celebrare. **-able**, ADJ.: lodabile, lodevole. **-ableness**, S.: laudabilità, laudevolezza, *f.* **-ably**, ADV.: lodabilmente, lodevolmente, con lode.
lâudanum, S.: laudano, *m.*
lâu-dative, **-datory**, ADJ.: lodante, laudante. **-d(e)s**, S. PL.: laudi, *m. pl.*
laugh 1 *lâf*, S.: riso, *m.*, risata, *f.* **laugh** 2, TR.: beffare, burlare; INTR.: ridere: — *at*, ridersi, burlarsi di; — *out*, ghignezzare; — *outright*, scoppiare dalle risa; — *in one's sleeves*, rider sotto i baffi.

rider di nascosto; — *one to scorn*, schernire (*or* scornare) uno. **-able**, ADJ.: risibile, ridicolo; faceto. **-er**, S.: che ride. **-ing**, ADJ.: ridente; S.: ridere, riso, *m.* **-ingly**, ADV.: con riso, in modo ridente; allegramente. **-ing-stock**, S.: ludibrio, trastullo, scherno, *m.* **-ter**, S.: riso, ridere, *m.*: *break out into* —, scoppiar dalle risa; *a fit of* —, una gran risata.

lâunch, TR.: lanciare; INTR.: slanciarsi: — *a ship*, varare un bastimento.

lâund, S.: landa, pianura fra boschi, *f.* **-er** 1, S.: truogo d' acqua, secchia, *f.* **-er** 2, TR.: lavare. **-erer**, S.: lavatore, lavandaio, *m.* **-ress**, S.: lavandaia, lavandara, *f.* **-ry**, S.: lavatoio, luogo da lavare, *m.*

lâureate, ADJ.: laureato, coronato di laurea.

lâurel, S.: laurea, *f.*, alloro, lauro, *m.* **-led**, ADJ.: coronato di laurea.

lâurestin, S.: (*bot.*) alloro selvatico, *m.*

lâva, S.: lava, *f.*

lavâtion, S.: lavazione, *f.*

lăvatory, S.: lavabo, lavatoio, *m.*; lavatura, *f.*

lâve, TR.: lavare; INTR.: lavarsi; bagnarsi.

lavēer, INTR.: (*nav.*) bordeggiare.

lăvender, S.: spigo, nardo, *m.*; lavanda, *f.*

lâver, S.: lavatoio, tino, *m.*

lăvish 1, ADJ.: prodigo, profuso, eccessivo. **lavish** 2, TR.: prodigalizzare, spendere profusamente, dissipare. **-er**, S.: spendereccio, prodigo, *m.* **-ing**, S.: scialacquamento, *m.* **-ly**, ADV.: prodigalmente, profusamente. **-ment**, **-ness**, S.: prodigalità, *f.*

lâw, S.: legge, *f.*; statuto; editto, *m.*; giurisprudenza, *f.*; processo; diritto, *m.*: *common* —, diritto comune; *statute* —, atti del parlamento, *m. pl.*; *doctor in* —, dottore di legge, *m.*; *become* —, passare in legge; *follow the* —, studiar la legge; *give* —*s*, dar leggi; *go to* —, formar processo, litigare, processare; *pass a* —, fare una legge; *take the* — *into one's own hands*, farsi giustizia da sè. **-day**, S.: giorno d' udienza, *m.* **-ful**, ADJ.: legittimo, legale, lecito; giusto. **-fully**, ADV.: secondo la legge, legalmente; giustamente. **-fulness**, S.: legalità; equità; giustizia, *f.* **-giver**, S.: legislatore, legista, *m.* **-giving**, ADJ.: legislativo. **-less**, ADJ.: senza legge; contrario alle leggi; illegale. **-lessly**, ADV.: in modo illegale. **-maker**, S.: legislatore, *m.*

lâwn, S.: pratellino, *m.*, pianura; rensa, *f.*

lâw-suit, S.: processo, *m.*, lite, causa, *f.* **-yer**, S.: avvocato; legista, giureconsulto, giurista, *m.*

lăx 1, ADJ.: molle; rilassato; debole, fiacco; vago. **lax** 2, S.: flusso di corpo, *m.*, soccorenza, *f.* **-ative**, ADJ.: lassativo; S.: (*med.*) lassativo, *m.* **-ativeness**, S.: allentamento; flusso, *m.* **-ity**, **-ness**, S.: lassità, lassitudine, rilassatezza; stanchezza, lentezza, *f.*

lây 1, ADJ.: laico, secolare. **lay** 2, S.: letto, *m.*; scommessa, *f.* **lay** 3, S.: canzone, *f.*, canto, *m.* **lay** 4, S.: terra erbosa, *f.* **lay** 5, IRR.; TR.: porre, mettere; posare; abbonacciare, calmare: disporre; scommettere; INTR.: fare una scommessa; fare delle uova: — *the cloth*, mettere la tavoglia; — *apart*, mettere da banda; rigettare; — *aside*, mettere da parte, metter da banda; deporre; omettere; lasciare, rinunziare, abbandonare; — *asleep*, addormentare, insonnare; — *out one's cards*, scartare; — *a charge against one*, incolpare alcuno; accusare alcuno; — *claim to*, pretendere; — *the dust*, abbattere la polvere; — *eggs*, fare delle uova; — *in heaps*, ammucchiare, ammassare; — *the heat*, abbattere il caldo; — *hold of*, afferrare, prendere, pigliare; — *out money*, sborsare, pagare danaro; — *open*, scoprire, spiegare, dichiarare; mostrare; — *in order*, mettere in ordine, ordinare; — *a punishment on one*, punire alcuno; — *a plot*, fare una congiura, tramare, macchinare; — *siege to*, mettere l' assiedo a; — *snares*, tendere insidie, insidiare; — *a tax*, imporre una tassa; — *a wager*, fare una scommessa; — *in wait for*, insidiare; — *waste*, desolare, distruggere, rovinare; — *wine*, mettere in cantina il vino; — *about*, battere, bastonare; — *against*, incolpare, accusare; — *at*, battere; mirare; — *away*, mettere da banda; rinunziare; — *before*, rappresentare, mostrare; — *by*, chiudere; serbare; — *down*, deporre; posare; riposare; — *forth*, distendersi; diffondere; — *in*, ammassare; — *in for*, sforzarsi di corrompere; — *on*, applicare; soprapporre; operare con vigore; — *out*, sborsare; spendere; disegnare; — *over*, coprire; incrostare; — *to*, imputare, accusare; — *together*, ammassare; comparare; confrontare; — *under*, sottomettere; — *up*, ammucchiare, accumulare; riserbare; — *upon*, soprapporre, imporre.

lây-days, S. PL.: (*nav.*) giorni di stallia, *m. pl.*

lây-er, S.: letto; strato; germoglio, *m.*; chioccia; crosta, incrostatura, *f.* **-land**, S.: (*agr.*) maggese, maggiatica, *f.*

lây-man, S.: laico, secolare; modello, *m.* **-priest**, S.: prete secolare, *m.*

lây-stall, S.: letamaio, *m.*

lâzer, S.: leproso, lebbroso, *m.* **-ĕtto**,

-house, S.: lazzaretto, *m.* **-wort**, S.: (*bot.*) belzuino, belgivino, *m.*
lāzi-ly, ADV.: lentamente, tardamente, pigramente. **-ness**, S.: tardezza, lentezza, pigrizia, *f.*
lăzuli, S.: lapislazzuli, *m.*
lāzy, ADJ.: lento, tardo; infingardo, neghittoso, pigro.
lēa, S.: prato chiuso intorno, *m.*
lēach 1, S.: ceneraccio, *m.* **leach** 2, TR.: imbucare.
lĕad 1, S.: piombo, *m.*: *black* —, miniera di piombo, *f.*; *white* —, biacca, *f.* **lead** 2, TR.: impiombare.
lēad 3, S.: direzione; condotta, *f.*; cominciamento (del giuoco); (*bill.*) acchitto, *m.*; (*fig.*) precedenza, superiorità, presidenza, *f.*: *take the* —, marciare alla testa, essere il primo; dominare; presidere; *have the* —, (*at cards*) aver la mano. **lead** 4, IRR.; TR.: menare, guidare, condurre; comandare; essere il capo: — *a dance*, guidare un ballo; — *by the hand*, menare per la mano (a mano); — *a good life*, menare buona vita; — *a sedentary life*, menare una vita sedentaria; — *by the nose*, menare pel naso; — *out of the way*, sviare; — *along*, condurre, accompagnare; — *away*, menare via; trarre seco; — *back*, rimenare, ricondurre; — *in*, introdurre; — *out*, menar fuora; *this road* —*s to R.*, questa strada conduce a R.
lĕaden, ADJ.: di piombo, piombino; pesante, goffo.
lēad-er, S.: conduttore; capo, capitano; articolo di fondo, *m.*; (*nav.*) marinaro di prua, *m.* **-ing**, ADJ.: primo, principale: — *article*, articolo di fondo, *m.*; — *hand*, mano, *m.*; — *horse*, cavallo da sella, *m.*; — *man*, capo, principale, *m.*; — *wind*, (*nav.*) vento largo, *m.* **-ing-strings**, S. PL.: stringhe, *f. pl.*; laccio, menaiuolo, *m.*: *be in* —, essere in istato di dipendenza (vassallaggio). **-man**, S.: direttore di ballo, *m.*
lĕad-ore, S.: miniera di piombo, *f.* **-pencil**, S.: lapis, *m.*, matita, *f.*
lēaf 1, S.: foglia, *f.*, foglio; battente, *m.*: *little* —, fogliolina, *f.*; — *of gold*, foglia d'oro; *turn over the leaves of a book*, sfogliettare un libro. **leaf** 2, INTR.: coprirsi di foglie, produr foglie, frondire. **-gold**, S.: oro in foglia, *m.* **-less**, ADJ.: sfrondato, senza frondi. **-let**, S.: fogliolina, *f.* **-y**, ADJ.: frondoso, frondifero, fogliato.
lēagu-e 1, S.: lega; unione; fazione, *f.*: *enter into a* —, far lega, legarsi. **-e** 2, INTR.: legarsi; confederarsi. **-ed**, ADJ.: legato; confederato. **-er**, S.: confederato; assedio; blocco, *m.*
lēak 1, S.: fessura, crepatura; (*nav.*) falla, *f.*: *stop a* —, stagnare una falla.
leak 2, INTR.: fare acqua, trapelare; colare. **-age**, S.: colatura, *f.*; scolo, *m.* **-y**, ADJ.: fesso, squarciato.
lēam, S.: (*hunt.*) guinzaglio, *m.*
lēan 1, ADJ.: magro, smunto, affilato, macilente: *grow* —, smagrire; *make* —, dimagrare. **lean** 2, (IR)R.; INTR.: appoggiarsi; inclinare; pendere: — *against*, appoggiarsi a; — *back in one's chair*, sedere dinoccolato; — *over*, sporgere; — *upon*, riposarsi sopra, fidarsi. **-ing**, S.: l'appoggiarsi, appoggiamento, *m.*; inclinazione, propensione, *f.* **-ing-staff**, S.: bastone per appoggiarsi, *m.*
lēan-ly, ADV.: magramente. **-ness**, S.: magrezza; estenuazione, *f.*
lēap 1, S.: salto, balzo, *m.*: *take a* —, fare un salto, spiccar un salto; *at a* —, ad un salto. **leap** 2, (IR)R.; TR.: coprire, montare; INTR.: saltare; lanciarsi; palpitare: — *over a ditch*, scavalcare una fossa; — *for joy*, saltare di gioia. **-er**, S.: saltatore, balzatore, *m.* **-frog**, S.: giuoco fanciullesco, *m.* **-year**, S.: anno bisestile, *m.*
lēarn, (IR)R.; (IN)TR.: insegnare; imparare, apprendere: — *by heart*, imparare a mente; — *wit*, scozzonarsi. **-ed**, ADJ.: istrutto, dotto, letterato, saputo, intelligente: *a* — *man*, un dotto, un erudito. **-edly**, ADV.: dottamente, eruditamente. **-er**, S.: scolare; principiante, *m.* **-ing**, S.: erudizione; scienza, dottrina, *f.*
lēase 1, S.: affitto, *m.*: *take a* —, *take on* —, pigliare in affitto. **lease** 2, TR.: dare in affitto, affittare. **lēase**† 3, INTR.: spigolare; ristoppare. **-hold**, S.: affitto, *m.* **-holder**, S.: fituaiuolo, fermiere, *m.* **-er**†, S.: spigolatore, *m.*
lēash 1, S.: guinzaglio, *m.*, lassa, *f.*, legame, legaccio, *m.* **leash** 2, TR.: legare, avvinchiare.
lēasing†, S.: spigolare, *m.*; menzogna, bugia, falsità, *f.*
lēasor, S.: affittatore, *m.*
lēast 1, ADJ., ADV.: minimo, più piccolo; meno; in minimo modo: *at* —, almeno; *not in the* —, in niun modo. **least** 2, S.: atomo, *m.*
lĕather, S: cuoio, *m.*, pelle, *f.*: *lose* —, scorticarsi. **-bottle**, S.: otre, otro, *m.* **-dresser**, S.: conciatore di pelli, *m.* **-n**, ADJ.: di cuoio, di pelle. **-seller**, S.: pelliciaio, pelliciere, *m.* **-y**, ADJ.: della qualità del cuoio; tiglioso, duro.
lēave 1, S.: permissione; licenza, libertà, *f.*; congedo, *m.*: *by your* —, *with your* —, con vostra licenza; *take* — *of*, prender congedo da, accommitarsi (congedarsi) di. **leave** 2, IRR.; TR.: lasciare; abbandonare; finire; INTR.: cessare; discontinuare: — *off*, abbandonare; — *off crying*,

mĕr-ciful, ADJ.: compassionevole, pietoso, clemente. **-cifully**, ADV.: misericordiosamente, compassionevolmente. **-cifulness**, S.: compassione, misericordia; pietà; clemenza, benignità, *f.* **-ciless**, ADJ.: spietato, inumano. **-cilessly**, ADV.: spietatamente, duramente, crudelmente. **-cilessness**, S.: spietatezza, inumanità, crudeltà, *f.*
mer-cūrial, ADJ.: mercuriale; vivace.
mĕr-cury, S.: mercurio, argento vivo, *m.*; vivacità, *f.*
mĕrcy, S.: misericordia, compassione; pietà; grazia, *f.*: *show* —, usar misericordia; *cry* —, domandar perdono; *for —'s sake*, di grazia. **-seat**, S.: propizitorio, *m.*
mēre 1, ADJ.: mero, puro, pretto; franco.
mere 2, S.: lago, pantano; limite, *m.* **-ly**, ADV.: solamente, semplicemente.
meretricious, ADJ.: meretricio, di meretrice, falso, vano. **-ly**, ADV.: a foggia di meretrice. **-ness**, S.: carezze di meretrice, *f. pl.*
mergănser, S.: mergo, *m.*
mĕrge, TR.: mergere.
merīdi-an, ADJ.: meridiano, di mezzo giorno; S.: meridiano; mezzodì, *m.* **-onal**, ADJ.: meridionale, australe. **-onally**, ADV.: meridionalmente; in faccia al mezzodì.
merīno, S.: merino, *m.*
mĕrit 1, S.: merito; pregio, valore; guiderdone; diritto, *m.*; ricompensa, *f.* **-merit** 2, TR.: meritare, essere degno di. **-ōrious**, ADJ.: meritorio, meritevole. **-ōriously**, ADV.: meritevolmente, in modo meritorio. **-ōriousness**, S.: merito, meritare, *m.*
mĕrlin, S.: smeriglio, *m.* (uccello).
mĕrmaid, S.: sirena, *f.*
mĕr-rily, ADV.: allegramente, lietamente, gaiamente. **-rimake** = *-ry-make.* **-riment**, S.: divertimento, festeggiamento, *m.*; allegria, *f.* **-riness**, S.: allegria, gaiezza, *f.* **-ry**, ADJ.: allegro, giocondo, gioioso, gaio, lieto; piacevole, grato, ameno: *make* —, divertirsi; beffarsi; *live a — life*, passar la vita in allegria. **-ry-Andrew**, S.: buffone, zanni, *m.* **-go-round**, S.: carosello, *m.* **-ry-make** 1, S.: festa. **-ry-make** 2, INTR.: festare. **-ry-making**, S.: festare, divertimento, *m.* **-ry-thought**, S.: forchetta del petto, *f.*
meseems, V. IMP.: mi pare, pare a me, io penso.
mes-entĕric, ADJ.: (*anat.*) mesenterico.
mĕs-entery, S.: (*anat.*) mesenterio, *m.*
mĕsh 1, S.: maglia, *f.*, buco (di rete, ecc.), *m.* **mesh** 2, TR.: prendere nella rete, inlacciare; accalappiare. **-y**, ADJ.: intrecciato.

mĕslin, S.: grano mescolato, *m.*
mĕsmerism, S.: mesmerismo, *m.*
mesprise†, S.: disprezzo, *m.*, disistima, *f.*
mĕss 1, S.: vivanda, *f.*, piatto, *m.*, pietanza; compagnia; (*nav.*) gamella, *f.*: *in a* —, in un imbroglio; sporco, infangato.
mess 2, INTR.: mangiare, vivere insieme.
mĕs-sage, S.: messaggio, *m.*, ambasciata, *f.* **-enger**, S.: messagiere; messaggio, *m.*
Messiah, S.: Messia, *m.* **-ship**, S.: missione di Messia, *f.*
mĕssieurs, S. PL.: Signori, *m. pl.*
mĕssmate, S.: commensale; (*nav.*) compagno di gamella, *m.*
mĕssuage, S.: podere affittato, *m.*; villa, *f.*
mētage, S.: misuramento (del carbone), *m.*
mĕt-al, S.: metallo; (*fig.*) spirito, *m.* **-ăllic(al)**, ADJ.: metallico, di metallo. **-alliferous**, ADJ.: metallifero. **-alline**, ADJ.: metallino, di metallo. **-allist**, S.: metalliere, *m.* **-allŏgraphy**, S.: metallografia, *f.* **-allurgist**, S.: metallurgo, *m.* **-allurgy**, S.: metallurgia, *f.*
metamŏrpho-se, TR.: trasformare. **-sis**, S.: metamorfosi, trasformazione, *f.*
mĕta-phor, S.: metafora, *f.*; tropo, *m.* **-phŏric(al)**, ADJ.: metaforico. **-phŏrically**, ADV.: metaforicamente.
mĕta-phrase, S.: metafrasi; versione, traduzione, *f.* **-phrast**, S.: metafraste, traduttore letterale, *m.*
metaphўsic(al), ADJ.: metafisico. **-ician**, S.: matafisico, *m.* **-ics**, S. PL.: metafisica, *f.*
metăstasis, S.: metastasi, *f.*
metăthesis, S.: metatesi, mutazione, *f.*
mēte, TR.: misurare.
metempsychōsis, S.: metempsicosi, *f.*
mēte-or, S.: meteora, *f.* **-orolŏgical**, ADJ.: meteorologico. **-orŏlogist**, S.: meteorologico, *m.* **-orŏlogy**, S.: meteorologia, *f.* **-ŏroscope**, S.: meteoroscopo, *m.* (strumento). **-ŏrous**, ADJ.: meteorico.
mēter, S.: misuratore, *m.*; = *metre.*
mēte-wand, **-yard**†, S.: misura, *f.*, braccio, *m.*, canna, *f.*
methĕglin, S.: idromele, *m.*, bevanda d' acqua e di mele, *f.*
methinks, V. IMP.: mi pare, io penso.
mĕth-od, S.: metodo; ordine, *m.*; maniera, *f.* **-ŏdical**, ADJ.: metodico. **-ŏdically**, ADV.: metodicamente, con metodo. **-odist**, S.: metodista, *m.* **-odize**, TR.: metodizzare.
methought *-thăt*, V. IMP.: mi pareva, mi parve, credevo.
me-tonўmic(al), ADJ.: metonimico. **-tonўmically**, ADV.: metonimicamente. **-tŏnymy**, S.: metonimia, *f.*
mētre, S.: metro, *m.*; misura (di versi), *f.*

-en, TR.: allungare, stendere; INTR.: allungarsi; distendersi. -ening, S.: allungamento, m. -wise, ADV.: in lungo.
lēnient, ADJ.: leniente, lenificativo; S.: medicina lenificativa, f.
lĕn-ify, TR.: lenificare, addolcire. -itive, ADJ.: lenitivo; mitigante; molcente; S.: lenificamento, m. -ity, S.: lenità; dolcezza, affabilità, umanità, f.
lĕns, S.: lente, m. (vetro).
Lĕnt, S.: quaresima, m.: *keep* —, osservare la quaresima. -en, ADJ.: quaresimale, di quaresima.
len-ticular, ADJ.: lenticolare. -tiginous, ADJ.: lentigginoso. lĕn-til, S.: lente, m.; lenticchia; lentiggine, f.
lĕntisk†, S.: lentischio, m.
lĕn-titude†, S.: lentezza, tardità, f. -tor, S.: tenacità, viscosità; lentezza, f. -tous, ADJ.: tenace, viscoso.
lēo, S.: (*astr.*) leone, m. -nine, ADJ.: leonino, di leone.
lĕopard, S.: leopardo, m.
lĕper, S.: lebbra, f. -ous = *leprous*.
lĕp-id, ADJ.: gaio, scherzevole, allegro. -idity, S.: lepidezza, gaiezza, f.
lĕporine, ADJ.: leporino, di lepre.
lĕp-rosy, S.: lebbra, f. -rous, ADJ.: lebbroso.
lēsion, S.: (*med.*) lesione, f.
lĕss, ADJ.: minore; inferiore; ADV.: meno, non tanto: *more or* —, più o meno; — *rich than*, meno ricco di.
lessēe, S.: pigionale, affituale, m.
lĕssen, TR.: render più piccolo, impicciolire, diminuire; scemare; INTR.: divenire più piccolo.
lĕsses†, S. PL.: sterco (di animali rapaci), m.
lĕsson 1, S.: lezione, ripetizione, f.; insegnamento, precetto; rimprovero, m. lesson 2, TR.: istruire, ammaestrare, addottrinare.
lĕssor, S.: affittatore, m.
lĕst, CONJ.: per tema, per paura (timore) che.
lĕt 1, S.: ostacolo, impedimento, m. let 2, IRR.; TR.: lasciare; permettere; ritenere, impedire; affittare, appigionare; IRR.: lasciar stare; soffrire; ritenersi, astenersi: — *alone*, lasciare in pace; — *blood*, cavare sangue; — *loose*, sciogliere; metter in libertà; — *down*, abbassare, calare; discendere; — *in* (*into*), introdurre, ammettere; — *off*, sparare, tirare; — *see*, far vedere; — *out*, far uscire; affittare; — *us speak English*, parliamo inglese; — *me speak*, lasciatemi parlare.
lēthal, ADJ.: letale, mortale, funesto. lethălity, S.: mortalità, f.
lethărgic, ADJ.: letargico. lĕthargy, S.: letargo, m.

lethiferous, ADJ.: letale, mortale.
lĕtter 1, S.: lettera, epistola, f.; carattere, m.: *capital* —, lettera maiuscula; *to the* —, alla lettera, esattamente; — *stamps*, bollini delle lettere; — *of attorney*, procura, f.; — *of mark*, lettera di marco, f.; —s, lettere, f. pl.; letteratura, scienza, f.; —*s patent*, patente, f.; —*s of respite*, arresto di rispitto, m. letter 2, TR.: soprascrivere. -bearer = -*carrier*. -box, S.: cassetta delle lettere. -carrier, S.: portalettere, m. -case, S.: portafogli, m. -ed, ADJ.: letterato, dotto. -founder, S.: fonditore di caratteri, m. -foundery, S.: fonderia di caratteri, f. -paper, S.: carta di lettere, f. -press, S.: torchio, m., stampa, f.
lĕt-tice, -tuce -*tis*, S.: lattuga, f.: *cabbage* —, lattuga cappuccia, f.
levănt, S.: levante, oriente, m. -ine, ADJ.: levantino, del Oriente.
lĕvee, S.: levata, f.; ricevimento, m.; diga, riva, f., argine, m.
lĕvel 1, ADJ.: a livello, livellato, piano; S.: livello, piano, m.; livella, f.: *make* —, lievellare, spianare, levigare; *on a* — *with*, al livello di, del pari; *above the* — *of the sea*, sopra il livello del mare. level 2, TR.: livellare, spianare, appianare; INTR.: mirare; comparare, conghietturare; tentare: — *a house with the ground*, spianare una casa; — *at*, mirare. -ler, S.: livellatore, m. -ness, S.: livello; spianamento, m.; uguaglianza, f.
lĕven = *leaven*.
lĕver, S.: lieva, stanga (da sollevare), f.
lĕveret, S.: leprettino, leprottino, lepratto, m.
lĕviable, ADJ.: che si può levare.
leviathan, S.: leviatan, m.
lĕvi-gate 1, ADJ.: levigato; polverizzato. -gate, TR.: levigare; polverizzare; stritolare. -gătion, S.: levigazione, f.; polverizzamento, m. -ty, S.: levità, leggerezza; volubilità, incostanza, f.
lĕvy 1, S.: colletta; leva (di soldati); levata; tassa, f.: — *of troops*, leva di truppe; — *of taxes*, levata di tasse. levy 2, TR.: levare; guerreggiare.
lēwd, ADJ.: dissoluto, lascivo; libidinoso, impudico. -ly, ADV.: dissolutamente, licenziosamente, impudicamente. -ness, S.: dissolutezza, f.; libertinaggio, m.; oscenità, f. -ster, S.: voluttuoso, m.
lexi-cŏgrapher, S.: lessicografo, m. -cŏgraphy, S.: lessicografia, f. -con, S.: lessico, dizionario, m.
lia-bility, S.: obbligazione, risponsabilità, f. lia-ble, ADJ.: soggetto, esposto; responsabile. -bleness = *liability*.
liar, S.: mentitore, bugiardo, m.

libātion, S.: libazione, *f.*
libel 1, S.: libello infamatorio, *m.*; satira, *f.* **libel** 2, (IN)TR.: diffamare, screditare in iscritto, calunniare. **-er**, S.: scrittore di libelli infami, diffamatore, calunniatore, *m.* **-lous**, ADJ.: diffamatorio, infamatorio.
liber-al, ADJ.: liberale, generoso, magnanimo, munificente: — *arts*, arti liberali, *m. pl.* **-alism**, S.: liberalismo, *m.* **-ălity**, S.: liberalità, generosità, magnanimità, *f.* **-alise**, TR.: render liberale. **-ally**, ADV.: liberalmente, generosamente, nobilmente. **-ate**, TR.: liberare; dare libertà. **-ātion**, S.: liberazione, *f.*, liberamento, *m.* **-ator**, S.: liberatore, *m.* **-tinage**, S.: vita licenziosa, sfrenatezza, *f.* **-tine**, ADJ.: licenzioso; S.: libertino, *m.* **-tinism**, S.: libertinismo, libertinaggio, *m.* **-ty**, S.: libertà; immunità, esenzione, *f.*; privilegio, *m.*: — *of the press*, libertà della stampa, *f.*; — *of trade*, libertà del commercio, *f.*; — *of will*, libero arbitrio, *m.*; voluntà, *f.*; *I take the* —, prendo la libertà; *shall you be at — this evening?* sarete disimpegnato questa sera?
libĭdinous, ADJ.: libidinoso, lascivo, voluttuoso. **-ly**, ADV.: libidinosamente, lascivamente. **-ness**, S.: libidine, voluttà, *f.*
libral, ADJ.: del peso d' una libbra.
li-brārian, S.: libraio; bibliotecario, *m.* **-brary**, S.: libreria; biblioteca, *f.*: *circulating* —, biblioteca circolante, *f.*; gabinetto di lettura, *m.* **-brary-keeper**, S.: bibliotecario, *m.*
li-brate, TR.: librare, equilibrare, pesare. **-brātion**, S.: libramento, *m.* **-bratory**, ADJ.: bilanciante, oscillatorio.
lice, PL. di *louse*.
licen-ce = **-se**, S.: licenza; permissione, autorizzazione, *f.*; privilegio, *m.*: *poetical* —, licenza poetica; *take out a* —, riportare una patente. **-se**, TR.: licenziare, dar licenza, autorizzare. **-ser**, S.: che da permissione; censore, *m.*
licĕn-tiate, S.: licenziato, graduato, *m.* **-tiate**, TR.: licenziare, permettere; autorizzare. **-tious**, ADJ.: licenzioso, dissoluto, sfrenato. **-tiously**, ADV.: licenziosamente, sfrenatamente. **-tiousness**, S.: licenziosità, sregolatezza, dissolutezza, *f.*
lichen, S.: (*bot.*) lichene, *m.*
licit, ADJ.: lecito.
licitātion, S.: vendita pubblica, *f.*, incanto, *m.*
licit-ly, ADV.: lecitamente. **-ness**, S.: liceitezza, legalità, *f.*
lick 1, S.: colpo, *m.*, botta, percossa; leccatura, *f.* **lick** 2, TR.: leccare, lambire: — *up*, leccare; ingoiare. **-dish**, S.: ghiottone, *m.* **-er**, S.: leccatore, *m.* **-erish**, ADJ.: delicato, leccardo, goloso. **-erishness**, S.: ghiottornia, golosità, *f.* **-erous** = *lickerish*. **-erousness** = *lickerishness*.
licorice, S.: regolizia, *f.*
lictor, S.: littore, birro, bidello, *m.*
lid, S.: coperchio, coverchio, *m.*; palpebra, *f.*
lie 1, S.: bugia, menzogna; falsità; bucata, *f.*: *give the* —, smentire; *tell —s*, dire delle menzogne, mentire. **lie** 2, INTR.: mentire, dire bugie. **lie** 3, IRR.; INTR.: giacere; esser situato; dimorare, restare; stare, essere: *here —s*, qui giace; — *close*, tenersi chiuso; — *lurking*, tenersi nascosto; — *under a mistake*, sbagliare; — *open*, essere aperto; — *sick a-bed*, stare malato in letto; — *about*, essere sparso in qua e in là; — *at*, importunare, vessare; — *by*, riposarsi; starsene quieto; — *down*, coricarsi, addormentarsi; riposarsi; — *in*, partorire: — *open*, essere esposto; — *out*, dormire fuor di casa; — *under*, essere soggetto; — *upon*, riposare; dipendere da.
lief, ADJ.: benamato, diletto; ADV.: volentieri, di buon grado; piuttosto: *I had as — go as stay*, è tutto uno per me l' andare o lo stare.
liege, ADJ.: ligio, suddito; fido; S.: vassallo, ligio, *m.*: — *lord*, sovrano signore. **-man**, S.: vassallo, *m.*
lieger, S.: ambasciadore residente, *m.*
lien, S.: diritto di ritenzione, *m.*
lientĕr-ic, ADJ.: di lienteria. **-y** *li-*, S.: lienteria, *f.*
lieu, S.: luogo, *m.*: *in — of*, in vece di.
lieutĕn-ancy, S.: luogotenenza, *f.* **-ant**, S.: luogotenente, tenente; governatore, *m.*: — *colonel*, tenente colonnello, *m.*; — *general*, tenente generale, *m.* **-ancy**, **-antship**, S.: luogotenenza, *f.*
life, S.: vita; esistenza, vivacità; condotta, *f.*: *for* —, a vita; *to the* —, al naturale; *give* —, animare; *lose one's* —, perder la vita, morire; *your — is at stake*, vi va della vita; *pension for* —, pensione vitalizia. **-blood**, S.: sangue, *m.* **-boat**, S.: batello da salvamento, *m.* **-giving**, ADJ.: vivificante. **-guard**, S.: guardia del corpo, *f.* **-less**, ADJ.: senza vita, inanimato. **-lessly**, ADV.: senza vigore. **-lessness**, S.: mancanza di vita, *f.* **-preserver**, S.: apparecchio di salvamento, *m.* **-rent**, S.: pensione a vita, *f.* **-time**, S.: tempo della vita; vita, *f.*: *in his* —, nella sua vita. **-weary**, ADJ.: stanco di vivere; miserabile, misero.
lift 1, S.: alzamento; sforzo (per levar); aiuto; ascensore, *m.*: *at one* —, alla pri-

ma, in un subito; *give one a* —, assistere alcuno, aiutare alcuno. **lift** 2, IRR.; TR.: levare, alzare; inalzare; sollevare; INTR.: sforzarsi di sollevare: — *away*, portar via; depredare. **-er**, S.: che alza. **-ing**, S.: elevazione, alzata, *f.*
liga-ment, S.: ligamento, vincolo, *m.* **-mĕntal**, **-mĕntous**, ADJ.: ligamentoso. **-ture**, S.: legatura; benda, *f.*
light 1, ADJ.: leggiero; agile, attivo, veloce; frivolo; incostante. **light** 2, ADJ.: chiaro, luminoso; biondo; (*nav.*) scaricato, alleggerito; ADV.: leggiermente; facilmente; agilmente: — *hair*, capelli biondi, *m. pl.*; — *as a feather*, leggiero quanto una piuma; — *of belief*, credulo; *make* — *of*, far poco conto di. **light** 3, S.: lume; splendore; faro, *m.*; chiarezza; intelligenza, conoscenza, *f.*: *it begins to be* —, comincia a farsi giorno; *bring to* —, metter in chiaro; *stand in one's* —, impedire il lume ad uno; far torto ad uno. **light** 4, IRR.; TR.: accendere, allumare; illuminare; dichiarare; scaricare. **light** 5, IRR.; INTR.: venire per accidente, incontrare; arrivare; succedere; scendere, montar da cavallo; posarsi, poggiarsi: — *upon*, imbattersi in.
light-armed, ADJ.: armato alla leggiera. **-brained**, ADJ.: scervellato.
light-coloured, ADJ.: chiaro. **-en**, TR.: illuminare; alleggerire; INTR.: balenare; lampeggiare: *it* —*s*, lampeggia. **-ening**, S.: alleggerimento; baleno, *m.*
lighter, S.: alleggio; batello, *m.*, chiatta, scafa, *f.* **-man**, S.: navalestro, *m.*
light-fingered, ADJ.: leggiero alla mano, inclinato a rubare. **-footed**, ADJ.: leggiero alla corsa, veloce. **-headed**, ADJ.: delirante, stordito. **-headedness**, S.: delirio, *m.* **-hearted**, ADJ.: gaio, giocondo, allegro. **-horse**, S.: cavalleria leggiera, *f.*
light-house, S.: faro, fanale, *m.* **-ing**, S.: illuminazione, *f.*
light-legged, ADJ.: veloce; leggiero.
lightless, ADJ.: oscuro, tenebroso, fosco.
light-ly, ADV.: leggiermente; facilmente; un poco. **-minded**, ADJ.: incostante, instabile.
light-ness, S.: leggerezza, agilità; prestezza, *f.* **-ning**, S.: baleno, lampo; bagliore, *m.* **-ning-rod**, S.: parafulmine, *m.* **-s**, S. PL.: polmoni (d'un animale), *m. pl.* **-some**, ADJ.: chiaro; allegro, gaio, gioioso. **-someness**, S.: chiarezza; gaiezza, *f.*
lignáloes, S.: legno aloè, *m.*
lig-neous, ADJ.: ligneo, di legno.
lik-e 1, ADJ.: simile, somigliante; pari; medesimo; probabile, verisimile; ADV.: come, da, alla maniera di: *be* —, esser somigliante a; esser sul punto; *in* — *manner*, parimente; *I had* — *to have forgotten it*, l'avevo quasi dimenticato; — *an honest man*, da galantuomo; — *master*, — *man*, qual padrone, tal servo; — *a man*, da valent'uomo; — *a madman*, da matto. **-e** 2, S.: pariglia; somiglianza; cosa simile, *f.*: *give* — *for* —, render la pariglia, render pane per focaccia. **-e** 3, TR.: amare; approvare; aggradire; INTR.: avere gusto, essere a grado, compiacersi; *how do you* — *it?* come vi piace? *I should* — *to see it*, vorrei vederlo; *as you* —, come vi piace (*or* aggrada). **-elihood**, **-eliness**, S.: probabilità; apparenza, *f.* **-ely**, ADJ.: probabile, verisimile, credibile; apparente; ADV.: probabilmente, verisimilmente. **-en**, TR.: comparare, paragonare; rassomigliare. **-eness**, S.: sembianza, somiglianza; apparenza; conformità; immagine, *f.*, ritratto, *m.*: *good* — ritratto rassomigliante; *in the* — *of*, all'immagine di. **-ewise**, ADV.: parimente, similmente, anche; pure; d'altrove, altresì. **-ing** 1, ADJ.: paffuto, grassetto. **-ing** 2, S.: grassezza, *f.*; genio, gusto; consenso, *m.*: *that is to my* —, ciò mi va a genio, ciò mi quadra; *take a* — *to a thing*, prendere diletto, dilettarsi di qualche cosa.
lilach, S.: lillà, ghianda unguentaria, *f.*
lil-ied, ADJ.: ornato di gigli. **-y**, S.: giglio; fiordaliso, *m.*: — *of the valley*, mughetto, *m.* **-y-livered**, ADJ.: codardo, pauroso.
limātion, S.: limare, *m.* **limature**, S.: limatura, *f.*
limb 1, S.: membro, *m.*; estremità; parte, *f.* **limb** 2, TR.: dare membra; smembrare, sbranare.
limbeck, S.: limbicco, lambicco, *m.*
limbed, ADJ.: membruto.
limber 1, ADJ.: flessibile, pieghevole, arrendevole; agevole. **limber** 2, S.: (*nav.*) anguilla, *f.* **-board**, S.: (*nav.*) apertura della tromba, *f.* **-hole**, S.: (*nav.*) anguilla, *f.* **-ness**, S.: flessibilità, *f.*
limbo, S.: limbo, *m.*; prigione, *f.*
lime 1, S.: calcina; calce, *f.*; lemone; tiglio, *m.*: *quick*—, calcina viva, *f.*
lime 2, TR.: invischiare; cimentare; incalcinare. **-burner**, S.: fornaciaio, *m.*
lime-hound, S.: bracco da sangue, *m.*
lime-juice, S.: acqua di cedro, *f.*
lime-kiln, S.: fornace (da calcinare), *f.* **-pit**, S.: buca della calcina, *f.*
limer = *lime-hound*.
lime-stone, S.: pietra da calcina, alberese, *f.* **-twig**, S.: fuscello impaniato, *m.* **-water**, S.: acqua impregnata di calce; acqua cedrata, *f.*
limit 1, S.: limite, termine, confine, *m.*

sione, *f.* **-pan**, s.: patella del ginocchio, *f.* **-tribute**, s.: genuflessione, *f.*
knĕll, s.: suono della campana funebre, *m.*, *f.*, suono funebre, *m.*
knife, s.: coltello, *m.*: *carving* —, coltello da trinciare; *pruning* —, roncone, falcetto, *m.*; *table* —, coltello da tavola; *sharpen a* —, arrotare (affilare) un coltello.
knight 1, s.: cavaliere, *m.*: — *of the garter*, cavaliere della giarrettiera. **knight** 2, TR.: creare cavaliere. **-errant**, s.: cavaliere errante, *m.* **-ĕrrantry**, s.: cavalleria errante, *f.* **-hood**, s.: dignità di cavaliere, *f.*; ordine di cavalleria, *m.* **-ly**, ADJ.: cavalleresco, di cavaliere. **-marshal**, s.: maresciallo di corte, *m.* **-service**, s.: servizio di cavaliere, *m.* **-templar**, s.: templario, tempiere, *m.*
knit 1, s.: lendine, *f.* **knit** 2, s.: lavoro a maglie, *m.* **knit** 3, (IR)R.; TR.: legare, annodare; unire; INTR.: lavorare all' ago: — *the brows*, increspar la fronte; — *stockings*, far (lavorar) calze; — *a net*, fare un rete, intrecciare. **-ter**, s.: lavoratore a maglie, lavoratore all' ago, *m.* **-ting-needle**, s.: gucchia, *f.*, ago da lavorare a maglie, *m.* **-ting-sheath**, s.: cannello per le gucchie, *m.* **-ting-yarn**, s.: filo da fare calzette, *m.* **-tle**, s.: cordicella, *f.*, cordoncino (di borsa), *m.* **-work**, s.: lavoro a maglie, *m.*
knŏb, s.: tumore; nodo, *m.*; bozza, *f.* **-bed**, ADJ.: nodoso, nocchioso. **-biness**, s.: nodosità; callosità, *f.* **-by**, ADJ.: nodoso, nocchioso; calloso.
knŏck 1, s.: colpo, *m.*, percossa, botta, *f.*; picchio (alla porta), *m.* **knock** 2, TR.: battere; colpire, picchiare; urtare, bussare; INTR.: urtarsi: — *away*, seguitar a picchiare; — *down*, atterrare; ammazzare; — *in*, ficcare dentro per forza; — *off*, rompere; far saltare; cessare di lavorare; — *out*, cacciare fuori per forza; — *under*, arrendersi, sommettersi; cedere; — *up*, risvegliare; straccare; *I am —ed up*, sono stracco. **-er**, s.: martello (di porta), *m.* **-ing**, s.: picchio; strepito, fracasso, romore, *m.*
knōll, TR.: sonare (la campana); sonare a morto.
knŏt 1, s.: nodo; nocchio; gruppo, *m.*; banda, brigata, *f.*; stormo; intrigo, imbroglio, *m.*, difficoltà, *f.*: *Gordian* —, nodo gordiano; *run nine —s an hour*, fare nove nodi per ora. **knot** 2, TR.: annodare; imbrogliare, intrigare; INTR.: annodarsi; germogliare; spuntare. **-grass**, s.: sanguinaria, *f.* **-ted**, ADJ.: annodato; nodoso, nocchioso. **-tiness**, s.: nodosità; difficoltà, *f.*, imbroglio, intrigo, *m.* **-ty**, ADJ.: nodoso, nocchiuto; difficile, intricato: — *question*, quistione intralciata.
knōut, s.: frusta russa (per punire), *f.*
knōw, IRR.; TR.: sapere, conoscere; INTR.: essere informato; sapere: — *one's self*, conoscersi; *let* —, far sapere, dar avviso, avvisare; — *by experience*, saper per prova; — *by sight*, conoscere di vista; — *thoroughly*, sapere a fondo; *that I* —, che io sappia. **-able**, ADJ.: conoscibile; che si può sapere. **-er**, s.: conoscitore, sapiente, *m.* **-ing** 1, ADJ.: sapevole, saputo, intelligente, accorto. **-ing** 2, s.: sapere, *m.*, notizia, scienza, *f.* **-ingly**, ADV.: sapevolmente, a bello studio. **knŏwledge**, s.: conoscenza; scienza; notizia; abilità, *f.*: *to my* —, a mia saputa; *without my* —, senza la mia saputa; *get* — *of*, informarsi. **-n**, ADJ.: cognito, conosciuto, saputo: *well* —, conosciutissimo.
knŭb, **-ble**, TR.: battere, schiaffeggiare.
knŭckle 1, s.: congiuntura, *f.*; garretto di vitella, *m.* **knuckle** 2, TR.: battere; INTR.: arrendersi, sommettersi. **-d**, ADJ.: nocchiuto, nocchieruto.
knur = *knar*. **-ry**, ADJ.: nodoso.
kōdak, s.: macchina fotografica per dilettanti, *f.*
kōran, s.: alcorano, *m.*

L

l *ell (the letter)*, s.: l, *m. or f.*
lā†, INTERJ.: là: ecco! vedi! guarda!
lăbdanum, s.: ladano, laudano, *m.*
lab-efăction, s.: debilitamento, *m.* **-efy**, TR.: indebolire.
lābel 1, s.: cartello, *m.*; inscrizione, etichetta, *f.* **label** 2, TR.: notare, segnare.
lā-bial, ADJ.: labiale; di viva voce. **-biated**, ADJ.: (*bot.*) labbiato.
lābor = *labour*.
lăboratory, s.: laboratorio, *m.*; fonderia, *f.*
labōrious, ADJ.: laborioso, faticoso, difficile; assiduo. **-ly**, ADV.: laboriosamente, con fatica. **-ness**, s.: fatica; difficoltà; diligenza, assiduità, *f.*
lābour 1, s.: lavoro, travaglio, *m.*; fatica, pena, opera, *f.*: *be in* —, aver le doglie. **labour** 2, TR.: lavorare; affaticare, tormentare; affliggere; battere; INTR.: affaticarsi, impiegarsi; esercitarsi: — *with child*, aver le doglie; — *for an office*, cercare una carica; — *under a mistake*, sbagliarsi; — *under many difficulties*, aver molte difficoltà a vincere. **-er**, s.: lavorante; operaio, *m.* **-less**, ADJ.: senza fatica. **-some**, ADJ.: laborioso, faticoso, difficile, arduo.

lăbyrinth, S.: laberinto, *m.*
lăc, S.: lacca, *f.*
lāce 1, S.: stringa, *f.*; merletto; nastro, *m.* **lace** 2, TR.: allacciare; gallonare, guarnire di merletto; bastonare. **-maker**, S.: facitore di merletto, *m.* **-man**, S.: che fa i passamani, fabbricatore di merletti, *m.* **-merchant**, S.: mercante di merletti, *m.* **-pillow**, S.: tombolo, *m.*
lăcer-able, ADJ.: lacerabile, che può lacerarsi. **-ăte**, TR.: lacerare; stracciare. **-ātion**, S.: lacerazione, *f.*, laceramento; stracciamento, *m.*
lāce-woman, S.: donna che fa merletti con piombini, *f.* **-work**, S.: passamano, merletto, *m.*
lăch-rymal, ADJ.: lagrimale, lacrimale. **-rymātion**, S.: lagrimazione, *f.* **-rymatory**, S.: lacrimatoio, *m.*
lăck 1, S.: mancanza, *f.*, bisogno, *m.*: *be in — of*, mancare di, di fettare. **lack** 2, TR.: mancare, avere bisogno. **-a-day!** INTERJ.: cappita! capperi! **-brain**, S.: scioccone, minchione, *m.*
lăcker 1, S.: vernice della Cina, lacca, *f.* **lacker** 2, TR.: vernicare, verniciare, inverniciare.
lăckey 1, S.: lacchè, staffiere, *m.* **lackey** 2, INTR.: servire vilmente.
lăck-lustre, ADJ.: senza splendore.
lacŏnic(al), ADJ.: laconico, conciso. **-ally**, ADV.: laconicamente, strettamente, brevemente.
lăconism, S.: laconismo, *m.*
lăc-tary 1, ADJ.: latteo, lattifero. **-tary** 2, S.: cascina, *f.*; latticini, *m. pl.* **-tātion**, S.: allattamento, *m.* **-teal**, ADJ.: latteo, lattifero, latticinoso: — *veins*, vene lattee, *f. pl.* **-teous**, ADJ.: latteo, chiloso. **-tĕscence**, S.: formazione del latte, *f.* **-tĕscent**, ADJ.: latteggiante, chilificante. **-tiferous**, ADJ.: (*anat.*) lattifero, latteo.
lacūna, S.: lacuna, *f.*, vuoto in un manoscritto, *m.*
lăd, S.: giovanetto, adolescente; garzone, *m.*
lădanum = *labdanum*.
lădder, S.: scala a piuoli; gradazione, *f.*, digradamento, *m.* **-rope**, S.: (*nav.*) guardamano, *m.* **-stop**, S.: piuolo, *m.*
lād-e 1, S.: bocca; imboccatura d' un fiume, *f.* **-e** 2, (IR)R.; TR.: caricare; colmare. **-en**, ADJ.: carico, aggravato, oppresso. **-ing**, S.: caricamento, caricare; noleggio, *m.*: *bill of —*, polizza di carico, *f.*
lādle, S.: cucchiaione, *m.*, mestola, *f.*; romaiuolo, *m.* **-ful**, S.: cucchiaiata, *f.*
lādy, S.: dama, signora, *f.*; padrona di casa; donna nobile (contessa, ecc.): *Our —*, nostra Signora, la Madonna; *young —*, damigella; *young married —*, giovine signora. **-bird**, **-cow**, S.: coccinella, *f.* (insetto). **-day**, S.: annunziazione, *f.* **-like**, ADJ.: donnesco; gentile, elegante. **-ship**, S.: qualità di donna; Signoria, Eccellenza, *f.*
lăg 1, ADJ.: ultimo; tardo, pigro; negligente. **lag** 2, S.: ultimo, *m.*; ultima classe, *f.*; rifiuto, *m.* **lag** 3, INTR.: restare dietro; muoversi pigramente; tentennare: — *behind*, star indietro, indugiare. **-gard**, **-ger**, S.: infingardo, pigro; tentennone; indugiatore, *m.*
lāger, **-beer**, S.: birra fermentata alla tedesca, *f.*
la-gōon, **-gūne**, S.: laguna, palude, *f.*
lāic(al), ADJ.: laico, secolare.
lāid, PART.: messo, posto; ordinato (cf. *lay*).
lāin, PART.: stato, giaciuto (cf. *lie*).
lāir, S.: ricettacolo; covile, *m.*; tana, *f.*
lāird, S.: signore d' un feudo, *m.*
lāity, S.: laici, secolari, *m. pl.*
lāke, S.: lago, *m.*; lacca, *f.*
lăm, TR.: bastonare, battere.
lămb 1, S.: agnello, *m.* **lamb** 2, INTR.: far un agnello.
lăm-bative, S.: (*med*) lambitivo, *m.* **-bent**, ADJ.: lambente, leccante; leggiere
lămb-kin, S.: agnellino, agnelletto, *m.* **-s'-wool**, S.: lana d' agnello; sorta di birra, *f.*
lāme 1, ADJ.: zoppo, storpiato; imperfetto: — *of one leg*, storpiato d' una gamba; *go —*, zoppicare. **lame** 2, TR.: storpiare, stroppiare; troncare, guastare.
lămellated, ADJ.: lamellato.
lāme-ly, ADV.: stortamente; imperfettamente; contra voglia. **-ness**, S.: storpiatura; imperfezione, *f*
lamĕnt 1, S.: lamento, *m.*, lamentazione, *f.*, compianto; gemito, *m.* **lament** 2, TR.: deplorare, compiangere; INTR.: lamentarsi, dolersi. **-able**, ADJ.: lamentevole, lamentabile, compassionevole, deplorabile. **-ably**, ADV.: lamentevolmente. **-ātion**, S.: lamentazione, *f.*, lamento, pianto, *m.* **-er**, S.: che si lamenta, che si deplora, lamentatore, *m.* **-ing**, S.: lamento, *m.*
lămi-na, S.: lamina, lama; piastra di metallo, *f.* **-nated**, ADJ.: ridotto laminoso.
lămm = *lam*.
lămmas, S.: primo giorn
lămp, S.: lampada, lampa
little —, lampionino, lamp
—, lampione, *m* **-black**
fummo, *m.*
lămpern, S.: lampreda, *f.*,
to, *m.*
lămp-maker, S.: lampanaio

lampòon, s.: satira, f., libello satirico, m. **lampoon** 2, TR.: far una satira, satireggiare, diffamare. **-er**, s.: scrittore di satire, m.
lamprey, s.: lampreda, f.
lampril, s.: lampredotto, m.
lamp-wick, s.: lucignolo, m.
lâ-nary, s.: magazzino della lana, m. **-nate(d)**, ADJ.: lanuto, lanoso.
lânce, s.: lancia, asta, f. **-e** 2, TR.: tagliare con lancetta, aprire. **-eolated**, ADJ.: lanceolato. **-e-shaped**, ADJ.: in forma di lancia. **-e-pesade**, s.: milite lancia spezzata, f. **-er**, s.: lanciere, m. **-et**, s.: (chir.) lancetta, lanciuola, f.
lânch = launch.
lancêr = lancer.
lânci-nate, TR.: stracciare, lacerare. **-nàtion**, s.: stracciamento, laceramento, m.
lând, s.: terra, regione, f., paese, m.: arable — terra arativa, aratoria, f.; foreign — paese straniero; native — terra natale; promised — terra promessa; Holy — Terra Santa; by —, per terra; make the — approdare, prender terra. **land** 2, INTR.: sbarcare, prender terra.
lândau, s.: carrozza a soffietto, f.
lând-cape, s.: promontorio, m. **-captain**, s.: capitano che serve per terra, m. **-chain**, s.: catena del misuratore, f. **-ed**, ADJ.: che possiede terre: — property, proprietà fondiaria. **-fall**, s.: eredità inaspettata, f. **-flood**, s.: inondazione, f. **-forces**, s. PL.: forze terrestri, f. pl. **-grave**, s.: langravio, m. **-gràviate**, s.: langraviato, m. **-holder**, s.: padrone di fondi, m. **-ing**, **-ing-place**, s.: sbarcatoio; pianerottolo, m. **-jobber**, s.: sensale, mezzano, m. **-lady**, s.: padrona di terre, ostessa, f. **-less**, ADJ.: senza terre, senza poderi. **-loper** = -lubber. **-lord**, s.: padrone di poderi; oste, m. **-lubber**, s.: uomo terragnolo; pellegrino, vagabondo, poltrone, m. **-mark**, s.: limite, m. **-measurer**, s.: agrimensore, misuratore, m. **-measuring**, s.: agrimensura, f. **-scape**, s.: paesaggio, paese, m. **-tax**, s.: taglia, gravezza sopra le terre, f. **-trade**, s.: traffico di terra, m. **-waiter**, s.: doganiere, m. **-ward(s)**, ADV.: verso terra.
lâne, s.: vico, vicolo, passaggio, m.; strada stretta, f.
lânęret, s.: laniere, m.
lângrel, s.: palla incatenata, f.
lânguage, s.: lingua, f., linguaggio; idioma, m.: *the English* —, la lingua inglese; *the — of birds*, il linguaggio degli uccelli; *give one good* —, dar delle buone parole ad uno; *give one ill* —, ingiurare uno. **-d**, ADJ.: che possiede diverse lingue, dotto in diverse lingue. **-master**, s.: maestro di lingua, m.
lânguid, ADJ.: languido, debole, fiacco. **-ly**, ADV.: languidamente, debolmente, fiaccamente. **-ness**, s.: languidezza, fiacchezza, f.
lânguish, INTR.: languire, infievolire; svanire, svenire. **-ing**, ADJ.: languente, languido, debole; addolorato. **-ingly**, ADV.: con languidezza. **-ment**, s.: languidezza, f.; debilitamento, m.
lânguor, s.: languore, m. **-ous**, ADJ.: languido; noioso.
lâniard, s.: (nar.) drizza, scotta, f.
lâniate, TR.: laniare, lacerare.
lânifice, s.: lanificio, m.
lanigerous, ADJ.: lanifero, lanuginoso.
lânk 1, ADJ.: magro, stenuato, gracile, debile, fiacco, languido; molle. **lank** 2, INTR.: smagrire. **-ness**, s.: magrezza, macilenza, fiacchezza, f.
lânner, **-et**, s.: laniere, m.
lânsquenet, s.: lanzichenecco, m.
lântern, s.: lanterna, f.; faro, fanale, m.: *dark* —, lanterna cieca (sorda), f.; *large* —, lanternone, m.; *small* —, lanternetta, f.; *magic* —, lanterna magica. **-jaws**, s. PL.: viso magro, viso asciutto, m. **-maker**, s.: lanternaio, m.
lanùginous, ADJ.: lanuginoso, lanoso.
lâp 1, s.: grembo, m.; falda, piega, f.: *on her* —, in grembo; — *of the ear*, punta dell' orecchio, f. **lap** 2, TR.: inviluppare, involgere. **lap** 3, TR.: leccare, lambire.
lâp-dog, s.: cagnolino, m. **-eared**, ADJ.: che ha gli orecchi pendenti. **-ful**, s.: grembiata, grembialata, f., grembiale pieno, m.
lapèl, s.: rivolta (dell' abito), m.
lâp-idary, s.: lapidario, gioielliere, m. **-idate**, TR.: lapidare, uccidere con sassi. **-idâtion**, s.: lapidazione, f. **-ideous**, ADJ.: lapideo, di lapide. **-idéscence**, s.: impietramento, m., lapidificazione, f. **-idific**, ADJ.: lapidescente. **-idificâtion**, s.: lapidificazione, f. **-idist**, s.: venditore di lapide, lapidario, m.
lâpis-lâzuli, s.: lapislazzalo, m.
lâppet, s.: falda, f.
lâpse 1, s.: cascata, f., scorrimento; errore, m.; mancanza, piccola colpa, f. **lapse** 2, INTR.: cascare; scorrere; mancare, errare.
lâpwing, s.: pavoncella, f.
lârboard, s.: (nar.) babordo, lato sinistro d' una nave, m.
lârceny, s.: furto, ladroneccio, rubamento, latrocinio, m.
lârch, **-tree**, s.: larice, m.
lârd 1, s.: lardo, grasso di porco, m.

lard 2, TR.: lardare, lardellare, ingrassare. **-er**, S.: dispensa; guardavivande, *f.* **-ing-pin**, S.: (*cook.*) lardatoio, *m.*
lârdon, S.: lardello, lardellino, *m.*
lâr-ge, ADJ.: largo, grosso, grande, ampio, spazioso, vasto; liberale: — *dog*, grosso cane; — *field*, campo spazioso; — *city*, città grande; — *man*, omone; *at* —, ampiamente; *set at* —, liberare. **-gely**, ADV.: largamente; copiosamente, abbondantemente; diffusamente. **-geness**, S.: larghezza, grandezza, ampiezza, *f.* **-gess**, S.: largità, liberalità; larghezza, *f.* **-gition**†, S.: dono, donativo, *m.*
lârk, S.: allodola, lodola, *f.*: *have a* —, fare un tiro da biricchino. **-er**, S.: uccellatore d'allodole, *m.* **-spur**, S.: (*bot.*) consolida reale, *f.*
lârum, S.: allarme, *m.*; campana a stormo, *f.*
lâr-va, S.: larva, *f.*, spettro, *m.* **-vated**, ADJ.: larvato, mascherato.
lărynx, S.: laringe, *f.*
lasciv-iency† = *lasciviousness.* **-ious**, ADJ.: lascivo, lussurioso; impudico. **-iously**, ADV.: lascivamente; impudicamente. **-iousness**, S.: lascivia, lascività, impudicità, *f.*
lăsh 1, S.: sferzata, frustata; cinghia, *f.*; (*fig.*) motto pungente; ciglio, *m.* **lash** 2, TR.: sferzare, frustare; cinghiare; (*fig.*) censurare aspramente. **-er**, S.: sferzatore, frustatore, *m.* **-ing**, S.: (*nav.*) aghetto, *m.*
lâss, S.: zitella, fanciulla, ragazza, *f.*
lâssitude, S.: lassezza, stanchezza; fatica, *f.*
lâsslorn, ADJ.: abbandonato dalla sua ragazza.
lăsso, S.: laccio, *m.*
lâst 1, ADJ.: ultimo; passato; ADV.: ultima volta, finalmente: — *night*, iersera; — *week*, settimana passata; *at* —, in fine; finalmente; *to the* —, sino alla fine; — *but one* (*two*), penultimo, antepenultimo; *the* — *time*, l'ultima volta, finalmente. **last** 2, S.: fine, estremità. **last** 3, S.: (*shoe*) forma, *f.* **last** 4, S.: (*nav.*) lasto, *m.* **last** 5, INTR.: durare, continuare; sussistere.
lâstage, S.: lassa sopra le mercanzie; (*nav.*) zavorra, *f.*
lâst-ing, ADJ.: durevole, duraturo, permanente. **-ingly**, ADV.: durevolmente, perpetuamente. **-ingness**, S.: durevolezza; continuazione, *f.* **-ly**, ADV.: in fine, alla fine, finalmente; in somma.
lătch 1, S.: saliscendo, *m.* **latch** 2, TR.: chiudere con saliscendo. **-et**, S.: correggia; cintura, *f.*
lāt-e, ADJ., ADV.: lento, tardo; ultimo: *of* —, ultimamente, non ha guari; *of* — *years*, da qualche anno, in questi ultimi anni; *the* — *king*, il re defunto; *the* — *minister*, l'ex-ministro. **-ed**†, ADJ.: sorpreso dalla notte.
latēen, ADJ.: (*nav.*) latino: — *sail*, vela latina, *f.*
lātely, ADV.: ultimamente, poco fa; non è gran tempo; poco stante.
lātency, S.: oscurità, *f.*, nascondimento, *m.*
lāteness, S.: tempo più tardo, *m.*; tardezza, *f.*; indugio, *m.*
lātent, ADJ.: latente, segreto, occulto.
lāter, ADJ.: posteriore; susseguente; ADV.: più tardi; dopo.
lăteral, ADJ.: laterale, da' fianchi. **-ly**, ADV.: lateralmente, da' fianchi.
lā-test, ADJ.: ultimo, più tardo. **-teward**†, ADV.: alquanto tardo.
lăth 1, S.: panconcello, *m.*, assicella, *f.*
lăth 2, TR.: inchiodare i panconcelli, coprire di assicelle.
lāthe, S.: tornio, *m.*
lăther 1, S.: saponata, schiuma di sapone, *f.* **lather** 2, TR.: insaponare; INTR.: schiumare, spumare.
Lăt-in, S.: lingua latina, *f.* **-inism**, S.: latinismo, *m.* **-inist**, S.: latinista, *m.* **-inity**, S.: latinità, lingua latina, *f.* **-inize**, TR.: latinizzare; dire in latino.
lātish, ADJ.: alquanto tardo, tardetto, tardivo.
lātitant†, ADJ.: nascosto, celato.
lătitud-e, S.: latitudine; larghezza, *f.*; spazio, *m.* **-inārian**, ADJ.: latitudinario; non limitato; S.: libertino, *m.*
lătten 1, S.: ottone, *m.*; latta, *f.* **latten** 2, ADJ.: d' ottone: — *wire*, fil d' ottone, *m.*
lătter, ADJ.: ultimo; recente; moderno; questi. **-ly**, ADV.: ultimamente, finalmente, poco fa, non è gran tempo.
lăttice 1, S.: graticciata, *f.*, graticcio, *m.* **lattice** 2, TR.: ingraticciare, ingraticolare; cancellare. **-d**, ADJ.: ingraticciato, chiuso con graticcio. **-window**, S.: inferriata, gelosia, *f.* **-work**, S.: inferriata, *f.*
lâud 1, S.: lode, laude; commendazione, *f.* **-laud** 2, TR.: lodare; commendare; celebrare. **-able**, ADJ.: lodabile, lodevole. **-ableness**, S.: laudabilità, laudevolezza, *f.* **-ably**, ADV.: lodabilmente, lodevolmente, con lode.
lăudanum, S.: laudano, *m.*
lâu-dative, **-datory**, ADJ.: lodante, laudante. **-d(e)s**, S. PL.: laudi, *m. pl.*
laugh 1 *lâf*, S.: riso, *m.*, risata, *f.* **laugh** 2, TR.: beffare, burlare; INTR.: ridere: — *at*, ridersi, burlarsi di; — *out*, ghignezzare; — *outright*, scoppiare dalle risa; — *in one's sleeves*, rider sotto i baffi

-house, S.: lazzaretto, *m.* **-wort**, S.: (*bot.*) belzuino, belgivino, *m.*

lāzi-ly, ADV.: lentamente, tardamente, pigramente. **-ness**, S.: tardezza, lentezza, pigrizia, *f.*

lăzuli, S.: lapislazzuli, *m.*

lāzy, ADJ.: lento, tardo; infingardo, neghittoso, pigro.

lēa, S.: prato chiuso intorno, *m.*

lēach 1, S.: ceneraccio, *m.* **leach** 2, TR.: imbucare.

lĕad 1, S.: piombo, *m.*: *black* —, miniera di piombo, *f.*; *white* —, biacca, *f.* **lead** 2, TR.: impiombare.

lēad 3, S.: direzione; condotta, *f.*; cominciamento (del giuoco); (*bill.*) acchitto, *m.*; (*fig.*) precedenza, superiorità, presidenza, *f.*: *take the* —, marciare alla testa, essere il primo; dominare; presidere; *have the* —, (*at cards*) aver la mano. **lead** 4, IRR.; TR.: menare, guidare, condurre; comandare; essere il capo: — *a dance*, guidare un ballo; — *by the hand*, menare per la mano (a mano); — *a good life*, menare buona vita; — *a sedentary life*, menare una vita sedentaria; — *by the nose*, menare pel naso; — *out of the way*, sviare; — *along*, condurre, accompagnare; — *away*, menare via; trarre seco; — *back*, rimenare, ricondurre; — *in*, introdurre; — *out*, menar fuora; *this road* —*s to R.*, questa strada conduce a R.

lĕaden, ADJ.: di piombo, piombino; pesante, goffo.

lēad-er, S.: conduttore; capo, capitano; articolo di fondo, *m.*; (*nav.*) marinaro di prua, *m.* **-ing**, ADJ.: primo, principale: — *article*, articolo di fondo, *m.*; — *hand*, mano, *m.*; — *horse*, cavallo da sella, *m.*; — *man*, capo, principale, *m.*; — *wind*, (*nav.*) vento largo, *m.* **-ing-strings**, S. PL.: stringhe, *f. pl.*; laccio, menaiuolo, *m.*: *be in* —, essere in istato di dipendenza (vasallaggio). **-man**, S.: direttore di ballo, *m.*

lĕad-ore, S.: miniera di piombo, *f.* **-pencil**, S.: lapis, *m.*, matita, *f.*

lēaf 1, S.: foglia, *f.*, foglio; battente, *m.*: *little* —, fogliolina, *f.*; — *of gold*, foglia d'oro; *turn over the leaves of a book*, sfogliettare un libro. **leaf** 2, INTR.: coprirsi di foglie, produr foglie, frondire. **-gold**, S.: oro in foglia, *m.* **-less**, ADJ.: sfrondato, senza frondi. **-let**, S.: fogliolina, *f.* **-y**, ADJ.: frondoso, frondifero, fogliato.

lēagu-e 1, S.: lega; unione; fazione, *f.*: *enter into a* —, far lega, legarsi. **-e** 2, INTR.: legarsi; confederarsi. **-ed**, ADJ.: legato; confederato. **-er**, S.: confederato; assedio; blocco, *m.*

lēak 1, S.: fessura, crepatura; (*nav.*) falla, *f.*: *stop a* —, stagnare una falla. **leak** 2, INTR.: fare acqua, trapelare; colare. **-age**, S.: colatura, *f.*; scolo, *m.* **-y**, ADJ.: fesso, squarciato.

lēam, S.: (*hunt.*) guinzaglio, *m.*

lēan 1, ADJ.: magro, smunto, affilato, macilente: *grow* —, smagrire; *make* —, dimagrare. **lean** 2, (IR)R.; INTR.: appoggiarsi; inclinare; pendere: — *against*, appoggiarsi a; — *back in one's chair*, sedere dinoccolato; — *over*, sporgere; — *upon*, riposarsi sopra, fidarsi. **-ing**, S.: l'appoggiarsi, appoggiamento, *m.*; inclinazione, propensione, *f.* **-ing-staff**, S.: bastone per appoggiarsi, *m.*

lēan-ly, ADV.: magramente. **-ness**, S.: magrezza; estenuazione, *f.*

lēap 1, S.: salto, balzo, *m.*: *take a* —, fare un salto, spiccar un salto; *at a* —, ad un salto. **leap** 2, (IR)R.; TR.: coprire, montare; INTR.: saltare; lanciarsi; palpitare: — *over a ditch*, scavalcare una fossa; — *for joy*, saltare di gioia. **-er**, S.: saltatore, balzatore, *m.* **-frog**, S.: giuoco fanciullesco, *m.* **-year**, S.: anno bisestile, *m.*

lēarn, (IR)R.; (IN)TR.: insegnare; imparare, apprendere: — *by heart*, imparare a mente; — *wit*, scozzonarsi. **-ed**, ADJ.: istrutto, dotto, letterato, saputo, intelligente: *a* — *man*, un dotto, un erudito. **-edly**, ADV.: dottamente, eruditamente. **-er**, S.: scolare; principiante, *m.* **-ing**, S.: erudizione; scienza, dottrina, *f.*

lēase 1, S.: affitto, *m.*: *take a* —, *take on* —, pigliare in affitto. **lease** 2, TR.: dare in affitto, affittare. **lēase**† 3, INTR.: spigolare; ristoppare. **-hold**, S.: affitto, *m.* **-holder**, S.: fituaiuolo, fermiere, *m.* **-er**†, S.: spigolatore, *m.*

lēash 1, S.: guinzaglio, *m.*, lassa, *f.*, legame, legaccio, *m.* **leash** 2, TR.: legare, avvinchiare.

lēasing†, S.: spigolare, *m.*; menzogna, bugia, falsità, *f.*

lēaser, S.: affittatore, *m.*

lēast 1, ADJ., ADV.: minimo, più piccolo; meno; in minimo modo: *at* —, almeno; *not in the* —, in niun modo. **least** 2, S.: atomo, *m.*

lĕather, S: cuoio, *m.*, pelle, *f.*: *lose* —, scorticarsi. **-bottle**, S.: otre, otro, *m.* **-dresser**, S.: conciatore di pelli, *m.* **-n**, ADJ.: di cuoio, di pelle. **-seller**, S.: pelliciaio, pelliciere, *m.* **-y**, ADJ.: della qualità del cuoio; tiglioso, duro.

lēave 1, S.: permissione; licenza, libertà, *f.*; congedo, *m.*: *by your* —, *with your* —, con vostra licenza; *take* — *of*, prender congedo da, accommitarsi (congedarsi) di. **leave** 2, IRR.; TR.: lasciare; abbandonare; finire; INTR.: cessare; discontinuare: — *off*, abbandonare; — *off crying*

mŭf-fle, TR.: camuffare, incapperucciare, imbacuccare. **-fler**, S.: cappuccio, *m.*; benda, *f.*

mŭfti, S.: mufti, *m.*

mŭg, S.: ciotola, brocca, *f.*; boccale, *m.*: *little* —, boccaletto, *m.*; — *of beer*, boccale di birra.

mŭg-gish, **-gy**, ADJ.: muffato, bagnato, umido, acquoso.

mŭgwort, S.: artemisia, *f.*

mulătto, S.: mulatto, meticcio, *m.*

mŭlberry, S.: mora, *f.* **-tree**, S.: moro; gelso, *m.*

mŭlct 1, S.: multa, ammenda, *f.* **mulct** 2, TR.: punire; sottoporre a multa, condannare all' ammenda.

mūl-e, S.: mulo, *m.*; mula, *f.* **-e-driver**, **-etēer**, S.: mulattiere, *m.* **-ish**, ADJ.: ostinato, caparbio.

mŭll, TR.: riscaldare (del vino); abbruciare.

mŭller, S.: macinello, macinatore, *m.*

mŭllein, S.: (*bot.*) verbena, *f.*, tassobarbasso, *m.*

mŭllet, S.: triglia, *f.* (pesce).

mŭlse, S.: mulsa, *f.*, vino cotto con miele, *m.*

multăngular, ADJ.: moltilatero, poligono.

multi-: **-căpsular**, ADJ.: di molti cassule. **-fārious**, ADJ.: vario, differente; frequente, comune. **-fāriously**, ADV.: multiplicatamente, in modo variato. **-fāriousness**, S.: varietà, diversità, multiplicità, *f.* **-form**, ADJ.: multiforme. **-lăteral**, ADJ.: moltilatero, di più angoli. **-loquous** *multĭ-*, ADJ.: moltiloquace. **-nŏminal**, ADJ.: che ha molti nomi. **-parous** *multĭ-*, ADJ.: moltiparo. **-ped**, S.: porcellino terrestre, *m.* **-ple**, ADJ.: moltiplice; moltiplicato. **-pliable**, **-plicable**, ADJ.: moltiplicabile. **-plicănd**, S.: moltiplicando, *m.* **-plicate**, ADJ.: moltiplicato. **-plicātion**, S.: moltiplicazione, *f.* **-plicator**, S.: moltiplicatore, *m.* **-plicity**, S.: moltiplicità, *f.* **-plier**, S.: moltiplicatore, *m.* **-ply**, (IN)TR.: moltiplicare; crescere. **-plying-glass**, S.: occhiale a faccette, *m.* **-syllable**, S.: moltisillabo, *m.* **-tude**, S.: moltitudine, *f.*; gran numero; volgo, *m.* **-tūdinous**, ADJ.: numeroso.

mŭm! 1, INTERJ.: zitto! silenzio! **mum** 2, S.: specie di birra, *f.*

mŭm-ble, TR.: pronunziare indistintamente; INTR.: mormorare; borbottare. **-bler**, S.: borbottone, tartaglione, *f.* **-blingly**, ADV.: in modo mormorante.

mŭmm, INTR.: mascherarsi; dissimulare, fingere. **-er**, S.: maschera; persona mascherata, *f.* **-ery**, S.: mascherata, *f.*

mŭm-mify, TR.: mummificare. **-mificātion**, S.: mummificazione, *f.* **-my**, S.: mummia, *f.*: *beat to a* —, bastonare ben bene.

mŭmp, TR.: mangiucchiare; acchiappare; ingannare, mendicare. **-er**, S.: scroccone; mendico; pezzente, *m.* **-ish**, ADJ.: di cattivo umore. **-ishness**, S.: cattivo umore, *m.* **-s**, S.: cattivo umore, *m.*; schinanzia, gonfiatura delle ghiandole, *f.*

mŭnch, (IN)TR.: mangiare ingordamente. **-er**, S.: mangiatore, mangione, *m.* **-ing**, S.: masticatura, *f.*

mŭn-dane, ADJ.: mondano, di mondo. **-dănity**, S.: vanità mondana; cosa mondana, *f.*

mundŭngus, S.: tabacco puzzoso, *m.*

mūner-ary†, ADJ.: rimunerativo. **-ate**†, TR.: munerare. **-ātion**†, S.: munerazione, rimunerazione, *f.*

mŭngrel = *mongrel*.

munĭci-pal, ADJ.: municipale. **-pălity**, S.: municipalità, *f.*

munĭficen-ce, S.: munificenza, liberalità, *f.* **-t**, ADJ.: munificente, liberale. **-tly**, ADV.: munificentemente, liberalmente.

mūniment†, S.: fortificazione, *f.*; riparo; (*leg.*) titolo, *m.*

munĭtion, S.: munizione; fortificazione; provvisione, *f.* **-bread**, S.: pane di munizione, *m.*

mū-rage, S.: dazio per mantenere le mura, *m.* **-ral**, ADJ.: murale, di muro: — *crown*, corona murale, *f.*

mŭrder 1, S.: omicidio; assassinio, *m.*: —*!* all' assassino! aiuto! **murder** 2, TR.: assassinare; ammazzare. **-er**, S.: micidiale, omicida, *m.* **-ess**, S.: omicidiale, omicida, *f.* **-ing**, S.: assassinamento, omicidio, *m.* **-ous**, ADJ.: micidiale; crudele. **-ously**, ADV.: crudelmente.

mū-re† 1, S.: muro, *m.* **-re** 2, TR.: murare. **-renger**, S.: inspettore delle mura, *m.*

muriătic, ADJ.: muriatico.

mŭrk, S.: oscurità, *f.*, tenebre, *f. pl.* **-y**, ADJ.: oscuro, tenebroso, buio.

mŭrmur 1, S.: mormorio, bisbiglio, susurro, *m.* **murmur** 2, TR.: mormorare, brontolare, borbottare. **-er**, S.: mormoratore, *m.* **-ing**, S.: mormoramento, mormorio, bisbiglio, *m.* **-ingly**, ADV.: con mormorio.

mŭrrain, S.: mortalità fra 'l bestiame, *f.*

mŭrrey, ADJ.: di color rosso oscuro.

mŭrrion, S.: morione, *m.*

Mŭsca-del, **-dine**, **-t**, S.: moscadello, *m.*

mŭscle, S.: muscolo, *m.*

muscŏsity, S.: esser muschioso, *m.*

mŭscu-lar, ADJ.: muscolare, di muscolo. **-lous**, ADJ.: muscoloso, pieno di muscoli.

mūs-e 1, S.: contemplazione, meditazione profonda; (*myth.*) musa, *f.*: *be in a* —, star pensieroso. **-e** 2, TR.: meditare; ruminare; pensare. **-eful**, ADJ.: pensa-

-en, TR.: allungare, stendere; INTR.: allungarsi; distendersi. -ening, S.: allungamento, *m.* -wise, ADV.: in lungo.
lēnient, ADJ.: leniente, lenificativo; S.: medicina lenificativa, *f.*
lĕn-ify, TR.: lenificare, addolcire. -itive, ADJ.: lenitivo; mitigante; molcente; S.: lenificamento, *m.* -ity, S.: lenità; dolcezza, affabilità, umanità, *f.*
lĕns, S.: lente, *m.* (vetro).
Lĕnt, S.: quaresima, *m.*: *keep* —, osservare la quaresima. -en, ADJ.: quaresimale, di quaresima.
len-ticular, ADJ.: lenticolare. -tiginous, ADJ.: lentigginoso. **lĕn-til**, S.: lente, *m.*; lenticchia; lentiggine, *f.*
lĕntisk†, S.: lentischio, *m.*
lĕn-titude†, S.: lentezza, tardità, *f.* -tor, S.: tenacità, viscosità; lentezza, *f.* -tous, ADJ.: tenace, viscoso.
lĕo, S.: (*astr.*) leone, *m.* -nine, ADJ.: leonino, di leone.
lĕopard, S.: leopardo, *m.*
lĕper, S.: lebbra, *f.* -ous = *leprous.*
lĕp-id, ADJ.: gaio, scherzevole, allegro. -idity, S.: lepidezza, gaiezza, *f.*
lĕporine, ADJ.: leporino, di lepre.
lĕp-rosy, S.: lebbra, *f.* -rous ADJ.: lebbroso.
lĕsion, S.: (*med.*) lesione, *f.*
lĕss, ADJ.: minore; inferiore; ADV.: meno, non tanto: *more or* —, più o meno; — *rich than*, meno ricco di.
lessēe, S.: pigionale, affituale, *m.*
lĕssen, TR.: render più piccolo, impicciolire, diminuire; scemare; INTR.: divenire più piccolo.
lĕssest†, S. PL.: sterco (di animali rapaci), *m.*
lĕsson 1, S.: lezione, ripetizione, *f.*; insegnamento, precetto; rimprovero, *m.*
lesson 2, TR.: istruire, ammaestrare, addottrinare.
lĕssor, S.: affittatore, *m.*
lĕst, CONJ.: per tema, per paura (timore) che.
lĕt 1, S.: ostacolo, impedimento, *m.* **let** 2, IRR.; TR.: lasciare; permettere; ritenere, impedire; affittare, appigionare; IRR.: lasciar stare; soffrire; ritenersi, astenersi: — *alone*, lasciare in pace; — *blood*, cavare sangue; — *loose*, sciogliere; metter in libertà; — *down*, abbassare, calare; discendere; — *in* (*into*), introdurre, ammettere; — *off*, sparare, tirare; — *see*, far vedere; — *out*, far uscire; affittare; — *us speak English*, parliamo inglese; — *me speak*, lasciatemi parlare.
lēthal, ADJ.: letale, mortale, funesto.
lethălity, S.: mortalità, *f.*
lethârgic, ADJ.: letargico. **lĕthargy**, S.: letargo, *m.*
lethiferous, ADJ.: letale, mortale.
lĕtter 1, S.: lettera, epistola, *f.*; carattere, *m.*: *capital* —, lettera maiuscula; *to the* —, alla lettera, esattamente; — *stamps*, bollini delle lettere; — *of attorney*, procura, *f.*; — *of mark*, lettera di marco, *f.*; —*s*, lettere, *f. pl.*; letteratura, scienza, *f.*; —*s patent*, patente, *f.*; —*s of respite*, arresto di rispitto, *m.* **letter** 2, TR.: soprascrivere. -bearer = -*carrier*. -box, S.: cassetta delle lettere. -carrier, S.: portalettere, *m.* -case, S.: portafogli, *m.* -ed, ADJ.: letterato, dotto. -founder, S.: fonditore di caratteri, *m.* -foundery, S.: fonderia di caratteri, *f.* -paper, S.: carta di lettere, *f.* -press, S.: torchio, *m.*, stampa, *f.*
lĕt-tice, -tuce -*tis*, S.: lattuga, *f.*: *cabbage* —, lattuga cappuccia, *f.*
levănt, S.: levante, oriente, *m.* -ine, ADJ.: levantino, del Oriente.
lĕvee, S.: levata, *f.*; ricevimento, *m.*; diga, riva, *f.*, argine, *m.*
lĕvel 1, ADJ.: a livello, livellato, piano; S.: livello, piano, *m.*; livella, *f.*: *make* —, lievellare, spianare, levigare; *on a — with*, al livello di, del pari; *above the — of the sea*, sopra il livello del mare.
level 2, TR.: livellare, spianare, appianare; INTR.: mirare; comparare, conghietturare; tentare: — *a house with the ground*, spianare una casa; — *at*, mirare. -ler, S.: livellatore, *m.* -ness, S.: livello; spianamento, *m.*; uguaglianza, *f.*
lĕven = *leaven.*
lĕver, S.: lieva, stanga (da sollevare), *f.*
lĕveret, S.: leprettino, leprottino, lepratto, *m.*
lĕviable, ADJ.: che si può levare.
leviathan, S.: leviatan, *m.*
lĕvi-gate 1, ADJ.: levigato; polverizzato. -gate, TR.: levigare; polverizzare; stritolare. -gātion, S.: levigazione, *f.*; polverizzamento, *m.* -ty, S.: levità, leggerezza; volubilità, incostanza, *f.*
lĕvy 1, S.: colletta; leva (di soldati); levata; tassa, *f.*: — *of troops*, leva di truppe; — *of taxes*, levata di tasse.
levy 2, TR.: levare; guerreggiare.
lēwd, ADJ.: dissoluto, lascivo; libidinoso, impudico. -ly, ADV.: dissolutamente, licenziosamente, impudicamente. -ness, S.: dissolutezza, *f.*; libertinaggio, *m.*; oscenità, *f.* -ster, S.: voluttuoso, *m.*
lexi-cŏgrapher, S.: lessicografo, *m.* -cŏgraphy, S.: lessicografia, *f.* -con, S.: lessico, dizionario, *m.*
lia-bility, S.: obbligazione, risponsabilità, *f.* **lia-ble**, ADJ.: soggetto, esposto, responsabile. -bleness = *liability.*
liar, S.: mentitore, bugiardo, *m.*

-tificātion, S.: mistificazione, *f.* **-tify**, TR.: confondere, rendere perplesso.
mȳth-ic(al), ADJ.: mitico, favoloso. **-ológical**, ADJ.: mitologico. **-ológical-ly**, ADV.: in modo mitologico. **-ŏlogist**, S.: mitologista, mitologo, *m.* **-ŏlogize**, INTR.: spiegare le favole. **-ŏlogy**, S.: mitologia, *f.*

N

n ĕn (*the letter*), S.: n, *f.* (*m.*).
năb, TR.: aggrappare, accaffare.
nābob, S.: nabob, *m.* (principe indiano).
nācre, S.: madreperla, *f.*
nādir, S.: (*astr.*) nadir, *m.*
năg, S.: bidetto, cavallino, *m.*
nāiad, S.: naiade, *f.*
nāil 1, S.: unghia; branca, *f.;* chiodo; ottavo, *m.* (misura): *the —s of the fingers*, le unghie delle dita; *—brush*, spazzalino per le unghie; (*up*)*on the —*, danari contanti; *tooth and —*, con ogni forza; *hit the — on the head*, dar nel segno; colpir nel brocco. **nail** 2, TR.: inchiodare, conficcare con chiodi: *— up a cannon*, inchiodare un cannone; *— a horse*, chiovare un cavallo. **-er**, S.: chiodaiuolo, *m.* **-ery**, S.: chioderia, *f.* **-smith**, S.: chiodaio, *m.* **-trade**, S.: chioderia, *f.*
nāked, ADJ.: nudo, ignudo; scoperto; evidente: *stark —*, affatto ignudo; *strip —*, nudare, spogliar nudo. **-ly**, ADV.: nudamente; semplicemente. **-ness**, S.: nudità; chiarezza, *f.*
nāmby-pāmby, ADJ.: sentimentale in modo imbecille, affettato.
nām-e 1, S.: nome, *m.;* fama, riputazione, *f.*, credito; colore, pretesto, *m.: Christian —*, nome di battesimo; *proper —*, nome proprio; *in God's —*, in nome di Dio; *what's your —?* come vi chiamate? *call —s*, ingiuriare; *go by the — of*, esser conosciuto sotto il nome di. **-e** 2, TR.: nomare, appellare; chiamare; mentovare. **-ed**, ADJ.: nomato; mentovato, nominato, chiamato: *the above-—*, il sullodato. **-eless**, ADJ.: senza nome, anonimo. **-ely**, ADV.: specialmente, particolarmente. **-er**, S.: nominatore, *m.* **-esake**, S.: che ha il medesimo nome, omonimo, *m.*
nankēen, S.: nanchino, *m.*, stoffa di Cina, *f.*
năp 1, S.: sonnellino, *m.;* lanugine, *f.* **nap** 2, TR.: cardare; INTR.: sonnecchiare, dormigliare.
nāpe, S.: nuca, coppa, *f.*
nāpery, S.: biancheria di tavola, *f.*
năphtha, S.: nafta, *f.*
năpkin, S.: tovagliolo, *m.*, salvietta, *f.*
năp-less, ADJ.: spelato, raso, logoro. **-piness**, S.: qualità pelosa, *f.* **-ping**, S.: cardatura, *f.* **-py**, ADJ.: spumoso, fumoso.
napōleon, S.: napoleone, *m.* (moneta).
narcissus, S.: (*bot.*) narcisso, *m.*, tazzetta, *f.*
narcŏtic 1, ADJ.: narcotico, sonnifero. **narcotic** 2, S.: medicina narcotica, *f.*
nârd, S.: nardo, *m.*
nâre, S.: narice, *f.*
năr-rable†, ADJ.: raccontabile. **-rate**, TR.: narrare, raccontare. **-rātion**, S.: narramento, racconto, *m.* **-rative** 1, S.: narrativa, narrazione; storia, *f.* **-rative** 2, ADJ.: narrativo, narratorio. **-ratively**, ADV.: in modo narrativo. **-rātor**, S.: narratore, raccontatore, *m.*
nărrow 1, ADJ.: stretto, angusto; scarso; avaro; vile, basso; esatto, attento: *— means*, angustia, *f.;* *— mind*, animo gretto; *bring in a — compass*, ristringere. **narrow** 2, TR.: stringere, limitare. **-breasted**, ADJ.: che ha il petto stretto. **-heeled**, ADJ.: che ha il calcagno stretto. **-ly**, ADV.: strettamente, angustamente; minutamente. **-mindedness**, S.: grettezza, *f.;* bigotismo, *m.* **-ness**, S.: strettezza, angustia; incapacità; povertà, stitichezza, *f.: — of heart*, avarizia, *f.*
nârwhal, S.: narvalo, *m.*
nāsal, ADJ.: nasale, del naso.
născent, ADJ.: nascente.
năs-tily, ADV.: sporcamente, bruttamente. **-tiness**, S.: sporcizia, sporchezza, bruttezza; oscenità; viltà, *f.* **-ty**, ADJ.: sporco, sordido; osceno.
nātal, ADJ.: natale, nativo.
natātion, S.: nuotare, nuoto, *m.*
nāthless†, ADV.: nulladimeno, con tutto ciò.
nātion, S.: nazione, gente, *f.*, popolo, *m.*
nătion-al, ADJ.: nazionale; generale. **-ălity**, S.: carattere nazionale, *m.*, nazionalità, *f.* **-ally**, ADV.: di tutta la nazione. **-alness**, S.: nazionalità, *f.*
nātive 1, ADJ.: nativo, natio, naturale: *— land* (*country*), patria, *f.* **native** 2, S.: nativo, originario, *m.: —s*, aborigeni, primi abitatori, *m. pl.* **-ness**, S.: naturalezza, *f.*
nativity, S.: natività; nascita, *f.*
nătty, ADJ.: elegante, attrattivo.
nătu-ral 1, ADJ.: naturale; semplice, facile; illegittimo. **-ral** 2, S.: sciocco, idiota, *m.* **-ralist**, S.: naturalista; fisico, *m.* **-rălity**, S.: stato naturale, *m.* **-ralizātion**, S.: diritto di naturalità, *f.* **-ralize**, TR.: naturalizzare; adottare. **-rally**, ADV.: naturalmente; semplicemente; spontaneamente; agevolmente. **-ralness**, S.: stato naturale, *m.*, naturalità, naturalezza; semplicità, *f.*

ma, in un subito; *give one a* —, assistere alcuno, aiutare alcuno. **lift** 2, IRR.; TR.: levare, alzare; inalzare; sollevare; INTR.: sforzarsi di sollevare: — *away*, portar via; depredare. **-er**, S.: che alza. **-ing**, S.: elevazione, alzata, *f.*
liga-ment, S.: ligamento, vincolo, *m.* **-mĕntal**, **-mĕntous**, ADJ.: ligamentoso. **-ture**, S.: legatura; benda, *f.*
light 1, ADJ.: leggiero; agile, attivo, veloce; frivolo; incostante. **light** 2, ADJ.: chiaro, luminoso; biondo; (*nav.*) scaricato, alleggerito; ADV.: leggiermente; facilmente; agilmente: — *hair*, capelli biondi, *m. pl.*; — *as a feather*, leggiero quanto una piuma; — *of belief*, credulo; *make* — *of*, far poco conto di. **light** 3, S.: lume; splendore; faro, *m.*; chiarezza; intelligenza, conoscenza, *f.*: *it begins to be* —, comincia a farsi giorno; *bring to* —, metter in chiaro; *stand in one's* —, impedire il lume ad uno; far torto ad uno. **light** 4, IRR.; TR.: accendere, allumare; illuminare; dichiarare; scaricare. **light** 5, IRR.; INTR.: venire per accidente, incontrare; arrivare; succedere; scendere, montar da cavallo; posarsi, poggiarsi: — *upon*, imbattersi in.
light-armed, ADJ.: armato alla leggiera. **-brained**, ADJ.: scervellato.
light-coloured, ADJ.: chiaro. **-en**, TR.: illuminare; alleggerire; INTR.: balenare; lampeggiare: *it* —*s*, lampeggia. **-ening**, S.: alleggerimento; baleno, *m.*
lighter, S.: alleggio; batello, *m.*, chiatta, scafa, *f.* **-man**, S.: navalestro, *m.*
light-fingered, ADJ.: leggiero alla mano, inclinato a rubare. **-footed**, ADJ.: leggiero alla corsa, veloce. **-headed**, ADJ.: delirante, stordito. **-headedness**, S.: delirio, *m.* **-hearted**, ADJ.: gaio, giocondo, allegro. **-horse**, S.: cavalleria leggiera, *f.*
light-house, S.: faro, fanale, *m.* **-ing**, S.: illuminazione, *f.*
light-legged, ADJ.: veloce; leggiero.
lightless, ADJ.: oscuro, tenebroso, fosco.
light-ly, ADV.: leggiermente; facilmente; un poco. **-minded**, ADJ.: incostante, instabile.
light-ness, S.: leggerezza, agilità; prestezza, *f.* **-ning**, S.: baleno, lampo; bagliore, *m.* **-ning-rod**, S.: parafulmine, *m.* **-s**, S. PL.: polmoni (d'un animale), *m. pl.* **-some**, ADJ.: chiaro; allegro, gaio, gioioso. **-someness**, S.: chiarezza; gaiezza, *f.*
lignăloes, S.: legno aloè, *m.*
lig-neous, ADJ.: ligneo, di legno.
lik-e 1, ADJ.: simile, somigliante; pari; medesimo; probabile, verisimile; ADV.: come, da, alla maniera di: *be* —, esser somigliante a; esser sul punto; *in* — *manner*, parimente; *I had* — *to have forgotten it*, l'avevo quasi dimenticato; — *an honest man*, da galantuomo; — *master*, — *man*, qual padrone, tal servo; — *a man*, da valent' uomo; — *a madman*, da matto. **-e** 2, S.: pariglia; somiglianza; cosa simile, *f.*: *give* — *for* —, render la pariglia, render pane per focaccia. **-e** 3, TR.: amare; approvare; aggradire; INTR.: avere gusto, essere a grado, compiacersi; *how do you* — *it?* come vi piace? *I should* — *to see it*, vorrei vederlo; *as you* —, come vi piace (*or* aggrada). **-elihood**, **-eliness**, S.: probabilità; apparenza, *f.* **-ely**, ADJ.: probabile, verisimile, credibile; apparente; ADV.: probabilmente, verisimilmente. **-en**, TR.: comparare, paragonare; rassomigliare. **-eness**, S.: sembianza, somiglianza; apparenza; conformità; immagine, *f.*, ritratto, *m.*: *good* — ritratto rassomigliante; *in the* — *of*, all'immagine di. **-ewise**, ADV.: parimente, similmente, anche; pure; d'altrove, altresì. **-ing** 1, ADJ.: paffuto, grassetto. **-ing** 2, S.: grassezza, *f.*; genio, gusto; consenso, *m.*: *that is to my* —, ciò mi va a genio, ciò mi quadra; *take a* — *to a thing*, prendere diletto, dilettarsi di qualche cosa.
lilach, S.: lillà, ghianda unguentaria, *f.*
lil-ied, ADJ.: ornato di gigli. **-y**, S.: giglio; fiordaliso, *m.*: — *of the valley*, mughetto, *m.* **-y-livered**, ADJ.: codardo, pauroso.
limātion, S.: limare, *m.* **limature**, S.: limatura, *f.*
limb 1, S.: membro, *m.*; estremità; parte, *f.* **limb** 2, TR.: dare membra; smembrare, sbranare.
limbeck, S.: limbicco, lambicco, *m.*
limbed, ADJ.: membruto.
limber 1, ADJ.: flessibile, pieghevole, arrendevole; agevole. **limber** 2, S.: (*nav.*) anguilla, *f.* **-board**, S.: (*nav.*) apertura della tromba, *f.* **-hole**, S.: (*nav.*) anguilla, *f.* **-ness**, S.: flessibilità, *f.*
limbo, S.: limbo, *m.*; prigione, *f.*
lime 1, S.: calcina; calce, *f.*; lemone; tiglio, *m.*: *quick*—, calcina viva, *f.*
lime 2, TR.: invischiare; cimentare; incalcinare. **-burner**, S.: fornaciaio, *m.*
lime-hound, S.: bracco da sangue, *m.*
lime-juice, S.: acqua di cedro, *f.*
lime-kiln, S.: fornace (da calcinare), *f.* **-pit**, S.: buca della calcina, *f.*
limer = *lime-hound.*
lime-stone, S.: pietra da calcina, alberese, *f.* **-twig**, S.: fuscello impaniato, *m.* **-water**, S.: acqua impregnata calce; acqua cedrata, *f.*
limit 1, S.: limite, termine, confine

m.; pack —, ago per cucire sacchi, *m.* **-case**, S.: agoraio da tenere gli aghi, *m.* **-fish**, S.: aguglia, *f.* (pesce). **-ful**, S.: aguglìata, *f.* **-gun**, S.: fucile ad ago, *m.* **-maker**, S.: agoraio, *m.*

nēedless, ADJ.: inutile; superfluo. **-ly**, ADV.: senza necessità, inutilmente. **-ness**, S.: inutilità; superfluità, *f.*

nēedle-work, S.: lavoro d' ago, *m.*

nēed-ş, ADV.: necessariamente; assolutamente: *it must — be so*, bisogna che sia così. **-y**, ADJ.: necessitoso, povero, indigente.

nē'er†, ADV.: mai, unque mai.

nēf, S.: nave, navata (d' una chiesa), *f.*

nefăndous†, ADV.: nefando, scellerato.

nefārious, ADJ.: nefario, scellerato, abbominevole.

negātion, S.: negazione, *f.*, negamento, *m.*

nĕga-tive, ADJ.: negativo, rifiutante; S.: (*phot.*) negativa; negazione, *f.* **-tively**, ADV.: negativamente. **-tory**, ADJ.: negativo.

neglĕct 1, S.: negligenza, trascuranza, *f.*

neglect 2, TR.: negligere, trascurare, mancare. **-er**, S.: negligente; trascurato, *m.* **-ful**, ADJ.: negligente. **-fully**, ADV.: negligentemente. **-ion**, †-t-, S.: negligenza, *f.* **-ive**, ADJ.: negligente.

nĕgligen-ce, S.: negligenza, trascuraggine, trascuranza, *f.* **-t**, ADJ.: negligente, trascurato. **-tly**, ADV.: con negligenza.

negō-tiable, ADJ.: che si può negoziare. **-tiate**, TR.: negoziare, trafficare; trattare. **-tiātion**, S.: negoziazione, *f.*; traffico, affare, *m.* **-tiater**, S.: negoziatore, negoziante; mediatore, *m.* **-tiatrix**, S.: negoziatrice; mediatrice, *f.*

nē-gress, S.: negra; mora, *f.* **-gro**, S.: negro, moro, *m.*

nēigh 1, S.: nitrito, nitrire, *m.* **neigh** 2, INTR.: nitrire.

nēighbo(u)r 1, S.: vicino, *m.*, vicina, *f.*

neighbo(u)r 2, TR.: confinare, conterminare. **-hood**, S.: vicinanza, *f.*: *near* —, prossimità, vicinanza, *f.* **-ing**, ADJ.: vicino, contiguo, prossimo. **-ly** 1, ADJ.: sociabile, amichevole. **-ly** 2, ADV.: da buon vicino; amichevolmente, da amico: *be* —, agire da buon vicino, essere buon vicino.

nēighing, S.: nitrito, *m.*

nēither 1, CONJ.: nè; nè più: — *more nor less*, nè più, nè meno. **neither** 2, PRON.: nè l' uno nè l' altro, nè l' una nè l' altra.

nĕmorous†, ADJ.: boscoso.

nĕnu-far, **-phar**, S.: nenufar, *m.*

ne-olŏgic(al), ADJ.: neologico. **-ŏlogy**, *s.: neologia, f.* **-ŏlogism**, S.: neologi*smo, m.* **-ŏlogist**, S.: neologista, *m.* **-ŏlogy**, *s.*: neologia, *f.*

nēophyte, *s.*: neofito, convertito, *m.*

neotĕric, ADJ.: moderno; recente.

nĕp, S.: nepitella, *f.*

nepĕnthe, S.: nepente, *m.* (panacea).

nĕ'phew, S.: nipote, *m.*: *little* (*young*) —, nipotino, *m.*; *grand* —, bisnipote, *m.*

ne-phritic, ADJ.: nefritico. **-phritis**, S.: nefritide, *f.*

nĕpotism, S.: nepotismo, *m.*

nēreid, S.: nereide, *f.*

nĕr-val, ADJ.: nervoso. **-ve**, S.: nervo, nerbo; tendine, *m.* **-veless**, ADJ.: enervato, fiacco. **-vŏsity**, S.: nervosità, *f.* **-vous**, ADJ.: nervoso, nerboso; robusto: — *disease*, malattia, nervosa. **-vously**, ADV.: nervosamente; con vigore (forza). **-vousness**, S.: nervosità, *f.* **-vy**, ADJ.: nervoso, vigoroso, robusto.

nĕscience, S.: ignoranza, *f.*

nĕst 1, S.: nido, *m.*, nidiata, *f.*; ricettacolo, rifugio, ricovero, asilo, *m.*: — *of birds*, nidiata, nidata di uccelli. **nest** 2, INTR.: nidificare, fare nido. **-egg**, S.: guardanidio, endice, *m.* **-le**, TR.: accarezzare; INTR.: annidarsi; fermare sua stanza. **-ling**, S.: uccello nidiace, *m.*

nĕt, S.: rete, *m.*, reticella, *f.*

nĕther, ADJ.: basso, inferiore: *in this — world*, quaggiù. **-most**, ADJ.: infimo, estremo.

nĕtting, S.: (*nav.*) filaretti, *m. pl.*

nĕt-tle 1, S.: ortica, *f.* **-tle** 2, TR.: pungere; esasperare. **-tle-rash**, S.: orticaria, *f.*

nĕt-wise, ADJ.: retato. **-work**, S.: reticella; tessitura.

neurălg-ia, S.: nevralgia, *f.* **-ic**, ADJ.: nevralgico.

neu-rŏlogy, S.: neurologia, *f.* **-rŏtomy**, S.: neurotomia, *f.*

neūter, ADJ.: neutro; indifferente; neutrale; S.: neutro, *m.*; neutrale, *m.*, *f.* **-tral**, ADJ.: neutrale; indifferente. **-trălity**, S.: neutralità; indifferenza, *f.* **-trally**, ADV.: neutralmente; in senso neutro.

nĕver, ADV.: mai, giammai, unque mai: — *a one*, nemmeno uno; — *a whit*, niente affatto. **-ceasing**, ADJ.: incessante, continuo. **-ending**, ADJ.: eterno, perpetuo. **-failing**, ADJ.: infallibile. **-theless**, CONJ.: nulladimeno, non pertanto, tuttavia.

new 1, ADJ.: nuovo, fresco; novello; moderno: *bran(d)* —, nuovo di zecca; — *Testament*, nuovo testamento; — *year*, *etc.*, *cf. below.* **new** 2, ADV.: nuovamente, novellamente. **-comer**, S.: forestiero, *m.* **-fangle**, TR.: formare di nuovo; inventare di fresco. **-fangled**, ADJ.: di nuovo genere, appariscente. **-fangledness**, S.: mania di novità, *f.* **-fashioned**, ADJ.: moderno, alla moda. **-ish**,

him do what he —*s*, faccia quel che vuole. **-ed**, ADJ.: strisciato, listato; ingaggiato.
listen, INTR.: ascoltare, udire, attendere, porgere orecchio. **-er**, S.: ascoltatore, *m.*
list-ful, ADJ.: attento. **-less**, ADJ.: trascurato; svogliato, indifferente. **-less-ly**, ADV.: trascuratamente, senza cura. **-lessness**, S.: trascuraggine, negligenza; svogliatezza, *f.*
litany, S.: letane, letanie, *f. pl.*
liter-al, ADJ.: litterale, letterale: — *fault*, errore di stampa, *m.* **-ălity**, S.: senso letterale, *m.* **-ally**, ADV.: letteralmente. **-ary**, ADJ.: letterario: — *man*, letterato. **-ate**, ADJ.: letterato; scienziato, dotto. **-ăti**, S. PL.: letterati, uomini dotti, *m. pl.* **-ature**, S.: letteratura, *f.*
litharge, S.: litargirio, *m.*
lith-e, ADJ.: pieghevole, flessibile; arrendevole. **-ness**, S.: flessibilità, arrendevolezza, *f.* **-er**, ADJ.: molle; lento; S.: lentezza, tardezza, *f.* **-esome**, ADJ.: pieghevole, arrendevole.
lith-ograph, S.: litografia, *f.* **-ŏgrapher**, S.: litografo, *m.* **-ográphic**, ADJ.: litografico. **-ŏgraphy**, S.: litografia, *f.* **-ŏlogy**, S.: litologia, *f.* **-ŏtomist**, S.: litotomista, litotomo, *m.* **-ŏtomy**, S.: litotomia, *f.*
lithy, ADJ.: pieghevole, arrendevole.
lit-igant, ADJ.: litigante; S.: litigante, litigatore, *m.* **-igate**, INTR.: litigare, contendere, contrastare. **-igātion**, S.: litigamento, *m.*, lite, contesa, *f.* **-igious**, ADJ.: litigioso, rissoso, brigoso. **-igiously**, ADV.: litigiosamente. **-igiousness**, S.: umore litigioso, *m.*
litmus, S.: oricello, *m.*
litoral = *littoral.*
litter I, S.: lettiga, *f.*, letto portabile, *m.*; paglia; ventrata, *f.*: *make a* —, mettere in disordine. **litter** 2, TR.: figliare; scompigliare, disordinare.
little I, ADJ.: piccolo, poco; S.: poco, *m.*; poca cosa, *f.*: *a* —, un poco; *a* — *one*, un fanciullo; *very* —, piccolissimo; piccino, piccinino. **little** 2, ADV.: poco, non molto, quasi nulla: *by* — *and* —, a poco a poco; *never so* —, un pochettino; *too* —, troppo poco; *however* —, per quanto poco. **-ness**, S.: piccolezza; poca importanza; bassezza, viltà, *f.*
littoral, ADJ.: littorale, del mare.
litŭrgic(al), ADJ.: liturgico.
liturgy, S.: liturgia, *f.*
live, ADJ.: vivo; attivo.
live, INTR.: vivere, sussistere; dimorare: *as long as I* —, tanto che (*or* finchè) vivrò; *where do you* —? dove state di casa? dove dimorate? — *from hand to mouth*, vivere dì per dì; — *upon good terms with one*, essere d' accordo con uno; — *on* (*upon*), nutrirsi, cibarsi.
live-d, ADJ.: di ... vita: *long* —, di vita lunga. **-lihood**, S.: vita, *f.*; vitto; mestiere, *m.*, arte, *f.*: *get one's* —, guadagnarsi il vitto. **-liness**, S.: vivacità, *f.*; vigore, *m.*
livelong, ADJ.: lungo, tedioso; durevole, eterno: *the* — *day*, tutto il giorno.
live-lily, ADV.: vivamente, in modo vivace. **-ly**, ADJ.: vivace, vivo, spiritoso, gaio: — *youth*, ragazzo svegliato.
liver, S.: vivente; fegato, *m.* **-colour**, ADJ.: di color di fegato, bruno. **-wort**, S.: (*bot.*) epatica, *f.*
livery, S.: livrea, *f.*; vestimento; possesso, *m.*: *keep horses at* —, tener cavalli d' affitto; *receive* —, esser messo in possesso; *wear* —, portar la livrea. **-horse**, S.: cavallo d' affitto, *m.* **-man**, S.: membro del corpo municipale, *m.* **-men**, PL.: gente di livrea, *f.* **-stable**, S.: scuderia di cavalli d' affitto, *f.*
live-stock, S.: (*agr.*) copia di bestiame, *f.*, bestiame, *m.*
liv-id, ADJ.: livido, nericcio; nericante. **-idity**, **-idness**, S.: lividezza, *f.*, lividore, *m.*; discolorazione, *f.*
living, ADJ.: vivente, vivo; S.: vita, *f.*, vivere; vitto, nutrimento; beneficio, *m.*, cura, *f.*: — *language*, lingua vivente; — *faith*, fede viva. **-ly**, ADV.: durante la vita.
livre, S.: lira, *f.* (moneta).
lixivium, S.: (*chem.*) lisciva, *f.*, ranno, *m.*
lizard, S.: lucertola, lucerta, *f.*
llâma, S.: lama, *f.*
lŏ! INTERJ.: ecco! ecco qui!
lōach, S.: ghiozzo, *m.* (pesce).
lōad I, S.: carica, soma, *f.*; peso, fardello, *m.*; mina, miniera, *f.*: — *of wood*, misura di legnami, *f.* **load** 2, (IR)R.; TR.: caricare; imbarazzare; ingombrare: — *the dice*, falsare i dadi. **-er**, S.: caricatore, *m.* **-ing**, S.: carica, *f.*, fardello, *m.*
lōad-sman†, S.: pilota, piloto; conduttore, *m.* **-star**, S.: cinosura, orsa minore, *f.* **-stone**, S.: calamita, *f.*
lōaf (pl. *loaves*), S.: pane; cibo, *m.*: — *of sugar*, pane di zucchero, *m.*
lōam I, S.: terra grassa; creta; marna, *f.* **loam** 2, TR.: concimare colla marna; imbrattare di creta. **-y**, ADJ.: argilloso; di marna.
lōan I, S.: prestito, presto, *m.*, prestanza *f.*: *put out to* —, dar in prestito, prestare **loan** 2, TR.: prestare. **-office**, S.: monte di pietà, *m.*
lōa-th, ADJ.: mal disposto; repugnante. **-the**, TR.: odiare; detestare, stomacare, nauseare; INTR.: nausearsi, recare

nine, ADJ.: nove. **-fold**, ADJ.: nove volte più. **-holes**, S.: giuoco fatto con pallottoline, *m*. **-pins**, S. PL.: birilli, sbrigli, *m. pl*. **-score**, ADJ.: centottanta. **-teen**, ADJ.: diecinove. **-teenth**, ADJ.: decimo nono. **-tieth**, ADJ.: novantesimo. **-ty**, ADJ.: novanta.

ninny, **-hammer**, S: sciocco, gonzo, merendone, *m*.

ninth, S., ADJ.: nono. **-ly**, ADV.: in nono luogo.

nip 1, S.: pizzico, pizzicotto, tagliuzzo, *m*.; burla, *f*. **nip** 2, TR.: pizzicare; motteggiare; annebbiare: — *off*, tagliare; guastare. **-pers**, S. PL.: pinzette, molette; (*nav*.) salmastre, *f. pl*. **-ping**, ADJ.: pungente, mordace; acerbo. **-pingly**, ADV.: mordacemente; satirescamente.

nipple, S.: capezzolo, *m*.

nit, S.: lendine, *f*.

nitency, S.: nitore, *m*.

nithing†, S.: poltrone, codardo, *m*.

nitid, ADJ.: nitido; lucente.

ni-tre, S.: (*chem*.) nitro, salnitro, *m*. **-tric**, ADJ.: nitrico. **-trificātion**, S.: nitrificazione, *f*. **-trogen**, S.: nitrogeno, azoto, *m*. **-troglycerine**, S.: nitroglicerina, *f*. **-trŏsity**, S.: nitrosità, *f*. **-trous**, **-try**, ADJ.: nitroso.

nitty, ADJ.: lendinoso, pieno di lendini.

nival†, **niveous**, ADJ.: nevoso, pieno di neve.

nō, ADJ.: nessuno, niuno, veruno; ADV.: no, non: — *such matter*, niente affatto; — *matter*, non importa; — *more*, non più; —*where*, in nessuno luogo; *to — purpose*. invano; *I have — pens*, non ho penne; — *man*, niun uomo, niuno.

nobili-tate†, TR.: nobilitare, fare nobile. **-tātion**†, S.: nobilitare, *m*. **-ty**, S.: nobilità, *f*.; nobili, *m. pl*.

nōbl-e, ADJ.: nobile, illustre; liberale; S.: nobile, *m*. **-eman**, S.: nobile, gentiluomo, *m*. **-eness**, S.: nobiltà, grandezza; sublimità, *f*. **-ĕss**, S.: nobili, *m. pl*.; ordine de nobili, *m*. **-ewoman**, S.: donna nobile, *f*. **-y**, ADV.: nobilmente; liberalmente.

nōbody, S.: nessuno, niuno, veruno, *m*.

nō-cent, ADJ.: nocente; colpevole, criminale. **-cive**, ADJ.: nocivo, nocevole.

nŏck, S.: tacca; intaccatura, *f*.

noctăm-bule, **-bulist**, S.: nottambulo, sonnambulo, *m*.

nocti-ferous†, ADJ.: che induce la notte. **-lūcous**, ADJ.: che splende nella notta. **-vagant**, ADJ.: nottivago.

nŏc-tuary, S.: ricordanze notturne, *f. pl*. **-turn**, S.: notturno, *m*. **-tŭrnal** 1, *ADJ.: notturno*, di notte. **-turnal** 2, S.: *notturlabio, m*. (strumento).

nŏcuous, *ADJ.*: nocivo.

nŏd 1, S.: cenno, segno, *m*.: *give a* —, fare cenno. **nod** 2, INTR.: accennare; dormicchiare; tentennare. **-ding**, S.: accennamento, *m*. **-dle**, S.: testa; zucca, *f*. **-dy**, S.: sciocco, minchione, *m*.

nŏd-e, S.: nodo; tumore, callo, *m*. **-ŏsity**, S.: nodosità, *f*.; nodo, *m*. **-ous**, ADJ.: nodoso, nocchioso.

nŏdule, S.: nodetto, piccol nodo, *m*.

nŏggin, S.: ciotola, *f*.; boccaletto, *m*.

nŏi-se 1, S.: strepito, romore, fracasso; susurro, ronzo; fischiamento, *m*.: *make a* —, far strepito, far romore. **-se** 2, TR.: divulgare, pubblicare. **-seful**, ADJ.: romoroso, strepitoso. **-seless**, ADJ.: senza strepito, silenzioso. **-se-maker**, S.: schiamazzatore, *m*. **-siness**, S.: gran strepito, tumulto. **-some**, ADJ.: nauseoso, disgustoso. **-somely**, ADV.: in modo nauseante; sporcamente. **-someness**, S.: nauseare, *m*.; sporchezza, *f*. **-sy**, ADJ.: turbolento, tumultuoso.

nolition, S.: ripugnanza, *f*.

nŏm-ad, S.: nomade, *m*., *f*. **-ăd(ic)**, ADJ.: nomade. **-adism**, S.: vita nomade, *f*.

nŏmen-clator, S.: nomenclatore, *m*. **-clāture**, S.: nomenclatura, *f*.

nŏmi-nal, ADJ.: nominale, titolare. **-nally**, ADV.: nominatamente; spezialmente. **-nate**, TR.: nominare, nomare; intitolare. **-nately**, ADV.: nominatamente, spezialmente. **-nātion**, S.: nomina; presentazione, *f*. **-native**, S.: (*gram*.) nominativo, *m*. **-nātor**, S.: nominatore, *m*.

nŏn-, PREF.: non-, in-, mancanza di. **-ability**, S.: inabilità, *f*. **-age**, S.: minorità, *f*. **-attĕndance**, S.: incuria, *f*.

nŏnce, S.: intento, disegno, *m*.

nonchalănce, S.: indifferenza, *f*.

non-compliance, S.: rifiuto, *m*. **-confôrmist**, S.: nonconformista, *m*. **-confôrmity**, S.: nonconformità, discordanza, *f*.

nŏndescript, ADJ.: indescrivibile.

nōne, ADJ.: niuno, nessuno, veruno: *I will have — of it*, io non ne voglio; *it is — of my fault*, non è mia colpa.

non-ĕntity, **-existence**, S.: nichilità, *f*. **-jūror**, S.: che non giura. **-parĕil**, S.: (*print*.) nompariglia, *f*. **-pāyment**, S.: mancanza di pagamento, *f*. **-perfôrmance**, S.: mancanza d' effezione, *f*. **-plus**, TR.: confondere, imbarazzare: *be at a* —, non saper più che dire, restar confuso. **-rĕsidence**, S.: assenza della residenza, *f*. **-rĕsident**, S.: assente della residenza, *m*. **-resistance**, S.: ubbidienza pronta, *f*.

nŏn-sense, S.: assurdità, *f*., spropositi, *m. pl*.; anfanamento, *m*.: *talk* —, anfanare, spropositare; dire sciocchezze. **-sĕnsical**, ADJ.: assurdo, ridicoloso, sproposita-

lungo tempo dopo; — *ago*, — *since*, lungo tempo fa; *not* — *before*, non molto prima; *ere* —, in breve, fra poco; *as* — *as*, tanto che, tanto quanto; *as* — *as I live*, finchè vivrò; *all this day* —, tutt' oggi; *shall you be out* —? starete di molto a tornare? *how* —? quanto tempo? **-g** 3, INTR.: desiderare; appetire, avere gran voglia: — *for*, bramare ardentemente. **-ganimity**, s.: longanimità, sofferenza, *f.* **-g-boat**, s.: scialuppa, *f.*; schifo, *m.* **-ger**, ADJ., ADV.: più lungo. **-gĕvity**, s.: longevità, lunga vita, *f.* **-g-headed**, ADJ.: che ha la testa appuntata; astuto. **-gimanous**, ADJ.: che ha le mani lunghe. **-gimetry**, s.: longimetria, *f.* **-ging**, s.: desiderio intenso, *m.*; impazienza, *f.* **-gingly**, ADV.: con desiderio intenso, bramosamente. **-ginquity**, s.: lontananza, distanza, *f.* **-gish**, ADJ.: alquanto lungo, lunghetto. **-gitude**, s.: longitudine; lunghezza, *f.* **-gitūdinal**, ADJ.: longitudinale. **-gitūdinally**, ADV.: in lungo. **-g-legged**, ADJ.: che ha le gambe lunghe. **-g-lived**, ADJ.: longevo. **-g-shanked** = *longlegged*. **-g-sighted**, ADJ.: che vede di lontano, che ha la vista lunga. **-g-sightedness**, s.: vista lontana, *f.* **-gsomet**†, ADJ.: lungo; tedioso, noioso. **-gsomeness**†, s.: noiosità, *f.* **-gsŭfferance**, s.: longanimità, pazienza, *f.* **-gsŭffering**, ADJ.: sofferente; paziente. **-gways**, ADV.: pel lungo. **-gwinded**, ADJ.: lungo, tedioso, noioso. **-gwise** = *longways*.

lōo, s.: bestia (*ad cards*).

lōo-bily, ADJ.: scimunito, sciocco. **-by**, s.: balordo, minchione, goffo, *m.*

lōof 1, s.: (*nav.*) sopravento, *m.* **loof** 2, TR.: (*nav.*) serrare il vento, andare all' orza.

lóok 1, s.: guardo; aspetto, *m.*; occhiata, *f.* **look!** 2, INTERJ.: ecco! vedi! **look** 3, TR.: vedere, guardare; cercare; INTR.: mirare, considerare, guardare; parere, sembrare; aver aspetto di: — *annoyed*, sembrare tediato; — *back*, riflettere sopra, ruminare; — *big*, braveggiare, pavoneggiare; — *like*, aver la cera, rassomigliare; — *well*, avere buon viso, avere buona cera; — *out of the window*, affacciarsi alla finestra; — *young again*, ringiovanire; — *about*, invigilare; badare; — *after*, aver cura di; aver l'occhio a; — *at*, considerare; osservare; — *down*, guardar con isdegno, avere a sdegno; — *for*, cercare; aspettare; — *into*, considerare; esaminare; — *on*, mirare; pregiare; — *out*, cercare; ricercare; scoprire; (*nav.*) tener vendetta; — *over*, esaminare; — *there!* mirate là! — *to*, badare; prender guardia; — *up*, guardare in alto; — *upon*, mirare; stimare. **-er**, **-er-on**, s.: spettatore; riguardante, *m.* **-ing-glass**, s.: specchio, *m.*; bambola, *f.* **-ing-glass-maker**, s.: specchiaio, *m.* **-out**, s.: veletta, vedetta; sentinella: *to be on the* —, spiare; osservare; *keep a good* —, stare all' erta

lōom 1, s.: telaio di tessitore, *m.* **loom** 2, INTR.: (*nav.*) apparire in lontananza, parere. **-gale**, s.: (*nav.*) venticello fresco, *m.* **-ing**, s.: (*nav.*) apparenza (d' un vascello), *f.*

lōon, s.: tuffetto (anatra); furfante, birbone, *m.*

lōop, s.: trina, *f.*; cordoncino, affibbiaglio, *m.* **-ed**, ADJ.: bucato, pieno di buchi, foracchiato. **-hole**, s.: buco; spiraglio; rigiro, sotterfugio; (*art.*) cannoniera, balestriera, *f.* **-holed**, ADJ.: bucato, pieno di spiragli. **-lace**, s.: gabbano, *m.* **-maker**, s.: nastraio, *m.*

lōord†, s.: poltrone, *m.*

lōose† 1, ADJ.: sciolto, slegato; lento; dissoluto, licenzioso, sviato: — *style*, stile bislacco; *be* —, essere sciolto; esser in libertà; *be in a* — *condition*, esser libero, vivere a suo modo; *get* —, scatenarsi; *get* — *from one*, liberarsi da uno; *hang* —, strascinare per terra; *grow* —, slegarsi, allontanarsi; *let* —, scatenare. **loose** 2, s.: libertà, *f.*, stato di libertà, *m.*; emanzipazione, *f.* **loose** 3, TR.: slegare, slacciare, rilasciare; sprigionare, liberare; INTR.: spiegare le vele, levar l' ancora; partire. **-ly**, ADV.: senza fermezza; dissolutamente, licenziosamente. **-n**, TR.: slegare, sciogliere, distaccare; rilassare, rallentare; INTR.: distaccarsi; separarsi. **-ness**, s.: allentamento; flusso di corpo, *m.* **-ning**, ADJ.: lassativo, mollificativo; s.: allentamento, *m.*

lŏp 1, s.: taglio; ramo tagliato, *m.*; pulce, *f.* **lop** 2, TR.: diramare, scapezzare, troncare; INTR.: pendere. **-per**, s.: che dirama; potatore, *m.* **-ping**, s.: potagione, *f.*, potamento, *m.* **-sided**, ADJ.: (*nav.*) abboccato.

lo-quācious, ADJ.: loquace; ciarliero. **-quăcity**, s.: loquacità; ciarlieria, ciancia, *f.*

lôrd 1, s.: signore; padrone; Iddio; lord, *m.*: *house of* —*s*, camera dei Lordi, *f.*; — *chancellor*, gran cancelliere, *m.*; — *chamberlain*, gran ciambellano, *m.*; — *chief justice*, gran giudice, *m.*; — *mayor of London*, podestà di Londra, *m.* **lord** 2, INTR.: signoreggiare, dominare: — *it over*, dominare, tiraneggiare. **-ing**† = *-ling*. **-liness**, s.: altezza; superbia, alterigia, *f.* **-like**, ADJ.: da signore, di gran signore; altiero. **-ling**, s.: sign

prima d' ora; — *and then*, di quando in quando; *every* — *and then*, ogni poco, ogni tanto. **now** 2, S.: tempo presente, *m.*; ora, *f.* **-adays**, ADV.: oggidì, al presente.
nōwes†, S.: nodo matrimoniale, *m.*
nō-way(s), ADV.: in niuna maniera. **-where** *-hwâr*, ADV.: in niun luogo, in nessuna parte. **-wise**, ADV.: in niun modo, per niente, in conto alcuno.
nŏxious, ADJ.: nocivo, pernizioso. **-ly**, ADV.: nocevolmente. **-ness**, S.: qualità nociva, *f.*, nocumento, *m.*
nŏzzle, S.: capezzolo, naso, *m.*; punta, *f.*
nūbi-le, ADJ.: nubile; maritale, da marito. **-lous**, ADJ.: nubiloso, nuvoloso.
nūcleus, S.: nucleo, nocciuolo, *m.*
nū-date, TR.: nudare. **-dātion**, S.: denudare; spogliamento, *m.* **-de**, ADJ.: nudo.
nŭdge, TR.: toccare col gomito (per chiamare l' attenzione).
nūdity, S.: nudità; semplicità, *f.*
nugăcity, S.: frivolezza, bagattella, beffa, *f.*; passatempo, *m.*
nūgatory, ADJ.: nugatorio, frivolo.
nŭgget, S.: pepite, pezzo d' oro o argento (in istato puro), *m.*
nūisance, S.: nocumento; incomodo, *m.*
nūke, S.: nuca, *m.*
nŭll 1, ADJ.: nullo; invalido. **null** 2, TR.: annullare; invalidare; cassare. **null** 3, S.: inefficacia; mancanza di forza, *f.* **-ify**, TR.: cancellare, cassare. **-ity**, S.: nullità, *f.*, niente, nulla, *m.*; invalidità, *f.*
nŭmb 1, ADJ.: torpido, intirizzito. **numb** 2, TR.: intirizzire; stupefare. **-(ed)ness**† = *numbness*.
nŭmber 1, S.: numero, *m.*, quantità, *f.* **number** 2, TR.: numerare; contare. **-er**, S.: numeratore; calcolatore, *m.* **-ful**, ADJ.: numeroso. **-less**, ADJ.: innumerabile.
nŭmbles, S. PL.: interiora (d' un cervo, ecc.), *f. pl.*
nŭmbness, S.: torpore; stupore; intirizzamento, *m.*
nūmer-able, ADJ.: numerabile. **-al**, ADJ.: numerale, di numero. **-ally**, ADV.: numeralmente. **-ary**, ADJ.: numerario, numerico. **-ate**, TR.: numerare. **-ātion**, S.: numerazione, *f.* **-ator**, S.: (*arith.*) numeratore, *m.*
numĕric, **-al**, ADJ.: numerico; numerale. **-ally**, ADV.: in modo numerico.
nūmerist, S.: calcolatore, computista, *m.*
nūmer-o, S.: numero; marca, *f.* **-ŏsity**, S.: numerosità; armonia, *f.* **-ous**, ADJ.: numeroso; armonioso, *f.* **-ousness**, S.: moltitudine; armonia, *f.*
numismătic, ADJ.: numismatico. **-s**, S. PL.: numismatica, scienza delle monete e medaglie, *f.*
nŭmmary, ADJ.: di moneta, danaioso.
nŭmskull, S.: minchione, goffo, *m.* **-ed**, ADJ.: stupido, goffo, balocco.
nŭn, S.: monaca; religiosa regolare; monacella, *f.*
nŭnchion, S.: merenda, *f.*
nŭn-ciature, S.: nunziatura, *f.* **-cio**, S.: nunzio; ambasciadore del papa, *m.*
nŭn-cupate, TR.: nunziare. **-cūpative**, **-cūpatory**, ADJ.: nuncupativo, verbale: — *will*, testamento verbale, *m.*
nŭndi-nal, **-nary**, ADJ.: di nundine, di fiera.
nŭnnery, S.: convento (di monache), *m.*
nŭptial, ADJ.: nuziale; coniugale: — *song*, epitalamio, *m.* **-s**, S. PL.: nozze, *f.*, matrimonio, *m.*
nŭr-se 1, S.: nutrice; balia, *f.* **-se** 2, TR.: nutrire, nutricare, allevare, fomentare; incoraggiare: — *a sick person*, aver cura d' un ammalato. **-se-child**, S.: bambino lattante, allievo, *m.* **-ser**, S.: nutritore, nutricatore; promotore, fautore, *m.* **-sery**, S.: camera della balia, *f.*: — *of learning*, seminario, *m.*; — *of plants*, semenzaio, *m.*; — *of trees*, semenzaio, *m.*, nestaiuola, *f.* **-sery-man**, S.: giardiniere che fa semenza, *m.* **-ing**, S.: nutrizione, *f.* **-sling**, S.: bambino di latte; favorito, *m.* **-ture** 1, S.: nutricamento, *m.*; educazione, *f.* **-ture** 2, TR.: nutricare, allevare; educare.
nŭstle†, TR.: vezzeggiare, lusingare.
nŭt, S.: noce, nocciuola, *f.*; (*nav.*) orecchio (dell' ancora), *m.* **-brown**, ADJ.: castagnino. **-cracker**, S.: acciaccanoci, schiaccianoci, *m.* **-gall**, S.: noce di galla, galla, *f.* **-hatch**, **-pecker**, S.: sorta di merlo, *f.* **-hook**, S.: uncinetto (da pigliare le noci), *m.* **-meg**, S.: noce moscada, *f.* **-peach**, S.: noce persica, *f.*
nū-triment, S.: nutrimento; cibo, *m.* **-trimĕntal**, ADJ.: nutrimentale. **-trition**, S.: nutrizione, *f.*, nutrimento, *m.* **-tritious**, **-tritive**, ADJ.: nutritivo.
nŭt-shell, S.: scorza di noce, *f.*; guscio, *m.* **-ting**, PART.: *go a*-—, andare a cogliere delle nocciuole. **-tree**, S.: albero di noce, nocciuole, noce, *m.*
nŭzzle, TR.: allattare, allevare; INTR.: annasare; nascondersi.
nȳe, S.: stormo di fagiani, *m.*
nўmph, S.: ninfa; giovinetta, *f.* **-omā-nia**, S.: ninfomania, *f.* **-ous**, ADJ.: di ninfa.

O

ō (*the letter*), S.: o, *m.* (*f.*).
O! ō, INTERJ.: o! o bravo! viva!
ōaf, S.: merendone, baccellone, *m.* **-ish**,

piccolezza; bassezza, viltà; sommessione, depressione, *f.* **-spirited**, ADJ.: malinconico, depresso, abbattuto. **-spiritedness**, S.: malinconia, tristezza, *f.* **-thoughted**, ADJ.: di pensieri vili.

loxodrŏmic, S.: lossodromia, *f.*

lŏyal, ADJ.: leale; fedele; onesto: — *party*, partito della corte. **-ist**, S.: aderente del re. **-ly**, ADV.: lealmente, fedelmente. **-ty**, S.: lealtà, fedeltà; aderenza, *f.*

lŏzenge, S.: rombo, *m.*; pastiglia, *f.*

lŭb-bard, S.: infingardaccio, poltrone, *m.* **-ber**, S.: infingardo, rusticone; poltrone, *m.* **-berly** 1, ADJ.: grossolano, villano; ozioso, pigro. **-berly** 2, ADV.: in modo villano, grossamente.

lū-bric, **-brical**, ADJ.: lubrico; leggiero; lascivo. **-bricate**, **-bricitate**, TR.: lubricare. **-bricity**, S.: lubricità; volubilità, leggerezza; incertezza; lascività, *f.* **-bricous**, ADJ.: lubrico; incerto. **-brification**, S.: azione lubricante, *f.*

lū-cent, ADJ.: lucente, luminoso; splendido. **-cid**, ADJ.: lucido, luminoso, chiaro; lucente, risplendente. **-cidity**, **-cidness**, S.: lucidezza; chiarezza, *f.*

Lū-cifer, S.: (*astr.*) Lucifero, *m.* (*pop.*) fiammifero, zolfanello, *m.* **-ciferous**, **-cific**, ADJ.: lucifero, luminoso.

lŭck, S.: caso, accidente, *m.*; fortuna, ventura, *f.*: *good* —, buona fortuna; *ill* —, mala fortuna, sventura; *by good* —, per buona ventura. **-ily**, ADV.: fortunatamente; avventurosamente. **-iness**, S.: buona ventura, fortuna, *f.* **-less**, ADJ.: sfortunato, sventurato, infelice. **-y**, ADJ.: fortunato, benavventurato.

lū-crative, ADJ.: lucrativo, profittevole. **-cre**, S.: lucro, guadagno, profitto, *m.*

luctātion, S.: sforzo, *m.*; contesa, *f.*

lūcu-brate, TR.: vegliare studiando; elaborare. **-brātion**, S.: elucubrazione, *f.*, studio notturno, *m.*; elaboratezza, *f.* **-bratory**, ADJ: composto a lume di candela.

lūculent, ADJ.: luculento, evidente, certo.

lūdicrous, ADJ.: burlesco, comico; piacevole, divertente, risibile. **-ly**, ADV.: in modo burlesco, comicamente. **-ness**, S.: ridicolosità, *f.*; scherzo, *m.*

lu-dificātion, S.: ludificazione, burla, *f.* **-dificatory**†, ADJ.: burlesco, piacevole.

lŭff 1, S.: palma della mano, *f.*, (*nav.*) sopravvento, *m.* **luff** 2, TR.: (*nav.*) tenersi col vento, orzare. **-tackle**, S.: (*nav.*) paranco portatile, *m.*

lŭg 1, S.: punta dell' orecchio; pertica, *f.* (misura). **lug** 2, TR.: tirare, strascinare; INTR.: restare indietro, star a bada.

lŭggage, S.: bagaglio; arredo, *m.*, salmeria, *f.* **-room**, S.: (*rail.*) loggia da mercanzie, *f.* **-train**, S.: (*rail.*) convoglio delle mercanzie, *m.* **-waggon**, S.: (*rail.*) vagone (da trasportar mercanzie), *m.*

lŭg-ger, S.: (*nav.*) traboccolo, *m.* **-sail**, S.: (*nav.*) vela al vento, *f.*

lugūbrious, ADJ.: lugubre, tristo, mest .

lūkewarm, ADJ.: tiepido; indifferente. **-ly**, ADV.: tiepidamente; indifferentemente. **-ness**, S.: tiepidezza; indifferenza, *f.*

lŭll, TR.: cullare; quetare: — *asleep*, addormentare. **-aby**, S.: ninnerella, *f.*

lumbāgo, S.: reumatismo lombare, *m.*

lŭmbary, ADJ.: lombare.

lŭmber 1, S.: arnesi inutili, *m. pl.* **lumber** 2, TR.: ammucchiare senza ordine; INTR.: muoversi lentamente.

lūmi-nary, S.: luminare, lume, *m.* **-nate**†, TR.: illuminare. **-nātion**†, S.: illuminazione, *f.* **-nous**, ADJ.: luminoso, fulgente. **-nousness**, S.: lucidezza, *f.*, splendore, *m.*

lŭmp 1, S.: massa, *f.*; pezzo; grosso, mucchio, *m.*: *by the* (*in the*) —, all' ingrosso, in blocco. **lump** 2, TR.: prendere il tutto senza badare. **-er**, S.: (*nav.*) navalestro, *m.* **-ing**, ADJ.: grosso, massiccio. **-ish**, ADJ.: pesante, grosso; rozzo; stupido. **-ishly**, ADV.: pesantemente: scioccamente. **-ishness**, S.: sciocchezza, stupidità, *f.* **-sugar**, S.: zucchero rosso, *m.* **-y**, ADJ.: grumoso.

lū-nacy, S.: follia, pazzia, frenezia, *f.* **-nar**, **-nary**, ADJ: lunare, della luna: — *eclipse*, eclisse lunare. **-nated**, ADJ.: lunato; di forma curva. **-natic**, ADJ.: lunatico; S.: matto, pazzo, *m.*: — *asylum*, manicomio, *m.* **-nātion**, S.: lunazione, *f.*; lunare, *m.*

lŭnch, **-eon**, S.: merenda, *f.*; mangiare, *m.*

lū-ne, S.: mezza luna; pazzia, frenesia, *f.* **-nĕtte**, S.: mezza luna piccola; (*fort.*) lunetta, *f.*

lŭng, S.: polmone, *m.* **-wort**, S.: (*bot.*) polmonaria, *f.*

lŭnt, S.: miccia, *f.*

lŭpine, S.: (*bot.*) lupino, *m.*

lŭrch 1, S.: stato derelitto, *m.*; (*gam.*) posta doppia, *f.*; (*nav.*) guinata, *f.*: *leave one in the* —, lasciare uno in nasso, abbondare alcuno; *lie upon the* —, insidiare, tendere insidie. **lurch** 2, TR.: deludere, truffare; INTR.: guadagnare posta doppia. **-er**, S.: truffatore, insidiatore; bassetto, *m.* **-ing**, S.: guadagnar il marcio; agguato, *m.*, insidia, *f.*

lūre 1, S.: logoro; allettamento, *m.* **lure** 2, allettare, adescare.

lūrid, ADJ.: squallido, livido; tristo.

lŭrk, INTR: nascondersi, appiattarsi. -

bilmente. **-vance**, S.: osservanza; riverenza; sommessione, *f.* **-vant**, ADJ.: osservante, obbediente; rispettoso: sommesso; attento. **-vā́tion**, S.: osservazione; cura, *f.* **-vatọr**, S.: osservatore, *m.* **-vatory**, S.: osservatorio, *m.* **-ve**, TR.: osservare, notare, servare: considerare; INTR.: essere attento. **-vẹr**, S.: osservatore, osservante, *m.*: osservatrice, *f.* **-ving**, S.: osservamento, *m.* **-vingly**, ADV.: attentamente.

ob-séss†, TR.: assediare. **-séssion**†, S.: assedio, *m.*

obsidional, ADJ.: ossidionale, d' assedio.

obsig-nate†, TR.: sigillare, ratificare. **-nā́tion**†, S.: ratificazione, *f.*

obso-léscent, ADJ.: che comincia ad essere disusato o vecchio. **-lẹte**, ADJ.: disusato, vecchio. **-lẹteness**, S.: disusanza, *f.*, disuso, *m.*

óbstacle, S.: ostacolo, impedimento, *m.*: difficoltà, *f.*

obs-tétric, ADJ.: obstetricio. **-s**, S. PL.: obstetricia, *f.* **-tẹtrícian**, S.: ostetrico, *m.*

ónsti-nacy, S.: ostinazione, caparbietà, *f.* **-nạte**, ADJ.: ostinato, caparbio, ritroso. **-nạtely**, ADV.: ostinatamente, pertinacemente. **-nạteness**, S.: ostinazione, pertinacia, caparbietà, *f.*

obstrépẹrous, ADJ.: strepitoso, turbolento: *be* —, fare un gran chiasso (fracasso). **-ly**, ADV.: strepitosamente, in modo turbolento. **-ness**, S.: strepito, romore, fracasso, *m.*

obstriction, S.: obbligamento, legame, vincolo, *m.*

obstrúc-t, TR.: ostruire, stoppare: impedire. **-tẹr**, S.: impeditore, *m.* **-tion**, S.: ostruzione, oppilazione, *f.*; impedimento, *m.* **-tive**, **-t**, ADJ.: ostruttivo, oppilativo; impeditivo.

óbstrụent = *obstructive*.

obtáin, TR.: ottenere, conseguire, acquistare, guadagnare; INTR.: prevalere: stabilirsi: *a use that —s everywhere*, un uso che prevale (che regna) da per tutto. **-able**, ADJ.: ottenibile; conseguibile. **-ẹr**, S.: che ottiene, che procura. **-ing**, **-ment**, S.: ottenimento, conseguimento, *m.*

obténd†, TR.: addurre incontro, opporre.

obténẹ-brạte†, TR.: oscurare, offuscare. **-brā́tion**†, S.: ottenebrazione, oscurazione, *f.*

obténtion, S.: opposizione, contraddizione, *f.*; ostacolo, *m.*

obtést, TR.: supplicare, scongiurare. **-ā́tion**, S.: supplica, preghiera, istanza, *f.*

obtrúd-e, TR.: intrudere; imporre: — *one's self*, intromettersi; — *one's opinions*, presentare le proprie opinioni in modo insistente. **-ẹr**, S.: intruso, importuno, *m.*

obtrún-cate, TR.: troncare. **-cā́tion**, S.: troncamento, *m.*

obtrú-sion, S.: intrusione; importunità, *f.* **-sive**, ADJ.: intruso, importuno.

obtúnd†, TR.: rintuzzare; spuntare.

obtúse, ADJ.: ottuso, spuntato; stupido. **-angled**, ADJ.: ad angulo ottuso. **-ly**, ADV.: ottusamente; stupidamente. **-ness**, ottusità: stupidezza, *f.*

obúm-brạte, TR.: adombrare, oscurare. **-brā́tion**, S.: adombramento, *m.*, oscurazione, *f.*

obvéntion, S.: imposizione ecclesiastica, *f.*

obvért, TR.: volgere indietro.

óbviạte, TR.: ovviare; prevenire; impedire: — *a danger*, scampare un pericolo.

óbvious, ADJ.: aperto, esposto; evidente: *that is* —, ciò va senza dire. **-ly**, ADV.: chiaramente, evidentemente. **-ness**, S.: chiarezza, evidenza: dimostrazione, *f.*

occásion 1, S.: occasione, occorrenza, opportunità; causa, cagione, *f.*, motivo, *m.*; necessità, *f.* **occasion** 2, TR.: cagionare, causare; eccitare. **-al**, ADJ.: occasionale, accidentale, casuale. **-ally**, ADV.: occasionalmente, accidentalmente. **-ẹr**, S.: cagionatore, *m.*

occẹcā́tion, S.: acciecamento, *m.*

ócci-dent, S.: occidente, occaso; ponente, *m.* **-déntal**, ADJ.: occidentale, d' occidente.

occiput, S.: occipizio, *m.*, collottola, *f.*

occlúde, TR.: chiudere, serrare.

occlú-se†, ADJ.: chiuso, serrato. **-sion**, S.: chiudimento, *m.*

occúlt, ADJ.: occulto, celato, nascoso, nascosto. **-ā́tion**, S.: occultazione, *f.* **-ness**, S.: occultezza, *f.*, occultamento; celamento, *m.*

óccụ-pancy, S.: occupazione, *f.* **-pant**, S.: occupatore; possessore, *m.* **-pạte**†, TR.: occupare; possedere. **-pā́tion**, S.: occupazione, *f.*: impiego, negozio, affare, *m.*: — *of land*, possessione, *f.*, possesso, *m.* **-pier**, S.: occupatore, posseditore, possessore, *m.* **-py**, TR.: occupare; godere; tenere luogo, possedere: impiegare; INTR.: negoziare, trafficare: — *one's self*, occuparsi; — *an apartment*, tenere (godere) un appartamento.

oc-cúr, INTR.: occorrere, accadere; farsi incontro. **-cúrrence**, S.: occorrenza, *f.*: evento, *m.* **-cúrrent**, ADJ.: occorrente, accidentale. **-sion**†, S.: occorsione, *f.*: incontro, *m.*

ō-cean, S.: oceano, alto mare, *m.* **-ceán(ic)**, ADJ.: oceanico.

ō-chre, S.: ocra, ocria, *f.* **-chrẹous**, ADJ.: ocraceo, d' ocra.

octaédron, S.: ottaedro, *m.*

óc-tagon, S.: (*geom.*) ottangolo, *m.*

mad-efăction, S.: immollamento, *m.* **-efy**, TR.: immollare; bagnare.
măd-house, S.: manicomio, spedale pe' matti, *m.* **-ly**, ADV.: pazzamente, follemente, stoltamente. **-man**, S.: pazzo, matto, *m.* **-ness**, S.: pazzia, follezza, furia, stravaganza, *f.*
mădrigal, S.: madrigale, *m.*
măd-woman, S.: pazza, matta, *f.*
măf-fle, INTR.: balbettare, scilinguare. **-fler**, S.: balbo, scilinguato, *m.*
magazine, S.: magazzino, *m.*; rivista periodica, *f.*: *powder* —, (*nav.*) Santa Barbara.
măgdalen, S.: meretrice pentita, *f.*
măge, S.: mago, *m.*
măggot, S.: baco, bruco; ghiribizzo, capriccio, *m.* **-iness**, S.: stato verminoso; capriccio, *m.* **-y**, ADJ.: bacato; capriccioso, bisbetico.
măgian, S.: mago, *m.*
mă-gic, S.: magia; stregoneria, *f.* **-gic(al)**, ADJ.: magico: — *lantern*, lanterna magica, *f.* **-gically**, ADV.: magicamente, per magia. **-gician**, S.: mago; stregone, *m.*
magistêrial, ADJ.: magistrale, imperioso. **-ly**, ADV.: magistralmente, imperiosamente. **-ness**, S.: imperiosità, *f.*
măgis-tery, S.: magisterio; precipitato, *m.* **-tracy**, S.: magistratura, *f.*, magistrato, *m.* **-tral**, ADJ.: magistrale. **-trally**, ADV.: magistralmente. **-trate**, S.: magistrato, *m.*
măgna-chârta, S.: magna carta (degli inglesi), *f.*
mag-nanimity, S.: magnanimità, grandezza d'animo, *f.* **-nănimous**, ADJ.: magnanimo, generoso, nobile; liberale. **-nănimously**, ADV.: con magnanimità, magnanimamente.
magnê-sia, S.: magnesia, *f.* **-sium**, S.: magnesio, *m.*
măg-net, S.: magnete, calamita, *f.* **-nĕtic(al)**, ADJ.: magnetico, di magnete: — *needle*, ago magnetico. **-netiser**, S.: magnetizzatore, *m.* **-netism**, S.: magnetismo, *m.*: *animal* —, magnetismo animale. **-netise**, TR.: magnetizzare.
mag-nific, ADJ.: magnifico; illustre. **-nificence**, S.: magnificenza, *f.*; splendore, *m.* **-nificent**, ADJ.: magnificente, pomposo, splendido, superbo. **-nificently**, ADV.: con magnificenza, con pompa. **-nifico**, S.: grande di Venezia, *m.*
măgni-fier, S.: magnificatore; lodatore; microscopio, *m.* **-nify**, TR.: magnificare; esaggerare, esaltare. **-nifying-glass**, S.: microscopio, *m.* **-nitude**, S.: magnitudine; grandezza, *f.*
măgpie, S.: gazza, pica, *f.* (uccello).
mahŏgany, S.: legno acagiù, m(ag)ogano, *m.*
Mahŏmetan, S.: maomettano, *m.* **-ism**, S.: religione di Maometto, *f.*, maomettismo, *m.*
măid, S.: squadro, *m.* (pesce). **-(en)** 1, S.: vergine; fanciulla, zitella, donzella, *f.*: *servant*-—, serva; *chamber*-—, cameriera; *old* —, vecchia zitella; *the* — *of Orleans*, la Pulcella d'Orleans; —*en speech*, primo discorso; —*en lady*, zitella. **-en** 2, ADJ.: di vergine; (*fig.*) fresco. **-enhair**, S.: capelvenere, *m.* **-enhead**, S.: verginità; imene, *f.* **-enly**, ADJ.: verginale, pudico; modesto, delicato. **-hood**, S.: verginità; purità, *f.* **-servant**, S.: serva; fante, *f.*
măil 1, S.: maglia; valigia; posta delle lettere, *f.*: *by the next* —, col primo corriere. **-able**, ADJ.: che si può mandare per la posta. **mail** 2, TR.: armare; proteggere. **-coach**, S.: carrozza di posta, diligenza, *f.* **-horse**, S.: cavallo di posta, *m.*
măim 1, S.: mutilamento, storpiamento; difetto, *m.*; offesa, *f.* **maim** 2, TR.: mutilare, storpiare. **-ed**, ADJ.: mutilato, mozzo. **-ing**, S.: mutilamento, troncamento, *m.*
măin 1, ADJ.: principale, capitale, essenziale; forte: — *battle*, corpo di battaglia, *m.*; — *body*, grosso, *m.*; — *flood*, marea alta, *f.*; — *road*, strada maestra; *by* — *force*, a viva forza. **main** 2, S.: grosso, totale; corpo principale; oceano, alto mare, *m.*; forza, *f.*: *in the* —, in somma, in generale, in fondo; *hydraulic* —, cilindro idraulico. **-guard**, S.: gran guardia, *f.* **-land**, S.: terra ferma, *f.*, continente, *m.* **-ly**, ADV.: principalmente, soprattutto. **-mast**, S.: albero maestro, grand' albero, *m.*
măinper-nable, ADJ.: che si può mallevare. **-nor**, S.: mallevadore, *m.*
măinprise, S.: malleveria, sicuranza, *f.*
măinsail, S.: vela di maestra, grande vela, *f.* **-sea**, S.: alto mare, oceano, *m.* **-sheets**, S. PL.: (*nav.*) scotte di maestra, *f. pl.* **-stay**, S.: (*nav.*) straglio di maestra, *m.*
main-tăin, TR.: mantenere, dare il vitto; difendere; INTR.: sostenere; affirmare; provare. **-tăinable**, ADJ.: sostenibile; provabile. **-tăiner**, S.: mantenitore; difensore, *m.* **-tenance**, S.: mantenimento; sostegno, *m.*; protezione, difesa, *f.*
măin-topmast, S.: grand' albero di gabbia, *m.* **-yard**, S.: antenna grande, *f.*
măize, S.: granturco, frumentone, *m.*
majĕstic(al), ADJ.: maestoso, grande. **-ally**, ADV.: maestosamente, con maestà.
măjesty, S.: maestà; grandezza; dignità, *f.*: *his* (*her*) —, sua maestà.

-mill, s.: macinatoio, *m.* **-miller**, s.: spremitore d' olio, *m.* **-painting**, s.: pittura a olio, *f.*; quadro dipinto a olio, *m.* **-shop**, s.: bottega d' oliandolo, *f.* **-tree** = *olive-tree.* **-y**, ADJ.: olioso, oleaceo; untuoso.

ŏint, TR.: ungere. **-ment**, s.: untume, unguento, *m.*

ōker, s.: ocra, ocria, *f.* (terra di color giallo).

ōld, ADJ.: vecchio, attempato; antico; annoso: *very* —, anziano; — *man*, vegliardo, vecchio, vecchione, *m.*; — *woman*, vecchia, *f.*; *poor little* — *woman*, vecchierella, *f.*; — *age*, vecchiaia, *f.*; — *oak*, quercia annosa; — *castle*, castello antico; — *Testament*, vecchio Testamento; *of* —, altre volte, anticamente; — *age*, vecchiaia, vecchiezza, *f.*; — *times*, tempi antichi, tempi passati, *m. pl.*; *how — are you?* quanti anni avete? *grow* —, diventar vecchio, vecchiare. **-en**, ADJ.: vecchio, antico. **-fashioned**, ADJ.: antico, all' antica. **-ish**, ADJ.: alquanto vecchio. **-ness**, s.: antichità; vecchiezza, vetustà, *f.*

oleáginous, ADJ.: olioso, oleaceo. **-ness**, s.: oleosità, *f.*

oleánder, s.: oleandro, rododendro, *m.*

oleáster, s.: oleastro, ulivo salvatico, *m.*

olfáct, TR.: fiutare, odorare. **-ory**, ADJ.: olfattorio.

ŏlid†, **-ous**†, ADJ.: fetido, puzzolente.

oligárchical, ADJ.: oligarchico. **ŏligarchy**, s.: oligarchia, *f.*

ŏlitory, ADJ.: olitorio.

olivăster, ADJ.: olivastro, di color d' oliva.

ŏlive, s.: oliva, uliva, *f.*: *Mount of the —s*, monte Oliveto. **-branch**, s.: ramo d' ulivo, *m.* **-grove**, s.: oliveto, *m.* **-harvest**, s.: raccolta delle olive, *f.* **-tree**, s.: olivo, ulivo, *m.*

olўm-piad, s.: olimpiade, *f.* **-pian**, **-pic**, ADJ.: olimpico: — *games*, giuochi olimpici. **-pus**, s.: olimpo, *m.*

ŏmbre, s.: ombre, *m.* (giuoco).

omēga, s.: omega, *f.*

ŏmelet, s.: frittata, *f.*

ōmen, s.: augurio, presagio, *m.* **-ed**, ADJ.: auguroso, di pronostico.

ŏmi-nate†, TR.: pronosticare, presagire. **-nātion**†, s.: augurio, pronostico, *m.* **-nous**, ADJ.: malauguroso, sinistro. **-nously**, ADV.: in modo auguroso; sinistramente. **-nousness**, s.: presagio, pronostico, *m.*

o-mission, s.: omissione, *f.*, tralasciamento, *m.* **-mit**, TR.: omettere, tralasciare. **-mittance**, s.: omissione, *f.*, tralasciamento, *m.*; astinenza, *f.*

ŏmnibus, s.: omnibus, *m.*

omnifárious, ADJ.: di tutte le specie.

omniferous, ADJ.: che produce tutte le cose.

ŏmniform, ADJ.: di tutte le forme.

omnipoten-ce, **-cy**, s.: onnipotenza, *f.* **-t**, ADJ.: onnipotente, onnipossente.

omniprēsen-ce, s.: onnipresenza, *f.* **-t**, ADJ.: presente dappertutto.

omni-science, **-sciency**, s.: onniscienza, *f.* **-scient**, **-scious**, ADJ.: onnisciente. **-vorous**, ADJ.: onnivoro.

ŏmoplate, s.: spalla, *f.*, omero, *m.*

ŏn, PREP., ADV.: sopra, su; a (al, alla, ecc.); successivamente: — *the ground*, sopra la terra; — *the desk*, sullo scrittoio; *and so* —, e così del resto; — *the contrary*, al contrario; — *foot*, a piedi; — *high*, in su, in alto; — *horseback*, a cavallo; — *the left*, alla man manca, alla sinistra; — *and off*, saltuariamente, a salti; — *my part*, dal canto mio; — *pain of death*, sotto pena di morte; — *purpose*, a bello studio; — *the right*, alla man dritta; — *a sudden*, in un batter d' occhio; *be* — *one's way*, esser in cammino; *go* —, passare avanti; *he had* — *a red coat*, egli indossava un abito rosso.

ŏnager, s.: (*zoöl.*) onagro, *m.*

ōnanism, s.: onanismo, *m.*

once *wŭns*, ADV.: una volta, un tempo, altra volta; tempo fa: *at* —, alla prima, in un colpo; *all at* —, in un subito, a un tratto; — *for all*, una volta per sempre; — *more*, un' altra volta.

one 1 *wŭn*, ADJ.: uno, una, un: — *by* —, uno ad uno; *any* —, chiunque, che si sia; *every* —, ciascheduno, ognuno; — *another*, l' un l' altro; —*'s self*, sè stesso, sè stessa; *such a* —, un tale, una tale; *it is all — to me*, è tutt' uno, non fa caso; *such a* —, un tale, il tale. **one** 2, PRON.: si. **-eyed**, ADJ.: monocolo, cieco d' un occhio. **-handed**, ADJ.: monco, moncherino.

oneirocritic, s.: interpretatore di sogni, *m.*

oneness *wŭn-*, s.: unità, *f.*

ŏner-ary, ADJ.: onerario, di peso. **-ate**†, TR.: caricare, aggravare. **-ātion**†, s.: caricamento, carico; peso, *m.* **-ous**, ADJ.: oneroso; incomodo.

ŏnion, s.: cipolla, *f.*: *young* —, cipolletta, *f.* **-bed**, s.: aiuola di cipolle, *f.* **-sauce**, s.: salsa cipollina, *f.*

ŏnlooker, s.: spettatore, *m.*

ōnly 1, ADJ.: solo, unico; semplice: *an — child*, figlio unico. **only** 2, ADV.: solamente; semplicemente; non . . . che, soltanto: *not* —, non solo, non solamente; *I have — one*, non ne ho che uno, ne ho uno soltanto.

onomatopœia, s.: onomatopeia, *f.*

le; flessibile, trattabile. **-leableness** = *malleability*. **-leate**, TR.: stendere col martello.
mállet, S.: maglio; martello di legno, *m.*
mállows, S.: malva, *f.*
mâlmsey, S.: malvagia, *f.* (vino).
malpráctice, S.: cattiva condotta, furberia, *f.*; cattivo servizio d' un medico o d' un chirurgo, *m.*
mâlt 1, S.: orzo macinato per far della birra, *m.* **malt** 2, INTR.: macerare o preparare l' orzo per far la birra. **-floor**, S.: suolo da seccare l' orzo, *m.* **-house**, luogo da preparare l' orzo, *m.* **-kiln**, S.: S.: forno da seccare l' orzo, *m.* **-man**, S.: mercante d' orzo preparato, *m.* **-mill**, S.: mulino da macinare l' orzo, *m.*
maltrëat, TR.: maltrattare.
malversátion, S.: trasgressione, cattiva condotta, *f.*
măměluke, S.: mammalucco, *m.*
mămma, S.: mamma, *f.* (voce fanciullesca).
mămmal, S.: mammifero.
mămmet, S.: fantoccio, bamboccino, *m.*
măm-miform, ADJ.: a guisa di mammella. **-millary**, ADJ.: mammillare.
mămmock† 1, S.: frammento, pezzo grosso, *m.* **mammock**† 2, TR.: spezzare, rompere, stracciare.
mămmon, S.: mammone, *m.*
mămmoth, S.: mammut, *m.*
măn 1, S.: uomo; servo, domestico, *m.*; pedina (agli scacchi); dama (alle tavole): *big* (*large*) —, omone; *little* —, ometto, omicciattolo; *bad little* —, ommattaccio; *stout* —, omaciotto; *every* —, ciascheduno; *no* —, nessuno; *like a* —, da uomo; — *of war*, nave da guerra, *m.*; *be one's own* —, non dipender da nessuno; — *and wife*, marito e moglie. **man** 2, TR.: fornire d' uomini, armare; presidiare: — *one's self*, rincorarsi.
mănacle, TR.: mettere le manette, catenare. **-s**, S. PL.: manette, *f. pl.*
mănage-e 1, S.: maneggio, *m.*; condotta, *f.*; governo, *m.* **-e** 2, maneggiare; condurre; governare; INTR.: invigilare. **-eable**, ADJ.: maneggiabile, agevole, trattabile. **-eableness**, S.: agevolezza; trattabilità, docilità, *f.* **-ement**, S.: maneggiamento, maneggio, *m.*; condotta; direzione, *f.* **-er**, S.: maneggiatore, direttore, amministratore; economo, *m.* **-ery**, S.: maneggio, *m.*; condotta; economia; frugalità, *f.*
mánchet†, S.: pan buffetto, pan morbido, *m.*
mánci-pate†, TR.: porre in schiavitù; sottomettere. **-pátion**†, S.: schiavitudine; soggezione, *f.* **-ple**, S.: dispensiere, provveditore, *m.*

mandâmus, S.: mandamento, mandato, ordine, *m.*
mandarín, S.: mandarino, *m.*
măn-datary, S.: mandatario; deputato, *m.* **-date**, S.: mandato, *m.*; commessione, *f.* **-dător**, S.: mandatore, *m.* **-datory**, ADJ.: comandativo, imperativo.
măn-dible, S.: mascella, mandibula, *f.* **-dibular**, ADJ.: della mascella.
mandíllion, S.: casacca (di lacchè), *f.*
măndolin, S.: mandolino, *m.* (strumento).
măndrake, S.: (*bot.*) mandragola, *f.*
măndu-cable, ADJ.: buono a mangiare, comestibile. **-cate**, TR.: manducare, masticare. **-cátion**, S.: manducazione, *f.*
măne, S.: criniera, giubba, chioma, *f.*
măn-eater, S.: antropofago, *m.*
măned, ADJ.: crinuto, chiomato.
manège, S.: maneggio, *m.*
mănes, S. PL.: anime de' morti, *f. pl.*
manœ̆uver 1, S.: manovra, *f.* **manœuver** 2, TR.: manovrare.
măn-ful, ADJ.: valoroso, bravo, coraggioso. **-fully**, ADV.: valorosamente, bravamente. **-fulness**, S.: valore, *m.*, bravura, *f.*, coraggio, *m.*
manganèse, S.: manganese, *f.*
mănge, S.: stizza; rogna, scabbia (di cane), *f.*
mănger, S.: mangiatoia, *f.*: *live at reck and* —, vivere prodigalmente.
mănginess, S.: stizza; rogna, *f.*
măn-gle 1, S.: mangano, *m.* **-gle** 2, TR.: lacerare, stroppiare; manganeggiare, manganare. **-gler**, S.: mutilatore, troncatore, *m.*; che manganeggia.
măngonise†, TR.: manganare.
măngy, ADJ.: scabbioso, rognoso.
măn-hater, S.: misantropo, *m.* **-hood**, S.: virilità, *f.*; valore, *m.*, fermezza, *f.*; coraggio, *m.*
mă-nia, S.: mania, pazzia, *f.* **-niac**, S.: pazzo, *m.* **-niac(al)**, ADJ.: maniaco, furioso, pazzo.
măni-fest 1, ADJ.: evidente, manifesto. **-fest** 2, TR.: manifestare, mostrare. **-festo**, S.: manifesto, *m.* **-festátion**, S.: manifestazione, *f.*, manifestamento, *m.* **-festly**, ADV.: manifestamente. **-festness**, S.: evidenza, chiarezza, *f.*
mănifold, ADJ.: parecchi, diversi. **-ly**, ADV.: di maniere diverse. **-ness**, S.: moltiplicità, *f.*
mănikin, S.: picool uomo, nano, *m.*
măn-iple, S.: manipolo, *m.*; manata; piccola truppa, *f.* **-ipular**, ADJ.: manipolare. **-ipulátion**, S.: manipolazione, *f.*
măn-killer, S.: omicida, *m.* **-kind**, S.: genere umano, *m.* **-less**, ADJ.: senza uomini. **-like**, ADJ.: degno d' un uomo, umano; valente. **-liness**, S.: aspet-

to maschile, *m.*, maschiezza, *f.*; coraggio, *m.* **-ly**, ADJ.: maschio; nobile; grande. **-midwife**, S.: raccoglitore (del parto), *m.*

mănna, S.: manna, *f.*

mănner, S.: maniera, guisa; forma, foggia; specie, sorta, *f.*; modo, *m.*; **—s**, costumi, *m. pl.*; costumanza; civiltà, buona creanza, *f.*: *in the same* (*like*) —, nello stesso modo, parimente, similmente; *all — of things*, cose di ogni maniera. **-ed**, ADJ.: manierato, ammanierato: *well* —, di belle maniere. **-liness**, S.: civiltà, politezza, *f.* **-ly**, ADJ.: manieroso, civile; ADV.: civilmente, con politezza.

mănnish, ADJ.: d'uomo, virile; bravo, coraggioso; impudente.

manœŭvre = *maneuver*.

manŏmeter, S.: manometro, *m.*

mănor, S.: castello, *m.*; signoria, *f.* **-house**, S.: casa del signore, *f.*, castello del signore, *m.*

mănsion 1, S.: dimora, abitazione; stanza, *f.* **mansion** 2, INTR.: dimorare, abitare. **-house**, S.: villa del padrone, casa, *f.*

măn-slaughter, S.: omicidio, *m.* **-slayer**, S.: omicida, omicidiale, *m.*

mănsue-tet†, ADJ.: mansueto; agevole, affabile, dolce. **-tude**, S.: mansuetudine: dolcezza, *f.*

măntel, S.: capanna di cammino, *f.* **-et**, S.: mantelletta, *f.*, mantelletto, *m.*

măn-tiger, S.: manticora, *f.*; babbuino, *m.*

mantilla, S.: mantiglia, *f.*

măntle 1, S.: mantello, manto, *m.* **-mantle** 2, TR.: mantellare; coprire; INTR.: schiumare; stender le ali. **-piece**, S.: cappa di camino, *f.*; caminetto, *m.*

măntua, S.: veste, roba da donna, *f.* **-maker**, S.: sarta (da donne), *f.*

mănual, ADJ.: manuale; S.: manuale; libretto, *m.* **-ist**, S.: artigiano, operaio, *m.*

manu-dŭction†, S.: guida, scorta, *f.*; soccorso, *m.* **-dŭctor**, S.: conduttore, guida, *m.* **-făctory**, S.: manifattura, fabbrica, *f.*; stabilimento, *m.* **-făcture** 1, S.: opera di manifattore, manifattura, fabbrica; fabbricazione, *f.* **-facture** 2, TR.: fabbricare. **-făcturer**, S.: manifattore, lavoratore, fabbricatore, *m.* **-făcturing**, S.: manifattura, *f.* **-mission**, S.: liberazione da servità, *f.* **-mit**, TR.: metter in libertà, affrancare.

manŭ-rable, ADJ.: arabile, coltivabile. **-rance**, S.: agricoltura, coltura, *f.* **-re**, S.: letame, concime, *m.* **-rement**, S.: letaminamento, *m.*; agricoltura, coltura, **-rer**, S.: agricoltore; lavoratore, *m.*

mănuscript, S.: manoscritto, *m.*

măny, ADJ.: molti, gran numero di: — *persons*, molte persone; — *times*, molte volte, sovente; — *a man*, molti uomini, *m. pl.*; — *a time*, molte volte; *twice as* —, due volte più; *a good* (*great*) —, parecchi; moltissimi; *how* —! quanti! *so* —, tanti; *as* — *as you like*, quanti ne volete; *too* —, troppi; *so* — *men*, *so* — *minds*, quanti uomini, tanti consigli. **-coloured**, ADJ.: di molti colori. **-cornered**, ADJ.: di più angoli, poligono. **-headed**, ADJ.: di molti capi. **-languaged**, ADJ.: che sa molte lingue. **-peopled**, ADJ.: popoloso.

măp 1, S.: carta geografica, *f.*: — *of the world*, mappamondo, *m.* **map** 2, TR.: delineare; descrivere.

măple, **-tree**, S.: acero, *m.*, acera, *f.* (albero).

măppery, S.: arte topografica, *f.*

mâr, TR.: guastare; corrompere.

marăsmus, S.: marasmo, *m.*, magrezza, consunzione, *f.*

marăud-er, S.: predatore, saccheggiatore, *m.* **-ing**, S.: scorreria, *f.*, saccheggiamento, *m.*

mârble 1, S.: marmo, *m.*; marmoreo, di marmo, marmorato. **marble** 2, TR.: marmorare, marezzare. **-cutter**, S.: marmorario, statuario, *m.* **-hearted**, ADJ.: duro, crudele. **-quarry**, S.: cava del marmo, *f.* **-worker**, S.: marmista, *m.* **-works**. **-yard**, S.: stabilimento di marmoraio, *m.*

Mârch, S.: marzo, *m.*

mârch 1, S.: marcia, *f.*: *begin one's* —, mettersi a marciare. **march** 2, INTR.: marciare, andare; avanzare; TR.: far marciare, mettere in marcia, dirigere: — *back*, far ritornare; — *in the rear*, andare dietro, seguire; — *in*, entrare; — *off*, andare via; levare campo; (*fig.*) morire; — *on*, camminare; avanzare; — *out*, andare fuora, uscire; far uscire.

mârch 3, S. (*us'ly pl. -es*): frontiera (d'un paese), *f.* **-er**, S.: comandante delle frontiere, *m.*

mârchioness, S.: marchesa, marchesana, *f.*

mârchpane†, S.: marzapane, *m.*

mârcid, ADJ.: marcio, fracido; magro.

măre, S.: cavalla, giumenta, *f.*

mâreschal = *marshal*.

măre's-nest, S.: scoperta creduta (cosa ridicola), *f.*

mârgarite, S.: margarita, *f.*

mârgin, S.: margine, *f.*; orlo, *m.*; marca; estremità, *f.* **-al**, ADJ.: marginale. **-ate**, TR.: orlare. **-ated**, ADJ.: provveduto d' una margine.

mâr-grave, S.: margravio, *m.* **-grăvi**

-ate, S.: stato del margravio, margraviato, *m.*
mări-ets, S. PL.: (*bot.*) specie di violetta, *f.* **-gold**, S.: fiorrancio, *m.*
măr-inate, TR.: marinare. **-ine** 1, S.: marina, nautica, *f.*; soldato di marina, *m.* **-ine** 2, ADJ.: marino, di mare. **-ine-officer**, S.: uffiziale di marina, *m.* **-iner**, S.: marinaio, marinaro; navigatore; soldato di marina, *m.*: *—'s compass*, bussola, *f.*; *—'s needle*, ago magnetico, *m.*
marionětte, S.: marionetta, *f.*
mărish 1, S.: pantano, palude, *m.* **marish** 2, ADJ.: pantanoso, paludoso, palustre.
mărital, ADJ.: maritale, congiugale.
măritime, ADJ.: marittimo, marino.
mârjoram, S.: maiorana, persa, *f.*
mârk 1, S.: marco, segno; contrassegno; indizio, *m.*; nota, *f.*; vestigio, *m.*, traccia, *f.*; attestato, testimonio, *m.*: *hit the —*, dar nel segno; *miss the —*, mancare il colpo; *shoot above the —*, tirare troppo alto; *shoot below the —*, tirare troppo basso. **mark** 2, TR.: marcare; indicare; contrassegnare; INTR.: osservare, considerare; stare attento; esaminare: *— out*, mostrare, fare vedere. **-er**, S.: segnatore; osservatore, *m.*
mârket 1, S.: mercato, *m.*; piazza di mercato, *f.* **market** 2, TR.: comprare; vendere; INTR.: mercantare. **-able**, ADJ.: vendibile; ben condizionato. **-day**, S.: giorno di mercato, *m.* **-folks**, S.: gente che bazzica continuamente in mercato, *f.* **-house**, S.: casa della piazza, *f.* **-man**, S.: che frequenta il mercato, venditore; compratore, *m.* **-place**, S.: piazza, *f.*; mercato, *m.* **-price**, **-rate**, S.: prezzo corrente, *m.* **-town**, S.: borgo, *m.*; terra, *f.* **-woman**, S.: venditrice nel mercato, mercatina, *f.*
mârk-ing, S.: marcare, *m.* **-ing-iron**, S.: marchio, *m.* -(s)**man**, S.: tiratore; cacciatore, *m.*
mârl 1, S.: marna, marga, terra grassa, *f.* **marl** 2, TR.: concimare colla marga, letamare con terra grassa; (*nav.*) ralingare. **-er**, S.: scavatore di marga o di marna, *m.*
mârline, S.: merlino, *m.*
mârl-pit, S.: cava di marna o di marga, *f.* **-y**, ADJ.: pieno di marga, pieno di marna.
mârma-lade, **-let**, S.: marmellata, conserva, *f.*
mar-morâtion, S.: incrostatura di marmo, *f.* **-mörean**, ADJ.: marmoreo, di marmo.
marmŏt(**to**), S.: marmotta, *f.*, marmotto, *m.*
marō(*o*)**n**, S.: marrone (castagno grosso), *m.*; ADJ.: di colore castagno.
mârquetry, S.: tarsia, intarsiatura, *f.*
mârquis, S.: marchese, *m.* **-ate**, S.: marchesato, *m.*
mârrer, S.: guastatore, danneggiatore, *m.*
măr-riage, S.: matrimonio, coniugio, *m.*; nozze, *f. pl.* **-riageable**, ADJ.: nubile; da marito. **-riageableness**, S.: età nubile; età da marito, *f.* **-riage-bed**, S.: talamo, *m.* **-riage-chamber**, S.: camera nuziale, *f.* **-riage-dress**, S.: abito di sposa, *m.* **-riage-song**, S.: epitalamio, *m.* **-riage-supper**, S.: festino nuziale, *m.* **-ried**, ADJ.: maritato, ammogliato; congiugale: *— man*, uomo ammogliato; *— woman*, donna maritata.
mărrow, S.: midolla, *f.*, midollo, *m.*; grassezza, *f.* **-bone**, S.: osso midolloso; ginocchio, *m.* **-less**, ADJ.: senza midolla. **-y**, ADJ.: midolloso; pastoso.
mărry 1, TR.: maritare, sposare; INTR.: maritarsi, sposarsi: *— a son*, ammogliare (*or* accasare) un figlio; *— a daughter*, maritare una figlia; *— (to) a girl*, sposare una fanciulla; *— again*, rimaritarsi.
marry† 2, INTERJ.: veramente.
mârsh, S.: palude, pantano, *m.*
mârshal 1, S.: maresciallo, *m.*: *field —*, maresciallo di campo, *m.* **marshal** 2, TR.: regolare, ordinare; schierare. **-ler**, S.: regolatore, ordinatore, *m.* **-sea**, S.: nome d' una prigione in Londra. **-ship**, S.: uffizio di maresciallo, *m.*
mârsh-mallow, S.: (*bot.*) bismalva, *f.* **-y**, ADJ.: paludoso, pantanoso.
mârt 1, S.: fiera, *f.*, traffico, *m.* **mart** 2, TR.: trafficare, mercare, mercatantare.
mârten, S.: martora, *f.* (animale).
mârtial, ADJ.: marziale; guerriero, bravo: *— law*, codice marziale, *m.* **-ist**, S.: guerriero, *m.*
mârtin(**et**), S.: rondone, *m.*
mârting-al, **-ale**, S.: striscia di cuoio; pastoia, *f.*
Mârtinmas, S.: festa di San Martino, *f.*
mârtlet = *martinet.*
mârtyr 1, S.: martire, *m.* **martyr** 2, TR.: martirizzare, martirare. **-dom**, S.: martirio, martirizzamento, *m.* **-ŏlogist**, S.: martirologista, *m.* **-ŏlogy**, S.: martirologio, *m.*
mârvel 1, S.: maraviglia, *f.*, prodigio, *m.* **marvel** 2, INTR.: maravigliare, istupidirsi, esser attonito. **-lous**, ADJ.: maraviglioso. **-lously**, ADV.: maravigliosamente. **-lousness**, S.: maravigliamento, *m.*, maraviglia, *f.*
măscarade = *masquerade.*
măsculine, ADJ.: mascolino; virile. **-ly**, ADV.: da uomo, virilmente; coraggioso. **-ness**, S.: maschiezza, virilità; aspetto nobile, *m.*
măsh 1, S.: mescuglio, *m.*, mescolan

volare più velocemente, sorpassare nel volo. **-fōol**, TR.: sorpassare in follia. **-form**, S.: esteriore, *m.*; apparenza, *f.* **-gate**, S.: uscita, *f.*, esito, *m.* **-give**, IRR.; TR.: superare in liberalità. **-gō**, IRR.; TR.: oltrapassare, andar più presto; precedere. **-gōing**, S.: uscità; spesa, *f.* **-grōw**, IRR.; TR.: crescere (*or* devenir) troppo grande per. **-guard**, S.: guardia avanzata, *f.* **-house**, S.: rimessa; casipola, *f.* **-knāve**, TR.: sorpassare in furberia. **-lăndish**, ADJ.: straniero, forestiero. **-lăst**, TR.: durare più lungamente. **-law**, S.: proscritto, bandito, *m.* **-law**, TR.: proscrivere, bandire. **-lawry**, S.: proscrizione, *f.*, bando, *m.* **-lay**, S.: sborso; gasto, *m.*, spese, *f. pl.* **-leap**, S.: impeto, *m.*; scappata, *f.* **-lēap**, TR.: strabalzare. **-lēarn**, TR.: superare nell' imparare. **-let**, S.: uscita, *f.*, esito; passaggio, *m.* **-line**, S.: contorno; schizzo, *m.* **-live**, TR.: sopravvivere. **-liver**, S.: sopravvivente; superstite, *m.* **-living**, S.: sopravvivere, *m.* **-look**, S.: vigilanza, *f.* **-lōok**, TR.: guardare con cipiglio. **-lying**, ADJ.: confinante; ulteriore. **-mărch**, INTR.: precedere nella marcia. **-mĕasure**, TR.: eccedere in misura. **-most**, ADJ.: estremo, ulteriore, rimotissimo. **-nŭmber**, TR.: sorpassare in numero. **-pāce**, TR.: precedere. **-parish**, S.: parrocchia fuor della città, *f.* **-part**, S.: parte esterna, *f.* **-post**, S.: guardia avanzata, *f.* **-put**, S.: produzione, quantità prodotta, *f.*

ŏut-rage, S.: oltraggio, *m.*; offesa, ingiuria; violenza, *f.* **-rāge**, TR.: oltraggiare, maltrattare. **-rāgeous**, ADJ.: oltraggioso, ingiurioso; atroce. **-rāgeously**, ADV.: oltraggiosamente, atrocemente, fieramente. **-rāgeousness**, S.: oltraggio, *m.*; violenza; atrocità, *f.*

ŏut-rē'ach, (IR)R.; TR.: oltrapassare; ingannare. **-ride**, IRR.; TR.: anticorrere a cavallo. **-right**, ADV.: subitamente, incontinente; schietto e netto. **-road**, S.: incursione, *f.* **-rōar**, TR.: eccedere in rugghiamenti. **-rōot**, TR.: sradicare, estirpare. **-rŭn**, INTR.; TR.: avanzare nel correre, precedere nel correre; eccedere. **-sāil**, TR.: avanzare alla vela, navigare più presto. **-scōrn**, TR.: braveggiare, dispregiare. **sĕll**, IRR.; TR.: sopravvendere. **-set**, S.: cominciamento, principio, *m.* **-shine**, IRR.; TR.: sorpassare in splendore. **-shōot**, IRR.; TR.: tirare di là del segno. **-side**, S.: superficie, *f.*, esteriore, *m.*, apparenza, *f.* **-sit**, IRR.; TR.: dimorare di là del tempo. **-skirt**, S.: sobborgo, *m.* **-slēep**, IRR.; TR.: dormire troppo lungo tempo. **-spēak**, *IRR.; TR.*: parlare troppo. **-spoken**, ADJ.: franco, ingenuo. **-sprĕad**, IRR.; TR.: spandere, diffondere. **-stănd**, IRR.; INTR.: mantenere, far fronte, resistere. **-stāre**, TR.: guardare con cipiglio; sconcertare. **-strĕtch**, TR.: distendere, spandere. **-strip**, TR.: antecorrere, avanzare, superare. **-swēar**, IRR.; TR.: giurare più di. **-vălue**, TR.: sorpassare in pregio. **-vĕnom**, TR.: essere più velenoso. **-vie**, TR.: sorpassare, superare; eccedere. **-villain**, TR.: eccedere in scelleratezza. **-vōte**, TR.: avere la pluralità de' voti. **-wălk**, TR.: camminare più presto. **-wall**, S.: antimuro; muro esteriore, *m.* **-ward** 1, ADJ.: esteriore, esterno; S.: esteriore, *m.*; forma esterna: — *show*, ostentazione, *f.*; —*bound*, diretto all' estero. **-ward(ly)** 2, ADV.: esteriormente, esternamente; in apparenza. **-wards**, ADV.: al di fuori, fuor del paese. **-wēar**, IRR.; TR.: durare più; annoiare. **-wēed**, TR.: svellere; sradicare. **-wēigh**, TR.: pesare più, sbilanciare. **-wit**, TR.: ingannare, truffare. **-work**, S.: edificio esteriore, *m.* **-wōrn**, ADJ.: usato, logoro. **-wórth**, TR.: eccedere in valore. **-wrought**, ADJ.: lavorato troppo.

ŏuz-e, S.: terra melmosa, *f.* **-y**, ADJ.: umido, pantanoso.

ō-val, ADJ.: ovale, di forma d' uovo, ellittico; S.: ovale, *m.*: — *window*, finestra tonda, *f.*; occhio, *m.* **-vărious**, ADJ.: fatto d' uova. **-vary**, S.: ovaia, *f.*; ovario, *m.*

ovātion, S.: ovazione, *f.*, piccol trionfo, *m.*

ŏven, S.: forno, *m.* **-fork**, S.: forchetto (da forno), *m.* **-ful**, S.: fornata, infornata, *f.* **-peel**, S.: pala (da forno), *f.* **-tender**, S.: fornaio, *m.*

ōver, PREP., ADV. PREF. (*with adjectives both members accented*): sopra, di sopra, su, sopra di; troppo, oltre: — *and* —, molte volte; — *and above*, oltre; — *again*, di nuovo, da capo; — *against*, in faccia, dirimpetto; — *night*, la notte passata; *be* —, esser finita; cessare; restare; *give* —, tralasciare; finire; *turn* —, voltare. **-abŏund**, INTR.: soprabbondare. **-ăct**, TR.: eccedere. **-ărch**, TR.: voltare; fabbricare a volta. **-āwe**, TR.: tenere in timore, tenere in rispetto. **-bălance** 1, S.: sovrappiù; eccesso, *m.* **-balance** 2, TR.: sbilanciare, tracollare, preponderare. **-bēar**, IRR.; TR.: sormontare; riprimere; vincere. **-bēaring**, ADJ.: insolente, altiero. **-bid**, IRR.; TR.: offerire all' incanto; incarire. **-board**, ADV.: fuor della nave. **-bŏil**, TR.: bollire troppo. **-bōld**, ADJ.: troppo temerario. **-bŭlk**, TR.: sopraccaricare, aggravare. **-bŭrden**, TR.: sopraggravare; opprimere.

lungo tempo dopo; — *ago*, — *since*, lungo tempo fa; *not* — *before*, non molto prima; *ere* —, in breve, fra poco; *as* — *as*, tanto che, tanto quanto; *as* — *as I live*, finchè vivrò; *all this day* —, tutt' oggi; *shall you be out* —? starete di molto a tornare? *how* —? quanto tempo? **-g** 3, INTR.: desiderare; appetire, avere gran voglia: — *for*, bramare ardentemente. **-ganimity**, S.: longanimità, sofferenza, *f.* **-g-boat**, S.: scialuppa, *f.*; schifo, *m.* **-ger**, ADJ., ADV.: più lungo. **-gěvity**, S.: longevità, lunga vita, *f.* **-g-headed**, ADJ.: che ha la testa appuntata; astuto. **-gimanous**, ADJ.: che ha le mani lunghe. **-gimetry**, S.: longimetria, *f.* **-ging**, S.: desiderio intenso, *m.*; impazienza, *f.* **-gingly**, ADV.: con desiderio intenso, bramosamente. **-ginquity**, S.: lontananza, distanza, *f.* **-gish**, ADJ.: alquanto lungo, lunghetto. **-gitude**, S.: longitudine; lunghezza, *f.* **-gitūdinal**, ADJ.: longitudinale. **-gitūdinally**, ADV.: in lungo. **-g-legged**, ADJ.: che ha le gambe lunghe. **-g-lived**, ADJ.: longevo. **-g-shanked** = *longlegged*. **-g-sighted**, ADJ.: che vede di lontano, che ha la vista lunga. **-g-sightedness**, S.: vista lontana, *f.* **-gsome**†, ADJ.: lungo; tedioso, noioso. **-gsomeness**†, S.: noiosità, *f.* **-gsŭfferance**, S.: longanimità, pazienza, *f.* **-gsŭffering**, ADJ.: sofferente; paziente. **-gways**, ADV.: pel lungo. **-gwinded**, ADJ.: lungo, tedioso, noioso. **-gwise** = *longways*.

lŏo, S.: bestia (*ad cards*).

lŏo-bily, ADJ.: scimunito, sciocco. **-by**, S.: balordo, minchione, goffo, *m.*

lŏof 1, S.: (*nav.*) sopravento, *m.* **loof** 2, TR.: (*nav.*) serrare il vento, andare all' orza.

lŏok 1, S.: guardo; aspetto, *m.*; occhiata, *f.* **look!** 2, INTERJ.: ecco! vedi! **look** 3, TR.: vedere, guardare; cercare; INTR.: mirare, considerare, guardare; parere, sembrare; aver aspetto di: — *annoyed*, sembrare tediato; — *back*, riflettere sopra, ruminare; — *big*, braveggiare, pavoneggiare; — *like*, aver la cera, rassomigliare; — *well*, avere buon viso, avere buona cera; — *out of the window*, affacciarsi alla finestra; — *young again*, ringiovanire; — *about*, invigilare; badare; — *after*, aver cura di; aver l' occhio a; — *at*, considerare; osservare; — *down*, guardar con isdegno, avere a sdegno; — *for*, cercare; aspettare; — *into*, considerare; esaminare; — *on*, mirare; pregiare; — *out*, cercare; ricercare; scoprire; (*nav.*) tener vendetta; — *over*, esaminare; — *there!* mirate là! — *to*, badare; prender guardia; — *up*, guardare in alto; — *upon*, mirare; stimare. **-er**, **-er-on**, S.: spettatore; riguardante, *m.* **-ing-glass**, S.: specchio, *m.*; bambola, *f.* **-ing-glass-maker**, S.: specchiaio, *m.* **-out**, S.: veletta, vedetta; sentinella: *to be on the* —, spiare; osservare; *keep a good* —, stare all' erta

lŏom 1, S.: telaio di tessitore, *m.* **loom** 2, INTR.: (*nav.*) apparire in lontananza, parere. **-gale**, S.: (*nav.*) venticello fresco, *m.* **-ing**, S.: (*nav.*) apparenza (d' un vascello), *f.*

lŏon, S.: tuffetto (anatra); furfante, birbone, *m.*

lŏop, S.: trina, *f.*; cordoncino, affibbiaglio, *m.* **-ed**, ADJ.: bucato, pieno di buchi, foracchiato. **-hole**, S.: buco; spiraglio; rigiro, sotterfugio; (*art.*) cannoniera, balestriera, *f.* **-holed**, ADJ.: bucato, pieno di spiragli. **-lace**, S.: gabbano, *m.* **-maker**, S.: nastraio, *m.*

lŏord†, S.: poltrone, *m.*

lŏose† 1, ADJ.: sciolto, slegato; lento; dissoluto, licenzioso, sviato: — *style*, stile bislacco; *be* —, essere sciolto; esser in libertà; *be in a* — *condition*, esser libero, vivere a suo modo; *get* —, scatenarsi; *get* — *from one*, liberarsi da uno; *hang* —, strascinare per terra; *grow* —, slegarsi, allontanarsi; *let* —, scatenare. **loose** 2, S.: libertà, *f.*, stato di libertà, *m.*; emanzipazione, *f.* **loose** 3, TR.: slegare, slacciare, rilasciare; sprigionare, liberare; INTR.: spiegare le vele, levar l' ancora; partire. **-ly**, ADV.: senza fermezza; dissolutamente, licenziosamente. **-n**, TR.: slegare, sciogliere, distaccare; rilassare, rallentare; INTR.: distaccarsi; separarsi. **-ness**, S.: allentamento; flusso di corpo, *m.* **-ning**, ADJ.: lassativo, mollificativo; S.: allentamento, *m.*

lŏp 1, S.: taglio; ramo tagliato, *m.*; pulce, *f.* **lop** 2, TR.: diramare, scapezzare, troncare; INTR.: pendere. **-per**, S.: che dirama; potatore, *m.* **-ping**, S.: potagione, *f.*, potamento, *m.* **-sided**, ADJ.: (*nav.*) abboccato.

lo-quācious, ADJ.: loquace; ciarliero. **-quăcity**, S.: loquacità; ciarlieria, ciancia, *f.*

lôrd 1, S.: signore; padrone; Iddio; lord, *m.*: *house of* —*s*, camera dei Lordi, *f.*; — *chancellor*, gran cancelliere, *m.*; — *chamberlain*, gran ciambellano, *m.*; — *chief justice*, gran giudice, *m.*; — *mayor of London*, podestà di Londra, *m.* **lord** 2, INTR.: signoreggiare, dominare: — *it over*, dominare, tiraneggiare. **-ing**† = *-ling*. **-liness**, S.: altezza; superbia, alterigia, *f.* **-like**, ADJ.: da signore, di gran signore; altiero. **-ling**, S.: signo-

IRR.; TR.: sopravvendere, stravendere. **-sĕt**, IRR.; TR.: rovesciare, rovinare; INTR.: abbattersi, demolirsi. **-shāde**, **-shădow**, TR.: adombrare, ombreggiare, proteggere. **-shōe**, S.: galoscia, soprascarpa di gomma, *f.* **-shōot**, IRR.; TR.: tirare di là del segno: — *one's self*, innoltrarsi troppo. **-sight**, S.: ispezione, cura, *f.*; errore, sbaglio, *m.* **-skip**, TR.: oltrepassare; trascurare, omettere. **-slēep**, IRR.; INTR.: dormir troppo. **-slip**, TR.: omettere; trascurare, lasciare. **-snōw**, TR.: coprire di neve. **-sōld**, ADJ.: sopravvenduto, stravenduto. **'-sōon**, ADV.: troppo presto. **-spĕnt**, ADJ.: affaticato, esausto. **-sprĕad**, IRR.; TR.: spandere; allargare, dilatare. **-stănd**, IRR.; TR.: stare troppo sulle condizioni. **-stāte**, TR.: esagerare. **-stŏck**, TR.: empiere troppo; calcare. **-strāin**, TR.: sforzare, raffinare troppo; INTR.: sforzarsi. **-strĕtch**, TR.: stendere troppo, stiracchiare. **-strēw**, IRR.; TR.: spargere. **-swāy**, TR.: predominare, prevalere. **-swĕll**, IRR.; TR.: rigonfiare; traboccare.

ōvert, ADJ.: aperto, pubblico.

over-tāke, IRR.; TR.: giungere; acchiappare; sorprendere: *I will soon — you*, presto vi raggiungerò; *—n by a storm*, colto da un temporale. **-tălk**, INTR.: parlare troppo. **-tâsk**, TR.: sopraggravare (con lavoro, ecc.). **-tăx**, TR.: tassare troppo, esigere troppo. **-thrōw**, S.: sovvertimento, *m.*, sconfitta, rovina, rotta, *f.* **-thrōw**, IRR.; TR.: rovesciare, rovinare, disfare. **-thrōwer**, S.: sovvertitore, rovinatore; vincitore, *m.* **'-thwărt**, ADJ.: opposito, avverso; ostinato. **'-thwartly†**, ADV.: a traverso, obbliquamente; tortamente; pertinacemente. **'-thwartness†**, S.: pertinacia, caparbieria, *f.* **-tire**, TR.: faticare troppo.

ōvertly, ADV.: apertamente.

over-tŏp, TR.: soprastare, sorpassare. **-trip**, TR.: camminare sopra pian piano.

ōverture, S.: apertura, scoperta; proposizione, offerta; (*mus.*) sinfonia, *f.*

over-tûrn, TR.: sovvertere, rovinare. **-tûrner**, S.: sovvertitore, distruttore, *m.* **-tûrning**, S.: sovvertimento, *m.*, rovina, *f.* **-vălue**, TR.: stimare troppo. **-vēil**, TR.: velare, coprire con un velo. **-violent**, ADJ.: troppo violento. **-vōte**, TR.: avere la pluralità delle voci. **-wătch**, TR.: affaticare con eccessive veglie. **-wēak**, ADJ.: troppo debole. **-wēary**, TR.: faticare troppo, stancare all' eccesso. **-wēen**, INTR.: pensare troppo bene di sè. **-wēening**, ADJ.: presuntuoso; S.: presunzione, arroganza, *f.* **-wēeningly**, ADV.: arrogantemente. **-wēigh**, TR.: pesare più, essere più pesante. **-wêight**, S.: preponderanza, *f.*; soprappiù, *m.* **-whĕlm** *-hwĕlm*, sommergere; opprimere, ricolmare, innondare; aggravare. **-whĕlming**, S.: sommergente, ecc., che sommerge, ecc. **-whĕlmingly**, ADV.: in modo oppressivo. **-wīse**, ADJ.: troppo savio, troppo accorto. **-wōrn**, ADJ.: oppresso, affaticato, usato. **-wrought** *-răt*, ADJ.: troppo lavorato, troppo studiato. **'-zēalous**, ADJ.: troppo zeloso.

ōviform, ADJ.: ovale, di forma d' uovo.

ōwe, (IR)R.; TR.: dovere; essere obbligato, esser tenuto: *I — my life to you*, vi son tenuto della vita. **-ing**, ADJ.: dovuto, imputabile: *that is — to*, ciò proviene da, ciò è cagionato da (*or* l' effetto di); è da attribuirsi a.

ōwl, S.: gufo; barbagianni, *m.*; civetta, *f.* **-er**, S.: contrabbandiere, *m.* **-et**, S.: civetta, *f.* **-ing**, S.: contrabbando, *m.*

ōwn 1, ADJ.: proprio: *my —*, il mio, la mia, i miei; *my — self*, io medesimo; *be one's —*, essere padrone di sè stesso.

own 2, TR.: confessare, concedere; riconoscere; possedere, essere proprietario di: — *a fact*, accusare un fatto. **-er**, S.: proprietario, padrone, *m.* **-ership**, S.: proprietà; signoria, *f.*

ŏx (pl. *oxen*), S.: bue, bove, *m.* **-eye**, S.: (*bot.*, *nav.*) occhio di bue, *m.* **-fly**, S.: tafano, *m.* **-heal**, S.: radice dell' elleboro, *f.* **-like**, ADJ.: come un bue. **-lip**, S.: (*bot.*) tassobarbasso, *m.* **-stall**, S.: stalla da buoi, *f.* **-tongue**, S.: (*bot.*) buglossa, *f.*

oxălic, ADJ.: ossalico: — *acid*, acido ossalico.

ŏxid-e, S.: ossido, *m.* **-ize**, TR.: ossidare.

ŏxycrate, S.: ossicrato, *m.*

ŏx-ygen, S.: ossigeno, *m.* **-ўgenate**, TR.: ossigenare. **-ygenātion**, S.: ossigenazione. **-ўgenous**, ADJ.: di ossigeno.

ōyer, S.: corte di giustizia decisiva, *f.*

ōyes! INTERJ.: ascoltate! udite!

ōyster, S.: ostrica, *f.* **-man**, S.: venditore d' ostriche, *m.* **-shell**, S.: conchiglia d' ostrica, *f.* **-wench**, **-woman**, S.: venditrice d' ostriche, *f.*

ozaēna, S.: (*surg.*) ozena, *f.*

ōzone, S.: ozono, *m.*

P

p *pē* (*the letter*), S.: p, *m.*

păb-ular, ADJ.: che da pascolo, erboso, nutritivo. **-ulātion**, S.: pascimento, pascolo, *m.* **-ulous** = *pabular*. **-ulŭm**, S.: pascolo, nutrimento, *m.*

pāc-e 1, S.: passo; andamento; ambio, *m.*: *at a slow —*, a passo lento; *keep — with*, camminare del pari con; *mend one's*

mégrim, S.: emicrania, magrana, *f.*
mělancho-lic, ADJ.: malinconico, malinconoso, stizzoso. **-lily**, ADV.: in modo malinconico. **-list†**, S.: malinconico; visionario, *m.* **-ly**, ADJ.: malinconico, tristo, afflitto; S.: malinconia; tristezza, *f.*
mêlée (*Engl. accents*) *mělě*, S.: zuffa, *f.*
mělilot, S.: (*bot.*) meliloto, *m.*
mē-liorate, TR.: migliorare, ammendare; INTR.: migliorarsi. **-lioration**, S.: miglioramento, *m.* **-lĭŏrity†**, S.: miglioranza, *f.*
měl-leous, ADJ.: melato. **-liferous**, ADJ.: mellifero. **-lificātion**, S.: fare il mele, *m.* **-lifluence**, S.: abbondanza di mele, *f.* **-lifluent**, **-lifluous**, ADJ.: mellifluo; dolce.
měllow 1, ADJ.: maturo; tenero, molle. **mellow** 2, TR.: maturare; INTR.: maturarsi, divenir maturo. **-ness**, S.: maturità, maturezza, *f.*
mel-ŏdious, ADJ.: melodioso, armonioso. **-ŏdiously**, ADV.: melodiosamente. **-ŏdiousness**, S.: melodia, armonia, *f.* **-odrâma**, S.: melodramma, *m.* **-ody**, S.: melodia; armonia, *f.*
mělon, S.: mellone, popone, *m.* **-bed**, S.: mellonaio, poponaio, *m.*
mělt, IRR.; TR.: fondere; liquefare; intenerire; (*fig.*) placare; INTR.: fondersi; liquefarsi; intenerirsi: — *away*, fondersi, dileguarsi; — *into tears*, disciogliersi in lagrime. **-er**, S.: fonditore, *m.* **-ing**, S.: liquefazione, *f.* **-ing-house**, S.: fonderia, *f.* **-ingly**, ADV.: in modo liquefattivo.
měmber, S.: membro, *m.*; parte, *f.*
měm-brane, S.: (*anat.*) membrana; tunica, *f.* **-brāneous**, ADJ.: membranoso.
memĕnto, S.: rimembranza, ricordanza, *f.*
měm-oir *-wor*, S.: ricordo (di fatti storici), *m.*, annotazione, *f.* **-orable**, ADJ.: memorabile, memorevole. **-orably**, ADV.: memorabilmente, degno di memoria. **-orăndum**, S.: annotazione, *f.*; ricordo, *m.* **-orative**, ADJ.: memorativo. **-ŏrial**, ADJ.: memorativo; della memoria; S.: memoriale, ricordo, *m.*, memoria; supplica, *f.* **-ŏrialist**, S.: autore di memorie, *m.* **-orize**, TR.: ricordare, memorare, ridurre a memoria. **-ory**, S.: memoria, ricordanza, *f.*; ricordo, *m.*: *by* —, a memoria; *of blessed* —, di santa memoria; *call to* —, ricordarsi; *have a poor* (*short*) —, aver la memoria labile (corta), aver poca memoria; *within the* — *of man*, a memoria d' uomo.
měn, S. PL.: uomini, *m. pl.*
měnace 1, S.: minaccia, *f.*, minacciamento, *m.* **-ce** 2, TR.: minacciare; fare temere. **-cer**, S.: minacciatore, minacciante, *m.* **-cing** 1, ADJ.: minacciante, minaccevole. **-cing** 2, S.: minacciare, minacciamento, *m.*
men-āge†, **-āgerie** *g* = *ž or g*, S.: serraglio (collezione d' animali, *f.*), *m.*
měnd, TR.: racconciare, rappezzare, rimendare, emendare; migliorare; correggere; ristaurare, riparare; INTR.: riformarsi; emendarsi: — *a coat*, tapezzare un vestito; — *one's fortune*, migliorare la sua condizione. **-able**, ADJ.: che si può riparare, corrigibile.
men-dācious, ADJ.: mendace. **-dăcity**, S.: menzogna, bugia, *f.*
měnder, S.: acconciatore, racconciatore, rappezzatore, *m.*
měn-dicancy, S.: mendicità, *f.* **-dicant**, ADJ.: mendico, povero; mendicante; S.: mendicante; barone, *m.* **-dicate**, INTR.: mendicare, limosinare. **-dicity**, S.: mendicità, mendicanza, *f.*
měnding, S.: racconciamento, racconciare, *m.*: *be on the* — *hand*, andar migliorando, esser convalescente.
měndment = *amendment*.
mēnial, ADJ.: domestico; servile.
men-inges, S.: (*anat.*) meninge, *f.* **-ingītis**, S.: meningite, *f.*
menŏlogy, S.: menologio, calendario, *m.*
měnsal, ADJ.: mensale, della mensa.
měns-trual, **-truous**, ADJ.: mestruale, mestruo, mensuale. **-truum**, S.: (*chem.*) mestruo, dissolvente, *m.*
mensurability, S.: misurabilità.
měnsu-rable, ADJ.: misurabile; atto a misurarsi. **-rate**, TR.: misurare; regolare. **-rātion**, S.: misuramento, misurare, *m.*
měntal, ADJ.: mentale, di mente, intellettuale. **-ly**, ADV.: mentalmente, colla mente.
měntion 1, S.: menzione, commemorazione, memoria, *f.*: *make* — *of one*, far menzione d' alcuno. **mention** 2, TR.: mentovare, menzionare: *don't* — *it, pray*, non ne parlate, prego. **-ing**, S.: menzione, *f.*
mephitic(al), ADJ.: mefitico.
me-rācious†, ADJ.: spiritoso, forte; puro; gustoso, saporoso.
měrcantile, ADJ.: mercantile: — *town*, città mercantile, *f.*
měrcena-riness, S.: venalità, *f.* **-ry**, ADJ.: mercenario, venale; S.: mercenario; interessato, *m.*
měrcer, S.: merciaio; setaiuolo, *m.* **-y**, S.: merceria, mercanzia da taglio, *f.*
měr-chandise, S.: mercanzia, *f.*; traffico, negozio, *m.* **-chandise**, INTR.: trafficare, negoziare, fare commercio. **-chandry**, S.: traffico, *m.* **-chant**, S.: mercante, mercatante, negoziante, *m.* **-chantable**, ADJ.: ben condizionato. **-chantlike**, ADJ.: mercatantesco. **-chantman**, S.: vascello mercantile, *m.*

parĕn-thesis, S.: parentesi, *f.* **-thĕtical**, ADJ.: tra parentesi. **-thĕtically**, ADV.: tra parentesi; incidentalmente.
parĕnticide, S.: parricida, *m.*
pârer, S.: rosolo, *f.*, incastro, *m.*
pârget 1, S.: intonacato, *m.* **parget** 2, TR.: intonacare. **-er**, S.: intonacatore, *m.*
parhēlion, S.: pareglio, *m.*
parietal, ADJ.: murale.
pâring, S.: ritaglio, *m.*; scorza, *f.* **-knife**, S.: trinciante di calzolaio, *m.*
păr-ish 1, S.: parrocchia, *f.*: *—church*, chiesa parrocchiale, *f.*; *—priest*, parroco, *m.*; *be on the —*, essere nella lista dei poveri. **-ish** 2, ADJ.: parrocchiale, di parrocchia. **-ishioner**, S.: parrocchiano, *m.*
parisyllăbic(al), ADJ.: parasillabico.
păritor, S.: cursore, bidello, *m.*
părity, S.: parità, ugualità, similitudine, simiglianza, *f.*
pârk 1, S.: parco, serraglio d' animali, *m.* **park** 2, TR.: mettere in un parco, rinchiudere. **-er**, **-keeper**, S.: custode di parco, *m.*
pâr-lance, S.: conversazione, conferenza, *f.* **-ley** 1, S.: conferenza, *f.*; parlamento, *m.*: *beat a —*, *sound a —*, suonare la chiamata. **-ley** 2, INTR.: parlamentare; conferire. **-liament**, S.: parlamento; senato, *m.*: *act of —*, legge, *f.*; *the houses of —*, le due camere (dei Comuni e dei Lordi). **-liamĕntary**, ADJ.: parlamentario. **-liament-man**, S.: membro di parlamento, *m.*
pârlo(u)r, S.: sala, *f.*; parlatorio, *m.*: *little —*, salottino, *m.*
pârlous†, ADJ.: attivo, vivace; gaio; astuto. **-ness**†, S.: vivacità, prontezza, *f.*
Parmesăn, S.: parmigiano, *m.* (cacio).
parō-chial, **-chian**, ADJ.: parrocchiale, della parrocchia.
părody 1, S.: parodia, *f.* **parody** 2, TR.: parodiare, travestire.
parōle, S.: parola; promessa, *f.*
paro-nomăsia, **-nŏmasy**, S.: paranomasia, *f.*
păroquet, S.: parrocchetto, specie di piccolo pappagallo, *m.*
parōtis, S.: (*anat.*) parotide, *f.*
păroxysm, S.: parossismo, *m.*
părri-cide, S.: parricida, *m.* **-cidal**, **-cidious**, ADJ.: di parricida.
părrot, S.: pappagallo, *m.*
părry, TR.: parare; evitare.
pârse, TR.: spiegare le parti d' orazione.
parsimō-nious, ADJ.: parco, economo. **-niously**, ADV.: con parsimonia. **-niousness**, **pârsimo-ny**, S.: parsimonia, *f.*; risparmio, *m.*; economia, *f.*
pârsley, S.: petrosemolo, petrosello, *m.*
pârsnip, S.: pastinaca, *f.*: *wild —*, sisaro, *m.*; *yellow —*, carota, *f.*

pârson, S.: ministro, curato, *m.* **-age**, S.: beneficio (d' una parrocchia), *m.*; casa del curato, *f.*
pârt 1, S.: parte, porzione, *f.*; personaggio; dovere, debito, *m.*: *—s*, mezzi, talenti, *m. pl.*; *the greater —*, la maggior parte; *the —s of speech*, le parti del discorso; *— by —*, partitamente; *for my —*, per me, in quanto a me; *for the most —*, la maggior parte del tempo, ordinariamente; *in some —*, in qualche parte; *on all —s*, da per tutto; *man of —s*, uomo garbato, uomo di talento, *m.*; *do the — of one*, tenere la vece d' uno; *take one's —*, pigliar le parti d' uno; *take in good —*, pigliare in buona parte; *take in ill —*, pigliare in cattiva parte. **part** 2, TR.: disunire, separare, dividere; INTR: separarsi; partirsi: *— asunder*, bipartirsi; *— a fray*, spartire una contesa. **-able**, ADJ.: partibile, spartibile. **-age**, S.: spartimento, *m.*; divisione, *f.*
partăk-e, IRR.; (IN)TR.: participare, avere parte: *— of a thing*, avere (prendere) parte di una cosa. **-er**, S.: participatore, *m.*
pârter, S.: partitore, *m.*
partĕrre, S.: giardino da fiori a aiuole, *m.*
pâr-tial, ADJ.: parziale; favorevole. **-tiălity**, S.: parzialità, *f.* **-tialize**, TR.: parzialeggiare, favorire; INTR.: esser parziale. **-tially**, ADV.: parzialmente, con parzialità.
partibility, S.: divisibilità, separabilità, *f.* **pârtible**, ADJ.: partibile, divisibile.
partici-pable, ADJ.: che può esser participato. **-pant**, ADJ.: participante. **-pate**, TR.: participare, aver parte. **-pă-tion**, S.: participazione, *f.*, participamento, *m.*
particip-ial, ADJ.: di participio. **-ially**, ADV.: a modo di participio. **pârticip-le**, S.: participio, *m.*
pâr-ticle, S.: particola; particella, *f.* **-ticular**, ADJ.: particolare, singolare, speciale; individuale; S.: particolare, *m.*, particolarità, *f.*: *—s*, particolari, *m. pl.*, circostanze, particolarità, *f. pl.*; *in —*, in ispecie, particolarmente; *— of an estate*, inventario, *m.* **-ticulărity**, S.: particolarità, singolarità, *f.* **-ticularize**, TR.: particolarizzare, distinguere particolarmente. **-ticularly**, ADV.: particolarmente, distintamente.
pârting, S.: partimento, spartimento, *m.*; partita, partenza, *f.*: *— cup*, buona mano, mancia, *f.*
pârtisan, S.: partigiana, *f.*; partigiano, *m.*
par-tition 1, S.: partizione, *f.*, spartimento, *m.*: *— wall*, muro di mezzo, *m.* **-tition** 2, TR.: dividere in parti distinti.
pâr-titive, ADJ.: partitivo.

mĕtric(al), ADJ.: metrico.
me-trŏpolis, S.: metropoli, *f.* **-tropŏl-itan**, ADJ.: metropolitano: — *church*, chiesa metropolitana, *f.*; S.: metropolitano, *m.*
mĕttle, S.: vivacità, foga, *f.*, spirito, coraggio, *m.* **-d**, **-some**, ADJ.: focoso, vivace. **-somely**, ADV.: spiritosamente, con foga. **-someness**, S.: vivacità, foga, *f.*
mew 1, S.: gabbia, *f.*; gabbiano, *m.* (uccello): —*s*, stalle (di cavalli), *f. pl.*
mew 2, TR.: rinchiudere; INTR.: mudare; miagolare.
mewl, INTR.: gridare (come un bambino).
miasm(a), S.: (*med.*) miasma, *f.* **-ătic**, ADJ.: (*med.*) miasmatico.
mica, S.: mica, specie di talco, *f.*
mice, PL. di *mouse*.
Michaelmas, S.: festa di san Michele, *f.*
mich-(e)†, INTR.: appiattarsi; nascondersi. **-er**†, S.: infingardo, furfante, perdigiorno, *m.*
mickle, ADJ.: molto, grande; assai: *many a — makes a muckle*, molti pochi fanno un assai.
mi-crobe, S.: microbo, *m.* **-crocosm**, S.: microcosmo, *m.* **-crŏmeter**, S.: micrometro, *m.* **-croscope**, S.: microscopio, *m.* **-croscŏpic(al)**, ADJ.: microscopico.
mid, ADJ.: mezzo; ugualmente distante. **-age**, S.: mezza età, *f.* **-course**, S.: mezza via, mezza strada, *f.* **-day**, S.: mezzodì, mezzogiorno, *m.* **-dle** 1, ADJ.: mezzo, mezzano; mediocre. **-dle** 2, S.: mezzo, centro; cuore, *m.* **-dle-aged**, ADJ.: di mezzana età. **-dle-ages**, S.: medio evo, *m.* **-dle-man**, S.: agente, mediatore, *m.* **-dlemost**, ADJ.: posto nel mezzo; del mezzo.. **-dle-sized**, ADJ.: di mezzana statura. **-dling**, ADJ.: mediocre; mezzano.
midge, S.: zanzara, *f.* (insetto).
mid-hĕaven, S.: centro de' cieli, *m.* **-land**, ADJ.: mediterraneo. **-leg**, S.: mezza gamba, *f.* **-lent**, S.: metà della quaresima, *f.* **-most**, ADJ.: posto nel mezzo, del mezzo. **-night**, S.: mezza notte, *f.*; ADJ.: di mezza notte. **-riff**, S.: diaframma, *m.* **-sea**, S.: mare mediterraneo, *m.* **-ship**, S.: mezzania, *f.* **-shipman**, S.: guardia marina, *f.*; sotto-luogotenente di nave, *m.* **-st**, ADJ.: mezzo, mezzano; S.: mezzo, centro; cuore, *m.* **-summer**, S.: mezzo della state, *m.*; festa di san Giovanni, *f.* **-way** 1, ADJ., ADV.: nel mezzo cammino. **-way** 2, S.: mezza strada, *f.*, mezzo cammino, *m.*
mid-wife, S.: levatrice, ricoglitrice, mammana, *f.* **-wifery**, S.: mestiere di levatrice, *m.*, ostetricia, *f.*
midwinter, S.: mezzo del verno, cuore del verno, *m.*
mien, S.: aria, ciera, *f.*; aspetto; portamento, *m.*: *dignified* —, aria distinta (dignitosa).
might, S.: potere, *m.*, potenza, possanza, forza, *f.*: *with — and main*, con ogni forza, vigorosamente; *with all one's* —, a tutto potere. **-ily**, ADV.: con forza; molto. **-iness**, S.: potenza, possanza, *f.*, potere, *m.* **-y**, ADJ.: potente; grande; forte; ADV.: molto, estremamente.
mignonĕtte *miny-*, S.: amorino, *m.*; reseda odorata, *f.*
mi-grate, INTR.: migrare. **-grātion**, S.: migrazione, *f.*, dipartimento, *m.*
milch, ADJ.: lattante; lattifero. **-cow**, S.: vacca lattante, *f.*
mild, ADJ.: dolce, mite, ameno; piacevole; moderato; indulgente: — *weather*, tempo dolce.
mil'dew 1, S.: nebbia; golpe, *f.*, carbone, *m.* **mildew** 2, TR.: annebbiare, involpare.
mild-ly, ADV.: dolcemente, mitemente, placidamente. **-ness**, S.: dolcezza; clemenza, indulgenza, *f.*
mile, S.: miglio, *m.* **-stone**, S.: pietra migliare, *f.*
mi'lfoil, S.: (*bot.*) millefoglie, *f.*
miliary, ADJ.: piccolo; simile al miglio: —*fever*, febbre miliare, *m.*
milice = *militia*.
mil-itant, ADJ.: militante. **-itary**, ADJ.: militare, da soldato. **-itia**, S.: milizia, *f.*; soldati nazionali, *m. pl.* **-itiaman**, S.: milite della guardia nazionale.
milk 1, S.: latte, *m.*: *thick* —, latte quagliato; *cow's* —, latte di vacca; *give* —, allattare. **milk** 2, TR.: mungere, trarre il latte. **-cow**, S.: vacca lattante, *f.* **-en**, ADJ.: latteo, di latte. **-food**, S.: latticinio, *m.*; vivanda di latte, *f.* **-house**, S.: cascina, *f.* **-iness**, S.: qualità latticinosa, *f.* **-livered**, ADJ.: poltrone, codardo. **-maid**, S.: lattaia, lattivendola, *f.* **-man**, S.: uomo che vende latte, *m.* **-pail**, S.: secchia da latte, *f.* **-pan**, S.: terrina, *f.*, piatto (da latte), *m.* **-pottage**, S.: zuppa di latte, *f.*, latteruolo, *m.* **-score**, S.: tacca; taglia (da latte), *f.* **-sop**, S.: effemminato, codardo, *m.* **-thistle**, S.: (*bot.*) titimalo, euforbio, *m.* **-tooth**, S.: dente lattaiuolo, *m.* **-weed**, S.: (*bot.*) titimalo, *m.* **-white**, ADJ.: del colore di latte. **-woman**, S.: lattaia, *f.* **-y**, ADJ.: lattifero, latteo: (*astr.*) — *way*, via lattea, *f.*
mill 1, S.: mulino, *m.*: *coffee* —, mulinello da caffè, *m.*; *hand* —, mulinello, *m.*; *oil* —, macinatoio, *m.*; *paper* —, cartiera, *f.* *water* —, mulino da acqua, *m.*; *wind* —

păten, S.: patena, *f.* (vaso sacro); piatto, *m.*
pătent 1, ADJ.: patente; privilegiato; S.: patente, lettera patente, *f.*; brevetto, *m.* **patent** 2, TR.: accordare una patente a. **-cap**, S.: capsula, *f.* **-ed**, ADJ.: brevettato. **-ēe**, S.: che riceve una patente. **-office**, S.: ufficio di brevetti, *m.*
patĕr-nal, ADJ.: paternale, paterno. **-nity**, S.: paternità, *f.*
păth, S.: sentiero, calle, *m.*; via, strada, *f.*
pathĕtic(al), ADJ.: patetico, energico. **-ly**, ADV.: in modo patetico, energicamente. **-ness**, S.: energia; sensibilità, *f.*
păthless, ADJ.: senza sentiero, impraticabile.
pa-thǫlŏgical, ADJ.: patologico. **-thŏlogy**, S.: patologia, *f.*
păthos, S.: energia movente le passioni, *f.*
păthway, S.: sentiero, *m.*; via, strada, *f.*
pătible†, ADJ.: passabile, tollerabile.
patĭbulary, ADJ.: di patibolo, di forca.
pātien-ce, S.: pazienza, sofferenza, tolleranza, *f.*: *be out of* —, rinnegar la pazienza; *take* —, prender pazienza; *tire out one's* —, far perder la pazienza ad uno. **-t**, ADJ.: paziente; sofferente; S.: paziente, ammalato, *m.* **-tly**, ADV.: pazientemente, con pazienza.
pătin(*e*), S.: patena, *f.*, coperchio del calice, *m.*
păt-ly, ADV.: convenevolmente, comodamente, a proposito. **-ness**, S.: adattamento, *m.*, comodità, *f.*
pātri-arch, S.: patriarca, *m.* **-ārchal**, ADJ.: patriarcale, di patriarca. **-ārchate**, **-archship**, S.: patriarcato, *m.*
patri-cian, ADJ.: patrizio, senatorio; S.: patrizio, uomo nobile, *m.* **-ciate**, S.: patriziato, *m.*
pătricide, S.: patricida; patricidio, *m.*
patrimō-nial, ADJ.: patrimoniale, di patrimonio. **-nially**, ADV.: di patrimonio.
pătrimo-ny, S.: patrimonio, *m.*
pātri-ot, S.: patriotta; paesano, *m.* **-ŏtic**, ADJ.: patriottico. **-otism**, S.: patriottismo, amor di patria, *m.*
patrŏci-nate, TR.: patrocinare, proteggere. **-nātion**, S.: patrocinio, *m.*, protezione, *f.*
patrōl 1, S.: pattuglia, ronda, *f.* **patrol** 2, TR.: fare la ronda.
pātron, S.: padrone, protettore, difensore, *m.*: — *saint*, santo protettore.
patron-age 1, S.: padronaggio; padronato, *m.* **-age** 2, TR.: patrocinare, proteggere, difendere: *under the* — *of*, sotto il patronato di. **-al**, ADJ.: di padrone. **-ess**, S.: padronezza, protettrice, *f.* **-ize**, TR.: patrocinare, favorire; difendere. **-izer**, S.: patrocinatore, *m.* **-less** *pā-*, ADJ.: senza protettore. **-ship** *pā-*, S.: protettorato, *m.*, protezione, *f.*
patronўmic, ADJ.: patronimico.
pătten, S.: zoccolo; pattino; basamento (di colonna), *m.* **-maker**, S.: zoccolaio, *m.*
pătter, INTR.: scalpitare, strepitare.
păttern, S.: modello, esempio, *m.*
pătty, S.: pasticcietto, *m.*
pāucity, S.: pochezza, *f.*, piccolo numero, *m.*
pāunch 1, S.: pancia, *f.* **paunch** 2, TR.: sventrare, sbudellare. **-bellied**, ADJ.: panciuto.
pāuper, S.: povero, indigente, *m.* **-ism**, S.: povertà, *f.*
pāuse 1, S.: pausa, fermata, *f.* **-e** 2, INTR.: pausare; fermarsi, pensare, riflettere. **-er**, S.: che pausa. **-ing**, S.: pausa; meditazione, considerazione, *f.*
pāv-e, TR.: lastricare; appianare: — *with bricks*, ammattonare; — *with pebbles*, selciare. **-ement**, S.: pavimento, lastricato, *m.* **-er**, **-ier**, S.: lastricatore, *m.*
pavilion 1, S.: padiglione, *m.*, tenda, *f.*; (*nav.*) stendardo, *m.* **pavilion** 2, TR.: fornire di tende; alloggiare.
pāving, S.: lastricare, *m.* **-beetle**, S.: battipalo, *m.*, mazzeranga, *f.*
pāw 1, S.: zampa, *f.* **paw** 2, (IN)TR.: zampettare, zampare; stazzonare, maneggiare; carezzare.
pāwn 1, S.: pegno, gaggio, *m.*; pedona, pedina, *f.*: *lend upon* —, prestar con pegno. **pawn** 2, TR.: impegnare, dare in pegno. **-broker**, S.: che impresta col pegno, prestatore, *m.* **-shop**, S.: monte di pietà, *m.*
pāy 1, S.: paga, *f.*, pagamento, soldo, salario, *m.* **pay** 2, TR.: pagare; rimunerare; soddisfare; scontare: — *in advance*, pagare anticipatamente; — *one's debts*, pagare i suoi debiti; — *one's respects*, salutare, riverire; — *a rope*, impeciare una fune; — *a visit*, rendere una visita; — *back*, restituire il pagato; — *down*, pagare contanti; — *off*, bastonare; punire. **-able**, ADJ.: pagabile, da pagarsi. **-day**, S.: giorno di pagamento, *m.* **-er**, S.: pagatore, *m.* **-ing** = *payment*. **-master**, S.: pagatore; tesoriere, *m.* **-ment**, S.: pagamento, salario, *m.*
pēa, S.: pisello, *m.*
pēace 1, S.: pace; tranquillità, quiete; riconciliazione, *f.*; accordo, *m.*: *hold your* —! tacete! zitto! *the king's* —, l'ordine publico; *justice of the* —, giudice di pace. **peace** 2, INTERJ.: silenzio, tacete! **-able**, ADJ.: pacifico, tranquillo. **-ableness**, S.: umore pacifico, *m.*, tranquillità, *f.* **-ably**, ADV.: tranquillamente. **-break-**

TR.: monetare, battere la moneta. **-age**, S.: monetaggio; conio, *m.* **-er, -man**, S.: monetiere, zecchiere, *m.* **-master**, S.: direttore della zeccha, *m.*
minuet, S.: minuetto, *m.*
minus, ADV.: meno.
minute 1, ADJ.: minuto, piccolo, piccolissimo; tenue.
minute 2 *-it*, S.: minuto; momento, istante, *m.* **minute** 3, TR.: abbozzare; disegnare. **-book**, S.: giornale, registro, *m.* **-glass**, S.: oriuolo, *m.* **-hand**, S.: ago di minuti, *m.*
minute-ly, ADV.: esattamente, precisamente. **-ness**, S.: minutezza, minuzia, esiguità, *f.*
minute-watch *-it*, S.: oriuolo che mostra i minuti, *m.*
minutia, S.: minuzia; cosa di nulla, *f.*
minx, S.: vanarella, civettola, sfacciatella, *f.*
mir-acle, S.: miracolo, *m.*, maraviglia, *f.: by a —*, per miracolo. **-acle-monger**, S.: spacciatore di miracoli, *m.* **-ăculous**, ADJ.: miracoloso, maraviglioso, stupendo. **-ăculously**, ADV.: miracolosamente, per miracolo. **-ăculousness**, S.: qualità miracolosa, *f.*, mirabile, *m.*
mirâge *-aj*, S.: miraggio, *m.*
mire 1, S.: fango, limo, *m.*, melma, *f.*
mire 2, INTR.: coprire di fango; imbrattare.
mirifical, ADJ.: mirifico, maraviglioso.
miriness, S.: fanghiglia, sporcizia, *f.*
mirk(some)†, ADJ.: buio, tenebroso. **-ness**†, S.: oscurità, *f.*
mirror, S.: specchio; (*fig.*) esemplare, modello, *m.*
mirth, *f.*: gioia, allegria, *f.*; contento, *m.* **-ful**, ADJ.: gioioso, gaio, giocondo, allegro. **-fully**, ADV.: gioiosamente, allegramente. **-fulness**, S.: gioia, allegria, *f.* **-less**, ADJ.: mesto, tristo.
miry, ADJ.: fangoso, melmoso, lotoso.
misacceptātion, S.: mala intelligenza, *f.*; errore; equivoco, *m.*
misadvĕnture, S.: disavventura, *f.*, infortunio, *m.* **-d**, ADJ.: sventurato; infelice.
misadvi-ce, S.: cattivo consiglio, *m.* **-se**, TR.: mal avvisare.
misaffĕcted, ADJ.: mal disposto.
misāimed, ADJ.: mal preso di mira.
mis-anthrope, S.: misantropo, *m.* **-anthrŏpic, -anthrŏpical**, ADJ.: misantropico. **-ănthropy**, S.: misantropia, *f.*
misap-plicātion, S.: cattiva applicazione, *f.* **-plȳ**, TR.: applicare male.
misappre-hĕnd, TR.: intendere male, non intendere. **-hĕnsion**, S.: errore; sbaglio, *m.*

misascribe, TR.: ascrivere falsamente; attribuire.
misassign, TR.: assegnare erroneamente.
misbecŏm-e, IRR.; INTR.: sconvenire; disdirsi. **-ing**, ADJ.: disdicevole; indecente. **-ingness**, S.: sconvenevolezza, indecenza, *f.*
misbegŏt(ten), ADJ.: illegittimo.
misbehā-ve, IRR.; INTR.: condursi male. **-viour**, S.: cattiva condotta, *f.*
misbe-lief, S: miscredenza, mala credenza, *f.* **-lieve**, INTR.: miscredere, discredere, essere incredulo. **-liever**, S.: miscredente; infedele, *m.* **-lieving**, ADJ.: miscredente, eretico.
miscălcu-late, TR.: calcolare male, computare male. **-lătion**, S.: cattivo calcolo, *m.*
miscall, TR: chiamare impropriamente.
miscăr-riage, S.: cattiva condotta, *f.*; cattivo successo; aborto, *m.* **-ry**, INTR.: fallire; abortire; smarrirsi, perdersi, non pervenire.
miscâst, IRR.; TR.: contar male; far errore.
miscellā-neous, ADJ.: miscellaneo. **-neousness**, S.: raccolta; varietà, *f.* **-ny** *mis-*, S.: miscellanea, *f.*; opere diverse, *f. pl.*
mischânce, S.: sventura, *f.*, disastro, infortunio, *m.*
mischief 1, S.: male; danno, *m.*; disgrazia, *f.*, infortunio, *m.* **mischief** 2, TR.: ingiurare; offendere, nuocere. **-maker**, S.: facimale, *m.* **-making**, ADJ.: malizioso.
mischievous, ADJ.: nocivo, pericoloso; maligno, malizioso. **-ly**, ADV.: maliziosamente, cattivamente. **-ness**, S.: malignità, malizia; ribalderia, *f.*
miscible, ADJ.: mescibile.
mis-citātion, S.: citazione falsa, *f.* **-cite**, TR.: fare falsa citazione.
misclāim, S.: domanda erronea, domanda mal fondata, *f.*
miscom-putātion, S.: calcolo false, *m.* **-pūte**, TR.: mal calcolare.
miscon-cēit, -cĕption, S.: concepimento erroneo, *m.*
miscŏn-duct 1, S.: cattiva condotta, *f.* **-dŭct**, TR.: mal condurre.
misconjĕcture, S.: congettura falsa, *f.*
mis-construction, S.: falsa costruzione, cattiva interpretazione, *f.* **-construe**, TR.: interpretare male.
miscontinuance, S.: tralasciamento, intermissione, *f.*
miscŏunsel, TR.: dare cattivo consiglio.
miscŏunt, TR.: calcolare male, contare male.
miscrean-ce, -cy, S.: miscredenza, **-t**, S.: miscredente, infedele, *m.*

miscreāte(d), ADJ.: mal formato.
misdāte 1, S.: falsa data, *f.* **misdate** 2, TR.: marcare con falsa data.
misdēed, S.: misfatto, delitto, crime, *m.*
misdēem, TR.: giudicare male, sbagliare.
misdemēan, INTR.: condursi male. **-er**, S.: cattiva condotta, *f.*; misfatto, *m.*
misdevōtion, S.: falsa pietà, *f.*
misdō, IRR.; TR.: far male, misfare; danneggiare.
misdōubt 1, S.: sospetto; dubbio, *m.* **misdoubt** 2, TR.: sospettare; disfidare.
mise, S.: spesa; tassa, *f.*
misemplöy, TR.: impiegare male. **-ment**, S.: cattivo impiego, *m.*
miser, S.: avaro, spilorcio; misero, *m.*
miser-able, ADJ.: miserabile, meschino; infelice; avaro. **-ableness**, S.: miserabilità; infelicità; spilorceria, avarizia, *f.* **-ably**, ADV.: miserabilmente; meschinamente, avaramente. **-y**, S.: miseria, indigenza; calamità, infelicità, *f.*
misestēem, S.: disprezzo, *m.*
misfāll, IRR.: TR.: accadere sfortunatamente.
misfāre, S.: infortunio, *m.*
misfāshion, TR.: formare male, sfigurare.
misfōrm, TR.: difformare; sfigurare.
misfôrtune, S.: infortunio, *m.*, calamità, *f.*
misgive, IRR.; TR.: mal presagire, presentire; temere. **-ing**, S.: sospetto; presentimento, *m.*
misgòvern, TR.: governare male, reggere male. **-ment**, S.: cattivo governo, disordine, *m.*
misgui-dance, S.: cattivo guidamento, *m.*, mala direzione, *f.*; errore, *m.* **-de**, TR.: guidare male, menare male.
mishāp, S.: contrattempo; accidente sinistro, *m.*, fatalità, *f.* **-pen**, INTR.: misavvenire, succedere male.
mishēar, IRR., INTR.: male intendere, frantendere.
mishmash, S.: mescuglio, guazzabuglio, *m.*
misinfēr, TR.: inferire male; dedurre falsamente.
misinfôrm, TR.: dare avviso erroneo. **-ātion**, S.: falsa informazione, *f.*
misintèlligence, S.: discordia, *f.*
misintērpret, TR.: interpretare male. **-ātion**, S.: falsa interpretazione, *f.*, storcimento del senso, *m.*
misjōin, TR.: giungere male.
misjūdge, TR.: giudicare male, giudicare falsamente. **-ment**, S.: giudizio temerario, *m.*
mislāy, IRR.; TR.: smarrire; rimuovere.
misle, INTR.: piovigginare.
mislēad, IRR.; TR.: sviare, traviare; sedurre. **-er**, S.: seduttore, *m.*

mislēam, S.: grano [illegible]
mislīk-e 1, S.: [illegible] voglienza, *f.*; disgusto, [illegible] provare; biasimare. [illegible] vatore, biasimatore, *m.*
mislive, INTR.: vivere una vita cattiva, cond[illegible]
mismānage, TR.: [illegible] vernare male. **-ment**, [illegible] neggio, *m.*
mismātch, TR.: assor[illegible] gere.
misnāme, TR.: nomina[illegible]
misnōmer, S.: nome [illegible]
misobsērve, TR.: osse[illegible]
misō-gamist, S.: miso[illegible] S.: odio al matrimonio, [illegible] che odia le donne. [illegible] sesso femminino, *m.*
misôrder 1, TR.: condu[illegible] nare. **misorder** 2, S.: [illegible] regolarità, *f.* **-ly**, ADJ [illegible] regolare.
mispersuāsion, S.: f[illegible] re, *m.*
misplāce, TR.: slogare, [illegible] sare.
mispōinting, S.: falsa [illegible]
misprint 1, S.: errore [illegible] **misprint** 2, TR.: fare er[illegible]
mis-prise, TR.: disprez[illegible] sprezzare. **-prision**, [illegible] glio, errore, *m.*; neglige[illegible]
mispronōunce, TR.: p[illegible]
misproportion, TR.: pr[illegible]
mis-quotātion, S.: ci[illegible] **-quōte**, TR.: citare fals[illegible]
misrecite, TR.: recitare [illegible]
misrēckon, TR.: cont[illegible] narsi nel conto. **-ing**, [illegible] conto, *m.*
misre-lāte, TR.: racco[illegible] narrare male. **-lātion** [illegible] zione, inesatta informazi[illegible]
misremember, TR.: ri[illegible]
misrepōrt 1, S.: falso r[illegible] **misreport** 2, TR.: far[illegible] porto.
misrepresent, TR.: rap[illegible] fare falsa relazione. -[illegible] relazione, *f.*
misrūle, S.: tumulto, *m.* [illegible] fracasso, *m.*
miss 1, S.: damigella, sig[illegible] *jest.*) madamigella: [illegible] signorina; *boarding-scho*[illegible]
miss 2, S.: sbaglio, [illegible]
miss 3, TR.: [illegible] dere; INTR.: errare, [illegible] sim, mancare il colpo; [illegible] *fire*, mancare; — e [illegible] garsi dell' assenza d' una [illegible]

I — a volume, mi accorgo che mi manca un volume.

missal, S.: missale, *m.*

missāy, IRR.; TR.: misdire, dire male.

missēem†, INTR.: sconvenire; disdirsi.

missērve, TR.: servire male, disservire.

misshāpe, TR.: difformare, disfigurare. **-ment**, S.: difformità, *f.* **-n**, ADJ.: disfigurato, deforme.

missile, ADJ.: dardeggiato.

missing, ADJ.: smarrito, perduto.

mission, S.: missione; ambasciata, *f.* **-ary**, **-er**, S.: missionario, *m.*

missive, ADJ.: missivo; S.: lettera, epistola, *f.*

misspēak, IRR.; TR.: parlare male; diffamare.

misspĕll, TR.: compitare male, ortografizzare male.

misspĕnd, TR.: spendere male, consumare il suo. **-er**, S.: dissipatore, prodigo, *m.*

mist, S.: nebbia, *f.*: *Scotch* —, gran pioggia, *f.*; *be in a* —, esser al buio, non sapere che fare.

mistāk-e, S.: errore, fallo, sbaglio; senso erroneo, *m.*: *make a* —, fare uno sbaglio. **-e**, IRR.; TR.: non intendere, non comprendere; INTR., IRR.: sbagliare; ingannarsi; *you* —, voi vi ingannate; — *the road*, smarrire la strada. **-en**, ADJ.: sbagliato; erroneo, falso; *be* —, ingannarsi, errare; *you are greatly* —, vi ingannate a partito. **-ingly**, ADV.: erroneamente, falsamente.

mistēach, IRR.; TR.: insegnare male; sviare.

mistĕll, IRR.; TR.: narrare falsamente, dire falsamente.

mistĕmper, TR.: temperare male, mischiare male.

mister, S.: signore, *m.*

mistĕrm, TR.: nominare erroneamente, appellare male.

mistful, ADJ.: nebuloso.

misthink, IRR.; TR.: pensare male.

mistime, TR.: fare a contrattempo.

mistiness, S.: nuvolosità, *f.*; offuscamento, *m.*

mistletoe, S.: vischio, *m.*

mistlike, ADJ.: folto come nebbia, oscuro, fosco.

mistress, S.: signora, padrona; madama; innamorata, *f.*

mistrŭst 1, S.: diffidenza, *f.*; sospetto, *m.* **mistrust** 2, TR.: diffidare; sospettare, dubitare. **-ful**, ADJ.: diffidente; sospettoso, dubbioso. **-fully**, ADV.: sospettosamente. **-fulness**, S.: diffidenza, *f.*; sospetto, *m.* **-less**, ADJ.: non sospettoso.

mistūne, INTR.: accordare male.

misty, ADJ.: nebbioso; oscuro.

misunder-stănd, IRR.; TR.: intendere male. **-stănding**, S.: mala intelligenza, discordia, *f.*; errore, *m.* **-stŏod**, PART. del v. *misunderstand*.

mis-ūsage, S.: cattivo uso, abuso, *m.*; villania, *f.* **-ūse** 1, S.: abuso; cattivo trattamento, *m.* **-ūse** 2, TR.: abusare; maltrattare; svillaneggiare.

mite, S.: tonchio, gorgoglione, *m.*; ventesima parte d' un grano, *f.*

miter = *mitre*.

mithridate, S.: mitridato, *m.*

miti-gant, ADJ.: mitigante, lenitivo. **-gate**, TR.: mitigare; raddolcire, placare, quietare. **-gātion**, S.: mitigazione, *f.*, mitigamento; raddolcimento, *m.* **-gator**, S.: mitigatore, *m.*

mitre, S.: mitra, *f.* (ornamento pontificale). **-d**, ADJ.: che porta la mitra.

mitten, S.: guanto senza dita, *m.*

mittimus, S.: (*leg.*) mandato di cattura, ordine per imprigionare, *m.*

mix, TR.: mischiare, mescolare; INTR.: mischiarsi, mescolarsi.

mixen, S.: letamaio, *m.*

mix-ing, S.: mischiamento, mescolamento, *m.* **-t**, ADJ.: mischiato, mescolato; confuso. **-tion**† = *-ture*. **-tly**, ADV.: mischiamente; confusamente. **-ture**, S.: mescolanza, mistura, *f.*

mizmaze†, S.: laberinto; imbroglio, *m.*

mizzen, S.: (*nav.*) mezzana, *f.* **-top-mast**, S.: albero di contramezzana, *m.* **-top-sail**, S.: contramezzana, *f.*

mizzle 1, S.: poca pioggia, spruzzaglia, *f.*

mizzle 2, INTR.: piovigginare, spruzzolare.

mizzy†, S.: pantano, *m.*

mnemŏnics, S. PL.: arte d' assistere la memoria, *f.*

mōan 1, S.: pianto, lamento, gemito, *m.*

moan 2, INTR.: piangere, gemere; dolersi; TR.: lamentarsi di. **-ful**, ADJ.: lamentevole, dolente. **-fully**, ADV.: lamentevolmente, con gemiti.

mōat 1, S.: canale d' acqua per difesa, *m.*

moat 2, TR.: far un canale d' acqua per difesa.

mŏb 1, S.: folla, turba; canaglia, *f.*

mob 2, TR.: tumultuare, insurgere. **-bish**, ADJ.: del popolazzo; tumultuoso. **-by**, S.: bevanda americana, *f.*

mō-bile, S.: popolazzo, *m.*, plebe, plebaglia, marmaglia, *f.* **-bility**, S.: mobilità; plebaglia, *f.*

mŏck 1, ADJ.: falso, contrafatto, finto; burlesco: — *turtle-soup*, cibreo alla tartaruga. **mock** 2, S.: derisione; beffa, *f.*, ludibrio, *m.*: *make a — of one*, burlarsi di alcuno. **mock** 3, (IN)TR.: imitare; burlare, beffare, deridere. **-able**, ADJ.: esposto alla derisione. **-er**, S.: beffatore schernitore, *m.* **-ery**, S.: scherno, *m.*

-bag [illegible]

-broker. **-changer**. [illegible] **-ed**. [illegible] **-less**. [illegible] **-matter**. [illegible]

[illegible] prodotto fra due specie.

[illegible] ammonire, avvertire.

[illegible] ammonitore, esortatore, [illegible]

-ition, S.: ammonizione, *f.*; avvertimento, *m.*, esortazione, *f.* **-itor**, S.: monitore, ammonitore, *m.* **-itórial**, ADJ.: monitorio. **-itory**, S.: monitorio, *m.*; ammonizione, *f.*

mónk, S.: monaco, frate, *m.* **-ery**, S.: monacato, *m.*

mónkey, S.: scimmia, bertuccia, *f.*, babbuino, *m.*

mónk-hood, S.: vita monastica, *f.*, monachismo, *m.* **-ish**, ADJ.: monastico, monacale. **-'s-hood**, S.: (*bot.*) aconito, *m.*

mŏn-ochord, S.: monocordo, *m.* **-ŏcular**, **-ŏculous**, ADJ.: monocolo, losco. **-ody**, S.: monodia, *f.* **-ŏgamist**, S.: monogamo, *m.* **-ŏgamy**, S.: monogamia, *f.* **-ogram**, S.: monogramma, *f.* **-ŏgraphy**, S.: monografia, *f.* **-ologue**, S.: monologo, soliloquio, *m.* **-ŏmachy**, S.: monomachia, *f.*, duello, *m.* **-ome**, S.: monomio, *m.* **-opĕtalous**, ADJ.: (*bot.*) monopetalo. **-ŏpolist**, S.: monopolista; incettatore, *m.* **-ŏpolize**, TR.: far monopolio, incettare. **-ŏpoly**, S.: monopolio, *m.* **-osyllăbic(al)**, ADJ.: monosillabo. **-osyllable**, S.: monosillabo, *m.*, monosillaba, *f.* **-otheism**, S.: monoteismo, *m.* **-ŏtonous**, ADJ.: monotono. **-ŏtony**, S.: monotonia, *f.*

monsŏon, S.: monsone, *m.*

mŏn-ster, S.: mostro, *m.*; singolarità, *f.* **-strŏsity**, S.: mostruosità, *f.* **-strous**, ADJ.: mostruoso, prodigioso. **-strously**, ADV.: mostruosamente. **-strousness**, S.: mostruosità; deformità, *f.*

montĕro, S.: montiera, *f.* (berretta).

mónth, S.: mese, *m.* **-ly** 1, ADJ.: d'ogni mese, mensuale. **-ly** 2, ADV.: una volta il mese, di mese in mese, ogni mese. **-lies**, S. PL.: mestrui, *m. pl.* **-'s-mind**†, S.: ardente desiderio, *m.*

mŏnu-ment, S.: monumento; memoriale; sepolcro, *m.* **-mĕntal**, ADJ.: di monumento.

mŏod, S.: modo; umore, capriccio, temperamento, *m.*: *in a merry* —, allegro; *in the right* —, ben disposto. **-y**, ADJ.: capriccioso.

mŏon, S.: luna, *f.*; mese, *m.*: *full* —, luna piena; plenilunio; *half* —, mezza luna; crescente; *new* —, luna nuova; *the phases of the* —, le fasi della luna. **-beam**, S.: raggio della luna, *m.* **-calf**, S.: mola, *f.*; mostro; minchione, balordo, *m.* **-eyed**, ADJ.: lunatico; di corta vista. **-less**, ADJ.: senza chiaro di luna. **-light**, S.: chiaro di luna, *m.* **-light**, ADJ.: illuminato dalla luna. **-shine**, S.: chiarezza della luna, *f.* **-shine**, **-shiny**, ADJ.: illuminato dalla luna. **-struck**, ADJ.: lunatico, pazzo.

mŏor 1, TR.: (*nav.*) gettare l'ancora; dare fondo. **moor** 2, S.: palude, pantano. **moor** 3, S.: moro, *m.* **-cock**, S.: gallo di palude, *m.* **-hen**, S.: folaga, *f.* (uccello).

mŏor-ing, S.: gettare l'ancora, *m.*

mŏor-ish, ADJ.: paludoso, pantanoso, melmoso; moresco. **-land**, S.: palude, pantano, *m.*

mŏose, S.: daino americano, *m.*

mŏot 1, S.: disputa di qualche materia legale, *f.* **moot** 2, TR.: disputare di qualche materia legale. **-case**, S.: questione legale, *f.* **-ed**, ADJ.: sradicato, estirpato. **-er**, S.: disputante in legge, *m.* **-hall**, S.: sala dove si disputa in legge, *f.*

mŏp 1, S.: spazzatoio, *m.* **mop** 2, TR.: spazzare; nettare il solaio: — *and mow*, fare il grugno.

mŏp-e, TR.: rendere stupido; INTR.: stupidire, divenire stupido. **-e-eyed**, ADJ.: cieco d'un' occhio, losco. **-ish**, ADJ.: abbattuto, tristo. **-ishness**, S.: abbattimento, *m.*, tristizia, *f.*

mŏppet, **mŏpsey**, S.: fantoccio di cenci, *m.*

mŏpus, S.: infingardo, pigro, *m.*

mŏr-al, ADJ.: morale; S.: dottrina morale, *f.*; costume buono, *m.*: — *philosopher* (*writer*), moralista, *m.*; *good* —*s*, buoni costumi. **-alist**, S.: moralista, *m.* **-ălity**, S.: moralità, *f.*; senso morale, *m.* **-alizātion**, S.: moralizzazione, *f.* **-alize**, (IN)TR.: moralizzare. **-alizer**, S.: moralista, predicatore, *m.* **-ally**, ADV.: moralmente. **-als**, S. PL.: buoni costumi, *m. pl.*

morăss, S.: palude, pantano, *m.* **-y**, ADJ.: paludoso, pantanoso.

mŏr-bid, ADJ.: morbido, malaticcio. **-bĭdity**, **-bidness**, S.: morbidezza; infermità, *f.* **-bĭfic(al)**, ADJ.: morbifico, morbifero.

mor-dācious, ADJ.: mordace; pungente. **-dăcity**, S.: mordacità; acutezza, *f.*

mŏr-dant, ADJ., S.: mordante. **-dicancy**, S.: mordacità; maldicenza, *f.* **-dicant**, ADJ.: mordente; pungente. **-dicate**, TR.: mordere; censurare. **-dicātion**, S.: mordicamento, *m.*; acrità, *f.*

mŏre 1, ADJ., ADV.: più; di più, di vantaggio maggiore, in maggior numero (*or* quantità): — *and* —, di più in più; *a great deal* —, molto più, vieppiù; *once* —, un' altra volta, ancora una volta; — *than enough*, più che non bisogna; *will you have some* —? ne volete più? *so much the* —, tanto più. **more** 1, S.: maggior parte, maggior quantità, *f.*

mŏrel(le), S.: morella, *f.* (pianta).

mŏreland, S.: paese montagnoso, *m.*

moreŏver, ADV., CONJ.: di più, oltre ciò, oltre a questo.

meán-der1, S.: meandro, laberinto; giro, rigiro, *m.* **-der**2, TR.: andare in giramento tortuoso. **-drous**, ADJ.: sinuoso, flessuoso; avviluppato.

mēaning, S.: disegno, *m.*, intenzione, *f.*, intento, *m.*; significazione, *f.*, significato, senso, sentimento, *m.*

mēan-ly, ADV.: mediocremente; cattivamente, poveramente: — *born*, di bassa nascita. **-ness**, S.: mediocrità; bassezza; povertà, *f.* **-spirited**, ADJ.: da animo basso.

mēan-time, **-while**, ADV.: frattanto: *in the* —, frattanto; in questo mentre.

mēa-sled, ADJ.: infettato della rosolia. **-sles**, S. PL.: rosolia, *f.*: — *of swine*, malore de' porci, *m.*; — *of trees*, rogna degli alberi, *f.* **-sly**, ADJ.: rognoso, scabbioso.

mĕasu-rable, S.: misurabile; moderato. **-rableness**, S.: misurabilità, *f.* **-rably**, ADV.: moderatamente. **-re**1, S.: misura; dimensione; mediocrità; moderazione; (*mus.*) misura, *f.*, tempo, *m.*, battuta; cadenza, *f.*: *beyond* —, oltre misura, eccessivamente; *in a great* —, grandemente, molto; *in some* —, in qualche maniera. **-re**2, TR.: misurare; aggiustare; INTR.: avere una misura. **-reless**, ADJ.: smisurato, immenso. **-rement**, S.: misuramento, misurare, *m.* **-rer**, S.: misuratore, *m.*: — *of land*, agrimensore, *m.* **-ing** = *measurement*.

mēat, S.: carne, *f.*; nutrimento, alimento; cibo, *m.*: *dish* —, piatto di carne, *m.*; *boiled* —, lesso, *m.*, vivanda lessata, *f.*; *minced* —, manicaretto, *m.*; *roast* —, vivanda arrostita, *f.*, arrosto, *m.* **-ball**, S.: polpetta, -ttina, *f.*

mēath(*e*)†, S.: bevanda, *f.*, beveraggio, *m.*

mēaty, ADJ.: carnoso, carneo; polposo.

mechăn-ic, S.: meccanico; manifattore, *m.* **-ic(al)**, ADJ.: meccanico; vile. **-ically**, ADV.: in modo meccanico. **-icalness**, S.: qualità meccanica, *f.* **-ician**, S.: meccanico, professore di meccanica, *m.* **-ics**, S. PL.: meccanica, *f.* **-ism** *mĕ-*, S.: mecanismo, *m.*, struttura, *f.*

mĕd-al, S.: medaglia; moneta antica, *f.* **-ăllion**, S.: medaglione, *m.*, medaglia grande, *f.* **-alist**, S.: medaglista, *m.*

mĕd-dle, INTR.: mescolarsi, impacciarsi, intromettersi: — *with*, maneggiare, toccare. **-dler**, S.: mezzano, affannone; impacciatore, *m.* **-dlesome**, ADJ.: affaccendato; intrigante; importuno. **-dlesomeness**, S.: importunità, *f.* **-dling**, S.: mescolamento, *m.*

mediaēval, ADJ.: medioevale.

mēdian, ADJ.: mediano, mezzano.

mēdi-ate, ADJ.: mediato, interposto. **-ate**, TR.: mediare, interporre, limitare: INTR.: stramezzare. **-ately**, ADV.: me-

diatamente, pe
S.: mediazione
sione, *f.* **-ato**
sore, *m.* **-atō**
S.: uffizio di me
di mediatore.
mĕd-icable,
ADJ.: medico, n
per via di medi
dicamento, rim
ADJ.: medicinal
S.: medicastro,
TR.: medicare.
zione, *f.*, medic
medichevole, m
medicinale, da
ADV.: medicinal
dicina, *f.*; medi
medicinare, me
dicina, *f.*
mediŏcrity,
moderazione, *f.*
mĕdi-tate, TR
ditare; conside
sopra. **-tātio**
templazione, *f.*
tivo; meditante
mediterrā-ne
terraneo: *Medi*
terraneo, *m.*
mēdium, S.:
zanità, medioc
mezzo: *observe*
mezzo; *the* —
mĕdlar, S.: ne
S.: nespolo, *m.*
mĕdley1, ADJ.
so. **medley**2
f., miscuglio, *m.*
mĕdullar(y),
medūsa, S.: m
mēed, S.: ricor
regalo, *m.*
mēek, ADJ.: d
affabile, benign
dolcire; mitiga
mente, benigna
mente. **-ness**,
za; modestia;
mēer, S.: la
-schaum, S.:
mēet1, ADJ.: co
cio, idoneo, att
contrare, aduna
trarsi, adunarsi
trare; affronta
all' incontro d'
fronte alle spes
assemblea, conf
house, S.: co
convenevolment
S.: convenevol

mĕgrim, S.: emicrania, magrana, *f.*

mĕlancho-lic, ADJ.: malinconico, malinconoso, stizzoso. **-lily**, ADV.: in modo malinconico. **-list†**, S.: malinconico; visionario, *m.* **-ly**, ADJ.: malinconico, tristo, afflitto; S.: malinconia; tristezza, *f.*

mêlée (*Engl. accents*) *mĕlĕ*, S.: zuffa, *f.*

mĕlilot, S.: (*bot.*) meliloto, *m.*

mē-liorate, TR.: migliorare, ammendare; INTR.: migliorarsi. **-liorātion**, S.: miglioramento, *m.* **-liŏrity†**, S.: miglioranza, *f.*

mĕl-leous, ADJ.: melato. **-liferous**, ADJ.: mellifero. **-lificātion**, S.: fare il mele, *m.* **-lifluence**, S.: abbondanza di mele, *f.* **-lifluent**, **-lifluous**, ADJ.: mellifluo; dolce.

mĕllow 1, ADJ.: maturo; tenero, molle. **mellow** 2, TR.: maturare; INTR.: maturarsi, divenir maturo. **-ness**, S.: maturità, maturezza, *f.*

mel-ŏdious, ADJ.: melodioso, armonioso. **-ŏdiously**, ADV.: melodiosamente. **-ŏdiousness**, S.: melodia, armonia, *f.* **-odrâma**, S.: melodramma, *m.* **-ody**, S.: melodia; armonia, *f.*

mĕlon, S.: mellone, popone, *m.* **-bed**, S.: mellonaio, poponaio, *m.*

mĕlt, IRR.; TR.: fondere; liquefare; intenerire; (*fig.*) placare; INTR.: fondersi; liquefarsi; intenerirsi: — *away*, fondersi, dileguarsi; — *into tears*, discioglìersi in lagrime. **-er**, S.: fonditore, *m.* **-ing**, S.: liquefazione, *f.* **-ing-house**, S.: fonderia, *f.* **-ingly**, ADV.: in modo liquefattivo.

mĕmber, S.: membro, *m.*; parte, *f.*

mĕm-brane, S.: (*anat.*) membrana; tunica, *f.* **-brāneous**, ADJ.: membranoso.

memĕnto, S.: rimembranza, ricordanza, *f.*

mĕm-oir *-wor*, S.: ricordo (di fatti storici), *m.*, annotazione, *f.* **-orable**, ADJ.: memorabile, memorevole. **-orably**, ADV.: memorabilmente, degno di memoria. **-orăndum**, S.: annotazione, *f.*; ricordo, *m.* **-orative**, ADJ.: memorativo. **-ōrial**, ADJ.: memorativo; della memoria; S.: memoriale, ricordo, *m.*, memoria; supplica, *f.* **-ōrialist**, S.: autore di memorie, *m.* **-orize**, TR.: ricordare, memorare, ridurre a memoria. **-ory**, S.: memoria, ricordanza, *f.*; ricordo, *m.*: *by* —, a memoria; *of blessed* —, di santa memoria; *call to* —, ricordarsi; *have a poor* (*short*) —, aver la memoria labile (corta), aver poca memoria; *within the* — *of man*, a memoria d' uomo.

mĕn, S. PL.: uomini, *m. pl.*

mĕnace 1, S.: minaccia, *f.*, minacciamento, *m.* **-ce** 2, TR.: minacciare; fare temere. **-cer**, S.: minacciatore, minacciante, *m.* **-cing** 1, ADJ.: minacciante, minaccevole. **-cing** 2, S.: minacciare, minacciamento, *m.*

men-āge†, **-āgerie** *g* = *s or g*, S.: serraglio (collezione d' animali, *f.*), *m.*

mĕnd, TR.: racconciare, rappezzare, rimendare, emendare; migliorare; correggere; ristaurare, riparare; INTR.: riformarsi; emendarsi: — *a coat*, tapezzare un vestito; — *one's fortune*, migliorare la sua condizione. **-able**, ADJ.: che si può riparare, corrigibile.

men-dācious, ADJ.: mendace. **-dăcity**, S.: menzogna, bugia, *f.*

mĕnder, S.: acconciatore, racconciatore, rappezzatore, *m.*

mĕn-dicancy, S.: mendicità, *f.* **-dicant**, ADJ.: mendico, povero; mendicante; S.: mendicante; barone, *m.* **-dicate**, INTR.: mendicare, limosinare. **-dicity**, S.: mendicità, mendicanza, *f.*

mĕnding, S.: racconciamento, racconciare, *m.*: *be on the* — *hand*, andar migliorando, esser convalescente.

mĕndment = *amendment*.

mēnial, ADJ.: domestico; servile.

men-inges, S.: (*anat.*) meninge, *f.* **-ingitis**, S.: meningite, *f.*

menŏlogy, S.: menologio, calendario, *m.*

mĕnsal, ADJ.: mensale, della mensa.

mĕns-trual, **-truous**, ADJ.: mestruale, mestruo, mensuale. **-truum**, S.: (*chem.*) mestruo, dissolvente, *m.*

mensurability, S.: misurabilità.

mĕnsu-rable, ADJ.: misurabile; atto a misurarsi. **-rate**, TR.: misurare; regolare. **-rātion**, S.: misuramento, misurare, *m.*

mĕntal, ADJ.: mentale, di mente, intellettuale. **-ly**, ADV.: mentalmente, colla mente.

mĕntion 1, S.: menzione, commemorazione, memoria, *f.*: *make* — *of one*, far menzione d' alcuno. **mention** 2, TR.: mentovare, menzionare: *don't* — *it, pray*, non ne parlate, prego. **-ing**, S.: menzione, *f.*

mephitic(al), ADJ.: mefitico.

me-rācious†, ADJ.: spiritoso, forte; puro; gustoso, saporoso.

mĕrcantile, ADJ.: mercantile: — *town*, città mercantile, *f.*

mĕrcena-riness, S.: venalità, *f.* **-ry**, ADJ.: mercenario, venale; S.: mercenario; interessato, *m.*

mĕrcer, S.: merciaio; setaiuolo, *m.* **-y**, S.: merceria, mercanzia da taglio, *f.*

mĕr-chandise, S.: mercanzia, *f.*; traffico, negozio, *m.* **-chandise**, INTR.: trafficare, negoziare, fare commercio. **-dry**, S.: traffico, *m.* **-chant**, S.: mercante, mercatante, negoziante, *m.* **-able**, ADJ.: ben condizionato. **-like**, ADJ.: mercatantesco. **-man**, S.: vascello mercantile, *m.*

pigmy, s.: pimmeo, nano, *m.*
pignorātion, s.: pegnorazione, *f.*, pignoramento, *m.*
pignut, s.: tartufo nero, *m.*
pig-sty, s.: porcile, *m.* **-tail**, s.: codino, *m.*
pike, s.: luccio, *m.* (pesce); picca, *f.*: *young* —, luccetto, *m.* **-d**, ADJ.: acuto, puntato, puntaguto. **-man**, s.: picchiere, *m.* **-staff**, s.: asta di picca, *f.*
pilăster, s.: (*arch.*) pilastro, *m.*; colonna, *f.*
pilcher, s.: pelliccia; saracca, *f.* (pesce).
pil-e 1, s.: palo; mucchio; fascio; —*s*, cf. *below*; edificio; pelo, *m.*, lanugine, *f.*: *funeral* —, rogo, *m.*, pira, *f.* **-e** 2, TR.: ammassare, ammucchiare; — *up*, accatastare. **-ęated**, ADJ.: fatto a foggia di cappello. **-ęr**, s.: ammassatore, accumulatore, *m.* **-ęs**, s. PL.: emorroidi, morici, *f. pl.* **-e-work**, s.: palafitta, *f.* **-ewǫrt**, s.: (*bot.*) scrofularia, *f.*
pilfęr, TR.: rubare, furare. **-ęr**, s: involatore, ladro, *m.* **-ing**, s.: rubamento, ladroneccio, *m.* **-ingly**, ADV.: in modo ladronesco, da scroccone. **-y**, s.: ruberia, truffa, frode, *f.*
pilgrim 1, s.: pellegrino, pellegrinante, *m.* **pilgrim** 2, TR.: peregrinare, vagare; andare errando. **-age**, s.: pellegrinaggio; viaggio, *m.*
pill 1, s.: pillola, *f.*: *blue* —, pillola mercuriale. **pill** 2, TR.: rubare, predare; INTR.: scorticarsi, pelarsi. **-age** 1, s.: predamento, *m.*, ruberia, *f.* **-age** 2, TR.: saccheggiare, predare, rubare. **-ager**, s.: saccheggiatore, predatore, *m.* **-aging**, s.: saccheggiamento, predamento, *m.*
pillar, s.: pilone, pilastro, *m.*: *small* —, colonnetta, *f.*; *Hercules'* —*s*, le colonne d'Ercole; colonna, *f.*; appoggio, *m.* **-ed**, ADJ.: sostenuto da pilastri.
pil-lęr, s.: predatore, ladro, *m.* **-lery**, **-ling**, s.: ruberia, *f.*, ladroneccio, *m.*
pilliǫn, s.: guancialetto, *m.*; sella da donna, *f.*
pillǫry 1, s.: berlina, gogna, *f.* **-pillory**, TR.: mettere alla berlina.
pillǫw 1, s.: guanciale, *m.* **pillow** 2, TR.: posare sur un guanciale. **-case**, s.: fodera di guanciale, *f.*
pi-lōse, ADJ.: peloso. **-lŏsity**, s.: pelosità, *f.*
pilǫt 1, s.: pilota, piloto, *m.* **pilot** 2, TR.: guidare; governare, reggere. **-age**, s.: uffizio del piloto; salario del piloto, *m.* **-boat**, s.: battello piloto, *m.*
pilous, ADJ.: piloso.
pimĕnta, s.: pepe d'India, *m.*
pimp 1, s.: ruffiano, lenone, mezzano, *m.* **pimp** 2, TR.: fare il ruffiano, arruffianare.
pimpęrnel, s.: (*bot.*) pimpinella, *f.*
pimping 1, ADJ.: piccolo, meschino, vile; povero. **pimping** 2, s.: ruffianeria, *f.*
pimple, s.: pustula, pustuletta, bolla, *f.*; cosso, *m.* **-d**, ADJ.: pieno di pustulette, barnoccoluto.
pin 1, s.: spilla, *f.*, spillo, *m.*; punta, *f.*; chiavistello, *m.*; caviglia, cavicchia, *f.*; ago, stile (d'oriuolo a sole); sbriglio; birillo, *m.*: —*-cushion*, guancialino da spille, torsello, buzzo, *m.*; *crisping* —, calamistro, *m.*; *larding* —, lardaruola, *f.*; *rolling* —, matterello (di pasticciere), *m.*; *I care not a* —, non me ne curo niente; *it is not worth a* —, non vale un frullo. **pin** 2, TR.: appuntare (con una spilla); serrare: — *cattle*, rinchiudere il bestiame; — *up*, succingere; — *one's self to*, attaccarsi a. **-case**, s.: scatola da spille, *f.*
pin-cer, s.: cavadenti, cane, *m.* (strumento). **-cęrs**, s. PL.: tanaglie, *f. pl.* **-ch** 1, s.: pizzico, *m.*; strettezza, difficoltà, *f.*: — *of snuff*, presa di tabacco, *f.*; *be at a* —, essere in pena. **-ch** 2, TR.: pizzicare; stringere; sparagnare, risparmiare; strappare; svellere; INTR.: ridurre in istrettezza: — *one's self*, privarsi del necessario; vivere stentatamente; — *with hunger*, affamare; *these shoes* — *me*, queste scarpe mi stringono troppo (mi fanno male).
pinchbeck, s.: orpello, tombacco, *m.*
pinch-fist, **-penny**, s.: avaro, taccagno, *m.*
pin-cushion, s.: cuscinetto; torsello, *m.* **-dust**, s.: limatura, *f.*
pine 1, s.: pino, *m.* (albero). **pine** 2, TR.: deplorare; affiggere; INTR.: languire, struggersi: — *away*, languire, deperire; — *for*, anelare, essere smanioso di, bramare; — *one's self to death*, morire d'affano; — *cone*, pigna, *f.* **-apple**, s.: ananasso, *m.*; pina, *f.* **pinę-al**, ADJ.: pineale. **-wood**, s.: legno del pino, *m.*
pin-feathered, ADJ.: non ancor pennuto.
pinfold, s.: parco; ovile; pecorile, *m.*
pinguid, ADJ.: pingue, grasso.
pin-hole, s.: bucco di spilla, *m.*
pining, ADJ.: languente, languido.
pinion 1, s.: rocchetto (d'oriuolo), *m.*; ala; estremità dell'ala, *f.* **pinion** 2, TR.: legare le braccia, incatenare; inchiodare.
pink 1, s.: garofano, *m.* **pink** 2, s.: barca, *f.* **pink** 3, TR.: distagliare, tagliuzzare, frastagliare. **pink** † 4, INTR.: ammiccare; battere gli occhi. **pink** † 5, ADJ.: mezzo chiuso. **-ęr**, s.: tagliuzzatore, *m.* **-eye**, s.: occhio piccolo, *m.* **-eyed**, ADJ.: che ha gli occhi piccoli. **-ing** 1, s.: taglio, frastaglio, *m.* **-ing** 2, ADJ.: che batte gli occhi, che ammicca.

mĕtric(al), ADJ.: metrico.
me-trŏpolis, S.: metropoli, *f.* **-tropŏl-itan**, ADJ.: metropolitano: — *church*, chiesa metropolitana, *f.*; S.: metropolitano, *m.*
mĕttle, S.: vivacità, foga, *f.*, spirito, coraggio, *m.* **-d**, **-some**, ADJ.: focoso, vivace. **-somely**, ADV.: spiritosamente, con foga. **-someness**, S.: vivacità, foga, *f.*
mew 1, S.: gabbia, *f.*; gabbiano, *m.* (uccello): —*s*, stalle (di cavalli), *f. pl.*
mew 2, TR.: rinchiudere; INTR.: mudare; miagolare.
mewl, INTR.: gridare (come un bambino).
miasm(a), S.: (*med.*) miasma, *f.* **-ătic**, ADJ.: (*med.*) miasmatico.
mica, S.: mica, specie di talco, *f.*
mice, PL. di *mouse*.
Michaelmas, S.: festa di san Michele, *f.*
mich-(e)†, INTR.: appiattarsi; nascondersi. **-er†**, S.: infingardo, furfante, perdigiorno, *m.*
mickle, ADJ.: molto, grande; assai: *many a — makes a muckle*, molti pochi fanno un assai.
mi-crobe, S.: microbo, *m.* **-crocosm**, S.: microcosmo, *m.* **-crŏmeter**, S.: micrometro, *m.* **-croscope**, S.: microscopio, *m.* **-croscŏpic(al)**, ADJ.: microscopico.
mid, ADJ.: mezzo; ugualmente distante. **-age**, S.: mezza età, *f.* **-course**, S.: mezza via, mezza strada, *f.* **-day**, S.: mezzodì, mezzogiorno, *m.* **-dle** 1, ADJ.: mezzo, mezzano; mediocre. **-dle** 2, S.: mezzo, centro; cuore, *m.* **-dle-aged**, ADJ.: di mezzana età. **-dle-ages**, S.: medio evo, *m.* **-dle-man**, S.: agente, mediatore, *m.* **-dlemost**, ADJ.: posto nel mezzo; del mezzo.. **-dle-sized**, ADJ.: di mezzana statura. **-dling**, ADJ.: mediocre; mezzano.
midge, S.: zanzara, *f.* (insetto).
mid-hĕaven, S.: centro de' cieli, *m.* **-land**, ADJ.: mediterraneo. **-leg**, S.: mezza gamba, *f.* **-lent**, S.: metà della quaresima, *f.* **-most**, ADJ.: posto nel mezzo, del mezzo. **-night**, S.: mezza notte, *f.*; ADJ.: di mezza notte. **-riff**, S.: diaframma, *m.* **-sea**, S.: mare mediterraneo, *m.* **-ship**, S.: mezzania, *f.* **-shipman**, S.: guardia marina, *f.*; sotto-luogotenente di nave, *m.* **-st**, ADJ.: mezzo, mezzano; S.: mezzo, centro; cuore, *m.* **-summer**, S.: mezzo della state, *m.*; festa di san Giovanni, *f.* **-way** 1, ADJ., ADV.: nel mezzo cammino. **-way** 2, S.: mezza strada, *f.*, mezzo cammino, *m.*
mid-wife, S.: levatrice, ricoglitrice, mammana, *f.* **-wifery**, S.: mestiere di levatrice, *m.*, ostetricia, *f.*
midwinter, S.: mezzo del verno, cuore del verno, *m.*
mien, S.: aria, ciera, *f.*; aspetto; portamento, *m.*: *dignified* —, aria distinta (dignitosa).
might, S.: potere, *m.*, potenza, possanza, forza, *f.*: *with — and main*, con ogni forza, vigorosamente; *with all one's* —, a tutto potere. **-ily**, ADV.: con forza; molto. **-iness**, S.: potenza, possanza, *f.*, potere, *m.* **-y**, ADJ.: potente; grande; forte; ADV.: molto, estremamente.
mignonĕtte *miny-*, S.: amorino, *m.*; reseda odorata, *f.*
mi-grate, INTR.: migrare. **-grātion**, S.: migrazione, *f.*, dipartimento, *m.*
milch, ADJ.: lattante; lattifero. **-cow**, S.: vacca lattante, *f.*
mild, ADJ.: dolce, mite, ameno; piacevole; moderato; indulgente: — *weather*, tempo dolce.
mĭ'ldew 1, S.: nebbia; golpe, *f.*, carbone, *m.* **mildew** 2, TR.: annebbiare, involpare.
mild-ly, ADV.: dolcemente, mitemente, placidamente. **-ness**, S.: dolcezza; clemenza, indulgenza, *f.*
mile, S.: miglio, *m.* **-stone**, S.: pietra migliare, *f.*
mĭ'lfoil, S.: (*bot.*) millefoglie, *f.*
miliary, ADJ.: piccolo; simile al miglio: — *fever*, febbre miliare, *m.*
milice = *militia*.
mil-itant, ADJ.: militante. **-itary**, ADJ.: militare, da soldato. **-itia**, S.: milizia, *f.*; soldati nazionali, *m. pl.* **-itiaman**, S.: milite della guardia nazionale.
milk 1, S.: latte, *m.*: *thick* —, latte quagliato; *cow's* —, latte di vacca; *give* —, allattare. **milk** 2, TR.: mungere, trarre il latte. **-cow**, S.: vacca lattante, *f.* **-en**, ADJ.: latteo, di latte. **-food**, S.: latticinio, *m.*; vivanda di latte, *f.* **-house**, S.: cascina, *f.* **-iness**, S.: qualità latticinosa, *f.* **-livered**, ADJ.: poltrone, codardo. **-maid**, S.: lattaia, lattivendola, *f.* **-man**, S.: uomo che vende latte, *m.* **-pail**, S.: secchia da latte, *f.* **-pan**, S.: terrina, *f.*, piatto (da latte), *m.* **-pottage**, S.: zuppa di latte, *f.*, latteruolo, *m.* **-score**, S.: tacca; taglia (da latte), *f.* **-sop**, S.: effemminato, codardo, *m.* **-thistle**, S.: (*bot.*) titimalo, euforbio, *m.* **-tooth**, S.: dente lattaiuolo, *m.* **-weed**, S.: (*bot.*) titimalo, *m.* **-white**, ADJ.: del colore di latte. **-woman**, S.: lattaia, *f.* **-y**, ADJ.: lattifero, latteo: (*astr.*) — *way*, via lattea, *f.*
mill 1, S.: mulino, *m.*: *coffee* —, mulinello da caffè, *m.*; *hand* —, mulinello, *m.*; *oil* —, macinatoio, *m.*; *paper* —, cartiera, *f.*; *water* —, mulino da acqua, *m.*; *wind* —,

pla-cărd, s.: editto; bando, affisso, cartellone, *m.*
plăcąte, TR.: placare, pacificare.
plă-ce 1, s.: luogo; sito; posto, uffizio; grado, *m.*: *in another* —, altrove; *trading* —, piazza di negozio, *f.*; *give* —, dar luogo, cedere; *take* —, aver luogo, accadere; sedersi; *in* — *of*, in luogo (vece) di; *in the next* —, in seguito. **-ce** 2, TR.: mettere, collocare; allocare, assegnare.
placĕnta, s.: placenta, *f.*
plăcer, s.: che mette, che assegna il luogo.
plă-cid, ADJ.: placido, quieto, mite. **-cidity**, s.: placidezza, *f.* **-cidly**, ADV.: placidamente; piacevolmente. **-cidnĕss** = *placidity*.
plăcit, s.: placito, decreto, giudizio; ordine, *m.*
plăcket, s.: gonna, gonnella, *f.*
plăgiar-ism, s.: plagio, ladrocinio letterario, *m.* **-ist, -y**, s.: plagiario, *m.*
plăg-ue 1, s.: peste; contagione; pena, *f.* **-ue** 2, TR.: infettare, appestare; tormentare, affliggere. **-ue-sore**, s.: gavocciolo, *m.* **-uily**, ADV.: affannosamente. **-uing**, ADJ.: fastidioso, noioso. **-uy**, ADJ.: affannoso, molesto; pericoloso.
plăice, s.: passere, *m.* (pesce).
plăid, s.: ciarpa de' Scozzesi, *f.*
plăin 1, ADJ.: piano, liscio, uguale; chiaro, evidente; franco, sincero; ADV.: chiaramente, distintamente: — *clothes*, abito ordinario; — *food*, cibo (nutrimento) semplice; *the* — *truth*, la pura verità; *in* — *terms*, chiaramente, distintamente. **plain** 2, s.: pianura; campagna rasa, *f.*; piano, *m.* **plain** 3, TR.: appianare, uguagliare; INTR.: compiangere, lamentarsi. **-dĕaler**, s.: uomo dabbene, uomo franco, *m.* **-dĕaling**, ADJ.: onesto, franco, sincero; s.: buona fede; sincerità, *f.* **-hearted**, ADJ.: sincero, franco. **-heartedness**, s.: sincerità, *f.* **-ly**, ADV.: semplicemente; schiettamente; francamente. **-ness**, s.: livello, *m.*; ugualità; semplicità; chiarezza, *f.*
plăint, s.: lamento, *m.*, querela, *f.* **-ful**, ADJ.: lamentoso, querulo. **-iff**, s.: dimandatore, *m.* **-ive**, ADJ.: dolente, querulo. **-ively**, ADV.: dolentemente. **-iveness**, s.: doglianza, *f.*
plăin-work, s.: lavoro d' ago, *m.*
plăit 1, s.: piega, *f.*, doppio, *m.*, treccia, *f.* **plait** 2, TR.: piegare; intrecciare. **-er**, s.: piegatore, *m.* **-ing**, s.: piegamento; intrecciare, *m.*
plăn 1, s.: piano, disegno, *m.* **plan** 2, TR.: disegnare; progettare; formare un disegno.
plănch, TR.: intavolare. **-ing**, s.: intavolatura, *f.*
plăne 1, s.: piano, *m.*; piana superficie; pianura; pialla, *f.*: *small* —, pialluzza, *f.* **plane** 2, TR.: piallare; appianare.
plănet, s.: pianeta, *m.* **-ărium**, s.: planetario, *m.* **-ary**, ADJ.: planetario, di pianeta.
plăne-tree, s.: platano, *m.*
plănet-struck, ADJ.: golpato, attonito.
planimetry, s.: planimetria, *f.*
plănish, TR.: adeguare, lisciare.
plănisphere, s.: planisferio, *m.*
plănk 1, s.: tavola, asse, *f.*; pancone, *m.* **plank** 2, TR.: tavolare, impalcare con tavole.
plănner, s.: disegnatore, *m.*
plănt 1, s.: pianta, *f.*; ramicello, *m.* **plant** 2, TR.: piantare; stabilire; INTR.: piantarsi.
plăntain, s.: piantaggine, *f.*
plăn-tal, ADJ.: vegetabile, vegetativo. **-tătion**, s.: piantagione; colonia, *f.* **-ter**, s.: piantatore; colono, *m.* **-ing**, s.: piantamento, piantare, *m.*
plăsh 1, s.: guazzo; pantano, palude, *m.* **plash** 2, TR.: spruzzare; piegare; rimescolare. **-y**, ADJ.: pantanoso, melmoso.
plăsm(a), s.: plasma, forma; matrice, *f.* **-ătical**, ADJ.: plastico, formativo.
plăster 1, s.: impiastro; calcistruzzo, intonaco, *m.*: *give a coat of* —, dar un intonaco, intonacare. **plaster** 2, TR.: impiastrare; ingessare; porre un impiastro medicinale: — *up*, rintonacare. **-er**, s.: muratore che intonica; statuario in gesso, *m.* **-ing**, s.: intonicatura, *f.* **-stone**, s.: pietra da gesso, *f.*
plăstic, ADJ.: plastico; s.: plastica, *f.*
plăstron, s.: piastrone; pettorale, *m.*
plăt 1, s.: campicello, camperello, *m.* **plat** 2, TR.: intrecciare, tessere.
plătan(e), s.: platana, *m.*
plătband, s.: aiuola; (*arch.*) fascia, *f.*
plăt-e 1, s.: piastra; argenteria; lamina, lama, *f.*; tondo, *m.* **-te** 2, TR.: inargentare, indorare; ridurre in lamina. **-ed**, ADJ.: inargentato: — *ware*, merci in placche, *f. pl.*
plăten, s.: pirrone, *m.*; (*print.*) piastretta, *f.*
plătform, s.: piattaforma; terrazza, *f.*
plăti-na, s.: platina, *f.* (metallo). **-num**, s.: platino, *m.*
plătitude, s.: frase altisonante, inezia, *f.*
Platŏnic, ADJ.: platonico.
Plā-tonism, s.: platonismo, *m.* **-tonist**, s.: platonico, *m.*
platŏon, s.: (*mil.*) squadrone, *m.*, schiera; banda, *f.*
plătten, s.: terrina, *f.*, gran piatto (di terra), *f.*
plăudit, s.: applauso, *m.*, acclamazione, *f.*

TR.: monetare, battere la moneta. **-age**, s.: monetaggio; conio, *m*. **-er**, **-man**, s.: monetiere, zecchiere, *m*. **-master**, s.: direttore della zecca, *m*.
minuet, s.: minuetto, *m*.
minus, ADV.: meno.
minûte 1, ADJ.: minuto, piccolo, piccolissimo; tenue.
minute 2 *-it*, s.: minuto; momento, istante, *m*. **minute** 3, TR.: abbozzare; disegnare. **-book**, s.: giornale, registro, *m*. **-glass**, s.: oriuolo, *m*. **-hand**, s.: ago di minuti, *m*.
minûte-ly, ADV.: esattamente, precisamente. **-ness**, s.: minutezza, minuzia, esiguità, *f*.
minute-watch *-it*, s.: oriuolo che mostra i minuti, *m*.
minûtia, s.: minuzia; cosa di nulla, *f*.
minx, s.: vanarella, civettola, sfacciatella, *f*.
mir-acle, s.: miracolo, *m*., maraviglia, *f.: by a —*, per miracolo. **-aclemonger**, s.: spacciatore di miracoli, *m*. **-ăculous**, ADJ.: miracoloso, maraviglioso, stupendo. **-ăculously**, ADV.: miracolosamente, per miracolo. **-ăculousness**, s.: qualità miracolosa, *f*., mirabile, *m*.
mirâge *-aj*, s.: miraggio, *m*.
mire 1, s.: fango, limo, *m*., melma, *f*.
mire 2, INTR.: coprire di fango; imbrattare.
mirifical, ADJ.: mirifico, maraviglioso.
miriness, s.: fanghiglia, sporcizia, *f*.
mirk(some)†, ADJ.: buio, tenebroso. **-ness**†, s.: oscurità, *f*.
mirror, s.: specchio; (*fig*.) esemplare, modello, *m*.
mirth, *f*.: gioia, allegria, *f*.; contento, *m*. **-ful**, ADJ.: gioioso, gaio, giocondo, allegro. **-fully**, ADV.: gioiosamente, allegramente. **-fulness**, s.: gioia, allegria, *f*. **-less**, ADJ.: mesto, tristo.
miry, ADJ.: fangoso, melmoso, lotoso.
misacceptâtion, s.: mala intelligenza, *f*.; errore; equivoco, *m*.
misadvĕnture, s.: disavventura, *f*., infortunio, *m*. **-d**, ADJ.: sventurato; infelice.
misadvi-ce, s.: cattivo consiglio, *m*. **-se**, TR.: mal avvisare.
misaffĕcted, ADJ.: mal disposto.
misâimed, ADJ.: mal preso di mira.
mis-anthrope, s.: misantropo, *m*. **-anthrŏpic**, **-anthrŏpical**, ADJ.: misantropico. **-ănthropy**, s.: misantropia, *f*.
misap-plicâtion, s.: cattiva applicazione, *f*. **-plў**, TR.: applicare male.
misappre-hĕnd, TR.: intendere male, non intendere. **-hĕnsion**, s.: errore; sbaglio, *m*.
misascrîbe, TR.: ascrivere falsamente; attribuire.
misassign, TR.: assegnare erroneamente.
misbecŏm-e, IRR.; INTR.: sconvenire; disdirsi. **-ing**, ADJ.: disdicevole; indecente. **-ingness**, s.: sconvenevolezza, indecenza, *f*.
misbegŏt(ten), ADJ.: illegittimo.
misbehâ-ve, IRR.; INTR.: condursi male. **-viour**, s.: cattiva condotta, *f*.
misbe-lief, s: miscredenza, mala credenza, *f*. **-lieve**, INTR.: miscredere, discredere, essere incredulo. **-liever**, s.: miscredente; infedele, *m*. **-lieving**, ADJ.: miscredente, eretico.
miscălcu-lâte, TR.: calcolare male, computare male. **-lâtion**, s.: cattivo calcolo, *m*.
miscall, TR: chiamare impropriamente.
miscăr-riage, s.: cattiva condotta, *f*.; cattivo successo; aborto, *m*. **-ry**, INTR.: fallire; abortire; smarrirsi, perdersi, non pervenire.
miscâst, IRR.; TR.: contar male; far errore.
miscellâ-neous, ADJ.: miscellaneo. **-neousness**, s.: raccolta; varietà, *f*. **-ny** *mis-*, s.: miscellanea, *f*.; opere diverse, *f. pl.*
mischânce, s.: sventura, *f*., disastro, infortunio, *m*.
mischief 1, s.: male; danno, *m*.; disgrazia, *f*., infortunio, *m*. **mischief** 2, TR.: ingiurare; offendere, nuocere. **-maker**, s.: facimale, *m*. **-making**, ADJ.: malizioso.
mischievous, ADJ.: nocivo, pericoloso; maligno, malizioso. **-ly**, ADV.: maliziosamente, cattivamente. **-ness**, s.: malignità, malizia; ribalderia, *f*.
miscible, ADJ.: mescibile.
mis-citâtion, s.: citazione falsa, *f*. **-cite**, TR.: fare falsa citazione.
misclâim, s.: domanda erronea, domanda mal fondata, *f*.
miscom-putâtion, s.: calcolo false, *m*. **-pûte**, TR.: mal calcolare.
miscon-ceit, **-cĕption**, s.: concepimento erroneo, *m*.
miscŏn-duct 1, s.: cattiva condotta, *f*. **-dŭct**, TR.: mal condurre.
misconjĕcture, s.: congettura falsa, *f*.
mis-construction, s.: falsa costruzione, cattiva interpretazione, *f*. **-construe**, TR.: interpretare male.
miscontinuance, s.: tralasciamento, intermissione, *f*.
miscounsel, TR.: dare cattivo consiglio.
miscount, TR.: calcolare male, contare male.
miscrean-ce, **-cy**, s.: miscredenza, **-t**, s.: miscredente, infedele, *m*.

miscreāte(d), ADJ.: mal formato.
misdāte 1, S.: falsa data, *f.* **misdate** 2, TR.: marcare con falsa data.
misdēed, S.: misfatto, delitto, crime, *m.*
misdēem, TR.: giudicare male, sbagliare.
misdemēan, INTR.: condursi male. **-or**, S.: cattiva condotta, *f.*; misfatto, *m.*
misdevōtion, S.: falsa pietà, *f.*
misdō, IRR.; TR.: far male, misfare; danneggiare.
misdoubt 1, S.: sospetto; dubbio, *m.* **misdoubt** 2, TR.: sospettare; disfidare.
mise, S.: spesa; tassa, *f.*
misemplōy, TR.: impiegare male. **-ment**, S.: cattivo impiego, *m.*
miser, S.: avaro, spilorcio; misero, *m.*
miser-able, ADJ.: miserabile, meschino; infelice; avaro. **-ableness**, S.: miserabilità; infelicità; spilorceria, avarizia, *f.* **-ably**, ADV.: miserabilmente; meschinamente, avaramente. **-y**, S.: miseria, indigenza; calamità, infelicità, *f.*
misestēem, S.: disprezzo, *m.*
misfall, IRR.: TR.: accadere sfortunatamente.
misfāre, S.: infortunio, *m.*
misfāshion, TR.: formare male, sfigurare.
misfōrm, TR.: difformare; sfigurare.
misfōrtune, S.: infortunio, *m.*, calamità, *f.*
misgive, IRR.; TR.: mal presagire, presentire; temere. **-ing**, S.: sospetto; presentimento, *m.*
misgovern, TR.: governare male, reggere male. **-ment**, S.: cattivo governo, disordine, *m.*
misguidance, S.: cattivo guidamento, *m.*, mala direzione, *f.*; errore, *m.* **-de**, TR.: guidare male, menare male.
mishāp, S.: contrattempo; accidente sinistro, *m.*, fatalità, *f.* **-pen**, INTR.: misavvenire, succedere male.
mishēar, IRR., INTR.: male intendere, frantendere.
mishmash, S.: mescuglio, guazzabuglio, *m.*
misinfēr, TR.: inferire male; dedurre falsamente.
misinfōrm, TR.: dare avviso erroneo. **-ātion**, S.: falsa informazione, *f.*
misintēlligence, S.: discordia, *f.*
misintērpret, TR.: interpretare male. **-ātion**, S.: falsa interpretazione, *f.*, storcimento del senso, *m.*
misjōin, TR.: giungere male.
misjūdge, TR.: giudicare male, giudicare falsamente. **-ment**, S.: giudizio temerario, *m.*
mislāy, IRR.; TR.: smarrire; rimuovere.
misle, INTR.: piovigginare.
mislēad, IRR.; TR.: sviare, traviare; sedurre. **-er**, S.: seduttore, *m.*

misleen, S.: grano mescolato, *m.*
mislike 1, S.: disapprovazione, [illegible] volenza, *f.*; disgusto, *m.* **-e** 2, TR.: [illegible] provare; biasimare. **-er**, S.: disap[illegible] vatore, biasimatore, *m.*
mislive, INTR.: vivere malamente, [illegible] una vita cattiva, condursi male.
mismānage, TR.: maneggiare male, [illegible] vernare male. **-ment**, S.: cattivo [illegible] neggio, *m.*
mismātch, TR.: assortire male; [illegible] gere.
misnāme, TR.: nominare impropriament[illegible]
misnōmer, S.: nome scorretto, *m.*
misobsērve, TR.: osservare male.
misō-gamist, S.: misogamo, *m.* **-gam**[illegible] S.: odio al matrimonio, *m.* **-gynist**, [illegible] che odia le donne. **-gyny**, S.: odio [illegible] sesso femminino, *m.*
misōrder 1, TR.: condurre male; [illegible] nare. **misorder** 2, S.: disordine, *m.*, [illegible] regolarità, *f.* **-ly**, ADJ.: disordinato; [illegible] regolare.
mispersuāsion, S.: falsa idea, *f.*, [illegible] re, *m.*
misplāce, TR.: slogare, rimuovere; [illegible] sare.
mispōinting, S.: falsa interpunzione, [illegible]
misprint 1, S.: errore della stampa, [illegible] **misprint** 2, TR.: fare errori nella stamp[illegible]
mis-prise, TR.: dispregiare, vilipendi[illegible] spreзzare. **-prision**, S.: disprezzo, [illegible] glio, errore, *m.*; negligenza, *f.*
mispronōunce, TR.: pronunciare mal[illegible]
misproportion, TR.: proporzionare mal[illegible]
mis-quotātion, S.: citazione falsa. **-quōte**, TR.: citare falsamente.
misrecite, TR.: recitare male.
misrēckon, TR.: contare male, [illegible] narsi nel conto. **-ing**, S.: errore [illegible] conto, *m.*
misre-lāte, TR.: raccontare malamen[illegible] narrare male. **-lātion**, S.: falsa [illegible] zione, inesatta informazione, *f.*
misremēmber, TR.: ricordarsi male.
misrepōrt 1, S.: falso rapportamento, [illegible] **misreport** 2, TR.: fare un falso [illegible] porto.
misrepresent, TR.: rappresentare [illegible] fare falsa relazione. **-ātion**, S.: [illegible] relazione, *f.*
misrūle, S.: tumulto, *m.*; confusione, fracasso, *m.*
miss 1, S.: damigella, signorina, *f.*, (ti[illegible] *jest.*) madamigella: *young* —, gio[illegible] signorina; *boarding-school* —, educand[illegible]
miss 2, S.: sbaglio, errore, fallo, [illegible]
miss 3, TR.: mancare; omettere, [illegible] dere; INTR.: errare, sbagliarsi: — c[illegible] sia, mancare il colpo; non riuscire; [illegible] *fire*, mancare; — *a person* (*thing*), ac[illegible] gersi dell' assenza d' una persona (co[illegible]

I — a volume, mi accorgo che mi manca un volume.
missal, S.: missale, *m*.
missay, IRR.; TR.: misdire, dire male.
misseem†, INTR.: sconvenire; disdirsi.
misserve, TR.: servire male, disservire.
misshape, TR.: difformare, disfigurare. **-ment**, S.: difformità, *f*. **-n**, ADJ.: disfigurato, deforme.
missile, ADJ.: dardeggiato.
missing, ADJ.: smarrito, perduto.
mission, S.: missione; ambasciata, *f*. **-ary**, **-er**, S.: missionario, *m*.
missive, ADJ.: missivo; S.: lettera, epistola, *f*.
misspeak, IRR.; TR.: parlare male; diffamare.
misspell, TR.: compitare male, ortografizzare male.
misspend, TR.: spendere male, consumare il suo. **-er**, S.: dissipatore, prodigo, *m*.
mist, S.: nebbia, *f*.: *Scotch* —, gran pioggia, *f*.; *be in a* —, esser al buio, non sapere che fare.
mistak-e, S.: errore, fallo, sbaglio; senso erroneo, *m*.: *make a* —, fare uno sbaglio. **-e**, IRR.; TR.: non intendere, non comprendere; INTR., IRR.: sbagliare; ingannarsi; *you* —, voi vi ingannate; — *the road*, smarrire la strada. **-en**, ADJ.: sbagliato; erroneo, falso; *be* —, ingannarsi, errare; *you are greatly* —, vi ingannate a partito. **-ingly**, ADV.: erroneamente, falsamente.
misteach, IRR.; TR.: insegnare male; sviare.
mistell, IRR.; TR.: narrare falsamente, dire falsamente.
mistemper, TR.: temperare male, mischiare male.
mister, S.: signore, *m*.
misterm, TR.: nominare erroneamente, appellare male.
mistful, ADJ.: nebuloso.
misthink, IRR.; TR.: pensare male.
mistime, TR.: fare a contrattempo.
mistiness, S.: nuvolosità, *f*.; offuscamento, *m*.
mistletoe, S.: vischio, *m*.
mistlike, ADJ.: folto come nebbia, oscuro, fosco.
mistress, S.: signora, padrona; madama; innamorata, *f*.
mistrust 1, S.: diffidenza, *f*.; sospetto, *m*. **mistrust** 2, TR.: diffidare; sospettare, dubitare. **-ful**, ADJ.: diffidente; sospettoso, dubbioso. **-fully**, ADV.: sospettosamente. **-fulness**, S.: diffidenza, *f*.; sospetto, *m*. **-less**, ADJ.: non sospettoso.
mistune, INTR.: accordare male.
misty, ADJ.: nebbioso; oscuro.
misunder-stand, IRR.; TR.: intendere male. **-standing**, S.: mala intelligenza, discordia, *f*.; errore, *m*. **-stood**, PART. del v. *misunderstand*.
mis-usage, S.: cattivo uso, abuso, *m*.; villania, *f*. **-use** 1, S.: abuso; cattivo trattamento, *m*. **-use** 2, TR.: abusare; maltrattare; svillaneggiare.
mite, S.: tonchio, gorgoglione, *m*.; ventesima parte d' un grano, *f*.
miter = *mitre*.
mithridate, S.: mitridato, *m*.
miti-gant, ADJ.: mitigante, lenitivo. **-gate**, TR.: mitigare; raddolcire, placare, quietare. **-gation**, S.: mitigazione, *f*., mitigamento; raddolcimento, *m*. **-gator**, S.: mitigatore, *m*.
mitre, S.: mitra, *f*. (ornamento pontificale). **-d**, ADJ.: che porta la mitra.
mitten, S.: guanto senza dita, *m*.
mittimus, S.: (*leg*.) mandato di cattura, ordine per imprigionare, *m*.
mix, TR.: mischiare, mescolare; INTR.: mischiarsi, mescolarsi.
mixen, S.: letamaio, *m*.
mix-ing, S.: mischiamento, mescolamento, *m*. **-t**, ADJ.: mischiato, mescolato; confuso. **-tion**† = *-ture*. **-tly**, ADV.: mischiamente; confusamente. **-ture**, S.: mescolanza, mistura, *f*.
mizmaze†, S.: laberinto; imbroglio, *m*.
mizzen, S.: (*nav*.) mezzana, *f*. **-top-mast**, S.: albero di contramezzana, *m*. **-top-sail**, S.: contramezzana, *f*.
mizzle 1, S.: poca pioggia, spruzzaglia, *f*.
mizzle 2, INTR.: piovigginare, spruzzolare.
mizzy†, S.: pantano, *m*.
mnemonics, S. PL.: arte d' assistere la memoria, *f*.
moan 1, S.: pianto, lamento, gemito, *m*.
moan 2, INTR.: piangere, gemere; dolersi; TR.: lamentarsi di. **-ful**, ADJ.: lamentevole, dolente. **-fully**, ADV.: lamentevolmente, con gemiti.
moat 1, S.: canale d' acqua per difesa, *m*.
moat 2, TR.: far un canale d' acqua per difesa.
mob 1, S.: folla, turba; canaglia, *f*.
mob 2, TR.: tumultuare, insurgere. **-bish**, ADJ.: del popolazzo; tumultuoso. **-by**, S.: bevanda americana, *f*.
mo-bile, S.: popolazzo, *m*., plebe, plebaglia, marmaglia, *f*. **-bility**, S.: mobilità; plebaglia, *f*.
mock 1, ADJ.: falso, contrafatto, finto; burlesco: — *turtle-soup*, cibreo alla tartaruga. **mock** 2, S.: derisione; beffa, *f*., ludibrio, *m*.: *make a — of one*, burlarsi di alcuno. **mock** 3, (IN)TR.: imitare; burlare, beffare, deridere. **-able**, AD esposto alla derisione. **-er**, S.: beffa schernitore, *m*. **-ery**, S.: scherno,

no, *m.* (figura di più lati). '**-gonal**, ADJ.: poligono. **-gram**, S.: poligramma, *m.* **-graph**, S.: poligrafo, *m.* '**-graphy**, S.: poligrafia, *f.* '**-mathy**, S.: cognizione generale, *f.* **-p**, S.: polpo, polipo, *m.* **-pous**, ADJ.: di molti piedi; del polipo. **-pus** = *polyp.* **-scope**, S.: occhiale a faccette, *m.* **-syllăbic(al)**, ADJ.: polisillabo. **-syllable**, S.: polisillabo, *m.* **-těchnic**, ADJ.: politecnico. **-theism**, S.: politeismo, *m.* **-theist**, S.: politeista, *m.* **-theistic(al)**, ADJ.: politeistico.

po-māceous, ADJ.: pieno di pomi. **-māde**, S.: pomato, manteca, *f.* **-mănder**, S.: saponetto profumato, *m.* **-mātum**, S.: pomata, *f.*

pómegranate, S.: melagrana, *f.*

pomiferous, ADJ.: pomifero, fruttifero.

pómmel 1, S.: pomo della spada, *f.* **pommel** 2, TR.: battere; stregghiare.

pŏmp, S.: pompa, *f.*, splendore, *m.* **-ătic**†, ADJ.: pomposo.

pómpion, S.: zucca, *f.*

pompŏsity, S.: aria pomposa, ostentazione, *f.*

pŏmpous, ADJ.: pomposo, fastoso, tronfio. **-ly**, ADV.: pomposamente, con pompa. **-ness**, S.: pompa, ostentazione, *f.*, splendore, *m.*

pŏnd, S.: stagno, vivaio, pescaio, *m.*

pŏnder, (IN)TR.: ponderare, pesare; considerare. **-able**, ADJ.: che può essere pesato. **-al**, ADJ.: stimato dal peso. **-ātion**, S.: pesare; peso, *m.* **-er**, S.: pesatore; pensatore, *m.* **-ing**, S.: ponderare, *m.* **-ingly**, ADV.: ponderatamente. **-ŏsity**, S.: ponderosità, *f.*; peso, *m.* **-ous**, ADJ.: ponderoso, pesante; grave. **-ously**, ADV.: pesantemente; gravemente. **-ousness**, S.: gravezza, gravita, *f.*, pondo, peso, *m.*

pŏnent, ADJ.: occidentale.

pŏniard 1, S.: pugnale, stiletto, *m.*: *stab with a* —, pugnalata, *f.* **poniard** 2, TR.: pugnalare, stilettare.

pŏnk†, S.: folletto, *m.*

pŏn-tiff, S.: pontefice, papa, *m.*: *sovereign* —, sovrano pontefice. **-tifical**, ADJ.: pontificale, di pontefice; S.: pontificale, *m.* (libro). **-tifically**, ADV.: pontificalmente, a maniera di pontefice. **-tificate**, S.: pontificato, papato, *m.* **-tificial**, ADJ.: pontificio.

pontōon, S.: pontone, *m.*: — *train*, equipaggio da ponti, *m.*

pōny, S.: bidetto, ronzino, *m.*

pōodle, S.: cane maltese, *m.*

pōol, S.: pozzanghera, *f.*; posta (al giuoco), *f.*; sorta di biliardo, *m.*

pōop, S.: poppa (della nave), *f.*

pōor, ADJ.: povero, misero, indigente, necessitoso; sterile: — *man*, povero, *m.*; — *woman*, povera, *f.*; — *fellow!* poveretto! *m.*; — *woman* (*girl*), poveretta, *f.*; *the* —, i poveri, *pl.*; poveraglia, *f.* **-house**, S.: asilo dei poveri, *m.* **-john**, S.: merluzzo, *m.* (pesce). **-law**, S.: legge sul pauperismo, *f.* **-ly**, ADV.: poveramente, meschinamente, vilmente. **-ness**, S.: povertà, indigenza, *f.* **-rate**, S.: contributo alla tassa dei poveri. **-spirited**, ADJ.: codardo, vile. **-spiritedness**, S.: dappocaggine, codardia, viltà, *f.*

pŏp 1, S.: piccolo romore acuto, piccolo strepito subito, *m.* **pop** 2, TR.: porre destramente; INTR.: sopravvenire all' improvviso: — *in*, entrare all' improvviso; — *off*, lanciare; sparare; scappare; fuggire; — *out*, andar via, uscire.

pōp-e, S.: papa, *m.* **-edom**, S.: pontificato, *m.* **-ery**, S.: papismo, *m.*

pŏp-gun, S.: buffo; cannello, *m.*

pŏpinjay, S.: pappagallo; minchioncello, parigino, *m.*

pōpish, ADJ.: del papa; Cattolico Romano. **-ly**, ADV.: a modo di papa, da papista. **-ness**, S.: papismo, *m.*

pŏplar, S.: pioppo, oppio, *m.*: *trembling* —, tremula, alberella, *f.*

pŏppy, S.: papavero, *m.*

pŏppycock, S.: (*slang*) pettegolezze, *f. pl.*

pŏpu-lace, S.: volgo, *m.*, plebaglia, *f.* **-lar**, ADJ.: popolare, popolano; comune. **-lărity**, S.: popolarità, *f.*; favore pubblico, *m.* **-larize**, TR.: popolarizzare. **-larly**, ADV.: popolarmente; comunemente. **-larness**, S.: popolarità, *f.* **-late**, TR.: popolare. **-lātion**, S.: popolazione, *f.*; popolo, *m.* **-lŏsity**, S.: popolazione, *f.* **-lous**, ADJ.: popoloso, popolato. **-lousness** = *populosity.*

pôrcelain, S.: porcellana, *f.*; vasi di porcellana, *m. pl.*

pōrch, S.: portico, *m.*, piazza, *f.*

pôrcupine, S.: porcospino, *m.*

pōre 1, S.: poro, *m.* **pore** 2, INTR.: riguardare fissamente, fissare; esaminare: — *over a book*, avere gli occhi fissi sopra un libro. **-blind**, ADJ.: corto di vista, miope. **-blindness**, S.: vista corta, miopia, *f.*

pōriness, S.: porosità, *f.*

pōrk, S.: porco, *m.*; carne di porco, *f.* **-chop**, S.: costoletta di porco, *f.* **-eater**, S.: che mangia carne di porco. **-er**, S.: porcellotto, porchetto, *m.* **-et**, S.: porcello, porcellino, *m.* **-ling**, S.: porco di latte, *m.*

porŏsity, S.: porosità, *f.*

pōrous, ADJ.: poroso, pieno di pori. **-ness** = *porosity.*

pôr-phyre, **-phyry**†, S.: porfido, *m.*

pôr-poise, **-pus**, S.: porco marino, *m.* (pesce).

-ĭtion, S.: ammonizione, *f.*; avvertimento, *m.*, esortazione, *f.* **-itor**, S.: monitore, ammonitore, *m.* **-itōrial**, ADJ.: monitorio. **-itory**, S.: monitorio, *m.*; ammonizione, *f.*

mónk, S.: monaco, frate, *m.* **-ery**, S.: monacato, *m.*

mónkey, S.: scimmia, bertuccia, *f.*, babbuino, *m.*

mónk-hood, S.: vita monastica, *f.*, monachismo, *m.* **-ish**, ADJ.: monastico, monacale. **-'s-hood**, S.: (*bot.*) aconito, *m.*

mŏn-ochord, S.: monocordo, *m.* **-ŏcular**, **-ŏculous**, ADJ.: monocolo, losco. **-ody**, S.: monodia, *f.* **-ŏgamist**, S.: monogamo, *m.* **-ŏgamy**, S.: monogamia, *f.* **-ogram**, S.: monogramma, *f.* **-ŏgraphy**, S.: monografia, *f.* **-ologue**, S.: monologo, soliloquio, *m.* **-ŏmachy**, S.: monomachia, *f.*, duello, *m.* **-ome**, S.: monomio, *m.* **-opĕtalous**, ADJ.: (*bot.*) monopetalo. **-ŏpolist**, S.: monopolista; incettatore, *m.* **-ŏpolize**, TR.: far monopolio, incettare. **-ŏpoly**, S.: monopolio, *m.* **-osyllăbic(al)**, ADJ.: monosillabo. **-osyllable**, S.: monosillabo, *m.*, monosillaba, *f.* **-otheism**, S.: monoteismo, *m.* **-ŏtonous**, ADJ.: monotono. **-ŏtony**, S.: monotonia, *f.*

monsōon, S.: monsone, *m.*

mŏn-ster, S.: mostro, *m.*; singolarità, *f.* **-strŏsity**, S.: mostruosità, *f.* **-strous**, ADJ.: mostruoso, prodigioso. **-strously**, ADV.: mostruosamente. **-strousness**, S.: mostruosità; deformità, *f.*

montēro, S.: montiera, *f.* (berretta).

mónth, S.: mese, *m.* **-ly** 1, ADJ.: d'ogni mese, mensuale. **-ly** 2, ADV.: una volta il mese, di mese in mese, ogni mese. **-lies**, S. PL.: mestrui, *m. pl.* **-'s-mind**†, S.: ardente desiderio, *m.*

mŏnu-ment, S.: monumento; memoriale; sepolcro, *m.* **-mĕntal**, ADJ.: di monumento.

mōod, S.: modo; umore, capriccio, temperamento, *m.*: *in a merry* —, allegro; *in the right* —, ben disposto. **-y**, ADJ.: capriccioso.

mōon, S.: luna, *f.*; mese, *m.*: *full* —, luna piena; plenilunio; *half* —, mezza luna; crescente; *new* —, luna nuova; *the phases of the* —, le fasi della luna. **-beam**, S.: raggio della luna, *m.* **-calf**, S.: mola, *f.*; mostro; minchione, balordo, *m.* **-eyed**, ADJ.: lunatico; di corta vista. **-less**, ADJ.: senza chiaro di luna. **-light**, S.: chiaro di luna, *m.* **-light**, ADJ.: illuminato dalla luna. **-shine**, S.: chiarezza della luna, *f.* **-shine**, **-shiny**, ADJ.: illuminato dalla luna. **-struck**, ADJ.: lunatico, pazzo.

mōor 1, TR.: (*nav.*) gettare l'ancora; dare fondo. **moor** 2, S.: palude, pantano. **moor** 3, S.: moro, *m.* **-cock**, S.: gallo di palude, *m.* **-hen**, S.: folaga, *f.* (uccello).

mōor-ing, S.: gettare l'ancora, *m.*

mōor-ish, ADJ.: paludoso, pantanoso, melmoso; moresco. **-land**, S.: palude, pantano, *m.*

mōose, S.: daino americano, *m.*

mōot 1, S.: disputa di qualche materia legale, *f.* **moot** 2, TR.: disputare di qualche materia legale. **-case**, S.: questione legale, *f.* **-ed**, ADJ.: sradicato, estirpato. **-er**, S.: disputante in legge, *m.* **-hall**, S.: sala dove si disputa in legge, *f.*

mŏp 1, S.: spazzatoio, *m.* **mop** 2, TR.: spazzare; nettare il solaio: — *and mow*, fare il grugno.

mōpe, TR.: rendere stupido; INTR.: stupidire, divenire stupido. **-e-eyed**, ADJ.: cieco d'un' occhio, losco. **-ish**, ADJ.: abbattuto, tristo. **-ishness**, S.: abbattimento, *m.*, tristizia, *f.*

mŏppet, **mŏpsey**, S.: fantoccio di cenci, *m.*

mōpus, S.: infingardo, pigro, *m.*

mŏr-al, ADJ.: morale; S.: dottrina morale, *f.*; costume buono, *m.*: — *philosopher* (*writer*), moralista, *m.*; *good* —*s*, buoni costumi. **-alist**, S.: moralista, *m.* **-ălity**, S.: moralità, *f.*; senso morale, *m.* **-alizātion**, S.: moralizzazione, *f.* **-alize**, (IN)TR.: moralizzare. **-alizer**, S.: moralista, predicatore, *m.* **-ally**, ADV.: moralmente. **-als**, S. PL.: buoni costumi, *m. pl.*

morăss, S.: palude, pantano, *m.* **-y**, ADJ.: paludoso, pantanoso.

môr-bid, ADJ.: morbido, malaticcio. **-bĭdity**, **-bidness**, S.: morbidezza; infermità, *f.* **-bĭfic(al)**, ADJ.: morbifico, morbifero.

mor-dāçious, ADJ.: mordace; pungente. **-dăcity**, S.: mordacità; acutezza, *f.*

môr-dant, ADJ., S.: mordante. **-dicancy**, S.: mordacità; maldicenza, *f.* **-dicant**, ADJ.: mordente; pungente. **-dicate**, TR.: mordere; censurare. **-dicātion**, S.: mordicamento, *m.*; acrità, *f.*

mōre 1, ADJ., ADV.: più; di più, di vantaggio maggiore, in maggior numero (*or* quantità): — *and* —, di più in più; *a great deal* —, molto più, vieppiù; *once* —, un' altra volta, ancora una volta: — *than enough*, più che non [illegible]
have some —? [illegible]
—, tanto [illegible]
te, [illegible]
mŏr-[illegible]
[illegible]

f. **-late** 2, TR.: domandare; supporre; avanzare. **-lātion**, S.: domanda, richiesta, *f.* **-latory**, ADJ.: supposto. **-lātum**, S.: postulato, supposto, *m.*
pŏsture 1, S.: postura, positura; situazione, *f.*; stato, *m.*, condizione, *f.*; ordine, *m.* **posture** 2, TR.: mettere in positura, ordinare; assettare. **-master**, S.: ciurmadore, giocolare, *m.*
pōsy, S.: mazzetto di fiori; motto, *m.*
pŏt 1, S.: vaso, boccale, orciuolo; ramino; orinale, *m.*; pentola, *f.*: *flower-—*, testo, *m.*; *watering-—*, annaffiatoio, *m.* **pot** 2, TR.: mettere in vaso; insalare.
pōtable, ADJ.: potabile, bevibile. **-ness**, S.: qualità potabile, *f.*
pŏtage = *pottage.* **-er**†, S.: pentola, *f.*; romaiuolo, *m.*
pŏtash, S.: potassa, *f.*, sale alcalino, *m.*
potăssium, S.: potassio, *m.*
potātion, S.: beveria, *f.*, svebazzamento, *m.*
potāto, S.: patata, *f.*, pomo di terra, *m.*: *mashed —*, sugo di patate; *sweet —*, patata dolce, batata.
pŏt-bellied, ADJ.: panciuto. **-belly**, S.: grossa pancia, *f.* **-butter**, S.: butirro salato, *m.*
pŏtch†, TR.: bollire; spingere.
pŏt-companion, S.: scialacquatare, beone, *m.*
pō-tency, S.: potenza, possanza; forza; efficacia, *f.* **-tent**, ADJ.: potente, possente; efficace. **-tentate**, S.: potentato, monarca, *m.* **-tĕntial**, ADJ.: potenziale; virtuale, efficace. **-tentiălity**, S.: possibilità; efficacia, *f.* **-tĕntially**, ADV.: con virtù potenziale. **-tently**, ADV.: potentemente, potenzialmente; con molto vigore. **-tentness**, S.: potere, forza, *f.*; vigore, *m.*; efficacia, *f.*
pŏt-full, S.: pentola piena; pignatta piena, *f.* **-gun**, S.: cannoniera, *f.* **-hanger**, S.: catena del cammino, *f.*
pŏthecary†, S.: speziale, *m.*
pŏther 1, S.: tumulto, strepito, romore, *m.* **pother** 2, TR.: schiamazzare senza effetto, far molto strepito.
pŏt-herb, S.: erbaggio, *m.*; erba da mangiare, *f.* **-hook**, S.: catena da fuoco, *f.*; manico d' un vaso, *m.*
pōtion, S.: pozione, bevanda, *f.*, beveraggio, *m.*
pŏt-lid, S.: coperchio d'un vaso, *m.* **-sherd**, S.: pezzo di vaso rotto, coccio, *m.* **-tage**, S.: minestra, zuppa, *f.* **-ter**, S.: pentolaio, vasellaio, figulo, *m.*: *—'s clay*, argilla, *f.*; *—'s ware*, vasellame di terra, *m.* **-tery**, S.: stoviglie, *f. pl.*; vasellame di terra; magazzino di pentole, *m.*
pŏttle, S.: quattro fogliette, *f. pl.* (misura).
pŏtvaliant, ADJ.: valoroso dopo d'aver bevuto.
pouch 1, S.: tasca, scarsella, borsa, *f.*; zaino, *m.*; (*fig.*) pancia, *f.* **pouch** 2, TR.: intascare; ingoiare.
pōule, S.: puglia, *f.*
pōult, S.: pollastrino, pollastrello, *m.* **-erer**, S.: pollaiuolo, pollinaro, *m.*
pōultice 1, S.: cataplasma, impiastro, *m.* **poultice** 2, TR.: applicare un cataplasma.
pōultry, S.: pollame, *m.*, polli, *m. pl.* **-yard**, S.: bassa corte, polleria, *f.*
pounce 1, S.: artiglio, *m.*; unghia. **pounce** 2, S.: polvere di pumice, *f.* **pounce** 3, TR.: spolverizzare; artigliare; sforacchiare. **-d**, ADJ.: artigliato.
pounce-box, S.: polverino, *m.*, scatoletta, *f.*
pound 1, S.: libbra, *f.*; parco, *m.*: *— sterling*, lira sterlina, *f.*; *by the* (*a*) *—*, alla libbra, per libbra. **pound** 2, S.: prigione per le bestie, *f.* **pound** 3, TR.: pestare; rinchiudere; staggire. **pound** 4, TR.: imprigionare. **-age**, S.: un tanto per lira, scellino per lira, *m.* **-er**, S.: pestello, *m.*; sorta di grossa pera, *f.*: *twelve-—*, cannone di dodici libbre di portata, *m.* **-ing**, S.: pestamento, tritamento, *m.*
pour, TR.: versare; spandere, effondere; INTR.: scorrere: *— down*, piovere strabocchevolmente, diluviare; *— out*, trasvasare; diffondere; *— me out a cup*, versatemi una tazza; *it —s*, diluvia, piove a secchie. **-er**, S.: versatore; diffonditore, *m.*
pourtrāy = *portray.*
pout 1, S.: merluzzo (pesce); francolino, *m.* (uccello). **pout** 2, TR.: fare il grugno, fare un mal viso. **-ing**, S.: stizza, *f.*; cattivo umore, *m.* **-ingly**, ADV.: burberamente; tronfiamente.
pŏverty, S.: povertà, indigenza; miseria, *f.*
powder 1, S.: polvere; polvere da cannone, *f.*: *reduce to —*, ridurre in polvere; *Jesuit's —*, chinachina, *f.* **powder** 2, TR.: polverizzare; salare. **-box**, S.: polverino, *m.* **-cart**, S.: cassone della polvere, *m.* **-chests**, S. PL.: cassoni di poppa, *m. pl.* **-horn**, S.: borsa da polvere, *f.* **-ing-tub**, S.: vaso da salarvi la carne, *m.* **-magazine**, S.: magazzino da polvere, *m.* **-ink**, S.: polvere per far l' inchiostro, *f.* **-mill**, S.: mulino da polvere, *m.* **-room**, S.: (*nav.*) Santa Barbara, *f.* **-y**, ADJ.: polveroso.
power, S.: potere, *m.*, forza, possanza; armata; autorità, influenza, *f*: *motive —*, forza motrice; *locomotive —*, forza locomotiva, *f.*; *of a hundred horse —*, della forza di cento cavalli; *love of —*, amor

montare un cannone; — *guard*, montar la guardia; — *on horseback*, montare a cavallo; *he is well —ed*, ha una bella cavalcatura.

möųntain, s.: montagna, *f.*, monte, *m.*; ADJ.: di montagna, montanaro: *little* —, montagnetta, *f.*; *make —s of molehills*, fare d' una mosca un elefante. **-ëer**, s.: montanaro, *m.* **-ous**, ADJ.: montagnoso. **-ousness**, s.: stato montagnoso, *m.* **-stream**, s.: torrente di montagna, *m.*

möųntębank 1, s.: ciarlatano, saltimbanco, *m.* **mountebank** 2, TR.: ciurmare; barare. **-ęry**, s.: ciarlataneria, *f.*

mŏurn, TR.: piangere, deplorare; INTR.: portare bruno; affiggersi. **-ęr**, s.: piangitore, piagnone, *m.* **-fųl**, ADJ.: piangevole, lugubre, tristo, dolente.

möų-se, s.: sorcio, topo, *m.*: *field*—, sorcio campestre, *m.*; *young* —, topolino, *m.* **-se** 2, TR.: prendere sorci. **-se-ear**, s.: (*bot.*) orecchia di topo, *f.* **-se-hole**, s.: buco di topo, *m.* **-ęer**, s.: pigliatore di topi, *m.* **-se-trap**, s.: trappola (da topi), *f.*

möų-th 1, s.: bocca; imboccatura; entrata, *f.*: *large ugly* —, boccaccia, *f.*; *pretty little* —, bel bocchino, *m.*; *by word of* —, a viva voce; *live from hand to* —, vivere alla giornata; *make a* —, *make —s*, fare smorfie; *stop one's* —, chiuder la bocca ad uno. **-th** 2, TR.: masticare; INTR.: parlare, gridare ad alta voce. **-thed**, ADJ.: dalla bocca, che ha la bocca. **-th-friend**, s.: amico falso, *m.*; amica falsa, *f.* **-thfųl**, s.: boccone, *m.*, boccata, *f.* **-th-honour**, s.: buone parole, *f. pl.*, complimenti, *m. pl.* **-thless**, ADJ.: senza bocca. **-thpiece**, s.: bocciuolo, *m.*

mō-vable, ADJ.: mobile, movibile. **-vableness**, s.: mobilità, *f.* **-vableş**, s. PL.: beni mobili, suppellettili, *m. pl.* **-vably**, ADV.: in modo movevole. **-ve** 1, s.: mossa, *f.*: *whose — is it?* a chi tocca a muovere? *it is my* —, tocca a me a muovere. **-ve** 2, TR.: muovere; agitare, commuovere, eccitare, sollecitare; indurre, persuadere; disturbare, stizzire, provocare; intenerire, toccare; proporre; raccomandare; INTR.: muoversi, darsi moto; dimenarsi, agitarsi: — *to laughter*, muover le risa; — *off*, fuggire, dar delle calcagna. **-veless**, ADJ.: immobile. **-vement**, s.: moto, movimento, *m.*; mozione, *f.*: — *of a watch*, macchina d' un oriuolo. **-vęr**, s.: motore, movitore, *m.* **-viņg**, ADJ.: movitivo, toccante; s.: movimento, *m.* **-viņgly**, ADV.: in modo patetico.

möw 1, s.: mucchio, cumulo, *m.*, bica, *f.* **mow** 2, IRR.; (IN)TR.: segare con falce, falciare, mietere; fare il grugno.

möwbųrn, INTR.: abbrucciarsi nella bica.

mōw-ęr, s.: falciatore, segatore (di fieno), mietitore, *m.* **-iņg**, s.: segamento; tagliamento (di fieno); grugno, *m.* **-iņg-time**, s.: stagione del falciare; segatura, mietitura; ricolta, *f.*

mŭch 1, ADJ., ADV.: molto, considerevole, assai; spesso; grandemente: — *richer*, molto più ricco; — *less*, molto meno; — *more*, assai più, molto più, vieppiù; *as* —, tanto, altrettanto; *as — as*, tanto quanto; *as — again*, una volta più, doppio; *by* —, di molto, vieppiù; *how* —, quanto; *too* —, di soverchio, troppo; *thus* —, tanto; *very* —, moltissimo; in gran quantità; *with — ado*, a grande stento; *make — of*, fare mille carezze, accarezzare; *make — of one*, far grande stima d' alcuno; *make — of one's self*, trattarsi bene; *make — of one's time*, impiegar bene il suo tempo. **much** 2, s.: molto, *m.*, gran copia, *f.* **-what†**, ADV.: presso a poco.

mŭcid, ADJ.: mucido, viscoso, tenace. **-ness**, s.: viscosità, *f.*; tanfo, *m.*

mŭci-lage, s.: mucilaggine, *f.* **-lăginous**, ADJ.: mucilagginoso, viscoso.

mŭck 1, s.: letame, concime; fimo, *m.*: *run a*—, correre all' impazzata. **muck** 2, TR.: letamare, concimare, ingrassare. **-ęr†**, INTR.: accumulare danari con sordidezza. **-hill**, s.: letamaio, *m.* **-iness**, s.: sporcizia, bruttura, lordura, *f.*

mŭckle, ADJ.: molto; cf. *mickle*.

mŭck-worm, s.: verme di letamaio, *m.* **-y**, ADJ.: sporco, sucido, lordo.

mŭcous, ADJ.: mucoso, mucilagginoso. **-ness**, s.: mucosità, mucilaggine, *f.*

mŭcrǫ, s.: punta, *f.* **-nąted**, ADJ.: mucronato.

mū-cųlency, s.: viscosità, *f.* **-cųlent**, ADJ.: viscoso, mucido. **-cus**, s.: muco, moccio, umore viscoso, *m.*

mŭd 1, s.: fango; limaccio, *m.*; melma, *f.*: *fall into the* —, cadere nel fango, infangarsi. **mud** 2, TR.: coprire di fango; intorbidare. **-cart**, s.: carro da letame, *m.* **-fish**, s.: chiozzo, *m.* **-hole**, s.: buco di fango, *m.*; melma, *f.* **-dily**, ADV.: fangosamente, torbidamente. **-diness**, s.: torbidezza, fangosità; feccia, *f.*; sedimento, *m.* **-dle**, TR.: intorbidare, innebbriare. **-dy** 1, s.: limoso, melmoso, fangoso, torbido. **-dy** 2, TR.: intorbidare; disturbare. **-wall**, s.: muro costrutto di fango e paglia, *m.* **-walled**, ADJ.: cinto d' un muro di 'ango e paglia.

mūe, INTR.: mudare.

mŭff, s.: manicotto, manichino, *m.*

mŭffin, s.: sorta di focaccia, *f.*

inconsiderazione, temerità, *f.* **-cipitator**, S.: precipitatore, *m.* **-cipitous**, ADJ.: precipitoso, temerario. **-cipitously**, ADV.: precipitosamente. **-cipitousness** = *precipitation.*

pre-cise, ADJ.: preciso, esatto. **-cisely**, ADV.: precisamente, esattamente. **-ciseness**, S.: precisione, esattezza, *f.* **-cisiant**†, S.: rigorista, *m.* **-cisianism**, S.: rigorismo, *m.* **-cision**, S.: precisione, esattezza, *f.*; limite, *m.* **-cisive**, ADJ.: precisivo; positivo.

preclū-de, TR.: precludere; impedire: — *the necessity of*, rendere non necessario. **-sion**, S.: impedimento, *m.* **-sive**, ADJ.: impeditivo.

pre-cōcious, ADJ.: precoce, prematuro. **-cōciousness**, **-cŏcity**, S.: maturità prima del tempo, *f.*

precŏgitate, TR.: premeditare.

precognition, S.: preconoscenza, *f.*

precompōse, TR.: comporre anticipatamente.

preconcĕit, S.: pregiudizio, *m.*; prevenzione, *f.*

precon-cĕive, TR.: prevedere; indovinare. **-cĕption**, S.: pregiudizio, *m.*

preconcĕrt, TR.: deliberare anticipatamente.

preconisātion, S.: preconizzazione, *f.*

prĕconize, TR.: preconizzare.

precŭr-se, S.: precorrimento; presagio, augurio, *m.* **-sor**, S.: precursore; annunzio, *m.* **-sory**, S.: introduzione, *f.*

predācious, ADJ.: predace.

prĕdatory, ADJ.: predatorio, rapace.

predecĕased, ADJ.: morto innanzi.

predecĕssor, S.: predecessore, antecessore, *m.*; antenati, progenitori, *m. pl.*

pre-destinārian, S.: che crede alla predestinazione. **-dĕstinate**, TR.: predestinare. **-dĕstinātion**, S.: predestinazione, *f.* **-dĕstinator** = *predestinarian.* **-dĕstine**, (IN)TR.: predestinare; decretare.

prede-terminātion, S.: predeterminazione, *f.* **-tĕrmine**, TR.: predeterminare.

prĕdial, ADJ.: prediale.

prĕ-dicable, S.: (*log.*) predicabile, *m.* **-dicament**, S.: predicamento, *m.*, categoria, *f.*: *in a bad* —, in mal passo. **-dicant**, S.: predicante, predicatore, *m.* **-dicate** 1, S.: predicato, predicamento, *m.* **-dicate**, TR.: affermare; dichiarare, manifestare, pubblicare. **-dicātion**, S.: affermazione, *f.* **-dicatory**, ADJ.: affermativo.

predic-t, TR.: predire; profetizzare. **-tion**, S.: predizione, *f.*, predicimento, *m.* **-tive**, ADV.: profetico. **-tor**, S.: pronosticatore, profeta, *m.*

predilĕction, S.: predilezione, *f.*

predis-pōse, TR.: disporre avanti, ordinare avanti. **-position**, S.: disposizione anteriore, *f.*

predŏmi-nance, **-nancy**, S.: superiorità, *f.* **-nant**, ADJ.: predominante, superiore. **-nate**, INTR.: predominare.

pre-elĕct, TR.: eleggere avanti.

pre-ĕminen-ce, S.: preeminenza; superiorità, *f.* **-t**, ADJ.: preeminente; superiore.

pre-ĕmption, S.: compra anticipata, *f.*; diritto di comprare avanti, *m.*

pre-engāge, TR.: impegnare precedentemente. **-ment**, S.: obbligo anteriore, *m.*

pre-estăblish, TR.: stabilire avanti. **-ment**, S.: stabilimento anteriore, *m.*

pre-exăminātion, S.: previa esaminazione, *f.* **-exămine**, TR.: esaminare avanti.

pre-exist, INTR.: preesistere, esistere avanti. **-ence**, S.: preesistenza, *f.* **-ent**, ADJ.: preesistenza, *f.*

prĕf-ace 1, S.: prefazione, *f.*, preambolo; proemio, *m.* **-ace** 2, (IN)TR.: dire avanti, introdurre. **-acer**, S.: scrittore d'una prefazione, *m.* **-atory**, ADJ.: introduttivo, preliminare.

prē-fect, S.: prefetto, preposto, governatore, *m.* **-fĕcture**, S.: prefettura, *f.*

prefĕr, TR.: preferire, preporre; promuovere, avanzare: — *a law*, proporre una legge.

prĕfer-able, ADJ.: preferibile; desiderabile. **-ableness**, S.: preferimento, *m.* **-ably**, ADV.: per preferenza. **-ence**, S.: preferenza, prelazione, *f.*

prefĕr-ment, S.: avanzamento, *m.*; promozione, *f.*; impiego, uffizio, *m.*: *come to* —, avanzarsi, aggrandirsi. **-rer**, S.: preferitore, promotore; delatore, accusatore, *m.*

prefigu-rate, TR.: significare avanti. **-rātion**, S.: prefiguramento, *m.* **-re** = *prefigurate.*

prefine, TR.: prefinire.

prē-fix 1, S.: (*gram.*) prefisso, *m.* **-fix** 2, TR.: prefiggere; stabilire. **-fixion**, S.: prefiggimento; tempo fissato, *m.*

prefŏrm, TR.: formare avanti, figurarsi.

prĕg-nable, ADJ.: espugnabile. **-nancy**, S.: pregnezza; inventiva, *f.* **-nant**, ADJ.: pregnante; fertile. **-nantly**, ADV.: fertilmente; pienamente, grandemente.

pregustātion, S.: assaggiamento anteriore, *m.*

prehĕnsi(b)le, ADJ.: prendibile.

prehistŏric, ADJ.: preistorico.

prejŭdge, **-jūdicate**, TR.: giudicare innanzi. **-jūdicate**, ADJ.: giudicato innanzi. **-judicātion**, S.: giudizio anticipato, *m.*

nā́tų-re, S.: natura; proprietà, essenzia; specie, *f.*; umore; genio, temperamento, *m.*: *by* —, secondo natura; naturalmente, per indole. **-red**, ADJ.: di . . . natura, di . . . naturale: *good-*—, d' un buon naturale.
nā́ufrągef†, S.: naufragio, *m.*
nā́ught 1, ADJ.: cattivo, malvagio, depravato, disonesto. **naught** 2, S.: niente, *m.*, nessuna cosa, *f.* **-ily**, ADV.: cattivamente; malamente. **-iness**, S.: cattivezza; tristizia, *f.* **-y**, ADJ.: cattivo, malvagio, corrotto; tristo.
nā́umachy, S.: naumachia, *f.*
nā́u-şęąte, TR.: nauseare, disgustare; recere; odiare. **-şeous**, ADJ.: nauseoso, disgustoso. **-şeously**, ADV.: in modo nauseoso. **-şeousness**, S.: nauseamento; nauseare, *m.*; abbominazione, *f.*
nā́utic, **-al**, ADJ.: nautico, di nave.
nā́utilus, S.: nautilo, *m.* (mollusco).
nā́val, ADJ.: navale; di marina: — *officer*, ufficiale della marina, *m.*
nā́ve, S.: mozzo (d'una ruota), *m.*; navata (d' una chiesa), *f.*
nā́vel, S.: bellico, ombilico; mezzo, *m.* **-string**, S.: tralcio, *m.* **-wǫrt**, S.: (*bot.*) bellico di venere, *m.*
nắvi-gable, ADJ.: navigabile. **-gąte**, (IN)TR.: navigare, veleggiare. **-gā́ţiǫn**, S.: navigazione, *f.*, navigare, *m.*, nautica, *f.* **-gątǫr**, S.: navigatore; marinaro, marinaio, *m.*
nā́vy, S.: armata navale, flotta, *f.* **-board**, S.: consiglio della marina, *m.* **-office**, S.: uffizio della marina. **-yard**, S.: arsenale di marina, *m.*
nā́y, ADV.: no; non solo; di più, inoltre. **nay**, S.: (*word*) negativa, *f.*, rifuto, *m.*, ripulsa, *f.*
Nazarḗne, ADJ.: nazzareno.
nē̆af, S.: pugno, *m.*
nē̆al, TR.: ricuocere, temperare.
nē̆ap, ADJ.: decrescente; basso: —*-tide*, S.: marea bassa, *f.*
nē̆ar, PREP., ADJ., ADV.: presso; appresso; vicino a, prossimo a, intimo, stretto; pressochè, poco meno, quasi: *very* —, vicinissimo, vicin vicino, pressochè; — *Rome*, vicino a Roma; — *at hand*, a mano, in pronto; *draw* —, approssimare, accostare; avvicinarsi; — *relation*, stretto parente; *they were* — *coming to blows*, poco mancò non venissero alle mani. **-ly**, ADV.: da vicino, presso; meschinamente, … …ssimità, pro… …ela, *f.* …ther, …

nē̆at-herd, S.: boare, vaccaio, bifolco, *m.* **-house**, S.: stalla da buoi, *f.*
nē̆at-ly, ADV.: pulitamente, elegantemente. **-ness**, S.: pulitezza, nettezza, eleganza, *f.*
nĕb, S.: becco, *m.*; punta, *f.*
nĕbụla, S.: nebula; macchia sull' occhio, *f.* **-ųlŏsity**, S.: nuvolosità, *f.* **-ųlous**, ADJ.: nebuloso, nuvoloso, nebbioso.
nĕcessą-rieş, S. PL.: necessario, bisognevole, *m.* **-rily**, ADV.: necessariamente. **-riness**, S.: esser necessario, *m.*; necessità, *f.* **-ry**, ADJ.: necessario; indispensabile; S.: guardaroba, *f.*; luogo comune, *m.* **-ry-house**, S.: necessario, agiamento, *m.*
nęcĕssi-tąte, TR.: necessitare, costringere; violentare, sforzare. **-tā́ţiǫn**, S.: urgenza, forza, *f.*, costringimento, *m.* **-tous**, ADJ.: necessitoso, bisognoso; indigente. **-tousness**, **-tụde**, S.: necessità, indigenza, *f.* **-ty**, S.: necessità; forza, violenza; povertà, *f.*: *of* —, necessariamente.
nĕck, S.: collo, *m.*: — *of land*, braccio di terra fra due mari, *m.*; — *of mutton*, collo di castrato, *m.*; — *of a violin*, manico d' un violino, *m.*; *take one about the* —, abbracciare alcuno. **-band**, S.: collare (d' una camicia), *m.* **-beef**, S.: grossa carne di manzo, *f.* **-cloth**, S.: cravatta, *f.*; fazzoletto da collo, *m.* **-ęrchief**, S.: fazzoletto da collo, *m.* **-lace**, S.: collana, *f.*; vezzo, *m.* **-piece**, S.: gorgiera, *f.* **-tie**, S.: cravatta, *f.* **-weed**, S.: canapa, *f.*
nĕc-rǫlogue, S.: necrologo, *m.* **-rŏlǫgy**, S.: necrologia, *f.*
nĕcrǫ-mancęr, S.: negromante, *m.*, negromantessa, *f.* **-mancy**, S.: negromanzia, *f.* **-măntic**, ADJ.: necromantico.
nĕc-tąr, S.: nettare, *m.* **-tąred**, ADJ.: misto con nettare. **-tā́ręous**, **-tąrine** 1, ADJ.: nettario, dolce. **-tarine** 2, S.: sorta di susina dolce, *f.*
nē̆ed 1, S.: bisogno, *m.*, necessità; esigenza, *f.*: *if* — *be*, se sarà necessario, al bisogno; *in* — *of*, necessitoso di; *stand in* — *of*, avere bisogno di; *at* —, all' uopo.
need 2, TR.: avere bisogno; mancare; INTR.: esser necessario; *you* — *but tell him*, ditegli solamente; *it* —*s not*, non è necessario. **-ęr**, S.: che ha bisogno; che manca. **-fụl**, ADJ.: necessario; requisito. **-fụlly**, ADV.: necessariamente. **-fụlness**, S.: necessità, *f.*; bisogno, *m.* **-ily**, ADV.: in indigenza; poveramente. **-iness**, …: indigenza, povertà; miseria, *f.*
…le, S.: ago, *m.*; aguglia, *f.*: *large* …ne, *m.*; *sewing* —, ago da cucire,

prē-script, ADJ.: prescritto; S.: prescritto, comando, *m.* **-cription**, S.: prescrizione; ordinazione, *f.*
prěsence, S.: presenza; aria, *f.*, aspetto, *m.*: — *of mind*, prontezza di spirito, *f.* **-chamber**, **-room**, S.: camera di presenza, *f.*
presensātion, **-sěnsion**†, S.: presentimento, *m.*
prěsent 1, ADJ.: presente; attento: — *month*, corrente mese; — *tense*, tempo presente, *m.*; *at* —, al presente, presentemente. **present** 2, S.: presente, dono, regalo, *m.* **presěnt** 3, TR.: presentare, far un presente, regalare a; offerire; conferire: — *arms*, presentare le armi; — *my compliments to*, presentate i miei complimenti a. **presěnt-able**, ADJ.: che può presentarsi. **-āneous**, ADJ.: presentaneo. **-ātion**, S.: presentazione, *f.* **-ēe**, S.: che è presentato a un beneficio. **presěnt-er**, S.: presentatore, presentante, *m.*
presěn-tial, ADJ.: presenziale; presente. **-tiálity**, S.: presenza reale, *f.* **-tially**, ADV.: presenzialmente.
presěntiment, S.: presentimento, *m.*
prěsently, ADV.: presentemente, al presente.
presěntment, S.: rappresentamento, *m.*; accusa, denunzia, *f.*
prěsentness, S.: acutezza d' ingegno, prontezza di spirito, *f.*
pre-servātion, S.: preservazione, *f.* **-sěrvative**, S.: preservativo, antidoto, *m.* **-sěrve** 1, S.: confettura, conserva, *f.*, confetti, *m. pl.* **-serve** 2, TR.: preservare, conservare; confettare. **-sěrver**, S.: conservatore, protettore, *m.* **-sěrvers**, S. PL.: occhiali di conserva, *m. pl.* **-sěrving**, S.: preservamento; preservare; confettare, *m.*
preside, INTR.: presedere; aver la direzione; soprantendere.
prěsiden-cy, S.: presidenza, soprantendenza, *f.* **-t**, S.: presidente; capo, *m.*: — *of a college*, rettore d' un collegio, *m.* **-tship**, S.: uffizio di presidente, *m.*
presidial, ADJ.: di presidio, di guernigione.
pre-significātion, S.: previa significazione, *f.* **-signify**, TR.: dimostrare previamente.
prěss 1, S.: torchio, torcolo; strettoia, *m.*; calca, folla; moltitudine, *f.*: — *for clothes*, guardaroba, *f.*; *my book is in the* —, il mio libro è sotto il torchio. **press** 2, TR.: premere, spremere, stringere; sollecitare, affrettare; importunare; INTR.: affrettarsi; mettere piede; ricercare con premura: — *grapes*, pigiar le uve; — *soldiers*, levar soldati per forza; — *on*, spingersi, ficcarsi avanti, affrettarsi; — *upon*, presentarsi, esporsi; — *out the juice*, spremere il sugo; — *each other's hands*, stringersi la mano. **-bed**, S.: letto in forma di guardaroba, *m.* **-er**, S.: torcoliere, *m.* **-gang**, S.: truppa da forzare marinari, *f.* **-ing**, ADJ.: urgente; importuno; S.: pressione; istanza, *f.* **-ingly**, ADV.: istantemente, violentemente. **-ion** *-shun*, S.: pressione, impressione, compressione, *f.* **-man**, S.: stampatore (di libri), torcoliere, *m.* **-money**, S.: danaro d' arrolamento, *m.* **-ure** *-shur*, S.: pressura; pressione, *f.*: *high* (*low*) —, alta (bassa) pressione. **-work**, S.: torchio, *m.*; tiratura, *f.*
prěst, ADJ.: presto, pronto, destro.
prestātion, S.: prestazione, *f.*
prěstige, S.: prestigio, *m.*
prěsto, ADV.: presto, prontamente.
pre-sūmably, ADV.: in modo presumabile, senza esaminare. **-sūme**, TR.: presumere; presupporre. **-sūmer**, S.: presuntuoso, *m.* **-sūmption**, S.: presunzione, arroganza, *f.* **-sūmptive**, ADJ.: presuntivo, presupposto. **-sūmptuous**, ADJ.: presuntuoso, arrogante. **-sūmptuously**, ADV.: presuntuosamente. **-sūmptuousness**, S: presuntuosità, *f.*
presuppō-se, TR.: presupporre, supporre. **-sition**, S.: presupposizione, *f.*
presurmise, S.: previo sospetto, *m.*
pre-těnce, S.: pretenzione, *f.*; pretesto; argomento falso, *m.*; apparenza, *f.* **-těnd**, (IN)TR.: pretendere; imaginarsi, piccarsi; fingere, far le viste: — *business*, far l' affaccendato. **-těnder**, S.: pretenditore, *m.*, -trice, *f.*; pretendente, *m.*, *f.* **-těndingly**, ADV.: presuntuosamente. **-těnsion**, S.: pretensione, *f.*; pretesto, *m.*
prěter-ite, ADJ.: preterito, passato: — *tense*, preterito, *m.* **-itness**, **-ition**, S.: omissione, *f.*
preterlāpsed, ADJ.: passato, scorso.
preter-mission, S.: pretermissione, omissione, *f.* **-mit**, TR.: pretermettere, lasciare, tralasciare, omettere.
preternātural, ADJ.: soprannaturale. **-ly**, ADV.: in modo soprannaturale. **-ness**, S.: modo soprannaturale, *m.*
prētext, S.: pretesto, colore, *m.*
prē-tor, S.: pretore, *m.* **-tōrial**, **-tōrian**, ADJ.: pretorio, di pretore. **-torship**, S.: pretoria, *f.*
prět-tily *prit-*, ADV.: d' una maniera piacevole, acconciamente. **-tiness**, S.: bellezza, leggiadria, *f.* **-ty** 1, ADJ.: bello, bellino, leggiadro, vago, grazioso: *rather* —, piuttosto bello, belluccio; — *trick*, bel tiro. **-ty** 2, ADV.: assai, così così; quasi.

ADJ.: alquanto nuovo. **-ly**, ADJ.: nuovamente, di fresco. **-ness**, S.: cosa nuova; novità, *f.*

news, S.: nuova, notizia (fresca), *f.*; avviso, *m.*: *what —?* che si dice di nuovo? **-monger**, S.: propagatore di nuove, *m.* **-paper**, S.: gazzetta, *f.* **-writer**, S.: novellista, gazzettiere, *m.* **-y**, ADJ.: (*coll.*) pieno di nuove.

new-year, S.: nuovo anno, *m.*; ADJ.: dal nuovo anno: *I wish you a happy —*, buon capo d' anno! **-year's day**, S.: capo d' anno, *m.* **-year's gift**, S.: strenna, *f.*

newt, S.: ramarro, *m.*

next 1, ADJ.: prossimo, contiguo: *the — day*, il giorno seguente. **next** 2, ADV.: dopo; in secondo luogo: (*the*) *— day*, il dì susseguente, l' indomani; *— chapter*, seguente capitolo; *— house*, casa contigua, prima porta; *— to*, dopo ciò, dopo di che.

nib, S.: becco, *m.*, becca (degli uccelli); punta, *f.* **-bed**, ADJ.: che ha un becco.

nib-ble, TR.: mordere; riprendere; INTR.: morsecchiare. **-bler**, S.: morditore; riprensore, *m.* **-blings**, S. PL.: morsecchiature, *f. pl.*

nice, ADJ.: raffinato, delicato, delizioso; esatto, accurato, studiato; difficile, scrupoloso; scimunito, sciocco: *— girl*, fanciulla vaga (vezzosa, simpatica). **-ly**, ADV.: delicatamente; esattamente; difficilmente. **-ness**, S.: delicatezza, delizia; esattezza, accuratezza; finezza, *f.* **-ties**, S. PL.: delizie, delicatezze, *f. pl.* **-ty**, S.: accuratezza; finezza; gentilezza, vezzosità; ghiottornia, cosa ghiotta, *f.*

niche, S.: nicchia; alcova, *f.*

nick 1, S.: tempo comodo, *m.*; opportunità, intaccatura, *f.*, taglio, *m.*: *old —*, diavolo, *m.*; *in the very — of time*, opportunamente, appunto. **nick** 2, TR.: toccare leggermente; intaccare; incontrare: *— the time*, incontrare il tempo.

nickel, S.: nichel, *m.*; ADJ.: di nichel. **-ed**, ADJ.: nichelato.

nickname 1, S.: soprannome, *m.* **nickname** 2, TR.: dare un soprannome.

nic-tate, TR.: ammiccare. **-tation**, S.: ammiccare, cenno cogli occhi, *m.*

nide†, S.: nidiata; covata, *f.*

nidifi-cate, TR.: nidificare, fare nido. **-cation**, S.: nidificare, fare nido, *m.*

[illegible]**ng†**, ADJ.: basso, vile, abbietto.

[illegible]**te**, TR.: nidificare. **-lation**, S.: [illegible]imaner nel nido, *m.*

[illegible]ote, *f.*

[illegible] taccagno, spilorcio, *m.*

[illegible]accagno, sordido, ava-

[illegible]ristringere; limi-

[illegible] taccagno, al-

quanto avaro. **-liness**, S.: spilorceria, avarizia, sordidezza, *f.* **-ly**, ADJ.: spilorcio, avaro, sordido; ADV.: avaramente, sordidamente; grettamente. **-ness**, S.: avarizia; parsimonia, *f.*

nigger, S.: negro, *m.*, negra, *f.*

nig-gle, INTR.: giullare, beffare. **-gler**, S.: buffone, zanni, *m.*

nigh, ADJ., PREP.: vicino, contiguo; accosto; PREP., ADV.: qui vicino, qui accanto: *well —*, quasi, pressochè; *draw —*, avvicinarsi; *write —*, scrivere stretto. **-ly**, ADV.: presso a poco. **-ness**, S.: vicinità; prossimità, contiguità, *f.*

night, S.: notte; sera, serata, *f.*: *at* (*by*) *—*, nottetempo, di notte tempo; *last —*, iersera, la notte scorsa; *— falls*, annotta; *in the dead of —*, a notte inoltrata, nel silenzio della notte. **-brawler**, S.: perturbatore della quiete, *m.* **-cap**, S.: berretta da notte, *f.* **-dew**, S.: sereno, *m.*; rugiada, *f.* **-dress**, S.: cuffia da notte, *f.*; vestimenti da notte, *m. pl.* **-ed**, ADJ.: fosco, nuvoloso, bruno. **-fall**, S.: crepuscolo, imbrunire, *m.* **-faring**, ADJ.: viaggiante di notte tempo. **-fire**, S.: fuoco, fatuo, *m.* **-fly**, S.: farfalla notturna, *f.* **-foundered**, ADJ.: sviato di notte tempo. **-gown**, S.: veste da camera, zimarra, *f.* **-hag**, S.: maga notturna *f.* **-hawk**, S.: allocco, *m.* (uccello). **-ingale**, S.: rusignuolo, usignuolo, *m.*, filomela, *f.* **-ly**, ADJ.: notturno, di notte; ADV.: di notte tempo, ogni notte. **-man**, S.: vuotacesso, *m.* **-mare**, S.: incubo, fantasima, *m.* **-piece**, S.: (*paint.*) pittura di notte, *f.* **-rail**, S.: capuccio, *m.*, mantellina, *f.* **-raven**, S.: gufaccio, *m.* (uccello). **-revelling**, S. PL.: stravizzi notturni, divertimenti notturni, *m. pl.* **-robber**, S.: ladrone di notte, *m.* **-rule**, S.: tumulto notturno, *m.* **-shade**, S.: (*bot.*) solano, *m.* **-shining**, ADJ.: lucente di notte. **-studies**, S. PL.: veglie, *f. pl.* **-walker**, S.: nottivago, nottolone, *m.* **-watch**, S.: guardia notturna, *f.*

nigrescent, ADJ.: nereggiante, bruno.

nigrification, S.: nereggiamento, *m.*, anneritura, *f.*

nihil-ism, S.: nichilismo, *m.* **-ist**, S.: nichilista, *m.*

nihil-ity, S.: nulla, *m.*

nill 1, S.: scintille, *f. pl.* **nill†** 2, INTR.: non volere: *will he — he*, buon grado, mal grado.

nim-ble, ADJ.: agile; lesto, leggiero. **-bleness**, S.: agilità; leggierezza; sveltezza, *f.* **-ble-witted**, ADJ.: pronto d' ingegno. **-bly**, ADV.: agilmente; leggiermente, prestamente.

nincompoop, S.: sciocco, balordo, *m.*

sovranità, *f.* **-pally**, ADV.: principalmente; soprattutto. **-palness**, S.: principale; essenziale, *m.* **-pate**, S.: principato, *m.*

principiation†, S.: analisi, *f.*

principle 1, S.: principio, fondamento; motivo, *m.*, causa, *f.*: *sound* —*s*, sani (sodi) principi; *from a* — *of*, per un principio di. **principle** 2, TR.: dare i principi; istruire. **-d**, ADJ.: che ha dei principi.

prin-cock† **-cox**†, S.: saccentone, saccentino, *m.*

prink, TR.: ornare; abbellire; INTR.: ornarsi, adornarsi.

print 1, S.: impressione; stampa, *f.*; carattere, *m.*, lettera, *f.*: *in* —, stampato; *out of* —, esaurito, che non si trova più a comprare; *come out in* —, venire alla luce (de' libri); *beautiful* —, bella impressione. **print** 2, TR.: imprimere; stampare. **-er**, S.: stampatore, tipografo, *m.* **-ing**, S.: impressione; stampa, *f.* **-ing-house**, **-ing-office**, S.: stamperia, *f.* **-ing-paper**, S.: carta da stampa, *f.*, fioretto, *m.* **-ing-press**, S.: torchio (da stampare), *m.* **-less**, ADJ.: senza impressione. **-shop**, S.: bottega, *f.*

prior 1, ADJ.: primo, anteriore, precedente. **prior** 2, S.: priore; superiore, *m.* **-ate**, S.: priorato, *m.* **-ess**, S.: priora; superiora, *f.* **priŏr-ity**, S.: priorità; precedenza, *f.* **-ship**, S.: dignità di priore, *f.*, priorato, *m.* **-y**, S.: priorato, *m.*

prism, S.: prisma, *m.* **-ătic(al)**, ADJ.: prismatico. **-ătically**, ADV.: in modo prismatico.

prison 1, S.: prigione, *f.*, carcere, *m.*: *keeper of a* —, carceriere, *m.* **prison** 2, TR.: imprigionare, incarcerare. **-base**, S.: barriera, *f.* (giuoco). **-er**, S.: prigioniere, prigionero; prigione, *m.*: *take* —, far prigione (prigioniere), arrestare; — *at the bar*, accusato, reo, *m.* **-house**, S.: prigione, *f.*, carcere, *m.* **-ment**, S.: prigionia, incarcerazione, *f.*

pristine, ADJ.: pristino, prisco; originale.

prithee, ti prego, di grazia.

prittle-prattle, S.: cicaleria, *f.*

pri-vacy, S.: segretezza; retiratezza, solitudine, *f.* **-vădo**†, S.: amico intimo, confidente, *m.* **-vate**, ADJ.: privato, particolare; segreto, nascosto: *in* —, privatamente; — *interview*, abboccamento segreto, *m.*; — *man*, uomo privato, *m.*; — *stairs*, scala segreta, *f.*

privateer 1, S.: corsale, *m.* **privateer** 2, INTR.: corseggiare.

privately, ADV.: privatamente, particolarmente; segretamente. **-ness**, S.: ritiratezza, oscurità, *f.*

privation, S.: privazione; mancanza, *f.*

privative, ADJ.: privativo, esclusivo; negativo. **-ly**, ADV.: privativamente. **-ness**, S.: mancanza; privazione, *f.*

privet, S.: rovistico, *m.* (arbore).

privilege 1, S.: privilegio, *m.*, prerogativa, *f.*, vantaggio, *m.* **privilege** 2, TR.: privilegiare; esentare, esimere.

pri-vily, ADV.: privatamente; in segreto. **-vity**, S.: partecipazione; confidenza; notizia, *f.* **-vy** 1, ADJ.: privato, particolare; famigliare; segreto; nascosto: — *council*, consiglio privato, *m.*; — *purse*, borsa privata, *f.* **-vy** 2, S.: privato, cesso, *m.*

priz-e 1, S.: prezzo; premio, *m.*; presa, *f.* **-e** 2, TR.: apprezzare, stimare, valutare. **-e-fighter**, S.: pugilato (di mestiere), *m.* **-e-fighting**, S.: pugilato, *m.* **-e-money**, S.: preda, *f.* **-er**, S.: prezzatore, stimatore, *m.* **-ing**, S.: stimazione, stima; valuta, *f.*

prŏ, PREP.: per: — *and con*, pro e contra.

probability, S.: probabilità, verisimilitudine, *f.*

prŏba-ble, ADJ.: probabile, verisimile. **-bly**, ADV.: probabilmente, verisimilmente.

prŏbate, S.: (*jur.*) verificazione (d'un testamento), *f.*

probation, S.: prova, *f.*; esperimento, *m.* **-al**, **-ary**, ADJ.: per prova. **-er**, S.: scolare che fa la sua prova; novizio, *m.* **-ership**, S.: noviziato, *m.*

prŏba-tive, **-tory**, ADJ.: provativo, per prova.

prŏbe 1, S.: (*surg.*) tenta, *f.* **probe** 2, TR.: tentare, toccare colla tenta. **-scissors**, S. PL.: forbici di chirurgo, *f. pl.*

prŏbity, S.: probità, sincerità; integrità, *f.*

prŏblem, S.: problema, *m.*; proposta, proposizione, *f.* **-ătic(al)**, ADJ.: problematico, incerto. **-ătically**, ADV.: in modo problematico.

proboscis, S.: proboscide; tromba (dell' elefante), *f.*

pro-cacious, ADJ.: procace; insolente, protervo. **-căcity**, S.: insolenza; petulanza; arroganza, *f.*

procedure, S.: procedimento; progresso, *m.*

proceed 1, S.: prodotto, guadagno, *m.* **proceed** 2, INTR.: procedere, derivare; provenire; comportarsi; andare avanti. **-er**, S.: che procede. **-ing**, S.: procedimento, procedere; atto; processo verbale, *m.*: *institute* —*s*, cominciare una lite; *the* —*s of the legislature*, gli atti del corpo legislativo.

prŏcess, S.: processo; progresso, *m.*: — *of time*, processo di tempo, *m.*; — *verbal*, processo informativo, *m.*

to. **-sĕnsically**, ADV.: in modo assurdo, spropositatamente. **-sĕnsicalness**, S.: assurdità, sciocchezza, stupidezza, *f.*
non-sŏlvent, ADJ.: insolvente.
nŏnsuit 1, S.: (*jur.*) desistimento di lite, *m* **-suit** 2, TR.: (*jur.*) condannare per desistimento di lite.
nŏodle, S.: sciocco, gonzo, *m.*; sorta di maccheroni, *m. pl.*
nòok, S.: angolo, cantone; ridotto, *m.*
nōon, S.: mezzodì, mezzo giorno, *m.* **-day** 1, S.: mezzodì, mezzo giorno, *m.*: *at* —, sul mezzodì. **-day** 2, ADJ.: di mezzodì; meridionale. **-ing**, S.: meriggiana, *f.*; tempo di mezzodì, *m.* **-tide** = *noonday*.
nōose 1, S.: nodo scorsoio; legame; laccio; inganno, *m.*: — *of matrimony*, nodo matrimoniale, *m.* **nōose** 2, TR.: legare, allacciare.
nôr, CONJ.: nè, nè più: *neither* . . . *nor*, nè . . . nè.
nôrmal, ADJ.: normale.
nôrth 1, S.: nord, norte, *m.*; settentrione, *m.*, tramontana, *f.* **north** 2, ADJ.: settentrionale. **-ĕast**, S.: nordest, *m.*; greco volturno, *m.* (vento). **-erly**, **-ern**, ADJ.: settentrionale. **-pole**, S.: polo artico, polo settentrionale, *m.* **-star**, S.: stella polare, *f.* **-ward**, **-wards**, ADV.: verso settentrione. **-wĕst**, S.: nordovest, *m.*; quarta di maestro, *f.* **-wind**, S.: aquilone, vento di tramontana, *m.*
nōse 1, S.: naso; sentore, *m.*: *big* (*large*) —, nasone, nasaccio, *m.*; *little* —, nasetto, *m.*; *flat* —, naso schiacciato; *turn up one's* —, arricciare il naso; *speak through the* —, parlare nel naso; *lead one by the* —, menar altrui pel naso; *Roman* —, naso aquilino. **nose** 2, TR.: sentire, fiutare; pavoneggiarsi; bravare. **-band**, S.: musoliera, *f.* **-bleed**, S.: millefoglie, *f.* (pianta). **-gay**, S.: mazzolino di fiori, *m.* **-less**, ADJ.: senza naso.
nosŏlogy, S.: nosologia, *f.*
nŏstril, S.: narice, nare, *f.*
nŏstrum, S.: rimedio finto, *m.*; medicina brevettata, *f.*
nŏt, ADV.: non, no: — *at all*, in niun modo, niente affatto; — *in the least*, niente affatto, per nulla.
nō-table, ADJ.: notabile, considerabile, insigne. **-tableness**, S.: notabilità, singolarità, *f.* **-tably**, ADV.: notabilmente. **-tārial**, ADJ.: notariale, autenticato da un notaio. **-tary**, S.: notaio, notaro, *m.* **-tātion**, S.: notare, *m.*; significazione, *f.*
nŏtch 1, S.: tacca; intaccatura, *f.* **notch** 2, TR.: intaccare, fare tacca. **-ing**, S.: tacca, *f.*
[illegible]**e** 1, S.: nota, annotazione; osserva[illegible]: distinzione, *f.*; merito, *m.*, importanza, *f.*; biglietto, *m.*, letterina, *f.*: *take* —*s*, far degli appunti; *promissory* —, pagherò; *foot*-—, nota a piè di pagina; *bank* —, biglietto di banco, banconota; — *of interrogation*, punto interrogativo, *m.* **-e** 2, TR.: notare; osservare, considerare; attendere. **-e-book**, S.: libretto d' annotazioni, *m.* **-ed**, ADJ.: notato; famoso, rinomato, eminente, illustre. **-edness**, S.: cospicuità, *f.* **-er**, S.: annotatore, osservatore, *m.*
nŏthing, S.: niente, nulla, *m.*; nullità, *f.*: *good for* —, buono a niente; *next to* —, quasi niente; — *venture*, — *have*, chi non risica non rosica; *make* — *of one*, disprezzare alcuno. **-ness**, S.: nichilità, *f.*, nulla, *m.*; bassezza, *f.*
nō-tice, S.: notizia, *f.*, avviso, *m.*; osservazione; attenzione, *f.*: *give* —, dar notizia, avvisare; *take* — *of a thing*, far attenzione a qualche cosa. **-tificātion**, S.: notificamento, notificare, *m.* **-tify**, TR.: notificare, significare. **-tion**, S.: nozione; idea, *f.*, pensiero, *m.*, opinione, *f.* **-tional**, ADJ.: immaginario, ideale. **-tionălity**, S.: opinione chimerica, *f.* **-tionally**, ADV.: per idea, mentalmente. **-toriety**, S.: notorietà; pubblicità, *f.* **-tōrious**, ADJ.: notorio, pubblico. **-tōriously**, ADV.: notoriamente, pubblicamente, evidentemente. **-tōriousness**, S.: fama pubblica; evidenza, *f.*
Nŏtus, S.: noto, *m.* (vento).
notwithstănding, CONJ.: non ostante, sebbene.
nought *nât*, S.: niente, nulla, *m.*: *set at* —, disprezzare, non far conto, sdegnare.
nŏun, S.: nome, *m.*
nŏurish, TR.: nutrire, alimentare; incoraggiare. **-able**, ADJ.: nutribile. **-er**, S.: nutritore, *m.* **-ing**, ADJ.: nutritivo. **-ment**, S.: nutrimento, *m.*, nutritura, *f.*, alimento, *m.*
no-vātion †, S.: innovazione; novità, *f.* **-vātor** †, S.: innovatore, novatore, *m.*
nŏvel 1, ADJ.: novello, nuovo. **novel** 2, S.: romanzo, *m.*, novella, narrazione favolosa, *f.*: — *writer*, romanziere, *m. f.*; *tell* --*s*, novellare. **-ist**, S.: innovatore, novellatore; novellista, *m.*; romanziere, *m.*, *f.* **-ize**, TR.: innovare. **-ty**, S.: novità; cosa nuova, *f.*
Novĕmber, S.: novembre, *m.*
nŏv-enary, S.: nove, *m.* **-ĕnnial**, ADJ.: di novennio.
novĕrcal, ADJ.: di noverca.
nŏv-ice, S.: novizio, *m.*; novizia, *f.* **-iceship**, **-iciate**, S.: noviziato, *m.*
nŏvity †, S.: novità, cosa nuova, *f.*
nŏw 1, ADV.: al presente, adesso, ora; attualmente: *just* —, testè, pur ora, in questo punto; *till* —, fin adesso; *before* —,

profū-se, ADJ.: profuso; esuberante, eccessivo; prodigo. **-sely**, ADV.: profusamente; prodigamente. **-seness**, **-sion**, S.: profusione; prodigalità; esuberanza, *f.*

prŏg 1, S.: vettovaglia, *f.*; provvisioni, *f. pl.* **prog** 2, INTR.: ingegnarsi, affaticarsi; rubare, involare.

progĕn-erate, TR.: generare; propagare. **-erātion**, S.: generazione; propagazione, *f.* **-itor**, S.: progenitore, *m.* **-iture**, **prŏgen-y**, S.: progenie, stirpe, schiatta, *f.*

prognŏstic 1, ADJ.: che pronostica. **prognostic** 2, S.: pronostico, presagio, *m.* **-ate**, TR.: pronosticare, predire. **-ātion**, S.: pronosticamento, pronostico, *m.* **-ator**, S.: pronosticatore, indovino, *m.*

prŏgram(me), S.: programma, avviso, *m.*

progrĕss 1, INTR.: progredire, andar innanzi. **prŏ-gress** 2, S.: progresso, processo; viaggio, *m.*: *in* —, di corso, avviato. **-grĕssion**, S.: progressione, *f.*; processo, *m.* **-grĕssional**, **-grĕssive**, ADJ.: progressivo. **-grĕssively**, ADV.: progressivamente. **-grĕssiveness**, S.: progresso, avanzamento, *m.*

prohib-it, TR.: proibire, impedire, vietare. **-iter**, S.: proibitore, vietatore, *m.* **-ition**, S.: proibizione, *f.*, proibire, *m.*; difesa, *f.* **-itionist**, S.: proibizionista, *m.* **-itive**, **-itory**, ADJ.: proibitivo, proibente.

prŏin †, TR.: rimondare; diramare.

pro-jĕct 1, TR.: disegnare; progettare; macchinare; INTR.: proporsi: (*rail.*) *—ed line*, strada ferrata progettata, *f.* **prŏject** 2, S.: disegno, progetto; divisamento; soggetto, *m.*: *form a* —, far progetto. **-jĕctile**, S.: proietto, *m.* **-jĕcting**, ADJ.: inventivo. **-jĕction**, **-jĕctment**, S.: proiezione, proiettura, *f.*; disegno, *m.* **-jĕctor**, S.: disegnatore, inventore, *m.* **-jĕcture**, S.: proiettura, *f.*; sporto, *m.*

prolegŏmena, S.: prolegomeni, *m. pl.*

prolĕp-sis, S.: prolepsi, *f.* **-tic(al)**, ADJ.: precedente, antecedente.

proletārian, ADJ.: proletario, plebeo; abbietto.

prolif-ic(al), ADJ.: prolifico, fecondo. **-ically**, ADV.: fecondamente. **-icātion**, S.: generazione, *f.* **-icness**, S.: fecondità, *f.*

prolix, ADJ.: prolisso, diffuso; tedioso. **-ity**, S.: prolissità; lunghezza, *f.* **-ly**, ADV.: prolissamente, lungamente, distesamente. **-ness** = *-ity*.

prolocūtor, S.: presidente (d'un' assemblea), *m.* **-ship**, S.: uffizio di presidente, *m.*

prŏ-loguize, **-logue** 1, (IN)TR.: prologare, prologizzare. **-logue** 2, S.: prologo, proemio, preambolo, *m.*

prolŏn-g, TR.: prolungare; allungare; differire. **-gātion**, **-ging**, S.: prolungamento; indugio, *m.*

prolūsion, S.: prolusione, *f.*; preludio, *m.*

promenāde 1, S.: spasseggiata, *f.* **promenade** 2, INTR.: spasseggiare.

prŏminen-ce, **-cy**, S.: prominenza, *f.*; risalto, *m.* **-t**, ADJ.: prominente; sporgente. **-tly**, ADV.: in modo prominente.

promiscuous, ADJ.: promiscuo, confuso. **-ly**, ADV.: promiscuamente, confusamente. **-ness**, S.: promiscuità; confusione, *f.*

prŏmis-e 1, S.: promessa; speranza, *f.*: *keep one's* —, tener (attener) la promessa; *breach of* —, violazione della promessa. **-e** 2, TR.: promettere, far sperare; affermare: — *wonders*, promettere mari e monti; — *one's self*, ripromettersi, lusingarsi, sperare. **-e-breach**, S.: mancanza di promessa, *f.* **-e-breaker**, S.: mancatore, violatore della promessa, *m.* **-er**, S.: promettitore, promettente, *m.* **-ing**, ADJ.: di buona indole; buono, bello; S.: promessa, *f.*: *very* —, che promette molto. **-sorily**, ADV.: per via di promessa, in modo promissorio. **-sory**, ADJ.: promissorio, di promessa.

prŏmontory, S.: promontorio, *m.*

pro-mōte, TR.: promuovere; stendere; far fiorire; conferire un grado. **-mōter**, S.: promotore; protettore, *m.* **-mōtion**, S.: promovimento; avanzamento; aggrandimento, *m.*; esaltazione, *f.* **-mōve** †, TR.: promuovere, avanzare; favorire

prŏmpt 1, ADJ.: pronto, lesto; apparecchiato; contante. **prompt** 2, TR.: suggerire, insinuare; eccitare. **-er**, S.: suggeritore, ammonitore, *m.* **-ing**, S.: suggestione, *f.* **-itude**, **-ness**, S.: prontezza, lestezza, speditezza, *f.* **-ly**, ADV.: prontamente, lestamente, prestamente. **-uary**, S.: magazzino, *m.*; dispensa, *f.*

promŭl-gate, TR.: promulgare, pubblicare. **-gātion**, S.: promulgazione, *f.* **-gator** *prō-*, S.: promulgatore, *m.* **-ge** = *promulgate*. **-ger** = *promulgator*.

prōne, ADJ.: prono, inclinato, dedito; disposto: *be* — *to*, esser dedito (inclinato) a. **-ness**, S.: propensione; inclinazione, *f.*

prŏng, S.: forchetta, forca, *f.*

pronŏminal, ADJ.: pronominale, di pronome.

prō'noun, S.: pronome, *m.*

pro-nounce, TR.: pronunziare; dichiarare. **-nounceable**, ADJ.: che può esser pronunziato. **-nouncer**, S.: pronunziatore, *m.* **-nouncing**, **-nunciātion**, S.: pronunzia, *f.*; pronunziare, *m.*: — *dictionary*, dizionario di pronunzia. **-nunciative**, ADJ.: pronunziativo; positivo.

prōof 1, ADJ.: a tutta prova; superiore. **proof** 2, S.: prova, *f.*, esperimento, *m.*; testimonianza, *f.*; segno, *m.*: *be* — *against*,

ADJ.: sciocco, balordo, goffo. **-ishness**, S.: stupidezza; imbecillità, *f.*

ōak, S.: quercia, querce, *f.*: *young* —, querciuola, *f.* **-apple**, S.: galla, *f.* **-en**, ADJ.: di quercia; fatto di quercia. **-grove**, S.: querceto, *m.* **-ling**, S.: querciuola, *f.*

ōakum, S.: stoppa, *f.*, corde sfilate, *f. pl.*

ōar 1, S.: remo, *m.* **oar** 2, TR.: remare; vogare; INTR.: andare a remi. **-handle**, S.: manico di remo, *m.* **-y**, ADJ.: fatto a foggia di remo.

ōasis, S.: oasi, *f.*

ōat-cake, S.: focaccia di vena, *f.* **-en**, ADJ.: di vena.

ōath, S.: giuramento, giurare, *m.*: *false* —, spergiuro, *m.*; *take one's* —, pigliare giuramento; *administer an — to, put on his* —, deferire il giuramento a. **-breaking**, S.: pergiuro, spergiuro, *m.*

ōat-meal, S.: farina di vena; avena móndata, *f.*, panico, *m.* **-s**, S. PL.: avena, vena, *f.*

obāmbulate†, INTR.: spasseggiare.

ŏb-duracy, S.: durezza di cuore, *f.*, induramento, *m.* **-durate**, ADJ.: indurito, duro; impenitente. **-durate**, TR.: indurire, rendere duro. **-durately**, ADV.: duramente, inflessibilmente. **-durateness**, **-durātion**, S.: induramento, *m.*, ostinazione, *f.* **-dūred**, ADJ.: indurito, inflessibile. **-dūredness**, S.: induramento, *m.*

obēdien-ce, S.: ubbidienza, *f.* **-t**, ADJ.: ubbidiente; sommesso. **-tly**, ADV.: ubbidientemente.

obēisance, S.: riverenza, *f.*; saluto, *m.*

ŏbelisk, S.: obelisco, *m.*; aguglia, *f.*

obĕqui-tate†, INTR.: cavalcare. **-tātion**†, S.: cavalcamento, *m.*

obēs-e, ADJ.: grasso, paffuto. **-eness**, **-ity**, S.: grassezza estrema, *f.*

obēy, TR.: obbedire, ubbidire: *he must be —ed*, bisogna ubbidirgli.

obfŭscate, TR.: offuscare.

ōbit, S.: funerale, *m.*, esequie, *f. pl.*

obituary, S.: necrologia, *f.*; libro de' morti, *m.*

ŏb-ject 1, S.: obietto, oggetto; soggetto, *m.*, materia, *f.*; motivo, *m.* **-jĕct** 2, TR.: obiettare; opporre, rimproverare, incolpare. **-jĕction**, S.: obiezione; opposizione, *f.*; rimprovero, *m.*: *have no* —, non aver nulla in contrario, non eccepire accusa, *f.* **-jĕctionable**, ADJ.: soggetto al obiezione. **-jĕctive**, ADJ.: oggettivo. **-jĕctively**, ADV.: in modo oggettivo. **-jĕctiveness**, S.: oggettività, *f.*, obiettare, *m.* **-jĕctor**, S.: oppositore, *m.*

objūr-gate, TR.: rimproverare, riprendere; bravare. **-gātion**, S.: riprensione, ripassata; bravata, *f.* **-gatory**, ADJ.: riprensivo, riprensorio.

ob-lāte, S.: oblato, *m.*; ADJ.: piatto dal canto de' poli. **-lātion**, S.: obblazione, offerta, *f.*; sacrifizio, *m.*

oblĕc-tate†, TR.: dilettare, rallegrare. **-tātion**, S.: diletto, *m.*, giocondità, *f.*

ŏbli-gate, TR.: obbligare, costringere. **-gātion**, S.: obbligazione, *f.*, obbligo; contratto, *m.*: *be under* —, esser obbligato. **-gatory**, ADJ.: obbligatorio.

oblig-e, TR.: obbligare, costringere, sforzare; beneficare: *you will — me*, mi obbligherete, mi farete favore. **-ed**, ADJ.: obbligato; ricordevole, grato; *much* —, obbligatissimo. **-ement**, S.: obbliganza, obbligazione, *f.* **-er**, S.: obbligatore; mallevadore, *m.* **-ing**, ADJ.: obbligante; gentile, cortese. **-ingly**, ADV.: obbligantemente. **-ingness**, S.: cortesia; compiacenza, *f.*

ob-liquātion, S.: obbliquità, *f.* **-lique**, ADJ.: obbliquo; indiretto. **-liquely**, ADV.: obbliquamente; tortamente. **-liqueness**, **-liquity**, S.: obbliquità, *f.*

oblitĕr-ate, TR.: obliterare; scancellare. **-ātion**, S.: cancellazione; estinzione, dimenticanza, *f*

obliv-ion, S.: obblivione, dimenticanza, *f.*: *act of* —, perdono generale, amnistia, *f.* **-ious**, ADJ.: smemorato, dimentico.

ŏblong, ADJ.: oblungo, bislungo. **-ness**, S.: forma bislunga, *f.*

ŏbloquy, S.: maldicenza, *f.*; biasimo, *m.*

obmutĕscence, S.: perdita della voce, *f.*

obnŏxious, ADJ.: odioso; soggetto; colpevole. **-ness**, S.: odiosità; soggezione, *f.*

obnūbi-late†, TR.: annebbiare, annuvolare, oscurare. **-lātion**, S.: oscuramento, *m.*

ŏbole, S.: obolo, *m.* (moneta).

obrĕption†, S.: insinuazione, *f.*

ob-scēne, ADJ.: osceno, impudico; offensivo. **-scēnely**, ADV.: oscenamente, impudicamente, immodestamente. **-scēneness**, **-scĕnity**, S.: oscenità, impudicizia, *f.*

ob-scurātion, S.: oscuramento, *m.*, oscurazione, *f.* **-scūre** 1, ADJ.: oscuro, tenebroso, buio; difficile. **-scure** 2, TR.: oscurare, offuscare; denigrare, intrigare. **-scūrely**, ADV.: oscuramente. **-scūreness**, S.: oscurità, *f.*, oscuramento, *m.*

ŏbse-crate, TR.: pregare, supplicare, congiurare. **-crātion**, S.: preghiera, *f.*, scongiuro, *m.*

ŏb-sequies, S. PL.: esequie, *f. pl.*, mortorio, *m.* **-sēquious**, ADJ.: ossequioso; cortese, civile. **-sēquiously**, ADV.: ossequiosamente, cortesemente. **-sēquiousness**, S.: ossequio, *m.*, osservanza, ubbidienza, *f.* **-sequy**†, SING. di *-sequies*; ossequio, *m.*

obsĕr-vable, ADJ.: osservabile; notabile, considerabile. **-vably**, ADV.: osserva-

prŏs-per, TR.: rendere felice; INTR.: prosperare; riuscire. **-pŏrity**, S.: prosperità; buona fortuna, *f.* **-perous**, ADJ.: prospero, felice; propizio. **-perously**, ADV.: prosperamente, con successo. **-perousness**, S.: prosperità, *f.*, successo, *m.*

prospicience, S.: prevedenza, *f.*, antivedimento, *m.*

prosternātion, S.: prosternazione, *f.*

prŏsti-tute 1, ADJ.: prostituito, mercenario; S.: prostituta, *f.* **-tute** 2, TR.: prostituire. **-tūtion**, S.: prostituzione, *f.* **-tuter**, S.: prostitutore, *m.*

prŏs-trate, ADJ.: prostrato, disteso a terra. **-trate**, TR.: prostrare, distendere a terra: — *one's self*, prostrarsi; cadere boccone. **-trātion**, S.: prostrazione, *f.*

prŏsy, ADJ.: prosaico; insulso: — *fellow*, prosaico, seccatore, *m.*

prŏtasis, S.: protasi; proposizione, *f.*, argomento, *m.*

protătic, ADJ.: previo.

protĕc-t, TR.: proteggere, difendere. **-tion**, S.: protezione, difesa, *f.*; protezionismo; passaporto, *m.*: *take one into* —, avere alcuno in protezione. **-tionist**, S.: protezionista, *m.* **-tive**, ADJ.: difensivo. **-tor**, S.: protettore, difensore; amministratore (d'uno stato), *m.*, -trice, *f.* **-torate**, **-torship**, S.: protettorato, *m.*; reggenza, *f.* **-tress**, S.: protettrice, *f.*

protĕnd, TR.: protendere, porgere.

protĕrvity, S.: protervia, protervità, petulanza, *f.*

prŏtest, S.: protesto, *m.*; protestazione, *f.*: *enter a* —, far inscrire una protesta.

protĕst, TR.: confessare; provare; pubblicare; INTR.: protestare; attestare, certificare, assicurare: — *a bill*, protestare una cambiale.

Prŏtestant, ADJ.: protestante; S.: protestante, *m.*, *f.* **-ism**, S.: religione protestante, *f.*

pro-testātion, S.: protestazione, *f.*; giuramento, *m.* **-tĕster**, S.: che protesta, che solennemente dichiara.

prothŏnotary, S.: protonotario, *m.*

prŏtocol, S.: protocollo, *m.*

protomârtyr, S.: protomartire, *m.*

prŏto-plasm, S.: protoplasma, *m.* **-plast**, S.: primo formato; protoplasto, *m.* **-plăstic**, ADJ.: protoplastico.

prŏtotype, S.: prototipo; originale, primo modello, *m.*

protrăc-t, TR.: protrarre, prolungare. **-ter**, S.: che protrae; (*geom.*) quadrante, *m.* **-tion**, S.: protrazione, *f.*, protrarre, *m.* **-tive**, ADJ.: protraente, dilatorio, indugevole.

protrū-de, (IN)TR.: sporgere, spingere; uscire di linea. **-sion**, S.: proietto, sporto; impeto, *m.* **-sive**, ADJ.: spingente.

protūber-ance, S.: protuberanza, *f.*, gonfiamento, tumore, *m.* **-ant**, ADJ.: prominente; tumido. **-ate**, INTR.: gonfiare, gonfiarsi. **-ātion**, S.: gonfiamento, *m.* **-ous** = *protuberant*.

proud, ADJ.: orgoglioso, superbo, altiero; arrogante: — *flesh*, carne morta, *f.*; — *horse*, cavallo fiero, *m.* **-ly**, ADV.: superbamente, altieramente, arrogantemente. **-ness**, S.: orgoglio, *m.*; arroganza, *f.*

prŏv-able, ADJ.: provabile. **-ably**, ADV.: provabilmente. **-e**, TR.: provare, esperimentare; dimostrare addurre le prove di; cimentare; INTR.: divenire; accadere: — *true*, verificare; verificarsi, esser vero. **-eable** = *provable*.

prŏvedore, S.: provveditore, munizioniere, *m.*

prŏvender, S.: foraggio, *m.*; vettovaglia, *f.*

prŏver, S.: provatore, *m.*

prŏverb, S.: proverbio, detto, motto, *m.*: *become a* —, divenire proverbiale; passare in proverbio.

provĕrbial, ADJ.: proverbiale, di proverbio. **-ly**, ADV.: proverbialmente, per motto.

provid-e, (IN)TR.: provvedere; fornire; munire: — *for*, fare provvedimento di, aver cura di, provvedere a' bisogni di; — *against*, cautelarsi; provvedersi (munirsi) contro, prepararsi per. **-ed**, ADJ.: provveduto, provisto, munito, preparato: — *that*, purchè, a condizione che.

prŏvi-dence, S.: providenza, *f.*; prevedimento, *m.*; circospezione, cautela; economia, *f.* **-dent**, ADJ.: provvidente; prudente, cauto; economo. **-dĕntial**, ADJ.: della providenza. **-dĕntially**, ADV.: per cura della providenza. **-dently**, ADV.: prudentemente, cautamente.

provider, S.: provveditore, *m.*

prŏvince, S.: provincia, regione; incombenza, cura, *f.*, affare, *m.*: *that is not within my* —, non è della mia portata, non mi tocca.

provin-cial, ADJ.: provinciale, di provincia; S.: provinciale; superiore, *m.* **-cialism**, S.: provincialismo, dialetto della provincia, *m.*

provision 1, S.: provvisione, *f.*; viveri, *m. pl.*: *make* — *for*, provvedere a. **provision** 2, TR.: provvisionare. **-al**, ADJ.: provvisionale. **-ally**, ADV.: provisionalmente.

provi-so, S.: condizione; stipulazione, *f.*, patto, *m.* **-sor**, S.: provveditore; rettore (d' un collegio), *m.* **-sory**, ADJ.: provisorio; condizionale.

provŏ-cative, ADJ.: provocativo; S.:

-tăgonal, -tăngular, ADJ.: ottangolare. **-tave**, S.: ottava, *f.* **-tāvo**, S.: libro in ottavo; ottavo, *m.* **-tĕnnial**, ADJ.: ottennio. **Oc-tōber**, S.: ottobre, *m.* **-togenārian, -tŏgenary**, ADJ.: ottuagenario. **-tonary**, ADJ.: ottonario, d'otto. **-topus**, S.: specie di seppia, *f.* **-tosÿllable**, ADJ.: ottonario, di otto sillabe. **-tuple**, ADJ.: ottuplo.

ŏcu-lar, ADJ.: oculare, di veduta. **-larly**, ADV.: ocularmente, di veduta. **-list**, S.: oculista, *m.*

ōdalisk, S.: odalisca, *f.*

ŏdd, ADJ.: impari, dispari; bizzarro, fantastico; cattivo: — *looking*, singolare d'aspetto; — *number*, numero caffo; *play at even and* —, giuocare a pari; *thirty pounds* —, trenta lire sterline e più. **-ity**, S.: singolarità, *f.* **-ly**, ADV.: in modo straordinario, fantasticamente. **-ness**, S.: inegualità; singolarità, stranezza; fantastichezza, *f.* **-s**, S.: disparità; differenza, *f.*; vantaggio, *m.*; superiorità, *f.*: *be at* — *with one*, contendere con uno; *have the* — *of one*, aver l'avvantaggio sopra uno; *fight against* —, battersi con un più forte; — *and ends*, bocconcini, *m. pl.*

ōde, S.: oda, ode, *f.*

ōdi-ous, ADJ.: odioso, detestabile. **-ously**, ADV.: odiosamente. **-ousness**, S.: odiosità; atrocità, enormità, *f.* **-um**, S.: odio, *m.*; colpa, *f.*

ōdour, S.: odore; profumo, *m.*, fragranza, *f.* **-ate**, ADJ.: odorante; odorato. **-iferous**, ADJ.: odorifero, odoroso. **-iferousness**, S.: odoramento, odore, *m.*

oe-conŏmic, ADJ.: economico. **-conŏmics**, S. PL.: economia, *f.* **-cŏnomy**, S.: economia; frugalità, *f.*

oecumĕnical, ADJ.: ecumenico, universale.

oe-dēma, S.: (*surg.*) edema, *m.* **-demătic, -dĕmatous**, ADJ.: edematico.

oeilliad†, S.: occhiata, *f.*, sguardo; segno, *m.*

oesŏphagus, S.: esofago, *m.*

ō'er = *over.*

ŏf ŏr, PREP.: di: — *the*, del (dello, della, dei, delle).

ŏff 1, ADV.: lontano, lunge, lungi; via: *well* —, benestante, comodo; *be* —*!* anda via! *far* —, lontano, lungi; — *with your hat!* giù col cappello! *be* — *and on*, esser in bilancia; *go* —, andar via, scoppiare; *push* —*!* scosta! allarga! **off** 2, INTERJ.: via via! andate via! **-hand**, ADJ.: improvviso, espontaneo; ADV.: all'improvvista, senza preparazione.

ŏffal, S.: rimasuglio; avanzo, *m.*

offĕn-ce, S.: offesa; colpa, *f.*; affronto, oltraggio, delitto, *m.*: *give* —, offendere; *take* — *at*, tenersi offeso di. **-ceful**, ADJ.: ingiurioso, offensivo. **-celess**, ADJ.: innocente. **-d**, TR.: offendere; dispiacere; nuocere; INTR.: fallire, peccare: *be* —*ded at*, esser in collera contro. **-der**, S.: offenditore, delinquente, criminale, *m.* **-ding**, S.: offendimento, *m.* **-dress**, S.: offenditrice; malfattrice, *f.* **-sive**, ADJ.: offensivo, ingiurioso; S.: offensiva, *f.*: — *arms*, armi offensive. **-sively**, ADV.: offensivamente. **-siveness**, S.: offesa, ingiuria, *f.*; dispiacere, male, *m.*

ŏffer 1, S.: offerta; profferta, *f.*; tentativo, *m.* **offer** 2, TR.: offerire, presentare; tentare; INTR.: offerirsi, presentarsi; obbligarsi: — *one's self*, esporsi; — *violence*, far violenza; *if you* — *to do it*, si vi provate di farlo. **-er**, S.: offeritore, *m.* **-ing**, S.: offerta, profferta; obblazione, *f.* **-tory**, S.: offertorio, *m.* **-ture**, S.: offerta, profferta, *f.*

ŏffi-ce, S.: ufficio, uffizio; studio; impiego, carico, servizio, *m.*: *high in* —, che copre alto impiego. **-cer**, S.: ufficiale, officiale; funzionario, agente, *m.* **-cered**, ADJ.: *be* — *by*, aver per ufficiali.

offic-ial 1, ADJ.: ufficiale; conducevole; idoneo. **-ial** 2, S.: ufficiale, officiale, *m.* **-ially**, ADV.: ufficialmente, d'ufficio. **-iality**, S.: carica, *f.*; ufficio d'un ufficiale, *m.* **-iate**, TR.: distribuire; INTR.: ufficiare.

officinal, ADJ.: officinale.

officious, ADJ.: officioso; obbligante; affabile. **-ly**, ADV.: officiosamente, cortesemente. **-ness**, S.: prontezza; cortesia; affabilità, *f.*

ŏffing, S.: largo, alto mare, *m.*

ŏff-scouring, S.: lavatura, *f.*; fecce, *f. pl.* **-set**, S.: germoglio, rampollo, *m.* **-spring**, S.: progenie, *f.*, discendenti, *m. pl.*

offŭs-cate, TR.: offuscare, adombrare. **-cātion**, S.: offuscazione, oscurazione, adombrazione, *f.*

ŏft, ŏften, ADV.: spesso, sovente: *how* —, quante volte.

oft(en)times, ADV.: spesse volte.

ogēe, S.: (*arch.*) festone, *m.*

ō-gle 1, S.: occhiata, *f.*, sguardo, *m.* **-gle** 2, TR.: occhieggiare; vagheggiare. **-gler**, S.: vagheggiatore. **-gling**, S.: vagheggiare, *m.*

ŏglio, S.: guazzabuglio, *m.*

ōgre, S.: orco, mostro antropofago, *m.*

ōh! INTERJ.: oh! o!

ŏil 1, S.: olio, *m.*: — *of roses*, olio rosato, *m.*; *paint in* —, dipingere a olio. **oil** 2, TR.: ungere con olio: *castor* —, olio di ricino. **-bottle**, S.: oliera, *f.* **-cloth**, S.: tela cerata, *f.* **-colour**, S.: colore a olio, colore misto con olio. **-iness**, S.: oleosità, *f.* **-man**, S.: oliandolo, *m.*

pŭg, s.: cagnolino da signora; scimmiotto; cuor mio†, *m.*
pŭgh! INTERJ.: oibò!
pŭgilt†, s.: pugillo; pizzicotto, *m.* **-ism**, s.: pugilato, *m.* **-ist**, s.: pugilatore, *m.*
pug-nācious, ADJ.: pugnace. **-năcity**, s.: pugnazione, *f.*
pūisne†, ADJ.: cadetto, piccolo, inferiore; vano.
pūissan-ce, s.: potenza, possanza, *f.* **-t**, ADJ.: potente, possente. **-tly**, ADV.: potentemente, con forza.
pu-ke 1, INTR.: vomitare, vomire. **-ke** 2, **-ker**, s.: emetico, vomitivo, *m.*
pŭlchritude, s.: bellezza, venustà, *f.*
pūle, INTR.: pigolare, piare; rammaricarsi.
pūlic, s.: (*bot.*) pulicaria, *f.*, psillo, *m.*
pūlicose, ADJ.: pieno di pulci.
pūling, ADJ.: malaticcio.
pull 1, s.: tirata; scossa, *f.*; tiramento, *m.* **pull** 2, TR.: tirare, stracciare, svellere; remare, vogare: — *the bell*, suonare il campanello; — *off one's hair*, strappare i capelli; — *in pieces*, metter in pezzi, sbranare; — *away*, svellere; sconficcare; — *back*, tirare indietro; — *down*, abbattere, atterrare; — *in*, tirare a sè; rintuzzare; — *off*, cavare; levare; — *off one's boots*, cavar gli stivali; — *out*, stracciare, tirare; — *to*, tirare a sè; stringere; — *up*, alzare; sradicare. **-back**, s.: impedimento, ostacolo, *m.*
pullen, s.: pollame, *m.*
puller, s.: che tira, che spinge con isforza.
pullet, s.: gallinella, *f.*, pollastro, *m.*
pulley, s.: girella; carrucola, *f.*
pŭllu-late, TR.: pullulare, germogliare. **-lātion**, s.: pullulare, *m.*
pŭl-monary 1, s.: (*bot.*) polmonaria, *f.* **-monary** 2, **-mŏnic**, ADJ.: polmonario.
pulp, s.: polpa, *f.*
pulpit, s.: pulpito, pergamo, *m.*; catedra, *f.*: — *orator*, predicatore, *m.*
pŭl-pous, ADJ.: polposo, polputo. **-pousness**, s.: qualità polposa, *f.* **-py** = *pulpous.*
pŭl-sate, INTR.: pulsare, palpitare. **-sātion**, s.: pulsazione, *f.*; battimento, *m.* **-satory**, ADJ.: pulsatorio. **-se** 1, s.: polso; legume, *m.*: *feel one's* —, toccare il polso ad uno. **-se** 2, INTR.: battere, pulsare. **-sion**, s.: pulsare, *m.*; impulsione, *f.*
pŭlver-able, ADJ.: polverizzabile. **-izātion**, s.: polverizzamento, polverizzare, *m.* **-ize**, TR.: polverizzare.
pŭmice(-stone), s.: pomice, *f.*
pŭmp 1, s.: tromba (di tirar acqua); scarpetta, *f.* **pump** 2, TR.: cavare l' acqua colla tromba; lavare; scalzare. **-brake**, **-break**, s.: manovella di tromba, *f.* **-dale**, s.: maniche di tromba, *f. pl.* **-er**, s.: pompiere, *m.* **-ion**, s.: zucca, *f.*
pŭn 1, s.: bisticcio, equivoco, *m.* **pun** 2, INTR.: bisticciare, equivocare.
pŭnch 1, s.: punteruolo, stampo, *m.* **punch** 2, s.: pulcinella, *f.* **punch** 3, s.: poncio, *m.* (bevanda). **punch** 4, TR.: forare, pertugiare. **-bowl**, s.: piatto da poncio, *m.* **-eon**, s.: punteruolo, stampo, *m.* **-er**, s.: succhio, *m.*
punchinĕllo, s.: pulcinella, *f.*, arlecchino, *m.*
pŭnch-ladle, s.: cucchiaio da poncio, *m.*
punctil-io, s.: puntiglio, *m.*, esattezza affettata, *f.* **-ious**, ADJ.: puntiglioso, troppo esatto, scrupoloso. **-iousness**, s.: stare sul puntiglio, *m.*; puntualità esatta, scrupolosità, *f.*
pŭnction, s.: puntura, *f.*
pŭncto, s.: ceremoniale, *m.*
pŭnc-tual, ADJ.: puntuale, esatto. **-tuălity**, s.: puntualità, esattezza, *f.* **-tually**, ADV.: puntualmente, esattamente. **-tualness** = *punctuality.* **-tuate**, TR.: punteggiare, puntare. **-tuātion**, s.: interpunzione; punteggiatura, *f.* **-tulate** = *punctuate.* **-ture** 1, s.: puntura, *m.* **-ture** 2, TR.: pungere.
pŭndle†, s.: (*fig.*) baldracca, *f.*
pŭngen-cy, s.: qualità pungente; punta; acutezza, *f.* **-t**, ADJ.: pungente; acuto.
Pūnic, ADJ.: punico; ingannevole.
pūniness, s.: piccolezza; magrezza, *f.*
pŭnish, TR.: punire, gastigare. **-able**, ADJ.: punibile; degno di punizione. **-er**, s.: punitore, gastigatore, *m.* **-ment**, s.: punimento, *m.*, punizione, *f.*; gastigo, *m.*; pena, *f.*: *ignominious* —, pena infamante.
pūni-tive, **-tory**, ADJ.: punitivo.
pŭnk, s.: prostituta, *f.*; esca, *f.*
pŭnster, s.: bisticciere; motteggiatore, *m.*
pŭnt 1, s.: barca piatta, *f.* **punt** 2, TR.: giuocare a bassetta, *m.* **-er**, s.: giuocatore a bassetta, *m.*
pūny, ADJ.: piccolo; giovane; inferiore; malsano, malaticcio.
pūp, INTR.: fare i catellini, figliare.
pūpa, s.: crisalide, *f.*
pūpil, s.: pupillo, scolare, *m.*; pupilla, *f.* **-age**, s.: minorità; tutela, *f.* **-lary**, ADJ.: pupillare, di pupillo.
pŭppet, s.: burattino, bamboccino, *m.* **-man**, **-player**, s.: ciarlatano, cantambanco, *m.* **-ry**, s.: affettazione, *f.*, smancerie, *f. pl.* **-show**, s.: commedia di burattini, *f.*
pŭppy 1, s.: cagnolino; sciocco, *m.* **puppy** 2, INTR.: fare i catellini, figliare. **-ism**, s.: estrema affettazione, *f.*
pūr = *purr.*

nātu-re, S.: natura; proprietà, essenzia; specie, *f.*; umore; genio, temperamento, *m.*: *by* —, secondo natura; naturalmente, per indole. **-red**, ADJ.: di ... natura, di ... naturale: *good-—*, d' un buon naturale.
nāufrage†, S.: naufragio, *m.*
nāught 1, ADJ.: cattivo, malvagio, depravato, disonesto. **naught 2**, S.: niente, *m.*, nessuna cosa, *f.* **-ily**, ADV.: cattivamente; malamente. **-iness**, S.: cattivezza; tristizia, *f.* **-y**, ADJ.: cattivo, malvagio, corrotto; tristo.
nāumachy, S.: naumachia, *f.*
nāu-seate, TR.: nauseare, disgustare; recere; odiare. **-seous**, ADJ.: nauseoso, disgustoso. **-seously**, ADV.: in modo nauseoso. **-seousness**, S.: nauseamento; nauseare, *m.*; abbominazione, *f.*
nāutic, **-al**, ADJ.: nautico, di nave.
nāutilus, S.: nautilo, *m.* (mollusco).
nāval, ADJ.: navale; di marina: — *officer*, ufficiale della marina, *m.*
nāve, S.: mozzo (d'una ruota), *m.*; navata (d' una chiesa), *f.*
nāvel, S.: bellico, ombilico; mezzo, *m.* **-string**, S.: tralcio, *m.* **-wort**, S.: (*bot.*) bellico di venere, *m.*
nāvi-gable, ADJ.: navigabile. **-gate**, (IN)TR.: navigare, veleggiare. **-gātion**, S.: navigazione, *f.*, navigare, *m.*, nautica, *f.* **-gator**, S.: navigatore; marinaro, marinaio, *m.*
nāvy, S.: armata navale, flotta, *f.* **-board**, S.: consiglio della marina, *m.* **-office**, S.: uffizio della marina. **-yard**, S.: arsenale di marina, *m.*
nāy, ADV.: no; non solo; di più, inoltre. **nay**, S.: (*word*) negativa, *f.*, rifiuto, *m.*, ripulsa, *f.*
Nazarēne, ADJ.: nazzareno.
nēaf, S.: pugno, *m.*
nēal, TR.: ricuocere, temperare.
nēap, ADJ.: decrescente; basso: *—-tide*, S.: marea bassa, *f.*
nēar, PREP., ADJ., ADV.: presso; appresso; vicino a, prossimo a, intimo, stretto; pressochè, poco meno, quasi: *very* —, vicinissimo, vicin vicino, pressochè; — *Rome*, vicino a Roma; — *at hand*, a mano, in pronto; *draw* —, approssimare, accostare; avvicinarsi; — *relation*, stretto parente; *they were — coming to blows*, poco mancò non venissero alle mani. **-ly**, ADV.: da vicino, presso; meschinamente, avaramente. **-ness**, S.: prossimità, propinquità, vicinità; affinità, parentela, *f.*
nēat 1, S.: bue, *m.*, vacca, *f.*: *—'s leather*, cuoio di bue, *m.* **neat 2**, ADJ.: netto, puro, pulito; vago, elegante; astuto. **-handed**, ADJ.: destro, abile. **-handedness**, S.: destrezza, abilità; sagacità, *f.*
nēat-herd, S.: boare, vaccaio, bifolco, *m.* **-house**, S.: stalla da buoi, *f.*
nēat-ly, ADV.: pulitamente, elegantemente. **-ness**, S.: pulitezza, nettezza, eleganza, *f.*
nĕb, S.: becco, *m.*; punta, *f.*
nĕbula, S.: nebula; macchia sull' occhio, *f.* **-ulŏsity**, S.: nuvolosità, *f.* **-ulous**, ADJ.: nebuloso, nuvoloso, nebbioso.
nĕcessa-ries, S. PL.: necessario, bisognevole, *m.* **-rily**, ADV.: necessariamente. **-riness**, S.: esser necessario, *m.*; necessità, *f.* **-ry**, ADJ.: necessario; indispensabile; S.: guardaroba, *f.*; luogo comune, *m.* **-ry-house**, S.: necessario, agiamento, *m.*
necĕssi-tate, TR.: necessitare, costringere; violentare, sforzare. **-tātion**, S.: urgenza, forza, *f.*, costringimento, *m.* **-tous**, ADJ.: necessitoso, bisognoso; indigente. **-tousness**, **-tude**, S.: necessità, indigenza, *f.* **-ty**, S.: necessità; forza, violenza; povertà, *f.*: *of* —, necessariamente.
nĕck, S.: collo, *m.*: — *of land*, braccio di terra fra due mari, *m.*; — *of mutton*, collo di castrato, *m.*; — *of a violin*, manico d' un violino, *m.*; *take one about the* —, abbracciare alcuno. **-band**, S.: collare (d' una camicia), *m.* **-beef**, S.: grossa carne di manzo, *f.* **-cloth**, S.: cravatta, *f.*; fazzoletto da collo, *m.* **-erchief**, S.: fazzoletto da collo, *m.* **-lace**, S.: collana, *f.*; vezzo, *m.* **-piece**, S.: gorgiera, *f.* **-tie**, S.: cravatta, *f.* **-weed**, S.: canapa, *f.*
nĕc-rologue, S.: necrologo, *m.* **-rŏlogy**, S.: necrologia, *f.*
nĕcro-mancer, S.: negromante, *m.*, negromantessa, *f.* **-mancy**, S.: negromanzia, *f.* **-măntic**, ADJ.: necromantico.
nĕc-tar, S.: nettare, *m.* **-tared**, ADJ.: misto con nettare. **-tāreous**, **-tarine 1**, ADJ.: nettario, dolce. **-tarine 2**, S.: sorta di susina dolce, *f.*
nēed 1, S.: bisogno, *m.*, necessità; esigenza, *f.*: *if — be*, se sarà necessario, al bisogno; *in — of*, necessitoso di; *stand in — of*, avere bisogno di; *at* —, all' uopo. **need 2**, TR.: avere bisogno; mancare; INTR.: esser necessario; *you — but tell him*, ditegli solamente; *it —s not*, non è necessario. **-er**, S.: che ha bisogno; che manca. **-ful**, ADJ.: necessario; requisito. **-fully**, ADV.: necessariamente. **-fulness**, S.: necessità, *f.*; bisogno, *m.* **-ily**, ADV.: in indigenza; poveramente. **-iness**, S.: indigenza, povertà; miseria, *f.*
nēedle, S.: ago, *m.*; aguglia, *f.*: *large* —, agone, *m.*; *sewing* —, ago da cucio

m.; *pack* —, ago per cucire sacchi, *m.* **-case**, S.: agoraio da tenere gli aghi, *m.* **-fish**, S.: aguglia, *f.* (pesce). **-ful**, S.: agugliata, *f.* **-gun**, S.: fucile ad ago, *m.* **-maker**, S.: agoraio, *m.*

nēedless, ADJ.: inutile; superfluo. **-ly**, ADV.: senza necessità, inutilmente. **-ness**, S.: inutilità; superfluità, *f.*

nēedle-work, S.: lavoro d' ago, *m.*

nēed-s, ADV.: necessariamente; assolutamente: *it must — be so*, bisogna che sia così. **-y**, ADJ.: necessitoso, povero, indigente.

nē'er†, ADV.: mai, unque mai.

nēf, S.: nave, navata (d' una chiesa), *f.*

nefăndous†, ADV.: nefando, scellerato.

nefārious, ADJ.: nefario, scellerato, abbominevole.

negātion, S.: negazione, *f.*, negamento, *m.*

nĕga-tive, ADJ.: negativo, rifiutante; S.: (*phot.*) negativa; negazione, *f.* **-tively**, ADV.: negativamente. **-tory**, ADJ.: negativo.

neglĕct 1, S.: negligenza, trascuranza, *f.*

neglect 2, TR.: negligere, trascurare, mancare. **-er**, S.: negligente; trascurato, *m.* **-ful**, ADJ.: negligente. **-fully**, ADV.: negligentemente. **-ion**, †**-t**, S.: negligenza, *f.* **-ive**, ADJ.: negligente.

nĕgligen-ce, S.: negligenza, trascuraggine, trascuranza, *f.* **-t**, ADJ.: negligente, trascurato. **-tly**, ADV.: con negligenza.

negō-tiable, ADJ.: che si può negoziare. **-tiate**, TR.: negoziare, trafficare; trattare. **-tiātion**, S.: negoziazione, *f.*; traffico, affare, *m.* **-tiator**, S.: negoziatore, negoziante; mediatore, *m.* **-tiatrix**, S.: negoziatrice; mediatrice, *f.*

nē-gress, S.: negra; mora, *f.* **-gro**, S.: negro, moro, *m.*

nēigh 1, S.: nitrito, nitrire, *m.* **neigh** 2, INTR.: nitrire.

nēighbo(u)r 1, S.: vicino, *m.*, vicina, *f.*

neighbo(u)r 2, TR.: confinare, conterminare. **-hood**, S.: vicinanza, *f.*: *near* —, prossimità, vicinanza, *f.* **-ing**, ADJ.: vicino, contiguo, prossimo. **-ly** 1, ADJ.: sociabile, amichevole. **-ly** 2, ADV.: da buon vicino; amichevolmente, da amico: *be* —, agire da buon vicino, essere buon vicino.

nēighing, S.: nitrito, *m.*

nēither 1, CONJ.: nè; nè più: — *more nor less*, nè più, nè meno. **neither** 2, PRON.: nè l' uno nè l' altro, nè l' una nè l' altra.

nĕmorous†, ADJ.: boscoso.

nēnu-far, **-phar**, S.: nenufar, *m.*

neo-lŏgic(al), ADJ.: neologico. **-ŏlogy**, S.: neologia, *f.* **-ŏlogism**, S.: neologismo, *m.* **-ŏlogist**, S.: neologista, *m.* **-ŏlogy**, S.: neologia, *f.*

nēophyte, S.: neofito, convertito, *m.*

neotĕric, ADJ.: moderno; recente.

nĕp, S.: nepitella, *f.*

nepĕnthe, S.: nepente, *m.* (pianta).

nĕ'phew, S.: nipote, *m.*: *little* (*great*) —, nipotino, *m.*; *grand* —, bisnipote, *m.*

ne-phritic, ADJ.: nefritico. **-phritis**, S.: nefritide, *f.*

nĕpotism, S.: nepotismo, *m.*

nĕreid, S.: nereide, *f.*

nĕr-val, ADJ.: nervoso. **-ve**, S.: nervo, nerbo; tendine, *m.* **-veless**, ADJ.: snervato, fiacco. **-vŏsity**, S.: nervosità, *f.* **-vous**, ADJ.: nervoso, nerboso; nervoso: — *disease*, malattia, nervosa. **-vously**, ADV.: nervosamente; con vigore (forza). **-vousness**, S.: nervosità, *f.* **-vy**, ADJ.: nervoso, vigoroso, robusto.

nĕscience, S.: ignoranza, *f.*

nĕst 1, S.: nido, *m.*, nidiata, *f.*; ricettacolo, rifugio, ricovero, covile, *m.*; — *of birds*, nidiata, nidata di uccelli. **nest** 2, INTR.: nidificare, fare nido. **-egg**, S.: guardanidio, endice, *m.* **-le**, TR.: accarezzare; INTR.: annidarsi; fermare sua stanza. **-ling**, S.: uccello nidiace, *m.*

nĕt, S.: rete, *m.*, reticella, *f.*

nĕther, ADJ.: basso, inferiore: *in the* — *world*, quaggiù. **-most**, ADJ.: infimo, estremo.

nĕtting, S.: (*nav.*) filaretti, *m. pl.*

nĕt-tle 1, S.: ortica, *f.* **-tle** 2, TR.: pungere; esasperare. **-tle-rash**, S.: orticaria, *f.*

nĕt-wise, ADJ.: retato. **-work**, S.: reticella; tessitura.

neurălg-ia, S.: nevralgia, *f.* **-ic**, ADJ.: nevralgico.

neu-rŏlogy, S.: neurologia, *f.* **-rŏtomy**, S.: neurotomia, *f.*

neūter, ADJ.: neutro; indifferente; neutrale; S.: neutro, *m.*; neutrale, *m.*, *f.* **-tral**, ADJ.: neutrale; indifferente. **-trălity**, S.: neutralità; indifferenza, *f.* **-trally**, ADV.: neutralmente; in senso neutro.

nĕver, ADV.: mai, giammai, unque mai: — *a one*, nemmeno uno; — *a whit*, niente affatto. **-ceasing**, ADJ.: incessante, continuo. **-ending**, ADJ.: eterno, perpetuo. **-failing**, ADJ.: infallibile. **-theless**, CONJ.: nulladimeno, non pertanto, tuttavia.

new 1, ADJ.: nuovo, fresco; novello; moderno: *bran(d)* —, nuovo di zecca; — *Testament*, nuovo testamento; — *year*, *etc.*, *cf. below*. **new** 2, ADV.: nuovamente, novellamente. **-comer**, S.: forestiero, *m.* **-fangle**, TR.: formare di nuovo; inventare di fresco. **-fangled**, ADJ.: di nuovo genere, appariscente. **-fangledness**, S.: mania di novità, *f.* **-fashioned**, ADJ.: moderno, alla moda. **-ish**,

ADJ.: alquanto nuovo. **-ly**, ADJ.: nuovamente, di fresco. **-ness**, S.: cosa nuova; novità, *f.*
news, S.: nuova, notizia (fresca), *f.*; avviso, *m.*: *what —?* che si dice di nuovo? **-monger**, S.: propagatore di nuove, *m.* **-paper**, S.: gazzetta, *f.* **-writer**, S.: novellista, gazzettiere, *m.* **-y**, ADJ.: (*coll.*) pieno di nuove.
new-year, S.: nuovo anno, *m.*; ADJ.: dal nuovo anno: *I wish you a happy —*, buon capo d'anno! **-year's day**, S.: capo d'anno, *m.* **-year's gift**, S.: strenna, *f.*
newt, S.: ramarro, *m.*
nĕxt 1, ADJ.: prossimo, contiguo: *the — day*, il giorno seguente. **next** 2, ADV.: dopo; in secondo luogo: (*the*) *— day*, il dì susseguente, l' indomani; *— chapter*, seguente capitolo; *— house*, casa contigua, prima porta; *— to*, dopo ciò, dopo di che.
nib, S.: becco, *m.*, becca (degli uccelli); punta, *f.* **-bed**, ADJ.: che ha un becco.
nib-ble, TR.: mordere; riprendere; INTR.: morsecchiare. **-bler**, S.: morditore; riprensore, *m.* **-blings**, S. PL.: morsecchiature, *f. pl.*
nice, ADJ.: raffinato, delicato, delizioso; esatto, accurato, studiato; difficile, scrupoloso; scimunito, sciocco: *— girl*, fanciulla vaga (vezzosa, simpatica). **-ly**, ADV.: delicatamente; esattamente; difficilmente. **-ness**, S.: delicatezza, delizia; esattezza, accuratezza; finezza, *f.* **-ties**, S. PL.: delizie, delicatezze, *f. pl.* **-ty**, S.: accuratezza; finezza; gentilezza, vezzosità; ghiottornia, cosa ghiotta, *f.*
niche, S.: nicchia; alcova, *f.*
nick 1, S.: tempo comodo, *m.*; opportunità, intaccatura, *f.*, taglio, *m.*: *old —*, diavolo, *m.*; *in the very — of time*, opportunamente, appunto. **nick** 2, TR.: toccare leggermente; intaccare; incontrare: *— the time*, incontrare il tempo.
nickel, S.: nichel, *m.*; ADJ.: di nichel. **-ed**, ADJ.: nichelato.
nickname 1, S.: soprannome, *m.* **nickname** 2, TR.: dare un soprannome.
nic-tate, TR.: ammiccare. **-tātion**, S.: ammiccare, cenno cogli occhi, *m.*
nide†, S.: nidiata; covata, *f.*
nidifi-cate, TR.: nidificare, fare nido. **-cātion**, S.: nidificare, fare nido, *m.*
niding†, ADJ.: basso, vile, abbietto.
nidu-late, TR.: nidificare. **-lātion**, S.: tempo di rimaner nel nido, *m.*
niece, S.: nipote, *f.*
niggard 1, S.: taccagno, spilorcio, *m.* **niggard** 2, ADJ.: taccagno, sordido, avaro. **niggard** 3, TR.: ristringere; limitare. **-ish**, ADJ.: alquanto taccagno, alquanto avaro. **-liness**, S.: spilorceria, avarizia, sordidezza, *f.* **-ly**, ADJ.: spilorcio, avaro, sordido; ADV.: avaramente, sordidamente; grettamente. **-ness**, S.: avarizia; parsimonia, *f.*
nigger, S.: negro, *m.*, negra, *f.*
nig-gle, INTR.: giullare, beffare. **-gler**, S.: buffone, zanni, *m.*
nigh, ADJ., PREP.: vicino, contiguo; accosto; PREP., ADV.: qui vicino, qui accanto: *well —*, quasi, pressochè; *draw —*, avvicinarsi; *write —*, scrivere stretto. **-ly**, ADV.: presso a poco. **-ness**, S.: vicinità; prossimità, contiguità, *f.*
night, S.: notte; sera, serata, *f.*: *at* (*by*) *—*, nottetempo, di notte tempo; *last —*, iersera, la notte scorsa; *— falls*, annotta; *in the dead of —*, a notte inoltrata, nel silenzio della notte. **-brawler**, S.: perturbatore della quiete, *m.* **-cap**, S.; berretta da notte, *f.* **-dew**, S.: sereno, *m.*; rugiada, *f.* **-dress**, S.: cuffia da notte, *f.*; vestimenti da notte, *m. pl.* **-ed**, ADJ.: fosco, nuvoloso, bruno. **-fall**, S.: crepuscolo, imbrunire, *m.* **-faring**, ADJ.: viaggiante di notte tempo. **-fire**, S.: fuoco, fatuo, *m.* **-fly**, S.: farfalla notturna, *f.* **-foundered**, ADJ.: sviato di notte tempo. **-gown**, S.: veste da camera, zimarra, *f.* **-hag**, S.: maga notturna *f.* **-hawk**, S.: allocco, *m.* (uccello). **-ingale**, S.: rusignuolo, usignuolo, *m.*, filomela, *f.* **-ly**, ADJ.: notturno, di notte; ADV.: di notte tempo, ogni notte. **-man**, S.: vuotacesso, *m.* **-mare**, S.: incubo, fantasima, *m.* **-piece**, S.: (*paint.*) pittura di notte, *f.* **-rail**, S.: capuccio, *m.*, mantellina, *f.* **-raven**, S.: gufaccio, *m.* (uccello). **-revelling**, S. PL.: stravizzi notturni, divertimenti notturni, *m. pl.* **-robber**, S.: ladrone di notte, *m.* **-rule**, S.: tumulto notturno, *m.* **-shade**, S.: (*bot.*) solano, *m.* **-shining**, ADJ.: lucente di notte. **-studies**, S. PL.: veglie, *f. pl.* **-walker**, S.: nottivago, nottolone, *m.* **-watch**, S.: guardia notturna, *f.*
nigrĕscent, ADJ.: nereggiante, bruno.
nigrificātion, S.: nereggiamento, *m.*, anneritura, *f.*
nihil-ism, S.: nichilismo, *m.* **-ist**, S.: nichilista, *m.*
nihil-ity, S.: nulla, *m.*
nill 1, S.: scintille, *f. pl.* **nill**† 2, INTR.: non volere: *will he — he*, buon grado, mal grado.
nim-ble, ADJ.: agile; lesto, leggiero. **-bleness**, S.: agilità; leggierezza; sveltezza, *f.* **-ble-witted**, ADJ.: pronto d'ingegno. **-bly**, ADV.: agilmente; leggiermente, prestamente.
nincompoop, S.: sciocco, balordo, *m.*

nine, ADJ.: nove. **-fold**, ADJ.: nove volte più. **-holes**, S.: giuoco fatto con pallottoline, m. **-pins**, S. PL.: birilli, sbrigli, m. pl. **-score**, ADJ.: centottanta. **-teen**, ADJ.: diecinove. **-teenth**, ADJ.: decimo nono. **-tieth**, ADJ.: novantesimo. **-ty**, ADJ.: novanta.

ninny, **-hammer**, S: sciocco, gonzo, merendone, m.

ninth, S., ADJ.: nono. **-ly**, ADV.: in nono luogo.

nip 1, S.: pizzico, pizzicotto, tagliuzzo, m.; burla, *f.* **nip** 2, TR.: pizzicare; motteggiare; annebbiare: — *off*, tagliare; guastare. **-pers**, S. PL.: pinzette, molette; (*nav.*) salmastre, *f. pl.* **-ping**, ADJ.: pungente, mordace; acerbo. **-pingly**, ADV.: mordacemente; satirescamente.

nipple, S.: capezzolo, m.

nit, S.: lendine, *f.*

nitency, S.: nitore, m.

nithing†, S.: poltrone, codardo, m.

nitid, ADJ.: nitido; lucente.

ni-tre, S.: (*chem.*) nitro, salnitro, m. **-tric**, ADJ.: nitrico. **-trification**, S.: nitrificazione, *f.* **-trogen**, S.: nitrogeno, azoto, m. **-troglycerine**, S.: nitroglicerina, *f.* **-trósity**, S.: nitrosità, *f.* **-trous**, **-try**, ADJ.: nitroso.

nitty, ADJ.: lendinoso, pieno di lendini.

nival†, **niveous**, ADJ.: nevoso, pieno di neve.

nō, ADJ.: nessuno, niuno, veruno; ADV.: no, non: — *such matter*, niente affatto; — *matter*, non importa; — *more*, non più; — *where*, in nessuno luogo; *to — purpose*, invano; *I have — pens*, non ho penne; — *man*, niun uomo, niuno.

nobili-tate†, TR.: nobilitare, fare nobile. **-tátion**†, S.: nobilitare, m. **-ty**, S.: nobilità, *f.*; nobili, m. *pl.*

nōbl-e, ADJ.: nobile, illustre; liberale; S.: nobile, m. **-eman**, S.: nobile, gentiluomo, m. **-eness**, S.: nobiltà, grandezza; sublimità, *f.* **-ēss**, S.: nobili, m. *pl.*; ordine de nobili, m. **-ewoman**, S.: donna nobile, *f.* **-y**, ADV.: nobilmente; liberalmente.

nōbody, S.: nessuno, niuno, veruno, m.

nō-cent, ADJ.: nocente; colpevole, criminale. **-cive**, ADJ.: nocivo, nocevole.

nōck, S.: tacca; intaccatura, *f.*

noctám-bule, **-bulist**, S.: nottambulo, sonnambulo, m.

nocti-ferous†, ADJ.: che induce la notte. **-lúcous**, ADJ.: che splende nella notte. **-vagant**, ADJ.: nottivago.

nōc-tuary, S.: ricordanze notturne, *f. pl.* **-turn**, S.: notturno, m. **-túrnal** 1, ADJ.: notturno, di notte. **-turnal** 2, S.: notturlabio, m. (strumento).

nocuous, ADJ.: nocivo.

nŏd 1, S.: cenno, segno, m.: give (…) fare cenno. **nod** 2, INTR.: a[…] dormicchiare; tentennare. **-din[…]** accennamento, m. **-dle**, S.: test[…] ca, *f.* **-dy**, S.: sciocco, minchion[…]

nŏd-e, S.: nodo; tumore, callo, m. **-ō[…]** S.: nodosità, *f.*; nodo, m. **-ous**, [ADJ.:] nodoso, nocchioso.

nŏdule, S.: nodetto, piccol nodo, m.

nŏggin, S.: ciotola, *f.*; boccaletto, (…)

nŏi-se 1, S.: strepito, romore, fra[…] susurro, ronzo; fischiamento, m.: — […] —, far strepito, far romore. **-se** 2 […] divulgare, pubblicare. **-seful**, ADJ[…] moroso, strepitoso. **-seless**, ADJ.: [senza] strepito, silenzioso. **-se-maker**[…] schiamazzatore, m. **-siness**, S.: strepito, tumulto. **-some**, ADJ.: n[…]so, disgustoso. **-somely**, ADV.: in[…] nauseante; sporcamente. **-some[ness]** S.: nauseare, m.; sporchezza, *f.* […] ADJ.: turbolento, tumultuoso.

nolition, S.: ripugnanza, *f.*

nŏm-ad, S.: nomade, m., *f.* **-ădic[al]**, […] nomade. **-adism**, S.: vita nomade, […]

nŏmen-clator, S.: nomenclator[e] […] **-clāture**, S.: nomenclatura, *f.* —[…]

nŏmi-nal, ADJ.: nominale, titolare. **-[nal]ly**, ADV.: nominatamente; special[mente] **-nate**, TR.: nominare, nomare; inti[tola]re. **-nately**, ADV.: nominatam[ente]; spezialmente. **-nātion**, S.: no[mina;] presentazione, *f.* **-native**, S.: (gram.) [no]minativo, m. **-nātor**, S.: nomina[tore] […]

nŏn-, PREP.: non-, in-, mancanza di. **-[ab]ility**, S.: inabilità, *f.* **-age**, S.: mi[norità,] *f.* **-attĕndance**, S.: incuria, *f.*

nŏnce, S.: intento, disegno, m.

nonchalance, S.: indifferenza, *f.*

non-compliance, S.: rifiuto, m. **-[con]fŏrmist**, S.: nonconformista, m. **-[con]fŏrmity**, S.: nonconformità, discr[epan]za, *f.*

nŏndescript, ADJ.: indescrivibile.

nŏne, ADJ.: niuno, nessuno, verun[o] […] *will have — of it*, io non ne voglio; […] — *of my fault*, non è mia colpa.

non-ĕntity, **-existence**, S.: nie[nte], *f.* **-jūror**, S.: che non giura. **-par[eil]**, S.: (*print.*) nompariglia, *f.* **-paym[ent]**, S.: mancanza di pagamento, *f.* **-[per]fŏrmance**, S.: mancanza d' effett[o] […] **-plus**, TR.: confondere, imbarazzare […] *at a —*, non saper più che dire, e[ssere] confuso. **-rĕsidence**, S.: assenza (…) residenza, *f.* **-rĕsident**, S.: […] della residenza, m. **-resistance**, […] ubbidienza pronta, *f.*

nŏn-sense, S.: assurdità, *f.*, sproposit[i, m.] *pl.*; anfanamento, m.: *talk —*, anfa[nare,] spropositare; dire sciocchezze. **-sĕn[sic]al**, ADJ.: assurdo, ridicoloso, sprop[ositato] […]

to. **-sĕnsically**, ADV.: in modo assurdo, spropositatamente. **-sĕnsicalness**, S.: assurdità, sciocchezza, stupidezza, *f.*
non-sŏlvent, ADJ.: insolvente.
nŏnsuit 1, S.: (*jur.*) desistimento di lite, *m* **-suit** 2, TR.: (*jur.*) condannare per desistimento di lite.
nŏodle, S.: sciocco, gonzo, *m.*; sorta di maccheroni, *m. pl.*
nóok, S.: angolo, cantone; ridotto, *m.*
nōon, S.: mezzodì, mezzo giorno, *m.* **-day** 1, S.: mezzodì, mezzo giorno, *m.*: *at* —, sul mezzodì. **-day** 2, ADJ.: di mezzodì; meridionale. **-ing**, S.: meriggiana, *f.*; tempo di mezzodì, *m.* **-tide** = *noonday.*
nōose 1, S.: nodo scorsoio; legame; laccio; inganno, *m.*: — *of matrimony*, nodo matrimoniale, *m.* **nōose** 2, TR.: legare, allacciare.
nôr, CONJ.: nè, nè più: *neither . . . nor*, nè . . . nè.
nôrmal, ADJ.: normale.
nôrth 1, S.: nord, norte, *m.*; settentrione, *m.*, tramontana, *f.* **north** 2, ADJ.: settentrionale. **-ēast**, S.: nordest, *m.*; greco volturno, *m.* (vento). **-erly**, **-ern**, ADJ.: settentrionale. **-pole**, S.: polo artico, polo settentrionale, *m.* **-star**, S.: stella polare, *f.* **-ward**, **-wards**, ADV.: verso settentrione. **-wĕst**, S.: nordovest, *m.*; quarta di maestro, *f.* **-wind**, S.: aquilone, vento di tramontana, *m.*
nōse 1, S.: naso; sentore, *m.*: *big* (*large*) —, nasone, nasaccio, *m.*; *little* —, nasetto, *m.*; *flat* —, naso schiacciato; *turn up one's* —, arricciare il naso; *speak through the* —, parlare nel naso; *lead one by the* —, menar altrui pel naso; *Roman* —, naso aquilino. **nose** 2, TR.: sentire, fiutare; pavoneggiarsi; bravare. **-band**, S.: musoliera, *f.* **-bleed**, S.: millefoglie, *f.* (pianta). **-gay**, S.: mazzolino di fiori, *m.* **-less**, ADJ.: senza naso.
nosŏlogy, S.: nosologia, *f.*
nŏstril, S.: narice, nare, *f.*
nŏstrum, S.: rimedio finto, *m.*; medicina brevettata, *f.*
nŏt, ADV.: non, no: — *at all*, in niun modo, niente affatto; — *in the least*, niente affatto, per nulla.
nō-table, ADJ.: notabile, considerabile, insigne. **-tableness**, S.: notabilità, singolarità, *f.* **-tably**, ADV.: notabilmente. **-tārial**, ADJ.: notariale, autenticato da un notaio. **-tary**, S.: notaio, notaro, *m.* **-tātion**, S.: notare, *m.*; significazione, *f.*
nŏtch 1, S.: tacca; intaccatura, *f.* **notch** 2, TR.: intaccare, fare tacca. **-ing**, S.: tacca, *f.*
nōt-e 1, S.: nota, annotazione; osservazione; distinzione, *f.*; merito, *m.*, importanza, *f.*; biglietto, *m.*, letterina, *f.*: *take* —*s*, far degli appunti; *promissory* —, pagherò; *foot-*—, nota a piè di pagina; *bank* —, biglietto di banco, banconota; — *of interrogation*, punto interrogativo, *m.* **-e** 2, TR.: notare; osservare, considerare; attendere. **-e-book**, S.: libretto d' annotazioni, *m.* **-ed**, ADJ.: notato; famoso, rinomato, eminente, illustre. **-edness**, S.: cospicuità, *f.* **-er**, S.: annotatore, osservatore, *m.*
nóthing, S.: niente, nulla, *m.*; nullità, *f.*: *good for* —, buono a niente; *next to* —, quasi niente; — *venture*, — *have*, chi non risica non rosica; *make* — *of one*, disprezzare alcuno. **-ness**, S.: nichilità, *f.*, nulla, *m.*; bassezza, *f.*
nō-tice, S.: notizia, *f.*, avviso, *m.*; osservazione; attenzione, *f.*: *give* —, dar notizia, avvisare; *take* — *of a thing*, far attenzione a qualche cosa. **-tificātion**, S.: notificamento, notificare, *m.* **-tify**, TR.: notificare, significare. **-tion**, S.: nozione; idea, *f.*, pensiero, *m.*, opinione, *f.* **-tional**, ADJ.: immaginario, ideale. **-tionălity**, S.: opinione chimerica, *f.* **-tionally**, ADV.: per idea, mentalmente. **-toriety**, S.: notorietà; pubblicità, *f.* **-tōrious**, ADJ.: notorio, pubblico. **-tōriously**, ADV.: notoriamente, pubblicamente, evidentemente. **-tōriousness**, S.: fama pubblica; evidenza, *f.*
Nōtus, S.: noto, *m.* (vento).
notwithstănding, CONJ.: non ostante, sebbene.
nought *nāt*, S.: niente, nulla, *m.*: *set at* —, disprezzare, non far conto, sdegnare.
nŏun, S.: nome, *m.*
nŏurish, TR.: nutrire, alimentare; incoraggiare. **-able**, ADJ.: nutribile. **-er**, S.: nutritore, *m.* **-ing**, ADJ.: nutritivo. **-ment**, S.: nutrimento, *m.*, nutritura, *f.*, alimento, *m.*
no-vātion †, S.: innovazione; novità, *f.* **-vātor** †, S.: innovatore, novatore, *m.*
nŏvel 1, ADJ.: novello, nuovo. **novel** 2, S.: romanzo, *m.*, novella, narrazione favolosa, *f.*: — *writer*, romanziere, *m. f.*; *tell* —*s*, novellare. **-ist**, S.: innovatore, novellatore; novellista, *m.*; romanziere, *m.*, *f.* **-ize**, TR.: innovare. **-ty**, S.: novità; cosa nuova, *f.*
Novĕmber, S.: novembre, *m.*
nŏv-enary, S.: nove, *m.* **-ĕnnial**, ADJ.: di novennio.
novĕrcal, ADJ.: di noverca.
nŏv-ice, S.: novizio, *m.*; novizia, *f.* **-iceship**, **-iciate**, S.: noviziato, *m.*
nŏvity †, S.: novità, cosa nuova, *f.*
nŏw 1, ADV.: al presente, adesso, ora; attualmente: *just* —, testè, pur ora, in questo punto; *till* —, fin adesso; *before* —,

prima d'ora; — *and then*, di quando in quando; *every* — *and then*, ogni poco, ogni tanto. **now** 2, S.: tempo presente, *m.*; ora, *f.* **-adays**, ADV.: oggidì, al presente.

nōwes†, S.: nodo matrimoniale, *m.*

nō-way(s), ADV.: in niuna maniera. **-where** *-hwār*, ADV.: in niun luogo, in nessuna parte. **-wise**, ADV.: in niun modo, per niente, in conto alcuno.

nŏxious, ADJ.: nocivo, pernizioso. **-ly**, ADV.: nocevolmente. **-ness**, S.: qualità nociva, *f.*, nocumento, *m.*

nŏzzle, S.: capezzolo, naso, *m.*; punta, *f.*

nūbi-le, ADJ.: nubile; maritale, da marito. **-lous**, ADJ.: nubiloso, nuvoloso.

nūcleus, S.: nucleo, nocciuolo, *m.*

nū-date, TR.: nudare. **-dātion**, S.: denudare; spogliamento, *m.* **-de**, ADJ.: nudo.

nŭdge, TR.: toccare col gomito (per chiamare l' attenzione).

nūdity, S.: nudità; semplicità, *f.*

nugăcity, S.: frivolezza, bagattella, beffa, *f.*; passatempo, *m.*

nūgatory, ADJ.: nugatorio, frivolo.

nŭgget, S.: pepite, pezzo d' oro o argento (in istato puro), *m.*

nūisance, S.: nocumento; incomodo, *m.*

nūke, S.: nuca, *m.*

nŭll I, ADJ.: nullo; invalido. **null** 2, TR.: annullare; invalidare; cassare. **null** 3, S.: inefficacia; mancanza di forza, *f.* **-ify**, TR.: cancellare, cassare. **-ity**, S.: nullità, *f.*, niente, nulla, *m.*; invalidità, *f.*

nŭmb I, ADJ.: torpido, intirizzito. **numb** 2, TR.: intirizzire; stupefare. -(**ed**)**ness**† = *numbness.*

nŭmber I, S.: numero, *m.*, quantità, *f.* **number** 2, TR.: numerare; contare. **-er**, S.: numeratore; calcolatore, *m.* **-ful**, ADJ.: numeroso. **-less**, ADJ.: innumerabile.

nŭmbles, S. PL.: interiora (d' un cervo, ecc.), *f. pl.*

nŭmbness, S.: torpore; stupore; intirizzamento, *m.*

nūmer-able, ADJ.: numerabile. **-al**, ADJ.: numerale, di numero. **-ally**, ADV.: numeralmente. **-ary**, ADJ.: numerario, numerico. **-ate**, TR.: numerare. **-ātion**, S.: numerazione, *f.* **-ator**, S.: (*arith.*) numeratore, *m.*

numĕric, **-al**, ADJ.: numerico; numerale. **-ally**, ADV.: in modo numerico.

nūmerist, S.: calcolatore, computista, *m.*

nūmer-o, S.: numero; marca, *f.* **-ŏsity**, S.: numerosità; armonia, *f.* **-ous**, ADJ.: numeroso; armonioso, *f.* **-ousness**, S.: moltitudine; armonia, *f.*

numismătic, ADJ.: numismatico. **-s**, S. PL.: numismatica, scienza delle monete e medaglie, *f.*

nŭmmary, ADJ.: di moneta, danaioso.

nŭmskull, S.: minchione, goffo, *m.* **-ed**, ADJ.: stupido, goffo, balocco.

nŭn, S.: monaca; religiosa regolare; monacella, *f.*

nŭnchion, S.: merenda, *f.*

nŭn-ciature, S.: nunziatura, *f.* **-cio**, S.: nunzio; ambasciadore del papa, *m.*

nŭn-cupate, TR.: nunziare. **-cūpative**, **-cūpatory**, ADJ.: nuncupativo, verbale: — *will*, testamento verbale, *m.*

nŭndi-nal, **-nary**, ADJ.: di nundine, di fiera.

nŭnnery, S.: convento (di monache), *m.*

nŭptial, ADJ.: nuziale; coniugale: — *song*, epitalamio, *m.* **-s**, S. PL.: nozze, *f.*, matrimonio, *m.*

nŭr-se I, S.: nutrice; balia, *f.* **-se** 2, TR.: nutrire, nutricare, allevare, fomentare; incoraggiare: — *a sick person*, aver cura d' un ammalato. **-se-child**, S.: bambino lattante, allievo, *m.* **-ser**, S.: nutritore, nutricatore; promotore, fautore, *m.* **-sery**, S.: camera della balia, *f.*: — *of learning*, seminario, *m.*; — *of plants*, semenzaio, *m.*; — *of trees*, semenzaio, *m.*, nestaiuola, *f.* **-sery-man**, S.: giardiniere che fa semenza, *m.* **-ing**, S.: nutrizione, *f.* **-sling**, S.: bambino di latte; favorito, *m.* **-ture** I, S.: nutricamento, *m.*; educazione, *f.* **-ture** 2, TR.: nutricare, allevare; educare.

nŭstle†, TR.: vezzeggiare, lusingare.

nŭt, S.: noce, nocciuola, *f.*; (*nav.*) orecchio (dell' ancora), *m.* **-brown**, ADJ.: castagnino. **-cracker**, S.: acciaccanoci, schiaccianoci, *m.* **-gall**, S.: noce di galla, galla, *f.* **-hatch**, **-pecker**, S.: sorta di merlo, *f.* **-hook**, S.: uncinetto (da pigliare le noci), *m.* **-meg**, S.: noce moscada, *f.* **-peach**, S.: noce persica, *f.*

nū-triment, S.: nutrimento; cibo, *m.* **-trimĕntal**, ADJ.: nutrimentale. **-trition**, S.: nutrizione, *f.*, nutrimento, *m.* **-tritious**, **-tritive**, ADJ.: nutritivo.

nŭt-shell, S.: scorza di noce, *f.*; guscio, *m.* **-ting**, PART.: *go a-—*, andare a cogliere delle nocciuole. **-tree**, S.: albero di noce, nocciuole, noce, *m.*

nŭzzle, TR.: allattare, allevare; INTR.: annasare; nascondersi.

nye, S.: stormo di fagiani, *m.*

nўmph, S.: ninfa; giovinetta, *f.* **-omānia**, S.: ninfomania, *f.* **-ous**, ADJ.: di ninfa.

O

ō (*the letter*), S.: o, *m.* (*f.*).

O! *ō*, INTERJ.: o! o bravo! viva!

ōaf, S.: merendone, baccellone, *m.* **-ish**,

ADJ.: sciocco, balordo, goffo. **-ishness**, S.: stupidezza; imbecillità, *f.*
ōak, S.: quercia, querce, *f.*: *young* —, querciuola, *f.* **-apple**, S.: galla, *f.* **-en**, ADJ.: di quercia; fatto di quercia. **-grove**, S.: querceto, *m.* **-ling**, S.: querciuola, *f.*
ōakum, S.: stoppa, *f.*, corde sfilate, *f. pl.*
ōar 1, S.: remo, *m.* **oar** 2, TR.: remare; vogare; INTR.: andare a remi. **-handle**, S.: manico di remo, *m.* **-y**, ADJ.: fatto a foggia di remo.
ōasis, S.: oasi, *f.*
ōat-cake, S.: focaccia di vena, *f.* **-en**, ADJ.: di vena.
ōath, S.: giuramento, giurare, *m.*: *false* —, spergiuro, *m.*; *take one's* —, pigliare giuramento; *administer an* — *to, put on his* —, deferire il giuramento a. **-breaking**, S.: pergiuro, spergiuro, *m.*
ōat-meal, S.: farina di vena; avena móndata, *f.*, panico, *m.* **-s**, S. PL.: avena, vena, *f.*
obămbulate†, INTR.: spasseggiare.
ŏb-duracy, S.: durezza di cuore, *f.*, induramento, *m.* **-durate**, ADJ.: indurito, duro; impenitente. **-durate**, TR.: indurire, rendere duro. **-durately**, ADV.: duramente, inflessibilmente. **-durateness**, **-durātion**, S.: induramento, *m.*, ostinazione, *f.* **-dūred**, ADJ.: indurito, inflessibile. **-dūredness**, S.: induramento, *m.*
obēdien-ce, S.: ubbidienza, *f.* **-t**, ADJ.: ubbidiente; sommesso. **-tly**, ADV.: ubbidientemente.
obēisance, S.: riverenza, *f.*; saluto, *m.*
ŏbelisk, S.: obelisco, *m.*; aguglia, *f.*
obĕqui-tate†, INTR.: cavalcare. **-tātion†**, S.: cavalcamento, *m.*
obēs-e, ADJ.: grasso, paffuto. **-eness**, **-ity**, S.: grassezza estrema, *f.*
obēy, TR.: obbedire, ubbidire: *he must be* —*ed*, bisogna ubbidirgli.
obfŭscate, TR.: offuscare.
ŏbit, S.: funerale, *m.*, esequie, *f. pl.*
obĭtuary, S.: necrologia, *f.*; libro de' morti, *m.*
ŏb-ject 1, S.: obietto, oggetto; soggetto, *m.*, materia, *f.*; motivo, *m.* **-jĕct** 2, TR.: obiettare; opporre, rimproverare, incolpare. **-jĕction**, S.: obiezione; opposizione, *f.*: rimprovero, *m.*: *have no* —, non aver nulla in contrario, non eccepire accusa, *f.* **-jĕctionable**, ADJ.: soggetto ad obiezione. **-jĕctive**, ADJ.: oggettivo. **-jĕctively**, ADV.: in modo oggettivo. **-jĕctiveness**, S.: oggettività, *f.*, obiettare, *m.* **-jĕctor**, S.: oppositore, *m.*
objŭr-gate, TR.: rimproverare, riprendere; bravare. **-gātion**, S.: riprensione, ripassata; bravata, *f.* **-gatory**, ADJ.: riprensivo, riprensorio.

ob-lāte, S.: oblato, *m.*; ADJ.: piatto dal canto de' poli. **-lātion**, S.: obblazione, offerta, *f.*; sacrifizio, *m.*
oblĕc-tate†, TR.: dilettare, rallegrare. **-tātion**, S.: diletto, *m.*, giocondità, *f.*
ŏbli-gate, TR.: obbligare, costringere. **-gātion**, S.: obbligazione, *f.*, obbligo; contratto, *m.*: *be under* —, esser obbligato. **-gatory**, ADJ.: obbligatorio.
oblig-e, TR.: obbligare, costringere, sforzare; beneficare: *you will* — *me*, mi obbligherete, mi farete favore. **-ed**, ADJ.: obbligato; ricordevole, grato; *much* —, obbligatissimo. **-ement**, S.: obbliganza, obbligazione, *f.* **-er**, S.: obbligatore; mallevadore, *m.* **-ing**, ADJ.: obbligante; gentile, cortese. **-ingly**, ADV.: obbligantemente. **-ingness**, S.: cortesia; compiacenza, *f.*
ob-liquātion, S.: obbliquità, *f.* **-lîque**, ADJ.: obbliquo; indiretto. **-lîquely**, ADV.: obbliquamente; tortamente. **-lîqueness**, **-liquity**, S.: obbliquità, *f.*
oblĭter-ate, TR.: obliterare; scancellare. **-ātion**, S.: cancellazione; estinzione, dimenticanza, *f*
obliv-ion, S.: obblivione, dimenticanza, *f.*: *act of* —, perdono generale, amnistia, *f.* **-ious**, ADJ.: smemorato, dimentico.
ŏblong, ADJ.: oblungo, bislungo. **-ness**, S.: forma bislunga, *f.*
ŏbloquy, S.: maldicenza, *f.*; biasimo, *m.*
obmutĕscence, S.: perdita della voce, *f.*
obnŏxious, ADJ.: odioso; soggetto; colpevole. **-ness**, S.: odiosità; soggezione, *f.*
obnūbi-late†, TR.: annebbiare, annuvolare, oscurare. **-lātion**, S.: oscuramento, *m.*
ŏbole, S.: obolo, *m.* (moneta).
obrĕption†, S.: insinuazione, *f.*
ob-scēne, ADJ.: osceno, impudico; offensivo. **-scēnely**, ADV.: oscenamente, impudicamente, immodestamente. **-scēneness**, **-scĕnity**, S.: oscenità, impudicizia, *f.*
ob-scurātion, S.: oscuramento, *m.*, oscurazione, *f.* **-scūre** 1, ADJ.: oscuro, tenebroso, buio; difficile. **-scure** 2, TR.: oscurare, offuscare; denigrare, intrigare. **-scūrely**, ADV.: oscuramente. **-scūreness**, S.: oscurità, *f.*, oscuramento, *m.*
ŏbse-crate, TR.: pregare, supplicare, congiurare. **-crātion**, S.: preghiera, *f.*, scongiuro, *m.*
ŏb-sequies, S. PL.: esequie, *f. pl.*, mortorio, *m.* **-sēquious**, ADJ.: ossequioso; cortese, civile. **-sēquiously**, ADV.: ossequiosamente, cortesemente. **-sēquiousness**, S.: ossequio, *m.*, osservanza, ubbidienza, *f.* **-sequy†**, SING. di *-sequies*; ossequio, *m.*
obsĕr-vable, ADJ.: osservabile; notabile, considerabile. **-vably**, ADV.: osserva-

-er, S.: sottile fetta di presciutto, *f.* **-ly**, ADV.: temerariamente. **-ness**, S.: temerità; imprudenza, *f.*

rásp 1, S.: raspa, lima grossa, scuffina, *f.* **rasp** 2, TR.: raspare, raschiare; limare; scrostare (pane). **-atery**, S.: rastiatoio, *m.* **rásp-berry**, S.: lampone, *m.* **-berry-bush**, S.: lampone (pianta), *m.* **-ing**, S.: raschiatura, rastiatura, *f.*

rásure, S.: rasura, raschiatura, cancellatura, *f.*

rát, S.: ratto; topo, sorcio; *m.*: *little* —, topolino; *smell a* —, aver un qualche sentore di suspicare.

ráta-ble, ADJ.: soggetto ad essere tassato. **-bly**, ADV.: per rata; proporzionalmente.

ratafia, S.: amarasco, *m.* (bevanda).

rá-te 1, S.: prezzo, valore, *m.*; tassa, assisa, imposizione; maniera; sfera, *f.*, grado, *m.*: (*of the*) *first* —, di prima sfera; di primo rango (ordine): *at low* —, a vil prezzo, a buon mercato: *at this* —, in questa maniera; *at the old* —, al solito, all'ordinario; *at any* —, comunque siasi; *at the* — *of*, al prezzo di; *second* —, di secondo ordine. **-te** 2, TR.: tassare, apprezzare, stimare, valutare; biasimare, rabbuffare. **-ter**, S.: stimatore, *m.*

rá-th(*e*)†, ADJ.: primaticcio, prematuro. **-ther**, ADV.: piuttosto, anzi; meglio; innanzi: — *cold*, alquanto freddo, piuttosto freddo; — *spiteful*, sdegnosetto; — *than*, anzi che; *the* —, tanto più che; *have* —, amare meglio, preferire.

ratificátion, S.: ratificazione, *f.*

ráti-fier, S.: confermatore, approvatore, *m.* **-fy**, TR.: ratificare; confermare, approvare.

ráting, S.: stimazione, *f.*, apprezzamento, *m.*; riprensione, *f.*

rátio, S.: razione; proporzione, *f.*

ratióci-nate, INTR.: raziocinare. **-nátion**, S.: raziocinio, ragionamento, *m.* **-native**, ADJ.: discorsivo.

rátion, S.: razione; proporzione, *f.*

rátion-al, ADJ.: razionale, ragionevole. **-alism**, S.: ragionalismo, *m.* **-alist**, S.: razionalista, filosofo, *m.* **-álity**, S.: razionalità, ragionevolezza; giustezza, *f.* **-ally**, ADV.: ragionevolmente, con ragione. **-alness** = *rationality*.

rát's-bane, S.: arsenico, *m.* **rát-trap**, S.: trappola da prender topi, *f.*

rattán, S.: sorta di canna (dalle Indie), *f.*

rattéen, S.: rovescio, *m.* (panno).

rátt-le 1, S.: sonaglio, strepito, fracasso: *child's* —, sonaglio, *m.*; *death* —, rantolo (della morte), *m.* **-e** 2, TR.: fare strepito, romoreggiare; riprendere; INTR.: parlare presto; strepitare: — *in the throat*, gorgogliare; — *away*, chiacchierare, non rifinire di parlare. **-e-brained**, **-e-headed**, ADJ.: cervello balzano, scervellato, pazzaccio. **-esnake**, S.: serpente a sonagli, *m.* **-ing**, S.: strepito, fracasso, romore, *m.*

rattóon, S.: volpe delle Indie occidentali, *f.*

ráucity, S.: raucedine, fiocaggine, *f.*

rávag-e 1, S.: strage, rovina, *f.*, guasto, *m.* **-e** 2, TR.: guastare, rovinare, saccheggiare. **-er**, S.: guastatore, saccheggiatore, predatore, *m.*

ráve, INTR.: delirare; esser fuor di sè: — *and tear*, disperarsi.

rável, TR.: imbrogliare, avviluppare, confondere; INTR.: filacciarsi, lambiccarsi il cervello: — *out*, sfilare.

rávelin, S.: (*fort.*) rivellino, *m.*

ráven 1, S.: corvo, corbo, *m.*: *sea* —, corvo marino, *m.*; *young* —, corbicino, *m.* **raven** 2, (IN)TR.: divorare, mangiare con avidità; rapacemente predare. **-ing**, ADJ.: vorace; S.: voracità, *f.*; predamento, *m.*

rávenous, ADJ.: vorace, goloso, ingordo. **-ly**, ADV.: con voracità, ingordamente, avidamente. **-ness**, S.: voracità furiosa; ingordigia, avidità, *f.*

ráver, S.: farnetico, *m.*

rávin, S.: rapina, preda, *f.*

ravíne, S.: borro, *m.*

ráving, ADJ.: delirante; frenetico; S.: delirio, *m.*, frenesia, *f.* **-ly**, ADV.: freneticamente, mattamente.

rávish, TR.: rapire; incantare. **-er**, S.: rapitore; stupratore, *m.* **-ing**, ADJ.: rapace; incantevole; estatico. **-ingly**, ADV.: in modo incantevole. **-ment**, S.: ratto, rapimento; stupro, *m.*; estasi, *f.*

ráw, ADJ.: crudo, fresco; indigesto, novizio: — *leather*, pelle cruda; — *meat*, carne cruda; — *silk*, seta greggia; — *troops*, truppe nuove; — *weather*, tempo freddo e umido. **-boned**, ADJ.: magro, macilento. **-head**, S.: biliorsa, *f.* **-ly**, ADV.: crudamente; sconciamente. **-ness**, S.: crudità; inesperienza; semplicità, *f.*

rây 1, S.: raggio; splendore, *m.* **ray** 2, S.: razza, *f.* (pesce): — *of gold*, foglia d'oro, *f.* **ray** 3, INTR.: raggiare, radiare; splendere. **-less**, ADJ.: senza raggio, oscuro.

rá-ze, TR.: scalfire; rovinare, distruggere: — *out*, cancellare; — *to the ground*, far radere al suolo. **-zor**, S.: rasoio, *m.* **-zor-pouch**, S.: fastello di barbiere, *m.* **-zor-strop**, S.: cuoio, *m.*; correggia da rasoio, *f.* **-zure**, S.: rasura; cancellatura, *f.*

reabsôrb, TR.: riassorbire.

reaccéss, S.: riaccesso, riaccozzamento, *m.*; rivisita, *f.*

-tăgonal, **-tăngular**, ADJ.: ottangolare. **-tave**, S.: ottava, *f.* **-tāvo**, S.: libro in ottavo; ottavo, *m.* **-tĕnnial**, ADJ.: ottennio. **Oc-tōber**, S.: ottobre, *m.* **-togenārian**, **-tŏgenary**, ADJ.: ottuagenario. **-tonary**, ADJ.: ottonario, d' otto. **-topus**, S.: specie di seppia, *f.* **-tosyllable**, ADJ.: ottonario, di otto sillabe. **-tuple**, ADJ.: ottuplo.

ŏcu-lar, ADJ.: oculare, di veduta. **-larly**, ADV.: ocularmente, di veduta. **-list**, S.: oculista, *m.*

ŏdalisk, S.: odalisca, *f.*

ŏdd, ADJ.: impari, dispari; bizzarro, fantastico; cattivo: — *looking*, singolare d' aspetto; — *number*, numero caffo; *play at even and* —, giuocare a pari; *thirty pounds* —, trenta lire sterline e più. **-ity**, S.: singolarità, *f.* **-ly**, ADV.: in modo straordinario, fantasticamente. **-ness**, S.: inegualità; singolarità, stranezza; fantastichezza, *f.* **-s**, S.: disparità; differenza, *f.*; vantaggio, *m.*; superiorità, *f.*: *be at* — *with one*, contendere con uno; *have the* — *of one*, aver l' avvantaggio sopra uno; *fight against* —, battersi con un più forte; — *and ends*, bocconcini, *m. pl.*

ŏde, S.: oda, ode, *f.*

ŏdi-ous, ADJ.: odioso, detestabile. **-ously**, ADV.: odiosamente. **-ousness**, S.: odiosità; atrocità, enormità, *f.* **-um**, S.: odio, *m.*; colpa, *f.*

ŏdour, S.: odore; profumo, *m.*, fragranza, *f.* **-ate**, ADJ.: odorante; odorato. **-iferous**, ADJ.: odorifero, odoroso. **-iferousness**, S.: odoramento, odore, *m.*

oe-conŏmic, ADJ.: economico. **-conŏmics**, S. PL.: economia, *f.* **-cŏnomy**, S.: economia; frugalità, *f.*

oecumĕnical, ADJ.: ecumenico, universale.

oe-dēma, S.: (*surg.*) edema, *m.* **-demătic**, **-dĕmatous**, ADJ.: edematico.

oeilliad†, S.: occhiata, *f.*, sguardo; segno, *m.*

oesŏphagus, S.: esofago, *m.*

ō'er = *over.*

ŏf ŏv, PREP.: di: — *the*, del (dello, della, dei, delle).

ŏff 1, ADV.: lontano, lunge, lungi; via: *well* —, benestante, comodo; *be* —*!* anda via! *far* —, lontano, lungi; — *with your hat!* giù col cappello! *be* — *and on*, esser in bilancia; *go* —, andar via, scoppiare; *push* —*!* scosta! allarga! **off** 2, INTERJ.: via via! andate via! **-hand**, ADJ.: improvviso, espontaneo; ADV.: all' improvvista, senza preparazione.

ŏffal, S.: rimasuglio; avanzo, *m.*

offĕn-ce, S.: offesa; colpa, *f.*; affronto, oltraggio, delitto, *m.*: *give* —, offendere; *take* — *at*, tenersi offeso di. **-ceful**, ADJ.: ingiurioso, offensivo. **-celess**, ADJ.: innocente. **-d**, TR.: offendere; dispiacere; nuocere; INTR.: fallire, peccare: *be* —*ded at*, esser in collera contro. **-der**, S.: offenditore, delinquente, criminale, *m.* **-ding**, S.: offendimento, *m.* **-dress**, S.: offenditrice; malfattrice, *f.* **-sive**, ADJ.: offensivo, ingiurioso; S.: offensiva, *f.*: — *arms*, armi offensive. **-sively**, ADV.: offensivamente. **-siveness**, S.: offesa, ingiuria, *f.*; dispiacere, male, *m.*

ŏffer 1, S.: offerta; profferta, *f.*; tentativo, *m.* **offer** 2, TR.: offerire, presentare; tentare; INTR.: offerirsi, presentarsi; obbligarsi: — *one's self*, esporsi; — *violence*, far violenza; *if you* — *to do it*, si vi provate di farlo. **-er**, S.: offeritore, *m.* **-ing**, S.: offerta, profferta; obblazione, *f.* **-tory**, S.: offertorio, *m.* **-ture**, S.: offerta, profferta, *f.*

ŏffi-ce, S.: ufficio, uffizio; studio; impiego, carico, servizio, *m.*: *high in* —, che copre alto impiego. **-cer**, S.: ufficiale, officiale; funzionario, agente, *m.* **-cered**, ADJ.: *be* — *by*, aver per ufficiali.

offic-ial 1, ADJ.: ufficiale; conducevole; idoneo. **-ial** 2, S.: ufficiale, officiale, *m.* **-ially**, ADV.: ufficialmente, d'ufficio. **-iality**, S.: carica, *f.*; ufficio d'un ufficiale, *m.* **-iate**, TR.: distribuire; INTR.: ufficiare.

officinal, ADJ.: officinale.

officious, ADJ.: officioso; obbligante; affabile. **-ly**, ADV.: officiosamente, cortesemente. **-ness**, S.: prontezza; cortesia; affabilità, *f.*

ŏffing, S.: largo, alto mare, *m.*

ŏff-scouring, S.: lavatura, *f.*; fecce, *f. pl.* **-set**, S.: germoglio, rampollo, *m.* **-spring**, S.: progenie, *f.*, discendenti, *m. pl.*

offŭs-cate, TR.: offuscare, adombrare. **-cātion**, S.: offuscazione, oscurazione, adombrazione, *f.*

ŏft, **ŏften**, ADV.: spesso, sovente: *how* —, quante volte.

oft(en)times, ADV.: spesse volte.

ogēe, S.: (*arch.*) festone, *m.*

ō-gle 1, S.: occhiata, *f.*, sguardo, *m.* **-gle** 2, TR.: occhieggiare; vagheggiare. **-gler**, S.: vagheggiatore. **-gling**, S.: vagheggiare, *m.*

ŏglio, S.: guazzabuglio, *m.*

ōgre, S.: orco, mostro antropofago, *m.*

ōh! INTERJ.: oh! o!

ŏil 1, S.: olio, *m.*: — *of roses*, olio rosato, *m.*; *paint in* —, dipingere a olio. **oil** 2, TR.: ungere con olio: *castor* —, olio di ricino. **-bottle**, S.: oliera, *f.* **-cloth**, S.: tela cerata, *f.* **-colour**, S.: colore a olio, colore misto con olio. **-iness**, S.: oleosità, *f.* **-man**, S.: oliandolo, *m.*

bellante, che si è ribellato, *m.* **-lion**, S.: ribellione, *f.*, ribellamento, *m.* **-lious**, ADJ.: ribello, ribellante. **-liously**, ADV.: in modo ribellante. **-liousness**, S.: ribellamento, *m.*

rebéllow, TR.: rimugghiare, remuggire.

rebóil, INTR.: ribollire.

rebóund 1, S.: rimbalzo, balzo, *m.* **rebound** 2, (IN)TR.: rimbalzare, ribalzare.

rebréathe, INTR.: respirare di nuovo.

rebúff 1, S.: ripercussione, *f.* **rebuff** 2, TR.: ripercuotere; rifiutare.

rebuild, IRR.; TR.: fabbricare di nuovo, rifabbricare.

rebú-kable, ADJ.: riprensibile, biasimevole. **-ke** 1, S.: rimprovero, *m.*, bravata, *f.* **-ke** 2, TR.: riprendere, ripigliare, sgridare. **-keful**, ADJ.: agro, severo. **-kefully**, ADV.: agramente, severamente. **-ker**, S.: riprenditore, rimproveratore, *m.*

rebullítion, S.: ribollimento, *m.*

rébus, S.: rebus, geroglifico, *m.*

rebút, TR.: ributtare, rispingere. **-ter**, S.: replica, risposta, *f.*

recálcitrant, ADJ.: ostinato, ribelle.

recáll 1, S.: richiamo, *m.* **recall** 2, TR.: richiamare, fare ritornare.

recánt, TR.: ritrattare, disdire; INTR.: ritrattarsi, disdirsi. **-átion**, S.: ritrattazione, disdetta, *f.* **-er**, S.: che si ritratta.

recapácitate, TR.: qualificare di nuovo.

recapitu-late, TR.: ricapitolare. **-látion**, S.: ricapitolazione, *f.*

recápture 1, S.: cattura ricuperata, *f.* **recapture** 2, TR.: ricuperare una cattura.

recárry, TR.: riportare, portare indietro.

recást, IRR.; TR.: rigettare.

recéde, INTR.: recedere, tornare indietro, ritirarsi.

recéipt 1, S.: ricevuta, ricetta; quitanza, *f.*, ricevimento, *m.*; riscossione, riscossa, *f.* **receipt** 2, TR.: quitanzare, mettere il saldo a: *—ed*, pagato, soldato.

recéi-vable, ADJ.: accettabile, ammissibile. **-ve**, TR.: ricevere, accettare, ammettere, pigliare; accogliere: — *kindly*, accogliere amorevolmente, fare buona accoglienza a; — *a loss*, fare una perdita; — *an opinion*, abbracciare un' opinione; — *taxes*, riscuotere le tasse. **-vedness**, S.: ammissione generale, *f.* **-ver**, S.: ricevitore, ricettatore, *m.*

recélebrate, TR.: celebrare di nuovo.

récency, S.: novità; freschezza, *f.*

recén-se, TR.: rivedere, esaminare. **-sion**, S.: rivista; enumerazione, *f.*

récent, ADJ.: recente, nuovo, fresco. **-ly**, ADV.: recentemente; frescamente; poco tempo fa. **-ness**, S.: novità; freschezza, *f.*

recép-tacle, S.: ricettacolo; ricovero, *m.*

récep-tary†, S.: ricevuta, *f.* **-tibility**, S.: possibilità di ricevere, *f.* **-tion**, S.: ricevuta; accoglienza, *f.* **-tive**, ADJ.: ricettivo. **-tory**, ADJ.: ammesso, ricevuto.

re-céss, S.: recesso, ritiro; luogo ritirato, vano, *m.*, solitudine, *f.*; vacanze: *Easter* —, vacanze di Pasqua. **-céssion**, S.: recedimento, ritiramento, *m.*

rechánge, TR.: cangiare di nuovo.

rechárge, TR.: raccusare; ricominciare l' attacco, rassalire.

rechéat, S.: (*hunt.*) chiamata, *f.*

récipe, S.: recipe, *m.*, ricetta, prescrizione medica, *f.*

recípient, S.: recipiente, *m.*

recípro-cal, ADJ.: reciproco, vicendevole. **-cally**, ADV.: reciprocamente, vicendevolmente, mutualmente. **-calness**, S.: vicendevolezza, *f.*; cambio, *m.* **-cate**, (IN)TR.: operare a vicenda, render la pariglia, alternare. **-cátion**, S.: reciprocazione; vicenda, *f.* **reciprócity**, S.: scambievolezza, *f.*, contraccambio, cambio, *m.*

recísion, S.: tagliamento, mozzamento, *m.*, mutilazione, *f.*

re-cítal, S.: repetizione; narrazione, relazione, *f.* **-citátion**, S.: recitazione; narrazione, *f.* **-citatíve**, **-citativo**, S.: (*mus.*) recitativo, *m.* **-cite**, TR.: recitare; raccontare, narrare. **-citer**, S.: recitatore, narratore, *m.*

réck, TR.: curare, pigliar cura; INTR.: curarsi; inquietarsi. **-less**, ADJ.: negligente, trascurato, indifferente. **-lessness**, S.: negligenza, trascuraggine, *f.* **-on**, TR.: contare; stimare; riputare; INTR.: pensare; calcolare, computare; dipendere: *don't — your chickens before they are hatched*, non dir quattro se tu non l' hai nel sacco; — *without one's host*, fare i conti senza l' oste. **-oner**, S.: calcolatore, computista, *m.* **-oning**, S.: conto, *m.*, computa, *f.*; scotto; giudizio, *m.*: *dead* —, rotta stimata, *f.*; *off* —, disconto, *m.*; diduzione, *f.*

re-cláim, TR.: richiamare; riformare; correggere; INTR.: riformarsi; correggersi. **-cláimable**, ADJ.: che si può ricuperare. **-cláimant**, S.: contraddicente, *m.* **-clamátion**, S.: richiamo; ricuperamento, *m*

recline 1, ADJ.: reclinante; chinato. **recline** 2, TR.: inclinare; riposare.

reclú-se 1, ADJ.: ritirato, richiuso, solitario; S.: solitario, *m.* **-se** 2, TR.: rinchiudere. **-sely**, ADV.: ritiratamente. **-seness**, **-sion**, S.: ritiratezza, *f.* **-sive**, ADJ.: ritirato, solitario; privato, segreto.

re-cógnisance, S.: scrittura d' obbligo, *f.* **-cognítion**, S.: ricognizione; confes-

ŏnset 1, s.: assalto, attacco, *m.* **onset** 2, TR.: assaltare, attacare.
ŏnslaught, s.: attacco impetuoso, *m.*
ontŏl-ogist, s.: metafisico, *m.* **-ogy**, s.: ontologia, metafisica, *f.*
ŏnward, ADV.: avanti: *go* —, avanzarsi.
ŏnyx, s.: onice, *m.*
ōoz-e, s.: malta; melma, *f.*; fango, *m.* **-e** 2, INTR.: trapelare, gocciolare. **-y**, ADJ.: melmoso, fangoso.
o-pācate†, TR.: rendere opaco; oscurare; annuvolare. **-păcity**, s.: opacità; spessezza, *f.* **-pācous**, ADJ.: opaco, oscuro; denso. **-pācousness** = opacity.
ōpal, s.: opalo, *m.*
ōpe = *open.* **-n** 1, ADJ.: aperto, scoperto; evidente, chiaro; sincero: *a little* —, mezzo aperto; *wide* —, spalancato; *in the* — *air*, a cielo scoperto; — *weather*, tempo sereno, tempo moderato, *m.*; *keep* — *table*, tener corte bandita; *lay* —, esporre, palesare; *with* — *arms*, a braccia aperto; *keep* — *bowels*, tenere pervie le vie. **-n** 2, TR.: aprire, scoprire; INTR.: aprirsi; fendersi: — *a letter*, dissuggellare; — *a bottle*, sturare una bottiglia; — *a vein*, cavare sangue. **-ner**, s.: apritore; espositore, *m.* **-n-eyed**, ADJ.: vigilante, attento. **-n-handed**, ADJ.: generoso, liberale. **-n-hearted**, ADJ.: franco, sincero; generoso. **-n-heartedness**, s.: franchezza, liberalità; generosità, *f.* **-ning**, ADJ.: aperitivo; lassativo; s.: apertura, *f.*; principio, *m.* **-nly**, ADV.: apertamente; evidentemente; liberamente, francamente. **-n-mouthed**, ADJ.: vorace, goloso. **-nness**, s.: chiarezza; franchezza, sincerità, *f.*
ŏper-a, s.: opera (musicale), *f.*: *comic* —, opera buffa. **-able**, ADJ.: operabile, praticabile. **-a-glass**, s.: occhialino, piccol occhiale, *m.* **-ate**, INTR.: operare; produrre. **-ātion**, s.: operazione, *f.*; effetto, *m.* **-ative**, ADJ.: operativo, efficiente. **-ator**, s.: operatore; agente, fattore; cerretano, *m.* **-ose**, ADJ.: operoso, laborioso, faticoso.
ŏphites, s.: ofite, serpentino, *m.*
ophthăl-mic, ADJ.: oftalmico, ottalmico. **-my**, s.: oftalmia, *f.*
ōpiate, s.: (*phar.*) oppiato, medicamento narcotico, *m.*
opin-e, INTR.: opinare, pensare; immaginarsi. **-er**, s.: opinante, *m.*
opin-iative, ADJ.: immaginato. **-iatively**, ADV.: ostinatamente, pertinacemente. **-iativeness**, s.: ostinazione, caparbietà, *f.* **-iātor**, s.: caparbio; protervo, *m.* **-iātre**†, ADJ.: ostinato, pertinace. **-iātetry**†, **-iatry**†, s.: ostinazione, pertinacia, caparbietà, *f.* **-ion**, s.: opinione, *f.*; pensiero, sentimento, *m.*; stima, *f.* **-ionat(ed)**, ADJ.: ostinato, pertinace. **-ionist**, s.: caparbio, protervo, *m.*
ōpium, s.: oppio, *m.*
opŏssum, s.: 'opossum,' *m.*, sariga, *f.*
ŏppidan, s.: borghese, cittadino, *m.*
oppignerate†, TR.: impegnare.
ŏppi-late†, TR.: oppilare, costipare, ostruire. **-lātion**, s.: oppilazione, *f.*, turamento, *m.* **-lative**†, ADJ.: oppilativo, costipativo, ostruttivo.
oppō-ne†, TR.: opporre, ripugnare. **-nent**, ADJ.: opponente; contrario; s.: opponente, avversario, *m.*
opportūn-e, ADJ.: opportuno, conveniente. **-ely**, ADV.: opportunamente, a tempo. **-ity**, s.: opportunità; occasione; comodità, *f.*: *avail one's self of an* —, profittare di un' occazione, approfittarsi dell' opportunità.
oppō-sal, s.: opponimento, *m.* **-se**, TR.: opporre; resistere, contrariare; INTR.: opporsi; contraddire. **-seless**, ADJ.: irresistibile. **-ser**, s.: oppositore, avversario, *m.*
ŏppo-site, ADJ.: opposito, contrario, avverso; s.: avversario, antagonista, *m.* **-sitely**, ADV.: faccia a faccia, dirimpetto, di rincontro. **-siteness**, s.: opposto, *m.*, contrarietà, *f.* **-sition**, s.: opposizione, resistenza, contrarietà, *f.*
op-prĕss, TR.: opprimere, soggiogare. **-prĕssion**, s.: oppressione; severità, *f.* **-prĕssive**, ADJ.: oppressivo, crudele. **-prĕssively**, ADV.: in modo oppressivo. **-prĕssor**, s.: oppressore; perseguitatore, *m.*
opprō-brious, ADJ.: obbrobrioso, vituperoso; ignominioso. **-briously**, ADV.: obbrobriosamente. **-briousness**, **-brium**, s.: obbrobrio, *m.*; ignominia; infamia, *f.*
op-pūgn, TR.: oppugnare, resistere; assalire. **-pŭgnancy**, s.: oppugnamento; contrasto, *m.* **-pūgner**, s.: oppugnatore; opponente, *m.*
ŏpta-ble†, ADJ.: desiderabile. **-tive**, ADJ.: ottativo; s.: (*gram.*) modo ottativo, *m.*
ŏp-tic(al), ADJ.: ottico, visuale. **-tician**, s.: ottico, *m.*, che sa l'ottica. **-tics**, s. PL.: ottica, *f.*
ŏpti-macy, s.: ottimato, *m.*, nobilità, *f.* **-mism**, s.: ottimismo, *m.* **-mist**, s.: ottimista, *m.*
ŏption, s.: scelta; volontà, *f.*, arbitrio, *m.* **-al**, ADJ.: libero a scegliersi: *be* — *with*, avere la scelta, avere la facoltà di scegliere.
ŏpulen-ce, s.: opulenza; ricchezza, *f.* **-t**, ADJ.: opulento, ricco. **-tly**, ADV.: opulentemente, riccamente.

recubation, S.: inclinazione, *f.*; riposamento, *m.*
recumben-ce, **-cy**, S.: giacimento, *m.* **-t**, ADJ.: giacente, riposante.
recuper-able, ADJ.: ricuperabile. **-ate**, TR.: ricuperare, ricoverare. **-ation**, S.: ricuperazione, *f.*, ricovero, *m.* **-ative**, ADJ.: ricuperante.
re-cur, INTR.: ricorrere, ritornare; rifuggire; accadere; aver ricorso. **-currence**, **-currency**, S.: ritorno, ricorrimento, *m.* **-current**, ADJ.: ricorrente; periodico.
recursion, S.: ricorso, ritorno, *m.*
recur-vate, TR.: curvare, incurvare. **-vation**, S.: curvità; curvatura, *f.* **-vous**, ADJ.: ricurvo, incurvato.
recu-sant, S.: ricusante; non conformista, *m.* **-sation†**, S.: ricusazione, *f.*; rifiuto, *m.* **-se**, TR.: ricusare; rifiutare.
red 1, ADJ.: rosso, vermiglio: — *face*, viso bernoccoluto, *m.*; — *lips*, labbra vermiglie, *f. pl.*; *get* —, diventar rosso. **red** 2, S.: rosso, color rosso; belletto, *m.* **-breast**, S.: pettirosso, *m.* (uccello). **-coat**, S.: soldato inglese, *m.* (scherz.). **-deer**, S.: salvaggina, *f.* **-den**, (IN)TR.: arrossire, divenire rosso. **-dish**, ADJ.: rossiccio, alquanto rosso. **-dishness**, S.: color rossiccio, *m.*
red-dition, S.: rendimento, *m.*, restituzione, *f.* **red-ditive**, ADJ.: risponsivo.
reddle, S.: sanguigna, *f.*
rede 1, S.: avviso, avvertimento, consiglio, *m.* **rede** 1, TR.: dar consiglio, consigliare.
redeem, TR.: redimere, riscattare, ricomprare. **-able**, ADJ.: redimibile. **-ableness**, S.: redimibilità, *f.* **-er**, S.: redentore; salvatore, *m.*
redeliberate, TR.: deliberare di nuovo.
redeliver, TR.: liberare di nuovo; restituire. **-y**, S.: liberazione di nuovo; restituzione, *f.*
redemand, TR.: ridomandare; richiedere.
redemp-tion, S.: redenzione, *f.*; riscatto, *m.* **-tory**, S.: redentorio, *m.*
redescend, INTR.: discendere di nuovo.
red-haired, **-headed**, ADJ.: rosso crinito, dai capelli rossi. **-hot**, ADJ.: infocato, rovente.
redinte-grate 1, TR.: reintegrare, rinnovare. **-grate** 2, ADJ.: reintegrato, rinnovato. **-gration**, S.: reintegrazione, *f.*; ristauro, *m.*
red-lead, S.: minio, *m.* **-ness**, S.: rossore, *m.*, rossezza, *f.* **-letter**, ADJ.: stampare in lettere rosse: — *day*, giorno di felicità, di festa, *m.*
redolen-ce, **-cy**, S.: profundo, buon odore, *m.*; ADJ.: profumato, odoroso.
redoubl-e, (IN)TR.: raddoppiare; reiterare; aumentare. **-ing**, S.: raddoppiamento; aumento, *m.*
redoubt, S.: ridotto, fortino, *m.* **-able**, **-ed**, ADJ.: formidabile, terribile.
redound, INTR.: ridondare; ribalzare; risultare.
redress 1, S.: riforma, correzione, emendazione, *f.*, rimedio, *m.*; riparazione del danno, *m.* **redress** 2, TR.: (rad)drizzare, riformare; correggere; rimediare; aggiustare: — *one's self*, farsi giustizia di sua mano; — *a grievance*, rimediare (*or* correggere) un abuso. **-er**, S.: riformatore; correttore, *m.* **-ive**, ADJ.: riformante; che conforta. **-less**, ADJ.: irremediabile.
red-sear, INTR.: rompersi al batter del martello. **-skin**, S.: pelirosso, *m*, pelle rossa, *f.* **-tail**, S.: codirosso, *m.* (uccello). **-tape**, **-tapism**, S.: burocrazia, *f.*
redu-ce, TR.: ridurre; ristorare; costringere, domare; abbassare: — *to ashes*, ridurre in polvere. **-cement**, S.: riducimento, *m.* **-cer**, S.: riducitore, riduttore, *m.* **-cible**, ADJ.: riducibile. **-cibleness**, S.: possibilità di ridurre, *f.*
reduc-t = *reduce*. **-tion**, S.: riduzione, *f.*, riducimento, *m.* **-tive**, ADJ.: riduttivo, riducente. **-tively**, ADV.: per riduzione.
redundan-ce, **-cy**, S.: ridondanza, superfluità, *f.* **-t**, ADJ.: ridondante, superfluo. **-tly**, ADV.: soprabbondantemente.
redupli-cate, TR.: raddoppiare; aumentare, crescere. **-cation**, S.: raddoppiamento; aumento, *m.* **-cative**, ADJ.: reduplicativo.
red-wing, S.: tordo rosso, *m.* (uccello). **-wood**, S.: albero gigante di California, *m.*
re-echo, INTR.: echeggiare.
reechy†, ADJ.: fumoso, caliginoso.
reed, S.: canna; saetta, *f.*
re-edification, S.: riedificazione, *f.* **-edify**, TR.: riedificare, rifabbricare.
reed-less, ADJ.: senza canne. **-plot**, S.: canneto, *m.* **-y**, ADJ.: cannoso, pieno di canne.
reef 1, TR.: ammainare le vele. **reef** 2, S.: scoglio (a fior d' acqua), *m.*
reek 1, S.: fumo, vapore; mucchio (di fieno), *m.* **reek** 2, INTR.: fumare; svaporare. **-ing**, ADJ.: fumante; fumoso. **-y**, ADJ.: fumoso; nero.
reel 1, S.: aspo, naspo; guindolo, *m.* **reel** 2, TR.: innaspare, aggomitolare; INTR.: traballare, barcollare: — *off*, aguindolare; *my head* —*s*, mi gira il capo. **-ing**, S.: barcollamento; vacillamento, *m.*
re-election, S.: rielezione, *f.*

rę-embârk, (IN)TR.: imbarcare; imbarcarsi di nuovo.
rę-enăct, TR.: ordinare di nuovo.
rę-enfōrce, TR.: rinforzare, fortificare. **-ment**, S.: rinforzamento, *m.*; rinforzata, *f.*
rę-engāge, TR.: impegnare di nuovo; attacar di nuovo (la battaglia). **-ment**, S.: obbligo nuovo, *m.*
rę-enjŏy, TR.: rigodere; possedere di nuovo.
rę-enkĭndle, TR.: riaccendere.
rę-ĕntęr, TR.: rientrare, entrare di nuovo.
rę-enthrōne, TR.: rimettere in trono.
rę-ĕntrance, S.: rientramento, *m.*
rēermouse, S.: pipistrello, *m.*
rę-estăblish, TR.: ristabilire, ristaurare. **-estăblishęr**, S.: riparatore, ristoratore, *m.* **-estăblishment**, S.: ristabilimento, *m.*
rēeve 1, S.: fattore; guardiano (d'un feudo), *m.* **reeve** 2, TR.: tirare una corda.
rę-ęxamināţion, S.: seconda esaminazione, *f.* **-ęxămine**, TR.: esaminare di nuovo.
rę-exchānge, S.: (*com.*) ricambio, contraccambio, *m.*
ręfĕc-t†, INTR.: rifarsi; ristaurarsi. **-ţion**, S.: refezione, *f.*; ristoro, *m.* **-tọry**, S.: refettorio, *m.*
ręfĕl†, TR.: confutare, riprovare.
ręfĕr, TR.: riferire; rimettere; rimandare; INTR.: rapportarsi: *I — it to you*, lo riferisco (*or* rimetto) a voi.
rĕfęr-able, ADJ.: riferibile. **-ĕe**, S.: arbitro; compromissario, *m.* **-ence**, S.: relazione, *f.*; rapporto; arbitrato, *m.*: *in — to*, in quanto a, in relazione a, a proposito di. **-ĕndary**, S.: referendario, *m.*
ręfęr-mĕnt, TR.: fermentare di nuovo.
ręfĕr-rible, ADJ.: riferibile. **-ring**, S.: riferimento, rapporto, *m.*
ręfind, IRR.; TR.: ritrovare.
ręfi-ne, TR.: raffinare, purificare; INTR.: raffinarsi, purificarsi. **-ned**, ADJ.: raffinato; affinato, purificato, puro; colto, elegante. **-nedly**, ADV.: raffinatamente; con eleganza troppo studiata. **-nement**, S.: raffinamento, *m.*; eleganza, *f.* **-nęr**, S.: raffinatore, affinatore, *m.* **-nęry**, S.: raffinatura, *f.*
ręfit, TR.: riparare; racconciare. **-ting**, S.: racconciamento, ammannamento, *m.*
ręflĕc-t, TR.: ripercuotere; rimandare; INTR.: riflettere, meditare; cascare: *— upon one*, criticare (biasimare) uno. **-tent**†, ADJ.: riflettente; ripercussivo. **-ting**, **-ţion**, S.: riflessione; meditazione, *f.*; riverbero, *m.* **-tive**, ADJ.: riflessivo, meditativo. **-tọr**, S.: meditante, consideratore; riverberatore, *m.*

rē-flex, ADJ.: riflesso; riverberato; S.: riflessione; riverberazione, *f.* **-flexibility**, S.: riflessibilità, *f.* **-flĕxible**, ADJ.: riflessibile. **-flĕxion** = *reflection*. **-flĕxive**, ADJ.: riflessivo; ripercussivo. **-flĕxively**, ADV.: per riflessione.
ręflōat, S.: riflusso, *m.*
ręflŏurish, INTR.: rifiorire, fiorire di nuovo.
ręflōw, IRR.; INTR.: rifluire; ritornare.
rĕfluent, ADJ.: refluo; che fluisce di nuovo.
rēflux, S.: riflusso, *m.*
ręfôrm 1, S.: riforma, *f.* **reform** 2, TR.: riformare; sbandare; INTR.: riformarsi. **-āţion**, S.: riformazione, *f.* **-ęr**, S.: riformatore, *m.* **-ist**, S.: riformato, Protestante, *m.*
ręfŏund, TR.: rifondere.
ręfrăc-t, TR.: rifrangere, riflettere. **-ţion**, S.: rifrangimento, *m.*, rifrazione, *f.* **-tive**, ADJ.: rifrattivo. **-tọrily**, ADV.: ostinatamente. **-tọriness**, S.: caparbieria, ostinazione, *f.* **-tọry**, ADJ.: rifrattario, caparbio, ostinato.
rĕfragable, ADJ.: refragabile.
ręfrāin 1, S.: (*mus.*) ritornello, *m.* **refrain** 2, TR.: raffrenare, reprimere; INTR.: raffrenarsi, astenersi, contenersi: *I could not — from*, non potei restarmi di.
ręfrangibility, S.: rifrangibilità, *f.* **-frăngible**, ADJ.: rifrangibile.
ręfrĕsh, TR.: rinfrescare; ristorare; rifocillare: *— one's self*, rinfrescarsi; ricrearsi, ristorarsi. **-ęr**, S.: rifrigerante; ricreatore, *m.* **-ing** 1, S.: rinfrescamento; conforto, *m.* **-ing** 2, ADJ.: rinfrescativo. **-ment**, S.: rinfrescamento; riposo, ristoro, *m.*
ręfrigęr-ant, ADJ.: refrigerante, refrigerativo. **-ate**, TR.: refrigerare, rinfrescare. **-āţion**, S.: refrigerazione, *f.*, rinfresco, *m.* **-ątive**, **-atọry** 1, ADJ.: refrigerativo, refrigerante. **-atory** 2, S.: refrigeratorio, *m.*
rĕfų-ge 1, S.: rifugio; asilo; sostegno, *m.*: *take — with*, rifugiarsi presso. **-ge** 2, TR.: dare rifugio, dare asilo, proteggere. **-ģēe**, S.: rifuggito, rifuggente, *m.*
ręfŭlgen-ce, **-cy**, S.: splendore, lustro, *m.* **-t**, ADJ.: rifulgente, lucido.
ręfŭnd, TR.: rifondere; restituire; rendere.
ręfū-ṣable, ADJ.: rifiutabile. **-ṣal**, S.: rifiuto, *m.*, ripulsa; scelta; preferenza, *f.*: *— meet with a —*, esser rifiutato, esser ributtato. **rĕfųse**, S.: rifiuto; resto, *m.*; feccia, *f.* **refū-ṣe**, TR.: rifiutare; rigettare, ributtare; ricusare. **-ṣęr**, S.: rifiutatore, rifiutante, *m.* **-ṣing**, S.: rifiuto, *m.*

refū-table, ADJ.: rifiutabile. **-tātion**, S.: confutazione, *f.* **-te**, TR.: confutare; riprovare. **-ter**, S.: confutatore, *m.*
regāin, TR.: riguadagnare; ricuperare.
rēgal, ADJ.: regale, reale; regio.
regāle 1, S.: banchetto, festino; convito, *m.* **regale** 2, TR.: regalare, far festa. **-ment** = *regale.*
regālia, S.: insegne reali, *f. pl.*, regalia, *f.*
regālity, S.: dignità reale, sovranità, *f.*
rēgally, ADV.: regalmente, da re.
regard 1, S.: riguardo, rispetto, *m.*, considerazione; stima, *f.*: *in* —, per riguardo, per rispetto; *in* — *of*, in quanto a, per rispetto di; *in* — *to*, in paragone di; *my kind* —*s to your uncle*, i miei complimenti al vostro signor zio. **regard** 2, TR.: riguardare, rispettare, aver riguardo: *as* —*s*, riguardo a; per quel che riguarda; quanto a. **-able**, ADJ.: riguardevole; osservabile. **-er**, S.: riguardatore; osservatore, *m.* **-ful**, ADJ.: attento, accurato, diligente. **-fully**, ADV.: attentamente; con rispetto. **-less**, ADJ.: senza riguardo, negligente, indifferente. **-lessly**, ADV.: disattentamente; indifferentemente. **-lessness**, S.: negligenza, trascurataggine; inattenzione, *f.*
regātta, S.: regata, corsa di barche, *f.*
rēgency, S.: reggenza, *f.*; governo, *m.*
regēner-acy, S.: rigenerazione, *f.* **-ate** 1, ADJ.: rigenerato. **-ate** 2, TR.: rigenerare, riprodurre. **-ātion**, S.: rigenerazione, *f.*
rēgent, ADJ.: reggente; S.: reggente, *m.* **-ess**, S.: reggente, *f.* **-ship**, S.: dignità di reggente, *f.*
regērmi-nate, TR.: rigermogliare. **-nātion**, S.: rigermogliare, *m.*
regēst†, S.: registro, *m.*
rēgicide, S.: regicida; regicidio, *m.*
régime (*Engl. acc.*) *rezím*, S.: reggimento, *m.*, amministrazione, *f.*
rēgimen, S.: dieta, *f.*; modo di vivere, *m.*
rēgi-ment, S.: reggimento, governo, *m.*; condotta, *f.* **-mēntal**, ADJ.: di reggimento. **-mēntals**, S. PL.: abito uniforme, *m.*
rēgion, S.: regione; provincia, *f.*; paese, *m.*: — *of the heart*, sede del cuore, *f.*
rēgis-ter 1, S.: registro; cancelliere, *m.* **-ter** 2, TR.: registrare; notare nel registro. **-tering**, S.: registratura, *f.* **-trar**, S.: registratore, cancelliere; archivista; secretario, *m.* **-trātion**, S.: registratura, *f.* **-try**, S.: registratura; cancelleria, *f.*
rēglet, S.: (*typ.*) riga, *f.*
rēgnant, ADJ.: regnante, predominante.
regōrge, TR.: ringorgare, vomitare.
regrāde, INTR.: ritirarsi.
regrāft, TR.: innestare di nuovo.
regrānt, TR.: concedere di nuovo.
regrāte, TR.: incettare; offendere. **-er**, S.: rigattiere, incettatore, monopolista, *m.*
regrēet 1, S.: risalutazione, *f.* **regreet** 2, TR.: risalutare, salutare di nuovo.
rē-gress, S.: regresso, ritorno, *m*; uscita, *f.* **-grēss**, INTR.: tornare indietro. **-grēssion**, S.: rigressione, *f.*
regrēt, S.: rammarico; dolore, *m.*: *with* —, mal volentieri. **regret** 2, TR.: rincrescere, compiangere; dolersi. **-ful**, ADJ.: rincrescevole. **-fully**, ADV.: rincrescevolmente.
reguērdon†, S.: guiderdone, *m.*, ricompensa, *f.*
rēgu-lar 1, ADJ.: regolare; ordinato, esatto: *in a* — *way*, secondo le regole, regolarmente. **-lar** 2, regolare, religioso, *m.* **-lărity**, S.: regolarità, *f.*, ordine, *m.*; esattezza, *f.* **-larly**, ADV.: regolarmente, secondo le regole. **-late**, TR.: regolare, ordinare; dirigere, governare. **-lātion**, S.: regolamento, ordinamento, *m.* **-later**, S.: regolatore; bilanciere, *m.*
regūrgi-tate, (IN)TR.: regurgitare, ringorgare. **-tātion**, S.: regurgitamento, *m.*
rehabili-tate, TR.: riabilitare. **-tātion**, S.: riabilitazione, *f.*
rehāsh, TR.: rifare goffamente.
rehēar, IRR.; TR.: riudire, udire di nuovo.
rehēar-sal, S.: ripetizione; relazione, narrazione; prova, *f.* **-se**, TR.: ripetere, recitare; provare. **-ser**, S.: recitatore, repetitore, *m.*
rêign 1, S.: regno, governo, dominio, *m.* **reign** 2, INTR.: regnare, dominare; prevalere. **-ing**, ADJ.: regnante, dominante.
reimbŏdy, TR.: incorporare di nuovo.
reimbūrse, TR.: rimborsare; restituire. **-ment**, S.: rimborsazione, *f.*, rimborso, *m.*
reimportūne, TR.: importunare di nuovo.
reimprēgnate, TR.: rimpregnare, ringravidare.
re-imprēssion, S.: ristampa; edizione nuova, *f.* **-imprint**, TR.: ristampare.
rêin 1, S.: redina, redine, *f.*: *give the* —*s*, *let loose the* —*s*, sciorre la briglia. **rein** 2, TR.: raffrenare, restringere; governare: *keep a tight* —, tener il freno. **-deer**, S.: renna, *f.*
reinfōrce, TR.: rinforzare. **-ment**, S.: rinforzamento, *m.*
reingrātiate, INTR.: rimettersi nella buona grazia.
rêinless, ADJ.: senza redine.
rêin-moss, S.: lichene delle renne, *m.*
rêins, S.: reni, lombi, *m. pl.*; schiena, *f.*
reinsērt, TR.: inserire di nuovo.
reinspire, TR.: inspirare di nuovo.
reinstāll, TR.: rimettere in possesso.

-buy, IRR.; TR.: comprare troppo caro. **-cărry**, TR.: portare troppo innanzi. **-căst**, IRR.; TR.: offuscare, oscurare, adombrare; INTR.: offuscarsi, adombrarsi: *become* —, annuvolarsi, oscurarsi. **'-cău-tious**, ADJ.: troppo cauto. **-charge**, S.: sopraccarico; rincarimento, *m*. **-chârge**, TR.: caricare troppo; opprimere; rincarire. **-clŏud**, TR.: annuvolare, oscurare. **-cloy**, TR.: satollare. **-coat**, S.: soprabito, *m*. **-cóme**, IRR.; TR.: superare, soverchiare, sormontare; vincere. **-cómer**, S.: superatore; vincitore, *m*. **'-cŏnfident**, ADJ.: troppo ardito, presuntuoso. **-cŏunt**, TR.: domandare troppo. **'-cūrious**, ADJ.: troppo curioso. **-dō**, IRR.; TR.: fare troppo, eccedere; faticar troppo; opprimere: — *one's self*, fatticarsi troppo. **-dóne**, ADJ.: esagerato; troppo cotto, stracotto. **-dose**, S.: dose troppo forte, *f*. **-drăw**, TR.: esagerare; fare una tratta che eccede il credito. **-drĕss**, TR.: vestire con troppa pompa; INTR.: adornarsi troppo. **-drive**, IRR.; TR.: fare andare troppo presto, stimolare troppo. **'-dūe**, ADJ.: (*com.*) scaduto; (*post.*) in ritardo. **'-ēager**, ADJ.: troppo ardente. **'-ēagerly**, ADV.: troppo ardentemente. **'-ēagerness**, S.: troppo grande ardore, *m*. **-ēat**, IRR.; INTR.: — *one's self*, mangiar troppo. **-ēye**, TR.: invigliare, osservare. **-făll**, S.: cateratta, cascata d'acquata, *f*. **-fill**, TR.: empiere troppo. **-fine**, ADJ.: strafino. **-flōat**, INTR.: fiottare; galleggiare. **-flow**, S.: inondazione, *f*. **-flōw**, IRR.; (IN)TR.: inondare, traboccare. **-flōwing**, S.: soprabbondanza, *f*.; eccesso, *m*. **-flōwingly**, ADV.: soprabbondantemente. **-flȳ**, IRR.; INTR.: sopravvolare. **-fŏnd**, ADJ.: troppo affezionato. **-fŏrward**, ADJ.: troppo sollecito, troppo frettoloso. **-fŏrwardness**, S.: troppa premura, *f*. **-frĕight**, TR.: caricare troppo, sopraccaricare. **-glânce**, TR.: dare un' occhiata. **-gĕt**, IRR.; TR.: sopraggiungere; arrivare. **-gō**, IRR.; TR.: sorpassare. **-gŏrge**, TR.: satollare; impinzare. **'-grêat**, ADJ.: troppo grande, eccessivo. **-grōw**, IRR.; INTR.: crescere troppo grande: —*n with*, coperto di. **-grōwth**, S.: accrescimento eccessivo, *m*. **-hāle**, TR.: (*nav.*) esaminare di nuovo. **-hăng**, IRR.; (IN)TR.: pendere in fuori, aggettare. **'-hăppy**, ADJ.: troppo felice. **-hărden**, TR.: indurire troppo. **-hāsten**, TR.: affrettar troppo. **-hāstiness**, S.: fretta soverchia, *f*. **'-hāsty**, ADJ.: troppo affrettato, frettoloso, precipitoso. **-hâul** = *overhale*. **-hĕad**, ADV.: in alto, sopra, in su. **-hēar**, IRR.; TR.: udire senza essere osservato. **-hēat**, TR.: scaldare soverchio, infiammare: — *one's self*, scaldarsi troppo. **-joy**, S.: estasi, *f*., eccesso di gioia, *m*. **-jŏy**, TR.: inondare di gioia, deliziare: *I am —ed at it*, me ne rallegro sommamente. **-lābour**, TR.: faticare; INTR.: affaticarsi. **-lāde**, IRR.; TR.: sopraccaricare; aggravare. **'-lârge**, ADJ.: troppo largo, troppo ampio. **-lāy**, IRR.; TR.: affogare, soffolcare, incrostare; coprire: — *with silver*, coprire di argento. **-lēap**, IRR.; TR.: saltare di là; trapassare. **-leather**, S.: tomaio, *m*. **-live**, (IN)TR.: sopprayvivere, vivere più di. **-liver**, S.: sopravvivente, *m*. **-lōad**, TR.: sopraccaricare; aggravare. **'-lŏng**, ADJ.: troppo lungo. **-lóok**, TR.: aver l'ispezione; soprastare, dominare; invigilare; esaminare; chiudere gli occhi; trascurare; tenere a sdegno, disprezzare; rivedere: *the hill —s the town*, il colle domina la città. **-looker**, S.: soprantendente; soprastante, *m*. **-mâster**, TR.: governare da padrone. **-mătch**, S.: partita ineguale, *f*. **-match**, TR.: sormontare; vincere. **-mĕasure**, S.: soverchio, soprappiù, *m*. **-mŭch**, ADJ.: superfluo, eccessivo; ADV.: soprammisura, troppo. **-nāme**, TR.: nominare uno dopo l'altro. **-nice**, ADJ.: troppo delicato, troppo difficile. **-night**, S.: notte passata, *f*. **'-offícious**, ADJ.: troppo officioso. **-păss**, TR.: trapassare; preterire, omettere; sdegnare. **-pāy**, TR.: strapagare, soprappagare. **-plus**, S.: soprappiù, soperchio, *m*. **-plȳ**, TR.: sopraggravare, sopraccaricare. **-poise**, S.: preponderanza, *f*.; peso, *m*. **-pŏise**, TR.: contrabilanciare. **-pŏwer**, TR.: predominare, prevalere; sopraffare, vincere, superare: —*ed by numbers*, oppresso dal numero. **-prĕss**, TR.: opprimere; ammaccare. **-prize**, TR.: stimare troppo. **-rate**, S.: prezzo eccessivo, *m*. **-rāte**, TR.: stimare troppo; domandare troppo. **-rēach**, (IR)REG.; TR.: prevenire; ingannare, eludere; INTR.: tagliarsi; ammaccarsi. **-rēacher**, S.: ingannatore, truffatore, *m*. **-rēad**, IRR.; TR.: leggere; esaminare. **-rĕckon**, TR.: contare troppo, computare troppo. **-ride**, IRR.; TR.: passare sopra; sopprimere; oltrapassare†; faticare, strappazzare (un cavallo). **'-ripe**, ADJ.: troppo maturo. **-ripen**, TR.: far troppo maturo. **-rōast**, TR.: arrostire troppo. **-rūle**, TR.: dominare, governare. **-rūler**, S.: governatore, *m*. **-rŭn**, IRR.; TR.: stracorrere, correre in là di; (*mil.*) invadere, percorrere; coprire; inondare; predare; INTR.: essere troppo pieno. **-scrūpulous**, ADJ.: troppo scrupoloso. **-sea**, ADV.: d' oltre mare. **-sēe**, IRR.; TR.: soprantendere; omettere. **-sēer**, S.: soprantendente, *m*. **-sĕll**,

chevole; osservabile, considerabile. **-ableness**, S.: cosa notabile; singolarità, importanza, *f.* **-ably**, ADV.: in modo rimarchevole. **-er**, S.: osservatore, *m.*

remarry, TR.: rimaritare.

remediable, ADJ.: rimediabile, curabile.

remediless, ADJ.: irremediabile, incurabile. **-dilessness**, S.: stato incurabile, *m.*, incurabilità, *f.* **-dy** 1, S.: rimedio; riparo, ricorso, mezzo, *m.*: *past* —, irremediable, incurabile. **-dy** 2, TR.: rimediare; riparare.

remember, TR.: ricordarsi, sovvenire: — *me to him*, salutatelo da mia parte; *if I — right*, se ben mi ricordo; *I don't — his name*, non mi ricordo del suo nome; — *me to your brother*, ricordatemi al vostro signor fratello. **-berer**, S.: ricordatore, *m.* **-brance**, S.: rimembranza, ricordanza, *f.*: *put in* —, ridurre a memoria. **-brance-book**, S.: libro di memoria, *m.* **-brancer**, S.: ammonitore; attuario, *m.*

rememoration, S.: rimembranza, *f.*

remigrate, INTR.: migrare di nuovo; ritornare. **-gration**, S.: ritorno, *m.*

remind, TR.: ridurre a memoria, ricordare, rammemorare.

reminiscence, S.: reminiscenza, rimembranza, *f.* **-cential**, ADJ.: appartenente alla reminiscenza.

remiss, ADJ.: rimesso, lento; pigro. **-missible**, ADJ.: remissibile, perdonabile. **-mission**, S.: remissione, *f.*; allentamento; perdono, *m.* **-missly**, ADV.: negligentemente; lentamente; pigramente. **-missness**, S.: negligenza, trascuraggine; infingardia, pigrizia, *f.*

remit, TR.: rimettere, rimandare; sminuire; perdonare; riferire; INTR.: diminuirsi; mitigarsi. **-ment**, S.: incarcerare nuovamente; perdono, *m.* **-tance**, S.: rimessa (di danari), *f.*: *make a* —, fare una rimessa. **-tent**, ADJ.: remittente: — *fever*, febbre remittente. **-ter**, S.: rimettitore; (*com.*) mittente, speditore, *m.*

remnant, ADJ.: rimanente: —*s*, restante, residuo; avanzo, *m.*

remodel, TR.: modellare di nuovo.

remolten, ADJ.: rifonduto.

remonstrance, S.: rimostranza, dichiarazione, ammonizione, *f.* **-strate**, TR.: rimostrare; rappresentare. **-stration** = *remonstrance*.

remora, S.: remora, *f.*, (pesce); (*fig.*) impedimento, ostacolo, *m.*

remorse, S.: rimorso, rimordimento, *m.* **-ful**, ADJ.: pieno di rimorsi, pentito. **-less**, ADJ.: senza rimorso, insensibile, crudele.

remote, ADJ.: rimoto, lontano. **-tely**, ADV.: rimotamente, lontanamente. **-teness**, S.: lontananza; distanza, *f.* **-tion**, S.: rimozione, *f.*

remount, (IN)TR.: rimontare, montare di nuovo.

removable, ADJ.: rimovibile, amovibile. **-al**, S.: rimozione, *f.*, rimovimento; cambiamento, *m.* **-e** 1, S.: cambiamento; trasporto, *m.*; partenza; poca distanza, *f.* **-e** 2, (IN)TR.: rimuovere; scomberare; mutare domicilio: — *a difficulty*, levare una difficoltà; — *one out of the way*, disfarsi d' alcuno. **-ed**, ADJ.: rimoto; separato. **-edness**, S.: rimovimento, *m.*, distanza, *f.* **-er**, S.: rimovitore, *m.* **-ing**, S.: rimovimento, *m.*, rimozione, *f.*; trasporto, *m.*

remunerable, ADJ.: degno di ricompensa. **-ate**, TR.: rimunerare, ricompensare. **-ation**, S.: rimunerazione, ricompensa, *f.* **-ative**, ADJ.: rimunerativo. **-ator**, S.: rimuneratore, *m.* **-atory** = *remunerative*.

remurmur, INTR.: rimormorare; risonare.

renal, ADJ.: renale.

renard, S.: volpe, *f.*

renascency, S.: rinascenza, *f.* **-cent**, ADJ.: rinascente. **-cible**, ADJ.: che si può rigenerare.

renavigate, TR.: rinavigare; rimbarcarsi.

rencounter 1, S.: riscontro, incontro; conflitto, *m.* **rencounter** 2, INTR.: scontare; abbattersi; raffrontarsi.

rend, IRR.; TR.: stracciare, lacerare, mettere in pezzi.

render, TR.: rendere; restituire; liberare; traslatare: — *like for like*, render pan per focaccia; — *thanks*, render grazie, ringraziare.

rendezvous 1, S.: appuntamento, *m.*, posta, assegnazione; piazza d' arme, *f.* **rendezvous** 2, TR.: trovarsi alla posta.

rendition, S.: arrendimento, *m.*, resa, *f.*

renegade, **-gado**, S.: rinnegato, apostata, *m.*

renege †, TR.: negare, rinnegare.

renew, TR.: rinnovare, rinnovellare; ricominciare. **-able**, ADJ.: che si può rinnovare. **-al**, S.: rinnovallamento, *m.* **-er**, S.: rinnovatore, *m.*

renitence, **-ey**, S.: renitenza; resistenza, *f.* **-t**, ADJ.: renitente; resistente.

rennet 1, S.: caglio, *m.* **rennet** 2, **-ing**, S.: appiuola, *f.* (mela).

renounce, TR.: rinunziare; rigettare; abbandonare: — *a thing*, rinunziare ad una cosa. **-cement**, S.: rinunziamento, *m.*, rinunzia, *f.*; rifiuto, *m.* **-cer**, S.: rinunziatore, *m.*

renovate, TR.: rinnovare, rinnovellare. **-vation**, S.: rinnovazione, *f.*

-tăgonal, -tăngular, ADJ.: ottangolare. **-tave**, S.: ottava, *f.* **-tāvo**, S.: libro in ottavo; ottavo, *m.* **-tĕnnial**, ADJ.: ottennio. **Oc-tōber**, S.: ottobre, *m.* **-togenārian, -tōgenary**, ADJ.: ottuagenario. **-tonary**, ADJ.: ottonario, d'otto. **-topus**, S.: specie di seppia, *f.* **-tosyllable**, ADJ.: ottonario, di otto sillabe. **-tuple**, ADJ.: ottuplo.
ŏcu-lar, ADJ.: oculare, di veduta. **-larly**, ADV.: ocularmente, di veduta. **-list**, S.: oculista, *m.*
ōdalisk, S.: odalisca, *f.*
ŏdd, ADJ.: impari, dispari; bizzarro, fantastico; cattivo: — *looking*, singolare d'aspetto; — *number*, numero caffo; *play at even and* —, giuocare a pari; *thirty pounds* —, trenta lire sterline e più. **-ity**, S.: singolarità, *f.* **-ly**, ADV.: in modo straordinario, fantasticamente. **-ness**, S.: inegualità; singolarità, stranezza; fantastichezza, *f.* **-s**, S.: disparità; differenza, *f.;* vantaggio, *m.;* superiorità, *f.:* *be at — with one*, contendere con uno; *have the — of one*, aver l'avvantaggio sopra uno; *fight against* —, battersi con un più forte; — *and ends*, bocconcini, *m. pl.*
ōde, S.: oda, ode, *f.*
ōdi-ous, ADJ.: odioso, detestabile. **-ously**, ADV.: odiosamente. **-ousness**, S.: odiosità; atrocità, enormità, *f.* **-um**, S.: odio, *m.;* colpa, *f.*
ōdour, S.: odore; profumo, *m.*, fragranza, *f.* **-ate**, ADJ.: odorante; odorato. **-iferous**, ADJ.: odorifero, odoroso. **-iferousness**, S.: odoramento, odore, *m.*
oe-conŏmic, ADJ.: economico. **-conŏmics**, S. PL.: economia, *f.* **-cŏnomy**, S.: economia; frugalità, *f.*
oecumĕnical, ADJ.: ecumenico, universale.
oe-dēma, S.: (*surg.*) edema, *m.* **-demătic, -dĕmatous**, ADJ.: edematico.
oeilliad†, S.: occhiata, *f.*, sguardo; segno, *m.*
oesŏphagus, S.: esofago, *m.*
ō'er = *over.*
ŏf ŏv, PREP.: di: — *the*, del (dello, della, dei, delle).
ŏff 1, ADV.: lontano, lunge, lungi; via: *well* —, benestante, comodo; *be —!* anda via! *far* —, lontano, lungi; — *with your hat!* giù col cappello! *be — and on*, esser in bilancia; *go* —, andar via, scoppiare; *push —!* scosta! allarga! **off** 2, INTERJ.: via via! andate via! **-hand**, ADJ.: improvviso, espontaneo; ADV.: all'improvvista, senza preparazione.
ŏffal, S.: rimasuglio; avanzo, *m.*
offĕn-ce, S.: offesa; colpa, *f.;* affronto, oltraggio, delitto, *m.:* *give* —, offendere; *take — at*, tenersi offeso di. **-ceful**, ADJ.: ingiurioso, offensivo. **-celess**, ADJ.: innocente. **-d**, TR.: offendere; dispiacere; nuocere; INTR.: fallire, peccare: *be —ded at*, esser in collera contro. **-der**, S.: offenditore, delinquente, criminale, *m.* **-ding**, S.: offendimento, *m.* **-dress**, S.: offenditrice; malfattrice, *f.* **-sive**, ADJ.: offensivo, ingiurioso; S.: offensiva, *f.:* — *arms*, armi offensive. **-sively**, ADV.: offensivamente. **-siveness**, S.: offesa, ingiuria, *f.;* dispiacere, male, *m.*
ŏffer 1, S.: offerta; profferta, *f.;* tentativo, *m.* **offer** 2, TR.: offerire, presentare; tentare; INTR.: offerirsi, presentarsi; obbligarsi: — *one's self*, esporsi; — *violence*, far violenza; *if you — to do it*, si vi provate di farlo. **-er**, S.: offeritore, *m.* **-ing**, S.: offerta, profferta; obblazione, *f.* **-tory**, S.: offertorio, *m.* **-ture**, S.: offerta, profferta, *f.*
ŏffi-ce, S.: ufficio, uffizio; studio; impiego, carico, servizio, *m.:* *high in* —, che copre alto impiego. **-cer**, S.: ufficiale, officiale; funzionario, agente, *m.* **-cered**, ADJ.: *be — by*, aver per ufficiali.
offic-ial 1, ADJ.: ufficiale; conducevole; idoneo. **-ial** 2, S.: ufficiale, officiale, *m.* **-ially**, ADV.: ufficialmente, d'ufficio. **-iality**, S.: carica, *f.;* ufficio d'un ufficiale, *m.* **-iate**, TR.: distribuire; INTR.: ufficiare.
officinal, ADJ.: officinale.
officious, ADJ.: officioso; obbligante; affabile. **-ly**, ADV.: officiosamente, cortesemente. **-ness**, S.: prontezza; cortesia; affabilità, *f.*
ŏffing, S.: largo, alto mare, *m.*
ŏff-scouring, S.: lavatura, *f.;* fecce, *f. pl.* **-set**, S.: germoglio, rampollo, *m.* **-spring**, S.: progenie, *f.*, discendenti, *m. pl.*
offŭs-cate, TR.: offuscare, adombrare. **-cātion**, S.: offuscazione, oscurazione, adombrazione, *f.*
ŏft, ŏften, ADV.: spesso, sovente: *how* —, quante volte.
oft(en)times, ADV.: spesse volte.
ogēe, S.: (*arch.*) festone, *m.*
ō-gle 1, S.: occhiata, *f.*, sguardo, *m.* **-gle** 2, TR.: occhieggiare; vagheggiare. **-gler**, S.: vagheggiatore. **-gling**, S.: vagheggiare, *m.*
ōglio, S.: guazzabuglio, *m.*
ōgre, S.: orco, mostro antropofago, *m.*
ōh ! INTERJ.: oh! o!
ŏil 1, S.: olio, *m.:* — *of roses*, olio rosato, *m.;* *paint in* —, dipingere a olio. **oil** 2, TR.: ungere con olio: *castor* —, olio di ricino. **-bottle**, S.: oliera, *f.* **-c**[...] S.: tela cerata, *f.* **-colour**, S.: [...] olio, colore misto con olio. **-in**[...] oleosità, *f.* **-man**, S.: olian[...]

repŏur, TR.: riversare.
reprehĕn-d, TR.: riprendere, rimproverare. **-der**, S.: riprenditore, riprensore, *m.* **-ding**, S.: riprensione, *f.*, rimprovero, *m.* **-sible**, ADJ.: riprensibile, biasimevole. **-sibleness**, S.: biasimo, rimprovero, *m.* **-sibly**, ADV.: in modo riprendevole. **-sion**, S.: riprensione, *f.*, biasimo, *m.*, ammonizione, *f.* **-sive**, ADJ.: riprensivo.
represĕnt, TR.: rappresentare, figurare, far conoscere, descrivere. **-ance** = *representation*. **-ant**, S.: rappresentante, *m.* **-ātion**, S.: rappresentazione, *f.* **-ative**, ADJ.: rappresentativo; S.: rappresentante, *m.* **-atively**, ADV.: rappresentativamente. **-er**, S.: rappresentatore, *m.* **-ment**, S.: rappresentamento, *m.*
re-prĕss, TR.: reprimere; raffrenare; moderare. **-prĕssion**, S.: reprimento, reprimere, *m.* **-prĕssive**, ADJ.: reprimente.
reprie-val, -ve 1, S.: sospensione, *f.*, differimento, rispitto, *m.*, prolungazione, *f.* **-ve** 2, TR.: sospendere, differire.
rĕprimand 1, S.: riprensione; ripassata, *f.* **reprimand** 2, TR.: riprendere, biasimare.
rē-print, S.: ristampa, *f.* **-print**, TR.: ristampare. **-printing**, S.: ristampa; edizione nuova, *f.*
repri-sal, S.: rappresaglia, *f.*: *make —s, make use of —s*, usar rappresaglie. **-se** 1, S.: ripresa; rappresaglia, *f.* **-se** 2, TR.: riprendere.
reprōach 1, S.: rimprovero, obbrobrio, vituperio, *m.* **reproach** 2, INTR.: rimproverare; rinfacciare; accusare. **-able**, ADJ.: biasimevole, vituperevole. **-ful**, ADJ.: ingiurioso, oltraggioso. **-fully**, ADV.: ingiuriosamente, oltraggiosamente.
rĕpro-bate 1, S.: reprobo, malvagio, *m.* **-bate** 2, TR.: riprovare, rifiutare. **-bateness, -bātion**, S.: riprovazione; dannazione, *f.*
repro-dūce, TR.: riprodurre. **-dūcer**, S.: riproduttore, *m.* **-dŭction**, S.: riproduzione, rigenerazione, *f.* **-dŭctive**, ADJ.: riproduttivo.
re-prōof, S.: rimprovero, *m.* riprensione, *f.* **-prōvable**, ADJ.: riprensibile, biasimevole. **-prōvableness**, S.: riprensibilità, *f.* **-prōve**, TR.: riprendere, rimproverare. **-prōver**, S.: riprenditore, *m.*
rĕptile, S.: rettile, *m.*
repŭblic, S.: repubblica, *f.*: *the — of letters*, la repubblica letteraria. **-an**, S.: repubblicano, *m.* **-anism**, S.: repubblicanismo, *m.* **-anize**, TR.: render repubblicano.
re-publicātion, S.: seconda pubblicazione, *f.* **-pŭblish**, TR.: pubblicare di nuovo.
repū-diable, ADJ.: degno d' essere ripudiato. **-diate**, TR.: ripudiare, rifiutare. **-diātion**, S.: ripudio, ripudiare; divorzio, *m.*
re-pūgn, TR.: ripugnare, contrariare. **-pŭgnance, -pŭgnancy**, S.: ripugnanza, avversione: controversia, *f.* **-pŭgnant**, ADJ.: ripugnante; contrario. **-pŭgnantly**, ADV.: con ripugnanza, di mala voglia.
repŭllulate, TR.: repullulare, germogliare.
repŭl-se 1, S.: ripulsa; sconfitta, negativa, *f.*; rabuffo, *m.* **-se** 2, TR.: ripulsare, repellere, respingere; regettare. **-sion**, S.: ripulsione, ripulsa, *f.* **-sive**, ADJ.: ripulsivo. **-sory**, ADJ.: ripulsante, ripulsivo.
repūrchase 1, S.: ricompra, *f.* **repurchase** 2, TR.: ricomprare, comprare di nuovo.
rĕp-utable, ADJ.: onorevole, onorato. **-utableness** = *reputation*. **-utably**, ADV.: onorevolmente. **-utātion, -ute** 1, S.: riputazione, fama, *f.*: *be in good —*, esser in buon concetto. **-ute** 2, TR.: riputare; stimare, credere. **-ūteless**, ADJ.: senza riputazione; infame; abietto.
requĕst 1, S.: richiesta, domanda; supplica, *f.*; credito, *m.*: *comply with a —*, accondiscendere ad una richiesta; *at your —*, a vostra richiesta; *make a — of one*, fare una domanda ad uno; *be in —*, esser in voga, essere ricercato. **request** 2, TR.: richiedere, pregare. **-er**, S.: richieditore, supplicante, *m.*
requicken, TR.: rianimare, ravvivare.
rēquiem, S.: orazione pe' morti; pace, *f.*
requi-rable, ADJ.: atto ad esser ricercato. **-re**, TR.: chiedere, richiedere; domandare; ricercare; esigere. **-rer**, S.: richieditore, *m.*
rĕqui-site 1, ADJ.: requisito, necessario. **-site** 2, S.: requisito, *m.*, cosa necessaria, *f.* **-sitely**, ADV.: necessariamente. **-siteness**, S.: necessità; esigenza, *f.* **-sition**, S.: requisizione; domanda, *f.* **-sitive, -sitory** *requi-*, ADJ.: requisitorio.
requi-tal, S.: ricompensa, *f.*; contraccambio, *m.* **-te**, TR.: ricompensare, rimunerare. **-ter**, S.: compensatore, rimuneratore, *m.* **-ting**, S.: ricompensa, *f.*; contraccambio, *m.*
rēremouse, S.: pipistrello, *m.*
rēreward, S.: retroguardia, rietroguardia, *f.*
resāil, TR.: rinavigare, navigare indietro.
resa-lutātion, S.: risalutare, *m.* **-lūte**, TR.: risalutare, rendere il saluto.
re-scind, TR.: rescindere; cassare. **-scis-**

ŏnset 1, s.: assalto, attacco, *m.* **onset** 2, TR.: assaltare, attacare.
ŏnslaught, s.: attacco impetuoso, *m.*
ontŏl-ogist, s.: metafisico, *m.* **-ogy**, s.: ontologia, metafisica, *f.*
ŏnward, ADV.: avanti: *go —*, avanzarsi.
ŏnyx, s.: onice, *m.*
ōoz-e, s.: malta; melma, *f.*; fango, *m.* **-e** 2, INTR.: trapelare, gocciolare. **-y**, ADJ.: melmoso, fangoso.
o-pāqate†, TR.: rendere opaco; oscurare; annuvolare. **-păcity**, s.: opacità; spessezza, *f.* **-pāqous**, ADJ.: opaco, oscuro; denso. **-pāqousness** = opacity.
ōpal, s.: opalo, *m.*
ōpe = *open.* **-n** 1, ADJ.: aperto, scoperto; evidente, chiaro; sincero: *a little —*, mezzo aperto; *wide —*, spalancato; *in the — air*, a cielo scoperto; *— weather*, tempo sereno, tempo moderato, *m.*; *keep — table*, tener corte bandita; *lay —*, esporre, palesare; *with — arms*, a braccia aperte; *keep — bowels*, tenere pervie le vie. **-n** 2, TR.: aprire, scoprire; INTR.: aprirsi; fendersi: *— a letter*, dissuggellare; *— a bottle*, sturare una bottiglia; *— a vein*, cavare sangue. **-ner**, s.: apritore; espositore, *m.* **-n-eyed**, ADJ.: vigilante, attento. **-n-handed**, ADJ.: generoso, liberale. **-n-hearted**, ADJ.: franco, sincero; generoso. **-n-heartedness**, s.: franchezza, liberalità; generosità, *f.* **-ning**, ADJ.: aperitivo; lassativo; s.: apertura, *f.*; principio, *m.* **-nly**, ADV.: apertamente; evidentemente; liberamente, francamente. **-n-mouthed**, ADJ.: vorace, goloso. **-nness**, s.: chiarezza; franchezza, sincerità, *f.*
ŏper-a, s.: opera (musicale), *f.*: *comic —*, opera buffa. **-able**, ADJ.: operabile, praticabile. **-a-glass**, s.: occhialino, piccol occhiale, *m.* **-ate**, INTR.: operare; produrre. **-ātion**, s.: operazione, *f.*; effetto, *m.* **-ative**, ADJ.: operativo, efficiente. **-ator**, s.: operatore; agente, fattore; cerretano, *m.* **-ose**, ADJ.: operoso, laborioso, faticoso.
ŏphites, s.: ofite, serpentino, *m.*
ophthăl-mic, ADJ.: oftalmico, ottalmico. **-my**, s.: oftalmia, *f.*
...**ate**, s.: (*phar.*) oppiato, medicamento ...rcotico, *m.*
...**e**, INTR.: opinare, pensare; immagi-... **-er**, s.: opinante, *m.*
...**s.** ADJ.: immaginato. **-ia-**
...tinatamente, pertinace-
... s.: ostinazione,
... caparbio; pro-
...nato, perti-
... ostina-
... s.:
... *m.*;

stima, *f.* **-ionat(ed)**, ADJ.: ostinato, pertinace. **-ionist**, s.: caparbio, protervo, *m.*
ōpium, s.: oppio, *m.*
opŏssum, s.: 'opossum,' *m.*, sariga, *f.*
ŏppidan, s.: borghese, cittadino, *m.*
oppignerate†, TR.: impegnare.
ŏppi-late†, TR.: oppilare, costipare, ostruire. **-lātion**, s.: oppilazione, *f.*, turamento, *m.* **-lative†**, ADJ.: oppilativo, costipativo, ostruttivo.
oppō-ne†, TR.: opporre, ripugnare. **-nent**, ADJ.: opponente; contrario; s.: opponente, avversario, *m.*
opportūn-e, ADJ.: opportuno, conveniente. **-ely**, ADV.: opportunamente, a tempo. **-ity**, s.: opportunità; occasione; comodità, *f.*: *avail one's self of an —*, profittare di un' occazione, approfittarsi dell' opportunità.
oppō-sal, s.: opponimento, *m.* **-se**, TR.: opporre; resistere, contrariare; INTR.: opporsi; contraddire. **-seless**, ADJ.: irresistibile. **-ser**, s.: oppositore, avversario, *m.*
ŏppo-site, ADJ.: opposito, contrario, avverso; s.: avversario, antagonista, *m.* **-sitely**, ADV.: faccia a faccia, dirimpetto, di rincontro. **-siteness**, s.: opposto, *m.*, contrarietà, *f.* **-sition**, s.: opposizione, resistenza, contrarietà, *f.*
op-prĕss, TR.: opprimere, soggiogare. **-prĕssion**, s.: oppressione; severità, *f.* **-prĕssive**, ADJ.: oppressivo, crudele. **-prĕssively**, ADV.: in modo oppressivo. **-prĕssor**, s.: oppressore; perseguitatore, *m.*
opprō-brious, ADJ.: obbrobrioso, vituperoso; ignominioso. **-briously**, ADV.: obbrobriosamente. **-briousness**, **-brium**, s.: obbrobrio, *m.*; ignominia; infamia, *f.*
op-pūgn, TR.: oppugnare, resistere; assalire. **-pŭgnancy**, s.: oppugnamento; contrasto, *m.* **-pūgner**, s.: oppugnatore; opponente, *m.*
ŏpta-ble†, ADJ.: desiderabile. **-tive**, ADJ.: ottativo; s.: (*gram.*) modo ottativo, *m.*
ŏp-tic(al), ADJ.: ottico, visuale. **-tician**, s.: ottico, *m.*, che sa l'ottica. **-tics**, s. PL.: ottica, *f.*
ŏpti-macy, s.: ottimato, *m.*, nobilità, *f.* **-mism**, s.: ottimismo, *m.* **-mist**, s.: ottimista, *m.*
ŏption, s.: scelta; volontà, *f.*, arbitrio, *m.* **-al**, ADJ.: libero a scegliersi: *be — with*, avere la scelta, avere la facoltà di scegliere.
ŏpulen-ce, s.: opulenza; ricchezza, *f.* **-t**, ADJ.: opulento, ricco. **-tly**, ADV.: opulentemente, riccamente.

resource, S.: mezzo, espediente, *m.* **-less**, ADJ.: senza rimedio, abbandonato.

resow, IRR.; TR.: riseminare, seminare di nuovo.

respeak, IRR.; INTR.: parlare di nuovo; far risposta.

respect 1, S.: rispetto, riguardo; motivo, *m.;* considerazione, stima, *f.: in some* —, in qualche modo; *with* —, con rispetto, con riverenza; *in* — *of*, in rispetto, a rispetto, in comparazione; *out of* — *to you*, per rispetto vostro; —*s*, complimenti, baciamenti, *m. pl.; pay one's* — *to one*, salutare alcuno, riverire uno. **respect** 2, TR.: rispettare, riguardare; onorare, riverire: — *the person*, aver riguardo alla persona. **-able**, ADJ.: rispettabile. **-ably**, ADV.: con rispetto, riguardevolmente. **-er**, S.: che rispetta. **-ful**, ADJ.: rispettoso; sommesso, umile. **-fully**, ADV.: rispettosamente. **-fulness**, S.: rispetto, riguardo, *m.;* deferenza, *f.* **-ive**, ADJ.: rispettivo, relativo. **-ively**, ADV.: rispettivamente, in rispetto. **-less**, ADJ.: senza rispetto, irreverente. **-lessness**, S.: irreverenza, *f.*

resperse†, TR.: rispergere.

respirable, ADJ.: respirabile. **-spiration**, S.: respirazione, *f.;* fiato, *m.* **-spire**, INTR.: respirare; ricrearsi.

respite 1, S.: rispitto, indugio; rescritto di dilazione, *m.* **respite** 2, TR.: sospendere, differire.

resplendence, **-cy**, S.: risplendenza, *f.*, splendore, lustro, *m.* **-t**, ADJ.: risplendente, brillante. **-tly**, ADV.: con grande splendore.

respond, INTR.: rispondere; corrispondere; convenire. **-dent**, S.: rispondente; difendente, *m.* **-se**, S.: risponso, *m.*, risposta; rifiutazione, *f.* **-sibility**, S.: risponsabilità; sicurtà, *f.* **-sible**, ADJ.: risponsabile; obbligato. **-sibleness**, S.: mallevadoria, cauzione, sicurtà, *f.* **-sion**, S.: risponzione, risposta, *f.* **-sive**, **-sory**, ADJ.: risponsivo, corrispondente.

rest 1, S.: riposo, sonno; resto, residuo, *m.* **rest** 2, S.: pausa, fermata; resta (di lancia), *f.: be at* —, esser in pace; *take* —, prender riposo; *among the* —, fra gli altri; *as to the* —, del resto. **rest** 3, TR.: riposare; appoggiare; posare; dar pace; INTR.: riposarsi; appoggiarsi; stare; dormire; morire: — *on*, appoggiarsi; far capitale; *it* —*s with him to decide*, spetta a lui il decidere.

restagnant, ADJ.: stagnante. **-nate**, INTR.: ristagnare; fermarsi. **-nation**, S.: ristagnamento, *m.*

restaurant, S.: ristorante, *m.* **-ation**, S.: ristorazione, *f.;* ristoro, *m.*

restem, TR.: andare contro la corrente.

restful, ADJ.: quieto; placido. **-ly**, ADV.: quietamente, riposatamente.

restily, ADV.: ostinatamente. **-iness**, S.: restio; ostinazione, caponeria, pertinacia, *f.* **-ing**, S.: riposo; sollievo, *m.;* quiete, *f.* **-ing-place**, S.: luogo di riposo, *m.*

restitute, TR.: restituire. **-tution**, S.: restituzione, *f.*, ristabilire, *m.* **-tutor**, S.: restitutore, *m.*

restive, ADJ.: restio, ricalcitrante, ritroso, caparbio.

restless, ADJ.: senza dormire; inquieto. **-ly**, ADV.: senza riposo; inquietamente. **-ness**, S.: mancanza di riposo; inquietudine, agitazione, *f.*

restorable, ADJ.: che può ricoverarsi. **-ration**, S.: ristorazione, *f.*, ristoramento, *m.* **-rative**, ADJ.: ristorativo, corroborativo; S.: ristorativo, *m.* (rimedio). **-re**, TR.: ristorare, ristabilire, rinnovare: — *to favour*, rimettere in grazia. **-rement**, S.: ristorazione, *f.*, ristauro, *m.* **-rer**, S.: ristoratore, *m.* **-ring**, S.: ristoramento, *m.;* restituzione, *f.*

restrain, TR.: ristringere, reprimere; raffrenare, ritenere. **-able**, ADJ.: atto ad essere ristretto. **-edly**, ADV.: con ristringimento, con ritegno. **-er**, S.: che ristringe, raffrenatore, *m.* **-t**, S.: costringimento, raffrenamento, *m.;* violenza, forza, *f.: without* —, senza ritegno (*or* freno).

restrict, TR.: ristringere, limitare. **-tion**, S.: limitazione, *f.* **-tive**, ADJ.: restrittivo, limitativo. **-tively**, ADV.: ristrettamente, in modo restrittivo.

restringe, TR.: ristringere, affrenare; limitare, confinare. **-gency**, S.: ristringimento, *m.* **-gent**, ADJ.: ristringente; astringente; S. (*med.*) astringente, *m.*

resty, ADJ.: quieto, inerte.

resublime, TR.: sublimare di nuovo, raffinare.

result 1, S.: risulta, *f.*, esito, fine, *m.* **result** 2, INTR.: risultare; seguire; provenire, venir per conseguenza. **-ance**, S.: risultamento, *m.;* risulta, *f.* **-ing**, ADJ.: risultante, provegnente.

resumable, ADJ.: che si può ripigliare. **-sume**, TR.: resumere, ripigliare; rifare; rinovellare. **-sumption**, S.: ripigliamento; ricominciamento, *m.* **-sumptive**, ADJ.: ripigliante.

resurrection, S.: risurrezione, *f.*

resurvey, TR.: rivedere, esaminare di nuovo.

resuscitate, TR.: risuscitare, ravvivare. **-tation**, S.: risuscitazione, *f.* **-tative**, ADJ.: risuscitante.

retail 1, S.: ritaglio, minuto, *m.: sell by*

ôrphan, ADJ.: orfano; S.: orfano, *m.*; orfana, *f.*: —*boy*, orfanello, *m.*; —*girl*, orfanella, *f.* **-age**, S.: orfanità, *f.*

ôrpiment, S.: orpimento, *m.* **-pine**, S.: (*bot.*) favagello, *m.*

ôrrery, S.: (*astr.*) planetario, *m.*

ôrthodox, ADJ.: ortodosso. **-ly**, ADV.: in modo ortodosso. **-y**, S.: ortodossia, *f.*

ôrthoe-pist, S.: ortoepista, *m.* **-py**, S.: ortoepia, retta pronunziazione, *f.*

ortho-gonal, ADJ.: rettangolo. **-grapher**, S.: versato nell' ortografia, *m.* **-gráphical**, ADJ.: ortografico, d' ortografia. **-gráphically**, ADV.: ortograficamente, in modo ortografico. **-graphize**, TR.: ortografizzare. **-graphy**, S.: ortografia, *f.* **-logy**, S.: ortologia, *f.*

ôrtive, ADJ.: (*astr.*) ortivo.

ôrtolan, S.: ortolano, *m.*

ôrval, S.: (*bot.*) clarea, *f.*

ŏscil-late, INTR.: oscillare. **-lation**, S.: oscillazione, vibrazione, *f.* **-latory**, ADJ.: oscillatorio, vibrativo.

ŏscitan-cy, S.: sbaviglio, *m.*, negligenza, incuria, *f.* **-t**, ADJ.: sbavigliante, infingardo. **-tly**, ADV.: negligentemente.

ŏşier, S.: vinco, vimine, *m.*

ŏsprey, S.: frosone, ossifrago, *m.*

ŏs-seous, ADJ.: osseo. **-sicle**, S.: osserello, ossetto, *m.* **-sific**, ADJ.: che trasforma in osso. **-sificátion**, S.: ossificazione, *f.* **-sifrage**, S.: ossifrago, *m.* **-sify**, TR.: fare divenir osso; INTR.: ossificarsi. **-sivorous**, ADJ.: ossivoro.

ostĕn-sible, ADJ.: ostensibile, apparente. **-sive**, ADJ.: ostensivo. **-t**, S: aspetto; prodigio, portento, *m.* **-tátion**, S.: ostentazione, *f.*, fasto, *m.* **-tátious**, ADJ.: pomposo, fastoso. **-tátiously**, ADV.: pomposamente, fastosamente, vanamente. **-tátiousness**, S.: pompositā, vanità, *f.* **-tator ŏs-**, S.: ostentatore, vantatore, *m.*

osteŏlogy, S.: osteologia, *f.*

ŏstiary, S.: ostiario, portinaio, *m.*

ŏstler, S.: stalliere, stabulario, *m.*

ŏstra-cism, S.: ostracismo, *m.* **-cites**, S.: ostracite, *f.* **-cize**, TR.: espellere dalla società.

ŏstrich, S.: struzzo, struzzolo, *m.*

ŏther, PRON.: altro: *any* —, qualunque altro; *every* — *day*, un giorno sì, un giorno no; *on the* — *side*, dall' altra parte; —*s*, gli altri; *each* —, l' un l' altro (gli uni gli altri). **-gates†**, ADV.: (*prov.*) [...]mente, in altro modo. **-guess**, [...]e, ADJ.: (*prov.*) d' un'altra sorta. [...]e, ADV.: in un altro luogo, al[...] **-while**, ADV.: in un altro tempo. [...]: altrimente. [...], *f.* (animale anfibio e ra-

ought I *ât*, IRR.; INTR.: *it* — *to be so*, dovrebbe esser così; *I* — *to go thither*, dovrei andarvi; *he* — *to have come*, egli avrebbe dovuto venire. **ought** 2 = *aught*.

ounce I, S.: oncia, *f.* **ounce** 2, S.: lince, *m.*, pantera, *f.*

ouphe†, S.: folletto, spirito aereo, *m.* **-n†**, ADJ.: di folletto, di spirito aereo.

our, PRON.: nostro (nostra, nostri, nostre). **-s**, PRON.: il nostro (la nostra, i nostri): *a friend of* —, un nostro amico. **-sĕlves**, PRON. PL.: noi, noi stessi, noi stesse.

ousel, S.: merlo, *m.* (uccello).

oust, TR.: portare via; privare; spingere.

out I, ADV., PREP.: fuori, fuora, fuor di; fuor di casa; uscito; spento, finito, terminato: — *of danger*, fuor di pericolo; — *of envy*, per invidia; — *of favour*, disgraziato; — *of hand*, subito; — *of hatred*, per odio; — *of hope*, senza speranza; — *of humour*, di cattivo umore; — *of order*, in disordine; indisposto, ammalato; — *of place*, senza impiego; — *of sight*, a perdita di vista; — *of spite*, per dispetto, per invidia; — *of tune*, discordante; — *of use*, inusitato; *be* —, sbagliare, errare; esser finito; esser spento, esser estinto; esser vuoto; *read* —, leggere tutto.

out! 2, INTERJ.: uscite di qui! **out** 3, TR.: spogliare, privare. **-act**, (IN)TR.: oltrepassare, eccedere, andare all' eccesso. **-bálance**, TR.: sbilanciare; preponderare. **-bid**, IRR.; INTR.: alzar il prezzo (all' incanto), incarire. **-bidder**, S.: maggior offerente, *m.* **-blŏwed**, ADJ.: gonfio, empito di fiato. **-born**, ADJ.: straniero, forestiero. **-bound**, ADJ.: caricato, destinato fuori. **-bráve**, TR.: braveggiare, affrontare. **-brázen**, TR.: bravare, affrontare, minacciare altieramente. **-break**, S.: eruzione; uscita, *f.* **-brĕathe**, TR.: spirare; faticare. **-burst**, S.: scoppio, *m.*; eruzione, *f.* **-cast**, ADJ.: esiliato, sbandito; di rifiuto; S.: esiliato, sbandito, *m.* **-class**, TR.: superare, soprastare. **-cráft**, TR.: superare in astuzia. **-cry**, S.: romore; schiamazzo, *m.*; vendita pubblica, *f.*, incanto, *m.* **-dáre**, IRR.; TR.: sfidare, braveggiare. **-dáte**, TR.: antidatare; invecchiare; disusare. **-dŏ**, IRR.; TR.: superare; soprastare. **-dŏer**, S.: superatore, *m.* **-dŏing**, S.: superamento, *m.* **-dóne**, ADJ.: superato, vinto. **-drink**, IRR.; TR.: eccedere nel bere. **-dwĕll**, TR.: restare indietro. **-er**, ADJ.: esteriore, esterno. **-erly**, ADV.: esteriormente, esternamente. **-ermost**, ADJ.: estremo, ultimo. **-fáce**, TR.: mantenere in faccia. **-fáwn**, TR.: lodare all' eccesso. **-fit**, S.: approvigionamento, *m.* **-fly̆**, IRR.; TR.:

volare più velocemente, sorpassare nel volo. **-fōol**, TR.: sorpassare in follia. **-form**, S.: esteriore, *m.*; apparenza, *f.* **-gate**, S.: uscita, *f.*, esito, *m.* **-give**, IRR.; TR.: superare in liberalità. **-gō**, IRR.; TR.: oltrapassare, andar più presto; precedere. **-gōing**, S.: uscità; spesa, *f.* **-grōw**, IRR.; TR.: crescere (*or* devenir) troppo grande per. **-guard**, S.: guardia avanzata, *f.* **-house**, S.: rimessa; casipola, *f.* **-knâve**, TR.: sorpassare in furberia. **-lăndish**, ADJ.: straniero, forestiero. **-lâst**, TR.: durare più lungamente. **-law**, S.: proscritto, bandito, *m.* **-law**, TR.: proscrivere, bandire. **-lawry**, S.: proscrizione, *f.*, bando, *m.* **-lay**, S.: sborso; gasto, *m.*, spese, *f. pl.* **-leap**, S.: impeto, *m.*; scappata, *f.* **-lēap**, TR.: strabalzare. **-lēarn**, TR.: superare nell' imparare. **-let**, S.: uscita, *f.*, esito; passaggio, *m.* **-line**, S.: contorno; schizzo, *m.* **-live**, TR.: sopravvivere. **-liver**, S.: sopravvivente; superstite, *m.* **-living**, S.: sopravvivere, *m.* **-look**, S.: vigilanza, *f.* **-lōok**, TR.: guardare con cipiglio. **-lying**, ADJ.: confinante; ulteriore. **-mârch**, INTR.: precedere nella marcia. **-mĕasure**, TR.: eccedere in misura. **-most**, ADJ.: estremo, ulteriore, rimotissimo. **-nŭmber**, TR.: sorpassare in numero. **-pâce**, TR.: precedere. **-parish**, S.: parrocchia fuor della città, *f.* **-part**, S.: parte esterna, *f.* **-post**, S.: guardia avanzata, *f.* **-put**, S.: produzione, quantità prodotta, *f.*

ŏut-rage, S.: oltraggio, *m.*; offesa, ingiuria; violenza, *f.* **-rāge**, TR.: oltraggiare, maltrattare. **-rāgeous**, ADJ.: oltraggioso, ingiurioso; atroce. **-rāgeously**, ADV.: oltraggiosamente, atrocemente, fieramente. **-rāgeousness**, S.: oltraggio, *m.*; violenza; atrocità, *f.*

ŏut-rē'ach, (IR)R.; TR.: oltrapassare; ingannare. **-ride**, IRR.; TR.: anticorrere a cavallo. **-right**, ADV.: subitamente, incontinente; schietto e netto. **-road**, S.: incursione, *f.* **-rōar**, TR.: eccedere in rugghiamenti. **-rōot**, TR.: sradicare, estirpare. **-rŭn**, INTR.; TR.: avanzare nel correre, precedere nel correre; eccedere. **-sâil**, TR.: avanzare alla vela, navigare più presto. **-scôrn**, TR.: braveggiare, dispregiare. **sĕll**, IRR.; TR.: sopravvendere. **-set**, S.: cominciamento, principio, *m.* **-shine**, IRR.; TR.: sorpassare in splendore. **-shōot**, IRR.; TR.: tirare di là del segno. **-side**, S.: superficie, *f.*, esteriore, *m.*, apparenza, *f.* **-sit**, IRR.; TR.: dimorare di là del tempo. **-skirt**, S.: sobborgo, *m.* **-slēep**, IRR.; TR.: dormire troppo lungo tempo. **-spēak**, IRR.; TR.: parlare troppo. **-spoken**, ADJ.:

franco, ingenuo. **-sprĕa**
spandere, diffondere. **-stân**
mantenere, far fronte, resis
TR.: guardare con cipiglio;
-strĕtch, TR.: distende
-strip, TR.: antecorrere, a
rare. **-swēar**, IRR.; TR.
di. **-vălue**, TR.: sorpass
-vĕnom, TR.: essere più ve
TR.: sorpassare, superare; ec
lain, TR.: eccedere in
-vōte, TR.: avere la plur
-wâlk, TR.: camminare
-wall, S.: antimuro; muro
-ward 1, ADJ.: esteriore,
esteriore, *m.*; forma estern
ostentazione, *f.*; —*bound*, d
stero. **-ward(ly)** 2, ADV.:
te, esternamente; in apparenz
ADV.: al di fuori, fuor del pae
IRR.; TR.: durare più; annoiar
TR.: svellere; sradicare. **-w**
pesare più, sbilanciare. **-wi**
gannare, truffare. **-work**,
esteriore, *m.* **-wôrn**, ADJ.:
goro. **-wôrth**, TR.: eccedere
-wrought, ADJ.: lavorato tro

ōuz-e, S.: terra melmosa, *f.*
umido, pantanoso.

ō-val, ADJ.: ovale, di forma d'
tico; S.: ovale, *m.*: — *windo*
tonda, *f.*; occhio, *m.* **-vârio**
fatto d'uova. **-vary**, S.: ovai
rio, *m.*

ovâtion, S.: ovazione, *f.*, pico
fo, *m.*

ŏven, S.: forno, *m.* **-fork**, S.:
to (da forno), *m.* **-ful**, S.: fo
fornata, *f.* **-peel**, S.: pala (da
-tender, S.: fornaio, *m.*

ōver, PREP., ADV. PREF. (*with a*
both members accented): sopra,
su, sopra di; troppo, oltre: —
molte volte; — *and above*, ol
again, di nuovo, da capo; — *ag*
faccia, dirimpetto; — *night*,
passata; *be* —, esser finita; cess
stare; *give* —, tralasciare; finir
—, voltare. **-abōund**, INTR.:
bondare. **-ăct**, TR.: eccedere.
TR.: voltare; fabbricare a volta.
TR.: tenere in timore, tenere in
-bălance 1, S.: sovrappiù; ecc
-balance 2, TR.: sbilanciare, tr
preponderare. **-bēar**, IRR.; TR
montare; riprimere; vincere. **-bĕ**
ADJ.: insolente, altiero. **-bĭd**, IR
offerire all' incanto; incarire. -
ADV.: fuor della nave. **-bŏil**, TR.
troppo. **-bōld**, ADJ.: troppo te
-bŭlk, TR.: sopraccaricare, ag
-bŭrden, TR.: sopraccaricare; op

-**buy**, IRR.; TR.: comprare troppo caro. -**cărry**, TR.: portare troppo innanzi. -**cást**, IRR.; TR.: offuscare, oscurare, adombrare; INTR.: offuscarsi, adombrarsi: *become* —, annuvolarsi, oscurarsi. '-**cāutious**, ADJ.: troppo cauto. -**charge**, S.: sopraccarico; rincarimento, *m*. -**chárge**, TR.: caricare troppo; opprimere; rincarire. -**clŏud**, TR.: annuvolare, oscurare. -**clŏy**, TR.: satollare. -**coat**, S.: soprabito, *m*. -**cóme**, IRR.; TR.: superare, soverchiare, sormontare; vincere. -**cómer**, S.: superatore; vincitore, *m*. '-**cŏnfident**, ADJ.: troppo ardito, presuntuoso. -**cŏunt**, TR.: domandare troppo. '-**cūrious**, ADJ.: troppo curioso. -**dō**, IRR.; TR.: fare troppo, eccedere; faticar troppo; opprimere: — *one's self*, fatticarsi troppo. -**dóne**, ADJ.: esagerato; troppo cotto, stracotto. -**dose**, S.: dose troppo forte, *f*. -**drăw**, TR.: esagerare; fare una tratta che eccede il credito. -**drĕss**, TR.: vestire con troppa pompa; INTR.: adornarsi troppo. -**drive**, IRR.; TR.: fare andare troppo presto, stimolare troppo. '-**dūe**, ADJ.: (*com.*) scaduto; (*post.*) in ritardo. '-**ēager**, ADJ.: troppo ardente. '-**ēagerly**, ADV.: troppo ardentemente. '-**ēagerness**, S.: troppo grande ardore, *m*. -**ēat**, IRR.; INTR.: — *one's self*, mangiar troppo. -**eȳe**, TR.: invigliare, osservare. -**făll**, S.: cateratta, cascata d'acquata, *f*. -**fill**, TR.: empiere troppo. -**fine**, ADJ.: strafino. -**flōat**, INTR.: fiottare; galleggiare. -**flow**, S.: inondazione, *f*. -**flŏw**, IRR.; (IN)TR.: inondare, traboccare. -**flŏwing**, S.: soprabbondanza, *f*.; eccesso, *m*. -**flŏwingly**, ADV.: soprabbondantemente. -**flȳ**, IRR.; INTR.: sopravvolare. -**fŏnd**, ADJ.: troppo affezionato. -**fŏrward**, ADJ.: troppo sollecito, troppo frettoloso. -**fŏrwardness**, S.: troppa premura, *f*. -**frèight**, TR.: caricare troppo, sopraccaricare. -**glânce**, TR.: dare un' occhiata. -**gĕt**, IRR.; TR.: sopraggiungere; arrivare. -**gō**, IRR.; TR.: sorpassare. -**gôrge**, TR.: satollare; impinzare. '-**grêat**, ADJ.: troppo grande, eccessivo. -**grŏw**, IRR.; INTR.: crescere troppo grande: —*n with*, coperto di. -**grŏwth**, S.: accrescimento eccessivo, *m*. -**hāle**, TR.: (*nav.*) esaminare di nuovo. -**hăng**, IRR.; (IN)TR.: pendere in fuori, aggettare. '-**hăppy**, ADJ.: troppo felice. -**hărden**, TR.: indurire troppo. -**hāsten**, TR.: affrettar troppo. -**hāstiness**, S.: fretta soverchia, *f*. '-**hāsty**, ADJ.: troppo affrettato, frettoloso, precipitoso. -**hăul** = *overhale*. -**hĕad**, ADV.: in alto, sopra, in su. -**hĕar**, IRR.; TR.: udire senza essere osservato. -**hĕat**, TR.: scaldare soverchio, infiammare: — *one's self*, scaldarsi troppo. -**joy**, S.: estasi, *f*., eccesso di gioia, *m*. -**jŏy**, TR.: inondare di gioia, deliziare: *I am —ed at it*, me ne rallegro sommamente. -**lābour**, TR.: faticare; INTR.: affaticarsi. -**lāde**, IRR.; TR.: sopraccaricare; aggravare. '-**lărge**, ADJ.: troppo largo, troppo ampio. -**lāy**, IRR.; TR.: affogare, soffolcare, incrostare; coprire: — *with silver*, coprire di argento. -**lĕap**, IRR.; TR.: saltare di là; trapassare. -**leather**, S.: tomaio, *m*. -**live**, (IN)TR.: soppravvivere, vivere più di. -**liver**, S.: sopravvivente, *m*. -**lōad**, TR.: sopraccaricare; aggravare. '-**lŏng**, ADJ.: troppo lungo. -**lŏok**, TR.: aver l'ispezione; soprastare, dominare; invigilare; esaminare; chiudere gli occhi; trascurare; tenere a sdegno, disprezzare; rivedere: *the hill —s the town*, il colle domina la città. -**lŏoker**, S.: soprantendente; soprastante, *m*. -**mâster**, TR.: governare da padrone. -**mătch**, S.: partita ineguale, *f*. -**match**, TR.: sormontare; vincere. -**mĕasure**, S.: soverchio, soprappiù, *m*. -**mŭch**, ADJ.: superfluo, eccessivo; ADV.: soprammisura, troppo. -**nāme**, TR.: nominare uno dopo l'altro. -**nice**, ADJ.: troppo delicato, troppo difficile. -**night**, S.: notte passata, *f*. '-**officious**, ADJ.: troppo officioso. -**păss**, TR.: trapassare; preterire, omettere; sdegnare. -**pāy**, TR.: strapagare, soprappagare. -**plus**, S.: soprappiù, soperchio, *m*. -**plȳ**, TR.: sopraggravare, sopraccaricare. -**poise**, S.: preponderanza, *f*.; peso, *m*. -**pŏise**, TR.: contrabilanciare. -**pŏwer**, TR.: predominare, prevalere; sopraffare, vincere, superare: —*ed by numbers*, oppresso dal numero. -**prĕss**, TR.: opprimere; ammaccare. -**prize**, TR.: stimare troppo. -**rate**, S.: prezzo eccessivo, *m*. -**rāte**, TR.: stimare troppo; domandare troppo. -**rēach**, (IR)REG.; TR.: prevenire; ingannare, eludere; INTR.: tagliarsi; ammaccarsi. -**rēacher**, S.: ingannatore, truffatore, *m*. -**rēad**, IRR.; TR.: leggere; esaminare. -**rĕckon**, TR.: contare troppo, computare troppo. -**ride**, IRR.; TR.: passare sopra; sopprimere; oltrapassare†; faticare, strappazzare (un cavallo). '-**ripe**, ADJ.: troppo maturo. -**ripen**, TR.: far troppo maturo. -**rōast**, TR.: arrostire troppo. -**rūle**, TR.: dominare, governare. -**rūler**, S.: governatore, *m*. -**rŭn**, IRR.; TR.: stracorrere, correre in là di; (*mil.*) invadere, percorrere; coprire; inondare; predare; INTR.: essere troppo pieno. -**scrŭpulous**, ADJ.: troppo scrupoloso. -**sea**, ADV.: d'oltre mare. -**sēe**, IRR.; TR.: soprantendere; omettere. -**sēer**, S.: soprantendente, *m*. -**sĕll**,

IRR.; TR.: sopravvendere, stravendere. **-sĕt**, IRR.; TR.: rovesciare, rovinare; INTR.: abbattersi, demolirsi. **-shāde**, **-shădōw**, TR.: adombrare, ombreggiare, proteggere. **-shōe**, S.: galoscia, soprascarpa di gomma, *f.* **-shōot**, IRR.; TR.: tirare di là del segno: — *one's self*, innoltrarsi troppo. **-sight**, S.: ispezione, cura, *f.*; errore, sbaglio, *m.* **-skip**, TR.: oltrepassare; trascurare, omettere. **-slēep**, IRR.; INTR.: dormir troppo. **-slip**, TR.: omettere; trascurare, lasciare. **-snōw**, TR.: coprire di neve. **-sōld**, ADJ.: sopravvenduto, stravenduto. ′**-sōon**, ADV.: troppo presto. **-spĕnt**, ADJ.: affaticato, esausto. **-sprĕad**, IRR.; TR.: spandere; allargare, dilatare. **-stănd**, IRR.; TR.: stare troppo sulle condizioni. **-stāte**, TR.: esagerare. **-stŏck**, TR.: empiere troppo; calcare. **-strāin**, TR.: sforzare, raffinare troppo; INTR.: sforzarsi. **-strĕtch**, TR.: stendere troppo, stiracchiare. **-strēw**, IRR.; TR.: spargere. **-swāy**, TR.: predominare, prevalere. **-swĕll**, IRR.; TR.: rigonfiare; traboccare.

ōvert, ADJ.: aperto, pubblico.

over-tāke, IRR.; TR.: giungere; acchiappare; sorprendere: *I will soon — you*, presto vi raggiungerò; *—n by a storm*, colto da un temporale. **-tălk**, INTR.: parlare troppo. **-tăsk**, TR.: sopraggravare (con lavoro, ecc.). **-tăx**, TR.: tassare troppo, esigere troppo. **-thrōw**, S.: sovvertimento, *m.*, sconfitta, rovina, rotta, *f.* **-thrōw**, IRR.; TR.: rovesciare, rovinare, disfare. **-thrōwer**, S.: sovvertitore, rovinatore; vincitore, *m.* ′**-thwărt**, ADJ.: opposito, avverso; ostinato. ′**-thwart-ly†**, ADV.: a traverso, obbliquamente; tortamente; pertinacemente. ′**-thwart-ness†**, S.: pertinacia, caparbieria, *f.* **-tire**, TR.: faticare troppo.

ōvertly, ADV.: apertamente.

over-tŏp, TR.: soprastare, sorpassare. **-trip**, TR.: camminare sopra pian piano.

ōverture, S.: apertura, scoperta; proposizione, offerta; (*mus.*) sinfonia, *f.*

over-tŭrn, TR.: sovvertere, rovinare. **-tŭrner**, S.: sovvertitore, distruttore, *m.* **-tŭrning**, S.: sovvertimento, *m.*, rovina, *f.* **-vălue**, TR.: stimare troppo. **-vēil**, TR.: velare, coprire con un velo. **-violent**, ADJ.: troppo violento. **-vōte**, TR.: avere la pluralità delle voci. **-wătch**, TR.: affaticare con eccessive veglie. **-wēak**, ADJ.: troppo debole. **-wēary**, TR.: faticare troppo, stancare all' eccesso. **-wēen**, INTR.: pensare troppo bene di sè. **-wēening**, ADJ.: presuntuoso; S.: presunzione, arroganza, *f.* **-wēeningly**, ADV.: arrogantemente. **-wēigh**, TR.: pesare più, essere più pesante. **-wēight**,

S.: preponderanza, *f.*; sopra[...]
-whĕlm *-hwĕlm*, sommergere; [...]re, ricolmare, inondare; [...]
-whĕlming, S.: sommergente, [...] sommerge, ecc. **-whĕlming**[...] in modo oppressivo. **-wīse**, AD[...] po, savio, troppo accorto. **-wŏ**[...] oppresso, affaticato, usato. [...]
-rāt, ADJ.: troppo lavorato, [...]diato. ′**-zēalous**, ADJ.: troppo[...]

ōviform, ADJ.: ovale, di forma [...]

ōwe, (IR)R.; TR.: dovere; [...]gato, esser tenuto: *I — my life* [...] son tenuto della vita. **-ing**, ADJ.: imputabile: *that is — to*, ciò pro[...] ciò è cagionato da (*or* l' effetto [...] attribuirsi a.

ŏwl, S.: gufo; barbagianni, *m.*; [...] *f.* **-er**, S.: contrabbandiere, *m.* [...] civetta, *f.* **-ing**, S.: contrabban[...]

ōwn[1], ADJ.: proprio: *my —*, [...] mia, i miei; *my — self*, io mede[...] *one's —*, essere padrone di s[...]

own[2], TR.: confessare, conced[...] conoscere: possedere, essere p[...]rio di: — *a fact*, accusare un fat[...] S.: proprietario, padrone, *m.* [...] S.: proprietà; signoria, *f.*

ŏx (pl. *oxen*), S.: bue, bove, *m.* [...] (*bot.*, *nav.*) occhio di bue, *m.* [...]fano, *m.* **-heal**, S.: radice dell'[...] *f.* **-like**, ADJ.: come un bue. [...] (*bot.*) tassobarbasso, *m.* **-stall**, [...] da buoi, *f.* **-tongue**, S.: (*bot.*) bu[...]

oxălic, ADJ.: ossalico: — *aci*[...] ossalico.

ŏxid-e, S.: ossido, *m.* **-ize**, TR.: [...]

ŏxycrate, S.: ossicrato, *m.*

ŏx-ygen, S.: ossigeno, *m.* **-yg**[...] TR.: ossigenare. **-ygenātion**, [...]genazione. **-ygenous**, ADJ.: di [...]

ōyer, S.: corte di giustizia decisiv[...]

ōyes! INTERJ.: ascoltate! udite!

ōyster, S.: ostrica, *f.* **-man**, S. [...]tore d' ostriche, *m.* **-shell**, S.: [...]glia d' ostrica, *f.* **-wench**, **-w**[...] S.: venditrice d' ostriche, *f.*

ozæna, S.: (*surg.*) ozena, *f.*

ōzone, S.: ozono, *m.*

P

p *pē* (*the letter*), S.: p, *m.*

păb-ular, ADJ.: che dà pascolo, nutritivo. **-ulātion**, S.: pa[...] pascolo, *m.* **-ulous** = pabular. [...] S.: pascolo, nutrimento, *m.*

păce [...] *m.*: *a*[...] *with*, [...]

—, raddoppiare i passi. **-e** 2, TR.: misurare co' passi; INTR.: andare passo a passo; andar l'ambio. **-er**, S.: cavallo ambiante, *m.*

pa-cific, ADJ.: pacifico. **-cification**, S.: pacificamento, fare pace, *m.* **-cificator**, S.: pacificatore, *m.* **-cificatory**, ADJ.: pacifico. **-cifier**, S.: pacificatore, mediatore, *m.* **-cify**, TR.: pacificare; placare.

păck 1, S.: balla, balletta, *f.*; fardello, *m.*; muta (di cani), *f.*: — *of cards*, mazzo di carte, *m.*; — *of hounds*, muta di cani da caccia, *f.*; — *of knaves*, mano di ladri, *m.* **pack** 2, TR.: imballare; affardellare; imbastare: — *the cards*, accozzare le carte; — *a jury*, scegliere giurati corrotti; — *away*, fare fagotto; — *off*, andare via; tirar le calze; (*fig.*) morire. **-age**, S.: balla, *f.* **-cloth**, S.: tela di sacco, *f.* **-er**, S.: imballatore, *m.* **-et** 1, S.: fascio, fardello, fastello; piego (di lettere); ballotto, *m.*; *steam* —, vascello a vapore, *m.* **-et** 2, TR.: imballare, fare un piego. **-et-boat**, S.: pacchebotto, vapore postale, *m.* **-horse**, S.: cavallo da basta, *m.* **-ing**, S.: imballare, *m.*: *send* —, mandare via; congedare. **-ing-paper**, S.: carta da invoglio, *f.* **-needle**, S.: ago per cucire sacchi, *m.* **-saddle**, S.: basto, *m.* **-thread**, S.: spago, *m.*, cordicina, *f.*

păc-t, **-tion**, S.: patto, *m.*, convenzion, *f.* **-tional**, **-titious**, ADJ.: patteggiato, convenuto.

păd 1, S.: strada battuta, *f.*; sentiero; cavallo portante; ladro. **pad** 2, S.: guancialetto; cercine, *m.*: — *of straw*, pagliaccio, *m.* **pad** 3, INTR.: rubare le strade; riempiere di borra. **-der**, S.: ladro di strada, *m.*

păddl-e 1, S.: remo corto e largo, *m.* **-e** 2, INTR.: remigare; maneggiare; guazzare: — *wheel*, ruota d'albero, *f.* **-box**, S.: carriola, *f.* **-er**, S.: rematore, *m.* **-e-steamer**, S.: vapore a ruote, *m.*

păddock, S.: botta, *f.*; parco, *m.*

păddy, S.: (*pop.*) irlandese, *m.*

pădlock 1, S.: cattenaccio, lucchetto, *m.* **padlock** 2, TR.: chiudere con lucchetto.

paēan, S.: pean, *m.*, peana, *f.*

pāgan, ADJ.: pagano, infedele; S.: pagano, *m.* **-ism**, S.: paganesimo, *m.*; idolatria, *f.* **-ize**, TR.: paganizzare.

pāge 1, S.: pagina; facciata (di carta), *f.*: *at the bottom of the* —, al piè della pa-[...] **page** 2, S.: paggio, servidore, *m.*: —. pagetto. **page** 3, TR.: numera-[...] (d' un libro).

[...] ADJ.: pomposo, splendido. [...] spettacolo, *m.*, pompa, *f.* [...] dare uno spettacolo; rappresentare. **-ry**, S.: fasto, *m.*, pompa, *f.*

pagōda, S.: pagode; tempio indiano, *m.*; pagoda, *f.*

pāil, S.: secchia, *f.* **-ful**, S.: secchiata, secchia piena, *f.*

pāin 1, S.: pena, *f.*; dolore, *m.*; punizione, affizione, *f.*: —*s*, doglie nel parto, *f. pl.*; *a — in the head*, mal di testa. **pain** 2, TR.: dolere, dar pena. **-ful**, ADJ.: doloroso, penoso, faticoso. **-fully**, ADV.: dolorosamente, con pena, penosamente. **-fulness**, S.: pena, affizione; difficoltà, *f.*

pāinim, ADJ.: pagano, infedele; S.: pagano, *m.*

pāin-less, ADJ.: senza pena, senza affizione. **-staker**, S.: che affatica molto, persona laboriosa, *f.* **-staking**, ADJ.: laborioso, industrioso; S.: industria, *f.*

pāint 1, S.: colore; liscio, belletto, *m.* **paint** 2, TR.: dipingere, rappresentare; INTR.: imbellettarsi: — *in oil*, dipingere ad olio; — *in water colours*, dipingere in acquarello. **-er**, S.: pittore, dipintore, *m.* **-ing**, S.: pintura; dipintura, *f.*; quadro; liscio, belletto, *m.*: — *in oil*, pittura in olio, *f.* **-ure**†, S.: pittura, *f.*

pāir 1, S.: paio, *m.*, coppia, *f.*: — *of gloves*, paio di guanti; — *of horses*, pariglia; *happy* —, coppia felice; — *royal*, zara, *f.* (al giuoco de' dadi). **pair** 2, appaiare; accoppiare, accompagnare; INTR.: accoppiarsi. **-ing**, S.: appaiamento, accoppiamento, *m.*: — *time*, stagione del appaiamento.

păl-ace, S.: palazzo, *m.* **-ācious**, ADJ.: maestoso, magnifico.

păladin, S.: paladino, *m.*

palanquin, S.: palanchino, *m.*

păla-table, ADJ.: grato al gusto, saporito. **-ableness**, S.: buon sapore, *m.* **-e**, S.: palato; gusto, *m.*

palātial, ADJ.: di palazzo; sontuoso; del palato.

Pălatine 1, ADJ.: palatino, di principe; S.: palatino, *m.* (titolo). **Palatine** 2, S.: palatinato, *m.*

palāver, S.: ciarla, ciarleria, *f.*

pāle 1, ADJ.: pallido, smorto: *rather* —, pallidetto, pallidiccio; *grow* —, impallidire. **pale** 2, S.: palo, *m.*; palata, palafitta, *f.*; riparo; grembo (della chiesa), *m.*: *within the* —, nel grembo. **pale** 3, TR.: palificare; stecconare; INTR.: fare impallidire. **-eyed**, ADJ.: di vista fosca. **-faced**, ADJ.: pallido, smorto. **-ly**, ADV.: pallidamente; languidamente. **-ness**, S.: pallidezza; bianchezza livida, *f.*

paleŏgraphy, S.: paleografia, *f.*

pālous, ADJ.: paglioso.

pălette, S.: (*paint.*) tavolozza, assicella, *f.*

Rō-mish, ADJ.: romano, papistico. **-mist**, S.: papista, *m.*
rŏmp 1, S.: ragazzaccia grossolana, *f.* **romp** 2, INTR.: trescare; scherzare grossolanamente. **-ishness**, S.: rustichezza, *f.*
rondeau *-dō*, S.: poesia francese col ritornello, *f.*
rŏndure†, S.: rotondo, cerchio, *m.*
rŏn-ion, -yon, S.: persona rognosa, *f.*
rŏnt, S.: animale bistorto, animale sformato, *m.*
rōod, S.: quarta parte d' una bifolca; croce, *f.*
rōof 1, S.: tetto; sommo, colmo, *m.;* coperta, *f.: — of a coach*, cielo d' una carrozza, *m.; — of the mouth*, palato, *m.* **roof** 2, TR.: coprire con un tetto. **-less**, ADJ.: senza tetto; scoperto. **-tile**, S.: tegola, *f.* **-y**, ADJ.: coperto d' un tetto.
rŏok 1, S.: cornacchia, *f.;* barattiere, furfante; rocco, *m.* (*at chess*). **rook** 2, TR.: truffare, ingannare. **-ery**, S.: luogo pieno di cornacchie, *m.* **-ing**, S.: mariuoleria, *f.*, inganno, *m.* **-y**, ADJ.: pieno di cornacchie.
rōom, S.: spazio, luogo, *m.;* camera, stanza; occasione, cagione, ragione, *f.: dining —*, sala da mangiare, *f.; drawing —*, camera d' assemblea, *f.; there is no — to doubt it*, non v' è luogo da dubitarne. **-age**† = *-iness*. **-ful**, ADJ.: abbondante di camere. **-iness**, S.: spazio, luogo, *m.;* larghezza, *f.* **-y**, ADJ.: spazioso, vasto, ampio.
rōost 1, S.: posatoio, *m.* **roost** 2, INTR.: appollaiarsi; albergare (ironicamente). **-er**, S.: gallo, *m.*
rōot 1, S.: radice; origine, *f.*, principio, *m.;* cagione, *f.: cube —*, radice cubica, *f.; take —*, radicarsi. **root** 2, (IN)TR.: abbarbicare, far radice, pigliar radice; grufolare: *— up, — out*, sbarbicare, sradicare. **-ed**, ADJ.: abbarbicato, radicato; inveterato: *— up, — out*, sbarbicato, sradicato. **-edly**, ADV.: profondamente; fortemente. **-ing** (*up, out*), S.: diradicamento, sradicamento, *m.* **-less**, ADJ.: senza radice. **-y**, ADJ.: pieno di radici.
rō-pe 1, S.: corda, fune, *f.;* laccio, *m.: — of onions*, resta di cipolle, *f.; — of pearls*, filo di perle, *m.* **-pe** 2, INTR.: scorrere con lentezza; filare, far filo. **-pe-dancer**, S.: ballerino da corda, *m.* **-pe-ladder**, S.: scala di corde, *f.* **-pe-maker, -er**, S.: funaio, funaiuolo, *m.* **-pe-trick, -pery**, S.: bricconeria, *f.* **-pe-walk**, S.: corderia, *f.* **-piness**, S.: viscosità, tenacità, *f.* **-py**, ADJ.: viscoso, tenace.
rŏquelaure *-lōr*, S.: mantello, pastrano, *m.*
rō-ral, -rid, ADJ.: pieno di rugiada. **-riferous**, ADJ.: rugiadoso.

rōsary, S.: rosario, rosaio, *m.*
rōscid, ADJ.: rugiadoso.
rō-se, S.: rosa, *f.: monthly —*, rosa di tutti i mesi; *moss —*, rosa muscosa; *no — without a thorn*, non v' è rosa senza spine; *oil of —*, olio rosato, *m.; under the —*, privatamente, in segreto. **-seate**, ADJ.: rosato, roseo. **-se-bud**, S.: bottone di rosa, *m.* **-se-bush**, S.: rosaio, *m.* **-sed**, ADJ.: rosso, vermiglio.
rōsemary, S.: rosmarino, ramerino, *m.*
rō-set, S.: creta rossa, *f.* **-se-tree**, S.: rosaio, *m.* **-sette**, S.: rosetta, *f.* **-se-water**, S.: acqua rosata, acqua rosa, *f.* **-sewood**, S.: legno rosa; palissandro, *m.* **-sier**†, S.: roseto, *m.*
rŏsin 1, S.: resina, ragia, gomma, *f.: hard —*, colofonia, *f.* **rosin** 2, TR.: stropicciare con ragia. **-y**, ADJ.: resinoso, gommifero, *m.*
rŏs-ter, S.: regolamento del servizio, *m.;* lista d' ufficiali, *f.* **-tral**, S.: rostrale, *m.* **-trated**, ADJ.: rostrato. **-trum**, S.: rostro; becco, *m.;* prua, *f.*
rōsy, ADJ.: roseo, vermiglio: *— cheeks*, guance rosee; *— lips*, labbra vermiglie.
rŏt 1, S.: moria; putrefazione, *f.* **rot** 2, TR.: infracidare; putrefare; INTR.: infracidarsi; putrefarsi.
rōta, S.: rota, *f.*
rō-tary, ADJ.: rotante, che ruota; girativo. **-tated**, ADJ.: rotato, rotante. **-tātion**, S.: rotazione, *f.*, rotamento, *m.* **-tātor**, S.: rotatore, *m.* **-tatory**, ADJ.: rotante.
rōte 1, S.: uso, *m.;* pratica, *f.: learn by —*, imparare per pratica (a mente). **rote** 2, TR.: imparare per pratica.
rŏther-beasts†, S. PL.: bestiame grosso, *m.*
rŏtten, ADJ.: infracidato, putrefatto: *— apple*, mela fracida, *f.; — egg*, uovo imputridito, *m.; — wood*, legno fracido, *m.; — at the core*, maganato, marcio, falso, perfido. **-ness**, S.: fracidezza, putrefazione; corruzione, *f.;* marciume, *m.*
rotŭnd, ADJ.: rotondo, circolare. **-ity**, S.: rotondità, sfericità, *f.* **-a**, S.: rotonda, *f.*, rotondo, *m.* (edifizio).
rouge 1 *rōş*, S.: liscio, belletto, *m.* **rouge** 2, TR.: imbellettare; INTR.: imbellettarsi.
rough *rŭf*, ADJ.: ruvido, aspro, rozzo; scabro: *— diamond*, diamante greggio, diamante grezzo, *m.; — draft*, primo abbozzo, schizzo; *— sea*, mar tempestoso, *m.; — style*, stile rozzo, *m.* **-cast** 1, S.: intonaco, modello abbozzato, *m.* **-cast** 2, TR.: intonacare; arricciare. **-draught**, S.: schizzo, abbozzo, *m.: — of a deed*, primo abbozzo, *m.* **-draw**, IRR.; TR.: schizzare, abbozzare. **-en**, TR.: rendere

papăverous, ADJ.: di papavero; sonnifero.

păper 1, S.: carta, *f.*; giornale, *m.*: *blotting* —, carta sugante, *f.*; —*s*, scritture, *f. pl.*, giornali, *m. pl.* **paper** 2, TR.: coprire di carta. **-currency**, S.: carta moneta, *f.* **-cutter**, S.: tagliacarta, *m.* **-hanger**, S.: paratore, tapezziere, *m.* **-maker**, S.: cartaio, cartaro, *m.* **-manufactory**, S.: fabbrica di carta, *f.* **-manufacturer**, S.: fabricatore di carta, *m.* **-mill**, S.: cartiera (da fabbricare la carta), *f.* **-money**, S.: carta moneta, *f.* **-seller**, S.: cartaio, *m.* **-staining**, S.: marezzo, *m.* **-windows**, S. PL.: impannate, *f. pl.*

papilio†, S.: farfalla, *f.*, papiglione, *m.* **-năceous**, ADJ.: papilionaceo.

păpil-lary, **-lous**, ADJ.: papillare.

pă-pism, S.: papismo, *m.* **-pist**, S.: papista, *m.* **-pistic(al)**, ADJ.: papistico, de' papisti. **-pistry**, S.: papismo, *m.*; religione Romana, *f.*

papŏose, S.: bambino indiano, *m.*

păppous, ADJ.: papposo.

păppy, ADJ.: molle, morbido, sugoso.

papўrus, S.: papiro, *m.*

păpulous, ADJ.: pieno di pustule.

păr, ADJ.: pari, uguale; S.: pari, *m.*, ugualità, *f.*; equivalente, *m.*: *above* —, sopra il pari; *be at* —, esser uguale; *on a — with*, uguale a.

păr-able, S.: parabola, allegoria, similitudine, *f.* **-ăbola**, S.: parabola, *f.* **-abŏlic(al)**, ADJ.: parabolico, di parabola. **-abŏlically**, ADV.: in maniera di parabola. **-ăbolism**, S.: parabolismo, *m.*

parăchronism, S.: paracronismo, *m.*

pârachute, S.: paracadute, *m.*

Păraclete, S.: Spirito Santo, *m.*

parăde, S.: parata; ostentazione, mostra; piazza d'arme, *f.*: *make a — of*, fare sfoggio di.

păradigm, S.: modello, esempio, *m.*

păra-dise, S.: paradiso, *m.* **-disiacal**, **-disian**, ADJ.: di paradiso.

păra-dox, S.: paradosso, *m.* **-dŏxical**, ADJ.: paradosso, strano. **-dŏxically**, ADV.: in modo paradosso.

păragon 1, S.: capo d'opera; modello perfetto. **paragon** 2, TR.: paragonare, comparare.

păra-graph, S.: paragrafo, *m.* **-grăphically**, ADV.: in paragrafi, a paragrafi.

parallăctic(al), ADJ.: parallatico.

părallax, S.: paralasse, *f.*

păral-lel 1, ADJ.: paralello, equidistante: *line*, linea paralella, *f.* **-lel** 2, S.: linea paralella; comparazione, *f.* **-lel** 3, TR.: paragonare, assomigliare. **-lelism**, S.: parallelismo, *m.* **-lĕlogram**, S.: parallelogrammo, *m.*

parăl-ogism, S.: paralogismo, *m.* **-ogise**, TR.: sottilizzare, sofisticare.

par-ălysis, S.: paralisia, *f.* **-alўtic**, S.: paralitico, *m.* **-alўtic(al)**, ADJ.: paralitico. **-alyze**, TR.: paralizzare, privare di moto.

pă'ramŏunt 1, ADJ.: superiore; sovrano, supremo, primo. **paramount** 2, S.: capo, padrone, *m.*

păramour, S: amante, innamorato, *m.*

păranymph, S.: paraninfo, *m.*

părapet, S.: parapetto, *m.*; sponda, *f.*

paraphernălia, S.: paraferna, sopraddota, *f.*

păra-phrase 1, S.: parafrasi, interpretazione, *f.* **-phrase** 2, TR.: commentare. **-phrast**, S.: parafraste, commentatore, *m.* **-phrăstic(al)**, ADJ.: parafrastico. **-phrăstically**, ADV.: parafrasticamente.

părasang, S.: parasanga, *f.* (misura di cinquanta stadi).

păra-site, S.: parasito; ghiottone, *m.* **-sitic(al)**, ADJ.: parasitico, di parasito. **-sitically**, ADV.: in modo parasitico.

părasol, S.: parasole, *m.*, ombrella, *f.*

păravaunt†, ADV.: in fronte, pubblicamente.

pârboil, TR.: sobbollire, mezzobollire.

pârcel 1, S.: particella, picciola porzione, *f.*: *by* —*s*, a minuto; — *of rogues*, brigata di furfanti, *f.*; *be part and — of*, far parte integrante di; *make up a* —, fare un pacco (involto). **parcel** 2, TR.: dividere; spartire, sminuzzare. **-ling**, S.: spartimento, *m.*

pârcener, S.: (*jur.*) coerede, *m.*

pârch, TR.: abbruciare, seccare; INTR.: essere abbruciato. **-ed**, ADJ.: secco, adusto. **-edness**, S.: secchezza, adustione, *f.* **-ing**, S.: seccamento, *m.*, adustione, *f.*

pârchment, S.: pergamena, carta pecora, *f.* **-maker**, S.: pergamenaio, *m.*

pârd, **-ale**†, S.: leopardo, liopardo, *m.*

pârdon 1, S.: perdono, *m.*; grazia, *f.*: *general* —, amnistia, *f.*; *I beg your* —, vi chieggo perdono. **pardon** 2, TR.: perdonare; far grazia: — *me*, mi perdoni, perdoni, perdonatemi. **-able**, ADJ.: perdonabile, scusabile. **-ably**, ADV.: in modo scusabile. **-er**, S.: perdonatore, scusatore, *m.*

pâre, TR.: pareggiare, scortecciare, scrostare (pane); affilare: — *the nails*, tagliare le unghie.

paregŏric(al), ADJ.: paregorico, lenitivo.

parĕnchyma, S.: parenchima, *m.*

pâr-ent, S.: padre, genitore, *m.*; madre, *f.*: — *state*, madre patria, *f.* **-entage**, S.: parentado, *m.*; stirpe, *f.* **-ĕntal**, ADJ.: paterno, di parenti; materno.

parentătion†, S.: parentazione, *f.*

rŭf-fle 1, s.: manichino; disturbo, tumulto, *m.* **-fle** 2, TR.: increspare, piagare; disordinare, disturbare, agitare; INTR.: divenire turbolento, agitarsi. **-fler**, s.: sgherro, *m.* **-fling**, s.: tumulto, *m.*
rŭfterhood, s.: (*falc.*) cappello, *m.*
rŭg, s.: tappettino, *m.*; pelosa coperta da letto, *f.*; can barbone, *m.*
rugged, ADJ.: ruvido, rozzo, rigido; brutale, brusco. **-ly**, ADV.: ruvidamente, rozzamente, aspramente. **-ness**, s.: ruvidezza, rozzezza, asprezza, *f.*
rūgine, s.: (*surg.*) raspa, *f.*
rugōse, ADJ.: rugoso, grinzo.
rūin 1, s.: rovina, ruina; decadenza, *f.*: *come to* —, rovinarsi; cadere in rovina. **ruin** 2, TR.: rovinare; distruggere; INTR.: rovinarsi, decadere: — *one's self*, rovinarsi, distruggersi. **-ous**, ADJ.: ruinoso, distruttivo; pericoloso. **-ously**, ADV.: rovinosamente; cattivamente. **-ousness**, s.: stato rovinoso, *m.*, rovina, *f.*
rūl-e 1, s.: regolo, *m.*; regola, *f.*; ordine, precetto; governo; modello, esempio, *m.*; usanza, *f.*, costume, *m.*: *the — of three*, la regola aurea; *bear* —, comandare, governare; *make it a* —, aver per regola; *there is no — without exceptions*, non v' è regola senza eccezioni. **-e** 2, (IN)TR.: rigare; regolare, ordinare; guidare; soggiogare, domare; umiliare: — *paper*, rigare della carta; — *over*, governare, dominare; signoreggiare. **-er**, s.: regolo; regolatore, governatore, *m.* **-ing**, ADJ.: regnante, dominante. **-y**, ADV.: regolato, moderato.
rŭm 1, ADJ.: strambo, strano. **rum** 2, s.: rum, *m.* (acquavite).
rŭm-ble, TR.: rombare; strepitare; mormorare. **-bler**, s.: borbottatore, bisbigliatore, *m.* **-bling**, ADJ.: rombante; s.: borboglio, mormorio, *m.*
rūmi-nant, ADJ.: ruminante. **-nate**, (IN)TR.: ruminare, riconsiderare. **-nātion**, s.: rugumazione, meditazione, *f.* **-nator**, s.: ruminatore, rugumatore, *m.*
rŭmmage, TR.: scompigliar cercando, cercare; predare.
rŭmmer, s.: bicchiere grande, *m.*
rūmour 1, s.: romore, *m.*; fama, voce, *f.* **rumour** 2, TR.: fare romore; divolgare: *it is —ed that*, corre voce che. **-er**, s.: divolgatore, promulgatore, *m.*
rŭmp, s.: groppone, *m.*; groppa, *f.*
rŭmple 1, s.: piega, grinza, riga, *f.* **rumple** 2, TR.: increspare, raggrinzare; rugare.
rŭn 1, s.: corsa, carriera, *f.*; corso, *m.*; fuga, *f.*: *in the long* —, a lungo andare; *the common* —, il comune, la maggior parte; *have a long* —, avere lungo successo; *take a* —, prender una corsa. **run** 2, INTR.: correre; passare; fuggire; gocciolare, colare; TR.: far correre, correre, figgere, spingere; dirigere, governare: — *aground*, dare in secco, arrenare; — *apace*, correre velocemente; — *through a book*, leggere tutto un libro; — *one's self out of breath*, correre fino a perder il fiato; — *one's country*, abbandonare il paese; — *in debt*, indebitarsi; — *a full gallop*, correre a briglia sciolta, galoppare; — *the gantlet*, passare per le bacchette; — *a hazard*, correr rischio; — *all hazards*, esporsi ad ogni rischio; — *out in length*, stendersi in lunghezza; — *mad*, impazzire; — *a race*, correre il palio; — *to seed*, andare in semenza, semenzire; — *out of one's wits*, impazzire, perder il senno; — *about*, andare attorno; — *after*, correre dietro; ambire; — *against*, incontrarsi; — *away*, scappare; fuggire; passare; — *away with*, portare via; — *back*, ritornare indietro; — *counter*, ripugnare; — *down*, scorrere; colare, stillare; vilipendere, disprezzare; — *for it*, darla a gambe; — *in (into)*, gettarsi, precipitarsi; concorrere; — *a nail into one's foot*, infilzarsi un chiodo nel piede; — *in with*, accordarsi, convenire; — *on*, continuare; seguitare; — *out*, finire; stendersi; — *over*, traboccare; trascorrere; — *over a book*, dare una scorsa ad un libro, sfiorare un libro; *be — over*, cadere sotto carrozza; — *through*, passare da banda a banda; infilare; — *through one's fortune*, scialacquare tutto il suo; — *to*, accorrere; — *up*, montare, alzarsi; — *up and down*, andare qua e là; — *upon*, lanciarsi sopra. **-agate**, s.: rinnegato; vagabondo, *m.* **-away**, s.: disertore, fuggitivo, *m.*
rŭn-dle, s.: piuolo di scala, *m.* **-dlet**, s.: bariletto, barlotto; piuolo di scala, *m.*
rŭng, s.: piuolo (d' una scala), *m.*; (*nav.*) costola, *f.*, fasciame, *m.*
rŭn-nel, s.: ruscelletto, ruscellettino, *m.* **-ner**, s.: corridore, corritore; sensale; germoglio, *m.*: — *of a mill*, mola di sopra d'un mulino, *f.* **-net**, s.: gaglio, coagulo; presame, *m.* **-ning**, s.: corrimento, corso, *m.*: — *footman*, lacchè, *m.*; — *knot*, cappio, *m.*; — *of the nose*, cimurro, *m.*; — *place*, carriera, *f.*; corso, *m.*; — *sore*, piaga che cola, *f.*; — *water*, acqua corrente, *f.*
rŭnnion = *ronion*.
rŭnt, s.: animale imbozzacchito, piccol animale, *m.*
rŭp-tion, s.: rottura, fessura, *f.* **-ture** 1, s.: rottura, crepatura; ernia, *f.* **-ture** 2, TR.: rompere, fracassare. **-turewort**, s.: (*bot.*) erniaria, *f.*
rūral, ADJ.: rurale, rustico; campestre. **-ly**, ADV.: secondo l' uso campestre.
ruricolist, s.: abitatore della campagna, *m.*

părt-ly, ADV.: in parte, in qualche modo. **-ner** 1, S.: associato, socio, compagno, *m.*: *managing* —, socio gerente; *sleeping* —, socio accomandante. **-ner** 2, (IN)TR.: associare; associarsi. **-nership**, S.: società; associazione, *f.*: *enter into — with*, entrare in società con; *take one into* —, associarsi uno.

părtridge, S.: pernice, *f.*: *young* —, perniciotto, *m.*

partū-rient, ADJ.: partoriente. **-rition**, S.: parto, *m.*

părty, S.: parte; fazione; persona, *f.*; (*pol.*) partito, *m.*, fazione, *f.*; (*mil.*) distaccamento, *m.*: *evening* —, veglia, serata, conversazione, *f.*; *dinner* —, pranzo, *m.*; *be a — to a thing*, *make one's self — in a thing*, prender parte in qualche cosa, interessarsi. **-coloured**, ADJ.: di più colori. **-jury**, S.: giurati spartiti, *m. pl.* **-man**, S.: fazioso; sedizioso, *m.* **-wall**, S.: muro divisorio, *m.*

părvenu, S.: nuovo ricco, *m.*

păs, S.: passo, *m.*; precedenza, *f.*

păschal, ADJ.: pasquale.

păsh 1 †, S.: capo; colpo, *m.* **pash** 2, TR.: ammaccare.

pasigraphy, S.: pasigrafia, *f.*

păsque-flower, S.: anemone, *f.*

păsquinade, S.: pasquinata, *f.*

păss 1, S.: passo; passaggio: grado, stato, *m.*, situazione, *f.*; stretto; colpo, *m.*, botta, *f.*; passaporto, *m.*: *come to* —, accadere, avvenire. **pass** 2, (IN)TR.: passare, trapassare; trasferire; fuggire; morire: — *a compliment upon one*, fare un complimento ad uno; — *a judgment*, — *a sentence*, sentenziare, giudicare; — *the time*, consumare il tempo: — *one's word*, dar sua parola, impegnarsi; — *along*, passare per; — *away*, andare via; consumare; — *by*, passare sotto silenzio; perdonare; negligere; — *for*, essere supposto; — *on*, trapassare; sfuggirsi; — *over*, omettere, trascurare; — *round*, far circolare. **-able**, ADJ.: passabile; tollerabile

passădo, S.: botta, *f.*, colpo, *m.*

păssage, S.: passaggio, trapasso; evento, caso, accidente; affare, *m.* **-money**, S.: prezzo del tragitto, *m.*

păssenger, S.: passeggiere, viandante, *m.*: *effects of —s*, roba di passeggiere, *f.*; (*rail.*) *—s' room*, stanza de' passaggieri, [illegible] **-carriage**, S.: (*rail.*) vagone da [illegible]e, *m.* **-train**, S.: treno di per-[illegible]

[illegible]: passatore, viandante, *m.*

[illegible]S.: passibilità, *f.*

[illegible]passibile. **-ness** = *pas-*[illegible]

[illegible], eminente, eccellente. **passing** 2, ADV.: estremamente. **-bell**, S.: campana a mortorio, *f.*

păssion, S.: passione, *f.*, affetto; amore, *m.*: *be in a* —, essere in collera; *get into a* —, mettersi in collera; *vent one's* —, sfogare la collera. **-ate**, ADJ.: appassionato, collerico. **-ate**, TR.: passionare. **-ately**, ADV.: iratamente, ardentemente. **-ateness**, S.: disposizione alla collera, *f.*, ardore, *m.*; impazienza, *f.* **-flower**, S.: fior della passione, *m.* **-less**, ADJ.: senza passione, tranquillo. **-week**, S.: settimana della passione, *f.*

păs-sive, ADJ.: passivo. **-sively**, ADV.: passivamente. **-siveness**, **-sivity**, S.: passività, *f.*

Păss-over, S.: pasqua de' giudei, *f.*

păssport, S.: passaporto, *m.*

păst 1, ADJ.: passato, scorso, scaduto, andato: *in times* —, altre volte; *be — shame*, esser sfacciato; — *all doubt*, oltre ogni dubbio; — *one o'clock*, un'ora passata; *a quarter — one*, un'ora e un quarto. **past** 2, PREP.: al di là, sopra, fuori.

păste 1, S.: pasta, colla, *f.* **paste** 2, TR.: impastare, incollare. **-board**, S.: cartone, *m.* **-board**, ADJ.: fatto di cartone. **-board-maker**, S.: cartolaio, *m.*

pastĕl, S.: (*paint.*) pastello, *m.*

păstern, S.: pastoia, *f.*, garretto (del cavallo), *m.*

păs-til, **-tille**, S.: pastiglia, *f.*

păstime, S.: passatempo; diporto, divertimento, *m.*

păstor, S.: pastore, rettore, curato, *m.* **-al**, ADJ.: pastorale; di pastore; S.: pastorale, egloga, *f.* **-ate**, S.: pastorato, uffizio di pastore, *m.* **-like**, ADJ.: pastorale, di pastore. **-ship** = *pastorate*.

păstry, S.: pasticceria, *f.* **-cook**, S.: pasticciere, *m.*

păstur-able, ADJ.: proprio a pasturare. **-age**, **-e**, S.: pastura, *f.*; pasto, pascolo, *m.*; TR.: pasturare, pascolare; pascere. **-e-ground**, S.: pastura, *f.*, pascolo, *m.*

păsty, S.: pasticcio, *m.*

păt 1, ADJ.: convenevole, proprio, opportuno. **pat** 2, S.: piccol colpo, *m.*, botta leggiera, *f.* **pat** 3, TR.: dare una percossa leggiera: — *at the door*, picchiare alla porta.

pătch 1, S.: pezza; toppa, *f.*; pezzo, pezzetto (sul viso), *m.* **patch**, TR.: rappezzare, rattoppare: — *one's face*, mettere nei sul viso; — *up*, stuccare (un muro); racconciare. **-er**, S.: racconciatore, rappezzatore, *m.* **-work**, S.: rappezzatura, *f.*, rappezzamento; racconciamento, *m.*

pāte, S.: testa; zucca, *f.*; capo; goffo, *m.*

patefaction, S.: dichiarazione, manifestazione, *f.*

brutto, m. **-den**, TR.: attristare, affliggere; INTR.: avere una cera mesta.
săddle 1, S.: sella, *f.*: — *of mutton*, coda di castrato, *f.*; *pack* —, basto, *m.* **saddle** 2, TR.: sellare, mettere il basto, imbastare: *be —d with*, avere indosso. **-backed**, ADJ.: sellato. **-bag**, S.: bisaccia, *f.* **-bow**, S.: arcione di sella, *m.* **-cloth**, S.: gualdrappa, covertina, *f.* **-maker**, **săddler**, S.: sellaio, *m.* **-tree**, S.: arcione di sella, *m.*
săd-ly, ADV.: tristamente; miserabilmente, cattivamente. **-ness**, S.: tristezza, *f.*, affanno, dolore, *m.*
sāfe 1, ADJ.: salvo, sicuro; felice; fuor di pericolo; fido, fidato: — *and sound*, sano e salvo; — *conduct*, salvacondotto, *m.*; — *return*, felice ritorno. **safe** 2, S.: guardavivande, *m.*, dispensa, *f.* **-guard** 1, TR.: conservare sano e salvo, guardare; proteggere. **-keeping**, S.: custodia, guardia, *f.* **-ly**, ADV.: salvamente; senza pericolo. **-ness**, S.: sicurezza, sicurtà, *f.* **-ty**, S.: salvezza; sicurezza; salute; custodia, *f.* **-ty-valve**, S.: valvola di sicurtà, *f.*
săffron 1, S.: zafferano, croco, *m.*: — *colour*, colore di zafferano, *m.* **saffron** 2, ADJ.: di color di zafferano, giallo. **saffron** 3, TR.: zafferanare. **-flower**, S.: fiore di zefferano, croco, *m.*
săg, TR.: caricare; INTR.: esser pesante, pesare.
sa-gāçious, ADJ.: sagace; astuto. **-gāçiously**, ADV.: sagacemente; astutamente. **-gāçiousness**, S.: acutezza d' ingegno, *f.* **-găcity**, S.: sagacità; astuzia, *f.*
sāge 1, ADJ.: savio, saggio; circospetto; S.: savio, uomo savio, *m.* **sage** 2, S.: (*bot.*) salvia, *f.* **-ly**, ADV.: saviamente, prudentemente. **-ness**, S.: saviezza, prudenza, *f.*
săgit-tal, ADJ.: (*anat.*) sagittale. **-tary**, S.: (*astr.*) sagittario, arciere, *m.*
sāgo, S.: sagu, *m.* **-tree**, S.: spezie di palmizio, *f.*
sāgy, ADJ.: pieno di salvia, *f.*
sāil 1, S.: vela; nave; ala, *f.*: *be under* —, esser alla vela; *hoist up* —, *set* —, far vela; *make* —, spiegar le vele; *shorten* —, diminuire le vele; *strike* —, ammainare le vele. **sail** 2, (IN)TR.: veleggiare, fare vela, navigare; imbarcarsi: — *along the coast*, costeggiare; — *back*, approdare, pigliare terra; — *in the main*, veleggiare in alto mare. **-able**, ADJ.: navigabile. **-er**, S.: vascello, naviglio, *m.* **-ing**, S.: navigazione, *f.*; veleggiamento, *m.* **-maker**, S.: fattore di vele, *m.* **-or**, S.: marinaro, marinaio, *m.* **-yard**, S.: antenna, *f.*
sāim, S.: saime, lardo grasso, *m.*
sāinfoin, S.: (*bot.*) cedrangola, *f.*, trifoglio, *m.*
sāint 1, ADJ.: santo; S.: santo, *m.*, santa, *f.*: *All —s' day*, il giorno di Ognissanti. **saint** 2, TR.: far il santo; INTR.: canonizzare. **-ed**, ADJ.: canonizzato, santo, sacro; pio. **-like**, ADJ.: da santo. **-ly**, ADV.: santamente; piamente. **-ship**, S.: santità; vita santa, *f.*
sāke, S.: causa, cagione; fine, *f.*; amore, *m.*: *for God's* —, per l' amor di Dio; *for your* —, per rispetto vostro.
sāker, S.: sagro, *m.* (falcone). **-et**, S.: maschio del falcone, *m.*
săl, S.: (*phar.*) sale, *m.*
săl-able, ADJ.: vendibile, da vendersi. **-ableness**, S.: essere vendibile, *m.* **-ably**, ADV.: in modo vendibile; in buona condizione.
sal-āçious, ADJ.: salace; lascivo, lussurioso. **-āçiously**, ADV.: lascivamente, lussuriosamente. **-ăcity**, S.: lascivia, lussuria, *f.*
sălad, S.: insalata, *f.* **-dish**, S.: piatto per l' insalata, *m.* **-oil**, S.: olio d' uliva, *m.*
salâm, S.: salamalecha, *f.*
salamăn-der, S.: salamandra, *f.* **-drine**, ADJ.: di salamandra.
sălary, S.: salario, *m.*, mercede, *f.*
sāle, S.: vendita, *f.*; incanto pubblico, *m.*: *ready* —, smercio rapido; *bill of* —, fattura, *f.*; *on (for)* —, vendibile; da vendersi; *make an open* —, vendere all' incanto. **-able**, ecc. = *salable*, ecc. **-sman**, S.: barattatore, rigattiere, *m.* **-swoman**, S.: barattatora, *f.* **-work**, S.: abiti fatti per vendere, *m. pl.*
sălic, ADJ.: salico.
sălient, ADJ.: sagliente; palpitante.
salificātion, S.: salificazione, *f.*
sā-line, **-linous**, ADJ.: salino, di sale.
sal-iva, S.: saliva, scialiva, *f.* **-ival**, **-ivary**, ADJ.: salivale. **-ivate**, TR.: rendere saliva. **-ivātion**, S.: salivazione, *f.*, salivare, *m.* **-ivous**, ADJ.: di saliva; pituitoso.
săllow 1, S.: salce, salcio, *m.* **sallow** 2, ADJ.: pallido, smorto. **-ness**, S.: pallidezza, *f.*, pallore, *m.* **-tree**, S.: salce, salcio, *m.*
sălly 1, S.: sortita, scappata; escursione, scorsa; stravaganza, *f.*; bollore, *m.* **sally** 2, INTR.: fare una sortita; uscire; (*mil.*) uscir de' ripari: — *forth*, uscire di slancio.
salmagŭndi, S.: manicaretto, *m.*
sălmon, S.: sermone, salmone, *m.* (pesce): *young* —, piccol sermone, *m.* **-pipe**, S.: macchina da prender salmoni, *f.* **-trout**, S.: trota del sapore del sermone, *f.*
salōon, S.: salone, *m.*, sala grande; birreria, osteria, *f.*

er, S.: che turba la pace. **-ful**, ADJ.: pacifico, tranquillo. **-fully**, ADV.: pacificamente, in pace. **-fulness**, S.: pace; tranquillità, *f.*; riposo, *m.* **-maker**, S.: pacificatore, riconciliatore; mediatore, *m.* **-offering**, S.: sacrificio propiziatorio, *m.*; offerta propiziatoria.

pēach I, S.: pesca, *f.*; persico, *m.* **peach** 2, accusare, dinunziare. **-coloured**, ADJ.: di color di pesca.

pēacher, S.: accusatore, *m.*

pēachick, S.: pavoncello, *m.*

pēach-tree, S.: persico, pesco, *m.*

pēa-cock, S.: pavone, paone, *m.* **-hen**, S.: pavonessa, *f.*

pēak I, S.: sommità, cima; estremità, *f.* **peak** 2, TR.: avere l'aria d'esser ammalato; esser malaticcio. **-ing**, ADJ.: malaticcio. **-ingness**, S.: stato malaticcio, *m.*

pēal I, S.: scampanata, *f.*; schiamazzo, *m.*: — *of hail*, burrasca di gragnuola, *f.*; — *of thunder*, scroscio, scoppio di tuono, *m.* **peal** 2, TR.: assalire con istrepito; INTR.: scampanare.

pēanut, S.: sorta di noci americani, *m. pl.*

pēar, S.: pera, *f.*

pēarl I, S.: perla; maglia nell'occhio; (*print.*) parigina, *f.*; *mother of* —, madre perla, *f.* **pearl** 2, TR.: perlare, ornare di perle. **-eyed**, ADJ.: che ha una maglia nell'occhio. **-y**, ADJ.: pieno di perle; perlato.

pēar-tree, S.: pero, *m.*

pēasant, S.: contadino, *m.*; contadina, *f.*: — *boy*, contadinello; — *girl*, contadinella. **-like**, ADJ.: rustico, rozzo. **-ry**, S.: contadini, campagnuoli, *m. pl.*

pēas-cod, S.: baccello di piselli, *m.* **-e-porridge**, S.: zuppa di piselli, *f.*

pēat, S.: terra di torba, torba, *f.* **-bog**, S.: torbera, *f.*

pĕb-ble, S.: selce, selice, *f.* **-bled**, ADJ.: pieno di selci. **-ble-stone** = *pebble*. **-bly** = *pebbled*.

peccability, S.: peccabilità, *f.*

pĕccable, ADJ.: peccabile.

peccadillo, S.: peccadiglio, peccatuzzo, *m.*

pĕccan-cy, S.: cattiva qualità, *f.*; difetto, *m.* **-t**, ADJ.: peccante; colpevole; (*med.*) nocivo.

...ck I, S.: profenda, *f.*; quarto di staio, ... **peck** 2, TR.: beccare; percuotere; ...re, riprendere. **-er**, S.: picco ...ello).

...acchiato, taccato.

...orale; stomacale.

...imedio petto-

...ro pub-

-le-

tor, S.: rubatore del danaro pubblico, concussionario, *m.*

pecū-liar, ADJ.: peculiare, particolare, singolare; proprio. **-liărity**, S.: particolarità, singolarità, *f.* **-liarize**, TR.: render peculiare, appropriare. **-liarly**, ADV.: peculiarmente, particolarmente, singolarmente, segnatamente. **-liarness**, S.: appropriazione, *f.*

pecū-niary, ADJ.: pecuniario. **-nious**, ADJ.: pecunioso, ricco.

pedagŏgic(al), ADJ.: da pedagogo.

pĕd-agogue, S.: pedagogo, pedante, *m.* **-agogy**, S.: pedagogia; istruzione, *f.*

pĕdal, ADJ.: di piede, col piede.

pĕdals, S. PL.: pedali, *m. pl.*

pedāneous, ADJ.: pedaneo, pedestre.

pĕd-ant, S.: pedante; pedagogo, *m.* **-ăntic(al)**, ADJ.: pedantesco, di pedante. **-ăntically**, ADV.: in modo pedantesco. **-antlike**, ADJ.: pedantescamente, da pedante. **-antism**, S.: pedantismo, *m.* **-antry**, S.: pedanteria, *f.*

pĕddle, INTR.: fare il merciaiuolo; baloccare.

pĕdestal, S.: piedestallo, *m.*

pedĕs-trian, ADJ.: pedestre, *m.*, pedone. **-trious**, ADJ.: pedestre.

pĕdicle, S.: pedicciuolo, *m.*

pedicular, ADJ.: pediculare, pidocchioso.

pĕdigree, S.: genealogia; stirpe, *f.*

pĕdiment, S.: (*arch.*) frontone, *m.*

pĕd-lar, **-ler**, S.: merciaiuolo, mercantuzzo ambulante, *m.* **-lery**, S.: mercanziuole; bagatelle, *f. pl.*

pedobăptism, S.: battesimo de' bambini, *m.*

pedŏmeter, S.: odometro, *m.*

pedŭncle, S.: (*bot.*) pedoncolo, *m.*

pēek I, S.: rancore, livore; (*nav.*) picco, *m.* **peek** 2, TR.: (*nav.*) drizzare, imbroncare.

pēel I, S.: scorza, pelle. **peel** 2, S.: (*bak.*) pala, *f.* **peel** 3, TR.: scortecciare, mondare, sbucciare; rubare: — *barley*, mondare dell'orzo; — *an egg*, sbucciare un uovo; — *hemp*, maciullare della canapa; — *off*, scorticarsi, scortecciarsi. **-er**, S.: scorticatore; rubatore, *m.*

pēep I, S.: spuntare del giorno, *m.*; occhiata, *f.* **peep** 2, INTR.: spuntare; guardare di segreto; pigolare: — *in*, guardare dentro; far capolino; — *out*, spuntare; — *over*, morire. **-er**, S.: pulcino; vagheggiatore, *m.* **-hole**, **-ing-hole**, S.: buco da spiare, *m.*

pēer I, INTR.: apparire; spiare. **peer** 2, S.: pari; ottimato; uguale, compagno, *m.* **-age**, **-dom**, S.: dignità di pari, *f.*; dominio d'un pari, *m.* **-ess**, S.: moglie d'un pari; donna nobile, *f.* **-less**, ADJ.: senza pari, incomparabile. **-lessness**, S.: incomparabilità, *f.*

Săn-scrit, -skrit, s.: sanscrito, *m.*
săp 1, s.: succhio, succo, sugo; alburno. **sap** 2, s.: umore, *m.* **sap** 3, TR.: minare; zappare; distruggere.
săp-id, ADJ.: saporito, gustoso. **-ĭdity, -idness,** s.: sapore, savore; gusto, *m.*
săpien-ce, s.: sapienza, saviezza, *f.*; conoscimento, *m.* **-t,** ADJ.: sapiente, savio, saputo.
săp-less, ADJ.: senza succhio, secco. **-ling,** s.: arbuscello, piantone, *m.*
sap-onāceous, -onary, ADJ.: saponaceo.
săper, s.: sapore, savore, *m.*; saporosità, *f.* **-ific,** ADJ.: saporifico, savoroso.
săpper, s.: zappatore, *m.*
Săpphic, ADJ.: saffico.
săp-phire, s.: zaffiro, *m.* **-phirine,** ADJ.: zaffirino.
săp-piness, s.: abbondanza di sugo, *f.* **-py,** ADJ.: pieno di succhio, vigoroso; giovane.
sărabаnd, s.: sarabanda, *f.* (ballo spagnuolo).
săr-casm, s.: sarcasmo, *m.* **-căstic(al),** ADJ.: sarcastico, satirico, pungente. **-căstically,** ADV.: satiricamente, di satira.
sărcenet, s.: taffetà, *f.*
sărcle, TR.: sarchiare.
sarc-ōma, s.: sarcoma, scirro, *m.* **-ŏphagous,** ADJ.: caustico, corrosivo. **-ŏphagus,** s.: sarcofago, *m.* **-ŏphagy,** s.: pascersi di carne, *m.* **-ŏtic,** s.: sarcotico, incarnativo, *m.*
sarculātion, s.: sarchiatura, *f.*, sarchiamento, *m.*
săr-del, -dine, s.: sardina, sardella, *f.*
sardŏnic, ADJ.: sardonico: — *laughter*, riso sardonico, *m.*
sărdonyx, s.: sardonico, *m.*
sarsaparilla, s.: (*phar.*) salsapariglia, *f.*
sărse 1, s.: staccio, *m.* **sarse** 2, TR.: stacciare.
sartŏrious, ADJ.: sartorio.
săsh, s.: cinto di seta, *m.*, cintura, *f.*: **-frame,** s.: intelaiatura, *f.* **-window,** s.: finestra a ghigliottina, *f.*
săssafras, s.: (*phar.*) sassafrasso, *m.*
săsse, s.: cateratta, *f.*
Să-tan, s.: Satan, diavolo, *m.* **-tănic(al),** ADJ.: satanico, diabolico. **-tănically,** ADV.: diabolicamente, da diavolo.
sătchel, s.: sacchetto, sacchettino, *m.*
săt-e, TR.: saziare, satollare. **-ed,** ADJ.: satollo, sazio, saziato. **-eless,** ADJ.: insaziabile.
sătellite, s.: satellite, *m.*
să-tiate 1, TR.: saziare, satollare; soddisfare. **-tiate** 2, ADJ.: satollo, saziato. **-tiātion, -tiety,** s.: sazietà, satollezza, sazievolezza, *f.*
sătin, s.: raso, *m.* (drappo). **-ribbon,** s.: nastro col lustro del raso, *m.*
să-tire, s.: satira, *f.* **-tiric(al),** ADJ.: satirico; mordace. **-tirically,** ADV.: satiricamente. **-tirist,** s.: satirico, scrittore di satire, *m.* **-tirize,** TR.: satireggiare, far satire.
satisfăc-tion, s.: soddisfazione; ragione, *f.*; piacere, *m.* **-tive,** ADJ.: soddisfacente. **-torily,** ADV.: d'una maniera soddisfacente. **-toriness,** s.: soddisfacimento, *m.* **-tory,** ADJ.: soddisfattorio.
sătisfy, (IN)TR.: soddisfare, dar soddisfazione; contentare; pagare; saziare: — *of*, convincere. **-ing,** ADJ.: soddisfacente.
sătrap, s.: satrapo, *m.* **-y,** s.: satrapia, *f.*, governo satrapico, *m.*
sătu-rable, ADJ.: che si può saturare. **-rate,** TR.: saturare, satollare, saziare. **-rătion,** s.: saturazione, *f.*
Săturday, s.: sabato, sabbato, *m.*
Săturn, s.: (*astr.*) saturno, *m.* **-ālia,** s. PL.: saturnali, *m. pl.* **-ālian,** ADJ.: saturnale. **-als** = *Saturnalia.* **-ian** *satŭrn-*, ADJ.: saturnino; felice, beato. **-ine,** ADJ.: saturnino; malinconico, tristo.
sătyr, s.: (*myth.*) satiro, *m.*
săuce 1, s.: condimento, *m.*; salsa, *f.*: *butter* —, salsa bianca, *f.* **-e** 2, TR.: condire; acconciare con salsa. **-e-box,** s.: sfacciato, sfrontato, *m.* **-e-pan,** s.: padellino, *m.* **-er,** s.: piattello; scodellino, *m.* **-ily,** ADV.: sfacciatamente, impertinentemente. **-iness,** s.: sfacciataggine, impudenza, *f.* **-y,** ADJ.: sfacciato, insolente, presuntuoso.
săunter, INTR.: battere le strade, vagabondare, andar ramingo. **-er,** s.: ozioso, vagabondo, *m.*
săusage, s.: salsiccia, *f.*, salame, *m.*
săvage 1, ADJ.: salvatico, fiero; crudele; s.: selvaggio, *m.* **-ge** 2, TR.: render salvatico. **-gely,** ADV.: alla salvatica; fieramente, crudelmente. **-geness, -gery,** s.: salvatichezza, rozzezza; crudeltà, barbarie, *f.*
savănna, s.: prateria, *f.*
săv-e 1, PREP., ADV.: salvo, eccettuato; eccetto che, tolto che, fuorchè. **-e** 2, TR.: salvare; risparmiare, conservare; INTR.: essere a buon mercato: *God — the king!* viva il re! Dio salvi il re! — *money*, risparmiare danari; *to — time*, per non perder tempo. **-eall,** s.: canello, *m.* **-er,** s.: salvatore, liberatore; risparmiatore, *m.*
săvin, s.: (*bot.*) savina, sabina, *f.*
săving 1, ADJ.: economo, parco; frugale; salvatore, -trice; s.: salvamento; risparmio, *m.*; economia, *f.*: — *faith*, fede salvatrice; *be* —, usar economia. **saving** 2, PREP.: salvo, eccetto, fuorchè, se non. **-ly,** ADV.: con risparmio, parcamente;

pĕn-wiper, S.: nettapenna, *m.*

pēony, S.: (*bot.*) peonia, *f.*

pēople 1, S.: popolo, *m.*, nazione, gente, *f.*: *common* —, bassa gente, *f.*, volgo, popolaccio, *m.*, plebe, *f.*; *fashionable* —, il bel mondo; *many* —, molta gente, molte persone; *of the* —, popolano; *throng of* —, calca di gente, *f.*; — *say*, si dice. **people** 2, TR.: popolare, mettere popolo; INTR.: popolarsi.

pĕpper 1, S.: pepe, *m.* **pepper** 2, TR.: impepare, condire con pepe. **-box**, S.: pepaiuola, *f.* **-corn**, S.: seme di pepe, *m.*; (*fig.*) bagatella, *f.* **-mint**, S.: (*bot.*) menta piperina, *f.*

pĕpsine, S.: pepsina, *f.*

pĕptic, ADJ.: (*med.*) digestivo.

pĕr, PREP.: per.

peracūte, ADJ.: acutissimo.

peradvĕnture, ADV.: per avventura, a caso: *without* —, senza dubbio, senza fallo.

perămbu-late, TR.: andare attorno, girare. **-lātion**, S.: andare attorno, giro, *m.* **-lator**, S.: odometro, *m.* (strumento); carrozzetta da bambino, *f.*

percĕi-vable, ADJ.: percettibile; sensibile. **-vably**, ADV.: percettibilmente, visibilmente. **-ve**, TR.: concepire, comprendere; osservare; scoprire, accorgersi: — *beforehand*, presentire.

percĕntage, S.: quantità per cento, *f.*

per-cĕptibility, S.: qualità percettibile, percezione, *f.* **-cĕptible**, ADJ.: percettibile; sensibile. **-cĕptibleness** = *perceptibility*. **-cĕptibly**, ADV.: in modo percettibile. **-cĕption**, S.: percezione, comprensione; capacità; intelligenza, *f.* **-cĕptive**, ADJ.: percettibile, intelligente. **-cĕptivity**, S.: facoltà da comprendere, percezione, *f.*

pĕrch 1, S.: pertica, *f.* **perch** 2, INTR.: alberare.

perchânce, ADV.: forse, per avventura, a caso.

percipient, ADJ.: percipiente.

pĕrco-late, TR.: feltrare, colare. **-lātion**, S.: feltrazione, *f.*, colamento, *m.*

per-cŭss, TR.: percuotere; bussare. **-cŭssion**, S.: percussione, percossa, *f.*: — *cap*, capsula di fucile a percussione, *f.*; — *gun*, fucile a percussione, schioppo a percussione, schioppo a capsula, *m.*

perdĭtion, S.: perdizione, rovina, *f.*

per-dū 1, S.: sentinella avanzata, *f.* **-du** 2, **-dūe**, ADV.: in aguato; occultamente.

perdū-rable †, ADJ.: perdurabile, permanente. **-rably** †, ADV.: perdurabilmente; sempre. **-rātion** †, S.: durazione, lunga [illegible]ta. continuazione, *f.*

-nate, INTR.: peregrinare, viaggiatore, *m.* **-tion**, S.: peregrinazione, *f.*, **-nator**, S.: peregrinatore, viaggiatore, *m.* **-ne**, ADJ.: peregrino, straniero.

perĕmp-t, TR.: uccidere; ammazzare. **-tion**, S.: (*jur.*) estinzione, *f.*

pĕremptọ-rily, ADV.: perentoriamente, decisivamente. **-riness**, S.: decisione, determinazione, *f.* **-ry**, ADJ.: perentorio, decisivo.

perĕn-nial, ADJ.: perenne, perpetuo. **-nity**, S.: perpetuità; continuanza, *f.*

pĕr-fect 1, ADJ.: perfetto, compiuto; puro; S.: (*gram.*) perfetto, *m.* **-fect** 2, TR.: perfezionare; compire, terminare, finire. **-fecter**, S.: perfezionatore, *m.* **-fĕctible**, ADJ.: perfettibile. **-fĕcting**, S.: compimento, *m.* **-fĕction**, S.: perfezione, *f.*, compimento, *m.*; eccellenza, *f.* **-fĕctionate**, TR.: perfezionare; finire. **-fĕctionist**, S.: puritano, *m.* **-fĕctive**, ADJ.: perfettivo, perfezionativo. **-fĕctively**, ADV.: in modo perfetto. **-fectly**, ADV.: perfettamente; esattamente. **-fectness**, S.: compimento, *m.*; bontà, *f.*

perfĭdious, ADJ.: perfido, disleale. **-ly**, ADV.: perfidamente. **-ness**, S.: perfidia, *f.*

pĕrfĭdy = *perfidiousness*.

pĕrfọ-rate, TR.: perforare; trafiggere. **-rātion**, S.: perforamento, *m.* **-rator**, S.: foratoio, succhiello, *m.*

perfōrce, ADV.: per forza, forzatamente; di viva forza.

perfōrm, (IN)TR.: operare, effettuare, fare, eseguire, compire; (*theat.*) agire; recitare, cantare: — *one's devotion*, dire le sue divozioni; — *one's promise*, effettuare la promessa. **-able**, ADJ.: eseguibile, praticabile, fattibile. **-ance**, S.: esecuzione, *f.*; eseguimento, compimento, *m.*; opera, azione; (*theat.*) rappresentazione, recita, *f.* **-er**, S.: esecutore, compitore, attore, *m.*, esecutrice, ecc., *f.* **-ing**, S.: compimento, effetto, *m.*

per-fūmatory, ADJ.: che profuma.

pĕr-fume 1, S.: profumo, odore soave, *m.* **-fūme** 2, TR.: profumare. **-fūmer**, S.: profumiere; unguentario, *m.* **-fūming**, S.: profumare, *m.* **-fūming-pan**, S.: profumiera, *f.*, turibile, *m.*

perfŭnctọ-rily, ADV.: negligentemente, leggiermente. **-riness**, S.: negligenza, trascuranza, *f.* **-ry**, ADJ.: trascurante, negligente.

perfūse, TR.: tingere, imbevere; aspergere.

pĕrgọla, S.: pergola, *f.*

perhăps, ADV.: forse, per avventura.

pĕrianth, S.: (*bot.*) perianto, *m.*

peri-cardītis, S.: pericardite, *f.* **-căr-dium**, S.: (*anat.*) pericardio, *m.*

pĕricarp, S.: (*bot.*) pericarpo, *m.*

pericrănium, S.: (*anat.*) pericraneo, *m.*

scăpu-la, s.: omero, m.: paletta della spalla, f. **-lar**, **-lary**, ADJ.: delle spalle. **-lary**, s.: scapolare, m.

scar 1, s.: cicatrice, f. **scar** 2, TR.: cicatrizzare, far una cicatrice; INTR.: formarsi in cicatrice.

scărab-ee, s.: scarafaggio, scarabeo, m.

scăramouch, s.: zanni, buffone, m.

scârce, ADJ.: scarso, raro. **-ce-ly**, ADV.: scarsamente, appena, a fatica, a stento. **-ceness**, **-city**, s.: scarsezza, scarsità, f.

scâre, TR.: [illegible], spaventare, far paura. **-crow**, s.: spauracchio, spaventacchio, m. **-d**, ADJ.: [illegible], spaventato.

scârf 1, s.: ciarpa, banda, cintura, f. **scarf** 2, TR.: [illegible] di ciarpa; incastrare, congiungere. **-ed**, ADJ.: vestito di ciarpa. **-skin**, s.: epidermide, cuticola, f.

scarificâtion, s.: scarificazione, f.

scari-ficator, **-fier**, s.: scarificatore, m. **-fy**, TR.: scarificare, scarnare. **-fying**, s.: scarificazione, f.

scar-latina, s.: febbre scarlattina, f. **-let**, ADJ.: scarlattino, scarlatto; — s.: scarlatto, m.: — fever, febbre scarlattina, f.; — [illegible], m.; — [illegible] di scarlatto, f.

scârp, s.: [illegible] scarpa, f.

scar-red, **-ry**, ADJ.: cicatrizzato.

scâtch, s.: morso di cavallo, m.

scâth 1, s.: perdita, f., danno, m. **scath** 2, **scâthe**, INTR.: danneggiare, guastare, rovinare. **-ful**, ADJ.: dannoso, distruttivo. **-less**, ADJ.: senza danno.

scătter, TR.: spandere, sparpagliare, dissipare. **-edly** = scatteringly. **-ing**, s.: sparpagliamento, m. **-ingly**, ADV.: sparsamente; confusamente. **-ling**, s.: vagabondo, m.

scăvenger, s.: spazzino, m.

scĕlerat†, s.: scellerato, briccone, m.

scĕn-e, s.: scena, f., teatro, m.: [illegible] —, [illegible], m.; [illegible] s. scene laterali, [illegible] pl. **-ery**, s.: vista, rappresentazione; scena, f.

scĕn-ic-al(1), ADJ.: scenico; teatrale. **-ográphic-al**(1), ADJ.: scenografico. **-ográphically**, ADV.: in modo scenografico; in prospettiva. **-ógraphy**, s.: scenografia; prospettiva, f.

scĕnt 1, s.: odore, sentore, odorato; fiuto, m.: lose by the —, [illegible] il fiuto. **scent** 2, TR.: odorare; fiutare, annasare; profumare: — out, rintracciare al fiuto, subodorare, scoprire. **-bottle**, s.: boccetta d'odore, f. **-ful**, ADJ.: odoroso. **-less**, ADJ.: inodorabile; senza fiuto.

scĕpti-c(al)(1), ADJ.: scettico. **-cism**, s.: scetticismo, m.

scĕptre, s.: scettro, m. **-bearer**, s.: che porta lo scettro, mazziere, f. **-d**, ADJ.: scettrato.

schĕdule, s.: cedola; cartuccia; polizza, f.

schē-matism, s.: figura, forma, f. **-me** 1, s.: piano, disegno; modello; sistema, m.: *wild* —, progetto stravagante. **-me** 2, TR.: progettare, disegnare. **-mer**, s.: disegnatore, inventore, m. **-ming**, ADJ.: progettante, astuto, artifizio; s.: progetto, il progettare, m.

schism, s.: scisma; divisione, separazione, f. **-atic**, s.: scismatico, m. **-átic-al**, ADJ.: scismatico, di scisma. **-átic-ally**, ADV.: in modo scismatico. **-atize**, TR.: fare uno scisma.

schŏlar, s.: scolare; dotto, erudito, letterato, m.: *Latin* —, latinista, m.; *Greek* —, grecista, m.; *day* —, scolare esterno; *fellow* —, condiscepolo, m. **-like**, ADJ.: da scolare. **-ship**, s.: dottrina, scienza, f.

scholásti-c-al(1), ADJ.: scolastico. **-cally**, ADV.: in modo scolastico.

schó-liast, s.: scoliaste, chiosatore, m. **-lion**, **-lium**, s.: scolio, breve commentario, m. **-ly**†, INTR.: fare scoli.

schŏol 1, s.: scuola, f.: *girl's* —, scuola femminile: *go to* —, andare alla scuola; *keep* —, tenere scuola. **school** 2, TR.: istruire, insegnare; riprendere. **-boy**, s.: scolare; studente, m. **-dame**, s.: maestra di scuola, f. **-divinity**, s.: teologia scolastica, f. **-fellow**, s.: condiscepolo; compagno di scuola, m. **-girl**, s.: ragazza di scuola, f. **-house**, s.: scuola, f. **-man**, s.: scolastico, m. **-master**, s.: maestro di scuola, m. **-mate**, s.: condiscepolo, compagno di scuola, m. **-mistress**, s.: maestra di scuola, f. **-room**, s.: classe, scuola, f.

schŏoner, s.: vascello a due alberi, m.

sciát-ic-a(1), s.: sciatica, f., aspro dolore, m. **-ic-al**(1), ADJ.: sciatico.

sciĕn-ce, s.: scienza; dottrina; letteratura, f. **-tific-al**(1), ADJ.: scientifico, dotto. **-tifically**, ADV.: scientificamente.

scimitar, s.: scimitarra, storta, f.

scintil-lant, ADJ.: scintillante. **-late**, INTR.: scintillare, sfavillare. **-lation**, s.: scintillazione, f.

scio-list, s.: saccentone, semidotto, m. **-lous**, ADJ.: sciolo, saputello.

scion, s.: rimessiticcio, ramicello, m.

scir-rhous, ADJ.: scirroso, indurato. **-rhus**, s.: scirro, induramento, m.

scis-sible, **-sile**, ADJ.: scissile. **-sion**, s.: scissione; separazione, f. **-sors**, S. PL.: forbici, f. pl.: *large* —, cesoie, f. pl.; *a pair of* —, un paio di forbici. **-sure**, s.: scissura; fessura, f.

sclerótic, s.: pannicolo duro, m.

-ence, -ency, S.: persistenza, perseveranza, fermezza, *f.* **-ive**, ADJ.: persistente, fermo, costante.

pĕr-son, S.: persona; figura, *f.*; esteriore, *m.*: —*s*, persone; gente, *f.*; *in* —, in persona, personalmente; *in a —'s place*, in persona di uno. **-sonable**, ADJ.: ben fatto, grazioso. **-sonage**, S.: personaggio; esteriore; carattere, *m.* **-sonal**, ADJ.: personale; peculiare, particolare, proprio: — *goods*, beni mobili, *m. pl.* **-sonăl(i)ty**, S.: personalità, *f.*; individuo, *m.* **-sonally**, ADV.: personalmente, in persona. **-sonate**, TR.: rappresentare, imitare. **-sonātion**, S.: rappresentazione, *f.*; carattere, *m.* **-sonificātion**, S.: personificazione, *f.* **-sŏnify**, TR.: personificare.

per-spĕctive 1, ADJ.: prospettivo, ottico, visivo. **-spective** 2, S.: prospettiva, vista, *f.*; paesaggio, *m.* **-spicācious**, ADJ.: perspicace; intelligente. **-spicāciousness**, **-spicăcity**, S.: perspicacità, penetrazione (d' ingegno), acutezza, *f.* **-spicience** †, S.: osservazione acuta, *f.*

per-spicūity, S.: perspicuità, trasparenza; chiarezza, evidenza, *f.* **-spicuous**, ADJ.: chiaro, evidente. **-spicuously**, ADV.: chiaramente. **-spicuousness**, S.: chiarezza, evidenza, *f.*

perspi-rable, ADJ.: perspirabile, traspirabile. **-spirātion**, S.: perspirazione, traspirazione, *f.* **-spirative**, ADJ.: traspirante, sudatorio. **-spire**, INTR.: traspirare, sudare.

persuā-dable, ADJ.: persuasibile, suadevole. **-de**, TR.: persuadere; convincere: — *one's self*, persuadersi. **-der**, S.: persuadente, *m.* **-sible**, ADJ.: persuasibile, suadevole. **-sion**, S.: persuasione; istigazione, *f.* **-sive**, ADJ.: persuasivo. **-sively**, ADV.: in modo persuasivo. **-siveness**, S.: facoltà di persuadere, *f.* **-sory**, ADJ.: persuasorio, persuasivo.

pĕrt, ADJ.: lesto, agile; impertinente, impronto.

pertāin, INTR.: appartenere, concernere, spettare.

perti-nācious, ADJ.: pertinace, ostinato. **-nāciously**, ADV.: pertinacemente. **-nāciousness**, **-năcity**, S.: pertinacia, caparbietà, ostinazione, *f.*

pĕrti-nacy †, S.: ostinazione, caparbieria, *f.* **-nence**, **-cy**, S.: pertinenza, appartenenza: convenevolezza, *f.* **-nent**, ADJ.: [...]porzionato, convenevole: *be* [...]roposito, cader in accon[...] [...]DV.: convenevolmen[...] **-nentness**, S.: [...]

[...] vivacemen[...] [...]temente.

-ness, S.: vivacità, attività; insolenza, impertinenza, *f.*

pertūrb, TR.: perturbare. **-ātion**, S.: perturbazione, *f.*; commovimento, *m.*, alterazione, *f.* **-ator**, S.: perturbatore, *m.*

pertūsion, S.: perforazione, *f.*

pĕruke, S.: parrucca, *f.*; capelli posticci, *m. pl.* **-maker**, S.: parrucchiere, *m.*

perū-sal, S.: lettura, *f.*, leggere, *m.* **-se**, TR.: leggere; esaminare. **-ser**, S.: lettore, leggitore, *m.*

Perūvian-bark, S.: chinachina, *f.*

pervā-de, TR.: passare oltre, penetrare, compenetrare, permeare, regnare in. **-sion**, S.: trapasso; penetramento, *m.* **-sive**, ADJ.: trapassante; penetrante.

pervĕr-se, ADJ.: perverso; ostinato, caparbio. **-sely**, ADJ.: perversamente, con perversità. **-seness**, S.: perversità, *f.*; cattivo umore, *m.* **-sion**, S.: perversione, *f.*, pervertimento, *m.* **-sity** = *perverseness*. **-sive**, ADJ.: pervertente. **-t**, TR.: pervertire, sconvolgere; corrompere. **-ter**, S.: pervertitore, corruttore, *m.* **-tible**, ADJ.: che può esser pervertito.

pĕrvious, ADJ.: pervio, passabile. **-ness**, S.: penetrabilità, *f.*

pesāde, S.: (*horse.*) pesata, *f.*

pĕssim-ism, S.: pessimismo, *m.* **-ist**, S.: pessimista, *m.*

pĕst, S.: peste, pestilenza; contagione, *f.*

pĕster, TR.: noiare, affannare, affliggere, inquietare, disturbare. **-er**, S.: importuno, seccatore, tormentatore, *m.* **-ous**, ADJ.: incomodo, annoioso. **-ousness**, S.: incomodità, *f.*

pĕst-house, S.: lazzaretto, spedale, *m.* **-iferous**, ADJ.: pestifero, contagioso.

pĕsti-lence, S.: pestilenza, peste, contagione, *f.* **-lent**, **-lĕntial**, ADJ.: pestilenziale. **-lently**, ADV.: in modo contagioso.

pestillātion, S.: pestimento, polverizzamento, *m.*

pĕstle, S.: pestello, *m.*

pĕt 1, S.: collera, *f.*; dispetto, sdegno; favorito, *m.*: — *bird*, uccellino; — *lamb*, agnello allevato a mano, agnello favorito; *be in a* —, essere in collera; *take* — *at a thing*, offendersi di qualche cosa. **pet** 2, TR.: vezzeggiare soverchiamente.

pĕtal, S.: (*bot.*) petalo, *m.*

pe-tār †, **-tārd**, S.: petardo, *m.*

Pēter-wort, S.: (*bot.*) tassobarbasso, *m.*

petition 1, S.: supplica, *f.*, memoriale, *m.* **petition** 2, TR.: supplicare, pregare; domandare. **-ary**, ADJ.: petitorio, supplicante. **-er**, S.: supplicante, *m.* **-ing**, S.: supplicare, pregare, *m.*

pĕtitory, ADJ.: petitorio, supplicatorio.

pētre, S.: nitro, salnitro, *m.*

pĕtrel, S.: procellaria, *f.* (uccello).

[illegible] [illegible] formant [illegible]

[illegible] [illegible] formula [illegible]

[illegible] formula [illegible] opposite form [illegible]

[illegible] [illegible] mezia [illegible]

[illegible] phil [illegible] formula

[illegible] [illegible]

-rilous, ADJ.: ingiurioso; vile, basso. **-rilously**, ADV.: in modo abusivo, ingiuriosamente. **-rilousness** = *scurrility*.

scŭr-vily, ADV.: bruttamente, vilmente, grossolanamente. **-viness**, S.: cattivezza, malignità, viltà, *f.* **-vy** 1, S.: scorbuto, *m.* **-vy** 2, ADJ.: cattivo, ribaldo, vile; tristo: — *trick*, tiro da briccone, *m.* **-vy-grass**, S.: gramigna, *f.*

scŭt, S.: coda (d'una lepre, d'un coniglio), *f.*

scŭtcheon, S.: scudo, *m.*; (*lock.*) toppa, *f.*

scŭtiform, ADJ.: a modo di scudo.

scŭttle 1, S.: graticola, *f.*; gran paniere, *m.* **scuttle** 2, S.: tramoggia di mulino, *f.* **scuttle** 3, S.: (*nav.*) boccaporto, *m.*: *coal* —, paniera pel carbone. **scuttle** 4, INTR.: andare qua e là.

scȳthe, S.: falce, *f.*

Scȳthian, ADJ.: Scita, degli Sciti; S.: scita, *m.*, *f.*

sēa, S.: mare, oceano, *m.*; onda, *f.*: *by — and land*, per mare e per terra; *main* —, alto mare; *heavy* —, mare grosso; *a* —, un cavallone; *be at* —, trovarsi in mare; *go to* —, andar sul mare; *put out to* —, far vela. **-bar**, S.: rondine di mare, *f.* **-beach**, S.: spiaggia, *f.*, lido, *m.* **-beat(en)**, ADJ.: agitato dal mare. **-boat**, S.: nave, *f.*, naviglio, legno, *m.* **-born**, ADJ.: nato dal mare. **-boy**, S.: mozzo di nave, *m.* **-breach**, S.: rottura del mare, *f.* **-breeze**, S.: vento impetuoso, *m.* **-calf**, S.: vitello marino, *m.* **-captain**, S.: capitano di naviglio, *m.* **-chart**, S.: carta da navigare, *f.* **-coast**, S.: costa del mare, *f.* **-compass**, S.: bussola, *f.* **-cow**, S.: vacca marina, *f.* (pesce). **-dog**, S.: pesce cane, *m.* **-fārer**, S.: marinaro, *m.* **-fāring**, ADJ.: andando per mare: — *man*, marinaro, *m.* **-fennel**, S.: finocchio marino, *m.* **-fight**, S.: combattimento navale, *m.* **-fowl**, S.: uccello marino, *m.* **-green**, ADJ.: del colore del mare. **-gull**, S.: mugnaio, *m.* (uccello). **-hog**, S.: porcello marino, *m.* **-horse**, S.: cavallo marino, *m.*

sēal 1, S.: sigillo, suggello; vitello marino, *m.* **seal** 2, S.: *under hand and* —, segnato e sigillato; *under the — of secrecy*, sotto sigillo di confessione; *affix one's — to*, porre la firma a. **seal** 3, TR.: sigillare, suggellare; confermare. **-er**, S.: sigillatore, *m.* **-ing-wax**, S.: ceralacca, cera di Spagna, *f.* **-ring**, S.: anello da sigillare, *m.*

sēam 1, S.: cucitura; congiuntura; cicatrice, *f.* **seam** 2, TR.: cucire; giungere; cicatrizzare.

sēa-maid, S.: sirena, *f.* **-man**, S.: marinaio, *m.* **-manship**, S.: (arte di) navigazione, *f.* **-mark**, S.: (*nav.*) segnale, *m.* **-mew**, S.: gabbiano, mugnaio, *m.* (uccello).

sēamless, ADJ.: senza sutura.

sēa-monster, S.: mostro marino, *m.*

sēam-stress, S.: cucitrice, sartora, *f.* **-y**, ADJ.: pieno di cuciture, cucito.

sēan†, S.: sagena, rete da pescare, *f.*

sēa-nymph, S.: ninfa del mare, *f.* **-onion**, S.: squilla, *f.* **-ooze**, S.: melma del mare, *f.* **-piece**, S.: marina; veduta di mare, *f.* **-pool**, S.: lago d'acque salse, *m.* **-port**, S.: porto di mare, *m.*

sēar 1, ADJ.: secco, arido; morto. **sear** 2, TR.: arrossare con ferro rovente.

sēarch 1, S.: inchiesta, ricerca; inquisizione, *f.* **search** 2, TR.: cercare, visitare; esaminare; frugare, frugacchiare; provare: — *a wound*, tentare una ferita; — *after*, ricercare, cercare, inchiedere; — *for*, cercare, buscare; — *into*, inchiedere; esaminare; penetrare; — *out*, fare una ricerca esatta. **-able**, ADJ.: che si può cercare. **-er**, S.: ricercatore; visitatore, *m.* **-ing**, ADJ.: penetrativo; pronto; S.: cerca, ricerca, *f.* **-less**, ADJ.: inscrutabile.

sēar-cloth, S.: impiastro, cerotto, *m.*

sēaredness, S.: secchezza, aridità; sterilità; insensibilità, *f.*

sēa-room, S.: alto mare, largo, *m.* **-rover**, S.: corsale, pirata, *m.* **-serpent**, S.: serpe di mare, *f.* **-service**, S.: servizio navale, *m.* **-shark**, S.: pesce cane, *m.* **-shell**, S.: guscio di pesce marino, *m.* **-shore**, S.: spiaggia, costa del mare, *f.* **-sick**, ADJ.: mareggiato: *be* —, mareggiarsi. **-sickness**, S.: mal di mare, *m.* **-side**, S.: lido del mare, *m.*, spiaggia, *f.*

sēason 1, S.: stagione, *f.*; tempo opportuno; condimento, *m.*: *in the mean* —, nulladimeno; *out of* —, fuori di stagione, intempestivo, inopportuno. **season** 2, TR.: condire; accostumare; INTR.: essere opportuno. **-able**, ADJ.: di stagione; opportuno. **-ableness**, S.: opportunità, occasione, *f.* **-ably**, ADV.: opportunamente; acconciamente; a proposito. **-er**, S.: stagionatore; che infonde, *m.* **-ing**, S.: stagionamento; condimento, *m.*

sēa-surgeon, S.: chirurgo di nave, *m.*

sēat 1, S.: sedia, *f.*; seggio; banco, *m.*; scena; tribuna; situazione, *f.*: *bishop's* —, seggio vescovile, *m.*; — *of justice*, tribunale, *m.*; *take a* —, sedetevi, accomodatevi. **seat** 2, TR.: situare; collocare; stabilire: — *one's self* (*be seated*), sedersi; stare seduto; *pray, be —ed*, s'accomodi.

sēa-term, S.: termine marinaresco, ter-

mine di marina, *m.* **-urchin,** S.: echino, *m.* **-voyage,** S.: viaggio per mare, *m.*
séavy, ADJ.: giuncoso.
séaward, ADV.: in alto mare, verso il mare. **-water,** S.: acqua marina, acqua salsa, *f.* **-weed,** S.: (*bot.*) alga, *f.*
sebáceous, ADJ.: sebaceo.
sécant, S.: (*geom.*) secante, *f.*
secéd-e, INTR.: ritirarsi; separarsi, dividersi. **-er,** S.: che si ritira; discordante, *m.*
secérn, TR.: separare; mettere da banda; INTR.: separarsi.
secéssion, S.: separazione, *f.*
seclú-de, TR.: escludere; eccettuare. **-sion,** S.: esclusione, *f.*
sécond 1, ADJ.: secondo: — *hand*, usato; di riscontro; — *sight*, preconoscenza del futuro, *f.*; *he is* — *to none*, egli non la cede a nessuno. **second** 2, S.: secondo; difensore, protettore, *m.*; sessantesima parte (d' un minuto, d' un grado), *f.* **second** 3, TR.: secondare, aiutare, proteggere, favorire: — *a motion*, appoggiare una mozione. **-arily,** ADV.: nel secondo ordine. **-ary** 1, ADJ.: secondario, accessorio: — *cause*, causa accessoria, *f.* **-ary** 2, S.: deputato, delegato, *m.* **-hand,** ADJ.: usato, non nuovo; inferiore; antiquario: — *clothes*, abiti usati; — *dinner*, pranzo riscaldato. **-ly,** ADV.: secondamente, in secondo luogo. **-rate,** ADJ.: di secondo grado (*or* ordine), inferiore.
sé-crecy, S.: segretezza; solitudine, *f.* **-cret** 1, ADJ.: segreto, occulto; privato: *in* —, in segreto, segretamente. **-cret** 2, S.: segreto, misterio, *m.* **-cret** 3, TR.: tener segreto.
sécretary, S.: segretario, secretario: —'*s office*, segreteria, *f.* **-ship,** S.: uffizio di segretario.
secré-te, TR.: nascondere, celare; separare. **-tion,** S.: secrezione, separazione, *f.*
sécret-ist, S.: ciarlatano, *m.* **-ly,** ADV.: segretamente, con segretezza. **-ness,** S.: segretezza, *f.*; misterio, *m.*
secrétory, ADJ.: secretorio, di secrezione.
sect, S.: setta, *f.* **-árian,** ADJ.: di setta; S.: settario, *m.* **-árianism, -arism**†, S.: spirito di fare setta, *m.* **-ary,** S.: settario, *m.* **-átor,** S.: settatore; discepolo, *m.*
séction, S.: sezione, divisione, *f.*: *conic* —*s*, sezioni coniche. **-alism,** S.: regionalismo, *m.*
séctor, S.: settore; compasso di proporzione, *m.*
sécu-lar, ADJ.: secolare; temporale, mondano; laico. **-lárity,** S.: secolarità, *f.*; cose mondane, *f. pl.* **-larizátion,** S.: secolarizzazione, *f.* **-larize,** TR.: secolarizzare. **-larly,** ADV.: in modo secolaresco, mondanamente. **-larness,** S.: vanità mondana, *f.*
sécundine, S.: secondina, *f.*
secú-re 1, ADJ.: sicuro, salvo; assicurato. **-re** 2, TR.: salvare; preservare; assicurare; proteggere; arrestare, imprigionare: — *one's self*, salvarsi. **-rely,** ADV.: sicuramente. **-rement,** S.: assicuramento, *m.*; protezione, difesa, *f.* **-reness,** S.: sicurezza; fiducia, fidanza, *f.* **-rity,** S.: sicurtà, sicurezza; malleveria, difesa, *f.*
sedán, -chair, S.: seggiola, sedia portatile, *f.*
sedáte, ADJ.: sedato, quieto, tranquillo, riposato. **-ly,** ADV.: tranquillamente. **-ness,** S.: tranquillità; moderazione, *f.*, sangue freddo, *m.*
sédative, ADJ.: sedativo, calmante.
sédenta-riness, S.: vita sedentaria, *f.* **-ry,** ADJ.: sedentario: — *life*, vita sedentaria, *f.*
séd-ge, S.: giunco, *m.* **-gy,** ADJ.: pieno di giunchi.
sédiment, S.: sedimento, *m.*; posatura, feccia, *f.*
sedí-tion, S.: sedizione, sollevazione, *f.*, scompiglio, *m.*; fazione, *f.* **-tionary,** ADJ.: sedizioso. **-tious,** ADJ.: sedizioso, fazioso. **-tiously,** ADV.: sediziosamente, tumultuariamente. **-tiousness,** S.: dispostezza a sedizione, *f.*
se-dúce, TR.: sedurre; corrompere. **-dúcement,** S.: seducimento, *m.*, seduzione, *f.* **-dúcer,** S.: seduttore, corruttore, *m.* **-dúcible,** ADJ.: seducibile. **-dúcing,** S.: sedurre, *m.*, seduzione, *f.* **-dúction,** S.: seduzione, *f.*, seducimento, *m.* **-dúctive,** ADJ.: seducente.
sedúlity, S.: sedulità, diligenza; esattezza, *f.*
sédulous, ADJ.: assiduo, diligente; esatto, accurato. **-ly,** ADV.: assiduamente, con diligenza. **-ness,** S.: assiduità, diligenza, *f.*
sée 1, S.: sede, sedia; dignità episcopale, *f.*: *bishop's* —, seggio episcopale, *m.*; *holy* —, sede apostolica, santa sede.
see 2, IRR.; TR.: vedere; comprendere, conoscere; osservare; scoprire; INTR.: aver l' occhio; informarsi; esser attento: *let me* — *it*, mostratemelo, lasciatemelo vedere; *I will come and* — *you*, verrò a vedervi; *I will* — *you off*, vi accompagnerò alla stazione (ecc.); *I shall* — *you home*, vi condurrò; — *what he wants*, domandategli quel che vuole; — *one another*, vedersi; visitarsi; *let* —, far vedere, mostrare; *go to* —, andare a vedere, visitare; — *for*, ricercare, cercare; —

pin-maker, S.: spillettaio, *m.* **-money**, S.: spille, *f. pl.*, danaro lampante, *m.*
pinnace, S.: scappavia, *f.* (barca).
pin-nacle, S.: pinnacolo; colmo, *m.* **-nated**, ADJ.: (*bot.*) pennuto. **-ner**, S.: spillettaio, *m.*; barba di cuffia, *f.*
pint, S.: foglietta; mezza bottiglia, *f.*
pioneer, S.: pioniere; marraiuolo; guastatore, *m.*
piony, S.: (*bot.*) peonia, *f.*
pious, ADJ.: pio, religioso, divoto, **-ly**, ADV.: piamente, religiosamente. **-ness**, S.: pietà, divozione, *f.*
pip I, S.: pipita, *f.* **pip** 2, INTR.: pigolare; garrire.
pip-e I, S.: tubo; condotto, *m.*; pippa; zampogna, *f.*; zufolo; ruolo, catalogo, *m.*; (*fig.*) voce; cantatrice, *f.*: — *of wine*, botte di vino, *f.* **-e** 2, (IN)TR.: zampognare; aver la voce acuta. **-er**, S.: zampognatore, suonator di flauto, *m.* **-e-tree**, S.: ghianda unguentaria, *f.* **-ing**, ADJ.: fiacco, malaticcio; fervido.
pipkin, S.: pignata; pentola, *f.*
pippin, S.: mela appiuola, *f.*
piqu-ancy, S.: acutezza, asprezza, sottigliezza, *f.* **-ant**, ADJ.: pungente, acuto. **-antly**, ADV.: in modo pungente. **-e**, S.: briga; offesa, *f.*; puntiglio, *m.* **-e**, TR.: piccare; irritare, offendere; REFL.: piccarsi: — *one's self upon*, picarsi di.
piquet, S.: picchetto, *m.* (giuoco di carte).
pi-racy, S.: pirateria, ruberia, *f.* **-rate** I, S.: pirato, corsale, *m.* **-rate** 2, (IN)TR.: corseggiare, rubare; contraffare (libri): —*d edition*, ristampa furtiva, *f.* **-rătical**, ADJ.: piratico. **-rătically**, ADV.: da pirato.
pirouette I, S.: giravolta, *f.* **pirouette** 2, INTR.: fare giravolta, piroettare.
pis-cary, S.: privilegio della pesca, *m.* **-catory**, ADJ.: pescatorio. **-ces**, S. PL.: (*astr.*) pesci, *m. pl.* **-cine**, S.: pescina, *f.*; serbatoio, *m.* **-civorous**, ADJ.: che si pasce di pesce.
pish I, INTERJ.: saetta! via! **pish** 2, INTR.: braveggiare, esprimere disprezzo.
pismire, S.: formica, formicola, *f.*
piss I, S.: orina, *f.* **piss** 2, INTR.: orinare, fare acqua. **-abed**, S.: (*bot.*) macerone, *m.*
pistāchio, S.: pistacchio, *m.* **-tree**, S.: pistacchio, *m.*
piste, S.: pesta, traccia, *f.*, vestigio, *m.*
-til, S., (*bot.*) pistillo, *m.*
' a —, scari-
·r pisto-
-tol-
f.

piston, S.: stantuffo; pistone, *m.*
pit I, S.: fossa, *f.*, fosso; abbisso; sepolcro; (*theat.*) pianterreno, *m.*, platea, *f.*: *arm*—, ascella, *f.*; *coal*—, miniera di carbone, *f.*; *gravel*—, cava di renella, ghiaia, *f.*; *sand*—, renaio, *m.* **pit** 2, TR.: scavare, incavare; INTR.: cavarsi.
pitapat, S.: palpitamento del cuore, *m.*: *my heart goes* —, il cuore mi palpita.
pitch I, S.: pece, *f.* **pitch** 2, S.: altezza; cima, *f.*; grado, *m.* **pitch** 3, IRR.; TR.: impeciare; ficcare, piantare; lanciare; (*nav.*) spalmare; INTR.: arrestarsi, fermarsi: — *a camp*, porsi a campo; — *a ship*, spalmare un bastimento; — *into one*, dar addosso a uno; — *upon*, sciegliere; — *upon one's head*, cimbottolare. **-ed**, ADJ.: impeciato, ecc. (cf. *pitch*): — *battle*, battaglia campale. **-er**, S.: brocca, *f.* **-fork**, S.: forca, *f.*, forcone, *m.* **-iness**, S.: oscurità, *f.* **-ing**, S.: (*nav.*) l'attuffarsi; il ficcare, il rollare. **-tree**, S.: pino, *m.* (albero). **-y**, ADJ.: impeciato; oscuro, fosco.
pit-coal, S.: carbone di miniera, *m.*
piteous, ADJ.: dolente, tristo, misero. **-ly**, ADV.: tristamente, miseramente. **-ness**, S.: miseria; compassione, tristezza, *f.*
pitfall, S.: trabocchetto, *m.*
pith, S.: midollo, *m.*, midolla; energia, *f.*: — *of a quill*, anima della penna, *f.* **-ily**, ADV.: vigorosamente, con energia. **-iness**, S.: vigore, *m.*, energia, *f.* **-less**, ADJ.: senza midolla; senza energia. **-y**, ADJ.: midolloso; energico, spiritoso.
piti-able, ADJ.: degno di compassione, misero. **-ableness**, S.: stato degno di compassione, *m.* **-ful**, ADJ.: compassionevole, miserabile. **-fully**, ADV.: compassionevolmente. **-fulness**, S.: compassione; pietà, misericordia, *f.* **-less**, ADJ.: spietato, fiero, crudele. **-lessly**, ADV.: spietatamente, crudelmente. **-lessness**, S.: spietatezza, crudeltà, *f.*
pit-saw, S.: sega grande, *f.*
pittance, S.: pietanza, porzioncella, *f.*
pitted, ADJ.: butterato.
pit-ūitary, ADJ.: pituitario, della pituita. **pit-uite**, S.: pituita; flemma, *f.*; umor pituitoso, *m.* **-ūitous**, ADJ.: pituitoso.
pity I, S.: pietà, compassione, *f.*: *'tis a* —, è un danno, è un peccato; *for —'s sake, out of* —, per pietà, per carità; *what a —!* che peccato! **pity** 2, TR.: compatire, compiangere.
pivot, S.: perno, cardine, *m.*
pix, S.: pisside, *f.*
placability, S.: clemenza, *f.*
plăcable, ADJ.: placabile; clemente.
-ness = placability.

pla-cárd, S.: editto; bando, affisso, cartellone, *m.*
plácate, TR.: placare, pacificare.
plá-ce 1, S.: luogo; sito; posto, uffizio; grado, *m.*: *in another* —, altrove; *trading* —, piazza di negozio, *f.*; *give* —, dar luogo, cedere; *take* —, aver luogo, accadere; sedersi; *in* — *of*, in luogo (vece) di; *in the next* —, in seguito. **-ce** 2, TR.: mettere, collocare; allocare, assegnare.
placénta, S.: placenta, *f.*
plácer, S.: che mette, che assegna il luogo.
plá-cid, ADJ.: placido, quieto, mite. **-cídity**, S.: placidezza, *f.* **-cidly**, ADV.: placidamente; piacevolmente. **-cidnéss** = *placidity*.
plácit, S.: placito, decreto, giudizio; ordine, *m.*
plácket, S.: gonna, gonnella, *f.*
plágiar-ism, S.: plagio, ladrocinio letterario, *m.* **-ist**, **-y**, S.: plagiario, *m.*
plág-ue 1, S.: peste; contagione; pena, *f.* **-ue** 2, TR.: infettare, appestare; tormentare, affliggere. **-ue-sore**, S.: gavocciolo, *m.* **-uily**, ADV.: affannosamente. **-uing**, ADJ.: fastidioso, noioso. **-uy**, ADJ.: affannoso, molesto; pericoloso.
pláice, S.: passere, *m.* (pesce).
pláid, S.: ciarpa de' Scozzesi, *f.*
pláin 1, ADJ.: piano, liscio, uguale; chiaro, evidente; franco, sincero; ADV.: chiaramente, distintamente: — *clothes*, abito ordinario; — *food*, cibo (nutrimento) semplice; *the* — *truth*, la pura verità; *in* — *terms*, chiaramente, distintamente. **plain** 2, S.: pianura; campagna rasa, *f.*; piano, *m.* **plain** 3, TR.: appianare, uguagliare; INTR.: compiangere, lamentarsi. **-déaler**, S.: uomo dabbene, uomo franco, *m.* **-déaling**, ADJ.: onesto, franco, sincero; S.: buona fede; sincerità, *f.* **-hearted**, ADJ.: sincero, franco. **-heartedness**, S.: sincerità, *f.* **-ly**, ADV.: semplicemente; schiettamente; francamente. **-ness**, S.: livello, *m.*; ugualità; semplicità; chiarezza, *f.*
pláint, S.: lamento, *m.*, querela, *f.* **-ful**, ADJ.: lamentoso, querulo. **-iff**, S.: dimandatore, *m.* **-ive**, ADJ.: dolente, querulo. **-ively**, ADV.: dolentemente. **-iveness**, S.: doglianza, *f.*
pláin-work, S.: lavoro d'ago, *m.*
pláit 1, S.: piega, *f.*, doppio, *m.*, treccia, *f.* **plait** 2, TR.: piegare; intrecciare. **-er**, S.: piegatore, *m.* **-ing**, S.: piegamento; intrecciare, *m.*
plán 1, S.: piano, disegno, *m.* **plan** 2, TR.: disegnare; progettare; formare un disegno.
plánch, TR.: intavolare. **-ing**, S.: intavolatura, *f.*
pláne 1, S.: piano, *m.*; pianura; pialla, *f.*: [illegible] —, **plane** 2, TR.: piallare; [illegible]
plánet, S.: pianeta, *m.* -[illegible] planetario, *m.* **-ary**, ADJ.: di pianeta.
pláne-tree, S.: platano, *m.*
plánet-struck, ADJ.: [illegible]
planímetry, S.: planimetria, [illegible]
plánish, TR.: adeguare, [illegible]
plánisphere, S.: planisferio, [illegible]
plánk 1, S.: tavola, asse, *f.*; [illegible] **plank** 2, TR.: tavolare, [illegible] tavole.
plánner, S.: disegnatore, *m.*
plánt 1, S.: pianta, *f.*; [illegible] **plant** 2, TR.: piantare; stabi[illegible] piantarsi.
plántain, S.: piantaggine, *f.*
plán-tal, ADJ.: vegetabile, [illegible] **-tátion**, S.: piantagione; [illegible] **-ter**, S.: piantatore; colono, [illegible] S.: piantamento, piantare, *m.*
plásh 1, S.: guazzo; pantano, [illegible] **plash** 2, TR.: spruzzare; pieg[illegible] scolare. **-y**, ADJ.: pantanoso, [illegible]
plásm(a), S.: plasma, forma; [illegible] **-ática**l, ADJ.: plastico, formati[illegible]
pláster 1, S.: impiastro; calcin[illegible] tonaco, *m.*: *give a coat of* —, [illegible] naco, intonacare. **plaster** 2, T[illegible] strare; ingessare: porre un [illegible] medicinale: — *up*, rintonacare. [illegible] muratore che intonica; [illegible] so, *m.* **-ing**, S.: intonicatura, *f.* S.: pietra da gesso, *f.*
plástic, ADJ.: plastico; S.: pla[illegible]
plástron, S.: piastrone; pettie[illegible]
plát 1, S.: campicello, campi[illegible] **plat** 2, TR.: intrecciare, tessere.
plátan(e), S.: platano, *m.*
plátband, S.: aiuola; (*arch.*) f[illegible]
plát-e 1, S.: piastra; argenteria [illegible] lama, *f.*; tondo, *m.* **-te** 2, TR.: [illegible] tare, indorare; ridurre in lami[illegible] ADJ.: inargentato: — *ware*, placche, *f. pl.*
pláten, S.: pirrone, *m.*: (*pri*[illegible] stretta, *f.*
plátform, S.: piattaforma; ter[illegible]
pláti-na, S.: platina, *f.* (metallo), [illegible] S.: platino, *m.*
plátitude, S.: frase altisonante, [illegible]
Platónic, ADJ.: platonico.
Plá-tonism, S.: platonismo, [illegible] **-nist**, S.: platonico, *m.*
platóon, S.: (*mil.*) squadrone, [illegible] ra; banda, *f.*
plátter, S.: terrina, *f.*, gran [illegible] terra), *f.*
pláudit, S.: applauso, *m.*, [illegible] ne, *f.*

plausibility, S.: plausibilità; apparenza, *f.*
plausibl-e, ADJ.: plausibile; apparente. **-eness** = *plausibility*. **-y**, ADV.: in modo plausibile, con applauso.
play1, S.: giuoco, divertimento; spettacolo, *m.*, commedia, *f.*: *fair* —, libero giuoco, giuoco senza inganni; *give one fair* —, lasciar fare ad uno; *foul* —, frode, truffa, *f.*; *go to the* —, andare alla commedia; *keep one in* —, tenere uno a bada. **play**2, (IN)TR.: giuocare; scherzare; rappresentare; beffare; burlare, burlarsi: — *away*, perdere (il giuoco); — *at cards*, giuocare alle carte; — *fair*, giuocare onestamente; — *the fool*, fare il pazzo; — *foul*, truffare, ingannare; — *a game*, giuocare una partita; — *the knave*, fare delle furfanterie; — *pranks*, fare delle sue; — *sure*, giuocare a giuoco sicuro; — *one a trick*, fare una burla; — *the truant*, fuggir la scuola; — *upon an instrument*, suonare uno strumento; — *upon a person*, farsi giuoco di alcuno; — *the wanton*, trastullare. **-book**, S.: libro di commedie, *m.* **-day**, S.: giorno di festa, giorno di vacanza, *m.* **-debt**, S.: debito d' onore, *m.* **-er**, S.: giuocatore, attore, *m.* **-fellow**, S.: compagno di giuoco, *m.* **-ful**, ADJ.: giocoso, scherzevole. **-fulness**, S.: facezia, burla, *f.* **-house**, S.: teatro, *m.* **-some**, ADJ.: scherzevole; allegro, gaio. **-someness**, S.: scherzo, giuoco; trastullo, *m.* **-thing**, S.: trastullo, *m.*; bagatella, *f.* **-wright**, S.: facitore di commedie, *m.*
plea, S.: difesa; scusa, *f.*; pretesto, colore, *m.*
pleach, TR.: piegare.
plead, TR.: difendere; allegare; INTR.: litigare, piatire: — *guilty*, confessarsi reo; — *not guilty*, dichiararsi innocente, respingere l' accusa; — *ignorance*, allegare causa d' ignoranza. **-able**, ADJ.: che può essere litigato. **-er**, S.: litigante, avvocato; piatitore, *m.* **-ing**, S.: litigare, piatire: —*s*, *pl.*, dibattimento, *m.*
pleasan-ce, S.: gaiezza; piacevolezza; baia, *f.* **-t**, ADJ.: piacevole, affabile, cortese; grato; gaio: *a — voyage!* buon viaggio! **-tly**, ADV.: piacevolmente; cortesemente; gaiamente. **-tness**, S.: piacevolezza, amenità, affabilità, cortesia. **-try**, S.: facezia, gaiezza; piacevolezza, *f.*
pleas-e, TR.: piacere; contentare, soddisfare; compiacere a: — *one's self*, compiacersi, dilettarsi; far da modo suo; *as you* —, come vi piacerà; *if you* —, se v' è grato; *be well —d with*, compiacersi in (*or* di); esser contento di; — *tell me*, piacciavi di dirmi; *do as you* —, fate quel che vi piace; *hard to* —, di difficile contentatura. **-ed**, ADJ.: contento, felice. **-ing**, ADJ.: grato, gustoso; accetto. **-ingly**, ADV.: con piacere, piacevolmente. **-ingness**, S.: piacevolezza, *f.*
pleasur-able, ADJ.: piacevole, delizioso, ameno. **-ableness**, S.: piacevolezza, *f.* **-ably**, ADV.: piacevolmente. **-e**1, S.: piacere, divertimento, diletto, *m.*; voglia, *f.*: *at* —, a piacere, a piacimento; *your* —*?* che domanda? **-e**2, TR.: piacere; contentare, soddisfare. **-boat**, S.: battello di piacere, *m.* **-ground**, S.: giardino inglese, *m.*
plebeian, S.: plebeo, volgare; S.: uomo plebeo, *m.*
plebiscite, S.: plebiscito, *m.*
plectrum, S.: plettro, *m.*
pledg-e1, S.: pegno; mallevadore, *m.*, sicurtà; testimonianza, *f.*; ostaggio, *m.* **-e**2, TR.: impegnare, dare in pegno: — *one's self*, impegnarsi, obbligarsi; — *in drinking*, fare ragione. **-et**, S.: (*surg.*) piumacciuolo, *m.*
Ple-iads, -iades, S. PL.: (*astr.*) pleiadi, *f. pl.*
plena-rily, ADV.: pienamente, totalmente. **-riness**, S.: ripienezza; plenitudine, *f.* **-ry**, ADJ.: plenario, intero.
plenilu-nary, ADJ.: plenilunare. **-ne** *plen-*, S.: plenilunio, *m.*
plenipo-tence, S.: plenipotenza, *f.* **-tent**, ADJ.: plenipotenziale. **-tentiary**, S.: plenipotenziario, *m.*
plen-ish†, TR.: riempire. **-itude**, S.: plenitudine, pienezza, *f.*
plen-teous, ADJ.: abbondante, copioso; fertile. **-teously**, ADV.: abbondantemente, in copia. **-teousness**, S.: abbondanza, copia; fertilità, *f.* **-tiful**, ADV.: abbondevole. **-tifully**, ADV.: in abbondanza, copiosamente. **-tifulness**, S.: abbondanza, copia; fertilità, *f.* **-ty**, S.: abbondanza, copia, quantità, *f.*
pleo-nasm, S.: pleonasmo, *m.* **-nastic**, ADJ.: pleonastico.
plesh†, S.: pantano, *m.*
pleth-ora, S.: pletora, abbondanza di sangue, *f.* **-oretic, -oric**, ADJ.: pletorico. **-ory** = *plethora*.
pleu-risy, S.: (*med.*) pleurisia, *f.* **-ritic(al)**, ADJ.: pleuritico.
plevin, S.: (*jur.*) permissione di vendere i beni, *f.*
pliability, S.: pieghevolezza, flessibilità, *f.*
pli-able, ADJ.: pieghevole, flessibile. **-ableness, -ancy**, S.: flessibilità; docilità, *f.* **-ant**, ADJ.: pieghevole, flessibile; arrendevole. **-antness**, S.: pieghevolezza, flessibilità, *f.*
plica, S.: (*med.*) plica polonica, *f.*
plic-ation, plic-ature, S.: piega, riga, *f.*

tree, S.: sorbo, *m.* **-vile**, ADJ.: servile; basso, abietto. **-vilely**, ADV.: servilmente; bassamente. **-vileness**, **-vility**, S.: servilità; bassezza, *f.* **-ving-maid**, S.: serva, *f.* **-ving-man**, S.: servidore; servo, *m.* **-vitor**, S.: servidore; povero studente, *m.* **-vitude**, S.: servitù, schiavitù, *f.*

sěsame, S.: sesamo, sisamo, *m.*

sesquiălter, ADJ.: sesquialtro.

sesquipedal, ADJ.: sesquipedale.

sěss†, S.: tassa, imposizione; imposta, *f.*

sěssion, S.: sessione; assemblea de' giudici, *f.*: *quarter —s*, assise tremestrali; *keep the —s*, tenere l' assise. **-hall**, S.: corte di giustizia, *f.*

sěsterce, S.: sesterzio, *m.*

sět 1, S.: assortimento, *m.*; partita (di giuoco), *f.*; pollone; ornamento, abbellimento, *m.*: — *of books*, collezione di libri; — *of buttons*, guarnizione di bottoni; — *of china*, servigio di porcellana; — *of diamonds*, guarnimento di diamanti; — *of a dog*, ferma; — *of horses*, tiro di cavalli; muta di cavalli; — *of men*, banda di persone; — *of plate*, apparato d' argenteria; — *of rascals*, mano di furfanti; — *of the sun*, occaso del sole; — *of teeth*, dentatura, *f.* **set** 2, ADJ.: posto, messo, fisso (cf. verbo *set*): — *battle*, battaglia formale, *f.*; — *hour*, ora fissa; — *meal*, pasto regolato; — *price*, prezzo fisso, prezzo stabilito; *on — purpose*, a bella posta, a bello studio; — *resolution*, ferma risoluzione; — *speech*, discorso studiato; — *visit*, visita formale. **set** 3, IRR.; (IN)TR.: mettere, collocare, porre; fissare, stabilire; affermare; tramontare; coagulare, rappigliarsi; applicarsi; — *a bone*, rimettere un osso slogato; — *up a cry*, mettersi a gridare; — *at defiance*, sfidare; bravare; — *a dog at*, aizzare un cane contro; — *a good example*, dare buon esempio; — *on fire*, dar fuoco a; incendiare; — *free*, mettere in libertà; — *on foot*, mettere in piedi, stabilire; — *a-going*, porre in moto, far andare; — *one's hand to*, sottoscrivere; — *up a laugh*, sganasciare delle risa; — *to music*, mettere in musica; — *nets*, tender reti; — *at nought*, non far conto, dispregiare; — *in order*, mettere in ordine, ordinare; — *a page*, comporre una pagina; — *apart*, porre da parte, riserbare; — *a razor*, affilare un rasoio; — *to rights*, raddirizzare; — *sail*, far vele, spiegar le vele; — *on shore*, mettere a terra, sbarcare; — *up a snare*, tendere insidie; — *up a tavern*, aprir taverna; — *a time*, stabilire il tempo, determinare; — *tools*, affilare ordigni; — *one at (to) work*, dar da lavorare ad uno; — *one's self to work*, mettersi a lavorare; — *about*, mettersi a fare; — *again*, rimettere; — *against*, incitare contro; opporsi; — *aside*, mettere da banda; — *away*, metter da parte; rimuovere; — *by*, considerare; omettere; — *down*, fissare, stabilire; scrivere; — *forth*, esporre, far vedere; — *forward*, avanzare, promuovere; andare via, partire; — *off*, abbellire, adornare; — *on*, incitare, animare; assaltare; cominciare; — *out*, esporre; partire, andarsene; dar risalto a, abbellire; — *up*, ergere; edificare; stabilire; mostrare; adirare; lodare, vantare; — *up again*, rimettere; — *up for*, darsi per; — *up for one's self*, stabilirsi, aprire bottega.

setāceous, ADJ.: setoloso, ispido.

sět-foil, S.: (*bot.*) tormentilla, *f.*

sět-off, S.: guernizione, *f.*, ornamento, *m.*

sěton, S.: setone, *m.*

set-tēe, S.: canapè, *m.* **-ter**, S.: spia; cane da ferma; truffatore, furbo, *m.* **-ter-on**, S.: istigatore, *m.* **-ting**, S.: il porre, il mettere; collocazione; incastonatura; (*nav.*) abbriva, tendenza, *f.*; — *dog*, cane da ferma; — *up*, stabilimento, *m.*; — *of the sun*, occaso del sole. **-ting-dog**, S.: cane da ferma; spia, *m.* **-ting-out**, S.: partire; cominciamento, *m.* **-ting-stick**, S.: piuolo; (*print.*) compositoio, *m.* **-tle** 1, S.: seggio; banco, lettiociuolo, *m.* **-tle** 2, TR.: stabilire; fermare, fissare; ordinare, aggiustare; INTR.: posarsi, rassettarsi; accasarsi, stanziarsi; andare a fondo; fissarsi, determinarsi; calmarsi, appaciarsi: — *an account*, saldare un conto; — *one's concerns*, regolare i suoi affari; — *one's mind*, quietare la sua mente; — *one's spirits*, acchetarsi; — *upon*, assegnare; costituire. **-tledness**, S.: stabilità, stabilezza, permanenza, *f.* **-tlement**, S.: stabilimento, *m.*; abitazione, *f.*, domicilio, *m.*; colonia, *f.*; patto, accordo, *m.*; feccia, *f.*: *make a — upon one*, assegnare ad uno un' entrata fissa. **-tler**, S.: colono, *m.* **-tling**, S.: fondigliuolo, *m.*, posatura, feccia, *f.*

sěven, ADJ.: sette. **-fold**, ADJ., ADV.: doppio sette volte; a sette doppi. **-night**, S.: settimana, *f.*, sette giorni, *m. pl.* **-score**, ADJ.: sette volte venti, cenquaranta. **-teen**, ADJ.: diecisette, diciasette. **-teenth**, ADJ.: diecisettimo, diciasettesimo. **-th**, ADJ.: settimo. **-thly**, ADV.: in settimo luogo. **-tieth**, ADJ.: settantesimo. **-ty**, ADJ.: settanta.

sěver, TR.: sceverare, separare, partire, dividere; INTR.: fare una separazione. **-al** 1, ADJ.: molti, diversi, parecchi: — *times*, molte volte, spesse volte; ADV.: in particolare. **-al** 2, S.: individuo, ricinto, *m.*; particolarità, *f.* **-alize**, TR.: parti-

pĕn-wiper, S.: nettapenna, *m*.
pēony, S.: (*bot.*) peonia, *f*.
pēople 1, S.: popolo, *m*., nazione, gente, *f*.: *common* —, bassa gente, *f*., volgo, popolaccio, *m*., plebe, *f*.; *fashionable* —, il bel mondo; *many* —, molta gente, molte persone; *of the* —, popolano; *throng of* —, calca di gente, *f*.; — *say*, si dice. **people** 2, TR.: popolare, mettere popolo; INTR.: popolarsi.
pĕpper 1, S.: pepe, *m*. **pepper** 2, TR.: impepare, condire con pepe. **-box**, S.: pepaiuola, *f*. **-corn**, S.: seme di pepe, *m*.; (*fig.*) bagatella, *f*. **-mint**, S.: (*bot.*) menta piperina, *f*.
pĕpsine, S.: pepsina, *f*.
pĕptic, ADJ.: (*med.*) digestivo.
pĕr, PREP.: per.
peracūte, ADJ.: acutissimo.
peradvĕnture, ADV.: per avventura, a caso: *without* —, senza dubbio, senza fallo.
perămbu-late, TR.: andare attorno, girare. **-lātion**, S.: andare attorno, giro, *m*. **-lator**, S.: odometro, *m*. (strumento); carrozzetta da bambino, *f*.
percēi-vable, ADJ.: percettibile; sensibile. **-vably**, ADV.: percettibilmente, visibilmente. **-ve**, TR.: concepire, comprendere; osservare; scoprire, accorgersi: — *beforehand*, presentire.
percĕntage, S.: quantità per cento, *f*.
per-cĕptibility, S.: qualità percettibile, percezione, *f*. **-cĕptible**, ADJ.: percettibile; sensibile. **-cĕptibleness** = *perceptibility*. **-cĕptibly**, ADV.: in modo percettibile. **-cĕption**, S.: percezione, comprensione; capacità; intelligenza, *f*. **-cĕptive**, ADJ.: percettibile, intelligente. **-cĕptivity**, S.: facoltà da comprendere, percezione, *f*.
pĕrch 1, S.: pertica, *f*. **perch** 2, INTR.: alberare.
perchânce, ADV.: forse, per avventura, a caso.
percipient, ADJ.: percipiente.
pĕrco-late, TR.: feltrare, colare. **-lātion**, S.: feltrazione, *f*., colamento, *m*.
per-cŭss, TR.: percuotere; bussare. **-cŭssion**, S.: percussione, percossa, *f*.: — *cap*, capsula di fucile a percussione, *f*.; — *gun*, fucile a percussione, schioppo a percussione, schioppo a capsula, *m*.
perdĭtion, S.: perdizione, rovina, *f*.
per-dū 1, S.: sentinella avanzata, *f*. **-du** 2, **-dūe**, ADV.: in aguato; occultamente.
perdū-rable†, ADJ.: perdurabile, permanente. **-rably**†, ADV.: perdurabilmente; sempre. **-rātion**†, S.: durazione, lunga durata, continuazione, *f*.
pĕregri-nate, INTR.: peregrinare, viaggiare. **-nātion**, S.: peregrinazione, *f*., viaggio, *m*. **-nator**, S.: peregrinatore, viaggiatore, *m*. **-ne**, ADJ.: peregrino, straniero.
perĕmp-t, TR.: uccidere; ammazzare. **-tion**, S.: (*jur.*) estinzione, *f*.
pĕremptq-rily, ADV.: perentoriamente, decisivamente. **-riness**, S.: decisione, determinazione, *f*. **-ry**, ADJ.: perentorio, decisivo.
perĕn-nial, ADJ.: perenne, perpetuo. **-nity**, S.: perpetuità; continuanza, *f*.
pĕr-fect 1, ADJ.: perfetto, compiuto; puro; S.: (*gram.*) perfetto, *m*. **-fect** 2, TR.: perfezionare; compire, terminare, finire. **-fecter**, S.: perfezionatore, *m*. **-fĕctible**, ADJ.: perfettibile. **-fĕcting**, S.: compimento, *m*. **-fĕction**, S.: perfezione, *f*., compimento, *m*.; eccellenza, *f*. **-fĕctionate**, TR.: perfezionare; finire. **-fĕctionist**, S.: puritano, *m*. **-fĕctive**, ADJ.: perfettivo, perfezionativo. **-fĕctively**, ADV.: in modo perfetto. **-fectly**, ADV.: perfettamente; esattamente. **-fectness**, S.: compimento, *m*.; bontà, *f*.
perfĭdious, ADJ.: perfido, disleale. **-ly**, ADV.: perfidamente. **-ness**, S.: perfidia, *f*.
pĕrfidy = *perfidiousness*.
pĕrfo-rate, TR.: perforare; trafiggere. **-rātion**, S.: perforamento, *m*. **-rator**, S.: foratoio, succhiello, *m*.
perfōrce, ADV.: per forza, forzatamente; di viva forza.
perfôrm, (IN)TR.: operare, effettuare, fare, eseguire, compire; (*theat.*) agire; recitare, cantare: — *one's devotion*, dire le sue divozioni; — *one's promise*, effettuare la promessa. **-able**, ADJ.: eseguibile, praticabile, fattibile. **-ance**, S.: esecuzione, *f*.; eseguimento, compimento, *m*.; opera, azione; (*theat.*) rappresentazione, recita, *f*. **-er**, S.: esecutore, compitore, attore, *m*., esecutrice, ecc., *f*. **-ing**, S.: compimento, effetto, *m*.
per-fūmatory, ADJ.: che profuma.
pĕr-fume 1, S.: profumo, odore soave, *m*. **-fūme** 2, TR.: profumare. **-fūmer**, S.: profumiere; unguentario, *m*. **-fūming**, S.: profumare, *m*. **-fūming-pan**, S.: profumiera, *f*., turibile, *m*.
perfŭnctq-rily, ADV.: negligentemente, leggiermente. **-riness**, S.: negligenza, trascuranza, *f*. **-ry**, ADJ.: trascurante, negligente.
perfūse, TR.: tingere, imbevere; aspergere.
pĕrgola, S.: pergola, *f*.
perhăps, ADV.: forse, per avventura.
pĕrianth, S.: (*bot.*) perianto, *m*.
peri-cardītis, S.: pericardite, *f*. **-cardium**, S.: (*anat.*) pericardio, *m*.
pĕricarp, S.: (*bot.*) pericarpo, *m*.
pericrānium, S.: (*anat.*) pericraneo.

perilous [illegible] pericoloso, rischioso.
péri-gee, -géum. s. [illegible] perigeo, m.
-hélium. s. [illegible] m.
péril s. [illegible] pericolo, rischio, m.; [illegible] a vostro rischio e pericolo. **peril** [illegible] pericolare. **-ous.** [illegible] pericoloso, periglioso, [illegible] **-ously.** [illegible] pericolosamente [illegible] **-ousness.** s. pericolo, [illegible] m.
perimeter. s. [illegible] perimetro, m., [illegible]
périod. s. [illegible] spazio di tempo; [illegible] m. [illegible] fine, f.; termine, m. [illegible] **-ódic al.** [illegible] **-ódically.** [illegible]
peri-ósteum. s. [illegible] **-patétic.** [illegible] **-phery.** s. [illegible] **-phrase** [illegible] **-phrasis** [illegible] **-phrástical.** [illegible] **-phrástically.** [illegible] **-plus** [illegible] **-scians** [illegible]
pérish. [illegible] **-able.** [illegible] **-ableness.** s. [illegible] **-ing.** [illegible]
peristáltic. [illegible]
péri-style. s. [illegible] **-tonéum.** s. [illegible] **-tonitis.** s. [illegible]
périwig s. [illegible] **periwig** [illegible]
périwinkle. s. [illegible]
pér-jure. [illegible] **-jurer.** s. [illegible] **-jurious.** [illegible] **-jury.** s. [illegible]
pérk. [illegible]
perlustrátion. s. [illegible]
pérmanen-ce, -cy. s. [illegible] **-t.** [illegible] **-tly.** [illegible]
pérme-able. [illegible] **-ant.** [illegible] **-ate.** [illegible] **-átion.** s. [illegible]
permiscible. [illegible]
per-míssible. [illegible] **-míssion.** s. [illegible]

missi[illegible] perm[illegible] sivan[illegible]
perm[illegible] scola[illegible]
pér-[illegible] *f.* [illegible] offri[illegible] io vi [illegible] indul[illegible]
per-[illegible] perm[illegible] camb[illegible] muta[illegible]
perm[illegible] **-ly.** [illegible] te.
pera[illegible]
perp[illegible]
perp[illegible]
perp[illegible]
perp[illegible]
perp[illegible]
perp[illegible] **-al** [illegible]
perp[illegible]
pérq[illegible]
pérr[illegible]
pérs[illegible]
pers[illegible]

-ence, **-ency**, S.: persistenza, perseveranza, fermezza, *f.* **-ive**, ADJ.: persistente, fermo, costante.

pĕr-son, S.: persona; figura, *f.*; esteriore, *m.*: **—s**, persone; gente, *f.*; *in —*, in persona, personalmente; *in a —'s place*, in persona di uno. **-sonable**, ADJ.: ben fatto, grazioso. **-sonage**, S.: personaggio; esteriore; carattere, *m.* **-sonal**, ADJ.: personale; peculiare, particolare, proprio: *— goods*, beni mobili, *m. pl.* **-sonăl(i)ty**, S.: personalità, *f.*; individuo, *m.* **-sonally**, ADV.: personalmente, in persona. **-sonate**, TR.: rappresentare, imitare. **-sonātion**, S.: rappresentazione, *f.*; carattere, *m.* **-sonification**, S.: personificazione, *f.* **-sŏnify**, TR.: personificare.

per-spĕctive 1, ADJ.: prospettivo, ottico, visivo. **-spective** 2, S.: prospettiva, vista, *f.*; paesaggio, *m.* **-spicācious**, ADJ.: perspicace; intelligente. **-spicāciousness**, **-spicăcity**, S.: perspicacità, penetrazione (d' ingegno), acutezza, *f.* **-spicience** †, S.: osservazione acuta, *f.*

per-spicūity, S.: perspicuità, trasparenza; chiarezza, evidenza, *f.* **-spicuous**, ADJ.: chiaro, evidente. **-spicuously**, ADV.: chiaramente. **-spicuousness**, S.: chiarezza, evidenza, *f.*

perspi-rable, ADJ.: perspirabile, traspirabile. **-spirātion**, S.: perspirazione, traspirazione, *f.* **-spirative**, ADJ.: traspirante, sudatorio. **-spire**, INTR.: traspirare, sudare.

persuā-dable, ADJ.: persuasibile, suadevole. **-de**, TR.: persuadere; convincere: *— one's self*, persuadersi. **-der**, S.: persuadente, *m.* **-sible**, ADJ.: persuasibile, suadevole. **-sion**, S.: persuasione; istigazione, *f.* **-sive**, ADJ.: persuasivo. **-sively**, ADV.: in modo persuasivo. **-siveness**, S.: facoltà di persuadere, *f.* **-sory**, ADJ.: persuasorio, persuasivo.

pĕrt, ADJ.: lesto, agile; impertinente, impronto.

pertāin, INTR.: appartenere, concernere, spettare.

perti-nācious, ADJ.: pertinace, ostinato. **-nāciously**, ADV.: pertinacemente. **-nāciousness**, **-năcity**, S.: pertinacia, caparbietà, ostinazione, *f.*

pĕrti-nacy †, S.: ostinazione, caparbieria, **-nence**, **-cy**, S.: pertinenza, apparconvenevolezza, *f.* **-nent**, ADJ.: [illegible]porzionato, convenevole: *be* [illegible]proposito, cader in accon[illegible] [illegible]DV.: convenevolmen[illegible] **-nentness**, S.: [illegible]

[illegible]vivacemen[illegible] [illegible]samente.

-ness, S.: vivacità, attività; insolenza, impertinenza, *f.*

pertŭrb, TR.: perturbare. **-ātion**, S.: perturbazione, *f.*; commovimento, *m.*, alterazione, *f.* **-ator**, S.: perturbatore, *m.*

pertūsion, S.: perforazione, *f.*

pĕruke, S.: parrucca, *f.*; capelli posticci, *m. pl.* **-maker**, S.: parrucchiere, *m.*

perū-sal, S.: lettura, *f.*, leggere, *m.* **-se**, TR.: leggere; esaminare. **-ser**, S.: lettore, leggitore, *m.*

Perūvian-bark, S.: chinachina, *f.*

pervā-de, TR.: passare oltre, penetrare, compenetrare, permeare, regnare in. **-sion**, S.: trapasso; penetramento, *m.* **-sive**, ADJ.: trapassante; penetrante.

pervĕr-se, ADJ.: perverso; ostinato, caparbio. **-sely**, ADJ.: perversamente, con perversità. **-seness**, S.: perversità, *f.*; cattivo umore, *m.* **-sion**, S.: perversione, *f.*, pervertimento, *m.* **-sity** = *perverseness.* **-sive**, ADJ.: pervertente. **-t**, TR.: pervertire, sconvolgere; corrompere. **-ter**, S.: pervertitore, corruttore, *m.* **-tible**, ADJ.: che può esser pervertito.

pĕrvious, ADJ.: pervio, passabile. **-ness**, S.: penetrabilità, *f.*

pesāde, S.: (*horse.*) pesata, *f.*

pĕssim-ism, S.: pessimismo, *m.* **-ist**, S.: pessimista, *m.*

pĕst, S.: peste, pestilenza; contagione, *f.*

pĕster, TR.: noiare, affannare, affliggere, inquietare, disturbare. **-er**, S.: importuno, seccatore, tormentatore, *m.* **-ous**, ADJ.: incomodo, annoioso. **-ousness**, S.: incomodità, *f.*

pĕst-house, S.: lazzaretto, spedale, *m.* **-iferous**, ADJ.: pestifero, contagioso.

pĕsti-lence, S.: pestilenza, peste, contagione, *f.* **-lent**, **-lĕntial**, ADJ.: pestilenziale. **-lently**, ADV.: in modo contagioso.

pestillātion, S.: pestimento, polverizzamento, *m.*

pĕstle, S.: pestello, *m.*

pĕt 1, S.: collera, *f.*; dispetto, sdegno; favorito, *m.*: *— bird*, uccellino; *— lamb*, agnello allevato a mano, agnello favorito; *be in a —*, essere in collera; *take — at a thing*, offendersi di qualche cosa. **pet** 2, TR.: vezzeggiare soverchiamente.

pĕtal, S.: (*bot.*) petalo, *m.*

pe-tār †, **-tārd**, S.: petardo, *m.*

Pēter-wort, S.: (*bot.*) tassobarbasso, *m.*

petition 1, S.: supplica, *f.*, memoriale, *m.* **petition** 2, TR.: supplicare, pregare; domandare. **-ary**, ADJ.: petitorio, supplicante. **-er**, S.: supplicante, *m.* **-ing**, S.: supplicare, pregare, *m.*

pĕtitory, ADJ.: petitorio, supplicatorio.

pētre, S.: nitro, salnitro, *m.*

pĕtrel, S.: procellaria, *f.* (uccello).

pe-tréscent, ADJ.: pietrificante. **-trifáction**, S.: pietrificazione, *f.*, impietramento, *m.* **-trifáctive**, **-tríffic**, ADJ.: petrifico. **-trificátion**, S.: pietrificazione, *f.* **pé-trify**, TR.: impietrare, convertire in pietra; INTR.: divenir pietra, impietrire.
petróleum, S.: petrolio, *m.*
pétronel, S.: piccol archibuso, *m.*, pistola, *f.*
pétticoat, S.: gonnella, gonnellina, *f.*
péttifog, TR.: fare il [illegible]. **-ger**, S.: leguleio, mozzorecchi; procuratorello, *m.* **-gery**, **-ging**, S.: lite, controversia, *f.*
péttiness, S.: piccolezza, *f.*
péttish, ADJ.: stizzoso, fantastico. **-ly**, ADV.: fantasticamente. **-ness**, S.: fantasticaggine, *f.*, cattivo umore, *m.*
pét-titoes, S.: piedi di porcello, *m. pl.* **-ty**, ADJ.: piccolo; piccino; meschino; di poco pregio; inferiore: — *jury*, giurì del ceto medio; — *patties*, pasticcetti, *m. pl.*
pétulan-ce, **-cy**, S.: petulanza, protervia, *f.* **-t**, ADJ.: petulante, protervo. **-tly**, ADV.: protervamente, con petulanza.
pew, S.: banco di chiesa, *m.*
péwit, S.: bubbola, upupa, *f.*
péwter, S.: peltro, *m.* **-er**, S.: peltraio, *m.*
phaéton, S.: faeton, *m.*
phálanx, S.: falange, *f.*
phan-tásm(a), S.: fantasima, *f.* **-tasmagória**, S.: fantasmagoria, *f.* **-tástical**, ADJ.: fantastico, chimerico. **phán-tasy**, S.: fantasia, *f.*
phántom, S.: fantasma; apparizione, *f.*
phare, **pharo**, S.: faro, *m.*
Pharisáical, ADJ.: farisaico.
Phárisee, S.: fariseo, *m.*
pharma-céutic(al), ADJ.: farmaceutico. **-cólogy**, S.: farmacologia, scienza della farmacia, *f.* **-copœia**, S.: farmacopea, *f.* **-cópolist**, S.: speziale, *m.* **-cy phár-**, S.: farmacia, *f.*
pháros, S.: faro, *m.*
phárynx, S.: faringe, *f.*
phase, **-sis**, S.: fase, *f.*: *the —s of the moon*, le fasi della luna.
pháseols, S. PL.: fagiuoli, *m. pl.*
phásm(a), S.: fantasma, apparizione,
phéasant, S.: fagiano, *m.*: *hen* —, [fa]giana, *f.*; *young* —, fagianotto, *m.*
S.: fagianaia, *f.*
phéese, TR.: pettinare; streggiare.
phénix, S.: fenice, *f.*
phenóme-nal, ADJ.: fenomenale. **-non**, S.: fenomeno, *m.*
phial, S.: fiala, caraffa, *f.*
phil-anthrópic(al), ADJ.: filantropico, umano, ben[efico] **-thropist**, S.: filan-

tropo, *m.* **-ánthropy**, S.: filan[tropia] umanità; ..., *f.*
phíllip, S.: buffetto, biscottino, *m.*
-ip, TR.: dare un buffetto.
philíppic, S.: filippica, *f.*
philólogy, S.: filologia, ...
-lógic(al), **-ly**, ADJ.: filologico, ...
-ogist, S.: filologo, ... **-ogy**, S.: filologia, *f.*; ... lettere, *m.*
philo-mel, **-méla**, S.: ...
philó-sopháte, TR.: filosofare ...
S.: filosofo, ...
fisime; fisima, *m.*; *—'s stone*, pie[tra] ... **-sóphical**, ADJ.: fi[losofico] **-sóphically**, ADV.: filosoficamente. **-sóphize**, INTR.: filosof[are] **-sophy**, S.: filosofia, *f.*: ... —, fisica, *f.*
philter¹, S.: filtro, *m.*, bevand[a amorosa], *f.* **philter²**, TR.: ammali[are con] un filtro.
phiz, S.: viso, visuccio, *m.*
phlebót-omist, S.: flebotomi[sta] ... **-omize**, TR.: flebot[omizzare] **-omy**, S.: flebotomia, *f.*
phlegm, S.: flemma; pituita; ...
phlegmátic, ADJ.: flemmatico, ...
phléme, S.: (vet.) fiamma, *f.*
phlogis-tic, ADJ.: (chem.) infiamm[ato] **-ton**, S.: (chem.) flogisto, *m.*
pho-nétic, ADJ.: fonetico. **-nétic[ally]**, ADV.: foneticamente. **-nólogy**, S.: fonologia, *f.* **phó-nograph**, S.: fonografo, *m.*
phósphate, S.: fosfato, *m.*
phós-phor = phosphorus. **-pho[rescence]**, S.: fosforescenza, *f.* **-pho[rescent]**, ADJ.: fosforescente. **-phoric**, ADJ.: fosforico, di fosforo. **-phorus**, S.: fosforo, *m.*
phó-tograph¹, S.: fotografia, *f.* **-tograph²**, TR.: fotografare. **-tógrapher**, S.: fotografo, *m.* **-tógraphy**, S.: fotografia, *f.* **-tómeter**, S.: fotometro, *m.*
phrase, S.: frase; ...

medicare, sanare. **-ical**, ADJ.: fisico; sanativo, medicinale; naturale. **-ically**, ADV.: fisicamente; naturalmente. **-ician**, S.: medico, *m.* **-ics**, S. PL.: fisica, filosofia naturale, *f.* **-icotheŏlogy**, S.: teologia fisica, *f.* **-iŏgnomer**, **-iŏgnomist**, S.: fisionomo, *m.* **-iŏgnomy**, S.: fisionomia, *f.* **-iolŏgical**, ADJ.: fisiologico. **-iŏlogist**, S.: fisiologico, *m.* **-iŏlogy**, S.: fisiologia, metafisica, *f.*

phytŏ-graphy, S.: fitografia, descrizione delle piante, *f.* **-logy**, S.: fitologia, *f.*

pi, S.: (*typ.*) refusi, *m. pl.*

piăc-ular, **-ulous**, ADJ.: espiatorio, purgativo.

pia-măter, S.: (*anat.*) piamadre, *f.*

pi-ănist, S.: pianista, *m.* **-ăno**, S.: pianoforte, piano, *m.*: *grand* —, pianoforte a coda; *square* —, piano quadrato; *upright* —, piano ritto. **-ăno-maker**, S.: fabbricatore di pianoforti, *m.*

piăster, S.: piastra, *f.* (moneta).

piăzza, S.: colonnato, portico, *m.*

pica, S.: voglia di donna gravida, *f.*; (*print.*) cicerone, *m.*

picarŏon, S.: rubatore, ladro, *m.*

piccage, S.: dazio che pagasi nei mercati, *m.*

piccolo, S.: flauto piccolo, *m.*

pick 1, S.: mazzuolo, *m.*; scelta, *f.* **pick** 2, TR.: cogliere, scegliere; nettare, mondare; INTR.: mangiare delicatamente: — *a bird*, spennare un uccello; — *a bone*, rosicchiare un osso; — *a lock*, aprire una serratura col grimaldello; — *pockets*, truffare, giuntare; — *a quarrel with one*, attacarla con uno; — *one's teeth*, nettarsi i denti; —*wool*, cardare, spilluccherare; — *out*, svellere; togliere; stentare; — *up*, beccare, pigliar su; raccogliere, raccattare; trovare.

pickaninny, S.: bambino negro, *m.*

pick-aback, **-apack**, ADV.: a modo di balla addosso. **-ax(e)**, S.: zappa, *f.*, piccone, *m.* **-back**, ADJ.: addossato. **-ed**, ADJ.: puntuto; scelto (cf. *pick*). **-edness**, S.: affettazioni, *f. pl.*

picker, S.: coglitore; sceglitore, *m.*: ... —, stuzzicorecchi, *m.*; *tooth* —, stuzzicadenti, *m.*; — *of quarrels*, accatta- ... *m.*

... S.: luccetto, *m.* (pesce).

... picchetto, *m.*

... -amoia, *f.*; stato, *m.*: *be* ... al acconciato; essere ... **pickle** 2, TR.: ... tare. **-d**, ADJ.: ... **-herring**, S.:

... ladro, *m.* ... taglia-

borse, *m.* **-thanks**, S.: affannone; adulatore, *m.* **-tooth**, S.: stuzzicadenti, *m.*

pic(k)nic(k), S.: festa campestre, *f.*, pranzo nel campo (dove ciascuno contribuisce la sua parte), *m.*

pictŏrial, ADJ.: illustrato, ornato.

pictur-e 1, S.: pittura, *f.*; ritratto, quadro, *m.*: *sit for one's* —, farsi ritrarre. **-e** 2, TR.: dipingere, rappresentare. **-e-drawer**, S.: pittore, dipintore, *m.* **-e-drawing**, S.: arte del dipingere; pittura, *f.* **-e-frame**, S.: cornice (di un quadro), *f.* **-e-gallery**, S.: galleria dei quadri, pinacoteca, *f.* **-ĕsque**, ADJ.: pittoresco.

piddl-e, INTR.: spilluzzicare; baloccare. **-er**, S.: che spilluzzica. **-ing**, S.: bagattella, cosa frivola, *f.*

pie 1, S.: pasticcio, *m.* **pie** 2, S.: pica, gazza, *f.* **pie** 3 = *pi.* **-bald**, ADJ.: pezzato, nero e bianco.

piec-e, S.: pezzo; frammento, *m.*; pezza, parte, *f.*; tozzo; moccolo, moccolino; cannone, *m.*: *a*—, ciascuno; — *of bread*, tozzo di pane; — *of cloth*, pezza di panno; — *of ordnance*, cannone, *m.*; *break to* —*s*, spezzare, infrangere; — *of wit*, detto arguto, *m.* **-e** 2, TR.: rappezzare, racconciare; metter un pezzo, giungere; INTR.: giungersi, unirsi. **-eless**, ADJ.: intero, senza pezzo. **-emeal**, ADJ.; ADV.: solo, distinto; separato; pezzo a pezzo, poco a poco. **-er**, S.: rappezzatore, racconciatore, *m.*

pied, ADJ.: pezzato, di vari colori. **-ness**, S.: varietà di colori, *f.*

pier, S.: pilastro da ponti; molo, *m.*

pierc-e, TR.: forare, pertugiare; penetrare; muovere.. **-er**, S.: foratoio, succhio, *m.* **-ing**, ADJ.: pungente; penetrante; acuto; sottile. **-ingly**, ADV.: in modo pungente, acutamente; sottilmente. **-ingness**, S.: acutezza; sottigliezza; vivacità, *f.*

pier-glass, S.: specchio grande, *m.*

pi-etism, S.: pietismo, *m.* **-etist**, S.: pietista, *m.* **-ety**, S.: pietà; religione, divozione, *f.*

pig 1, S.: porco, porcello, porcastro, porchetto, *m.*: — *of lead*, lastra di piombo, *f.* **pig** 2, INTR.: fare i porcelli, figliare. **-badger**, S.: tasso porco, *m.*

pigeon, S.: colombo, piccione, *m.*: *young* —, piccioncino, piccioncello, *m.*; *wild* —, piccione selvatica. **-house**, S.: colombaio, *m.*, colombaia, *f.* **-hole**, S.: cestino, *m.* **-pie**, S.: pasticcio di piccioni, *m.* **-livered**, ADJ.: mite; affabile, timido.

piggin, S.: orciuolo, *m.*, secchia, *f.*

pig-headed, ADJ.: balordo, stupido.

pigment, S.: belletto, liscio; colore, *m.*

omicciattolo, *m.* **shrub** 2, TR.: battere, bastonare. **-bery**, S.: luogo piantato d' arbusti, *m.* **-by**, ADJ.: pieno d' arbuscelli.

shrŭg 1, S.: ristringimento delle spalle, *m.* **shrug** 2, TR.: stringere; INTR.: ristringersi: — *the shoulders*, crollare le spalle.

shrŭnk(en), ADJ.: scorciato, ritirato.

shŭd-der, INTR.: tremare di paura, abbrividare. **-der(ing)**, S.: tremore, tremito, *m.*

shŭf-fle 1, S.: scompiglio, *m.*; truffa, furberia, *f.*; sotterfugio, *m.* **-fle** 2, TR.: mescolare; confondere; ingannare, truffare; usare di sotterfugi; INTR.: sforzarsi: — *cards*, mescolare le carte: — *one off*, disfarsi d' alcuno. **-fler**, S.: furbo, truffatore, ingannatore, *m.* **-fling**, ADJ.: che spinge; evasivo, rancante: S.: sotterfugio, *m.*; furberia, *f.*, artifizio, *m.*, astuzia, *f.* **-flingly**, ADV.: sconciamente, con astuzia.

shŭn, TR.: evitare; scampare, fuggire. **-less**, ADJ.: inevitabile.

shŭt 1, ADJ.: chiuso: sciolto (cf. *shut*). **shut** 2, S.: chiuso, luogo chiuso, *m.*; portella, *f.* **shut** 3, IRR.: TR.: chiudere, rinchiudere, riserrare; INTR.: chiudersi: — *in*, rinchiudere; — *out*, escludere; chiudere la porta ad uno; — *up*, conchiudere; rinchiudere. **-ter**, S.: che chiude; paravento, *m.*

shŭttle, S.: spola, spuola, *f.* **-cock**, S.: volante, *m.* (giuoco).

shȳ 1, ADJ.: ritroso, schifo, contegnoso. **shy** 2, INTR.: pigliar ombra, rincularsi. **-ly**, ADV.: con ritrosia, vergognosamente. **-ness**, S.: ritrosia; peritanza, *f.*

sib†, S.: parente, consanguinea, *m.*

sibi-lant, ADJ.: sibilante, sibiloso. **-lā-tion**, S.: sibilo, fischio, *m.*

sibyl, S.: sibilla; indovinatrice, *f.* **-line**, ADJ.: sibillino.

sicamore, S.: sicomoro, *m.*

sic-cate, TR.: seccare. **-cātion**, S.: seccare. **-city**, S.: siccità, secchezza, aridità, *f.*

sice, S.: due sei (al giuoco de' dadi).

sick, ADJ.: ammalato, indisposto, infermo; fastidito: *feel* —, sentirsi male: — *of*, disgustato di. **-bed**, S.: letto dell' infermo, *m.* **-en**, TR.: render ammalato, render debole; INTR.: ammalarsi. **-ish**, ADJ.: poco ammalato.

sickl-e, S.: falce, falcinola, *f.*, falcetto, *m.* **-eman**, **-er**, S.: falciatore, mietitore, *m.*

sick-liness, S.: disposizione inferma, *f.* **-ly**, ADJ.: malaticcio, infermiccio: — *weather*, tempo malsano, *m.* **-ness**, S.: malattia, infermità, *f.*: *falling* —, mal caduco, *m.*, epilessia, *f.*; *great* —, peste, contagione, *f.*; *green* —, itterizia, *f.*

side 1, S.: lato, canto; fianco, *m.*; pagina, facciata (d' un libro); parte; fazione, *f.*: *the weak* —, il lato debole; *on all* —*s*, per ogni lato; *on that* —, da quella banda; *on the other* —, dall' altra banda, dall' altra parte; *on this* — *of*, di qua di; *on both* —*s*, dalle due bande; *right* —, dritto (d' un panno), *m.*; *wrong* —, verso, rovescio (d' un panno), *m.*; — *of a hill*, pendio d' un colle, *m.*; — *of a river*, sponda d' un fiume, *f.*; *speak on one's* —, parlare in favore d' alcuno; *take one's* —, pigliar le parti d' uno; *walk by one's* —, caminare a lato di uno. **side** 2, ADJ.: laterale; obbliquo. **side** 3, INTR.: pigliare la parte. **-blow**, S.: rovescione, *m.* **-board**, S.: buffetto, *m.*, credenza, *f.* **-box**, S.: palchetto (*m.*) o loggia da canto del teatro, *f.* **-face**, S.: testa del profilo, *f.* **-glance**, S.: occhiata obbliqua, *f.* **-long**, ADJ.: laterale, da canto; ADV.: a traverso, obbliquamente.

sider, S.: partigiano, *m.*

sideral, **sidēreal**, ADJ.: siderale, astrale.

side-saddle, S.: sella da donna, *f.* **-sman**, S.: assistente del sacristano, *m.* **-motion**, S.: movimento obbliquo, *m.* **-walk**, S.: marciapiede, *m.* **-ways**, **-wise**, ADV.: a traverso, a sghembo; da canto, lateralmente. **-wind**, S.: (*mar.*) vento in fianco, *m.*

sidle, INTR.: camminare per fianco.

siege 1, S.: assedio: seggio, *m.* **siege** 2, TR.: assediare, mettere l' assedio a.

siĕsta, S.: meriggiana, *f.*, sonnicello (dopo il pranzo), *m.*: *take a* —, meriggiare, far la meriggiana.

sieve, S.: staccio, crivello, vaglio, *m.* **-maker**, S.: stacciaio, *m.*

sift, TR.: stacciare, crivellare, vagliare; investigare; esaminare; scovare: — *out*, procurare di scoprire. **-er**, S.: vagliatore; esaminatore, *m.* **-ing**, S.: stacciatura, vagliatura; inchiesta, *f.*

sigh 1, S.: sospiro, *m.*: *heave a* —, mandar fuori un sospiro. **sigh** 2, INTR.: sospirare. **-er**, S.: sospiratore, *m.* **-ing**, ADJ.: sospirante, sospiroso; S.: sospiro, *m.*

sight, S.: vista; prospettiva; mira, *f.*; spettacolo, *m.*; occhi, *m. pl.*: *at* —, a vista; *at first* —, a prima vista, subito; *by* —, di vista; *in the* — *of*, in presenza di; *come in* —, apparire; *dazzle the* —, abbagliare la vista; *know one by* —, conoscer alcuno di vista; *lose* — *of*, perder di vista; *vanish out of* —, svanire; *out of* —, *out of mind*, fuori di vista, fuori di mente. **-fulness**, S.: acutezza di vista, *f.* **-less**, ADJ.: cieco. **-liness**, S.: bell' aspetto, *m.* **-ly**, ADJ.: vistoso, di bella presenza.

sigil, S.: sigillo, suggello, *m.*

pin-maker, S.: spillettaio, *m.* **-money**, S.: spille, *f. pl.*, danaro lampante, *m.*
pinnace, S.: scappavia, *f.* (barca).
pin-nacle, S.: pinnacolo; colmo, *m.* **-nated**, ADJ.: (*bot.*) pennuto. **-ner**, S.: spillettaio, *m.*; barba di cuffia, *f.*
pint, S.: foglietta; mezza bottiglia, *f.*
pionéer, S.: pioniere; marraiuolo; guastatore, *m.*
piony, S.: (*bot.*) peonia, *f.*
pious, ADJ.: pio, religioso, divoto, **-ly**, ADV.: piamente, religiosamente. **-ness**, S.: pietà, divozione, *f.*
pip 1, S.: pipita, *f.* **pip** 2, INTR.: pigolare; garrire.
pip-e 1, S.: tubo; condotto, *m.*; pippa; zampogna, *f.*; zufolo; ruolo, catalogo, *m.*; (*fig.*) voce; cantatrice, *f.*: — *of wine*, botte di vino, *f.* **-e** 2, (IN)TR.: zampognare; aver la voce acuta. **-er**, S.: zampognatore, suonator di flauto, *m.* **-e-tree**, S.: ghianda unguentaria, *f.* **-ing**, ADJ.: fiacco, malaticcio; fervido.
pipkin, S.: pignata; pentola, *f.*
pippin, S.: mela appiuola, *f.*
piqu-ancy, S.: acutezza, asprezza, sottigliezza, *f.* **-ant**, ADJ.: pungente, acuto. **-antly**, ADV.: in modo pungente. **-e**, S.: briga; offesa, *f.*; puntiglio, *m.* **-e**, TR.: piccare; irritare, offendere; REFL.: piccarsi: — *one's self upon*, picarsi di.
piquét, S.: piochetto, *m.* (giuoco di carte).
pi-racy, S.: pirateria, ruberia, *f.* **-rate** 1, S.: pirato, corsale, *m.* **-rate** 2, (IN)TR.: corseggiare, rubare; contraffare (libri): —*d edition*, ristampa furtiva, *f.* **-rát-ical**, ADJ.: piratico. **-ráticallly**, ADV.: da pirato.
pirouétte 1, S.: giravolta, *f.* **pirouette** 2, INTR.: fare giravolta, piroettare.
pis-cary, S.: privilegio della pesca, *m.* **-catory**, ADJ.: pescatorio. **-ces**, S. PL.: (*astr.*) pesci, *m. pl.* **-cine**, S.: pescina, *f.*; serbatoio, *m.* **-cívorous**, ADJ.: che si pasce di pesce.
pish 1, INTERJ.: saetta! via! **pish** 2, INTR.: braveggiare, esprimere disprezzo.
pismire, S.: formica, formicola, *f.*
piss 1, S.: orina, *f.* **piss** 2, INTR.: orinare, fare acqua. **-abed**, S.: (*bot.*) macerone, *m.*
pistáchio, S.: pistacchio, *m.* **-tree**, S.: pistacchio, *m.*
piste, S.: pesta, traccia, *f.*, vestigio, *m.*
pistil, S.. (*bot.*) pistillo, *m.*
pis-tol 1, S.: pistola, *f.*: *fire a* —, scaricare una pistola. **-tol** 2, TR.: tirar pistolettate, ammazzare con pistolettate. **-tol-bag**, **-tol-case**, S.: fonda di pistola, *f.* **-tóle**, S.: doppia, *f.* (moneta). **-tolet**, S.: pistoletto, *m.* **-tol-shot**, S.: pistolettata, *f.*, colpo di pistola, *m.*
piston, S.: stantuffo; pistone, *m.*
pit 1, S.: fossa, *f.*, fosso; abbisso; sepolcro; (*theat.*) pianterreno, *m.*, platea, *f.*: *arm*—, ascella, *f.*; *coal*—, miniera di carbone, *f.*; *gravel*—, cava di renella, ghiaia, *f.*; *sand*—, renaio, *m.* **pit** 2, TR.: scavare, incavare; INTR.: cavarsi.
pitapat, S.: palpitamento del cuore, *m.*: *my heart goes* —, il cuore mi palpita.
pitch 1, S.: pece, *f.* **pitch** 2, S.: altezza; cima, *f.*; grado, *m.* **pitch** 3, IRR.; TR.: impeciare; ficcare, piantare; lanciare; (*nav.*) spalmare; INTR.: arrestarsi, fermarsi: — *a camp*, porsi a campo; — *a ship*, spalmare un bastimento; — *into one*, dar addosso a uno; — *upon*, sciegliere; — *upon one's head*, cimbottolare. **-ed**, ADJ.: impeciato, ecc. (cf. *pitch*): — *battle*, battaglia campale. **-er**, S.: brocca, *f.* **-fork**, S.: forca, *f.*, forcone, *m.* **-iness**, S.: oscurità, *f.* **-ing**, S.: (*nav.*) l' attuffarsi; il ficcare, il rollare. **-tree**, S.: pino, *m.* (albero). **-y**, ADJ.: impeciato; oscuro, fosco.
pit-coal, S.: carbone di miniera, *m.*
piteous, ADJ.: dolente, tristo, misero. **-ly**, ADV.: tristamente, miseramente. **-ness**, S.: miseria; compassione, tristezza, *f.*
pitfall, S.: trabocchetto, *m.*
pith, S.: midollo, *m.*, midolla; energia, *f.*: — *of a quill*, anima della penna, *f.* **-ily**, ADV.: vigorosamente, con energia. **-iness**, S.: vigore, *m.*, energia, *f.* **-less**, ADJ.: senza midolla; senza energia. **-y**, ADJ.: midolloso; energico, spiritoso.
piti-able, ADJ.: degno di compassione, misero. **-ableness**, S.: stato degno di compassione, *m.* **-ful**, ADJ.: compassionevole, miserabile. **-fully**, ADV.: compassionevolmente. **-fulness**, S.: compassione; pietà, misericordia, *f.* **-less**, ADJ.: spietato, fiero, crudele. **-lessly**, ADV.: spietatamente, crudelmente. **-lessness**, S.: spietatezza, crudeltà, *f.*
pit-saw, S.: sega grande, *f.*
pittance, S.: pietanza, porzioncella, *f.*
pitted, ADJ.: butterato.
pit-úitary, ADJ.: pituitario, della pituita. **pit-uite**, S.: pituita; flemma, *f.*; umor pituitoso, *m.* **-úitous**, ADJ.: pituitoso.
pity 1, S.: pietà, compassione, *f.*: *'tis a* —, è un danno, è un peccato; *for —'s sake, out of* —, per pietà, per carità; *what a —!* che peccato! **pity** 2, TR.: compatire, compiangere.
pivot, S.: perno, cardine, *m.*
pix, S.: pisside, *f.*
placability, S.: clemenza, *f.*
plácable, ADJ.: placabile; clemente. **-ness** = placability.

simulatore; ipocrita, *m.* **-late**, INTR.: simulare. **-lātion**, S.: simulazione, *f.*
simultāneous, ADJ.: simultaneo. **-ly**, ADV.: unitamente, tutti insieme. **-ness**, S.: simultaneità, *f.*, sincronismo, *m.*
sin 1, S.: peccato, fallo, *m.;* colpa, *f.*
sin 2, INTR.: peccare, commettere peccato, fallire.
sinapism, S.: (*med*) senapismo, *m.*
since, PREP., ADV.: di poi, dopo; da, da ... in qua; poichè: *long* —, molto tempo fa; *not long* —, non è lungo tempo, poco fa; *many years* —, molti anni sono; *a while* —, non ha guari, poco fa; — *yesterday*, da ieri in qua; — *when?* da quando in qua?
sin-cēre, ADJ.: sincero, franco; schietto, onesto. **-cērely**, ADV.: sinceramente; schiettamente. **-cēreness**, **-cĕrity**, S.: sincerità; schiettezza, *f.*
sine, S.: (*geom.*) sino, seno, *m.*
sinecure, S.: beneficio senza cura, *m.*
si'new, S.: nervo, nerbo; tendine, *m.* **-ed**, ADJ.: nervoso, nerboso; vigoroso. **-less**, ADJ.: senza nervi, debole. **-y**, ADJ.: nervoso, nerboso; vigoroso, forte.
sinful, ADJ.: criminale, vizioso, corrotto **-ly**, ADV.: criminalmente, viziosamente. **-ness**, S.: corruzione; trasgressione, *f.*
sing, IRR.; TR.: cantare, canterellare; lodare, celebrare; IRR.; INTR.: cantare; garrire.
singe, TR.: abbruciacchiare, abbrustiare.
sing-er, S.: cantante, cantatore, *m.* **-ing**, S.: canto, cantare; garrire, *m.* **-ing-book**, S.: libro di canti, *m.* **-ing-boy**, S.: ragazzo che canta in coro, *m.* **-ing-man**, S.: cantore, corista, *m.* **-ing-master**, S.: maestro di musica, *m.*
sin-gle 1, ADJ.: solo, unico; semplice: — *combat*, duello, *m.;* — *game*, semplice partita, *f.;* — *life*, celibato, *m.;* — *man*, scapolo, smogliato, *m.;* — *woman*, zitella; donna nubile, *f.; live* —, viver nel celibato. **-gle** 2, TR.: separare, scegliere; segnare. **-gle-handed**, ADJ.: monco d'una mano; solo, senza soccorso. **-gle-hearted**, ADJ.: sincero, franco, schietto. **-gleness**, S.: semplicità; sincerità, schiettezza, *f.* **-gly**, ADV.: separatamente; onestamente.
sing-song, S.: canto monotono, *m.*
singu-lar, ADJ.: singolare, particolare; raro; bizzarro: — *number*, numero singolare, *m.* **-lărity**, S.: singolarità, particolarità; rarità, *f.* **-larize**, TR.: singolarizzare; separare. **-larly**, ADV.: singolarmente, particolarmente.
singult†, S.: singulto, *m.*
sinis-ter, ADJ.: sinistro; cattivo, ingiusto; malizioso; infelice, funesto. **-trous**, ADJ.: sinistro; assurdo, perverso. **-trously**, ADV.: sinistramente; assurdamente, perversamente.
sink 1, S.: sentina, cloaca, *f.;* lavatoio, *m.*
sink 2, IRR.; TR.: sommergere, affondare; scavare; opprimere; disfare, distruggere, rovinare; avventurare; IRR.; TR.: attuffarsi, andare a fondo; abbassarsi, abbattersi; soccombere; cadere, decrescere; penetrare: — *a ship*, mandare a fondo un vascello. **-ing**, ADJ.: cadente, ecc.; S.: affondare, abbassamento, *m.:* — *fund*, cassa d'ammortizzazione, *f.* **-ing-paper**, S.: carta che beve l'inchiostro, *f.*
sin-less, ADJ.: senza peccato, immacolato. **-lessness**, S.: esenzione da peccato, impeccabilità, *f.* **-ner**, S.: peccatore, offenditore; peccatrice, *f.* **-ning**, S.: peccare, *m.* **-offering**, S.: offerta espiatoria, *f.*
sin-oper, **-ople**, S.: sinopia, senopia, *f.*
sin-uate, TR.: rendere sinuoso; INTR.: serpere. **-uātion**, **-uŏsity**, S.: sinuosità; circuito; seno, *m.* **-uous**, ADJ.: sinuoso, torto.
sinus, S.: seno (di mare), golfo, *m.*
sip 1, S.: sorso, centellino, *m.* **sip** 2, (IN)TR.: sorsare, bere a sorsi; gocciare.
siphon, S.: sifone, tubo, *m.*
sipid, ADJ.: gustoso.
sipper, S.: che sorseggia, che beve a piccoli sorsi.
sippet, S.: fettolina, fetticella (di pane), *f.*
sir, S.: signore, *m.*
sire, S.: sire, *m.*, maestà, *f.;* (*poet.*) padre.
siren, S.: sirena, ninfa del mare, *f.* **-ize**, TR.: far da sirena, incantare.
Sirius, S.: (*astr.*) sirio, *m.*, canicola, *f.*
sirloin, S.: lonza, lombata, *f.*
sirŏcco, S.: scilocco, *m.*
sirrah, S.: briccone, mariuolo, *m.*
sirup, S.: siroppo, sciroppo, *m.* **-ed**, ADJ.: dolce come lo sciroppo. **-y**, ADJ.: assomigliante allo sciroppo.
siskin, S.: lucherino, *m.* (uccello).
sister, S.: sorella, sirocchia, *f.: little* —, sorellina, *f.* **-hood**, S.: qualità di sorella; affinità di sorella, *f.;* sorelle, *f. pl.* **-in-law**, S.: cognata, *f.* **-ly**, ADJ.: di sorella, sirocchevole.
sit, IRR.; TR.: posare, collocare; TR.: sedere; stare; esser situato; essere; riposarsi; adunarsi: — *close to one's work*, lavorare assiduamente; — *for one's picture*, farsi dipingere; — *in the sun*, stare al sole; — *still*, stare fermo; non muoversi; — *at table*, sedersi a tavola; — *well*, andare bene; — *down*, sedersi; restare; — *out*, essere senza impiego; — *up*, levarsi; — *up in bed*, tenersi assiso sul letto.
sit-e, S.: sito, *m.;* situazione, positura, *f.* **-ed**†, ADJ.: situato.

plausibility, S.: plausibilità; apparenza, *f.* **pläusibl-e**, ADJ.: plausibile; apparente. **-eness** = *plausibility*. **-y**, ADV.: in modo plausibile, con applauso.

play1, S.: giuoco, divertimento; spettacolo, *m.*, commedia, *f.*: *fair* —, libero giuoco, giuoco senza inganni; *give one fair* —, lasciar fare ad uno; *foul* —, frode, truffa, *f.*; *go to the* —, andare alla commedia; *keep one in* —, tenere uno a bada. **play**2, (IN)TR.: giuocare; scherzare; rappresentare; beffare; burlare, burlarsi: — *away*, perdere (il giuoco); — *at cards*, giuocare alle carte; — *fair*, giuocare onestamente; — *the fool*, fare il pazzo; — *foul*, truffare, ingannare; — *a game*, giuocare una partita; — *the knave*, fare delle furfanterie; — *pranks*, fare delle suo; — *sure*, giuocare a giuoco sicuro; — *one a trick*, fare una burla; — *the truant*, fuggir la scuola; — *upon an instrument*, suonare uno strumento; — *upon a person*, farsi giuoco di alcuno; — *the wanton*, trastullare. **-book**, S.: libro di commedie, *m.* **-day**, S.: giorno di festa, giorno di vacanza, *m.* **-debt**, S.: debito d' onore, *m.* **-er**, S.: giuocatore, attore, *m.* **-fellow**, S.: compagno di giuoco, *m.* **-ful**, ADJ.: giocoso, scherzevole. **-fulness**, S.: facezia, burla, *f.* **-house**, S.: teatro, *m.* **-some**, ADJ.: scherzevole; allegro, gaio. **-someness**, S.: scherzo, giuoco; trastullo, *m.* **-thing**, S.: trastullo, *m.*; bagatella, *f.* **-wright**, S.: facitore di commedie, *m.*

plĕa, S.: difesa; scusa, *f.*; pretesto, colore, *m.*

plĕach, TR.: piegare.

plĕad, TR.: difendere; allegare; INTR.: litigare, piatire: — *guilty*, confessarsi reo; — *not guilty*, dichiararsi innocente, respingere l' accusa; — *ignorance*, allegare causa d' ignoranza. **-able**, ADJ.: che può essere litigato. **-er**, S.: litigante, avvocato; piatitore, *m.* **-ing**, S.: litigare, piatire: —*s*, *pl.*, dibattimento, *m.*

plĕasan-ce, S.: gaiezza; piacevolezza; baia, *f.* **-t**, ADJ.: piacevole, affabile, cortese; grato; gaio: *a* — *voyage!* buon viaggio! **-tly**, ADV.: piacevolmente; cortesemente; gaiamente. **-tness**, S.: piacevolezza, amenità, affabilità, cortesia. **-try**, S.: facezia, gaiezza; piacevolezza, *f.*

plĕas-e, TR.: piacere; contentare, soddisfare; compiacere a: — *one's self*, compiacersi, dilettarsi; far da modo suo; *as you* —, come vi piacerà; *if you* —, se v' è grato; *be well* —*d with*, compiacersi in ... esser contento di; — *tell me*, *do as you* —, fate quel ... —, di difficile con... contento, felice. **-ing**, ADJ.: grato, gustoso; accetto. **-ingly**, ADV.: con piacere, piacevolmente. **-ingness**, S.: piacevolezza, *f.*

plĕasur-able, ADJ.: piacevole, delizioso, ameno. **-ableness**, S.: piacevolezza, *f.* **-ably**, ADV.: piacevolmente. **-e**1, S.: piacere, divertimento, diletto, *m.*; voglia, *f.*: *at* —, a piacere, a piacimento; *your* —*?* che domanda? **-e**2, TR.: piacere; contentare, soddisfare. **-boat**, S.: battello di piacere, *m.* **-ground**, S.: giardino inglese, *m.*

plebĕian, S.: plebeo, volgare; S.: uomo plebeo, *m.*

plĕbiscite, S.: plebiscito, *m.*

plĕctrum, S.: plettro, *m.*

plĕd-ge1, S.: pegno; mallevadore, *m.*, sicurtà; testimonianza, *f.*; ostaggio, *m.* **-ge**2, TR.: impegnare, dare in pegno: — *one's self*, impegnarsi, obbligarsi; — *in drinking*, fare ragione. **-get**, S.: (*surg.*) piumacciuolo, *m.*

Plē-iads, **-iades**, S. PL.: (*astr.*) pleiadi, *f. pl.*

plĕna-rily, ADV.: pienamente, totalmente. **-riness**, S.: ripienezza; plenitudine, *f.* **-ry**, ADJ.: plenario, intero.

plenilū-nary, ADJ.: plenilunare. **-ne** *plĕn-*, S.: plenilunio, *m.*

plenipo-tence, S.: plenipotenza, *f.* **-tent**, ADJ.: plenipotenziale. **-tĕntiary**, S.: plenipotenziario, *m.*

plĕn-ish†, TR.: riempire. **-itude**, S.: plenitudine, pienezza, *f.*

plĕn-teous, ADJ.: abbondante, copioso; fertile. **-teously**, ADV.: abbondantemente, in copia. **-teousness**, S.: abbondanza, copia; fertilità, *f.* **-tiful**, ADV.: abbondevole. **-tifully**, ADV.: in abbondanza, copiosamente. **-tifulness**, S.: abbondanza, copia; fertilità, *f.* **-ty**, S.: abbondanza, copia, quantità, *f.*

plĕo-nasm, S.: pleonasmo, *m.* **-năstic**, ADJ.: pleonastico.

plĕsh†, S.: pantano, *m.*

plĕth-ora, S.: pletora, abbondanza di sangue, *f.* **-orĕtic**, **-ŏric**, ADJ.: pletorico. **-ory** = *plethora*.

pleū-risy, S.: (*med.*) pleurisia, *f.* **-ritic(al)**, ADJ.: pleuritico.

plĕvin, S.: (*jur.*) permissione di vendere i beni, *f.*

pliability, S.: pieghevolezza, flessibilità, *f.*

pli-able, ADJ.: pieghevole, flessibile. **-ableness**, **-ancy**, S.: flessibilità; docilità, *f.* **-ant**, ADJ.: pieghevole, flessibile; arrendevole. **-antness**, S.: pieghevolezza, flessibilità, *f.*

plica, S.: (*med.*) plica polonica, *f.*

plic-ation, **plic-ature**, S.: piega, riga, *f.*

do. **-colour**, S.: azzurro, turchino, *m.* **-coloured**, ADJ.: azzurrigno. **-dyed**, ADJ.: tinto d' azzurro. **-ed**, ADJ.: circondato da cieli. **-ey**, ADJ.: etereo. **-ish**, ADJ.: azzurriccio, turchiniccio. **-lark**, S.: allodola, *f.* **-light**, S.: abbaino, *m.* **-rocket**, S.: razzo, *m.* **-scraper**, S.: piccola vela sopra al pappafico, *f.;* molto alto edifizio.

slăb 1, ADJ.: glutinoso, viscoso, tenace. **slab** 2, S.: fango, limo, *m.*, melma; belletta, *f.:* — *of marble*, tavola di marmo, *f.*

slăb-ber, (IN)TR.: bavare; sporcare, imbrattare; effondere. **-ber-chops**, **-berer**, S.: bavoso, *m.* **-bering**, ADJ.: bavoso, sporco; S.: sporcare, *m.*

slăb-biness, S.: stato melmoso, *m.* **-by**, ADJ.: fangoso, viscoso, umido.

slăck 1, ADJ.: sciolto, lento; negligente, infingardo: — *in payment*, lento nel pagare. **slack** 2, S.: bracia, brace; valletta, *f.* **slack(en)** 3, TR.: slegare, allentare; ritardare; negligere; stemperare; estinguere; (IN)TR.: allentarsi, rallentarsi; diminuire: — *one's hand*, prendere riposo, ricrearsi; — *the rein*, allargare il freno; — *one's speed*, rallentare i passi. **-ly**, ADV.: lentamente; trascuratamente, pigramente. **-ness**, S.: rilassamento, *m.;* tardezza, negligenza, *f.*

slāde†, S.: valletta, *f.*

slăg, S.: scoria, *f.*, rosticci (de' metalli), *m. pl.*

slāle, S.: (*weav.*) spola, spuola, *f.*

slāk-e 1, S.: fiocco di neve, *m.* **-e** 2, TR.: estinguere; stemperare; liquefare: — *one's thirst*, smorzarsi la sete. **-ing**, S.: stemperamento, *m.*

slăm 1, S.. cappotto, *m.* (al giuoco delle carte). **slam** 2, TR.: macellare; fare tutte le bazze.

slămkin †, S.: donna sudicia, *f.*

slănder 1, S.: calunnia, maldicenza, diffamazione, *f.* **slander** 2, TR.: calunniare, diffamare. **-er**, S.: calunniatore, maldicente, diffamatore, *m.* **-ing**, ADJ.: calunnioso; S.: calunnia, maldicenza, *f.* **-ous**, ADJ.: calunnioso, maldicente. **-ously**, ADV.: calunniosamente. **-ousness**, S.: calunnia, maldicenza, *f.*

slăng, S.: gergo, parlare corrotto, *m.*

slănk, S.: alga marina, *f.*

slănt 1, TR.: volgere obbliquamente. **slant(ing)** 2, ADJ.: traverso, obbliquo. **-ingly**, **-wise**, ADV.: di scancio, obbliquamente.

slăp 1, ADV.: con un colpo subito e violento. **slap** 2, S.: colpo, schiaffo, *m.*, guanciata, *f.* **slap** 3, TR.: schiaffeggiare, battere; percuotere: — *up*, inghiottire, ingoiare. **-dash**, ADV.: in un colpo, in un subito, a un tratto.

slāpe, ADJ.: sdrucciolo, liscio.

slăppy, ADJ.: melmoso, pantanoso.

slăsh 1, S.: ferita, staffilata, *f.*, sguarcio, sfregio, taglio, *m.:* — *of a whip*, sferzata ben applicata, *f.* **slash** 2, TR.: staffilare, tagliare, sfregiare.

slătch, S.: (*nav.*) corda sciolta, *f.;* vento momentaneo, *m.*

slāt-e 1, S.: lavagna, *f.* **-e** 2, TR.: coprire di lavagne. **-quarry**, S.: cava della lavagna, *f.* **-er**, S.: conciatetti, *m.*

slătter(n) 1, (IN)TR.: esser neghittoso; perdere per negligenza. **slattern** 2, S.: donna neghittosa, donna sudicia, *f.* **-ly**, ADJ.: neghittoso, sudicio; ADV.: neghittosamente.

slāty, ADJ.: lavagnoso, di lavagna.

slăughter 1, S.: strage, *f.*, macello, *m.* **slaughter** 2, TR.: ammazzare, macellare, trucidare. **-er**, S.: uccisore, assassino, *m.* **-house**, S.: macello, *m.*, beccheria, *f.* **-man**, S.: beccaio, macellaio, *m.* **-ous**, ADJ.: micidiale.

slāve 1, S.: schiavo, *m.* **slave** 2, TR.: affaticarsi, stentare. **-driver**, S.: aguzzino di schiavi, *m.*

slăver 1, S.: bava, *f.* **slaver** 2, TR.: fare bava, sporcare di bava. **-er** 3, S.: bavoso; minchione, *m.* **-ingly**, ADV.: con bava.

slāve-holder, **-owner**, S.: possessore di schiavi, *m.*

slā-very, S.: schiavitù, servitù, *f.* **-veship**, S.: bastimento da schiavi, *m.* **-vetrade**, S.: tratta dei schiavi (*or* negri), *f.* **-vish**, ADJ.: schiavesco, servile. **-vishly**, ADV.: da schiavo, servilmente. **-vishness**, S.: servilità; bassezza, *f.*

Slavŏnic, ADJ.: slavo; S.: slavo, *m.;* lingua slava, *f.*

slāy 1, S.: pettine (di tessitore), *m.* **slay** 2, IRR.; TR.: uccidere, ammazzare, trucidare. **-er**, S.: ammazzatore, trucidatore, *m.*

slēave, TR.: separare in fila: —*d silk*, seta non lavorata, *f.*

slēazy, ADJ.: rado, tenue, sottile.

slĕd = *sledge*. **-ded**, ADJ.: montato sur una slitta.

slĕdge 1, S.: slitta, treggia, *f.;* traino, *m.* **slĕdge** 2, **-hammer**, S.: martello (di fabbro), *m.*

slēek 1, ADJ.: liscio, pulito; morbido, **sleek** 2, TR.: lisciare, pulire, lustrare. **-ly**, ADV.: pulitamente, lisciamente. **-ness**, S.: lisciamento, *m.* **-stone**, S.: lisciatoio, brunitoio, *m.*

slēep 1, S.: sonno; riposo, *m.*, quiete, *f.* **sleep** 2, IRR.; TR.: dormire; riposarsi: — *again*, raddormentarsi; — *away*, fare passare (per sonno); — *upon*, non darsi briga di. **-er**, S.: dormitore; tentennone, *m.;* (*rail.*) traversa, *f.* **-ful**, ADJ.: oppresso del sonno. **-fulness**, S.: sopore, *m.* **-ily**, ADV.: dormendo; in modo

podĕsta, S.: podestà, *m.* (magistrato).
pŏdge, S.: lagume; pantano, palude, *m.*
pō-em, S.: poema, *m.* **-ęsy**, S.: poesia, *f.* **-et**, S.: poeta; verseggiatore, *m.* **-etăstęr**, S.: poetastro, poetaccio, *m.* **-etess**, S.: poetessa, *f.* **-ĕtic(al)**, ADJ.: poetico, di poesia. **-ĕtically**, ADV.: poeticamente. **-ĕtics**, S. PL.: poetica, *f.* **-etize**, TR.: comporre poesie. **-etry**, S.: poesia, *f.*
pöignan-cy, S.: acutezza, mordacità, *f.* **-t**, ADJ.: acuto, pungente; mordace, satirico. **-tly**, ADV.: acutamente; pungentemente.
pöint 1, S.: punta, *f.*; capo; promontorio; punto, passo; momento; stato; (*rail.*) ago, *m.*: *at all —s*, totalmente; *in — of*, in caso di; *— of honour*, punto d' onore, *m.*; *— of time*, momento, *m.*; *be on* (*upon*) *the — of*, stare sul punto, essere per; *hit the —*, dar nel punto; *make it a —*, avere per regola. **point** 2, TR.: appuntare; aguzzare; puntare; INTR.: punteggiare; mostrare col dito: *— a cannon*, appuntare (voltare) il cannone; (*nav.*) *— a sail*, mettere le rizze ad una vela; *— at*, indicare, mostrare; *— one's finger at*, mostrare a dito. **-blank**, ADV.: di punto in bianco; direttamente; *shoot —*, tirare nel punto. **-ed**, ADJ.: appuntato, acuto, puntuto. **-edly**, ADV.: espressamente; chiaramente. **-edness**, acutezza; arguzia, *f.* **-ęr**, S.: appuntatore; cane da fermo, *m.* **-ing**, S.: puntuazione, *f.*; punteggiare, *m.* **-ing-stock**, S.: trastullo, scherzo, *m.* **-less**, ADJ.: spuntato, ottuso. **-sman**, S.: (*rail.*) guardiano, *m.*
pöi-çe 1, S.: equilibrio; peso, *m.*, gravezza; bilancia, *f.*, bilanciere, *m.* **-se** 2, TR.: pesare, contrappesare; bilanciare: *— down*, opprimere, aggravare.
pöişon 1, S.: veleno, tossico, *m.* **poison** 2, avvelenare, attossicare; infettare, contaminare. **-ęr**, S.: avvelenatore; corrompitore, *m.* **-ing**, S.: attossicamento, *m.* **-ous**, ADJ.: velenoso, nocivo, **-ously**, ADV.: velenosamente, in modo distruttivo. **-ousness**, S.: qualità velenosa, *f.*
[...]**k-e** 1, S.: tasca, borsa, *f.*; sacchetto, [...]: *buy a pig in a —*, comprare gatta [...] sacco. **-e** 2, TR.: cercare al tasto; [...], frugacchiare; mettere in sacco: [...]*re*, attizzare il fuoco. **-ęr** 1, S.: [...] attizzare il fuoco), forcone, *m.*
[...] di carte americano, *m.*
[...]: *— bear*, orso bian-[...]
[...]olarità, *f.* **-larizā-**[...]
[...] *f.* **-larize**,
[...]
[...] pertica,
[...] *m.*:

barber's —, insegna di barbiere, *f.*; *beat down with a —*, batacchiare. **pole** 3, TR.: ficcare pali in terra. **-axe**, S.: scure, azza, *f.* **-cat**, S.: puzzola, faina, *f.* **-edge**, S.: pergolato, *m.*
polĕm-ic, S.: polemico; controvertista, *m.* **-ic(al)**, ADJ.: polemico. **-ęscope**, S.: polemoscopio, *m.*
pōle-star, S.: stella polare, *f.*
polīce, S.: polizia, *f.*, governo civile, *m.*, amministrazione (d' una città), *f.* **-d**, ADJ.: regolato. **-man**, S.: agente della polizia; (*disp.*) poliziotto, *m.* **-officer**, S.: agente di polizia, *m.*
pŏlicy, S.: politica; accortezza, astuzia, *f.*: *— of insurance*, polizza di sicurtà, *f.*
pŏlish 1, S.: pulimento, *m.*, pulitura, *f.* **polish** 2, TR.: pulire, lisciare; limare; INTR.: divenire pulito. **-able**, ADJ.: che si può pulire. **-edness**, S.: pulitura; eleganza, *f.* **-ęr**, S.: pulitore, lisciatore, *m.* **-ing**, S.: pulimento, *m.*
polīte, ADJ.: pulito, garbato; civile, cortese: *— learning*, le belle lettere. **-ly**, ADV.: pulitamente, cortesemente, civilmente. **-ness**, S.: politezza; garbatezza; cortesia, civiltà, *f.*
politi-c(al), ADJ.: politico, civile, circospetto, prudente. **-cally**, ADV.: politicamente; con artifizio. **-căstęr**, S.: politicastro, *m.*
politịçian, S.: politico; uomo astuto, *m.*
pŏlitic-ly, ADV.: astutamente, accortamente. **-s**, S. PL.: politica, *f.*
pŏliture, S.: pulitura, *f.*, polimento, *m.*
pŏlity, S.: governo civile; ordine, *m.*
pŏlka, S.: polca, *f.*
pōll 1, S.: testa; lista, *f.*; suffragio, *m.*: *demand a —*, domandare uno squittino. **poll** 2, TR.: scapezzare; tosare; votare, squittinare. **poll** 3, S.: pappagallo, *m.*
pŏllard, S.: albero scapezzato; ghiozzo, *m.* (pesce).
pŏllen, S.: cruschello, *m.*, farina; stacciatura, *f.*; (*bot.*) polline, *f.*
pōllęr, S.: tosatore; rubatore; squittinatore, *m.*
pollicitāṭion, S.: promessa, *f.*
pōll-tax, S.: capitazione, *f.*
pollū-te, TR.: sporcare; corrompere. **-tedness**, S.: macchia; contaminazione, *f.* **-tęr**, S.: imbrattatore, corruttore, *m.* **-ṭion**, S.: polluzione, *f.*; contaminamento, *m.*
poltrōon, S.: poltrone, codardo, *m.* **-ęry**, S.: codardia, *f.*
poly-ēdron, S.: poliedro, *m.*
polўgamist, S.: poligamo, *m.* **-gamy**, S.: poligamia.
pŏly-glot, ADJ.: poliglotto: *— bible*, *m.*, poliglotta, *f.* (bibbia). **-gon**, S.: poligo-

no, m. (figura di più lati). '-gonal, ADJ.: poligono. -gram, S.: poligramma, m. -graph, S.: poligrafo, m. '-graphy, S.: poligrafia, f. '-mathy, S.: cognizione generale, f. -p, S.: polpo, polipo, m. -pous, ADJ.: di molti piedi; del polipo. -pus = *polyp*. -scope, S.: occhiale a faccette, m. -syllăbic(al), ADJ.: polisillabo. -syllable, S.: polisillabo, m. -tĕchnic, ADJ.: politecnico. -theism, S.: politeismo, m. -theist, S.: politeista, m. -theistic(al), ADJ.: politeistico.

po-mâceous, ADJ.: pieno di pomi. -mâde, S.: pomato, manteca, f. -mânder, S.: saponetto profumato, m. -mâtum, S.: pomata, f.

pómegranate, S.: melagrana, f.

pomĭferous, ADJ.: pomifero, fruttifero.

pómmel 1, S.: pomo della spada, f. pommel 2, TR.: battere; stregghiare.

pŏmp, S.: pompa, f., splendore, m. -ătic †, ADJ.: pomposo.

pómpion, S.: zucca, f.

pompŏsity, S.: aria pomposa, ostentazione, f.

pŏmpous, ADJ.: pomposo, fastoso, tronfio. -ly, ADV.: pomposamente, con pompa. -ness, S.: pompa, ostentazione, f., splendore, m.

pŏnd, S.: stagno, vivaio, pescaio, m.

pŏnder, (IN)TR.: ponderare, pesare; considerare. -able, ADJ.: che può essere pesato. -al, ADJ.: stimato dal peso. -âtion, S.: pesare; peso, m. -er, S.: pesatore; pensatore, m. -ing, S.: ponderare, m. -ingly, ADV.: ponderatamente. -ŏsity, S.: ponderosità, f.; peso, m. -ous, ADJ.: ponderoso, pesante; grave. -ously, ADV.: pesantemente; gravemente. -ousness, S.: gravezza, gravità, f., pondo, peso, m.

pŏnent, ADJ.: occidentale.

pŏniard 1, S.: pugnale, stiletto, m.: *stab with a* —, pugnalata, f. poniard 2, TR.: pugnalare, stilettare.

pŏnk †, S.: folletto, m.

pŏn-tiff, S.: pontefice, papa, m.: *sovereign* —, sovrano pontefice. -tĭfical, ADJ.: pontificale, di pontefice; S.: pontificale, m. (libro). -tĭfically, ADV.: pontificalmente, a maniera di pontefice. -tĭficate, S.: pontificato, papato, m. -tĭficial, ADJ.: pontificio.

pontōon, S.: pontone, m.: — *train*, equipaggio da ponti, m.

pŏny, S.: bidetto, ronzino, m.

pōodle, S.: cane maltese, m.

pōol, S.: pozzanghera, f.; posta (al giuoco), f.; sorta di biliardo, m.

— woman, povera, f.; — [illegible] to! m.; — woman (girl, [illegible] the —, i poveri, [illegible] -house, S.: asilo dei poveri [illegible] S.: merluzzo, m. (pesce). [illegible] ge sul pauperismo, f. -ly, ADV.: [illegible] mente, meschinamente, [illegible] S.: povertà, indigenza, f. [illegible] tributo alla tassa dei poveri. [illegible] ADJ.: codardo, vile. -spirited[illegible] dappocaggine, codardia, viltà, f.

pŏp 1, S.: piccolo romore [illegible] strepito subito, m. pop 2, TR.: [illegible] stramente; INTR.: sopravvenir[illegible] provviso: — *in*, entrare all' [illegible] — *off*, lanciare; sparare; [illegible] gire; — *out*, andar via, uscire.

pōpe, S.: papa, m. -dom, S.: [illegible] cato, m. -ery, S.: papismo, [illegible]

pŏp-gun, S.: buffo; cannello, [illegible]

pŏpinjay, S.: pappagallo; [illegible] parigino, m.

pōpish, ADJ.: del papa; Cattoli[illegible] no. -ly, ADV.: a modo di papa, [illegible] sta. -ness, S.: papismo, m.

pŏplar, S.: pioppo, oppio, m.: [illegible] —, tremula, alberella, f.

pŏppy, S.: papavero, m.

pŏppycock, S.: (*slang*) pettegol[illegible]

pŏpu-lace, S.: volgo, m., [illegible] -lar, ADJ.: popolare, popolano[illegible] -lărity, S.: popolarità, f.: [illegible] blico, m. -larize, TR.: [illegible] -larly, ADV.: popolarmente; [illegible] te. -larness, S.: popolarità, [illegible] TR.: popolare. -lâtion, S.: [illegible] ne, f.; popolo, m. -lŏsity, S.: [illegible] ne, f. -lous, ADJ.: popoloso, [illegible] -lousness = *populosity*.

pôrcelain, S.: porcellana, f. [illegible] porcellana, m. *pl.*

pôrch, S.: portico, m., piazza, f. [illegible]

pôrcupine, S.: porcospino, m. [illegible]

pōre 1, S.: poro, m. pore 2, [illegible] guardare fissamente, fissare; [illegible] — *over a book*, avere gli occhi [illegible] un libro. -blind, ADJ.: corto [illegible] miope. -blindness, S.: [illegible] miopia, f.

pōriness, S.: porosità, f.

pōrk, S.: porco, m.; carne di [illegible] -chop, S.: costoletta di porco, f. [illegible] S.: che mangia carne di porco, [illegible] porcellotto, porchetto, m. -et, [illegible] cello, porcellino, m. -ling, S.: [illegible] latte, m.

porŏsity, S.: porosità, f.

pōrous, ADJ.: poroso, pieno di pori [illegible] = *porosity*.

porrāçeous, ADJ.: porraceo, prassino.
pŏrret, S.: cipollina, *f.*, cipollino, *m.*
pŏrri-dge, S.: minestra, zuppa, *f.* **-dge-plate**, S.: piattello da zuppa, *m.* **-nger**, S.: scodella; acconciatura, *f.* **-ngerful**, S.: scodella piena, *f.*
pōrt 1, S.: porto, *m.* **port** 2, S.: (*nav.*) cannoniera, *f.* **-able**, ADJ.: portabile, portatile; sopportabile. **-ableness**, S.: attezza ad essere portato; portatura, *f.* **-age**, S.: porto; portamento, *m.* **-al**, S.: portone, *m.* **-ance†**, S.: portamento; aspetto, *m.*, aria, *f.* **-ative**, ADJ.: portativo. **-crāyon**, S.: matitatoio, *m.*
portcŭllis, S.: (*fort.*) saracinesca, *f.*
pōrte, S.: porta ottomana, *f.*
portĕn-d, TR.: presagire, augurare. **-tion**, S.: presagio, augurio, *m.* **-t**, S.: portento; mostro, *m.* **-tous**, ADJ.: portentoso, prodigioso.
pōrter, S.: portinaio; facchino, *m.*; birra forte, *f.* **-age**, S.: prezzo del portare, *m.*
portfōlio, S.: portafogli, portalettere, *m.*
pōrt-hole, S.: cannoniera (di vascello), *f.*
pōrtico, S.: portico, luogo coperto, *m.*; piazza, *f.*
pōrtion 1, S.: porzione; parte; fortuna, *f.*: *woman's* —, dote, *f.* **portion** 2, TR.: dividere, spartire; (*jur.*) dotare. **-er**, S.: che divide.
pōrt-liness, S.: aria maestosa, dignità, *f.* **-ly**, ADJ.: maestoso, grande; nobile: — *mien*, ariona, *f.*
pōrtman, S.: borghese, cittadino, *m.*
portmănteau *-to*, S.: portamantello, *m.*, valigia, *f.*
pōrtrait, **-ure**, S.: ritratto, *m.*, pittura, *f.*: *have one's* — *taken*, farsi ritrarre. **-painter**, S.: ritrattista, *m.*
portrāy, TR.: dipingere, far ritratti, rappresentare. **-er**, S.: ritrattista, *m.*
pōrtress, S.: portinaia, guardiana, *f.*
pōrt-reve, S.: magistrato d' un porto, *m.* **-sale**, S.: vendita pubblica, *f.*
pōry, ADJ.: poroso.
pōṣ-e, TR.: imbarazzare, confondere, imbrogliare. **-er**, S.: che confonde, che imbarazza. **pōṣ-it**, TR.: posare, disponere, ordinare. **-ition**, S.: posizione; situazione; proposta; tesi, *f.*
pŏṣiti-ve, ADJ.: positivo, assoluto; vero, certo; ostinato. **-vely**, ADV.: positivamente, assolutamente, certamente. **-veness**, S.: certezza; determinazione, *f.* **-vism**, S.: positivismo, *m.*
pŏṣiture, S.: positura, situazione, *f.*
pŏṣnet, S.: bacinella, *f.*
pŏsse, S.: adunanza del popolo armato, *f.*
posṣĕss, TR.: possedere; ottenere; godere: — *one's self of a thing*, impossessarsi di qualche cosa; — *one with an opinion*, preoccupare alcuno d' una opinione. **-ṣĕssed**, ADJ.: preoccupato. **-ṣĕssion**, S.: possessione, *f.*, possesso, possedimento; godimento, *m.*; —*s*, possessioni, *f. pl.*, poderi, *m. pl.* **-ṣĕssive**, ADJ.: (*gram.*) possessivo. **-ṣĕssor**, S.: posseditore, possessore, *m.* **-ṣĕssory**, ADJ.: possessorio.
pŏsset, S.: bevanda di latte, cervogia, ecc., *f.*
possibĭlity, S.: possibilità, *f.*, possibile, *m.*
pŏssi-ble, ADJ.: possibile. **-bly**, ADV.: in modo possibile, forse.
pŏssum = *opossum*.
pōst 1, S.: corriere; posto, luogo, uffizio, impiego, *m.*; posta, *f.*: *by* —, per posta; *by this day's* —, col corriere di oggi; *by return of* —, a posta corriente; *in* — *haste*, in gran fretta. **post** 2, TR.: porre, mettere; (*merch.*) trascrivere; INTR.: andare in posta, correre la posta. **-age**, S.: porto, danaro (delle lettere), francobollo, *m.* **-age-label**, S.: marca da francare, *f.* **-age-stamp**, S.: francobollo (postale), bollino di posta, *m.* **-bag**, S.: bolgetta, *f.* **-boy**, S.: postiglione, *m.*
pōst-date 1, S.: data posteriore; data falsa, *f.* **-date** 2, TR.: mettere una data posteriore. **-dilūvian**, ADJ.: diluviano.
pōster, S.: che corre la posta, corriere; affisso, cartellone, *m.*
pos-tērior, ADJ.: posteriore; deretano. **-teriŏrity**, S.: posteriorità, *f.*; esser posteriore, *m.* **-tĕrity**, S.: posterità, *f.*; discendenti, *m. pl.*
pōstern, S.: porticciuola, porticella, *f.*
post-exĭstence, S.: esistenza futura, *f.*
post-haste, S.: gran fretta; posta, *f.*: *make* —, correre a briglia sciolta, far ogni diligenza possibile. **-horse**, S.: cavallo di posta, *m.* **-house**, S.: posta, *f.*; uffizio della posta, *m.*
pōsthu-me, **-mous**, ADJ.: postumo: — *child*, postumo, *m.*
pōstil 1, S.: postilla, *f.* **postil** 2, TR.: postillare, fare postille. **-ler**, S.: postillatore, comentatore, *m.*
postillion, S.: postiglione, *m.*
postlim-inar, **-inous**, ADJ.: fatto dopo.
pōst-master, S.: maestro della posta, *m.*: —*-general*, capo della posta, *m.*
post-meridian, ADJ.: del dopo mezzogiorno. **-mōrtem examination**, S.: inspezione del cadavere, *f.*
pōst-office, S.: uffizio della posta, *m.* **-paid**, ADJ.: franco, porto pagato.
postpōne, TR.: posporre; differire; disprezzare. **-ment**, S.: posposizione, *f.*
pōstscript, S.: poscritto, *m.*, poscritta, *f.*
pōst-stamp = *postage-stamp*.
pōstu-late 1, S.: postulato, *m.*; domanda

-er, S.: sgridatore, rampognatore, *m.* **-ing**, ADJ.: ringhioso, stizzoso.
snāry, ADJ.: insidioso.
snāst†, S.: moccolo di candela, *m.*
snătch 1, S.: pezzo; accesso, *m.*; scappata, *f.*: *by —es*, a salti. **snatch** 2, TR.: afferrare, arraffare, acchiappare; portare via. **-er**, S.: arraffatore, arrapatore, *m.*: *body-—*, dissotterratore di cadaveri, *m.* **-ingly**, ADV.: con moto subito, in fretta.
snēak, INTR.: rampiccare, andare alle belle: *— along, — away*, andare colla testa bassa. **-er**, S.: piccol bacino, *m.* **-ing**, ADJ.: servile, basso, abietto, meschino, povero. **-ingly**, ADV.: servilmente, bassamente, meschinamente, poveramente. **-ingness**, S.: bassezza; miseria; spilorceria, *f.* **-cup**, S.: birbone, codardo, *m.*
snēap† 1, S.: ripassata, *f.* **sneap†** 2, **snĕb†**, TR.: riprendere, fare un rabbuffo; sgridare.
snēer 1, S.: ghigno, *m.*, ghignata, *f.*, riso di dispregio; scherno, *m.* **sneer** 2, INTR.: sogghignare; burlare: *— at*, farsi beffa di. **-er**, S.: ghignatore; burlatore, *m.* **-ing**, S.: ghignata, *f.* **-ingly**, ADV.: con disprezzo.
snēeze 1, S.: starnuto, starnutamento, *m.* **sneeze** 2, INTR.: starnutare, starnutire. **-wort**, S.: starnutatoria, *f.*
snick, S.: taglio, *m.*: *— and snee*, combattimento a' coltelli, *m.*
snicker, INTR.: ghignare, sorridere.
sniff 2, S.: respirazione pel naso, *f.* **sniff** 2, INTR.: respirare pel naso, tirare il fiato; torcere il grifo.
snip 1, S.: taglio; scampolo; avanzo, *m.*: *go —s with one*, far a metà con uno. **snip** 1, TR.: troncare con forbici, mozzare.
snipe, S.: beccaccino (uccello); minchione, *m.*
snip-per, S.: che mozza. **-pet**, S.: piccola parte, *f.*, pezzetto, *m.*
snipsnap, S.: contesa, disputa, *f.*
snipt off, ADJ.: mozzato, troncato.
snivel 1, S.: moccio, *m.*, gocciola (del naso), *f.* **snivel** 2, INTR.: moccicare. **-ler**, S.: moccicone; piagnucolone, *m.* **-ling**, ADJ.: moccicoso, moccioso.
snōok†, INTR.: acquattarsi.
snŏr-e 1, S.: russare, russo, *m.* **-e** 2, INTR.: russare. **-er**, S.: russatore, *m.*, -trice, *f.* **-ing**, S.: russare, russo, *m.*
snôrt, (IN)TR.: sbuffare, soffiare forte, russare. **-er**, S.: che sbuffa. **-ing**, S.: sbuffare, russare, *m.*
snŏt, S.: moccio, *m.*, gocciola, *f.* **-ter**, TR.: piangere come un bambino. **-ty**, ADJ.: moccioso.
snōut, S.: grugno, muso, grifo, *m.*; tromba (d'un elefante), *f.*: *— of bellows*, cannello d'un soffietto, *m.* **-ed**, ADJ.: che ha il grugno in fuora.
snōw 1, S.: neve, *f.*: *heavy fall of —*, nevata, *f.* **snow** 2, INTR.: nevicare, nevare, fioccare: *— very hard*, fioccare foltamente. **-ball**, S.: palla di neve, *f.* **-capped**, ADJ.: coronato di neve. **-covered**, ADJ.: coperto di neve. **-drift**, S.: ammasso di neve, *m.*; falda di neve, nevata, *f.* **-drop**, S.: pianterella primaticcia, *f.* **-flake**, S.: fiocco di neve, *m.* **-line**, S.: limite della neve, *m.* **-man**, S.: figura d'uomo fatta di neve, *f.* **-shoes**, S. PL.: sandali a rete de' selvaggi del nord, *m. pl.* **-storm**, S.: tempesta di neve, *f.* **-water**, S.: acqua di neve, *f.* **-white**, ADJ.: bianco come la neve. **-y**, ADJ.: nevoso, nevicoso.
snŭb 1, S.: bozzolo, nodo, *m.* **snub** 2, TR.: riprendere, rabbuffare; INTR.: singhiozzare†. **-nosed**, ADJ.: camoscio.
snŭdge 1, S.: taccagno, spilorcio, *m.* **snudge** 2, INTR.: *— along*, andar musando.
snŭff 1, S.: tabacco (in polvere); collera, *f.*, rancore, *m.*: *take —*, pigliare tabacco; *take a —*, prendere in mala parte. **snuff** 2, S.: lucignolo (d'una candela). **snuff** 3, TR.: prendere del tabacco, pigliare tabacco. **snuff** 4, INTR.: respirare, tirare il fiato: *— the candle*, smoccolare la candela; *— at one*, andare in collera contro alcuno; *— up*, respirare; sentire. **-box**, S.: tabacchiera, scatola da tabacco, *f.*
snŭffer, S.: smoccolatore, *m.* **-s**, S. PL.: smoccolatoio, *m.*, smoccolatoie, *f. pl.* **-'s-pan**, S.: piattello da smoccolatoie, *m.*
snŭffle, TR.: parlare col naso. **-er**, S.: che parla col naso.
snŭff-taker, S.: che prende tabacco, prenditore di tabacco, *m.* **-y**, ADJ.: sucido di tabacco.
snŭg 1, ADJ.: serrato, compatto, ben fatto, comodo; nascosto: *lie —*, stringersi, accosciarsi. **snug** 2, INTR.: stringersi; accostarsi. **-gle**, INTR.: stringersi nel letto, avvicinarsi. **-ly**, ADV.: unitamente; comodamente. **-ness**, S.: comodità, *f.*, agio, *m.*
sō 1, ADV.: così, in questa maniera; sì, talmente; lo: *I believe —*, lo credo; *— that*, di maniera che, talmente che; *— forth*, e così del resto; *— much*, tanto, tanti. **so!** 2, INTERJ.: ben! ora!
sōak, TR.: ammollare, inzuppare; INTR.: imbeversi: inzupparsi: *— in*, imbevere, succiare; *— through*, penetrare, insinuarsi. **-er**, S.: beone, bevitore, *m.* **-ing**, S.: inzuppamento, *m.*, infusione, *f.*
sōap 1, S.: sapone, *m.* **soap** 2, TR.: insaponare; nettare col sapone: *— manu-*

del potere. **-ful**, ADJ.: potente; efficace. **-fully**, ADV.: potentemente, con forza. **-fulness**, S.: vigore, *m.*; efficacia; energia, *f.* **-less**, ADJ.: senza potere, impotente. **-lessness**, S.: impotenza, debolezza, *f.*

pŏw-wow, S.: indovino, *m.*, cagnara, *f.*

pŏx, S.: morbo gallico, *m.*: *chicken* —, vaiuolo benigno, *m.*; *cow* —, vaccina, *f.*; *small* —, vaiuolo, *m.*; bolle, *f. pl.*

pŏy, S.: contrappeso (de' ballerini di corda), *m.*

pōse, TR.: confondere, imbarazzare.

prac-ticability = *practicableness.*

prăc-ticable, ADJ.: praticabile, fattevole. **-ticableness**, S.: possibilità d'essere praticato, *f.* **-ticably**, ADV.: in modo praticabile. **-tical**, ADJ.: pratico. **-tically**, ADV.: praticamente; realmente. **-ticalness**, S.: effettività; esperienza, *f.* **-tice**, S.: pratica, *f.*; uso, costume; metodo; (*mil.*) esercizio, *m.*: —*s*, pratiche segrete, *f. pl.*: *put in* —, mettere in pratica. **-tise**, (IN)TR.: praticare; esercitare, professare: — *physic*, esercitare la medicina. **-tiser**, S.: praticante; medico, *m.* **-titioner**, S.: artista; pratico; medico, *m.*

pragmătic(al), ADJ.: prammatico; affaccendato. **-ly**, ADV.: in modo protervo, arrogantemente. **-ness**, S.: protervia, arroganza, impertinenza, *f.*

prāirie, S.: prato, *m.*, prateria, *f.*

prāise 1, S.: lode, *f.*, elogio, *m.*; gloria, *f.*: *fulsome* —, nauseose lodi. **-e** 2, TR.: lodare, commendare; celebrare. **-er**, S.: lodatore, commendatore, *m.* **-eworthiness**, S.: lodabilità, *f.* **-eworthy**, ADJ.: laudevole, laudabile. **-ing**, S.: elogio; commendamento, *m.*

prāme, S.: barca con fondo piatto, *f.*

prânce, INTR.: impennarsi; cavalcare con brio. **-cer**, S.: cavallo a mano, cavallo di parata, *m.* **-cing-horse**, S.: cavallo che s'impenna, *m.*

prănk 1, S.: beffa; scappata, *f.*, tiro, *m.*: *play one a* —, accordarla ad uno; *he plays his* —*s*, ne fa delle sue. **prank** 2, TR.: ornare, adornare.

prăt-e 1, S.: ciarla, ciancia, *f.* **-e** 2, INTR.: čicalare, ciarlare. **-er**, S.: ciarlone, chiacchierone, *m.* **-ing**, S.: ciarla, loquacità, *f.* **-ingly**, ADV.: da ciarlone.

prătique, S.: prattica, *f.*

prăt-tle 1, S.: ciarleria, ciancia, *f.* **-tle** 2, INTR.: ciarlare, chiacchierare. **-tler**, S.: ciarlone, chiaccherone, *m.* **-tling**, S.: ciarleria, ciancia, *f.*

prăvity, S.: pravità, corruzione; malizia, *f.*

prăwn, S.: granchiolino, *m.*

prāy, INTR.: pregare, supplicare: — *to God*, pregare Iddio; — *tell me*, ditemi di grazia.

prâyer, S.: preghiera, domanda, richiesta; orazione, *f.*: *Lord's* —, orazione Domenicale, *f.* **-book**, S.: libro di preghiere, *m.* **-ful**, ADJ.: supplichevole, pio. **-fully**, ADV.: con molte preghiere.

prāyingly, ADV.: supplichevolmente.

prēach, INTR.: predicare; evangelizzare: — *up*, esaltare, vantare; — *the Gospel*, evangelizzare. **-er**, S.: predicatore, *m.* **-ership**, S.: uffizio d'un predicatore, *m.* **-ment**, S.: predica, *f.*, predicamento, *m.*

preacquāintance, S.: preconoscenza, *f.*

preădamite, ADJ.: preadamitico.

prē-amble, S.: preambolo, *m.*, prefazione, *f.* **-ămbulous**, ADJ.: previo.

preapprehĕnsion, S.: preconoscenza, *f.*

prĕb-end, S.: prebenda, *f.* **-ĕndal**, ADJ.: di prebenda. **-endary**, S.: prebendario, benefiziato, *m.* **-endaryship**, S.: canonicato, *m.*

precārious, ADJ.: precario, incerto. **-ly**, ADV.: precariamente, in modo precario. **-ness**, S.: incertezza; dipendenza, *f.*

prĕca-tive, **-tory**, ADJ.: supplichevole.

precâution 1, S.: precauzione; cautela, *f.* **precaution** 2, TR.: dare avviso, avvertire.

pre-cedāneous†, ADJ.: antecedente, precedente. **-cēde**, TR.: precedere, andare avanti, sopravanzare. **-cēdence**, **-cēdency**, S.: precedenza, *f.* **-cēdent**, ADJ.: precedente; anteriore. **prĕ-cedent**, S.: esempio; uso stabilito, *m.*; scrittura originale, *f.* **-cedent-book**, S.: protocollo, formulario, *m.* **-cēdently**, ADV.: precedentemente, da prima.

precĕntor, S.: precentore, *m.*

prē-cept, S.: precetto; comandamento, *m.*; regola, *f.*, ordine, *m.* **-cĕptial**†, ADJ.: istruttivo. **-cĕptive**, ADJ.: precettivo. **-cĕptor**, S.: precettore, maestro, *m.* **-cĕptory**, ADJ.: precettivo, istruttivo; S.: seminario, *m.*

precĕssion, S.: precessione, precedenza, *f.*

prēcinct, S.: precinto, circuito, *m.*

prĕcious, ADJ.: prezioso, di gran valore. **-ly**, ADV.: preziosamente. **-ness**, S.: preziosità, *f.*, gran pregio, *m.*

prĕ-cipice, S.: precipizio, *m.* **-cĭpitance**, **-cipitancy**, S.: precipitamento, *m.*, fretta temeraria, *f.* **-cipitant**, ADJ.: precipitante, affrettoso. **-cipitantly**, ADV.: con precipitazione, con gran fretta. **-cipitate** 1, ADJ.: precipitato, affrettoso; S.: precipitato, *m.* **-cipitate** 2, TR.: precipitare, affrettare, accelerare; INTR.: precipitarsi, affrettarsi. **-cipitately**, ADV.: precipitatamente, con fretta. **-cipitātion**, S.: precipitazione;

cio; durabile; vero, reale. **-id** 2, s.: solido, corpo solido, *m.*: *become* —, solidificarsi, assodarsi. **-idate**, TR.: solidare. **-idity**, s.: solidità; fermezza, durezza; verità, *f.* **-idly**, ADV.: solidamente; fermamente. **-idness** = *solidity*.

solilo-quize, INTR.: fare un soliloquio. **-quy**, s.: soliloquio, monologo, *m.*

solitâire, s.: solitario; eremita; monile, *m.* (ornamento).

sŏli-tarily, ADV.: solitariamente. **-tariness**, s.: solitudine, vita ritirata, ritiratezza, *f.* **-tary**, ADJ.: solitario, ritirato, deserto; unico; s.: solitario, eremita, *m.* **-tude**, s.: solitudine, *f.*, luogo deserto, *m.*; vita solitaria, *f.*

sŏllar, s.: granaio, *m.*

sollicit = *solicit*, ecc.

solmizâtion, s.: (*mus.*) solfeggio, *m.*

sŏlo, s.: sonata a solo, *f.*

sŏl-stice, s.: solstizio, *m.* **-stitial**, ADJ.: solstiziale, solstiziario.

solubility, s.: solubilità, *f.*

sŏl-uble, ADJ.: solubile. **-ūtion**, s.: soluzione, risoluzione, *f.*, scioglimento, *m.* **-utive**, ADJ.: solutivo; lassativo.

sŏl-vable, ADJ.: solvibile, solvente. **-ve**, TR.: solvere; dichiarare. **-vency**, s.: facoltà di pagare, *f.* **-vent**, ADJ.: solvente, che può pagare. **-ver**, s.: solvitore, *m.* **-vible**, ADJ.: solubile.

somatŏlogy, s.: somatologia, *f.*

sŏm-bre, **-brous**, ADJ.: oscuro.

sôme 1, ART.: del, dello, della; dei, degli, delle. **some** 2, PRON.: qualche; qualcheduno, alcuno; alcuni, certi, *pl.*; PART. ART.: del (dello, ecc.), ne: — *say*, alcuni dicono; — *bread*, (del) pane; — *apples*, (delle) mela; *give me* — (*of it*), datemene; *I have* —, ne ho. **-body**, s.: qualcheduno, qualcuno, *m.* **-how**, ADV.: in qualche maniera.

sômerset, s.: soprassalto; salto del carpione, *m.*

sôme-thing, s.: qualche cosa, *f.*; ADV.: un poco, alquanto. **-time**, ADV.: un tempo, altre volte: — *or other*, un giorno o l'altro. **-times**, ADV.: qualchevolta, talvolta. **-what**, s.: qualche cosa, *f.*; ADV.: un poco, alquanto. **-where**, ADV.: in qualche luogo: — *else*, altrove; *from* — *else*, altronde. **-while**, ADV.: qualche tempo.

somnăm-bulism, s.: sonnambulismo, *m.* **-bulist**, **-bule**, s.: sonnambulo, nottambulo, *m.*

som-niferous, **-nific**, ADJ.: sonnifero. **-nolence**, **-nolency**, s.: sonnolenza, *f.*, letargo, *m.*

sôn, s.: figlio, figliuolo; discendente, *m.* **-in-law**, s.: genero, *m.*

sonâta, s.: sonata, *f.*

sŏng, s.: canzona, canzone, aria, *f.*; cantare, *m.*: *little* —, canzonetta, canzoncina, *f.*; *plain* —, canto fermo; *Solomon's* —, Cantico dei Cantici; *old* —, cosa di poco, bagatella, *f.* **-book**, s.: canzoniere, *m.* **-ish**, ADJ.: pieno di canzoni. **-ster**, s.: cantatore, canterino, *m.* **-stress**, s.: cantatrice, canterina, *f.*

soniferous = *sonorific*.

sŏnnet, s.: sonnetto, *m.* **-tēer**, **-writer**, s.: poetastro, poetuzzo, *m.*

sonōrous, ADJ.: sonoro, canoro. **-ly**, ADV.: sonoramente, con sonorità. **-ness**, s.: sonorità; risonanza, *f.*

sônship, s.: figliuolanza, *f.*

sōon, ADV.: tosto, presto, quanto prima, subito: *very* —, ben tosto, quanto prima; — *after*, non molto dopo; *as* — *as*, subito che, tosto che; *too* —, troppo tosto, troppo presto. **-er**, ADV.: più tosto, meglio; anzi: — *than*, anzi che; *the* — *the better*, il più presto sarà il meglio; — *or later*, tosto o tardi. **-est**, ADJ.: il più tosto: *at the* —, al più tosto, al più presto. **-ly**, ADV.: prontamente.

sōot, s.: fuliggine, caligine, *f.* **-ed**, ADJ.: imbrattato di fuliggine.

sōo-th 1, ADJ.: piacevole, dilettevole; grato. **-th** 2, s.: verità; realtà, *f.*: *in* —, in realtà. **-the**, TR.: adulare, lusingare; addolcire, calmare. **-ther**, s.: adulatore, lusinghiere, *m.* **-thing**, s.: adulazione, lusinga, *f.*; carezze, *f. pl.* **-thingly**, ADV.: lusinghevolmente. **-thly**†, ADV.: realmente, veramente. **-thsay** 1, s.: predizone, *f.*, pronostico, *m.* **-thsay** 2, (IN)TR.: predire, pronosticare. **-thsayer**, s.: indovinatore, indovino, *m.* **-thsaying**, s.: indovinazione, predizione, *f.*

sōot-iness, s.: qualità fuligginosa, fuliggine, *f.* **-y** 1, ADJ.: fuligginoso, caliginoso. **-y** 2, TR.: tingere di fuliggine.

sŏp 1, s.: zuppa, *f.*, pan unto, *m.* **sop** 2, TR.: inzuppare, intingere (pane).

sŏph = *-ister* (Ingl.), o *-omore* (Am.).

sŏph-ism, s.: sofisma, *f.*, sofismo, *m.* **-ist**, s.: sofista; filosofo, *m.* **-ister**, s.: sofista, *m.*; studente del secondo (*junior s.*) o del terzo anno (*senior s.*), al collegio ingl. **-istical**, ADJ.: sofistico, capzioso. **-istically**, ADV.: sofisticamente, in modo sofistico. **-isticate**, ADJ.: sofisticato, falsificato. **-isticate**, TR.: sofisticare, falsificare, adulterare. **-isticâtion**, s.: sofisticheria, *f.*, fatturare, *m.* **-isticator**, s.: che sofistica, che falsifica. **-istry**, s.: sofisticheria, *f.* **-omore**, s.: studente del secondo anno (al collegio amer.), *m.*

sŏpo-rate, INTR.: addormentire. **-riferous**, ADJ.: soporifero, sonnifero. **-riferousness**, s.: qualità soporifera, *f.* **-rific**, **-rous** = *soporiferous*.

prĕju-dice 1, S.: pregiudizio, *m.*, prevenzione, *f.*; detrimento, danno, *m.* **-dice** 2, TR.: pregiudicare; nuocere. **-dicial**, ADJ.: pregiudizioso, nocivo. **-dicialness**, S.: pregiudizio, nocumento; torto, *m.*

prĕ-lacy, S.: prelatura, *f.* **-late**, S.: prelato, *m.* **-lateship**, S.: prelatura, *f.* **-látical**, ADJ.: prelatizio, di prelato. **-lātion**, S.: prelazione, preferenza, *f.* **-lature(ship)**, S.: dignità di prelato, *f.*

prelĕc-t, TR.: preleggere. **-tion**, S.: previa lettura, *f.*; discorso, *m.* **-tor**, S.: prelettore, *m.*

prelibātion, S.: prelibazione, *f.*; previo gusto, *m.*

preliminary, ADJ.: preliminare.

prē-lude, S.: preludio; proemio, *m.* **-lūde**, TR.: suonare un preludio; introdurre. **-lūdious**, **-lūsive**, **-lusory**, ADJ.: prelusivo introduttivo.

prematūr-e, ADJ.: prematuro, primaticcio. **-ely**, ADV.: prematuramente. **-eness**, **-ity**, S.: maturità avanti il tempo, *f.*

premĕdi-tate, (IN)TR.: premeditare, pensare avanti, appensare. **-tātion**, S.: premeditazione, *f.*

premĕrit, TR.: meritare innanzi.

prĕmices, S. PL.: primizie, *f. pl.*, primi frutti, *m. pl.*

prĕmier, ADJ.: primiero, principale; S.: primo ministro, *m.* **-ship**, S.: dignità d' un primo ministro, *f.*

premise, TR.: spiegare in primo luogo.

prĕm-ises, S. PL.: (*log.*) premesse; (*leg.*) case, *f. pl.*; beni terreni, *m. pl.* **-iss**, S.: proposizione antecedente, *f.*

prĕmium, S.: premio, *m.*; ricompensa, *f.*

pre-mŏnish, TR.: avvertire avanti, ammonire avanti. **-mŏnishment**, **-monition**, S.: premonizione, *f.* **-mŏnitory**, ADJ.: che ammonisce anticipatamente.

premŏn-strate, TR.: premostrare. **-strātion**, S.: premostrazione, *f.*

premunire, S.: (*leg.*) confiscazione di beni, *f.*

premunition, S.: premonizione; anticipazione (d' obbiezioni), *f.*

prenŏmi-nate, TR.: nominare avanti. **-nātion**, S.: prima nominazione, *f.*

prenŏtion, S.: prescienza, *f.*

prĕntice†, S.: novizio, principiante, *m.* **-ship**†, S.: tempo d' imparare un' arte, garzonaggio, *m.*

prenunciātion, S.: annunzio, *m.*

preŏc-cupancy, S.: previa possessione, *f.* **-cupate**, TR.: preoccupare, anticipare. **-cupātion**, S.: preoccupazione, prevenzione, *f.* **-cupy**, TR.: preoccupare, prevenire.

preopinion, S.: pregiudizio, *m.*; prevenzione, *f.*

preŏption, S.: (*jur.*) diritto della prima scelta, *m.*

pre-ordāin, TR.: preordinare, predestinare. **-ôrdinance**, **-ordinātion**, S.: decreto antecedente, *m.*

pre-parātion, S.: preparazione, *f.*, preparativo; apparecchio, *m.* **-părative**, ADJ.: preparativo, preparatorio; S.: preparamento, apparato, *m.* **-părativety**, ADV.: in modo preparativo, precedentemente. **-păratory**, ADJ.: preparatorio, preparativo, preparante. **-pâre**, TR.: preparare; apparecchiare; INTR.: prepararsi; apparecchiarsi. **-pâredness**, S.: preparazione, disposizione; convenevolezza, *f.* **-pârer**, S.: preparatore; apparecchiatore, *m.*

prepāy, TR.: pagare anticipatamente.

prepĕn-se, INTR.: premeditare. **-se(d)**, ADJ.: premeditato.

prepŏllency, S.: prevalenza, prepotenza, *f.*

prepŏnder, TR.: preponderare, prevalere. **-ance**, **-ancy**, S.: preponderanza, *f.* **-ant**, ADJ.: preponderante. **-ate**, INTR.: preponderare; superare. **-ātion**, S.: preponderanza, *f.*

prepō-se, TR.: preporre, mettere avanti. **-sition**, S.: preposizione, *f.*

prepŏsi-tive, ADJ.: prepositivo; preponente. **-tor**, S.: preposto, proposto; osservatore, *m.*

prepos-sĕss, TR.: preoccupare; prevenire; cattivarsi. **-sessing**, ADJ.: insinuante; attraente: *a very — young lady*, una damigella molto avvenente. **-sĕssion**, S.: preoccupazione; prevenzione, *f.* **-sĕssor**, S.: preoccupatore, *m.*

prepŏsterous, ADJ.: prepostero; assurdo. **-ly**, ADV.: in modo prepostero, a rovescio, assurdamente. **-ness**, S.: assurdità, *f.*

prepŏ-tency, S.: prepotenza, *f.* **-tent**, ADJ.: prepotente, superiore.

prēpuce, S.: prepuzio, *m.*

pre-require, TR.: esigere innanzi. **-rĕquisite**, ADJ.: richiesto avanti.

prerŏgative, S.: prerogativa, *f.*; privilegio, vantaggio, *m.*

prē-sage, S.: presagio, augurio, *m.* **-sāge**, TR.: presagire, augurare. **-sāgeful**, ADJ.: pronosticante. **-sāgement**, S.: presentimento, pronostico, *m.* **-sāger**, S.: indovino, *m.*

prĕsby-ter, S.: ministro presbiteriano, prete, *m.* **-tērian**, ADJ.: presbiteriano. **-tērianism**, S.: presbiterianismo, Calvinismo, *m.* **-tery**, S.: presbitero, *m.*

prĕscien-ce, S.: prescienza, preconoscenza, *f.* **-t**, ADJ.: presciente; profetico.

prescind, TR.: prescindere; astrarre.

prescribe, (IN)TR.: prescrivere; dirigere, ordinare.

prē script, ADJ.: prescritto; S.: prescritto, comando, *m.* **-scrip̧tion**, S.: prescrizione; ordinazione, *f.*

prēsence, S.: presenza; aria, *f.*, aspetto, *m.*: — *of mind*, prontezza di spirito, *f.* **-chamber**, **-room**, S.: camera di presenza, *f.*

pre-sensātion, **-sĕnsion†**, S.: presentimento, *m.*

prēsent 1, ADJ.: presente; attento: — *month*, corrente mese; — *tense*, tempo presente, *m.*; *at* —, al presente, presentemente. **present** 2, S.: presente, dono, regalo, *m.* **present** 3, TR.: presentare, far un presente, regalare a; offerire; conferire: — *arms*, presentare le armi; — *my compliments to*, presentate i miei complimenti a. **presĕnt-able**, ADJ.: che può presentarsi. **-āneous**, ADJ.: presentaneo. **-ātion**, S.: presentazione, *f.* **-ēe**, S.: che è presentato a un beneficio. **presĕnt-er**, S.: presentatore, presentante, *m.*

presĕn-tial, ADJ.: presenziale; presente. **-tiălity**, S.: presenza reale, *f.* **-tially**, ADV.: presenzialmente.

presĕntiment, S.: presentimento, *m.*

prēsently, ADV.: presentemente, al presente.

presĕntment, S.: rappresentamento, *m.*; accusa, denunzia, *f.*

prēsentness, S.: acutezza d' ingegno, prontezza di spirito, *f.*

pre-servātion, S.: preservazione, *f.* **-sĕrvative**, S.: preservativo, antidoto, *m.* **-sĕrve** 1, S.: confettura, conserva, *f.*, confetti, *m. pl.* **-serve** 2, TR.: preservare, conservare; confettare. **-sĕrver**, S.: conservatore, protettore, *m.* **-sĕrvers**, S. PL.: occhiali di conserva, *m. pl.* **-sĕrving**, S.: preservamento; preservare; confettare, *m.*

preside, INTR.: presedere; aver la direzione; soprantendere.

prēsiden-cy, S.: presidenza, soprantendenza, *f.* **-t**, S.: presidente; capo, *m.*: — *of a college*, rettore d' un collegio, *m.* **-tship**, S.: uffizio di presidente, *m.*

presidial, ADJ.: di presidio, di guernigione.

pre-significātion, S.: previa significazione, *f.* **-signify**, TR.: dimostrare previamente.

prēss 1, S.: torchio, torcolo; strettoia, *m.*; calca, folla; moltitudine, *f.*: — *for clothes*, guardaroba, *f.*; *my book is in the* —, il mio libro è sotto il torchio. **press** 2, TR.: premere, spremere, stringere; sollecitare, affrettare; importunare; INTR.: affrettarsi; mettere piede; ricercare con premura: — *grapes*, pigiar le uve; — *soldiers*, levar soldati per forza; —

on, spingersi, fi
— *upon*, presen
juice, spremere
hands, stringer
letto in forma
S.: torcoliere, *m*
forzare marinari
te; importuno;
-ingly, ADV.:
mente. **-ion** **-sh**
sione, compressi
patore (di libri),
S.: danaro d' arr
S.: pressura; p
—, alta (bassa)
torchio, *m.*; tira

prēst, ADJ.: pre
prestātion, S.:
prēstige, S.: pr
prēsto, ADV.: pr
pre-sūmably,
bile, senza esamir
sumere; presupp
suntuoso, *m.* -
zione, arroganza,
presuntivo, presu
ADJ.: presuntuoso
ously, ADV.: pre
tuousness, S:
presuppōse, TR.
-sition, S.: pres
presurmise, S.:
pre-tĕnce, S.: p
argomento falso, *m*
(IN)TR.: pretender
fingere, far le v
l' affaccendato. -
tore, *m.*, -trice, *f*
-tĕndingly, AD
-tĕnsion, S.: p
sto, *m.*

prēter-ite, ADJ.:
tense, preterito,
S.: omissione, *f.*
preterlāpsed, A
preter-mission
omissione, *f.* -mi
lasciare, tralasciar
preternātural,
-ly, ADV.: in
-ness, S.: modo
prētext, S.: prete
prē-tor, S.: pretc
rian, ADJ.: pretc
ship, S.: pretoria
prēt-tily *prit-*,
piacevole, acconci
bellezza, leggiadria
bellino, leggiadro,
—, piuttosto bell
bel tiro. **-ty** 2, A
quasi.

prevāil, INTR.: prevalere; avere la superiorità; eccedere: — *against*, resistere; opporsi; — *on* (*upon*, *with*), persuadere; — *over*, superare, vincere. **-ing**, ADJ.: predominante, potente, generale. **-ment**, S.: prevalenza, potenza; efficacia, *f.*

prĕvalen-ce, **-cy** = *prevailment*. **-t**, ADJ.: potente; efficace. **-tly**, ADV.: potentemente; efficacemente.

prevári-cāte, INTR.: prevaricare; colludere. **-cātion**, S.: prevaricazione; collusione, *f.* **-cator**, S.: prevaricatore, *m.*

pre-vēne†, TR.: prevenire; impedire. **-vēnient**, ADJ.: preveniente. **-vĕnt**, TR.: prevenire, anticipare; ovviare, impedire. **-vĕnter**, S.: che previene, impeditore, *m.* **-vĕntingly**, ADV.: preventivamente. **-vĕntion**, S.: prevenzione, anticipazione; preoccupazione, *f.*: *for the* — *of*, per prevenire; onde prevenire. **-vĕntional**, **-vĕntive**, ADJ.: preveniente; preservativo. **-ventive**, S.: preservativo, antidoto, *m.* **-vĕntively**, ADV.: preventivamente, in modo preventivo.

prēvious, ADJ.: previo, precedente. **-ly**, ADV.: precedentemente, da prima. **-ness**, S.: precedenza, antecedenza, anteriorità, *f.*

prevision, S.: previsione, *f.*, antivedimento, *m.*

prewārn, TR.: avvertire avanti.

prêy 1, S.: preda, rapina, *f.*; bottino, *m.*: *bird of* —, uccello di rapina, *m.*; *a* — *to*, in preda a. **prey** 2, INTR.: predare; rubare: — *upon* (= *eat*), mangiare; *jealousy* —*s upon health*, la gelosia mina la salute. **-er**, S.: predatore, rubatore, *m.*

price 1, S.: prezzo, valore, *m.*, valuta; ricompensa, *f.*: *current* —, *market* —, prezzo corrente; *fixed* —, prezzo fisso; *what's your* —? quanto vale? *at any* —, a qualunque prezzo. **price** 2, TR.: dar il giusto prezzo.

prick 1, S.: puntura, ferita, *f.*; bersaglio, rimorso, *m.* **prick** 2, TR.: pungere; stimolare, spronare: — *a cask*, spillare una botte; — *one's ears*, stare cogli occhi tesi, (*of horses*) drizzare le orrecchie; — *music*, notare (un' aria); (*nav.*) — *the sails*, ricucire le vele. **-er**, S.: bracchiere a cavallo, *m.* **-et**, S.: cerbiatto, *m.* **-ing**, S.: pungimento; pizzicore, *m.* **-le**, S.: punta; spina, *f.* **-liness**, S.: spinosità, *f.* **-ly**, ADJ.: pieno di spine, spinoso. **-wood**, S.: fusaggine, *f.*

pride 1, S.: orgoglio, *m.*, superbia, alterigia, vanità, *f.*: *take* — *in*, vanagloriarsi, vantarsi: — *one's self on*, vantarsi di, pregiarsi di. **pride** 2, INTR.: vantarsi, glorificarsi; pregiarsi. **-ful**, ADJ.: orgoglioso, altiero, vanaglorioso.

prier, S.: spione, spia, *m.*

priest, S.: prete, sacerdote, ministro, *m.* **-craft**, S.: fraude ecclesiastica, *f.* **-ess**, S.: sacerdotessa, *f.* **-hood**, S.: sacerdozio, *m.* **-like**, ADJ.: da prete, pretesco. **-liness**, S.: aria di prete, *f.* **-ly**, ADJ.: di prete, pretesco; sacerdotale. **-ridden**, ADJ.: governato da preti.

prig 1, S.: presuntuoso, pazzo, *m.* **prig** 2, TR.: mariolare, truffare. **-gish**, ADJ.: impertinente, arrogante.

prill, S.: rombo, *m.* (pesce).

prim 1, ADJ.: affettato, ricercato, studiato. **prim** 2, TR.: ornare a bella posta; INTR.: esser affettato, civettare.

prima-cy, S.: primato, *m.* **-rily**, ADV.: primieramente, da prima. **-riness**, S.: primato; primo luogo, *m.* **-ry**, ADJ.: primario, primo, principale.

primate, S.: primate; capo, *m.* **-ship**, S.: primazia, dignità di primate, *f.*

prime 1, ADJ.: primo, principale, originale; precoce; S.: principio; fiore, *m.*; primavera, *f.*: — *of life* (*age*), fiore dell' età, *m.*; — *of the moon*, novilunio, *m.* **prime** 2, TR.: mettere il polverino; preparare. **-ly**, ADV.: da prima†; eccellentemente. **-ness**, S.: primato, *m.*; eccellenza, *f.*

primer, S.: piccolo libretto; breviario, *m.*: *long* —, garamone, *m.*, dieci punti, *m. pl.*; *great* —, carattere di diciotto punti, *m.*

primē-val, **-vous**, ADJ.: primordiale, primitivo.

priming, S.: polverino da focone, *m.*; capsula di fucile, *f.* **-iron**, S.: spillo da nettare il focone, *m.*

primitial, ADJ.: delle primizie.

primitive, ADJ.: primitivo, originale. **-ly**, ADV.: primitivamente, in principio. **-ness**, S.: originalità; antichità, *f.*

prim-ly, ADJ.: con affettazione. **-ness**, S.: affettazione, *f.*

primo-gĕnial, ADJ.: primogenito. **-gĕniture**, S.: primogenitura, *f.*

primôr-dial, **-diate**, ADJ.: primordiale.

primrose, S.: margheritina, *f.*

prin-ce, S.: principe; sovrano, *m.*: *live like a* —, vivere da principe. **-cedom**, S.: principato, *m.* **-celike**, ADJ.: di principe, da principe, nobile. **-celiness**, S.: dignità di principe, *f.* **-cely**, ADJ.: principesco; nobile; ADV.: da principe, principesco; nobilmente. **-cess**, S.: principessa, *f.*

princi-pal, ADJ.: principale, primario, essenziale; S.: principale; capitale, *m.*: *pay off the* —, rimborsare il principale (il capitale). **-pălity**, S.: principato, *m.*;

sovranità, *f.* **-pally**, ADV.: principalmente; soprattutto. **-palness**, S.: principale; essenziale, *m.* **-pate**, S.: principato, *m.*

principiàtion†, S.: analisi, *f.*

principle 1, S.: principio, fondamento; motivo, *m.*, causa, *f.*: *sound —s*, sani (sodi) principi; *from a — of*, per un principio di. **principle** 2, TR.: dare i principi; istruire. **-d**, ADJ.: che ha dei principi.

prin-cock† **-cox**†, S.: saccentone, saccentino, *m.*

prink, TR.: ornare; abbellire; INTR.: ornarsi, adornarsi.

print 1, S.: impressione; stampa, *f.*; carattere, *m.*, lettera, *f.*: *in —*, stampato; *out of —*, esaurito, che non si trova più a comprare; *come out in —*, venire alla luce (de' libri); *beautiful —*, bella impressione. **print** 2, TR.: imprimere; stampare. **-er**, S.: stampatore, tipografo, *m.* **-ing**, S.: impressione; stampa, *f.* **-ing-house**, **-ing-office**, S.: stamperia, *f.* **-ing-paper**, S.: carta da stampa, *f.*, fioretto, *m.* **-ing-press**, S.: torchio (da stampare), *m.* **-less**, ADJ.: senza impressione. **-shop**, S.: bottega, *f.*

prior 1, ADJ.: primo, anteriore, precedente. **prior** 2, S.: priore; superiore, *m.* **-ate**, S.: priorato, *m.* **-ess**, S.: priora; superiora, *f.* **priŏr-ity**, S.: priorità; precedenza, *f.* **-ship**, S.: dignità di priore, *f.*, priorato, *m.* **-y**, S.: priorato, *m.*

prism, S.: prisma, *m.* **-àtic(al)**, ADJ.: prismatico. **-àtically**, ADV.: in modo prismatico.

prison 1, S.: prigione, *f.*, carcere, *m.*: *keeper of a —*, carceriere, *m.* **prison** 2, TR.: imprigionare, incarcerare. **-base**, S.: barriera, *f.* (giuoco). **-er**, S.: prigioniere, prigionero; prigione, *m.*: *take —*, far prigione (prigioniere), arrestare; *— at the bar*, accusato, reo, *m.* **-house**, S.: prigione, *f.*, carcere, *m.* **-ment**, S.: prigionia, incarcerazione, *f.*

pristine, ADJ.: pristino, prisco; originale.

prithee, ti prego, di grazia.

prittle-prattle, S.: cicaleria, *f.*

pri-vacy, S.: segretezza; retiratezza, solitudine, *f.* **-vàdo**†, S.: amico intimo, confidente, *m.* **-vate**, ADJ.: privato, particolare; segreto, nascosto: *in —*, privatamente; *— interview*, abboccamento segreto, *m.*; *— man*, uomo privato, *m.*; *— stairs*, scala segreta, *f.*

privatĕer 1, S.: corsale, *m.* **privateer** 2, INTR.: corseggiare.

private-ly, ADV.: privatamente, particolarmente; segretamente. **-ness**, S.: ritiratezza, oscurità, *f.*

privàtion, S.: privazione; mancanza, *f.*

prize 1, S.: prezzo; premio, *m.*;

probabile, ...

probabilmente, ...

prŏbate, S.: (*jur.*) verificazion... testamento), *f.*

: prova, *f.*; esper...

, ADJ.: per prova...

fa la sua prova; ...

m. **-ership**, S.: noviziato, *m.*

prŏba-tive,

sors, S. PL.:

proces̈sion, S.: processione, *f.* **-al**, **-ary**, ADJ.: di processione.
prŏchronism, S.: procronismo, *m.*
procinct, S.: preparamento, *m.*
pro-claim, TR.: proclamare; pubblicare; bandire. **-claimer**, S.: proclamatore; banditore, *m.* **-clamation**, S.: proclama, *f.*; bando, *m.*
procliv-ity, S.: proclività, propensione, *f.* **-ous**, ADJ.: proclive; inclinato.
procŏnsul, S.: proconsolo, *m.* **-ar**, ADJ.: proconsolare. **-ate**, **-ship**, S.: proconsolato, *m.*
procrásti-nate, TR.: procrastinare; indugiare. **-nation**, S.: procrastinazione, *f.*
prŏcre-ant, ADJ.: procreante, produttivo. **-ate**, TR.: procreare; produrre. **-ation**, S.: procreamento, procreare, *m.* **-ative**, ADJ.: generativo, produttivo. **-ativeness**, S.: potere di procreare, *m.*, facoltà generativa, *f.* **-ator**, S.: procreatore; generatore, *m.*
prŏctor, S.: procuratore; fattore, *m.*: *—s*, moderatori, *m. pl.* **-ship**, S.: uffizio di procuratore, *m.*
procumbent, ADJ.: disteso, prono, inclinato.
procurable, ADJ.: che si può procurare.
prŏcuracy, S.: amministrazione; condotta, *f.*
procuration, S.: procurazione, procura, *f.*
prŏcura-tor, S.: procuratore; agente, *m.* **-torship**, S.: uffizio del procuratore, *m.* **-tory**, ADJ.: di procurazione.
procur-e, TR.: procurare; ottenere; fare il ruffiano. **-ement**, S.: procurazione, *f.* **-er**, S.: procuratore; mezzano, mediatore, *m.* **-ess**, S.: procuratrice, mezzana, *f.*
prŏd, TR.: pungere; instigare, stimolare.
prŏdi-gal, ADJ.: prodigo, spendereccio; S.: prodigo, *m.*: — *son*, figliuol prodigo. **-gality**, S.: prodigalità, *f.* **-galize**, INTR.: prodigalizzare. **-gally**, ADV.: prodigamente, profusamente. **-galness**, S.: prodigalità, *f.*
prodigious, ADJ.: prodigioso, mostruoso, stupendo; straordinario. **-ly**, ADV.: prodigiosamente. **-ness**, S.: mostruosità; maraviglia, *f.*
prŏdigy, S.: prodigio, portento, *m.*
prodition†, S.: prodizione, *f.*, tradimento, *m.*
prŏdi-tor†, S.: traditore; perfido, *m.* **-tŏrious†**, **-tory†**, ADJ.: proditorio, traditoresco.
prŏdrome, S.: prodromo, *m.*
produce 1, TR.: produrre; causare. **prŏduce** 2, S.: prodotto; profitto, guadagno, *m.* **-cement**, S.: producimento, *m.*, produzione, *f.* **-cer**, S.: produttore, generatore, *m.* **-cible**, ADJ.: producibile, producente. **-cibleness**, S.: facoltà producibile; produzione, *f.* **-cing**, S.: producimento, produrre, *m.*
prŏ-duct, S.: prodotto; effetto, *m.*; opera, *f.* **-duction**, S.: produzione, *f.*, prodotto, *m.* **-ductiveness**, S.: produttività; fertilità, *f.*
prō-em 1, S.: proemio, *m.*, prefazione, *f.* **-em** 2, TR.: proemiare. **-ēmial**, ADJ.: proemiale, introduttivo.
pro-fanation, S.: profanazione, *f.*, profanamento, *m.* **-fāne** 1, ADJ.: profano, secolare; impuro, polluto. **-fane** 2, TR.: profanare, violare, abusare. **-fānely**, ADV.: profanamente, con profanità. **-fāneness**, S.: profanità; irreverenza a cose sacre, *f.* **-fāner**, S.: profanatore, violatore, *m.* **-fānity** = *profaneness*.
pro-fĕss, (IN)TR.: professare; esercitare, mantenere, seguitare: *—ed monk*, frate professo, *m.* **-fĕssedly**, ADV.: pubblicamente, apertamente. **-fĕssion**, S.: professione, *f.*; mestiere, arte; protesto, *m.*: *by* —, per (*or* di) professione. **-fĕssional**, ADJ.: di professione. **-fĕssor**, S.: professore; lettore pubblico, *m.*; chi professa, *m.*, *f.* **-fessŏrial**, ADJ.: professoriale. **-fĕssorship**, S.: impiego di professore, professorato, *m.*, cattedra, *f.*
prŏffer 1, S.: profferenza, profferta, offerta; tentativa, *f.* **proffer** 2, TR.: profferire, offerire; proporre. **-er**, S.: profferitore, offerente, *m.*
proficien-ce, **-cy**, S.: avanzamento; progresso, *m.* **-t**, ADJ.: proficiente; avanzato.
prōfile, S.: proffilo, *m.*
prŏfit 1, S.: profitto, guadagno; vantaggio; frutto, *m.* **profit** 2, TR.: avvantaggiare; essere utile; INTR.: profittare; far progressi: *what —s it?* che giova? a che serve? **-able**, ADJ.: profittabile, profittevole, vantaggioso, utile. **-ableness**, S.: profitto, guadagno, giovamento; utile, *m.* **-ably**, ADV.: profittevolmente; con profitto. **-ing**, S.: profitto; progresso, avanzamento, *m.* **-less**, ADJ.: di niuno profitto; inutile.
prŏfli-gacy, S.: scelleratezza, dissolutezza, *f.* **-gate** 1, ADJ.: scellerato, malvagio. **-gate** 2, INTR.: abbandonare. **-gately**, ADV.: scelleratamente; con dissolutezza. **-gateness**, S.: scelleratezza, malvagità, *f.*
prŏfluen-ce, S.: profluvio; progresso; corso, *m.* **-t**, ADJ.: scorrente, fluido.
pro-fŏund 1, S.: abisso; alto mare, *m.* **-found** 2, ADJ.: profondo, alto; insigne, eminente: — *sleep*, alto sonno. **-fŏundly**, ADV.: profondamente, profondo. **-fŏundness**, **-fŭndity**, S.: profondità; penetrazione, *f.*

sgorgante. -ing 2, s.: sgorgamento, sgorgo, *m.*
sprăg, s.: giovane salmone, *m.*
sprāin 1, s.: storcimento, *m.*, stortilatura, *f.* **sprain** 2, TR.: storcere, dislogare, sconciare: — *one's foot*, storcersi un piede.
sprăt, s.: laterino, *m.* (pesce).
sprâwl, INTR.: stendersi (per terra), dimenarsi, agitarsi.
sprāy 1, s.: ramicello, *m.*; frasca, *f.* **spray** 2, s.: spuma (del mare), *f.*
sprĕad 1, ADJ.: steso; divolgato. **spread** 2, s.: estensione, espansione, *f.*, spandimento, *m.* **spread** 3, IRR.; (IN)TR.: stendere, spandere, sparpagliare, spargere; stendersi, spargersi; aprirsi: — *the cloth*, metter la tovaglia; — *sail*, spiegare le vele; — *abroad*, divolgare, pubblicare; — *over*, coprire. **-er**, s.: spargitore; divolgatore, *m.*
sprig, s.: ramuscello, *m.* **-gy**, ADJ.: pieno di ramuscelli.
spright, s.: spirito†, *m.*; fantasma, *m.*, apparizione, *f.* **-ful**, ADJ.: gaio, allegro, vivace, spiritoso. **-fully**, ADV.: gaiamente, con ardore. **-fulness**, **-liness**, s.: vivacità, allegria, *f.* **-ly**, ADJ.: leggiadro, lieto, gaio, spiritoso.
spring 1, s.: salto, slancio, balzo, *m.*; sorgente, fonte; origine, causa, *f.*; principio, *m.*; forza elastica, molla; (*season*) primavera, *f.*: *take a* —, spiccare un salto; — *water*, acqua di sorgente; *main* —, molla principale; *in* (*the*) —, nella primavera. **spring** 2, IRR.; TR.: fare levare; scoprire; far scoppiare; saltare, scavalcare; INTR.: sorgere, scaturire, sboccare; lanciarsi; saltare; spuntare, germogliare; uscire, procedere, derivare: — *a leak*, fare acqua; — *a light*, accendere; — *a mine*, fare scoppiare una mina; — *a well*, cavare un pozzo; — *forward*, lanciarsi; avventarsi; — *out*, zampillare, sgorgare; — *over a ditch*, saltare una fossa. **-al**†, s.: giovanotto, giovinotto, *m.* **-box**, s.: (*watch.*) bariletto, tamburo, *m.* **spring-e** 1, s.: lacciuolo, galappio, *m.* **-e** 2, TR.: tendere lacciuoli. **spring-er**, s.: battitore, *m.* **-halt**, s.: (*vet.*) granchio, *m.* **-head**, s.: sorgente, fonte, *f.* **-iness**, s.: elasticità, forza elastica, *f.* **-tide**, s.: alta marea, *f.* **-water**, s.: acqua sorgente, *f.* **-wheat**, s.: fromento estivo, *m.* **-y**, ADJ.: elastico.
sprin-kle 1, s.: aspersorio, *m.* **-kle** 2, (IN)TR.: spruzzare, aspergere, spazzare; spargere, dispergere: — *with salt*, aspergere di sale. **-kler**, s.: chi *or* che sparge; spruzza, *f.*; aspergitore; aspersorio, *m.* **-kling**, s.: aspersione, *f.*; spruzzolo, spruzzo, *m.*: — *of rain*, spruzzaglia, pioggerella, *f.*

sprit 1, s.: rampollo, germoglio; brocco, *m.* **sprit** 2, TR.: cacciar fuori, espurgare; INTR.: germogliare.
sprite, ecc. = *spright*, ecc.
sprit-sail, s.: (*nav.*) trinchetto, *m.*
sprout 1, s.: cavolino; germoglio, broccolo, *m.* **sprout** 2, INTR.: cestire, germogliare. **-ing**, ADJ.: germogliante.
sprūce 1, ADJ.: attillato, pulito, lindo, vago. **spruce** 2, INTR.: attillarsi, pararsi. **spruce** 3, s.: abete, *m.*: — *beer*, birra d'abete, *f.* **-leather**, s.: cuoio di Prussia, *m.* **-ly**, ADV.: attillatamente, pulitamente, lindamente, vagamente. **-ness**, s.: attillatura, lindezza, *f.*
sprŭnt 1, ADJ.: vivace, lesto. **sprunt** 2, s.: pezzo corto, *m.* **sprunt** 3, INTR.: germogliare.
sprȳ, ADJ.: attivo, vivo, presto.
spŭd, s.: coltello corto, coltellaccio, *m.*
spū-me 1, s.: spiuma, spuma, schiuma, *f.* **-me** 2, INTR.: spiumare, schiumare. **-mous**, **-my**, ADJ.: spumoso.
spŭnge = *sponge*.
spŭnk, s.: esca, miccia, *f.*, legno insolfato, coraggio, *m.*
spûr 1, s.: sprone; incentivo, stimolo, *m.*: *upon the* —, nella fretta di; *be upon the* —, esser in gran fretta. **spur** 2, TR.: spronare; eccitare, incitare, affrettare, animare; INTR.: affrettarsi. **-gall**, s.: piaga fatta cogli sproni, *f.* **-galled**, ADJ.: piagato cogli sproni.
spûrge, s.: (*bot.*) catapuzza, *f.* **-laurel**, **-olive**, s.: timelea, *f.*
spūrious, ADJ.: spurio, falso, falsificato. **-ly**, ADV.: falsamente. **-ness**, s.: falsificamento, *m.*, falsità, *f.*
spûr-leather, s.: cuoio dello sprone, *m.*
spûrling, s.: laterino, *m.* (pesce).
spûrn 1, s.: celcio; dispregio, vilipendio, *m.* **spurn** 2, TR.: calcitrare; sprezzare, sdegnare: — *away*, scacciare a calci.
spûr-red, ADJ.: spronato; eccitato, istigato. **-rer**, s.: spronatore; eccitatore, *m.* **-rier**, s.: spronaio, *m.* **-ring**, s.: spronare; incitamento, eccitamento, *m.* **-rowel**, s.: spronella, *f.*
spûrt 1, s.: capriccio, ghiribizzo, *m.*; fantasia, *f.*: — *of wind*, soffio di vento, buffo, *m.* **spurt** 2, INTR.: schizzare; zampillare: — *up*, scaturire con impeto.
sputātion, s.: sputare, *m.*; espurgazione, *f.*
spŭtter 1, s.: strepito, romore, fracasso, *m.* **sputter** 2, INTR.: sputacchiare; borbottare; barbugliare. **-er**, s.: che sputacchia; borbottone, *m.*
spȳ 1, s.: spia, *f.*, spione; esploratore, *m.* **spy** 2, TR.: spiare, investigare, osservare; vedere, discernere: — *into*, ricercare; — *out*, scoprire; trovare. **-boat**, s.: cor-

essere a prova di. **-less**, ADJ.: senza prova, senza segno.

prŏp 1, S.: sostegno, puntello; appoggio, aiuto, *m.* **prop** 2, TR.: sostenere, appuntellare; aiutare; favorire.

prŏpa-gable, ADJ.: che si può propagare. **-gănda**, S.: propaganda, *f.* **-gate**, TR.: propagare; multiplicare; divolgare; INTR.: propagarsi; multiplicarsi. **-gātion**, S.: propagazione; multiplicazione, *f.* **-gator**, S.: propagatore, *m.*

propĕl, TR.: cacciare avanti, spingere avanti; impellere. **-ler**, S.: elice; nave ad elice, *f.*

propĕnd, INTR.: propendere; inclinare. **-ency**, S.: propensione; tendenza, inclinazione, *f.*

propĕn-se, ADJ.: inclinato, prono; dedito. **-sion**, **-sity**, S.: propensione; tendenza, *f.*

prŏper, ADJ.: proprio, propio; convenevole, competente; esatto: — *owner*, proprietario, padrone, *m.* **-ly**, ADV.: propiamente; giustamente. **-ness**, S.: convenevolezza; attezza, *f.* **-ty** 1, S.: proprietà; qualità, *f.*: *man of* —, uomo facoltoso, proprietario; *real* —, beni stabili. **-ty** 2, TR.: appropriare; INTR.: appropriarsi.

prŏph-ecy, S.: profezia, predizione, *f.* **-esier**, S.: profeta, *m.* **-esy**, TR.: profeteggiare, predire; INTR.: predire il futuro; predicare. **-et**, S.: profeta, *m.* **-etess**, S.: profetessa, *f.* **-ĕtic(al)**, ADJ.: profetico, di profeta. **-ĕtically**, ADV.: profeticamente. **-etize**, TR.: profetizzare, profeteggiare, predire.

prophylăctic, ADJ.: (*med.*) profilattico.

propinquity, S.: propinquità, vicinità; affinità, *f.*

propi-tiable, ADJ.: conciliabile. **-tiate**, TR.: rendere propizio. **-tiātion**, S.: propiziazione, *f.* **-tiator**, S.: propiziatore; mediatore, *m.* **-tiatory**, ADJ.: propiziatorio. **-tious**, ADJ.: propizio, favorevole. **-tiously**, ADV.: propiziamente, favorevolmente. **-tiousness**, S.: benignità, bontà, *f.*; favore, *m.*

prō-plasm, S.: forma, *f.*, modello, *m.*, matrice, *f.* **-plăstice**, S.: arte di far modelli, *f.*

prŏpolis, S.: propoli, *f.*

propōnent, S.: proponente, *m.*

propōrtion 1, S.: proporzione, simmetria; conformità; porzione, *f.*: *in* — *as*, a misura che. **proportion** 2, TR.: proporzionare, aggiustare. **-able**, ADJ.: proporzionale, proporzionato. **-ableness**, S.: proporzionalità, *f.* **-ably**, ADV.: proporzionalmente. **-al**, ADJ.: proporzionale, proporzionato. **-ălity**, S.: proporzionalità, *f.* **-ally**, ADV.: proporzionalmente, con proporzione. **-ate** 1, ADJ.: proporzionato. **-ate** 2, TR.: proporzionare, aggiustare, adattare. **-ately**, ADV.: proporzionatamente. **-ateness**, S.: proporzionalità, *f.* **-less**, ADJ.: sproporzionato.

propō-sal, S.: proposizione; proposta, offerta, *f.* **-se**, TR.: proporre, offerire; intendere; statuire: *what do you* — *to do?* che intendete di fare? **-ser**, S.: proponente; che propone, *m.*

propositīon, S.: proposizione; offerta, *f.* **-al**, ADJ.: proposto; di proposizione.

propŏund, TR.: proporre; mettere in campo. **-er**, S.: proponente; incettatore, *m.*

prŏpped, ADJ.: puntellato, sostenuto.

proprie-tary, **-tor**, S.: proprietario, padrone, *m.*: *joint* —, comproprietario. **-tress**, S.: proprietaria, padrona, *f.* **-ty**, S.: proprietà; convenevolezza, *f.*

prŏpt = *propped.*

pro-pūgn, TR.: propugnare; difendere. **-pugnātion**, S.: propugnazione; difesa, *f.* **-pūgner**, S.: difenditore, *m.*

propŭl-se, TR.: propulsare. ribattere. **-sion**, S.: espulsione, *f.*

prōre, S.: prora, prua, *f.*

pro-rogātion, S.: proroga, *f.*, allungamento di tempo, *m.* **-rōgue**, TR.: prorogare, prolungare, differire.

prorŭption, S.: prorompimento, *m.*

prosāic, ADJ.: prosaico, di prosa, in prosa.

prōsaist, S.: prosaista, prosatore, *m.*

pro-scribe, TR.: proscrivere, esiliare. **-scriber**, S.: che esilia, condannatore, *m.* **-script**, S.: esiliato, bandito, *m.* **-scription**, S.: proscrizione, *f.*

prōse 1, S.: prosa, *f.* **prose** 2, TR.: prosare, scrivere in prosa.

prŏse-cute, TR.: proseguire, proseguitare: — *at law*, perseguitare in giustizia; processare. **-cūtion**, S.: proseguimento, *m.*; continuazione, *f.* **-cuter**, S.: attore; postulante, *m.*

prŏse-lyte 1, S.: proselito, convertito, *m.* **-lyte** = *proselytize.* **-lytism**, S.: proselitismo, *m.* **-lytize**, TR.: far proseliti, convertire.

prō-ser, S.: prosatore; scrittore tedioso, *m.* **-siness**, S.: carattere prosaico, *m.*; noia, *f.*, tedio, *m.*

pro-sodiacal, ADJ.: di prosodia. **-sōdian**, S.: che è versato nella prosodia.

prŏ-sody, S.: prosodia, *f.*

prosopopœia, S.: (*rhet.*) prosopopea, *f.*

prŏs-pect 1, S.: prospettiva; vista, *f.*; disegno, intento. *m.*: *in* —, in mira. **-pect** 2, INTR.: prospettare, guardare, mirare. **-pĕctive**, ADJ.: prospettivo, provido. **-pĕctive-glass**, S.: cannocchiale, *m.* **-pĕctus**, S.: prospetto, programma, *m.*

stădthọldẹr, S.: statoder, *m.*
stăff, S.: bastone; bordone; spiedo (da caccia), *m.*; asta, *f.*; sostegno, appoggio; versetto, *m.*, stanza, *f.*; stato maggiore, *m.*; autorità, possanza, *f.*: *pilgrim's* —, bordone, *m.*; *bishop's* —, pastorale, *m.*; — *of command*, bastone di comando, *m.* **-ish†**, ADJ.: rigido, aspro. **-officer**, S.: uffiziale dello stato maggiore, *m.* **-tree**, S.: (*bot.*) ligustro, *m.*
stăg, S.: cervo, *m.* **-beetle**, S.: cervo volante, *m*
stāge 1, S.: teatro, *m.*, scena; osteria; posta, *f.*: *get up for the* —, mettere in iscena, sceneggiare; *come to the* —, arrivar alla posta. **stage** 2, TR.: rappresentare pubblicamente. **-box**, S.: palco, palchetto, *m.* **-coach**, S.: carrozza di viaggio, *f.* **-horse**, S.: cavallo di posta, *m.* **-play**, S.: opero di teatro, commedia, *f.* **-player**, S.: commediante, attore, *m.* **-r -ẹr**, S.: attore; praticone, *m.* **-writer**, S.: che scrive commedie.
stăggạrd, S.: cervo di quattro anni, *m.*
stăggẹr, S.: vacillamento, *m.*; TR.: scuotere; allarmare; INTR.: barcollare, traballare; titubare, star dubbioso. **-ing**, ADJ.: vacillante; S.: vacillamento, varcollone, *m.* **-ingly**, ADV.: barcollone. **-ṣ**, S. PL.: vertigine (di cavallo); imbarazzo†, *m.*
stăg-nancy, S.: stagnamento, ristagno, *m.* **-nant**, ADJ.: stagnante. **-nate**, TR.: stagnare. **-nā̆tiọn** = *stagnancy.*
stāid, ADJ.: sobrio; grave; regolare. **-ness**, S.: sobrietà; gravità; regolarità, *f.*
stāin 1, S.: macchia; infamia, *f.* **stain** 2, TR.: macchiare; diffamare. **-ed**, ADJ.: macchiato; tinto, colorato, dipinto; infamato. **-ẹr**, S.: che macchia. **-less**, ADJ.: senza macchia; immacolato, incontaminato.
stāir, S.: grado; scalino, scaglione, *m.*: *flight of* —*s*, ramo di scala, *m.*, scalinata, *f.*; *one pair of* —*s* (*first floor*), primo piano, *m.*; *two pair of* —*s*, secondo appartamento, *m.*; —*s*, scala, *f.*; *go up* —*s*, andar su, montare su. **-case**, S.: scala, *f.*: *winding* —, scala a chiocciola.
stāke 1, S.: steccone, palo, *m.*; palanca; posta; scommessa, *f.*, pericolo, *m.*: *be at* —, esser in pericolo; *lay all at* —, mettere il tutto a ripentaglio; *sweep* —*s*, tirar la posta. **stake** 2, TR.: steccare, guarnire di pali; scommettere; venturare, giocare.
stalăctịte, S.: stalattite, *f.*
stāle 1, ADJ.: stantio, vecchio; vieto, passo, sventato; vapido: — *beer*, birra vecchia, *f.*; — *bread*, pane duro, *m.*; — *wine*, vino vecchio, *m.*; *grow* —, divenire stantio; invecchiare. **stale** 2, S.: manico, *m.*
stale 3, S.: allettamento, *m.*; cosa vecchia. **stale** 4, (IN)TR.: invecchiare; consumarsi. **-ly**, ADV.: già da gran tempo, anticamente. **-ness**, S.: vecchiezza; lunghezza di tempo, *f.*
stâlk 1, S.: stelo, gambo, *m.*; stoppia (di grano, ecc.), *f.*, torso, torsolo (di cavolo), *m.*; andata pomposa, *f.*: — *of corn*, stoppia, *f.* **stalk** 2, INTR.: camminare pomposamente. **-ing-horse**, S.: artifizio, mezzo, pretesto, *m.* **-y**, ADJ.: fibroso, duro.
stâll 1, S.: stalla; mangiatoia; botteghetta; mostra di bottega, *f.*; sedile (nel coro), *m.*: *butcher's* —, desco di beccaio, *m.*; *cobbler's* —, desco di ciabattino, *m.* **stall** 2, TR.: mettere nella stalla, stabilire. **-age**, S.: stallaggio; diritto di poter aprir bottega, *m.* **-fed**, ADJ.: allevato nella stalla. **stâll-iọn**, S.: stallone, *m.*
stâlwạrt, ADJ.: robusto, gagliardo, vigoroso.
stāmen, S.: (*bot.*) stame, *m.*; (*fig.*) origine, *f.*
stăm-ina, S. PL.: stami (de' fiori), primi principi, *m. pl.* **-ĭneous**, ADJ.: composto di stami.
stămmẹr, INTR.: tartagliare, balbettare; esitare: — *out*, profferire balbettando. **-ẹr**, S.: tartaglione, *m.* **-ing**, S.: tartagliare, *m.*, balbuzie, *f.* **-ingly**, ADV.: tartagliando, con balbuzie.
stămp 1, S.: stampa, impronta; impressione, *f.*; segno, *m.*: *postage* —, francobollo, *m.*; *bear the* — *of*, portare l'impronta di.
stamp 2, TR.: stampare, improntare, battere; imprimere; bollare; INTR.: pestare i piedi, colpire col piede, scalpitare, scalpicciare: — *under foot*, calpestare; conculcare; — *with one's foot*, battere col piede in terra. **-act**, S.: legge sul bollo, *f.* **-ẹr**, S.: pastello, pestatoio, *m.* **-fee**, S.: diritto di bollo, *m.* **-ing**, S.: scalpitamento, calpestare, *m.* **-mill**, S.: mulino a pestone, pestone, *m.* **-office**, S.: uffizio di bollo, *m.* **-paper**, S.: carta bollata, *f.*
stânch 1, ADJ.: solido, fermo; onesto, sincero, franco: — *commodity*, mercanzia ben condizionata, *f.*; — *knave*, vero briccone, *m.* **stanch** 2, (IN)TR.: stagnare, ristagnare; stagnarsi.
stânchiọn, S.: sostegno; puntello, *m.*
stânch-less, ADJ.: che non si può stagnare. **-ness**, S.: buona qualità, bontà (d' una mercanzia); fermezza, *f.*
stănd 1, S.: stazione; posta; piazza, *f.*; stato, grado, *m.*; pausa, fermata, *f.*, alto; lucerniere, candelabro; indugio, imbroglio, *m.*; difficoltà, *f.*: *be at a* —, stare irresoluto, esser impacciato, esser imbarazzato; *make a* —, far alto, fermarsi; opporsi, far testa; *put to a* —, imbarazzare; intriga-

rimedio provocativo, *m.* **-cativeness,** S.: qualità provocativa, *f.;* eccitamento, *m.* **-catory,** S.: provocazione, *f.* **-ke,** TR.: provocare, appellare. **-ker,** S.: provocatore, promotore, *m.* **-king,** ADJ.: provocante, irritante: *it is really* —, fa rabbia davvero. **-kingly,** ADV.: in modo provocativo.

prŏvost, S.: proposto, prevosto, *m.:* — *marshal,* proposto della milizia. **-ship,** S.: propostato, *m.*, propositura, *f.*

prŏw 1, ADJ.: valente, valoroso, animoso.

prow 2, S.: prora, prua, proda, *f.*

prŏwess, S.: prodessa, *f.*, valore, *m.;* azioni valorose, *f. pl.*

prŏwl, TR.: cercare di rubare; rubare, saccheggiare: — *about,* andare intorno. **-er,** S.: vagabondo, rubatore; truffatore, *m.*

prŏx-imate, ADJ.: prossimo, vicino; immediato. **-imately,** ADV.: prossimamente; immediatamente. **-ime†** = *proximate.* **-imity,** S.: prossimità, vicinanza, *f.*

prŏxy, S.: deputato; procuratore, *m.;* procura, *f.: be married by* —, esser maritato per procura. **-ship,** S.: uffizio d' un procuratore, *m.*

prū-de, S.: che fa la modesta, affettatuzza, *f.* **-dence,** S.: prudenza, saviezza, *f.* **-dent,** ADJ.: prudente, savio, accorto, circospetto. **-dĕntial,** ADJ.: prudenziale. **-dĕntially, -dently,** ADV.: prudentemente, con prudenza. **-dery,** S.: modestia affettata, affettazione, *f.* **-dish,** ADJ.: di modestia affettata, affettato.

prūne 1, S.: susina secca, prugna, *f.*

prune 2, TR.: dibruscare, diramare; rimondare, potare: — *up,* abbellirsi, adornarsi.

prú-nelle, -nĕllo, S.: prugnola, *f.*

prūner, S.: che scapezza, potatore, *m.*

pruniferous, ADJ.: producente prugne.

prūning, S.: potamento, scapezzare, *m.* **-hook, -knife,** S.: falcetto, *m.*

prūrien-ce, -cy, S.: prudore, pizzicore, **-t,** ADJ.: pizzicante.

pru-riginous, ADJ.: pruriginoso, pizzicante. **-rigo,** S.: prurito, *m.*, prurigine, *f.*

prȳ, INTR.: spiare, investigare, cercare diligentemente. **-ing** (*into*), S.: investigamento, spiamento, *m.*

psâlm, S.: salmo, *m.*, canzone sacra, *f.* **-ist,** S.: salmista, *m.* **-ody,** S.: salmodia, *f.*

psâlter, S.: saltero, libro di salmi, *m.* **-y,** S.: saltero, salterio, *m.* (strumento).

pseū-do, ADJ.: falso, supposto. **-dŏgrapher,** S.: pseudografo, *m.* **-dŏgraphy,** S.: pseudografia, *f.*, scritto supposto, *m.* **-dŏlogy,** S.: falsezza, menzogna, *f.* **-donym,** S.: pseudonimo, *m.*

pshâw! INTERJ.: via via! oibò!

psōra, S.: rogna, *f.*

psȳ-che, S.: (*fig.*) anima; vita, *f.;* spirito, *m.* **-chologic(al),** ADJ.: psicologico. **-chŏlogy,** S.: psicologia, *f.*, trattato sopra l' anima, *m.*

ptisan, S.: tisana, bevanda d' orzo, *f.*

pū-berty, S.: pubertà, adolescenza, *f.* **-bĕscence,** S.: età pubescente, *f.* **-bĕscent,** ADJ.: pubescente, di pubertà.

pŭb-lic 1, ADJ.: pubblico, manifesto, comune, generale: — *house,* osteria, bettola, *f.* **-lic** 2, S.: pubblico, comune, *m.* **-lican,** S.: pubblicano, gabelliere, *m.* **-licā-tion,** S.: pubblicazione, edizione, *f.* **-licist,** S.: pubblicista, *m.* **-licity,** S.: pubblicità, notorietà, *f.* **-licly,** ADV.: pubblicamente, manifestamente, apertamente. **-licness** = *publicity.* **-lic-spirited,** ADJ.: devoto al bene pubblico. **-lic-spiritedness,** S.: devozione al bene pubblico. **-lish,** TR.: pubblicare, manifestare; divolgare, bandire. **-lisher,** S.: pubblicatore; editore, *m.* **-lishing,** S.: pubblicazione, *f.*, pubblicare, *m.*

pūce, ADJ.: del color di pulce.

pūcelage, S.: pulcellaggio, *m.;* virginità, *f.*

pŭck, S.: folletto, diavoletto, *m.* **-ball,** S.: vescia, *f.* (fungo).

pŭcker 1, S.: piega, grinza, *f.* **pucker** 2, TR.: piegare, raggrinzare.

pŭdder 1, S.: romore, strepito, schiamazzo, *m.* **pudder** 2, (IN)TR.: schiamazzare; disturbare.

pŭdding, S.: podingo; sanguinaccio, *m.* **-pie,** S.: torta di carne, *f.* **-time†,** S.: ora di pranzo, *f.: in* —, a tempo.

pŭd-dle 1, S.: guazzo; fango, limo, *m.* **-dle** 2, TR.: sguazzare; imbrattare. **-dle-water,** S.: acqua fangosa, *f.* **-dly,** ADJ.: fangoso, pantanoso.

pū-dency, S.: pudicizia, *f.*, pudore, *m.* **-dĕnda, -dĕndum,** S.: pudenda, *f.* **-dicity,** S.: pudicizia, castità, *f.*

pūer-ile, ADJ.: puerile, fanciullesco. **-ility,** S.: puerizia, fanciullezza, *f.*

puĕrperal, ADJ.: (*med.*) di puerperio.

pūet, S.: upupa, bubbola, *f.*

pŭff 1, S.: soffio; fungo; fiocco, *m.:* — *of smoke,* boccata di fumo. **puff** 2, TR.: soffiare, gonfiare; esaltare; INTR.: gonfiarsi, sbuffare: *huff and* —, anelare, ansare; — *away,* dissipare con un soffio, soffiare violentemente; — *up,* gonfiare; lodare strabocatamente; — *up with pride,* fare insuperbire. **-ball,** S.: vescia, *f.* **-er,** S.: soffiatore, vantatore, *m.* **-in,** S.: smergo marino, *m.* **-iness,** S.: gonfiezza, tumidezza, *f.* **-ingly,** ADV.: tumidamente, in modo gonfio. **-paste,** S.: pasta a foglie, *f.* **-y,** ADJ.: gonfiato, enfiato.

m. **-ing** 2, S.: saltare, *m.*; scossa, *f.* **-ing-hole**, S.: scusa, *f.*, sotterfugio, *m.* **-ingly**, ADV.: a scosse, interrottamente. **-ing-place**, S.: mosse, *f. pl.* **-ish**, ADJ.: alquanto ombroso, un poco pauroso. **-le** 1, S.: salto improvviso, *m.*; subita impressione di paura, *f.* **-le** 2, TR.: spaventare, fare paura; INTR.: tremar di paura, strabiliare. **-up**, S.: uomo da nulla arricchito, *m.*

starvation, S.: morte cagionata dalla fame, *f.*

stârve, TR.: far morire di fame, affamare; INTR.: avere fame; morire di fame: — *with cold*, morire di freddo. **-ling**, S.: animale affamaticcio, *m.*

stârwort, S.: astere, -ro, *m.*

stāte 1, S.: stato; grado, rango, *m.*; ordine; condizione; situazione, *f.*; governo, dominio, *m.*; grandezza, magnificenza, pompa; dignità, *f.*; orgoglio, *m.*, alterigia, *f.*: *bed of* —, letto di rispetto, *m.*; *council of* —, consiglio di stato, *m.*; *live in great* —, vivere splendidamente. **state** 2, TR.: stabilire; regolare, ordinare, determinare. **-craft**, S.: politica, *f.*; maneggio, *m.* **-liness**, S.: pompa, grandezza; maestà; alterigia, *f.* **-ly** 1, ADJ.: grande; magnifico, pomposo; superbo, altero. **-ly** 2, ADV.: pomposamente; superbamente. **-ment**, S.: racconto circostanziato, *m.* **-railway**, S.: strada ferrata dello stato, *f.* **-room**, S.: camerino di vapore, *m.*; camera di ricevimento, *f.* **-sman**, S.: politico; ministro di stato, *m.* **-smanlike**, ADJ.: da uomo di stato. **-smanship**, S.: scienza del governo; politica, *f.* **-swoman**, S.: politica, *f.*

stăt-ic(al), ADJ.: statico. **-ics**, S. PL.: statica, *f.*

stātion 1, S.: posto; staggio, *m.*; stazione; abitazione, *f.*; grado, *m.*, condizione; (*rail.*) stazione, *f.*, atrio (della strada ferrata), *m.* **station** 2, TR.: porre in un posto; dar un impiego. **-ary**, ADJ.: stazionario; fermo. **-er**, S.: cartolaio; che vende carta; libraio, *m.* **-ery**, S.: cartoleria, *f.*, merci di cartolaio, *m. pl.* **-house**, S.: (*rail.*) casa di stazione (per prendere acqua), *f.*

stătist, S.: statista, politico, *m.*

statistic(al), ADJ.: statistico.

stă-tuary, S.: statuario, scultore, *m.* **-tue**, S.: statua, *f.*: *little* —, statuetta, *f.* **-tuĕtte**, S.: statuetta, piccola statua, *f.* **-ture**, S.: statura, *f.* **-tutable**, ADJ.: conforme agli statuti. **-tute**, S.: statuto, *m.*, legge, *f.*

stāve 1, (IN)TR.: fendere, spaccare; sfondare (un barile): — *off*, togliere, respingere, scartare, eliminare. **stave** 2, S.: doga (di botte), *f.*; versetto, rigo, *m.* **-s**, PL. di *staff* o *stave*.

stāy 1, S.: soggiorno; indugio, *m.*, dimora, *f.*; appoggio, sostegno; legaccio, cordoncino, *m.* **-s**, S. PL.: busto (da donna), *m.*: *keep at a* —, tener in freno; *make* —, fermarsi, tardare. **stay** 2, IRR.; TR.: ritenere, fermare; indugiare; appoggiare; appuntellare; placare, calmare; INTR.: stare; fermarsi; soggiornare; indugiare, aspettare: — *a little longer*, trattenersi un po' più; — *away*, assentarsi, scostarsi; — *on* (*upon*), fare capitale, riposarsi. **-band**, S.: cuffietta, *f.* **-ed**, ADJ.: fisso, fermo; discreto, cauto. **-edly**, ADV.: seriamente; discretamente, prudentemente. **-edness**, S.: solidità; prudenza; moderazione, *f.* **-er**, S.: che ferma, che appoggia, *f.* **-lace**, S.: stringa, *f.*, lacciuolo, *m.* **-maker**, S.: fabbricante di busti, *m.* **-s**, S. PL.: busto (da donna), *m.*

stĕad 1, S.: luogo, *m.*; vece, *f.*: *stand in good* —, render servizio; *be in* —, esser utile, servire. **stead** 2, TR.: render servizio, aiutare; sostenere. **-fast**, ADJ.: fermo, sodo, fisso; risoluto. **-fastly**, ADV.: fermamente, costantemente; risolutamente. **-fastness**, S.: fermezza; solidità; costanza, *f.* **-ily**, ADV.: con fermezza, costantemente, saldamente. **-iness**, S.: solidità; fermezza, *f.* **-y** 1, ADJ.: fermo, saldo; posato; sicuro, discreto, cauto. **-y** 2, TR.: render fermo; render sicuro.

stêak, S.: braciuola, fetta sottile di carne, *f.*

stēal, IRR.; (IN)TR.: rubare, involare: — *a thing from one*, involare una cosa ad alcuno, derubare alcuno di una cosa; — *a marriage*, maritarsi clandestinamente; — *away*, involarsi; svignare; — *away from*, distornare, distrarre; — *into*, insinuarsi; — *on*, cattivarsi; — *upon*, sorprendere; ingannare; cogliere al improvisto. **-er**, S.: ladro, rubatore, *m.* **-ing**, S.: rubamento, *m.*, ruberia, *f.* **-ingly**, ADV.: astutamente, clandestinamente, segretamente.

stĕalth, S.: furto, *m.*, ruberia; pratica segreta, *f.*: *by* —, di soppiatto, di nascosto; furtivamente. **-y**, ADJ.: clandestino, segreto, occulto.

stēam 1, S.: vapore, fumo, *m.* **steam** 2, INTR.: vaporare, fumare; esalare. **-bath**, S.: bagno a vapore, *m.* **-boat**, S.: battello a vapore, vascello a vapore, *m.* **-carriage**, S.: vettura a vapore; locomotiva, *f.* **-chimney**, S.: (*loc.*) cammino a vapore, *m.* **-coach**, S.: carrozza a vapore, *m.* **-engine**, S.: macchina a vapore, *f.* **-er**, S.: battello a vapore, vascello a vapore, *m.* **-mill**, S.: mulino a vapore, *m.* **-navigation**, S.: naviga-

pūrblind, ADJ.: di corta vista. **-ness**, S.: corta vista, miopia, *f.*

pūrcha-sable, ADJ.: che si può comprare. **-se** 1, S.: acquisto, *m.*, compra, *f.*; bottino, *m.*: *make a* —, far un acquisto (una compra). **-se** 2, TR.: comprare, acquistare. **-ser**, S.: compratore, acquistatore, *m.*

pūre, ADJ.: puro, mero, chiaro; casto; squisito, eccellente. **-ly**, ADV.: puramente; solamente, semplicemente. **-ness**, S.: purità; innocenza, *f.*

pūrfile, S.: testura d'oro; ricamatura, *f.*

pūr-fle 1, TR.: ricamare. **-fle** 2, **-'flew**, S.: ricamatura, *f.*

purgātion, S.: purgazione, purga; giustificazione, *f.*

pūr-gative, ADJ.: purgativo, evacuativo; S.: medicamento purgativo, *m.*, purga, *f.* **-gatory**, ADJ.: purgativo, purgante; S.: purgatorio, *m.* **-ge** 1, S.: purga; medicina, *f.* **-ge** 2, TR.: purgare; giustificare; INTR.: evacuare; mandare fuori: — *one's self of a suspicion*, purgarsi da un sospetto. **-ger**, S.: purgatore, purgante, *m.* **-ging**, ADJ.: purgativo; S.: purgare, *m.*

purificātion, S.: purificazione, *f.*

pū-rificative, **-rificatory** 1, ADJ.: purificante. **-rificatory** 2, S.: purificatoio, *m.* **-rifier**, S.: che purifica, affinatore, *m.* **-rify**, TR.: purificare; nettare; raffinare; correggere; INTR.: purificarsi. **-rism**, S.: purismo, *m.* **-rist**, S.: purista, *m.* **-ritan**, S., ADJ.: puritano. **-ritānical**, ADJ.: puritano. **-ritanism**, S.: puritanismo, *m.*, credenza presbiteriana, *f.* **-rity**, S.: purità; innocenza, *f.*

pūrl 1, S.: smerlatura; cervogia con assenzio, *f.* **purl** 2, TR.: ornare di frange; INTR.: gorgogliare, mormorare.

pūrlieu, S.: terreno confinante con una foresta, *m.*

pūrling, S.: gorgoglio, mormorio, *m.*

purlōin, TR.: involare, rubare. **-er**, S.: involatore, rubatore, *m.*

pūrpl-e 1, S.: porpora, *f.*; color di porpora, *m.* **-e** 2, ADJ.: porporino: — *colour*, porpora, color di porpora. **-e** 3, TR.: imporporare, tingere colla porpora, invermigliare. **-e-dye**, S.: colore porporino, *m.* **-es**, S. PL.: febbre petecchiale, *f.* **-ish**, ADJ.: porporeggiante, porporino.

pūrport 1, S.: obbietto; tenore, contenuto (d'una scrittura); senso, *m.*, significazione, *f.* **purport** 2, INTR.: intendere; significare.

pūrpose 1, S.: proposito; intento *m.*, intenzione, *f.*, disegno; soggetto; effetto, *m.*, conseguenza; utilità, *f.*: *on* —, a bello studio, a bella posta; *to no* —, in vano, inutilmente; *for what* —? a che fine? a che serve? *for that* —, a questo effetto; *change one's* —, cangiar consiglio; *speak to the* —, parlar a proposito; *to all intents and* —*s*, interamente, affatto. **purpose** 2, (IN)TR.: intendere; proporre; far proposito; deliberare; disegnare. **-less**, ADJ.: inutile. **-ly**, ADV.: a bella posta, deliberatamente.

pūrprise, S.: ricinto, *m.*, chiusura, *f.*

pūrr 1, S.: allodola di mare, *f.* **purr** 2, INTR.: far le fusa (come fa il gatto), tornire. **-ing**, S.: tornire (del gatto), *m.*

pūr-se 1, S.: borsa, *f.*: *little* —, borsellino. **-se** 2, TR.: imborsare, mettere nella borsa. **-se-cutter**, S.: tagliaborse, *m.* **-se-maker**, S.: borsaio, *m.* **-se-net**, S.: tagliuola, *f.* **-se-proud**, ADJ.: fiero delle sue ricchezze. **-ser**, S.: provveditore d'un vascello; commissario de' viveri, *m.* **-siness**, **-siveness**, S.: bolsaggine, *f.*, asma, *m.*

pūrslain, S.: (*bot.*) porcellana, *f.*

pur-sūable, ADJ.: che si può perseguitare. **-sūance**, S.: conseguenza, *f.*; processo, *m.*: *in* — *of*, in seguito a, in conseguenza di. **-sūant**, ADJ.: conforme; secondo; in conseguenza di. **-sūe**, TR.: seguitare, perseguitare; INTR.: continuare. **-sūer**, S.: seguitatore, persecutore, *m.* **-sūit**, S.: persecuzione; caccia; sollecitazione, istanza; diligenza, *f.*: *in the* — *of truth*, nella ricerca del vero; *literary* —*s*, lavori letterari; *mercantile* —*s*, occupazioni mercantili.

pūrsuivant, S.: messaggiere del araldo, *m.*

pūrsy, ADJ.: bolso, asmatico.

pūrtenance, S.: frattaglie, *f. pl.*

pūrulen-ce, **-cy**, S.: purulenza, *f.*, marcidume, *m.* **-t**, ADJ.: purulento, marcioso.

purvēy, (IN)TR.: provvedere, procacciare, procurare. **-ance**, S.: provvisione, *f.*; viveri, *m. pl.* **-er**, S.: provveditore, provvisore, *m.*

pŭs, S.: marcia, materia, *f.*; marciume, *m.*

pŭsh 1, S.: spinta, *f.*, urto, colpo; assalto; sforzo, *m.*; bollicola, pustula, *f.*; termine, fine, *m.*: *bring to the last* —, condurre a fine; *give one a* —, dare una spinta ad uno. **push** 2, TR.: spingere, urtare, cacciare; eccitare; INTR.: portare una botta; sforzarsi: — *one's self forward*, ficcarsi avanti; — *at*, assalire; — *back*, rispingere; — *down*, cacciare abbasso; — *forward*, sospingere, cacciar avanti; — *in*, ficcar dentro; — *on*, seguitare; continuare; urgere; spronare. **-er**, S.: spingitore, *m.* **-ing**, ADJ.: coraggioso, animoso; intraprendente. **-pin**, S.: spingere le spille, *m.* (giuoco).

pusil-lanimity, S.: pusillanimità, timidità, *f.* **-lānimous**, ADJ.: pusillanimo,

ostinato, caparbio. **-ness**, s.: rigidezza, saldezza, durezza; caparbietà, *f.*
sti-fle, TR.: soffocare; sopprimere. **-fling** 1, ADJ.: soffocante. **-fling** 2, s.: soffocamento, affogamento, *m.*
stig-ma, s.: segno d' infamia; disonore, *m.*, infamia, *f.* **-mătic(al)**, ADJ.: ignominioso, infame. **-matize**, TR.: stimatizzare, segnare con ferro caldo; diffamare.
stile 1, s.: barriera, *f.*; gnomone. **stile** 2, s.: stilo, *m.*
stilétto, s.: stiletto, *m.*
still 1, ADJ.: quieto, tranquillo; cheto; stagnante: — *water*, acqua cheta. **still** 2, ADV.: fin adesso, ancora, sempre. **still** 3, s.: calma, *f.*, silenzio. **still** 4, TR.: far tacere, calmare, tranquillare. **still** 5, s.: lambicco, *m.* **-atitious**, ADJ.: gocciolante, distillato. **-atory**, s.: distillatoio, *m.*
still-born, ADJ.: morto nato.
still-icide†, s.: stillicidio, *m.* **-ing**, s.: distillazione, *f.*
still-ness, s.: calma, bonaccia; quiete, *f.*; silenzio, *m.* **-y**, ADV.: in silenzio, tranquillamente, quietamente.
stilts, s. PL.: trampoli, *m. pl.*
stimu-late, TR.: stimolare, spronare; incitare, animare. **-lating**, s.: eccitamento, *m.* **-lātion**, s.: stimolazione, *f.*; stimolo, *m.* **-lative**, ADJ.: stimolativo. **-lator**, s.: stimolatore, *m.*
sting 1, s.: spina, *f.*, ago; stimolo; rimorso, *m.* **sting** 2, IRR.; TR.: pungere, trafiggere.
stingi-ly, ADV.: avaramente, sordidamente. **-ness**, s.: avarizia, sordidezza, spilorceria; miseria, *f.*
sting-ing, s.: pungimento, *m.*, puntura, morsicatura, *f.* **-less**, ADJ.: senza pungiglione. **-o**, s.: birra vecchia e forte, *f.*
stingy, ADJ.: avaro, taccagno, sordido, spilorcio.
stink 1, s.: puzzo, fetore, *m.*, puzza, *f.* **stink** 2, IRR.; INTR.: puzzare, putire. **-ard**, s.: uomo sordido, taccagno, spilorcio, *m.* **-er**, s.: cosa che ha cattivo odore, *f.* **-ing**, ADJ.: puzzolente, puzzoso: — *fellow*, uomo vile, *m.* **-ingly**, ADV.: fetidamente. **-pot**, s.: composto di cattivo odore, *m.*
stint 1, s.: limite, confine, *m.*; porzione, *f.*: *go beyond the* —, passare i limiti. **stint** 2, TR.: limitare; ristringere, frenare, raffrenare, reprimere; INTR.: cessare, tralasciare.
sti-pend, s.: stipendio, salario, *m.*, paga, *f.* **-pĕndiary** 1, ADJ.: stipendiario, stipendiato. **-pendiary** 2, s.: stipendiario, *m.*
stipple, TR.: incidere con punteggio.
stiptic(al), ADJ.: (*med.*) stiptico, astringente.

stipu-late, INTR.: stipulare, fare contratto. **-lātion**, s.: stipulazione, *f.*, contratto, *m.* **-lator**, s.: stipulante, *m.*
stir 1, s.: strepito, romore, fracasso, scompiglio, *m.* **stir** 2, TR.: muovere; agitare, scuotere; INTR.: muoversi; agitarsi, scuotersi: — *the corn*, voltare il grano; — *the fire*, attizzare il fuoco; — *the humours*, provocare gli umori; — *about*, andare attorno; imbrigarsi, industriarsi; — *up*, suscitare, eccitare.
stirp†, s.: stirpe, progenie, *f.*
stir-rage†, s.: movimento, *m.* **-rer**, s.: che è in moto; che si leva di buon' ora; stimolatore; sedizioso, *m.* **-ring**, ADJ.: muovente, in moto; affaccendato, attivo; sedizioso; s.: movimento, *m.*, sollevazione, *f.*
stirrup, s.: staffa, *f.* **-cup**, **-glass**, s.: mancia, benandata, *f.* **-leather**, s.: striscia della staffa, *f.*, staffile, *m.* **-stockings**, s. PL.: calze a staffa, *f. pl.*
stitch 1, s.: punto (fatto coll' ago); dolore pungente, *m.*; maglia, *f.*: *take up a* —, pigliare (riprendere) una maglia. **stitch** 2, TR.: appuntare; cucire (un libro); pungere: — *up*, racconciare, risarcire. **-ed**, ADJ.: cucito; legato alla rustica. **-er**, s.: cucitore, *m.*, cucitrice *f.* **-ery**, s.: lavoro d' ago, *m.* **-ing**, s.: appuntare, cucire, *m.* **-ing-silk**, s.: seta grossa, *f.* **-wort**, s.: camomilla, *f.*
stithy, s.: ancudine, *f.*
stive, TR.: stufare, riscaldare.
stōak, TR.: turare.
stōat, s.: ermellino (d' estate), *m.*
stoccā-de, **-do**, s.: stoccata, *f.*
stŏck 1, s.: tronco, gambo; stelo, fusto; manico, *m.*; azione, *f.*; fondo, capitale, principale, *m.*; razza, schiatta, famiglia, *f.*; garofano, *m.*; cravatta, *f.*, collare; minchione, sciocco; monte (delle carte): —*s*, ceppi; fondi pubblici, *m. pl.*; — *of a gun*, cassa d' uno schioppo, *f.*; *large* — *of goods*, buona quantità di mercanzie; *laughing*—, ludibrio, zimbello, *m.*; *leaning* —, appoggio, sostegno, *m.* **stock** 2, TR.: empiere; fornire, provvedere, munire; sbarbare; svellere, estirpare. **-broker**, s.: agente di cambio, *m.* **-dove**, s.: colombo, *m.* **-fish**, s.: baccalà, *f.* **-gillyflower**, s.: garafano, *m.*, viola, *f.* **-holder**, s.: azionario, *m.* **-ing**, s.: calza, calzetta, *f.* **-ing-frame**, s.: telaio di calzettaio, *m.* **-ing-mender**, s.: conciacalzette, *f.* **-ing-weaver**, s.: calzettaio, *m.* **-ish**, s.: stupido, sciocco. **-jobber**, s.: sensale di fondi pubblici, *m.* **-jobbing**, s.: senseria, *f.* **-lock**, s.: serratura fissa in legno, *f.* **-still**, ADJ.: immobile; fermo.
stŏi-c, s.: stoico, *m.* **-cal**, ADJ.: stoico,

quàdr-: **-agènary**, ADJ.: quadragenario. **-agèsima**, S.: digiuno di quaranta giorni, *m.* **-agèsimal**, ADJ.: quaresimale, di quaresima. **-angle**, S.: quadrangolo, *m.* **-àngular**, ADJ.: quadrangolare. **-ant**, S.: quadrante, *m.*; quarta parte, *f.* **-ate** 1, ADJ.: quadrato, quadro; convenevole; S.: quadrato, *m.* **-ate** 2, INTR.: quadrare; accomodarsi. **-àtic**, ADJ.: quadratico, di quattro lati. **-ature**, S.: quadratura, *f.* **-ènnial**, ADJ.: quadriennio. **-ifid**, ADJ.: (*bot.*) quadrifido. **-ilàteral**, ADJ.: quadrilatero. **-ille**, S.: quadriglia (ballo). **-inòmial**, S.: quadrinomio, *m.* **-ipartite**, ADJ.: quadripartito. **-ipartìtion**, S.: quadripartizione, *f.* **-ireme**, ADJ.: con quattro ordini di remi. **-isỳllable**, S.: quadrisillabo, *m.* **-òon**, S.: quadrone, meticcio, *m.*, quadrona, *f.* **-uped**, ADJ.: quadrupede; S.: quadrupede, quadrupedo, *m.* **-uple**, S.: quadruplo. **-ùplicate**, TR.: quadruplicare, multiplicare per quadruplo. **-uplicàtion**, S.: quadruplicazione, *f.* **-uply**, ADV.: per quattro volte più.

quàff, INTR.: sbevazzare, trincare. **-er**, S.: bevitore, beone, *m.* **-ing**, S.: beveria, bevuta, *f.*

quàg-gy, ADJ.: melmoso, fangoso. **-mire**, S.: pantano, marese, *m.*

quàil 1, S.: quaglia, *f.* (uccello): *water* —, gallina regina, *f.* **quail** 2, INTR.: quagliare; languire, svenire. **-ing**, S.: languore, debilitamento, *m.* **-pipe**, S.: richiamo da tentar le quaglie, *m.*

quàint, ADJ.: bello† (squisito); scrupoloso† (esatto); strano, singolare, bizzarro, fantastico. **-ly**, ADV.: squisitamente†; bizzarramente, stranamente. **-ness**, S.: leggiadria†; eleganza†; bizzarria, stranezza, singolarità, *f.*

quàk-e 1, S.: tremito, tremore, *m.* **-e** 2, INTR.: tremare; scuotersi. **Quàk-er**, S.: quacchero, *m.* **-erism**, S.: quacchedrismo, *m.* **-ing** 1, S.: tremito, tremore, *m.* **-ing** 2, ADJ.: tremante; tremoloso.

qual-ificàtion, S.: qualificazione, qualità, *f.*, talento, *m.* **-ificator**, S.: qualificatore, *m.* **-ified**, ADJ.: capace; idoneo, propio. **-ifier**, S.: qualificatore, *m.* **-ify**, TR.: qualificare, adattare; temperare, moderare; quietare: — *one's self*, rendersi capace, capacitarsi; addattarsi; *be qualified*, aver le qualità volute; aver il diritto. **-ity**, S.: qualità; condizione; natura; nobilità, *f.*: *man of* —, gentiluomo, *m.*; *in his* — *of*, nella sua qualità di.

quàlm, S.: nausea, *f.*; mal di cuore, *m.* **-ish**, ADJ.: nauseato, disposto a recere.

quàndary, S.: dubbio, *m.*, esitazione, *f.*: *be in a* —, non sapere che fare.

quàn-titative, **-titive**, ADJ.: quantitativo. **-tity**, S.: quantità, *f.*, gran numero, *m.* **-tum**, S.: quantità, *f.*; totale, *m.*

quàrantine, S.: quarantina, *f.*: *pass* —, *perform* —, far la quarantina.

quàrrel 1, S.: disputa, contesa, lite, *f.*: — *of a cross-bow*, freccia, saetta, *f.*; *breed* —*s*, eccitare lite; *pick up a* — *with one*, appiccar lite con alcuno. **quarrel** 2, INTR.: contendere, litigare, rabbuffare: — *with*, trovare a ridire. **-er**, contenditore, beccalite, *m.* **-ing**, S.: lite, *f.* **-some**, ADJ.: riottoso, rissoso. **-somely**, ADV.: riottosamente. **-someness**, S.: umore rissoso, *m.*

quàrry 1, S.: quadrato, quadrello, *m.*; petraia; preda degli uccelli di rapina, *f.* **quarry** 2, TR.: scavare le pietre; (*hunt.*) vivere di rapina. **-man**, S.: lavoratore nelle petraie, *m.*

quàrt, S.: boccale, *m.* (misura); quarta, *f.* **-an**, S.: febbre quartana, *f.* **-er** 1, S.: quarto, *m.*, quarta parte, *f.*; quartiere, *m.*; dimora, grazia, *f.*: — *of an hour*, quarto d' ora; — *of a pound*, quarto di libbra; —*s of the moon*, quarti della luna; *winter* —*s*, alloggiamenti d' inverno; *it is a* — *past two*, sono le due ed un quarto; *cry* —, domandar la vita; *give* —, dar quartiere; *take* —, pigliar quartiere; *have free* —*s*, esser alloggiato a discrezione; *take up one's* —, acquartierarsi. **-er** 2, TR.: squartare; alloggiare; INTR.: esser alloggiato. **-erage**, S.: salario d' ogni quarto d' anno, *m.* **-er-day**, S.: ultimo giorno del quartiere, *m.* **-er-deck**, S.: cassero d' un vascello, *m.* **-erly**, ADJ.: di quarto, trimestrale; ADV.: per quartiere; ogni tre mesi; — *review*, rivista trimestrale. **-er-master**, S.: quartiermastro, *m.* **-ern**, S.: mezza foglietta, *f.* (misura). **-er-piece**, S.: quartiere di scarpa, *m.* **-er-staff**, S.: bastone lungo da battersi, *m.* **-ile**, ADJ.: (*astr.*) della quadratura. **-èt**, S.: (*mus.*) quartetto, *m.* **-o**, ADJ.: in quarto; S.: libro in quarto, *m.*: — *volume*, volume (libro) in quarto.

quàrtz, S.: quarzo, *m.*

quàsh, TR.: conquassare, fracassare, rovinare; annullare; disfare.

quassàtion, S.: scossa, *f.*

quàssia, S.: (*phar.*) quassia, *f.*

quàt†, S.: pustula, *f.*

quàter-cousins, S. PL.: buoni amici, *m. pl.*

quatèr-nary, **-nion**, S.: quaternità, *f.*

quàtrain, S.: quadernario, *m.*

quàver 1, S.: (*mus.*) croma, *f.*; trillo, tremore, *m.* **quaver** 2, INTR.: gorgheggiare, trillare: — *a note*, trillare una nota. **-ing**, S.: trillo, gorgheggiare, *m.*

—, dirizzare; levare su; *make — again*, ridirizzare. **-en**, TR.: dirizzare, far diritto. **-forth**, ADV.: direttamente, immediatamente. **-ly**, ADV.: in linea retta. **-ness**, S.: rettitudine, dirittura, *f.* **-way(s)**, ADV.: immediate, subito.

străin 1, S.: razza, schiatta; disposizione, *f.*; umore, *m.* **strain** 2, S.: sforzo; storcimento, *m.*; suono, *m.*; canzone, aria, *f.*; stile; grado; carattere; qualità, *f.*: *high — of speech*, stile sublime, *m.*; *take too high —*, alzarsi troppo; *melodious —*, concenti armoniosi, *m. pl.* **strain** 3, TR.: spremere, premere, stringere; colare, filtrare; violentare; INTR.: sforzarsi, fare ogni sforzo, ingegnarsi; *— out*, spremere, estrarre; *— one's voice*, sforzare la voce; *— one's eyes*, aguzzare gli occhi; sforzarsi per vedere; *— every nerve*, far ogni sforzo. **-er**, S.: colatoio, *m.* **-ing**, S.: colamento, *m.*; tensione; forza, violenza, *f.*

străit 1, ADJ.: stretto, angusto; intimo, intrinseco; rigoroso, rigido; penoso. **strait** 2, S.: stretto, *m.*; difficoltà; angustia, penuria, *f.*: *be in great —s*, trovarsi in grandi strette (grandi angustie); essere molto travagliato. **strait** 3, TR.: imbarazzare; travagliare. **-en**, TR.: stringere, ristringere, angustiare; serrare, violentare. **-ened**, ADJ.: angustiato, travagliato. **-handed**, ADJ.: avaro, taccagno. **-handedness**, S.: avarizia, *f.* **-jacket**, S.: camicia di forza, *f.* **-laced**, ADJ.: allacciato, ristretto. **-ly**, ADV.: strettamente; rigidamente. **-ness**, S.: strettezza; angustia, difficoltà, necessità; intimità, intrinsichezza, *f.*; rigore, *m.*

străke†, S.: striscia, *f.*

stramineous, ADJ.: di paglia.

strănd 1, S.: piaggia, sponda, *f.*, lido, *m.* **strand** 2, S.: filo di corda, *m.* **strand** 3, INTR.: dare sulle secche. **-ed**, ADJ.: naufragato sulla piaggia.

străn-ge 1, ADJ.: strano, straordinario, bizzarro: *look — upon one*, far cattiva cera ad uno. **-ge** 2, INTERJ.: maraviglia! stranezza! **-ge!** 3, TR.: alienare; INTR.: maravigliarsi. **-gely**, ADV.: stranamente; maravigliosamente. **-geness**, S.: stranezza; singolarità, rarità, *f.* **-ger** 1, S.: straniero, forestiero, *m.*: *be a — to*, non sapere nulla di; ignorare, non essere conosciuto; *you are quite a —*, voi non vi fate mai vedere. **-ger** 2, TR.: allontanare, alienare.

străn-gle, TR.: strangolare; strozzare. **-gler**, S.: che strangola. **-gles**, S. PL.: stranguglioni, *m. pl.* **-gle-weed**, S.: (*bot.*) orobanche, *f.* **-gulātion**, S.: strozzatura, *f.*

străngury, S.: stranguria, *f.*

străp 1, S.: coreggia, *f.*, striscia di cuoio, *f.* **strap** 2, TR.: scoreggiare.

strappădo, S.: strappata, *f.*, tratto di corda, *m.*

străpping, ADJ.: grande, grosso: *— girl*, giovinastra, *f.*

străta, S. PL.: strati, suoli, *m. pl.*

străta-gem, S.: stratagemma, *m.*, astuzia, furberia, *f.* **-gĕmical**, ADJ.: pieno di stratagemme; astuto, furbo.

strat-ificātion, S.: stratificazione, *f.* **-ify**, TR.: stratificare.

străt-um (pl. *strata*), S.: strato; letto; pavimento, *m.*

strâw, S.: paglia, *f.*; festuco; filo di paglia; niente, *m.*: *stack of —*, pagliaio, *m.*; *man of —*, uomo di paglia, uomo da nulla, *m.*; *it isn't worth a —*, non vale un fico. **-bed**, S.: letto di paglia, pagliaccio, paglierìccio, *m.* **-berry**, S.: fragola, *f.* **-berry-plant**, S.: pianta di fragola, *f.* **-built**, ADJ.: fatto di paglia, coperto di paglia. **-coloured**, ADJ.: di color di paglia. **-hat**, S.: cappello di paglia, *m.* **-stuffed**, ADJ.: riempito di paglia. **-worm**, S.: baco di paglia, *m.* **-y**, ADJ.: fatto di paglia.

strāy 1, ADJ.: sviato, travviato. **stray** 2, S.: sviamento; vagabondo, *m.* **stray** 3, INTR.: sviare, travviare.

strēak 1, S.: striscia, riga, *f.*; cerchio (d'una ruota), *m.* **streak** 2, TR.: strisciare, rigare. **-y**, ADJ.: strisciato, rigato.

strēam 1, S.: corrente, *f.*, ruscello; rivolo, ruscelletto; corso, *m.*: *little —*, ruscelletto, *m.*; *— of light*, raggio di lume, *m.*; *— of words*, abbondanza di parole, *f.*; *go with the —*, andare a seconda. **stream** 2, TR.: strisciare, rigare; INTR.: scorrere, zampillare; sorgere, uscire; gettare raggi. **-er**, S.: pennoncello, *m.*, banderuola, *f.* **-let**, S.: ruscelletto, ruscello, *m.* **-y**, ADJ.: scorrente; fluido.

strēet, S.: strada, via; contrada, *f.* **-door**, S.: porta di dinanzi, *f.* **-walker**, S.: squaldrina, bagascia, *f.*

strĕngth, S.: forza, possanza, *f.*; vigore; energia; fortificazione, *f.*, forte, *m.*: *gather —*, ripigliar le forze, rimettersi. **-en**, TR.: fortificare, afforzare; dar vigore; INTR.: fortificarsi; rinforzarsi. **-ener**, S.: corroborante, *m.* **-less**, ADJ.: privo di forza; impotente, inefficace. **-ner** = *strengthener*.

strĕnuous, ADJ.: strenuo, valoroso, bravo; attivo. **-ly**, ADV.: strenuamente, valorosamente; attivamente. **-ness**, S.: forza, arditezza, *f.*, valore; coraggio, *m.*

strĕperous, ADJ.: strepitoso, romoroso.

strĕss, S.: punto principale, *m.*; importanza; forza, *f.*: *— of the voice*, sforzo

quinary, ADJ.: quinario.
quince, S.: melacotogna, *f.* **-tree**, S.: cotogno, *m.*
quinine, S.: chinina, *f.*
quinqua-gēnary, ADJ.: quinquagenario. **-gēsima**, S.: quinquagesima; pentecoste, *f.*
quinquángular, ADJ.: di cinque angoli.
quinquénnial, ADJ.: quinquennale, di cinque anni.
quinquina†, S.: (*phar.*) chinachina, *f.*
quinsy, S.: squinanzia, *f.*
quint, S.: quinta, *f.* (al giuoco di picchetto). **-ain**, S.: quintana, *f.* (giuoco). **-al**, S.: quintale, *m.* **-éssence**, S.: quintessenza, *f.*, estratto, *m.* **-ĕt**, S.: quintetto, *m.* **-in** = *quintain*. **-uple**, ADJ.: quintuplo.
quip 1, S.: burla, *f.*, motteggio, *m.*, botta, *f.*, bottone, *m.* **quip** 2, INTR.: burlare; esser sarcastico.
quire 1, S.: coro (di chiesa); quinterno (di carta), *m.* **quire** 2, INTR.: cantare in coro.
quirk, S.: cavillo; accesso; bottone, *m.* **-ish**, ADJ.: cavilloso, sottile.
quit 1, ADJ.: libero, liberato: *go* —, esser fuor d' impaccio. **quit** 2, TR.: abbandonare, lasciare; uscire di; rinunziare, desistere, cessare, far quitanza; liberare; giustificare: — *one's ground*, andare via; — *one's self of*, liberarsi, sbrigarsi di; — *a design*, desistere da un' impresa; — *a siege*, levare l' assedio. **-claim** 1, S.: rinunziazione, *f.* **-claim** 2, INTR.: rinunziare, desistere.
quite, ADV.: affatto, intieramente: — *well*, benissimo, benone; *not* —, non al tutto.
quit-rent, S.: censo, *m.*; rendita, *f.* **-s!** INTERJ.: pace! pagati del tutto! **-tal**, **-tance** 1, S.: quitanza, ricevuta; ricompensa, *f.* **-tance** 2, TR.: rimunerare, ricompensare; riconoscere. **-ter**, S.: scoria di latta, *f.*
quiver 1, INTR.: tremare; trillare. **quiver** 2, S.: faretra, *f.*, turcasso, *m.* **-ed**, ADJ.: faretrato. **-ing**, S.: tremamento, *m.*
quixōtic, ADJ.: chisciottesco.
quiz 1, S.: mistificazione, *f.*; burlone, *m.* **quiz** 2, TR.: mistificare; burlare, sbirciare. **-ical**, ADJ.: scherzevole, faceto.
quŏb, TR.: battere, palpitare.
quŏdlibet, S.: motto, *m.*; sottigliezza, *f.*
quoif†, **-fure** = *coif*, *-fure*.
...**n**, S.: (*arch.*) cantone, *m.*, cantonata,
...) cuneo, *m.*
... S.: disco, *m.*; piastrella, *f.*
... (IN)TR.: giuocare alle morelle.
... ADJ.: d' altre volte, vetusto.
...numero sufficiente, *m.*: *form*
...numero per deliberare.
quōta, S.: contingente, *m.*, parte, *f.*
quotātion, S.: citazione, allegazione, *f.*: — *points*, virgolette.
quō-te, TR.: citare, allegare; addurre; (*typ.*) virgolettare. **-ter**, S.: che allega, citatore, *m.* **-th**, DEF. VERB: — *I*, dico io; dissi io; — *he*, dice egli; disse egli.
quotídian, ADJ.: quotidiano, cotidiano; S.: febbre quotidiana, *f.*
quōtient, S.: (*arith.*) quoziente, *m.*
quōting, S.: citazione, *f.*

R

r âr (*the letter*), S.: r, *f.* (*m.*).
rabāte, TR.: (*falc.*) ricovrare (il falcone).
răbbet 1, S.: scanalatura, incastratura, *f.* **rabbet** 2, TR.: scanalare, incastrare.
răb-bi, S.: rabbi, rabbino, *m.* **-binical**, ADJ.: rabbinico, di rabbino. **-binist**, S.: rabbinista, *m.*
răbbit, S.: coniglio, *m.*: *young* —, coniglietto, *m.*; *Welch* —, fetta di pane con cacio, *f.*; —'*s nest*, tana de' conigli, *f.*; — *warren*, conigliera, *f.*
răbble, S.: plebe, *f.*, popolaccio, *m.* **-ment**, S.: folla di popolaccio, *f.*, popolaccio tumultuante, *m.*
răbid, ADJ.: rabbioso, stizzoso. **-ness**, S.: rabbia, *f.*
raccōon, S.: tasso americano, *m.*
rāc-e 1, S.: razza, stirpe. **race** 2, S.: corsa, *f.*, patio, *m.*: *foot* —, corsa a piedi, *f.* **race** 3, INTR.: contendere al corso. **-horse**, S.: cavallo da corsa, corsiere, corridore; barbero, *m.*
racemātion, S.: grappolo, racemo, racimolo, *m.* **-miferous**, ADJ.: racemifero, racemoso.
rācer, S.: corsiere, corridore, *m.*
răch†, S.: cane da caccia, *m.*
rāciness, S.: gusto piccante (del vino), *m.*
răck 1, S.: tortura, corda; rastrelliera, *f.*, rastrello (di cucina), *m.*; rocca, *f.*; stanghe (d' un carro), *f. pl.*: — *of mutton*, collo di castrato, *m.*; *put to the* —, collare, dare la corda, mettere alla tortura. **rack** 2, TR.: dar la corda, tormentare; travasare; tramutare (il vino, ecc.): — *one's brains*, lambiccarsi il cervello. **-er**, S.: tormentatore, *m.*
răcket 1, S.: rumore, *m.* **racket** 2, S.: racchetta, *f.* **-maker**, S.: facitore di racchette, *m.*
răcking, S.: tortura, *f.*
răckrent, S.: affitto sforzato, *m.* **-er**, S.: livellario sopraggravato, *m.*
rācy, ADJ.: piccante; saporoso, gustoso (del vino).
răddle, TR.: intrecciare.

agognare a; — *with* (*against*), lottare (combattere) con. **-gler**, s.: contenditore; opponente, *m.* **-gling**, s.: scossa, lotta; contesa, *f.*

strū-ma, s.: struma, scrofola, *f.* **-mous**, ADJ.: scrofoloso.

strŭmpet, s.: cattiva donna, *f.*

strŭt 1, s.: camminare affettato, *m.* **strut** 2, INTR.: pavoneggiarsi, ringalluzzarsi. **-tingly**, ADV.: pavoneggiante; affettatamente.

strȳchnine, s.: stricnina, *f.*

stŭb 1, s.: ceppo, tronco, *m.* **-stub** 2, TR.: sradicare, svellere. **-bed**, ADJ.: membruto, robusto, forte. **-bedness**, s.: qualità d' esser corto e robusto; figura corta e spessa, *f.*

stŭbble, s.: stoppia, *f.* **-goose**, s.: oca d' autunno, *f.*

stŭbborn, ADJ.: ostinato, ritroso, pertinace, caparbio. **-ly**, ADV.: ostinatamente, pertinacemente, con caparbietà. **-ness**, s.: ostinazione, pertinacia, caparbietà, *f.*

stŭb-by, ADJ.: corto e grosso, paffuto. **-nail**, s.: chiodo usato, chiodo rotto, *m.*

stŭcco 1, s.: stucco, *m.* **stucco** 2, TR.: stuccare.

stŭckle, s.: quantità di covoni, *f.*

stŭd 1, s.: borchia, *f.*; palo, *m.*; razza (di cavalli), *f.*, bottone, bottoncino, *m.*: *gold —s*, bottoncini di oro. **stud**, TR.: guarnire di borchie.

stūdent, s.: studente, scolare; letterato, *m.*: *fellow-—*, camerata di studio, *m.*: *medical —*, studente di medicina, *m.*

stŭd-ied, ADJ.: studiato, letterato; versato. **-ier**, s.: studiante, studente, *m.*

stūdio, s.: studio (d' artista), *m.*

stūdious, ADJ.: studioso; attento: *live a — life*, passar la vita studiando. **-ly**, ADV.: studiosamente, con diligenza. **-ness**, s.: applicazione allo studio; attenzione, *f.*

stŭdy 1, s.: studio, *m.*; applicazione, diligenza, *f.*; studiuolo, gabinetto, *m.*: *be in a brown —*, star pensieroso; esser malinconico. **study** 2, TR.: studiare; osservare; INTR.: studiarsi; applicarsi, ingegnarsi. **-ing**, s.: studiare, studio, *m.*

stŭff 1, s.: stoffa; materia, *f.*; drappo, *m.*: *household —*, mobili, *m. pl.*; masserizie, *f. pl.*; *kitchen —*, grascia di cucina, *f.*: *silk —s*, tessuti di seta. **stuff!** 2, INTERJ.: bagattella! *what —!* che robaccia! **stuff** 3, TR.: riempire, riempiere, stivare; satollare; INTR.: mangiare con voracità: — *up*, turare, stoppare; soffocare. **-ing**, s.: stivamento, *m.*; borra, *f.*

stŭket, s.: stucco, *m.*

stŭltify, TR.: istupidire.

stultiloquence, **-quy**, s.: stoltiloquio, vaniloquio, *m.*; assurdità, *f.*

stŭm 1, s.: mosto, *m.* **stum** 2, TR.: fare fermentare di nuovo (il vino).

stŭm-ble 1, s.: passo falso; errore, fallo, *m.* **-ble** 2, TR.: fare inciampare; INTR.: inciampare; errare, fallire: — *at*, farsi scrupolo di; fallire; — *upon*, rincontrare a caso, intoppare, imbattersi in. **-bler**, s.: che inciampa, che fa un passo falso. **-bling**, s.: inciampo, intoppo, *m.* **-bling-block**, s.: inciampo, intoppo; ostacolo, *m.* **-bling-horse**, s.: cavallo che inciampa, *m.* **-blingly**, ADV.: con inciampo. **-bling-stone** = *stumbling-block*.

stŭmp 1, s.: tronco, ceppo, toppo; moncone, moncherino, *m.* **stump** 2, TR.: stralciare; INTR.: camminare come un villano. **-footed**, ADJ.: che ha il piè storto. **-y**, ADJ.: pieno di ceppi; duro, sodo.

stŭn, TR.: stordire, sbalordire.

stŭng, impf. e part. del v. *sting*.

stŭnning, ADJ.: assordante; (*pop.*) splendido, elegante; s.: stordimento, *m.*; sorpresa, *f.*

stŭnt, TR.: impedire l' accrescimento; fare intristire. **-ed**, ADJ.: mal cresciuto: *grow —*, intristire, provenire male.

stūpe 1, s.: fomento, *m.*, fomentazione, *f.* **stupe** 2, TR.: fomentare; spruzzare.

stūpefac-tion, s.: stupefazione, *f.*, stupore, *m.* **-tive**, ADJ.: stupefattivo.

stupĕndous, ADJ.: stupendo, maraviglioso. **-ly**, ADV.: maravigliosamente. **-ness**, s.: stupore, *m.*, maraviglia, *f.*

stū-pid, ADJ.: stupido, sciocco, scempiato, goffo. **-pidity**, s.: stupidità, stupidezza, *f.* **-pidly**, ADV.: stupidamente, goffamente. **-pidness** = *stupidity*. **-pifier**, s.: rimedio sonnifero, *m.* **-pify**, TR.: stupefare. **-por**, s.: stupore; intormentimento, *m.*

stū-prate, TR.: stuprare, violare. **-prátion**, s.: stupro, *m.*

stŭr-dily, ADV.: bruscamente, stizzosamente, ostinatamente. **-diness**, s.: caparbietà, insolenza; rigidezza, robustezza, forza, *f.* **-dy**, ADJ.: caparbio; robusto, gagliardo, forte.

stŭrgeon, s.: storione, *m.* (pesce).

stŭrk, s.: giovenco, bue giovane, *m.*; giovenca, *f.*

stŭtter, INTR.: tartagliare, balbettare. **-er**, s.: tartaglione, borbottone, *m.* **-ing**, s.: balbettare, barbugliamento, *m.* **-ingly**, ADV.: in modo balbettante.

stȳ 1, s.: porcile, *m.*, stia, *f.* **sty** 2, TR.: chiudere nel porcile.

Stȳgian, ADJ.: stigio, inferno.

stȳ-le 1, s.: stile; titolo, *m.*; forma, *f.*; modo, *m.*; pratica, *f.*: *in the Roman —*, ad uso de' Romani. **-le** 2, s.: chiamare, appellare: — *one's self*, nominarsi, chiamarsi. **-let**, s.: stiletto, *m.*

rambōose†, S.: bevanda di vino, cervogia e zucchero, *f.*
rămekin, S.: fetta di pane e cacio, *f.*
rami-ficātion, S.: ramificazione, *f.*
rămify, INTR.: ramificare; diramarsi.
rămmer, S.: mazzeranga; bacchetta da schioppo, *f.*
rămmish, ADJ.: che sente del becco. **-ness**, S.: odore del becco, *m.*
rāmous, ADJ.: ramoso, frondoso.
rămp 1, S.: salto, *m.*; scossa, *f.*. **ramp** 2, TR.: rampicare, montare; saltare con gran forza. **-ălliant**†, S.: furfantone, briccone, *m.* **-ancy**, S.: esuberanza; prevalenza, superiorità, *f.* **-ant**, ADJ.: esuberante, soprabbondante.
răm-part 1, **-pire**, S.: baluardo, riparo, *m.* **-part** 2, **-pire**, TR.: fortificare con bastioni.
rămpion, S.: raperonzolo, *m.*
rămrod, S.: bacchetta (da schioppo), *f.*
rănch 1, TR.: storcere; sforzare. **ranch** 2, S.: (*Am.*) rancio (tratto di terra di pastura), *m.* **-o**, S.: (*Am.*) capanna di pastori, *f.*; = *ranch* 2.
răn-cid, ADJ.: rancido, stantio, putrido. **-cidity**, **-cidness**, S.: rancidezza, *f.*
răn-corous, ADJ.: maligno, malizioso. **-corously**, ADV.: con rancore, malignamente. **-cour**, S.: rancore, sdegno, *m.*; malignità; animosità, *f.*
rănd, S.: cucitura delle scarpe, *f.*
răndom 1, S.: caso, accidente, *m.*: *at* —, a caso, alla cieca; *speak at* —, parlare alla cieca, anfanare, sconnettere. **random** 2, ADJ.: fatto a caso, inconsiderato: — *shot*, colpo a caso, *m.*
rān-ge 1, S.: ordine, classe; metà, *f.*; giro, *m.*; corsa, scorsa; graticola (per la cucina), *f.*; timone (d' una carrozza), *m.*: — *of mountains*, catena di montagne, *f.*; *within the* — *of*, nel cerchio di, entro il raggio di; alla portata di. **-ge** 2, TR.: ordinare; schierare; INTR.: vagabondare, vagare. **-ger** 1, S.: maestro di caccia, *m.* **-ger** 2, S.: bracco, cane che bracca, *m.*
rănk 1, S.: ordine, grado; posto, *m.*; dignità, *f.*: — *of soldiers*, fila di soldati, *f.*; *break the* —*s*, rompere le file; *of high* —, di alto grado. **rank** 2, TR.: mettere in ordine, mettere nel numero; INTR.: putrefarsi, corrompersi: — *high*, essere di alto grado, esser alto locato, esser di alto affare. **rank** 3, ADJ.: abbondante, super-[illegible]; rancido, stantio. **-ish**, ADJ.: al-[illegible]-rancido. **-le**, INTR.: putrefarsi, [illegible]i. **-ly**, ADV.: in modo grosso-[illegible]nte. **-ness**, S.: esuberanza [illegible] rancidezza, puzza, *f.*
[illegible]scheggiare, predare.
[illegible]tatore, *m.* **-ing**,

rănsom 1, S.: riscatto, *m.*; taglia, *f.* **ransom** 2, TR.: riscattare, ricomperare. **-er**, S.: riscattatore, *m.* **-less**, ADJ.: senza riscatto.
rănt 1, S.: discorso troppo ampolloso, *m.* **rant** 2, INTR.: parlare troppo ampollosamente. **-er**, S.: smaniatore, *m.* **-ing**, ADJ.: smaniante parlando.
răntipole, ADJ.: stordito, scapestrato, stravagante.
rănula, S.: ranella, *f.*, tumore sotto la lingua, *m.*
ranŭnculus, S.: ranuncolo, *m.*
răp 1, S.: scapezzone; colpo forte; picchio, *m.*: — *on the nose*, buffetto sul naso, *m.* **rap** 2, (IN)TR.: bossare, picchiare, battere: — *at the door*, picchiare alla porta.
ra-pācious, ADJ.: rapace; predace. **-pāciously**, ADV.: con rapacità. **-pāciousness**, **-păcity**, S.: rapacità, ingordigia, avidità, *f.*
rāpe 1, S.: rapimento, ratto; stupro, *m.* **rape** 2, S.: (*bot.*) ravizzone, *m.*
răp-id, ADJ.: rapido, veloce, prestissimo. **-idity**, S.: rapidità, impetuosità, velocità, *f.* **-idly**, ADV.: rapidamente, velocemente. **-idness** = *rapidity*.
rāpier, S.: stocco, *m.*
răpine 1, S.: rapina; violenza, forza, *f.* **rapine** 2, TR.: rapinare, predare.
răpper, S.: che picchia; bussatore, *m.*
rappōrt, S.: relazione, *f.*
răpsody†, S.: rassodia; raccolta, *f.*
răpt, ADJ.: rapito, estatico. **-ture**, S.: rapimento, ratto, *m.*; estasi, *f.*; furor poetico, *m.* **-tured**, ADJ.: rapito, trasportato, estatico. **-turous**, ADJ.: estatico.
rār-e, ADJ.: raro, straordinario, eccellente, prezioso; non denso, rado; scarso; poco cotto. **-ee-show**, S.: piccolo spettacolo, *m.*
rarefăction, S.: rarefazione, *f.*
rār-efiable, ADJ.: che si può rarefare. **-efy**, TR.: rarefare; diradare; INTR.: divenir raro, rarificarsi. **rār-ely**, ADV.: raramente, non sovente; di rado. **rār-eness**, S.: rarezza, singolarità; eccellenza, *f.* **-ity**, S.: rarità, cosa rara, curiosità; scarsezza, rarezza, radezza; qualità rarefatta, *f.*
răs-cal, S.: furfante, briccone, *m.*: — *deer*, cervo magro; cervo castrato, *m.* **-cality**, S.: furfanteria; canaglia, feccia del popolo, *f.* **-căllion**, S.: birbone, briccone, *m.* **-cally**, ADJ.: furfantesco, bricconesco.
rāse = *raze*.
răsh 1, ADJ.: temerario, precipitoso. **rash** 2, S.: eruzione; uscita, *f.*; raso, *m.* (specie di drappo). **rash** 3, TR.: tagliare in pezzi.

agognare a; — *with* (*against*), lottare (combattere) con. **-gler**, s.: contenditore; opponente, *m.* **-gling**, s.: scossa, lotta; contesa, *f.*

strū-ma, s.: struma, scrofola, *f.* **-mous**, ADJ.: scrofoloso.

strŭmpet, s.: cattiva donna, *f.*

strŭt 1, s.: camminare affettato, *m.* **strut** 2, INTR.: pavoneggiarsi, ringalluzzarsi. **-tingly**, ADV.: pavoneggiante; affettatamente.

strўchnine, s.: stricnina, *f.*

stŭb 1, s.: ceppo, tronco, *m.* **-stub** 2, TR.: sradicare, svellere. **-bed**, ADJ.: membruto, robusto, forte. **-bedness**, s.: qualità d' esser corto e robusto; figura corta e spessa, *f.*

stŭbble, s.: stoppia, *f.* **-goose**, s.: oca d' autunno, *f.*

stŭbborn, ADJ.: ostinato, ritroso, pertinace, caparbio. **-ly**, ADV.: ostinatamente, pertinacemente, con caparbietà. **-ness**, s.: ostinazione, pertinacia, caparbietà, *f.*

stŭb-by, ADJ.: corto e grosso, paffuto. **-nail**, s.: chiodo usato, chiodo rotto, *m.*

stŭcco 1, s.: stucco, *m.* **stucco** 2, TR.: stuccare.

stŭckle, s.: quantità di covoni, *f.*

stŭd 1, s.: borchia, *f.*; palo, *m.*; razza (di cavalli), *f.*, bottone, bottoncino, *m.*: *gold —s*, bottoncini di oro. **stud**, TR.: guarnire di borchie.

stūdent, s.: studente, scolare; letterato, *m.*: *fellow-—*, camerata di studio, *m.*; *medical —*, studente di medicina, *m.*

stŭd-ied, ADJ.: studiato, letterato; versato. **-ier**, s.: studiante, studente, *m.*

stūdio, s.: studio (d' artista), *m.*

stūdious, ADJ.: studioso; attento: *live a — life*, passar la vita studiando. **-ly**, ADV.: studiosamente, con diligenza. **-ness**, s.: applicazione allo studio; attenzione, *f.*

stŭdy 1, s.: studio, *m.*; applicazione, diligenza, *f.*; studiuolo, gabinetto, *m.*: *be in a brown —*, star pensieroso; esser malinconico. **study** 2, TR.: studiare; osservare; INTR.: studiarsi; applicarsi, ingegnarsi. **-ing**, s.: studiare, studio, *m.*

stŭff 1, s.: stoffa; materia, *f.*; drappo, *m.*: *household —*, mobili, *m. pl.*; masserizie, *f. pl.*; *kitchen —*, grascia di cucina, *f.*: *silk —s*, tessuti di seta. **stuff!** 2, INTERJ.: bagattella! *what —!* che robaccia! **stuff** 3, TR.: riempire, riempiere, stivare; satollare; INTR.: mangiare con voracità: — *up*, turare, stoppare; soffocare. **-ing**, s.: stivamento, *m.*; borra, *f.*

stŭket, s.: stucco, *m.*

stŭltify, TR.: istupidire.

stultilo-quence, **-quy**, s.: stoltiloquio, vaniloquio, *m.*; assurdità, *f.*

stŭm 1, s.: mosto, *m.* **stum** 2, TR.: fare fermentare di nuovo (il vino).

stŭm-ble 1, s.: passo falso; errore, fallo, *m.* **-ble** 2, TR.: fare inciampare; INTR.: inciampare; errare, fallire: — *at*, farsi scrupolo di; fallire; — *upon*, rincontrare a caso, intoppare, imbattersi in. **-bler**, s.: che inciampa, che fa un passo falso. **-bling**, s.: inciampo, intoppo, *m.* **-bling-block**, s.: inciampo, intoppo; ostacolo, *m.* **-bling-horse**, s.: cavallo che inciampa, *m.* **-blingly**, ADV.: con inciampo. **-bling-stone** = *stumbling-block*.

stŭmp 1, s.: tronco, ceppo, toppo; moncone, moncherino, *m.* **stump** 2, TR.: stralciare; INTR.: camminare come un villano. **-footed**, ADJ.: che ha il piè storto. **-y**, ADJ.: pieno di ceppi; duro, sodo.

stŭn, TR.: stordire, sbalordire.

stŭng, impf. e part. del v. *sting*.

stŭnning, ADJ.: assordante; (*pop.*) splendido, elegante; s.: stordimento, *m.*; sorpresa, *f.*

stŭnt, TR.: impedire l' accrescimento; fare intristire. **-ed**, ADJ.: mal cresciuto: *grow —*, intristire, provenire male.

stūpe 1, s.: fomento, *m.*, fomentazione, *f.* **stupe** 2, TR.: fomentare; spruzzare.

stupefăc-tion, s.: stupefazione, *f.*, stupore, *m.* **-tive**, ADJ.: stupefattivo.

stupĕndous, ADJ.: stupendo, maraviglioso. **-ly**, ADV.: maravigliosamente. **-ness**, s.: stupore, *m.*, maraviglia, *f.*

stū-pid, ADJ.: stupido, sciocco, scempiato, goffo. **-pidity**, s.: stupidità, stupidezza, *f.* **-pidly**, ADV.: stupidamente, goffamente. **-pidness** = *stupidity*. **-pifier**, s.: rimedio sonnifero, *m.* **-pify**, TR.: stupefare. **-por**, s.: stupore; intormentimento, *m.*

stū-prate, TR.: stuprare, violare. **-prā-tion**, s.: stupro, *m.*

stŭr-dily, ADV.: bruscamente, stizzosamente, ostinatamente. **-diness**, s.: caparbietà, insolenza; rigidezza, robustezza, forza, *f.* **-dy**, ADJ.: caparbio; robusto, gagliardo, forte.

stŭrgeon, s.: storione, *m.* (pesce).

stŭrk, s.: giovenco, bue giovane, *m.*; giovenca, *f.*

stŭtter, INTR.: tartagliare, balbettare. **-er**, s.: tartaglione, borbottone, *m.* **-ing**, s.: balbettare, barbugliamento, *m.* **-ingly**, ADV.: in modo balbettante.

stȳ 1, s.: porcile, *m.*, stia, *f.* **sty** 2, TR.: chiudere nel porcile.

Stȳgian, ADJ.: stigio, inferno.

stȳ-le 1, s.: stile; titolo, *m.*; forma, *f.*; modo, *m.*; pratica, *f.*: *in the Roman —*, ad uso de' Romani. **-le** 2, s.: chiamare, appellare: — *one's self*, nominarsi, chiamarsi. **-let**, s.: stiletto, *m.*

rēach 1, S.: tiro, *m.*, tirata; estensione; capacità; possa, autorità; penetrazione; perspicacità, sagacità; sottigliezza, *f.*; inganno, *m.*: *that is not in my* —, *it is out of my* —, non posso arrivarsi, non è in poter mio. **reach** 2, IRR.; TR.: porgere; giungere; INTR.: arrivare; stendersi; penetrare; spettare: — *forth* (*out*), protendere; — *a place*, arrivare (pervenire) ad un luogo; *your letter —ed me yesterday*, la vostra lettera mi pervenne ieri.

reăc-t, INTR.: repellere. **-tion**, S.: reazione; azione reciproca, *f.* **-tionary**, ADJ.: reazionario.

rĕad 1, ADJ.: letto, letterato, saputo; S.: sentenza, *f.* **read** 2, IRR.; TR.: leggere; studiare; congetturare; fare letture: — *about*, leggere a vicenda; — *again*, leggere di nuovo; — *on*, continuare a leggere; — *out*, — *aloud*, leggere ad alta voce; — *over*, leggere tutto; scorrere; — *through*, leggere tutto; *well* — (*part.*), che ha letto molto, dotto, erudito. **-able**, ADJ.: leggibile.

readĕption, S.: ricoveramento, ricuperamento, *m.*

rĕader, S.: lettore, leggitore, *m.* **-ship**, S.: uffizio di lettore, *m.*

rĕadi-ly, ADV.: prontamente, prestamente; volontiermente; a memoria; a mente. **-ness**, S.: prontezza; diligenza; acutezza, *f.*: — *of speech*, facondia; eloquenza, *f.*; — *of wit*, prontezza di spirito, *f.*

rĕading, S.: lettura, *f.*; discorso, *m.* **-desk**, S.: leggio, *m.* **-lamp**, S.: lampada da studiare, *f.* **-room**, S.: studio, scrittoio, *m.*

readjŏurn, TR.: prorogare di nuovo; differire. **-ing**, S.: allungamento di tempo, *m.*

readjŭst, TR.: aggiustare di nuovo.

read-mission, S.: ammettere di nuovo. **-mit**, TR.: ammettere di nuovo, ricevere di nuovo.

readŏrn, TR.: adornare di nuovo.

rĕady 1, ADJ.: pronto, preparato, apparecchiato, acconcio; inclinato: — *at hand*, in ordine, apparecchiato; — *money*, danari contanti, *m. pl.*; — *wit*, acutezza d'ingegno, *f.*, spirito vivace, *m.*; *get* —, metter in ordine, apparecchiare; *get* (*one's self*) —, prepararsi; mettersi in punto; vestirsi. **ready** 2, ADV.: già, di già; adesso: —*made clothes*, abiti fatti.

[illegible]affirm, TR.: confermare di nuovo. **[illegible]ce, -ation**, S.: seconda conferma-[illegible]

[illegible] : (*chem.*) reagente, *m.*

[illegible]o, *m.*: *play* —*s*, braveg-[illegible]

[illegible]fettivo: — *estate*, [illegible] *m. pl.*

reălgar, S.: realgale, *m.* (arsenico).

reăl-ity, S.: realtà; verità, *f.*; effetto, *m.* **-ization**, S.: effettuare, effetto, *m.*

rēal-ize, TR.: effettuare, mandare ad effetto.

reallĕge, TR.: allegare di nuovo.

rēally, ADV.: realmente, in realtà; veramente, certamente.

rĕalm, S.: regno, reame, *m.*

rĕalty, S.: lealtà, *f.*

rĕam, S.: risma di carta, *f.*; venti quaderni, *m. pl.*

reănimate, TR.: rianimare, rincorare.

reannĕx, TR.: unire di nuovo.

rĕap, TR.: mietere; ricogliere. **-er**, S.: mietitore, *m.* **-ing**, S.: mietitura, *f.* **-ing-hook**, S.: falciuola, *f.*, falcetto, *m.* **-ing-time**, S.: tempo del mietere, *m.*

reappĕar, INTR.: riapparire.

rĕar 1, S.: retroguardia; ultima classe, *f.* **rear** 2, ADJ.: crudo, mezzo cotto. **rear** 3, TR.: levare; innalzare, ergere: — *a child*, allevare un figliuolo. **-admiral**, S.: contr'ammiraglio, *m.* **-guard**, S.: retroguardia, *f.*

rĕarmouse, S.: pipistrello, *m.*

rĕarward, S.: ultima schiera, *f.*

reascĕnd, (IN)TR.: rimontare; risalire.

rĕason 1, S.: ragione, intellettiva; cagione, causa, *f.*, motivo, *m.*: *by — of*, a cagione di; *by — that*, perchè, a causa che; *what is the — that?* per che ragione? *from another* —, altronde; *bring one to* —, mettere alcuno alla ragione; *bring to* —, mettere alla ragione; *have* —, avere ragione; *speak* —, parlar sensatamente; *yield to* —, sottomettersi alla ragione. **reason** 2, (IN)TR.: ragionare; disputare, discorrere. **-able**, ADJ.: ragionevole, giusto; convenevole. **-ableness**, S.: ragione; giustezza, *f.* **-ably**, ADV.: ragionevolmente, con ragione, giustamente. **-er**, S.: ragionatore, *m.* **-ing**, S.: ragionamento, ragionare, *m.* **-less**, ADJ.: senza ragione, irragionevole.

reassĕm-blage, S.: riadunanza, *f.* **-ble**, TR.: riadunare, adunare nuovamente.

reassĕrt, TR.: affermare di nuovo.

reassŭme, TR.: assumere di nuovo.

reassŭre, TR.: riassicurare, assicurare di nuovo.

rĕave†, IRR.; TR.: portar via per forza.

rebap-tisātion, S.: ribattezzamento, ribattezzare, *m.* **-tize**, TR.: battezzare di nuovo. **-tizer**, S.: ribattezzatore, *m.*

rebāte 1, S.: scanalatura, *f.* **rebate** 2, TR.: scanalare; spuntare; ribattere, abbattere. **-ment**, S.: deduzione; diminuzione, *f.*

rĕbec, S.: ribeca, *f.*

rebĕl 1, INTR.: ribellarsi; sollevarsi. **rĕb-el** 2, S.: ribello, rubello, *m.* **-ler**, S.: ri-[illegible]

f.; abbonamento, *m.*: — *pay one's* —, pagare l'abbonamento. **-sĕcutive**, ADJ.: sussecutivo. **-sĕcutively**, ADV.: sussecutivamente. **-sĕptuple**, ADJ.: d'una settima parte. **-sequence, -sequency**, S.: susseguenza; conseguenza, *f.* **-sequent**, ADJ.: susseguente, posteriore. **-sequently**, ADV.: susseguentemente. **-sĕrve**, TR.: aiutare, secondare; servire. **-sĕrvience, -sĕrviency**, S.: assistenza; utilità, *f.* **-sĕrvient**, ADJ.: ausiliario, utile, vantaggioso: *make* — *to*, far servire a. **-sĕxtuple**, ADJ.: d'una sesta parte. **-side**, TR.: abbassarsi; calmarsi; andar a fondo. **-sidence, -cy**, posatura, feccia, *f.* **-sidiary**, ADJ.: sussidiario, ausiliario. **-sidy**, S.: sussidio, aiuto; soccorso (di danari), *m.* **-sign**, TR.: sottoscrivere, segnare sotto. **-signātion**, S.: sottoscrizione, *f.* **-sist**, INTR.: sussistere, esistere; mantenersi, vivere. **-sistence**, S.: sussistenza, esistenza, *f.*; cibo, *m.* **-sistent**, ADJ.: sussistente, esistente. **-soil**, S.: sottosuolo, *m.* **-stance**, S.: sostanza, sustanza; essenza, quiddità, *f.*; contenuto, *m.* **-stăntial**, ADJ.: sustanziale, essenziale, reale; forte. **-stantiălity**, S.: sustanzialità, sostanzialità; realità; forza, *f.* **-stăntially**, ADV.: sustanzialmente. **-stăntialness** = *substantiality*. **-stăntiate**, TR.: sostanziare, fare esistere; avverare, provare. **-stantive**, ADJ.: sostantivo; S.: (*gram.*) sostantivo, *m.* **-stantively**, ADV.: sostantivamente. **-stitute** 1, S.: sostituto; vicario, *m.* **-stitute** 2, TR.: sostituire, sustituire. **-stitūtion**, S.: sostituzione, *f.* **-strŭction**, S.: fondamento, *m.*, base, *f.* **-sŭltive**, ADJ.: saltellante, balzellante. **-sŭltorily**, ADV.: in modo saltellante. **-sŭltory** = *subsultive*. **-tăngent**, S.: sottangente, *f.* **-tĕnd**, INTR.: sottendersi, stendersi sotto. **-tĕnse**, S.: sottendente, *f.*

subtĕrflu-ent, -ous, ADJ.: colando sotto; superfluo, soperchio.

sŭbterfuge, S.: sotterfugio, scampo, *m.*

subter-rānean, -rāneous, ADJ.: sotterraneo. **-rănity**, S.: sotterraneo, *m.*

sŭb-tile, ADJ.: sottile; fino, delicato; acuto; penetrante, penetrativo. **-tilely**, ADV.: sottilmente, ingegnosamente, astutamente. **-tileness**, S.: sottigliezza, astuzia, *f.* **-tiliate**, TR.: sottigliare, rendere tenue. **-tiliātion, -tilizātion**, S.: sottigliamento, *m.* **-tility**, S.: sottigliezza, delicatezza, *f.* **-tilize**, TR.: assottigliare, affinare, sottilizzare. **-tilty**, S.: sottigliezza; astuzia, finezza, *f.*

sŭb-tle, ADJ.: sottile; penetrativo; astuto, furbesco. **-tlety**, S.: sottigliezza, astuzia, accortezza, *f.* **-tly**, ADV.: sottilmente; astutamente, sagacemente.

sub-trăct, TR.: sottrarre. **-trăction**, S.: sottrazione, *f.* **-trahĕnd**, S.: numero da sottrarsi, *m.* **-tūtor**, S: sottomaestro, *m.* **'-urb**, S.: borgo, sobborgo, *m.* **-ŭrban, -ŭrbian**, ADJ.: suburbano. **-vĕntion**, S.: sovvenimento, sussidio, *m.* **-vĕrse**, TR.: sovvertire. **-vĕrsion**, S.: sovversione, rovina, *f.* **-vĕrsive**, ADJ.: sovversivo, sovvertente. **-vĕrt**, TR.: sovvertere, guastare, rovinare. **-vĕrter**, S.: sovvertitore, distruggitore, *m.* **-vicar**, S.: sottovicario, *m.* **-vicarship**, S.: sottovicariato, *m.* **-wŏrker**, S.: operaio subordinato, *m.*

suc-cedāneous, ADJ.: succedaneo, successivo. **-cedāneum**, S.: succedaneo, sostituto, *m.* **-cēed**, TR.: succedere, seguire; INTR.: riuscire; venire dopo; accadere, avvenire: — *in doing*, riuscire a fare. **-cēeder**, S.: succeditore, successore, *m.* **-cēeding**, ADJ.: succedente, seguente. **-cĕss**, S.: successo, evento, avvenimento, *m.*: *have* —, riuscire bene. **-cĕssful**, ADJ.: fortunato, propizio, felice. **-cĕssfully**, ADV.: con successo, felicemente. **-cĕssfulness**, S.: buon successo, evento fortunato, *m.* **-cĕssion**, S.: successione; eredità; serie, *f.*: *in* —, per successione. **-cĕssive**, ADJ.: successivo. **-cĕssively**, ADV.: successivamente, *m.* **-cĕssiveness**, S.: continuazione, progressione; serie, *f.* **-cĕssless**, ADJ.: sgraziato, infelice, sfortunato. **-cĕsslessness**, S.: disgrazia, sventura, *f.* **-cĕssor**, S.: successore, *m.*

succinct, ADJ.: succinto, conciso. **-ly**, ADV.: succintamente, compendiosamente, con brevità. **-ness**, S: concisione, brevità, *f.*

sŭc-cory, S.: cicorea, *f.*, radicchio, *m.* **-co(u)r** 1, S.: soccorso, aiuto, sussidio, *m.*; assistenza, *f.* **-co(u)r** 2, TR.: soccorrere, aiutare, assistere; sovvenire. **-co(u)rer**, S.: soccorritore, aiutatore, *m.* **-co(u)rless**, ADJ.: privo di soccorso.

sŭccubus, S.: succubo, *m.*

sŭcculen-ce, -cy, S.: sugosità, *f.* **-t**, ADJ.: sugoso, pieno di sugo.

succŭmb, INTR.: soccombere; soggiacere.

succŭssion, S.: scossa, *f.*, scotimento, *m.*

sŭch, PRON.: tale, simile: — *a*, un tal; *in* — *a way*, in tale modo; *and* — *like*, e altri simili; — *a thing*, tal cosa; *for* — *a man as I*, per un uomo della mia fatta; *I am not* — *a fool*, non sono così sciocco; — *as*, quei che.

sŭck 1, S.: sugare, succiamento, *m.*: *give* —, allattare. **suck** 2, (IN)TR.: succiare; attrarre: — *in*, imbevere; essere imbevuto; — *out (up)*, succiare. **-er**, S.: suc-

sione, *f.* **rĕ-cognize**, TR.: riconoscere; confessare. **-cognizée**, S.: a chi un' obbligazione è fatta, *m.* **rĕ-cognizer**, S.: riconoscitore, *m.*

recoil 1, S.: rinculamento, *m.; ritirata, f.* **recoil** 2, INTR.: rinculare; venir meno.

recoin, TR.: stampare di nuovo (la moneta). **-age**, S.: rinnovamento della moneta, *m.*

recollĕc-t, TR.: ricordarsi, sovvenirsi; riflettere, pensare; radunare: *I don't* —, non mi raccapezzo; *I cannot* — *his name*, non posso ricordarmi il suo nome. **-tion**, S.: ricordanza, reminiscenza; riflessione, *f.*

recombine, TR.: combinare di nuovo.

recómfort, TR.: riconfortare, rincorare.

recommĕnce, TR.: ricominciare.

recommĕnd, TR.: raccomandare; lodare. **-able**, ADJ.: commendabile, lodevole, stimabile. **-ătion**, S.: raccomandazione, *f.: letter of* —, lettera di raccomandazione, commendatizia, *f.* **-atory**, ADJ.: raccomandatorio, di raccomandazione. **-er**, S.: raccomandatore, *m.*

recommit, TR.: commettere di nuovo.

recompensătion, S.: ricompensazione, ricompensa, *f.*

rĕcompense 1, S.: ricompensa, rimunerazione, *f.* **recompense** 2, TR.: ricompensare, rimunerare.

recompilement, S.: compilamento nuovo, *m.*, nuova compilazione, *f.*

recompŏ-se, TR.: ricomporre; rimettere insieme. **-sition**, S.: nuova composizione, *f.*

rĕcon-cilable, ADJ.: che si può riconciliare. **-cilableness**, S.: aggiustamento, *m.* **-cile**, TR.: riconciliare; raccordare, metter pace: *I was —d to my fate*, mi rassegnai al mio destino. **-cileable** = *reconcilable.* **-cilement**, S.: riconciliamento, *m.*, riconciliazione, *f.* **-ciler**, S.: riconciliatore, mediatore, *m.* **-ciliătion**, S.: riconciliazione, *f.* **-ciliatory**, ADJ.: riconciliante.

recondĕnse, TR.: ricondensare.

rĕcondite, ADJ.: ricondito, profondo.

recondŭct, TR.: ricondurre, rimenare.

reconfirm, TR.: confermare di nuovo.

recŏnnoissance, S.: (*mil.*) riconoscenza, *f.*

reconnŏi-ter, -tre, TR.: (*mil.*) riconoscere.

reconjŏin, TR.: ricongiungere.

recŏnquer, TR.: riconquistare, ricuperare.

-cŏnsecrate, TR.: concecrare di nuovo.

-nsider, TR.: riconsiderare.

-olate, TR.: riconsolare.

-uct, TR.: ricostruire.

TR.: adunare di nuovo.

reconvĕy, TR.: ricondurre, riportare.

rĕcord, S.: registro, testimonio autentico, *m.: —s*, archivi, annali, *m. pl.; bear* —, far testimonianza; *public —s*, archivi, *m. pl.; keeper of the —s*, archivista, *m.*

recŏrd, TR.: registrare, iscrivere, ricordare, arrolare. **-ătion†**, S.: ricordamento, ricordo, *m.* **-er**, S.: attuario; flauto, *m.*

recoŭnt, TR.: raccontare; riferire. **-ment**, S.: raccontamento, *m.*, narrazione, relazione, *f.*

recoŭp, INTR.: ricuperare.

recoŭrse, S.: ricorso, ricovero; rifugio: concorso; accesso (di febbre), *m.: have — to*, ricorrere a.

recóver, TR.: ricuperare; racquistare; INTR.: ricoverarsi; rimettersi, rifarsi; star meglio, guarire, risanare: — *a loss*, riparare una perdita; — *from sickness*, ricuperar la salute, riaversi; — *one's self*, ricuperare gli spiriti. **-able**, ADJ.: ricuperabile. **-y**, S.: ricoveramento, *m.: past* —, incurabile, irremediabile.

rĕcreant, S.: poltrone, codardo; miscredente, apostata, *f.*

rĕcre-ate 1, TR.: ricreare; dilettare, divertire. **recre-ăte** 2, TR.: ricreare, creare di nuovo. **-ătion**, S.: ricreazione, *f.; divertimento, m.* **-ative**, ADJ.: ricreativo, dilettevole, piacevole. **-atively**, ADV.: in modo ricreativo, piacevolmente. **-ativeness**, S.: sollievo; passatempo, spasso, *m.*

rĕcre-ment, S.: recremento, *m.;* feccia, spuma, *f.* **-mĕntal, -mentitious**, ADJ.: feccioso, spumoso,

recrimi-nate, TR.: incolpare (l' accusante), rimproverare. **-nătion**, S.: accusa reciproca, *f.* **-nator**, S.: che accusa l' accusante. **-natory**, ADJ.: recriminatorio.

recrŭit 1, S.: rinforzo; recluta; soldato reclutato, *m.* **recruit** 2, TR.: reclutare; rinforzare; supplire: — *one's self*, rimettersi in piedi, ristorarsi.

rĕct-angle, S.: (*geom.*) rettangolo, *m.* **-ăngular**, ADJ.: rettangolo, di quattro angoli retti.

rĕcti-fiable, ADJ.: rettificabile, che può rettificarsi. **-ficătion**, S.: rettificamento, *m.* **-fy**, TR.: rettificare, aggiustare, correggere.

recti-linear, -lineous, ADJ.: rettilineo.

rĕctitude, S.: rettitudine; dirittura; bontà, *f.*

rĕc-tor, S.: rettore; capo di collegio; parroco, curato; piovano (d' una parrocchia), *m.* **-tórial**, ADJ.: di piovano (d' una parrocchia). **-torship**, S.: rettoria; dignità di rettore, *f.*, uffizio di rettore, *m.* **-tory**, S.: rettoria; parrocchia, *f.*

rĕctum, S.: (*anat.*) retto, *m.*

sŭl-triness, S.: afa, *f.*, calore soffocante, caldo soverchio, *m.* **-try**, ADJ.: fervido, fervoroso; soffocante.
sŭm 1, S.: somma, *f.*; totale, montante; compendio; risultamento, *m.* **sum** 2, TR.: sommare, numerare; annoverare: — *up*, ricapitolare, comprendere; — *up all*, in somma, in conclusione.
sŭmach, S.: sommaco, *m.*
sŭmage, S.: soma, *m.*
sŭmless, ADJ.: innumerabile; infinito.
sŭmma-rily, ADV.: sommariamente, in sommario. **-ry**, ADJ.: sommario, compendioso. **-ry**, S.: sommario, compendio; breve ristretto, *m.*
sŭmmer 1, S.: state, estate; (*arch.*) trave principale, *f.* **summer** 2, TR.: passar la state. **-house**, S.: gabinetto di verdura, *m.*
sŭmmer-sault, **-set**, S.: salto mortale, sbalzo alto, *m.*
sŭmmer-quarters, S. PL.: quartieri di state, *m. pl.* **-suit**, S.: abito di state, *m.*
sŭmmit, S.: sommità, cima, *f.*; colmo, *m.*
sŭmmon, TR.: citare, chiamare in giudizio; intimare. **-er**, S.: sergente, birro, *m.* **-s**, S.: citazione, *f.*, comandamento, *m.*
sŭmpter, S.: somiere, *m.*, bestia da soma, *f.* **-saddle**, S.: basto, *m.*
sŭmption, S.: presa, cattura, *f.*, arresto, *m.*
sŭmp-tuary, ADJ.: suntuario. **-tuŏsity**, S.: suntuosità, splendidezza, magnificenza, *f.* **-tuous**, ADJ.: suntuoso, dispendioso; splendido, magnifico. **-tuously**, ADV.: suntuosamente; splendidamente, magnificamente. **-tuousness**, S.: spesa; magnificenza, *f.*
sŭn 1, S.: sole, *m.*: *the — rises*, il sole si alza; *under the —*, sotto il sole; nel mondo. **sun** 2, TR.: soleggiare, porre al sole. **-beam**, S.: raggio di sole, *m.* **-beat**, ADJ.: esposto al sole, battuto dal sole. **-bright**, ADJ.: lucente; risplendente. **-burning**, S.: caldura, *f.*, abbronzare, *m.* **-burnt**, ADJ.: bruciato dal sole, abbronzato, bronzino.
Sŭnday, S.: domenica, *f.*
sŭnder, TR.: separare; partire.
sŭn-dial, S.: orologio a sole, orologio solare, *m.* **-dried**, ADJ.: seccato dal sole.
sŭndry, ADJ.: diversi, molti.
sŭnflower, S.: tornasole, eliotropio, *m.*
sŭnk, part. del v. *sink*.
sŭn-less, ADJ.: privo di sole. **-light**, S.: lume del sole, *m.* **-like**, ADJ.: simile al sole. **-ny**, ADJ.: di sole, lucente come il sole; aprico, esposto al sole, solatio. **-proof**, ADJ.: impervio al lume del sole. **-rise**, **-rising**, S.: levar del sole, *m.* **-set**, S.: tramontare del sole, *m.* **-shine**, S.: chiarezza del sole, *f.* **-shiny**, ADJ.: illuminato dal sole, splendente col sole: — *day*, giorno radiante; giorno glorioso, *m.* **-stroke**, S.: colpo di sole, *m.*; sol(in)ata, *f.*
sŭp 1, S.: sorso, centellino, *m.* **sup** 2, TR.: sorsare, bere a sorsi. **sup** 3, (IN)TR.: dare da cena; cenare.
sūper-able, ADJ.: superabile. **-ableness**, S.: possibilità di superare, *f.* **-ably**, ADV.: in modo superabile.
super-abound, (IN)TR.: soprabbondare, sopravanzare. **-abŭndance**, S.: soprabbondanza, *f.* **-abŭndant**, ADJ.: soprabbondante. **-abŭndantly**, ADV.: con soprabbondanza. **-ădd**, TR.: aggiungere di più. **-addition**, S.: aggiunta, *f.*; soprappiù, *m.* **-ănnuate**, (IN)TR.: rendere vecchio; divenir vecchio. **-ănnuated**, ADJ.: vecchio, troppo vecchio; stantio. **-annuātion**, S.: vecchiaia, vecchiezza, *f.*
supērb, ADJ.: superbo, pomposo. **-ly**, ADV.: superbamente, pomposamente.
super-cârgo, S.: sopraccarico, *m.* **-celĕstial**, ADJ.: sopraceleste. **-ciliary**, ADJ.: sopraccigliare. **-cilious**, ADJ.: altiero, austero; arrogante, burbero. **-ciliously**, ADV.: altieramente, fieramente; burbantemente, arrogantemente, con isprezzo. **-ciliousness**, S.: alterezza, *f.*, orgoglio, *m.*, arroganza, *f.*; sprezzo, *m.* **-crĕscence**, S.: escrescenza, *f.* **-ĕminence**, **-ĕminency**, S.: preeminenza, *f.* **-ĕminent**, ADJ.: eminente; eccellente. **-ĕminently**, ADV.: eccellentemente. **-ĕrogate**, TR.: strafare, far più del debito. **-erogātion**, S.: supererogazione, *f.* **-erŏgative**, **-erŏgatory**, ADJ.: di supererogazione, soprabbondante. **-exălt**, TR.: sopraesaltare. **-exaltātion**, S.: sopraesaltazione, *f.* **-ĕxcellent**, ADJ.: eccellentissimo. **-excrĕscence**, S.: escrescenza, *f.* **-fētate**, INTR.: superfetare. **-fetātion**, S.: superfetazione, *f.* **-fice** † sŭ-, S.: superficie, *f.*; esteriore, *m.* **-ficial**, ADJ.: superficiale; esteriore. **-ficiălity**, ADJ.: superficialità, *f.* **-ficially**, ADV.: superficialmente. **-ficialness**, S.: superficialità; superficiale notizia, tintura, *f.* **-ficies**, S.: superficie, *f.* **-fine** sŭ-, ADJ.: sopraffino, sopraffine, finissimo.
supĕr-fluence, S.: superfluità, *f.* **-fluitant**, ADJ.: galleggiante. **-fluity**, S.: superfluità, soprabbondanza, *f.* **-supĕrfluous**, ADJ.: superfluo, soperchio; inutile. ′**-fluously**, ADV.: soperchiamente, con superfluità. ′**-fluousness**, S.: superfluità, *f.*; eccesso, *m.* **-hūman**, ADJ.: soprumano. **-impregnātion**, S.: superfetazione, *f.* **-incŭmbent**, ADJ.: disteso sopra. **-indūce**, TR.: soprainddurre; aggiungere. **-indŭction**, S.:

stўp-tic(al), ADJ.: (*med.*) stiptico, astringente. **-tĭcity**, S.: qualità molto astringente, *f.*

suāge†, TR.: mitigare, raddolcire.

suā-sive, ADJ.: suasivo, persuasivo. **-sory** = *suasive.*

suāve, ADJ.: dolce, blando, gentile. **suāv-ity**, S.: suavità, dolcezza; benignità, *f.*

sub-ăcid, ADJ.: alquanto acido. **-ăcrid**, ADJ.: alquanto acre.

sub-ăct, TR.: sottomettere, soggiogare; conquistare. **-ăction**, S.: soggiogazione, riduzione, *f.*

subăl-tern 1, ADJ.: subalterno, subordinato, inferiore. **-tern** 2, S.: uffiziale subalterno, subalterno, *m.* **-tĕrnate**, ADJ.: subordinato. **-ternātion**, S.: subordinazione, *f.*

sŭb-: **-astringent**, ADJ.: alquanto astringente. **-brigadier**, S.: sottobrigadiere, *m.* **-celĕstial**, ADJ.: terrestre, mondano. **-chănter**, S.: sotto precentore, *m.* **-constellātion**, S.: costellazione secondaria, *f.* **-cutāneous**, ADJ.: (*anat.*) subcutaneo. **-dēacon**, S.: soddiacono, suddiacono, *m.* **-dēaconry**, **-dēaconship**, S.: soddiaconato, *m.* **-dean**, S.: suddecano, *m.* **-dēanery** = *sub-deaconry.* **-dĕlegate** 1, S.: suddelegato, sostituto, *m.* **-delegate** 2, TR.: suddelegare, sostituire. **-delegātion**, S.: suddelegazione, *f.* **-ditĭtious**, ADJ.: supposto, sostituto. **-divide**, TR.: suddividere. **-division**, S.: suddivisione, *f.* **-dolous**, ADJ.: doloso, fraudolente; astuto, ingannoso. **-dūal**, S.: soggiogamento, *m.* **-dūce**, **-dŭct**, TR.: involare; (*arith.*) sottrarre. **-dŭction**, S.: sottrazione, *f.* **-dūe**, TR.: soggiogare, superare, vincere; mortificare. **-dūement**, S.: soggiogazione, *f.* **-dūer**, S.: soggiogatore, vincitore, *m.* **-indicātion**, S.: significazione, *f.* **-ingrĕssion**, S.: entrata segreta, *f.* **-itāneous**, ADJ.: subitaneo, repentino. **-jăcent**, ADJ.: soggiacente. **-ject** 1, ADJ.: soggetto, esposto, suddito; dedito, portato. **-ject** 2, S.: soggetto; suddito, *m.*; materia, *f.*: *dwell upon a —*, estendersi sopra un soggetto. **-jĕct** 3, soggettare, costringere, obbligare; esporre. **-jĕcted**, ADJ.: soggetto, sottomesso, esposto. **-jĕction**, S.: soggezione, sottomessione; dipendenza; condizione; necessità, *f.* **-jĕctive**, ADJ.: soggettivo. **-jŏin**, TR.: soggiungere, aggiungere. **-jugate**, TR.: soggiogare, superare. **-jugātion**, S.: soggiogazione; conquista, *f.* **-jŭnction**, S.: soggiunzione, *f.* **-jŭnctive**, ADJ.: soggiuntivo; S.: soggiuntivo, *m.* **-lātion**, S.: rapimento, ratto, *m.* **-levātion**, S.: sollevazione, *f.*, alzamento, *m.* **-limable**, ADJ.: che si può sublimare. **-limableness**, S.: raffinamento, *m.* **sŭb-limate** 1, S.: solimato, *m.* **sŭb-limate** 2, TR.: sublimare; raffinare. **-limātion**, S.: sublimazione, *f.* **-lime** 1, ADJ.: sublime; alto, eccelso. **-lime** 2, S.: sublime; stile nobile, *m.* **-lime** 3, TR.: (*chem.*) sublimare, volatilizzare; innalzare; sublimarsi. **-limely**, ADV.: in modo sublime; altamente, grandemente. **-limeness**, **-limity**, S.: sublimità, altezza, grandezza, eccellenza, *f.* **-lingual**, ADJ.: sublinguale. **-lūnar**, **-lunary**, ADJ.: sullunare, terrestre. **-marine**, ADJ.: sottomarino. **-mĕrge**, TR.: sommergere, immergere, allegare; INTR.: immergersi, tuffarsi. **-mĕrse**, TR.: immergere. **-mĕrsion**, S.: sommersione, *f.*, allagamento, *m.* **-minister**, **-istrate**, INTR.: somministrare; servire, esser utile. **-ministrātion**, S.: somministrazione, *f.* **-miss**, ADJ.: sommesso, rispettoso, ossequioso, umile. **-mission**, S.: sommessione, obbedienza, ubbidienza, umiltà, *f.* **-missive**, ADJ.: sommessivo, sommesso, umile. **-missively**, ADV.: con sommessione, umilmente. **-missiveness**, S.: sommessione, umiltà, *f.* **-missly**, ADV.: con sommessione, umilmente. **-missness**, S.: sommessione, umiliazione, *f.* **-mit**, TR.: sommettere, soggettare; INTR.: sommettersi, rimettersi; conformarsi. **-mŭltiple**, S.: numero sottomoltiplice, *m.* **-ôrdinacy**, **-nancy**, S.: subordinamento, *m.*, subordinazione, *f.* **-ôrdinate** 1, ADJ.: subordinato; inferiore. **-ôrdinate** 2, TR.: subordinare. **-ôrdinately**, ADV.: subordinatamente. **-ôrdinātion**, S.: subordinazione; dipendenza, *f.* **-ôrn**, TR.: subornare, persuadere, sedurre. **-ornātion**, S.: subornazione, *f.*, subornamento, sodducimento, *m.* **-ôrner**, S.: subornatore, seduttore, *m.* **-poēna** 1, S.: citazione sotto pena, *f.* **-poena** 2, TR.: citare sotto pena. **-quădruple**, ADJ.: d' una quarta parte. **-quintuple**, ADJ.: d' una quinta parte. **-rĕctor**, S.: sottorettore, vicerettore, *m.* **-rĕ**[illegible]
surrezione; sorpresa, *f.* **-**[illegible]
ADJ.: surrettizio, furtivo.
ly, ADV.: in modo sur[illegible]
tive, ADJ.: surrettizio.
surrogato, sostituto. [illegible]
surrogare, sostitui[illegible]
surrogazione, sor[illegible]
TR.: soscrive[illegible]
INTR.: co[illegible]
newspaper
to an [illegible]
-scribe[illegible]
newspa[illegible]
-scrip[illegible]

sūral, ADJ.: surale.
sūrance†, S.: sicurtà, assicuranza; malleveria, *f.*
surbāte 1, S.: spedatura, *f.*, straccare, *m.* **surbate** 2, TR.: affaticare, straccare.
surcēase 1, S.: cessazione; sospensione, dilazione, *f.* **surcease** 2, TR.: sospendere; INTR.: cessare; tralasciare.
surchârge 1, S.: sopraccarico, soverchio carico, *m.* **surcharge** 2, TR.: sopraccaricare, caricare troppo.
sūrcingle, S.: cintura, cintola, *f.*
sūrcoat, S.: saltambarco, *m.*, sopravvesta, *f.*
surd, ADJ.: sordo. **-ity**, S.: sordità, sordaggine, *f.*
sūre 1, ADJ.: certo, sicuro, assicurato; fermo, stabile: *be* —, esser certi; *to be —!* certamente, senza dubbio! — *enough!* ben certo! **sure** 2, ADV.: certamente, senza dubbio. **-footed**, ADJ.: che cammina con piede fermo. **-ly**, ADV.: certamente, sicuramente. **-ness**, S.: certezza, sicurezza, *f.* **-tiship**, S.: malleveria, cauzione, *f.* **-ty**, S.: sicurezza, certezza, *f.*; mallevadore, *m.*
sūrf, S.: cavalloni, *m. pl.*, onde (del mare), *f. pl.*
sūrface, S.: superficie, *f.*; esteriore, *m.*
sūrfeit 1, S.: indigestione; sazietà, *f.*; disgusto, fastidio, *m.* **surfeit** 2, (IN)TR.: satollare, impinzare; saziarsi. **-er**, S.: mangione, ghiottone, *m.* **-ing**, S.: stucchevolezza, sazievolezza, sazietà, *f.* **-water**, S.: acqua stomacale, *f.*
sūrge 1, S.: onda, *f.*, cavallone; flutto, *m.* **surge** 2, INTR.: fare cavalloni, gonfiarsi.
sūr-geon, S.: chirurgo, cerusico, *m.* **-gery**, S.: cirurgia, chirurgia, *f.* **-gical**, ADJ.: chirurgico.
sūrgy, ADJ.: fluttuoso, tempestoso.
sūr-lily, ADV.: burberamente, aspramente; orgogliosamente. **-liness**, S.: cattivo umore, *m.*; caponeria, *f.* **-ly**, ADJ.: arcigno, burbero, sdegnoso.
surmise 1, S.: sospetto, *m.*; supposizione; immaginazione, opinione, *f.* **surmise** 2, TR.: sospettare; immaginarsi, pensare; credere.
surmōunt, TR.: sormontare, superare; avanzare. **-able**, ADJ.: sormontabile.
sūrmulet, S.: triglia, *f.* (pesce).
sūrname 1, S.: soprannome, cognome, *m.* **surname** 2, TR.: soprannomare, cognominare.
surpâss, TR.: sorpassare; superare, soprastare, sovranzare, avanzare, eccedere. **-able**, ADJ.: sorpassabile. **-ing**, ADJ.: sorpassante; eccellente, maraviglioso. **-ingly**, ADV.: straordinariamente, *eccellentemente.*
sūrplice, S.: cotta (d' ecclesiastico), *f.*
sūrplus(age), S.: sovrappiù, soverchio, *m.*
surpri-sal, **-se** 2, S.: sorpresa, *f.*, stupore, *m.*, maraviglia, *f.* **-se** 2, TR.: sorprendere, maravigliare: *I am* —*d at it*, ne sono sorpreso; *you* — *me*, mi fate stupire. **-sing**, ADJ.: stupendo, maraviglioso. **-singly**, ADV.: in modo stupendo, stranamente.
surrĕnder 1, (IN)TR.: cedere; arrendersi. **surrender** 2, S.: resa, *f.*, rendimento, *m.*
surrĕp-tion, S.: sorpresa, *f.* **-titious**, ADJ.: surrettizio, fraudolento. **-titiously**, ADV.: surrettiziamente.
sŭrro-gate 1, S.: surrogato, sostituto, *m.* **-gate** 2, TR.: surrogare, sostituire. **-gātion**, S.: surrogazione, sostituzione, *f.*
surrŏund, TR.: circondare; chiudere intorno, stringere intorno.
sursŏlid, S.: (*geom.*) quarta potenza, *f.*
surtŏut, S.: soprabito, *m.*, zimara, *f.*
survēne, TR.: sopravvenire, venire per aggiunta.
survĕillance *-ly-*, S.: sorveglianza, *f.*
survĕy 1, S.: rivista; descrizione, *f.*: — *of land*, agrimensura, *f.* **survey** 2, TR.: osservare; esaminare; misurare: — *land*, misurare terreno. **-ing**, S.: misurare il terreno, *m.* **-or**, S.: soprantendente; misuratore, agrimensore, *m.*: — *of the customs*, inspettore, *m.* **-orship**, S.: uffizio del soprantendente, *m.*
survi-vance, S.: sopravvivere, *m.* **-ve**, (IN)TR.: sopravvivere, vivere più di. **-ver**, **-vor**, S.: sopravvivente; superstite, *m.* **-vorship**, S.: sopravvivenza, *f.*
sus-ceptibility, S.: suscettibilità, *f.* **-cĕptible**, ADJ.: suscettibile, suscettivo. **-cĕptibleness** = *susceptibility*. **-cĕption**, S.: suscezione, *f.* **-cĕptive**, ADJ.: suscettibile. **-ceptivity**, S.: suscettibilità, *f.* **-cĕptor**, S.: impresario; padrino, *m.* **-cipiency**, S.: ricevimento, *m.*
sŭsci-tate, TR.: suscitare, incitare. **-tā-tion**, S.: suscitamento, incitamento, *m.*
suspĕct 1, ADJ.: sospetto, dubbioso. **suspect** 2, (IN)TR.: sospettare; diffidarsi; dubitare: *I — him*, sospetto di lui; *I — the truth of the story*, dubito se la storia sia vera. **-able**, ADJ.: sospettevole. **-edness**, S.: sospizione, diffidenza, *f.* **-ful**, ADJ.: sospettoso, diffidente. **-less**, ADJ.: senza sospetto.
suspĕn-d, TR.: sospendere, differire, prolungare: — *one's judgment*, tenere sospeso il suo giudizio: — *an officer*, sospendere un uffiziale. **-ders**, S. PL.: bretelle, *f. pl.* **-sion**, S.: sospensione, dilazione, *f.* **-se** 1, ADJ.: sospeso; incerto, dubbioso. **-se** 2, S.: dubbio, *m.*, incertezza; dilazione, *f.*: *remain in* —, star sospeso, star in forse; *keep in* —, tenere nell' incertezza.

reinstāt-e, TR.: ristabilire. **-ing**, S.: ristabilimento, *m.*
reintegrate, TR.: rintegrare, ristabilire.
reinthrōne = *reënthrone*.
reinvĕst, TR.: rimettere in possesso, ristabilire.
reinvite, TR.: invitare di nuovo.
reiter-ate, TR.: reiterare; rifare. **-ātion**, S.: reiterazione, *f.*
rejĕc-t, TR.: rigettare, ributtare. **-tion**, S.: rigettamento; rifiuto, *m.*
rejŏi-ce, TR.: rallegrare; divertire; INTR.: rallegrarsi; divertirsi: *I — at it*, me ne rallegro. **-cer**, S.: rallegratore, *m.* **-cing**, S.: rallegramento, *m.*; allegrezza, *f.* **-cingly**, ADV.: allegramente.
rejŏin, TR.: rigiungere; INTR.: rispondere, replicare. **-der** 1, S.: replica, seconda risposta, *f.* **-der** 2, TR.: far una seconda risposta.
rejŏlt, S.: scossa, *f.*
rejŭdge, TR.: giudicare di nuovo, esaminare di nuovo.
rejŭvenate, TR.: far ringiovanire.
rekindle, INTR.: raccendere, rallumare.
relăpse 1, S.: ricadimento, *m.*; recidiva, ricascata, *f.* **relapse** 2, INTR.: ricadere, ricascare.
relā-te, TR.: recitare, raccontare; dire; INTR.: rapportarsi; rassomigliarsi; partenere. **-ted**, PART.: recitato, ecc.; che ha relazione a (con), parente: *be — to*, essere parente di; avere rapporto a. **-ter**, S.: relatore, narratore, *m.* **-tion**, S.: relazione; somiglianza; affinità, *f.*, parente, coniunto, *m.*: *in — to*, in riguardo, in quanto a. **-tionship**, S.: affinità, parentela, *f.*
rĕlative, ADJ.: relativo; S.: parente; consanguineo, *m.* **-ly**, ADV.: relativamente. **-ness**, S.: relazione, *f.*
relăx, TR.: rilassare, rallentare; sbattere; moderare, mitigare; divertire; INTR.: rilassarsi; moderarsi; divertirsi: *— one's mind*, ricrearsi. **-ātion**, S.: rilassamento, *m.*; remissione, *f.*, debilitamento, *m.*; ricreazione, *f.*, divertimento, riposo, *m.* **-ative**, ADJ.: rilassante.
relāy, S.: posta, *f.*: *—s*, cavalli freschi; cavalli di ricambio, *m. pl.*
relēa-se 1, S.: liberazione; libertà, *f.*; scarico, *m.* **-se** 2, TR.: mettere in libertà; dispensare, esentare. **-ser**, S.: liberatore, *m.* **-sement**, S.: liberazione, *f.*, scarico, *m.*
…e, TR.: relegare, esiliare. **-gā-** …legazione, *f.*, esilio, *m.*
…entare; mollificare; miti- …rsi, intenerirsi, miti- …; fondersi. **-ing**, …nessione, *f.*
…edele.

rĕlevan-ce, **-cy**, S.: rilevamento, *m.*; comodità, *f.* **-t**, ADJ.: soccorrevole, aiutativo.
relevātion, S.: alzamento, rilevamento, *m.*
reli-able, ADJ.: degno di fiducia. **-ance**, S.: confidenza, fiducia, *f.*: *place — on*, fiarsi di; porre fiducia in.
rĕlic, S.: reliquia; rimembranza, *f.*: *—s*, reliquie, ceneri, *f. pl.*
rĕlict, S.: vedova, donna vedovata, *f.*
relie-f, S.: sollievo, alleggiamento; conforto; rilievo, *m.*: *feel —*, sentirsi alleggerito. **-vable**, ADJ.: atto ad essere aiutato. **-ve**, TR.: alleviare; confortare; mitigare; soccorrere, aiutare: *— guard*, rilevare la guardia. **-ver**, S.: alleggiatore, confortatore, *m.* **-vo**, S.: rilievo, *m.*
relight, TR.: riaccendere, raccendere.
relig-ion, S.: religione; fede; pietà, *f.* **-ionary**, ADJ.: religioso. **-ionist**, S.: fanatico, *m.* **-iŏsity**, S.: religiosità, *f.* **-ious**, ADJ.: religioso, pio, divoto; esatto. **-iously**, ADV.: religiosamente; piamente; esattamente. **-iousness**, S.: religiosità, *f.*
relinquish, TR.: abbandonare, lasciare, desistere da. **-er**, abbandonatore, *m.* **-ment**, S.: abbandono, *m.*
rĕlish 1, S.: buon gusto, sapore; diletto, *m.*: *give a —*, rendere saporito. **relish** 2, TR.: gustare, dar gusto; INTR.: avere buon gusto; piacere. **-able**, ADJ.: gustoso, saporoso. **-ing**, ADJ.: di buon gusto; S.: approbazione, *f.*
relive, INTR.: rivivere.
relūcent, ADJ.: rilucente; trasparente, chiaro, lucido.
relŭct, INTR.: resistere, contrastare, ripugnare. **-ance**, **-ancy**, S.: ripugnanza; avversione, *f.* **-ant**, ADJ.: ripugnante; avverso: *be — to*, aver ripugnanza a. **-antly**, ADV.: con ripugnanza, a contraggenio, contro cuore. **-ate**† = *reluct.* **-ātion**†, S.: resistenza, opposizione, ripugnanza, *f.*
relū-me, **-mine**, TR.: ralluminare; ravvivare.
relȳ, INTR.: fidarsi, far capitale, rimettersi in.
remāin, INTR.: rimanere, restare; avanzare, continuare. **-der**, S.: resto, residuo, restante, rimasuglio; avanzo, *m.* **-s**, S. PL.: reliquie, *f. pl.*; avanzi, *m. pl.*
remāke, IRR.; TR.: rifare, fare di nuovo.
remănd, TR.: rimandare; richiamare.
rĕmanent, S.: rimanente; resto, *m.*
remārk 1, S.: nota, osservazione, notizia, *f.*; conto, *m.*: *make a —*, far un' osservazione. **remark** 2, TR.: notare, osservare; distinguere. **-able**, ADJ.: rimar-

swĕll 1, s.: gonfiezza, *f.*; tumore, *m.*; uomo gonfio, pallone, elegante, *m.*; cavalloni, *m. pl.*; onde, *f. pl.*: *a regular* —, un milordino. **swell** 2, IRR.; TR.: enfiare, gonfiare; ingrossare; aggravare; INTR.: enfiarsi; gonfiarsi; crescere: — *out*, far sacco (d' un muro); — *up*, ingrossare, aumentare. **-ing** 1, ADJ.: enfiato, tumido. **-ing** 2, s.: gonfiamento, tumore, *m.*

swĕl-tęr, (IN)TR.: opprimere (affogare) di caldo. **-tęring, -try,** ADJ.: che affoga; molto caldo.

swĕrve, INTR.: sviarsi, stornarsi; andar vagando, errare.

swift 1, ADJ.: veloce, pronto, presto. **swift** 2, s.: rondone (uccello); corrente, corso (d' un ruscello), *m.* **-footed,** ADJ.: spedito, veloce. **-ly,** ADV.: velocemente, con rapidità. **-ness,** s.: velocità, prestezza; rapidità, *f.*

swig, INTR.: bere a gran sorsi; tracannare.

swill 1, s.: gran sorso, *m.* **swill** 2, TR.: trangugiare; INTR.: bere molto; imbriacarsi. **-ęr,** s.: tracannatore, bevitore, *m.* **-ing,** s.: imbriachezza; crapula, *f.*

swim 1 = *swim-bladder.* **swim** 2, IRR.; (IN)TR.: passare a nuoto, nuotare; abbondare: — *with the tide*, andare colla marea; — *across*, passar a nuoto; *his head* —*s*, è vertiginoso. **-bladder,** s.: vessica del pesce, *f.* **-mer,** s.: nuotatore, *m.* **-ming,** s.: nuoto, andare a nuoto, *m.*: *by* —, a nuoto; — *of the head*, vertigine, *f.*, capogiro, *m.* **-mingly,** ADV.: dolcemente, ben bene.

swin-dle, TR.: ingannare, truffare, abbindolare: *he* —*d me out of ten francs*, mi ha scroccato dieci franchi. **-dlęr,** s.: ingannatore, truffatore, *m.*

swine, s.: porco, *m.* **-bread,** s.: tartufo, *m.* (fungo). **-grass,** s.: (*bot.*) piantaggine, *f.* **-herd,** s.: porcaro, porcaio, *m.* **-hull, -sty,** s.: porcile, *m.*

swing 1, s.: altalena, *f.*; dondolare, *m.*: *full* —, campo libero, briglia sciolta. **swing** 2, IRR.; TR.: altalenare, dondolare, agitare; INTR.: dondolarsi; agitarsi: — *about*, aggirare, andare attorno.

swinge, TR.: sferzare, frustare, bastonare, tartassare. **-buckler,** s.: bravaccio, *m.*

swing-ęr, s.: che si dondola; lanciatore, *m.* **-gate,** s.: altalena; porta (di steccato), *f.* **-ing** 1, ADJ.: grande, vasto. **-ing** 2, s.: barcollamento, dondolare, *m.* **-ingly,** ADV.: grandemente, vastamente.

swingle, TR.: scotolare; maciullare. **-bar, -tree,** s.: bilancino (di carrozze).

-inish, ADJ.: di porco; brutale.

-ink † 1, s.: travaglio, *m.*, fatica, *f.* **-ink** † 2, TR.: schiaccare; affaticare; INTR.: *faticarsi*, lavorare.

swipe, s.: altaleno, *m.*

switch 1, s.: bacchetta, verga; (*rail.*) macchina di baratto, *f.* **switch** 2, TR.: battere con bacchetta, sferzare.

swivel, s.: perno; piccol pezzo d' artiglieria, *m.*

swŏbbęr, s.: mozzo (di vascello), *m.*

swóon 1, s.: svenimento, deliquio, *m.* **swoon** 2, INTR.: svenire; venir meno. **-ing,** s.: svenimento, deliquio, tramortimento, *m.*

swōop 1, s.: piombare (d' un uccello rapace), *m.*: *at one* —, ad un tratto. **swoop** 2, TR.: afferrare, piombare addosso.

swŏp, TR.: barattare, cambiare. **-ping,** s.: baratto, cambio, *m.*

swōrd, s.: spada, *f.*: *by dint of* —, per forza d' arme; *put to the* —, metter a fil di spada. **-cutter,** s.: spadaio, *m.* **-ed,** ADJ.: armato d' una spada. **-ęr,** s.: ammazzatore; soldato, *m.* **-fish,** s.: spada, *f.* (pesce). **-handle,** s.: impugnatura di spada, *f.* **-knot,** s.: nastro di spada, *m.* **-law,** s.: violenza; oppressione, *f.* **-man,** s.: soldato, *m.* **-player,** s.: schermidore, gladiatore, *m.* **-șman,** s.: spadaccino, schermitore, *m.* **-șmanship,** s.: scherma, arte di scherma, *f.*

sўbarite, s.: sibarita, *m.*

sўcamǫre, s.: sicomoro, *m.*

sўcǫ-phant, s.: parassito; adulatore, *m.* **-phăntic, -phăntical,** ADJ.: parassitico.

syllăbic(al), ADJ.: sillabico, di sillaba.

sўlla-ble 1, s.: sillaba, *f.* **-ble** 2, TR.: sillabare; pronunziare distintamente. **-bus,** s.: estratto; compendio, sommario, *m.*

sўllǫ-gism, s.: sillogismo, *m.* **-gistic-(al),** ADJ.: sillogistico. **-gistically,** ADV.: in forma di sillogismo. **-gize,** TR.: sillogizzare, far sillogismi.

silph, -phid, s.: spirito aereo, *m.*

sўl-van 1, ADJ.: silvano; rustico. **-van** 2, s.: silvano; satiro, *m.* **-vătic,** ADJ.: silvestre, salvatico.

sўm-bol, s.: simbolo, *m.* **-bŏlical,** ADJ.: simbolico, allegorico. **-bŏlically,** ADV.: in maniera simbolica. **-bolizătion,** s.: simbolizzare, *m.*; immagine, figura, *f.* **-bolize,** (IN)TR.: simbolizzare. **-bolizing,** ADJ.: simbolico.

sym-mĕtrical, ADJ.: simmetrico, fatto con simmetria. **sўm-mętrize,** TR.: simmetrizzare, porre in simmetria. **-mętry,** s.: simmetria; proporzione, *f.*

sym-pathĕtic(al), ADJ.: simpatico, di simpatia. **-pathĕtically,** ADV.: simpaticamente, in modo simpatico. **-pathize,** INTR.: simpatizzare; compatire. **-pathy,** s.: simpatia; compassione, *f.*

sym-phōnious, ADJ.: armonioso. **-phon-**

renöwn 1, s.: fama, rinomanza, celebrità, *f.* **renown** 2, TR.: rinomare; celebrare, laudare. **-ed**, ADJ.: rinomato, celebre, illustre. **-edly**, ADV.: famosamente. **-less**, ADJ.: senza rinomanza.

rĕnt 1, s.: stracciatura, *f.*; squarcio, *m.*; rendita, entrata. **rent** 2, s.: pigione (di casa, ecc.), *f.*: — *of a house*, pigione, fitto, *m.*; — *of land*, fitto, terratico, *m.* **rent** 3, TR.: appigionare, torre a pigione una casa: — *a farm*, prendere in affitto un podere. **-able**, ADJ.: che si può torre a pigione. **-age**, s.: pigione, *f.* **-al**, s.: conto di rendite, *m.* **-er**, s.: affittuale, *m.* **-roll**, s.: ruolo delle rendite, *m.* **-service**, s.: rendita feudale, *f.*

renunciātion, s.: rinunzia, *f.*, rinunziamento, *m.*

re-ordáin, TR.: ordinare di nuovo. **-ordinātion**, s.: riordinare, *m.*

re-organizātion, s.: riorganizzazione, *f.* **-organize**, TR.: riorganizzare.

repăcify, TR.: rappacificare.

repáir 1, s.: riparo, ristauro; ricovero, rifugio; viaggio, *m.*, camminata, *f.*; (*nav.*) racconciamento, *m.*: *keep a house in* —, riparare una casa. **repair** 2, TR.: riparare; (*nav.*) racconciare; INTR.: andare; rendersi. **-er**, s.: riparatore, che ripara, *m.*

rĕ-parable, ADJ.: riparabile; rimediabile. **-parably**, ADV.: in modo riparabile. **-parātion**, s.: riparazione, *f.*; riparo, ristauro, *m.* **-părative**, ADJ.: ristaurante.

repartée 1, s.: risposta pronta e acuta, *f.* **repartee** 2, TR.: dare pronta risposta, ripiccare.

repartition, s.: spartizione, divisione, *f.*

repâss, INTR.: ripassare, passare di nuovo.

repâst 1, s.: pasto, cibo, *m.*; viveri, *m. pl.* **repast** 2, INTR.: banchettare. **-ure**, s.: festino banchetto, pasto, *m.*

repáy, TR.: pagare un' altra volta, rimborsare, rendere. **-ment**, s.: ripagare, *m.*

repéal 1, s.: rivocazione, *f.*; annullamento, *m.* **repeal** 2, TR.: rivocare; annullare, cassare, abolire. **-able**, ADJ.: rivocabile. **-er**, s.: che abolisce, che annul[illegible] **-ing**, s.: rivocamento; abolire, *m.*

[illegible]**ăt**, TR.: ripetere; replicare. **-edly**, [illegible]: spesso, spesse volte. **-er**, s.: ri[illegible], recitatore; oriuolo a ripetizione, [illegible]: ripetizione, *f.*

[illegible]ellere, scacciare; rispin[illegible] **-lent**, s.: repulsivo, [illegible] s.: scacciatore, *m.* [illegible]affliggersi; TR.: [illegible]imento, *m.*, [illegible]itante; [illegible]ato.

-er, s.: ripentitore, *m.* **-ing**, s.: ripentimento, *m.* **-ingly**, ADV.: con ripentimento.

repéople, TR.: popolare di nuovo.

reper-cúss, TR.: ripercuotere; riflettere. **-cússion**, s.: ripercussione; riflessione, *f.* **-cússive**, ADJ.: ripercussivo; riflessivo.

rĕpertory, s.: repertorio, indice, *m.*

repetition, s.: ripetizione, reiterazione, *f.*

repin-e, INTR.: rincrescere, dolersi; rimbrottare. **-er**, s.: rimbrottatore, mormoratore, *m.* **-ing**, s.: dispiacere; travaglio, *m.*, noia, *f.*, fastidio, *m.* **-ingly**, ADV.: in modo rimbrottevole.

replā-ce, TR.: collocare di nuovo, rilogare, rimpiazzare. **-cement**, **-cing**, s.: collocamento; rimpiazzare, *m.*

repláit, TR.: ripiegare, rincrespare.

replănt, TR.: ripiantare, piantare di nuovo. **-ātion**, s.: ripiantamento, *m.*, piantata nuova, *f.*

repléad, INTR.: litigare di nuovo.

replĕnish, TR.: riempiere, empiere di nuovo.

replē-te, ADJ.: pieno, riempito: — *with*, pieno (zeppo) di. **-tion**, s.: replezione, ripienezza, *f.* **-tive**, ADJ.: riempitivo.

replĕv-iable, ADJ.: (*jur.*) che può ricuperarsi. **-in** 1, **-y** 1, s.: (*jur.*) reintegrazione, *f.* **-in** 2, **-y** 2, TR.: ricoverare, riottenere.

replicātion, s.: ribalzo, *m.*; replica, risposta, *f.*

re-plier, s.: che replica. **-plý** 1, s.: replica, risposta, *f.* **-ply** 2, (IN)TR.: replicare, rispondere; soggiungere. **-plýer** = *replier*. **-plýing**, s.: replica, *f.*

repŏlish, TR.: pulire di nuovo.

repŏrt 1, s.: voce; fama, *f.*; romore, strepito; bisbiglio, *m.*; relazione, *f.*: *make a* —, riferire, narrare; *there is a* —, corre voce; — *of a gun*, rimbombo di un cannone (d' un fucile). **report** 2, TR.: rapportare, raccontare; dichiarare; dar conto; scoppiare, far romore: *it is* —*ed*, corre voce; si dice. **-er**, s.: relatore, raccontatore; giornalista (portanotizie), *m.* **-ingly**, ADV.: secondo la fama comune, per avere inteso dire.

re-pōsal, s.: confidenza, *f.*; deposito, *m.* **-pōse** 1, s.: riposo, *m.*; tranquillità, *f.* **-pose** 2, TR.: riposare; depositare; INTR.: riposarsi sopra; fidarsi; dormire. **-pōsed**, ADJ.: riposato, tranquillo. **-pōsedly**, ADV.: ripostamente; quietamente. **-pōsedness**, s.: essere in riposo, essere quieto, *m.* **-pŏsit**, TR.: riporre, mettere in deposito. **-position**, s.: ristabilimento, collocamento, *m.* **-pŏsitory**, s.: ripostiglio, ripositorio, *m.*

repossĕss, TR.: rientrare in possesso.

sū̆ral, ADJ.: surale.
sū̆ranee†, S.: sicurtà, assicuranza; malleveria, *f.*
surbāte 1, S.: spedatura, *f.*, straccare, *m.*
surbate 2, TR.: affaticare, straccare.
surcēase 1, S.: cessazione; sospensione, dilazione, *f.* **surcease** 2, TR.: sospendere; INTR.: cessare; tralasciare.
surchârge 1, S.: sopraccarico, soverchio carico, *m.* **surcharge** 2, TR.: sopraccaricare, caricare troppo.
sûrcingle, S.: cintura, cintola, *f.*
sŭrcoat, S.: saltambarco, *m.*, sopravvesta, *f.*
surd, ADJ.: sordo. **-ity**, S.: sordità, sordaggine, *f.*
sûre 1, ADJ.: certo, sicuro, assicurato; fermo, stabile: *be* —, esser certi; *to be* —*!* certamente, senza dubbio! — *enough!* ben certo! **sure** 2, ADV.: certamente, senza dubbio. **-footed**, ADJ.: che cammina con piede fermo. **-ly**, ADV.: certamente, sicuramente. **-ness**, S.: certezza, sicurezza, *f.* **-tiship**, S.: malleveria, cauzione, *f.* **-ty**, S.: sicurezza, certezza, *f.*; mallevadore, *m.*
sûrf, S.: cavalloni, *m. pl.*, onde (del mare), *f. pl.*
sûrface, S.: superficie, *f.*; esteriore, *m.*
sûrfeit 1, S.: indigestione; sazietà, *f.*; disgusto, fastidio, *m.* **surfeit** 2, (IN)TR.: satollare, impinzare; saziarsi. **-er**, S.: mangione, ghiottone, *m.* **-ing**, S.: stucchevolezza, sazievolezza, sazietà, *f.* **-water**, S.: acqua stomacale, *f.*
sûrge 1, S.: onda, *f.*, cavallone; flutto, *m.* **surge** 2, INTR.: fare cavalloni, gonfiarsi.
sûr-geon, S.: chirurgo, cerusico, *m.* **-gery**, S.: cirurgia, chirurgia, *f.* **-gical**, ADJ.: chirurgico.
sûrgy, ADJ.: fluttuoso, tempestoso.
sûr-lily, ADV.: burberamente, aspramente; orgogliosamente. **-liness**, S.: cattivo umore, *m.*; caponeria, *f.* **-ly**, ADJ.: arcigno, burbero, sdegnoso.
surmise 1, S.: sospetto, *m.*; supposizione; immaginazione, opinione, *f.* **surmise** 2, TR.: sospettare; immaginarsi, pensare; credere.
surmöunt, TR.: sormontare, superare; avanzare. **-able**, ADJ.: sormontabile.
sûrmulet, S.: triglia, *f.* (pesce).
sûrname 1, S.: soprannome, cognome, *m.* **surname** 2, TR.: soprannomare, cognominare.
surpáss, TR.: sorpassare; superare, soprastare, sovranzare, avanzare, eccedere. **-able**, ADJ.: sorpassabile. **-ing**, ADJ.: sorpassante; eccellente, maraviglioso. **-ingly**, ADV.: straordinariamente, eccellentemente.
-ce, S.: cotta (d' ecclesiastico), *f.*

sŭrp
surp
m.,
re, n
no s
-cin
-cin
ment
surr
surr
surr
ADJ.:
ly, A
sŭrr
-gat
tion.
surrō
torno,
surcō
surtō
survē
aggiu
survē
survē
of la
osser
misur
terren
misur
custo
fizio d
survi-
(IN)TR
-vor,
-vors
sus-ce
-cĕpt
vo.
-cĕpt
ADJ.:
scettil
padrin
to, *m.*
sŭsci-
tion,
suspĕ
pect
dubita
the tr
sia ve
ness,
ADJ.:
senza
suspĕ
lungar
so il s
re un
f. pl.
f. -se
-se 2,
f.: *re*
forse;

sion, S.: rescissione, *f.;* abolimento, *m.* **-scissory**, ADJ.: rescissorio.

-scribe, TR.: riscrivere; rispondere.

-script, S.: rescritto, editto, *m.*

-cuable, ADJ.: che può essere liberato. **-cue** 1, S.: liberamento, scampo; soccorso, *m.: to the* —, alla riscossa. **-cue** 2, TR.: liberare, scampare; venir in soccorso. **-cuer**, S.: liberatore, soccorritore, *m.*

research 1, S.: ricerca, inchiesta, *f.* **research** 2, TR.: ricercare, inchiedere; esaminare. **-er**, S.: ricercatore, inchieditore, *m.*

reseat, TR.: posare, rimettere; INTR.: riporsi a sedere.

reseize, TR.: sequestrare di nuovo. **-zure**, S.: nuova sequestrazione, *f.*

resell, TR.: rivendere.

resemblance, S.: somiglianza, *f.* **-ble**, INTR.: rassomigliare, esser simile. **-bling**, ADJ.: somigliante, simile.

resend, IRR.; TR.: rimandare, mandare indietro.

resent, TR.: pigliare in (buona† o) mala parte; risentirsi; offendersi: — *an insult*, risentirsi di una ingiuria. **-er**, S.: che si risente d'un' ingiuria. **-ful**, ADJ.: pieno di risentimento. **-ingly**, ADV.: risentitamente, con risentimento. **-ment**, S.: risentimento, risentirsi, *m.*

re-servation, S.: riserva, riserba; restrizione, *f.: mental* —, restrizione mentale. **-servative**, ADJ.: riserbante. **-servatory**, S.: riserbatoio, serbatoio, *m.;* conserva, *f.* **-serve** 1, S.: riserva; limitazione, eccezione; modestia, *f.: mental* —, restrizione mentale, intenzione occulta; *without* —, senza riserba; interamente. **-serve** 2, TR.: riservare; conservare. **-served**, ADJ.: riservato; modesto, discreto. **-servedly**, ADV.: con riserba, con riguardo. **-servedness**, S.: riserba; circospezione, discrezione, *f.* **-server**, S.: riserbatore, servatore, *m.*

reservoir *-vwor*, S.: serbatoio, *m.*

reset, TR.: rifiggere; (*typ.*) ricomporre.

resettle, TR.: ristabilire. **-ment**, S.: ristabilimento, *m.*

reship, TR.: rimbarcare. **-ment**, S.: rimbarco, *m.*

resiance† = *residence.*

reside, INTR.: risedere, dimorare.

resi-dence, **-dency**, S.: residenza; dimora, *f.* **-dent** 1, ADJ.: residente, dimorante. **-dent** 2, S.: residente; ambasciadore, deputato, *m.* **-dentiary**, ADJ.: residente.

-ual, **-uary**, ADJ.: del residuo, *re-* — *heir*, S.: erede universale, *m.* **-ue**, S.: residuo, restante, resto, *m.* residuo, *m.*

re-sign, (IN)TR.: rassegnare; cedere; deporre; disfarsi; sommettersi; dare la propria dimissione: *be* —*ed*, essere rassegnato; *the ministers have* —*ed*, i ministri hanno dato la loro dimissione. **-signation**, S.: rassegnazione; cessione; demissione, *f.* **-signed**, ADJ.: rassegnato. **-signedly**, ADV.: con rassegnazione. **-signer**, S.: rassegnante, che rassegna, *m.* **-signing**, **-signment**, S.: rassegnazione; demissione, *f.*

resi-lience, **-liency**, S.: resilienza, *f.*, ribalzo, *m.* **-lient**, ADJ.: che risalta, zampillante. **-lition**, S.: zampillio, ribalzo, *m.*

resin, S.: resina, gomma, *f.* **-acious**, **-ous**, ADJ.: resinoso, ragioso, gommifero. **-ousness**, S.: qualità resinosa, *f.*

resipiscence, S.: risipiscenza, *f.*, pentimento, *m.*

resist, TR.: resistere; opporsi. **-ance**, S.: resistenza, opposizione, *f.;* ostacolo, *m.* **-ant**, S.: resistente, *m.* **-ence** = *resistance.* **-ibility**, S.: resistibilità, *f.* **-ible**, ADJ.: resistibile. **-less**, ADJ.: irresistibile; insuperabile. **-lessly**, ADV.: irresistibilmente. **-lessness**, S.: irresistibilità, *f.*

reso-luble, ADJ.: dissolubile, solubile. **-lute**, ADJ.: risoluto, determinato. **-lutely**, ADV.: determinatamente, intrepidamente. **-luteness**, S.: determinazione; arditezza, *f.* **-lution**, S.: risoluzione; determinazione; fermezza, intrepidezza; decomposizione, analisi, *f.* **-lutive**, ADJ.: (*med.*) risolutivo, solutivo.

resol-vable = *resoluble.* **-ve** 1, S.: risoluzione; determinazione, *f.* **-ve** 2, TR.: risolvere; sciogliere, solvere; determinare; liquefare; INTR.: risolversi; determinarsi, decidersi. **-vedly**, ADV.: risolutamente; fermamente. **-vedness**, S.: risoluzione, *f.;* fermo proposito, *m.*, fermezza, *f.* **-vent**, S.: dissolvente, solutivo, *m.* **-ver**, S.: risolvente, *m.* **-ving**, S.: soluzione, *f.;* scioglimento, *m.;* dichiarazione, *f.*

resonan-ce, S.: risonanza, *f.* **-t**, ADJ.: risonante, rimbombante.

resorb, TR.: assorbire. **-ent**, ADJ.: assorbente.

resort 1, S.: concorso, *m.;* folla, calca, *f.;* ricorso, rifugio, *m.;* forza elastica, *f.* **resort** 2, INTR.: avere ricorso; frequentare, capitare, bazzicare: — *to a person*, aver ricorso ad una persona; — *to other means*, appigliarsi ad altri mezzi. **-er**, S.: frequentatore (d' un luogo), *m.*

resound, TR.: ripetere; celebrare; INTR.: risonare, rimbombare. **-ing**, ADJ.: risonante, rimbombante; S.: risonanza, *f.*, rimbombo, *m.*

tattŏo 1, s.: (*mil.*) ritirata, *f.* **tattoo** 2, TR.: tatuare. **-ing**, s.: tat(t)uaggio, *m.*
tâught 1, PRET., PART. di *teach*. **taught** 2 = *taut*.
tâunt 1, s.: motteggio, *m.*, burla, *f.* **taunt** 2, TR.: motteggiare, burlare, beffare; insultare. **-er**, s.: motteggiatore, buffatore, *m.* **-ing**, s.: motteggio, *m.*, burla, *f.* **-ingly**, ADJ.: in modo scherzevole, da scherzo, in burla.
tâut, ADJ.: (*nav.*) duro, steso.
tau-tŏlogist, s.: tautologo, *m.* **-tŏlogy**, s.: tautologia, *f.*
tăvern, s.: taverna, osteria, bettola, *f.* **-er** = *tavern-keeper*. **-hunter**, s.: frequentatore di taverne, *m.* **-keeper**, **-man**, s.: tavernaio, ostiere, bettoliere, *m.*
tâw 1, s.: palla di marmo (da giuocare), *f.* **taw** 2, TR.: conciare (con allume).
tâw-drily, ADV.: sfoggiatamente. **-driness**, s.: sfoggio, *m.*, pompa senza eleganza, abbigliamento fastoso, *m.* **-dry**, ADJ.: fastoso, sfoggiato.
tâwer, s.: conciatore (con allume), *m.* **-y**, s.: arte di conciare con allume, *f.*
tâwny, ADJ.: bruno, abbronzato, fosco.
tăx 1, s.: tassa, imposizione, gabella; censura, *f.* **tax** 2, TR.: tassare; censurare, accusare. **-able**, ADJ.: soggetto al catasto. **-ātion**, s.: tassagione, tassazione, tassa, *f.* **-er**, s.: che impone le tasse. **-gatherer**, s.: collettore delle tasse, *m.* **-ing**, s.: tassazione, tassa, *f.*
tēa, s.: tè, *m.* **-board**, s.: vassoio (da servire il tè), *m.* **-canister**, s.: scatola da tè, *f.*
tēach, IRR.: (IN)TR.: insegnare, ammaestrare, istruire, mostrare: — *wit*, scaltrire, fare astuto. **-able**, ADJ.: docile, atto ad apprendere. **-ableness**, s.: docilità, attitudine ad imparare; capacità, *f.* **-er**, s: insegnatore, *m.* **-ing**, s.: insegnamento, ammaestramento, *m.*
tēacup, s.: tazza da tè, *f.*
tēal, s.: farchetola, *f.* (uccello).
tēam 1, s.: tirata, muta, *f.*, tiro, *m.* **team** 2, TR.: attaccare (a cavalli).
tēa-pot, s.: cocoma per il tè, *f.*
tēar 1, s.: lagrima, gocciola, *f.*; pianto, *m.*: *shed —s*, versar lagrime, lagrimare.
târ 2, s.: stracciatura, *f.*, squarcio, *m.* **tear** 3, IRR.; TR.: lacerare; stracciare, squarciare; INTR.: adirarsi, montar in collera. **-er**, s.: stracciatore, laceratore, *m.* **-falling**, ADJ.: tenero di cuore, pronto a piangere. **-ful**, ADJ.: lagrimoso, piangente. **-less**, ADJ.: senza lagrime.
târing, s.: stracciamento, *m.*, stracciatura, *f.*
tēa-saucer, s.: sottocoppa, *f.*
tēa-se, TR.: pettinare, cardare; infastidire, importunare. **-sel**, s.: cardo, scardasso, *m.* **-seler**, s.: cardatore, *m.* **-ser**, s.: importuno, *m.*
tēaspoon, s.: cucchiaino, *m.*
tēat, s.: tetta, poppa, *f.*
tēa-water, s.: acqua da tè, *f.*
tĕch-ily, ADV.: petulantemente. **-iness**, s.: petulanza, *f.*; cattivo umore, *m.*
tĕch-nical, ADJ.: tecnico. **-nŏlogy**, s.: tecnologia, *f.*
tĕchy, ADJ.: di cattivo umore, stizzoso.
tĕd, TR.: spandere l'erba frescamente mietuta.
tĕdder 1, s.: pastoia, *f.*, ritegno, *m.* **tedder** 2, TR.: ristringere, legare.
tēdious, ADJ.: tedioso, noioso; lento. **-ly**, ADV.: tediosamente, noiosamente. **-ness**, s.: tedio, rincrescimento, *m.*, spiacevolezza, noia, *f.*
tēem, TR.: produrre; INTR.: esser gravida. **-er**, s.: produttrice, generatrice, *f.* **-ful**, ADJ.: prolifico, fecondo; gravido. **-less**, ADJ.: infecondo, infruttuoso.
tēen 1, s.: dolore, affanno, *m.*, pena, *f.* **teen** 2, TR.: eccitare, incoraggiare.
tēens, s. PL.: anni 13–19 (numeri colla desinenza *-teen*, -'dici'), *m. pl.*, giovanezza, *f.*
tēe-th 1, PL. di *tooth*. **-th** 2, INTR.: mettere i denti, essere nella dentizione. **-thing**, s.: mettere de' denti, *m.*, dentizione, *f.*
teetōtal(l)er, s.: bevilacqua, *m.*
tĕgument, s.: integumento, coprimento, *m.*
tĕil(-tree), s.: tiglio, *m.*
tĕl-egraph 1, s.: telegrafo, *m.* **-egraph** 2, TR.: telegrafare, dar segnali (mediante il telegrafo). **-egrăphic(al)**, ADJ.: telegrafico. **-ĕgraphy**, s.: telegrafia, *f.*
tĕle-phone 1, s.: telefono, *m.* **-phone** 2, INTR.: telefonare. **-phŏnic**, ADJ.: telefonico. **-scope**, s.: telescopio, *m.* **-scŏpic(al)**, ADJ.: telescopico, di telescopio.
tĕll, IRR.: (IN)TR.: dire; dichiarare, mostrare; numerare; dettare, comunicare; raccontare: — *abroad*, pubblicare, divolgare; — *again*, ridire, ricontare; *I can (could) not — you*, non saprei dirvi; *I am told*, mi si dice. **-er**, s.: dicitore, raccontatore; cassiere, computista, *m.*: *fortune-—*, astrologo. **-tale**, s.: maldicente, *m.*
te-merārious, ADJ.: temerario, inconsiderato. **-merāriously**, ADV.: temerariamente, con temerità. **-mĕrity**, s.: temerità, audacia, *f.*
tĕmper 1, s.: tempera, tempra, *f.*; temperamento, *m.*, disposizione, *f.*, umore, *m.*: *be in good —*, essere in buona tempra; *be out of —*, essere di cattivo umore, esser fuori de' gangheri. **temper** 2, TR.: tem-

—, vendere a minuto; — *trade*, vendetta al minuto (a ritaglio). **-tâil** 2, TR.: vendere a minuto, rivendere. **-tâiler**, S.: venditore a minuto, *m.*

retâin, (IN)TR.: ritenere; tenere a mente. **-er**, S.: aderente, *m.*; persona salariata, *f.*, stipendiato, *m.* **-ing**, S.: ritenimento, ritegno, *m.*

retâke, IRR.; TR.: ripigliare.

retâl-iate, TR.: rendere la pariglia. **-iâtion**, S.: pariglia, *f.*; contraccambio, *m.*: *by way of* —, per vendetta.

retârd, (IN)TR.: ritardare; differire. **-âtion**, S.: ritardamento, *m.* **-er**, S.: ritardatore, indugiatore, *m.* **-ing**, **-ment**, S.: ritardamento, *m.*

rětch, INTR.: aver voglia di recere, vomitare, recere.

retěn-tion, S.: ritenzione; custodia, *f.* **-tive**, ADJ.: ritentivo, ritenitivo, *m.* **-tiveness**, S.: facoltà ritentiva, tenacità di memoria, *f.*

rěticence, S.: reticenza, *f.*

rět-icle, S.: rete piccola, *f.*; sacchetto, *m.* **-icular**, ADJ.: reticolare, reticolato. **-iculated**, ADJ.: reticolato. **-icule**, S.: borsa da donna, *f.* **-iform**, ADJ.: retiforme. **-ina**, S.: retina (dell' occhio), *f.*

rětinue, S.: corteggio; accompagnamento, *m.*

reti-re 1, S.: ritirata, *f.*; ritiro, rifugio, *m.* **-re** 2, TR.: ritirare; INTR.: ritirarsi. **-red**, ADJ.: ritirato, solitario: — *life*, vita ritirata; *on the —d list*, giubilato, in quiescenza. **-redly**, ADV.: solitariamente; privatamente. **-redness**, S.: ritiratezza, vita privata; solitudine, *f.* **-rement**, S.: ritiratezza; solitudine, *f.* **-ring**, ADJ.: che si ritira; che ama la solitudine; schivo, riservato: — *manners*, modi riservati (schivi, timidi).

retôrt 1, S.: storta; risposta, *f.* **retort** 2, TR.: ritorcere; replicare. **-er**, S.: che ritorce. **-ing**, **-tion**, S.: ritorcimento, *m.*; confutazione, *f.*

retôss, TR.: far balzare indietro; rigettare, rispingere.

retôuch, TR.: ritoccare; ripulire.

retrâce, TR.: delineare di nuovo: — *one's steps*, tornare indietro.

[illegible]**-t**, TR.: ritrattare; INTR.: ritrattarsi, disdirsi. **-(tâ)tion**, S.: rittratta[illegible], *f.*; ritrattare, *m.* **-tive**, ADJ.: ri[illegible]

[illegible] S.: (*leg.*) rinunzia, *f.*

[illegible]: ritirata; solitudine, *f.*:

—, suonare la ritirata.

[illegible]arsi; andare via.

[illegible] tagliare, scema-

[illegible] (*fort.*) trin-

[illegible]acierarsi:

[illegible]omis-

zare. **-ment**, S.: scemamento; sminuimento, *m.*; economia; (*fort.*) trincea, *f.*

retrib-ute, TR.: retribuire; ricompensare. **-uter**, S.: retribuitore, *m.* **-ûtion**, S.: retribuzione; ricompensa, *f.* **-utive**, **-utory**, ADJ.: retribuente; rimunerativo.

retrie-vable, ADJ.: ricuperabile. **-ve**, TR.: ricoverare; ricuperare: — *one's honour*, ricoverare il suo onore; — *a loss*, riparare una perdita. **-ver**, S.: ricoveratore, *m.*, -trice, *f.*; cane barbone scozzese, *m.*

retroâc-tion, S.: retroazione, *f.* **-tive**, ADJ.: retroattivo.

retro-cêde, INTR.: retrocedere. **-cěssion**, S.: retrocedimento; ritirarsi, *m.*

retro-gradâtion, S.: retrogradazione, *f.* **rětro-grade** 1, ADJ.: retrogrado. **-grade** 2, INTR.: retrogradare. **-grading**, **-grěssion**, S.: retrocedere, *m.*

rětro-spect, **-spěction**, S.: guardare indietro, mirar indietro, *m.* **-spěctive**, ADJ.: che guarda indietro; passato: — *glance*, colpo d' occhio sul passato.

retrûde, INTR.: spingere indietro.

retŭnd, TR.: rintuzzare; attutire.

retûrn 1, S.: ritorno, *m.*; ricaduta; ricompensa; risposta, *f.*: — *of money*, rimessa di danari, *f.*; *make a* —, render la pariglia. **return** 2, TR.: rendere; rimettere, restituire; ricompensare; contraccambiare; INTR.: ritornare, rimettersi: — *an answer*, rispondere, render risposta; — *a letter*, rimandare una lettera; — *good for evil*, ricambiare il male col bene; — *a favour*, reciprocare una gentilezza; — *thanks*, render grazie. **-able**, ADJ.: di rimando. **-er**, S.: che rimette danaro.

reû-nion, S.: reunione, riconciliazione, *f.* **-nite**, TR.: riunire, riconciliare; INTR.: riunirsi, ricongiungersi, riconciliarsi. **-niting**, S.: riunimento, *m.*, riconciliazione, *f.*

rêve, S.: guardiano d' un feude, *m.*

revêal, TR.: rivelare, scoprire, manifestare. **-er**, S.: rivelatore, scopritore, *m.* **-ing**, S.: rivelamento, svelamento, *m.*

revêille *-lye*, S.: (*mil.*) battere la diana, *m.*

rěvel 1, S.: gozzoviglia, festa romorosa, *f.*

revel 2, TR.: ritrattare; INTR.: gozzovigliare, festeggiare.

revelâtion, S.: rivelazione, *f.*, palesamento, *m.*

rěvel-ler, S.: gozzovigliante, festeggiante, *m.* **-ling**, S.: gozzoviglia; allegrezzza, *f.* **-ry**, S.: gozzoviglia, festa romorosa, *f.* **-rout**†, S.: assemblea illegale, *f.*

revěn-ge 1, S.: vendetta; rivincita (alle carte), *f.*: *take one's* —, prendere una rivincita; *glut one's* —, sfogare la propria vendetta. **-ge** 2, (IN)TR.: vendicare, vendicarsi. **-geful**, ADJ.: vendicativo. **-gefully**, ADV.: d' una maniera vendicativa.

tepefáction, S.: tepefare, *m.*
tĕp-id, ADJ.: tiepido, freddo; indifferente; lento. **-ídity**, S.: tiepidezza; freddezza, indifferenza, *f.*
tĕr-ce, S.: terzo (d' una botte di vino), *m.* **-cet**, S.: (*mus.*) mezzana, *f.*
tĕre-binth, S.: terebinto, *m.* **-binthinate**, **-binthine**, ADJ.: terebintinato.
tĕre-brate, TR.: forare, bucare, pertugiare, *m.* **-brátion**, S.: forare, pertugiare, *m.*
tergéminous, ADJ.: tergemino, triplice, triforme.
tergiver-sate, INTR.: tergiversare, scansare. **-sátion**, S.: tergiversazione, *f.*
tĕrm 1, S.: termine, confine; tempo, *m.*; espressione, locuzione; condizione, *f.*, grado, stato, *m.*: **—s**, termini, *m. pl.*; condizioni, *f. pl.*; stato, *m.*; *a — of ten years*, un termine di dieci anni; *be on* (*upon*) *good — with*, esser del pari con; essere amico intrinseco di. **term** 2, TR.: nominare, chiamare.
tĕrmagan-cy, S.: torbidezza d' animo, *f.*; strepito, *m.* **-t**, ADJ.: torbido, tumultuante; S.: litigioso, *m.*; sgridatrice, megera, *f.*: *— wife*, moglie irrequieta (diavolessa).
tĕrmi-nable, ADJ.: terminabile. **-nate**, TR.: terminare, limitare; mettere fine; INTR.: terminarsi, finirsi. **-nately**, ADV.: terminatamente. **-nátion**, S.: terminazione, conclusione, *f.*
terminthus, S.: (*surg.*) tumore, *m.*
tĕrm-inus, S.: atrio (della strada ferrata), *m.* **-less**, ADJ.: illimitato. **-ly**, ADV.: ogni termine successivo. **-time**, S.: giorni curiali, *m. pl.*
tĕrnary, S.: ternario, *m.*
tĕr-race, S.: terrazzo, *m.* **-ráqueous**, ADJ.: terracqueo, di terra ed acqua. **-rēne**, ADJ.: terreno, terrestre. **-reous**, ADJ.: terroso, misto di terra. **-rĕstrial**, ADJ.: terrestre, di terra.
tĕrri-ble, ADJ.: terribile; spaventevole. **-bleness**, S.: terribilità, *f.*; terrore, *m.* **-bly**, ADV.: terribilmente, spaventevolmente; estremamente.
tĕrrier, S.: bassetto; succhiello, *m.*
ter-rífic, ADJ.: terrifico, spaventevole.
tĕr-rify, TR.: atterrire, spaventare.
territórial, ADJ.: territoriale. **tĕrritory**, S.: territorio; dominio, *m.*
tĕrror, S.: terrore, spavento, *m.*
tĕrse, ADJ.: terso, pulito, elegante. **-ly**, ADV.: pulitamente, elegantemente. **-ness**, S: pulitezza, eleganza, *f.*
tĕr-tian, S.: terzana, febbre terzana, *f.* **-tiate**, TR.: (*agr.*) terzare.
tĕsselated, ADJ.: commesso a scacchi.
tĕst, S.: coppella; prova, *f.*; saggio; cimento, *m.*: *put to the —*, mettere in prova; *take the —*, stare la prova; *religious —*, dichiarazione di fede. **-able**, ADJ.: testabile.
testáceous, ADJ.: testaceo, crostaceo.
tĕst-act, S.: legge di giuramento di professione religiosa, *f.*
tĕs-tament, S.: testamento, *m.*; scrittura sacra, *f.*: *new* (*old*) *—*, n(u)ovo (vecchio) testamento. **-tamĕntary**, ADJ.: testamentario **-tate**, ADJ.: testato, che ha fatto testamento. **-tátion**, S.: testimonianza, *f.* **-tátor**, S.: testatore, *m.* **-tátrix**, S.: testatrice, *f.*
tĕsted, ADJ.: saggiato, provato.
tĕster, S.: sei soldi, *m. pl.*; cielo del letto, *m.*
tĕsticle, S.: testicolo, *m.*
tes-tificátion, S.: testificazione; testimonianza, *f.* **'-tificator**, **-tifier**, S.: testificatore, *m.* **'-tify**, TR.: testificare; certificare, assicurare.
tĕstily, ADV.: con caponeria, in modo arcigno.
tes-timōnial, S.: testimoniale, *m.* **tĕstimony** 1, S.: testimonio, *m.*; testimonianza; sicurtà; prova, *f.*; ordine, *m.*: *in — whereof*, in fede di che; *bear —*, far testimonianza. **-timony** 2, TR.: testimoniare.
tĕstiness, S.: ostinatezza, caparbietà, *f.*; cattivo umore, *m.*
tĕston, S.: testone, *m.* (moneta).
tĕsty, **tĕtchy**, ADJ.: stizzoso, irascibile; ostinato, caparbio.
tête-à-tête (*Eng. acc.*), S.: conversazione segreta, *f.*; ADV.: testa a testa, a solo a solo.
tĕther 1, S.: pastoia, *f.*; ritegno, *m.*: *be brought to a —*, venire in potere d' altri; *hold one to his —*, tener uno in freno. **tether** 2, TR.: impastoiare.
tĕtra-gon, S.: tetragono, *m.* **-gonal** **-ă-**, ADJ.: tetragono, tetragonico. **-rch** *tĕtra-*, S.: tetrarca, *m.* **-chate**, **-chy** *tetrā-*, S.: tetrarchia, *f.* **-stich** **-ă-**, S.: (*poet.*) tetrastico, *m.* **-syllable**, S.: tetrasillaba, *f.*
tĕtri-c(al), **-cous**, ADJ.: tetrico, di cattivo umore.
tĕtter, S.: empettigine, volatica, *f.*
tew† 1, S.: materiale, *m.* **tew**† 2, TR.: lavorare, strappare, tirare.
tĕxt, S.: testo, *m.* **-ile**, ADJ.: che può essere tessuto. **-letter**, S.: (*print.*) testo, *m.* **-ual**, ADJ.: testuale. **-uarist**, S.: teologo versato nella scrittura, *m.* **-uary**, ADJ.: contenuto nel testo. **-ure**, S.: tessitura, *f.*; tessuto, *m.*
thăn, CONJ.: che, di; che non; anzi che.
thāne, S.: baronetto, *m.*
thănk, TR.: ringraziare, render grazie. **-ful**, ADJ.: grato, riconoscente. **-fully**,

rhūbarb, S.: rabarbaro, reobarbaro, *m.*
rhym-e 1, S.: rima; poesia, *f.* **-e** 2, INTR.: rimare; accordarsi. **-eless**, ADJ.: senza rima. **-er**, **-ester**, S.: rimatore, poetastro, *m.*
rhythm, S.: ritmo, *m.;* misura; armonia, *f.* **-ical**, ADJ.: ritmico, armonioso. **-us** = *rhythm.*
rib, S.: costola, *f.*
ribald, S.: ribaldo, libertino, *m.: play the* —, ribaldeggiare. **-ry**, S.: ribalderia; oscenità, disonestà, *f.*
riband, S.: nastro, *m.*, fettuccia, *f.* **-weaver**, S.: nastraio, *m.*
ribbed, ADJ.: fornito di costole.
ribble-răbble, S.: canaglia, *f.*, popolaccio, *m.*
ribbon, S.: nastro, *m.*, fettuccia, *f.* **-trade**, S.: traffico di nastri, *m.* **-weaver**, S.: nastraio, *m.*
ribwort, S.: piantaggine, petacciuola, *f.*
rice, S.: riso, *m.*
rich, ADJ.: ricco, opulento; copioso, abbondante; fertile, ubertoso; sontuoso: — *wine*, vino gagliardo, *m.;* — *soil*, suolo ubertoso. **-es**, S. PL.: ricchezze, dovizie, *f. pl.* **-ly**, ADV.: riccamente; copiosamente. **-ness**, S.: ricchezza, opulenza; abbondanza, copia; magnificenza, *f.*
rick, S.: cumulo, mucchio, *m.*
ricket-s, S. PL.: rachitide, *f.* **-y**, ADJ.: rachitico; tentennante, zoppo.
ricochĕt, S.: rimbalzo, *m.*, riscossa, *f.*
rid 1, ADJ.: liberato, sbrogliato, sbrigato: *get — of*, liberarsi, disfarsi, sbrigarsi di.
rid 2, IRR.; TR.: liberare, sbrogliare; disimpegnare: — *one of his money*, scroccare ad uno il suo danaro. **-dance**, S.: sbarazzare; scioglimento, *m.*
rid-dle 1, S.: enimma, *m.* **-dle** 2, S.: staccio, *m.* **-dle** 3, TR.: spiegare (un enimma). **-dle** 4, TR.: stacciare; INTR.: parlare oscuramente. **-dlingly**, ADV.: in modo enimmatico.
rid-e 1, S.: corso a cavallo, *m.*, cavalcata, *f.* **-e** 2, IRR.; TR.: andare a cavallo; andare in carrozza; maneggiare; governare; (*nav.*) esser all' ancora: — *hard*, andare in posta; — *a horse*, montare a cavallo; *learn to* —, imparare a montare a cavallo; — *about*, fare una girata a cavallo; — *away*, scampare a cavallo; — *back*, ritornare a cavallo. **-er**, S.: cavalcatore; cavaliere, *m.*
... 1, S.: cima, sommità, *f.;* solco, *m.;* ...ch.) scanalatura, *f.* **-ge** 2, TR.: ...h.) scanalare. **-ge-band**, ... **-ge-bone**, S.: spina ... **-e**, S.: tegola, *f.*, te... ...mina del tetto, ...che ha gio-

ri-dicule 1, S.: ridicolo, *m.*, cosa ridicola, *f.* **-dicule** 2, TR.: rendere ridicolo, beffare: *turn into* —, mettere in ridicolo. **-diculer**, S.: beffeggiatore, *m.* **-diculous**, ADJ.: ridicolo. **-diculously**, ADV.: ridicolosamente. **-diculousness**, S.: ridicolosaggine, *f.;* ridicolo, *m.*
riding 1, ADJ.: viaggiante a cavallo. **riding** 2, S.: andare a cavallo, *m.:* — *for pleasure*, passeggio a cavallo, *m.* **-cap**, S.: beretta per la campagna, *f.* **-coat**, S.: abito da cavalcare, gabbano, *m.* **-habit**, S.: abito da cavalcare, *m.*, ammazone, *f.* **-hood**, S.: mantello da donna da cavalcare, *m.* **-master**, S.: cavallerizzo, cavalcatore valente, *m.* **-rod**, S.: bacchetta, verga, *f.* **-school**, S.: scuola di cavallerizza, *f.*
ridŏtto, S.: ridotto, ballo; concerto, *m.*
rife, ADJ.: frequente, comune. **-ly**, ADV.: comunemente, abbondantemente. **-ness**, S.: prevalenza, abbondanza, *f.*
riff-raff, S.: robaccia, *f.;* cattive cose, *f. pl.*
rifle 1, TR.: rubare, saccheggiare; scanalare, rigare. **rifle** 2, **-gun**, S.: schioppo rigato, *m.* **-man**, S.: carabiniere, *m.*
rifler, S.: predatore, rubatore, *m.*
rift 1, S.: crepatura, apertura, *f.* **rift** 2, TR.: fendere, spaccare; (*nav.*) ammainare; INTR.: fendersi, spaccarsi.
rig 1, S.: cima, sommità. **rig** 2, S.: burla. **rig** 3, TR.: addobbare, ornare; (*nav.*) arredare, allestire.
rigadōon, S.: rigodone, *m.* (ballo).
rigātion, S.: innaffiamento, adacquare, *m.*
rig-ger, S.: (*nav.*) apparecchiatore, *m.* **-ging**, S.: (*nav.*) attrezzi, arredi, *m. pl.*
riggish†, ADJ.: dissoluto, lascivo.
riggle, INTR.: dimenarsi, agitarsi.
right 1, ADJ.: dritto, diritto, destro; retto, in linea retta; giusto, equo; franco; mero, puro; opportuno: — *hand*, mano destra, *f.;* — *line*, linea retta, *f.;* — *truth*, pura verità, *f.;* — *way*, strada dritta, *f.;* vero mezzo, *m.; as is* —, como è di ragione; *be* —, aver ragione; *set* —, rettificare; *be in one's — senses*, essere in buon senno. **right** 2, INTERJ.: bella! ben bene! **right** 3, ADV.: bene, giustamente: — *or wrong*, bene o male; a dritto o torto; *very* —, molto bene; — *learned*, molto dotto; — *over against*, dirimpetto, in faccia; *be* —, avere ragione; *you say* —, dite bene. **right** 4, S.: diritto, *m.;* giustizia; ragione, *f.;* privilegio, *m.*, prerogativa, *f.; to the* —, a destra; *be in the* —, aver ragione; *do — to, do one* —, rendere giustizia ad alcuno; *maintain one's* —, mantenere il suo diritto; *set one to* —, trarre alcuno d' errore; *set to* —*s*, aggiustare, metter in ordine,

thick-lipped, ADJ.: che ha le labbra grosse. **-ly**, ADV.: spessamente, foltamente; in gran numero. **-ness**, S.: spessezza, densità, grossezza, *f.*: — *of hearing*, durezza d' orecchie, *f.* **-set**, ADJ.: spesso, folto. **-skin**, S.: pelle dura, pelle grossa, *f.* **-skinned**, ADJ.: che ha la pelle dura. **-skulled**, ADJ.: che ha la testa dura; stupido.

thie-f, S.: ladro, rubatore, *m.*: *little* (*petty*) —, ladroncello, *m.*; *set a — to catch a* —, carne di lupo, zanne di cane; *stop —!* al ladro! *play the* —, rubare. **-f-catcher**, **-f-taker**, S.: birro, sergente, *m.* **-ve**, TR.: rubare, involare. **-very**, S.: ruberia, *f.*, furto, latrocinio, *m.* **-ving**, S.: rubamento, *m.*, ruberia, *f.*, ladroneccio, *m.* **-vish**, ADJ.: inclinato a rubare. **-vishly**, ADV.: da ladro. **-vishness**, S.: inclinazione a rubare, *f.*

thigh, S.: coscia, *f.*

thill, S.: timone (di carro), *m.* **-er**, **-horse**, S.: cavallo delle stanghe, *m.*

thimble, S.: ditale, *m.*

thin 1, ADJ.: magro, smunto, smilzo; leggiero; sottile, raro; tenue, fievole; chiaro; ADV.: radamente, in piccol numero; chiaramente: *grow* —, divenir magro, smagrire; — *cloth*, panno sottile (leggiero); — *hair*, capelli rari; — *audience*, uditorio poco numeroso. **thin** 2, TR.: diradare, rarefare, attenuare; schiarare; diramare.

thine, PRON.: tuo, tuoi, tue; il tuo, la tua, i tuoi, le tue.

thing, S.: cosa, *f.*, oggetto, affare, *m.*: —*s*, cose, *f. pl.*, affari; effetti, bauli, *m. pl.*, bagaglio, *m.*; *another* —, altra cosa; *poor little* —, poveretto, poverino; *above all —s*, principalmente.

think, IRR.; (IN)TR.: pensare, immaginare; meditare, considerare; stimare; osservare; esaminare; immaginarsi: *I — so*, credo così; *what do you — of it?* che ve ne pare? — *light of*, far poco conto di; — *much of*, stimare, pregiare; — *well of one's self*, aver buona opinione di sè stesso; *I will — the matter over*, ci rifletterò sopra, ci penserò. **-er**, S.: pensatore, meditante, *m.* **-ing** 1, ADJ.: giudizioso, savio. **-ing** 2, TR.: pensamento, pensiero, *m.*, opinione, *f.*, giudizio, *m.*

thin-ly, ADV.: radamente; in piccol numero. **-ness**, S.: radezza, rarità, tenuità; magrezza, *f.*

third 1, ADJ.: terzo: *every — day*, di tre in tre giorni. **third** 2, S.: terzo, *m.*, terza parte, *f.* **-borough**, S.: sottoconestabile, *m.* **-ly**, ADV.: terzamente, nel terzo luogo.

thirl, TR.: forare, bucare.

thirst, S.: sete; voglia, *f.*, desiderio, *m.*: *quench one's* —, dissetarsi. **thirst** 2, INTR.: aver sete; desiderare, bramare. **-iness**, S.: sete; appetito ardente, *m.* **-y**, ADJ.: assetato, sitibondo; bramoso, desideroso: *be* (*very*) —, aver (gran) sete.

thir-teen, ADJ.: tredici, *m.* **-teenth**, ADJ.: tredicesimo. **-tieth**, ADJ.: trentesimo. **-ty**, ADJ.: trenta.

this, PRON.: questo, questa; questa cosa: *from — place*, da qui; *by — time*, a quest' ora, adesso; — *way*, da qui, per di qua, costì, in questo luogo.

this-tle, S.: cardo, cardone, *m.* **-tle-down**, S.: cottone di cardone, *m.* **-tly**, ADJ.: pieno di cardoni.

thither, ADV.: lì, là, a questo luogo. **-to**, ADV.: fin là. **-ward**, ADV.: verso là, verso quella parte.

thō' = *though.*

thōle 1, S.: schermo (per i remi), *m.* **thole**† 2, INTR.: soffrire.

thŏng, S.: coreggia, striscia di cuoio, *f.*

tho-răcic, ADJ.: toracico. **-rax**, S.: (*anat.*) torace, petto, *m.*

thôrn, S.: spina, *f.*, spino; travaglio, *m.* **-back**, S.: razza, *f.* (pesce). **-bush**, S.: spineto, *m.* **-y**, ADJ.: spinoso; afflittivo.

thŏrough 1, ADJ.: intero, compiuto, perfetto; profondo, radicale. **thorough** 2, PREP.: per traverso, a traverso. **-bred**, ADJ.: di puro sangue. **-fare**, S.: passaggio aperto, corso, *m.*; strada larga, via pubblica, *f.* **-ly**, ADV.: interamente, a fondo, affatto, perfettamente. **-paced**, **-sped**, ADJ.: perfetto, compiuto, finito. **-stitch**†, ADV.: interamente, affatto.

thōse, PRON.: quelli, quei, quegli; quelle; coloro.

thou 1, PRON.: tu. **thou** 2, TR.: dare del tu a.

though, CONJ.: benchè, ancorchè, quantunque, nonostante: *as* —, come se; *even* —, ancorchè, quand' anche; — *it were so*, supposto fosse così.

thought *thăt*, S.: pensiero, *m.*, opinione, riflessione; cura; intenzione, *f.*: *a — strikes me*, mi viene un' idea. **-ful**, ADJ.: pensieroso, pensoso, meditativo. **-fully**, ADV.: con viso pensoso. **-fulness**, S.: pensiero profondo, *m.* **-less**, ADJ.: spensierato, trascurato, negligente. **-lessly**, ADV.: spensieratamente, negligentemente. **-lessness**, S.: spensierataggine, inavvertenza; stolidezza, *f.* **-sick**, ADJ.: pieno di pensieri.

thousand, ADJ.: mille: *a* —, mille; *two* —, due mila; *by —s*, a migliaia. **-th**, ADJ.: millesimo.

thrăck, TR.: caricare.

thrăldom, S.: servitù, schiavitù, *f.*

thrăll 1, S.: schiavo, *m.*; servitù, *f.* **thrall** 2, TR.: porre in schiavitù, sottomettere.

perare, temprare; moderare; dare la tempera; stagionare: — *colours*, temperare colori. **-ament**, S.: temperamento, *m.*, complessione, *f.*; mezzo; modo; termine, *m.* **-amĕntal**, ADJ.: costituzionale. **-ance**, S.: temperanza; moderazione, *f.* **-ate**, ADJ.: temperato, moderato; sobrio. **-ately**, ADV.: temperatamente, moderatamente. **-ateness**, S.: moderazione; mediocrità, *f.* **-ative**, ADJ.: temperativo. **-ature**, S.: temperie; tempra; moderazione d' animo; mediocrità, *f.* **-ed**, ADJ.: temperato, moderato.

tĕm-pest 1, S.: tempesta, procella, *f.*; scompiglio, *m.* **-pest** 2, TR.: tempestare, perturbare, inquietare, infuriare. **-pest-beaten**, ADJ.: agitato dalla tempesta. **-pĕstive**, ADJ.: tempestivo, opportuno. **-pĕstively**, ADV.: tempestivamente, opportunamente. **-pestivity**, S.: tempo opportuno, *m.*; stagione, *f.* **-pest-tossed**, ADJ.: tormentato dalla tempesta. **-pĕstuous**, ADJ.: tempestoso, procelloso. **-pĕstuously**, ADV.: tempestosamente.

Tĕmplar, S.: templare, *m.*

tĕmple, S.: tempio, templo, *m.*; tempia, *f.*

tĕmpo-ral, ADJ.: temporale; secolare, mondano; caduco. **-rălity**, S.: temporalità, *f.* **-rally**, ADV.: temporalmente, mondanamente. **-rals** = *temporality*. **-ralty**, S.: temporale, *m.*; beni secolari, *m. pl.* **-rariness**, S.: stato temporaneo, *m.* **-rary**, ADJ.: temporaneo. **-rizătion**, S.: temporizzare, *m.* **-rize**, INTR.: indugiare, differire. **-rizer**, S.: indugiatore, *m.* **-rizing**, S.: temporeggiare; indugio, *m.*

tĕmpt, TR.: tentare; eccitare, provocare; importunare. **-able**, ADJ.: soggetto alla tentazione. **-ătion**, S.: tentazione, *f.* **-er**, S.: tentatore, seduttore, *m.* **-ing**, ADJ.: tentante, seducente; S.: tentamento, *m.* **-ress**, S.: tentatrice, *f.*

tĕmulen-cy, S.: ubbriacchezza, *f.* **-t**, ADJ.: ebrio, imbriaco.

tĕn, ADJ.: dieci.

tĕnable, ADJ.: tenibile, sostenibile.

te-năcious, ADJ.: tenace, viscoso. **-năciously**, ADV.: tenacemente, con tenacità. **-năciousness**, **-năcity**, S.: tenacità, viscosità; avarizia, *f.*

tĕnan-cy, S.: possesso temporario, *m.* **-t** 1, S.: fittaiuolo, fittuario, feudatario, ...ale, *m* **-t** 2, TR.: tenere a pigione, ... fitto. **-table**, ADJ.: abitabile. ...: non affittato, disabitato. ... degli affittuali, *m.* ... *f.* (pesce). ... guardare; INTR.: ten... — *upon*, scortare;

tĕndance, S.: aspettativa; cura, *f.*; servizio, *m.*

tĕnden-ce, **-cy**, S.: tendenza; propenzione, inclinazione, *f.*

tĕnder 1, ADJ.: tenero, delicato; sensibile. **tender** 2, S.: offerta, profferta, *f.* **tender** 3, S.: battello; alleggeritore; (*rail.*) tender, *m.*: *make a — of*, far l' offerta di. **tender** 4, TR.: offrire, presentare; stimare. **-hearted**, ADJ.: compassionevole, affettuoso, tenero. **-heartedness**, S.: tenerezza, *f.*, affetto, *m.* **-ling**, S.: prime corna d'un cervo, *f. pl.* **-ly**, ADV.: teneramente; dolcemente. **-ness**, S.: tenerezza, compassione, sensibilità, *f.*

tĕn-dinous, ADJ.: tendinoso, nervoso. **-don**, S.: tendine; nervo, *m.* **-dril**, S.: tenerume, rampollo, *m.*

tĕ-nebriæ *-bre*, S.: (*eccl.*) tenebre. **-nĕbrious**, **-nebrose** = *-nebrous*. **-nebrŏsity**, S.: tenebrosità, oscurità, *f.* **-nebrous**, ADJ.: tenebroso, oscuro.

tĕnement, S.: tenimento, *m.*, tenuta, *f.*

tenĕrity†, S.: tenerità, tenerezza, *f.*

tĕnet, S.: dottrina; opinione, *f.*

tĕnfold, ADJ.: decuplo, dieci volte tanto.

tĕnnis, S.: pallacorda, *f.* (giuoco). **-court**, S.: luogo da giocare alla palla, *m.* **-play**, S.: giuoco della pallacorda, *m.*

tĕn-or, **-our**, S.: tenore; soggetto, contenuto, *m.*; forma, *f.*

tĕn-se 1, S.: (*gram.*) tempo, *m.* **-se** 2, ADJ.: teso, esteso; rigido. **-seness**, S.: tensione, rigidezza, *f.* **-sible**, **-sile**, ADJ.: tensile; elastico. **-sion**, **-sure**, S.: tensione, *f.*

tĕnt 1, S.: tenda, *f.*, padiglione; ricovero, *m.*; tasta, *f.*; vino d'Alicante, *m.*: *pitch —s*, accamparsi, drizzare le tende. **tent** 2, TR.: mettere una tasta nella piaga; INTR.: attendarsi; campeggiare. **-age**, S.: accampamento, *m.*

tentătion, S.: tentativo, assaggio, *m.*, prova, *f.*; sforzo, *m.*

tĕntative, ADJ.: tentante.

tĕn-ted, ADJ.: coperto di tende; accampato. **-ter** 1, S.: uncino, rampino, *m.*: *be on the —s*, essere irresoluto; *keep upon the —s*, tenere a bada. **-ter** 2, (IN)TR.: distendere con uncini; appiccare, attaccare. **-ter-hook**, S.: uncino, *m.* **-ter-ground**, S.: campo per stendere i panni, *m.*

tĕnth 1, S.: decima parte; decima, *f.*: *the — of May*, il dieci maggio. **tenth** 2, ADJ.: decimo: *the — part*, la decima parte. **-ly**, ADV.: in decimo luogo.

tenŭity, S.: tenuità; sottigliezza, *f.*

tĕn-uous, ADJ.: tenue, sottile, scarso.

tĕnure, S.: tenuta, dipendenza (d' un feudo), *f.*: *freehold —*, possesso in franco allodio; *copyhold —*, possesso in feudo.

ADJ.: grosso, grande. **-ing** 2, S.: battimento, percuotere, *m.*
thŭndęr 2, S.: tuono; romore, *m.: the — roars*, mugghia il tuono. **thunder** 2, TR.: fulminare; gridare; INTR.: tuonare; far un romore grande. **-bolt,** S: fulmine, folgore, *m.;* scomunica, *f.* **-clap,** S.: scoppio di tuono, scoppio di fulmine, *m.* **-ęr,** S.: fulminatore, *m.* **-ing,** ADJ.: tonante; terribile, strepitoso; grande: *— noise*, romore grande, *m.; — voice*, voce strepitosa, *f.* **-ous,** ADJ.: tonante, fulminante. **-shower,** S.: piaggia accompagnata da lampi e tuoni, tempesta, *f.* **-stone,** S.: fulmine, folgore, *m.* **-strike,** TR.: uccidere col fulmine, fulminare.
thū-rible, S.: turibolo, *m.* **-rifęrous,** ADJ.: producente del incenso. **-rificā-tįon,** S.: incensamento, *m.*
Thŭrsdąy, S.: giovedì, *m.: Maundy —*, giovedì santo, *m.*
thŭs, ADV.: così, in questo modo, in questa maniera: *— far*, sin qui, sin adesso; *— much*, tanto.
thwăck 1, S.: percossa, *f.*, colpo, *m.;* sferza, frusta, *f.* **thwack** 2, TR.: percuotere; sferzare, frustare.
thwârt 1, ADJ.: traverso, obbliquo, sghembo, bistorto; perverso, malizioso. **thwart** 2, ADV.: a traverso, obbliquamente, a sghembo. **thwart** 3, TR.: attraversare, contrariare, contrastare, contendere; INTR.: opporsi, esser opposto. **-ing** 1, ADJ.: contrario, avverso, opposto. **-ing** 2, S.: contrarietà, contraddizione, opposizione, *f.* **-ingly,** ADV.: in modo opposto, con opposizione. **-ness,** S.: contrarietà, perversità, *f.*
thȳ, PRON.: tuo, tua; tuoi, tue, *pl.*
thȳ-me, S.: timo, *m.. wild —*, sermolino, serpillo, *m.* **-my,** ADJ.: pieno di timo.
thyself, PRON.: te stesso, te stessa.
tiăr(a), S.: tiara, *f.;* diadema, *m.*
tick 1, S.: conto; credito, *m.* **tick** 2, S.: fodera (di piumaccio); fodera d'un guanciale, *f.* **tick** 3, S.: ghiribizzo, *m.;* zecca, *f.* (insetto): *go upon —*, pigliar a credito. **tick** 4, INTR.: pigliar a credito. **-en,** S.: traliccio, *m.* **-et** 1, S.: biglietto, *m.;* bulletta, *f.*, bullettino, *m.: round trip —*, biglietto d'andata e ritorno. **-et** 2, TR.: mettere delle bullette. **-ing** = *ticken.*
tĭck-le 1, ADJ.: vacillante, barcollante; incerto, istabile. **-le** 2, TR.: solleticare, dileticare; piacere; INTR.: solleticarsi, dilettarsi. **-leness,** S.: vacillamento, *m.;* incertezza, *f.* **-lęr,** S.: lusingatore, adulatore, *m.* **-ling,** S.: solleticamento, *m.* **-lish,** ADJ.: soggetto al solletico, solleticoso; delicato. **-lishness,** S.: solletico, *m.;* incertezza; difficoltà, *f.*
ticktack, S.: giuoco alle tavole, tavoliere, *m.*
tid, ADJ.: delicato, schifo. **-bit,** S.: boccone delicato, *m.* **-dęr, -dle,** TR.: accarezzare.
tide 1, S.: marea, *f.*, flusso del mare; tempo, *m.*, stagione, *f.: — of flood*, riflusso, *m.; go with the —*, andare a seconda della marea. **tide** 2, TR.: sospingere col flutto. **tide** 3, INTR.: andare a seconda della marea. **-gate,** S.: cateratta; pescaia, *f.* **-ęman, -waiter,** S.: doganiere, *m.*
ti-dily, ADV.: pulitamente, acconciatamente, destramente. **-diness,** S.: pulitezza; destrezza, acconcezza, nettezza, *f.*
tidingş, S. PL.: nuove, novelle, *f. pl.*
tidy, ADJ.: pulito, netto, acconcio, destro.
ti-e 1, S.: legame, nodo; patto, accordo, *m.: —s of friendship*, vincoli (legami) dell' amicizia. **-e** 2, TR.: legare, attaccare, serrare; obbligare, impegnare; forzare: *— a knot*, fare un nodo, annodare; *— one's self*, obbligarsi con voto. **-e-beam,** S.: tirante, *m.;* chiave, *f.* **-ęr,** S.: fila, *f.:* filare; numero, *m.*
tier-ce, S.: terzo, *m.;* terza, *f.* **-cel,** S.: terzuolo, *m.* (falcone). **-cet,** S.: terzetto, *m.*
tiff 1, S.: bevanda; collera, stizza, *f.* **tiff** 2, INTR.: essere in collera, adirarsi.
tiffany, S.: velo, *m.;* tocca, *f.*
tigęr, S.: tigre, *f.*
tigh, S.: chiusura, *f.*
tight, ADJ.: tirato, teso, stretto; pulito, acconcio, attillato; attivo: *— coat*, abito stretto (giusto); *— rope*, corda tesa. **-en,** INTR.: tirare, stringere. **-ly,** ADV.: strettamente; attillatamente. **-ness,** S.: strettezza; attillatura, nettezza, *f.*
tigress, S.: tigre, *f.*
til-e 1, S.: tegola, *f.*, tegolo, *m.* **-e** 2, TR.: coprire con tegole. **-ekiln,** S.: fornace da tegole, *f.* **-ęr,** S.: facitor di tegole; conciatetti, *m.* **-ing,** S.: letto coperto di tegole, *m.*
till 1, PREP., CONJ.: fino, infino, sino, insino; finchè: *— now*, fin adesso; *— then*, fin allora; *— Monday*, sino a lunedì. **till** 2, S.: piccolo tiratoio, *m.;* cassettina; tavoletta, *f.* **till** 3, TR.: arare, lavorare, coltivare. **-able,** ADJ.: arabile, coltivabile. **-age,** S.: aramento, *m.;* coltura, agricoltura, *f.* **-ęr** 1, S.: aratore, lavoratore; cassettino, salvadanaio; piccolo albero.
tillęr 2, S.: timone (d'una barca), *m.*
till-ing, S.: aramento, *m.;* coltura, agricoltura, *f.* **-man†,** S.: agricoltore, aratore, *m.*
tilt 1, S.: giostra, *f.*, torneamento, *m.* **tilt** 2, S.: tenda, coperta, *f.;* riparo, *m.:*

...uvido, render aspro; INTR.: divenir ruvido. **-hew**, IRR.; TR.: abbozzare, schizzare. **-ly**, ADV.: rozzamente, aspramente; incivilmente, zoticamente. **-ness**, S.: ruvidezza, rozzezza, asprezza; zotichezza; violenza, *f.* **-rider**, S.: scozzone, cavalerizzo, *m.* **-work**, IRR.; TR.: lavorare grossolanamente; acciarpare, acciabattare.

roulette, S.: roletta, *f.* (giuoco).

round 1, ADJ.: tondo, rotondo; circolare, sferico; franco, candido: *in — numbers*, a un di presso, un po' più un po' meno; — *sum*, buona somma (di danari), *f.*; *fight ten —s*, riprendere dieci volte la lotta; *three —s of applause*, tre salvi di applausi. **round** 2, ADV.: da ogni banda, all' intorno, al giro: — *about*, tutto all' intorno, da ogni banda; *all the year* —, tutto l' anno; *drink* —, bere a vicenda in giro; *look* —, guardare attorno; *turn* —, voltarsi in giro. **round** 3, S.: giro, cerchio; corso, *m.*; ronda, *f.*: *take a* —, fare un giro. **round** 4, TR.: rotondare, fare tondo; INTR.: divenire tondo; soffiare negli orecchi, bisbigliare. **-about**, ADJ.: ampio; vago; indiretto. **-el**, **-elay**, S.: strambotto, *m.* **-er**, S.: circonferenza, *f.*; ricinto, *m.* **-head**, S.: testa tonda, *f.* **-house**, S.: carcere, *m.*, prigione, *f.* **-ish**, ADJ.: rotondetto. **-let**, S.: piccolo cerchio, *m.* **-ly**, ADV.: rotondamente; schiettamente; apertamente, francamente. **-ness**, S.: rotondità, rotondezza, *f.* **-robin**, S.: petizione sottoscritta da varie persone in un cerchio, *f.*

rouse, TR.: svegliare, destare; eccitare, far uscire; INTR.: svegliarsi, destarsi; eccitarsi. **-ser**, S.: svegliatore; istigatore, *m.*

rout 1, S.: folla, pressa, rotta, *f.*; tracasso, strepito, *m.*; (*hunt.*) traccia, *f.*: *put to* —, cf. *rout*. **rout** 2, TR.: mettere in rotta; sconfiggere; imbarazzare, imbrogliare.

route, S.: via, strada, *f.*, sentiero, *m.* **-tine**, S.: pratica, *f.*, costume, uso, *m.*

rove, INTR.: andare attorno, girare, vagare. **-ver**, S.: vagabondo; corsale, *m.*: *at —s*, a caso, inconsideratamente.

row 1, S.: fila, filata, *f.*, filare; ordine, *m.*: — *of houses*, filare di case, *m.*; *set in a* —, mettere in fila. **row** 2, S.: baruffa, ...a, *f.*; tafferuglio, *m.*: *get into a* —, ... addosso un tafferuglio; *have a* — ... scenata a; *keep up a* —, far ... **row** 3, INTR.: remigare, rema... andar d' accordo.

...e, *m.*

...llo sprone), *f.*; se... applicare un

rower, S.: rematore, vogatore, *m.* **-ing**, S.: remare, remigare, *m.* **-lock**, S.: rinforzo, *m.*

royal, ADJ.: reale, regale, regio; nobile, magnifico. **-ist**, S.: regalista, *m.* **-ize**, TR.: rendere reale. **-ly**, ADV.: realmente, da re. **-ty**, S.: dignità reale, *m.*; regalia, *f.*

roynish †, ADJ.: abietto, misero.

roytish †, ADJ.: selvatico.

rub 1, S.: fregamento; intoppo, ostacolo, impedimento; bottone, *m.* **rub** 2, TR.: fregare; strofinare, stropicciare, grattare: — *down* (*a horse*), stropicciare (un cavallo); — *off*, levare il fango; ripulire; — *out*, spungere, cancellare; — *over*, ritoccare; ripulire; — *up*, rinfrescare; eccitare; — *one up*, dare ad uno un bottone. **-ber**, S.: strofinaccio, *m.*; lima grossa, *f.*: (*at whist*), partita, *f.*; *India* —, gomma elastica, *f.* **-bing**, S.: fregamento, *m.* **-bing-cloth**, S.: strofinaccio, strofinacciolo, *m.* **-bish**, S.: stracci, *m. pl.*, robe vecchie; rovine, *f. pl.*; marame, *m.*

rubicund, ADJ.: rubicondo. **-bied**, ADJ.: del colore del rubino. **-bific**, ADJ.: rubificativo, rubificante. **-bify**, TR.: rubificarsi, divenire rosso. **-bious**, ADJ.: rosso.

rubric, S.: rubrica, *f.* **-ated**, ADJ.: macchiato di rosso; rosso.

rub-stone, S.: pietra per ripulire, *f.*

ruby 1, S.: rubino (pietra); carbonchio, *m.* **ruby** 2, ADJ.: rubinoso, vermiglio.

ruck, INTR.: appiattarsi.

ructation, S.: rutto, ruttare, *m.*

rudder, S.: timone, *m.*

ruddiness, S.: freschezza di carnagione, *f.* **-dle**, S.: sinopia, *f.* **-dock**, S.: pettirosso, *m.* (uccello). **-dy**, ADJ.: rosso, rosseggiante, rubicondo: — *complexion*, viso fresco, *m.*

rude, ADJ.: rozzo, grossolano, scortese, incivile; turbolento. **-ly**, ADV.: grossolanamente, incivilmente; insolentemente. **-ness**, S.: rozzezza, inciviltà; insolenza, *f.*

rudenture, S.: (*arch.*) cannellatura, *f.*

rudesby †, S.: uomo rozzo, *m.*

rudiment, TR.: fondare, stabilire. **-mental**, ADJ.: de' rudimenti. **-ments**, S. PL.: rudimenti, elementi, principi, *m. pl.*

rue 1, S.: (*bot.*) ruta, *f.* **rue** 2, TR.: dolersi, pentirsi. **-ful**, ADJ.: lamentevole compassionevole, dolente; tristo. **-fully**, ADV.: lamentevolmente; tristamente. **-fulness**, S.: affanno, cordoglio, *m.*; tristezza, *f.*

ruelle †, S.: cerchio, *m.*; assemblea, *f.*

ruff, S.: gala, *f.*; collare, *m.*

ruffian, ADJ.: brutale; crudele; S.: malandrino, assassino di strada, *m.* **-like**, ADJ.: brutale, crudele.

straccarsi, noiarsi: — *out one's patience*, far scappare la pazienza ad uno. **-d**, ADJ.: stanco, affaticato, seccato: *rather* —, stanchetto, lasso; *very* —, stracco; — *to death*, annoiatissimo. **-dness**, S.: fatica, stanchezza, *f.* **-some**, ADJ.: noioso, tedioso, importuno, incomodo. **-someness**, S.: noia, *f.*; fastidio, *m.*; molestia, seccaggine, *f.* **-woman**, S.: acconciatrice; cameriera, *f.*

tiring-house, -room, S.: camera da vestirsi, *f.*

'tis, egli è, gli è.

tisic, S.: tisichezza, *f.* **-al**, ADJ.: tisico.

tissue 1, S.: tessuto, *m.*; ordine, organizzazione, *f.* **tissue** 2, TR.: intrecciare; variare.

tit, S.: cavallino; pezzo, *m.*; cingallegra, *f.*

Tī-tan, S.: Titano. **ti-tānic**, ADJ.: titanico.

titbit, S.: boccone delicato, *m.*

tith-able = *titheable.* **-e** 1, S.: decima, *f.* **-e** 2, TR.: decimare, riscuotere le decime; tassare. **-eable**, ADJ.: decimabile. **-efree**, ADJ.: esente della decima. **-er**, S.: riscuotitore delle decime, *m.* **-ing**, S.: decina; società di dieci, *f.* **-ingman**, S.: capodieci, capo d' una decina; caporale, *m.*

titil-late, TR.: titillare, solleticare. **-lātion**, S.: titillamento, solletico, *m.*

titlark, S.: allodola di prato, *f.*

title 1, S.: titolo, *m.*; denominazione, iscrizione; ragione; dignità, *f.*: *by a good* —, a buon titolo. **title** 2, TR.: titolare, intitolare; nominare. **-less**, ADJ.: senza titolo, senza nome. **-page**, S.: titolo, frontispizio (d' un libro), *m.*

titmouse, S.: cingallegra, *f.*

titter 1, S.: sorriso, riso ristretto, *m.* **titter** 2, INTR.: sorridere.

tittle, S.: punto (sopra la lettera); segno, *m.*; particella, *f.* **-tattle**, S.: cicalamento; cicalone, *m.* **-tattle** 2, INTR.: cicalare, chiacchierare.

titu-bate, INTR.: titubare, vacillare. **-bātion**, S.: titubazione, *f.*, vacillamento, *m.*

titu-lar, ADJ.: titolare, nominale. **-lărity**, S.: dignità titolare, *f.* **-lary**, ADJ.: titolario, titolato; S.: titolario, *m.*

tō, PREP.: a, verso, fino a: — *the*, al; (allo, alla; ai, agli; alle); — *and fro*, qua e là; — *the end that*, affinchè, acciocchè; *he was like — die*, egli fu per morire; *go — school*, andare alla scuola; *count — ten*, contare fino a dieci.

tōad, S.: rospo, *m.*, botta, *f.* **-eater**, S.: parassito, *m.* **-stone**, S.: chelonite, *f.* **-stool**, S.: specie di fungo (*agaricus*), *m.*

tōast 1, S.: pane abbrustolito, *m.*; salute; *donna celebre*, *f.*: *buttered* —, pane abbrustolito con burro. **toast** 2, TR.: abbrustolire; bere alla salute, far brindisi: —*ed bread*, pane abbrustolito. **-er**, S.: bevitore alla salute di qualcheduno, *m.*

tobăcco, S.: tabacco, *m.*: *smoke* —, fumare del tabacco. **-box**, S.: tabacchiera, scatola da tabacco, *f.* **-nist**, S.: tabaccaio; venditore di tabacco, *m.* **-pipe**, S.: pipa, *f.* **-pouch**, S.: borsa da tabacco, *f.* **-shop**, S.: bottega d' un tabaccaio, *f.* **-smell**, S.: odore di tabacco, *m.* **-smoke**, S.: fumo di tabacco, *m.* **-spinner**, S.: filatore di tabacco, *m.*

tŏcsin, S.: campana d' allarme, *f.*

tŏd, S.: cespuglio; peso di venti otto libbre (di lana), *m.*

to-dāy, ADV.: oggi.

tŏddle, INTR.: vacillare.

tōe, S.: dito del piede, *m.*: *from top to* —, da capo a piedi.

tofōre, ADV.: avanti, innanzi, prima.

tŏft, S.: boschetto, *m.*

tō-ga, S.: toga, *f.* **-ged†**, ADJ.: togato, vestito di toga.

togĕther, ADV.: insieme: — *with*, in compagnia di, unitamente a.

tŏil 1, S.: pena, fatica. **toil** 2, S.: lungaiuola, *f.* (rete). **toil** 3, TR.: lavorare, faticare, penare; INTR.: affaticarsi, affannarsi.

tŏilet, S.: tavolino da acconciarsi, *m.*

tŏil-ing, S.: pena, fatica, *f.*, travaglio, stento, *m.* **-some**, ADJ.: faticoso, penoso, laborioso. **-someness**, S.: fatica, *f.*, lavoro, stento, *m.*

tōken 1, S.: segno; presente, regalo; pegno, *m.* **token** 2, INTR.: far conoscer (per un segno).

tōle, TR.: trarre poco a poco.

tŏler-able, ADJ.: tollerabile, sopportabile; mediocre. **-ableness**, S.: esser tollerabile, *m.*; mediocrità, *f.* **-ably**, ADV.: tollerabilmente, così così. **-ance**, S.: tolleranza, pazienza, *f.* **-ant**, ADJ.: tollerante. **-ate**, TR.: tollerare, sopportare, soffrire. **-ātion**, S.: tolleranza, *f.*

tōll 1, S.: pedaggio, *m.* **toll** 2, TR.: fare pagare il pedaggio; INTR.: suonare una campana a tocchi: — *on*, incitare; spronare. **-bar**, S.: barriera, *f.* **-booth**, S.: casotto di pedaggio, *m.*; prigione, *f.*, carcere, *m.* **-bridge**, S.: ponte ove si paga il pedaggio, *m.* **-free**, ADJ.: franco di pedaggio. **-gate**, S.: ponte ove si paga il pedaggio, *f.* **-gatherer**, S.: collettore del pedaggio, pedaggiere, *m.* **-money**, S.: pedaggio, *m.*

tōmb 1, S.: tomba, sepoltura, *f.* **tomb** 2, TR.: seppellire. **-less**, ADJ.: privo di tomba. **-stone**, S.: lapide, *f.*; monumento, *m.*

tŏm-boy, S.: ragazzaccia, *f.* **-cat**, S.: gatto, gattone, *m.*

sion, S.: rescissione, *f.;* abolimento, *m.* **-scissory**, ADJ.: rescissorio.
rescribe, TR.: riscrivere; rispondere.
rescript, S.: rescritto, editto, *m.*
res-cuable, ADJ.: che può essere liberato. **-cue** 1, S.: liberamento, scampo; soccorso, *m.: to the —*, alla riscossa. **-cue** 2, TR.: liberare, scampare; venir in soccorso. **-cuer**, S.: liberatore, soccorritore, *m.*
research 1, S.: ricerca, inchiesta, *f.* **research** 2, TR.: ricercare, inchiedere; esaminare. **-er**, S.: ricercatore, inchieditore, *m.*
reseat, TR.: posare, rimettere; INTR.: riporsi a sedere.
reseize, TR.: sequestrare di nuovo. **-zure**, S.: nuova sequestrazione, *f.*
resell, TR.: rivendere.
resem-blance, S.: somiglianza, *f.* **-ble**, INTR.: rassomigliare, esser simile. **-bling**, ADJ.: somigliante, simile.
resend, IRR.; TR.: rimandare, mandare indietro.
resent, TR.: pigliare in (buona† o) mala parte; risentirsi; offendersi: *— an insult*, risentirsi di una ingiuria. **-er**, S.: che si risente d' un' ingiuria. **-ful**, ADJ.: pieno di risentimento. **-ingly**, ADV.: risentitamente, con risentimento. **-ment**, S.: risentimento, risentirsi, *m.*
re-servation, S.: riserva, riserba; restrizione, *f.: mental —*, restrizione mentale. **-servative**, ADJ.: riserbante. **-servatory**, S.: riserbatoio, serbatoio, *m.;* conserva, *f.* **-serve** 1, S.: riserva; limitazione, eccezione; modestia, *f.: mental —*, restrizione mentale, intenzione occulta; *without —*, senza riserba; interamente. **-serve** 2, TR.: riservare; conservare. **-served**, ADJ.: riservato; modesto, discreto. **-servedly**, ADV.: con riserba, con riguardo. **-servedness**, S.: riserba; circospezione, discrezione, *f.* **-server**, S.: riserbatore, servatore, *m.*
reservoir *-vwor*, S.: serbatoio, *m.*
reset, TR.: rifiggere; (*typ.*) ricomporre.
resettle, TR.: ristabilire. **-ment**, S.: ristabilimento, *m.*
reship, TR.: rimbarcare. **-ment**, S.: rimbarco, *m.*
resiance† = *residence.*
reside, INTR.: risedere, dimorare.
resi-dence, **-dency**, S.: residenza; dimora, *f.* **-dent** 1, ADJ.: residente, dimorante. **-dent** 2, S.: residente; ambassadore, deputato, *m.* **-dentiary**, ADJ.: residente.
resid-ual, **-uary**, ADJ.: del residuo, restante: *— heir*, S.: erede universale, *m.*
resid-ue, S.: residuo, restante, resto, *m.* **-uum**, S.: residuo, *m.*

re-sign, (IN)TR.: rassegnare; cedere; deporre; disfarsi; sommettersi; dare la propria dimissione: *be —ed*, essere rassegnato; *the ministers have —ed*, i ministri hanno dato la loro dimissione. **-signation**, S.: rassegnazione; cessione; demissione, *f.* **-signed**, ADJ.: rassegnato. **-signedly**, ADV.: con rassegnazione. **-signer**, S.: rassegnante, che rassegna, *m.* **-signing**, **-signment**, S.: rassegnazione; demissione, *f.*
resi-lience, **-liency**, S.: resilienza, *f.*, ribalzo, *m.* **-lient**, ADJ.: che risalta, zampillante. **-lition**, S.: zampillio, ribalzo, *m.*
resin, S.: resina, gomma, *f.* **-aceous**, **-ous**, ADJ.: resinoso, ragioso, gommifero. **-ousness**, S.: qualità resinosa, *f.*
resipiscence, S.: risipiscenza, *f.*, pentimento, *m.*
resist, TR.: resistere; opporsi. **-ance**, S.: resistenza, opposizione, *f.;* ostacolo, *m.* **-ant**, S.: resistente, *m.* **-ence** = *resistance.* **-ibility**, S.: resistibilità, *f.* **-ible**, ADJ.: resistibile. **-less**, ADJ.: irresistibile; insuperabile. **-lessly**, ADV.: irresistibilmente. **-lessness**, S.: irresistibilità, *f.*
reso-luble, ADJ.: dissolubile, solubile. **-lute**, ADJ.: risoluto, determinato. **-lutely**, ADV.: determinatamente, intrepidamente. **-luteness**, S.: determinazione; arditezza, *f.* **-lution**, S.: risoluzione; determinazione; fermezza, intrepidezza; decomposizione, analisi, *f.* **-lutive**, ADJ.: (*med.*) risolutivo, solutivo.
resol-vable = *resoluble.* **-ve** 1, S.: risoluzione; determinazione, *f.* **-ve** 2, TR.: risolvere; sciogliere, solvere; determinare; liquefare; INTR.: risolversi; determinarsi, decidersi. **-vedly**, ADV.: risolutamente; fermamente. **-vedness**, S.: risoluzione, *f.;* fermo proposito, *m.*, fermezza, *f.* **-vent**, S.: dissolvente, solutivo, *m.* **-ver**, S.: risolvente, *m.* **-ving**, S.: soluzione, *f.;* scioglimento, *m.;* dichiarazione, *f.*
resonan-ce, S.: risonanza, *f.* **-t**, ADJ.: risonante, rimbombante.
resorb, TR.: assorbire. **-ent**, ADJ.: assorbente.
resort 1, S.: concorso, *m.;* folla, calca, *f.;* ricorso, rifugio, *m.;* forza elastica, *f.* **resort** 2, INTR.: avere ricorso; frequentare, capitare, bazzicare: *— to a person*, aver ricorso ad una persona; *— t[o] means*, appigliarsi ad altri mezzi. frequentatore (d' un luogo), *m.*
resound, TR.: ripetere; celebrare risonare, rimbombare. **-ing**, AD[J.] nante, rimbombante; S.: risona[nza] rimbombo, *m.*

torto, pregiudiziale. **-tive,** ADJ.: tortuoso, attorcigliato.

tôrtoise, S.: testuggine, *f.* **-shell,** S.: tartaruga, *f.*

tortuŏsity, S.: tortuosità, sinuosità, *f.*

tôrtuous, ADJ.: tortuoso, sinuoso. **-ness** = *tortuosity.*

tôrtur-e 1, S.: tortura, *f.*, tormento; dolore, *m.*: *put to the* —, porre alla tortura. **-e** 2, TR.: dare la tortura, tormentare. **-er,** S.: che da la tortura, carnefice, *m.* **-ing,** S.: tortura, *f.*, tormento, *m.* **-ingly,** ADV.: tormentosamente. **-ous,** ADJ.: tormentoso.

tôr-vity †, S.: torvità, *f.*; viso arcigno, *m.* **-vous** †, ADJ.: torvo, arcigno, austero.

Tōry, S.: tori, *m.*

tōse †, TR.: scardassare.

tŏss 1, S.: scossa, gettata, *f.*, sbalzo, crollo, *m.*: *give a thing a* —, dare una scossa ad una cosa; *it is a —-up*, è affatto incerto. **toss** 2, TR.: sbalzare, scuotere, agitare, gettare; tormentare, penare, affannare; palleggiare; INTR.: agitarsi, dimenarsi; affannarsi: — *a ball*, rimandare una palla; — *about*, gettar qua e là; — *up*, giuocar a cappelletto. **-er,** S.: che scuote, che agita. **-ing,** S.: scossa; agitazione, commozione, *f.*, tempellamento, movimento, *m.*: *the — of the waves*, l' agitarsi de' flutti; *the — of the ship*, il tempellamento della nave. **-pot,** S.: bevitore, trincatore, *m.*

tō-tal, ADJ.: totale, tutto, intero: — *sum*, somma totale, *f.* **-tălity,** S.: totalità; somma totale, *f.* **-tally,** ADV.: totalmente, interamente, affatto. **-talness** = *totality.*

t'ŏther, PRON.: l' altro.

tŏtter, INTR.: vacillare, traballare, barcollare. **-ing,** ADJ.: vacillante, barcollante; S.: vacillamento, *m.* **-ingly,** ADV.: in modo vacillante, a onde. **-y** †, ADJ.: vacillante, barcollante; vertiginoso.

tŏuch 1, S.: tocco, tatto; tratto (di pennello), *m.*; tintura, *f.*; saggio, *m.*; prova, *f.*, cimento, esame; detto acuto, *m.*: — *of disease*, attacco di malattia, *m.*; *give one a* —, toccare alcuno; *give a — by the by*, sbottonare alcuno. **touch** 2, TR.: toccare, tastare; provare; INTR.: essere vicino; appigliarsi; aspettarsi: — *a musical instrument*, suonare qualche strumento musicale; — *with pity*, muovere a compassione; — *at*, approdare, pigliare porto; — *on*, toccare; parlare brevemente di; — *up*, ritoccare; — *to the quick*, toccare al vivo. **-able,** ADJ.: toccabile, palpabile. **-hole,** S.: focone (d' un' arma da fuoco), *m.* **-iness,** S.: stizza, *f.*, mal umore, *m.* **-ing** 1, PREP.: circa, intorno, concernente. **-ing** 2, ADJ.: toccante; commovente, patetico; compassionevole. **-ing** 3, S.: toccamento, tatto, *m.* **-ingly,** ADV.: in modo commovente (patetico). **-me-not,** S.: (*bot.*) noli me tangere, *m.* **-pan,** S.: focone (d' un' arma da fuoco), *m.* **-stone,** S.: pietra di paragone, *f.*; criterio, esame, *m.* **-wood,** S.: legno putrido; agarico, *m.* **-y,** ADJ.: stizzoso, ritroso; litigioso, irascibile.

tough *tŭf*, ADJ.: tiglioso, viscoso, tenace; duro; forte, robusto; crudele. **-en,** INTR.: diventare duro, diventare tiglioso. **-ness,** S.: durezza; viscosità, tenacità, inflessibilità, *f.*

toupêt, S.: ciuffetto, toppè, *m.*

tŏur, S.: giro, *m.*, girata; scorsa, spasseggiata, *f.*: *little* —, viaggetto, giro, *m.*, gitta, *f.*; *grand* —, giro. **-ist,** S.: turista, gitante; viaggiatore, *m.*

tŏur-nament, -ney 1, S.: torneamento, *m.*, giostra, *f.* **-ney** 2, INTR.: far torneamento, giostrare. **-niquet,** S.: (*surg.*) tornaquette, compressore, *m.*

tŏu-se, TR.: straccinare, strascinare. **-ser,** S.: mastino (cane); furioso, *m.*

tōw 1, S.: stoppa, *f.* **tow** 2, S.: fune, alzana, *f.*; filo della canapa, *m.* **tow** 3, TR.: rimorchiare, rimurchiare. **-age,** S.: rimorchio, *m.*

tōward 1, PREP.: verso, inverso: — *the right hand*, a man dritta. **toward** 2, ADJ.: dedito, inclinato, prono; docile. **-liness,** S.: attitudine, dispostezza; docilità, *f.* **-ly** 1, ADJ.: disposto ad imparare, docile. **-ly** 2, ADV.: destramente. **-ness** = *towardliness*. **-s** = *toward, prep.*

tōw-boat, S.: rimorchiatore, *m.*

tŏwel, S.: tovaglia, salvietta, *f.*; tovagliuolo, *m.*

tŏwer 1, S.: torre; fortezza, *f.* **tower** 2, torreggiare; alzarsi alto: *little* —, torretta, *f.* **-ed,** ADJ.: munito da torri.

tōw-ing, S.: rimorchiare, *m.* **-line,** S.: (*nav.*) corda da rimorchiare, *f.*

tŏwn, S.: città, *f.*; borgo grosso, *m.*; borgata, *f.*: *little* —, borguccio, borghetto; *fortified* —, piazza forte, *f.*; *go to* —, andare in città. **-clerk,** S.: segretario della città, *f.* **-dues,** S.: dazi di consumo, *m. pl.* **-house,** S.: casa della città, *f.* **-ship,** S.: corporazione d' una città; giurisdizione d' una città, *f.* **-sman,** S.: borghese, concittadino, *m.* **-talk,** S.: romore, bisbiglio generale, *m.*: *'tis the* —, così si dice per la città.

tŏxic(al), ADJ.: tossicoso, velenoso.

tŏy 1, S.: bagatella, frascheria, *f.* **toy** 2, INTR.: scherzare, trastullare. **-er,** S.: trastullatore, *m.* **-ful,** ADJ.: trastullevole. **-ing,** S.: burla, *f.*, scherzo, *m.* **-ish,** ADJ.: scherzoso, burlevole. **-ish-**

—, vendere a minuto; — *trade*, vendetta al minuto (a ritaglio). **-tāil** 2, TR.: vendere a minuto, rivendere. **-tāiler**, S.: venditore a minuto, *m.*

retāin, (IN)TR.: ritenere; tenere a mente. **-er**, S.: aderente, *m.*; persona salariata, *f.*, stipendiato, *m.* **-ing**, S.: ritenimento, ritegno, *m.*

retāke, IRR.; TR.: ripigliare.

retāl-iate, TR.: rendere la pariglia. **-iātion**, S.: pariglia, *f.*; contraccambio, *m.*: *by way of* —, per vendetta.

retārd, (IN)TR.: ritardare; differire. **-ātion**, S.: ritardamento, *m.* **-er**, S.: ritardatore, indugiatore, *m.* **-ing**, **-ment**, S.: ritardamento, *m.*

rětch, INTR.: aver voglia di recere, vomitare, recere.

retěn-tion, S.: ritenzione; custodia, *f.* **-tive**, ADJ.: ritentivo, ritenitivo, *m.* **-tiveness**, S.: facoltà ritentiva, tenacità di memoria, *f.*

rěticence, S.: reticenza, *f.*

rět-icle, S.: rete piccola, *f.*; sacchetto, *m.* **-icular**, ADJ.: reticolare, reticolato. **-iculated**, ADJ.: reticolato. **-icule**, S.: borsa da donna, *f.* **-iform**, ADJ.: retiforme. **-ina**, S.: retina (dell' occhio), *f.*

rětinue, S.: corteggio; accompagnamento, *m.*

reti-re 1, S.: ritirata, *f.*; ritiro, rifugio, *m.* **-re** 2, TR.: ritirare; INTR.: ritirarsi. **-red**, ADJ.: ritirato, solitario: — *life*, vita ritirata; *on the* —*d list*, giubilato, in quiescenza. **-redly**, ADV.: solitariamente; privatamente. **-redness**, S.: ritiratezza, vita privata; solitudine, *f.* **-rement**, S.: ritiratezza; solitudine, *f.* **-ring**, ADJ.: che si ritira; che ama la solitudine; schivo, riservato: — *manners*, modi riservati (schivi, timidi).

retôrt 1, S.: storta; risposta, *f.* **retort** 2, TR.: ritorcere; replicare. **-er**, S.: che ritorce. **-ing**, **-tion**, S.: ritorcimento, *m.*; confutazione, *f.*

retôss, TR.: far balzare indietro; rigettare, rispingere.

retôuch, TR.: ritoccare; ripulire.

retrāce, TR.: delineare di nuovo: — *one's steps*, tornare indietro.

retrăc-t, TR.: ritrattare; INTR.: ritrattarsi, disdirsi. **-(tā)tion**, S.: rittrattazione, *f.*; ritrattare, *m.* **-tive**, ADJ.: ritrattivo.

retrăxit, S.: (*leg.*) rinunzia, *f.*

retrēat 1, S.: ritirata; solitudine, *f.*: *sound (beat) the* —, suonare la ritirata. **-eat** 2, TR.: ritirarsi; andare via.

-ch, TR.: levare; tagliare, scemare: sopprimere; (*fort.*) trinceristringersi; trincierarsi: ...ire le spese, economizzare. **-ment**, S.: scemamento; sminuimento, *m.*; economia; (*fort.*) trincea, *f.*

retrib-ute, TR.: retribuire; ricompensare. **-uter**, S.: retribuitore, *m.* **-ūtion**, S.: retribuzione; ricompensa, *f.* **-utive**, **-utory**, ADJ.: retribuente; rimunerativo.

retrīe-vable, ADJ.: ricuperabile. **-ve**, TR.: ricoverare; ricuperare: — *one's honour*, ricoverare il suo onore; — *a loss*, riparare una perdita. **-ver**, S.: ricoveratore, *m.*, -trice, *f.*; cane barbone scozzese, *m.*

retroāc-tion, S.: retroazione, *f.* **-tive**, ADJ.: retroattivo.

retro-cēde, INTR.: retrocedere. **-cěssion**, S.: retrocedimento; ritirarsi, *m.*

retro-gradātion, S.: retrogradazione, *f.* **rětro-grade** 1, ADJ.: retrogrado. **-grade** 2, INTR.: retrogradare. **-grading**, **-grěssion**, S.: retrocedere, *m.*

rětro-spect, **-spěction**, S.: guardare indietro, mirar indietro, *m.* **-spěctive**, ADJ.: che guarda indietro; passato: — *glance*, colpo d' occhio sul passato.

retrūde, INTR.: spingere indietro.

retŭnd, TR.: rintuzzare; attutire.

retûrn 1, S.: ritorno, *m.*; ricaduta; ricompensa; risposta, *f.*: — *of money*, rimessa di danari, *f.*; *make a* —, render la pariglia. **return** 2, TR.: rendere; rimettere, restituire; ricompensare; contraccambiare; INTR.: ritornare, rimettersi: — *an answer*, rispondere, render risposta; — *a letter*, rimandare una lettera; — *good for evil*, ricambiare il male col bene; — *a favour*, reciprocare una gentilezza; — *thanks*, render grazie. **-able**, ADJ.: di rimando. **-er**, S.: che rimette danaro.

reū-nion, S.: reunione, riconciliazione, *f.* **-nite**, TR.: riunire, riconciliare; INTR.: riunirsi, ricongiungersi, riconciliarsi. **-niting**, S.: riunimento, *m.*, riconciliazione, *f.*

rēve, S.: guardiano d' un feude, *m.*

revēal, TR.: rivelare, scoprire, manifestare. **-er**, S.: rivelatore, scopritore, *m.* **-ing**, S.: rivelamento, svelamento, *m.*

revěille *-lye*, S.: (*mil.*) battere la diana, *m.*

rěvel 1, S.: gozzoviglia, festa romorosa, *f.* **revel** 2, TR.: ritrattare; INTR.: gozzovigliare, festeggiare.

revelātion, S.: rivelazione, *f.*, palesamento, *m.*

rěvel-ler, S.: gozzovigliante, festeggiante, *m.* **-ling**, S.: gozzoviglia; allegrezzza, *f.* **-ry**, S.: gozzoviglia, festa romorosa, *f.* **-rout**†, S.: assemblea illegale, *f.*

revěn-ge 1, S.: vendetta; rivincita (alle carte), *f.*: *take one's* —, prendere una rivincita; *glut one's* —, sfogare la propria vendetta. **-ge** 2, (IN)TR.: vendicare, vendicarsi. **-geful**, ADJ.: vendicativo. **-gefully**, ADV.: d' una maniera vendicativa.

trám-road, -way, S.: tramvia, *f.*, tramway, *m.*
tránce, S.: estasi, *f.*, rapimento, *m.* **-d,** ADJ.: in estasi, estatico.
trănnel†, S.: spilla acuta, *f.*; spilletto acuto, *m.*
trán-quil, ADJ.: tranquillo, quieto, non agitato. **-quillize,** TR.: tranquillare, abbonacciare. **-quillity,** S.: tranquillità, quiete; bonaccia, *f.* **-quilly,** ADV.: tranquillamente. **-quilness,** S.: tranquillità, *f.*
transăc-t, TR.: maneggiare; negoziare, trattare. **-tion,** S.: transazione, negoziazione, convenzione, *f.*; atto: *the —s of the Royal Society*, gli atti della Società Reale. **-tor,** S.: negoziatore; fattore, *m.*
transăni-mate†, TR.: transanimare; transmigrare. **-mātion,** S.: transmigrazione, *f.*
transcĕnd, TR.: trascendere, eccedere, superare. **-ence, -ency,** S.: superiorità, eccellenza, *f.* **-ent,** ADJ.: trascendente. **-ĕntal,** ADJ.: trascendentale. **-ĕntally,** ADV.: in modo sopreminente, straordinariamente.
trănscolate†, TR.: colare, feltrare, passare.
tran-scribe, INTR.: trascrivere, copiare. **-scriber,** S.: trascrittore, copista. **-script,** S.: copia, *f.*; apografo, *m.* **-scription,** S.: trascrivere, copiare, *m.* **-scriptively†,** ADV.: in modo trascritto, in modo copiato.
transcŭr†, TR.: trascorrere, vagare. **-sion†,** S.: trascorrere, vagamento, *m.*
trănse = *trance.*
trăns-fer 1, S.: trasferimento, trasportamento, *m.* **-fĕr** 2, TR.: trasferire, trasportare. **-fĕrable,** ADJ.: trasferibile, trasportabile. **-fĕrrer,** S.: che trasferisce.
trans-figurate = *transfigure.* **-figurātion,** S.: trasfigurazione, *f.* **-figure,** TR.: trasfigurare, mutare figura.
transfix, TR.: trafiggere, trapassare.
trans-fôrm, TR.: trasformare; mutar forma; INTR.: trasformarsi, cangiarsi. **-formātion,** S.: trasformazione, *f.* **-fôrming,** S.: trasformamento, *m.*
transfretātion†, S.: viaggio d' oltramare, *m.*
transfū-se, TR.: trasfondere, travasare. **-sible,** ADJ.: trasfondibile. **-sion,** S.: trasfondimento, *m.*
trans-grĕss, (IN)TR.: trasgredire; disubbidire; violare: — *a law*, violare una legge. **-grĕssion,** S.: trasgressione, *f.* **-grĕssive,** ADJ.: trasgressivo; colpevole. **-grĕssor,** S.: trasgreditore, peccatore, *m.*, -trice, *f.*
trănsient, ADJ.: transitorio; labile; passeggiero. **-ly,** ADV.: in modo transitorio, di passaggio. **-ness,** S.: poca durabilità, *f.*
transilien-ce†, -cy†, S.: salto di cosa in cosa, *m.*
trăn-sit, S.: transito; passare, *m.* **-sition,** S.: passaggio; mutamento, cambiamento, *m.* **-sitive,** ADJ.: transitivo. **-sitorily,** ADV.: transitoriamente. **-sitoriness,** S.: poca durabilità, *f.* **-sitory,** ADJ.: transitorio, passeggiero.
trans-lātable, ADJ.: traducibile; trasportabile. **-lāte,** TR.: traslatare; tradurre: — *literally*, tradurre letteralmente (alla lettera). **-lāting, -lātion,** S.: traduzione; traslazione, *f.* **-lātor,** S.: traduttore; traslatore, *m.* **-lātory,** ADJ.: traslatorio.
trans-lūcency, S.: trasparenza, diafanità, *f.* **-lūcent, -lūcid†,** ADJ.: trasparente.
transmarine, ADJ.: oltramarino.
trăns-migrate, TR.: trasmigrare, passare da un luogo all' altro. **-migrātion,** S.: trasmigrazione, *f.*
trans-mission, S.: trasmissione, *f.*, trasporto, *m.* **-missive,** ADJ.: trasmesso. **-mit,** TR.: trasmettere, fare passare. **-mittal†,** S.: trasmissione, *f.*; trasporto, *m.* **-mitter,** S.: trasmettitore, *m.*
trans-mūtable, ADJ.: trasmutabile. **-mūtably,** ADV.: in modo trasmutabile. **-mutātion,** S.: trasmutazione, *f.*, trasmutamento, *m.* **-mūte,** TR.: trasmutare, trasformare. **-mūter,** S.: trasmutatore, cambiatore, *m.*
trănsom, S.: traversa; imposta di porta, *f.*
transpāren-cy, S.: trasparenza, diafanità, *f.* **-t,** ADJ.: trasparente, diafano. **-tly,** ADV.: in modo trasparente. **-tness** = *transparency.*
transpáss†, INTR.: trapassare.
transpicuous, ADJ.: trasparente.
transpierce, TR.: trafiggere; trapassare.
trans-pirable, ADJ.: traspirabile. **-pirātion,** S.: traspirazione, *f.* **-pire,** INTR.: traspirare; esalare.
translāce†, TR.: rimuovere, dislogare.
trans-plănt, TR.: traspiantare; trasferire. **-plantātion,** S.: traspiantamento, *m.* **-plănter,** S.: che traspianta. **-plănting,** S.: traspiantamento, *m.*
transplĕndent†, ADJ.: tralucente.
trăns-port, S.: trasporto; rapimento, *m.*, estasi, *f.*: *—s of joy*, estasi, *f.* **-pŏrt,** TR.: trasportare; trasferire; metter fuor di sè. **-pŏrtance†,** S.: trasporto, trasportare, *m.* **-portātion,** S.: trasportazione, *f.*, trasporto, *m.* **-pŏrtedly,** ADV.: in modo estatico. **-pŏrter,** S.: trasportatore, *m.* **-pŏrting,** ADJ.: estatico, maraviglioso. **-pŏrtment†,** S.: traspor-

frugalmente. **-ness**, S.: frugalità; economia, *f.* **-s-bank**, S.: banco di risparmio, *m.*; cassa di risparmio, *f.*
sāviour, S.: salvatore, redentore, *m.*
sāvour 1, S.: sapore, savore; gusto; odore, *m.* **savour** 2, TR.: saporare, assaporare; sentire: *it —s of*, sa di, sente di. **-ily**, ADV.: saporitamente, con gusto. **-iness**, S.: sapore, buon gusto; odore, *m.* **-less**, ADJ.: senza sapore. **-rous**, ADJ.: saporoso. **-y**, ADJ.: saporito, saporoso, di buon sapore.
sāvoury, S.: (*bot.*) santoreggia, timbra, *f.*
savōy, S.: cavolo capuccio, *m.*
sāw 1, S.: sega, *f.*: *little —, hand —*, seghetta, *f.* **saw** 2, S.: proverbio, motto, *m.* **saw** 3, TR.: segare. **-dust**, S.: segatura, *f.* **-er** = *sawyer*. **-fish**, S.: segamarina, *f.* (pesce). **-ing**, S.: segare, segamento, *m.* **-mill**, S.: mulino da segare, *m.* **-pit**, S.: fossa de' segatori, *f.* **-yer**, S.: segatore, *m.*
săx-ifrage, S.: (*bot.*) sassifraga, *f.* **-ifragous**, ADJ.: litontritico.
sāy 1, S.: saga (panno); mostra, *f.* **say** 2, IRR.; INTR.: dire; narrare, raccontare: *that is to —*, cioè a dire, cioè; *— by heart*, recitare a mente; *— over again*, dire di nuovo, ridire; *— on!* dite su! *I —!* dimmi un po'! *no sooner said than done*, detto, fatto. **-ing**, S.: dicimento; proverbio, motto, *m.*: *as the — is*, come dice il proverbio.
scăb, S.: scabbia, rogna, *f.*; birbone, *m.*
scăbbard, S.: fodero, *m.*; guaina, *f.*
scăb-bed, ADJ.: scabbioso, rognoso, lebbroso. **-bedness**, **-biness**, S.: rogna, *f.* **-by** = *scabbed*.
scăbious, ADJ.: scabbioso, rognoso; S.: scabbiosa, gallinella, *f.*
scăbrous, ADJ.: scabroso; rozzo; senza armonia. **-ness**, S.: scabrosità, *f.*
scăbwort, S.: (*bot.*) scabbiosa, *f.*
scăffold 1, S.: palco, catafalco, *m.* **scaffold** 2, TR.: impalcare. **-age**, **-ing**, S.: struttura di palchi; galleria, *f.*
[illegible]**-de**, **-do**, S.: scalata, *f.*, scalamen-[illegible]
[illegible], S.: uomo da niente, furbo, *m.*
[illegible] ADJ.: misero, cattivo, spregievole.
[illegible] S.: tigna, *f.* **scald** 3, TR.: scot-[illegible] con acqua calda. **-head**, [illegible], *f.* **-ing-hot**, ADJ.: [illegible] **-ing-house**, S.: luo-[illegible] *m.*
[illegible] *m.*; (*mus.*)
[illegible] bilan-
[illegible] —*s.*

pesare; INTR.: scagliarsi; scorticarsi: *— the walls*, scalare le mura, dare la scalata alle mura. **-ed**, ADJ.: scaglioso, squamoso. **-eless**, ADJ.: senza scaglie.
scalēne, S.: scaleno, *m.*
scāliness, S.: essere scaglioso, *m.*, squamosità, *f.*
scāling, S.: scalata, *f.*: *— ladders*, scale da scalare, *f. pl.*
scăll, S.: lebbra, lepra, tigna, *f.* **-ed**, ADJ.: tignoso,
scăllion, S.: scalogno, *m.*, cipollina, *f.*
scăllop 1, S.: petonchio, *m.* (conchiglia). **scallop** 2, TR.: tagliare a festone.
scălp 1, S.: capellatura, *f.*; pericranio, *m.* **scalp** 2, TR.: levare via il pericranio. **-el**, **-ing-iron**, S.: scalpello, *m.*
scāly, ADJ.: scaglioso, squamoso.
scăm-ble, (IN)TR.: moversi goffamente; esser turbolento, tumultuare. **-bler**, S.: sfacciato, leccappiatti, parasito, *m.* **-bling**, ADJ.: turbolento, tumultuante. **-blingly**, ADV.: con romore; sfacciatamente.
scam-mōniate, ADJ.: di scamonea. **scămmony**, S.: (*bot.*) scamonea, *f.*
scămper, TR.: scampare, fuggire via: *— away* (*off*), darla a gambe, scappare, scampare. **-er**, S.: fuggitivo, *m.*
scăn, TR.: scandere, misurare un verso; esaminare, ponderare.
scăndal 1, S.: scandalo, scandolo, *m.*; ignominia, infamia, *f.*: *bring a — upon*, scandalizzare; *lie under a —*, aver cattivo nome, esser in cattiva riputazione. **scandal** 2, TR.: diffamare, accusare falsamente. **-ize**, TR.: scandalizzare, dare scandalo. **-ous**, ADJ.: scandaloso, diffamatorio, infame. **-ously**, ADV.: scandalosamente. **-ousness**, S.: scandalo pubblico, *m.*
scăn-ned, ADJ.: scandito, misurato. **-ning**, S.: scandere, misurare (i versi), *m.* **-sion**, S.: scansione, misura (di versi), *f.*
scănt 1, ADJ.: parco, stretto; meschino; ADV.: appena. **scant** 2, TR.: limitare, ristringere; INTR.: (*nav.*) mancare: *the wind —s*, il vento manca. **-ily**, ADV.: parcamente; meschinamente. **-iness**, S.: scarsezza, strettezza; insufficienza, *f.*
scănt-le, TR.: dividere in piccoli pezzi; INTR.: mancare. **-let**, S.: pezzetto, *m.*; quantità piccola, *f.* **-ling**, S.: pezzetta; misura, grandezzia, *f.*
scănt-ly, ADV.: strettamente, parcamente; meschinamente. **-ness**, S.: strettezza; scarsezza, parcità, *f.* **-y**, ADJ.: stretto, parco; sordito.
scāpe 1, S.: scappata, fuga, *f.* **scape** 2, TR.: scappare, fuggire; evitare. **-goat**, S.: becco di espiazione, capro emissario. **-grace**, S.: birichino, monello, cattiggetto, bricconcello, *m.*

trĕnch 1, s.: fosso, *m.*; fossa; (*mil.*) trincea, *f.*: — *about*, circondare di trincee. **trench** 2, TR.: tagliare; scavare: — *about*, circondare con trincee. **-ant**, ADJ.: trinciante; tagliente, affilato. **-er**, s.: tagliere, *m.*; tavola, *f.* **-erfly** †, s.: parassito, scroccone, *m.* **-erman**, s.: gran mangiatore, ghiottone, *m.* **-ermate**, s.: compagno di tavola, *m.*
trĕnd 1, s.: direzione, *f.* **trend** 2, TR.: tendere; tirare.
trĕndle, s.: viluppo; cilindro, *m.*
trepăn 1, s.: trapano; stratagemma, *m.* **trepan** 2, TR.: trapanare; adescare, allettare, lusingare. **-ner**, s.: furbo; ingannatore, *m.*
trĕp-id †, ADJ.: tremante, timoroso. **-idā-tion**, s.: trepidazione, *f.* **-idity** †, s.: trepidazione, *f.*, terrore, *m.*
trĕspass 1, s.: trasgressione, *f.*, misfatto, *m.*, offesa, *f.*; delitto, *m.* **trespass** 2, INTR.: trasgredire; offendere, violare: — *upon*, infringere, violare; abusare di: *I fear to — upon your time*, temo di abusare del vostro tempo. **-er**, s.: trasgreditore; offenditore, *m.*
trĕss, s.: treccia di capelli, *f.*: *golden —es*, trecce d' oro. **-ed**, ADJ.: intrecciato, annodato in treccia. **-es**, s. PL.: trecce di capelli, *f. pl.*
trĕs-tle, s.: cavalletto; trespolo, *m.*
trĕt, s.: (*com.*) tara, *f.*
trĕvet, s.: treppiede, treppiè, *m.*
trêy, s.: tre, *m.* (alle carte o a' dadi).
triable, ADJ.: che si può provare.
triad, s.: unità di tre, *f.*
trial, s.: saggio, esame, *m.*; prova, *f.*; attentato, sforzo, *m.*: *on —*, alla prova; *by way of —*, per via di saggio; — *at law*, causa, *f.*, processo, *m.*; *make a — of a thing*, far prova di qualche cosa.
tri-angle, s.: triangolo, *m.* **-ăngular**, ADJ.: triangolare.
tribe, s.: tribù; razza, stirpe, *f.*
tribulātion, s.: tribolazione, afflizione, *f.*; affanno, *m.*
tribūnal, s.: tribunale, *m.*
tribu-ne, s.: tribuno, *m.* **-neship**, s.: uffizio di tribuno, *m.* **-nitial**, **-nitious** †, ADJ.: tribunizio.
tribu-tary, s.: tributario; dipendente. **-te** 1, s.: tributo, censo, *m.*, tassa, *f.*: (*fig.*) *pay — to nature*, pagare il tributo alla natura, morire. **-te** 2, TR.: pagare come tributo.
trice, s.: momento, istante, attimo, *m.*: *in a —*, in un istante, in un attimo.
trick 1, s.: furberia; sottigliezza; malizia; beffa, burla, *f.*; artifizio, giuoco di mano, *m.*; abitudine, costume; mano, bazza, *f.* (alle carte): *play a —*, fare una burla; ingannare; *ugly —*, brutto scherzo, *m.*, villania, *f.*; *odd —s*, stramberia, *f. pl.*; *full of —s*, pieno di maliziette. **trick** 2, TR.: burlare; ingannare, gabbare: — *up*, abbellire, ornare. **-er**, s.: grillo (d' uno schioppo), *m.* **-ery**, s.: artifizio, *m.* **-ing**, s.: ornamento; abbigliamento, vestimento, *m.* **-ing-fellow**, s.: impostore, truffatore, *m.* **-ish**, ADJ.: artifizioso, scaltro. **-ishness**, s.: furberia, *f.*
trickle 1, s.: gocciola, *f.* **trickle** 2, INTR.: gocciolare, cascare a gocciole.
trickment †, s.: abbigliamento, vestimento, *m.*
trick-ster, s.: furbo, *m.* **-sy**, ADJ.: astuto.
ticktrack, s.: giuoco alle tavole, *m.*
tricolo(u)r, s.: tricolore, *m.*
tricôrporal, ADJ.: tricorporeo.
tride, ADJ.: (*hunt.*) corto e pronto.
trident, s.: tridente, *m.*
triĕnnial, ADJ.: triennale, di triennio.
trier, s.: saggiatore, provatore, *m.*
trifallow, TR.: (*agr.*) terzare, arare la terza volta.
trifid, ADJ.: trifido.
tri-fle 1, s.: bagattella, baia, frasca, frascheria, *f.*: *dispute about —s*, disputare dell' ombra dell' asino. **-fle** 2, INTR.: cianciare, scherzare; beffare, dileggiare: — *away one's time*, spender il tempo in vano, stare a bada; — *with*, scherzare con, burlarsi di. **-fler**, s.: bagattelliere, baione, *m.* **-fling**, ADJ.: frivolo, da nulla, di poca importanza; s.: bagattella, ciancia, burla, *f.* **-flingly**, ADV.: di nessun' importanza; vano, da nulla. **-flingness**, s.: vanità, leggierezza, *f.*
trifōliate, ADJ.: trifogliato.
trig † 1, ADJ.: pulito, netto. **trig** 2, TR.: incatenare (una ruota); INTR.: (una ruota); INTR.: riempiere.
trigamy, s.: trigamia, *f.*
trigger, s.: pezzo di ferro da fermar le ruote; grillo, cane (d' uno schioppo), *m.*
trigintals, s. PL.: trenta messe una dopo l' altra, *f. pl.*
triglyph, s.: (*arch.*) triglifo, *m.*
trigon, s.: trigono, triangolo, *m.*
trigo-nal, ADJ.: triangolare. **-nomĕtrical**, ADJ.: trigonometrico. **-nŏmetry**, s.: trigonometria, *f.*
trilăteral, ADJ.: trilatero, di tre lati.
trill 1, s.: trillo, *m.*, cadenza, *f.* **trill** 2, (IN)TR.: trillare, gorgheggiare; gocciolare.
trillion, s.: trilione, *m.*
trilūmi-nar †, **-nous** †, ADJ.: di tre lumi.
trim 1, ADJ.: pulito, attillato, bello, ben fatto, assettato. **trim** 2, s.: abbigliamento, abito, ornamento, *m.* **trim** 3, TR.: guarnire, guernire; radere; INTR.: temporeggiare, esitare: — *a boat*, mettere una barca in istiva; — *up*, adornare; ag-

scŏat, TR.: fermare una ruota.
scŏbs, S. PL.: limatura d' avorio, *f.*
scŏff 1, S.: scherno, *m.*, beffa, burla, *f.* **scoff** 2, TR.: schernire, beffare, burlare: — *at*, deridere. **-er**, S.: schernitore, beffatore, beffardo, *m.* **-ing** 1, ADJ.: scherzevole; contumelioso. **-ing** 2, S.: scherno, *m.*, burla, baia, *f.* **-ingly**, ADV.: in modo burlevole, burlescamente.
scŏld 1, S.: garritrice, riottosa, *f.* **scold** 2, (IN)TR.: rabbuffare; borbottare, contendere. **-ing**, S.: contesa, *f.*, contendimento; sgridamento, *m.*
scŏllop, S.: petonchio, *m.* (conchiglia).
scŏnce 1, S.: forte, baluardo; candelabro, *m.*; elmo, casco, *m.*; (*coll.*) testa, *f.* **sconce** 2, TR.: fare ammenda, sottoporre a multa.
scŏop 1, S.: paletta; gotazza a mano, *f.* **scoop** 2, TR.: votare, scavare.
scōpe, S.: scopo; segno; disegno; fine, *m.*; libertà, *f.*, campo, *m.*: *free* —, libero campo.
scŏpulous†, ADJ.: pieno di scogli.
scôr-bute, S.: scorbuto, *m.* **-bûtic(al)**, ADJ.: scorbutico.
scôree, S.: cambio, baratto, *m.*
scôrch, (IN)TR.: riardere; abbruciare: —*ed by the sun*, abbronzato. **-ing**, ADJ.: ardente: —*fire*, gran fuoco, *m.*; S.: riardimento, *m.*, adustione, *f.*
scôrdium, S.: (*bot.*) scordio, *m.*
scōre 1, S.: conto; scotto, *m.*; taglia; ventina, *f.*; risguardo, rispetto, *m.*; ragione, *f.*: *upon a new* —, da capo, di nuovo; *upon the* —, in risguardo; *upon what* —? per che ragione? *quit* —*s*, saldare il conto. **score** 2, TR.: segnare, notare; mettere in conto: — *out*, cassare, cancellare; — *a writing*, rigare una scrittura.
scō-ria, S.: scoria, *f.*; rosticci, *m. pl.* **-rious**, ADJ.: pieno di rosticci, schiumoso.
scôrn 1, S.: sdegno, disprezzo; scorno: *laugh to* —, mettere in derisione, farsi beffe di. **scorn** 2, (IN)TR.: sdegnare, dispregiare, vilipendere, sprezzare. **-er**, S.: dispregiatore, beffatore, *m.* **-ful**, ADJ.: sdegnoso, sprezzante, spregioso. **-fully**, ADV.: disprezzevolmente, sdegnosamente. **-ing**, S.: dispregiamento, disprezzo, *m.*
scôrpion, S.: scorpione, *m.*
scôrse = *scorce*.
scŏt, S.: scotto, *m.*; parte, porzione, *f.*: — *and lot*, diritti della parrocchia, *m. pl.*
Scŏtch 1, ADJ. *or* S. (*m.*, *f.*): scozzese.
scŏtch 2, S.: picciol taglio, tagliuzzo, *m.* **scotch** 3, TR.: far un picciol taglio, tagliare la superfizie. **-(ed)-collops**, S. PL.: (*cook.*) braciuola di carne fritta, *f.*
Scŏtchman, S.: scozzese, *m.*
scŏtfree, ADJ.: franco, immune.
scŏtomy, S.: scotomia, *f.*
scŏundrel, S.: briccone, gaglioffo, *m.*
scŏur 1, (IN)TR.: forbire; nettare; fregare: — *the country*, battere la strada; — *the woods*, perlustrare i boschi; — *about*, vagare, vagabondare; — *away*, fuggire via, svignare. **-er**, S.: cavamacchie, *m.*; guattera, *f.*; perdigiorno, *m.*
scóur-ge 1, S.: sferza, frusta, *f.*; flagello, gastigo, *m.*: *the* — *of*, il flagello di. **-ge** 2, TR.: sferzare, frustare; punire. **-ger**, S.: sferzatore, flagellatore, gastigatore, *m.* **-ging**, S.: flagellamento, *m.*, gastigazione, *f.*
scŏuring, S.: forbire, *m.*; uscita; soccorrenza, *f.*
scŏut 1, S.: corridore; battistrada, *m.*; vedetta, veletta, *f.* **scout** 2, INTR.: battere le strade; fare la scoperta.
scóvel, S.: spazzatoio, *m.*
scŏw, S.: chiatta, *f.*
scŏwl 1, S.: cipiglio, guardo arcigno, *m.* **scowl** 2, INTR.: increspare le ciglia; mostrar un viso arcigno: — *upon*, guardar con cipiglio. **-ing**, S.: increspamento; guardo arcigno, *m.* **-ingly**, ADV.: con viso arcigno, ritrosamente.
scrăbble, TR.: palpeggiare, tastare; graffiare; INTR.: andar tastone, brancolare.
scrăg, S.: collo mozzato; scheletro, *m.* **-ged**, ADJ.: ruvido, scabroso; rozzo; ineguale. **-gedness**, **-giness**, S.: macilenza, magrezza; ruvidezza, *f.* **-gy**, ADJ.: molto magro, scarno.
scrăm-ble 1, S.: aggrappamento, rampicare, *m.* **-ble** 2, INTR.: aggrappare, rampicare: —*for*, procurare di ghermire, acchiappare, arraffare: — *up*, inerpicarsi sopra. **-bler**, S.: che aggrappa, che rampica.
scrănch, TR.: sgretolare, rompere co' denti.
scrănnel†, ADJ.: aspro; indigente, povero.
scrăp, S.: pezzo, frammento; rimasuglio, *m.*: — *of paper*, pezzetto di carta, *m.* **-book**, S.: libro di squarci, *m.*
scrăp-e 1, S.: difficoltà, *f.*; impaccio, *m.*; saluto sgraziato, *m.* **-e** 2, TR.: raschiare, grattare, rastiare; INTR.: strimpellare, raspare, razzolare: — *at the door*, raschiare alla porta; — *out*, radere, cancellare; — *up*, accumulare, ammassare. **-epenny**, S.: spilorcio, avaro, *m.* **-er**, S.: rastiatoio; cattivo suonatore, *m.* **-ing**, S.: rastiatura, raschiatura, *f.*; piccol profitto, *m.*
scrăt†, S.: ermafrodito, *m.*
scrătch 1, S.: graffiatura, *f.*, graffio, *m.* **scratch** 2, TR.: grattare, graffiare; cancellare: — *one's self*, grattarsi; — *out*, cancellare. **-er**, S.: sgraffiatore, *m.* **-es**,

dar di trotto, *m.* **-ting-horse**, S.: cavallo che va di trotto, *m.*
troubadour, S.: trovatore, poeta provenzale, *m.*
troub-le 1, S.: disturbanza; inquietudine; pena, fatica, *f.*, affanno, travaglio, *m.*; afflizione, *f.*, cordoglio; infortunio, *m.*: *be a — to*, incomodare, importunare; *bring into —s*, dar travaglio, travagliare; *put to —*, disturbare, molestare, importunare; *pray, take the —*, abbiate la gentilezza. **-le** 2, TR.: disturbare, incomodare, importunare, vessare; inquietare; interrompere, impedire; intrigare, affliggere: *— one's self*, incomodarsi, infastidirsi; turbarsi; *I am sorry to — you*, mi rincresce di sturbarvi; *may I — you for the salt?* mi favorisca il sale. **-le-feast**, S.: importuno, perturbatore, *m.* **-ler**, S.: turbatore; perturbatore, *m.* **-lesome**, ADJ.: noioso, affannoso, fastidioso, penoso; importuno: *— guest*, guastafeste, *m.* **-lesomely**, ADV.: importunamente. **-lesomeness**, S.: importunità; molestia, fatica, pena, *f.*, affanno, *m.* **-le-state** †, S.: disturbatore dello stato, *m.* **-lous**, ADJ.: tumultuoso, confuso.
trough *tróf*, S.: truogo, trogolo, *m.*: *kneading —*, madia, *f.*
troul, INTR.: muoversi; parlare volubilmente.
trounce, TR.: punire con dar un' accusa; maltrattare.
trousers, S. PL.: calzoni lunghi, *m. pl.*
trout, S.: trota, *f.* (pesce); sciocco, *m.*
trow †, INTR.: credere; immaginare.
trowel, S.: cazzuola, mestola, *f.* **-ful**, S.: cazzuola piena, *f.*
trowsers = *trousers*.
troy, **-weight**, S.: peso di dodici once la libbra, *m.*
truant 1, ADJ.: infingardo, scioperato, ozioso. **truant** 2, S.: vagabondo, perdigiorno, *m.*: *play the —*, fuggire la scuola. **truant** † 3, INTR.: scioperarsi; fuggire la scuola. **-ly**, ADV.: da vagabondo. **-ship**, S.: infingardia, pigrizia, *f.*
truce, S.: tregua; sospensione, *f.*
truchman †, S.: turcimano, interprete, *m.*
trucidation †, S.: trucidamento, *m.*
truck 1, S.: baratto, cambio, *m.* **truck** 2, S.: carretta, *f.*, carro di trasporto, *m.* **truck** 3, INTR.: barattare, cambiare, permutare. **-age**, S.: baratto, *m.* **-er**, S.: barattiere, *m.* **-ing** = *truckage*. **-le** 1, S.: girella, picciola ruota, *f.*
truck-le 2, INTR.: sommettersi, rendersi. **-le-bed**, S.: carriuola, *f.* **-ling**, S.: sommessione, *f.*
truculen-ce, **-cy**, S.: aspetto truculento, *m.*, ferocità, *f.* **-t**, ADJ.: truculento, feroce; crudele.

trud-ge, INTR.: andare attorno; affaticarsi. **-ging**, S.: travaglio, affanno, *m.*, fatica, *f.*
true, ADJ.: vero, certo, sincero, esatto: *be —*, esser fedele; *speak —*, dire la verità. **-born**, ADJ.: per diritto di nascita, legittimo. **-bred**, ADJ.: di buona razza. **-hearted**, ADJ.: franco, sincero. **-heartedness**, S.: sincerità, schiettezza, buona fede, *f.* **-knave**, S.: pretto furbo, *m.* **-love**, S.: (*bot.*) uva di volpe, *f.* **-ness**, S.: sincerità, franchezza, schiettezza, *f.* **-penny**, S.: uomo fidato, *m.*
truffle, S.: tartufo nero, *m.*
trug, S.: truogo (di muratore), *m.*
truism, S.: verità evidente, *f.*
trull, S.: sgualdrina, *f.*
truly, ADV.: veramente, sinceramente.
trump 1, S.: tromba, *f.* **trump** 2, S.: trionfo (alle carte), *m.*: *play —s*, giuocare trionfo; *be put to one's —s*, esser ridotto all' estremità. **trump** 3, TR.: prendere con un trionfo (al giuoco delle carte): *— about*, giuocare trionfo; esaltare; *— up*, inventare; fabbricare, acciabattare.
trumpery, S.: bagattella; falsità, *f.*
trumpet 1, S.: tromba, *f.*: *speaking —*, portavoce, *m.*; tromba parlante, *f.*; *sound the —*, suonare la tromba. **trumpet** 2, TR.: suonare la tromba; pubblicare, proclamare, divulgare. **-er**, S.: trombettiere, *m.*
trun-cate, TR.: troncare, mozzare. **-cation**, S.: troncamento, *m.*
truncheon 1, S.: bastone, frugone, *m.* **truncheon** 2, TR.: bastonare. **-eer**, S.: bastoniere, mazziere, *m.*
trundle 1, S.: carriuola, *f.*; cilindro, *m.* **trundle** 2, INTR.: ruotolare; volgere. **-tail**, S.: berghinella, *f.*
trunk 1, S.: tronco; ceppo; busto; cofano, forziere, baule, *m.*, cassa; doccia; cerbottana; tromba, proboscide: *pack up one's —*, fare il baule; *unpack one's —*, disfare il baule. **trunk** 2, TR.: troncare, mozzare. **-breeches**, S. PL.: brache alla svizzera, *f. pl.* **-hose**, S.: brache larghe, *f. pl.*, calzoni, *m. pl.* **-light**, S.: abbaino, spiraglio, *m.* **-maker**, S.: cofanaio, baulaio, *m.*
trunnion, S.: orecchione (di cannone); cardine, *m.*
trusion †, S.: spingimento; moto, *m.*
truss 1, S.: fascio, fastello, fardello; bracchiere, *m.* **truss** 2, TR.: imballare; legare, attaccare, annodare: *— up one's clothes*, succingersi i vestimenti; *— up one's hair*, legarsi i capelli.
trust 1, S.: fiducia, fede, confidenza, *f.*; credito, *m.*: *breach of —*, abuso di fiducia; *on —*, a credito; *hold in —*, tenere

-rilous, ADJ.: ingiurioso; vile, basso. **-rilously**, ADV.: in modo abusivo, ingiuriosamente. **-rilousness** = *scurrility*.

scŭr-vily, ADV.: bruttamente, vilmente, grossolanamente. **-viness**, S.: cattivezza, malignità, viltà, *f.* **-vy** 1, S.: scorbuto, *m.* **-vy** 2, ADJ.: cattivo, ribaldo, vile; tristo: — *trick*, tiro da briccone, *m.* **-vy-grass**, S.: gramigna, *f.*

scŭt, S.: coda (d' una lepre, d' un coniglio), *f.*

scŭtcheon, S.: scudo, *m.*; (*lock.*) toppa, *f.*

scŭtiform, ADJ.: a modo di scudo.

scŭttle 1, S.: graticola, *f.*; gran paniere, *m.* **scuttle** 2, S.: tramoggia di mulino, *f.* **scuttle** 3, S.: (*nav.*) boccaporto, *m.*: *coal* —, paniera pel carbone. **scuttle** 4, INTR.: andare qua e là.

scy̆the, S.: falce, *f.*

Scy̆thian, ADJ.: Scita, degli Sciti; S.: scita, *m.*, *f.*

sēa, S.: mare, oceano, *m.*; onda, *f.*: *by — and land*, per mare e per terra; *main* —, alto mare; *heavy* —, mare grosso; *a* —, un cavallone; *be at* —, trovarsi in mare; *go to* —, andar sul mare; *put out to* —, far vela. **-bar**, S.: rondine di mare, *f.* **-beach**, S.: spiaggia, *f.*, lido, *m.* **-beat(en)**, ADJ.: agitato dal mare. **-boat**, S.: nave, *f.*, naviglio, legno, *m.* **-born**, ADJ.: nato dal mare. **-boy**, S.: mozzo di nave, *m.* **-breach**, S.: rottura del mare, *f.* **-breeze**, S.: vento impetuoso, *m.* **-calf**, S.: vitello marino, *m.* **-captain**, S.: capitano di naviglio, *m.* **-chart**, S.: carta da navigare, *f.* **-coast**, S.: costa del mare, *f.* **-compass**, S.: bussola, *f.* **-cow**, S.: vacca marina, *f.* (pesce). **-dog**, S.: pesce cane, *m.* **-fārer**, S.: marinaro, *m.* **-fāring**, ADJ.: andando per mare: — *man*, marinaro, *m.* **-fennel**, S.: finocchio marino, *m.* **-fight**, S.: combattimento navale, *m.* **-fowl**, S.: uccello marino, *m.* **-green**, ADJ.: del colore del mare. **-gull**, S.: mugnaio, *m.* (uccello). **-hog**, S.: porcello marino, *m.* **-horse**, S.: cavallo marino, *m.*

sēal 1, S.: sigillo, suggello; vitello marino, *m.* **seal** 2, S.: *under hand and* —, segnato e sigillato; *under the — of secrecy*, sotto sigillo di confessione; *affix one's — to*, porre la firma a. **seal** 3, TR.: sigillare, suggellare; confermare. **-er**, S.: sigillatore, *m.* **-ing-wax**, S.: ceralacca, cera di Spagna, *f.* **-ring**, S.: anello da sigillare, *m.*

sēam 1, S.: cucitura; congiuntura; cicatrice, *f.* **seam** 2, TR.: cucire; giungere; cicatrizzare.

sēa-maid, S.: sirena, *f.* **-man**, S.: marinaio, *m.* **-manship**, S.: (arte di) navigazione, *f.* **-mark**, S.: (*nav.*) segnale, *m.* **-mew**, S.: gabbiano, mugnaio, *m.* (uccello).

sēamless, ADJ.: senza sutura.

sēa-monster, S.: mostro marino, *m.*

sēam-stress, S.: cucitrice, sartora, *f.* **-y**, ADJ.: pieno di cuciture, cucito.

sēan†, S.: sagena, rete da pescare, *f.*

sēa-nymph, S.: ninfa del mare, *f.* **-onion**, S.: squilla, *f.* **-ooze**, S.: melma del mare, *f.* **-piece**, S.: marina; veduta di mare, *f.* **-pool**, S.: lago d' acque salse, *m.* **-port**, S.: porto di mare, *m.*

sēar 1, ADJ.: secco, arido; morto. **sear** 2, TR.: arrossare con ferro rovente.

sēarch 1, S.: inchiesta, ricerca; inquisizione, *f.* **search** 2, TR.: cercare, visitare; esaminare; frugare, frugacchiare; provare: — *a wound*, tentare una ferita; — *after*, ricercare, cercare, inchiedere; — *for*, cercare, buscare; — *into*, inchiedere; esaminare; penetrare; — *out*, fare una ricerca esatta. **-able**, ADJ.: che si può cercare. **-er**, S.: ricercatore; visitatore, *m.* **-ing**, ADJ.: penetrativo; pronto; S.: cerca, ricerca, *f.* **-less**, ADJ.: inscrutabile.

sēar-cloth, S.: impiastro, cerotto, *m.*

sēaredness, S.: secchezza, aridità; sterilità; insensibilità, *f.*

sēa-room, S.: alto mare, largo, *m.* **-rover**, S.: corsale, pirata, *m.* **-serpent**, S.: serpe di mare, *f.* **-service**, S.: servizio navale, *m.* **-shark**, S.: pesce cane, *m.* **-shell**, S.: guscio di pesce marino, *m.* **-shore**, S.: spiaggia, costa del mare, *f.* **-sick**, ADJ.: mareggiato: *be* —, mareggiarsi. **-sickness**, S.: mal di mare, *m.* **-side**, S.: lido del mare, *m.*, spiaggia, *f.*

sēason 1, S.: stagione, *f.*; tempo opportuno; condimento, *m.*: *in the mean* —, nulladimeno; *out of* —, fuori di stagione, intempestivo, inopportuno. **season** 2, TR.: condire; accostumare; INTR.: essere opportuno. **-able**, ADJ.: di stagione; opportuno. **-ableness**, S.: opportunità, occasione, *f.* **-ably**, ADV.: opportunamente; acconciamente; a proposito. **-er**, S.: stagionatore; che infonde, *m.* **-ing**, S.: stagionamento; condimento, *m.*

sēa-surgeon, S.: chirurgo di nave, *m.*

sēat 1, S.: sedia, *f.*; seggio; banco, *m.*; scena; tribuna; situazione, *f.*: *bishop's* —, seggio vescovile, *m.*; — *of justice*, tribunale, *m.*; *take a* —, sedetevi, accomodatevi. **seat** 2, TR.: situare; collocare; stabilire: — *one's self* (*be seated*), sedersi; stare seduto; *pray, be —ed*, s' accomodi.

sēa-term, S.: termine marinaresco, ter-

lo, *m.* **tunnel** 2, TR.: pigliar (uccelli) col tramaglio.
tŭnny, S.: tonno, *m.* (pesce).
tŭp 1, S.: ariete, montone, *m.* **tup** 2, TR.: cozzare; urtare.
tŭrban, S.: turbante, *m.* **-ed**, ADJ.: che porta il turbante. **-t**† = *turban.*
tŭrbid, ADJ.: torbido, fangoso; denso. **-ly**, ADV.: torbidamente; orgogliosamente. **-ness**, S.: torbidezza; spessezza, *f.*
tŭrbi-nal, **-nated**, ADJ.: turbinato, attortigliato. **-ne**, S.: turbina, *f.*
tŭrbot, S.: rombo, *m.* (pesce).
tŭrbulen-ce, **-cy**, S.: turbolenza, perturbazione, *f.*, romore, *m.* **-t**, ADJ.: turbolento, tumultuoso, sedizioso. **-tly**, ADV.: con turbolenza.
tŭrf 1, S.: erbuccia; zólla d'erba, *f.* **turf** 1, TR.: coprire d'erbuccia. **-iness**, S.: abbondanza di zolle d'erba, *f.* **-y**, ADJ.: pieno di zolle d'erba.
tŭr-gent, ADJ.: turgido, ampolloso. **-gĕscence**, **-gĕscency**, S.: turgenza, *f.*, enfiato, *m.* **-gid**, ADJ.: turgido, enfiato. **-gidity**, **-gidness**, S.: turgidezza, enfiatura; alterigia, *f.*, orgoglio, *m.*
Tŭrk, S.: turco, *m.*, -ca, *f.*
tŭrkey, S.: tacchino, gallo d'India; gallinaccio, *m.* **-hen**, S.: tacchina, gallina d'India, *f.* **-wheat**, S.: grano d'India, *m.*, meliga, *f.*
Tŭrkish, ADJ.: turco, turchesco; S.: turco, *m.*, lingua turca, *f.*
tŭrm†, S.: turma, truppa, banda, *f.*
tŭrmeric, S.: titimaglio, *m.* (radice).
tŭrmoil 1, S.: tumulto, strepito, romore; affanno, *m.* **turmoil** 2, INTR.: strepitare; agitare, disturbare; molestare.
tŭrn 1, S.: giro, rigiro, *m.*; girata, passeggiata, *f.*; tiro; tornio; servizio, uffizio; cangiamento, *m.*: *by* —*s*, a vicenda, in giro; *at every* —, ad ogni tratto, ad ogni momento; *in the* — *of a hand*, in un batter d'occhio, in un momento; *every one in his* —, ognuno in giro; *do one a good* —, render un buon uffizio ad uno; *take a* —, far una girata; *serve one's* —, far per uno; *one good* — *deserves another*, una buon' azione merita il contraccambio. **turn** 2, TR.: voltare, volgere; cambiare; torniare, formare; tradurre; esaminare; INTR.: andar in giro, voltarsi, muoversi; cambiarsi; frastornare; diventare; convertirsi; guastarsi: — *one's back*, voltar le spalle; abbandonare; — *fair*, divenir bello; — *home*, ritornare a casa; — *over a new leaf*, cangiare costumi; cangiare vita; — *the milk*, guastare il latte; — *in one's mind*, riflettere; — *physician*, farsi medico; — *into ridicule*, beffare, uccellare; beffarsi, farsi beffe; — *the scale*, dar il trabocco alla bilancia; — *the wrong side*, ritornare, tornare; — *sour*, divenir agro, inacerirsi, incerconarsi; — *one's stomach*, sconvolgere lo stomaco; — *into stone*, impietrarsi; — *tables*, rendere la pariglia; — *tail*, rigirare, trovar giri e rigiri; — *about*, muoversi in giro; — *away*, licenziare, mandare via; stornarsi, frastornarsi; — *away from*, abbandonare il partito; — *back*, tornare, ritornare; — *back upon*, rimandare; riflettere; — *down*, piegare; spianare; — *in*, ripiegare; rimboccare; — *in and out*, serpeggiare; — *into*, cangiare, mutare; cangiarsi; convertirsi; — *off*, rimandare; liberarsi da; stornare; — *out*, mandare via, deporre; — *over*, riferire; — *over to*, rimettere; trasferire; — *to*, abbracciare il partito di; — *to* (*into*), cangiarsi, trasformarsi; — *to and fro*, andar girando in qua e in là; — *up*, vangare; zappare; — *upside down*, rovesciare; sconvolgere. **-back**, S.: codardo, vigliacco, *m.* **-bench**, S.: tornio, *m.* **-broach**, S.: menarrosto, *m.* **-coat**, S.: voltacasacca, rinnegato, *m.* **-er**, S.: torniaio, tornitore, *m.* **-ery**, S.: arte del torniaio, *f.* **-ing**, S.: giro; circuito, *m.*: *in the* — *of a hand*, in un attimo. **-ingness**†, S.: sotterfugio; abbindolamento, *m.* **-ing-table**, S.: tavola girante, *f.*
tŭrnip, S.: rapa, *f.*, navone, napo, *m.*
tŭrn-key, S.: servitore del carceriere, *m.* **-pike**, S.: arganello; steccato, *m.* **-pikeman**, S.: riscuotitore del dazio, *m.* **-sole**, S.: girasole, eliotropio, *m.* **-spit**, S.: menarrosto, girarrosto, *m.* **-stile**, S.: arganello, cancello, *m.* **-table**, S.: (*rail.*) piattaforma (che volta la locomotiva), *f.*
tŭrpentine, S.: trementina, *f.* **-tree**, S.: terebinto, *m.* (albero).
tŭrpitude, S.: turpitudine; infamia, *f.*
tŭrquoise, S.: turchina, *f.* (pietra preziosa).
tŭrrel, S.: succhio, succhiello, *m.*
tŭrret, S.: torricciuola, torricella, *f.* **-ed**, ADJ.: fatto a modo di torre.
tŭrtle 1, S.: testuggine (di mare), *f.* **turtle** 2 (**-dove**), S.: tortora, tortorella, *f.* **-shell**, S.: tartaruga, scaglia della testuggine, *f.*
tŭsh! INTERJ.: oibò!
tŭsk 1, S.: zanna, sanna (di cignale), *f.* **tusk**† 2, INTR.: digrignare i denti. **-ed**, **-y**, ADJ.: zannuto.
tŭsle, S.: lotta, contesa, *f.*
tŭssuck†, S.: ciuffo d'erba, *m.*
tŭt, INTERJ.: oibò! via via!
tūtela-ge, S.: tutela; minorità, *f.* **-r**(**y**), ADJ.: tutelare, dal tutore; di guardiano.
tūtor 1, S.: tutore; precettore, maestro, *m.* **tutor**, TR.: insegnare, addottrinare, disciplinare; correggere, riprendere.

into, penetrare, investigare; — *through*, penetrare, indovinare, sventare; — *to*, pensare, meditare. **see!** 3, INTERJ.: ecco! ecco qui!

sēed 1, S.: seme, semente, *m.*, sementa, semenza; (*fig.*) cagione, *f.*: *run to* —, fare il tallo, tallire. **seed** 2, TR.: granare, far il granello, tallire. **-cake**, S.: focaccia di semi aromatici, *f.* **-ling**, S.: pianticella, *f.* **-ling-bed**, S.: semenzaio, *m.* **-lip**, **-lop**, S.: sacco da porvi il grano, *m.* **-pearl**, S.: semenza di perla, *f.* **-plot**, S.: semenzaio, *m.* **-sman**, S.: mercante di semi, *m.* **-time**, S.: tempo del seminare, *m.*; sementa, *f.* **-y**, ADJ.: granoso, pieno di granelli.

sēeing 1, S.: vedere, *m.*; vista, *f.* **seeing** 2, GER.: vedendo: — *that*, vedendo che; CONJ.: considerando che, poichè, mentre che.

sēek, IRR.; TR.: cercare, ricercare; domandare; INTR.: informarsi; sforzarsi: — *one's ruin*, tramare l'altrui rovina; — *after*, cercare, chiedere ardentemente; — *for*, adoperarsi per ottenere; — *out*, andar cercando; — *to*, ricorrere, aver ricorso. **-er**, S.: cercatore, ricercatore, *m.* **-ing**, S.: cerca; perquisizione, *f.* **-sorrow**, S.: tormentatore di sè stesso, *m.*

sēel 1, TR.: accigliare (un falcone); (*nav.*) barcollare. **sēel** 2, **-ing**, S.: (*nav.*) barcollamento, *m.*

sēem, INTR.: parere, sembrare, apparire: *it —s to me*, mi pare. **-er**, S.: dissimulatore, ipocrita, *m.* **-ing**, ADJ.: apparente; S.: sembianza, apparenza, *f.* **-ingly**, ADV.: in apparenza, verisimilmente. **-ingness**, S.: apparenza; plausibilità, verisimiglianza, *f.* **-less**, ADJ.: indecente, indecoro. **-lily**, ADV.: decentemente. **-liness**, S.: decenza, grazia, *f.* **-ly**, ADJ.: decente; convenevole; ADV.: decentemente, convenevolmente; propriamente.

sēer, S.: profeta, indovino, *m.* **-wood**, S.: legno secco, *m.*

sēesaw 1, S.: altalena, *f.*, barcollamento reciproco, *m.* **seesaw** 2, INTR.: altalenare; tracollare.

sēeth, IRR.; (IN)TR.: fare bollire; bollire: — *over*, bollire fuor; fervere. **-er**, S.: pentola, pignatta, *f.* **-ing** 1, ADJ.: bogliente, bollente; cocente. **-ing** 2, S.: bollimento, *m.*; lessatura, *f.* **-ing-pot**, S.: pentola, pignatta, *f.*

sĕgment, S.: semmento, *m.*

sĕgre-gate, TR.: segregare, spartire. **-gātion**, S.: separazione, *f.*

seigneūrial, ADJ.: signoresco, di signore.

sēignior, S.: signore, *m.* **-age**, S.: signoraggio, *m.* **-ize**, TR.: signoreggiare; dominare. **-y**, S.: signoria, *f.*; diritto feodale, *m.*

sēine, S.: scorticaria, *f.*

sēi-zable, ADJ.: che si può staggire. **-ze**, TR.: prendere, pigliare, acchiappare; usurpare; staggire, sequestrare; assalire: — *the opportunity*, cogliere l' occasione; *be —d of*, essere possessore di; — *upon*, impossessarsi di. **-zin**, S.: pigliar possessione, *m.*; possessione, *f.* **-zure**, S.: staggina, *f.*, sequestro, *m.*

sēlcouth†, ADJ.: raro.

sĕldom, ADV.: raramente, di rado. **-ness**, S.: rarezza, rarità, singolarità, *f.*

selĕc-t 1, ADJ.: scelto; eccellente: — *pieces*, squarci scelti. **-t** 2, TR.: scegliere, eleggere. **-tion**, **-tness**, S.: scelta, *f.*, sceglimento, *m.*: *make a* —, fare una scelta. **-tor**, S.: sceglitore, *m.*

sĕle-nite, S.: selenite, *m.* **-nográphic(al)**, ADJ.: selenografico. **-nŏgraphy**, S.: selenografia, descrizione della luna, *f.*

sĕlf, PRON.: medesimo, stesso, proprio: *one's* —, sè stesso; *ourselves*, noi medesimi; *the —same*, lo stesso, gli stessi; desso, dessi; *be one's — again*, rientrare in sè (in sè stesso). **-abāsing**, ADJ.: umiliante. **-abūse**, S.: abuso di sè stesso, *m.*; illusione, *f.* **-accūsing**, ADJ.: che si accusa da sè. **-ăcting**, ADJ.: automatico. **-admirātion**, S.: ammirazione di sè medesimo. **-admiring**, S.: che ammira sè stesso. **-combŭstion**, S.: combustione spontanea, *f.* **-commănd**, S.: padronanza di sè, *f.* **-concēit**, S.: presunzione, vanagloria, *f.* **-concēited**, ADJ.: presuntuoso, arrogante: *be* —, aver gran fava. **-concēitedness**, S.: presunzione, arroganza, ostentazione, *f.* **-contrōl**, S.: padronanza di sè, *f.*, sangue freddo, *m.* **-defĕnce**, S.: difesa propria, *f.* **-denial**, S.: astinenza; mortificazione, *f.* **-destrŭction**, S.: distruzione propria, *f.* **-ends**, S.: interesse proprio, *m.* **-estēem**, S.: stima di sè medesimo, *f.*, amor proprio, *m.* **-ĕvident**, ADJ.: chiaro, manifesto. **-ĕxcellence**, S.: eccellenza naturale, *f.* **-heal**, S.: (*phar.*) sanicula, *f.* **-interest**, S.: interesse proprio, *m.* **-ish**, ADJ.: egoistico; interessato: — *man*, egoista, *m.* **-ishly**, ADV.: in modo interessato. **-ishness**, S.: egoismo; amor proprio, *m.* **-love**, S.: amor proprio, amor di sè stesso, *m.* **-loving**, ADJ.: che ama sè stesso. **-mōved**, ADJ.: volontario, spontaneo. **-mŭrder**, S.: omicidio di sè stesso, *m.* **-mŭrderer**, S.: omicida di sè stesso, *m.* **-possĕssion**, S.: calma, *f.*, sangue freddo, *m.* **-preservātion**, S.: conservazione propria, *f.* **-same**, PRON.: desso, quello stesso. **-sufficiency**, S.: presuntuosità, arroganza, *f.* **-sufficient**,

U

ū *yū* (*the letter*), s.: u, *m.*

ū'ber-ous†, ADJ.: ubertoso; abbondante; copioso. **-ty**†, s.: ubertà; abbondanza, *f.*

ubiqui-tary, ADJ.: esistente dappertutto. **-ty**, s.: ubiquità, onnipresenza, *f.*

ŭdder, s.: poppa, tetta, tettola (di vacca, ecc.), *f.*

ŭg-lily, ADV.: bruttamente, sozzamente, laidamente. **-liness**, s.: bruttezza, sozzezza, laidezza, deformità, *f.* **-ly**, ADJ.: brutto, laido, deforme; vergognoso, cattivo: *rather* —, bruttino; *grow* —, diventare brutto.

ŭlcer, s.: ulcera, *f.*, ulcero, *m.* **-ate**, INTR.: ulcerare, ulcerarsi, esulcerare. **-ātion**, s.: ulcerazione, *f.*, ulceramento, *m.* **-ed**, ADJ.: ulcerato. **-ous**, ADJ.: ulceroso, pieno d'ulcere. **-ousness**, s.: ulcerazione, *f.*

uliginous†, ADJ.: uliginoso, fangoso.

ŭlster, s.: sobrabito lungo, *m.*

ultĕrior†, ADJ.: ulteriore.

ŭl-timate, ADJ.: ultimo, finale. **-timately**, ADV.: ultimamente, finalmente, alla fine. **-timātum**, s.: ultima offerta, *f.* **-tĭmity**†, s.: fine, *f.*

ultra-marine 1, ADJ.: oltramarino, d'oltre mare. **-marine** 2, s.: oltramarino, azzurro, *m.* **-mŏntane**, ADJ.: oltramontano. **-mŭndane**, ADJ.: oltramondano, celeste.

ŭlulate, INTR.: ululare.

ŭmbel, s.: umbella, *f.* **-lated**, **-liferous**, ADJ.: (*bot.*) umbellato.

ŭmber, s.: terra d'ombra; ombrina, *f.* (pesce). **-ed**, ADJ.: ombreggiato, annuvolato, offuscato.

umbilic, s.: umbilico, *m.* **-al**, ADJ.: ombelicale.

ŭmbles, S. PL.: coratella di cervo o daino, *f.*

ŭm-brage, s.: ombra, *f.*; pretesto, colore, *m.*, scusa, *f.*; sospetto, *m.* **-brāgeous**, ADJ.: ombroso. **-brāgeousness**, s.: ombrosità, *f.*, ombramento, *m.* **-brĕl(la)**, s.: ombrello, *m.* **-briere**†, s.: visiera, *f.* **-brŏsity**†, s.: ombrosità; oscurità, *f.*

ŭm-pirage, s.: arbitrato, *m.* **-pire** 1, s.: arbitro; mediatore, *m.* **-pire** 2, TR.: decidere da arbitro.

un-abăshed, ADJ.: impudente, impudico, sfacciato. **-ability**, s.: inabilità, incapacità, *f.* **-āble**, ADJ.: inabile, incapace: *she is — to pay*, ella non può pagare; le è impossibile di pagare. **-āblenesss**†, s.: inabilità, incapacità, *f.* **-abŏlishable**, inabolibile. **-abŏlished**, ADJ.: non **-accĕnted**, ADJ.: non accentuato. **-accĕptable**, ADJ.: dispiacente, spiacevole. **-accĕptableness**, s.: dispiacenza, spiacevolezza, *f.* **-accĕpted**, ADJ.: non accettato. **-accĕssible**, ADJ.: inaccessibile; inaccesso. **-accĕssibleness**, s.: esser inaccessibile, *m.* **-accŏmmodated**, ADJ.: sfornito; inconveniente. **-accŏmpanied**, ADJ.: senza compagnia, solo. **-accŏmplished**, ADJ.: incompiuto, imperfetto, inelegante. **-accoŭntable**, ADJ.: inesplicabile; strano, bizzarro. **-accoŭntableness**, s.: singolarità, stranezza, *f.* **-accoŭntably**, ADV.: in modo inesplicabile, stranamente. **-ăccurate**, ADJ.: inesatto. **-ăccurateness**†, s.: inesattezza, trascuranza, *f.* **-accŭstomed**, ADJ.: insolito, non comune. **-acknŏwledged**, ADJ.: sconosciuto, non confessato. **-acquāintance**, s.: ignoranza, *f.* **-acquāinted**, ADJ.: ignorante, non versato. **-acquāintedness**†, s.: poca conoscenza, ignoranza, *f.* **-ăctive**†, ADJ.: non attivo, ozioso, infingardo. **-admīred**, ADJ.: non ammirato; poco stimato. **-admŏnished**, ADJ.: non avvertito. **-adôrned**, ADJ.: non ornato, indecorato. **-adŭlterated**, ADJ.: puro, immisto. **-advīsed**, ADJ.: sconsigliato, mal avvisato; imprudente. **-advīsedly**, ADV.: imprudentemente, inconsideratamente. **-advīsedness**, s.: imprudenza, inconsiderazione, *f.* **-affĕcted**, ADJ.: senza affettazione, semplice. **-affĕctedly**, ADV.: naturalmente, schiettamente. **-affĕctedness**, s.: semplicità, schiettezza, *f.* **-affĕcting**, ADJ.: spassionato. **-agrēeable**, ADJ.: inconveniente. **-āided**, ADJ.: senza aiuto. **-āliénable**†, ADJ.: inalienabile. **-allied**, ADJ.: senza parenti. **-allŏwed**, ADJ.: illecito. **-ălterable**, ADJ.: inalterabile, immutabile. **-ălterableness**, s.: immutabilità, *f.* **-ălterably**, ADV.: inalterabilmente. **-amāzed**, ADJ.: intrepido. **-amāzedly**, ADJ.: intrepidamente. **-amāzedness**, s.: intrepidità, *f.* **-amĕndable**, ADJ.: incorregibile. **-āmiable**, ADJ.: spiacevole, dispiacente.

un-animity, s.: unanimità, concordia, *f.* **-ănimous**, ADJ.: unanime, concorde. **-ănimously**, ADV.: unanimamente.

un-ănswerable, ADJ.: incontestabile, incontrastabile. **-ănswered**, ADJ.: senza risposta. **-appālled**, ADJ.: non spaventato, intrepido. **-appēalable**, ADJ.: non appellabile. **-appēasable**, ADJ.: implacabile. **-apprehĕnsible**, ADJ.: incomprensibile. **-apprehĕnsive**, ADJ.: non intelligente. **-apprōachable**, ADJ.: inaccessibile. **-apprŏved**, ADJ.: disapprovato, rigettato. **-ăpt**, ADJ.: inetto, inabile. **-ăptly**, ADV.: mal a proposito, male. **-ăptness**, s.: sconvenevolezza;

salsŭginous, ADJ.: salsugginoso, salmastro.
sălt 1, S.: sale; (*fig.*) senno, genio, *m.*: *mineral* —, salgemma, *f.*; *attic* —, sale attico; *Epsom* —, sal d' Inghilterra. **salt** 2, ADJ.: salato: — *meat*, carne salata; — *water*, acqua di mare. **salt** 3, TR.: salare.
saltātion, S.: saltazione, *f.*, saltare, *m.*
sălt-beef, S.: bue salato, *m.* **-box**, S.: cassa da conservare il sale, *f.* **-cat**, S.: pezzo di sale, *m.* **-cellar**, S.: saliera, *f.* **-er**, S.: venditore di sale, *m.* **-ern**, **-house**, S.: salina, fabbrica di sale, *f.*
saltimbănco†, S.: saltimbanco, cerretano, *m.*
sălt-ish, ADJ.: salsetto, salaticcio. **-less**, ADJ.: senza sale; insipido. **-ly**, ADV.: con sale. **-maker**, S.: lavorante al sale, *m.* **-marsh**, S.: salina, *f.* **-meat**, S.: carne salata fecca, *f.* **-mine**, S.: salina, *f.* **-ness**, S.: salsezza, salsuggine, *f.* **-pan** = *salt-pit.* **-pĕtre**, S.: salnitro, nitro, *m.* **-pĕtre-house**, S.: fabbrica del salnitro, *f.* **-pĕtre-maker**, S.: che lavora al salnitro. **-pillar**, S.: statua di sale, *f.* **-pit**, S.: salina, *f.*; pozzo d' acqua salsa, *m.* **-spring**, S.: sorgente d' acqua salmastra, *f.* **-tub**, S.: vaso da salarvi dentro la carne, *m.*; saliera, *f.* **-water**, S.: acqua salsa, *f.* **-work**, S.: salina, *f.* **-y**, ADJ.: salso.
salūbri-ous, ADJ.: salubre, salutifero. **-ously**, ADV.: salubremente. **-ty**, S.: salubrità, sanità, *f.*
sălutar-iness, S.: salubrità; sanità, *f.* **-y**, ADJ.: salutevole, salutare.
sa-lutātion, S.: salutazione, *f.*; salutare, saluto, *m.* **-lūte** 1, S.: saluto, salutare, *m.*, riverenza, *f.*; bacio, *m.* **-lute** 2, TR.: salutare, chinare la testa, baciare: — *each other*, salutarsi l' un l' altro. **-lūter**, S.: salutatore; baciatore, *m.* **-lutiferous**, ADJ.: salutifero, salubre.
sal-vability, S.: possibilità di salvarsi, *f.*
săl-vable, ADJ.: che può essere sàlvato.
săl-vage, S.: premio per salvar da un naufragio, *m.* **-vātion**, S.: salvamento, *m.*; eterna salute, *f.*: *eternal* —, l' eterna salute; — *Army*, esercito della salute. **-vatory**, S.: ricettacolo; conservatorio, *m.*; guardaroba, *f.*
sălve 1, S.: unguento, impiastro; rimedio. **salve** 2, TR.: salvare; medicare; aiutare.
săl-ver, S.: vassoio, *m.*; sottocoppa, *f.* **-vo**, S.: riserbazione; scusa, *f.*
samăr, S.: zimarra, *f.*
săme, ADJ.: medesimo, stesso; simile: *it is the — to me*, per me è lo stesso; *it is the very* —, questo è desso. **-ness**, S.: medesimezza, cosa medesima, *f.*
sămlet, S.: piccol salmone, *m.* (pesce).
sămphire, S.: (*bot.*) finocchio marino, *m.*
săm-ple 1, S.: esemplare, modello; esempio, *m.*; mostra, *f.* **-ple** 2, TR.: mostrare l' esempio. **-pler**, S.: saggio, *m.*, mostra, *f.*, modello, *m.*
săn-able, ADJ.: sanabile. **-ātion**, S.: sanazione, *f.*, guarimento, *m.* **-ative**, ADJ.: sanativo. **-ativeness**, S.: virtù di sanare, virtù di guarire, *f.*
săno-tificate, TR.: santificare. **-tificātion**, S.: santificazione, *f.* **-tifier**, S.: santificatore, *m.* **-tify**, TR.: santificare, fare santo. **-tifying**, S.: santificamento, santificare, *m.* **-timōnious**, ADJ.: da santo; santo, ipocrito: — *person*, bacchettone, *m.*, bacchettona, *f.* **-timōniously**, ADV.: con santimonia. **-timōniousness**, **-timony**, S.: santimonia; santità, *f.* **-tion** 1, S.: sanzione, *f.*, decreto, *m.*, legge, *f.*: *pragmatical* —, prammatica sanzione, *f.* **-tion** 2, TR.: dar sanzione. **-titude**, S.: santità, *f.* **-tity**, S.: santità; vita religiosa, *f.* **-tuarise**†, TR.: dar santuario, dare un asilo. **-tuary**, S.: santuario; asilo, *m.*
sănd 1, S.: arena, rena, sabbia, *f.*; sabbione, *m.*: *fine* —, rena, sabbioncella, *f.*; *drift* —, arena mobile. **sand** 2, TR.: coprire di rena, coprire di sabbia.
săndal, S.: sandalo, zoccolo, *m.* **-tree**, S.: sandalo, *m.* **-wood**, S.: sandalo, *m.*
săndarack, S.: sandaraca, *f.* (*gomma*).
sănd-bank, S.: banco di rena, *m.*, secca, *f.*
săndblind, ADJ.: vedente fosco.
sănd-box, S.: polverino, *m.* **-cart**, S.: carro da sabbia, *m.* **-ed**, ADJ.: coperto di sabbia, sabbionoso. **-hill**, S.: mucchio di sabbia, *m.*, monticella di rena, *f.* **-iness**, S.: stato sabbionoso, *m.*, arenosità, *f.* **-ish**, ADJ.: alquanto sabbionoso. **-paper**, S.: carta vetro, *f.* **-pit**, S.: cava di sabbione, *f.* **-stone**, S.: pietra arenaria, *f.*
săndwich, S.: panino gravido, *m.*
săndy, ADJ.: sabbioso, arenoso.
săne, ADJ.: sano, in buona sanità.
săn-guifier, S.: sanguificante, *m.* **-guify**, INTR.: generare sangue. **-guinary**, ADJ.: sanguinario; crudele. **-guine**, ADJ.: sanguigno, sanguineo. **-guinely**, ADV.: ardentemente. **-guineness**, S.: ardore, *m.* **-guineous**, ADJ.: sanguineo, sanguigno. **-guinity**, S.: ardore, *m.*; confidenza, *f.* **-guinolent**, ADJ.: sanguinolento, crudele.
Sănhedrim, S.: sanedrim, sinedrio, *m.*
sănicle, S.: (*bot.*) sanicula, *f.*
săni-es, S.: sanie, marcia, *f.* **-ous** sanioso, marcioso.
sănity, S.: sanità, *f.*; stato per mente, *m.*

rial., spirituale. **-cëase**, TR.: cavar fuori dallo staccio; divestire; scorticare. **-caught**, ADJ.: non ancora preso. **-caused**, ADJ.: senza causa. **-cautious**, ADJ.: incauto, imprudente; trascurato. **-ceasing**, ADJ.: incessante, continuo. **-ceremonious**, ADJ.: senza cerimonie, poco cerimonioso, alla buona. **-ceremoniously**, ADV.: senza cerimonie, poco cerimoniosamente. **-certain**, ADJ.: incerto, dubbioso; incostante, variabile. **-certainly**, ADV.: incertamente. **-certainty**, S.: incertezza, irresoluzione, dubbiezza, *f.* **-cessant** = *unceasing*. **-cessantly**, ADV.: incessantemente, continuamente. **-chain**, TR.: scatenare. **-changeable**, ADJ.: immutabile, permanente. **-changeableness**, S.: immutabilità, costanza, *f.* **-changeably**, ADV.: immutabilmente, costantemente. **-changed**, ADJ.: inalterato; inalterabile. **-changing**, ADJ.: invariabile, costante. **-charge**, TR.: ritrattare (un' accusazione); negare. **-charitable**, ADJ.: non caritatevole. **-charitableness**, S.: mancanza di carità, *f.* **-charitably**, ADV.: senza carità. **-charm**, TR.: romper la malia. **-chary**, ADJ.: non circospetto, incauto. **-chaste**, ADJ.: incasto, impudico, disonesto. **-chastely**, ADV.: impudicamente, immodestamente. **-chasteness**, **-chastity**, S.: incontinenza, immodestia, *f.* **-checked**, ADJ.: non frenato, irrefrenato, non ristretto, illimitato. **-cheerful†**, ADJ.: malinconico, tristo. **-cheerfulness†**, S.: malinconia; tristezza, *f.* **-chewed**, ADJ.: non masticato. **-child**, TR.: privare d' infanti. **-christened†**, ADJ.: non ancora battezzato. **-Christian**, ADJ.: indegno d' un cristiano. **-Christianlike**, ADJ.: in modo poco cristiano. **-Christianly**, ADV.: poco cristianamente. **-church**, TR.: scomunicare. **-circumcised**, ADJ.: incirconciso. **-circumcision**, S.: incirconcisione, *f.* **-circumscribed**, ADJ.: incircoscritto, illimitato. **-circumspect**, ADJ.: inavvertito, indiscreto, imprudente. **-circumstantial**, ADJ.: di poco rilievo, di poca importanza. **-civil**, ADJ.: incivile, scortese. **-civilized**, ADJ.: grossolano, rozzo, villano. **-civilly**, ADV.: incivilmente, rusticamente. **-clarified**, ADJ.: non purificato. **-clasp**, TR.: sfibbiare. **-classic(al)**, ADJ.: non classico.

uncle, S.: zio, *m.*

un-clean, ADJ.: immondo, sporco; incasto, impudico. **-cleanliness**, S.: sporcizia, bruttura, immondizia; impudicizia, *f.* **-cleanly**, ADJ.: sporcamente; impudicamente. **-cleanness**, S.: immondizia, bruttura; impudicizia, *f.* **-cleansed**, ADJ.: non purgato, sporco. **-clench**, TR.: aprire (il pugno). **-clew**, TR.: disfare, slegare. **-clinch** = *unclench*. **-clipped**, ADJ.: non mozzato, non tagliato, intero. **-clog**, TR.: sbrogliare; liberare. **-cloister**, TR.: affrancare, porre in libertà. **-close**, TR.: schiudere, aprire. **-closed**, ADJ.: schiuso, aperto. **-clothe**, TR.: svestire; spogliare. **-clouded**, ADJ.: senza nuvole, sereno, chiaro. **-cloudedness**, S.: serenità, chiarezza, *f.* **-cloudy** = *unclouded*. **-clutch**, TR.: schiudere, aprire. **-coif**, TR.: levare la cuffia dalla testa. **-coil**, TR.: sviluppare; svolgere. **-coined**, ADJ.: non coniato, non monetato. **-collected**, ADJ.: sparso, disperso. **-colored**, ADJ.: non colorito. **-combed**, ADJ.: non pettinato. **-comeatable†**, ADJ.: inaccessibile. **-comeliness**, S.: sconvenevolezza, indecenza, ineleganza, *f.* **-comely**, ADJ.: sconvenevole, indecente, inelegante. **-comfortable**, ADJ.: inconsolabile; sconsolato; misero. **-comfortableness**, S.: disagio, *m.*; tristizia, *f.* **-comfortably**, ADV.: malagevolmente, tristamente. **-commanded**, ADJ.: non comandato; non lodato. **-common**, ADJ.: raro, straordinario. **-commonly**, ADV.: raramente, straordinariamente. **-commonness**, S.: rarità; singolarità, *f.* **-communicated**, ADJ.: non communicato. **-compact(ed)**, ADJ.: non compatto, non sodo. **-companied†**, ADJ.: scompagnato, solo. **-compelled**, ADJ.: non sforzato, volontario, spontaneo. **-complaisant**, ADJ.: incivile. **-complaisantly**, ADV.: incivilmente. **-complete†**, ADJ.: incompiuto, imperfetto. **-compounded**, ADJ.: non misto, semplice. **-compoundedness**, S.: semplicità, *f.* **-comprehensive**, ADJ.: incomprensibile. **-compressed**, ADJ.: non compresso. **-conceivable†**, ADJ.: inconcepibile, incomprensibile. **-conceivableness†**, S.: incomprensibilità, *f.* **-conceived**, ADJ.: non concepito. **-concern**, S.: indifferenza; negligenza; spassionatezza, *f.* **-concerned**, ADJ.: indifferente; insensibile; spassionato. **-concernedly**, ADV.: indifferentemente; spassionatamente. **-concernedness**, S.: indifferenza, freddezza, *f.* **-concerning†**, ADJ.: non interessante. **-concocted**, ADJ.: inconcotto, indigesto. **-conditional**, ADJ.: senza condizione, assoluto. **-confined**, ADJ.: illimitato, libero. **-confinedly**, ADV.: illimitatamente. **-confirmed**, ADJ.: non confirmato, incerto. **-conform**, ADJ.: differente, dissimile. **-conformable**, ADJ.: non conforme, incongruo. **-conformity†**, S.: dissimiglianza, differenza, *f.* **-confused**,

frugalmente. **-ness**, S.: frugalità; economia, *f.* **-ş-bank**, S.: banco di risparmio, *m.*; cassa di risparmio, *f.*

Săviour, S.: salvatore, redentore, *m.*

săvour 1, S.: sapore, savore; gusto; odore, *m.* **savour** 2, TR.: saporare, assaporare; sentire: *it —s of*, sa di, sente di. **-ily**, ADV.: saporitamente, con gusto. **-iness**, S.: sapore, buon gusto; odore, *m.* **-less**, ADJ.: senza sapore. **-rous**, ADJ.: saporoso. **-y**, ADJ.: saporito, saporoso, di buon sapore.

săvoury, S.: (*bot.*) santoreggia, timbra, *f.*

Savöy, S.: cavolo capuccio, *m.*

săw 1, S.: sega, *f.*: *little —*, *hand —*, seghetta, *f.* **saw** 2, S.: proverbio, motto, *m.* **saw** 3, TR.: segare. **-dust**, S.: segatura, *f.* **-er** = *sawyer*. **-fish**, S.: segamarina, *f.* (pesce). **-ing**, S.: segare, segamento, *m.* **-mill**, S.: mulino da segare, *m.* **-pit**, S.: fossa de' segatori, *f.* **-yer**, S.: segatore, *m.*

săx-ifrage, S.: (*bot.*) sassifraga, *f.* **-ifragous**, ADJ.: litontritico.

săy 1, S.: saga (panno); mostra, *f.* **say** 2, IRR.; INTR.: dire; narrare, raccontare: *that is to —*, cioè a dire, cioè; *— by heart*, recitare a mente; *— over again*, dire di nuovo, ridire; *— on!* dite su! *I —!* dimmi un po'! *no sooner said than done*, detto, fatto. **-ing**, S.: dicimento; proverbio, motto, *m.*: *as the — is*, come dice il proverbio.

scăb, S.: scabbia, rogna, *f.*; birbone, *m.*

scăbbard, S.: fodero, *m.*; guaina, *f.*

scăb-bed, ADJ.: scabbioso, rognoso, lebbroso. **-bedness**, **-biness**, S.: rogna, *f.* **-by** = *scabbed*.

scăbious, ADJ.: scabbioso, rognoso; S.: scabbiosa, gallinella, *f.*

scăbrous, ADJ.: scabroso; rozzo; senza armonia. **-ness**, S.: scabrosità, *f.*

scăbwort, S.: (*bot.*) scabbiosa, *f.*

scăffold 1, S.: palco, catafalco, *m.* **scaffold** 2, TR.: impalcare. **-age**, **-ing**, S.: struttura di palchi; galleria, *f.*

scală-de, **-do**, S.: scalata, *f.*, scalamento, *m.*

scălawag, S.: uomo da niente, furbo, *m.*

[illegible]**ld** 1, ADJ.: misero, cattivo, spregievole. [illegible]**ld** 2, S.: tigna, *f.* **scald** 3, TR.: scot[illegible]; **sciacquare** con acqua calda. **-head**, [illegible] **tigna**, forfora, *f.* **-ing-hot**, ADJ.: [illegible] **fervente**. **-ing-house**, S.: luo[illegible] la scottatura, *m.*

[illegible]**cia**, *f.*; guscio, *m.*; (*mus.*) [illegible]**vinolo**, *m.*: *—s*, bilan[illegible] **libra**; *pair of —s*, [illegible]**ala** d' una car[illegible] **squame** di [illegible]**ferro**, *f.* [illegible]**are**;

pesare; INTR.: scagliarsi; scorticarsi: *— the walls*, scalare le mura, dare la scalata alle mura. **-ed**, ADJ.: scaglioso, squamoso. **-eless**, ADJ.: senza scaglie.

scalēne, S.: scaleno, *m.*

scăliness, S.: essere scaglioso, *m.*, squamosità, *f.*

scăling, S.: scalata, *f.*: *— ladders*, scale da scalare, *f. pl.*

scăll, S.: lebbra, lepra, tigna, *f.* **-ed**, ADJ.: tignoso,

scăllion, S.: scalogno, *m.*, cipollina, *f.*

scăllop 1, S.: petonchio, *m.* (conchiglia). **scallop** 2, TR.: tagliare a festone.

scălp 1, S.: capellatura, *f.*; pericranio, *m.* **scalp** 2, TR.: levare via il pericranio. **-el**, **-ing-iron**, S.: scalpello, *m.*

scăly, ADJ.: scaglioso, squamoso.

scăm-ble, (IN)TR.: moversi goffamente; esser turbolento, tumultuare. **-bler**, S.: sfacciato, leccappiatti, parasito, *m.* **-bling**, ADJ.: turbolento, tumultuante. **-blingly**, ADV.: con romore; sfacciatamente.

scam-mōniate, ADJ.: di scamonea. **scămmony**, S.: (*bot.*) scamonea, *f.*

scămper, TR.: scampare, fuggire via: *— away* (*off*), darla a gambe, scappare, scampare. **-er**, S.: fuggitivo, *m.*

scăn, TR.: scandere, misurare un verso; esaminare, ponderare.

scăndal 1, S.: scandalo, scandolo, *m.*; ignominia, infamia, *f.*: *bring a — upon*, scandalizzare; *lie under a —*, aver cattivo nome, esser in cattiva riputazione. **scandal** 2, TR.: diffamare, accusare falsamente. **-ize**, TR.: scandalizzare, dare scandalo. **-ous**, ADJ.: scandaloso, diffamatorio, infame. **-ously**, ADV.: scandalosamente. **-ousness**, S.: scandalo pubblico, *m.*

scăn-ned, ADJ.: scandito, misurato. **-ning**, S.: scandere, misurare (i versi), *m.* **-sion**, S.: scansione, misura (di versi), *f.*

scănt 1, ADJ.: parco, stretto; meschino; ADV.: appena. **scant** 2, TR.: limitare, ristringere; INTR.: (*nav.*) mancare: *the wind —s*, il vento manca. **-ily**, ADV.: parcamente; meschinamente. **-iness**, S.: scarsezza, strettezza; insufficienza, *f.*

scănt-le, TR.: dividere in piccoli pezzi; INTR.: mancare. **-let**, S.: pezzetto, *m.*; quantità piccola, *f.* **-ling**, S.: pezzetta; misura, grandezzia, *f.*

scănt-ly, ADV.: strettamente, parcamente; meschinamente. **-ness**, S.: strettezza; scarsezza, parcità, *f.* **-y**, ADJ.: stretto, parco; sordito.

scăpe 1, S.: scappata, fuga, *f.* **scape** 2, TR.: scappare, fuggire; evitare. **-goat**, S.: becco di espiazione, capro emissario, *m.* **-grace**, S.: birichino, monello, cattivo soggetto, bricconcello, *m.*

tion, s.: azione subordinata, azione inferiore, *f.* **-age**†, s.: minorità, età di pubertà, *f.* **-bear**, IRR.; TR.: sopportare, tollerare. **-bid**, IRR.; TR.: offrire meno del giusto valore. **-bind**, IRR.; TR.: legar per di sotto. **-butler**, s.: sottobottigliere, *m.* **-clerk**, s.: sottosegretario, sottoproposto; sostituto, *m.* **-dō**, IRR.; TR.: fare meno, trascurare. **-dóne**, ADJ.: troppo poco cotto, non ben cotto; cuocere troppo poco: *this roast beef is* —, quest' arrosto è troppo poco cotto (alquanto crudo). **-fellow**, s.: briccone, guidone, *m.* **-furnish**, TR.: non provvedere d' assai. **-gird**, IRR.; TR.; cingere per di sotto. **-gō**, IRR.; TR.: soffrire; sostenere. **-governor**, s.: sottogovernatore. **-ground**, s.: cavità, *f.*, sotterraneo, *m.* **-growth**, s.: bosco ceduo, *m.* **-hand** 1, ADJ.: clandestino, segreto: — *dealings*, pratiche segrete, *f. pl.* **-hand** 2, ADV.: sottomano, di soppiatto. **-labourer**, s.: manovale, *m.* **-lāy**, IRR.; TR.: sottoporre; appuntellare. **-lāyer**, s.: puntello, sostegno, *m.* **-lieutĕnant**, s.: sottoluogotenente, *m.* **-line**, TR.: interlineare; scrivere sotto. **-ling**, s.: piccol agente; partigiano vile, *m.* **-lip**, s.: labbro di sotto, *m.* **-master**, s.: sottomaestro, *m.* **-mine**, TR.: minare, contramminare, distruggere. **-miner**, s.: minatore; marraiuolo, *m.* **-most**, ADJ.: infimo, più basso. **-nēath**, PREP.: di sotto, sotto. **-ŏfficer**, s.: uffiziale subordinato, *m.*

underŏgatory, ADJ.: non derogatorio.

ŭnder-part, s.: parte subordinata, *f.* **-pĕtticoat**, s.: gonnellino, *m.*, sottana, *f.* **-pin**, TR.: puntellare. **-plot**, s.: intreccio d' una commedia, episodio, *m.*; cospirazione, *f.* **-prāise**, TR.: spregiare, disprezzare. **-prior**, s.: soppriore, *m.* **-prize**, TR.: stimar poco, vilipendere. **-prŏp**, TR.: puntellare, sostenere. **-propŏrtioned**, ADJ.: sproporzionato. **-rate**, s.: vil prezzo, prezzo basso, *m.* **-rāte**, TR.: disprezzare; vilipendere, avvilire; non bastantemente apprezzare. **-sāy**†, IRR.; TR.: contraddire. **-sĕcretary**, s.: sottosegretario, *m.* **-sĕll**, IRR.; TR.: vendere per meno. **-sĕlling**, s.: vendita fatta a vil prezzo, *f.* **-servant**, s.: servitore basso, *m.* **-sĕt**†, IRR.; TR.: mettere di sotto; puntellare, appoggiare, sostenere. **-sĕtter**, s.: puntello, sostegno; piedestallo, *m.* **-sheriff**, s.: sottosciriffo, *m.* **-sheriffry**, s.: uffizio di sottosciriffo, *m.* **-shot**, ADJ.: mosso dall' acqua di sotto. **-sign**, TR.: sottoscrivere: —*ed*, il sottoscritto. **-soil**, s.: sottosuolo, *m.* **-song**, s.: (*mus.*) ritornello, *m.* **-stănd**, IRR.; TR.: intendere, capire, comprendere; esser avviso o informato; INTR.: comprendere; capire, intendere; aver notizia: *do you — what I say?* intendete ciò che dico? *I have understood that*, ho sentito dire che; *give to* —, dare ad intendere; — *one's self*, conoscersi. **-stănding** 1, ADJ.: intelligente, saputo. **-standing** 2, s.: intelletto; intendimento, *m.*; intelligenza; corrispondenza, *f.*: *come to an — with*, intendersi con; *man of* —, uomo d' intelletto (di ricapito). **-stăndingly**, ADV.: intelligibilmente, con giudizio. **-stóod**, ADJ.: inteso, compreso; capito. **-strapper**, s.: piccol agente; uomo da poco, *m.* **-tāke**, IRR., TR.: intraprendere; impegnarsi; INTR.: ingerirsi, intromettersi, impacciarsi: — *to prove*, impegnarsi di provare. **-tāker**, s.: intraprenditore; agente; impresario di pompe funebri, becchino, *m.* **-tāking**, s.: impresa, *f.*, intraprendimento, *m.* **-tenant**, s.: sottopigionale, *m.* **-treasurer**, s.: vicetesoriere, *m.* **-valuation**, s.: svilimento del prezzo, *m.* **-vălue**, s.: vil prezzo; sprezzamento, biasimo, *m.* **-value**, TR.: disprezzare, vilipendere. **-vălner**, s.: disprezzatore, spregiatore, *m.* **-wood**, s.: bosco ceduo, *m.*, arbusti piccoli, *m. pl.* **-work**, s.: affari di poco momento, *m. pl.* **-wŏrk**, IRR.; TR.: contramminare, spiantare. **-workman**, s.: artigiano inferiore, manovale, *m.* **-write**, IRR.; TR.: sottoscrivere. **-writer**, s.: assicuratore, mallevadore, *m.* **-written**, ADJ.: sottoscritto.

un-described, ADJ.: non descritto. **-desĕrved**, ADJ.: immeritevole. **-desĕrvedly**, ADV.: immeritamente. **-desĕrvedness**, s.: indegnità, *f.* **-desĕrving**, ADJ.: non meritevole, indegno. **-desĕrvingly**, ADV.: immeritamente. **-designed**, ADJ.: non progettato, senza intento; involontario. **-designedness**, s.: schietezza, sincerità, *f.* **-designing**, ADJ.: schietto, sincero. **-desirable**, ADJ.: da non desiderarsi. **-desired**, ADJ.: non desiderato. **-destrŏyable**, ADJ.: da non distruggersi. **-destrŏyed**, ADJ.: non distrutto. **-detĕrminable**†, ADJ.: da non determinarsi. **-detĕrminate**, ADJ.: indeterminato; irresoluto. **-detĕrminateness**†, **-determinātion**†, s.: incertezza, dubbiezza, *f.* **-detĕrmined**, ADJ.: indeterminato, indeciso; incerto. **-devŏted**, ADJ.: non dedicato. **-devŏutly**, ADV.: indivotamente. **-digĕsted**, ADJ.: indigesto, crudo. **-diminished**, ADJ.: non diminuito. **-dipped**, ADJ.: non tuffato. **-dirĕcted**, ADJ.: non diretto, indiretto. **-discĕrned**, ADJ.: inosservato. **-discĕrnedly**, ADV.: impercettibilmente. **-discĕrnible**, ADJ.: impercettibile, invisibile. **-discĕrnible-**

padrone di pecore; pastore, *m.* **-shearer**, S.: tosatore di pecore, *m.* **-shearing**, S.: tonditura delle pecore, *f.* **-skin**, S.: pelle di pecora, *f.;* diploma, *m.* **-walk**, S.: parco di pecore, *m.*

shēer 1, ADJ.: puro, chiaro; naturale, semplice; ADV.: affatto, del tutto; alla prima: — *through*, da banda a banda. **sheer** 2, INTR.: (*nav.*) andare alla banda: — *off*, involarsi, fuggire via di nascosto. **-hook**, S.: grappino a mano, *m.* **-ing**, S.: (*nav.*) tempellamento, *m.* **-ly**, ADV.: affatto, subito. **-s** = *shears*.

shēet 1, S.: lenzuolo; foglio (di carta), *m.: book in —s*, libro non legato, libro sciolto, *m.;* — *of ice*, lastra, *f.*, blocco di ghiaccio, *m.;* — *of water*, estensione di agua, *f.* **sheet** 2, TR.: porre le lenzuola, involgere in un lenzuolo; coprire leggermente. **-anchor**, S.: ancora maestra, grande ancora, *f.* **-ing**, S.: lino da lenzuolo, panno lino, *m.* **-iron**, S.: piastra di ferro, *m.*

shĕkel, S.: siclo, *m.* (moneta).

shĕld, ADJ.: maculato.

shĕldrake, S.: fringuello, *m.;* specie di anatra, *f.*

shĕlf (pl. *shelves*), S.: scaffale, *m.*, scansia; secca (in mare), *f.* **-y**, ADJ.: pieno di scogli, pieno di secche pericolose.

shĕll 1, S.: scaglia; conchiglia, conca, *f.;* nicchio (di pesce), *m.;* scorza, corteccia; buccia (di nave), *f.:* — *of a sword*, fodero della spada, *m.* **shell** 2, TR.: sgusciare, scorzare; sgranare; INTR.: sgusciarsi, scagliarsi: — *off*, sgusciarsi, scagliarsi. **-fish**, S.: pesce di nicchio, *m.* **-work**, S.: lavoro in conchiglie, *m.* **-y**, ADJ.: coperto di scaglie, squamoso.

shĕlter 1, S.: coperto; rifugio, asilo, *m.;* sicurtà, *f.* **shelter** 2, TR.: dare il coperto, ricevere in casa sua; proteggere; INTR.: mettersi a coperto. **-less**, ADJ.: senza asilo, derelitto.

shĕl-ves, PL. di *shelf*. **-ving**, ADJ.: pendente; declive. **-vy**, ADJ.: poco profondo, pieno di scogli.

shĕnd†, IRR.; TR.: rovinare, guastare; disonorare; sorpassare.

shĕpherd, S.: pastore, pecoraio, *m.: —'s dog*, cane guardagregge, *m.* **-boy**, S.: pastorello, *m.* **-ess**, S.: pastorella, pecoraia, *f.: young* (*or pretty*) —, pastorella, *f.* **-girl**, S.: pastorella, *f.* **-ish**, ADJ.: pastorellesco, pastorale; rustico.

[illegible] ..., *m.*

[illegible] vaso rotto), coccio,

[illegible] ...y, -dom, S.:

[illegible] ...'li Xe-

shew *shō* = *show*. **-bread** = *show-bread*.

shield 1, S.: scudo, *m.;* difesa; protezione, *f.* **shield** 2, TR.: difendere, proteggere. **-bearer**, S.: scudiere, *m.*

shift 1, S.: camicia, camiscia (da donna), *f.;* spediente, mezzo, *m.;* scusa, *f.;* pretesto, *m.;* astuzia, *f.: last* —, ultimo spediente, ultima risorsa; *put one to his —s*, imbarazzare alcuno, confondere alcuno. **shift** 2, TR.: mutare; cambiare; trasportare; INTR.: andare da un lungo ad un altro; mutar di casa; usare astuzie; — *one's self*, cambiare di camicia; — *for one's self*, ingegnarsi; fuggirsene; — *one off*, strigarsi d' uno; — *one's clothes*, cambiar d' abiti; — *the scene*, cambiar la scena. **-er**, S.: mariuolo, truffatore, *m.* **-ing**, ADJ.: cambiante; S.: cambiamento, *m.* **-ing-fellow**, S.: ingannatore, mariuolo, *m.* **-ingly**, ADV.: artatamente, con astuzia. **-less**, ADJ.: povero di mezzi: — *fellow*, povero diavolo, dappoco.

shilling, S.: scellino, *m.* (moneta).

shilly-shally, ADV.: in modo irresoluto, dubbiosamente; INTR.: esitare; frivoleggiare: *stand* —, stare in dubbio.

shily, ADV.: con ritrosia; timidamente; freddamente.

shin, S.: stinco, *m.:* — *of beef*, garretto di bue, *m.*

shine 1, S.: splendore, lustro, *m.;* chiarezza, *f.: moon*—, chiaro della luna, *m;* — *forth*, rifulgere, brillare, ruggiare. **shine** 2, IRR.; INTR.: rilucere, risplendere; brillare.

shin-gle 1, S.: assicella, *f.* **-gle** 2, TR.: coprire con assicelle. **-gler**, S.: facitor d' assicelle, *m.* **-gles**, S.PL.: (*med.*) fuoco salvatico, *m.*

shi-ning, ADJ.: luminoso, risplendente; S.: luce, *f.;* splendore, *m.* **-ningness**, S.: rilucentezza, *f.* **-ny**, ADJ.: rilucente, lucido; brillante.

ship 1, S.: nave, *f.*, naviglio, vascello, bastimento, *m.:* — *of the line*, vascello di linea, *m.;* — *of war*, nave da guerra, *f.;* —*'s lantern*, fanale, *m.; iron-clad* —, nave corazzata; *merchant* —, bastimento mercantile; *fit out a* —, equipaggiare (armare) un bastimento; *take* —, imbarcarsi. **ship** 2, TR.: imbarcare. **-board**, S.: bordo di vascello, *m.; go to* —, imbarcarsi. **-boat**, S.: schifo, *m.* **-boy**, S.: mozzo, *m.* **-building**, S.: architettura navale, *f.* **-carpenter**, S.: carpentiere navale, *m.* **-lead**, S.: carico di bastimento, *m.* **-man**, S.: marinaio, *m.* **-master**, S.: padrone di bastimento, *m.* **-ment**, S.: imbarcamento, *m.* **-owner**, S.: padrone d' una nave, *m.* **-ping**, ADJ.: navale, maritimo; S.: imbarcamento, *m.;*

hausted, ADJ.: non esausto. **-expănded**, ADJ.: non disteso, non dilatato. **-expĕcted**, ADJ.: inaspettato, non immaginato; inopinato, improvviso. **-expĕctedly**, ADV.: inopinatamente, all' improvviso. **-expĕctedness**, S.: prontezza inaspettata, *f.*, caso subito, *m.* **-expēdient**†, ADJ.: inopportuno, inconveniente. **-expērienced**, ADJ.: non sperimentato. **-expērt**†, ADJ.: inesperto, senza pratica. **-expērtly**†, ADV.: in modo inesperto, da novizio. **-expērtness**, S.: inesperienza, imperizia, *f.* **-ĕxplicable**, ADJ.: inesplicabile. **-explōred**, ADJ.: non esplorato, non esaminato. **-expōsed**, ADJ.: non esposto. **-exprĕssible**†, **-exprĕssive**, ADJ.: inesprimibile, ineffabile. **-extĕnded**, ADJ.: non disteso. **-extĭnguishable**, ADJ.: inestinguibile. **-extĭnguished**, ADJ.: non estinto, non ammortito. **-făded**, ADJ.: non sfiorito, non appassito. **-făding**, ADJ.: sempre florido. **-făilable**†, ADJ.: infallibile. **-făilableness**†, S.: infallibilità, *f.* **-făiling**, ADJ.: infallibile, sicuro. **-făilingness**, S.: infallibilità, *f.* **-făir**, ADJ.: ingiusto, disonesto. **-făirly**, ADV.: ingiustamenmente, disonestamente. **-făirness**, S.: ingiustizia, *f.* **-făithful**, ADJ.: perfido, infedele. **-făithfully**, ADV.: perfidamente, infedelmente. **-făithfulness**, S.: perfidia, infedeltà, *f.* **-familiar**, ADJ.: non comune, straordinario. **-făshionable**, ADJ.: non alla moda. **-făshionableness**, S.: deviamento dalla moda, *m.* **-făshionably**, ADJ.: non secondo la moda. **-făshioned**, ADJ.: informe, sformato. **-făsten**, TR.: sciorre, disfare, disunire. **-făthered**†, ADJ.: senza padre. **-făthomable**, ADJ.: senza fondo; impenetrabile. **-făthomably**, ADV.: in modo impenetrabile. **-făthomed**, ADJ.: che non è scandagliato. **-fatigued**, ADJ.: indefesso, non stancato. **-făvourable**, ADJ.: disfavorevole; avverso. **-făvourably**, ADV.: disfavorevolmente, avversamente. **-fēared**†, ADJ.: intrepido, non temuto. **-fēasible**, ADJ.: impraticabile. **-fēathered**, ADJ.: non piumato. **-fĕd**, ADJ.: non pasciuto. **-fēed**, ADJ.: non pagato, senza salario. **-fēeling**, ADJ.: insensibile, duro di cuore. **-fēelingly**, ADV.: insensibilmente. **-fēelingness**, S.: insensibilità, *f.* **-fēigned**, ADJ.: non finto; sincero. **-fēignedly**, ADV.: sinceramente, veramente. **-fēignedness**, S.: sincerità, schiettezza, *f.* **-fĕlt**, ADJ.: non sentito; insensibile. **-fĕnced**, *ADJ.*: *senza siepe*; non fortificato. **-fermĕnted**, ADJ.: non fermentato. **-fĕrtile**, *ADJ.*: *infertile*, infecondo, sterile.

-fĕtter, TR.: togliere i ceppi, scatenare; liberare. **-figured**, ADJ.: non figurato. **-filial**, ADJ.: indegno d' un figliuolo. **-filled**, ADJ.: non empiuto, vuoto. **-finished**, ADJ.: non finito, incompiuto, imperfetto. **-fĭrm**, ADJ.: infermo, debole. **-fĭt** 1, ADJ.: inetto, incapace, inabile; improprio, sconvenevole: *it is* —, non conviene. **-fĭt** 2, TR.: rendere incapace, disabilitare. **-fĭtly**, ADV.: sconvenevolmente, impropriamente, malamente. **-fĭtness**, S.: incapacità; sconvenevolezza, *f.* **-fĭtting**, ADJ.: sconvenevole, disdicevole. **-fĭx**, TR.: slegare, distaccare; render fluido, liquefare. **-fĭxed**, ADJ.: non fisso; errante. **-flĕdged**, ADJ.: senza piume. **-foiled**, ADJ.: non sottomesso, non vinto. **-fōld**, TR.: spiegare, sviluppare; aprire: — *sheep*, fare uscire le pecore dell' ovile. **-fōol**, TR.: render savio. **-forbĭdden**, ADJ.: non proibito, permesso. **-fōrced**, ADJ.: non sforzato, libero. **-fōrcedly**, ADV.: liberamente, volontariamente. **-fōrcible**, ADJ.: senza forza, debole. **-foreknōwn**, ADJ.: non preconosciuto, non preveduto. **-foreseen**, ADJ.: non previsto; inopinato. **-forewârned**, ADJ.: non ammonito, non avvertito. **-fôrfeited**, ADJ.: non confiscato, non sequestrato. **-forgiving**, ADJ.: implacabile, inesorabile. **-forgŏtten**, ADJ.: non dimentico. **-fôrmed**, ADJ.: sformato, informe. **-forsāken**, ADJ.: non abbandonato. **-fôrtified**, ADJ.: non fortificato. **-fôrtunate**, ADJ.: sfortunato, sventurato, infelice. **-fôrtunately**, ADV.: sfortunatamente. **-fôrtunateness**, S.: sfortuna, *f.*, infortunio, *m.* **-fought** *-fât*, ADJ.: non combattuto. **-fouled**, ADJ.: non contaminato. **-fōund**, ADJ.: non trovato, non incontrato. **-frāmable**†, ADJ.: che non può formarsi. **-frāmed**, ADJ.: non formato; senza cornice. **-frēquent**, ADJ.: infrequente. **-frequĕnted**, ADJ.: non frequentato, non visitato. **-frēquently**, ADV.: radamente, raramente. **-friĕnded**, ADJ.: senza amici; non protetto. **-friĕndliness**, S.: poca benevolenza, *f.* **-friĕndly**, ADJ.: non amichevole, scortese; ADV.: scortesemente. **-frŏck**, TR.: spogliare. **-frōzen**, ADJ.: non gelato; non rappreso. **-frūitful**, ADJ.: infruttuoso, infecondo. **-frūitfulness**, S.: sterilità, infecondità, *f.* **-fulfilled**, ADJ.: non adempito, non colmo. **-fūrl**, TR.: spandere, spiegare, aprire. **-fūrnish**, ADJ.: sfornire; spogliare. **-fūrnished**, ADJ.: non arredato, non (am)mobiliato, senza mobili; sfornito, sprovvisto: — *apartments*, camere non ammobiliate. **-gāge**, TR.: disimpegnare. **-gāinly**, ADJ.: scon-

memoria labile, *f.* **-nosed**, s.: dal naso corto. **-ribs**, s. pl.: costoline, coste false, *f. pl.* **-sighted**, adj.: di corta vista, miope. **-sightedness**, s.: corta vista, miopia, *f.* **-waisted**, adj.: corto di taglia, di piccola statura. **-winded**, adj.: bolso, asmatico. **-winged**, adj.: di corte ali.

shōry, adj.: litorale, vicino al lido del mare.

shŏt, s.: colpo, tiro, sparo, *m.*; palla (di schioppo), *f.*; pallini, *m. pl.*; scotto, pagamento; tiratore: *bar* —, *chain* —, balla ramata, *f.*; *bow* —, tratto d' arco, *m.*; *cannon* —, tiro di cannone, *m.*; *within cannon* —, a tiro di cannone; *within a musket* —, a tiro di moschetto; *great* —, palla di cannone, *f. pl.*; *small* —, pallini, *m. pl.*, migliaruola, *f.*; *at a* —, a un tratto, in una volta; *be a good* —, esser buon tiratore; *pay one's* —, pagare il suo scotto. **-free**, adj.: franco, senza pagare nulla, a bardotto. **-gun**, s.: schioppo, leggiero fucile, *m.*

shŏtten, adj.: andato in frega; sporgente.

shŏugh, s.: barbone; mucchio, *m.*

shōulder 1, s.: spalla, *f.*, omero, *m.* **shoulder** 2, tr.: mettere sopra le spalle: — *one up*, spalleggiare alcuno. **-belt**, s.: ciarpa, *f.*, budriere, *m.* **-blade**, s.: scapula, *f.* **-bone**, s.: ossa della spalla, *m.* **-knot**, s.: spallaccio, *m.* **-piece**, s.: armadura della spalla, *f.*, spallaccio, *m.* **-clapper**, s.: che affetta familiarità. **-shotten**, adj.: spallato. **-slip**, s.: dislocamento di spalla, *m.*

shōut 1, s.: clamore, grido, *m.*: — *for joy*, grido d' allegrezza, *m.* **shout** 2, intr.: gridare; far applauso. **-er**, s.: gridatore, applauditore, *m.* **-ing**, s.: acclamazione, *f.*

shŏve 1, s.: colpo, urto, *m.*; spinta, *f.* **shove** 2, (in)tr.: spingere, urtare; assalire: — *along*, spingere avanti; — *backward*, spingere indietro.

shŏvel 1, s.: pala, paletta, *f.* **shovel** 2, tr.: gettare colla pala, ammucchiare. **-board**, s.: morella, *f.* (giuoco). **-ful**, s.: palata, *f.* **-ler**, s.: pellicano, *m.*

shŏve-net, s.: ritrosa, *f.* (rete).

... 1, s.: mostra; apparenza, *f.*; spetta...; pretesto, *m.*: — *of friendship*, sem... d' amicizia, *f.*; *make a fine* —, fare ... figura. **show** 2, irr.; tr.: mostra... vedere; manifestare, scoprire; intr.: parere, sembrare, ... *one's self*, mostrarsi; — ... *heels*, voltare le cal... fare giuochi ... annunzia... ; — *her* ... di

shŏwer 1, s.: rovescio, nembo, *m.*: *great* —, acquazzone, *m.*; *light* —, acquetta, *f.* **shower** 2, intr.: piovere a rovescio, strapiovere. **-bath**, s.: doccia, *f.* **-y**, adj.: piovoso.

shōw-ily, adv.: con pompa. **-iness**, s.: pompa, *f.*, fasto, *m.* **-ish**, adj.: splendido, fastoso, pomposo, vano. **-y** = *showish*.

shrĕd 1, s.: ritaglio; pezzo, *m.* **shred** 2, tr.: sminuzzare, tagliare minuto; (*gard.*) potare. **-ding**, s.: piccolo pezzo, frammento, *m.*

shrew *shrū*, s.: sgridatrice, *f.* **-d**, adj.: astuto, arguto, perspicace, fino; maligno. **-ly**, adv.: astutamente, argutamente, sagacemente; maliziosamente. **-dness**, s.: astuzia; sottigliezza, sagacità, *f.* **-ish**, adj.: ritroso; petulante. **-ishly**, adv.: in modo garrulo; petulantemente. **-ishness**, s.: cattivo umore, *m.*; petulanza, *f.* **-mouse**, s.: topo campestre, *m.*

shriek 1, s.: strillo, grido acuto, *m.* **shriek** 2, intr.: strillare, stridere: — *out*, mettere grida, schiamazzare.

shrie-valty, s.: uffizio di sciriffo, *m.* **-ve†**, s.: sciriffo, *m.*

shrift 1, part. del v. *shrive*. **shrift** 2, s.: confessione (fatta al confessore), *f.*

shrill 1, adj.: squillante, risonante; sottile; acuto. **shrill** 2, intr.: squillare, strillare; risonare. **-ness**, s.: acutezza di voce; sottigliezza, *f.* **-y**, adj.: squillante, acuto; adv.: squillantemente.

shrimp 1, s.: squilla, *f.* (gamberetto marino); nano, *m.* **shrimp** 2, tr.: scorciare.

shrine, s.: reliquiario, *m.*

shrink 1, s.: stringimento, *m.*; contrazione, *f.* **shrink** 2, irr.; tr.: scorciare, scortare, diminuire; irr.; intr.: scorciarsi, ritirarsi; rinculare; soccombere: — *away*, dare dietro, svignare via; accartocciarsi; — *with cold*, tremar di freddo. **-age**, s.: contrazione, *f.*, restringimento, *m.* **-er**, s.: codardo; infingardo, *m.* **-ing**, s.: stringimento; scorciamento, *m.*

shrive, irr.; tr.: (*shrove*; *shriven*, *shrift*) stare a udire in confessione, confessarsi (al confessore).

shrivel, tr.: aggrinzare; intr.: raggrinzarsi.

shri-ver, s.: confessore, *m.* **-ving** = *shrift*.

shrōud 1, s.: coperto; panno funebre, *m.* **shroud** 2, tr.: coprire; seppellire; difendere, proteggere; intr.: mettersi al coperto; rifugiarsi.

Shrōve-tide, s.: carnasciale, carnavale. **-Tuesday**, s.: martedì grasso, giorno innanzi le ceneri, *m.*

shrŭb 1, s.: arbuscello, arbusto; nano,

me (de' soldati), *m.* **-förmity**, S.: uniformità; conformità, *f.* **-formly**, ADV.: uniformemente.

un-imáginable, ADJ.: non immaginabile. **-imáginably**, ADV.: in modo inimmaginabile. **-imitable**†, ADJ.: inimitabile, da non imitarsi. **-immôrtal**, ADJ.: non immortale, mortale. **-impáired**, ADJ.: non diminuito, inalterato; buono. **-impáirable**, ADJ.: inalterabile. **-impássioned**, ADJ.: non collerico, tranquillo. **-impéached**, ADJ.: non accusato, intatto. **-impôrtant**, ADJ.: che non è d' importanza; senza orgoglio, modesto. **-importūned**, ADJ.: non importunato, non sollecitato. **-impróvable**, ADJ.: che non si può migliorare. **-impróvableness**, S.: incapacità di miglioramento, *f.* **-impróved**, ADJ.: non migliorato, non perfezionato; incolto, senza coltura; senza approfittarne. **-indifferent**, ADJ.: parziale, favorevole. **-indústrious**, ADJ.: pigro, ozioso. **-inféoted**, ADJ.: non infettato. **-inflámed**, ADJ.: non acceso, non infiammato. **-infôrmed**, ADJ.: non istrutto, non addottrinato, ignorante. **-ingénuous**, ADJ.: illiberale; finto, falso. **-inhábitable**, ADJ.: non abitabile. **-inhábitableness**, S.: essere inabitabile, *m.* **-inhábited**, ADJ.: disabitato, deserto. **-injured**, ADJ.: illeso, non offeso; senza danno. **-inscribed**, ADJ.: senza iscrizione. **-inspired**, ADJ.: non ispirato. **-instrúcted**, ADJ.: non istrutto, ignorante. **-instrúctive**, ADJ.: non istruttivo. **-intélligent**, ADJ.: non intelligente, ignorante. **-intelligibility**, S.: inintelligibilità, *f.* **-intélligible**, ADV.: inintelligibile. **-intélligibleness** = *unintelligibility*. **-intélligibly**, ADV.: in modo inintelligibile. **-inténtional**, ADJ.: non premeditato. **-interessed**†, **-interested**, ADJ.: disinteresssato. **-interesting**, ADJ.: non interessante. **-intermitted**, ADJ.: continuo, perpetuo. **-intermixed**, ADJ.: non intermisto. **-interrúpted**, ADJ.: non interrotto, continuo. **-interrúptedly**, ADV.: senza interruzione. **-intrénched**, ADJ.: non trincierato. **-invénted**, ADJ.: non inventato. **-invéstigable**, ADJ.: imperscrutabile; incomprensibile. **-invited**, ADJ.: non invitato.

ūnion, S.: unione, concordia, *f.*; accoppiamento, *m.*: *American* —, l' Unione americana, *f.*

uníque, ADJ.: unico, solo; singolare.

unîparous, ADJ.: uniparo.

ūnison, S.: unisono, accordo, *m.*: *in* —, *all' unisono*, d' accordo, insieme.

ūnit, *S.*: unità, *f.*

Unitárian u, S.: Unitario, Sociniano, *m.*

uni-te, TR.: unire, congiungere; collegare; accoppiare; adunare; INTR.: unirsi, congiungersi; adunarsi. **-ted**, ADJ.: unito, ecc. (cf. *unite*): *the* — *States*, gli Stati Uniti; *the* — *Kingdom*, il Regno Unito. **-tedly**, ADV.: congiuntamente, insieme. **-ter**, S.: unitore, congiungitore, *m.*

ūni-tive†, ADJ.: unitivo. **-ty**, S.: unità; concordia; uniformità, *f.*

univér-sal 1, ADJ.: universale, generale. **-sal** 2, S.: universale, sistema generale, *m.* **-sálity**, S.: universalità, generalità, *f.* **-sally**, ADV.: universalmente. **-salness**† = *universality*. **-se**, S.: universo, tutto il mondo, *m.* **-sity**, S.: università, *f.*; collegio, *m.*

univo-cal, ADJ.: univoco. **-cally**, ADV.: univocamente.

un-jóin†, TR.: disgiungere, separare, dislogare. **-jóint**, TR.: dislogare, disgiungere. **-jóyful**, **-jóyous**, ADJ.: non gioioso, tristo, malinconico. **-júdged**, ADJ.: non giudicato, non determinato. **-júst**, ADJ.: ingiusto, iniquitoso. **-jústifiable**, ADJ.: inammissibile, illecito. **-jústifiably**, ADV.: illecitamente. **-jústly**, ADV.: ingiustamente. **-kémpt**, ADJ.: non pettinato. **-kénnel**, TR.: fare uscire. **-képt**, ADJ.: non tenuto; non osservato, non ubbidito. **-kind**, ADJ.: non benigno, inamabile, non benevolo; scortese, incivile, duro. **-kindliness**, S.: scortesia, inciviltà, *f.* **-kindly** 1, ADJ.: non favorevole, con poca gentilezza; duramente: *part* —, separarsi freddamente; *take it* —, aversene a male. **-kindly** 2, ADV.: scortesemente, incivilmente. **-kindness**, S.: malignità; scortesia, *f.* **-king**†, TR.: privare della dignita reale. **-knightly**, ADJ.: indegno d' un cavaliere. **-knit**, TR.: disfare, snodare. **-knótty**, ADJ.: senza nodi. **-knówable**, ADJ.: che non si può sapere. **-knówing**, ADJ.: ignorante. **-knówingly**, ADV.: ignorantemente. **-knówn**, ADJ.: sconosciuto; incognito: — *to me*, senza mia saputa; *he is* — *to me*, non lo conosco. **-láboured**, ADJ.: non coltivato; volontario, spontaneo. **-láce**, TR.: dislacciare. **-láde**, IRR.; TR.: scaricare; alleggerire. **-láid**†, ADJ.: non posto, non collocato; non quietato, non pacificato. **-laménted**, ADJ.: non compianto. **-látch**, TR.: aprire il saliscendo. **-láwful**, ADJ.: illegittimo, illecito. **-láwfully**, ADV.: illegittimamente, illecitamente. **-láwfulness**, S.: stato illegittimo, *m.* **-léarn**, TR.: disimparare, disapprendere. **-léarned**, ADJ.: illetterato, ignorante. **-léarnedly**, ADV.: da ignorante, ignorantemente. **-léave**, TR.: levar via le foglie, sfrondare. **-léav-**

sign 1, S.: segno; indizio, *m.*; insegna, *f.*; vestigio, *m.*, traccia, *f.* **sign** 2, TR.: segnare, far segno; accennare; significare, rappresentare: — *a letter*, sottoscrivere una lettera.

sig-nal 1, ADJ.: segnalato, egregio, eccellente, illustre. **-nal** 2, S.: segnale, segno; contrassegno, *m.* **-nal** 3, TR.: segnalare; commandare. **-nal-gun**, S.: colpo di cannone tirato per segnale, colpo di segnale, *m.* **-năllty**, S.: celebrità, *f.* **-nalize**, TR.: signalare; rendere famoso: — *one's self*, signalarsi. **-nal-lamp**, S.: (*rail.*) lampada di segnale, *f.* **-nal-light**, S.: fanale, *m.* **-nally**, ADV.: segnalatamente; illustremente.

signature, S.: soscrizione; firma, prova; (*print.*) segnatura, *f.*

signer, S.: segnatore, *m.*

signet, S.: suggello (del re), *m.*

sig-nificance, **-nificancy**, S.: significanza, importanza, *f.* **-nificant**, ADJ.: significante; espressivo. **-nificantly**, ADV.: in modo espressivo. **-nificâtion**, S.: significazione, *f.*; senso, *m.* **-nificative**, ADJ.: significativo. **-nificatively**, ADV.: significativamente. **-nificâtor**, S.: significatore, *m.* **-nificatory**, ADJ.: emblematico. **-nify**, TR.: significare; avvisare; esprimere; INTR.: essere energico.

signior, S.: signore, *m.* **-ize†**, INTR.: signoreggiare, dominare. **-y**, S.: signoria, *f.*; dominio, *m.*

signpost, S.: palo d' insegna, *m.*

silen-ce 1, S.: silenzio; segreto, *m.*: *put one to* —, imporre silenzio ad uno; — *gives consent*, chi tace acconsente. **-ce** 2, INTERJ.: silenzio! zitto! **-ce** 3, TR.: imporre silenzio, far tacere; interdire. **-t**, ADJ.: silente, taciturno, cheto. **-tly**, ADV.: tacitamente, senza parlare, pian piano.

silicious, ADJ.: di cilicio.

siliculose, ADJ.: pieno di lolle, baccelluto.

siliginose, ADJ.: fatto di siligine.

sili-qua, S.: siliqua, *f.*, baccello, *m.* **-quose**, **-quous**, ADJ.: baccelluto, cassulare.

silhouĕtte, S.: siluetta, *f.*

silk, S.: seta, *f.*: —*s*, seterie, *f. pl.* **-en**, ADJ.: setoso, di seta. **-floss**, S.: fiocchi di seta, *m. pl.* **-iness**, S.: qualità setacea. **-manufactory**, S.: fabbrica di seta, *f.* **-mercer**, S.: mercante di seteria, *m.* **-stockings**, S. PL.: calzette di seta, *f. pl.* **-stuff**, S.: drappo di seta, *m.* **-thread**, S.: filo di seta, *m.* **-throwster**, S.: torcitore di seta, *m.* **-wares**, S. PL.: mercanzie di seta, *f. pl.* **-weaver**, S.: tessitore di drappi, *m.* **-worm**, S.: baco filugello, bigatto, *m.* **-y**, ADJ.: (fatto) di seta, setaceo; setoso, morbido.

sill, S.: soglio, limitare, *m.*

sillabub, S.: limonea vinosa, *f.*; capo di latte, *m.*

sil-lily, ADV.: scioccamente, goffamente. **-liness**, S.: sciocchezza, goffaggine, *f.* **-ly**, ADJ.: sciocco, goffo; semplice: — *fellow*, semplicione, imbecille, *m.*; — *look*, aria da scimunito, *f.*; — *thing*, sciocchezza, *f.*

silt S.: fango, limo, *m.*, melma, *f.*

silvan, ADJ.: silvano.

silver 1, S.: argento, *m.*; moneta d' argento, *f.* **silver** 2, ADJ.: d'argento, argentino. **silver** 3, TR.: argentare, inargentare. **-beater**, S.: battitore d' argento, *m.* **-coin**, S.: moneta d' argento, *f.* **-lace**, S.: gallone d' argento, *m.* **-ly**, ADJ.: argentino, d' argento. **-mine**, S.: miniera d' argento, *f.* **-plate**, S.: vasellame d' argento, *m.* **-smith**, S.: argentiere, orefice, orafo, *m.* **-spoon**, S.: cucchiaio d' argento, *m.* **-thistle**, S.: brancorsina, *f.* **-weed**, S.: argentina, *f.* **-wire**, S.: argento filato, *m.* **-y**, ADJ.: argenteo, argentino.

simâr, S.: zimarra, *f.*

sim-ilar, ADJ.: similare, simigliante; omogeneo. **-ilărity**, S.: simiglianza, similitudine, *f.* **-ilarly**, ADV.: similmente, parimente. **-ile**, S.: simile, *m.*, similitudine, *f.*; esempio, paragone, *m.* **-ilitûde**, S.: similitudine; conformità, *f.*

simitar, S.: scimitarra, *f.*

simmer, INTR.: grillare, bollire dolcemente, bollire a fuoco lento. **-ing**, S.: bollire a fuoco lento, *m.*

simō-niac, S.: simoniaco, *m.* **-niacal**, ADJ.: simoniaco. **simony**, S.: simonia, *f.*

simper 1, S.: sorriso, sorridere degli sciocchi, *m.* **simper** 2, INTR.: sorridere scioccamente. **-ing**, ADJ.: che sorride scioccamente, affettato; S.: sorriso, sciocco. **-ingly**, ADV.: con sorriso sciocco.

sim-ple 1, ADJ.: semplice; puro, ingenuo; inesperto, goffo: — *fellow*, semplicione, *m.* **-ple** 2, S.: semplice, *m.*, droga, erba medicinale, *f.* **-ple** 3, INTR.: erborare, cogliere degli semplici. **-ple-minded**, ADJ.: candido, sincero. **-ple-mindedness**, S.: candore, *m.*, sincerità, *f.* **-pleness**, S.: semplicità; sciocchezza, *f.* **-pler**, S.: semplicista, botanico, *m.* **-pless†**, S.: semplicità, ingenuità, *f.* **-pleton**, S.: semplicione, sciocco, *m.* **-ple-witted**, ADJ.: ingenuo, sempliciotto. **-plicity**, S.: semplicità; purità, ingenuità; sciocchezza, *f.* **-plificâtion**, S.: simplificazione, *f.* **-plify**, TR.: simplificare, rendere men complesso. **-plist** = *simpler*. **-ply**, ADV.: semplicemente, solamente.

simu-lacre, S.: simulacro, *m.* **-lar**, S.:

ADJ.: non navigabile. -**nĕcessarily**, ADV.: senza necessità, inutilmente. -**nĕcessariness**, S.: inutilità, *f.* -**nĕcessary**, ADJ.: non necessario, inutile. -**nēedful**, ADJ.: non necessario. -**nêighbourly** 1, ADJ.: non da vicino, scortese. -**neighbourly** 2, ADV.: incivilmente. -**nĕrve**, TR.: snervare, indebolire. -**nĕrved**, ADJ.: snervato, debole. -**nō̆ble**, ADJ.: ignobile, basso. -**nōbly**, ADV.: ignobilmente, bassamente. -**nōted**, -**nōticed**, ADJ.: inosservato. -**nŭmbered**, ADJ.: non numerato, innumerabile. -**obēdient**†, ADJ.: disubbidiente. -**obêyed**, ADJ.: disubbidito. -**obnŏxious**, ADJ.: non esposto ad un male. -**obsēquiousness**, S.: disubbidienza, *f.* -**obsĕrvable**, ADJ.: inosservabile, impercettibile. -**obsĕrvant**, ADJ.: disattento, disubbidiente. -**sĕrved**, ADJ.: non osservato, negletto. -**obsĕrving**, ADJ.: disattento, trascurato. -**obstrŭcted**, ADJ.: non ostrutto; non impedito. -**obstrŭctive**, ADJ.: non ostruttivo. -**obtāined**, ADJ.: non ottenuto, non acquistato. -**ŏbvious**, ADJ.: non evidente, non chiaro. -**ŏccupied**, ADJ.: non occupato, senza possessore; incolto, sodo; disponibile. -**offĕnding**†, -**offĕnsive**†, ADJ.: innocente, senza peccato. -**officious**, ADJ.: inofficioso; scortese. -**ōpening**, ADJ.: non aperiente. -**ŏperative**†, ADJ.: inefficace, senza effetto. -**oppōsed**, ADJ.: non opposto. -**ôrderly**†, ADJ.: irregolare; disordinato, confuso. -**ôrdinary**, ADJ.: raro, straordinario. -**ôrganized**, ADJ.: non organizzato. -**original**, -**originated**, ADJ.: senza origine; non generato, increato. -**ôrthodox**, ADJ.: non ortodosso, eterodosso. -**ōwned**, ADJ.: non riconosciuto, non richiamato. -**păcified**, ADJ.: non pacificato, non calmato. -**păck**, TR.: sballare; spiegare. -**pāid**, ADJ.: non pagato, da pagarsi. -**pāined**, ADJ.: senza pena, senza dolore. -**pāinful**, ADJ.: non doloroso. -**pălatable**, ADJ.: nauseoso, spiacevole. -**păragoned**, ADJ.: senza paragone, impareggiabile. -**părallelled**, ADJ.: incomparabile. -**pârdonable**, ADJ.: imperdonabile, irremissibile. -**pârdonably**, ADV.: irremissibilmente. -**pârdoned**, ADJ.: non perdonato. -**pârdoning**, ADJ.: implacabile, inesorabile. -**parliamĕntary**, ADJ.: contrario all' uso del parlamento. -**pârtable**, ADJ.: inseparabile, indivisibile. -**pârtably**, ADV.: inseparabilmente. -**pârted**, ADJ.: indiviso. -**pârtial**, ADJ.: imparziale. -**pârtially**, ADV.: senza parzialità, con imparzialità. -**păssable**, ADJ.: che non può passarsi; impraticabile. -**păssionate**†, ADJ.: spassionato, tranquillo. -**pâthed**, ADJ.: non battuto, non frequentato. -**pāve**, TR.: levare i selici, smattonare. -**pāwned**, ADJ.: non impegnato. -**pēaceable**, ADJ.: turbolento, tumultuoso, agitato. -**pēaceably**, ADV.: con turbolenza, in disordine. -**pĕg**, TR.: togliere via la cavicchia. -**pĕnsioned**, ADJ.: senza pensione. -**pēople**, TR.: spopolare; desolare. -**percēivable**, ADJ.: impercettibile. -**percēivably**, ADV.: impercettibilmente. -**percēived**, ADJ.: non osservato. -**percēivedly**, ADV.: impercettibilmente, appoco appoco. -**pĕrfect**†, ADJ.: imperfetto, incompiuto. -**pĕrfectly**†, ADV.: imperfettamente. -**pĕrfectness**†, S.: imperfezione, *f.*; difetto, *m.* -**perfôrmed**, ADJ.: non messo ad effetto. -**pĕrishable**†, ADJ.: che non può perire, incorruttibile. -**pĕrjured**, ADJ.: non spergiurato. -**perplĕxed**†, ADJ.: non perplesso, non imbrogliato. -**perspirable**, ADJ.: non traspirabile. -**persuādable**, ADJ.: impersuasibile, inesorabile. -**pĕtrified**, ADJ.: non petrificato. -**philosŏphical**, ADJ.: non filosofico, poco filosofico. -**philosŏphically**, ADV.: non da filosofo, poco filosoficamente. -**philosŏphicalness**, S.: incongruità con la filosofia, filosofia falsa, *f.* -**pīerced**, ADJ.: non perforato, non penetrato. -**pillared**, ADJ.: senza colonne. -**pillowed**, ADJ.: senza guanciale. -**pin**, ADJ.: togliere via le spille. -**pitied**, ADJ.: non compatito, non compianto. -**pitiful**, ADJ.: non compassionevole, spietato. -**pitifully**, ADV.: senza compassione, spietatamente. -**pitying**, ADJ.: non compassionevole. -**plăcable**†, ADJ.: implacabile. -**plāced**, ADJ.: non impiegato, senza posto. -**plāgued**, ADJ.: non tormentato. -**plāit**, TR.: spiegare, torre le pieghe. -**plănted**, ADJ.: non piantato. -**plāusible**, ADJ.: non plausibile. -**plāusive**, ADJ.: discordante, dissenziente. -**plĕasant**, ADJ.: spiacevole, ingrato. -**plĕasantly**, ADV.: spiacevolmente. -**plĕasantness**, S.: spiacevolezza, *f.* -**plēased**, ADJ.: spaciuto, non soddisfatto, malcontento. -**plēasing**, ADJ.: spiacevole; offensivo. -**plēasingness**, S.: spiacevolezza, *f.* -**pliant**, ADJ.: inflessibile; indocile. -**pliantness**, S.: inflessibilità, *f.* -**ploughed**, ADJ.: non arato, non coltivato. -**plūme**, TR.: pennare, spiumare. -**poĕtic(al)**, ADJ.: non poetico. -**pŏison**, TR.: levar via il veleno. -**pŏlished**, ADJ.: non ripulito, rozzo, ruvido. -**polite**†, ADJ.: incivile, scortese. -**politeness**†, S.: inciviltà, scortesia, *f.* -**pollūted**, ADJ.: non polluto, intemerato. -**pŏpular**, ADJ.: non popolare.

cio, svenevole, sciamannato; ADV.: disacconciamente, svenevolmente. **-gălled**, ADJ.: non piagato, non ferito, illeso. **-gârtered**, ADJ.: senza giarrettiere. **-găthered**, ADJ.: non raccolto. **-gĕnerated**, ADJ.: non generato, increato. **-gĕnerative**, ADJ.: non fruttifero, sterile. **-gĕnerous**, ADJ.: non generoso, ignobile, illiberale. **-gĕnial**, ADJ.: non geniale; malsano. **-gentēel**, ADJ.: incivile, scortese. **-gentēelly**, ADV.: incivilmente, scortesemente, grossolanamente, rozzamente. **-gentēelness**, S.: scortesia; rozzezza, zotichezza, *f.* **-gĕntle**, ADJ.: indocile, intrattabile; duro, rigoroso. **-gĕntlemanlike**, **-gĕntlemanly**, ADJ.: incivile, illiberale. **-gĕntleness**, S.: indocilità; rigidezza, severità, *f.* **-gĕntly**, ADV.: aspramente, severamente; rozzamente. **-gĭlded**, ADJ.: non dorato. **-gird**, IRR.; TR.: sciogliere la cintura. **-girt**, ADJ.: scinto. **-giving**†, ADJ.: illiberale; non benevolo. **-glāzed**, ADJ.: senza vetro; senza fenestre. **-glŏrified**†, ADJ.: non glorificate. **-glŏve**, TR.: levare i guanti **-glŏved**, TR.: senza guanti. **-glūe**, TR.: scollare. **-gŏdlily**, ADV.: in modo empio, empiamente; senza religione. **-gŏdliness**, S.: empietà; irreligione, *f.* **-gŏdly**, ADJ.: empio, irreligioso. **-gōred**, ADJ.: non piagato, non ferito. **-gôrged**, ADJ.: non empiuto, non sazio. **-gŏt**, ADJ.: non acquistato; non generato. **-gŏvernable**, ADJ.: indomabile; sfrenato. **-gŏvernableness**, S.: sfrenatezza, *f.* **-gŏvernably**, ADV.: sfrenatamente. **-gŏverned**, ADJ.: sfrenato, licenzioso. **-grāceful**, ADJ.: sgraziato, svenevole. **-grācefully**, ADV.: sgraziatamente, svenevolmente. **-grācefulness**, S.: sgraziataggine, svenevolezza, *f.* **-grācious**, ADJ.: sgraziato, svenevole; scortese. **-grāciously**, ADV.: sgraziatamente; scortesemente. **-grāciousness**, S.: sgarbatezza; inciviltà, *f.* **-grammătical**, ADJ.: sgrammaticato. **-grănted**, ADJ.: non dato, non concesso. **-grāteful**, ADJ.: ingrato, sconoscente; noioso. **-grātefully**, ADV.: ingratamente, sconoscentemente. **-grātefulness**, S.: ingratitudine, sconoscenza, *f.* **-grătified**, ADJ.: non gratificato. **-grăvel**, TR.: levar la ghiaia; (*fig.*) rimuovere gli scrupoli. **-grāvely**†, ADV.: [illegible] gravità, non seriamente. **-grōunded**, [illegible]: malfondato. **-grŭdgingly**, [illegible] invidia, di buon cuore, lieta-[illegible] **-[illegible]rded**†, ADJ.: non guardato, [illegible]liente, poco misurato, **-[illegible]dly**†, ADV.: ne-

un-guĕssed, ADJ.: non conghietturato. **-guīded**, ADJ.: non guidato. **-guiltiness**, S.: innocenza, *f.* **-guilty**, ADJ.: innocente. **-hăbitable**†, ADJ.: inabitabile. **-hăft**, TR.: levar il manico. **-hăllow**, TR.: profanare. **-hălter**, TR.: levar la cavezza. **-hănd**, TR.: lasciare andare le mani. **-hăndsome**, ADJ.: laido, deforme. **-hăndsomely**, ADV.: bruttamente, incivilmente; malamente. **-hăndsomeness**, S.: laidezza, bruttezza, deformità, *f.* **-hăndy**, ADJ.: non destro; goffo, sgraziato. **-hăppily**, ADV.: infelicemente, sfortunatamente. **-hăppiness**, S.: infelicità, miseria, *f.* **-hăppy**, ADJ.: infelice, sfortunato, misero. **-hârmed**, ADJ.: non guastato, non piagato. **-hârmful**, ADJ.: non nocivo; innocente. **-harmōnious**, ADJ.: disarmonico, discordante. **-hârness**, TR.: levare gli arnesi. **-hăsp**, TR.: sfibbiare. **-hăzarded**, ADJ.: non azzardato, non arrischiato. **-hĕalthful**, ADJ.: malsano, malaticcio, morbido; insalubre. **-hĕalthfulness**, S.: mala sanità; aria cattiva, *f.* **-hĕalthy**, ADJ.: malsano, malaticcio; insalubre: *rather* —, malaticcio, infermiccio. **-hĕard** (*of*), ADJ.: inaudito, straordinario. **-heârt**†, TR.: discoraggiare. **-hēated**, ADJ.: non riscaldato. **-hēeded**, ADJ.: non curato; negletto; di poca importanza. **-hēedful**, ADJ.: negligente, incauto. **-hēediness**, S.: negligenza, trascuraggine, *f.* **-hēeding**, ADJ.: negligente, trascurato. **-hēedy**†, ADJ.: subito, precipitoso. **-hĕlped**, ADJ.: non aiutato, non protetto. **-hĕlpful**, ADJ.: non aiutante; inutile. **-hidebound**†, ADJ.: di stomaco ampio. **-hinge**, TR.: sgangherare; sconnettere, disordinare. **-hōliness**, S.: empietà, profanità, *f.* **-hōly**, ADV.: empio, profano. **-hŏnoured**, ADJ.: non onorato. **-hŏod**, TR.: discappellare, trar di cappello. **-hŏok**, TR.: spiocare dall' uncino, sfibbiare. **-hōop**, TR.: levare via i cerchi. **-hōped**, ADJ.: inaspettato. **-hōpeful**, ADJ.: che non da buona speranza. **-hōrse**, TR.: scavalcare; levare di sella. **-hŏspitable**, ADJ.: inospitale, scortese. **-hŏstile**, ADJ.: non ostile; amichevole. **-hōuse**, TR.: cacciare di casa. **-hōused**, ADJ.: senza casa; senza rifugio. **-hŭmbled**, ADJ.: non umiliato. **-hûrt**, ADJ.: non ferito, illeso, salvo. **-hûrtful**, ADJ.: innocente; non nocivo. **-hûrtfully**, ADV.: innocentemente. **-hŭsbanded**, ADJ.: non coltivato. **-hŭsk**, TR.: sgranare, sgusciare.

ūni-corn, ADJ.: liocorno, unicorno, *m.* **-form** 1, ADJ.: uniforme; conforme, eguale, regolare. **-form** 2, S.: abito unifor-

to, sbrigliato. **-rĕlatively**, ADV.: senza connessione. **-relĕnting**, ADJ.: inflessibile; inesorabile. **-relievable**, ADJ.: senza soccorso, senza alleviamento. **-relieved**, ADJ.: non soccorso, non alleviato. **-remârkable**, ADJ.: non rimarchevole, non notabile. **-remĕdiable**, ADJ.: irremediabile. **-remĕmbering**, ADJ.: smemorato. **-remitted**, ADJ.: non perdonato. **-remōvable**†, ADJ.: non amovibile, immobile. **-remōvableness**†, S.: immobilità, *f.* **-remōvably**†, ADV.: senza rimovimento, immobilmente. **-remōved**, ADJ.: non rimosso, immobile; fermo. **-repâid**, ADJ.: non rimunerato. **-repâirable**, ADJ.: irreparabile, senza riparo. **-repâired**, ADJ.: non riparato, non risarcito. **-rĕparable**† = *unrepairable.* **-repēalable**†, ADJ.: irrevocabile. **-repēaled**, ADJ.: non rivocato, non abolito. **-repĕntance**†, S.: impenitenza, *f.* **-repĕntant**, ADJ.: impenitente. **-repĕnted**, ADJ.: non pentito. **-repĕnting**, ADJ.: impenitente. **-repining**, ADJ.: senza compiangere. **-replĕnished**, ADJ.: non riempiuto. **-reprievable**, ADJ.: da non sospendersi. **-reprōached**†, ADJ.: non reprobato, non rimproverato, non censurato. **-reprōved**†, ADJ.: non ripreso, non corretto. **-repŭgnant**, ADJ.: non repugnante, compatibile. **-rĕputable**, ADJ.: poco onorabile, diffamante. **-requĕsted**, ADJ.: non domandato. **-requitable**, ADJ.: irremunerabile. **-requited**, ADJ.: irremunerato. **-resĕnted**, ADJ.: senza risentimento, non risentito. **-resĕrved**, ADJ.: senza riserva, franco. **-resĕrvedly**, ADV.: senza riserva, francamente. **-resĕrvedness**, S.: franchezza, sincerità, *f.* **-resisted**, ADJ.: non opposto. **-resistible**†, ADJ.: irresistibile. **-resisting**, ADJ.: non resistente. **-resŏlvable**†, ADJ.: irresolubile, insolubile. **-resŏlved**, ADJ.: non determinato, irresoluto, dubbioso. **-resŏlving**, ADJ.: irresoluto, incerto. **-respĕctful**, ADJ.: irreverente; incivile, scortese. **-respĕctfully**, ADV.: irreverentemente. **-respĕctfulness**, S.: irreverenza; inciviltà, *f.* **-rĕst**, S.: inquietudine, *f.*; affanno, *m.* **-restōred**, ADJ.: non restituito. **-restrâined**, ADJ.: non ritenuto, non limitato. **-retrăcted**, ADJ.: non rivocato. **-revēaled**, ADJ.: non rivelato. **-revĕnged**, ADJ.: invendicato, inulto. **-rĕverend**, ADJ.: irreverente, senza rispetto. **-rĕverently**†, ADV.: irreverentemente. **-revōked**, ADJ.: non rivocato, non abrogato. **-rewârded**, ADJ.: non rimunerato. **-riddle**, TR.: *spiegare, scoprire,* dichiarare. **-rig**, TR.: *togliere le sarte.* **-righteous**, ADJ.: ingiusto, iniquo. **-righteously**, ADV.: ingiustamente. **-righteousness**, S.: iniquità; empietà, *f.* **-rightful**, ADJ.: ingiusto, iniquo. **-ring**, TR.: pigliare via l' anello. **-rip**, (IN)TR.: scucire; sguarciare. **-ripe(ned)**, ADJ.: immaturo, crudo. **-ripeness**, S.: immaturità, crudezza, *f.* **-rivalled**, ADJ.: senza rivale, impareggiabile. **-rōbe**, TR.: spogliare. **-rōll**, TR.: sviluppare, spiegare, svolgere. **-rōof**, TR.: levar via il tetto. **-rōost**, (IN)TR.: snidiare. **-rōot**, TR.: sradicare; estirpare. **-rōyal**, ADJ.: indegno d' un re. **-rŭffle**, INTR.: calmarsi, abbonacciarsi, tranquillarsi. **-rŭffled**, ADJ.: calmo, tranquillo, quieto. **-rūled**, ADJ.: non regolato. **-rūlily**, ADV.: sregolatamente, in modo sregolato. **-rūliness**, S.: sregolatezza, turbolenza, *f.* **-rūly**, ADJ.: sregolato, turbolento. **-săddle**, TR.: levare la sella. **-sâfe**, ADJ.: non sicuro, pericoloso. **-sâfely**, ADJ.: pericolosamente. **-sâid**, ADJ.: non pronunziato, non mentovato; disdetto. **-săl(e)able**, ADJ.: non vendibile. **-sâlted**, ADJ.: non salato. **-salūted**, ADJ.: non salutato. **-sănctified**, ADJ.: non santificato. **-sâtiable**†, ADJ.: insaziabile, insaturabile. **-satisfăctoriness**†, S.: mancanza di dare soddisfazione, scontentezza, *f.* **-satisfăctory**, ADJ.: non soddisfattorio; imperfetto. **-sătisfied**, ADJ.: non soddisfatto, scontento. **-sătisfiedness**, S.: scontento; cattivo umore, *m.* **-sătisfying**, ADJ.: non soddisfacente. **-sâvourily**, ADV.: insipidamente, in modo insipido. **-sâvouriness**, S.: insipidezza, *f.* **-sâvoury**, ADJ.: non saporito; non saporoso; insipido; stomachevole. **-sây**, IRR.; (IN)TR.: disdirsi; ritrattarsi, negare. **-scâle**, TR.: levar le scaglie, scagliare. **-scâly**, ADJ.: senza scaglie. **-scănned**, ADJ.: non misurato. **-scârred**, ADJ.: senza cicatrici. **-scholăstic**, ADJ.: non scolastico, illetterato. **-schōoled**, ADJ.: non addottrinato, non educato, non dotto. **-scôrched**, ADJ.: non abbruciato. **-screēned**, ADJ.: non coperto, non difeso. **-screw** *scrū*, TR.: svolgere la vite, svitare. **-scriptural**, ADJ.: non fondato nella bibbia. **-scrūpulous**, ADJ.: senza scrupoli. **-sēal**, TR.: levar il sigillo di, dissigillare, dissuggellare; aprire: — *a letter*, dissigillare (aprire) una lettera. **-sēaled**, ADJ.: dissuggellato; non sigillato. **-sēam**, TR.: scuscire, scucire. **-sēarchable**, ADJ.: imperscrutabile. **-sēarchableness**, S.: qualità imperscrutabile; incomprensibilità, *f.* **-sēasonable**, ADJ.: fuor(i) di stagione, intempestivo, improprio: — *hour*, ora indebita, *f.*; — *weather*, tempo

ened, ADJ.: non fermentato: — *bread*, pane azzimo.

ŭnless, CONJ.: a meno che, fuorchè; eccetto, eccettuato che, se non: — *you study more*, a meno che non studiate di più.

un-lĕttered, ADJ.: non letterato, ignorante. **-lĕvelled**, ADJ.: non spianato, ineguale. **-licensed**, ADJ.: senza licenza. **-licked**, ADJ.: non leccato, sformato. **-lighted**, ADJ.: non acceso, non illuminato. **-like**, ADJ.: differente, dissimile, diverso; improbabile. **-likelihood**, **-likeliness**, S.: improbabilità, *f.* **-likely**, ADJ.: improbabile. **-likely**, ADV.: improbabilmente. **-likeness**, S.: dissimiglianza, differenza, *f.* **-limitable**†, ADJ.: che non può esser limitato, immenso. **-limited**, ADJ.: illimitato. **-limitedly**, ADV.: illimitatamente, senza limiti. **-limitedness**, S.: illimitazione, *f.* **-line**, TR.: levar via la fodera, sfoderare. **-lineal**, ADJ.: collaterale. **-link**, TR.: storcere, svolgere, spiegare, aprire. **-liquified**, ADJ.: non liquefatto. **-lōad**, IRR.; TR.: scaricare, alleggerire. **-lōading**, S.: scaricamento, *m.* **-lŏck**, TR.: schiavare; sfogarsi. **-looked** (*for*), ADJ.: inaspettato, inopinato. **-lōose**, TR.: sciorre, slegare, disfare; INTR.: sciorsi, slegarsi, disfarsi. **-lŏved**†, ADJ.: disamato, odiato. **-lŏvely**, ADJ.: non amabile; svenevole. **lŭckily**, ADV.: per mala fortuna, per disgrazia, *f.* **-lŭckiness**, S.: disavventura; disgrazia, *f.* **-lŭcky**, ADJ.: sfortunato, sinistro. **-lūte**, TR.: togliere il loto. **-māde**, ADJ.: non ancora fatto, non finito. **-māimed**, ADJ.: non mutilato, non troncato. **-mākable**†, ADJ.: che non si può fare. **-māke**, IRR.; TR.: disfare, distruggere; mettere in pezzi. **-măn**, TR.: effeminare; degradare; disarmare (un vascello). **-mănageable**, ADJ.: intrattabile, indocile. **-mănaged**, ADJ.: non addestrato, non educato. **-mănliness**, S.: condotta indegna d' un uomo, *f.* **-mănly**, ADJ.: indegno d'un uomo. **-mănnered**, ADJ.: incivile, scortese; rozzo, ruvido. **-mănnerliness**, S.: scortesia, inciviltà; rozzezza, ruvidezza, *f.* **-măn-** [illegible] **ly** [1], ADJ.: incivile, rozzo, grossolano. [illegible] **-nnerly** [2], ADV.: incivilmente, rozza- [illegible] **-manūred**, ADJ.: non coltivato, [illegible] **-mārked**, ADJ.: non osservato. [illegible] ADJ.: senza marito; senza [illegible] smogliato, *m.*; — [illegible] *f.* **-mărry**†, [illegible] **-māsk**, [illegible] cherarsi. [illegible]

invincibile. **-māstered**, ADJ.: indomito; invincibile. **-măt**, TR.: disfare le trecce. **-mătch**, TR.: dispaiare. **-mătchable**, ADJ.: impareggiabile, incomparabile. **-mătched**, ADJ.: senza pari. **-mĕaning**, ADJ.: senza senso, insignificante. **-mĕant**†, ADJ.: non proposto, non disegnato. **-mĕasurable**†, ADJ.: che non può misurarsi, smisurato, immenso. **-mĕasurableness**†, S.: smisuratezza, immensità, *f.* **-mĕasurably**†, ADV.: senza misura, eccessivamente. **-mĕasured**, ADJ.: non misurato, immenso. **-mĕditated**, ADJ.: non premeditato. **-mĕddled**, ADJ.: immisto, inalterato. **-mēet**, ADJ.: non conveniente, sconvenevole. **-mēetly**, ADV.: sconvenevolmente, incongruentemente. **-mēetness**, S.: sconvenevolezza, incongruità, *f.* **-melōdious**, ADJ.: non melodioso. **-mĕlted**, ADJ.: non liquefatto. **-mĕntioned**, ADJ.: non mentovato, omesso. **-mĕrchantable**, ADJ.: non vendibile. **-mĕrciful**, ADJ.: spietato; inumano, crudele. **-mĕrcifully**, ADV.: spietatamente; inumanamente. **-mĕrcifulness**, S.: inumanità, crudeltà, *f.* **-mĕritable**, ADJ.: immeritevole. **-mĕrited**, ADJ.: non meritato, ingiusto. **-milked**, ADJ.: non munto. **-minded**, ADJ.: non osservato, negletto. **-mindful**, ADJ.: negligente, trascurato. **-mindfully**, ADV.: negligentemente, trascuratamente. **-mindfulness**, S.: negligenza, trascuraggine, *f.* **-mingle**, TR.: separare. **-mingled**, ADJ.: immisto, semplice. **-mistākable**, ADJ.: che non può sbagliarsi, evidente. **-mitigated**, ADJ.: non mitigato, implacabile; completo, perfetto. **-mixed**, **-mixt**, ADJ.: immisto, schietto, puro. **-mōaned**, ADJ.: non deplorato, non compianto. **-moistened**, ADJ.: non umettato, inumidito. **-molĕsted**, ADJ.: non molestato. **-mōor**, TR.: (*nav.*) sarpare, levare l' ancora. **-môrtgaged**, ADJ.: non dato in ipoteca, **-môrtified**, ADJ.: immortificato. **-mōv(e)able**†, ADJ.: immobile, fermo. **-mōv(e)ably**†, ADV.: immobilmente, fermamente. **-mōved**, ADJ.: immoto, fermo. **-mōving**, ADJ.: immobile. **-mōuld**, TR.: mutare la forma. **-mōurned**, ADJ.: non deplorato, non lamentato. **-mŭffle**, TR.: smascherare. **-mūsical**, ADJ.: non armonioso, discordante. **-mŭzzle**, TR.: torre la museruola. **-nāil**, TR.: schiodare. **-nāmed**, ADJ.: innominato, senza nome. **-nātive**, ADJ.: non nativo. **-nătural**, ADJ.: non naturale, contra natura, snaturato, crudele; sforzato, ricercato. **-năturally**, ADV.: contra natura; inumanamente, crudelmente. **-năturalness**, S.: inumanità, brutalità, *f.* **-năvigable**,

s.: incostanza, leggerezza, *f.* **-stĕadily**, ADV.: incostantemente, leggermente. **-stĕadiness**, s.: incostanza, leggerezza, *f.* **-stĕady**, ADJ.: incostante; irresoluto, leggiero. **-stēeped**, ADJ.: non tuffato, non macerato. **-stinted**, ADJ.: non limitato. **-stirred**, ADJ.: non mosso. **-stitch**, TR.: scucire; disfare. **-stŏck**, TR.: smontare (uno schioppo). **-stōoping**, ADJ.: inflessibile; non condiscendente. **-stŏp**, TR.: sturare; aprire. **-strāined**, ADJ.: non forzato; non colato; facile. **-strāitened**, ADJ.: non contratto, non ristretto. **-strĕngthened**†, ADJ.: non rinforzato; non difeso. **-string**, TR.: levare le corde; slegare. **-strŭck**, ADJ.: non rimosso: — *with horror*, non atterrito. **-strŭng**, ADJ.: scordato, slegato. **-stŭdied**, ADJ.: non istudiato, non premeditato. **-stŭffed**, ADJ.: non ripieno. **-subdūed**, ADJ.: non soggiogato, indomito. **-substăntial**, ADJ.: non sostanziale, poco solido. **-succēeded**†, ADJ.: non succeduto, non seguitato. **-succĕssful**, ADJ.: senza successo, malaguroso, infelice. **-succĕssfully**, ADV.: senza successo, senza riuscita. **-succĕssfulness**, s.: cattivo successo, *m.*; sventura, *f.* **-sŭcked**, ADJ.: non succiato, non allattato. **-sŭfferable**†, ADJ.: insopportabile, intollerabile. **-sŭfferably**†, ADV.: insopportabilmente, intollerabilmente. **-sufficient**†, ADJ.: insufficiente. **-sŭgared**, ADJ.: non zuccherato. **-sūitable**, ADJ.: non adattato, non idoneo, disadatto, sconvenevole; indecente; incongruo. **-sūitableness**, s.: sconvenevolezza; incongruità, *f.* **-sŭllied**, ADJ.: immacolato; intatto, puro. **-sŭng**, ADJ.: non celebrato in versi. **-sŭnned**, ADJ.: non aprico, non esposto al sole. **-supĕrfluous**†, ADJ.: non superfluo. **-supplănted**, ADJ.: non soppiantato. **-supplied**, ADJ.: sprovveduto, sfornito. **-suppōrtable**†, ADJ.: insopportabile. **-suppōrtableness**†, s.: stato insopportabile, *m.* **-suppōrtably**†, ADV.: insopportabilmente. **-suppōrted**, ADJ.: non sostenuto, non aiutato. **-sūre**, ADJ.: incerto, non sicuro. **-surmŏuntable**, ADJ.: insormontabile. **-suscĕptible**, ADJ.: non suscettibile. **-suspĕcted**, ADJ.: non sospetto. **-suspĕcting**, **-suspicious**, ADJ.: non sospettoso, non sospicioso. **-sustāinable**, ADJ.: non sostenibile. **-sustāined**, ADJ.: non sostenuto. **-swāthe** TR.: sfasciare (un bambino). **-swāyed**, ADJ.: non maneggiabile; restio. **-swĕar**, IRR.; INTR.: abgiurare, ritrattarsi. **-swĕar**†, INTR.: rilassarsi; riposarsi. **-swōrn**, ADJ.: non affermato con giuramento. **-tāinted**, ADJ.: non macchiato, non corrotto. **-tāintedness**, s.: incorruzione, *f.* **-tălked** (*of*), ADJ.: non menzionato; non rinomato, incelebre. **-tām(e)able**, ADJ.: indomabile; intrattabile. **-tāmed**, ADJ.: indomito. **-tăngle**, TR.: sviluppare; distrigare. **-tāsted**, ADJ.: non gustato, non assaggiato. **-tāsting**, ADJ.: senza gusto. **-tāught**, ADJ.: non insegnato; ignorante. **-tēach**, IRR.; TR.: fare disimparare. **-tēachable**, ADJ.: che non vuole imparare; indocile. **-tĕmpered**, ADJ.: non temperato. **-tĕmpted**, ADJ.: non tentato, non allettato. **-tĕnable**, ADJ.: da non tenersi, non difensibile. **-tĕnanted**, ADJ.: non affittato, senza pigionale. **-tĕnded**, ADJ.: senza seguito. **-tĕnder**, ADJ.: non tenero; insensibile. **-tĕrrified**, ADJ.: intrepido. **-thănked**, ADJ.: non ringraziato. **-thănkful**, ADJ.: sconoscente, ingrato. **-thănkfully**, ADV.: sconoscentemente, ingratamente. **-thănkfulness**, s.: sconoscenza, ingratitudine, *f.* **-thāwed**, ADJ.: non dighiacciato. **-think**, IRR.; TR.: dimenticare, dimettere il pensiero. **-thinking**, ADJ.: spensierato, indiscreto. **-thought** *-thăt* (*of*), ADJ.: impensato, inopinato. **-thrĕad**, TR.: sfilare; sciorre. **-thrĕatened**, ADJ.: non minacciato. **-thrift**†, ADJ.: stravagante, profuso, prodigo. **-thriftly**, ADV.: profusamente, prodigamente. **-thriftiness**, s.: prodigalità, *f.*, scialacquo, *m.* **-thrifty**, ADJ.: prodigo, profuso. **-thriving**, ADJ.: che non cresce; senza successo. **-thrōne**, TR.: privare del trono. **-tidy**, ADJ.: non pulito, non ornato. **-tie**, TR.: slegare, snodare, sciogliere, sciorre: — *a knot*, sciorre un nodo.

until, PREP., CONJ.: sino a, sino a che, infino a: — *now*, finora, sinora; — *then*, fin' allora; — *next week*, sino alla settimana ventura; — *he arrive*, finchè egli non arrivi.

un-tilled, ADJ.: incolto, non coltivato. **-timbered**, ADJ.: non sostenuto da travi. **-timed**, ADJ.: fatto fuor di tempo. **-timely** 1, ADJ.: intempestivo, inopportuno: — *hour*, fuor d' ora. **-timely** 2, ADV.: intempestivamente. **-tinged**, ADJ.: non tinto, non scolorito; non infettato. **-tirable**, ADJ.: infaticabile; indefesso. **-tired**, ADJ.: non istancato, non faticato. **-titled**, ADJ.: senza titolo.

untō, PREP.: a, ad, in; per.

un-tōld, ADJ.: non detto, non contato. **-tōmb**, TR.: dissotterrare. **-tŏuched**, ADJ.: intatto, non toccato. **-tōward**, ADJ.: sfavorevole, contrario; caparbio, ostinato, perverso. **-tōwardly** 1, ADJ.: disaddatto, sgraziato, perverso. **-tōwardly** 2, ADV.: sinistramente, infelicemente.

-pórtable, ADJ.: non portabile. **-possessed**, ADJ.: non posseduto. **-possessing**, ADJ.: non possedente. **-práctio-able**†, ADJ.: impraticabile, da non farsi. **-práctised**, ADJ.: non praticato, inesperto. **-práised**†, ADJ.: non lodato. **-precárious**, ADJ.: indipendente. **-précedented**, ADJ.: senza esempio. **-precise**, ADJ.: non preciso, non esatto. **-preférred**, ADJ.: non avanzato, non promosso. **-préjudiced**, ADJ.: spregiudicato, non preoccupato, non prevenuto. **-premeditated**, ADJ.: non premeditato. **-prepáred**, ADJ.: non preparato, impreparato. **-prepáredness**, S.: esser impreparato, *m.* **-prepossessed**, ADJ.: non preoccupato, non prevenuto. **-prepossessing**, ADJ.: non avvenente. **-préssed**, ADJ.: non spremuto. **-presúmptuous**, ADJ.: non presuntuoso. **-preténding**, ADJ.: poco ambizioso. **-preváiling**, ADJ.: inefficace. **-prevénted**, ADJ.: non impedito, non opposto. **-príncely**†, ADJ.: indegno d' un principe. **-principled**, ADJ.: senza principi. **-printed**, ADJ.: non stampato. **-prizable**†, ADJ.: di poco valore, inestimabile. **-prisoned**, ADJ.: non imprigionato, libero. **-prized**†, ADJ.: non apprezzato, inestimato. **-procláimed**, ADJ.: non proclamato. **-prodúctive**, ADJ.: improduttivo, infruttifero: — *capital*, capitale infruttifero. **-prodúctively**, ADJ.: improduttivamente, senza profitto. **-prodúctiveness**, S.: improduttività, infertilità, *f.* **-proféssional**, ADJ.: non della professione. **-proféssionally**, ADV.: non professionalmente. **-profáned**, ADJ.: non profanato. **-prófitable**, ADJ.: non profittevole; inutile, vano. **-prófitableness**, S.: inutilità, *f.* **-prófitably**, ADV.: senza profitto; inutilmente. **-prófited**, ADJ.: senza profitto, senza guadagno, senza vantaggio. **-prolific**, ADJ.: infecondo, sterile. **-próper**†, ADJ.: improprio; non particolare. **-próperly**†, ADV.: impropriamente. **-propítious**, ADJ.: non propizio, non favorevole. **-propórtionable**, **-propórtioned**, ADJ.: sproporzionato. **-própped**, ADJ.: non puntellato, non sostenuto. **-propósed**, ADJ.: non proposto. **-prósperous**, ADJ.: non fortunato, infelice. **-prósperously**, ADV.: [illegible]mente. **-prósperousness**, S.: in[illegible] **-[illegible]ted**, ADJ.: non pro[illegible] **-[illegible]wed**, ADJ.: non [illegible] **-provide**†, [illegible] **-provided**, [illegible] **-[illegible]ned**, [illegible] **-[illegible]ib-**[illegible]

ADJ.: non pubblicato, non divolgato; inedito. **-púnished**, ADJ.: impunito. **-púrchased**, ADJ.: non comprato. **-púrged**, **-púrified**, ADJ.: non purificato, impuro. **-púrposed**, ADJ.: non progettato. **-pursúed**, ADJ.: non perseguito. **-quálified**, ADJ.: inabile, inetto. **-quálifiedness**, S.: inabilità, incapacità, *f.* **-quálify**†, TR.: rendere incapace. **-quárrelable**†, ADJ.: incontrastabile, indisputabile. **-quéen**, TR.: deporre una regina. **-quénchable**, ADJ.: inestinguibile. **-quénchableness**, S.: qualità inestinguibile. **-quéstionable**, ADJ.: indubitabile, incontrastabile; certo. **-quéstionableness**, S.: certezza, *f.* **-quéstionably**, ADV.: indubitabilmente, certamente. **-quéstioned**, ADJ.: non domandato, indubitato. **-quick**, ADJ.: immobile. **-quiet**, ADJ.: inquieto, agitato. **-quietly**, ADV.: inquietamente. **-quietness**, **-quietude**†, S.: inquietudine, *f.*; travaglio, *m.* **-rácked**, ADJ.: non travasato. **-ránsacked**, ADJ.: non saccheggiato. **-ránsomed**, ADJ.: non riscattato, non redento. **-rável**, TR.: sviluppare, schiarire. **-rásored**, ADJ.: non raso. **-réached**, ADJ.: non arrivato, non ottenuto. **-réad**, ADJ.: non letto; ignorante. **-réadiness**, S.: inabilità, *f.* **-réady**, ADJ.: non parato; pesante; restio. **-réal**, ADJ.: non reale, senza realità. **-réasonable**, ADJ.: irragionevole; esorbitante. **-réasonableness**, S.: poca ragione; esorbitanza, enormità, *f.* **-réasonably**, ADV.: irragionevolmente; eccessivamente. **-réave**†, TR.: sviluppare; disfare. **-rebúkable**, ADJ.: irreprensibile. **-recéived**, ADJ.: non ricevuto, non pigliato. **-récompensed**, ADJ.: non compensato, non rimunerato. **-reconcilable**, ADJ.: irreconciliabile. **-réconciled**, ADJ.: non reconciliato. **-recórded**, ADJ.: non mentovato; non trasmesso alla posterità. **-recóverable**, ADJ.: irrecuperabile. **-recóvered**, ADJ.: non ricuperato. **-recóunted**, ADJ.: non raccontato. **-recrúitable**, ADJ.: da non reclutarsi. **-recúring**†, ADJ.: irremediabile, senza rimedio. **-redéemable**†, ADJ.: non redimibile. **-redéemed**†, ADJ.: non redento, disimpegnato. **-redúced**, ADJ.: non ridotto; non sottomesso. **-refíned**, ADJ.: non raffinato. **-refórmable**, ADJ.: incorrigibile; inalterabile. **-refórmed**, ADJ.: non riformato. **-refrácted**, ADJ.: non rifratto. **-refréshed**, ADJ.: non riconfortato, non ricreato. **-regárded**, ADJ.: negletto, disprezzato. **-regárdful**, ADJ.: non curante, negligente. **-regénerate**, ADJ.: non regenerato. **-réined**, ADJ.: sfrena-

vertentemente. **-witty** †, ADJ.: sciocco, stupido. **-wónted**, ADJ.: insolito; non comune, raro. **-wŏrking**, ADJ.: senza lavorare. **-wŏrshipped**, ADJ.: non adorato. **-wŏrthily**, ADV.: indegnamente. **-wŏrthiness**, S.: indegnità, mancanza di merito, *f.* **-wŏrthy**, ADJ.: indegno, immeritevole. **-wŏund**, ADJ.: distrigato, sviluppato. **-wŏunded**, ADJ.: non piagato. **-wrăp**, TR.: sviluppare, sciogliere. **-wrēathe**, TR.: storcere; svoltare. **-wrinkle**, TR.: levar via le rughe. **-written**, ADJ.: non iscritto. **-rought** *-răt*, ADJ.: non lavorato, crudo. **-yielded**, ADJ.: non ceduto. **-yielding**, ADJ.: restio; inflessibile. **-yōke**, TR.: sciorre dal giogo, disgiogare; disgiungere. **-yōked**, ADJ.: sfrenato, dissoluto.

ŭp 1, PREP.: su, sur, sopra, sovra, di sopra. **up** 2, ADV.: su, in su, da basso in alto, in alto; sopra: — *there*, colassù; *the sun is* —, il sole è sorto; — *stairs*, di sopra; — *and down*, su e giù; qua e là; — *on end*, in piedi ritto; *be* —, essere in piedi, esser levato dal letto; esser finito; *not be* — *to a thing*, non ci arrivare; *look* —, guardare in su; *get* —, montare, salire; *do* — *a letter*, piegare una lettera; *rise* —, levarsi; *stand* —, stare in piedi, levarsi; *stand* —*!* alzatevi in piedi! **up**3, INTERJ.: su! levatevi! **-bêar**, IRR.; TR.: sostenere in alto, alzare; sopportare. **-brăid**, TR.: rimproverare, rinfacciare; vilipendere. **-brăider**, S.: rimproveratore, *m.* **-brăiding**, S.: rimproveramento, *m.* **-brăidingly**, ADV.: in modo riprendevole. **-brought** *-brăt*, ADJ.: allevato, nutrito; educato. **-căst** 1, ADJ.: lanciato, mandato in alto. **-cast** 2, S.: gettata, *f.*; tiro, *m.* **-drăw**, IRR.; TR.: tirare su. **-găther** †, TR.: ristringere, contrarre. **-hĕld**, ADJ.: sostenuto, mantenuto, sopportato. **-hill**, ADJ.: difficile; penoso, laborioso. **-hōard** †, TR.: accumulare, ammucchiare. **-hōld**, IRR.; TR.: sostenere; mantenere; proteggere, favorire. **-hōlder**, S.: fautore; somministratore, *m.* **-hōlding**, S.: sostegno, appoggio, mantenimento, *m.*; difesa, *f.* **-hōlsterer**, S.: tappezziere, *m.* **-hōlstery**, S.: tappezzeria, *f.* **-land** 1, S.: paese montagnoso, *m.*; montagne, *f. pl.* **-land** 2, ADJ.: montagnoso; alto. **-lander** †, S.: montanaro, *m.* **-landish** †, ADJ.: montagnoso, montanino. **-lāy** †, IRR.; TR.: ammucchiare, ammassare. **-lift**, TR.: alzare, inalzare, elevare. **-most** †, ADJ.: il più alto, superiore. **-ŏn**, PREP.: su, sopra; per: — *my conscience*, in coscienza mia; — *my word*, sulla mia parola; — *the whole*, in complesso, in sostanza, in fine; — *the right hand*, a man dritta; — *any occasion*, in ogni occasione; — *pain of death*, sotto pena della vita; — *this*, su questo punto, con ciò; — *trial*, a prova; — *the whole*, del resto, in fine; *depend* —, dipendere da, contare su. **-per**, ADJ.: superiore, più alto, di sopra: *have the* — *hand*, avere il sopravvento, avere il di su. **-permost**, ADJ.: superiore; predominante: *be* —, restare superiore. **-pish**, ADJ.: arrogante, altiero. **-pishness**, S.: arroganza, alterezza, *f.* **-răise**, TR.: elevare; esaltare. **-rēar**, TR.: alzare, innalzare. **-right**, ADJ.: eretto, ritto; dritto, giusto; sincero, onesto. **-rightly**, ADV.: dirittamente; giustamente; sinceramente, onestamente. **-rightness**, S.: dirittezza; sincerità, onestà, *f.* **-rise** 1, S.: sorgere, apparire all' orizzonte. **-roar** 1, S.: tumulto, romore, fracasso, *m.* **-rōar** † 2, TR.: mettere in confusione. **-rōll**, TR.: involgere. **-rōot**, INTR.: sradicare, estirpare. **-rōuse**, TR.: svegliare; eccitare, stimolare, incoraggiare. **-sĕt**, IRR.; TR.: rovesciare. **-shot**, S.: esito; evento, successo, *m.*; fine, *f.* **-side-down**, ADV.: sossopra, sozzopra. **-stănd** †, IRR.; INTR.: stare in piedi; esser eretto. **-start** 1, S.: villano rifatto, *m.* **-stârt** 2, INTR.: saltare su repentinamente. **-stāy**, IRR.; TR.: sostenere; spalleggiare, puntellare; sopportare. **-swărm** †, TR.: bulicare; abbondare. **-têar**, IRR.; TR.: stracciare. **-trăin** †, TR.: allevare, educare. **-tûrn**, TR.: gettare su; solcare. **-ward**, ADJ.: alzato, elevato. **-ward(s)**, ADV.: in su, in alto: — *of*, più di, oltre, sopra; *ten and* —*s*, dieci e più.

uranŏgraphy, S.: uranografia, *f.*

ŭr-bane, ADJ.: urbano, cortese, civile. **-bănity**, S.: urbanità, cortesia, civiltà, *f.* **-banise** †, TR.: render urbano, render cortese.

ŭrchin, S.: riccio; bambino restio, birichino, *m.*: *sea* —, riccio marino, echino, *m.*

ūre †, S.: uso, costume, *m.*; pratica, *f.*: *keep in* —, esercitare, metter in pratica.

urēthra, S.: (*anat.*) uretra, *f.*

ŭr-ge, TR.: sollecitare, eccitare, stimolare, istigare, provocare; pregare con istanza: — *a reason*, adoperare un argomento; — *on*, sospingere, incalzare. **-gency**, S.: urgenza, necessità urgente, *f.* **-gent**, ADJ.: urgente, cogente. **-gently**, ADV.: urgentemente, istantemente, con istanza. **-ger**, S.: importuno, stimolatore, *m.*

ūri-nal, S.: orinale, *m.* **-nary**, ADJ.: urinario, orinale. **-nate**, **-ne** † 1, INTR.: orinare. **-ne** 2, S.: orina, *f.* **-nous**, ADJ.: orinoso, di orina.

ŭrn, S.: urna, *f.*

ŭs, PRON.: noi, per noi, ci: *he told* —, ci disse.

fuor di stagione. **-sèasonableness**, S.: inconvenienza, *f.* **-sèasonably**, ADV.: intempestivamente, fuor di stagione. **-sèasoned**, ADJ.: non condito; inopportuno, intempestivo; irregolare. **-sěconded**, ADJ.: non assistito. **-sècret**†, ADJ.: non secreto, non fidato. **-sęcūre**†, ADJ.: non sicuro, non certo. **-sędūced**, ADJ.: non sedotto, non corrotto. **-sèeing**, ADJ.: senza vedere, cieco. **-sèem**, TR.: non parere, non sembrare. **-sèemliness**, S.: sconvenevolezza, indecenza, *f.* **-sèemly**, ADJ.: sconvenevole, indecente; ADV.: sconvenevolmente, indecentemente. **-sèen**, ADJ.: non veduto; invisibile. **-sělfish**, ADJ.: disinteressato, senza interesse. **-sěnt**, ADJ.: non mandato: — *for*, non mandato a cercare. **-sěparable**†, ADJ.: inseparabile, indivisibile. **-sěparated**, ADJ.: non separato, indiviso. **-sěrviceable**, ADJ.: che non può servire, inutile. **-sěrviceableness**, S.: inutilità, *f.* **-sěrviceably**, ADV.: inutilmente. **-sět**, ADJ.: non messo; non piantato. **-sěttle**, TR.: rendere incerto; disordinare. **-sěttled**, ADJ.: non fisso; irresoluto, incostante: — *state*, perturbazione, disordine. **-sěttledness**, S.: irresoluzione, incostanza, *f.* **-sěvered**, ADJ.: non separato, non diviso. **-sew** *-sō*, scuscire, scucire. **-shăckle**, TR.: scatenare; sciorre i ceppi. **-shāded**, **-shādowed**, ADJ.: non ombrato, scoperto. **-shāken**, ADJ.: non smosso, fermo, costante. **-shāmed**, ADJ.: non svergognato. **-shāmefaced**, ADJ.: sfacciato, sfrontato. **-shamefacedness**, S.: sfacciataggine, *f.* **-shāpen**, ADJ.: sformato, deformo, malfatto. **-shāred**, ADJ.: non spartito. **-shāved**, **-shāven**, ADJ.: non raso, non barbato. **-shèathe**, INTR.: sguainare, cavar dalla guaina. **-shěd**, ADJ.: non effuso, non versato. **-shěltered**, ADJ.: non protetto, senza difesa. **-ship**, TR.: sbarcare: — *the rudder*, torre il timone. **-shŏcked**, ADJ.: non offeso. **-shŏd**, ADJ.: scalzo, senza scarpe; sferrato. **-shŏe**, TR.: sferrare (un cavallo). **-shŏrn**, ADJ.: non tonduto, non tosato. **-shŏt**, ADJ.: non tirato, mancato. **-shrinking**, ADJ.: intimidito, intrepido. **-shrinkingly**, ADV.: intrepidamente. **-shŭnnable**, ADJ.: inevitabile. **-shŭt**†, ADJ.: non chiuso, aperto. **-sifted**, ADJ.: non crivellato; non sperimentato. **-sight**, ADJ.: senza vedere. **-sighted**†, ADJ.: invisibile; impercettibile. **-sightliness**, S.: difformità, laidezza, *f.* **-sightly**, ADJ.: spia- ole alla vista, difforme. **-sincère**†, non sincero, dissimulato. **-sincèr-** dissimulazione, falsità, *f.* .: snervare, debilitare.

-si'nèwed, ADJ.: snervato, debilitato, debole. **-singed**, ADJ.: non abbrustiato, non iscottato. **-sinning**, ADJ.: senza peccato, impeccabile. **-skilful**, ADJ.: inesperto, inetto, ignorante. **-skilfully**, ADV.: disadattamente; da ignorante. **-skilfulness**, S.: disadattaggine; ignoranza, *f.* **-skilled**, ADJ.: inesperto, inetto, ignorante. **-slāin**, ADJ.: non ucciso. **-slāked**, ADJ.: non estinto. **-slèeping**, ADJ.: senza dormire, sempre vigilante. **-slipping**, ADJ.: fermo, stretto, serrato. **-smirched**, ADJ.: non isporcato, immacolato. **-smōked**, ADJ.: non affumato. **-sōciable**, ADJ.: insociabile; non benevolo. **-sōciableness**, S.: disposizione insociabile, *f.*, umore solitario, *m.* **-sōciably**, ADV.: in modo insociabile. **-sŏdden**, ADJ.: non bollito. **-sōiled**, ADJ.: non macchiato. **-sold**, ADJ.: non venduto. **-sŏlder**, TR.: levare la saldatura. **-sōldierlike**, **-sōldierly**, ADJ.: non da soldato. **-sōle**, TR.: levare le suole. **-solicited**, ADJ.: non sollecitato. **-sŏlid**, ADJ.: non solido; fluido; non coerente. **-sŏlved**, ADJ.: non soluto, non ispiegato. **-sophisticated**, ADJ.: non falsificato, puro, verace, innocente; semplice. **-sought** *sât*, ADJ.: non ricercato. **-sōund**, ADJ.: non sano, malsano, malaticcio; corrotto, guasto, non onesto; erroneo, falso; insano. **-sōunded**, ADJ.: non scandagliato. **-sōundness**, S.: miscredenza; mancanza di solidità, *f.* **-sōured**, ADJ.: non acido; non arcigno. **-sōwn**, ADJ.: non seminato. **-spāred**, ADJ.: non risparmiato. **-spāring**, ADJ.: non sordido, liberale. **-spèakable**, ADJ.: ineffabile; inesprimibile. **-spèakably**, ADV.: indicibilmente, in modo ineffabile. **-spěcified**, ADJ.: non ispecificato. **-spěculative**, ADJ.: non ispeculativo. **-spěd**†, ADJ.: non ispedito, non fatto. **-spěnt**, ADJ.: non ispeso, non consumato. **-spied**, ADJ.: non ispiato; non iscoperto. **-spilt**, ADJ.: non versato, non isparso. **-spirit**†, TR.: discoraggiare, scoraggire. **-spiritualize**, TR.: privare di spiritualità. **-spōiled**, ADJ.: non saccheggiato, non guasto. **-spŏtted**, ADJ.: non contaminato, immacolato, puro. **-spŏttedness**, S.: incontaminatezza, *f.* **-stability**, S.: incostanza, *f.* **-stāble**, ADJ.: instabile, incostante. **-stāid**, ADJ.: incostante; mutabile. **-stāidness**, S.: incostanza, volubilità, *f.* **-stāined**, ADJ.: non macchiato, puro. **-stāte**†, TR.: mettere fuor di stato. **-stătutable**, ADJ.: contrario agli statuti. **-stâunched**, ADJ.: non ristagnato, non arrestato. **-stèadfast**, ADJ.: non fisso, non solido. **-stèadfastly**, ADV.: senza fermezza. **-stèadfastness**,

vălance 1, S.: pendaglio; drappellone, *m.* **valance** 2, TR.: ornare con degli arazzi.
vāle, S.: valle, vallatta; caparra, *f.*
valedic-tion, S.: addio; commiato, *m.*; licenza, *f.* **-tory**, ADJ.: d'addio; di commiato, di licenza.
vălentine, S.: valentino, *m.*
valērian, S.: (*bot.*) valeriana, *f.*
vălet, S.: servo, servitore; fante, *m.*
vale-tudinārian, **-tūdinary** 1, ADJ.: valetudinario, malaticcio. **-tudinary** 2, S.: infermeria, *f.*
valian-ce, **-cy**, S.: valore, *m.*, forza, *f.*, coraggio, *m.* **-t**, ADJ.: valoroso, coraggioso. **-tly**, ADV.: valorosamamente, con coraggio. **-tness**, S.: valore, *m.*, virtù; bravura, *f.*
văl-id, ADJ.: valido; efficace. **-idāte**, TR.: render valido. **-idātion** †, S.: corroborazione, *f.* **-idity**, S.: validità; forza, *f.*, valore, *m.*
valise, S.: portamantello, *m.*
vallātion, S.: vallata, trincea, *f.*
vălley, S.: valle, vallata, *f.*: *little* —, valletta, vallicella, *f.*; *large* —, vallone, *m.*
vălo(u)r, S.: valore, *m.*; forza, *f.* **-ous**, ADJ.: valoroso, coraggioso.
vălu-able, ADJ.: di gran prezzo, prezioso. **-ableness**, S.: valore, prezzo, *m.* **-ātion**, S.: valuta; stima, *f.*, prezzo, *m.* **-ator**, S.: stimatore, apprezzatore, *m.* **-e** 1, S.: valore, *m.*; valuta; stimazione, considerazione, *f.*: *for — received*, per valuta avuta; *be of some* —, valer qualche cosa; *set a great* —, fare grande stima. **-e** 2, TR.: valutare; stimare, apprezzare. **-ed**, ADJ.: pregiato, apprezzato, stimato: *highly* —, molto apprezzato, stimatissimo. **-eless**, ADJ.: di nessun valore. **-er**, S.: stimatore, apprezzatore, *m.* **-ing**, S.: valuta; stima, *f.*
văl-ve, S.: porta a due imposte; coperchio, *m.*; valvola, *f.*: *steam* —, valvola a vapore, *f.* **-vule**, S.: valvula, *f.*
vămp 1, S.: tomaio, *m.* **vamp** 2, TR.: rappezzare; aggiustare. **-er**, S.: rappezzatore, racconciatore, *m.*
vămpire, S.: vampiro, *m.*
văn 1, S.: vanguardia, *f.* **van** 2, S.: vaglio, *m.* **van** 3, TR.: vagliare.
vancōurier, S.: precursore; corriere; foriero, *m.*
văndalism, S.: vandalismo, *m.*
vāne, S.: girella, banderuola, *f.*
vănguard, S.: vanguardia, *f.*
vanilla, S.: vainiglia, *f.*
vănish, INTR.: svanire, sparire.
vănity, S.: vanità; inutilità; vanagloria, alterigia, *f.*
vănquish, TR.: vincere; soggiogare, domare. **-able**, ADJ.: vincibile. **-er**, S.: vincitore, *m.*

vântage 1 †, S.: vantaggio, profitto, *m.* **vantage** 2, INTR.: esser vantaggioso. **-ground**, S.: posizione vantaggiosa, *f.*, sopravvento, *m.*
văntbrass †, S.: bracciale, *m.*
văp-id, ADJ.: vapido, svaporato, insipido. **-idity**, **-idness**, S.: vapidezza, insipidezza, *f.*
vāpor, ecc. = *vapour*, ecc.
văpor-ate †, INTR.: evaporare. **-ātion** †, S.: vaporazione, *f.*; svaporare, *m.*
vā-perer, S.: millantatore, *m.* **-perous**, ADJ.: vaporoso. **-porousness**, S.: vaporosità, *f.* **-pour** 1, S.: vapore, *m.*; esalazione, *f.* **-pour** 2, TR.: vaporare, esalare; INTR.: svaporarsi; millantarsi, bravare. **-pour-bath**, S.: bagno a vapore, *m.* **-pouring**, S.: millanteria, iattanza, *f.*
vāri-able, ADJ.: variabile, mutabile; incostante. **-ableness**, S.: variazione; mutabilità, *f.* **-ably**, ADV.: variamente, mutabilmente; incostantemente. **-ance**, S.: differenza, dissensione, discordia; lite, *f.* **-ate**, (IN)TR.: variare, mutare. **-ātion**, S.: variazione, *f.*, cangiamento, *m.* **-egate**, TR.: variare, screziare. **-egātion**, S.: screzio, *m.*; varietà di colori, *f.* **vari-ety**, S.: varietà, diversità, *f.* **-ous**, ADJ.: vario, diverso; differente. **-ously**, ADV.: variamente, diversamente; differentemente. **-ousness** = *variety*.
vârlet, S.: briccone, furfante, *m.* **-ry**, S.: popolaccio, *m.*, canaglia, *f.*
vârnish 1, S.: vernice, *f.* **varnish** 2, TR.: verniciare, inverniciare. **-er**, S.: che fa la vernice, che dà la vernice. **-ing**, S.: verniciare, *m.*
vāry, TR.: variare, mutare, diversificare; INTR.: variarsi, mutarsi; differire; contrastare.
văscular, ADJ.: vascolare, vascoloso.
vāse, S.: vaso, *m.*
văssal 1, S.: vassallo, suddito, *m.* **vassal** 2, TR.: render vassallo, sottomettere. **-age**, S.: vassallaggio, *m.*; servitù, *f.*
vâst 1, ADJ.: vasto, immenso; ADV.: vastamente, eccessivamente. **vast** 2, S.: luogo vasto, terreno vasto, *m.* **-ātion** †, S.: desolazione, rovina, *f.* **-idity** †, S.: vastità, immensità, *f.* **-ly**, ADV.: vastamente, eccessivamente. **-ness**, S.: vastità, immensità; grandezza, ampiezza, *f.* **-y**, ADJ.: vasto, ampio; largo.
văt, S.: tino, *m.*
Vătican, S.: vaticano, *m.*
vatici-nate, INTR.: profetizzare, predire. **-nātion**, S.: vaticinio, *m.*
vâult 1, S.: volta; cantina, *f.*; arco, *m.* **vault** 2, TR.: voltare; INTR.: saltare, volteggiare. **-age** †, S.: cantina fatta a volta, *f.* **-er**, S.: che volteggia, saltatore, *m.* **-y** †, ADJ.: voltato, fatto a volta.

-tòwardness, S.: ostinazione, caponeria, perversità, *f.* -tràced, ADJ.: non tracciato; senza vestigi. -tràctable†, ADJ.: intrattabile; indocile. -tràctableness, S.: intrattabilità; indocilità, *f.* -tràding, ADJ.: non trafficante. -tràined, ADJ.: non disciplinato. -transfèrable, ADJ.: non trasferibile. -translàtable, ADJ.: intraducibile. -transpàrent, ADJ.: non trasparente. -tràvelled, ADJ.: non viaggiato. -trèad, TR.: tornare indietro, ritornare. -trèasured, ADJ.: non tesaurizzato. -trèatable, ADJ.: non trattabile; impraticabile. -tried, ADJ.: non provato, non tentato, intentato. -trimmed, non ornato, non raso. -tròd(den), ADJ.: non calpestato, non battuto. -tròubled, ADJ.: non torbidato, non perturbato. -trùe, ADJ.: falso, infedele; disleale. -trùly, ADV.: falsamente, infedelmente. -trùss, TR.: sciogliere; lasciare andare. -trùstiness, S.: perfidia, infedeltà, *f.* -trùsty, ADJ.: perfido, falso, non onesto. -trùth, S.: falsità; menzogna, *f.* -tùck, TR.: slegare, sciogliere. -tùnable, ADJ.: scordante, non armonioso. -tùnableness, S.: mancanza d' armonia, *f.* -tùne, TR.: scordare; disordinare. -tùrned, ADJ.: non voltato. -tùtored, ADJ.: senza istruzione, rudo. -twine, -twist, TR.: storcere, sviluppare, svolgere: *get —ed*, storcigliarsi, sfilacciarsi. -tye = *untie*. -ùniform, ADJ.: non conforme. -ùrged, ADJ.: non istigato, non sollecitato. -ùsed, ADJ.: non usato, inusitato. -ùseful, ADJ.: inutile. -ùsual, ADJ.: inusitato, non comune; straordinario, raro. -ùsually, ADV.: inusitatamente, raramente; di rado. -ùsualness, S.: rarità; radezza, *f.* -ùtterable, ADJ.: ineffabile, inenarrabile. -vàil, TR.: svelare; scoprire. -vàluable†, ADJ.: inestimabile; senza prezzo. -vàlued, ADJ.: inestimato, disprezzato, negletto. -vànquished, ADJ.: invitto. -vàriable†, ADJ.: invariabile, immutabile. -vàriableness, S.: invariabilità, immutabilità, *f.* -vàriably, ADV.: invariabilmente, immutabilmente. -vàried, ADJ.: non variato. -vàrnished, ADJ.: non inverniciato; semplice. -vàrying, ADJ.: invariato; costante. -vèil, TR.: svelare; scoprire. -vèiledly, ADV.: apertamente; senza maschera; chiaramente. -vèntilated, ADJ.: non ventilato. -vèritable, ADJ.: non vero, non verace, falso. -vèrsed, ADJ.: non versato, inesperto. -vèxed, [illegible] non tormentato, quie- [illegible] inviolato, intero. [illegible] incasto, [illegible] visita-

to, non frequentato. -vùlnerable†, ADJ.: invulnerabile. -wàkened, ADJ.: non svegliato, addormentato. -wàlled, ADJ.: senza mura. -wàres†, ADV.: inaspettamente, all' improvviso, subitamente. -wàrily, ADV.: imprudentemente, inconsideratamente. -wàriness, S.: imprudenza, sconsideratezza, *f.* -wàrlike, ADJ.: non guerriero, non agguerrito. -wàrned, ADJ.: non avvertito, non ammonito. -wàrrantable, ADJ.: da non giustificarsi. -wàrrantably, ADV.: in modo non giustificabile. -wàrranted, ADJ.: non assicurato, non accertato. -wàry, ADJ.: incauto, improvvido, imprudente, sconsiderato. -wàshed, -wàshen, ADJ.: non lavato, sporco. -wàsted, ADJ.: non consumato. -wàsting, ADJ.: senza venire meno. -wàtered, ADJ.: non adacquato, non irrigato. -wàvering, ADJ.: non vacillante, fermo. -wèakened, ADJ.: non debilitato, indebolito. -wèaponed, ADJ.: non armato. -wèariable, ADJ.: infaticabile, instancabile; indefesso. -wèariably, ADV.: infaticabilmente. -wèaried, ADJ.: infaticabile; continuo. -wèariedly, ADV.: infaticabilmente. -wèariness, S.: diligenza infaticabile, *f.* -wèary 1, ADJ.: non affaticato, non stanco. -weary 2, TR.: torre la stanchezza. -wèd(ded), ADJ.: non maritato. -wèeded, ADJ.: non sarchiato. -wèeting†, ADJ.: ignorante, illetterato. -wèighed, ADJ.: non pesato; sconsiderato. -wèighing, ADJ.: sconsiderato, trascurato. -wèlcome, ADJ.: non ben venuto; spiacevole; fastidioso, noioso. -wèll, ADJ.: non bene, male; malaticcio. -wèpt, ADJ.: non deplorato. -whipped, ADJ.: non frustato, non punito. -whòlesome, ADJ.: malsano, nocivo. -whòlesomeness, S.: qualità insalubre, qualità nociva, *f.* -wieldiness, S.: pesantezza, gravezza, *f.* -wieldy, ADJ.: pesante, lento. -willing, ADJ.: non voglioso, ricalcitrante, ripugnante; mal disposto: *willing or* —, volere o non volere; vogliate o non vogliate, a contraggenio; *be* —, non volere. -willingly, ADV.: mal volentieri. -willingness, S.: ripugnanza, ritrosia, *f.* -wind, IRR.; TR.: distrigare; svolgere. -wiped, ADJ.: non asciugato, non ripulito. -wise, ADJ.: poco accorto, imprudente; stupido. -wisely, ADV.: imprudentemente, mal accortamente. -wished, ADJ.: non desiderato. -withdràwing, ADJ.: sempre liberale. -withstòod, ADJ.: non opposto. -witnessed, ADJ.: senza testimoni. -wittily, ADV.: scioccamente, pazzamente, stupidamente. -wittingly, ADV.: senza saperlo, inav-

tura. -*ousness*, s.: arditezza, *f.*, arrischiare, *m.*
věnue, s.: (*leg.*) vicinato, *m.*
ve-răcious, ADV.: verace; sincero, veritiero, veridico. **-răcity**, s.: veracità; sincerità, *f.*
verănda, s.: veranda, *f.*
věrb, s.: verbo, *m.* **-al**, ADJ.: verbale; litterale. **-ălity** †, s.: verbosità, loquacità, *f.* **-ally**, ADV.: verbalmente, di bocca a bocca; letteralmente. **-ătim**, ADV.: parola per parola.
věrber-ate †, TR.: percuotere, battere, sferzare. **-ătion**, s.: percussione, *f.*, battimento, *m.*
věr-biage, s.: loquacità, *f.* **-bōse**, ADJ.: verboso, prolisso. **-bŏsity**, s.: verbosità, loquacità, *f.*
věr-dancy, s.: verdura, *f.* **-dant**, ADJ.: verdeggiante, verde. **-dantness** = *verdancy.* **-derer**, s.: guardaboschi, *m.*
věrdict, s.: giudizio, sentimento; verdetto, *m.*, sentenza, *f.*: *the jury gave in their* —, i giurati pronunciarono il loro verdetto.
věr-digris, s.: verderame, *m.* **-diter**, s.: verdeporro, *m.*
věrdur-e, s.: verdura, *f.*, verdume, *m.* **-ous**, ADJ.: coperto di verzura, verde, verdeggiante.
verecŭn-d(ious) †, ADJ.: verecondo, modesto. **-dity** †, s.: verecondia, *f.*
věr-ge 1, s.: verga, bacchetta; estremità, *f.*, orlo, margine, *m.*; giurisdizione, *f.*: *on the — of the tomb*, sull'orlo della tomba. **-ge** 2, TR.: inclinare, piegare; tendere. **-ger**, s.: mazziere, bidello, *m.*
verĭdical †, ADJ.: veridico, vero.
verificătion, s.: verificazione; prova, *f.*
věri-fier, s.: che verifica. **-fy**, TR.: verificare, certificare; provare. **-fying**, s.: verificazione, *f.* **-ly**, ADV.: in verità, in vero, certamente, realmente. **-simi-lar** †, ADJ.: verisimile, probabile. **-si-militude**, **-simility** †, s.: verisimiglianza, *f.* **-similous** = *verisimilar.* **-table**, ADJ.: veritevole. **-tably**, ADV.: veramente, in verità. **-ty**, s.: verità; sincerità, *f.*
věrjuice, s.: agresto, *m.*
ver-micělli, s. PL.: vermicelli, *m. pl.* **-micular**, ADJ.: vermicolare; tortuoso. **-miculate**, TR.: intarsiare. **-micule** †, s.: vermicello, vermicciuolo, *m.* **-micu-lous**, ADJ.: vermicoloso. **-miform**, ADJ.: vermiforme. **-mifuge**, ADJ.: vermifugo, antelmintico; s.: (*med.*) medicina antelmintica, *f.*
vermil(ion) 1, s.: vermiglione, cinabro, *m.* **vermilion** 2, TR.: colorire di vermiglio.
věrmin, s.: vermi, vermini, *m. pl.* **-ate**, TR.: produrre vermi. **-ous**, ADJ.: verminoso.
vermĭparous, ADJ.: producente vermi.
vernăcular, ADJ.: vernacolo, nativo: — *tongue*, lingua vernacola, *f.*
věr-nal, ADJ.: vernale, di primavera: — *season*, primavera, *f.* **-nant** †, ADJ.: fiorente, florido.
vernility †, s.: condotta da schiavo, bassezza, *f.*
versability †, s.: versabilità, *f.*
věrsable = *versatile.* **-ness** = *versability.*
věrsal †, ADJ.: universale; intero.
věrsa-tile, ADJ.: versatile; flessibile. **-tileness**, **-tility**, s.: versatilità, *f.*
věr-se, s.: verso, versetto, *m.*: *blank* —, versi sciolti, *m. pl.*; — *of a chapter*, versetto, *m.*; *turn into* —, versificare. **-sed**, ADJ.: versato, sperimentato. **-seman**, s.: versificatore, *m.* **-sicle**, s.: piccol verso, versetto, *m.* **-sificătion**, s.: versificazione, *f.*, versificare, *m.* **-sificator**, **-sifier**, s.: versificatore, *m.* **-sify**, TR.: verseggiare, versificare.
věrsion, s.: versione, traduzione, *f.*
věrt, s.: fogliame, *m.*, foglie, *f. pl.*
věrte-bra, s.: vertebra, *f.* **-bral**, ADJ.: vertebrale. **-brate**, s., ADJ.: vertebrato.
věr-tex, s.: vertice, *m.*; cima, sommità, *f.* **-tical**, ADJ.: verticale, perpendicolare. **-ticalness**, **-ticălity** †, s.: sommo, apice, *m.* **-tically**, ADV.: verticalmente. **-ticillate**, ADJ.: verticillato. **-ticity** †, s.: circonvoluzione, *f.*
vert-iginous, ADJ.: vertiginoso, girativo. **věrt-igo**, s.: vertigine, *f.*, capogiro, *m.*
věr-vain, **-vine**, s.: (*bot.*) verbena, *f.*
věry 1, ADJ.: vero; mero, pretto; medesimo, stesso. **very** 2, ADV.: molto; assai, grandemente; bene, esattamente; ADJ.: vero, esatto, stesso, identico: — *much*, in gran quantità; moltissimo; — *well*, benissimo; — *many*, moltissimi; *it is the — same*, egli è desso.
věs-icate †, TR.: applicare un vescicante. **-icatory**, s.: vescicatorio, *m.* **-icle**, s.: vescichetta, *f.* **-icular**, ADJ.: vescicolare.
věsper, s.: vespro, *m.*, sera, *f.* **-s**, s. PL.: vespro, vespero, *m.* (uffizio divino). **-tine**, ADJ.: vespertino, della sera.
věssel 1, s.: vaso; vascello, *m.*, nave, barca, *f.*, bastimento; (*anat.*) vaso, *m.* **vessel** 2, TR.: porre in una botte, imbottare.
věst 1, s.: camiciuola, sottoveste, *f.* **vest** 2, TR.: investire, porre in possesso.
věs-tal 1, ADJ.: vestale; verginale. **-tal** 2, s.: verginella, *f.*
věstiary, s.: vestiario, *m.*
věstibule, s.: vestibulo, *m.*

ū-sage, S.: uso; costume; trattamento, *m.* **-sance**, S.: uso, *m.*, usanza, usura, *f.*; interesse, *m.*

ūse 1, S.: uso, servigio, *m.*; utilità, *f.*; costume, *m.*; pratica, *f.*: *make — of*, servirsi; *put into —*, mettere in uso, mettere in pratica; *what —?* a che serve? *it is of no —*, è inutile; *out of —*, smesso. **ūse** 2, TR.: usare, adoperare, servirsi; frequentare; praticare; INTR.: solere, esser solito: *— ill*, abusare; oltraggiare; *— well*, trattare bene. **-ful**, ADJ.: utile, profittevole. **-fully**, ADV.: utilmente, profittevolmente. **-fulness**, S.: utilità, *f.*, profitto, comodo, vantaggio, *m.* **-less**, ADJ.: inutile, buono a nulla. **-lessly**, ADV.: inutilmente, di niuna utilità. **-lessness**, S.: inutilità, *f.* **-money**, S.: interesse, *m.* **ūse-r**, S.: che usa, che fa uso di.

ŭsher 1, S.: bracciere; sottomaestro; usciere, portinaio, *m.* **usher** 2, TR.: introdurre; precedere.

ŭsquebaugh, S.: sorta d' acquavite, *f.*

ŭstion, S.: ustione, *f.*

ūsual, ADJ.: comune, ordinario, consueto, solito: *as —*, al solito; *in the — manner*, al modo usato. **-ly**, ADV.: ordinariamente, comunemente, generalmente. **-ness**, S.: frequenza; abitudine, *f.*

usucăption, S.: (*jur.*) usucapione, *f.*

ūsu-fruct, S.: usufrutto, *m.* **-frŭctuary**, S.: (*jur.*) usufruttuario, *m.*

ū-sure†, INTR.: dare ad usura. **-surer**, S.: usuraio, che presta ad usura, *m.* **-sūrious**, ADJ.: usurario, usuraio.

usūrp, TR.: usurpare, occupare ingiustamente. **-ātion**, S.: usurpazione, *f.* **-er**, S.: usurpatore, *m.* **-ing**, S.: usurpamento, *m.* **-ingly**, ADV.: usurpativamente, senza dritto.

ūsury, S.: usura, *f.*: *lend upon —*, dar ad usura, usureggiare; *practice —*, far l' usuraio, usureggiare.

utĕnsil, S.: utensile; ordigno, strumento, *m.*

ū-terine, ADJ.: uterino. **-terus**, S.: (*anat.*) utero, *m.*, matrice, *f.*

util-ity, S.: utilità, *f.*; profitto, *m.*: *of —*, utile; *of no —*, inutile. **ūtil-ize**, TR.: utilizzare.

ŭt-most 1, ADJ.: estremo, ultimo, massimo. **-most** 2, S.: ogni sforzo; possibile, *m.*: *the —*, il più possibile; *at the —*, al più, tutto al più; *to the —*, con ogni sforzo; *I'll do my —*, farò ogni mio sforzo; farò ogni sforzo possibile. **-ter** 1, ADJ.: [illegible]riore, estremo, tutto, intero: *— dark*[illegible]le tenebre più profonde; *— ruin*, [illegible] **-tera**[illegible] [illegible]nferire, pronunziare; ma[illegible] **-able**, ADJ.: proffe-ribile. **-ance**, pronunziare, *m.*; espressione; vendita, *f.*: *give — to*, esprimere, proferire, palesare. **-er**, S.: pronunziatore; divolgatore, *m.*

ŭtter-ly, ADV.: affatto, interamente, totalmente. **-most** 1, ADJ.: estremo, ultimo. **-most** 2, S.: estremo; possibile, *m.*: *to the —*, al più alto grado, all' ultimo grado.

ūvula, S.: ugola, *f.*

uxōrious, ADJ.: innamorato e schiavo della moglie. **-ness**, S.: amore soverchio per la moglie.

V

v *vē* (*the letter*), S.: v, *m.*

vā-cancy, S.: vuoto, *m.*; vacanza, vacazione, *f.*, riposo, *m.* **-cant**, ADJ.: vacante; vuoto, vacuo: *— hours*, ore di ozio; *— space*, spazio vuoto; *be —*, essere vacanto, vacare. **-cate**, TR.: vuotare; annullare, cassare. **-cātion**, S.: vacazione, vacanza, intermissione, *f.*; riposo, *m.*

văcchary, S.: pascolo da vacche, *m.*; stalla da vacche, *f.*

văcci-nate, TR.: vaccinare. **-nātion**, S.: vaccinazione, *f.* **-ne**, ADJ.: vaccino; di vacca: *— inoculation*, vaccinazione, *f.*

văcil-lancy†, S.: vacillamento, *m.* **-late**, INTR.: vacillare, barcollare. **-lation**, S.: vacillazione, *f.*, vacillamento, *m.*; titubazione, *f.*

văc-uate†, TR.: vacuare, vuotare. **-uātion**, S.: evacuazione, *f.*; vuotamento, *m.* **-uist**, S.: vacuista, *m.* **-ūity**, S.: vacuità, *f.*, spazio vacuo, *m.* **-uous**, ADJ.: vacuo, vuoto. **-uousness** = *vacuity*. **-uum**, S.: vacuo, *m.*

vāfrous†, ADJ.: astuto, scaltrito.

văgabond 1, ADJ.: vagabondo, vagante; errante. **vagabond** 2, S.: vagabondo, *m.* **-ry**, S.: vita vagabonda, vagabondità, *f.*

vagāry, S.: fantasia, *f.*; capriccio, *m.*

vāgran-cy, S.: vita vagabonda, *f.* **-t**, ADJ.: vagabondo, vagante.

vāgue, ADJ.: vago, vagabondo: *in a — manner*, in modo indeterminato. **-ly**, ADV.: vagamente. **-ness**, S.: vago, *m.*, incertezza, *f.*

vāil 1, S.: cortina, *f.*; velo, *m.*; arra, caparra, *f.* **vail** 2, TR.: velare; lasciare cadere; INTR.: dar luogo, cedere.

vāin, ADJ.: vano; frivolo; orgoglioso, altiero; inutile: *in —*, invano, inutilmente; *be — of*, andar vanitoso di. **-glōrious**, ADJ.: vanaglorioso, orgoglioso. **-glōry**, S.: vanagloria, *f.*; orgoglio, *m.* **-ly**, ADV.: vanamente, inutilmente. **-ness**, S.: vanità, frivolezza, inutilità, *f.*

s.: contadino, villano, *m.* **-ry**, s.: territorio di villaggio, *m.*
vil-lain, s.: briccone, furfante, *m.* **-lanage**, s.: ignobilità, bassezza, *f.* **-lanize**, TR.: degradare; disprezzare. **-lanous**, ADJ.: villano, basso, cattivo, infame. **-lanously**, ADV.: bassamente, indegnamente, infamemente. **-lanousness**, s.: bassezza; scelleratezza, infamia, *f.* **-lany**, s.: villania, indegnità, ingiuria, *f.*
villàtic, ADJ.: villeresco, villesco, campestre.
villous, ADJ.: velloso, peloso.
viminęous, ADJ.: vimineo, di vimini.
vinâçeous, ADJ.: vinario.
vincible, ADJ.: vincibile, superabile. **-ness**, s.: possibilità d' esser vinto, *f.*
vinctųre†, s.: legatura, *f.*
vindē-mial, ADJ.: di vendemmia. **-miątє**†, TR.: vendemmiare. **-mātįǫn**†, s.: vendemmia, *f.*
vindi-cąte, TR.: vendicare, giustificare, difendere: — *one's self*, giustificarsi. **-câtįǫn**, s.: giustificazione, difesa, *f.* **-cątive**, ADJ.: vendicativo, vendichevole; vindicatore, *m.*, -trice, *f.* **-cątǫr**, s.: vendicatore; giustificatore, difensore, *m.* **-catǫry**, ADJ.: vendicativo, giustificativo.
vindictive, ADJ.: vendicativo; implacabile. **-ly**, ADV.: vendicativamente. **-ness**, s.: vendicamento, *m.*
vine, s.: vite, vigna, *f.* **-branch**, s.: pampano, *m.*, pampana, *f.* **-dresser**, s.: vignaio, vignaiuolo, *m.*
vinęgąr, s.: aceto, vinagro, *m.* **-cruet**, s.: caraffa per l' aceto, *f.*
vine-leaf, s.: pampino, *m.* **-reaper**, s.: vendemmiatore, *m.* **-shoot**, s.: tralcio, sarmento, *m.*
vin-yard, s.: vigneto, vignaio, *m.*
vinǫlen-cy†, s.: vinolenza, *f.* **-t**, ADJ.: vinolento.
vinŏsity, s.: vinosità, qualità vinosa, *f.*
vinous, ADJ.: vinoso, di vino.
vintą-ge, s.: vendemmia, *f.* **-gęr**, s.: **-ge-time**, s.: tempo della vendemmia, *m.*
vint-nęr, s.: tavernaio; mercante di vino, *m.* **-ry**†, s.: luogo dove si vende vino.
viǫl, s.: viola, *f.*
viǫlable, ADJ.: violabile.
viǫlâçeous, ADJ.: violaceo.
viǫ-late, TR.: violare; infringere, trasgredire. **-lâtįǫn**, s.: violazione, *f.*, trasgredimento, *m.* **-lątǫr**, s.: violatore, trasgreditore, *m.* **-lence**, s.: violenza, veemenza, impetuosità, *f.* **-lent**, ADJ.: violento; impetuoso: *lay — hands upon one's self*, ammazzarsi. **-lently**, ADV.: violentemente, con violenza.
viǫlet, s.: viola, violetta, *f.* **-colour**, s.: colore violetto, *m.*
viǫl-in, s.: violino, *m.*: *play on the —*, suonare il violino. **-inist**, s.: suonatore di violino, violinista, *m.* **-oncellǫ**, s.: violoncello, *m.*
vipęr, s.: vipera, *f.*: *little-—*, viperetta, *f.* **-grass**, s.: (*bot.*) scorzonera, *f.* **-ine**, ADJ.: viperino. **-ous**, ADJ.: vipereo, di vipera.
virâgǫ, s.: viragine, amazone, gigantessa, *f.*
viręlay, s.: strambotto, *m.*
virent†, ADJ.: virente, verdeggiante.
virge†, s.: verga, mazza portata innanzi al decano, *f.*
vir-gin 1, ADJ.: virgineo, di vergine. **-gin** 2, s.: vergine, zitella, donzella, *f.*: *Holy —*, Santa Vergine. **-ginal** 1, ADJ.: verginale, vergineo, di vergine; puro. **-ginal**† 2, s.: verginale, *m.* **-gin-honey**, s.: miele vergine, *m.* **-ginity**, s.: verginità; purità, *f.* **-gin-wax**, s.: cera vergine, *f.*
viridity, s.: verdezza, *f.*
vi-rile, ADJ.: virile, mascolino. **-rility**, s.: virilità, *f.*; coraggio, *m.*
virtù, s.: gusto; amore, *m.*
vir-tųal, ADJ.: virtuale; efficace, effettivo. **-tųâlity**†, s.: virtualità; efficacia, *f.* **-tųally**, ADV.: virtualmente; efficacemente. **-tųe**, s.: virtù; efficacia; forza, *f.*, vigore, *m.*, possanza, *f.*: *by — of*, in virtù di, per la virtù di, per mezzo di: *make a — of necessity*, far della necessità virtù. **-tųeless**, ADJ.: senza virtù; inefficace, impotente. **-tųôsǫ**, s.: (pl. *virtuosi*) dilettante, *m.* **-tųous**, ADJ.: virtuoso; efficace. **-tųously**, ADV.: virtuosamente. **-tųousness**, s.: castità; purità, *f.*
virųlen-ce, **-cy**, s.: virulenza, *f.* **-t**, ADJ.: virulento, velenoso; mordente, maligno. **-tly**, ADV.: in modo maligno, mordacemente.
viṣąge, s.: visaggio, volto, *m.*, faccia, *f.*
viscęr-al, ADJ.: viscerale, delle viscere. **-ąte**, TR.: sviscerare, sbudellare.
vis-cid, ADJ.: viscido, viscoso, tenace. **-cidity**, **-cŏsity**, s.: viscidità, viscosità, *f.*
viscount, s.: visconte, *m.* **-ess**, s.: viscontessa, *f.* **-y**, s.: viscontado, *m.*, viscontea, *f.*
viscous, ADJ.: viscoso, glutinoso, tenace. **-ness**, s.: viscosità, tenacità, *f.*
vise 1, s.: tenaglia, *f.*
viṣé, s.: visto (d' un passaporto), *m.*
viṣibility, s.: visibilità, *f.*
vi-ṣible, ADJ.: visibile; percettibile; evidente. **-ṣibleness**, s.: visibilità; apparenza, *f.* **-ṣibly**, ADV.: visibilmente; evidentemente.
viṣįǫn, s.: visione, apparizione, *f.* **-ary** 1,

vâunt 1, S.: vanto, vantamento, *m.*, millanteria, *f.* **vaunt** 2, INTR.: vantarsi, gloriarsi. **-er**, S.: vantatore, millantatore, *m.* **-ful**†, ADJ.: vanaglorioso. **-ing**, S.: millanteria, iattanza, *f.* **-ingly**, ADV.: con vanto, in modo vantevole.
vâward†, S.: (*mil.*) vanguardia, *f.*
vēal, S.: vitello, *m.*, carne di vitello, *f.* **-cutlet**, S.: costoletta di vitello, *f.*
vēcture†, S.: vettura; condotta, *f.*
vēer, TR.: voltare; girare; (*nav.*) mollare; INTR.: cangiarsi; voltarsi.
vegetability†, S.: natura vegetabile, *f.*
vēge-table 1, ADJ.: vegetabile, vegetativo: — *kingdom*, regno vegetale, *m.* **-table** 2, S.: vegetale, *m.*; INTR.: vegetabili, *m. pl.* **-tate**, INTR.: vegetare. **-tātion**, S.: vegetazione, *f.*, vegetare, *m.* **-tative**, ADJ.: vegetativo, vegetante. **-tativeness**, S.: vegetazione, *f.*
vēhemen-ce, -cy†, S.: veemenza, violenza, forza, *f.* **-t**, ADJ.: veemente, violento, impetuoso. **-tly**, ADV.: veementemente, con forza, con impeto.
vēhicle, S.: veicolo, *m.*, vettura, *f.*
vēil 1, S.: velo; pretesto, *m.*, maschera, *f.* **veil** 2, TR.: velare; coprire, celare.
vēin 1, S.: vena; cavità, *f.*; umore, *m.* **vein** 2, TR.: screziare, marezzare. **-ed, -y**, ADJ.: venoso, pieno di vene.
velitātion†, S.: contesa, disputa, *f.*
vellēity, S.: velleità, *f.*
vělli-cate, TR.: pizzicare, titillare. **-cātion**, S.: pizzico, vellicamento, *m.*
věllum, S.: pergamena, cartapecora, *f.*
velōci-pēde, S.: velocipede, *m.* **-ty**, S.: velocità, celerità, *f.*
vělvet 1, S.: velluto, *m.* **-velvet** 2, ADJ.: di velluto, vellutato; (*fig.*) molle, delicato. **-maker**, S.: tessitore di velluto, *m.*
vē-nal, ADJ.: venale, mercenario. **-nālity**, S.: venalità, *f.*
vēnary, ADJ.: venatorio.
venātion, S.: venagione, caccia, *f.*
věnd, TR.: vendere, spacciare. **-ěe**, S.: compratore, acquistatore, *m.* **-er**, S.: venditore, *m.* **-ible**, ADJ.: vendibile, vendevole; venale. **-ibleness**, S.: qualità vendevole, *f.*, esser vendibile, *m.* **-ibly**, ADV.: in modo vendibile. **-ing**, S.: vendita, *f.*, spaccio, *m.* **-ition**, S.: vendimento, *m.*, vendita, *f.*
veněer, TR.: intarsiare. **-ing**, S.: intarsiatura, *f.*
věne-fice†, S.: veneficio, avvelenamento, *m.* **-ficial**†, ADJ.: velenoso; incantevole. **-ficiously**†, ADV.: velenosamente. **-nous**†, ADJ.: venenifero, venenoso. **-nate** 1, ADJ.: avvelenato. **-nate** 2, TR.: avvelenare. **-nātion**, S.: attossicamento; veneno, *m.* **-nōse**†, ADJ.: venenoso, velenoso.

venerability†, S.: venerabilità, *f.*
věner-able, ADJ.: venerabile, venerando. **-ableness** = *venerability*. **-ably**, ADV.: venerabilmente, in modo venerabile. **-ate**, TR.: venerare; onorare. **-ātion**, S.: venerazione, *f.*; onore, *m.* **-ator**, S.: veneratore, *m.*
venē-real, -rean, ADJ.: venereo, libidinoso: — *disease*, mal francese.
věnery, S.: venagione; libidine, *f.*
venesěction, S.: cavata di sangue, flebotomia, *f.*
Venētian, ADJ., S.: veneziano: — *blind*, gelosia, persiana, gratticciata, *f.*
věn-cy, -ēw, S.: (*fenc.*) assalto, colpo, *m.*
věn-get, TR.: vendicare; punire. **-geable**†, ADJ.: vendicativo. **-geance**, S.: vendetta; punizione, *f.*: *take* —, fare vendetta, vendicarsi. **-geful**, ADJ.: vendicativo. **-ger**†, S.: vendicatore, *m.*
vēnial, ADJ.: veniale, perdonabile: — *sin*, peccato veniale. **-ness**, S.: mancamento leggiero, *m.*
věnison, S.: salvaggina, *f.*, salvaggiume, *m.*
věnom 1, S.: veneno, veleno, tossico, *m.* **venom** 2, TR.: avvelenare, attossicare. **-ous**, ADJ.: venenoso, velenoso; maledico, mordace. **-ously**, ADV.: in modo velenoso; in modo malizioso. **-ousness**, S.: velenosità; malignità, *f.*
věnt 1, S.: vento, *m.*; aria; fessura; vendita, *f.*, spaccio, *m.*: *give* — *to*, dare sfogo (libero corso) a, sfogare, sventare, esalare. **vent** 2, TR.: sventare; flutare, esalare; divulgare, scoprire, palesare: — *one's passion*, sfogare la sua passione. **-age**†, S.: spiraglio; piccol buco (di flauto), *m.* **-ail**, S.: visiera (d'un elmo), *f.* **-āna**†, S.: finestra, *f.*
věnter, S.: ventre, addomine, *m.*
věnt-hole, S.: spiraglio, sfogatoio, *m.*
věntiduct, S.: condotto di vento, *m.*
věnti-late, TR.: ventilare, sventare; esaminare. **-lātion**, S.: ventilazione, *f.* **-lator**, S.: ventilatore, ventilatoio, *m.*
ventŏsity, S.: ventosità, *f.*, vento, *m.*
věntricle, S.: ventricolo, *m.*
ventrilo-quism, S.: ventriloquio, *m.* **-quist**, S.: ventriloquo, *m.* **-quy** = *ventriloquism*. **-quize**, INTR.: parlare come ventriloquo.
věntur-e 1, S.: ventura, *f.*; rischio; sorte, *m.*: *at a* —, alla ventura, per sorte; *put to* —, mettere alla ventura. **-e** 2, TR.: avventurare, arrischiare; INTR.: avventurarsi, arrischiarsi: — *a wager*, fare una scommessa; — *at* (*on, upon*), intraprendere; arrischiarsi; *nothing* — *nothing win*, chi non risica non rosica. **-er**, S.: venturiere, *m.* **-esome, -ous**, ADJ.: ardito, coraggioso. **-ously**, ADV.: alla ven-

volūte, s.: (*arch.*) voluta, *f.*
vŏm-ica, s.: vomica, postema suppurata, *f.*: **nux** —, or **-ic-nut**, s.: noce vomica, *f.* **-it** 1, s.: vomitivo, vomito, *m.* **-it** 2, TR.: vomitare, recere. **vom-ĭtion**, s.: vomizione, *f.* **-itive**, **-itory** 1, ADJ.: vomitivo, vomitorio. **-itory** 2, s.: vomitivo, *m.*
vo-rācious, ADJ.: vorace; ingordo, avido. **-rāciously**, ADV.: voracemente; avidamente. **-rāciousness**, **-răcity**, s.: voracità, *f.*
vôrtex (pl. *vortices*), s.: vortice, gorgo, *m.*
vō-taress, s.: devota, religiosa, *f.* **-tarist**, **-tary**, s.: devoto; amante, *m.*; amanza, *f.* **-te** 1, s.: voto, suffragio, *m.*: *put to the* —, raccogliere le voci. **-te** 2, (IN)TR.: dare la sua voce, dare il suo suffragio; stabilire; conchiudere: — *in*, eleggere; scegliere. **-ter**, s.: votante, *m.* **-tive**, ADJ.: votivo, offerto in voto.
vouch 1, s.: testimonio; affermamento, *m.* **vouch** 2, TR.: affermare, accertare; asserire: — *one*, chiamare uno in giudizio; — *for one*, entrar mallevadore per qualcheduno. **-er**, s.: sicurtà; testimonianza, *f.*, garante, *m.* **-sāfe**, TR.: concedere, accordare; INTR.: degnarsi, compiacersi. **-sāfement**, s.: condiscendenza, *f.*
vŏw 1, s.: voto, *m.*; promessa solenne, *f.*: *make a* —, fare un voto. **vow** 2, TR.: votare; dedicare, consecrare; INTR.: fare un voto; giurare.
vŏwel, s.: vocale, *f.*
vŏwer, s.: votatore, *m.*
vŏyage 1, s.: viaggio (per mare), *m.* **voyage** 2, INTR.: fare viaggio per mare, *m.*
vŭl-gar 1, ADJ.: volgare, comune; popolare. **-gar** 2, s.: volgo, popolaccio, *m.* **-gărity**, s.: volgarità, bassezza, *f.* **-garize**, TR.: render volgare, render vile. **-garly**, ADV.: volgarmente, comunemente, trivialmente.
Vŭlgate, s.: vulgata, *f.*
vŭlner-able, ADJ.: vulnerabile. **-ary**, ADJ.: vulnerario; s.: rimedio vulnerario, *m.* **-ate**†, TR.: vulnerare; fare male. **-ātion**†, s.: vulnerare, *m.*
vŭlpine, ADJ.: volpino; astuto, furbo.
vŭltur-e, s.: avoltoio, avoltore, *m.* (uccello). **-ine**, **-ous**, ADJ.: d' avoltoio; vorace.

W

w *dŭbl-ū* (*the letter*), s.: w, *m.*
wăbble, TR.: ondeggiare, dondolarsi; zoppicare, barcollare.
wăd 1, s.: fascio (di paglia, ecc.); stoppaccio, *m.* **wad** 2, TR.: mettere lo stoppaccio.
wādable, ADJ.: guadabile.
wădd, s.: piombaggine, *f.*
wădding, s.: bambagia, borra (di lana, ecc.), *f.*
wăddle, INTR.: zoppicare, barcollare.
wāde, INTR.: guadare, passare con difficoltà: — *into*, penetrare; ingolfarsi; — *over*, traversare.
wăd-hook, s.: tirapalle, *m.*
wāfer, s.: cialda, ostia, *f.* **-iron**, s.: ferro da cialde, *m.* **-maker**, s.: cialdonaio, *m.*
wăft 1, s.: ondulazione, *f.*; (*nav.*) segnale, *m.* **waft** 2, TR.: condurre per; convogliare; far cenno, segnare; INTR.: fiottare, galleggiare. **-age**, s.: trasporto per mare o aria, *m.* **-er**, s.: fregata di convoglio, *f.* **-ure**†, s.: ondeggiamento, *m.*
wăg 1, s.: trastullatore, uomo giocoso, *m.* **wag** 2, TR.: scuotere, muovere, agitare leggermente; INTR.: scuotersi, muoversi, agitarsi: — *the tail*, scuotere la coda.
wā-ge† 1, s.: pegno, *m.*: —*s*, salario, *m.*; paga, mercede, *f.*, stipendio, *m.* **-ge** 2, TR.: venturare, tentare, provare; litigare: — *war*, muover guerra. **-ger** 1, s.: scommessa, *f.*: *lay a* —, scommettere; fare una scommessa. **-ger** 2, TR.: scommettere, fare una scommessa.
wăg-gery, s.: trastullo, scherzo, *m.* **-gish**, ADJ.: scherzevole, solazzevole: — *trick*, tiro da burlone. **-gishly**, ADV.: scherzevolmente, da scherzo. **-gishness**, s.: scherzo, sollazzo, *m.*
wăggle, INTR.: dimenarsi, muoversi; agitare.
wăggon, s.: carro, *m.*, carretta, *f.*; (*rail.*) vagone, vagone da trasportar mercanzie, *m.* **-age**, s.: paga del trasporto nel carro, *f.* **-er**, s.: carrettaio, carrettiere, *m.*; (*astr.*) orsa maggiore, *f.* **-maker**, s.: carradore, carpentiere, *m.*
wăgtail, s.: cutretta, cutrettola, *f.* (uccello).
wāid†, ADJ.: schiacciato.
wāif, **-t**, s.: cosa perduta, *f.*
wāil 1, s.: lamento, compianto, *m.* **wail** 2, TR.: deplorare; INTR.: lamentare; piangere. **-ful**, ADJ.: deplorabile, lamentabile. **-ing** = *wail.*
wāin, s.: carro, *m.*; carretta, *f.*: (*astr.*) *Charles'* —, orsa maggiore, *f.* **-driver**, s.: carrettaio, carrettiere, *m.* **-load**, s.: carrettata, *f.* **-rope**, s.: corda del carro, *f.*
wāinscot 1, s.: tavolato; palco, *m.* **wainscot** 2, TR.: intavolare; soffittare. **-ting**, s.: intavolato, *m.*, impiallacciatura, *f.*
wāist, s.: cintura; parte più stretta del corpo, *f.*; (*nav.*) ponte di mezzo, *m.*

vĕstige, S.: vestigio, *m.*, pedata, traccia, orma, *f.*
vĕstment, S.: vestimento, abito, *m.*
vĕstry, S.: sagrestia, *f.* **-keeper**, S.: sagrestano, *m.* **-room**, S.: sagrestia, *f.*
vĕsture, S.: vestimento, abito, *m.*; vestitura, *f.*
vĕtch, S.: veccia, *f.*: *full of* —, veccioso. **-y**, ADJ.: veccioso.
vĕteran 1, ADJ.: veterano, sperimentato.
veteran 2, S.: veterano, reduce, *m.*
veteri-nărian, ADJ.: veterinario. **vĕter-inary**, S.: veterinario, *m.*
vĕx, TR.: vessare, travagliare, molestare, affannare; INTR.: affannarsi, affliggersi. **-ătion**, S.: affanno; travaglio, *m.*, sollecitudine, molestia, *f.* **-ătious**, ADJ.: affannoso, molesto, incomodo. **-ătiously**, ADV.: affannosamente, molestamente. **-ătiousness**, S.: vessamento, travaglio, *m.*, sollecitudine, *f.*, disturbo, *m.* **-er**, S.: vessatore, travagliatore, *m.* **-ingly** = *vexatiously*.
viaduct, S.: viadotto, *m.*
vial, S.: boccia; fiala, caraffina, *f.*
viand, S.: vivanda, *f.*; cibo, *m.*
viăticum, S.: viatico, *m.*
vi-brate, TR.: render tremolo, brandire; INTR.: vibrare, muoversi. **-brātion**, S.: vibrazione, *f.*
vicar, S.: vicario, piovano; sostituto, *m.* **-age**, S.: beneficio di vicario, vicariato, *m.*
vicā-rial, ADJ.: di vicario. **-riate**, S.: vicariato, *m.* **-rious**, ADJ.: di vicario, deputato, sostituito.
vicarship, S.: vicariato, *m.*
vice 1, S.: vizio, *m.*; colpa; vite; tanaglia, morsa, *f.*; buffone, zanni, *m.* **vice** 2, TR.: stringere con una vite, stringere con una morsa.
vice-ădmiral, S.: viceammiraglio, *m.* **-ădmiralty**, S.: viceammiragliato, *m.* **-āgent**, S.: agente, sostituto, *m.* **-chăncellor**, S.: vicecancelliere, *m.* **-chăncellorship**, S.: uffizio del vicecancelliere, *m.* **-cŏnsul**, S.: viceconsolo, proconsolo, *m.*
viced †, ADJ.: vizioso, corrotto.
vice-gērency, S.: vicegerenza, luogotenenza, *f.* **-gērent**, S.: vicegerente, luogotenente, *m.* **-prĕsident**, S.: vicepresidente, *m.* **-rēgent**, S.: vicereggente, *m.* **-roy**, S.: vicerè, *m.* **-rŏyalty**, S.: dignità di vicerè, *f.*
viciate, TR.: corrompere, depravare, viziare, magagnare.
vic-inage = *vicinity*. **-inal**, **-ine**, ADJ.: vicino, vicinale, prossimo. **-inity**, S.: vicinanza, vicinità, prossimità, *f.*, dintorni, *m.*: *in the — of*, nei dintorni di.
vicious, ADJ.: vizioso, corrotto. **-ly**, ADV.: viziosamente. **-ness**, S.: corruttela, *f.*
vicissitude, S.: vicissitudine, *f.*
victim, S.: vittima, *f.*, sacrifizio, *m.* **-ate**, TR.: sacrificare.
vic-tor, S.: vincitore, conquistatore, *m.* **-toress** †, S.: vincitrice, *f.* **-tōrious**, ADJ.: vittorioso. **-tōriously**, ADV.: vittoriosamente. **-tory**, S.: vittoria, *f.*; trionfo, *m.*: *get the* —, ottenere la vittoria, trionfare. **-tress**, S.: vincitrice, *f.*
victual, TR.: vettovagliare, provvedere. **-ler**, S.: provveditore (di vettovaglie), *m.* **-ling**, S.: vettovagliare, munire di vettovaglie, *m.* **-ling-house**, S.: osteria, bettola, *f.* **-s**, S. PL.: vettovaglie, provvisioni, *f. pl.*
vidēlicet, ADV.: cioè, vale a dire.
vid-ual †, ADJ.: vedovile. **-ūity** †, S.: viduità, *f.*, vedovaggio, *m.*
vie, (IN)TR.: invitare †; contendere, contestare; sforzarsi: — *with*, fare a gara; — *with each other*, gareggiare insieme, rivalizzare.
view 1, S.: vista, veduta, *f.*, aspetto, *m.*; prospettiva, *f.*; esame, *m.*; traccia (di cervo), *f.*: *at one* —, alla prima, ad un' occhiata; *at first* —, a prima vista; *at a* —, ad un colpo d' occhio; *my* —, a parer mio; *with a* — *to*, col disegno di; *field of* —, campo di vista; *bird's-eye* —, vista a volo d' uccello; *take a* — *of*, riguardare, riconoscere; esaminare. **view** 2, TR.: vedere, riguardare; osservare, considerare; riconoscere; esaminare. **-er**, S.: che vede, che risguarda; ispettore, *m.* **-less**, ADJ.: non veduto, non visto; impercettibile.
vigil, S.: vigilia, veglia, *f.* **-ance**, **-ancy** †, S.: vigilanza, attenzione, cura, *f.* **-ant**, ADJ.: vigilante, attento, diligente. **-antly**, ADV.: vigilantemente, con attenzione, diligentemente.
vignette *vinyĕt*, S.: vignetta, *f.*
vigo(u)r, S.: vigore, *f.*, robustezza; energia, *f.* **-ous**, ADJ.: vigoroso, gagliardo, robusto. **-ously**, ADV.: vigorosamente, con vigore. **-ousness**, S.: vigorosità, *f.*
viking, S.: corsaro scandinavo antico, *m.*
vile, ADJ.: vile, basso, abietto: — *commodity*, mercanzia di vil prezzo, *f.* [illegible] ADJ.: oltraggioso, diffamante [illegible] vilmente, abiettamente [illegible] bassezza, abie[illegible]
vilificati[illegible]
vili-fier [illegible] avvilire, [illegible] TR.: vil[illegible] za, *f.*
vill, S. [illegible]
villa, [illegible]
villag[illegible]

la, *f.* **ward** 2, TR.: guardare, far la guardia; parare; eludere; proteggere, difendere: — *off*, parare, stornare. **-en**, S.: custode, guardiano; governatore, rettore: — *of a prison*, carceriere, *m.* **-enship**, S.: uffizio di guardiano, *m.*; tutoreria, *f.* **-er**, S.: guardia, *f.*; bastone di comando, *m.* **-mote**, S.: assemblea de' magistrati del rione, *f.* **-robe**, S.: guardaroba, *f.* **-ship**, S.: carica del guardiano, tutela, *f.*

wāre 1, S.: mercanzia, roba, merce, *f.*: *China*—, porcellana, *f.*; *Dutch* —, maiolica, *f.*; *earthen*—, vasellame di terra, *m.*; *small* —, merceria, *f.* **ware** † 2, INTR.: prendere guardia, guardarsi; badare. **ware**3(**ful**)†, ADJ.: circospetto, accorto. **-fulness**†, S.: circospezione, cautela, *f.*

wārehouse, S.: magazzino, *m.* **-keeper**, S.: magazziniere, *m.*

wāre-less†, ADJ.: incauto. **-ly**, ADV.: cautamente, accortamente.

wăr-fare 1, S.: vita militare; guerra, *f.* **-fare** 2, INTR.: vivere da militare. **-faring**, ADJ.: militare, guerriero. **-horse**, S.: cavallo da guerra, *m.*

wāri-ly, ADV.: prudentemente, accortamente, sagacemente. **-ness**, S.: cautela, prudente, accortezza, *f.*; risparmio, *m.*

wărlike, ADJ.: bellicoso, guerriero, militare. **-ness**, S.: carattere bellicoso, *m.*

wăr-lock, **-luck**, S.: stregone, maliardo, *m.*

wărm 1, ADJ.: caldo; zeloso, furioso: *be* — (*of weather*), far caldo; (*of persons*) avere caldo; *grow* —, divenire caldo, scaldarsi; *make* —, far caldo, scaldare. **warm** 2, TR.: scaldare: — *again*, riscaldare; — *one's self*, scaldarsi; — *up again*, riscaldare. **-ing**, S.: riscaldamento, *m.* **-ing-pan**, S.: scaldaletto, *m.* **-ing-place**, S.: scaldatoio, *m.* **-ly**, ADV.: caldamente; passionatamente. **-ness**, **-th**, S.: caldezza, *f.*; ardore, zelo, *m.*

wărn, TR.: ammonire; avvertire, avvisare; citare: — *away*, licenziare, dare congedo. **-er**, S.: ammonitore; avvisatore, *m.* **-ing**, S.: avvertimento, avviso; congedo, *m.*: *give* —, avvertire; dar congedo; *take* —, stare avvertito; pigliar esempio.

wăr-office, S.: ministerio della guerra, *m.*

wărp 1, S.: (*weav.*) ordito, *m.* **warp** 2, TR.: ordire; piegare; stornare; (*nav.*) rimorchiare; INTR.: piegarsi, incurvarsi. **-ed**, ADJ.: piegato, curvato, storto. **-ing**, S.: piegamento; (*weav.*) orditoio, *m.*, orditura, *f.* **-ing-loom**, S.: orditoio, *m.*

wăr-proof, S.: bravura, *f.*

wárrant 1, S.: ordine; potere, *m.*, autorità; permissione, *f.*; brevetto, patente, *m.*: — *of attorney*, procura, *f.*; *give a* —, dare un brevetto; *have a* —, aver un ordine d' arrestare. **warrant** 2, TR.: assicurare, accertare, mantenere; mallevare. **-able**, ADJ.: giustificabile, difendevole. **-ableness**, S.: giustificazione; autorità, *f.* **-ably**, ADV.: giustificatamente, in modo difendevole. **-er**, S.: mallevadore, *m.*, sicurtà, *f.* **-ise**†, S.: sicurtà; cauzione, malleveria, *f.* **-y**, S.: sicurtà; obbligazione, *f.*

wárren, S.: conigliera, *f.* **-er**, S.: guardiano di conigliera, *m.*

wărrior, S.: guerriero, soldato, *m.*

wărt, S.: porro, *m.*, verruca, *f.* **-wort**, S.: verrucaria, *f.* **-y**, ADJ.: pieno di porri.

wărworn, ADJ.: consumato dalla guerra.

wāry, ADJ.: circospetto, prudente, cauto, accorto; parco, frugale.

wăsh 1, S.: lavazione, lavatura; lisciva, bucata, broda, *f.*; imbratto; pantano, palude; acquerello, vinello, *m.* **wash** 2, IRR.; TR.: lavare, bagnare; bianchire, pulire; INTR.: lavarsi; nettarsi: — *away* (*off*), nettare, purgare; — *over*, colorare; coprire. **-ball**, S.: palla di sapone, *f.* **-er**, S.: lavatore; guattero, *m.* **-erwoman**, S.: lavandaia, *f.* **-hand-basin**, S.: bacino, bacile, *m.* **-house**, S.: lavatoio, *m.*, stanza da lavare, *f.* **-ing**, S.: lavamento, *m.*; imbiancatura, *f.* **-ing-machine**, S.: macchina da lavare, *f.* **-ing-place**, S.: lavatoio, *m.* **-stand**, S.: portacatino, *m.* **-tub**, S.: tino, *m.* **-y**, ADJ.: umido, inumidito.

wăsp, S.: vespa, *f.* **-ish**, ADJ.: dispettoso, fastidioso, fantastico, stizzoso. **-ishly**, ADV.: fastidiosamente, fantasticamente, stizzosamente. **-ishness**, S.: cattivo umore, *m.*, fantasticaggine, *f.*, fastidio, *m.*

wăssail, S.: gozzoviglia, *f.* **-er**, S.: briacone, beone, *m.*

wāste 1, ADJ.: inutile; incolto; distrutto, desolato: *lay* —, distruggere, desolare, rovinare. **waste** 2, S.: distruzione, desolazione; profusione; consunzione; terra deserta, *f.*: *go to* —, andare in malora. **waste** 3, TR.: guastare, desolare, distruggere; spendere, scialacquare; consumare, scemare; diminuire; INTR.: consumarsi, scemarsi: — *away*, deperire, consumarsi. **-ful**, ADJ.: rovinoso, distruttivo; prodigo, spendereccio; deserto, inculto. **-fully**, ADV.: prodigamente, profusamente. **-fulness**, S.: prodigalità, *f.* **-goods**, S.: prodigo, spendereccio, *m.* **-ground**, S.: terra inculta, terra deserta, *f.* **-paper**, S.: carta straccia, *f.* **-r -er**, S.: distruggitore; prodigo, consumatore, *m.*

wătch 1, S.: veglia, guardia; sentinella, *f.*; oriuolo, *m.*; mostra, *f.*: *be upon*

ADJ.: visionario, immaginario. **-ary** 2, **-ist**, S.: visionario, *m.*
visit 1, S.: visita, *f.*, visitamento, *m.*: *pay a —*, fare una visita, visitare; *return a —*, rendere una visita; *on a —*, in visita. **visit** 2, TR.: visitare, far la visita, andare a vedere; far ricadere. **-able**, ADJ.: soggetto ad esser visitato. **-ant**, S.: visitante; visitatore, *m.* **-ātion**, S.: visitazione, *f.*, visitamento, *m.* **-atōrial**, ADJ.: di visitatore. **-er**†, S.: visitatore, *m.* **-ing**, S.: visitamento, *m.*, visita, *f.*: *go a—*, andare in visita. **-ing-day**, S.: giorno di visite, *m.* **-or**, S.: visitatore, *m.*
visor, S.: maschera; visiera (d'un elmo), *f.* **-ed**, ADJ.: mascherato.
vista, S.: vista; prospettiva, *f.*
visual, ADJ.: visuale, visivo.
vi-tal, ADJ.: vitale; essenziale. **-tăl-ity**, S.: vitalità, *f.* **-tally**, ADV.: vitalmente, in modo vitale. **-tals**, S. PL.: parti vitali, *f. pl.*
vi-tiate, TR.: viziare; guastare, corrompere. **-tiātion**, S.: depravazione, corruzione, corruttela, *f.*
vitiliti-gate†, INTR.: contendere in legge, cavillare. **-gātion**†, S.: contenzione, cavillazione, *f.*
vitiŏsity, S.: viziosità, corruttela, *f.*
vitious, ADJ.: vizioso, corrotto. **-ly**, ADV.: viziosamente. **-ness**, S.: depravazione, corruzione, *f.*
vit-reous, ADJ.: vitreo, di vetro. **-rif-icable**†, ADJ.: convertibile in vetro. **-rificātion**, S.: vetrificazione, *f.* **-rify**, TR.: vetrificare; INTR.: vetrificarsi. **-riol**, S.: vitriolo, *m.* **-riolate(d)**†, ADJ.: vitriolato. **-riŏlic**, **-riolous**, ADJ.: vitriolico.
vituline, ADJ.: vitellino, di vitello.
vitŭper-able, ADJ.: vituperabile, vituperevole. **-ate**, TR.: vituperare, censurare, biasimare, svergognare. **-ātion**, S.: vituperazione, *f.* **-ative**, ADJ.: vituperativo.
vi-vācious, ADJ.: vivace; svegliato, brioso. **-vāciousness**, **-văcity**, S.: vivacità; vita; attività, *f.*
vives, S. PL.: (*vet.*) viole, *f. pl.*
vivid, ADJ.: vivido, vivace, spiritoso. **-ly**, ADV.: vivamente, vivacemente. **-ness**, S.: vivezza; vivacità, attività, *f.*, vigore, *m.*
vivifi-c(al)†, ADJ.: vivifico, vivificante. **-cate**† = *vivify*. **-cātion**, S.: vivificazione, *f.*
vivify, TR.: vivificare, animare.
viviparous, ADJ.: viviparo.
vixen, S.: volpe femmina; garritrice, *f.*
viz, ADV.: cioè, vale a dire.
vizard 1, S.: maschera, *f.* **vizard** 2, TR.: mascherare.
vizier, S.: visire, *m.*
vō-cable, S.: vocabolo, *m.* **-căbulary**, S.: vocabolario, dizionario, *m.* **-cal**, ADJ.: vocale, di voce. **-calize**, TR.: vocalizzare. **-cally**, ADV.: vocalmente, articolatamente. **-cātion**, S.: vocazione, *f.*; impiego, *m.* **-cative vŏ-**, S.: (*gram.*) vocativo, caso vocativo, *m.* **-cif-erate**, INTR.: vociferare. **-ciferation**, S.: vociferazione, *f.* **-ciferous**, ADJ.: vociferante; romoroso.
vōgue, S.: voga; moda, foggia; stima, *f.*, credito, *m.*
vōice 1, S.: voce, *f.*; suffragio, *m.*: *in a loud —*, ad alta voce; *in a low —*, sotto voce, con voce sommessa. **voice** 2, TR.: pubblicare. **-d**, ADJ.: dalla voce: *shrill —*, dalla voce stridula.
vōid 1, ADJ.: vuoto, vacuo, nullo: *— of reason*, privo di ragione; *make —*, annullare. **void** 2, S.: vacuo, *m.*, vacuità; nullità; lacuna, *f.* **void** 3, TR.: votare; abbandonare. **-er**, S.: canestro, *m.* **-ness**, S.: vacuità; nullità, *f.*
vōiture†, S.: vettura, *f.*
vōlant, ADJ.: volante; veloce.
vŏla-tile, ADJ.: volatile; volubile. **-tile-ness**, **-tility**, S.: volatilità, *f.* **-tilizātion**, S.: volatilizzazione, *f.* **-tilize**, TR.: volatilizzare.
vol-cānic, ADJ.: vulcanico. **-cāno**, S.: vulcano, *m.*
vōle, S.: tutte le basi, tutte le mani (al giuoco delle carte), *f. pl.*
vōlery, S.: brigata d'uccelli, uccelliera, *f.*
volition, S.: volontà, *f.*, volere, *m.*
vōlitive, ADJ.: volitivo, vogliente.
vŏlley 1, S.: salva (di moschettate); brigata; acclamazione, *f.*, grido, *m.* **volley** 2, TR.: scaricare, sparare.
vōlt 1, S.: (*horse.*) volta, *f.* **volt** 2, S.: unità per misurare la forza elettrica, *f.* **-āic**, ADJ.: voltaico: *— pile*, pila voltaica.
volubility, S.: volubilità; mutabilità; prestezza di lingua, *f.*
vŏlu-ble, ADJ.: volubile; leggiero; presto. **-bly**, ADV.: volubilmente, leggiermente.
vŏl-ume, S.: volume; libro, *m.* **-ūminous**, ADJ.: voluminoso, copioso. **-ūminously**, ADV.: in molti volumi.
vŏlun-tarily, ADV.: volontariamente, spontaneamente. **-tary** 1, ADJ.: volontario, spontaneo. **-tary** 2, S.: (*mus.*) capriccio, *m.*, fantasia, *f.*
voluntēer 1, S.: soldato volontario; avventuriere, *m.* **volunteer** 2, TR.: farsi soldato volontario; arrolarsi.
volŭptu-ary, S.: uomo voluttuoso, *m.* **-ous**, ADJ.: voluttuoso, lussurioso, sensuale. **-ously**, ADV.: voluttuosamente, sensualmente. **-ousness**, S.: voluttà, lussuria, *f.*

viandante, viaggiatore, *m.* **-faring**, ADJ.: viaggiante. **-goer**, S.: ambulante; vagabondo, *m.* **-lāy**, TR.: insidiare, tendere insidie. **-layer**, S.: insidiatore, *m.* **-less**, ADJ.: senza via; non frequentato. **-mark**, S.: indice; palo d' insegna, *m.* **-side**, S.: margine della strada, *m.* **-wanderer**, S.: viandante, *m.*

wāyward, ADJ.: ostinato, ritroso; fastidioso. **-ly**, ADV.: ostinatamente, ritrosamente. **-ness**, S.: ostinatezza; caparbietà; fantasticaggine, *f.*

wē, PRON. PL.: noi.

wēak, ADJ.: debole, infermo; soro: *get* —, indebolirsi, infiacchirsi. **-en**, TR.: debilitare, affievolire; INTR.: debilitarsi, affievolirsi. **-ening**, S.: debilitamento, *m.* **-ling**, S.: deboletto, sparuto, *m.* **-ly** 1, ADJ.: debole, spossato; dilicato. **-ly** 2, ADV.: debolmente. **-ness**, S.: debolezza, infermità, fiacchezza, *f.* **-side**, S.: debole, *m.*, debolezza, *f.*

wēal, S.: bene, *m.*, felicità; prosperità, *f.*

wēald, S.: foresta, selva, *f.*; bosco, *m.*

wĕalth, S.: ricchezze, dovizie, *f. pl.*, beni, *m. pl.* **-ily**, ADV.: riccamente, opulentemente. **-iness**, S.: opulenza, ricchezza, *f.* **-y**, ADJ.: opulento, ricco, dovizioso.

wēan, INTR.: svezzare, spoppare. **-el**, **-ling**, S.: bestiuola spoppata, creaturina slattato, *f.*

wĕapon, S.: arma, *f.* **-ed**, ADJ.: armato. **-less**, ADJ.: senza arme, disarmato.

wêar 1, S.: abiti, vestimenti, *m. pl.*; serbatoio; servizio, *m.*: *the — and tear*, il lograre e lo sdruscire, deterioramento, guastamento. **wear** 2, IRR.; TR.: usare; portare; consumare; INTR.: usarsi; consumarsi: — *away*, logorare, consumare a poco a poco; venir meno, consumarsi; — *off*, logorarsi, usarsi; — *out*, allassare; logorarsi, sdrucirsi; — *well*, essere di buona durata. **-able**, ADJ.: portabile.

wēard†, S.: vigilanza, cura, *f.*

wêarer, S.: portatore, *m.*

wēar-ied, ADJ.: faticato, disgustato. **-iness**, S.: fatica; stanchezza, stracchezza, *f.*; fastidio, *m.*

wêaring, S.: abiti, vestimenti, *m. pl.*: — *apparel*, vestiario, abiti, vestimenti, panni, *m. pl.*

wēa-rish†, ADJ.: pantanoso, melmoso. **-risome**, ADJ.: tedioso, noioso, importuno, incomodo. **-risomely**, ADV.: tediosamente, noiosamente, molestamente. **-risomeness**, S.: tedio, fastidio, *m.*; noia, molestia, *f.* **-ry** 1, ADJ.: lasso, faticato, stracco; infastidito: *grow* —, stufarsi, straccarsi. **-ry** 2, TR.: stufare, straccare, fastidire, noiare.

wēasand, S.: (*anat.*) trachea, *f.*

wēasel, S.: donnola, *f.*

wĕather 1, S.: tempo, *m.*, disposizione dell' aria: *be fine* —, far bel tempo, far bello; *rainy* —, tempo piovoso, *m.*; *stormy* —, tempo procelloso, *m.* **weather** 2, TR.: esporre all' aria; trapassare: — *out*, soffrire, sopportare; — *the storm*, resistere alla tempesta. **-beaten**, ADJ.: sbattuto dal mal tempo. **-board**, S.: parte del vascello esposta al vento, *f.* **-cock**, S.: banderuola, *f.* **-driven**, ADJ.: spinto dalla burrasca. **-gauge**, **-glass**, S.: barometro, termometro, *m.* **-spy**, S.: astrologo, astrolago, *m.* **-wise**, ADJ.: che prevede il tempo che farà.

wēav-e, IRR.; TR.: tessere; intrecciare: — *into*, interporre; far entrare. **-er**, S.: tessitore, *m.*; tesserandolo, *m.*: —*'s beam*, subbio, *m.*; —*'s loom*, telaio, *m.* **-ing**, S.: tessitura; intrecciatura, *f.*

wĕb, S.: tela; tessitura, *f.*; tessuto, *m.*; maglia, macchia (nell' occhio), *f.*: — *of lead*, foglia di piombo, *f.* **-bed**, ADJ.: coperto d' una pellicola. **-footed**, ADJ.: palmipede. **-ster**, S.: tessitore, *m.*

wĕd, TR.: sposare; INTR.: ammogliarsi, unirsi in matrimonio. **-ded**, ADJ.: maritato, sposato. **-ding**, S.: sposalizio, *m* **-ding-day**, S.: giorno nuziale, *m.* **-ding-feast**, S.: festino nuziale, *m.* **-ding-garment**, S.: abito nuziale, *m.* **-ding-guest**, S.: convitato alle nozze, *m.* **-ding-song**, S.: epitalamio, *m.*

wĕdge 1, S.: conio, *m.*: — *of gold*, verga d' oro, *f.*; — *of lead*, spola, spuola, *f.* (strumento). **wedge** 2, TR.: serrare, premere.

wĕdlock, S.: matrimonio, coniugio, *m.*

Wĕdnesday, S.: mercoledì, *m.*

wēe, ADJ.: piccolo, piccino.

wēed 1, S.: abito, *m.*: *black* —*s*, abito lugubre, bruno, *m.*; *friar's* —, abito monacale, *m.* **weed** 2, S.: mal' erba, *f.* **weed** 3, TR.: sarchiare; estirpare. **-er**, S.: sarchiatore; estirpatore, *m.* (**-ing**)**-hook**, S.: sarchiello, sarchio, *m.* **-less**, ADJ.: libero dalle gramigne. **-y**, ADJ.: pieno di cattive erbe.

wēek, S.: settimana, *f.*: *by the* —, a (per) settimana; *next* —, la settimana ventura; *a — from to-morrow*, domani a otto. **-day**, S.: giorno feriale, *m.* **-ly** 1, ADJ.: d' ogni settimana, ebdomadario. **-ly** 2, ADV.: ogni settimana, per settimana.

wēel, S.: nassa; voragine, *f.*

wēen†, INTR.: pensare, immaginare; credere. **-ing**, S.: pensiero, *m.*, opinione; credenza, *f.*

wēep, IRR.; (IN)TR.: piangere, lagrimare. **-er**, S.: piangitore, lagrimante, *m.* **-ers**, S. PL.: strisce di mossolina bianca, *f. pl.* **-ing**, S.: piangimento, pianto, *m.* **-ingly**, ADV.: con pianto. **-ing-willow**, S.: salcio lagrimante, *m.*

-belt, S.: cintola, *f.*, cinturino, *m.* **-coat,** S.: camiciuola, sottoveste, *f.*
wāit 1, S.: agguato; inganno, *m.*, insidia, *f.*: *lie in* —, essere in agguato; spiare; *lie in* — *for one, lay* — *for one,* tendere insidie ad alcuno. **wait** 2, INTR.: aspettare, stare ad aspettare; attendere; dimorare; TR.: aspettarsi a, attendere: — *for,* aspettare; — *on* (*upon*), servire; andare a vedere; — *at table,* servire a tavola. **-er,** S.: servo, garzone di caffè, *m.* **-es,** S. PL.: musici di notte, *m. pl.*; mattinata, *f.* **-ing,** S.: aspettamento, *m.*, guardia, *f.*; attesa: *in* —, in attesa; *lady in* —, dama di onore. **-ing-gentleman,** S.: cameriere, *m.* **-ing-maid, -ing-woman,** S.: cameriera, damigella, *f.* **-ing-room,** S.: sala di attesa (di aspetto), *f.*
wāive, TR.: lasciare, abbandonare, rinunciare a, passar sopra: — *a privilege,* rinunciare ad un privilegio; — *an objection,* passar sopra un' obiezione.
wāk-e 1, S.: vigilia, veglia, *f.* **-e** 2, IRR.; (IN)TR.: destare; vegliare, svegliare. **-eful,** ADJ.: vigilante, svegliato. **-efully,** ADV.: vigilantemente. **-efulness,** S.: poca disposizione a dormire, *f.*; svegliare, *m.* **-en,** (IN)TR.: svegliare; svegliarsi. **-ener,** S.: eccitatore, *m.* **-ing,** S.: svegliamento, *m.*
wāle, S.: parte vellosa (di drappo), *f.*
wālk 1, S.: camminata, passeggiata, *f.*, viale, *m.*: *take a* —, fare una passeggiata. **walk** 2, (IN)TR.: andare, camminare; passeggiare: — *the rounds,* far la ronda; — *the streets,* battere le strade; — *after,* seguitare, seguire; — *in,* entrare; — *off,* andarsene, scappare; — *out,* uscire; venire fuora; — *up,* salire. **-er,** S.: camminatore, camminante, *m.* **-ing,** S.: passeggiata, *f.*: *go a-*—, andare a spasso. **-ing-place,** S.: passeggio, viale, *m.* **-ing-staff,** S.: bastone, bordone; sostegno, *m.* **-ing-stick,** S.: bacchetta, *f.*, bastoncino, *m.*
wāll 1, S.: muro, *m.*, muraglia; parete, *f.*: *city* —*s,* mura della città; *partition* —, parete, *f.*; *go to the* —, soccombere; *give one the* —, dar la dritta ad alcuno. **wall** 2, TR.: murare; circondare con un muro. **-creeper,** S.: picchio, *m.* (uccello).
wāllet, S.: valigia, bisaccia, tasca, *f.*
wāll-eyed, ADJ.: che ha gli occhi bianchi. **-flower,** S.: garofano, *m.* **-fruit,** S.: frutto di spalliera, *m.*
wāllop, INTR.: bollire; (*pop.*) battere, bastonare.
wāllow, INTR.: voltolare, voltolarsi nel fango: — *in the mire,* avvoltolarsi nel fango.
wāllow-ish†, ADJ.: sporco, scipito.
wāll-tree, S.: spalliera, *f.* **-wort,** S.: (*bot.*) parietaria, *f.*
wālnut, S.: noce, *f.* **-shell,** S.: scorza di noce, *f.* **-tree,** S.: noce, *m.*
wāltron†, **wālrus,** S.: morsa (foca zannuta), *f.*
wāltz 1, S.: valzer, *m.* **waltz** 2, INTR.: ballare il valzer. **-er,** S.: valzista, *m.*
wām-ble, INTR.: gorgogliare, romoreggiare; bollire. **-bling,** S.: gorgogliamento, *m.*
wān, ADJ.: pallido, smorto; macilente: *grow* —, impallidire.
wānd, S.: verga; bacchetta magica, *f.*
wānder, (IN)TR.: vagare, vagabondare: — *out of the way,* errare la strada, smarrirsi. **-er,** S.: vagabondo, *m.* **-ing** 1, ADJ.: errante, errabondo, vagabondo; distratto: — *life,* vita girovaga. **-ing** 2, S.: l' errare, il vagare; scorsa, *f.*; sviamento, *m.*
wāne 1, S.: scemo (della luna), *m.*; decadenza, *f.* **wane** 2, INTR.: scemarsi; declinare.
wān-ned, ADJ.: impallidito, scolorito. **-ness,** S.: pallidezza; macilenza, *f.* **-nish,** ADJ.: pallidetto.
wānt 1, S.: mancanza, *f.*, mancamento; difetto, *m.*, deficienza, *f.*; bisogno, *m.*; necessità; indigenza, povertà, *f.*: *for* — *of,* per mancanza (deficienza) di; *be in* — *of,* aver bisogno di. **want** 2, TR.: avere bisogno di, abbisognare; mancare; INTR.: mancare; essere deficiente; volere, desiderare, domandare: *what do you* —? che vi manca? che cercate? che volete? *I* — *a hat,* ho bisogno di un cappello; *you are* —*ed,* qualcheduno vi domanda. **-ing** 1, ADJ.: manchevole, che manca, mancante, assente: *be* —, difettare, mancare; venir meno; *he is not* — *in courage,* non gli manca il coraggio. **-ing** 2, S.: mancamento, bisogno, *m.*, necessità, *f.* **-less,** ADJ.: che non manca, abbondante.
wānton 1, ADJ.: scherzevole; libidinoso, lascivo. **wanton** 2, S.: scherzoso, *m.*, persona lasciva, *f.* **wanton** 3, INTR.: scherzare, gozzovigliare, pazzeggiare. **-ly,** ADV.: scherzevolmente; lascivamente, impudicamente. **-ness,** S.: scherzo, trastullo, *m.*; lascivia, impudicizia, *f.*
wāntwit†, S.: baccello, minchione, *m.*
wār 1, S.: guerra; ostilità, *f.*: *man of* —, uomo di guerra, soldato, *m.*; nave da guerra, *f.*; *make* —, fare guerra, muover guerra; *at* —, in guerra. **war** 2, INTR.: guerreggiare, fare guerra.
wār-ble, TR.: gorgheggiare; trillare. **-bler,** S.: che gorgheggia, che trilla. **-bling,** S.: garrito (degli uccelli), trillo, *m.*
wārd 1, S.: guardia, custodia; prigione *f.*, carcere; quartiere; pupillo, *m.*; **tuts**

whàt, PRON. REL.: ciò che, quel che; INT.: che? che cosa? come? quale? — *you learn, learn well*, ciò che imparate, imparatelo bene; *I don't understand — you say*, non intendo quel che dite; *know —'s —*, saper distinguere; — *do you say?* che dite? che cosa dite? — *a beautiful woman!* che bella donna! — *is your name?* come vi chiamate? **-ĕvẹr, -sǫĕvẹr**, PRON.: qualunque, qual si sia; qualche, checche.

whēal, S.: ciccione, cosso, *m.*, bolla, *f.*

whēat, S.: grano, frumento, *m.*, biada, *f.*: *spring* —, frumento marzuolo. **-en**, ADJ.: di grano.

whēe-dle, TR.: allettare, lusingare; ingannare. **-dlẹr**, S.: allettatore, lusingatore, *m.* **-dling** 1, ADJ.: lusinghevole. **-dling** 2, S.: allettamento, blandimento, *m.*

whēel 1, S.: ruota; volta, *f.*: *spinning* —, filatoio, *m.*; *turner's* —, tornio, *m.*; — *of fortune*, ruota della fortuna. **wheel** 2, TR.: voltolare, rotolare; INTR.: voltarsi, aggirarsi; voltar faccia. **-age**, S.: tassa che pagano i carri, *f.* **-barrǫw**, S.: carriuola, *f.*, carrettino, *m.* **-ẹr**, S.: facitore di ruote, *m.* **-track**, S.: rotaia, *f.* **-work**, S.: ruote (d' una macchina), *f. pl.* **-wright**, S.: facitore di ruote, *m.* **-y**†, ADJ.: rotatorio, circolare.

whēeze, INTR.: respirare, rifiatare con difficoltà.

whĕlk, S.: pustula; protuberanza, *f.* **-y**, ADJ.: gonfio, tumido.

whĕlm, TR.: coprire, occultare; seppellire.

whĕlp 1, S.: cagnuolino, cagnolino; lupicino, *m.* **whelp** 2, INTR.: figliare; fare i cagnuolini.

whĕn, ADV.: quando; mentre; allorchè: — *will you come?* quando verrete? *since —?* di quando in qua? — *you were in F.*, allorchè eravate in F.

whĕn-ce, ADV.: onde, donde. **-ceĕvẹr, -cesǫĕvẹr**, ADV.: dondechè. **-ĕvẹr, -sǫĕvẹr**, ADV.: quando, ogni volta che.

whêre, ADV.: dove, in qual luogo: *any-* —, ovunque; *every*—, dappertutto, pertutto. **-about(s)**, ADJ.: dove, in che luogo: *let us know your* —, fateci sapere dove siete. **-ăs**, ADV.: in luogo che; perchè, stante che. **-ăt**, ADV.: al che, del che. **-bȳ**, ADV.: per il quale, per cui. **-fǫre**, ADV.: per la qual causa, perciò. **-frŏm**, ADV.: donde. **-in**, ADV.: in che, nel quale; dove. **-intō**, ADV.: nel quale. **-ŏf**, PRON.: del quale; delle quali. **-ŏn**, ADV.: sopra di che, sul che, sul quale. **-sǫĕvẹr**, ADV.: in qualunque luogo. **-tō**, **-untō**, ADV.: al che, al quale. **-upŏn**, ADV.: nel che, in questo mentre. **-vẹr ĕvẹr**, ADV.: ovunque, in qualunque luogo. **-with(ăl)**, ADV.: con che, con quale.

whĕrret† 1, S.: schiaffo, *m.* **wherret**† 2, TR.: dare schiaffi; affrettare.

whĕrry, S.: barchetta, *f.*

whĕt 1, S.: aguzzamento; sorso, *m.* **whet** 2, TR.: aguzzare, affilare; (*fig.*) eccitare: — *a knife*, aguzzare (affilare) un coltello; — *the appetite*, aguzzare l' appetito.

whĕthẹr, PRON.: quale, quale de' due; CONJ.: se, sia, sia che, che: — *he come or not*, che (*or* se) venga o non; — *he will or no*, voglia o non voglia.

whĕt-stone, S.: cote, *f.* **-tẹr**, S.: affilatore, arrotino, *m.* **-ting**, S.: agguzzamento, affilare, *m.*

whêy, S.: siero, *m.* **-ey, -ish**, ADJ.: sieroso, di siero.

which, PRON. REL.: che, il quale (la quale, i quali, le quali), il (lo) che *or* quale; INTERR.: quale (quali)? *the book* —, il libro che; *the horses* —, i cavalli che; *take — you please*, prendete qual volete; *you have lied, — displeases me*, voi avete mentito, il che mi dispiace; *of* —, del quale; *from* —, dal quale; — *will you have?* qual volete? **-sǫĕvẹr**, PRON.: qualunque, l' uno o l' altro.

whiff, S.: alito, fiato, soffiamento, *m.*: — *of tobacco*, soffio di tabacco, *m.* **-le**, TR.: soffiare; INTR.: muoversi ad ogni vento; dondolarsi. **-lẹr**, S.: soffiatore; piffero; uomo da niente, *m.* **-ling**, ADJ.: di niun valore, frivolo.

Whig 1, S.: repubblicano, *m.* **whig**† 2, S.: siero, *m.* **-gish**, ADJ.: repubblicano. **-gism**, S.: fazione inglese di repubblicani, *f.*

whil-e 1, S.: tempo, spazio di tempo, *m.*; volta, *f.*: *a little* —, poco tempo, un momentino; *a — after*, qualche tempo dopo; *all the* —, per tutto il tempo; *for a* —, per qualche tempo; *in the mean*—, frattanto; *between —s*, di quando in quando; *it is not worth the* —, non monta il pregio; non vale la pena. **-e** 2, CONJ.: mentre che, tanto che. **-e** 3, INTR.: indugiare, procrastinare: — *away one's time*, perder il suo tempo. **-ǫm**, ADV.: tempo fu, altre volte, anticamente. **-st**, CONJ.: mentre che.

whim, S.: capriccio, *m.*, fantasia, *f.*

whimpẹr, INTR.: gemere, dolersi. **-ing**, S.: lamento, *m.*, doglianza, *f.*

whim-sey, S.: capriccio, ghiribizzo, *m.* **-sical**, ADJ.: capriccioso, ghiribizzoso, fantastico. **-sically**, ADV.: a capriccio, fantasticamente. **-sicalness**, S.: capricciosità, *f.* **-wham**, S.: bagattella, *f.*

whin, S.: (bot.) agrifoglio, alloro spinoso, *m.*

wēet †, INTR.: sapere, essere informato. **-less** †, ADJ.: senza sapere, ignorante.
wēevil, S.: punteruolo, gorgoglione, tonchio, *m.*
wēezel, S.: donnola, *f.*
wĕft †, S.: tessuto, *m.*, tessitura; treccia (di capelli), *f.* **-age** †, S.: tessuto, *m.*; connessione, *f.*
wēigh, TR.: pesare, ponderare; considerare; esaminare; INTR.: pesare, essere pesante, essere di peso: — *anchor*, salpare, sarpare l'ancora; — *every word*, ponderare ogni parola; — *down*, prevalere, superare; — *upon*, pesare; affiggere. **-er**, S.: pesatore, *m.* **-ing**, S.: pesare, *m.* **-t**, S.: peso, *m.*; gravezza; importanza, *f.*, momento, *m.*: —*s*, *pair of* —*s*, bilancia, *f.*; *net* —, peso netto; *stamped* —, peso aggiustato; *standard* —, peso regolato; *make good* —, far buon peso; *matters of little* —, cose di poca rilevanza. **-tily**, ADV.: pesantemente, gravemente. **-tiness**, S.: peso, *m.*, gravezza; importanza, *f.* **-tless**, ADJ.: non pesante, leggiero; di poca importanza. **-ty**, ADJ.: pesante; grave, importante.
wēird, ADJ.: fatidico, fatale; spaventevole.
wĕlaway! †, INTERJ.: ohimè!
Wĕlch-rabbit, S.: fetta di pane con cacio, *f.*
wĕlcom-e 1, ADJ.: ben venuto; grato, piacevole: *bid* —, fare buona accoglienza; *you are* —, ben venuto; *if you like it you are* —, se vi aggrada, è a vostro comando. **-e!** 2, INTERJ.: siate ben venuto! **-e** 3, S.: buona accoglienza, *f.* **-e** 4, TR.: fare buona accoglienza, accogliere con amorevolezza. **-eness**, S.: piacevolezza, accettatezza, *f.* **-er**, S.: che fa buona accoglienza. **-ing**, S.: buona accoglienza, *f.*
wĕld 1, S.: guado, *m.*, erba guada, *f.* **weld** 2, TR.: battere il ferro caldo; giungere, unire.
wĕlfare, S.: salute, prosperità, *f.*
wĕlk 1, S.: ruga, grinza, crespa, *f.* **welk** 2, TR.: oscurare, adombrare. **-ed**, ADJ.: rugoso, aggrinzato, piegato.
wĕlkin, S.: etere, cielo, fermamento, *m.*
wĕll 1, S.: pozzo, *m.*, sorgente, fontana, *f.* **well** 2, INTR.: zampillare, scaturire. **well** 3, ADJ.: sano, in buona salute; felice; ADV.: bene, molto: *be* —, esser bene; — *and good*, alla buon' ora; *as* — *as*, tanto bene che, così bene come; *grow* — *again*, ricuperare la salute; *all's* — *that ends* —, la fine corona l'opera. **-aday!** INTERJ.: cappita! capperi! **-affected**, ADJ.: ben intenzionato. **-becoming**, ADJ.: convenevole, dicevole. **-being**, S.: prosperità, felicità, *f.* **-beloved**, ADJ.: molto amato, dilettissimo. **-born**, ADJ.: di buona nascita. **-bred**, ADJ.: ben allevato, ben creato. **-disposed**, ADJ.: caritatevole. **-doing**, S.: benignità, *f.* **-done**, ADJ.: ben fatto; ben cotto. **-formed**, ADJ.: ben formato.
wĕllhead, S.: sorgente, fontana, *f.*
wĕll-looking, ADJ.: avvenente, avvistato. **-meaning** 1, ADJ.: ben intenzionato. **-meaning** 2, S.: buona intenzione, *f.* **-met!** INTERJ.: mi rallegro di vedervi. **-nātured**, ADJ.: di buon naturale. **-nigh**, ADV.: presso a poco, quasi. **-pump**, S.: sentina, *f.* **-spring**, S.: sorgente, fontana, *f.* **-water**, S.: acqua di pozzo, *f.*
wĕll-willer †, S.: benevogliente, benevolo, *m.* **-wish**, S.: buona volontà, benevolenza, *f.* **-wisher**, S.: che desidera bene; amico, *m.*
wĕlt 1, S.: orlo, lembo, *m.*; margine, *f.* **welt** 2, TR.: orlare, fregiare.
wĕlter, INTR.: voltolarsi; impantanarsi.
wĕm † 1, S.: macchia; pancia, *f.* **wem** 2, TR.: macchiare.
wĕn, S.: tumore calloso, gozzo, enfiamento, *m.*
wĕnch, S.: zitella, ragazza, *f.*
wĕnd, INTR.: andare, andar via; volgersi.
wĕn-nish, **-ny**, ADJ.: gozzuto, gonfio; di gozzo.
wēre (di *be*): *as it* —, per così dire, quasi che; *if I* — *rich*, s'io fossi rico.
wēr(e)wolf, S.: lupo uomo, lupo mannaro, *m.*
wē-sand, **-sil** = *weasand*.
wĕst 1, ADJ.: occidentale. **west** 2, ADV.: al ponente, all'occidente. **west** 3, S.: ovest, ponente, occidente, occaso, *m.* **-ering**, ADJ.: andante verso l'occidente, tramontante. **-erly**, **-ern**, ADJ.: occidentale, d'occidente. **-ward**, **-wardly**, ADV.: verso l'ovest, all'occidente.
wĕt 1, ADJ.: umido, bagnato; molle: — *weather*, tempo piovoso, *m.*; *make* —, bagnare. **wet** 2, S.: umidità; mollezza, *f.* **wet** 3, TR.: umettare, bagnare, adacquare.
wĕther, S.: montone, castrato, *m.*
wĕt-ness, S.: umidezza, umidità; mollezza, *f.* **-nurse**, S.: balia, allevatrice, *f.* **-ting**, S.: bagnamento, bagnare, *m.* **-tish** †, ADJ.: alquanto umido.
wĕx †, INTR.: crescere, ingrandirsi.
whāl-e, S.: balena, *f.* **-ebone**, S.: osso di balena, *m.* **-er**, S.: pescatore delle balene, *m.*
whălly, ADJ.: strisciato, vergato.
whăng 1, S.: coreggia, *f.* **whang** 2, TR.: frustrare, battere.
whăp, S.: colpo, *m.*
whārf, S.: porto; molo, *m.* **-age**, S.: diritto del ripaggio, *m.* **-inger**, S.: guardiano d'un molo, *m.*

mente. **-ness**, S.: iniquità, malvagità, perversità, *f.*
wicker, ADJ.: di vinco.
wicket, S.: sportello, portello, *m.*
widdle-waddle, ADV.: barcollando.
wide, ADJ.: largo, ampio, vasto; grande; ADV.: largamente, lontano; affatto: *far and* —, dappertutto, da ogni banda; *throw* — *open*, spalancare. **-ly**, ADV.: largamente, ampiamente; molto. **-n**, (IN)TR.: allargare, distendere. **-ness**, S.: larghezza, ampiezza, *f.*
widgeon, S.: folaga, *f.* (uccello); sciocco, *m.*
widow 1, S.: vedova, *f.* **widow** 2, TR.: privare del marito. **-er**, S.: vedovo, *m.* **-hood**, S.: vedovaggio, stato vedovile, *m.* **-hunter**, S.: che amoreggia vedove per la dote.
width, S.: larghezza, ampiezza, *f.*
wield, TR.: maneggiare, trattare; governare. **-ing**, S.: maneggiare, maneggio, *m.* **-less**, ADJ.: non maneggiabile. **-y**, ADJ.: maneggevole, maneggiabile.
wiery†, ADJ.: fatto di fili di metallo; umido.
wife, S.: moglie, sposa, *f.* **-hood**, S.: stato coniugale, *m.* **-less**, ADJ.: senza moglie.
wig, S.: parrucca; ciambella, *f.*
wight 1, S.: uomo, *m.*; donna; creatura, *f.* **wight**† 2, ADJ.: veloce, presto. **-ly**†, ADV.: velocemente.
wigwam, S.: capanna indiana, *f.*
wild 1, ADJ.: salvatico; deserto; intrattabile, indomito, feroce: — *animals*, animali selvatici; — *flowers*, fiori silvestri; — *country*, paese incolto (silvestre); — *passions*, passioni sfrenati; — *project*, progetto insensato; — *beast*, fiera, *f.*; — *oats*, avena sterile; *sow one's* — *oats*, scapricciarsi; *lead one a* — *goose chase*, tenere uno a bada con belle promesse.
wild 2, S.: deserto, paese solitario, *m.*
wilder, TR.: imbarazzare.
wilderness, S.: deserto, *m.*, solitudine, *f.*
wild-fire, S.: fuoco greco, *m.* **-goose-chase**, S.: abbaiare alla luna, *m.* **-ing** 1, S.: corbezzola, *f.*: —*s*, frutti salvatici, *m. pl.* **-ing** 2, ADJ.: salvatico. **-ing-tree**, S.: corbezzolo, *m.* **-look**, S.: aria stravolta, *f.* **-ly**, ADV.: salvaticamente; confusamente. **-ness**, S.: salvatichezza; ferocia, *f.*
wile 1, S.: furberia, sottigliezza, *f.* **wile**† 2, TR.: ingannare.
wilful, ADJ.: caparbio, ostinato. **-ly**, ADV.: caparbiamente, ostinatamente. **-ness**, S.: caparbietà; ostinazione, *f.*
wili-ly, ADV.: astutamente, fraudolosamente, ingannevolmente. **-ness**, S.: astuzia, sottigliezza, *f.*
will 1, S.: volontà, inclinazione, *f.*; volere, piacere; desiderio, piacimeno, *m.*: *free* —, libero arbitrio, *m.*; *good* —, benevolenza, *f.*; *ill* —, malevolenza, malignità, *f.*; *last* —, ultima volontà, *f.*, testamento, *m.*; *against one's* —, malvolentieri, malgrado; *at* —, a volontà, a piacere, a piacimento; *bear one good* (*bad*) —, volere bene (male) ad uno. **will** 2, IRR.; TR.: volere, desiderare; comandare; ordinare; legare (per testamento); *as aux.* = *Fut.* ecc.; *I* — *go*, voglio andare; *he* — *go*, andrà; — *he, nill he*, buon grado mal grado. **-ing**, ADJ.: inclinato, pronto: *with a* — *mind*, di buon grado. **-ingly**, ADV.: volentiermente, volentieri, di buon grado. **-ingness**, S.: buona volontà, prontezza, *f.*
will-o'-the-wisp, S.: fuoco fatuo, *m.*
willow, S.: salce, sàlice, *m.* **-plot**, S.: salceto, *m.* **-y**, ADJ.: pieno di salci.
wilsome†, ADJ.: ostinato, caparbio.
wily, ADJ.: astuto, scaltrito, fino.
wimble 1, S.: foratoio, succhio, succhiello, *m.* **wimble** 2, ADJ.: agile, destro.
wimple, S.: banderuola, *f.*, pennoncello; capperone, *m.*
win, IRR.; TR.: vincere, guadagnare; acquistare: — *the day*, ottenere la vittoria; — *back*, riacquistare, riguadagnare.
wince, **winch** 1, INTR.: calcitrare, tirare de' calci. **winch** 2, S.: vite; chiocciola; manovella, *f.*, manubrio, *m.*
wind 1, S.: vento; alito, fiato, respiro; odore, *m.*; vanità, *f.*: *the* — *blows*, fa vento; *gust of* —, folata, *f.*; *break* —, tirar corregge; *fetch one's* —, respirare; *go down the* —, venire in peggiore stato; *have the* —, avere l'avvantaggio; *sail before the* —, aver il vento in poppa.
wind 2, IRR.; TR.: voltare; variare, mutare; serpeggiare; torcigliare; avvolgere, inviluppare; aggomitolare; fiutare; annasare; INTR.: attorcigliarsi; avvolgersi: — *a horn*, suonare un corno; — *up a watch*, caricare un oriuolo; — *off*, annaspare; — *out*, spacciare, sgomberare; — *up*, accordare; alzare; finire, conchiudere.
wind-bound, ADJ.: (*nav.*) trattenuto dal vento contrario.
winder, S.: aggomitolatore; arcolaio, *m.*
wind-fall, S.: accidente prospero, *m.*, buona fortuna, *f.* **-flower**, S.: anemone, *f.* **-gall**, S.: (*vet.*) tumore acqueo, *m.* **-gun**, S.: schioppo da vento, *m.* **-iness**, S.: ventosità, flatuosità, *f.*
winding, S.: giramento, *m.*; sinuosità, *f.*: —*s of a river*, andirivieni di un fiume. **-sheet**, S.: palio di morto, *m.* **-stairs**, S. PL.: scala a chiocciola, *f.*
windlass, S.: argano, *m.*
wind-mill, S.: mulino a vento, mulino da vento, *m.*

whin-e 1, s.: lamento, rammarico, *m.* **-e** 2, INTR.: dolersi, rammaricarsi, lagnarsi. **-ing** 1, ADJ.: lamentevole, dolente. **-ing** 2, s.: lamento, rammarico; dolore, *m.*

whinny, INTR.: nitrire, annitrire.

whip 1, s.: frusta, sferza, *f.* **whip** 2, TR.: frustare, sferzare: — *away*, cacciare a furia di sferzate; — *in*, entrare subitamente; — *off*, afferrare; spedire; — *out*, uscir subitamente; — *up*, salire prontamente; — *up and down*, andare qua e là. **-cord**, s.: corda da frusta, *f.* **-hand**, s.: vantaggio, *m.*, superiorità, *f.* **-lash**, s.: punta della frusta, *f.* **-per**, s.: frustatore, *m.* **-ping**, s.: il frustare, il flagellare, *m.*; sferzata, frustatura, bastonata, staffilata, *f.*: *give a* —, dare una staffilata, bastonare. **-ping-post**, s.: palo da frustare, *m.* **-saw**, s.: pialla, *f.* **-staff**, s.: timone, *m.*, manovella, *f.* **-ster**, s.: giovanotto svelto, *m.* **-stock**, s.: manico della sferza, *f.* **-t**, impf. e part. del v. *whip*.

whirl 1, s.: giramento, turbine, *m.* **whirl** 2, (IN)TR.: girare con impeto; aggirarsi. **-bone**, s.: padella del ginocchio, *f.* **-igig**, s.: zurlo, *m.*, trottola, *f.* **-pool**, s.: voragine, *f.*; abisso, *m.* **-wind**, s.: turbine, *m.*

whirry† = *whirl.*

whisk 1, s.: spazzola, scopetta, *f.* **whisk** 2, TR.: spazzolare, nettare colla spazzola: — *away*, spacciarsi, spedirsi. **-er**, s.: mustacchio, *m.*; basetta, *f.*

whisk(e)y, s.: orzo stillato, *m.*

whisper 1, s.: bisbiglio, mormorio, *m.* **whisper** 2, s.: bisbigliare, susurrare. **-er**, s.: bisbigliatore, susurrone, *m.* **-ing**, s.: bisbiglio, *m.*

whist 1, INTERJ.: zitto! silenzio! **whist** 2, s.: giuoco di carte, *m.*

whis-tle 1, s.: fischio, *m.* **-tle** 2, INTR.: zufolare, fischiare. **-tler**, s.: fischiatore; sibilatore, *m.* **-tling**, ADJ.: fischiante; sibilante. **-tling**, s.: fischio, zufolio, sibilo, *m.*

whit, s.: poco, tantino, punto, *m.*; nulla, *f.*: *every* —, affatto, pertutto; *not a* —, niente affatto.

white 1, ADJ.: bianco; bigio, puro. **white** 2, s.: bianco, color bianco; belletto; bersaglio; albume (d'un' uovo), *m.*: *hit the* —, dar nel bersaglio. **white** 3, TR.: imbiancare, far divenire bianco. **-lead**, s.: piombo calcinato, *m.*, cerussa, *f.* **-lime**, s.: calcina, calce bianca, *f.* **-livered**, ADJ.: poltrone, malizioso, codardo. **-ly**†, ADJ.: alquanto bianco, bianchiccio. **-meat**, s.: biancomangiare, *m.* **-n**, INTR.: imbiancare. **-ner**, s.: imbiancatore; purgatore, *m.* **-ness**, s.: bianchezza; pallidezza, *f.* **-ning**, s.: bianchimento; curare, *m.* **-pot**, s.: tarta, *f.*, pasticetto, *m.* **-thorn**, s.: spina alba, *f.*, bianco spino, *m.* **-wash** 1, s.: liscio; belletto, *m.* **-wash** 2, TR.: intonicare; colorire. **-wine**, s.: vino bianco, *m.* **-wort**, s.: (*bot.*) matricale, *f.*

whither, ADV.: dove, ove. **-soever**, ADV.: in qualunque luogo, dovunque.

whiting, s.: nasello, merluzzo, *m.* (pesce).

whitish, ADJ.: bianchetto, biancastro. **-ness**, s.: bianchezza, *f.*

whitlow, s.: panereccio, *m.*

whitster†, s.: imbiancatore, curandaio, *m.*

Whitsun-day, s.: pentecoste, *f.* **-tide**, s.: stagione della pentecoste, *f.*

whitten-tree, s.: oppio, *m.* (albero).

whittle 1, s.: vesta bianca (da donna), mantellina, *f.*; coltellino, *m.* **whittle** 2, INTR.: scorzare, tagliuzzare.

whiz 1, INTR.: ronzare; sibilare. **-whiz(zing)** 2, s.: ronzio; fischio, sibilo, susurro, *m.*

whō, PRON. INTERR.: chi? PRON. REL.: che, il quale. **-ŏver**, PRON.: chiunque, qualunque.

whōle 1, ADJ.: tutto, intero, totale: — *and sound*, bello e buono; *a — year*, un anno intero. **whole** 2, s.: tutto, *m.*, totalità, *f.*: *in the* —, in tutto e per tutto; *upon the* —, ogni cosa ben pesata, in somma, in sostanza; *sell by the* —, vendere all' ingrosso. **-ness**, s.: stato intero, *m.*, integrità, *f.* **-sale**, s.: vendita all' ingrosso, *f.*: — *dealer*, — *merchant*, venditore all' ingrosso, *m.* **-some**, ADJ.: sano; salutifero, salubre. **-somely**, ADV.: sanamente; salubremente. **-someness**, s.: sanità; salubrità, *f.*

whŏlly, ADV.: interamente, affatto.

whōm, PRON.: che. **-soĕver**, PRON.: chiunque, qualunque.

whōobub†, s.: tumulto, romore, *m.*; rissa, *f.*

whōop 1, s.: upupa, *f.* (uccello); grido, *m.* **whoop** 2, TR.: gridare: — *at*, insultare.

whōre, s.: cattiva donna, *f.*

whŏrtleberry, s.: mora prugnola, *f.*

whō-se, PRON. INTERR.: di chi? di quale? PRON. REL.: di cui, di chi, a chi, da chi. **-so(ĕver)**, PRON.: chiunque, qualunque.

whŭr, INTR.: ringhiare (come un cane).

whŭrt†, s.: mora prugnola, mora del rogo, *f.*

whȳ, ADV.: perchè, per che causa, per che ragione: — *not?* perchè non? — *truly*, veramente.

wick, s.: stoppino, lucignolo, *m.*

wicked, ADJ.: cattivo, maligno; tristo: *the* —, gli cattivi, gli dannati, *pl.* **-ly** ADV.: cattivamente, malamente; tristi

witcracker†, S.: beffatore, *m.*
with, PREP.: con; da, di, a: — *me*, con me, meco; — *child*, incinta; *meet* —, incontrare; abbattersi in. **-āl** 1, PREP.: con, fra, infra, tra. **-al** 2, ADV.: anche, ancora, di più. **-drāw**, IRR.; TR.: ritirare; levare; INTR.: ritirarsi, andarsene; partire, uscire. **-drāwing-room**, S.: retrocamera, *f.*
withe, S.: ramicello di salcio, vinco; ramo, *m.*
wither, TR.: fare seccare; appassare; INTR.: sfiorire; disseccarsi, appassarsi. **-ed**, ADJ.: sfiorito; appassato, passo. **-ing**, S.: sfiorire, *m.*; aridezza, *f.* **-edness**, S.: smarrimento, *m.*; aridezza, *f.*
withers, S. PL.: garrese (del cavallo), *m.* **-wrung**, S.: morso di cavallo, *m.*
with-held, ADJ.: ritenuto; impedito. **-hōld**, IRR.; TR.: ritenere, impedire; ricusare; arrestare: — *a thing from*, rifiutare una cosa a. **-hōlden**, ADJ.: ritenuto; ricusato. **-hōlder**, S.: ritenitore, detentore, *m.* **-hōlding**, S.: ritenimento ritegno, *m.* **-in**, PREP.: in, fra, dentro; ADV.: indentro, interiormente; a casa, in casa: — *and without*, per entro e fuor; — *reach*, alla portata. **-out**, PREP.: fuor, fuori di; ADV.: fuori, al di fuori, fuora; esteriormente; fuorchè, a meno che, se non che: — *the city*, fuori della città; — *book*, a mente; — *doubt*, senza dubbio; — *much ado*, senza soverchia difficoltà; *a fine house* —, una bella casa al di fuori. **-stănd**, IRR.; TR.: resistere, opporsi. **-stănder**, S.: resistente, oppositore, *m.* **-stănding**, S.: resistenza, opposizione, *f.*
withy, S.: vinco, vinciglio, *m.*
witless ADJ.: sciocco, scimunito. **-ly**, ADV.: scioccamente, inconsideratamente. **-ness**, S.: sciocchezza, inconsideratezza, *f.*
witling, S.: saccentuzzo, *m.*
witness 1, S.: testimonio, testimone, *m.*; testimonianza, *f.*: *with a* —, effettivamente; *bear* —, testificare; *call to* —, chiamare in testimonio. **witness** 2, (IN)TR.: testificare, attestare. **-ing**, S.: testimonianza, *f.*
wit-snapper†, S.: che studia di dar belle risposte. **-ted**, ADJ.: d' ingegno. **-ticism**, S.: concetto spiritoso, *m.* **-tily**, ADV.: ingegnosamente, con ispirito. **-tiness**, S.: acutezza d' ingegno, *f.*, spirito, *m.* **-tingly**, ADV.: a posta, a posta fatta, a bello studio. **-ty**, ADJ.: ingegnoso, spiritoso: *be* —, motteggiare.
wive, INTR.: ammogliarsi, prender moglie. **-hood**†, S.: stato coniugale, *m.* **-less**†, ADV.: senza moglie. **-ly**†, ADJ.: mogliereccio, mogliesco. **-s**, PL. di *wife*.
wizard, S.: indovino, mago, *m.* **-y**, S.: stregoneria, malia, *f.*
wizen, INTR.: seccarsi.
wō†, ecc. = *woe*, ecc.
wōad 1, S.: guado, *m.* **woad** 2, TR.: tingere con guado.
wōe 1, S.: guaio, dolore, *m.*; miseria, *f.* **woe !** 2, INTERJ.: guai! **-begone**, ADJ.: immerso in guai, addoloratissimo. **-ful**, ADJ.: dolente; mesto, misero. **-fully**, ADV.: dogliosamente, miseramente. **-fulness**, S.: miseria, tristezza, calamità, *f.*
wōld, S.: rasa campagna, campagna aprica e montagnosa, *f.*
wolf *wŭlf* (pl. *wolves*), S.: lupo, *m.*: *young* —, lupacchino, lupicino, *m.*; *she*—, lupa, *f.* **-dog**, S.: mastino, *m.* **-ish**, ADJ.: di lupo; goloso. **-s'-bane**, S.: (*bot.*) aconito, *m.* **-'s-milk**, S.: (*bot.*) titimalo, titimaglio, *m.*
wŏman, S.: femmina, donna, *f.* **-ed**, ADJ.: accompagnato con donna. **-hater**, S.: odiatore del sesso femmineo, *m.* **-hood**, S.: stato di donna, *m.*, condizione di donna, *f.* **-ish**, ADJ.: di donna; femminile; effeminato. **-ishly**, ADV.: donnescamente. **-ize**†, TR.: snervare, effemminare. **-kind**, S.: sesso femmineo, *m.*; donne, *f. pl.* **-like**, ADJ.: femmineo, femminino. **-ly** 1, ADJ.: di donna, donnesco, effemminato, debile. **-ly** 2, ADV.: da donna; effemminatamente; mollemente.
wōmb, S.: matrice, *f.*, utero, *m.*
wŏn 1, impf. e part. del v. *win*. **won**† 2, S.: dimora, abitazione, *f.* **won**† 3, INTR.: dimorare, stare.
wŏnder 1, S.: maraviglia, *f.*; stupore, *m.* **wonder** 2, INTR.: maravigliarsi; stupirsi (di, *at*): *I* — *what that is*, vorrei sapere che cosa è questa. **-er**, S.: ammiratore, *m.* **-ful**, ADJ.: maraviglioso, straordinario. **-fully**, ADV.: maravigliosamente, straordinariamente. **-fulness**, S.: qualità maravigliosa, *f.*, mirabile, *m.* **-ing**, S.: maravigliare; stupore, *m.* **-ment**, S.: ammirazione, sorpresa, *f.* **-struck**, ADJ.: maravigliato, sbalordito, attonito.
wŏndrous, ADJ.: maraviglioso, ammirabile. **-ly**, ADV.: maravigliosamente.
wōn't = *will not*.
wŏnt 1, ADJ.: accostumato, solito: *be* —, solere; costumare. **wont** 2, S.: uso, costume, *m.*; usanza, *f.* **-ed**, ADJ.: accostumato, solito. **-edness**†, S.: avvezzamento, abito, costume, uso, *m.* **-less**†, ADJ.: non accostumato, non avvezzo.
wōo, TR.: fare l' amore, amoreggiare.
wŏod, S.: legno, legname; bosco, *m.*, selva, foresta, *f.* **-bine**, S.: madreselva, *f.* **-chuck**, S.: marmotta americana, *f.* **-cleaver**, S.: falegname, taglialegno, *m.* **-cock**, S.: beccaccia, *f.* (uccello).

-culver, s.: colembaccio, *m.* **-cut**, s.: intaglio in legno, *m.*; riproduzione silografica, *f.* **-cutter**, s.: taglialegna, *m.* **-ed**, ADJ.: fornito di legna. **-en**, ADJ.: di legno, fatto di legno. **-fretter**, s.: gorgoglione, *m.* **-hole**, **-house**, s.: legnaia, *f.* **-iness**, s.: stato boscoso, *m.* **-land**, s.: paese boscoso, *m.* **-lark**, s.: mattolina, *f.* **-less**, ADJ.: senza boschi o foreste. **-louse**, s.: centogambe, *m.* **-man**, s.: cacciatore, amatore della caccia, *m.* **-monger**†, s.: mercante di legna, *m.* **-note**†, s.: canto d'uccelli, *m.* **-nymph**, s.: ninfa de' boschi, *f.* **-pecker**, s.: picchio, *m.* (uccello). **-pigeon**, s.: colombo salvatico, *m.* **-pile**, s.: catasta di legna, *f.* **-reve**, s.: guardiano de' boschi, *m.* **-sorrel**, s.: (*bot.*) acetosa salvatica, *f.* **-stock**, s.: mucchio di legna, *m.* **-ward**, s.: guardiano de' boschi, uffiziale di foresta, *m.* **-y**, ADJ.: boscoso, selvoso. **-yard**, s.: cortile da tenervi le legna, *m.*

wōoer, s.: amante, innamorato, *m.*

wōof, s.: trama; tessitura, *f.*

wōoingly, ADV.: in modo amoroso, in modo carezzoso.

wool, s.: lana, *f.*: *lamb's* —, lana di agnello. **-carder**, s.: scardassiere, pettinatore di lana, *m.* **-clothes**, s. PL.: panno lino, *m.* **-comber**, s.: scardassiere, *m.* **-len**, ADJ.: di lana, fatto di lana. **-len-cloth**, s.: panno, *m.*; pannina, *f.* **-len-draper**, s.: pannaiuolo, *m.* **-len-stockings**, s. PL.: calzette di lana, *f. pl.* **-ly**, ADJ.: lanoso, peloso. **-market**, s.: mercato di lana, *m.* **-pack**, **-sack**, s.: sacco di lana, fascio di lana, *m.* **-shearing**, s.: tosare, *m.* **-spinner**, s.: filatore di lana, *m.* **-staple** = *wool-market*. **-trade**, s.: traffico di lana, *m.* **-ware**, s.: panno lino, *m.* **-weaver**, s.: lanaiuolo, *m.*

wōrd 1, s.: parola, *f.*; termine; discorso, *m.*; promessa; notizia, *f.*: *the* —, (*theol.*) il verbo; *by* — *of mouth*, di bocca; *at a* —, *in a* —, in una parola; *in few* —*s*, in poche parole; *high* —*s*, alterchi, *m. pl.*; contesa di parole, *f.*; *soft* —*s*, parole melate, *f. pl.*; *upon my* —, sulla mia parola; *fail of one's* —, mancar di parola; *keep one's* —, mantenere la parola; *pass one's* —, dar parola; *send* —, mandare a dire.

word 2, TR.: esprimere, scrivere; INTR.: disputare. **-catcher**, s.: critico severo, *m.* **-catching**, s.: critica, censura, *f.* **-iness**, s.: verbosità, *f.* **-less**, ADJ.: silenzioso. **-y**, ADJ.: verboso.

wōrk 1, s.: lavoro, travaglio, *m.*; opera; faccenda; fatica, pena, *f.*; effetto, *m.*: —*s*, movimiento; fabbrica, *f.*; opere, *f. pl.*, scritti, *m. pl.*; *hard* —, lavoro penoso; *open* —, ricamo a giorno; *piece of* —, lavoro, travaglio; *out of* —, senza lavoro, senza padrone; *be at* —, esser al lavoro; *be hard at* —, lavorare assiduamente.

work 2, IRR.; (IN)TR.: lavorare, operare, effettuare; fabbricare; fare; fermentare, bollire; eccitare, stimolare: — *out of error*, disingannare; — *hard*, lavorare assiduamente; — *a hat*, follare un cappello; — *a mine*, scavare una mina; — *a stone*, tagliare una pietra; — *one's way*, farsi strada; parvenire; — *again*, lavorare di nuovo, rifare; — *in*, far entrare, ficcar dentro; — *off*, consumare, usare, terminare; pagare lavorando; — *out*, finire, compire; effettuare; venire a capo; — *up*, innalzare, elevare; — *upon*, penetrare; toccare, muovere. **-bag**, s.: sacchetto, necessario, *m.* **-day**, s.: giorno di lavoro, *m.* **-er**, s.: lavoratore, lavorante, *m.* **-fellow**, s.: compagno nel lavoro, *m.* **-house**, s.: casa da lavorare, *f.*, lavoratoio, *m.*: *hatter's* —, gualchiera, *f.* **-ing** 1, ADJ.: laborioso; effettivo: — *classes*, classi operaie, *f. pl.*; —*day*, giorno di lavoro, *m.*; *hard*— *man*, uomo travagliativo, affacchinatore, *m.* **-ing** 2, s.: lavoro, *m.*; opera; agitazione (del mare), *f.* **-ing-house** = *workhouse*. **-man**, s.: operaio, artefice; lavoratore, garzone, *m.* **-manlike**, ADJ.: ben fatto, ben lavorato. **-manly**, ADJ.: ben fatto. **-manship**, s.: manufattura; arte dell' artefice, *f.*: *fine piece of* —, capo d' opera, *m.* **-master**†, s.: artigiano, artefice, *m.* **-shop**, s.: lavoratoio, *m.*; lavoranti, *m. pl.* **-woman**, s.: artigiana, lavoratrice, *f.* **-yday**†, s.: giorno di lavoro, *m.*

wōrld, s.: mondo; universo, *m.*; terra; vita; quantità immensa, *f.*: *in the* —, al mondo, nel mondo; *in this* —, in questo mondo, quaggiù; *learned* —, letterati, dotti, *m. pl.*; *polite* —, persone civili, *f. pl.*; *fashionable* —, bel mondo; *begin the* —, stabilirsi. **-liness**, s.: mondanità; avarizia, cupidità, *f.* **-ling**, s.: mondano, uomo interessato, *m.* **-ly**, ADJ.: mondano; vano. **-ly-minded**, ADJ.: mondano.

wōrm, s.: verme, vermine; baco, *m.*: *little* —, vermicciuolo, *m.*: — *of conscience*, verme divoratore, *m.*; — *of a screw*, chiocciola d' una vite, *f.* **worm** 2, (IN)TR.: soppiantare; minare; lavorare secretamente: — *a secret out of one*, cavare il segreto ad uno; cavargli il verme del naso. **-eaten**, ADJ.: bucato, mangiato da' vermi: *grow* —, tarlarsi. **-holes**, s. PL.: intarlamento, *m.* **-seed**, s.: rimedio antelmintico, *m.* **-wood**, s.: assenzio, *m.* **-y**, ADJ.: verminoso, pieno di vermi, bucato.

wōrry, TR.: stracciare, sbranare; t mentare; opprimere.

wŏrse 1, ADJ., ADV.: peggiore; in modo peggiore, peggio: *be — off*, star peggio; *grow — (and —)*, peggiorare; *get —*, star più male; *so much the —*, tanto peggio. **worse** 2, S.: peggio, disavvantaggio, *m.* **worse** 3, TR.: cagionare disavvantaggio.
wŏrship 1, S.: culto divino, *m.;* adorazione, *f.: your —*, vostra riverenza, vostra eccellenza (titolo). **worship** 2, TR.: adorare; onorare: *— one*, prostrarsi innanzi ad uno. **-ful**, ADJ.: riverendo, rispettabile. **-fully**, ADV.: rispettosamente, con rispetto. **-er**, S.: adoratore, *m.*, adorazione, *f.* **-(p)ing**, S.: adorare, *m.*, adorazione, *f.*
wŏrst 1, ADJ.: il più cattivo, il peggiore. **worst** 2, S.: peggiore, peggio, *m.;* estremità, *f.: let the — come to the —*, al peggio de' peggi; *have the — of it*, averla peggio. **worst** 3, TR.: soperchiare, superare; vincere.
wŏrsted, S.: lana filata, *f.*, stame, *m.*
wŏrt 1, S.: erba, pianta, *f.; pl.* cavoli. **wort** 2, S.: mosto, *m.*, birra nuova, *f.*
wŏr-th 1, ADJ.: degno, meritante: *be — something*, essere d' un certo valore, valere; avere; *it is not — worth the while*, non vale la pena (*or* lo sconcio). **-th** 2, S.: prezzo, valore, *m.;* valuta, *f.* **-thily**, ADV.: degnamente, meritamente. **-thiness**, S.: merito, *m.;* importanza, dignità; eccellenza, *f.* **-thless**, ADJ.: indegno, di poco valore. **-thlessness**, S.: indegnità; viltà, *f.* **-thy** 1, ADJ.: degno, meritevole. **-thy** 2, S.: uomo illustre, *m.*
wŏt†, 1, 3 pers. sing. Pres. di *wit* 2: *God —*, Iddio sa.
wŏuld-be, ADJ.: pretendente. **-ing**†, S.: desiderio, *m.*, inclinazione, *f.*
wŏund 1, S.: ferita, piaga, percossa, *f.* **wound** 2, TR.: ferire, piagare. **-less**, ADJ.: senza ferite; sano. **-wort**, S.: vulneraria, *f.*
wrăck† = *wreck.*
wrăn-gle 1, S.: rissa, contesa, disputa, *f.* **-gle** 2, INTR.: rissare, contendere, disputare, contrastare. **-gler**, S.: contenditore, garritore, *m.* **-gling** 1, ADJ.: rissoso, riottoso. **-gling** 2, S.: rissa, contesa, disputa, *f.*
wrăp, TR.: involgere, inviluppare, attorcigliare; trasportare: *be —ped up in*, amare perdutamente. **-per**, S.: che inviluppa, *m.;* coperta, *f.* **-t**, ADJ.: inviluppato, involto (cf. *wrap*).
wrăth, S.: collera, stizza, *f.;* sdegno, *m.* **-ful**, ADJ.: irato, collerico, stizzoso. **-fully**, ADV.: iratamente, iracondamente, stizzosamente. **-fulness**, S.: iracondia, *f.* **-less**, ADJ.: esente di collera; calmato.
wrăwl†, INTR.: miagolare.
wrēak 1†, S.: vendetta; rabbia, *f.*, furore, *m.* **wreak** 2, TR.: vendicare; sfogare. **-ful**, ADJ.: vendicativo, rabbioso.
wrēa-th, S.: corona, ghirlanda, *f.;* cercine, *m.* **-the**, TR.: torcere, attorcigliare, intrecciare; inghirlandare, coronare. **-then**, ADJ.: attorcigliato. **-thless**, ADJ.: senza ghirlanda. **-thy**, ADJ.: attorcigliato, intrecciato.
wrĕck 1, S.: naufragio, *m.;* distruzione, *f.: go to —*, andare in rovina. **wreck** 2, TR.: rompere; rovinare; INTR.: naufragare, far naufragio. **-ful**, ADJ.: rovinoso.
wrĕn, S.: reatino, luì, *m.* (uccello).
wrĕnch 1, S.: dislogamento, storcimento, *m.;* (*mec.*) madriente. **wrench** 2, TR.: slogare, storcere; rompere a forza.
wrĕst 1, S.: storcimento, *m.;* violenza, *f.* **wrest** 2, TR.: storcere, stravolgere; strappare; levare via con violenza. **-er**, S.: che storce, che leva via con violenza.
wrĕstl-e, INTR.: lottare; contendere. **-er**, S.: lottatore; combattitore, *m.* **-ing**, S.: lotta, lutta; contesa, *f.* **-ing-place**, S.: palestra, *f.;* ginnasio, *m.*
wrĕtch, S.: misero, meschino, furfante, scellerato, *m.* **-ed**, ADJ.: misero, povero, meschino, sventurato, tristo. **-edly**, ADV.: miseramente, meschinamente, vilmente. **-edness**, S.: miseria, meschinità, bassezza, *f.* **-less**†, ADJ.: trascurato, negligente.
wrig-gle, TR.: ficcare; INTR.: agitare, dimenarsi; piegarsi. **-gling**, S.: dimenio; giro e rigiro, *m.*
wright, S.: artigiano, artefice; lavorante, *m.*
wrin-g, IRR.; TR.: torcere, storcere; premere; strappare, levare via; tormentare, affliggere; INTR.: esser molto afflitto: *— money from*, cavare (*or* carpire) danaro da. **-er**, S.: che spreme l' acqua de' panni, *m.*
wrinkle 1, S.: piega, ruga, grinza, *f.* **wrinkle** 2, TR.: piegare, rugare, grinzare; INTR.: piegarsi, rugarsi, grinzarsi.
wrist, S.: giuntura della mano, *f.;* polso, *m.* **-band**, S.: polsino, *m.*
writ, S.: ordine in iscritto; citazione, *f.; Holy —*, scrittura sacra, *f.; — of execution*, mandato esecutivo, *m.; issue a —*, dare ordine.
writ-e, IRR.; TR.: scrivere; comporre: *— back again*, far risposta, rispondere; *— down*, mettere in iscritto; *— out*, trascrivere, copiare; *— a good hand*, aver una bella scrittura. **-er**, S.: scrittore, autore; copista, *m.*
writh-e, TR.: torcere, piegare; strappare; INTR.: soffrire. **-ing**, S.: torcimento; travaglio, *m.*
writing, S.: scrittura, *f.;* scritto, *m.: art of —*, arte di scrivere, *f.; put down*

in —, mettere in iscritto. **-book**, S.: quaderno, *m.* **-desk**, S.: scrittoio, tavolino, *m.* **-error**, S.: errore di penna, *m.* **-lesson**, S.: lezione di scrittura, *f.* **-master**, S.: maestro di scrittura, *m.* **-paper**, S.: carta da scrivere, *f.* **-school**, S.: scuola dove s' insegna a scrivere, *f.* **-s**, S. PL.: scritture, *f. pl.*, scritti. *m. pl.* **-stand**, S.: calamaio, *m.*

wrizzled †, ADJ.: rugato, grinzato.

wrŏng 1, ADJ.: falso; indiretto; ADV.: torto, ingiustamente: — *side*, rovescio, *m.*; *the* — *side out*, alla rovescia; *right or* —, a diritto o a torto; *be* —, avere torto. **wrong** 2, S.: torto; errore, *m.*; ingiustizia, *f.*: *be in the* —, avere torto; ingannarsi. **wrong** 3, TR.: fare torto, ingiurare, oltraggiare. **-doer**, S.: uomo ingiusto, persona ingiuriosa, *f.* **-er**, S.: che fa torto, ingiuratore, *m.* **-ful**, ADJ.: ingiusto, ingiurioso. **-fully**, ADV.: a torto; ingiustamente. **-headed**, ADJ.: ostinato, perverso. **-headedness**, S.: ostinatezza, perversità, *f.* **-lessly** †, ADV.: senza fare ingiuria. **-ly**, ADV.: a torto, ingiustamente; male. **-ness**, S.: ingiustizia; perversità, *f.*

wrŏth, ADJ.: irato, stizzato, corrucciato.

wrŭng, impf. e part. del v. *wring*.

wrȳ 1, ADJ.: storto, bistorto, curvo; sghembo: *make* — *faces*, far il grugno. **wry** † 2, TR.: torcere; INTR.: torcersi. **-face**, S.: smorfia, *f.*, visaccio, *m.* **-ly**, ADV.: tortamente, a traverso, biecamente, a sghembo. **-mouthed**, ADJ.: che torce la bocca. **-neck**, S.: torcicollo, *m.* (uccello). **-ness**, S.: contorsione; deviazione, *f.*

X

x ĕks (*the letter*), S.: x, *f.*

xylŏ-grapher *z*-, S.: silografo, *m.* **-grăphic(al)**, ADJ.: silografico. **-graphy**, S.: silografia, *f.*

xȳster *z*-, S.: (*surg.*) rastiatoio, *m.*

Y

y wī (*the letter*), S.: y, *m.*

yăcht, S.: iachetto, *m.*, saettia, *f.*

yăp, INTR.: abbaiare.

yärd, S.: cortile, *m.*, bassa corte; verga (misura di tre piedi); antenna (d' una nave), *f.* **-stick**, S.: canna di iarda (di tre piedi).

yāre †, ADJ.: agile, destro; ardente, avido. **-ly** †, ADV.: agilmente, destramente; bravamente; ardentemente.

yärn, S.: stame, *m.*, lana filata, *f.*: *spin a* —, far un filo; sciorinare una lunga filastrocca.

yărr †, INTR.: ringhiare.

yărrow, S.: millefoglie, *f.*

yăwl, S.: barchetta, *f.*, battello, *m.*

yăwn 1, S.: sbavigliamento, sbadiglio, *m.* **yawn** 2, INTR.: sbavigliare, sbadigliare. **-er**, S.: sbadigliante, *m.* **-ing** 1, ADJ.: sonnolento. **-ing** 2, S.: spavigliamento, spadigliamento, *m.*

yclăd †, ADJ.: vestito, abbigliato.

yclĕp(e)d †, ADJ.: nominato, chiamato.

yē, PRON.: voi.

yēa, ADV.: sì, in verità.

yēan, TR.: figliare, far agnelli. **-ling**, S.: agnello, pecorino, *m.*, pecorella, *f.*

yēar, S.: anno, *m.*; annata, *f.*: *a* —, per anno, annualmente; *by the* —, all' anno; *every* —, d' anno in anno; *every third* —, di tre in tre anni; *be in* —*s*, esser avanzato in età; *grow in* —*s*, diventar vecchio, invecchiare. **-book**, S.: annali, fasti, *m. pl.* **-ling**, ADJ.: che non ha che un anno. **-ly**, ADJ.: annuale, d' un anno; ADV.: annualmente, d' anno in anno, ogni anno.

yēarn, TR.: affliggere, travagliare; INTR.: esser molto affannato. **-ful** †, ADJ.: commosso, intenerito. **-fully** †, ADV.: compassionevolmente, pietosamente. **-ing**, S.: compassione, pietà, *f.*

yēast, S.: fermento; lievito, *m.*, feccia (della birra), *f.* **-y**, ADJ.: spumoso.

yĕlk, S.: tuorlo, rosso d' uovo, *m.*

yĕll 1, S.: ululo, urlamento, grido, *m.* **yell** 2, INTR.: ululare, urlare, abbaiare.

yĕllow, ADJ.: giallo; S.: giallo, color giallo, *m.*: — *fever*, febbre gialla, *f.*; — *earth*, terra gialla, *f.* **-boy**, S.: ghinea, *f.* (moneta d'oro). **-haired**, ADJ.: da' biondi capelli. **-hammer**, S.: rigogolo, *m.* (uccello). **-ish**, ADJ.: gialliccio, giallognolo. **-ishness**, S.: colore gialliccio, *m.* **-ness**, S.: giallezza, *f.*, color giallo, *m.* **-s**, S.: (*vet.*) itterizia, *f.*

yĕlp, INTR.: abbaiare, squittire. **-ing**, S.: gagnolo, squittire, *m.*

yeōman, S.: contadino ricco, *m.*: — *of the guards*, guardia a piedi, *f.*; — *of the pantry*, panattiere (del re), *m.*; — *of the scullery*, guardavasellame, *m.* **-ry**, S.: guardie a piedi, *f. pl.*; contadini, *m. pl.*

yĕrk 1, S.: percossa, *f.*, urto, *m.* **yerk** 2, TR.: gettare a terra; scuotere, calcitrare.

yĕs, ADV.: sì; veramente, in vero: *say* —, dire di sì; —, —, sì, sì; già, già.

yēst = *yeast*.

yĕster, ADJ.: di ieri. **-day**, ADJ.: ieri, di ieri: — *evening*, ieri sera, iersera; — *morning*, ieri mattina, iermattina; *day before* —, ier l' altro. **-night**, S.: iersera, iernotte, notte passata, *f.*

yĕt, CONJ.: nondimeno, nulladimeno, però, tuttavia; ADV.: ancora, più innanzi: *as —*, per anco.
yēw, S.: tasso, nasso, *m.* (albero).
yĕx† 1, S.: singhiozzo, *m.* **yex** 2, INTR.: singhiozzare.
yield, TR.: rendere, produrre; fruttare; permettere, accordare, dare; INTR.: rendersi, sottomettersi; soccombere: *— up*, cedere; concedere; *— up the ghost*, render l' anima; *— to the times*, cedere al tempo; *— to temptation*, soccombere a tentazione. **-ablenees†**, S.: disposizione di concedere, *f.* **-ance**, S.: produzione; concessione, *f.* **-er**, S.: che cede, che si sottomette. **-ing** 1, ADJ.: facile; comodo; condiscendente. **-ing** 2, S.: sommessione, *f.*; cedere, *m.* **-ingly**, ADV.: con compiacenza, francamente. **-ingness**, S.: facilità; condiscendenza, *f.*
yōke 1, S.: giogo; paio, *m.*, coppia; servitù, *f.*: *bring under the —*, soggiogare; *shake off the —*, scuotere il giogo. **yoke** 2, TR.: accoppiare al giogo; soggiogare. **-elm**, S.: carpino, carpine, *m.* **-fellow**, **-mate**, S.: compagno nel lavoro, *m.*
yōlk, S.: tuorlo, rosso d' uovo, *m.*
yŏn, ADV.: là, in vista.
yŏnd†, ADJ.: furibondo, furioso.
yŏnder = *yon*.
yōre, ADV.: (*in times*) *of —*, altre volte, anticamente, ab antico.
yoū, PRON.: voi, vi: (*respectful address*) Ella (*or* Lei; PL.: Loro, Lor signori, Lor signore).
yoŭng 1, ADJ.: giovane, giovine; novizio; nuovo: *— man* (*fellow*), giovine, giovinotto, giovanetto, *m.*; *— woman*, giovine, *f.*; *— girl*, fanciulla, ragazza, *f.*; *— lady*, damigella, signorina, *f.*; *— age*, età giovanile, *f.*; *— beginner*, cominciante; novizio, *m.*; *— fellow*, giovinotto, giovanotto, *m.*; *— shoot*, germoglio, rampollo, *m.* **young** 2, S.: figliuolino (d' animale), *m.*: *bear —*, figliare; portare. **yoŭng-er**, ADJ.: più giovane, minore. **-ish**, ADJ.: alquanto giovane. **-ling**, S.: figliuolino, animal giovine, *m.* **-ly†** 1, ADJ.: giovanile. **-ly†** 2, ADV.: giovanilmente; inespertamente. **-ster**, **yoŭnker†**, S.: giovanastro, giovanotto, *m.* **-th**, S.: gioventù, *f.*
yoūr, PRON.: vostro, vostra; vostri, vostre. **-s**, PRON.: il vostro, la vostra, i vostri: *this is —*, questo è vostro. **-self**, PRON.: voi stesso, voi medesimo: *yourselves*, voi stessi, voi stesse; *help —, and heaven will help you*, aiutatevi, che il cielo vi aiuterà; *you deceive —, yourselves*, voi v' ingannate.
yoūth, S.: giovanezza, gioventù, *f.*; giovincello, giovane, *m.*: *in the prime of —*, nel fior degli anni. **-ful**, ADJ.: giovane, giovanile: *— days*, gioventù. **-fully**, ADV.: giovanilmente, da giovane. **-fulness**, S.: giovanezza, gioventù, *f.*
yŭck 1, S.: rogna, *f.* **yuck** 2, INTR.: aver la rogna.
yūle, S.: Natale, *m.* **-log**, S.: ceppo di Natale, *m.* **-tide**, S.: (tempo di) Natale, *m.*

Z

z *zē* (*the letter*), S.: z, *f.*
zāny 1, S.: zanni, buffone, *m.* **zany†** 2, TR.: far il buffone.
zēal 1, S.: zelo, ardore; affetto, *m.* **zeal†** 2, INTR.: esser zelante. **-less**, ADJ.: senza zelo.
zĕal-ot, S.: zelatore, zelante, *m.* **-ous**, ADJ.: zeloso, zelante. **-ously**, ADV.: zelosamente, con zelo. **-ousness**, S.: zelo, fervore; ardore, *m.*
zēbra, S.: zebra, *f.*
zēbu, S.: zebu, *m.*
zĕcchin, S.: zecchino, *m.*
zĕdoary, S.: zettovario, zenzevero, *m.*
zēnith, S.: zenitte; colmo, sommo, *m.*
zĕphyr(us), S.: zeffiro, *m.*
zēro, S.: zero; niente, nulla, *m.*
zĕst 1, S.: frullo; pezzetto (di scorza); gusto, sapore, *m.* **zest** 2, TR.: rendere gustoso, rendere saporevole.
zetĕtic, ADJ.: zetetico, inquisitivo.
zeŭgma, S.: (*rhet.*) zeugma, *f.*
zigzag 1, S.: zigzag; serpeggiamento, *m.*; ADJ.: tutto a zigzag, pieno di angoli e giri. **zigzag** 2, INTR.: fare (andare) a zigzag.
zinc, S.: zinco, *m.*
zĭther, S.: cetra, *f.*
zōcle, S.: zocco, zoccolo, *m.*
zō-diac, S.: (*astr.*) zodiaco. **-diacal**, ADJ.: zodiacale.
zōne, S.: zona; fascia, cintura, *f.*
zoŏ-graphĕr, S.: zoografo, *m.* **-grăphical**, ADJ.: zoografico. **-graphy**, S.: zoografia, *f.* **-lŏgic(al)**, ADJ.: zoologico. **-logist**, S.: zoologo, *m.* **-logy**, S.: zoologia, *f.* **-phŏric**, ADJ.: zooforico, **-phite**, S.: zoofito, piantanimale, *m.* **-tomist**, S.: zootomista, *m.* **-tomy**, S.: zootomia, anatomia degli animali, *f.*
zouāve, S.: zuavo, *m.*
zoŭnds! INTERJ.: cancheri! cappita!

GEOGRAPHICAL NAMES AND NAMES OF NATIONALITIES

A

Abbeville, Abbevilla.
Abdēra, Abdera.
Aberdeen, Aberdonia.
Abrŭzzi, Abruzzi.
Âbukir, Abuchiro.
Abyssinia, Abissinia.
Abyssinian, Abissino.
Acādia, Acadia.
Achāia, Acaia.
Achāian, Acaico.
Ăcheron, Acheronte.
Adrianōple, Adrianopoli.
Adriătic, Adriatico.
Aegēan, Egeo.
Ăfrica, Affrica, Africa.
Ăfrican, Affricano, Africano.
Âgra, Agra.
Âix, Aix.
Aix-la-Chapĕlle, Aquisgrana.
Âlbion, Albione.
Âlexăndria, Alessandria.
Algârve, Algarvia.
Algârvian, Algarvese.
Ălgiers, Algeri.
Ălgerine, Algerino.
Ălps, Alpi.
Alsâce, Alsazia.
Alsâcian, Alsazio.
Amĕrica, America.
Amĕrican, Americano.
Ămsterdăm, Amsterdamo.
Andalŭsia, Andalusia.
Andalŭsian, Andalusiano
Ăndes, Ande, Cordigliere.
Ănglesea, Anglesia.
Ăngoulême, Angoleme.
Ânjou, Angio.

Antībes, Antibo.
Antĭlles, Antille.
Antioch, Antiochia.
Ăntwerp, Anversa.
Ăpennines, Appennini.
Arābia, Arabia.
Arābian, Arabico, Arabo.
Arcādia, Arcadia.
Archăngel, Arcangelo.
Archipĕlago, Arcipelago.
Ărgolis, Argolide.
Armâgh, Armacco.
Ărragon, Aragona.
Āsia, Asia.
Asiătic Asiatico.
Assisi, Assisi.
Assyria, Assiria.
Assyrian, Assiriano.
Astrachăn, Astracan.
Athēnian, Ateniense, Atenese.
Ăthens, Atene.
Atlăntic, Atlantico.
Ătlas, Atlante.
A'ugsburgh, Augusta.
Auvĕrgne ō-, Alvergna.
Avignŏn -nyon, Avignone.
Azōres, Azzorre.

B

Băbel, Babele.
Băbylon, Babilonia.
Băctria, Battria.
Bactriāna, Battriana.
Bāden, Bada, Badena.
Bălcan, Balcano.
Baleāres, Baleari.
Băltic, Mare Baltico.

Băltimore, Baltimora.
Barbādoes, Barbada.
Bârbary, Barbaria.
Bavāria, Baviera.
Bavārian, Bavarese, Bavaro.
Bĕlgian, Belgio, Belgioo.
Bĕlgium, Belgio.
Belgrāde, Belgrado.
Bellinzōna, Bellinzona.
Bellisle, Bellisola.
Bengâl, Bengala.
Bĕrgen-op-Zōom, Bergopsom.
Bĕrlin, Berlino.
Berlinian, Berlinese.
Bermūdas, Bermude.
Bĕrn, Berna.
Besânçon, Besanzone.
Bĕthlehem, Betlemme.
Biscay, Biscaglia.
Bithŷnia, Bitinia.
Bithŷnian, Bitinio.
Bohēmia, Boemia.
Bohēmian, Boemo.
Bordeaux -dō, Bordo.
Bŏsphorus, Bosforo.
Bŏthnia, Botnia.
Brâbant, Brabante.
Brâbantine, Brabanzese.
Brăndenburgh, Brandemburgo.
Brazil, Brasile.
Brazilian, Brasilese, Brasiliano.
Brēmen, Brema.
Brĕslaw, Breslavia.
Britain, **Britany**, Bretagna.
British, Britannico; **Channel**, la Manica.

Brŭnswick, Brunsvigo, Brunswich.
Brussēlian, Brussellese.
Brŭssels, Brusselle.
Bŭcharest, Bucoresia.
Bŭckingham, Buckingamo.
Burgŭndian, Burgognese.
Bŭrgundy, Burgogna.
Byzăntium, Bisanzio.

C

Cădiz, Cadice.
Căffre, Caffro.
Calābrian, Calabrese.
Călais, Calé, Calese.
Călmuc, Calmucco.
Cămbridge, Cambrigge.
Cānaan, Cana.
Canāry Islands, Canarie.
Căntęrbury *-bĕrry*, Cantorberi.
Cāpe, Capo; — *of Good Hope*, Capo di Buona Speranza; — *Horn*, Capo Horn; — *Verde*, Capo Verde; — *St. Vincent*, Capo S. Vincenzo.
Căpua, Capua.
Caramānia, Caramania.
Căribbee Islands, Isole de' Cannibali.
Carinthia, Carintia.
Carlisle, Carlilla.
Cārmarthen, Carmarten.
Cārmel, Carmelo.
Cārpum, Carpi.
Cārthage, Cartagine.
Carthagēna, Cartagena.
Carthaginian, Cartaginese.
Căspian, Caspio.
Castīle, Castiglia.
Castilian, Castigliano.
Căucasus, Caucaso.
Cayĕnne *Kī-en*, Caienna.
Cĕlebes, Celebi.
Cevĕnnes, Cevenne.
Cēylon, Ceilan.
Charўbdis, Cariddi.
Chili, Chili.
China, Cina.
Chinēse, Cinese.
Circăssia, Circassia.
Circăssian, Circasso.
Clermŏnt, Clermonte.
Clēves, Clives, Clivia.
Cŏblentz, Coblenza.
Cŏlchester, Colchester.
Colŏgne, Cologna, Colonia.
Cŏnstance, Costanza.
Constantinŏple, Costantinopoli.
Copenhāgen, Copenaghen.
Cŏrinth, Corinto.
Corinthian, Corintiano.
Cŏrnwall, Cornovaglia.
Corrēgium, Correggio.
Cosēntia, Cosenza.
Cŏssack, Cossacco.
Crăcow, Cracovia.
Crētan, Cretese.
Crēte, Creta.
Croātia, Croazia.
Cŭmberland, Cumberlandia.
Curaçōa, Curazzao.
Cŭrland, Curlandia.
Curlăndian, Curlandese.
Cўclades, Cicladi.
Cўprus, Cipro.

D

Dalmātia, Dalmazia.
Damăscus, Damasco.
Damiĕtta, Damiata.
Dāne, Danese.
Dăntzick, Danzica.
Dănube, Danubio, Istro.
Dardanĕlls, Dardanelli.
Dĕlphos, Delfo.
Dĕnmark, Danimarca.
Diĕppe, Dieppe.
Dniēper, Neper.
Dniēster, Niester.
Dōver; *the Straits of* —, Passo di Calè.
Dōwns, Dune.
Drĕsden, Dresda.
Dŭblin, Dublino.
Dŭnkirk, Duncherche, Dunquerque.
Dŭrham, Duram.
Dwina, Duina.

E

Ēastern, Orientale.
Ĕdinburgh, Edimburgo.
Ĕger, Egra.
Ēgypt, Egitto.
Egўptian, Egizio.
England *ing-*, Inghilterra.
English *ing-*, Inglese.
Englishman *ing-*, Inglese.
Ephēsian, Efesino.
Ĕphesus, Efeso.
Epidāurus, Epidauro.
Ēpirus, Epiro.
Ĕri'danus, Eridano, Po.
Ĕsquimaux *-mō*, Eschimesi, -ali.
Esthōnia, Estonia.
Euphrātes, Eufrate.
Eūripus, Euripo.
Eūrope, Europa.
Europēan, Europeo.

F

Fălmouth, Falmout.
Făyance, Faenza.
Flănders, Fiandra.
Flŏrence, Firenze.
Flŏrida, Florida.
Fontainebleau *-blō*, Fontanablo.
Frănce, Francia.

Franconia, Franconia.
Franconian, Franconiano.
Frankfort, Francoforte.
French, Francese.
Friburgh, Friburgo.
Friesland, Frisia.
Frieslander, Frisio.
Frozen Ocean, Oceano Settentrionale.

G

Galatia, Galazia.
Galilee, Galilea.
Galloway, Gallovai.
Ganges, Gange.
Garonne, Garonna
Gascon, Gascone.
Gascony, Gascogna.
Geneva, Ginevra.
Genoa, Genova.
Genoese, Genovese.
Georgian, Georgio.
German, Germano, Tedesco.
Germany, Germania.
Ghent, Gand.
Gibraltar, Gibilterra.
Glasgow, Glasgovia.
Gothard, Gottardo.
Gothia, Gotia, Gozia.
Great Britain, Gran-Bretagna.
Greece, Grecia.
Grecian, Greek, Greco.
Greenland, Gronlandia.
Greenlander, Gronlandese.
Grenoble, Grenoble
Grisons, Grigioni.
Guadaloupe, Guadalupa.
Guelderland, Gheldria.
Guienne, Guienna.
Guinea, Guinea.

H

Hague, Aia.
Hainault -o, Ain.
Hamburg, Amburgo.
Hanover, Annovera, Annover.
Havana, Avana.
Hecla, Ecla.
Heidelberg, Eidelberga.
Hellespont, Ellesponto.
Hereford, Ereford.
Hertford, Ertford.
Hessian, Assiaco.
Hibernia, Ibernia.
Hindostan, Indostan.
Holland, Olanda.
Hollander, Olandese.
Holstein, Holstein, Olsazia.
Hottentots, Ottentoti.
Hungarian, Ungaro, Ungherese, Unghero.
Hungary, Ungaria, Ungheria.

I

Iceland, Islandia.
Icelander, Islandese.
Illyrian, Illirico.
Illyricum, Illiria, Illirica.
Indies, le Indie.
Irishman, Irelander, Irlandese.
Ireland, Irlanda.
Iroquois, Irocco.
Italian, Italiano.
Italy, Italia.
Ithaca, Itaca.
Ivrea, Ivrea.

J

Jamaica, Giamaica.
Japan, Giappone.
Japanese, Giapponese.
Java, Giava.
Jersey, Gersei.
Jerusalem, Gerusalemme.
Jordan, Giordano.
Judea, Giudea.

L

Lancaster, Lancastro.
Lapland, Lapponia.
Laplander, Lappone, Lapponese.
Latin, Latino.
Latium, Lazio.
Laurence, S. Lorenzo.
Laybach, Lubiana.
Lebanon, Libano.
Leghorn, Livorno.
Leipsic, Lipsia.
Lemnos, Lemno.
Leon, Leone.
Lesbos, Lesbo.
Liege, Liegi.
Limburg, Limburgo.
Lintz, Linz.
Lisbon, Lisbona.
Lisbonian, Lisbonese.
Lisle, Lilla.
Liverpool, Liverpula.
Loire *lwär*, Loira.
Lombard, Lombardo.
Lombardy, Lombardia.
London, Londra.
Lorrain, Lorena.
Louisiana, Luigiana.
Lubeck, Lubecca.
Lucern, Lucerna.
Lucernian, Lucernese.
Lund, Lunda.
Lusatia, Lusazia.
Luxemburg, Lussemburgo.
Lyons, Lione.

M

Madeira, Madera.
Magdeburg, Maddeburgo.
Maine, Maina.
Manchester, Manchester.
Mantua, Mantoa, Mantova.
Mantuan, Mantoano, Mantovano.
Marathon, Maratoa

Mârch, Marca.
Mârne, Marna.
Marseilles, Marsiglia.
Martinique, Martinicca.
Măryland, Marilandia.
Măurice, St., S. Maurizio.
Meănder, Meandro.
Mĕcklenburg, Meclemburgo.
Mĕmphis, Menfi.
Mĕntz, Magonza.
Mĕxican, Messicano.
Mĕxico, Messico.
Mĭlan, Milano.
Milētus, Mileto.
Moldāvia, Moldavia.
Molŭcca Islands, Molucche.
Mŏnmouth, Monmutto.
Montauban *-tobŏn*, Montalbano.
Mont Blânc, Monte Bianco.
Montgŏmery, Montgommeri.
Montreăl, Montereale.
Mŏrat, Morato.
Mŏscovite, Moscovita.
Mŏscow, Mosca.
Mosĕlla, Mosella.
Mozambique, Mozambico.
Mŭnich, Monaco.

N

Nankin, Nankin, Nanchino.
Năples, Napoli.
Napŏlitan, Napolitano.
Narbŏnne, Narbona.
Năssau, Nassau, Nassovia.
Navârre, Navarra.
Năzareth, Nazaret.
Nĕtherlands, Paesi Bassi.
Nĕwcastle, Newcastle.
Nĕw-Foundland, Terra Nuova.
Nĕw-Yôrk, Nuova York.
Nice, *Nizza*.
Nicŏpolis, Nicopoli.
Nieper, Dnieper.
Nile, Nilo.
Nimĕguen, Nimega.
Ninevĕh, Ninive.
Nismes, Nimes.
Nôrmandy, Normandia.
Northămpton, Nortamton.
Northŭmberland, Nortumbria.
Nôrway, Norvegia.
Norwĕgian, Norvegio.
Nŏttingham, Nottingamo.
Număntia, Numanzia.
Nŭremberg, Norimberga.

O

Ŏder, Odera, Viadro.
Oise, Oise.
Olmŭtz, Olmuzza.
Onĕlia, Oneglia.
Ôrkneys, Orcadi.
Ostĕnd, Ostenda.
Otahaiti, Otaiti.
Ŏttoman, Ottomano.
Ŏxford, Osfordia.

P

Pădua, Padova.
Păduan, Padoano, Padovano.
Palătinate, Palatinato.
Pălestine, Palestina.
Palmўra, Palmira.
Paraguāy, Paraguai.
Păris, Parigi.
Parisian, Parigino.
Parnăssus, Parnasso.
Pătmos, Patmo.
Patrâs, Patrasso.
Peking, Pechino.
Peloponnēsus, Peloponneso, Morea.
Pennsylvānia, Pensilvania.
Pennsylvānian, Pensilvaniano.
Perpignan *-nyŏn*, Perpignano.
Pĕsth, Pesto.
Pĕtersbŭrg, Pietroburgo.
Phœnicia, Fenicia.
Philadĕlphia, Filadelfia.
Philippine Islands, Isole Filippine.
Phrўgia, Frigia.
Piedmont, Piemonte.
Pindus, Pindo.
Placĕntia, Piacenza.
Plўmouth, Plimuto.
Podŏlia, Podolia.
Pŏland, Polonia.
Pōle, Polonese, Polacco.
Pŏlish, Polonese.
Polynēsia, Polinesia.
Pŏntus, Ponto.
Pŏrto, Oporto.
Pŏrto Rico, Portoricco.
Pŏrtugal, Portogallo.
Portuguēse, Portoghese.
Pŏsen, Posna, Posnania.
Pŏtsdam, Posdammo.
Prăgue, Praga.
Provence *-văn*, Provenza.

Q

Quebĕc, Quebecco.

R

Rătisbon, Ratisbona.
Rhĕims, Reims, Remi.
Rhine, Reno.
Rhŏdes, Rodi.
Rhŏdian, Rodiano.
Rhŏne, Rodano.
Richmond, Richmond
Rochĕlle, Roccella
Rōman, Romano.
Romānian, Romanesco.
Rōme, Roma.
Rŏtterdam, Roterdammo
Rouen *-ŏn*, Roano.

Rūbicon, Rubicone.
Rŭtland, Rutlandia.

S

Sabine, Sabino.
Sălamis, Salamina.
Săliṣbury *-beri*, Salisburi.
Samăritan, Samaritano.
Sāmos, Samo.
Saône, Saona.
Sardinia, Sardegna, Sardigna.
Săvoy, Savoia.
Săvoyard, Savoiardo.
Săxon, Sassone.
Săxony, Sassonia.
Schaffhäusen, Scaffusa.
Scheld, Scelda.
Sclavonia, Schiavonia.
Scotch, **Scotchman**, Scozzese, Scotto.
Scotland, Scozia.
Scylla, Scilla.
Scythia, Scizia.
Seine, Senna.
Senegal, Senegallo.
Sĕvern, Severna.
Seville, Siviglia.
Siamese, Siamese.
Sicily, Sicilia.
Silesia, Slesia.
Silesian, Slesiano.
Smyrna, Smirna.
Sound, Sund.
Southerland, Suterlandia.
Spain, Spagna.
Spaniard, Spagnuolo.
Stafford, Stafford.
Stettin, Stettino.
Stockolm, Stocolma.
Străsburg, Strasburgo.
Stŭtgart, Stutgardia.
Suăbia, Suevia.
Sudetes, Sudeti.
Surăt, Surate.
Surinăm, Surinamo.
Swēde, Svedese.
Swēden, Suezia.
Swiss, Svizzero.
Switzerland, Svizzera.
Sȳracuse, Siracusa.

T

Tāgus, Tago.
Tărtary, Tartaria.
Tăuris, Tauri.
Tăurus, Tauro.
Terceira, Tercera.
Thāmes, Tamigi.
Thēban, Tebano.
Thēbes, Tebe.
Thermŏpylae, Termopili.
Thessalōnian, Tessaliano.
Thessalōnic, Salonico.
Thĕssaly, Tessaglia.
Thrāce, Tracia.
Thrăcian, Trace.
Thuringia, Turingia.
Thuringian, Turingiano.
Tiber, Tevere.
Tigris, Tigri.
Tipperāry, Tipperari.
Tobŏlsk, Tobol.
Toulŏn, Tolone.
Toulouse, Tolosa.
Touraine, Turenne.
Trĕbizond, Trabisonda.
Trĕnt, Trento.
Trēves, Treveri, Treviri.
Trŏy, Troia.
Tūnis, Tunisi.
Turcomānia, Turcomania.
Tŭrk, Turco.
Tŭrkey, Turchia.
Tŭscan, Toscano.
Tŭscany, Toscana.
Tŭsculum, Tusculo.
Tȳre, Tiro.
Tȳrol, Tirolo.

U

Ukraine *ī*, Ucrania.
United States *ī*, Stati Uniti.
Úpsal, Upsala.
Ūtrĕcht, Utretto.

V

Valence, Valencia.
Valĕncian, Valenzano.
Vendée *von-*, Vendea.
Venĕtian, Veneziano.
Vĕnice, Venezia.
Vĕra-Cruz, Veracroce.
Verdŭn, Verduno.
Versăilles, Versaglia.
Vesŭvius, Vesuvio.
Visigoth, Visigoto.
Vistula, Vistola.
Vivière, Vivierse.
Volhȳnia, Volinia.

W

Wāles, Galles.
Wallōnian, Vallano.
Wārsaw, Varsavia.
Wallăchia, Vallachia.
Wārwick, Warwick.
Wēsel, Vesalia.
Wēser, Weser.
Westphālia, Vestfalia.
Westphālian, Vestfalo.
Wilna, Vilna.
Wŏrms, Vormes.
Wŭrtemberg, Virtemberga.
Wŭrtzburg, Vurtsburgo.

Y

Yŏrk, Jorca.
Ŷpres, Ipra.

Z

Zēaland, Zelandia.
Zŭrich, Zurigo.
Zuȳder-Zēe, Zuidersè.

PERSONAL NAMES

A

Ābel, Abele.
Ăbelard, Abelardo.
Ābraham, Abramo.
Achillēs, Achille.
Adeline, Adelina.
Adŏlphus, Adolfo.
Ăgnes, Agnese.
Ălaric, Alarico.
Ălban, Albano.
Ălbert, Alberto.
Ălbin, Albīnus, Albino.
Alexănder, Alessandro.
Alĕxis, Alessio.
Ălice, Adelaide.
Alphŏnsus, Alfonso.
Ălwin, Alvino.
Ămbrose, Ambrogio.
Āmy, Amedea.
Anastāsius, Anastasio.
Ăndrew *-drų*, Andrea.
Āngel, Angelo.
Ănselm, Anselmo.
Ănthony, Antonio.
Ârchibald, Arcibaldo.
Ârmand, Armando.
Ârnold, Arnoldo.
Ăssy, Adelaide.
Augŭ'stus, Augusto, Agosto.
Aurē'lius, Aurelio.
Austin, Agostino.
Austī'na, Agostina.

B

Băb = *Barbara*.
Balthăsar, Baltasarre.
Băptist, Batista.
Bărnaby, Barnaba.
Barthŏ'lomew, Bartolommeo.
Băsil, Basilio.
Băt = *Bartholomew*.
Bĕn = *Benjamin*.
Bĕnedict, Benedetto.
Benedicta, Benedetta.
Bĕnjamin, Beniamino.
Bĕnnet = *Benedict*.
Bĕrnard, Bernardo.
Bĕrtha, Berta.
Bĕrtram, Bertrando.
Bĕss, Bĕt, Bĕtty = *Elisabeth*.
Biddy = *Bridget*.
Bill, Billy = *William*.
Blăno, Bianco.
Blănche, Bianca.
Blāse, Biasio, Biagio.
Bŏnifāce, Bonifazio.
Bridget, Brigit, Brigida.
Brūno, Brunone.

C

Cæsar, Cesare.
Căjetan, Gaetano.
Camillus, Camillo.
Căroline, Carolina.
Căsimir, Casimiro.
Cătharine, Cătherine, Caterina.
Cĕlestine, Celestino.
Cĕlsus, Celso.
Chârles, Carlo.
Chârlotte, Carlotta.
Christopher, Cristoforo.
Chrysŏstom, Crisostomo, Grisostomo.
Cíprian, Cipriano.
Clāre, Chiara.
Clăudius, Claudio.
Clĕment, Clemente.
Cŏnrad, Corrado.
Cŏnstance, Costanza.
Cŏnstantine, Costantino.
Cornēlius, Cornelio.
Cŏsmus, Cosimo.
Crispin, Crispino.
Cunigŭnda, Cunigonda.
Cyrïacus, Ciriaco.
Cyril, Cirillo.
Cyrus, Ciro.

D

Dăgobert, Dagoberto.
Dămian, Damiano.
Dăniel, Daniele.
Dăvid, Davidde.
Debŏrah, Debora.
Dĕcius, Decio.
Dĕ(n)nis, Dionigi
Deodātus, Diodato.
Dĕrric, Diterico.
Desidĕrius, Desiderio.
Dionysius, Dionisio, Dionigi.
Dŏll, Dŏlly = *Dorothy*.
Dŏminic, Domenico.
Donātus, Donato.
Dŏrothy, Dorotea.

E

Ĕdmund, Edemondo.
Ēdith, Editta.
Ĕdward, Edoardo.
Ĕdwin, Edovino.
Ĕleanor, Eleonora.
Elisabeth, Elisabetta.
Emilius, Emilio.

Ĕmmy, Emilia, Emmi.
Erăsmus, Erasmo.
Ĕric, Erico.
Ĕrnest, Ernesto.
Ĕrnestine, Ernestina.
Eugēne, ***Eugēnius***, Eugenio.
Eusēbius, Eusebio.
Eustăchius, ***Eustăthius***, Eustachio, Eustazio.
Ĕverard, Everardo.

F

Fābian, Fabiano.
Fabricius, Fabrizio.
Fănny, Franceschina, Francesca.
Făustus, Fausto.
Felicia, **Fēlice**, Felicia.
Fēlix, Felice.
Fĕrdinand, Ferdinando.
Flāvian, Flaviano.
Florentīna, Fiorentina.
Flŏrentine, Fiorentino.
Flōrian, Floriano.
Fortunātus, Fortunato.
Frănces = *Fanny*.
Frăncis, **Frănk**, Francesco.
Frĕderic, Federico, Federigo.
Frederica, Federica, Federiga.
Fulgentius, Fulgenzio.

G

Gābriel, Gabrielle.
Gabriēla, Gabriella.
Găspar, Gasparo, Gaspare, Gasparre.
Găston, Gastone.
Genēva, Ginevra.
Genevieve, Genoveffa.
George, Giorgio.
Gĕrard, Gerardo.
Gertrude, Gertrude.
Gervas, Gervasio.
Gideon, Gedeone.
Gŏdard, Godardo.
Grătian, Graziano.
Grĕgory, Gregorio.
Gustāvus, Gustavo.
Guy, Guido.

H

Hărriet, Enrichetta.
Hĕlen, **Hĕlena**, Elena.
Hĕnry, Enrico, Arrico.
Heraclius, Eraclio.
Herminius, Erminio.
Hilărion, Ilarione.
Hĭlary, Ilario.
Honōrius, Onorato.
Hŏrtense, Ortencia.
Hubāldus, Ubaldo.
Hūgh, **Hūgo**, Ugo, Ugone.

I

Ignātia, Ignazia.
Ignātius, Ignazio.
Immănuel, Emanuele.
Irenæus, Ireneo.
Īsaac, Isacco.

J

Jacintha, Giacinta.
Jacinthus, Giacinto.
Jăck, Giovanni.
Jāmes, Giacomo.
Jāne, Giovanna.
Jănuary, Gennaro.
Jĕff, ***Jĕffery***, ***Jĕffrey***, Goffredo.
Jĕnny, Giovannia, Nuccia.
Jeremīah, Geremia.
Jerōme, Geronimo, Girolamo.
Jōachim, Gioacchino.
Jōb, Giobbe.
Jocundus, Giocondo.
Jŏhn, **Jŏhnny**, Giovanni, Nuccio.
Jōseph, Giuseppe.
Josephīne, Giuseppina.
Jŏshua, Giosuè.
Jūdith, Giuditta.
Jūlia, Giulia.
Jūlian, Giuliano.
Jūlius, Giulio.
Justinus, Giustino.

K

Kāte = *Catherine*.

L

Lactantius, Lattanzio.
Lămbert, Lamberto.
Laurence, Lorenzo.
Lawrence = *Laurence*.
Lāzarus, Lazzaro.
Leănder, Leandro.
Lĕn = *Leonard*.
Lēo, Leone.
Lĕonard, Leonardo.
Lĕopold, Leopoldo.
Lewis Louis, *Luigi*, *Ludovico*.
Lĭvy, Livio.
Lĭzzy = *Lisette*.
Louisa, Luigia.
Lūcian, Luciano.
Lūcius, Lucio.
Lucrētia, Lucrezia.
Lūcy, Lucia.
Ludŏlphus, Ludolfo.
Lūke, Luca.

M

Mădeline, ***Măgdalen***, Maddalena.
Măg = *Margaret*.
Marcellīnus, Marcellino.
Marcĕllus, Marcello.
Mărgaret, ***Mărgery***, Margarita, Margherita.

Mărian, Marianna.
Mârk, Marco.
Mârtin, Martino.
Măry, Maria.
Măt = *Martha.*
Mathilda, Matilda, Metilde.
Mă'tthew, Matteo.
Matthias, Mattia.
Măud = *Mathilda.*
Măurice, Maurizio.
Maximilian, Massimiliano.
Măximus, Massimo.
Mĕlchior, Melchiorre.
Mike, **Michael**, Michele.
Mŏll, **Mŏlly**, Mariuccia, Marietta.
Mŏrris = *Maurice.*
Mōses, Mosè.

N

Năncy, **Nănny**, Annina.
Napōleon, Napoleone.
Nĕd = *Edward.*
Nehemiah, Neemia.
Nĕll = *Eleanor.*
Nēro, Nerone.
Nicodēmus, Nicodemo.
Nicol, **Nicholas**, Niccola, Nicolao.
Nōah, Noè, Noè.

O

Octăvia, Ottavia.
Octaviānus, Ottaviano.
Octăvius, Ottavio.
Ŏliver, Oliviero.
Onûphrius, Onofrio.
Ōtho, Ottone.

P

Păncras, Pancrazio.
Pătrick, Patrizio.
Păul, Paolo.
Paulīna, Paola, Paolina.
Paulīnus, Paolino.
Pĕg = *Margaret.*
Pēter, Pietro.
Petrōnius, Petronio.
Philibert, Filiberto.
Philibērta, Filiberta.
Philip, Filippo, Felipe.
Philippa, Filippa.
Pīus, Pio.
Pŏlly = *Margaret.*
Pŏmpey, Pompeo.
Priscus, Prisco.

R

Răchel, Rachele, Rachelle.
Rălph, Radolfo.
Răndolph, Randolfo.
Răphael *-fyel*, Raffaelle, Raffaello.
Răymund, Raimondo.
Reinhard, Reinardo.
Rĕmy, Remigio.
Reynaud *-nō*, **Rĕynold**, Rinaldo.
Richard, Riccardo.
Rŏb, **Rŏbert**, **Rŏbin**, Roberto.
Rŏderich, Roderico.
Rŏger, **Rŏgers**, Rugiero.
Rŏsamund, Rosamonda, Rosmunda.
Rōsary, Rosaura.
Rōse, Rosetta, Rosa.
Rōwland, Rolando, Orlando.
Rudŏlphus, Rodolfo.
Rūfus, Rufo.
Rūpert, Ruperto.

S

Săl, **Sălly** = *Sarah.*
Sămuel, Samuele.
Scipio, Scipione.
Sārah, Sara.
Sebăstian, Sebastiano.
Semiramis, Semiramide.
Semprōnius, Sempronio.
Seraphīnus, Serafino.
Sibyl, Sibilla.
Simeon, Simeone.
Simon, Simone.
Simson, Sansone.
Sixtus, Sisto.
Sŏlomon, Salomone.
Sophia, **Sophy**, Sofia.
Stanislāus, Stanislao.
Stēphen, Stefano.
Sulpicius, Sulpizio.
Sūsan, **Susănnah**, Susanna.
Sūsy, Susetta.
Sylvānus, Silvano.
Sylvĕster, Silvestro.

T

Tăcitus, Tacito.
Tăncred, Tancredi.
Thăddeus, Taddeo.
Thēobald, Teobaldo.
Theodōra, Teodora.
Thēodore, Teodoro.
Theodōsia, Teodosia.
Theodōsius, Teodosio.
Theŏphilus, Teofilo.
Thŏmas, Tommaso.
Tibērius, Tiberio.
Tibŭrtius, Tiburzio.
Tim, **Timothy**, Timoteo.
Titian, Tiziano.
Tobias, **Tōby**, Tobia.
Tŏm, **Tŏmmy** = *Thomas.*
Tōny = *Anthony.*

U

Ūlric, Udalrico.
Ŭlrica, Udalrica.
Ulўsses u-, Ulisse.
Ŭrsula, Orsola.

V

Vălentine, Valentino.
Valĕrian, Valeriano.
Valĕrius, Valerio.
Victor, Vittore.
Victŏria, Vittoria.
Vincent, Vincenzo.
Vitĕllius, Vitale.
Vivian, Viviano.

W

Wălter, Gualtiero.
Wilfred, Vilfredo.
Will, **William**, Guglielmo.

X

Xavĕrius, Saverio.

Z

Zăch, **Zacharias**, **Zăchary**, Zaccaria, Zaccheria.
Zacchĕus, Zaccheo.
Zēno, Zenone.
Zĕphirus, Zeffiro, Zeffirino.
Zoroăster, Zoroastro.

VERBI IRREGOLARI

☛ **Le forme in stampa grassa son solamente irregolari; le altre son regolari o irregolari.**

Infinitivo	*Preterito*	*Partic. Pass.*
abide	**abode**	**abode**
be	**was**	**been**
pres.		
am, art, is		
are	were	
conj. be	were	
bear	**bore**	**borne**
	(bare)	**born**
beat	**beat**	**beaten**
begin	**begun**	**begun**
	begun	
bend	bent	bent
beseech	**besought**	**besought**
bid	**bade**	**bidden**
	bid	
bind	**bound**	**bound**
		bounden
bite	**bit**	**bitten**
		bit
bleed	**bled**	**bled**
blow	**blew**	**blown**
break	**broke**	**broken**
	(brake)	
breed	**bred**	**bred**
bring	**brought**	**brought**
build	built	built
burn	burnt	burnt.
burst	**burst**	**burst**
buy	**bought**	**bought**
pres. **can**	**could**	———
cast	**cast**	**cast**
catch	**caught**	**caught**
chide	**chid**	**chidden**
	(chode)	**chid**
choose	**chose**	**chosen**
cleave	clove	cloven
	clave	cleft
	cleft	

Infinitivo	*Preterito*	*Partic. Pass.*
cling	**clung**	**clung**
clothe	clad	clad
come	**came**	**come**
cost	**cost**	**cost**
creep	**crept**	**crept**
crow	**crew**	**crowed**
cut	**cut**	**cut**
dare	durst	**dared**
deal	**dealt**	**dealt**
dig	dug	dug
do	**did**	**done**
draw	**drew**	**drawn**
dream	dreamt	dreamt
drink	**drank**	**drunk**
	drunk	**drunken**
drive	**drove**	**driven**
dwell	dwelt	dwelt
eat	**ate**	**eaten**
	eat	
fall	**fell**	**fallen**
feed	**fed**	**fed**
feel	**felt**	**felt**
fight	**fought**	**fought**
find	**found**	**found**
flee	**fled**	**fled**
fling	**flung**	**flung**
fly	**flew**	**flown**
forsake	**forsook**	**forsaken**
freeze	**froze**	**frozen**
freight	**freighted**	fraught
get	**got**	**gotten**
	(gat)	**got**
gild	gilt	gilt
gird	girt	girt
give	**gave**	**given**
go	**went**	**gone**
grave	**graved**	graven

Infinitivo	*Preterito*	*Partic. Pass.*	*Infinitivo*	*Preterito*	*Partic. Pass.*
grind	**ground**	**ground**	**ring**	**rang**	**rung**
grow	**grew**	**grown**		**rung**	
hang	hung	hung	**rise**	**rose**	**risen**
have	**had**	**had**	**rive**	**rived**	riven
pres.			**rot**	**rotted**	rotten
have, hast, has			**run**	**ran**	**run**
hear	**heard**	**heard**	**saw**	**sawed**	**sawn**
heave	hove	**heaved**	**say**	**said**	**said**
hew	**hewed**	hewn	**see**	**saw**	**seen**
hide	**hid**	**hidden**	**seek**	**sought**	**sought**
		hid	**seethe**	sod	sodden
hit	**hit**	**hit**	**sell**	**sold**	**sold**
hold	**held**	**held**	**send**	**sent**	**sent**
		(holden)	**set**	**set**	**set**
hurt	**hurt**	**hurt**	**shake**	**shook**	**shaken**
keep	**kept**	**kept**	*pres.* **shall**	**should**	———
kneel	knelt	knelt	**shape**	**shaped**	shapen
knit	knit	knit	**shave**	**shaved**	shaven
know	**knew**	**known**	**shear**	**sheared**	shorn
lade	**laded**	laden	**shed**	**shed**	**shed**
lead	**led**	**led**	**shine**	shone	shone
lean	leant	leant	**shoe**	**shod**	**shod**
leap	leapt	leapt	**shoot**	**shot**	**shot**
learn	learnt	learnt	**show**	**showed**	shown
leave	**left**	**left**	**(show)**	**(showed)**	(shown)
lend	**lent**	**lent**	**shred**	**shred**	**shred**
let	**let**	**let**	**shrink**	**shrank**	**shrunk**
lie	**lay**	**lain**		**shrunk**	**shrunken**
light	lit	lit	**shut**	**shut**	**shut**
lose	**lost**	**lost**	**sing**	**sang**	**sung**
make	**made**	**made**		**sung**	
pres. **may**	**might**	———	**sink**	**sank**	**sunk**
mean	**meant**	**meant**		**sunk**	**sunken**
meet	**met**	**met**	**sit**	**sat**	**sat**
melt	**melted**	molten	**slay**	**slew**	**slain**
mow	**mowed**	mown	**sleep**	**slept**	**slept**
pres. **must**	———	———	**slide**	**slid**	**slid**
pres. **ought**	———	———			**slidden**
pen	pent	pent	**sling**	**slung**	**slung**
put	**put**	**put**		**slung**	
quit	quit	quit	**slink**	**slunk**	**slunk**
———	**quoth**	———	**slit**	slit	slit
read	**read**	**read**	**smell**	**smelt**	**smelt**
reave	reft	reft	**smite**	**smote**	**smitten**
rend	rent	rent	**sow**	**sowed**	**sown**
rid	**rid**	**rid**	**speak**	**spoke**	**spoken**
ride	**rode**	**ridden**		**(spake)**	

Infinitivo	*Preterito*	*Partic. Pass.*
speed	sped	sped
spell	spelt	spelt
spend	**spent**	**spent**
spill	spilt	spilt
spin	**spun** (**span**)	**spun**
spit	**spat** **spit**	**spit**
split	**split**	**split**
spoil	spoilt	spoilt
spread	**spread**	**spread**
spring	**sprang** **sprung**	**sprung**
stand	**stood**	**stood**
stave	stove	**staved**
steal	**stole**	**stolen**
stick	**stuck**	**stuck**
sting	**stung**	**stung**
stink	**stank**	**stunk**
stride	**strode**	**stridden**
strike	**struck**	**struck** (**stricken**)
string	**strung**	**strung**
strive	**strove**	**striven**
strow	**strowed**	strown
strew	**strewed**	strewn
swear	**swore** (**sware**)	**sworn**
sweat	sweat	sweat
sweep	**swept**	**swept**
swell	**swelled**	swollen

Infinitivo	*Preterito*	*Partic. Pass.*
swim	**swam** **swum**	**swum**
swing	**swung**	**swung**
take	**took**	**taken**
teach	**taught**	**taught**
tear	**tore** (**tare**)	**torn**
tell	**told**	**told**
think	**thought**	**thought**
thrive	throve	thriven
throw	**threw**	**thrown**
thrust	**thrust**	**thrust**
tread	**trod**	**trodden**
wake	woke	woke
wax	**waxed**	(waxen)
wear	**wore** (**ware**)	**worn**
weave	**wove**	**woven**
weep	**wept**	**wept**
wet	wet	wet
whet	whet	whet
pres. **will**	**would**	———
win	**won**	**won**
wind	**wound**	**wound**
wit	**wist**	———
pres. wot		
work	wrought	wrought
wring	**wrung**	**wrung**
write	**wrote**	**written**

Lightning Source UK Ltd.
Milton Keynes UK
UKHW022224081218
333475UK00009B/1194/P

9 780266 664970